O'CONNOR'S TE
CIVIL TRIALS

UPDATED BY
JOHN ZAVITSANOS

O'CONNOR'S TEXAS LITIGATION SERIES
Suggested cite form: O'Connor's Texas Rules * Civil Trials (2021)

For Customer Assistance Call 1-800-328-4880

Mat #42698170

O'CONNOR'S

Print date: January 12, 2021
Printed in the United States of America

ISBN 978-1-53929-045-2

This book is intended to provide attorneys with current information about selected Texas cases, rules, and statutes. The information in this book, however, may not be sufficient in dealing with a client's particular legal problem, and O'Connor's and John Zavitsanos do not warrant or represent its suitability for this purpose. Attorneys using this book do so with the understanding that the information published in it should not be relied on as a substitute for independent research using original sources of authority.

Thank you for subscribing to this product. We welcome your feedback and suggestions at editors.us-legal@tr.com. Our reference attorneys are available to answer product questions and provide research assistance at 1-800-733-2889. To learn about related products or to place an order, visit legalsolutions.thomsonreuters.com.

2021 EDITION HIGHLIGHTS

What's New in This Edition

This year's edition of **O'Connor's Texas Rules ★ Civil Trials** has been updated to reflect 2020 rule and case-law changes. We have also revised and reorganized parts of the commentaries to improve clarity and add further explanation. Here are some of the changes we made this year:

- We revised "Expedited Actions," ch. 2-C, to reflect the 2021 amendments to TRCP 169 and 190, which broaden the applicability of the expedited-actions process and modify the discovery period and certain limitations under the Level 1 discovery-control plan.
- We revised "Types of service," ch. 2-I, § 4.3.1(2)(b), to reflect that substituted service via electronic means such as social media, e-mail, or other technology is permissible based on the 2021 amendments to TRCP 106.
- We revised and reorganized "TRCP 109—service by publication," ch. 2-I, § 4.3.2(1), to explain that, under the 2021 amendments to TRCP 116, service by publication is accomplished by publication on the newly created Public Information Internet Website and, in most cases, publication in a local newspaper.
- We revised "Review after interlocutory order," ch. 4-C, § 8.3.1, based on **Bonsmara Nat. Beef Co. v. Hart of Tex. Cattle Feeders, LLC**, 603 S.W.3d 385 (Tex.2020), to clarify that a party's decision not to pursue an interlocutory appeal of an order denying a motion to compel arbitration does not affect its right to appeal the order after final judgment.
- We revised "Discovery-control plans," ch. 6-A, § 7, to reflect the changes in applicability of the Level 1 discovery-control plan based on the 2021 amendments to TRCP 169 and 190. We also revised "Discovery periods," ch. 6-A, § 8, to reflect the changes to the length of the discovery periods in Level 1 and Level 2 cases based on the 2021 amendments to TRCP 190.
- We significantly revised and reorganized "Disclosures," ch. 6-E, to reflect the changes in procedure for discovering the information and material specified in TRCP 194 and 195 based on the 2021 amendments to these rules.
- We revised "Motion or indication in record," ch. 7-B, § 6.9.3(2), and "Filing late evidence," ch. 7-B, § 6.9.4, based on **B.C. v. Steak N Shake Opers., Inc.**, 598 S.W.3d 256 (Tex.2020), to clarify that for an appellate court to find that a party was granted leave to file a late summary-judgment response or late summary-judgment evidence, there must be a ruling on a motion for leave or an affirmative indication in the record that the trial court considered the late filing.

Emergency Orders Related to COVID-19

In 2020, the Texas Supreme Court issued several emergency orders addressing procedures and deadlines during the COVID-19 pandemic. To familiarize yourself with the COVID-19 emergency orders that are currently in effect, visit www.txcourts.gov/court-coronavirus-information/emergency-orders/.

2024 EDITION HIGHLIGHTS

What's New in This Edition

This year's edition of O'Connor's Texas Rules * Civil Trials has been updated to reflect 2023 rules and case law changes. We have also revised and reorganized parts of the commentary to improve clarity and further explanation. Here are some of the changes [illegible] to the [illegible]

- We revised "Expedited Actions," ch. 2-C, to reflect the 2023 amendments to TRCP 169 and 190, which broaden the applicability of the expedited-actions process and modify the discovery period and certain provisions under the [illegible] control plan.
- We revised "Types of service," ch. 2-H, §4.1.4, for revisions that substituted service via electronic means such as social media, email, or other technology [illegible] based on the 2021 amendments to TRCP 106.
- We revised and reorganized TRCP 106—service by publication, ch. 2-H, [illegible] to explain that under the 2021 amendments to TRCP, the service by publication as accomplished by publication on the newly created Public Information Internet Website and, in most cases, publication in a local newspaper.
- We revised "Review of [illegible] order," ch. [illegible], based on [illegible] [illegible] [illegible] [illegible] *Cattle Feeders*, [illegible] [illegible] to clarify that a party is [illegible] not required to pursue an interlocutory appeal of an order [illegible] [illegible] [illegible] does not affect its right to appeal the order [illegible] final judgment.
- We revised "Discovery control plans," ch. 6-A, [illegible] to reflect the changes [illegible] [illegible] of the Level [illegible] discovery-control plan based on the 2023 amendments to TRCP 169 and 190. We also revised "Discovery periods," ch. 6-A, [illegible] to reflect the changes to the length of the discovery periods in Level 1 and Level [illegible] based on the 2023 amendments to TRCP 190.
- We [illegible] revised and reorganized "Disclosures," ch. 6-B, to reflect the changes [illegible] procedure for discovering the information and material specified in TRCP 194 and 195 based on the 2021 amendments to those rules.
- We revised "Motion for new trial," [illegible] ch. [illegible] and "[illegible]" [illegible] [illegible] [illegible] [illegible] *Stock* [illegible] [illegible] [illegible] [illegible] to clarify that [illegible] [illegible] [illegible] [illegible] [illegible] [illegible] leave to file a late summary-judgment response or a supplementary summary-judgment evidence [illegible] [illegible] [illegible] a motion for leave or an affirmative indication in the record that the trial court considered the late filing.

Emergency Orders Related to COVID-19

In 2020, the Texas Supreme Court issued several emergency orders addressing procedural [illegible] during the COVID-19 pandemic. To implement the end of [illegible] COVID-19 emergency orders that are [illegible] in effect, [illegible] [illegible] governing [illegible] [illegible] [illegible] [illegible] orders.

INTRODUCTION

Conventions

In writing this book, we have tried to produce a plain-English reference gui for attorneys and judges to use. To this end, we should point out a few things a First, the rules are in double columns so they can be instantly distinguish commentaries. Second, we supply page headers for quick reference. Third, whe tions of this and other books are relevant, we cross-reference them. Fourth, w practice tips and caution notes that are separate from the main text so they can spotted. Fifth, to save space we have eliminated the history notes to all but the most amended TRAPs. Finally, we include timetables for certain pretrial, trial, and po procedures.

Throughout this book, we refer to forms in the companion volume **O'Connor's Texas Forms** (2020). The forms are numbered to match the chapter in this book where each t is discussed.

To reduce gender-specific language, we refer to trial judges as the "trial court" and to mos parties as "it" as if the parties were corporations, which they often are. When gender-specific language cannot be avoided, we use the feminine pronoun. To save space when making textual references to certain rules and statutes, we abbreviate the name of the Texas Rules of Civil Procedure to TRCP, the Texas Rules of Evidence to TRE, the Texas Rules of Appellate Procedure to TRAP, the Texas Rules of Judicial Administration to TRJA, the Texas Civil Practice & Remedies Code to CPRC, and the Texas Revised Civil Statutes to TRCS.

All websites cited or referenced in this book are current through October 2020.

Suggestions

Thank you for subscribing to this product. We welcome your feedback and suggestions at editors.us-legal@tr.com.

Caveat

This book provides citations to important opinions that interpret the Texas Rules of Civil Procedure and Texas Rules of Evidence through December 2020. You may disagree with our explanations of the rules and cases cited in this book. You should therefore use this book only as a research guide. Read the rules and cases yourself and make your own evaluation of them.

HOW TO USE THIS BOOK

Use the page corners to quickly find topics listed in the index or cross-referenced within the commentaries. The index entries and cross-references refer to specific sections in the book, and the section identifiers located on the top outside corners of the commentaries pages indicate the sections that can be found on each page. The left-hand page corner identifier indicates the first section on the left-hand page, and the right-hand page corner identifier indicates the last section on the right-hand page. Navigate to the correct page by finding the range of section identifiers containing the relevant index entry or cross-reference.

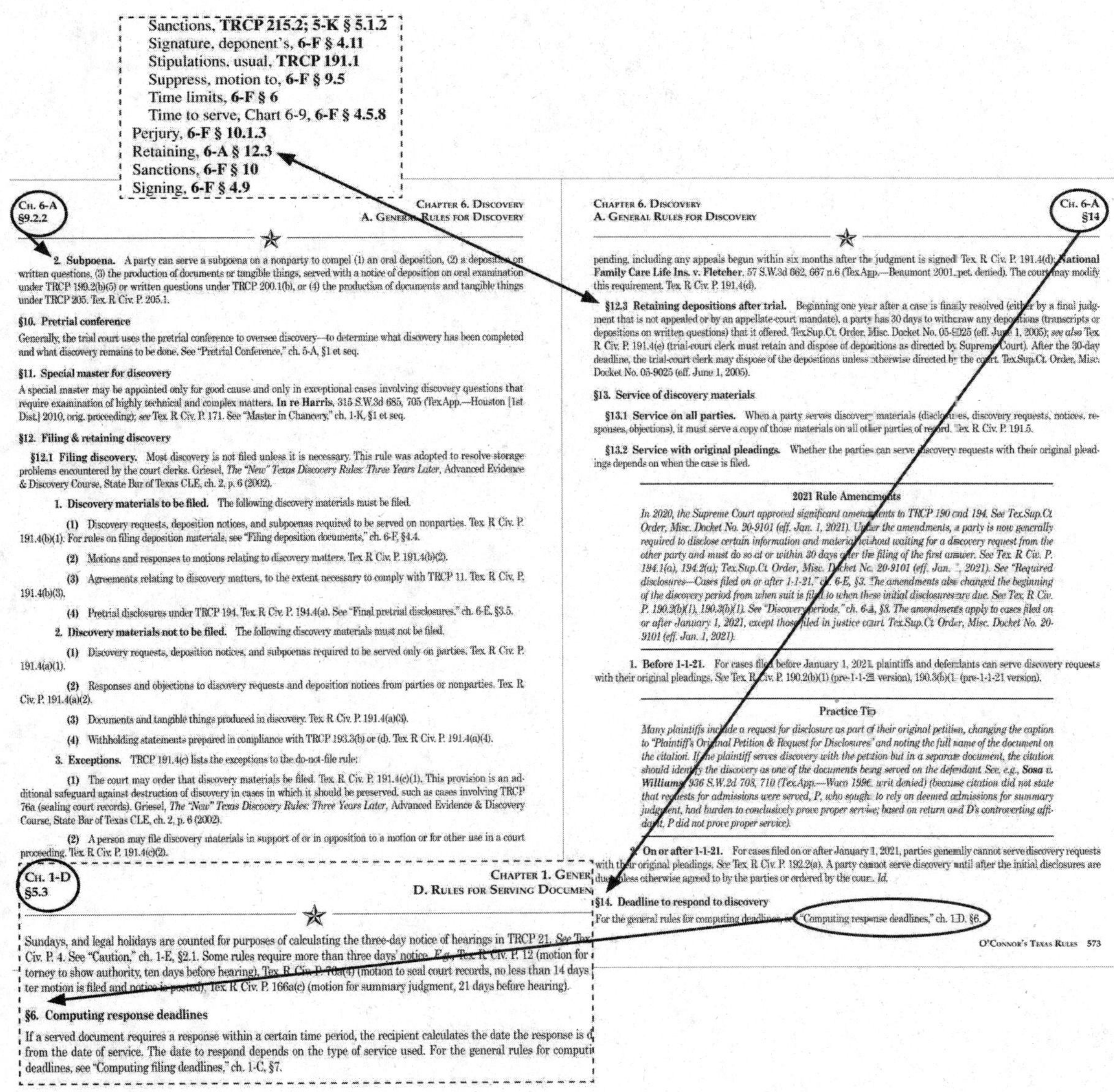

ABOUT THE EDITORS

John Zavitsanos is a highly regarded trial lawyer who loves trying cases and loves winning. He has achieved success for a multitude of clients—both defendants and plaintiffs, from big energy companies to lone whistleblowers battling the odds. He is co-founder of AZA. He has tried more than 75 cases to verdict in litigation, including cases involving financial services, oil and gas, healthcare, construction, complex commercial disputes, director and officer liability, noncompete agreements, and trade-secret disputes. He is board-certified in civil trial law by both the Texas Board of Legal Specialization and the National Board of Trial Advocacy. He has given numerous continuing legal education seminars on trial techniques, depositions, voir dire, cross-examination, and other civil-trial specialty areas. He has been included in *The Best Lawyers in America*, has been recognized for his commercial litigation work in Texas by Chambers USA: America's Leading Lawyers for Business, and has the highest possible peer rating from Martindale-Hubbell. He was named a *Benchmark Litigation* Star from 2016 to 2020 and is also a Litigation Counsel of America Fellow.

Jane Langdell Robinson is an appellate lawyer with extensive practice in state and federal courts. She handles a wide variety of civil appellate matters, including mandamus proceedings, interlocutory appeals, and appeals of final judgments in Texas, other state appellate courts, numerous federal circuits, the Court of Appeals for Veterans Claims, and the United States Supreme Court. Ms. Robinson is board-certified in civil appellate law by the Texas Board of Legal Specialization, a distinction held by less than one percent of licensed lawyers in Texas. She has also been recognized by attorneys across the country in *The Best Lawyers in America* for her appellate work. Ms. Robinson is a life fellow of the Texas Bar Foundation.

STAFF INFORMATION

As always, the staff of O'Connor's worked hard to prepare this publication, both in its substance and in its layout. The people who worked on this edition of **O'Connor's Texas Rules ★ Civil Trials** are listed below.

EXECUTIVE ATTORNEY EDITOR
Douglas Rosenzweig, J.D.

MANAGING ATTORNEY EDITOR
Kristen N. Ellis, J.D.

ASSISTANT MANAGING ATTORNEY EDITOR
Victoria R. Guzman, J.D.

CONTRIBUTING ATTORNEY EDITORS
Eun-Jeong Choi, J.D.
Kalina Dalal, J.D.
Mathew Kone, J.D.
Sarah Arocha Ostriyznick, J.D.
Kathryn A. Ritcheske, J.D.

EDITORIAL OPERATIONS
Jennifer L. Foster
Nicole E. Hammond
Marc A. Kashiwagi, J.D.

COPYEDITOR
David W. Schultz, J.D.

PRODUCT LIST

TEXAS LITIGATION SERIES

O'Connor's Texas Rules ★ Civil Trials

O'Connor's Texas Civil Forms

O'Connor's Texas Civil Appeals

TEXAS EXPERT SERIES

O'Connor's Texas Causes of Action

O'Connor's Texas Causes of Action Pleadings

O'Connor's Texas Crimes & Consequences

O'Connor's Texas Family Law Handbook

O'Connor's Texas Family Law Forms

O'Connor's Texas Probate Law Handbook

O'Connor's Texas Probate Forms

Davis's Texas Estate Planning Forms

Texas Rules of Evidence Handbook

Texas Forms ★ Real Estate

FEDERAL LITIGATION SERIES

O'Connor's Federal Rules ★ Civil Trials

O'Connor's Federal Civil Forms

CALIFORNIA SERIES

O'Connor's California Practice ★ Civil Pretrial

California Guide to Criminal Evidence

PRACTICE RESOURCES

Illustrated Guide to Criminal Law

Typography for Lawyers

TEXAS ANNOTATED CODES SERIES

O'Connor's Texas Business & Commerce Code Plus

O'Connor's Texas Business Organizations Code Plus

O'Connor's Texas Civil Practice & Remedies Code Plus

O'Connor's Texas Criminal Codes Plus

O'Connor's Texas Employment Codes Plus

O'Connor's Texas Estates Code Plus

O'Connor's Texas Family Code Plus

O'Connor's Texas Oil & Gas Statutes & Regulations

O'Connor's Texas Property Code Plus

FEDERAL ANNOTATED CODES SERIES

O'Connor's Federal Criminal Rules & Codes Plus

O'Connor's Federal Employment Codes Plus

O'Connor's Federal Intellectual Property Codes Plus

CALCULATORS

O'Connor's Texas Pretrial Deadlines Calculator

O'Connor's Federal Deadlines Calculator

Table of Contents

Chapter 1. General

A. Introduction to the Texas Rules

In 1939, the Texas Legislature gave the Supreme Court rulemaking power in civil actions. The Legislature placed two limits on the Court's authority over the rules: (1) the Court cannot enact rules that "abridge, enlarge, or modify the substantive rights of a litigant," and (2) the Legislature retains the power to disapprove of the Court's rules. Tex. Gov't Code §22.004(a), (b). The Court must file a copy of all rule changes with the Secretary of State and identify which statutes the rules repeal or modify. Tex. Gov't Code §22.004(b), (c). On receipt of a written request from a member of the Legislature, the Secretary of State must provide the member with electronic notifications when the Supreme Court promulgates rules or amendments to the rules. Tex. Gov't Code §22.004(b).

§1. Texas Rules of Civil Procedure (TRCPs)

In 1941, the Supreme Court adopted the Texas Rules of Civil Procedure. *See* Tex. Gov't Code §22.004; Tex. R. Civ. P. 2, 814. The TRCPs have the same force and effect as statutes. **Missouri Pac. R.R. v. Cross**, 501 S.W.2d 868, 872 (Tex.1973). When a rule of procedure conflicts with a substantive statute or a statute passed after the rule, the statute prevails. *See* Tex. Gov't Code §22.004(c); **In re M.N.**, 262 S.W.3d 799, 802 (Tex.2008).

§2. Texas Rules of Evidence (TREs)

In 1983, the Supreme Court adopted the Texas Rules of Evidence for civil cases. 641–642 S.W.2d (Tex.Cases) xxxv (1983). In 1988, it renamed them the "Texas Rules of Civil Evidence." 733–734 S.W.2d (Tex.Cases) lxxxv (1987). In 1998, the Supreme Court and the Court of Criminal Appeals merged the civil and criminal rules and renamed them the "Texas Rules of Evidence." 960 S.W.2d (Tex.Cases) xxix (1998). See Brown & Rondon, **Texas Rules of Evidence Handbook** (2021 ed.) (Introduction). In 2015, the Supreme Court restyled the TREs to make them as consistent as possible with the Federal Rules of Evidence (FREs), without effecting any substantive change in Texas evidence law other than the amendments to TRE 511 and 613. Tex.Sup.Ct. Order, Misc. Docket No. 15-9048, §2, ¶¶1, 2 (eff. Apr. 1, 2015). The revisions were designed to make the TREs more easily understood and to make style and terminology consistent throughout. Tex.Sup.Ct. Order, Misc. Docket No. 15-9048, §2, ¶1 (eff. Apr. 1, 2015). The TREs apply to most civil and criminal proceedings in Texas courts. Tex. R. Evid. 101(b).

§3. Texas Rules of Appellate Procedure (TRAPs)

In 1986, the Supreme Court and the Court of Criminal Appeals adopted the Texas Rules of Appellate Procedure. 707–708 S.W.2d (Tex.Cases) xxix (1986). As part of that process, the appellate rules in the TRCPs were repealed. In 1997, the Supreme Court and the Court of Criminal Appeals adopted a new set of TRAPs. 948–949 S.W.2d (Tex.Cases) lxi (1997).

§4. Local rules

TRCP 3a permits the trial courts to establish local rules consistent with the TRCPs. Local rules cannot impose restrictions on or conflict with the TRCPs. *See* **Jamar v. Patterson**, 868 S.W.2d 318, 318 n.2 (Tex.1993); **Approximately $14,980.00 v. State**, 261 S.W.3d 182, 188–89 (Tex.App.—Houston [14th Dist.] 2008, no pet.); *see also* **Kenley v. Quintana Pet. Corp.**, 931 S.W.2d 318, 321 (Tex.App.—San Antonio 1996, writ denied) (local rule, which stated it constituted notice that cases on file for more than six months would be set for dismissal hearing, contradicted TRCP 165a notice requirements). Local rules also cannot be applied to determine the merits of any matter. Tex. R. Civ. P. 3a(6); **Approximately $1,589.00 v. State**, 230 S.W.3d 871, 874 (Tex.App.—Houston [14th Dist.] 2007, no pet.).

§4.1 Notice of local rules. Litigants are charged with knowledge of local rules. **Mayad v. Rizk**, 554 S.W.2d 835, 838–39 (Tex.App.—Houston [14th Dist.] 1977, writ ref'd n.r.e.); **In re Estate of Stanton**, No. 12-05-00041-CV, 2006 WL 343907 (Tex.App.—Tyler 2006, pet. denied) (memo op.; 2-15-06); **Zarosky v. State**, No. 03-03-00116-CV, 2004 WL 1114539 (Tex.App.—Austin 2004, no pet.) (memo op.; 5-20-04). TRCP 3a requires the trial courts to file copies of their local rules with the Supreme Court for approval and to publish them at least 30 days before they become effective. Tex. R. Civ. P. 3a(3), (4).

§4.2 Effect of local rules. Litigants should pay particular attention to local rules. Some local rules provide that failure to file a response to a motion indicates acquiescence to the relief sought in the motion. *E.g.*, Harris Cty. Loc. R. 3.3.2 (district courts); *see* **Cire v. Cummings**, 134 S.W.3d 835, 844 (Tex.2004). Some local rules require a specific request for oral argument; without a proper request, no argument will be permitted. *E.g.*, Smith Cty. Loc. R. 2.3 (oral argument on motion for summary judgment); **Rorie v. Goodwin**, 171 S.W.3d 579, 583 (Tex.App.—Tyler 2005, no pet.) (same).

B. Rules of Pleading

§1. General

§1.1 Rules. Tex. R. Civ. P. 21, 21b, 22 to 24, 45 to 71, 74 to 98, 166(b), 169, 190.2.

§1.2 Purpose. The purpose of the pleadings is to define the issues for trial. **Murray v. O&A Express, Inc.**, 630 S.W.2d 633, 636 (Tex.1982).

§1.3 Forms. **O'Connor's Texas Civil Forms**, FORMS 1B:1 et seq. (2020 ed.); **O'Connor's Texas Civil Appeals**, FORM 1D:13 (2020 ed.).

§1.4 Other references. Judicial Committee on Information Technology (JCIT) Technology Standards, version 6.5 (Oct. 11, 2019) (referred to as JCIT Tech. Stds., v. 6.5); **O'Connor's Texas Causes of Action** (2021 ed.); **O'Connor's Texas Civil Appeals** (2020 ed.); Brown & Rondon, **Texas Rules of Evidence Handbook** (2021 ed.).

Note

As of the publication of this book, version 6.5 is the most recent version of the technology standards promulgated by the JCIT and approved by the Texas Supreme Court. See Tex.Sup.Ct. Order, Misc. Docket No. 20-9012 (Jan. 14, 2020). To check for newer versions of the technology standards, see the JCIT's website at www.txcourts.gov/jcit or the Court's website at www.txcourts.gov/supreme.

§2. Types of documents filed with court

It is important to distinguish the different types of documents filed with the court and to understand their functions.

§2.1 Pleading. The Texas system of pleadings is composed of petitions and answers. **Elliott v. Elliott**, 797 S.W.2d 388, 391–92 (Tex.App.—Austin 1990, no writ); *see* Tex. R. Civ. P. 45(a). The pleadings define the suit, give notice of the facts and legal theories of the case, guide the trial court in admitting evidence and in charging the jury, restrict the trial court in rendering the judgment, and form the basis for appellate review. *See* **Erisman v. Thompson**, 167 S.W.2d 731, 733 (Tex.1943) (pleadings define lawsuit and determine issues for trial); **Crain v. San Jacinto Sav. Ass'n**, 781 S.W.2d 638, 639 (Tex.App.—Houston [14th Dist.] 1989, writ dism'd) (pleadings give notice of evidence to be introduced). The controversy described in the pleadings is resolved by a judgment. **Lindley v. Flores**, 672 S.W.2d 612, 614 (Tex.App.—Corpus Christi 1984, no writ).

§2.2 Motion. A motion is a request for an order from the court. **Durbin v. Culberson Cty.**, 132 S.W.3d 650, 656 (Tex.App.—El Paso 2004, no pet.); **Elliott v. Elliott**, 797 S.W.2d 388, 392 (Tex.App.—Austin 1990, no writ); **Lindley v. Flores**, 672 S.W.2d 612, 614 (Tex.App.—Corpus Christi 1984, no writ). Most motions are resolved by an order. When a motion requesting a judgment (e.g., a motion for summary judgment) is granted, the motion is resolved by a judgment; when it is denied, it is resolved by an order. See **O'Connor's Texas Civil Forms**, FORMS 1B:1, 1G:1 (2020 ed.).

§2.3 Plea. "Plea" is an archaic term referring to certain defensive pleadings. *See* **Bland ISD v. Blue**, 34 S.W.3d 547, 554 (Tex.2000). In most instances, the TRCPs replaced the term "plea" with "motion." *See, e.g.*, **Toliver v. Dallas Fort Worth Hosp. Council**, 198 S.W.3d 444, 447 (Tex.App.—Dallas 2006, no pet.) ("plea of privilege" is now motion to transfer venue). But some of the rules continue to refer to pleas. For example, TRCP 85 lists the pleas that may be included in the defendant's answer. In this book, most pleas are cast as motions (e.g., a motion to abate instead of a plea in abatement).

§2.4 Bill. A bill is a formal, written declaration, complaint, or statement of particular issues (e.g., a bill of review or a bill of exception).

§3. Pleading practice

§3.1 Local requirements. In drafting and filing pleadings, the parties must comply with the requirements of local rules. Some local rules have specific requirements for the form and organization of the pleadings. For example, under Dallas County Civil Court Local Rule 2.04, a pleading must include a footer at the bottom of each page with the document's caption and page number, and judgments and orders must be separate documents.

§3.2 Formal requirements.

1. In writing. All pleadings must be in writing unless they are made in open court and transcribed by the court reporter. *See* **Pennington v. Gurkoff**, 899 S.W.2d 767, 771 (Tex.App.—Fort Worth 1995, writ denied).

(1) Format for paper pleadings. Pleadings that are filed in paper form must be on 8½-by-11-inch paper. Tex. R. Civ. P. 45. Parties are "strongly encouraged" to use recycled paper. *Id.*

(2) Format for e-filed pleadings. Pleadings that are electronically filed (e-filed) must comply with TRCP 21(f) and the technology standards promulgated by the JCIT and approved by the Supreme Court. *See* Tex. R. Civ. P. 21(f)(8). An e-filed pleading must meet the following requirements:

(a) The document must be in text-searchable portable document format (PDF). Tex. R. Civ. P. 21(f)(8)(A).

(b) The document must be directly converted to PDF. Tex. R. Civ. P. 21(f)(8)(B). Scanning should be avoided if possible. *Id.*

(c) If a document must be scanned, it must have a resolution of 300 dots per inch and should be made searchable using optical-character-recognition software. JCIT Tech. Stds., v. 6.5, §3.1.C.

(d) The PDF must be an 8½-by-11-inch page size with the content appropriately rotated. *Id.* §3.1.A.

(e) The PDF should not be embedded within another PDF or contain embedded fonts. *Id.* §3.1.E. Each document must be a single PDF, but an appellate court may require that multiple PDFs be combined into one PDF document with bookmarks used to separate the material. *Id.*

(f) The document must not be locked. Tex. R. Civ. P. 21(f)(8)(C).

(g) The document cannot have any security or feature restrictions (e.g., password protection) and cannot contain embedded multimedia video, audio, or programming. JCIT Tech. Stds., v. 6.5, §3.1.D.

(h) The document's filename should have only alphanumeric characters that are part of the Latin1_General character set; no special characters are allowed. *Id.* §3.1.F. The filename should not exceed 50 characters. *Id.*

(i) The document must include a standardized filing code, which depends on the type of case filed. *See id.* §§4.1–4.5. Standardized codes have been issued for the following types of cases: civil, family, probate, multidistrict litigation, and juvenile. *See id.*

2. Style. The style is the heading of the pleading. It contains the cause number, the names of the parties, the court, and the county of suit. See **O'Connor's Texas Civil Forms**, FORM 1B:2 (2020 ed.).

(1) Cause number. The clerk assigns the cause number. Tex. R. Civ. P. 23. The parties should make sure all pleadings are filed with the correct cause number. However, filing a document with the wrong cause number is generally not considered a jurisdictional defect. *See, e.g.,* **Curtis v. Gibbs**, 511 S.W.2d 263, 268 (Tex.1974) (mistake in cause number of original petition was "irrelevant").

(2) List of parties. In the style of the original petition and the answer, all the parties should be listed by their full names. In later pleadings, the list of parties in the style may be shortened by naming the first party and using the inclusive term "et al." *See, e.g.,* **Abramcik v. U.S. Home Corp.**, 792 S.W.2d 822, 824 (Tex.App.—Houston [14th Dist.] 1990, writ denied) (generic reference to Ps using term "et al." in style of sixth amended petition was sufficient to maintain cause of action for individually named Ps in previous petition).

3. Caption. The caption is the title of the pleading.

Note

Courts and practitioners are inconsistent in what they consider the "style" and "caption" of a case, and many use the terms interchangeably. This book uses "style" to refer to the entire heading and "caption"

to refer only to the title.

(1) Correct title. The title of a pleading should be useful to the court, the clerk, and the attorney's files. The title should include the version of the pleading, such as "Plaintiff's First Supplemental Petition." Tex. R. Civ. P. 78, 83; *see* Tex. R. Civ. P. 64.

(2) Incorrect title. If the party makes an error in the caption of the pleading, the court will treat the pleading as if it had been properly named. Tex. R. Civ. P. 71. The clerk will file a pleading using the caption the party provides, but the court may order the document redesignated. *Id.*

4. Party information.

(1) Name. Generally, the full names of all parties should be included in the body of all petitions (amended and supplemental) and in any other documents that must be served with citation. Pleadings should not rely on "et al." to refer to the parties. *See* Tex. R. Civ. P. 79. In an amended petition, the omission of a party's name and the claims asserted against that party normally indicates an intent to nonsuit that party. *See* **American Petrofina, Inc. v. Allen**, 887 S.W.2d 829, 831 (Tex.1994); **Woodruff v. Wright**, 51 S.W.3d 727, 731–32 (Tex.App.—Texarkana 2001, pet. denied). If the party was omitted from an amended pleading but renamed in a later pleading, the later pleading may relate back to the earlier pleading as long as the earlier omission was inadvertent, temporary, and not prejudicial to the other parties. *See* **American Petrofina**, 887 S.W.2d at 831; **Woodruff**, 51 S.W.3d at 733. But if a party's name was not included in the original petition and is mentioned for the first time in an amended or supplemental pleading, the amended or supplemental pleading does not relate back to the original pleading for limitations purposes. *See* **Alexander v. Turtur & Assocs.**, 146 S.W.3d 113, 121 (Tex.2004). See "Amended or supplemental pleading," **O'Connor's Texas Causes of Action**, ch. 52, §4.4 (2021 ed.).

(2) Residence. Any pleading that must be served with citation must identify the residence of the party to be served, if it is known. *See* Tex. R. Civ. P. 79; *see, e.g.,* **Graham v. Huff**, 384 S.W.2d 904, 905 (Tex.App.—Dallas 1964, no writ) (petition did not include Ds' addresses or state they were unknown). The parties' residences are important for purposes of service, personal jurisdiction, venue, and forum non conveniens. *See* **Kelly v. Demoss Owners Ass'n**, 71 S.W.3d 419, 424 (Tex.App.—Amarillo 2002, no pet.).

(3) ID number. The initial pleading filed in district court, county court, or statutory county court must include the last three digits of the filing party's driver's license number and the last three digits of her Social Security number. Tex. Civ. Prac. & Rem. Code §30.014(a). A court may, on its own motion or on the motion of a party, order a party to amend a pleading to include this information. Tex. Civ. Prac. & Rem. Code §30.014(b). If the party does not amend the pleading as ordered, the court may find the party in contempt. *Id.*

5. Fair notice. The pleadings must give fair notice of the claims, defenses, and relief sought. **In re Lipsky**, 460 S.W.3d 579, 590 (Tex.2015); *see* Tex. R. Civ. P. 21(a) (pleadings must state grounds and relief sought), Tex. R. Civ. P. 45(b) (pleadings must state claims and defenses), Tex. R. Civ. P. 47(a) (pleading must contain statement sufficient to give fair notice of claim); **DeRoeck v. DHM Ventures, LLC**, 556 S.W.3d 831, 835 (Tex.2018) (pleading is sufficient if it gives fair and adequate notice of facts that claim is based on). See "Fair notice of claim," ch. 2-B, §7.2.

6. Numbered paragraphs. The paragraphs in pleadings must be numbered, and each paragraph should be limited to a single set of circumstances. Tex. R. Civ. P. 50. Arabic numerals (e.g., 1, 2, 3) should be used, and Roman numerals (e.g., I, II, III) should be avoided.

7. Separate counts or defenses. The pleading should divide the allegations into counts or defenses. Tex. R. Civ. P. 48, 50. Headings and subheadings are useful in separating the sections of the pleading.

8. Relief sought.

(1) Statement of damages. An original pleading that states a claim for relief must contain a statement that the damages sought are within the jurisdictional limits of the court. Tex. R. Civ. P. 47(b). See "Damages," ch. 2-B, §9.

(2) Specific statement of relief.

(a) Generally. All original pleadings that set forth a claim for relief—whether an original petition, counterclaim, cross-claim, or third-party claim—generally must contain a specific statement of the relief the party seeks. *See*

Tex. R. Civ. P. 47(c) & cmt. (2013) (statement of relief requires parties to plead into or out of expedited-actions process in TRCP 169).

2021 Rule Amendments

In 2020, the Supreme Court approved amendments to TRCP 47 and 169. See Tex.Sup.Ct. Order, Misc. Docket No. 20-9153 (eff. Jan. 1, 2021). The amendments increased the limit on the monetary relief that can be sought in an expedited action from $100,000 to $250,000. See Tex. R. Civ. P. 169(a). The statements of relief in TRCP 47 were amended to correspond to this change. See Tex. R. Civ. P. 47(c). The amendments apply to cases filed on or after January 1, 2021, except those filed in justice court. Tex.Sup.Ct. Order, Misc. Docket No. 20-9153 (eff. Jan. 1, 2021).

[1] Specific statements. The pleading must include one of the following statements:

[a] The party seeks only monetary relief of $250,000 or less, excluding interest, statutory or punitive damages and penalties, and attorney fees and costs. Tex. R. Civ. P. 47(c)(1). A suit in which the pleading contains a specific statement of relief under TRCP 47(c)(1) is governed by the expedited-actions process in TRCP 169 and the discovery limitations in TRCP 190.2. *See* Tex. R. Civ. P. 169(a), (d)(1), 190.2(a)(1), 47 cmt. (2021). See "Expedited Actions," ch. 2-C, §1 et seq.

2021 Rule Amendments

For cases filed before January 1, 2021, the calculation of the monetary relief sought included damages of any kind, penalties, costs, expenses, prejudgment interest, and attorney fees. See Tex. R. Civ. P. 47(c)(1) (pre-1-1-21 version), Tex. R. Civ. P. 169(a)(1) (pre-1-1-21 version). For cases filed on or after January 1, 2021, most of these elements are excluded from the calculation of the monetary relief sought. See Tex.Sup.Ct. Order, Misc. Docket No. 20-9153 (eff. Jan. 1, 2021).

[b] The party seeks monetary relief of $250,000 or less and nonmonetary relief. Tex. R. Civ. P. 47(c)(2).

[c] The party seeks monetary relief over $250,000 but not more than $1,000,000. Tex. R. Civ. P. 47(c)(3).

[d] The party seeks monetary relief over $1,000,000. Tex. R. Civ. P. 47(c)(4).

[e] The party seeks only nonmonetary relief. Tex. R. Civ. P. 47(c)(5).

Note

The specific statements of relief under TRCP 47(c)(2) to (5) provide information on the nature of the case and do not affect a party's substantive rights. See Tex. R. Civ. P. 47 cmt. (2013).

[2] Effect of noncompliance—no discovery. If a party does not comply with TRCP 47(c), the party cannot conduct discovery until its pleading is amended to comply. Tex. R. Civ. P. 47. If the party has already sent discovery requests to the opposing party, the party is not required to reissue the requests after amending its pleading. **In re Greater McAllen Star Props., Inc.**, 444 S.W.3d 743, 751 (Tex.App.—Corpus Christi 2014, orig. proceeding). Once an amended pleading that complies with TRCP 47 is filed, the time to respond to the discovery requests begins to run. *See* **In re Greater McAllen Star**, 444 S.W.3d at 751.

[3] Special exceptions. If a party does not specify the maximum amount claimed, the opposing party can specially except to require the pleading party to amend its pleading to specify the maximum amount. Tex. R. Civ. P. 47. See "Special Exceptions—Challenging the Pleadings," ch. 3-G, §1 et seq.

(b) Exceptions.

[1] Guardianship & probate proceedings. Pleadings in guardianship and probate proceedings do not require a specific statement of relief. Tex. Est. Code §53.107(1) (probate), §1053.105(1) (guardianship).

[2] **Family Code.** Pleadings in suits governed by the Family Code do not require a specific statement of relief. Tex. R. Civ. P. 47(c).

[3] **Justice court.** Pleadings in suits filed in justice court do not require a specific statement of relief. Tex.Sup.Ct. Order, Misc. Docket No. 20-9153 (eff. Jan. 1, 2021); Tex.Sup.Ct. Order, Misc. Docket No. 13-9022 (eff. Mar. 1, 2013).

(3) **All other relief.** The pleading must contain a demand for judgment for all other relief to which the party is entitled. Tex. R. Civ. P. 47(d).

9. **Alternative claims or defenses.** A party can plead alternative or hypothetical theories, allege inconsistent claims or defenses, and allege claims or defenses based on legal grounds, equitable grounds, or both. Tex. R. Civ. P. 48; *see* Tex. R. Civ. P. 47 (party may plead for alternative relief); **Gunn v. McCoy**, 554 S.W.3d 645, 678 (Tex.2018) (party may plead alternative defenses); **JLG Trucking, LLC v. Garza**, 466 S.W.3d 157, 164 (Tex.2015) (party may plead conflicting claims and defenses and alternative, inconsistent theories of relief); **Delaney v. Davis**, 81 S.W.3d 445, 452 (Tex.App.—Houston [14th Dist.] 2002, no pet.) (party may plead and prove inconsistent claims). There must be a reasonable basis in fact or law for each alternative theory pleaded. **JLG Trucking**, 466 S.W.3d at 164; **Low v. Henry**, 221 S.W.3d 609, 615 (Tex.2007). Generally, a pleading does not state a cause of action if it states inconsistent, contradictory facts that are material to the cause of action without alleging an alternative theory. **Vinklarek v. Vinklarek**, 596 S.W.2d 197, 199 (Tex.App.—Houston [1st Dist.] 1980, writ dism'd).

10. **Adoption by reference.** A party can adopt statements by reference from another pleading that has not been superseded by an amended pleading. Tex. R. Civ. P. 58; *see* **Texas Gas Utils. Co. v. Barrett**, 460 S.W.2d 409, 416 (Tex.1970). Similarly, a party can attach and adopt exhibits by reference or copy them into the body of the pleading. Tex. R. Civ. P. 59. A party should not adopt by reference from a superseded pleading, but if it does, the adopted material is not void and must be challenged by a special exception. *See* **Hawkins v. Anderson**, 672 S.W.2d 293, 295 (Tex.App.—Dallas 1984, no writ).

11. **Prayer.** At the end of the pleading, under the heading "Prayer," the party should state exactly what relief it seeks. The prayer for relief should match the purpose of the pleading. See "Prayer," ch. 2-B, §15.

12. **Signature block.** The signature block identifies the person signing the pleading and provides that person's contact information. See **O'Connor's Texas Civil Forms**, FORM 1B:3 (2020 ed.).

(1) **Who must sign.** A pleading must be signed by the party's attorney or by the party if not represented by an attorney. Tex. R. Civ. P. 45; *see* Tex. R. Civ. P. 57. The lack of a signature does not alter the legal effect of the pleading. **W.C. Turnbow Pet. Co. v. Fulton**, 194 S.W.2d 256, 257 (Tex.1946); **Frank v. Corbett**, 682 S.W.2d 587, 588 (Tex.App.—Waco 1984, no writ). A pleading that is e-filed must contain an electronic signature. *See* Tex. R. Civ. P. 21(f)(7).

(a) **Attorney.** When a pleading is signed by an attorney, the pleading must identify the attorney by name, State Bar number, address, telephone number, e-mail address, and fax number (if any). Tex. R. Civ. P. 57; *see* Tex. R. Civ. P. 21(f)(2), 191.3(a)(1). The signature fixes responsibility for the allegations and identifies the party the attorney represents. **Ingram v. Card Co.**, 540 S.W.2d 803, 804 (Tex.App.—Corpus Christi 1976, no writ); *see* Tex. Civ. Prac. & Rem. Code §§9.011, 10.001; Tex. R. Civ. P. 13. The attorney whose signature first appears on the initial pleading for any party is the "attorney in charge," unless another attorney is specifically designated. Tex. R. Civ. P. 8. See "Designation of attorneys," ch. 1-H, §3. Pleadings must be signed by at least one attorney of record; there is no requirement that the attorney in charge sign and file all pleadings. *See* Tex. R. Civ. P. 57; **Sunbeam Envtl. Servs. v. Texas Workers' Comp. Ins. Facility**, 71 S.W.3d 846, 851 (Tex.App.—Austin 2002, no pet.).

(b) **Pro se party.** An unrepresented (pro se) party must sign a pleading. A pro se party's signature block must include its address, telephone number, e-mail address, and fax number (if any). Tex. R. Civ. P. 57; *see* Tex. R. Civ. P. 21(f)(2), 191.3(a)(2); **Kelly**, 71 S.W.3d at 424.

(2) **Form of signature.**

(a) **Paper signature.** A pleading filed with the court in paper form must be signed by the attorney or pro se party. Tex. R. Civ. P. 45; *see* Tex. R. Civ. P. 57.

(b) Electronic signature. A pleading that is e-filed or e-served must contain an electronic signature. *See* Tex. R. Civ. P. 21(f)(7).

[1] Attorney's or party's signature. The pleading must contain one of the following signature substitutes: (1) an "/s/" with the attorney's or party's typed name in the same place where the signature would otherwise appear or (2) an electronic or scanned image of the attorney's or party's signature. Tex. R. Civ. P. 21(f)(7).

[2] Notarized or sworn documents. If the pleading is notarized or sworn, it must include an electronic or scanned image of the necessary signatures. *See* Tex. R. Civ. P. 21(f)(7).

(3) Certification by signature. A person who signs a pleading (or motion) represents that the pleading is not frivolous or groundless. Tex. R. Civ. P. 13. The court can impose sanctions on the signer of a frivolous or groundless pleading, a party represented by the signer, or both. See "Groundless or frivolous pleadings," ch. 1-B, §3.3; "Groundless or frivolous pleadings, motions, or other papers," ch. 5-K, §5.2.

(a) Under CPRC ch. 10. Under CPRC §10.001, signing a pleading (or motion) constitutes a certificate that to the signatory's best knowledge, information, and belief, formed after a reasonable inquiry, the following is true:

[1] The matters in the pleading are not presented for an improper purpose, including to harass or to cause unnecessary delay or needless increase in the cost of litigation. Tex. Civ. Prac. & Rem. Code §10.001(1). A pleading is "presented" to a court when the person signs, files, submits, or later advocates it. *Cf.* Fed. R. Civ. P. 11(b) (representations to federal court).

[2] Each claim, defense, or other legal contention is warranted by existing law or by a nonfrivolous argument for the extension, modification, or reversal of existing law or the establishment of new law. Tex. Civ. Prac. & Rem. Code §10.001(2). Filing a general denial does not violate CPRC §10.001(2). Tex. Civ. Prac. & Rem. Code §10.004(f).

[3] Each allegation or factual contention has evidentiary support or, for a specifically identified allegation or factual contention, is likely to have evidentiary support after a reasonable opportunity for further investigation or discovery. Tex. Civ. Prac. & Rem. Code §10.001(3); **Low**, 221 S.W.3d at 614–15.

[4] Each denial of a factual contention is warranted by the evidence or, for a specifically identified denial, is reasonably based on a lack of information or belief. Tex. Civ. Prac. & Rem. Code §10.001(4).

(b) Under TRCP 13. Under TRCP 13, signing a pleading (or motion or other paper) constitutes a certificate that (1) the signatory has read the document and (2) to the signatory's best knowledge, information, and belief, formed after reasonable inquiry, the document is not groundless and is not brought in bad faith, brought for the purpose of harassment, or false when made.

(c) Under CPRC ch. 9. Under CPRC §9.011, signing a pleading (or motion) constitutes a certificate that to the signatory's best knowledge, information, and belief, formed after reasonable inquiry, the pleading (1) is not groundless, (2) is not brought in bad faith or for the purpose of harassment, and (3) is not brought for any improper purpose, such as to cause unnecessary delay or expense. CPRC chapter 9 does not alter the TRCPs. Tex. Civ. Prac. & Rem. Code §9.003.

(d) Under TRCP 191.3. The discovery rules impose obligations on the attorney (or pro se party) who signs written discovery. See "Certification by signature," ch. 6-A, §4.1.

13. Certificate of service. All pleadings required to be served under TRCP 21 (except those served with citation) must contain a certificate of service in the document itself. *See* Tex. R. Civ. P. 21(d), 21a(a). See **O'Connor's Texas Civil Forms**, FORM 1B:13 (2020 ed.).

(1) Contents. The certificate should contain the recipient's physical address and e-mail address, a statement that the document was served on opposing counsel (or pro se party) by a certain method (e.g., by mail, by delivery, or electronically) on a certain date, and the signature of the attorney of record (or party, if pro se). *See* Tex. R. Civ. P. 21(d), 21a(a), 57. See "Attorneys of record," ch. 1-H, §3.2.

(2) Method of service. The certificate should identify the method of service. *See* **Dunn v. Menassen**, 913 S.W.2d 621, 626 (Tex.App.—Corpus Christi 1995, writ denied). Although TRCP 21a does not require that the certificate

include the method of service, it can be important for determining the deadline for the response. For example, when a document is served by mail, the deadline is determined by adding three days to the date the document was sent. Tex. R. Civ. P. 21a(c). See "Computing response deadlines," ch. 1-D, §6.

14. Exhibits. A pleading must identify and incorporate by reference the exhibits attached to it and those filed separately. Tex. R. Civ. P. 59. Simply attaching documents to a pleading does not make the documents admissible as evidence. **United Rentals, Inc. v. Smith**, 445 S.W.3d 808, 814 (Tex.App.—El Paso 2014, no pet.); **Ceramic Tile Int'l v. Balusek**, 137 S.W.3d 722, 725 (Tex.App.—San Antonio 2004, no pet.). If a pleading does not incorporate the exhibits by reference, the exhibits do not add anything to the pleading. **Street v. Cunningham**, 156 S.W.2d 541, 542 (Tex.App.—Fort Worth 1941, no writ). TRCP 59 lists the following exhibits that may be attached to a pleading, filed separately, or copied into the body of a pleading: notes, accounts, bonds, mortgages, records, and all other written instruments, in whole or in part, constituting the claim or defense. No other document may be attached as an exhibit to a pleading. Tex. R. Civ. P. 59; *see, e.g.*, **Texas Elec. Serv. v. Commercial Std. Ins.**, 592 S.W.2d 677, 684 (Tex.App.—Fort Worth 1979, writ ref'd n.r.e.) (improper to attach deposition as exhibit to pleading).

15. Verification. When a pleading contains facts outside the record, the party may be required to verify the pleading. A verification is a signed and notarized statement attached to a pleading by which a witness swears that the statements in the pleading are true and correct. *See* Verification, *Black's Law Dictionary* (11th ed. 2019). See **O'Connor's Texas Civil Forms**, FORM 1B:7 (2020 ed.). Some formal pleadings must be verified. See "Verified pleas," ch. 3-E, §4.

Note

Under CPRC §132.001, an unsworn declaration can be used instead of a verification. See "Unsworn declaration," ch. 1-B, §3.2.17.

---

16. Affidavits. When a pleading contains facts outside the record, the party may be required to verify the facts with an affidavit. An affidavit is a written, factual statement signed by the person making it, sworn to before an officer authorized to administer oaths, and officially certified by the officer under seal of office. Tex. Gov't Code §312.011(1); **Mansions in the Forest, L.P. v. Montgomery Cty.**, 365 S.W.3d 314, 316 (Tex.2012); **Ford Motor Co. v. Leggat**, 904 S.W.2d 643, 645–46 (Tex.1995). See **O'Connor's Texas Civil Forms**, FORM 1B:8 (2020 ed.).

Note

Under CPRC §132.001, an unsworn declaration can be used instead of an affidavit. See "Unsworn declaration," ch. 1-B, §3.2.17.

---

(1) Form of affidavit.

(a) Caption. The affidavit should contain a caption, such as "Affidavit of ________." *See* **Acme Brick v. Temple Assocs.**, 816 S.W.2d 440, 441 (Tex.App.—Waco 1991, writ denied).

(b) Venue. The affidavit should state the county and state in which it was made. *See* **Acme Brick**, 816 S.W.2d at 441.

(c) Body. The affidavit should contain the facts in the body of the instrument. *See* **Acme Brick**, 816 S.W.2d at 441.

(d) Affiant's signature. The affidavit must contain the affiant's signature. Tex. Gov't Code §312.011(1). If the affidavit is not signed by the affiant, the affidavit provides no support for the motion and is fatally defective. *See* **Hawthorne v. Guenther**, 917 S.W.2d 924, 929 (Tex.App.—Beaumont 1996, writ denied).

(e) Jurat. The affidavit must contain a jurat or other evidence that it was sworn to before an authorized officer. **Mansions in the Forest**, 365 S.W.3d at 316–17. A jurat is a certification under seal by an authorized officer (generally a notary public) stating that the writing was sworn to before the officer. *Id.* at 316. The jurat identifies the officer, the af-

fiant, and the date the affidavit was made. *See* Jurat, *Black's Law Dictionary* (11th ed. 2019). See **O'Connor's Texas Civil Forms**, FORM 1B:10 (2020 ed.). Gov't Code §312.011(1) requires that an affidavit be sworn to, but it does not specifically require a jurat. **Mansions in the Forest**, 365 S.W.3d at 316. Normally, an affiant includes a jurat to prove that the written statement was made under oath before an authorized officer. *Id.* at 316–17. If the written statement does not include a jurat, there must be other evidence in the record to show that the written statement was sworn to before an authorized officer; otherwise, the statement is not an affidavit. *Id.* at 317.

(f) Officer's seal & signature. The affidavit must contain the authorized officer's seal and signature. *See* Tex. Gov't Code §312.011(1); **Mansions in the Forest**, 365 S.W.3d at 316; **Leggat**, 904 S.W.2d at 645–46; **Griffin v. Baylor Coll. of Med.**, 945 S.W.2d 158, 159–60 (Tex.App.—Houston [1st Dist.] 1997, no pet.).

(2) Competency of witness. An affidavit must show that it was made by a person who is competent to testify. *See* Tex. R. Evid. 601(a) (every person, including a child, is presumed competent to testify unless person is determined to be insane or found to lack sufficient intellect). The affiant must be able to accurately perceive, recall, and recount. Brown & Rondon, **Texas Rules of Evidence Handbook**, Rule 601 (2021 ed.) (n.13). Competency is determined by the trial court, which is not bound by the rules of evidence other than those relating to privilege. Tex. R. Evid. 104(a); Brown & Rondon, **Texas Rules of Evidence Handbook**, Rule 601 (2021 ed.) (n.23). Competency refers to the person's ability to be a witness—for example, is the witness too young, too old, or too mentally unstable to testify? Competency does not refer to the sufficiency of the specific testimony, which is an issue of personal knowledge. *See* Tex. R. Evid. 602; Brown & Rondon, **Texas Rules of Evidence Handbook**, Rule 601 (2021 ed.) (nn.26–27). However, the courts sometimes incorrectly treat the affiant's competency and personal knowledge as the same issue. *See, e.g.*, **Laidlaw Waste Sys. v. City of Wilmer**, 904 S.W.2d 656, 661 (Tex.1995) (witness was found not competent to testify about property metes and bounds because he made only conclusory statements); **First Nat'l Bank v. Lubbock Feeders, L.P.**, 183 S.W.3d 875, 881 (Tex.App.—Eastland 2006, pet. denied) (affiant was found competent to testify because affidavit established he had personal knowledge of the transactions).

(3) Factual statements.

(a) Personal knowledge. An affidavit must be based on the affiant's personal knowledge and must state that the facts in it are true. **Humphreys v. Caldwell**, 888 S.W.2d 469, 470 (Tex.1994); *see* Tex. R. Evid. 602 (evidence must show witness has personal knowledge); *see, e.g.*, **Agar Corp. v. Electro Circuits Int'l**, 580 S.W.3d 136, 148 (Tex.2019) (affidavit stating that it was taken on affiant's oath and that facts were based on his personal knowledge was sufficient); **Kerlin v. Arias**, 274 S.W.3d 666, 668 (Tex.2008) (affidavit that did not show how witness could have personal knowledge of events from the 1840s was insufficient). Personal knowledge is whether the witness knows enough about the subject to testify. *See* Tex. R. Evid. 104(b), 602. Any qualifying statement about the affiant's personal knowledge makes the affidavit legally invalid. *See, e.g.*, **Ryland Grp. v. Hood**, 924 S.W.2d 120, 122 (Tex.1996) (affiant's statement about his "understanding" was conclusory and would not support summary judgment); **Humphreys**, 888 S.W.2d at 470–71 (affiant's statement that information was based on personal knowledge acquired from inquiry made affidavit invalid). The affidavit must contain direct and unequivocal statements that, if false, would be grounds for perjury. **Burke v. Satterfield**, 525 S.W.2d 950, 955 (Tex.1975); **Hall v. Stephenson**, 919 S.W.2d 454, 466 (Tex.App.—Fort Worth 1996, writ denied). For a discussion of the personal-knowledge requirement and summary-judgment affidavits, see "Personal knowledge," ch. 7-B, §9.4.4.

(b) Knowledge & belief. By statute or rule, some affidavits may be made on "knowledge and belief." *See, e.g.*, Tex. R. Civ. P. 18a(a)(4)(A) (motion to recuse or disqualify judge), Tex. R. Civ. P. 93(7), (8), (13), (15) (certain verified denials). An affidavit cannot be based on "knowledge and belief" unless it is authorized by a special statute or rule. **Burke**, 525 S.W.2d at 954–55; **Slater v. Metro Nissan**, 801 S.W.2d 253, 254 (Tex.App.—Fort Worth 1990, writ denied); *see, e.g.*, **Noriega v. Mireles**, 925 S.W.2d 261, 263–64 (Tex.App.—Corpus Christi 1996, writ denied) (expert's affidavit made on his "best knowledge and belief" was not fatally defective because TRE 702 and 703 contemplate that experts bring more to court than their personal knowledge of facts). TRCP 166a does not authorize an affidavit made on knowledge and belief to be used as summary-judgment proof. *See, e.g.*, **Kerlin**, 274 S.W.3d at 668 (affiant's statement "to the best of my personal knowledge and belief" would not support summary judgment).

(4) Executed by party or agent. TRCP 14 provides that whenever an affidavit is required, it may be made by either the party or the party's agent or attorney. However, before assuming that an affidavit may be made by someone else, the party should check the statutes and rules. *E.g.*, Tex. R. Civ. P. 197.2(d) & cmt. 2 (certain interrogatories must be signed by party under oath).

(5) Copy of affidavit. If a copy of an affidavit is admitted, the copy does not need to be authenticated unless (1) a question is raised about the original's authenticity or (2) the circumstances make it unfair to admit the copy. Tex. R. Evid. 1003; *see* **Leggat**, 904 S.W.2d at 646.

(6) Exhibits. If there are exhibits attached to an affidavit, the affidavit must show they are authentic and admissible. *See* Tex. R. Evid. 901(a).

(a) Authentic. To authenticate the exhibit, the affidavit should state that the attached exhibit is a true and correct copy of the original or that it is self-proving. *See* **Kleven v. TDCJ-Inst. Div.**, 69 S.W.3d 341, 345 (Tex.App.—Texarkana 2002, no pet.). An exhibit attached to an affidavit is not competent summary-judgment evidence unless the exhibit is self-proving or the affidavit proves the exhibit is true. *See* **Republic Nat'l Leasing Corp. v. Schindler**, 717 S.W.2d 606, 607 (Tex.1986) (documents submitted as summary-judgment proof must be sworn or certified); **Norcross v. Conoco, Inc.**, 720 S.W.2d 627, 632 (Tex.App.—San Antonio 1986, no writ) (documents submitted as summary-judgment proof must be authenticated by affidavit). See "Authenticity," ch. 8-C, §8.4.

(b) Admissible. To show the admissibility of the exhibit, the affidavit should overcome any objection to the exhibit's admissibility. For example, invoices attached as exhibits are not admissible without the statements required by TRE 803(6) and 902(10). *See* **Norcross**, 720 S.W.2d at 632. See "Introducing documents," ch. 8-C, §8.

17. Unsworn declaration.

(1) Generally. When an affidavit, verification, written sworn declaration, certification, or oath is required, any person can instead make an unsworn declaration. Tex. Civ. Prac. & Rem. Code §132.001(a). See **O'Connor's Texas Civil Forms**, FORM 1B:9 (2020 ed.).

(a) Format—generally. The unsworn declaration must (1) be in writing, (2) be subscribed by the declarant as true and correct under penalty of perjury, and (3) include a jurat with the declarant's name, date of birth, and address. Tex. Civ. Prac. & Rem. Code §132.001(c), (d); *see, e.g.*, **Hays St. Bridge Restoration Grp. v. City of San Antonio**, 570 S.W.3d 697, 702 & n.15 (Tex.2019) (declaration that stated it was made under penalty of perjury but did not include declarant's date of birth in jurat could not support party's motion). At least one court has held that a declaration made under federal perjury penalties is sufficient. **United Rentals**, 445 S.W.3d at 813. The jurat must substantially comply with the format in CPRC §132.001(d).

Note

A guardian may use an unsworn declaration instead of the affidavit or declaration required by Estates Code §1163.101 when filing an annual report, but the unsworn declaration must comply with the requirements in Estates Code §1163.1011(b); an unsworn declaration authorized by CPRC §132.001 cannot be used. Tex. Est. Code §1163.1011.

(b) Format—inmate. If an inmate makes an unsworn declaration, the declaration must (1) be in writing, (2) be subscribed by the declarant as true and correct under penalty of perjury, and (3) include a jurat with the declarant's name, date of birth, inmate identification number, if any, and the name and address of the corrections unit. Tex. Civ. Prac. & Rem. Code §132.001(c), (e). The jurat must substantially comply with the format in CPRC §132.001(e).

(c) Format—state employee. If an employee of a state agency or political subdivision makes an unsworn declaration in the course of her duties, the declaration must (1) be in writing, (2) be subscribed by the declarant as true and correct under penalty of perjury, and (3) include a jurat with the declarant's name and the name of the government agency that employs the declarant. Tex. Civ. Prac. & Rem. Code §132.001(c), (f). The jurat must substantially comply with the format in CPRC §132.001(f).

(2) Exceptions. A person cannot make an unsworn declaration for the following:

(a) A lien filed with a county clerk. Tex. Civ. Prac. & Rem. Code §132.001(b).

(b) An instrument concerning property filed with a county clerk. *Id.*

(c) An oath of office. *Id.*

(d) An oath before a specified official other than a notary public. *Id.*

(e) A self-proved will executed on or after January 1, 2014. *See* Tex. Est. Code §21.005; Acts 2013, 83rd Leg., R.S., ch. 1136, §1, eff. Jan. 1, 2014.

18. Notice of party's name & address. Each party's name and address must be provided in writing to the clerk when the party files its initial pleading or within seven days after the clerk requests the information, and whenever the party changes its address. Tex. Civ. Prac. & Rem. Code §30.015(a), (c), (d). To comply with CPRC §30.015, an attorney—when filing the first pleading in the case—should file a one-page notice, titled "Notice of Current Address," that contains the caption of the case, the party's name and current address, and the attorney's signature. See **O'Connor's Texas Civil Forms**, FORM 1B:14 (2020 ed.).

19. Notice to Attorney General.

(1) Suits involving the State. If a party files suit in certain cases involving the State of Texas, the party must mail a copy of the petition to the Attorney General. *See* Tex. Civ. Prac. & Rem. Code §30.004(a), (b). The party must mail a copy of the petition for suits in which (1) the State of Texas is named as a party, (2) an agency in the legislative or executive department is named as a party, or (3) the Attorney General may represent a party based on state liability for conduct of a public servant under CPRC chapter 104. Tex. Civ. Prac. & Rem. Code §30.004(a). The petition must be mailed to the Attorney General's office in Austin, Texas by certified mail, return receipt requested. Tex. Civ. Prac. & Rem. Code §30.004(b). Mailing the petition does not relieve the party from serving process on any named party in the case. Tex. Civ. Prac. & Rem. Code §30.004(c). See "Serving the Defendant with Suit," ch. 2-I, §1 et seq. If the required notice is not given, any default judgment in the case can be set aside without costs. Tex. Civ. Prac. & Rem. Code §30.004(d). See "After notice to Attorney General," ch. 7-A, §3.9.1(4).

(2) Suits involving constitutional challenge.

(a) Generally. If a party files a petition, motion, or other pleading challenging the constitutionality of a Texas statute, the party must also file a form with the court in which the suit is pending that identifies which pleading contains the constitutional challenge. *See* Tex. Gov't Code §402.010(a), (a-1). See **O'Connor's Texas Civil Forms**, FORM 2B:25 (2020 ed.). The form, Challenge to Constitutionality of a State Statute, is available at www.txcourts.gov/rules-forms/forms. The court must then serve notice of the constitutional challenge and a copy of the pleading on the Attorney General, unless the Attorney General is a party to or counsel in the suit. Tex. Gov't Code §402.010(a); *see also* Tex. Const. art. 5, §32(1) (Legislature is authorized to require court to provide notice to Attorney General). Notice must be sent either by certified or registered mail or electronically to an e-mail address designated by the Attorney General. Tex. Gov't Code §402.010(a). Even if the party does not file the form with the court or the court does not properly serve notice, the court retains jurisdiction over the case and any timely filed claim or defense based on the constitutional challenge is not forfeited. Tex. Gov't Code §402.010(c). However, a court cannot enter a final judgment holding a Texas statute unconstitutional until 45 days after the date notice is served on the Attorney General. Tex. Gov't Code §402.010(b); *see also* Tex. Const. art. 5, §32(2) (Legislature is authorized to prescribe period of up to 45 days during which court cannot enter final judgment).

(b) Declaratory action. If a party files an action for declaratory relief that challenges the constitutionality of a statute, an ordinance, or a franchise, the Attorney General must be served with a copy of the pleadings. Tex. Civ. Prac. & Rem. Code §37.006(b); *see* **Scurlock Permian Corp. v. Brazos Cty.**, 869 S.W.2d 478, 483 (Tex.App.—Houston [1st Dist.] 1993, writ denied) (trial court has no jurisdiction if Attorney General is not notified of declaratory-judgment action based on constitutional challenge to statute, ordinance, or franchise). See "Declaratory Judgment," ch. 2-E, §1 et seq.

20. Case-information sheet. A party is no longer required to file a civil-case-information sheet. TRCP 78a, which required all original petitions and applications filed in district and county-level courts to include a case-information

sheet, was repealed effective December 11, 2018. *See* Tex.Sup.Ct. Order, Misc. Docket No. 18-9163 (eff. Dec. 11, 2018). Similarly, TRCP 502.2(b), which required a case-information sheet to be included with all original petitions filed in justice court, was repealed effective February 26, 2019. *See* Tex.Sup.Ct. Order, Misc. Docket No. 19-9017 (eff. Feb. 26, 2019). Filing a case-information sheet is no longer necessary because the required information is recorded in the e-filing system. Tex.Sup.Ct. Order, Misc. Docket No. 18-9163 (eff. Dec. 11, 2018).

§3.3 Groundless or frivolous pleadings. A party or attorney who files groundless or frivolous pleadings may be sanctioned under CPRC chapter 9 (frivolous pleadings), CPRC chapter 10 (frivolous pleadings), and TRCP 13 (groundless pleadings).

1. Purpose. The purpose of CPRC chapter 9, CPRC chapter 10, and TRCP 13 is to curb abuses in the pleading process so that when a pleading is filed, the litigant's position is factually well-grounded and legally tenable. *See* **Skepnek v. Mynatt**, 8 S.W.3d 377, 381–82 (Tex.App.—El Paso 1999, pet. denied) (CPRC ch. 10 and TRCP 13); **Falk & Mayfield L.L.P. v. Molzan**, 974 S.W.2d 821, 827 (Tex.App.—Houston [14th Dist.] 1998, pet. denied) (TRCP 13); **Herrmann & Andreas Ins. Agency, Inc. v. Appling**, 800 S.W.2d 312, 320 (Tex.App.—Corpus Christi 1990, no writ) (CPRC §9.012).

2. Sanctions. For a discussion of a motion for sanctions for frivolous or groundless pleadings, see "Motion for Sanctions," ch. 5-K, §1 et seq.

§3.4 Vexatious litigant. CPRC chapter 11 provides a procedure to restrict the filing of vexatious litigation.

1. Applicability. CPRC chapter 11 applies to pro se plaintiffs. *See* Tex. Civ. Prac. & Rem. Code §11.001(5); **Morgan v. Talley**, 597 S.W.3d 607, 610 (Tex.App.—El Paso 2020, no pet.); *see, e.g.*, **1901 NW 28th St. Trust v. Lillian Wilson, LLC**, 535 S.W.3d 96, 98–100 (Tex.App.—Fort Worth 2017, no pet.) (even though case was styled in name of trust, pro se individual commenced suit and thus was P under statute). It does not apply to attorneys licensed in Texas unless the attorney appears pro se. Tex. Civ. Prac. & Rem. Code §11.002(a). It also does not apply to municipal-court proceedings. Tex. Civ. Prac. & Rem. Code §11.002(b).

2. Types of motions. The statute provides two different methods for restricting a plaintiff from filing vexatious litigation: (1) a motion by the defendant requesting that the plaintiff in a current lawsuit be declared a vexatious litigant and be required to furnish security and (2) a motion by any party or the court on its own initiative requesting that a person be prohibited from filing new litigation without the permission of the local administrative judge. *See* Tex. Civ. Prac. & Rem. Code §§11.051, 11.101(a).

Note

For practical purposes, a defendant may choose to file a single motion requesting that the plaintiff be declared a vexatious litigant and that the plaintiff be prohibited from filing new litigation. See ***O'Connor's Texas Civil Forms**, FORM 1B:16 (2020 ed.).*

---

(1) Motion for vexatious-litigant determination and for security. A defendant can file a motion asking the court to determine that the plaintiff is a vexatious litigant and to require the plaintiff to furnish security. Tex. Civ. Prac. & Rem. Code §11.051. See **O'Connor's Texas Civil Forms**, FORM 1B:16 (2020 ed.).

(a) Deadline. The defendant must file the motion within 90 days after it files its original answer or makes its special appearance. Tex. Civ. Prac. & Rem. Code §11.051; **Spiller v. Spiller**, 21 S.W.3d 451, 454 (Tex.App.—San Antonio 2000, no pet.).

(b) Grounds. The defendant must first show there is no reasonable probability that the plaintiff will prevail in the litigation. Tex. Civ. Prac. & Rem. Code §11.054; **1901 NW 28th St. Trust**, 535 S.W.3d at 99; **Amir-Sharif v. Quick Trip Corp.**, 416 S.W.3d 914, 919 (Tex.App.—Dallas 2013, no pet.); **Douglas v. American Title Co.**, 196 S.W.3d 876, 880 (Tex.App.—Houston [1st Dist.] 2006, no pet.). The defendant must then show one of the following:

[1] Multiple lawsuits. In the seven years before the motion, the plaintiff (while acting pro se) commenced, prosecuted, or maintained at least five lawsuits that were (1) decided against the plaintiff, (2) pending for at least

two years without being brought to trial or hearing, or (3) determined by a trial or appellate court to be frivolous or groundless. Tex. Civ. Prac. & Rem. Code §11.054(1); *e.g.*, **Yazdchi v. Jones**, 499 S.W.3d 564, 569–70 (Tex.App.—Houston [1st Dist.] 2016, pet. denied) (independent executor was litigant under §11.054 because she was party to suit; cases in which P had acted as pro se executor counted toward five-case requirement in §11.054(1)); *see, e.g.*, **1901 NW 28th St. Trust**, 535 S.W.3d at 101–02 (case in which P was initially represented by attorney but then maintained suit pro se after attorney withdrew counted toward five-case requirement in §11.054(1)).

[2] Relitigation. Another lawsuit between the parties was finally determined against the plaintiff, and the plaintiff (while acting pro se) repeatedly relitigated or attempted to relitigate the cause of action, claim, controversy, issues of fact, issues of law, or validity of the final judgment against the same defendant. Tex. Civ. Prac. & Rem. Code §11.054(2); **Akinwamide v. Transportation Ins.**, 499 S.W.3d 511, 531 (Tex.App.—Houston [1st Dist.] 2016, pet. denied).

[3] Declared vexatious litigant. The plaintiff was already declared a vexatious litigant by a state or federal court in an action or proceeding based on the same or substantially similar facts, transactions, or occurrences. Tex. Civ. Prac. & Rem. Code §11.054(3).

(c) Stay of litigation. A motion filed under CPRC §11.051 stays the litigation until the trial court rules on the motion. Tex. Civ. Prac. & Rem. Code §11.052; **Douglas**, 196 S.W.3d at 880.

(d) Response. A plaintiff is not required to file a response; however, if the plaintiff chooses to respond, she should refute the defendant's arguments and file the response before the hearing. See **O'Connor's Texas Civil Forms**, FORM 1B:17 (2020 ed.).

(e) Hearing. The court, after notice to all parties, must conduct a hearing on the motion. Tex. Civ. Prac. & Rem. Code §11.053(a); **Akinwamide**, 499 S.W.3d at 531 (on court's own motion).

[1] Notice. Notice must be served on all parties at least three days before the hearing. Tex. R. Civ. P. 21(b).

[2] Evidence. The court can consider written or oral evidence and testimony presented by witnesses or by affidavits. Tex. Civ. Prac. & Rem. Code §11.053(b).

(f) Order. If the defendant meets its burden, the court may declare that the plaintiff is a vexatious litigant. *See* Tex. Civ. Prac. & Rem. Code §11.054; **Leonard v. Abbott**, 171 S.W.3d 451, 458–59 (Tex.App.—Austin 2005, pet. denied). If the court finds that the plaintiff is a vexatious litigant, it must order the plaintiff to furnish security to cover reasonable expenses incurred by the defendant, including costs and attorney fees, that will be recoverable by the defendant if the litigation is dismissed on the merits. *See* Tex. Civ. Prac. & Rem. Code §§11.055, 11.057. See **O'Connor's Texas Civil Forms**, FORM 1B:18 (2020 ed.). If the plaintiff does not furnish security within the time period ordered by the court, the litigation will be dismissed. Tex. Civ. Prac. & Rem. Code §11.056.

(2) Motion for prefiling order to prohibit new litigation. Any party, or a court on its own initiative, can move to prohibit a person from filing new litigation as a pro se party. Tex. Civ. Prac. & Rem. Code §11.101(a); **Devoll v. State**, 155 S.W.3d 498, 501–02 (Tex.App.—San Antonio 2004, no pet.); *see, e.g.*, **In re Douglas**, 333 S.W.3d 273, 280 (Tex.App.—Houston [1st Dist.] 2010, pet. denied) (on court's own motion).

(a) Grounds. The motion must show that the person (1) is a vexatious litigant and (2) has not obtained permission to file new litigation from the appropriate local administrative judge. *See* Tex. Civ. Prac. & Rem. Code §11.101(a); **Akinwamide**, 499 S.W.3d at 531; **Devoll**, 155 S.W.3d at 502; *see also* Tex. Civ. Prac. & Rem. Code §11.102(a) (determining appropriate local administrative judge). For the criteria for declaring a person a vexatious litigant, see "Grounds," ch. 1-B, §3.4.2(1)(b).

(b) Prefiling order—litigation prohibited. If the person has been declared a vexatious litigant after notice and a hearing under CPRC §11.053, the court can issue a prefiling order prohibiting the person from filing new litigation as a pro se party unless the person obtains permission from the appropriate local administrative judge. Tex. Civ. Prac. & Rem. Code §11.101(a); *see also* Tex. Civ. Prac. & Rem. Code §11.102(a) (determining appropriate local administrative judge).

If a district or statutory county court enters the order, the order applies to all Texas state courts. Tex. Civ. Prac. & Rem. Code §11.101(e). If a justice court or constitutional county court enters the order, the order applies only to the court that entered the order. Tex. Civ. Prac. & Rem. Code §11.101(d).

Note

The Office of Court Administration must post on its website a list of vexatious litigants subject to a prefiling order under CPRC §11.101(a). Tex. Civ. Prac. & Rem. Code §11.104(b). If requested by the person designated as a vexatious litigant, the list must indicate whether an appeal of that designation has been filed. Id. See "Appeal," ch. 1-B, §3.4.2(3)(b).

(c) Request for permission to file. Even if a prefiling order has been entered prohibiting the vexatious litigant from filing new litigation as a pro se party, she can request permission from the local administrative judge to file the proposed litigation. *See* Tex. Civ. Prac. & Rem. Code §§11.101(a), 11.102(a).

[1] Request.

[a] File with local administrative judge. A vexatious litigant who wishes to file litigation should file a request with the appropriate local administrative judge. *See* Tex. Civ. Prac. & Rem. Code §11.102. If the vexatious litigant intends to file the proposed litigation in a justice or constitutional county court, she must get the permission of the local administrative judge of the county where the court sits. Tex. Civ. Prac. & Rem. Code §11.102(a)(2). If the vexatious litigant intends to file in any other court, she must get the permission of the local administrative judge of the type of court in which she intends to file. Tex. Civ. Prac. & Rem. Code §11.102(a)(1).

[b] Provide copies. The vexatious litigant must provide a copy of the request to all defendants named in the proposed litigation. Tex. Civ. Prac. & Rem. Code §11.102(b).

[2] Hearing. The local administrative judge has discretion to decide whether to hold a hearing to determine whether the vexatious litigant can proceed with the proposed litigation. Tex. Civ. Prac. & Rem. Code §11.102(c). If the judge decides to hold a hearing, the judge can require that the litigant provide notice of the hearing to all named defendants in the proposed litigation. *Id.*

[3] Local administrative judge's determination.

[a] Deny request. If the local administrative judge denies the request for permission to file the proposed litigation, the vexatious litigant cannot file the litigation. *See* Tex. Civ. Prac. & Rem. Code §11.102(a).

[b] Grant request. The local administrative judge may grant the request for permission to file the proposed litigation if the judge finds that the litigation has merit and has not been filed to harass or cause delay. Tex. Civ. Prac. & Rem. Code §11.102(d). The judge may condition the permission on the vexatious litigant furnishing adequate security for the defendant's benefit. Tex. Civ. Prac. & Rem. Code §11.102(e).

(d) Mistaken filing after order. If a court clerk mistakenly files pro se litigation subject to a prefiling order, any party can file with the clerk and serve on all parties to the litigation a notice showing that the plaintiff is a vexatious litigant. Tex. Civ. Prac. & Rem. Code §11.1035(a). See **O'Connor's Texas Civil Forms**, FORM 1B:19 (2020 ed.). Within one business day after receiving the notice, the clerk must notify the court that the litigation was mistakenly filed, and the court must immediately stay the litigation. Tex. Civ. Prac. & Rem. Code §11.1035(b). If the vexatious litigant does not receive permission to file from the appropriate local administrative judge under CPRC §11.102(a) within ten days of the filing of the notice, the litigation will be dismissed. Tex. Civ. Prac. & Rem. Code §11.1035(b).

(3) Review.

(a) Standard of review. The court's determination of whether a person is a vexatious litigant is reviewed for abuse of discretion. **Morgan**, 597 S.W.3d at 609; **1901 NW 28th St. Trust**, 535 S.W.3d at 99; **Akinwamide**, 499 S.W.3d at 530.

(b) Appeal. A person may appeal an order under CPRC §11.101(a) designating her as a vexatious litigant and prohibiting her from filing new litigation. Tex. Civ. Prac. & Rem. Code §11.101(c). But a local administrative judge's decision under CPRC §11.102 to deny a person permission to file new litigation or to condition permission on furnishing security cannot be appealed. Tex. Civ. Prac. & Rem. Code §11.102(f).

(c) Mandamus. A person may file a writ of mandamus with the court of appeals to review a local administrative judge's decision under CPRC §11.102 to deny the person permission to file new litigation or to condition permission on furnishing security. Tex. Civ. Prac. & Rem. Code §11.102(f). The writ of mandamus must be filed within 30 days after the local administrative judge's decision. *Id.* If the writ of mandamus is denied, the person cannot seek relief in the Supreme Court. *Id.*

§3.5 Defective pleadings.

1. Waiver of pleading defect. There are two types of pleading defects that the opponent must object to: (1) defects in form (e.g., failure to include a verification) and (2) defects in substance (e.g., failure to plead a cause of action or defense with sufficient specificity). **Aquila Sw. Pipeline, Inc. v. Harmony Expl., Inc.**, 48 S.W.3d 225, 233 (Tex.App.—San Antonio 2001, pet. denied). If the opponent does not object to these pleading defects by special exception before the charge to the jury, or in nonjury cases before the judgment is signed, the defects are waived. Tex. R. Civ. P. 90; *see* **Shoemake v. Fogel, Ltd.**, 826 S.W.2d 933, 937 (Tex.1992). For example, when a plaintiff claims that a defendant's action caused injury but does not use the term "negligence," the error is waived unless the defendant objects to the petition by special exception. *See* **Roark v. Allen**, 633 S.W.2d 804, 810 (Tex.1982). See "Special Exceptions—Challenging the Pleadings," ch. 3-G, §1 et seq. If the pleadings are defective, the party should immediately move to amend. See "Amending or supplementing pleadings," ch. 1-B, §3.6; "Options for plaintiff," ch. 3-G, §9.3. An objection to a pleading defect is not necessary in a case resolved by a default judgment. Tex. R. Civ. P. 90; **Stoner v. Thompson**, 578 S.W.2d 679, 684–85 (Tex.1979).

2. Trial by consent. Generally, a party cannot obtain discovery, offer evidence, or submit jury questions on issues that were not pleaded. However, an issue that is not included in the pleadings is "tried by consent" when it is supported by evidence at trial and is submitted to the jury without objection. See "Issue tried by consent," ch. 8-F, §2.4.2(1). If the opponent objects to evidence on the ground that the issue was not pleaded, or objects to the submission of the jury question for the same reason, the issue is not tried by consent. See "Issue not tried by consent," ch. 8-F, §2.4.2(2).

§3.6 Amending or supplementing pleadings.

1. Two methods. The rules permit the parties to change, correct, revise, or explain filed pleadings by filing amended or supplemental pleadings. The statute of limitations is tolled and the amended or supplemental pleading relates back to the original pleading unless the amended or supplemental pleading alleges a wholly new, distinct, or different transaction. Tex. Civ. Prac. & Rem. Code §16.068; **Alexander v. Turtur & Assocs.**, 146 S.W.3d 113, 121 (Tex.2004). See "Amended or supplemental pleading," **O'Connor's Texas Causes of Action**, ch. 52, §4.4 (2021 ed.).

(1) Amended pleadings. An amended pleading adds or withdraws matters to correct or change the previous pleading. Tex. R. Civ. P. 62; **J.M. Huber Corp. v. Santa Fe Energy Res.**, 871 S.W.2d 842, 844 (Tex.App.—Houston [14th Dist.] 1994, writ denied); *see* **Retzlaff v. TDCJ**, 135 S.W.3d 731, 737 (Tex.App.—Houston [1st Dist.] 2003, no pet.) (amended pleading appropriate to add new cause of action or affirmative defense); **Tex-Hio Prtshp. v. Garner**, 106 S.W.3d 886, 890 (Tex.App.—Dallas 2003, no pet.) (amended pleading appropriate to bring new parties into suit). The amended pleading must comply with the rules that applied to the original pleading (e.g., if the original pleading was verified, the amended pleading must also be verified). The last amended pleading filed is called the "live" pleading.

(a) Effect on previous pleading. An amended pleading completely replaces and supersedes the previous pleading. **Phifer v. Nacogdoches Cty. Cent. Appr. Dist.**, 45 S.W.3d 159, 172 (Tex.App.—Tyler 2000, pet. denied); *see* Tex. R. Civ. P. 65; **Bos v. Smith**, 556 S.W.3d 293, 306 (Tex.2018); **University of Tex. Health Sci. Ctr. v. Rios**, 542 S.W.3d 530, 538 (Tex.2017). Once an amended pleading is filed, the previous pleading is no longer part of the proceedings. Tex. R. Civ. P. 65; **University of Tex. Health Sci. Ctr.**, 542 S.W.3d at 538; *see* **Drake Ins. v. King**, 606 S.W.2d 812, 817 (Tex.1980). This fact does not, however, nullify the filing of the earlier pleading and does not allow the party to avoid any consequences resulting from that filing. *E.g.*, **University of Tex. Health Sci. Ctr.**, 542 S.W.3d at 538 (P brought tort claims against both D and its doctor-employees; D filed motion to dismiss and triggered right to dismissal under CPRC §101.106(e), which P could not avoid by amending petition to drop tort claims against D).

(b) Effect on omitted party or cause of action. Filing an amended pleading that omits a party or cause of action that was included in the previous pleading effectively nonsuits or voluntarily dismisses that omitted party or cause of action when the amended pleading is filed. **Bos**, 556 S.W.3d at 306 (cause of action); **FKM Prtshp. v. Board of Regents**, 255 S.W.3d 619, 632–33 (Tex.2008) (cause of action); **Randolph v. Jackson Walker L.L.P.**, 29 S.W.3d 271, 274 (Tex.App.—Houston [14th Dist.] 2000, pet. denied) (party).

(c) Effect on statements as judicial admissions. After an amendment, statements in the earlier pleadings are no longer judicial admissions. **Sosa v. Central Power & Light**, 909 S.W.2d 893, 895 (Tex.1995). See "Pleadings as judicial admissions," ch. 1-B, §3.7.

(2) Supplemental pleadings. A supplemental or reply pleading is made in response to an adverse party's last pleading. Tex. R. Civ. P. 69; **Sixth RMA Partners v. Sibley**, 111 S.W.3d 46, 53 (Tex.2003); **J.M. Huber Corp.**, 871 S.W.2d at 844. It adds to, but does not supersede or replace, the previous pleading. The plaintiff's supplemental petition may contain the following matters in reply to what the defendant alleges: special exceptions, general denials, and the allegation of new matters not already alleged. Tex. R. Civ. P. 80. A supplemental pleading should restate only the matters from the previous pleading that are necessary to introduce the things being changed, added, or challenged. *See* Tex. R. Civ. P. 69; **Sibley**, 111 S.W.3d at 53. When a supplemental pleading contains matters outside the scope of TRCP 69, the adverse party must object or it waives the error. *See* **Sibley**, 111 S.W.3d at 54.

Practice Tip

Avoid using supplemental pleadings. If you amend pleadings instead of supplementing them, the case file will contain fewer live pleadings and will be less confusing. See ***Alert Synteks, Inc. v. Jerry Spencer, L.P.****, 151 S.W.3d 246, 253 (Tex.App.—Tyler 2004, no pet.).*

---

2. Procedure for amending pleadings. The procedure for amending pleadings at various stages of the trial is discussed in other sections of this book.

(1) Amending pleadings before trial. See "Motion to Amend Pleadings—Pretrial," ch. 5-F, §1 et seq.

(2) Amending pleadings in a summary-judgment case. See "Amending the petition or answer," ch. 7-B, §8.

(3) Amending pleadings during trial and after verdict. See "Motion to Amend Pleadings—Trial & Post-trial," ch. 8-F, §1 et seq.

3. Appellate review of amended pleadings. On appeal, the court reviews the trial court's rulings on amendments under the abuse-of-discretion standard. **Hardin v. Hardin**, 597 S.W.2d 347, 349–50 (Tex.1980); **Dunnagan v. Watson**, 204 S.W.3d 30, 38 (Tex.App.—Fort Worth 2006, pet. denied). Whether an amendment is appropriate is a function of three factors: the nature of the amendment, the evidence introduced at trial, and the timeliness of the amendment.

(1) Nature of amendment.

(a) Amendment is procedural. If the amendment corrected a procedural defect in the pleadings, it was less likely to cause surprise and should have been permitted, even if late in the trial. *See* **Stephenson v. LeBoeuf**, 16 S.W.3d 829, 839 (Tex.App.—Houston [14th Dist.] 2000, pet. denied) (trial court has no discretion to refuse amendment that is merely procedural); *see, e.g.*, **Chapin & Chapin, Inc. v. Texas Sand & Gravel Co.**, 844 S.W.2d 664, 665 (Tex.1992) (trial court should have permitted D to add verified denial to its answer). See "Procedural change," ch. 5-F, §3 2.3(1); "TRCP 63 & 66," ch. 8-F, §2.4.1.

(b) Amendment is substantive. If the amendment made a substantive change and altered the nature of the trial itself, the trial court had the discretion to deny leave to amend. **Chapin & Chapin**, 844 S.W.2d at 665; *see, e.g.*, **Hardin**, 597 S.W.2d at 350 (trial court had discretion to deny amendment offered on day of trial to add affirmative defenses). On appeal, an appellant who objected to the amendment must show that the amendment (1) caused surprise or prejudice or (2) asserted a new cause of action or defense and thus was prejudicial on its face. **State Bar v. Kilpatrick**, 874 S.W.2d 656,

658 (Tex.1994); **Chapin & Chapin**, 844 S.W.2d at 665; **Stephenson**, 16 S.W.3d at 839. See "Substantive change," ch. 5-F, §3.2.3(2); "TRCP 63 & 66," ch. 8-F, §2.4.1; "Prove surprise or prejudice," ch. 8-F, §3.2.

(2) Evidence introduced at trial. If the amendment conforms the pleadings to the evidence, the trial court should have permitted the amendment. See "TRCP 63 & 66," ch. 8-F, §2.4.1.

(3) Timeliness of amendment. If the amendment was filed as soon as the party realized it was necessary, the trial court should have permitted the amendment because it was unlikely to have surprised or prejudiced the other party. See "Rules for amending pleadings before trial," ch. 5-F, §3; "Motion for leave to amend," ch. 8-F, §2.

§3.7 Pleadings as judicial admissions.

1. Pleading assertions of fact. Assertions of fact in a party's live pleadings that are not pleaded in the alternative are regarded as formal judicial admissions. **Holy Cross Ch. of God in Christ v. Wolf**, 44 S.W.3d 562, 568 (Tex.2001); **Houston First Am. Sav. v. Musick**, 650 S.W.2d 764, 767 (Tex.1983). To be a judicial admission, a statement in a pleading must be deliberate, clear, and unequivocal. **Mapco, Inc. v. Carter**, 817 S.W.2d 686, 687 (Tex.1991); **Charles Brown, L.L.P. v. Lanier Worldwide, Inc.**, 124 S.W.3d 883, 900 (Tex.App.—Houston [14th Dist.] 2004, no pet.); *see* **PPG Indus. v. JMB/Houston Ctrs. Partners**, 146 S.W.3d 79, 95 (Tex.2004). A party may plead alternative theories without judicially admitting them. **Dowling v. NADW Mktg., Inc.**, 631 S.W.2d 726, 729 (Tex.1982); *see* Tex. R. Civ. P. 48.

(1) Effect. A judicial admission is conclusive against the party making it, relieves the opposing party of the burden of proving the admitted fact, and bars the admitting party from disputing it. **Mendoza v. Fidelity & Guar. Ins. Underwriters, Inc.**, 606 S.W.2d 692, 694 (Tex.1980); **Charles Brown, L.L.P.**, 124 S.W.3d at 900; **Frazer v. Texas Farm Bur. Mut. Ins.**, 4 S.W.3d 819, 825 (Tex.App.—Houston [1st Dist.] 1999, no pet.). Once a fact is conclusively established by judicial admission, no jury questions on the fact need to be submitted. **Horizon/CMS Healthcare Corp. v. Auld**, 34 S.W.3d 887, 905 (Tex.2000).

(2) Waiver of judicial admission. A party relying on an opponent's pleadings as judicial admissions of fact must protect the record by objecting both to the introduction of controverting evidence and to the submission of a jury question on the admitted fact. **Marshall v. Vise**, 767 S.W.2d 699, 700 (Tex.1989); **Musick**, 650 S.W.2d at 769; *e.g.*, **Hurlbut v. Gulf Atl. Life Ins.**, 749 S.W.2d 762, 765 (Tex.1987) (admission waived because Ds did not object to submission of jury question). See "Making & Preserving Objections," ch. 1-F, §1 et seq.

(3) Not in superseded pleadings. Statements in superseded pleadings are not conclusive or indisputable judicial admissions. **Sosa v. Central Power & Light**, 909 S.W.2d 893, 895 (Tex.1995); **Drake Ins. v. King**, 606 S.W.2d 812, 817 (Tex.1980). *But see* **H2O Solutions, Ltd. v. PM Rlty. Grp.**, 438 S.W.3d 606, 620 (Tex.App.—Houston [1st Dist.] 2014, pet. denied) (D could rely on statements in affidavit attached to P's earlier petition as judicial admissions when D objected to contrary factual allegations in P's fourth amended petition). Statements in superseded pleadings may, however, be admitted into evidence against the pleader. *See* **Bay Area Healthcare Grp. v. McShane**, 239 S.W.3d 231, 235 (Tex.2007). Because a superseded statement is not conclusive, the pleader may dispute it. **Quick v. Plastic Solutions**, 270 S.W.3d 173, 185 (Tex.App.—El Paso 2008, no pet.).

2. Compared to testimonial admissions. A party's testimonial declarations that are contrary to its position are quasi-admissions, but they are not conclusive. **Hennigan v. I.P. Pet. Co.**, 858 S.W.2d 371, 372 (Tex.1993); **Mendoza**, 606 S.W.2d at 694. Quasi-admissions are distinguishable from true judicial admissions, which are a formal waiver of proof usually found in pleadings or the parties' stipulations. **Mendoza**, 606 S.W.2d at 694. For a party's testimonial quasi-admission to be treated as a conclusive judicial admission, the following must be true: (1) the relied-on declaration was made during a judicial proceeding, (2) the declaration is contrary to a fact that is essential to the testifying person's claim or defense, (3) the declaration was deliberate, clear, and unequivocal, (4) allowing the declaration to have conclusive effect would be consistent with public policy, and (5) the declaration is not destructive to the other party's claim. *Id.*; **Griffin v. Superior Ins.**, 338 S.W.2d 415, 419 (Tex.1960).

Note

An attorney's statements on behalf of a client can serve as judicial admissions if the requirements set out above are shown. ***In re M.M.O.****, 981 S.W.2d 72, 84 (Tex.App.—San Antonio 1998, no pet.);* ***Sepulveda v. Krishnan****, 839 S.W.2d 132, 135 (Tex.App.—Corpus Christi 1992), aff'd, 916 S.W.2d 478 (Tex.1995).*

§4. Motion practice

§4.1 Drafting motions.

1. In writing. Most motions must be in writing. *E.g.*, Tex. R. Civ. P. 86 (motion to transfer venue); **McConnell v. Southside ISD**, 858 S.W.2d 337, 343 n.7 (Tex.1993) (special exceptions); **City of Houston v. Clear Creek Basin Auth.**, 589 S.W.2d 671, 677 (Tex.1979) (motion for summary judgment). Motions that are electronically filed must meet certain additional requirements. See "Format for e-filed pleadings," ch. 1-B, §3.2.1(2).

2. Style. The style is the heading of the motion. It contains the cause number, the names of the parties, the court, and the county of suit. See **O'Connor's Texas Civil Forms**, FORM 1B:2 (2020 ed.).

(1) Cause number. The clerk assigns a cause number to each suit. Tex. R. Civ. P. 23. The parties should make sure all documents are filed with the correct cause number. However, filing a document with the wrong cause number generally should not be considered a jurisdictional defect. *See, e.g.*, **Blankenship v. Robins**, 878 S.W.2d 138, 138–39 (Tex.1994) (motion for new trial with wrong cause number was effective); **McRoberts v. Ryals**, 863 S.W.2d 450, 454–55 (Tex.1993) (same); **City of San Antonio v. Rodriguez**, 828 S.W.2d 417, 418 (Tex.1992) (notice of appeal with wrong cause number was effective). *But see* **Philbrook v. Berry**, 683 S.W.2d 378, 379 (Tex.1985) (motion for new trial was ineffective because of wrong cause number). The **Philbrook** holding on this issue has been distinguished, explained, and questioned into irrelevance. *See* **Paselk v. Rabun**, 293 S.W.3d 600, 606 (Tex.App.—Texarkana 2009, pet. denied) (**Philbrook** has been all but expressly overruled); **In re Old Am. Cty. Mut. Fire Ins.**, No. 13-13-00644-CV, 2014 WL 1633098 (Tex.App.—Corpus Christi 2014, orig. proceeding) (memo op.; 4-23-14) (same).

(2) List of parties. In motions, the list of parties in the style may be shortened by naming the first party and using the inclusive term "et al." *Cf.* **Abramcik v. U.S. Home Corp.**, 792 S.W.2d 822, 824 (Tex.App.—Houston [14th Dist.] 1990, writ denied) (term "et al." can be used in later pleadings). If a party misnames itself or another party in a motion, the error is misnomer and can be corrected by amendment. *E.g.*, **In re Greater Houston Orthopaedic Specialists, Inc.**, 295 S.W.3d 323, 325–26 (Tex.2009) (misnomer when P omitted part of its name from motion for nonsuit). See "Misnomer," ch. 2-B, §4.3.1(2)(a).

3. Caption. The caption is the title of the motion.

(1) Correct title. The title of a motion should be useful to the court, the clerk, and the attorney's files. The title should identify the party who filed the motion and the type of motion (e.g., "Defendant's Motion to Extend Time to . . ."). If there are multiple parties, the title should use an abbreviated name for the party (e.g., "Bank's Motion to . . ."). The title should indicate if a motion is agreed (e.g., "Agreed Motion to . . .") or has been made before (e.g., "Bank's Second Motion to . . .").

(2) Incorrect title. If the party makes an error in the caption of the motion, the court will treat the motion as if it had been properly named. *See* Tex. R. Civ. P. 71; **In re J.Z.P.**, 484 S.W.3d 924, 925 (Tex.2016); **Speer v. Stover**, 685 S.W.2d 22, 23 (Tex.1985). A misnomer of the motion does not make it ineffective. *See* **General Motors Acceptance Corp. v. Harris Cty. MUD**, 899 S.W.2d 821, 824 n.3 (Tex.App.—Houston [14th Dist.] 1995, no writ). The court will look to the substance of a motion to determine its nature. *E.g.*, **In re J.Z.P.**, 484 S.W.3d at 924–25 (motion to reopen and vacate order was treated as motion to extend postjudgment deadlines); **State Bar v. Heard**, 603 S.W.2d 829, 833 (Tex.1980) (motion for summary judgment was actually motion to suspend law license under special statute); *see, e.g.*, **Speer**, 685 S.W.2d at 23 (plea in abatement was actually plea to the jurisdiction); **In re Bokeloh**, 21 S.W.3d 784, 789–90 (Tex.App.—Houston [14th Dist.] 2000, orig. proceeding) (motion to retain was not motion to reinstate because it did not address reinstatement).

4. Contents. A motion must state the relief sought and the grounds for the relief. Tex. R. Civ. P. 21(a).

5. Numbered paragraphs. The paragraphs should be numbered, and each paragraph should be limited to a single set of circumstances. *Cf.* Tex. R. Civ. P. 50 (numbered paragraphs for petitions and answers). Arabic numerals (e.g., 1, 2, 3) should be used, and Roman numerals (e.g., I, II, III) should be avoided.

6. Adoption by reference. Parties may adopt statements by reference from another motion. Tex. R. Civ. P. 58.

7. Prayer. At the end of the motion, under the heading "Prayer," the party should state exactly what relief it seeks. The prayer for relief should match the purpose of the motion. *See, e.g.*, **Finley v. J.C. Pace Ltd.**, 4 S.W.3d 319, 320 (Tex.App.—Houston [1st Dist.] 1999, order) (motion for rehearing was actually motion for new trial because prayer requested relitigation of issues); **Mercer v. Band**, 454 S.W.2d 833, 835–36 (Tex.App.—Houston [14th Dist.] 1970, no writ) (motion for new trial was actually motion for judgment because prayer asked for different judgment, not new trial). See "Prayer," ch. 2-B, §15.

8. Signature block. The requirements for a signature block for motions are the same as for pleadings. See "Signature block," ch. 1-B, §3.2.12.

9. Certificate of conference. All motions relating to discovery should contain a certificate that the party made a reasonable attempt to resolve the discovery dispute without court intervention but failed. Tex. R. Civ. P. 191.2. See "Certificate of conference," ch. 6-A, §4.2; **O'Connor's Texas Civil Forms**, FORM 1B:12 (2020 ed.). Some local rules require a certificate of conference on other motions as well. *E.g.*, Tarrant Cty. Loc. R. 3.06(b) (no motion will be set for hearing without a certificate of conference).

10. Certificate of service. All documents required to be served under TRCP 21 (except those served with citation) must contain a certificate of service in the document itself. *See* Tex. R. Civ. P. 21(d), 21a(a). See "Certificate of service," ch. 1-B, §3.2.13; **O'Connor's Texas Civil Forms**, FORM 1B:13 (2020 ed.).

(1) Pleadings. All pleadings, motions, responses, or applications to the court for an order, unless served with citation or presented during a hearing or trial, must contain a certificate of service. *See* Tex. R. Civ. P. 21(d).

(2) Orders & judgments. All proposed orders and judgments sent to the court separately from a motion or response must contain a certificate of service. See "Certificate of service," ch. 1-G, §4.1.9.

11. Exhibits. Although no rule specifies the method for attaching exhibits to motions, parties should follow the rules for attaching exhibits to pleadings. A motion should identify and incorporate by reference the exhibits attached to it and those filed separately. *See* **Hooks v. Davis**, No. 03-03-00739-CV, 2004 WL 1686551 (Tex.App.—Austin 2004, pet. denied) (memo op.; 7-29-04). See "Exhibits," ch. 1-B, §3.2.14.

12. Verification & affidavits. When a motion contains facts outside the record, the party may be required to verify the motion by attaching a verification or an affidavit. *See* **In re General Agents Ins.**, 254 S.W.3d 670, 676 (Tex.App.—Houston [14th Dist.] 2008, orig. proceeding); **Raymond v. Raymond**, 190 S.W.3d 77, 82 (Tex.App.—Houston [1st Dist.] 2005, no pet.). See "Verification," ch. 1-B, §3.2.15; "Affidavits," ch. 1-B, §3.2.16. For the procedure for using an unsworn declaration instead of a verification or an affidavit, see "Unsworn declaration," ch. 1-B, §3.2.17.

13. Notice to Attorney General. If a party files a motion (or a petition or other pleading) challenging the constitutionality of a Texas statute, the Attorney General must be notified unless the Attorney General is a party to or counsel in the suit. *See* Tex. Gov't Code §402.010(a). For a discussion of this procedure, see "Generally," ch. 1-B, §3.2.19(2)(a).

§4.2 Serving & filing motions. All written motions must be served on all parties. Tex. R. Civ. P. 21(a). See "Rules for Serving Documents," ch. 1-D, §1 et seq. All motions should generally be filed. See "Rules for Filing Documents," ch. 1-C, §1 et seq.

§4.3 Hearing on motions. The court will not always hold a hearing before ruling on a motion. See "Hearing on motion," ch. 1-E, §4.

C. Rules for Filing Documents

§1. General

§1.1 Rules. Tex. R. Civ. P. 4, 5, 21, 21a, 21b, 21c, 23 to 27, 45, 74, 502.1. See Tex. Gov't Code §311.014; Tex. R. App. P. 4.1, 5, 9.

§1.2 Purpose. Documents are filed to put them into the court's record of the lawsuit. Filing documents should not be confused with serving documents. Documents are filed with the clerk; they are served on the other parties in the lawsuit. The rules for filing and serving are different. *Compare* Tex. R. Civ. P. 21 (filing and serving of pleadings and motions) *with* Tex. R. Civ. P. 21a (methods of service). See "Rules for Serving Documents," ch. 1-D, §1 et seq.

Note

Local rules cannot impose additional restrictions on what constitutes a "filing" under the TRCPs (or the TRAPs). ***Jamar v. Patterson,*** *868 S.W.2d 318, 318 n.2 (Tex.1993).*

---

§1.3 Forms. **O'Connor's Texas Civil Forms**, FORMS 1C:1 et seq. (2020 ed.).

§1.4 Other references. Judicial Committee on Information Technology (JCIT) Technology Standards, version 6.5 (Oct. 11, 2019) (referred to as JCIT Tech. Stds., v. 6.5); Jefferson, *Trends & Traps in Rules of Civil Procedure*, Litigation Update Institute, State Bar of Texas CLE, ch. 3.2 (2015); Spencer, *Filing Accepted! Best Practices for E-filing in Texas*, Family Law Technology 360: Everything You Need to Know for Your 21st Century Practice, State Bar of Texas CLE, ch. 5 (2014).

Note

As of the publication of this book, version 6.5 is the most recent version of the technology standards promulgated by the JCIT and approved by the Texas Supreme Court. See Tex.Sup.Ct. Order, Misc. Docket No. 20-9012 (Jan. 14, 2020). To check for newer versions of the technology standards, see the JCIT's website at www.txcourts.gov/jcit or the Court's website at www.txcourts.gov/supreme.

---

§2. What to file

File all pleadings, motions, and other documents unless a rule explicitly states otherwise. *See, e.g.*, Tex. R. Civ. P. 191.4(a) (list of discovery materials that must not be filed).

§2.1 Pleadings. The party should file the signed original of its petition or answer with the court.

§2.2 Motions. The party should file the signed original of any motion or response.

§2.3 Exhibits. The party can attach the original or a copy of an exhibit to the pleading filed with the court. Tex. R. Civ. P. 59. However, an original negotiable financial document should never be filed with the court; instead, a copy should be attached to the pleadings.

§3. With whom to file

§3.1 E-filing. Documents that are electronically filed should be submitted to the party's electronic-filing service provider, which sends the documents through efiletexas.gov to the court clerk. See "How to e-file," ch. 1-C, §4.1.1(3).

§3.2 Paper filing. Documents are considered filed when they reach the court. **Jamar v. Patterson**, 868 S.W.2d 318, 319 (Tex.1993); **In re Smith**, 263 S.W.3d 93, 95 (Tex.App.—Houston [1st Dist.] 2006, orig. proceeding); *see* **Stokes v. Aberdeen Ins.**, 917 S.W.2d 267, 268 (Tex.1996) (mailing document to proper court address controls over naming correct court representative). Documents must be filed with the court clerk unless they are presented during a trial or hearing or given to the judge for filing. *See* Tex. R. Civ. P. 21(a), 74.

1. Clerk. Generally, documents should be presented to the court clerk for filing. Tex. R. Civ. P. 21(a), 74. When the courthouse is closed, documents may be filed with the clerk wherever she can be located, generally at her residence. *See* **Miller Brewing Co. v. Villarreal**, 829 S.W.2d 770, 771 (Tex.1992).

2. Judge. Documents may be filed with the trial judge during a trial or hearing. *See* Tex. R. Civ. P. 21(a), 74. When the courthouse is closed, documents may be filed with the trial judge—with her permission—wherever she can be located, generally at her residence. *See* Tex. R. Civ. P. 74; **Miller Brewing**, 829 S.W.2d at 771. When the trial judge is unavailable, documents may be filed with another judge occupying the same type of bench in the same county. *See, e.g.*, **In re Cuban**, 24 S.W.3d 381, 383 (Tex.App.—Dallas 2000, orig. proceeding) (motion to recuse judge in County Court at Law No. 2 filed with judge of County Court at Law No. 3). The judge must note the date and time of filing on the document and forward it to the clerk's office. Tex. R. Civ. P. 74.

§4. How to file

§4.1 Methods of filing. Traditionally, documents could be filed by mail, by delivery, by fax, or electronically. Now, most documents must be e-filed—as of July 1, 2016, e-filing is mandatory for all nonjuvenile civil cases in most courts in all counties. *See* Tex. R. Civ. P. 21 cmt.; Tex.Sup.Ct. Order, Misc. Docket No. 13-9164 (Dec. 9, 2013). Parties required to e-file cannot use alternative means of electronic filing, including fax filing, unless there is an emergency. Tex.Sup.Ct. Order, Misc. Docket No. 13-9164 (Dec. 9, 2013).

1. E-filing. E-filing allows a party to file a document with a court through the online computer transmission of an electronic form of the document. *See* Tex. R. Civ. P. 21(f)(3). E-filing is now mandatory in all nonjuvenile civil cases, including family and probate cases, in a district court, statutory county court, constitutional county court, or statutory probate court. Tex.Sup.Ct. Order, Misc. Docket No. 13-9164 (Dec. 9, 2013); *see* Tex. R. Civ. P. 21(f)(1) (attorneys must e-file except in juvenile cases under Family Code title 3 and truancy cases under Family Code title 3A). E-filing is optional in a justice court if that court permits it. *See* Tex. R. Civ. P. 502.1. For a list of justice courts that permit e-filing, see www.efiletexas.gov/active-courts/dcpj-courts.htm. E-filing in any district, county, or justice court is governed by TRCP 21. *See* Tex. R. Civ. P. 21(f), 502.1. All other district, county, and justice-court e-filing rules and local rules based on e-filing templates have been superseded. Tex.Sup.Ct. Order, Misc. Docket No. 13-9165 (eff. Jan. 1, 2014).

Note

E-filing facilitates access to court documents that is more efficient for judges, clerks, attorneys, and parties, reducing costs to taxpayers, attorneys, and litigants. Tex.Sup.Ct. Order, Misc. Docket No. 17-9025, ¶3 (eff. Feb. 21, 2017). An attorney has permission to access case-index information and all e-filed documents for any case in which she is the attorney of record or has made an appearance. Id. at ¶4; see also Tex.Sup.Ct. Order, Misc. Docket No. 18-9132, ¶4 (eff. Oct. 2, 2018) (licensed attorneys can access case-index information and all publicly available e-filed documents relating to any case in which they may have an interest).

---

(1) Who e-files.

(a) Required parties. Any party represented by an attorney must e-file most documents in the courts where mandatory e-filing has been implemented. Tex. R. Civ. P. 21(f)(1).

(b) Optional parties. The following parties are not required to e-file but may do so if e-filing is available:

[1] A party not represented by an attorney. Tex. R. Civ. P. 21(f)(1).

[2] A party, whether represented by an attorney or not, filing in a justice court. *See* Tex. R. Civ. P. 502.1.

(2) What to e-file.

(a) Generally—documents. A party generally must e-file any document that can be filed in paper form. *See* Tex. R. Civ. P. 21(f)(1). An attorney or pro se party must include her e-mail address on the e-filed document. Tex. R. Civ. P. 21(f)(2). Unless required by local rule, a party does not need to file paper copies of an e-filed document. Tex. R. Civ. P. 21(f)(9).

(b) Exceptions.

[1] **Documents not required to be e-filed.** A party is not required to e-file a will. Tex. R. Civ. P. 21(f)(4)(A).

Note

If a party e-files an application to probate an original will, the party must file the original will with the clerk within three business days after filing the application. Tex. R. Civ. P. 21(f)(12). The clerk must retain the original will in a numbered file folder. Tex. R. Civ. P. 21(f)(13).

[2] Documents not allowed to be e-filed. A party cannot e-file the following documents: (1) documents filed under seal, (2) documents presented to the court in camera, and (3) documents that have their access restricted by law or court order. Tex. R. Civ. P. 21(f)(4)(B); *see* JCIT Tech. Stds., v. 6.5, §4.8.3 (clerk cannot accept e-filed document that is under seal, that is presented in camera, or from e-filer who is vexatious litigant who has not received permission to e-file). See "Vexatious litigant," ch. 1-B, §3.4; "Motion to Seal Court Records," ch. 5-L, §1 et seq.

[3] Other documents—good cause. A party may be able to file certain documents in paper form in a particular case on a showing of good cause. Tex. R. Civ. P. 21(f)(4)(C); *see also* Tex.Sup.Ct. Order, Misc. Docket No. 13-9164 (Dec. 9, 2013) (court cannot accept, file, or docket document that does not comply with e-filing mandate in Order unless there is an emergency).

(3) How to e-file. E-filing is done through efiletexas.gov, which is the e-filing manager (EFM) established by the Office of Court Administration. *See* Tex. R. Civ. P. 21(f)(3). The EFM controls the flow of electronic information among e-filers, court clerks, and judges. *See* www.efiletexas.gov/faqs.htm (select "How does e-filing work?"). Before e-filing, a party must select and register with a certified electronic-filing service provider (EFSP). *See* Tex. R. Civ. P. 21(f)(3); www.efiletexas.gov/service-providers.htm. The EFSP collects filing information and documents from e-filers and submits them to the EFM. *See* Tex. R. Civ. P. 21(f)(3); www.efiletexas.gov/faqs.htm (select "What is an EFSP?"). The party does not e-file directly with the court but instead submits a document to its EFSP, which sends the document through the EFM to the particular court. *See* www.efiletexas.gov/faqs.htm (select "How does e-filing work?"). The court clerk will review the document and either (1) accept the filing, (2) reject the filing, if the document is one that cannot be e-filed, or (3) request that the filing party make corrections to the document before the court accepts the filing. *See id.* See "Documents not allowed to be e-filed," ch. 1-C, §4.1.1(2)(b)[2]; "Nonconforming documents," ch. 1-C, §4.1.1(3)(d). If the clerk accepts the filing, she will provide the filing party with an electronic time-stamp notification. www.efiletexas.gov/faqs.htm (select "How does e-filing work?"); *see also* JCIT Tech. Stds., v. 6.5, §3.1.G (once filing is accepted, it is available for download by filing party for 30 days); *cf.* Tex. R. Civ. P. 21a(b)(3) (confirmation of service sent by EFM). For more information on how to e-file through the EFM, see efiletexas.gov.

Note

The EFM limits the size of an individual uploaded document to 25 MB and the total size of an uploaded file to 35 MB. Spencer, Filing Accepted! Best Practices for E-filing in Texas, Family Law Technology 360: Everything You Need to Know for Your 21st Century Practice, State Bar of Texas CLE, ch. 5, p. 2 (2014). Certain EFSPs may also have caps on document and file size that differ from the EFM's caps. Check with your specific EFSP to make sure you do not exceed any size limits for your files. See www.efiletexas.gov/service-providers.htm.

(a) Filing format. Documents that are e-filed must comply with TRCP 21(f) and the technology standards promulgated by the JCIT and approved by the Supreme Court. *See* Tex. R. Civ. P. 21(f)(8). See "Format for e-filed pleadings," ch. 1-B, §3.2.1(2).

(b) Signing documents. Any document that is e-filed must contain an electronic signature. *See* Tex. R. Civ. P. 21(f)(7). See "Electronic signature," ch. 1-B, §3.2.12(2)(b).

(c) Service of citation. When service of citation is needed for an e-filed document filed through efiletexas.gov, the filing party must select "Issue Citation" as an additional service. JCIT Tech. Stds., v. 6.5, §4.8.2.1.

(d) Nonconforming documents. Generally, if a document does not conform with TRCP 21(f), the clerk cannot refuse to file it. Tex. R. Civ. P. 21(f)(11). But the clerk can refuse to file certain documents that are prohibited from be-

ing e-filed under TRCP 21(f)(4)(B). See "Documents not allowed to be e-filed," ch. 1-C, §4.1.1(2)(b)[2]. For a document that otherwise does not conform with TRCP 21(f), the clerk may identify the error and provide a deadline for the party to resubmit a properly formatted document. Tex. R. Civ. P. 21(f)(11). Types of errors that may require a document to be resubmitted include the following:

[1] The document is formatted incorrectly. JCIT Tech. Stds., v. 6.5, §4.8.4.

[2] The document is illegible. *Id.*

[3] The document contains incorrect or incomplete case information. *Id.*

[4] The document is addressed to the wrong clerk's office. *Id.*

[5] Multiple documents are submitted for filing in a single PDF. *Id.*

[6] The filing requesting a new case duplicates an existing case. *Id.*

(e) E-filing fees. A party who e-files a document must pay e-filing fees, which include fees paid to the EFSP and convenience fees for credit-card processing. *See* www.efiletexas.gov/faqs.htm (select "Is there a fee to use eFileTexas.gov?"). The party must also pay the standard court filing fees. See "Filing fees," ch. 1-C, §6. If the fees submitted are insufficient or the party's credit card was declined for insufficient funds, the clerk may identify the error and provide a deadline for the party to resubmit a properly e-filed document. *See* JCIT Tech. Stds., v. 6.5, §4.8.4.

(4) When to e-file. For a document to be timely filed, a party generally must e-file it before midnight (in the court's time zone) on the day of the filing deadline. Tex. R. Civ. P. 21(f)(5). If a document must be filed by a certain time of day, the party must e-file it by that time for it to be considered timely filed. *Id.*

(a) Deemed filed.

[1] Generally—when document transmitted. An e-filed document is generally deemed filed when it is transmitted to the party's EFSP. Tex. R. Civ. P. 21(f)(5); *e.g.*, **Cummings v. Billman**, __ S.W.3d __, 2020 WL 938172 (Tex.App.—Fort Worth 2020, order) (No. 02-20-00034-CV; 2-27-20) (motion to reinstate was deemed filed when transmitted to party's EFSP even though transaction was canceled by party before clerk processed and file-stamped document; deemed filing thus extended deadline for filing notice of appeal); **High Rev Power, L.L.C. v. Freeport Logistics, Inc.**, No. 05-13-01360-CV, 2016 WL 6462392 (Tex.App.—Dallas 2016, no pet.) (memo op.; 10-31-16) (motion for new trial was deemed filed when transmitted to party's EFSP even though motion was never forwarded to clerk). The document is deemed filed when it is transmitted to the party's EFSP even if it is returned for not conforming with TRCP 21(f) and must be resubmitted. *See* Tex. R. Civ. P. 21(f)(11). See "Nonconforming documents," ch. 1-C, §4.1.1(3)(d).

[2] Exceptions.

[a] Saturday, Sunday, or legal holiday. If a document is transmitted to the EFSP on a Saturday, Sunday, or legal holiday, the document is deemed filed on the next day that is not a Saturday, Sunday, or legal holiday. Tex. R. Civ. P. 21(f)(5)(A).

[b] Filing requires order. If a document cannot be filed without a motion and court order, the document is deemed filed on the date the motion is granted. Tex. R. Civ. P. 21(f)(5)(B).

(b) Technical failure. If a document is transmitted but a technical failure or system outage prevents it from being timely delivered, the party may seek appropriate relief from the court. Tex. R. Civ. P. 21(f)(6). If the missed deadline is one under the TRCPs, the court must give the party a reasonable extension of time to complete the filing. *Id.*

Note

TRCP 21 does not define "technical failure" or "system outage." It is uncertain whether a technical failure or system outage that affects the party's equipment (e.g., the party's hard drive crashes) would allow the party to seek relief under TRCP 21(f)(6). See Jefferson, Trends & Traps in Rules of Civil Proce-

dure, Litigation Update Institute, State Bar of Texas CLE, ch. 3.2, p. 9 n.127 (2015). Most likely, a technical failure or system outage refers to that of the EFM or the party's EFSP. Id. at 9.

(5) Documents as official record. The clerk can designate an e-filed document or a scanned paper document as the official court record. Tex. R. Civ. P. 21(f)(13).

2. Filing documents in paper form. Under certain circumstances, a document may be filed with the court in paper form instead of being e-filed. See "Optional parties," ch. 1-C, §4.1.1(1)(b); "Exceptions," ch. 1-C, §4.1.1(2)(b). When permitted, a party may be able to file a document in paper form by mail, delivery, or fax.

(1) Mail. A party may file a document in paper form by mailing it to the clerk on or before the date it is due. Tex. R. Civ. P. 5; **Ramos v. Richardson**, 228 S.W.3d 671, 673 (Tex.2007); *see, e.g.*, **Beard v. Beard**, 49 S.W.3d 40, 54 (Tex.App.—Waco 2001, pet. denied) (motion for new trial deposited in mail on day it was due was timely). When a party files a document by mail, it invokes the "mailbox rule" in TRCP 5, which provides a ten-day grace period for a document that arrives at the clerk's office after the deadline. *See* Tex. R. Civ. P. 5. A document mailed to the clerk is considered filed on the day it is deposited with the U.S. Postal Service (USPS) if all the following conditions are met.

(a) The document was sent by first-class U.S. mail. Tex. R. Civ. P. 5; **Ramos**, 228 S.W.3d at 673. If the document is sent to the trial court by FedEx, UPS, or any other commercial delivery service, the mailbox rule in TRCP 5 does not apply. **Fountain Parkway, Ltd. v. Tarrant Appr. Dist.**, 920 S.W.2d 799, 802–03 (Tex.App.—Fort Worth 1996, writ denied); *see* **Carpenter v. Town & Country Bank**, 806 S.W.2d 959, 960 (Tex.App.—Eastland 1991, writ denied). By comparison, under TRAP 9.2(b)(1)(A), a document sent to an appellate clerk by commercial delivery service does invoke the mailbox rule.

(b) The document was properly stamped with the correct postage. *See* Tex. R. Civ. P. 5; **Ramos**, 228 S.W.3d at 673.

(c) The document was addressed to the proper clerk or court and sent to the correct address. Tex. R. Civ. P. 5; **Ramos**, 228 S.W.3d at 673; **Stokes v. Aberdeen Ins.**, 917 S.W.2d 267, 268 (Tex.1996); *see, e.g.* **Desai v. Chambers Cty. Appr. Dist.**, 376 S.W.3d 295, 301–02 (Tex.App.—Houston [14th Dist.] 2012, no pet.) (mailing petitions to district clerk's physical address, rather than mailing address, was proper under TRCP 5). An incorrect or omitted zip code does not make the address improper. **Judkins v. Davenport**, 59 S.W.3d 689, 691 (Tex.App.—Amarillo 2000, no pet.).

(d) The document was mailed on or before the due date. Tex. R. Civ. P. 5; **Ramos**, 228 S.W.3d at 673; *e.g.*, **Milam v. Miller**, 891 S.W.2d 1, 2 (Tex.App.—Amarillo 1994, writ ref'd) (answer mailed at post office at 8:30 a.m. on due date, 90 minutes before answer deadline, was timely filed). A legible USPS postmark on the envelope is prima facie evidence of the date of mailing. Tex. R. Civ. P. 5; *e.g.*, **Landers v. State Farm Lloyds**, 257 S.W.3d 740, 745 & n.5 (Tex.App.—Houston [1st Dist.] 2008, no pet.) (private postage meter stamp did not establish date of mailing). See "Proving date of filing," ch. 1-C, §11.1.

(e) The document or a copy was received by the clerk within ten days after the due date. Tex. R. Civ. P. 5; **Ramos**, 228 S.W.3d at 673; *e.g.*, **Stokes**, 917 S.W.2d at 267–68 (party sent original motion to clerk using FedEx overnight service and mailed copy to judge; clerk's copy was received within ten days and considered timely filed). If the document arrives on the 11th day, it is not considered timely filed unless the party files, and the court grants, a motion to extend the time for filing. *See* Tex. R. Civ. P. 5. See "Motion to extend time," ch. 1-C, §9.1.

(2) Delivery. A party may file a document in paper form by delivering it to the clerk of the trial court. *See* Tex. R. Civ. P. 21(a), 74. Anyone—the party's attorney, a member of the attorney's office staff, or a commercial delivery service (e.g., FedEx or UPS)—may deliver a document, as long as it is delivered on or before the date it is due. *See, e.g.*, **Carpenter**, 806 S.W.2d at 960 (under TRCP 5, motion for new trial sent by UPS was late when received by clerk six days after deadline; ten-day period under mailbox rule does not apply to UPS delivery). A party may also file a document with the judge; for example, while in court, an attorney may personally hand a document to the judge for filing. *See* Tex. R. Civ. P. 74.

(3) Fax in emergency. A party represented by an attorney may file a document in paper form with the clerk by fax only in an emergency. Tex.Sup.Ct. Order, Misc. Docket No. 13-9164 (eff. Dec. 9, 2013); *see* Tex. Gov't Code §51.807 (Supreme Court can adopt county's local rules for fax filing); *see also* Tex. R. Civ. P. 21(f)(1) (pro se party not required to e-file).

The fax machine used for the filing should be set to produce a transmission-verification report confirming the date and time the document was sent and received. The party should attach the transmission-verification report to the file copy of the document as proof of the date and time of filing.

Note

Because a pro se party is not required to e-file, the party may be able to file a document in paper form by fax in a nonemergency situation if the county's local rules permit fax filing. See Tex. Gov't Code §51.807; Tex. R. Civ. P. 21(f)(1).

§4.2 Documents with sensitive data—privacy protection. TRCP 21c provides measures for protecting certain sensitive data that is included in a filed document.

1. Application.

(1) Generally. Generally, sensitive data appearing in any electronic or paper document must be redacted before the document is filed. Tex. R. Civ. P. 21c(b).

(a) Sensitive data. Any of the following is considered sensitive data:

[1] A driver's license number, passport number, social-security number, taxpayer-identification number, or similar government-issued personal identification number. Tex. R. Civ. P. 21c(a)(1).

[2] A bank-account number, credit-card number, or other financial-account number. Tex. R. Civ. P. 21c(a)(2).

[3] A birth date. Tex. R. Civ. P. 21c(a)(3).

[4] A home address. *Id.*

[5] The name of any person who was a minor when the underlying suit was filed. *Id.*

(b) Redaction. To redact sensitive data, a party must do either of the following:

[1] Use the letter "X" in place of each omitted digit or character. Tex. R. Civ. P. 21c(c).

[2] Remove the sensitive data in a manner indicating that it has been redacted. *Id.*

(2) Exceptions. Sensitive data appearing in an electronic or paper document does not have to be redacted in either of the following circumstances:

(a) Sensitive data is specifically required by a statute, a court rule, or an administrative regulation. Tex. R. Civ. P. 21c(b). When a document must include sensitive data, the filing party must notify the clerk in the following manner:

[1] If the document is e-filed, designate the document as having sensitive data. Tex. R. Civ. P. 21c(d)(1).

[2] If the document is not e-filed, include the following on the upper left-hand side of the first page: "NOTICE: THIS DOCUMENT CONTAINS SENSITIVE DATA." Tex. R. Civ. P. 21c(d)(2).

(b) The document is a will or is filed under seal. Tex. R. Civ. P. 21c(b).

2. Nonconforming documents. If a document contains sensitive data that violates TRCP 21c, the clerk cannot refuse to file it. Tex. R. Civ. P. 21c(e). The clerk may identify the error and provide a deadline for the party to redact the sensitive data and submit a substitute document. *Id.*; *see* JCIT Tech. Stds., v. 6.5, §4.8.4. A document containing sensitive data in violation of TRCP 21c must not be posted on the Internet. Tex. R. Civ. P. 21c(f).

3. Retain unredacted copy. The filing party must keep an unredacted version of the document while the case is pending and during any related appellate proceedings filed within six months after the judgment is signed. Tex. R. Civ. P. 21c(c).

§5. When to file

Documents must be filed by the deadlines provided in the statutes, TRCPs, local rules, pretrial docketing orders, or other orders of the court.

§5.1 By deadline. A document is timely filed if it is filed on or before the deadline. See "Computing filing deadlines," ch. 1-C, §7.

§5.2 Premature. Occasionally, a document is filed before the filing period begins. A prematurely filed document is deemed filed on the date of, but after, the event that begins the filing period. *See* Tex. R. Civ. P. 306c (motion for new trial, request for findings of fact); Tex. R. App. P. 27.1 (notice of appeal); **Padilla v. LaFrance**, 907 S.W.2d 454, 458 (Tex.1995) (motion to modify judgment); **In re Estate of Ayala**, 19 S.W.3d 477, 479–80 (Tex.App.—Corpus Christi 2000, pet. denied) (creditor suit filed before claim was rejected by representative of estate); **Perez v. Texas Empls. Ins.**, 926 S.W.2d 425, 426–27 (Tex.App.—Austin 1996, order) (verified motion to reinstate).

§6. Filing fees

§6.1 Due when filed. Some filing fees must be paid when a document is filed. For example, in district courts, a fee is required when filing a suit, a cross-claim, a counterclaim, an intervention, a motion for contempt, a motion for new trial, or a third-party petition, or for requesting issuance of a citation or other writ. Tex. Gov't Code §51.317(a), (b).

§6.2 Amount for filing suit.

1. Generally.

(1) District courts. Generally, the fees for filing a suit in district court are as follows:

(a) $50 for filing a suit with ten or fewer plaintiffs. Tex. Gov't Code §51.317(b)(1).

(b) Between $75 and $200 for filing a suit with more than ten plaintiffs, depending on the number of plaintiffs. Tex. Gov't Code §51.317(b-1).

(c) $15 for filing a cross-claim, a counterclaim, an intervention, a motion for contempt, a motion for new trial, or a third-party petition. Tex. Gov't Code §51.317(b)(2).

(d) $8 for requesting issuance of a citation or other writ. Tex. Gov't Code §51.317(b)(3).

(2) County & justice courts. The fees for filing a suit in a county court or justice court vary depending on the particular court in which the suit is filed. For the specific fees, a party should check the website for the court in which the party is filing.

2. Additional fees. The clerk in certain courts must collect fees in addition to those for filing suit.

Note

Before September 1, 2019, a county or appellate court that used the statewide e-filing system could charge $2 for each e-filing transaction under certain circumstances. See Tex. Gov't Code §72.031(c) (pre-9-1-19 version). Gov't Code §72.031(c), authorizing the e-filing transaction fee, expired September 1, 2019. See Tex. Gov't Code §72.031(c-1) (pre-9-1-19 version); Acts 2013, 83rd Leg., R.S., ch. 1290, §3, eff. Sept. 1, 2013.

---

(1) For electronic-filing-system fund. The clerk of a district court, county court, statutory county court, or statutory probate court must collect an additional $30 ($10 in justice court) on the filing of any civil action or proceeding, cross-action, counterclaim, intervention, interpleader, or third-party action that requires a filing fee. *See* Tex. Gov't Code §51.851(b), (c). This additional fee is deposited into the statewide electronic-filing-system fund, which will be used to offset the cost of implementing the statewide e-filing system. *See* Tex. Gov't Code §§51.851(g), (i), 51.852. For information on statewide e-filing, see "E-filing," ch. 1-C, §4.1.1.

(2) For court-records archiving. The clerk of a district court must collect a court-records archiving fee for filing a suit, including an appeal from an inferior court, or a cross-action, counterclaim, intervention, contempt action, motion for new trial, or third-party petition. Tex. Gov't Code §51.317(b)(5). The fee is set by the county commissioners court and cannot exceed $10. *Id.*

(3) For judicial & court personnel training fund. The clerk of a district court, county court, statutory county court, statutory probate court, or justice court must collect a $5 fee on the filing of any civil action or proceeding—including an appeal—and on the filing of any counterclaim, cross-action, intervention, interpleader, or third-party action that requires a filing fee. Tex. Gov't Code §51.971(a). If the filing party is indigent, the court may waive payment of the fee. Tex. Gov't Code §51.971(b). This additional fee is deposited into the judicial and court personnel training fund to be used in accordance with Gov't Code §56.003. *See* Tex. Gov't Code §§51.971(a), (e), 56.001.

§6.3 Filing complete when paid. If a document is filed without the payment of the required fee, it is considered "conditionally filed" on the date it was tendered to the clerk. **Tate v. E.I. DuPont de Nemours & Co.**, 934 S.W.2d 83, 84 (Tex.1996); *see* **Jamar v. Patterson**, 868 S.W.2d 318, 319 (Tex.1993). When the filing fee is paid, the document is deemed filed on the date it was originally tendered. *See* **Jamar**, 868 S.W.2d at 319.

Note

When the filing fee for a motion for new trial is paid after the trial court loses plenary power, the motion does not preserve error for those issues that must be preserved in a motion for new trial. See, e.g., ***Garza v. Garcia****, 137 S.W.3d 36, 38 (Tex.2004) (trial court was not required to review factual-sufficiency complaint in motion for new trial because fee was never paid). See "Paid after loss of plenary power," ch. 10-B, §4.2.2(2).*

§7. Computing filing deadlines

A document that is filed or served late is not effective. Thus, calculating the time limits is extremely important. There are two rules on computation of time: TRCP 4, "Computation of Time," and TRCP 5, "Enlargement of Time." Gov't Code §311.014 also discusses computation of time.

§7.1 Computing time limits—days. Most deadlines are based on days.

1. General rules.

(1) First day. Begin counting the day after the period begins. Tex. Gov't Code §311.014(a); Tex. R. Civ. P. 4. The day the time period begins (e.g., the date of filing, the date of service) is not counted. For example, if a judgment is signed on Friday and a party has 30 days to file a motion for new trial, Friday is "day 0," Saturday is "day 1," and Sunday is "day 2." Similarly, if a plaintiff is served with interrogatories on Friday and has 30 days to answer, Friday is "day 0," Saturday is "day 1," and Sunday is "day 2."

(2) Counted days. Count every day after the first day—including Saturdays, Sundays, and legal holidays—until the last day. *See* Tex. Gov't Code §311.014(a); Tex. R. Civ. P. 4.

(3) Last day. Count the last day unless it is a Saturday, Sunday, or legal holiday. Tex. R. Civ. P. 4; **Lewis v. Blake**, 876 S.W.2d 314, 315–16 (Tex.1994). If the last day is a Saturday, Sunday, or legal holiday, the deadline is the next regular business day. Tex. Gov't Code §311.014(b); Tex. R. Civ. P. 4; **Melendez v. Exxon Corp.**, 998 S.W.2d 266, 275 (Tex.App.—Houston [14th Dist.] 1999, no pet.); *see, e.g.,* **Williams v. Flores**, 88 S.W.3d 631, 632 (Tex.2002) (motion for new trial was timely filed on 32nd day after judgment because 30th day was Sunday and 31st day was legal holiday). See "Legal holidays," ch. 1-C, §8.

Note

For time periods that are counted backward (e.g., a response to a summary-judgment motion must be filed at least seven days before the hearing), when the last day is a Saturday, Sunday, or legal holiday, the next regular business day—counting forward—is the deadline. See, e.g., ***Hammonds v. Thomas****, 770 S.W.2d 1, 2–3 (Tex.App.—Texarkana 1989, no writ) (when summary-judgment hearing was set for July 11, court should have considered nonmovant's affidavits in response to motion filed on July 5 because the seventh day before the hearing was July 4, a national holiday); see also* ***Lewis****, 876 S.W.2d*

*at 316 (Supreme Court approved conclusion in **Hammonds** and applied TRCP 4 to 21-day notice requirement in TRCP 166a(c)). TRCP 4 applies to any time period under the TRCPs, not just time periods running "after" a specific event. **Hammonds**, 770 S.W.2d at 3; see **Lewis**, 876 S.W.2d at 316.*

2. Exception. There is an exception to the general rules for computing deadlines—and to make matters more confusing, the exception has its own exception.

(1) Period to act is 5 days or less. If the period to act is five days or less, do not count the intervening Saturdays, Sundays, and legal holidays for any purpose. Tex. R. Civ. P. 4. That is, start counting the day after the period begins, skip any Saturday, Sunday, or legal holiday, and count until the last day that is not a Saturday, Sunday, or legal holiday.

Caution

*Unlike TRCP 4, Gov't Code §311.014 has no provision for calculating time periods of five days or less. When computing statutory deadlines involving five days or less, ignore TRCP 4—that is, start counting the day after the period begins, do not skip any Saturday, Sunday, or legal holiday, and file on or before the last day that is not a Saturday, Sunday, or legal holiday. See **Peacock v. Humble**, 933 S.W.2d 341, 342-43 (Tex.App.—Austin 1996, orig. proceeding).*

(2) Exception to the exception. The three-day extension of time in TRCP 21a(c) when service is made by mail is counted in the same way as under the general rules. *See* Tex. R. Civ. P. 4. That is, count Saturdays, Sundays, and legal holidays for purposes of TRCP 21a unless the last day is a Saturday, Sunday, or legal holiday. Tex. R. Civ. P. 4; *see* Tex. Gov't Code §311.014(b). It is not clear, however, whether Saturdays, Sundays, and legal holidays are counted for purposes of calculating the three-day notice of hearings in TRCP 21. See "Caution," ch. 1-E, §2.1.

§7.2 Computing time limits—months. Some deadlines are based on months, not days. *E.g.*, Tex. R. Civ. P. 190.3(b)(1)(B)(ii) (discovery period of nine months in Level 2 nonfamily cases). If a number of months is to be computed, the period ends on the same numerical day in the last month as the day the period began in the first month. Tex. Gov't Code §311.014(c). If this is impossible because there are fewer days in the last month, the period ends on the last day of that month. *Id.* Thus, if the discovery period in a Level 2 nonfamily case began on December 31, the period would end on September 30, the last day of the ninth and last month, regardless of the number of days in the period. If the last day is a Saturday, Sunday, or legal holiday, the deadline is extended to the next regular business day. Tex. Gov't Code §311.014(b).

§7.3 Computing time limits—years. Statute-of-limitations deadlines are based on years. These deadlines are computed in the same way as deadlines based on months. **Medina v. Lopez-Roman**, 49 S.W.3d 393, 398 (Tex.App.—Austin 2000, pet. denied); *see, e.g.*, **Salahat v. Kincaid**, 195 S.W.3d 342, 344 (Tex.App.—Fort Worth 2006, no pet.) (two-year statute of limitations for cause of action that accrued February 25, 2002, ended February 25, 2004); *see also* Tex. Civ. Prac. & Rem. Code §16.072 (if last day of limitations period is Saturday, Sunday, or legal holiday, period for filing suit is extended to next regular business day that county offices are open).

§7.4 Problems in computing deadlines. Computing deadlines is confusing. The rules do not describe the deadlines with uniform phrasing, and some rules apply the deadline to both filing and service, some only to filing, and some only to service. For example, TRCP 166a(c) requires a party to file and serve a motion for summary judgment "at least" 21 days before the hearing; TRCP 197.2(a) requires a party to serve responses to interrogatories "within" 30 days after service; TRCP 93(13) requires a party to file a verified denial of an Industrial Accident Board award "not less than" 7 days before the case proceeds to trial.

§8. Legal holidays

The issue of "legal holidays" in relation to filing deadlines is more confusing than most appellate opinions acknowledge because the appellate courts have interpreted TRCP 4 as adopting the list of legal holidays from Gov't Code §662.003. Section 662.003 was not enacted to explain the impact of legal holidays on filing deadlines; it was enacted to inform state-paid

employees which days are paid holidays. Section 662.003 does not address legal holidays for county employees. Legal holidays are a budget issue decided at both the state and county levels. The holidays for state employees are determined by the Legislature and published in the Government Code every other year. The holidays for county employees, on the other hand, are determined by the counties every year and published in their annual budgets. Because legal holidays are different for state and county employees, they are different for the different types of courts—the appellate courts follow the holiday schedule set by the Legislature, while the county courts and district courts follow the counties' holiday schedules.

§8.1 Definition of legal holiday. A "legal holiday," as used in TRCP 4, includes all days the courthouse is officially closed. *See* **Miller Brewing Co. v. Villarreal**, 829 S.W.2d 770, 772 (Tex.1992). Whether a holiday is a legal holiday for purposes of TRCP 4 generally depends on the type and location of the court.

1. Legal holidays for trial courts.

(1) County courts. Because a county court's personnel (e.g., the judge, clerk, and bailiff) are paid by the county, their paid holidays are set by the county commissioners court. For county courts, the term "legal holidays" in TRCP 4 includes only those days designated by the commissioners court. **Miller Brewing**, 829 S.W.2d at 772; *see also* **Walles v. McDonald**, 889 S.W.2d 236, 237 (Tex.1994) (when courthouse is closed for local holiday, time to file under Election Code is extended). See the shaded parts of the last column in "Multiple-county districts," ch. 1-C, §8.1.1(2)(b). Most counties observe most of the holidays listed in Gov't Code §662.003(a). However, if a holiday listed in Gov't Code §662.003 is not designated as a holiday by the commissioners court, it is not a legal holiday for purposes of TRCP 4 in that county, and the courthouse will be open. *See, e.g.*, **Lowe v. Rivera**, 60 S.W.3d 366, 369–70 & n.3 (Tex.App.—Dallas 2001, no pet.) (Dallas County commissioners court did not designate Presidents' Day as a legal holiday).

Practice Tip

To determine whether a certain day is a legal holiday for a particular county, call the court clerk or go to the county's website and search for "holidays." Do not rely on assurances from courthouse personnel (other than those in the clerk's office) that a certain day is an official holiday. See, e.g., ***Seismic & Digital Concepts, Inc. v. Digital Res.****, 583 S.W.2d 442, 442 (Tex.App.—Houston [1st Dist] 1979, no writ) (mistake of courthouse telephone operator, who told attorney that courthouse would be closed, did not extend time for filing).*

(2) District courts. The judge of a district court is paid by the State, and the district court's other personnel (e.g., the clerk and bailiff) are paid by the county. However, the county-paid employees, not the judge, determine whether the courthouse will be open. A district judge cannot operate the courtroom without a clerk and bailiff. So the rule for district courts is the same as for county courts—the term "legal holidays" in TRCP 4 includes only the days designated as holidays by the commissioners court.

(a) Single-county districts. Generally, district courts located in metropolitan areas are contained within the borders of one county. For example, the 11th District Court has jurisdiction and sits solely in Harris County. That court will close for the same holidays as the county courts in Harris County.

(b) Multiple-county districts. District courts in other areas of the state often have jurisdiction and sit in a number of counties. For example, the 155th District Court serves Waller, Austin, and Fayette Counties. That court will be closed for holidays in each county according to that county's commissioners court.

1-1. Legal Holidays for Filing*

Name of holiday		Date of holiday	Gov't Code provision	Appellate courts	District & county courts
1	New Year's Day	January 1	§662.003(a)(1)	Closed	Closed
2	MLK Day	January, 3rd Monday	§662.003(a)(2)	Closed	Call clerk
3	Confederate Heroes Day	January 19	§§662.003(b)(1), 662.004	Skeleton staff	Call clerk

1-1. Legal Holidays for Filing*					
Name of holiday		Date of holiday	Gov't Code provision	Appellate courts	District & county courts
4	Presidents' Day	February, 3rd Monday	§662.003(a)(3)	Closed	Call clerk
5	Texas Independence Day	March 2	§§662.003(b)(2), 662.004	Skeleton staff	Call clerk
6	San Jacinto Day	April 21	§§662.003(b)(3), 662.004	Skeleton staff	Call clerk
7	Memorial Day	May, last Monday	§662.003(a)(4)	Closed	Closed
8	Emancipation Day in Texas	June 19	§§662.003(b)(4), 662.004	Skeleton staff	Call clerk
9	Independence Day	July 4	§662.003(a)(5)	Closed	Closed
10	LBJ Day	August 27	§§662.003(b)(5), 662.004	Skeleton staff	Call clerk
11	Labor Day	September, 1st Monday	§662.003(a)(6)	Closed	Closed
12	Veterans Day	November 11	§662.003(a)(7)	Closed	Call clerk
13	Thanksgiving Day	November, 4th Thursday	§662.003(a)(8)	Closed	Closed
14	Day after Thanksgiving	Friday after Thanksgiving Day	§§662.003(b)(6), 662.004	Closed	Call clerk
15	Christmas Eve	December 24	§§662.003(b)(7), 662.004	Closed	Call clerk
16	Christmas Day	December 25	§662.003(a)(9)	Closed	Closed
17	Day after Christmas	December 26	§§662.003(b)(8), 662.004	Closed	Call clerk

* The Government Code lists Rosh Hashanah, Yom Kippur, and Good Friday as optional holidays. Tex. Gov't Code §662.003(c).

2. Legal holidays for appellate courts. For appellate courts, legal holidays in TRCP 4 include the "legal holidays" listed in Gov't Code §662.003(a) (national holidays) and (b)(1) through (b)(6) (specified state holidays). *See* Tex. Gov't Code §662.021 (defining "legal holiday"). But because the employees of appellate courts (i.e., the Supreme Court and the courts of appeals) are paid by the State, they are entitled to paid holidays on the national holidays and all of the state holidays recognized by the Legislature, which include the days before and after Christmas. *See* Tex. Gov't Code §662.003(a), (b)(1) to (8). Thus, the days when appellate-court employees are generally off include the days before and after Christmas in addition to those defined as legal holidays. *See* Tex. Gov't Code §§662.003(b)(7), (8), 662.021. Not all holidays listed in §662.003 extend filing deadlines, however, because Gov't Code §662.004 requires skeleton staffing for some, but not all, state holidays. The cumulative effect of these statutes is as follows:

(1) Closed. Appellate courts are closed, and no employees are present to accept filings, on all the federal holidays listed in §662.003(a) and the three state holidays listed in §662.003(b)(6) through (b)(8). *See* Tex. Gov't Code §§662.004(b), 662.021, 662.022. When a court is closed on a state holiday, that day is considered a legal holiday for purposes of TRCP 4, which extends the date for filing. See the shaded cells in the "Appellate courts" column in chart 1-1, above.

(2) Not closed. Appellate courts must leave a skeleton staff on duty to accept filings on the five state holidays listed in §662.003(b)(1) through (b)(5). *See* Tex. Gov't Code §662.004(a). When a skeleton staff is on duty, that day is not considered a legal holiday for purposes of TRCP 4 and does not extend the date for filing. See the unshaded cells in the "Appellate courts" column in chart 1-1, above.

3. Emergency. When a clerk's office is closed on a day not designated as a holiday (e.g., for a hurricane), that day is considered a legal holiday for purposes of TRCP 4 and extends the deadline for filing. *See* **Miller Brewing**, 829 S.W.2d at 772; *see also* **Boone v. St. Paul Fire & Mar. Ins.**, 968 S.W.2d 468, 470 (Tex.App.—Fort Worth 1998, pet. denied) (two-hour

delay in opening county clerk's office because of inclement weather did not make entire day a legal holiday and did not extend filing deadline).

Practice Tip

If the issue of whether a trial court was closed on a particular day is critical on appeal, the attorney can direct the appellate court to the county's website that lists the court's holidays or file an affidavit from the clerk of the trial court stating that the day was a legal holiday.

§8.2 After hours. If a party is facing a nonextendable deadline to file a document (e.g., a motion for new trial) and it is after 5:00 p.m., the party may still be able to timely file the document.

1. When document is e-filed. When a party e-files a document, the party may generally file it until 11:59 p.m. on the day of the filing deadline. *See* Tex. R. Civ. P. 21(f)(5). See "When to e-file," ch. 1-C, §4.1.1(4).

2. When document is not e-filed. When a party is not required to e-file or a document cannot be e-filed, the party may file by other methods. See "Filing documents in paper form," ch. 1-C, §4.1.2.

(1) U.S. mail. A party may file a document when the courthouse is closed by mailing it. *See* **Miller Brewing Co. v. Villarreal**, 829 S.W.2d 770, 771 (Tex.1992). A document is considered filed the day it is mailed if it is sent to the proper clerk at the correct address, is sent by first-class U.S. mail, and gets to the courthouse within ten days after the day it was due. Tex. R. Civ. P. 5. A document is "mailed" when it is deposited into a U.S. Postal Service (USPS) mailbox (not a party's own mailbox), left in a receptacle for mail at the post office, or given to a USPS mail carrier. *See id.*; *cf.* Tex. R. Civ. P. 21a(b)(1) (service by mail is complete when document is deposited in mail). The postmark date on the envelope will be prima facie evidence of the day it was mailed. Tex. R. Civ. P. 5. See "Mail," ch. 1-C, §11.1.2(1). Even without a postmark, a party can prove the date of mailing by filing an affidavit of an attorney, the clerk, or some other person. See "Any method—by affidavit," ch. 1-C, §11.1.3.

(2) Court drop box. Some counties provide a drop box for filing after hours or on holidays. Most drop boxes are located inside the courthouse, and a party who wants to file a document must contact the guard for access. Some counties provide a date-stamp device so the party filing the document can date-stamp it before dropping it into the box.

(3) Fax. Because a pro se party is not required to e-file, the party may be able to file a document in paper form by fax if the county's local rules permit fax filing. *See* Tex. Gov't Code §51.807; Tex. R. Civ. P. 21(f)(1). Some counties allow after-hours fax filing until 11:59 p.m. on the day of the filing deadline.

Note

Although a represented party is generally required to e-file, she can file a document in paper form by fax, but only in an emergency. See "Fax in emergency," ch. 1-C, §4.1.2(3).

(4) Delivery to clerk or judge. An attorney or pro se party may call the court clerk and take the document to the clerk's residence to file. See "Clerk," ch. 1-C, §3.2.1. If the attorney or pro se party cannot locate the clerk, she can call the trial judge and, with permission, take the document to the judge's residence to file. If neither the clerk nor the trial judge is available, the attorney or pro se party can file the document with another judge occupying the same type of bench in the same county. See "Judge," ch. 1-C, §3.2.2.

§9. Securing additional time

If a party needs more time to file a document or to prepare for a hearing, the party should ask for it in advance.

§9.1 Motion to extend time. A motion to extend time is a request to extend the time to do some act that the rules or the court require to be done within a specified time. See **O'Connor's Texas Civil Forms**, FORM 1C:1 (2020 ed.). TRCP 5 governs motions to extend time for all matters except discovery, which is governed by TRCP 191.1. For motions to extend

time in discovery matters, see "Court order to extend," ch. 6-A, §15.2; **O'Connor's Texas Civil Forms**, FORM 6A:2 (2020 ed.). A motion to extend time should be filed as soon as it becomes apparent that more time is necessary. The longer a party waits to ask for an extension, the harder it is to get one.

1. **Before deadline.** When the party asks for additional time before the deadline, TRCP 5 permits the court to grant an extension of time for "cause shown," with or without a motion or notice. The party is not required to show "good cause," a higher burden, if the party files the motion before the deadline. Tex. R. Civ. P. 5. *But cf.* Tex. R. Civ. P. 191.1 (all motions to extend discovery deadlines require good cause). Even though a motion is not required, the party should always file a motion or make the request in open court on the record.

2. **After deadline.** When the party asks for additional time after the deadline, TRCP 5 requires the party to file a motion and show good cause for not acting before the deadline. *See* **Remington Arms Co. v. Canales**, 837 S.W.2d 624, 625 (Tex.1992).

§9.2 Agreement to extend time. To extend the time for responding to a motion, the party seeking an extension should secure a signed agreement from the other party. *See* Tex. R. Civ. P. 11. See "Modifying discovery by agreement," ch. 6-A, §6.1; **O'Connor's Texas Civil Forms**, FORMS 1H:13, 6A:3 (2020 ed.).

Caution

The deadline to file a motion for new trial cannot be extended by the court or by agreement. See Tex. R. Civ. P. 5.

---

§9.3 Motion for continuance. A motion for continuance is a request to postpone or delay a trial or hearing. *See* Tex. R. Civ. P. 252. See "Motion for Continuance," ch. 5-D, §1 et seq.

§10. Filed documents

§10.1 Clerk's endorsement. The clerk must endorse each document presented for filing with the file number, the date and time the document was presented, and the clerk's name. Tex. R. Civ. P. 24. If for any reason the clerk believes a document should not be filed, the clerk must still accept the document and note on it the date it was presented for filing. If a party files a document with the judge instead of the clerk, the judge must endorse it, sign it, and give it to the clerk. *See* Tex. R. Civ. P. 21(a), 24, 74.

§10.2 Deemed filed.

1. **E-filing.** For a discussion of when an e-filed document is deemed filed, see "When to e-file," ch. 1-C, §4.1.1(4).

2. **Filing by mail, delivery, or fax.** A document is deemed filed when it is put in the clerk's custody and control. **Warner v. Glass**, 135 S.W.3d 681, 684 (Tex.2004); **Jamar v. Patterson**, 868 S.W.2d 318, 319 (Tex.1993); **Standard Fire Ins. v. LaCoke**, 585 S.W.2d 678, 680 (Tex.1979). If the clerk refuses to file a document or file-marks it late, the document is considered filed on the date it was presented for filing. *See* **Jamar**, 868 S.W.2d at 318–19; **Mr. Penguin Tuxedo Rental & Sales, Inc. v. NCR Corp.**, 787 S.W.2d 371, 372 (Tex.1990). A party that has satisfied its duty of putting a document in the clerk's custody and control should not be penalized for filing errors made by the clerk. **Warner**, 135 S.W.3d at 684. If the date of filing becomes an issue, the party relying on the document must prove the date the document was tendered to the clerk. *See* **Biffle v. Morton Rubber Indus.**, 785 S.W.2d 143, 144 (Tex.1990) (affidavit stating date document was delivered to clerk's office). See "Proving date of filing," ch. 1-C, §11.1. If a document is mailed to the clerk and the party meets all the requirements of TRCP 5, the document is considered filed on the day it was mailed. *See* Tex. R. Civ. P. 5; *see also* **Warner**, 135 S.W.3d at 684 (pro se inmate's document placed in properly addressed and stamped envelope is deemed filed when prison authorities receive document to be mailed). See "Filing documents in paper form," ch. 1-C, §4.1.2.

Practice Tip

*When you present a document to the clerk for filing, the clerk cannot refuse to file it because of a procedural shortcoming. See **Jamar**, 868 S.W.2d at 318–19. The clerk must file whatever document you present as long as it is in writing and properly identifies the suit in which it should be filed. When a clerk refuses to file a document, insist that the clerk take the document, note on the document that it was presented for filing, note the date and the time it was presented, and sign it. Once the clerk notes on the document that it was presented for filing, address the issue of whether it should be filed with the judge, not the clerk. See **In re Bernard**, 993 S.W.2d 453, 455 (Tex.App.—Houston [1st Dist.] 1999, orig. proceeding) (O'Connor, J., concurring).*

§10.3 Withdrawing pleadings. The clerk will not permit a party to withdraw a pleading from the court's file without a court order. Tex. R. Civ. P. 75.

§10.4 Lost pleadings. If a pleading is lost or destroyed during the prosecution of the suit, the parties can replace it with a copy. Tex. R. Civ. P. 77; **Coke v. Coke**, 802 S.W.2d 270, 275 (Tex.App.—Dallas 1990, writ denied); *see* Tex. R. Evid. 1004(a). Replacing lost or destroyed papers or records requires notice, a sworn motion, and a hearing. Tex. R. Civ. P. 77; *see* **In re Taylor**, 113 S.W.3d 385, 391 (Tex.App.—Houston [1st Dist.] 2003, orig. proceeding). However, the court can order a document replaced even if one of the parties does not agree to the replacement. *See* Tex. R. Civ. P. 77(b) (lost papers or records during suit); Tex. R. App. P. 34.5(e) (clerk's record lost or destroyed); *see also* **Hackney v. First State Bank**, 866 S.W.2d 59, 61–62 (Tex.App.—Texarkana 1993, no writ) (refusal of one party to agree to replace exhibits does not automatically require new trial).

§11. Proving filing

§11.1 Proving date of filing.

1. E-filing. To prove the date of an e-filing, a party may introduce a transaction receipt or confirmation notice of the filing sent to the party from the EFM. *Cf.* Tex. R. Civ. P. 21a(b)(3) (confirmation of service sent by EFM). The party may also introduce a file-stamped copy of the filing, which may be attached with the confirmation notice or may appear on the website of the party's EFSP within a short time after filing. *See* www.efiletexas.gov/faqs.htm (select "How does e-filing work?"). See "How to e-file," ch. 1-C, §4.1.1(3).

2. Paper filing. The easiest way to prove the filing date of a document that is filed in paper form is with the file-stamped copy. When mailing or delivering a document, include an extra copy, a self-addressed stamped envelope, and a request that the clerk file-stamp and return the extra copy. When a dispute arises about the filing date of a document, however, the date the document was tendered to the clerk controls, even over the file-stamp date on the document. **Coastal Banc SSB v. Helle**, 988 S.W.2d 214, 216 (Tex.1999); **Jamar v. Patterson**, 868 S.W.2d 318, 319 (Tex.1993).

(1) Mail. When a document is mailed with the correct address and proper postage, there is a presumption that it was received. *Cf.* **Thomas v. Ray**, 889 S.W.2d 237, 238 (Tex.1994) (case involved service of document, not filing).

(a) U.S. postmark. To prove that a document was filed by mail, a party may introduce a copy of the envelope with the postmark affixed. The date of the postmark stamped on an envelope by the USPS is prima facie proof of filing. Tex. R. Civ. P. 5; **Alvarez v. Thomas**, 172 S.W.3d 298, 301 (Tex.App.—Texarkana 2005, no pet.).

Practice Tip

*The date marked by a private postage meter is not prima facie proof of the date a document was mailed. **Landers v. State Farm Lloyds**, 257 S.W.3d 740, 745 n.5 (Tex.App.—Houston [1st Dist.] 2008, no pet.). When you use a private postage meter, you must introduce some evidence besides the envelope to prove the date it was mailed. See **Texas Beef Cattle Co. v. Green**, 862 S.W.2d 812, 813–14 (Tex.App.—Beaumont 1993, order); see, e.g., **Doyle v. Grady**, 543 S.W.2d 893, 894 (Tex.App.—Texarkana 1976, no writ) (party filed affidavit from post-office employee that envelope was processed on postage-meter*

date); see also ***Ector Cty. ISD v. Hopkins****, 518 S.W.2d 576, 583 & n.1 (Tex.App.—El Paso 1974, no writ) (private postage meter is some evidence of date of mailing but is not conclusive).*

(b) Green card. To prove that a document was filed by certified mail, return receipt requested, a party may introduce the "green card" returned from the post office, which shows the date the document was received by the clerk, and the bar-coded, white-and-green postal receipt bearing the USPS cancellation. *See* USPS Forms 3800, 3811. See "Return receipt—green card," ch. 1-D, §7.1.3(1).

(c) Domestic-mail return receipt. To prove that a document was filed when the green card is lost or not returned, a party may introduce a domestic-mail return receipt. *See* USPS Form 3811-A ("Request for Delivery Information/ Return Receipt"). The receipt establishes the date of delivery and the recipient according to the post office's records. *See id.*

(d) White slip. To prove that a document was mailed (not received), a party may introduce a USPS certificate of mailing (i.e., the "white slip"). *See* USPS Form 3817. See "Certificate of mailing," ch. 1-D, §7.1.3(3).

(2) Delivery. To prove that a document was filed by delivery, a party may introduce a copy of the pleading presented to the clerk when the original was filed, with the clerk's date-stamp on it, or a signed receipt from a commercial delivery service such as FedEx or UPS.

(3) Fax. To prove that a document was filed by fax, a party may introduce the transmission-verification report confirming the date and time the document was sent and received. Evidence showing a fax to the recipient's current fax number raises a presumption that the document was received by the addressee. *Cf.* **American Paging v. El Paso Paging, Inc.**, 9 S.W.3d 237, 240 (Tex.App.—El Paso 1999, pet. denied) (case involved service of notice, not filing).

3. Any method—by affidavit. To prove the date a document was filed electronically or by mail, delivery, or fax, the party may be able to file an affidavit of an attorney or the court clerk. *See, e.g.*, **Coastal Banc**, 988 S.W.2d at 216 (date of filing was established by uncontroverted affidavits of court clerk and attorney, even though file-stamp indicated that document was filed on different date); **Lofton v. Allstate Ins.**, 895 S.W.2d 693, 693–94 (Tex.1995) (attorney's uncontroverted affidavit stating date document was mailed to trial court was allowed as evidence of date of mailing); *cf.* Tex. R. Civ. P. 21a(e) (proof of service). When relying on office routine or custom to support the inference that a document was sent, the party must provide corroborating evidence that the practice was actually carried out. **Wembley Inv. v. Herrera**, 11 S.W.3d 924, 928 (Tex.1999).

§11.2 Proving untimely filing. The presumption of receipt disappears when verified evidence is introduced that the document was not received. *Cf.* **Thomas v. Ray**, 889 S.W.2d 237, 238–39 (Tex.1994) (case involved service of document, not filing; party claiming nonreceipt did not present verified evidence).

1. Testimony of clerk. To prove that a document was not filed, the party should present sworn testimony from the clerk that the document was not received. If the clerk's office has any procedure for logging documents as they are received, the log should be produced.

2. Affidavit by USPS claims clerk. To disprove the date on a green card, a party can secure an affidavit from the USPS claims clerk. *Cf.* **Ogunboyejo v. Prudential Prop. & Cas. Co.**, 844 S.W.2d 860, 862 (Tex.App.—Texarkana 1992, writ denied) (case involved service of discovery requests; D introduced postal clerk's affidavit to show P's attorney had altered number on green card to reflect earlier mailing date). The USPS keeps a record of each certified-mail delivery by date and number. *See id.*

§12. Court's dockets

The TRCPs require the clerk to keep five dockets.

§12.1 Clerk's file docket—TRCP 25. The clerk's file docket must show the cause number of the suit, the attorneys' names, the parties' names, the nature of the suit, the officer's return on the process (in brief form), and all proceedings in the case with the dates of each proceeding. Tex. R. Civ. P. 25.

1. Order of cases. The clerk must place cases on the docket as they are filed. Tex. R. Civ. P. 27. A case is "docketed" when the clerk places the case on the list of cases pending in the court. **Bigham v. Dempster**, 901 S.W.2d 424, 431 (Tex.1995).

2. Order of pleadings. The clerk must note on the docket every pleading, plea, motion, or application to the court for an order, regardless of its form. Tex. R. Civ. P. 21(a). The clerk must docket pleadings according to the title designated by the parties (e.g., motion for new trial). Tex. R. Civ. P. 71. If the court orders a pleading to be redesignated, the clerk must modify the docket and all other records to reflect the redesignation. *Id.* See "Incorrect title," ch. 1-B, §3.2.3(2); "Incorrect title," ch. 1-B, §4.1.3(2).

§12.2 Clerk's court docket—TRCP 26. Each clerk must keep a court docket in a permanent record that includes the cause number of the case and the parties' names, the attorneys' names, the nature of the action, the pleas, the motions, and the court's rulings. Tex. R. Civ. P. 26. The clerk's docket entries of rulings are made only for the clerk's convenience and are not considered rulings of the court. **Miller v. Kendall**, 804 S.W.2d 933, 944 (Tex.App.—Houston [1st Dist.] 1990, no writ). In only a few situations can the appellate courts consider docket entries to determine a trial court's ruling. *See, e.g.*, **Escobar v. Escobar**, 711 S.W.2d 230, 232 (Tex.1986) (to determine whether court had authority to correct judgment by nunc pro tunc); **Pruet v. Coastal States Trading, Inc.**, 715 S.W.2d 702, 705 (Tex.App.—Houston [1st Dist.] 1986, no writ) (to determine clerical error in nunc pro tunc proceeding); **Buffalo Bag Co. v. Joachim**, 704 S.W.2d 482, 484 (Tex.App.—Houston [14th Dist.] 1986, writ ref'd n.r.e.) (to determine whether motion for new trial that was lost by clerk had been filed).

§12.3 Jury docket—TRCP 218. The court clerk must keep a docket, titled "The Jury Docket," to list the cases in which jury fees were paid or affidavits were filed instead of fees. Tex. R. Civ. P. 218; *see* **Higginbotham v. Collateral Prot., Inc.**, 859 S.W.2d 487, 488 n.1 (Tex.App.—Houston [1st Dist.] 1993, writ denied).

§12.4 Nonjury docket—TRCP 249. Cases not set on the jury docket are set on the nonjury docket. *See* Tex. R. Civ. P. 249.

§12.5 Dismissal docket—TRCP 165a(2). Any case not disposed of within the time standards set by the Supreme Court under its Administrative Rules may be placed on a dismissal docket. Tex. R. Civ. P. 165a(2); **In re Seals**, 83 S.W.3d 870, 874 (Tex.App.—Texarkana 2002, no pet.).

D. Rules for Serving Documents

§1. General

§1.1 Rules. Tex. R. Civ. P. 21, 21a.

§1.2 Purpose. The purpose of serving documents is to give the other party a copy of the documents filed with the court. Recall the distinction between filing and serving: documents are filed with the clerk and served on other parties. This subchapter discusses serving documents after the suit has been filed. It does not discuss service of citation. TRCP 21 and 21a, which govern service of all documents other than citation, provide less formal service requirements than the rules for service of citation. **Texas Nat. Res. Conserv. Comm'n v. Sierra Club**, 70 S.W.3d 809, 813 (Tex.2002). For a discussion of service of citation, see "Serving the Defendant with Suit," ch. 2-I, §1 et seq.

§1.3 Forms. **O'Connor's Texas Civil Forms**, FORMS 1B:13 to 1B:15 (2020 ed.).

§2. What to serve

An attorney should serve all parties with a copy of each document filed with the court and copies of all other communications with the court about the lawsuit. *See* Tex. R. Civ. P. 21(a); *see also* Tex. R. Civ. P. 21(e) (served party can get additional copies by making reasonable payment for copies and delivery). Any communication with the court about the lawsuit that is not served on opposing counsel is an improper ex parte communication unless there is a specific exception. *See* Tex. Disciplinary R. Prof'l Conduct 3.05(b)(2). Certain documents that are not filed may also need to be served on the parties. *See, e.g.*, Tex. R. Civ. P. 197.1 (interrogatories).

§3. Whom to serve

§3.1 Party or attorney? If a party is represented by an attorney, all documents must be served on the attorney. *See* Tex. R. Civ. P. 8, 21a(a). The rules of ethics prohibit an attorney from communicating about a lawsuit with a party who is represented by counsel. Tex. Disciplinary R. Prof'l Conduct 4.02(a). Only when a party is not represented by counsel should an attorney serve documents on the party. Once a party secures an attorney, all communications must be sent to the attorney. **Lester v. Capital Indus.**, 153 S.W.3d 93, 96 (Tex.App.—San Antonio 2004, no pet.); **Morin v. Boecker**, 122 S.W.3d 911, 914 (Tex.App.—Corpus Christi 2003, no pet.); **In re Household Fin. Corp. III**, No. 14-08-00673-CV, 2008 WL 5220542 (Tex.App.—Houston [14th Dist.] 2008, orig. proceeding) (memo op.; 12-11-08). *But see* **Trevino v. Hidalgo Publ'g**, 805 S.W.2d 862, 863 (Tex.App.—Corpus Christi 1991, no writ) (service of notice of summary-judgment hearing on party was not improper even though party was represented by attorney); **Krchnak v. Fulton**, 759 S.W.2d 524, 528 (Tex.App.—Amarillo 1988, writ denied) (same), *disapproved on other grounds*, **Carpenter v. Cimarron Hydrocarbons Corp.**, 98 S.W.3d 682 (Tex.2002).

§3.2 Which attorney? If a party is represented by more than one attorney, all documents must be served on the attorney in charge, generally the attorney who signed the first pleading or who has been specifically designated as the attorney in charge. Tex. R. Civ. P. 8; *see also* Tex. R. Civ. P. 21(c) (service on each attorney in charge when multiple parties are represented by different attorneys). Service on an attorney other than the attorney in charge is not considered service. *See* Tex. R. Civ. P. 8; **Reichhold Chems., Inc. v. Puremco Mfg.**, 854 S.W.2d 240, 245–46 (Tex.App.—Waco 1993, writ denied); *cf.* **Kenley v. Quintana Pet. Corp.**, 931 S.W.2d 318, 321 (Tex.App.—San Antonio 1996, writ denied) (clerk's notice of dismissal to local counsel did not comply with TRCP 8, which requires notice to attorney in charge). See "Attorney in charge," ch. 1-H, §3.1.

§3.3 How many parties? A copy of each document filed with the court must be served on the attorney in charge for each party, no matter how many parties there are. *See* Tex. R. Civ. P. 21(c) (copy of each pleading must be served on each attorney in charge). If there are so many parties that serving them all is burdensome, a party can ask the court for relief under TRCP 166, the pretrial-conference rule. The court may then designate certain key parties to receive documents on behalf of other parties. *See* Tex. R. Civ. P. 166.

§4. How to serve

§4.1 Who can serve. The following persons can serve documents: the attorney of record, the party, a sheriff, a constable, or any other person competent to testify. Tex. R. Civ. P. 21a(d); **State v. Bristol Hotel Asset Co.**, 65 S.W.3d 638, 642 (Tex.2001).

§4.2 Methods of service. The method of service depends on whether a document was e-filed. For a detailed discussion of e-filing, see "E-filing," ch. 1-C, §4.1.1.

1. Document was e-filed.

(1) Generally—e-service. If a document was e-filed, a party must serve it electronically (e-service) through the electronic-filing manager (EFM), as long as the EFM has on file the e-mail address of the attorney or pro se party to be served. Tex. R. Civ. P. 21a(a)(1).

(a) Service complete. E-service is complete when the document is sent to the serving party's electronic-filing service provider (EFSP). Tex. R. Civ. P. 21a(b)(3); *cf.* Tex. R. App. P. 9.5(c)(4) (same, for appeals). *But cf.* Tex. R. Civ. P. 501.4(a)(4) (in justice courts, document served by e-mail after 5:00 p.m. local time of recipient is deemed served on following day). The EFM will send a confirmation notice of service to the e-serving party. Tex. R. Civ. P. 21a(b)(3).

(b) Signing documents. Any document that is e-served must contain an electronic signature. *See* Tex. R. Civ. P. 21(f)(7). See "Electronic signature," ch. 1-B, §3.2.12(2)(b).

(c) Fees. Depending on the EFSP, a party may have to pay transaction and service fees. *See* www.efiletexas.gov/faqs.htm (select "Is there a fee to use eFileTexas.gov?").

(2) Exception—e-mail not on file. If a document was e-filed but the e-mail address of the attorney or pro se party to be served is not on file with the EFM, a party may serve the document as if it had not been e-filed—that is, by any method under TRCP 21a(a)(2). Tex. R. Civ. P. 21a(a)(1).

2. Document was not e-filed. If a document was not e-filed, a party may serve it by any of the following methods.

Note

Certain documents, such as discovery requests on a party, are generally not e-filed or filed by other traditional methods. See "Filing discovery," ch. 6-A, §12.1. Parties required to serve unfiled documents can use the EFM to serve those documents as long as the e-mail address of the attorney or pro se party to be served is on file with the EFM. See www.efiletexas.gov/faqs.htm (select "Can I use e-service without filing a document with the court?"). If the e-mail address of the attorney or pro se party is not on file with the EFM, the party can use the methods identified below.

(1) Mail. A party may serve documents by mail. Tex. R. Civ. P. 21a(a)(2). Service by mail is complete upon mailing. *See* Tex. R. Civ. P. 21a(b)(1); *cf.* Tex. R. App. P. 9.5(c)(1) (for appeals, same). When a party serves a document by mail, it invokes the "mailbox rule" in TRCP 21a. A document is considered served on the day it is deposited in the mail if all the following conditions are met:

(a) The document was sent by U.S. mail, which includes regular mail or certified or registered mail. *See* Tex. R. Civ. P. 21a(a)(2), (b)(1).

(b) The document was properly addressed to the other party and mailed with postage paid. Tex. R. Civ. P. 21a(b)(1). Under TRCP 21a, a document that is properly addressed and mailed with postage paid is presumed to have been received by the addressee. **Thomas v. Ray**, 889 S.W.2d 237, 238 (Tex.1994); *see* Tex. R. Civ. P. 21a(b)(1).

(c) The attorney of record or the party signed a certificate of service stating that the filed document was served in compliance with TRCP 21a. Tex. R. Civ. P. 21a(e). The certificate is prima facie evidence of the date of service. **Shaw v. National Cty. Mut. Fire Ins.**, 723 S.W.2d 236, 237 (Tex.App.—Houston [1st Dist.] 1986, no writ); *see* Tex. R. Civ. P. 21a(e) (certificate is prima facie evidence of service); **State v. Bristol Hotel Asset Co.**, 65 S.W.3d 638, 642 (Tex.2001) (same).

Caution

The mailbox rule for filing with the clerk differs from the mailbox rule for serving a document on the other party. The most important difference is that the ten-day grace period for receipt in TRCP 5 does

not apply to service of documents on parties. ***Salazar v. Canales****, 85 S.W.3d 859, 863–64 (Tex.App.—Corpus Christi 2002, no pet.). See "Mail," ch. 1-C, §4.1.2(1). Thus, when a document is mailed to the other party on the date it is due, it is considered served on the other party on the date it was mailed, no matter when the other party receives it.*

(2) Delivery. A party may serve documents by personal delivery or commercial delivery service. Tex. R. Civ. P. 21a(a)(2).

(a) Personal delivery. Service by personal delivery may be accomplished by the party, the attorney, or a member of the attorney's office staff. *See* Tex. R. Civ. P. 21a(a)(2), (d). Service of a document by personal delivery is complete when it is delivered to the party or the party's authorized agent or attorney of record. *See* Tex. R. Civ. P. 21a(a).

(b) Commercial delivery. Service by commercial delivery may be accomplished by a commercial delivery service (e.g., FedEx, UPS). *See* Tex. R. Civ. P. 21a(a)(2). Service of a document by commercial delivery is complete when it is deposited with the commercial delivery service. Tex. R. Civ. P. 21a(b)(1); *cf.* Tex. R. App. P. 9.5(c)(2) (for appeals, documents are served when placed in control of commercial delivery service). The document must be properly addressed and deposited with shipping fees paid. Tex. R. Civ. P. 21a(b)(1).

(3) Fax. A party may serve documents by fax. Tex. R. Civ. P. 21a(a)(2). Service by fax is complete on receipt. Tex. R. Civ. P. 21a(b)(2); *cf.* Tex. R. App. P. 9.5(c)(3) (for appeals, same). A document served by fax is considered served on the day the fax is sent if it is received before 5:00 p.m. local time of the recipient. *See* Tex. R. Civ. P. 21a(b)(2). If the document is received after 5:00 p.m. local time of the recipient, it is considered served on the next day. *Id.* The sender's fax machine should be set to produce a transmission-verification report confirming the date and time the document was sent and received. The report should be attached to the attorney's file copy of the document in case it becomes necessary to prove the date and time of service.

(4) E-mail. A party may serve documents by e-mail. Tex. R. Civ. P. 21a(a)(2). The party can use the e-mail address identified on a party's pleading. *See* Tex. R. Civ. P. 57 (every pleading signed by attorney or pro se party must include e-mail address). Although not specified under TRCP 21a, service by e-mail is presumably complete on transmission of the document to the receiving party. *Cf.* Tex. R. Civ. P. 21a(b)(3) (e-service is complete on transmission of document to party's EFSP).

(5) According to order. A party may use some other type of service if it can prove to the court that another method is necessary and the court signs an order to that effect. *See* Tex. R. Civ. P. 21a(a)(2).

§4.3 Certificate of service. Once the defendant has been served with process and is before the court, all other documents filed with the court and served on other parties or nonparties should contain a certificate of service, signed by the attorney of record or the party. *See* Tex. R. Civ. P. 21(d), 21a(e); **State v. Bristol Hotel Asset Co.**, 65 S.W.3d 638, 642 (Tex.2001). The certificate of service should identify the person on whom it was served and, although not required, the method of service used. *See* Tex. R. Civ. P. 21a(a), (e); **Approximately $14,980.00 v. State**, 261 S.W.3d 182, 187 (Tex.App.—Houston [14th Dist.] 2008, no pet.). For the proper contents of the certificate, see "Contents," ch. 1-B, §3.2.13(1); **O'Connor's Texas Civil Forms**, FORM 1B:13 (2020 ed.).

§5. When to serve

§5.1 With filing. Every document that must be filed must be served on all other parties at the same time it is filed. Tex. R. Civ. P. 21(a).

§5.2 By deadline to respond. A party should serve a document before the deadline to respond established by the TRCPs, statutes, or court order. See "Computing response deadlines," ch. 1-D, §6.

§5.3 Before hearing on motion. Motions presented to the court for an order (unless presented during a hearing or trial) must be served on all other parties at least three days before the hearing. Tex. R. Civ. P. 21(b). In some situations (e.g., an application for a TRO), the court can shorten the three-day notice requirement. *See id.* It is not clear whether Saturdays,

Sundays, and legal holidays are counted for purposes of calculating the three-day notice of hearings in TRCP 21. *See* Tex. R. Civ. P. 4. See "Caution," ch. 1-E, §2.1. Some rules require more than three days' notice. *E.g.*, Tex. R. Civ. P. 12 (motion for attorney to show authority, ten days before hearing), Tex. R. Civ. P. 76a(4) (motion to seal court records, no less than 14 days after motion is filed and notice is posted), Tex. R. Civ. P. 166a(c) (motion for summary judgment, 21 days before hearing).

§6. Computing response deadlines

If a served document requires a response within a certain time period, the recipient calculates the date the response is due from the date of service. The date to respond depends on the type of service used. For the general rules for computing deadlines, see "Computing filing deadlines," ch. 1-C, §7.

§6.1 E-service. For a document served electronically, service is complete when the document is sent to the serving party's EFSP. Tex. R. Civ. P. 21a(b)(3). See "Service complete," ch. 1-D, §4.2.1(1)(a). To determine the date to respond, count from the date the document was served. *See* Tex. R. Civ. P. 21a(b)(3).

§6.2 Mail. For a document served by mail, service is complete when the document is mailed. *See* Tex. R. Civ. P. 21a(b)(1). To determine the date to respond, add three days to whatever time the party has to respond to the document, counting from the date of mailing. *See* Tex. R. Civ. P. 21a(c). For example, TRCP 21a extends the minimum notice for a hearing on a motion for summary judgment from 21 to 24 days when the motion is served by mail. **Lewis v. Blake**, 876 S.W.2d 314, 315–16 (Tex.1994); *see also* **Cherry v. North Am. Lloyds**, 770 S.W.2d 4, 5 (Tex.App.—Houston [1st Dist.] 1989, writ denied) (when party receives request for admissions by mail, TRCP 21a adds three days to 30 days permitted by TRCP 198.2(a), formerly TRCP 169, to serve answers). The three-day grace period presumes that the post office delivered the document within three days after it was mailed. If there is an unusual delay, the recipient should file a motion with the court before the response is due, stating that the recipient did not receive the document within three days and needs additional time to respond. *See* Tex. R. Civ. P. 5, 21a(e); **Cudd v. Hydrostatic Transmission, Inc.**, 867 S.W.2d 101, 103 (Tex.App.—Corpus Christi 1993, no writ).

§6.3 Delivery.

1. Personal delivery. For a document served by personal delivery, service is complete when the document is delivered. *See* Tex. R. Civ. P. 21a(a)(2). To determine the date to respond, count from the date the document was delivered. *See id.*

2. Commercial delivery. For a document served by commercial delivery (e.g., FedEx, UPS), service is complete when the document is deposited with the commercial delivery service. Tex. R. Civ. P. 21a(b)(1). See "Commercial delivery," ch. 1-D, §4.2.2(2)(b). To determine the date to respond, count from the date the document was deposited with the commercial delivery service. *See* Tex. R. Civ. P. 21a(b)(1).

§6.4 Fax. For a document served by fax, service is complete when the document is received, if before 5:00 p.m. local time of the recipient. *See* Tex. R. Civ. P. 21a(b)(2). When a fax is received after 5:00 p.m. local time of the recipient, the document is deemed served on the next day, even if it is a Saturday, Sunday, or legal holiday. *See* Tex. R. Civ. P. 4, 21a(b)(2); **Amaya v. Enriquez**, 296 S.W.3d 781, 784 (Tex.App.—El Paso 2009, pet. denied). To determine the date to respond, count from the date the document was served. *See* Tex. R. Civ. P. 21a(b)(2).

Note

Three days are not added to a party's response time when served by fax; three days are added only when service is by mail. See Tex. R. Civ. P. 21a(c); Tex.Sup.Ct. Order, Misc. Docket No. 13-9165 (eff. Jan. 1, 2014). See "Mail," ch. 1-D, §6.2.

§6.5 E-mail. For a document served by e-mail, service is presumably complete when the document is sent to the receiving party. *Cf.* Tex. R. Civ. P. 21a(b)(3) (e-service is complete on transmission to party's EFSP). To determine the date to respond, count from the date the document was e-mailed.

1-2. Computing Response Deadlines		
Document served by		Deadline
1	E-service	Date of e-service + number of days to respond
2	Mail	Date of mailing (generally, postmark date) + 3 days + number of days to respond
3	Personal delivery	Date of delivery + number of days to respond
4	Commercial delivery	Date of deposit with commercial delivery service + number of days to respond
5	Fax before 5 p.m.	Date of fax + number of days to respond
6	Fax after 5 p.m.	Date of fax + 1 day + number of days to respond
7	E-mail	Date of e-mail + number of days to respond

§7. Proving service

TRCP 21a creates a presumption that a properly sent document was received by the addressee. **Mathis v. Lockwood**, 166 S.W.3d 743, 745 (Tex.2005); **Thomas v. Ray**, 889 S.W.2d 237, 238 (Tex.1994); *see* Tex. R. Civ. P. 21a(e). The presumption disappears when opposing evidence is introduced. **In re E.A.**, 287 S.W.3d 1, 5 (Tex.2009); **Wembley Inv. v. Herrera**, 11 S.W.3d 924, 927 (Tex.1999).

§7.1 Proving receipt.

1. Proving all methods of service.

(1) Certificate of service. To prove the receipt of a served document, a party should call the court's attention to the certificate of service attached to the served document, signed by the attorney of record or the party. *See* Tex. R. Civ. P. 21a(e); **State v. Bristol Hotel Asset Co.**, 65 S.W.3d 638, 642 (Tex.2001). The certificate of service on the document is prima facie evidence of service. Tex. R. Civ. P. 21a(e); **In re E.A.**, 287 S.W.3d 1, 5 (Tex.2009); **Jacobs v. Jacobs**, 448 S.W.3d 626, 632 (Tex.App.—Houston [14th Dist.] 2014, no pet.); **Limestone Constr., Inc. v. Summit Commercial Indus. Props., Inc.**, 143 S.W.3d 538, 544 (Tex.App.—Austin 2004, no pet.).

(2) Affidavit. To prove the receipt of a served document, a party can file the affidavit of any person describing the type and date of service. *See* Tex. R. Civ. P. 21a(e); **Bristol Hotel**, 65 S.W.3d at 642; **Thomas v. Ray**, 889 S.W.2d 237, 238 (Tex.1994). The affidavit is prima facie evidence of service. Tex. R. Civ. P. 21a(e); **Jacobs**, 448 S.W.3d at 632. When relying on office routine or custom to support an inference that the document was sent, the party must provide corroborating evidence that the practice was actually carried out. **Wembley Inv. v. Herrera**, 11 S.W.3d 924, 928 (Tex.1999); **Mocega v. Urquhart**, 79 S.W.3d 61, 65 (Tex.App.—Houston [14th Dist.] 2002, pet. denied).

2. Proving e-service. To prove the receipt of a document served electronically, a party can introduce the confirmation of service sent to the party by the EFM. *See* Tex. R. Civ. P. 21a(b)(3). See "Service complete," ch. 1-D, §4 2.1(1)(a).

3. Proving service by mail. To prove the receipt of a document served by mail, a party can introduce certain documents from the U.S. Postal Service. The party should verify the contents of the document by either attaching it to an affidavit or presenting sworn proof at a hearing.

(1) Return receipt—green card. To prove the receipt of a document served by mail, a party can introduce a domestic-mail return receipt (the "green card") which establishes the date of delivery and the person who received the delivery. *See* USPS Form 3811; *see, e.g.*, **Ruiz v. Nicolas Trevino Forwarding Agency, Inc.**, 888 S.W.2d 86, 88 (Tex.App.—San Antonio 1994, no writ) (when green card was not produced and other party swore document was not received, presumption of service was rebutted); *cf.* Tex. R. App. P. 9.2(b)(2)(B) (appellate courts will accept USPS-endorsed receipt for registered or certified mail as conclusive proof of date of mailing). Alternatively, a party can introduce an electronic return receipt to establish the date of delivery and who received the delivery. *See* about.usps.com/publications/pub370.pdf. To obtain return-receipt service, the party must send the document by (1) certified mail, (2) collect on delivery (COD), (3) insured mail, or (4) registered mail. *Id.*; *see* USPS Forms 3800 (certified mail), 3806 (registered mail). Although certified mail can be placed in a post-office mail drop, a party should present the document to a USPS employee and have a round-date applied to the form to

show the date the article was accepted by the USPS.

Practice Tip

When using certified mail, an attorney should type the certified-mail identification number on the document so certified-mail receipts can easily be matched to the document. This prevents opposing counsel from claiming that the receipt was for some other communication.

(2) Return receipt after mailing. To prove the receipt of a document served by mail when the green card is lost or not returned or when the party did not request a return receipt at the time of mailing, a party can introduce a domestic-mail return receipt. *See* USPS Form 3811-A ("Request for Delivery Information/Return Receipt"). The receipt establishes the date of delivery and the person who received the delivery according to the post office's records. *See id.*

(3) Certificate of mailing. To prove the receipt of a document served by mail, a party can introduce a USPS certificate of mailing. *See* USPS Form 3817; *cf.* Tex. R. App. P. 9.2(b)(2)(C) (appellate courts will accept USPS certificate of mailing as conclusive proof of date of mailing). The certificate of mailing provides evidence that a document was presented to the USPS for mailing; it does not provide a record of delivery. *See* USPS Form 3817.

4. Proving service by delivery. To prove the receipt of a document served by delivery, a party can introduce a signed and dated receipt from the person served or the commercial delivery service. *See* Tex. R. Civ. P. 21a(b)(1); *cf.* Tex. R. App. P. 9.2(b)(2)(D) (appellate courts will accept receipt endorsed by commercial delivery service as conclusive proof of date of mailing).

5. Proving service by fax. To prove the receipt of a document served by fax, a party can introduce the transmission-verification report. *See* **American Paging v. El Paso Paging, Inc.**, 9 S.W.3d 237, 240 (Tex.App.—El Paso 1999, pet. denied) (evidence showing fax to recipient's current fax number raises presumption that document was received by addressee). See "Fax," ch. 1-D, §4.2.2(3). The report must be attached to an affidavit.

6. Proving service by e-mail. To prove the receipt of a document served by e-mail, a party can introduce a transmission report verifying when the document was e-mailed. *See* Tex. R. Civ. P. 21a(a)(2). See "E-mail," ch. 1-D, §4.2.2(4).

7. Proving constructive service. To prove constructive service, a party can prove the other party refused to accept service. **Etheredge v. Hidden Valley Airpark Ass'n**, 169 S.W.3d 378, 382 (Tex.App.—Fort Worth 2005, pet. denied); *see* **Jacobs**, 448 S.W.3d at 632; *see, e.g.*, **Roberts v. Roberts**, 133 S.W.3d 661, 663 (Tex.App.—Corpus Christi 2003, no pet.) (P had constructive notice of judgment because she refused to accept certified mail).

Practice Tip

*An addressee cannot obstruct service by refusing to accept delivery of or refusing to retrieve certified mail after notice by the post office. See **Jacobs**, 448 S.W.3d at 633; **Osborn v. Osborn**, 961 S.W.2d 408, 412–13 (Tex.App.—Houston [1st Dist.] 1997, pet. denied); **Gonzales v. Surplus Ins.**, 863 S.W.2d 96, 101–02 (Tex.App.—Beaumont 1993, writ denied), disapproved on other grounds, **Carpenter v. Cimarron Hydrocarbons Corp.**, 98 S.W.3d 682 (Tex.2002).*

§7.2 Proving nonreceipt. The presumption of receipt in TRCP 21a disappears when verified evidence is introduced that the document was not received. *E.g.*, **Wembley Inv. v. Herrera**, 11 S.W.3d 924, 927 (Tex.1999) (attorneys provided affidavits stating they never received nonsuit motion or judgment); **Thomas v. Ray**, 889 S.W.2d 237, 238–39 (Tex.1994) (party claiming nonreceipt did not present any verified evidence); **Cliff v. Huggins**, 724 S.W.2d 778, 779–80 (Tex.1987) (party and attorney swore they did not receive notice of trial setting); *see* Tex. R. Civ. P. 21a(e); *see also* **Mathis v. Lockwood**, 166 S.W.3d 743, 745 (Tex.2005) (presumption did not apply because record contained no certificate of service, no return receipt of certified or registered mail, and no affidavit certifying service).

1. Affidavit by USPS claims clerk. To disprove the date on a green card, a party can secure an affidavit from the USPS claims clerk. *See, e.g.*, **Ogunboyejo v. Prudential Prop. & Cas. Co.**, 844 S.W.2d 860, 862 (Tex.App.—Texarkana

1992, writ denied) (D introduced postal clerk's affidavit to show P's attorney had altered number on green card to reflect earlier mailing date). The USPS keeps a record of each certified-mail delivery by date and number. *See id.*

2. Testimony of attorney & party. To prove that a document was not received, a party can present sworn testimony that neither the attorney nor the party received the document. *See* **Cliff**, 724 S.W.2d at 779; *see, e.g.,* **Smith v. Holmes**, 53 S.W.3d 815, 817–18 (Tex.App.—Austin 2001, no pet.) (pro se inmate submitted declaration denying he had received document). The attorney in charge of the case at the time the document was sent should testify that the document was not received. *See* Tex. R. Civ. P. 8; **Wembley Inv.**, 11 S.W.3d at 927. The testimony of another attorney in the same firm will not rebut the presumption that the document was received. *See* **Gonzalez v. Stevenson**, 791 S.W.2d 250, 252 (Tex.App.—Corpus Christi 1990, no writ).

§8. Sanctions for failure to serve

TRCP 21b authorizes sanctions under TRCP 215.2(b) for failure to serve copies of pleadings and motions. See "Failure to serve—TRCP 21b," ch. 5-K, §5.3; **O'Connor's Texas Civil Forms**, FORM 5K:3 (2020 ed.).

E. Types of Hearings

§1. General

§1.1 Rule. Tex. R. Civ. P. 21.

§1.2 Purpose. A hearing brings the parties before the court to argue and sometimes to present evidence.

§1.3 Forms. **O'Connor's Texas Civil Forms**, FORMS 1E:1 et seq. (2020 ed.).

§1.4 Other references. **O'Connor's Texas Civil Appeals** (2020 ed.).

§2. Notice of hearing

§2.1 First setting. The party scheduling a hearing on a motion for an order must serve notice of the hearing on all parties at least three days before the hearing, unless the rules provide otherwise or the court shortens the period. Tex. R. Civ. P. 21(b). See **O'Connor's Texas Civil Forms**, FORM 1E:1 (2020 ed.). In determining whether to shorten the notice period, the court should consider the exigent circumstances of the particular case. **Cotten v. Briley**, 517 S.W.3d 177, 185 (Tex.App.—Texarkana 2017, no pet.).

Caution

TRCP 4 seems to say that Saturdays, Sundays, and legal holidays "shall be counted for purposes of the three-day periods in Rules 21 and 21a . . . ." If the courts interpret it that way, a party may give notice on a Friday for a hearing the next Monday. But there is an ambiguity created by the qualifying phrase in TRCP 4 after the reference to the three-day periods in Rules 21 and 21a—"extending other periods by three days when service is made by mail." The qualifying phrase seems to indicate that Saturdays, Sundays, and legal holidays are not counted for the three days' notice for the hearing in TRCP 21(b) because the notice requirement is not "extending other periods by three days." See "Computing time limits—days," ch. 1-C, §7.1.

---

§2.2 Resetting. When a hearing on a motion is reset, the three-day notice requirement in TRCP 21 does not apply if the parties had proper notice of the original hearing. *See* **Magnuson v. Mullen**, 65 S.W.3d 815, 824 (Tex.App.—Fort Worth 2002, pet. denied).

§3. Duties of court reporter

The duties of the court reporter are prescribed by TRAP 13 and Gov't Code §52.046. For a detailed discussion of the court reporter's duties, see "Duties of court reporter & court recorder," **O'Connor's Texas Civil Appeals**, ch. 6-C, §2 (2020 ed.).

§3.1 Attend court & make record.

1. TRAP 13.1. Under TRAP 13.1, the court reporter must attend all sessions of the court and make a full record of the proceedings unless excused by agreement of the parties. Tex. R. App. P. 13.1(a); **Michiana Easy Livin' Country, Inc. v. Holten**, 168 S.W.3d 777, 783 (Tex.2005); **Rittenhouse v. Sabine Valley Ctr. Found.**, 161 S.W.3d 157, 161 (Tex.App.—Texarkana 2005, no pet.); *see* **Palmer v. Espey Huston & Assocs.**, 84 S.W.3d 345, 350–51 (Tex.App.—Corpus Christi 2002, pet. denied); *see also* Tex. Fam. Code §105.003(c) (court reporter must record all suits affecting the parent-child relationship unless parties waive record with court's consent). In a pretrial hearing, the court reporter must make a record only if evidence is introduced in open court. **Michiana**, 168 S.W.3d at 781–82.

2. Gov't Code §52.046. Under Gov't Code §52.046, the court reporter must, on request, attend all sessions of the court and take shorthand notes of oral testimony and, if requested by a party's attorney, closing arguments. Tex. Gov't Code §52.046(a)(1) to (a)(3).

Caution

Although TRAP 13.1(a) requires a court reporter to attend all sessions of the court and make a full record of all proceedings unless excused by agreement of the parties, Gov't Code §52.046(a) requires a court reporter to attend and make a full record of the proceedings only if requested by a party. Thus, it is unclear whether a party who wants a record made must request that a court reporter attend and make a record. In ***Michiana****, the Supreme Court followed TRAP 13.1(a) without addressing the apparent conflict between the rule and the statute. See* ***Michiana****, 168 S.W.3d at 783 & n.20. Some courts of appeals, however, have held that the statute controls. See, e.g.,* ***Nicholson v. Fifth Third Bank****, 226 S.W.3d 581, 583 (Tex.App.—Houston [1st Dist.] 2007, no pet.) (party must request record; Gov't Code §52.046(a) controls); see also* ***Nabelek v. District Atty. of Harris Cty.****, 290 S.W.3d 222, 231–32 (Tex.App.—Houston [14th Dist.] 2005, pet. denied) (applying Gov't Code §52.046; error not preserved because P did not request that court reporter record hearing and did not object to reporter's failure to record hearing); cf.* ***Langford v. State****, 129 S.W.3d 138, 139 (Tex.App.—Dallas 2003, no pet.) (criminal case; Gov't Code §52.046(a) controls, so party must request record). Until this conflict is resolved, the best practice is to request that a court reporter attend and make a full record of the proceedings. See* ***O'Connor's Texas Civil Forms****, FORM 1E:2 (2020 ed.). If a court reporter does not record a hearing or part of a trial, the party must object to preserve error. See* ***Nabelek****, 290 S.W.3d at 231–32.*

§3.2 Accept & file exhibits. The court reporter must accept and mark all exhibits offered as evidence during a hearing or trial and file them with the court clerk. Tex. R. App. P. 13.1(b), (c).

§3.3 Preserve notes. On request, a court reporter must preserve the notes from a hearing or trial for three years from the date they were taken. Tex. Gov't Code §52.046(a)(4). See **O'Connor's Texas Civil Forms**, FORM 1E:2 (2020 ed.). After three years, even if the case is still pending, the court reporter can destroy stale notes if no party has requested that they be preserved or transcribed. **Piotrowski v. Minns**, 873 S.W.2d 368, 371 (Tex.1993); **Ganesan v. Vallabhaneni**, 96 S.W.3d 345, 349 (Tex.App.—Austin 2002, pet. denied). Once a lawsuit has been pending for three years, a party should either ask the court reporter to transcribe the record or file a motion with the court to require the court reporter to preserve all notes from hearings and the trial. See **O'Connor's Texas Civil Forms**, FORM 1E:3 (2020 ed.).

§3.4 Prepare reporter's record. The court reporter must prepare the reporter's record for appeal when requested by a party. *See* Tex. R. App. P. 13.1(d); *see also* Tex. Gov't Code §52.046(a)(5) (if requested, court reporter must furnish transcript of reported evidence or other proceedings); Tex. R. App. P. 35.3(b) (responsibility for filing reporter's record).

§4. Hearing on motion

The court will not always hold a hearing before ruling on a motion. The term "hearing" does not necessarily mean a personal appearance before the court or an oral presentation to the court. **Martin v. Martin, Martin & Richards, Inc.**, 989 S.W.2d 357, 359 (Tex.1998). If the court conducts a hearing, it will not always permit the parties to introduce evidence. Some rules provide for a hearing or submission date as a way of creating a deadline for filing the response (e.g., motion for summary judgment).

§4.1 Hearing for argument only. If a rule prohibits oral testimony at the hearing, the hearing is for argument only. When the hearing is for argument only, the party can submit a motion for the court's decision without actually making an appearance to argue the motion in court. For example, the summary-judgment rule states: "No oral testimony shall be received . . . ." Tex. R. Civ. P. 166a(c). Because no evidence is presented at a summary-judgment hearing, the court can decide the motion on the pleadings, without an appearance by the attorneys before the court. See "On submission," ch. 7-B, §11.1.2. A hearing for argument only does not need to be recorded by a court reporter. See "Reporter's record not necessary," **O'Connor's Texas Civil Appeals**, ch. 6-C, §3.2 (2020 ed.).

§4.2 Hearing for evidence. When a hearing is for the receipt of evidence, it should be recorded.

1. Hearing required. A few rules require the trial court to hold a hearing to receive evidence before ruling. For example, TRCP 165a requires the court to conduct a hearing on a motion to reinstate a case after dismissal for want of prosecution. See "Hearing," ch. 10-F, §7.

2. Hearing requested. If a rule authorizes a hearing for the receipt of evidence and the party asks for a hearing, the court must conduct one. For example, when a party objects to a legislative continuance on due-process grounds, the trial court cannot refuse the party a hearing. **Waites v. Sondock**, 561 S.W.2d 772, 776 (Tex.1977).

§4.3 Submitted on pleadings & proof. Courts tend not to hold full evidentiary hearings in open court for most pretrial matters. **Michiana Easy Livin' Country, Inc. v. Holten**, 168 S.W.3d 777, 782 (Tex.2005). The Supreme Court encourages the submission of written proof when testimony and evidence can fairly resolve factual issues. *See id.* at 782–83. The Rules of Judicial Administration approve the submission of motions on written pleadings instead of by a personal appearance for a hearing. *See* Tex. R. Jud. Admin. 7(a)(6)(b); **Koslow's v. Mackie**, 796 S.W.2d 700, 703 (Tex.1990). Some motions requiring evidence may be submitted on a verified motion and affidavits, without oral testimony.

Practice Tip

If in doubt whether a particular motion may be submitted on the pleadings, file a written agreement stating that the parties agree to submit the motion for a ruling based on the motion, the response, and the evidence attached to the motion and response. Make sure the agreement meets the requirements of TRCP 11. See "Agreements between attorneys—Rule 11," ch. 1-H, §9.

§4.4 Telephone hearing. The Rules of Judicial Administration permit a telephone hearing on a motion instead of a personal appearance. Tex. R. Jud. Admin. 7(a)(6)(b); **Gulf Coast Inv. v. NASA 1 Bus. Ctr.**, 754 S.W.2d 152, 153 (Tex.1988). Some courts have adopted local rules permitting telephone hearings on motions that do not require evidence. *E.g.*, **Xu v. Davis**, 884 S.W.2d 916, 918 n.2 (Tex.App.—Waco 1994, orig. proceeding) (Brazos County).

§5. Evidence for motions

§5.1 Live testimony. When a motion requires live testimony at the hearing, the parties must present evidence with all the formalities of a trial—the witnesses must be sworn, and the documents must be identified on the record, authenticated, and admitted into evidence. Statements made by an attorney during the hearing are not evidence. See "Attorney's appearance before court," ch. 1-H, §5.2.

§5.2 Affidavit & other sworn proof. Some motions that require evidence and are generally supported with live testimony (e.g., a motion to abate) can be submitted on a motion and sworn proof, without live testimony. Motions that do not permit live testimony must be submitted on pleadings and sworn proof (e.g., a motion for summary judgment or motion to transfer venue). See "Affidavits," ch. 1-B, §3.2.16.

§6. Waiver

§6.1 Type of hearing. If a party appears for what it assumes is a hearing for argument only but instead is a hearing to receive evidence, the party must object on the record to preserve the error for appeal. **Lemons v. EMW Mfg.**, 747 S.W.2d 372, 373 (Tex.1988). Similarly, if a party appears for what it assumes is a hearing for evidence but instead is a hearing for argument only, the party must object on the record. *See, e.g.*, **Union Carbide Corp. v. Moye**, 798 S.W.2d 792, 793 (Tex.1990) (D's attorney filed motion for continuance and asked for additional time to file affidavits when he discovered that no evidence would be received). The party should tell the trial court on the record that it expected to present argument (or evidence) and is not prepared to go forward. The party should file a handwritten, verified motion for continuance and describe the type of notice that was sent. *See* **Lemons**, 747 S.W.2d at 373. See "Verification," ch. 1-B, §3.2.15; "Making & Preserving Objections," ch. 1-F, §1 et seq.; "Motion for Continuance," ch. 5-D, §1 et seq.

§6.2 Order signed without hearing. To preserve error when the trial court signs an order without holding a hearing, a party who is entitled to a hearing and has properly requested one must file a motion asking the court to set aside the order and hold a hearing. *See, e.g.*, **State v. Owens**, 907 S.W.2d 484, 486 (Tex.1995) (party waived right to hearing to contest master's recommendations). See "Making & Preserving Objections," ch. 1-F, §1 et seq.

§6.3 Motion waived. If the movant does not present evidence when a rule permits it, in some cases the movant waives the motion. For example, when a party files a sworn motion to abate and attaches affidavits, the party must still ask for a

hearing and present testimony. **Atkinson v. Reid**, 625 S.W.2d 64, 67 (Tex.App.—San Antonio 1981, no writ). If the party does not ask for a hearing and present evidence, the court will overrule the motion.

§7. Securing attendance of witness

When a party plans to introduce evidence at a hearing on a motion, the party may subpoena a witness to attend the hearing. *See* Tex. R. Civ. P. 176.2. See "Subpoenas," ch. 1-L, §1 et seq.

§8. Review

The presumption on appeal is that pretrial hearings are nonevidentiary. **Michiana Easy Livin' Country, Inc. v. Holten**, 168 S.W.3d 777, 783 (Tex.2005). This presumption controls unless there is a specific indication or assertion to the contrary. *Id.* The presumption does not apply when the appellate court determines there was an evidentiary hearing because of the type of proceeding below, the trial court's order, or a specific assertion showing that an evidentiary hearing took place. *Id.* When an evidentiary hearing took place, the appellant must present a record of the hearing to the appellate court to establish harmful error. *Id.*

F. Making & Preserving Objections

§1. General

§1.1 Rules. Tex R Evid. 103; Tex R App. P. 33.1, 44.

§1.2 Purpose. There are two reasons to make objections. The first and most important reason is to convince the trial court of the merits of the party's position. The second reason is to make a record of the objection so that the party will be able to argue the objection on appeal as a ground for error. *See generally* Tex R App. P. 33.1 (preservation of complaints).

§1.3 Forms. None.

§1.4 Other references. Yeates et al., *Preservation of Error*, Advanced Evidence & Discovery Course, State Bar of Texas CLE, ch. 20 (2012).

§2. Grounds for objection

Almost every rule of procedure can be a ground for an objection. When a rule requires action by a party or by the court, the beneficiary of the rule may object to nonperformance or inadequate performance of the required action.

§3. Types of error

The type of objection and the timing of the objection depend on the type of error. If the error is committed by the jury in evaluating the facts, the objection must be made in writing, in either a motion for new trial or a motion for judgment notwithstanding the verdict. *See* Tex R Civ. P. 300, 320. If the error is committed by the trial judge in applying the law, the party may complain by making an oral objection in open court or by filing a written motion. See "Preserving error," ch. 1-F, §4. Thus, the objecting party must first decide who made what type of error.

§3.1 Role of jury. The jury's task is simple: it listens to the evidence and answers the questions the trial court submits to it by returning a verdict. The jury is the fact-finder. **Chitsey v. National Lloyds Ins.**, 738 S.W.2d 641, 643 (Tex 1987). Thus, a mistake by the jury is a mistake in evaluating the evidence.

§3.2 Role of trial judge. The trial judge can make mistakes in applying the law or in evaluating the evidence.

1. In jury trial. The trial judge plays two roles in a jury trial. During the trial, the judge decides which facts are admissible into evidence. After the judge admits the evidence and the jury resolves the fact issues by the verdict, the judge renders the final judgment. With one exception, the judge does not have fact-finding power in either role. For the exception, see "Incomplete claim or defense submitted," ch. 8-I, §7.2. The judge is authorized only to apply the appropriate law to the established facts and sign the appropriate judgment. The judge has no discretion when applying the law. **Walker v. Packer**, 827 S.W.2d 833, 840 (Tex 1992).

2. In nonjury trial. In a nonjury trial, the judge is the substitute for the jury and has the same fact-finding power as the jury. Thus, in a nonjury trial, the judge plays three roles: (1) the judge decides which facts are admissible into evidence, (2) relying on the admitted evidence, the judge resolves the fact issues, and (3) relying on the resolution of the fact issues, the judge applies the law and signs the appropriate judgment.

§3.3 Appealable error. In broad terms, there are three kinds of error made during a trial: (1) error in applying the law, (2) error in weighing the evidence, and (3) abuse of discretion. The third type of error is the most difficult to reverse on appeal.

1. Error in applying law. The trial court errs in applying the law when it misinterprets the law, applies the wrong law, ignores the law, exercises power it does not have, or refuses to exercise power it is required to exercise. *See* **Walker v. Packer**, 827 S.W.2d 833, 840 (Tex 1992) (trial court has no discretion to decide what the law is or how to apply it to the facts). Because the trial court has no discretion in these matters, appellate courts review these rulings de novo, without deference to the trial court's legal determinations. See "Review of legal issues," ch. 1-G, §5.2.1.

2. Error in weighing evidence.

(1) Evaluating evidence. The fact-finder—either the jury or, in a nonjury trial, the judge—errs when it incorrectly evaluates the evidence. This error is challenged on appeal by allegations that the evidence is legally and factually insufficient. See "Review of fact issues," ch. 1-G, §5.2.2.

(2) Deciding if fact issue exists. The trial court errs when it does not recognize that there is a fact issue. A fact issue exists when a party has introduced some evidence on an issue but has not proved the issue conclusively as a matter of law. Deciding if there is a fact issue is one of the most difficult tasks for the trial court.

(a) Fact issue. When there is a fact issue, the trial court must submit the contested issue to the jury and cannot grant a motion for summary judgment, a motion for directed verdict, or a motion for judgment notwithstanding the verdict. *See* **White v. Southwestern Bell Tel. Co.**, 651 S.W.2d 260, 262 (Tex.1983).

(b) No fact issue. When the facts on an issue are uncontested, they are established conclusively. When there are no contested issues to submit to the jury, the trial court should grant a motion for summary judgment, a motion for directed verdict, or a motion for judgment notwithstanding the verdict. *See* **Massey v. Houston Baptist Univ.**, 902 S.W.2d 81, 83 (Tex.App.—Houston [1st Dist.] 1995, writ denied).

For example, assume fact A is important to the outcome of a case. Before the trial starts, there is no evidence of fact A. After the plaintiff begins presenting evidence on fact A, there is some evidence of it, perhaps somewhere between no evidence and a preponderance of the evidence. Once the plaintiff makes a solid case on fact A, the plaintiff crosses the line marking preponderance of the evidence and is headed toward the great weight of the evidence. If the plaintiff produces indisputable evidence of fact A, the fact has been proved as a matter of law. The evidence of fact A went from one absolute (no evidence) through all the sufficiency stages to the other absolute (proved as a matter of law). The graph of fact A's progress looks like this:

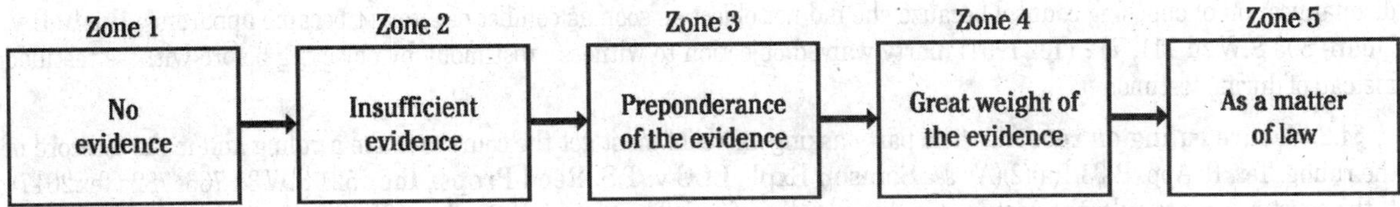

Think of the trial as a modified football game. A party scores in this game by taking the football, which represents the party's burden of proof on each one of its fact issues, beyond the 50-yard line, Zone 3. The party and its opponent face each other from opposite ends of the field, and both have the same objectives: (1) take the ball as far as possible past Zone 3 and (2) prevent the opponent from carrying the ball past Zone 3. The farther the party carries the ball down the field, the better the party proves its case. Each party wants to establish all the facts it needs by the strongest evidence it can produce, and it wants to prevent its opponent from crossing into Zone 3. If a party reaches its opponent's end zone, Zone 5, the party has proved an issue as a matter of law and there is no longer a fact issue.

The appellant should think of the trial as a football game that it lost. Its objective on appeal is to convince the appellate court of two things: (1) it carried the ball farther than the jury believed, far beyond Zone 3, and (2) its opponent never made it to Zone 3, as the jury thought it did. The appellant wants to demonstrate to the appellate court that the jury misunderstood the sufficiency of the evidence.

3. Abuse of discretion. The most nebulous type of error, and the most difficult to reverse on appeal, is the trial court's abuse of discretion. A trial court abuses its discretion when it (1) renders an arbitrary and unreasonable decision or (2) acts without reference to any guiding rules and principles. **Butnaru v. Ford Motor Co.**, 84 S.W.3d 198, 211 (Tex.2002); **Beaumont Bank v. Buller**, 806 S.W.2d 223, 226 (Tex.1991). A mere error in judgment is not an abuse of discretion. **Loftin v. Martin**, 776 S.W.2d 145, 146 (Tex.1989). Appellate courts will not reverse the trial court simply because they disagree with the trial court; they will reverse only if they find that the trial court acted in an unreasonable or arbitrary manner. See "Review of court's discretion," ch. 1-G, §5.2.3.

§4. Preserving error

Preserving error is governed by TRAP 33.1.

§4.1 Make proper objection. To make a proper objection, a party must do the following:

1. Assert valid complaint. The party must make a valid, timely, and specific request, motion, or objection. Tex. R. App. P. 33.1(a); Tex. R. Evid. 103(a)(1); **Samson Expl., LLC v. T.S. Reed Props., Inc.**, 521 S.W.3d 766, 782 (Tex.2017); **Till v. Thomas**, 10 S.W.3d 730, 734 (Tex.App.—Houston [1st Dist.] 1999, no pet.); *see* **In re Bates**, 555 S.W.2d 420, 432 (Tex.1977). Generally, if the party does not make an objection during trial, it cannot make the objection for the first time on appeal. **City of Fort Worth v. Zimlich**, 29 S.W.3d 62, 73 (Tex.2000); *e.g.*, **Alphonso v. Deshotel**, 417 S.W.3d 194, 199 (Tex.App.—El Paso 2013, no pet.) (constitutional challenge to CPRC ch. 27 could not be made for first time on appeal), *disapproved on other grounds*, **In re Lipsky**, 460 S.W.3d 579 (Tex.2015); **Mandell v. Mandell**, 214 S.W.3d 682, 691 (Tex.App.—Houston [14th Dist.] 2007, no pet.) (complaint against award of attorney fees could not be made for first time on appeal). However, in a civil nonjury case, a complaint about the legal or factual sufficiency of the evidence may be made for the first time on appeal. Tex. R. App. P. 33.1(d). Any complaint made must comply with the TREs, TRCPs, or TRAPs. Tex. R. App. P. 33.1(a)(1)(B); **Samson Expl.**, 521 S.W.3d at 782.

2. Properly support it. When necessary, the party must support its objection or motion with evidence. Many motions and some objections require support in the form of affidavits or sworn testimony. *See, e.g.*, **Dillard Dept. Stores v. Hall**, 909 S.W.2d 491, 491–92 (Tex.1995) (D's objection to P's discovery request for all similar complaints filed against D was supported with affidavit stating that D had 227 stores in 20 states).

3. Make it timely. The party must request relief within the time permitted by the rules and case law. *See* Tex. R. App. P. 33.1(a)(1); **Samson Expl.**, 521 S.W.3d at 782; *see, e.g.*, **Zimlich**, 29 S.W.3d at 73 (city waived pleading error because it did not object before case was submitted to jury); **Vaughan v. Walther**, 875 S.W.2d 690, 690–91 (Tex.1994) (party waived disqualification of opposing counsel because she did not object as soon as conflict of interest became apparent); **Bushell v. Dean**, 803 S.W.2d 711, 712 (Tex.1991) (party waived objection to witness's testimony by objecting before witness testified instead of during testimony).

§4.2 Secure ruling on record. The party asking for relief must get the court to make a ruling and make a record of the ruling. Tex. R. App. P. 33.1(a)(2)(A); *see* **Samson Expl., LLC v. T.S. Reed Props., Inc.**, 521 S.W.3d 766, 782 (Tex.2017). If the court refuses to rule, the party must object to the refusal. Tex. R. App. P. 33.1(a)(2)(B). See "Rulings of the Court," ch. 1-G, §1 et seq.

§4.3 Exception—fundamental error. It is not necessary to make a timely objection to preserve "fundamental error," which is an extremely rare form of error. Fundamental error occurs only when the record shows that the court lacked jurisdiction or that the public interest, as declared in the Texas Constitution or statutes, is directly and adversely affected. **Pirtle v. Gregory**, 629 S.W.2d 919, 920 (Tex.1982).

§5. Summary chart for motions

Chart 1-3, below, summarizes some of the requirements for various motions—when a motion must be in writing, when it must be verified, when affidavits should be attached, and what type of hearing should be requested. The last column indicates where in this book the motions are discussed.

1-3. Summary Chart for Motions

	Motion	File written motion	Verify motion	Attach affidavits	Hearing for evidence or argument	Cross-reference
1	Special appearance	Yes	Yes	Yes	Evidence	ch. 3-B, §1 et seq.
2	Motion to transfer venue, generally	Yes	No	Yes	Argument	ch. 3-C, §1 et seq.
3	Motion to change venue, local prejudice	Yes	No	Yes	Uncertain	ch. 3-C, §3
4	Motion to transfer venue, Family Code	Yes	No	Yes	Evidence	ch. 3-C, §5.4.2
5	Forum non conveniens	Yes	Yes	Yes	Argument	ch. 3-D, §1 et seq.

1-3. Summary Chart for Motions

	Motion	File written motion	Verify motion	Attach affidavits	Hearing for evidence or argument	Cross-reference
6	Plea to the jurisdiction	Yes	No	Sometimes	Either	ch. 3-F, §1 et seq.
7	Special exceptions	Yes	No	No	Argument	ch. 3-G, §1 et seq.
8	Motion to dismiss—baseless cause of action	Yes	No	No	Either	ch. 3-H, §1 et seq.
9	Motion to abate	Yes	Yes	Yes	Evidence	ch. 3-I, §1 et seq.
10	Motion to dismiss—anti-SLAPP motion	Yes	No	Yes	Evidence	ch. 3-K, §1 et seq.
11	Motion for continuance	Yes	Yes	Yes	Evidence	ch. 5-D, §1 et seq.
12	Motion in limine	Yes	No	No	Argument	ch. 5-E, §1 et seq.
13	Motion for additional resources	Yes	No	No	Evidence, hearing is cptional	ch. 5-H, §1 et seq.
14	Motion for sanctions	Yes	Yes	Yes	Evidence	ch. 5-K, §1 et seq.
15	Motion for no-answer default judgment	Not necessary	No	For damages	Evidence for unliquidated damages	ch. 7-A, §3
16	Motion for summary judgment, Tex. R. Civ. P. 166a(a), (b)	Yes	No	Yes, in most cases	Argument	ch. 7-B, §1 et seq.
17	No-evidence motion for summary judgment, Tex. R. Civ. P. 166a(i)	Yes	No	No	Argument	ch. 7-D, §1 et seq.
18	Motion for nonsuit	Not necessary	No	No	Neither	ch. 7-F, §1 et seq.
19	Motion for JNOV	Yes	No	No	Argument	ch. 9-B, §1 et seq.
20	Unsworn motion for new trial	Yes	No	No	Argument	ch. 10-B, §1 et seq.
21	Sworn motion for new trial	Yes	Yes	Yes	Evidence	ch. 10-B, §1 et seq.
22	Motion to reinstate after DWOP	Yes	Yes	Yes	Evidence	ch. 10-F, §1 et seq.

G. Rulings of the Court

§1. General

§1.1 Rule. Tex R. App. P. 33.1.

§1.2 Purpose. The purpose of a ruling is to announce the court's decision on a matter pending for resolution. The party seeking a ruling on a motion or objection must get the court to (1) make a ruling and (2) make a record of the ruling to preserve the issue for appeal. Tex R. App. P. 33.1(a)(2); *see* **Volume Millwork, Inc. v. West Houston Airport Corp.**, 218 S.W.3d 722, 734 (Tex.App.—Houston [1st Dist.] 2006, pet. denied).

§1.3 Form. **O'Connor's Texas Civil Forms**, FORM 1G:1 (2020 ed.).

§1.4 Other references. **O'Connor's Texas Causes of Action** (2021 ed.); **O'Connor's Texas Civil Appeals** (2020 ed.).

§2. Court's ruling

§2.1 Judgment vs. order. A judgment is the documentation of the court's ruling that resolves the lawsuit. *See* **Lindley v. Flores**, 672 S.W.2d 612, 614 (Tex.App.—Corpus Christi 1984, no writ). In contrast, an order is the documentation of the court's ruling that resolves a motion or objection. *See id.* If an order resolves all the issues in a lawsuit, the order is a "judgment." *See* **Stewart v. USA Custom Paint & Body Shop, Inc.**, 870 S.W.2d 18, 20 (Tex.1994) (order of dismissal is a judgment). For a discussion of judgments, see "Judgment," ch. 9-C, §1 et seq.

§2.2 Types of rulings. Under TRAP 33.1(a)(2), error is preserved by an express ruling, an implicit ruling, or a refusal to rule.

1. Express ruling. A party should attempt to secure an express ruling (i.e., a ruling on the record, either in open court or in writing, that specifically states the court's ruling) on each of its motions, objections, or offers of evidence. *See* Tex. R. App. P. 33.1(a)(2)(A). If an express ruling is ambiguous, the party should ask the court to clarify it. When a ruling is susceptible to two constructions, the appellate court will adopt the construction that correctly applies the law. **MacGregor v. Rich**, 941 S.W.2d 74, 75 (Tex.1997).

Practice Tip

If, in response to an objection, the trial judge makes a statement that does not rule on the objection (e.g., "let's move on"), the polite way to secure a ruling is to say, "I am sorry, your Honor, did you sustain my objection?" The judge must then say yes or no.

2. Implicit ruling. If the court does not make an express ruling but takes other action that implicitly overrules the motion or objection, error is preserved. *See* Tex. R. App. P. 33.1(a)(2)(A); **In re Z.L.T.**, 124 S.W.3d 163, 165 (Tex.2003); *see, e.g.*, **Rosemond v. Al-Lahiq**, 331 S.W.3d 764, 767 (Tex.2011) (ruling on motion to dismiss for inadequate expert report implicitly overruled motion to dismiss for untimely service of report because court could rule on report's adequacy only if it was timely served); **Chilkewitz v. Hyson**, 22 S.W.3d 825, 828 (Tex.1999) (by rendering judgment on verdict, court "impliedly" overruled motion for JNOV); **Salinas v. Rafati**, 948 S.W.2d 286, 288 (Tex.1997) (ruling granting one party's motion, which was opposite of other party's motion, "automatically" denied other party's motion); **Woods v. Woods**, 193 S.W.3d 720, 723 (Tex.App.—Beaumont 2006, pet. denied) (objection to commissioner's report on division of property was implicitly overruled when court accepted the report); **Lopez v. Lopez**, 55 S.W.3d 194, 201 (Tex.App.—Corpus Christi 2001, no pet.) (ruling granting divorce implicitly overruled motion to reopen); **Amalgamated Acme Affiliates, Inc. v. Minton**, 33 S.W.3d 387, 392 n.2 (Tex.App.—Austin 2000, no pet.) (constitutional arguments in motion to dissolve injunction were implicitly overruled when court refused to consider motion). For a discussion of implicit rulings in summary-judgment cases, see "Secure ruling on objections," ch. 7-B, §10.2.

3. Refusal to rule + objection. The trial court does not have the discretion to refuse to rule. **In re Shredder Co.**, 225 S.W.3d 676, 679 (Tex.App.—El Paso 2006, orig. proceeding); **Barnes v. State**, 832 S.W.2d 424, 426 (Tex.App.—

Houston [1st Dist.] 1992, orig. proceeding). If the trial court refuses to rule, the party must (1) object to the court's refusal to rule and (2) make sure all of the following appear in the appellate record: the request for a ruling, the court's refusal to rule, and the objection to the court's refusal to rule. *See* Tex. R. App. P. 33.1(a)(2)(B), 33.2; *see, e.g.*, **In re Shredder Co.**, 225 S.W.3d at 679–80 (D attempted to secure ruling on motion to compel arbitration at five separate hearings, but court refused to rule); **Goodchild v. Bombardier-Rotax GMBH**, 979 S.W.2d 1, 6–7 (Tex.App.—Houston [14th Dist.] 1998, pet. denied) (error was waived because P did not object to court's refusal to rule); **O'Donnell v. Roger Bullivant of Tex., Inc.**, 940 S.W.2d 411, 416 (Tex.App.—Fort Worth 1997, writ denied) (error was preserved because P objected to court's refusal to rule), *overruled on other grounds*, **Perry Homes v. Alwattari**, 33 S.W.3d 376 (Tex.App.—Fort Worth 2000, pet. denied). See "Offer of Proof & Bill of Exception," ch. 8-E, §1 et seq.

Practice Tip

Another way to secure a ruling from a judge who refuses to rule is to reurge the objection in a motion for new trial, along with an objection to the judge's refusal to rule. Even if the judge refuses to rule on the motion for new trial, the motion will be automatically overruled by operation of law. See Tex. R. Civ. P. 329b(c). See "Deadline to sign order on MNT," ch. 10-B, §8.4.

4. Nonruling.

(1) Ruling deferred. If the trial court states that it will rule on the objection later or invites the party to reurge the objection later, the statement is not a ruling and does not preserve error. *See* **Bushell v. Dean**, 803 S.W.2d 711, 712 (Tex.1991).

(2) No ruling. If the trial court does not make either an express or an implicit ruling on a motion or objection, error is not preserved. *See, e.g.*, **Wal-Mart Stores v. Reece**, 32 S.W.3d 339, 347–48 (Tex.App.—Waco 2000) (D's objection to sidebar comments was not preserved because court's response asking parties to abide by motion in limine was too indefinite to constitute implicit ruling), *rev'd on other grounds*, 81 S.W.3d 812 (Tex.2002); **Martin v. Uvalde S&L Ass'n**, 773 S.W.2d 808, 814 (Tex.App.—San Antonio 1989, no writ) (because D did not secure ruling on motion to strike, error was waived).

§2.3 Timing of ruling. The trial court must consider and rule on a motion or objection within a reasonable time. **In re Kleven**, 100 S.W.3d 643, 644 (Tex.App.—Texarkana 2003, orig. proceeding). The trial court abuses its discretion if it refuses to rule on a pending motion. **Eli Lilly & Co. v. Marshall**, 829 S.W.2d 157, 158 (Tex.1992); *e.g.*, **In re Rodriguez**, 196 S.W.3d 454, 459 (Tex.App.—El Paso 2006, orig. proceeding) (trial judge did not abuse discretion by leaving on month-long vacation before ruling). When a motion is pending before a trial court, the act of giving it consideration and ruling on it is a ministerial act. **In re Kleven**, 100 S.W.3d at 644; **Safety-Kleen Corp. v. Garcia**, 945 S.W.2d 268, 269 (Tex.App.—San Antonio 1997, orig. proceeding). A party can seek a writ of mandamus from an appellate court if the trial court refuses to rule within a reasonable time. **In re Shredder Co.**, 225 S.W.3d 676, 679 (Tex.App.—El Paso 2006, orig. proceeding); *see, e.g.*, **Marshall**, 829 S.W.2d at 158 (appellate court conditionally issued mandamus to compel ruling on TRCP 76a motion).

Practice Tip

If you realize after the judgment is signed that the court did not make a record of some ruling, you can ask the court to reduce the ruling to writing before its plenary power expires. See ***Crocker v. Paulyne's Nursing Home, Inc.****, 95 S.W.3d 416, 421 (Tex.App.—Dallas 2002, no pet.).*

§3. Record of ruling

To be effective, all orders and rulings must be made on the record, either in writing or in open court and transcribed by the court reporter. *See* Tex. R. App. P. 33.1(a)(2); **State Farm Ins. v. Pults**, 850 S.W.2d 691, 693 (Tex.App.—Corpus Christi 1993, no writ). The type of ruling required generally depends on the type of motion or objection. If the motion is in writing, the party should always ask the court to sign a written order. If the motion or objection is made orally during the trial, an oral ruling is usually sufficient.

§3.1 In writing.

1. Written order. The trial court should sign a written order that clearly reflects the ruling. *See, e.g.,* **McAdams v. Capitol Prods.**, 810 S.W.2d 290, 292 (Tex.App.—Fort Worth 1991, writ denied) (court's notations on motion that special exceptions were "or." or "sus." were not effective as rulings).

(1) Required by law. When the rules place a deadline on the court's jurisdiction to act on a matter, the court must make a written ruling; an oral ruling is not effective. **Walker v. Harrison**, 597 S.W.2d 913, 915 (Tex.1980); *see, e.g.,* Tex. R. Civ. P. 165a(3) (order granting motion to reinstate must be in writing); Tex. R. Civ. P. 329b(c) (order granting new trial or modifying, correcting, or reforming judgment must be in writing); **Faulkner v. Culver**, 851 S.W.2d 187, 188 (Tex.1993) (oral order granting new trial was ineffective); **Emerald Oaks Hotel/Conf. Ctr., Inc. v. Zardenetta**, 776 S.W.2d 577, 578 (Tex.1989) (oral order reinstating case was ineffective).

(2) Not transcribed by reporter. When the trial court makes an oral ruling that the court reporter does not transcribe, the party must insist that the judge sign a written order. *Cf.* **In re Bledsoe**, 41 S.W.3d 807, 811 (Tex.App.—Fort Worth 2001, orig. proceeding) (when party files mandamus action without a signed written order, oral order will be considered only if it is clear, specific, enforceable, and shown by the record).

2. Signature. The trial judge should sign her name to her orders and judgments. However, the trial judge may direct a person under her immediate authority to affix the judge's signature using a rubber stamp. **In re Barber**, 982 S.W.2d 364, 366–67 (Tex.1998). For electronic or digital court documents, including orders, judgments, rulings, notices, commissions, or precepts, the judge can sign electronically, digitally, or through another secure method. Tex. Gov't Code §21.011.

§3.2 In open court. When the trial court makes an oral ruling in open court that is transcribed by the court reporter, the statement of the court's ruling in the reporter's record preserves the ruling for appeal. **Pride Pet. Servs. v. Criswell**, 924 S.W.2d 720, 721 (Tex.App.—El Paso 1996, writ denied) (construing former TRAP 52, now TRAP 33.1); *see* Tex. R. App. P. 33.2(b), (c); **State Farm Ins. v. Pults**, 850 S.W.2d 691, 693 (Tex.App.—Corpus Christi 1993, no writ).

§3.3 Docket entries. A party should not rely on a docket entry as a ruling on a motion; a party should always get the trial court to sign an order. *See* **Bailey-Mason v. Mason**, 122 S.W.3d 894, 897 (Tex.App.—Dallas 2003, pet. denied) (docket entry by itself cannot constitute judgment or decree by the court). Because many judges use their own shorthand for their rulings and their docket notations are often unintelligible to others, docket entries are inherently unreliable. *See* **Guyot v. Guyot**, 3 S.W.3d 243, 246 (Tex.App.—Fort Worth 1999, no pet.); **Energo Int'l v. Modern Indus. Heating, Inc.**, 722 S.W.2d 149, 151 n.2 (Tex.App.—Dallas 1986, no writ). In some cases, the court clerk makes the docket entries. *See* **State Farm Ins. v. Pults**, 850 S.W.2d 691, 693 (Tex.App.—Corpus Christi 1993, no writ). The docket sheet's function is limited to correcting clerical mistakes. *See* **Energo Int'l**, 722 S.W.2d at 151 n.2.

1. Not an order. A docket entry cannot contradict or take the place of a written order or judgment. *See, e.g.,* **Smith v. McCorkle**, 895 S.W.2d 692, 692 (Tex.1995) (docket entry indicating that affidavit of indigence was denied was not effective as order); **Faulkner v. Culver**, 851 S.W.2d 187, 188 (Tex.1993) (docket entry granting new trial was not effective); **Taack v. McFall**, 661 S.W.2d 923, 924 (Tex.1983) (docket entry and oral ruling granting motion for new trial were not effective); **N-S-W Corp. v. Snell**, 561 S.W.2d 798, 799 (Tex.1977) (docket entry granting motion to reinstate could not contradict order); **First Nat'l Bank v. Birnbaum**, 826 S.W.2d 189, 190 (Tex.App.—Austin 1992, no writ) (docket entry denying turnover relief was not order); **Grant v. American Nat'l Ins.**, 808 S.W.2d 181, 184 (Tex.App.—Houston [14th Dist.] 1991, no writ) (docket notation dismissing case was not appealable order); **Miller v. Kendall**, 804 S.W.2d 933, 943–44 (Tex.App.—Houston [1st Dist.] 1990, no writ) (docket entry denying motion was not order and did not preserve error).

2. Supplement to rendition of judgment. The trial court's notation on the docket sheet can sometimes be used as evidence to support the trial judge's testimony that judgment was orally rendered on a certain date. *See* **Bailey-Mason**, 122 S.W.3d at 897 (for docket sheet to constitute a judgment, record must show that court called docket notation to parties' attention in open court or filed docket sheet with clerk as the judgment); *see, e.g.,* **Dearing v. Johnson**, 947 S.W.2d 641, 643 (Tex.App.—Texarkana 1997, no writ) (judge's affidavit that he orally rendered judgment and docket-sheet notation of "divorce granted" amounted to rendition of judgment); **Oak Creek Homes, Inc. v. Jones**, 758 S.W.2d 288, 290–91 (Tex.App.—Waco 1988, no writ) (judge's announcement that "I'll grant all the relief you've asked for" and docket notation of

"default judgment," followed by judge's signature, amounted to rendition); *see also* Tex. Fam. Code §101.026 (rendition of judgment may be accomplished by docket notation for suits affecting parent-child relationship). See "Rendering, signing & entering judgment," ch. 9-C, §3.

§3.4 Letters. A letter from the trial court announcing the ruling is generally not the equivalent of a signed order or a rendition of judgment, except in certain circumstances.

1. Order. For a letter to be the equivalent of a signed order, the judge must have intended the letter to be a final, appealable order. *See* **Goff v. Tuchscherer**, 627 S.W.2d 397, 398 (Tex.1982). For example, a draft, directive, or subsequent order indicates that the judge did not intend the letter itself to be the order. *See* **Schaeffer Homes, Inc. v. Esterak**, 792 S.W.2d 567, 569 (Tex.App.—El Paso 1990, no writ); *see, e.g.*, **Goff**, 627 S.W.2d at 398–99 (letter was not intended as appealable order because it directed attorney to submit draft of final order). Even if it appears that the judge intended the letter to be an order, the letter still must meet the requirements for a valid order. *See* **Schaeffer Homes**, 792 S.W.2d at 569. Specifically, the letter must (1) be filed with the clerk, (2) be written in the present tense (i.e., must not indicate an intent to be effectuated in the future), (3) be signed and dated and include the cause number and the parties' names, and (4) contain the command language that identifies an order. *See* **Gregory v. Foster**, 35 S.W.3d 255, 256–57 (Tex.App.—Texarkana 2000, no pet.); **Schaeffer Homes**, 792 S.W.2d at 569; *see, e.g.*, **Barron v. Vanier**, 190 S.W.3d 841, 846 (Tex.App.—Fort Worth 2006, no pet.) (although letter used "present language," included cause number and parties' names, and was signed and dated, it did not constitute appealable order because it was not filed with clerk); **In re Fuentes**, 960 S.W.2d 261, 264–65 (Tex.App.—Corpus Christi 1997, orig. proceeding) (letter granting new trial was not valid because it required future action and was not filed with clerk).

2. Rendition of judgment. For a letter to be the equivalent of a rendition of judgment, the letter must (1) qualify as a written memorandum, (2) be filed with the clerk, and (3) clearly indicate the court's intent to render judgment at the present time rather than in a certain way in the future. *See* **Genesis Prod'g Co. v. Smith Big Oil Corp.**, 454 S.W.3d 655, 659 (Tex.App.—Houston [14th Dist.] 2014, no pet.); **Abarca v. Roadstar Corp.**, 647 S.W.2d 327, 327–28 (Tex.App.—Corpus Christi 1982, no writ); *see, e.g.*, **Greene v. State**, 324 S.W.3d 276, 282–83 (Tex.App.—Austin 2010, no pet.) (letter served as rendition of judgment because it qualified as memorandum, was filed with clerk, and was written in present tense, stating "judgment is rendered for the plaintiffs on all claims"); **Ex parte Gnesoulis**, 525 S.W.2d 205, 209 (Tex.App.—Houston [14th Dist.] 1975, orig. proceeding) (letter outlining terms of divorce was not rendition of judgment because it was not filed with clerk and was intended as guideline for proposed judgments). See "Rendition," ch. 9-C, §3.1; "Form of judgment," ch. 9-C, §4. A letter to the parties that describes the court's findings and asks the parties to prepare a judgment can serve as a rendition of judgment if it is filed with the clerk. **Greene**, 324 S.W.3d at 282; *see, e.g.*, **Abarca**, 647 S.W.2d at 327–28 (summary judgment). Although a letter can serve as a rendition, it is not a final judgment for purposes of appeal. *See* **Greene**, 324 S.W.3d at 281–82. The judgment is not final, and appellate deadlines do not begin to run, until the judgment is signed. *See* Tex. R. Civ. P. 306a(1); **In re Bennett**, 960 S.W.2d 35, 38 (Tex.1997); *see also* **Greene**, 324 S.W.3d at 282 (judge who retired after rendering judgment in letter, but before signing final judgment, retained judicial capacity to sign judgment because doing so was ministerial act that merely recorded rendition). See "Signing," ch. 9-C, §3.2.

Note

At least one court has suggested that an e-mail from a trial court can be the equivalent of a rendition of judgment in the same manner as a letter. See ***Genesis Prod'g****, 454 S.W.3d at 660 (e-mail stating court's ruling on parties' summary-judgment motions was not rendition of judgment because there was no indication on record that it was filed with clerk or otherwise publicly announced).*

§4. Order

§4.1 Form of order. When a party submits an order to the trial court, the order should contain certain items. See **O'Connor's Texas Civil Forms**, FORM 1G:1 (2020 ed.).

1. Party names. The order should contain the full names of the parties. *Cf.* Tex. R. Civ. P. 306 (judgment must contain full names of parties).

2. Identification of motion. The order should identify the motion, the party that made the motion, whether the court held a hearing, and whether the hearing was for the receipt of evidence or for argument only.

3. Ruling. The order should resolve the issues presented in the motion.

4. Findings. Some rules require findings to be included in the order. *E.g.*, Tex. R. Civ. P. 13 (order must contain findings of good cause for sanctions). Other rules prohibit findings from being included in the order or judgment. *E.g.*, Tex. R. Civ. P. 299a (findings of fact cannot be included in the judgment).

5. Costs. Some rules permit the trial court to award costs as part of the relief granted on a motion. See "Court Costs," **O'Connor's Texas Causes of Action**, ch. 44, §1 et seq. (2021 ed.).

6. Date. The order should include a line that reads, "Signed on __________, 20__," which appears immediately above the signature line for the trial judge. The Supreme Court has asked authors of legal form books to tell attorneys to draft orders and judgments that say "signed" on a certain date, not rendered or entered. **Burrell v. Cornelius**, 570 S.W.2d 382, 384 (Tex.1978).

7. Signature line for judge. The order must contain a signature line for the trial judge.

8. Signature line for attorneys. Most orders do not contain signature lines for the attorneys to approve the form of the order. Some judges, however, may require the attorneys to approve the form of the order. Approving the form of the order does not waive complaints about the ruling in the order. See "Signature line for attorneys," ch. 9-C, §4.13.

9. Certificate of service. If the order is sent to a party or the court separately from a motion or response, the order must contain a certificate of service; however, if the order is served on the other party with a motion or response, the order does not need to have a separate certificate of service. *See* Tex. R. Civ. P. 21(d). The certificate of service on the motion or response must list the order as one of the documents served on the other party. See **O'Connor's Texas Civil Forms**, FORM 1B:13 (2020 ed.).

§4.2 Changing the order. For the time limits for changing orders, see "Power to change judgment," ch. 9-C, §7; "Deadline to change order on MNT," ch. 10-B, §8.5.

§5. Review

§5.1 Challenging ruling. There are three ways to challenge a ruling of the trial court.

1. Appeal after final judgment. Most rulings are challenged after the trial court renders a final judgment. See "Appeals from final judgments or orders," **O'Connor's Texas Civil Appeals**, ch. 1-B, §2.1 (2020 ed.).

2. Interlocutory appeal. An interlocutory (i.e., nonfinal) order can generally be appealed before final judgment if the appeal is authorized by statute or rule. See "Appeals from interlocutory orders," **O'Connor's Texas Civil Appeals**, ch. 1-B, §2.4 (2020 ed.). The majority of interlocutory appeals are authorized by CPRC §51.014. See "Motion for Interlocutory Appeal & Stay Pending Appeal," **O'Connor's Texas Civil Appeals**, ch. 3-P, §1 et seq. (2020 ed.).

3. Mandamus. Any ruling that cannot be reviewed by either an appeal after final judgment or an interlocutory appeal can be challenged by mandamus. See "Writ of Mandamus," **O'Connor's Texas Civil Appeals**, ch. 10-B, §1 et seq. (2020 ed.).

§5.2 Standards of review.

1. Review of legal issues. Legal issues are reviewed de novo, without deference to the trial court's decision. **Interstate Northborough Prtshp. v. State**, 66 S.W.3d 213, 220 (Tex.2001); **State v. Heal**, 917 S.W.2d 6, 9 (Tex.1996). The trial court has no discretion to decide what the law is or how to apply it to the facts. **Walker v. Packer**, 827 S.W.2d 833, 840 (Tex.1992). See "De novo," **O'Connor's Texas Civil Appeals**, ch. 1-G, §6.1 (2020 ed.).

2. Review of fact issues. Appellate courts will defer to the trial court's discretionary rulings when reviewing issues of fact. *See* **Walker**, 827 S.W.2d at 839–40; **Williams v. Chisolm**, 111 S.W.3d 811, 815 (Tex.App.—Houston [1st Dist.]

2003, no pet.). The appellate court cannot substitute its judgment for that of the trial court. **Walker**, 827 S.W.2d at 839. See "Legal & factual sufficiency," **O'Connor's Texas Civil Appeals**, ch. 1-G, §6.3 (2020 ed.).

3. Review of court's discretion. A trial court abuses its discretion when it (1) renders an arbitrary and unreasonable decision or (2) acts without reference to any guiding rules and principles. **Butnaru v. Ford Motor Co.**, 84 S.W.3d 198, 211 (Tex.2002); **Beaumont Bank v. Buller**, 806 S.W.2d 223, 226 (Tex.1991). Appellate courts will not reverse the trial court simply because they disagree with the trial court; they will reverse only if they find that the trial court acted in an unreasonable or arbitrary manner. **Butnaru**, 84 S.W.3d at 211; **Beaumont Bank**, 806 S.W.2d at 226. See "Abuse of discretion," **O'Connor's Texas Civil Appeals**, ch. 1-G, §6.2 (2020 ed.).

H. The Attorney

§1. General

§1.1 Rules. Tex. R. Civ. P. 7 to 14. See Tex. Gov't Code §81.102 (requirement of state-bar membership).

§1.2 Purpose. A party has the right to be represented by the counsel of its choice. **Spinks v. Brown**, 103 S.W.3d 452, 459 (Tex.App.—San Antonio 2002, pet. denied); *see* Tex. R. Civ. P. 7. Unless there is a compelling reason, courts should not deprive litigants of this right. **Keller Indus. v. Blanton**, 804 S.W.2d 182, 185 (Tex.App.—Houston [14th Dist.] 1991, orig. proceeding).

§1.3 Forms. **O'Connor's Texas Civil Forms**, FORMS 1H:1 et seq. (2020 ed.); **O'Connor's Texas Causes of Action Pleadings**, FORMS 45:1 et seq. (2020 ed.).

§1.4 Other references. **O'Connor's Texas Causes of Action** (2021 ed.); **O'Connor's Texas Civil Appeals** (2020 ed.); **O'Connor's Texas Civil Practice & Remedies Code Plus** (2020–21 ed.).

§2. Appearing before Texas courts

§2.1 Requirements. To practice law in Texas state courts, an attorney must be a member of the State Bar of Texas, which is governed by the State Bar Act and is administratively controlled by the Texas Supreme Court. Tex. Gov't Code §81.102; **Daves v. State Bar**, 691 S.W.2d 784, 786 (Tex.App.—Amarillo 1985, writ ref'd n.r.e.). The Board of Law Examiners, appointed by the Supreme Court, is empowered to investigate the fitness and moral character of each license applicant. Tex. Gov't Code §82.028(a); *see* **Board of Law Exam'rs v. Stevens**, 868 S.W.2d 773, 776 (Tex.1994); *see also* Tex. Gov't Code §82.001 (composition and appointment of Board).

§2.2 Limited practice of law. The Supreme Court has the authority to make rules prescribing the procedure for limited practice of law by attorneys (including military attorneys) licensed in another jurisdiction, law students, unlicensed law-school graduates who are attending or have attended a law school approved by the Supreme Court, and foreign legal consultants. Tex. Gov't Code §81.102(b) (attorneys licensed in other jurisdiction, students, and unlicensed graduates), §82.036 (foreign attorneys); *see, e.g.*, Tex. Rules Govern. Bar Adm'n R. 14 (foreign legal consultants), 22 (military attorneys), 23 (spouses of military members).

1. Nonresident attorneys.

(1) Definition. A nonresident attorney is a person who resides in and is licensed to practice law in a state other than Texas or in a foreign jurisdiction and who is not a member of the State Bar of Texas. *See* Tex. Gov't Code §82.0361(a); Tex. Rules Govern. Bar Adm'n R. 19(a).

(2) Appearance in Texas court. A nonresident attorney may apply for permission to appear in a Texas state court by a sworn motion requesting admission to the court "pro hac vice," which means "for this one particular occasion." *See* **Keller Indus. v. Blanton**, 804 S.W.2d 182, 184 (Tex.App.—Houston [14th Dist.] 1991, orig. proceeding); **Commercial Credit & Control Data Corp. v. Wheeler**, 756 S.W.2d 769, 770–71 (Tex.App.—Corpus Christi 1988, writ denied). The procedure is governed by the Rules Governing Admission to the Bar of Texas, Rule 19, "Requirements for Participation in Texas Proceedings by a Non-Resident Attorney," which can be found on the Texas Board of Law Examiners website at ble.texas.gov/home, by selecting "Rulebook" from the main menu. The nonresident attorney must file two motions.

(a) Motion by nonresident attorney. The nonresident attorney must file a sworn motion containing (1) her office address, telephone number, fax number, and e-mail address, (2) the name and State Bar card number of an attorney licensed in Texas with whom she will be associated in the trial, and that attorney's office address, telephone number, fax number, and e-mail address, (3) a list of all Texas cases, including cause numbers and captions, in which she has appeared or sought leave to appear or participate within the past two years, (4) a list of jurisdictions in which she is licensed, and a statement whether she is an active member in good standing in each of those jurisdictions, (5) a statement whether she has been the subject of disciplinary action during the last five years by the bar or courts of any jurisdiction in which she is licensed, and a description of any such actions, (6) a statement that she has not been denied admission to the courts of any

state or to any federal court during the last five years, and (7) a statement that she is familiar with the rules of the State Bar of Texas governing the conduct of its members and will comply with those rules as long as the trial or hearing is pending and she has not withdrawn as counsel in the case. Tex Rules Govern. Bar Adm'n R 19(a); *see* **Keller Indus.**, 804 S.W.2d at 184 (requirements 2, 5–7). See **O'Connor's Texas Civil Forms**, FORM 1H:2 (2020 ed.).

(b) Motion by Texas attorney. The nonresident attorney must also attach a sworn motion from the Texas attorney with whom she will be associated in the trial. Tex Rules Govern. Bar Adm'n R 19(b). The motion must state that the Texas attorney (1) is associated with the nonresident attorney on the case, is employed as an attorney on the case, and will personally participate in the hearings and trial, (2) is a practicing attorney and a member in good standing of the State Bar of Texas, and (3) finds the nonresident attorney to be a reputable attorney and recommends that the nonresident attorney be permitted to practice in this proceeding before the court. *See id.* See **O'Connor's Texas Civil Forms**, FORM 1H:3 (2020 ed.).

(3) Fees. A nonresident attorney requesting permission to appear in a Texas state court must pay a $250 fee for each case in which the attorney wants to participate. Tex Gov't Code §82.0361(b). The nonresident attorney must pay the fee to the Board of Law Examiners before filing the pro hac vice motion and must provide proof of payment to the court in which the attorney wants to participate. *See* Tex Gov't Code §82.0361(b), (f). The fee may be waived or reduced for a nonresident attorney who represents an indigent. Tex Gov't Code §82.0361(e).

2. Nonresident military attorneys. Under Rule 22 of the Rules Governing Admission to the Bar of Texas, military attorneys who are full-time, active-duty military officers stationed in Texas but licensed in another state, a U.S. territory, or the District of Columbia, can represent military servicemembers or their dependents in limited civil proceedings. Tex Rules Govern. Bar Adm'n R 22, §§1, 6. This rule does not prevent a military attorney from applying for permission to appear pro hac vice. Tex Rules Govern. Bar Adm'n R 22, §1. See "Motion by nonresident attorney," ch. 1-H, §2.2.1(2)(a).

3. Nonresident military spouses. Effective December 1, 2019, under Rule 23 of the Rules Governing Admission to the Bar of Texas, the spouse of an active-duty military servicemember stationed in Texas is eligible for a three-year temporary license to practice law in Texas if the spouse is admitted to practice law in another state, a U.S. territory, or the District of Columbia, and satisfies certain conditions. Tex Rules Govern. Bar Adm'n R 23, §1; Tex.Sup.Ct. Order, Misc. Docket No. 19-9109 (eff. Dec. 1, 2019).

4. Law students & law-school graduates. Under Gov't Code §81.102(b) and the Rules Governing the Supervised Practice of Law by Qualified Law Students & Qualified Unlicensed Law School Graduates in Texas, law students and unlicensed law-school graduates have a limited ability to participate in the practice of law. *See* Tex.Sup.Ct. Order, Misc. Docket No. 20-9069 (eff. May 20, 2020). See **O'Connor's Texas Civil Forms**, FORM 1H:5 (2020 ed.).

5. Foreign legal consultants. Under Rule 14 of the Rules Governing Admission to the Bar of Texas, foreign attorneys have a limited ability to participate in the practice of law as foreign legal consultants.

§2.3 Pro se representation.

1. Individual. An individual litigant has the right to represent herself without an attorney. Tex R Civ. P. 7; **Ayres v. Canales**, 790 S.W.2d 554, 557 (Tex1990); **Thomas v. Anderson**, 861 S.W.2d 58, 61 n.1 (Tex.App.—El Paso 1993, no writ); **Nichols v. Martin**, 776 S.W.2d 621, 623 (Tex.App.—Tyler 1989, no writ). A court cannot deny a party the right to self-representation, nor can it order a party to be represented by an attorney. *See* **In re Commitment of Bluitt**, 605 S.W.3d 199, 203 (Tex2020); **Ex parte Shaffer**, 649 S.W.2d 300, 302 (Tex1983). A party acting pro se must comply with substantive law and procedural rules. **Martinez v. Leeds**, 218 S.W.3d 845, 848 (Tex.App.—El Paso 2007, no pet.). A party represented by an attorney cannot also proceed pro se. **Posner v. Dallas Cty. Child Welfare Unit**, 784 S.W.2d 585, 588 (Tex.App.—Eastland 1990, writ denied). A person not licensed as an attorney cannot represent another person as a "next friend" under TRCP 44. **Jimison v. Mann**, 957 S.W.2d 860, 861 (Tex.App.—Amarillo 1997, no writ).

2. Sole proprietorship. A sole proprietorship can be represented pro se by its sole proprietor; the sole proprietor does not have to be an attorney. *See* **In re Gerstner**, No. 02-15-00315-CV, 2015 WL 6444797 (Tex.App.—Fort Worth 2015, orig. proceeding) (memo op.; 10-23-15); **Professional Res. Plus v. University of Tex., Austin**, No. 03-10-00524-CV, 2011 WL 749352 (Tex.App.—Austin 2011, no pet.) (memo op.; 3-4-11) (footnote 1); *see also* **Holberg & Co. v. Citizens Nat'l Assur. Co.**, 856 S.W.2d 515, 518 (Tex.App.—Houston [1st Dist.] 1993, no writ) (unincorporated sole proprietorship does not exist apart from its owner).

3. Corporation. A corporation generally cannot be represented pro se by an officer who is not an attorney. **Dell Dev. Corp. v. Best Indus. Unif. Sup. Co.**, 743 S.W.2d 302, 303 (Tex.App.—Houston [14th Dist.] 1987, writ denied); *see* **Kunstoplast of Am., Inc. v. Formosa Plastics Corp., USA**, 937 S.W.2d 455, 456 (Tex.1996) (although corporation must generally be represented by attorney, nonattorney may perform specific ministerial tasks, like depositing cash with clerk in lieu of cost bond). A corporation must appear and be represented by an attorney. **Electronic Data Sys. v. Tyson**, 862 S.W.2d 728, 737 (Tex.App.—Dallas 1993, orig. proceeding). The one exception is that a corporation may appear pro se in justice court. Tex. R. Civ. P. 500.4(b)(1).

4. Partnership. A partnership generally cannot be represented pro se by a partner who is not an attorney. **Simmons, Jannace & Stagg, L.L.P. v. Buzbee Law Firm**, 324 S.W.3d 833, 833 (Tex.App.—Houston [14th Dist.] 2010, no pet.). The one exception is that a partnership may appear pro se in justice court. *See* Tex. R. Civ. P. 500.4(b)(1).

5. Joint venture. A joint venture generally cannot be represented pro se by a joint venturer who is not an attorney. *See* **Cypresswood Land Partners I v. Beirne, Maynard & Parsons, LLP**, No. 14-16-00389-CV, 2016 WL 6465778 (Tex.App.—Houston [14th Dist.] 2016, no pet.) (memo op.; 11-1-16). The one exception is that a joint venture may appear pro se in justice court. *See* Tex. R. Civ. P. 500.4(b)(1).

§3. Designation of attorneys

§3.1 Attorney in charge. The attorney whose signature appears first on a party's first pleading is the "attorney in charge," unless another attorney is specifically designated. Tex. R. Civ. P. 8; **In re K.L.R.**, 162 S.W.3d 291, 299 (Tex.App.—Tyler 2005, no pet.); **Joyner v. Commission for Lawyer Discipline**, 102 S.W.3d 344, 347 (Tex.App.—Dallas 2003, no pet.). The attorney in charge, also called lead counsel, is responsible for the lawsuit. Tex. R. Civ. P. 8; **Palmer v. Cantrell**, 747 S.W.2d 39, 41 (Tex.App.—Houston [1st Dist.] 1988, no writ); *see* Tex. R. Civ. P. 21(c). All communications from the court or other attorneys must be sent to the attorney in charge. Tex. R. Civ. P. 8; **City of Tyler v. Beck**, 196 S.W.3d 784, 787 (Tex.2006); *see, e.g.*, **Reichhold Chems., Inc. v. Puremco Mfg.**, 854 S.W.2d 240, 246 (Tex.App.—Waco 1993, writ denied) (service on cocounsel to attorney in charge was not effective). However, another attorney may file a motion or take other action on behalf of the party. *E.g.*, **City of Tyler**, 196 S.W.3d at 787 (motions filed by attorney not designated as attorney in charge were not void).

§3.2 Attorneys of record. The attorneys of record are all the attorneys who have made an appearance in the case or whose names appear in the pleadings, including the attorney in charge. The following rules of procedure refer to the attorney of record: Tex. R. Civ. P. 21, 21a, 44, 57, 119a, 130, 165a, 176, 237a, 306a, 315, 500.8, 501.4, 655, and 791.

Note

There is a difference between "attorney in charge" and "attorney of record." While there can be only one attorney in charge for each party, a party may be represented by many attorneys of record. See Tex. R. Civ. P. 21(c), 21a.

§4. Authority of attorney

§4.1 Representing an individual. A party must authorize an attorney to bring suit. *See* Tex. R. Civ. P. 12; **Vela v. Vela**, 763 S.W.2d 601, 602 (Tex.App.—San Antonio 1988, writ denied).

§4.2 Representing a corporation. A corporation's board of directors must authorize the hiring of an attorney. **Square 67 Dev. Corp. v. Red Oak State Bank**, 559 S.W.2d 136, 138 (Tex.App.—Waco 1977, writ ref'd n.r.e.); *see* Bus. Orgs. Code §21.401. Unless permitted by the bylaws or a directors' resolution, the president of the corporation has no authority to conduct litigation for the corporation. **Kaspar v. Thorne**, 755 S.W.2d 151, 154 (Tex.App.—Dallas 1988, no writ); **Valley Int'l Props., Inc. v. Brownsville S&L Ass'n**, 581 S.W.2d 222, 227 (Tex.App.—Corpus Christi 1979, no writ); *see* Bus. Orgs. Code §§3.101, 3.103, 21.401(a).

§4.3 Representing other entities. The authority to represent other business entities (e.g., joint ventures) depends largely on the agreements that formed the entity. *See, e.g.*, **Miller v. Stout**, 706 S.W.2d 785, 787 (Tex.App.—San Antonio 1986, no writ) (joint-venture agreement did not require all members to approve filing of suit).

§4.4 Challenging authority. If a party believes that a suit is being prosecuted or defended without the other party's authority, the party should challenge the authority of the attorney under TRCP 12. *See* **In re Murrin Bros. 1885, Ltd.**, 603 S.W.3d 53, 61 (Tex.2019). The rule requires the challenging party to file a sworn motion, before the parties announce ready for trial, alleging that the suit is being prosecuted or defended without the other party's authority. Tex. R. Civ. P. 12. See **O'Connor's Texas Civil Forms**, FORM 1H:8 (2020 ed.). However, if a new attorney is substituted after the parties announce ready, a Rule 12 motion may be brought to challenge that attorney. *See* **Air Park-Dallas Zoning Cmte. v. Crow-Billingsley Airpark, Ltd.**, 109 S.W.3d 900, 905–06 (Tex.App.—Dallas 2003, no pet.) (Rule 12 motion can be brought when new attorney appears after trial is over and files motion for new trial). The challenged attorney is entitled to ten days' notice before the hearing. Tex. R. Civ. P. 12. At the hearing, the challenged attorney has the burden to show sufficient authority to prosecute or defend the suit on the party's behalf. *Id.*; **In re Murrin Bros.**, 603 S.W.3d at 61; **Boudreau v. Federal Trust Bank**, 115 S.W.3d 740, 741 (Tex.App.—Dallas 2003, pet. denied). The challenged attorney's testimony is sufficient to support a ruling that the attorney has the authority to represent the party. *See* **Boudreau**, 115 S.W.3d at 742. If the challenged attorney does not show authority, the court cannot allow the attorney to appear and must strike the pleadings if no other authorized person appears. Tex. R. Civ. P. 12; **In re Murrin Bros.**, 603 S.W.3d at 61; **Boudreau**, 115 S.W.3d at 741.

§5. Communications with court

§5.1 No ex parte communications. Ex parte communications with the judge involve fewer than all of the parties. **In re S.A.G.**, 403 S.W.3d 907, 914 (Tex.App.—Texarkana 2013, pet. denied); **In re Thoma**, 873 S.W.2d 477, 496 (Tex.Rev.Trib.1994, no appeal). Except in limited circumstances, a judge cannot directly or indirectly initiate, permit, or consider ex parte or other private communications about the merits of a pending or upcoming judicial proceeding. Tex. Code Jud. Conduct, Canon 3(B)(8); **U.S. Gov't v. Marks**, 949 S.W.2d 320, 325 (Tex.1997); **Barnes v. Whittington**, 751 S.W.2d 493, 495 n.1 (Tex.1988); **In re Thoma**, 873 S.W.2d at 496. A judge cannot conduct private proceedings involving the adjudication of causes. **In re Thoma**, 873 S.W.2d at 496. The prohibition on communications with the court about the merits of the case extends to communications with the court's staff. *See, e.g.*, **In re J.B.K.**, 931 S.W.2d 581, 583–84 (Tex.App.—El Paso 1996, order) (attorney should not have asked staff person what the chances were and if he should settle case).

§5.2 Attorney's appearance before court. An attorney's unsworn statements are not evidence. **U.S. Gov't v. Marks**, 949 S.W.2d 320, 326–27 (Tex.1997). However, an attorney's unsworn statement can be considered as evidence on appeal if the other side did not object at trial. **Banda v. Garcia**, 955 S.W.2d 270, 272 (Tex.1997). Texas Disciplinary Rule of Professional Conduct 3.03 forbids an attorney from making false statements of material fact or law to a tribunal.

1. To argue. The attorney does not need to be sworn when she is merely arguing the facts or the law. *See* **Las Palmas Med. Ctr. v. Moore**, 349 S.W.3d 57, 67 (Tex.App.—El Paso 2010, pet. denied).

2. To present evidence. An attorney's statement of fact must be under oath to be considered as evidence. **Banda**, 955 S.W.2d at 272; *see, e.g.*, **Casino Magic Corp. v. King**, 43 S.W.3d 14, 20 (Tex.App.—Dallas 2001, pet. denied) (in garnishment action, attorney's unsworn statement that D was ex-husband's employer and thus liable for failing to withhold child support was not evidence).

(1) Objection to lack of oath. When an attorney who is not under oath presents facts as evidence to the court, the other party should object and ask that the attorney be sworn and subjected to cross-examination. *See* **Banda**, 955 S.W.2d at 272.

(2) Waiver of oath. When the other party is aware the attorney is testifying and does not object, the administration of the oath is waived. **Banda**, 955 S.W.2d at 272; **Knie v. Piskun**, 23 S.W.3d 455, 463 (Tex.App.—Amarillo 2000, pet. denied); *see, e.g.*, **Fullenwider v. American Guar. & Liab. Ins.**, 821 S.W.2d 658, 662 (Tex.App.—San Antonio 1991, writ denied) (when issue was timely supplementation of interrogatory answers, attorney's statements were clearly regarded as evidence). However, if the other party is not in a position to object (e.g., in a default-judgment case), the administration of the oath is not waived. *See* **De La Garza v. Salazar**, 851 S.W.2d 380, 383 (Tex.App.—San Antonio 1993, no writ).

§6. Communications from court

§6.1 Sent to attorney or pro se party.

1. Attorney. When a party is represented by an attorney, notices and other communications must be sent to the attorney. *See* Tex. R. Civ. P. 21a(a). If the party is represented by more than one attorney, notices and other communications must be sent to the attorney in charge. *See* Tex. R. Civ. P. 8 (all communications must be sent to attorney in charge); **Lofland Bros. v. Downey**, 822 S.W.2d 249, 251 (Tex.App.—Houston [1st Dist.] 1991, orig. proceeding) (same); *cf.* Tex. R. Civ. P. 21(c) (service on each attorney in charge when multiple parties are represented by different attorneys). Two rules require notices to be sent to all attorneys of record, not just the attorney in charge: TRCP 165a (notice of dismissal) and TRCP 306a (notice of signing of a final judgment or an appealable order). **Cannon v. ICO Tubular Servs.**, 905 S.W.2d 380, 388 (Tex.App.—Houston [1st Dist.] 1995, no writ), *overruled on other grounds*, **Lane Bank Equip. Co. v. Smith S. Equip., Inc.**, 10 S.W.3d 308 (Tex.2000).

2. Pro se party. When a party is pro se, notices and other communications must be sent to the party. *See* Tex. R. Civ. P. 21a(a); *see, e.g.*, **General Elec. Co. v. Falcon Ridge Apts., Jt.V.**, 811 S.W.2d 942, 943 (Tex.1991) (notice to dismiss).

§6.2 Methods of communication.

A court, judge, justice, magistrate, or clerk may send any notice or document by mail or electronic mail. Tex. Gov't Code §80.002; *see* Tex. R. Civ. P. 21(f)(10) (clerk may send notices, orders, or other communications to the party electronically). But a notice or document must be delivered if an applicable statute requires proof of delivery. *See* Tex. Gov't Code §80.004(b)(1); Senate Cmte. on State Affairs, Bill Analysis, Tex. S.B. 1116, 84th Leg., R.S. (2015).

Caution

To stay apprised of all communications from the court, attorneys and pro se parties must update the court with not only changes to their physical addresses but also changes to their e-mail addresses. See ***O'Connor's Texas Civil Forms****, FORMS 1B:14 to 1B:15 (2020 ed.).*

1. Mail. Any notice or document can be sent to an attorney or pro se party by mail. *See* Tex. Gov't Code §80.002.

(1) Methods of delivering mail. Proper methods of delivering a notice or document by mail are the following: (1) first-class mail, (2) first-class U.S. mail, (3) ordinary or regular mail, and (4) international first-class mail. Tex. Gov't Code §80.004(a). Some rules require notices to be sent by first-class mail. *E.g.*, Tex. R. Civ. P. 165a(1) (clerk must mail notice of intent to dismiss and must send notice of dismissal according to TRCP 306a), Tex. R. Civ. P. 306a(3) (clerk must use first-class mail to send notice of judgment). Methods of delivering mail that are not authorized include the following: (1) any form of mail that requires proof of delivery, (2) certified mail, (3) mail delivered by a commercial delivery service (e.g., FedEx, UPS), (4) first-class mail, return receipt requested, (5) mail that is personally served or hand-delivered, and (6) registered mail. Tex. Gov't Code §80.004(b).

(2) Attorney or pro se party's current address. An attorney or pro se party must include a physical address in the signature block of all pleadings and discovery. *See* Tex. R. Civ. P. 21(f)(2), 57. See "Signature block," ch. 1-B, §3.2.12. Whether a party's last filing contains the attorney's or pro se party's most current address can, at times, be difficult to determine.

(a) Attorney. Although the TRCPs do not state how the clerk should determine the attorney's current address, the attorney in charge has a continuing duty to inform the court of any change to her address. *See* **Withrow v. Schou**, 13 S.W.3d 37, 41 (Tex.App.—Houston [14th Dist.] 1999, pet. denied).

(b) Pro se party. Although the TRCPs do not state how the clerk should determine a pro se party's current address, a party's current address and any change of address must be provided to the court. Tex. Civ. Prac. & Rem. Code §30.015(a), (d). See "Notice of party's name & address," ch. 1-B, §3.2.18.

2. Electronic mail. Any notice or document can be sent to an attorney or pro se party by electronic mail. *See* Tex. Gov't Code §80.002. If a document is issued electronically by the court or the clerk, it must be electronically signed in the same manner as for an e-filing or e-serving party. *See* Tex. R. Civ. P. 21(f)(7); *see also* Tex. Gov't Code §21.011 (for electronic or

digital court documents, including orders, judgments, rulings, notices, commissions, or precepts, judge can sign electronically, digitally, or through another secure method). See "Electronic signature," ch. 1-B, §3.2.12(2)(b). A court seal may be electronic as well. Tex. R. Civ. P. 21(f)(10).

(1) Methods of delivering electronic mail. Proper methods of delivering a notice or document by electronic mail are the following: (1) electronic notice through the e-filing system on efiletexas.gov, (2) electronic notice, (3) electronic mail messages, (4) e-mail, and (5) secure electronic mail. Tex. Gov't Code §80.005(a). See "How to e-file," ch. 1-C, §4.1.1(3). Methods of electronic mail that are not authorized are the following: (1) faxes, (2) instant messages, (3) messages through a social network (e.g., Facebook), (4) telegraphs, (5) telephone messages, (6) text messages, (7) videoconferences, (8) voice messages, and (9) webcams. Tex. Gov't Code §80.005(b).

(2) Proper e-mail address. When sending a notice or document by e-mail to an attorney or pro se party who is registered with the electronic-filing service provider (EFSP) through efiletexas.gov, the court or authorized person must use the attorney's or pro se party's e-mail address that is on file with the EFSP, if the court uses that e-filing system. Tex. Gov't Code §80.003(a). If the attorney or pro se party is not registered with an EFSP or if the court does not use the e-filing system, the clerk must use the e-mail address provided by the attorney or pro se party. *See* Tex. Gov't Code §80.003(b); *see also* Tex. R. Civ. P. 57 (every pleading signed by attorney or pro se party must include e-mail address).

§7. Withdrawal

The parties must give the trial court specific and unambiguous notice when an attorney withdraws or is substituted. **Palkovic v. Cox**, 792 S.W.2d 743, 745 (Tex.App.—Houston [14th Dist.] 1990, writ denied) (signing amended petition is not a substitution of counsel).

§7.1 Termination by client. A client may discharge its attorney at any time, even without cause. **Rogers v. Clinton**, 794 S.W.2d 9, 10 n.1 (Tex.1990). Once an attorney is discharged, she must withdraw from the case and cannot continue to appear or file motions for the party. *See, e.g.*, **Bloom v. Graham**, 825 S.W.2d 244, 247–48 (Tex.App.—Fort Worth 1992, writ denied) (discharged attorney was sanctioned under TRCP 13 for filing groundless pleadings after discharge).

§7.2 Withdrawal by attorney. An attorney cannot withdraw from a case without satisfying the requirements of TRCP 10. **Rogers v. Clinton**, 794 S.W.2d 9, 10 n.1 (Tex.1990); **Moss v. Malone**, 880 S.W.2d 45, 49–50 (Tex.App.—Tyler 1994, writ denied).

1. Motion. To withdraw, the attorney must file a written motion showing good cause. Tex. R. Civ. P. 10. See **O'Connor's Texas Civil Forms**, FORM 1H:6 (2020 ed.). TRCP 10 does not define good cause, but courts generally view the Texas Disciplinary Rules of Professional Conduct as guidance for determining whether withdrawal is appropriate. *E.g.*, **In re Marriage of Harrison**, 557 S.W.3d 99, 115–16 (Tex.App.—Houston [14th Dist.] 2018, pet. denied) (good cause for withdrawal based on Tex. Disciplinary R. Prof'l Conduct 1.15 when attorney alleged that continued representation of client would cause her to violate disciplinary rules); **In re Daniels**, 138 S.W.3d 31, 33 (Tex.App.—San Antonio 2004, orig. proceeding) (good cause for withdrawal based on Tex. Disciplinary R. Prof'l Conduct 1.15 when client did not fulfill obligations under agreement, including payment of attorney fees, and continued representation would have been financially burdensome to attorney). Depending on whether an attorney is to be substituted, the motion must also state the following:

(1) Substitute attorney. If another attorney is to be substituted, the motion must state (1) the new attorney's name, address, telephone and fax numbers, and State Bar of Texas number, (2) that the client approves of the substitution, and (3) that the withdrawal is not for delay only. Tex. R. Civ. P. 10; *see* **Spinks v. Brown**, 103 S.W.3d 452, 459–60 (Tex.App.—San Antonio 2002, pet. denied).

(2) No substitute attorney. If no attorney is to be substituted, the motion must state (1) that a copy of the motion was delivered to the client, (2) that the client was notified in writing of its right to object to the motion, (3) whether the client consents to the motion, (4) the client's last known address, and (5) all pending settings and deadlines. Tex. R. Civ. P. 10; **Moss**, 880 S.W.2d at 49; *see also* **Williams v. Bank One**, 15 S.W.3d 110, 113–14 (Tex.App.—Waco 1999, no pet.) (granting of motion to withdraw, which did not inform client of right to object, was harmless error because client had 42 days to hire new attorney).

2. Ruling. If the court denies the motion to withdraw, the attorney must continue her representation in the case. *See* Tex. R. Civ. P. 10. If the court grants the motion to withdraw, the attorney must immediately notify the party in writing of any additional settings or deadlines that the attorney has knowledge of at the time of withdrawal and that the attorney has not already notified the party about. *Id.* The court can impose further conditions if it grants the motion. *Id.*

3. Review. The standard of review for a motion to withdraw is abuse of discretion. **In re Marriage of Harrison**, 557 S.W.3d at 112.

§8. Disqualification

Because disqualification of a party's attorney is a severe remedy, the courts must follow exacting standards when considering motions to disqualify. **In re RSR Corp.**, 568 S.W.3d 663, 666 (Tex.2019); **In re Nitla S.A. de C.V.**, 92 S.W.3d 419, 422 (Tex.2002); **Spears v. Fourth Ct. of Appeals**, 797 S.W.2d 654, 656 (Tex.1990).

§8.1 Timely filed motion. A motion to disqualify an attorney must be timely filed or else the complaint is waived. **In re RSR Corp.**, 568 S.W.3d 663, 666 (Tex.2019); **In re George**, 28 S.W.3d 511, 513 (Tex.2000); **Vaughan v. Walther**, 875 S.W.2d 690, 690 (Tex.1994). See **O'Connor's Texas Civil Forms**, FORM 1H:11 (2020 ed.). In determining whether waiver has occurred, the court should consider the following:

1. The length of time between when the movant learned of the conflict of interest or other ground for disqualification and when she filed the motion to disqualify. **In re Kahn**, 533 S.W.3d 387, 391 (Tex.App.—Houston [14th Dist.] 2015, orig. proceeding); **Wasserman v. Black**, 910 S.W.2d 564, 568 (Tex.App.—Waco 1995, writ dism'd); *e.g.*, **In re Trujillo**, 511 S.W.3d 726, 729–30 (Tex.App.—El Paso 2015, orig. proceeding) (motion to disqualify, filed 16 months after movant learned of conflict and shortly after opposing party set hearing date, was not timely); *see, e.g.*, **Vaughan**, 875 S.W.2d at 690–91 (motion to disqualify, filed more than six months after alleged conflict was discovered and on day of final hearing in child-custody case, was not timely). A delay by one party in filing a motion to disqualify cannot be attributed to another party. *See, e.g.*, **In re Kahn**, 533 S.W.3d at 392 (couple's motion to disqualify, filed three months after wife joined suit but ten months after suit was originally filed by husband, was not untimely; court considered only time that elapsed after wife joined suit).

2. Whether the evidence indicates that the motion is being used as a dilatory trial tactic. *Id.* at 391–92; *e.g.*, **Wasserman**, 910 S.W.2d at 568–69 (facts did not indicate that two-month delay in filing motion to disqualify was a dilatory tactic by movant).

3. Whether there has been significant discovery in the case. **In re Kahn**, 533 S.W.3d at 392.

4. Whether the delay in filing the motion has prejudiced the other party. *Id.*

§8.2 Grounds for disqualification. To disqualify an attorney, the movant must show that (1) the attorney violated the Texas Disciplinary Rules of Professional Conduct (the "Rules") or (2) other circumstances justify the attorney's disqualification.

1. Violation of disciplinary rules. An attorney can be disqualified from representing a client if she violates the Texas Disciplinary Rules of Professional Conduct. *See* **In re Murrin Bros. 1885, Ltd.**, 603 S.W.3d 53, 57 (Tex.2019); **In re Users Sys. Servs.**, 22 S.W.3d 331, 334 (Tex.1999); **In re Epic Holdings, Inc.**, 985 S.W.2d 41, 48 (Tex.1998); *see also* **National Med. Enters. v. Godbey**, 924 S.W.2d 123, 132 (Tex.1996) (disciplinary rules do not determine whether attorney is disqualified, but they do provide guidelines and suggest considerations). The violation must be established with specificity; mere allegations of unethical conduct or evidence showing a remote possibility of a violation is not enough to support disqualification. **In re Sanders**, 153 S.W.3d 54, 57 (Tex.2004); **Spears v. Fourth Ct. of Appeals**, 797 S.W.2d 654, 656 (Tex.1990); *see* **In re Thetford**, 574 S.W.3d 362, 373–74 (Tex.2019). The party seeking disqualification must also show that the attorney's representation of the adverse party will cause the party prejudice. **In re Murrin Bros.**, 603 S.W.3d at 57; *see* **In re Sanders**, 153 S.W.3d at 57 (Tex. Disciplinary R. Prof'l Conduct 3.08); **In re Duke**, No. 09-16-00185-CV, 2016 WL 4040128 (Tex.App.—Beaumont 2016, orig. proceeding) (memo op.; 7-28-16) (Tex. Disciplinary R. Prof'l Conduct 7.03); *see, e.g.*, **Busby v. Harvey**, 551 S.W.3d 184, 189 (Tex.App.—Fort Worth 2017, no pet.) (court did not address question of whether attorney violated any disciplinary rules because fact that party did not show actual prejudice was dispositive); *see also* **In re Nitla S.A. de C.V.**, 92 S.W.3d 419, 422 (Tex.2002) (although case did not involve violation of disciplinary rules, Court stated in dicta that, even if

disciplinary rule is violated, party must still show actual prejudice). Some courts, however, have held that when an attorney violates Texas Disciplinary Rule of Professional Conduct 1.09, no specific showing of prejudice is required. *See* **Cimarron Agric., Ltd. v. Guitar Holding Co.**, 209 S.W.3d 197, 203–04 (Tex.App.—El Paso 2006, no pet.); **In re Innovation Res. Solution, LLC**, No. 12-15-00254-CV, 2016 WL 1254058 (Tex.App.—Tyler 2016, orig. proceeding) (memo op.; 3-31-16); see, e.g., **Hendricks v. Barker**, 523 S.W.3d 152, 159–60 (Tex.App.—Houston [14th Dist.] 2016, no pet.) (because party established violation of Tex. Disciplinary R. Prof'l Conduct 1.09(a)(3), no showing of actual prejudice was required).

Practice Tip

The party seeking disqualification may also want to address any prejudice the nonmovant may suffer, such as the financial burden of replacing her attorney with someone unfamiliar with the case, which the court may be a consider in determining whether disqualification is proper. See ***In re Murrin Bros.****, 603 S.W.3d at 57.*

(1) Rule 1.09—attorney conflict of interest.

(a) Attorney. An attorney can be disqualified from representing a client if (1) she personally represented a former client, (2) she currently represents the client in question in a matter adverse to the former client, (3) she does not have the former client's consent to represent the other client, and (4) the representation results in a conflict of interest under Texas Disciplinary Rule of Professional Conduct 1.09. *See* Tex. Disciplinary R. Prof'l Conduct 1.09(a).

Note

At least one court has held that, although the wording of Rule 1.09(a) indicates that it was designed primarily to address situations where an attorney seeks to represent a new client in litigation against a former client, it also applies when an attorney represents multiple parties and a conflict arises among them. E.g., ***In re Kahn****, 533 S.W.3d 387, 392–93 (Tex.App.—Houston [14th Dist.] 2015, orig. proceeding) (attorney represented multiple Ds who were adverse because one D had claims it could bring against other Ds based on allegedly fraudulent transfer; court disqualified attorney from representing Ds under Rule 1.09(a)(3)); see* ***Wasserman v. Black****, 910 S.W.2d 564, 567 (Tex.App.—Waco 1995, writ dism'd).*

[1] Personally represented former client. An attorney personally represents a client under Rule 1.09(a) if she is exposed to the client's case and confidential information; she does not need to have personally and substantially participated in the case. *See* **Henderson v. Floyd**, 891 S.W.2d 252, 253–54 (Tex.1995).

[2] Current matter adverse to former client. A current matter is adverse to a former client under Rule 1.09(a) if the attorney's representation could harm the former client; it is not necessary that the former client be an opposing party in the matter. *See* **Cimarron Agric.**, 209 S.W.3d at 201–02 (court should focus on effect attorney's representation may have on former client's interests, not solely on former client's relationship with pending litigation); *see, e.g.*, **National Med.**, 924 S.W.2d at 132–33 (representation was adverse even though former client was not party to suit); **In re Roseland Oil & Gas, Inc.**, 68 S.W.3d 784, 787 (Tex.App.—Eastland 2001, orig. proceeding) (adversity has nothing to do with sides of suit; representation was adverse even though parties were both Ds). To determine if the attorney should be disqualified based on adversity, the court should consider the likelihood that harm will occur and the seriousness of the harm. **National Med.**, 924 S.W.2d at 132; *see* **In re Thetford**, 574 S.W.3d at 375. If the possible harm is severe, an attorney should be disqualified even if the likelihood of the harm is small. *E.g.*, **National Med.**, 924 S.W.2d at 132–33 (threat of criminal prosecution is serious enough to require disqualification even if risk of prosecution is small); *see* **In re Kahn**, 533 S.W.3d at 393.

[3] No consent. A former client waives a conflict of interest under Rule 1.09(a) only if the client gives informed consent to the representation. *See* Tex. Disciplinary R. Prof'l Conduct 1.09 cmt. 10; *see, e.g.*, **In re Cerberus Capital Mgmt.**, 164 S.W.3d 379, 382–83 (Tex.2005) (disqualification improper when attorneys for former client sought and obtained valid written waiver of conflict). An attorney should not ask a former client to waive the conflict if a disinterested attorney would conclude that the former client should not agree to the conflicting representation. *See* Tex. Disciplinary R. Prof'l Conduct 1.06 cmt. 7, 1.09 cmt. 10.

[a] Degree of disclosure. Consent is valid only if the attorney has fully disclosed the relevant circumstances, including her past or intended role on behalf of the former and current clients. Tex. Disciplinary R. Prof'l Conduct 1.09 cmt. 10. The degree of disclosure necessary for informed consent will vary depending on the client's level of sophistication. *See* Tex. Disciplinary R. Prof'l Conduct 1.06 cmt. 8.

[b] Form of consent. Although consent can be given orally, it is not advisable to obtain oral consent. **In re Cerberus Capital**, 164 S.W.3d at 383; *see* Tex. Disciplinary R. Prof'l Conduct 1.06 cmt. 8. In most cases, the attorney should obtain a written, signed conflict-of-interest waiver that discloses the following: (1) the proposed representation, (2) the subject matter of the work performed for the former client, (3) the time period involved, (4) the attorney involved, (5) the nature of discussions with the former client, and (6) how the earlier representation concluded. *See* **In re Cerberus Capital**, 164 S.W.3d at 382–83.

[4] Conflict of interest. An attorney's representation of a new client creates a conflict of interest with a former client under Rule 1.09(a) when the representation (1) may cause the current client to question the validity of the attorney's work for the former client, (2) will, in reasonable probability, require the attorney to reveal or use the former client's confidential information, or (3) involves a matter that is the same as or substantially related to the subject of the earlier representation. Tex. Disciplinary R. Prof'l Conduct 1.09(a).

[a] Makes client question validity of prior work. An attorney must be disqualified if her current client questions the validity of her services or work product—or those of her firm while she was employed there—for a former client. *See* Tex. Disciplinary R. Prof'l Conduct 1.09(a)(1); **In re Basco**, 221 S.W.3d 637, 638–39 (Tex.2007).

[b] Reveals or uses confidential information. An attorney must be disqualified if there is a reasonable probability the representation will involve a violation of Rule 1.05, which governs an attorney's duty to preserve a client's confidential information. Tex. Disciplinary R. Prof'l Conduct 1.09(a)(2); *see, e.g.*, **In re Hoar Constr., L.L.C.**, 256 S.W.3d 790, 803–04 (Tex.App.—Houston [14th Dist.] 2008, orig. proceeding) (firm disqualified when former client's confidential information would be useful in current client's case).

[c] Involves substantially related matter. An attorney must be disqualified if she represents her current client in a matter that is the same as or substantially related to the subject of her representation of the former client. Tex. Disciplinary R. Prof'l Conduct 1.09(a)(3); **Metropolitan Life Ins. v. Syntek Fin. Corp.**, 881 S.W.2d 319, 320 (Tex.1994); *see* **NCNB Tex. Nat'l Bank v. Coker**, 765 S.W.2d 398, 399–400 (Tex.1989). To satisfy the substantial-relationship test, the movant must show that the facts of the previous representation are so related to those in the pending litigation that there is a genuine threat the confidences revealed to the former counsel will be divulged to a present adversary. **In re Thetford**, 574 S.W.3d at 374; **Metropolitan Life**, 881 S.W.2d at 320–21; *see* Tex. Disciplinary R. Prof'l Conduct 1.09 cmt. 4A; *see also* **Hendricks**, 523 S.W.3d at 159 (if movant shows substantial relationship, she is entitled to conclusive presumption that she revealed confidences to attorney). Conclusory statements that the matters are substantially related or mere facial similarities between the current matter and the previous representation are insufficient. *E.g.*, **In re Thetford**, 574 S.W.3d at 374–75 (current guardianship proceeding was only facially similar to previous representation for estate-planning services).

Note

Although there is some overlap between Rule 1.09(a)(2) and Rule 1.09(a)(3) because each involves the threatened revelation of a former client's confidences, the two are distinct and alternative grounds for disqualification. See ***In re Butler****, 987 S.W.2d 221, 226 n.3 (Tex.App.—Houston [14th Dist.] 1999, orig. proceeding).*

(b) Attorney's current firm. An attorney's current firm can be disqualified from representing a client when any of the members or associates of the firm, if practicing alone, would be disqualified from representing that client under Rule 1.09. Tex. Disciplinary R. Prof'l Conduct 1.09(b); **In re Basco**, 221 S.W.3d at 638–39. See "Attorney," ch. 1-H, §8.2.1(1)(a).

(c) Attorney's former firm. The partners and associates of an attorney's former firm who were associated with the attorney at the time she left can be disqualified from representing a client if the attorney would be disqualified from

representing that client under Rule 1.09(a)(1) or (a)(2). Tex. Disciplinary R. Prof'l Conduct 1.09(c) & cmt. 6, 7; **In re Basco**, 221 S.W.3d at 638–39. See "Makes client question validity of prior work," ch. 1-H, §8.2.1(1)(a)[4][a]; "Reveals or uses confidential information," ch. 1-H, §8.2.1(1)(a)[4][b].

Note

Disqualification based on previous government employment is governed by the Texas Disciplinary Rule of Professional Conduct 1.10.

(2) Rule 5.03—responsibility for nonattorney employee. An attorney and her firm can be disqualified from representing a client in a current matter if a nonattorney employee of the firm (1) obtained confidences about the matter while previously working for another firm and (2) shared those confidences with her current firm. **In re Turner**, 542 S.W.3d 553, 555–56 (Tex.2017); *see* **In re Guaranty Ins. Servs.**, 343 S.W.3d 130, 134 (Tex.2011). In this situation, disqualification is based on the attorney's duty to ensure that the conduct of her nonattorney employees is compatible with the professional obligations of the attorney; the attorney cannot allow a nonattorney employee to engage in conduct that would, if engaged in by the attorney, subject the attorney to discipline. Tex. Disciplinary R. Prof'l Conduct 5.03; **In re Columbia Valley Healthcare Sys.**, 320 S.W.3d 819, 827 (Tex.2010); **Phoenix Founders, Inc. v. Marshall**, 887 S.W.2d 831, 834 (Tex.1994). Thus, disciplinary rules prohibiting the attorney from revealing confidential information also prohibit the attorney from allowing a nonattorney employee to reveal such information. **In re Columbia Valley Healthcare**, 320 S.W.3d at 827; **Phoenix Founders**, 887 S.W.2d at 834. In determining whether the requirements for disqualification have been met, the following presumptions apply.

Note

Whether the standards and presumptions that apply to former nonattorney employees of opposing counsel (e.g., paralegals, legal assistants) also apply to former nonattorney employees of the opposing party depends on the following criteria: (1) whether the nonattorney employee was hired specifically for litigation purposes and (2) whether the employee reported directly to the opposing party's attorneys. See ***In re RSR Corp.****, 475 S.W.3d 775, 776 (Tex.2015). In determining whether to apply these standards and presumptions, a court will look not only to the employee's former job title but also to her former duties. See id. at 780–81. If the employee performed the same duties that a full-time legal assistant of a law firm or a party's legal department would, then the same standards and presumptions applicable to nonattorney employees of opposing counsel would apply; however, if the duties are not the same, then the employee is likely to be considered merely a fact witness, and the standards and presumptions would not apply. See, e.g., id. (D's former finance manager, whose duties included ensuring cash flow and securing company financing, was considered fact witness because his position was created independently of litigation and his primary function was not to report to D's attorneys). When a nonattorney employee is considered a fact witness, but she has disclosed a former employer's privileged and confidential information, the court should instead consider the factors in* ***In re Meador****, 968 S.W.2d 346, 351–52 (Tex.1998) to determine whether disqualification is proper. See* ***In re RSR Corp.****, 475 S.W.3d at 776. See "Outside discovery process," ch. 1-H, §8.2.2(2)(a).*

(a) Obtained confidences—conclusive presumption. If the nonattorney employee actually worked on the matter in question at another firm, it is conclusively presumed that she obtained confidences about the matter while working for the other firm. **In re Turner**, 542 S.W.3d at 556; **In re Guaranty Ins.**, 343 S.W.3d at 134; *see* **Phoenix Founders**, 887 S.W.2d at 834. Even if the nonattorney employee did not actually work on the matter in question, disqualification may still be proper if the party seeking disqualification shows that the nonattorney employee otherwise obtained confidences about the matter during her previous employment. *See* **In re Turner**, 542 S.W.3d at 555–56.

(b) Shared confidences—rebuttable or conclusive presumption. If the nonattorney employee obtained confidences while working for the previous firm, it is presumed that she shared the information with her current

firm. **In re Turner**, 542 S.W.3d at 556; **In re Guaranty Ins.**, 343 S.W.3d at 134. This presumption can be rebuttable or conclusive, depending on the circumstances. **In re Turner**, 542 S.W.3d at 556.

[1] General rule—rebuttable. The presumption of shared confidences is generally rebuttable. **In re Turner**, 542 S.W.3d at 556. To rebut the presumption, the attorney or the current firm must show that (1) the nonattorney employee was instructed not to work on the matter and (2) formal, institutionalized screening measures (e.g., removing the file from the employee's access, having the employee sign a confidentiality agreement) were put in place to limit the possibility of the employee having contact with the suit. *See id.*; **In re Guaranty Ins.**, 343 S.W.3d at 134; **Phoenix Founders**, 887 S.W.2d at 835. The attorney or firm must have instructed the nonattorney employee not to work on any matter that she worked on during her previous employment, even if the attorney or firm was not aware of the specific conflict in question. **In re Turner**, 542 S.W.3d at 557. If the attorney or firm shows that the instruction was given, the court will then consider whether the screening measures were effective. *See id.* at 556–57. The court can consider the following factors to determine whether the screening was effective: (1) the substantiality of the relationship between the former and current matters, (2) the time elapsing between the matters, (3) the size of the firm, (4) the number of individuals presumed to have confidential information, (5) the nature of their involvement in the former matter, and (6) the timing and features of any measures taken to reduce the danger of disclosure. *Id.* at 556; **In re Guaranty Ins.**, 343 S.W.3d at 134–35; **Phoenix Founders**, 887 S.W.2d at 836.

[2] Exceptions—conclusive. The presumption of shared confidences can become conclusive if the party seeking disqualification shows that (1) the nonattorney employee did in fact share confidences with her current firm, (2) the employee actually performed work, including clerical work, on the matter in question at the attorney's directive, and the attorney reasonably should have known about the conflict of interest, (3) screening the employee from the matter was or would be ineffective, or (4) the employee would necessarily be required to work on the matter in question. **In re Guaranty Ins.**, 343 S.W.3d at 135; **In re Columbia Valley Healthcare**, 320 S.W.3d at 828; *see* **In re Turner**, 542 S.W.3d at 557 n.3; **Phoenix Founders**, 887 S.W.2d at 835.

(3) Rule 3.08—attorney as witness. An attorney can be disqualified if (1) she is or may be a witness necessary to establish a disputed, essential fact for her client (other than attorney fees) or (2) she will or may be called to give testimony that is substantially adverse to her client without the client's consent. **Spears**, 797 S.W.2d at 657–58; *see* Tex. Disciplinary R. Prof'l Conduct 3.08(a), (b); **In re Keenan**, 501 S.W.3d 74, 76–77 (Tex.2016); **In re Sanders**, 153 S.W.3d at 56–57. The party requesting disqualification must show that the attorney's dual role as advocate-witness will cause the party actual prejudice. **Ayres v. Canales**, 790 S.W.2d 554, 558 (Tex.1990); **In re Guidry**, 316 S.W.3d 729, 738 (Tex.App.—Houston [14th Dist.] 2010, orig. proceeding); **In re VSDH Vaquero Venture, Ltd.**, No. 05-15-01513-CV, 2016 WL 2621073 (Tex.App.—Dallas 2016, orig. proceeding) (memo op.; 5-6-16); *e.g.*, **In re Sanders**, 153 S.W.3d at 57 (no actual prejudice when party could use evidentiary sources other than attorney testimony); *see* Tex. Disciplinary R. Prof'l Conduct 3.08 cmt. 10; *see, e.g.*, **In re Bahn**, 13 S.W.3d 865, 874 (Tex.App.—Fort Worth 2000, orig. proceeding) (testimony from trial counsel could cause jury confusion). An attorney who will be a witness at trial can still participate in out-of-court matters such as preparing and signing pleadings, planning strategy, and negotiating settlement. **Anderson Prod'g Inc. v. Koch Oil Co.**, 929 S.W.2d 416, 422 (Tex.1996); **In re Guidry**, 316 S.W.3d at 738; *see* Tex. Disciplinary R. Prof'l Conduct 3.08 cmt. 8. Another attorney in the testifying attorney's firm may act as trial counsel if the client gives informed consent. **Anderson Prod'g**, 929 S.W.2d at 424; *see* Tex. Disciplinary R. Prof'l Conduct 3.08(c).

Caution

An attorney should not testify as an expert in a case in which she is legal counsel. Everything an expert reviews is subject to discovery. See "Securing Discovery from Experts," ch. 6-D, §1 et seq. The attorney-client privilege will probably shield some of the information the expert-attorney reviews, but other information may need to be turned over to the opposing party.

---

2. Other circumstances.

(1) Attorney assumed duty to preserve nonclient's confidences. An attorney can be disqualified from a suit if she has assumed a duty to preserve the confidential information of a nonclient. *E.g.*, **In re Mitcham**, 133 S.W.3d 274,

276–77 (Tex.2004) (attorney was disqualified when he had entered into conflicts-of-interest agreement in which he agreed not to share any information regarding nonclient's use of asbestos); **National Med.**, 924 S.W.2d at 130–31 (attorney was disqualified when suit was substantially related to earlier suit in which attorney was part of joint-defense agreement). This duty arises most often in the context of providing a joint defense in a multiparty case because the attorney either expressly agrees in writing to maintain a nonclient's confidences or impliedly agrees by participating in a joint defense, which creates a joint-defense privilege. *See* **In re Skiles**, 102 S.W.3d 323, 327 (Tex.App.—Beaumont 2003, orig. proceeding); *see also* Tex. R. Evid. 503(b)(1)(C) (joint-defense privilege). To disqualify an attorney based on a joint-defense privilege, the party seeking disqualification must show (1) confidential information has been shared and (2) the matter in which the information was shared is substantially related to the matter in which disqualification is sought. **In re Skiles**, 102 S.W.3d at 327; **Rio Hondo Implement Co. v. Euresti**, 903 S.W.2d 128, 132 (Tex.App.—Corpus Christi 1995, orig. proceeding). For example, if an attorney represents a defendant, D1, in a suit with other defendants, D2 and D3, and the defendants shared information about their defense, the attorney cannot later represent a plaintiff against D2 or D3 in a suit substantially related to the earlier suit. *See* **National Med.**, 924 S.W.2d at 129–30. This disqualification extends to the attorney's firm, even if the attorney does not work on the later suit. *Id.* at 131–32.

(2) Attorney received privileged materials. When an attorney receives an opponent's privileged materials, the attorney can be disqualified from continuing to represent the client. **In re Nitla**, 92 S.W.3d at 422–23; **In re Meador**, 968 S.W.2d at 351.

(a) Outside discovery process. When an attorney receives privileged materials outside the normal discovery process, through no wrongdoing of her own, the attorney may be disqualified based on the following factors: (1) whether the attorney knew or should have known the materials were privileged, (2) the promptness with which the attorney notified opposing counsel, (3) the extent to which the attorney reviewed and digested the information, (4) the significance of the privileged information, (5) the extent to which the movant may be at fault for the disclosure, and (6) the extent to which the nonmovant will suffer prejudice from the disqualification. **In re Meador**, 968 S.W.2d at 351–52; *e.g.*, **In re RSR Corp.**, 475 S.W.3d at 779 (when D's former finance manager, who was considered fact witness, disclosed privileged and confidential information to Ps' attorneys, **Meador** factors should have controlled trial court's determination on disqualification).

Note

Although the Texas Disciplinary Rules of Professional Conduct do not specifically address an attorney's obligations when she receives an opponent's confidential information, an attorney who does not take action on receipt of the information could violate disciplinary rules directed at criminal, fraudulent, dishonest, and misleading conduct, depending on the specific facts and circumstances of the case. See Tex. Cmte. on Prof'l Ethics, Op. 664 (2016); see, e.g., Tex. Disciplinary R. Prof'l Conduct 4.01(b) (attorney must not knowingly fail to disclose material fact to third person when necessary to avoid making attorney assist in client's criminal or fraudulent act), Tex. Disciplinary R. Prof'l Conduct 8.04(a)(3) (attorney must not knowingly engage in dishonest, fraudulent, deceitful, or misleading conduct).

(b) Through discovery process. When an attorney receives privileged materials through the normal discovery process (e.g., from the trial court after in camera review), the movant seeking to disqualify the attorney must show the following: (1) the attorney's review of the privileged materials caused the movant actual harm, and (2) the attorney's disqualification is necessary because there are no lesser means to remedy the harm. **In re Nitla**, 92 S.W.3d at 423.

§8.3 Disqualified attorney's file. When an attorney is disqualified, the successor attorney will want access to two types of information in the file.

1. Public materials. The successor attorney can have access to and use of the pleadings, discovery, correspondence, and other public materials from the disqualified attorney's file. **In re George**, 28 S.W.3d 511, 514 (Tex.2000).

2. Work product. A successor attorney's access to the disqualified attorney's work product is restricted or denied "to the extent that such a remedy furthers the purposes underlying the disqualification." **In re George**, 28 S.W.3d at 512. When an attorney has been disqualified for representing an opposing party in an earlier suit, the presumption that the dis-

qualified attorney's work product contains confidential information arises once the former client establishes that the two representations are substantially related. *Id.* at 518. The burden then shifts to the current client to rebut the presumption by demonstrating there is not a substantial likelihood that the work product contains confidential information. *Id.* Once the successor attorney moves for access to the work product or the former client moves to restrict access, the court should order the disqualified attorney to produce an inventory of the work product describing (1) the type of work, (2) the subject matter of the items, (3) the claims they relate to, and (4) any other relevant factors. *Id.* The court may also conduct an in camera inspection. *Id.* at 519.

§9. Agreements between attorneys—Rule 11

The purpose of TRCP 11 is to avoid disputes over the terms of oral agreements made between attorneys in a pending lawsuit. *See* **Padilla v. LaFrance**, 907 S.W.2d 454, 461 (Tex.1995); **Kennedy v. Hyde**, 682 S.W.2d 525, 529–30 (Tex.1984). See **O'Connor's Texas Civil Forms**, FORM 1H:13 (2020 ed.).

§9.1 Agreements about pending suits. To be enforceable, an agreement about any matter in a pending lawsuit must meet the requirements of TRCP 11. **Knapp Med. Ctr. v. De La Garza**, 238 S.W.3d 767, 768 (Tex.2007); **London Mkt. Cos. v. Schattman**, 811 S.W.2d 550, 552 (Tex.1991); **Meza v. Hooker Contracting Co.**, 104 S.W.3d 111, 114–15 (Tex.App.—San Antonio 2003, no pet.). The agreement may be written or oral.

Caution

Any agreements made between parties that may affect statutorily mandated deadlines must be expressly stated in a docket-control order or other written agreement (e.g., a Rule 11 agreement); otherwise, the parties' agreed terms will not be upheld. See ***Crosstex Energy Servs. v. Pro Plus, Inc.****, 430 S.W.3d 384, 395 (Tex.2014). See "Pretrial order," ch. 5-A, §5.*

1. Written agreement. To be enforceable, a written agreement about a pending lawsuit must be in writing, signed, and filed with the court. Tex. R. Civ. P. 11; **Padilla v. LaFrance**, 907 S.W.2d 454, 460 (Tex.1995) (written settlement agreement); *e.g.*, **Knapp Med. Ctr.**, 238 S.W.3d at 768–69 (oral settlement agreement was unenforceable); **London Mkt.**, 811 S.W.2d at 552 (oral agreement to extend time for discovery was unenforceable); **Meza**, 104 S.W.3d at 115 (oral agreement to delay service was unenforceable).

(1) In writing. The "in writing" requirement is satisfied if all essential terms of the agreement are in writing. **Padilla**, 907 S.W.2d at 460; *see* **Shamrock Psychiatric Clinic, P.A. v. Texas Dept. of H&HS**, 540 S.W.3d 553, 561 (Tex.2018); **Neasbitt v. Warren**, 105 S.W.3d 113, 116 (Tex.App.—Fort Worth 2003, no pet.). This requirement may be satisfied by a series of documents as long as the agreement can be ascertained from the documents without resorting to oral testimony. **Padilla**, 907 S.W.2d at 460; *see* **Shamrock Psychiatric Clinic**, 540 S.W.3d at 561; *see, e.g.*, **Green v. Midland Mortg. Co.**, 342 S.W.3d 686, 691–92 (Tex.App.—Houston [14th Dist.] 2011, no pet.) (series of e-mails was sufficient to satisfy Rule 11).

(2) Signed. The "signed" requirement is satisfied if the agreement includes the signatures of the attorneys entering into the agreement. *See* Tex. R. Civ. P. 11.

Note

If attorneys enter into a Rule 11 agreement electronically, the Uniform Electronic Transactions Act (UETA) may apply. See Tex. Bus. & Com. Code §322.001 et seq.; ***Cunningham v. Zurich Am. Ins.****, 352 S.W.3d 519, 529 (Tex.App.—Fort Worth 2011, pet. denied). Courts disagree on what is sufficient to constitute a signature under the UETA. Compare* ***Khoury v. Tomlinson****, 518 S.W.3d 568, 576–78 (Tex.App.—Houston [1st Dist.] 2017, no pet.) (breach-of-contract case not involving Rule 11 agreement; automatically generated e-mail signature block and name in "From" field constitute signatures under UETA), with* ***Cunningham****, 352 S.W.3d at 530 (no valid Rule 11 agreement because automatically generated e-mail signature block does not constitute signature under UETA).*

(3) Filed with court. The "filed with the court" requirement is satisfied if the agreement is filed with the court anytime before it is to be enforced. **Padilla**, 907 S.W.2d at 461; *see, e.g.*, **Southwestern Bell Tel. Co. v. Perez**, 904 S.W.2d 817, 822 (Tex.App.—San Antonio 1995, orig. proceeding) (letter agreement extending deadlines that was filed as exhibit to party's motion to compel met filing requirement of TRCP 11).

2. Oral agreement in court. To be enforceable, an oral agreement about a pending lawsuit must be made in open court and entered into the record. Tex. R. Civ. P. 11; **Youngkin v. Hines**, 546 S.W.3d 675, 678 n.1 (Tex.2018); **Sitaram v. Aetna U.S. Healthcare**, 152 S.W.3d 817, 824 (Tex.App.—Texarkana 2004, no pet.); *e.g.*, **Ronin v. Lerner**, 7 S.W.3d 883, 886 (Tex.App.—Houston [1st Dist.] 1999, no pet.) (oral settlement agreement met requirements of TRCP 11). All material terms of the agreement must be included in the record. **Sitaram**, 152 S.W.3d at 824; **Neasbitt**, 105 S.W.3d at 116.

3. Agreement recorded in deposition. An agreement between attorneys about a pending lawsuit that is made part of the record of a deposition is enforceable to the extent that it affects the oral deposition. Tex. R. Civ. P. 191.1. Other agreements recorded in a deposition and filed with the court may be enforceable as TRCP 11 agreements. The courts disagree on the enforceability of agreements made during a deposition about matters not related to the deposition. *Compare* **Tindall v. Bishop, Peterson & Sharp, P.C.**, 961 S.W.2d 248, 251 (Tex.App.—Houston [1st Dist.] 1997, no writ) (settlement agreement dictated during deposition was not enforceable under TRCP 11 but was enforceable as exception to statute of frauds), *with* **Kosowska v. Khan**, 929 S.W.2d 505, 508 (Tex.App.—San Antonio 1996, writ denied) (settlement agreement dictated during deposition, not signed by parties or attorneys, was enforceable under TRCP 11).

§9.2 Exceptions to Rule 11. There are exceptions to the strict requirements of TRCP 11. **Kennedy v. Hyde**, 682 S.W.2d 525, 529 (Tex.1984). For example, a nonconforming Rule 11 agreement may be given effect if the terms are undisputed. *Id.*; *e.g.*, **Anderson v. Cocheu**, 176 S.W.3d 685, 689 (Tex.App.—Dallas 2005, pet. denied) (oral settlement agreement was enforced because it was not disputed). A nonconforming Rule 11 agreement may also be enforced for equitable reasons. **Kennedy**, 682 S.W.2d at 529; *e.g.*, **Massey v. Galvan**, 822 S.W.2d 309, 317–18 (Tex.App.—Houston [14th Dist.] 1992, writ denied) (nonconforming agreement to arbitrate was enforced because party's conduct indicated existence of agreement and because agreement to arbitrate was not challenged until after unfavorable result was rendered); *see* **Williams v. Huling**, 43 Tex. 113, 120 (1875). A conforming Rule 11 agreement can be challenged on grounds of fraud or mistake. **Kennedy**, 682 S.W.2d at 529; *see* **Burnaman v. Heaton**, 240 S.W.2d 288, 291 (Tex.1951).

§9.3 Agreements before suit filed. An agreement about a potential lawsuit does not need to be in writing. TRCP 11 applies only to agreements about pending suits. *E.g.*, **Estate of Pollack v. McMurrey**, 858 S.W.2d 388, 393 (Tex.1993) (oral presuit agreement to settle was enforceable as contract but not under TRCP 11); *see also* **Belleza-Gonzalez v. Villa**, 57 S.W.3d 8, 12 (Tex.App.—Houston [14th Dist.] 2001, no pet.) (presuit agreement to postpone service was not enforceable because it should have been reduced to writing once suit was filed). See "Presuit settlement agreement," ch. 7-I, §3.1.1.

§10. Attorney fees from adverse party

The general rule in Texas is that each litigant must pay its own attorney fees. **Rohrmoos Venture v. UTSW DVA Healthcare, LLP**, 578 S.W.3d 469, 483 (Tex.2019). But in certain situations, a party may be able to recover attorney fees from the adverse party. For a detailed discussion of recovering attorney fees from an adverse party, see "Attorney Fees," **O'Connor's Texas Causes of Action**, ch. 45-A, §1 et seq. (2021 ed.).

Note

As part of the recovery of attorney fees, a party may be able to recover costs expended for paralegals and legal assistants. See "Evidence about paralegals," ***O'Connor's Texas Causes of Action****, ch. 45-A, §4.1.4 (2021 ed.).*

§10.1 Prerequisites for recovery of attorney fees.

1. Party pleaded for fees. To recover attorney fees, the party must plead for them, unless fees are mandated by statute. **Alan Reuber Chevrolet, Inc. v. Grady Chevrolet, Ltd.**, 287 S.W.3d 877, 884 (Tex.App.—Dallas 2009, no pet.); **Swate v. Medina Cmty. Hosp.**, 966 S.W.2d 693, 701 (Tex.App.—San Antonio 1998, pet. denied); *see* **Wells Fargo Bank v.**

Murphy, 458 S.W.3d 912, 915 (Tex.2015). The party should identify the specific authority for attorney fees in its pleadings; if it does not, the party is still entitled to fees if it pleads facts that support a claim for them or if the defendant does not object to the failure to identify the authority. *See* **Whallon v. City of Houston**, 462 S.W.3d 146, 165 (Tex.App.—Houston [1st Dist.] 2015, pet. denied); **Mitchell v. LaFlamme**, 60 S.W.3d 123, 130 (Tex.App.—Houston [14th Dist.] 2000, no pet.); **O'Connell v. Hitt**, 730 S.W.2d 16, 18 (Tex.App.—Corpus Christi 1987, no writ). See "Plaintiff pleaded for attorney fees," **O'Connor's Texas Causes of Action**, ch. 45-A, §2.1 (2021 ed.); "No identification of authority," **O'Connor's Texas Causes of Action**, ch. 45-A, §3.3.1 (2021 ed.); **O'Connor's Texas Causes of Action Pleadings**, FORMS 45B:2, 45C:1, 45D:1 (2020 ed.). If the plaintiff pleads a specific authority for attorney fees, it is limited to that authority and cannot recover attorney fees under a different, unpleaded authority. **Heritage Gulf Coast Props., Ltd. v. Sandalwood Apts., Inc.**, 416 S.W.3d 642, 660 (Tex.App.—Houston [14th Dist.] 2013, no pet.).

2. Party represented by attorney. To recover attorney fees, the party must have been represented by an attorney. **Rohrmoos Venture v. UTSW DVA Healthcare, LLP**, 578 S.W.3d 469, 488 (Tex.2019). See "Plaintiff represented by attorney," **O'Connor's Texas Causes of Action**, ch. 45-A, §2.3 (2021 ed.).

3. Party complied with conditions precedent. To recover attorney fees, the party must plead and prove that it complied with all conditions precedent to recovery. See "Plaintiff complied with conditions precedent," **O'Connor's Texas Causes of Action**, ch. 45-A, §2.4 (2021 ed.).

4. Claim was authorized. To recover attorney fees, the party must show that the claim for fees is authorized by a statute or a rule of procedure, by a contract between the parties, or under equity. *See* Tex. R. Civ. P. 215.2(b)(8) (attorney fees as sanctions); **Rohrmoos Venture**, 578 S.W.3d at 487 (recovery of attorney fees is allowed if authorized by statute or contract between parties); **In re National Lloyds Ins.**, 532 S.W.3d 794, 809 (Tex.2017) (same); **In re Nalle Plastics F.L.P.**, 406 S.W.3d 168, 172 (Tex.2013) (same); **1/2 Price Checks Cashed v. United Auto. Ins.**, 344 S.W.3d 378, 382 (Tex.2011) (same); **Knebel v. Capital Nat'l Bank**, 518 S.W.2d 795, 799 (Tex.1974) (attorney fees can be awarded under equity). See **O'Connor's Texas Civil Forms**, FORM 1H:14 (2020 ed.).

(1) Attorney fees under statute. Generally, a party can recover attorney fees under a statute if (1) the statute authorizes attorney fees and (2) the party met the requirements of the statute. See "By statute," **O'Connor's Texas Causes of Action**, ch. 45-A, §2.5.1 (2021 ed.).

Note

Some statutes that permit the recovery of attorney fees require that the party recover actual damages as a prerequisite to a fee award. See ***Ortiz v. State Farm Lloyds**, 589 S.W.3d 127, 134–35 (Tex.2019); see, e.g., Tex. Ins. Code §541.152(a)(1) (prevailing party can recover actual damages plus costs and attorney fees). Under such a statute, the party must be claiming that it suffered other damages in addition to attorney fees to be entitled to a fee award because attorney fees incurred in the prosecution or defense of a claim are not considered damages. See **Ortiz**, 589 S.W.3d at 135.*

(a) CPRC ch. 38. CPRC chapter 38 is the general attorney-fees statute. For a detailed discussion of attorney fees under chapter 38, see "Attorney Fees Under CPRC ch. 38," **O'Connor's Texas Causes of Action**, ch. 45-B, §1 et seq. (2021 ed.).

Note

*If a written contract provides for the recovery of attorney fees, the contractual provisions will trump the statutory provisions in CPRC chapter 38. See **Intercontinental Grp. v. KB Home Lone Star L.P.**, 295 S.W.3d 650, 653 (Tex.2009). See "Claims under contract vs. claims under CPRC ch. 38," **O'Connor's Texas Causes of Action**, ch. 45-C, §1.3 (2021 ed.).*

[1] Requirements. To be entitled to attorney fees under CPRC §38.001, a party must show that the following requirements have been met:

[a] The party is a proper party to bring a claim for attorney fees. A plaintiff who successfully prosecutes a claim for which attorney fees are available under CPRC chapter 38 is a proper party. A defendant who successfully brings a counterclaim for which attorney fees are available under CPRC chapter 38 may also be a proper party if the counterclaim arises from the same transaction as the original claim and the same facts required to assert the original claim are required to defend against the counterclaim. *See* **Brockie v. Webb**, 244 S.W.3d 905, 910 (Tex.App.—Dallas 2008, pet. denied). See "For counterclaim," **O'Connor's Texas Causes of Action**, ch. 45-B, §2.2.1(2)(a) (2021 ed.). But a defendant who successfully defends a suit in which the plaintiff sought attorney fees under CPRC chapter 38 is not entitled to recover attorney fees. *See* **Brockie**, 244 S.W.3d at 910. See "Not for defense," **O'Connor's Texas Causes of Action**, ch. 45-B, §2.2.1(2)(b) (2021 ed.).

[b] The party pleaded facts sufficient to support a claim for attorney fees. See "Plaintiff pleaded for attorney fees," **O'Connor's Texas Causes of Action**, ch. 45-B, §2.1 (2021 ed.).

[c] The underlying claim is a CPRC §38.001 claim. *See* **1/2 Price Checks**, 344 S.W.3d at 383; **Coward v. Gateway Nat'l Bank**, 525 S.W.2d 857, 858–59 (Tex.1975) (citing former TRCS art. 2226); **London v. London**, 94 S.W.3d 139, 147–48 (Tex.App.—Houston [14th Dist.] 2002, no pet.). Section 38.001 lists the following claims that qualify for attorney fees: (1) rendered services, (2) performed labor, (3) furnished materials, (4) freight or express overcharges, (5) lost or damaged freight or express, (6) killed or injured livestock, (7) a sworn account, or (8) an oral or written contract. See "Authorized claims," **O'Connor's Texas Causes of Action**, ch. 45-B, §2.2.2 (2021 ed.).

[d] The party was represented by an attorney. Tex. Civ. Prac. & Rem. Code §38.002(1); **1/2 Price Checks**, 344 S.W.3d at 383; **Great Am. Ins. v. North Austin MUD**, 908 S.W.2d 415, 427 n.10 (Tex.1995). See "Plaintiff represented by attorney," **O'Connor's Texas Causes of Action**, ch. 45-A, §2.3 (2021 ed.).

[e] The party against whom attorney fees are to be assessed is an individual or a corporation. Tex. Civ. Prac. & Rem. Code §38.001; *e.g.*, **Fleming & Assocs. v. Barton**, 425 S.W.3d 560, 574 (Tex.App.—Houston [14th Dist.] 2014, pet. denied) (partnership is not corporation or individual and thus is not liable for attorney fees under CPRC §38.001); **Harris Cty. MUD v. Mitchell**, 915 S.W.2d 859, 865–66 (Tex.App.—Houston [1st Dist.] 1995, writ denied) (same, for a municipal utility district); **Base-Seal, Inc. v. Jefferson Cty.**, 901 S.W.2d 783, 786–87 (Tex.App.—Beaumont 1995, writ denied) (same, for a county). See "Defendant was individual or corporation," **O'Connor's Texas Causes of Action**, ch. 45-B, §2.4 (2021 ed.).

[f] The §38.001 claim was presented to the opposing party or its agent. Tex. Civ. Prac. & Rem. Code §38.002(2); **1/2 Price Checks**, 344 S.W.3d at 383; **Great Am. Ins.**, 908 S.W.2d at 427 n.10. The demand should include (1) the assertion of a debt or a claim and (2) a request for payment. *See* **Jones v. Kelley**, 614 S.W.2d 95, 100 (Tex.1981). The demand may be made orally or in writing. *Id.*; **Honeycutt v. Billingsley**, 992 S.W.2d 570, 581 (Tex.App.—Houston [1st Dist.] 1999, pet. denied). See "Plaintiff presented claim to defendant," **O'Connor's Texas Causes of Action**, ch. 45-B, §2.5 (2021 ed.).

[g] The opposing party either did not tender payment of the claim or did not tender it on time (i.e., within 30 days after the claim was presented). Tex. Civ. Prac. & Rem. Code §38.002(3); **1/2 Price Checks**, 344 S.W.3d at 383; **Great Am. Ins.**, 908 S.W.2d at 427 n.10. See "Defendant did not tender payment," **O'Connor's Texas Causes of Action**, ch. 45-B, §2.6 (2021 ed.).

[h] The party prevailed and recovered damages on a cause of action for which attorney fees are recoverable. **In re Nalle Plastics F.L.P.**, 406 S.W.3d at 173; **MBM Fin. Corp. v. Woodlands Oper. Co.**, 292 S.W.3d 660, 666 (Tex.2009); *e.g.*, **Green Int'l v. Solis**, 951 S.W.2d 384, 390 (Tex.1997) (prevailing party was not entitled to attorney fees because it was not awarded damages); **State Farm Life Ins. v. Beaston**, 907 S.W.2d 430, 437 (Tex.1995) (same); **Stevens v. Anatolian Shepherd Dog Club**, 231 S.W.3d 71, 77–78 (Tex.App.—Houston [14th Dist.] 2007, pet. denied) (party was not entitled to attorney fees because she did not prevail on undecided claim); *see* **Ashford Partners v. ECO Res.**, 401 S.W.3d 35, 40 (Tex.2012). The courts of appeals are split on the issue of whether other, non-monetary relief—such as specific performance or an injunction—that has financial value to the party is considered a favorable finding on damages. See "Liability & damages," **O'Connor's Texas Causes of Action**, ch. 45-B, §2.7.1 (2021 ed.). A net recovery is not required. See "Net recovery not required," **O'Connor's Texas Causes of Action**, ch. 45-B, §2.7.2 (2021 ed.).

Note

A party that prevails in the trial court can also ask the court to award conditional appellate attorney fees. See ***Ventling v. Johnson****, 466 S.W.3d 143, 154 (Tex.2015). In most cases, a prevailing party in the trial court seeks recovery of appellate attorney fees for successfully defending a judgment on appeal; however, a prevailing party can recover appellate attorney fees for successfully prosecuting an appeal as well. See id. at 154–55. To be entitled to appellate attorney fees, the party must at least partially prevail on appeal. See id. at 155. For details on proving appellate attorney fees, see "Note," ch. 1-H, §10.2.1(1).*

[i] The party requesting attorney fees established the elements of proof for the recovery of attorney fees, either by judicial notice or by evidence. See "Plaintiff incurred reasonable attorney fees," **O'Connor's Texas Causes of Action**, ch. 45-B, §2.8 (2021 ed.).

[2] Judicial notice. Judicial notice of attorney fees can be taken only when (1) the claim is a CPRC §38.001 claim and (2) the claim is tried on the merits. *See* Tex. Civ. Prac. & Rem. Code §38.004. The trial court, without receiving evidence, can take judicial notice of (1) the usual and customary attorney fees and (2) the contents of the file. *Id.* The usual and customary fees are presumed reasonable. Tex. Civ. Prac. & Rem. Code §38.003. See "By judicial notice," **O'Connor's Texas Causes of Action**, ch. 45-B, §2.8.2(2)(b) (2021 ed.).

Caution

In ***Rohrmoos Venture****, the Texas Supreme Court clarified that the lodestar method is the standard for calculating reasonable and necessary attorney fees in Texas and stated that this method applies in any situation where an objective calculation of reasonable hours worked multiplied by a reasonable hourly rate can be used.* ***Rohrmoos Venture****, 578 S.W.3d at 497–98. See "Proving reasonableness & necessity of attorney fees," ch. 1-H, §10.2. Although the Court noted the judicial-notice provision and statutory presumption of reasonableness for CPRC §38.001 claims, it remains unclear whether a party must present evidence of reasonableness and necessity using the lodestar method for these claims. See* ***Rohrmoos Venture****, 578 S.W.3d at 490 n.9; see also* ***Barnett v. Schiro****, 579 S.W.3d 73, 74 (Tex.2019) (court remanded issue of attorney fees under CPRC §38.001 for redetermination consistent with* ***Rohrmoos Venture****);* ***Scott Pelley P.C. v. Wynne****, 578 S.W.3d 694, 705 (Tex.App.—Dallas 2019, no pet.) (court of appeals determined that party's evidence satisfied* ***Rohrmoos Venture*** *standard but also stated that fee award should be sustained because trial court properly took judicial notice of fees under CPRC ch. 38 and thus no further evidence was needed).*

[a] Section 38.001 claim. The claim must be a CPRC §38.001 claim. **Charette v. Fitzgerald**, 213 S.W.3d 505, 514 (Tex.App.—Houston [14th Dist.] 2006, no pet.); *see* Tex. Civ. Prac. & Rem. Code §38.004; **Coward**, 525 S.W.2d at 858–59 (analyzing predecessor statute). If the claim is not included in CPRC §38.001, the court cannot take judicial notice of the fees. *E.g.*, **Dilston House Condo. Ass'n v. White**, 230 S.W.3d 714, 719 (Tex.App.—Houston [14th Dist.] 2007, no pet.) (no judicial notice for violation of Property Code); **Pheng Invs. v. Rodriquez**, 196 S.W.3d 322, 333 (Tex.App.—Fort Worth 2006, no pet.) (no judicial notice for fraudulent misrepresentation), *overruled on other grounds*, **Hoskins v. Hoskins**, 497 S.W.3d 490 (Tex.2016); **Gorman v. Gorman**, 966 S.W.2d 858, 866–67 (Tex.App.—Houston [1st Dist.] 1998, pet. denied) (no judicial notice in declaratory-judgment case); **Richards v. Mena**, 907 S.W.2d 566, 573–74 (Tex.App.—Corpus Christi 1995, writ dism'd) (no judicial notice in redistricting and voting-rights case); **Smith v. Smith**, 757 S.W.2d 422, 425 (Tex.App.—Dallas 1988, writ denied) (no judicial notice in DTPA case). *But see* **Matelski v. Matelski**, 840 S.W.2d 124, 130 (Tex.App.—Fort Worth 1992, no writ) (court took judicial notice of attorney fees in family-law case).

[b] Tried on merits. The claim must be tried on the merits; that is, for the court to take judicial notice of attorney fees, there must be either (1) a proceeding before the court or (2) a jury case in which the amount of attorney fees is submitted to the court by agreement. Tex. Civ. Prac. & Rem. Code §38.004. The term "proceeding before the court" is not defined in CPRC §38.004. The Supreme Court has said the trial judge may take judicial notice of attorney fees only "in

his role of trier of fact in the conventional trial of a nonjury case but not in passing on a motion for summary judgment." **Coward**, 525 S.W.2d at 859; *see* **Garcia v. Martinez**, 894 S.W.2d 806, 807 (Tex.App.—Corpus Christi 1994, no writ) (dicta; trial court cannot adjudicate attorney fees based on judicial notice without hearing evidence); **General Elec. Sup. v. Gulf Electroquip, Inc.**, 857 S.W.2d 591, 601 (Tex.App.—Houston [1st Dist.] 1993, writ denied) (in summary-judgment case, fact issue about attorney fees cannot be resolved by judicial notice). *But see* **Purvis Oil Corp. v. Hillin**, 890 S.W.2d 931, 939 (Tex.App.—El Paso 1994, no writ) (in summary-judgment case, fact issue about attorney fees can be resolved by judicial notice).

(b) Other statutes. Various statutes provide for the recovery of attorney fees from an adverse party, but their wording and rationales are different. For lists of such statutes, see "Statutory Attorney Fees—Private Litigants," **O'Connor's Texas Civil Practice & Remedies Code Plus**, chart 2 (2020–21 ed.); "Statutory Attorney Fees—Attorney General," **O'Connor's Texas Civil Practice & Remedies Code Plus**, chart 3 (2020–21 ed.). For a discussion of mandatory and discretionary statutory attorney fees, see "Mandatory or discretionary," **O'Connor's Texas Causes of Action**, ch. 45-A, §5.1 (2021 ed.).

(2) Attorney fees under contract. A party can recover attorney fees if a written contract provides for them. See "Attorney Fees Under Written Contract," **O'Connor's Texas Causes of Action**, ch. 45-C, §1 et seq. (2021 ed.).

(3) Attorney fees under equity. Attorney fees may be awarded on equitable grounds even when there is no statute or contract providing for them. See "Attorney Fees Under Equity," **O'Connor's Texas Causes of Action**, ch. 45-D, §1 et seq. (2021 ed.).

5. Fees were incurred. To recover attorney fees, the party must prove that it either incurred attorney fees or that it must be awarded attorney fees to be made whole, depending on the basis for the claim. *See* **Rohrmoos Venture**, 578 S.W.3d at 489–90. If the statute or contract that authorizes attorney fees requires the fees to be incurred, or if the party is seeking attorney fees under equity, the party must prove that it incurred or will incur fees. *See id.* at 489; **Turner v. Turner**, 385 S.W.2d 230, 234 (Tex.1964), *overruled on other grounds*, **Bounds v. Caudle**, 560 S.W.2d 925 (Tex.1977). Generally, fees are incurred when a party becomes liable for them. **Rohrmoos Venture**, 578 S.W.3d at 489. The amount incurred is not, however, conclusive evidence of a reasonable and necessary fee; those elements must still be established by the party requesting the attorney fees. *Id.* at 488. See "Proving reasonableness & necessity of attorney fees," ch. 1-H, §10.2. If the statute or contract does not require attorney fees to be incurred, the party should instead offer evidence showing that the fee award is reasonable and necessary to compensate the party for losses resulting from the litigation process. *See* **Rohrmoos Venture**, at 489–90 (court will not imply incurred requirement). See "Plaintiff incurred attorney fees," **O'Connor's Texas Causes of Action**, ch. 45-A, §2.6 (2021 ed.).

Note

A prevailing party is entitled to conditional appellate attorney fees, even though those fees have not yet been incurred, if it can prove the fees are reasonable and necessary. See ***Yowell v. Granite Oper. Co.***, *__ S.W.3d __, 2020 WL 2502141 (Tex.2020) (No. 18-0841; 5-15-20);* ***Ventling***, *466 S.W.3d at 154. See "Note," ch. 1-H, §10.1.4(1)(a)[1][h]. For details on proving appellate attorney fees, see "Note," ch. 1-H, §10.2.1(1).*

6. Fees were reasonable & necessary. To recover attorney fees, the party must prove that the fees were reasonable and necessary. **Rohrmoos Venture**, 578 S.W.3d at 489; *see* **Arthur Andersen & Co. v. Perry Equip. Corp.**, 945 S.W.2d 812, 818–19 (Tex.1997). See "Proving reasonableness & necessity of attorney fees," ch. 1-H, §10.2.

7. Fees were segregated. To recover attorney fees, the party must segregate recoverable fees when necessary. *See* **Tony Gullo Motors I, L.P. v. Chapa**, 212 S.W.3d 299, 311 (Tex.2006). Whether attorney fees are required to be segregated is a question of law. **McCarty v. Montgomery**, 290 S.W.3d 525, 540 (Tex.App.—Eastland 2009, pet. denied); **Clearview Props., L.P. v. Property Tex. SC One Corp.**, 287 S.W.3d 132, 143 (Tex.App.—Houston [14th Dist.] 2009, pet. denied). The extent to which claims can or cannot be segregated is a mixed question of law and fact. **Tony Gullo Motors**, 212 S.W.3d at 313.

(1) Segregation required. If a party is entitled to attorney fees from the adverse party on one claim but not another, the party claiming attorney fees must segregate the recoverable fees from the unrecoverable fees. **Kinsel v. Lindsey**, 526 S.W.3d 411, 427 (Tex.2017); **Tony Gullo Motors**, 212 S.W.3d at 313; **Clearview Props.**, 287 S.W.3d at 143. Even if the underlying facts are the same for different claims, attorney fees are not necessarily recoverable for all the claims or "inseparable." *See* **Tony Gullo Motors**, 212 S.W.3d at 313. Attorney fees must be segregated even if an attorney spent only a nominal amount of time on a claim for which fees are unrecoverable. **Home Comfortable Sups. v. Cooper**, 544 S.W.3d 899, 910 (Tex.App.—Houston [14th Dist.] 2018, no pet.); *see* **Tony Gullo Motors**, 212 S.W.3d at 313. An attorney is not required to keep separate records documenting the exact amount of time spent on each claim; she can establish segregation if she presents evidence of a reliable estimate of the percentage of time spent on each claim. *See* **Tony Gullo Motors**, 212 S.W.3d at 314; *see, e.g.*, **State Farm Lloyds v. Hanson**, 500 S.W.3d 84, 102 (Tex.App.—Houston [14th Dist.] 2016, pet. dism'd) (attorney's estimate that 95% of time was spent on contract claim and 5% on bad-faith claim sufficiently segregated fees).

(2) Segregation not required.

(a) Recoverable-fee claims only. If a party pursued only claims for which attorney fees are recoverable, the attorney is not required to segregate attorney fees between claims. *See* **Tony Gullo Motors**, 212 S.W.3d at 311.

(b) Inseparable legal services. If a party incurred attorney fees related to claims for which attorney fees are both recoverable and unrecoverable, but the legal services provided were necessary for all the claims in the suit, the party is not required to segregate attorney fees between claims. **A.G. Edwards & Sons, Inc. v. Beyer**, 235 S.W.3d 704, 710 (Tex.2007); **Tony Gullo Motors**, 212 S.W.3d at 313–14. That is, when the legal services are so intertwined with both the recoverable and unrecoverable claims, the attorney fees do not need to be segregated. **Kinsel**, 526 S.W.3d at 427; **Tony Gullo Motors**, 212 S.W.3d at 313–14; *see* **Varner v. Cardenas**, 218 S.W.3d 68, 69 (Tex.2007). For example, depositions of critical witnesses, discovery motions, and voir dire may be necessary whether a recoverable claim is filed by itself or with other unrecoverable claims; as long as the services were necessary for all the claims, segregation of fees for those services is not required. *See* **Tony Gullo Motors**, 212 S.W.3d at 313.

(3) Objections. The adverse party must object to an unsegregated fee award; otherwise, the issue of segregation is waived on appeal. **Green Int'l**, 951 S.W.2d at 389; **Arthur J. Gallagher & Co. v. Dieterich**, 270 S.W.3d 695, 705 (Tex.App.—Dallas 2008, no pet.); *see* **In re M.G.N.**, 491 S.W.3d 386, 409 (Tex.App.—San Antonio 2016, pet. denied).

(a) Timing of objection.

[1] Jury trial. In a jury trial, a complaint about a failure to segregate is preserved if raised in an objection to the jury charge—that is, before the case is submitted to the jury. **Home Comfortable**, 544 S.W.3d at 908; *see* **Editorial Caballero, S.A. de C.V. v. Playboy Enters.**, 359 S.W.3d 318, 341 (Tex.App.—Corpus Christi 2012, pet. denied).

[2] Nonjury trial. In a nonjury trial, a complaint about a failure to segregate is preserved if raised at the time that the fee testimony and billing records are offered as evidence. *See* **In re M.G.N.**, 491 S.W.3d at 409; **McCalla v. Ski River Dev. Inc.**, 239 S.W.3d 374, 383 (Tex.App.—Waco 2007, no pet.); **Lost Creek Ventures, LLC v. Pilgrim**, No. 01-15-00375-CV, 2016 WL 3569756 (Tex.App.—Houston [1st Dist.] 2016, no pet.) (memo op.; 6-30-16) (footnote 1).

Caution

Some courts have held that, in a nonjury trial, a complaint about failure to segregate is preserved as long as it is raised at some point before the case is submitted to the fact-finder. See ***Lawson v. Keene***, *No. 03-13-00498-CV, 2016 WL 767772 (Tex.App.—Austin 2016, pet. denied) (memo op.; 2-23-16); see, e.g.,* ***Home Comfortable***, *544 S.W.3d at 909–10 (error preserved when attorney objected to failure to segregate fees in closing argument). At least one court has also found that error was preserved when the complaint was raised in a postjudgment motion.* ***Clearview Props.***, *287 S.W.3d at 143 n.4. Because courts disagree about the proper time to bring this objection, the best practice is to raise the complaint when the fee testimony and billing records are offered as evidence.*

(b) Improper trial-court ruling. If the trial court overrules an objection and awards attorney fees based on unsegregated fees but the appellate court finds that the fees should have been segregated, the appellate court must remand the issue of attorney fees to the trial court for a new hearing. **Stewart Title Guar. Co. v. Sterling**, 822 S.W.2d 1, 11–12 (Tex.1991), *modified on other grounds*, **Tony Gullo Motors I, L.P. v. Chapa**, 212 S.W.3d 299 (Tex.2006); *see* **Kinsel**, 526 S.W.3d at 428; **Tony Gullo Motors**, 212 S.W.3d at 314. On remand, the party should present detailed information on attorney fees; if contemporaneous fee records are unavailable, the trial court may allow for reconstruction of the attorney's work and consideration of evidence to demonstrate the time spent and tasks performed. **Kinsel**, 526 S.W.3d at 428.

§10.2 Proving reasonableness & necessity of attorney fees. To recover attorney fees, the party must prove that the fees were reasonable and necessary. **Rohrmoos Venture v. UTSW DVA Healthcare, LLP**, 578 S.W.3d 469, 489 (Tex.2019); *see* **Arthur Andersen & Co. v. Perry Equip. Corp.**, 945 S.W.2d 812, 818–19 (Tex.1997). The party must prove reasonableness and necessity even if the statute or contract authorizing attorney fees does not explicitly require both; there is no material distinction between provisions requiring proof of "reasonable" fees and provisions requiring proof of "reasonable and necessary" fees. *See* **Rohrmoos Venture**, 578 S.W.3d at 488–89.

1. Lodestar method. The party must present evidence that the attorney fees were reasonable and necessary by using the lodestar method. *See* **Rohrmoos Venture**, 578 S.W.3d at 496. When attorney fees are calculated using this method and supported by sufficient evidence, there is a presumption that the fees are reasonable and necessary. *Id.* at 499; **Scott Pelley P.C. v. Wynne**, 578 S.W.3d 694, 704 (Tex.App.—Dallas 2019, no pet.).

Caution

For claims brought under CPRC §38.001, there is a presumption that the usual and customary attorney fees are reasonable. Tex. Civ. Prac. & Rem. Code §38.003. This presumption can be rebutted. Id. See "Presumption of reasonableness," ***O'Connor's Texas Causes of Action****, ch. 45-B, §2.8.2(1) (2021 ed.). After* ***Rohrmoos Venture****, however, it is unclear how the statutory presumption in CPRC §38.003 is affected by the Court's broad statements supporting the application of the lodestar calculation in most, if not all, situations. See* ***Rohrmoos Venture****, 578 S.W.3d at 497–98; see also* ***Barnett v. Schiro****, 579 S.W.3d 73, 74 (Tex.2019) (remanding issue of attorney fees under CPRC §38.001 for redetermination consistent with* ***Rohrmoos Venture****).*

(1) Applicability. The lodestar method should be applied to any situation or fee arrangement in which the calculation can be used. *See* **Rohrmoos Venture**, 578 S.W.3d at 498–99 & n.10; **Jardon v. Pfister**, 593 S.W.3d 810, 838 (Tex.App.—El Paso 2019, no pet.); **Scott Pelley P.C.**, 578 S.W.3d at 704–05. This includes situations where the party and its attorney enter into a specific contractual fee arrangement. *See* **Rohrmoos Venture**, 578 S.W.3d at 498. In such a situation, the party cannot rely solely on the contract as proof to support a fee award; the party must still prove that the fees contracted for were reasonable and necessary using the lodestar method. *See id.*; **Jardon**, 593 S.W.3d at 837–38.

Note

The lodestar method should not be used to calculate contingent appellate attorney fees because, at the time of the calculation, it is uncertain who will represent the party on appeal, what the attorney's hourly rate will be, and what services will be necessary. ***Yowell v. Granite Oper. Co.****, __ S.W.3d __, 2020 WL 2502141 (Tex.2020) (No. 18-0841; 5-15-20). Instead, the calculation should be based on testimony about the services that the party reasonably believes will be necessary to defend the appeal and a reasonable hourly rate for those services. Id.*

(a) Hourly fee. When the contract between the party and its attorney states the fee in terms of an hourly rate, attorney fees can be recovered from the adverse party based on that rate if the rate was reasonable. *See* **Rohrmoos Venture**, 578 S.W.3d at 498–99. The rate contracted for between the party and its attorney is not conclusively reasonable; the party claiming the attorney fees must still establish that the fee was reasonable and necessary under the lodestar

method. *Id.* at 488; *see* **Toledo v. KBMT Oper. Co.**, 581 S.W.3d 324, 329 (Tex.App.—Beaumont 2019, pet. denied). See "Hourly fee," **O'Connor's Texas Causes of Action**, ch. 45-A, §2.7.1(2)(a) (2021 ed.).

(b) Contingent fee. When the contract between the party and its attorney provides for a contingent award of attorney fees (i.e., attorney fees based on a percentage of the plaintiff's recovery), attorney fees cannot be recovered from the adverse party based solely on evidence of the fee agreement. **Arthur Andersen**, 945 S.W.2d at 818; *see* **Rohrmoos Venture**, 578 S.W.3d at 498; **Toledo**, 581 S.W.3d at 329. The party must still offer evidence that the attorney fees were reasonable and necessary under the lodestar method. *See* **Rohrmoos Venture**, 578 S.W.3d at 498. Because there will not be evidence of a particular hourly rate billed in such a situation, the party has the burden to show, generally through expert testimony, that the rate claimed for purposes of the lodestar calculation reflects a reasonable market rate. *Id.* at 499 n.10. See "Contingent fee," **O'Connor's Texas Causes of Action**, ch. 45-A, §2.7.1(2)(b) (2021 ed.).

(c) Fixed fee. When the contract between the party and its attorney states the fee in terms of a fixed amount for reaching certain stages of litigation, attorney fees cannot be recovered based solely on the contract. *See* **Rohrmoos Venture**, 578 S.W.3d at 498. The party must still offer evidence that the attorney fees were reasonable and necessary under the lodestar method. *See id.* Because there will not be evidence of a particular hourly rate billed in such a situation, the party has the burden to show, generally through expert testimony, that the rate claimed for purposes of the lodestar calculation reflects a reasonable market rate. *Id.* at 499 n.10. See "Fixed fee," **O'Connor's Texas Causes of Action**, ch. 45-A, §2.7.1(2)(c) (2021 ed.).

(2) Calculation. Under the lodestar method, first the lodestar figure (i.e., the base amount) is calculated; that number can then be adjusted up or down based on certain considerations not already accounted for in the base amount. *See* **Rohrmoos Venture**, 578 S.W.3d at 496. The lodestar calculation is generally based on the **Arthur Andersen** considerations, which include the following: (1) the time and labor required, the novelty and difficulty of the questions involved, and the skill required to perform the legal service properly, (2) the likelihood that the acceptance of the particular employment will preclude other employment by the attorney, (3) the fee customarily charged in the locality for similar legal services, (4) the amount involved and the results obtained, (5) the time limitations imposed by the client or the circumstances, (6) the nature and length of the professional relationship with the client, (7) the experience, reputation, and ability of the attorney performing the services, and (8) whether the fee is fixed or contingent on results obtained (i.e., the uncertainty of collection before the legal services have been rendered). *See* Tex. Disciplinary R. Prof'l Conduct 1.04(b); **Rohrmoos Venture**, 578 S.W.3d at 494; **Arthur Andersen**, 945 S.W.2d at 818.

Note

The Texas Supreme Court has clarified that the lodestar method developed as a shorthand version of the ***Arthur Andersen*** *considerations that Texas courts have traditionally used to determine the reasonableness of attorney fees.* ***Rohrmoos Venture****, 578 S.W.3d at 496. The* ***Arthur Andersen*** *considerations were never intended as a separate method or test.* ***Rohrmoos Venture****, 578 S.W.3d at 496. Because the lodestar method incorporates most of the traditional* ***Arthur Andersen*** *considerations, the lodestar amount is presumptively reasonable and necessary. See* ***Rohrmoos Venture****, 578 S.W.3d at 496.*

(a) Determining base lodestar amount. The base lodestar amount is determined by multiplying the number of hours reasonably worked on the case by the reasonable hourly rate for that work. **Rohrmoos Venture**, 578 S.W.3d at 498; **El Apple I, Ltd. v. Olivas**, 370 S.W.3d 757, 760 (Tex.2012). The base lodestar amount generally takes into account at least the following **Arthur Andersen** considerations: (1) the time and labor required, the novelty and difficulty of the questions involved, and the skill required to perform the legal service properly, (2) the fee customarily charged in the locality for similar legal services, (3) the amount involved, (4) the results obtained up to trial, (5) the experience, reputation, and ability of the attorney performing the services, and (6) whether the fee is fixed or contingent on results obtained (i.e., the uncertainty of collection before the legal services have been rendered). **Rohrmoos Venture**, 578 S.W.3d at 500 & n.12.

[1] Number of hours. The party should offer evidence of the number of hours reasonably worked on the party's claim. **Rohrmoos Venture**, 578 S.W.3d at 498; **Sullivan v. Abraham**, 488 S.W.3d 294, 299 (Tex.2016); **El**

Apple, 370 S.W.3d at 762–63. Sufficient evidence of the number of hours worked includes, at a minimum, (1) the particular services performed, (2) who performed the services, (3) approximately when the services were performed, and (4) the reasonable amount of time required to perform the services. **Rohrmoos Venture**, 578 S.W.3d at 498; **Jardon**, 593 S.W.3d at 839; **Toledo**, 581 S.W.3d at 329; *see* **El Apple**, 370 S.W.3d at 762–63 (evidence should include basic facts underlying lodestar amount, including nature of the work, services each attorney performed, dates and times each service was performed, and number of hours worked). The number of hours submitted should not include any duplicative, excessive, or inadequately documented work. **El Apple**, 370 S.W.3d at 762. The party should include in its lodestar calculation only the hours worked on claims for which fees are recoverable or inseparable. See "Fees were segregated," ch. 1-H, §10.1.7; "Number of hours," **O'Connor's Texas Causes of Action**, ch. 45-A, §4.1.2(2)(b)[1][a] (2021 ed.).

[2] Hourly rate. The party should offer evidence of a reasonable hourly rate for the work done on the party's claim. **Rohrmoos Venture**, 578 S.W.3d at 498; *see* **City of Laredo v. Montano**, 414 S.W.3d 731, 736 (Tex.2013); **El Apple**, 370 S.W.3d at 763–64. Specifically, to show the reasonableness of the hourly rate, the attorney should offer evidence based on the **Arthur Andersen** considerations, including the attorney's experience and expertise, the novelty and complexity of the questions involved, any special skill required for the representation, the attorney's risk in accepting the representation, and any other considerations that would factor into the attorney's fee negotiations. *See* **Rohrmoos Venture**, 578 S.W.3d at 499 n.10. If the claim involves a fee agreement other than hourly billing (e.g., a contingent fee arrangement), the party has the burden to show the hourly rate used in the lodestar calculation is a reasonable market rate based on these same **Arthur Andersen** considerations. **Rohrmoos Venture**, 578 S.W.3d at 499 n.10; *see, e.g.*, **Bailey v. Smith**, 581 S.W.3d 374, 397–98 (Tex.App.—Austin 2019, pet. denied) (reasonable hourly rate for assistant attorney general was based on hourly billing rates published in *Texas Lawyer* for lawyers practicing in relevant practice areas in same county).

(b) Adjusting lodestar amount. Once the base lodestar amount is determined, the court may adjust the amount up or down if the presumption of reasonableness is overcome by other considerations not already accounted for. **Rohrmoos Venture**, 578 S.W.3d at 500–01; *see* **Jardon**, 593 S.W.3d at 839. That is, any **Arthur Andersen** considerations not factored into the base lodestar amount can be used to adjust that amount in the second step of the lodestar calculation, but the adjustment cannot be based on any considerations that would duplicate those used in calculating the base lodestar amount. *See* **Rohrmoos Venture**, 578 S.W.3d at 500–01; **Jardon**, 593 S.W.3d at 839. If a fee claimant seeks an increase in the fee award, it must produce specific evidence showing that a higher amount is necessary for the fee award to be reasonable. **Rohrmoos Venture**, 578 S.W.3d at 501. Similarly, if the opposing party seeks a reduction of the fee award, it must product specific evidence to overcome the presumptive reasonableness of the base lodestar figure. *Id.* Because the base lodestar amount is presumptively reasonable, an adjustment to a fee award should be made only in rare or exceptional circumstances. *See* **Perdue v. Kenny A.**, 559 U.S. 542, 552 (2010); **El Apple**, 370 S.W.3d at 765. See "Step 2—Adjusting base lodestar amount," **O'Connor's Texas Causes of Action**, ch. 45-A, §4.1.2(2)(b)[2] (2021 ed.).

[1] *Arthur Andersen* considerations. The base lodestar amount may be adjusted based on the following **Arthur Andersen** considerations, which are not factored into the base amount: (1) the likelihood that the acceptance of the particular employment will preclude other employment by the attorney, (2) the results obtained during or after trial, (3) the time limitations imposed by the client or the circumstances, or (4) the nature and length of the professional relationship with the client. *See* **Rohrmoos Venture**, 578 S.W.3d at 494, 500 & n.12. Specific evidence of these considerations can generally be used to enhance or reduce the base lodestar amount and overcome the presumption that the base lodestar amount reflects reasonable and necessary attorney fees. *See id.* at 501.

[2] Other factors. The **Arthur Andersen** considerations are not exclusive. **In re National Lloyds Ins.**, 532 S.W.3d 794, 809 (Tex.2017). Courts can consider other factors in adjusting the base lodestar amount, including the following: (1) the entire record, (2) the common knowledge of the attorneys and judges, (3) the relative success of the parties, (4) the client's interest that is at stake, and (5) the responsibility imposed on the attorney. *See* **Smith v. Patrick W.Y. Tam Trust**, 296 S.W.3d 545, 547 (Tex.2009); **Rapid Settlements, Ltd. v. Settlement Funding, LLC**, 358 S.W.3d 777, 786 (Tex.App.—Houston [14th Dist.] 2012, no pet.).

2. Evidence.

(1) Introduce evidence through expert. In most cases, the party must offer evidence of reasonableness and necessity through an attorney who testifies as an expert. *See* **Lesikar v. Rappeport**, 33 S.W.3d 282, 308 (Tex.App.—

Texarkana 2000, pet. denied). The expert can be (1) an attorney who has not worked on the party's claim and bases her testimony on information such as the trial attorney's file and timesheets or (2) the party's trial attorney, who can testify based on her personal knowledge of the claim. *See* **Garcia v. Gomez**, 319 S.W.3d 638, 641 (Tex.2010); **Rhey v. Redic**, 408 S.W.3d 440, 455–56 (Tex.App.—El Paso 2013, no pet.).

Note

In certain cases, the party may be able to rely on judicial notice to establish attorney fees. See "Judicial notice," ch. 1-H, §10.1.4(1)(a)[2].

(2) Specific testimony or documentation. To prove the reasonableness and necessity of the attorney fees using the lodestar method, the party must offer specific testimony or other evidence about the details of the work performed that substantiates the claim for fees. *See* **Rohrmoos Venture**, 578 S.W.3d at 499; **El Apple**, 370 S.W.3d at 764; *see, e.g.*, **Long v. Griffin**, 442 S.W.3d 253, 255 (Tex.2014) (affidavit that provided generalities about hours spent and nature of attorney's work without evidence of time spent on specific tasks was insufficient to support attorney-fees award). In most cases, the party should support the claim with detailed and contemporaneous billing records or other specific documentary evidence. **El Apple**, 370 S.W.3d at 763; *see* **Rohrmoos**, 578 S.W.3d at 502 (billing records are not required but are strongly encouraged); **Jardon**, 593 S.W.3d at 839 (same). General testimony about an attorney's experience, the total amount of fees, and the reasonableness of those fees is insufficient to support an award of attorney fees. **Rohrmoos**, 578 S.W.3d at 496; *see* **Jardon**, 593 S.W.3d at 839. If more than one attorney worked on the plaintiff's claim, the documentation should indicate which attorney performed each task or category of tasks. **El Apple**, 370 S.W.3d at 763. Time spent on tasks for which the defendant's attorney was also present may be verifiable without documentation. *See, e.g.*, **City of Laredo**, 414 S.W.3d at 737 (time attorney spent at trial was compensable even when billing records for those hours had not yet been prepared).

Practice Tip

The attorney should make sure to document her time just as she would when billing her own clients. ***El Apple**, 370 S.W.3d at 763. Whenever possible, the attorney should document her time with contemporaneous billing records or other documentation recorded reasonably close in time to when the work was performed.* ***City of Laredo**, 414 S.W.3d at 736;* ***El Apple**, 370 S.W.3d at 763. If the attorney does not provide sufficient details of the work performed and an appellate court reverses because the evidence is insufficient to support the award of attorney fees, on remand the attorney may have to reconstruct her work to provide the trial court with sufficient information to review the attorney-fees claim.* ***El Apple**, 370 S.W.3d at 764; see* ***Long**, 442 S.W.3d at 255–56.*

§11. Review

§11.1 Disqualification.

1. Standard of review. The standard of review for a disqualification motion is abuse of discretion. *See* **In re Murrin Bros. 1885, Ltd.**, 603 S.W.3d 53, 57 (Tex.2019) (mandamus); **In re Turner**, 542 S.W.3d 553, 555 (Tex.2017) (mandamus); **In re Meador**, 968 S.W.2d 346, 351 (Tex.1998) (mandamus); **Metropolitan Life Ins. v. Syntek Fin. Corp.**, 881 S.W.2d 319, 321 (Tex.1994) (appeal).

2. Appeal. Disqualification issues are subject to review on appeal. *See* **Metropolitan Life**, 881 S.W.2d at 320–21; *see also* **Hall v. Birchfield**, 718 S.W.2d 313, 322 n.1 (Tex.App.—Texarkana 1986) (mandamus would be better procedure than awaiting outcome of main trial), *rev'd on other grounds sub nom.* **Birchfield v. Texarkana Mem'l Hosp.**, 747 S.W.2d 361 (Tex.1987).

3. Mandamus. Mandamus review is appropriate when a trial judge erroneously grants or denies a motion to disqualify an attorney or law firm. *See* **In re Murrin Bros.**, 603 S.W.3d at 56–57; **In re Turner**, 542 S.W.3d at 555. See "Disqualification of attorney," **O'Connor's Texas Civil Appeals**, ch. 10-B, §5.1.2(2) (2020 ed.).

Note

Depending on the facts of the case, mandamus may be appropriate to review the ruling on a motion to show authority under TRCP 12. See ***In re Murrin Bros.****, 603 S.W.3d at 61–62 & n.3 (under facts of case, party could not show lack of adequate appellate remedy, but Court did not foreclose possibility of mandamus review in appropriate cases).*

§11.2 Attorney fees. The standard for reviewing whether an award of attorney fees was reasonable and necessary is sufficiency of the evidence. **Brazos Elec. Power Coop. v. Weber**, 238 S.W.3d 582, 583 (Tex.App.—Dallas 2007, no pet.); **Doncaster v. Hernaiz**, 161 S.W.3d 594, 606 (Tex.App.—San Antonio 2005, no pet.). A party can preserve error by complaining for the first time in a motion for judgment notwithstanding the verdict that the opposing party is not entitled to attorney fees. *See* **Holland v. Wal-Mart Stores**, 1 S.W.3d 91, 94 (Tex.1999) (statute did not permit attorney fees).

I. Guardian Ad Litem Under TRCP 173

§1. General

§1.1 Rules. Tex. R. Civ. P. 44, 173.

§1.2 Purpose. The purpose of appointing a guardian ad litem under TRCP 173 is to protect the interest of an incapacitated party—generally a minor or other person incapable of self-representation—when that party's next friend or guardian has an adverse interest in the division of settlement proceeds. **Jocson v. Crabb**, 196 S.W.3d 302, 305–06 (Tex.App.—Houston [1st Dist.] 2006, no pet.); Tex. R. Civ. P. 173 cmt. 3; *see* **Land Rover U.K., Ltd. v. Hinojosa**, 210 S.W.3d 604, 607 (Tex.2006) (guardian ad litem is appointed to assist court in protecting child's interest); **Goodyear Dunlop Tires v. Gamez**, 151 S.W.3d 574, 584 (Tex.App.—San Antonio 2004, no pet.) (guardian ad litem has duty to evaluate settlement offer from minor's perspective). The term "ad litem" means "for the suit." **Brownsville-Valley Reg'l Med. Ctr., Inc. v. Gamez**, 894 S.W.2d 753, 756 (Tex.1995); Ad Litem, *Black's Law Dictionary* (11th ed. 2019). TRCP 173 does not apply to an appointment of a guardian ad litem governed by statutes, such as the Family Code or the Estates Code, or by other rules, such as the Parental Notification Rules. Tex. R. Civ. P. 173.1 & cmt. 2.

Note

In this subchapter, "incapacitated party" refers to a person who needs a guardian ad litem.

§1.3 Forms. **O'Connor's Texas Civil Forms**, FORMS 1I:1 et seq. (2020 ed.).

§1.4 Other references. Anton, Comment, *The Ambiguous Role & Responsibilities of a Guardian Ad Litem in Texas in Personal Injury Litigation*, 51 SMU L.Rev. 161 (1997); Wood, *The Duties of Guardians & Attorneys Ad Litem*, The New Guardianship Laws in Texas, State Bar of Texas CLE, ch. F (1994); **O'Connor's Texas Causes of Action** (2021 ed.); **O'Connor's Texas Family Law Handbook** (2021 ed.).

§2. Comparison of guardian ad litem & attorney ad litem

The term "guardian ad litem" is often confused with the term "attorney ad litem" because both are used in the TRCPs, the Estates Code, the Family Code, and other statutes. *See, e.g.,* **International Dairy Queen, Inc. v. Matthews**, 126 S.W.3d 629, 630 (Tex.App.—Beaumont 2004, no pet.) (parties used terms interchangeably); **Brownsville-Valley Reg'l Med. Ctr., Inc. v. Gamez**, 871 S.W.2d 781, 784 (Tex.App.—Corpus Christi 1994) (court referred to guardian ad litem as attorney ad litem), *rev'd on other grounds*, 894 S.W.2d 753 (Tex.1995). Because the roles of a guardian ad litem and an attorney ad litem are different, attorneys should understand the differences and insist on correct references in all court documents.

§2.1 Guardian ad litem. A guardian ad litem is an officer appointed by the court to assist in protecting the settlement interest of an incapacitated party who is represented by a next friend or guardian who appears to have an interest adverse to the incapacitated party. **Ford Motor Co. v. Stewart, Cox & Hatcher, P.C.**, 390 S.W.3d 294, 297 (Tex.2013); **Ford Motor Co. v. Chacon**, 370 S.W.3d 359, 361 (Tex.2012); **Ford Motor Co. v. Garcia**, 363 S.W.3d 573, 577 (Tex.2012); *see* Tex. R. Civ. P. 173.2(a)(1) (court must appoint guardian ad litem for incapacitated party if represented by next friend or guardian who appears to have adverse interest), Tex. R. Civ. P. 173 cmt. 3 (guardian ad litem will be appointed when incapacitated party's next friend or guardian appears to have interest adverse to incapacitated party because of division of settlement proceeds). A guardian ad litem acts as an officer of and adviser to the court. Tex. R. Civ. P. 173.4(a). Although a guardian ad litem may be a licensed attorney, she is the personal representative of the incapacitated party, not an attorney for the incapacitated party. **Land Rover U.K., Ltd. v. Hinojosa**, 210 S.W.3d 604, 607 (Tex.2006); **American Gen. Fire & Cas. Co. v. Vandewater**, 907 S.W.2d 491, 493 n.2 (Tex.1995); *see* **Garcia**, 363 S.W.3d at 577 (duty of guardian ad litem is different from duty of incapacitated party's attorney); *see also* Tex. R. Civ. P. 173.4(d)(3) (guardian ad litem cannot participate in litigation except by court order). See "Guardian ad litem," **O'Connor's Texas Family Law Handbook**, ch. 4-C, §4 (2021 ed.).

Note

A guardian ad litem appointed under TRCP 173, acting as an adviser to and officer of the court, has derived judicial immunity—that is, she has a common-law defense to being sued in her individual capacity for performing judicial acts. See Tex. R. Civ. P. 173 cmt. 5. See generally ***Dallas Cty. v. Halsey****, 87 S.W.3d 552, 554–57 (Tex.2002) (discussing applicability of derived judicial immunity to court reporters). See "Judicial Immunity,"* ***O'Connor's Texas Causes of Action****, ch. 46-C, §1 et seq. (2021 ed.). But the guardian ad litem can be sanctioned for violating TRCP 173. Tex. R. Civ. P. 173 cmt. 8.*

§2.2 Attorney ad litem. An attorney ad litem performs the same services as any attorney—giving legal advice, doing research, and conducting litigation—for an incapacitated party. **City of Houston v. Woods**, 138 S.W.3d 574, 582 (Tex.App.—Houston [14th Dist.] 2004, no pet.); **Coleson v. Bethan**, 931 S.W.2d 706, 713 (Tex.App.—Fort Worth 1996, no writ); *see, e.g.*, Tex. Fam. Code §107.003 (duties of attorney ad litem for child in family-law cases include, among other things, investigation, reviewing copies of relevant records, interviewing parties, and participating in litigation). See "Attorney ad litem," **O'Connor's Texas Family Law Handbook**, ch. 4-C, §2 (2021 ed.).

Chart 1-4, below, shows when a guardian ad litem or an attorney ad litem should be appointed.

1-4. Comparison of Ad Litems		
	Guardian ad litem	**Attorney ad litem**
TRCP		
1	In civil litigation, guardian ad litem must be appointed to represent person whose guardian or next friend has adverse interest. Tex. R. Civ. P. 173.2(a)(1).	In default-judgment proceedings against D who was served by publication but did not answer or appear, attorney ad litem must be appointed to represent D. Tex. R. Civ. P. 244.
Estates Code		
2		In probate proceeding, attorney ad litem may be appointed to represent any person, including person with legal disability under state or federal law, nonresident, unborn or unascertained person, unknown or missing heir, or unknown or missing person for whom cash is deposited into court's registry. Tex. Est. Code §53.104.
3		In heirship proceedings, attorney ad litem may be appointed to represent incapacitated person if appointment is necessary to protect that person's interest. Tex. Est. Code §202.009(b); *see* Tex. Est. Code §22.016.
4		In heirship proceedings, attorney ad litem must be appointed to represent interest of unknown or missing heir. Tex. Est. Code §202.009(a).

1-4. Comparison of Ad Litems		
	Guardian ad litem	**Attorney ad litem**
5	In guardianship proceedings, guardian ad litem may be appointed to: • Represent best interest of incapacitated person. Tex. Est. Code §§1002.013, 1054.051. •Investigate proposed ward's conditions and circumstances to determine whether person is incapacitated and guardianship is necessary. Tex. Est. Code §1102.001(a).	In guardianship proceedings, attorney ad litem may be appointed to represent: • Proposed ward. Tex. Est. Code §§1002.002, 1054.007(a)(2). • Incapacitated person. Tex. Est. Code §§1002.002, 1054.007(a)(1). • Unborn person. Tex. Est. Code §§1002.002, 1054.007(a)(4). • Legally disabled person. Tex. Est. Code §§1002.002, 1054.007(a)(1). • Nonresident. Tex. Est. Code §§1002.002, 1054.007(a)(3). • Unascertained person. Tex. Est. Code §§1002.002, 1054.007(a)(4). • Unknown or missing potential heir. Tex. Est. Code §§1002.002, 1054.007(a)(5). • Ward when settling guardianship. Tex. Est. Code §§1204.001(e), 1204.002.
6	In proceedings to remove a guardian, guardian ad litem must be appointed in certain circumstances. Tex. Est. Code §1203.051(b).	In guardianship proceedings, attorney ad litem must be appointed to represent ward when: • Appointing guardian. Tex. Est. Code §1054.001. • Modifying guardianship. Tex. Fam. Code §1202.101. • Restoring ward's capacity. *Id.* • Removing guardian (in certain circumstances). Tex. Fam. Code §1203.051(b). • Guardian wants to buy ward's property. Tex. Fam. Code §1158.653(b). • Removing community administrator (incapacitated spouse). Tex. Fam. Code §1353.151(a).
7	Guardian ad litem may be appointed to represent minor for limited purpose of applying for order to sell minor's interest in property if net value of interest does not exceed $100,000. Tex. Est. Code §1351.001.	Attorney ad litem may be appointed to represent minor for limited purpose of applying for order to sell minor's interest in property if net value of interest does not exceed $100,000. Tex. Est. Code §1351.001.
Family Code		
8	Guardian ad litem may be appointed in suit in which best interest of child is at issue. Tex. Fam. Code §107.021(a)(3).	Attorney ad litem may be appointed in suit in which best interest of a child is at issue. Tex. Fam. Code §107.021(a)(2).
9	In suit brought by government seeking termination of parent-child relationship or appointment of a conservator for child, guardian ad litem must be appointed to represent interest of child. Tex. Fam. Code §107.011(a).	In suit brought by government seeking termination of parent-child relationship or appointment of a conservator for child, attorney ad litem must be appointed to represent interest of child. Tex. Fam. Code §107.012.
10		In suit brought by government seeking termination of parent-child relationship or appointment of a conservator for child, attorney ad litem must be appointed to represent interest of (1) indigent parent of child if parent opposes termination or appointment, (2) parent served with citation by publication, (3) alleged father who did not register with paternity registry and whose identity or whereabouts are unknown, or (4) alleged father who has registered with paternity registry but cannot be served. Tex. Fam. Code §107.013(a).

1-4. Comparison of Ad Litems

	Guardian ad litem	Attorney ad litem
11		In suit seeking termination of parent-child relationship that is not brought by government, attorney ad litem must be appointed if interest of child is not adequately represented. Tex. Fam. Code §107.021(a-1)(2).
12		In suit to determine parentage, attorney ad litem must be appointed to represent a minor or incapacitated child if interest of child is not adequately represented. Tex. Fam. Code §160.612(b).
13		In suit seeking order removing the disabilities of minority, amicus attorney or attorney ad litem must be appointed for minor. Tex. Fam. Code §31.004.

§3. Appointing a guardian ad litem under TRCP 173

§3.1 Appointment of guardian ad litem.

1. When required.

(1) Adverse interest. The court must appoint a guardian ad litem for an incapacitated party represented by a next friend or guardian when the next friend or guardian appears to the court to have an interest adverse to the incapacitated party. Tex. R. Civ. P. 173.2(a)(1); *see* **Ford Motor Co. v. Stewart, Cox & Hatcher, P.C.**, 390 S.W.3d 294, 297 (Tex.2013). TRCP 173 specifically applies when the incapacitated party's next friend or guardian appears to have an interest adverse to the incapacitated party with respect to division of settlement proceeds. Tex. R. Civ. P. 173. However, the rule may also apply in other situations. *See* **In re KC Greenhouse Patio Apts., LP**, 445 S.W.3d 168, 176 (Tex.App.—Houston [1st Dist.] 2012, orig. proceeding). For example, a parent or guardian may have a conflict of interest in handling a minor's settlement fund, in receiving compensation for services as managing conservator, or in a minor's inheritance if the minor predeceases the parent or guardian. *Id.*; *see* **McGough v. First Ct. of Appeals**, 842 S.W.2d 637, 640 (Tex.1992). Also, when a parent appears as next friend for a child who has sustained serious injuries requiring medical treatment, an adverse interest may arise because the claim for the child's medical expenses belongs to the parent, while the claim for personal injuries belongs to the child. **In re KC Greenhouse Patio Apts.**, 445 S.W.3d at 176. But a parent's obligation to provide her child with medical care does not, by itself, create a conflict of interest. **Stewart, Cox & Hatcher, P.C.**, 390 S.W.3d at 298.

(2) Agreement of parties. The court must appoint a guardian ad litem for an incapacitated party represented by a next friend or guardian if the parties agree to the appointment. Tex. R. Civ. P. 173.2(a)(2).

2. Same ad litem for similarly situated parties. The court must appoint the same guardian ad litem for similarly situated parties unless the court finds that the appointment of different guardians ad litem is necessary. Tex. R. Civ. P. 173.2(b). For example, when a settlement is to be divided between parents and their two children, the court must appoint the same guardian ad litem for both children.

§3.2 Qualifications. TRCP 173 does not provide a list of qualifications for a guardian ad litem. Although Estates Code §§1104.351 to 1104.357 do not apply to a guardian ad litem appointed under TRCP 173, the statute gives broad guidelines for determining when a person is not qualified. *Cf.* **Gallegos v. Clegg**, 417 S.W.2d 347, 352 (Tex.App.—Corpus Christi 1967, writ ref'd n.r.e.) (former Prob. Code §110, later renumbered as §681, was applied to decide if next friend was disqualified).

Practice Tip

Some courts might require an attorney to have certain training or certification to qualify for an appointment as a guardian ad litem. Thus, an attorney should check with the local or state bar association about available seminars or CLEs that would qualify her for appointment.

§3.3 Procedure to appoint.

1. Motion. Any party who believes a guardian ad litem is necessary may file a motion for the court to appoint one. Tex. R. Civ. P. 173.3(a). The court may also appoint a guardian ad litem on its own initiative. *Id.*

2. Selection. Courts located in counties with populations of 25,000 or more are required to maintain a list of all attorneys and other persons who are qualified to serve as guardians ad litem and are registered with the court. Tex. Gov't Code §§37.001, 37.003(a)(2). The court must annually post this list of qualified guardians ad litem at the county courthouse where the court is located and on the court's website. Tex. Gov't Code §37.005. Unless an exemption applies under Gov't Code §37.002, the process for selecting a guardian ad litem from the list is as follows:

(1) Generally—first on list. In each case in which the appointment of a guardian ad litem is necessary, the court, using a rotation system, must appoint the person whose name appears first on the list. Tex. Gov't Code §37.004(a).

(2) Exceptions. The court may appoint a person whose name does not appear first on the list or who is not included on the list—but meets statutory or other requirements to serve—for any of the following reasons:

(a) The appointment is agreed on by the parties and approved by the court. Tex. Gov't Code §37.004(c).

(b) On a finding of good cause, a guardian ad litem is required on a complex matter because she (1) has specialized education, skill, knowledge, training, certification, or language proficiency relevant to the subject matter of the case, (2) has relevant past involvement with the parties or the case, or (3) is in a relevant geographic location. Tex. Gov't Code §37.004(d).

(c) An initial declaration of a state of disaster is made for the area served by the court within 30 days before the date of appointment. Tex. Gov't Code §37.004(d-1); *see also* Tex. Gov't Code §37.004(g) (defining "declaration of a state of disaster").

(3) After appointment. Once a guardian ad litem has been appointed, the court must put that person's name at the end of the list. Tex. Gov't Code §37.004(f).

Note

Unless an exemption applies, the court clerk must prepare a monthly report on the court's appointments for guardians ad litem that includes (1) the name of the guardian ad litem, (2) the name of the judge and date of the order approving compensation to be paid to the guardian ad litem, (3) the case number and style for each case and the number of cases in which the guardian ad litem was appointed, and (4) the total compensation paid to the guardian ad litem, plus, if the compensation exceeds $1,000, information related to the case on the number of hours and expenses billed. See Tex. Gov't Code §36.004(a); see also Tex. Gov't Code §36.003 (listing exemptions from reporting requirements of Gov't Code §36.004).

3. Order. The appointment must be made by written order. Tex. R. Civ. P. 173.3(b); *e.g.*, **Ford Motor Co. v. Chacon**, 370 S.W.3d 359, 362 (Tex.2012) (order for appointment of guardian ad litem specifically limited guardian ad litem's appointment to representing minor's interest as to settlement with D1; no order in record appointing guardian ad litem to represent minor's interest in settlement with D2). An improper designation in the trial court's order does not control the nature of the appointment. *E.g.*, **Ford Motor Co. v. Garcia**, 363 S.W.3d 573, 577–78 (Tex.2012) (although motion used "attorney ad litem" in one sentence and order stated ad litem was appointed "to serve as Attorney Ad Litem," his appointment was requested only after division of settlement with D created a conflict; appointment was as guardian ad litem).

§3.4 Objections to appointment. Any party may object to the appointment of a guardian ad litem. Tex. R. Civ. P. 173.3(c). Objections to the appointment could include the following:

1. Unnecessary. The appointment of a guardian ad litem is not necessary because there is no conflict between the incapacitated party and the next friend or guardian. *See* Tex. R. Civ. P. 173.2(a)(1); *see also* **Ford Motor Co. v. Stewart, Cox & Hatcher, P.C.**, 390 S.W.3d 294, 298 (Tex.2013) (guardian ad litem should have been removed once he had determined there was no conflict).

2. Unqualified. The person appointed as guardian ad litem is not qualified to serve in that capacity. See "Qualifications," ch. 1-I, §3.2.

3. Dual appointment. The court should not appoint more than one guardian ad litem for similarly situated incapacitated parties. *See* Tex. R. Civ. P. 173.2(b).

§4. Role of guardian ad litem

Once appointed, the guardian ad litem displaces the next friend or guardian—to the limited extent of protecting the incapacitated party's interest that appears to be adverse to the next friend's or guardian's interest—and becomes the personal representative of the incapacitated party. **City of Houston v. Woods**, 138 S.W.3d 574, 579 (Tex.App.—Houston [14th Dist.] 2004, no pet.); *see* **In re KC Greenhouse Patio Apts., LP**, 445 S.W.3d 168, 176 (Tex.App.—Houston [1st Dist.] 2012, orig. proceeding). The guardian ad litem is not an attorney for the incapacitated party but an officer appointed by the court to assist in protecting the incapacitated party's interest. See "Guardian ad litem," ch. 1-I, §2.1. The guardian ad litem has the burden to ensure that her services do not exceed the scope of her appointed role. **Ford Motor Co. v. Chacon**, 370 S.W.3d 359, 362 (Tex.2012); **Ford Motor Co. v. Garcia**, 363 S.W.3d 573, 577 (Tex.2012).

Practice Tip

A guardian ad litem who is an attorney may choose to become involved in litigation beyond her role as a guardian ad litem (e.g., review the file or attend proceedings when it is unnecessary), but she will not be compensated for these expenses or services. Tex. R. Civ. P. 173 cmt. 3. See "Outside scope of duties," ch. 1-I, §6.1.3(2)(a).

§4.1 Role during trial.

1. Adverse-interest proceeding. A guardian ad litem must participate in any proceeding before the court that is intended to determine whether an incapacitated party's next friend or guardian has an interest adverse to the incapacitated party. Tex. R. Civ. P. 173.4(d)(2). The guardian ad litem must advise the court whether the incapacitated party's next friend or guardian has an interest adverse to the incapacitated party. Tex. R. Civ. P. 173.4(b); *see* **Ford Motor Co. v. Stewart, Cox & Hatcher, P.C.**, 390 S.W.3d 294, 297 (Tex.2013).

2. Settlement proceedings.

(1) Advise on settlement offer. When an offer has been made to settle the claim of an incapacitated party represented by a next friend or guardian, a guardian ad litem has the limited duty to determine whether the settlement is in the incapacitated party's best interest and make a recommendation to the trial court. Tex. R. Civ. P. 173.4(c); *see* **Ordonez v. Abraham**, 545 S.W.3d 655, 669 (Tex.App.—El Paso 2017, no pet.); **Jocson v. Crabb**, 196 S.W.3d 302, 308 (Tex.App.—Houston [1st Dist.] 2006, no pet.). When a settlement is proposed, the guardian ad litem must do the following:

(a) Evaluate settlement offer. The guardian ad litem must determine whether the settlement offer is fair and reasonable to the incapacitated party. *See* **Jocson**, 196 S.W.3d at 308; **Byrd v. Woodruff**, 891 S.W.2d 689, 707 (Tex.App.—Dallas 1994, writ dism'd). To determine the adequacy of a settlement agreement, the guardian ad litem should evaluate (1) the damages suffered by the incapacitated party, (2) the proposed apportionment of the settlement proceeds among the parties, (3) the proposed manner of disbursing the settlement proceeds, and (4) the amount of attorney fees charged by the incapacitated party's attorney. **Jocson**, 196 S.W.3d at 308; **Goodyear Dunlop Tires v. Gamez**, 151 S.W.3d 574, 584 (Tex.App.—San Antonio 2004, no pet.); **Byrd**, 891 S.W.2d at 707.

(b) Attend settlement hearing. The guardian ad litem must participate in any proceeding before the court that is intended to determine whether a settlement of the incapacitated party's claim is in the party's best interest. Tex. R. Civ. P. 173.4(d)(2).

(c) Make recommendation. The guardian ad litem must make a recommendation to the trial court on the incapacitated party's behalf. **Goodyear**, 151 S.W.3d at 584; **Byrd**, 891 S.W.2d at 707; *see* **Ordonez**, 545 S.W.3d at 661 n.7.

(d) Review final judgment. The guardian ad litem should review the final settlement documents and judgment submitted to the court. Wood, *The Duties of Guardians & Attorneys Ad Litem*, The New Guardianship Laws in Texas, State Bar of Texas CLE, ch. F, p. F-19 (1994).

(2) Participate in mediation proceeding. The guardian ad litem may, but is not required to, participate in mediation or similar proceedings to attempt to reach a settlement. Tex. R. Civ. P. 173.4(d)(1). Unless the guardian ad litem's presence is required at the mediation proceeding, there is some question whether she can claim compensation for attending. *See* Tex. R. Civ. P. 173 cmt. 7.

3. Discovery & trial proceeding.

(1) General rule—no participation in litigation. Generally, the guardian ad litem must not participate in discovery, trial, or any other part of the litigation. Tex. R. Civ. P. 173.4(d)(3); *see, e.g.*, **Jocson v. Crabb**, 133 S.W.3d 268, 270–71 (Tex.2004) (court remanded to permit Ds to challenge award compensating guardian ad litem for attending 50 depositions and for other work).

(2) Exception—necessary to protect party's interest. The guardian ad litem can participate in discovery, trial, or any other part of the litigation only if the participation is (1) necessary to protect the incapacitated party's interest that is adverse to the next friend's or guardian's and (2) directed by the court in a written order stating sufficient reasons. Tex. R. Civ. P. 173.4(d)(3); *see* Tex. R. Civ. P. 173 cmt. 4.

(a) Limited role. Even when the guardian ad litem participates in discovery, trial, or another part of the litigation, the guardian ad litem's function is to determine whether an incapacitated party's next friend or guardian has an interest adverse to the party that should be considered by the court under TRCP 44. Tex. R. Civ. P. 173 cmt. 4.

(b) No representation. Even when the guardian ad litem participates in discovery, trial, or another part of the litigation, the guardian ad litem may never supervise or supplant the next friend or undertake to represent the incapacitated party while serving as guardian ad litem. Tex. R. Civ. P. 173 cmt. 4; *see* **Ordonez**, 545 S.W.3d at 669 (appointment of guardian ad litem does not trump parents' statutory right to represent child in legal action).

Practice Tip

A guardian ad litem appointed under TRCP 173 should not take any action that requires a bar card. If she does, the other parties should object. A guardian ad litem cannot be paid for work performed outside the scope of that role unless the court signs an order under TRCP 173.4(d)(3). If the guardian ad litem believes that an incapacitated party needs an attorney ad litem, the guardian ad litem should petition the court to appoint one. See "Attorney ad litem," ch. 1-I, §2.2.

---

§4.2 Role after trial. A guardian ad litem is appointed only for the duration of the case. After the judgment is signed, the guardian ad litem usually has no further responsibilities. *See* **Brownsville-Valley Reg'l Med. Ctr., Inc. v. Gamez**, 894 S.W.2d 753, 755 (Tex.1995). Once the conflict ends, the guardian ad litem should be removed. *Id.* However, at the conclusion of the case, the guardian ad litem should be expected to do the following:

1. The guardian ad litem should provide her address and telephone number to the incapacitated party and the next friend or guardian in case the incapacitated party needs help in the future. Anton, Comment, *The Ambiguous Role & Responsibilities of a Guardian Ad Litem in Texas in Personal Injury Litigation*, 51 SMU L.Rev. 161, 193 (1997).

2. The guardian ad litem should retain the incapacitated party's file. *Id.*

3. The guardian ad litem should expect, on a no-fee basis, to assist the incapacitated party in securing funds from the court registry when the incapacity is lifted (e.g., when the minor becomes an adult). Wood, *The Duties of Guardians & Attorneys Ad Litem*, The New Guardianship Laws in Texas, State Bar of Texas CLE, ch. F, p. F-20 (1994); *see* **Brownsville-Valley Reg'l**, 894 S.W.2d at 756–57 (guardian ad litem cannot recover fees for services rendered after resolution of conflict for which she was appointed).

§5. Guardian ad litem communications

§5.1 With parties. Communications between the guardian ad litem and the incapacitated party, the next friend, the guardian, or their attorneys are privileged just as if the guardian ad litem were the attorney for the incapacitated party. Tex. R. Civ. P. 173.5.

§5.2 With court. A guardian ad litem cannot have ex parte communications with the court, even though she is an adviser to the court. Tex. R. Civ. P. 173 cmt. 6; *see* Tex. Code Jud. Conduct, Canon 3(B)(8).

§6. Compensation

A guardian ad litem may be reimbursed for reasonable and necessary expenses incurred and may receive a reasonable hourly fee for her services. Tex. R. Civ. P. 173.6(a). The determination of guardian ad litem fees is within the sound discretion of the trial court. **Ford Motor Co. v. Chacon**, 370 S.W.3d 359, 362 (Tex.2012); **Ford Motor Co. v. Garcia**, 363 S.W.3d 573, 578 (Tex.2012); **Land Rover U.K., Ltd. v. Hinojosa**, 210 S.W.3d 604, 607 (Tex.2006). However, a guardian ad litem has a limited role in the litigation and thus may be compensated only for limited types of activities. **Garcia**, 363 S.W.3d at 579; *see* Tex. R. Civ. P. 173 cmt. 7. A guardian ad litem cannot receive, directly or indirectly, anything of value in consideration of the appointment other than as provided by TRCP 173. Tex. R. Civ. P. 173.6(d).

§6.1 Application for fees. If the guardian ad litem intends to request reimbursement for expenses and compensation for service, she may file an application for compensation at the conclusion of the appointment. Tex. R. Civ. P. 173.6(b).

Note

Filing an application (1) allows other parties to see the exact compensation requested and the reasons the compensation is appropriate and (2) gives the parties a better opportunity to agree to a fee and avoid a hearing. ***Ford Motor Co. v. Garcia****, 363 S.W.3d 573, 575 n.1 (Tex.2012). See "Agreed application," ch. 1-I, §6.1.2; "Hearing on application," ch. 1-I, §6.3. At a minimum, filing an application will provide specifics of the fee request and allow the parties and the court to better prepare for the hearing.* ***Garcia****, 363 S.W.3d at 575 n.1.*

1. Verified. The application must be verified. Tex. R. Civ. P. 173.6(b).

2. Agreed application. The guardian ad litem should ask the parties to agree to the application. If the parties agree, the court can render judgment on the application. *See* Tex. R. Civ. P. 173.6(b).

3. Fees. The application must describe in detail the basis for the compensation requested. Tex. R. Civ. P. 173.6(b).

(1) Fees permitted.

(a) For services of guardian ad litem. Generally, only the person appointed as a guardian ad litem can be compensated for services under TRCP 173. **Garcia**, 363 S.W.3d at 580. The guardian ad litem may (1) be reimbursed for reasonable and necessary expenses incurred and (2) receive a reasonable hourly fee for necessary services performed. Tex. R. Civ. P. 173.6(a); **Ford Motor Co. v. Chacon**, 370 S.W.3d 359, 362 (Tex.2012). For the guardian ad litem's necessary services, see "Role of guardian ad litem," ch. 1-I, §4.

[1] Expenses. The guardian ad litem should list the reasonable and necessary expenses incurred. *See* Tex. R. Civ. P. 173.6(b).

[2] Hourly fees. The guardian ad litem should identify (1) a reasonable hourly fee for services performed, (2) the services performed as a guardian ad litem by date and amount of time spent on each task, (3) why each task was necessary, and (4) the total amount claimed. *See* Tex. R. Civ. P. 173.6. A reasonable fee for a guardian ad litem is a reasonable hourly rate multiplied by the number of hours spent performing services within the guardian ad litem's role. **Garcia**, 363 S.W.3d at 580; **Land Rover U.K., Ltd. v. Hinojosa**, 210 S.W.3d 604, 608 (Tex.2006).

(b) For services of person other than guardian ad litem. A guardian ad litem may be compensated for services performed by a person other than the designated guardian ad litem. **Garcia**, 363 S.W.3d at 580. If claiming

compensation for time spent by another person, the guardian ad litem should identify that person and prove (1) unusual circumstances required the services of that person to fulfill the guardian ad litem's duties, (2) the specific services that were performed, (3) when the services were performed, (4) the amount of time spent on each task, (5) why each task was necessary in light of the guardian ad litem's appointment, (6) a reasonable hourly rate for the person, and (7) the total amount claimed. *See id.* The following are examples of when unusual circumstances may occur: • A paralegal supervised by the guardian ad litem could perform tasks necessary to fulfill the guardian ad litem's appointed role, but at a lower hourly rate. *Id.* • An emergency arises that requires an attorney familiar with the matter, rather than the guardian ad litem, to make an appearance at a hearing. *Id.* • An actuary or accountant is necessary to evaluate the finances of a structured settlement. *Id.* at 580 n.5.

Practice Tip

Although nothing in TRCP 173 precludes awarding compensation based on services performed by a person other than a guardian ad litem, the guardian ad litem should, if possible, get the trial court's authorization for using those services before any expenses are actually incurred. ***Garcia****, 363 S.W.3d at 580 & n.5.*

(2) Fees not permitted.

(a) Outside scope of duties. A guardian ad litem cannot be paid for work performed outside the scope of her duties as a guardian ad litem. **Garcia**, 363 S.W.3d at 580; **Land Rover**, 210 S.W.3d at 607.

[1] Determining scope. In determining the scope of the guardian ad litem's appointment, courts look to the context of the appointment and the duties assigned to the guardian ad litem. **Chacon**, 370 S.W.3d at 362; **Garcia**, 363 S.W.3d at 577. Specifically, a court may examine the timing of the appointment, the grounds in the motion for appointment, and the order granting the appointment. *E.g.*, **Chacon**, 370 S.W.3d at 362–63 (motion and order for appointment of guardian ad litem specifically limited guardian ad litem's appointment to representing minor's interest as to settlement with D1; guardian ad litem's work on settlement with D2 was beyond scope of his appointment and was not compensable).

[2] Examples. The following are examples of services performed outside the scope of the guardian ad litem's duties: • Reviewing the litigation file or attending trial proceedings, unless those services are necessary to protect the incapacitated party's interest. *See* Tex. R. Civ. P. 173 cmt. 3; *see, e.g.*, **Garcia**, 363 S.W.3d at 582 (no compensation for reviewing motions to transfer venue, various discovery requests and responses, correspondence about postponed hearings, and pleadings on already-settled claims). See "Discovery & trial proceeding," ch. 1-I, §4.1.3. • Consulting daily with plaintiff's attorney about trial strategy. **Land Rover**, 210 S.W.3d at 609. • Conducting independent legal research or similar services more appropriate for the incapacitated party's attorney. *See, e.g.*, **Youngstown Area Jewish Fed'n v. Dunleavy**, 223 S.W.3d 604, 609–10 (Tex.App.—Dallas 2007, no pet.) (no compensation for legal research, review of case law, and telephone calls and letters to obtain medical records).

(b) After determination that there is no conflict. A guardian ad litem cannot be awarded fees for services performed after it is determined that there is no conflict of interest. *E.g.*, **Ford Motor Co. v. Stewart, Cox & Hatcher, P.C.**, 390 S.W.3d 294, 297–98 (Tex.2013) (guardian ad litem should have been removed once it became clear there was no conflict and should only have been awarded fees for work performed in making that determination).

(c) After conflict is resolved. A guardian ad litem cannot be awarded fees for services to be performed after the conflict of interest that necessitated her appointment has been resolved. **Frank A. Smith Sales, Inc. v. Flores**, 907 S.W.2d 487, 488 (Tex.1995); **Brownsville-Valley Reg'l Med. Ctr., Inc. v. Gamez**, 894 S.W.2d 753, 757 (Tex.1995).

(d) For guardian ad litem's own interest. A guardian ad litem cannot be awarded fees for representing her own interest, such as researching and preparing fee statements, attending a fee hearing, or defending her fees on appeal. **Goodyear Dunlop Tires v. Gamez**, 151 S.W.3d 574, 587–88 (Tex.App.—San Antonio 2004, no pet.); *see* **Harris Cty. Children's Prot. Servs. v. Olvera**, 77 S.W.3d 336, 342–43 (Tex.App.—Houston [14th Dist.] 2002, pet. denied). *But see* **DeSai v. Islas**, 884 S.W.2d 204, 206 (Tex.App.—Eastland 1994, writ denied) (court affirmed contingent fee awarded if guardian ad litem had to defend original fee on appeal).

§6.2 Objection to fees. To complain about the guardian ad litem fees on appeal, a party must make its objection known to the trial court either orally (on the record during the litigation or at the hearing on guardian ad litem fees) or in writing (in a motion or response filed with the court). *See, e.g.,* **Jocson v. Crabb**, 133 S.W.3d 268, 269–70 (Tex.2004) (Ds preserved issue by objecting at final fee hearing); **Goodyear Dunlop Tires v. Gamez**, 151 S.W.3d 574, 582 (Tex.App.—San Antonio 2004, no pet.) (same). Objections to the award could include the following:

1. Excessive amount. The amount of the award sought by the guardian ad litem is excessive. *See* **Goodyear**, 151 S.W.3d at 588–89.

2. Outside scope. The guardian ad litem should not be compensated for work performed outside the scope of her duties as a guardian ad litem. See "Outside scope of duties," ch. 1-I, §6.1.3(2)(a).

3. Overbilling. The guardian ad litem should not be compensated for overbilling her expenses and services. *See, e.g.,* **Goodyear**, 151 S.W.3d at 588–89 (guardians ad litem billed for more than 24 hours in one day and charged for time spent sleeping while out of town).

4. Unreasonable hourly rate. The guardian ad litem should not be compensated at the hourly rate requested because it is an unreasonable hourly rate. *See, e.g.,* **Goodyear**, 151 S.W.3d at 590–91 (court of appeals found hourly rate of $400 to $500 excessive).

5. Percent of recovery. The guardian ad litem is not entitled to a percentage of the judgment or settlement. Tex. R. Civ. P. 173.6(b).

6. Lost opportunity. Unless there are exceptional circumstances, the guardian ad litem is not entitled to be compensated for lost opportunity for other employment. *See* **Land Rover U.K., Ltd. v. Hinojosa**, 210 S.W.3d 604, 608–09 (Tex.2006).

§6.3 Hearing on application. If the parties do not agree to the guardian ad litem's application for fees, the court must conduct an evidentiary hearing to determine the total amount of reasonable and necessary fees and expenses. Tex. R. Civ. P. 173.6(b). The hearing is for the receipt of evidence to determine the amount of the guardian ad litem's fees. *See* **Jocson v. Crabb**, 133 S.W.3d 268, 270 (Tex.2004); **Garcia v. Martinez**, 988 S.W.2d 219, 221–22 (Tex.1999); **Daimler-Chrysler Corp. v. Brannon**, 67 S.W.3d 294, 299 (Tex.App.—Texarkana 2001, no pet.). A party can raise any objections to an application for fees at the hearing. *See* **Goodyear Dunlop Tires v. Gamez**, 151 S.W.3d 574, 582 (Tex.App.—San Antonio 2004, no pet.) (D does not have to object that guardian ad litem's services are outside scope of her duties until final fee hearing); *see, e.g.,* **Jocson**, 133 S.W.3d at 270 (complaint that guardian ad litem unnecessarily attended depositions, made at final fee hearing, was timely).

§6.4 Taxed as costs. The court may tax a guardian ad litem's compensation as court costs. Tex. R. Civ. P. 173.6(c); **Ford Motor Co. v. Garcia**, 363 S.W.3d 573, 577 (Tex.2012); **City of Houston v. Woods**, 138 S.W.3d 574, 581 (Tex.App.—Houston [14th Dist.] 2004, no pet.).

1. Unsuccessful party. The guardian ad litem fees should be taxed as costs against the unsuccessful party in the suit. *See* Tex. R. Civ. P. 131; **Woods**, 138 S.W.3d at 581; **Borden, Inc. v. Martinez**, 19 S.W.3d 469, 471 (Tex.App.—San Antonio 2000, no pet.).

2. Prevailing party. As a rule, the guardian ad litem fees should not be taxed against the prevailing party. *See* Tex. R. Civ. P. 131. The court can tax costs against the prevailing party only when the court finds good cause and states it on the record. Tex. R. Civ. P. 141; *e.g.,* **Rogers v. Walmart Stores**, 686 S.W.2d 599, 601 (Tex.1985) (good cause to assess part of guardian ad litem fees against prevailing party for prolonging trial); **Price Constr., Inc. v. Castillo**, 147 S.W.3d 431, 443 (Tex.App.—San Antonio 2004, pet. denied) (remanded case to determine whether there was good cause to assess guardian ad litem fees against prevailing party based on unsuccessful parties' inability to pay); **Davis v. Henley**, 471 S.W.2d 883, 884–85 (Tex.App.—Houston [1st Dist.] 1971, writ ref'd n.r.e.) (good cause to assess guardian ad litem fees against prevailing parties because unsuccessful parties had no assets or income to pay the fee). Without evidence of good cause, the court abuses its discretion by taxing the guardian ad litem fees against the prevailing party. *See, e.g.,* **Suiter v. Woodard**, 635 S.W.2d 639, 641 (Tex.App.—Waco 1982, writ ref'd n.r.e.) (court could not tax costs against P, who was neither adverse to nor on the same side as minor Ps).

3. **Both parties.** Without a finding of good cause, the court cannot split the guardian ad litem fees between the parties. *See* **Roberts v. Williamson**, 111 S.W.3d 113, 124 (Tex.2003).

§6.5 Separate order. The order awarding a fee to the guardian ad litem should be recorded in a written order, separate from the judgment. *See* Tex.Sup.Ct. Order, Misc. Docket No. 07-9188, §2 (eff. Oct. 30, 2007). The district and county court clerks must report to the Supreme Court all fees of $500 or more paid to any person appointed by each court by listing the amount of the fees and the names of the persons receiving them. *Id.* §5.

§7. Review

§7.1 Record. If any party plans to challenge the appointment of the guardian ad litem or the fees awarded to the guardian ad litem, that party must ensure that a record is made of the hearing at which those issues are heard and resolved. *See* **City of Houston v. Woods**, 138 S.W.3d 574, 580 (Tex.App.—Houston [14th Dist.] 2004, no pet.). Without a record, the appellate court will assume the evidence was sufficient to support the trial court's ruling. *Id.*

§7.2 Right of review. Any party may seek mandamus review of an order appointing a guardian ad litem or directing a guardian ad litem's participation in the litigation. Tex. R. Civ. P. 173.7(a); *see* **Magna Donnelly Corp. v. DeLeon**, 267 S.W.3d 108, 114 (Tex.App.—San Antonio 2008, no pet.). Any party or the guardian ad litem may appeal an order awarding fees to the guardian ad litem. Tex. R. Civ. P. 173.7(a).

§7.3 Severance. If the order awarding fees to a guardian ad litem is included in the judgment, on the motion of the guardian ad litem or any party, the court must sever it to create a final, appealable order. Tex. R. Civ. P. 173.7(b).

§7.4 Finality not affected. Appellate proceedings to review an order pertaining to a guardian ad litem do not affect the finality of a settlement or judgment. Tex. R. Civ. P. 173.7(c).

J. Associate Judge

§1. General

§1.1 Rules. Tex Gov't Code §§54A.101 to 54A.118.

§1.2 Purpose. Gov't Code chapter 54A enables counties to create positions for associate judges who can preside over civil matters. *See* Tex. Gov't Code §§54A.101, 54A.102(a). A district or statutory county court judge can refer some or all of a civil case, including a trial, to an associate judge for resolution as long as an associate-judge position has been authorized by the county commissioners court and filled by appointment. *See* Tex. Gov't Code §§54A.102(a), 54A.106(a).

Note

This subchapter covers the standards for associate judges who preside over civil matters. It does not cover the standards for associate judges who preside over criminal, juvenile, family, or probate matters.

§1.3 Forms. **O'Connor's Texas Civil Forms**, FORMS 1J:1 et seq. (2020 ed.).

§2. Creating & appointing

§2.1 Creating associate-judge positions. Before a matter can be referred to an associate judge, the county commissioners court must authorize the creation of an associate-judge position for a district or statutory county court. Tex. Gov't Code §54A.102(a); *see* Tex. Gov't Code §54A.101.

1. District court has jurisdiction in more than one county. For district courts that have jurisdiction in more than one county, the commissioners courts for those counties must designate each county where the associate judge may serve. *See* Tex. Gov't Code §54A.102(b).

2. County has more than one court. For counties with more than one district court, statutory county court, or both, the county commissioners court may either create an associate-judge position for each court or authorize one or more associate judges to serve the courts. Tex. Gov't Code §54A.102(c).

§2.2 Appointing associate judges. Once an associate-judge position is created, a district or statutory county court judge can appoint an associate judge to perform the duties granted under Gov't Code §54A.101 et seq. *See* Tex. Gov't Code §54A.102(a). If the associate judge serves more than one court, however, the judge's appointment must be made as established by local rule, and requires at least a vote of two-thirds of the judges under whom the associate judge serves. Tex. Gov't Code §54A.102(d).

§3. Referring cases

§3.1 Scope of referral. A district or statutory county court judge can refer any civil case or part of a civil case to an associate judge for resolution. Tex. Gov't Code §54A.106(a).

§3.2 Order of referral. A case can be referred to an associate judge by an order of referral in a specific case or by an omnibus order. Tex. Gov't Code §54A.107(a). Unless otherwise specified, the associate judge can do any of the following under the order of referral:

1. Conduct hearings. Tex. Gov't Code §54A.108(a)(1).
2. Regulate proceedings in a hearing. Tex. Gov't Code §54A.108(a)(12).
3. Conduct trials. Tex. Gov't Code §54A.106(b). See "Objection to referral," ch. 1-J, §3.3.
4. Hear evidence. Tex. Gov't Code §54A.108(a)(2).
5. Compel production of relevant evidence. Tex. Gov't Code §54A.108(a)(3).
6. Rule on the admissibility of evidence. Tex. Gov't Code §54A.108(a)(4).

7. Issue summonses for the appearance of witnesses, examine witnesses, and swear witnesses for hearings. Tex Gov't Code §54A.108(a)(5) to (7).

8. Order the attachment of a witness or party who fails to obey a subpoena. Tex Gov't Code §54A.108(a)(13). See "Enforcing subpoenas," ch. 1-L, §5.

9. Make findings of fact on evidence. Tex Gov't Code §54A.108(a)(8).

10. Formulate conclusions of law. Tex Gov't Code §54A.108(a)(9).

11. Rule on pretrial motions. Tex Gov't Code §54A.108(a)(10).

12. Recommend the rulings, orders, or judgment to be made in a case. Tex Gov't Code §54A.108(a)(11).

13. Take action as necessary and proper for the efficient performance of the duties required by the order of referral. Tex Gov't Code §54A.108(a)(14).

§3.3 Objection to referral. A party can file an objection to an associate judge hearing a trial on the merits or presiding at a jury trial. Tex Gov't Code §54A.106(c). The party must file the objection no later than ten days after the party receives notice that the associate judge will hear the trial. *Id.* If an objection is filed, the referring court must hear the trial on the merits or preside at the jury trial. *Id.*

§3.4 Referral back. An associate judge can, in the interest of justice, refer a case back to the referring court regardless of whether a party has made a timely objection to the associate judge hearing the trial on the merits or presiding at a jury trial. Tex Gov't Code §54A.108(b).

§4. Proceedings

§4.1 Hearing. Hearings before an associate judge are performed in the same manner as hearings before the referring court.

1. Waiving de novo review. Before the hearing begins, a party can waive its right to de novo review of the associate judge's decision by the referring court either in writing or on the record. Tex Gov't Code §54A.112(c). See "To referring court—de novo hearing," ch. 1-J, §9.1.

2. Preserving the record. A court reporter can be provided—whether by a party, the associate judge, the referring court, or otherwise—during a hearing held by an associate judge. Tex Gov't Code §54A.110(a), (b). If there is no court reporter, or if the parties agree, the record may be preserved by any means approved by the associate judge. Tex Gov't Code §54A.110(c). If other means are used, the referring court or associate judge can assess the expense of preserving the record as costs. Tex Gov't Code §54A.110(d).

Caution

If the record is not taken by a court reporter, the referring court will not be able to consider the record on appeal from the associate judge's decision. See Tex. Gov't Code §§54A.110(e), 54A.115(f).

§4.2 Trial. Trials before an associate judge are performed in the same manner as trials before the referring court. A "trial on the merits" is any final adjudication from which an appeal can be taken to a court of appeals. Tex Gov't Code §54A.106(b). Unlike with hearings before an associate judge, a court reporter must be provided when the associate judge presides over a jury trial. Tex Gov't Code §54A.110(a).

§4.3 Witnesses. Witnesses who appear before an associate judge are subject to the same penalties of perjury as other witnesses in civil matters. Tex Gov't Code §54A.109(a). The referring court—not the associate judge—can fine or imprison a witness if the witness does not appear after being summoned or improperly refuses to answer questions and the refusal has been certified by the associate judge. Tex Gov't Code §54A.109(b).

§5. Notice of right to de novo hearing

The referring court or the associate judge must give all parties notice of the right to a de novo hearing before the referring court. *See* Tex. Gov't Code §54A.112(a). The notice can be given (1) by oral statement in open court, (2) by posting inside or outside the courtroom of the referring court, or (3) as otherwise directed by the referring court. Tex. Gov't Code §54A.112(b).

§6. Decision

An associate judge can take actions, render decisions, and propose orders or judgments in civil matters referred to her. An associate judge's decision has the same force and effect as an order of the referring court, unless a party appeals the decision. Tex. Gov't Code §54A.111(a). See "Effect of request on order or judgment only," ch. 1-J, §9.1.2. If the decision is not rendered in open court after hearing the matter, the associate judge must notify each attorney participating in the hearing of the decision. *See* Tex. Gov't Code §54A.111(a).

§6.1 Temporary restraining orders. A temporary restraining order issued by an associate judge is effective immediately and expires 15 days later unless, after a hearing, the order is modified or extended by the associate judge or referring judge. Tex. Gov't Code §54A.111(c).

§6.2 Temporary injunctions. A temporary injunction issued by an associate judge is effective immediately and continues during the trial unless, after a hearing, the order is modified by the referring judge. Tex. Gov't Code §54A.111(d).

§6.3 Orders for detention or incarceration. An order for the temporary detention or incarceration of a witness or party issued by an associate judge must be presented to the referring court on the day the witness or party is detained or incarcerated. Tex. Gov't Code §54A.113(c). The referring court, without prejudice to the right to a de novo hearing, can approve the temporary detention or incarceration or can order the release of the witness or party, with or without bond, pending a de novo hearing. *Id.* If the referring court is not immediately available, the associate judge can order the release of the witness or party, with or without bond, pending a de novo hearing or can continue the detention or incarceration for up to 72 hours. *Id.* See "To referring court—de novo hearing," ch. 1-J, §9.1.

§7. Consideration of decision

The referring court can take certain actions on the associate judge's decision, but those actions will depend on whether the decision was in the nature of an "action taken" or a proposed order or judgment.

§7.1 Action taken. If the associate judge has taken an action in the matter, the referring court has 30 days after the action was taken to modify, correct, reject, reverse, or recommit for further information the action taken. Tex. Gov't Code §54A.117(a). If the referring court does not do so, the associate judge's action becomes the decree of the court. Tex. Gov't Code §54A.117(b).

§7.2 Proposed order or judgment. If the associate judge has proposed an order or judgment and no party has filed a written request for a de novo hearing (or the parties have waived the right to a de novo hearing), the referring court can (1) adopt, modify, or reject the associate judge's proposed order or judgment, (2) hear additional evidence, or (3) recommit the matter to the associate judge for further proceedings. Tex. Gov't Code §54A.114; *see* Tex. Gov't Code §54A.113(b). When the referring court signs the proposed order or judgment, it becomes the order or judgment of the referring court. Tex. Gov't Code §54A.113(b).

§8. Reconsideration of order or judgment—Postjudgment motions

A party can file a motion for new trial, a motion for judgment notwithstanding the verdict, or other postjudgment motions after the referring court signs the associate judge's proposed order or judgment. *See* Tex. Gov't Code §§54A.113(b), 54A.115(g). See "Postjudgment Motions," ch. 10-A, §1 et seq.

§9. Appeal

A party can appeal the associate judge's decision to either the referring court or an appellate court. *See* Tex. Gov't Code §§54A.111(b), 54A.116(a). A party does not lose the right to appeal to or request other relief from a court of appeals or the Texas Supreme Court if it does not request or otherwise waives its right to a de novo hearing before the referring court. Tex. Gov't Code §54A.116(a).

§9.1 To referring court—de novo hearing. When an appeal is made to the referring court, the referring court holds a de novo hearing. Tex. Gov't Code §54A.111(e). A de novo hearing is a new hearing without deference to the associate judge's decision. *See* Tex. Gov't Code §54A.115; Hearing De Novo, *Black's Law Dictionary* (11th ed. 2019).

1. Request hearing.

(1) Deadline. A party must file an appeal in the referring court within seven working days after the date the party receives notice of the associate judge's decision unless the request is for a hearing to modify a temporary restraining order (TRO) or temporary injunction, which can be made anytime before the TRO or injunction expires. *See* Tex. Gov't Code §54A.111(b). If a request for a de novo hearing is timely made, any other party can file its own request for a de novo hearing before the referring court and must do so within seven working days after the date the initial request was filed. Tex. Gov't Code §54A.115(d). See "Temporary restraining orders," ch. 1-J, §6.1; "Temporary injunctions," ch. 1-J, §6.2; "Orders for detention or incarceration," ch. 1-J, §6.3.

(2) Where to file. The party should file a request for a de novo hearing with the clerk of the referring court. Tex. Gov't Code §54A.115(a).

(3) What to file. The request must be in writing and must specify the issues that will be presented to the referring court. Tex. Gov't Code §54A.115(a), (b). The de novo hearing is limited to the specified issues. Tex. Gov't Code §54A.115(b).

Note

If a party requests a de novo hearing to review the associate judge's proposed order or judgment after a jury trial, the party cannot demand a second jury to review that order or judgment. Tex. Gov't Code §54A.115(h).

(4) Notice. Notice of a request for a de novo hearing before the referring court must be given to the opposing attorney in the manner provided by TRCP 21a. Tex. Gov't Code §54A.115(c). See "How to serve," ch. 1-D, §4.

2. Effect of request on order or judgment only. A proposed order issued or a judgment rendered by an associate judge, except for an order providing for the appointment of a receiver, remains in full force and effect and is enforceable as an order or judgment of the referring court while the de novo hearing is pending. Tex. Gov't Code §54A.113(a).

3. Hearing.

(1) Deadline. The referring court, after notice to the parties, must hold a de novo hearing no later than 30 days after the initial request for a de novo hearing was filed. Tex. Gov't Code §54A.115(e).

(2) Scope. The de novo hearing is limited to only those matters specified in the appeal. Tex. Gov't Code §54A.111(e). Except on leave of court, a party cannot submit any additional evidence or pleadings. *Id.*

(3) Evidence. The parties can present witnesses on the issues specified in the request for hearing. Tex. Gov't Code §54A.115(f). If a record of the hearing before the associate judge was taken by a court reporter, the referring court can consider it, including the charge to and verdict returned by a jury. *Id.*

4. Order. The referring court should issue a written order on its ruling. *See* **Klentzman v. Brady**, 312 S.W.3d 886, 908 (Tex.App.—Houston [1st Dist.] 2009, no pet.). This order can be appealed to the appellate court. *See id.* at 908 & n.21.

5. Reconsideration of order or judgment—postjudgment motions. A party can file a motion for new trial, a motion for judgment notwithstanding the verdict, or other postjudgment motions if the referring court denies relief after a de novo hearing and signs the associate judge's proposed order or judgment. *See* Tex. Gov't Code §54A.115(g); *see also* Tex. Gov't Code §54A.116(b) (date order or judgment was signed by referring court is controlling date for purposes of appeal). See "Postjudgment Motions," ch. 10-A, §1 et seq.

§9.2 To appellate court. The procedure and deadline for appealing to the court of appeals or the Texas Supreme Court is the same as with other judgments or orders. See "Calculating appellate deadlines," ch. 9-C, §9.1. Generally, the date an order or judgment is signed by the referring court is the controlling date for appellate deadlines. Tex. Gov't Code §54A.116(b). If the order is an agreed order or a default order, the date the order is signed by an associate judge is the controlling date for appellate deadlines. Tex. Gov't Code §54A.116(c).

K. Master in Chancery

§1. General

§1.1 Rule. Tex. R. Civ. P. 171.

§1.2 Purpose. A master in chancery, sometimes called a special master, is a person designated by a judicial officer to hear certain matters. *See, e.g.*, **Simpson v. Canales**, 806 S.W.2d 802, 806 (Tex.1991) (master appointed for discovery). The theory underlying the use of masters is that, by delegating certain matters to them, the trial judge is free to devote more time to trials and substantive decisions, thus expediting the trial docket. *Id.* at 809 n.9. For a discussion of the historical development of the office of masters and an explanation of the courts' inherent distrust of them, read **Simpson**.

§1.3 Forms. **O'Connor's Texas Civil Forms**, FORMS 1K:1 et seq. (2020 ed.).

§1.4 Other references. Furgeson et al., *E-Discovery & the Use of Special Masters*, Litigation Update Institute, State Bar of Texas CLE, ch. 3 (2011); **O'Connor's Texas Civil Appeals** (2020 ed.).

§2. Authority for referral to master

There are three sources of authority for a master: TRCP 171, statutes, and the consent of the parties.

§2.1 TRCP 171. Every referral to a master must comply with TRCP 171 unless authorized by statute or consented to by the parties. **Simpson v. Canales**, 806 S.W.2d 802, 810 (Tex.1991); **Hansen v. Sullivan**, 886 S.W.2d 467, 469 (Tex.App.—Houston [1st Dist.] 1994, orig. proceeding).

§2.2 Statutes. The Legislature has created certain types of masters, limited to specific subjects and counties. For example, the following matters may be referred to a master: family-law matters (Family Code §§201.101 to 201.113); juvenile matters in certain counties (e.g., Gov't Code §§54.801 to 54.820 (Harris County)); and criminal matters in certain counties (e.g., Gov't Code §§54.301 to 54.312 (Dallas County)). These provisions for the appointment of masters contain their own procedures for appointing and compensating masters and for appealing their decisions.

§2.3 Consent. The parties may consent to the referral of a case to a master, even when there is no authority under TRCP 171 or any statute. **Simpson v. Canales**, 806 S.W.2d 802, 810–11 (Tex.1991); **In re Polybutylene Plumbing Litig.**, 23 S.W.3d 428, 439 (Tex.App.—Houston [1st Dist.] 2000, pet. dism'd). Consent to the referral of a matter to a master demonstrates a party's intent to be bound on the matters referred. *See* **In re Sheets**, 971 S.W.2d 745, 747 (Tex.App.—Dallas 1998, orig. proceeding). When parties consent to the appointment of a master, the appointment is not subject to the same limitations as one imposed by the court under TRCP 171. **Simpson**, 806 S.W.2d at 811.

§3. Motion for referral to master under TRCP 171

§3.1 Written. A motion for referral to a master should be in writing. See **O'Connor's Texas Civil Forms**, FORM 1K:1 (2020 ed.).

§3.2 Grounds. A motion for referral to a master under TRCP 171 should include the following allegations:

1. Specific, pending matter. The motion should identify a specific, pending matter that the party requests be referred to a master. The motion should not ask the trial court to refer all present and future issues of a particular type to a master. *See* **Academy of Model Aeronautics, Inc. v. Packer**, 860 S.W.2d 419, 419 (Tex.1993).

2. Exceptional matter. The matter should be referred to a master because it is exceptional. Tex. R. Civ. P. 171; **Simpson v. Canales**, 806 S.W.2d 802, 811 (Tex.1991). For example, the court may appoint a master with technical knowledge to conduct a comprehensive analysis of highly technical data. *E.g.*, **In re Harris**, 315 S.W.3d 685, 705–06 (Tex.App.—Houston [1st Dist.] 2010, orig. proceeding) (court abused discretion by referring electronic-discovery matter to special master when case was not of a highly technical nature); **TransAmerican Nat. Gas Corp. v. Mancias**, 877 S.W.2d 840, 843 (Tex.App.—Corpus Christi 1994, orig. proceeding) (geologist appointed to assist in review of documents); *see also* **Chapa v. Garcia**, 848 S.W.2d 667, 668 (Tex.1992) (Supreme Court suggested that trial court appoint a master with special expertise to assist in review of documents). Referral to a master is not justified just because a case is complicated or time-consuming or

because the court is busy. **Simpson**, 806 S.W.2d at 811; **In re Sheets**, 971 S.W.2d 745, 747 (Tex.App.—Dallas 1998, orig. proceeding); **In re King**, No. 01-13-00434-CV, 2013 WL 4007798 (Tex.App.—Houston [1st Dist.] 2013, orig. proceeding) (memo op.; 8-6-13).

3. Good cause. The court has good cause to refer the matter to a master. Tex. R. Civ. P. 171; **Simpson**, 806 S.W.2d at 811; **Owens-Corning Fiberglas Corp. v. Caldwell**, 830 S.W.2d 622, 626 (Tex.App.—Houston [1st Dist.] 1991, orig. proceeding); *see* **In re Harris**, 315 S.W.3d at 705–06 (presence of electronic discovery alone is not good cause for appointing special master). The "good cause" requirement has not been precisely defined. *See generally* **Simpson**, 806 S.W.2d at 811–12 (discussing difficulty in defining "good cause" requirement of TRCP 171).

§4. Order of referral to master

The decision to appoint a master is within the trial court's discretion. **Simpson v. Canales**, 806 S.W.2d 802, 811 (Tex.1991); **Tollett v. Carmona**, 915 S.W.2d 562, 564 (Tex.App.—Houston [14th Dist.] 1995, orig. proceeding). See **O'Connor's Texas Civil Forms**, FORM 1K:3 (2020 ed.).

§4.1 Findings. To refer a case to a master without the parties' consent, the trial court must find that (1) the case is an exceptional one and (2) there is good cause for the appointment. Tex. R. Civ. P. 171; **Simpson v. Canales**, 806 S.W.2d 802, 811 (Tex.1991); **In re Sheets**, 971 S.W.2d 745, 747 (Tex.App.—Dallas 1998, orig. proceeding).

§4.2 Scope of referral. The order referring a matter to a master should identify the scope and limits of the master's authority. Tex. R. Civ. P. 171. The order should specify the master's powers and direct the master to report only on particular matters, perform only particular acts, or receive and report evidence only. *Id.*

§4.3 No blanket referral. The court cannot make a blanket referral of all discovery matters to a master. *See* **Academy of Model Aeronautics, Inc. v. Packer**, 860 S.W.2d 419, 419 (Tex.1993) (trial court could not refer all present and future discovery disputes to master); **Simpson v. Canales**, 806 S.W.2d 802, 811–12 (Tex.1991) (even in exceptional case, court would be reluctant to refer all discovery matters to master); **Owens-Corning Fiberglas Corp. v. Caldwell**, 830 S.W.2d 622, 626 (Tex.App.—Houston [1st Dist.] 1991, orig. proceeding) (same).

§4.4 Appointee. The master must be a citizen of Texas and cannot be related to or be an attorney for any of the parties. Tex. R. Civ. P. 171.

§4.5 Time & place. The order of referral may set the time and place for the hearings and the time for the filing of the master's report. Tex. R. Civ. P. 171.

§5. Objection to master's appointment

§5.1 Types of objections. A party must make its objections when the court refers a matter to a master, or it waives them. *See* **Tollett v. Carmona**, 915 S.W.2d 562, 564–65 (Tex.App.—Houston [14th Dist.] 1995, orig. proceeding) (party must object to appointment either before participating in any proceedings in front of master, or before parties, master, and trial court have relied on appointment); **Owens-Corning Fiberglas Corp. v. Caldwell**, 830 S.W.2d 622, 625 (Tex.App.—Houston [1st Dist.] 1991, orig. proceeding) (same). See "Making & Preserving Objections," ch. 1-F, §1 et seq.; **O'Connor's Texas Civil Forms**, FORM 1K:2 (2020 ed.). Objections include the following:

1. This is not the type of matter that should be referred to a master because it is not exceptional, and the referral is without good cause. Tex. R. Civ. P. 171; **Simpson v. Canales**, 806 S.W.2d 802, 811 (Tex.1991). See "Grounds," ch. 1-K, §3.2.

2. The scope of the appointment and the master's duties are not clearly defined in the order of referral. Tex. R. Civ. P. 171.

3. The referral is a blanket referral, in violation of TRCP 171. **Academy of Model Aeronautics, Inc. v. Packer**, 860 S.W.2d 419, 419 (Tex.1993); **Simpson**, 806 S.W.2d at 812; **Owens-Corning**, 830 S.W.2d at 626.

4. The person appointed to serve as a master is not qualified to serve because she is not a citizen of Texas, is related to one of the parties, or is an attorney for one of the parties. Tex. R. Civ. P. 171.

§5.2 Deadline to object. TRCP 171 does not specify the deadline for a party to object to the appointment of a master. A party must object to the appointment either before participating in any proceedings in front of the master or before the parties, master, and trial court act in reliance on the appointment. **Tollett v. Carmona**, 915 S.W.2d 562, 564–65 (Tex.App.—Houston [14th Dist.] 1995, orig. proceeding); *see* **Owens-Corning Fiberglas Corp. v. Caldwell**, 830 S.W.2d 622, 624–25 (Tex.App.—Houston [1st Dist.] 1991, orig. proceeding).

§6. Hearing before master

§6.1 Record of hearing. When requested, the master must make a record of the evidence just as if the case were tried before the court. Tex. R. Civ. P. 171. When a party wants the proceeding recorded, the party should file a written request as soon as the appointment is made. See **O'Connor's Texas Civil Forms**, FORM 1K:4 (2020 ed.). If a court reporter is not present, any party who wants the hearing recorded should object in writing.

§6.2 Attendance of witnesses. The parties may procure the attendance of witnesses by the issuance and service of process as provided by the same rules as for a trial before a judge. Tex. R. Civ. P. 171. See "Subpoenas," ch. 1-L, §1 et seq.

§6.3 Scope of hearing. The scope of the hearing is determined by the trial court's order referring the matter to the master. See "Scope of referral," ch. 1-K, §4.2.

§6.4 Authority of master. Subject to the limitations stated in the order, the master may regulate the hearing and take all measures necessary or proper for the efficient performance of the duties specified in the order. The master may require the production of evidence, including books, papers, vouchers, documents, and other writings; may rule on the admissibility of evidence; and may place parties and witnesses under oath and examine them. Tex. R. Civ. P. 171.

§7. Master's report

§7.1 Report. The master's report should conform to the instructions in the order of referral. If the order instructed the master to receive evidence and settle factual disputes, the master should file findings of fact just as if the case were tried to a court without a jury. The master does not have the authority to render judgment. **Hansen v. Sullivan**, 886 S.W.2d 467, 469 (Tex.App.—Houston [1st Dist.] 1994, orig. proceeding).

§7.2 Notice. Once the master files the report with the trial court, the parties are entitled to notice and an opportunity to object.

§8. Objection to master's report

§8.1 No objection. When issues are referred to a master under TRCP 171, the master's report is conclusive on all issues to which the parties do not object. **Lesikar v. Moon**, 237 S.W.3d 361, 371 (Tex.App.—Houston [14th Dist.] 2007, pet. denied); **Young v. Young**, 854 S.W.2d 698, 701 (Tex.App.—Dallas 1993, writ denied).

§8.2 Objection. To the extent that a party objects to the master's report, the report is not binding. **Lesikar v. Moon**, 237 S.W.3d 361, 371 (Tex.App.—Houston [14th Dist.] 2007, pet. denied); **Young v. Young**, 854 S.W.2d 698, 701 (Tex.App.—Dallas 1993, writ denied). See **O'Connor's Texas Civil Forms**, FORM 1K:5 (2020 ed.).

1. Timely. A party must object to the master's report before the trial court adopts it. **Robles v. Robles**, 965 S.W.2d 605, 612 (Tex.App.—Houston [1st Dist.] 1998, pet. denied). However, if the trial court adopts the report before a party has notice of the report, the party does not waive its objections. **Republic Ins. v. Davis**, 856 S.W.2d 158, 160 (Tex.1993).

2. Specific. An objection to the report must be specific. **Lesikar**, 237 S.W.3d at 371; *see, e.g.*, **Young**, 854 S.W.2d at 700–01 (wife objected to finding that she executed agreement voluntarily). A party does not need to support its objection with evidence; only a formal objection is necessary. *See* **Young**, 854 S.W.2d at 703. See "Making & Preserving Objections," ch. 1-F, §1 et seq.

3. Effect of objection. An objection to the master's findings raises a fact issue. **Young**, 854 S.W.2d at 701.

§9. Trial court's review of master's report

§9.1 Court review of report. The court may confirm, modify, correct, reject, reverse, or recommit the report after it is filed. Tex. R. Civ. P. 171. If the court makes a finding without specifically rejecting a master's finding on the same issue, the

court's finding supersedes the master's. **Hyundai Motor Am. v. O'Neill**, 839 S.W.2d 474, 481 (Tex.App.—Dallas 1992, orig. proceeding). The court can review only the matters that were specifically referred to the special master. *See, e.g.*, **In re Polybutylene Plumbing Litig.**, 23 S.W.3d 428, 439–42 (Tex.App.—Houston [1st Dist.] 2000, pet. dism'd) (trial court had no jurisdiction to modify terms of fully performed attorney-fee agreement when master was appointed solely to implement parties' agreement and to determine whether parties' proposed formula accomplished that agreement).

§9.2 Trial de novo. The fact issues raised by the objections are tried de novo. **Hyundai Motor Am. v. O'Neill**, 839 S.W.2d 474, 480 (Tex.App.—Dallas 1992, orig. proceeding). That is, each party has the right to present evidence on the issues specified in the objections and have the court or jury decide those issues based on the evidence presented in court. **Young v. Young**, 854 S.W.2d 698, 701 (Tex.App.—Dallas 1993, writ denied).

§9.3 Jury or nonjury trial? If one of the parties properly requested a jury, the court must conduct a jury trial on the fact issues raised by the objections to the master's report. **Young v. Young**, 854 S.W.2d 698, 701 (Tex.App.—Dallas 1993, writ denied); **Minnich v. Jones**, 799 S.W.2d 327, 328 (Tex.App.—Texarkana 1990, orig. proceeding); *see also* **Mann v. Mann**, 607 S.W.2d 243, 246 (Tex.1980) (request for jury trial in divorce proceeding does not prevent appointment of master). If no jury was requested, the court will conduct a nonjury trial on those issues.

§10. Payment of master

§10.1 Reasonable compensation. The trial court will award the master reasonable compensation, which will be taxed as a cost of the suit. Tex. R. Civ. P. 171; **TransAmerican Nat. Gas Corp. v. Mancias**, 877 S.W.2d 840, 844 (Tex.App.—Corpus Christi 1994, orig. proceeding). Fees for masters are not necessarily determined by the stringent requirements of proof for attorney fees. **Frost v. Frost**, 695 S.W.2d 279, 282 (Tex.App.—San Antonio 1985, no writ). A fee awarded to the master will be reversed only on a showing of a clear abuse of discretion. **Mann v. Mann**, 607 S.W.2d 243, 246 (Tex.1980); **Texas Bank & Trust Co. v. Moore**, 595 S.W.2d 502, 511 (Tex.1980).

§10.2 Not in advance. The trial court cannot require the parties to deposit funds into the court's registry to cover the master's fee. **TransAmerican Nat. Gas Corp. v. Mancias**, 877 S.W.2d 840, 844 (Tex.App.—Corpus Christi 1994, orig. proceeding). The Supreme Court has not addressed this issue. **Simpson v. Canales**, 806 S.W.2d 802, 812 n.14 (Tex.1991).

§11. Review

§11.1 Appeal.

1. Master's appointment. Generally, when the trial court grants a motion to appoint a master, the order cannot be appealed until after a final judgment is rendered in the case. *See* **Moyer v. Moyer**, 183 S.W.3d 48, 58 (Tex.App.—Austin 2005, no pet.).

2. Master's report. If the court overrules an objection to the master's report, the party may appeal and challenge the ruling after a final judgment is rendered.

§11.2 Mandamus. If the court improperly overrules a party's objection to the order of referral to a master, the party can file a petition for writ of mandamus. *See* **Simpson v. Canales**, 806 S.W.2d 802, 812 (Tex.1991); **Tollett v. Carmona**, 915 S.W.2d 562, 564 (Tex.App.—Houston [14th Dist.] 1995, orig. proceeding). Appointment of a master will be reversed only on a showing of a clear abuse of discretion. **Simpson**, 806 S.W.2d at 811; **In re Harris**, 315 S.W.3d 685, 704 (Tex.App.—Houston [1st Dist.] 2010, orig. proceeding).

L. Subpoenas

§1. General

§1.1 Rules. Tex. R. Civ. P. 176, 199.3, 205. See Tex. Civ. Prac. & Rem. Code §§22.001, 22.002.

§1.2 Purpose. A subpoena is a process or writ that commands a person either to appear and give testimony or to produce or permit inspection and copying of documents or other tangible things. Tex. R. Civ. P. 176.2; *see* Tex. R. Civ. P. 199.3, 205.3; **In re Z.A.T.**, 193 S.W.3d 197, 207 (Tex.App.—Waco 2006, pet. denied).

§1.3 Forms. **O'Connor's Texas Civil Forms**, FORMS 1L:1 et seq., 6A:13 to 6A:14 (2020 ed.).

§1.4 Other references. Buccieri, *Texas Trial Handbook* §8:15 (3d ed.); Griesel, *The "New" Texas Discovery Rules: Three Years Later—Are Old Dogs Learning New Tricks?*, Advanced Evidence & Discovery Course, State Bar of Texas CLE, ch. 2, §IV (2002).

§2. Types of subpoenas

Subpoenas may be issued to command a person (1) to attend and give testimony, (2) to produce and permit inspection of books, papers, documents, or tangible things designated in the subpoena, or (3) to do both. Tex. R. Civ. P. 176.2.

§2.1 Discovery subpoena. A discovery subpoena is a writ by which a court, at the request of a party, commands a person to appear or produce documents or other things for discovery. Tex. R. Civ. P. 176.2. A person commanded to produce documents or other things does not need to appear in person unless the subpoena commands the person to attend and give testimony. Tex. R. Civ. P. 176.6(c). A subpoena cannot be used for discovery in a manner or time other than as provided by the rules of discovery. Tex. R. Civ. P. 176.3(b); **Prestige Ford Co. v. Gilmore**, 56 S.W.3d 73, 80 (Tex.App.—Houston [14th Dist.] 2001, pet. denied). In most cases, a discovery subpoena is issued to compel a nonparty to attend a deposition and produce documents. See "Securing things from a nonparty," ch. 6-I, §5.

§2.2 Trial subpoena. A subpoena for a hearing or trial commands a witness to attend and give testimony or to produce documents or things at a hearing or trial, and to remain there from day to day until discharged by either the court or the party issuing the subpoena. Tex. R. Civ. P. 176.2(a), 176.6(a), (f). Attorneys may issue their own trial subpoenas. Tex. R. Civ. P. 176.4(b). See "Who may issue subpoenas," ch. 1-L, §3.3. A party cannot secure a trial subpoena by making an oral request to the court. **Holleman v. West End Cab Co.**, No. 07-99-0232-CV, 2000 WL 898003 (Tex.App.—Amarillo 2000, pet. denied) (no pub.; 7-6-00).

Practice Tip

If the witness to be subpoenaed can be characterized as "friendly," the attorney may include in the trial subpoena a request that the witness call the attorney to set up a date and time for the witness to appear at trial.

1. Time for issuance. TRCP 176 does not state how much advance notice should be allowed for issuing a subpoena for a hearing or trial. The only rule is that the party who issued the subpoena should be "diligent" in procuring the witness's testimony. *See, e.g.*, **Hatteberg v. Hatteberg**, 933 S.W.2d 522, 526 (Tex.App.—Houston [1st Dist.] 1994, no writ) (continuance denied; attempted service of subpoena nine days before trial was not diligent); **Victor M. Solis Underground Util. & Paving Co. v. City of Laredo**, 751 S.W.2d 532, 537 (Tex.App.—San Antonio 1988, writ denied) (continuance denied; subpoena issued for out-of-town witness only three days before trial was not diligent); **Dairyland Cty. Mut. Ins. v. Keys**, 568 S.W.2d 457, 460 (Tex.App.—Tyler 1978, writ ref'd n.r.e.) (continuance denied; party waited to have subpoena issued on day of trial rather than two weeks earlier at time of docket call).

2. Discharging the witness. The court or the summoning party may discharge a witness summoned for a hearing or trial. Tex. R. Civ. P. 176.6(a). A discharged witness may be subpoenaed again to appear and give testimony. **Burttschell v. Sheppard**, 69 S.W.2d 402, 404 (Tex.1934).

§3. Formal requirements for subpoenas

The subpoena must meet the formal requirements of TRCP 176.1 and any additional requirements imposed by local district or county rules that apply where the case is pending.

§3.1 Form of subpoena. The subpoena must (1) be issued in the name of "The State of Texas," (2) include the style and cause number of the suit, (3) identify the court where the suit is pending, (4) state the date the subpoena is issued, (5) identify the person to whom the subpoena is directed, (6) state the time, place, and nature of the action required of the person being subpoenaed, (7) identify the party who secured the subpoena, (8) include the text of TRCP 176.8(a) regarding contempt, (9) be signed by the person issuing the subpoena, and (10) command a person (a) to attend and give testimony, (b) to produce and permit inspection of the books, papers, documents, or tangible things designated in the subpoena, or (c) to do both. Tex. R. Civ. P. 176.1, 176.2. See **O'Connor's Texas Civil Forms**, FORM 1L:1 (2020 ed.).

§3.2 Range of subpoena. Both TRCP 176.3 and CPRC §22.002 limit the geographic reach of subpoenas to 150 miles, but the range of a subpoena is broader under TRCP 176.3 than under CPRC §22.002. Other statutes, however, may modify the 150-mile range in TRCP 176.3 and CPRC §22.002.

1. TRCP 176.3. A witness may be required by subpoena to appear or produce documents in any county within 150 miles of the place where the witness resides or was served. Tex. R. Civ. P. 176.3(a). To determine the range of a subpoena under TRCP 176.3, trace a circle with a radius of 150 miles from the place where the witness resides or was served. The witness may be required to appear or produce documents at any place in any county that is even partially in that circle. TRCP 176.3 does not restrict the places for deposition listed in TRCP 199.2(b)(2) for parties and other witnesses who can be compelled to appear by notice alone.

2. CPRC §22.002. A witness may be required by subpoena to appear for a trial or hearing in the county of suit if the witness resides or was served within 150 miles of that county. Tex. Civ. Prac. & Rem. Code §22.002. To determine the range under CPRC §22.002, trace a circle around the county of suit with a radius of 150 miles out from the county line. If the witness resides or was served within that circle, the witness can be compelled to attend.

Practice Tip

An attorney may be able to use online tools to determine whether a subpoenaed person is located within the 150-mile radius required by TRCP 176.3 and CPRC §22.002. See, e.g., Radius Around Point Map, www.freemaptools.com/radius-around-pointhtm.

1-5. Distance Nonparty Can Be Compelled to Travel

	Authority	Residence	Where served
1	Tex. R. Civ. P. 176.3	To any county, if part of county is within radius of 150 miles from witness's residence	To any county, if part of county is within radius of 150 miles from place served
2	Tex. Civ. Prac. & Rem. Code §22.002	To county of suit, if witness's residence is within 150 miles of that county	To county of suit, if witness was served within 150 miles of that county

3. Other statutes. Other statutes may modify the 150-mile subpoena range in TRCP 176.3 and CPRC §22.002 for particular suits. For example, in a suit to prohibit restraint on trade, a witness located anywhere in the state may be required by subpoena to appear for a trial or hearing. Tex. Bus. & Com. Code §15.11; *see also* Tex. Bus. & Com. Code §17.57 (in DTPA suits, witness residing or served within 100 miles of courthouse, or, for suits pending in Travis County, within 100 miles of courthouse of county where suit could have been brought, can be subpoenaed to appear or produce documents).

§3.3 Who may issue subpoenas. Subpoenas may be issued by the court clerk, an attorney, or a deposition officer. Tex. R. Civ. P. 176.4. For the definition of "deposition officer," see "Deposition officer," ch. 6-F, §3. When a subpoena is issued by the clerk, the clerk must provide the party requesting the subpoena with an original and a copy (both to be completed by the party) for each witness. Tex. R. Civ. P. 176.4(a).

§3.4 Who may serve subpoenas. Subpoenas may be served by the sheriff, constable, or any other person who is not a party and is at least 18 years old. Tex. R. Civ. P. 176.5(a). Generally, when a witness is subpoenaed for a deposition, the court reporter serves the subpoena with the notice of deposition. *See* Tex. R. Civ. P. 176.4(c). For detailed information about who may serve subpoenas, see "Who may serve process," ch. 2-I, §3.

§3.5 Who may be subpoenaed. Subpoenas may require the attendance of parties and nonparties (e.g., witnesses, custodians of records). Tex. R. Civ. P. 176.2, 199.3, 205.1; *see* **St. Luke's Episcopal Hosp. v. Garcia**, 928 S.W.2d 307, 311 (Tex.App.—Houston [14th Dist.] 1996, orig. proceeding) (a subpoena is the instrument that compels nonparties to respond to a deposition); **Cheatham v. Rogers**, 824 S.W.2d 231, 234 (Tex.App.—Tyler 1992, orig. proceeding) (nonparty witness can be subpoenaed to attend deposition). When securing documents from a custodian of records, the subpoena does not need to name the person; the subpoena can be addressed to the "custodian of records" of the business entity. When securing documents from a party, it is not necessary to serve a subpoena. See "Securing things from a party," ch. 6-I, §3.

§3.6 Notice to other parties. A party is not required to give other parties notice of its trial subpoenas, but it must give other parties notice of its discovery subpoenas. *See* Tex. R. Civ. P. 191.5. A party cannot secure discovery by using a trial subpoena to avoid the notice requirements of TRCP 191.5. *See* Tex. R. Civ. P. 176.3(b) (prohibiting use of subpoena to circumvent discovery rules); **Prestige Ford Co. v. Gilmore**, 56 S.W.3d 73, 80 (Tex.App.—Houston [14th Dist.] 2001, pet. denied) (same).

§3.7 Manner of service. A subpoena is served by delivering a copy of the subpoena, with the subpoena fee, to the witness. Tex. R. Civ. P. 176.5(a). If the witness is a party and is represented by an attorney, the subpoena and fee may be served on the witness's attorney of record. *Id.* When a discovery subpoena requires the witness to attend a deposition, the notice of deposition may be served with the subpoena. Tex. R. Civ. P. 176.4(c).

§3.8 Subpoena fee. The subpoena fee is $10 for each day the witness is required to attend trial or discovery. Tex. Civ. Prac. & Rem. Code §22.001(a); **Tex. Atty. Gen. Op.** No. DM-342 (1995). When a person is subpoenaed to attend, the person is entitled to receive payment of one day's witness fee at the time the subpoena is served. Tex. Civ. Prac. & Rem. Code §22.001 ($10 per day, first day payable at service). Subpoena fees are recoverable as court costs. Tex. Civ. Prac. & Rem. Code §22.001(c); *see* **Shenandoah Assocs. v. J&K Props., Inc.**, 741 S.W.2d 470, 487 (Tex.App.—Dallas 1987, writ denied).

§3.9 Proof of service. Proof of service must be made by filing with the court (1) the witness's signed written memorandum or (2) a statement by the person who served the subpoena stating the date, time, and manner of service and the name of the person served. Tex. R. Civ. P. 176.5(b).

§4. Objecting to trial & discovery subpoenas

§4.1 Who can challenge. The subpoena can be challenged by the person being subpoenaed, the parties, or any other person affected by the subpoena. *See* Tex. R. Civ. P. 176.6(d) to (f). Each of these persons have an independent right to challenge the subpoena—that is, a ruling on one person's challenge to the subpoena will not affect another's right to bring her own challenge. *See, e.g.*, **In re Garza**, 544 S.W.3d 836, 841–42 (Tex.2018) (nonparty custodians of records were permitted to seek protection from discovery subpoena even though P had already sought and been denied protection from same request).

1. Person subject to subpoena. A subpoenaed person may challenge the subpoena by filing (1) a motion for protective order or (2) an objection to the subpoena. *See* Tex. R. Civ. P. 176.6(d) to (f), 192.6; **In re Diversicare Gen. Partner, Inc.**, 41 S.W.3d 788, 794 (Tex.App.—Corpus Christi 2001, orig. proceeding), *overruled on other grounds*, **In re Arriola**, 159 S.W.3d 670 (Tex.App.—Corpus Christi 2004, orig. proceeding). See "Filing motion for protective order or objection," ch. 1-L, §4.3.1. A subpoenaed person may also withhold material or information claimed to be privileged. See "Asserting privileges," ch. 1-L, §4.3.2.

2. Party or other person. A party or any other person affected by the subpoena may challenge the subpoena by filing a motion for protective order. *See* Tex. R. Civ. P. 176.6(e), 192.6. See "Motion for protective order," ch. 1-L, §4.3.1(1).

§4.2 Deadline to challenge.

1. Trial subpoena. If possible, a person challenging a trial subpoena should make the challenge before the time specified for appearing in court. Tex. R. Civ. P. 176.6(d), (e). However, the person may wait to challenge the subpoena until the witness appears in court. Tex. R. Civ. P. 176.6(f).

2. Discovery subpoena. A person challenging a discovery subpoena must make the challenge before the time specified for compliance in the subpoena, or the challenge will be waived. Tex. R. Civ. P. 176.6(d), (e); **In re University of Tex. Health Ctr.**, 198 S.W.3d 392, 395 (Tex.App.—Texarkana 2006, orig. proceeding).

§4.3 Types of challenges.

1. Filing motion for protective order or objection. The subpoena may be challenged by filing a motion for protective order or an objection to the subpoena.

Note

Under TRCP 176.6(d) to (f), a person can challenge a subpoena by filing a motion for protective order or an objection to the subpoena; nothing in the rule provides for filing a motion to quash the subpoena. See ***In re K.L.&J. L.P.****, 336 S.W.3d 286, 293 n.3 (Tex.App.—San Antonio 2010, orig. proceeding). However, some parties still file—and courts may review—a motion to quash the subpoena issued under TRCP 176. See, e.g.,* ***In re Rabb****, 293 S.W.3d 865, 866–67 (Tex.App.—Dallas 2009, orig. proceeding) (persons subject to trial subpoena filed motion to quash).*

---

(1) Motion for protective order. The person challenging the subpoena can file a motion for protective order. The motion can be brought in either the court in which the action is pending or the county where the subpoena was served. Tex. R. Civ. P. 176.6(e).

(a) To challenge procedural defect. If a subpoena is procedurally defective, the person challenging the subpoena should file a motion for protective order. *See* Tex. R. Civ. P. 176.6(e), 192.6. See "Motion for protective order," ch. 6-A, §20; **O'Connor's Texas Civil Forms**, FORM 6A:13 (2020 ed.) (motion for protection from discovery subpoena). The following are examples of challenges a person can make to a subpoena that is procedurally defective: • The subpoena was not dated and signed by a person authorized under TRCP 176.4 to issue subpoenas. Tex. R. Civ. P. 176.1(h). • The subpoena was not served by a sheriff, constable, or other person authorized by law. Tex. R. Civ. P. 176.5(a). • There was no witness fee attached to the subpoena. Tex. R. Civ. P. 176.8(b); **Kieffer v. Miller**, 560 S.W.2d 431, 432 (Tex.App.—Beaumont 1977, writ ref'd n.r.e.); *see* Tex. Civ. Prac. & Rem. Code §22.001. • Only one subpoena was issued for two or more witnesses, including the subpoenaed person. *See* Tex. R. Civ. P. 176.1(d). • Nonparty witness was served with a subpoena to appear more than 150 miles from both the place where she was served with the subpoena and the place where she resides. Tex. R. Civ. P. 176.3(a).

(b) To challenge discovery request. If a subpoena requests information that is unduly burdensome or expensive, harassing, annoying, or invasive of a protected right, the person challenging the subpoena should file a motion for protective order. *See* Tex. R. Civ. P. 176.7, 192.6. See "Grounds to limit scope of discovery," ch. 6-A, §20.1.

(2) Objection. If the person challenging the subpoena is the person being subpoenaed, the person can file an objection to the subpoena rather than a motion for protective order. Tex. R. Civ. P. 176.6(d).

2. Asserting privileges. A subpoenaed person may withhold any material or information claimed to be privileged, but that person must comply with TRCP 193.3. Tex. R. Civ. P. 176.6(c). When an assertion of privilege is appropriate, a person should not seek a protective order; however, a motion for protective order will not waive the privilege. Tex. R. Civ. P. 192.6(a). The privilege claim must be asserted before the deadline for complying with the subpoena. See "Asserting privileges," ch. 6-A, §18.2; "When necessary," ch. 6-A, §18.7.1.

§5. Enforcing subpoenas

The court may impose a fine or confine the subpoenaed person for contempt of court for not complying with a subpoena. Tex. R. Civ. P. 176.8(a). If a subpoenaed witness does not appear for trial, the trial court may issue a writ of attachment to compel her attendance. **In re Z.A.T.**, 193 S.W.3d 197, 207 (Tex.App.—Waco 2006, pet. denied). The court cannot impose a fine or issue a writ of attachment in a civil suit until the summoning party provides an affidavit stating that all lawful fees were paid or tendered to the witness. Tex. R. Civ. P. 176.8(b); **Kieffer v. Miller**, 560 S.W.2d 431, 432 (Tex.App.—Beaumont 1977, writ ref'd n.r.e.); **Tex. Atty. Gen. Op.** No. DM-342 (1995). The trial court has no authority to issue a writ of attachment for a witness discharged by the summoning party. **Alcocer v. Travelers Ins.**, 446 S.W.2d 927, 928–29 (Tex.App.—Houston [14th Dist.] 1969, no writ).

Chapter 2. Plaintiff's Lawsuit

A. Prefiling Considerations

§1. General

§1.1 Rule. Tex. R. Civ. P. 54.

§1.2 Purpose. Before filing suit, the plaintiff should check appropriate statutes and any document on which the suit is based to determine whether there are any prerequisites to filing suit.

§1.3 Forms. **O'Connor's Texas Civil Forms**, FORMS 2A:1 et seq. (2020 ed.).

§1.4 Other references. **O'Connor's Federal Rules * Civil Trials** (2021 ed.); **O'Connor's Texas Causes of Action** (2021 ed.).

§2. Notices & demands

The plaintiff should consider whether it must give the defendant notice or make a pretrial demand before filing suit.

§2.1 Statutory notice. Before plaintiffs can file certain types of suits against certain defendants, they must give written notice. *See, e.g.*, Tex. Civ. Prac. & Rem. Code §74.051(a) (before filing suit against health-care provider, P must give 60 days' written notice of claim); Tex. Civ. Prac. & Rem. Code §101.101(a) (under Texas Tort Claims Act, P should give written notice to state entity within six months after date of incident giving rise to claim). See "Presuit notice of claim," **O'Connor's Texas Causes of Action**, ch. 8, §6 (2021 ed.) (DTPA); "Presuit notice of claim," **O'Connor's Texas Causes of Action**, ch. 13-C, §6 (2021 ed.) (deceptive insurance practice); "Presuit notice of claim," **O'Connor's Texas Causes of Action**, ch. 20-A, §7.1 (2021 ed.) (medical malpractice); "Presuit notice," **O'Connor's Texas Causes of Action**, ch. 20-C, §6.1.2(1) (2021 ed.) (negligence by managed care entity); "Notice of claim," **O'Connor's Texas Causes of Action**, ch. 24-A, §2.7 (2021 ed.) (suits against the government); "Notice of claim," **O'Connor's Texas Causes of Action**, ch. 25-A, §2.7 (2021 ed.) (Texas Tort Claims Act); "Presuit notice," **O'Connor's Texas Causes of Action**, ch. 31, §6.2 (2021 ed.) (usury); "Presuit notice," **O'Connor's Texas Causes of Action**, ch. 32-I, §6.2.1 (2021 ed.) (RCLA). The time limits for most statutory notices are substantially shorter than limitations periods. In some cases, the suit is barred if the plaintiff does not give the required statutory notice. *See, e.g.*, **Cathey v. Booth**, 900 S.W.2d 339, 340–41 (Tex.1995) (suit under Texas Tort Claims Act barred because Ps did not give written notice and governmental unit did not have actual notice). In other cases, the plaintiff's failure to give notice is merely a reason to abate, not dismiss. *See, e.g.*, Tex. Bus. & Com. Code §17.505(c) to (e) (DTPA claim); **De Checa v. Diagnostic Ctr. Hosp., Inc.**, 852 S.W.2d 935, 939 (Tex.1993) (health-care-liability claim). See **O'Connor's Texas Civil Forms**, FORMS 2A:1 et seq. (2020 ed.).

§2.2 Statutory demand. Under some statutes, before filing suit, a plaintiff must make a written demand stating the extent of the plaintiff's damages, attorney fees, and costs. *E.g.*, Tex. Bus. & Com. Code §17.505(a) (60 days before filing DTPA suit); Tex. Ins. Code §541.154 (60 days before filing suit for deceptive acts). See **O'Connor's Texas Civil Forms**, FORMS 2A:1 et seq. (2020 ed.).

§2.3 Conditions precedent in contracts. Many contracts contain provisions that are conditions precedent to filing suit. Typically, the provisions require the plaintiff to give notice of the claim and notice of its intent to sue. See "Conditions precedent," ch. 2-B, §12; **O'Connor's Texas Civil Forms**, FORM 2B:2 (2020 ed.).

§2.4 Preservation letter for electronic discovery. To ensure that all parties to a potential suit are aware of electronic-discovery intentions, a letter should be sent to each of them outlining the type of information to be preserved. See "Preservation letter," ch. 6-C, §3.2.2(2); **O'Connor's Texas Civil Forms**, FORM 2A:1 (2020 ed.).

§2.5 Consent to sue. In some situations, a party must obtain consent to sue. *See, e.g.*, **State Farm Mut. Auto. Ins. v. Azima**, 896 S.W.2d 177, 177–78 (Tex.1995) (some insurance contracts require consent from insurer before suit can be filed against uninsured motorist).

§3. Filing considerations

§3.1 State vs. federal court. Some cases must be filed in federal court (e.g., patent and copyright), some may be filed only in state court (e.g., suits with no federal question or diversity), and others may be filed in either state or federal court. In

the last situation, the plaintiff should decide where it has an advantage and file in that jurisdiction. If the plaintiff wants to avoid removal to federal court, it should include a local defendant if possible. For information about federal jurisdiction and removal to federal court, see "Choosing the Court—Jurisdiction," **O'Connor's Federal Rules * Civil Trials**, ch. 2-F, §1 et seq. (2021 ed.); "Defendant's Notice of Removal," **O'Connor's Federal Rules * Civil Trials**, ch. 4-A, §1 et seq. (2021 ed.).

§3.2 Administrative procedure. Before filing a claim against a governmental unit, the plaintiff should determine whether it must first submit the dispute to an administrative procedure. *See* **Texas DOT v. Jones Bros. Dirt & Paving Contractors, Inc.**, 92 S.W.3d 477, 484 (Tex.2002); **General Servs. Comm'n v. Little-Tex Insulation Co.**, 39 S.W.3d 591, 597 (Tex.2001). When an agency has exclusive jurisdiction (not just primary jurisdiction) over a dispute, a party must exhaust all administrative remedies before seeking judicial review of the agency's action. **Forest Oil Corp. v. El Rucio Land & Cattle Co.**, 518 S.W.3d 422, 428 (Tex.2017); **Subaru of Am., Inc. v. David McDavid Nissan, Inc.**, 84 S.W.3d 212, 221 (Tex.2002); **Cash Am. Int'l v. Bennett**, 35 S.W.3d 12, 15 (Tex.2000). See "Administrative agency has exclusive jurisdiction," ch. 3-F, §3.6; "Administrative remedies," **O'Connor's Texas Causes of Action**, ch. 24-A, §2.8 (2021 ed.).

§3.3 ADR. Sometimes the plaintiff is required by either statute or contract to submit a dispute to some form of dispute resolution. See "The ADR System," ch. 4-A, §1 et seq.

§3.4 Statutes of limitations. The plaintiff should consider any limitations periods that may affect its planned causes of action. See "Limitations," **O'Connor's Texas Causes of Action**, ch. 52, §1 et seq. (2021 ed.); "Statutes of Limitations," **O'Connor's Texas Civil Practice & Remedies Code Plus**, chart 1 (2020–21 ed.).

§4. Miscellaneous

Before filing suit, the plaintiff should consider other miscellaneous matters.

§4.1 Internet research. Information about a defendant can be found on the Internet. For example, to find information about a corporation (e.g., registered agent, officers, directors), go to the website of the Texas Comptroller of Public Accounts, mycpa.cpa.state.tx.us/coa/search.do, or the Texas Secretary of State, www.sos.state.tx.us. Information about property appraisal can be found on county appraisal district websites. *See, e.g.*, hcad.org (Harris County). Other Internet companies can, for a fee, provide comprehensive information about individuals, including location, family members, nearest neighbors with listed telephone numbers, judgments, and bankruptcies. *See, e.g.*, ussearch.com.

§4.2 Presuit discovery. A plaintiff may secure discovery before filing suit. A plaintiff can file a verified motion and obtain an order authorizing the taking of depositions before suit. Tex. R. Civ. P. 202.1, 202.2. Presuit discovery is useful to preserve evidence when a critical witness is elderly, infirm, or about to leave the jurisdiction. It can also be used to investigate a case before filing suit to avoid penalties under TRCP 13 and CPRC §§9.012 and 10.004 for groundless and frivolous lawsuits. See "Deposition before suit," ch. 6-F, §16; **O'Connor's Texas Civil Forms**, FORMS 6F:8 to 6F:11 (2020 ed.).

§4.3 Appointment of legal representative. When a party is incompetent to represent herself in court (e.g., a minor, an incapacitated person), the attorney should determine whether the party has a legal representative with the capacity to file or defend the suit. See "Minor as P," ch. 2-B, §4.4.2; "Minor as D," ch. 2-B, §4.5.4.

§4.4 Lis pendens notice. In cases involving a direct interest in real property, the plaintiff may file a lis pendens notice. *See* Tex. Prop. Code §12.007; **In re Collins**, 172 S.W.3d 287, 292–93 (Tex.App.—Fort Worth 2005, orig. proceeding). For there to be a direct interest in real property, the action must involve (1) title to the property, (2) the establishment of an interest in the property, or (3) the enforcement of an interest in the property. *See* Tex. Prop. Code §12.007(a); **In re Collins**, 172 S.W.3d at 292–93. The filing of a lis pendens notice puts the public on notice that the property is involved in litigation. **In re Collins**, 172 S.W.3d at 292; **Prappas v. Meyerland Cmty. Imprv. Ass'n**, 795 S.W.2d 794, 795 (Tex.App.—Houston [14th Dist.] 1990, writ denied); *see* Tex. Prop. Code §13.004(a). The notice warns a prospective buyer that any interest the buyer may acquire in the property is subject to the outcome of the litigation. **Gene Hill Equip. Co. v. Merryman**, 771 S.W.2d 207, 209 (Tex.App.—Austin 1989, no writ); *see* **Cherokee Water Co. v. Advance Oil & Gas Co.**, 843 S.W.2d 132, 135 (Tex.App.—Texarkana 1992, writ denied). Although the Property Code requires service, the notice is effective regardless of whether the parties to the proceedings were served. *See* Tex. Prop. Code §§12.007(d), 13.004(a); **In re Collins**, 172 S.W.3d at 293. The notice does not prevent transfer of the property during the litigation. **Cherokee**, 843 S.W.2d at 135.

B. Plaintiff's Original Petition

§1. General

§1.1 Rules. Tex. R. Civ. P. 45 to 61, 78 to 82, 190.

§1.2 Purpose. The plaintiff's petition defines the issues for trial. **Murray v. O&A Express, Inc.**, 630 S.W.2d 633, 636 (Tex.1982). The petition should give fair notice of the facts relied on, enabling the defendant to prepare a defense. **Horizon/CMS Healthcare Corp. v. Auld**, 34 S.W.3d 887, 897 (Tex.2000); **Garvey v. Vawter**, 795 S.W.2d 741, 742 (Tex.1990); **Roark v. Allen**, 633 S.W.2d 804, 810 (Tex.1982); *see* Tex. R. Civ. P. 45(b).

§1.3 Forms. O'Connor's Texas Civil Forms, FORMS 2B:1 et seq. (2020 ed.); **O'Connor's Texas Causes of Action Pleadings** (2020 ed.).

§1.4 Other references. Reese, *Misnomer & Misidentification: Suing the Wrong Defendant*, 60 Tex.B.J. 548 (June 1997); **O'Connor's Federal Rules * Civil Trials** (2021 ed.); **O'Connor's Texas Causes of Action** (2021 ed.); **O'Connor's Texas Civil Practice & Remedies Code Plus** (2020–21 ed.).

§2. Discovery-control plans

In the first numbered paragraph of its petition, the plaintiff must allege whether discovery is intended to be conducted under Level 1, 2, or 3 of TRCP 190. Tex. R. Civ. P. 190.1. See "Discovery-control plans," ch. 6-A, §7. The level designated for the discovery-control plan must relate to the type of suit and the amount of damages. See "Damages," ch. 2-B, §9. The plaintiff must also include the statement about the discovery level in any amended pleading. If the plaintiff does not plead a discovery level as required by TRCP 190.1, the defendant may file special exceptions. *See* Tex. R. Civ. P. 190 cmt. 1 (1999). See "Special Exceptions—Challenging the Pleadings," ch. 3-G, §1 et seq.

2021 Rule Amendments

In 2020, the Supreme Court approved significant amendments to TRCP 190. See Tex.Sup.Ct. Order, Misc. Docket No. 20-9153 (eff. Jan. 1, 2021). The amendments increased the limit on monetary relief sought in cases to which Level 1 discovery applies to $250,000. See Tex. R. Civ. P. 169(a), 190.2(a). The amendments apply to cases filed on or after January 1, 2021, except those filed in justice court. Tex.Sup.Ct. Order, Misc. Docket No. 20-9153 (eff. Jan. 1, 2021). For cases filed before January 1, 2021, the monetary limit for Level 1 discovery in suits for divorce is $50,000, and the monetary limit for the expedited-actions process to apply is $100,000. See Tex. R. Civ. P. 169(a)(1) (pre-1-1-21 version); Tex. R. Civ. P. 190.2(a)(2) (pre-1-1-21 version).

---

§2.1 Level 1. If the plaintiff intends discovery to be conducted under Level 1, its petition should allege one of the following:

1. Suits for monetary damages. "Plaintiff intends that discovery be conducted under Level 1 and affirmatively pleads that this suit is governed by the expedited-actions process in TRCP 169." *See* Tex. R. Civ. P. 169(a), (d)(1), 190.2(a)(1). See "Expedited Actions," ch. 2-C, §1 et seq.; "Level 1," ch. 6-A, §7.2; **O'Connor's Texas Civil Forms**, FORM 2B:1 (2020 ed.).

2. Suits for divorce. "Plaintiff intends that discovery be conducted under Level 1 and affirmatively pleads this is a suit for divorce in which there are no children and the value of the marital estate is more than zero but no more than $250,000." Tex. R. Civ. P. 190.2(a)(2) & cmt. (2021).

§2.2 Level 2. Level 2 is the default discovery level if neither Level 1 nor Level 3 applies. *See* Tex. R. Civ. P. 190.3(a). If the plaintiff intends discovery to be conducted under Level 2, its petition should allege one of the following:

1. Suits in which expedited-actions process does not apply. "Plaintiff intends that discovery be conducted under Level 2." *See* Tex. R. Civ. P. 190.3(a). See "Level 2," ch. 6-A, §7.3; **O'Connor's Texas Civil Forms**, FORM 2B:1 (2020 ed.). The plaintiff can explain why the suit is not an expedited action governed by Level 1 discovery. See "Level 1," ch. 2-B, §2.1.

2. Suits for divorce.

(1) Children. "Plaintiff intends that discovery be conducted under Level 2 and affirmatively pleads this is a suit for divorce in which there are children." Discovery for a divorce involving children cannot be conducted under Level 1. *See* Tex. R. Civ. P. 190.2(a)(2), 190.3(a) & cmt. 2 (1999).

(2) Estate over $250,000. "Plaintiff intends that discovery be conducted under Level 2 and affirmatively pleads this is a suit for divorce in which the value of the marital estate is more than $250,000." *See* Tex. R. Civ. P. 190.2(a)(2), 190.3(a).

(3) Parties' agreement. "Plaintiff intends that discovery be conducted under Level 2 and affirmatively pleads that the parties have agreed Level 2 should apply, even though this is a suit for divorce in which there are no children and the value of the marital estate is more than zero but no more than $250,000." *See* Tex. R. Civ. P. 190.2(a)(2).

§2.3 Level 3. If the plaintiff intends that discovery be conducted under Level 3, its petition should allege the following: "Plaintiff intends that discovery be conducted under Level 3." *See* Tex. R. Civ. P. 190.4(a). A plaintiff should plead Level 3 when a discovery-control plan must be tailored to the circumstances of the specific suit. *Id.* A plaintiff's allegation that the case is to be governed by Level 3 does not make Level 3 applicable; a case can be conducted under Level 3 only by court order. Tex. R. Civ. P. 190 cmt. 1 (1999).

§3. Specific statement of relief

The plaintiff generally must include a specific statement of the relief it seeks after the paragraph in the petition alleging the level for the discovery-control plan. *See* Tex. R. Civ. P. 47(c) & cmt. (2013) (statement of relief ensures that parties will plead into or out of expedited-actions process in TRCP 169). See "Specific statement of relief," ch. 1-B, §3.2.8(2).

§4. Parties

§4.1 General rule.

1. Named party. A person or entity is not a party to a lawsuit unless named as a party. *See* Tex. R. Civ. P. 79; **Mapco, Inc. v. Carter**, 817 S.W.2d 686, 687 (Tex.1991); *see also* **Zanchi v. Lane**, 408 S.W.3d 373, 377 (Tex.2013) (under Texas Medical Liability Act, "party" means person named in filed pleading regardless of whether person has been served with process). See "Parties & Claims," ch. 2-F, §1 et seq.; **O'Connor's Texas Civil Forms**, FORMS 2B:9 to 2B:19 (2020 ed.). A suit may be maintained only by and against parties who have an actual or legal existence. **Bailey v. Vanscot Concrete Co.**, 894 S.W.2d 757, 759 (Tex.1995), *disapproved on other grounds*, **Chilkewitz v. Hyson**, 22 S.W.3d 825 (Tex.1999).

2. Virtual party. Under the virtual-representation doctrine, persons who are not joined by name as parties may still be parties in substance and legal effect. **New Boston Gen. Hosp., Inc. v. Texas Workforce Comm'n**, 47 S.W.3d 34, 39 (Tex.App.—Texarkana 2001, no pet.). To claim virtual representation, an unnamed party must show the following: (1) it is bound by the judgment, (2) its privity of estate, title, or interest is apparent from the record, and (3) there is a common interest between the unnamed party and a named party. **State v. Naylor**, 466 S.W.3d 783, 789 (Tex.2015); **In re Lumbermens Mut. Cas. Co.**, 184 S.W.3d 718, 722 (Tex.2006); **City of San Benito v. Rio Grande Valley Gas Co.**, 109 S.W.3d 750, 755 (Tex.2003); **Motor Vehicle Bd. of Tex. DOT v. El Paso Indep. Auto. Dealers Ass'n**, 1 S.W.3d 108, 110 (Tex.1999). The unnamed party must take some timely action to attain named-party status (e.g., filing a postjudgment motion to intervene in the trial court or court of appeals). **In re Lumbermens**, 184 S.W.3d at 722. An unnamed party cannot appeal unless it is virtually represented. *See* **Naylor**, 466 S.W.3d at 789 (unnamed party may appeal if it satisfies elements of virtual-representation doctrine unless postjudgment intervention would be unjust to existing parties); **Motor Vehicle Bd.**, 1 S.W.3d at 110 (generally, appeal is available only to parties of record); *see, e.g.*, **City of San Benito**, 109 S.W.3d at 754–55 (unnamed class members who would be bound by judgment approving settlement were "parties" for purposes of appeal).

Note

In a recent Supreme Court case, the plaintiff argued that the virtual-representation doctrine is limited to situations where a named party whose interest would otherwise overlap with that of the virtual party has abandoned its position. ***Chambers-Liberty Cty. Nav. Dist. v. State****, 575 S.W.3d 339, 355 (Tex.2019). Although the Court declined to address whether the virtual-representation doctrine applies only when the named party has abandoned its position, the Court stated that the party's request for virtual-representation status would have been stronger if the named party had abandoned its litigation position, leaving the virtual party without appellate review of arguments necessary to preserve its interest in defending the validity of a lease executed between the virtual party and the named party. Id.*

§4.2 Standing & capacity. Before filing suit, the plaintiff should ensure that (1) it has standing and capacity to file the suit and (2) the correct defendant is sued in the correct capacity.

1. Standing. Standing is a constitutional prerequisite to filing suit. **Jefferson Cty. v. Jefferson Cty. Constables Ass'n**, 546 S.W.3d 661, 666 (Tex.2018); **Heckman v. Williamson Cty.**, 369 S.W.3d 137, 150 (Tex.2012); **City of Houston v. Williams**, 353 S.W.3d 128, 145 (Tex.2011). A court does not have jurisdiction over a claim made by a plaintiff who does not have standing to assert it. **Heckman**, 369 S.W.3d at 150; *e.g.*, **State v. Naylor**, 466 S.W.3d 783, 791–92 (Tex.2015) (court of appeals did not have jurisdiction over State's claims because State did not attempt to intervene until after judgment had been rendered and did not satisfy elements of virtual representation; thus, State did not have standing). Because standing is a component of subject-matter jurisdiction, it cannot be waived and can be raised for the first time on appeal. **Teal Trading & Dev., LP v. Champee Springs Ranches Prop. Owners Ass'n**, 593 S.W.3d 324, 331 (Tex.2020); **Meyers v. JDC/Firethorne, Ltd.**, 548 S.W.3d 477, 484 (Tex.2018); **West Orange-Cove Consol. ISD v. Alanis**, 107 S.W.3d 558, 583 (Tex.2003); **Texas Ass'n of Bus. v. Texas Air Control Bd.**, 852 S.W.2d 440, 445 (Tex.1993). A court can—and, if standing is in doubt, must—raise the issue of standing on its own at any time. **Meyers**, 548 S.W.3d at 484; **Finance Comm'n v. Norwood**, 418 S.W.3d 566, 580 (Tex.2013).

Note

When standing is raised for the first time on appeal, the plaintiff generally will not have had the opportunity to replead or develop the record on the jurisdictional issue. ***RSL Funding, LLC v. Pippins****, 499 S.W.3d 423, 429 (Tex.2016). In such a situation, the appellate court will construe the pleadings in favor of the plaintiff and, if necessary, review the record for evidence supporting jurisdiction. Id. If standing has not been shown, the case will be remanded to the trial court and the plaintiff will be given an opportunity to replead and develop the record on the jurisdictional issue, as long as the pleadings and the record do not demonstrate an incurable jurisdictional defect. Id.*

(1) Individual plaintiff's standing. Generally, a court must analyze each individual plaintiff's standing to bring each individual claim she alleges. **Patel v. Texas Dept. of Licensing & Regulation**, 469 S.W.3d 39, 77 (Tex.2015); **Heckman**, 369 S.W.3d at 152; *see* **In re Abbott**, 601 S.W.3d 802, 807 (Tex.2020). But if there are multiple plaintiffs suing individually who are all seeking the same injunctive or declaratory relief, the court is required to analyze standing for only one of the plaintiffs, as long as that plaintiff has standing to pursue as much or more relief than any of the other plaintiffs. **Patel**, 469 S.W.3d at 77; **Heckman**, 369 S.W.3d at 152 n.64.

(a) Requirements—generally. Generally, for a plaintiff to have standing, there must be a concrete injury to the plaintiff and a real controversy between the parties that will be resolved by the court. **Farmers Tex. Cty. Mut. Ins. v. Beasley**, 598 S.W.3d 237, 241 (Tex.2020); **Meyers**, 548 S.W.3d at 484; **Linegar v. DLA Piper LLP (US)**, 495 S.W.3d 276, 279 (Tex.2016); **Morath v. Texas Taxpayer & Student Fairness Coalition**, 490 S.W.3d 826, 847 (Tex.2016); **Heckman**, 369 S.W.3d at 154. That is, there must be an injury that is traceable to the defendant's conduct and is likely to be redressed by the requested relief. **Meyers**, 548 S.W.3d at 485; **Heckman**, 369 S.W.3d at 154.

[1] Injury. The plaintiff must show she is suffering or has suffered an actual or threatened injury. **Farmers Tex. Cty. Mut.**, 598 S.W.3d at 241; **Heckman**, 369 S.W.3d at 155; *see* **Meyers**, 548 S.W.3d at 485. The injury must be

concrete, particularized, and actual or imminent; it cannot be hypothetical. **Teal Trading & Dev.**, 593 S.W.3d at 331; **Linegar**, 495 S.W.3d at 279; **Heckman**, 369 S.W.3d at 155; **DaimlerChrysler Corp. v. Inman**, 252 S.W.3d 299, 304–05 (Tex.2008); *e.g.*, **Garcia v. City of Willis**, 593 S.W.3d 201, 206 (Tex.2019) (P lacked standing to seek prospective relief based on constitutionality and enforcement of city's red-light ordinance because he paid requisite fine and did not argue that he would violate ordinance in future; P did, however, have standing to seek retrospective relief based on argument that fine he already paid was unlawful penalty). The injury must be personal to the plaintiff, rather than be suffered by a third party or the public at large. **Meyers**, 548 S.W.3d at 485; **Linegar**, 495 S.W.3d at 279; **Heckman**, 369 S.W.3d at 155; *see* **Jefferson Cty.**, 546 S.W.3d at 666; **Lance v. Robinson**, 543 S.W.3d 723, 740 (Tex.2018). When a plaintiff challenges a statute, these same general requirements for injury must be met to confer standing; that is, the plaintiff must suffer actual or threatened injury and must contend that the statute unconstitutionally restricts her rights. **Patel**, 469 S.W.3d at 77.

Note

A citizen generally lacks standing to bring a suit challenging the lawfulness of governmental acts. ***Finance Comm'n**, 418 S.W.3d at 580;* ***Andrade v. NAACP**, 345 S.W.3d 1, 7 (Tex.2011); see* ***In re Abbott**, 601 S.W.3d at 808. A plaintiff must be able to show more than a generalized grievance. See* ***NAACP**, 345 S.W.3d at 7–8 (Ps cannot sue solely as citizens who insist that government follow the law). In certain exceptional circumstances, a citizen may be able to show a particularized injury sufficient to confer standing. See, e.g.,* ***Finance Comm'n**, 418 S.W.3d at 581–82 (injury was sufficient to confer standing in homeowners' suit to challenge Finance and Credit Union Commissions' interpretations of home-equity provisions in Texas Constitution);* ***NAACP**, 345 S.W.3d at 10–11 (injury was sufficient to confer standing in voters' equal-protection suit against Secretary of State).*

[2] Traceability. The plaintiff must show the injury can fairly be traced to the defendant's conduct and is not the result of an independent action of a third party. **In re Abbott**, 601 S.W.3d at 808; **Heckman**, 369 S.W.3d at 155; *see* **Meyers**, 548 S.W.3d at 485; **Linegar**, 495 S.W.3d at 279.

[3] Redressability. The plaintiff must show there is a substantial likelihood that the requested relief will remedy the alleged injury. **Meyers**, 548 S.W.3d at 485; **Heckman**, 369 S.W.3d at 155; *see* **Linegar**, 495 S.W.3d at 279. Whether a plaintiff has sufficiently pleaded that the requested relief will remedy the alleged injury can turn on whether the plaintiff has shown that the defendant has authority to respond to any requested relief. *See* **Meyers**, 548 S.W.3d at 487. Thus, the plaintiff must establish redressability for each form of relief sought. **Heckman**, 369 S.W.3d at 155. For example, if a party requests injunctive relief as well as damages, but the injunctive relief could not possibly remedy her injury, she lacks standing to bring the claim for injunctive relief. **Meyers**, 548 S.W.3d at 485; **Heckman**, 369 S.W.3d at 155.

(b) Exceptions.

[1] Statutory standing. When standing is conferred by statute, the plaintiff does not have to show she suffered a particularized injury distinct from the general public. **Andrade v. Venable**, 372 S.W.3d 134, 137 (Tex.2012); *see* **SCI Tex. Funeral Servs. v. Hijar**, 214 S.W.3d 148, 154 (Tex.App.—El Paso 2007, pet. denied) (legislature may by statute exempt Ps from proving "special injury" required for common-law standing); **Everett v. TK-Taito, L.L.C.**, 178 S.W.3d 844, 850–51 (Tex.App.—Fort Worth 2005, no pet.) (statute itself serves as proper framework for standing analysis). Instead, the plaintiff must establish how she has been injured within the parameters of the statutory language. **OAIC Commercial Assets, L.L.C. v. Stonegate Village, L.P.**, 234 S.W.3d 726, 736 (Tex.App.—Dallas 2007, pet. denied); **SCI Tex. Funeral**, 214 S.W.3d at 154; **Everett**, 178 S.W.3d at 851; *see, e.g.*, **In re H.S.**, 550 S.W.3d 151, 155 (Tex.2018) (standing to file SAPCR under Fam. Code §102.003).

[2] Taxpayer standing. When a taxpayer sues to enjoin the illegal expenditure of public funds, she does not have to show she suffered a particularized injury. **Andrade**, 372 S.W.3d at 137; **Williams v. Lara**, 52 S.W.3d 171, 179 (Tex.2001). Instead, to establish standing, the plaintiff must show that (1) she is a taxpayer and (2) public funds are expended on the allegedly illegal activity. **Andrade**, 372 S.W.3d at 137; **Williams**, 52 S.W.3d at 179; *see, e.g.*, **South Tex. Water Auth. v. Lomas**, 223 S.W.3d 304, 307–08 (Tex.2007) (taxpayer lacked standing under taxpayer exception because

funds used did not derive from taxes). The taxpayer must demonstrate that the expenditure is illegal, rather than just unwise or indiscreet. **Lomas**, 223 S.W.3d at 308; *see* **Williams**, 52 S.W.3d at 180. Further, the taxpayer must plead facts showing that the government is actually spending money on the alleged illegal activity, not on a related activity. **Andrade**, 372 S.W.3d at 138; **Williams**, 52 S.W.3d at 181. The expenditure must be significant and measurable, and it must be an added expenditure—not one that would have been made in spite of the alleged illegal activity. **Andrade**, 372 S.W.3d at 138.

(2) Standing to sue on behalf of others.

(a) Shareholder derivative standing.

[1] Generally. A shareholder of a corporation has standing to sue on behalf of the corporation if the shareholder (1) was a shareholder of the corporation at the time of the act or omission complained of or became a shareholder by operation of law originating from a person that was a shareholder at the time of the act or omission complained of and (2) fairly and adequately represents the interests of the corporation in enforcing the corporation's rights. Tex. Bus. Orgs. Code §21.552(a).

Note

In derivative actions instituted on or after September 1, 2019, the shareholder of a converted entity that is a corporation does not have standing to sue on behalf of the corporation for an act or omission that took place as to the converted entity before the date of conversion unless (1) the shareholder was an equity owner of the converting entity at the time of the act or omission and (2) the shareholder fairly and adequately represents the interests of the corporation in enforcing the rights of the corporation. See Tex. Bus. Orgs. Code §21.552(b); HB. 3603, §§1, 31, 32, 86th Leg., R.S., eff. Sept. 1, 2019; see also Tex. Bus. Orgs. Code §1.002(11) (defining "converted entity").

[2] Closely held corporations. A shareholder of a closely held corporation has standing to sue on behalf of the corporation. **Sneed v. Webre**, 465 S.W.3d 169, 181 (Tex.2015); **Ritchie v. Rupe**, 443 S.W.3d 856, 880–81 (Tex.2014); *see also* Tex. Bus. Orgs. Code §21.563(a) (defining "closely held corporation"). Likewise, a shareholder of a closely held parent corporation has standing to bring suit on behalf of a fully owned subsidiary of the corporation. **Sneed**, 465 S.W.3d at 192 & n.14. This is referred to as "double-derivative standing." *See id.* at 192.

Note

For derivative proceedings filed on or after September 1, 2019, the proceeding can be treated as a direct action brought by the shareholder for her own benefit only if justice requires and if Business Organizations Code §§21.552 to 21.560 do not apply because the derivative proceeding is against a director, an officer, or a shareholder of the corporation. See Tex. Bus. Orgs. Code §21.563(b), (c). For derivative proceedings filed before September 1, 2019, the only requirement for treating the derivative proceeding as a direct action brought by the shareholder for her own benefit is that justice requires it. See Tex. Bus. Orgs. Code §21.563(c) (pre-9-1-19 version).

(b) Associational standing. An association has standing to sue on behalf of its constituents if (1) the constituents are considered "members" of the association and (2) the association meets the test for suing on behalf of those members (the "associational-standing test"). *See* **Texas Ass'n of Bus.**, 852 S.W.2d at 447; **City of Westworth Vill. v. Texas Voices for Reason & Justice, Inc.**, 520 S.W.3d 652, 656 (Tex.App.—Fort Worth 2017, pet. granted, judgm't vacated w.r.m.).

[1] Members. An association is considered to have "members" for purposes of associational standing if it is either a traditional voluntary-membership organization or the functional equivalent of one. *E.g.*, **City of Westworth Vill.**, 520 S.W.3d at 657–58 (because nonprofit corporation's certificate of formation indicated it would have no members, corporation was not traditional membership organization). If an association is a traditional voluntary-membership organiza-

tion, then no further inquiry into the issue of membership is necessary. *Id.* If the association is not a traditional voluntary-membership organization, then it can still establish membership for purposes of associational standing by showing it is the functional equivalent of a traditional voluntary-membership organization. *Id.* at 658. To do so, the association must establish the following:

[a] It serves a specialized segment of the community. *Id.* at 659.

[b] Its constituents possess all the "indicia of membership" in an organization. *Id.* What a court may consider as indicia of membership includes whether the constituents have voting rights or other direct influence or control over who the association's directors are and whether the constituents are required to contribute financially to the association. *See id.* at 660–61.

[c] Its fortunes are closely tied to those of its constituency. *Id.* at 659.

[2] Standing to sue on members' behalf. If an association has members, it has standing to sue on their behalf if all the following are true:

[a] The members would otherwise have standing to sue on their own. **Texas Ass'n of Bus.**, 852 S.W.2d at 447; *see* **Lomas**, 223 S.W.3d at 308.

[b] The interests the association seeks to protect are germane to its purpose. **Texas Ass'n of Bus.**, 852 S.W.2d at 447; *see* **Lomas**, 223 S.W.3d at 308.

[c] Neither the nature of the claim nor the relief sought requires the participation of the individual members in the suit. **Texas Ass'n of Bus.**, 852 S.W.2d at 447; *see* **Lomas**, 223 S.W.3d at 308. Determining whether the participation of individual members is required can be difficult. **Big Rock Investors Ass'n v. Big Rock Pet., Inc.**, 409 S.W.3d 845, 849 (Tex.App.—Fort Worth 2013, pet. denied). Typically, individual members must be parties to the suit when (1) claims for damages have not been assigned to an association, (2) the association seeks monetary damages for alleged injuries to individual members, and (3) the damages claimed are not common to the entire membership or shared equally by all members. *Id.* at 850. But if an association seeks equitable relief, the participation of individual members will likely not be required. *See id.* at 850–51 (if association seeks equitable relief, members that were actually injured are presumed to benefit from relief sought; although some individualized evidence from representative injured members is permissible, claims must be resolvable without fact-intensive individual inquiry).

(c) Class-action standing. A named plaintiff in a class action must have individual standing to assert the claim at the time suit is filed. **Heckman**, 369 S.W.3d at 151; *see* **Garcia**, 593 S.W.3d at 208. See "Requirements—generally," ch. 2-B, §4.2.1(1)(a). When multiple plaintiffs asserting multiple claims seek to represent a class, the court must assess standing plaintiff by plaintiff and claim by claim. **Heckman**, 369 S.W.3d at 153. A plaintiff does not need to have standing on each of the class's claims; as long as she has standing as an individual plaintiff on some claim, she has standing to pursue class certification on that claim. *Id.* at 154. Standing is a threshold inquiry that must be determined before the court can consider whether (1) the named plaintiff is a proper class representative and (2) it can certify the putative class. *See id.* at 151; **M.D. Anderson Cancer Ctr. v. Novak**, 52 S.W.3d 704, 710 (Tex.2001).

2. Capacity. A party has capacity to file or defend a suit if it has the legal authority to act, regardless of whether it has a justiciable interest. **Austin Nursing Ctr., Inc. v. Lovato**, 171 S.W.3d 845, 848–49 (Tex.2005); **Coastal Liquids Transp. v. Harris Cty. Appr. Dist.**, 46 S.W.3d 880, 884 (Tex.2001); **Nootsie, Ltd. v. Williamson Cty. Appr. Dist.**, 925 S.W.2d 659, 661 (Tex.1996); *see, e.g.*, **Christi Bay Temple v. GuideOne Specialty Mut. Ins.**, 330 S.W.3d 251, 253 (Tex.2010) (church that had always operated as unincorporated religious association had capacity to bring suit). A court can render judgment for or against a party only in the capacity in which the party sued or was sued. *See, e.g.*, **Werner v. Colwell**, 909 S.W.2d 866, 870 (Tex.1995) (because D was sued only in individual capacity, judgment could not be rendered against her as trustee); **Gracia v. RC Cola-7-Up Bottling Co.**, 667 S.W.2d 517, 519–20 (Tex.1984) (because P brought first suit only as next friend, she was not a party and thus res judicata did not bar second suit by her individually). Unlike standing, an objection to a party's capacity to file or defend a suit can be waived. **Nootsie, Ltd.**, 925 S.W.2d at 662; *see* **Pike v. Texas EMC Mgmt.**, ___ S.W.3d ___, 2020 WL 3405812 (Tex.2020) (No. 17-0557; 6-19-20); **Austin Nursing**, 171 S.W.3d at 849.

3. Distinction between standing & capacity. It is sometimes difficult to distinguish between a party's standing to sue and its capacity to sue. *See* **Austin Nursing**, 171 S.W.3d at 848. A person has standing if she is personally ag-

grieved, regardless of whether she has legal authority to file suit; a person has capacity if she has the authority to file suit, regardless of whether she has a justiciable interest in the suit. *See* **Pike**, __ S.W.3d at __, 2020 WL 3405812; **Austin Nursing**, 171 S.W.3d at 848–49; **Nootsie, Ltd.**, 925 S.W.2d at 661. One way of looking at the distinction between standing and capacity is this: when a party to a suit has an interest in the suit but needs a surrogate to bring or defend the suit, the party does not have capacity. For example, capacity is a problem for a minor who attempts to file suit. *See* **Austin Nursing**, 171 S.W.3d at 849; **Byrd v. Woodruff**, 891 S.W.2d 689, 704 (Tex.App.—Dallas 1994, writ dism'd). Even though the minor has an interest in the litigation, the suit must be filed by a surrogate.

§4.3 Party identification.

1. Full name. The petition should state the full names of the parties and allege the suing party's capacity in one of the early paragraphs under a section titled "Parties." *See* Tex. R. Civ. P. 79; **Austin Nursing Ctr., Inc. v. Lovato**, 171 S.W.3d 845, 852 (Tex.2005).

(1) Misspelled name. Under the rule of *idem sonans* (Latin for "sounding the same"), a misspelled name is sufficient identification if it sounds practically identical to the correct name. *E.g.*, "Mantis" **Mantis v. Resz**, 5 S.W.3d 388, 391 & n.5 (Tex.App.—Fort Worth 1999, pet. denied) (sounds like "Mantas"), *overruled on other grounds*, **Sheldon v. Emergency Med. Consultants, I, P.A.**, 43 S.W.3d 701 (Tex.App.—Fort Worth 2001, no pet.); **Chumney v. Craig**, 805 S.W.2d 864, 866 (Tex.App.—Waco 1991, writ denied) ("Damond" sufficiently similar to "Damon").

(2) Misnomer vs. misidentification.

(a) Misnomer. A misnomer occurs when a plaintiff misnames itself or another party but the correct parties are involved. **Exxon Mobil Corp. v. Rincones**, 520 S.W.3d 572, 594 (Tex.2017); **Reddy Prtshp./5900 N. Freeway, L.P. v. Harris Cty. Appr. Dist.**, 370 S.W.3d 373, 376 (Tex.2012); **In re Greater Houston Orthopaedic Specialists, Inc.**, 295 S.W.3d 323, 325 (Tex.2009). A misnomer can be corrected by amendment even after the statute of limitations expires. **In re Greater Houston**, 295 S.W.3d at 326; **Enserch Corp. v. Parker**, 794 S.W.2d 2, 4–5 (Tex.1990); *see* **Exxon Mobil**, 520 S.W.3d at 594. The amendment containing the correct name relates back to the original filing date. **In re Greater Houston**, 295 S.W.3d at 326; **Pierson v. SMS Fin. II, L.L.C.**, 959 S.W.2d 343, 347 (Tex.App.—Texarkana 1998, no pet.); *see* **Reddy Prtshp.**, 370 S.W.3d at 377. Courts generally allow parties to correct a misnomer as long as it is not misleading. **Reddy Prtshp.**, 370 S.W.3d at 377.

[1] Misnaming D. If a plaintiff sues and serves the correct defendant but misnames the defendant, the error is misnomer. **Chilkewitz v. Hyson**, 22 S.W.3d 825, 828 (Tex.1999); **Charles Brown, L.L.P. v. Lanier Worldwide, Inc.**, 124 S.W.3d 883, 894 (Tex.App.—Houston [14th Dist.] 2004, no pet.); *see, e.g.*, **Barth v. Bank of Am.**, 351 S.W.3d 875, 876–77 (Tex.2011) (misnomer when P sued Bank of America Corporation instead of Bank of America, N.A.; Bank of America, N.A. answered, agreed it had not been misled, and had representative testify that it was the entity involved in the dispute). "John Doe" is not a misnomer for a person or entity. **Riston v. Doe**, 161 S.W.3d 525, 528 (Tex.App.—Houston [14th Dist.] 2004, pet. denied). When the error is misnomer, service is proper on the correct defendant, and the defendant then has the burden of pleading misnomer and seeking an abatement. **Charles Brown, L.L.P.**, 124 S.W.3d at 894. See "Name," ch. 2-I, §2.5.1(1).

[2] Misnaming P. If a plaintiff sues and serves the correct defendant but misnames itself, the error is misnomer. *E.g.*, **Reddy Prtshp.**, 370 S.W.3d at 376–77 (misnomer when P misnamed itself as "Reddy Partnership, ETAL," rather than "Reddy Partnership/5900 North Freeway, L.P."); **Pierson**, 959 S.W.2d at 347 (misnomer when P mistakenly named a related corporate entity rather than itself as P); *cf.* **In re Greater Houston**, 295 S.W.3d at 325 (misnomer when P omitted part of its name in motion for nonsuit).

(b) Misidentification. If the plaintiff sues and serves a party that does not have an interest in the suit, the error is misidentification. *See* **Diamond v. Eighth Ave. 92, L.C.**, 105 S.W.3d 691, 695 (Tex.App.—Fort Worth 2003, no pet.). Misidentification occurs when there are two separate individuals or legal entities with similar names, and the plaintiff sues the wrong one. **Exxon Mobil**, 520 S.W.3d at 594; **Reddy Prtshp.**, 370 S.W.3d at 376; **Chilkewitz**, 22 S.W.3d at 828; *see, e.g.*, **Continental S. Lines, Inc. v. Hilland**, 528 S.W.2d 828, 829–30 (Tex.1975) (P sued Continental Trailways, Inc., instead of Continental Southern Lines, Inc., which did business as "Continental Trailways"); **Cortinas v. Wilson**, 851

S.W.2d 324, 327 (Tex.App.—Dallas 1993, no writ) (P sued and served mother of intended D). A suit mistakenly filed against the wrong defendant imposes no duty on the correct defendant to intervene and point out the plaintiff's error. **Matthews Trucking Co. v. Smith**, 682 S.W.2d 237, 239 (Tex.1984). Misidentification generally does not toll limitations. *See* **Exxon Mobil**, 520 S.W.3d at 594; **Enserch Corp.**, 794 S.W.2d at 5. However, limitations can be tolled in a misidentification case if (1) there were two separate but related entities (not individuals) using a similar name, (2) the correct entity had notice of the suit, and (3) the correct entity was not misled or disadvantaged (prejudiced) by the mistake. **Flour Bluff ISD v. Bass**, 133 S.W.3d 272, 274 (Tex.2004); **Chilkewitz**, 22 S.W.3d at 830; *see* **Diamond**, 105 S.W.3d at 695; **McCord v. Dodds**, 69 S.W.3d 230, 234 (Tex.App.—Corpus Christi 2001, pet. denied); *see also* Tex. R. Civ. P. 28 (permits suits against entities under their trade names). As soon as the plaintiff discovers a misidentification, it should serve the correct defendant with citation, even if the entities are related. *See* **Wilkins v. Methodist Health Care Sys.**, 108 S.W.3d 565, 570 (Tex.App.—Houston [14th Dist.] 2003), *rev'd on other grounds*, 160 S.W.3d 559 (Tex.2005); *see also* Tex. R. Civ. P. 124 (no judgment may be rendered against D without proper service).

Practice Tip

Always file an answer for your client, even when you believe the client is misidentified. First, you could be wrong and the defendant could have been properly identified, which could subject you to a malpractice case. Second, if a default judgment is rendered and execution of judgment is attempted, your client will incur substantial costs in setting aside the judgment. Third, it is easier to dispose of a case by filing an answer and a motion for summary judgment than by challenging a final judgment.

2. Estate. Because the estate of a decedent is not a legal entity, a suit by or against an estate must be brought in the name of its personal representative. **Embrey v. Royal Ins.**, 22 S.W.3d 414, 415 n.2 (Tex.2000); **Price v. Estate of Anderson**, 522 S.W.2d 690, 691 (Tex.1975); *see* **Austin Nursing**, 171 S.W.3d at 849; **Henson v. Estate of Crow**, 734 S.W.2d 648, 649 (Tex.1987). The personal representative is the plaintiff or defendant. If a suit names the estate rather than the personal representative, the trial court may still have jurisdiction if the personal representative is served with citation and participates in the suit. **Miller v. Estate of Self**, 113 S.W.3d 554, 557 (Tex.App.—Texarkana 2003, no pet.); *see* **Embrey**, 22 S.W.3d at 415 n.2 (if unnamed personal representative participated in case, judgment involving estate may be valid).

(1) Personal representative qualified in Texas. A personal representative of an estate must be qualified by a Texas court to bring or defend a suit relating to the estate in a Texas court. **Minga v. Perales**, 603 S.W.2d 240, 242 (Tex.App.—Corpus Christi 1980, no writ); *see, e.g.*, **McAdams v. Capitol Prods.**, 810 S.W.2d 290, 293 (Tex.App.—Fort Worth 1991, writ denied) (administrator appointed by Arkansas court was not qualified to bring suit in Texas until she was appointed by Texas court); *see also* Tex. Est. Code §501.006 (qualification of foreign executor).

(2) Death of plaintiff during suit. When a plaintiff dies after suit is filed, the personal representative of the estate—or the heirs, if there is no personal representative—should file a "suggestion of death" with the court, stating that the person has died and naming the personal representative or heirs of the person's estate. Tex. R. Civ. P. 151. If the cause of action survives the plaintiff's death, the personal representative or heirs may then enter an appearance and prosecute the suit in their own names. Tex. R. Civ. P. 150, 151; *see* **Kenseth v. Dallas Cty.**, 126 S.W.3d 584, 596 (Tex.App.—Dallas 2004, pet. denied). If, within a reasonable time, the personal representative or heirs do not file a suggestion of death and appear to prosecute the suit, the defendant should file a suggestion of death and ask the court clerk to issue and serve a writ of scire facias—similar to a citation—on the personal representative or heirs. Tex. R. Civ. P. 151; **Gracey v. West**, 422 S.W.2d 913, 917 (Tex.1968); *see also* Tex. R. Civ. P. 154 (requisites of scire facias). If the personal representative or heirs do not appear and prosecute the suit by 10:00 a.m. on the first Monday after the expiration of 20 days from the date the scire facias is served, the defendant can ask the court to dismiss the suit for want of prosecution. *See* Tex. R. Civ. P. 99(b), 151, 154; **Gracey**, 422 S.W.2d at 917.

(3) Death of defendant during suit. When a defendant dies after suit is filed, if the cause of action survives the defendant's death, the plaintiff must amend the suit to name the estate's personal representative or, if the representative is unavailable, the estate's heirs. *See* Tex. R. Civ. P. 152; **Rooke v. Jenson**, 838 S.W.2d 229, 230 (Tex.1992); **Price**, 522 S.W.2d at 691. Once the plaintiff has petitioned the court, or if a suggestion of death is filed, the court clerk must issue a writ

of scire facias, requiring the personal representative or heirs to appear and defend the suit. Tex. R. Civ. P. 152. On the return of service, the plaintiff may proceed with the suit against the personal representative or heirs. *Id.*

Note

The filing of a suggestion of death for a defendant does not, on its own, constitute a general appearance in the suit. ***Hegwer v. Edwards****, 527 S.W.3d 337, 340 (Tex.App.—Dallas 2017, no pet.).*

(4) Death or replacement of personal representative. If a personal representative dies, resigns, or is removed while party to a suit, the suit then proceeds in the name of the successor personal representative (or the heirs, if there is no successor). Tex. R. Civ. P. 153. The procedure for substituting the successor personal representative or heirs into the suit is similar to that for the death of a plaintiff or defendant. *Id.*

(5) Real property. In a suit against an estate of a decedent that involves title to real property, the executor or administrator of the estate, if any, and the heirs to the estate must be made party-defendants. Tex. Civ. Prac. & Rem. Code §17.002.

3. Trust. Because a trust is not a legal entity, a suit by or against a trust must be brought in the name of the trustee. **Ray Malooly Trust v. Juhl**, 186 S.W.3d 568, 570 (Tex.2006); *see* **Huie v. DeShazo**, 922 S.W.2d 920, 926 (Tex.1996).

4. Corporation. A corporation may sue or be sued as a corporate entity. In most situations, a shareholder cannot file suit individually for damages owed to the corporation because the shareholder lacks both standing (the shareholder was not personally aggrieved) and capacity (the shareholder is not the right surrogate) to bring suit for damages to the corporation. *See* **Emmett Props., Inc. v. Halliburton Energy Servs.**, 167 S.W.3d 365, 371 (Tex.App.—Houston [14th Dist.] 2005, pet. denied). For the situations where a shareholder may have standing to sue individually, see "Shareholder derivative standing," ch. 2-B, §4.2.1(2)(a). If the corporation is the defendant, individual shareholder liability may be imposed only if the plaintiff is able to show that the corporate form was abused. See "Piercing the Corporate Veil," **O'Connor's Texas Causes of Action**, ch. 38-F, §1 et seq. (2021 ed.).

5. Assumed name. A person or business entity (i.e., a partnership, an unincorporated association, or a private corporation) doing business under an assumed name may sue or be sued in its assumed or common name. Tex. R. Civ. P. 28; **Chilkewitz**, 22 S.W.3d at 828–29; *see* **Christi Bay Temple v. GuideOne Specialty Mut. Ins.**, 330 S.W.3d 251, 253 (Tex.2010). A person or business entity doing business under an assumed name must file an assumed-name certificate. *See* Tex. Bus. & Com. Code §§71.051 to 71.054, 71.101 to 71.104; **Sixth RMA Partners v. Sibley**, 111 S.W.3d 46, 55 (Tex.2003) (under former Bus. & Com. Code §36.11). The court may abate an action until the certificate is filed. **Sibley**, 111 S.W.3d at 55; *see* Tex. Bus. & Com. Code §71.201(a). Before judgment is rendered, the person or entity's correct legal name must be substituted for its assumed name. **Sibley**, 111 S.W.3d at 53; *see* Tex. R. Civ. P. 28. The correct name may be substituted by motion of a party or the court, by an amended pleading, or, if there is no objection, by a supplemental pleading. *See* Tex. R. Civ. P. 28; **Sibley**, 111 S.W.3d at 53. When a person is doing business under an assumed name, a judgment rendered against the unincorporated association is binding on that person. **Holberg & Co. v. Citizens Nat'l Assur. Co.**, 856 S.W.2d 515, 517 (Tex.App.—Houston [1st Dist.] 1993, no writ).

(1) Unincorporated for-profit association. Members of an unincorporated for-profit association are individually liable for the act of an agent or employee of the association if the act is committed within the scope of the agent's or employee's authority. *See* **Hutchins v. Grace Tabernacle United Pentecostal Ch.**, 804 S.W.2d 598, 599 (Tex.App.—Houston [1st Dist.] 1991, no writ).

(2) Unincorporated nonprofit association. Unincorporated nonprofit associations (e.g., churches, property owners' groups) are legal entities liable for their contracts and torts. *See* Tex. Bus. Orgs. Code §252.006(a). The members of an unincorporated nonprofit association are relieved from individual responsibility. Tex. Bus. Orgs. Code §252.006(b).

6. County or city. A suit by or against a county or incorporated city must be in the entity's corporate name. Tex. R. Civ. P. 33.

§4.4 Plaintiff.

1. P's residence. The petition must state the residence of each party, if it is known. Tex. R. Civ. P. 79. The plaintiff should include its county of residence in the petition; a street address is not necessary. *See* **Isaacson v. Anderson**, 982 S.W.2d 39, 40 (Tex.App.—Houston [1st Dist.] 1998, no pet.).

2. Minor as P. In Texas, a minor is an unmarried person under age 18. *See* Tex. Civ. Prac. & Rem. Code §129.001; Tex. Est. Code §22.022. A minor does not have the legal capacity to employ an attorney or anyone else to watch over her interests. **Byrd v. Woodruff**, 891 S.W.2d 689, 704 (Tex.App.—Dallas 1994, writ dism'd). A minor cannot bring a cause of action on her own behalf unless her disability has been removed. **Sax v. Votteler**, 648 S.W.2d 661, 666 (Tex.1983); *see* Tex. Civ. Prac. & Rem. Code §16.001(b) (tolling limitations period while person is under legal disability). However, a lawsuit may be filed on behalf of a minor by (1) the guardian of the minor, (2) the guardian of the estate of the minor, or (3) if the minor has no guardian, by a next friend or by a representative appointed by the court. *See* Tex. Est. Code §1151.104 (guardian of estate); Tex. Fam. Code §102.003(a)(2) (representative authorized by court), §102.003(a)(4) (guardian of person or estate); Tex. R. Civ. P. 44 (next friend); *see also* **In re Bridgestone Americas Tire Opers., LLC**, 459 S.W.3d 565, 570 (Tex.2015) (if minor has guardian who was appointed in another jurisdiction but who lacks authority to sue on minor's behalf in Texas, minor "has no guardian" for purposes of TRCP 44 and may be represented by next friend). A parent is a proper next friend, although any competent adult may act as a next friend. *See* Tex. Fam. Code §102.003(a)(1) (parent may file suit for child).

3. Death actions. The proper plaintiff in a survival action is the legal representative of the decedent's estate. *See* Tex. Civ. Prac. & Rem. Code §71.021. See "Survival," **O'Connor's Texas Causes of Action**, ch. 7-A, §1 et seq. (2021 ed.). The proper plaintiffs in a wrongful-death case are the decedent's spouse, children, and parents. Tex. Civ. Prac. & Rem. Code §71.004(b). See "Wrongful Death," **O'Connor's Texas Causes of Action**, ch. 7-B, §1 et seq. (2021 ed.).

§4.5 Defendant.

The petition (and the citation) should designate as the defendant the person or entity against whom the plaintiff can collect the judgment. See **O'Connor's Texas Civil Forms**, FORMS 2B:10 to 2B:19 (2020 ed.). This can be confusing when the defendant must be sued through a representative. For example, because an estate is not a legal entity, the petition, citation, and judgment should name the representative of the estate as the defendant on behalf of the estate, not the decedent. See "Estate," ch. 2-B, §4.3.2. A judgment is void if the trial court did not have personal jurisdiction over the defendant. **American Gen. Fire & Cas. Co. v. Vandewater**, 907 S.W.2d 491, 492 (Tex.1995).

1. D's address for service. For purposes of service, the petition must state the address, if known, of the defendant or the defendant's agent. *See* Tex. R. Civ. P. 79. See "Address for service," ch. 2-I, §2.5.1(3).

2. D's agent for service. When the defendant is a corporation or another entity served through an agent, the petition must identify the defendant's agent for service and its address. *See* **Harmon & Reid v. Quin**, 258 S.W.2d 441, 442 (Tex.App.—San Antonio 1953, orig. proceeding); *see also* **Interaction, Inc. v. State**, 17 S.W.3d 775, 779–80 (Tex.App.—Austin 2000, pet. denied) (corporation doing business in Texas must maintain current name and address of its registered agent on file with Secretary of State).

3. Agency. If a principal is liable for the acts of its agent, the plaintiff should sue the principal and allege the agency relationship. *See* **Southern Cty. Mut. Ins. v. First Bank & Trust**, 750 S.W.2d 170, 172 (Tex.1988).

4. Minor as D. Generally, a minor who is sued must be personally served with process. **Wright v. Jones**, 52 S.W.2d 247, 251 (Tex.Comm'n App.1932, holding approved); **In re Estate of Bean**, 120 S.W.3d 914, 920 (Tex.App.—Texarkana 2003, pet. denied). This is because the minor lacks the capacity to waive service of process, and no one can waive it for the minor. **Wheeler v. Ahrenbeak**, 54 Tex. 535, 539 (Tex.1881); **Wright**, 52 S.W.2d at 251; **In re M.W.**, 523 S.W.2d 513, 515 (Tex.App.—El Paso 1975, no writ). Once the minor has been served, the court has personal jurisdiction over the minor and can appoint a guardian ad litem to represent the minor's interests. **Sprague v. Haines**, 4 S.W. 371, 373 (Tex.1887); **Wright**, 52 S.W.2d at 251; *see also* Tex. R. Civ. P. 173 (guardian ad litem rule). See "Guardian Ad Litem Under TRCP 173," ch. 1-I, §1 et seq. There are two exceptions to the rule that a minor must be served directly:

(1) Guardian of estate. If, before suit is filed, the minor has a guardian of the estate appointed under the Estates Code, the plaintiff should sue and serve the guardian as defendant instead of the minor ward. *See* Tex. Est. Code §1151.101(a)(4); **Peek v. DeBerry**, 819 S.W.2d 217, 218 (Tex.App.—San Antonio 1991, writ denied).

(2) Minor as claimant. If the minor, even though named as a defendant, is actually a claimant through a parent-next friend, the plaintiff can sue and serve the minor's parent as the minor's next friend. *See, e.g.,* **Vandewater**, 907 S.W.2d at 492 (settlement of minor's personal-injury claim was followed by declaratory-judgment action to determine insurance-policy limits); **Orange Grove ISD v. Rivera**, 679 S.W.2d 482, 483 (Tex.1984) (workers' compensation award to minor was followed by appeal of award to district court).

Note

Neither the rules of civil procedure nor case law specifies a different method of serving process on minors from the method for serving it on adults. Some methods of service, however, may be inappropriate for use with minors, especially infants and young children. See "Methods of service," ch. 2-I, §4. Rather than attempting a "crib drop" to serve an infant by personal delivery, a plaintiff should consider serving the minor by another method, such as by mail, and if necessary, petitioning the court to permit service on the minor through a parent or guardian. See "Substituted service," ch. 2-I, §4.3.

5. Partnership. A petition against a partnership should allege that there is a partnership, state the name of the partnership, list all the partners, and state that the partners are sued as members of the partnership. *See, e.g.,* **Ben Fitzgerald Rlty. Co. v. Muller**, 846 S.W.2d 110, 115 (Tex.App.—Tyler 1993, writ denied) (petition did not allege partnership or that Ds were partners). If the petition names all the partners and citation is served on each partner individually, a judgment may be entered against the partnership and each partner. *See* Tex. Civ. Prac. & Rem. Code §31.003 (court may enter judgment only against partners actually served); *see also* Tex. Bus. Orgs. Code §152.304(a) (all partners are jointly and severally liable for all obligations of partnership unless otherwise agreed by claimant or provided by law). If the petition names only the partnership, a judgment may be entered only against the partnership. *See* Tex. Civ. Prac. & Rem. Code §§17.022, 31.003; **Kao Holdings, L.P. v. Young**, 261 S.W.3d 60, 64 (Tex.2008). See "Partnership," **O'Connor's Texas Causes of Action**, ch. 39-A, §1 et seq. (2021 ed.).

Note

Although a judgment may generally be entered against both the partnership and each partner who is named in the citation and served, there are certain situations where liability against the partners may be limited. See Tex. Bus. Orgs. Code §152.801(a) (partners are generally not liable for obligations of limited-liability partnership), §153.102 (limited partners are generally not liable for obligations of limited partnership).

6. Corporation.

(1) Privileges forfeited. In a suit against a corporation whose right to sue was forfeited for non-payment of taxes, the plaintiff should name the corporation and all the stockholders. *See* **Humble Oil & Ref. Co. v. Blankenburg**, 235 S.W.2d 891, 894 (Tex.1951). If a domestic or foreign corporation does not pay its assessed franchise tax within 45 days after notice of forfeiture is mailed, the comptroller will forfeit its corporate privileges. Tex. Tax Code §171.251(2). Upon forfeiture of corporate privileges, the corporation is denied the right to sue or defend in a Texas court. Tex. Tax Code §171.252(1); **G. Richard Goins Constr. Co. v. S.B. McLaughlin Assocs.**, 930 S.W.2d 124, 127-28 (Tex.App.—Tyler 1996, writ denied); *see also* **Humble Oil**, 235 S.W.2d at 894 (when corporation's charter is forfeited, stockholders may defend actions to protect their property rights); **M&M Constr. Co. v. Great Am. Ins.**, 747 S.W.2d 552, 555 (Tex.App.—Corpus Christi 1988, no writ) (same). For the difference between forfeiture of privilege to sue and forfeiture of corporate charter, see "Stages of Corporate Decay" in **El T. Mexican Rests., Inc. v. Bacon**, 921 S.W.2d 247, 252-53 (Tex.App.—Houston [1st Dist.] 1995, writ denied).

(2) Corporate merger. In a suit against a corporation that was merged with another corporation, the plaintiff should name the surviving corporation and, to be safe, the merged corporation. When a merger takes effect, the separate existence of the corporations ceases, except for any surviving or new domestic corporation. Tex. Bus. Orgs. Code §10.008(a)(1); **Bailey v. Vanscot Concrete Co.**, 894 S.W.2d 757, 759 (Tex.1995), *disapproved on other grounds,* **Chilkewitz v. Hyson**, 22 S.W.3d 825 (Tex.1999). In a merger, the privileges, powers, rights, and duties of the corporation are transferred to the surviving corporation. **Bailey**, 894 S.W.2d at 759.

7. Governmental unit. For the substantive law on suits against the State of Texas or other governmental units, see "The Doctrines of Sovereign & Governmental Immunity," **O'Connor's Texas Causes of Action**, ch. 24-A, §1 et seq. (2021 ed.).

§4.6 Necessary parties. The plaintiff should sue all defendants for all claims necessary to avoid the preclusive effects of res judicata. See "Multiple defendants," ch. 2-F, §4; "Res Judicata & Collateral Estoppel," ch. 9-D, §1 et seq.

§5. Jurisdiction

Unlike the federal rules, the Texas rules of pleading do not require a plaintiff to allege the court has jurisdiction over the case. However, the plaintiff must plead enough facts to affirmatively demonstrate the trial court has jurisdiction over the suit. **TDCJ v. Miller**, 51 S.W.3d 583, 587 (Tex.2001); **Texas Ass'n of Bus. v. Texas Air Control Bd.**, 852 S.W.2d 440, 446 (Tex.1993). See **O'Connor's Texas Civil Forms**, FORM 2B:20 (2020 ed.). To render a binding judgment, the trial court must have (1) jurisdiction over the parties or property, (2) jurisdiction over the subject matter of the suit, (3) jurisdiction to enter the particular judgment, and (4) capacity to act as a court. **State Bar v. Gomez**, 891 S.W.2d 243, 245 (Tex.1994); *see* **State v. Owens**, 907 S.W.2d 484, 485 (Tex.1995). See "Personal jurisdiction," ch. 2-B, §5.1; "Subject-matter jurisdiction," ch. 2-B, §5.2; "Choosing the Court—Jurisdiction," ch. 2-G, §1 et seq.; "Plea to the Jurisdiction—Challenging the Court," ch. 3-F, §1 et seq. Before filing suit, the plaintiff should examine its petition to determine whether it has made sufficient jurisdictional allegations to satisfy due-process requirements under the U.S. Constitution and to require the defendant to answer. *See* **Paramount Pipe & Sup. Co. v. Muhr**, 749 S.W.2d 491, 496 (Tex.1988). Unless the pleadings demonstrate the absence of jurisdiction or the defendant challenges jurisdiction, the court will assume it has jurisdiction over the case. **Peek v. Equipment Serv.**, 779 S.W.2d 802, 804–05 (Tex.1989); see **Beacon Nat'l Ins. v. Montemayor**, 86 S.W.3d 260, 266 (Tex.App.—Austin 2002, no pet.). For jurisdictional challenges the defendant can make, see "Special Appearance—Challenging Personal Jurisdiction," ch. 3-B, §1 et seq.; "Plea to the Jurisdiction—Challenging the Court," ch. 3-F, §1 et seq.

§5.1 Personal jurisdiction. Jurisdiction over the defendant concerns whether the defendant is properly before the court, as authorized by procedural statutes and rules, within the limits of due process. **Perry v. Ponder**, 604 S.W.2d 306, 322 (Tex.App.—Dallas 1980, no writ); *see* Tex. Civ. Prac. & Rem. Code ch. 17. The plaintiff should draft its petition to support a default judgment in case the defendant does not file an answer. See **O'Connor's Texas Civil Forms**, FORM 2B:1 (2020 ed.).

1. Over resident. When the petition states the defendant is a resident of Texas and provides an address in Texas where the defendant can be served, it satisfies the threshold requirement for jurisdiction over a resident defendant.

2. Over nonresident. When a plaintiff files suit against a nonresident defendant, the plaintiff should allege facts that, if true, would make the nonresident defendant subject to the in personam jurisdiction of a Texas court. *See* **Paramount Pipe & Sup. Co. v. Muhr**, 749 S.W.2d 491, 496 (Tex.1988); *see, e.g.*, **Frank A. Smith Sales, Inc. v. Atlantic Aero, Inc.**, 31 S.W.3d 742, 746 (Tex.App.—Corpus Christi 2000, no pet.) (P did not allege facts showing actions in Texas); **Biotrace Int'l v. Wilwerding**, 937 S.W.2d 146, 147 (Tex.App.—Houston [1st Dist.] 1997, no writ) (default judgment reversed because P did not allege any activity in Texas); *see also* **Temperature Sys. v. Bill Pepper, Inc.**, 854 S.W.2d 669, 673 (Tex.App.—Dallas 1993, writ dism'd) (even though P did not allege facts to support general jurisdiction in petition, issue was tried by consent at special-appearance hearing). The plaintiff should allege facts showing that the defendant "purposefully availed" itself of the privilege of conducting activities in Texas. *See* **Kelly v. General Interior Constr., Inc.**, 301 S.W.3d 653, 660–61 (Tex.2010); **Guardian Royal Exch. Assur., Ltd. v. English China Clays, P.L.C.**, 815 S.W.2d 223, 226 (Tex.1991). The petition should state how, when, and where each nonresident defendant made itself subject to the jurisdiction of Texas courts. When the facts for personal jurisdiction fall within one of the provisions of the Texas long-arm statute, the plaintiff should track the language of the section that confers personal jurisdiction; however, the list in CPRC chapter 17 is not exclusive. *See* Tex. Civ. Prac. & Rem. Code ch. 17; **BMC Software Belg., N.V. v. Marchand**, 83 S.W.3d 789, 795 (Tex.2002). See "Long-arm service," ch. 2-I, §5.3; "Special Appearance—Challenging Personal Jurisdiction," ch. 3-B, §1 et seq.

§5.2 Subject-matter jurisdiction. Subject-matter jurisdiction concerns the kinds of controversies a court has the authority to resolve. **Davis v. Zoning Bd.**, 865 S.W.2d 941, 942 (Tex.1993). Subject-matter jurisdiction requires that the

party bringing suit have standing, that there be a live controversy between the parties, and that the case be justiciable. **State Bar v. Gomez**, 891 S.W.2d 243, 245 (Tex.1994). See "Standing," ch. 2-B, §4.2.1. Subject-matter jurisdiction cannot be granted by consent and cannot be waived. **Carroll v. Carroll**, 304 S.W.3d 366, 367 (Tex.2010).

1. Common-law claims. In most civil cases, a trial court's jurisdiction is based on the allegations in the petition about the amount in controversy. **Continental Coffee Prods. v. Cazarez**, 937 S.W.2d 444, 449 (Tex.1996). If jurisdiction depends on the amount in controversy, the plaintiff's petition must allege facts showing the court has jurisdiction. *See* **Richardson v. First Nat'l Life Ins.**, 419 S.W.2d 836, 839 (Tex.1967). This is often accomplished by the statement that the plaintiff pleads for damages within the court's jurisdiction. *See* Tex. R. Civ. P. 47(b). See "Statement of damages," ch. 1-B, §3.2.8(1). Many of the trial courts have overlapping monetary jurisdiction. For example, a suit for $500 can be brought in any trial court. See "Monetary jurisdiction," ch. 2-G, §2.3.

2. Statutory claims.

(1) Not dependent on amount in controversy. If a statute that creates a cause of action identifies the court in which the suit must be brought, the suit must be brought in that court. *See, e.g.*, **In re Burlington N. & Santa Fe Ry.**, 12 S.W.3d 891, 899 (Tex.App.—Houston [14th Dist.] 2000, orig. proceeding) (statute conferred jurisdiction on Fort Bend county court at law for eminent-domain cases). When a statute that creates a claim specifies the court in which the claim must be brought, a plaintiff is not required to allege an amount in controversy. *Id.* In such a case, the plaintiff should plead the statute.

(2) Dependent on amount in controversy. If a statute that creates a cause of action does not identify the court in which the suit must be brought, the court's jurisdiction depends on the amount in controversy. *See* **In re Burlington**, 12 S.W.3d at 899. In such a case, the plaintiff should plead both the statute and that the amount in controversy is within the court's jurisdiction. For example, Gov't Code §§501.007 and 501.008, which authorize a suit by an inmate for lost or damaged property, do not specify the court in which the suit must be filed; thus, the suit may be filed in district, county, or justice court, depending on the amount in controversy.

Note

Occasionally, the statute that creates the cause of action may identify the court in which the suit must be brought but may also specify that the court's jurisdiction depends on the amount in controversy. See, e.g., Tex. Gov't Code §25.1032(c) (condemnation claims in Harris County must be brought in county court at law in Harris County if amount in controversy is within jurisdictional limits provided by Gov't Code §25.0003(c); if amount in controversy exceeds those limits, party may file condemnation petition in district court).

---

§5.3 Nonremovable claim. If, by statute, a case filed in state court is not removable to federal court (e.g., FELA or Jones Act case), the plaintiff should expressly plead that the suit is not removable. If a defendant attempts to remove to federal court a case that is not removable, and the plaintiff's pleadings state that the case is not removable, the defendant could face sanctions in federal court under FRCP 11 or in state court under TRCP 13 and CPRC §§9.012 and 10.004. To prevent a suit from being removed to federal court when filing suit against a non-Texas corporation doing business in Texas, the plaintiff should consider suing one of the corporation's employees who resides in Texas. See "Diversity jurisdiction," **O'Connor's Federal Rules * Civil Trials**, ch. 2-F, §3 (2021 ed.).

§6. Venue

The Texas rules of pleading do not require a plaintiff to plead the basis for venue in the county of suit. *See* **Electronic Data Sys. v. Pioneer Elecs. (USA) Inc.**, 68 S.W.3d 254, 260 (Tex.App.—Fort Worth 2002, no pet.) (dicta). However, the plaintiff's original petition should state enough facts about the cause of action to establish venue in the county where the suit is filed. Pleading specific venue facts in the petition and citing the venue statute may prevent a defendant from pursuing a fruitless motion to transfer venue. *See* Tex. Civ. Prac. & Rem. Code ch. 15; Tex. R. Civ. P. 86, 87. If a particular venue statute is cited in

the petition, it does not limit the plaintiff to that ground. *See* **Electronic Data**, 68 S.W.3d at 260 (dicta). See "Choosing the Court—Venue," ch. 2-H, §1 et seq.; "Motion to Transfer—Challenging Venue," ch. 3-C, §1 et seq.; **O'Connor's Texas Civil Forms**, FORM 2B:21 (2020 ed.).

§7. Pleading a cause of action

A cause of action consists of a plaintiff's primary right and the defendant's act or omission that violated that right. **Jones v. Ray**, 886 S.W.2d 817, 821 (Tex.App.—Houston [1st Dist.] 1994, orig. proceeding). For a cause of action to be adequately pleaded, the trial court must be able to determine with reasonable certainty the elements of the cause of action and the relief sought. **Stoner v. Thompson**, 578 S.W.2d 679, 683 (Tex.1979). For the elements of many causes of action, see **O'Connor's Texas Causes of Action** (2021 ed.).

§7.1 Essential allegations. At a minimum, the pleaded facts must show (1) the plaintiff's right and the defendant's duty, (2) the defendant's breach of its duty, and (3) the plaintiff's injury as a result of the defendant's breach. *See* **Crosstex N. Tex. Pipeline, L.P. v. Gardiner**, 505 S.W.3d 580, 601 (Tex.2016); *see, e.g.*, **Greater Houston Transp. v. Phillips**, 801 S.W.2d 523, 525 (Tex.1990) (elements of common-law negligence).

§7.2 Fair notice of claim. The pleadings must give a short statement of the cause of action sufficient to give the defendant fair and adequate notice of the claim involved and to enable it to prepare a defense. Tex. R. Civ. P. 45(b), 47(a); **Kopplow Dev., Inc. v. City of San Antonio**, 399 S.W.3d 532, 536 (Tex.2013); **Garvey v. Vawter**, 795 S.W.2d 741, 742 (Tex.1990); *see* **First United Pentecostal Ch. v. Parker**, 514 S.W.3d 214, 224–25 (Tex.2017); *see, e.g.*, **DeRoeck v. DHM Ventures, LLC**, 556 S.W.3d 831, 835–36 (Tex.2018) (although claim was not actually named in petition, P pleaded facts sufficient to provide D with fair notice of claim); **Bos v. Smith**, 556 S.W.3d 293, 305–06 (Tex.2018) (live pleading referring to statements D made about P, D's former son-in-law, did not provide D with fair notice that P's children from previous marriage were also seeking to bring defamation claim against D). Texas follows the "fair-notice" standard for pleading, which requires that the opposing party be able to ascertain from the pleading the nature and basic issues of the controversy and what type of evidence might be relevant. **First United Pentecostal Ch.**, 514 S.W.3d at 224; **Low v. Henry**, 221 S.W.3d 609, 612 (Tex.2007); **Horizon/CMS Healthcare Corp. v. Auld**, 34 S.W.3d 887, 896 (Tex.2000). The fair-notice requirement does not require the pleader to plead evidentiary matters with meticulous particularity. **State Fid. Mortg. Co. v. Varner**, 740 S.W.2d 477, 480 (Tex.App.—Houston [1st Dist.] 1987, writ denied); *see* **Low**, 221 S.W.3d at 612 (fair-notice standard is relatively liberal).

Caution

A plaintiff must ensure that its petition contains sufficient allegations to support its cause of action so that the defendant has fair and adequate notice of the claim. See ***Roark v. Allen****, 633 S.W.2d 804, 810 (Tex.1982). Otherwise, the plaintiff may be subject to a motion to dismiss under TRCP 91a for asserting a cause of action that has no basis in law or fact. See "Motion to Dismiss—Baseless Cause of Action," ch. 3-H, §1 et seq.*

1. Alleging facts. The petition must state enough facts to inform the defendant of the nature of the claim. The petition does not need to include the evidence the plaintiff intends to rely on. **Paramount Pipe & Sup. Co. v. Muhr**, 749 S.W.2d 491, 494–95 (Tex.1988). The petition is sufficient if it alleges facts generally. *See* Tex. R. Civ. P. 45(b), 47(a); **Willock v. Bui**, 734 S.W.2d 390, 392 (Tex.App.—Houston [1st Dist.] 1987, no writ). The plaintiff should evaluate its petition to determine whether it would support a default judgment in the event the defendant does not answer. See "Sufficiency of plaintiff's petition," ch. 7-A, §3.2.

Practice Tip

If you are unsure of the exact date when something happened, you should allege that the event occurred "on or about" the date. See ***Winfield v. Renfro****, 821 S.W.2d 640, 646–47 (Tex.App.—Houston [1st Dist.] 1991, writ denied);* ***Fortner v. Merrill Lynch, Pierce, Fenner & Smith, Inc.****, 687 S.W.2d 8, 11 (Tex.App.—Dallas 1984, writ ref'd n.r.e.). The courts have upheld as much as a three-month vari-*

ance in dates between a plaintiff's allegation of when an event occurred and the proof of when it occurred. ***Winfield****, 821 S.W.2d at 647.*

2. Alleging legal theories. The plaintiff must identify the legal basis for the defendant's liability for the injury. A plaintiff has no right to recover against a defendant if the defendant did not breach a legal duty it owed to the plaintiff. *See, e.g.,* **El Chico Corp. v. Poole**, 732 S.W.2d 306, 311 (Tex.1987) (duty in negligence suit). A duty represents a legally enforceable obligation to conform to a particular standard of conduct. *Prosser & Keeton on Torts* §53, at 356 (5th ed. 1984 & Supp.1988).

3. Inferring legal theories from facts. A court may infer a legal theory from the facts presented, but the facts must be expressly stated. *See, e.g.,* **Troutman v. Traeco Bldg. Sys.**, 724 S.W.2d 385, 387 (Tex.1987) (P cited section of DTPA and alleged facts that made obvious its theory that D made a false representation). A court cannot infer facts from legal theories. *See, e.g.,* **White v. Jackson**, 358 S.W.2d 174, 178 (Tex.App.—Waco 1962, writ ref'd n.r.e.) (court would not infer facts to support bare allegation that D was negligent).

§7.3 General vs. specific allegations. A petition may allege a cause of action generally or specifically. Often, plaintiffs will plead a cause of action generally and follow it with specific allegations. A specific allegation controls over a general one. **Bos v. Smith**, 556 S.W.3d 293, 306 (Tex.2018); **Monsanto Co. v. Milam**, 494 S.W.2d 534, 536 (Tex.1973); *e.g.,* **Chuck Wagon Feeding Co. v. Davis**, 768 S.W.2d 360, 364 (Tex.App.—El Paso 1989, writ denied) (specific pleadings based on contract precluded proof on collateral note). If a petition contains specific causes of action, the court will not infer another cause of action unless the petition gives fair notice of that cause of action. *See* **Boyles v. Kerr**, 855 S.W.2d 593, 601 (Tex.1993).

Practice Tip

As a plaintiff, always describe your cause of action with general allegations. If you plead specific acts of breach of duty, you will be limited to proving those specific acts at trial. See ***Mobil Chem. Co. v. Bell****, 517 S.W.2d 245, 254 (Tex.1974). As a defendant, consider filing special exceptions to limit the plaintiff's proof at trial. See "Special Exceptions—Challenging the Pleadings," ch. 3-G, §1 et seq.*

1. Tort cases. Certain theories of tort law must be specifically pleaded.

(1) Negligence per se. Negligence per se is a common-law doctrine in which a duty is imposed based on a standard of conduct created by a penal statute rather than on the "reasonably prudent person" standard used in ordinary-negligence claims. **Smith v. Merritt**, 940 S.W.2d 602, 607 (Tex.1997). See "Negligence Per Se," **O'Connor's Texas Causes of Action**, ch. 21-B, §1 et seq. (2021 ed.); **O'Connor's Texas Causes of Action Pleadings**, FORMS 21B:1 et seq. (2020 ed.). Under the doctrine of negligence per se, the unexcused violation of a statute setting the standard of care constitutes negligence as a matter of law if the statute was designed to prevent injuries to a class of persons that the plaintiff belongs to. **El Chico Corp. v. Poole**, 732 S.W.2d 306, 312 (Tex.1987). A plaintiff relying on negligence per se must specifically plead it and should identify the specific statute that applies. **Daugherty v. Southern Pac. Transp.**, 772 S.W.2d 81, 83 (Tex.1989). If the plaintiff does not specifically plead negligence per se and makes only a general allegation of negligence, the defendant should challenge the pleading by a special exception. *See* **Murray v. O&A Express, Inc.**, 630 S.W.2d 633, 636–37 (Tex.1982).

(2) Res ipsa loquitur. Res ipsa loquitur is a rule of evidence that allows the jury to infer negligence. **Haddock v. Arnspiger**, 793 S.W.2d 948, 950 (Tex.1990). A general allegation of negligence includes an allegation of res ipsa loquitur. *See* **Farm Servs. v. Gonzales**, 756 S.W.2d 747, 751 (Tex.App.—Corpus Christi 1988, writ denied). If a petition alleges specific acts of negligence, it excludes res ipsa loquitur unless the petition (1) gives fair notice it is not relying solely on specific acts or (2) alleges res ipsa loquitur in the alternative. *See* **Mobil Chem.**, 517 S.W.2d at 254. The doctrine of res ipsa loquitur is applicable only when (1) the character of the injury is such that it would not have occurred without negligence and (2) the instrumentality that caused the injury is shown to have been under the sole management and control of the defendant. **Gaulding v. Celotex Corp.**, 772 S.W.2d 66, 68 (Tex.1989); *see* **Haddock**, 793 S.W.2d at 950. See "Res ipsa loquitur," **O'Connor's Texas Causes of Action**, ch. 21-A, §7.6 (2021 ed.).

2. Contract cases. Certain theories of relief must be specifically pleaded in a contract case. See "Contract Actions," **O'Connor's Texas Causes of Action**, ch. 5-A, §1 et seq. (2021 ed.).

(1) Rescission. Rescission must be specifically pleaded, or the trial court cannot grant it. **Argee Corp. v. Solis**, 932 S.W.2d 39, 66 (Tex.App.—Beaumont 1995), *rev'd on other grounds sub nom.* **Green Int'l v. Solis**, 951 S.W.2d 384 (Tex.1997); **Burnett v. James**, 564 S.W.2d 407, 409 (Tex.App.—Dallas 1978, writ dism'd); *see also* **Perez v. Briercroft Serv.**, 809 S.W.2d 216, 218 (Tex.1991) (because D raised rescission as defense, it was not necessary for P to plead it). See "Rescission," **O'Connor's Texas Causes of Action**, ch. 5-B, §3.5.2 (2021 ed.).

(2) Modification. New consideration to support modification of a contract must be specifically pleaded. *See* **Barnhill v. Moore**, 630 S.W.2d 817, 820 (Tex.App.—Corpus Christi 1982, no writ). See "New consideration for modification," **O'Connor's Texas Causes of Action**, ch. 5-A, §2.5.2 (2021 ed.).

(3) Quantum meruit. Quantum meruit is an equitable theory of recovery based on an implied agreement to pay for benefits received. **Heldenfels Bros. v. City of Corpus Christi**, 832 S.W.2d 39, 41 (Tex.1992). Quantum meruit must be specifically pleaded and is often pleaded in the alternative to a contract claim. *See* **Centex Corp. v. Dalton**, 840 S.W.2d 952, 955 & n.7 (Tex.1992). See "Quantum Meruit," **O'Connor's Texas Causes of Action**, ch. 5-C, §1 et seq. (2021 ed.); **O'Connor's Texas Causes of Action Pleadings**, FORMS 5C:1 et seq. (2020 ed.).

§7.4 Notice allegation. Some causes of action require the plaintiff to plead and prove notice. See **O'Connor's Texas Civil Forms**, FORMS 2A:1 et seq. (2020 ed.). For example, a DTPA plaintiff must plead that it gave the defendant notice before filing suit. **Hines v. Hash**, 843 S.W.2d 464, 467 (Tex.1992). See "Statutory notice," ch. 2-A, §2.1.

§7.5 Alternative claims. The plaintiff may plead alternative theories of recovery, even if they are inconsistent. Tex. R. Civ. P. 48; *see* Tex. R. Civ. P. 47. See "Alternative claims or defenses," ch. 1-B, §3.2.9.

§7.6 Joinder of multiple claims. See "Parties & Claims," ch. 2-F, §1 et seq.

§8. Anticipating defenses

Before filing the original petition, the plaintiff should check the affirmative defenses listed in TRCP 94 to see whether any defenses should be pleaded to support its cause of action. See "Affirmative defenses," ch. 3-E, §5. TRCP 94 applies to plaintiffs as well as to defendants. **Simmons v. Compania Financiera Libano, S.A.**, 830 S.W.2d 789, 792 (Tex.App.—Houston [1st Dist.] 1992, writ denied). For example, if the plaintiff must rely on estoppel to establish its cause of action, the plaintiff must plead it. **Nicholson v. Memorial Hosp. Sys.**, 722 S.W.2d 746, 749 (Tex.App.—Houston [14th Dist.] 1986, writ ref'd n.r.e.). If the plaintiff knows the defendant will challenge the suit based on limitations, it should plead the discovery rule in its original petition. **Woods v. William M. Mercer, Inc.**, 769 S.W.2d 515, 518 (Tex.1988). See "Discovery rule," **O'Connor's Texas Causes of Action**, ch. 52, §2.4.1 (2021 ed.).

§9. Damages

The damages alleged in the petition must be within the level designated for the discovery-control plan. See "Discovery-control plans," ch. 2-B, §2. A party's pleadings limit the damages it can recover; the party cannot recover damages it did not request in its pleadings. *See, e.g.,* **Fubar, Inc. v. Turner**, 944 S.W.2d 64, 66 (Tex.App.—Texarkana 1997, no writ) (P, who pleaded for net revenues, waived recovery for gross revenues). Whether the damages are liquidated or unliquidated, the party's pleading must contain a statement that the damages sought are within the jurisdictional limits of the court. *See* Tex. R. Civ. P. 47(b); *see also* **Peek v. Equipment Servs.**, 779 S.W.2d 802, 805 (Tex.1989) (if P does not plead amount in controversy, omission is pleading defect that D can challenge by special exception). For definitions of liquidated and unliquidated damages, see "Hearing on damages," ch. 7-A, §3.13. The pleading must also contain a specific statement of the relief sought. *See* Tex. R. Civ. P. 47(c). For the specific request for relief a party must make in its pleading, see "Specific statement of relief," ch. 1-B, §3.2.8(2).

§9.1 Definition. Damages are defined as compensation in money imposed by law for loss or injury. **Geters v. Eagle Ins.**, 834 S.W.2d 49, 50 (Tex.1992). Damages are also defined as "legal injuries," which are invasions of the plaintiff's legally protected interests. **American Med. Elecs., Inc. v. Korn**, 819 S.W.2d 573, 577 n.3 (Tex.App.—Dallas 1991, writ denied).

§9.2 Types of damages. For a detailed discussion of damages, see "Damages," **O'Connor's Texas Causes of Action**, ch. 41-A, §1 et seq. (2021 ed.).

1. Actual damages. Actual damages are damages recoverable under common law. **Arthur Andersen & Co. v. Perry Equip. Corp.**, 945 S.W.2d 812, 816 (Tex.1997). Actual damages are classified as either direct (general damages) or

consequential (special damages). *Id.*; *see* **J&D Towing, LLC v. American Alt. Ins.**, 478 S.W.3d 649, 655 (Tex.2016). The distinction is important because general damages do not need to be specifically pleaded, but special damages must be pleaded. Tex. R. Civ. P. 56. *See generally* Cagle et al., Comment, *The Classification of General & Special Damages for Pleading Purposes in Texas*, 51 Baylor L.Rev. 629 (1999).

Practice Tip

Rule 56 does not define which damages are special. Because the courts do not always agree on which damages are special (and must be specifically pleaded), the plaintiff should plead all damages, general and special.

(1) General damages. General damages are damages that naturally and necessarily flow from a wrongful act and would normally compensate for the loss, damage, or injury that is presumed to have been foreseen or contemplated by the party as a consequence of its wrongful act. **Arthur Andersen**, 945 S.W.2d at 816; *see* **J&D Towing**, 478 S.W.3d at 655. The plaintiff does not have to specifically plead general damages. **Green v. Allied Interests, Inc.**, 963 S.W.2d 205, 208 (Tex.App.—Austin 1998, pet. denied). The following are examples of general damages: • In a personal-injury suit, damages for pretrial pain and suffering. *See* **Pecos & N.T. Ry. v. Huskey**, 166 S.W. 493, 494 (Tex.App.—Amarillo 1914, writ ref'd). • In a negligent-misrepresentation case, damages for benefit of the bargain and out-of-pocket expenses. **Airborne Freight Corp. v. C.R. Lee Enters.**, 847 S.W.2d 289, 296 (Tex.App.—El Paso 1992, writ denied). • In a breach-of-contract case, the difference between the cost of a substitute product from another company and the original contract price. **Hess Die Mold, Inc. v. American Plasti-Plate Corp.**, 653 S.W.2d 927, 929 (Tex.App.—Tyler 1983, no writ).

(2) Special damages. Special damages, which compensate a party for a loss that arises naturally but not necessarily from the defendant's wrongful act, must be foreseeable and be directly traceable to and result from the defendant's wrongful act. **J&D Towing**, 478 S.W.3d at 655; *see* **Arthur Andersen**, 945 S.W.2d at 816; **Stuart v. Bayless**, 964 S.W.2d 920, 921 (Tex.1998); **Haynes & Boone v. Bowser Bouldin, Ltd.**, 896 S.W.2d 179, 182 (Tex.1995). Because special damages vary from person to person, a party must specifically plead for them. *See* Tex. R. Civ. P. 56; **Harkins v. Crews**, 907 S.W.2d 51, 61 (Tex.App.—San Antonio 1995, writ denied). See chart 41-1, under "Pleading exemplary damages," **O'Connor's Texas Causes of Action**, ch. 41-A, §3.4 (2021 ed.). The following are examples of special damages: • Loss of use of personal property. *See* **J&D Towing**, 478 S.W.3d at 655 (loss-of-use damages are often appropriately characterized as special damages). • Loss of investment. **Haynes & Boone**, 896 S.W.2d at 182. • Loss of family companionship. *See* **Reagan v. Vaughn**, 804 S.W.2d 463, 466 (Tex.1990) (loss of parental companionship); **Sanchez v. Schindler**, 651 S.W.2d 249, 252–53 (Tex.1983) (loss of companionship of child). • Loss of credit reputation. **Mead v. Johnson Grp.**, 615 S.W.2d 685, 688 (Tex.1981); **Boat Superstore, Inc. v. Haner**, 877 S.W.2d 376, 379 (Tex.App.—Houston [1st Dist.] 1994, no writ). • Cost of repairs. *See* **Kissman v. Bendix Home Sys.**, 587 S.W.2d 675, 677 (Tex.1979). • Loss of earning capacity. **Peshak v. Greer**, 13 S.W.3d 421, 427 (Tex.App.—Corpus Christi 2000, no pet.); **Weingartens, Inc. v. Price**, 461 S.W.2d 260, 264 (Tex.App.—Houston [14th Dist.] 1970, writ ref'd n.r.e.). • Lost profits. **Naegeli Transp. v. Gulf Electroquip, Inc.**, 853 S.W.2d 737, 739 (Tex.App.—Houston [14th Dist.] 1993, writ denied).

2. Exemplary damages. Exemplary (or punitive) damages are designed to penalize and deter conduct that is outrageous, malicious, or morally culpable. **Owens-Corning Fiberglas Corp. v. Malone**, 972 S.W.2d 35, 40 (Tex.1998); *see* Tex. Civ. Prac. & Rem. Code §41.001(5); **Horizon Health Corp. v. Acadia Healthcare Co.**, 520 S.W.3d 848, 873 (Tex.2017); **Transportation Ins. v. Moriel**, 879 S.W.2d 10, 16 (Tex.1994). Exemplary damages are not compensatory. Tex. Civ. Prac. & Rem. Code §41.001(5); **Owens-Corning**, 972 S.W.2d at 39–40. Exemplary damages, like special damages, must be specifically pleaded. *See* **Al Parker Buick Co. v. Touchy**, 788 S.W.2d 129, 130 (Tex.App.—Houston [1st Dist.] 1990, orig. proceeding). For a detailed discussion of exemplary damages, see "Exemplary Damages," **O'Connor's Texas Causes of Action**, ch. 42-A, §1 et seq. (2021 ed.).

§9.3 Damages not permitted. Some claims do not entitle the plaintiff to damages, only to equitable relief. *See, e.g.*, **City of Beaumont v. Bouillion**, 896 S.W.2d 143, 149 (Tex.1995) (no monetary damages for violation of Texas Constitution). See "Injunctive Relief," ch. 2-D, §1 et seq.

§10. Court costs & interest

The plaintiff should always plead for court costs and prejudgment and postjudgment interest, even though pleading for them is not always necessary. See "Prejudgment interest," ch. 9-C, §4.5; "Postjudgment interest," ch. 9-C, §4.6; "Interest," **O'Connor's Texas Causes of Action**, ch. 43, §1 et seq. (2021 ed.); **O'Connor's Texas Causes of Action Pleadings**, FORMS 43:1, 44:1 (2020 ed.).

§11. Attorney fees

For information on pleading a claim for attorney fees, see "Attorney fees from adverse party," ch. 1-H, §10; **O'Connor's Texas Causes of Action Pleadings**, FORMS 45B:1 et seq. (2020 ed.). For lists of statutes that authorize attorney fees, see "Statutory Attorney Fees—Private Litigants," **O'Connor's Texas Civil Practice & Remedies Code Plus**, chart 2 (2019-20 ed.); "Statutory Attorney Fees—Attorney General," **O'Connor's Texas Civil Practice & Remedies Code Plus**, chart 3 (2019-20 ed.). For a detailed discussion of attorney fees, see "Attorney Fees," **O'Connor's Texas Causes of Action**, ch. 45-A, §1 et seq. (2021 ed.).

§12. Conditions precedent

In its petition, the plaintiff should always allege that "all conditions precedent have been performed or have occurred." Tex. R. Civ. P. 54. A condition precedent is an event that must occur or be performed before a plaintiff can sue to enforce an obligation. **Solar Applications Eng'g v. T.A. Oper. Corp.**, 327 S.W.3d 104, 108 (Tex.2010); **Centex Corp. v. Dalton**, 840 S.W.2d 952, 956 (Tex.1992). A plaintiff who makes the TRCP 54 allegation is not required to prove that it complied with any conditions precedent unless the defendant specifically denies them. Tex. R. Civ. P. 54; **Associated Indem. Corp. v. CAT Contracting, Inc.**, 964 S.W.2d 276, 283 n.6 (Tex.1998); *see* **Community Bank & Trust v. Fleck**, 107 S.W.3d 541, 542 (Tex.2002); **Greathouse v. Charter Nat'l Bank-Sw.**, 851 S.W.2d 173, 176–77 (Tex.1992) (TRCP 54 allegation prevails against general denial); *see, e.g.*, **Knupp v. Miller**, 858 S.W.2d 945, 955 (Tex.App.—Beaumont 1993, writ denied) (in suit that provided for statutory attorney fees, unchallenged TRCP 54 allegation was sufficient to support attorney fees). See "Denial of conditions precedent," ch. 3-E, §6.1. The TRCP 54 allegation shifts the burden of pleading (not of proof) to the defendant to specifically deny those conditions precedent that have not occurred. **Trevino v. Allstate Ins.**, 651 S.W.2d 8, 11 (Tex.App.—Dallas 1983, writ ref'd n.r.e.). If a plaintiff does not include the TRCP 54 allegation in its petition and the defendant makes a general denial, the plaintiff will need to prove the performance of all conditions precedent. *See* **Grimm v. Grimm**, 864 S.W.2d 160, 162 (Tex.App.—Houston [14th Dist.] 1993, no writ).

Practice Tip

The TRCP 54 allegation should be pleaded generally and should not identify any specific claim. When pleaded specifically for a claim, the allegation is limited to that claim. See ***Cook Composites, Inc. v. Westlake Styrene Corp.****, 15 S.W.3d 124, 138 (Tex.App.—Houston [14th Dist.] 2000, pet. dism'd).*

§13. Jury demand

If the plaintiff wants a jury trial, it should include a request for a jury in its petition. For the request to be effective, the plaintiff must pay the appropriate jury fees. See "Request for Jury Trial," ch. 5-B, §1 et seq.

§14. Request for disclosure

For cases filed before January 1, 2021, a request for disclosure could be included in the plaintiff's original petition. *See* Tex. R. Civ. P. 194.1 (pre-1-1-21 version). For cases filed on or after January 1, 2021, a party is generally required to disclose certain information automatically without waiting for a discovery request from the other party. *See* Tex. R. Civ. P. 194.1(a); Tex.Sup.Ct. Order, Misc. Docket No. 20-9153 (eff. Jan. 1, 2021). See "Required disclosures—Cases filed on or after 1-1-21," ch. 6-E, §3. Thus, for cases filed on or after January 1, 2021, the original petition should not include a disclosure request.

§15. Prayer

The plaintiff's petition should include a demand for judgment for all the relief sought. Tex. R. Civ. P. 47(d).

§15.1 General prayer. A general prayer for relief requests "all other relief to which plaintiff is entitled." *See* **Kelso v. Hanson**, 388 S.W.2d 396, 399 (Tex.1965); **City of McKinney v. Hank's Rest. Grp.**, 412 S.W.3d 102, 118 (Tex.App.—Dallas

2013, no pet.). A general prayer will support any relief raised by the evidence and consistent with the claims asserted in the petition. **Nelson v. Najm**, 127 S.W.3d 170, 177 (Tex.App.—Houston [1st Dist.] 2003, pet. denied); **Khalaf v. Williams**, 814 S.W.2d 854, 858 (Tex.App.—Houston [1st Dist.] 1991, no writ); *see* **Kissman v. Bendix Home Sys.**, 587 S.W.2d 675, 677 (Tex.1979); **Stoner v. Thompson**, 578 S.W.2d 679, 683–84 (Tex.1979). A general prayer for relief for "other sums as shall be found due" or for "other and further relief to which plaintiff may be entitled at law or in equity" does not enlarge a specific request for relief or permit relief for claims not alleged in the pleadings. *See* **Richardson v. First Nat'l Life Ins.**, 419 S.W.2d 836, 837, 839 (Tex.1967); **Victory Energy Corp. v. Oz Gas Corp.**, 461 S.W.3d 159, 176 (Tex.App.—El Paso 2014, pet. denied); **Moore v. Collins**, 897 S.W.2d 496, 500 (Tex.App.—Houston [1st Dist.] 1995, no writ).

§15.2 Special prayer. If a party wants relief other than damages (e.g., injunctive relief, rescission of a contract, attorney fees, court costs, appointment of a receiver), the party should specifically plead for it in the prayer. *See* **Gause v. Gause**, 430 S.W.2d 409, 413 (Tex.App.—Austin 1968, no writ); *see, e.g.*, **City of McKinney v. Hank's Rest. Grp.**, 412 S.W.3d 102, 118 (Tex.App.—Dallas 2013, no pet.) (attorney fees).

§16. Signature

The attorney (or party if pro se) must sign the pleading, which must contain an address, telephone number, e-mail address, and, if available, a fax number. Tex. R. Civ. P. 57; *see* Tex. R. Civ. P. 45. See "Signature block," ch. 1-B, §3.2.12. Pleadings that are e-filed must contain an electronic signature. *See* Tex. R. Civ. P. 21(f)(7).

§17. Exhibits

If exhibits are attached to the petition, the petition must identify them and incorporate them by reference. *See* Tex. R. Civ. P. 59. TRCP 59 lists the types of documents that may be properly attached as exhibits to pleadings. See "Exhibits," ch. 1-B, §3.2.14.

§18. Verification & affidavits

Some pleadings must be verified, and some require affidavits. Verification may be necessary to assert certain defenses when the issue is not apparent on the face of the plaintiff's pleadings. If a plaintiff does not verify a pleading that requires it, the trial court should permit an amendment to add the verification. *See* **Chapin & Chapin, Inc. v. Texas Sand & Gravel Co.**, 844 S.W.2d 664, 665 (Tex.1992). See "Verification," ch. 1-B, §3.2.15; "Affidavits," ch. 1-B, §3.2.16; "Verified pleas," ch. 3-E, §4; **O'Connor's Texas Civil Forms**, FORMS 1B:7 to 1B:8 (2020 ed.). For the requirements for using an unsworn declaration in place of a verification or an affidavit, see "Unsworn declaration," ch. 1-B, §3.2.17.

§19. Responding to defendant's pleadings

Once the defendant files its answer, the plaintiff should review the answer to determine whether it needs to file any additional pleadings.

§19.1 Defense to defense. The plaintiff should determine whether it needs to plead a defense to the defendant's defense. For example, to avoid the defendant's defense of statute of limitations, a plaintiff must plead the discovery rule. **Woods v. William M. Mercer, Inc.**, 769 S.W.2d 515, 518 (Tex.1988). The plaintiff is not required to plead affirmative defenses when a defendant files only a general denial. *See* **Berry v. Berry**, 786 S.W.2d 672, 673 n.3 (Tex.1990).

§19.2 Response to counterclaim. The plaintiff is not required to file a general denial in response to a counterclaim. *See* Tex. R. Civ. P. 92. But the plaintiff should file an answer in some situations. First, if the plaintiff intends to assert an affirmative defense (TRCP 94) or a defensive theory that must be verified (TRCP 93), it must file an answer. *See* **Greater Fort Worth & Tarrant Cty. Cmty. Action Agency v. Mims**, 627 S.W.2d 149, 152 (Tex.1982); **$191,452 v. State**, 827 S.W.2d 430, 432 (Tex.App.—Corpus Christi 1992, writ denied). See "Verified pleas," ch. 3-E, §4; "Affirmative defenses," ch. 3-E, §5. Second, the plaintiff must assert all of its compulsory counterclaims to the defendant's counterclaim, or they will be barred in a later suit. The compulsory-counterclaim rule applies to a party against whom a counterclaim has been filed. See "Compulsory joinder of claims," ch. 2-F, §6.

§19.3 Special exceptions. The plaintiff must obey the same rules for special exceptions in objecting to pleading defects in the defendant's answer that the defendant follows in objecting to the plaintiff's petition. *See, e.g.*, **Shoemake v.**

Fogel, Ltd., 826 S.W.2d 933, 937 (Tex.1992) (counter-P failed to specially except to affirmative defense that counter-D was not liable "as a matter of law," and thus waived objection to defense of parental immunity). See "Special Exceptions—Challenging the Pleadings," ch. 3-G, §1 et seq.

C. Expedited Actions

§1. General

§1.1 Rules. Tex. R. Civ. P. 169. See Tex. R. Civ. P. 47 (pleading specific damages), Tex. R. Civ. P. 190.2 (discovery limitations).

§1.2 Purpose. TRCP 169, the expedited-actions rule, provides a procedure for the prompt, efficient, and cost-effective resolution of certain civil actions. *See* Tex. R. Civ. P. 169 cmt. (2021); Tex.Sup.Ct. Order, Misc. Docket No. 20-9153 (eff. Jan. 1, 2021). TRCP 169 limits discovery, mandates a quick trial setting, provides for an abbreviated trial, and restricts the court's ability to require alternative dispute resolution (ADR).

§1.3 Forms. O'Connor's Texas Civil Forms, FORMS 2C:1 et seq. (2020 ed.).

§2. Applicability

Parties must plead into or out of the expedited-actions process. *See* Tex. R. Civ. P. 47(c) & cmt. (2013). See "Specific statement of relief," ch. 1-B, §3.2.8(2). The expedited-actions process applies to actions filed in district courts, county courts at law, and statutory probate courts. Tex. Gov't Code §22.004(h); *see* Tex. R. Civ. P. 169 cmt. (2021) (TRCP 169's application is not limited to county courts at law).

2021 Rule Amendments

In 2020, the Supreme Court approved significant amendments to TRCP 169 that broaden the applicability of the expedited-actions process. See Tex.Sup.Ct. Order, Misc. Docket No. 20-9153 (eff. Jan. 1, 2021). The amendments apply to cases filed on or after January 1, 2021, except those filed in justice court. Id.

---

§2.1 Claimant's pleadings. The following rules apply to suits filed by all claimants other than counterclaimants. *See* Tex. R. Civ. P. 169(a), (c)(1)(B).

1. TRCP 169 mandatory. The expedited-actions process is mandatory for any suit filed by a claimant that qualifies as an expedited action. Tex. R. Civ. P. 169 cmt. 2 (2013). The requirements for a suit to qualify as an expedited action depend on when the suit was filed.

(1) Before 1-1-21. For cases filed before January 1, 2021, TRCP 169 applies if both of the following are true: (1) only monetary relief is sought and (2) the aggregate of the relief requested by all claimants, other than counterclaimants, is $100,000 or less. Tex. R. Civ. P. 169(a)(1) (pre-1-1-21 version). This aggregate includes damages of any kind, penalties, costs, expenses, prejudgment interest, and attorney fees. *Id.* It does not include postjudgment interest. *See* Tex. R. Civ. P. 169(a)(1), (b) (pre-1-1-21 version).

(2) On or after 1-1-21. For cases filed on or after January 1, 2021, TRCP 169 applies if both of the following are true: (1) only monetary relief is sought and (2) the aggregate of the relief requested by all claimants, other than counterclaimants, is $250,000 or less. Tex. R. Civ. P. 169(a). This aggregate does not include interest, statutory or punitive damages and penalties, or attorney fees and costs. *Id.*

2. TRCP 169 inapplicable. TRCP 169 does not apply to the following:

(1) A claim for nonmonetary relief. *See* Tex. R. Civ. P. 169(a) (rule applies when claimant seeks only monetary relief).

(2) A suit that is exempt from TRCP 169's application by statute. Tex. R. Civ. P. 169 cmt. (2021); *see, e.g.*, Tex. Est. Code §53.107 (TRCP 169 does not apply to probate proceedings), Tex. Est. Code §1053.105 (TRCP 169 does not apply to guardianship proceedings).

2021 Rule Amendments

Before the 2021 amendments to TRCP 169, claims governed by the Family Code, the Property Code, the Tax Code, and CPRC chapter 74 (the Medical Liability Act) were specifically exempt from the expedited-actions process. See Tex. R. Civ. P. 169(a)(2) (pre-1-1-21 version). For cases filed on or after January 1, 2021, the expedited-actions process can apply to these claims if they meet the requirements of TRCP 169 and are not otherwise exempt. See Tex. R. Civ. P. 169 & cmt (2021).

(3) A suit brought in justice court. *See* Tex.Sup.Ct. Order, Misc. Docket No. 20-9153 (eff. Jan. 1, 2021); Tex.Sup.Ct. Order, Misc. Docket No. 13-9022 (eff. Mar. 1, 2013).

§2.2 Counterclaimant's pleadings. A counterclaimant can include in its pleadings demands for monetary relief in excess of $250,000 and nonmonetary relief. *See* Tex. R. Civ. P. 169(a), (c)(1)(B). See "TRCP 169 mandatory," ch. 2-C, §2.1.1. To determine whether the expedited-actions process applies, the court will look only at the claimant's pleadings; any pleadings filed by counterclaimants do not affect the applicability of TRCP 169.

§3. Removal from TRCP 169 procedure

§3.1 Removal by motion. A court must remove a suit from the expedited-actions process if a party files a motion to remove and makes a showing of good cause. Tex. R. Civ. P. 169(c)(1)(A). See **O'Connor's Texas Civil Forms**, FORM 2C:1 (2020 ed.).

1. Deadline for motion. TRCP 169 does not specify a deadline to file a motion to remove. A party should, however, file the motion as soon as possible.

2. Factors. To show there is good cause to remove the suit from the expedited-actions process, the movant should address the following factors:

(1) Whether the total damages sought by multiple claimants against the same defendant exceed the monetary relief allowed under TRCP 169(a). Tex. R. Civ. P. 169 cmt. 3 (2013); *see* Tex. R. Civ. P. 169(a). See "TRCP 169 mandatory," ch. 2-C, §2.1.1.

(2) Whether a defendant has in good faith filed a compulsory counterclaim that seeks relief other than what is allowed in TRCP 169(a). Tex. R. Civ. P. 169 cmt. 3 (2013); *see* Tex. R. Civ. P. 169(a). See "Compulsory-counterclaim rule," ch. 2-F, §6.1.

(3) The number of parties and witnesses. Tex. R. Civ. P. 169 cmt. 3 (2013).

(4) The complexity of the legal and factual issues. *Id.*

(5) Whether an interpreter is necessary. *Id.*

§3.2 Removal by pleading. A court must remove a suit from the expedited-actions process if any claimant, other than a counterclaimant, files a pleading or an amended or supplemental pleading that seeks relief other than the monetary relief allowed under TRCP 169(a). Tex. R. Civ. P. 169(c)(1)(B). See "TRCP 169 mandatory," ch. 2-C, §2.1.1. A claimant can file a pleading, amended pleading, or supplemental pleading that removes a suit from the expedited-actions process without leave of court if the claimant files the pleading no later than 30 days after the discovery period is closed or at least 30 days before the date set for trial, whichever is earlier. Tex. R. Civ. P. 169(c)(2). If leave to amend is required, the claimant must show that there is good cause for filing the pleading and that it outweighs any prejudice to the opposing party. *Id.*

§3.3 Effect of removal. If the suit is removed from the expedited-actions process, the court must reopen discovery under TRCP 190.2(c). Tex. R. Civ. P. 169(c)(3). See "Period reopens," ch. 6-A, §8.1.1(2). Thus, the Level 1 discovery-control plan would no longer apply, and the suit would then be governed by a Level 2 or 3 discovery-control plan. *See* Tex. R. Civ. P. 190.2(a)(1), (c).

§4. Discovery

§4.1 Level 1. Discovery in an expedited action is governed by the Level 1 discovery-control plan. *See* Tex. R. Civ. P. 169(d)(1), 190.2(a)(1). See "Level 1," ch. 6-A, §7.2.

§4.2 Discovery period. The length of the discovery period in Level 1 depends on when the case was filed. If the suit is removed from the expedited-actions process, the court must reopen discovery under TRCP 190.2(c). Tex. R. Civ. P. 169(c)(3). See "Effect of removal," ch. 2-C, §3.3.

2021 Rule Amendments

In 2020, the Supreme Court approved significant amendments to TRCP 190 and 194. See Tex.Sup.Ct. Order, Misc. Docket No. 20-9153 (eff. Jan. 1, 2021). Under the amendments, a party is generally required to make certain initial disclosures without waiting for a discovery request from the other party. See Tex. R. Civ. P. 194.1(a), 194.2(b). See "Required disclosures—Cases filed on or after 1-1-21," ch. 6-E, §3. The beginning and end of the discovery period in Level 1 are now tied to the due date of the first initial disclosures. See Tex. R. Civ. P. 190.2(b)(1). The amendments apply to cases filed on or after January 1, 2021, except those filed in justice court. Tex.Sup.Ct. Order, Misc. Docket No. 20-9153 (eff. Jan. 1, 2021).

1. Before 1-1-21. For cases filed before January 1, 2021, the discovery period begins when suit is filed and ends 180 days after the first discovery request is served. Tex. R. Civ. P. 190.2(b)(1) (pre-1-1-21 version).

2. On or after 1-1-21. For cases filed on or after January 1, 2021, the discovery period begins when the first initial disclosures under TRCP 194 are due and continues for 180 days. Tex. R. Civ. P. 190.2(b)(1). The first initial disclosures are generally due within 30 days after the filing of the first answer or general appearance. Tex. R. Civ. P. 194.2(a). See "Deadline," ch. 6-E, §3.3.1.

§4.3 Types of discovery. Under the Level 1 discovery-control plan, limitations apply to certain types of discovery.

2021 Rule Amendments

In 2020, the Supreme Court approved significant amendments to TRCP 190, 194, and 195. See Tex.Sup.Ct. Order, Misc. Docket No. 20-9153 (eff. Jan. 1, 2021). The amendments increased the number of hours a party has to conduct depositions under the Level 1 discovery-control plan and changed the procedure for requesting disclosures. See id. The amendments apply to cases filed on or after January 1, 2021, except those filed in justice court. Id.

1. Oral depositions. Discovery can be conducted through oral depositions; however, the amount of time allowed for depositions depends on when the case was filed. The court can modify the hours so that no party is given an unfair advantage. Tex. R. Civ. P. 190.2(b)(2). See "Oral depositions," ch. 6-A, §7.2.2(2).

(1) Before 1-1-21. For cases filed before January 1, 2021, each party may take no more than six hours to examine and cross-examine all witnesses in oral depositions. Tex. R. Civ. P. 190.2(b)(2) (pre-1-1-21 version). The parties may agree to extend this time, but they cannot extend it beyond ten hours without a court order. *Id.*

(2) On or after 1-1-21. For cases filed on or after January 1, 2021, each party may take no more than 20 hours to examine and cross-examine all witnesses in oral depositions. Tex. R. Civ. P. 190.2(b)(2).

2. Interrogatories. Discovery can be conducted through interrogatories; however, parties are limited to serving 15 questions. Tex. R. Civ. P. 190.2(b)(3). See "Interrogatories," ch. 6-A, §7.2.2(3)(a).

3. Requests for production. Discovery can be conducted through requests for production; however, parties are limited to serving 15 requests. Tex. R. Civ. P. 190.2(b)(4). See "Requests for production," ch. 6-A, §7.2.2(3)(b).

4. Requests for admissions. Discovery can be conducted through requests for admissions; however, parties are limited to serving 15 requests. Tex. R. Civ. P. 190.2(b)(5). See "Requests for admissions," ch. 6-A, §7.2.2(3)(c).

5. Disclosures. Whether discovery can be conducted through requests for disclosure depends on when the case was filed.

(1) Before 1-1-21. For cases filed before January 1, 2021, requests for disclosure can be used to require the production of all documents, electronic information, and tangible items that the other party may use to support its claims or defenses. *See* Tex. R. Civ. P. 190.2(b)(6) (pre-1-1-21 version). See "Disclosures," ch. 6-A, §7.2.2(3)(d).

(2) On or after 1-1-21. For cases filed on or after January 1, 2021, parties are required to disclose certain information and materials described in TRCP 194 and 195. *See* Tex. R. Civ. P. 194.1(a), 194.3, 190 cmt. (2021); Tex.Sup.Ct. Order, Misc. Docket No. 20-9153 (eff. Jan. 1, 2021). The party seeking discovery does not have to serve a request for disclosure to trigger the opposing party's duty to produce the information. *See* Tex. R. Civ. P. 194.1(a). See "Required disclosures—Cases filed on or after 1-1-21," ch. 6-E, §3.

§4.4 Additional discovery. Expedited actions are not subject to the mandatory additional-discovery provisions of TRCP 190.5, but the court may allow additional discovery if the conditions of TRCP 190.5(a) are met. Tex. R. Civ. P. 190 cmt. (2013). See "Modification of discovery periods," ch. 6-A, §8.2.

§5. Challenging expert testimony

§5.1 Pretrial challenges.

1. Nonsponsoring party. The nonsponsoring party cannot challenge the testimony of the other party's expert before trial other than by making an objection to summary-judgment evidence. *See* Tex. R. Civ. P. 169(d)(5). TRCP 169(d)(5) does not, however, prevent the nonsponsoring party from filing a motion to strike an expert for an untimely designation. See "Deadlines for securing discovery from experts," ch. 6-D, §6.

2. Sponsoring party. The party sponsoring the expert can request a pretrial **Daubert-Robinson** hearing on the expert's admissibility. *See* Tex. R. Civ. P. 169(d)(5). See "Motion to Exclude Expert," ch. 5-N, §1 et seq.

§5.2 Summary judgment & trial challenges. Any party can challenge the admissibility of expert testimony as an objection to summary-judgment evidence under TRCP 166a or during the trial on the merits. *See* Tex. R. Civ. P. 169(d)(5). See "Motion to Exclude Expert," ch. 5-N, §1 et seq.; "Objections to summary-judgment evidence," ch. 7-B, §10.

§6. Time limits for trial

§6.1 Trial date.

1. Request for trial setting. The court must, on any party's request, set a trial date that is within 90 days after the discovery period ends. Tex. R. Civ. P. 169(d)(2); *see also* Tex. R. Civ. P. 190.2(b)(1) (length of Level 1 discovery period is 180 days). See "Level 1," ch. 6-A, §8.1.1. Thus, the latest the case can be set for trial is 270 days after the discovery period begins. *See* Tex. R. Civ. P. 169(d)(2), 190.2(b)(1).

Caution

A party should request a trial setting no later than 45 days after the discovery period ends. Because TRCP 245 requires that the parties have 45 days' notice of the first trial setting, any request made more than 45 days after the discovery period ends would cause the trial setting to exceed the 90-day limit under TRCP 169(d)(2). See "Trial setting," ch. 5-A, §3.3.

---

2. Request for continuance. The court may continue the case twice for no more than a total of 60 days. Tex. R. Civ. P. 169(d)(2).

§6.2 Time limits during trial.

1. Generally. Each side is allowed no more than eight hours to complete jury selection, opening statements, presentation of evidence, examination and cross-examination of witnesses, and closing arguments. Tex. R. Civ. P. 169(d)(3). The term "side" has the same meaning as that used in TRCP 233. Tex. R. Civ. P. 169(d)(3)(A). See "Side," ch. 6-A, §2.7; "Are parties properly aligned?," ch. 8-A, §7.2.2(1). Time spent on objections, bench conferences, bills of exception, and challenges for cause to a juror under TRCP 228 are not included in the time limit. Tex. R. Civ. P. 169(d)(3)(B).

2. **Motion for extension.** On a motion and showing of good cause by any party, the court may extend the time limit to no more than 12 hours per side. Tex. R. Civ. P. 169(d)(3). See **O'Connor's Texas Civil Forms**, FORM 2C:2 (2020 ed.).

(1) **Deadline.** TRCP 169 does not specify a deadline to file a motion to extend the time limit. A party should, however, file the motion as soon as possible.

(2) **Factors.** To show good cause, the movant should address some of the factors the trial court considers when determining whether there is good cause to remove a suit from the expedited-actions process. *See* Tex. R. Civ. P. 169 cmt. 3 (2013). See "Factors," ch. 2-C, §3.1.2 (factors 2–5).

§7. Alternative dispute resolution

§7.1 Limitations. The ADR procedure for TRCP 169 cases is limited as follows:

1. **No forced ADR.** The court cannot require the parties to participate in ADR if they agreed not to engage in ADR. *See* Tex. R. Civ. P. 169(d)(4)(A).

2. **One referral.** The court can refer a TRCP 169 case to ADR only once. Tex. R. Civ. P. 169(d)(4)(A).

3. **Length.** The ADR procedure cannot be longer than a half-day, excluding scheduling time. Tex. R. Civ. P. 169(d)(4)(A)(i).

4. **Cost.** The ADR procedure cannot cost more than twice the amount of applicable civil filing fees. Tex. R. Civ. P. 169(d)(4)(A)(ii).

5. **Timing.** The ADR procedure must be completed at least 60 days before the initial trial setting. Tex. R. Civ. P. 169(d)(4)(A)(iii).

§7.2 Objections to referral. A party can object to the ADR referral unless prohibited by statute. *See* Tex. R. Civ. P. 169(d)(4)(B).

§7.3 Parties' agreement. The parties can agree to engage in a type of ADR different than that provided for in TRCP 169(d)(4)(A) or agree not to participate in ADR. *See* Tex. R. Civ. P. 169(d)(4)(A), (d)(4)(C).

§8. Judgment

§8.1 Limits on final judgment. TRCP 169 places a monetary limit on the judgment a plaintiff can recover; this limit, however, does not apply to the jury's verdict. *See* Tex. R. Civ. P. 169(b).

2021 Rule Amendments

The 2021 amendments to TRCP 169 increased the monetary limit on judgments in expedited actions and excluded additional elements from the calculation of the judgment amount. See Tex. R. Civ. P. 169(b); Tex.Sup.Ct. Order, Misc. Docket No. 20-9153 (eff. Jan. 1, 2021).

1. **Plaintiff's recovery.** The monetary limit on the plaintiff's recovery depends on when the case was filed. If the jury awards damages greater than the limit in TRCP 169(b), the plaintiff cannot move to amend the pleadings to conform to the higher damages award. *See* **Cross v. Wagner**, 497 S.W.3d 611, 614 (Tex.App.—El Paso 2016, no pet.) (under pre-1-1-21 version of TRCP 169); Tex. R. Civ. P. 169 cmt. 4 (2013). See "Amendments conforming pleadings to damages award," ch. 8-F, §3.2.1(1).

(1) **Before 1-1-21.** For cases filed before January 1, 2021, a party who prosecutes a suit under TRCP 169 cannot recover a judgment greater than $100,000, excluding postjudgment interest. Tex. R. Civ. P. 169(b) (pre-1-1-21 version); **Cross**, 497 S.W.3d at 613 (under pre-1-1-21 version of TRCP 169).

(2) **On or after 1-1-21.** For cases filed on or after January 1, 2021, a party who prosecutes a suit under TRCP 169 cannot recover a judgment greater than $250,000, excluding interest, statutory or punitive damages and penalties, and attorney fees and costs. Tex. R. Civ. P. 169(b).

2. Counterclaimant's recovery. The recovery limitations in TRCP 169(b) do not apply to a counterclaimant who seeks relief other than that allowed under TRCP 169(a). Tex. R. Civ. P. 169 cmt. 4 (2013). See "Counterclaimant's pleadings," ch. 2-C, §2.2.

§8.2 No limit on jury verdict. Unlike a final judgment, the jury's verdict is not limited by TRCP 169(b). *See* **Cross v. Wagner**, 497 S.W.3d 611, 615 (Tex.App.—El Paso 2016, no pet.) (under pre-1-1-21 version of TRCP 169). This distinction can be important in cases when the jury is asked to assess the plaintiff's proportionate responsibility. *See id.* at 614. In such a case, TRCP 169 does not require the trial court to cap the jury's award before reducing it by the proportionate responsibility of the parties; only the ultimate recovery must be capped at the TRCP 169(b) limit. *E.g.*, **Cross**, 497 S.W.3d at 614 (under pre-1-1-21 version of TRCP 169; jury awarded $170,225, which trial court reduced to judgment of $92,718 based on P's percentage of responsibility). As long as the plaintiff's petition seeks relief less than or equal to the amount in TRCP 169(b), the rule does not prevent the plaintiff from asking the jury to award damages totaling more than the TRCP 169(b) amount. **Cross**, 497 S.W.3d at 614–15 (under pre-1-1-21 version of TRCP 169).

D. Injunctive Relief

§1. General

§1.1 Rules. Tex. R. Civ. P. 680 to 693a. See Tex. Civ. Prac. & Rem. Code ch. 65.

§1.2 Purpose. There are two general types of injunctive relief: prohibitory and mandatory. **RP&R, Inc. v. Territo**, 32 S.W.3d 396, 400 (Tex.App.—Houston [14th Dist.] 2000, no pet.). Most injunctions are prohibitory—that is, they prohibit a party from continuing certain conduct. Shannon et al., *Temporary Restraining Orders & Temporary Injunctions in Texas—A Ten Year Survey, 1975–1985*, 17 St. Mary's L.J. 689, 736 (1986). In some cases, a party may need a mandatory injunction—that is, one requiring another party to act affirmatively rather than merely to refrain from certain conduct. *Id.*; *e.g.*, **Territo**, 32 S.W.3d at 400 (injunction required P to give weekly paychecks to D). There are three types of injunctive orders: temporary restraining orders, temporary injunctions, and permanent injunctions.

1. **TRO.** The purpose of a temporary restraining order (TRO) is to preserve the status quo of the subject matter of the litigation until a preliminary hearing can be held on an application for a temporary injunction. Moore, *The Ingenious Use of Injunctive Remedies in Texas*, 18 S.Tex.L.J. 87, 89 (1977); *see* **Cannan v. Green Oaks Apts., Ltd.**, 758 S.W.2d 753, 755 (Tex.1988). The status quo is the last actual, peaceable, noncontested status that preceded the controversy. **In re Newton**, 146 S.W.3d 648, 651 (Tex.2004); **Big Three Indus. v. Railroad Comm'n**, 618 S.W.2d 543, 548 (Tex.1981); **State v. Southwestern Bell Tel. Co.**, 526 S.W.2d 526, 528 (Tex.1975).

2. **Temporary injunction.** The purpose of a temporary injunction is to preserve the status quo of the subject matter of the litigation until a trial on the merits. **Clint ISD v. Marquez**, 487 S.W.3d 538, 555 (Tex.2016); **Butnaru v. Ford Motor Co.**, 84 S.W.3d 198, 204 (Tex.2002); *see* **Walling v. Metcalfe**, 863 S.W.2d 56, 58 (Tex.1993).

3. **Permanent injunction.** The purpose of a permanent injunction is to grant the injunctive relief the applicant is entitled to as part of the final judgment after a trial on the merits. **NMTC Corp. v. Conarroe**, 99 S.W.3d 865, 868 (Tex.App.—Beaumont 2003, no pet.); *see* **Elizondo v. Williams**, 643 S.W.2d 765, 767 (Tex.App.—San Antonio 1982, orig. proceeding).

§1.3 Forms. **O'Connor's Texas Civil Forms**, FORMS 2D:1 et seq. (2020 ed.).

§1.4 Other references. Thomas et al., *TRO's & TI's: Still Extraordinary?*, Advanced Civil Trial Course, State Bar of Texas CLE, ch. 19 (2010); Urquhart, *The Most Extraordinary Remedy: The Injunction*, 45 Tex.B.J. 358 (Mar.1982); Moore, *The Ingenious Use of Injunctive Remedies in Texas*, 18 S.Tex.L.J. 87 (1977); **O'Connor's Texas Causes of Action** (2021 ed.); **O'Connor's Texas Civil Appeals** (2020 ed.).

§2. Overview of injunction process

Before getting into the pleading requirements for the three types of injunctions, it is necessary to have a general idea of the procedure for obtaining an injunctive order. Because injunction procedures vary somewhat from county to county, the following is not intended to be representative of every county but is merely a general guide to the process of obtaining injunctive relief—from the ex parte TRO to the permanent injunction.

§2.1 Prepare petition & application. The plaintiff should prepare the petition for suit and include with it an application for the type or types of injunction order requested—TRO, temporary injunction, or permanent injunction. See "Application," ch. 2-D, §5.1 (TRO); "Application," ch. 2-D, §6.2 (temporary injunction); "Application," ch. 2-D, §7.1 (permanent injunction). The application for injunctive relief can be filed as a separate instrument. If the plaintiff seeks an ex parte TRO, the application must state why a TRO is necessary. See "Ex parte allegations," ch. 2-D, §5.1.4. Many local rules require the plaintiff to certify, as part of the application for an ex parte TRO, one of the following: (1) to the best of its knowledge, the defendant is unrepresented, (2) the defendant is represented but her counsel does not want to be heard or could not be reached, or (3) notifying the defendant or its counsel would cause irreparable harm to the plaintiff. *E.g.*, Bexar Cty. Loc. R. 6(C) (district courts); *see, e.g.*, Dallas Cty. Loc. R. 2.02(b); Tarrant Cty. Loc. R. 3.30(c).

§2.2 Prepare for bond. Before filing the petition and application, the plaintiff should call the court clerk to ask what type of bond and surety the court might require. See "Bond," ch. 2-D, §5.4.

§2.3 File petition & application. In some counties, the plaintiff must file the application for a TRO with the clerk, who will assign the case to a court and forward the papers to the presiding judge of that court. *E.g.*, Collin Cty. Loc. R. 1.4(a) (unless clerk's office is closed, application must first be filed and assigned to a court); Dallas Cty. Loc. R. 2.01(a) (same); El Paso Cty. Loc. R. 1.05(A) (same); Tarrant Cty. Loc. R. 3.30(a) (unless impossible, application must be filed with clerk and assigned to a court before it can be presented to judge). In other counties, the plaintiff can take the application for a TRO directly to the judge designated to hear TROs without filing it with the clerk. *See, e.g.*, Bexar Cty. Loc. R. 6(C) (district courts). In Harris County, the plaintiff must present the application to an ancillary court that is designated for hearing TRO applications. *See* Harris Cty. Loc. R. 3.5.1(a) (district courts).

§2.4 Notify defendant. Unless the application seeks an ex parte TRO, the plaintiff should notify the defendant of its intent to ask for a TRO and the time and place for the hearing. *See* Tex. R. Civ. P. 680.

§2.5 TRO hearing. The plaintiff must present the petition and application to the trial court. If both sides are present, the court will hear arguments. Generally, the court reviews the application and issues a ruling immediately. If the court grants the TRO, the court will set the amount of the bond and set the hearing on the temporary injunction at the earliest possible date, but no later than 14 days after the TRO is signed. *See* Tex. R. Civ. P. 680, 684. See "Bond," ch. 2-D, §5.4.

§2.6 Service on defendant. If the court grants the TRO, the court's clerk will deliver the original petition, TRO application, and signed TRO to the district or county clerk's office for preparation of the service of process, precept (notice of TRO injunction), and writ. Once the plaintiff posts the bond with the clerk, the clerk will issue a citation for the original petition, the notice of TRO injunction, and the writ of injunction. See "Serving the TRO," ch. 2-D, §5.3.3. The defendant must be given an opportunity to present evidence, raise defenses, and be heard at the temporary-injunction hearing. See "Notice," ch. 2-D, §6.3.

§2.7 Temporary-injunction hearing. At the temporary-injunction hearing, the court will hear arguments and receive evidence. See "Hearing," ch. 2-D, §6.4. If the court grants the injunction, the court will set an amount for a bond for the temporary injunction (or, if the court authorizes it, the bond can be a continuation of the bond set for the TRO). See "Bond," ch. 2-D, §5.4. Unless the petitioner needs to post a new bond, the clerk will issue the writ of injunction when it receives the temporary-injunction order. The temporary-injunction order must specify a date for trial. Tex. R. Civ. P. 683. See "Order," ch. 2-D, §6.5.

§2.8 Trial on merits. If the plaintiff asked for permanent injunctive relief, the court may grant the relief after the trial on the merits. See "Application," ch. 2-D, §7.1. If the court grants permanent injunctive relief, a bond is no longer required, and the applicant may request the return of its bond. See "Bond," ch. 2-D, §7.4. Although a writ of permanent injunction is not necessary, the petitioner can ask the court to instruct the clerk to issue one. *See* Tex. R. Civ. P. 688 (permanent injunction not listed as requiring a writ).

§3. Where to file

§3.1 Jurisdiction. The district and county courts have jurisdiction to hear applications for injunctions. *See* Tex. Const. art. 5, §8 (district court), art. 5, §16 (county court); Tex. Civ. Prac. & Rem. Code §65.021(a) (district and county courts); Tex. Gov't Code §24.007 (district courts), §25.0026 (statutory probate courts), §26.051 (county courts). See "Choosing the Court—Jurisdiction," ch. 2-G, §1 et seq. An application for injunctive relief invokes a court's equity jurisdiction. **In re Gamble**, 71 S.W.3d 313, 317 (Tex.2002).

§3.2 Venue. The basis for determining venue depends on whether the request for injunctive relief is ancillary to the lawsuit or is the primary reason for it. *See* **In re Fox River Real Estate Holdings, Inc.**, 596 S.W.3d 759, 765–66 (Tex.2020); **Brown v. Gulf TV Co.**, 306 S.W.2d 706, 708 (Tex.1957). See "Choosing the Court—Venue," ch. 2-H, §1 et seq.

1. Ancillary relief. When injunctive relief is ancillary to the lawsuit, venue is determined by the lawsuit, not by the request for injunction. *See* **O'Quinn v. Hall**, 77 S.W.3d 452, 456 (Tex.App.—Corpus Christi 2002, orig. proceeding) (when injunctive relief is ancillary, venue is determined by venue statutes, not injunction statutes); *see, e.g.*, **In re Fox River**, 596 S.W.3d at 765–66 (because injunctive relief was ancillary to suit, venue was determined by CPRC §15.020, which governs major transactions, not CPRC §65.023, which governs injunctions).

2. Primary relief. When injunctive relief is the primary relief requested in the petition, CPRC §65.023 determines venue. **In re Fox River**, 596 S.W.3d at 765; **In re Continental Airlines, Inc.**, 988 S.W.2d 733, 736 (Tex.1998); *e.g.*, **Karagounis v. Bexar Cty. Hosp. Dist.**, 70 S.W.3d 145, 147 (Tex.App.—San Antonio 2001, pet. denied) (because primary relief was contractual, not injunctive, venue not governed by §65.023); *see, e.g.*, **Billings v. Concordia Heritage Ass'n**, 960 S.W.2d 688, 692–93 (Tex.App.—El Paso 1997, pet. denied) (because primary relief was to enjoin Ds from exhuming body, venue was governed by §65.023). Primary, in this context, means first in order of rank or importance. **In re Fox River**, 596 S.W.3d at 765.

(1) Venue generally. Generally, a suit for injunctive relief against a Texas resident must be tried in the county of the defendant's domicile. Tex. Civ. Prac. & Rem. Code §65.023(a).

(2) Venue for writ to stay proceeding or execution of judgment. If the writ is to stay either a proceeding in a suit or the execution of a judgment, it must be tried in the court where the suit is pending or where the judgment was rendered. Tex. Civ. Prac. & Rem. Code §65.023(b); *see also* Tex. Civ. Prac. & Rem. Code §15.012 (under mandatory-venue statute, venue for injunction to stay proceedings must be in county where suit is pending), §15.013 (under mandatory-venue statute, venue for injunction to stay execution of judgment must be in county where judgment was rendered). CPRC §65.023(b) applies if the injunctive relief cannot be granted independently of the judgment. *See* **Campbell v. Wilder**, 487 S.W.3d 146, 149–50 (Tex.2016) (purpose of §65.023(b) is to protect judgment and processes of one court from direct attack by another court); *see, e.g.*, **Gardner v. Stewart**, 223 S.W.3d 436, 438 (Tex.App.—Amarillo 2006, pet. denied) (CPRC §65.023(b) applied when parties sought to enjoin execution of judgment granting third party possession of land).

Note

In construing CPRC §65.023(b) in ***Campbell***, *the Supreme Court assumed, without deciding, that the statute is jurisdictional even though §65.023(b) is captioned "Place for Trial," which suggests that it is a venue provision.* ***Campbell***, *487 S.W.3d at 149 n.13; see also* ***In re Continental Airlines***, *988 S.W.2d at 736 (referring to §65.023 as injunction venue statute). Some courts of appeals have construed CPRC §65.023(b) as controlling both venue and jurisdiction. See, e.g.,* ***Shor v. Pelican Oil & Gas Mgmt.***, *405 S.W.3d 737, 744 (Tex.App.—Houston [1st Dist.] 2013, no pet.);* ***Gardner***, *223 S.W.3d at 438;* ***Hageman/Fritz, Byrne, Head & Harrison, L.L.P. v. Luth***, *150 S.W.3d 617, 629 (Tex.App.—Austin 2004, no pet.).*

---

§4. Grounds for injunctive relief

To determine whether a party is entitled to injunctive relief, two questions must be answered. First, what are the grounds for the injunctive relief sought? Second, has the party made the appropriate showing of each prerequisite for obtaining injunctive relief?

§4.1 Grounds for injunctive relief.

Several statutes authorize injunctive relief.

1. CPRC §65.011. The most common statutory grounds for injunctive relief are found in CPRC §65.011, the general injunction statute, which authorizes injunctive relief in the following situations:

(1) When the applicant is entitled to the relief demanded, and all or part of the relief requires the restraint of some act prejudicial to the applicant. Tex. Civ. Prac. & Rem. Code §65.011(1); *see* **Coastal Mar. Serv. v. City of Port Neches**, 11 S.W.3d 509, 515 (Tex.App.—Beaumont 2000, no pet.); *see, e.g.*, **Dallas Cty. v. Sweitzer**, 881 S.W.2d 757, 769 (Tex.App.—Dallas 1994, writ denied) (P sought injunction to prevent enforcement of unconstitutional fee-collection statute). Although earlier cases suggested CPRC §65.011(1) does not require a showing of lack of an adequate legal remedy, the Supreme Court held it does. **Town of Palm Valley v. Johnson**, 87 S.W.3d 110, 111 (Tex.2001).

(2) When a party performs or is about to perform, or is procuring or allowing the performance of, an act relating to the subject of pending litigation, in violation of the applicant's rights, and the act would tend to render the judgment in that litigation ineffectual. Tex. Civ. Prac. & Rem. Code §65.011(2). Types of injunctions under CPRC §65.011(2) include the following:

(a) An injunction to preserve the subject matter of the suit until the suit is resolved by a judgment. *See* **City of Dallas v. Wright**, 36 S.W.2d 973, 975 (Tex.1931); *see, e.g.*, **PILF Invs. v. Arlitt**, 940 S.W.2d 255, 258–59 (Tex.App.—San Antonio 1997, no writ) (to prevent forced sale of property); **Vannerson v. Vannerson**, 857 S.W.2d 659, 674 (Tex.App.—Houston [1st Dist.] 1993, writ denied) (to safeguard property during divorce).

(b) An antisuit injunction to (1) address a threat to the court's jurisdiction, (2) prevent the evasion of important public policy, (3) prevent a multiplicity of suits, or (4) protect a party from vexatious or harassing litigation. **Frost Nat'l Bank v. Fernandez**, 315 S.W.3d 494, 512 (Tex.2010); **Golden Rule Ins. v. Harper**, 925 S.W.2d 649, 651 (Tex.1996); **AVCO Corp. v. Interstate Sw., Ltd.**, 145 S.W.3d 257, 262 (Tex.App.—Houston [14th Dist.] 2004, no pet.). The courts of appeals disagree on whether the **Golden Rule** test applies only during the trial court's plenary power or whether it also applies after the trial court loses plenary power. *Compare* **Panda Energy Corp. v. Allstate Ins.**, 91 S.W.3d 29, 35 (Tex.App.—Dallas 2002, pet. granted, judgm't vacated w.r.m.) (applies only while court has plenary jurisdiction), *with* **Bridas Corp. v. Unocal Corp.**, 16 S.W.3d 887, 890 (Tex.App.—Houston [14th Dist.] 2000, pet. dism'd) (applies while case is on appeal).

(3) When the applicant is entitled to a writ of injunction under the principles of equity and the laws of Texas relating to injunctions. Tex. Civ. Prac. & Rem. Code §65.011(3); *see* **Butnaru v. Ford Motor Co.**, 84 S.W.3d 198, 210 (Tex.2002).

(4) When real property is being sold under an execution against a party having no interest in the real property at the time of sale and would result in a cloud being placed on the title. Tex. Civ. Prac. & Rem. Code §65.011(4); **Citizens State Bank v. Caney Invs.**, 733 S.W.2d 581, 585–86 (Tex.App.—Houston [1st Dist.] 1987), *rev'd on other grounds*, 746 S.W.2d 477 (Tex.1988).

(5) When irreparable injury to real or personal property is threatened, irrespective of any remedy at law. Tex. Civ. Prac. & Rem. Code §65.011(5).

2. Other statutory grounds. Other statutes that authorize injunctive relief include the following: Business & Commerce Code §15.51(a) (injunction to enforce covenant not to compete), §24.008(a)(3)(A) (injunction to prevent further disposition of assets in suit for fraudulent transfer); CPRC §134A.003 (injunctive relief for actual or threatened misappropriation of trade secret); and Property Code §21.064(a) (injunctive relief in eminent-domain suits).

§4.2 Prerequisites for injunctive relief. Unless excepted by statute, the following prerequisites must be pleaded and proved before a party can obtain injunctive relief:

1. Valid cause of action. The applicant must plead a valid cause of action against the defendant and request some form of permanent relief, such as a permanent injunction or damages. *See* **Abbott v. Anti-Defamation League**, __ S.W.3d __, 2020 WL 6295076 (Tex.2020) (No. 20-0846; 10-27-20); **Butnaru v. Ford Motor Co.**, 84 S.W.3d 198, 204 (Tex.2002); **Walling v. Metcalfe**, 863 S.W.2d 56, 57 (Tex.1993). If the applicant pleads a cause of action that is not recognized in Texas, the trial court cannot grant an injunction. *See, e.g.*, **Valenzuela v. Aquino**, 853 S.W.2d 512, 513 (Tex.1993) (because Texas has no cause of action for negligent infliction of emotional distress, trial court could not enjoin picketers). For the elements of various causes of action, see **O'Connor's Texas Causes of Action** (2021 ed.).

2. Probable right to relief. The applicant must show it has a probable right to the relief it seeks on final hearing. **Abbott**, __ S.W.3d at __, 2020 WL 6295076; **Butnaru**, 84 S.W.3d at 204; **Walling**, 863 S.W.2d at 58; **Sun Oil Co. v. Whitaker**, 424 S.W.2d 216, 218 (Tex.1968). To establish a probable right to relief, the applicant must show that it has standing to bring the claims and that it is likely to succeed on the merits of its lawsuit. **Abbott**, __ S.W.3d at __, 2020 WL 6295076; *see* **DeSantis v. Wackenhut Corp.**, 793 S.W.2d 670, 686 (Tex.1990); **Southwestern Bell Tel. Co. v. Public Util. Comm'n**, 571 S.W.2d 503, 506 (Tex.1978). It is not necessary for the applicant to prove it will ultimately prevail. **Walling**, 863 S.W.2d at 58; **Sun Oil**, 424 S.W.2d at 218; *see* **Abbott**, __ S.W.3d at __, 2020 WL 6295076.

3. Probable injury. The applicant must plead it will suffer a probable injury. **Abbott**, __ S.W.3d at __, 2020 WL 6295076; **Butnaru**, 84 S.W.3d at 204; **Universal Health Servs. v. Thompson**, 24 S.W.3d 570, 577 (Tex.App.—Austin 2000, no pet.). Probable injury requires a showing that the harm is imminent, the injury would be irreparable, and the applicant has no other adequate legal remedy. **Henry v. Cox**, 483 S.W.3d 119, 137 (Tex.App.—Houston [1st Dist.] 2015), *rev'd on other grounds*, 520 S.W.3d 28 (Tex.2017); **Harbor Perfusion, Inc. v. Floyd**, 45 S.W.3d 713, 716 (Tex.App.—Corpus

Christi 2001, no pet.).

Note

Courts disagree on whether contractual stipulations of injury are sufficient to show irreparable injury or an inadequate remedy at law. Compare ***W.R. Grace & Co.-Conn v. Taylor****, No. 14-06-01056-CV, 2007 WL 1438544 (Tex.App.—Houston [14th Dist.] 2007, no pet.) (memo op.; 5-17-07) (footnote 7; stipulations are insufficient to show irreparable injury), with* ***Henderson v. KRTS, Inc.****, 822 S.W.2d 769, 776 (Tex.App.—Houston [1st Dist.] 1992, no writ) (finding of no adequate remedy upheld when parties' agreement stipulated that any breach of agreement would result in inadequate remedy at law and that injunctive relief could be granted without proof of actual damages).*

(1) Imminent harm. The applicant must plead the harm is imminent. *See* **Abbott**, __ S.W.3d at __, 2020 WL 6295076 (temporary injunction); **Operation Rescue-Nat'l v. Planned Parenthood**, 975 S.W.2d 546, 554 (Tex.1998) (permanent injunction); *see, e.g.*, **Surko Enters. v. Borg-Warner Acceptance Corp.**, 782 S.W.2d 223, 225 (Tex.App.—Houston [1st Dist.] 1989, no writ) (temporary injunction; in suit over collateral, P showed imminent harm because D was insolvent and transferring property to another). An injunction will not be issued unless it is shown that the respondent will otherwise engage in the activity enjoined. **State v. Morales**, 869 S.W.2d 941, 946 (Tex.1994). An applicant's fear or apprehension of the possibility of injury is not sufficient; the applicant must prove the respondent has attempted or intends to harm the applicant. **Jones v. Jefferson Cty.**, 15 S.W.3d 206, 213 (Tex.App.—Texarkana 2000, pet. denied); *see* **Matrix Network, Inc. v. Ginn**, 211 S.W.3d 944, 947–48 (Tex.App.—Dallas 2007, no pet.); **EMSL Analytical, Inc. v. Younker**, 154 S.W.3d 693, 697 (Tex.App.—Houston [14th Dist.] 2004, no pet.).

(2) Irreparable injury. The applicant must plead that, if the injunction is not issued, the harm that will occur is irreparable. **Butnaru**, 84 S.W.3d at 204 (temporary injunction); **Town of Palm Valley v. Johnson**, 87 S.W.3d 110, 111 (Tex.2001) (permanent injunction); *see* **State v. Hollins**, __ S.W.3d __, 2020 WL 5919729 (Tex.2020) (No. 20-0729; 10-7-20) (temporary injunction). An injury is irreparable if the injured party cannot be adequately compensated in damages or if the damages cannot be measured by any certain pecuniary standard. **Hollins**, __ S.W.3d at __, 2020 WL 5919729; **Butnaru**, 84 S.W.3d at 204; *e.g.*, **Wright v. Sport Sup. Grp.**, 137 S.W.3d 289, 294 (Tex.App.—Beaumont 2004, no pet.) (irreparable injury because P's damages were not presently ascertainable or easily calculated); **Haq v. America's Favorite Chicken Co.**, 921 S.W.2d 728, 730–31 (Tex.App.—Corpus Christi 1996, writ dism'd) (no irreparable injury because P did not prove damages it might suffer pending trial were different from damages recoverable for breach of contract); *see also* **Liberty Mut. Ins. v. Mustang Tractor & Equip. Co.**, 812 S.W.2d 663, 666 (Tex.App.—Houston [14th Dist.] 1991, no writ) (disruption of business can be irreparable harm). The courts disagree on whether cost and delay are sufficient injuries to be considered irreparable. *Compare* **Niemeyer v. Tana Oil & Gas Corp.**, 952 S.W.2d 941, 945 (Tex.App.—Austin 1997, no pet.) (costs and delay alone were not sufficient injuries), *and* **Reynolds, Shannon, Miller, Blinn, White & Cook v. Flanary**, 872 S.W.2d 248, 252 (Tex.App.—Dallas 1993, no writ) (same), *with* **In re Estate of Dilasky**, 972 S.W.2d 763, 767 (Tex.App.—Corpus Christi 1998, no pet.) (costs and delay can be factors in irreparable harm). The following are some exceptions to the irreparable-injury requirement:

(a) Restrictive covenant. An applicant seeking an injunction to enforce a restrictive covenant is not required to prove irreparable injury. **Jim Rutherford Invs. v. Terramar Beach Cmty. Ass'n**, 25 S.W.3d 845, 849 (Tex.App.—Houston [14th Dist.] 2000, pet. denied); **Munson v. Milton**, 948 S.W.2d 813, 815 (Tex.App.—San Antonio 1997, pet. denied). An applicant needs to show only that the nonmovant intends to do an act that would breach the covenant. **Marcus v. Whispering Springs Homeowners Ass'n**, 153 S.W.3d 702, 707 (Tex.App.—Dallas 2005, no pet.); **Munson**, 948 S.W.2d at 815.

(b) Zoning violation. A city seeking to enjoin the violation of a zoning ordinance is not required to prove the violation would cause injury to it or its residents. **San Miguel v. City of Windcrest**, 40 S.W.3d 104, 108 (Tex.App.—San Antonio 2000, no pet.).

(c) Covenant not to compete. An applicant seeking a permanent injunction to enforce a covenant not to compete is not required to prove irreparable injury. **Butler v. Arrow Mirror & Glass, Inc.**, 51 S.W.3d 787, 795 (Tex.App.—

Houston [1st Dist.] 2001, no pet.); *see also* **Wright**, 137 S.W.3d at 294 (employee's breach of covenant not to compete creates rebuttable presumption of irreparable injury). But an applicant seeking a temporary injunction to enforce a covenant not to compete must prove irreparable injury. *See* **EMS USA, Inc. v. Shary**, 309 S.W.3d 653, 657 (Tex.App.—Houston [14th Dist.] 2010, no pet.). See "Injunctive relief," **O'Connor's Texas Causes of Action**, ch. 5-I, §3.3.1 (2021 ed.).

(3) Inadequate remedy.

(a) Generally. The applicant generally must plead that there is no adequate remedy at law. **Pike v. Texas EMC Mgmt.**, __ S.W.3d __, 2020 WL 3405812 (Tex.2020) (No. 17-0557; 6-19-20); **Synergy Ctr., Ltd. v. Lone Star Franchising, Inc.**, 63 S.W.3d 561, 567 (Tex.App.—Austin 2001, no pet.); **Fasken v. Darby**, 901 S.W.2d 591, 592 (Tex.App.—El Paso 1995, no writ). A court will not issue a temporary injunction when there is a plain and adequate remedy at law. **McGlothlin v. Kliebert**, 672 S.W.2d 231, 232 (Tex.1984); *see* **Campbell v. Wilder**, 487 S.W.3d 146, 152 (Tex.2016). For a legal remedy to be adequate, it must give the applicant complete, final, and equal relief. **Henderson**, 822 S.W.2d at 773; *see* **Universal Health**, 24 S.W.3d at 577. For purposes of injunctive relief, there is no adequate remedy at law if (1) damages cannot be calculated or (2) the defendant will be unable to pay damages. **Texas Indus. Gas v. Phoenix Metallurgical Corp.**, 828 S.W.2d 529, 533 (Tex.App.—Houston [1st Dist.] 1992, no writ); *see* **Pike**, __ S.W.3d at __, 2020 WL 3405812; **Surko Enters.**, 782 S.W.2d at 225; *cf.* **Butnaru**, 84 S.W.3d at 204 (irreparable injury if damages cannot be measured by any certain pecuniary standard).

Practice Tip

A plaintiff who seeks only damages as relief is not necessarily barred from establishing an inadequate remedy at law for the purpose of obtaining a temporary injunction. ***Walling****, 863 S.W.2d at 58. But if you are seeking temporary injunctive relief, you should also request a permanent injunction or other permanent equitable relief (e.g., specific performance) in your petition and not damages alone. See "Request for permanent injunction," ch. 2-D, §7. Otherwise, you might have difficulty persuading the court that your legal remedy is inadequate.*

(b) Exceptions. The following are some exceptions to the requirement of no adequate remedy at law.

[1] Statutory right. An applicant who has a statutory right to an injunction does not have to prove that there is no adequate remedy at law. **Butnaru**, 84 S.W.3d at 210.

[2] City ordinance. An applicant seeking to enjoin the violation of a city ordinance does not have to prove that there is no adequate remedy at law. **San Miguel**, 40 S.W.3d at 108.

[3] Cloud on title. An applicant seeking to prevent a cloud from being cast on the title to real property does not have to prove that there is no adequate remedy at law. Tex. Civ. Prac. & Rem. Code §65.011(4).

[4] Irreparable injury to property. An applicant seeking to prevent irreparable injury to real or personal property does not have to prove that there is no adequate remedy at law. Tex. Civ. Prac. & Rem. Code §65.011(5).

§5. Request for temporary restraining order (TRO)

§5.1 Application.

1. Grounds. The application for a TRO must identify one or more of the grounds for injunction. See "Grounds for injunctive relief," ch. 2-D, §4.1.

2. Prerequisites. The application for a TRO must plead the prerequisites for injunctive relief. See "Prerequisites for injunctive relief," ch. 2-D, §4.2. The applicant must plead all of the necessary facts supporting the issuance of injunctive relief; legal conclusions are not sufficient. **Texas State Bd. of Med. Exam'rs v. McKinney**, 315 S.W.2d 387, 390 (Tex.App.—Waco 1958, no writ).

3. Request for injunction. The application for a TRO must include a request for a temporary injunction. *See* Tex. R. Civ. P. 680; Urquhart, *The Most Extraordinary Remedy: The Injunction*, 45 Tex.B.J. 358, 359 (Mar.1982). See "Request for temporary injunction," ch. 2-D, §6.

4. Ex parte allegations. If an applicant is seeking a TRO without notice to the other party, the application must identify specific facts showing why the order should be entered ex parte. Tex. R. Civ. P. 680. The application must show (1) the applicant will suffer irreparable injury, loss, or damage if the TRO is not granted and (2) there is not enough time to serve notice on the respondent and hold a hearing. *See id.* Some local rules may require an additional written certificate. *See, e.g.*, Dallas Cty. Loc. R. 2.02(b); Tarrant Cty. Loc. R. 3.30(c).

5. Bond. The application for a TRO must state the applicant's willingness to post bond. *See* Tex. R. Civ. P. 684.

6. Relief. The application for a TRO must identify the relief sought. **Fairfield v. Stonehenge Ass'n**, 678 S.W.2d 608, 611 (Tex.App.—Houston [14th Dist.] 1984, no writ). A trial court can grant only the injunctive relief an applicant specifically requests. *Id.*; *see* Tex. R. Civ. P. 682; **Colorado River Valley Co. v. Schiavone**, 476 S.W.2d 368, 370 (Tex.App.—Austin 1972, writ ref'd n.r.e.). A general prayer for relief does not allow injunctive relief beyond what is specifically requested. **Fairfield**, 678 S.W.2d at 611.

7. Verified. The application for a TRO must be verified or supported with affidavits. Tex. R. Civ. P. 680, 682. Affidavits must be based on the personal knowledge of the affiant. *See* **Williams v. Bagley**, 875 S.W.2d 808, 810 (Tex.App.—Beaumont 1994, no writ).

§5.2 Hearing. The court should conduct a hearing on the TRO, but the TRO can be granted ex parte, without a hearing. *See* Tex. R. Civ. P. 680.

§5.3 TRO.

1. Form. A TRO must be in writing. *See* Tex. R. Civ. P. 680, 683 (both rules assume, but do not state, that order must be in writing); **Ex parte Lesikar**, 899 S.W.2d 654, 654 (Tex.1995) (TRO extension order must be in writing). Until the TRO is signed by the judge, it is not enforceable by contempt. *See* **Ex parte Price**, 741 S.W.2d 366, 367 (Tex.1987). The order must make certain specific statements. *See* Tex. R. Civ. P. 680, 683. See "Order," ch. 2-D, §6.5. In its order, the court must do the following:

(1) Identify the person or entity to be restrained. *See* Tex. R. Civ. P. 683.

(2) State why the TRO was granted without notice if it is granted ex parte. Tex. R. Civ. P. 680.

(3) State the reasons for the issuance of the TRO by defining the injury and describing why it is irreparable. *Id.*; *see* Tex. R. Civ. P. 683.

(4) Define, in reasonable detail, the act to be restrained. Tex. R. Civ. P. 683. The act to be restrained cannot be described by reference to the pleadings or other documents. *Id.*

(5) State the date and hour of issuance if it was granted ex parte. Tex. R. Civ. P. 680. The trial court cannot hold a party in contempt for an act that occurred before the date and time of issuance. *See* **Ex parte Guetersloh**, 935 S.W.2d 110, 111 (Tex.1996) (appeal of temporary injunction).

(6) State the date the order expires. Tex. R. Civ. P. 680. The court can grant a TRO for only 14 days. *Id.* The 14-day time limit does not consist of 14 24-hour periods that begin running at the time the TRO is signed; the TRO expires at midnight 14 calendar days after it is signed. *E.g.*, **In re Walkup**, 122 S.W.3d 215, 217–18 (Tex.App.—Houston [1st Dist.] 2003, orig. proceeding) (TRO granted on 1-30-03 at 2:30 p.m. expired at midnight, not at 2:30 p.m., on 2-13-03).

(7) State the date for the hearing on the temporary injunction. Tex. R. Civ. P. 680. The injunction hearing must be set at the earliest possible time. *Id.* The hearing on the temporary injunction takes precedence over other matters. *Id.*

(8) Fix the amount of the TRO bond. Tex. R. Civ. P. 684. See "Bond," ch. 2-D, §5.4.

2. Extending the TRO. An order extending a TRO must be in writing. An oral order extending a TRO is not effective. **Ex parte Lesikar**, 899 S.W.2d at 654.

(1) On motion & order. The applicant may ask the trial court to extend the TRO by filing a motion, before the TRO expires, showing good cause. *See* Tex. R. Civ. P. 680; **In re Texas Nat. Res. Conserv. Comm'n**, 85 S.W.3d 201, 203 (Tex.2002). The court can grant one extension of the TRO for an additional 14 days. Tex. R. Civ. P. 680; **In re Texas Nat. Res.**, 85 S.W.3d at 204–05.

(2) By agreement. If the respondent agrees, the TRO may be extended for more than 14 days. Tex. R. Civ. P. 680.

3. Serving the TRO. Once the clerk has received the original petition and application for TRO, and the bond has been filed into the registry of the court, the clerk will issue a precept for the TRO and a notice of the hearing on the temporary injunction. The precept will be served with the citation and writ of injunction. All the documents are served on the defendant by the sheriff or constable or by a private process server as authorized by court order. *See* Tex. R. Civ. P. 686, 688. See "Who may serve process," ch. 2-I, §3.

§5.4 Bond. The order for temporary injunctive relief must set the amount for the bond. Tex. R. Civ. P. 684. If the order does not set the bond, the order is void and not enforceable. **Qwest Comms. v. AT&T Corp.**, 24 S.W.3d 334, 337 (Tex 2000) (temporary injunction); *see* **Ex parte Jordan**, 787 S.W.2d 367, 368 (Tex 1990) (TRO). The bond protects the respondent from any harm it may sustain as a result of the TRO. **DeSantis v. Wackenhut Corp.**, 793 S.W.2d 670, 686 (Tex 1990).

1. Setting the bond.

(1) Bond required. To protect the respondent, the amount of the bond must have some relation to the potential harm the respondent could suffer as a result of the injunction. *See, e.g.*, **Franklin Sav. Ass'n v. Reese**, 756 S.W.2d 14, 16 (Tex App.—Austin 1988, no writ) ($10,000 bond was not adequate for debt accruing $300,000 per month in interest); **El Paso Dev. Co. v. Berryman**, 729 S.W.2d 883, 888–89 (Tex App.—Corpus Christi 1987, no writ) ($15,000 bond was adequate for debt of over $7 million because there was sufficient collateral). A bond for a TRO does not continue on and act as security for a temporary injunction unless expressly authorized by the court. **Bay Fin. Sav. Bank v. Brown**, 142 S.W.3d 586, 591 (Tex App.—Texarkana 2004, no pet.).

(2) Bond amount discretionary. If the suit is against the State or its agency or subdivision, or against a city in its governmental capacity, and the governmental unit has no pecuniary interest in the suit and no monetary damages can be shown, the court may set the amount in its discretion. Tex. R. Civ. P. 684.

(3) Bond not required. The court may not require an indigent party to post a bond for a TRO or an injunction if (1) the applicant submits an affidavit that meets the requirements of CPRC §65.043 and (2) the court finds the order is intended to restrain the adverse party from foreclosing on the applicant's residence. Tex. Civ. Prac. & Rem. Code §§65.041, 65.042(a).

2. Posting bond. The applicant must post the bond before the clerk issues the writ. *See* **Goodwin v. Goodwin**, 456 S.W.2d 885, 885 (Tex 1970) (temporary injunction); **Williams v. Bagley**, 875 S.W.2d 808, 810 (Tex App.—Beaumont 1994, no writ) (TRO).

3. Challenging bond. The party restrained by the injunction may challenge the adequacy of the bond by filing a motion to increase the bond. *See* **Maples v. Muscletech, Inc.**, 74 S.W.3d 429, 430 (Tex App.—Amarillo 2002, no pet.). The party must make a "clear showing" that its potential losses are greater than the amount of the bond. *See id.* at 432.

§5.5 Writ.

1. Form. The court clerk will prepare the writ of injunction for issuance. *See* Tex. R. Civ. P. 688. The clerk is responsible for ensuring the form of the writ complies with TRCP 687.

2. Service. The writ of injunction must be served on the respondent by a sheriff or constable of the county of the respondent's residence or by a person authorized by court order. *See* Tex. R. Civ. P. 103, 688, 689. See "Who may serve process," ch. 2-I, §3. The applicant should ensure that copies of the writ are also served on any other persons acting in concert with the respondent or the respondent's officers, agents, servants, employees, or attorneys. *See* Tex. R. Civ. P. 683.

3. Return of service. The officer or authorized person serving the writ of injunction must complete and file a return of service for the writ that meets the requirements of TRCP 107. Tex. R. Civ. P. 689.

4. Copy in court's file. The clerk must keep a copy of the TRO (or temporary injunction) in the court's file. Tex. R. Civ. P. 688.

§6. Request for temporary injunction

§6.1 Parties. Under TRCP 39, the applicant must join all parties who are indispensable in the injunction proceeding before the court can grant temporary injunctive relief. *See* **Henry v. Cox**, 520 S.W.3d 28, 34 (Tex.2017). See "Parties to be joined," ch. 2-F, §6.2. The following parties have been held to be indispensable to an injunction proceeding:

1. Those whose rights will be directly affected by the writ. *See* **Ladner v. Reliance Corp.**, 293 S.W.2d 758, 764–65 (Tex.1956); **Scott v. Graham**, 292 S.W.2d 324, 327 (Tex.1956).

2. All parties to a contract if the applicant is seeking to restrain enforcement of the contract. **McCharen v. Bailey**, 87 S.W.2d 284, 285 (Tex.App.—Eastland 1935, no writ).

3. Any state, county, or city if the applicant is seeking to restrain a public official acting on behalf of the state, county, or city. *See* **Davis v. Wildenthal**, 241 S.W.2d 620, 621–22 (Tex.App.—El Paso 1951, writ ref'd n.r.e.).

§6.2 Application. When the applicant's original petition includes a request for a TRO, its request for a temporary injunction is merely an additional paragraph asking the court to set a hearing for a temporary injunction. When the applicant seeks a temporary injunction without a TRO, its petition must meet all the pleading requirements for a TRO except the request for ex parte relief. That is, the petition for a temporary injunction must be verified and must allege the following: (1) a cause of action, (2) a probable right to relief, (3) a probable injury in the interim (which includes proof of imminent and irreparable injury and no adequate remedy at law), and (4) a willingness to post bond. *See* Tex. R. Civ. P. 682 (verified petition), Tex. R. Civ. P. 684 (bond). See "Prerequisites for injunctive relief," ch. 2-D, §4.2.

§6.3 Notice. The party to be enjoined is entitled to notice and an opportunity to be heard. **PILF Invs. v. Arlitt**, 940 S.W.2d 255, 259–60 (Tex.App.—San Antonio 1997, no writ); **City of Houston v. Houston Lighting & Power Co.**, 530 S.W.2d 866, 869 (Tex.App.—Houston [14th Dist.] 1975, writ ref'd n.r.e.); *see* Tex. R. Civ. P. 681. When a request for injunction is ancillary to a pending suit, notice through service by citation is not necessary; when a request is independent of a pending suit, the defendant must be served by citation. *See* **In re Poe**, 996 S.W.2d 281, 282–83 (Tex.App.—Amarillo 1999, orig. proceeding). The party must be given three days' notice of the temporary-injunction hearing. *See* Tex. R. Civ. P. 21(b).

§6.4 Hearing.

1. Priority of setting. The setting of the hearing on the temporary injunction will be given preference over certain other matters pending in the trial court. *See* Tex. Gov't Code §23.101(a)(1).

2. Scope of proceeding. The only issue presented at the temporary-injunction hearing is the need for immediate relief pending the trial on the merits. **Transport Co. v. Robertson Transps.**, 261 S.W.2d 549, 552 (Tex.1953); **Coastal Mar. Serv. v. City of Port Neches**, 11 S.W.3d 509, 515 (Tex.App.—Beaumont 2000, no pet.).

3. Appearance.

(1) Applicant does not appear. If the applicant does not appear for the hearing on the temporary injunction, any TRO granted earlier will be dissolved, and the injunction will be denied.

(2) Respondent does not appear. If the respondent does not appear for the hearing on the temporary injunction, the petitioner is not entitled to a default judgment; a full evidentiary hearing is still required. *See* **Millwrights Local Un. v. Rust Eng'g**, 433 S.W.2d 683, 686–87 (Tex.1968).

4. Evidence.

(1) Applicant's burden. At the hearing, the applicant must introduce competent evidence to support a probable right to recovery and a probable injury. **Letson v. Barnes**, 979 S.W.2d 414, 417 (Tex.App.—Amarillo 1998, pet. denied); *see* **Bay Fin. Sav. Bank v. Brown**, 142 S.W.3d 586, 589–90 (Tex.App.—Texarkana 2004, no pet.). See "Prerequisites for injunctive relief," ch. 2-D, §4.2. An injunction cannot be upheld without evidence. **Atkinson v. Arnold**, 893 S.W.2d 294, 297 (Tex.App.—Texarkana 1995, no writ); *see* **Millwrights Local Un.**, 433 S.W.2d at 687 (conduct of hearing under TRCP 680 implies evidence will be offered). The court cannot consider the affidavits attached to the application for temporary injunc-

tion unless the parties agree or no one objects. **Millwrights Local Un.**, 433 S.W.2d at 686 (no agreement); **Ahmed v. Shimi Ventures, L.P.**, 99 S.W.3d 682, 684 n.2 (Tex.App.—Houston [1st Dist.] 2003, no pet.) (no objection).

(2) Limitation on evidence. The trial court can impose reasonable limits on the parties' presentation of evidence in a temporary-injunction hearing. **Reading & Bates Constr. Co. v. O'Donnell**, 627 S.W.2d 239, 244 (Tex.App.—Corpus Christi 1982, writ ref'd n.r.e.); **City of Houston v. Houston Lighting & Power Co.**, 530 S.W.2d 866, 869 (Tex.App.—Houston [14th Dist.] 1975, writ ref'd n.r.e.); *see, e.g.*, **Birds Constr., Inc. v. Gonzalez**, 595 S.W.2d 926, 928–29 (Tex.App.—Corpus Christi 1981, no writ) (court did not abuse discretion in granting temporary injunction based on stipulated facts, argument, and summary of other expected evidence from both parties). The court's limitations, however, cannot deprive the parties of their right to be heard. *E.g.*, **Houston Lighting & Power**, 530 S.W.2d at 869 (court's ruling deprived D of right to offer any evidence at hearing); **Oertel v. Gulf States Abrasive Mfg.**, 429 S.W.2d 623, 623 (Tex.App.—Houston [1st Dist.] 1968, no writ) (court refused to allow D to call any witnesses).

§6.5 Order. To be valid, an injunction order must be in writing, signed by the judge, and entered into the minutes of the court. *See* **Ex parte Price**, 741 S.W.2d 366, 367–68 (Tex.1987) (permanent injunction). The order must make certain specific statements. Tex. R. Civ. P. 683. The requirements of TRCP 683 are mandatory and must be strictly followed. **Qwest Comms. v. AT&T Corp.**, 24 S.W.3d 334, 337 (Tex.2000). An injunction order that does not comply with TRCP 683 is subject to being declared void and dissolved. **Qwest Comms.**, 24 S.W.3d at 337. In its order, the court must do the following:

1. State the reasons for the issuance of the injunction by defining the injury and describing why it is irreparable. *See* Tex. R. Civ. P. 683; **State v. Cook United, Inc.**, 464 S.W.2d 105, 106 (Tex.1971). TRCP 683 requires the injunction order to state the reasons an injury will be suffered if the interlocutory relief is not granted. **Cook United**, 464 S.W.2d at 106; **Kotz v. Imperial Capital Bank**, 319 S.W.3d 54, 56 (Tex.App.—San Antonio 2010, no pet.); **International Bhd. of Elec. Workers Local Un. v. Becon Constr. Co.**, 104 S.W.3d 239, 243 (Tex.App.—Beaumont 2003, no pet.); **Fasken v. Darby**, 901 S.W.2d 591, 592–93 (Tex.App.—El Paso 1995, no writ). The reasons must be stated because the appellate court cannot infer them from the evidence, the pleadings, or the court's oral pronouncement at the hearing. **Moreno v. Baker Tools, Inc.**, 808 S.W.2d 208, 211 (Tex.App.—Houston [1st Dist.] 1991, no writ).

2. Define, in reasonable detail and without reference to the pleadings or to other documents, the act to be restrained. Tex. R. Civ. P. 683; *see, e.g.*, **Maloy v. City of Lewisville**, 848 S.W.2d 380, 385 (Tex.App.—Fort Worth 1993, no writ) (when order described acts to be enjoined in reasonable detail, it was not error to refer to a city ordinance), *disapproved on other grounds*, **Schleuter v. City of Fort Worth**, 947 S.W.2d 920 (Tex.App.—Fort Worth 1997, pet. denied). The injunction should not be so broad as to preclude a party from lawful activities that are a proper exercise of its rights. *See* **Coyote Lake Ranch, LLC v. City of Lubbock**, 498 S.W.3d 53, 65 (Tex.2016); **Campbell v. Wilder**, 487 S.W.3d 146, 153 (Tex.2016). When an injunction is granted to protect confidential information and trade secrets, the order can refer to sealed exhibits as long as the activity to be enjoined is described in reasonable detail. **Rugen v. Interactive Bus. Sys.**, 864 S.W.2d 548, 553 (Tex.App.—Dallas 1993, no writ).

3. Include an order setting the case for a trial on the merits. Tex. R. Civ. P. 683; **Qwest Comms.**, 24 S.W.3d at 337; **InterFirst Bank San Felipe v. Paz Constr. Co.**, 715 S.W.2d 640, 641 (Tex.1986). If the injunction does not set the case for a trial on the merits, it is void. **Qwest Comms.**, 24 S.W.3d at 337; **InterFirst Bank**, 715 S.W.2d at 641; **City of Sherman v. Eiras**, 157 S.W.3d 931, 931 (Tex.App.—Dallas 2005, no pet.); **EOG Res. v. Gutierrez**, 75 S.W.3d 50, 52–53 (Tex.App.—San Antonio 2002, no pet.).

4. Fix the amount of the bond. Tex. R. Civ. P. 684; **Qwest Comms.**, 24 S.W.3d at 337. See "Bond," ch. 2-D, §5.4.

§6.6 Writ. See "Writ," ch. 2-D, §5.5.

§7. Request for permanent injunction

§7.1 Application. When the applicant's original petition includes pleadings for other injunctive relief (a TRO or temporary injunction), its request for a permanent injunction is merely an additional paragraph asking the court to grant a permanent injunction after the trial on the merits. When the applicant seeks a permanent injunction without other injunctive relief, its petition must meet all the requirements for a TRO except (1) a request for ex parte relief, (2) a statement of

willingness to post bond, and (3) verification or affidavits. *See* **Town of Palm Valley v. Johnson**, 17 S.W.3d 281, 288 (Tex.App.—Corpus Christi 2000) (verification not necessary), *pet denied*, 87 S.W.3d 110 (Tex.2001). That is, the petition for a permanent injunction must allege the following: (1) a cause of action, (2) a probable right to the relief, and (3) a probable injury (which includes imminent and irreparable injury and no adequate remedy at law). See "Prerequisites for injunctive relief," ch. 2-D, §4.2.

§7.2 Hearing. The hearing on the permanent injunction is a full trial of the issues in the applicant's petition. The applicant is entitled to a jury at the hearing. **Citizens State Bank v. Caney Invs.**, 746 S.W.2d 477, 478 (Tex.1988).

§7.3 Judgment. A judgment for a permanent injunction must describe in reasonable detail the acts to be restrained and should not be so broad as to preclude a party from lawful activities that are a proper exercise of its rights. **Computek Computer & Office Sups. v. Walton**, 156 S.W.3d 217, 220–21 (Tex.App.—Dallas 2005, no pet.); *see* **San Antonio Bar Ass'n v. Guardian Abstract & Title Co.**, 291 S.W.2d 697, 702 (Tex.1956); **Adust Video v. Nueces Cty.**, 996 S.W.2d 245, 249–50 (Tex.App.—Corpus Christi 1999, no pet.). The judgment does not need to describe in detail the reasons for its issuance. **Adust Video**, 996 S.W.2d at 249–50. The requirement in TRCP 683 that the order contain detailed explanations of the reasons for the issuance of the injunction does not apply to a permanent injunction when the injunction is the only relief sought by the action. **Adust Video**, 996 S.W.2d at 249; *see* **Qaddura v. Indo-European Foods, Inc.** 141 S.W.3d 882, 891–92 (Tex.App.—Dallas 2004, pet. denied); **Shields v. State**, 27 S.W.3d 267, 273 (Tex.App.—Austin 2000, no pet.); **City of Houston v. Morgan Guar. Int'l Bank**, 666 S.W.2d 524, 536 (Tex.App.—Houston [1st Dist.] 1983, writ ref'd n.r.e.). *But see* **Pauli v. Hayes**, No. 04-17-00026-CV, 2018 WL 3440767 (Tex.App.—San Antonio 2018, no pet.) (memo op.; 6-18-18) (requirements in TRCP 683 apply to all injunctions).

§7.4 Bond. A bond is not required for a permanent injunction. **Citizens State Bank v. Caney Invs.**, 733 S.W.2d 581, 585 (Tex.App.—Houston [1st Dist.] 1987), *rev'd on other grounds*, 746 S.W.2d 477 (Tex.1988); *see* **Canteen Corp. v. Republic of Tex. Props., Inc.**, 773 S.W.2d 398, 400 (Tex.App.—Dallas 1989, no writ).

§7.5 Writ. A writ of injunction is not issued after a permanent injunction. *See* Tex. R. Civ. P. 688 (refers only to writs for TROs and temporary injunctions).

§8. Response

§8.1 Defenses to request for injunction. Defenses to injunctive relief include the following: (1) the applicant has an adequate remedy at law, (2) a temporary injunction will accomplish the whole object of the suit, (3) a temporary injunction will destroy, rather than preserve, the status quo, (4) the applicant is not entitled to equitable relief because it is guilty of inequitable conduct (e.g., laches, unclean hands), and (5) the applicant's verification is insufficient. **McGlothlin v. Kliebert**, 672 S.W.2d 231, 232 (Tex.1984) (#1); **Texas Foundries, Inc. v. International Moulders & Foundry Workers' Un.**, 248 S.W.2d 460, 464 (Tex.1952) (#2); **Friona ISD v. King**, 15 S.W.3d 653, 659 (Tex.App.—Amarillo 2000, no pet.) (#2); **Landry's Seafood Inn & Oyster Bar-Kemah, Inc. v. Wiggins**, 919 S.W.2d 924, 927 (Tex.App.—Houston [14th Dist.] 1996, no writ) (#4); **Crystal Media, Inc. v. HCI Acquisition Corp.**, 773 S.W.2d 732, 734 (Tex.App.—San Antonio 1989, no writ) (#5); **Ballenger v. Ballenger**, 668 S.W.2d 467, 469–70 (Tex.App.—Corpus Christi 1984, writ dism'd) (#3).

§8.2 Motion to modify or dissolve.

1. Ex parte TRO. The respondent can move to modify or dissolve an ex parte TRO. The respondent must give the applicant two days' notice (unless the notice period is shortened by court order) of the hearing on the motion. Tex. R. Civ. P. 680; *see, e.g.*, **Forestier v. San Antonio Sav. Ass'n**, 564 S.W.2d 160, 163–64 (Tex.App.—El Paso 1978, writ ref'd n.r.e.) (hearing on motion to dissolve held same day TRO was issued).

2. TRO & temporary injunction.

(1) Modify. The respondent can move to modify a temporary injunction on the following grounds: • The injunction is overbroad. **Harbor Perfusion, Inc. v. Floyd**, 45 S.W.3d 713, 718 (Tex.App.—Corpus Christi 2001, no pet.). • The injunction granted more relief than requested. **Easton v. Brasch**, 277 S.W.3d 558, 560 (Tex.App.—Houston [1st Dist.] 2009, no pet.). • The claimed injury is speculative. **Fox v. Tropical Warehouses Inc.**, 121 S.W.3d 853, 861 (Tex.App.—Fort

Worth 2003, no pet.). • An injunction would be an unconstitutional prior restraint on speech. **Texas Mut. Ins. v. Surety Bank**, 156 S.W.3d 125, 131 (Tex.App.—Fort Worth 2005, no pet.).

(2) Dissolve. The respondent can move to dissolve a temporary injunction on the grounds that the injunction order is void. A TRO or temporary injunction is void if it does not comply with the requirements of TRCP 683 and 684. **Qwest Comms. v. AT&T Corp.**, 24 S.W.3d 334, 337 (Tex.2000); *e.g.*, **InterFirst Bank San Felipe v. Paz Constr. Co.**, 715 S.W.2d 640, 641 (Tex.1986) (injunction order void because it did not set case for trial on merits); **Goodwin v. Goodwin**, 456 S.W.2d 885, 885 (Tex.1970) (injunction order void because bond was not filed before injunction issued); **Beckham v. Beckham**, 672 S.W.2d 41, 43 (Tex.App.—Houston [14th Dist.] 1984, no writ) (injunction order void because it did not set out reasons for issuance); *see* **In re Office of the Atty. Gen.**, 257 S.W.3d 695, 697 (Tex.2008) (injunction order void if it does not comply with TRCP 680 and 684). Most courts have held that a party cannot waive an objection to a temporary injunction that does not comply with TRCP 683 because the rule's requirements are mandatory and must be strictly followed. *E.g.*, **International Bhd. of Elec. Workers Local Un. v. Becon Constr. Co.**, 104 S.W.3d 239, 243 (Tex.App.—Beaumont 2003, no pet.); **EOG Res. v. Gutierrez**, 75 S.W.3d 50, 52–53 (Tex.App.—San Antonio 2002, no pet.); **Evans v. C. Woods, Inc.**, 34 S.W.3d 581, 582–83 (Tex.App.—Tyler 1999, no pet.); **Big D Props., Inc. v. Foster**, 2 S.W.3d 21, 23 (Tex.App.—Fort Worth 1999, no pet.); **360 Degree Comms. v. Grundman**, 937 S.W.2d 574, 575 (Tex.App.—Texarkana 1996, no writ); **Fasken v. Darby**, 901 S.W.2d 591, 593 (Tex.App.—El Paso 1995, no writ). *But see* **Texas Tech Univ. Health Sci. Ctr. v. Rao**, 105 S.W.3d 763, 768 (Tex.App.—Amarillo 2003, pet. dism'd) (error waived); **Emerson v. Fires Out, Inc.**, 735 S.W.2d 492, 493–94 (Tex.App.—Austin 1987, no writ) (same).

3. Temporary & permanent injunction. The respondent can move to modify or dissolve a temporary or permanent injunction on the grounds of either changed circumstances or fundamental error. **Universal Health Servs. v. Thompson**, 24 S.W.3d 570, 580 (Tex.App.—Austin 2000, no pet.); *see* **City of San Antonio v. Singleton**, 858 S.W.2d 411, 412 (Tex.1993) (changed circumstances for permanent injunction); **Smith v. O'Neill**, 813 S.W.2d 501, 502 (Tex.1991) (same); **Murphy v. McDaniel**, 20 S.W.3d 873, 877 (Tex.App.—Dallas 2000, no pet.) (changed circumstances for temporary injunction). The respondent must present new evidence showing changed circumstances or fundamental error. **Universal Health**, 24 S.W.3d at 580. The respondent cannot use the motion to modify or dissolve to relitigate the basis for the injunction when that basis has not changed. **Chase Manhattan Bank v. Bowles**, 52 S.W.3d 871, 879 (Tex.App.—Waco 2001, no pet.).

(1) Changed circumstances. Changed circumstances are conditions that either alter the status quo after the issuance of the injunction or make the injunction unnecessary or improper. **Bowles**, 52 S.W.3d at 879. Changed circumstances can include changes in the law, newly revealed facts, or an agreement of the parties. **Murphy**, 20 S.W.3d at 878; *see* **Pidgeon v. Turner**, 538 S.W.3d 73, 84 (Tex.2017) (changes in law); **Kubala Pub. Adjusters, Inc. v. Unauthorized Practice of Law Cmte.**, 133 S.W.3d 790, 794–95 (Tex.App.—Texarkana 2004, no pet.) (changes in law or facts); **Bowles**, 52 S.W.3d at 878–79 (changes in law).

Note

Generally, the dissolution of an injunction prohibits a second application for injunctive relief. ***Pidgeon***, *538 S.W.3d at 84. But if a second application is based on changed circumstances unknown to the movant when the first application was filed, the court can consider the second application in light of the changed circumstances. Id.*

(2) Fundamental error. Fundamental error, which is rare, occurs when the record shows either the trial court did not have jurisdiction or the error directly and adversely affects the public interest as that interest is declared in a statute or the Texas Constitution. **In re C.O.S.**, 988 S.W.2d 760, 765 (Tex.1999); **Universal Health**, 24 S.W.3d at 580.

§8.3 Answer to the lawsuit

1. Special appearance & venue. If the temporary-injunction hearing was held before the respondent's deadline under TRCP 99 to answer the suit, the respondent does not waive any objection to personal jurisdiction or venue by participating at the hearing or by filing an answer to the application for temporary injunction or a motion for continuance of the

hearing. *See, e.g.*, **Valsangiacomo v. Americana Juice Imp., Inc.**, 35 S.W.3d 201, 204 n.3 (Tex.App.—Corpus Christi 2000, no pet.) (participation in temporary-injunction hearing did not waive special appearance); **Gentry v. Tucker**, 891 S.W.2d 766, 768 (Tex.App.—Texarkana 1995, no writ) (filing motion for continuance did not waive venue challenge); **Perkola v. Koelling & Assocs.**, 601 S.W.2d 110, 111–12 (Tex.App.—Dallas 1980, writ dism'd) (appearance at temporary-injunction hearing did not waive venue challenge); **Gibson v. State**, 288 S.W.2d 577, 578 (Tex.App.—Waco 1956, writ dism'd) (answer to application for temporary injunction did not waive venue challenge).

2. Answer. The respondent should remember to file an answer to the underlying suit. Once the deadline to file an answer has expired, the petitioner can take a default judgment against a nonanswering respondent, even if the respondent appeared at the injunction hearing. *See* **Borrego v. del Palacio**, 445 S.W.2d 620, 621 (Tex.App.—El Paso 1969, no writ).

§9. Enforcing the injunction

An injunction is binding on (1) the parties, (2) the parties' officers, agents, servants, employees, and attorneys, and (3) any other person who acts in concert with the parties or their agents and who receives actual notice of the order. Tex. R. Civ. P. 683.

§9.1 Motion for contempt. The trial court may enforce an injunction by holding the enjoined party in contempt for violating the injunction order. Tex. R. Civ. P. 692; **Ex parte Blasingame**, 748 S.W.2d 444, 447 (Tex.1988); *see also* **State v. Credit Bureau of Laredo, Inc.**, 530 S.W.2d 288, 290–91 (Tex.1975) (distinguishing between proceedings for contempt and civil penalty). The trial court may punish the contemnor for violating an injunction by imposing a fine or imprisonment. **Ex parte Blasingame**, 748 S.W.2d at 447; **Southwest Prof'l Indem. Corp. v. Texas Dept. of Ins.**, 914 S.W.2d 256, 265 (Tex.App.—Austin 1996, writ denied). For a discussion of fines and imprisonment for contempt, see "Section 21.002," ch. 5-K, §7.6.1. The order cannot punish the contemnor for actions taken before the court signed its order or, in the case of an ex parte TRO, before the respondent had notice of the order. *See* **Ex parte Guetersloh**, 935 S.W.2d 110, 111 (Tex.1996) (action taken before court signed order); **Ex parte Conway**, 419 S.W.2d 827, 828 (Tex.1967) (for contempt order to be valid, contemnor must have notice or knowledge of order that she is charged with violating); *see, e.g.*, **Ex parte Lesikar**, 899 S.W.2d 654, 654 (Tex.1995) (contemnor must have had notice of written extension of TRO to be held in contempt for violating it).

§9.2 Suit to enforce penalty in injunction. The party who obtained the injunction may enforce it by filing a suit to enforce a penalty within the injunctive order. **Transcontinental Gas Pipe Line Corp. v. American Nat'l Pet. Co.**, 763 S.W.2d 809, 824 (Tex.App.—Texarkana 1988), *rev'd on other grounds*, 798 S.W.2d 274 (Tex.1990); *see also* **State v. Credit Bureau of Laredo, Inc.**, 530 S.W.2d 288, 290–91 (Tex.1975) (distinguishing between proceedings for contempt and civil penalty).

§9.3 Other means of enforcement. It is unclear whether the party who obtained the injunction may sue the enjoined party for damages, without an independent cause of action, because of a violation of the injunction. *See* **Cannan v. Green Oaks Apts., Ltd.**, 758 S.W.2d 753, 755 (Tex.1988).

§10. Relief from wrongful injunction

A person who wrongfully obtained a TRO or temporary injunction is liable for damages caused by the injunction. **DeSantis v. Wackenhut Corp.**, 793 S.W.2d 670, 685 (Tex.1990). There are two types of actions for wrongful injunction.

§10.1 Suit on bond. To prevail on a cause of action on a bond, the claimant must prove the injunction was issued or perpetuated when it should not have been and that it was later dissolved. **DeSantis v. Wackenhut Corp.**, 793 S.W.2d 670, 685–86 (Tex.1990). Damages are limited to the amount of the bond. *Id.* at 686.

§10.2 Malicious prosecution. To prevail on a cause of action for malicious prosecution of an injunction, the claimant must prove that the injunction suit was (1) prosecuted maliciously, (2) prosecuted without probable cause, and (3) terminated in the claimant's favor. **DeSantis v. Wackenhut Corp.**, 793 S.W.2d 670, 686 (Tex.1990); **Sweezy Constr., Inc. v. Murray**, 915 S.W.2d 527, 531 (Tex.App.—Corpus Christi 1995, orig. proceeding). The suit should be brought as a counterclaim in the same lawsuit. *See* **Sweezy Constr.**, 915 S.W.2d at 531–32. The claimant is entitled to all actual damages. **DeSantis**, 793 S.W.2d at 686. See "Malicious Civil Prosecution," **O'Connor's Texas Causes of Action**, ch. 19-B, §1 et seq. (2021 ed.).

§11. Review

§11.1 TRO. A TRO cannot be appealed. **In re Texas Nat. Res. Conserv. Comm'n**, 85 S.W.3d 201, 205 (Tex.2002); **Ex parte Tucci**, 859 S.W.2d 1, 2 n.4 (Tex.1993); *see* Tex. R. Civ. P. 680 (TRO "shall expire by its terms"). However, if the issues are sufficiently serious, a TRO can be challenged by mandamus because there is no remedy by appeal. *See, e.g.*, **In re Office of the Atty. Gen.**, 257 S.W.3d 695, 698 (Tex.2008) (Attorney General presented evidence that Texas could lose federal funding if forced to comply with TRO; mandamus review granted).

§11.2 Temporary injunction. An order that grants or denies a temporary injunction, or grants or overrules a motion to dissolve a temporary injunction as provided by CPRC chapter 65, is an appealable interlocutory order. Tex. Civ. Prac. & Rem. Code §51.014(a)(4); *see* **Pidgeon v. Turner**, 538 S.W.3d 73, 81 (Tex.2017); **In re Texas Nat. Res. Conserv. Comm'n**, 85 S.W.3d 201, 205 (Tex.2002); **Qwest Comms. v. AT&T Corp.**, 24 S.W.3d 334, 338 (Tex.2000). If the trial court modifies the temporary-injunction order during the appeal of the original order, the appellate court has jurisdiction to review the modified order if it concerns the same subject matter as the original order. Tex. R. App. P. 29.6(a)(1); **Ahmed v. Shimi Ventures, L.P.**, 99 S.W.3d 682, 689 (Tex.App.—Houston [1st Dist.] 2003, no pet.). The interlocutory appeal of any order under CPRC §51.014(a)(4) does not stay the commencement of the trial. Tex. Civ. Prac. & Rem. Code §51.014(b). Appellate review of a temporary injunction cannot be used to secure an advance ruling on the merits. **Iranian Muslim Org. v. City of San Antonio**, 615 S.W.2d 202, 208 (Tex.1981).

Note

In 2017, the Legislature repealed Gov't Code §22.225(b), which prohibited a party from filing a petition for review in the Supreme Court after an appeal of an order granting or denying a temporary injunction or of an order granting or overruling a motion to dissolve a temporary injunction. See Acts 2017, 85th Leg., R.S., ch. 150, §4(3), eff. Sept. 1, 2017. Now, a party can file a petition for review after a court of appeals' decision on a temporary-injunction order. See id.

1. Accelerated appeal. Appeals of interlocutory orders are accelerated appeals. Tex. R. App. P. 28.1(a); **In re Gorman**, 1 S.W.3d 894, 895 (Tex.App.—Fort Worth 1999, orig. proceeding). The deadlines for perfecting the appeal (20 days), filing the record (10 days after filing the notice of appeal), and filing the briefs (20 days after filing the record) are much shorter than for regular appeals. *See* Tex. R. App. P. 26.1(b), 35.1(b), 38.6(a). The deadlines in TRAP 26.1(b) are mandatory and jurisdictional. **State v. Gibson's Distrib. Co.**, 436 S.W.2d 122, 123 (Tex.1968) (discussing former TRCP 385). See "Motion to Accelerate Appeal or to Give Appeal Precedence," **O'Connor's Texas Civil Appeals**, ch. 3-C, §1 et seq. (2020 ed.).

2. Motion for new trial. A party may file a motion for new trial after an interlocutory order. *See* Tex. R. App. P. 28.1(b). The motion does not extend the time to file the notice of appeal, which is only 20 days. *See* Tex. R. App. P. 26.1(b), 28.1(b).

3. Necessity of brief. Although TRAP 28.1(e) permits the appellate court to proceed without a brief, the courts are reluctant to do so. *See* **Lagrone v. John Robert Powers Sch., Inc.**, 841 S.W.2d 34, 37–38 (Tex.App.—Dallas 1992, no writ) (under former TRAP 42(c), now TRAP 28.1(e)).

4. Standard of review. Appellate review of the temporary injunction is limited to deciding whether the trial court clearly abused its discretion. **Henry v. Cox**, 520 S.W.3d 28, 33–34 (Tex.2017); **Butnaru v. Ford Motor Co.**, 84 S.W.3d 198, 204 (Tex.2002); **Davis v. Huey**, 571 S.W.2d 859, 861–62 (Tex.1978); *see* **State v. Hollins**, __ S.W.3d __, 2020 WL 5919729 (Tex.2020) (No. 20-0729; 10-7-20). The trial court abuses its discretion when it misapplies the law to established facts or when it concludes the applicant has a probable right of recovery and the conclusion is not reasonably supported by the evidence. **State v. Southwestern Bell Tel. Co.**, 526 S.W.2d 526, 528 (Tex.1975). The trial court does not abuse its discretion when it bases its decision on conflicting evidence presented by the parties. **Davis**, 571 S.W.2d at 862. The appellate court should not substitute its judgment for the trial court's unless the court's action was so arbitrary that it exceeded the bounds of reasonable discretion. **Henry**, 520 S.W.3d at 33–34; **Butnaru**, 84 S.W.3d at 204.

5. Mootness. The appellate courts cannot review a temporary injunction that is moot; such a review constitutes an impermissible advisory opinion. **NCAA v. Jones**, 1 S.W.3d 83, 86 (Tex.1999). A temporary injunction becomes moot when

a change in the status of the parties or the passage of time makes the injunction inoperative or when the objective of the injunction is accomplished. *See* **Jones**, 1 S.W.3d at 86; *see, e.g.*, **Reagan Nat'l Adver. v. Vanderhoof Family Trust**, 82 S.W.3d 366, 371 (Tex.App.—Austin 2002, no pet.) (threat to P of loss of property was no longer an issue). If the trial court renders a final judgment during the pendency of the appeal of the temporary injunction, the case becomes moot on appeal. **Isuani v. Manske-Sheffield Radiology Grp.**, 802 S.W.2d 235, 236 (Tex.1991); **Jordan v. Landry's Seafood Rest., Inc.**, 89 S.W.3d 737, 741 (Tex.App.—Houston [1st Dist.] 2002, pet. denied). When a case becomes moot on appeal, the appellate court must set aside all orders pertaining to the temporary injunction and dismiss the case. **Isuani**, 802 S.W.2d at 236.

§11.3 Permanent injunction. The granting or denial of a permanent injunction is reviewed for abuse of discretion. **ORIX Capital Mkts., LLC v. La Villita Motor Inns, J.V.**, 329 S.W.3d 30, 44 (Tex.App.—San Antonio 2010, pet. denied); **City of Round Rock v. Rodriguez**, 317 S.W.3d 871, 891 (Tex.App.—Austin 2010), *rev'd on other grounds*, 399 S.W.3d 130 (Tex.2013); *see* **Pike v. Texas EMC Mgmt.**, ___ S.W.3d ___, 2020 WL 3405812 (Tex.2020) (No. 17-0557; 6-19-20); **Operation Rescue-Nat'l v. Planned Parenthood**, 975 S.W.2d 546, 560 (Tex.1998); **TMRJ Holdings, Inc. v. Inhance Techs.**, 540 S.W.3d 202, 208 (Tex.App.—Houston [1st Dist.] 2018, no pet.); **Parham F.L.P. v. Morgan**, 434 S.W.3d 774, 790 (Tex.App.—Houston [14th Dist.] 2014, no pet.).

E. Declaratory Judgment

§1. General

§1.1 Rules. No rule of procedure deals directly with declaratory judgments; only a few rules even mention them. See Tex. R. Civ. P. 42(b)(2), 166a(a), (b). The authority for declaratory actions is found in the Declaratory Judgments Act (DJ Act), located in CPRC chapter 37.

§1.2 Purpose. The purpose of a declaratory action is to establish existing rights, status, or other legal relationships. **Loya Ins. v. Avalos**, __ S.W.3d __, 2020 WL 2089752 (Tex.2020) (No. 18-0837; 5-1-20); **City of El Paso v. Heinrich**, 284 S.W.3d 366, 370 (Tex.2009); **City of Garland v. Dallas Morning News**, 22 S.W.3d 351, 357 (Tex.2000) (plurality op.); **Bonham State Bank v. Beadle**, 907 S.W.2d 465, 467 (Tex.1995). A declaratory action is an additional and cumulative remedy and does not supplant any existing remedy. **Creative Thinking Sources, Inc. v. Creative Thinking, Inc.**, 74 S.W.3d 504, 513 (Tex.App.—Corpus Christi 2002, no pet.) (presence of another adequate remedy does not bar declaratory action). A declaratory action cannot be used as an affirmative ground of recovery to alter rights, status, or relationships. **Republic Ins. v. Davis**, 856 S.W.2d 158, 164 (Tex.1993). The DJ Act is "remedial" only. Tex. Civ. Prac. & Rem. Code §37.002(b); **Texas Nat. Res. Conserv. Comm'n v. IT-Davy**, 74 S.W.3d 849, 855 (Tex.2002) (plurality op.); **Bonham State Bank**, 907 S.W.2d at 467. The DJ Act is a procedural device for deciding cases that are already within the trial court's jurisdiction and cannot independently establish jurisdiction. **City of Dallas v. Albert**, 354 S.W.3d 368, 378 (Tex.2011); **Chenault v. Phillips**, 914 S.W.2d 140, 141 (Tex.1996); **State v. Morales**, 869 S.W.2d 941, 947 (Tex.1994); *see* **In re Dow**, 481 S.W.3d 215, 226 (Tex.2015).

§1.3 Forms. O'Connor's Texas Civil Forms, FORMS 2E:1, 3E:9 (2020 ed.).

§1.4 Other references. O'Connor's Texas Causes of Action (2021 ed.).

§2. Availability of declaratory judgment

An action for declaratory judgment is neither legal nor equitable but is sui generis—that is, of its own kind. **Texas Liquor Control Bd. v. Canyon Creek Land Corp.**, 456 S.W.2d 891, 895 (Tex.1970).

§2.1 When available. A declaratory judgment is appropriate only when there is a justiciable controversy about the rights and status of the parties, and the declaration would resolve the controversy. **Loya Ins. v. Avalos**, __ S.W.3d __, 2020 WL 2089752 (Tex.2020) (No. 18-0837; 5-1-20); **Southwestern Elec. Power Co. v. Lynch**, 595 S.W.3d 678, 685 (Tex.2020); **Bonham State Bank v. Beadle**, 907 S.W.2d 465, 467 (Tex.1995). The controversy must be real and substantial, involving a genuine conflict of tangible interests and not merely a theoretical dispute. **Bonham State Bank**, 907 S.W.2d at 467; *e.g.*, **Southwestern Elec. Power**, 595 S.W.3d at 684–85 (DJ appropriate to determine scope of easements); *see* **City of Dallas v. VSC, LLC**, 347 S.W.3d 231, 240 (Tex.2011); *see, e.g.*, **Farmers Tex. Cty. Mut. Ins. v. Griffin**, 955 S.W.2d 81, 84 (Tex.1997) (DJ appropriate to determine whether insurance carrier had duty to defend when pedestrian was shot by occupant of insured vehicle); **Holmes v. Morales**, 924 S.W.2d 920, 922 (Tex.1996) (DJ appropriate to determine whether DA was required to turn over "closed" criminal-litigation files under Open Records Act, now Public Information Act); **Davis v. Shanks**, 898 S.W.2d 285, 286 (Tex.1995) (DJ appropriate to determine whether word "contents" in will was ambiguous). The controversy does not need to be fully ripe, but it must indicate that imminent litigation seems unavoidable. *See* **Unauthorized Practice of Law Cmte. v. Nationwide Mut. Ins.**, 155 S.W.3d 590, 595 (Tex.App.—San Antonio 2004, pet. denied); **Texas DPS v. Moore**, 985 S.W.2d 149, 153–54 (Tex.App.—Austin 1998, no pet.).

1. Under CPRC ch. 37. CPRC chapter 37 lists suits that are appropriate for declaratory relief; however, the list is not exhaustive. Tex. Civ. Prac. & Rem. Code §37.003(c). Situations in which a person—as defined in CPRC §37.001—can seek declaratory relief under CPRC chapter 37 include the following:

(1) Construction or validity of written instrument. A person interested under a deed, will, written contract, or other writings constituting a contract can seek a declaratory judgment to determine any question of construction or validity arising under the instrument and obtain a declaration of rights, status, or other legal relationships. Tex. Civ. Prac. & Rem. Code §37.004(a); *see* **Southwestern Elec. Power**, 595 S.W.3d at 684; *see, e.g.*, **Transportation Ins. v. WH Cleaners, Inc.**, 372 S.W.3d 223, 228–29 (Tex.App.—Dallas 2012, no pet) (DJ appropriate to determine insurance carrier's contractual duty to defend); **Roberson v. City of Austin**, 157 S.W.3d 130, 135 (Tex.App.—Austin 2005, pet. denied) (DJ ap-

propriate to determine validity of easement). A person can seek declaratory relief to construe a contract either before or after there has been a breach. Tex. Civ. Prac. & Rem. Code §37.004(b).

(2) Construction or validity of statute, ordinance, contract, or franchise. A person whose rights, status, or other legal relationships are affected by a statute, municipal ordinance, contract, or franchise can seek a declaratory judgment to determine any question of construction or validity arising under the statute, ordinance, contract, or franchise and obtain a declaration of rights, status, or other legal relationships. Tex. Civ. Prac. & Rem. Code §37.004(a); *see, e.g.*, **City of Ingleside v. City of Corpus Christi**, 469 S.W.3d 589, 590 (Tex.2015) (city could seek DJ to interpret relevant boundary ordinances).

(3) Determination of proper boundary line between adjoining properties. Notwithstanding Property Code §22.001 (trespass-to-try-title statute), a person interested under a deed, will, written contract, or other writings constituting a contract, or a person whose rights, status, or other legal relationships are affected by a statute, municipal ordinance, contract, or franchise, can seek a declaratory judgment to determine the sole issue of the proper boundary line between adjoining properties. Tex. Civ. Prac. & Rem. Code §37.004(a), (c).

(4) Rights relating to trust or estate. A person interested as or through an executor or administrator, including an independent executor or administrator, a trustee, guardian, other fiduciary, creditor, devisee, legatee, heir, next of kin, or cestui que trust (i.e., beneficiary) in the administration of a trust or estate of a decedent, infant, mentally incapacitated person, or insolvent can seek a declaratory judgment for the trust or estate to do any of the following:

(a) To ascertain any class of creditors, devisees, legatees, heirs, next of kin, or others. Tex. Civ. Prac. & Rem. Code §37.005(1).

(b) To direct the executors, administrators, or trustees to do or abstain from doing a particular act in their fiduciary capacity. Tex. Civ. Prac. & Rem. Code §37.005(2).

(c) To determine any question arising in the trust's or estate's administration, including questions of construction of wills and other writings. Tex. Civ. Prac. & Rem. Code §37.005(3).

(d) To determine rights or legal relationships of an independent executor or independent administrator about fiduciary fees and the settling of accounts. Tex. Civ. Prac. & Rem. Code §37.005(4).

2. Counterclaims. When a counterclaim for declaratory relief will have greater ramifications than the original suit, declaratory relief is appropriate. **BHP Pet. Co. v. Millard**, 800 S.W.2d 838, 842 (Tex.1990); **McGehee v. Endeavor Acquisitions, LLC**, 603 S.W.3d 515, 529 (Tex.App.—El Paso 2020, no pet.); **Georgiades v. Di Ferrante**, 871 S.W.2d 878, 880 (Tex.App.—Houston [14th Dist.] 1994, writ denied); *e.g.*, **Winslow v. Acker**, 781 S.W.2d 322, 328 (Tex.App.—San Antonio 1989, writ denied) (in Ps' suit for recovery of royalty interests assigned to Ds, Ds' counterclaim for declaratory relief was appropriate because it would settle all future royalty disputes).

§2.2 When not available. A declaratory judgment is not available in the following instances:

1. No justiciable conflict. A declaratory judgment is not available when there is no justiciable conflict. **Bonham State Bank v. Beadle**, 907 S.W.2d 465, 467 (Tex.1995); *e.g.*, **Di Portanova v. Monroe**, 229 S.W.3d 324, 329 (Tex.App.—Houston [1st Dist.] 2006, pet. denied) (beneficiary could not bring DJ action to resolve dispute over how trustee should exercise discretion given to trustee in trust instrument); **Paulsen v. Texas Equal Access to Justice Found.**, 23 S.W.3d 42, 44–45 (Tex.App.—Austin 1999, pet. denied) (parties agreed on constitutionality of challenged statute and desired the same result); **Barcroft v. State**, 900 S.W.2d 370, 372 (Tex.App.—Texarkana 1995, no writ) (P could not bring suit to be declared "Private State Citizen of Texas").

2. Potential tort liability. Generally, a defendant cannot use a declaratory-judgment action to determine potential tort liability. *E.g.*, **In re Houston Specialty Ins.**, 569 S.W.3d 138, 140–41 (Tex.2019) (legal malpractice); **Abor v. Black**, 695 S.W.2d 564, 566 (Tex.1985) (personal injury), *overruled on other grounds*, **In re J.B. Hunt Transp.**, 492 S.W.3d 287 (Tex.2016); **Trantham v. Isaacks**, 218 S.W.3d 750, 756 (Tex.App.—Fort Worth 2007, pet. denied) (defamation); **Stein v. First Nat'l Bank**, 950 S.W.2d 172, 174–75 (Tex.App.—Austin 1997, no writ) (fraud); *see also* **Texas State Bank v. Amaro**,

87 S.W.3d 538, 545 (Tex.2002) (trustee tort liability).

Note

*In **In re Houston Specialty**, the party requesting declaratory relief argued that courts have discretionary jurisdiction over declaratory actions seeking to determine potential tort liability and that a court can retain such a case on its docket if the tortfeasor-plaintiff also requests declarations that do not expressly ask for a determination of liability. **In re Houston Specialty**, 569 S.W.3d at 140–41. The Court rejected this argument and emphasized that there is no recognized exception to the rule that a potential tort defendant cannot use a declaratory-judgment action to determine potential tort liability. Id.*

3. Future controversy. A declaratory judgment is not available to resolve issues that are not yet mature and are subject to change. *See, e.g.*, **City of Garland v. Louton**, 691 S.W.2d 603, 605 (Tex.1985) (parties not entitled to DJ on constitutionality of referendum statute before election); **California Prods. v. Puretex Lemon Juice, Inc.**, 334 S.W.2d 780, 783 (Tex.1960) (P not entitled to advisory opinion on whether proposed bottle design would violate injunction); **Paulsen**, 23 S.W.3d at 47 (parties not entitled to advisory opinion on how broadly a U.S. Supreme Court opinion could be read); **Lane v. Baxter Healthcare Corp.**, 905 S.W.2d 39, 41–42 (Tex.App.—Houston [1st Dist.] 1995, no writ) (P not entitled to resolve issue of ownership of trade secrets before any dispute). The DJ Act does not permit litigants to "fish in judicial ponds for legal advice." **California Prods.**, 334 S.W.2d at 781.

4. In another court. Generally, a declaratory judgment is not available to resolve an issue that will be adjudicated by a separate proceeding involving the same parties. **Texas Liquor Control Bd. v. Canyon Creek Land Corp.**, 456 S.W.2d 891, 895 (Tex.1970); **Creative Thinking Sources, Inc. v. Creative Thinking, Inc.**, 74 S.W.3d 504, 513 (Tex.App.—Corpus Christi 2002, no pet.).

5. In same suit. Generally, a declaratory judgment is not available to resolve issues already pending in the same suit before the court. *See* **Kyle v. Strasburger**, 522 S.W.3d 461, 467 n.10 (Tex.2017); **BHP Pet. Co. v. Millard**, 800 S.W.2d 838, 841 (Tex.1990); **Hageman/Fritz, Byrne, Head & Harrison, L.L.P. v. Luth**, 150 S.W.3d 617, 627 (Tex.App.—Austin 2004, no pet.); *see, e.g.*, **Boatman v. Lites**, 970 S.W.2d 41, 43 (Tex.App.—Tyler 1998, no pet.) (DJ action to determine rights under Water Code §11.086 requested no greater or different relief from that requested in pending suit); **Staff Indus. v. Hallmark Contracting, Inc.**, 846 S.W.2d 542, 547–48 (Tex.App.—Corpus Christi 1993, no writ) (counterclaim for declaratory relief concerning amount due under purchase order presented no issues beyond those in underlying suit).

6. No jurisdiction over underlying dispute. A declaratory judgment is not available if the court does not have jurisdiction over the underlying cause of action. **Chenault v. Phillips**, 914 S.W.2d 140, 141 (Tex.1996); **Southwest Airlines Co. v. Texas High-Speed Rail Auth.**, 863 S.W.2d 123, 125–26 (Tex.App.—Austin 1993, writ denied); *see, e.g.*, **State Bar v. Gomez**, 891 S.W.2d 243, 246 (Tex.1994) (district court had no jurisdiction over suit to compel mandatory pro bono).

7. Earlier judgment. A declaratory judgment is not available to seek a judicial interpretation of an earlier judgment. **Samedan Oil Corp. v. Louis Dreyfus Nat. Gas Corp.**, 52 S.W.3d 788, 792 (Tex.App.—Eastland 2001, pet. denied) (dicta); **Martin v. Dosohs I, Ltd.**, 2 S.W.3d 350, 354 (Tex.App.—San Antonio 1999, pet. denied); **Cohen v. Cohen**, 632 S.W.2d 172, 173 (Tex.App.—Waco 1982, no writ).

8. Criminal issue. A declaratory judgment is not available to determine the rights, status, or other legal relationships arising under a penal statute. *E.g.*, **State v. Morales**, 869 S.W.2d 941, 947 (Tex.1994) (court could not decide constitutionality of sodomy law).

9. Suit against the government. Generally, a declaratory judgment is not available to (1) circumvent a government's sovereign immunity by having a suit for monetary damages characterized as a suit to determine rights or (2) determine the rights of the parties under a contract when a contractual dispute with the government must be submitted to an administrative procedure. *See* **City of Dallas v. Albert**, 354 S.W.3d 368, 378 (Tex.2011) (#1); **City of El Paso v. Heinrich**, 284 S.W.3d 366, 371 (Tex.2009) (#1); **Texas DOT v. Jones Bros. Dirt & Paving Contractors, Inc.**, 92 S.W.3d 477,

484–85 (Tex.2002) (#2). See "Declaratory Judgments Act," **O'Connor's Texas Causes of Action**, ch. 24-A, §2.4.1(2)(c)[1] (2021 ed.); "Other issues," **O'Connor's Texas Causes of Action**, ch. 24-B, §6 (2021 ed.).

§3. Procedure

§3.1 Court. Only a court of record that has jurisdiction may hear an action for declaratory relief. Tex. Civ. Prac. & Rem. Code §37.003(a); **Wilson v. Wilson**, 378 S.W.2d 156, 160 (Tex.App.—Tyler 1964, no writ).

§3.2 Parties. The petition should name as parties all persons or entities who have a claim or interest that would be affected by the declaration. Tex. Civ. Prac. & Rem. Code §37.006(a); **Musgrave v. Owen**, 67 S.W.3d 513, 521 (Tex.App.—Texarkana 2002, no pet.); **Dahl v. Hartman**, 14 S.W.3d 434, 436 (Tex.App.—Houston [14th Dist.] 2000, pet. denied); *see* **Brooks v. Northglen Ass'n**, 141 S.W.3d 158, 162 (Tex.2004). The court does not have jurisdiction to issue a declaratory judgment for parties who are not before the court. *See* **Brooks**, 141 S.W.3d at 162–63; *see also* Tex. Civ. Prac. & Rem. Code §37.006(a) (declaration does not prejudice rights of person who is not a party to the proceeding). When a suit challenges the validity of a municipal ordinance or franchise, the municipality must be made a party. Tex. Civ. Prac. & Rem. Code §37.006(b). When a suit challenges the constitutionality of a statute, an ordinance, or a franchise, the Attorney General must be served and is entitled to be heard. *Id.*

Note

A party seeking to compel joinder of other persons in a declaratory-judgment action must show that the requirements of TRCP 39 are met. See ***Crawford v. XTO Energy, Inc.****, 509 S.W.3d 906, 911 n.3 (Tex.2017). See "Parties to be joined," ch. 2-F, §6.2.*

§3.3 Jurisdiction. The court in which the declaratory-judgment action is brought must have subject-matter jurisdiction over the claims. *See* **Southwestern Elec. Power Co. v. Lynch**, 595 S.W.3d 678, 683 (Tex.2020). The DJ Act does not enlarge the existing jurisdiction of the court or create new jurisdiction. **Texas Nat. Res. Conserv. Comm'n v. IT-Davy**, 74 S.W.3d 849, 855 (Tex.2002) (plurality op.); **State v. Morales**, 869 S.W.2d 941, 947 (Tex.1994); **Kadish v. Pennington Assocs.**, 948 S.W.2d 301, 304 (Tex.App.—Houston [1st Dist.] 1995, no writ). The DJ Act is not a grant of jurisdiction, but merely a procedural device for deciding cases already within the court's jurisdiction. **Chenault v. Phillips**, 914 S.W.2d 140, 141 (Tex.1996); *see* **Frasier v. Yanes**, 9 S.W.3d 422, 427 (Tex.App.—Austin 1999, no pet.).

§3.4 Venue. Venue for a declaratory-judgment action is governed by the rules relating to civil actions generally. **Bonham State Bank v. Beadle**, 907 S.W.2d 465, 471 (Tex.1995); **Stiba v. Bowers**, 756 S.W.2d 835, 837 (Tex.App.—Corpus Christi 1988, no writ). Thus, to determine venue for a suit requesting a declaratory judgment, a party must look to the facts of the underlying cause of action. See "Choosing the Court—Venue," ch. 2-H, §1 et seq.

§3.5 Relief. The petition may ask for affirmative or negative relief. Tex. Civ. Prac. & Rem. Code §37.003(b). The declaratory action may ask for relief in questions of construction or validity arising under a deed, will, written contract, or other instrument, or arising under another relation affected by a statute, municipal ordinance, contract, or franchise. Tex. Civ. Prac. & Rem. Code §37.004(a). The declaratory action may also ask for relief regarding a trust or estate. Tex. Civ. Prac. & Rem. Code §37.005. The lists in §§37.004 and 37.005 do not limit the power of the court to grant declaratory relief. Tex. Civ. Prac. & Rem. Code §37.003(c).

§3.6 Jury trial. The parties are entitled to a jury trial, as in other civil cases. *See* Tex. Civ. Prac. & Rem. Code §37.007. The jury can decide any disputed fact issues. *See id.*; **Hot-Hed, Inc. v. Safehouse Habitats (Scotland), Ltd.**, 333 S.W.3d 719, 728 (Tex.App.—Houston [1st Dist.] 2010, pet. denied).

§3.7 Judgment. The declaration has the force and effect of a final judgment or decree. Tex. Civ. Prac. & Rem. Code §37.003(b); *see* **Brooks v. Northglen Ass'n**, 141 S.W.3d 158, 162 (Tex.2004).

§3.8 Costs & attorney fees. The trial court has the discretion to award costs and attorney fees as part of a declaratory judgment. Tex. Civ. Prac. & Rem. Code §37.009; **Yowell v. Granite Oper. Co.**, ___ S.W.3d ___, 2020 WL 2502141 (Tex.2020) (No. 18-0841; 5-15-20); **Kachina Pipeline Co. v. Lillis**, 471 S.W.3d 445, 455 (Tex.2015); **John G. & Marie Stella Kenedy**

Mem'l Found. v. Dewhurst, 90 S.W.3d 268, 289 (Tex.2002); **Bocquet v. Herring**, 972 S.W.2d 19, 20 (Tex.1998). The court can award attorney fees in any proceeding under the DJ Act, even if the court has not rendered judgment on the merits of the claim. **Yowell**, __ S.W.3d at __, 2020 WL 2502141; *see* Tex. Civ. Prac. & Rem. Code §37.009; **Falls Cty. v. Perkins & Cullum**, 798 S.W.2d 868, 871 (Tex.App.—Fort Worth 1990, no writ). Attorney fees can be awarded to any party, not just a prevailing party. *See* **Morath v. Texas Taxpayer & Student Fairness Coalition**, 490 S.W.3d 826, 885 (Tex.2016); **Barshop v. Medina Cty. Underground Water Conserv. Dist.**, 925 S.W.2d 618, 637 (Tex.1996); **SAVA gumarska in kemijska industria d.d. v. Advanced Polymer Sci., Inc.**, 128 S.W.3d 304, 323–24 (Tex.App.—Dallas 2004, no pet.); *see also* **West Beach Marina, Ltd. v. Erdeljac**, 94 S.W.3d 248, 270 (Tex.App.—Austin 2002, no pet.) (because CPRC §37.009 controls over TRCP 131, showing of good cause is not required when prevailing party is not awarded costs). For a discussion of attorney fees generally, see "Attorney fees from adverse party," ch. 1-H, §10.

Practice Tip

Because the court has the discretion to award attorney fees to any party, a party seeking a declaration under the DJ Act should be mindful of the possibility that fees could be awarded against it. Even if the party seeking a declaration files a nonsuit of the DJ Act claim, that party may not be able to avoid an award of attorney fees against it. See ***Falls Cty.****, 798 S.W.2d at 871–72.*

---

1. Requirements. There are four requirements for an award of attorney fees under the DJ Act—the fees must be reasonable, necessary, equitable, and just. Tex. Civ. Prac. & Rem. Code §37.009; **Yowell**, __ S.W.3d at __, 2020 WL 2502141; **Kinsel v. Lindsey**, 526 S.W.3d 411, 427 (Tex.2017); **Wells Fargo Bank v. Murphy**, 458 S.W.3d 912, 915 (Tex.2015); **GuideOne Elite Ins. v. Fielder Rd. Baptist Ch.**, 197 S.W.3d 305, 311 (Tex.2006). The issue of the amount of attorney fees (the reasonable and necessary requirements) is an issue for the trier of fact; the issue of whether to award attorney fees (the equitable and just requirements) is a question of law for the trial court. **GuideOne Elite**, 197 S.W.3d at 311; **Ridge Oil Co. v. Guinn Invs.**, 148 S.W.3d 143, 161 (Tex.2004); **Bocquet**, 972 S.W.2d at 21; *see* **Kinsel**, 526 S.W.3d at 427; **Morath**, 490 S.W.3d at 885. However, CPRC §37.009's "equitable and just" language authorizes the court to award attorney fees in an amount less than what was determined by the jury to be reasonable and necessary. **Ridge Oil Co.**, 148 S.W.3d at 162. See "Proving reasonableness & necessity of attorney fees," ch. 1-H, §10.2.

2. Not available.

(1) Duplicative or incidental claim for declaratory relief. A party cannot recover attorney fees under the DJ Act if the claim for declaratory relief merely duplicates or repleads an existing claim or is only incidental to other claims for relief. *See* **Etan Indus. v. Lehmann**, 359 S.W.3d 620, 624 (Tex.2011); **MBM Fin. Corp. v. Woodlands Oper. Co.**, 292 S.W.3d 660, 669–70 (Tex.2009); **Dewhurst**, 90 S.W.3d at 289; *see, e.g.*, **Jackson v. State Office of Admin. Hearings**, 351 S.W.3d 290, 301 (Tex.2011) (declaratory relief was incidental to central claim for relief under the Texas Public Information Act). Attorney fees are also not available when the declaratory-judgment claim is a subset of an invalid claim. *See* **MBM Fin. Corp.**, 292 S.W.3d at 670; *see, e.g.*, **Sharyland Water Sup. v. City of Alton**, 354 S.W.3d 407, 424 (Tex.2011) (P could not recover fees under DJ Act when claim for declaratory relief was subset of breach-of-contract claim and D had immunity from that claim).

Note

Similarly, a party generally cannot recover attorney fees under the DJ Act by bringing a counterclaim for declaratory relief when the counterclaim involves only issues that were raised by the original claims. ***Save Our Springs Alliance, Inc. v. Lazy Nine MUD****, 198 S.W.3d 300, 318 (Tex.App.—Texarkana 2006, pet. denied); see* ***McGehee v. Endeavor Acquisitions, LLC****, 603 S.W.3d 515, 528–29 (Tex.App.—El Paso 2020, no pet.). But if the original claims were brought as DJ Act claims, a counterclaim for declaratory relief will support an award of attorney fees even if it duplicates the claims already raised.* ***McGehee****, 603 S.W.3d at 529;* ***Save Our Springs Alliance****, 198 S.W.3d at 318. In a situation where the DJ Act was invoked by the original claimant, the counterclaim is not being used solely to facilitate an award of attorney fees under the Act.* ***McGehee****, 603 S.W.3d at 529; see*

Save Our Springs Alliance, 198 S.W.3d at 318.

(2) Statutes other than the DJ Act. When declaratory judgment claims are brought under statutes that independently authorize declaratory relief but do not incorporate the DJ Act and do not authorize fees, attorney fees are not available. *See* **In re Allcat Claims Serv.**, 356 S.W.3d 455, 472 (Tex.2011).

§3.9 Motion to enforce judgment. The DJ Act empowers the trial court to make supplemental rulings to aid in the enforcement of a declaratory judgment. **In re Crow-Billingsley Air Park, Ltd.**, 98 S.W.3d 178, 179 (Tex.2003); *see* Tex. Civ. Prac. & Rem. Code §37.011. The trial court may hear a motion to enforce its final judgment, even while the judgment is on appeal, if the judgment was not superseded. *See* **In re Crow-Billingsley**, 98 S.W.3d at 179.

§3.10 Answer. To file an answer to a declaratory-judgment action, a party must follow the same steps it would for filing any other answer. See "The Answer—Denying Liability," ch. 3-E, §1 et seq.; **O'Connor's Texas Civil Forms**, FORM 3E:9 (2020 ed.).

§4. Review

§4.1 Standard of review. Declaratory judgments are reviewed under the same standards as other judgments and decrees. **Roberts v. Squyres**, 4 S.W.3d 485, 488 (Tex.App.—Beaumont 1999, pet. denied); **FDIC v. Projects Am. Corp.**, 828 S.W.2d 771, 772 (Tex.App.—Texarkana 1992, writ denied). Thus, if the declaratory judgment was granted on a motion for summary judgment, the review is governed by the rules for summary judgment; if the declaratory judgment was granted on an agreed statement of facts under TRCP 263, review is governed by the rules for agreed statements of facts. *See, e.g.*, **In re Marriage of I.C. & Q.C.**, 551 S.W.3d 119, 121–22 (Tex.2018) (case submitted on summary judgment); **Kachina Pipeline Co. v. Lillis**, 471 S.W.3d 445, 449 (Tex.2015) (case submitted on summary judgment); **Roberts**, 4 S.W.3d at 488 (case submitted on agreed statement); **Unauthorized Practice of Law Cmte. v. Jansen**, 816 S.W.2d 813, 814–15 (Tex.App.—Houston [14th Dist.] 1991, writ denied) (case submitted on agreed statement and on summary judgment). See "Review," ch. 7-C, §7; "Review," ch. 7-E, §6.

§4.2 Appeal. The trial court's decision, which is a conclusion of law, will be upheld on appeal if it can be sustained on any legal theory supported by the evidence. **Alma Invs. v. Bahia Mar Co-Owners Ass'n**, 999 S.W.2d 820, 823 (Tex.App.—Corpus Christi 1999, pet. denied); **FDIC v. Projects Am. Corp.**, 828 S.W.2d 771, 772 (Tex.App.—Texarkana 1992, writ denied). If reversal is warranted, the appellate court can render the judgment the trial court should have rendered, unless a remand for further proceedings is necessary. **FDIC**, 828 S.W.2d at 772; *see also* **Kachina Pipeline Co. v. Lillis**, 471 S.W.3d 445, 455 (Tex.2015) (when appellate court reverses DJ, it can also reverse attorney-fees award).

F. Parties & Claims

§1. General

§1.1 Rules. Tex. R. Civ. P. 28 to 44, 51, 174. See Tex. Civ. Prac. & Rem. Code ch. 33 (proportionate responsibility).

§1.2 Purpose. For the sake of judicial economy, the rules encourage parties to combine multiple claims and parties into a single lawsuit. There are, however, limits to what claims and parties can be joined.

§1.3 Forms. **O'Connor's Texas Civil Forms**, FORMS 2B:9 to 2B:19, 3E:12 to 3E:17, 5I:1 et seq., 5J:1 et seq. (2020 ed.).

§1.4 Other references. **O'Connor's Texas Causes of Action** (2021 ed.).

§2. Methods for joining parties & claims

Parties and claims are brought into a lawsuit by any of the following methods:

§2.1 Petition. The plaintiff initially decides who the parties are and what the claims are. *See* Tex. R. Civ. P. 22. See "Plaintiff's Original Petition," ch. 2-B, §1 et seq.

§2.2 Cross-actions.

1. Counterclaim. A counterclaim is an affirmative claim for relief filed against an opposing party. *See* Tex. R. Civ. P. 97(a), (b). A counterclaim is most often raised by the defendant, although it may be raised by a plaintiff in response to a defendant's or other party's pleading. Counterclaims are either compulsory or permissive. Tex. R. Civ. P. 97(a), (b). For the difference between them, see "Compulsory joinder of claims," ch. 2-F, §6; "Permissive joinder of claims," ch. 2-F, §7.

2. Cross-claim. A cross-claim is an affirmative claim for relief filed by one party against its coparty. Tex. R. Civ. P. 97(e). For example, if a counterclaim is brought against a plaintiff, the plaintiff may file a cross-claim against another plaintiff. See "Cross-claims," ch. 3-E, §7.2.

§2.3 Third-party practice. Third-party practice, also called impleader, is the procedure by which a defendant can bring an additional party into the suit who may be liable for all or part of the plaintiff's claim. Tex. R. Civ. P. 38. See "Third-party petitions," ch. 3-E, §7.3. A plaintiff may implead an additional party in response to a counterclaim by the defendant. Tex. R. Civ. P. 38(b).

§2.4 Responsible third party. Under CPRC §33.004, the defendant can designate a person as a responsible third party who is alleged to have caused or contributed to causing the harm for which recovery of damages is sought. See "RTP," ch. 3-E, §7.4.

§2.5 Intervention. A plea in intervention is the procedure for a person to join a lawsuit already in progress. *See* Tex. R. Civ. P. 60, 61. See "Petition in intervention," ch. 5-J, §2.

§2.6 Interpleader. A bill of interpleader is the procedure for a person in possession of property claimed by others to transfer the property and the dispute to the court. *See* Tex. R. Civ. P. 43. See "Interpleader suit," ch. 5-J, §3.

§2.7 Consolidation. A motion to consolidate asks the court to consolidate two or more suits with a common question of law or fact. Tex. R. Civ. P. 174(a). The consolidated suit will have one cause number and be resolved by a single judgment. See "Motion to consolidate," ch. 5-J, §4.

§2.8 Joint trial. A motion for joint trial asks the court to hold one trial for two or more suits. *See* Tex. R. Civ. P. 174(a). The cases are joined for trial only, are tried at the same time but under separate cause numbers, and are resolved by separate judgments.

§3. General rules for joinder of claims

§3.1 Single plaintiff & single defendant. There can be no misjoinder of claims when there is only one plaintiff and one defendant. *See* Tex. R. Civ. P. 51(a); *see, e.g.*, **Twyman v. Twyman**, 855 S.W.2d 619, 625 (Tex.1993) (tort claims could be

joined with divorce). The plaintiff can bring as many claims as it may have against the defendant, and the defendant can bring as many claims as it may have against the plaintiff. The claims do not need to arise from the same transaction or occurrence and may be entirely unrelated. *See* Tex. R. Civ. P. 51(a).

§3.2 Multiple parties. When there are multiple parties in the suit, the parties can bring as many claims as they may have against each other as long as the claims arise from the same transaction, occurrence, or series of transactions or occurrences and have a common question of law or fact. *See* Tex. R. Civ. P. 39(a), 40(a), 43, 51(a). When there are multiple plaintiffs in a pending suit, they should consider the effect of the venue provisions that require each plaintiff to justify venue in the county. *See* Tex. Civ. Prac. & Rem. Code §15.003. See "Multiple plaintiffs," ch. 2-H, §7.1.

§4. Multiple defendants

Multiple defendants may be joined in a suit when (1) a right to relief relating to or arising from the same transaction or occurrence is asserted against them jointly, severally, or in the alternative, and (2) any questions of law or fact common to all of them will arise in the action. Tex. R. Civ. P. 40(a); **In re Caballero**, 53 S.W.3d 391, 397 (Tex.App.—Amarillo 2001, pet. denied).

§4.1 Joint liability. Joint liability is when a defendant is liable with another defendant for damages to the plaintiff. *See* Joint Liability, *Black's Law Dictionary* (11th ed. 2019).

§4.2 Several liability. Several liability is when a defendant is liable separately and distinctly from another defendant. Several Liability, *Black's Law Dictionary* (11th ed. 2019). The term "several" implies that each defendant is liable alone.

§4.3 Joint & several liability. Joint and several liability refers to a defendant who is liable both jointly with other defendants and separately. When the acts of two or more wrongdoers join to produce an indivisible injury, all the wrongdoers are jointly and severally liable for the entire amount of damages. **Amstadt v. U.S. Brass Corp.**, 919 S.W.2d 644, 654 (Tex.1996); **Landers v. East Tex. Salt Water Disposal Co.**, 248 S.W.2d 731, 734 (Tex.1952). The plaintiff has the option to sue all the defendants responsible for an indivisible injury in one suit, or any one defendant separately. **Morgan v. Compugraphic Corp.**, 675 S.W.2d 729, 733 (Tex.1984). *But see* **Jones v. Ray**, 886 S.W.2d 817, 822 (Tex.App.—Houston [1st Dist.] 1994, orig. proceeding) (severing P's claims against jointly and severally liable Ds was inequitable because suits were intertwined). There can be only one recovery for one injury. **Stewart Title Guar. Co. v. Sterling**, 822 S.W.2d 1, 8 (Tex.1991), *modified on other grounds*, **Tony Gullo Motors I, L.P. v. Chapa**, 212 S.W.3d 299 (Tex.2006); *see* **Crown Life Ins. v. Casteel**, 22 S.W.3d 378, 390 (Tex.2000). This rule applies even though more than one defendant may have caused the injury or there may be more than one theory of liability. **Stewart Title**, 822 S.W.2d at 8; *see* **Casteel**, 22 S.W.3d at 390. See "Defendant jointly & severally liable," **O'Connor's Texas Causes of Action**, ch. 51, §6.2 (2021 ed.).

§5. Proportionate responsibility for damages

For a more detailed discussion of proportionate responsibility, see "Proportionate Responsibility & Contribution," **O'Connor's Texas Causes of Action**, ch. 51, §1 et seq. (2021 ed.).

§5.1 Plaintiff's bar. The claimant (usually the plaintiff) is barred from recovering damages if its responsibility is found to be greater than 50% in any cause of action based on tort. *See* Tex. Civ. Prac. & Rem. Code §§32.001(a), 33.001; **Nabors Well Servs. v. Romero**, 456 S.W.3d 553, 560 (Tex.2015).

Note

The Supreme Court has held that relevant evidence of a plaintiff's nonuse of a seat belt may be considered when assessing each party's percentage of responsibility if the nonuse caused or contributed in any way to the plaintiff's damages. E.g., ***Nabors Well****, 456 S.W.3d at 562–63 (Ps' failure to wear seat belts contributed to severity of injuries sustained in truck accident and could be admissible to apportion responsibility even though failure to wear seat belts did not contribute to causation of accident itself); see Tex. Civ. Prac. & Rem. Code §33.003(a). A jury question seeking percentage-of-responsibility findings can be submitted only if the pleadings and evidence raise the issue of a party's liability. See "Determining percentages of responsibility,"* ***O'Connor's Texas Causes of Action****, ch. 51, §4 (2021*

ed.).

§5.2 Among defendants.

1. Most cases. A defendant is generally liable only for the percentage of damages equal to the defendant's own percentage of responsibility. Tex. Civ. Prac. & Rem. Code §33.013(a). But a defendant will be held jointly and severally liable for the entire amount of damages (after a reduction for the plaintiff's percentage or for any settlement credit) when its responsibility with respect to the cause of action is found to be greater than 50%. *See* Tex. Civ. Prac. & Rem. Code §33.013(b)(1).

2. Intentional criminal acts. If the jury finds the defendant engaged in intentional conduct constituting any of the Penal Code offenses listed in CPRC §33.013(b)(2), the defendant will be held jointly and severally liable. Tex. Civ. Prac. & Rem. Code §33.013(b)(2).

3. Indivisible injury. If the responsibility for the plaintiff's injury is indivisible such that liability cannot be apportioned with reasonable certainty among the defendants and other responsible parties, CPRC ch. 33 does not apply, and the defendants will be held jointly and severally liable. **Lakes of Rosehill Homeowners Ass'n v. Jones**, 552 S.W.3d 414, 420 (Tex.App.—Houston [14th Dist.] 2018, no pet.); *see* **Amstadt v. U.S. Brass Corp.**, 919 S.W.2d 644, 654 (Tex.1996).

§5.3 Third-party responsibility. The defendant can designate a person as a responsible third party who is alleged to have caused or contributed to causing the harm for which recovery of damages is sought. See "RTP," ch. 3-E, §7.4.

§6. Compulsory joinder of claims

The parties should join to the suit all claims that are compulsory. A claim is compulsory only if it meets all the criteria in TRCP 97(a) and (d). **Ingersoll-Rand Co. v. Valero Energy Corp.**, 997 S.W.2d 203, 207 (Tex.1999), *overruled on other grounds*, **In re J.B. Hunt Transp.**, 492 S.W.3d 287 (Tex.2016); **Wyatt v. Shaw Plumbing Co.**, 760 S.W.2d 245, 247 (Tex.1988), *overruled on other grounds*, **In re J.B. Hunt Transp.**, 492 S.W.3d 287 (Tex.2016). See "Criteria," ch. 2-F, §6.1.1. If a compulsory claim is not brought in the suit, the party with the claim is barred from asserting it in a later suit. **Wyatt**, 760 S.W.2d at 247; **Tindle v. Jackson Nat'l Life Ins.**, 837 S.W.2d 795, 800 (Tex.App.—Dallas 1992, no writ); *see* Tex. R. Civ. P. 97(a).

§6.1 Compulsory-counterclaim rule. The compulsory-counterclaim rule is designed to avoid piecemeal or duplicative litigation. **Bard v. Charles R. Myers Ins. Agency, Inc.**, 839 S.W.2d 791, 796 (Tex.1992). The sole compelling interest underlying the rule is judicial economy (i.e., to prevent multiple suits arising from the same transaction or occurrence). *Id.*

Note

Although this rule is called the "compulsory-counterclaim rule," it is not limited to defendants. The rule also applies to plaintiffs, cross-claim defendants, and third-party defendants. Although the plaintiff may initially choose the claims it wants to bring against the defendant, if the defendant asserts claims against the plaintiff, the plaintiff must then assert all of its compulsory counterclaims, or they will be barred in a later suit.

1. Criteria.

(1) Within jurisdiction. The claim must be within the court's subject-matter jurisdiction. Tex. R. Civ. P. 97(a); **Ingersoll-Rand Co. v. Valero Energy Corp.**, 997 S.W.2d 203, 207 (Tex.1999), *overruled on other grounds*, **In re J.B. Hunt Transp.**, 492 S.W.3d 287 (Tex.2016); **Wyatt v. Shaw Plumbing Co.**, 760 S.W.2d 245, 247 (Tex.1988), *overruled on other grounds*, **In re J.B. Hunt Transp.**, 492 S.W.3d 287 (Tex.2016). A court can reach below its minimum jurisdictional limits if the claim arises from the same transaction or occurrence as the plaintiff's claim. If the damages are above the court's maximum jurisdictional limits, the claim is permissive, not compulsory, and the court should dismiss it. *See* Tex. R. Civ. P. 97(a); **Pinckard v. Associated Popcorn Distribs.**, 611 S.W.2d 491, 492 (Tex.App.—Dallas 1981, no writ); **Kitchen Designs, Inc. v. Wood**, 584 S.W.2d 305, 307 (Tex.App.—Texarkana 1979, writ ref'd n.r.e.). See "Permissive joinder of claims," ch. 2-F, §7. The counterclaims of multiple defendants are not aggregated when determining whether the amount in

controversy exceeds the court's maximum statutory jurisdictional limit and divests the court of jurisdiction. **Smith v. Clary Corp.**, 917 S.W.2d 796, 798–99 (Tex.1996). See "Multiple parties," ch. 2-G, §2.3.1(2); "Counterclaims," ch. 2-G, §2.3.1(3).

(2) Not filed elsewhere. The claim must not have been the subject of a pending action in another court at the time the original suit was commenced. **In re J.B. Hunt Transp.**, 492 S.W.3d 287, 293 (Tex.2016); *see* Tex. R. Civ. P. 97(a).

Note

Before ***In re J.B. Hunt Transp.****, both the* ***Ingersoll-Rand*** *and* ***Wyatt*** *opinions interpreted TRCP 97(a) to mean that a counterclaim was compulsory if the claim was not the subject of a pending action at the time the defendant filed its answer. See* ***In re J.B. Hunt Transp.****, 492 S.W.3d at 292 & n.5. The Court's opinion in* ***In re J.B. Hunt Transp.*** *clarified two mistakes in that interpretation. Id. at 292. First, the Court pointed out that the rule refers to the time of filing the "pleading"—not the answer. Id. Second, the Court held that the proper inquiry is whether the claim was the subject of a pending action at the time the original suit was commenced—not at the time the party asserting the counterclaim filed its pleading. Id. at 292–93. Under the Court's earlier interpretation of TRCP 97(a), a litigant could have avoided the compulsory-counterclaim rule by filing a second suit asserting the claim before filing its pleading in the original suit. Id. at 293; see* ***Commint Tech. Servs. v. Quickel****, 314 S.W.3d 646, 652 (Tex.App.—Houston [14th Dist.] 2010, no pet.).*

(3) Mature. The claim must be mature and owned by the pleader when it files its answer. **Ingersoll-Rand**, 997 S.W.2d at 207; **Wyatt**, 760 S.W.2d at 247; **Compass Expl., Inc. v. B-E Drilling Co.**, 60 S.W.3d 273, 277 (Tex.App.—Waco 2001, no pet.); *see* Tex. R. Civ. P. 97(d). Claims that are speculative and premature at the time the answer is filed are not considered compulsory counterclaims. *See, e.g.*, **Ingersoll-Rand**, 997 S.W.2d at 208 (claim for indemnity did not mature until date of judgment). Claims for attorney fees, however, are compulsory even though they are contingent on the outcome of the suit. **Fidelity Mut. Life Ins. v. Kaminsky**, 820 S.W.2d 878, 882 (Tex.App.—Texarkana 1991, writ denied).

(4) Same transaction or occurrence. The claim must arise from the same transaction or occurrence as the opposing party's claim. Tex. R. Civ. P. 97(a); **Ingersoll-Rand**, 997 S.W.2d at 207; **Wyatt**, 760 S.W.2d at 247; **Compass Expl.**, 60 S.W.3d at 277–78. Texas applies the "logical-relationship" test to determine whether claims arise from the same transaction or occurrence. **Commint Tech. Servs.**, 314 S.W.3d at 653; **Community State Bank v. NSW Invs.**, 38 S.W.3d 256, 258 (Tex.App.—Texarkana 2001, pet. dism'd); **Jack H. Brown & Co. v. Northwest Sign Co.**, 718 S.W.2d 397, 399–400 (Tex.App.—Dallas 1986, writ ref'd n.r.e.). Under this test, a transaction is flexible and may be a series of many occurrences logically related to one another. **Community State Bank**, 38 S.W.3d at 258; **Tindle v. Jackson Nat'l Life Ins.**, 837 S.W.2d 795, 798 (Tex.App.—Dallas 1992, no writ). For the claims to arise from the same transaction, at least some of the facts must be relevant to both claims. **Community State Bank**, 38 S.W.3d at 258; **Tindle**, 837 S.W.2d at 798. The Supreme Court has drawn a parallel between the transactional approach embodied in the compulsory-counterclaim rule and the transactional approach to res judicata. **Barr v. Resolution Trust Corp.**, 837 S.W.2d 627, 630–31 (Tex.1992); **Weiman v. Addicks-Fairbanks Rd. Sand Co.**, 846 S.W.2d 414, 419 (Tex.App.—Houston [14th Dist.] 1992, writ denied). Under **Barr**, factors to consider in determining whether events constitute the same transaction include (1) whether they are related in time, space, origin, or motivation, (2) whether, taken together, they form a convenient unit for trial purposes, and (3) whether their treatment as a trial unit conforms to the parties' expectations or business understanding or usage. **Barr**, 837 S.W.2d at 631; *see* **Getty Oil Co. v. Insurance Co. of N. Am.**, 845 S.W.2d 794, 798–99 (Tex.1992); *see also* Restatement Second, Judgments §24, comment b ("transaction" connotes natural grouping or common nucleus of operative facts).

(5) In same capacity. The claim must be against the opposing party in the same capacity in which that party filed its claim. **Ingersoll-Rand**, 997 S.W.2d at 207; **Wyatt**, 760 S.W.2d at 247; **Compass Expl.**, 60 S.W.3d at 277–78; *see* Tex. R. Civ. P. 97(a); *see also* **Encore Enters. v. Borderplex Rlty. Trust**, 583 S.W.3d 713, 723 (Tex.App.—El Paso 2019, no pet.) (phrase "opposing party in the same capacity" is not included in TRCP 97(a) but instead has been added by courts interpreting the rule). For example, when the plaintiff files suit in only a representative capacity, any claim against the plaintiff in its individual capacity is not compulsory. For a discussion of capacity, see "Capacity," ch. 2-B, §4.2.2.

(6) All parties available. The claim must not require the presence of additional parties over whom the court cannot acquire personal jurisdiction. Tex. R. Civ. P. 97(a); **Ingersoll-Rand**, 997 S.W.2d at 207; **Wyatt**, 760 S.W.2d at 247;

Compass Expl., 60 S.W.3d at 277–78.

Caution

A default judgment bars any claim the defendant could have asserted as a compulsory counterclaim if the defendant had answered. ***Jack H Brown & Co.****, 718 S.W.2d at 400.*

2. Cross-claim. When parties are coparties rather than opposing parties, the compulsory-counterclaim rule acts as a bar to a coparty's claim in a later suit only if the coparties had "issues drawn between them" in the first suit. **State & Cty. Mut. Fire Ins. v. Miller**, 52 S.W.3d 693, 696 (Tex.2001); **Getty Oil**, 845 S.W.2d at 800. For purposes of res judicata, coparties have issues drawn between them and become adverse when one coparty files a cross-claim against another coparty. **Miller**, 52 S.W.3d at 696.

§6.2 Parties to be joined. The parties should join all persons and entities needed for the just adjudication of the claims. *See* Tex. R. Civ. P. 39(a).

1. Feasible parties. The parties should join all feasible parties. Tex. R. Civ. P. 39(a). Before the 1971 amendment to TRCP 39, the courts used the phrase "necessary parties"; now the preferred phrase is "persons to be joined if feasible." **Wyatt v. Shaw Plumbing Co.**, 760 S.W.2d 245, 248 & n.2 (Tex.1988), *overruled on other grounds*, **In re J.B. Hunt Transp.**, 492 S.W.3d 287 (Tex.2016).

(1) Primary parties. A party subject to service of process should be joined if either one of the following applies:

(a) Without the absent party, complete relief cannot be given to those who are already parties. Tex. R. Civ. P. 39(a); **Henry v. Cox**, 520 S.W.3d 28, 34 (Tex.2017); **Wilchester W. Concerned Homeowners LDEF, Inc. v. Wilchester W. Fund, Inc.**, 177 S.W.3d 552, 559 (Tex.App.—Houston [1st Dist.] 2005, pet. denied); *see* **Brooks v. Northglen Ass'n**, 141 S.W.3d 158, 162 (Tex.2004).

(b) The absent party claims an interest in the subject matter of the action and its absence from the suit may either (1) prevent it from protecting this interest or (2) leave the parties already joined subject to a substantial risk of multiple liability or inconsistent obligations to the absent party. Tex. R. Civ. P. 39(a); **Crawford v. XTO Energy, Inc.**, 509 S.W.3d 906, 911 (Tex.2017); **Brooks**, 141 S.W.3d at 162–63; *see also* **Cooper v. Texas Gulf Indus.**, 513 S.W.2d 200, 204 (Tex.1974) (no precise standard for determining whether a person falls within provisions of TRCP 39(a)). TRCP 39(a) requires joinder for an absent party who actually claims an interest in the subject matter of the action; joinder is not required for an absent party who could potentially claim an interest in the subject matter of the action. **Crawford**, 509 S.W.3d at 913–14.

(2) Secondary parties.

(a) Sureties. A plaintiff can sue a surety without suing the principal only if judgment has already been taken against the principal or a statute (such as the CPRC or the UCC) authorizes the suit. Tex. R. Civ. P. 31; *see* Tex. Civ. Prac. & Rem. Code §17.001.

(b) Contracts with several obligors. A judgment can be rendered against a person who is not primarily liable on a contract only if judgment is also rendered against the principal obligor. Tex. Civ. Prac. & Rem. Code §17.001(a). There are four exceptions. An assignor, endorser, guarantor, or surety on a contract may be sued individually if the principal obligor (1) is a nonresident or resides where she cannot be reached by the ordinary process of law, (2) resides in an unknown place that cannot be ascertained by reasonable diligence, (3) is dead, or (4) is actually or notoriously insolvent. Tex. Civ. Prac. & Rem. Code §17.001(b).

(c) Under UCC. Assignors, endorsers, and other parties not primarily liable on commercial paper may be sued with the principal obligor or sued alone when permitted by statute. Tex. R. Civ. P. 30; *see* Tex. Bus. & Com. Code ch. 3.

2. Indispensable parties. If a feasible party cannot be joined, the court must decide whether the absent person is an indispensable party and the case should be dismissed. Tex. R. Civ. P. 39(b). Seldom is a person's presence in a suit so indispensable that the person's absence will deprive the court of jurisdiction to adjudicate the dispute between the parties al-

ready joined. **Cooper**, 513 S.W.2d at 204; *e.g.*, **Cox v. Johnson**, 638 S.W.2d 867, 868 (Tex.1982) (failure to join joint payee in suit on note was not fundamental error); *see, e.g.*, **Allison v. National Un. Fire Ins.**, 703 S.W.2d 637, 638 (Tex.1986) (failure of P-attorneys to join their clients in declaratory-judgment action against insurance companies that insured clients was not fundamental error). But if a party is truly indispensable, it is fundamental error for the court to proceed without that party. **Vondy v. Commissioners Ct.**, 620 S.W.2d 104, 106 (Tex.1981); *see, e.g.*, **Henry**, 520 S.W.3d at 35–36 (error for trial court to issue temporary injunction against county judge because Commissioners Court was not named as party to requested injunction but was indispensable). Instead, the court should dismiss the case. *See, e.g.*, **Gilmer ISD v. Dorfman**, 156 S.W.3d 586, 588–89 (Tex.App.—Tyler 2003, no pet.) (trial court erred in denying plea to the jurisdiction in suit contesting constitutionality of Educ. Code provisions because Commissioner of Education was indispensable party). To determine whether a person is an indispensable party, the court must consider the following factors:

(1) The extent to which a judgment rendered in the person's absence might be prejudicial to it or to those already parties. Tex. R. Civ. P. 39(b).

(2) The extent to which the prejudice can be lessened or avoided by protective provisions in the judgment, by the shaping of relief, or by other measures. *Id.*

(3) Whether a judgment rendered in the person's absence will be adequate. *Id.*

(4) Whether the plaintiff will have an adequate remedy if the action is dismissed for nonjoinder. *Id.*

§7. Permissive joinder of claims

§7.1 General. Any claim that involves some or all of the same parties to an ongoing suit and has common issues of fact and law, but does not satisfy the compulsory-counterclaim test, is a permissive claim in that suit. *See* Tex. R. Civ. P. 40, 174(a); *see, e.g.*, **Valley Forge Ins. v. Ryan**, 824 S.W.2d 236, 239 (Tex.App.—Fort Worth 1992, no writ) (because claim between same parties was not compulsory, it was permissive); *see also* **Getty Oil Co. v. Insurance Co. of N. Am.**, 845 S.W.2d 794, 800 (Tex.1992) (cross-claim under TRCP 97(e) against coparty is permissive). The compulsory-counterclaim rule does not bar the assertion of a permissive counterclaim in a later lawsuit. *See, e.g.*, **Brown Lex Real Estate Dev. Corp. v. American Nat'l Bank-S.**, 736 S.W.2d 205, 206–07 (Tex.App.—Corpus Christi 1987, writ ref'd n.r.e.) (because D admitted counterclaim was permissive, he conceded that denial of leave to file it was not error).

§7.2 Joining & separating permissive claims. There are four rules of procedure to consider in determining whether permissive claims should be tried together or separately: TRCP 40 (permissive joinder of parties), TRCP 41 (misjoinder and nonjoinder of parties), TRCP 51 (joinder of claims and remedies), and TRCP 174 (consolidation and separate trials). The relevant inquiry is whether a joint (or separate) trial of the claims will prevent manifest injustice and will not prejudice the rights of the parties. **Womack v. Berry**, 291 S.W.2d 677, 683 (Tex.1956); *see* Tex. R. Civ. P. 40(b) (prevent embarrassment, delay, or additional expense), Tex. R. Civ. P. 174(b) (further convenience and avoid prejudice); *see also* **Jones v. Ray**, 886 S.W.2d 817, 822 (Tex.App.—Houston [1st Dist.] 1994, orig. proceeding) (separate trials would permit Ds to make "empty chair" argument); **Dal-Briar Corp. v. Baskette**, 833 S.W.2d 612, 616–17 (Tex.App.—El Paso 1992, orig. proceeding) (joint trial would create unacceptable probability of unfair result). The judicial economy and convenience that may be gained by consolidation must be weighed against the likelihood that consolidation may result in delay, prejudice, or jury confusion. *See* **Dal-Briar Corp.**, 833 S.W.2d at 616–17.

§8. Remedies

§8.1 For misjoinder. If there is misjoinder of claims or parties (e.g., in a multiparty action, claims are added that are not part of the same transaction or occurrence), the court should drop or add parties, consolidate separate actions, sever actions improperly joined, or order separate trials within the same case. Tex. R. Civ. P. 41; *see* Tex. R. Civ. P. 40(b), 174. The court cannot dismiss all or part of the suit. Tex. R. Civ. P. 41.

1. Drop or add parties. A court may order that parties be added or dropped from the suit. Tex. R. Civ. P. 41.

2. Consolidate actions. A court may order consolidation of two or more suits with common questions of law or fact. Tex. R. Civ. P. 174(a). The consolidated suit will have one cause number and be resolved by a single judgment. See "Motion to consolidate," ch. 5-J, §4.

3. Sever claims. A court may order severance of claims into two or more suits from what was originally one suit. *See* Tex. R. Civ. P. 41. Each suit will be given its own cause number and be resolved by a separate judgment. See "Motion for severance," ch. 5-I, §3.

4. Separate trials. A court may order separate trials of issues in one case for reasons of convenience or to avoid prejudice or embarrassment. *See* Tex. R. Civ. P. 40(b), 174(b). The claims remain part of the same suit and are resolved by a single judgment. See "Motion for separate (bifurcated) trial," ch. 5-I, §4.

§8.2 For absent party. If a party that should be joined is absent, the complaining party should file a motion to abate. See "Motion to Abate—Challenging the Suit," ch. 3-I, §1 et seq.

G. Choosing the Court—Jurisdiction

§1. General

§1.1 Rules. None. See Tex. Const. art. 5; Tex. Civ. Prac. & Rem. Code chs. 51, 61 to 64; Tex. Est. Code ch. 32, §34.001, ch. 1022; Tex. Fam. Code §§51.04, 51.0413; Tex. Gov't Code chs. 24 to 27; Tex. Prop. Code §115.001.

§1.2 Purpose. Before filing suit, the plaintiff must decide in which of the Texas trial courts the lawsuit should be filed. That decision is made by choosing the court with both jurisdiction over the dispute and proper venue. For venue, see "Choosing the Court—Venue," ch. 2-H, §1 et seq. To challenge the subject-matter jurisdiction of the court, see "Plea to the Jurisdiction—Challenging the Court," ch. 3-F, §1 et seq.

§1.3 Form. **O'Connor's Texas Civil Forms**, FORM 2B:20 (2020 ed.).

§1.4 Other references. Texas Judicial Branch, *Overview of the Texas Judicial System*, www.txcourts.gov/about-texas-courts; Pargaman, *Probate, Guardianship, and Trust Law*, 72 Tex.B.J. 674 (Sept.2009).

§2. Jurisdiction of Texas trial courts

The jurisdiction of Texas courts is conferred solely by the Texas Constitution and state statutes. **Chenault v. Phillips**, 914 S.W.2d 140, 141 (Tex.1996).

§2.1 Types of trial courts. In Texas, there are district, county, justice-of-the-peace, and various other courts established by legislative enactment. Each type of court has jurisdiction over specific types of cases and amounts in controversy. *See* **In re United Servs. Auto. Ass'n**, 307 S.W.3d 299, 303 (Tex.2010). Although all courts can render a judgment for damages, not all courts can render a judgment for other types of relief (e.g., injunctive relief).

§2.2 Nonmonetary jurisdiction. Some claims do not depend on the amount of damages sought to establish jurisdiction (e.g., divorce suits, defamation suits, forcible-entry-and-detainer suits).

§2.3 Monetary jurisdiction. Most claims depend on the amount of damages sought to establish jurisdiction (e.g., breach-of-contract suits, personal-injury suits). See "Damages," ch. 2-B, §9.

1. Computing amount in controversy. The amount in controversy is determined by the plaintiff's good-faith pleadings. **Smith Detective Agency & Nightwatch Serv. v. Stanley Smith Sec., Inc.**, 938 S.W.2d 743, 747 (Tex.App.—Dallas 1996, writ denied); *see also* **Tune v. Texas DPS**, 23 S.W.3d 358, 362 (Tex.2000) (amount in controversy determined by subjective value of rights asserted by P, if asserted in good faith).

(1) Single plaintiff vs. single defendant. When one plaintiff asserts multiple claims against a single defendant, jurisdiction is determined by adding the amounts together. **Texas City Tire Shop, Inc. v. Alexander**, 333 S.W.2d 690, 693 (Tex.App.—Houston 1960, no writ); *see also* **Tejas Toyota, Inc. v. Griffin**, 587 S.W.2d 775, 776 (Tex.App.—Waco 1979, writ ref'd n.r.e.) (cross-actions are treated as separate suits; sum of damages in cross-action exceeded jurisdiction of trial court). When a plaintiff asserts claims based on alternative theories, jurisdiction is determined according to the theory that would yield the highest award. **Lucey v. Southeast Tex. Emerg. Physicians Assocs.**, 802 S.W.2d 300, 302 (Tex.App.—El Paso 1990, writ denied).

(2) Multiple parties.

(a) By multiple plaintiffs. When multiple plaintiffs assert claims against a defendant, their claims are aggregated to determine the amount in controversy. Tex. Gov't Code §24.009; **Dubai Pet. Co. v. Kazi**, 12 S.W.3d 71, 75 n.4 (Tex.2000). Thus, a class action with 100 plaintiffs each suing for $10 would have $1,000 in controversy and could be filed in district court.

(b) Against multiple defendants. When a plaintiff asserts separate, independent, and distinct claims against multiple defendants, jurisdiction is determined by looking at the claims separately, and the amounts are not aggregated. **Borrego v. del Palacio**, 445 S.W.2d 620, 622 (Tex.App.—El Paso 1969, no writ). Thus, one plaintiff suing 100 defendants for $10 each would have only $10 in controversy and would file the suit in justice court.

(3) Counterclaims. Counterclaims, whether permissive or compulsory, are judged on their own merits and must be within the court's jurisdiction. **Color Tile, Inc. v. Ramsey**, 905 S.W.2d 620, 623 (Tex.App.—Houston [14th Dist.] 1995, no writ); *see* Tex. R. Civ. P. 97; **Smith v. Clary Corp.**, 917 S.W.2d 796, 798 (Tex.1996). A permissive or compulsory counterclaim can be for an amount within or below the court's minimum jurisdiction, but it cannot be for an amount above the court's maximum jurisdiction. *See, e.g.*, **Dykes v. Crausbay**, 214 S.W.3d 200, 202 (Tex.App.—Amarillo 2007, no pet.) (claim above jurisdictional limit not a compulsory counterclaim); **Kitchen Designs, Inc. v. Wood**, 584 S.W.2d 305, 307 (Tex.App.—Texarkana 1979, writ ref'd n.r.e.) (same); **Watkins v. Cossaboom**, 204 S.W.2d 56, 57–58 (Tex.App.—Galveston 1947, writ dism'd) (compulsory counterclaim below jurisdictional limit). If a counterclaim is above the jurisdictional limit of the court, the trial court should dismiss the counterclaim. **Kitchen Designs**, 584 S.W.2d at 307. Counterclaims of multiple defendants are not aggregated under the aggregating statute. **Smith**, 917 S.W.2d at 798; *see* Tex. Gov't Code §24.009.

(4) Actions other than for damages. When the action is to recover or foreclose on personal property, the amount in controversy is either the fair market value of the property or the amount of the underlying debt, whichever is higher. If the suit is for injunctive relief, and there is no amount in controversy, jurisdiction is in the district court based on residual jurisdiction. *See* **Super X Drugs v. State**, 505 S.W.2d 333, 336 (Tex.App.—Houston [14th Dist.] 1974, no writ); *see also* **Martin v. Victoria ISD**, 972 S.W.2d 815, 818 (Tex.App.—Corpus Christi 1998, pet. denied) (county court cannot hold injunction hearing unless amount in controversy is alleged). See "General jurisdiction," ch. 2-G, §3.1.

(5) Other related claims. A court can assert jurisdiction over claims that are below its minimum jurisdictional limits if those claims arise from the same transaction or occurrence as a claim that the court has jurisdiction over. **Watkins**, 204 S.W.2d at 57. A court cannot assert jurisdiction over a claim that is above its maximum jurisdictional limits. **Hawkins v. Anderson**, 672 S.W.2d 293, 296 (Tex.App.—Dallas 1984, no writ).

(6) Amendments in excess of jurisdictional limits. Generally, once jurisdiction is properly acquired, no later fact or event can defeat the court's jurisdiction. **Continental Coffee Prods. v. Cazarez**, 937 S.W.2d 444, 449 (Tex.1996); **Dallas ISD v. Porter**, 709 S.W.2d 642, 643 (Tex.1986); **Weidner v. Sanchez**, 14 S.W.3d 353, 360–61 (Tex.App.—Houston [14th Dist.] 2000, no pet.). If the plaintiff's original petition was properly brought in a particular court, but an amendment increases the amount in controversy above the court's jurisdictional limits, the court will continue to have jurisdiction if the additional damages accrued as a result of the passage of time. **Continental Coffee**, 937 S.W.2d at 449; **Mr. W. Fireworks, Inc. v. Mitchell**, 622 S.W.2d 576, 577 (Tex.1981). If an amendment adds a claim for damages that existed at the time the suit was filed but was not included in the original petition, and if the additional claim is outside the court's jurisdiction, the additional claim should be dismissed on a plea to the jurisdiction. *See* **Hawkins**, 672 S.W.2d at 296.

(7) Interest. Interest is seldom included in the amount in controversy. The courts distinguish between interest eo nomine (interest as interest), which is excluded, and interest as damages, which is included. **Weidner**, 14 S.W.3d at 362; *see also* Tex. Gov't Code §25.0003(c)(1) (specifically excludes interest eo nomine in determining the amount in controversy in suits filed in county courts at law); **Smith**, 917 S.W.2d at 798 (same). Interest eo nomine is interest as provided for by agreement or by statute; it is part of the debt. Interest as damages is interest that is added to the debt for not paying a sum certain at the time the debt was due. For example, prejudgment interest is usually considered interest as damages, but if it is provided for by contract or statute it is interest eo nomine. **Weidner**, 14 S.W.3d at 362; *see* **Barnes v. U.S. Fid. & Guar. Co.**, 279 S.W.2d 919, 921 (Tex.App.—Waco 1955, no writ).

(8) Attorney fees & exemplary damages. Attorney fees are generally included in the amount in controversy. **Johnson v. Universal Life & Acc. Ins.**, 94 S.W.2d 1145, 1146 (Tex.1936); **Long v. Fox**, 625 S.W.2d 376, 378 (Tex.App.—San Antonio 1981, writ ref'd n.r.e.). But in suits filed in county courts at law, attorney fees, penalties, and statutory or punitive damages are specifically excluded from the amount in controversy. Tex. Gov't Code §25.0003(c)(1); **Smith**, 917 S.W.2d at 798.

(9) Costs. Court costs are not included in the amount in controversy.

2. Amending to correct amount in controversy.

(1) Liquidated damages. If a pleading makes a claim for nonseverable liquidated damages that are outside the trial court's jurisdiction (either above or below), the party cannot amend its damages to state an amount within the court's jurisdiction. *See* **Smith Detective Agency**, 938 S.W.2d at 747.

(2) Unliquidated damages. TRCP 47 requires a pleading to contain the specific range of monetary relief the party seeks. *See* Tex. R. Civ. P. 47(c). Thus, it is unclear whether a party whose pleading makes a claim for unliquidated damages that are outside the trial court's jurisdiction (either above or below) can amend its damages to state an amount within the court's jurisdiction. See "Specific statement of relief," ch. 1-B, §3.2.8(2).

§3. District courts

§3.1 General jurisdiction. The district courts are the primary trial courts of Texas. *See* **Dubai Pet. Co. v. Kazi**, 12 S.W.3d 71, 75 (Tex.2000). District courts are courts of general jurisdiction. *See* Tex. Gov't Code §24.008. That is, the Constitution gives district courts exclusive, appellate, and original jurisdiction over all actions, proceedings, and remedies, except in cases in which jurisdiction is conferred by the Texas Constitution or other law on another court, tribunal, or administrative body. Tex. Const. art. 5, §8; **Dubai Pet.**, 12 S.W.3d at 75; *see* Tex. Gov't Code §§24.007(a), 24.008, 24.011. District courts have jurisdiction over all types of claims over which justice and county courts do not. *See* Tex. Const. art. 5, §8; Tex. Gov't Code §24.008. District courts have concurrent jurisdiction with each other over the same cases in the same county. *See* Tex. Gov't Code §24.003(b); **Pinnacle Gas Treating, Inc. v. Read**, 160 S.W.3d 564, 566 (Tex.2005). But a district court generally cannot transfer a case or proceeding to the docket of another district court without the consent of the judge of the court receiving the transfer. Tex. Gov't Code §24.003(b-1). See "Transfer of cases & exchange of benches," ch. 2-G, §3.5.

§3.2 Specialized jurisdiction. The Constitution gives the Legislature the power to "establish such other courts as it may deem necessary," to prescribe the jurisdiction of those legislative courts, and to "conform the jurisdiction of the district and other inferior courts thereto." Tex. Const. art. 5, §1. Examples of the most common types of courts with specialized jurisdiction are the following:

1. Family district courts. The Legislature created family district courts with jurisdiction equal to that of constitutional district courts but with primary responsibility for family-law matters such as divorce, annulment, child conservatorship, and child support. Tex. Gov't Code §24.601(a), (b); *see* **Beach v. Beach**, 912 S.W.2d 345, 347 n.3 (Tex.App.—Houston [14th Dist.] 1995, no writ). The family district courts have concurrent jurisdiction with other district courts in the county where they are located. Tex. Gov't Code §24.601(a).

2. Juvenile-court designation. A district court is one of the courts that may be designated as a juvenile court. *See* Tex. Gov't Code §23.001 (other courts that may be designated are a county court or a statutory county court that is exercising jurisdiction of district or county court); Tex. Fam. Code §51.04(b) (other courts that may be designated are a criminal district court, domestic-relations court, juvenile court, county court, or county court at law). The designation as a juvenile court is made by the county's juvenile board. Tex. Fam. Code §51.04(b), (i). Juvenile courts have original, exclusive jurisdiction over proceedings under the Juvenile Justice Code. Tex. Fam. Code §51.04(a). Under certain circumstances, juvenile courts can simultaneously exercise jurisdiction over proceedings under the Juvenile Justice Code and under Family Code title 5, subtitle E (child-abuse cases). Tex. Fam. Code §51.0413(a).

§3.3 Amount in controversy. District courts have original jurisdiction in civil cases in which the amount in controversy exceeds $500, excluding interest. Tex. Gov't Code §24.007(b). There is no upper limit to their amount-in-controversy jurisdiction. *See generally* Tex. Const. art. 5, §8 (jurisdiction of district court); Tex. Gov't Code §§24.007, 24.008 (same). See "Summary chart of amount in controversy," ch. 2-G, §6.

§3.4 Relief available. A district court can grant all types of relief, including writs of injunction, mandamus, sequestration, attachment, garnishment, certiorari, and supersedeas, and all other writs necessary to enforce its jurisdiction. *See* Tex. Const. art. 5, §8; Tex. Gov't Code §§24.008, 24.011.

§3.5 Transfer of cases & exchange of benches. District judges may transfer cases to or exchange benches with another district court in the same county. Tex. Gov't Code §24.003(b); Tex. R. Civ. P. 330(e); *see* Tex. Const. art. 5, §11; *see also* Tex. Gov't Code §24.003(b-1) (district judge may not transfer case without consent of judge of court receiving transfer). The rules for transferring cases and exchanging benches apply to counties with two or more district courts. Tex. Gov't Code §24.003(a); Tex. R. Civ. P. 330(e).

Note

When a case is transferred from one district court to another, all processes, writs, bonds, and other obligations that are issued by the transferring court can be returned to the court to which the case is being transferred as if that court had originally issued the obligation. Tex. Gov't Code §24.023.

1. Judge's power to transfer & exchange. Unless local rules of administration provide otherwise, a district judge in a county with two or more district courts can do the following:

(1) Transfer any civil case or proceeding on the court's docket, other than a case governed by Family Code chapter 155 (jurisdiction over suits affecting the parent-child relationship), to the docket of another district court in the county, as long as the judge of the court receiving the transfer has consented to it. Tex. Gov't Code §24.003(b)(1), (b-1); *see* Tex. R. Civ. P. 330(e).

(2) Hear and determine any case or proceeding, or any part or question of a case or proceeding, pending in another district court in the county without having the case transferred. Tex. Gov't Code §24.003(b)(2), (d); *see* Tex. Gov't Code §74.094(a) (district judge may hear and determine matter pending in any district court in county regardless of whether matter is preliminary or final and may sign judgment or order regardless of whether case is transferred); Tex. R. Civ. P. 330(e) (district judge may, in her own courtroom, try and determine case or proceeding pending in another district court).

(3) Sit for another district court in the county and hear and determine any case or proceeding pending in that court. Tex. Gov't Code §24.003(b)(3); Tex. R. Civ. P. 330(e).

(4) Temporarily exchange benches with the judge of another district court in the county. Tex. Gov't Code §24.003(b)(4); *see* Tex. R. Civ. P. 330(e).

(5) Try different cases in the same court at the same time. Tex. Gov't Code §24.003(b)(5); Tex. R. Civ. P. 330(e).

(6) Occupy the judge's own courtroom or the courtroom of another district court in the county. Tex. Gov't Code §24.003(b)(6); Tex. R. Civ. P. 330(e).

2. Absent judge. If a district judge in the county is sick or otherwise absent, another district judge in the county can hold court for that judge. Tex. Gov't Code §24.003(c).

3. Matters to be heard & determined. Under Gov't Code §24.003, a district judge can hear and determine the following matters in a case or proceeding pending in another court without transferring the case or proceeding:

(1) Motions, including motions for new trial. Tex. Gov't Code §24.003(d).

(2) Petitions for injunctive relief. *Id.*

(3) Applications for the appointment of a receiver. *Id.*

(4) Petitions in intervention. *Id.*

(5) Pleas in abatement or other dilatory pleas. *Id.*

(6) All preliminary matters, questions, and proceedings. *Id.*

4. Judgment or order.

(1) Restraining order or injunction. A district judge can issue a restraining order or an injunction that is returnable to any other district court. Tex. Gov't Code §24.003(d); Tex. R. Civ. P. 330(e).

(2) Rendition of judgment. A district judge who hears and determines certain matters in a case or proceeding pending in another district court can render judgment in the case or proceeding. *See* Tex. Gov't Code §24.003(d); Tex. R. Civ. P. 330(e). See "Judge's power to transfer & exchange," ch. 2-G, §3.5.1(3). The district judge in whose court a matter is pending can also hear, complete, and determine the matter, or all or any part of another matter, and render a final judgment.

Tex. Gov't Code §24.003(d). If a district judge hears and determines any part or question of a pending case or proceeding, any other district judge can then complete the hearing and render judgment. *Id.*

(3) Entry of judgment or order. A district judge who hears and determines a matter can enter a judgment or an order on that matter without transferring the case or proceeding. Tex. Gov't Code §24.003(d). Any judgment or order must be entered in the minutes of the court where the case is pending. Tex. Gov't Code §24.003(e); Tex. R. Civ. P. 330(e); *see* Tex. Gov't Code §24.003(d).

5. No limitation of powers. Gov't Code §24.003 does not limit a district judge's powers when that judge is acting for another judge because of the transfer of a case or proceeding, the exchange of benches, or any other reason under Gov't Code §24.003. *See* Tex. Gov't Code §24.003(f).

§4. County courts

There are various types of county courts with different types of jurisdiction. The most complicated aspect of county-court jurisdiction is probate jurisdiction. As the Supreme Court noted, "Texas probate jurisdiction is, to say the least, somewhat complex." **Palmer v. Coble Wall Trust Co.**, 851 S.W.2d 178, 180 n.3 (Tex.1992).

§4.1 Constitutional county courts. Every county has a constitutional county court, which is the office of the chief administrator of the county. *See* Tex. Const. art. 5, §§15, 16. In some counties the constitutional county judge exercises probate jurisdiction, and in others the judge acts only as the county's administrator and takes no action as a trial judge. The Texas Constitution states that the jurisdiction of the constitutional county court is "as provided by law." Tex. Const. art. 5, §16. Its jurisdiction, therefore, is governed by statutes. *See* Tex. Civ. Prac. & Rem. Code §§51.001, 51.002, 61.021; Tex. Gov't Code §§26.041 to 26.044, 26.048, 26.050, 26.051.

1. Amount in controversy. The constitutional county courts have concurrent jurisdiction with (1) the justice courts in civil cases in which the amount in controversy exceeds $200 but does not exceed $20,000, excluding interest, and (2) the district courts in civil cases in which the amount in controversy exceeds $500 but does not exceed $5,000, excluding interest. Tex. Gov't Code §26.042(a), (d). The amount in controversy does not limit the court's probate jurisdiction. **Womble v. Atkins**, 331 S.W.2d 294, 299 (Tex.1960). See "Summary chart of amount in controversy," ch. 2-G, §6.

Note

For causes of action filed before September 1, 2020, the constitutional county courts had concurrent jurisdiction with justice courts in civil cases in which the amount in controversy exceeded $200 but did not exceed $10,000, excluding interest. See Tex. Gov't Code §26.042(a) (pre-9-1-20 version); Acts 2019, 86th Leg., R.S., ch. 696, §§31, 36, 37, eff. Sept. 1, 2020.

---

2. Probate & guardianship matters.

(1) Original jurisdiction. Except in the counties where probate jurisdiction rests exclusively in other courts, constitutional county courts have original jurisdiction over probate and guardianship proceedings. *See* Tex. Est. Code §32.002(a) (probate), §1022.002(a) (guardianship).

(2) Matters related to probate proceeding. Constitutional county courts with original probate jurisdiction also have jurisdiction over certain matters "related to" probate proceedings. *See* Tex. Est. Code §32.001(a).

(a) County without county court at law. If the constitutional county court is located in a county that does not have a county court at law, the court has jurisdiction over the following matters related to a probate proceeding:

[1] An action against a personal representative or former personal representative arising from the representative's performance of the duties of a personal representative. Tex. Est. Code §§31.002(a)(1), 32.001(a).

[2] An action against a surety of a personal representative or former personal representative. Tex. Est. Code §§31.002(a)(2), 32.001(a).

[3] A claim brought by a personal representative on behalf of the estate. Tex. Est. Code §§31.002(a)(3), 32.001(a).

[4] An action brought against a personal representative in the representative's capacity as personal representative. Tex. Est. Code §§31.002(a)(4), 32.001(a).

[5] An action for trial of title to real property that is estate property, including the enforcement of a lien against the property. Tex. Est. Code §§31.002(a)(5), 32.001(a).

[6] An action for trial of the right of property that is estate property. Tex. Est. Code §§31.002(a)(6), 32.001(a).

(b) County with county court at law. If the constitutional county court is located in a county that also has a county court at law, the constitutional county court has jurisdiction over the following matters related to a probate proceeding:

[1] An action against a personal representative or former personal representative arising from the representative's performance of the duties of a personal representative. Tex. Est. Code §§31.002(a)(1), (b)(1), 32.001(a).

[2] An action against a surety of a personal representative or former personal representative. Tex. Est. Code §§31.002(a)(2), (b)(1), 32.001(a).

[3] A claim brought by a personal representative on behalf of the estate. Tex. Est. Code §§31.002(a)(3), (b)(1), 32.001(a).

[4] An action brought against a personal representative in the representative's capacity as personal representative. Tex. Est. Code §§31.002(a)(4), (b)(1), 32.001(a).

[5] An action for trial of title to real property that is estate property, including the enforcement of a lien against the property. Tex. Est. Code §§31.002(a)(5), (b)(1), 32.001(a).

[6] An action for trial of the right of property that is estate property. Tex. Est. Code §§31.002(a)(6), (b)(1), 32.001(a).

[7] The interpretation and administration of a testamentary trust if the will creating the trust has been admitted to probate in the court. Tex. Est. Code §§31.002(b)(2), 32.001(a).

[8] The interpretation and administration of an inter vivos trust created by a decedent whose will has been admitted to probate in the court. Tex. Est. Code §§31.002(b)(3), 32.001(a).

(3) Pendent & ancillary jurisdiction for probate estate. A constitutional county court with original jurisdiction over probate proceedings may exercise pendent and ancillary jurisdiction as necessary to promote judicial efficiency and economy. *See* Tex. Est. Code §32.001(b) ("probate court" may exercise pendent and ancillary jurisdiction); *see also* Tex. Est. Code §22.007(b) ("probate court" is any court exercising original probate jurisdiction).

(4) Matters related to guardianship proceeding. Constitutional county courts have jurisdiction over matters that are "related to" a guardianship proceeding. *See* Tex. Est. Code §§1021.001(a), 1022.001(a), 1022.002(a). Specifically, these matters include:

(a) The granting of letters of guardianship. Tex. Est. Code §1021.001(a)(1).

(b) The settling of a guardian's account and all other matters relating to the settlement, partition, or distribution of a ward's estate. Tex. Est. Code §1021.001(a)(2).

(c) A claim by or against a guardianship estate. Tex. Est. Code §1021.001(a)(3).

(d) An action for trial of title to land that is guardianship-estate property, including the enforcement of a lien against the property. Tex. Est. Code §1021.001(a)(4).

(e) An action for trial of the right of property that is guardianship-estate property. Tex. Est. Code §1021.001(a)(5).

(f) After a guardianship of a ward's estate is required to be settled under Estates Code §1204.001:

[1] An action by or on behalf of the former ward against a former guardian of the ward for alleged misconduct arising from the performance of the person's duties as guardian. Tex. Est. Code §1021.001(a)(6)(A).

[2] An action calling on the surety of a guardian or former guardian to perform in place of the guardian or former guardian, which may include the award of a judgment against the guardian or former guardian in favor of the surety. Tex. Est. Code §1021.001(a)(6)(B).

[3] An action against a former guardian of the former ward that is brought by a surety called on to perform in place of the former guardian. Tex. Est. Code §1021.001(a)(6)(C).

[4] A claim for the payment of compensation, expenses, and court costs, and any other matter authorized under Estates Code chapter 1155. Tex. Est. Code §1021.001(a)(6)(D).

[5] A matter related to an authorization made or duty performed by a guardian under Estates Code chapter 1204. Tex. Est. Code §1021.001(a)(6)(E).

(g) The appointment of a trustee for a trust created under Estates Code §1301.053 or §1301.054, the settling of an account of the trustee, and all other matters related to the trust. Tex. Est. Code §1021.001(a)(7).

3. Juvenile matters. A constitutional county court may be designated as a juvenile court. Tex. Fam. Code §51.04(b); Tex. Gov't Code §23.001; *see* Tex. Gov't Code §26.042(b) (county court has juvenile jurisdiction as provided by §23.001). See "Juvenile-court designation," ch. 2-G, §3.2.2. If a county court is designated as a juvenile court, at least one other court must also be designated as a juvenile court. Tex. Fam. Code §51.04(c). If the judge of the county court is not a licensed attorney, an alternate court must be designated. Tex. Fam. Code §51.04(d).

4. Appellate jurisdiction. Constitutional county courts have appellate jurisdiction over cases originating in the justice courts when the amount in controversy or the judgment exceeds $250, not including costs. Tex. Civ. Prac. & Rem. Code §51.001(a); Tex. Gov't Code §26.042(e); *see* Tex. R. Civ. P. 506.3. The standard of review in the constitutional county court is de novo. Tex. R. Civ. P. 506.3, 509.8(e), 510.10(c).

5. Additional jurisdiction. The Legislature has given some constitutional county courts limited jurisdiction over other matters. *See, e.g.*, Tex. Gov't Code §26.134 (Cass County constitutional county court has the power to receive and enter guilty pleas in misdemeanor cases).

6. Relief available. A constitutional county court can grant all types of relief, including writs of injunction, mandamus, sequestration, attachment, garnishment, certiorari, and supersedeas, and all other writs necessary to enforce its jurisdiction. *See* Tex. Const. art. 5, §16; Tex. Gov't Code §§26.044, 26.051; **Martin v. Victoria ISD**, 972 S.W.2d 815, 817 (Tex.App.—Corpus Christi 1998, pet. denied).

7. Cases excluded. Constitutional county courts do not have jurisdiction over suits for (1) recovery of damages for defamation, (2) enforcement of liens on land, (3) escheat on behalf of the State, (4) divorce, (5) forfeiture of a corporate charter, (6) the trial of the right to property valued at $500 or more and levied under a writ of execution, sequestration, or attachment, (7) eminent domain, or (8) recovery of land. Tex. Gov't Code §26.043.

§4.2 County courts at law. Every county court at law (also called a statutory county court) has the same jurisdiction as the constitutional county court in that county, unless modified by (1) the statute that created the county court at law or (2) a statute that applies to all county courts at law. *See* Tex. Gov't Code §§25.0001(a), 25.0003(a), 25.0004(c); *see also* Tex. Const. art. 5, §1 (Legislature may establish other courts as it deems necessary); Tex. Gov't Code ch. 25, subchs. D, F (multicounty statutory county courts). *See generally* Tex. Gov't Code ch. 25, subch. C (jurisdictional provisions for particular county courts at law).

1. Amount in controversy. The county courts at law have concurrent jurisdiction with the district courts for cases in which the amount in controversy exceeds $500 but does not exceed $250,000, excluding mandatory damages and penalties, attorney fees, interest, and court costs. Tex. Gov't Code §25.0003(c)(1). The amount in controversy includes all

damages the plaintiff seeks to recover, not the amount of damages the plaintiff is likely to recover. **United Servs. Auto. Ass'n v. Brite**, 215 S.W.3d 400, 402–03 (Tex.2007). Because county courts at law have the same jurisdiction as constitutional county courts, the actual dollar range of the amount in controversy for county courts at law starts as low as $200.01 and goes as high as $250,000, depending on which statute governs that court's jurisdiction. *See* Tex. Gov't Code §§25.0003(a), 26.042(a). Although some county courts at law have very limited jurisdiction, others have about the same jurisdiction as the district courts. *E.g.*, Tex. Gov't Code §25.0592(a) (Dallas County), §25.0732(a) (El Paso County), §25.0862(a) (Galveston County); *see, e.g.*, **Weinberger v. Longer**, 222 S.W.3d 557, 560–61 (Tex.App.—Houston [14th Dist.] 2007, pet. denied) (because Galveston County court at law had concurrent jurisdiction with district court regardless of amount in controversy, county court had jurisdiction over counterclaim exceeding $100,000; decided under former Gov't Code §25.003(c)(1) with amount-in-controversy ceiling of $100,000); **Schuld v. Dembrinski**, 12 S.W.3d 485, 489 (Tex.App.—Dallas 2000, no pet.) (because Dallas County court at law had concurrent jurisdiction with district court in civil cases regardless of amount in controversy, county court had jurisdiction over partition suit). See "Summary chart of amount in controversy," ch. 2-G, §6. A county court may have exclusive jurisdiction over certain claims regardless of the amount in controversy. *E.g.*, **AIC Mgmt. v. Crews**, 246 S.W.3d 640, 644 (Tex.2008) (Harris County court at law had exclusive jurisdiction over eminent-domain proceedings regardless of amount in controversy).

Note

For causes of action filed before September 1, 2020, the county courts at law had concurrent jurisdiction with the district courts for cases in which the amount in controversy exceeded $500 but did not exceed $200,000, excluding mandatory damages and penalties, attorney fees, interest, and court costs. See Tex. Gov't Code §25.0003(c)(1) (pre-9-1-20 version); Acts 2019, 86th Leg., R.S., ch. 696, §§2, 36, 37, eff. Sept. 1, 2020.

2. Probate & guardianship matters.

(1) Original jurisdiction. Gov't Code §25.0003(d) authorizes county courts at law to exercise original probate jurisdiction, unless there is a statutory probate court in the same county. *See* Tex. Gov't Code §25.0003(e); *see also* Tex. Est. Code §32.002(b) (probate), §1022.002(b) (guardianship). However, a county court at law does not have the same jurisdiction granted to statutory probate courts under the Estates Code. Tex. Gov't Code §25.0003(f); **Carroll v. Carroll**, 304 S.W.3d 366, 368 (Tex.2010); *see* **In re G.C.**, 66 S.W.3d 517, 522 (Tex.App.—Fort Worth 2002, no pet.) (county court at law does not become statutory probate court merely by exercising its probate jurisdiction). Instead, a county court at law has the general probate jurisdiction of a constitutional county court over probate and guardianship proceedings. *See* Tex. Est. Code §32.002(b) (probate), §1022.002(b) (guardianship); Tex. Gov't Code §25.0003(d).

(2) Matters related to probate proceeding. A county court at law has jurisdiction over the same matters "related to" probate proceedings as do the constitutional county courts located in the same county. *See* Tex. Est. Code §§31.002(b), 32.001(a), 32.002(b). See "County with county court at law," ch. 2-G, §4.1.2(2)(b).

(3) Pendent & ancillary jurisdiction for probate estate. A county court at law with original jurisdiction over probate proceedings may exercise pendent and ancillary jurisdiction as necessary to promote judicial efficiency and economy. *See* Tex. Est. Code §32.001(b) ("probate court" may exercise pendent and ancillary jurisdiction); *see also* Tex. Est. Code §22.007(b) ("probate court" is any court exercising original probate jurisdiction).

(4) Matters related to guardianship proceeding. A county court at law has jurisdiction over the same matters "related to" guardianship proceedings as do the constitutional county courts. *See* Tex. Est. Code §§1021.001(a), 1022.001(a), 1022.002(b). See "Matters related to guardianship proceeding," ch. 2-G, §4.1.2(4).

3. Civil & criminal. County courts at law have jurisdiction over all civil and criminal causes prescribed by law for constitutional county courts. Tex. Gov't Code §25.0003(a); **Weeks v. Hobson**, 877 S.W.2d 478, 480 n.1 (Tex.App.—Houston [1st Dist.] 1994, orig. proceeding).

4. Relief available. A county court at law can grant all types of relief, including writs of injunction, mandamus, sequestration, attachment, garnishment, certiorari, and supersedeas, and other writs necessary to enforce its jurisdiction.

See Tex. Gov't Code §25.0004(a), (c); **In re Burlington N. & Santa Fe Ry.**, 12 S.W.3d 891, 896 (Tex.App.—Houston [14th Dist.] 2000, orig. proceeding); **Martin v. Victoria ISD**, 972 S.W.2d 815, 817 (Tex.App.—Corpus Christi 1998, pet. denied).

5. Juvenile matters. A county court at law may be designated as a juvenile court. Tex. Fam. Code §51.04(b); Tex. Gov't Code §23.001. See "Juvenile-court designation," ch. 2-G, §3.2.2.

6. Matters pending in another court. A judge in a county court at law can hear and determine a matter pending in any county court at law in the county, regardless of whether the matter is preliminary or final. Tex. Gov't Code §74.094(a); **Rodriguez v. EMC Mortg. Corp.**, 94 S.W.3d 795, 797–98 (Tex.App.—San Antonio 2002, no pet.). The judge can also sign a judgment or an order in any of the county courts at law, regardless of whether the case is transferred. Tex. Gov't Code §74.094(a).

7. Matters excluded. A county court at law does not have jurisdiction over county business of the commissioners court or over matters excluded from the jurisdiction of the constitutional county court. *See* Tex. Gov't Code §25.0003(b) (county-business exclusion), §26.043 (exclusions for constitutional county courts); *see, e.g.*, **Matherne v. Carre**, 7 S.W.3d 903, 906 (Tex.App.—Beaumont 1999, pet. denied) (county court at law does not have jurisdiction over suit for enforcement of lien on land); **Loville v. Loville**, 944 S.W.2d 818, 819 (Tex.App.—Beaumont 1997, writ denied) (like constitutional county court, county court at law does not have jurisdiction over suit to recover land). *But see* Tex. Gov't Code §25.1032(c), (d) (Harris County civil court at law has jurisdiction over eminent-domain proceedings in which amount in controversy is within jurisdictional limits for county courts at law, as well as over certain other matters excluded from constitutional county court). See "Cases excluded," ch. 2-G, §4.1.7.

§4.3 Statutory probate courts. Certain courts are designated as "statutory probate courts" under Gov't Code chapter 25. Tex. Est. Code §22.007(c); Tex. Gov't Code §21.009(4).

1. Original jurisdiction. In a county with a statutory probate court, all probate and guardianship matters must be heard in the statutory probate court, whether contested or not. Tex. Est. Code §32.005(a) (probate), §1022.005(a) (guardianship); *see* Tex. Est. Code §1022.002(c) (guardianship). Statutory probate courts have general probate jurisdiction under the Estates Code. *See* Tex. Gov't Code §25.0021(b)(1); **Schuld v. Dembrinski**, 12 S.W.3d 485, 487 (Tex.App.—Dallas 2000, no pet.); **Green v. Watson**, 860 S.W.2d 238, 242 (Tex.App.—Austin 1993, no writ). Gov't Code §25.0021(a) does, however, limit the jurisdiction of statutory probate courts to matters in probate, guardianship, mental health, and eminent domain, superseding any other Government Code provisions that give additional jurisdiction to statutory probate courts in specific counties.

2. Matters related to probate proceeding. Unless a statutory probate court's jurisdiction is concurrent with that of the district court, all matters "related to" a probate proceeding must be brought in the statutory probate court. Tex. Est. Code §32.005(a); **King v. Deutsche Bank Nat'l Trust Co.**, 472 S.W.3d 848, 852 (Tex.App.—Houston [1st Dist.] 2015, no pet.). The statutory probate court has jurisdiction over the same matters related to probate proceedings as do county courts at law and constitutional county courts located in a county with a county court at law. *See* Tex. Est. Code §31.002(c)(1). See "County with county court at law," ch. 2-G, §4.1.2(2)(b); "Matters related to probate proceeding," ch. 2-G, §4.2.2(2). If any estate is pending in a statutory probate court, the court also has jurisdiction over any action in which the personal representative of that estate is a party in her capacity as personal representative. Tex. Est. Code §31.002(c)(2).

3. Matters related to guardianship proceeding. Unless a statutory probate court's jurisdiction is concurrent with that of the district court, all matters "related to" a guardianship proceeding must be brought in the statutory probate court. Tex. Est. Code §1022.005(b). The statutory probate court has jurisdiction over the same matters related to guardianship proceedings as do constitutional county courts and county courts at law. *See* Tex. Est. Code §1021.001(b)(1). See "Matters related to guardianship proceeding," ch. 2-G, §4.1.2(4); "Matters related to guardianship proceeding," ch. 2-G, §4.2.2(4). The statutory probate court also has jurisdiction over (1) a suit, action, or application filed against or on behalf of a guardianship or a trustee of a trust created under Estates Code §1301.053 or §1301.054 and (2) a cause of action in which a guardian in a guardianship pending in the statutory probate court is a party. Tex. Est. Code §1021.001(b)(2), (b)(3).

4. Trust matters. Statutory probate courts have concurrent jurisdiction with district courts in actions involving inter vivos, testamentary, and charitable trusts, and in actions brought by or against a trustee. Tex. Est. Code §32.007(2), (3); *see* Tex. Est. Code §32.006(1), (2); *see also* **Warren v. Weiner**, 462 S.W.3d 140, 143–44 (Tex.App.—Houston [1st Dist.] 2015,

no pet.) (probate court had jurisdiction to hear dispute over management of child's trust under divorce decree because trust decree, not divorce decree, governed administration of trust's assets). Constitutional county courts and county courts at law do not have jurisdiction over trusts. *See* Tex. Prop. Code §115.001(a) (with some exceptions, district court generally has exclusive jurisdiction over trusts); **Carroll v. Carroll**, 304 S.W.3d 366, 368 (Tex.2010) (same).

Note

A statutory probate court's jurisdiction over trust matters is independent of its probate jurisdiction—that is, the court can exercise its jurisdiction over trust matters regardless of whether there is a pending probate proceeding. See **Lee v. Lee**, *528 S.W.3d 201, 212 (Tex.App.—Houston [14th Dist.] 2017, pet. denied).*

5. Actions by, against, or involving personal representative or guardian. Statutory probate courts have concurrent jurisdiction with district courts in (1) all personal-injury, survival, or wrongful-death actions by or against a person in her capacity as a personal representative or a guardian and (2) all actions involving a personal representative of an estate or a guardian in which no other party aligned with the personal representative or guardian is an interested person in that estate or guardianship. Tex. Est. Code §32.007(1), (4) (probate), §1022.006 (guardianship).

6. Power-of-attorney matters. Statutory probate courts have concurrent jurisdiction with district courts in actions (1) to determine the validity of a power of attorney, (2) to determine an agent's rights, powers, or duties under a power of attorney, and (3) against an agent or former agent under a power of attorney arising from the agent's performance of its duties. Tex. Est. Code §32.007(5), (6); *see* Tex. Est. Code §32.006(3), (4). Statutory probate courts also have exclusive jurisdiction over actions by an agent or former agent under a power of attorney arising from the agent's performance of its duties. Tex. Est. Code §32.006(3); *see* Tex. Est. Code §32.005(a).

7. Pendent & ancillary jurisdiction. Statutory probate courts may exercise pendent and ancillary jurisdiction as necessary to promote judicial efficiency and economy. Tex. Est. Code §32.001(b) (probate), §1022.001(b) (guardianship). Generally, probate courts exercise pendent or ancillary jurisdiction when there is a close relationship between the nonprobate claims and the claims against the estate. **Shell Cortez Pipeline Co. v. Shores**, 127 S.W.3d 286, 294 (Tex.App.—Fort Worth 2004, no pet.). Other courts exercising probate jurisdiction do not have pendent and ancillary jurisdiction.

§4.4 Contested matters—assignment or transfer from constitutional county court. If the constitutional county court retains probate jurisdiction in a particular county and a party contests any matter in a probate or guardianship case before that court, the contested matter or the entire proceeding may be assigned or transferred. Tex. Est. Code §§32.003, 32.004 (probate), §§1022.003, 1022.004 (guardianship).

1. Assignment to statutory probate judge. In a county that does not have a statutory probate court or a county court at law exercising original probate jurisdiction, either the contested matter or the entire proceeding can be assigned to a statutory probate judge. *See* Tex. Est. Code §§32.003(a)(1), (b-1), 1022.003(a), (c).

(1) Assignment of contested matter.

(a) On party's motion or court's own initiative. If any party moves for a statutory probate judge to be assigned to hear the contested matter, the constitutional county court must grant the motion. Tex. Est. Code §§32.003(a)(1), 1022.003(a)(1); *see* Tex. Est. Code §§32.003(b), 1022.003(b). The motion can be made at any time before or after the matter is contested. Tex. Est. Code §§32.003(c), 1022.003(d). Even if no party moves to assign the contested matter to a statutory probate judge, the constitutional county court may assign the contested matter on its own initiative. Tex. Est. Code §§32.003(a), 1022.003(a). After the court grants the motion or assigns the matter on its own initiative, the presiding statutory probate judge will then assign a current or former statutory probate judge to hear the contested matter. *See* Tex. Gov't Code §25.0022(h).

(b) Later-filed contested matter. After a contested matter has been assigned to a statutory probate judge, any other contested matter that is later filed in the proceeding must also be assigned to that judge. Tex. Est. Code §§32.003(h), 1022.003(i).

(c) Statutory probate judge's power. The statutory probate judge has all the jurisdictional tools of a statutory probate court available when hearing the contested matter, including the power to transfer other pending matters under Estates Code §§34.001 and 1022.007. *See* Tex. Est. Code §§32.003(e), 1022.003(f); Tex. Gov't Code §25.0022(i). Unless a party objects, the statutory probate judge can hear ancillary motions in that judge's home county, but the trial on the merits must be conducted in the county where the probate proceeding is pending. Tex. Gov't Code §25.0022(n).

(d) Constitutional county court's jurisdiction. The constitutional county court retains jurisdiction over the estate or guardianship, except for the contested matter. Tex. Est. Code §§32.003(g), 1022.003(h). Once the statutory probate judge resolves the contested matter, including any appeals, the matter is transferred back to the constitutional county court for further proceedings. Tex. Est. Code §§32.003(e), 1022.003(f).

(2) Assignment of entire proceeding. If any party, or the judge of the constitutional county court on her own initiative, moves for a statutory probate judge to be assigned to hear the contested matter, the judge may request, on her own initiative or on a party's motion, that the statutory probate judge be assigned to the entire proceeding. Tex. Est. Code §§32.003(b-1), 1022.003(c). The statutory probate judge has all the jurisdictional tools of a statutory probate court available when hearing the entire proceeding, including the power to transfer other pending matters under Estates Code §§34.001 and 1022.007. *See* Tex. Est. Code §§32.003(e), 1022.003(f); Tex. Gov't Code §25.0022(i). Once the statutory probate judge resolves the contested matter, including any appeals, the entire proceeding is transferred back to the constitutional county court for further proceedings. Tex. Est. Code §§32.003(e), 1022.003(f).

2. Transfer to district court. In a county that does not have a statutory probate court or a county court at law exercising original probate jurisdiction, the contested matter and any matter related to the proceeding can be transferred to the district court. Tex. Est. Code §§32.003(a)(2), (g), 1022.003(a)(2), (h).

(1) Transfer of contested matter.

(a) On party's motion or court's own initiative. If any party moves to transfer a contested matter to the district court, the constitutional county court must grant the motion. Tex. Est. Code §§32.003(a)(2), 1022.003(a)(2). Even if no party moves to transfer a contested matter to the district court, the constitutional county court may transfer the contested matter on its own initiative. Tex. Est. Code §§32.003(a)(2), 1022.003(a)(2). After the court grants the motion or transfers the matter on its own initiative, the district court can then hear the contested matter as if it had originally been filed there. Tex. Est. Code §§32.003(a)(2), 1022.003(a)(2).

(b) Motion to assign controls. A motion to assign a statutory probate judge to the contested matter controls over a motion to transfer the matter to the district court. *See* Tex. Est. Code §§32.003(b), 1022.003(b). Thus, a motion to assign a statutory probate judge must be granted, unless the motion is withdrawn or the constitutional county court has already transferred the contested matter to a district court. *See* Tex. Est. Code §§32.003(b), 1022.003(b).

(c) Later-filed contested matter. Once a contested matter has been transferred to the district court, any other contested matter that is later filed in the proceeding must also be transferred to that court. Tex. Est. Code §§32.003(h), 1022.003(i).

(d) District court's power. The district court has all the jurisdictional tools of a statutory probate court available when hearing the contested matter, including the power to transfer other pending matters under Estates Code §§34.001 and 1022.007. *See* Tex. Est. Code §§32.003(f), 1022.003(g); Tex. Gov't Code §25.0022(i).

(e) Constitutional county court's jurisdiction. The constitutional county court retains jurisdiction over the estate or guardianship, except for the contested matter. Tex. Est. Code §§32.003(g), 1022.003(h). Once the district court resolves the contested matter, including any appeals, the matter is transferred back to the constitutional county court for further proceedings. Tex. Est. Code §§32.003(f), 1022.003(g).

(2) Transfer of related matter. Any matter related to a probate or guardianship proceeding in which a contested matter is transferred to a district court may be brought in the district court. Tex. Est. Code §§32.003(g), 1022.003(h). The district court may, on its own initiative or on any party's motion, find that the related matter is not a contested matter and transfer the matter to the constitutional county court with jurisdiction over the management of the estate or guardianship. Tex. Est. Code §§32.003(g), 1022.003(h).

3. Transfer to county court at law. In a county that does not have a statutory probate court but does have a county court at law exercising original probate jurisdiction, either the contested matter or the entire proceeding can be transferred to the county court at law. Tex. Est. Code §§32.004(a), 1022.004(a).

(1) Transfer of contested matter. If any party moves to transfer the contested matter to the county court at law, the constitutional county court must grant the motion. Tex. Est. Code §§32.004(a), 1022.004(a). The county court at law then hears the contested matter as if it had originally been filed there. Tex. Est. Code §§32.004(b), 1022.004(b). Even if no party moves to transfer a contested matter to the county court at law, the constitutional county court may transfer the contested matter on its own initiative. Tex. Est. Code §§32.004(a), 1022.004(a). Once the county court at law resolves the contested matter, including any appeals, the matter is transferred back to the constitutional county court for further proceedings. *See* Tex. Est. Code §§32.004(b), 1022.004(b).

(2) Transfer of entire proceeding. If any party moves to transfer the entire proceeding to the county court at law, the constitutional county court may grant the motion. Tex. Est. Code §§32.004(a), 1022.004(a). The county court at law then hears the proceeding as if it had originally been filed there. Tex. Est. Code §§32.004(b), 1022.004(b). Even if no party moves to transfer the proceeding to the county court at law, the constitutional county court may transfer it on its own initiative. Tex. Est. Code §§32.004(a), 1022.004(a).

§4.5 Transfer to statutory probate court.

1. Matter related to probate proceeding. On the motion of a party or person interested in an estate, a statutory probate court may transfer to itself from a district court, constitutional county court, or county court at law a cause of action (1) related to a probate proceeding pending in the statutory probate court or (2) in which the personal representative of an estate pending in the statutory probate court is a party. Tex. Est. Code §34.001(a); *see also* Tex. Est. Code §31.002 (identifying matters related to probate proceedings). See "Matters related to probate proceeding," ch. 2-G, §4.3.2. The court can consolidate the transferred cause of action with any other proceedings related to the estate. Tex. Est. Code §34.001(a).

2. Matter related to guardianship proceeding. On the motion of a party or person interested in a guardianship, a statutory probate court may transfer to itself from a district court, constitutional county court, or county court at law a cause of action related to a guardianship proceeding pending in the statutory probate court, including one in which a guardian, ward, or proposed ward in the pending guardianship proceeding is a party. Tex. Est. Code §1022.007(a)(1); *see also* Tex. Est. Code §1021.001 (identifying matters related to guardianship proceedings); **In re CC&M Garza Ranches L.P.**, 409 S.W.3d 106, 109 (Tex.App.—Houston [1st Dist.] 2013, orig. proceeding) (action to try title to real property of guardianship estate was "related to" guardianship proceeding; thus, transfer to statutory probate court was proper). See "Matters related to guardianship proceeding," ch. 2-G, §4.3.3. The court can consolidate the transferred cause of action with the related guardianship proceeding and any other proceedings related to the guardianship proceeding. Tex. Est. Code §1022.007(a)(2).

3. Venue. For an action by or against a personal representative or a guardian, ward, or proposed ward for personal injury, death, or property damage, venue is determined under CPRC §15.007. Tex. Est. Code §33.003 (personal representative), §34.001(b) (same), §1022.007(b) (guardian, ward, or proposed ward); *see* Tex. Civ. Prac. & Rem. Code §15.007 (in suits for personal injury, death, or property damage brought by or against executor, administrator, or guardian, venue under CPRC overrides venue provisions in Estates Code). When a party timely objects, a statutory probate court cannot transfer a suit for personal injury, death, or property damage to itself if venue for the suit under CPRC chapter 15 is not proper in the county where the probate court is located. **Gonzalez v. Reliant Energy, Inc.**, 159 S.W.3d 615, 621 (Tex.2005); *see* Tex. Civ. Prac. & Rem. Code §15.007. Thus, a statutory probate court's authority to transfer cases is limited by the venue provisions in CPRC chapter 15 for claims for personal injury, death, and property damage. **Gonzalez**, 159 S.W.3d at 621.

§5. Justice courts

The justice courts were created by the Texas Constitution. *See* Tex. Const. art. 5, §19. Jury trials are available in justice courts. Tex. R. Civ. P. 504.1(a). Parties, including corporations, may represent themselves or may choose to be represented by attorneys. Tex. R. Civ. P. 500.4.

§5.1 Amount in controversy. Justice courts have jurisdiction over cases in which the amount in controversy is not more than $20,000, including attorney fees, but excluding interest and court costs. Tex. R. Civ. P. 500.3(a) to (d); *see* Tex. Gov't

Code §27.031(a)(1). The justice courts have original exclusive jurisdiction over civil cases in which the amount in controversy is $200 or less. Tex. Const. art. 5, §19. Their original jurisdiction is concurrent with the district and county courts in civil cases in which the amount in controversy exceeds $200 but does not exceed $20,000. *See* Tex. Gov't Code §27.031(a)(1). See "Summary chart of amount in controversy," ch. 2-G, §6.

Note

For causes of action filed before September 1, 2020, justice courts had jurisdiction over cases in which the amount in controversy was not more than $10,000, excluding interest. See Tex. Gov't Code §27.031(a)(1) (pre-9-1-20 version); Tex. R. Civ. P. 500.3(a) to (d) (pre-9-1-20 version), Acts 2019, 86th Leg., R.S., ch. 696, §§31, 32, 36, 37, eff. Sept. 1, 2020.

§5.2 Types of cases. Justice courts have jurisdiction over the following types of cases:

1. **Small claims.** A small-claims case is a suit brought to recover money damages, civil penalties, personal property, or other relief allowed by law. Tex. R. Civ. P. 500.3(a). Small-claims cases are governed by TRCP 500 to 507. Tex. R. Civ. P. 500.3(a).

2. **Debt claims.** A debt-claim case is a suit brought to recover a debt by an assignee of a claim, a debt collector or collection agency, a financial institution, or a person or entity primarily engaged in the business of lending money at interest. Tex. R. Civ. P. 500.3(b). Debt-claim cases in justice court are governed by TRCP 500 to 508. Tex. R. Civ. P. 500.3(b).

3. **Repair & remedy.** A repair-and-remedy case is a suit filed by a residential tenant under Property Code chapter 92, subchapter B, to enforce the landlord's duty to repair or remedy a condition materially affecting the physical health or safety of an ordinary tenant. Tex. R. Civ. P. 500.3(c). Repair-and-remedy cases are governed by TRCP 500 to 507 and 509. Tex. R. Civ. P. 500.3(c).

4. **Eviction.** An eviction case is a suit brought to recover possession of real property under Property Code chapter 24 (forcible entry and detainer), often by a landlord against a tenant. Tex. R. Civ. P. 500.3(d). Eviction suits include forcible-entry-and-detainer and forcible-detainer suits. Tex. Prop. Code §24.004(a). Justice courts in the precinct where the real property is located generally have original, exclusive jurisdiction over eviction suits. *See* Tex. Gov't Code §27.031(a)(2); Tex. Prop. Code §24.004(a). Although the only issue tried and determined in an eviction suit is the right to possession, a claim for rent may be joined with an eviction suit if the amount of due and unpaid rent is not more than the jurisdictional limits of the justice court. *See* Tex. R. Civ. P. 500.3(d), 510.3(d), (e). An eviction suit cannot be used to determine title to real property. Tex. R. Civ. P. 510.3(e).

5. **Expunction.** Justice courts have concurrent jurisdiction with district courts and municipal courts of record over expunction proceedings involving the arrest of a person for an offense punishable only by fine. Tex. Gov't Code §27.031(e).

§5.3 Cases excluded. Justice courts do not have jurisdiction over the following suits: (1) on behalf of the State to recover penalties, forfeitures, and escheats, (2) for divorce, (3) for slander or defamation, (4) for title to land, and (5) to enforce liens on land. Tex. Gov't Code §27.031(b). Unless expressly permitted by the Legislature, justice courts cannot issue writs of mandamus or injunction. *See* **Malmgren v. Inverness Forest Residents Civic Club, Inc.**, 981 S.W.2d 875, 879 (Tex.App.—Houston [1st Dist.] 1998, no pet.); **Bowles v. Angelo**, 188 S.W.2d 691, 693 (Tex.App.—Galveston 1945, no writ).

§5.4 Application of rules. The TRCPs and TREs do not apply to justice courts except when a judge determines that a particular rule must be followed to ensure fairness to all parties, or when otherwise specifically provided by law or by TRCP 500 to 510. Tex. R. Civ. P. 500.3(e); *see* Tex. R. Evid. 101(f).

§5.5 Relief available. In addition to the jurisdiction provided by the Texas Constitution and other law, justice courts have original jurisdiction to (1) foreclose mortgages and enforce liens on personal property when the amount in controversy is within their jurisdictional limits, (2) issue writs of attachment, garnishment, and sequestration in cases within their jurisdiction, and (3) enforce deed restrictions that do not involve a structural change to a dwelling. Tex. Gov't Code §27.031(a)(3) (#1), §27.032 (#2), §27.034(a) (#3). When a statute provides that the jurisdiction of the justice court is concurrent with that of

a superior court, the justice court has all the authority of the superior court. *See, e.g.*, **Malmgren v. Inverness Forest Residents Civic Club, Inc.**, 981 S.W.2d 875, 879 (Tex.App.—Houston [1st Dist.] 1998, no pet.) (because Gov't Code §27.034 states that justice court's jurisdiction is concurrent with jurisdiction of district court in suits to enforce deed restrictions, justice court can issue injunctions).

§5.6 Right to appeal. A party may appeal from a justice court to a county court if the amount in controversy or the judgment exceeds $250, not including costs. Tex. Gov't Code §26.042(e). The standard of review in the county court is de novo. Tex. R. Civ. P. 506.3, 509.8(e), 510.10(c). The county court's appellate jurisdiction is restricted to the jurisdictional limits of the justice court. **Kendziorski v. Saunders**, 191 S.W.3d 395, 409 (Tex.App.—Austin 2006, no pet.). A county court cannot award damages that exceed the jurisdictional limits of the justice court unless additional damages have been incurred because of the passage of time (e.g., attorney fees). *See, e.g., id.* at 409–10 (portion of county court's award that exceeded justice court's jurisdictional limit was void because additional amount was not result of passage of time).

§6. Summary chart of amount in controversy

Chart 2-1, below, shows the overlapping monetary jurisdiction of the trial courts.

2-1. Overlapping Monetary Jurisdiction of Trial Courts

Amount	District courts	Constitutional county courts	County courts at law	Justice courts
$250,000+	District courts			
$250,000			County courts at law	
$20,000		Constitutional county courts		Justice courts
$500.01 +	See ch. 2-G, §3.3			
$200.01 +		See ch. 2-G, §4.1.1	See ch. 2-G, §4.2.1	
$.01 +				See ch. 2-G, §5.1

§7. Summary chart of jurisdiction

Chart 2-2, below, shows the various levels of civil courts in Texas and their jurisdiction. This chart is derived from the Texas Judicial Branch, *Court Structure Chart*, at www.txcourts.gov/about-texas-courts.

2-2. Civil Jurisdiction of Texas Courts

SUPREME COURT

– Statewide Jurisdiction –
Final appellate jurisdiction in civil and juvenile cases.

COURTS OF APPEALS

14 courts
– Regional Jurisdiction –
Immediate appeals from trial courts in their respective courts-of-appeals districts.

DISTRICT COURTS

478 courts
– Jurisdiction –
- Original jurisdiction in civil actions from $500.01,[1] divorce, title to land, and contested elections.
- Juvenile matters.

COUNTY-LEVEL COURTS

Constitutional County Courts
254 courts
– Jurisdiction –
- Original jurisdiction in civil actions between $200.01[2] and $20,000.[3]
- Probate, mental health, and guardianship. (Contested matters can be transferred to district court.)
- Juvenile matters.
- Appeals de novo from lower courts or on the record from municipal courts of record.

County Courts at Law
250 courts
– Jurisdiction –
- All civil, original, and appellate actions prescribed by law for constitutional county courts.
- Jurisdiction over civil matters between $200.01[2] and $250,000[4] (some courts may have higher maximum jurisdiction amounts).

Probate Courts
18 courts
– Jurisdiction –
- Limited primarily to probate, mental-health, and guardianship matters.

MUNICIPAL COURTS

945 courts
Most are not courts of record.
– Jurisdiction –
- Limited civil jurisdiction.
- Magistrate functions.

JUSTICE COURTS

802 courts
None are courts of record.
– Jurisdiction –
- Civil actions $20,000[5] and under.
- Small claims.
- Magistrate functions.

1 Based on Tex. Gov't Code §24.007(b) (eff. 1-1-12). See "Amount in controversy," ch. 2-G, §3.3.

2 Amount in controversy must exceed $200. See "Amount in controversy," ch. 2-G, §4.1.1; "Amount in controversy," ch. 2-G, §4.2.1.

3 See "Amount in controversy," ch. 2-G, §4.1.1.

4 See "Amount in controversy," ch. 2-G, §4.2.1.

5 See "Amount in controversy," ch. 2-G, §5.1.

H. Choosing the Court—Venue

§1. General

§1.1 Rules. Tex. R. Civ. P. 85 to 89. See Tex. Civ. Prac. & Rem. Code ch. 15.

§1.2 Purpose. Before filing the suit, the plaintiff must decide in which of the 254 Texas counties the lawsuit should be filed. Venue is different from jurisdiction—it deals with the propriety of prosecuting a suit in a particular county, not the power of a court to determine the dispute and render judgment.

Note

To challenge the venue of the suit, see "Motion to Transfer—Challenging Venue," ch. 3-C, §1 et seq.

§1.3 Form. O'Connor's Texas Civil Forms, FORM 2B:21 (2020 ed.).

§1.4 Other references. O'Connor's Texas Causes of Action (2021 ed.); **O'Connor's Texas Family Law Handbook** (2021 ed.).

§2. Definitions

§2.1 Principal office. "Principal office" means a Texas office of a corporation, unincorporated association, or partnership, in which the decision-makers for the organization within Texas conduct the daily affairs of the organization. Tex. Civ. Prac. & Rem. Code §15.001(a). The mere presence of an organization's agency or representative in a county does not establish a principal office in that county. *Id.*; *see, e.g.*, **In re Missouri Pac. R.R.**, 998 S.W.2d 212, 221 (Tex.1999) (Ps did not show D's office in Tarrant County was a principal office as compared to responsibility and authority exercised by company officials in Harris County office). A business may have more than one principal office in Texas. *See* Tex. Civ. Prac. & Rem. Code §15.001(a) (code says "a" principal office, not "the" principal office).

§2.2 Residence. Residence is established if the party (1) possessed a fixed place of abode and (2) occupied or intended to occupy it over a substantial period of time in a permanent, rather than temporary, manner. **Snyder v. Pitts**, 241 S.W.2d 136, 140 (Tex.1951); **In re S.D.**, 980 S.W.2d 758, 760 (Tex.App.—San Antonio 1998, pet. denied). The term "residence" is not limited to natural persons. *E.g.*, **In re Transcontinental Rlty. Investors, Inc.**, 271 S.W.3d 270, 272 (Tex.2008) (corporation can be sued where it "resides" under Property Code §21.013(a)). A person may have more than one residence for venue purposes. **GeoChem Tech v. Verseckes**, 962 S.W.2d 541, 543 (Tex.1998). However, venue is fixed at whichever residence the party was occupying when the cause of action accrued. *See* Tex. Civ. Prac. & Rem. Code §15.002(a)(2) (D's residence at time of accrual), §15.002(a)(4) (P's residence at time of accrual), §15.006 (court shall determine venue on facts existing at time of accrual).

§2.3 When cause accrues. Venue is determined by facts as they existed when the cause of action accrued. Tex. Civ. Prac. & Rem. Code §15.006. Generally, a cause of action accrues when a wrongful act causes a legal injury, even if the fact of injury is not discovered until later and all resulting damages have not yet occurred. **In re Travelers Prop. Cas. Co.**, 485 S.W.3d 921, 926 (Tex.App.—Dallas 2016, orig. proceeding); *see* **S.V. v. R.V.**, 933 S.W.2d 1, 4 (Tex.1996) (limitations case).

§2.4 Where cause accrues. A cause of action accrues in a county in which all or a substantial part of the events or omissions that give rise to the claim occurred. *See* Tex. Civ. Prac. & Rem. Code §15.002(a)(1); *see, e.g.*, **KW Constr. v. Stephens & Sons Concrete Contractors, Inc.**, 165 S.W.3d 874, 882–83 (Tex.App.—Texarkana 2005, pet. denied) (events that occurred in Lamar County pertaining to two out of four elements of P's breach-of-contract claim qualified as substantial part of cause of action). A substantial part of the act or omission may occur in more than one county. **Velasco v. Texas Kenworth Co.**, 144 S.W.3d 632, 635 (Tex.App.—Dallas 2004, pet. denied); **Southern Cty. Mut. Ins. v. Ochoa**, 19 S.W.3d 452, 458 (Tex.App.—Corpus Christi 2000, no pet.). The phrase "a substantial part" restricts venue choices to fewer counties than other venue provisions. *Compare* Tex. Civ. Prac. & Rem. Code §15.002(a)(1) ("in the county in which all or a substantial part of the events or omissions giving rise to the claim occurred") *with* §101.102(a) (under TTCA, "in the county in which the cause of action or a part of the cause of action arises"). The parties may stipulate that all or a substantial part of the cause of action occurred in a particular county. *See* **In re Omni Hotels Mgmt.**, 159 S.W.3d 627, 628–29 (Tex.2005).

§3. County of proper venue

Under CPRC §15.001(b), all lawsuits must be brought in a county of "proper venue" according to the following venue scheme:

§3.1 Mandatory-venue provisions. If there is a mandatory-venue provision, a suit must be filed in the county of mandatory venue, as required by CPRC chapter 15, subchapter B, or other statutes prescribing mandatory venue. Tex. Civ. Prac. & Rem. Code §15.001(b)(1). *See generally* Tex. Civ. Prac. & Rem. Code §§15.011 to 15.020 (mandatory-venue provisions). See "Mandatory-venue provisions," ch. 2-H, §4.

§3.2 No mandatory-venue provisions. If there is no mandatory-venue provision, then venue may be proper under either the general venue rule or a permissive-venue provision. **Shamoun & Norman, LLP v. Yarto Int'l Grp.**, 398 S.W.3d 272, 287–88 (Tex.App.—Corpus Christi 2012, pet. dism'd); *see* Tex. Civ. Prac. & Rem. Code §15.001(b)(2).

Note

If a plaintiff files suit in a county of proper venue either under the general rule or under a permissive exception, the defendant cannot transfer the case unless (1) a mandatory-venue provision controls or (2) the court transfers the case for convenience and in the interest of justice. See "Venue convenient elsewhere," ch. 3-C, §2.3.5.

---

1. No mandatory venue, but permissive venue. If there is no mandatory-venue provision but a permissive-venue provision applies, the plaintiff can choose to file suit in a county that is proper under either the applicable permissive-venue provision or the general venue rule. *See* Tex. Civ. Prac. & Rem. Code §§15.001(b)(2), 15.002(a). See "Permissive-venue provisions," ch. 2-H, §5; "General venue rule," ch. 2-H, §6.

2. No mandatory or permissive venue. If there is no mandatory or permissive venue, the general venue rule applies. *See* Tex. Civ. Prac. & Rem. Code §15.002(a); **Double Diamond-Del., Inc. v. Alfonso**, 487 S.W.3d 265, 270 (Tex.App.—Corpus Christi 2016, no pet.); **Chiriboga v. State Farm Mut. Auto. Ins.**, 96 S.W.3d 673, 678 (Tex.App.—Austin 2003, no pet.). See "General venue rule," ch. 2-H, §6.

§4. Mandatory-venue provisions

Mandatory venue is compulsory only if a defendant properly objects to the plaintiff's choice of venue. Most of the mandatory-venue provisions are listed in CPRC chapter 15, subchapter B. *See* **In re Sosa**, 370 S.W.3d 79, 81 (Tex.App.—Houston [14th Dist.] 2012, orig. proceeding). An action governed by any other statute prescribing mandatory venue outside of CPRC chapter 15 must be brought in the county required by that other statute. Tex. Civ. Prac. & Rem. Code §15.016.

§4.1 Mandatory venue in CPRC ch. 15.

1. Land dispute. A suit involving a land dispute must be filed in the county where all or part of the land is located. Tex. Civ. Prac. & Rem. Code §15.011; **In re Applied Chem. Magnesias Corp.**, 206 S.W.3d 114, 117 (Tex.2006). Suits involving land disputes are suits to (1) recover real property, (2) recover an estate or interest in real property, (3) partition real property, (4) remove encumbrances on title to real property, (5) recover damages to real property, and (6) quiet title to real property. *See* Tex. Civ. Prac. & Rem. Code §15.011. Two venue facts must be established to invoke the mandatory-venue provision for land: (1) all or part of the land is located in the county of suit and (2) the nature of the claim is enumerated in CPRC §15.011. **In re Stroud Oil Props., Inc.**, 110 S.W.3d 18, 24 (Tex.App.—Waco 2002, orig. proceeding); *e.g.*, **Sustainable Tex. Oyster Res. Mgmt. v. Hannah Reef, Inc.**, 491 S.W.3d 96, 107 (Tex.App.—Houston [1st Dist.] 2016, pet. denied) (suit to determine validity of lease providing right to harvest oysters in area covered by lease was suit involving interest in real property); *see, e.g.*, **In re Applied Chem.**, 206 S.W.3d at 117 (suit to determine whether D had right to mine marble on P's land based on agreement was suit involving interest in real property); **Kilgore v. Black Stone Oil Co.**, 15 S.W.3d 666, 670 (Tex.App.—Beaumont 2000, pet. denied) (suit for conversion of oil and gas and title to minerals was suit for recovery of land). The dominant purpose of the suit determines whether this venue provision controls; the provision is inapplicable when the action involves title only incidentally or secondarily and not directly. **Stiba v. Bowers**, 756 S.W.2d 835, 839 (Tex.App.—Corpus Christi 1988, no writ); *see* **Sustainable Tex. Oyster**, 491 S.W.3d at 107 (CPRC §15.011 controls venue when essence of dispute involves interest in real property).

2. Landlord-tenant. A suit between a landlord and a tenant arising under a lease must be brought in the county where all or part of the real property is located. Tex. Civ. Prac. & Rem. Code §15.0115(a). If another provision prescribes mandatory venue, that provision controls over the landlord-tenant provision in CPRC §15.0115(a). The term "lease" includes any written or oral agreement between the landlord and tenant that establishes or modifies the terms, conditions, or other provisions relating to the use and occupancy of the real property. Tex. Civ. Prac. & Rem. Code §15.0115(b). See "Landlord-Tenant Actions," **O'Connor's Texas Causes of Action**, ch. 16-A, §1 et seq. (2021 ed.).

3. Injunction against suit. An action to stay a proceeding in a suit must be filed in the county where the suit is pending. Tex. Civ. Prac. & Rem. Code §15.012; **O'Quinn v. Hall**, 77 S.W.3d 452, 455 (Tex.App.—Corpus Christi 2002, orig. proceeding); *see also* Tex. Civ. Prac. & Rem. Code §65.023(b) (writ of injunction to stay proceedings must be tried in the court in which suit is pending or judgment was rendered).

4. Injunction against execution of judgment. An action to restrain the execution of a judgment based on the invalidity of the judgment or writ of execution must be filed in the county where the judgment was rendered. Tex. Civ. Prac. & Rem. Code §15.013; *see also* Tex. Civ. Prac. & Rem. Code §65.023(b) (writ of injunction to stay execution of judgment must be tried in the court in which suit is pending or judgment was rendered).

5. Mandamus against State. A petition for a writ of mandamus against the head of a department of the State of Texas must be filed in Travis County. Tex. Civ. Prac. & Rem. Code §15.014.

6. Suit against county. A suit against a county must be filed in that county. Tex. Civ. Prac. & Rem. Code §15.015; **Wichita Cty. v. Hart**, 917 S.W.2d 779, 781 (Tex.1996); *e.g.*, **In re Fort Bend Cty.**, 278 S.W.3d 842, 844–45 (Tex.App.—Houston [14th Dist.] 2009, orig. proceeding) (in suit under TTCA, CPRC §15.015 controlled over CPRC §101.102(a)). A suit against a county official only in that person's individual capacity is not a suit against the county for purposes of CPRC §15.015. *See* **McIntosh v. Copeland**, 894 S.W.2d 60, 63–64 (Tex.App.—Austin 1995, writ denied).

7. Suit against political subdivisions. A suit filed against a political subdivision that is located in a county with a population of 100,000 or less must be brought in the county where the political subdivision is located. Tex. Civ. Prac. & Rem. Code §15.0151(a).

8. Defamation or invasion of privacy. A suit for libel, slander, or invasion of privacy must be filed in one of the following: (1) the county where the plaintiff resided when the action accrued, (2) the county where the defendant resided when the suit was filed, (3) the county where any of the defendants reside, or (4) the domicile of any corporate defendant. Tex. Civ. Prac. & Rem. Code §15.017; **Rodriguez v. Printone Color Corp.**, 982 S.W.2d 69, 71 (Tex.App.—Houston [1st Dist.] 1998, pet. denied); **Acker v. Denton Publ'g**, 937 S.W.2d 111, 114 (Tex.App.—Fort Worth 1996, no writ). See "Defamation," **O'Connor's Texas Causes of Action**, ch. 18-A, §1 et seq. (2021 ed.).

9. FELA & Jones Act. A suit brought under the Federal Employers' Liability Act (FELA) (45 U.S.C. §51) or the Jones Act (46 U.S.C. §30104) must be brought in one of the following counties: (1) the county where all or a substantial part of the events or omissions giving rise to the claim occurred, (2) the county where the defendant's principal office in Texas is located, or (3) the county where the plaintiff resided when the cause of action accrued. Tex. Civ. Prac. & Rem. Code §15.018(b) (FELA), §15.0181(c) (Jones Act); **In re Missouri Pac. R.R.**, 998 S.W.2d 212, 214 (Tex.1999) (FELA). However, under the Jones Act, if a substantial part of the event or omission giving rise to the claim occurred on inland waters, ashore in Texas or a Gulf Coast state, or during an erosion-response project in Texas or a Gulf Coast state, suit may need to be brought in a different county. Tex. Civ. Prac. & Rem. Code §15.0181(d), (e); *see also* Tex. Civ. Prac. & Rem. Code §15.0181(a)(4), (a)(5) (defining "Gulf Coast state" and "inland waters").

10. Inmate litigation. A suit brought by an inmate for an action that accrued while the inmate was in a Texas prison operated by the Texas Department of Criminal Justice must be filed in the county where the facility is located. Tex. Civ. Prac. & Rem. Code §15.019(a); **In re Travelers Prop. Cas. Co.**, 485 S.W.3d 921, 925 (Tex.App.—Dallas 2016, orig. proceeding).

11. Contractual agreement for venue—major transaction. Under CPRC §15.020, parties may contractually agree to venue in a suit that arises from a "major transaction." *See* Tex. Civ. Prac. & Rem. Code §15.020(b), (c); **In re Fox**

River Real Estate Holdings, Inc., 596 S.W.3d 759, 763–64 (Tex.2020); **Pinto Tech. Ventures, L.P. v. Sheldon**, 526 S.W.3d 428, 446 (Tex.2017); **In re Fisher**, 433 S.W.3d 523, 529 (Tex.2014). That is, the suit must be filed in a certain county determined according to a written agreement signed before suit. *See* Tex. Civ. Prac. & Rem. Code §15.020(b), (c). Except for major transactions, the parties cannot contractually agree before suit to a venue contrary to a mandatory-venue provision or a specific venue statute. *See, e.g.*, **Leonard v. Paxson**, 654 S.W.2d 440, 441–42 (Tex.1983) (settlement agreement could not override venue in Fam. Code); **Fidelity Un. Life Ins. v. Evans**, 477 S.W.2d 535, 537 (Tex.1972) (contract agreement on venue could not override venue provision in injunction statute).

Note

When the language in an agreed venue-selection clause indicates that the parties' choice of venue is mandatory, permissive language about submitting to the forum court's "nonexclusive jurisdiction" does not necessarily control over the mandatory language; the permissive language is a consent-to-jurisdiction clause and does not affect the mandatory-venue provision. E.g., ***In re Fisher****, 433 S.W.3d at 532–33 (agreed venue provision specifying that any suit would be brought in Tarrant County and not in any other court controlled over permissive language that parties would submit to Tarrant County district court's nonexclusive jurisdiction).*

(1) Major transaction. A major transaction is one in which the consideration has an aggregate value of at least $1 million. Tex. Civ. Prac. & Rem. Code §15.020(a); *e.g.*, **In re Texas Ass'n of Sch. Bds., Inc.**, 169 S.W.3d 653, 656 (Tex.2005) (insurance-premium payment of $41,973, not coverage amount of $17 million, was aggregate value of consideration for insurance-coverage agreement; not major transaction); **Spin Doctor Golf, Inc. v. Paymentech, L.P.**, 296 S.W.3d 354, 358–59 (Tex.App.—Dallas 2009, pet. denied) ($5 million in annual credit-card sales was aggregate value of consideration for contract in which D agreed to process P's credit-card sales; major transaction). By definition, it does not include a transaction for personal, family, or household purposes or for settlement of a personal-injury or wrongful-death suit. Tex. Civ. Prac. & Rem. Code §15.020(a).

(2) Arises from. Whether a suit "arises from" a major transaction is determined by a commonsense examination of the substance of the claims. **In re Fisher**, 433 S.W.3d at 529–30. The suit must arise from a major transaction, as defined by the statute, to which the venue-selection clause applies; it does not have to arise directly from the agreement containing the venue-selection clause. *See id.* at 531; *see, e.g.*, **Pinto Tech.**, 526 S.W.3d at 447 (CPRC §15.020 did not apply because parties agreed to venue for disputes arising from shareholder's agreement, not for disputes arising from financing agreement that was major transaction on which suit was based).

(3) Controlling provision. If a contractual agreement for venue meets the requirements of CPRC §15.020, that provision controls over any other mandatory-venue provision in CPRC title 2, chapters 5 to 52. *See* Tex. Civ. Prac. & Rem. Code §15.020(c) (§15.020 applies to action arising from major transaction "[n]otwithstanding any other provision of this title"); **In re Fox River**, 596 S.W.3d at 764 (§15.020 is not "super mandatory" venue statute overriding all other mandatory-venue provisions; §15.020 controls only over mandatory-venue provisions in CPRC title 2); *see, e.g.*, **In re Fisher**, 433 S.W.3d at 533–34 (venue agreement under CPRC §15.020 controlled over mandatory-venue provision in CPRC §15.017 for defamation suits); **In re Group 1 Rlty., Inc.**, 441 S.W.3d 469, 472–73 (Tex.App.—El Paso 2014, orig. proceeding) (venue agreement under CPRC §15.020 controlled over mandatory-venue provision in CPRC §15.0115 for suit between landlord and tenant arising from lease).

12. Counterclaims, cross-claims, or third-party claims. Venue for a counterclaim, cross-claim, or properly joined third-party claim is established by the venue for the original suit. Tex. Civ. Prac. & Rem. Code §15.062(a); *see* **Perryman v. Spartan Tex. Six Capital Partners**, 546 S.W.3d 110, 132 (Tex.2018) (venue under CPRC §15.062(a) is mandatory).

§4.2 Other mandatory-venue provisions.

1. CPRC.

(1) TTCA. The Texas Tort Claims Act (TTCA) provides that a suit under the TTCA "shall" be brought in the county where "the cause of action or a part of the cause of action arises." Tex. Civ. Prac. & Rem. Code §101.102(a); *e.g.*, **In re**

Texas DOT, 218 S.W.3d 74, 76 (Tex.2007) (suit should have been transferred from county where negligence was alleged to county of accident because Ps pleaded only premises-liability claim, not negligence claim).

(2) Receivership. An action to have a receiver appointed for a corporation with property in Texas must be brought in the county where the corporation's principal office is located. Tex. Civ. Prac. & Rem. Code §64.071.

(3) Injunction suit against Texas resident. CPRC §65.023(a) provides that, except as mandated by subsection (b), injunction suits against a resident party must be tried in a district or county court in the county where the party is domiciled. Tex. Civ. Prac. & Rem. Code §65.023(a); **In re Continental Airlines, Inc.**, 988 S.W.2d 733, 736 (Tex.1998). For venue under CPRC §65.023(b), see "Injunction against suit," ch. 2-H, §4.1.3; "Injunction against execution of judgment," ch. 2-H, §4.1.4.

(4) Arbitration. Where to file an initial application in an arbitration proceeding depends on whether the arbitration agreement specifies the county of venue, whether the arbitration hearing has already taken place, and whether a suit involving an issue referable to arbitration is already pending in the court.

(a) Generally. A party generally must file an initial application in the county in which an adverse party resides or has a place of business, or, if an adverse party does not have a residence or place of business in Texas, in any county. Tex. Civ. Prac. & Rem. Code §171.096(a).

(b) By contract. If the agreement to arbitrate specifies that an arbitration hearing be held in a particular Texas county, a party must file the initial application in that county. Tex. Civ. Prac. & Rem. Code §171.096(b).

(c) After hearing. If an arbitration hearing has been held, a party must file an initial application for a proceeding arising from the arbitration in the county in which the hearing was held. Tex. Civ. Prac. & Rem. Code §171.096(c); *e.g.*, **In re Lopez**, 372 S.W.3d 174, 175–76 (Tex.2012) (although arbitration agreement specified venue in Victoria County, parties disregarded agreement and arbitrated in Travis County; thus, under mandatory-venue provision in CPRC §171.096(c), proper venue for application to vacate arbitration award was Travis County).

(d) Pending proceeding. If there is a proceeding pending in a court that involves an issue that is referable to arbitration, a party must file an initial application in that court. Tex. Civ. Prac. & Rem. Code §§171.024(a), 171.096(d).

2. Other statutes.

(1) Attorney disciplinary action. In a suit against an attorney for disciplinary action, venue is in the district court (1) in the county of the attorney's principal place of practice, (2) in the county of the attorney's residence if the attorney does not have a place of practice in Texas, or (3) in the county where the misconduct occurred in whole or in part if the attorney maintains neither a residence nor a place of practice in Texas. Tex. R Disciplinary P. 3.03; *see* **State Bar v. McGee,** 972 S.W.2d 770, 774 (Tex.App.—Corpus Christi 1998, no pet.). In all other instances, venue is in Travis County. Tex. R Disciplinary P. 3.03.

(2) Condemnation. In a condemnation proceeding, if the owner resides in a county where part of the property is located, venue is in the county where the owner resides. Tex. Prop. Code §21.013(a). Otherwise, venue is in any county where at least part of the property is located. *Id.*

(3) Probate & guardianship. Estates Code §§33.001, 33.051 to 33.055, and chapter 1023 establish venue for the probate of wills, letters testamentary or letters of administration, and appointments of guardians. Tex. Est. Code §§33.001(a), 33.051 to 33.055, 1023.001; *see also* Tex. Est. Code §33.002 (any cause of action related to probate proceeding pending in statutory probate court), §33.004 (proceeding to determine heirship), §33.005 (proceeding alleging breach of fiduciary duty by charitable entity). However, in suits brought by or against a personal representative or a guardian, ward, or proposed ward for personal injury, death, or property damage, proper venue is determined under CPRC §15.007. Tex. Est. Code §33.003 (personal representative), §34.001(b) (same), §1022.007(b) (guardian, ward, or proposed ward). See "Venue," ch. 2-G, §4.5.3. Venue for probate depends largely on where the decedent was domiciled or where the majority of the estate is located. *See* Tex. Est. Code §§33.001(a). Venue for guardianship of a minor depends largely on where the parents reside. *See* Tex. Est. Code §1023.001.

(4) **Trust.**

(a) **Noncorporate trustees.**

[1] **No principal office in Texas.** For suits involving a trust in which there is either a single noncorporate trustee or multiple trustees, none of whom is a corporate trustee, and the trustees do not maintain a principal office in Texas, venue is in any county where, during the four-year period before the suit was filed, a trustee resided or the trust was maintained. Tex. Prop. Code §115.002(b) (single trustee), §115.002(b-2) (multiple trustees).

[2] **Principal office in Texas.** For suits involving a trust in which there are multiple trustees, none of whom is a corporate trustee, and the trustees maintain a principal office in Texas, venue is in any county where (1) the trustees maintain the principal office or (2) the trust was maintained during the four-year period before the suit was filed. Tex. Prop. Code §115.002(b-1).

(b) **Corporate trustees.** For suits involving one or more corporate trustees, venue is in any county where (1) any trustee maintains its principal office or (2) the trust was maintained during the four-year period before the suit was filed. Tex. Prop. Code §115.002(c).

(c) **Administration of inter vivos or testamentary trust.** If the settlor is deceased and an administration of the settlor's estate is pending in Texas, an action for the interpretation and administration of an inter vivos trust created by the settlor or a testamentary trust created by the settlor's will may be brought in a county where (1) venue is generally proper for suits involving a trust under Property Code §115.002(b), (b-1), (b-2), or (c), or (2) the administration of the settlor's estate is pending. Tex. Prop. Code §115.002(c-1).

(d) **Transfer.** Venue may be transferred to another county for the convenience of the parties and witnesses, or if all parties agree. Tex. Prop. Code §115.002(d), (e).

(5) **Family law.** The Family Code has its own rules and procedures governing mandatory venue. For example, in an original suit affecting the parent-child relationship (SAPCR), venue is in the county where the child resides, unless an exception applies. Tex. Fam. Code §103.001. See "Where to file SAPCR," **O'Connor's Texas Family Law Handbook**, ch. 4-A, §3 (2021 ed.).

(6) **Insurance contract.** In a suit against an insurance company regarding coverage, Insurance Code §1952.110 provides two mandatory venues: (1) in the county where the policyholder or beneficiary who instituted the suit resided at the time of the accident or (2) in the county where the accident involving the uninsured or underinsured motorist's vehicle occurred. Tex. Ins. Code §1952.110. For the types of insurance suits to which permissive venue applies, see "Insurance contract," ch. 2-H, §5.1.5.

§4.3 Miscellaneous rules governing mandatory venue.

1. **Two counties of mandatory venue.**

(1) **Both venue provisions under CPRC ch. 15.**

(a) **Generally.** When there are two counties of mandatory venue and both mandatory provisions are under CPRC chapter 15, the plaintiff generally has the right to choose between the two provisions. *See* **In re Fisher**, 433 S.W.3d 523, 533 (Tex.2014); **Marshall v. Mahaffey**, 974 S.W.2d 942, 947 (Tex.App.—Beaumont 1998, pet. denied)

(b) **Exceptions.**

[1] **Major transaction.** When there are two counties of mandatory venue under CPRC chapter 15 but one of the mandatory provisions is under CPRC §15.020, involving a contractual agreement for venue arising from a major transaction, that section controls over the other mandatory provision. *See* **In re Fisher**, 433 S.W.3d at 533–34; **In re Group 1 Rlty., Inc.**, 441 S.W.3d 469, 472–73 (Tex.App.—El Paso 2014, orig. proceeding). See "Controlling provision," ch. 2-H, §4.1.11(3).

[2] **Counterclaim, cross-claim, or third-party claim.** When there are two counties of mandatory venue under CPRC chapter 15 but one of the mandatory provisions is under CPRC §15.062(a), involving a counterclaim,

cross-claim, or properly joined third-party claim, that section controls over the other mandatory provision. *See, e.g.*, **Perryman v. Spartan Tex. Six Capital Partners**, 546 S.W.3d 110, 132–33 (Tex.2018) (CPRC §15.062(a) controls over other mandatory-venue provisions, such as CPRC §15.011, because it requires venue for properly joined third-party claims to be same as venue for original suit and thus it honors general rule that P makes first choice of appropriate venue).

(2) Both venue provisions outside CPRC ch. 15. When there are two counties of mandatory venue and both mandatory provisions are outside CPRC chapter 15, at least one court has held that the court must resolve the conflict by analyzing the two statutes. *See* **In re Sosa**, 370 S.W.3d 79, 81 (Tex.App.—Houston [14th Dist.] 2012, orig. proceeding) (because no venue statute gives P the right to choose between two conflicting mandatory-venue provisions, court must resolve conflict by statutory-construction analysis; examination of mandatory venue under CPRC §§65.023 and 171.096).

(3) One venue provision under CPRC ch. 15 and one outside it.

(a) Generally. When there are two counties of mandatory venue but one mandatory provision is under CPRC chapter 15 and the other is outside it, suit must be brought in the county required by the mandatory-venue provision outside CPRC chapter 15. Tex. Civ. Prac. & Rem. Code §15.016; *e.g.*, **In re J.P. Morgan Chase Bank**, 373 S.W.3d 615, 617–18 (Tex.App.—San Antonio 2012, orig. proceeding) (mandatory venue in Prop. Code §115.002 controlled over CPRC §15.011); **In re Adan Volpe Props., Ltd.**, 306 S.W.3d 369, 375 (Tex.App.—Corpus Christi 2010, orig. proceeding) (mandatory venue in CPRC §65.023 controlled over CPRC §15.017, but court ultimately determined that §65.023 did not apply to the case); *see, e.g.*, **In re Fox River Real Estate Holdings, Inc.**, 596 S.W.3d 759, 765 (Tex.2020) (mandatory venue in CPRC §65.023 controlled over CPRC §15.020, but Court ultimately determined that §65.023 did not apply to the case).

(b) Exception—suit against county. When there are two counties of mandatory venue and one of the mandatory provisions involves a suit against a county under CPRC §15.015 and the other is outside CPRC chapter 15, the mandatory-venue provision under CPRC §15.015 controls over the other mandatory provision. *See* **In re Fort Bend Cty.**, 278 S.W.3d 842, 844–45 & n.1 (Tex.App.—Houston [14th Dist.] 2009, orig. proceeding). See "Suit against county," ch. 2-H, §4.1.6.

2. Permissive & mandatory counties. When there is a county of mandatory venue and a county of permissive venue, the suit should be brought in—and on motion must be transferred to—the county of mandatory venue. *See* Tex. Civ. Prac. & Rem. Code §15.004; Tex. R. Civ. P. 86(3)(b); **In re Fisher**, 433 S.W.3d at 534; *see, e.g.*, **Wichita Cty. v. Hart**, 917 S.W.2d 779, 781 (Tex.1996) (whistleblower suit against county was governed by mandatory provision, not by permissive-venue provision).

3. Multiple claims. If any claim in a suit is controlled by a mandatory-venue provision, all properly joined claims arising from the same transaction, occurrence, or series of transactions or occurrences are controlled by the same provision. Tex. Civ. Prac. & Rem. Code §15.004; **In re Fisher**, 433 S.W.3d at 534; **Madera Prod. v. Atlantic Richfield Co.**, 107 S.W.3d 652, 658 (Tex.App.—Texarkana 2003, pet. denied); *see* **Pinto Tech. Ventures, L.P. v. Sheldon**, 526 S.W.3d 428, 447 (Tex.2017). See "Multiple parties & claims," ch. 2-H, §7.

§5. Permissive-venue provisions

If no mandatory-venue provision applies, the plaintiff can decide where to file the suit according to an applicable permissive-venue provision. *See* Tex. Civ. Prac. & Rem. Code §§15.001(b)(2), 15.002(a). The permissive-venue provisions provide venue alternatives to the general venue rule. *See* Tex. Civ. Prac. & Rem. Code §15.002(a). See "General venue rule," ch. 2-H, §6. Most of the permissive-venue provisions are listed in CPRC chapter 15, subchapter C.

§5.1 Permissive venue in CPRC ch. 15.

1. Executor, administrator, or guardian. CPRC §15.031 is a permissive-venue provision that governs suits against an executor, administrator, or guardian. The provisions in CPRC §15.031 control over any conflicting venue provisions in the Estates Code in a suit against an executor, administrator, or guardian for personal injury, death, or property damage. Tex. Civ. Prac. & Rem. Code §15.007.

(1) Negligent act. In a suit against an executor, administrator, or guardian for a negligent act or omission of the person whose estate is being represented, venue is permissive in the county where the negligent act or omission occurred. Tex. Civ. Prac. & Rem. Code §15.031.

(2) Debt of estate. In a suit for a debt of an estate, venue is permissive in the county where the estate is being administered. Tex. Civ. Prac. & Rem. Code §15.031.

2. Breach of warranty. In a suit against a manufacturer of consumer goods for breach of warranty, venue is permissive in any of the following counties: (1) the county where all or a substantial part of the events or omissions giving rise to the claim occurred, (2) the county where the manufacturer has its principal office in Texas, or (3) the county where the plaintiff resided when the cause of action accrued. Tex. Civ. Prac. & Rem. Code §15.033.

3. Written contract.

(1) County of performance. In a suit on a written contract that states the contract is to be performed in a certain county or a definite place in that county, venue is permissive either in the specified county or in the county of the defendant's domicile. Tex. Civ. Prac. & Rem. Code §15.035(a); **Killeen v. Lighthouse Elec. Contractors, L.P.**, 248 S.W.3d 343, 347 (Tex.App.—San Antonio 2007, pet. denied).

(2) Contract in consumer transaction. In a suit by a creditor involving a consumer transaction, venue is permissive in the county where the defendant signed the contract or where the defendant resided when the suit was filed. Tex. Civ. Prac. & Rem. Code §15.035(b). Subsection (b) of CPRC §15.035 controls over subsection (a) and cannot be waived. *See* Tex. Civ. Prac. & Rem. Code §15.035(b). Thus, if a consumer contract identifies the creditor's home county as the place of payment, the creditor cannot sue there unless it is also the county where the defendant signed the contract or the county of the defendant's residence.

Note

It is a false, misleading, or deceptive act under the DTPA to file suit based on a consumer transaction involving a written contract signed by the defendant-consumer in any county other than the county (1) where the defendant-consumer resides at the time the suit is brought or (2) where the defendant-consumer signed the contract. Tex. Bus. & Com. Code §17.46(b)(23).

4. Oral contract. In a suit on an oral contract, the venue rules in CPRC chapter 15 apply. *See, e.g.*, Tex. Civ. Prac. & Rem. Code §15.092(b) (for justice-of-the-peace cases, suit on oral contract for labor actually performed may be brought in county and precinct where labor was performed); **KW Constr. v. Stephens & Sons Concrete Contractors, Inc.**, 165 S.W.3d 874, 880 (Tex.App.—Texarkana 2005, pet. denied) (in suit for breach of oral contract, CPRC §15.002(a) applied).

5. Insurance contract. CPRC §15.032 provides two permissive venues for suits on insurance policies: (1) in a suit against a fire, marine, or inland insurance company, venue is permissive in the county where the insured property is located, or (2) in a suit against any life, accident, or health-insurance company, venue is permissive in the county where the insurance company's principal office is located, in the county where the loss occurred, or in the county where the policyholder or beneficiary resided when the cause of action accrued. Tex. Civ. Prac. & Rem. Code §15.032. Suits against an insurance company regarding coverage are governed by mandatory-venue provisions in the Insurance Code. See "Insurance contract," ch. 2-H, §4.2.2(6).

§5.2 Other permissive-venue statutes. An action governed by any other statute prescribing permissive venue may be brought in the county allowed by that statute. Tex. Civ. Prac. & Rem. Code §15.038. Other permissive-venue provisions include the following:

1. DTPA. A suit under the DTPA may be filed only in a county (1) where venue is proper under CPRC chapter 15 (except in a suit against an insurer relating to uninsured or underinsured motorist coverage) or (2) where the defendant or its authorized agent solicited the transaction that forms the basis of the suit. *See* Tex. Bus. & Com. Code §17.56; Tex. Ins. Code §1952.110.

2. Whistleblower. The venue provision in a whistleblower suit is permissive. **City of Fort Worth v. Zimlich**, 29 S.W.3d 62, 72 (Tex.2000); **Wichita Cty. v. Hart**, 917 S.W.2d 779, 782 (Tex.1996).

(1) State. When the plaintiff is an employee of the State of Texas, suit may be filed either in the county where the cause of action arose or in Travis County. Tex. Gov't Code §554.007(a).

(2) Local government. When the plaintiff is an employee of a local-governmental unit, suit may be brought either in the county where the cause of action arose or in a county in the same geographic area that has established a council of governments or a regional-planning commission with the county where the cause of action arose. Tex. Gov't Code §554.007(b).

§6. General venue rule

§6.1 Applicability. If no mandatory-venue provision or permissive-venue provision applies, the plaintiff should file the suit according to the general venue rule; if a permissive-venue provision does apply, the plaintiff can choose to file suit under either the permissive-venue provision or the general venue rule. *See* Tex. Civ. Prac. & Rem. Code §§15.001(b)(2), 15.002(a); **Shamoun & Norman, LLP v. Yarto Int'l Grp.**, 398 S.W.3d 272, 287–88 (Tex.App.—Corpus Christi 2012, pet. dism'd). See "Permissive-venue provisions," ch. 2-H, §5.

§6.2 Proper counties. Under the general venue rule, a suit must be brought in one of the following counties:

1. In the county where all or a substantial part of the events giving rise to the claim occurred. Tex. Civ. Prac. & Rem. Code §15.002(a)(1).

2. In the county of the defendant's residence when the cause of action accrued, if the defendant is a natural person. Tex. Civ. Prac. & Rem. Code §15.002(a)(2).

3. In the county of the defendant's principal office in Texas, if the defendant is not a natural person (i.e., if the defendant is a corporation). Tex. Civ. Prac. & Rem. Code §15.002(a)(3).

4. In the county where the plaintiff resided when the action accrued, if none of the other provisions apply. Tex. Civ. Prac. & Rem. Code §15.002(a)(4). The purpose of CPRC §15.002(a)(4) is to provide venue for a plaintiff's suit against a nonresident defendant when the cause of action arises outside Texas.

§7. Multiple parties & claims

§7.1 Multiple plaintiffs. In a suit with multiple plaintiffs, a plaintiff or intervenor may remain in the suit only if it is able to establish one of the following:

1. **Proper venue.** Venue in the county of suit is proper for that plaintiff, independent of every other plaintiff. Tex Civ. Prac. & Rem. Code §15.003(a); **Surgitek v. Abel**, 997 S.W.2d 598, 600 (Tex.1999); **Sustainable Tex. Oyster Res. Mgmt. v. Hannah Reef, Inc.**, 491 S.W.3d 96, 105 (Tex.App.—Houston [1st Dist.] 2016, pet. denied); **Shell Oil Co. v. Baran**, 258 S.W.3d 719, 721 (Tex.App.—Beaumont 2008, pet. dism'd); **O'Quinn v. Hall**, 77 S.W.3d 438, 448 (Tex.App.—Corpus Christi 2002, no pet.).

2. **Proper joinder.** Venue in the county of suit meets the requirements for proper joinder of multiple plaintiffs under CPRC §15.003(a)(1) to (4). **Surgitek**, 997 S.W.2d at 600; **Sustainable Tex. Oyster**, 491 S.W.3d at 105; **Shell Oil**, 258 S.W.3d at 721; **O'Quinn**, 77 S.W.3d at 448. See "Joinder proper," ch. 3-C, §2.6.4(2).

§7.2 Multiple claims. If a plaintiff properly joins two or more claims arising from the same transaction, occurrence, or series of transactions or occurrences, and one of the claims is governed by a mandatory-venue provision in CPRC chapter 15, subchapter B, the mandatory-venue provision controls venue for the suit. Tex. Civ. Prac. & Rem. Code §15.004; **In re Fisher**, 433 S.W.3d 523, 534 (Tex.2014); **In re Stroud Oil Props., Inc.**, 110 S.W.3d 18, 23 (Tex.App.—Waco 2002, orig. proceeding).

§7.3 Multiple defendants.

1. **Venue against all.** In a suit with multiple defendants, if the plaintiff establishes proper venue against one defendant, then venue is proper for all defendants as long as the claims arise from the same transaction, occurrence, or series of transactions or occurrences. Tex. Civ. Prac. & Rem. Code §15.005; **American Home Prods. v. Clark**, 38 S.W.3d 92, 94 (Tex.2000).

2. **No waiver.** A waiver of venue by one defendant does not prevent another defendant from appropriately challenging venue. Tex. Civ. Prac. & Rem. Code §15.0641; **Brookshire Grocery Co. v. Smith**, 99 S.W.3d 819, 821–22 (Tex.App.—Beaumont 2003, pet. denied); **Hyundai Motor Co. v. Alvarado**, 989 S.W.2d 32, 37 (Tex.App.—San Antonio 1998, pet. granted, judgm't vacated w.r.m.).

§7.4 Counterclaim, cross-claim, or third-party claim. Venue for the main action establishes venue for a defendant's counterclaim or cross-claim or for a third-party claim properly joined under the TRCPs or any applicable statute. Tex. Civ. Prac. & Rem. Code §15.062(a); *see also* Tex. R. Civ. P. 38 (parties can bring in third parties who may be liable for all or part of claims involved in suit). Venue under CPRC §15.062(a) is mandatory and controls over other mandatory-venue provisions. **Perryman v. Spartan Tex. Six Capital Partners**, 546 S.W.3d 110, 132–33 (Tex.2018). When the original defendant joins a third-party defendant, venue for the main action establishes venue for any claim by the plaintiff against that third-party defendant arising from (1) the same transaction, occurrence, or series of transactions or occurrences and (2) the same subject matter as the plaintiff's claim against the original defendant. Tex. Civ. Prac. & Rem. Code §15.062(b); *e.g.* **Perryman**, 546 S.W.3d at 132 (CPRC §15.062(b) did not apply because Ps did not bring any claims against third-party D, only original D did).

I. Serving the Defendant with Suit

§1. General

§1.1 Rules. Tex. R. Civ. P. 15 to 17, 99, 103, 105 to 109a, 118 to 124, 237. See Tex. Civ. Prac. & Rem. Code ch. 17; Tex. Bus. Orgs. Code §§5.201, 5.251 to 5.257.

§1.2 Purpose.

1. Generally. "Service of citation" is a term that describes the formal process by which a plaintiff gives a defendant notice that it has been sued. **Texas Nat. Res. Conserv. Comm'n v. Sierra Club**, 70 S.W.3d 809, 813 (Tex.2002). The purpose of the citation is to give the court jurisdiction over the defendant, to satisfy due-process requirements, and to give the defendant the opportunity to appear and defend. **Cockrell v. Estevez**, 737 S.W.2d 138, 140 (Tex.App.—San Antonio 1987, no writ). The citation and a copy of the plaintiff's petition, which is attached, are collectively referred to as the "process." Service of process is accomplished when the citation and a copy of the petition are delivered to the defendant, or the defendant is given notice of the suit through some other authorized means. *See* Tex. R. Civ. P. 99(a). The plaintiff, not the process server, is responsible for ensuring that service is properly accomplished. *Id.*; **Primate Constr., Inc. v. Silver**, 884 S.W.2d 151, 153 (Tex.1994); *see, e.g.*, **In re Buggs**, 166 S.W.3d 506, 508 (Tex.App.—Texarkana 2005, orig. proceeding) (P's duty, not clerk's, to locate newspaper and pay for service by publication).

2. Default judgment. The rules for the issuance of citation, the service of process, and the return of process are especially important when the court renders a default judgment. A judgment cannot be rendered against a defendant unless the defendant was served with process, accepted or waived service, or made an appearance. Tex. R. Civ. P. 124; **Werner v. Colwell**, 909 S.W.2d 866, 869–70 (Tex.1995); **Mapco, Inc. v. Carter**, 817 S.W.2d 686, 687 (Tex.1991). Because the ordinary presumptions of valid service do not apply in an appeal of a no-answer default judgment, the judgment will be reversed unless there is strict compliance with the rules. **Primate Constr.**, 884 S.W.2d at 152. See "Sufficiency of service," ch. 7-A, §3.4.

§1.3 Timetables & forms. Appendix IV, Timetable 8, Pretrial motions; Appendix IV, Timetable 11, No-answer default judgment; **O'Connor's Texas Civil Forms**, FORMS 2B:10 to 2B:19, 2I:1 et seq. (2020 ed.).

§1.4 Other references. Anderson, *Transnational Litigation Involving Mexican Parties*, 25 St. Mary's L.J. 1059 (1994); Miller, Comment, *Misnomers: Default Judgments & Strict Compliance with Service of Process Rules*, 46 Baylor L.Rev. 633 (1994); Jones, *International Judicial Assistance: Procedural Chaos & a Program for Reform*, 62 Yale L.J. 515 (1953); **O'Connor's Federal Rules * Civil Trials** (2021 ed.); **O'Connor's Texas Family Law Handbook** (2021 ed.).

§2. Requirements for the citation

The citation, which is issued by the court clerk after payment of a fee, must comply with TRCP 15 and 99. The clerk must keep a copy of the citation in the court's file. Tex. R. Civ. P. 99(a).

Practice Tip

Before the court clerk will issue the citation, the plaintiff may need to complete and file with its pleading a Civil Process Request Form identifying the person to be served and the method of service. Check the court's website for specific requirements and to obtain a copy of the form.

---

§2.1 Style of process. The style of the process must be "The State of Texas." Tex. R. Civ. P. 15, 99(b)(1). The process must be directed to any sheriff or constable in the State of Texas. Tex. R. Civ. P. 15.

§2.2 Information about suit. The citation must identify the suit by showing the cause number. Tex. R. Civ. P. 99(b)(6) (called "file" number). If the citation omits the cause number or contains the wrong number, the citation is fatally defective. **Martinez v. Wilber**, 810 S.W.2d 461, 463 (Tex.App.—San Antonio 1991, writ denied). Service of process with one cause number will not support a suit with a different cause number. *See, e.g.*, **Finlay v. Jones**, 435 S.W.2d 136, 137 (Tex.1968) (D was served under cause number 144,608 instead of 144,607).

§2.3 Information about court. The citation must contain the following information about the court:

1. Identification of court. The citation must contain the name and location of the court and the address of the clerk who issued the citation. Tex. R. Civ. P. 99(b)(3), (b)(11).

2. Signature & seal. The citation must be signed by the clerk and issued under the seal of the court. Tex. R. Civ. P. 15, 99(b)(2); **Midstate Envtl. Servs. v. Peterson**, 435 S.W.3d 287, 290 (Tex.App.—Waco 2014, no pet.) *see* **Paramount Credit, Inc. v. Montgomery**, 420 S.W.3d 226, 233 (Tex.App.—Houston [1st Dist.] 2013, no pet.).

§2.4 Information about P. The citation must contain the following information about the plaintiff:

1. Identification of P. The citation must contain the name of the plaintiff. Tex. R. Civ. P. 99(b)(7); *e.g.*, **Patrick O'Connor & Assocs. v. Hall**, No. 01-15-00661-CV, 2016 WL 4440665 (Tex.App.—Houston [1st Dist.] 2016, pet. denied) (memo op.; 8-23-16) (citation that named P as "Patrick OConnor Associates" instead of "Patrick O'Connor & Associates, LP" was invalid).

2. P's attorney. The citation must contain the name and address of the plaintiff's attorney. Tex. R. Civ. P. 99(b)(9). If the plaintiff is pro se, the citation must contain the plaintiff's address. *Id.*

§2.5 Information about D.

1. Identification of D.

(1) Name. The citation must contain the defendant's correct name. Tex. R. Civ. P. 99(b)(7); *see* **Amato v. Hernandez**, 981 S.W.2d 947, 949 (Tex.App.—Houston [1st Dist.] 1998, pet. denied). If the correct defendant was incorrectly named in the petition, the error is a misnomer, and a default judgment against that defendant will be affirmed if (1) the correct defendant was actually served and (2) the petition describes the facts in such a way that the correct defendant knows it is the intended defendant. *See* **Union Pac. Corp. v. Legg**, 49 S.W.3d 72, 78 (Tex.App.—Austin 2001, no pet.). If the wrong defendant was named in the petition, the error is a misidentification, and a default judgment must be reversed. *See, e.g., id.* (P named and served Union Pacific Railroad, not Union Pacific Corp.). See "Misnomer vs. misidentification," ch. 2-B, §4.3.1(2).

(2) Capacity. When the defendant is sued in a representative capacity, the defendant must be identified in the petition by that capacity (e.g., trustee, executor). *See, e.g.,* **Werner v. Colwell**, 909 S.W.2d 866, 870 (Tex.1995) (judgment could not be rendered against D as trustee when she was sued only as individual). See "Capacity," ch. 2-B, §4.2.2. Similarly, the defendant should be identified by the correct capacity in the citation. *Cf.* **Price v. Dean**, 990 S.W.2d 453, 454–55 (Tex.App.—Corpus Christi 1999, no pet.) (return that does not identify D by correct capacity renders service invalid).

(3) Address for service. The citation should include the defendant's address for service of process. *See* Tex. R. Civ. P. 99(b), 106(a). When the defendant is a nonresident, the petition should use the exact language from the long-arm statute, TRCP 108, or other applicable statute to describe the place for service. The general long-arm statute requires that the petition and citation to be served on the Secretary of State include a statement of the nonresident's name and home or home-office address where the process is to be served. Tex. Civ. Prac. & Rem. Code §17.045(a). See "Service on Secretary of State," ch. 2-I, §5.

2. Citation directed to D. The citation must "be directed to the defendant." Tex. R. Civ. P. 99(b)(8); *see, e.g.,* **Plains Chevrolet, Inc. v. Thorne**, 656 S.W.2d 631, 632–33 (Tex.App.—Waco 1983, no writ) (service was void because citation was directed to General Motors Corporation, not Plains Chevrolet). TRCP 15, however, also requires the process to "be directed to any sheriff or any constable within the State of Texas." Two courts of appeals have harmonized these rules and determined that the citation must be expressly directed to the defendant under TRCP 99 and may also be addressed to the sheriff or constable under TRCP 15. **Williams v. Williams**, 150 S.W.3d 436, 445 (Tex.App.—Austin 2004, pet. denied); *see, e.g.,* **Barker CATV Constr., Inc. v. Ampro, Inc.**, 989 S.W.2d 789, 792–93 (Tex.App.—Houston [1st Dist.] 1999, no pet.) (overruling other First Court of Appeals cases that held citation defective because it was directed to sheriff as well as D). The omission of directions to the sheriff or constable on the form of the citation will not render it void. **Williams**, 150 S.W.3d at 445.

§2.6 Identification of D's agent for service. The citation must name the agent for service and state the address for service on the agent if the defendant is to be served through an agent. Even though an agent is to be served for the defendant,

the citation must be directed to the defendant and not to the agent. *See* **Barker CATV Constr., Inc. v. Ampro, Inc.**, 989 S.W.2d 789, 792 (Tex.App.—Houston [1st Dist.] 1999, no pet.). If the citation is directed to the agent, it does not confer jurisdiction over the defendant. **Dan Edge Motors, Inc. v. Scott**, 657 S.W.2d 822, 823 (Tex.App.—Texarkana 1983, no writ); *see, e.g.*, **Verlander Enters. v. Graham**, 932 S.W.2d 259, 261 (Tex.App.—El Paso 1996, no writ) (citation was directed to a vice president instead of the corporation). When the citation names one person as agent for service, but the return of the citation shows it was served on another person, the trial court does not acquire jurisdiction over the defendant. **Pharmakinetics Labs. v. Katz**, 717 S.W.2d 704, 706 (Tex.App.—San Antonio 1986, no writ).

1. Corporation. When the defendant is a corporation, the citation should be directed to the corporation and name as agent for service the president, any vice president, or the registered agent. **Dan Edge Motors**, 657 S.W.2d at 823.

2. Partnership. When the defendant is a partnership, the citation should be directed to the defendant-partnership and name the individual partners for service. *See* Tex. Civ. Prac. & Rem. Code §17.022; **Shawell v. Pend Oreille Oil & Gas Co.**, 823 S.W.2d 336, 337–38 (Tex.App.—Texarkana 1991, writ denied); **Fincher v. B&D Air Conditioning & Heating Co.**, 816 S.W.2d 509, 513 (Tex.App.—Houston [1st Dist.] 1991, writ denied). If a claim is also brought against a partner in her individual capacity, the citation must be directed to the individual partner. *See* **Kao Holdings, L.P. v. Young**, 261 S.W.3d 60, 64 (Tex.2008).

§2.7 Critical dates. The citation must contain the following dates:

1. Date petition filed. The citation must state the date the plaintiff filed the petition. Tex. R. Civ. P. 99(b)(4). If the petition's filing date is omitted, the defect is fatal. *See* **Hance v. Cogswell**, 307 S.W.2d 277, 278–79 (Tex.App.—Austin 1957, no writ). If the citation states an impossible date for filing, the defect is fatal. *E.g.*, **McGraw-Hill, Inc. v. Futrell**, 823 S.W.2d 414, 417 (Tex.App.—Houston [1st Dist.] 1992, writ denied) (date of service was 17 days before suit filed); **George v. Elledge**, 261 S.W.2d 201, 201 (Tex.App.—San Antonio 1953, no writ) (date of service was seven months before suit filed).

2. Date citation issued. The citation must state the date it was issued. Tex. R. Civ. P. 15, 99(b)(5); **London v. Chandler**, 406 S.W.2d 203, 204 (Tex.1966). The date the citation is issued may be different from the date the clerk signs and seals the citation. **London**, 406 S.W.2d at 204. The citation is issued when the clerk authorizes delivery and gives the citation to an officer or other authorized person for service. *Id.* If the date the citation was issued is omitted, the citation is not invalid and may be amended. *Id.*; *see* Tex. R. Civ. P. 118.

3. Time to answer. The citation for district and county courts must state that the defendant is required to file a written answer by 10:00 a.m. on the first Monday after the expiration of 20 days from the date of service. Tex. R. Civ. P. 15, 99(b), (c). This requirement must be stated in the exact language of TRCP 99(c). If the 20th day falls on a Monday, the answer must be filed by the next Monday. The citation for justice courts must be stated in the exact language of TRCP 501.1(c), which has a shorter deadline—14 days.

4. Date of delivery. If the citation is personally served on the defendant, it must state the date that it was delivered. *See* Tex. R. Civ. P. 106(a)(1).

§2.8 Warning of default. The citation must notify the defendant that if it does not file an answer, judgment by default may be rendered for the relief demanded in the petition. Tex. R. Civ. P. 99(b)(12). This notice must be stated in the exact language of TRCP 99(c).

§2.9 Notice of required disclosures. For cases filed on or after January 1, 2021, the citation must notify the defendant that it may be required to make initial disclosures of certain information generally within 30 days after filing its answer. *See* Tex. R. Civ. P. 99(b)(13). This notice must be stated in the exact language of TRCP 99(c).

2021 Rule Amendments

In 2020, the Supreme Court approved significant amendments to TRCP 194. See Tex.Sup.Ct. Order, Misc. Docket No. 20-9153 (eff. Jan. 1, 2021). Under the amendments, a party is generally required to make certain initial disclosures without waiting for a discovery request from the other party. See Tex. R. Civ. P. 194.1(a), 194.2(b). See "Required disclosures—Cases filed on or after 1-1-21," ch. 6-E, §3. The

amendments apply to cases filed on or after January 1, 2021, except those filed in justice court. Tex.Sup.Ct. Order, Misc. Docket No. 20-9153 (eff. Jan. 1, 2021).

§2.10 Copy of petition. A copy of the plaintiff's original petition must be served with the citation. Tex. R. Civ. P. 106(a); *see* Tex. R. Civ. P. 99(a). If the plaintiff amends the petition before service by adding parties, claims, or damages, the amended petition must be served with the citation. *See, e.g.*, **Primate Constr., Inc. v. Silver**, 884 S.W.2d 151, 152–53 (Tex.1994) (default J reversed because D served with original petition, which did not name it as D, instead of amended petition); **Seeley v. KCI USA, Inc.**, 100 S.W.3d 276, 277–78 (Tex.App.—San Antonio 2002, no pet.) (same). See "Description of documents," ch. 2-I, §9.4.3; "Amending the petition," ch. 2-I, §10.1.

§2.11 Endorsement on process. The officer or other authorized person serving process must endorse on it the day and hour when she received it. Tex. R. Civ. P. 16, 105; **In re Z.J.W.**, 185 S.W.3d 905, 907 (Tex.App.—Tyler 2006, no pet.); *see, e.g.*, **Melendez v. John R. Schatzman, Inc.**, 685 S.W.2d 137, 138 (Tex.App.—El Paso 1985, no writ) (officer did not endorse day and hour he received process). See "Who may serve process," ch. 2-I, §3. When process is served, the officer or other authorized person must also endorse on the process the manner in which she issued it and the time and place it was served. Tex. R. Civ. P. 16. See "Methods of service," ch. 2-I, §4.

§3. Who may serve process

The plaintiff should make sure that service is accomplished by a person who is authorized by rule, statute, or court order to serve process. *See* Tex. R. Civ. P. 103. Service of process by a person who is not authorized is invalid and will not support a default judgment. Process includes citation and other notices, writs, orders, and papers issued by the court. *Id.*

§3.1 Court clerk. The court clerk is authorized to serve process by registered or certified mail and to serve citation by publication. Tex. R. Civ. P. 103.

§3.2 Officers. A sheriff, constable, or other person authorized by law may serve process in Texas. Tex. R. Civ. P. 103; *see* Tex. Loc. Gov't Code §85.021(a) (sheriff), §86.021(c) (constable). Sheriffs may serve process anywhere in Texas; nothing in Local Gov't Code §85.021 limits sheriffs to serving process only in their own counties. Constables, however, may serve process only in their own and contiguous counties. Tex. Loc. Gov't Code §86.021(c), (d). Only a sheriff or constable can serve the following types of process without a court order: for an action for forcible entry and detainer; for a writ that requires taking actual possession of a person, property, or thing; and for an enforcement action that must be physically performed by the person delivering process. Tex. R. Civ. P. 103 & cmt.

§3.3 Authorized by court order. TRCP 103 permits service of process by persons authorized by court order.

1. Trial-court order. A person may serve process if she has no interest in the lawsuit, is at least 18 years old, and is authorized by law or a written court order. Tex. R. Civ. P. 103; *see* **Mayfield v. Dean Witter Fin. Servs.**, 894 S.W.2d 502, 505 (Tex.App.—Austin 1995, writ denied); *cf.* Tex. Ins. Code §804.201(b) (service on insurance company). See "Not interested person," ch. 2-I, §3.4. The process must include a copy of the court order that authorized the person to serve process; without it, the person cannot effectuate service. *See, e.g.*, **HB & WM, Inc. v. Smith**, 802 S.W.2d 279, 281 (Tex.App.—San Antonio 1990, no writ) (no order authorizing commercial process server).

2. Supreme Court order. A person who is certified by order of the Supreme Court may serve process. Tex. R. Civ. P. 103. The Supreme Court has adopted guidelines in Judicial Branch Certification Commission Rule 8.0 for a person to be certified to serve process. *See* Tex.Sup.Ct. Order, Misc. Docket No. 14-9168 (eff. Sept. 1, 2014); *see also* Tex.Sup.Ct. Order, Misc. Docket No. 14-9186 (eff. Sept. 1, 2014) (person certified by Judicial Branch Certification Commission to serve process is certified by order of Supreme Court under TRCP 103). The Judicial Branch Certification Commission Rules and other information on process-server certification can be found on the Judicial Branch Certification Commission website at www.txcourts.gov/jbcc.

§3.4 Not interested person. Generally, no person who is a party or who is interested in the outcome of the suit may serve process. Tex. R. Civ. P. 103. A person who is "interested in the outcome of a suit" includes the party, the party's attorney, and their agents and employees. *See, e.g.*, **Palomin v. Zarsky Lumber Co.**, 26 S.W.3d 690, 695 (Tex.App.—Corpus Christi

2000, pet. denied) (bookkeeper for P's attorney was not interested person because she was off duty when she served D and she received additional pay for service); **Jackson v. U.S.**, 138 F.R.D. 83, 87–88 (S.D.Tex.1991) (secretary who served process was interested person because she was employee of P's attorney). A party or its representative is permitted, however, to serve process on the Secretary of State. Tex. Civ. Prac. & Rem. Code §17.026(a). See "Service on Secretary of State," ch. 2-I, §5.

§4. Methods of service

Process may be served on the defendant according to several different methods. If the citation restricts service to a particular method, service must be made according to the citation's terms. *See, e.g.*, **Smith v. Commercial Equip. Leasing Co.**, 678 S.W.2d 917, 917–18 (Tex.1984) (service invalid because citation was restricted to personal service and process was served by certified mail).

Note

A citation cannot be served on Sunday, except in cases of injunction, attachment, garnishment, sequestration, or distress proceedings. Tex. R. Civ. P. 6; ***Nichols v. Nichols****, 857 S.W.2d 657, 658 & n.1 (Tex.App.—Houston [1st Dist] 1993, no writ).*

§4.1 Service by U.S. mail. Service by certified mail, return receipt requested, is the most popular method of service. It is much less expensive and time-consuming than any other method of service. Service by certified mail may be made by (1) the court clerk, (2) the sheriff or constable or any other person authorized by law, (3) any person 18 years of age or older, authorized by law or by order of court, or (4) any person certified by order of the Supreme Court. *See* Tex. R. Civ. P. 103, 106(a)(2); **P&H Transp. v. Robinson**, 930 S.W.2d 857, 859 (Tex.App.—Houston [1st Dist.] 1996, writ denied). CPRC §17.026(a) authorizes the court clerk or a party or its representative to serve the Secretary of State with process by certified mail, return receipt requested.

§4.2 Service by personal delivery. Any person who has the authority to serve process (by law or court order) may serve the defendant by delivering the process to the defendant personally. *See* Tex. R. Civ. P. 103, 106(a)(1); **Woodall v. Lansford**, 254 S.W.2d 540, 541 (Tex.App.—Fort Worth 1953, no writ). When the authorized person hands the citation to the defendant, the defendant must be made to understand that it is a lawsuit and that the defendant is being served. *See* **Texas Indus. v. Sanchez**, 521 S.W.2d 133, 135–36 (Tex.App.—Dallas 1975), *writ ref'd n.r.e.*, 525 S.W.2d 870 (Tex.1975).

§4.3 Substituted service.

1. Substituted service under TRCP 106. If personal service or service by mail was attempted but not successful, the court may authorize another method of service. Tex. R. Civ. P. 106(b); **State Farm Fire & Cas. Co. v. Costley**, 868 S.W.2d 298, 298–99 (Tex.1993); *see* **Hubicki v. Festina**, 226 S.W.3d 405, 408 (Tex.2007). When a court orders substituted service under TRCP 106, the only authority for the service is the order itself. **Creaven v. Creaven**, 551 S.W.3d 865, 870 (Tex.App.—Houston [14th Dist.] 2018, no pet.); **Dolly v. Aethos Comms. Sys.**, 10 S.W.3d 384, 388 (Tex.App.—Dallas 2000, no pet.). The order must contain specific instructions for the process server to follow or else it is defective. **Steinke v. Mann**, 276 S.W.3d 608, 610 (Tex.App.—Waco 2008, no pet.). Any deviation from the specifications in the order may result in improper service. **Steinke**, 276 S.W.3d at 610; **Dolly**, 10 S.W.3d at 388; *e.g.*, **Creaven**, 551 S.W.3d at 870 (service was improper when affidavit supporting return of service stated D was served at different address than what court's order directed); *see* Tex. R. Civ. P. 107(f) (when service is authorized under TRCP 106, proof of service must be made in manner ordered by court).

(1) Motion & sworn statement. Before the court can order substituted service, the plaintiff must file a motion for substituted service supported by a statement that is sworn to before a notary or made under penalty of perjury and that describes the unsuccessful attempts at service under TRCP 106(a)(1) or (a)(2) and lists a location where the defendant can probably be found. Tex. R. Civ. P. 106(b); *see* **Hubicki**, 226 S.W.3d at 408; **Costley**, 868 S.W.2d at 298–99 & n.1; **In re Sloan**, 214 S.W.3d 217, 222 (Tex.App.—Eastland 2007, orig. proceeding). The party should make multiple attempts at service before moving for substituted service; one attempt is insufficient. *See, e.g.*, **Hubicki**, 226 S.W.3d at 408 (single attempt at service by certified mail; substituted service ineffective); **Costley**, 868 S.W.2d at 298–99 (ten failed attempts at personal

service; substituted service effective). If the plaintiff does not file a statement verifying the unsuccessful efforts to serve the defendant, the court cannot order substituted service. *See* **Wilson v. Dunn**, 800 S.W.2d 833, 836 (Tex.1990). A party needs to show only that attempts failed under TRCP 106(a)(1) or (a)(2). **Costley**, 868 S.W.2d at 299 n.2.

2020 Rule Amendments

Before the 2020 amendments to TRCP 106, the plaintiff was required to support its motion for substituted service with an affidavit; now, a statement sworn before a notary or made under penalty of perjury is acceptable. See Tex. R. Civ. P. 106(b); Tex.Sup.Ct. Order, Misc. Docket No. 20-9148 (Dec. 18, 2020); Tex.Sup.Ct. Order, Misc. Docket No. 20-9103 (eff. Dec. 31, 2020).

(2) Types of service. Under TRCP 106(b), the following types of service are permissible:

(a) Delivery of process to any person older than 16 at a location where the defendant can probably be found, as specified in the statement supporting the motion. Tex. R. Civ. P. 106(b)(1); *see* **Olympia Marble & Granite v. Mayes**, 17 S.W.3d 437, 444–45 (Tex.App.—Houston [1st Dist.] 2000, no pet.); **Walker v. Brodhead**, 828 S.W.2d 278, 280 (Tex.App.—Austin 1992, writ denied).

(b) Service of process in any other manner—including electronically by social media, e-mail, or other technology—that the statement or other evidence shows will be reasonably effective to give the defendant notice of the suit. Tex. R. Civ. P. 106(b)(2); *see* **In re J.Z.P.**, 484 S.W.3d 924, 924 (Tex.2016); *see, e.g.*, **Costley**, 868 S.W.2d at 299 (first-class mail service); *see also* Tex. Civ. Prac. & Rem. Code §17.033(a) (court may order service by electronic communication sent to D through social-media presence). In determining whether to order electronic service of process, the court should consider whether the technology being considered actually belongs to the defendant and whether the defendant regularly uses or has recently used the technology. Tex. R. Civ. P. 106 cmt. (2020).

2020 Rule Amendments

In 2020, TRCP 106 was amended to specify that substituted service via electronic means such as social media, e-mail, or other technology is permissible. See Tex. R. Civ. P. 106(b)(2); Tex.Sup.Ct. Order, Misc. Docket No. 20-9148 (Dec. 18, 2020); Tex.Sup.Ct. Order, Misc. Docket No. 20-9103 (eff. Dec. 31, 2020).

2. Substituted service under TRCP 109 or 109a.

(1) TRCP 109—service by publication. Service by publication is a form of substituted service in which notice is published online and, generally, also in a local newspaper. *See* Tex. Gov't Code §72.034; Tex. R. Civ. P. 109, 116. Although this section discusses service by publication under TRCP 109, service by publication may also be authorized by court order under TRCP 106(b)(2).

(a) When service by publication is authorized.

[1] Unknown defendant. Service by publication is authorized for use in actions against an unknown defendant; if a defendant's identity is known, service by publication is generally inadequate. *See* **In re E.R.**, 385 S.W.3d 552, 560 (Tex.2012); *see, e.g.*, **Wood v. Brown**, 819 S.W.2d 799, 800 (Tex.1991) (attorney's affidavit did not satisfy TRCP 109 because it did not identify how defendant was unknown). Service by publication is authorized for use on the following parties:

[a] A defendant whose residence is unknown. Tex. R. Civ. P. 109.

[b] A defendant who is transient. *Id.*

[c] A defendant who is absent from the State or is a nonresident of the State and on whom the party serving citation has attempted to obtain personal service of nonresident notice under TRCP 108. Tex. R. Civ. P. 109.

[d] An unknown heir or stockholder of a defunct corporation. Tex. R. Civ. P. 111.

[e] An unknown owner or claimant of an interest in land. Tex. R. Civ. P. 112.

[f] An unknown defendant or unknown owner of any interest in property in a suit for delinquent ad valorem taxes. *See* Tex. R. Civ. P. 117a.

[2] Diligent search. The party serving citation must conduct a diligent search for the defendant before resorting to service by publication. **In re E.R.**, 385 S.W.3d at 564; *see* Tex. R. Civ. P. 109. A diligent search must include inquiries that someone who really wants to find the defendant would make and should be measured by the quality, rather than the quantity, of the search. **In re E.R.**, 385 S.W.3d at 565. A lack of diligence makes service by publication ineffective. *Id.* at 564.

(b) Form of citation. The form of the citation generally must comply with TRCP 15 and 99, except that the plaintiff should not include a copy of the petition with the citation. Tex. R. Civ. P. 114. See "Requirements for the citation," ch. 2-I, §2. Specifically, the citation must contain the following: (1) the names of the parties (or the parties' designations or classifications, as stated in the petition), (2) a brief statement of the nature of the suit, which does not need to include details about the claim, (3) a description of any property involved and the defendant's interest in the property, and (4) if the suit involves land, the specific statements required in TRCP 115. Tex. R. Civ. P. 114; *see* **Wiebusch v. Wiebusch**, 636 S.W.2d 540, 542 (Tex.App.—San Antonio 1982, no writ) (notice of nature of suit is necessary for service by publication).

Note

The deadline for the parties to answer and appear depends on whether the citation is issued from the district or county court or from the justice court. See Tex. R. Civ. P. 114. For the specific appearance requirements that must be included in the citation, see TRCP 114. A defendant served by publication who does not answer or appear must be represented by an attorney appointed by the court. Tex. R. Civ. P. 244. See "Trial," ch. 10-B, §10.1.

(c) Manner of service. Service by publication is accomplished by publishing notice online, via the Public Information Internet Website maintained by the Office of Court Administration (OCA), and in most cases, also in a local newspaper. *See* Tex. R. Civ. P. 116(b)(1); *see also* Tex. Gov't Code §72.034 (authorizing OCA to develop and maintain Website).

2020 Rule Amendments

In 2020, the Supreme Court amended TRCP 116 (and TRCP 117, which governs the return of citation) to require that service by publication be accomplished by publication on the newly created Public Information Internet Website in addition to publication in a local newspaper. See Tex.Sup.Ct. Order, Misc. Docket No. 20-9009 (eff. June 1, 2020); see also Tex.Sup.Ct. Order, Misc. Docket No. 20-9081 (eff. July 1, 2020) (final order approving amendments set forth in Misc. Docket No. 29-9009). The Website, which is maintained by the OCA, is the official statewide website that will provide for citation by publication and allow the public to access, search, and sort the public information. Tex. Gov't Code §72.034(a)(2), (c); see Tex. R. Civ. P. 116(a).

[1] Publication on Public Information Internet Website. The citation for service via the Public Information Internet Website must be served by the clerk of the court in which the case is pending. Tex. R. Civ. P. 116(d)(1). The citation must be published for at least 28 days before the return is filed and must follow any other guidelines established by the OCA. Tex. R. Civ. P. 116(d)(2), (3).

[2] Publication in newspaper. Publication in a newspaper is required in most cases. When required, the citation must be served by the clerk of the court in which the case is pending or any sheriff or constable. Tex. R. Civ. P. 116(c)(1).

[a] Required. Publication in a newspaper is required unless one of the circumstances under TRCP 116(b)(2) is met. The citation must be published once each week for four consecutive weeks, and the first publication must be

at least 28 days before the return is filed. Tex. R. Civ. P. 116(c)(2). If the suit does not involve the title to land or the partition of real estate, the citation must be published in a newspaper in the county where the suit is pending; in suits involving the title to land or the partition of real estate, the citation must be published in a newspaper where the land or a part of it is situated. Tex. R. Civ. P. 116(c)(3), (4).

[b] Not required. Publication in a newspaper is not required if any of the following are true: (1) the party requesting citation files a Statement of Inability to Afford Payment of Court Costs under TRCP 145, (2) the total cost of the publication is more than $200 each week or an amount set by the Supreme Court, whichever is greater, or (3) the county in which the publication is required does not publish, print, or generally circulate a newspaper. Tex. R. Civ. P. 116(b)(2). For a discussion of filing a Statement under TRCP 145, see "Suit by Indigent," ch. 2-J, §1 et seq.

(d) Return of service.

[1] Publication on Public Information Internet Website. When citation is served by publication on the Public Information Internet Website, the return of service must specify the dates of publication and be generated by the OCA. Tex. R. Civ. P. 117(b). See "Proof of service—The return," ch. 2-I, §9.

[2] Publication in newspaper. When citation is served by newspaper publication, the return of service must state how the citation was published, specify the dates of publication, be signed by the officer who served the citation, and be accompanied by an image of the publication. Tex. R. Civ. P. 117(a). See "Proof of service—The return," ch. 2-I, §9.

(e) Challenging service. A defendant served by publication can file a motion for new trial up to two years after the judgment. Tex. R. Civ. P. 329(a). See "MNT after service by publication," ch. 10-B, §10.

(2) TRCP 109a—other manner of service. If service by publication is authorized, a plaintiff can file a motion asking the court to allow for a different method of substituted service. Tex. R. Civ. P. 109a. For substituted service under TRCP 109a to be effective, the court must find and state in its order that the method of service would be as likely as service by publication to give the defendant actual notice of the suit. *Id.*; **In re E.D.**, 553 S.W.3d 101, 105 (Tex.App.—Fort Worth 2018, no pet.).

Note

Service under TRCP 109a is not invalid just because the defendant does not respond to it. Tex. R. Civ. P. 109a. A defendant served under TRCP 109a who does not answer or appear must be represented by an attorney appointed by the court. See Tex. R. Civ. P. 109a, 244. See "Trial," ch. 10-B, §10.1.

(a) Return of service. The return of service must specifically state the manner in which service was accomplished and attach any evidence (e.g., return receipt, returned mail) showing the result of the service. Tex. R. Civ. P. 109a. See "Proof of service—The return," ch. 2-I, §9.

(b) Challenging service. A defendant served under TRCP 109a can file a motion for new trial up to two years after the judgment. *See* Tex. R. Civ. P. 109a, 329(a). See "MNT after service by publication," ch. 10-B, §10.

§5. Service on Secretary of State

Several statutory provisions designate the Secretary of State as an agent for service of process. For the list of the statutes, see www.sos.state.tx.us/corp/statutes-service-of-process.shtml. The two most important of these involve service on a nonresident and service on a corporation. See "Long-arm service," ch. 2-I, §5.3; "Service on corporation," ch. 2-I, §5.4. The other statutes include CPRC §17.091 (nonresident in a delinquent-tax case), §101.102(c) (Tort Claims Act); Estates Code §§505.004 & 505.005 (foreign corporate fiduciary); and Insurance Code §§541.255(b)(3) & 804.301 (insurance company). For information about serving the Secretary of State, call the Citations Unit at (512) 463-5560.

§5.1 General rules. When serving the Secretary of State with process, the plaintiff should consult the specific statutes and observe the following general rules:

1. Service on Secretary. The plaintiff may accomplish service on the Secretary of State by certified mail, by delivery by a qualified officer or a private process server, or by any other means permitted by rule or statute. *See* Tex. Civ.

Prac. & Rem. Code §17.026 (certified mail can be sent by clerk or party). Personal service on the Secretary of State is not necessary. *See* **Capitol Brick, Inc. v. Fleming Mfg. Co.**, 722 S.W.2d 399, 401 (Tex.1986) (service under long-arm statute). Two copies of the process must be served on the Secretary of State. 1 Tex. Admin. Code §71.21(a). When process is served by a sheriff or constable, the plaintiff must include an additional copy of the process for the return. When process is served by a private process server, the plaintiff must include copies of the order appointing the process server. When process is served by mail, the citation should be sent to the Secretary of State's post-office address. When process is served by delivery, it should be delivered to the street address of the Citations Unit.

2. Necessary information. The citation must contain the following information: (1) the defendant's name, (2) the defendant's address for service, and (3) when specified in the statute, the proper identification of the address. *See* Tex. Civ. Prac. & Rem. Code §17.045(a); 1 Tex. Admin. Code §71.21(a). The citation should also identify the statute authorizing service. If the statute authorizing service identifies the address by name, the plaintiff should use the same language. For example, for service on a nonresident under CPRC §17.045(a), the plaintiff should identify the address as that of the nonresident's "home" or "home office." **World Distribs. v. Knox**, 968 S.W.2d 474, 477–78 (Tex.App.—El Paso 1998, no pet.); *see* **Wachovia Bank v. Gilliam**, 215 S.W.3d 848, 849–50 (Tex.2007). If the plaintiff does not state and the face of the record does not otherwise show that the address is the nonresident's home or home office, service is invalid. **Wachovia Bank**, 215 S.W.3d at 849–50; **World Distribs.**, 968 S.W.2d at 477–78.
Chart 2-3, below, lists some of the statutory identifications of the addresses for service on defendants through the Secretary of State.

2-3. Service Through Secretary of State

	Statute	Identify address as the
1	Tex. Bus. Orgs. Code §5.253(b)(1)	Most recent address of entity on file
2	Tex. Bus. Orgs. Code §9.011(b)(6)	Address of foreign entity
3	Long-Arm Statute—Tex. Civ. Prac. & Rem. Code §17.045(a)	Home or home office
4	Tex. Ins. Code §804.302	Last known home office or principal place of business

3. Fees. The fee payable to the Secretary of State is $40 per defendant for maintaining a record of service of process and $15 for the issuance of a certificate of service. Tex. Gov't Code §405.031(a)(1), (4).

4. Secretary forwards process. Once served, the Secretary of State will mail a copy of the citation and petition to the defendant by registered or certified mail, return receipt requested. *See* Tex. Civ. Prac. & Rem. Code §17.045(b), (d) (notice to nonresident). Service on the defendant is complete when the Secretary of State is served, not when the defendant receives notice. **Bonewitz v. Bonewitz**, 726 S.W.2d 227, 230 (Tex.App.—Austin 1987, writ ref'd n.r.e.). In other words, the Secretary is the agent for receiving process on the defendant's behalf, not for serving process. **Campus Invs. v. Cullever**, 144 S.W.3d 464, 466 (Tex.2004).

§5.2 Proof of service. Proof the citation was served on the Secretary of State is not enough to support jurisdiction over the defendant; the plaintiff must prove the Secretary of State forwarded the process to the defendant. **Whitney v. L&L Rlty. Corp.**, 500 S.W.2d 94, 96 (Tex.1973). To prove the Secretary forwarded the process, the plaintiff should secure a certificate (sometimes referred to as a "Whitney certificate") from the Secretary of State. *See* **Capitol Brick, Inc. v. Fleming Mfg. Co.**, 722 S.W.2d 399, 401 (Tex.1986). The certificate showing the Secretary forwarded process to the defendant is conclusive proof that process was served. **Campus Invs. v. Cullever**, 144 S.W.3d 464, 466 (Tex.2004); *see* **Wachovia Bank v. Gilliam**, 215 S.W.3d 848, 850 (Tex.2007); **Capitol Brick**, 722 S.W.2d at 401. Once the Secretary of State forwards process to the defendant, the defendant is considered served even if the process is returned to the Secretary of State. *See, e.g.*, **Campus Invs.**, 144 S.W.3d at 465–66 (D considered served when process returned marked "Attempted—Not Known"); **Zuyus v. No'Mis Comms.**, 930 S.W.2d 743, 746–47 (Tex.App.—Corpus Christi 1996, no writ) (D considered served when process returned with notation "unclaimed"); **BLS Limousine Serv. v. Buslease, Inc.**, 680 S.W.2d 543, 546 (Tex.App.—Dallas 1984, writ ref'd n.r.e.) (D considered served when process returned with notation "refused"); *see also* **Mahon v. Caldwell, Haddad, Skaggs, Inc.**, 783 S.W.2d 769, 772 (Tex.App.—Fort Worth 1990, no writ) (D considered served when D's agent, not D, signed return receipt). *But see* **GMR Gymnastics Sales, Inc. v. Walz**, 117 S.W.3d 57, 59 (Tex.App.—Fort

Worth 2003, pet. denied) (return labeled "not deliverable as addressed, unable to forward" was prima facie evidence that address P provided to Secretary of State was incorrect; thus D was not served). If the Secretary of State forwards the process to the wrong address because of a typographical error, the service is invalid. *E.g.*, **Royal Surplus Lines Ins. v. Samaria Baptist Ch.**, 840 S.W.2d 382, 383 (Tex.1992) (citation mailed to 1201 Bassie, instead of 1201 Bessie, was invalid).

Practice Tip

Before taking a default judgment, the plaintiff should contact the Secretary of State's Citations Unit at (512) 463-5560 and request a certificate of service. The certificate will show the date the Secretary of State's office received the process, the date it forwarded the process to the defendant, and the date it received the return receipt.

§5.3 Long-arm service.

1. Minimum contacts. The test for service on a nonresident is whether Texas has provisions for service on a defendant under the facts presented and, if so, whether service on the defendant violates the Due Process Clause of the U.S. Constitution. See "Grounds," ch. 3-B, §2.4.

2. Long-arm allegations in petition. When serving a nonresident defendant by service on the Secretary of State, the face of the plaintiff's petition must support long-arm service. *See* **McKanna v. Edgar**, 388 S.W.2d 927, 929 (Tex.1965). Thus, the petition must allege (1) the Secretary of State is the agent for service on the nonresident, (2) the nonresident engages in business in Texas, (3) the nonresident does not maintain a regular place of business in Texas, (4) the nonresident does not have a designated agent for service of process, and (5) the lawsuit arises from the nonresident's business in Texas. Tex. Civ. Prac. & Rem. Code §17.044(b); **Lozano v. Hayes Wheel Int'l**, 933 S.W.2d 245, 247–48 (Tex.App.—Corpus Christi 1996, no writ); **South Mill Mushrooms Sales, Inc. v. Weenick**, 851 S.W.2d 346, 350 (Tex.App.—Dallas 1993, writ denied). For other allegations regarding service on a nonresident, see CPRC §17.044(a), (c), (d). See **O'Connor's Texas Civil Forms**, FORMS 2B:14 to 2B:18 (2020 ed.).

§5.4 Service on corporation. Domestic and foreign corporations that do business in Texas must designate and maintain registered agents for service in Texas. Tex. Bus. Orgs. Code §5.201(a), (b); *see* **Ingram Indus. v. U.S. Bolt Mfg.**, 121 S.W.3d 31, 34 (Tex.App.—Houston [1st Dist.] 2003, no pet.); **Interaction, Inc. v. State**, 17 S.W.3d 775, 779 (Tex.App.—Austin 2000, pet. denied); *see also* Tex. Bus. Orgs. Code §9.004(b)(9) (foreign entity must provide name and address of agent in application to register business in Texas).

Note

A registered agent may be an individual or an organization. Tex. Bus. Orgs. Code §5.201(b)(2); ***Paramount Credit, Inc. v. Montgomery****, 420 S.W.3d 226, 230 (Tex.App.—Houston [1st Dist.] 2013, no pet.). If the registered agent is an organization, it must have an employee available at the registered office during normal business hours to receive service of process. Tex. Bus. Orgs. Code §5.201(d). Any employee may receive service. Id.*

1. Diligence. The record must show on its face that the plaintiff used reasonable diligence to serve the corporation's president, vice president, or registered agent at its registered office. *See* Tex. Bus. Orgs. Code §§5.251(1)(B), 5.255(1); **Wright Bros. Energy, Inc. v. Krough**, 67 S.W.3d 271, 274 (Tex.App.—Houston [1st Dist.] 2001, no pet.); **National Multiple Sclerosis Soc'y v. Rice**, 29 S.W.3d 174, 176 (Tex.App.—Eastland 2000, no pet.); **Maddison Dual Fuels, Inc. v. Southern Un. Co.**, 944 S.W.2d 735, 738 (Tex.App.—Corpus Christi 1997, no writ); *see, e.g.*, **Marrot Comms. v. Town & Country Prtshp.**, 227 S.W.3d 372, 378 (Tex.App.—Houston [1st Dist.] 2007, pet. denied) (record did not show reasonable diligence because affidavit describing attempted service was not made part of record until after trial court signed default J). To establish reasonable diligence, the record must reflect more than just a problem with the address. *See* **Wright Bros.**, 67 S.W.3d at 275 (return must explain why service was not accepted); *see, e.g.*, **Ingram Indus.**, 121 S.W.3d at 34 (return stated that registered agent was not at registered address and that location had been occupied by someone else for the past ten

years; one attempt at service constituted reasonable diligence). If the corporation's president, vice president, or registered agent cannot be found through reasonable diligence, the plaintiff can serve the Secretary of State. **Interaction, Inc.**, 17 S.W.3d at 779.

2. Secretary forwards process. Once served, the Secretary of State must immediately mail a copy of the citation and petition to the defendant by registered or certified mail, return receipt requested. *See* Tex. Bus. Orgs. Code §5.253. If the Secretary of State forwards the process to the wrong address because the corporation did not notify the Secretary of State of a change of address of its registered office, the service is still valid. **Tankard-Smith, Inc. Gen. Contractors v. Thursby**, 663 S.W.2d 473, 475–76 (Tex.App.—Houston [14th Dist.] 1983, writ ref'd n.r.e.).

§6. Who may be served

There are two issues regarding the proper person to serve. First, when the defendant is not an individual, who is the person authorized to receive service of process for the defendant? Second, when service on the defendant is not possible, who can be served as a substitute for the defendant? See chart 2-4, below.

2-4. Proper Person to Serve

If defendant is		Actual service is made on	Constructive service may be made on
1	Authorized foreign corporation	President, vice president, or registered agent. Tex. Bus. Orgs. Code §§5.201(a), (b), 5.255(1).	Sec'y of State. Tex. Civ. Prac. & Rem. Code §17.044; Tex. Bus. Orgs. Code §5.251.
2	Corporation	President, vice president, or registered agent. Tex. Bus. Orgs. Code §§5.201(a), (b), 5.255(1).	Sec'y of State. Tex. Civ. Prac. & Rem. Code §17.044; Tex. Bus. Orgs. Code §5.251.
3	County	County judge. Tex. Civ. Prac. & Rem. Code §17.024(a).	
4	Credit union	Registered agent. Tex. Civ. Prac. & Rem. Code §17.028(c).	President or vice president. Tex. Civ. Prac. & Rem. Code §17.028(c).
5	Customer of financial institution	Registered agent of financial institution. Tex. Fin. Code §59.008(a); *see* Tex. Civ. Prac. & Rem. Code §17.028(f).	
6	Estate	Executor or administrator. *See* Tex Est. Code §51.056. If suit involves title to land, executor or administrator and heirs must be served. Tex Civ. Prac. & Rem. Code §17.002.	Sec'y of State (only for estate of nonresident defendant). Tex. Civ. Prac. & Rem. Code §17.044(c).
7	Financial institution	Registered agent. Tex. Civ. Prac. & Rem. Code §17.028(b).	President or branch manager at any office located in the state. Tex. Civ. Prac. & Rem. Code §17.028(b).
8	Foreign country	Depends on U.S. treaties and laws of foreign country.	
9	Foreign insurance company	Agent for service. Tex. Ins. Code §804.103(b).	Comm'r of Insurance. Tex. Ins. Code §804.103(c); *see* Tex. Ins. Code §883.103(a)(3).
10	Foreign railway	Defendant. *See* Tex. R. Civ. P. 108.	Some train conductors, Tex. Civ. Prac. & Rem. Code §17.093(2); person in charge of Texas office, Tex. Civ. Prac. & Rem. Code §17.043; Sec'y of State, Tex. Civ. Prac. & Rem. Code §17.044.
11	Incorporated city, town, or village	Mayor, clerk, secretary, or treasurer. Tex. Civ. Prac. & Rem. Code §17.024(b).	

2-4. Proper Person to Serve

If defendant is		Actual service is made on	Constructive service may be made on
12	Individual	Defendant. Tex. R. Civ. P. 106(a).	Various persons by court order, Tex. R. Civ. P. 106(b), 109a; by publication, Tex. R. Civ. P. 109; agent or clerk at defendant's office, Tex. Civ. Prac. & Rem. Code §17.021.
13	Inmate	Employee who has been designated as agent for service at facility where defendant is confined. Tex. Civ. Prac. & Rem. Code §17.029(c).	
14	Insurance company	President, active vice president, secretary, or attorney-in-fact at home office or principal place of business, or by leaving copy of process at home office or principal place of business during business hours. Tex. Ins. Code §804.101(b).	Comm'r of Insurance. Tex. Ins Code §804.102(c).
15	Minor	Minor or guardian of minor's estate if one has been appointed. **In re Estate of Bean**, 120 S.W.3d 914, 920 (Texark. 2003, denied); *see* Tex. Est. Code §1151.101.	Same as permitted on an individual. See Individual, above.
16	Nonprofit corporation	President, vice president, registered agent, or members of executive committee. Tex. Bus. Orgs. Code §§5.201(a), (b), 5.255(1), (5).	Sec'y of State. Tex. Bus. Orgs. Code §5.251.
17	Nonresident or out-of-state defendant	Defendant. Tex. R. Civ. P. 108.	Various persons by court order, Tex. R. Civ. P. 106(b), 109a; by publication, Tex. R. Civ. P. 109; agent or clerk at defendant's office, Tex. Civ. Prac. & Rem. Code §17.021; person in charge of Texas office (only for nonresident defendant), Tex. Civ. Prac. & Rem. Code §17.043; Sec'y of State (only for nonresident defendant), Tex. Civ. Prac. & Rem. Code §17.044.
18	Nonresident defendant driver	Defendant. Tex. Civ. Prac. & Rem. Code §17.065(a); *see* Tex. R. Civ. P. 108.	Chair of the Texas Transportation Commission. Tex. Civ. Prac. & Rem. Code §17.062.
19	Out-of-U.S. defendant	Defendant. Tex. R. Civ. P. 108a(a).	Person in charge of Texas office, Tex. Civ. Prac. & Rem. Code §17.043; Sec'y of State, Tex. Civ. Prac. & Rem. Code §17.044. Service in foreign country depends on international agreements and foreign country's laws. *See* Tex. R. Civ. P. 108a(a).
20	Partnership	Partners. Tex. Civ. Prac. & Rem. Code §§17.022, 31.003.	Agent or clerk at partnership office, Tex. Civ. Prac. & Rem. Code §17.021(a); Sec'y of State, Tex. Civ. Prac. & Rem. Code §17.044.
21	Patient in inpatient mental-health facility	Administrator, superintendent, supervisor, or manager of mental-health facility. Tex. Health & Safety Code §571.010(a).	
22	School district	President of school board or superintendent. Tex. Civ. Prac. & Rem. Code §17.024(c).	

2-4. Proper Person to Serve			
If defendant is		Actual service is made on	Constructive service may be made on
23	Series of domestic limited-liability company (LLC) or series of foreign entity	Either (1) registered agent designated by the domestic LLC or foreign entity or (2) governing person of series. Tex. Bus. Orgs. Code §§5.302(a), 5.305; *see* Tex. Bus. Orgs. Code §101.608 (defining "governing authority" for LLC).	Sec'y of State. Tex. Bus. Orgs. Code §5.304(a).
24	State of Texas	Sec'y of State. Tex. Civ. Prac. & Rem. Code §101.102(c).	
25	Trust	Trustee. *See* Tex. Prop. Code §§114.083, 114.084. If charitable trust, also serve Att'y Gen. Tex. Prop. Code §115.011(c).	Sec'y of State (only for nonresident trustee). *Cf.* Tex. Civ. Prac. & Rem. Code §17.044(c) (constructive service on Sec'y of State for nonresident executor, administrator, or heir of nonresident decedent).
26	Unincorporated business association	President, secretary, treasurer, or general agent. Tex. Rev. Civ. Stat. art. 6134.	Agent or clerk at association's office, Tex. Civ. Prac. & Rem. Code §17.021(a); Sec'y of State, Tex. Civ. Prac. & Rem. Code §17.044.
27	United States	U.S. Atty. Gen. and either (1) U.S. Atty. for district where suit is brought, or designated Assistant U.S. Atty. or clerical employee, or (2) civil process clerk at U.S. Atty's Office. Fed. R. Civ. P. 4(i)(1).	

§7. Deadline for service

§7.1 Within limitations. The process should be served on the defendant within the limitations period.

§7.2 Outside limitations. Service outside the limitations period is valid only if both of the following conditions are met:

1. Petition filed. The petition was filed within the limitations period. **Gant v. DeLeon**, 786 S.W.2d 259, 260 (Tex.1990).

2. Diligence in service. The plaintiff exercised diligence in procuring service of process on the defendant. **Ashley v. Hawkins**, 293 S.W.3d 175, 179 (Tex.2009); **Gant**, 786 S.W.2d at 260; **Harrell v. Alvarez**, 46 S.W.3d 483, 485 (Tex.App.—El Paso 2001, no pet.); **Roberts v. Padre Island Brewing Co.**, 28 S.W.3d 618, 621 (Tex.App.—Corpus Christi 2000, pet. denied). When a plaintiff serves the defendant after limitations, the date of service relates back to the date of filing the suit if the plaintiff exercised diligence in effecting service. **Proulx v. Wells**, 235 S.W.3d 213, 215 (Tex.2007); **Gant**, 786 S.W.2d at 260. The test for diligence is whether the plaintiff (1) acted as an ordinary, prudent person would act under the same circumstances and (2) was diligent up until the time the defendant was served. **Ashley**, 293 S.W.3d at 179; **Proulx**, 235 S.W.3d at 216; *see, e.g.*, **Tarrant Cty. v. Vandigriff**, 71 S.W.3d 921, 925–26 (Tex.App.—Fort Worth 2002, pet. denied) (delay of service for over two years showed no due diligence as a matter of law). Repeated ineffective attempts at service do not constitute due diligence if easily available and more effective alternatives are ignored. **Carter v. MacFadyen**, 93 S.W.3d 307, 314–15 (Tex.App.—Houston [14th Dist.] 2002, pet. denied). If the plaintiff learns, or through the exercise of due diligence should have learned, that the clerk has not fulfilled her duty to issue citation in compliance with TRCP 99, the plaintiff must ensure that the defendant is served. *E.g.*, **Tarrant Cty.**, 71 S.W.3d at 926 (although error in clerk's office was reason for 28-month delay in serving D, P should have discovered through diligence that D was not properly served); **Boyattia v. Hinojosa**, 18 S.W.3d 729, 734 (Tex.App.—Dallas 2000, pet. denied) (after three months, clerk's duty to serve citation was replaced by P's duty to ensure that service was actually completed); *see* **Allen v. Rushing**, 129 S.W.3d 226, 230–31 (Tex.App.—Texarkana 2004, no pet.).

Practice Tip

To prove diligence, the plaintiff should keep a log of its attempts to serve the defendant. The log must show constant and continual attempts at service. Any period in which there are no attempts to serve the defendant may negate diligence. ***Ashley****, 293 S.W.3d at 179;* ***Proulx****, 235 S.W.3d at 216; see, e.g.,* ***Webster v. Thomas****, 5 S.W.3d 287, 291 (Tex.App.—Houston [14th Dist.] 1999, no pet.) (four-month delay in procuring service, when efforts were careless and not persistent, negated diligence);* ***Butler v. Ross****, 836 S.W.2d 833, 835–36 (Tex.App.—Houston [1st Dist.] 1992, no writ) (no activity for over five months after return of unserved original citation negated diligence);* ***Hansler v. Mainka****, 807 S.W.2d 3, 5 (Tex.App.—Corpus Christi 1991, no writ) (no request for process for over five months after suit was filed negated diligence). If there was a gap between service attempts, the plaintiff should explain the reason for the gap.* ***Ashley****, 293 S.W.3d at 179.*

§8. Waiver of service

§8.1 Voluntary appearance. A defendant who is legally competent may appear in open court and waive service of process in person, by an attorney, or by an authorized agent. Tex. R. Civ. P. 120; *see* **Gonzalez v. Phoenix Frozen Foods, Inc.**, 884 S.W.2d 587, 589 (Tex.App.—Corpus Christi 1994, no writ); *see also* **Shamrock Oil Co. v. Gulf Coast Nat. Gas, Inc.**, 68 S.W.3d 737, 739 (Tex.App.—Houston [14th Dist.] 2001, pet. denied) (appearance by corporate attorney did not waive service on corporate officers). Once a defendant makes a voluntary appearance, the court must note the appearance on the docket and enter it in the minutes. Tex. R. Civ. P. 120.

§8.2 Written waiver. A defendant who is legally competent may waive service of process in writing. Tex. R. Civ. P. 119. To be effective, the waiver must (1) expressly state that the defendant waives service, (2) acknowledge that the defendant received a copy of the plaintiff's petition, (3) be in writing, (4) be signed by the defendant or its authorized agent or attorney, (5) be verified before someone other than an attorney in the case, (6) be dated after the suit was filed, and (7) be filed among the papers of the case. Tex. R. Civ. P. 119; *see, e.g.,* **Deen v. Kirk**, 508 S.W.2d 70, 71 (Tex.1974) (waiver ineffective because it was signed before suit filed); **Dunn v. Wilson**, 752 S.W.2d 15, 17 (Tex.App.—Fort Worth 1988) (document ineffective because it did not state D waived service), *aff'd*, 800 S.W.2d 833 (Tex.1990). The requirements for waiving service under TRCP 119 do not apply in a suit for divorce. *See* Tex. Fam. Code §6.4035(d). See "Waives service of process," **O'Connor's Texas Family Law Handbook**, ch. 3-A, §2.4.1(2) (2021 ed.).

§8.3 Presuit waiver. There is one statutorily created exception that permits a presuit waiver of service. A waiver of service in an affidavit to relinquish parental rights, signed before suit is filed, effectively waives service of process. *See* Tex. Fam. Code §§102.009(a)(7), 161.103(c), 161.106(a); **Brown v. McLennan Cty. Children's Prot. Servs.**, 627 S.W.2d 390, 393 (Tex.1982).

§9. Proof of service—The return

The officer or other authorized person issuing the citation must complete a return of service. Tex. R. Civ. P. 107(a). The return is not a trivial, formulaic document. **Primate Constr., Inc. v. Silver**, 884 S.W.2d 151, 152 (Tex.1994); **Rivers v. Viskozki**, 967 S.W.2d 868, 870 (Tex.App.—Eastland 1998, no pet.). Unless the plaintiff strictly complies with the rules relating to proper service, the service is invalid. **Primate Constr.**, 884 S.W.2d at 152; **Union Pac. Corp. v. Legg**, 49 S.W.3d 72, 77 (Tex.App.—Austin 2001, no pet.); *see* **Insurance Co. of Pa. v. Lejeune**, 297 S.W.3d 254, 256 (Tex.2009). Strict compliance is determined by whether the exact procedural requirements have been met, not whether the intended party received notice of the lawsuit. **Union Pac.**, 49 S.W.3d at 78; *see* **In re Z.J.W.**, 185 S.W.3d 905, 908 (Tex.App.—Tyler 2006, no pet.) (strict compliance means literal compliance with the rules). The return should be construed fairly and reasonably so that its plain intent and meaning are given full effect. **Conseco Fin. Servicing Corp. v. Klein ISD**, 78 S.W.3d 666, 673 (Tex.App.—Houston [14th Dist.] 2002, no pet.).

§9.1 Endorsed or attached. The return may be, but does not have to be, endorsed on or attached to the citation. Tex. R. Civ. P. 107(a); *see* Tex. Civ. Prac. & Rem. Code §17.030(b)(1)(A).

§9.2 Verification. The return generally does not have to be verified. *See* Tex. Civ. Prac. & Rem. Code §17.030(c). The return must be verified, however, if it is signed by an authorized person other than a sheriff, constable, or court clerk and it is not signed under penalty of perjury. Tex. R. Civ. P. 107(e). See "Other authorized person," ch. 2-I, §9.6.2.

§9.3 Filing return. The return and any document to which it is attached must be filed and may be filed electronically or by fax, if those methods of filing are available. Tex. R. Civ. P. 107(g); *see* Tex. Civ. Prac. & Rem. Code §17.030(b)(1)(B).

§9.4 Recitation of due service. The plaintiff must make sure the court's record of the case reflects that the defendant was properly served. **Primate Constr., Inc. v. Silver**, 884 S.W.2d 151, 153 (Tex.1994). That responsibility involves checking the statements on the return, including the preprinted statements on the form used by the sheriff's or constable's office. *Id.* The return, together with any document to which it is attached, must include the following information:

1. Case information. The return must identify the case name, the cause number, and the court where the case is filed. Tex. R. Civ. P. 107(b)(1), (b)(2); **Dole v. LSREF2 APEX 2, LLC**, 425 S.W.3d 617, 622 (Tex.App.—Dallas 2014, no pet.).

2. Date of receipt of process by server. The return must show the date and time the officer or other authorized person received the process for service. Tex. R. Civ. P. 107(b)(4).

3. Description of documents. The return must include a description of what was served. Tex. R. Civ. P. 107(b)(3). That is, the return must state that a copy of the citation and a copy of the petition were served on the defendant. *See* Tex. R. Civ. P. 106(a). The return must correctly identify the petition served on the defendant. *See, e.g.*, **Primate Constr.**, 884 S.W.2d at 152 (recitation that original petition was served, instead of second petition, was fatal); **Shamrock Oil Co. v. Gulf Coast Nat. Gas, Inc.**, 68 S.W.3d 737, 738–39 (Tex.App.—Houston [14th Dist.] 2001, pet. denied) (recitation that "[blank] petition" was served was fatal); **Ortiz v. Avante Villa at Corpus Christi, Inc.**, 926 S.W.2d 608, 612 (Tex.App.—Corpus Christi 1996, writ denied) (recitation that "petition attached" was served was sufficient); **Herbert v. Greater Gulf Coast Enters.**, 915 S.W.2d 866, 871 (Tex.App.—Houston [1st Dist.] 1995, no writ) (recitation that "complaint" was served was sufficient); **Woodall v. Lansford**, 254 S.W.2d 540, 542–43 (Tex.App.—Fort Worth 1953, no writ) (recitation that "copy of the citation" was served instead of petition was fatal). The return must show that the defendant was named as a defendant in the petition. *See, e.g.*, **Primate Constr.**, 884 S.W.2d at 152–53 (default J reversed because return showed D served with original petition but not named as D until amended petition); **Seeley v. KCI USA, Inc.**, 100 S.W.3d 276, 277–78 (Tex.App.—San Antonio 2002, no pet.) (same).

4. Person or entity served. The return must identify the person or entity served. Tex. R. Civ. P. 107(b)(5).

(1) Fatal errors. The following mistakes in the name on the return made the return invalid: • The return did not include "Jr." **Uvalde Country Club v. Martin Linen Sup. Co.**, 690 S.W.2d 884, 885 (Tex.1985). • The citation named one person as agent for service on the defendant, but the return showed service on another person. **All Commercial Floors, Inc. v. Barton & Rasor**, 97 S.W.3d 723, 726–27 (Tex.App.—Fort Worth 2003, no pet.); *see* **Greystar, LLC v. Adams**, 426 S.W.3d 861, 867–68 (Tex.App.—Dallas 2014, no pet.). • The return did not identify the defendant-corporation as the entity served. **Benefit Planners, L.L.P. v. Rencare, Ltd.**, 81 S.W.3d 855, 861 (Tex.App.—San Antonio 2002, pet. denied); *see, e.g.*, **Barker CATV Constr., Inc. v. Ampro, Inc.**, 989 S.W.2d 789, 793 (Tex.App.—Houston [1st Dist.] 1999, no pet.) (return defective because name of "James Barker" alone on return did not establish he was D's agent for service or that D-corporation was actually served). • The return did not give the complete and correct name of the defendant. **Hercules Concrete Pumping Serv. v. Bencon Mgmt. & Gen. Contracting Corp.**, 62 S.W.3d 308, 310–11 (Tex.App.—Houston [1st Dist.] 2001, pet. denied); *see, e.g.*, **North Carolina Mut. Life Ins. v. Whitworth**, 124 S.W.3d 714, 720 (Tex.App.—Austin 2003, pet. denied) (return omitted "Life" from North Carolina Mutual Life Insurance Company). • The return did not indicate the person receiving process was served in her capacity as trustee. **Price v. Dean**, 990 S.W.2d 453, 454–55 (Tex.App.—Corpus Christi 1999, no pet.). • The return contained only the surname. **Exposition Apts. Co. v. Barba**, 630 S.W.2d 462, 465 (Tex.App.—Austin 1982, no writ). • The return did not include the correct middle initial. **Zaragoza v. Morales**, 616 S.W.2d 295, 296 (Tex.App.—Eastland 1981, writ ref'd n.r.e.). • The return did not identify the defendant as a corporation, as it was identified in the petition and citation. **Brown-McKee, Inc. v. J.F. Bryan & Assocs.**, 522 S.W.2d 958, 959 (Tex.App.—Texarkana 1975, no writ).

(2) Nonfatal errors. The following mistakes in the name on the return did not make the return invalid: • The return omitted "Group, L.L.C." **Myan Mgmt. Grp. v. Adam Sparks Family Revocable Trust**, 292 S.W.3d 750, 753–54 (Tex.App.—Dallas 2009, no pet.). • The return omitted an accent mark and the word "Inc." and substituted the

symbol "@" for the word "at." **Ortiz**, 926 S.W.2d at 613. • The return omitted "Ltd." after "Corp." **Stephenson v. Corporate Servs.**, 650 S.W.2d 181, 183–84 (Tex.App.—Tyler 1983, writ ref'd n.r.e.).

5. Service address. The return must show the address of service. Tex. R. Civ. P. 107(b)(6); *see* **Jacksboro Nat'l Bank v. Signal Oil & Gas Co.**, 482 S.W.2d 339, 341–42 (Tex.App.—Tyler 1972, no writ).

6. Manner of service or attempted service. The return must identify the manner of delivery of service or attempted service. Tex. R. Civ. P. 107(b)(8); **Camoco, LLC v. Terrazas**, 569 S.W.3d 270, 273 (Tex.App.—El Paso 2018, no pet.); *see also* **Dolly v. Aethos Comms. Sys.**, 10 S.W.3d 384, 388 (Tex.App.—Dallas 2000, no pet.) (return that stated D was served "in person," but also noted that process was "posted to front door," was inherently inconsistent). The requirement that the return identify the manner of delivery of service or attempted service is not satisfied if the return merely states that a person "was served" or that the citation was delivered "by serving" a particular person; however, language in the return stating that service was accomplished "by delivering" is sufficient. **Camoco, LLC**, 569 S.W.3d at 273–74; *see, e.g.*, **Curry Motor Freight, Inc. v. Ralston Purina Co.**, 565 S.W.2d 105, 106–07 (Tex.App.—Amarillo 1978, no writ) (return that merely said service was accomplished "by serving" person was defective). The return should also show that the citation was served on a person capable of accepting service. **Faggett v. Hargrove**, 921 S.W.2d 274, 277 (Tex.App.—Houston [1st Dist.] 1995, no writ), *overruled on other grounds*, **Barker CATV Constr., Inc. v. Ampro, Inc.**, 989 S.W.2d 789 (Tex.App.—Houston [1st Dist.] 1999, no pet.); *see, e.g.*, **Reed Elsevier, Inc. v. Carrollton-Farmers Branch ISD**, 180 S.W.3d 903, 905–06 (Tex.App.—Dallas 2005, pet. denied) (return did not show that person served was authorized to accept service).

7. Name of server. The return must identify the name of the person who served or attempted to serve the defendant. Tex. R. Civ. P. 107(b)(9).

(1) Sheriffs & constables. When public officials such as sheriffs and constables are authorized to effect service, they may personally serve process, or they may serve process through their deputies. **Pratt v. Moore**, 746 S.W.2d 486, 487 (Tex.App.—Dallas 1988, no writ). When citation is served by a deputy, the deputy must indicate who employed him as a deputy. **Houston Pipe Coating Co. v. Houston Freightways, Inc.**, 679 S.W.2d 42, 45 (Tex.App.—Houston [14th Dist.] 1984, writ ref'd n.r.e.). See "Officers," ch. 2-I, §3.2.

(2) Person authorized by trial court. If the trial court appointed a disinterested person to serve process, the return must show service by that person, and the name of the person in the order must match the name of the person who served process. *See, e.g.*, **Cates v. Pon**, 663 S.W.2d 99, 102 (Tex.App.—Houston [14th Dist.] 1983, writ ref'd n.r.e.) (invalid service because order appointed disinterested adult to serve process and return was signed by deputy constable); **Mega v. Anglo Iron & Metal Co.**, 601 S.W.2d 501, 504 (Tex.App.—Corpus Christi 1980, no writ) (invalid service because order appointed "A.R. 'Tony' Martinez" to serve process and the return was signed by "A.R. Martinez, Jr."). See "Trial-court order," ch. 2-I, §3.3.1.

(3) Process server certified by Supreme Court. If the Supreme Court, by order, has certified a person to serve process, the return must show her identification number and the expiration date of her certification. Tex. R. Civ. P. 107(b)(10). See "Supreme Court order," ch. 2-I, §3.3.2.

8. Date of service or attempted service. The return must show the date of service or attempted service. Tex. R. Civ. P. 107(b)(7). Although the return can also show the time of service or attempted service, it is not required. *See id.*; **Mandel v. Lewisville ISD**, 445 S.W.3d 469, 476–77 (Tex.App.—Fort Worth 2014, pet. denied). If there are typographical errors on the return about the date of service or attempted service, the court can determine if the proper date of service is apparent from the record. *E.g.*, **Dole**, 425 S.W.3d at 621–22 (although return indicated process server executed service before documents were received, verification of return and certificate from Secretary of State demonstrated correct date of service; return was valid); *see, e.g.*, **Goodman v. Oakley**, No. 14-01-01004-CV, 2003 WL 297517 (Tex.App.—Houston [14th Dist.] 2003, no pet.) (memo op.; 2-13-03) (although return indicated process server served citation 11 months before receiving it, proper date of service could be determined by viewing file stamps and citation as a whole; return was valid). When service is made by certified mail, the postmark is sufficient to show the latest date of delivery. **Nelson v. Remmert**, 726 S.W.2d 171, 172 (Tex.App.—Houston [14th Dist.] 1987, writ ref'd n.r.e.).

Note

Although the court can determine if the proper date of service is apparent from the record when there is a typographical error, the party requesting service ultimately must ensure that service is properly accomplished. See ***Primate Constr.****, 884 S.W.2d at 153. Thus, if the return has a typographical error, the party should consider amending the return rather than relying on the court to find that service is valid. See, e.g.,* ***TAC Americas, Inc. v. Boothe****, 94 S.W.3d 315, 320–22 (Tex.App.—Austin 2002, no pet.) (service was invalid when return indicated time process server delivered documents was before they were received; Ds should have amended return to correct error). See "Amending the return," ch. 2-I, §10.2.2.*

9. Filing date. The return must state the date on which it was filed; if it does not, the record cannot establish that the return was on file for ten days, which is necessary before a default judgment may be granted. *See* Tex. R. Civ. P. 107(h); **HB & WM, Inc. v. Smith**, 802 S.W.2d 279, 281–82 (Tex.App.—San Antonio 1990, no writ); *see, e.g.,* **Melendez v. John R. Schatzman, Inc.**, 685 S.W.2d 137, 138 (Tex.App.—El Paso 1985, no writ) (because clerk did not include date and file mark on citation, it was impossible to determine how long return had been on file). See "Filing return," ch. 2-I, §9.3; "In most cases," ch. 7-A, §3.9.1(1).

10. Diligence of attempted service. When service has not been accomplished, the return must show the following:

(1) The diligence used by the officer or other authorized person in attempting to serve process. Tex. R. Civ. P. 107(d).

(2) The reason service was not accomplished. *Id.*

(3) The defendant's location, if it is known. *Id.*

11. Other information. The return must include any other information that is required by rule or by law. Tex. R. Civ. P. 107(b)(11).

§9.5 Addressee's signature. When process is served by registered or certified mail, the return must contain the return receipt with the addressee's signature. Tex. R. Civ. P. 107(c); **Ramirez v. Consolidated HGM Corp.**, 124 S.W.3d 914, 916 (Tex.App.—Amarillo 2004, no pet.); **All Commercial Floors, Inc. v. Barton & Rasor**, 97 S.W.3d 723, 726 (Tex.App.—Fort Worth 2003, no pet.); **Fowler v. Quinlan ISD**, 963 S.W.2d 941, 943 (Tex.App.—Texarkana 1998, no pet.); *see* **Hubicki v. Festina**, 226 S.W.3d 405, 408 (Tex.2007); *see, e.g.,* **Union Pac. Corp. v. Legg**, 49 S.W.3d 72, 79 (Tex.App.—Austin 2001, no pet.) (return invalid because it was stamped with signature and no proof was offered to show signature was authorized). If the defendant is a corporation, the return receipt must be signed by the corporation's president, vice president, or registered agent. *See* Tex. Bus. Orgs. Code §§5.201(a), (b), 5.255(1); **Cox Mktg., Inc. v. Adams**, 688 S.W.2d 215, 217 (Tex.App.—El Paso 1985, no writ). When a return recites that the person served is a corporation's registered agent, it is prima facie evidence of that person's status. **Primate Constr., Inc. v. Silver**, 884 S.W.2d 151, 152 n.1 (Tex.1994). **Primate** overruled those cases that held the record must affirmatively show that the person served was in fact the registered agent. *See id.*

§9.6 Signature of server. The signature of the server must appear on the return. Tex. Civ. Prac. & Rem. Code §17.030(c); Tex. R. Civ. P. 107(e); **Hot Shot Messenger Serv. v. State**, 818 S.W.2d 905, 907 (Tex.App.—Austin 1991, no writ); **American Bankers Ins. v. State**, 749 S.W.2d 195, 197 (Tex.App.—Houston [14th Dist.] 1988, no writ).

1. Sheriff, constable, or court clerk. If the return is signed by a sheriff, constable, or court clerk, a stamped or printed signature is sufficient. *See, e.g.,* **Payne & Keller Co. v. Word**, 732 S.W.2d 38, 40 (Tex.App.—Houston [14th Dist.] 1987, writ ref'd n.r.e.) (constable).

2. Other authorized person. If the return is signed by an authorized person other than a sheriff, constable, or court clerk, the return must be verified or signed under penalty of perjury. Tex. R. Civ. P. 107(e); **Dole v. LSREF2 APEX 2,**

LLC, 425 S.W.3d 617, 622 (Tex.App.—Dallas 2014, no pet.); *see* Tex. Civ. Prac. & Rem. Code §17.030(c). If the return is signed under penalty of perjury, it must (1) contain a statement that includes the server's name, date of birth, and address, and (2) substantially comply with the form in TRCP 107(e). Tex. R. Civ. P. 107(e); *see, e.g.*, **Dole**, 425 S.W.3d at 622 (because return was verified, process server's country and date of birth were not required). For the complete statement that must be signed under penalty of perjury, see TRCP 107(e).

§9.7 Falsifying return. A person who knowingly or intentionally falsifies a return of service may be prosecuted under Penal Code chapter 37 for tampering with a governmental record. Tex. Civ. Prac. & Rem. Code §17.030(d).

§10. Amending the service documents

§10.1 Amending the petition. When the plaintiff amends the petition and the amended petition asks for a more onerous judgment, a nonanswering defendant must be served with the amended petition; the plaintiff does not need to serve the defendant with a new citation. **In re E.A.**, 287 S.W.3d 1, 6 (Tex.2009). See "Service of amended pleadings," ch. 5-F, §3.3; "Adding claims or damages—service required," ch. 7-A, §3.2.1(1).

§10.2 Amending the citation & return. The trial court may allow the process or proof of service to be amended at any time in the court's discretion and on such notice and terms as it deems just. Tex. R. Civ. P. 118. No other person has the authority to amend the citation or the return. *See, e.g.*, **Barker CATV Constr., Inc. v. Ampro, Inc.**, 989 S.W.2d 789, 793–94 (Tex.App.—Houston [1st Dist.] 1999, no pet.) (no proof trial court authorized amended return; amended return disallowed); **Plains Chevrolet, Inc. v. Thorne**, 656 S.W.2d 631, 633 (Tex.App.—Waco 1983, no writ) (serving officer not permitted to correct D's name in citation; amended citation disallowed). If the court signs an order permitting amendment of the citation or the return, the plaintiff does not need to re-serve the defendant with process.

1. **Amending the citation.** The court may permit the citation to be amended. Tex. R. Civ. P. 118; **London v. Chandler**, 406 S.W.2d 203, 204 (Tex.1966).

2. **Amending the return.** The court, at any time during its plenary power, may permit proof of service to be amended to reflect the actual service on the defendant. *See* Tex. R. Civ. P. 118; **Higginbotham v. General Life & Acc. Ins.**, 796 S.W.2d 695, 696 (Tex.1990); **Dawson v. Briggs**, 107 S.W.3d 739, 747 (Tex.App.—Fort Worth 2003, no pet.); *see, e.g.*, **Walker v. Brodhead**, 828 S.W.2d 278, 282 (Tex.App.—Austin 1992, writ denied) (verification of return added; amendment permitted); **Bavarian Autohaus, Inc. v. Holland**, 570 S.W.2d 110, 113 (Tex.App.—Houston [1st Dist.] 1978, no writ) (return amended and filed before judgment to reflect service on corporation by delivery to vice president; amendment permitted). The return cannot be amended without court approval. *See* **Barker CATV**, 989 S.W.2d at 793–94. A properly amended return relates back to and is considered filed on the date the original return was filed. **Brodhead**, 828 S.W.2d at 282; **Bavarian Autohaus**, 570 S.W.2d at 113.

§11. Service outside the United States

Service of process in a foreign country must give the defendant actual notice of the proceeding in time to answer and defend. Tex. R. Civ. P. 108a(a); **Hubicki v. Festina**, 226 S.W.3d 405, 407 (Tex.2007).

§11.1 Comity. Comity is the extent to which the laws of one nation are allowed to operate within the territory of another nation. **Hilton v. Guyot**, 159 U.S. 113, 163–64 (1895). No nation can demand that its laws have effect beyond the limits of its sovereignty. *See id.* at 163. Some countries consider service of judicial documents as requiring the performance of a judicial or "sovereign" act, and thus view service of judicial documents from another country within their borders as offensive to their sovereignty. *See* Jones, *International Judicial Assistance: Procedural Chaos & a Program for Reform*, 62 Yale L.J. 515, 537 (1953).

§11.2 Methods of service permitted. A person outside the United States may be served by any method permitted by TRCP 108a. **Hubicki v. Festina**, 226 S.W.3d 405, 407 (Tex.2007). A nonresident defendant may be served with process outside the United States as provided by (1) the foreign country's law, (2) foreign authority in response to a letter rogatory, (3) TRCP 106(a), (4) an international agreement, (5) the U.S. Department of State, or (6) other means that is not prohibited by international agreement or the foreign country's law, as ordered by the court. Tex. R. Civ. P. 108a(a).

Caution

Unless a plaintiff uses the appropriate method of service in a foreign country as required by a treaty with that country, a judgment rendered for the plaintiff may not be enforceable in that country. See ***Kreimerman v. Casa Veerkamp, S.A. de C.V.****, 22 F.3d 634, 643–44 (5th Cir.1994).*

§11.3 Preference for service according to international agreements. The preferred method of serving a defendant in another country is under the Hague Convention on the Service Abroad of Judicial & Extrajudicial Documents (Hague Convention), or under any other applicable treaty. 1993 Adv. Cmte. Notes to Fed. R. Civ. P. 4 at ¶41, **O'Connor's Federal Rules * Civil Trials**, Appendix V (2021 ed.); *see* **Volkswagenwerk A.G. v. Schlunk**, 486 U.S. 694, 706 (1988) (voluntary use of conventional procedures may be desirable even when service could constitutionally be made in another manner). Service abroad must be made under a treaty if (1) there is a treaty and (2) the treaty requires service to be made according to its terms. 1993 Adv. Cmte. Notes to Fed. R. Civ. P. 4 at ¶41, **O'Connor's Federal Rules * Civil Trials**, Appendix V (2021 ed.); *see* Fed. R. Civ. P. 4(f)(1). A convention or treaty does not necessarily preempt all other methods of service on a defendant who resides in a signatory country; preemption depends on the language, history, and purpose of the treaty. *See* **Kreimerman v. Casa Veerkamp, S.A. de C.V.**, 22 F.3d 634, 638, 644 (5th Cir.1994). The Hague Convention preempts inconsistent methods of service prescribed by state law in all cases to which it applies. **Volkswagenwerk A.G.**, 486 U.S. at 699; *see* **Ackermann v. Levine**, 788 F.2d 830, 840 (2d Cir.1986). By contrast, the Inter-American Convention on Letters Rogatory does not preempt other methods of service. **Kreimerman**, 22 F.3d at 647. For the procedure for service under the Hague Convention, see "Serving an individual abroad," **O'Connor's Federal Rules * Civil Trials**, ch. 2-H, §6.3 (2021 ed.).

Practice Tip

To determine whether a particular country is presently a signatory to the Hague Convention or any other treaty affecting service, contact the Office of Treaty Affairs, Department of State, www.state.gov/bureaus-offices/treaty-affairs/, or refer to the Hague Conference on Private International Law website, www.hcch.net.

J. Suit by Indigent

§1. General

§1.1 Rules. Tex. R. Civ. P. 145, 217, 502.3; Tex. R. App. P. 20. See Tex. Civ. Prac. & Rem. Code chs. 13, 14.

§1.2 Purpose. The Texas Constitution and the rules of procedure recognize that courts must be open to all persons with legitimate disputes, not just those who can afford to pay the court fees. **Griffin Indus. v. Thirteenth Ct. of Appeals**, 934 S.W.2d 349, 353 (Tex.1996); *see* Tex. Const. art. 1, §13; Tex. R. Civ. P. 145, 217; Tex. R. App. P. 20.1; **In re C.H.C.**, 331 S.W.3d 426, 429 (Tex.2011). TRCP 145 gives an indigent access to the courthouse without the payment of costs. **Spellmon v. Sweeney**, 819 S.W.2d 206, 208 (Tex.App.—Waco 1991, no writ). TRCP 217 gives an indigent the right to a jury trial without the payment of the jury fee. Although a litigant is not entitled to appointed counsel in a civil case, under exceptional circumstances, when public and private interests are at stake, the court may appoint an attorney to represent an indigent civil litigant. **Gibson v. Tolbert**, 102 S.W.3d 710, 712 (Tex.2003); *see* Tex. Fam. Code §107.013(a)(1), (d) (in suit by government to terminate parent-child relationship or to appoint conservator for child, court must appoint attorney ad litem to represent indigent parent who opposes termination or appointment); Tex. Gov't Code §24.016 (district judge has discretion to appoint attorney if party provides affidavit stating she cannot afford counsel).

2021 Rule Amendments

In 2020, the Supreme Court preliminarily approved amendments to TRCP 145. See Tex.Sup.Ct. Order, Misc. Docket No. 20-9154 (eff. Dec. 23, 2020). The amendments do the following, among other things: (1) clarify that certain categories of evidence are prima facie proof of a declarant's inability to afford costs and (2) require a court reporter's contest to meet the same conditions as a contest filed by the clerk or a party. See id. These amendments are subject to change based on public comments submitted by April 2, 2021. The Court will issue a final order approving the amendments at least 60 days after their publication in the February edition of the Texas Bar Journal. To view the orders related to these amendments, visit the Court's website at txcourts.gov/supreme.

---

§1.3 Timetable & forms. Appeal by Indigent Party to Court of Appeals, **O'Connor's Texas Civil Appeals**, Appendix IV, Timetable 3 (2020 ed.); **O'Connor's Texas Civil Forms**, FORMS 1B:9, 2J:1 et seq. (2020 ed.).

§1.4 Other references. **O'Connor's Texas Civil Appeals** (2020 ed.).

§2. Defining indigency

An indigent is a person who cannot afford to pay the costs for the suit. *See* Tex. R. Civ. P. 145(e) & cmt. (2016).

Note

TRCP 145 refers to the filing party as a "declarant" rather than as an "indigent." See Tex. R. Civ. P. 145(a). In this subchapter, both "indigent" and "declarant" refer to the filing party.

---

§2.1 Cannot afford to pay. When the court makes an indigency determination, the issue is not merely whether a person can pay costs but whether the person can afford to pay costs. Tex. R. Civ. P. 145 cmt. (2016); *see* **In re A.M.**, 557 S.W.3d 607, 610 (Tex.App.—El Paso 2016, n.p.h.) (court must consider monthly income as well as monthly expenses and outstanding debts to determine if party can afford to pay costs). A person may have sufficient cash on hand to pay filing fees, but the person cannot afford the fees if paying them would prevent the person from paying for basic needs, such as housing or food. Tex. R. Civ. P. 145 cmt. (2016). Generally, a person who is receiving a governmental entitlement, public assistance, or free legal services cannot afford to pay costs. *See* Tex. R. Civ. P. 145(e) & cmt. (2016); **Griffin Indus. v. Thirteenth Ct. of Appeals**, 934 S.W.2d 349, 351 (Tex.1996); *see, e.g.*, **Goffney v. Lowry**, 554 S.W.2d 157, 159–60 (Tex.1977) (party who received public assistance, had not been regularly employed, and was not able to obtain loans to pay for court costs was found indigent). See "Evidence," ch. 2-J, §3.3.

§2.2 Costs. A party who is indigent cannot be required to pay "costs," as defined by TRCP 145(c). *See* Tex. R. Civ. P. 145(a). Under the rule, costs are any fee charged by the court or an officer of the court that could be taxed in a bill of costs, including but not limited to filing fees, fees for issuance and service of process, fees for a court-appointed professional, and fees charged by the clerk or court reporter for preparing the appellate record. Tex. R. Civ. P. 145(c); *see also* Tex. R. Civ. P. 145 cmt. (2016) (whether particular fee is court cost covered by TRCP 145 is determined by text of the rule, CPRC §31.007, and case law).

Note

Although attorney fees are generally not considered costs, payment of an opposing party's attorney fees as a condition of a new trial is considered a "cost" under TRCP 145. ***Equitable Gen. Ins. v. Yates,*** *684 S.W.2d 669, 671 (Tex.1984);* ***Abrigo v. Ginez,*** *580 S.W.3d 416, 420–21 (Tex.App.—Houston [14th Dist.] 2019, no pet.). Thus, a court cannot require a declarant who has asserted an uncontested claim of indigence to pay attorney fees as a condition of a new trial. See* ***Equitable Gen.,*** *684 S.W.2d at 671;* ***Abrigo,*** *580 S.W.3d at 420–21.*

§3. Statement of inability to afford payment of costs

To make a claim of indigency, a party must file a Statement of Inability to Afford Payment of Court Costs. Tex. R. Civ. P. 145(a). A party who files the Statement is not required to pay costs unless the court orders otherwise as provided under TRCP 145. Tex. R. Civ. P. 145(a).

Note

In this subchapter, the Statement of Inability to Afford Payment of Court Costs is referred to as the "Statement."

§3.1 Form. The declarant must use the form Statement provided by the Supreme Court or file a statement that includes all the information required by the Court-approved form. Tex. R. Civ. P. 145(b); *e.g.,* **Abrigo v. Ginez,** 580 S.W.3d 416, 419–20 (Tex.App.—Houston [14th Dist.] 2019, no pet.) (although declarant did not use Court-approved form, her affidavit was sufficient because it included proper verification and explained her monthly income from public benefits, her monthly expenses and creditor payments, her property, and how many dependents she had). An electronic version of the Court-approved form Statement can be found on the Texas Office of Court Administration website, www.txcourts.gov/rules-forms/forms.

§3.2 Verification. The Statement must be sworn to before a notary or made under penalty of perjury, as permitted by CPRC §132.001. Tex. R. Civ. P. 145(a) & cmt. (2016); *see* Tex. Civ. Prac. & Rem. Code §132.001. See "Unsworn declaration," ch. 1-B, §3.2.17. The clerk may refuse to file a Statement that does not comply with this requirement. Tex. R. Civ. P. 145(d); **Abrigo v. Ginez,** 580 S.W.3d 416, 419 (Tex.App.—Houston [14th Dist.] 2019, no pet.).

§3.3 Evidence. The declarant must include in the Statement and, if available, in attachments to the Statement evidence of her inability to afford costs. Tex. R. Civ. P. 145(e). The form Statement does not ask the declarant to state what portion of costs she is able to afford, and there is no requirement that she do so. **Koehne v. Koehne,** __ S.W.3d __, 2017 WL 2375789 (Tex.App.—Houston [1st Dist.] 2017, order) (No. 01-17-00016-CV; 6-1-17). The declarant can include evidence of the following to show her inability to afford costs:

1. The declarant receives benefits from a government entitlement program, eligibility for which is dependent on the declarant's means. Tex. R. Civ. P. 145(e)(1).

2. The declarant is being represented in the case by an attorney who is providing free legal services to the declarant, without contingency, through (1) a provider funded by either the Texas Access to Justice Foundation or the Legal Services Corporation or (2) a nonprofit that provides civil legal services to individuals living at or below 200% of the federal poverty guidelines published annually by the U.S. Department of Health & Human Services. Tex. R. Civ. P. 145(e)(2); *see* **In re**

A.M., 557 S.W.3d 607, 608–09 (Tex.App.—El Paso 2016, n.p.h.). The declarant should attach to her Statement a certificate from the legal-aid provider as proof of her claim.

Note

Before the 2016 amendments to TRCP 145, if an affidavit of indigence was accompanied by an attorney's Interest on Lawyers' Trust Accounts (IOLTA) certificate confirming the party was screened by an IOLTA-funded program for income eligibility under IOLTA guidelines, then the affidavit could not be contested. See Tex. R. Civ. P. 145(c) (pre-9-1-16 version). Under the amended rule, the declarant can submit evidence that she is being represented through a legal-aid service provider, as defined in TRCP 145(e)(2), to support her claim that she is unable to afford costs; however, such evidence does not prohibit a contest of the claim, except in a suit filed in justice court. See Tex. R. Civ. P. 145(e)(2), (f), 502.3(c). See "Challenging claim of inability to afford payment of costs," ch. 2-J, §7.

3. The declarant has applied for free legal services for her case through a provider listed in TRCP 145(e)(2) but was declined representation although she was financially eligible. Tex. R. Civ. P. 145(e)(3). The declarant should attach to her Statement documentation from the legal-aid provider as proof of her claim.

4. The declarant does not have funds to afford payment of costs. Tex. R. Civ. P. 145(e)(4). Information the declarant is required to provide in her Statement (i.e., details about her monthly income and expenses, the value of her personal property, and her debts) can support the declarant's claim that she does not have funds to afford payment of costs. *See, e.g.,* **Koehne**, __ S.W.3d at __, 2017 WL 2375789 (trial court abused its discretion in sustaining challenge to declarant's Statement when evidence showed declarant had no current income, had no assets to sell to pay for costs, could not borrow money, and was in jail).

§3.4 Time to file & serve. TRCP 145 does not specify a deadline for filing and serving the Statement, but it should be filed along with the original petition and served on the defendant along with the citation. *See* **Baughman v. Baughman**, 65 S.W.3d 309, 312 (Tex.App.—Waco 2001, pet. denied) (under pre 9-1-16 version of TRCP 145). If the affidavit is not filed with the original petition, it must be served on the other parties under TRCP 21a.

§3.5 Amending the Statement. If there is a material defect or omission in the Statement, the court—on its own motion or on the motion of the clerk or any party—may direct the declarant to correct or clarify the Statement. Tex. R. Civ. P. 145(d); *see* **Abrigo v. Ginez**, 580 S.W.3d 416, 419 (Tex.App.—Houston [14th Dist.] 2019, no pet.).

§4. Suit by indigent inmate

§4.1 Statement of Inability to Afford Payment of Court Costs. An indigent inmate must file the Statement of Inability to Afford Payment of Court Costs required by TRCP 145. See "Statement of inability to afford payment of costs," ch. 2-J, §3.

§4.2 Additional documents. An indigent inmate must also file the affidavits or unsworn declarations and related documents required by CPRC §§14.004 (previous filings) and 14.005 (grievance-system claims).

1. Previous filings. The inmate must file (1) an affidavit or unsworn declaration that describes all actions (including any appeal or original proceeding but excluding actions under the Family Code) previously filed by the inmate in which the inmate was not represented by an attorney and (2) a certified copy of the inmate's trust-account statement. *See* Tex. Civ. Prac. & Rem. Code §§14.002(a), 14.004; *see also* **Light v. Womack**, 113 S.W.3d 872, 874 (Tex.App.—Beaumont 2003, no pet.) (inmate must disclose all pro se suits, not just suits filed as indigent). See **O'Connor's Texas Civil Forms**, FORM 2J:2 (2020 ed.).

(1) Information about previous actions. The inmate must include the following information about each previous action in the affidavit or unsworn declaration: (1) the operative facts for which relief was sought, (2) the case name, cause number, and court in which the action was brought, (3) the identity of each party named in the action (4) the results of the action, including whether the action or a claim that was the basis for it was dismissed as frivolous or malicious, and (5) if

a previous action or claim was dismissed as frivolous or malicious, the date of the final order affirming the dismissal. Tex. Civ. Prac. & Rem. Code §14.004(a)(2), (b). If an inmate does not file an affidavit or unsworn declaration or files an affidavit or unsworn declaration that does not provide the required information, the court must give the inmate an opportunity to amend the filing to cure the defect. **McLean v. Livingston**, 486 S.W.3d 561, 562 (Tex.2016); *see* **Peña v. McDowell**, 201 S.W.3d 665, 665–66 (Tex.2006). If, after an opportunity to cure the defect, the inmate still does not provide the required information, then the court may dismiss the suit. *See* **McLean**, 486 S.W.3d at 565; *see, e.g.*, **In re Jones**, 464 S.W.3d 874, 874–75 (Tex.App.—Beaumont 2015, orig. proceeding) (court dismissed suit after clerk notified inmate of his failure to file required documents, gave deadline to correct defects, and warned him that suit would be dismissed as frivolous if defects were not corrected).

(2) Trust-account statement. The inmate must provide a certified copy of the inmate's trust-account statement, which should be attached to the affidavit or unsworn declaration describing previous filings. Tex. Civ. Prac. & Rem. Code §14.004(c); *see* Tex. Civ. Prac. & Rem. Code §14.006(f); *see, e.g.*, **Remsburg v. Marquez**, 542 S.W.3d 823, 829 (Tex.App.—Amarillo 2018, no pet.) (inmate substantially complied with §14.004(c) when he filed certified copy of trust account on same day as affidavit of inability to pay). If the inmate does not file a copy of her trust-account statement, the court must request the trust-account information before ordering the inmate to pay the full amount of court fees and costs or dismissing the suit. *See* Tex. Civ. Prac. & Rem. Code §14.006(f) (court may request TDCJ or jail to provide trust-account information); **McLean**, 486 S.W.3d at 562 (inmate must be given opportunity to cure defects in CPRC ch. 14 filings before court dismisses suit); **Bonds v. TDCJ**, 953 S.W.2d 233, 233–34 (Tex.1997) (court cannot order payment of total fees and costs merely because inmate does not provide trust-account statement).

2. Grievance-system claims. Before filing suit in the trial court to resolve a claim that is subject to the grievance system established under Gov't Code §501.008, an inmate must exhaust her administrative remedies as provided by the grievance system. *See* Tex. Civ. Prac. & Rem. Code §14.005(a); Tex. Gov't Code §501.008(d). If the claim is subject to the grievance system, the inmate must file with the court an affidavit or unsworn declaration explaining that she exhausted her administrative remedies. *See* Tex. Civ. Prac. & Rem. Code §14.005(a); **Mahuron v. TDCJ**, 494 S.W.3d 377, 381 (Tex.App.—Waco 2015, no pet.).

(1) Requirements for affidavit or declaration. The affidavit or unsworn declaration must state the date the grievance was filed and the date the inmate received a written decision on the grievance. Tex. Civ. Prac. & Rem. Code §14.005(a)(1); **Bishop v. Lawson**, 131 S.W.3d 571, 574 (Tex.App.—Fort Worth 2004, pet. denied). See **O'Connor's Texas Civil Forms**, FORM 2J:3 (2020 ed.). The inmate must also attach a copy of the written decision to the affidavit or unsworn declaration. Tex. Civ. Prac. & Rem. Code §14.005(a)(2); **Bishop**, 131 S.W.3d at 574; *see also* **Garrett v. Borden**, 283 S.W.3d 852, 853 (Tex.2009) ("copy" is not limited to photocopies; hand-typed, verbatim reproduction of decision is sufficient). Although the inmate should strictly comply with the requirements of CPRC §14.005(a), some courts have held that substantial compliance is sufficient, as long as the inmate shows that she exhausted her administrative remedies and timely filed her suit. *See* **Mahuron**, 494 S.W.3d at 381–82 (inmate may substantially comply with §14.005 by providing affidavit or declaration stating filing dates and explaining why she cannot state date of grievance decision or provide written copy of decision); *see, e.g.*, **Camacho v. Rosales**, 511 S.W.3d 82, 87 (Tex.App.—El Paso 2014, no pet.) (inmate substantially complied with §14.005(a) by reciting date of grievance decision in petition and attaching administrative grievance form); **Francis v. TDCJ-CID**, 188 S.W.3d 799, 804 (Tex.App.—Fort Worth 2006, no pet.) (although inmate did not file affidavit or declaration, he filed copy of written grievance decision for particular claim that, on its face, provided information necessary for court to determine timeliness of claim; "hypertechnical application" of §14.005(a)(1) was unnecessary for that claim); *see also* **Conely v. Texas Bd. of Crim. Justice**, No. 03-10-00422-CV, 2011 WL 3890404 (Tex.App.—Austin 2011, no pet.) (memo op.; 8-31-11) (when inmate did not receive written decision, he could have satisfied §14.005(a) by stating date he filed grievance and showing that 180 days passed without receiving decision; affidavit did not comply because it did not state date he attempted to file grievance). *But see* **Hill v. Reilly**, 343 S.W.3d 447, 451–52 (Tex.App.—El Paso 2010, pet. denied) (statements in inmate's declaration that described written decision did not satisfy statutory requirement of "copy" of decision; court of appeals would have declined to follow **Francis** but was bound to apply Fort Worth precedent because case had been transferred).

(2) Deadline for filing with court. The inmate must file the claim in the trial court within 30 days after receiving the written decision or, if a written decision has not been received, at least 180 days after the grievance was filed.

See Tex. Civ. Prac. & Rem. Code §14.005(b) (inmate must file claim before the 31st day after the date inmate receives written grievance decision); Tex. Gov't Code §501.008(d)(2) (if inmate has not received written grievance decision, claim must be filed no earlier than 180th day after grievance was filed). If the inmate files the claim before the grievance-system procedure is complete, the court must stay the proceedings to allow for completion of the grievance-system procedure for a period of no more than 180 days. Tex. Civ. Prac. & Rem. Code §14.005(c); **Morgan v. Whitfield**, 547 S.W.3d 1, 3 (Tex.App.—El Paso 2017, no pet.). An indigent inmate's claim is deemed filed when the prison authorities receive the document to be mailed. **Warner v. Glass**, 135 S.W.3d 681, 684 (Tex.2004); *see* **Remsburg**, 542 S.W.3d at 828.

Caution

Although CPRC §14.005(b) says the claim must have been filed "before the 31st day" after the inmate receives the written grievance decision, some courts have interpreted the deadline as "within 31 days." See, e.g., ***Remsburg****, 542 S.W.3d at 828;* ***Moreland v. Johnson****, 95 S.W.3d 392, 395 (Tex.App.—Houston [1st Dist.] 2002, no pet.);* ***Retzlaff v. TDCJ****, 94 S.W.3d 650, 652 (Tex.App.—Houston [14th Dist.] 2002, pet. denied);* ***Perez v. TDCJ****, No. 06-14-00065-CV, 2015 WL 733257 (Tex.App.—Texarkana 2015, no pet.) (memo op.; 2-20-15). To avoid dismissal of a claim under CPRC §14.005, an inmate should follow the language of the statute and file before the 31st day—that is, within 30 days.*

§4.3 Other information. For additional information about the hearing, the costs, the submission of evidence, and the order of dismissal, see CPRC §§14.006 to 14.014.

§5. Duties of the clerk

§5.1 Accept filing of Statement. Generally, the clerk must accept the declarant's Statement for filing even if it is defective. *See* Tex. R. Civ. P. 145(d). The clerk may refuse to file the declarant's Statement only if the Statement is not sworn to before a notary or made under penalty of perjury; no other defect is a proper ground for refusing to file the Statement or requiring payment of costs. *Id.*

§5.2 Issue citation. Once the declarant files the Statement under TRCP 145, the clerk must docket the action, issue a citation, and provide any other service that is ordinarily provided to a party. Tex. R. Civ. P. 145(a). The clerk must issue a citation even though the court has not yet ruled on the claim of indigence. *See* **McDonald v. Houston Dairy**, 813 S.W.2d 238, 238 (Tex.App.—Houston [1st Dist.] 1991, no writ) (under pre 9-1-16 version of TRCP 145).

Note

If a declarant who has filed a Statement requests service of process in a county other than the county of suit, the clerk must indicate on the document to be served that a Statement has been filed, and the sheriff or constable must execute the service without requiring payment of a fee for serving process. Tex. R. Civ. P. 126(b).

§5.3 Give notice. The clerk will give the defendant notice of the filing of the Statement along with the service of the citation. *See* Tex. R. Civ. P. 145(a). There is no requirement for the indigent plaintiff to give the defendant notice of the suit and the Statement.

§6. Summary dismissal

Under CPRC §13.001(c) (indigents) and §14.003(a) (indigent inmates), the trial court has the authority to dismiss a suit before or after process is served. *See* **Black v. Jackson**, 82 S.W.3d 44, 53 (Tex.App.—Tyler 2002, no pet.); **Pedraza v. Tibbs**, 826 S.W.2d 695, 698 (Tex.App.—Houston [1st Dist.] 1992, writ dism'd). This action spares the prospective defendant the inconvenience and expense of answering a frivolous complaint.

§6.1 Motion. The court may dismiss the suit on its own motion or on a party's motion to dismiss. **Black v. Jackson**, 82 S.W.3d 44, 53 (Tex.App.—Tyler 2002, no pet.).

§6.2 Grounds for dismissal.

1. CPRC §13.001—indigents. The court has the authority to dismiss a suit filed by an indigent if the court finds any of the following:

(1) Not indigent. The allegation of poverty in the Statement is false. *See* Tex. Civ. Prac. & Rem. Code §13.001(a)(1). The court does not have to find that the allegation of poverty was false when it was made or that the Statement itself contains a false assertion; the court may dismiss the action if the allegation of poverty, although true when filed, later became inaccurate. **Poff v. Guzman**, 532 S.W.3d 867, 871 (Tex.App.—Houston [14th Dist.] 2017, no pet.).

(2) Action is frivolous or malicious. The action is frivolous or malicious. Tex. Civ. Prac. & Rem. Code §13.001(a)(2); **Johnson v. Lynaugh**, 796 S.W.2d 705, 706 (Tex.1990); **McDonald v. Houston Dairy**, 813 S.W.2d 238, 238 (Tex.App.—Houston [1st Dist.] 1991, no writ). In determining whether an action is frivolous or malicious, the court is limited to the standard under CPRC §13.001(b)(2), which permits the court to dismiss if the claim has no arguable basis in law or in fact. *See* **Johnson**, 796 S.W.2d at 706–07 (dismissal under CPRC §13.001(b)(3) is not appropriate); **Pedraza v. Tibbs**, 826 S.W.2d 695, 698 (Tex.App.—Houston [1st Dist.] 1992, writ dism'd) (dismissal under CPRC §13.001(b)(1) & (b)(3) is not appropriate). A claim that has no arguable basis in law or in fact does not constitute a cause of action. **Pedraza**, 826 S.W.2d at 698; **Spellmon v. Sweeney**, 819 S.W.2d 206, 210 (Tex.App.—Waco 1991, no writ).

2. CPRC §14.003—indigent inmates. The court has the authority to dismiss a suit filed by an indigent inmate if the court finds any of the following:

(1) Not indigent. The allegation of poverty in the Statement is false. *See* Tex. Civ. Prac. & Rem. Code §14.003(a)(1).

(2) Claim is frivolous or malicious. The claim is frivolous or malicious. Tex. Civ. Prac. & Rem. Code §14.003(a)(2). In determining whether an indigent inmate's claim is frivolous or malicious, the court may consider any of the following:

(a) Whether the realistic chance of ultimate success on the claim is slight. Tex. Civ. Prac. & Rem. Code §14.003(b)(1); **Lopez v. Serna**, 414 S.W.3d 890, 896 (Tex.App.—San Antonio 2013, no pet.); **Powell v. Clements**, 220 S.W.3d 138, 139 (Tex.App.—Waco 2007, pet. denied).

Caution

*Based on **Johnson v. Lynaugh**, 796 S.W.2d 705 (Tex.1990), some courts have questioned whether the grounds in CPRC §14.003(b)(1) and (b)(3)—which are substantively identical to the grounds in CPRC §13.001(b)(1) and (b)(3)—are still appropriate bases for dismissing an inmate's claim. See, e.g., **Lagaite v. Boland**, 300 S.W.3d 911, 913 (Tex.App.—Amarillo 2009, no pet.) (grounds in CPRC §14.003(b)(1) and (b)(3) are addressed by asking whether claim lacks arguable basis in law or fact under (b)(2)); **Vacca v. Farrington**, 85 S.W.3d 438, 439 (Tex.App.—Texarkana 2002, no pet.) (Supreme Court has discouraged reliance on grounds in CPRC §14.003(b)(1) and (b)(3)); see also **Powell**, 220 S.W.3d at 139 n.1 (court recognized that Supreme Court has cast doubt on whether claim can be dismissed based on §14.003(b)(1) alone, citing **Johnson**, but dismissal under (b)(1) was proper based on facts of case). See "Action is frivolous or malicious," ch. 2-J, §6.2.1(2).*

(b) Whether the claim has no arguable basis in law or fact. Tex. Civ. Prac. & Rem. Code §14.003(b)(2); **Nabelek v. District Atty. of Harris Cty.**, 290 S.W.3d 222, 227 (Tex.App.—Houston [14th Dist.] 2005, pet. denied).

(c) Whether it is clear that the inmate cannot prove facts to support the claim. Tex. Civ. Prac. & Rem. Code §14.003(b)(3). At least one court has questioned whether this ground is an appropriate basis for dismissal. See "Caution," ch. 2-J, §6.2.2(2)(a).

(d) Whether the claim is substantially similar to and arises from the same operative facts as a previous claim filed by the inmate. Tex. Civ. Prac. & Rem. Code §14.003(b)(4); **Vacca**, 85 S.W.3d at 439. If the inmate does not comply

with the procedural requirements in CPRC §14.004, the court may assume the suit is substantially similar to a previous suit and thus is frivolous. **Bell v. TDCJ**, 962 S.W.2d 156, 158 (Tex.App.—Houston [14th Dist.] 1998, pet. denied); *see* **Lilly v. Northrep**, 100 S.W.3d 335, 336 (Tex.App.—San Antonio 2002, pet. denied). See "Previous filings," ch. 2-J, §4.2.1.

Note

A dismissal for failure to comply with procedural requirements in CPRC chapter 14 generally should be without prejudice. ***Remsburg v. Marquez****, 542 S.W.3d 823, 826 (Tex.App.—Amarillo 2018, no pet.);* ***Hughes v. Massey****, 65 S.W.3d 743, 746 (Tex.App.—Beaumont 2001, no pet.). See "No amendment," ch. 2-J, §6.4.*

(3) False filing. The indigent inmate filed an affidavit or unsworn declaration required by CPRC chapter 14 that the inmate knew was false. Tex. Civ. Prac. & Rem. Code §14.003(a)(3); *see* Tex. Civ. Prac. & Rem. Code §14.004 (affidavit about previous filings).

§6.3 Hearing. The court may dismiss a suit without a hearing on factual issues only when there is no arguable basis in law for the suit. **Denson v. TDCJ-I.D.**, 63 S.W.3d 454, 459 (Tex.App.—Tyler 1999, pet. denied); **Leon Springs Gas Co. v. Restaurant Equip. Leasing Co.**, 961 S.W.2d 574, 579 (Tex.App.—San Antonio 1997, no pet.); **Hector v. Thaler**, 862 S.W.2d 176, 178 (Tex.App.—Houston [1st Dist.] 1993, no writ). Before the court can dismiss a suit for having no arguable basis in fact, it must hold a hearing. **Harrison v. TDCJ-Inst. Div.**, 164 S.W.3d 871, 875 (Tex.App.—Corpus Christi 2005, no pet.); **Hector**, 862 S.W.2d at 178. *But see* **Timmons v. Luce**, 840 S.W.2d 582, 586 (Tex.App.—Tyler 1992, no writ) (court is not required to hold hearing if action is frivolous).

§6.4 No amendment. The court is not required to give the indigent an opportunity to amend the petition before dismissing under CPRC §13.001 or §14.003. *See* **Kendrick v. Lynaugh**, 804 S.W.2d 153, 156 (Tex.App.—Houston [14th Dist.] 1990, no writ) (CPRC §13.001). However, if the court gives an indigent the opportunity to amend her pleadings and the indigent does not amend, the court can dismiss the indigent's suit with prejudice. **Lentworth v. Trahan**, 981 S.W.2d 720, 722–23 (Tex.App.—Houston [1st Dist.] 1998, no pet.); *see* **Hughes v. Massey**, 65 S.W.3d 743, 746 (Tex.App.—Beaumont 2001, no pet.) (if indigent not given opportunity to amend, dismissal should be without prejudice).

§6.5 No notice. Neither CPRC §13.001 nor §14.003 requires the court to give the indigent notice that it intends to dismiss the suit for "no arguable basis in law." *See* **Timmons v. Luce**, 840 S.W.2d 582, 586 (Tex.App.—Tyler 1992, no writ) (CPRC §13.001). But if there is a hearing, the indigent must be given notice.

§6.6 Order on summary dismissal. The court's order summarily dismissing the indigent's suit must state the reasons for the dismissal. *See* **Poff v. Guzman**, 532 S.W.3d 867, 872 (Tex.App.—Houston [14th Dist.] 2017, no pet.); **Dillon v. Ousley**, 890 S.W.2d 500, 502 (Tex.App.—Corpus Christi 1994, no writ). The court's order dismissing an inmate's suit should be based on CPRC chapter 14, not CPRC chapter 13. *E.g.*, **Thompson v. Henderson**, 927 S.W.2d 323, 324 (Tex.App.—Houston [1st Dist.] 1996, no writ) (remanded for trial court to consider provisions of CPRC ch. 14).

§6.7 Review. The declarant may challenge the court's order dismissing her suit by filing a notice of appeal. *See* **Spellmon v. Sweeney**, 819 S.W.2d 206, 207 (Tex.App.—Waco 1991, no writ). The dismissal is reviewed for abuse of discretion. **Remsburg v. Marquez**, 542 S.W.3d 823, 825 (Tex.App.—Amarillo 2018, no pet.) (dismissal under CPRC ch. 14); **Morgan v. Whitfield**, 547 S.W.3d 1, 2 (Tex.App.—El Paso 2017, no pet.) (same); **Poff v. Guzman**, 532 S.W.3d 867, 871 (Tex.App.—Houston [14th Dist.] 2017, no pet.) (dismissal under CPRC §13.001); **Pedraza v. Tibbs**, 826 S.W.2d 695, 698–99 (Tex.App.—Houston [1st Dist.] 1992, writ dism'd) (same).

§7. Challenging claim of inability to afford payment of costs

§7.1 Motion to challenge. The declarant's claim of inability to afford payment of costs may be challenged by motion in certain specified circumstances. *See* Tex. R. Civ. P. 145(f); *see also* Tex. R. Civ. P. 502.3(c) (in justice court, Statement accompanied by certificate of legal-aid provider cannot be contested). If no challenge is made, the Statement is conclusive as a matter of law. **Abrigo v. Ginez**, 580 S.W.3d 416, 419 (Tex.App.—Houston [14th Dist.] 2019, no pet.); *see* Tex. R. Civ. P. 145(a),

(f); **Campbell v. Wilder**, 487 S.W.3d 146, 151 (Tex.2016) (under pre 9-1-16 version of TRCP 145); **Equitable Gen. Ins. v. Yates**, 684 S.W.2d 669, 671 (Tex.1984) (same). The declarant's claim of inability to afford payment of costs can be challenged for the following reasons:

1. False Statement or changed circumstances.

(1) Motion by clerk or party. The clerk or any party may file a motion challenging a declarant's Statement and requesting that the declarant be required to pay costs if the motion contains sworn evidence (1) that the Statement was materially false when made or (2) that, because of changed circumstances, the Statement is no longer true in material respects. Tex. R. Civ. P. 145(f)(1) & cmt. (2016). A motion made on mere information or belief is insufficient. Tex. R. Civ. P. 145(f)(1).

Note

Because costs to access the court—that is, filing fees, fees for issuance of process and notices, and fees for service and return—are kept relatively low, the expense in challenging a claim of inability to afford payment of costs is likely to exceed the costs themselves. Tex. R. Civ. P. 145 cmt. (2016). Thus, TRCP 145 does not allow the clerk or a party to challenge a declarant's claim of inability to afford costs without sworn evidence that the claim is false or that there has been a change in the declarant's circumstances that makes the claim no longer true. See Tex. R. Civ. P. 145 cmt. (2016); see, e.g., ***In re A.M.****, 557 S.W.3d 607, 609 (Tex.App.—El Paso 2016, n.p.h.) (error for trial court to conduct hearing and rule on motion to challenge that was not supported by sworn evidence).*

(2) Motion by attorney ad litem. An attorney ad litem appointed to represent a parent under Family Code §107.013 may file a motion requesting that the parent be required to pay costs if the motion satisfies the requirements under TRCP 145(f)(1). Tex. R. Civ. P. 145(f)(2).

2. Inability to pay for reporter's record. The court reporter may file a motion requesting that the declarant be required to prove her inability to afford costs when the declarant requests the preparation of a reporter's record but cannot pay for the record. Tex. R. Civ. P. 145(f)(3); *see* Tex. R. Civ. P. 145 cmt. (2016) (reporter is always allowed to challenge claim of inability to afford costs before incurring substantial expense of preparing record).

3. Evidence of ability to afford costs. If the court learns of evidence showing the declarant may be able to afford costs, the court may require the declarant to prove her inability to afford costs. Tex. R. Civ. P. 145(f)(4).

4. Appointment of officer or professional. If an officer or professional must be appointed to the case, the court may require the declarant to prove her inability to afford costs. Tex. R. Civ. P. 145(f)(4) & cmt. (2016); *e.g.*, **In re A.M.**, 557 S.W.3d at 609 (court could require declarant to prove inability to afford costs after appointment of attorney ad litem).

§7.2 Hearing.

1. Oral hearing.

(1) Most cases. In most cases, the court must conduct an oral evidentiary hearing before it can require the declarant to pay costs. Tex. R. Civ. P. 145(f)(5); *see* **Koehne v. Koehne**, ___ S.W.3d ___, 2017 WL 2375789 (Tex.App.—Houston [1st Dist.] 2017, order) (No. 01-17-00016-CV; 6-1-17).

(2) Indigent inmate. A court may hold a hearing by video communications for an indigent inmate at a jail facility. Tex. Civ. Prac. & Rem. Code §14.008(a). A court may also consider the case on submission by requiring that written statements be submitted and copies be provided to the inmate. Tex. Civ. Prac. & Rem. Code §14.009.

2. Notice of hearing. The declarant must be given ten days' notice of the hearing. Tex. R. Civ. P. 145(f)(5); *see also* **Abrigo v. Ginez**, 580 S.W.3d 416, 420 (Tex.App.—Houston [14th Dist.] 2019, no pet.) (protection of notice provision applies to declarant, not opposing party). Notice must be in writing and served under TRCP 21a or given in open court. Tex. R. Civ. P. 145(f)(5). See "Rules for Serving Documents," ch. 1-D, §1 et seq.

3. Burden. At the hearing, the burden is on the declarant to prove her inability to afford costs. Tex. R. Civ. P. 145(f)(5). See "Evidence," ch. 2-J, §3.3. The proper consideration is the declarant's present ability to pay costs rather than a future, more speculative ability. **Brown v. Clapp**, 613 S.W.2d 78, 80 (Tex.App.—Tyler 1981, orig. proceeding) (under pre 9-1-16 version of TRCP 145).

§7.3 Order.

1. Declarant cannot afford costs. If the court finds that the declarant cannot afford costs, the suit will proceed, and the declarant will not be liable for costs. *See* Tex. R. Civ. P. 145(a).

2. Declarant can afford costs.

(1) Pay full costs. If the court finds that the declarant can afford costs or that the declarant's Statement was materially false when made or is no longer true in material respects, the court will order the declarant to pay costs. *See* Tex. R. Civ. P. 145(f). The order must be supported by detailed findings of the declarant's ability to afford costs. Tex. R. Civ. P. 145(f)(6); **In re A.M.**, 557 S.W.3d 607, 610 n.2 (Tex.App.—El Paso 2016, n.p.h.).

(2) Make partial or installment payments. If the court finds that the declarant can afford only part of the costs, the court may order the declarant to make partial payment. Tex. R. Civ. P. 145(f)(7). The court may also order the declarant to pay costs in installments. *Id.* If the court orders the declarant to make installment payments, the court cannot delay the case. *Id.*

§7.4 Review of order.

1. Who can challenge. Only the declarant can challenge the trial court's order issued under TRCP 145(f). Tex. R. Civ. P. 145(g)(1).

2. How to challenge. The declarant should challenge the trial court's order by filing a motion. Tex. R. Civ. P. 145(g)(1); *see also* **Koehne v. Koehne**, ___ S.W.3d ___, 2017 WL 2375789 (Tex.App.—Houston [1st Dist.] 2017, order) (No. 01-17-00016-CV; 6-1-17) (declarant filed timely notice of appeal that court construed as motion under TRCP 145(g)(1)).

3. Where to file. The declarant must file the motion in the court of appeals that has jurisdiction over an appeal from the judgment in the case. Tex. R. Civ. P. 145(g)(1); *see* **Koehne**, ___ S.W.3d at ___, 2017 WL 2375789.

4. Deadline. The declarant must file the motion within ten days after the trial court's order is signed. Tex. R. Civ. P. 145(g)(2). On a written showing of good cause, the court of appeals may extend the deadline by 15 days. *Id.*

5. Filing fees. The declarant is not required to pay any filing fees related to the motion. Tex. R. Civ. P. 145(g)(1).

6. Request for trial court's record. After the declarant files the motion, the court of appeals must promptly send notice to the trial-court clerk and court reporter requesting preparation of the record of all trial-court proceedings on the declarant's claim of indigence. Tex. R. Civ. P. 145(g)(3); *see* **Koehne**, ___ S.W.3d at ___, 2017 WL 2375789. The court of appeals may set a deadline for filing the record, and the record must be provided without charge. Tex. R. Civ. P. 145(g)(3).

7. Ruling. The court of appeals must rule on the declarant's motion at the earliest practicable time. Tex. R. Civ. P. 145(g)(4).

§8. Payment of costs in judgment

Generally, if the court finds under TRCP 145(f) that the declarant cannot afford costs, then any provision in the judgment requiring the declarant to pay costs is void. *See* Tex. R. Civ. P. 145(h). But the judgment may require the declarant to pay costs if (1) the court has issued an order to pay costs under TRCP 145(f) or (2) the declarant has recovered a monetary judgment from the defendant and the court orders the recovery to be applied toward payment of costs. *See* Tex. R. Civ. P. 145(h). See "Declarant can afford costs," ch. 2-J, §7.3.2.

§9. Appealing judgment as indigent

A party who filed a Statement in the trial court cannot be required to pay costs for an appeal of the judgment unless the trial court issued an order under TRCP 145(f) overruling the party's claim of indigence. Tex. R. App. P. 20.1(b)(1). See "Declarant

can afford costs," ch. 2-J, §7.3.2. If the trial court issued an order under TRCP 145(f) overruling the party's claim of indigence, the party can appeal without paying costs if she establishes that her financial circumstances have materially and substantially changed since the date of the trial court's order. Tex. R. App. P. 20.1(b)(3) & cmt. (2016). To do so, the party must file in the appellate court a motion alleging the change in circumstances and a current Statement under TRCP 145. Tex. R. App. P. 20.1(b)(3)(A).

Chapter 3. Defendant's Response & Pleadings

A. Defendant's Pleadings

§1. General

§1.1 Rules. Tex. R. Civ. P. 83 to 98.

§1.2 Purpose. Initially, the most important function of the defendant's pleadings in response to the suit is to avoid a default judgment. After that, the defendant's pleadings challenge the plaintiff's petition and answer its allegations.

§1.3 Timetables & forms. Appendix IV, Timetable 1, Special appearance; Appendix IV, Timetable 2, Motion to transfer venue—Wrong or inconvenient county; Appendix IV, Timetable 4, Motion to dismiss—Code forum non conveniens; Appendix IV, Timetable 7, Motion to abate; Appendix IV, Timetable 8, Pretrial motions; **O'Connor's Texas Civil Forms**, FORMS 1, 3 (2020 ed.).

§1.4 Other references. **O'Connor's Federal Rules * Civil Trials** (2021 ed.).

§2. Prefiling considerations

§2.1 Notice to carrier. If the claim is covered by insurance, the defendant should read its policy and give its insurance carrier all required notices. *See, e.g.*, **Harwell v. State Farm Mut. Auto. Ins.**, 896 S.W.2d 170, 173–74 (Tex.1995) (under policy's notice-of-suit provision, D was required to notify carrier; notice of claim sent to carrier by P's attorney was not sufficient); **Struna v. Concord Ins. Servs.**, 11 S.W.3d 355, 359 (Tex.App.—Houston [1st Dist.] 2000, no pet.) (under policy provisions, D was required to notify carrier whenever claim was made and to forward relevant documents).

§2.2 Offer to settle.

1. Presuit offer. If a potential defendant receives a demand notice before suit is filed, it should consider making a reasonable offer to settle. *See, e.g.*, Tex. Bus. & Com. Code §17.5052(a) (DTPA); Tex. Ins. Code §541.156(a) (unfair or deceptive insurance practices); Tex. Prop. Code §27.004(b) (RCLA).

2. Offer after suit filed.

(1) Limit damages. A defendant's offer to settle can limit the amount of damages. *See, e.g.*, Tex. Civ. Prac. & Rem. Code §38.002(3) (tendering payment bars recovery of attorney fees); Tex. Fin. Code §304.105 (settlement offer in wrongful-death, personal-injury, and property-damage cases may prevent accrual of prejudgment interest during period that offer may be accepted).

(2) Recover litigation costs. A defendant can recover litigation costs under CPRC chapter 42 and TRCP 167 if the plaintiff rejected an offer to settle a claim for monetary damages that was significantly more favorable than the judgment. See "Offer of Settlement," ch. 7-H, §1 et seq.

§2.3 State vs. federal court. Once the defendant is served with the suit, it should consider whether it would prefer to try the case in federal court and, if so, whether the case is removable. For a discussion about removing a case to federal court, see "Removal & Remand," **O'Connor's Federal Rules * Civil Trials**, ch. 4-A, §1 et seq. (2021 ed.).

§2.4 ADR. If the parties are required by statute or contract to submit a dispute to a form of alternative dispute resolution (ADR), the defendant should file a motion to abate and a motion to compel ADR after filing its answer. See "The ADR System," ch. 4-A, §1 et seq.

§3. Due order of pleading

§3.1 Order of filing. Under the due-order-of-pleading rule, a defendant must file certain pleadings or motions in a specific order. *See* **Exito Elecs. Co. v. Trejo**, 142 S.W.3d 302, 305 (Tex.2004). If the defendant files a pleading or motion out of order, it waives that pleading or motion. *See, e.g.*, **Allianz Risk Transfer Ltd. v. S.J. Camp & Co.**, 117 S.W.3d 92, 97 (Tex.App.—Tyler 2003, no pet.) (D filed motion to transfer venue and original answer one minute before filing special appearance; special appearance waived). The defendant must file pleadings and motions in the following order:

1. Special appearance. When challenging personal jurisdiction, the defendant must file a special appearance before any other pleading or motion. Tex. R. Civ. P. 120a(1); *see* Tex. R. Civ. P. 86(1); *see also* **Composite Cooling Solutions,**

L.P. v. Larrabee Air Conditioning, Inc., No. 02-17-00006-CV, 2017 WL 2979918 (Tex.App.—Fort Worth 2017, no pet.) (memo op.; 7-13-17) (compliance with due-order-of-pleading requirements does not defeat substantive challenge that D waived special appearance by making general appearance). See "Due order of pleading," ch. 3-B, §2.2.

2. Motion to transfer venue. When challenging venue, the defendant must file a motion to transfer venue after a special appearance (if any) and before or along with any other pleading or motion. Tex. R. Civ. P. 86(1), 120a(1); *see* **Massey v. Columbus State Bank**, 35 S.W.3d 697, 700 (Tex.App.—Houston [1st Dist.] 2000, pet. denied); **Antonio v. Rico Marino, S.A.**, 910 S.W.2d 624, 630 (Tex.App.—Houston [14th Dist.] 1995, no writ). See "Due order of pleading," ch. 3-C, §2.2.2.

3. All other pleadings or motions. After a special appearance (if any) or a motion to transfer venue (if any) is filed, the defendant can file any other pleading or motion without violating the due-order-of-pleading rule. *See* Tex. R. Civ. P. 86(1), 120a(1); **Exito Elecs.**, 142 S.W.3d at 305.

§3.2 Exceptions to due-order-of-pleading rule. A defendant can take the following actions without waiving the special appearance or the motion to transfer venue.

1. Removal to federal court. The defendant can file a notice of removal to federal court before the special appearance without waiving the special appearance or the motion to transfer venue. **Antonio v. Rico Marino, S.A.**, 910 S.W.2d 624, 629 (Tex.App.—Houston [14th Dist.] 1995, no writ).

2. Other motions. The defendant can file motions that are not related to the merits of the suit and do not invoke the court's general jurisdiction before the special appearance without waiving the special appearance or the motion to transfer venue. *See, e.g.*, **Gentry v. Tucker**, 891 S.W.2d 766, 768 (Tex.App.—Texarkana 1995, no writ) (D did not waive venue by filing motion to continue temporary-injunction hearing before answer date); **Perkola v. Koelling & Assocs.**, 601 S.W.2d 110, 112 (Tex.App.—Dallas 1980, writ dism'd) (D did not waive venue by contesting temporary injunction that did not resolve any issues of law or fact in main case).

3. Correspondence with court. Under certain circumstances, the defendant can correspond with the court without waiving the special appearance or the motion to transfer venue. *See, e.g.*, **Gales v. Denis**, 260 S.W.3d 22, 30 (Tex.App.—Houston [1st Dist.] 2008, no pet.) (pro se D's letter to court was answer, which waived special appearance because letter did not challenge jurisdiction); **N803RA, Inc. v. Hammer**, 11 S.W.3d 363, 367 (Tex.App.—Houston [1st Dist.] 2000, no pet.) (pro se D's letter to court was answer, but special appearance was not waived because letter also challenged jurisdiction); **Moore v. Elektro-Mobil Technik GmbH**, 874 S.W.2d 324, 327 (Tex.App.—El Paso 1994, writ denied) (German company did not waive special appearance when it wrote to court stating that service was improper, requesting that case be dismissed, and making objections to interrogatories).

4. Rule 11 agreement. The defendant can file a Rule 11 agreement without waiving the special appearance or the motion to transfer venue. *See* **Exito Elecs. Co. v. Trejo**, 142 S.W.3d 302, 305 (Tex.2004). See "Rule 11 agreement," ch. 3-B, §3.5.1(3).

§3.3 Ruling order.

1. General rule—due order of pleading. The defendant should ask the court to rule first on the special appearance, then on venue, and then on other motions. *See* Tex. Civ. Prac. & Rem. Code §15.063; Tex. R. Civ. P. 86(1), 120a(2); *see, e.g.*, **Landry v. Daigrepont**, 35 S.W.3d 265, 267 (Tex.App.—Corpus Christi 2000, no pet.) (special appearance waived because D asked for ruling on motion for new trial first).

2. Exceptions. The defendant can obtain a ruling on the following without violating the due-order-of-pleading rule:

(1) Motion for continuance. The defendant can obtain a ruling on (1) a motion for continuance of the hearing on a special appearance, on a motion to transfer venue, or on a motion for forum non conveniens, or (2) a motion to continue some preliminary motion filed by the plaintiff. *See* Tex. R. Civ. P. 120a(3) (rule permits continuance in special appearance); *see, e.g.*, **Gentry v. Tucker**, 891 S.W.2d 766, 768 (Tex.App.—Texarkana 1995, no writ) (D's motion for continuance of temporary-injunction hearing did not waive right to transfer venue).

(2) Plaintiff's motions. The defendant can ask the court to rule on the plaintiff's preliminary motions. *See* **Perkola v. Koelling & Assocs.**, 601 S.W.2d 110, 112 (Tex.App.—Dallas 1980, writ dism'd).

§4. Constructing the original answer

§4.1 Options. A defendant has three options for filing its answer and other pleas and motions: (1) file the answer and all other initial pleas and motions in one document, (2) file the answer and each of the other pleas and motions separately, or (3) file the answer and some of the pleas and motions in one document, and file the other pleas and motions separately. *See* Tex. R. Civ. P. 85. When filed separately, the items must be filed in the appropriate order; when included in one document, they should be listed in the appropriate order.

§4.2 Inclusive answer + some motions. The best practice is to file an original answer containing some of the defendant's pleas and motions, and to file other pleas and motions separately.

1. Original answer. The defendant should consider the following when preparing the original answer:

- Is the defendant a nonresident of Texas claiming it has not done business in Texas? If so, the first part of the answer must be a special appearance. See "Special Appearance—Challenging Personal Jurisdiction," ch. 3-B, §1 et seq.
- Is there another county in Texas where the defendant contends the suit should or could have been filed? If so, the next part of the answer must be a motion to transfer venue. See "Motion to Transfer—Challenging Venue," ch. 3-C, §1 et seq.
- Is there a court in another jurisdiction outside Texas that the defendant contends has jurisdiction over the suit and is a more appropriate forum? If so, the defendant must file a motion for forum non conveniens. See "Forum Non Conveniens—Challenging the Texas Forum," ch. 3-D, §1 et seq.
- The next part of the answer is the general denial. See "General denial," ch. 3-E, §3.
- Does the defendant want to assert any of the pleas listed in TRCP 93? If so, the defendant must specifically plead them and verify the answer. See "Verified pleas," ch. 3-E, §4.
- Does the defendant want to plead defenses establishing an independent reason why the plaintiff cannot prevail? If so, the defendant must affirmatively plead the defenses. See "Affirmative defenses," ch. 3-E, §5.
- Did the plaintiff plead that "all conditions precedent have been performed or have occurred" according to TRCP 54? If so, the defendant must specifically deny the statement, identify the specific conditions the plaintiff did not comply with, and verify the denial. See "Denial of conditions precedent," ch. 3-E, §6.1.
- Does the defendant have claims against the plaintiff or other persons? If so, the next part of the answer should identify the defendant's counterclaims, cross-claims, or third-party claims. *See* Tex. R. Civ. P. 38, 97. See "Cross-actions," ch. 2-F, §2.2.
- The last part of the answer is the conclusion, prayer, signature block, and if necessary, verification and affidavits.

2. Separate motions. The defendant should consider the following when deciding whether to file additional motions:

- *Motion 1:* Are there responsible third parties (RTPs), as defined in CPRC §33.011(6), that the defendant should designate? If so, the defendant should file a motion for leave to designate a person as an RTP. The motion must be filed at least 60 days before trial. See "RTP," ch. 3-E, §7.4.
- *Motion 2:* Are there defects in the court's subject-matter jurisdiction that prevent this particular court from hearing the case? If so, the defendant should file a plea to the jurisdiction. See "Plea to the Jurisdiction—Challenging the Court," ch. 3-F, §1 et seq.
- *Motion 3:* Are there defects in the plaintiff's suit that are apparent from the face of the plaintiff's petition? If so, the defendant should file special exceptions to object to the pleading defects and, if necessary, a motion for summary judgment. See "Special Exceptions—Challenging the Pleadings," ch. 3-G, §1 et seq.

• *Motion 4:* Is the plaintiff's suit based on a cause of action that has no basis in law or fact? If so, the defendant should file a motion to dismiss the cause of action. *See* Tex. R. Civ. P. 91a.1. See "Motion to Dismiss—Baseless Cause of Action," ch. 3-H, §1 et seq.

• *Motion 5:* Are there defects in the plaintiff's suit that are not apparent from the face of the petition? That is, must the defendant inform the court of facts not in the petition to illustrate the defect? If so, the defendant should file a verified motion to abate. Many of the matters that the defendant files as part of a verified answer should also be the subject of a motion to abate. See "Motion to Abate—Challenging the Suit," ch. 3-I, §1 et seq.

• *Motion 6:* Is the plaintiff's suit based on or in response to the defendant's exercise of the right of free speech, the right to petition, or the right of association? If so, the defendant should file a motion to dismiss under the Texas Citizens Participation Act (TCPA). *See* Tex. Civ. Prac. & Rem. Code §27.003(a). The motion must generally be filed within 60 days after service of the suit. Tex. Civ. Prac. & Rem. Code §27.003(b). See "Motion to Dismiss—Anti-SLAPP Motion," ch. 3-K, §1 et seq.

§5. Deadline to file defendant's answer & motions

See the appropriate subchapter of this chapter for deadlines to file. For example, for the deadline to file an answer, see "Deadline to answer," ch. 3-E, §2.

§6. Summary of defendant's pleadings

Chart 3-1, below, matches the challenges defendants can make with the proper procedural steps.

3-1. Summary of Defendant's Pleadings

	To urge this	File this
	Challenging jurisdiction	
1	The defendant, a nonresident, has never conducted business in Texas, and Texas courts do not have jurisdiction over the defendant or its property.	A special appearance with a prayer to dismiss.
2	The court does not have jurisdiction over the subject matter of this suit.	A plea to the jurisdiction with a prayer to dismiss.
	Challenging the court where the suit was filed	
3	The case should be tried in another county because this county is not a county of proper venue.	A motion to transfer venue.
4	The case should be tried in another county that is more convenient.	A motion to transfer venue.
5	The case should be tried in another county because of local prejudice.	A motion to change venue.
6	Another court outside Texas has jurisdiction and is more appropriate.	A motion to stay or dismiss for forum non conveniens with a prayer to stay or dismiss.
7	The same dispute between the same parties is pending in another court.	A verified denial and a motion to abate. If nothing is left to litigate in this suit after the other suit is litigated, file a motion to dismiss.
	Challenging the pleadings	
8	The plaintiff did not plead notice or proof of the claim, as required by statute.	Special exceptions.
9	The plaintiff should amend to delete an unspecified claim for damages and plead damages specifically.	Special exceptions.
10	The plaintiff did not verify its petition.	Special exceptions.
11	The pleadings do not state a cause of action (e.g., fraud) because they do not include the element of injury.	Special exceptions.

3-1. Summary of Defendant's Pleadings		
	To urge this	**File this**
12	The pleadings do not state a viable cause of action (e.g., pleadings state cause of action for death of unborn child).	Special exceptions, a motion to dismiss, and if necessary, a motion for summary judgment.
	Challenging the suit	
13	The government is immune from suit.	A plea to the jurisdiction and a motion to dismiss.
14	The government is immune from liability.	An affirmative defense and a motion for summary judgment.
15	The suit is barred by a statute of limitations.	An affirmative defense and a motion for summary judgment.
16	The suit is barred by laches.	An affirmative defense and a motion for summary judgment.
17	The same dispute was litigated and resolved by final judgment.	An affirmative defense and a motion for summary judgment.
18	The dispute is subject to arbitration.	A motion to abate and to compel arbitration.
19	The plaintiff's TRCP 54 conditions precedent were not met.	A verified denial listing conditions the plaintiff did not comply with.
20	The cause of action has no basis in law or fact.	A motion to dismiss under TRCP 91a.
21	The plaintiff's suit is based on or in response to the defendant's exercise of the right of free speech, the right to petition, or the right of association.	A motion to dismiss under CPRC chapter 27.
	Challenging the parties	
22	The plaintiff (or defendant) cannot sue (or be sued) in that capacity.	A verified denial and a motion to abate. If the matter cannot be cured by an amendment, file a motion for summary judgment.
23	The plaintiff lacks standing to bring suit.	A plea to the jurisdiction.
24	Another entity is a necessary party to this suit.	A verified denial and a motion to abate.
25	The defendant is secondarily liable, and the plaintiff has not sued the principal.	A verified denial and a motion to abate.
26	The plaintiff is a foreign corporation doing business in Texas, has not registered with the Secretary of State, and cannot bring a suit for relief.	A verified denial and a motion to dismiss.
27	The plaintiff did not file an assumed-name certificate.	A verified denial and a motion to abate.
28	The death of a party requires the substitution of a representative.	A motion to abate. If a representative is not substituted, the defendant must get a scire facias before moving to dismiss.
29	The plaintiff (or defendant) is not a corporation (or partnership), as pleaded.	A verified denial and a motion to abate. If the matter cannot be cured by amendment, file a motion for summary judgment.
30	The death of a party extinguished the cause of action.	A verified plea to the jurisdiction with a prayer to dismiss.
31	The defendant is a debtor in bankruptcy.	A notice of bankruptcy with a copy of the bankruptcy petition. The bankruptcy order acts as an automatic stay.
32	Misnomer of the defendant.	A motion to abate alleging the defendant was sued in the wrong name.
33	The plaintiff sued the wrong defendant.	A verified denial and a motion for summary judgment.

3-1. Summary of Defendant's Pleadings		
To urge this		File this
Challenging liability		
34	The defendant is not responsible for the plaintiff's injury.	A general denial and a motion for summary judgment.
35	Other persons are responsible for some or all of the plaintiff's injury.	A motion for leave to designate an RTP.
36	The defendant did not execute the contract as the plaintiff alleges.	A verified denial and a motion for summary judgment.
37	The endorsement on the note was not genuine.	A verified denial and a motion for summary judgment.
38	There was no consideration for the contract subject to the suit or the contract is usurious.	A verified denial and a motion for summary judgment.
39	A contingency in the contract precludes liability, the contract was modified, there was a failure of consideration, or there was a mutual mistake.	An affirmative defense and a motion for summary judgment.
40	The defendant's debts were discharged in bankruptcy.	An affirmative defense and a motion for summary judgment.
41	Duress, estoppel, illegality, license, payment, or waiver.	An affirmative defense and a motion for summary judgment.
42	The loss was within a specific exclusion in an insurance contract.	An affirmative defense and a motion for summary judgment.
43	Any other matter constituting avoidance.	An affirmative defense and a motion for summary judgment.

B. Special Appearance—Challenging Personal Jurisdiction

§1. General

§1.1 Rule. Tex. R. Civ. P. 120a. See Tex. Civ. Prac. & Rem. Code ch. 17.

§1.2 Purpose. A special appearance allows a nonresident defendant to challenge the court's personal jurisdiction over the defendant without becoming subject to the jurisdiction of Texas courts. Tex. R. Civ. P. 120a; **Kawasaki Steel Corp. v. Middleton**, 699 S.W.2d 199, 201 (Tex.1985). Texas courts have jurisdiction over a nonresident defendant only when jurisdiction is (1) proper under the Texas long-arm statute and (2) consistent with federal and state due-process guarantees. **Old Republic Nat'l Title Ins. v. Bell**, 549 S.W.3d 550, 558 (Tex.2018); **TV Azteca, S.A.B. de C.V. v. Ruiz**, 490 S.W.3d 29, 36 (Tex.2016); **Spir Star AG v. Kimich**, 310 S.W.3d 868, 872 (Tex.2010); *see also* Tex. Civ. Prac. & Rem. Code §§17.041 to 17.045 (long-arm statute). The Due Process Clause of the U.S. Constitution guarantees that a party cannot be bound by the judgment of a forum with which the party has established no meaningful contacts, ties, or relations. **National Indus. Sand Ass'n v. Gibson**, 897 S.W.2d 769, 772 (Tex.1995). The only question addressed in the special appearance is whether a Texas court can constitutionally exercise jurisdiction over the defendant. **Kawasaki Steel**, 699 S.W.2d at 202.

Practice Tip

To determine whether a defect in the petition regarding personal jurisdiction should be challenged by a special appearance or by a motion to quash, consider whether the defect is curable. If the defect is incurable (i.e., the defendant is a nonresident and not subject to the jurisdiction of Texas courts), challenge it with a special appearance; if the defect is curable and the defendant admits that Texas courts have personal jurisdiction (e.g., the defendant contracted with the plaintiff in Texas but was not properly served with suit), challenge it with a motion to quash. See ***Kawasaki Steel****, 699 S.W.2d at 202–03. See "Motion to Quash—Challenging the Service," ch. 3-J, §1 et seq. However, since the only remedy for a motion to quash is additional time to answer, a defendant who admits personal jurisdiction should just file a timely answer (instead of a motion to quash) and avoid the risk of a default judgment.*

§1.3 Timetables & forms. Appendix IV, Timetable 1, Special appearance; Appendix IV, Timetable 8, Pretrial motions; **O'Connor's Texas Civil Forms**, FORMS 3B:1 et seq. (2020 ed.).

§1.4 Other references. **O'Connor's Texas Causes of Action** (2021 ed.); **O'Connor's Texas Civil Appeals** (2020 ed.).

§2. Special appearance

§2.1 Deadline to file. The special appearance must be filed by the deadline for filing the answer. See "Deadline to answer," ch. 3-E, §2.

§2.2 Due order of pleading. The special appearance must be the first pleading the defendant files. See "Due order of pleading," ch. 3-A, §3. Every other pleading or motion is presumed to be subject to the court's ruling on the special appearance. **Dawson-Austin v. Austin**, 968 S.W.2d 319, 322 (Tex.1998). See "No waiver," ch. 3-B, §3.5.

§2.3 Due order of hearings. The special appearance must be heard and determined before a motion to transfer venue or any other pleading or motion. Tex. R. Civ. P. 120a(2); **Nationwide Distrib. Servs. v. Jones**, 496 S.W.3d 221, 224 (Tex.App.—Houston [1st Dist.] 2016, no pet.); **Wakefield v. British Med. Journal Publ'g Grp.**, 449 S.W.3d 172, 179 (Tex.App.—Austin 2014, no pet.); **Grynberg v. M-I L.L.C.**, 398 S.W.3d 864, 876 (Tex.App.—Corpus Christi 2012, pet. denied); *see* **In re Doe**, 444 S.W.3d 603, 608 (Tex.2014) (dicta). See "Requesting hearing," ch. 3-B, §2.7. If a defendant obtains a hearing on a motion that seeks affirmative relief unrelated to the special appearance before it obtains a hearing and ruling on the special appearance, the defendant has entered a general appearance and waived any challenge to personal jurisdiction. **Global Paragon Dallas, LLC v. SBM Rlty., LLC**, 448 S.W.3d 607, 612 (Tex.App.—Houston [14th Dist.] 2014, no pet.); **Trenz v. Peter Paul Pet. Co.**, 388 S.W.3d 796, 802 (Tex.App.—Houston [1st Dist.] 2012, no pet.); *see, e.g.*, **Klingenschmitt v. Weinstein**, 342 S.W.3d 131, 134–35 (Tex.App.—Dallas 2011, no pet.) (hearing and ruling on D's motion to dismiss P's

claims with prejudice before hearing on special appearance violated due-order-of-hearing requirement; special appearance waived). See "Ruling order," ch. 3-A, §3.3; "Waiver," ch. 3-B, §3.

§2.4 Grounds. The defendant must negate all grounds for personal jurisdiction alleged in the plaintiff's petition. **Old Republic Nat'l Title Ins. v. Bell**, 549 S.W.3d 550, 559 (Tex.2018); **TV Azteca, S.A.B. de C.V. v. Ruiz**, 490 S.W.3d 29, 36 n.4 (Tex.2016); **Kelly v. General Interior Constr., Inc.**, 301 S.W.3d 653, 658 (Tex.2010); **BMC Software Belg., N.V. v. Marchand**, 83 S.W.3d 789, 793 (Tex.2002). The defendant should plead and prove that (1) it is not a Texas resident, (2) it did not have minimum contacts with Texas, and (3) even if it had some contacts with Texas, the exercise of jurisdiction would offend the traditional notions of fair play and substantial justice. *See* **BMC Software**, 83 S.W.3d at 795; **Guardian Royal Exch. Assur., Ltd. v. English China Clays, P.L.C.**, 815 S.W.2d 223, 226 (Tex.1991). If the defendant produces sufficient evidence negating jurisdiction, the burden shifts to the plaintiff to show that the court has jurisdiction over the defendant. **M.G.M. Grand Hotel, Inc. v. Castro**, 8 S.W.3d 403, 408 (Tex.App.—Corpus Christi 1999, no pet.).

Note

When a presuit deposition is sought under TRCP 202, a potential defendant can file a special appearance if she does not have sufficient minimum contacts with Texas for the court to exercise personal jurisdiction over her. See ***In re Doe**, 444 S.W.3d 603, 605 (Tex.2014). A court must have personal jurisdiction over a potential defendant to grant a presuit deposition under TRCP 202.* ***In re Doe**, 444 S.W.3d at 610. See "Court's jurisdiction," ch. 6-F, §16.3.*

1. Not Texas resident. The defendant should state that it is not a Texas resident. If the plaintiff did not allege a basis for personal jurisdiction over the defendant (i.e., that the defendant committed or conspired to commit an act in Texas, or that the defendant's acts outside Texas had reasonably foreseeable consequences in Texas), then the defendant needs to prove only that it is a nonresident. *See* **Kelly**, 301 S.W.3d at 658–59; **Siskind v. Villa Found. for Educ., Inc.**, 642 S.W.2d 434, 438 & n.5 (Tex.1982); **Booth v. Kontomitras**, 485 S.W.3d 461, 476 (Tex.App.—Beaumont 2016, no pet.); **Perna v. Hogan**, 162 S.W.3d 648, 653 (Tex.App.—Houston [14th Dist.] 2005, no pet.). See **O'Connor's Texas Civil Forms**, FORM 3B:2 (2020 ed.).

2. No minimum contacts. The defendant should plead that it did not have sufficient minimum contacts with Texas to confer jurisdiction on Texas courts. *See* **CSR Ltd. v. Link**, 925 S.W.2d 591, 594–95 (Tex.1996); **Guardian Royal**, 815 S.W.2d at 226–27; **Schlobohm v. Schapiro**, 784 S.W.2d 355, 358 (Tex.1990). To negate minimum contacts for personal jurisdiction, the defendant must allege and prove a negative—that is, it did not have any (or enough) contacts with Texas to justify a Texas court's claim of personal jurisdiction over it or over the property subject to the suit. *See* **BMC Software**, 83 S.W.3d at 795; **Siskind**, 642 S.W.2d at 438. To prove it had no minimum contacts with Texas, the defendant must show that (1) it did not purposefully avail itself of the privilege of conducting activities within Texas and (2) any contacts it may have had with Texas do not give rise to specific or general jurisdiction. *See* **Moki Mac River Expeditions v. Drugg**, 221 S.W.3d 569, 575–76 (Tex.2007); **Commonwealth Gen. Corp. v. York**, 177 S.W.3d 923, 925 (Tex.2005); **BMC Software**, 83 S.W.3d at 795; **Guardian Royal**, 815 S.W.2d at 227–28; **Schlobohm**, 784 S.W.2d at 358. See **O'Connor's Texas Civil Forms**, FORM 3B:2 (2020 ed.).

(1) No purposeful availment. The purposeful-availment analysis seeks to determine whether a nonresident defendant's conduct and connection to Texas are such that the defendant could reasonably anticipate being brought into court there. **Searcy v. Parex Res.**, 496 S.W.3d 58, 67 (Tex.2016); **Moncrief Oil Int'l v. OAO Gazprom**, 414 S.W.3d 142, 152 (Tex.2013). In this analysis, (1) only the defendant's contacts with Texas are considered—the unilateral activity of another party or a third person cannot constitute purposeful availment by the defendant, (2) the defendant's acts must have been purposeful rather than random, fortuitous, or attenuated, and (3) the defendant must have sought some benefit, advantage, or profit by availing itself of the jurisdiction. **Old Republic Nat'l Title**, 549 S.W.3d at 559; **M&F Worldwide Corp. v. Pepsi-Cola Metro. Bottling Co.**, 512 S.W.3d 878, 886 (Tex.2017); **TV Azteca**, 490 S.W.3d at 37–38; **Moncrief Oil**, 414 S.W.3d at 151; *e.g.*, **Retamco Oper., Inc. v. Republic Drilling Co.**, 278 S.W.3d 333, 338–39 (Tex.2009) (D who purchased Texas real property purposefully availed itself of Texas forum); **Riverside Exps., Inc. v. B.R. Crane & Equip., LLC**, 362 S.W.3d 649, 652–53 (Tex.App.—Houston [14th Dist.] 2011, pet. denied) (P, a Texas resident, bought equipment

from nonresident D and then sued D in Texas for DTPA violations and breach of contract; D's e-mail correspondence and return of deposit to Texas were not sufficient to show purposeful availment); *see also* **American Type Culture Collection, Inc. v. Coleman**, 83 S.W.3d 801, 808 (Tex.2002) (nonresident D can avoid state's jurisdiction by purposefully structuring transactions to avoid benefits and protections of state's laws). The purposeful-availment analysis looks to the defendant's contacts with Texas itself, not its contacts with persons who reside there. **Old Republic Nat'l Title**, 549 S.W.3d at 561.

(a) Analyzing contacts—generally. When analyzing the defendant's contacts, the court should consider the quality and nature of the contacts, not the number of contacts or whether the contacts themselves were tortious. *See* **Moncrief Oil**, 414 S.W.3d at 151; **Retamco Oper.**, 278 S.W.3d at 339; **Michiana Easy Livin' Country, Inc. v. Holten**, 168 S.W.3d 777, 791–92 (Tex.2005); *see, e.g.*, **TV Azteca**, 490 S.W.3d at 38 (mere showing that D directed defamatory statements at P who lived in and allegedly suffered injuries in Texas, without more, was insufficient to establish jurisdiction; exercise of jurisdiction proper based on D's other contacts).

Note

Under the "effects test" for determining personal jurisdiction based on a nonresident defendant's tortious conduct, there must be intentional conduct by the defendant that connects the defendant to the Texas forum itself—not merely to the resident plaintiff—for the court to have jurisdiction over the defendant. See ***Old Republic Nat'l Title****, 549 S.W.3d at 564;* ***TV Azteca****, 490 S.W.3d at 42. Jurisdiction cannot turn on whether the defendant "directed a tort" at Texas or whether the plaintiff resided in Texas and felt the effects of the tort there. See* ***Michiana****, 168 S.W.3d at 791–92;* ***Vinmar Overseas Singapore PTE Ltd. v. PTT Int'l Trading PTE Ltd.****, 538 S.W.3d 126, 134 (Tex.App.—Houston [14th Dist.] 2017, pet. denied). Even if the defendant knows that the alleged harm would have effects in Texas, there is still not a sufficient basis for jurisdiction.* ***Old Republic Nat'l Title****, 549 S.W.3d at 565;* ***Searcy****, 496 S.W.3d at 68–69; see* ***Vinmar Overseas****, 538 S.W.3d at 134. The effects test supplements, but does not replace, the general guidelines for determining whether a defendant has purposefully availed itself of the Texas forum. See* ***Old Republic Nat'l Title****, 549 S.W.3d at 565.*

(b) Analyzing contacts—stream of commerce. A defendant can purposefully avail itself of the Texas forum by putting its products in the stream of commerce. For a defendant to purposefully avail itself of the Texas forum, the defendant must have more than mere knowledge that its products would reach Texas; there must also be evidence that the defendant had the intent or purpose to serve the Texas market. *See* **Spir Star AG v. Kimich**, 310 S.W.3d 868, 873 (Tex.2010).

[1] Knowledge. The defendant must have put products in the stream of commerce knowing that some of them would reach Texas. **Moki Mac**, 221 S.W.3d at 576–77; *see* **Spir Star**, 310 S.W.3d at 873; **Michiana**, 168 S.W.3d at 786; *see also* **Zinc Nacional, S.A. v. Bouché Trucking, Inc.**, 308 S.W.3d 395, 397–98 (Tex.2010) (knowledge that goods will end up in forum state is not sufficient; D must actually direct sales to forum state, not through it).

[2] Additional conduct—intent to serve Texas market. The defendant must have engaged in additional conduct that indicates an intent to serve the Texas market. **Spir Star**, 310 S.W.3d at 873; **Moki Mac**, 221 S.W.3d at 577; *see* **Michiana**, 168 S.W.3d at 786. Additional conduct can include:

[a] Designing the product for the Texas market. **Spir Star**, 310 S.W.3d at 873; **Moki Mac**, 221 S.W.3d at 577.

[b] Advertising in Texas. **Spir Star**, 310 S.W.3d at 873; **Moki Mac**, 221 S.W.3d at 577.

[c] Establishing channels of regular communication with Texas customers. **Spir Star**, 310 S.W.3d at 873; **Moki Mac**, 221 S.W.3d at 577.

[d] Marketing the product through a distributor who will sell the product in Texas. **Spir Star**, 310 S.W.3d at 873; *see* **Moki Mac**, 221 S.W.3d at 577; *see, e.g.*, **Semperit Technische Produkte GmbH v. Hennessy**, 508 S.W.3d 569, 576–77 (Tex.App.—El Paso 2016, no pet.) (Texas court had personal jurisdiction over nonresident D that sold product to New Jersey subsidiary that sold product to Oklahoma distributor that then resold product in Texas). When sales

of a product in Texas are conducted through a distributor, the actions of the nonresident-manufacturer defendant, not the distributor or affiliate, are analyzed to determine purposeful availment. *See* **Spir Star**, 310 S.W.3d at 874. Usually, when a nonresident manufacturer specifically targets Texas as a market for its products by using a distributor as an in-state sales agent, the manufacturer is subject to a products-liability suit in Texas based on a product sold in the state. *Id.* But there may be situations when the use of a Texas distributor will not support a finding that the nonresident manufacturer intended to serve the Texas market—for example, the manufacturer may have chosen to use the Texas distributorship to increase the manufacturer's bottom line through gained efficiencies and economies of scale rather than to serve the Texas market. *Id.* at 875.

(c) Analyzing contacts—defamatory broadcasts. A media defendant can purposefully avail itself of the Texas forum if a broadcast that originates outside Texas is viewed in the state. For a defendant to purposefully avail itself of the Texas forum, the defendant must have more than mere knowledge that its broadcasts could be viewed in Texas; there must also be evidence that the defendant had the intent or purpose to target the Texas market. **TV Azteca**, 490 S.W.3d at 46–47.

Note

In ***TV Azteca****, the Court applied a test similar to that used in stream-of-commerce cases to determine purposeful availment in the context of allegedly defamatory media broadcasts that originated outside Texas but were seen by Texas viewers. See* ***TV Azteca****, 490 S.W.3d at 46–47. The Court declined to address whether purposeful availment in the context of Internet publications should be analyzed under the same test applied to broadcasts. Id. at 44 n.8. See "Analyzing contacts—Internet activity," ch. 3-B, §2.4.2(1)(d).*

---

[1] Knowledge. The defendant must have known that its broadcasts could be viewed in Texas. **TV Azteca**, 490 S.W.3d at 46.

[2] Intentional targeting of Texas market. The defendant must have intentionally targeted the Texas market. **TV Azteca**, 490 S.W.3d at 47. A defendant can be found to have intentionally targeted the Texas market in either of the following ways:

[a] Subject-and-sources test. A defendant intentionally targets the Texas market if (1) the subject matter of the defendant's broadcasts involves events in Texas and (2) the defendant relied on Texas sources to prepare the broadcasts. *See, e.g.,* **TV Azteca**, 490 S.W.3d at 47–48 (broadcasts that were seen by Texas viewers but concerned people and events in Brazil and Mexico did not support finding of purposeful availment under subject-and-sources test); *cf.* **Calder v. Jones**, 465 U.S. 783, 788–89 (1984) (applying subject-and-sources test to determine purposeful availment in context of defamatory magazine article). In this situation, the defendant intentionally targets the Texas market by making Texas the focal point of its broadcasts. *See* **TV Azteca**, 490 S.W.3d at 49.

[b] Additional conduct—intent to serve Texas market. A defendant intentionally targets the Texas market if it engages in additional conduct that indicates an intent or purpose to serve the Texas market. *See* **TV Azteca**, 490 S.W.3d at 54. Additional conduct can include advertising in Texas and establishing channels of regular communication with Texas customers. *E.g., id.* (Ds "continuously and deliberately exploited" Texas market by physically entering Texas to produce and promote broadcasts, deriving substantial revenue by selling advertising time to Texas businesses, and making substantial efforts to distribute programs and increase their popularity in Texas).

(d) Analyzing contacts—Internet activity. To determine whether contacts arising from Internet activity are sufficient to establish personal jurisdiction, courts consider three categories of Internet activity: (1) websites used for transacting business, (2) passive websites used only for advertising, and (3) interactive websites that allow for the exchange of information. **All Star Enter. v. Buchanan**, 298 S.W.3d 404, 426–27 (Tex.App.—Houston [14th Dist.] 2009, no pet.); **Schexnayder v. Daniels**, 187 S.W.3d 238, 248 (Tex.App.—Texarkana 2006, pet. dism'd); **Reiff v. Roy**, 115 S.W.3d 700, 705–06 (Tex.App.—Dallas 2003, pet. denied); **Michel v. Rocket Eng'g**, 45 S.W.3d 658, 677 (Tex.App.—Fort Worth 2001, no pet.); **Daimler-Benz A.G. v. Olson**, 21 S.W.3d 707, 725 (Tex.App.—Austin 2000, pet. dism'd). The nature and quality of

these Internet contacts are evaluated on a sliding scale. **Experimental Aircraft Ass'n v. Doctor**, 76 S.W.3d 496, 506 (Tex.App.—Houston [14th Dist.] 2002, no pet.); *see* **Epicous Adventure Travel, LLC v. Tateossian, Inc.**, 573 S.W.3d 375, 387 (Tex.App.—El Paso 2019, no pet.). If the website is clearly used for business transactions, such as entering into contracts or repeatedly transmitting information, it will generally be sufficient to establish minimum contacts. **Schexnayder**, 187 S.W.3d at 248; **Exito Elecs. Co. v. Trejo**, 166 S.W.3d 839, 857–58 (Tex.App.—Corpus Christi 2005, no pet.); **Reiff**, 115 S.W.3d at 705–06; **Daimler-Benz**, 21 S.W.3d at 725. If the website is passive (i.e., used only to provide contact information or to advertise), it is insufficient to establish minimum contacts, even if it is accessible to Texas residents. **Riverside Exps.**, 362 S.W.3d at 655; **Schexnayder**, 187 S.W.3d at 248; **Exito Elecs.**, 166 S.W.3d at 858; **Reiff**, 115 S.W.3d at 706; *see* **Waterman S.S. Corp. v. Ruiz**, 355 S.W.3d 387, 412 (Tex.App.—Houston [1st Dist.] 2011, pet. denied). If the website is interactive and allows for the exchange of information between the potential customer and the person or company hosting the website, whether the court has personal jurisdiction is determined by evaluating the degree of interaction and the commercial nature of the information exchanged. **Epicous Adventure Travel**, 573 S.W.3d at 387; *see* **Schexnayder**, 187 S.W.3d at 248; **Exito Elecs.**, 166 S.W.3d at 858 n.16; **Reiff**, 115 S.W.3d at 706; **Experimental Aircraft**, 76 S.W.3d at 507. An interactive website alone may not be sufficient to establish personal jurisdiction, but courts will consider it along with a defendant's other contacts. *See* **Daimler-Benz**, 21 S.W.3d at 725. Whether Internet contacts are sufficient to establish personal jurisdiction is determined on a case-by-case basis. See chart 3-2, below, for examples.

Note

At least two courts have held that the sliding-scale test should not be used when the website is controlled by a third party and not the defendant. See, e.g., ***Wilkerson v. RSL Funding, L.L.C.****, 388 S.W.3d 668, 676–77 (Tex.App.—Houston [1st Dist.] 2011, pet. denied);* ***Moulton v. Shane****, No. 04-18-00338-CV, 2018 WL 6517395 (Tex.App.—San Antonio 2018, no pet.) (memo op.; 12-12-18); see also* ***Epicous Adventure Travel****, 573 S.W.3d at 387–88 (court expressed reservations about application of sliding scale to third-party websites, but determination of issue was not necessary for resolution of case).*

3-2. Internet Contacts

	Facts	Case
	Sufficient contacts	
1	D's products were available to Texas residents on its website, and D paid search engines to direct users to website to place orders.	**I & JC**, 164 S.W.3d 877, 889 (E.P. 2005, denied).
2	Interactive website had online shop with e-mail purchasing capabilities, encouraged people to become members online, and heavily promoted membership benefits, including insurance plans and discounted prices.	**Experimental Aircraft**, 76 S.W.3d 496, 507 (Hous. [14th] 2002, no pet.) (commercial nature of exchange of information was significant factor supporting personal jurisdiction).
3	Interactive website allowed customers to submit comments and questions to D's representatives and to receive e-mails from D.	**Daimler-Benz**, 21 S.W.3d 707, 725 (Aus. 2000, dism'd).
	Insufficient contacts	
4	Passive website provided contact information, but customers could not book cargo or enter into contracts through website and D could not respond to customer inquiries through website.	**Waterman S.S.**, 355 S.W.3d 387, 412 (Hous. [1st] 2011, denied).
5	Passive website posted D's telephone number, e-mail address, and a contact form.	**Jackson**, 312 S.W.3d 146, 155 (Hous. [14th] 2010, no pet.).
6	Website allowed visitors to submit online employment application but instructed them to contact Utah office for more information.	**All Star**, 298 S.W.3d 404, 427 (Hous. [14th] 2009, no pet.).

3-2. Internet Contacts

	Facts	Case
7	Website displayed D-doctor's biography, credentials, and job description, but did not allow doctors to interact about patient care online.	**Schexnayder**, 187 S.W.3d 238, 249 (Texark. 2006, dism'd).
8	Passive website identified catalog items and provided contact information for potentially interested customers.	**Exito Elecs.**, 166 S.W.3d 839, 858 (C.C. 2005, no pet.); *see* **Townsend**, 83 S.W.3d 913, 922 (Texark. 2002, denied).
9	Website did not allow D to directly respond over Internet to information provided by potential customers; sales representative followed up personally.	**Michel**, 45 S.W.3d 658, 678 (F.W. 2001, no pet.).
10	Website allowed customers to make room reservations with D-hotel/casino but did not allow customers to obtain line of credit.	**Riviera Oper.**, 29 S.W.3d 905, 910–11 (Beau. 2000, denied).

(e) Analyzing contacts—attributed actions.

[1] Agents. An agent's contacts can be attributed to its principal. **Olympia Capital Assocs. v. Jackson**, 247 S.W.3d 399, 412 (Tex.App.—Dallas 2008, no pet.); **Walker Ins. v. Bottle Rock Power Corp.**, 108 S.W.3d 538, 549 & n.4 (Tex.App.—Houston [14th Dist.] 2003, no pet.). The plaintiff must show (1) that the principal had the right to control both the means and the details of the agent's work, (2) evidence of actual or apparent authority, or (3) that the principal later ratified the agent's conduct. *See* **Stocksy United v. Morris**, 592 S.W.3d 538, 548 (Tex.App.—Houston [1st Dist.] 2019, no pet.); **Greenfield Energy, Inc. v. Duprey**, 252 S.W.3d 721, 734 (Tex.App.—Houston [14th Dist.] 2008, no pet.). See "Principal-Agent Liability," **O'Connor's Texas Causes of Action**, ch. 38-A, §1 et seq. (2021 ed.).

[2] Corporate subsidiaries. A parent corporation's contacts can be attributed to its subsidiary, or vice versa, if the parent corporation and the subsidiary can be "fused" for jurisdictional purposes (i.e., jurisdictional veil-piercing). *See* **Cornerstone Healthcare Grp. Holding, Inc. v. Nautic Mgmt. VI, L.P.**, 493 S.W.3d 65, 71–72 (Tex.2016); **PHC-Minden, L.P. v. Kimberly-Clark Corp.**, 235 S.W.3d 163, 174–75 (Tex.2007); **Semperit Technische**, 508 S.W.3d at 585. To fuse the parent corporation and its subsidiary, the plaintiff must prove that the parent controls the internal business operations and affairs of the subsidiary. **PHC-Minden**, 235 S.W.3d at 175; **BMC Software**, 83 S.W.3d at 799; *see also* **Cornerstone Healthcare**, 493 S.W.3d at 72–73 (although subsidiaries' contacts could not be attributed to parent corporation, parent corporation's contacts with Texas were "purposeful" because parent corporation directed creation of subsidiaries for purpose of purchasing Texas assets). The degree of control must be greater than is normally associated with common ownership and directorship; the evidence must show that the two entities are no longer separate and distinct and that the corporate identities should be fused to prevent fraud or injustice. **PHC-Minden**, 235 S.W.3d at 175; **BMC Software**, 83 S.W.3d at 799; **TMX Fin. Holdings, Inc. v. Wellshire Fin. Servs.**, 515 S.W.3d 1, 8 (Tex.App.—Houston [1st Dist.] 2016, pet. dism'd).

Note

Although jurisdictional veil-piercing is similar to substantive veil-piercing (i.e., holding an individual or corporate affiliate liable for the acts of a legally separate business entity under an alter-ego theory), the two theories are distinct and involve different elements of proof. See ***PHC-Minden****, 235 S.W.3d at 174–75. See "Piercing the Corporate Veil,"* ***O'Connor's Texas Causes of Action****, ch. 38-F, §1 et seq. (2021 ed.). This distinction exists in part because substantive veil-piercing is governed by statutes and common law but jurisdictional veil-piercing implicates due-process issues. See* ***PHC-Minden****, 235 S.W.3d at 174.*

[3] Corporate officers & employees. A corporation's contacts usually cannot be attributed to its employees. **Nichols v. Tseng Hsiang Lin**, 282 S.W.3d 743, 750 (Tex.App.—Dallas 2009, no pet.). Under the fiduciary-shield doctrine, a court cannot exercise jurisdiction over a nonresident corporate officer or employee if the only contacts with Texas

are those the defendant made on the employer's behalf. **Booth**, 485 S.W.3d at 482; **Garner v. Furmanite Austl. Pty., Ltd.**, 966 S.W.2d 798, 803 (Tex.App.—Houston [1st Dist.] 1998, pet. denied); *see* **Siskind**, 642 S.W.2d at 438; **Stull v. LaPlant**, 411 S.W.3d 129, 134 (Tex.App.—Dallas 2013, no pet.). The corporation's contacts can be considered if the plaintiff shows that (1) the defendant was using the corporate entity as a sham or (2) the corporation is the defendant's alter ego. **Wolf v. Summers-Wood, L.P.**, 214 S.W.3d 783, 790 (Tex.App.—Dallas 2007, no pet.); **J&J Mar., Inc. v. Le**, 982 S.W.2d 918, 927 (Tex.App.—Corpus Christi 1998, no pet.); *see* **Booth**, 485 S.W.3d at 482; **Nichols**, 282 S.W.3d at 750.

(2) Insufficient Texas contacts.

(a) Specific jurisdiction. To negate specific jurisdiction, the defendant should plead and prove that the plaintiff's cause of action did not arise from or relate to the defendant's contacts with Texas. *See* **Cornerstone Healthcare**, 493 S.W.3d at 73–74; **Moncrief Oil**, 414 S.W.3d at 156; **Kelly**, 301 S.W.3d at 659; **Moki Mac**, 221 S.W.3d at 579; **BMC Software**, 83 S.W.3d at 796; **Guardian Royal**, 815 S.W.2d at 227. The "arise from or relate to" requirement means the defendant's contacts must be substantially connected to the operative facts of the litigation. **M&F Worldwide**, 512 S.W.3d at 890; **Cornerstone Healthcare**, 493 S.W.3d at 74; **Spir Star**, 310 S.W.3d at 874; *see* **Bristol-Myers Squibb Co. v. Superior Ct.**, ___ U.S. ___, 137 S.Ct. 1773, 1780 (2017) (must be an activity or occurrence that takes place in forum state and is therefore subject to forum state's regulation); **Daimler AG v. Bauman**, 571 U.S. 117, 122 (2014) (specific jurisdiction is "conduct-linked"); **Guardian Royal**, 815 S.W.2d at 228 (focus is on relationship among D, forum, and litigation). If the defendant's contacts are not substantially connected to the operative facts of the litigation, the court cannot exercise specific jurisdiction, regardless of the extent of the defendant's unconnected activities in Texas. *See* **Bristol-Myers Squibb**, ___ U.S. at ___, 137 S.Ct. at 1781; *see, e.g.*, **Moki Mac**, 221 S.W.3d at 585 (although nonresident D purposefully availed itself of Texas forum by advertising and soliciting customers for out-of-state rafting trips, contacts did not substantially relate to P's suit, which was for negligence based on personal injury in Arizona). If a plaintiff brought multiple claims arising from different forum contacts of the defendant and alleged specific jurisdiction for each of those claims, the defendant must negate specific jurisdiction for each claim. *See* **M&F Worldwide**, 512 S.W.3d at 886 (courts must analyze jurisdiction on claim-by-claim basis unless all claims arise from same contacts); **Moncrief Oil**, 414 S.W.3d at 150–51 (same). Whether contacts are sufficient to establish specific jurisdiction is determined on a case-by-case basis. See chart 3-3, below, for examples.

3-3. Specific Jurisdiction

	Facts	Case
	Sufficient contacts	
1	Ds invested in Texas subsidiary created for purpose of purchasing chain of Texas hospitals.	**Cornerstone Healthcare**, 493 S.W.3d 65, 67 (Tex.2016).
2	Ds entered Texas to promote television broadcasts, derived substantial revenue by selling advertising time to Texas businesses, and made efforts to distribute programs and increase their popularity in Texas.	**TV Azteca**, 490 S.W.3d 29, 52 (Tex.2016).
3	Ds attended two meetings in Texas at which they accepted alleged trade secrets from P relating to proposed joint venture in Texas.	**Moncrief Oil**, 414 S.W.3d 142, 154 (Tex.2013).
4	D marketed products to Texas customers and sold them through its Texas distributor.	**Spir Star AG**, 310 S.W.3d 868, 874 (Tex.2010).
5	D received transfer of Texas oil and gas interests that were already subject of suit between two Texas companies.	**Retamco Oper.**, 278 S.W.3d 333, 341 (Tex.2009).
6	Joint venture between Florida and Texas companies, in which both shared control, contracted for elevators to be delivered to Texas.	**Zac Smith & Co.**, 734 S.W.2d 662, 664–65 (Tex.1987).
7	D had sales office in Texas and annual sales of $40–48 million worth of steel that reached Texas.	**Kawasaki Steel**, 699 S.W.2d 199, 201 (Tex.1985).
8	D-attorney applied for pro hac vice admission to Texas court, recruited Texas law firm to serve as local counsel and supervised its work, and drafted documents and filed them with Texas court.	**Nawracaj**, 524 S.W.3d 746, 754–55 (Hous. [14th] 2017, no pet.).

3-3. Specific Jurisdiction		
	Facts	Case
9	D purchased puppy located in Texas and traveled to Texas twice for training, observation, and receipt of puppy.	**Fleischer**, 270 S.W.3d 334, 338 (Dal. 2008, no pet.).
10	D purchased promissory notes executed by Texas residents, with knowledge that notes were subject of Texas litigation.	**Kelly Inv.**, 85 S.W.3d 371, 375–76 (Dal. 2002, no pet.).
11	Over five-year period, D audited Texas firm managed entirely in San Antonio, which later was subject of securities-fraud class action.	**Gutierrez**, 100 S.W.3d 261, 272–73 (S.A. 2002, dism'd).
12	D-sales agent contracted with Texas corporation, sent orders to Texas, received payments from Texas, and cashed checks drawn on Texas bank.	**Billingsley Parts**, 881 S.W.2d 165, 169–70 (Hous. [1st] 1994, denied).
Insufficient contacts		
13	P alleged that D participated in fraudulent-transfer scheme based on hundreds of phone calls that D had with friend who was Texas resident, series of loans that D made to friend, and proceeds from sale of friend's Texas residence that D accepted.	**Old Republic Nat'l Title**, 549 S.W.3d 550, 556–57 (Tex.2018).
14	P alleged that Ds negotiated tortious business plan in Texas based on two meetings in Texas and then developed plan through communications sent to Texas; transactions giving rise to alleged torts did not take place in Texas, and P never alleged that any torts were committed against Texas residents.	**M&F Worldwide**, 512 S.W.3d 878, 890 (Tex.2017).
15	D purchased shares that formed basis of tortious-interference claim from company that had operations in Texas, but D did not specifically seek out a Texas seller or Texas assets and did not seek to launch operations in Texas; seller's Texas presence was coincidental.	**Searcy**, 496 S.W.3d 58, 73–74 (Tex.2016).
16	P alleged that Ds' meeting with third party in California and Ds' establishment of competing enterprise in Texas constituted tortious interference with P's agreement with third party.	**Moncrief Oil**, 414 S.W.3d at 156–57.
17	D used third-party trucking service to transport goods through Texas to out-of-state customer.	**Zinc Nacional**, 308 S.W.3d 395, 397–98 (Tex.2010).
18	P bought RV from D-factory outlet located in Indiana; RV was constructed, equipped, and paid for outside Texas and was shipped by D to Texas at P's request and expense.	**Michiana**, 168 S.W.3d 777, 787–88 (Tex.2005).
19	D sent employees to Texas to attend corporate meetings during its purchase of insurance company headquartered in Texas.	**Commonwealth Gen.**, 177 S.W.3d 923, 925 (Tex.2005).
20	Officers of wholly owned Belgian subsidiary of Texas company had conversation in Texas about whether to offer employment and stock options to P, who was not present.	**BMC Software**, 83 S.W.3d 789, 796–97 (Tex.2002).
21	Foreign manufacturer knew product would be shipped to Texas but did not design product for use in Texas or market it there.	**CMMC**, 929 S.W.2d 435, 439 (Tex.1996).
22	P alleged conspiracy between D-Maryland organization and Texas corporation.	**National Indus.**, 897 S.W.2d 769, 774–76 (Tex.1995).
23	D-foreign reinsurer contracted with foreign primary insurer to pay primary insurer for claims paid to its insureds, some of whom lived in Texas.	**Malaysia British Assur.**, 830 S.W.2d 919, 921 (Tex.1992).

3-3. Specific Jurisdiction		
	Facts	**Case**
24	Ds previously represented nationwide class in suit filed in Illinois against Texas company; Texas residents made up 9% of class.	**National Fire**, 429 S.W.3d 806, 814 (Dal. 2014, no pet.).
25	D who was in auto accident in Virginia had no association with Texas other than fact that truck he drove was owned by Texas company and licensed in Texas.	**Jones**, 400 S.W.3d 684, 688 (Dal. 2013, no pet.).
26	D-doctor performed surgery on P in Michigan and prescribed follow-up care to take place at health-care facility in Texas.	**Brocail**, 132 S.W.3d 552, 562–63 & n.5 (Hous. [14th] 2004, denied).
27	D initiated and entered into contract with Texas corporation; contract was to be performed entirely outside Texas, and payments were forwarded to Texas.	**Blair Comm.**, 80 S.W.3d 723, 730 (Hous. [1st] 2002, no pet.).
28	One of Ps traveled to Texas for reasons unrelated to suit and made one telephone call to Ds' agent to confirm transaction.	**Al-Turki**, 958 S.W.2d 258, 262 (East. 1997, denied).

(b) General jurisdiction. Traditionally, to negate general jurisdiction, a defendant had to prove that it did not have continuous or systematic contacts with Texas. *See* **BMC Software**, 83 S.W.3d at 797. This standard required that all the defendant's contacts with Texas be carefully investigated, compiled, sorted, and analyzed for proof of a pattern of continuing and systematic activity—a more demanding minimum-contacts analysis than for specific jurisdiction. *See* **Spir Star**, 310 S.W.3d at 873; **American Type Culture**, 83 S.W.3d at 809; **BMC Software**, 83 S.W.3d at 797. In **Daimler AG**, however, the U.S. Supreme Court shifted the focus of the general-jurisdiction inquiry from whether a defendant has substantial "continuous and systematic" contacts with the forum state to whether a defendant's affiliations are so continuous and systematic as to render it essentially "at home" in the forum state. **Daimler AG**, 571 U.S. at 138–39 & n.20. See "General jurisdiction," **O'Connor's Federal Rules * Civil Trials**, ch. 3-B, §2.3.2(1)(b)[2] (2021 ed.). Thus, to negate general jurisdiction under **Daimler**, the defendant should plead and prove that its affiliations do not render it "at home" in Texas. *See* **Daimler AG**, 571 U.S. at 138–39; **Searcy**, 496 S.W.3d at 72; **Booth**, 485 S.W.3d at 478; **Bautista v. Trinidad Drilling Ltd.**, 484 S.W.3d 491, 499 (Tex.App.—Houston [1st Dist.] 2016, no pet.). The defendant's specific arguments depend on whether it is a corporate defendant or an individual defendant.

[1] Corporate defendants. A corporate defendant is considered "at home" where it is incorporated or where it has its principal place of business. *See* **BNSF Ry. v. Tyrrell**, __ U.S. __, 137 S.Ct. 1549, 1558 (2017); **Daimler AG**, 571 U.S. at 137; **Searcy**, 496 S.W.3d at 72; **Bautista**, 484 S.W.3d at 500; **In re Deutsche Bank Secs. Inc.**, No. 03-14-00744-CV, 2015 WL 4079280 (Tex.App.—Austin 2015, orig. proceeding) (memo op.; 7-3-15). A corporate defendant will be subject to general jurisdiction in a forum other than its place of incorporation or principal place of business only in exceptional cases in which its contacts with that forum are so substantial as to render it "at home" there. **BNSF Ry.**, __ U.S. at __, 137 S.Ct. at 1558; **Searcy**, 496 S.W.3d at 72; *see* **Daimler AG**, 571 U.S. at 139 n.19 (suggesting that cases such as **Perkins v. Benguet Consol. Mining Co.**, 342 U.S. 437 (1952), in which the Court found Ohio courts had general jurisdiction over D that was incorporated in the Philippines but temporarily moved its principal place of business to Ohio because of World War II, would qualify as "exceptional"); **Booth**, 485 S.W.3d at 479–80 (facts in **Perkins** illustrate type of continuous and systematic contacts by nonresident D that would suffice for general jurisdiction); *see, e.g.*, **In re Deutsche Bank Secs.**, No. 03-14-00744-CV, 2015 WL 4079280 (memo op.) (trial court abused its discretion by granting P's motion to compel jurisdictional discovery because request did not seek information (1) about whether D temporarily or permanently moved business operations to Texas or (2) that might otherwise establish exceptional case). Thus, to negate general jurisdiction, a corporate defendant should argue that it is not incorporated in Texas, that it does not have its principal place of business in Texas, and that this is not an exceptional case in which the defendant's contacts are so substantial as to render it "at home" in Texas.

[2] Individual defendants. An individual defendant is considered "at home" where she is domiciled. *See* **Daimler AG**, 571 U.S. at 137; *see, e.g.*, **Henkel v. Emjo Invs.**, 480 S.W.3d 1, 5–6 (Tex.App.—Houston [1st Dist.] 2015, no pet.) (parties agreed court did not have general jurisdiction because D was not domiciled or "at home" in Texas; court confined its analysis to specific jurisdiction). Thus, to negate general jurisdiction, an individual defendant should argue that

she is not domiciled in Texas.

Note

There is federal authority stating there may be exceptional cases in which an individual defendant will be considered "at home" in a forum outside of her domicile. ***Reich v. Lopez****, 858 F.3d 55, 63 (2d Cir.2017); see* ***Robatech Midwest, Inc. v. Leuthner****, No. 14-CV-1230-JPS, 2015 WL 1219642 (E.D.Wis.2015) (slip op.; 3-17-15). Texas authority, however, has been less clear on the issue. See, e.g.,* ***Loya v. Taylor****, No. 01-14-01014-CV, 2016 WL 6962312 (Tex.App.—Houston [1st Dist.] 2016, pet. denied) (memo op.; 11-29-16) (D, who was domiciled in England, argued—and court agreed—that D's contacts with Texas were not continuous and systematic enough to render him at home there); see also* ***Booth****, 485 S.W.3d at 479 n.8 (declining to address issue but questioning whether an individual's continuous and systematic contacts can be basis for general jurisdiction).*

3. Exercise of jurisdiction unfair. The defendant should state that the court's exercise of jurisdiction over the defendant and its property would offend traditional notions of fair play and substantial justice and would be inconsistent with the constitutional requirements of due process. **International Shoe Co. v. Washington**, 326 U.S. 310, 316 (1945); *see* **Moncrief Oil**, 414 S.W.3d at 154; **Spir Star**, 310 S.W.3d at 878–79; **Guardian Royal**, 815 S.W.2d at 231. The exercise of jurisdiction will rarely be deemed unfair when the defendant has established minimum contacts with the state. **TV Azteca**, 490 S.W.3d at 55; **Moncrief Oil**, 414 S.W.3d at 154–55; **Spir Star**, 310 S.W.3d at 878; **Guardian Royal**, 815 S.W.2d at 231.

Note

In ***Daimler****, the U.S. Supreme Court suggested that the "fair play and substantial justice" analysis is not required in cases involving general jurisdiction. See* ***Daimler AG****, 571 U.S. at 139 n.20. However, no Texas court has specifically addressed this issue.*

(1) U.S. defendant. If the defendant is a resident of the United States, the defendant should allege that the exercise of jurisdiction by the Texas court over the defendant would be unfair, considering the following factors:

(a) The burden on the defendant. **Guardian Royal**, 815 S.W.2d at 231; **Schexnayder**, 187 S.W.3d at 246; *e.g.*, **Small v. Small**, 216 S.W.3d 872, 879–80 (Tex.App.—Beaumont 2007, pet. denied) (D's status as graduate student at university in Virginia was insufficient to establish undue burden).

(b) The interest of Texas in adjudicating the dispute. **Guardian Royal**, 815 S.W.2d at 231; **Schexnayder**, 187 S.W.3d at 246.

(c) The plaintiff's interest in obtaining convenient and effective relief. **Guardian Royal**, 815 S.W.2d at 231; **Schexnayder**, 187 S.W.3d at 246.

(d) The interstate judicial system's interest in obtaining the most efficient resolution of controversies. **Guardian Royal**, 815 S.W.2d at 231; **Schexnayder**, 187 S.W.3d at 246.

(e) The shared interest of the states in furthering fundamental and substantive social policies. **Guardian Royal**, 815 S.W.2d at 231; **Schexnayder**, 187 S.W.3d at 246.

(2) Foreign defendant. If the defendant is a resident of a foreign country, the defendant should allege that the exercise of jurisdiction by the Texas court over the defendant would be unfair, considering the following factors:

(a) The burden on the defendant. **Moncrief Oil**, 414 S.W.3d at 155; **Spir Star**, 310 S.W.3d at 878; **Guardian Royal**, 815 S.W.2d at 232.

(b) The interest of Texas in adjudicating the dispute. **TV Azteca**, 490 S.W.3d at 55; **Moncrief Oil**, 414 S.W.3d at 155; **Spir Star**, 310 S.W.3d at 878; **Guardian Royal**, 815 S.W.2d at 232.

(c) The plaintiff's interest in obtaining convenient and effective relief. **Moncrief Oil**, 414 S.W.3d at 155; **Spir Star**, 310 S.W.3d at 878; **Guardian Royal**, 815 S.W.2d at 232.

(d) The international interest in obtaining the most efficient resolution of controversies. **TV Azteca**, 490 S.W.3d at 55–56; **Moncrief Oil**, 414 S.W.3d at 155; **Spir Star**, 310 S.W.3d at 878 & n.3.

(e) The shared interest of the nations in furthering fundamental and substantive social policies. **Moncrief Oil**, 414 S.W.3d at 155; **Spir Star**, 310 S.W.3d at 878.

§2.5 Verification. The special appearance must be verified—that is, made by sworn motion. Tex. R. Civ. P. 120a(1); **Exito Elecs. Co. v. Trejo**, 142 S.W.3d 302, 307 (Tex.2004); **Siemens AG v. Houston Cas. Co.**, 127 S.W.3d 436, 439 (Tex.App.—Dallas 2004, pet. dism'd); **International Turbine Serv. v. Lovitt**, 881 S.W.2d 805, 808 (Tex.App.—Fort Worth 1994, writ denied). The motion cannot be verified based on information and belief. *See* **International Turbine**, 881 S.W.2d at 808. An unverified special appearance can be amended to cure the defect, even after the trial court has ruled on the special appearance, as long as the amendment is filed before the defendant enters a general appearance. **Dawson-Austin v. Austin**, 968 S.W.2d 319, 322 (Tex.1998); *see* **Exito Elecs.**, 142 S.W.3d at 307 (unverified special appearance does not concede jurisdiction). See "Amending special appearance," ch. 3-B, §2.8. If the plaintiff does not object to an unverified special appearance, and sworn proof is presented at the hearing, the issue is tried by consent. **General Refractories Co. v. Martin**, 8 S.W.3d 818, 820 n.1 (Tex.App.—Beaumont 2000, pet. denied). If the special-appearance motion is not verified, and no sworn proof attests to the truth of the statements in the motion (either by affidavit or at the hearing), the court should deny the motion. *See* **Casino Magic Corp. v. King**, 43 S.W.3d 14, 18 (Tex.App.—Dallas 2001, pet. denied).

§2.6 Evidence. The defendant should file affidavits with the special appearance that provide evidentiary support for the factual allegations. See "Evidence," ch. 3-B, §9.3.

§2.7 Requesting hearing. The defendant must ask for and secure a hearing. **Milacron Inc. v. Performance Rail Tie, L.P.**, 262 S.W.3d 872, 876 (Tex.App.—Texarkana 2008, no pet.); **Bruneio v. Bruneio**, 890 S.W.2d 150, 154 (Tex.App.—Corpus Christi 1994, no writ). See "Evidentiary," ch. 3-B, §9.1.1. If the defendant does not secure a hearing, it waives the special appearance and effectively makes a general appearance. *See* **Bruneio**, 890 S.W.2d at 154. See "General appearance," ch. 3-B, §3.4.

§2.8 Amending special appearance. The defendant can amend a special appearance. Tex. R. Civ. P. 120a(1); *e.g.*, **Dawson-Austin v. Austin**, 968 S.W.2d 319, 322 (Tex.1998) (amendment to add verification permitted after hearing but before entering a general appearance); **Zamarron v. Shinko Wire Co.**, 125 S.W.3d 132, 139 (Tex.App.—Houston [14th Dist.] 2003, pet. denied) (D did not waive special appearance by submitting amended affidavit).

§3. Waiver

A defendant can waive objections to personal jurisdiction in Texas. *See* **RSR Corp. v. Siegmund**, 309 S.W.3d 686, 704 (Tex.App.—Dallas 2010, no pet.). Under such circumstances, the court's exercise of personal jurisdiction does not violate due process even without proof of minimum contacts. *See id.*

§3.1 Contractual consent. A defendant expressly consents to and waives its objection to personal jurisdiction if it executes a contract with a valid forum-selection clause submitting itself to the jurisdiction of the Texas courts. *See* **RSR Corp. v. Siegmund**, 309 S.W.3d 686, 704 (Tex.App.—Dallas 2010, no pet.); *see also* **Vak v. Net Matrix Solutions, Inc.**, 442 S.W.3d 553, 560 (Tex.App.—Houston [1st Dist.] 2014, no pet.) (agreed-on clause providing for exclusive venue in particular county can be treated as forum-selection clause; because agreement provided for exclusive venue in Harris County, trial court did not err in denying D's special appearance). See "Forum-selection clause," ch. 3-D, §6.

§3.2 No due order of pleading. A defendant waives its objection to personal jurisdiction if it files any other pleading before its special appearance. See "Due order of pleading," ch. 3-A, §3.

§3.3 No due order of hearings. A defendant waives its objection to personal jurisdiction if it obtains a hearing on a motion that seeks affirmative relief unrelated to the special appearance before it obtains a hearing and ruling on the special appearance. See "Due order of hearings," ch. 3-B, §2.3.

§3.4 General appearance. A defendant waives its objection to personal jurisdiction if it makes a general appearance. **Von Briesen, Purtell & Roper, S.C. v. French**, 78 S.W.3d 570, 575 (Tex.App.—Amarillo 2002, pet. dism'd); *see* **Global**

Paragon Dallas, LLC v. SBM Rlty., LLC, 448 S.W.3d 607, 611 (Tex.App.—Houston [14th Dist.] 2014, no pet.). Every appearance before judgment that does not comply with TRCP 120a is a general appearance. Tex. R. Civ. P. 120a(1); **Exito Elecs. Co. v. Trejo**, 142 S.W.3d 302, 304 (Tex.2004). A party makes a general appearance when it (1) invokes the trial court's judgment on any question other than the court's jurisdiction, (2) recognizes by its acts that an action is properly pending, or (3) seeks affirmative action from the court. **Exito Elecs.**, 142 S.W.3d at 304; **Dawson-Austin v. Austin**, 968 S.W.2d 319, 322 (Tex.1998); **Global Paragon Dallas**, 448 S.W.3d at 611.

Note

It may be possible for a defendant to make a general appearance after final judgment has been entered. See, e.g., ***Composite Cooling Solutions, L.P. v. Larrabee Air Conditioning, Inc.****, No. 02-17-00006-CV, 2017 WL 2979918 (Tex.App.—Fort Worth 2017, no pet.) (memo op.; 7-13-17) (D made general appearance when it filed and argued motion for attorney fees under Declaratory Judgments Act after special appearance was sustained and final judgment was entered); see also* ***Kaminetzky v. Newman****, No. 01-10-01113-CV, 2011 WL 6938536 (Tex.App.—Houston [1st Dist.] 2011, no pet.) (memo op.; 12-29-11) (TRCP 120a does not foreclose possibility that general appearance can be made after judgment is entered). If a defendant makes a general appearance after final judgment, the appearance has the effect of being a general appearance for all matters from that point on; it will not apply retroactively to validate a judgment entered when the court did not have personal jurisdiction over the defendant. See, e.g.,* ***Kaminetzky****, No. 01-10-01113-CV, 2011 WL 6938536 (memo op.) (default judgment based on defective service of citation was not validated by D's general appearance made after rendition of judgment).*

§3.5 No waiver.

1. Actions before filing special appearance. The defendant does not make a general appearance (and thus does not waive its objection to personal jurisdiction) if it takes the following actions before filing the special appearance:

(1) Notice of removal. The defendant can file a notice of removal to federal court before the special appearance without waiving the special appearance. **Antonio v. Rico Marino, S.A.**, 910 S.W.2d 624, 629 (Tex.App.—Houston [14th Dist.] 1995, no writ).

(2) Correspondence with court. Under certain circumstances, the defendant can correspond with the court without waiving the special appearance. See "Discovery," ch. 3-B, §7.

(3) Rule 11 agreement. A Rule 11 agreement that extends the time for the defendant to file its initial pleading in response to the plaintiff's petition is not a general appearance, even if the agreement is not expressly made subject to the ruling on the special appearance. **Exito Elecs. Co. v. Trejo**, 142 S.W.3d 302, 306 (Tex.2004); *see, e.g.*, **Crystalix Grp. Int'l v. Vitro Laser Grp. USA, Inc.**, 127 S.W.3d 425, 428 (Tex.App.—Dallas 2004, pet. denied) (Rule 11 agreement to extend TRO did not alter material components of TRO and was not general appearance); **Angelou v. African Overseas Un.**, 33 S.W.3d 269, 275–76 (Tex.App.—Houston [14th Dist.] 2000, no pet.) (Rule 11 agreement to extend answer date filed before special appearance was not general appearance because agreement did not seek affirmative action from court or recognize action as properly pending). A Rule 11 agreement is not by itself a request for enforcement or for any other affirmative action by the court. **Exito Elecs.**, 142 S.W.3d at 305. See "Agreements between attorneys—Rule 11," ch. 1-H, §9; **O'Connor's Texas Civil Forms**, FORM 1H:13 (2020 ed.).

2. Actions after filing special appearance. A defendant does not make a general appearance (and thus does not waive its objection to personal jurisdiction) if it asks for intermediate relief by filing other pleadings and motions after the special appearance, as long as the documents do not acknowledge the trial court's jurisdiction or seek court action that is inconsistent with the assertion that the court lacks jurisdiction. *See* **Dawson-Austin v. Austin**, 968 S.W.2d 319, 322–23 (Tex.1998) (statement that pleading is "subject to the ruling on the special appearance" is not required to avoid waiver); *see, e.g.*, **GFTA Trendanalysen v. Varme**, 991 S.W.2d 785, 786–87 (Tex.1999) (D did not consent to personal jurisdiction by challenging service in its special appearance); **Yuen v. Fisher**, 227 S.W.3d 193, 199 (Tex.App.—Houston [1st Dist.] 2007, no

pet.) (motion to set aside default judgment, in which D asked for sanctions subject to court's ruling on special appearance, did not waive special appearance). TRCP 120a(1) provides that any pleading or motion can be filed after the special appearance without waiving the special appearance. **Dawson-Austin**, 968 S.W.2d at 322–23. The defendant does not waive its special appearance by filing the following motions or engaging in the following activity:

(1) Motion for continuance. The defendant does not waive its special appearance by filing a motion for continuance. *See* **Dawson-Austin**, 968 S.W.2d at 323. See "Defendant," ch. 3-B, §8.2.

(2) Discovery. The defendant does not waive its special appearance by engaging in discovery related to the special appearance. Tex. R. Civ. P. 120a(1). See "Discovery," ch. 3-B, §7.

(3) Motion to dismiss for baseless cause of action. The defendant does not waive its special appearance by filing a motion to dismiss a cause of action on the ground that it has no basis in law or fact. Tex. R. Civ. P. 91a.8; *see* Tex. R. Civ. P. 91a.1. See "No waiver of special appearance or motion to transfer venue," ch. 3-H, §2.6.1. The defendant submits to the trial court's jurisdiction only in proceedings on the Rule 91a motion. Tex. R. Civ. P. 91a.8.

(4) Motion to dismiss under TCPA. The defendant does not waive its special appearance by filing an anti-SLAPP motion (i.e., a motion to dismiss under the Texas Citizens Participation Act (TCPA)). *See* **Wakefield v. British Med. Journal Publ'g Grp.**, 449 S.W.3d 172, 180 (Tex.App.—Austin 2014, no pet.). See "Motion to Dismiss—Anti-SLAPP Motion," ch. 3-K, §1 et seq.

Note

*The court of appeals in **Wakefield** suggested that a defendant may be able to pursue its rights under the TCPA without waiving its objection to personal jurisdiction. See **Wakefield**, 449 S.W.3d at 180; see also Tex. Civ. Prac. & Rem. Code §27.011(a) (TCPA does not abrogate or lessen any other defense, remedy, or privilege available under other statutory, case, or rule provisions). Even if a defendant's actions under the TCPA could constitute waiver of the special appearance, the court held that no such waiver occurred in the case. See **Wakefield**, 449 S.W.3d at 180–82 (nothing in record indicated that Ds requested continuance on anti-SLAPP hearing, that the hearing was delayed to further the merits of Ds' anti-SLAPP motion, or that Ds' request for briefing schedule required P to respond to anti-SLAPP motion before special-appearance hearing; Ds did not make general appearance).*

(5) Motion for new trial after default judgment. The defendant does not waive its special appearance by filing a motion for new trial with or after a special appearance. See "Special appearance after default judgment," ch. 3-B, §4.

§4. Special appearance after default judgment

If a nonresident defendant discovers that a default judgment was rendered against it before the deadline for filing a motion for new trial, the nonresident defendant can preserve the due order of pleading while challenging the default judgment by filing the documents in the following order: (1) a special appearance, (2) a motion for new trial, and (3) an answer. *See* Tex. R. Civ. P. 120a(1) (special appearance must be filed before any other pleading or motion); *see, e.g.*, **Lang v. Capital Res.**, 102 S.W.3d 861, 864 (Tex.App.—Dallas 2003, no pet.) (D filed special appearance and, subject to that, motion for new trial); **Puri v. Mansukhani**, 973 S.W.2d 701, 706–07 (Tex.App.—Houston [14th Dist.] 1998, no pet.) (same); **Koch Graphics, Inc. v. Avantech, Inc.**, 803 S.W.2d 432, 433 (Tex.App.—Dallas 1991, no writ) (D filed special appearance and, subject to that, motion to quash, motion for new trial, and answer). The defendant must request a ruling on the special appearance before a ruling on any other motion. *E.g.*, **Global Paragon Dallas, LLC v. SBM Rlty., LLC**, 448 S.W.3d 607, 612–13 (Tex.App.—Houston [14th Dist.] 2014, no pet.) (despite motion for new trial stating it was subject to special appearance, D waived special appearance by seeking and obtaining ruling on motion for new trial first); **Landry v. Daigrepont**, 35 S.W.3d 265, 267–68 (Tex.App.—Corpus Christi 2000, no pet.) (D waived special appearance by arguing motion for new trial first). A motion for new trial and a motion to quash service, filed with or after a special appearance, do not waive the special appearance; matters in the same or a later instrument are subject to the special appearance. Tex. R. Civ. P. 120a(1); **Dawson-Austin v. Austin**, 968 S.W.2d 319, 322 (Tex.1998). The defendant may include language in the motion for new trial that it is

ready to proceed to trial without waiving the special appearance as long as the motion does not acknowledge jurisdiction or ask for some action other than dismissal for lack of jurisdiction. *See* **Lang**, 102 S.W.3d at 864; **Puri**, 973 S.W.2d at 706–07.

§5. Response

The plaintiff may file a response challenging the defendant's allegations of lack of personal jurisdiction. See **O'Connor's Texas Civil Forms**, FORM 3B:3 (2020 ed.). The response should be verified and supported with affidavits. The plaintiff may respond to the defendant's special appearance in the following ways:

§5.1 Amend petition. If the defendant filed a bare-bones response and affidavit, alleging simply that it is a nonresident, the plaintiff should review its petition. See "Not Texas resident," ch. 3-B, §2.4.1. If the plaintiff finds that it did not allege any actions in Texas by the defendant, it should amend its pleading to include them. **Kelly v. General Interior Constr., Inc.**, 301 S.W.3d 653, 659 & n.6 (Tex.2010). See "Over nonresident," ch. 2-B, §5.1.2.

§5.2 Object to procedural errors. The plaintiff should object to any procedural errors in the defendant's special appearance. If the plaintiff does not object, it waives the error. *See, e.g.*, **International Turbine Serv. v. Lovitt**, 881 S.W.2d 805, 808 (Tex.App.—Fort Worth 1994, writ denied) (P waived error in inadequate affidavit).

§5.3 Allege waiver by defendant. The plaintiff should watch for any action the defendant takes that is inconsistent with a special appearance and that could be construed as a general appearance. In the response, the plaintiff should allege the defendant waived its special appearance because (as is appropriate to the case) the defendant did not observe the due order of pleading or hearings, the defendant made a general appearance, or the defendant did not limit the special appearance to the issue of personal jurisdiction.

§5.4 Challenge defendant's allegations. The plaintiff should challenge the defendant's factual grounds for denying jurisdiction and the defendant's legal interpretation of the factors that constitute jurisdiction over a nonresident.

1. Minimum contacts. The plaintiff should state that the court has jurisdiction over the defendant because the defendant purposefully established minimum contacts with Texas. **Schlobohm v. Schapiro**, 784 S.W.2d 355, 358 (Tex.1990); *see* **Guardian Royal Exch. Assur., Ltd. v. English China Clays, P.L.C.**, 815 S.W.2d 223, 232 (Tex.1991). In certain situations, the court can analyze the contacts of the defendant's parent corporation, agents, or corporate officers and employees. See "Analyzing contacts—attributed actions," ch. 3-B, §2.4.2(1)(e).

(1) Specific jurisdiction. To establish specific jurisdiction, the plaintiff should plead and prove that its cause of action arose from and relates to the nonresident defendant's contacts with Texas. **Schlobohm**, 784 S.W.2d at 358. See "Specific jurisdiction," ch. 3-B, §2.4.2(2)(a).

(2) General jurisdiction. To establish general jurisdiction, the plaintiff should plead and prove that the nonresident defendant's affiliations with Texas are so continuous and systematic as to render it essentially "at home" in Texas. See "General jurisdiction," ch. 3-B, §2.4.2(2)(b).

2. No issue of fair play. The plaintiff should plead and prove that the court's exercise of jurisdiction over the defendant and its property will not offend traditional notions of fair play and substantial justice and is consistent with the constitutional requirements of due process. *See* **Schlobohm**, 784 S.W.2d at 359. See "Exercise of jurisdiction unfair," ch. 3-B, §2.4.3.

§6. Reply

The defendant can file a reply, supported by evidence, that refutes the allegations in the plaintiff's response. *See* **Booth v. Kontomitras**, 485 S.W.3d 461, 474 (Tex.App.—Beaumont 2016, no pet.); **Bautista v. Trinidad Drilling Ltd.**, 484 S.W.3d 491, 496 (Tex.App.—Houston [1st Dist.] 2016, no pet.).

§7. Discovery

The parties may engage in discovery before the hearing on the special appearance. *See* Tex. R. Civ. P. 120a(1).

§7.1 Discovery related to special appearance. A defendant does not waive its special appearance by engaging in discovery related to the special appearance. **Exito Elecs. Co. v. Trejo**, 142 S.W.3d 302, 306–07 (Tex.2004). The defendant's

participation in the court's resolution of discovery matters related to the special appearance is not a request for affirmative relief or a recognition that the suit is properly pending. *Id.* at 307. Discovery conducted before the special appearance is resolved should be limited to issues related to the special appearance. *See* **In re Doe**, 444 S.W.3d 603, 608 (Tex.2014) (dicta); **Dawson-Austin v. Austin**, 968 S.W.2d 319, 323–24 (Tex.1998) (dicta).

Practice Tip

If a party has conducted discovery on an issue related to the special appearance, a request to conduct additional discovery must specify what additional jurisdictional facts the discovery will provide; otherwise, the discovery will likely be deemed cumulative and the request will be denied. See, e.g., ***Moncrief Oil Int'l v. OAO Gazprom**, 414 S.W.3d 142, 157–58 (Tex.2013) (P's motion to compel additional depositions was denied because P did not show what additional jurisdictional facts the depositions would provide about Texas contacts for tortious-interference claims);* ***In re Miscavige**, 436 S.W.3d 430, 439 (Tex.App.—Austin 2014, orig. proceeding) (P's motion to compel apex deposition was denied because P did not show what additional jurisdictional facts deposition would provide to establish specific or general jurisdiction).*

§7.2 Discovery unrelated to special appearance. Some courts of appeals have held that a defendant does not waive its special appearance by engaging in discovery unrelated to the special appearance, even if the discovery involves the merits of the case. *E.g.*, **Case v. Grammar**, 31 S.W.3d 304, 311 (Tex.App.—San Antonio 2000, no pet.) (nothing in TRCP 120a(1) limits discovery only to matters related to special appearance), *disapproved on other grounds*, **BMC Software Belg., N.V. v. Marchand**, 83 S.W.3d 789 (Tex.2002); **Minucci v. Sogevalor, S.A.**, 14 S.W.3d 790, 801 (Tex.App.—Houston [1st Dist.] 2000, no pet.) (same); *see, e.g.*, **Silbaugh v. Ramirez**, 126 S.W.3d 88, 93 (Tex.App.—Houston [1st Dist.] 2002, no pet.) (filing motions opposing discovery and serving nonjurisdictional discovery on P did not waive special appearance); **Gutierrez v. Deloitte & Touche**, 100 S.W.3d 261, 267–68 (Tex.App.—San Antonio 2002, pet. dism'd) (filing mandamus to challenge discovery order compelling production of allegedly privileged materials did not waive special appearance); *see also* **Wakefield v. British Med. Journal Publ'g Grp.**, 449 S.W.3d 172, 182 (Tex.App.—Austin 2014, no pet.) (although court did not decide if a D could always participate in discovery unrelated to general appearance, no waiver when Ds opposed P's discovery requests on Ds' anti-SLAPP motion and Ds participated only after the court ordered discovery). One appellate court, however, has clarified that even though a defendant does not waive its special appearance by participating in discovery on the merits, the trial court cannot compel merits-related discovery before ruling on the special appearance. *See* **In re Stern**, 321 S.W.3d 828, 839–40 (Tex.App.—Houston [1st Dist.] 2010, orig. proceeding) (other cases stating that TRCP 120a does not limit scope of discovery are in context of waiver, not motions to compel).

§8. Continuance

§8.1 Plaintiff. The court may grant a plaintiff's sworn motion for continuance if the plaintiff cannot present facts by affidavit to respond to the special appearance and needs time to secure affidavits, take depositions, or engage in other discovery. Tex. R. Civ. P. 120a(3). See **O'Connor's Texas Civil Forms**, FORM 3B:5 (2020 ed.).

1. Grounds. The plaintiff should show that (1) the information sought is material to establishing jurisdiction and (2) it acted diligently in trying to obtain the information. **Barron v. Vanier**, 190 S.W.3d 841, 847 (Tex.App.—Fort Worth 2006, no pet.); *see* **Lamar v. Poncon**, 305 S.W.3d 130, 139–40 (Tex.App.—Houston [1st Dist.] 2009, pet. denied).

2. Limited discovery—jurisdictional facts. When the court grants a continuance for the plaintiff to conduct additional discovery, the discovery is limited to the jurisdictional facts necessary to justify the plaintiff's opposition to the special appearance. **In re Stern**, 321 S.W.3d 828, 839 (Tex.App.—Houston [1st Dist.] 2010, orig. proceeding). Discovery irrelevant to the jurisdictional facts is not allowed; that type of discovery is limited to when the court considers whether a defendant waives a special appearance by engaging in discovery. *Id.* at 840. See "Discovery," ch. 3-B, §7.

§8.2 Defendant. A defendant may file a motion for continuance. *See, e.g.*, **Dawson-Austin v. Austin**, 968 S.W.2d 319, 323 (Tex.1998) (when P requested hearing on special appearance, D filed motion for continuance on day of hearing on grounds that she had been given inadequate notice, her counsel had just been hired and was in trial, and discovery was necessary).

1. Grounds. Although TRCP 120a does not identify the contents of a motion for continuance for a hearing on a special appearance, the defendant should probably follow the outline for a continuance based on the need for additional evidence. See "Continuance for additional discovery," ch. 5-D, §8; **O'Connor's Texas Civil Forms**, FORM 5D:1 (2020 ed.).

2. Discovery. When the court grants a continuance for the defendant, discovery should be limited to issues related to the special appearance. See "Discovery," ch. 3-B, §7.

§9. Hearing

§9.1 Type of hearing.

1. Evidentiary. The trial court must resolve a special appearance based on the evidence. *See* Tex. R. Civ. P. 120a(3). The evidence can be received in open court or by written submission. **Michiana Easy Livin' Country, Inc. v. Holten**, 168 S.W.3d 777, 782 (Tex.2005). See "Evidence," ch. 3-B, §9.3.

2. Nonjury. When the trial court holds a hearing in open court on a special appearance, the hearing is not before a jury. *See* **Roquemore v. Roquemore**, 431 S.W.2d 595, 601 (Tex.App.—Corpus Christi 1968, no writ).

§9.2 Defendant's burden.

At the hearing on a special appearance, the nonresident defendant must disprove jurisdiction by negating all alleged grounds for personal jurisdiction. **BMC Software Belg., N.V. v. Marchand**, 83 S.W.3d 789, 793 (Tex.2002); **Kawasaki Steel Corp. v. Middleton**, 699 S.W.2d 199, 203 (Tex.1985). If the defendant does not provide sufficient evidence in support of its special appearance, the court should deny the motion. *See* **Exito Elecs. Co. v. Trejo**, 142 S.W.3d 302, 307–08 (Tex.2004). A defect in the defendant's proof does not waive the special appearance. **Exito Elecs.**, 142 S.W.3d at 308 (issue of defective verification and affidavit relates to merits of appeal of ruling on special appearance; defect in proof is not waiver of issue).

§9.3 Evidence.

TRCP 120a(3) lists the types of proof that are allowed at the hearing on a special appearance.

1. Stipulations. Stipulations must meet the requirements of TRCP 11—they must be in writing and signed by the attorneys or parties and filed with the court, or made in open court and entered in the record. See "Agreements between attorneys—Rule 11," ch. 1-H, §9.

2. Discovery. Discovery submitted to the court at the special-appearance hearing may include depositions, requests for admissions, and information obtained through other discovery processes. *See* Tex. R. Civ. P. 120a(1), (3). See "Forms of discovery," ch. 6-A, §5.

2021 Rule Amendments

In 2020, the Supreme Court approved significant amendments to TRCP 190 and 194. See Tex.Sup.Ct. Order, Misc. Docket No. 20-9153 (eff. Jan. 1, 2021). Under the amendments, a party is now generally required to disclose certain information and material without waiting for a discovery request from the other party and must do so within 30 days after the filing of the first answer or general appearance. See Tex. R. Civ. P. 194.1(a), 194.2(a). See "Required disclosures—Cases filed on or after 1-1-21," ch. 6-E, §3. The amendments also changed the beginning of the discovery period from when suit is filed to when the first initial disclosures are due. See Tex. R. Civ. P. 190.2(b)(1), 190.3(b)(1). See "Discovery periods," ch. 6-A, §8. The deadline for filing a special appearance is the date when the answer is due. See Tex. R. Civ. P. 120a(1). Because the discovery period now begins within 30 days after the filing of the first answer or general appearance, it is unclear what effect, if any, the amendments will have on discovery related to a special-appearance hearing. The amendments apply to cases filed on or after January 1, 2021, except those filed in justice court. Tex.Sup.Ct. Order, Misc. Docket No. 20-9153 (eff. Jan. 1, 2021).

---

3. Oral testimony. The trial court can consider live testimony from witnesses at the hearing. Tex. R. Civ. P. 120a(3).

4. Affidavits. Affidavits and attachments must meet certain requirements. They must be filed and served at least seven days before the hearing on the special appearance. Tex. R. Civ. P. 120a(3); **Potkovick v. Regional Ventures, Inc.**, 904 S.W.2d 846, 850 (Tex.App.—Eastland 1995, no writ). They must be made on personal knowledge, set forth specific facts that would be admissible as evidence, and affirmatively show that the affiant is competent to testify. Tex. R. Civ. P. 120a(3); *see* **S.p.A. Giacomini v. Lamping**, 42 S.W.3d 265, 270 (Tex.App.—Corpus Christi 2001, no pet.); **International Turbine Serv. v. Lovitt**, 881 S.W.2d 805, 808 (Tex.App.—Fort Worth 1994, writ denied). See "Affidavits," ch. 1-B, §3.2.16.

Practice Tip

If you intend to object to any of the statements in an affidavit, you should object before the hearing on the ground that you will not have an opportunity to cross-examine the witness at the hearing. The court may require you to take a deposition of the witness. By objecting before the hearing, you will give the court and the other party notice that you intend to assert your right to cross-examine the witness.

§10. Ruling

After the court rules on a special appearance, it should sign the appropriate order. Tex. R. Civ. P. 120a(4). See **O'Connor's Texas Civil Forms**, FORM 3B:4 (2020 ed.). Without a ruling on the special appearance, the party cannot preserve error for review. **Wilson v. Chemco Chem. Co.**, 711 S.W.2d 265, 266 (Tex.App.—Dallas 1986, no writ).

§10.1 Sustains motion. If the court sustains the special appearance, it will sign an order of dismissal, which is a final and appealable judgment. *See* Tex. Civ. Prac. & Rem. Code §51.014(a)(7); Tex. R. Civ. P. 120a(4). When sustaining the special appearance, the court should not rule on the merits of the claims. *E.g.*, **Nguyen v. Desai**, 132 S.W.3d 115, 117 (Tex.App.—Houston [14th Dist.] 2004, no pet.) (in sustaining special appearance, court erred by ordering that Ps take nothing and by dismissing suit with prejudice). If the court hears other motions and sustains them at the same time it sustains the special appearance, the order should state that the other rulings are made in the alternative. *See, e.g.*, **Antonio v. Rico Marino, S.A.**, 910 S.W.2d 624, 626 (Tex.App.—Houston [14th Dist.] 1995, no writ) (trial court ordered dismissal based on special appearance and forum non conveniens and sustained D's venue challenge). If the order sustains the special appearance and dismisses the suit first, with the other rulings as alternative reasons to dismiss or transfer, the plaintiff is forced to challenge each ruling separately on appeal.

§10.2 Overrules motion. If the court overrules the special appearance, it will sign an order overruling the motion and continue with the trial of the case. Once the court overrules the defendant's special appearance, the defendant's participation in the trial does not waive its objection to jurisdiction. Tex. R. Civ. P. 120a(4); **Equitable Prod. v. Canales-Treviño**, 136 S.W.3d 235, 238 (Tex.App.—San Antonio 2004, pet. denied); **N.H. Helicopters, Inc. v. Brown**, 841 S.W.2d 424, 425 (Tex.App.—Dallas 1992, orig. proceeding).

§10.3 Sanctions. The court may impose sanctions for affidavits that violate TRCP 13 and CPRC chapter 10. *See* Tex. R. Civ. P. 120a(3); *see, e.g.*, **Skepnek v. Mynatt**, 8 S.W.3d 377, 381–82 (Tex.App.—El Paso 1999, pet. denied) (attorney fined $30,000 for filing special appearance that was groundless, presented for improper purposes, and based on false affidavit of corporation's president). See "Motion for Sanctions," ch. 5-K, §1 et seq.

§11. Findings of fact

The party who receives an adverse ruling on the special appearance should request findings of fact. **Goodenbour v. Goodenbour**, 64 S.W.3d 69, 75 (Tex.App.—Austin 2001, pet. denied); *see* Tex. R. Civ. P. 296; *see also* Tex. R. App. P. 28.1(c) (trial court may file findings of fact within 30 days after signing interlocutory order). But the court is not required to file findings of fact on the special appearance. **Niehaus v. Cedar Bridge, Inc.**, 208 S.W.3d 575, 579 n.5 (Tex.App.—Austin 2006, no pet.). See "Jurisdictional challenge," ch. 10-E, §2.2.2(2). When no findings of fact are filed, all facts necessary to support the judgment and supported by the evidence are implied. **M&F Worldwide Corp. v. Pepsi-Cola Metro. Bottling Co.**, 512 S.W.3d 878, 885 (Tex.2017); **TV Azteca, S.A.B. de C.V. v. Ruiz**, 490 S.W.3d 29, 36 n.4 (Tex.2016); **BMC Software Belg., N.V. v. Marchand**, 83 S.W.3d 789, 795 (Tex.2002).

§12. Review

§12.1 Record. If the trial court received evidence in open court, the reporter's record is necessary on appeal. **Michiana Easy Livin' Country, Inc. v. Holten**, 168 S.W.3d 777, 782 (Tex.2005). If nothing indicates the trial court received evidence

in open court, the reporter's record is not necessary. *Id.* On appeal, there is a presumption that no evidence was received in open court at a pretrial hearing. *Id.* at 783. See "Review," ch. 1-E, §8.

§12.2 Standard of review. The issue on appeal is whether the nonresident defendant negated all alleged grounds for personal jurisdiction. **Kawasaki Steel Corp. v. Middleton**, 699 S.W.2d 199, 203 (Tex.1985); **Minucci v. Sogevalor, S.A.**, 14 S.W.3d 790, 794 (Tex.App.—Houston [1st Dist.] 2000, no pet.). Whether the court can exercise personal jurisdiction over a nonresident defendant is a question of law that is reviewed de novo. **Old Republic Nat'l Title Ins. v. Bell**, 549 S.W.3d 550, 558 (Tex.2018); **M&F Worldwide Corp. v. Pepsi-Cola Metro. Bottling Co.**, 512 S.W.3d 878, 885 (Tex.2017); **Moncrief Oil Int'l v. OAO Gazprom**, 414 S.W.3d 142, 150 (Tex.2013). If the trial court issues findings of fact and conclusions of law, the court of appeals should review the trial court's factual findings for legal and factual sufficiency and review the trial court's legal conclusions de novo. **American Type Culture Collection, Inc. v. Coleman**, 83 S.W.3d 801, 806 (Tex.2002); **BMC Software Belg., N.V. v. Marchand**, 83 S.W.3d 789, 794 (Tex.2002).

§12.3 Interlocutory appeal.

1. Appeal. An order granting or denying a special appearance may be appealed immediately (except in a suit brought under the Family Code). Tex. Civ. Prac. & Rem. Code §51.014(a)(7); *see* **TV Azteca, S.A.B. de C.V. v. Ruiz**, 490 S.W.3d 29, 35 (Tex.2016); **In re E.I. du Pont de Nemours & Co.**, 92 S.W.3d 517, 521 (Tex.2002). See "Special appearance," **O'Connor's Texas Civil Appeals**, ch. 1-B, §2.4.1(6) (2020 ed.). Because interlocutory appeals are accelerated, the appellant must file a notice of appeal within 20 days after the trial court signs the order. *See* Tex. R. App. P. 26.1(b), 28.1(a). Filing a motion for new trial or any other post-trial motion or a request for findings of fact does not extend the time to perfect the appeal. Tex. R. App. P. 28.1(b). See "Generally," **O'Connor's Texas Civil Appeals**, ch. 5-A, §5.2.2(1) (2020 ed.).

2. Stay of trial. The interlocutory appeal of an order granting a special appearance automatically stays the commencement of trial during the appeal. *See* Tex. Civ. Prac. & Rem. Code §51.014(b). The interlocutory appeal of an order denying a special appearance, however, does not automatically stay the commencement of trial during the appeal; it will stay the commencement of trial only if the defendant timely filed and requested the special appearance for submission or hearing by the deadline in CPRC §51.014(c). See "Orders resulting in automatic stay after motion denied & deadlines met," **O'Connor's Texas Civil Appeals**, ch. 3-P, §3.1.2 (2020 ed.).

§12.4 Mandamus.

1. Family Code cases. Mandamus is the appropriate method for challenging the trial court's ruling on a special appearance in cases involving child-custody and child-support disputes because of the special interests involved and the unavailability of interlocutory appeal from those orders. **In re Barnes**, 127 S.W.3d 843, 846 (Tex.App.—San Antonio 2003, orig. proceeding) (child-custody suit); **In re Cannon**, 993 S.W.2d 354, 355 (Tex.App.—San Antonio 1999, orig. proceeding) (proceeding to enforce child support); *see also* Tex. Civ. Prac. & Rem. Code §51.014(a)(7) (order granting or denying special appearance is appealable except in suit brought under Family Code); *cf.* **Proffer v. Yates**, 734 S.W.2d 671, 672 (Tex.1987) (mandamus appropriate to review mandatory venue transfer in Family Code case).

2. Other cases. Mandamus is not an appropriate method for challenging orders granting or denying a special appearance in most other cases because those orders can be appealed immediately. *See* Tex. Civ. Prac. & Rem. Code §51.014(a)(7); **Raymond Overseas Holding, Ltd. v. Curry**, 955 S.W.2d 470, 471 (Tex.App.—Fort Worth 1997, orig. proceeding). See "Interlocutory appeal," ch. 3-B, §12.3.

C. Motion to Transfer—Challenging Venue

§1. General

§1.1 Rules. Tex. R. Civ. P. 85 to 89, 255, 257 to 259, 261. See Tex. Const. art. 3, §45; Tex. Civ. Prac. & Rem. Code ch. 15.

§1.2 Purpose. A motion to transfer venue is the procedure for transferring a case to another county in Texas. There are three types of motions to transfer: (1) improper county or convenience of the parties and witnesses, (2) local prejudice, and (3) consent of the parties. Only the defendant can file the first type; either the plaintiff or the defendant can file the second and third types. *See* **Tenneco, Inc. v. Salyer**, 739 S.W.2d 448, 449 (Tex.App.—Corpus Christi 1987, orig. proceeding). For the rules governing venue selection, see "Choosing the Court—Venue," ch. 2-H, §1 et seq.

Note

For a discussion of transferring a case to a jurisdiction outside of Texas, see "Forum Non Conveniens—Challenging the Texas Forum," ch. 3-D, §1 et seq.

§1.3 Timetables & forms. Appendix IV, Timetable 2, Motion to transfer venue—Wrong or inconvenient county; Appendix IV, Timetable 3, Motion to change venue—Local prejudice; **O'Connor's Texas Civil Forms**, FORMS 3C:1 et seq. (2020 ed.).

§1.4 Other references. **O'Connor's Texas Civil Appeals** (2020 ed.); **O'Connor's Texas Family Law Handbook** (2021 ed.).

§2. Improper county or convenience

Venue selection assumes that the parties to the suit have choices and preferences about where the case will be tried. **Wilson v. Texas Parks & Wildlife Dept.**, 886 S.W.2d 259, 260 (Tex.1994). "Proper venue" means venue under the mandatory-venue provisions or, if none apply, under the general venue rule or the permissive-venue provisions. Tex. Civ. Prac. & Rem. Code §15.001(b); **O'Quinn v. Hall**, 77 S.W.3d 438, 448-49 (Tex.App.—Corpus Christi 2002, no pet.).

§2.1 Plaintiff's choice of venue. The plaintiff chooses the venue by filing the suit in a proper county. **In re Team Rocket, L.P.**, 256 S.W.3d 257, 259 (Tex.2008); **In re Masonite Corp.**, 997 S.W.2d 194, 197 (Tex.1999).

§2.2 Defendant's motion to transfer venue. A defendant raises the question of proper venue by challenging the plaintiff's choice through a motion to transfer venue. **Wichita Cty. v. Hart**, 917 S.W.2d 779, 781 (Tex.1996); *see* Tex. R. Civ. P. 86(1). If venue is not proper in the county where the case is pending, the court must, on the defendant's timely filed motion, transfer the case to a county of proper venue. Tex. Civ. Prac. & Rem. Code §15.063(1). Without a motion, the court cannot transfer venue, even to a county of proper venue. **In re Masonite Corp.**, 997 S.W.2d 194, 198 (Tex.1999).

1. Deadline to file. A motion to transfer for improper venue is waived if it is made after any written motion (other than a special appearance) is filed. Tex. R. Civ. P. 86(1). The motion to transfer may be filed concurrently with the answer. Tex. R. Civ. P. 86(2); *see* Tex. Civ. Prac. & Rem. Code §15.063. See "Deadline to answer," ch. 3-E, §2.

2. Due order of pleading. The defendant must file a motion to transfer for improper venue before or along with all other pleadings or motions except the special appearance, which must be filed first. *See* Tex. R. Civ. P. 86(1). See "Due order of pleading," ch. 3-A, §3. The defendant waives its objection to improper venue if it files a motion to transfer after it files an answer. *See* Tex. R. Civ. P. 86(1); **Adame v. State Farm Lloyds**, 506 S.W.3d 96, 100 (Tex.App.—Corpus Christi 2016, pet. denied); **Kshatrya v. Texas Workforce Comm'n**, 97 S.W.3d 825, 832 (Tex.App.—Dallas 2003, no pet.).

Note

Although a motion to dismiss under TRCP 91a is not an exception to the due-order-of-pleading rule, a defendant can file a motion to dismiss without waiving a pending motion to transfer venue. Tex. R. Civ. P. 91a.8. See "No waiver of special appearance or motion to transfer venue," ch. 3-H, §2.6.1

3. Form. The motion to transfer venue must be in writing and may be made either as part of the defendant's first responsive pleading or as a separate document. Tex. R. Civ. P. 86(1), (2). See **O'Connor's Texas Civil Forms**, FORMS 3C:1 to 3C:3 (2020 ed.).

4. No affidavits necessary. The defendant may, but is not required to, support the motion with affidavits when it is filed. Tex. R. Civ. P. 86(3) (last paragraph); **GeoChem Tech v. Verseckes**, 962 S.W.2d 541, 543 (Tex.1998). The question of proper venue is raised by simply objecting to the plaintiff's venue choice through a motion to transfer venue. **Billings v. Concordia Heritage Ass'n**, 960 S.W.2d 688, 692 (Tex.App.—El Paso 1997, pet. denied). But once the plaintiff responds to the motion and denies the defendant's venue facts, the defendant must provide proof as required by TRCP 87(3). *See* Tex. R. Civ. P. 87(2).

5. Request hearing. The defendant must request a hearing, secure a setting for the hearing, and give the plaintiff at least 45 days' notice of the hearing. *See* Tex. R. Civ. P. 87(1); *see, e.g.*, **Carlile v. RLS Legal Solutions, Inc.**, 138 S.W.3d 403, 408 (Tex.App.—Houston [14th Dist.] 2004, no pet.) (14-month delay between filing motion to transfer and securing hearing showed lack of diligence); **Bristol v. Placid Oil Co.**, 74 S.W.3d 156, 159 (Tex.App.—Amarillo 2002, no pet.) (32-month delay between motion to transfer and ruling was not attributable to D because D's motion asked court to set hearing); **Grozier v. L-B Sprinkler & Plumbing Repair**, 744 S.W.2d 306, 311 (Tex.App.—Fort Worth 1988, writ denied) (D waived motion to transfer venue when he did not secure reset of hearing on motion after it was not heard at first setting, did not respond to venue-related discovery, and invoked jurisdiction of court by filing motion for new trial after summary judgment). See "Procedure for hearing," ch. 3-C, §2.11.

6. No codefendant waiver. Although a defendant can waive its own venue rights, it cannot waive the venue rights of a codefendant. No act or omission constituting waiver by one defendant impairs the right of any other defendant to challenge venue. Tex. Civ. Prac. & Rem. Code §15.0641; **WTFO, Inc. v. Braithwaite**, 899 S.W.2d 709, 718 (Tex.App.—Dallas 1995, no writ); *see, e.g.*, **Pearson v. Jones Co.**, 898 S.W.2d 329, 331–32 (Tex.App.—Eastland 1994, no writ) (waiver of venue when D1 and D2 filed answers did not waive D3's venue objection).

§2.3 Defendant's grounds. The defendant should ask the court to transfer the suit to another county for one of the following reasons:

1. Mandatory venue. The defendant should allege that venue is not proper in the county of suit because a mandatory-venue provision requires transfer to another county. *See* Tex. Civ. Prac. & Rem. Code §15.001(b)(1). The defendant must identify the mandatory-venue provision that requires transfer to a specific county. See "Mandatory-venue provisions," ch. 2-H, §4.

2. General venue rule. The defendant should allege that venue is not proper in the county of suit because the general venue rule requires transfer to another county. *See* Tex. Civ. Prac. & Rem. Code §15.002. The defendant must identify the specific part of the statute that was violated when the plaintiff filed suit and the specific county where the suit should be transferred. See "General venue rule," ch. 2-H, §6.

3. Permissive venue. The defendant should allege that venue is not proper in the county of suit, no mandatory provision applies, and venue is permissive in another county. The defendant must state why the plaintiff's choice of venue is not proper and identify the permissive-venue provision that permits transfer to a specific county. See "Permissive-venue provisions," ch. 2-H, §5.

4. Improper venue for some plaintiffs. In a suit with multiple plaintiffs, the defendant can challenge venue for one plaintiff without challenging it for the others. *See* Tex. Civ. Prac. & Rem. Code §15.003(a) (each P must, independently of every other P, establish proper venue). The defendant should allege that the plaintiff cannot establish proper venue through the usual methods (i.e., a mandatory-venue provision, the general venue rule, or a permissive-venue provision) or through the joinder elements of CPRC §15.003(a)(1) to (4). *See* Tex. Civ. Prac. & Rem. Code §15.003(a). See "Venue or joinder proper in multiple-plaintiff case," ch. 3-C, §2.6.4.

5. Venue convenient elsewhere. The defendant should allege that, although suit was filed in a county of proper venue, the court should transfer the suit to another county of proper venue in the interest of justice and for the convenience

of the parties and witnesses. Tex. Civ. Prac. & Rem. Code §15.002(b). A defendant may file a motion to transfer venue to another county of proper venue based on convenience whenever venue is not controlled by a mandatory-venue provision. *See id.* A defendant should include a request for a convenience transfer in every venue motion because a ruling granting (or denying) a convenience transfer is not subject to review. *See* Tex. Civ. Prac. & Rem. Code §15.002(c). See "No appeal of convenience transfer," ch. 3-C, §5.1.

(1) Allegations. The defendant should show that the parties and witnesses will be inconvenienced by maintaining the suit in the county where suit was filed and that transfer is proper by alleging the following:

(a) Hardship on defendant. Maintaining the suit in the original county will impose an economic and personal hardship on the defendant. Tex. Civ. Prac. & Rem. Code §15.002(b)(1). The defendant should state why litigation in the other county will not impose a hardship.

(b) Balance of interests. The balance of all the parties' interests weighs in favor of the suit being brought in the other county. Tex. Civ. Prac. & Rem. Code §15.002(b)(2). The defendant should list the factors that favor the other county.

(c) No hardship on other party. The transfer will not impose an injustice on any other party. Tex. Civ. Prac. & Rem. Code §15.002(b)(3). The defendant should state why the transfer would not impose an injustice on the plaintiff or any other party.

(d) Proper county. The original county is not a county of mandatory venue, and the other county is a county of proper venue. *See* Tex. Civ. Prac. & Rem. Code §15.002(b).

(2) Affidavits. The defendant should support all its factual allegations with affidavits or other properly authenticated proof. *See* Tex. R. Civ. P. 87(3)(a). The general rule is that a defendant is not required to support a motion to transfer with affidavits when it is filed. See "No affidavits necessary," ch. 3-C, §2.2.4. But because a motion to transfer for convenience is based on facts outside the plaintiff's petition, the defendant is probably required to file proof with its motion.

§2.4 Defendant's other allegations.

1. Deny plaintiff's venue facts. The defendant must specifically deny the venue facts in the plaintiff's petition, or else they are accepted as true. Tex. R. Civ. P. 87(3)(a). A specific denial requires more than just the words "we specifically deny." See "Denial of venue facts," ch. 3-C, §2.11.4(1).

2. Allege specific county. The motion to transfer venue must ask the court to transfer the case to a specific county and provide facts showing why venue is proper in that county. *See* Tex. R. Civ. P. 86(3). See "Prima facie proof," ch. 3-C, §2.11.4(2). Nothing in the venue rule or the CPRC prevents a defendant from alleging that two or more counties are counties of proper venue. *See* **GeoChem Tech v. Verseckes**, 962 S.W.2d 541, 543–44 (Tex.1998); **Rosales v. H.E. Butt Grocery Co.**, 905 S.W.2d 745, 748 (Tex.App.—San Antonio 1995, writ denied). The defendant does not admit that the plaintiff has a valid claim by filing a motion to transfer to the county where the cause of action accrued. Tex. R. Civ. P. 87(2)(b).

3. File motion to sever & transfer.

(1) Multiple plaintiffs. In a suit with multiple plaintiffs, a defendant may file a motion to sever and transfer a claim asserted against it if the claim was brought by a plaintiff who has not established proper venue. *See* Tex. Civ. Prac. & Rem. Code §15.003(a). See "Improper venue for some plaintiffs," ch. 3-C, §2.3.4; **O'Connor's Texas Civil Forms**, FORM 3C:2 (2020 ed.).

(2) Multiple defendants. In a suit with multiple defendants, a defendant may file a motion to sever and transfer a claim asserted against it if severance is proper. *See* Tex. R. Civ. P. 89; *see, e.g.*, **Jones v. Ray**, 886 S.W.2d 817, 823 (Tex.App.—Houston [1st Dist.] 1994, orig. proceeding) (because severance order for multiple Ds was improper, order transferring venue was also improper). Severance is proper if (1) the controversy involves more than one cause of action, (2) the severed cause is one that would be the proper subject of a suit if independently asserted, and (3) the severed and remaining causes are not so intertwined as to involve the same facts and issues. **Guaranty Fed. Sav. Bank v. Horseshoe Oper. Co.**,

793 S.W.2d 652, 658 (Tex.1990); **Jones**, 886 S.W.2d at 820. See "Motion for severance," ch. 5-I, §3.

Practice Tip

If a defendant in a suit with multiple defendants wants to sever and transfer the claims against it, the defendant should use a general motion to sever along with an appropriate motion to transfer. See ***O'Connor's Texas Civil Forms****, FORMS 3C:1 to 3C:3, 5I:1 (2020 ed.).*

4. Request court costs. The defendant should request that the court tax against the plaintiff all costs incurred before the case is transferred. *See* Tex. R. Civ. P. 89.

§2.5 Plaintiff's procedure. The plaintiff is not required to file a response to a motion to transfer unless proof is necessary. Tex. R. Civ. P. 86(4). But as a general rule, the plaintiff should file a response and address the grounds asserted in the defendant's motion. See "Plaintiff's proof," ch. 3-C, §2.7.

1. Deadline to file. The deadline to file a response to the motion to transfer, including any opposing affidavits and attachments, is 30 days before the venue hearing unless the plaintiff gets permission to file it later. Tex. R. Civ. P. 87(1); **Moriarty v. Williams**, 752 S.W.2d 610, 611 (Tex.App.—El Paso 1988, writ denied). See "Continuance," ch. 3-C, §2.10.3.

2. Form. The response to the motion to transfer venue must be in writing. *See* Tex. R. Civ. P. 86(1). See **O'Connor's Texas Civil Forms**, FORMS 3C:5 to 3C:7 (2020 ed.).

3. Affidavits & attachments. The plaintiff must file affidavits and any necessary discovery products to establish prima facie proof of its venue facts once the defendant has specifically denied those facts. The discovery products should be attached to affidavits verifying their authenticity. See "Procedure for securing evidence," ch. 3-C, §2.10.

§2.6 Plaintiff's response to defendant's grounds.

1. Venue not mandatory elsewhere. If the defendant alleged that a mandatory-venue provision requires transfer to another county, the plaintiff should argue that the defendant's county of choice is not a mandatory county for venue. *See* Tex. Civ. Prac. & Rem. Code §15.001(b)(1). *See generally* Tex. Civ. Prac. & Rem. Code §§15.011 to 15.020 (mandatory-venue provisions).

2. Venue proper under general rule. If the defendant alleged that the general venue rule requires a transfer, the plaintiff should argue that its county of choice complies with the general venue rule because (1) a substantial part of the events or omissions occurred in the county, (2) the defendant, a natural person, resided in the county at the time the cause of action accrued, (3) the defendant, a corporation or other organization, has its principal Texas office in the county, or (4) if no other provision in CPRC §15.002(a) applies, the suit is proper in the county because the plaintiff resided there when the cause of action accrued. Tex. Civ. Prac. & Rem. Code §15.002(a); *see, e.g.*, **In re Missouri Pac. R.R.**, 998 S.W.2d 212, 221 (Tex.1999) (Ps did not show D's office in county of suit was a principal office as compared to responsibility and authority exercised by company officials in another Texas county).

3. Venue not permissive elsewhere. If the defendant alleged that venue is not proper in the county of suit and is permissive in another county, the plaintiff should argue that (1) venue is proper and (2) the defendant's county of choice is not a permissive county for venue.

4. Venue or joinder proper in multiple-plaintiff case. If the defendant alleged that venue was improper for one of the plaintiffs, that plaintiff should establish, independently of every other plaintiff, either of the following:

(1) Venue proper. The plaintiff can establish proper venue under the general venue rule, a mandatory-venue provision, or a permissive-venue provision. **O'Quinn v. Hall**, 77 S.W.3d 438, 448–49 (Tex.App.—Corpus Christi 2002, no pet.); *see* Tex. Civ. Prac. & Rem. Code §§15.001(b), 15.003.

(2) Joinder proper. The plaintiff can establish venue by proving the following four elements:

(a) Joinder of the plaintiff or intervention by the plaintiff is proper under the TRCPs. Tex. Civ. Prac. & Rem. Code §15.003(a)(1); *see also* Tex. R. Civ. P. 40 (permissive joinder), Tex. R. Civ. P. 43 (interpleader), Tex. R. Civ. P. 60, 61 (intervention), Tex. R. Civ. P. 174(a) (consolidation). See "Joining Parties or Claims," ch. 5-J, §1 et seq.

(b) Maintaining venue for the plaintiff in the county of suit does not unfairly prejudice another party to the suit. Tex. Civ. Prac. & Rem. Code §15.003(a)(2).

(c) There is an essential need to have the plaintiff's claim tried in the county where the suit is pending. Tex. Civ. Prac. & Rem. Code §15.003(a)(3). The "essential need" requirement means that each plaintiff must demonstrate it is "indispensably necessary" to try its claims in that county; "essential" means that it is "necessary, such that one cannot do without it." **Surgitek v. Abel**, 997 S.W.2d 598, 604 (Tex.1999); *see* **O'Quinn**, 77 S.W.3d at 451; **American Home Prods. v. Burrough**, 998 S.W.2d 696, 699–700 (Tex.App.—Eastland 1999, no pet.); *see, e.g.*, **Sustainable Tex. Oyster Res. Mgmt. v. Hannah Reef, Inc.**, 491 S.W.3d 96, 112 (Tex.App.—Houston [1st Dist.] 2016, pet. denied) (potential for inconsistent judgments showed essential need to have claims tried in county where suit was pending).

(d) The county where the suit is pending is a fair and convenient venue for the plaintiff seeking to join in or maintain venue and for all persons against whom the suit is brought. Tex. Civ. Prac. & Rem. Code §15.003(a)(4).

5. Venue not convenient elsewhere. If the defendant alleged that venue is more convenient in another county, the plaintiff should argue that, in the interest of justice and for the convenience of the parties and witnesses, the suit should be maintained in the county where suit was originally filed. *See* Tex. Civ. Prac. & Rem. Code §15.002(b). The plaintiff should show how the parties and witnesses will be inconvenienced by the move and should identify the witnesses who will probably testify by deposition and thus will not be inconvenienced by maintaining the suit in the original county. In its response, the plaintiff should argue the following:

(1) No hardship on defendant. Maintaining the suit in the original county will not impose an economic or personal hardship on the defendant. Tex. Civ. Prac. & Rem. Code §15.002(b)(1). The plaintiff should include reasons why the suit will be no more inconvenient for the defendant in the original county than in the defendant's county of choice.

(2) Balance of interests. The balance of all the parties' interests weighs in favor of the suit remaining in the original county. Tex. Civ. Prac. & Rem. Code §15.002(b)(2). The plaintiff should list the factors that favor the original county.

(3) Hardship on plaintiff. The transfer to the other county will impose a hardship or injustice on the plaintiff or another party. Tex. Civ. Prac. & Rem. Code §15.002(b)(3). The plaintiff should include specific examples of the hardship or injustice.

(4) Improper county for transfer. The other county is not a county of proper venue. Tex. Civ. Prac. & Rem. Code §15.002(b).

6. Deny defendant's venue facts. When appropriate, the plaintiff should specifically deny the venue facts pleaded by the defendant. Unless the plaintiff specifically denies them, the defendant's venue facts will be accepted as true. Tex. R. Civ. P. 87(3)(a). See "Denial of venue facts," ch. 3-C, §2.11.4(1).

7. Allege waiver. When appropriate, the plaintiff should allege that the defendant waived a transfer of venue (e.g., the defendant waived venue by filing its motion to transfer after filing its answer). See "Due order of pleading," ch. 3-C, §2.2.2.

§2.7 Plaintiff's proof. The plaintiff should support all factual allegations in its response with affidavits or other proof.

1. Proof of denied venue facts. If the defendant specifically denied the plaintiff's venue facts, the plaintiff must make a prima facie case of the facts through affidavits and other authenticated proof. Tex. R. Civ. P. 87(3)(a); **In re Missouri Pac. R.R.**, 998 S.W.2d 212, 216 (Tex.1999); **GeoChem Tech v. Verseckes**, 962 S.W.2d 541, 543 (Tex.1998); *see, e.g.*, **Maranatha Temple, Inc. v. Enterprise Prods.**, 833 S.W.2d 736, 740 (Tex.App.—Houston [1st Dist.] 1992, writ denied) (because Ds did not specifically deny venue facts, P was not required to offer prima facie proof).

2. Proof of joinder elements. In a multiple-plaintiff case, if a plaintiff is unable to independently establish proper venue, that plaintiff is required to establish each of the four joinder elements of CPRC §15.003(a). **Surgitek v. Abel**, 997 S.W.2d 598, 602 (Tex.1999). See "Joinder proper," ch. 3-C, §2.6.4(2).

3. Proof of convenience issues. The plaintiff should support its allegations about the convenience of the forum with sworn proof. See "Venue not convenient elsewhere," ch. 3-C, §2.6.5.

4. No proof of cause of action. The plaintiff is not required to prove the existence of a cause of action. Tex. R. Civ. P. 87(2)(b), (3)(a). By its pleading, the plaintiff establishes all the elements of its cause of action, which the defendant cannot controvert for venue purposes. *See* Tex. R. Civ. P. 87(2)(b), (3)(a).

§2.8 Plaintiff's other options.

1. Amend petition. The plaintiff may add or drop claims from its original petition to establish proper venue. The plaintiff must file an amended petition at least seven days before the hearing on the motion to transfer. *See* Tex. R. Civ. P. 63; **Watson v. City of Odessa**, 893 S.W.2d 197, 200 (Tex.App.—El Paso 1995, writ denied). If the plaintiff timely amends its petition, the court must consider the amended petition at the hearing. *See, e.g.*, **Watson**, 893 S.W.2d at 199–200 (P amended petition to drop claim on which motion to transfer was based); **Moriarty v. Williams**, 752 S.W.2d 610, 611 (Tex.App.—El Paso 1988, writ denied) (P amended petition to add claims not addressed by D's motion to transfer).

2. Take nonsuit. In some circumstances, the plaintiff may be able to avoid an unfavorable venue ruling by taking a nonsuit of the entire case and refiling the case in another county. *See* **GeoChem Tech v. Verseckes**, 962 S.W.2d 541, 543 (Tex.1998). If the plaintiff nonsuits a case after the defendant files a motion to transfer and before the court rules on the motion, the dismissal does not fix venue in the county designated in the defendant's motion. *See id.* at 544. On refiling, the plaintiff still has the right to choose between two counties where mandatory venue is proper even though it filed its first suit in a county where venue was improper. *Id.* After the nonsuit, the court where the case is pending must sign the order of nonsuit; that court cannot transfer the suit to the defendant's county of choice. **Zimmerman v. Ottis**, 941 S.W.2d 259, 263 (Tex.App.—Corpus Christi 1996, orig. proceeding). See "Effect on venue," ch. 7-F, §6.4.

§2.9 Procedure for defendant's reply. The defendant is not required to file a reply to the plaintiff's response but may choose to do so. Tex. R. Civ. P. 87(1).

1. Deadline to file. The deadline to file a reply, including any affidavits and attachments, to the plaintiff's response is seven days before the venue hearing unless the defendant secures permission to file it later. Tex. R. Civ. P. 87(1).

2. Affidavits & attachments. If the plaintiff specifically denied the defendant's venue facts, the defendant must file affidavits and any necessary discovery products establishing prima facie proof of the facts. Tex. R. Civ. P. 87(3)(a).

§2.10 Procedure for securing evidence.

1. Affidavits. The parties may support their factual allegations with affidavits and properly authenticated proof attached to the affidavits. Affidavits must be made on personal knowledge, set forth specific facts that would be admissible as evidence, and affirmatively show that the affiant is competent to testify. Tex. R. Civ. P. 87(3)(a). For the requirements for the affidavit, see "Affidavits," ch. 1-B, §3.2.16. For the requirements for using an unsworn declaration in place of an affidavit, see "Unsworn declaration," ch. 1-B, §3.2.17.

2. Discovery. The parties may engage in discovery for the motion to transfer venue and for the case-in-chief without waiving the issue of venue. Tex. R. Civ. P. 88. Reasonable discovery is permitted to support or oppose the motion. Tex. R. Civ. P. 88, 258; **Beard v. Gonzalez**, 924 S.W.2d 763, 765 (Tex.App.—El Paso 1996, orig. proceeding) (motion under TRCP 257); **City of La Grange v. McBee**, 923 S.W.2d 89, 91 (Tex.App.—Houston [1st Dist.] 1996, writ denied) (same); *see also* **Double Diamond-Del., Inc. v. Alfonso**, 487 S.W.3d 265, 272–73 (Tex.App.—Corpus Christi 2016, no pet.) (party can use its own discovery responses as venue evidence). The parties must be given reasonable time to conduct discovery before the venue hearing. **Union Carbide Corp. v. Moye**, 798 S.W.2d 792, 793 (Tex.1990) (motion under TRCP 257); *see, e.g.*, **Bridgestone/Firestone, Inc. v. Thirteenth Ct. of Appeals**, 929 S.W.2d 440, 442 (Tex.1996) (five months and one continuance of hearing was reasonable time). To be considered at the venue hearing, the discovery must be attached to or incorporated by reference in an affidavit of a party, witness, or attorney who has knowledge of the discovery. Tex. R. Civ. P. 88. For the requirements for these affidavits, see "Affidavits," ch. 1-B, §3.2.16.

Note

Although TRCP 88 requires the discovery to be attached to or incorporated by reference in an affidavit, CPRC §132.001 allows for the use of an unsworn declaration instead of an affidavit. See Tex. Civ. Prac. & Rem. Code §132.001(a). For the requirements for using an unsworn declaration, see "Unsworn declaration," ch. 1-B, §3.2.17.

3. Continuance. If a party needs more time to collect affidavits and conduct discovery solely on the issue of venue, it should file a motion for continuance. **Beard**, 924 S.W.2d at 765 (motion under TRCP 257); *see* **McBee**, 923 S.W.2d at 91 (same). See "Continuance for additional discovery," ch. 5-D, §8.

§2.11 Procedure for hearing. The court cannot rule on the motion without proper notice and a hearing. *See* **Henderson v. O'Neill**, 797 S.W.2d 905, 905 (Tex.1990). The hearing must be held promptly and within a reasonable time before the beginning of the trial on the merits. Tex. R. Civ. P. 87(1).

1. Burden to ask for hearing. A defendant must request a hearing on its motion within a reasonable time. *E.g.*, **Whitworth v. Kuhn**, 734 S.W.2d 108, 111 (Tex.App.—Austin 1987, no writ) (one-year delay between filing motion to transfer and requesting hearing showed lack of diligence); *see* Tex. R. Civ. P. 87(1); *see, e.g.*, **Accent Energy Corp. v. Gillman**, 824 S.W.2d 274, 276–77 (Tex.App.—Amarillo 1992, writ denied) (three-year delay reasonable because P asked for continuance and filed amended pleadings after motion was set for hearing).

2. Notice of hearing. Each party is entitled to at least 45 days' notice of the hearing on the motion. Tex. R. Civ. P. 87(1); **HCA Health Servs. v. Salinas**, 838 S.W.2d 246, 247–48 (Tex.1992); **Henderson**, 797 S.W.2d at 905; **Bench Co. v. Nations Rent**, 133 S.W.3d 907, 908 (Tex.App.—Dallas 2004, no pet.); *cf.* **Beard v. Gonzalez**, 924 S.W.2d 763, 765 (Tex.App.—El Paso 1996, orig. proceeding) (45 days' notice required for motion under TRCP 257); **City of La Grange v. McBee**, 923 S.W.2d 89, 91 (Tex.App.—Houston [1st Dist.] 1996, writ denied) (same). To preserve an objection to lack of sufficient notice, the party must file a written objection and a motion for continuance. **Bench Co.**, 133 S.W.3d at 908; **Beard**, 924 S.W.2d at 765; **Gonzalez v. Nielson**, 770 S.W.2d 99, 101 (Tex.App.—Corpus Christi 1989, writ denied).

3. Hearing. The court may hold an oral hearing or decide the motion without oral argument. *See* Tex. R. Civ. P. 87(1); *see also* **Orion Enters. v. Pope**, 927 S.W.2d 654, 657–58 (Tex.App.—San Antonio 1996, orig. proceeding) (stating that TRCP 87 appears to contemplate hearing by written submission but declining to decide whether oral hearing is required). The hearing is not before a jury. Tex. R. Civ. P. 87(4); **Eddins v. Parker**, 63 S.W.3d 15, 18 (Tex.App.—El Paso 2001, pet. denied).

(1) Most cases. Generally, if the court holds an oral hearing on a motion to transfer, the hearing will be for argument only, and no evidence will be received. *See* Tex. Civ. Prac. & Rem. Code §15.064(a); **Jack B. Anglin Co. v. Tipps**, 842 S.W.2d 266, 269 n.4 (Tex.1992); **Eddins**, 63 S.W.3d at 18. The court will consider only the pleadings and affidavits in ruling on the motion. Tex. Civ. Prac. & Rem. Code §15.064(a).

(2) Joinder cases. If a plaintiff is establishing venue by proving the CPRC §15.003(a) joinder elements, the court may consider a broad range of evidence, including live testimony, in addition to the pleadings and affidavits. **Surgitek v. Abel**, 997 S.W.2d 598, 603 (Tex.1999); *see* **Sustainable Tex. Oyster Res. Mgmt. v. Hannah Reef, Inc.**, 491 S.W.3d 96, 106–07 (Tex.App.—Houston [1st Dist.] 2016, pet. denied). See "Joinder proper," ch. 3-C, §2.6.4(2). If the defendant rebuts the plaintiff's evidence on the joinder elements, the court may consider all available evidence to resolve the dispute. **Surgitek**, 997 S.W.2d at 603.

4. Burden of proof.

(1) Denial of venue facts. The court must accept as true any pleaded venue facts that are not specifically denied by the other party. Tex. R. Civ. P. 87(3)(a); **GeoChem Tech v. Verseckes**, 962 S.W.2d 541, 543 (Tex.1998); **Sanes v. Clark**, 25 S.W.3d 800, 803 (Tex.App.—Waco 2000, pet. denied). A global denial (e.g., "I specifically deny the venue facts") is not a specific denial. **Bleeker v. Villarreal**, 941 S.W.2d 163, 176 (Tex.App.—Corpus Christi 1996, writ dism'd) (denying "the fact that venue is proper" is not specific denial); **Maranatha Temple, Inc. v. Enterprise Prods.**, 833 S.W.2d 736, 740

(Tex.App.—Houston [1st Dist.] 1992, writ denied) (specific denial requires more than just the words "we specifically deny"). When a party's venue facts are not specifically denied, there is no burden on the party to submit proof of the facts. *See* **Bleeker**, 941 S.W.2d at 175. Undenied venue facts will not conclusively establish proper venue, however, if they would not support venue even if true. *See, e.g.*, **In re Fort Bend Cty.**, 278 S.W.3d 842, 845 (Tex.App.—Houston [14th Dist.] 2009, orig. proceeding) (D did not need to challenge Ps' venue facts because facts, even if true, did not establish proper venue).

(2) Prima facie proof. Once a venue fact has been specifically denied, the party pleading the venue fact has the burden to make prima facie proof of that fact. Tex. R. Civ. P. 87(2)(b); **GeoChem Tech**, 962 S.W.2d at 543; **In re Berry GP, Inc.**, 530 S.W.3d 201, 203 (Tex.App.—Beaumont 2016, orig. proceeding); **KW Constr. v. Stephens & Sons Concrete Contractors, Inc.**, 165 S.W.3d 874, 879 (Tex.App.—Texarkana 2005, pet. denied). Prima facie proof is made when the venue facts are properly pleaded and are supported by proper affidavit proof. Tex. R. Civ. P. 87(3)(a); **Sustainable Tex. Oyster**, 491 S.W.3d at 106; **Union Pac. R.R. v. Stouffer**, 420 S.W.3d 233, 239 (Tex.App.—Dallas 2013, pet. dism'd).

(a) No rebuttal.

[1] Most cases. Generally, prima facie proof is not subject to rebuttal, cross-examination, impeachment, or disproof. **Ruiz v. Conoco, Inc.**, 868 S.W.2d 752, 757 (Tex.1993); **Sustainable Tex. Oyster**, 491 S.W.3d at 106. The court should not weigh the credibility of the affiants when evaluating the venue proof. **Humphrey v. May**, 804 S.W.2d 328, 329 (Tex.App.—Austin 1991, writ denied).

[2] Exception—joinder cases. If a plaintiff is establishing venue by proving the CPRC §15.003(a) joinder elements, the defendant can introduce any admissible evidence to rebut the plaintiff's prima facie proof. **Surgitek**, 997 S.W.2d at 603; **Sustainable Tex. Oyster**, 491 S.W.3d at 106–07; **American Home Prods. v. Bernal**, 5 S.W.3d 344, 346–47 (Tex.App.—Corpus Christi 1999, no pet.). See "Joinder cases," ch. 3-C, §2.11.3(2).

(b) Defendant's burden if no prima facie proof. If the plaintiff does not present prima facie proof that venue is proper in the county where suit was filed, the defendant must prove that venue is proper in its chosen county. **In re Berry GP**, 530 S.W.3d at 205.

§2.12 Order. The court will decide venue based on the pleadings, motion, response, affidavits, and discovery filed in support of both the defendant's motion to transfer and the plaintiff's response. Tex. Civ. Prac. & Rem. Code §15.064(a); *see* Tex. R. Civ. P. 87(3)(b), 87(4), 88. The defendant has the burden to obtain a ruling, or else it waives its venue challenge. *See* **Marathon Corp. v. Pitzner**, 55 S.W.3d 114, 138 (Tex.App.—Corpus Christi 2001), *rev'd on other grounds*, 106 S.W.3d 724 (Tex.2003).

1. Transfer denied. If the court denies the motion to transfer, the case should proceed to trial.

2. Transfer granted. If the court grants the motion to transfer, the clerk will begin the process of transferring the case to the other county; the case will not be dismissed. Tex. R. Civ. P. 89. The order should tax court costs incurred before the suit is transferred against the plaintiff. *Id.*

Note

If the court grants a motion to transfer venue that includes a request to transfer for convenience, the order does not need to state that the case was or was not transferred for the convenience of the parties under CPRC §15.002(b). See ***Garza v. Garcia**, 137 S.W.3d 36, 39 (Tex.2004). The convenience-transfer order is not subject to appeal. See "No appeal of convenience transfer," ch. 3-C, §5.1.*

---

§2.13 Rehearing & later motions. Before the court rules on a timely motion to transfer venue, a defendant can file an amended motion to cure any defects. *See* **In re Pepsico, Inc.**, 87 S.W.3d 787, 794 (Tex.App.—Texarkana 2002, orig. proceeding) (amended motion relates back to and supersedes original motion). Once the court rules on the motion to transfer, it cannot consider any later motion to transfer, regardless of whether the movant was a party when the original motion was heard. Tex. R. Civ. P. 87(5); **UPS Ground Freight, Inc. v. Trotter**, 606 S.W.3d 781, 785 (Tex.App.—Tyler 2020, pet. filed 5-4-20). This rule does not bar a later-added defendant's motion based on grounds of either mandatory venue, if the earlier

defendants could not have filed such a motion, or local prejudice. Tex. R. Civ. P. 87(5). See "Local prejudice," ch. 3-C, §3. Similarly, TRCP 87(5) does not bar a later venue determination in a suit involving multiple plaintiffs under CPRC §15.003. *See* **UPS Ground Freight**, 606 S.W.3d at 787–88. See "Improper venue for some plaintiffs," ch. 3-C, §2.3.4.

1. Rehearing of initial motion. The court may reconsider its ruling granting the motion to transfer before the case is transferred to another county and while it still has plenary power. *See* **U.S. Res. v. Placke**, 682 S.W.2d 403, 405 (Tex.App.—Austin 1984, orig. proceeding). The court retains plenary power over the order transferring the case to another county for 30 days after it signs the transfer order. **In re Southwestern Bell Tel. Co.**, 35 S.W.3d 602, 605 (Tex.2000); **HCA Health Servs. v. Salinas**, 838 S.W.2d 246, 248 (Tex.1992). After those 30 days, the order is final for the transferring court, even though it is interlocutory for the parties. **In re Team Rocket, L.P.**, 256 S.W.3d 257, 260 (Tex.2008); **In re Southwestern Bell**, 35 S.W.3d at 605.

2. Motion by new defendant. A new defendant is limited to motions to transfer based on (1) local prejudice or (2) a ground of mandatory venue not available to the other defendants. Tex. R. Civ. P. 87(5). However, under CPRC §15.0641, no act or omission by one defendant impairs the rights of another defendant. Thus, it is uncertain whether a defendant is limited in its venue objections when it is brought into the suit after the court ruled on another defendant's motion to transfer venue.

3. Motion by third-party defendant. A third-party defendant can file a motion to transfer the claims against it. *See* **Perryman v. Spartan Tex. Six Capital Partners**, 546 S.W.3d 110, 130 (Tex.2018).

(1) Claims brought by defendant. Venue for the main action establishes venue for a defendant's third-party claim as long as the claim is properly joined under the TRCPs or other applicable statutes. Tex. Civ. Prac. & Rem. Code §15.062(a); **Perryman**, 546 S.W.3d at 131; *see also* Tex. R. Civ. P. 38 (parties can bring in third parties who may be liable for all or part of claims involved in suit). Thus, the third-party defendant can argue that the claim was not properly joined and move to transfer to another county.

(2) Claims brought by plaintiff against third-party defendant. When an original defendant joins a third-party defendant, venue for the main action establishes venue for any claim by the plaintiff against that third-party defendant arising from (1) the same transaction, occurrence, or series of transactions or occurrences and (2) the same subject matter as the plaintiff's claim against the original defendant. Tex. Civ. Prac. & Rem. Code §15.062(b); **Perryman**, 546 S.W.3d at 132. Thus, the third-party defendant can argue that the claim brought by the plaintiff does not arise from the same transaction or from the same subject matter as the plaintiff's claim against the original defendant and move to transfer to another county.

Note

CPRC §15.062(b) applies only to claims brought by the original plaintiff against the third-party defendant. Thus, venue can be established under CPRC §15.062(a) for a defendant's third-party claim regardless of whether the claim arises from the same transaction or occurrence and the same subject matter as the plaintiff's claim against the defendant. See ***Perryman**, 546 S.W.3d at 132.*

---

4. Motion by substituted defendant. A substituted defendant is bound by the actions of its predecessor and cannot change the venue status of the case. **First Heights Bank v. Gutierrez**, 852 S.W.2d 596, 618 (Tex.App.—Corpus Christi 1993, writ denied); *see* Tex. R. Civ. P. 87(5).

5. Motion by intervening party. An intervening party has the status of a plaintiff and is in no better position to contest venue than the plaintiff. **First Heights**, 852 S.W.2d at 618.

§3. Local prejudice

A motion to change venue because of local prejudice is different from a motion to transfer under the CPRC. A motion to change venue because of local prejudice is governed by TRCP 257 to 259.

§3.1 Purpose. The motion to change venue because of local prejudice allows the court to transfer a case from a county if trial in that county would be unfair to one or both parties. The allegation that a party cannot get a fair trial implicates the

Due Process Clause of the 14th Amendment to the U.S. Constitution and the "due course of law" provision of Texas Constitution article 1, §19. Most motions to change venue made under TRCP 257 to 259 involve prejudice generated by extensive pretrial publicity.

§3.2 Motion. Either party may make a motion to change venue because of local prejudice, even though the plaintiff chose the venue. Tex. R. Civ. P. 257; *e.g.*, **Carrasco v. Goatcher**, 623 S.W.2d 769, 771 (Tex.App.—El Paso 1981, no writ) (P filed motion). See **O'Connor's Texas Civil Forms**, FORM 3C:4 (2020 ed.).

Note

The due-order-of-pleading rule on filing venue motions before most other pleadings does not apply to a motion to change venue based on local prejudice for two reasons: (1) the local prejudice might arise or become known after the answer is due and (2) either party may file this type of motion.

§3.3 Grounds. The grounds for change of venue because of local prejudice include the following:

1. **Prejudice.** The prejudice against the party in the county of suit is so great that the party cannot get a fair trial. Tex. R. Civ. P. 257(a).

2. **Combination.** There is a "combination" (i.e., conspiracy) against the party instigated by influential persons in the county of suit that would prevent a fair trial. Tex. R. Civ. P. 257(b); *see* Combination, *Black's Law Dictionary* (11th ed. 2019).

3. **No impartial trial.** An impartial trial cannot be had in the county of suit. Tex. R. Civ. P. 257(c); **In re East Tex. Med. Ctr. Athens**, 154 S.W.3d 933, 935 (Tex.App.—Tyler 2005, orig. proceeding). The movant should also allege that local prejudice will deprive the movant of its due-process rights to a fair trial under both the U.S. and Texas Constitutions.

4. **Other reasons.** The party may assert any other relevant reasons to support the motion. *See* Tex. R. Civ. P. 257(d).

§3.4 Deadline to file. The motion to change venue should be filed as soon as the local prejudice becomes known. *See, e.g.*, **City of Abilene v. Downs**, 367 S.W.2d 153, 155–56 (Tex.1963) (motion to change venue filed after case reset for trial); **Lone Star Steel Co. v. Scott**, 759 S.W.2d 144, 146 (Tex.App.—Texarkana 1988, writ denied) (motion to change venue filed after D announced ready for trial). Although CPRC §15.063 includes the motion to transfer venue on grounds of local prejudice among those that must be filed before or with the defendant's answer, this inclusion is generally acknowledged as an error. *See* **Union Carbide Corp. v. Moye**, 798 S.W.2d 792, 797 & n.5 (Tex.1990) (Gonzalez, J., concurring) (CPRC §15.063 does not establish exclusive circumstances for transfer based on local prejudice).

§3.5 Affidavits. The movant must file its own affidavit and the affidavits of at least three credible residents of the county where the suit is pending to support the grounds for change of venue because of local prejudice. Tex. R. Civ. P. 257; **In re East Tex. Med. Ctr. Athens**, 154 S.W.3d 933, 935 (Tex.App.—Tyler 2005, orig. proceeding); **Acker v. Denton Publ'g**, 937 S.W.2d 111, 118 (Tex.App.—Fort Worth 1996, no writ).

§3.6 Discovery & continuance. Discovery is permitted to support or oppose the motion. Tex. R. Civ. P. 258. A continuance may be needed to obtain the necessary discovery. See "Procedure for securing evidence," ch. 3-C, §2.10.

§3.7 Response. By filing the affidavit of a credible person, the nonmovant may challenge the credibility of the movant's affiants and their means of knowing the truth of the facts stated in the motion. Tex. R. Civ. P. 258. If the party needs more time to respond, it must file a motion for continuance. See "Continuance for additional discovery," ch. 5-D, §8.

§3.8 Waiver. If the nonmovant does not file affidavits controverting the claim of local prejudice, the court must transfer the case. **City of Abilene v. Downs**, 367 S.W.2d 153, 155 (Tex.1963); **Lone Star Steel Co. v. Scott**, 759 S.W.2d 144, 146 (Tex.App.—Texarkana 1988, writ denied). If the movant waits too long to ask for a hearing, the court may find that the motion was waived. *See, e.g.*, **Whitworth v. Kuhn**, 734 S.W.2d 108, 111 (Tex.App.—Austin 1987, no writ) (one-year delay in asking for hearing was inconsistent with purpose of TRCP 87(1)).

§3.9 Notice of hearing. Each party is entitled to at least 45 days' notice of the hearing. See "Notice of hearing," ch. 3-C, §2.11.2.

§3.10 Hearing. If the credibility of the movant's affiants is attacked, the issue of local prejudice must be tried by the court. Tex. R. Civ. P. 258. It is not clear whether the court must hear live testimony. **Union Carbide Corp. v. Moye**, 798 S.W.2d 792, 793 n.1 (Tex.1990); *see* Tex. Civ. Prac. & Rem. Code §15.064(a) (court must determine venue on pleadings and affidavits). The Supreme Court did not address the issue when presented with the opportunity in **Moye**, and the concurring opinions reached different conclusions. *Compare* **Moye**, 798 S.W.2d at 794 (Hecht, J., concurring) (trial court may hear live testimony or may decide motion on affidavits), *with id.* at 795 (Gonzales, J., concurring) (trial court must hear live testimony).

Practice Tip

Until the Texas Supreme Court resolves the issue of whether a hearing under TRCP 258 is for live testimony or merely for argument, support a motion to transfer for local prejudice with affidavits and discovery products and ask for a hearing to present evidence. If the trial court refuses to give you a hearing, make an offer of proof to create the record you would have made if you had been given the opportunity to present evidence. See "Offer of Proof & Bill of Exception," ch. 8-E, §1 et seq.

§3.11 Ruling. If the court grants a motion to change venue under TRCP 257, it should transfer the suit according to the following rules:

1. If the transfer is from a district court, the court should transfer to any county of proper venue in the same or an adjoining district. Tex. R. Civ. P. 259(a).

2. If the transfer is from a county court, the court should transfer to any adjoining county of proper venue. Tex. R. Civ. P. 259(b).

3. If neither TRCP 259(a) nor (b) applies, the court should transfer to any county of proper venue. Tex. R. Civ. P. 259(c).

4. When there is no county of proper venue other than the county where suit was originally filed, the court should transfer according to the following guidelines:

(1) When the transfer is from a district court, the court should transfer to any county in the same or an adjoining district or to any district where an impartial trial can be had. Tex. R. Civ. P. 259(d)(1).

(2) When the transfer is from a county court, the court should transfer to any adjoining county or to any district where an impartial trial can be had. Tex. R. Civ. P. 259(d)(2).

5. If the parties agree to transfer venue to some other county, the court should transfer to that county. Tex. R. Civ. P. 259.

§4. Consent of the parties

The parties can agree to transfer the case to another county of proper venue. Tex. Civ. Prac. & Rem. Code §15.063(3); Tex. R. Civ. P. 255.

§4.1 Deadline to file. There is no deadline to file written consent to transfer venue. Tex. Civ. Prac. & Rem. Code §15.063(3); Tex. R. Civ. P. 86(1); *see* **Farris v. Ray**, 895 S.W.2d 351, 352 (Tex.1995).

§4.2 Filing. The agreement must be filed with the clerk of the court where the case is pending. *See* Tex. R. Civ. P. 86(1); **Farris v. Ray**, 895 S.W.2d 351, 352 (Tex.1995).

§5. Review

§5.1 No appeal of convenience transfer. The court's decision to grant or deny a motion to transfer based on convenience is not subject to review by appeal or mandamus and is not reversible error. Tex. Civ. Prac. & Rem. Code §15.002(c);

Garza v. Garcia, 137 S.W.3d 36, 39 (Tex.2004); *see* **In re Continental Airlines, Inc.**, 988 S.W.2d 733, 735 (Tex.1998); **Lopez v. Texas Workers' Comp. Ins. Fund**, 11 S.W.3d 490, 494 (Tex.App.—Austin 2000, pet. denied). The appellate court cannot review the order on a motion to transfer for convenience or the evidence to support the order. **Garza**, 137 S.W.3d at 39. When the trial court grants a motion to transfer based on convenience and another venue ground without stating in the order the basis for its decision, the appellate court cannot review either ground. *Id.* When the trial court overrules a motion to transfer based on convenience and another venue ground, the appellate court can review only the other ground. *Id.*

§5.2 Interlocutory appeal. For the rules on interlocutory appeal, see "Motion for Interlocutory Appeal & Stay Pending Appeal," **O'Connor's Texas Civil Appeals**, ch. 3-P, §1 et seq. (2020 ed.).

1. Most cases. Generally, there is no interlocutory appeal from trial-court rulings on venue motions. Tex. Civ. Prac. & Rem. Code §15.064(a); Tex. R. Civ. P. 87(6); **In re Team Rocket, L.P.**, 256 S.W.3d 257, 259 (Tex.2008); **UPS Ground Freight, Inc. v. Trotter**, 606 S.W.3d 781, 786 (Tex.App.—Tyler 2020, pet. filed 5-4-20); **Electronic Data Sys. v. Pioneer Elecs. (USA) Inc.**, 68 S.W.3d 254, 257 (Tex.App.—Fort Worth 2002, no pet.).

2. Exception—multiple plaintiffs. In suits involving more than one plaintiff—whether the plaintiffs are included by joinder, by intervention, because multiple plaintiffs began the suit, or otherwise—CPRC §15.003 allows an interlocutory appeal to contest the trial court's decision that (1) a plaintiff did or did not independently establish proper venue or (2) a plaintiff who did not independently establish proper venue did or did not establish the elements of CPRC §15.003(a)(1) to (4). Tex. Civ. Prac. & Rem. Code §15.003(b); **Sustainable Tex. Oyster Res. Mgmt. v. Hannah Reef, Inc.**, 491 S.W.3d 96, 106 (Tex.App.—Houston [1st Dist.] 2016, pet. denied); **Union Pac. R.R. v. Stouffer**, 420 S.W.3d 233, 236 (Tex.App.—Dallas 2013, pet. dism'd); **Shamoun & Norman, LLP v. Yarto Int'l Grp.**, 398 S.W.3d 272, 285 (Tex.App.—Corpus Christi 2012, pet. dism'd). See "Venue or joinder proper in multiple-plaintiff case," ch. 3-C, §2.6.4. Any party affected by the trial court's decision can file an interlocutory appeal. Tex. Civ. Prac. & Rem. Code §15.003(c); **Surgitek v. Abel**, 997 S.W.2d 598, 601 (Tex.1999). An interlocutory appeal under CPRC §15.003(b) stays the commencement of trial until the appeal has been resolved. Tex. Civ. Prac. & Rem. Code §15.003(d).

§5.3 Appeal after trial on merits. Most venue rulings must be appealed after a judgment is rendered on the merits. *See* **Montalvo v. Fourth Ct. of Appeals**, 917 S.W.2d 1, 2 (Tex.1995); **Mauro v. Banales**, 858 S.W.2d 651, 652–53 (Tex.App.—Corpus Christi 1993, orig. proceeding). For exceptions, see "Mandamus," ch. 3-C, §5.4.

1. Record.

(1) Entire reporter's record. To appeal the venue ruling, the appellant must present the entire reporter's record from the trial and from the venue hearing. See "Scope of review," ch. 3-C, §5.3.2.

(2) Limited reporter's record. One court of appeals has approved the appeal of a venue ruling with a limited reporter's record under TRAP 34.6(c). **Steger & Bizzell, Inc. v. VandeWater Constr., Inc.**, 811 S.W.2d 687, 689 (Tex.App.—Austin 1991, writ denied) (analysis under former TRAP 53(d)). Under this procedure, the appellant serves the court reporter and the appellee with a request to prepare part of the record along with a statement of points or issues to be presented on appeal. Tex. R. App. P. 34.6(c)(1). The appellee can designate any additions from the testimony to be incorporated into the reporter's record. Tex. R. App. P. 34.6(c)(2). If the appellant complies with the procedure, there is a presumption that nothing omitted from the reporter's record is relevant to the appeal. Tex. R. App. P. 34.6(c)(4). In **Steger & Bizzell**, the court noted that the trial on the merits lasted 22 days, so the limited record for venue was an appropriate use of the former TRAP 53(d) procedure. **Steger & Bizzell**, 811 S.W.2d at 689 & n.2. For a description of the procedure for limited appeals, see "Requesting a partial record under TRAP 34.6(c)," **O'Connor's Texas Civil Appeals**, ch. 6-C, §7 (2020 ed.).

2. Scope of review. When the trial court's venue ruling is challenged on appeal after a trial on the merits, the appellate court conducts an independent review of the entire record to determine whether the evidence introduced during the trial supports the venue ruling. Tex. Civ. Prac. & Rem. Code §15.064(b); **Wilson v. Texas Parks & Wildlife Dept.**, 886 S.W.2d 259, 261 (Tex.1994); **Ruiz v. Conoco, Inc.**, 868 S.W.2d 752, 758 (Tex.1993); *see* **Ford Motor Co. v. Miles**, 967 S.W.2d 377, 380 (Tex.1998). The appellate court may reverse a decision that was correct when it was made at the venue hearing but was erroneous in light of the evidence introduced at the trial on the merits. **Bleeker v. Villarreal**, 941 S.W.2d 163, 167 (Tex.App.—Corpus Christi 1996, writ dism'd). The requirement that the appellate court review the entire record

was designed to prevent fraud in pleading venue facts that might not be discoverable until after the trial on the merits. **Humphrey v. May**, 804 S.W.2d 328, 330 (Tex.App.—Austin 1991, writ denied).

3. Appellate court order.

(1) Other error. If the defendant presents arguments on appeal that entitle it to rendition of judgment—not just remand—the appellate court should consider those points first and, if it sustains them, reverse and render judgment for the defendant without reaching the venue issue. **Bradleys' Elec., Inc. v. Cigna Lloyds Ins.**, 995 S.W.2d 675, 677 (Tex.1999); *see* **CMH Homes, Inc. v. Daenen**, 15 S.W.3d 97, 99 (Tex.2000).

(2) Venue error.

(a) Uphold venue. If the record contains any probative evidence that venue was proper, even if the preponderance of the evidence is to the contrary, the appellate court must uphold the trial court's venue determination. **Bonham State Bank v. Beadle**, 907 S.W.2d 465, 471 (Tex.1995); **Ruiz**, 868 S.W.2d at 758; *see* Tex. Civ. Prac. & Rem. Code §15.064(b).

(b) Reverse venue. If the record contains no probative evidence that venue was proper, the appellate court must reverse the trial court's venue determination. **Ruiz**, 868 S.W.2d at 758; *see* Tex. Civ. Prac. & Rem. Code §15.064(b); **Bonham State Bank**, 907 S.W.2d at 471. When the appellate court reverses, it must determine whether to remand for trial in another county or for a new venue hearing.

[1] Remand for trial. If there is any probative evidence that venue is proper in the county where the defendant sought to transfer the case, the appellate court must instruct the trial court to transfer the case to that county. **Ruiz**, 868 S.W.2d at 758.

[2] Remand for hearing. If there is no probative evidence that venue is proper in the county of suit or the county to which transfer was sought, the appellate court must remand the case for further proceedings on the venue issue. **Ruiz**, 868 S.W.2d at 758.

§5.4 Mandamus. Most venue determinations are correctable on appeal and cannot be challenged by mandamus. **Montalvo v. Fourth Ct. of Appeals**, 917 S.W.2d 1, 2 (Tex.1995). But mandamus is appropriate in the following instances:

1. Mandatory venue in CPRC. A party may file a petition for writ of mandamus to enforce a mandatory-venue provision in CPRC chapter 15. Tex. Civ. Prac. & Rem. Code §15.0642; **In re Fisher**, 433 S.W.3d 523, 528–29 (Tex.2014); **In re Missouri Pac. R.R.**, 998 S.W.2d 212, 214–15 (Tex.1999). Under CPRC §15.0642, the relator is not required to show it lacks an adequate remedy on appeal. **In re Missouri Pac.**, 998 S.W.2d at 216; **KJ Eastwood Invs. v. Enlow**, 923 S.W.2d 255, 258 (Tex.App.—Fort Worth 1996, orig. proceeding). The petition must be filed before the later of the following dates: (1) the 90th day before the trial starts or (2) the 10th day after the party receives notice of the trial setting. Tex. Civ. Prac. & Rem. Code §15.0642.

2. Mandatory venue in Family Code. When a court has a mandatory duty to transfer a case under the Family Code, a party may seek mandamus relief to enforce the transfer. *See* **Proffer v. Yates**, 734 S.W.2d 671, 673 (Tex.1987) (under former Fam. Code §11.06(b), now §155.201); **In re Knotts**, 62 S.W.3d 922, 923 n.1 (Tex.App.—Texarkana 2001, orig. proceeding) (under Fam. Code §155.201); **In re Kramer**, 9 S.W.3d 449, 450 (Tex.App.—San Antonio 1999, orig. proceeding) (same). See "Challenging venue," **O'Connor's Texas Family Law Handbook**, ch. 4-B, §3 (2021 ed.).

3. Exceptional circumstances. Occasionally, a party may be entitled to mandamus relief from a venue order when "exceptional circumstances" make appeal an inadequate remedy. **In re Masonite Corp.**, 997 S.W.2d 194, 197 (Tex.1999); *see* **In re Berry GP, Inc.**, 530 S.W.3d 201, 206–07 (Tex.App.—Beaumont 2016, orig. proceeding) (mandamus proper when trial court uses blatantly improper venue procedure); *see, e.g.*, **HCA Health Servs. v. Salinas**, 838 S.W.2d 246, 247–48 (Tex.1992) (order transferring venue signed by mistake); **Union Carbide Corp. v. Moye**, 798 S.W.2d 792, 793 (Tex.1990) (trial court misled party about acceptable form of venue proof); **Henderson v. O'Neill**, 797 S.W.2d 905, 905 (Tex.1990) (no notice of hearing); *see also* **In re City of Irving**, 45 S.W.3d 777, 779 (Tex.App.—Texarkana 2001, orig. proceeding) (trial court's erroneous venue order that was eventually reversed on appeal was not exceptional circumstance warranting mandamus).

§5.5 Standard of review. The standard of review for venue rulings depends on the type of ruling being challenged.

1. Most venue rulings.

(1) Venue proper. If the record contains any probative evidence that venue was proper—even if the preponderance of the evidence is to the contrary—the appellate court must uphold the trial court's venue determination. **Bonham State Bank v. Beadle**, 907 S.W.2d 465, 471 (Tex.1995); **Ruiz v. Conoco, Inc.**, 868 S.W.2d 752, 758 (Tex.1993); *see* Tex. Civ. Prac. & Rem. Code §15.064(b).

(2) Venue improper. If the record contains no evidence that venue was proper, the appellate court must reverse the trial court's venue ruling and remand the case for a new trial without conducting the usual harm analysis under TRAP 44.1(a). **Bleeker v. Villarreal**, 941 S.W.2d 163, 167 (Tex.App.—Corpus Christi 1996, writ dism'd); *see* Tex. Civ. Prac. & Rem. Code §15.064(b); **Wichita Cty. v. Hart**, 917 S.W.2d 779, 781 (Tex.1996). Thus, venue is one of the rare situations where the harmless-error rule does not apply. If the trial court makes an erroneous venue ruling, the case must be reversed even if the appellant cannot show harm. **Wilson v. Texas Parks & Wildlife Dept.**, 886 S.W.2d 259, 261 (Tex.1994); **Maranatha Temple, Inc. v. Enterprise Prods.**, 833 S.W.2d 736, 740–41 (Tex.App.—Houston [1st Dist.] 1992, writ denied); *see* **Double Diamond-Del., Inc. v. Alfonso**, 487 S.W.3d 265, 269 (Tex.App.—Corpus Christi 2016, no pet.). The Legislature intended venue rulings to be exempt from the harmless-error rule to discourage the prosecution of meritless venue claims. **Maranatha Temple**, 833 S.W.2d at 741.

2. Mandamus under CPRC §15.0642. The standard of review for mandatory venue under CPRC §15.0642 is abuse of discretion. **In re Missouri Pac. R.R.**, 998 S.W.2d 212, 215 (Tex.1999); **In re Continental Airlines, Inc.**, 988 S.W.2d 733, 735 (Tex.1998).

3. Interlocutory appeal under CPRC §15.003. The standard of review for a venue determination made in a multiple-plaintiff case under CPRC §15.003 is de novo. **Surgitek v. Abel**, 997 S.W.2d 598, 603 (Tex.1999); **Sustainable Tex. Oyster Res. Mgmt. v. Hannah Reef, Inc.**, 491 S.W.3d 96, 107 (Tex.App.—Houston [1st Dist.] 2016, pet. denied). That is, the court of appeals will make an independent determination from the record—without any deference to the trial court's decision—of whether the trial court's order was proper. Tex. Civ. Prac. & Rem. Code §15.003(c)(1); **Shamoun & Norman, LLP v. Yarto Int'l Grp.**, 398 S.W.3d 272, 288 (Tex.App.—Corpus Christi 2012, pet. dism'd). If a party contends that it was improperly denied the opportunity to present proof, the standard of review for that complaint is abuse of discretion. **Surgitek**, 997 S.W.2d at 603.

4. Local prejudice. The standard of review for local prejudice is abuse of discretion. *See, e.g.*, **Union Carbide Corp. v. Moye**, 798 S.W.2d 792, 793 (Tex.1990) (court did not allow reasonable opportunity to supplement venue record); **Beard v. Gonzalez**, 924 S.W.2d 763, 764 (Tex.App.—El Paso 1996, orig. proceeding) (court did not allow reasonable discovery); **City of La Grange v. McBee**, 923 S.W.2d 89, 90 (Tex.App.—Houston [1st Dist.] 1996, writ denied) (same).

D. Forum Non Conveniens—Challenging the Texas Forum

§1. General

§1.1 Rules. None. See Tex. Civ. Prac. & Rem. Code §71.051.

§1.2 Purpose. A forum non conveniens (FNC) motion asks the court to dismiss or stay a suit because a court outside Texas that has jurisdiction over the dispute is a more appropriate forum. **A.P. Keller Dev., Inc. v. One Jackson Place, Ltd.**, 890 S.W.2d 502, 505 (Tex.App.—El Paso 1994, no writ). The FNC doctrine presumes at least two forums have jurisdiction over the dispute. **Gottwald v. de Cano**, 568 S.W.3d 241, 249 (Tex.App.—El Paso 2019, no pet.); *see* **In re ENSCO Offshore Int'l**, 311 S.W.3d 921, 925 (Tex.2010). FNC is an equitable doctrine that courts exercise to avoid imposing an inconvenient jurisdiction on a litigant, even if jurisdiction is supported by the long-arm statute and would not violate due process. **Tullis v. Georgia-Pac. Corp.**, 45 S.W.3d 118, 122 (Tex.App.—Fort Worth 2000, no pet.); *see* **Benz Grp. v. Barreto**, 404 S.W.3d 92, 96 (Tex.App.—Houston [1st Dist.] 2013, no pet.). A motion to stay or dismiss on FNC grounds is appropriate only when the defendant wants to defend the suit in another state or country.

Note

Forum non conveniens deals with whether a suit should be prosecuted in a forum outside of Texas, while venue deals with the proper county within Texas in which to bring a suit. For a discussion of how to challenge venue, see "Motion to Transfer—Challenging Venue," ch. 3-C, §1 et seq.

---

§1.3 Timetables & forms. Appendix IV, Timetable 4, Motion to dismiss—Code forum non conveniens; Appendix IV, Timetable 5, Motion to dismiss—Common-law forum non conveniens; **O'Connor's Texas Civil Forms**, FORMS 3D:1 et seq. (2020 ed.).

§1.4 Other references. Restatement Second, Conflict of Laws §84, comments a to f; **O'Connor's Texas Causes of Action** (2021 ed.).

§2. Types of motions

There are generally two types of FNC motions in Texas courts: (1) a motion to stay or dismiss under the CPRC when a plaintiff asserts a claim for personal injury or wrongful death and (2) a motion to dismiss for common-law FNC when the plaintiff asserts almost any other cause of action. FNC for cases under the CPRC will be referred to as "Code FNC." FNC for all other cases will be referred to as "common-law FNC." A party can also file a motion to enforce a forum-selection clause in a contract, which is related to an FNC motion. See "Forum-selection clause," ch. 3-D, §6.

§3. Code FNC motion

§3.1 Motion.

1. Applicability. For a Code FNC motion to apply, the plaintiff must have asserted a claim for personal injury or wrongful death. Tex. Civ. Prac. & Rem. Code §71.051(i). Although CPRC §71.051 does not define the term "personal injury," at least one court of appeals has interpreted the statute as covering only claims involving bodily injury and excluding claims for other torts. *See, e.g.,* **Gottwald v. de Cano**, 568 S.W.3d 241, 247–48 (Tex.App.—El Paso 2019, no pet.) (because claim for intentional infliction of emotional distress does not require manifestation of physical injury, it is not personal-injury claim under CPRC §71.051).

Note

CPRC §71.051 does not address whether it is limited to wrongful-death or survival claims under CPRC chapter 71 or whether it instead applies generally to all common-law and statutory personal-injury claims. See, e.g., ***In re Mahindra, USA Inc.***, *549 S.W.3d 541, 547 (Tex.2018) (Court did not determine whether CPRC §71.051 applied to common-law bystander claim).*

2. In writing. A Code FNC motion must be made in writing. Tex. Civ. Prac. & Rem. Code §71.051(b). See **O'Connor's Texas Civil Forms**, FORM 3D:1 (2020 ed.).

3. Deadline to file. The deadline to file a Code FNC motion is 180 days after the last date for filing a motion to transfer venue. Tex. Civ. Prac. & Rem. Code §71.051(d). Because the deadline to file a motion to transfer venue is the same as the deadline to file an answer, the deadline to file a Code FNC motion is approximately 200 days after the suit is served (180 days plus 20+ days). See "Motion to extend time," ch. 3-D, §3.4; "Deadline to answer," ch. 3-E, §2.

4. Grounds. A court must stay or dismiss a claim or an action for personal injury or wrongful death if the defendant can establish that (1) the plaintiff is not a "plaintiff" under CPRC §71.051 or the plaintiff is not a legal resident of Texas or a derivative claimant of a legal resident of Texas and (2) in the interest of justice and for the convenience of the parties, the claim or action would be more properly heard in a forum outside Texas. *See* Tex. Civ. Prac. & Rem. Code §71.051(b), (e), (h), (i).

(1) Not a "plaintiff," legal resident, or derivative claimant of legal resident. The defendant must allege that (1) the plaintiff is not a "plaintiff" as defined in CPRC §71.051(h)(2) or (2) one or more of the plaintiffs is not a legal resident of Texas or a derivative claimant of a legal resident of Texas. *See* Tex. Civ. Prac. & Rem. Code §71.051(e), (h). The trial court cannot stay or dismiss a plaintiff's claim if the plaintiff is a "plaintiff" as defined in CPRC §71.051(h)(2) and a legal resident of Texas or a derivative claimant of a legal resident of Texas. *See* Tex. Civ. Prac. & Rem. Code §71.051(e); **In re Mahindra, USA**, 549 S.W.3d at 545; *see also* **In re Bridgestone Americas Tire Opers., LLC**, 459 S.W.3d 565, 569 (Tex.2015) (if Texas-resident exception in CPRC §71.051(e) applies, case cannot be dismissed on FNC grounds no matter how tenuous P's connection to Texas is).

(a) Not a "plaintiff" under CPRC §71.051. The defendant can allege that the plaintiff whose claim or action the defendant is asking the court to stay or dismiss is not a "plaintiff" as defined in CPRC §71.051(h)(2). *See* Tex. Civ. Prac. & Rem. Code §71.051(e), (h)(2).

[1] Who is a plaintiff? A party seeking to recover damages for personal injury or wrongful death is a "plaintiff" under CPRC §71.051. Tex. Civ. Prac. & Rem. Code §71.051(h)(2); *e.g.*, **In re Mahindra, USA**, 549 S.W.3d at 546–47 (Ps were plaintiffs under CPRC §71.051 for bringing individual claims for loss of society, companionship, and inheritance and for mental anguish based on father's wrongful death).

[2] Who is not a plaintiff?

[a] Counterclaimant, cross-claimant, or third-party plaintiff. A party who files a counterclaim, cross-claim, or third-party claim is not a "plaintiff" under CPRC §71.051. Tex. Civ. Prac. & Rem. Code §71.051(h)(2)(A). To be excluded from the statutory definition, however, the party asserting the counterclaim, cross-claim, or third-party claim must be a defendant or characterized as a defendant; if the original plaintiff or a party characterized as a plaintiff is asserting the claim, that party is still considered a "plaintiff" under the statute. *See* **In re Ford Motor Co.**, 442 S.W.3d 265, 270 (Tex.2014).

[b] Intervenor—excluded as third-party plaintiff. Depending on the nature of its claims and interests, an intervenor can be excluded from being a "plaintiff" and instead can be considered a third-party plaintiff under CPRC §71.051(h)(2)(A) if the intervenor is properly characterized as a defendant. **In re Ford Motor**, 442 S.W.3d at 274. An intervenor will be considered a defendant if (1) the intervenor is closely aligned with the defendant, (2) the intervenor and the original plaintiff are directly antagonistic to each other, and (3) equitable factors weigh in favor of treating the intervenor as a defendant. *E.g.*, *id.* at 275–76 (wrongful-death beneficiaries intervened and asserted affirmative claims for relief, their interests were not in opposition to P's interests, and their claims were not closely aligned with D's claims; intervenors were characterized as Ps and thus were not excluded as third-party Ps).

[c] Assignee. A person who is assigned a cause of action for personal injury is not a "plaintiff" under CPRC §71.051. Tex. Civ. Prac. & Rem. Code §71.051(h)(2)(A).

[d] Representative, administrator, guardian, or next friend. A party who is a representative, administrator, guardian, or next friend is not a "plaintiff" under CPRC §71.051, as long as the party is not otherwise a derivative claimant of a legal resident of Texas. Tex. Civ. Prac. & Rem. Code §71.051(h)(2)(B); *e.g.*, **In re Mahindra, USA**, 549

S.W.3d at 546 (P was not plaintiff under CPRC §71.051 in his capacity as representative of estate but could qualify as plaintiff for individual claims); *see, e.g.*, **In re Bridgestone**, 459 S.W.3d at 572–73 (uncle, a Texas resident, sued as next friend for minors residing in Mexico; uncle's residency did not control and did not preclude dismissal because uncle was not a P under CPRC §71.051(h)(2)). See "Derivative claimant of legal resident," ch. 3-D, §3.1.4(1)(b)[2].

(b) Not a legal resident or derivative claimant of legal resident. The defendant can allege that the plaintiff whose claim or action the defendant is asking the court to stay or dismiss is not a legal resident of Texas or a derivative claimant of a legal resident of Texas. *See* Tex. Civ. Prac. & Rem. Code §71.051(e). To support the defendant's allegation that the suit should be stayed or dismissed, the defendant must identify each plaintiff who is not a legal resident or a derivative claimant of a legal resident and then address the CPRC §71.051(b) factors for each plaintiff. *See* Tex. Civ. Prac. & Rem. Code §71.051(e). See "Action should be heard in alternate forum," ch. 3-D, §3.1.4(2). The court will then make a determination of whether to stay or dismiss the claims of each of the plaintiffs individually based on the §71.051(b) factors, regardless of whether the claims of any other plaintiff in the suit may be stayed or dismissed under §71.051(b). *See* Tex. Civ. Prac. & Rem. Code §71.051(e). The plaintiff's country of citizenship or national origin is also irrelevant to the court's determination. *Id.*

[1] Legal resident. CPRC §71.051 does not define "legal resident," but the term generally refers to whether a person or corporation is a resident of Texas for legal purposes. *See* Acts 2015, 84th Leg., R.S., ch. 537, §1, eff. June 16, 2015 (eliminating statutory definition of legal resident in §71.051(h)(1)); Domicile, *Black's Law Dictionary* (11th ed. 2019) (listing "legal residence" as synonym of domicile); *see also* Senate Cmte. on State Affairs, Bill Analysis, Tex. H.B. 1692, 84th Leg., R.S. (2015) (statutory definition of legal resident was too broad).

[2] Derivative claimant of legal resident. A derivative claimant is a person whose damages were caused by personal injury to or the wrongful death of another person. Tex. Civ. Prac. & Rem. Code §71.051(h)(1). If a plaintiff brought claims as a derivative claimant and the plaintiff herself is not a Texas resident, the residency of the person whose injury or death the plaintiff's claims are based on controls for purposes of CPRC §71.051(e); thus, the defendant should allege that the person whose injury or death the plaintiff's claims are based on is not a legal resident of Texas. *See* Tex. Civ. Prac. & Rem. Code §71.051(e).

Note

In many cases, the party bringing suit will be considered both a plaintiff and a derivative claimant under CPRC §71.051. See ***In re Mahindra, USA****, 549 S.W.3d at 546–47. In such a case, if the plaintiff herself is a Texas resident, she can rely on this fact to prevent dismissal of her claim. See id. at 548 (Texas-resident exception is not merely Texas-decedent exception). Whether the person whose injury or death her claims are based on is a Texas resident would then be irrelevant. See id.; see also* ***In re Ford Motor****, 442 S.W.3d at 280 (wrongful-death beneficiaries and decedent are distinct Ps under statute). If the plaintiff is not a Texas resident, however, she will have to rely on her status as a derivative claimant, and she can prevent dismissal of her claims under the Texas-resident exception only if the injured or deceased person is a Texas resident. See* ***In re Mahindra, USA****, 549 S.W.3d at 548.*

---

(2) Action should be heard in alternate forum. The defendant must allege that the plaintiff's claim or action would be more properly heard in a forum outside Texas based on the interest of justice and for the convenience of the parties. *See* Tex. Civ. Prac. & Rem. Code §71.051(b); **In re Bridgestone**, 459 S.W.3d at 575; **In re ENSCO Offshore Int'l**, 311 S.W.3d 921, 924 (Tex.2010); **In re General Elec. Co.**, 271 S.W.3d 681, 686–87 (Tex.2008). "Interest of justice" and "convenience of the parties" are essentially defined by the factors in CPRC §71.051(b). **In re General Elec.**, 271 S.W.3d at 686. To support its motion to stay or dismiss, the defendant should address all the factors under CPRC §71.051(b).

Note

The defendant is not required to prove or present evidence on each factor under CPRC §71.051(b); the statute simply requires the trial court to consider the factors to the extent they apply. ***In re General Elec.****, 271 S.W.3d at 687. See "Burden of proof," ch. 3-D, §3.6.4; "Review of §71.051 factors," ch. 3-D, §3.7.1. At the very least, however, a defendant should argue that another forum is both available and adequate. Cf.* ***Piper Aircraft Co. v. Reyno****, 454 U.S. 235, 254 n.22 (1981) (common-law FNC; court required both factors before dismissing case).*

(a) Alternate forum available. The defendant must identify an alternate forum where the claim may be tried. Tex. Civ. Prac. & Rem. Code §71.051(b)(1). An alternate forum is available if the defendant would be amenable to service of process there. **In re ENSCO**, 311 S.W.3d at 924.

(b) Alternate forum adequate. The defendant must show that the alternate forum provides an adequate remedy. Tex. Civ. Prac. & Rem. Code §71.051(b)(2). An inadequate forum is one in which the remedies offered are so unsatisfactory they are the equivalent of no remedy at all. **In re Oceanografia, S.A. de C.V.**, 494 S.W.3d 728, 732 (Tex.2016); **In re ENSCO**, 311 S.W.3d at 924; **In re General Elec.**, 271 S.W.3d at 688; *see* **In re Pirelli Tire, L.L.C.**, 247 S.W.3d 670, 678 (Tex.2007) (fact that substantive law of alternate forum may be less favorable to P is entitled to little, if any, weight). If there is a question about the adequacy of the alternate forum's remedy, the defendant may have to compare the rights, remedies, and procedures available in each of the forums, but this comparative analysis is usually unnecessary. *See* **In re ENSCO**, 311 S.W.3d at 924–25; **In re General Elec.**, 271 S.W.3d at 688; *see, e.g.*, **In re BPZ Res.**, 359 S.W.3d 866, 873 (Tex.App.—Houston [14th Dist.] 2012, orig. proceeding) (because there was no evidence that Peru's courts are so corrupt as to provide inadequate remedy, no comparative analysis between Texas and Peru was necessary). If there is more than one alternate forum, the defendant is not required to pick one but may instead show how any or all of them are adequate. *See* **In re ENSCO**, 311 S.W.3d at 925.

(c) Substantial injustice imposed. The defendant must show how maintaining the action in Texas would impose a substantial injustice on the defendant. Tex. Civ. Prac. & Rem. Code §71.051(b)(3); *e.g.*, **In re ENSCO**, 311 S.W.3d at 925 (maintaining action in Texas would be substantially unjust when majority of witnesses could not be subpoenaed to appear in Texas and related suit for contractual indemnity against foreign party was already pending in Australia).

(d) Alternate forum can exercise jurisdiction. The defendant must show the alternate forum, as a result of the parties' submission or otherwise, can exercise jurisdiction over all the defendants properly joined to the plaintiff's claim. Tex. Civ. Prac. & Rem. Code §71.051(b)(4); *e.g.*, **In re ENSCO**, 311 S.W.3d at 925–26 (all Ds agreed to submit to jurisdiction in either of the alternate forums).

(e) Balance of private and public interests favors alternate forum. The defendant must show that the balance of the parties' private interests and the state's public interests favors the alternate forum. Tex. Civ. Prac. & Rem. Code §71.051(b)(5); **In re ENSCO**, 311 S.W.3d at 926. Most of the private and public interests originated in **Gulf Oil Corp. v. Gilbert**, 330 U.S. 501 (1947), and are called the **Gulf Oil** factors.

[1] Private interests. The defendant should establish that the private interests of the parties will be better served in the alternate forum by addressing the following:

[a] Whether access to sources of proof will be easier in the alternate forum than in Texas. *See* **Gulf Oil**, 330 U.S. at 508.

[b] Whether compulsory process for the attendance of unwilling witnesses is available in the alternate forum. *See id.*; **In re Mahindra, USA**, 549 S.W.3d at 549; *see, e.g.*, **In re ENSCO**, 311 S.W.3d at 926 (lack of compulsory process in Texas to secure production of witnesses and other documents weighed in favor of alternate forums); **In re Pirelli Tire**, 247 S.W.3d at 678–79 (compulsory process may have been available under Hague Convention, but D's evidence that process was time-consuming, uncertain as to result, and unlikely to be completed before trial weighed in favor of alternate forum).

[c] Whether the costs of securing the presence of willing witnesses will be lower in the alternate forum than in Texas. *See* **Gulf Oil**, 330 U.S. at 508.

[d] Whether viewing the relevant premises is necessary to the suit and whether the possibility of viewing the premises is better in the alternate forum than in Texas. *See id.*

[e] Whether the enforceability of the judgment in the alternate forum is as good as or better than in Texas. *See id.*

[f] All other practical problems that make trial easy, expeditious, and inexpensive. *See id.*; **In re ENSCO**, 311 S.W.3d at 926; *see also* **In re BPZ**, 359 S.W.3d at 879 (allegations of political unrest in alternate forum will generally not suffice to outweigh other factors favoring dismissal). For example, an alternate forum would be preferable if the cost, time, and scheduling difficulties necessary to obtain evidence and present witness testimony would be far greater in Texas than in the alternate forum. *See* **In re ENSCO**, 311 S.W.3d at 926.

[2] Public interests. The defendant should establish that the public interests will be better served in the alternate forum by addressing the following:

[a] Whether the administrative burden (e.g., congested docket, jury duty of citizens) on the alternate forum's court is less than the burden on the Texas court. *See* **Gulf Oil**, 330 U.S. at 508–09.

[b] The extent to which the interest in deciding the case in the alternate forum is greater than that in Texas. *See id.* at 509; *see, e.g.*, **In re ENSCO**, 311 S.W.3d at 927 (Texas had no significant relationship to case involving injury occurring in Singapore's territorial waters on Liberian-flagged vessel to Australian citizen employed by Australian company).

[c] Whether the law of the alternate forum will control the disposition of the case. *See* **Gulf Oil**, 330 U.S. at 509; *see, e.g.*, **In re BPZ**, 359 S.W.3d at 878 (Peruvian law applied and events giving rise to claim were more substantially connected with Peru than with Texas).

[d] Whether the law of the alternate forum must be applied to the facts of the case and, if so, whether that law is so dissimilar to Texas law that its enforcement in Texas will be difficult or impossible. **Gurvich v. Tyree**, 694 S.W.2d 39, 46 (Tex.App.—Corpus Christi 1985, no writ).

[3] No act or omission in Texas. The defendant must show the extent to which the plaintiff's personal injury or death did not result from acts or omissions that occurred in Texas. Tex. Civ. Prac. & Rem. Code §71.051(b)(5); *see* **In re ENSCO**, 311 S.W.3d at 926.

(f) No duplication or proliferation of litigation. The defendant must show that the stay or dismissal will not result in unreasonable duplication or proliferation of litigation. Tex. Civ. Prac. & Rem. Code §71.051(b)(6); **In re Mahindra, USA**, 549 S.W.3d at 549–50; **In re ENSCO**, 311 S.W.3d at 928; *see, e.g.*, **In re General Elec.**, 271 S.W.3d at 693 (D asked for dismissal of entire case, but even if court dismissed only part of case, fragmentation of litigation would not be unreasonable).

5. Verified. Because most of the defendant's factual allegations are outside the record, the defendant should probably verify the motion, even though nothing in CPRC §71.051 requires verification.

6. Request hearing. The defendant must request a hearing on the motion. Tex. Civ. Prac. & Rem. Code §71.051(d). See "Hearing," ch. 3-D, §3.6.

§3.2 Response.

1. Form.

(1) Written. The plaintiff should file a written response challenging the allegations in the defendant's motion. See **O'Connor's Texas Civil Forms**, FORM 3D:3 (2020 ed.).

(2) No verification required. The plaintiff is not required to provide verified evidence to support its response. *See* Tex. Civ. Prac. & Rem. Code §71.051(b). The plaintiff should, however, verify the response if it relies on facts outside the record. See "Verification & affidavits," ch. 1-B, §4.1.12.

(3) Deadline to file. There is no deadline in CPRC §71.051 for filing the plaintiff's response, but the plaintiff should file and serve a response far enough in advance of the hearing for the court to consider the arguments and any evidence.

2. Grounds. The plaintiff should negate the defendant's allegations and identify any exceptions to the application of CPRC §71.051.

Practice Tip

In addition to negating the defendant's allegations as discussed below, the plaintiff should address any conditions it would like for the court to include in the order should the court grant the defendant's FNC motion. See Tex. Civ. Prac. & Rem. Code §71.051(c). See "Code FNC," ch. 3-D, §5.1. For example, if the plaintiff's suit would be time-barred after dismissal, the plaintiff should provide evidence of this and argue that the alternate forum will not provide an adequate remedy unless the defendant agrees to waive any limitations defense in the alternate forum. See ***In re Mantle Oil & Gas, LLC****, 426 S.W.3d 182, 191 (Tex.App.—Houston [1st Dist.] 2012, orig. proceeding) (court may impose condition on dismissal that requires D to refrain from asserting any limitations defense when suit is filed in alternate forum); see, e.g.,* ***In re Bridgestone Americas Tire Opers., LLC****, 459 S.W.3d 565, 577 n.15 (Tex.2015) (because P did not raise limitations argument in trial court and record did not show that limitations would bar refiling in Mexico, Court did not consider whether limitations rendered Mexico an inadequate forum). Addressing any limitations argument is particularly important because CPRC §71.051 no longer explicitly requires the defendant to waive any limitations defense. See* ***Adams v. Baxter Healthcare Corp.****, 998 S.W.2d 349, 354 (Tex.App.—Austin 1999, no pet.) (under former CPRC §71.051(c)).*

(1) Plaintiff is a "plaintiff" under CPRC §71.051. The plaintiff can allege that, contrary to the defendant's allegation, the plaintiff is a "plaintiff" as defined in CPRC §71.051(h)(2). *See* Tex. Civ. Prac. & Rem. Code §71.051(e), (h)(2). See "Not a 'plaintiff' under CPRC §71.051," ch. 3-D, §3.1.4(1)(a).

(2) Plaintiff is legal resident or derivative claimant of legal resident. The plaintiff can allege that, contrary to the defendant's allegation, the plaintiff is a legal resident of Texas or a derivative claimant of a legal resident of Texas. *See* Tex. Civ. Prac. & Rem. Code §71.051(e). The trial court cannot stay or dismiss a plaintiff's claim under CPRC §71.051(b) if the plaintiff is a "plaintiff" as defined in CPRC §71.051(h)(2) and a legal resident of Texas or a derivative claimant of a legal resident of Texas. *See* Tex. Civ. Prac. & Rem. Code §71.051(e). See "Not a legal resident or derivative claimant of legal resident," ch. 3-D, §3.1.4(1)(b).

(3) No forum outside Texas. The plaintiff can allege that, contrary to the defendant's allegation, the plaintiff's claim or action would not be more properly heard in a forum outside Texas based on the following:

(a) No alternate forum. The plaintiff can allege that the defendant did not identify an alternate forum or, if it did, that the defendant is not amenable to service of process in that forum. *See* Tex. Civ. Prac. & Rem. Code §71.051(b)(1).

(b) No adequate remedy. The plaintiff can allege that the alternate forum does not provide an adequate remedy. *See* Tex. Civ. Prac. & Rem. Code §71.051(b)(2). See "Alternate forum adequate," ch. 3-D, §3.1.4(2)(b).

(c) No substantial injustice. The plaintiff can allege that maintaining the suit in Texas would not impose a substantial injustice on the defendant. *See* Tex. Civ. Prac. & Rem. Code §71.051(b)(3).

(d) No jurisdiction. The plaintiff can allege that the alternate forum does not have jurisdiction over the claim. *See* Tex. Civ. Prac. & Rem. Code §71.051(b)(4). The plaintiff can argue that the defendant has not submitted itself to the jurisdiction of the alternate forum and that the alternate forum has no other means of exercising personal jurisdiction over the defendant. *See id.*

(e) Balance of interests. The plaintiff can allege that the balance of private and public interests favors the Texas forum. *See* Tex. Civ. Prac. & Rem. Code §71.051(b)(5).

[1] ***Gulf Oil* factors.** The plaintiff should build its argument around the **Gulf Oil** factors. See "Balance of private and public interests favors alternate forum," ch. 3-D, §3.1.4(2)(e).

[2] Act or omission occurred in Texas. The plaintiff can allege that her claim for personal injury or wrongful death was the result of the defendant's act or omission that occurred in Texas. *See* Tex. Civ. Prac. & Rem. Code §71.051(b)(5).

(f) Duplication or proliferation. The plaintiff can allege that the stay or dismissal would result in unreasonable duplication or proliferation of litigation. *See* Tex. Civ. Prac. & Rem. Code §71.051(b)(6).

(4) Improper notice of hearing. If the defendant did not give proper notice, the plaintiff must challenge the notice, or else it waives the issue. The plaintiff can object if the defendant set the hearing within 30 days of trial or did not give the plaintiff 21 days' notice of the hearing. *See* Tex. Civ. Prac. & Rem. Code §71.051(d). See "Hearing," ch. 3-D, §3.6.

(5) Waiver. If the defendant filed its Code FNC motion after the deadline, the plaintiff should allege that the defendant waived the motion. See "Deadline to file," ch. 3-D, §3.1.3.

§3.3 Defendant's reply. If the plaintiff provides evidence to negate the defendant's allegations, the defendant should reply by supplying verified evidence to support its motion. See "No verification required," ch. 3-D, §3.2.1(2).

§3.4 Motion to extend time. The court may extend any time limit established under CPRC §71.051 at the request of any party for good cause. Tex. Civ. Prac. & Rem. Code §71.051(g). If a party needs more time to file a response or reply, it should file a motion for continuance. See "Motion for Continuance," ch. 5-D, §1 et seq.

§3.5 Discovery. The court must give the parties "ample opportunity" for discovery of information relevant to the Code FNC motion before the hearing on the motion. Tex. Civ. Prac. & Rem. Code §71.051(d). See "Discovery," ch. 6-A, §1 et seq. If a party needs more time for discovery, it should file a motion for continuance. See "Motion for Continuance," ch. 5-D, §1 et seq.

§3.6 Hearing. The court must hold a hearing before ruling on a Code FNC motion. Tex. Civ. Prac. & Rem. Code §71.051(d).

1. Notice. The court cannot rule on the motion unless the parties have at least 21 days' notice of the hearing. Tex. Civ. Prac. & Rem. Code §71.051(d).

2. Deadline. The hearing must be held a reasonable time before trial—at least 30 days. Tex. Civ. Prac. & Rem. Code §71.051(d).

3. Evidence. The parties should produce affidavits, deposition testimony, discovery responses, or other verified evidence. CPRC §71.051 does not explicitly prohibit oral testimony at the hearing.

4. Burden of proof. CPRC §71.051 does not place the burden of proof on either the plaintiff or the defendant to show whether the court should exercise jurisdiction. **In re ENSCO Offshore Int'l**, 311 S.W.3d 921, 927 (Tex.2010); **In re General Elec. Co.**, 271 S.W.3d 681, 687 (Tex.2008). The statute does not require that a party prove each of the §71.051(b) factors or that the factors "strongly" favor granting the FNC motion. *See* **In re ENSCO**, 311 S.W.3d at 929; **In re General Elec.**, 271 S.W.3d at 687.

§3.7 Ruling.

1. Review of §71.051 factors. In ruling on the Code FNC motion, the trial court must consider the CPRC §71.051(b) factors to the extent they apply. **In re General Elec. Co.**, 271 S.W.3d 681, 687 (Tex.2008). The trial court's determination of whether a claim should be stayed or dismissed under CPRC §71.051(b) must be made with respect to each plaintiff individually—whether the claims of any other plaintiff in the suit may be stayed or dismissed based on the §71.051(b) factors is irrelevant. Tex. Civ. Prac. & Rem. Code §71.051(e). If the statutory factors weigh in favor of the claim being heard in an alternate forum, the trial court must grant the FNC motion. **In re General Elec.**, 271 S.W.3d at 686. When evidence is necessary to support a party's position, the court will base its decision on the greater weight of the evidence. **In re ENSCO Offshore Int'l**, 311 S.W.3d 921, 927 (Tex.2010); **In re General Elec.**, 271 S.W.3d at 687; *see* **In re Mahindra, USA Inc.**, 549 S.W.3d 541, 550 (Tex.2018).

2. Timing.

(1) Generally—after resolving jurisdictional challenges. Generally, a court must determine whether it has jurisdiction over a defendant before ruling on an FNC motion. *Cf.* **Exxon Corp. v. Choo**, 881 S.W.2d 301, 302 n.2 (Tex.1994) (suit filed before effective date of CPRC §71.051). See "Due order of pleading," ch. 3-A, §3; "Special Appearance—Challenging Personal Jurisdiction," ch. 3-B, §1 et seq.

(2) Exception—jurisdictional challenges difficult to resolve. A court may take the less burdensome approach and resolve an FNC motion before a jurisdictional challenge if the jurisdictional challenge would be more difficult to resolve and the FNC considerations weigh heavily in favor of dismissal. **Sinochem Int'l Co. v. Malaysia Int'l Shipping Corp.**, 549 U.S. 422, 436 (2007); *see, e.g.*, **Schippers v. Mazak Props., Inc.**, 350 S.W.3d 294, 296 (Tex.App.—San Antonio 2011, pet. denied) (because FNC is a determination of whether merits of claim should be decided elsewhere rather than a determination of substantive law, court addressed FNC motion before special appearance); *cf.* **Vinmar Trade Fin., Ltd. v. Utility Trailers de Mex., S.A. de C.V.**, 336 S.W.3d 664, 671–72 (Tex.App.—Houston [1st Dist.] 2010, no pet.) (common-law FNC; court addressed FNC motion before special appearance because it enabled court to address issues involving both parties while special appearance involved only one party).

§4. Common-law FNC motion

In cases not involving personal injury or wrongful death, the court can decline to exercise its jurisdiction over the action to avoid imposing an inconvenient forum on a litigant and witnesses. *See* **Gottwald v. de Cano**, 568 S.W.3d 241, 246 (Tex.App.—El Paso 2019, no pet.); **Sarieddine v. Moussa**, 820 S.W.2d 837, 839–41 (Tex.App.—Dallas 1991, writ denied). A common-law FNC motion to dismiss asks the court to decline jurisdiction because a court outside Texas has jurisdiction over the dispute and the defendants and is a more appropriate forum. *See* **Van Winkle-Hooker Co. v. Rice**, 448 S.W.2d 824, 826 (Tex.App.—Dallas 1969, no writ). Unlike under Code FNC, dismissal in favor of an alternate forum may be appropriate under common-law FNC even if the plaintiff is a Texas resident. *See* **Gottwald**, 568 S.W.3d at 246–47. See "Not a 'plaintiff,' legal resident, or derivative claimant of legal resident," ch. 3-D, §3.1.4(1); "Plaintiff is legal resident or derivative claimant of legal resident," ch. 3-D, §3.2.2(2).

§4.1 Motion.

1. In writing. A common-law FNC motion should be made in writing and supported by evidence. *See* **RSR Corp. v. Siegmund**, 309 S.W.3d 686, 710 (Tex.App.—Dallas 2010, no pet.) (D bears burden of invoking doctrine of FNC in motion to dismiss); *see also* **Seung Ok Lee v. Ki Pong Na**, 198 S.W.3d 492, 495 (Tex.App.—Dallas 2006, no pet.) (there must be some evidence in record that allows trial court to balance FNC factors and determine whether they weigh in favor of trying case in another forum). See **O'Connor's Texas Civil Forms**, FORM 3D:2 (2020 ed.).

2. Deadline to file. Generally, there is no deadline for filing a motion for common-law FNC; however, the motion should be brought before trial. *See* **Flaiz v. Moore**, 359 S.W.2d 872, 875 (Tex.1962); **Direct Color Servs. v. Eastman Kodak Co.**, 929 S.W.2d 558, 567 (Tex.App.—Tyler 1996, writ dism'd).

3. Grounds. To be entitled to a dismissal, the defendant must assert the following grounds in the common-law FNC motion.

(1) Alternate forum available. For dismissal to be proper, there must be another forum that is both available and adequate. **Gottwald v. de Cano**, 568 S.W.3d 241, 249 (Tex.App.—El Paso 2019, no pet.). As a threshold matter, the defendant must show that the other forum is available. *See id.*; **Vinmar Trade Fin., Ltd. v. Utility Trailers de Mex., S.A. de C.V.**, 336 S.W.3d 664, 674 (Tex.App.—Houston [1st Dist.] 2010, no pet.). Another forum is "available" when the entire case and all the defendants can come within the jurisdiction of the forum. **Gottwald**, 568 S.W.3d at 249; **Sarieddine v. Moussa**, 820 S.W.2d 837, 841 (Tex.App.—Dallas 1991, writ denied); *see* **Benz Grp. v. Barreto**, 404 S.W.3d 92, 97 (Tex.App.—Houston [1st Dist.] 2013, no pet.). This requirement is satisfied if the defendant establishes that all defendants are amenable to process in the alternate forum. **Gottwald**, 568 S.W.3d at 249; **Direct Color**, 929 S.W.2d at 564. A defendant is amenable to process when (1) it has minimum contacts sufficient for a court to exercise jurisdiction over it or (2) it agrees to submit to the court's jurisdiction. **Direct Color**, 929 S.W.2d at 564; *see, e.g.*, **Seguros Comercial Am., S.A. de C.V. v. American**

President Lines, Ltd., 966 S.W.2d 652, 656 (Tex.App.—San Antonio 1998, no pet.) (Mexico was available forum because D was willing to submit to jurisdiction of Mexican court); **Sarieddine**, 820 S.W.2d at 842 (Abu Dhabi was available forum because Ds consented to jurisdiction there). If the defendant shows that the forum is available, the burden shifts to the plaintiff to show that the forum is not adequate. **RSR Corp.**, 309 S.W.3d at 710. See "Forum is not adequate," ch. 3-D, §4.2.3(1).

Note

Under Code FNC analysis, whether an alternate forum is available and adequate is one of several factors the court considers in making its determination. ***Gottwald****, 568 S.W.3d at 249; see Tex. Civ. Prac. & Rem. Code §71.051(b). See "Action should be heard in alternate forum," ch. 3-D, §3.1.4(2). But under common-law FNC analysis, whether the alternate forum is both available and adequate is a threshold question the court must answer before it weighs the private- and public-interest factors.* ***Gottwald****, 568 S.W.3d at 249.*

(2) *Gulf Oil* factors favor alternate forum. The defendant must show that the balance of the parties' private interests and the state's public interests favors the alternate forum. **Quixtar Inc. v. Signature Mgmt. Team, LLC**, 315 S.W.3d 28, 33–34 (Tex.2010); **RSR Corp.**, 309 S.W.3d at 710; **Yoroshii Invs. (Mauritius) Pte. Ltd. v. BP Int'l**, 179 S.W.3d 639, 643 (Tex.App.—El Paso 2005, pet. denied). See "Balance of private and public interests favors alternate forum," ch. 3-D, §3.1.4(2)(e).

(a) *Gulf Oil* factors. The private- and public-interest factors originated in **Gulf Oil Corp. v. Gilbert**, 330 U.S. 501 (1947), and are called the **Gulf Oil** factors.

[1] Private interests. The defendant should establish that the private interests of the parties will be better served in the alternate forum.

[a] The defendant should address whether access to sources of proof will be easier in the alternate forum than in Texas. **Quixtar**, 315 S.W.3d at 33; **RSR Corp.**, 309 S.W.3d at 710; **Yoroshii Invs.**, 179 S.W.3d at 643.

[b] The defendant should address whether compulsory process for the attendance of unwilling witnesses is available in the alternate forum. **Quixtar**, 315 S.W.3d at 33; **RSR Corp.**, 309 S.W.3d at 710; **Yoroshii Invs.**, 179 S.W.3d at 643.

[c] The defendant should address whether the costs of securing the presence of willing witnesses will be lower in the alternate forum than in Texas. **Quixtar**, 315 S.W.3d at 33; **RSR Corp.**, 309 S.W.3d at 710.

[d] The defendant should address whether viewing the relevant premises is necessary to the suit and whether the possibility of viewing the premises is better in the alternate forum than in Texas. **Quixtar**, 315 S.W.3d at 33.

[e] The defendant should address whether the enforceability of the judgment in the alternate forum is as good as or better than in Texas. *Id.*; **RSR Corp.**, 309 S.W.3d at 710; **Yoroshii Invs.**, 179 S.W.3d at 643.

[f] The defendant should address all other practical problems that make the trial of a case easy, expeditious, and inexpensive. **Quixtar**, 315 S.W.3d at 33; **RSR Corp.**, 309 S.W.3d at 710.

[2] Public interests. The defendant should establish that the public interests will be better served in the alternate forum.

[a] The defendant should address whether the burden of jury duty is more appropriately placed on the alternate forum's citizens rather than on Texas citizens. **Quixtar**, 315 S.W.3d at 34; *see* **RSR Corp.**, 309 S.W.3d at 710; **Yoroshii Invs.**, 179 S.W.3d at 643.

[b] The defendant should address whether the administrative burden (e.g., congested docket) on the alternate forum's court is less than the burden on the Texas court. **Quixtar**, 315 S.W.3d at 33–34; *see* **RSR Corp.**, 309 S.W.3d at 710; **Yoroshii Invs.**, 179 S.W.3d at 643.

[c] The defendant should address the extent to which the interest in deciding the case in the alternate forum is greater than that in Texas. *See* **Quixtar**, 315 S.W.3d at 33–34; **RSR Corp.**, 309 S.W.3d at 710; **Yoroshii Invs.**, 179 S.W.3d at 643.

[d] The defendant should address whether the law of the alternate forum will control the disposition of the case. *See* **Quixtar**, 315 S.W.3d at 34; **RSR Corp.**, 309 S.W.3d at 710; **Yoroshii Invs.**, 179 S.W.3d at 643.

(b) D's burden of persuasion & proof.

[1] Persuasion. The defendant must provide the court with enough information to enable the court to determine that the **Gulf Oil** factors support dismissal. **Quixtar**, 315 S.W.3d at 34. This burden of persuasion does not require, however, that the defendant make an "extensive investigation" to produce evidence for the dismissal hearing. *Id.*

[2] Proof. The defendant's burden of proof on the balance of the **Gulf Oil** factors depends on the plaintiff's status as a Texas resident.

[a] P is resident. If the plaintiff (either an individual or a corporation) is a Texas resident, the defendant must show the balance of factors "strongly favors" dismissal. *See* **Quixtar**, 315 S.W.3d at 33; **Vinmar Trade**, 336 S.W.3d at 678. But if the plaintiff is a Texas corporation that does extensive foreign business, the defendant must show the balance of factors simply "favors" dismissal. *See* **Vinmar Trade**, 336 S.W.3d at 678 (choice of forum for Texas corporation doing extensive foreign business is given less deference).

[b] P is nonresident. If the plaintiff is a nonresident, the defendant must show the balance of factors simply "favors" dismissal. *See* **Quixtar**, 315 S.W.3d at 32–33 (nonresident's choice of forum is entitled to less deference, and thus D's burden of proof is less stringent than if P were a resident).

§4.2 Response.

1. In writing. The plaintiff should file a written response challenging the allegations in the defendant's motion.

2. Deadline to file. Although there is no deadline for filing the response, the plaintiff should file (and serve) it far enough in advance of the hearing for the court to consider the arguments and evidence.

3. Grounds. The plaintiff should challenge the defendant's allegations raised in the motion. See **O'Connor's Texas Civil Forms**, FORM 3D:4 (2020 ed.).

(1) Forum is not adequate. If the defendant establishes that an alternate forum is available, the plaintiff must show that the forum is not adequate. **RSR Corp. v. Siegmund**, 309 S.W.3d 686, 710 (Tex.App.—Dallas 2010, no pet.); *see* **Vinmar Trade Fin., Ltd. v. Utility Trailers de Mex., S.A. de C.V.**, 336 S.W.3d 664, 674 (Tex.App.—Houston [1st Dist.] 2010, no pet.) (alternate forum's laws presumed adequate unless P makes contrary showing). An alternate forum is adequate when the parties will not be deprived of all remedies or treated unfairly. **Vinmar Trade**, 336 S.W.3d at 674; **RSR Corp.**, 309 S.W.3d at 710. An alternate forum is not adequate when the remedies it offers are so unsatisfactory that they essentially offer no remedy at all. **Gottwald v. de Cano**, 568 S.W.3d 241, 249 (Tex.App.—El Paso 2019, no pet.); *see* **RSR Corp.**, 309 S.W.3d at 710. But remedies that may merely be different or less advantageous will not make the alternate forum inadequate. **Gottwald**, 568 S.W.3d at 249.

(2) *Gulf Oil* factors favor Texas forum. The plaintiff should address the **Gulf Oil** factors and demonstrate how the balance of those factors favors the Texas forum. See "*Gulf Oil* factors," ch. 3-D, §4.1.3(2)(a).

§4.3 Hearing. The court must hold a hearing and allow for evidence to be presented before it can rule on a common-law FNC motion. **Garden City Boxing Club, Inc. v. 3425 Club, Inc.**, No. 05-08-00571-CV, 2009 WL 930460 (Tex.App.—Dallas 2009, no pet.) (memo op.; 4-8-09); *see* **Seung Ok Lee v. Ki Pong Na**, 198 S.W.3d 492, 495 (Tex.App.—Dallas 2006, no pet.). The court is not required to consider only evidence admitted at the evidentiary hearing; it may consider any evidence properly before it, including evidence attached to the defendant's FNC motion. **Crum & Forster Specialty Ins. v. Creekstone Builders, Inc.**, 489 S.W.3d 473, 481 (Tex.App.—Houston [1st Dist.] 2015, no pet.).

§4.4 Ruling. If the alternate forum is available and adequate and the balance of private- and public-interest factors either strongly favors or simply favors the alternate forum (depending on the plaintiff's status as a Texas resident), the trial

court must grant the common-law FNC motion to dismiss. *See* **Quixtar Inc. v. Signature Mgmt. Team, LLC**, 315 S.W.3d 28, 33–35 (Tex.2010). See "Proof," ch. 3-D, §4.1.3(2)(b)[2]. For a discussion of whether the ruling on the motion can be made before a ruling on any jurisdictional challenges, see "Timing," ch. 3-D, §3.7.2.

§5. Order

The court must sign a written order sustaining or overruling the motion.

§5.1 Code FNC.

1. Motion sustained. When the court sustains a motion for Code FNC, it can grant either a dismissal or a stay. The court must issue specific findings of fact and conclusions of law. Tex. Civ. Prac. & Rem. Code §71.051(f); **In re Mahindra, USA Inc.**, 549 S.W.3d 541, 545 (Tex.2018). The court may set terms and conditions for dismissing or staying a claim as the interest of justice requires. Tex. Civ. Prac. & Rem. Code §71.051(c). If a defendant violates the terms or conditions of the order of dismissal or stay, the court must withdraw the order and proceed as if it had never been issued, despite any other law on jurisdiction. *Id.*

Note

A Texas court does not have the power to transfer a case to another state's or country's court. See ***Accelerated Christian Educ., Inc. v. Oracle Corp.****, 925 S.W.2d 66, 70 (Tex.App.—Dallas 1996, no writ); Restatement Second, Conflict of Laws §84, comment e. Thus, a Texas court can only dismiss or stay the suit.*

2. Motion overruled. When the court overrules a motion for Code FNC, the suit will continue in the Texas court. The court is not required to issue specific findings of fact and conclusions of law. *See* Tex. Civ. Prac. & Rem. Code §71.051(f).

§5.2 Common-law FNC.

1. Motion sustained. When the court sustains a motion for common-law FNC, it will usually dismiss the case. *See* **Sarieddine v. Moussa**, 820 S.W.2d 837, 839 (Tex.App.—Dallas 1991, writ denied). The court may, however, consider granting a stay instead. If the court grants a dismissal under common law, it cannot later withdraw the order of dismissal as it can under CPRC §71.051(c). By granting a stay, the court retains the case on its docket in the event the defendant does not comply with its agreement to be sued in the alternate forum.

2. Motion overruled. When the court overrules a motion for common-law FNC, the suit will continue in the Texas court.

§6. Forum-selection clause

Forum-selection clauses are contractual provisions in which parties select in advance a particular jurisdiction for resolving their disputes. **Pinto Tech. Ventures, L.P. v. Sheldon**, 526 S.W.3d 428, 436 (Tex.2017); **Guam Indus. Servs. v. Dresser-Rand Co.**, 514 S.W.3d 828, 833 (Tex.App.—Houston [1st Dist.] 2017, no pet.); **RSR Corp. v. Siegmund**, 309 S.W.3d 686, 700 (Tex.App.—Dallas 2010, no pet.). Contractual forum-selection clauses are presumed to be valid and enforceable in Texas. **In re Laibe Corp.**, 307 S.W.3d 314, 316 (Tex.2010); **In re International Profit Assocs.**, 274 S.W.3d 672, 675 (Tex.2009); **In re Lyon Fin. Servs.**, 257 S.W.3d 228, 232 (Tex.2008). A motion to dismiss is the appropriate mechanism for enforcing a forum-selection clause. **RSR Corp.**, 309 S.W.3d at 709; **Deep Water Slender Wells, Ltd. v. Shell Int'l Expl. & Prod.**, 234 S.W.3d 679, 687 (Tex.App.—Houston [14th Dist.] 2007, pet. denied); *see also* **HMT Tank Serv. v. American Tank & Vessel, Inc.**, 565 S.W.3d 799, 805–06 & n.2 (Tex.App.—Houston [14th Dist.] 2018, no pet.) (general motion to dismiss is appropriate mechanism to enforce forum-selection clause; TRCP 91a motion to dismiss is generally not appropriate).

§6.1 Enforcement. A party seeking to enforce a forum-selection clause has the initial burden of establishing that there is a valid agreement to use an exclusive forum and that the party's claims fall within the scope of the forum-selection clause. **HMT Tank Serv. v. American Tank & Vessel, Inc.**, 565 S.W.3d 799, 805 (Tex.App.—Houston [14th Dist.] 2018, no pet.);

see **Phoenix Network Techs. (Eur.) Ltd. v. Neon Sys.**, 177 S.W.3d 605, 613–14 (Tex.App.—Houston [1st Dist.] 2005, no pet.). Once that burden is met, the burden shifts to the opposing party to overcome the presumed validity of the forum-selection clause. **HMT Tank Serv.**, 565 S.W.3d at 805; *see* **Phoenix Network**, 177 S.W.3d at 613–14.

1. Who can enforce.

(1) Signatories. Generally, a forum-selection clause can be enforced only by a party to the contract containing the clause. **Pinto Tech. Ventures, L.P. v. Sheldon**, 526 S.W.3d 428, 443 (Tex.2017).

(2) Nonsignatories. Nonsignatories can enforce a forum-selection clause under certain limited circumstances. *See* **Pinto Tech.**, 526 S.W.3d at 443.

(a) Clause's plain language. Nonsignatories may be able to enforce a forum-selection clause when the plain language indicates the parties' intent to extend enforcement rights to nonsignatories. *See, e.g.*, **Pinto Tech.**, 526 S.W.3d at 445 (language in forum-selection clause extended contractual rights and remedies only to parties and permitted successors and assignees, which did not include nonsignatory Ds); *cf.* **In re Rubiola**, 334 S.W.3d 220, 224–25 (Tex.2011) (in arbitration case, nonsignatories could compel arbitration when contract provided that "individual partners, affiliates, officers, directors, employees, agents, and/or representatives of any party" were considered parties to contract).

(b) Arbitration-related enforcement theories. Because forum-selection clauses and arbitration clauses are treated similarly, nonsignatories may be able to enforce a forum-selection clause under some of the same theories for enforcement of an arbitration clause by a nonsignatory. *See* **Chandler Mgmt. v. First Specialty Ins.**, 452 S.W.3d 887, 891 (Tex.App.—Dallas 2014, no pet.); **Smith v. Kenda Capital, LLC**, 451 S.W.3d 453, 458 (Tex.App.—Houston [14th Dist.] 2014, no pet.); **Phoenix Network**, 177 S.W.3d at 623–24. One such theory that may arise in the forum-selection context is equitable estoppel. *See* **Pinto Tech.**, 526 S.W.3d at 446; **Chandler Mgmt.**, 452 S.W.3d at 891; **Phoenix Network**, 177 S.W.3d at 623–24. See "Equitable estoppel," ch. 4-C, §5.1.2(6). Specifically, a nonsignatory may be able to enforce a forum-selection clause by alleging direct-benefits estoppel or concerted-misconduct estoppel. *See, e.g.*, **Pinto Tech.**, 526 S.W.3d at 446 (nonsignatories could not enforce forum-selection clause under concerted-misconduct estoppel; Court followed its earlier precedent that declined to adopt concerted-misconduct estoppel in arbitration cases because parties did not address or distinguish those cases); **Smith**, 451 S.W.3d at 458–59 (nonsignatory could enforce forum-selection clause under direct-benefits estoppel). For other theories of enforcement of an arbitration clause by a nonsignatory, see "Nonsignatory," ch. 4-C, §5.1.2.

Note

*At least one court has recognized an additional theory of enforcement besides those discussed in the arbitration context—the transaction-participant theory. See, e.g., **Carlile Bancshares, Inc. v. Armstrong**, No. 02-14-00014-CV, 2014 WL 3891658 (Tex.App.—Fort Worth 2014, no pet.) (memo op.; 8-7-14) (court recognized theory but determined it did not apply to case facts). Under this theory, a nonsignatory can enforce a forum-selection clause against a signatory if the nonsignatory is a transaction participant (e.g., an employee of one of the contracting parties who is individually named by another contracting party in a suit arising from the contract containing the forum-selection clause) and enforcement of the forum-selection clause would be foreseeable to the opposing party. See **Pinto Tech.**, 526 S.W.3d at 444; **Carlile Bancshares**, No. 02-14-00014-CV, 2014 WL 3891658 (memo op.). On two separate occasions, however, the Supreme Court has not addressed whether or under what circumstances this theory would apply because enforcement was not reasonably foreseeable in those cases. See **Rieder v. Woods**, 603 S.W.3d 86, 100–01 (Tex.2020); **Pinto Tech.**, 526 S.W.3d at 445.*

2. Mandatory vs. permissive. To be enforceable, a forum-selection clause must be mandatory, not permissive. *See* **Phoenix Network**, 177 S.W.3d at 615; **Mabon Ltd. v. Afri-Carib Enters.**, 29 S.W.3d 291, 297 (Tex.App.—Houston [14th Dist.] 2000, no pet.); **In re Agresti**, No. 13-14-00126-CV, 2014 WL 3408691 (Tex.App.—Corpus Christi 2014, orig. proceeding) (memo op.; 5-29-14). If the terms of a forum-selection clause are ambiguous, the court will apply principles of

contract law to determine the parties' intent. **In re Agresti**, No. 13-14-00126-CV, 2014 WL 3408691 (memo op.); *see* **RSR Corp. v. Siegmund**, 309 S.W.3d 686, 700 (Tex.App.—Dallas 2010, no pet.); **Phoenix Network**, 177 S.W.3d at 615.

(1) Mandatory. A mandatory clause states that a suit must be brought only in a designated forum; that is, there must be some language explicitly excluding other forums. **Mabon Ltd.**, 29 S.W.3d at 297; **In re Agresti**, No. 13-14-00126-CV, 2014 WL 3408691 (memo op.); *see, e.g.*, **Deep Water Slender Wells, Ltd. v. Shell Int'l Expl. & Prod.**, 234 S.W.3d 679, 687 (Tex.App.—Houston [14th Dist.] 2007, pet. denied) (forum-selection clause that stated designated forum had "exclusive jurisdiction" to resolve suits was mandatory); **Phoenix Network**, 177 S.W.3d at 615 (forum-selection clause that provided for United Kingdom as "the venue" for suit was mandatory; use of definite article "the" indicated exclusivity).

(2) Permissive. A permissive clause states that a suit may be brought in a designated forum; that is, the clause does not require that the suit be brought in that forum. **Ramsay v. Texas Trading Co.**, 254 S.W.3d 620, 629 (Tex.App.—Texarkana 2008, pet. denied); **Mabon Ltd.**, 29 S.W.3d at 297; **In re Agresti**, No. 13-14-00126-CV, 2014 WL 3408691 (memo op.). Although the term "shall" in a forum-selection clause is generally mandatory, without other exclusive language, the clause may be deemed permissive. *See* **Phoenix Network**, 177 S.W.3d at 615; *see, e.g.*, **Mabon Ltd.**, 29 S.W.3d at 297 (forum-selection clause was permissive even though it stated Nigeria "shall have venue"; term "shall" did not provide for exclusive jurisdiction but instead meant only that Nigeria was an acceptable forum); **Southwest Intelecom, Inc. v. Hotel Networks Corp.**, 997 S.W.2d 322, 325–26 (Tex.App.—Austin 1999, pet. denied) (forum-selection clause was permissive even though it stated that agreement "shall be governed" by laws of Minnesota and parties stipulated to jurisdiction and venue there; clause did not mandate exclusive jurisdiction in Minnesota but instead required parties to submit to jurisdiction in Minnesota only if suit was brought there).

3. Within scope. For a court to enforce a forum-selection clause, a plaintiff's claims must fall within the scope of the clause. *See* **In re Lisa Laser USA, Inc.**, 310 S.W.3d 880, 884–85 (Tex.2010); **Stokes Interest, G.P. v. Santo-Pietro**, 343 S.W.3d 441, 445 (Tex.App.—El Paso 2010, no pet.); *see, e.g.*, **Guam Indus. Servs. v. Dresser-Rand Co.**, 514 S.W.3d 828, 833 (Tex.App.—Houston [1st Dist.] 2017, no pet.) (litigation of claims on merits did not fall within scope of clause stating parties agreed to conduct arbitration in Texas). In determining whether a claim falls within the clause's scope, the court will focus on the substantive factual allegations; the causes of action alleged are not determinative. **Pinto Tech.**, 526 S.W.3d at 437.

(1) Clause's plain language. The particular language of the forum-selection clause will control its scope. *See* **Rieder**, 603 S.W.3d at 94; **Pinto Tech.**, 526 S.W.3d at 437; *see, e.g.*, **Marullo v. Apollo Associated Servs.**, 515 S.W.3d 902, 904–05 (Tex.App.—Houston [14th Dist.] 2017, no pet.) (claims based on employee's conduct before he signed contract containing forum-selection clause were covered by clause because clause stated it applied to claims arising from employment with company, not from only the contract itself); *see also* **In re International Profit Assocs.**, 274 S.W.3d 672, 677 (Tex.2009) (court should use "common sense" approach in determining whether forum-selection clause covers P's claims). Forum-selection clauses commonly state that they apply to any claims or disputes "arising out of" or "arising from" the contract that contains the forum-selection clause. *See* **In re Lisa Laser**, 310 S.W.3d at 882; *see, e.g.*, **Pinto Tech.**, 526 S.W.3d at 439 (clause applied to "any dispute arising out of" agreement, which is broader in scope than "any claims"). In **Pinto Tech.**, the Supreme Court set forth a two-part framework to use in considering whether a claim arises out of a contract and thus falls within the scope of the form-selection clause. *See* **Pinto Tech.**, 526 S.W.3d at 440.

(a) Same operative facts. The court will consider whether the claim involves the same operative facts as would a parallel claim for breach of contract—that is, whether the operative facts of the claim involve the validity, terms, or performance of the contract or are substantially connected to it. *See* **Pinto Tech.**, 526 S.W.3d at 440–41.

(b) But-for causation. The court will consider whether, but for the agreement, the plaintiff would have no basis for her claim. *See* **Pinto Tech.**, 526 S.W.3d at 440–41; **In re Lisa Laser**, 310 S.W.3d at 886.

Note

In an earlier opinion, the Supreme Court suggested that for a forum-selection clause to cover a certain claim based on the but-for standard, the obligations the party's claim was based on had to arise from

the contract and not from "general obligations imposed by law." See ***In re Lisa Laser****, 310 S.W.3d at 884. But in* ***Pinto Tech.****, the Court clarified that it is not always necessary that the obligation arise directly from the contract; depending on the language of the particular forum-selection clause, it is possible that a clause could apply to claims based on general obligations imposed by law. See* ***Pinto Tech.****, 526 S.W.3d at 442 (claim based on general obligations imposed by law can be within scope of clause that applies to any "dispute" arising from contract).*

(2) Other documents relevant to determining scope. In determining the scope of the forum-selection clause, the court may also examine any other documents that pertain to the same transaction as the document containing the clause. *See* **Rieder**, 603 S.W.3d at 94; **In re Lisa Laser**, 310 S.W.3d at 885; **In re Laibe Corp.**, 307 S.W.3d 314, 317 (Tex.2010). The documents do not need to have been executed at the same time or expressly refer to each other, as long as the court determines that they are part of a single, unified instrument. **Rieder**, 603 S.W.3d at 94; **In re Laibe Corp.**, 307 S.W.3d at 317. If the documents are construed as a single instrument, the forum-selection clause applies as if it were part of all the documents. *See* **Rieder**, 603 S.W.3d at 94; **In re Laibe Corp.**, 307 S.W.3d at 317; *see, e.g.*, **In re Lisa Laser**, 310 S.W.3d at 885 (agreement including multiple exhibits, one of which contained forum-selection clause applicable to sales between P and D-distributor, was read as multiple documents describing one transaction; forum-selection clause applied to all of P's claims under agreement).

4. No exception or waiver. If the plaintiff's claims fall within the scope of the forum-selection clause, the court must enforce the clause unless the party opposing it can show an exception to enforcement or a waiver by the other party.

(1) Exceptions. The party opposing the forum-selection clause has a heavy burden of proof. **Rieder**, 603 S.W.3d at 93; **In re Laibe Corp.**, 307 S.W.3d at 316; **In re International Profit**, 274 S.W.3d at 675. The party must clearly show that (1) enforcement of the clause would be unreasonable and unjust, (2) the clause is invalid because of fraud or overreaching, (3) enforcement would contravene a strong Texas public policy, or (4) the selected forum is seriously inconvenient for trial. **Rieder**, 603 S.W.3d at 93; **In re ADM Investor Servs.**, 304 S.W.3d 371, 375 (Tex.2010); **In re Lyon Fin. Servs.**, 257 S.W.3d 228, 231–32 (Tex.2008); *see* **In re Nationwide Ins.**, 494 S.W.3d 708, 712 (Tex.2016). See **O'Connor's Texas Civil Forms**, FORM 3D:8 (2020 ed.).

(a) Unreasonable & unjust. The party opposing the forum-selection clause may show that enforcement of the clause would be unreasonable and unjust. **In re Laibe Corp.**, 307 S.W.3d at 316; **In re ADM Investor**, 304 S.W.3d at 375; **In re International Profit**, 274 S.W.3d at 675; **In re AutoNation, Inc.**, 228 S.W.3d 663, 668 (Tex.2007); **In re AIU Ins.**, 148 S.W.3d 109, 112 (Tex.2004). Enforcement will be unreasonable and unjust only in extreme or exceptional circumstances. *See* **In re ADM Investor**, 304 S.W.3d at 376.

(b) Fraud or overreaching. The party opposing the forum-selection clause may show that the clause is invalid because it is the result of fraud or overreaching. **In re Laibe Corp.**, 307 S.W.3d at 316; **In re ADM Investor**, 304 S.W.3d at 375; **In re Lyon Fin.**, 257 S.W.3d at 231–32; **In re AutoNation, Inc.**, 228 S.W.3d at 668; *see, e.g.*, **In re International Profit Assocs.**, 286 S.W.3d 921, 923–24 (Tex.2009) (P claimed D did not show page of contract containing forum-selection clause to P's representative; no evidence of fraud or overreaching without some misrepresentation or fraudulent concealment of part of contract). Fraud in a forum-selection clause is shown by proving the usual elements of fraud. *See* **In re International Profit**, 274 S.W.3d at 678. See "Fraud," **O'Connor's Texas Causes of Action**, ch. 12-A, §1 et seq. (2021 ed.). The claim of fraud must relate to the forum-selection clause itself, not to the contract as a whole. *See* **In re Lyon Fin.**, 257 S.W.3d at 232. The courts analyze claims of overreaching by determining whether the forum-selection clause results in unfair surprise or oppression to the party opposing it. **In re International Profit**, 274 S.W.3d at 678; *see* **In re Lyon Fin.**, 257 S.W.3d at 232–33.

(c) Against public policy. The party opposing the forum-selection clause may show that enforcement of the clause would contravene a strong Texas public policy. **In re Laibe Corp.**, 307 S.W.3d at 316; **In re ADM Investor**, 304 S.W.3d at 375; **In re International Profit**, 274 S.W.3d at 675; **In re Lyon Fin.**, 257 S.W.3d at 231–32. A Texas statute that simply specifies the application of Texas law, but does not require that suit be brought in Texas, does not establish a public policy that would prevent enforcement of a forum-selection clause. *E.g.*, **In re Lyon Fin.**, 257 S.W.3d at 234 (P's inability to assert usury claim in Pennsylvania did not create public-policy reason to deny enforcement of forum-selection clause); *see* **In re AutoNation, Inc.**, 228 S.W.3d at 669.

(d) Seriously inconvenient. The party opposing the forum-selection clause may show that the selected forum would be seriously inconvenient such that enforcement of the clause would deprive the party of its day in court. **In re Laibe Corp.**, 307 S.W.3d at 316–17; **In re ADM Investor**, 304 S.W.3d at 375; *e.g.*, **In re Lyon Fin.**, 257 S.W.3d at 233–34 (Pennsylvania was not such an inconvenient forum that enforcing forum-selection clause would produce an "unjust result"). The party should show that special and unusual circumstances have developed that would make litigation in the selected forum extremely difficult and inconvenient. *E.g.*, **In re International Profit**, 274 S.W.3d at 680 (witnesses' residences in location other than where suit was brought was not special or unusual circumstance). Conclusory statements are insufficient to establish serious inconvenience. **In re Laibe Corp.**, 307 S.W.3d at 318; *e.g.*, **In re ADM Investor**, 304 S.W.3d at 375 (P's conclusory statements about her health problems were insufficient to establish inconvenience); *see* **In re Lyon Fin.**, 257 S.W.3d at 234 (party must do more than just state that change in financial or logistical conditions will preclude litigation in another state).

Note

The Court in **In re ADM Investor** *did not decide whether health problems would, in a different case, be sufficient grounds to establish inconvenience or what proof would be necessary to do so.* **In re ADM Investor**, *304 S.W.3d at 376 n.1. In the concurring opinion, one justice did suggest that, at a minimum, testimony from a medical provider is necessary, and the provider should state that the patient's condition makes travel to the agreed forum not only seriously inconvenient but also medically prohibited. Id. at 377 (Willett, J., concurring).*

(2) Waiver. The party opposing the forum-selection clause may show that the other party waived its right to rely on the clause. *See* **In re Nationwide Ins.**, 494 S.W.3d at 712; **In re AIU Ins.**, 148 S.W.3d at 121. To determine whether the forum-selection clause is waived, the court should apply the test for waiver of an arbitration clause—that is, whether a party substantially invoked the judicial process causing prejudice to the other party. **In re Boehme**, 256 S.W.3d 878, 884 (Tex.App.—Houston [14th Dist.] 2008, orig. proceeding); *e.g.*, **In re Nationwide Ins.**, 494 S.W.3d at 712–13 (filing motion to dismiss based on forum-selection clause after expiration of contractual limitations period was not prejudicial when D agreed to waive limitations); **In re ADM Investor**, 304 S.W.3d at 374 (filing answer and motion to transfer venue at same time as motion to dismiss based on forum-selection clause did not substantially invoke judicial process to P's detriment); *see* **In re AIU Ins.**, 148 S.W.3d at 115 (arbitration agreement is type of forum-selection clause). See "Implied waiver," ch. 4-C, §7.5.2.

§6.2 Effect of court's ruling. Dismissal is the appropriate remedy after granting a motion based on a forum-selection clause that identifies another state as the proper forum. **Accelerated Christian Educ., Inc. v. Oracle Corp.**, 925 S.W.2d 66, 70 (Tex.App.—Dallas 1996, no writ); *see* **Stokes Interest, G.P. v. Santo-Pietro**, 343 S.W.3d 441, 444 (Tex.App.—El Paso 2010, no pet.); **Greenwood v. Tillamook Country Smoker, Inc.**, 857 S.W.2d 654, 657 (Tex.App.—Houston [1st Dist.] 1993, no writ). The denial of a motion based on a valid, enforceable forum-selection clause that specifies another state as the chosen forum is reversible error. **In re AIU Ins.**, 148 S.W.3d 109, 118 (Tex.2004).

§7. Review

§7.1 Appealability.

1. Motion granted. A trial court's ruling granting a motion to dismiss for FNC or to enforce a forum-selection clause is generally a final order that can be appealed. *See* **In re Mahindra, USA Inc.**, 549 S.W.3d 541, 545 (Tex.2018) (Code FNC); **Quixtar Inc. v. Signature Mgmt. Team, LLC**, 315 S.W.3d 28, 31 (Tex.2010) (common-law FNC); **Stokes Interest, G.P. v. Santo-Pietro**, 343 S.W.3d 441, 444 (Tex.App.—El Paso 2010, no pet.) (forum-selection clause); *see also* **Martinez v. Bell Helicopter Textron, Inc.**, 49 S.W.3d 890, 891 (Tex.App.—Fort Worth 2001, pet. denied) (Code FNC order that dismissed suit pending resolution in foreign country was not appealable; order was not final because trial court maintained continuing jurisdiction to resolve potential discovery disputes).

2. Motion denied.

(1) No interlocutory appeal. A trial court's denial of a motion to stay or dismiss for FNC or to enforce a forum-selection clause cannot be appealed until after final judgment. *See* **In re Mahindra, USA**, 549 S.W.3d at 545 (Code FNC); **In re ENSCO Offshore Int'l**, 311 S.W.3d 921, 923 (Tex.2010) (Code FNC); **In re AIU Ins.**, 148 S.W.3d 109, 115–16 (Tex.2004) (forum-selection clause).

(2) Mandamus. A defendant can challenge the denial of a motion to stay or dismiss for FNC or to enforce a forum-selection clause by filing a petition for writ of mandamus. **In re Mahindra, USA**, 549 S.W.3d at 545 (Code FNC); **In re Nationwide Ins.**, 494 S.W.3d 708, 712 (Tex.2016) (forum-selection clause); **In re Bridgestone Americas Tire Opers., LLC**, 459 S.W.3d 565, 569 (Tex.2015) (Code FNC); **In re ADM Investor Servs.**, 304 S.W.3d 371, 374 (Tex.2010) (forum-selection clause); **In re Pirelli Tire, L.L.C.**, 247 S.W.3d 670, 676 (Tex.2007) (Code FNC).

§7.2 Standard of review.

1. FNC. A trial court's ruling on an FNC motion is reviewed for abuse of discretion. **In re Mahindra, USA Inc.**, 549 S.W.3d 541, 545 (Tex.2018); **In re Bridgestone Americas Tire Opers., LLC**, 459 S.W.3d 565, 569 (Tex.2015); **Quixtar Inc. v. Signature Mgmt. Team, LLC**, 315 S.W.3d 28, 31 (Tex.2010); **In re ENSCO Offshore Int'l**, 311 S.W.3d 921, 923 (Tex.2010). To determine whether the trial court abused its discretion, the appellate court must decide whether the trial court acted without reference to any guiding rules or principles—that is, whether the act was arbitrary or unreasonable. **In re Pirelli Tire, L.L.C.**, 247 S.W.3d 670, 676 (Tex.2007).

2. Forum-selection clause. A trial court's ruling on a motion to enforce a forum-selection clause is reviewed for abuse of discretion. **In re Lisa Laser USA, Inc.**, 310 S.W.3d 880, 883 (Tex.2010); **In re ADM Investor Servs.**, 304 S.W.3d 371, 374 (Tex.2010); **In re AIU Ins.**, 148 S.W.3d 109, 114–15 (Tex.2004). A trial court abuses its discretion when it improperly interprets or applies a forum-selection clause. **In re Lisa Laser**, 310 S.W.3d at 883. When reviewing a trial court's ruling on whether a claim comes within the scope of an unambiguous forum-selection clause, the appellate court will apply a de novo standard. *See* **Marullo v. Apollo Associated Servs.**, 515 S.W.3d 902, 904 (Tex.App.—Houston [14th Dist.] 2017, no pet.); **Stokes Interest, G.P. v. Santo-Pietro**, 343 S.W.3d 441, 444 (Tex.App.—El Paso 2010, no pet.); **RSR Corp. v. Siegmund**, 309 S.W.3d 686, 709 (Tex.App.—Dallas 2010, no pet.).

§7.3 Filing suit in another jurisdiction. After a dismissal based on an FNC order, the plaintiff can file the suit in another jurisdiction while pursuing an appeal in Texas. *See* **VE Corp. v. Ernst & Young**, 860 S.W.2d 83, 84 (Tex.1993).

E. The Answer—Denying Liability

§1. General

§1.1 Rules. Tex. R. Civ. P. 38, 83 to 85, 90 to 95, 97, 98.

§1.2 Purpose. With its answer, the defendant enters an appearance, denies the allegations in the plaintiff's petition, identifies its defenses, and avoids a default judgment. Once the defendant files an answer, it is entitled to notice of all proceedings in the case.

§1.3 Timetable & forms. Appendix IV, Timetable 8, Pretrial motions; **O'Connor's Texas Civil Forms**, FORMS 3E:1 et seq. (2020 ed.).

§1.4 Other references. McDonald & Carlson, *Texas Civil Practice* §7:17 (2d ed.); **O'Connor's Texas Causes of Action** (2021 ed.); **O'Connor's Texas Civil Appeals** (2020 ed.); **O'Connor's Texas Civil Practice & Remedies Code Plus** (2020–21 ed.).

§2. Deadline to answer

§2.1 Most cases. In district and county courts, the defendant must file its answer by 10:00 a.m. on the first Monday after the expiration of 20 days from the date the defendant was served with the citation. Tex. R. Civ. P. 99(b); **Solis v. Garcia**, 702 S.W.2d 668, 671 (Tex.App.—Houston [14th Dist.] 1985, no writ). An answer is timely if the defendant puts it in the custody of the U.S. Postal Service before 10:00 a.m. on the day it is due, as long as the clerk receives it no later than ten days after the due date. **Milam v. Miller**, 891 S.W.2d 1, 2 (Tex.App.—Amarillo 1994, writ ref'd). If the 20th day after service falls on a Monday, the answer is due on the next Monday. **Proctor v. Green**, 673 S.W.2d 390, 392 (Tex.App.—Houston [1st Dist.] 1984, no writ). If the first Monday after 20 days is a legal holiday, the answer is due on Tuesday. *See* Tex. R. Civ. P. 4; **Conaway v. Lopez**, 880 S.W.2d 448, 450 (Tex.App.—Austin 1994, writ ref'd); **Solis**, 702 S.W.2d at 671; **Proctor**, 673 S.W.2d at 392. In that situation, the defendant has until the end of the next day that is not a legal holiday to file the answer, not just until 10:00 a.m. *E.g.*, **Conaway**, 880 S.W.2d at 450 (default judgment granted on Tuesday afternoon was reversed).

Note

Although the Supreme Court has not addressed whether a motion to transfer venue affects the deadline for filing an answer, there is some authority suggesting that the deadline is delayed until after the court rules on the motion. See ***Glover v. Moser***, *930 S.W.2d 940, 943–44 (Tex.App.—Beaumont 1996, writ denied); McDonald & Carlson, Texas Civil Practice, §7:17 (2d ed.).*

§2.2 Service through Secretary of State. When a defendant is served through the Secretary of State, service of process on the Secretary is constructive service on the defendant and triggers the defendant's answer date. **Bonewitz v. Bonewitz**, 726 S.W.2d 227, 230 (Tex.App.—Austin 1987, writ ref'd n.r.e.). Thus, if the Secretary is served with process on May 8 and forwards it to the defendant on May 12, and the defendant receives it on May 16, the defendant starts counting from the day the Secretary received the process—May 8 is "day 0," May 9 is "day 1," May 10 is "day 2," and so on. See "Computing time limits—days," ch. 1-C, §7.1; "Service on Secretary of State," ch. 2-I, §5.

§2.3 Service by publication. When citation is served by publication, the deadline for filing the answer depends on where it will be filed. In district and county courts, the defendant must file its answer by 10:00 a.m. on the first Monday after the expiration of 42 days from the date the citation was issued. Tex. R. Civ. P. 114. In justice-of-the-peace courts, the defendant must file its answer on or before the first day of the first term of court that convenes after the expiration of 42 days from the date the citation was issued. *Id.* See "Substituted service," ch. 2-I, §4.3.

§2.4 After bankruptcy. When a case is in bankruptcy, the automatic stay tolls the time for a bankruptcy defendant to answer. The time for a bankruptcy defendant to answer in state court resumes running 30 days after the bankruptcy court lifts the stay, dismisses the case, or closes the case. 11 U.S.C. §108(c); *see* **HBA E., Ltd. v. JEA Boxing Co.**, 796 S.W.2d 534, 536 (Tex.App.—Houston [1st Dist.] 1990, writ denied).

§2.5 After remand. Once a case has been remanded to state court after removal to federal court, TRCP 237a gives the defendant 15 days to file its answer, counting from the date the defendant receives notice of the federal court's remand. *See* **HBA E., Ltd. v. JEA Boxing Co.**, 796 S.W.2d 534, 538 (Tex.App.—Houston [1st Dist.] 1990, writ denied). TRCP 237a places the burden on the plaintiff to file a copy of the remand order with the clerk of the state court and to give the defendant written notice of the remand. **HBA**, 796 S.W.2d at 538; *see* **Gonzalez v. Guilbot**, 315 S.W.3d 533, 538 (Tex.2010). Actual notice of the remand is irrelevant. **HBA**, 796 S.W.2d at 537. Until the plaintiff gives the defendant notice of the remand, the defendant's deadline to answer does not begin to run. *Id.* at 538. If the defendant filed an answer in federal court during removal, that answer will suffice in state court once the case is remanded. *See* Tex. R. Civ. P. 237a.

§3. General denial

Every answer should contain a general denial.

§3.1 Definition. A general denial is a statement that the defendant "generally denies all the allegations in the plaintiff's petition." By comparison, a special denial is one that must be specifically pleaded (i.e., when a general denial is insufficient). *See, e.g.*, Tex. R. Civ. P. 52 (denial of corporate status), Tex. R. Civ. P. 54 (conditions precedent), Tex. R. Civ. P. 93 (verified pleas), Tex. R. Civ. P. 94 (affirmative defenses).

§3.2 Effects. The effects of filing a general denial include the following:

1. Puts plaintiff's allegations at issue. A general denial puts at issue everything in the plaintiff's petition that is not required to be denied under oath or specially denied. Tex. R. Civ. P. 92; **Shell Chem. Co. v. Lamb**, 493 S.W.2d 742, 744 (Tex.1973); **Cadle Co. v. Castle**, 913 S.W.2d 627, 631 (Tex.App.—Dallas 1995, writ denied).

2. Prevents default. A general denial prevents the plaintiff from taking a default judgment, even if the answer is defective. See "Sufficiency of defendant's answer," ch. 7-A, §3.7.

3. No jury questions. A general denial does not permit the defendant to submit any questions to the jury. **Luther Transfer & Storage, Inc. v. Walton**, 296 S.W.2d 750, 754 (Tex.1956); *see also* Tex. R. Civ. P. 278 (court must submit questions raised by written pleadings and evidence). If the defendant intends to submit a jury question (e.g., on an affirmative defense), the defendant must plead it in the answer. See "Affirmative defenses," ch. 3-E, §5.

§4. Verified pleas

A general denial may not put all the plaintiff's allegations at issue because some matters must be specifically pleaded and verified by affidavit based on personal knowledge. *See* **Roark v. Stallworth Oil & Gas, Inc.**, 813 S.W.2d 492, 494 (Tex.1991). If the defendant does not verify a denial that must be verified under the rules, the plaintiff must object to the defect, or else it waives the error. *See* **Werner v. Colwell**, 909 S.W.2d 866, 870 (Tex.1995); **Southern Cty. Mut. Ins. v. Ochoa**, 19 S.W.3d 452, 461 (Tex.App.—Corpus Christi 2000, no pet.). A pleading may usually be amended to include a verification, even during trial. *E.g.*, **Chapin & Chapin, Inc. v. Texas Sand & Gravel Co.**, 844 S.W.2d 664, 664–65 (Tex.1992) (trial court should have permitted amendment on day of trial).

Practice Tip

If you need to file a verified plea under TRCP 93, you may also need to file a motion to abate on the same ground to avoid waiving the error. See "Motion to Abate—Challenging the Suit," ch. 3-I, §1 et seq.

§4.1 Verified pleas in TRCP 93. TRCP 93 contains a list of defenses, pleas, and other matters that must be verified "unless the truth of such matters appear[s] of record." **Apresa v. Montfort Ins.**, 932 S.W.2d 246, 248 n.2 (Tex.App.—El Paso 1996, no writ). Verification is thus necessary to assert certain defenses when the issue is not apparent on the face of the plaintiff's pleadings. *See* **Pledger v. Schoellkopf**, 762 S.W.2d 145, 146 (Tex.1988). If there is any doubt, the defendant should verify its answer. Under TRCP 93, the following pleas must be verified:

1. An attack on the legal capacity of either the plaintiff to sue or the defendant to be sued. Tex. R. Civ. P. 93(1); **Austin Nursing Ctr., Inc. v. Lovato**, 171 S.W.3d 845, 849 (Tex.2005); **Sixth RMA Partners v. Sibley**, 111 S.W.3d 46, 56 (Tex.2003); **Nootsie, Ltd. v. Williamson Cty. Appr. Dist.**, 925 S.W.2d 659, 662 (Tex.1996). See "Capacity," ch. 2-B, §4.2.2; "Defects in parties," ch. 3-I, §3.1.1.

2. An allegation that the plaintiff is not entitled to recover in the capacity in which it sues or that the defendant is not liable in the capacity in which it is sued. Tex. R. Civ. P. 93(2); **Pledger**, 762 S.W.2d at 146; **W.O.S. Constr. Co. v. Hanyard**, 684 S.W.2d 675, 676 (Tex.1985); *see* **Pike v. Texas EMC Mgmt.**, __ S.W.3d __, 2020 WL 3405812 (Tex.2020) (No. 17-0557; 6-19-20). Even though the failure to file a verified plea waives any complaint about a judgment rendered against a party in the capacity in which it was sued, the failure does not authorize a court to render a judgment against the party in any capacity in which it was not sued. **Werner v. Colwell**, 909 S.W.2d 866, 870 (Tex.1995). See "Defects in parties," ch. 3-I, §3.1.1.

3. An allegation that another suit is pending in Texas between the same parties involving the same claim. Tex. R. Civ. P. 93(3); **Southern Cty. Mut. Ins. v. Ochoa**, 19 S.W.3d 452, 461 (Tex.App.—Corpus Christi 2000, no pet.). See "Abate—same dispute in another Texas court," ch. 3-I, §3.2.

4. An allegation of any other defect of the parties. Tex. R. Civ. P. 93(4); **Cantu v. Holiday Inns, Inc.**, 910 S.W.2d 113, 115 (Tex.App.—Corpus Christi 1995, writ denied). Any defect of the parties not covered by some other section of TRCP 93 must be denied under oath under TRCP 93(4). *See, e.g.*, **Allison v. National Un. Fire Ins.**, 703 S.W.2d 637, 638 (Tex.1986) (D should have filed verified denial that necessary parties were not joined); **Beacon Nat'l Ins. v. Reynolds**, 799 S.W.2d 390, 395 (Tex.App.—Fort Worth 1990, writ denied) (D should have filed verified denial that it was not correct insurance company); *see also* **CHCA E. Houston, L.P. v. Henderson**, 99 S.W.3d 630, 633 (Tex.App.—Houston [14th Dist.] 2003, no pet.) (misidentification must be raised by verified pleading).

5. A denial of a partnership alleged in a pleading for any party to the suit. Tex. R. Civ. P. 93(5); **Cadle Co. v. Bankston & Lobingier**, 868 S.W.2d 918, 922–23 (Tex.App.—Fort Worth 1994), *writ denied*, 893 S.W.2d 949 (Tex.1994); *e.g.*, **Champion v. Wright**, 740 S.W.2d 848, 851 (Tex.App.—San Antonio 1987, writ denied) (D did not file verified denial that P did not have authority to recover damages to partnership). The failure to deny partnership status is an admission of the partnership that cannot be controverted at trial. **Washburn v. Krenek**, 684 S.W.2d 187, 191 (Tex.App.—Houston [14th Dist.] 1984, writ ref'd n.r.e.).

6. A denial that a party is incorporated as alleged. Tex. R. Civ. P. 93(6); *see* **Panama Ref. Co. v. Crouch**, 124 S.W.2d 988, 989 (Tex.1939); *see also* Tex. R. Civ. P. 52 (allegation of incorporation taken as true unless denied by adverse party's affidavit).

7. A denial that the defendant or a person under the defendant's authority executed a written instrument that is the subject of the suit. Tex. R. Civ. P. 93(7); **City of Oak Ridge N. v. Mendes**, 339 S.W.3d 222, 230 (Tex.App.—Beaumont 2011, no pet.); **Methodist Hosps. v. Corporate Communicators, Inc.**, 806 S.W.2d 879, 882 (Tex.App.—Dallas 1991, writ denied). To deny the execution of a document alleged to have been executed by a person now deceased, a party may state that it "has reason to believe and does believe that such instrument was not executed by the decedent or by his authority." Tex. R. Civ. P. 93(7). Without a verified denial, the document is fully proved. *Id.*; *e.g.*, **Boyd v. Diversified Fin. Sys.**, 1 S.W.3d 888, 891 (Tex.App.—Dallas 1999, no pet.) (documents were admissible because no verified denial was filed); *see also* **In re Estate of Guerrero**, 465 S.W.3d 693, 704–05 (Tex.App.—Houston [14th Dist.] 2015, pet. denied) (even if no verified denial is filed, document must still be authenticated to be admissible).

8. A denial of the genuineness of an indorsement or assignment of a written instrument that is the subject of the suit. Tex. R. Civ. P. 93(8). The denial may be made based on information and belief. *Id.* If no verified denial is filed, the indorsement is fully proved. *Id.*; *see also* **Overall v. Southwestern Bell Yellow Pages, Inc.**, 869 S.W.2d 629, 632 (Tex.App.—Houston [14th Dist.] 1994, no writ) (evidence contesting genuineness of contract was excluded because no verified denial was filed).

9. An allegation that a written instrument that is the subject of the suit is without consideration or that the consideration for the instrument failed in whole or in part. Tex. R. Civ. P. 93(9), 94; **Brown v. Aztec Rig Equip., Inc.**, 921 S.W.2d 835, 845 (Tex.App.—Houston [14th Dist.] 1996, writ denied); **Champion**, 740 S.W.2d at 851–52. If no verified plea is filed, the plaintiff is not required to prove consideration. See "Consideration defenses," **O'Connor's Texas Causes of Action**, ch. 5-B, §5.1.9 (2021 ed.).

Note

Although both a lack of consideration and a failure of consideration must be raised by a verified pleading, only an alleged failure of consideration must be pleaded as an affirmative defense. Because consideration is a required element for proving a valid contract, an alleged lack of consideration is not considered an affirmative defense. See "Affirmative defenses in TRCP 94," ch. 3-E, §5.2.8.

10. A denial of an account, supported by an affidavit. Tex. R. Civ. P. 93(10), 185; **Panditi v. Apostle**, 180 S.W.3d 924, 927 (Tex.App.—Dallas 2006, no pet.); **Powers v. Adams**, 2 S.W.3d 496, 498 (Tex.App.—Houston [14th Dist.] 1999, no pet.); *see* **Tedder v. Gardner Aldrich, LLP**, 421 S.W.3d 651, 653 (Tex.2013); *see, e.g.*, **Brown Found. Repair & Consulting, Inc. v. Friendly Chevrolet Co.**, 715 S.W.2d 115, 117–18 (Tex.App.—Dallas 1986, writ ref'd n.r.e.) (affidavit was not verified denial because D did not affirm under oath that statements made in trial pleadings were true; mere statement in jurat that affiant has subscribed and sworn to document is not sufficient). See "Suit on Sworn Account," **O'Connor's Texas Causes of Action**, ch. 5-E, §1 et seq. (2021 ed.). TRCP 185 presumes that the defendant has personal knowledge of the basis of the claim. **Tedder**, 421 S.W.3d at 653. Thus, a defendant is not required to file a verified denial of an account if she does not have personal knowledge of the account; a defendant cannot swear to what she does not and cannot know. *E.g., id.* at 654. (D who was stranger to account did not have to file sworn denial to contest liability). If a verified denial is required but not filed, the plaintiff does not need to introduce additional evidence. **Northeast Wholesale Lumber, Inc. v. Leader Lumber, Inc.**, 785 S.W.2d 402, 407 (Tex.App.—Dallas 1989, no writ); *see* Tex. R. Civ. P. 185. A general denial, even if it is verified, does not comply with the requirements of TRCP 93(10) and 185. **Andrews v. East Tex. Med. Ctr.-Athens**, 885 S.W.2d 264, 268 (Tex.App.—Tyler 1994, no writ).

11. An allegation that a contract is usurious. Tex. R. Civ. P. 93(11); **Powers**, 2 S.W.3d at 498 n.1. See "Usury," **O'Connor's Texas Causes of Action**, ch. 31, §1 et seq. (2021 ed.).

12. An allegation that notice and proof of the loss or claim were not given as alleged. Tex. R. Civ. P. 93(12); *see also* Tex. R. Civ. P. 54 (conditions precedent). The denial must be made with specificity. Tex. R. Civ. P. 93(12). If a verified denial is not filed, notice and proof are presumed, and no evidence to the contrary may be admitted. *Id.*; **Sanchez v. Jary**, 768 S.W.2d 933, 936 (Tex.App.—San Antonio 1989, no writ).

13. A denial of specific matters in an appeal from the Division of Workers' Compensation, Texas Department of Insurance (formerly the Industrial Accident Board). Tex. R. Civ. P. 93(13). TRCP 93(13) lists the allegations that must be denied. A defendant may make a denial based on information and belief under TRCP 93(13)(a) (notice of injury) and (13)(g) (P did not have good cause for filing claim after one-year deadline). Tex. R. Civ. P. 93(13) (second-to-last paragraph); **National Un. Fire Ins. v. Reyna**, 897 S.W.2d 777, 779 (Tex.1995).

14. A denial that a party is doing business under an assumed or trade name. Tex. R. Civ. P. 93(14); **Hyson v. Chilkewitz**, 971 S.W.2d 563, 569 (Tex.App.—Dallas 1998), *rev'd on other grounds*, 22 S.W.3d 825 (Tex.1999).

15. A denial of the occurrence or performance of a condition precedent in a suit by an insured against an auto insurer. Tex. R. Civ. P. 93(15); *see* Tex. R. Civ. P. 54. The denial may be made based on information and belief. Tex. R. Civ. P. 93(15).

16. An allegation of any other matter required by statute to be pleaded under oath. Tex. R. Civ. P. 93(16).

§4.2 Verified pleas in other rules. Other matters that must be verified include the following: a special appearance (TRCP 120a(1)), a confession of judgment (TRCP 314), a writ of certiorari to a county court (TRCP 577), a garnishee's answer (TRCP 665), a complaint seeking an injunction (TRCP 680 and 682), a request to dissolve an injunction before a final hearing (TRCP 690), a claimant's oath by a third party to reclaim personal property that has been levied (TRCP 717), and a claim of right of property (TRCP 717).

§5. Affirmative defenses

An affirmative defense is a reason why the plaintiff should not recover independent of the elements of the plaintiff's claim. *See* **MAN Engines & Components, Inc. v. Shows**, 434 S.W.3d 132, 137 (Tex.2014); **Texas Beef Cattle Co. v. Green**,

921 S.W.2d 203, 212 (Tex.1996). If the defense is successful, the defendant can avoid liability even if the plaintiff can establish the elements of its cause of action. *See* **Godoy v. Wells Fargo Bank**, 575 S.W.3d 531, 536 (Tex.2019) **Pathfinder Oil & Gas, Inc. v. Great W. Drilling, Ltd.**, 574 S.W.3d 882, 891 n.35 (Tex.2019); **Zorrilla v. Aypco Constr. II, LLC**, 469 S.W.3d 143, 155–56 (Tex.2015); **MAN Engines & Components**, 434 S.W.3d at 137. A general denial does not include any affirmative defenses. If a defendant wants to rely on an affirmative defense, it must specifically raise the defense in its pretrial pleadings. **MAN Engines & Components**, 434 S.W.3d at 137; *see* Tex. R. Civ. P. 94; **Zorrilla**, 469 S.W.3d at 155. If an affirmative defense is not timely raised in the trial court, it is waived and cannot be argued on appeal. *See* **Willacy Cty. Appr. Dist. v. Sebastian Cotton & Grain, Ltd.**, 555 S.W.3d 29, 50 (Tex.2018); **MAN Engines & Components**, 434 S.W.3d at 137.

Note

The defendant does not waive an affirmative defense by not pleading it if the plaintiff anticipated the defense in its pleading and the defense is established at trial as a matter of law. ***Shoemake v. Fogel, Ltd.****, 826 S.W.2d 933, 937 (Tex.1992) (parental immunity);* ***Phillips v. Phillips****, 820 S.W.2d 785, 789 (Tex.1991) (illegality). But the best practice is for the defendant to plead every affirmative defense that is supported by the facts.*

§5.1 Affirmative defense vs. counterclaim. Some claims (e.g., fraud) can be raised as either an affirmative defense or a counterclaim. *See* **Kuehnhoefer v. Welch**, 893 S.W.2d 689, 692 (Tex.App.—Texarkana 1995, writ denied); **Adams v. Tri-Continental Leasing Corp.**, 713 S.W.2d 152, 153 (Tex.App.—Dallas 1986, no writ). See "Counterclaims," ch. 3-E, §7.1. The test to determine which is appropriate is whether the defendant seeks affirmative relief. If the defendant asks for affirmative relief, it is a counterclaim; if the defendant does not ask for affirmative relief, it is an affirmative defense. *See* **My-Tech, Inc. v. University of N. Tex. Health Sci. Ctr.**, 166 S.W.3d 880, 884 (Tex.App.—Dallas 2005, pet. denied). For example, if a defendant alleges fraud and asks for damages, fraud is a counterclaim. *See* **Kuehnhoefer**, 893 S.W.2d at 692. If a defendant does not ask for damages, fraud is an affirmative defense.

§5.2 Affirmative defenses in TRCP 94. Many, but not all, of the affirmative defenses are listed in TRCP 94:

1. Accord and satisfaction. **Williams v. Colthurst**, 253 S.W.3d 353, 359 (Tex.App.—Eastland 2008, no pet.). See "Accord & satisfaction," **O'Connor's Texas Causes of Action**, ch. 5-B, §5.1.15 (2021 ed.).

2. Arbitration and award. **Transwestern Pipeline Co. v. Horizon Oil & Gas Co.**, 809 S.W.2d 589, 593 (Tex.App.—Dallas 1991, writ dism'd). See "Arbitration," ch. 4-C, §1 et seq.

3. Assumption of the risk. In products-liability cases, assumption of the risk is included under the defense of contributory negligence. **Duncan v. Cessna Aircraft Co.**, 665 S.W.2d 414, 428 (Tex.1984). The Supreme Court abolished assumption of the risk as an affirmative defense to most negligence actions; it is generally used only as a factor in assessing proportionate responsibility. *See* **Del Lago Partners v. Smith**, 307 S.W.3d 762, 772 (Tex.2010); **Farley v. M M Cattle Co.**, 529 S.W.2d 751, 758 (Tex.1975). However, assumption of the risk retains limited viability in the following instances:

(1) When the plaintiff knowingly and expressly consented (orally or in writing) to the dangerous activity or condition. **Farley**, 529 S.W.2d at 758; *see, e.g.*, **Newman v. Tropical Visions, Inc.**, 891 S.W.2d 713, 718–19 (Tex.App.—San Antonio 1994, writ denied) (by written agreement, P assumed risk of scuba diving). For example, participants in certain sports activities are deemed to accept the risk of being injured. See "Express consent," **O'Connor's Texas Causes of Action**, ch. 21-A, §5.5.1 (2021 ed.).

(2) When the plaintiff was injured while committing a felony or attempting suicide. Tex. Civ. Prac. & Rem. Code §93.001(a)(1), (a)(2). See "Felony or suicide," **O'Connor's Texas Causes of Action**, ch. 21-A, §5.5.2 (2021 ed.).

4. Contributory negligence. See "Proportionate Responsibility & Contribution," **O'Connor's Texas Causes of Action**, ch. 51, §1 et seq. (2021 ed.).

5. Discharge in bankruptcy. **Burnam v. Patterson**, 119 S.W.3d 12, 15 (Tex.App.—Amarillo 2003, pet. denied). An allegation that the defendant filed for bankruptcy is not sufficient; the defendant must plead that it was discharged in bankruptcy. **Seiffert v. Bowden**, 556 S.W.2d 406, 409 (Tex.App.—Corpus Christi 1977, no writ).

6. Duress. **Gooch v. American Sling Co.**, 902 S.W.2d 181, 186 (Tex.App.—Fort Worth 1995, no writ). See "Duress," **O'Connor's Texas Causes of Action**, ch. 5-B, §5.1.10 (2021 ed.).

7. Estoppel. **Loya Ins. v. Avalos**, __ S.W.3d __ n.3, 2020 WL 2089752 (Tex.2020) (No. 18-0837; 5-1-20) (collateral estoppel); **Phillips v. Flying J Inc.**, 375 S.W.3d 367, 369 (Tex.App.—Amarillo 2012, no pet.) (judicial estoppel); **Hennessey v. Vanguard Ins.**, 895 S.W.2d 794, 797–98 (Tex.App.—Amarillo 1995, writ denied) (equitable estoppel); **Huddleston v. Texas Commerce Bank-Dallas**, 756 S.W.2d 343, 346–47 (Tex.App.—Dallas 1988, writ denied) (estoppel by deed). See "Estoppel Defenses," **O'Connor's Texas Causes of Action**, ch. 49-A, §1 et seq. (2021 ed.).

8. Failure of consideration. **Burges v. Mosley**, 304 S.W.3d 623, 628 (Tex.App.—Tyler 2010, no pet.); *see* **Yanez v. Ducasson**, No. 01-12-00173-CV, 2012 WL 6645011 (Tex.App.—Houston [1st Dist.] 2012, n.p.h.) (memo op.; 12-20-12) (failure of consideration is affirmative defense under TRCP 94, but lack of consideration is not); *see also* Tex. R. Civ. P. 93(9) (verified plea). See "Consideration defenses," **O'Connor's Texas Causes of Action**, ch. 5-B, §5.1.9 (2021 ed.).

9. Fraud. **Texas Farmers Ins. v. Murphy**, 996 S.W.2d 873, 879–80 (Tex.1999). See "Fraud as affirmative defense," **O'Connor's Texas Causes of Action**, ch. 12-A, §7.1 (2021 ed.).

10. Illegality. **Jefferson Cty. v. Jefferson Cty. Constables Ass'n**, 546 S.W.3d 661, 666 (Tex.2018); **Phillips v. Phillips**, 820 S.W.2d 785, 789 (Tex.1991). The defendant does not need to plead illegality as a defense if (1) illegality is apparent on the face of the plaintiff's pleadings because the plaintiff anticipated the defense and (2) the defense is proved as a matter of law at trial. **Phillips**, 820 S.W.2d at 789; *see* **Lewkowicz v. El Paso Apparel Corp.**, 625 S.W.2d 301, 303 (Tex.1981). See "Illegality," **O'Connor's Texas Causes of Action**, ch. 5-B, §5.1.6 (2021 ed.).

11. Injury by a fellow servant. **City of San Antonio v. Mendoza**, 532 S.W.2d 353, 360 (Tex.App.—San Antonio 1975, writ ref'd n.r.e.).

12. Laches. **Knesek v. Witte**, 754 S.W.2d 814, 816 (Tex.App.—Houston [1st Dist.] 1988, writ denied); **Murray v. Murray**, 611 S.W.2d 172, 173 (Tex.App.—El Paso 1981, no writ). See "Laches," **O'Connor's Texas Causes of Action**, ch. 52, §3.2 (2021 ed.).

13. License. *See* **Moore v. Sedig**, 791 S.W.2d 556, 561 (Tex.App.—Dallas 1990, no writ) (absence of license is affirmative defense).

14. Loss within an exception to general liability. *See* **Venture Encoding Serv. v. Atlantic Mut. Ins.**, 107 S.W.3d 729, 733 (Tex.App.—Fort Worth 2003, pet. denied). When a plaintiff sues to collect on a general-hazards insurance policy that has provisions limiting general liability, the insurer-defendant must specifically allege that the loss was within a particular exception to general liability. *Id.* If the insurer pleads an exclusion under the policy, the plaintiff must then prove that the loss was not within the exclusion. **Southern Ins. v. Progressive Cty. Mut. Ins.**, 708 S.W.2d 549, 551 (Tex.App.—Houston [1st Dist.] 1986, writ ref'd n.r.e.).

15. Payment. **Southwestern Fire & Cas. Co. v. Larue**, 367 S.W.2d 162, 163 (Tex.1963); **Equitable Trust Co. v. Roland**, 644 S.W.2d 46, 53 (Tex.App.—San Antonio 1982, no writ); *see also* Tex. R. Civ. P. 93(10) (verified denial), Tex. R. Civ. P. 95 (plea of payment). When a defendant claims it paid the sums sued for, it should either (1) file with its answer an account that distinctly states the details of payment or (2) describe the payment in the answer so plainly and particularly as to give the plaintiff full notice of the character of the payment. Tex. R. Civ. P. 95. If the defendant does not do either, it will not be allowed to prove the payment at trial. *See id.*; **Jack Parker Indus. v. FDIC**, 769 S.W.2d 700, 702 (Tex.App.—El Paso 1989, no writ).

16. Release. **Dresser Indus. v. Page Pet., Inc.**, 853 S.W.2d 505, 508 (Tex.1993) (preinjury); **Williams v. Glash**, 789 S.W.2d 261, 264 (Tex.1990) (postinjury); *see* **National Prop. Holdings, L.P. v. Westergren**, 453 S.W.3d 419, 428 (Tex.2015). See "Release," ch. 7-I, §2.1.

17. Res judicata. **Texas Beef Cattle Co. v. Green**, 921 S.W.2d 203, 206–07 (Tex.1996); **Dardari v. Texas Commerce Bank**, 961 S.W.2d 466, 470 (Tex.App.—Houston [1st Dist.] 1997, no pet.). See "Res Judicata & Collateral Estoppel," ch. 9-D, §1 et seq.

18. Statute of frauds. **First Nat'l Bank v. Zimmerman**, 442 S.W.2d 674, 675–76 (Tex.1969); **Adams v. H&H Meat Prods.**, 41 S.W.3d 762, 776 (Tex.App.—Corpus Christi 2001, no pet.); *see* **Dynegy, Inc. v. Yates**, 422 S.W.3d 638, 641 (Tex.2013). See "Statute of Frauds," **O'Connor's Texas Causes of Action**, ch. 50, §1 et seq. (2021 ed.).

19. Statute of limitations. **Godoy v. Wells Fargo Bank**, 575 S.W.3d 531, 536 (Tex.2019); **Southwestern Energy Prod. v. Berry-Helfand**, 491 S.W.3d 699, 722 (Tex.2016); **In re United Servs. Auto. Ass'n**, 307 S.W.3d 299, 308 (Tex.2010). See "Statutes of Limitations," **O'Connor's Texas Civil Practice & Remedies Code Plus**, chart 1 (2020–21 ed.); "Limitations," **O'Connor's Texas Causes of Action**, ch. 52, §1 et seq. (2021 ed.).

20. Waiver. **Tenneco Inc. v. Enterprise Prods.**, 925 S.W.2d 640, 643 (Tex.1996); *see, e.g.*, **T.O. Stanley Boot Co. v. Bank of El Paso**, 847 S.W.2d 218, 223 (Tex.1992) (by not pleading waiver, P waived affirmative defense of waiver).

§5.3 Other avoidances or affirmative defenses. Any other matter constituting an avoidance or affirmative defense not listed in TRCP 94 must be specifically raised in the defendant's pretrial pleadings. *See* Tex. R. Civ. P. 94; *see also* **Zorrilla v. Aypco Constr. II, LLC**, 469 S.W.3d 143, 156 (Tex.2015) (courts often use "avoidance" and "affirmative defense" interchangeably although terms are historically distinct; avoidance admits cause of action but asserts other facts as justification or excuse). For a particular matter to constitute an avoidance or affirmative defense that must be specifically pleaded under TRCP 94, the defendant must have the burden of proof to present sufficient evidence to establish the defense and obtain the requisite jury findings. *See, e.g.*, **Zorrilla**, 469 S.W.3d at 156–57 (exemplary-damages cap under CPRC §41.008(b) is not avoidance or affirmative defense because cap applies automatically and does not place burden of proof on D). The following matters not specified in TRCP 94 have been found to be avoidances or affirmative defenses:

1. Contract-related actions.

(1) Ambiguity. See "Ambiguity," **O'Connor's Texas Causes of Action**, ch. 5-B, §7.2.2(3) (2021 ed.).

(2) Justification. See "Justification," **O'Connor's Texas Causes of Action**, ch. 5-G, §5.4.2 (2021 ed.).

(3) Mistake. See "Mistake," **O'Connor's Texas Causes of Action**, ch. 5-B, §5.1.11 (2021 ed.).

(4) Offset. See "Offset," **O'Connor's Texas Causes of Action**, ch. 5-B, §5.1.22 (2021 ed.).

(5) Penalty. See "Penalty," **O'Connor's Texas Causes of Action**, ch. 5-B, §5.1.23 (2021 ed.).

(6) Privilege. See "Privilege," **O'Connor's Texas Causes of Action**, ch. 5-G, §5.4.1 (2021 ed.).

(7) Ratification. See "Ratification," **O'Connor's Texas Causes of Action**, ch. 5-B, §5.1.19 (2021 ed.).

2. Criminal acts.

(1) By plaintiff. If the plaintiff was injured while committing an offense for which she was convicted, neither she nor those with derivative claims are entitled to recover for her injuries. Tex. Civ. Prac. & Rem. Code §§86.001 to 86.003; *see also* Tex. Civ. Prac. & Rem. Code §93.001(a) (P cannot recover if injured while attempting to commit felony or suicide). The defense in CPRC chapter 86 does not apply to injuries arising from traffic offenses and certain conduct involving criminal trespass. *See* Tex. Civ. Prac. & Rem. Code §§86.005, 86.007.

(2) By third person. As a general rule, a person has no duty to protect another from the criminal acts of a third person. **Walker v. Harris**, 924 S.W.2d 375, 377 (Tex.1996). If the defendant is negligent but the plaintiff is injured as the result of a criminal act by a third person, the criminal conduct is a superseding cause that relieves the defendant of liability unless the criminal act was a foreseeable result of the defendant's negligence. **El Chico Corp. v. Poole**, 732 S.W.2d 306, 313–14 (Tex.1987); **Wilson v. Brister**, 982 S.W.2d 42, 44–45 (Tex.App.—Houston [1st Dist.] 1998, pet. denied).

3. DTPA. See "Defenses," **O'Connor's Texas Causes of Action**, ch. 8, §5 (2021 ed.).

4. Disclaimer. See "Disclaimers of warranty," **O'Connor's Texas Causes of Action**, ch. 32-A, §4 (2021 ed.).

5. ERISA. The defendant may assert that the claim is preempted by the Employee Retirement Income Security Act of 1974, 29 U.S.C. §1001 et seq. **Gorman v. Life Ins. Co. of N. Am.**, 811 S.W.2d 542, 546 (Tex.1991).

6. Failure to mitigate. The defendant may assert that the plaintiff did not make reasonable efforts to mitigate its damages. *E.g.*, **Gunn Infiniti, Inc. v. O'Byrne**, 996 S.W.2d 854, 856–57 (Tex.1999) (DTPA claimant's duty to mitigate); **Austin Hill Country Rlty., Inc. v. Palisades Plaza, Inc.**, 948 S.W.2d 293, 294 (Tex.1997) (landlord's duty to mitigate); **Gulf Consol. Int'l v. Murphy**, 658 S.W.2d 565, 566 (Tex.1983) (discharged employee's duty to mitigate). When the defendant offers evidence showing that the plaintiff actually mitigated its damages, and thus that the plaintiff's damages are lower than the plaintiff claims, the evidence of the plaintiff's mitigation rebuts the plaintiff's evidence of damages and is admissible under a general denial. *See* **Austin Hill**, 948 S.W.2d at 300.

7. First Amendment. When a plaintiff's suit implicates a defendant's free exercise of rights, the defendant may assert the First Amendment as an affirmative defense. See "First Amendment," **O'Connor's Texas Causes of Action**, ch. 14, §5.7 (2021 ed.) (IIED claims); "First Amendment," **O'Connor's Texas Causes of Action**, ch. 21-E, §5.5 (2021 ed.) (negligent-misrepresentation claims); "First Amendment disclosure," **O'Connor's Texas Causes of Action**, ch. 33-A, §5.4 (2021 ed.) (criminal-wiretap claims).

8. Immunity.

(1) Attorney. An attorney is immune from liability to nonclients for actions taken within the scope of representing a client in litigation. **Bethel v. Quilling, Selander, Lownds, Winslett & Moser, P.C.**, 595 S.W.3d 651, 657 (Tex.2020); **Youngkin v. Hines**, 546 S.W.3d 675, 681 (Tex.2018); **Cantey Hanger, LLP v. Byrd**, 467 S.W.3d 477, 481 (Tex.2015). See "Attorney immunity," **O'Connor's Texas Causes of Action**, ch. 17, §5.3 (2021 ed.).

(2) Charitable. CPRC chapter 84 provides limited immunity for the acts of volunteers, employees, and charities, including the officers of charitable organizations and health-care providers.

(3) Governmental. The defendant may be immune from liability because it is a governmental unit. *See* **Tarrant Cty. v. Bonner**, 574 S.W.3d 893, 900 (Tex.2019); **Rosenberg Dev. Corp. v. Imperial Performing Arts, Inc.**, 571 S.W.3d 738, 746 (Tex.2019); **Kinnear v. Texas Comm'n on Human Rights**, 14 S.W.3d 299, 300 (Tex.2000). See "Suits Against the Government," **O'Connor's Texas Causes of Action**, ch. 24-A, §1 et seq. (2021 ed.); "Waivers of Governmental Immunity," **O'Connor's Texas Civil Practice & Remedies Code Plus**, chart 6 (2020–21 ed.). If the defendant is immune from suit, it should file a plea to the jurisdiction. See "Governmental immunity from suit," ch. 3-F, §3.7.

(4) Judicial. See "Judicial Immunity," **O'Connor's Texas Causes of Action**, ch. 46-C, §1 et seq. (2021 ed.).

(5) Legislative. See "Legislative Immunity," **O'Connor's Texas Causes of Action**, ch. 46-B, §1 et seq. (2021 ed.).

(6) Official. The common-law defense of official immunity protects individual officials from personal liability when they perform discretionary duties in good faith within the scope of their authority. See "Official Immunity," **O'Connor's Texas Causes of Action**, ch. 46-A, §1 et seq. (2021 ed.).

(7) Parental. See "Parental Immunity," **O'Connor's Texas Causes of Action**, ch. 48, §1 et seq. (2021 ed.).

(8) Professional employee of school district or charter school. A professional employee of a school district or charter school is immune from liability for any discretionary act committed within the scope of her duties. Tex. Educ. Code §12.1056 (charter school), §22.0511(a) (school district); *see* **Downing v. Brown**, 935 S.W.2d 112, 114 (Tex.1996); **LTTS Charter Sch., Inc. v. C2 Constr., Inc.**, 358 S.W.3d 725, 734 (Tex.App.—Dallas 2011, pet. denied). See "Employee immunity," **O'Connor's Texas Causes of Action**, ch. 47, §3.1 (2021 ed.).

(9) Volunteer. See "ADR volunteers," **O'Connor's Texas Causes of Action**, ch. 47, §1.3 (2021 ed.); "Volunteer firefighters or fire departments," **O'Connor's Texas Causes of Action**, ch. 47, §1.4 (2021 ed.); "Volunteer immunity," **O'Connor's Texas Causes of Action**, ch. 47, §3.2 (2021 ed.).

9. Statute of repose. **FDIC v. Lenk**, 361 S.W.3d 602, 609 (Tex.2012). See "Statute of repose," **O'Connor's Texas Causes of Action**, ch. 52, §2.7 (2021 ed.).

10. Suicide. It is an affirmative defense to a suit for personal injury or death that the plaintiff's suicide or attempted suicide was the sole cause of the injury. Tex. Civ. Prac. & Rem. Code §93.001(a)(2); **Kassen v. Hatley**, 887 S.W.2d 4, 12 (Tex.1994). See "Felony or suicide," **O'Connor's Texas Causes of Action**, ch. 21-A, §5.5.2 (2021 ed.).

11. Truth. In defamation suits brought by private individuals, truth is an affirmative defense. See "Substantial truth," **O'Connor's Texas Causes of Action**, ch. 18-A, §5.4 (2021 ed.).

§6. Other defensive matters

§6.1 Denial of conditions precedent. If the plaintiff alleges that "all conditions precedent have been performed or have occurred," the defendant must specifically deny any conditions that were not performed or have not occurred. Tex. R. Civ. P. 54; **Greathouse v. Charter Nat'l Bank-Sw.**, 851 S.W.2d 173, 174 (Tex.1992); *see also* Tex. R. Civ. P. 93(12) (requiring specific denial for notice and proof of loss or claim for damages). The defendant cannot simply deny that some conditions precedent have occurred. **Hill v. Thompson & Knight**, 756 S.W.2d 824, 826 (Tex.App.—Dallas 1988, no writ). By specifically denying the plaintiff's TRCP 54 allegations, the defendant forces the plaintiff to prove the conditions that were specifically denied. **Betty Leavell Rlty. Co. v. Raggio**, 669 S.W.2d 102, 104 (Tex.1984); **Phifer v. Nacogdoches Cty. Cent. Appr. Dist.**, 45 S.W.3d 159, 174 (Tex.App.—Tyler 2000, pet. denied); **Love of God Holiness Temple Ch. v. Union Std. Ins.**, 860 S.W.2d 179, 180 (Tex.App.—Texarkana 1993, writ denied). If the defendant does not identify the specific conditions the plaintiff did not comply with, it admits that all conditions precedent occurred. *See* **Greathouse**, 851 S.W.2d at 177. A specific denial under TRCP 54 should be verified, just like specific pleas under TRCP 93.

§6.2 Inferential rebuttals. An inferential rebuttal is a defensive theory used in negligence cases that rebuts one of the elements of the plaintiff's claim by proving certain other facts. **Dillard v. Texas Elec. Coop.**, 157 S.W.3d 429, 430 (Tex.2005); **Buls v. Fuselier**, 55 S.W.3d 204, 211 (Tex.App.—Texarkana 2001, no pet.). An inferential rebuttal is not an affirmative defense because it does not admit the truth of the plaintiff's claims, as an affirmative defense does. *See* **Buls**, 55 S.W.3d at 211. Inferential-rebuttal theories include act of God, unavoidable accident, new and independent cause, sole proximate cause, and sudden emergency. For a discussion of these inferential rebuttals, see "Inferential rebuttals," **O'Connor's Texas Causes of Action**, ch. 21-A, §5.12 (2021 ed.).

1. Pleading. It is not necessary for the defendant to plead an inferential rebuttal in its answer. The defendant may introduce evidence of an inferential rebuttal under a general denial because the evidence rebuts the plaintiff's cause of action. **Buls**, 55 S.W.3d at 211; *see* **Reinhart v. Young**, 906 S.W.2d 471, 475 (Tex.1995) (Hecht & Owen, JJ., concurring).

2. Jury charge. If the defendant introduces evidence that raises an inferential rebuttal, the inferential-rebuttal issue is submitted to the jury as an instruction, not as a question. See "Inferential-rebuttal instructions," ch. 8-I, §6.2.2(1).

§7. Defendant's claims

A defendant can make claims under several different authorities. *See, e.g.*, Tex. Civ. Prac. & Rem. Code §33.004 (D can designate person as responsible third party); Tex. R. Civ. P. 38 (parties can bring in third parties who may be liable for all or part of claims involved in suit), Tex. R. Civ. P. 85 (D can bring cross-action, which places D in the shoes of a P), Tex. R. Civ. P. 97 (parties can file counterclaims and cross-claims).

Practice Tip

If a defendant asserts a counterclaim or cross-claim that changes the discovery level, the defendant should probably allege a new discovery level in the first paragraph of its pleading, even though TRCP 190 does not mention defendants. See "Discovery-control plans," ch. 6-A, §7.

---

§7.1 Counterclaims. A defendant may file a claim against the plaintiff through a counterclaim. Tex. R. Civ. P. 97(a), (b). A counterclaim is an affirmative claim for relief filed against an opposing party. Generally, the term "counterclaim" denotes a defendant's claim against a plaintiff that will, in some way, defeat or reduce a judgment for the plaintiff. **Doyer v. Pitney Bowes, Inc.**, 80 S.W.3d 215, 218 (Tex.App.—Austin 2002, pet. denied); *see* Tex. R. Civ. P. 97(c).

1. Types of counterclaims. A counterclaim can be either compulsory or permissive.

(1) Compulsory. For the test for a compulsory counterclaim, see "Compulsory joinder of claims," ch. 2-F, §6.

(2) Permissive. Any counterclaim that does not satisfy the compulsory-counterclaim test is a permissive counterclaim. For the test for permissive claims, see "Permissive joinder of claims," ch. 2-F, §7.

2. Service of process not necessary. Service of process is not necessary when a counterclaim is filed against a party who has already made an appearance in the case; service under TRCP 21a is sufficient. Tex. R. Civ. P. 124; **In re A.L.H.C.**, 49 S.W.3d 911, 916–17 (Tex.App.—Dallas 2001, pet. denied); **Houston Crushed Concrete, Inc. v. Concrete Recycling Corp.**, 879 S.W.2d 258, 261 (Tex.App.—Houston [14th Dist.] 1994, no writ).

§7.2 Cross-claims. A cross-claim is an affirmative claim for relief filed against a coparty. A defendant may file a cross-claim against a codefendant if the claim arises from the same transaction or occurrence as the original action or any counterclaim. Tex. R. Civ. P. 97(e). The cross-defendant must assert its compulsory claims against the cross-claimant, or else its claims will be barred. *See* **Getty Oil Co. v. Insurance Co. of N. Am.**, 845 S.W.2d 794, 800 (Tex.1992). In such a case, the parties are no longer merely coparties but are opposing parties, and the compulsory-counterclaim rule applies. For example, if A sues B and C, and B files a cross-claim against C, C must file its compulsory counterclaims against A and B, or the claims will be barred in a later suit. Service of process is not necessary when a cross-claim is filed against a party who has already made an appearance in the case; service under TRCP 21a is sufficient. Tex. R. Civ. P. 124; **Mays v. Perkins**, 927 S.W.2d 222, 227 (Tex.App.—Houston [1st Dist.] 1996, no writ); *see* **Von Briesen, Purtell & Roper, S.C. v. French**, 78 S.W.3d 570, 575 (Tex.App.—Amarillo 2002, pet. dism'd). If the party has not made an appearance, service of process is necessary.

§7.3 Third-party petitions. A third-party petition is the procedure used by a defendant to bring into the suit a third party who is or may be liable to the defendant or the plaintiff for all or part of the plaintiff's claim. Tex. R. Civ. P. 38(a); **Perryman v. Spartan Tex. Six Capital Partners**, 546 S.W.3d 110, 132 (Tex.2018); **Omega Contracting, Inc. v. Torres**, 191 S.W.3d 828, 837 (Tex.App.—Fort Worth 2006, no pet.); *e.g.*, **Bennett v. Grant**, 525 S.W.3d 642, 653 (Tex.2017) (although trial court did not specify rule when granting joinder, joinder under TRCP 38(a) would have been improper because D did not allege that third party was liable to P for any part of P's slander claim against D). See **O'Connor's Texas Civil Forms**, FORM 3E:12 (2020 ed.). The third-party petition is limited to contribution and indemnification claims, making it more restrictive than the "same transaction or occurrence" test used for counterclaims and cross-claims.

1. Leave of court. The defendant may file a third-party petition without leave of court within 30 days after filing its answer; after 30 days, leave of court is required. Tex. R. Civ. P. 38(a); **Bilek & Purcell Indus. v. Paderwerk Gebr. Benteler GmbH**, 694 S.W.2d 225, 227 (Tex.App.—Houston [1st Dist.] 1985, no writ).

2. Service of citation. The defendant, as a third-party plaintiff, must serve the third-party defendant with citation and petition. Tex. R. Civ. P. 38(a).

§7.4 RTP. A defendant can designate a person who bears some responsibility for the plaintiff's injuries as a responsible third party (RTP) in the suit. *See* Tex. Civ. Prac. & Rem. Code §§33.004(a), 33.011(6); *see also* **In re CVR Energy, Inc.**, 500 S.W.3d 67, 75–76 (Tex.App.—Houston [1st Dist.] 2016, orig. proceeding) ("third party" means party not already in the suit; thus, person cannot be D and RTP at the same time).

1. Identifying an RTP.

(1) Who is an RTP. An RTP is any person who is alleged to have caused or contributed to the harm for which recovery of damages is sought, whether by (1) a negligent act or omission, (2) any defective or unreasonably dangerous product, or (3) other conduct or activity that violates an applicable legal standard. Tex. Civ. Prac. & Rem. Code §33.011(6); *see also* Tex. Gov't Code §311.005(2) ("person" includes corporation, organization, or other legal entity). The following persons can be designated as an RTP:

(a) A person who is immune from liability to the plaintiff. **In re Unitec Elevator Servs.**, 178 S.W.3d 53, 58 n.5 (Tex.App.—Houston [1st Dist.] 2005, orig. proceeding).

(b) A person who is not subject to the court's jurisdiction. *Id.*

(c) An unknown person. *See* Tex. Civ. Prac. & Rem. Code §33.004(j).

(d) An attorney. **In re Coppola**, 535 S.W.3d 506, 508–09 (Tex.2017).

(2) Who is not an RTP. A seller eligible for indemnity in a products-liability action under CPRC §82.002 cannot be designated as an RTP. Tex. Civ. Prac. & Rem. Code §33.011(6).

2. Designating an RTP. The defendant may designate a person as an RTP by filing a motion for leave to designate that person as an RTP. Tex. Civ. Prac. & Rem. Code §33.004(a). See "Motion for leave to designate," ch. 3-E, §7.4.2(2). If the RTP is an unknown criminal, the defendant must first file an amended answer before seeking leave to designate. A defendant that has entered into a settlement agreement with the plaintiff can still seek to designate a person as an RTP as long as the plaintiff has not filed a nonsuit against the defendant. **Flack v. Hanke**, 334 S.W.3d 251, 258 (Tex.App.—San Antonio 2010, pet. denied).

Note

The filing or granting of a motion for leave to designate a person as an RTP or the finding of fault against a person does not by itself impose liability on the RTP in the current suit or in any other proceeding. Tex. Civ. Prac. & Rem. Code §33.004(i); ***In re Mobile Mini, Inc.****, 596 S.W.3d 781, 784 (Tex.2020); see also* ***Galbraith Eng'g Consultants, Inc. v. Pochucha****, 290 S.W.3d 863, 868–69 (Tex.2009) (D can designate RTP even if RTP has defense to liability or cannot be formally joined as a defendant). The designation simply allows the jury to consider the third party's percentage of responsibility. Tex. Civ. Prac. & Rem. Code §33.003(a). By designating an RTP who shares the blame for the injury, the defendant can reduce its own percentage of responsibility. If the RTP is joined by the plaintiff, the RTP becomes a defendant and can be liable to the plaintiff. See* ***Flack****, 334 S.W.3d at 256. See "Plaintiff's joinder," ch. 3-E, §7.4.2(4).*

(1) Amended answer—RTP is unknown criminal. If the RTP is an unknown person alleged to have committed a criminal act, the defendant must file an amended answer before filing a motion for leave to designate the person as an RTP. *See* Tex. Civ. Prac. & Rem. Code §33.004(j). The amended answer must be filed no later than 60 days after the defendant filed its original answer. *Id.*; **In re Unitec Elevator**, 178 S.W.3d at 61; *see also* **In re Echols**, 569 S.W.3d 776, 780–81 (Tex.App.—Dallas 2018, orig. proceeding) (60-day deadline is mandatory; deadline in CPRC §33.004(a) is not alternative to deadline in §33.004(j) for situations involving unknown criminal). In the amended answer, the defendant must do the following:

(a) Allege that an unknown person committed a criminal act that caused the loss or injury that is the subject of the suit. Tex. Civ. Prac. & Rem. Code §33.004(j).

(b) Plead facts sufficient to show a reasonable probability that the person's act was criminal. Tex. Civ. Prac. & Rem. Code §33.004(j)(1).

(c) Plead all identifying characteristics of the person that are known at the time the amended answer is filed. Tex. Civ. Prac. & Rem. Code §33.004(j)(2).

(d) Plead facts about the person's responsibility sufficient to satisfy the pleading requirements of the TRCPs. Tex. Civ. Prac. & Rem. Code §33.004(j)(3).

(e) Refer to the person as "Jane Doe" or "John Doe" until the person's identity is known. Tex. Civ. Prac. & Rem. Code §33.004(k).

(2) Motion for leave to designate. The defendant may file a motion for leave to designate a person as an RTP. Tex. Civ. Prac. & Rem. Code §33.004(a). See **O'Connor's Texas Civil Forms**, FORM 3E:14 (2020 ed.).

(a) Deadline to file. The deadline for filing a motion for leave to designate an RTP depends on whether the limitations period for the underlying cause of action against the RTP has expired.

[1] Limitations period has not expired. If the limitations period against the RTP has not expired when the motion for leave to designate is to be filed, the deadline for filing the motion is at least 60 days before the trial date. *See* Tex. Civ. Prac. & Rem. Code §33.004(a), (d); **In re Coppola**, 535 S.W.3d at 507. If the trial date is reset, the motion must be filed at least 60 days before the new trial date. *See, e.g.*, **In re Coppola**, 535 S.W.3d at 507–08 (motion for leave to designate filed 76 days before third trial setting was timely). On a finding of good cause, the court may allow the motion for leave

to designate an RTP to be filed at a later date. Tex. Civ. Prac. & Rem. Code §33.004(a); *e.g.*, **In re CVR Energy**, 500 S.W.3d at 79 (good cause for D to file motion 29 days before trial date when RTP was a named co-D at 60-day deadline; D was not required to make RTP designation until after RTP was nonsuited by P).

[2] Limitations period has expired. If the limitations period against the RTP has expired when the motion for leave to designate is to be filed, the defendant cannot file the motion if the defendant knew but did not timely disclose that the person might be designated as an RTP (e.g., during discovery). *E.g.*, **In re Dawson**, 550 S.W.3d 625, 629 (Tex.2018) (D's supplemental response to request for disclosure that only included RTP's name and phone number was not sufficient disclosure); *see* Tex. Civ. Prac. & Rem. Code §33.004(d); *see, e.g.*, **In re CVR Energy**, 500 S.W.3d at 79 (D did not have duty to disclose that company already named as co-D might be designated as RTP). "Timely" disclosure means before the deadline to respond to discovery under the TRCPs, even if that deadline occurs after the limitations period has expired. *See* **In re Mobile Mini**, 596 S.W.3d at 784. If the defendant timely disclosed her intent to designate the RTP, the deadline for filing the motion is the same as if the limitations period had not expired. *See* Tex. Civ. Prac. & Rem. Code §33.004(a), (d).

(b) Grounds. The defendant must plead sufficient facts about the RTP's alleged responsibility to satisfy the pleading requirements of the TRCPs. *See* Tex. Civ. Prac. & Rem. Code §33.004(g)(1). The fair-notice pleading standard applies to a motion for leave to designate. **In re Greyhound Lines, Inc.**, No. 05-13-01646-CV, 2014 WL 1022329 (Tex.App.—Dallas 2014, orig. proceeding) (memo op.; 2-21-14); *see* **In re Bustamante**, 510 S.W.3d at 737; **In re CVR Energy**, 500 S.W.3d at 80. See "Fair notice of claim," ch. 2-B, §7.2.

(c) Amended answer—unknown criminal. If the RTP is an unknown criminal, the defendant should attach a copy of the amended answer to the motion. *See* Tex. Civ. Prac. & Rem. Code §33.004(j).

(d) Objection. Any party can file an objection to the motion for leave to designate an RTP. *See* Tex. Civ. Prac. & Rem. Code §33.004(f); **Flack**, 334 S.W.3d at 262. See **O'Connor's Texas Civil Forms**, FORM 3E:15 (2020 ed.).

[1] Deadline. A party must file the objection within 15 days after the motion is served. Tex. Civ. Prac. & Rem. Code §33.004(f).

[2] Grounds. To defeat the motion for leave to designate, the objecting party must assert certain grounds in the following objections:

[a] Initial objection. The objecting party must establish that the defendant did not plead sufficient facts about the RTP's alleged responsibility to satisfy the pleading requirements of the TRCPs. Tex. Civ. Prac. & Rem. Code §33.004(g)(1).

[b] Second objection. If the trial court sustains the initial objection, it must give the defendant an opportunity to replead. *See* Tex. Civ. Prac. & Rem. Code §33.004(g)(2); **In re Coppola**, 535 S.W.3d at 508; **In re Oncor Elec. Delivery Co.**, 355 S.W.3d 304, 306 (Tex.App.—Dallas 2011, orig. proceeding). See "Insufficient facts pleaded," ch. 3-E, §7.4.2(2)(e)[2][a]. After the defendant has had an opportunity to replead, the objecting party must establish that the defendant still did not satisfy the pleading requirements of the TRCPs. *See* Tex. Civ. Prac. & Rem. Code §33.004(g)(2).

(e) Ruling on motion. In ruling on a motion for leave to designate, the court should consider only the sufficiency of the facts pleaded by the defendant and should not consider evidence of the RTP's ultimate liability. **In re Greyhound Lines**, No. 05-13-01646-CV, 2014 WL 1022329 (memo op.).

[1] Grant. If the court grants the motion for leave to designate, the person named in the motion is designated as an RTP without any further action by the court or any party. Tex. Civ. Prac. & Rem. Code §33.004(h). The court must grant the motion for either of the following reasons:

[a] No objection. The court must grant the motion for leave to designate if a party does not object to it. Tex. Civ. Prac. & Rem. Code §33.004(f); *e.g.*, **In re Brokers Logistics, Ltd.**, 320 S.W.3d 402, 406 & n.4 (Tex.App.—El Paso 2010, orig. proceeding) (court granted motion because P filed objection after 15-day deadline); *see also* **Valverde v. Biela's Glass & Aluminum Prods.**, 293 S.W.3d 751, 755 (Tex.App.—San Antonio 2009, pet. denied) (even if no objection is filed, designation is not effective until court grants motion).

[b] Sufficient facts pleaded. The court must grant the motion for leave to designate if the defendant pleaded sufficient facts about the RTP's alleged responsibility to satisfy the pleading requirements of the TRCPs. *See* Tex. Civ. Prac. & Rem. Code §33.004(g).

[2] Deny. The court must deny the motion for either of the following reasons:

[a] Insufficient facts pleaded. The court must deny the motion for leave to designate if the objecting party establishes that the defendant did not plead sufficient facts about the RTP's alleged responsibility to satisfy the pleading requirements of the TRCPs. *See* Tex. Civ. Prac. & Rem. Code §33.004(g). Before the court can deny the motion for leave to designate, it must give the defendant an opportunity to replead after an initial objection is filed. *See* Tex. Civ. Prac. & Rem. Code §33.004(g)(2); **In re Coppola**, 535 S.W.3d at 508; **In re Oncor Elec.**, 355 S.W.3d at 306. If the defendant still has not satisfied the pleading requirements of the TRCPs after having had an opportunity to replead, only then can the court deny the motion. *See* Tex. Civ. Prac. & Rem. Code §33.004(g)(2); **In re Oncor Elec.**, 355 S.W.3d at 306.

[b] Motion or amended answer not timely. The court must deny the motion for leave to designate if the motion or amended answer was not timely filed. See "Amended answer—RTP is unknown criminal," ch. 3-E, §7.4.2(1); "Deadline to file," ch. 3-E, §7.4.2(2)(a).

[3] Review. Mandamus review is appropriate when the trial court erroneously grants or denies a motion for leave to designate. **In re Dawson**, 550 S.W.3d at 631; *see* **In re Mobile Mini**, 596 S.W.3d at 787–88; **In re Coppola**, 535 S.W.3d at 509. To be entitled to mandamus relief, the defendant is generally required to show only that the trial court abused its discretion in granting or denying the motion. *See* **In re Dawson**, 550 S.W.3d at 630; **In re Coppola**, 535 S.W.3d at 510.

(3) Motion to strike designation. After an adequate time for discovery, a party may move to strike the designation of an RTP if there is no evidence the designated person was responsible for any part of the plaintiff's injury or damages. Tex. Civ. Prac. & Rem. Code §33.004(l); *see* **In re Coppola**, 535 S.W.3d at 508. See **O'Connor's Texas Civil Forms**, FORM 3E:17 (2020 ed.). The court must grant the motion to strike unless the defendant presents sufficient evidence to raise a fact issue about the designated person's responsibility for the plaintiff's injury or damages. Tex. Civ. Prac. & Rem. Code §33.004(l).

(4) Plaintiff's joinder. Generally, a plaintiff may join a person as a defendant if that person has been designated as an RTP. See **O'Connor's Texas Civil Forms**, FORM 3E:16 (2020 ed.). The plaintiff must file an amended petition adding the RTP as a defendant. See "Motion to Amend Pleadings—Pretrial," ch. 5-F, §1 et seq.

Note

Even if the plaintiff does not join the RTP as a defendant, a jury charge on the responsibility for the injury among the plaintiff, the defendant, the designated RTP, and any settling person will be submitted to the jury. See Tex. Civ. Prac. & Rem. Code §33.003(a). A question about the conduct of any person cannot be submitted to the jury without sufficient evidence to support the submission. Tex. Civ. Prac. & Rem. Code §33.003(b). The defendant is liable for the percentage of responsibility attributed to it by the jury, as well as for the amounts it is jointly and severally liable for. Tex. Civ. Prac. & Rem. Code §33.013(a), (b). See "Determining what each defendant owes," ***O'Connor's Texas Causes of Action****, ch. 51, §6 (2021 ed.).*

(a) Deadline.

[1] Limitations period has not expired. If the limitations period for the underlying cause of action against the RTP has not expired, the plaintiff can join the RTP as a defendant anytime before the deadline for joinder set by the trial court or after the joinder deadline with leave of court. *See* Tex. R. Civ. P. 40(a), 41. See "Pleading deadlines," ch. 5-A, §3.4.

[2] Limitations period has expired. If the limitations period for the underlying cause of action against the RTP has expired, the plaintiff cannot join the RTP as a defendant. **In re Dawson**, 550 S.W.3d at 628; *see* Acts 2011, 82nd Leg., R.S., ch. 203, §5.02, eff. Sept. 1, 2011 (repeal of CPRC §33.004(e), which allowed for joinder after limitations period expired in cases filed before 9-1-11).

(b) Effect of joinder. When the RTP is joined, it becomes a party to the suit and is no longer an RTP, even if the claim against the designating defendant is later dismissed. *See* **Flack**, 334 S.W.3d at 262.

§8. Request for disclosure

For cases filed before January 1, 2021, a request for disclosure could be included in the defendant's original answer. *See* Tex. R. Civ. P. 194.1 (pre-1-1-21 version). For cases filed on or after January 1, 2021, a party is generally required to disclose certain information automatically without waiting for a discovery request from the other party. *See* Tex. R. Civ. P. 194.1(a); Tex.Sup.Ct. Order, Misc. Docket No. 20-9153 (eff. Jan. 1, 2021). See "Required disclosures—Cases filed on or after 1-1-21," ch. 6-E, §3. Thus, for cases filed on or after January 1, 2021, the original answer should not include a disclosure request.

§9. Drafting the answer

For a series of considerations that will help the defendant draft its original answer, see "Constructing the original answer," ch. 3-A, §4.

F. Plea to the Jurisdiction—Challenging the Court

§1. General

§1.1 Rule. Tex. R. Civ. P. 85. See Tex. Civ. Prac. & Rem. Code §16.064.

§1.2 Purpose. A plea to the jurisdiction is a procedural device used to challenge the court's subject-matter jurisdiction over a claim. **Texas Dept. of Parks & Wildlife v. Miranda**, 133 S.W.3d 217, 232 (Tex.2004); **Bland ISD v. Blue**, 34 S.W.3d 547, 554 (Tex.2000); *see* **City of Ingleside v. City of Corpus Christi**, 469 S.W.3d 589, 590 (Tex.2015). Without subject-matter jurisdiction, a court does not have authority to render judgment and must dismiss the claim without resolving the parties' substantive arguments. *See* **City of Houston v. Rhule**, 417 S.W.3d 440, 442 (Tex.2013); **DaimlerChrysler Corp. v. Inman**, 252 S.W.3d 299, 304 (Tex.2008); **Bland ISD**, 34 S.W.3d at 553–54. Thus, the defendant can use a plea to the jurisdiction to defeat a cause of action without regard to its merits. **Mission Consol. ISD v. Garcia**, 372 S.W.3d 629, 635 (Tex.2012); **Bland ISD**, 34 S.W.3d at 554.

Note

Subject-matter jurisdiction cannot be given or taken away by consent and cannot be waived. ***Carroll v. Carroll****, 304 S.W.3d 366, 367 (Tex.2010);* ***Parham F.L.P. v. Morgan****, 434 S.W.3d 774, 783 (Tex.App.—Houston [14th Dist.] 2014, no pet.); see* ***University of Houston v. Barth****, 313 S.W.3d 817, 818 (Tex.2010). Thus, parties cannot challenge or support a court's subject-matter jurisdiction on those grounds.*

§1.3 Timetable & forms. Appendix IV, Timetable 8, Pretrial motions; **O'Connor's Texas Civil Forms**, FORMS 3F:1 et seq. (2020 ed.); **O'Connor's Texas Causes of Action Pleadings** (2020 ed.).

§1.4 Other references. Simmons & Patton, *Plea to the Jurisdiction: Defining the Undefined*, 40 St. Mary's L.J. 627 (2009); **O'Connor's Texas Causes of Action** (2021 ed.); **O'Connor's Texas Civil Appeals** (2020 ed.).

§2. Plea to the jurisdiction

§2.1 Form. A plea to the jurisdiction may be included in the answer or filed as a separate motion. Tex. R. Civ. P. 85. If filed as a motion, it should be captioned as a motion to dismiss for lack of jurisdiction. See **O'Connor's Texas Civil Forms**, FORM 3F:1 (2020 ed.). Subject-matter jurisdiction can also be challenged in another procedural instrument, such as a traditional or no-evidence motion for summary judgment. **Town of Shady Shores v. Swanson**, 590 S.W.3d 544, 550–51 (Tex.2019); *see* **State v. Lueck**, 290 S.W.3d 876, 884 (Tex.2009); **Bland ISD v. Blue**, 34 S.W.3d 547, 554 (Tex.2000); *see, e.g.*, **City of Dallas v. Sanchez**, 494 S.W.3d 722, 725 (Tex.2016) (subject-matter jurisdiction challenged in motion to dismiss under TRCP 91a); *see also* **TDCJ v. Simons**, 140 S.W.3d 338, 349 (Tex.2004) (interlocutory appeal under CPRC §51.014(a)(8) can be taken from refusal to dismiss for lack of jurisdiction whether jurisdictional argument is made in plea to the jurisdiction or some other instrument).

Note

If the jurisdictional defect is a pleading defect that can be cured by amendment, it should be challenged by special exceptions. See "Curable defects in jurisdiction," ch. 3-G, §2.2.4.

§2.2 Evidence. The trial court may consider evidence in ruling on a plea to the jurisdiction and must consider evidence when necessary to resolve the jurisdictional issues raised. **Nettles v. GTECH Corp.**, 606 S.W.3d 726, ___ (Tex.2020); **Vernco Constr., Inc. v. Nelson**, 460 S.W.3d 145, 149 (Tex.2015); **Bland ISD v. Blue**, 34 S.W.3d 547, 555 (Tex.2000). Thus, when necessary, a defendant should attach affidavits, discovery, or other evidence to the plea.

1. Not necessary. Evidence is not necessary to resolve a plea to the jurisdiction when the plaintiff's petition (1) affirmatively demonstrates the court's jurisdiction, (2) affirmatively negates the court's jurisdiction, or (3) is insufficient to

determine jurisdiction but does not affirmatively demonstrate incurable defects (and thus may be amended). **Texas Dept. of Parks & Wildlife v. Miranda**, 133 S.W.3d 217, 226–27 (Tex.2004).

2. Necessary. The trial court must consider evidence on a plea to the jurisdiction when evidence is necessary to determine jurisdictional facts. **Nettles**, 606 S.W.3d at __; **Alamo Heights ISD v. Clark**, 544 S.W.3d 755, 770–71 (Tex.2018); **Heckman v. Williamson Cty.**, 369 S.W.3d 137, 150 (Tex.2012); **Miranda**, 133 S.W.3d at 227. See "Evidence to determine jurisdictional facts," ch. 3-F, §5.1. The trial court can allow the parties a reasonable opportunity for targeted discovery and time to gather evidence and prepare for a hearing. **Mission Consol. ISD v. Garcia**, 372 S.W.3d 629, 642–43 (Tex.2012); *see* **Miranda**, 133 S.W.3d at 229; *see, e.g.*, **Hearts Bluff Game Ranch, Inc. v. State**, 381 S.W.3d 468, 491–92 (Tex.2012) (court allowed limited discovery through which P served requests for production and obtained documents, but P did not take depositions and did not answer D's discovery requests until ordered by court; P's opportunity for discovery was sufficient); **Diocese of Galveston-Houston v. Stone**, 892 S.W.2d 169, 176–77 (Tex.App.—Houston [14th Dist.] 1994, orig. proceeding) (in suit against church by employee, discovery permitted to determine whether church could assert ecclesiastical privilege). See "Hearing," ch. 3-F, §5.

§2.3 No verification. No rule or statute requires that the plea to the jurisdiction be verified. **Ab-Tex Bev. Corp. v. Angelo State Univ.**, 96 S.W.3d 683, 688 (Tex.App.—Austin 2003, no pet.); *see* **Pakdimounivong v. City of Arlington**, 219 S.W.3d 401, 413–14 (Tex.App.—Fort Worth 2006, pet. denied) (because pleas to the jurisdiction are not listed in TRCP 93, they do not need to be verified). See "Verified pleas in TRCP 93," ch. 3-E, §4.1. If jurisdictional evidence is necessary, affidavits and other sworn proof should be attached to the plea.

§2.4 No deadline. There is no deadline for the plea to the jurisdiction. Lack of subject-matter jurisdiction is fundamental error and can be raised at any time. **Sivley v. Sivley**, 972 S.W.2d 850, 855 (Tex.App.—Tyler 1998, no pet.). The challenge can be raised for the first time on appeal. **American K-9 Detection Servs. v. Freeman**, 556 S.W.3d 246, 260 (Tex.2018); **Waco ISD v. Gibson**, 22 S.W.3d 849, 851 (Tex.2000); **Tullos v. Eaton Corp.**, 695 S.W.2d 568, 568 (Tex.1985). A court can inquire into its jurisdiction on its own initiative without a motion at any time. *See* **American K-9 Detection**, 556 S.W.3d at 260; **Texas Workers' Comp. Comm'n v. Garcia**, 893 S.W.2d 504, 517 n.15 (Tex.1995).

Note

The Supreme Court has clarified that, while governmental immunity "implicates" subject-matter jurisdiction and thus is properly raised in a plea to the jurisdiction, it does not equate to a lack of subject-matter jurisdiction for purposes of res judicata. ***Engelman Irrigation Dist. v. Shields Bros.**, 514 S.W.3d 746, 751 (Tex.2017); see **Rusk State Hosp. v. Black**, 392 S.W.3d 88, 95 (Tex.2012) (defense of governmental immunity implicates subject-matter jurisdiction and can be raised for first time on appeal). See "Res judicata—Claim preclusion," ch. 9-D, §3. Thus, a party cannot collaterally attack a final judgment by arguing that it is void due to lack of subject-matter jurisdiction based on the defense of immunity. See **Engelman Irrigation Dist.**, 514 S.W.3d at 755.*

§3. Grounds

§3.1 No justiciable issue. A plea to the jurisdiction is proper to challenge the lack of a justiciable issue. **State Office of Risk Mgmt. v. Rodriguez**, 355 S.W.3d 439, 446 (Tex.App.—El Paso 2011, pet. denied); *see* **American K-9 Detection Servs. v. Freeman**, 556 S.W.3d 246, 251 (Tex.2018). To present a justiciable issue, a suit must involve a real controversy that will be resolved by the judicial relief sought. *E.g.*, **State Bar v. Gomez**, 891 S.W.2d 243, 245–46 (Tex.1994) (district court did not have authority to compel State Bar or Supreme Court to implement mandatory pro bono); *see, e.g.*, **In re Nolo Press**, 991 S.W.2d 768, 777–78 (Tex.1999) (district court did not have authority to modify Supreme Court order).

§3.2 No standing. A plea to the jurisdiction is proper to challenge a party's lack of standing. *See* **Farmers Tex. Cty. Mut. Ins. v. Beasley**, 598 S.W.3d 237, 241 (Tex.2020); **Vernco Constr., Inc. v. Nelson**, 460 S.W.3d 145, 149 (Tex.2015); **M.D. Anderson Cancer Ctr. v. Novak**, 52 S.W.3d 704, 710–11 (Tex.2001). Standing focuses on who is the correct party to bring the suit. **Vernco Constr.**, 460 S.W.3d at 149; **Patterson v. Planned Parenthood**, 971 S.W.2d 439, 442 (Tex.1998). See "Standing," ch. 2-B, §4.2.1.

§3.3 Not ripe. A plea to the jurisdiction is proper to challenge the lack of ripeness. *See* **Southwestern Elec. Power Co. v. Lynch**, 595 S.W.3d 678, 681 (Tex.2020); **Waco ISD v. Gibson**, 22 S.W.3d 849, 851–52 (Tex.2000). Ripeness focuses on when an action may be brought. **Patterson v. Planned Parenthood**, 971 S.W.2d 439, 442 (Tex.1998); **American Nat'l Ins. v. Cannon**, 86 S.W.3d 801, 806 (Tex.App.—Beaumont 2002, no pet.). See "Ripeness," **O'Connor's Texas Causes of Action**, ch. 52, §3.4 (2021 ed.).

§3.4 Mootness.

1. Generally. A plea to the jurisdiction is generally proper to challenge a case that has become moot. *See* **Glassdoor, Inc. v. Andra Grp.**, 575 S.W.3d 523, 527 (Tex.2019) (when case is moot, court normally dismisses for lack of jurisdiction); **Heckman v. Williamson Cty.**, 369 S.W.3d 137, 162 (Tex.2012) (same); **Hansen v. JP Morgan Chase Bank**, 346 S.W.3d 769, 773 (Tex.App.—Dallas 2011, no pet.) (mootness implicates subject-matter jurisdiction); **Pantera Energy Co. v. Railroad Comm'n of Tex.**, 150 S.W.3d 466, 471 (Tex.App.—Austin 2004, no pet.) (same). A case becomes moot if (1) a party seeks a judgment based on a controversy that no longer exists (i.e., the controversy is not "live") or (2) the parties have no legally cognizable interest in the outcome. **State v. Harper**, 562 S.W.3d 1, 6 (Tex.2018); **City of Krum v. Rice**, 543 S.W.3d 747, 749 (Tex.2017); **Heckman**, 369 S.W.3d at 162; **Allstate Ins. v. Hallman**, 159 S.W.3d 640, 642 (Tex.2005); *see also* **Speer v. Presbyterian Children's Home & Serv. Agency**, 847 S.W.2d 227, 229 (Tex.1993) (courts have no jurisdiction to issue advisory opinions). A dismissal for mootness is not a ruling on the merits. **Speer**, 847 S.W.2d at 229.

Note

*In some situations, a claim for attorney fees will "breathe life" into a case that has otherwise become moot. **Harper**, 562 S.W.3d at 7. If a party seeks attorney fees under a statute that allows a nonprevailing party to recover fees under equitable principles, the claim for attorney fees will not be moot because the trial court must consider the relative merits of the parties' positions in exercising its discretion to award fees. Id.; see **Allstate Ins.**, 159 S.W.3d at 643. But if the party seeks attorney fees under a prevailing-party statute, the fee claim will be moot unless the party prevailed before the underlying substantive claim became moot. **Glassdoor, Inc.**, 575 S.W.3d at 530–31; e.g., **Harper**, 562 S.W.3d at 7–8 (because D prevailed on his motion to dismiss under Texas Citizens Participation Act before case became moot, he could still recover attorney fees as prevailing party under the Act); see **Speer**, 847 S.W.2d at 229; **Camarena v. Texas Empl. Comm'n**, 754 S.W.2d 149, 151 (Tex.1988).*

2. Exceptions. A court may have jurisdiction to decide the merits of a case, even if it is moot, based on certain exceptions. *See* **Heckman**, 369 S.W.3d at 163–64; **FDIC v. Nueces Cty.**, 886 S.W.2d 766, 767 (Tex.1994); **General Land Office v. OXY U.S.A., Inc.**, 789 S.W.2d 569, 571 (Tex.1990). For the specific exceptions, see "Exceptions," **O'Connor's Texas Civil Appeals**, ch. 3-E, §3.1.3(6)(a)[2] (2020 ed.).

§3.5 Another court has exclusive jurisdiction. A plea to the jurisdiction is proper to challenge a suit brought in one court when another court has continuing, exclusive jurisdiction. **Jansen v. Fitzpatrick**, 14 S.W.3d 426, 430–31 (Tex.App.—Houston [14th Dist.] 2000, no pet.); *see also* **Speer v. Stover**, 685 S.W.2d 22, 23 (Tex.1985) (district court did not have jurisdiction over case pending in probate court); **Howe State Bank v. Crookham**, 873 S.W.2d 745, 747–48 (Tex.App.—Dallas 1994, no writ) (same); *cf.* **Geary v. Peavy**, 878 S.W.2d 602, 604–05 (Tex.1994) (Minnesota court had exclusive jurisdiction over child-custody case). By comparison, when two courts have concurrent jurisdiction, the issue of dominant jurisdiction should be challenged by a plea in abatement. *E.g.*, **In re Puig**, 351 S.W.3d 301, 305 (Tex.2011) (county court at law exercising probate jurisdiction had concurrent jurisdiction with district court; plea to the jurisdiction was improper method for contesting dominant jurisdiction). See "Abate—same dispute in another Texas court," ch. 3-I, §3.2.

Note

For the rules governing the plaintiff's selection of a court, see "Choosing the Court—Jurisdiction," ch. 2-G, §1 et seq.

§3.6 Administrative agency has exclusive jurisdiction. A plea to the jurisdiction is proper to allege that an administrative agency has exclusive jurisdiction over the dispute. *See* **Oncor Elec. Delivery Co. v. Chaparral Energy, LLC**, 546 S.W.3d 133, 138 (Tex.2018); **In re Crawford & Co.**, 458 S.W.3d 920, 928–29 (Tex.2015); **City of Houston v. Rhule**, 417 S.W.3d 440, 442 (Tex.2013); *see also* **Klumb v. Houston Mun. Empls. Pension Sys.**, 458 S.W.3d 1, 8 (Tex.2015) (plea to the jurisdiction is proper to challenge judicial review of administrative order). When an agency's jurisdiction is exclusive, a party must exhaust all administrative remedies before seeking judicial review of a decision; until the party exhausts those remedies, a court lacks subject-matter jurisdiction, and dismissal is mandatory. **Forest Oil Corp. v. El Rucio Land & Cattle Co.**, 518 S.W.3d 422, 428 (Tex.2017); **Clint ISD v. Marquez**, 487 S.W.3d 538, 544 (Tex.2016); **Thomas v. Long**, 207 S.W.3d 334, 340 (Tex.2006); **In re Entergy Corp.**, 142 S.W.3d 316, 321–22 (Tex.2004); **Subaru of Am., Inc. v. David McDavid Nissan, Inc.**, 84 S.W.3d 212, 221 (Tex.2002). See "Administrative remedies," **O'Connor's Texas Causes of Action**, ch. 24-A, §2.8 (2021 ed.). But when an agency's jurisdiction is primary, not exclusive, abatement is appropriate. See "Abate—administrative agency has primary jurisdiction," ch. 3-I, §3.4.

§3.7 Governmental immunity from suit. A plea to the jurisdiction is proper to challenge a suit filed against a governmental unit when the governmental unit is immune from suit. **City of Conroe v. San Jacinto River Auth.**, 602 S.W.3d 444, 457 (Tex.2020); **Tarrant Reg'l Water Dist. v. Johnson**, 572 S.W.3d 658, 664 (Tex.2019); **City of Houston v. Houston Mun. Empls. Pension Sys.**, 549 S.W.3d 566, 575 (Tex.2018); **State v. Lueck**, 290 S.W.3d 876, 880 (Tex.2009); **Harris Cty. v. Sykes**, 136 S.W.3d 635, 638 (Tex.2004). When filing suit for damages against the government, the plaintiff must affirmatively demonstrate the court's jurisdiction to hear the suit under the Texas Tort Claims Act or another statute that waives the government's immunity from suit. **TDCJ v. Miller**, 51 S.W.3d 583, 587 (Tex.2001); *see* **Sampson v. University of Tex. at Austin**, 500 S.W.3d 380, 384 (Tex.2016); **Suarez v. City of Tex. City**, 465 S.W.3d 623, 627 (Tex.2015); **University of Tex. v. Hayes**, 327 S.W.3d 113, 115 (Tex.2010). For the elements of a suit against a governmental unit, see **O'Connor's Texas Causes of Action**, chs. 24 to 26 (2021 ed.); for the allegations to include in the petition, see **O'Connor's Texas Causes of Action Pleadings**, FORMS 24:1 et seq. to 26:1 et seq. (2020 ed.). If the government has immunity from suit but the plaintiff can cure the defect (e.g., obtain legislative consent to sue), the case should be abated until the defect is remedied. *See* **Texas A&M Univ. Sys. v. Koseoglu**, 233 S.W.3d 835, 839–40 (Tex.2007).

Note

The Supreme Court has clarified that, while governmental immunity "implicates" subject-matter jurisdiction and thus is properly raised in a plea to the jurisdiction, it does not equate to a lack of subject-matter jurisdiction for purposes of res judicata. See "Note," ch. 3-F, §2.4.

§3.8 Statutory jurisdictional requirements.

1. Suits generally. A plea to the jurisdiction is proper to challenge a statutory claim when the plaintiff did not comply with a statutory jurisdictional requirement. When a plaintiff does not comply with a jurisdictional requirement, it deprives the court of subject-matter jurisdiction. *See* **City of DeSoto v. White**, 288 S.W.3d 389, 393 (Tex.2009). Not all statutory requirements for filing suit are jurisdictional. *Id.* at 395; *see* **Crosstex Energy Servs. v. Pro Plus, Inc.**, 430 S.W.3d 384, 391 (Tex.2014); **Dubai Pet. Co. v. Kazi**, 12 S.W.3d 71, 76–77 (Tex.2000). When a statutory requirement is not jurisdictional, failure to comply is a defensive matter that should be raised in a different pleading. *See, e.g.*, Tex. Bus. & Com. Code §17.505(c) (when statutory notice is not received, D may file plea in abatement).

(1) Unambiguous. If a statute identifies a requirement as jurisdictional, the failure to comply with the requirement should be challenged by a plea to the jurisdiction. *See, e.g.*, **Sierra Club v. Texas Nat. Res. Conserv. Comm'n**, 26 S.W.3d 684, 688 (Tex.App.—Austin 2000) (requirements in §2001.174 of Administrative Procedure Act are jurisdictional because they restrict the kind of case a court may decide and the kind of relief a court may grant), *aff'd*, 70 S.W.3d 809 (Tex.2002). When a statute unambiguously identifies a requirement as jurisdictional, the statute's plain language controls unless that interpretation would lead to absurd results. *See* **TDPRS v. Mega Child Care, Inc.**, 145 S.W.3d 170, 177 (Tex.2004).

(2) Ambiguous. If a statute does not clearly identify a requirement as jurisdictional, the presumption is that it is not jurisdictional. *See* **In re United Servs. Auto. Ass'n**, 307 S.W.3d 299, 307 (Tex.2010); **City of DeSoto**, 288 S.W.3d

at 394. This presumption can be overcome only by clear legislative intent to the contrary. **In re United Servs. Auto.**, 307 S.W.3d at 307; **City of DeSoto**, 288 S.W.3d at 394. To determine legislative intent, the court begins with an analysis of the statute's text. **City of DeSoto**, 288 S.W.3d at 395; *see* **Texas Mut. Ins. v. Chicas**, 593 S.W.3d 284, 287–88 (Tex.2019). The court may also consider one or more of the following: (1) the object sought to be obtained, (2) the statute's legislative history, (3) the presence or absence of specific consequences for noncompliance with the statute, and (4) the consequences of each possible interpretation of the statute. *See* Tex. Gov't Code §311.023; **Texas Mut.**, 593 S.W.3d at 287; **Crosstex Energy**, 430 S.W.3d at 392; **City of DeSoto**, 288 S.W.3d at 396.

(a) Intended as jurisdictional. If the court determines that the Legislature intended the statutory requirement to be jurisdictional, failure to comply with the requirement should be challenged by a plea to the jurisdiction. *See, e.g.*, **Subaru of Am., Inc. v. David McDavid Nissan, Inc.**, 84 S.W.3d 212, 220–21 (Tex.2002) (failure to exhaust administrative remedies before filing suit is jurisdictional if administrative body has exclusive jurisdiction over dispute).

(b) Intended as defensive. If the court determines that the Legislature intended the statutory requirement to be defensive and not jurisdictional, failure to comply with the requirement cannot be challenged by a plea to the jurisdiction. *See, e.g.*, **Texas Mut.**, 593 S.W.3d at 291 (deadline under Lab. Code §410.252(a) to file suit for judicial review of appeals-panel decision in workers' compensation cases is not jurisdictional); **City of DeSoto**, 288 S.W.3d at 398 (notice provision in Fire Fighter & Police Officer Civil Service Act is not jurisdictional); **Hubenak v. San Jacinto Gas Transmission Co.**, 141 S.W.3d 172, 182–83 (Tex.2004) ("unable to agree" requirement in Prop. Code §21.012 is not jurisdictional); **Subaru of Am.**, 84 S.W.3d at 221 (failure to exhaust administrative remedies before filing suit is not jurisdictional if administrative body has only primary jurisdiction over dispute); **Dubai Pet.**, 12 S.W.3d at 76–77 (in wrongful-death case, statute's "equal treaty rights" provision is not jurisdictional).

2. Suits against governmental entity. In a suit against a governmental entity, a plea to the jurisdiction is proper to challenge certain statutory claims.

(1) Statutory prerequisites. In a suit against a governmental entity, a plea to the jurisdiction is proper to challenge a statutory claim when the plaintiff did not comply with a statutory prerequisite to filing suit. *See* Tex. Gov't Code §311.034; **City of Madisonville v. Sims**, __ S.W.3d __, 2020 WL 1898540 (Tex.2020) (No. 18-1047; 4-17-20); **Prairie View A&M Univ. v. Chatha**, 381 S.W.3d 500, 510 (Tex.2012); *see, e.g*, **Worsdale v. City of Killeen**, 578 S.W.3d 57, 61 (Tex.2019) (notice of claim is prerequisite to suit under Texas Torts Claim Act and thus properly challenged by plea to the jurisdiction; although City properly filed plea because timely, formal notice was lacking, court determined City had actual notice under statute and reversed judgment dismissing for lack of jurisdiction). To be a statutory prerequisite, the prerequisite must (1) appear in the statutory language, (2) be mandatory, and (3) be accomplished before suit is filed. **Prairie View A&M**, 381 S.W.3d at 511–12; *see* **City of Madisonville**, __ S.W.3d at __, 2020 WL 1898540. In all suits against a governmental entity, a statutory prerequisite—whether administrative (e.g., filing a charge of discrimination) or procedural (e.g., timely filing suit)—is a jurisdictional requirement. *E.g.*, **Prairie View A&M**, 381 S.W.3d at 515 (administrative filing requirement for employment-discrimination claim under Texas Commission on Human Rights Act is statutory prerequisite to suit under Gov't Code §311.034 and is jurisdictional); *see* Tex. Gov't Code §311.034; **City of Madisonville**, __ S.W.3d at __, 2020 WL 1898540.

(2) Statutory elements of a cause of action. In a suit against a governmental entity, a plea to the jurisdiction is proper to challenge a statutory claim when the statutory elements of a cause of action are jurisdictional and the plaintiff did not comply with those elements. *See* **Alamo Heights ISD v. Clark**, 544 S.W.3d 755, 784–85 (Tex.2018); *see, e.g.*, **University of Tex. Sw. Med. Ctr. v. Gentilello**, 398 S.W.3d 680, 682 (Tex.2013) (plea to the jurisdiction was proper to challenge suit by whistleblower-P who had reported only to internal supervisor, who was not "appropriate law enforcement authority" under Gov't Code §554.002(b)); **Mission Consol. ISD v. Garcia**, 372 S.W.3d 629, 637–38 (Tex.2012) (plea to the jurisdiction was proper to challenge whether P pleaded prima facie elements for age-discrimination claim under Texas Commission on Human Rights Act); **State v. Lueck**, 290 S.W.3d 876, 883–84 (Tex.2009) (elements under Gov't Code §554.002(a) that whistleblower-P must be public employee and must state good-faith report of violation of Whistleblower Act were jurisdictional; plea to the jurisdiction was proper). In such cases, the statutory elements can be considered to determine both jurisdiction and liability. **Lueck**, 290 S.W.3d at 883; *see* **Mission Consol.**, 372 S.W.3d at 636–37.

§3.9 Federal preemption. A plea to the jurisdiction is proper to challenge a suit preempted by a federal law requiring that the claim be tried in a federal court. *See* **Southland Life Ins. v. Estate of Small**, 806 S.W.2d 800, 801 (Tex.1991) (ERISA). But if federal law does not require that the claim be tried in federal court, preemption is merely an affirmative defense and does not deprive a state court of jurisdiction. **Mills v. Warner Lambert Co.**, 157 S.W.3d 424, 427 (Tex.2005).

§3.10 Death. A plea to the jurisdiction is proper to challenge the continuation of a suit when the claim is extinguished by a party's death. A suit for a claim such as divorce or usury should be dismissed if either party dies before the trial court renders judgment on the merits. *E.g.*, **Whatley v. Bacon**, 649 S.W.2d 297, 299 (Tex.1983) (divorce); **Turner v. Ward**, 910 S.W.2d 500, 503 (Tex.App.—El Paso 1994, no writ) (divorce); **Orr v. International Bank of Commerce**, 649 S.W.2d 769, 772 (Tex.App.—San Antonio 1983, no writ) (usury). If the claim survives the party's death, dismissal is not appropriate, and the suit should proceed to judgment. *See* Tex. R. Civ. P. 150. For example, a suit for wrongful acquisition of property by fraud survives the death of either party. **Pace v. McEwen**, 574 S.W.2d 792, 800 (Tex.App.—El Paso 1978, writ ref'd n.r.e.). Once a judgment is rendered, the death of one of the parties does not extinguish the claim. *See* Tex. R. App. P. 7.1(a)(1) (when party dies after trial court renders judgment, case may be appealed). See "Rendition," ch. 9-C, §3.1.

§3.11 Fabricated jurisdiction. A plea to the jurisdiction is proper to challenge fraudulent allegations of an amount in controversy. *See* **Texas Dept. of Parks & Wildlife v. Miranda**, 133 S.W.3d 217, 224 & n.4 (Tex.2004); *see, e.g.*, **Delk v. City of Dallas**, 560 S.W.2d 519, 520 (Tex.App.—Texarkana 1977, no writ) (in suit to foreclose lien, D argued that P made fraudulent allegation of property value). The defendant must plead and prove that the allegations of the amount in controversy in the plaintiff's pleadings are false and were made fraudulently for the purpose of conferring jurisdiction. **Delk**, 560 S.W.2d at 520.

§3.12 Religious matters. A plea to the jurisdiction is proper to challenge the court's jurisdiction over a religious or ecclesiastical matter. **Westbrook v. Penley**, 231 S.W.3d 389, 394 (Tex.2007); *see* **Thiagarajan v. Tadepalli**, 430 S.W.3d 589, 593–94 (Tex.App.—Houston [14th Dist.] 2014, pet. denied); **Green v. United Pentecostal Ch. Int'l**, 899 S.W.2d 28, 29–30 (Tex.App.—Austin 1995, writ denied); *see also* **Williams v. Gleason**, 26 S.W.3d 54, 59–60 & n.7 (Tex.App.—Houston [14th Dist.] 2000, pet. denied) (issue raised by motion for summary judgment). Secular courts do not have jurisdiction over theological controversies and cannot constitutionally determine the truth or falsity of religious matters. *See* **Serbian E. Orthodox Diocese v. Milivojevich**, 426 U.S. 696, 713 (1976); **Masterson v. Diocese of Nw. Tex.**, 422 S.W.3d 594, 605–06 (Tex.2013); **Tilton v. Marshall**, 925 S.W.2d 672, 678 (Tex.1996).

§3.13 Estate as defendant. A plea to the jurisdiction is proper when the plaintiff names an estate as the defendant without any reference to the personal representative. *See* **Henson v. Estate of Crow**, 734 S.W.2d 648, 649 (Tex.1987); **Miller v. Estate of Self**, 113 S.W.3d 554, 556 (Tex.App.—Texarkana 2003, no pet.); **Estate of C.M. v. S.G.**, 937 S.W.2d 8, 10 (Tex.App.—Houston [14th Dist.] 1996, no writ). *But see* **Estate of Crawford v. Town of Flower Mound**, 933 S.W.2d 727, 731 (Tex.App.—Fort Worth 1996, writ denied) (claim that estate lacks legal capacity to be sued must be raised in verified pleading). See "Estate," ch. 2-B, §4.3.2.

Note

When an estate is named as the plaintiff without any reference to the personal representative, the defendant should file a verified plea challenging the plaintiff's capacity. See Tex. R. Civ. P. 93(1); ***Austin Nursing Ctr., Inc. v. Lovato****, 171 S.W.3d 845, 849 (Tex.2005). See "Verified pleas," ch. 3-E, §4.*

§3.14 No viable takings claim. A plea to the jurisdiction is proper when the plaintiff cannot establish a viable takings claim. **City of Houston v. Carlson**, 451 S.W.3d 828, 830 (Tex.2014); **Texas DOT v. A.P.I. Pipe & Sup.**, 397 S.W.3d 162, 166 (Tex.2013); *see* **Harris Cty. Flood Control Dist. v. Kerr**, 499 S.W.3d 793, 797 (Tex.2016); **Texas DOT v. City of Sunset Valley**, 146 S.W.3d 637, 644 (Tex.2004); *see also* Tex. Const. art. 1, §17(a) (no person's property shall be taken, damaged, or destroyed for or applied to public use without adequate compensation unless the person consents). See "Violation of Texas Constitution," **O'Connor's Texas Causes of Action**, ch. 24-A, §2.3.2(1) (2021 ed.). For example, if the plaintiff does not own the land, a takings claim is not viable and the trial court does not have jurisdiction. **Texas DOT**, 397 S.W.3d at 166.

§4. Response

§4.1 Plea is not valid. If the plea to the jurisdiction is not valid, the plaintiff should file a response and contest the factual allegations in the plea. *See* **Alamo Heights ISD v. Clark**, 544 S.W.3d 755, 771 (Tex.2018); *see, e.g.*, **Southwestern**

Bell Tel., L.P. v. Emmett, 459 S.W.3d 578, 587–88 (Tex.2015) (P argued ultra vires exception to governmental immunity in response to Ds' plea to the jurisdiction). See "Grounds," ch. 3-F, §3; **O'Connor's Texas Civil Forms**, FORM 3F:2 (2020 ed.). The response should follow the format of the plea. For example, if the plea includes evidence and is verified, the response should also include evidence and be verified.

§4.2 Plea is valid. If the defendant's plea to the jurisdiction is valid and the plaintiff filed suit in the wrong court, the plaintiff should admit the validity of the plea and file the suit in a proper court that has jurisdiction. If the limitations period has run, the plaintiff must be careful to avoid losing the tolling benefits of CPRC §16.064. See "Dismissal & limitations," ch. 3-F, §6.2.

§4.3 Additional discovery necessary. If the plaintiff needs additional time to conduct discovery and gather evidence that supports the court's jurisdiction, the plaintiff should file a motion for continuance. *See* **Patten v. Johnson**, 429 S.W.3d 767, 775 (Tex.App.—Dallas 2014, pet. denied). See "Continuance for additional discovery," ch. 5-D, §8.

§5. Hearing

The trial court can rule on a plea to the jurisdiction by submission or after a hearing. **Vernco Constr., Inc. v. Nelson**, 460 S.W.3d 145, 149 (Tex.2015); *see* **F/R Cattle Co. v. State**, 866 S.W.2d 200, 201–02 (Tex.1993).

§5.1 Evidence to determine jurisdictional facts. The court must consider evidence on a plea to the jurisdiction when evidence is necessary to determine jurisdictional facts. **Nettles v. GTECH Corp.**, 606 S.W.3d 726, __ (Tex.2020); **Alamo Heights ISD v. Clark**, 544 S.W.3d 755, 770–71 (Tex.2018); **Vernco Constr., Inc. v. Nelson**, 460 S.W.3d 145, 149 (Tex.2015); **Texas Dept. of Parks & Wildlife v. Miranda**, 133 S.W.3d 217, 227 (Tex.2004). For a discussion of situations where evidence is not necessary to resolve a plea to the jurisdiction, see "Not necessary," ch. 3-F, §2.2.1.

1. Jurisdiction unrelated to merits. In most pleas to the jurisdiction, the court should limit the evidence to only what is relevant to the jurisdictional issue and avoid considering evidence that goes to the merits of the case. **Bland ISD v. Blue**, 34 S.W.3d 547, 555 (Tex.2000); **Harris Cty. v. Progressive Nat'l Bank**, 93 S.W.3d 381, 384 (Tex.App.—Houston [14th Dist.] 2002, pet. denied); *see* **Farmers Tex. Cty. Mut. Ins. v. Beasley**, 598 S.W.3d 237, 241 (Tex.2020); **Ryder Integrated Logistics, Inc. v. Fayette Cty.**, 453 S.W.3d 922, 928 (Tex.2015); **Miranda**, 133 S.W.3d at 223. When the jurisdictional issue is unrelated to the merits, any disputed fact issues will be resolved by the court. **Vernco Constr.**, 460 S.W.3d at 149; *see* **Miranda**, 133 S.W.3d at 226; **Bland ISD**, 34 S.W.3d at 554–55.

2. Jurisdiction related to merits. In some cases, jurisdiction involves the merits of the case. For example, to prove jurisdiction against the State under the Recreational Use Statute, the plaintiff must prove the State was grossly negligent. See "Injury While Engaged in Recreation," **O'Connor's Texas Causes of Action**, ch. 26-F, §1 et seq. (2021 ed.). When jurisdiction involves the merits of the case, the trial court must review the evidence to determine whether there is a fact issue. **Suarez v. City of Tex. City**, 465 S.W.3d 623, 632–33 (Tex.2015); **Miranda**, 133 S.W.3d at 227; *see* **Harris Cty. Flood Control Dist. v. Kerr**, 499 S.W.3d 793, 798 (Tex.2016); **Mission Consol. ISD v. Garcia**, 372 S.W.3d 629, 635 (Tex.2012). This standard mirrors the traditional summary-judgment procedure under TRCP 166a(c). **TDCJ v. Rangel**, 595 S.W.3d 198, 205 (Tex.2020); **Alamo Heights ISD**, 544 S.W.3d at 771; **Sampson v. University of Tex. at Austin**, 500 S.W.3d 380, 384 (Tex.2016); **Mission Consol.**, 372 S.W.3d at 635; **Miranda**, 133 S.W.3d at 228; *see also* **Town of Shady Shores v. Swanson**, 590 S.W.3d 544, 551 (Tex.2019) (jurisdictional challenges can also be raised in no-evidence motion for summary judgment). That is, the defendant must first present evidence to show that the court lacks subject-matter jurisdiction; if the defendant does so, the plaintiff must then show there is a disputed material fact on the jurisdictional issue. **Mission Consol.**, 372 S.W.3d at 635; **Miranda**, 133 S.W.3d at 228; *see* **Rangel**, 595 S.W.3d at 205; **Alamo Heights ISD**, 544 S.W.3d at 771. If the facts are disputed, the court cannot grant the plea to the jurisdiction, and the issue must be resolved by the fact-finder at trial; however, if the evidence is undisputed or if there is no fact question on the jurisdictional issue, the trial court will rule on the plea to the jurisdiction as a matter of law. **Rangel**, 595 S.W.3d at 205; **PHI, Inc. v. Texas Juvenile Justice Dept.**, 593 S.W.3d 296, 302 (Tex.2019); **Suarez**, 465 S.W.3d at 633; **Miranda**, 133 S.W.3d at 227–28. See "Ruling," ch. 3-F, §6.

§5.2 Form of evidence received. When a trial court holds an evidentiary hearing, it may receive evidence in the form of oral testimony, discovery, and exhibits. *See, e.g.*, **TDCJ v. Miller**, 51 S.W.3d 583, 586 (Tex.2001) (in Texas Tort

Claims Act suit, court considered deposition testimony); **Bland ISD v. Blue**, 34 S.W.3d 547, 550 (Tex.2000) (trial court conducted evidentiary hearing and received oral testimony); **State v. Sledge**, 36 S.W.3d 152, 155 (Tex.App.—Houston [1st Dist.] 2000, pet. denied) (trial court conducted hearing and received oral testimony, affidavits, exhibits, and stipulations).

§6. Ruling

§6.1 Order. If a claim is not within a court's jurisdiction and the impediment to jurisdiction cannot be removed, the claim must be dismissed; but if the impediment to jurisdiction can be removed, the court should abate the proceedings to allow the plaintiff a reasonable opportunity to cure the jurisdictional problem. **American Motorists Ins. v. Fodge**, 63 S.W.3d 801, 805 (Tex.2001); *see* **Thomas v. Long**, 207 S.W.3d 334, 338 (Tex.2006). A petition containing multiple claims should not be dismissed just because the court lacks jurisdiction over one of the claims. *See* **Thomas**, 207 S.W.3d at 338–39. The court may dismiss or abate the claims over which it does not have subject-matter jurisdiction and retain the claims over which it does have jurisdiction. *See id.*

1. Opportunity to amend. If the jurisdictional defect can be cured by an amendment, the court should allow the plaintiff to amend. **Westbrook v. Penley**, 231 S.W.3d 389, 395 (Tex.2007); **Texas Dept. of Parks & Wildlife v. Miranda**, 133 S.W.3d 217, 226–27 (Tex.2004); **County of Cameron v. Brown**, 80 S.W.3d 549, 555 (Tex.2002); *see, e.g.*, **Clint ISD v. Marquez**, 487 S.W.3d 538, 558–59 (Tex.2016) (dismissal proper when amendments would not change nature of Ps' claims that required administrative remedies to be exhausted before filing suit; jurisdictional bar arose from nature of Ps' claims, not from lack of factual allegations); *see also* **Harris Cty. v. Annab**, 547 S.W.3d 609, 616 (Tex.2018) (when jurisdictional defect is raised for first time on appeal, remand may be appropriate to give P opportunity to replead and develop record). A plaintiff is not entitled to amend if its petition affirmatively negates jurisdiction. **Meyers v. JDC/Firethorne, Ltd.**, 548 S.W.3d 477, 486 (Tex.2018); **Houston Belt & Terminal Ry. v. City of Houston**, 487 S.W.3d 154, 160 (Tex.2016); **Miranda**, 133 S.W.3d at 227.

2. Dismissal. If the pleadings affirmatively negate jurisdiction, the suit should be dismissed. **Meyers**, 548 S.W.3d at 486; **Rusk State Hosp. v. Black**, 392 S.W.3d 88, 96 (Tex.2012); *see* **Heckman v. Williamson Cty.**, 369 S.W.3d 137, 150 (Tex.2012). If the pleadings do not affirmatively negate jurisdiction, the court can dismiss only if the defendant has shown that (1) the plaintiff, despite having had the opportunity to amend the petition, still cannot establish jurisdiction or (2) the plaintiff would be unable to show that the claim is within the court's jurisdiction even if the case were remanded and the plaintiff had an opportunity to amend. **Annab**, 547 S.W.3d at 616; **Rusk State Hosp.**, 392 S.W.3d at 96; *see* **TDCJ-Cmty. Justice Assistance Div. v. Campos**, 384 S.W.3d 810, 815 (Tex.2012); **Miranda**, 133 S.W.3d at 226–27.

(1) Without prejudice—most pleas. Generally, if the court does not have jurisdiction over the subject matter of the suit, it must dismiss the suit for lack of jurisdiction without rendering a judgment on the merits. **Black v. Jackson**, 82 S.W.3d 44, 56 (Tex.App.—Tyler 2002, no pet.); *see* **Jansen v. Fitzpatrick**, 14 S.W.3d 426, 431 (Tex.App.—Houston [14th Dist.] 2000, no pet.). The dismissal must be without prejudice because a dismissal with prejudice is a final decision on the merits. *See* **Black**, 82 S.W.3d at 56; **Jansen**, 14 S.W.3d at 431.

(2) With prejudice—governmental immunity. If a plaintiff in a suit against a governmental entity has been given a reasonable opportunity to amend and the plaintiff's amended pleading still does not allege facts that would constitute a waiver of immunity, the court should dismiss the plaintiff's suit with prejudice. **Harris Cty. v. Sykes**, 136 S.W.3d 635, 639 (Tex.2004); **City of Carrollton v. Harlan**, 180 S.W.3d 894, 898 (Tex.App.—Dallas 2005, pet. denied); *see also* **Texas A&M Univ. Sys. v. Koseoglu**, 233 S.W.3d 835, 839–40 (Tex.2007) (P is not required to amend its pleading until after court rules on plea to the jurisdiction). The dismissal is with prejudice because a plaintiff should not be permitted to relitigate jurisdiction once a court has determined there is no waiver of governmental immunity. *See* **Harris Cty.**, 136 S.W.3d at 639; **City of Carrollton**, 180 S.W.3d at 898.

3. Transfer. Generally, if the court lacks subject-matter jurisdiction, it must dismiss the case. **Kormanik v. Seghers**, 362 S.W.3d 679, 693 (Tex.App.—Houston [14th Dist.] 2012, pet. denied). But if another court has subject-matter jurisdiction over the case and a statute authorizes a transfer of the case to that court, the original court can transfer the case to the court having jurisdiction instead of dismissing the case. *E.g., id.* (county court without subject-matter jurisdiction could transfer case to district court with subject-matter jurisdiction because transfer was authorized by Gov't Code §74.121(b)).

But see **State v. Benavides**, 772 S.W.2d 271, 273 (Tex.App.—Corpus Christi 1989, writ denied) (court without subject-matter jurisdiction does not have power to transfer case to proper court).

§6.2 Dismissal & limitations.

1. Refiling suit & tolling limitations. If the statute of limitations expired after the suit was filed in the first court and before the case was dismissed, the plaintiff may refile the suit in the proper court within 60 days after the dismissal of the first suit becomes final. Tex. Civ. Prac. & Rem. Code §16.064(a). CPRC §16.064(a) tolls the statute of limitations for the period between the date the plaintiff filed the suit in the first court and the date the plaintiff refiles the suit in the correct court. Tex. Civ. Prac. & Rem. Code §16.064(a)(2); *see also* **Nathan v. Whittington**, 408 S.W.3d 870, 875 (Tex.2013) (CPRC §16.064 tolls statute of limitations, not statute of repose). To defeat the plaintiff's use of CPRC §16.064(a), a defendant must show that either (1) the first suit was not dismissed for lack of jurisdiction or (2) the causes of action are not the same for purposes of the tolling provision. **Turner v. Texas Dept. of MHMR**, 920 S.W.2d 415, 418 (Tex.App.—Austin 1996, writ denied); *see, e.g.,* **Malmgren v. Inverness Forest Residents Civic Club, Inc.**, 981 S.W.2d 875, 879–80 (Tex.App.—Houston [1st Dist.] 1998, no pet.) (because P voluntarily dismissed suit, CPRC §16.064(a) did not apply).

2. No tolling—intentional disregard. If the plaintiff filed the suit in the first court with intentional disregard for proper jurisdiction, CPRC §16.064(a) does not toll limitations. Tex. Civ. Prac. & Rem. Code §16.064(b); *e.g.,* **In re United Servs. Auto. Ass'n**, 307 S.W.3d 299, 312–13 (Tex.2010) (even though P anticipated verdict within jurisdictional limits, he strategically decided to seek damages outside the county court at law's jurisdiction; limitations not tolled). The intent standard under §16.064(b) is similar to the **Craddock** requirement for setting aside a default judgment; a mistake of law may be a sufficient excuse. **In re United Servs. Auto.**, 307 S.W.3d at 313. See "Not intentional but accidental," ch. 10-B, §9.1.3(1). Once the defendant moves for relief under §16.064(b), the plaintiff has the burden of showing she did not intentionally disregard proper jurisdiction when filing the case. **In re United Servs. Auto.**, 307 S.W.3d at 312.

§6.3 Findings. Findings of fact are not necessary when the trial court rules on a motion to dismiss based on the face of the pleadings. *See* **Awde v. Dabeit**, 938 S.W.2d 31, 33 (Tex.1997). But findings of fact are helpful on appeal when the trial court considers evidence (e.g., in a plea based on fabricated jurisdiction). See "Jurisdictional challenge," ch. 10-E, §2.2.2(2).

§7. Review

§7.1 Record. A reporter's record is not necessary to appeal the trial court's ruling on subject-matter jurisdiction unless the court held an evidentiary hearing. *See* **Vernco Constr., Inc. v. Nelson**, 460 S.W.3d 145, 150–51 & n.4 (Tex.2015).

§7.2 Standard of review. Whether a court can exercise subject-matter jurisdiction over a claim is a question of law that is reviewed de novo. **EBS Solutions, Inc. v. Hegar**, 601 S.W.3d 744, 749 (Tex.2020); **Harris Cty. v. Annab**, 547 S.W.3d 609, 612 (Tex.2018); **City of Ingleside v. City of Corpus Christi**, 469 S.W.3d 589, 590 (Tex.2015).

Note

If the appellate court determines that the trial court lacked subject-matter jurisdiction, any orders or judgments rendered by the trial court are void, not just voidable. ***In re United Servs. Auto. Ass'n,*** *307 S.W.3d 299, 309 (Tex.2010);* ***Mapco, Inc. v. Forrest,*** *795 S.W.2d 700, 703 (Tex.1990).*

1. Challenge to pleadings. In the appeal of a case involving a jurisdictional challenge to the pleadings, the appellate court must accept as true all the factual allegations in the plaintiff's petition. *See* **Axtell v. University of Tex.**, 69 S.W.3d 261, 264 (Tex.App.—Austin 2002, no pet.); **Jansen v. Fitzpatrick**, 14 S.W.3d 426, 431 (Tex.App.—Houston [14th Dist.] 2000, no pet.). The court examines the pleader's intent and construes the pleadings in the plaintiff's favor. **Houston Belt & Terminal Ry. v. City of Houston**, 487 S.W.3d 154, 160 (Tex.2016); **Texas Dept. of Parks & Wildlife v. Miranda**, 133 S.W.3d 217, 226 (Tex.2004); **County of Cameron v. Brown**, 80 S.W.3d 549, 555 (Tex.2002). The court must determine if the pleader alleged facts that affirmatively demonstrate subject-matter jurisdiction. **Miranda**, 133 S.W.3d at 226. See "Not necessary," ch. 3-F, §2.2.1.

2. Challenge to existence of jurisdictional facts. In the appeal of a case involving a challenge to the existence of jurisdictional facts, the appellate court must consider relevant evidence submitted by the parties when necessary to

resolve the jurisdictional issues raised. *See* **Miranda**, 133 S.W.3d at 227; **Bland ISD v. Blue**, 34 S.W.3d 547, 554–55 (Tex.2000). See "Necessary," ch. 3-F, §2.2.2. The court applies a similar standard of review as it would to an appeal of a summary judgment—it takes as true all evidence favorable to the nonmovant, indulges every reasonable inference in favor of the nonmovant, and resolves any doubts in favor of the nonmovant. **Miranda**, 133 S.W.3d at 228.

§7.3 Interlocutory appeal.

1. Appeal.

(1) Plea to the jurisdiction—governmental unit. A party may appeal an interlocutory order granting or denying a plea to the jurisdiction filed by a governmental unit. Tex. Civ. Prac. & Rem. Code §51.014(a)(8); **Hughes v. Tom Green Cty.**, 573 S.W.3d 212, 216 (Tex.2019); **City of Houston v. Estate of Jones**, 388 S.W.3d 663, 666 (Tex.2012); *see* **University of the Incarnate Word v. Redus**, 602 S.W.3d 398, 402 (Tex.2020); **Harris Cty. v. Annab**, 547 S.W.3d 609, 612 (Tex.2018). See "Government's plea to the jurisdiction," **O'Connor's Texas Civil Appeals**, ch. 1-B, §2.4.1(7) (2020 ed.).

(2) Plea to the jurisdiction—all other parties.

(a) Generally prohibited. Generally, an order on a plea to the jurisdiction filed by a party other than a governmental unit cannot be appealed before final judgment. *See* Tex. Civ. Prac. & Rem. Code §51.014(a)(8).

(b) Exception. A trial court, on its own initiative or on a party's motion, can allow an interlocutory appeal from an order that is not otherwise appealable if the following conditions are met: (1) the order to be appealed involves a controlling question of law about which there is a substantial ground for difference of opinion and (2) an immediate appeal from the order may materially advance the ultimate termination of the litigation. Tex. Civ. Prac. & Rem. Code §51.014(d); Tex. R. Civ. P. 168. Permission must be stated in the order being appealed rather than in a separate order. Tex. R. Civ. P. 168 & cmt. Although the trial court can grant permission to appeal, the court of appeals has discretion to accept or refuse to hear the appeal. *See* Tex. Civ. Prac. & Rem. Code §51.014(f). See "Interlocutory appeal by permission," **O'Connor's Texas Civil Appeals**, ch. 3-P, §2.1 (2020 ed.).

2. Stay of trial & other proceedings.

(1) For governmental unit. The interlocutory appeal of an order granting a plea to the jurisdiction by a governmental unit automatically stays the commencement of trial during the appeal. *See* Tex. Civ. Prac. & Rem. Code §51.014(b). An interlocutory appeal under CPRC §51.014(a)(8) also stays all other proceedings in the trial court pending resolution of the appeal. Tex. Civ. Prac. & Rem. Code §51.014(b). The interlocutory appeal of an order denying a plea to the jurisdiction by a governmental unit does not automatically stay the commencement of trial during the appeal. Tex. Civ. Prac. & Rem. Code §51.014(c). For a discussion of when the defendant may be entitled to a stay after the denial of a motion, see "Orders resulting in automatic stay after motion denied & deadlines met," **O'Connor's Texas Civil Appeals**, ch. 3-P, §3.1.2 (2020 ed.).

(2) Under CPRC §51.014(d). The interlocutory appeal of an order under CPRC §51.014(d) stays proceedings in the trial court if (1) the parties agree to a stay or (2) the trial or appellate court orders a stay pending the appeal. Tex. Civ. Prac. & Rem. Code §51.014(e). See "Interlocutory appeal by permission," **O'Connor's Texas Civil Appeals**, ch. 3-P, §2.1 (2020 ed.).

§7.4 Mandamus.

1. Mandamus not available. In most cases, a party cannot challenge the trial court's lack of subject-matter jurisdiction by mandamus. **In re Bay Area Citizens Against Lawsuit Abuse**, 982 S.W.2d 371, 375 (Tex.1998); **Canadian Helicopters Ltd. v. Wittig**, 876 S.W.2d 304, 306 (Tex.1994); **Bell Helicopter Textron, Inc. v. Walker**, 787 S.W.2d 954, 955 (Tex.1990). Typically, remedy by appeal is adequate.

2. Mandamus available.

(1) Child custody. A party can challenge the trial court's ruling on a plea to the jurisdiction by mandamus when two trial courts issue conflicting child-custody orders. **Geary v. Peavy**, 878 S.W.2d 602, 603 (Tex.1994).

(2) Constitutional challenges to suit. If a constitutional issue is not resolved by the trial court, mandamus may be available to resolve the issue before a trial on the merits. *See, e.g.*, **Tilton v. Marshall**, 925 S.W.2d 672, 676 & n.4 (Tex.1996) (D challenged trial court's refusal to dismiss and refusal to bar discovery on grounds of free exercise of religion).

(3) Agency has exclusive jurisdiction. A party can challenge the trial court's denial of a plea to the jurisdiction by mandamus if an agency has exclusive jurisdiction over the suit. *See* **In re Crawford & Co.**, 458 S.W.3d 920, 928–29 (Tex.2015); **In re Southwestern Bell Tel. Co.**, 235 S.W.3d 619, 623–24 (Tex.2007); **In re Entergy Corp.**, 142 S.W.3d 316, 321 (Tex.2004).

(4) Failure to exhaust administrative remedies. A party can challenge the trial court's denial of a plea to the jurisdiction by mandamus if the opposing party has not exhausted its administrative remedies. *See* **In re Liberty Mut. Fire Ins.**, 295 S.W.3d 327, 328 (Tex.2009).

(5) Plea ruled on as matter of law. If the trial court erroneously concludes, solely as a matter of law, that it has subject-matter jurisdiction, its order is void and the party may be able to challenge the order by mandamus. **Qwest Microwave, Inc. v. Bedard**, 756 S.W.2d 426, 434 (Tex.App.—Dallas 1988, orig. proceeding); *see* **Miller v. Woods**, 872 S.W.2d 343, 346 (Tex.App.—Beaumont 1994, orig. proceeding). *But see* **Brown v. Herman**, 852 S.W.2d 91, 93 (Tex.App.—Austin 1993, orig. proceeding) (declining to follow **Qwest Microwave**). Mandamus is not available when jurisdiction is based on questions of fact or mixed questions of law and fact. **Qwest Microwave**, 756 S.W.2d at 433; **In re Kamstra**, No. 12-09-00017-CV, 2010 WL 708857 (Tex.App.—Tyler 2010, orig. proceeding) (memo op.; 3-2-10).

G. Special Exceptions—Challenging the Pleadings

§1. General

§1.1 Rules. Tex R Civ. P. 90, 91.

§1.2 Purpose. The purpose of special exceptions is to inform the opposing party of defects in its pleadings so it can cure them, if possible, by amendment. **Horizon/CMS Healthcare Corp. v. Auld**, 34 S.W.3d 887, 897 (Tex.2000). By filing special exceptions, the opposing party identifies defects that should be remedied before a substantive response is required. **O'Neal v. Sherck Equip. Co.**, 751 S.W.2d 559, 562 (Tex.App.—Texarkana 1988, no writ). Unless a party challenges curable pleading defects by special exceptions, the defects are waived. **Crosstex Energy Servs. v. Pro Plus, Inc.**, 430 S.W.3d 384, 395 (Tex.2014). See "Waiver," ch. 3-G, §6.

Note

Special exceptions may be filed by either party. See "Grounds," ch. 3-G, §5; ***O'Connor's Texas Civil Forms****, FORM 3G:1 (2020 ed.). Because most special exceptions are filed by the defendant, this subchapter uses "defendant" as the objecting party and "plaintiff" as the party with the challenged pleading.*

§1.3 Timetable & forms. Appendix IV, Timetable 8, Pretrial motions; **O'Connor's Texas Civil Forms**, FORMS 3G:1 et seq. (2020 ed.).

§1.4 Other references. **O'Connor's Texas Causes of Action** (2021 ed.).

§2. Types of pleading defects to challenge by special exceptions

There are two types of pleading defects that a defendant must object to before trial: defects in form and defects in substance. **Aquila Sw. Pipeline, Inc. v. Harmony Expl., Inc.**, 48 S.W.3d 225, 233 (Tex.App.—San Antonio 2001, pet. denied). Because special exceptions can be determined by reference to the pleadings only, any challenge to a pleading that requires reference to extrinsic facts should not be brought as a special exception. See "Limited to pleadings," ch. 3-G, §3.3.

Note

Special exceptions are not the correct procedure for addressing a misnomer (i.e., when the plaintiff misnames itself or another party but the correct parties are involved). In that case, the defendant should plead misnomer and seek an abatement. See "Misnomer," ch. 2-B, §4.3.1(2)(a).

§2.1 Defects in form.

1. Lack of verification. If the plaintiff does not verify its petition when necessary, the defendant may file special exceptions to require the plaintiff to correct the defect. *See* **Huddleston v. Western Nat'l Bank**, 577 S.W.2d 778, 781 (Tex.App.—Amarillo 1979, writ ref'd n.r.e.).

2. Failure to plead discovery level. If the plaintiff does not plead the discovery level in its original petition as required by TRCP 190.1, the defendant may file special exceptions to require the plaintiff to do so. *See* Tex. R. Civ. P. 190 cmt. 1 (1999).

3. Improper incorporation by reference. If the plaintiff files an amended petition that incorporates by reference exhibits to an earlier, superseded petition, the defendant may file special exceptions to require the plaintiff to attach the documents as exhibits to the amended petition. *See, e.g.,* **Fawcett v. Grosu**, 498 S.W.3d 650, 659 (Tex.App.—Houston [14th Dist.] 2016, pet. denied) (exhibits to superseded pleading that were improperly incorporated by reference into amended pleading could be considered by court because D did not specially except to defect).

§2.2 Defects in substance.

1. General allegations. If the plaintiff pleads a cause of action in general terms, the defendant may file special exceptions to require the plaintiff to plead specifically. **Subia v. Texas Dept. of Human Servs.**, 750 S.W.2d 827, 829

(Tex.App.—El Paso 1988, no writ). Texas follows the "fair notice" standard for pleading, which looks at whether the opposing party can ascertain from the pleading the nature and basic issues of the controversy and what testimony will be relevant. **Horizon/CMS Healthcare Corp. v. Auld**, 34 S.W.3d 887, 896 (Tex.2000); *see also* Tex. R. Civ. P. 45(b) (action must be stated in plain and concise language), Tex. R. Civ. P. 47(a) (action must be sufficient to give fair notice of claim). TRCP 45 does not require the plaintiff to describe the evidence in detail in its petition. **Paramount Pipe & Sup. Co. v. Muhr**, 749 S.W.2d 491, 494–95 (Tex.1988). If the plaintiff's petition does not give fair notice of the facts, the trial court can either require the plaintiff to amend its petition or require the defendant to obtain additional facts through discovery.

2. Inadequate allegations. If the plaintiff does not plead all the elements of its cause of action, the defendant may file special exceptions to require the plaintiff to plead specifically. *See* **Mowbray v. Avery**, 76 S.W.3d 663, 677 (Tex.App.—Corpus Christi 2002, pet. denied). The defendant must specifically identify the missing elements. *See* **Spencer v. City of Seagoville**, 700 S.W.2d 953, 957 (Tex.App.—Dallas 1985, no writ). The plaintiff's omission of an element of the cause of action does not deprive the court of jurisdiction; it is merely a defect in pleading subject to special exceptions and amendment. *E.g.*, **Peek v. Equipment Serv.**, 779 S.W.2d 802, 805 (Tex.1989) (P did not allege amount of damages). See "P pleads cause of action defectively—Special exceptions," ch. 3-G, §10.1.2. For the elements of various causes of action, see **O'Connor's Texas Causes of Action** (2021 ed.).

3. No viable cause of action. If the plaintiff's suit is not permitted by law, the defendant may file special exceptions and a motion to dismiss. **Wayne Duddlesten, Inc. v. Highland Ins.**, 110 S.W.3d 85, 96–97 (Tex.App.—Houston [1st Dist.] 2003, pet. denied); *see, e.g.*, **Trevino v. Ortega**, 969 S.W.2d 950, 951 (Tex.1998) (no cause of action for spoliation of evidence); **Friesenhahn v. Ryan**, 960 S.W.2d 656, 658 & n.1 (Tex.1998) (no cause of action for social-host liability); **Krishnan v. Sepulveda**, 916 S.W.2d 478, 479 (Tex.1995) (no cause of action for negligence to fetus, but mother may have had action for mental anguish). Another option is to file special exceptions and a motion for summary judgment. See "P has no viable cause of action—Dismissal or SJ," ch. 3-G, §10.1.1.

4. Curable defects in jurisdiction. If the plaintiff's pleadings do not affirmatively establish subject-matter jurisdiction or if they contain some other curable jurisdictional defect, the defendant should challenge the pleadings by special exceptions, not by a plea to the jurisdiction or a motion for summary judgment. *See* **Texas Dept. of Corr. v. Herring**, 513 S.W.2d 6, 9–10 (Tex.1974); **Texas DOT v. Beckner**, 74 S.W.3d 98, 104 (Tex.App.—Waco 2002, no pet.), *overruled on other grounds*, **Texas Mut. Ins. v. Chicas**, 593 S.W.3d 284 (Tex.2019); **Washington v. Fort Bend ISD**, 892 S.W.2d 156, 159 (Tex.App.—Houston [14th Dist.] 1994, writ denied). *But see* **Riner v. City of Hunters Creek**, 403 S.W.3d 919, 921–22 (Tex.App.—Houston [14th Dist.] 2013, no pet.) (typical procedural vehicle used to challenge sufficiency of jurisdictional allegations is plea to the jurisdiction; although D specially excepted to Ps' pleadings, court disregarded "misnomer" and treated D's special exceptions as plea to the jurisdiction). See "P pleads cause of action defectively—Special exceptions," ch. 3-G, §10.1.2. But if the pleadings demonstrate that the court lacks subject-matter jurisdiction or if the jurisdictional defect is otherwise not curable by amendment, the defendant can file a plea to the jurisdiction or a motion to dismiss the claim without first filing special exceptions. *See, e.g.*, **Crosstex Energy Servs. v. Pro Plus, Inc.**, 430 S.W.3d 384, 395 (Tex.2014) (failure to file certificate of merit with original petition under CPRC §150.002 was incurable defect; D could file motion to dismiss without first filing special exceptions); **Texas Dept. of Parks & Wildlife v. Miranda**, 133 S.W.3d 217, 225–26 (Tex.2004) (sovereign immunity was properly asserted in plea to the jurisdiction).

Note

A nonresident defendant who wants to challenge allegations of personal jurisdiction should not use special exceptions. Instead, the nonresident defendant should file a special appearance. See "Special Appearance—Challenging Personal Jurisdiction," ch. 3-B, §1 et seq.

5. Claims for relief. If the plaintiff seeks relief without specifying the maximum amount claimed, the defendant can file special exceptions. Tex. R. Civ. P. 47. TRCP 47 requires that the plaintiff's pleading contain a specific statement of relief sought; that is, the plaintiff must plead into or out of the expedited-actions process under TRCP 169. *See* Tex. R. Civ. P.

47(c) & cmt. (2013). See "Specific statement of relief," ch. 1-B, §3.2.8(2); "Expedited Actions," ch. 2-C, §1 et seq. Thus, if the plaintiff does not specify the maximum amount claimed, the defendant can specially except to require the plaintiff to specify the maximum amount. Tex. R. Civ. P. 47.

§3. Form

§3.1 Written. Special exceptions must be in writing. Tex. R. Civ. P. 90. An oral objection to pleadings does not comply with the TRCPs. **Nassar v. Hughes**, 882 S.W.2d 36, 38 (Tex.App.—Houston [1st Dist.] 1994, writ denied); **Hawkins v. Anderson**, 672 S.W.2d 293, 295 (Tex.App.—Dallas 1984, no writ).

§3.2 Specific. When drafting special exceptions, the defendant must identify the particular part of the plaintiff's pleading it challenges and point out the particular defect, omission, obscurity, duplicity, generality, or other insufficiency. Tex. R. Civ. P. 91; **Muecke v. Hallstead**, 25 S.W.3d 221, 224 (Tex.App.—San Antonio 2000, no pet.); **Gutierrez v. Karl Perry Enters.**, 874 S.W.2d 103, 105 (Tex.App.—El Paso 1994, no writ). The defendant should identify the defective paragraph by number, state why it is defective, and explain how it can be corrected. General allegations that the petition is vague, is indefinite, or does not state a cause of action are not sufficient to identify the defect. **Spillman v. Simkins**, 757 S.W.2d 166, 168 (Tex.App.—San Antonio 1988, writ dism'd); **Farrar v. Farrar**, 620 S.W.2d 801, 802 (Tex.App.—Houston [14th Dist.] 1981, no writ). If the special exception is not specific, it is a prohibited general demurrer and should be overruled. *See* Tex. R. Civ. P. 90; **Fuentes v. McFadden**, 825 S.W.2d 772, 778 (Tex.App.—El Paso 1992, no writ); **Spillman**, 757 S.W.2d at 168.

§3.3 Limited to pleadings. When drafting special exceptions, the defendant cannot challenge pleading defects by relying on facts outside the plaintiff's petition. **O'Neal v. Sherck Equip. Co.**, 751 S.W.2d 559, 562 (Tex.App.—Texarkana 1988, no writ) (referred to as a "speaking demurrer"); **Augustine v. Nusom**, 671 S.W.2d 112, 114 (Tex.App.—Houston [14th Dist.] 1984, writ ref'd n.r.e.) (same). If a defendant must rely on facts that are not in the petition to demonstrate the defect, the defendant should file some other type of pleading (e.g., a motion to abate or a motion for summary judgment). **Bader v. Cox**, 701 S.W.2d 677, 686–87 (Tex.App.—Dallas 1985, writ ref'd n.r.e.); **Augustine**, 671 S.W.2d at 114.

§3.4 Not verified. Special exceptions should not be verified. *See* Tex. R. Civ. P. 90, 91.

§3.5 Request hearing. The party challenging the pleadings must secure a hearing (either oral or by written submission) and a ruling on the special exceptions, or else they are waived. *See* **Shelton v. Kalbow**, 489 S.W.3d 32, 54 n.28 (Tex.App.—Houston [14th Dist.] 2016, pet. denied); **Brooks v. Housing Auth.**, 926 S.W.2d 316, 322 (Tex.App.—El Paso 1996, no writ). See "Hearing," ch. 3-G, §8; "Written order," ch. 3-G, §9.1.

§4. Deadline

As a general rule, special exceptions should be filed by the defendant either with its answer or shortly thereafter, and by the plaintiff shortly after the defendant files its answer. Special exceptions may also be raised during trial. In a jury trial, a party urging special exceptions must bring them to the trial court's attention before the charge is read to the jury; in a nonjury trial, they must be brought before the judgment is signed. Tex. R. Civ. P. 90. If special exceptions are not timely raised, the defect is waived (except in default-judgment cases). *Id.*; *see, e.g.*, **Hudspeth v. Hudspeth**, 756 S.W.2d 29, 34 (Tex.App.—San Antonio 1988, writ denied) (party waived error in pleadings by objecting only after trial court signed judgment).

§5. Grounds

§5.1 Proper objections to pleadings. For examples of special exceptions that are valid objections to the pleadings, see "Types of pleading defects to challenge by special exceptions," ch. 3-G, §2, and **O'Connor's Texas Civil Forms**, FORM 3G:1 (2020 ed.).

§5.2 Improper objections to pleadings. The following are examples of special exceptions that are not valid objections to the pleadings:

1. The pleadings, as a matter of law, do not state a cause of action. *See* **Spillman v. Simkins**, 757 S.W.2d 166, 168 (Tex.App.—San Antonio 1988, writ dism'd). General allegations that the pleadings do not state a cause of action are a general demurrer, which is prohibited by TRCP 90. *See* **Texas Dept. of Corr. v. Herring**, 513 S.W.2d 6, 10 (Tex.1974); **Spill-**

man, 757 S.W.2d at 168. See "Specific," ch. 3-G, §3.2.

Note

To challenge a cause of action that has no basis in law or fact, a defendant should timely file a motion to dismiss under TRCP 91a. See "Motion to Dismiss—Baseless Cause of Action," ch. 3-H, §1 et seq.

2. The pleadings do not allege all the elements necessary to support a cause of action. *See* **Spencer v. City of Seagoville**, 700 S.W.2d 953, 957 (Tex.App.—Dallas 1985, no writ). When a defendant objects that the plaintiff did not plead a complete cause of action, the defendant must list the specific elements the plaintiff omitted. *Id.*; *see* Tex. R. Civ. P. 91. See "Inadequate allegations," ch. 3-G, §2.2.2; "Specific," ch. 3-G, §3.2.

3. The plaintiff's pleadings allege matters that are immaterial, prejudicial, and inflammatory. **Pargas of Canton, Inc. v. Clower**, 434 S.W.2d 192, 196 (Tex.App.—Tyler 1968, no writ). These objections are too general. *See* Tex. R. Civ. P. 91 (special exceptions must point out insufficiencies with particularity).

4. The plaintiff did not attach a copy of the relevant contract to its pleadings. **Randolph Junior Coll. v. Isaacks**, 113 S.W.2d 628, 629 (Tex.App.—Eastland 1938, no writ).

5. The damages allegations do not specify the dollar value for each element of special damages. *See* **Phillips v. Vinson Sup.**, 581 S.W.2d 789, 791 (Tex.App.—Houston [14th Dist.] 1979, no writ) (TRCP 47 requires P to designate only the maximum amount claimed, not how much money is attributable to each element of damages).

§6. Waiver

§6.1 Unchallenged pleadings. When pleadings are not challenged by special exceptions, the court will construe them liberally in favor of the pleader. **Horizon/CMS Healthcare Corp. v. Auld**, 34 S.W.3d 887, 897 (Tex.2000); **Boyles v. Kerr**, 855 S.W.2d 593, 601 (Tex.1993). The court will look to the pleader's intent and will supply every fact "that can reasonably be inferred from what is specifically stated." *E.g.*, **Roark v. Allen**, 633 S.W.2d 804, 809 (Tex.1982) (when D did not specially except, P was not required to plead exactly how doctor used forceps; general allegation of negligent delivery was sufficient). Without special exceptions, the court will uphold the pleading even if an element of a cause of action is omitted. *Id.*

§6.2 Waiver on appeal. Every defect not specifically pointed out by special exception before the jury is charged (or in a nonjury case, before the judgment is signed) is waived by the party seeking reversal. Tex. R. Civ. P. 90. This rule does not apply, however, to default judgments. *Id.* See "Special exceptions & default judgments," ch. 3-G, §11.

1. Appellant. The party seeking reversal (the appellant) cannot urge any defects in the appellee's pleadings as a ground for reversal unless the appellant specially excepted to that defect. For example, if the plaintiff did not object to defects in the defendant's pleading of exclusions in an insurance policy, the plaintiff-appellant cannot complain about them for the first time on appeal. **Sherman v. Provident Am. Ins.**, 421 S.W.2d 652, 654 (Tex.1967); *see also* **Sixth RMA Partners v. Sibley**, 111 S.W.3d 46, 54–55 (Tex.2003) (P-appellant waived error by not objecting when D-appellee filed amended answer instead of supplemental answer); **Troutman v. Traeco Bldg. Sys.**, 724 S.W.2d 385, 387 (Tex.1987) (D-appellant waived error by not objecting when P-appellee did not properly plead DTPA violation); **Tullis v. Georgia-Pac. Corp.**, 45 S.W.3d 118, 124 (Tex.App.—Fort Worth 2000, no pet.) (P-appellant waived error by not objecting when D-appellee did not allege that P was nonresident in forum non conveniens motion).

2. Appellee. The party seeking affirmance (the appellee) can argue on appeal that defects in the appellant's pleadings are reasons to affirm, even if it did not specially except to them. TRCP 90 does not require the party seeking affirmance to have objected to a defect that is a basis for its argument on appeal. *See* **Ward v. Clark**, 435 S.W.2d 621, 624 (Tex.App.—Tyler 1968, no writ). For example, if the plaintiff pleads "all conditions precedent have occurred" under TRCP 54, and the defendant responds with a general (instead of specific) statement that the plaintiff did not meet all conditions precedent, the plaintiff-appellee can argue on appeal that the defendant's failure to make a specific denial is grounds for affirmance. *See, e.g.*, **Dairyland Cty. Mut. Ins. v. Roman**, 498 S.W.2d 154, 158–59 (Tex.1973) (P did not waive defects in D's general response to TRCP 54 allegation because P was urging affirmance).

§7. Response

If the plaintiff agrees the exceptions are valid, it should amend its pleadings without contesting the exceptions. If the plaintiff does not agree the exceptions are valid, it should file a response stating why the exceptions should be denied.

§8. Hearing

§8.1 Argument only. The hearing on special exceptions is for argument only. No evidence may be presented. See "Limited to pleadings," ch. 3-G, §3.3.

§8.2 Standard. When ruling on special exceptions, the court must accept as true all material factual allegations and all factual statements reasonably inferred from the allegations in the challenged pleadings. **Sorokolit v. Rhodes**, 889 S.W.2d 239, 240 (Tex.1994) (appellate court); **City of Austin v. Houston Lighting & Power Co.**, 844 S.W.2d 773, 783 (Tex.App.—Dallas 1992, writ denied) (trial court). The trial court has wide discretion in ruling on special exceptions. **LaRue v. GeneScreen, Inc.**, 957 S.W.2d 958, 961 (Tex.App.—Beaumont 1997, pet. denied); **City of Austin**, 844 S.W.2d at 783.

§9. Ruling

§9.1 Written order. The defendant must obtain a written ruling on its special exceptions, or else they are waived. *See* Tex. R. Civ. P. 90; **Shelton v. Kalbow**, 489 S.W.3d 32, 54 n.28 (Tex.App.—Houston [14th Dist.] 2016, pet. denied); **Smith v. Grace**, 919 S.W.2d 673, 678 (Tex.App.—Dallas 1996, writ denied); **In re Marriage of Moore**, 890 S.W.2d 821, 826–27 (Tex.App.—Amarillo 1994, no writ). When making its ruling, the court should not merely make margin notations on the special exceptions. *E.g.*, **McAdams v. Capitol Prods.**, 810 S,W.2d 290, 292 (Tex.App.—Fort Worth 1991, writ denied) (unclear whether notations "OR," "Sus.," or "withdrawn" constituted court's ruling on special exceptions). The defendant should insist that the judge sign a written order. *See id.* See **O'Connor's Texas Civil Forms**, FORM 3G:2 (2020 ed.).

§9.2 Options for court.

1. Court overrules special exceptions. When the court overrules the special exceptions, it will proceed with other matters. When exceptions are overruled, error regarding the defective pleadings is preserved. *See, e.g.*, **Johnson v. Willis**, 596 S.W.2d 256, 260 (Tex.App.—Waco 1980) (court held special exceptions were improperly overruled because pleading did not provide proper notice under DTPA), *writ ref'd n.r.e.*, 603 S.W.2d 828 (Tex.1980).

2. Court sustains special exceptions.

(1) Curable defect. Generally, when the court sustains the special exceptions, it must give the plaintiff a chance to amend its pleadings by ordering it to replead. *See* **Baylor Univ. v. Sonnichsen**, 221 S.W.3d 632, 635 (Tex.2007); **Parker v. Barefield**, 206 S.W.3d 119, 120 (Tex.2006); **Friesenhahn v. Ryan**, 960 S.W.2d 656, 658 (Tex.1998); **Texas Dept. of Corr. v. Herring**, 513 S.W.2d 6, 10 (Tex.1974). The court cannot dismiss the case at the same time it sustains the special exceptions. *See* **Texas Dept. of Corr.**, 513 S.W.2d at 10; **Mowbray v. Avery**, 76 S.W.3d 663, 678 (Tex.App.—Corpus Christi 2002, pet. denied). To dismiss without giving the plaintiff the opportunity to amend is the functional equivalent of a general demurrer, which is prohibited by TRCP 90. *See* **Texas Dept. of Corr.**, 513 S.W.2d at 10; **Hunter v. Johnson**, 25 S.W.3d 247, 249 (Tex.App.—El Paso 2000, no pet.).

(2) Incurable defect. The court is not required to give the plaintiff an opportunity to amend if the pleading defect is one that cannot be cured by amendment. *E.g.*, **Baylor Univ.**, 221 S.W.3d at 635 (petition alleging breach of contract could not be cured by amendment because P's allegations established there was no mutual assent and thus no binding written contract).

§9.3 Options for plaintiff. When special exceptions are sustained, the plaintiff may do any of the following:

1. Amend. The plaintiff may amend its pleadings to correct the defect. **Mowbray v. Avery**, 76 S.W.3d 663, 677 (Tex.App.—Corpus Christi 2002, pet. denied); **Butler Weldments Corp. v. Liberty Mut. Ins.**, 3 S.W.3d 654, 658 (Tex.App.—Austin 1999, no pet.); **Cameron v. University of Houston**, 598 S.W.2d 344, 345 (Tex.App.—Houston [14th Dist.] 1980, writ ref'd n.r.e.). In the amended pleading, the plaintiff may include new allegations.

2. Refuse to amend. The plaintiff may challenge the trial court's ruling by standing on the pleadings and refusing to amend. **Mowbray**, 76 S.W.3d at 677; **Muecke v. Hallstead**, 25 S.W.3d 221, 223–24 (Tex.App.—San Antonio 2000, no

pet.); **Butler Weldments**, 3 S.W.3d at 658.

Practice Tip

When the plaintiff believes it is entitled to the claim, the plaintiff should ask the court to sign an order striking the defective paragraphs; the plaintiff should not voluntarily amend its pleadings to delete the allegations. By refusing to amend, the plaintiff can test the validity of the court's ruling on appeal. ***Mowbray****, 76 S.W.3d at 677;* ***Muecke****, 25 S.W.3d at 223–24;* ***Butler Weldments****, 3 S.W.3d at 658. If the plaintiff amends its pleadings to delete the allegations, it waives the issue on appeal.* ***Long v. Tascosa Nat'l Bank****, 678 S.W.2d 699, 703 (Tex.App.—Amarillo 1984, no writ).*

3. Partially comply. If the trial court sustains a number of special exceptions, the plaintiff may agree to make some changes but refuse to make others. For example, assume that the court sustains two special exceptions: one to a bad-faith claim, and one that the plaintiff did not plead all the elements of fraud. If the plaintiff believes it has a cause of action for bad faith, it should amend the defective allegations of fraud but refuse to delete the bad-faith allegation. By reasserting the bad-faith allegation in the amended petition and having the court strike that part of the petition, the plaintiff preserves for appeal the issue of whether it has such a cause of action. *See* **Fuentes v. Texas Empls. Ins.**, 757 S.W.2d 31, 32–33 (Tex.App.—San Antonio 1988, no writ).

4. Request time to amend & obtain ruling. If the trial court sustains the special exceptions but does not give the plaintiff an opportunity to replead, the plaintiff must ask the court for time to amend and obtain a ruling on the record denying the requested opportunity to amend, or else the error is waived. *E.g.*, **Parker v. Barefield**, 206 S.W.3d 119, 120–21 (Tex.2006) (error preserved because record showed that Ps requested leave to amend and filed amended pleadings; court effectively denied request when it sustained special exceptions); **Inglish v. Prudential Ins.**, 928 S.W.2d 702, 705 (Tex.App.—Houston [1st Dist.] 1996, writ denied) (error waived because record did not reflect that Ps ever sought to amend their pleadings); *see* Tex. R. App. P. 33.1(a). If the court's ruling denying the plaintiff the opportunity to amend is not reflected in the record, the plaintiff should file a motion for new trial to preserve the error for appeal. **Inglish**, 928 S.W.2d at 705.

§9.4 Options for defendant.

1. If defect not cured. When special exceptions are sustained and the plaintiff is given an opportunity to amend but does not, or the plaintiff amends but does not cure the defect, the defendant may do any of the following:

(1) Move to dismiss. If the entire pleading is subject to a special exception, the defendant may file a motion to dismiss based on the plaintiff's failure to cure the defect. *See* **Baca v. Sanchez**, 172 S.W.3d 93, 96 (Tex.App.—El Paso 2005, no pet.). If the request for a dismissal is included in the special exceptions, the defendant may need to set a hearing on only the request to dismiss.

(2) Move to strike. If only part of the pleading is subject to a special exception, the defendant may file a motion to strike that part of the petition, not a motion to dismiss the entire suit. *See* **Ross v. Goldstein**, 203 S.W.3d 508, 513–14 (Tex.App.—Houston [14th Dist.] 2006, no pet.).

(3) Move for summary judgment. The defendant may file a motion for a partial or full summary judgment. *See* **Friesenhahn v. Ryan**, 960 S.W.2d 656, 658 (Tex.1998). For the defendant, a summary judgment is preferable to a dismissal without prejudice because it is a resolution on the merits and invokes res judicata. See "Special exceptions & summary judgments," ch. 3-G, §10.

2. If original defect cured but others created. When the plaintiff files an amended petition in response to special exceptions, the defendant should review the new allegations to determine whether it should file additional special exceptions to the new allegations. *See* **Geochem Labs. v. Brown & Ruth Labs.**, 689 S.W.2d 288, 290 (Tex.App.—Houston [1st Dist.] 1985, writ ref'd n.r.e.).

§9.5 Options for court after plaintiff given opportunity to replead.

1. Plaintiff amended & cured defect. If the plaintiff amends the pleadings and cures the defect, the trial court should allow the suit to go forward. If the plaintiff adds other allegations that are objectionable, the defendant must file

special exceptions to the new allegations, and the court must again give the plaintiff the opportunity to amend. *See* **Geochem Labs. v. Brown & Ruth Labs.**, 689 S.W.2d 288, 290 (Tex.App.—Houston [1st Dist.] 1985, writ ref'd n.r.e.).

2. Plaintiff amended but did not cure defect.

(1) Good-faith attempt to cure. If the plaintiff makes a good-faith attempt to cure the defect in an amended petition, the court cannot strike the objectionable allegations. **Humphreys v. Meadows**, 938 S.W.2d 750, 753 (Tex.App.—Fort Worth 1996, writ denied). Instead, the defendant must file new special exceptions, the court must sustain them, and the plaintiff must be given another opportunity to amend before the court can dismiss. *Id.* If the plaintiff amends the pleadings but does not make a good-faith attempt to cure the objectionable allegations, the court can strike the objectionable allegations. *See* **Ahmed v. Mallory**, No. 03-10-00405-CV, 2011 WL 2993298 (Tex.App.—Austin 2011, no pet.) (memo op.; 7-21-11); *cf.* **Cruz v. Morris**, 877 S.W.2d 45, 47 (Tex.App.—Houston [14th Dist.] 1994, no writ) (if P refuses to amend, court can strike objectionable allegations).

(2) No unlimited right to amend. A plaintiff's right to amend is not unlimited. **Ford v. Performance Aircraft Servs.**, 178 S.W.3d 330, 336 (Tex.App.—Fort Worth 2005, pet. denied); **Mowbray v. Avery**, 76 S.W.3d 663, 678 (Tex.App.—Corpus Christi 2002, pet. denied). The court may deny leave to amend if there is no reasonable probability that further amendment would state facts legally sufficient to sustain the cause of action. **Mowbray**, 76 S.W.3d at 678.

(3) No cause of action remains. If no cause of action is stated in the remainder of the petition, the trial court will dismiss the suit. **Ford**, 178 S.W.3d at 336; **Mowbray**, 76 S.W.3d at 678. See "No cause of action remains," ch. 3-G, §9.5.3(2).

3. Plaintiff refused to amend. If the plaintiff refuses to amend, the trial court should strike the objectionable allegations. *E.g.*, **Cruz**, 877 S.W.2d at 47 (court struck damages allegations after P refused to replead).

(1) Proceed on remainder of petition. The plaintiff may proceed to trial based on the rest of its pleadings.

(2) No cause of action remains. If no cause of action is stated in the remainder of the petition, the trial court will dismiss the suit. **Ford**, 178 S.W.3d at 336; **Mowbray**, 76 S.W.3d at 678. The issue then is whether the court should dismiss with or without prejudice.

(a) Dismissal without prejudice. In most cases, the dismissal after a refusal to amend is without prejudice. **Kutch v. Del Mar Coll.**, 831 S.W.2d 506, 508 (Tex.App.—Corpus Christi 1992, no writ). If the defect can be cured by amendment, dismissal should be without prejudice. **Hajdik v. Wingate**, 753 S.W.2d 199, 202 (Tex.App.—Houston [1st Dist.] 1988), *aff'd*, 795 S.W.2d 717 (Tex.1990); **Atkinson v. Reid**, 625 S.W.2d 64, 66 (Tex.App.—San Antonio 1981, no writ).

(b) Dismissal with prejudice. If the defect cannot be cured by amendment, dismissal may be with prejudice. *See, e.g.*, **Joseph E. Seagram & Sons, Inc. v. McGuire**, 814 S.W.2d 385, 386 (Tex.1991) (with prejudice; no cause of action because no duty to warn of alcoholism); **Hickman v. Myers**, 632 S.W.2d 869, 869–70 (Tex.App.—Fort Worth 1982, writ ref'd n.r.e.) (with prejudice; no cause of action because no recovery for healthy but unplanned child).

§9.6 Amendments after pleadings struck. After the court strikes a claim or defense in the pleadings, if the plaintiff needs to amend its pleadings for some reason unrelated to the special exceptions, the plaintiff should not include the struck paragraphs in its amended pleadings. Once the court strikes allegations in the pleadings, a party is not required to violate the court's order and include them in its amended pleadings. **Melendez v. Exxon Corp.**, 998 S.W.2d 266, 272 & n.1 (Tex.App.—Houston [14th Dist.] 1999, no pet.). In fact, there is some risk in repleading struck allegations. In **Duncan v. Cessna Aircraft Co.**, 665 S.W.2d 414, 433 (Tex.1984), after the trial court struck allegations in the defendant's pleadings, the defendant repleaded them in an amended pleading. On appeal, the court said the defendant waived the issues because it had not introduced evidence to support them. **Duncan**, 665 S.W.2d at 433.

§10. Special exceptions & summary judgments

§10.1 Defendant's options.

1. P has no viable cause of action—Dismissal or SJ. If the plaintiff has no viable cause of action and refuses to amend after special exceptions are sustained, the defendant has two options. First, it may ask the court to dismiss the

case with prejudice. See "Dismissal with prejudice," ch. 3-G, §9.5.3(2)(b). Second, it may move for summary judgment on the pleadings. **Friesenhahn v. Ryan**, 960 S.W.2d 656, 658 (Tex.1998); **Massey v. Armco Steel Co.**, 652 S.W.2d 932, 934 (Tex.1983); *see* **Pietila v. Crites**, 851 S.W.2d 185, 186 & n.2 (Tex.1993); *see, e.g.*, **Castleberry v. Goolsby Bldg. Corp.**, 617 S.W.2d 665, 666 (Tex.1981) (affirmed summary judgment on pleadings when P's pleadings showed that suit was barred by statute). See "Special exceptions in summary-judgment procedure," ch. 7-B, §5. A motion for summary judgment is more favorable to the defendant because it is a ruling on the merits; a dismissal is not, unless it is with prejudice. For causes of action that can be challenged as not viable, see chart 35-2, under "Causes of Action Not Recognized in Texas," **O'Connor's Texas Causes of Action**, ch. 35-B, §1 et seq. (2021 ed.).

2. P pleads cause of action defectively—Special exceptions. When the plaintiff has a viable cause of action but pleaded it defectively, the defendant should file special exceptions, not a motion for summary judgment. **Friesenhahn v. Ryan**, 960 S.W.2d 656, 659 (Tex.1998); *see* **Natividad v. Alexsis, Inc.**, 875 S.W.2d 695, 699 (Tex.1994). Because the summary-judgment procedure does not provide an opportunity to replead, it cannot be used to terminate a suit based on pleading defects. **Sixth RMA Partners v. Sibley**, 111 S.W.3d 46, 54–55 (Tex.2003); **Saenz v. Southern Un. Gas Co.**, 916 S.W.2d 703, 705 (Tex.App.—El Paso 1996, writ denied); *see, e.g.*, **Friesenhahn**, 960 S.W.2d at 658–59 (summary judgment reversed when Ps were not given opportunity to amend their claims for wrongful death of minor); **Peek v. Equipment Serv.**, 779 S.W.2d 802, 804–05 (Tex.1989) (failure to plead for damages in the jurisdictional amount should have been challenged by special exception, not summary judgment); **Texas Dept. of Corr. v. Herring**, 513 S.W.2d 6, 9–10 (Tex.1974) (summary judgment reversed when P did not correctly plead TTCA requirements). Summary judgment based on a pleading defect is proper if a plaintiff had an opportunity to amend after a special exception and refused to do so. **Natividad**, 875 S.W.2d at 699; *see* **Friesenhahn**, 960 S.W.2d at 658; **Pietila v. Crites**, 851 S.W.2d 185, 186 & n.2 (Tex.1993).

Practice Tip

If the defendant is uncertain whether the plaintiff has a viable cause of action or merely pleaded a cause of action defectively, the defendant should first file special exceptions and then, if the plaintiff is not able to plead a viable cause of action, file a motion for summary judgment. See ***Friesenhahn****, 960 S.W.2d at 658;* ***Pietila****, 851 S.W.2d at 186 & n.2.*

§10.2 Plaintiff's objection. If the defendant files a motion for summary judgment when it should have first filed special exceptions, the plaintiff must object to the defendant's motion for summary judgment on the ground that it is an attempt to circumvent the special-exception practice. **Vawter v. Garvey**, 786 S.W.2d 263, 264 (Tex.1990); **San Jacinto River Auth. v. Duke**, 783 S.W.2d 209, 209 (Tex.1990); **Dickey v. Jansen**, 731 S.W.2d 581, 583 (Tex.App.—Houston [1st Dist.] 1987, writ ref'd n.r.e.). If the plaintiff does not object, the issue is waived. **Duke**, 783 S.W.2d at 209–10.

§11. Special exceptions & default judgments

Special exceptions are not required to preserve pleading errors in default-judgment cases. Tex. R. Civ. P. 90; **Stoner v. Thompson**, 578 S.W.2d 679, 684 (Tex.1979); **Rose v. Burton**, 614 S.W.2d 651, 652 (Tex.App.—Texarkana 1981, writ ref'd n.r.e.).

§12. Review

§12.1 Appeal. The trial court's ruling on special exceptions can be appealed. **Low v. King**, 867 S.W.2d 141, 142 (Tex.App.—Beaumont 1993, orig. proceeding); **Hill v. Lopez**, 858 S.W.2d 563, 565 (Tex.App.—Amarillo 1993, orig. proceeding).

1. Complaint on appeal. An appellant who complains of the dismissal of a cause of action following special exceptions must attack both the trial court's decision to sustain the special exceptions and the decision to dismiss the cause of action. **Perry v. Cohen**, 272 S.W.3d 585, 588 (Tex.2008); **Mowbray v. Avery**, 76 S.W.3d 663, 678 (Tex.App.—Corpus Christi 2002, pet. denied); **Cole v. Hall**, 864 S.W.2d 563, 566 (Tex.App.—Dallas 1993, writ dism'd). The appellant must challenge both rulings, or else it waives the unchallenged issue. **Mowbray**, 76 S.W.3d at 678.

2. Standard of review. The appellate court reviews the trial court's ruling on special exceptions for abuse of discretion. **Muecke v. Hallstead**, 25 S.W.3d 221, 224 (Tex.App.—San Antonio 2000, no pet.); **LaRue v. GeneScreen, Inc.**,

957 S.W.2d 958, 961 (Tex.App.—Beaumont 1997, pet. denied). But the appellate court reviews the trial court's legal conclusions (e.g., whether a cause of action is legally valid) de novo. **Gatten v. McCarley**, 391 S.W.3d 669, 673–74 (Tex.App.—Dallas 2013, no pet.). The appellate court must construe the pleadings liberally and accept as true all factual allegations in the pleadings. *See* **Sorokolit v. Rhodes**, 889 S.W.2d 239, 240 (Tex.1994). The appellate court must ignore any factual propositions outside the petition that tend to contradict the petition. **Hur v. City of Mesquite**, 893 S.W.2d 227, 233 (Tex.App.—Amarillo 1995, writ denied); *see* **O'Neal v. Sherck Equip. Co.**, 751 S.W.2d 559, 562 (Tex.App.—Texarkana 1988, no writ).

3. Record. To appeal a dismissal based on refusal to amend pleadings after special exceptions, the appellant must request the clerk's record and file it with the court of appeals. The reporter's record is not necessary because the dismissal will be judged on the pleadings, not on the evidence. *See* **Holt v. Reproductive Servs.**, 946 S.W.2d 602, 604 (Tex.App.—Corpus Christi 1997, writ denied); **Cole**, 864 S.W.2d at 566. See "Limited to pleadings," ch. 3-G, §3.3.

§12.2 No mandamus. The trial court's ruling on special exceptions cannot be reviewed by mandamus. **Hill v. Lopez**, 858 S.W.2d 563, 565 (Tex.App.—Amarillo 1993, orig. proceeding).

H. Motion to Dismiss—Baseless Cause of Action

§1. General

§1.1 Rule. Tex. R. Civ. P. 91a.

§1.2 Purpose. TRCP 91a, which is similar to FRCP 12(b)(6), provides for the dismissal of a cause of action that has no basis in law or fact. *See* Tex. R. Civ. P. 91a cmt.; *see also* **GoDaddy.com, LLC v. Toups**, 429 S.W.3d 752, 754 (Tex.App.—Beaumont 2014, pet. denied) (dismissal is appropriate under FRCP 12(b)(6) if complaint does not state a claim on which relief can be granted). See "Motion to Dismiss for Failure to State a Claim—FRCP 12(b)(6)," **O'Connor's Federal Rules * Civil Trials**, ch. 3-F, §1 et seq. (2021 ed.). TRCP 91a allows the court to quickly dispose of a baseless cause of action as a matter of law without considering any evidence. *See* Tex. R. Civ. P. 91a cmt. TRCP 91a does not supersede or affect any other procedures authorizing dismissal. Tex. R. Civ. P. 91a.9; *see* **HMT Tank Serv. v. American Tank & Vessel, Inc.**, 565 S.W.3d 799, 805–06 & n.2 (Tex.App.—Houston [14th Dist.] 2018, no pet.) (general motion to dismiss is appropriate mechanism to enforce forum-selection clause; TRCP 91a motion is generally not appropriate).

§1.3 Timetable & forms. Appendix IV, Timetable 6, Motion to dismiss—Baseless cause of action; **O'Connor's Texas Civil Forms**, FORMS 3H:1 et seq. (2020 ed.).

§1.4 Other references. Chamberlain & Parker, *Rule 91a Motions to Dismiss*, Advanced Trial Strategies, State Bar of Texas CLE, ch. 1.2 (2016); Jefferson & Gibson, *New Rules—Dismissal & Expedited Actions: History & Practical Considerations*, Advanced Civil Trial Course, State Bar of Texas CLE, ch. 2 (2013); **O'Connor's Texas Civil Appeals** (2020 ed.).

§2. Motion

§2.1 Who can file.

1. Generally. Generally, any defendant can move to dismiss a baseless cause of action. *See* Tex. R. Civ. P. 91a.1.

Note

In this subchapter, "defendant" includes counterdefendants and third-party defendants.

2. Exceptions. A defendant cannot move to dismiss a baseless cause of action if the suit is brought under the Family Code or governed by CPRC chapter 14 (inmate litigation). Tex. R. Civ. P. 91a.1.

§2.2 In writing. The motion to dismiss must be in writing. *See* Tex. R. Civ. P. 91a.2.

§2.3 Deadline to file. The defendant must file the motion to dismiss within 60 days after being served with the first pleading containing the challenged cause of action. Tex. R. Civ. P. 91a.3(a).

§2.4 Contents. The defendant generally must do all the following in the motion to dismiss:

1. State under TRCP 91a. The defendant must state that the motion is made under TRCP 91a. Tex. R. Civ. P. 91a.2; *see* **HMT Tank Serv. v. American Tank & Vessel, Inc.**, 565 S.W.3d 799, 807 (Tex.App.—Houston [14th Dist.] 2018, no pet.).

2. Identify challenged cause of action. The defendant must identify each challenged cause of action. Tex. R. Civ. P. 91a.2; **HMT Tank**, 565 S.W.3d at 807.

3. Provide grounds for dismissal. The defendant must provide the reasons why the challenged cause of action has no basis in law, no basis in fact, or both. Tex. R. Civ. P. 91a.2; **HMT Tank Serv.**, 565 S.W.3d at 807; *see* **Wooley v. Schaffer**, 447 S.W.3d 71, 77 n.12 (Tex.App.—Houston [14th Dist.] 2014, pet. denied) ("magic words" are not required to satisfy TRCP 91a.2 as long as arguments are clearly stated in motion).

(1) No basis in law. A cause of action has no basis in law if the allegations, taken as true, together with inferences reasonably drawn from them, do not entitle the plaintiff to the relief sought. Tex. R. Civ. P. 91a.1; *e.g.*, **Bethel v. Quill-**

ing, Selander, Lownds, Winslett & Moser, P.C., 595 S.W.3d 651, 654–55 (Tex.2020) (cause of action had no basis in law when Ds could properly assert affirmative defense of attorney immunity); **In re Houston Specialty Ins.**, 569 S.W.3d 138, 139 & n.1 (Tex.2019) (cause of action for declaration of nonliability in tort under Uniform Declaratory Judgments Act had no basis in law); *see, e.g.*, **In re Essex Ins.**, 450 S.W.3d 524, 527–28 (Tex.2014) (P's cause of action directly against D's insurer for declaration of insurer's duty to indemnify D before D's liability had been determined had no basis in law). Generally, a cause of action is found to have no basis in law in two situations: (1) the petition alleges too few facts to demonstrate a viable, legally cognizable claim to relief or (2) the petition alleges additional facts that, if true, bar the plaintiff's recovery. **Stallworth v. Ayers**, 510 S.W.3d 187, 190 (Tex.App.—Houston [1st Dist.] 2016, no pet.); *see also* **Reaves v. City of Corpus Christi**, 518 S.W.3d 594, 608 (Tex.App.—Corpus Christi 2017, no pet.) (although court agreed with general substance of first situation, court disagreed to extent that it implies fair notice is not correct rule in Texas).

Note

If the court lacks subject-matter jurisdiction over a claim, the defendant may be able to use a TRCP 91a motion, rather than a plea to the jurisdiction, to argue that the claim has no basis in law and thus should be dismissed. See, e.g., ***City of Dallas v. Sanchez****, 494 S.W.3d 722, 724–25 (Tex.2016) (TRCP 91a motion based on governmental immunity);* ***Reaves****, 518 S.W.3d at 606–07 (same). See "Plea to the Jurisdiction—Challenging the Court," ch. 3-F, §1 et seq. In such a case, the court will apply the standards and procedures under Rule 91a to determine whether dismissal is proper; simply including a jurisdictional argument does not override the rule's requirements. See* ***Reaves****, 518 S.W.3d at 606–07.*

(2) No basis in fact. A cause of action has no basis in fact if no reasonable person could believe the facts pleaded. Tex. R. Civ. P. 91a.1; **Drake v. Chase Bank**, No. 02-13-00340-CV, 2014 WL 6493411 (Tex.App.—Fort Worth 2014, no pet.) (memo op.; 11-20-14); *e.g.*, **Drake v. Walker**, No. 05-14-00355-CV, 2015 WL 2160565 (Tex.App.—Dallas 2015, no pet.) (memo op.; 5-8-15) (negligence claim had basis in fact because reasonable person could believe P's allegations that D-dentist injured P when injecting him with pain medication and then refused to treat him).

4. Request hearing. Because the court must rule on the motion to dismiss within 45 days after it is filed, the defendant should request that the motion be set for hearing or submission as early as possible. *See* Tex. R. Civ. P. 91a.3(c). See "Ruling," ch. 3-H, §6. But the motion to dismiss cannot be set for hearing or submission any earlier than 21 days after the motion is filed. Tex. R. Civ. P. 91a.3(b). See "Hearing," ch. 3-H, §5.

5. Request attorney fees & costs. The defendant should ask the court to award reasonable and necessary attorney fees and all costs incurred if the motion is granted, either in whole or in part, unless the action was brought by or against (1) the State, (2) a governmental entity, or (3) a public official acting in her official capacity or under color of law. *See* Tex. Civ. Prac. & Rem. Code §30.021; Tex. R. Civ. P. 91a.7. See "Attorney fees from adverse party," ch. 1-H, §10; "Award of attorney fees & costs," ch. 3-H, §7.2; "Attorney Fees," **O'Connor's Texas Causes of Action**, ch. 45-A, §1 et seq. (2021 ed.). A request for attorney fees and costs should be supported by evidence, in the form of either affidavits or live testimony. *See* Tex. R. Civ. P. 91a.7. See "Extrinsic evidence," ch. 3-H, §6.1.1.

§2.5 No extrinsic materials. The defendant should not attach any affidavits, evidence, or other extrinsic materials to the motion, except to support an award of attorney fees and costs. *See* Tex. R. Civ. P. 91a.6, 91a.7. See "Matter considered," ch. 3-H, §6.1.

§2.6 Effect of motion on personal jurisdiction and venue.

1. No waiver of special appearance or motion to transfer venue. The defendant can file a motion to dismiss and obtain a ruling on it without waiving its right to a special appearance under TRCP 120a or a motion to transfer venue under TRCP 86. Tex. R. Civ. P. 91a.8; Chamberlain & Parker, *Rule 91A Motions to Dismiss*, at 5. See "Actions after filing special appearance," ch. 3-B, §3.5.2; "Due order of pleading," ch. 3-C, §2.2.2. But the filing of a motion to dismiss is not an exception to the due-order-of-pleading rule; that is, a special appearance or a motion to transfer venue must be filed before the motion to dismiss. *See* Tex. R. Civ. P. 91a.8; Chamberlain & Parker, *Rule 91A Motions to Dismiss*, at 5. See "Due order of pleading," ch. 3-A, §3.

2. Bound by court's ruling. By filing a motion to dismiss, the defendant submits to the court's jurisdiction only in proceedings on the motion and is bound by the court's ruling (i.e., whether or not the cause of action is dismissed), which can include an award of attorney fees and costs against the defendant. Tex. R. Civ. P. 91a.8. See "Order," ch. 3-H, §7.

§3. Response

The plaintiff has several options following a motion to dismiss under TRCP 91a.

§3.1 Respond. The plaintiff can file a response to the motion to dismiss. *See* Tex. R. Civ. P. 91a.4; *see also* **In re Estate of Savana**, 529 S.W.3d 587, 592–93 (Tex.App.—Houston [14th Dist.] 2017, no pet.) (no requirement that court grant motion to dismiss if P does not timely file response). See **O'Connor's Texas Civil Forms**, FORM 3H:2 (2020 ed.)

1. Deadline to file. The plaintiff must file its response at least seven days before the hearing date. Tex. R. Civ. P. 91a.4. See "Hearing," ch. 3-H, §5.

2. Contents.

(1) Grounds.

(a) Not timely. The plaintiff can argue that the defendant's motion to dismiss was not timely filed. *See* Tex. R. Civ. P. 91a.3. See "Deadline to file," ch. 3-H, §2.3.

(b) Basis in law or fact. The plaintiff can refute the defendant's grounds and show how each challenged cause of action has a basis in law or fact. *See* Tex. R. Civ. P. 91a.1, 91a.2. See "Provide grounds for dismissal," ch. 3-H, §2.4.3.

(2) Request for attorney fees & costs. The plaintiff should ask the court to award reasonable and necessary attorney fees and all costs incurred if the motion is denied, either in whole or in part, unless the action was brought by or against (1) the State, (2) a governmental entity, or (3) a public official acting in her official capacity or under color of law. *See* Tex. Civ. Prac. & Rem. Code §30.021; Tex. R. Civ. P. 91a.7. See "Award of attorney fees & costs," ch. 3-H, §7.2; "Attorney Fees," **O'Connor's Texas Causes of Action**, ch. 45-A, §1 et seq. (2021 ed.).

§3.2 Amend pleading. The plaintiff can file an amended pleading in addition to or instead of a response. *See* Tex. R. Civ. P. 91a.5(b); **In re Estate of Savana**, 529 S.W.3d 587, 592 (Tex.App.—Houston [14th Dist.] 2017, no pet.); *see, e.g.*, **In re Nationwide Ins.**, 494 S.W.3d 708, 713 (Tex.2016) (P amended pleadings to remove claims addressed in TRCP 91a motions and avoid formal dismissal). See "Amended pleading," ch. 3-H, §4.2. An amended pleading must be filed at least three days before the hearing date for the court to consider the amendment in ruling on the motion. *See* Tex. R. Civ. P. 91a.5(b), (c).

§3.3 Take nonsuit. The plaintiff can nonsuit the challenged cause of action. **In re Estate of Savana**, 529 S.W.3d 587, 592 (Tex.App.—Houston [14th Dist.] 2017, no pet.); *see* Tex. R. Civ. P. 91a.5(a). See "Voluntary Dismissal—Nonsuit," ch. 7-F, §1 et seq. The nonsuit must be filed at least three days before the hearing date to prevent the court from ruling on the cause of action. *See* Tex. R. Civ. P. 91a.5(a), (c).

§4. Reply

The defendant may have an opportunity to reply depending on the plaintiff's response to the motion.

§4.1 No amended pleading. If the plaintiff filed a response to the motion but did not file an amended pleading, the defendant can do either of the following:

1. Let court rule on motion. The defendant can do nothing and let the court rule on the motion. *See* Tex. R. Civ. P. 91a.3(c), 91a.5(c). See "Ruling required," ch. 3-H, §6.2.

2. Withdraw motion. The defendant can withdraw the motion but must do so at least three days before the hearing date. Tex. R. Civ. P. 91a.5(a). See "Withdrawal," ch. 3-H, §6.3.2; **O'Connor's Texas Civil Forms**, FORM 3H:3 (2020 ed.).

§4.2 Amended pleading. If the plaintiff filed an amended pleading at least three days before the hearing, the defendant can do any of the following:

1. Let court rule on motion. The defendant can do nothing and let the court rule on the original motion. *See* **Drake v. Walker**, No. 05-14-00355-CV, 2015 WL 2160565 (Tex.App.—Dallas 2015, no pet.) (memo op.; 5-8-15).

2. Withdraw motion. The defendant can withdraw the motion anytime before the hearing date. Tex. R. Civ. P. 91a.5(b). See **O'Connor's Texas Civil Forms**, FORM 3H:3 (2020 ed.).

3. Amend motion. The defendant can file an amended motion challenging the amended pleading anytime before the hearing date. Tex. R. Civ. P. 91a.5(b). If the defendant amends the motion, all time periods in TRCP 91a are reset. Tex. R. Civ. P. 91a.5(d). That is, the hearing must be reset to a date at least 21 days after the amended motion was filed, the plaintiff must be given an opportunity to file a response (at least 7 days before the hearing) to the amended motion, and the court must rule on the amended motion within 45 days after it is filed. *See* Tex. R. Civ. P. 91a.3, 91a.4 & cmt. See "Deadline to file," ch. 3-H, §3.1.1; "Ruling required," ch. 3-H, §6.2.

§5. Hearing

§5.1 Oral hearing or written submission. The court must conduct a hearing on the motion to dismiss. *See* Tex. R. Civ. P. 91a.6. The court can either conduct an oral hearing or issue a ruling based on the motion and response. *Id.*; *see* **In re Butt**, 495 S.W.3d 455, 461 (Tex.App.—Corpus Christi 2016, orig. proceeding) (court is not required to conduct oral hearing); **Wooley v. Schaffer**, 447 S.W.3d 71, 74 n.7 (Tex.App.—Houston [14th Dist.] 2014, pet. denied) (same); Tex. R. Civ. P. 91a cmt. (term "hearing" includes both oral hearing and written submission of motion).

§5.2 Notice. The parties must receive notice of the hearing at least 14 days before the hearing date. Tex. R. Civ. P. 91a.6; *e.g.*, **Gaskill v. VHS San Antonio Partners**, 456 S.W.3d 234, 238–39 (Tex.App.—San Antonio 2014, pet. denied) (error for court to rule on written submission without providing notice under TRCP 91a.6; no implied notice of hearing on 45th day after motion is filed).

§5.3 Timing. The hearing must be held at least 21 days after the motion is filed. Tex. R. Civ. P. 91a.3(b).

§6. Ruling

§6.1 Matter considered. The court must decide the motion based solely on the pleading of the cause of action, along with any pleading exhibits allowed under TRCP 59. Tex. R. Civ. P. 91a.6; **Bethel v. Quilling, Selander, Lownds, Winslett & Moser, P.C.**, 595 S.W.3d 651, 654 (Tex.2020); *e.g.*, **Koenig v. Blaylock**, 497 S.W.3d 595, 599–600 (Tex.App.—Austin 2016, pet. denied) (in ruling on motion to dismiss, court considered exhibits attached to P's response); *see* **ConocoPhillips Co. v. Koopmann**, 547 S.W.3d 858, 880 (Tex.2018). See "Exhibits," ch. 1-B, §3.2.14.

Note

In ***Bethel***, *the defendants moved to dismiss under TRCP 91a, arguing that the plaintiff's causes of action had no basis in law based on the defendants' assertion of the affirmative defense of attorney immunity.* ***Bethel***, *595 S.W.3d at 654. The plaintiff argued that an affirmative defense cannot be the basis of a TRCP 91a motion to dismiss because TRCP 91a.6 limits the court's consideration to the "pleading of a cause of action" (i.e., the plaintiff's pleading).* ***Bethel***, *595 S.W.3d at 654. The Supreme Court rejected this argument and held that TRCP 91a limits a court's factual inquiry to the plaintiff's pleadings, but not its legal inquiry; thus, a court may consider the defendant's pleadings in ruling on a motion to dismiss if doing so is necessary to make the legal determination of whether an affirmative defense applies.* ***Bethel***, *595 S.W.3d at 656. But because extrinsic evidence is generally not allowed, the affirmative defense must be conclusively established by the facts in the plaintiff's petition to form a proper basis for the motion to dismiss. See Tex. R. Civ. P. 91a.6;* ***Bethel***, *595 S.W.3d at 656.*

1. Extrinsic evidence. The court cannot consider any extrinsic evidence in ruling on the motion except when determining an award of attorney fees and costs. *See* Tex. R. Civ. P. 91a.6, 91a.7; *see, e.g.*, **In re Butt**, 495 S.W.3d 455, 462–63 (Tex.App.—Corpus Christi 2016, orig. proceeding) (because court generally cannot consider extrinsic evidence, Ds did not have to respond to Ps' discovery requests before court ruled on motion to dismiss); **Drake v. Chase Bank**, No. 02-13-00340-

CV, 2014 WL 6493411 (Tex.App.—Fort Worth 2014, no pet.) (memo op.; 11-20-14) (D's attorney submitted affidavit and presented live testimony to establish reasonable and necessary attorney fees). See "Award of attorney fees & costs," ch. 3-H, §7.2.

2. Defective or untimely amendments or nonsuit. The court cannot consider the effect of an amended pleading, an amended motion to dismiss, or a nonsuit that does not comply with TRCP 91a.5(a) or (b). *See* Tex. R. Civ. P. 91a.5(c).

§6.2 Ruling required. In most cases, the court must rule on the motion to dismiss. *See* Tex. R. Civ. P. 91a.5(c).

1. Deadline—generally. The court must rule on the motion to dismiss within 45 days after it is filed. Tex. Gov't Code §22.004(g); Tex. R. Civ. P. 91a.3(c) & cmt. There is not, however, any statutory consequence (e.g., denial by operation of law) for noncompliance with the deadline, and the court is not divested of its jurisdiction to issue a ruling after the deadline passes. *See* **Reaves v. City of Corpus Christi**, 518 S.W.3d 594, 602 (Tex.App.—Corpus Christi 2017, no pet.); **Koenig v. Blaylock**, 497 S.W.3d 595, 598–99 (Tex.App.—Austin 2016, pet. denied); **Walker v. Owens**, 492 S.W.3d 787, 790–91 (Tex.App.—Houston [1st Dist.] 2016, no pet.); *see also* **Aguilar v. Morales**, 545 S.W.3d 670, 682 (Tex.App.—El Paso 2017, pet. denied) (even if court rules on motion after deadline, party must still show harmful error to warrant reversal).

2. Deadline—amended motion. If the defendant files an amended motion to dismiss, the court must rule on the amended motion within 45 days after it is filed. Tex. R. Civ. P. 91a.5(d) & cmt. See "Amend motion," ch. 3-H, §4.2.3.

§6.3 Ruling not permitted. The court cannot rule on the motion to dismiss if any of the following occur:

1. Nonsuit. The court cannot rule on the motion to dismiss if the plaintiff timely files a nonsuit. Tex. R. Civ. P. 91a.5(a); **Thuesen v. Amerisure Ins.**, 487 S.W.3d 291, 301 (Tex.App.—Houston [14th Dist.] 2016, no pet.); *see* Tex. R. Civ. P. 91a.5(c) & cmt. See "Take nonsuit," ch. 3-H, §3.3.

2. Withdrawal. The court cannot rule on the motion to dismiss if the defendant withdraws the motion (1) at least three days before the hearing date or (2) anytime before the hearing if the plaintiff timely amended the challenged cause of action. *See* Tex. R. Civ. P. 91a.5 & cmt.

3. Parties' agreement. The court cannot rule on the motion to dismiss if the parties file an agreed motion to withdraw the motion to dismiss. *See* Tex. R. Civ. P. 91a.5(c).

§7. Order

§7.1 Ruling on motion. If the court denies the motion to dismiss, the plaintiff's case continues; if the court grants the motion to dismiss, it must dismiss all or part of the case. See "Involuntary Dismissal," ch. 7-G, §1 et seq.

§7.2 Award of attorney fees & costs. For actions commenced on or after September 1, 2019, an award of attorney fees and costs is discretionary. *See* Tex. Civ. Prac. & Rem. Code §30.021; Tex. R. Civ. P. 91a.7; Acts 2019, 86th Leg., R.S., ch. 885, eff. Sept. 1, 2019; Tex.Sup.Ct. Order, Misc. Docket No. 19-9108 (eff. Sept. 1, 2019). For actions commenced before September 1, 2019, an award of attorney fees and costs is generally mandatory. *See* Tex. Civ. Prac. & Rem. Code §30.021 (pre-9-1-19 version); Tex. R. Civ. P. 91a.7 (pre-9-1-19 version).

1. Who can be awarded fees & costs.

(1) Proper party. An award of attorney fees and costs to the prevailing party is proper whether the motion is granted or denied in whole or in part. *See* Tex. Civ. Prac. & Rem. Code §30.021; Tex. R. Civ. P. 91a.7. The party must prevail on the Rule 91a motion to be entitled to attorney fees; prevailing on a later summary-judgment motion does not entitle the party to attorney fees. *E.g.*, **ConocoPhillips Co. v. Koopmann**, 547 S.W.3d 858, 880 (Tex.2018) (D whose Rule 91a motion was denied but who was later granted summary judgment on same claims was not prevailing party entitled to attorney fees).

Note

If a plaintiff timely nonsuits a cause of action in response to a motion to dismiss, the defendant is not considered a prevailing party entitled to attorney fees and costs. ***Thuesen v. Amerisure Ins.****, 487 S.W.3d 291, 301 (Tex.App.—Houston [14th Dist.] 2016, no pet.). See "Take nonsuit," ch. 3-H, §3.3; "Nonsuit," ch. 3-H, §6.3.1. There must be a ruling on the motion to dismiss for a party to be considered a prevailing party.* ***Thuesen****, 487 S.W.3d at 301.*

(2) Improper party. An award of attorney fees and costs is not proper if the action was brought by or against (1) the State, (2) a governmental entity, or (3) a public official acting in her official capacity or under color of law. *See* Tex. Civ. Prac. & Rem. Code §30.021; Tex. R. Civ. P. 91a.7.

2. What fees & costs can be awarded. The court can award the prevailing party on the motion to dismiss all reasonable and necessary attorney fees and all costs. Tex. Civ. Prac. & Rem. Code §30.021; Tex. R. Civ. P. 91a.7; *see, e.g.*, **Weizhong Zheng v. Vacation Network, Inc.**, 468 S.W.3d 180, 187 (Tex.App.—Houston [14th Dist.] 2015, pet. denied) (because trial court determined Ds were no longer prevailing parties on claims, on remand, court ordered Ds to segregate attorney fees related to causes of action that appellate court affirmed dismissal of). Only fees and costs incurred as a result of the challenged cause of action can be awarded. Tex. R. Civ. P. 91a.7 & cmt. For example, the court can award fees incurred as a result of preparing or responding to the motion to dismiss or responding to a motion to reconsider the court's ruling on the motion to dismiss. *See* Tex. R. Civ. P. 91a cmt.; *see, e.g.*, **Drake v. Chase Bank**, No. 02-13-00340-CV, 2014 WL 6493411 (Tex.App.—Fort Worth 2014, no pet.) (memo op.; 11-20-14) (trial court properly awarded attorney fees and costs incurred in responding to motion to reconsider ruling on motion to dismiss). At least one court has held that attorney fees and costs under TRCP 91a.7 include those incurred on appeal. **Weizhong Zheng**, 468 S.W.3d at 188.

§7.3 No findings of fact & conclusions of law. The court should not make findings of fact or conclusions of law when ruling on the motion to dismiss because it does not consider any evidence. See "Matter considered," ch. 3-H, §6.1.

§8. Review

§8.1 Standard of review. The appellate court's standard of review for a trial court's determination of whether a cause of action has any basis in law or fact is de novo. **HMT Tank Serv. v. American Tank & Vessel, Inc.**, 565 S.W.3d 799, 808 (Tex.App.—Houston [14th Dist.] 2018, no pet.); **Stallworth v. Ayers**, 510 S.W.3d 187, 190 (Tex.App.—Houston [1st Dist.] 2016, no pet.); **Vasquez v. Legend Nat. Gas III, LP**, 492 S.W.3d 448, 451 (Tex.App.—San Antonio 2016, pet. denied); *see* **City of Dallas v. Sanchez**, 494 S.W.3d 722, 724 (Tex.2016). In conducting its review, the court must liberally construe the pleadings in favor of the plaintiff, look to the plaintiff's intent, and accept as true the factual allegations in the pleadings. **HMT Tank**, 565 S.W.3d at 808; **Aguilar v. Morales**, 545 S.W.3d 670, 677 (Tex.App.—El Paso 2017, pet. denied); *see* **City of Dallas**, 494 S.W.3d at 725; **Reaves v. City of Corpus Christi**, 518 S.W.3d 594, 604–05 (Tex.App.—Corpus Christi 2017, no pet.). In determining whether the petition sufficiently alleges a cause of action, most courts have applied Texas's fair-notice pleading standard. *E.g.*, **Thomas v. 462 Thomas Family Props., LP**, 559 S.W.3d 634, 639 (Tex.App.—Dallas 2018, pet. denied); **Cooper v. Trent**, 551 S.W.3d 325, 329 (Tex.App.—Houston [14th Dist.] 2018, pet. denied); **Skelton v. Gray**, 547 S.W.3d 272, 275 (Tex.App.—San Antonio 2018), *aff'd*, 595 S.W.3d 633 (Tex.2020); **Aguilar**, 545 S.W.3d at 677; **In re Butt**, 495 S.W.3d 455, 461–62 (Tex.App.—Corpus Christi 2016, orig. proceeding). See "Fair notice of claim," ch. 2-B, §7.2.

Note

Because TRCP 91a is analogous to FRCP 12(b)(6), some courts have looked at case law interpreting the federal rule as instructive and applied the federal "plausibility" standard in making their determination. See ***GoDaddy.com, LLC v. Toups****, 429 S.W.3d 752, 754 (Tex.App.—Beaumont 2014, pet. denied); see also* ***Weizhong Zheng v. Vacation Network, Inc.****, 468 S.W.3d 180, 186 (Tex.App.—Houston [14th Dist.] 2015, pet. denied) (in applying fair-notice pleading standard, court discussed federal standards and determined P's pleading was insufficient because it contained "threadbare recital" of elements of fraudulent inducement). For the standards for dismissal under FRCP 12(b)(6), see*

*"Ruling," **O'Connor's Federal Rules * Civil Trials**, ch. 3-F, §5 (2021 ed.).*

§8.2 Appeal.

1. Motion granted. If the motion to dismiss is granted and the trial court does not state the grounds on which it granted dismissal, the plaintiff must negate the validity of each ground alleged in the motion, similar to when an order granting summary judgment does not specify the grounds it was based on. **Parkhurst v. Office of the Atty. Gen.**, 481 S.W.3d 400, 402 (Tex.App.—Amarillo 2015, no pet.); *see* **In re Estate of Savana**, 529 S.W.3d 587, 592 (Tex.App.—Houston [14th Dist.] 2017, no pet.). See "When not identified in judgment," ch. 7-B, §14.3.1(2). If each ground is not negated, dismissal may be affirmed on any unchallenged ground. **Parkhurst**, 481 S.W.3d at 402.

(1) Motion granted, case dismissed. If the motion to dismiss is granted and the entire case is dismissed, the plaintiff can challenge the ruling after the order of dismissal is signed. *See* **Stewart v. USA Custom Paint & Body Shop, Inc.**, 870 S.W.2d 18, 20 (Tex.1994) (properly executed order of dismissal is a judgment).

(2) Motion granted in part. If the motion to dismiss is granted in part, or if the motion was filed for only some cause of action in the suit, the plaintiff or the defendant can challenge the ruling by asking permission to file an interlocutory appeal. *See* **City of Dallas v. Sanchez**, 449 S.W.3d 645, 647 (Tex.App.—Dallas 2014), *rev'd on other grounds*, 494 S.W.3d 722 (Tex.2016). See "Interlocutory appeal by permission," **O'Connor's Texas Civil Appeals**, ch. 3-P, §2.1 (2020 ed.).

2. Motion denied. If the motion to dismiss is denied, the defendant can challenge the ruling by asking permission to file an interlocutory appeal. *See* **GoDaddy.com, LLC v. Toups**, 429 S.W.3d 752, 753 (Tex.App.—Beaumont 2014, pet. denied). See "Interlocutory appeal by permission," **O'Connor's Texas Civil Appeals**, ch. 3-P, §2.1 (2020 ed.). If no interlocutory appeal is sought or if permission to file an interlocutory appeal is denied, then the defendant can challenge the ruling only after a final judgment is signed. See "Final judgment," ch. 9-C, §6.

Note

*If the defendant's motion to dismiss challenges the court's subject-matter jurisdiction, an interlocutory appeal may be available under CPRC §51.014(a)(8); under that section, "plea to the jurisdiction" refers to the substance of the issue raised, not the procedural vehicle used to raise the issue. See **City of Magnolia 4A Econ. Dev. Corp. v. Smedley**, 533 S.W.3d 297, 299 (Tex.2017); **City of Houston v. Estate of Jones**, 388 S.W.3d 663, 666 (Tex.2012); see, e.g., **City of Austin v. Liberty Mut. Ins.**, 431 S.W.3d 817, 822 & n.1 (Tex.App.—Austin 2014, no pet.) (interlocutory appeal under CPRC §51.014(a)(8) proper for Rule 91a motion used to challenge subject-matter jurisdiction). See "Form," ch. 3-F, §2.1; "Plea to the jurisdiction—governmental unit," ch. 3-F, §7.3.1(1).*

§8.3 Mandamus.

1. Court denies motion. If the motion to dismiss is denied, the defendant can challenge the ruling by filing a petition for writ of mandamus. *See* **In re Houston Specialty Ins.**, 569 S.W.3d 138, 141–42 (Tex.2019); **In re Essex Ins.**, 450 S.W.3d 524, 526 (Tex.2014); **In re Butt**, 495 S.W.3d 455, 460 (Tex.App.—Corpus Christi 2016, orig. proceeding).

2. Court does not rule on motion. If the court does not rule on the motion to dismiss by the 45-day deadline, mandamus may be available to compel the court to rule promptly. **Reaves v. City of Corpus Christi**, 518 S.W.3d 594, 602 (Tex.App.—Corpus Christi 2017, no pet.). See "Deadline—generally," ch. 3-H, §6.2.1.

I. Motion to Abate—Challenging the Suit

§1. General

§1.1 Rules. Tex. R. Civ. P. 85, 150 to 160, 175.

§1.2 Purpose. A defendant uses a motion to abate, also called a plea in abatement, to challenge the plaintiff's pleadings by alleging facts outside the pleadings that prove the suit cannot go forward in its present condition. **Lagow v. Hamon**, 384 S.W.3d 411, 418 (Tex.App.—Dallas 2012, no pet.); **Martin v. Dosohs I, Ltd.**, 2 S.W.3d 350, 354 (Tex.App.—San Antonio 1999, pet. denied). A motion to abate cannot be used to determine the merits of an action. **KSNG Architects, Inc. v. Beasley**, 109 S.W.3d 894, 898 (Tex.App.—Dallas 2003, no pet.). In a motion to abate, the defendant identifies some impediment to the continuation of the suit, identifies an effective cure, and asks the court to suspend the suit until the plaintiff cures the defect. **Martin**, 2 S.W.3d at 354; *see* **American Motorists Ins. v. Fodge**, 63 S.W.3d 801, 805 (Tex.2001). By granting the motion to abate, the court gives the plaintiff an opportunity to cure the defect. **Speer v. Stover**, 685 S.W.2d 22, 23 (Tex.1985). If the plaintiff cures the defect, the court will permit the suit to continue; if not, the court will dismiss the suit. *See* **Garcia-Marroquin v. Nueces Cty. Bail Bond Bd.**, 1 S.W.3d 366, 374 (Tex.App.—Corpus Christi 1999, no pet.).

§1.3 Timetable & forms. Appendix IV, Timetable 7, Motion to abate; **O'Connor's Texas Civil Forms**, FORMS 3I:1 et seq. (2020 ed.).

§1.4 Other references. O'Connor's Texas Causes of Action (2021 ed.); **O'Connor's Texas Civil Appeals** (2020 ed.).

§2. Motion

§2.1 Separate instrument. A defendant should ask for an abatement in a separate instrument from the answer. If a motion to abate is included in the answer, it is called a plea in abatement. *See* Tex. R. Civ. P. 85; **Southwestern Life Ins. v. Sanguinet**, 231 S.W.2d 727, 730 (Tex.App.—Fort Worth 1950, no writ).

§2.2 Specific allegations. A motion to abate must specify the improper grounds on which a suit is brought and show how the suit should have been brought. **Bryce v. Corpus Christi Area Convention & Tourist Bur.**, 569 S.W.2d 496, 499 (Tex.App.—Corpus Christi 1978, writ ref'd n.r.e.). The motion must inform the court and the other party exactly what is wrong and how to cure it. **M&M Constr. Co. v. Great Am. Ins.**, 747 S.W.2d 552, 554 (Tex.App.—Corpus Christi 1988, no writ).

§2.3 Verified. The motion to abate generally must be verified. **Sparks v. Bolton**, 335 S.W.2d 780, 785 (Tex.App.—Dallas 1960, no writ); *see* Tex. R. Civ. P. 93 (pleas that must be verified). *But see* **Southern Cty. Mut. Ins. v. Ochoa**, 19 S.W.3d 452, 461–62 (Tex.App.—Corpus Christi 2000, no pet.) (verification requirement excused when D filed verified answer and verified motion to transfer venue with plea in abatement). The movant may also file affidavits if necessary to support the allegations in the motion.

§2.4 Deadline to file. A motion to abate must be made in a timely manner, or else it is waived. **Wyatt v. Shaw Plumbing Co.**, 760 S.W.2d 245, 248 (Tex.1988), *overruled on other grounds*, **In re J.B. Hunt Transp.**, 492 S.W.3d 287 (Tex.2016); **In re King**, 478 S.W.3d 930, 933 (Tex.App.—Dallas 2015, orig. proceeding); **Lopez v. Texas Workers' Comp. Ins. Fund**, 11 S.W.3d 490, 493 (Tex.App.—Austin 2000, pet. denied); *see* **Lagow v. Hamon**, 384 S.W.3d 411, 417–18 (Tex.App.—Dallas 2012, no pet.) (if D does not request abatement before proceeding to trial, abatement is waived). The motion must be made while the purpose of the motion remains viable. *See* **Hines v. Hash**, 843 S.W.2d 464, 469 (Tex.1992) (when objecting to lack of notice under DTPA, D must request abatement with filing of answer or soon thereafter); **Garcia-Marroquin v. Nueces Cty. Bail Bond Bd.**, 1 S.W.3d 366, 374 (Tex.App.—Corpus Christi 1999, no pet.) (same, for provision under Local Gov't Code); *see, e.g.*, **Bluebonnet Farms, Inc. v. Gibraltar Sav. Ass'n**, 618 S.W.2d 81, 83–84 (Tex.App.—Houston [1st Dist.] 1980, writ ref'd n.r.e.) (motion to abate filed four years after suit filed and after limitations ran was too late).

Practice Tip

In deciding whether to file a motion to abate, a defendant should look at the verified denials in its original answer. Many of the matters that a party is required to deny under oath, listed in TRCP 93, are also matters that should be made the subject of a verified motion to abate. See "Verified pleas in TRCP 93," ch. 3-E, §4.1.

§3. Types of motions to abate

§3.1 Abate—defect in pleadings. A defendant should file a motion to abate when there is a defect in the pleadings that must be supported by extrinsic evidence. See **O'Connor's Texas Civil Forms**, FORM 3I:1 (2020 ed.). If the defect is apparent from the face of the pleadings, it can be challenged by special exceptions. See "Types of pleading defects to challenge by special exceptions," ch. 3-G, §2; "Limited to pleadings," ch. 3-G, §3.3. There are two types of pleading defects that can be challenged by a motion to abate: defects in parties and defects in allegations.

1. Defects in parties.

(1) Minor or incapacitated person. A motion to abate is appropriate to challenge a minor or incapacitated person who files suit in her own name, instead of a next friend's or guardian's name. **Sax v. Votteler**, 648 S.W.2d 661, 666 (Tex.1983). See "Minor as P," ch. 2-B, §4.4.2.

(2) Estate of decedent. A motion to abate is appropriate to challenge the following defects when the estate of a decedent is a party: • To challenge a suit brought on behalf of an estate by an individual, instead of by the estate's representative. *See* **Coakley v. Reising**, 436 S.W.2d 315, 317 (Tex.1968). • To contest the authority of an administrator to represent the estate, who must then file proof of authority (the bond and oath). **Shiffers v. Estate of Ward**, 762 S.W.2d 753, 755 (Tex.App.—Fort Worth 1988, writ denied). See "Estate," ch. 2-B, §4.3.2.

(3) Death-action beneficiary. A motion to abate is appropriate to challenge whether the plaintiff has the proper capacity to sue as the legal representative of an estate under the Texas Survival Statute and the Texas Wrongful Death Act. *See* **Ford Motor Co. v. Aguiniga**, 9 S.W.3d 252, 259 (Tex.App.—San Antonio 1999, pet. denied). If the plaintiff alleges that she is the personal representative of an estate and the defendant does not challenge that status in a motion to abate, the defendant waives any complaint about the plaintiff's capacity as personal representative. *See e.g., id.* (Ps were not required to prove capacity to sue as personal representatives because D did not challenge capacity by motion to abate or verified denial). See "Legal representative of estate," **O'Connor's Texas Causes of Action** ch. 7-A, §2.1.2 (2021 ed.); "Statutory beneficiaries," **O'Connor's Texas Causes of Action**, ch. 7-B, §2.1.2 (2021 ed.).

(4) Wrong representative of corporation. A motion to abate is appropriate to challenge whether a stockholder suing for damages to a corporation has standing and capacity to bring suit. Except in a derivative action, a stockholder lacks both standing (because the stockholder was not personally aggrieved) and capacity (because the stockholder is not the right surrogate) to bring suit for damages to a corporation. *See* **White v. Independence Bank**, 794 S.W.2d 895, 898 & n.3 (Tex.App.—Houston [1st Dist.] 1990, writ denied). See "Corporation," ch. 2-B, §4.3.4.

(5) Not corporation or partnership. A motion to abate is appropriate to challenge whether the plaintiff is a corporation or partnership, as it alleges. Tex. R. Civ. P. 52, 93(5), (6); *see* **Lighthouse Ch. v. Texas Bank**, 889 S.W.2d 595, 600 (Tex.App.—Houston [14th Dist.] 1994, writ denied).

(6) Unauthorized foreign corporation. A motion to abate is appropriate to challenge whether a foreign corporation is registered with the Secretary of State and can maintain an action for affirmative relief. *See* **Jay-Lor Textiles, Inc. v. Pacific Compress Whs. Co.**, 547 S.W.2d 738, 740 (Tex.App.—Corpus Christi 1977, writ ref'd n.r.e.).

(7) No assumed-name certificate. A motion to abate is appropriate to challenge the lack of an assumed-name certificate. **Sixth RMA Partners v. Sibley**, 111 S.W.3d 46, 55 (Tex.2003); *see* Tex. Bus. & Com. Code §71.201 (party is prohibited from prosecuting suit until it files assumed-name certificate).

(8) Necessary party absent. A motion to abate is appropriate to challenge the absence of a necessary party and force the plaintiff to add the missing party. *See, e.g.,* **Allison v. National Un. Fire Ins.**, 703 S.W.2d 637, 638 (Tex.1986)

(challenging absence of necessary parties from contract dispute); **Dahl v. Hartman**, 14 S.W.3d 434, 435–36 (Tex.App.—Houston [14th Dist.] 2000, pet. denied) (challenging absence of necessary parties in declaratory-judgment action); **Wolfe v. Schuster**, 591 S.W.2d 926, 931 (Tex.App.—Dallas 1979, no writ) (challenging P's failure to sue principal when D is surety and P has not already taken judgment against principal); *see also* Tex. R. Civ. P. 31 (surety), Tex. R. Civ. P. 32 (same).

(9) Misnomer of defendant. A motion to abate is appropriate to challenge the name under which the defendant was sued. *See* **Matthews Trucking Co. v. Smith**, 682 S.W.2d 237, 238–39 (Tex.1984) (if correct D sued in wrong name, D should file motion to abate); **Charles Brown, L.L.P. v. Lanier Worldwide, Inc.**, 124 S.W.3d 883, 894 (Tex.App.—Houston [14th Dist.] 2004, no pet.) (same).

2. Defects in allegations.

(1) Lack of notice. A motion to abate is generally appropriate to challenge the lack of notice or the allegation that the plaintiff gave proper presuit notice. In some cases, however, lack of notice subjects the suit to dismissal, not abatement. *See, e.g.*, **Reese v. Texas State Dept. of Hwys. & Pub. Transp.**, 831 S.W.2d 529, 530–31 (Tex.App.—Tyler 1992, writ denied) (lack of notice under TTCA was not subject to abatement; suit was perpetually barred). A motion to abate is appropriate in the following instances:

(a) To challenge notice of suit against a professional employee of a school district. Tex. Educ. Code §22.0513(c).

(b) To challenge notice of a DTPA claim. *See* **Hines v. Hash**, 843 S.W.2d 464, 469 (Tex.1992). Under the DTPA, a defendant must move to abate for lack of notice within 30 days after filing its answer. Tex. Bus. & Com. Code §17.505(c); **America Online, Inc. v. Williams**, 958 S.W.2d 268, 277 (Tex.App.—Houston [14th Dist.] 1997, no pet.). The abatement is automatic when a verified motion to abate is filed and lack of presuit notice is not controverted within 11 days after the motion was filed. Tex. Bus. & Com. Code §17.505(d); **America Online**, 958 S.W.2d at 273. See "Presuit notice of claim," **O'Connor's Texas Causes of Action**, ch. 8, §6 (2021 ed.).

(c) To challenge notice of a health-care-liability claim. *See* Tex. Civ. Prac. & Rem. Code §§74.051(a), 74.052(a). If a medical-authorization form is not attached to the notice, all proceedings against a physician or health-care provider must be abated until 60 days after the physician or health-care provider receives the authorization. Tex. Civ. Prac. & Rem. Code §74.052(a). See "Authorization form," **O'Connor's Texas Causes of Action**, ch. 20-A, §7.1.5 (2021 ed.).

(2) Lack of residency. A motion to abate is appropriate to challenge the lack of residency when there is a residency requirement for filing suit. **Cook v. Mayfield**, 886 S.W.2d 840, 841 (Tex.App.—Waco 1994, orig. proceeding); *see, e.g.*, Tex. Fam. Code §6.301(2) (one of the parties to a divorce must have been resident of county for 90 days); **Reynolds v. Reynolds**, 86 S.W.3d 272, 277 (Tex.App.—Austin 2002, no pet.) (divorce petition did not properly allege residency requirements under Fam. Code §6.301).

§3.2 Abate—same dispute in another Texas court. When two suits involving the same subject matter are filed in courts of concurrent jurisdiction, a party may file a motion to abate in one court, claiming the other court has dominant jurisdiction. **In re Puig**, 351 S.W.3d 301, 305 (Tex.2011); *see* **In re Red Dot Bldg. Sys.**, 504 S.W.3d 320, 322 (Tex.2016); **Wyatt v. Shaw Plumbing Co.**, 760 S.W.2d 245, 247–48 (Tex.1988), *overruled on other grounds*, **In re J.B. Hunt Transp.**, 492 S.W.3d 287 (Tex.2016); **In re Volkswagen Clean Diesel Litig.**, 557 S.W.3d 73, 75 (Tex.App.—Austin 2017, orig. proceeding); *cf.* **Miles v. Ford Motor Co.**, 914 S.W.2d 135, 139 (Tex.1995) (appeals filed by different parties in different courts of appeals). See **O'Connor's Texas Civil Forms**, FORM 3I:2 (2020 ed.). By comparison, if a suit is brought in one court when another court has continuing, exclusive jurisdiction, a party should challenge the issue of exclusive jurisdiction by a plea to the jurisdiction. See "Another court has exclusive jurisdiction," ch. 3-F, §3.5. If the movant can prove the grounds for abatement as set out below, the court generally must abate the suit because the other court has dominant jurisdiction. **In re Red Dot Bldg.**, 504 S.W.3d at 322; **In re Volkswagen Clean Diesel Litig.**, 557 S.W.3d at 77; *see* **Curtis v. Gibbs**, 511 S.W.2d 263, 267 (Tex.1974).

Note

When a claim asserted in a second suit is outside the jurisdictional limits of the court where the first suit was filed, the first court cannot assert dominant jurisdiction over the claim in the second suit. ***In re King****, 478 S.W.3d 930, 933 (Tex.App.—Dallas 2015, orig. proceeding).*

1. **Dominant jurisdiction.** To be entitled to an abatement based on dominant jurisdiction, the movant must file a motion to abate in the court where the other suit (the "second suit") was filed and must allege and prove the following:

(1) **Commenced.** The movant's suit (the "first suit") was commenced first. **In re King**, 478 S.W.3d at 933; *see* **In re Red Dot Bldg.**, 504 S.W.3d at 322; **In re Sims**, 88 S.W.3d 297, 303 (Tex.App.—San Antonio 2002, orig. proceeding). A suit is "commenced" when the petition is filed, unless the plaintiff has no intention to obtain service and prosecute the suit. **Russell v. Taylor**, 49 S.W.2d 733, 737 (Tex.Comm'n App.1932, judgm't adopted); *see* **Grimes v. Harris**, 695 S.W.2d 648, 651 (Tex.App.—Dallas 1985, orig. proceeding). See "Lack of intent to prosecute," ch. 3-I, §3.2.2(2).

(2) **Venue proper.** The first suit was filed in a county of proper venue. The court where the first suit was filed generally has dominant jurisdiction if venue is proper in that county. **In re Red Dot Bldg.**, 504 S.W.3d at 322; **Gonzalez v. Reliant Energy, Inc.**, 159 S.W.3d 615, 622 (Tex.2005); **Wyatt**, 760 S.W.2d at 248.

(3) **Pending.** The first suit is still pending in the other court. **In re King**, 478 S.W.3d at 933; **In re Sims**, 88 S.W.3d at 303; **Southern Cty. Mut. Ins. v. Ochoa**, 19 S.W.3d 452, 468 (Tex.App.—Corpus Christi 2000, no pet.).

(4) **Same parties & dispute.** The two suits involve the same parties and the same dispute. **In re King**, 478 S.W.3d at 933; **In re Sims**, 88 S.W.3d at 303; *see* **Wyatt**, 760 S.W.2d at 248; **Southern Cty.**, 19 S.W.3d at 468. That is, there must be an "inherent interrelation" of the subject matter in the two suits. **Wyatt**, 760 S.W.2d at 247; **In re Sims**, 88 S.W.3d at 303; *see* **In re Red Dot Bldg.**, 504 S.W.3d at 322. But the exact issues and all the parties do not need to be included in the first suit as long as the petition in the first suit can be amended to bring in all necessary parties and issues. **Wyatt**, 760 S.W.2d at 247; **In re Sims**, 88 S.W.3d at 303; *see* **In re King**, 478 S.W.3d at 933.

Note

At least two courts have held that, in determining whether two suits are inherently interrelated, a court should be guided in part by the test for evaluating whether a counterclaim is compulsory. E.g., ***Encore Enters. v. Borderplex Rlty. Trust****, 583 S.W.3d 713, 721–22 (Tex.App.—El Paso 2019, no pet.) (addressing elements of same transaction or occurrence and same parties in same capacity);* ***In re Texas Christian Univ.****, 571 S.W.3d 384, 389 (Tex.App.—Dallas 2019, orig. proceeding) (memo op.; addressing element of same transaction or occurrence). For a detailed discussion of the test for compulsory counterclaims, see "Criteria," ch. 2-F, §6.1.1.*

2. **Exceptions to dominant jurisdiction.** There are three exceptions to the dominant jurisdiction of the first court. **Wyatt**, 760 S.W.2d at 248; **Mission Res. v. Garza Energy Trust**, 166 S.W.3d 301, 328 (Tex.App.—Corpus Christi 2005), *rev'd on other grounds sub nom.* **Coastal Oil & Gas Corp. v. Garza Energy Trust**, 268 S.W.3d 1 (Tex.2008).

(1) **Estoppel.** A party can be estopped from asserting the dominant jurisdiction of the first court if both of the following occur:

(a) The party engaged in inequitable conduct. **In re J.B. Hunt Transp.**, 492 S.W.3d 287, 294 (Tex.2016); **Curtis**, 511 S.W.2d at 267; *see* **Wyatt**, 760 S.W.2d at 248. Examples of inequitable conduct include:

[1] Representing to the second court that it has jurisdiction. **Sweezy Constr., Inc. v. Murray**, 915 S.W.2d 527, 532 (Tex.App.—Corpus Christi 1995, orig. proceeding); *see* **Howell v. Mauzy**, 899 S.W.2d 690, 698 (Tex.App.—Austin 1994, writ denied).

[2] Not acting while the two courts issue conflicting orders. **Sweezy Constr.**, 915 S.W.2d at 532.

[3] Filing an unripe claim. **Perry v. Del Rio**, 66 S.W.3d 239, 252–53 (Tex.2001).

[4] Misrepresenting an intent to settle to prevent the adverse party from filing suit in another court first. *See* **In re Henry**, 274 S.W.3d 185, 191 (Tex.App.—Houston [1st Dist.] 2008, orig. proceeding).

(b) The party filing the second suit was prejudiced by the inequitable conduct. *E.g.*, **In re J.B. Hunt Transp.**, 492 S.W.3d at 295 (estoppel did not apply when parties filing second suit did not show how first-filing party's conduct caused them to delay filing second suit).

(2) Lack of intent to prosecute. A party's lack of intent to prosecute a suit deprives the first court of dominant jurisdiction. **In re J.B. Hunt Transp.**, 492 S.W.3d at 295; **Wyatt**, 760 S.W.2d at 248; **Mission Res.**, 166 S.W.3d at 328. The first suit does not confer dominant jurisdiction if the plaintiff was not diligent in serving process. *See* **In re J.B. Hunt Transp.**, 492 S.W.3d at 295–96; **Russell**, 49 S.W.2d at 737; *see, e.g.*, **Curtis**, 511 S.W.2d at 268 (delay of service for 26 days was not unreasonable; abatement of second suit should have been sustained); **Reed v. Reed**, 311 S.W.2d 628, 631 (Tex.1958) (delay of service for almost 15 months was unreasonable; second suit should not have been abated); **Southern Cty.**, 19 S.W.3d at 468 (delay of service for four months was unreasonable; denial of abatement of second suit affirmed). But a plaintiff that attempts to obtain a waiver of personal service or threatens to obtain a temporary restraining order in the court in which it has sued shows an intent to prosecute the suit. **In re J.B. Hunt Transp.**, 492 S.W.3d at 296.

(3) Lack of necessary parties. A party's inability to join necessary parties in the first suit because it is not feasible or is impossible deprives the first court of dominant jurisdiction. **Perry**, 66 S.W.3d at 252; **Wyatt**, 760 S.W.2d at 248.

3. Strategy. When two suits involving the same parties and the same dispute are on file in two counties, each party will want to abate the other party's suit. A party must make a strategic decision—whether to file a motion to abate the suit in which it is a defendant or to move the other suit forward and force the defendant in that suit to file a motion to abate.

§3.3 Abate—dispute subject to arbitration. A defendant may file a motion to abate requesting a suspension of the suit when the dispute should have been submitted to arbitration. See "Arbitration," ch. 4-C, §1 et seq.

§3.4 Abate—administrative agency has primary jurisdiction. A defendant may file a motion to abate requesting a suspension of the suit when an administrative agency has primary jurisdiction over the dispute (i.e., when both the agency and the court have authority to make an initial determination in the dispute). **In re Southwestern Bell Tel. Co.**, 226 S.W.3d 400, 403 (Tex.2007); **Subaru of Am., Inc. v. David McDavid Nissan, Inc.**, 84 S.W.3d 212, 221 (Tex.2002); *see* **Forest Oil Corp. v. El Rucio Land & Cattle Co.**, 518 S.W.3d 422, 429–30 (Tex.2017) (primary-jurisdiction doctrine does not apply to inherently judicial claims, such as trespass); *see also* **O'Neal v. Ector Cty. ISD**, 251 S.W.3d 50, 52 (Tex.2008) (abatement may also be appropriate if agency has exclusive jurisdiction over some claims but no jurisdiction over others). The movant should allege that the trial court should allow the administrative agency to initially hear the dispute because (1) the issues involved require the special competence of the agency's experts and (2) great benefit is derived from the agency's uniform interpretation of its laws and regulations. *See* **Forest Oil**, 518 S.W.3d at 429–30; **In re Southwestern Bell**, 226 S.W.3d at 403; **Subaru of Am.**, 84 S.W.3d at 221. When the primary-jurisdiction doctrine requires a trial court to defer to an agency to make an initial determination, the court should abate the suit until the agency has had an opportunity to act. **Forest Oil**, 518 S.W.3d at 430; **Subaru of Am.**, 84 S.W.3d at 221. But when an administrative agency has exclusive jurisdiction over the dispute, dismissal is mandatory, and the defendant should file a plea to the jurisdiction instead of a motion to abate. See "Administrative agency has exclusive jurisdiction," ch. 3-F, §3.6.

§3.5 Abate—insurance disputes. When breach-of-contract and bad-faith claims (i.e., contractual and extracontractual claims) are brought in the same suit, an insurer can seek to sever the claims and abate the bad-faith claim until liability on the insurance contract is determined. *See* **Liberty Nat'l Fire Ins. v. Akin**, 927 S.W.2d 627, 630 (Tex.1996); **In re Progressive Cty. Mut. Ins.**, 439 S.W.3d 422, 425 (Tex.App.—Houston [1st Dist.] 2014, orig. proceeding); **In re State Farm Mut. Auto. Ins.**, 395 S.W.3d 229, 233 (Tex.App.—El Paso 2012, orig. proceeding). See "Severing claims," **O'Connor's Texas Causes of Action**, ch. 13-B, §7.2 (2021 ed.).

§4. Motion to stay

§4.1 Motion to stay vs. motion to abate. A motion to stay is included in this subchapter, even though it is different in some respects from a motion to abate, because it is used instead of a motion to abate when the same suit is filed in a Texas court and in a court of another jurisdiction.

1. Comity. When a suit filed in a Texas court was first filed in a federal court or in another state's court, the defendant should file a motion to stay—not a motion to abate—in the Texas suit, requesting that the court suspend the Texas suit. A motion to abate contends that one court has dominant jurisdiction over the other court; a motion to stay recognizes that sister courts are foreign to each other, and the concept of dominant jurisdiction does not apply. **Crown Leasing Corp. v. Sims**, 92 S.W.3d 924, 927 (Tex.App.—Texarkana 2002, no pet.). As a matter of comity, it is customary for the second court to stay its proceedings for a reasonable time or until the first suit is resolved. *Id.* Many parties and even the appellate courts make the mistake of referring to a motion to stay as a motion to abate. *See, e.g.*, **VE Corp. v. Ernst & Young**, 860 S.W.2d 83, 84 (Tex.1993) (court's mistake); **Crown Leasing**, 92 S.W.3d at 926–27 (party's mistake).

2. Discretion. When a party makes a motion to stay in a Texas court because the same suit was first filed in a federal court or in another state's court, the court's ruling is within its discretion. The difference between the rulings on a motion to abate and a motion to stay is that the court must grant a proper motion to abate but can deny a proper motion to stay. **Williamson v. Tucker**, 615 S.W.2d 881, 886 (Tex.App.—Dallas 1981, writ ref'd n.r.e.). The court's ruling on a motion to stay will be reversed only if the court abuses its discretion by its ruling. *Id.*; *see* **In re State Farm Mut. Auto. Ins.**, 192 S.W.3d 897, 903 (Tex.App.—Tyler 2006, orig. proceeding) (trial court's ruling on motion to stay reversed for abuse of discretion). Because the granting of a motion to stay is within the trial court's discretion, the court can consider a number of factors before ruling on a motion to stay. *See* **In re State Farm**, 192 S.W.3d at 901.

(1) First suit. Which suit was filed first? **In re State Farm**, 192 S.W.3d at 901.

(2) Same parties. Are the parties the same in both suits? **In re State Farm**, 192 S.W.3d at 901; *see, e.g.*, **Williamson**, 615 S.W.2d at 886 (no abuse of discretion to deny motion to stay because federal suit involved numerous parties who were not parties to state suit).

(3) Same suit. Do the suits involve the same cause of action, concern the same subject matter, involve the same issues, and seek the same relief? **In re State Farm**, 192 S.W.3d at 901.

(4) Effect of judgment. What will be the effect of a judgment in the second suit on any order or judgment in the first suit? **In re State Farm**, 192 S.W.3d at 901.

§4.2 Stay—same dispute in another state's court. A defendant may file a motion to stay in a Texas court requesting that the court suspend the case because the same case was first filed in another state's court. *See, e.g.*, **In re State Farm Mut. Auto. Ins.**, 192 S.W.3d 897, 899 (Tex.App.—Tyler 2006, orig. proceeding) (first suit filed in Louisiana; D in first suit entitled to stay of Texas suit); **Crown Leasing Corp. v. Sims**, 92 S.W.3d 924, 927 (Tex.App.—Texarkana 2002, no pet.) (first suit filed in Florida; D in first suit entitled to stay of Texas suit). See **O'Connor's Texas Civil Forms**, FORM 3I:2 (2020 ed.).

Note

When the same case is filed in a Texas court and another state's court, a defendant may be able to file an application for an antisuit injunction in the Texas court to enjoin the plaintiff from proceeding with the suit in the other state's court. See ***Golden Rule Ins. v. Harper****, 925 S.W.2d 649, 651 (Tex.1996). See "CPRC §65.011," ch. 2-D, §4.1.1(2)(b). For details on the injunction process, see "Injunctive Relief," ch. 2-D, §1 et seq.*

§4.3 Stay—same dispute in federal court. A defendant may file a motion to stay in a Texas court requesting that the court suspend the case because the same case was first filed in a federal court. *See, e.g.*, **Space Master Int'l v. Porta-Kamp Mfg. Co.**, 794 S.W.2d 944, 946 (Tex.App.—Houston [1st Dist.] 1990, no writ) (first suit removed to federal court in Massachusetts; P in first suit entitled to stay of Texas suit); **Alpine Gulf, Inc. v. Valentino**, 563 S.W.2d 358, 359 (Tex.App.—Houston [14th Dist.] 1978, writ ref'd n.r.e.) (first suit filed in federal court in New York; D in first suit entitled to stay of Texas suit). See **O'Connor's Texas Civil Forms**, FORM 3I:2 (2020 ed.).

§5. Response

§5.1 Cure. The plaintiff may agree with the motion to abate and cure the defect. For example, when a motion to abate is filed in the second court on the ground that the first court has dominant jurisdiction, there is no longer a reason to abate if the plaintiff dismisses the first suit. *See* **Pleasants v. Emmons**, 871 S.W.2d 296, 298 (Tex.App.—Eastland 1994, no writ).

§5.2 Object. The plaintiff may file a response that challenges the factual matters alleged by the defendant. See **O'Connor's Texas Civil Forms**, FORM 3I:3 (2020 ed.). The response should follow the format of the motion to abate. It should be verified and, if necessary, include affidavits.

§6. Hearing

§6.1 Evidence. The hearing on a motion to abate is for the receipt of evidence, not just for argument. *See* **Upchurch v. Albear**, 5 S.W.3d 274, 277 & n.4 (Tex.App.—Amarillo 1999, pet. denied). The defendant must introduce evidence in support of its motion. **Bernal v. Garrison**, 818 S.W.2d 79, 82 (Tex.App.—Corpus Christi 1991, writ denied). When a defendant does not introduce evidence to support its motion to abate, the court must overrule it, unless the matters alleged in the motion appear on the face of the plaintiff's pleadings. *See id.* at 83; *see also* **Brazos Elec. Power Coop. v. Weatherford ISD**, 453 S.W.2d 185, 189 (Tex.App.—Fort Worth 1970, writ ref'd n.r.e.) (reversible error for abatement to be sustained without any evidence).

§6.2 No jury. The hearing is before the court, not a jury. **Union Pac. Fuels, Inc. v. Johnson**, 909 S.W.2d 130, 135 (Tex.App.—Houston [14th Dist.] 1995, orig. proceeding); **Miller v. Stout**, 706 S.W.2d 785, 787 (Tex.App.—San Antonio 1986, no writ).

§6.3 Waiver. A motion to abate is waived if it is not set for a hearing before the trial or made in a timely manner. *See* **Wyatt v. Shaw Plumbing Co.**, 760 S.W.2d 245, 248 (Tex.1988), *overruled on other grounds*, **In re J.B. Hunt Transp.**, 492 S.W.3d 287 (Tex.2016); **In re King**, 478 S.W.3d 930, 933 (Tex.App.—Dallas 2015, orig. proceeding); **Mekeel v. U.S. Bank**, 355 S.W.3d 349, 353 (Tex.App.—El Paso 2011, pet. dism'd).

§6.4 Burden of proof. The defendant has the burden of proof on the allegations in its motion to abate. **Flowers v. Steelcraft Corp.**, 406 S.W.2d 199, 199 (Tex.1966); **Southern Cty. Mut. Ins. v. Ochoa**, 19 S.W.3d 452, 469 (Tex.App.—Corpus Christi 2000, no pet.); **Lopez v. Texas Workers' Comp. Ins. Fund**, 11 S.W.3d 490, 493 (Tex.App.—Austin 2000, pet. denied). The defendant must prove the relevant facts by a preponderance of the evidence. **Lopez**, 11 S.W.3d at 493; **Bernal v. Garrison**, 818 S.W.2d 79, 82 (Tex.App.—Corpus Christi 1991, writ denied); **Brazos Elec. Power Coop. v. Weatherford ISD**, 453 S.W.2d 185, 188 (Tex.App.—Fort Worth 1970, writ ref'd n.r.e.). If the defendant does not disprove the facts in the plaintiff's petition, the court must accept the facts as true. **Bernal**, 818 S.W.2d at 82; **Seth v. Meyer**, 730 S.W.2d 884, 885 (Tex.App.—Fort Worth 1987, no writ).

§7. Order

§7.1 Motion overruled + determination of fact issue. In cases involving a question of dominant jurisdiction, the court where the second suit was filed will acquire dominant jurisdiction—and the case will proceed to trial in that court—if it determines that an exception to the dominant jurisdiction of the first court applies and overrules the defendant's motion to abate. *See* **Curtis v. Gibbs**, 511 S.W.2d 263, 267 (Tex.1974) (second court has jurisdiction to rule on motion to abate and fact issues raised by allegations in motion and in opposition to motion); **In re Henry**, 274 S.W.3d 185, 191 (Tex.App.—Houston [1st Dist.] 2008, orig. proceeding) (mere fact that second court is first to rule on motion to abate does not vest second court with dominant jurisdiction); **4M Linen & Unif. Sup. Co. v. W.P. Ballard & Co.**, 793 S.W.2d 320, 322 (Tex.App.—Houston [1st Dist.] 1990, writ denied) (second court acquires dominant jurisdiction if it resolves fact issue, such as estoppel, against D). The first court cannot enjoin the second court from proceeding to trial. **Johnson v. Avery**, 414 S.W.2d 441, 442–43 (Tex.1966). If the first court continues to issue conflicting orders in the case, that court is subject to mandamus. **Hall v. Lawlis**, 907 S.W.2d 493, 494 (Tex.1995), *overruled on other grounds*, **In re J.B. Hunt Transp.**, 492 S.W.3d 287 (Tex.2016). See "Mandamus," ch. 3-I, §8.3.

§7.2 Motion sustained. If the motion to abate is sustained, the case is abated until the obstacle to its prosecution is removed. **Texas Hwy. Dept. v. Jarrell**, 418 S.W.2d 486, 488 (Tex.1967). A court must set the terms for the abatement; a case cannot be abated indefinitely. **Gebhardt v. Gallardo**, 891 S.W.2d 327, 332 (Tex.App.—San Antonio 1995, orig. proceeding).

1. Suspending suit. The order sustaining a motion to abate suspends all action in the suit until the cause of the abatement is cured. **Permanente Med. Ass'n v. Johnson**, 917 S.W.2d 515, 517 (Tex.App.—Waco 1996, orig. proceeding);

see **America Online, Inc. v. Williams**, 958 S.W.2d 268, 272 (Tex.App.—Houston [14th Dist.] 1997, no pet.). The parties should not attempt to engage in discovery while an abatement is in effect; discovery requests filed during abatement are invalid and are not revived when the suit is revived. **Lumbermens Mut. Cas. Co. v. Garza**, 777 S.W.2d 198, 199 (Tex.App.—Corpus Christi 1989, orig. proceeding). The abatement prevents both the court and the parties from taking any action in the case. **In re Kimball Hill Homes**, 969 S.W.2d 522, 527 (Tex.App.—Houston [14th Dist.] 1998, orig. proceeding). But the abatement does not prevent the plaintiff from dismissing claims or taking a nonsuit. **United Oil & Minerals, Inc. v. Costilla Energy, Inc.**, 1 S.W.3d 840, 846 (Tex.App.—Corpus Christi 1999, pet. dism'd).

Practice Tip

If you want to continue with discovery, ask that the trial court's order state that discovery is exempt from the abatement. In other words, ask for a partial abatement.

2. Reviving suit. When the cause for the abatement is cured, the suit may be revived if anything remains to be litigated. **Texas Empls. Ins. v. Baeza**, 584 S.W.2d 317, 321 (Tex.App.—Amarillo 1979, no writ).

3. Dismissing suit. If the trial court grants a motion to abate and the plaintiff refuses to cure the defect, the court may dismiss the suit. The dismissal should be without prejudice. *See* **Gordon v. Jones**, 196 S.W.3d 376, 386 (Tex.App.—Houston [1st Dist.] 2006, no pet.); **M&M Constr. Co. v. Great Am. Ins.**, 747 S.W.2d 552, 555 (Tex.App.—Corpus Christi 1988, no writ). The court cannot dismiss the suit immediately after granting the motion to abate; it must give the party whose pleadings were attacked the opportunity to amend to cure the defect. **Martin v. Dosohs I, Ltd.**, 2 S.W.3d 350, 354 (Tex.App.—San Antonio 1999, pet. denied); **Lighthouse Ch. v. Texas Bank**, 889 S.W.2d 595, 600 (Tex.App.—Houston [14th Dist.] 1994, writ denied); **Polk v. Braddock**, 864 S.W.2d 78, 80 (Tex.App.—Dallas 1992, no writ).

§8. Review

§8.1 Interlocutory appeal.

1. Most orders. Generally, there is no interlocutory appeal from a ruling on a motion to abate. *See* Tex. Civ. Prac. & Rem. Code §51.014(a); **Serrano v. Union Planter's Bank**, 155 S.W.3d 381, 382 (Tex.App.—El Paso 2004, no pet.). However, a trial court can, on its own initiative or on a party's motion, allow an interlocutory appeal from an order that is not otherwise appealable if certain conditions are met. *See* Tex. Civ. Prac. & Rem. Code §51.014(d); Tex. R. Civ. P. 168. Although the trial court can grant permission to appeal, the court of appeals has discretion to accept or refuse to hear the appeal. *See* Tex. Civ. Prac. & Rem. Code §51.014(f). See "Interlocutory appeal by permission," **O'Connor's Texas Civil Appeals**, ch. 3-P, §2.1 (2020 ed.).

2. Order denying arbitration. An order denying a motion to abate for arbitration in a suit that is subject to the Texas Arbitration Act can be appealed before final judgment. See "Order denying motion," ch. 4-C, §8.3.1(1)(a).

§8.2 Appeal after final judgment. Generally, the order on a motion to abate is reviewable on appeal only after the case is terminated by a final judgment. **Johnson v. Avery**, 414 S.W.2d 441, 443 (Tex.1966); *see also* **Wyatt v. Shaw Plumbing Co.**, 760 S.W.2d 245, 248 (Tex.1988) (Supreme Court reversed judgment from Nueces County court, which denied D's plea in abatement, with instructions to abate until after suit was completed in Duval County), *overruled on other grounds*, **In re J.B. Hunt Transp.**, 492 S.W.3d 287 (Tex.2016).

1. Standard of review. On appeal, the standard of review on a motion to abate is for abuse of discretion. **Dolenz v. Continental Nat'l Bank**, 620 S.W.2d 572, 575 (Tex.1981); **Dahl v. Hartman**, 14 S.W.3d 434, 436 (Tex.App.—Houston [14th Dist.] 2000, pet. denied); *see* **In re J.B. Hunt Transp.**, 492 S.W.3d 287, 293 (Tex.2016).

2. Record. To properly present an allegation that the trial court erred in its ruling on a motion to abate, the complaining party must give the court of appeals a record of the hearing on the motion. **4M Linen & Unif. Sup. Co. v. W.P. Ballard & Co.**, 793 S.W.2d 320, 323 (Tex.App.—Houston [1st Dist.] 1990, writ denied). The reporter's record must contain the evidence from the hearing on the motion to abate and from the trial. *See* **In re Guardianship of Berry**, 105 S.W.3d 665, 667 (Tex.App.—Beaumont 2003, no pet.) (if trial court held evidentiary hearing and appellant does not provide

record, appellate court will presume evidence supported trial court's order); **Hartley v. Coker**, 843 S.W.2d 743, 748 (Tex.App.—Corpus Christi 1992, no writ) (same); *see, e.g.*, **Hiles v. Arnie & Co.**, 402 S.W.3d 820, 827–28 (Tex.App.—Houston [14th Dist.] 2013, pet. denied) (because nothing in record suggested evidentiary hearing took place, appellant was not required to present record of hearing on appeal).

§8.3 Mandamus. The appellate courts have granted mandamus to review abatement orders in the following situations: • The trial court abated the case indefinitely. **Texas Mut. Ins. v. Sonic Sys. Int'l**, 214 S.W.3d 469, 482 (Tex.App.—Houston [14th Dist.] 2006, orig. proceeding); **Gebhardt v. Gallardo**, 891 S.W.2d 327, 333 (Tex.App.—San Antonio 1995, orig. proceeding). • The trial court refused to sustain a proper plea in abatement when one court had obtained dominant jurisdiction. **In re Red Dot Bldg. Sys.**, 504 S.W.3d 320, 322 (Tex.2016); **In re J.B. Hunt Transp.**, 492 S.W.3d 287, 299–300 (Tex.2016); **Curtis v. Gibbs**, 511 S.W.2d 263, 267 (Tex.1974). • The trial court sustained a plea in abatement that suspended the suit, but no other court was willing to go forward. **Trapnell v. Hunter**, 785 S.W.2d 426, 429 (Tex.App.—Corpus Christi 1990, orig. proceeding); *see* **In re Sims**, 88 S.W.3d 297, 306 (Tex.App.—San Antonio 2002, orig. proceeding) (by granting plea in abatement, court effectively refused to proceed to trial). • The plaintiff did not give notice of the claim before suit was filed as required by statute. **Hines v. Hash**, 843 S.W.2d 464, 469 (Tex.1992) (DTPA); **In re Kimball Hill Homes**, 969 S.W.2d 522, 526–27 (Tex.App.—Houston [14th Dist.] 1998, orig. proceeding) (Residential Construction Liability Act); **Permanente Med. Ass'n v. Johnson**, 917 S.W.2d 515, 517 (Tex.App.—Waco 1996, orig. proceeding) (medical malpractice).

Note

In ***In re J.B. Hunt Transp.****, the Supreme Court clarified the standard for granting mandamus review of an improperly denied plea in abatement in dominant-jurisdiction cases. See* ***In re J.B. Hunt Transp.****, 492 S.W.3d at 299–300. The Court held that a defendant is required to show only that the trial court abused its discretion in denying the plea. Id.; see* ***In re Red Dot Bldg.****, 504 S.W.3d at 322. The Court clarified that, in an earlier opinion, it had expressly abrogated its opinion in* ***Abor v. Black****, 695 S.W.2d 564 (Tex.1985), which held that mandamus was proper to review the denial of a plea in abatement only when the two courts were directly interfering with each other by issuing conflicting orders or injunctions. See* ***In re J.B. Hunt Transp.****, 492 S.W.3d at 298–99.*

J. Motion to Quash—Challenging the Service

§1. General

Practice Tip

A defendant should avoid filing a motion to quash service. The benefit of a motion to quash (the delayed date for answering) is greatly outweighed by the risk of filing a late answer and having a default judgment rendered.

§1.1 Rule. Tex. R. Civ. P. 122.

§1.2 Purpose. A motion to quash is used to challenge defects in the citation or the service of process. **Kawasaki Steel Corp. v. Middleton**, 699 S.W.2d 199, 203 (Tex.1985); **Texas DPS v. Kreipe**, 29 S.W.3d 334, 336 (Tex.App.—Houston [14th Dist.] 2000, pet. denied). A successful motion to quash service merely delays the date when the defendant must answer the plaintiff's suit. **Kawasaki Steel**, 699 S.W.2d at 202; **In re Quinones**, 557 S.W.3d 647, 649 (Tex.App.—El Paso 2017, orig. proceeding); **Kreipe**, 29 S.W.3d at 336; *see* Tex. R. Civ. P. 122. A motion to quash service is like a motion to abate in that it delays but does not end the suit. But a motion to quash cannot be used to challenge the court's jurisdiction over the defendant. *See* **Wheat v. Toone**, 700 S.W.2d 915, 915 (Tex.1985); **Kawasaki Steel**, 699 S.W.2d at 202–03. In fact, because a party makes a general appearance when it files a motion to quash, the motion actually confers jurisdiction. *See* **In re Quinones**, 557 S.W.3d at 649; **Onda Enters. v. Pierce**, 750 S.W.2d 812, 813–14 (Tex.App.—Tyler 1988, orig. proceeding).

Caution

*The Corpus Christi Court of Appeals, relying on **Kawasaki Steel**, said in dicta that a defendant must challenge inadequate allegations of personal jurisdiction by a motion to quash. **Exito Elecs. Co. v. Trejo**, 99 S.W.3d 360, 367 (Tex.App.—Corpus Christi 2003), rev'd on other grounds, 142 S.W.3d 302 (Tex.2004). Until the Supreme Court clarifies the issue, a party should not challenge inadequate allegations of personal jurisdiction by a motion to quash. By doing so, the defendant subjects itself to the court's jurisdiction. See Tex. R. Civ. P. 122. **Kawasaki Steel** does not support the dicta in **Exito Elecs.** See **Ennis v. Loiseau**, 164 S.W.3d 698, 704–05 (Tex.App.—Austin 2005, no pet.) (**Kawasaki Steel** required motion to quash for challenging only curable, procedural defects with service of process; special appearance is proper tool for raising challenge that D is not amenable to service of process in Texas). The only jurisdictional defect discussed in **Kawasaki Steel** was the failure to bring a suit under the correct statute. See **Kawasaki Steel**, 699 S.W.2d at 202 ("an attempt to bring the defendant before the court under the wrong statute does not authorize the use of the special appearance" (quoting Thode, In Personam Jurisdiction, 42 Tex.L.Rev. 279, 312 (1964))).*

§1.3 Forms. None.

§2. Motion to quash

A defendant may challenge defective service of citation with a motion to quash or a motion for new trial, depending on whether a no-answer default judgment was rendered.

§2.1 Motion to quash—no default judgment.

1. Resident defendant. If, before filing an answer, a defendant discovers that service of process was defective, the defendant may file a motion to quash service. *See* **Onda Enters. v. Pierce**, 750 S.W.2d 812, 814 (Tex.App.—Tyler 1988, orig. proceeding). The effect of the motion to quash is to make an appearance before the court and, when the motion is granted, to delay the filing of the answer. **Alcala v. Williams**, 908 S.W.2d 54, 56 (Tex.App.—San Antonio 1995, no writ); *see* **Allright, Inc. v. Roper**, 478 S.W.2d 245, 247–48 (Tex.App.—Houston [14th Dist.] 1972, writ dism'd).

2. Nonresident defendant. A nonresident defendant who intends to challenge personal jurisdiction should not file a motion to quash. *See, e.g.*, **Onda Enters.**, 750 S.W.2d at 813–14 (D should have filed special appearance, not motion to

quash). A special appearance is the correct motion to challenge personal jurisdiction. See "Special Appearance—Challenging Personal Jurisdiction," ch. 3-B, §1 et seq. If the defendant alternatively contends that service of process was technically defective, it should file a motion to quash after it files the special appearance and ensure that the special appearance is set for hearing first. *See* Tex. R. Civ. P. 120a(2).

§2.2 Motion for new trial after default judgment. Once a no-answer default judgment is rendered, any challenge to service can be made in a motion for new trial, with affidavits attached proving defective service. See "MNT after default judgment," ch. 10-B, §9. A motion for new trial must be filed within 30 days after the date of the default judgment. Tex. R. Civ. P. 329b(a). If the court grants the motion for new trial, the defendant will have more time to answer, counting from the date of the ruling on the motion for new trial. See "Time to answer," ch. 3-J, §4.2.1. If the court denies the motion for new trial, the defendant should perfect its appeal.

1. Resident defendant. If a resident defendant discovers that the service of process was defective after a no-answer default judgment was rendered but before the deadline to file a motion for new trial has expired, the defendant should file a motion for new trial to challenge service. See "Improper service + no-answer default," ch. 10-B, §9.1.1.

2. Nonresident defendant. If a nonresident defendant discovers that the service of process was defective after a no-answer default judgment was rendered but before the deadline to file a motion for new trial has expired, the defendant should first file a special appearance (alleging no personal jurisdiction) and then file a motion for new trial (alleging defective service). *See* Tex. R. Civ. P. 120a(1); *see, e.g.,* **Puri v. Mansukhani**, 973 S.W.2d 701, 707 (Tex.App.—Houston [14th Dist.] 1998, no pet.) (D filed motion for new trial subject to special appearance); *see also* **Koch Graphics, Inc. v. Avantech, Inc.**, 803 S.W.2d 432, 433 (Tex.App.—Dallas 1991, no writ) (D filed special appearance and then filed motion to quash, motion for new trial, and answer, all subject to special appearance). The defendant must request a ruling on the special appearance before a ruling on the motion for new trial. *See* Tex. R. Civ. P. 120a(2); **Landry v. Daigrepont**, 35 S.W.3d 265, 267–68 (Tex.App.—Corpus Christi 2000, no pet.).

§3. Response

In most cases, the plaintiff should not contest the defendant's motion to quash service and should encourage the trial court to grant the motion and see if the defendant files an answer as required. If the defendant does not file an answer by the new answer date, the plaintiff may take a default judgment. Tex. R. Civ. P. 122; **Kawasaki Steel Corp. v. Middleton**, 699 S.W.2d 199, 202 (Tex.1985).

§4. Order

§4.1 Court denies motion. If the court denies the motion to quash, the time for the defendant to file its answer is not extended.

§4.2 Court grants motion.

1. Time to answer. If the court grants the defendant's motion to quash or a motion for new trial challenging service, the defendant must file an answer on the first Monday after the expiration of 20 days from the date of the order. Tex. R. Civ. P. 122; *see* **Kawasaki Steel Corp. v. Middleton**, 699 S.W.2d 199, 202 (Tex.1985) (remedy for defective service is additional time to answer). The plaintiff is not required to re-serve the defendant. *See* Tex. R. Civ. P. 122; **In re Quinones**, 557 S.W.3d 647, 649 (Tex.App.—El Paso 2017, orig. proceeding). The defendant is deemed served when the trial court quashes the service or citation. Tex. R. Civ. P. 122.

2. No dismissal. Dismissal is not an available remedy for service being quashed. *See* Tex. R. Civ. P. 122; **Kawasaki Steel**, 699 S.W.2d at 202; **Texas DPS v. Kreipe**, 29 S.W.3d 334, 336 (Tex.App.—Houston [14th Dist.] 2000, pet. denied).

§5. Review

If the trial court denies the motion to quash and grants a default judgment against the defendant, the defendant can appeal that order after judgment becomes final. If the appellate court decides the trial court erred in denying the motion to quash, the appellate court will reverse the judgment and remand the case to the trial court, which will give the defendant more time to answer the suit. *See* **Boreham v. Hartsell**, 826 S.W.2d 193, 197 (Tex.App.—Dallas 1992, no writ). On remand, the plaintiff does not need to reissue service. *See id.*

K. Motion to Dismiss—Anti-SLAPP Motion

§1. General

The Texas Citizens Participation Act (TCPA) allows for the dismissal of "SLAPP" actions—strategic lawsuits against public participation. *See* Senate Cmte. on State Affairs, Bill Analysis, Tex. H.B. 2973, 82nd Leg., R.S. (2011). The motion to dismiss such an action, which was created by the Legislature through the TCPA, is generally referred to as an "anti-SLAPP" motion. *Id.*; *see* **KBMT Oper. Co. v. Toledo**, 492 S.W.3d 710, 713 & n.6 (Tex.2016). The TCPA was enacted (1) to encourage and safeguard the constitutional rights of a person to petition, speak, and associate freely and otherwise participate in government as permitted by law and (2) to protect the rights of a person to file a meritorious lawsuit for a demonstrable injury. Tex. Civ. Prac. & Rem. Code §27.002. The TCPA does not abrogate or lessen any other defense, remedy, immunity, or privilege available under other constitutional, statutory, case, common-law, or rule provisions. Tex. Civ. Prac. & Rem. Code §27.011(a).

Note

In 2019, the Legislature approved significant amendments to the TCPA. See Acts 2019, 86th Leg., R.S., ch. 378, eff. Sept. 1, 2019. These amendments apply only to actions filed on or after September 1, 2019; actions filed before that date are governed by the former law. Acts 2019, 86th Leg., R.S., ch. 378, §§11, 12, eff. Sept. 1, 2019. Where appropriate, this subchapter addresses both the current and former law.

§1.1 Rules. None. See Tex. Civ. Prac. & Rem. Code ch. 27.

§1.2 Purpose. An anti-SLAPP motion is a mechanism for early dismissal of a lawsuit that threatens certain acts protected under the TCPA. *See* **Greer v. Abraham**, 489 S.W.3d 440, 442 (Tex.2016).

§1.3 Forms. See **O'Connor's Texas Civil Forms**, FORMS 3K:1 et seq. (2020 ed.).

§1.4 Other references. **O'Connor's Texas Civil Appeals** (2020 ed.).

§2. Defendant's burden

To prevail on an anti-SLAPP motion, the defendant must initially show that the plaintiff's action is a legal action under the TCPA and that there is a connection between the legal action and a protected act by the defendant. *See* Tex. Civ. Prac. & Rem. Code §27.005(b). Once the defendant has made the required showing, the burden shifts to the plaintiff to either (1) establish that the action is exempt from the TCPA or (2) establish by clear and specific evidence a prima facie case for each essential element of its claim. *See* Tex. Civ. Prac. & Rem. Code §§27.005(c), 27.010. See "Response," ch. 3-K, §4. If the plaintiff responds to the anti-SLAPP motion by establishing the essential elements of its claim, the defendant can still prevail by establishing a defense to the plaintiff's claim. *See* Tex. Civ. Prac. & Rem. Code §27.005(d). See "Reply," ch. 3-K, §5.

Note

Generally, a defendant files an anti-SLAPP motion in response to a plaintiff's legal action. See Tex. Civ. Prac. & Rem. Code §27.003(a); Senate Cmte. on State Affairs, Bill Analysis, Tex. H.B. 2973, 82nd Leg., R.S. (2011). But because a legal action can be a cross-claim or counterclaim from the defendant, the original plaintiff can also file an anti-SLAPP motion. See ***Hawxhurst v. Austin's Boat Tours****, 550 S.W.3d 220, 223 (Tex.App.—Austin 2018, no pet.). In this subchapter, "defendant" refers to the party who files an anti-SLAPP motion, and "plaintiff" refers to the party who files the legal action.*

§2.1 Legal action. To meet its burden under the TCPA, the defendant must show that it is seeking to dismiss a legal action. *See* Tex. Civ. Prac. & Rem. Code §27.003(a).

1. Definition.

(1) What is a legal action. For actions filed on or after September 1, 2019, a "legal action" includes the following: (1) a lawsuit, (2) a cause of action, (3) a petition, (4) a complaint, (5) a cross-claim, (6) a counterclaim, or (7) any

other judicial pleading or filing that requests legal, declaratory, or equitable relief. Tex. Civ. Prac. & Rem. Code §27.001(6); *see, e.g.*, **State v. Harper**, 562 S.W.3d 1, 8–9 (Tex.2018) (petition to remove D from hospital-board position sought legal relief and thus was a legal action under TCPA).

Note

Before the 2019 amendments to the TCPA, the definition of "legal action" did not expressly include judicial pleadings or filings that requested declaratory relief. See Tex. Civ. Prac. & Rem. Code §27.001(6) (pre-9-1-19 version).

(2) What is not a legal action. For actions filed on or after September 1, 2019, the term "legal action" does not include the following: (1) a procedural action taken or motion made in an action that does not amend or add a claim for legal, equitable, or declaratory relief, (2) alternative-dispute-resolution proceedings, or (3) postjudgment enforcement actions. Tex. Civ. Prac. & Rem. Code §27.001(6); *see, e.g.*, **Dow Jones & Co. v. Highland Capital Mgmt.**, 564 S.W.3d 852, 855–57 (Tex.App.—Dallas 2018, pet. denied) (third-party discovery subpoena is not a filing that seeks legal or equitable relief and thus is not a legal action under TCPA); **Roach v. Ingram**, 557 S.W.3d 203, 217–18 (Tex.App.—Houston [14th Dist.] 2018, pet. denied) (motion to dismiss under TCPA itself is not a legal action); *see also* **Amini v. Spicewood Springs Animal Hosp., LLC**, 550 S.W.3d 843, 844–45 (Tex.App.—Austin 2018, no pet.) (in context of TCPA as a whole, "legal action" contemplates trial-level proceedings; TCPA cannot be used to dismiss appeal).

Note

Before the 2019 amendments to the TCPA, the definition of "legal action" did not expressly exclude certain types of actions. See Tex. Civ. Prac. & Rem. Code. §27.001(6) (pre-9-1-19 version). Under the former definition, courts disagreed on whether a TRCP 202 petition for a presuit deposition was a legal action under the TCPA. Compare ***DeAngelis v. Protective Parents Coalition****, 556 S.W.3d 836, 849 (Tex.App.—Fort Worth 2018, no pet.) (TCPA applies because TRCP 202 petition is a "petition" or "other judicial pleading or filing that requests legal or equitable relief"), and* ***In re Elliott****, 504 S.W.3d 455, 463 (Tex.App.—Austin 2016, orig. proceeding) (same), with* ***Hughes v. Giammanco****, 579 S.W.3d 672, 678–79 (Tex.App.—Houston [1st Dist.] 2019, no pet.) (TRCP 202 petition asserts no substantive claim or cause of action on which relief can be granted and thus is not a legal action under TCPA). It is unclear whether courts will construe a TRCP 202 petition as being excluded from the amended definition of "legal action" under CPRC §27.001(6).*

2. Covered legal actions.

(1) Generally. If the defendant can meet its burden under the TCPA, any cause of action not expressly exempt from the statute can be dismissed. *See, e.g.*, **Young v. Krantz**, 434 S.W.3d 335, 344 (Tex.App.—Dallas 2014, no pet.) (intentional infliction of emotional distress), *disapproved on other grounds*, **In re Lipsky**, 460 S.W.3d 579 (Tex.2015); **United Food & Commercial Workers Int'l Un. v. Wal-Mart Stores**, 430 S.W.3d 508, 509–10 (Tex.App.—Fort Worth 2014, no pet.) (trespass); **Better Bus. Bur. v. BH DFW, Inc.**, 402 S.W.3d 299, 312 (Tex.App.—Dallas 2013, pet. denied) (breach of contract); *see also* **Cavin v. Abbott**, 545 S.W.3d 47, 65–66 (Tex.App.—Austin 2017, no pet.) (TCPA is implicated by "vast array of 'garden-variety tort claims'"; Ps' suit asserted theories of defamation, conversion, interference with existing contract, and abuse of process, among others).

(2) Actions described by CPRC §27.010(b). For actions filed on or after September 1, 2019, the legal actions described by CPRC §27.010(b) are specifically covered by the TCPA, notwithstanding the exemptions in CPRC §27.010(a)(2), (7), and (12). See "Acts described by CPRC §27.010(b)," ch. 3-K, §2.3.2; "Legal action is exempt from TCPA," ch. 3-K, §4.2.2(1)(d).

(3) Family-violence actions. For actions filed on or after September 1, 2019, the TCPA covers a legal action that is (1) against a victim or alleged victim of family violence or dating violence as defined by Family Code chapter 71 or of an offense under Penal Code chapter 20, 20A, 21, or 22 and (2) based on or in response to a public or private communication. Tex. Civ. Prac. & Rem. Code §27.010(c).

3. Exempt legal actions. Certain legal actions are exempt from the TCPA; however, the plaintiff—not the defendant—has the burden of proving that a legal action is exempt. *See* Tex. Civ. Prac. & Rem. Code §27.010; **Kirkstall Rd. Enters. v. Jones**, 523 S.W.3d 251, 253 (Tex.App.—Dallas 2017, no pet.); **Newspaper Holdings, Inc. v. Crazy Hotel Assisted Living, Ltd.**, 416 S.W.3d 71, 89 (Tex.App.—Houston [1st Dist.] 2013, pet. denied), *overruled on other grounds*, **Castleman v. Internet Money Ltd.**, 546 S.W.3d 684 (Tex.2018). See "Legal action is exempt from TCPA," ch. 3-K, §4.2.2(1)(d).

§2.2 Connection between legal action and protected act. To meet its burden under the TCPA, the defendant must show that there is a certain connection between the legal action and an act protected under the TCPA. *See* Tex. Civ. Prac. & Rem. Code §§27.003(a), 27.005(b).

1. Required connection.

(1) Before 9-1-19. For actions filed before September 1, 2019, the defendant must show by a preponderance of the evidence that the legal action is based on, relates to, or is in response to the defendant's protected act. *See* Tex. Civ. Prac. & Rem. Code §27.003 (pre-9-1-19 version), §27.005(b) (pre-9-1-19 version). See "Acts protected by right of free speech, right to petition, or right of association," ch. 3-K, §2.3.1. At a minimum, the "based on, related to, or in response to" language requires a legal action to be factually predicated on alleged conduct that could fall within the definition of a protected act. *E.g.*, **Cavin v. Abbott**, 545 S.W.3d 47, 65 (Tex.App.—Austin 2017, no pet.) (Ps' claims for defamation and tortious interference were factually predicated on Ds' statements about mental illness and abuse). Generally, all that is required is that there be some sort of connection, reference, or relationship between the legal action and a protected act. *See id.* at 69–70 ("relates to" and "in response to" are not limited by nature, directness, or strength of connections between legal action and protected act); *see also* **ExxonMobil Pipeline Co. v. Coleman**, 512 S.W.3d 895, 900 (Tex.2017) (communication "in connection with" matter of public concern under CPRC §27.001(3) does not require more than tangential or remote relationship for TCPA to apply).

(2) On or after 9-1-19. For actions filed on or after September 1, 2019, the defendant must demonstrate that the legal action is based on or is in response to (1) an act of the defendant protected by the right of free speech, right to petition, or right of association or (2) an act of the defendant described by CPRC §27.010(b). *See* Tex. Civ. Prac. & Rem. Code §§27.003(a), 27.005(b); **Youngblood v. Zaccaria**, ___ S.W.3d ___, 2020 WL 4606894 (Tex.App.—San Antonio 2020, pet. filed 9-25-20) (No. 04-19-00868-CV; 8-12-20). See "Protected act," ch. 3-K, §2.3; "On or after 9-1-19," ch. 3-K, §3.4.1(2). The TCPA no longer applies to actions that are merely "related to" a defendant's protected act. *See* Tex. Civ. Prac. & Rem. Code §§27.003(a), 27.005(b).

Note

Before the 2019 amendments to the TCPA, the defendant had to prove the requirements for dismissal by a preponderance of the evidence. See Tex. Civ. Prac. & Rem. Code §27.005(b) (pre-9-1-19 version). Under the amended statute, the defendant must simply "demonstrate" the requirements for dismissal. Tex. Civ. Prac. & Rem. Code §27.005(b). The TCPA does not elaborate on what it means to "demonstrate" the dismissal requirements.

2. Established by P's allegations. The basis of a legal action is determined by the plaintiff's allegations, not by the defendant's admissions or denials. **Hersh v. Tatum**, 526 S.W.3d 462, 467 (Tex.2017). Thus, even if the defendant asserts an actual-innocence defense—claiming it did not do the act that formed the basis of the legal action—it can still rely on the TCPA to obtain an order of dismissal. *See id.* at 463.

3. D's protected act. The defendant must show that its own protected act is the basis of the legal action; the defendant cannot use the TCPA to dismiss a legal action that interferes with the protected acts of third parties. *See* Tex. Civ. Prac. & Rem. Code §27.003(a) (if legal action is based on or is in response to party's protected act, that party may file motion to dismiss); *see, e.g.*, **LFMC Enters. v. Baker**, 546 S.W.3d 893, 897–98 (Tex.App.—Houston [1st Dist.] 2018, pet. denied) (TCPA did not apply when Ds, who owned nightclub premises, alleged that legal action was based on nightclub patrons' exercise of right of association); **Dolcefino v. Cypress Creek EMS**, 540 S.W.3d 194, 199–200 (Tex.App.—Houston [1st Dist.] 2017, no pet.) (TCPA did not apply when P sought declaration of its duty in response to request for information; legal action concerned P's own conduct and did not seek to prohibit any conduct or speech by D).

§2.3 Protected act. To meet its burden under the TCPA, the defendant must show that the plaintiff's legal action alleges an act that is protected by the TCPA. *See* Tex. Civ. Prac. & Rem. Code §§27.003(a), 27.005(b), 27.010(b).

1. Acts protected by right of free speech, right to petition, or right of association. To meet its burden under the TCPA, the defendant can show that the plaintiff's legal action alleges an act that is protected by the defendant's right of free speech, right to petition, or right of association. *See* Tex. Civ. Prac. & Rem. Code §§27.003(a), 27.005(b)(1).

Note

If the defendant alleges that the legal action involves an act protected by the defendant's right of free speech, right to petition, or right of association, the defendant must show only that the act is protected by one of those rights as defined by the TCPA; the defendant does not need to show that the act is constitutionally protected under the First Amendment. See ***Elite Auto Body LLC v. Autocraft Bodywerks, Inc.****, 520 S.W.3d 191, 203–04 (Tex.App.—Austin 2017, pet. dism'd) (constitutional concept of freedom of speech has no bearing when construing TCPA's plain-meaning definition of that term). But the plaintiff can offer proof that the defendant's act is not constitutionally protected as part of its prima facie case establishing each element of its claim. Id. at 204–05. See "P can establish prima facie case for legal action," ch. 3-K, §4.2.2(1)(f).*

(1) Right of free speech. To meet its burden, the defendant can show that the legal action alleges an act that is protected by the right of free speech. *See* Tex. Civ. Prac. & Rem. Code §27.005(b)(1)(A); *see also* **Sanchez v. Striever**, ___ S.W.3d ___, 2020 WL 5637879 (Tex.App.—Houston [14th Dist.] 2020, n.p.h.) (No. 14-19-00449-CV; 9-22-20) (TCPA does not protect assault as exercise of right of free speech). A communication made in connection with a matter of public concern is an act protected by the right of free speech. Tex. Civ. Prac. & Rem. Code §27.001(3); **Lippincott v. Whisenhunt**, 462 S.W.3d 507, 509 (Tex.2015).

(a) Communication. A communication is the making or submission of a statement or document in any form or medium, including oral, visual, written, audiovisual, or electronic. Tex. Civ. Prac. & Rem. Code §27.001(1); *see, e.g.*, **Better Bus. Bur. v. John Moore Servs.**, 441 S.W.3d 345, 353–54 (Tex.App.—Houston [1st Dist.] 2013, pet. denied) (ratings and reviews posted on nonprofit's website); **Newspaper Holdings, Inc. v. Crazy Hotel Assisted Living, Ltd.**, 416 S.W.3d 71, 81 (Tex.App.—Houston [1st Dist.] 2013, pet. denied) (newspaper articles), *overruled on other grounds*, **Castleman v. Internet Money Ltd.**, 546 S.W.3d 684 (Tex.2018). Protection is not limited to public communications; private communications may be protected as well. *E.g.*, **ExxonMobil Pipeline Co. v. Coleman**, 512 S.W.3d 895, 899 (Tex.2017) (TCPA applied to internal company communications); **Lippincott**, 462 S.W.3d at 509–10 (TCPA applied to internal company e-mails).

(b) Public concern.

[1] Before 9-1-19. For actions filed before September 1, 2019, the TCPA contains a nonexclusive list of issues that relate to a matter of public concern. *See* Tex. Civ. Prac. & Rem. Code §27.001(7) (pre-9-1-19 version). The TCPA requires only that the defendant's communication be "in connection with" a matter of public concern; it does not require that a communication specifically mention one of the matters of public concern listed in the statute, nor does it require more than a tangential relationship to those matters. **Coleman**, 512 S.W.3d at 900; **Cavin v. Abbott**, 545 S.W.3d 47, 62–63 (Tex.App.—Austin 2017, no pet.). A matter of public concern includes an issue related to the following:

[a] Health or safety. Tex. Civ. Prac. & Rem. Code §27.001(7)(A) (pre-9-1-19 version); **Coleman**, 512 S.W.3d at 899; *see, e.g.*, **Hersh v. Tatum**, 526 S.W.3d 462, 468 (Tex.2017) (online blog about suicide prevention and awareness was protected communication); **Lippincott**, 462 S.W.3d at 509–10 (internal e-mails about medical services provided by health-care professional were protected communications); *see also* **Cavin**, 545 S.W.3d at 63–64 (health and safety under TCPA includes that of private parties in private dispute).

[b] Environmental, economic, or community well-being. Tex. Civ. Prac. & Rem. Code §27.001(7)(B) (pre-9-1-19 version); *e.g.*, **Adams v. Starside Custom Builders, LLC**, 547 S.W.3d 890, 896 (Tex.2018) (e-mail alleging that homeowners' association did not follow city ordinance on tree preservation was protected communication); **Coleman**, 512

S.W.3d at 899 (internal communications about employee's failure to check levels in chemical storage tank were protected communications); **Deaver v. Desai**, 483 S.W.3d 668, 672–73 (Tex.App.—Houston [14th Dist.] 2015, no pet.) (website posts alleging P committed identity theft were protected communications); **Newspaper Holdings**, 416 S.W.3d at 81 (newspaper articles alleging licensing and code violations by assisted-living facility were protected communications).

[c] The government. Tex. Civ. Prac. & Rem. Code §27.001(7)(C) (pre-9-1-19 version); *e.g.*, **Shipp v. Malouf**, 439 S.W.3d 432, 438–39 (Tex.App.—Dallas 2014, pet. denied) (television broadcast about dentist's alleged Medicaid fraud was protected communication), *disapproved on other grounds*, **In re Lipsky**, 460 S.W.3d 579 (Tex.2015); **Avery v. Baddour**, No. 04-16-00184-CV, 2016 WL 4208115 (Tex.App.—San Antonio 2016, pet. denied) (memo op.; 8-10-16) (newspaper article about secessionist group was protected communication).

[d] A public official or figure. Tex. Civ. Prac. & Rem. Code §27.001(7)(D) (pre-9-1-19 version); *e.g.*, **Cruz v. Van Sickle**, 452 S.W.3d 503, 514–15 (Tex.App.—Dallas 2014, pet. denied) (judicial candidate was public figure under TCPA); *see, e.g.*, **Sloat v. Rathbun**, 513 S.W.3d 500, 508 (Tex.App.—Austin 2015, pet. dism'd) (wife of former high-ranking Scientology official was not public figure under TCPA).

[e] A good, product, or service in the marketplace. Tex. Civ. Prac. & Rem. Code §27.001(7)(E) (pre-9-1-19 version); *e.g.*, **Creative Oil & Gas, LLC v. Lona Hills Ranch, LLC**, 591 S.W.3d 127, 131 (Tex.2020) (private business discussions about oil-well production were not related to good or service in marketplace and thus were not protected communications); **Adams**, 547 S.W.3d at 894–95 (blog about homebuilder's business practices was protected communication); **Quintanilla v. West**, 534 S.W.3d 34, 45–46 (Tex.App.—San Antonio 2017) (filing of UCC financing statement was protected communication), *rev'd on other grounds*, 573 S.W.3d 237 (Tex.2019); **Deaver**, 483 S.W.3d at 672–73 (statements on website criticizing attorney's practices and ethics were protected communications); **Better Bus. Bur.**, 441 S.W.3d at 353–54 (ratings and reviews of area businesses posted on nonprofit's website for consumer use were protected communications).

[2] On or after 9-1-19. For actions filed on or after September 1, 2019, a matter of public concern is a statement or activity about one of the following:

[a] A public official, public figure, or other person who has drawn substantial public attention due to the person's official acts, fame, notoriety, or celebrity. Tex. Civ. Prac. & Rem. Code §27.001(7)(A).

[b] A matter of political, social, or other interest to the community. Tex. Civ. Prac. & Rem. Code §27.001(7)(B).

[c] A subject of concern to the public. Tex. Civ. Prac. & Rem. Code §27.001(7)(C).

(2) Right to petition. To meet its burden, the defendant can show that the legal action alleges an act that is protected by the right to petition. *See* Tex. Civ. Prac. & Rem. Code §27.005(b)(1)(B); **Creative Oil & Gas**, 591 S.W.3d at 137. Communications made in or about a judicial, legislative, executive, or other governmental proceeding are protected by the right to petition. *See* Tex. Civ. Prac. & Rem. Code §27.001(4); *see also* **Holcomb v. Waller Cty.**, 546 S.W.3d 833, 839–40 (Tex.App.—Houston [1st Dist.] 2018, pet. denied) (right to petition is protected regardless of whether petition merely complains or demands action). For the definition of a "communication," see "Communication," ch. 3-K, §2.3.1(1)(a). There is no requirement, however, that the subject matter of the proceeding must concern the government or a public interest for the protection to apply. *See* **Watson v. Hardman**, 497 S.W.3d 601, 606 (Tex.App.—Dallas 2016, no pet.). The following types of communication are acts protected by the right to petition:

(a) A communication in or about one of the following:

[1] A judicial proceeding. Tex. Civ. Prac. & Rem. Code §27.001(4)(A)(i); *e.g.*, **Youngkin v. Hines**, 546 S.W.3d 675, 680–81 (Tex.2018) (attorney's recitation of Rule 11 agreement in open court was communication made in judicial proceeding); *see, e.g.*, **Watson**, 497 S.W.3d at 606 (TRCP 202 petition was communication in or about judicial proceeding); *see also* **Johnson-Todd v. Morgan**, 480 S.W.3d 605, 611 (Tex.App.—Beaumont 2015, pet. denied) (person making the communication does not need to have been party to underlying judicial proceeding for protection to apply; protection extends to attorneys acting as agents for their clients when communications are made during judicial proceedings).

Note

It is unclear whether presuit communications fall within the scope of CPRC §27.001(4)(A)(i). Some courts have held that "judicial proceeding" means an actual, pending proceeding—not an anticipated or potential future proceeding—and thus that CPRC §27.001(4)(A)(i) does not protect presuit communications. E.g., ***QTAT BPO Solutions, Inc. v. Lee & Murphy Law Firm, G.P.****, 524 S.W.3d 770, 777–78 (Tex.App.—Houston [14th Dist.] 2017, pet. denied) (presuit communications with attorney);* ***Levatino v. Apple Tree Café Touring, Inc.****, 486 S.W.3d 724, 728–29 (Tex.App.—Dallas 2016, pet. denied) (presuit demand letters); see, e.g.,* ***Long Canyon Phase II & III Homeowners Ass'n v. Cashion****, 517 S.W.3d 212, 220 (Tex.App.—Austin 2017, no pet.) (presuit demand letter). One court, however, has held that a communication made in anticipation of litigation is protected under CPRC §27.001(4)(A)(i). See, e.g.,* ***Quintanilla****, 534 S.W.3d at 46 (demand letters showed that later-filed UCC financing statements were filed in context of impending litigation and statements were thus protected by right to petition); see also* ***Cuba v. Pylant****, 814 F.3d 701, 711–12 (5th Cir.2016) (communication that "pertained to" judicial proceeding was protected under TCPA even though there was no "live" proceeding when communication was made). Even if presuit communications are not protected under CPRC §27.001(4)(A)(i), they may be protected under §27.001(4)(E). See, e.g.,* ***Long Canyon****, 517 S.W.3d at 220 (presuit demand letters are protected under §27.001(4)(E));* ***Moricz v. Long****, No. 06-17-00011-CV, 2017 WL 3081512 (Tex.App.—Texarkana 2017, no pet.) (memo op.; 7-20-17) (same). See "Right to petition," ch. 3-K, §2.3.1(2)(e).*

[2] An official proceeding, other than a judicial proceeding, to administer the law. Tex. Civ. Prac. & Rem. Code §27.001(4)(A)(ii). An official proceeding is any type of administrative, executive, legislative, or judicial proceeding that may be conducted before a public servant. Tex. Civ. Prac. & Rem. Code §27.001(8). A public servant is a person elected, selected, appointed, employed, or otherwise designated as one of the following, even if the person has not yet qualified for office or assumed her duties: (1) an officer, employee, or agent of government, (2) a juror, (3) an arbitrator, referee, or other person who is authorized by law or private written agreement to hear or determine a case or controversy, (4) an attorney or notary public when participating in the performance of a governmental function, or (5) a person who is performing a governmental function under a claim of right but is not legally qualified to do so. Tex. Civ. Prac. & Rem. Code §27.001(9).

[3] An executive or other proceeding before a department or subdivision of the state or federal government. Tex. Civ. Prac. & Rem. Code §27.001(4)(A)(iii).

[4] A legislative proceeding, including a proceeding of a legislative committee. Tex. Civ. Prac. & Rem. Code §27.001(4)(A)(iv).

[5] A proceeding before an entity that requires by rule that public notice be given before its proceedings. Tex. Civ. Prac. & Rem. Code §27.001(4)(A)(v).

[6] A proceeding in or before a managing board of an educational or nonprofit institution supported directly or indirectly by public revenue. Tex. Civ. Prac. & Rem. Code §27.001(4)(A)(vi).

[7] A proceeding of the governing body of any political subdivision of the State. Tex. Civ. Prac. & Rem. Code §27.001(4)(A)(vii).

[8] A report of or debate and statements made in (1) an executive or other proceeding before a department or subdivision of the state or federal government, (2) a legislative proceeding, including a proceeding of a legislative committee, (3) a proceeding before an entity that requires by rule that public notice be given before its proceedings, (4) a proceeding in or before a managing board of an educational or nonprofit institution supported directly or indirectly by public revenue, or (5) a proceeding of the governing body of any political subdivision of the State. Tex. Civ. Prac. & Rem. Code §27.001(4)(A)(viii).

[9] A public meeting dealing with a public purpose, including statements and discussions at the meeting or other matters of public concern occurring at the meeting. Tex. Civ. Prac. & Rem. Code §27.001(4)(A)(ix). For the definition of "matters of public concern," see "Public concern," ch. 3-K, §2.3.1(1)(b).

(b) A communication in connection with an issue under consideration or review by a legislative, executive, judicial, or other governmental body or in another governmental or official proceeding. Tex. Civ. Prac. & Rem. Code §27.001(4)(B). A governmental proceeding is a proceeding, other than a judicial proceeding, by (1) an officer, official, or body of the State of Texas or a political subdivision of the State, including a board or commission, or (2) an officer, official, or body of the federal government. Tex. Civ. Prac. & Rem. Code §27.001(5). For the definition of an "official proceeding," see "Right to petition," ch. 3-K, §2.3.1(2)(a)[2].

(c) A communication reasonably likely to encourage consideration or review of an issue by a legislative, executive, judicial, or other governmental body or in another governmental or official proceeding. Tex. Civ. Prac. & Rem. Code §27.001(4)(C). For the definition of an "official proceeding," see "Right to petition," ch. 3-K, §2.3.1(2)(a)[2]; for the definition of a "governmental proceeding," see "Right to petition," ch. 3-K, §2.3.1(2)(b).

(d) A communication reasonably likely to secure public participation in an attempt to effect consideration of an issue by a legislative, executive, judicial, or other governmental body or in another governmental or official proceeding. Tex. Civ. Prac. & Rem. Code §27.001(4)(D). For the definition of an "official proceeding," see "Right to petition," ch. 3-K, §2.3.1(2)(a)[2]; for the definition of a "governmental proceeding," see "Right to petition," ch. 3-K, §2.3.1(2)(b).

(e) Any other communication that falls within the protection of the right to petition government under the U.S. or Texas Constitution. Tex. Civ. Prac. & Rem. Code §27.001(4)(E).

(3) Right of association. To meet its burden, the defendant can show that the legal action alleges an act that is protected by the right of association. *See* Tex. Civ. Prac. & Rem. Code §27.005(b)(1)(C).

(a) Before 9-1-19. For actions filed before September 1, 2019, a communication between individuals who join together to collectively express, promote, pursue, or defend common interests is an act protected by the right of association. Tex. Civ. Prac. & Rem. Code §27.001(2) (pre-9-1-19 version); *e.g.*, **Levatino**, 486 S.W.3d at 727–28 (attorney's communications with opposing counsel were not for purpose of promoting common interests and thus were not protected by right of association); **Backes v. Misko**, 486 S.W.3d 7, 20–21 (Tex.App.—Dallas 2015, pet. denied) (social-media discussions criticizing counter-P's business practices in horse-breeding industry were communications protected by right of association), *overruled on other grounds*, **Castleman v. Internet Money Ltd.**, 546 S.W.3d 684 (Tex.2018); *see also* **Kawcak v. Antero Res.**, 582 S.W.3d 566, 588 (Tex.App.—Fort Worth 2019, pet. denied) ("common" interest requires more than two tortfeasors conspiring to act tortiously for their own benefit). Protection applies to both public and private communications. **Fawcett v. Grosu**, 498 S.W.3d 650, 658 (Tex.App.—Houston [14th Dist.] 2016, pet. denied); **Fawcett v. Rogers**, 492 S.W.3d 18, 24–25 (Tex.App.—Houston [1st Dist.] 2016, no pet.); *see* **Lippincott**, 462 S.W.3d at 509 (right of free speech). For the definition of a "communication," see "Communication," ch. 3-K, §2.3.1(1)(a).

Note

*Before the 2019 amendments to the TCPA, some courts of appeals took a stringent approach when construing the right of association under the TCPA and suggested that a communication must involve public participation to be protected. See, e.g., **ExxonMobil Pipeline Co. v. Coleman**, 464 S.W.3d 841, 848–49 (Tex.App.—Dallas 2015), rev'd on other grounds, 512 S.W.3d 895 (Tex.2017); **Cheniere Energy, Inc. v. Lotfi**, 449 S.W.3d 210, 216 (Tex.App.—Houston [1st Dist.] 2014, no pet.).*

(b) On or after 9-1-19. For actions filed on or after September 1, 2019, the joining together to collectively express, promote, pursue, or defend common interests relating to a governmental proceeding or a matter of public concern is an act protected by the right of association. Tex. Civ. Prac. & Rem. Code §27.001(2). For what constitutes a matter of public concern, see "On or after 9-1-19," ch. 3-K, §2.3.1(1)(b)[2].

Note

Before the 2019 amendments to the TCPA, protection under the right of association applied to a communication between individuals. See Tex. Civ. Prac. & Rem. Code §27.001(2) (pre-9-1-19 version). The amended definition of the right of association does not include the "communication between individuals" language and requires that the association relate to a governmental proceeding or a matter of public concern. See Tex. Civ. Prac. & Rem. Code §27.001(2).

2. Acts described by CPRC §27.010(b). For actions filed on or after September 1, 2019, to meet its burden, the defendant can demonstrate that the legal action alleges an act described by CPRC §27.010(b). Tex. Civ. Prac. & Rem. Code §27.005(b)(2); *see* Tex. Civ. Prac. & Rem. Code §27.003(a). The following legal actions are protected under CPRC §27.010(b):

(1) A legal action that has all the following characteristics:

(a) The action arises from any act, whether public or private, of the person against whom the legal action is brought. Tex. Civ. Prac. & Rem. Code §27.010(b)(1).

(b) The action is related to the gathering, receiving, posting, or processing of information for communication to the public, whether or not the information is actually communicated. *Id.*

(c) The action is for the creation, dissemination, exhibition, or advertisement or other similar promotion of a dramatic, literary, musical, political, journalistic or otherwise artistic work, including audiovisual work regardless of the means of distribution, a motion picture, a television or radio program, or an article published in a newspaper, website, magazine, or other platform, no matter the method or extent of distribution. *Id.*

(2) A legal action against a person related to the communication, gathering, receiving, posting, or processing of consumer opinions or commentary, evaluations of consumer complaints, or reviews or ratings of businesses. Tex. Civ. Prac. & Rem. Code §27.010(b)(2).

§3. Motion

§3.1 Who can file. Generally, any person against whom a SLAPP action has been filed can file an anti-SLAPP motion. *See* Tex. Civ. Prac. & Rem. Code §27.003(a). A "person" can include a legal entity. Tex. Gov't Code §311.005(2). For actions filed on or after September 1, 2019, an anti-SLAPP motion cannot be brought by a governmental entity, an agency, or an official or employee acting in an official capacity. Tex. Civ. Prac. & Rem. Code §27.003(a). See **O'Connor's Texas Civil Forms**, FORM 3K:1 (2020 ed.).

§3.2 Deadline to file & serve.

1. Deadline to file.

(1) Generally—60 days after service of legal action. The anti-SLAPP motion generally must be filed within 60 days after service of the legal action. Tex. Civ. Prac. & Rem. Code §27.003(b). See "Computing filing deadlines," ch. 1-C, §7. This deadline is based on service of the original legal action that implicates the TCPA. **Estate of Check**, 438 S.W.3d 829, 837 (Tex.App.—San Antonio 2014, no pet.). If the defendant accepts or waives service of process by written memorandum under TRCP 119, the 60-day period will begin to run from the date the memorandum is filed with the trial-court clerk. **Grant v. Pivot Tech. Solutions, Ltd.**, 556 S.W.3d 865, 885 (Tex.App.—Austin 2018, pet. denied). If instead the defendant voluntarily appears by filing an answer before she receives service of the legal action, the 60-day period will begin to run on the date she appears. **Jordan v. Hall**, 510 S.W.3d 194, 198 (Tex.App.—Houston [1st Dist.] 2016, no pet.); *see* **Bacharach v. Garcia**, 485 S.W.3d 600, 602 (Tex.App.—Houston [14th Dist.] 2016, no pet.).

Note

The 60-day deadline for filing a motion to dismiss under the TCPA is tolled if the case is abated under the Defamation Mitigation Act. ***Hearst Newspapers, LLC v. Status Lounge Inc.****, 541 S.W.3d 881, 891 (Tex.App.—Houston [14th Dist.] 2017, no pet.). See "Defamation Mitigation Act,"* ***O'Connor's Texas Causes of Action****, ch. 18-A, §7 (2021 ed.).*

(2) Exceptions. The deadline for filing the anti-SLAPP motion may be extended in certain circumstances. For a general discussion of motions to extend time, see "Motion to extend time," ch. 1-C, §9.1.

(a) Amendment adds new parties or claims. The filing of an amended legal action (e.g., an amended counterclaim) may extend the deadline for filing the anti-SLAPP motion if the amendment adds new parties or claims. *See* **Jordan**, 510 S.W.3d at 198; **Estate of Check**, 438 S.W.3d at 837; **Better Bus. Bur. v. Ward**, 401 S.W.3d 440, 443 (Tex.App.—Dallas 2013, pet. denied). When an amendment adds new parties or claims, the deadline for filing an anti-SLAPP motion is reset for those claims and runs from the date the amended legal action was served. *See* **Estate of Check**, 438 S.W.3d at 837; *see, e.g.*, **Ward**, 401 S.W.3d at 443 (although original petition was served before enactment of TCPA, D was served with amended petition asserting new, individual claims after TCPA's effective date; deadline for filing anti-SLAPP motion to dismiss new claims was 60 days after amended petition was served).

(b) Good cause. The court may extend the deadline for filing an anti-SLAPP motion if the defendant shows good cause. Tex. Civ. Prac. & Rem. Code §27.003(b).

(c) Parties' agreement. For actions filed on or after September 1, 2019, the parties may agree to extend the deadline for filing an anti-SLAPP motion. Tex. Civ. Prac. & Rem. Code §27.003(b).

2. Deadline to serve. The TCPA does not specify a deadline for serving the anti-SLAPP motion, but local rules and TRCP 21(a) generally require any motions filed with the court to be served on opposing counsel on the same day.

§3.3 Hearing. See "Hearing," ch. 3-K, §6.

§3.4 Contents.

1. Grounds for TCPA's application.

(1) Before 9-1-19. For actions filed before September 1, 2019, the defendant must show by a preponderance of the evidence that the legal action is based on, related to, or in response to the defendant's exercise of its right of free speech, right to petition, or right of association. *See* Tex. Civ. Prac. & Rem. Code §27.003(a) (pre-9-1-19 version), §27.005(b) (pre-9-1-19 version). See "Defendant's burden," ch. 3-K, §2.

(2) On or after 9-1-19. For actions filed on or after September 1, 2019, the defendant must demonstrate that the legal action is based on or is in response to (1) an act of the defendant protected by the right of free speech, right to petition, or right of association or (2) an act of the defendant described by CPRC §27.010(b). *See* Tex. Civ. Prac. & Rem. Code §§27.003(a), 27.005(b). See "Defendant's burden," ch. 3-K, §2.

Caution

The 2019 amendments to CPRC §27.005(b) require a court to dismiss a legal action if a party demonstrates that the action is based on or in response to (1) the party's exercise of the right of free speech, right to petition, or right of association or (2) the act of a party described by CPRC §27.010(b). See Tex. Civ. Prac. & Rem. Code §27.005(b). The 2019 amendments to CPRC §27.003(a), however, allow a party to file a motion to dismiss if a legal action (1) is based on or in response to the party's exercise of the right of free speech, right to petition, or right of association or (2) arises from any act of the party in furtherance of the party's communication or conduct described by §27.010(b). See Tex. Civ. Prac. & Rem. Code §27.003(a). It is unclear whether the "arises from" language in §27.003(a) creates a

different burden for the movant than what is addressed in §27.005(b).

2. Evidence proving TCPA's application. The motion should be supported by admissible evidence in the form of pleadings and affidavits. Tex. Civ. Prac. & Rem. Code §27.006(a); *see* **Hersh v. Tatum**, 526 S.W.3d 462, 467 (Tex.2017) (when P's pleadings clearly show that legal action is covered by TCPA, D does not need to show more); **In re Elliott**, 504 S.W.3d 455, 462 (Tex.App.—Austin 2016, orig. proceeding) (movant is not required to present testimony or other evidence to meet her burden under TCPA). See "Verification & affidavits," ch. 1-B, §4.1.12. For actions filed on or after September 1, 2019, the motion can also be supported by any evidence that the court could consider under TRCP 166a. Tex. Civ. Prac. & Rem. Code §27.006(a). See "Summary-judgment evidence," ch. 7-B, §9.

3. Defenses to liability. Even if the plaintiff can prove the elements of its claim, the defendant can still prevail on the anti-SLAPP motion with evidence establishing a defense. *See* Tex. Civ. Prac. & Rem. Code §27.005(c), (d). See "P can establish prima facie case for legal action," ch. 3-K, §4.2.2(1)(f). If the defendant intends to claim such a defense, the defendant should raise the defense in its motion and attach sufficient affidavits and other evidence if necessary to establish the defense. *See* Tex. Civ. Prac. & Rem. Code §§27.005(d), 27.006(a); *see, e.g.*, **Youngkin v. Hines**, 546 S.W.3d 675, 683 (Tex.2018) (although D did not attach affidavit or other evidence to motion alleging attorney-immunity defense, memorandum that contained arguments required to support defense was sufficient). See "Verification & affidavits," ch. 1-B, §4.1.12. The defendant's burden depends on when the action was filed.

(1) Before 9-1-19. For actions filed before September 1, 2019, the defendant should establish by a preponderance of the evidence each essential element of any valid defenses to the plaintiff's claim. Tex. Civ. Prac. & Rem. Code §27.005(d) (pre-9-1-19 version); **D Mag. Partners v. Rosenthal**, 529 S.W.3d 429, 434 (Tex.2017); *e.g.*, **Youngkin**, 546 S.W.3d at 681 (D established defense of attorney immunity); *see, e.g.*, **Johnson-Todd v. Morgan**, 480 S.W.3d 605, 610 (Tex.App.—Beaumont 2015, pet. denied) (D established defense of judicial-communications privilege).

(2) On or after 9-1-19. For actions filed on or after September 1, 2019, the defendant should establish an affirmative defense or other grounds on which the defendant is entitled to judgment as a matter of law. Tex. Civ. Prac. & Rem. Code §27.005(d). See "Affirmative defenses," ch. 3-E, §5.

4. Request for attorney fees & costs. The defendant should request attorney fees and costs for bringing the anti-SLAPP motion. Tex. Civ. Prac. & Rem. Code §27.009(a)(1). The defendant should support its request with sufficient evidence establishing the amount of attorney fees and costs incurred in defending the legal action by either attaching documents to its motion or presenting affidavits at the hearing on the motion. *See* **Fawcett v. Grosu**, 498 S.W.3d 650, 665 (Tex.App.—Houston [14th Dist.] 2016, pet. denied). See "Evidence," ch. 1-H, §10.2.2.

5. Request for sanctions. The defendant should request sanctions against the plaintiff to deter the plaintiff from bringing similar actions. Tex. Civ. Prac. & Rem. Code §27.009(a)(2). See "Motion for Sanctions," ch. 5-K, §1 et seq.

§3.5 Effect of motion on discovery. The filing of an anti-SLAPP motion stays all discovery proceedings. Tex. Civ. Prac. & Rem. Code §27.003(c); *e.g.*, **In re Elliott**, 504 S.W.3d 455, 465 (Tex.App.—Austin 2016, orig. proceeding) (filing of anti-SLAPP motion should have stayed proceedings on petition to conduct presuit deposition under TRCP 202; trial court had no discretion to order TRCP 202 deposition before ruling on anti-SLAPP motion). The discovery stay remains in effect until the court grants or denies the anti-SLAPP motion. Tex. Civ. Prac. & Rem. Code §27.003(c). The court, on its own initiative or on a party's motion and for good cause shown, can order that specified and limited discovery relevant to the anti-SLAPP motion be conducted during the stay. Tex. Civ. Prac. & Rem. Code §27.006(b); *see* **Greer v. Abraham**, 489 S.W.3d 440, 443 (Tex.2016).

§4. Response

§4.1 Motion to conduct discovery. The plaintiff can respond to the anti-SLAPP motion by filing a motion asking the court to allow it to conduct discovery relevant to the anti-SLAPP motion. *See* Tex. Civ. Prac. & Rem. Code §27.006(b). See **O'Connor's Texas Civil Forms**, FORM 3K:2 (2020 ed.). The TCPA restricts the court to authorizing "specified and limited" discovery relevant to the motion. Tex. Civ. Prac. & Rem. Code §27.006(b); **In re SSCP Mgmt.**, 573 S.W.3d 464, 470 (Tex.App.—

Fort Worth 2019, orig. proceeding). Some merits-based discovery may be relevant to the extent that it helps the plaintiff present its prima facie case; however, the discovery should still be limited considering the prima facie standard requires only the minimum amount of evidence necessary to support a rational inference that a factual allegation is true. **In re SSCP Mgmt.**, 573 S.W.3d at 472. See "P can establish prima facie case for legal action," ch. 3-K, §4.2.2(1)(f).

Note

If discovery cannot be completed before the hearing on the anti-SLAPP motion, the plaintiff may file a motion to continue the hearing. See "Continuance for additional discovery," ch. 5-D, §8. Although there is no express authority in the TCPA for filing a motion for continuance, such authority is implied because a defendant can obtain a short delay of the dismissal hearing on a showing of good cause. See Tex. Civ. Prac. & Rem. Code §27.004(a). See "Deadline," ch. 3-K, §6.1.

1. Deadline to file & serve. The TCPA does not specify when to file and serve the motion to conduct discovery. Because the hearing on the anti-SLAPP motion must be set within 60 days after service of the motion, the plaintiff should file and serve the motion to conduct discovery as soon as possible after the anti-SLAPP motion is served. *See* Tex. Civ. Prac. & Rem. Code §27.004(a); *see, e.g.*, **Whisenhunt v. Lippincott**, 474 S.W.3d 30, 41 (Tex.App.—Texarkana 2015, no pet.) (motion to conduct discovery filed on day of hearing on anti-SLAPP motion was untimely), *overruled on other grounds*, **Castleman v. Internet Money Ltd.**, 546 S.W.3d 684 (Tex.2018). See "When to file," ch. 1-C, §5; "When to serve," ch. 1-D, §5.

Practice Tip

Because the plaintiff may file a response—and voluminous evidence—too close to the hearing for the defendant to fully process it, the defendant should consider asking the court to impose an evidence and briefing deadline when, for example, the parties are already before the court on a motion for continuance or motion to conduct discovery. See "Motion to conduct discovery," ch. 3-K, §4.1. Alternatively, an agreed briefing and evidentiary schedule could be a concession that the defendant seeks in exchange for consent to the plaintiff's request to reschedule a dismissal hearing. See "Hearing," ch. 3-K, §6.

2. Grounds. The plaintiff must show good cause to conduct discovery. Tex. Civ. Prac. & Rem. Code §27.006(b); *e.g.*, **In re SSCP Mgmt.**, 573 S.W.3d at 470–71 (good cause for discovery when P brought claim for fraud by nondisclosure and all documents and information relevant to P's prima facie case were in D's possession). Generalized, conclusory statements that discovery will help develop the plaintiff's claims are insufficient to show good cause. *See, e.g.*, **In re D.C.**, No. 05-13-00944-CV, 2013 WL 4041507 (Tex.App.—Dallas 2013, orig. proceeding) (memo op.; 8-9-13) (statement that P needed to conduct depositions to defend against motion to dismiss was insufficient to show good cause). Good cause can be difficult to prove, especially when the discovery sought is pertinent to only a few elements of a claim and the plaintiff cannot establish the other elements or cannot overcome an affirmative defense. *See, e.g.*, **Walker v. Schion**, 420 S.W.3d 454, 458 (Tex.App.—Houston [14th Dist.] 2014, no pet.) (denial of discovery of actual malice to prove defamation was affirmed because P lacked evidence of other elements).

§4.2 Response to anti-SLAPP motion. The plaintiff can oppose an anti-SLAPP motion by filing a response. *See* Tex. Civ. Prac. & Rem. Code §27.005(c). See **O'Connor's Texas Civil Forms**, FORM 3K:3 (2020 ed.).

1. Deadline to file & serve.

(1) Before 9-1-19. For actions filed before September 1, 2019, the TCPA does not specify when to file and serve the response. Because the hearing on the anti-SLAPP motion must be set within 60 days after service of the motion, the plaintiff should file and serve the response as soon as possible after the anti-SLAPP motion is served, unless local rules or a court order specifies otherwise. *See* Tex. Civ. Prac. & Rem. Code §27.004(a). See "When to file," ch. 1-C, §5; "When to serve," ch. 1-D, §5.

(2) On or after 9-1-19. For actions filed on or after September 1, 2019, the response must be filed no later than seven days before the date of the hearing on the anti-SLAPP motion unless otherwise provided by the parties' agree-

ment or a court order. Tex. Civ. Prac. & Rem. Code §27.003(e). The TCPA does not specify a deadline for serving the response, but local rules and TRCP 21(a) generally require any responses filed with the court to be served on opposing counsel on the same day.

2. Contents.

(1) Grounds. The plaintiff can oppose the anti-SLAPP motion on the following grounds:

(a) Motion is untimely. The plaintiff can oppose the anti-SLAPP motion on the ground that the motion was not timely filed and served. *See* Tex. Civ. Prac. & Rem. Code §27.003(b). See "Deadline to file & serve," ch. 3-K, §3.2.

(b) Hearing is untimely. The plaintiff can oppose the anti-SLAPP motion on the ground that the hearing was not timely. See "Hearing," ch. 3-K, §6.

(c) Evidence supporting motion is defective. The plaintiff can oppose the anti-SLAPP motion on the ground that some or all of the evidence submitted in support of the motion is inadmissible. *See* Tex. Civ. Prac. & Rem. Code §27.006(a). See "Objecting to Evidence," ch. 8-D, §1 et seq.

(d) Legal action is exempt from TCPA. The plaintiff can oppose the anti-SLAPP motion on the ground that the challenged legal action is exempt from the TCPA. *See* Tex. Civ. Prac. & Rem. Code §27.010; **Newspaper Holdings, Inc. v. Crazy Hotel Assisted Living, Ltd.**, 416 S.W.3d 71, 88 (Tex.App.—Houston [1st Dist.] 2013, pet. denied), *overruled on other grounds*, **Castleman v. Internet Money Ltd.**, 546 S.W.3d 684 (Tex.2018). The plaintiff has the burden to establish that a cause of action is exempt. *See* **Toth v. Sears Home Imprv. Prods.**, 557 S.W.3d 142, 152 (Tex.App.—Houston [14th Dist.] 2018, no pet.); **Kirkstall Rd. Enters. v. Jones**, 523 S.W.3d 251, 253 (Tex.App.—Dallas 2017, no pet.). The following legal actions are exempt from the TCPA:

[1] Enforcement actions. An enforcement action brought in the name of the State of Texas or a political subdivision of the State by the Attorney General, a district attorney, a criminal district attorney, or a county attorney is exempt from the TCPA. Tex. Civ. Prac. & Rem. Code §27.010(a)(1). Enforcement actions brought by a person or entity other than the Attorney General, a district attorney, a criminal district attorney, or a county attorney are not exempt. *See, e.g.*, **Commission for Lawyer Discipline v. Rosales**, 577 S.W.3d 305, 311–12 (Tex.App.—Austin 2019, pet. denied) (action brought by Commission for Lawyer Discipline was not exempt enforcement action). Although the TCPA does not explain what an enforcement action is, the Supreme Court has defined it as a "governmental attempt to enforce a substantive legal prohibition against unlawful conduct." *E.g.*, **State v. Harper**, 562 S.W.3d 1, 12–13 (Tex.2018) (action to remove hospital-board member from his position for incompetence was not enforcement action because removal was not based on any alleged unlawful conduct).

[2] Commercial-speech actions. A legal action involving certain commercial speech is generally exempt from the TCPA. *See* Tex. Civ. Prac. & Rem. Code §27.010(a)(2). The exemption applies to commercial speech that does no more than propose a commercial transaction (i.e., speech made for the purpose of securing sales of goods or services of the person making the statement). *See* **Castleman v. Internet Money Ltd.**, 546 S.W.3d 684, 690 (Tex.2018); **Toth**, 557 S.W.3d at 153. The TCPA does, however, specifically cover certain legal actions notwithstanding the exemptions in CPRC §27.010(a)(2). *See* Tex. Civ. Prac. & Rem. Code §27.010(b). See "Actions described by CPRC §27.010(b)," ch. 3-K, §2.1.2(2). For the commercial-speech exemption to apply, the cause of action must meet the following criteria.

Note

Some courts of appeals have used a four-part test based on the California anti-SLAPP statute to determine whether the exemption under the TCPA applies. ***Castleman****, 546 S.W.3d at 686. The Texas Supreme Court recently rejected relying on the California four-part test in construing the TCPA and set out its own test for determining application of the commercial-speech exemption. See id. at 687–88. Although the Court refused to rely on courts' construction of the California commercial-speech exemption, the Court determined that the exemption under the TCPA carries the same meaning. Id. at 687.*

[a] D primarily engaged in selling or leasing goods or services. The action is against a defendant primarily engaged in the business of selling or leasing goods or services. Tex. Civ. Prac. & Rem. Code §27.010(a)(2); **Castleman**, 546 S.W.3d at 688; **Toth**, 557 S.W.3d at 152; *e.g.*, **Hawkins v. Fox Corporate Hous., LLC**, 606 S.W.3d 41, 46–47 (Tex.App.—Houston [1st Dist.] 2020, no pet.) (sales executive who facilitated property rentals for corporate-housing company was considered to be engaged in business of selling or leasing goods or services; no requirement that D has to be the "actual business itself"); *see, e.g.*, **Whisenhunt v. Lippincott**, 474 S.W.3d 30, 42 (Tex.App.—Texarkana 2015, no pet.) (because nothing in record specified whether Ds actually sold or leased surgical services, Ds' titles as administrators, without more, did not suggest that they were primarily engaged in business of selling services for their company), *overruled on other grounds*, **Castleman v. Internet Money Ltd.**, 546 S.W.3d 684 (Tex.2018).

[b] D made statement or engaged in conduct as seller or lessor. The action is based on a statement that the defendant made or conduct in which the defendant engaged in her capacity as a seller or lessor of goods or services. **Hawkins**, 606 S.W.3d at 46; **Toth**, 557 S.W.3d at 152; *e.g.*, **Castleman**, 546 S.W.3d at 688 (exemption did not apply when D was primarily engaged in business of selling goods but statements were made in capacity as P's customer); *see* Tex. Civ. Prac. & Rem. Code §27.010(a)(2).

[c] Statement or conduct arose out of D's sale or lease. The action is based on a statement or conduct that arose out of a commercial transaction involving the kind of goods or services the defendant provides. **Castleman**, 546 S.W.3d at 688; **Hawkins**, 606 S.W.3d at 46; **Toth**, 557 S.W.3d at 152; **Grant v. Pivot Tech. Solutions, Ltd.**, 556 S.W.3d 865, 887 (Tex.App.—Austin 2018, pet. denied); *see* Tex. Civ. Prac. & Rem. Code §27.010(a)(2); *see, e.g.*, **Global Tel*Link Corp. v. Securus Techs.**, No. 05-16-01224-CV, 2017 WL 3275921 (Tex.App.—Dallas 2017, pet. dism'd) (memo op.; 7-31-17) (exemption did not apply in suit against business competitor based on e-mails sent to members of industry because e-mails did not arise from sale of goods or services or any other actual or contemplated commercial transaction).

[d] Intended audience is D's actual or potential customers. The defendant intended her statement or conduct to reach her actual or potential customers for the kind of goods or services the defendant provides. **Castleman**, 546 S.W.3d at 688; **Hawkins**, 606 S.W.3d at 46; **Toth**, 557 S.W.3d at 153; *see* Tex. Civ. Prac. & Rem. Code §27.010(a)(2). The exemption does not apply if the intended audience was the plaintiff's customers or the public at large. *See, e.g.*, **Castleman**, 546 S.W.3d at 688 (suit based on D's statements about quality of P's services was not commercial-speech action because D's intended audience was P's customers, not D's own customers); **Better Bus. Bur. v. BH DFW, Inc.**, 402 S.W.3d 299, 309 (Tex.App.—Dallas 2013, pet. denied) (suit based on ratings published by BBB was not commercial-speech action because intended audience was public consumer, not BBB's customer base of businesses seeking accreditation).

[3] Actions to recover for bodily injury, wrongful death, or survival. A legal action seeking recovery for bodily injury, wrongful death, or survival is exempt from the TCPA. Tex. Civ. Prac. & Rem. Code §27.010(a)(3); *e.g.*, **Cavin v. Abbott**, 545 S.W.3d 47, 56–57 (Tex.App.—Austin 2017, no pet.) (assault claim); **Kirkstall Rd.**, 523 S.W.3d at 253 (negligence claim seeking recovery for bodily injury). Likewise, statements about a legal action seeking recovery for bodily injury, wrongful death, or survival are not protected under the TCPA. Tex. Civ. Prac. & Rem. Code §27.010(a)(3).

[4] Insurance actions. A legal action brought under the Insurance Code or arising from an insurance contract is exempt from the TCPA. Tex. Civ. Prac. & Rem. Code §27.010(a)(4).

[5] Cyberbullying actions. A legal action brought under CPRC chapter 129A (cyberbullying of a child) is exempt from the TCPA. Tex. Civ. Prac. & Rem. Code §129A.004(b).

[6] Actions for misappropriation of trade secrets or enforcement of nondisparagement agreement. For actions filed on or after September 1, 2019, a legal action arising from an officer-director, employer-employee, or independent contractor relationship that seeks recovery for the misappropriation of trade secrets or corporate opportunities or seeks to enforce a nondisparagement agreement or a covenant not to compete is exempt from the TCPA. Tex. Civ. Prac. & Rem. Code §27.010(a)(5).

[7] Family Code actions. For actions filed on or after September 1, 2019, a legal action filed under Family Code title 1, 2, 4, or 5 is exempt from the TCPA. Tex. Civ. Prac. & Rem. Code §27.010(a)(6).

[8] Application for protective order. For actions filed on or after September 1, 2019, an application for a protective order under Code of Criminal Procedure chapter 7A is exempt from the TCPA. Tex. Civ. Prac. & Rem. Code §27.010(a)(6).

[9] DTPA actions. For actions filed on or after September 1, 2019, a legal action brought under Business & Commerce Code chapter 17, other than an action under Business & Commerce Code §17.49(a), is generally exempt from the TCPA. Tex. Civ. Prac. & Rem. Code §27.010(a)(7). But the TCPA does specifically cover certain legal actions notwithstanding this exemption. *See* Tex. Civ. Prac. & Rem. Code §27.010(b). See "Actions described by CPRC §27.010(b)," ch. 3-K, §2.1.2(2).

[10] Actions involving immunity for medical committees and medical peer-review committees. For actions filed on or after September 1, 2019, a legal action in which a moving party raises a defense under Occupations Code §160.010, Health & Safety Code §161.033, or the Health Care Quality Improvement Act of 1986 (42 U.S.C. §11101 et seq.) is exempt from the TCPA. Tex. Civ. Prac. & Rem. Code §27.010(a)(8).

[11] Eviction actions. For actions filed on or after September 1, 2019, an eviction suit brought under Property Code chapter 24 is exempt from the TCPA. Tex. Civ. Prac. & Rem. Code §27.010(a)(9).

[12] Disciplinary actions. For actions filed on or after September 1, 2019, a disciplinary action or proceeding brought under Gov't Code chapter 81 or the Texas Rules of Disciplinary Procedure is exempt from the TCPA. Tex. Civ. Prac. & Rem. Code §27.010(a)(10).

[13] Governmental retaliation actions. For actions filed on or after September 1, 2019, a legal action brought under Gov't Code chapter 554 is exempt from the TCPA. Tex. Civ. Prac. & Rem. Code §27.010(a)(11).

[14] Fraud actions. For actions filed on or after September 1, 2019, a legal action based on common-law fraud is generally exempt from the TCPA. Tex. Civ. Prac. & Rem. Code §27.010(a)(12). But the TCPA does specifically cover certain legal actions notwithstanding this exemption. *See* Tex. Civ. Prac. & Rem. Code §27.010(b). See "Actions described by CPRC §27.010(b)," ch. 3-K, §2.1.2(2).

(e) D did not show legal action involves protected act. The plaintiff can oppose the anti-SLAPP motion on the ground that the defendant did not meet its initial burden to show that the legal action is based on or is in response to the defendant's protected act. *See* Tex. Civ. Prac. & Rem. Code §27.005(b). See "Defendant's burden," ch. 3-K, §2.

(f) P can establish prima facie case for legal action. The plaintiff can oppose the anti-SLAPP motion, even if the defendant met its initial burden, on the ground that the plaintiff can establish by clear and specific evidence—which can include relevant circumstantial evidence—a prima facie case for each essential element of the challenged claim. *See* Tex. Civ. Prac. & Rem. Code §27.005(b), (c); **S&S Emerg. Training Solutions, Inc. v. Elliott**, 564 S.W.3d 843, 847 (Tex.2018); **Bedford v. Spassoff**, 520 S.W.3d 901, 904 (Tex.2017); **In re Lipsky**, 460 S.W.3d 579, 590–91 (Tex.2015). Prima facie evidence is the minimum amount of evidence necessary to support a rational inference that a factual allegation is true. **S&S Emerg. Training Solutions**, 564 S.W.3d at 847; **In re Lipsky**, 460 S.W.3d at 590; **Texas Campaign for the Env't v. Partners Dewatering Int'l**, 485 S.W.3d 184, 191–92 (Tex.App.—Corpus Christi 2016, no pet.). Conclusory statements are not sufficient to establish a prima facie case. *See* **In re Lipsky**, 460 S.W.3d at 592; **Texas Campaign for the Env't**, 485 S.W.3d at 192. Although the TCPA does not define "clear and specific" evidence, these terms are given their ordinary meaning—that is, unambiguous, easily understood, and explicit. *See* **S&S Emerg. Training Solutions**, 564 S.W.3d at 847; **In re Lipsky**, 460 S.W.3d at 590; *see also* **Serafine v. Blunt**, 466 S.W.3d 352, 358 (Tex.App.—Austin 2015, no pet.) ("clear and specific" refers to quality of evidence necessary to establish prima facie case; "prima facie" refers to amount of evidence necessary to satisfy P's burden). Thus, the plaintiff must do more than make general allegations that restate the elements of a cause of action—it must provide enough detail to show the factual basis for its claim. **In re Lipsky**, 460 S.W.3d at 590–91; *see* **D Mag. Partners v. Rosenthal**, 529 S.W.3d 429, 434 (Tex.2017); *see, e.g.*, **United Food & Commercial Workers Int'l Un. v. Wal-Mart Stores**, 430 S.W.3d 508, 513 (Tex.App.—Fort Worth 2014, no pet.) (in trespass case, cease-and-desist letters sent to Ds that prohibited demonstrations on P's property constituted clear and specific evidence that Ds were not authorized to enter and protest on P's property); **KTRK TV, Inc. v. Robinson**, 409 S.W.3d 682, 692 (Tex.App.—Houston [1st Dist.] 2013, pet. denied) (in defamation case, reports alleging financial mismanagement of charter school that did not explicitly accuse P-director of misconduct did not constitute clear and specific evidence of defamation per se).

Note

Although the TCPA initially requires more information about the underlying claim than the fair-notice pleading standard under TRCP 45(b) and 47(a), the Supreme Court in ***Lipsky*** *disapproved of cases interpreting "clear and specific evidence" as a heightened evidentiary standard and held that the TCPA does not categorically reject the use of circumstantial evidence. See* ***In re Lipsky****, 460 S.W.3d at 590–91.*

(2) Supporting evidence. The response should be supported by admissible evidence in the form of pleadings and affidavits stating the facts on which the defendant's liability is based. Tex. Civ. Prac. & Rem. Code §27.006(a). See "Verification & affidavits," ch. 1-B, §4.1.12. For actions filed on or after September 1, 2019, the response can also be supported by any evidence the court could consider under TRCP 166a. Tex. Civ. Prac. & Rem. Code §27.006(a). See "Summary-judgment evidence," ch. 7-B, §9.

(3) Request for costs & reasonable attorney fees. The plaintiff can argue that the anti-SLAPP motion is frivolous or solely intended to cause unnecessary delay and request that the plaintiff be awarded costs and reasonable attorney fees. Tex. Civ. Prac. & Rem. Code §27.009(b). The plaintiff should support its request with sufficient evidence establishing the amount of costs and attorney fees incurred in making the response. See "Evidence," ch. 1-H, §10.2.2.

§4.3 Amended petition. Although not explicitly provided for in the TCPA, a plaintiff may be able to respond to an anti-SLAPP motion by filing an amended petition. *Cf.* **Verizon Del., Inc. v. Covad Comms.**, 377 F.3d 1081, 1091 (9th Cir.2004) (granting anti-SLAPP motion without allowing P leave to amend would directly conflict with FRCP 15(a)). See "Motion to Amend Pleadings—Pretrial," ch. 5-F, §1 et seq. However, a plaintiff who amends to delete any cause of action after an anti-SLAPP motion has been filed will become liable for attorney fees and sanctions attributable to that cause of action. *See* Tex. Civ. Prac. & Rem. Code §27.009(a). See "Award of costs, fees & sanctions," ch. 3-K, §8.2.2.

Practice Tip

Because the TCPA provides for an award of attorney fees and sanctions to a defendant when a legal action is dismissed, litigants should be cautious when filing pleadings with multiple causes of action. See Tex. Civ. Prac. & Rem. Code §27.009(a). For example, a plaintiff may have clear and specific evidence to support a straightforward claim for defamation per se. But if the plaintiff has only weak evidence of special damages and chooses to also include claims for business disparagement, tortious interference, or other borderline theories, the plaintiff will likely emerge from the anti-SLAPP proceedings with one claim still standing but a large fee and sanction award owed to the defendant for the causes of action that were dismissed. Thus, if a suit is likely subject to the TCPA, plaintiffs should file only their strongest cause of action and, barring some compelling reason not to, omit all borderline alternative claims.

§4.4 Voluntary dismissal. A plaintiff may be able to respond to an anti-SLAPP motion by filing a voluntary dismissal. See "Voluntary Dismissal—Nonsuit," ch. 7-F, §1 et seq. But if the defendant's motion requests more relief than a nonsuit provides, the defendant is entitled to a ruling on its motion despite the plaintiff's nonsuit. *See* **Craig v. Tejas Promotions, LLC**, 550 S.W.3d 287, 293 (Tex.App.—Austin 2018, pet. denied); **Walker v. Hartman**, 516 S.W.3d 71, 80 (Tex.App.—Beaumont 2017, pet. denied); *see, e.g.*, **Rauhauser v. McGibney**, 508 S.W.3d 377, 382–83 (Tex.App.—Fort Worth 2014, no pet.) (although trial court granted Ps' motion for nonsuit without prejudice, D was still entitled to be heard on anti-SLAPP motion because motion sought dismissal with prejudice, attorney fees, and sanctions), *disapproved on other grounds*, **Hersh v. Tatum**, 526 S.W.3d 462 (Tex.2017). See "Effect on defendant's claims," ch. 7-F, §6.3. As a result, the plaintiff may still be liable for attorney fees and costs for work performed before the nonsuit and may be subject to sanctions. *See* **James v. Calkins**, 446 S.W.3d 135, 143 (Tex.App.—Houston [1st Dist.] 2014, pet. denied). See "Contents," ch. 3-K, §3.4; "Award of costs, fees & sanctions," ch. 3-K, §8.2.2.

Practice Tip

In some cases, a plaintiff may recognize only after receiving an anti-SLAPP motion that the TCPA applies to its claims, that all or some of its claims cannot be established by clear and specific evidence, and that it is likely to be liable for attorney fees and sanctions. In this situation, the plaintiff should consider quickly contacting the defendant's attorney about a "walk-away" settlement agreement. A walk-away settlement agreement may be particularly attractive to the defendant under these circumstances if it would be difficult to collect a fee judgment from the plaintiff. If the plaintiff instead continues to litigate the claims, seeks discovery, and incurs defense fees, the defendant will have less of a financial incentive to accept such an agreement later.

§5. Reply

Depending on when the plaintiff files a response and the content of that response, the defendant may choose to file a reply. See **O'Connor's Texas Civil Forms**, FORM 3K:4 (2020 ed.).

§5.1 Deadline to file & serve. The TCPA does not specify when to file and serve a reply. Because the hearing on the anti-SLAPP motion must be set within 60 days after service of the motion, the defendant should file and serve the reply as soon as possible after the plaintiff's response is served, unless local rules or a court order specifies otherwise. *See* Tex. Civ. Prac. & Rem. Code §27.004(a). See "When to file," ch. 1-C, §5; "When to serve," ch. 1-D, §5.

§5.2 Contents.

1. No prima facie case. The defendant should argue that the plaintiff has not established a prima facie case for each essential element of the plaintiff's claim. *See* Tex. Civ. Prac. & Rem. Code §27.005(c). See "P can establish prima facie case for legal action," ch. 3-K, §4.2.2(1)(f).

2. Defenses. The defendant should establish any defense to the plaintiff's claim. Tex. Civ. Prac. & Rem. Code §27.005(d). See "Defenses to liability," ch. 3-K, §3.4.3. If the defendant raised a defense in the anti-SLAPP motion and the plaintiff has responded to that defense, the defendant can address the plaintiff's response and further strengthen its arguments in favor of the defense. *See* Tex. Civ. Prac. & Rem. Code §27.005(d).

3. Supplement to request for attorney fees & sanctions. If additional attorney fees have been incurred since the anti-SLAPP motion was filed, or if new evidence has developed that strengthens the case for the amount of sanctions sought, the defendant should attach supplemental evidence on attorney fees and sanctions to the reply. See "Request for attorney fees & costs," ch. 3-K, §3.4.4.

§6. Hearing

The defendant has the burden to obtain a timely hearing on the anti-SLAPP motion or request an extension; the failure to obtain a timely hearing is a proper basis for the court to deny the motion. *See* **Grubbs v. ATW Invs.**, 544 S.W.3d 421, 425–26 (Tex.App.—San Antonio 2017, no pet.); **Morin v. Law Office of Kleinhans Gruber, PLLC**, No. 03-15-00174-CV, 2015 WL 4999045 (Tex.App.—Austin 2015, no pet.) (memo op.; 8-21-15).

§6.1 Deadline.

1. Generally—60 days. Generally, the hearing on the anti-SLAPP motion must be set within 60 days after service of the motion. Tex. Civ. Prac. & Rem. Code §27.004(a). See "Hearing on motion," ch. 1-E, §4.

2. Certain conditions—90 days. The hearing on the anti-SLAPP motion must occur within 90 days after service of the motion if (1) the court's docket conditions require a later hearing date (i.e., the court cannot hold a hearing within 60 days after service of the motion), (2) there is good cause shown, or (3) the parties agree. Tex. Civ. Prac. & Rem. Code §27.004(a). The court can take judicial notice that the court's docket conditions required the later hearing date. Tex. Civ. Prac. & Rem. Code §27.004(b).

3. Court allows discovery—120 days. If the court allows discovery under CPRC §27.006(b), the hearing on the anti-SLAPP motion must occur within 120 days after service of the motion. Tex. Civ. Prac. & Rem. Code §27.004(c).

§6.2 Notice. For actions filed on or after September 1, 2019, the defendant must provide written notice of the date and time of the hearing no later than 21 days before the hearing unless otherwise provided by the parties' agreement or by court order. Tex. Civ. Prac. & Rem. Code §27.003(d).

§6.3 Proof. In determining whether a legal action is subject to or should be dismissed under the TCPA, the court must consider certain types of proof. *See* Tex. Civ. Prac. & Rem. Code §27.006(a).

1. Pleadings & affidavits. The court must consider admissible evidence in the form of pleadings and supporting affidavits stating the facts on which the liability or defense is based. Tex. Civ. Prac. & Rem. Code §27.006(a); *see* **West v. Quintanilla**, 573 S.W.3d 237, 242 n.8 (Tex.2019) (pleadings are best evidence in determining whether claim should be dismissed); **Greer v. Abraham**, 489 S.W.3d 440, 446 (Tex.2016) (pleadings and affidavits are primary evidence for determining whether dismissal is proper); **In re Lipsky**, 460 S.W.3d 579, 587 (Tex.2015) (court must consider pleadings and any supporting and opposing affidavits).

2. Evidence under TRCP 166a. For actions filed on or after September 1, 2019, the court must consider any evidence it could consider under TRCP 166a. Tex. Civ. Prac. & Rem. Code §27.006(a). See "Summary-judgment evidence," ch. 7-B, §9.

Note

Before the 2019 amendments to the TCPA, courts disagreed on whether live testimony was permissible at the hearing. Compare ***Quintanilla v. West****, 534 S.W.3d 34, 42 (Tex.App.—San Antonio 2017) (court cannot hear live testimony), rev'd on other grounds, 573 S.W.3d 237 (Tex.2019), and* ***Pena v. Perel****, 417 S.W.3d 552, 556 (Tex.App.—El Paso 2013, no pet.) (same), with* ***Serafine v. Blunt****, 466 S.W.3d 352, 361–62 (Tex.App.—Austin 2015, no pet.) (court considered testimony at hearing), and* ***Bacharach v. Garcia****, No. 13-14-00693-CV, 2015 WL 5136192 (Tex.App.—Corpus Christi 2015, no pet.) (memo op.; 8-31-15) (same). Under the 2019 amendments, the court is directed to consider any evidence it could consider under TRCP 166a, which does not allow for oral testimony. See Tex. Civ. Prac. & Rem. Code §27.006(a); Tex. R. Civ. P. 166a(c).*

---

3. Limited discovery. The court must consider any limited discovery relevant to the anti-SLAPP motion that the court allowed. *See* Tex. Civ. Prac. & Rem. Code §27.006(b).

§7. Ruling

In ruling on an anti-SLAPP motion, the court must construe the TCPA liberally to fully effectuate its purpose and intent. Tex. Civ. Prac. & Rem. Code §27.011(b). In doing so, the court must look at the TCPA's plain language and, when the language is unambiguous, interpret the TCPA according to its plain meaning. **ExxonMobil Pipeline Co. v. Coleman**, 512 S.W.3d 895, 899 (Tex.2017); **Lippincott v. Whisenhunt**, 462 S.W.3d 507, 509 (Tex.2015); *see* **Elite Auto Body LLC v. Autocraft Bodywerks, Inc.**, 520 S.W.3d 191, 199 (Tex.App.—Austin 2017, pet. dism'd).

§7.1 Deadline. The court must rule on an anti-SLAPP motion within 30 days after the date the hearing concludes. Tex. Civ. Prac. & Rem. Code §27.005(a); *see also* **In re Panchakarla**, 602 S.W.3d 536, 539–40 (Tex.2020) (30-day deadline does not apply to trial court's power to reconsider its ruling on motion to dismiss; court can vacate ruling after 30-day deadline as long initial ruling was timely and court has plenary power to vacate). If the court does not rule within 30 days, the motion is considered denied by operation of law and the defendant may appeal. Tex. Civ. Prac. & Rem. Code §27.008(a); *e.g.*, **Inwood Forest Cmty. Imprv. Ass'n v. Arce**, 485 S.W.3d 65, 69–70 (Tex.App.—Houston [14th Dist.] 2015, pet. denied) (trial judge's oral statement that she intended to grant motions to dismiss did not constitute ruling; motions denied by operation of law after 30 days and written orders signed later had no effect). See "Appellate review," ch. 3-K, §10. The TCPA does not require the court to completely resolve all matters by the 30-day deadline; as long as the request for dismissal is ruled on within 30 days, other issues such as attorney fees and sanctions can be resolved at a later time. *See* **Eureka Holdings Acquisitions, L.P. v. Marshall Apts., LLC**, 597 S.W.3d 921, 924 (Tex.App.—Austin 2020, pet. denied); *see, e.g.*, **DeAngelis v. Protective Parents Coalition**, 556 S.W.3d 836, 859 (Tex.App.—Fort Worth 2018, no pet.) (motion not denied by operation of law when

court granted motion within 30 days but later determined attorney fees and sanctions).

Note

In 2019, CPRC §27.005(a) was amended to specify that the 30-day window for the court to rule on the motion to dismiss begins after the date the hearing concludes. See Tex. Civ. Prac. & Rem. Code §27.005(a). Before the 2019 amendment, the statute stated that the 30-day window began after "the date of the hearing." See Tex. Civ. Prac. & Rem. Code §27.005(a) (pre-9-1-19 version). The amendment clears up any potential confusion about whether the 30-day window begins after the day the hearing starts or after the hearing ends.

§7.2 Court's determination. In ruling on an anti-SLAPP motion, the court applies a three-step analysis. *See* Tex. Civ. Prac. & Rem. Code §27.005(b) to (d).

1. Determine whether D has met its burden. The court must first determine whether the defendant has met its burden. Tex. Civ. Prac. & Rem. Code §27.005(b). See "Defendant's burden," ch. 3-K, §2. If the defendant has not met its burden, the court must deny the motion; if the defendant has met its burden, the court must then determine whether the plaintiff has met its burden. *See* Tex. Civ. Prac. & Rem. Code §27.005(b), (c).

2. Determine whether P has met its burden. If the defendant has met its burden, the court must determine whether the plaintiff has established by clear and specific evidence a prima facie case for each essential element of its claim. Tex. Civ. Prac. & Rem. Code §27.005(c). If the plaintiff has not met its burden, the court must grant the motion; if the plaintiff has met its burden, the court must then determine whether the defendant has established a defense to the plaintiff's claims. *See* Tex. Civ. Prac. & Rem. Code §27.005(b) to (d).

Note

In determining whether the plaintiff has established a prima facie case, some courts consider only the pleadings and evidence in favor of the plaintiff's case and not any rebuttal evidence offered by the defendant. E.g., ***Fawcett v. Grosu****, 498 S.W.3d 650, 661 (Tex.App.—Houston [14th Dist.] 2016, pet. denied);* ***D Mag. Partners v. Rosenthal****, 475 S.W.3d 470, 480–81 (Tex.App.—Dallas 2015), rev'd in part on other grounds, 529 S.W.3d 429 (Tex.2017). But other courts consider all the pleadings and evidence and construe them in the light most favorable to the plaintiff. See, e.g.,* ***Robert B. James, DDS, Inc. v. Elkins****, 553 S.W.3d 596, 603 (Tex.App.—San Antonio 2018, pet. denied);* ***Warner Bros. Entm't, Inc. v. Jones****, 538 S.W.3d 781, 801 (Tex.App.—Austin 2017), aff'd, ___ S.W.3d ___, 2020 WL 2315280 (Tex.2020) (No. 18-0068; 5-8-20);* ***Cosmopolitan Condo. Owners Ass'n v. Class A Investors Post Oak, LP****, No. 01-16-00769-CV, 2017 WL 1520448 (Tex.App.—Houston [1st Dist.] 2017, pet. denied) (memo op.; 4-27-17).*

3. Determine whether D has established defense. If the plaintiff has met its burden, the court must determine whether the defendant has established a defense to the plaintiff's claims. Tex. Civ. Prac. & Rem. Code §27.005(d). See "Defenses to liability," ch. 3-K, §3.4.3. If the defendant has not met its burden, the court must deny the motion; if the defendant has met its burden, the court must dismiss the action. *See* Tex. Civ. Prac. & Rem. Code §27.005(d).

§7.3 Effect of ruling. For actions filed on or after September 1, 2019, neither the court's ruling on the motion nor the fact that the court made a ruling is admissible into evidence at any later stage of the case. Tex. Civ. Prac. & Rem. Code §27.0075. Further, the ruling does not affect any burden or degree of proof that is otherwise applicable. *Id.*

§8. Order

§8.1 Motion denied. If the court denies the motion to dismiss, the discovery stay is lifted and the legal action will continue unless the defendant files an interlocutory appeal. *See* Tex. Civ. Prac. & Rem. Code §§27.003(c), 27.008(a). See "Effect of motion on discovery," ch. 3-K, §3.5; "Order denying motion," ch. 3-K, §10.2.1(1). The court can award costs and reason-

able attorney fees to the plaintiff if the court finds that the motion was frivolous or solely intended to delay. Tex. Civ. Prac. & Rem. Code §27.009(b); **Caliber Oil & Gas, LLC v. Midland Visions 2000**, 591 S.W.3d 226, 243 (Tex.App.—Eastland 2019, no pet.); *e.g.*, **Sloat v. Rathbun**, 513 S.W.3d 500, 510 (Tex.App.—Austin 2015, pet. dism'd) (finding that motion was litigated in such a way as to cause delay was insufficient to support award of costs and fees; motion itself must be frivolous). A motion to dismiss is considered frivolous when it has no basis in law or fact and lacks a legal basis or legal merit. **Youngblood v. Zaccaria**, __ S.W.3d __, 2020 WL 4606894 (Tex.App.—San Antonio 2020, pet. filed 9-25-20) (No. 04-19-00868-CV; 8-12-20); **Caliber Oil & Gas**, 591 S.W.3d at 243. See "Request for costs & reasonable attorney fees," ch. 3-K, §4.2.2(3).

§8.2 Motion granted.

1. Dismissal with prejudice. If the court grants the motion, the legal action will be dismissed with prejudice. *See* Tex. Civ. Prac. & Rem. Code §27.005(b). Dismissal with prejudice constitutes a final determination on the merits. **Better Bus. Bur. v. John Moore Servs.**, 500 S.W.3d 26, 40 (Tex.App.—Houston [1st Dist.] 2016, pet. denied). See "Dismissal with prejudice," ch. 7-G, §6.3.1.

2. Award of costs, fees & sanctions. When the legal action is dismissed, the defendant may be entitled to an award of costs, attorney fees, and sanctions. *See* Tex. Civ. Prac. & Rem. Code §27.009.

Note

Courts disagree on whether the TCPA authorizes an award of attorney fees and sanctions when a party successfully challenges the underlying legal action on jurisdictional grounds—that is, whether the trial court can award costs, attorney fees, and sanctions even if it lacks jurisdiction over the "object" of the motion to dismiss. Compare ***Houston Forensic Sci. Ctr., Inc. v. Barette****, No. 01-19-00129-CV, 2019 WL 5792194 (Tex.App.—Houston [1st Dist] 2019, no pet.) (memo op.; 11-7-19) (trial court cannot award costs, attorney fees, and sanctions under TCPA when it lacks subject-matter jurisdiction over underlying claim), and* ***Shankles v. Gordon****, 05-16-00863-CV, 2018 WL 4100030 (Tex.App.—Dallas 2018, no pet.) (memo op.; 8-27-18) (same), with* ***de la Torre v. de la Torre****, __ S.W.3d __, 2020 WL 6018572 (Tex.App.—Austin 2020, n.p.h.) (No. 03-19-00597-CV; 10-9-20) (trial court should have granted motion to dismiss and allowed for determination of attorney fees and sanctions even though P did not have standing to bring claim that formed basis of motion to dismiss).*

(1) Costs, attorney fees & other expenses. When the legal action is dismissed, the defendant is generally entitled to an award of costs and reasonable attorney fees that are incurred in defending the legal action. Tex. Civ. Prac. & Rem. Code §27.009(a), (c); *see, e.g.*, **D Mag. Partners v. Rosenthal**, 529 S.W.3d 429, 441–42 (Tex.2017) (if case includes multiple legal actions and court dismisses some but not all of them, D can still recover attorney fees based on partial dismissal; Ds were entitled to attorney fees when court dismissed statutory claims even though defamation claim was not dismissed); **Cruz v. Van Sickle**, 452 S.W.3d 503, 522 (Tex.App.—Dallas 2014, pet. denied) (because Ds were represented pro bono, they did not incur any attorney fees and thus were not entitled to fee award). A successful defendant may be able to recover not only attorney fees incurred while defending the legal action, but also those incurred before the action is formally commenced or after dismissal has been granted. *See* **Cruz**, 452 S.W.3d at 526 (TCPA permits successful D to recover postdismissal attorney fees—such as those for reviewing dismissal order or opponent's motion for new trial—incurred in defending against claim); **American Heritage Capital, LP v. Gonzalez**, 436 S.W.3d 865, 879–80 (Tex.App.—Dallas 2014, no pet.) (TCPA permits successful D to recover attorney fees incurred in defending against claim even if fees were incurred before D was formally sued), *disapproved on other grounds*, **Hersh v. Tatum**, 526 S.W.3d 462 (Tex.2017). See "Request for attorney fees & costs," ch. 3-K, §3.4.4. Depending on when the underlying legal action was filed, the defendant may also be entitled to an award of other expenses if the legal action is dismissed.

(a) Before 9-1-19. For actions filed before September 1, 2019, when the legal action is dismissed, the court must award the defendant court costs, reasonable attorney fees, and other expenses incurred in defending against the legal action as justice and equity may require. Tex. Civ. Prac. & Rem. Code §27.009(a)(1) (pre-9-1-19 version); **Sullivan v. Abraham**, 488 S.W.3d 294, 296 (Tex.2016); *see* **D Mag.**, 529 S.W.3d at 441. The court has discretion to determine the amount

of reasonable attorney fees. **Sullivan**, 488 S.W.3d at 299. Even though the amount of reasonable attorney fees is subject to the court's discretion, the court cannot adjust what is reasonable based on considerations of justice and equity. *Id.*; **Tatum v. Hersh**, 559 S.W.3d 581, 584 (Tex.App.—Dallas 2018, no pet.). The court may consider justice and equity only when determining whether to award "other expenses" incurred in defending the legal action. *See* Tex. Civ. Prac. & Rem. Code §27.009(a)(1); **Sullivan**, 488 S.W.3d at 298–99. That is, other expenses incurred in defending the legal action are recoverable, but only if the court determines they are required based on considerations of justice and equity. *See* **Sullivan**, 488 S.W.3d at 298–99; *see also* **McGibney v. Rauhauser**, 549 S.W.3d 816, 821 (Tex.App.—Fort Worth 2018, pet. denied) (D is not limited to attorney fees "incurred in defending the legal action"; limitation applies only to other expenses).

Note

*Although **Sullivan** stated that the court has discretion to determine the amount of reasonable attorney fees, one court has determined that this language should not be interpreted as stating that the court has exclusive authority to assess attorney fees. **Pisharodi v. Columbia Valley Healthcare Sys.**, __ S.W.3d __, 2020 WL 2213951 (Tex.App.—Corpus Christi 2020, n.p.h.) (No. 13-18-00364-CV; 5-7-20). The court in **Pisharodi** held that the amount of reasonable attorney fees can be determined by a jury, on a proper request, because reasonableness is a question of fact and nothing in CPRC §27.009 prohibits the parties from having the jury determine the reasonableness of the attorney fees. **Pisharodi**, __ S.W.3d at __, 2020 WL 2213951.*

(b) On or after 9-1-19.

[1] Generally—award required. For actions filed on or after September 1, 2019, when the legal action is dismissed, the court generally must award the defendant court costs and reasonable attorney fees incurred in defending against the legal action. Tex. Civ. Prac. & Rem. Code §27.009(a)(1).

Note

After the 2019 amendments to the TCPA, when the legal action is dismissed, the defendant is no longer entitled to an award of other expenses incurred in defending against the legal action as justice and equity may require. See Tex. Civ. Prac. & Rem. Code §27.009(a)(1).

[2] Exception—award discretionary if frivolous counterclaim. For actions filed on or after September 1, 2019, if the court orders dismissal of a compulsory counterclaim, the court may, but is not required to, award the party moving for dismissal reasonable attorney fees incurred in defending against the counterclaim if the court finds that the counterclaim is frivolous or intended solely for delay. Tex. Civ. Prac. & Rem. Code §27.009(c).

(2) Sanctions. Depending on when the underlying legal action was filed, an award of sanctions may be mandatory or discretionary.

Note

*CPRC §27.009 does not authorize the use of nonmonetary sanctions. **McGibney**, 549 S.W.3d at 835.*

(a) Before 9-1-19. For actions filed before September 1, 2019, when the legal action is dismissed, the court must sanction the plaintiff sufficiently to deter the plaintiff from bringing similar actions and award the defendant those sanctions in addition to costs, attorney fees, and expenses. Tex. Civ. Prac. & Rem. Code §27.009(a) (pre-9-1-19 version); **Cox Media Grp. v. Joselevitz**, 524 S.W.3d 850, 864 (Tex.App.—Houston [14th Dist.] 2017, no pet.); **Serafine v. Blunt**, 466 S.W.3d 352, 364 (Tex.App.—Austin 2015, no pet.). As with costs, attorney fees, and expenses, the court's award of sanctions is mandatory if the defendant is successful; however, the court has discretion to determine what sanction is appropriate to deter the plaintiff from bringing similar future actions. **Rauhauser v. McGibney**, 508 S.W.3d 377, 389 (Tex.App.—Fort Worth 2014, no pet.), *disapproved on other grounds*, **Hersh v. Tatum**, 526 S.W.3d 462 (Tex.2017); *see, e.g.*, **American Heritage**

Capital, 436 S.W.3d at 881 (court looked at P's annual net profits and conduct during litigation to determine appropriate sanction).

Note

Before the 2019 amendments to the TCPA, at least two courts held that, while an award of sanctions is mandatory if the defendant is successful, the trial court has discretion to award a nominal sanction if it determines that the plaintiff does not need to be deterred from bringing a similar action. E.g., ***Tatum****, 559 S.W.3d at 587–88; see, e.g.,* ***Rich v. Range Res.****, 535 S.W.3d 610, 612–13 (Tex.App.—Fort Worth 2017, pet. denied). If the court determines that the plaintiff does not need deterrence, a failure to award a nominal sanction will be considered harmless error, unless the court abused its discretion in finding that no deterrence was necessary.* ***Tatum****, 559 S.W.3d at 588.*

(b) On or after 9-1-19. For actions filed on or after September 1, 2019, when the legal action is dismissed, the court may, but is not required to, sanction the plaintiff in an amount sufficient to deter the plaintiff from bringing similar future actions and award the defendant those sanctions in addition to costs and attorney fees. Tex. Civ. Prac. & Rem. Code §27.009(a). See "Request for sanctions," ch. 3-K, §3.4.5.

§9. Additional findings

The circumstances under which the court must issue findings depend on when the underlying legal action was filed.

§9.1 Before 9-1-19. For actions filed before September 1, 2019, if the defendant makes a request, the court must issue findings on whether the legal action was brought to deter or prevent the defendant from exercising its constitutional rights and whether the legal action was brought for an improper purpose, including to harass, cause unnecessary delay, or increase the cost of litigation. Tex. Civ. Prac. & Rem. Code §27.007(a) (pre-9-1-19 version); *see* **Greer v. Abraham**, 489 S.W.3d 440, 443 & n.3 (Tex.2016); *see, e.g.*, **McGibney v. Rauhauser**, 549 S.W.3d 816, 836–37 (Tex.App.—Fort Worth 2018, pet. denied) (because willfulness and malice are not tantamount to finding of improper purpose, request for additional findings on these issues was beyond scope of CPRC §27.007(a)).

Note

The TCPA does not specify a deadline for requesting additional findings. But the court must issue findings within 30 days after the defendant makes such a request. Tex. Civ. Prac. & Rem. Code §27.007(b). For the general deadline for requesting findings of fact, see "Requesting findings of fact," ch. 10-E, §3.

§9.2 On or after 9-1-19. For actions filed on or after September 1, 2019, if the court awards sanctions under CPRC §27.009(b), the court must issue findings on whether the legal action was brought to deter or prevent the defendant from exercising its constitutional rights and whether the legal action was brought for an improper purpose, including to harass, cause unnecessary delay, or increase the cost of litigation. Tex. Civ. Prac. & Rem. Code §27.007(a).

Note

Before the 2019 amendments to the TCPA, CPRC §27.007(a) required the court to issue findings at the request of the party making the motion to dismiss. Tex. Civ. Prac. & Rem. Code §27.007(a) (pre-9-1-19 version). CPRC §27.007(b) stated that the court had to issue findings within 30 days after such a request. Tex. Civ. Prac. & Rem. Code §27.007(b) (pre-9-1-19 version). Subsection (b) was not changed by the 2019 amendments; subsection (a), however, now states that the court must issue findings if it awards sanctions under CPRC §27.009(b) and no longer contains language requiring findings based on a party's request. See Tex. Civ. Prac. & Rem. Code §27.007. Thus, for actions filed on or after September 1, 2019, it is unclear whether a party is still required to make a request for findings.

§10. Appellate review

§10.1 Standard of review. A court's decision on whether a party has met its burden under the TCPA is reviewed de novo; for other issues under the TCPA, a court's decision is reviewed for abuse of discretion.

1. De novo.

(1) D established protected act. A court's decision on whether the defendant met its burden under CPRC §27.005(b) is reviewed de novo. **Dallas Morning News, Inc. v. Hall**, 579 S.W.3d 370, 377 (Tex.2019); **Warner Bros. Entm't, Inc. v. Jones**, 538 S.W.3d 781, 797 (Tex.App.—Austin 2017), *aff'd*, __ S.W.3d __, 2020 WL 2315280 (Tex.2020) (No. 18-0068; 5-8-20); **Better Bus. Bur. v. John Moore Servs.**, 500 S.W.3d 26, 39 (Tex.App.—Houston [1st Dist.] 2016, pet. denied); **Deaver v. Desai**, 483 S.W.3d 668, 672 (Tex.App.—Houston [14th Dist.] 2015, no pet.); **United Food & Commercial Workers Int'l Un. v. Wal-Mart Stores**, 430 S.W.3d 508, 511 (Tex.App.—Fort Worth 2014, no pet.). See "Defendant's burden," ch. 3-K, §2.

(2) P established elements of claim. A court's decision on whether the plaintiff met its burden under CPRC §27.005(c) to establish by clear and specific evidence a prima facie case for each essential element of the challenged claim is reviewed de novo. **Dallas Morning News**, 579 S.W.3d at 377; **Warner Bros. Entm't**, 538 S.W.3d at 797; **Texas Campaign for the Env't v. Partners Dewatering Int'l**, 485 S.W.3d 184, 192 (Tex.App.—Corpus Christi 2016, no pet.); *see* **Deaver**, 483 S.W.3d at 675–76. See "P can establish prima facie case for legal action," ch. 3-K, §4.2.2(1)(f).

(3) D established defense to claim. A court's decision on whether the defendant met its burden under CPRC §27.005(d) to establish a defense to the plaintiff's claim is reviewed de novo. **Dallas Morning News**, 579 S.W.3d at 377; **United Food**, 430 S.W.3d at 511; *see* **Deaver**, 483 S.W.3d at 674. See "Reply," ch. 3-K, §5.

(4) P established exemption from TCPA. A court's decision on whether the plaintiff established that the legal action is exempt from the TCPA under CPRC §27.010 is reviewed de novo. *See, e.g.*, **Better Bus. Bur. v. BH DFW, Inc.**, 402 S.W.3d 299, 304 (Tex.App.—Dallas 2013, pet. denied) (whether TCPA applies to business ratings made by BBB is question of statutory construction that is reviewed de novo). See "Legal action is exempt from TCPA," ch. 3-K, §4.2.2(1)(d).

2. Abuse of discretion.

(1) Denial of discovery. A court's decision to deny a motion for discovery under CPRC §27.006(b) is reviewed for abuse of discretion. **Walker v. Schion**, 420 S.W.3d 454, 458 (Tex.App.—Houston [14th Dist.] 2014, no pet.).

(2) Award of attorney fees or sanctions. A court's award of attorney fees or sanctions under CPRC §27.009 is reviewed for abuse of discretion. *See* **McGibney v. Rauhauser**, 549 S.W.3d 816, 820 (Tex.App.—Fort Worth 2018, pet. denied); **American Heritage Capital, LP v. Gonzalez**, 436 S.W.3d 865, 877, 880 (Tex.App.—Dallas 2014, no pet.) (attorney fees and sanctions), *disapproved on other grounds*, **Hersh v. Tatum**, 526 S.W.3d 462 (Tex.2017).

§10.2 Interlocutory appeal.

1. Appeal.

(1) Order denying motion. An order denying an anti-SLAPP motion—whether expressly or by operation of law—is reviewable by interlocutory appeal. *See* Tex. Civ. Prac. & Rem. Code §27.008(a) (motion denied by operation of law), §51.014(a)(12) (motion denied generally); **In re Lipsky**, 460 S.W.3d 579, 585 & n.2 (Tex.2015) (motion denied by express ruling); **Johnson-Todd v. Morgan**, 480 S.W.3d 605, 609 (Tex.App.—Beaumont 2015, pet. denied) (motion denied by operation of law); *see also* **Better Bus. Bur. v. John Moore Servs.**, 500 S.W.3d 26, 39 (Tex.App.—Houston [1st Dist.] 2016, pet. denied) (appellate court had jurisdiction to hear interlocutory appeal of denial of anti-SLAPP motion that was overruled by operation of law even though trial court later issued untimely order granting motion, which itself was not reviewable).

Note

One court has held that an appellate court does not have jurisdiction to hear an interlocutory appeal from an order denying an anti-SLAPP motion if the defendant has not shown that the TCPA applies

to the claims at issue. E.g., ***QTAT BPO Solutions, Inc. v. Lee & Murphy Law Firm, G.P.****, 524 S.W.3d 770, 779–80 (Tex.App.—Houston [14th Dist.] 2017, pet. denied) (even though trial court denied TCPA motion, court lacked jurisdiction over appeal because TCPA did not apply to breach-of-contract claims).*

(2) Order granting motion. An order granting an anti-SLAPP motion is not reviewable by interlocutory appeal. **Eureka Holdings Acquisitions, L.P. v. Marshall Apts., LLC**, 597 S.W.3d 921, 923 (Tex.App.—Austin 2020, pet. denied); **Trane US, Inc. v. Sublett**, 501 S.W.3d 783, 786 (Tex.App.—Amarillo 2016, no pet.); **Fleming & Assocs. v. Kirklin**, 479 S.W.3d 458, 460 (Tex.App.—Houston [14th Dist.] 2015, pet. denied); **Schlumberger Ltd. v. Rutherford**, 472 S.W.3d 881, 887 (Tex.App.—Houston [1st Dist.] 2015, no pet.). If an order fully grants an anti-SLAPP motion, the order can be appealed after final judgment if the order disposes of all claims and parties. See "Final judgment," ch. 9-C, §6

Note

When a partial grant of an anti-SLAPP motion is included in the same order as a partial denial, the partial denial does not provide a means for the interlocutory appeal of the partial grant. See ***Schlumberger Ltd.****, 472 S.W.3d at 890–91;* ***Walker v. Pegasus Eventing, LLC****, No. 05-19-00252-CV, 2020 WL 3248476 (Tex.App.—Dallas 2020, n.p.h.) (memo op.; 6-16-20);* ***Moricz v. Long****, No. 06-17-00011-CV, 2017 WL 3081512 (Tex.App.—Texarkana 2017, no pet.) (memo op.; 7-20-17).*

(3) Other orders.

(a) Denial of motion seeking leave or extension of time. An interlocutory appeal is not allowed to challenge the court's denial of a motion seeking leave or a motion for extension of time to file an anti-SLAPP motion. *See* **Summersett v. Jaiyeola**, 438 S.W.3d 84, 90–91 (Tex.App.—Corpus Christi 2013, pet. denied).

(b) Denial of attorney fees. An interlocutory appeal is not allowed to challenge the court's denial of attorney fees under the TCPA if the denial of attorney fees is ancillary to the granting of an anti-SLAPP motion. *See* **Paulsen v. Yarrell**, 455 S.W.3d 192, 195–96 (Tex.App.—Houston [1st Dist.] 2014, no pet.). But if the court's order at least partially denies the anti-SLAPP motion, the denial of attorney fees can be challenged as part of the interlocutory appeal of the denial of the anti-SLAPP motion. *See* **D Mag. Partners v. Rosenthal**, 529 S.W.3d 429, 441 (Tex.2017).

2. Stay of trial & other proceedings. An interlocutory appeal of an order denying an anti-SLAPP motion stays the commencement of trial. Tex. Civ. Prac. & Rem. Code §51.014(a)(12), (b); **In re Geomet Recycling LLC**, 578 S.W.3d 82, 86 (Tex.2019). An interlocutory appeal also stays all other proceedings in the trial court until the appeal is resolved. Tex. Civ. Prac. & Rem. Code §51.014(a)(12), (b); **In re Geomet Recycling**, 578 S.W.3d at 86. The court of appeals does not have discretion to lift the stay, even for a limited purpose; the stay must remain in place until the resolution of the appeal. **In re Geomet Recycling**, 578 S.W.3d at 86–87; *see* Tex. Civ. Prac. & Rem. Code §51.014(b).

Note

Although the stay is mandatory, the parties may waive its application by agreement. ***In re Geomet Recycling****, 578 S.W.3d at 87 n.1.*

§10.3 Expedited. An appeal or other writ from a trial court order on a motion to dismiss, whether interlocutory or not, must be expedited by the appellate court. Tex. Civ. Prac. & Rem. Code §27.008(b). The appeal or writ is expedited whether the trial court issues an order on a motion to dismiss or the motion is denied by operation of law. *Id.* See "Appeals that must be given precedence," **O'Connor's Texas Civil Appeals**, ch. 3-C, §5 (2020 ed.).

Chapter 4. Alternative Dispute Resolution

A. The ADR System

The alternative-dispute-resolution (ADR) system is a method of privatizing justice. The parties are taken out of the public justice system by agreement or by court order and are sent to resolve their dispute before a private tribunal.

§1. General

§1.1 Rules. None. See Tex. Civ. Prac. & Rem. Code ch. 154.

§1.2 Purpose. The purpose of ADR is to encourage the peaceable resolution of civil disputes and the early settlement of litigation through voluntary settlement procedures. Tex. Civ. Prac. & Rem. Code §154.002; **Keene Corp. v. Gardner**, 837 S.W.2d 224, 232 (Tex.App.—Dallas 1992, writ denied); **Downey v. Gregory**, 757 S.W.2d 524, 525 (Tex.App.—Houston [1st Dist.] 1988, orig. proceeding).

§1.3 Forms. O'Connor's Texas Civil Forms, FORMS 4A:1 et seq. (2020 ed.).

§1.4 Other references. Prather and Palmer, *Texas Practice Guide, Alternative Dispute Resolution* (2019–20 ed.); Skinner, *Alternative Dispute Resolution Expands into Pre-trial Practice: An Introduction to the Role of E-Neutrals*, 13 Cardozo J. Conflict Resol. 113 (2011); Evans & Wettman, *Managed Dispute Resolution: Designing a Dispute Resolution Process for Efficiency & Affordability*, Alternative Dispute Resolution Course, State Bar of Texas CLE, ch. 2.2 (2010); Lopez, *Alternative Dispute Resolution*, 71 Tex.B.J. 36 (Jan.2008); Kovach, *Mediation: Principles & Practice* (3d ed. 2004); **O'Connor's Texas Family Law Handbook** (2021 ed.).

§2. Types of ADR

§2.1 By agreement, motion, or order. The following types of ADR are available by agreement of the parties, by motion of one of the parties, or by order of the court.

1. Mediation. Most cases referred to ADR are referred to mediation. Mediation is a nonbinding procedure in which an impartial person (the mediator) facilitates communication between the parties to promote reconciliation, settlement, or understanding. Tex. Civ. Prac. & Rem. Code §154.023(a); *see* Mediation, *Black's Law Dictionary* (11th ed. 2019). See "Mediation," ch. 4-B, §1 et seq.; **O'Connor's Texas Civil Forms**, FORMS 4B:1 et seq. (2020 ed.).

2. Moderated settlement conference. A moderated settlement conference is a nonbinding procedure in which the case is submitted to a panel of impartial third parties for an evaluation of the case intended to lead to realistic settlement negotiations. Tex. Civ. Prac. & Rem. Code §154.025(a), (b), (d). This procedure requires each party and its attorney to present the party's position before a panel of impartial third parties (often three attorneys). Tex. Civ. Prac. & Rem. Code §154.025(b). The parties may be asked to give the panel a written memorandum of the issues before the proceeding begins. The typical conference starts with an introduction from the panel and a presentation from each party. The panel will ask questions, and each party will get an opportunity to summarize its case. After the panel deliberates, it will issue a nonbinding advisory opinion on liability, damages, or both. Tex. Civ. Prac. & Rem. Code §154.025(c), (d). Opinions on damages often take the form of ranges based on the panel's experience with similar suits. See **O'Connor's Texas Civil Forms**, FORMS 4A:1, 4A:5 (2020 ed.).

3. Early neutral evaluation. Early neutral evaluation is a nonbinding procedure in which the case is submitted to an evaluator with expertise in the subject matter. *See* Lopez, *Alternative Dispute Resolution*, 71 Tex.B.J. 36, 36 (Jan.2008). The parties present summaries of their positions and evidence, possibly including witness testimony, to the evaluator while all parties are present. *Id.* The evaluator provides a written evaluation after questioning the parties. *Id.* The parties can have the evaluator present the evaluation to them, or they can engage in further settlement negotiations with the evaluator's assistance. *Id.* at 37. Any agreement the parties reach can be finalized in writing. *Id.* If the parties do not reach an agreement, the evaluator can help develop a plan for how to move forward in the case, including specifying the issues, identifying witnesses, and exchanging documentary evidence. *Id.*

4. Summary jury trial. A summary jury trial is a nonbinding procedure in which the case is submitted to a panel of jurors drawn from the county's jury pool. *See* Judge Brown, *The Summary Jury Trial: Perspectives of Bench and*

Bar, Parts I & II, 38 Houston Lawyer 5, p. 32 (Mar./Apr. 2001) and 38 Houston Lawyer 6, p. 16 (May/June 2001). The jury is not told that it is not providing a binding verdict. This procedure requires each party and its attorney to present the party's position before a panel of six jurors (unless the parties agree to a different number). Tex. Civ. Prac. & Rem. Code §154.026(b), (c). After deliberations, the jury will issue a nonbinding advisory opinion on liability, damages, or both. Tex. Civ. Prac. & Rem. Code §154.026(d), (e). A summary jury trial uses a format similar to a regular jury trial, but the rules of procedure and evidence are relaxed. The supervising court will establish guidelines for voir dire, opening statements, summary of admissible evidence, closing arguments, jury deliberations, verdict, and final discussion. The final discussion takes place between the jurors and the parties outside the presence of the judge. See **O'Connor's Texas Civil Forms**, FORMS 4A:1, 4A:6 (2020 ed.).

5. Arbitration. In arbitration, each party and its attorney present the party's position to an impartial third party or panel, who renders a specific award. *See* Tex. Civ. Prac. & Rem. Code §154.027. See "Arbitration," ch. 4-C, §1 et seq.; **O'Connor's Texas Civil Forms**, FORMS 4A:1, 4A:7 (2020 ed.).

(1) Binding arbitration. There are three types of binding arbitration: (1) agreed, in which the parties agree to settle a particular dispute by binding arbitration, (2) contractual, in which the parties agree as part of a contract to refer all disputes to arbitration, and (3) statutory, in which a statute requires the parties to arbitrate their disputes instead of litigating them. *See* Tex. Civ. Prac. & Rem. Code §154.027(b). See **O'Connor's Texas Civil Forms**, FORMS 4C:1 et seq. (2020 ed.).

(2) Nonbinding arbitration. If the parties do not agree in advance that the award will be binding, the award will be nonbinding. Tex. Civ. Prac. & Rem. Code §154.027(b). A nonbinding arbitration award is advisory only and provides the basis for further settlement negotiations between the parties. *Id.*

§2.2 By agreement only. The court can order the following types of ADR only when all parties agree to participate.

1. Minitrial. A minitrial is a nonbinding settlement procedure that uses several dispute-resolution processes. In a minitrial, each party and its attorney present the party's position to an impartial third party or to selected representatives of the parties. Tex. Civ. Prac. & Rem. Code §154.024(b). The impartial third party may issue a nonbinding advisory opinion on the merits of the case. Tex. Civ. Prac. & Rem. Code §154.024(c), (d). The advisory opinion becomes binding if the parties agree and enter into a written settlement agreement. Tex. Civ. Prac. & Rem. Code §154.024(d). In most cases, the procedure for a minitrial is as follows: (1) each party makes an opening statement summarizing the facts and legal arguments, (2) each party has an opportunity to respond to the other parties' opening statements, (3) the parties are questioned by the impartial third party or the parties' selected representatives, (4) the parties negotiate, and, if necessary, (5) an advisory opinion is issued. See **O'Connor's Texas Civil Forms**, FORMS 4A:8 to 4A:9 (2020 ed.).

2. Special-judge trial. In a trial by a special judge, the parties try their case before a retired or former judge who is selected by the parties to hear the case. The procedure is described in CPRC chapter 151. See "Special Judge," ch. 4-D, §1 et seq.; **O'Connor's Texas Civil Forms**, FORMS 4D:1 et seq. (2020 ed.).

3. Expert panel. Many cases hinge on issues involving highly technical, scientific, medical, or other specialized concepts or theories that cannot be established without expert testimony. An expert panel provides an ADR forum in which one expert or a group of experts serves as a neutral third-party decision-maker to review and evaluate the merits of a case and make a determination based on the facts and evidence presented. *See* Kovach, *Mediation: Principles & Practice*, p. 10 (3d ed. 2004). The expert determination may be either binding or advisory. *See id.* If the parties decide to be bound by the expert panel's opinions, the parties must agree in advance that the expert panel's evaluation of the issues presented is conclusive. *Id.* If the expert panel's opinion is merely advisory, the parties can agree that a trial court or subsequent decision-maker is free to reach new, independent conclusions about the evidence and that the expert panel's decision is not controlling. *See id.*

4. Jury-determined settlement. Jury-determined settlement (JDS) combines the ADR procedures of a summary jury trial and arbitration into one proceeding. Kovach, *Mediation: Principles & Practice*, p. 18 (3d ed. 2004). Under a JDS approach, a jury is impaneled and the trial moves forward like a summary jury trial. *Id.* The JDS participants retain some control over the outcome of the process by setting exposure limits through a high-low settlement agreement. *See id.* Once the JDS proceeding is completed, the jury does not render a verdict; instead, it issues a settlement decision that is binding on the JDS participants. *Id.*

5. Collaborative-law agreement. In suits for dissolution of marriage or suits affecting the parent-child relationship (SAPCRs), the parties may agree to enter into a collaborative-law agreement. *See* Tex. Fam. Code §§15.001 to 15.116. For a detailed discussion of the collaborative-law process, see "Collaborative law," **O'Connor's Texas Family Law Handbook**, ch. 3-A, §13.1.2 (2021 ed.).

§3. Referral procedures for ADR

§3.1 Procedure for proposing ADR

1. By agreement. The parties may agree to submit a dispute to ADR.

(1) Presuit agreements. The parties may agree by contract to submit any future disputes to ADR.

(2) Pretrial agreements. Once the parties are in litigation, they may agree to take all or part of the dispute out of litigation and submit it to another form of dispute resolution. *See* **Massey v. Galvan**, 822 S.W.2d 309, 318 (Tex.App.—Houston [14th Dist.] 1992, writ denied); *see, e.g.*, Tex. Est. Code §1055.151(a) (parties can execute agreement to submit contested guardianship proceeding to mediation); Tex. Fam. Code §153.0071(a), (c) (parties can execute agreement to submit SAPCR to arbitration or mediation). The ADR agreement should (1) be signed by the parties and their attorneys, (2) identify which part of the lawsuit is subject to the agreement, (3) state whether the ADR result is binding or nonbinding, and (4) be filed with the court.

2. On party's motion. A party may ask the court to refer the suit to ADR at any time during the trial or appellate process. **Downey v. Gregory**, 757 S.W.2d 524, 525 (Tex.App.—Houston [1st Dist.] 1988, orig. proceeding); *see* Tex. Civ. Prac. & Rem. Code §154.021(a).

3. On court's motion. The court may, on its own initiative, refer a suit to ADR. Tex. Civ. Prac. & Rem. Code §154.021(a); **Beldon Roofing Co. v. Sunchase IV Homeowners' Ass'n**, 494 S.W.3d 231, 238 (Tex.App.—Corpus Christi 2015, no pet.); **Texas Parks & Wildlife Dept. v. Davis**, 988 S.W.2d 370, 375 (Tex.App.—Austin 1999, no pet.); **Decker v. Lindsay**, 824 S.W.2d 247, 250 (Tex.App.—Houston [1st Dist.] 1992, orig. proceeding); *see, e.g.*, Tex. Est. Code §1055.151(a) (referral of contested guardianship proceeding to mediation); Tex. Fam. Code §153.0071(c) (referral of SAPCR to mediation). The court may refer a case to ADR at any time during the trial. **Downey**, 757 S.W.2d at 525. Even an appellate court can refer a case to ADR. *See, e.g.*, **In re Cassey D.**, 783 S.W.2d 592, 598 (Tex.App.—Houston [1st Dist.] 1990, no writ) (court of appeals referred case to ADR after reversing trial court's denial of visitation privileges to parent).

§3.2 Pre-referral issues for the court

1. Considerations for referral. The court may consider several factors in deciding whether to refer a case to ADR, including (1) the nature of the dispute, (2) the complexity of the issues, (3) the number of parties, (4) the extent of past settlement discussions, (5) the positions of the parties, and (6) whether there has been sufficient discovery to permit an accurate evaluation of the case. **Walton v. Canon, Short & Gaston, P.C.**, 23 S.W.3d 143, 150 (Tex.App.—El Paso 2000, no pet.); **Downey v. Gregory**, 757 S.W.2d 524, 525 (Tex.App.—Houston [1st Dist.] 1988, orig. proceeding).

2. Consultation with parties. The court must "confer" with the parties to determine the most appropriate ADR procedure. Tex. Civ. Prac. & Rem. Code §154.021(b). This does not mean the court must give the parties an oral hearing. *See* **Downey**, 757 S.W.2d at 525 (trial court may, but is not required to, hold a hearing before making a decision about referral to ADR). The court cannot order mediation in an action that is subject to the Federal Arbitration Act (FAA) unless the parties agree. Tex. Civ. Prac. & Rem. Code §154.021(c).

3. Notice of intent to refer. When the court decides that a case should go to ADR, it must notify the parties that it intends to send the case to ADR. Tex. Civ. Prac. & Rem. Code §154.022(a). The trial court cannot require ADR without giving at least ten days' notice. *E.g.*, **Keene Corp. v. Gardner**, 837 S.W.2d 224, 232 (Tex.App.—Dallas 1992, writ denied) (24 hours' notice to mediate violated statute); *see* Tex. Civ. Prac. & Rem. Code §154.022(b).

§4. Objecting to ADR

§4.1 Written.

An objection to ADR must be in writing. Tex. Civ. Prac. & Rem. Code §154.022(b). See **O'Connor's Texas Civil Forms**, FORMS 4A:2 to 4A:3 (2020 ed.). The objection should be verified if it includes any statement of facts outside the record.

§4.2 Deadline. To object to ADR, a party must file its objections within ten days after the referral. Tex. Civ. Prac. & Rem. Code §154.022(b); **Beldon Roofing Co. v. Sunchase IV Homeowners' Ass'n**, 494 S.W.3d 231, 238 (Tex.App.—Corpus Christi 2015, no pet.); **Keene Corp. v. Gardner**, 837 S.W.2d 224, 232 (Tex.App.—Dallas 1992, writ denied).

§4.3 Grounds. To avoid ADR, the objections must state a "reasonable basis." Tex. Civ. Prac. & Rem. Code §154.022(c). Nothing in the ADR statute provides guidance for making objections that have a "reasonable basis." The following are some possible objections to a referral to ADR:

1. Too broad. A party should challenge the court's referral if the court's order is too broad and goes beyond the statute. *See* **In re Acceptance Ins.**, 33 S.W.3d 443, 451 (Tex.App.—Fort Worth 2000, orig. proceeding). For example, while a court may compel the parties to participate in mediation, it cannot compel them to negotiate in good faith or to settle their dispute. **Avary v. Bank of Am.**, 72 S.W.3d 779, 797 (Tex.App.—Dallas 2002, pet. denied); **In re Acceptance Ins.**, 33 S.W.3d at 451–52; **Texas Parks & Wildlife Dept. v. Davis**, 988 S.W.2d 370, 375 (Tex.App.—Austin 1999, no pet.); *see* **Decker v. Lindsay**, 824 S.W.2d 247, 251–52 (Tex.App.—Houston [1st Dist.] 1992, orig. proceeding).

2. No conference with parties. A party may challenge the court's referral if the court did not "confer" with the parties to determine the most appropriate ADR procedure, as required by CPRC §154.021(b). *See, e.g.*, **Decker**, 824 S.W.2d at 248–49 (parties did not object to lack of conference).

3. Less than 10 days' notice. A party may challenge the court's referral if the court did not give the parties at least ten days' notice of the referral. **Keene Corp. v. Gardner**, 837 S.W.2d 224, 232 (Tex.App.—Dallas 1992, writ denied).

4. Case not appropriate. A party may challenge the court's referral if the case is not appropriate for ADR. So far, challenges of this nature have not been successful. *See* **Decker**, 824 S.W.2d at 249–50 (not reasonable to object on grounds that mediation will not resolve lawsuit).

5. Other ADR procedure. After the court refers the case to ADR, a party may file a written proposal suggesting a more appropriate ADR procedure. **Paul v. Paul**, 870 S.W.2d 349, 350 (Tex.App.—Waco 1994, no writ).

6. Mediation order in FAA case. A party may challenge the court's referral if a case is subject to the FAA and the court ordered mediation without the parties' agreement. *See* Tex. Civ. Prac. & Rem. Code §154.021(c).

7. Multiple referrals in same case. A party may challenge the court's referral if the case has already been submitted to ADR. Some trial courts repeatedly send the same case to ADR.

§5. Order for ADR

§5.1 Ruling on objection. If the trial court finds there is a reasonable basis for an objection, the court cannot refer the dispute to ADR. Tex. Civ. Prac. & Rem. Code §154.022(c).

§5.2 Order. The court may require the parties to attend ADR; however, the court cannot compel the parties to negotiate in good faith because doing so violates the "open-courts" provision of the Texas Constitution. **Hansen v. Sullivan**, 886 S.W.2d 467, 469 (Tex.App.—Houston [1st Dist.] 1994, orig. proceeding); *see* **Beldon Roofing Co. v. Sunchase IV Homeowners' Ass'n**, 494 S.W.3d 231, 240 (Tex.App.—Corpus Christi 2015, no pet.) (court has authority to compel parties to participate in ADR proceedings after time to object has passed). An order requiring good-faith negotiations is void. **In re Acceptance Ins.**, 33 S.W.3d 443, 452 (Tex.App.—Fort Worth 2000, orig. proceeding).

§5.3 ADR providers. Under CPRC §154.021(a), a court is authorized to refer a case to any of the following ADR providers:

1. County-sponsored ADR system. A court can refer a case to a county-sponsored ADR system established under CPRC chapter 152. *See* Tex. Civ. Prac. & Rem. Code §§152.002, 154.021(a)(1). An ADR system is an informal forum using mediation, conciliation, or nonbinding arbitration to resolve disputes among individuals, entities, or governmental units. Tex. Civ. Prac. & Rem. Code §152.001.

(1) Establishing ADR system. To establish and maintain an ADR system, each county has the authority to tax and collect money as a cost of suit (up to $15 per case). Tex. Civ. Prac. & Rem. Code §152.004(a). A county may contract

with a private nonprofit corporation, a political subdivision, a public corporation, or any combination of these entities to establish a dispute-resolution center (DRC). *See* Tex. Civ. Prac. & Rem. Code §152.002(b)(1). For a list of DRCs in Texas and their contact information, see law.utexas.edu/cppdr/resources/texas-community-dispute-resolution-centers/.

(2) Managing ADR system. Management of the ADR system may be vested in a committee selected by the county bar association. Tex. Civ. Prac. & Rem. Code §152.002(b)(3). For example, in Harris County, the Harris County DRC is sponsored by the Houston Bar Association. *See* drc.harriscountytx.gov/en-usa/Pages/Default.aspx.

(3) Collecting fees. A DRC may collect a reasonable fee as set by the commissioners court. Tex. Civ. Prac. & Rem. Code §152.006.

2. Dispute-resolution organization. A court can refer a case to a dispute-resolution organization, which is a private for-profit or nonprofit corporation, political subdivision, or public corporation that offers ADR services to the public. *See* Tex. Civ. Prac. & Rem. Code §§154.001(2), 154.021(a)(2).

3. Impartial third party. A court can refer a case to a nonjudicial and informally conducted forum for the voluntary settlement of citizens' disputes through the intervention of an impartial third party. Tex. Civ. Prac. & Rem. Code §154.021(a)(3). See "Appointment of impartial third party," ch. 4-A, §6.

4. Other ADR providers. A court can refer a case to any other ADR provider the court deems appropriate. *See* Tex. Civ. Prac. & Rem. Code §154.021(a) (uses the term "including" before list of ADR providers).

§6. Appointment of impartial third party

If the court refers a dispute to ADR, the court may appoint one or more impartial third parties agreed on by the parties to facilitate the ADR. Tex. Civ. Prac. & Rem. Code §154.051.

§6.1 Qualifications.

1. Generally. To qualify for appointment as an impartial third party, the person must have completed 40 classroom hours of training provided by an ADR system or other organization approved by the court. Tex. Civ. Prac. & Rem. Code §154.052(a).

2. For parent-child disputes. To qualify for appointment in a dispute relating to the parent-child relationship, a person must have—in addition to the 40 classroom hours of general ADR training—24 hours of training in family dynamics, child development, and family law, including a minimum of 4 hours of family-violence dynamics training developed in consultation with a statewide family-violence advocacy organization. Tex. Civ. Prac. & Rem. Code §154.052(b).

3. Exceptions. A court has the discretion to appoint a person who does not otherwise qualify, as long as the court bases its appointment on the person's legal or other professional training or experience. Tex. Civ. Prac. & Rem. Code §154.052(c). For example, the court could appoint a former judge who has not satisfied the training requirement.

§6.2 Standards & duties. A person appointed as an impartial third party must encourage and assist the parties in reaching a settlement but cannot compel or coerce the parties to settle. Tex. Civ. Prac. & Rem. Code §154.053(a). The third party's role is to facilitate communication between the parties, to encourage reconciliation, settlement, and understanding, and to avoid further litigation. **In re Marriage of Ames**, 860 S.W.2d 590, 592 (Tex.App.—Amarillo 1993, no writ). Impartial third parties cannot alter the agreement between the parties or interject their own terms into the agreement. *See* **In re Marriage of McIntosh**, 918 S.W.2d 87, 89 (Tex.App.—Amarillo 1996, no writ).

§6.3 Fees. The court may set a reasonable fee for the services of an impartial third party appointed to facilitate an ADR procedure. Tex. Civ. Prac. & Rem. Code §154.054(a); **Decker v. Lindsay**, 824 S.W.2d 247, 249–50 (Tex.App.—Houston [1st Dist.] 1992, orig. proceeding). Unless otherwise agreed by the parties, the court must tax the fee as a cost of the suit. Tex. Civ. Prac. & Rem. Code §154.054(b); **Paul v. Paul**, 870 S.W.2d 349, 350 (Tex.App.—Waco 1994, no writ).

§7. Confidentiality

Any communication about the subject matter of a dispute made by a participant in an ADR procedure is confidential, is not subject to disclosure, and cannot be used as evidence against the participant in any judicial or administrative proceeding.

Tex. Civ. Prac. & Rem. Code §154.073(a); **In re M.S.**, 115 S.W.3d 534, 543 (Tex.2003); **In re Cartwright**, 104 S.W.3d 706, 713–14 (Tex.App.—Houston [1st Dist.] 2003, orig. proceeding); *see* Tex. R. Evid. 408(a)(2) (evidence of statements in compromise negotiations is generally not admissible); *see, e.g.*, **Rabe v. Dillard's, Inc.**, 214 S.W.3d 767, 769 (Tex.App.—Dallas 2007, no pet.) (statement made by attorney during mediation was not competent summary-judgment evidence).

§7.1 No disclosure by impartial third party. The impartial third party cannot disclose the following:

1. To any party, the information given in confidence by the other party, unless authorized by the disclosing party. Tex. Civ. Prac. & Rem. Code §154.053(b).

2. To any person, including the court, any matter relating to the settlement process, including the conduct and demeanor of the parties and their attorneys, unless the parties agree otherwise. Tex. Civ. Prac. & Rem. Code §154.053(c); *see also* **In re Cartwright**, 104 S.W.3d 706, 714 (Tex.App.—Houston [1st Dist.] 2003, orig. proceeding) (improper for mediator to later serve as arbitrator of same or related dispute between same parties). Mediators generally cannot testify about the bargaining sessions they attend. **In re Anonymous**, 283 F.3d 627, 639–40 (4th Cir.2002); **NLRB v. Joseph Macaluso, Inc.**, 618 F.2d 51, 53 (9th Cir.1980). The complete exclusion of mediator testimony is necessary to preserve an effective system of mediation. **NLRB**, 618 F.2d at 56; *see also* **Wilson v. Attaway**, 757 F.2d 1227, 1245 (11th Cir.1985) (trial court did not abuse its discretion by refusing to admit report of community mediator who witnessed a riot).

§7.2 Confidential record. Any record made at an ADR procedure is confidential; the participants and the impartial third party cannot be required to testify in any proceeding relating to or arising from the matter in dispute and cannot be subject to process requiring disclosure of confidential information or data relating to or arising from the matter in dispute. Tex. Civ. Prac. & Rem. Code §154.073(b).

§7.3 Exceptions. There are several exceptions to the general rule of confidentiality for communications made in an ADR procedure.

1. **Independently discoverable.** A communication made in an ADR procedure is discoverable and admissible if the same information is discoverable independently of the ADR procedure. Tex. Civ. Prac. & Rem. Code §154.073(c); **In re Learjet Inc.**, 59 S.W.3d 842, 845 (Tex.App.—Texarkana 2001, orig. proceeding).

2. **Legal requirements for disclosure.** If CPRC §154.073 conflicts with other legal requirements for disclosure of communications or materials, the confidential information may be presented to the court for an in camera determination of whether it is discoverable. Tex. Civ. Prac. & Rem. Code §154.073(e); **Avary v. Bank of Am.**, 72 S.W.3d 779, 796 (Tex.App.—Dallas 2002, pet. denied); **In re Acceptance Ins.**, 33 S.W.3d 443, 453 (Tex.App.—Fort Worth 2000, orig. proceeding); *see also* Tex. R. Evid. 408(b) (permitting in-court disclosure of evidence of compromise negotiations if offered for purpose listed in TRE 408).

3. **Report of abuse.** CPRC §154.073 does not affect the requirements for reporting abuse under Family Code chapter 261 or Human Resources Code chapter 48. Tex. Civ. Prac. & Rem. Code §154.073(f).

4. **Unrelated to dispute.** When a communication does not relate to or arise from the subject matter of a dispute, it may not be confidential under CPRC §154.073(a) and (b). **Avary**, 72 S.W.3d at 794; *see, e.g.*, **In re Daley**, 29 S.W.3d 915, 918 (Tex.App.—Beaumont 2000, orig. proceeding) (deposition questions about whether participant attended mediation and whether he had permission to leave did not relate to subject matter of underlying suit and thus were not confidential).

§8. Sanctions

§8.1 Sanctions. The trial court may impose sanctions for refusal to participate in court-ordered ADR. *See, e.g.*, **In re K.A.R.**, 171 S.W.3d 705, 715 (Tex.App.—Houston [14th Dist.] 2005, no pet.) (sanctions appropriate against party who canceled court-ordered mediation); **Roberts v. Rose**, 37 S.W.3d 31, 34–35 (Tex.App.—San Antonio 2000, no pet.) (attorney who misinformed client about need to appear at ADR was sanctioned, but client was not); **Texas DOT v. Pirtle**, 977 S.W.2d 657, 658 (Tex.App.—Fort Worth 1998, pet. denied) (sanctions appropriate against prevailing party for not filing written objections to ADR and for refusing to participate); **Luxenberg v. Marshall**, 835 S.W.2d 136, 141 (Tex.App.—Dallas 1992, orig. proceeding) (trial court struck D's pleadings because D did not comply with numerous pretrial orders, including an order to mediate).

The court cannot dismiss a case or render a default judgment for failure to observe court-imposed ADR deadlines unless it first applies the test for death-penalty sanctions. *See* **Wal-Mart Stores v. Butler**, 41 S.W.3d 816, 817–18 (Tex.App.—Dallas 2001, no pet.). See "Death-penalty sanctions," ch. 5-K, §3.2.

§8.2 No sanctions. The trial court cannot impose sanctions for refusal to settle a case in court-ordered ADR. *See* **Hansen v. Sullivan**, 886 S.W.2d 467, 469 (Tex.App.—Houston [1st Dist.] 1994, orig. proceeding). The court also cannot impose sanctions for failure to negotiate in good faith. **Avary v. Bank of Am.**, 72 S.W.3d 779, 797 (Tex.App.—Dallas 2002, pet. denied); *see* **Texas Parks & Wildlife Dept. v. Davis**, 988 S.W.2d 370, 375 (Tex.App.—Austin 1999, no pet.); **Gleason v. Lawson**, 850 S.W.2d 714, 717 (Tex.App.—Corpus Christi 1993, no writ). Once the case is settled, the trial court cannot impose sanctions for failure to pay the settlement agreement. *E.g.*, **Island Entm't, Inc. v. Castaneda**, 882 S.W.2d 2, 5 (Tex.App.—Houston [1st Dist.] 1994, writ denied) (written settlement agreement after mediation).

§9. Settlement weeks

In every county with a population of at least 150,000, the ADR statute requires two weeks—law week and judicial-conference week—to be set aside each year for the courts to facilitate the voluntary settlement of pending cases. Tex. Civ. Prac. & Rem. Code §155.001. Any licensed attorney may serve as a mediator during settlement weeks under the terms, conditions, and training required by the administrative judge of the judicial district. Tex. Civ. Prac. & Rem. Code §155.003.

§10. Settlement agreement

§10.1 Agreement reached. If the parties execute a written agreement disposing of the dispute through ADR, the agreement is enforceable like any other written contract. Tex. Civ. Prac. & Rem. Code §154.071(a); **Mantas v. Fifth Ct. of Appeals**, 925 S.W.2d 656, 658 (Tex.1996); **Castano v. San Felipe Agric., Mfg., & Irrigation Co.**, 147 S.W.3d 444, 448 (Tex.App.—San Antonio 2004, no pet.); **Davis v. Wickham**, 917 S.W.2d 414, 416 (Tex.App.—Houston [14th Dist.] 1996, no writ). If the agreement complies with TRCP 11 or contract law, one of the parties can enforce it without the other parties' consent. **Davis**, 917 S.W.2d at 416; **Stevens v. Snyder**, 874 S.W.2d 241, 243 (Tex.App.—Dallas 1994, writ denied). As with any enforceable contract, a party who signs a settlement agreement disposing of a dispute through ADR cannot unilaterally repudiate the agreement. **In re Marriage of Banks**, 887 S.W.2d 160, 163 (Tex.App.—Texarkana 1994, no writ); **In re Marriage of Ames**, 860 S.W.2d 590, 591 (Tex.App.—Amarillo 1993, no writ). See "Settlement of the Suit," ch. 7-I, §1 et seq.

§10.2 Action to enforce. The court cannot take action on a settlement agreement without a request to do so, such as a motion for summary judgment based on the agreement or an amended pleading that requests relief or proposes a defense based on the agreement. **Pickell v. Guaranty Nat'l Life Ins.**, 917 S.W.2d 439, 441–42 (Tex.App.—Houston [14th Dist.] 1996, no writ). The court may incorporate the terms of the agreement into the final decree disposing of the case. Tex. Civ. Prac. & Rem. Code §154.071(b). The terms of the settlement agreement can be enforced as contract rights regardless of whether they were incorporated into the judgment. **McFarland v. Bridges**, 104 S.W.3d 906, 910 (Tex.App.—El Paso 2003, no pet.). The court cannot modify the agreement reached in ADR without the consent of all parties. See "Enforcing settlement agreement," ch. 7-I, §3.2.

§10.3 Mediated settlement agreement. If the parties reach a settlement, they can dispose of their dispute by executing a written mediated settlement agreement (MSA). *See* Tex. Civ. Prac. & Rem. Code §154.071.

1. Family-law cases. In certain family-law suits, the parties can make the MSA binding at the time of its execution if the agreement (1) includes a prominently displayed statement, in boldfaced type or in capital letters or underlined, that the agreement is not subject to revocation, (2) is signed by each party to the agreement, and (3) is signed by the party's attorney, if any, who is present when the agreement is signed. Tex. Fam. Code §6.602(b) (divorce cases), §153.0071(d) (SAPCRs); **Highsmith v. Highsmith**, 587 S.W.3d 771, 774 (Tex.2019) (divorce case); **In re A.C.**, 560 S.W.3d 624, 632 (Tex.2018) (SAPCR). If the parties entered into a binding MSA that is not illegal or procured by dishonest means, a party to the MSA is entitled to judgment on the agreement even if the other party withdraws her consent. *See* Tex. Fam. Code §6.602(c) (divorce cases), §153.0071(e) (SAPCRs); **In re Calderon**, 96 S.W.3d 711, 718 (Tex.App.—Tyler 2003, orig. proceeding); **Boyd v. Boyd**, 67 S.W.3d 398, 402–03 (Tex.App.—Fort Worth 2002, no pet.). See "Binding agreement," **O'Connor's Texas Family Law Handbook**, ch. 3-A, §13.1.1(7)(b)[1] (2021 ed.); "Illegality, public policy & fraud," **O'Connor's Texas Family Law Handbook**, ch. 4-D, §10.1.1(7)(a)[4] (2021 ed.). In SAPCRs, a court may decline to enter a judgment on the MSA if the court

finds that the agreement is not in the child's best interest and that either (1) a party to the agreement was a victim of family violence and that circumstance impaired the party's ability to make decisions, or (2) the agreement would allow a person who is required to register as a sex offender or who otherwise has a pattern of past or present physical or sexual abuse against another to either reside in the same household as the child or have unsupervised access to the child. Tex. Fam. Code §153.0071(e-1). A court cannot, however, decline to enter a judgment on the MSA based on a broad best-interest-of-the-child inquiry. **In re Lee**, 411 S.W.3d 445, 447 (Tex.2013) (majority op., Parts I-III, V, and VII); *see id.* at 461 & n.1 (Guzman, J., concurring). See "Limited review," **O'Connor's Texas Family Law Handbook**, ch. 4-D, §10.1.1(7)(a) (2021 ed.).

2. Guardianship proceedings. In guardianship proceedings, the parties can make the MSA binding at the time of its execution if the agreement (1) includes a prominently displayed statement, in boldfaced type or in capital letters or underlined, that the agreement is not subject to revocation by the parties, (2) is signed by each party to the agreement, and (3) is signed by the party's attorney, if any, who is present when the agreement is signed. Tex. Est. Code §1055.151(b). If the parties entered into a binding MSA, a party to the MSA is entitled to judgment on the agreement notwithstanding TRCP 11 or another rule or law. Tex. Est. Code §1055.151(c); *cf.* **Boyd**, 67 S.W.3d at 402 (in divorce suits, "notwithstanding rule 11 or another rule of law" means a party is entitled to judgment even when the opposing party withdraws consent as long as MSA is not illegal or procured by dishonest means). A court may decline to enter a judgment on the MSA if the court finds that the agreement is not in the best interests of the ward or proposed ward. Tex. Est. Code §1055.151(d).

§10.4 Collaborative-law agreement. Parties in certain family-law suits can resolve their dispute through the collaborative-law process. *See* Tex. Fam. Code §§15.001 to 15.116. A collaborative-law agreement is enforceable in the same manner as a written settlement agreement under CPRC §154.071. Tex. Fam. Code §15.105(a). For a detailed discussion of the collaborative-law process, see "Collaborative law," **O'Connor's Texas Family Law Handbook**, ch. 3-A, §13.1.2 (2021 ed.).

B. Mediation

§1. General

§1.1 Rules. None. See Tex. Civ. Prac. & Rem. Code §154.023.

§1.2 Purpose. The purpose of mediation is to provide a forum in which an impartial person—the mediator—facilitates communication among the parties to promote reconciliation, settlement, or understanding. Tex. Civ. Prac. & Rem. Code §154.023(a); *see* **In re Jones**, 55 S.W.3d 243, 247 (Tex.Spec.Ct.Rev.2000) (CPRC contemplates mediation only in family or civil context).

§1.3 Forms. **O'Connor's Texas Civil Forms**, FORMS 4A:1 to 4A:4, 4B:1 et seq. (2020 ed.).

§1.4 Other references. Prather and Palmer, *Texas Practice Guide, Alternative Dispute Resolution* (2019–20 ed.); Kovach, *Ethical Considerations in the Practice of Mediation*, Alternative Dispute Resolution Course, State Bar of Texas CLE, ch. 1.1 (2012); Bayer & VanBuren, *Mediation*, Advanced Personal Injury Course, State Bar of Texas CLE, ch. 8 (2011); *Ethical Guidelines for Mediators*, Tex.Sup.Ct. Order, Misc. Docket No. 11-9062 (eff. June 1, 2011); Lowry & Robinson, *Advanced Mediation Skills for the Negotiation & Closing Stages*, Advanced Mediation: Skills & Techniques Course, State Bar of Texas CLE, ch. 1 (2009); Kovach, *Mediation: Principles & Practice* (3d ed. 2004); **O'Connor's Texas Causes of Action** (2021 ed.).

§2. Agreements to mediate

See "By agreement," ch. 4-A, §3.1.1.

§3. Compulsory mediation

§3.1 DTPA claims. A party can file a motion to compel mediation within 90 days after service of a pleading requesting relief under the DTPA. Tex. Bus. & Com. Code §17.5051(a). A claim for damages less than $15,000 cannot be forced into mediation unless the party moving for mediation (1) files a motion to compel within 90 days of service and (2) agrees to pay the costs of the mediation. Tex. Bus. & Com. Code §17.5051(a), (f). Section 17.5051 does not apply to a suit for a restraining order brought by the Texas Attorney General. Tex. Bus. & Com. Code §17.5051(h).

1. Order. The court has 30 days after the motion is filed to sign an order setting the time and place of the mediation. Tex. Bus. & Com. Code §17.5051(b). The mediation must be held within 30 days after the date the order is signed, unless the parties agree otherwise or the court determines that additional time, not to exceed an additional 30 days, is warranted. Tex. Bus. & Com. Code §17.5051(d).

2. Fees. Unless the parties agree otherwise, the parties share the mediation fees. Tex. Bus. & Com. Code §17.5051(e).

§3.2 By local rule. Some courts require mediation by local rule. For example, the Harris County family courts require all disputed custody or visitation matters that are set for a temporary hearing to be submitted for mediation to Family Court Services or another private mediator agreed on by the parties and their attorneys. Harris Cty. Fam. Ct. Loc. R. 7.1; *see also* Travis Cty. Loc. R. 13.3(a) (provides for automatic referral of most civil cases to pretrial mediation).

§4. Mediator

§4.1 Procedure to appoint.

1. Generally. Most of the rules governing mediation are contained in the general ADR statutes. *See* Tex. Civ. Prac. & Rem. Code §§154.001 to 154.073. For rules on the appointment, qualifications, standards, duties, and compensation of an impartial third party, see "Appointment of impartial third party," ch. 4-A, §6.

2. Selection. Courts located in counties with populations of 25,000 or more are required to maintain a list of all persons registered with the court to serve as a mediator. *See* Tex. Gov't Code §§37.001(a), 37.003(a)(3). The court must annually post this list of qualified mediators at the county courthouse where the court is located and on the court's website. Tex. Gov't Code §37.005. Unless an exemption applies under Gov't Code §37.002, the process for selecting a mediator from the list is as follows:

(1) Generally—first on list. If the parties cannot agree on a mediator, the court, using a rotation system, must appoint the person whose name appears first on the mediator list under Gov't Code §37.003. *See* Tex. Gov't Code §§37.002, 37.004(b).

(2) Exceptions. The court may appoint a person whose name does not appear first on the list or who is not included on the list—but meets statutory or other requirements to serve—for either of the following reasons:

(a) The court finds that there is good cause and that a mediator is required on a complex matter because she (1) has relevant specialized education, training, certification, skill, language proficiency, or knowledge of the subject matter of the case, (2) has relevant past involvement with the parties or the case, or (3) is in a relevant geographic location. Tex. Gov't Code §37.004(d).

(b) An initial declaration of a state of disaster is made for the area served by the court within 30 days before the date of appointment. Tex. Gov't Code §37.004(d-1); *see also* Tex. Gov't Code §37.004(g) (defining "declaration of a state of disaster").

(3) After appointment. Once a mediator has been appointed, the court must put that person's name at the end of the list. Tex. Gov't Code §37.004(f).

Note

Unless an exemption applies, the court clerk must prepare a monthly report on the court's mediator appointments that includes (1) the name of each appointed mediator, (2) the name of the judge and the date of the order approving compensation to be paid to each mediator, (3) the case number and style for each case and the number of cases in which each mediator was appointed, and (4) the total compensation paid to each mediator, plus, if the compensation for any one appointed case exceeds $1,000, information related to the case on the number of hours and expenses billed. See Tex. Gov't Code §36.004(a); see also Tex. Gov't Code §36.003 (listing exemptions from reporting requirements of Gov't Code §36.004).

§4.2 Conduct. A mediator should protect the integrity and confidentiality of the mediation process. *Ethical Guidelines for Mediators*, Tex.Sup.Ct. Order, Misc. Docket No. 11-9062, §2 (eff. June 1, 2011). This duty is continuous and does not end when the mediation is over. *Id.*

§4.3 Resolution. The mediator cannot substitute her own judgment on the issues for that of the parties. Tex. Civ. Prac. & Rem. Code §154.023(b); **Decker v. Lindsay**, 824 S.W.2d 247, 251 (Tex.App.—Houston [1st Dist.] 1992, orig. proceeding). The mediator cannot alter any resulting agreement or interject her own terms into the agreement. **In re Marriage of McIntosh**, 918 S.W.2d 87, 89 (Tex.App.—Amarillo 1996, no writ).

§5. Preparing for mediation

§5.1 Have authority to settle. Mediation can be successful only if a party or its representative with settlement authority attends the mediation. *See, e.g.*, **Suarez v. Jordan**, 35 S.W.3d 268, 273 (Tex.App.—Houston [14th Dist.] 2000, no pet.) (mediated settlement agreement signed by son did not bind father because son did not have settlement authority). The ADR statute is silent on the issue of who must attend, but there are cases addressing this issue. *See, e.g.*, **In re Vinson**, ___ S.W.3d ___, 2019 WL 2417441 (Tex.App.—El Paso 2019, orig. proceeding) (No. 08-18-00207-CV; 6-10-19) (although court could require that an insurance representative with full settlement authority attend mediation, court could not mandate that a particular representative attend); **Nueces Cty. v. De Pena**, 953 S.W.2d 835, 836–37 (Tex.App.—Corpus Christi 1997, orig. proceeding) (county judge could not be ordered to attend mediation because he had no authority to settle case without agreement of commissioners court); **Hur v. City of Mesquite**, 893 S.W.2d 227, 232–34 (Tex.App.—Amarillo 1995, writ denied) (city agreed during mediation to settle for specific amount but later claimed agreement was subject to city council's approval; court held that P could sue city for breach of oral agreement to settle).

§5.2 Send documents to mediator. Most mediations begin when the parties send the mediator copies of the pleadings and other important documents and copies of any legal authority necessary to resolve the issues. In some cases, the parties also send the mediator a short position paper explaining their version of the issues.

§5.3 Send documents to other parties. Each party should send the other parties copies of all the materials it sent to the mediator, except for confidential materials.

§5.4 Review file. The attorneys should review their files thoroughly and be prepared to argue the facts, the issues, and the law.

§5.5 Prepare the party. The attorneys should explain the mediation process to the parties and explain their roles. *See* Prather and Palmer, *Texas Practice Guide, Alternative Dispute Resolution* §6.4 (2019–20 ed.). The attorneys should review all the documents the parties sent to the mediator and make each party aware of the other parties' positions. *See id.*

§5.6 Take documents to mediation. If possible, the attorney should take the entire file to mediation. The documents a party will most likely need will be those sent to the mediator, but a party may want to refer to additional documents and discovery during mediation. As the parties review their positions in the mediation, it is sometimes necessary to refer to the documents and discovery to verify the accuracy of a party's memory of events and discovery concessions.

§6. Mediation session

§6.1 Mediator's opening statement. The mediator will begin the session by explaining the procedure for mediation. In most cases, the mediator will require the parties to sign an acknowledgment that the mediation procedure is confidential.

§6.2 Parties' opening statements. Each party is given an opportunity to make an opening statement explaining its position on the issues. The attorneys, as well as the parties, may make an opening statement. An attorney should determine whether allowing the party to make the opening statement will enhance the presentation of the case. A party who is articulate and who will make a good witness should probably be allowed to participate in the opening statement. A party's opening statement allows the opposition to assess that party's understanding of the lawsuit and its determination to proceed with settlement or trial, and it helps the attorneys evaluate the party as a witness in case mediation fails.

§7. Caucusing

After the joint session, the parties normally separate into different rooms, and "shuttle diplomacy" begins. The mediator spends time with each party, learning about the case and conveying settlement ideas back and forth without disclosing confidential information. *See* Tex. Civ. Prac. & Rem. Code §§154.053(b), (c), 154.073. Some mediators ask each party to submit a written "wish list" and a list of nonnegotiable matters. From that point, the mediator tries to move the parties toward settlement.

§8. Duration

Most mediations are set for one day. Mediation rarely ends at 5:00 p.m., and it can go on into the night. It is often late in the afternoon before the parties start making serious efforts to settle the case. In cases involving child custody and visitation, several shorter sessions are probably more appropriate than a single extended one. The parties in these cases should not be pushed to exhaustion because financial issues are not the most important issues to be resolved.

§9. Sanctions

See "Sanctions," ch. 4-A, §8.

§10. Settlement agreement

See "Settlement agreement," ch. 4-A, §10.

C. Arbitration

§1. General

§1.1 Rules. None. See the Federal Arbitration Act, U.S.C. title 9 (FAA); the Texas Arbitration Act (TAA), Tex. Civ. Prac. & Rem. Code ch. 171; and the Alternative Dispute Resolution Code, CPRC title 7 (ADR Act).

§1.2 Purpose. Arbitration is an efficient method for settling a dispute outside the courtroom. *See* **Rachal v. Reitz**, 403 S.W.3d 840, 842 (Tex.2013). One purpose behind arbitration is to avoid large litigation expenses, particularly the costs of longer proceedings, complicated appeals, discovery, investigations, fees, and expert witnesses. **In re Olshan Found. Repair Co.**, 328 S.W.3d 883, 894 (Tex.2010). Federal and state laws strongly favor arbitration. **In re FirstMerit Bank**, 52 S.W.3d 749, 753 (Tex.2001); **EZ Pawn Corp. v. Mancias**, 934 S.W.2d 87, 90 (Tex.1996); **Cantella & Co. v. Goodwin**, 924 S.W.2d 943, 944 (Tex.1996). There are three kinds of arbitration: ADR arbitration, statutory arbitration, and contractual arbitration under the FAA or TAA.

§1.3 Forms. **O'Connor's Texas Civil Forms**, FORMS 4C:1 et seq. (2020 ed.).

§1.4 Other references. Bayer & VanBuren, *Evidence & Discovery in Arbitration, Advanced Evidence & Discovery Course*, State Bar of Texas CLE, ch. 18 (2010); Levinson, *Lawyering Skills, Principles & Methods Offer Insight as to Best Practices for Arbitration*, 60 Baylor L.Rev. 1 (2008); Hecht, *Arbitration & the Vanishing Jury Trial*, 69 Tex.B.J. 852 (Oct.2006); Stilwell, *Correcting Errors: Imperfect Awards in Texas Arbitration*, 58 Baylor L.Rev. 467 (2006); **O'Connor's Federal Rules * Civil Trials** (2021 ed.); **O'Connor's Texas Causes of Action** (2021 ed.); **O'Connor's Texas Civil Appeals** (2020 ed.).

§2. Motion to compel ADR arbitration

§2.1 Types of ADR arbitration. ADR arbitration applies to court-ordered referrals to arbitration, which can be nonbinding or binding. *See* Tex. Civ. Prac. & Rem. Code §154.027(b); **Beldon Roofing Co. v. Sunchase IV Homeowners' Ass'n**, 494 S.W.3d 231, 239 (Tex.App.—Corpus Christi 2015, no pet.).

Note

Although ADR arbitration can be nonbinding or binding, arbitration under the TAA, which applies to enforce parties' private agreements to arbitrate, contemplates only binding arbitration that is subject to limited judicial review. ***Beldon Roofing****, 494 S.W.3d at 239; see* ***In re Cartwright****, 104 S.W.3d 706, 711 (Tex.App.—Houston [1st Dist.] 2003, orig. proceeding). See "Motion to compel contractual arbitration under TAA," ch. 4-C, §6; "TAA," ch. 4-C, §8.3.1(1).*

1. Nonbinding. A party may file a motion to refer its case to nonbinding arbitration as part of an ADR procedure. *See* Tex. Civ. Prac. & Rem. Code §§152.003(a), 154.021, 154.027(a).

2. Binding. If the parties stipulate in advance that court-ordered arbitration will be binding, the award is binding and enforceable like any contract obligation. Tex. Civ. Prac. & Rem. Code §154.027(b); **Beldon Roofing**, 494 S.W.3d at 239.

§2.2 Procedure for ADR arbitration. See "Referral procedures for ADR," ch. 4-A, §3.

§3. Motion to compel statutory arbitration

§3.1 Statutes requiring arbitration. A number of statutes require parties to arbitrate disputes instead of litigating them. *See, e.g.*, Tex. Agric. Code ch. 64 (seed-performance disputes); Tex. Alco. Bev. Code §102.77 (intra-industry disputes); Tex. Tax Code §42.225 (property owner's appeal of appraisal-review-board order).

§3.2 Procedure for statutory arbitration. When a case is referred to arbitration under a specific code provision, the attorney should check the provisions in that code for the procedures to follow.

§4. Motion to compel contractual arbitration—FAA or TAA?

Parties that agree to arbitrate can be compelled to arbitrate under the Federal Arbitration Act (FAA), the Texas Arbitration Act (TAA), or both, depending on the terms of the agreement and the nature of the claim. When both acts apply, the FAA preempts the TAA to the extent that they conflict. See "FAA preemption of TAA," ch. 4-C, §4.5. Many of the same substantive principles apply regardless of whether cases are governed by the FAA or the TAA, and courts rely on FAA and TAA cases interchangeably. **Forest Oil Corp. v. McAllen**, 268 S.W.3d 51, 56 n.10 (Tex.2008).

Note

Even if the parties' arbitration agreement falls outside the scope of the FAA and the TAA, the agreement may be enforceable under common law. See ***Hoskins v. Hoskins****, 497 S.W.3d 490, 495 (Tex.2016);* ***Blue Cross Blue Shield v. Juneau****, 114 S.W.3d 126, 134 n.5 (Tex.App.—Austin 2003, no pet.); see, e.g.,* ***Jefferson Cty. v. Jefferson Cty. Constables Ass'n****, 546 S.W.3d 661, 665 (Tex.2018) (because TAA does not apply to collective-bargaining agreements, arbitration award was reviewed under common law);* ***L.H. Lacy Co. v. City of Lubbock****, 559 S.W.2d 348, 350 (Tex.1977) (because construction contracts were exempt under former version of TAA, arbitration award was reviewed under common law).*

§4.1 Agreement specifies FAA. If an agreement requires arbitration under the FAA, a party can be compelled to arbitrate under the FAA regardless of whether the transaction involved or affected interstate commerce. **Teel v. Beldon Roofing & Remodeling Co.**, 281 S.W.3d 446, 449 (Tex.App.—San Antonio 2007, pet. denied); **In re Kellogg Brown & Root**, 80 S.W.3d 611, 617 (Tex.App.—Houston [1st Dist.] 2002, orig. proceeding); *see* **In re Rubiola**, 334 S.W.3d 220, 223 (Tex.2011). Texas courts have the power to compel arbitration under the FAA. **USX Corp. v. West**, 781 S.W.2d 453, 454 (Tex.App.—Houston [1st Dist.] 1989, orig. proceeding).

§4.2 Agreement specifies TAA. If an agreement requires arbitration under the TAA, a party can be compelled to arbitrate under the TAA regardless of whether the transaction involved or affected interstate commerce. *See* **In re Olshan Found. Repair Co.**, 328 S.W.3d 883, 890–91 (Tex.2010); **In re L&L Kempwood Assocs.**, 9 S.W.3d 125, 127–28 (Tex.1999). An arbitration clause specifically invoking the TAA designates the TAA to govern all aspects of the arbitration agreement. *See* **In re Olshan Found.**, 328 S.W.3d at 890–91. The FAA is not part of the TAA and is thus excluded when the TAA is specifically invoked. *Id.* at 891; *see* **In re L&L Kempwood**, 9 S.W.3d at 127–28. The FAA, however, is part of "the arbitration laws in your state." See "Law of the place," ch. 4-C, §4.4.2. The parties' intent should be the focus when determining whether the TAA or FAA applies. *See* **In re Olshan Found.**, 328 S.W.3d at 891.

§4.3 Agreement specifies FAA & TAA. If the agreement provides for arbitration under both the FAA and the TAA or if the agreement can be interpreted as invoking both acts, both the FAA and the TAA may apply. *See* **In re D. Wilson Constr. Co.**, 196 S.W.3d 774, 778–79 (Tex.2006). When both acts apply, preemption becomes an issue. See "FAA preemption of TAA," ch. 4-C, §4.5.

§4.4 Agreement does not specify either FAA or TAA.

1. Interstate commerce. If an agreement requires arbitration and involves interstate commerce but does not specify either the FAA or the TAA, both acts may apply. *See* **In re D. Wilson Constr. Co.**, 196 S.W.3d 774, 778–79 (Tex.2006); *see, e.g.,* **Sporran Kbusco, Inc. v. Cerda**, 227 S.W.3d 288, 291 (Tex.App.—San Antonio 2007, pet. denied) (agreement did not specify FAA or TAA; both applied because contract involved interstate commerce and TAA was not preempted). When both the FAA and the TAA apply, preemption becomes an issue. See "FAA preemption of TAA," ch. 4-C, §4.5.

2. Law of the place. If an agreement requires arbitration and does not specify either the FAA or the TAA but states that arbitration is under "the arbitration laws in your state" or that it "shall be governed by the law of the place where the Project is located" or uses similar language, both the FAA and the TAA may apply. **In re Olshan Found. Repair Co.**, 328 S.W.3d 883, 890 (Tex.2010); *see* **In re D. Wilson Constr.**, 196 S.W.3d at 778–79; **In re L&L Kempwood Assocs.**, 9 S.W.3d 125, 127–28 (Tex.1999). The Texas Supreme Court has interpreted a law-of-the-place provision to include both federal

and state laws. **In re L&L Kempwood**, 9 S.W.3d at 127–28; *see* **In re Olshan Found.**, 328 S.W.3d at 890 (FAA is part of "arbitration laws of Texas"). Thus, if the contract has a law-of-the-place provision, it is not necessary to show the contract involved interstate commerce to invoke the FAA. To apply only the TAA, a law-of-the-place provision must contain language that specifically excludes application of the FAA. **In re Olshan Found.**, 328 S.W.3d at 890.

3. No interstate commerce or law-of-the-place provision. If an agreement requires arbitration and (1) does not specify either the FAA or the TAA, (2) does not involve interstate commerce, and (3) does not contain a law-of-the-place provision, only the TAA applies. See "Motion to compel arbitration under TAA," ch. 4-C, §6.2.

§4.5 FAA preemption of TAA. If an agreement refers to both the FAA and the TAA, or if it does not refer to either act, both acts may apply, raising the issue of preemption. *See* **In re D. Wilson Constr. Co.**, 196 S.W.3d 774, 778–79 (Tex.2006).

1. When FAA preempts. When both acts apply, courts use the four-part test set out in **In re Nexion Health**, 173 S.W.3d 67 (Tex.2005), to determine whether the TAA thwarts the goals and policies of the FAA and is thus preempted. For the FAA to preempt the TAA, the following must be true:

(1) In writing. The agreement is in writing. **Nafta Traders, Inc. v. Quinn**, 339 S.W.3d 84, 98 (Tex.2011); **In re D. Wilson Constr.**, 196 S.W.3d at 780; **In re Nexion Health**, 173 S.W.3d at 69.

(2) Interstate commerce. The agreement involves interstate commerce. **Nafta Traders**, 339 S.W.3d at 98; **In re Olshan Found. Repair Co.**, 328 S.W.3d 883, 888 (Tex.2010); **In re D. Wilson Constr.**, 196 S.W.3d at 780; **In re Nexion Health**, 173 S.W.3d at 69; *see* 9 U.S.C. §2. Under the FAA, "commerce" is read broadly, and almost anything can bring a dispute under the FAA. *See, e.g.,* **In re Nexion Health**, 173 S.W.3d at 69 (Medicare payments made to health-care center on D's behalf established interstate commerce); **In re L&L Kempwood Assocs.**, 9 S.W.3d 125, 127 (Tex.1999) (contract involved interstate commerce because parties resided in different states); **In re Nasr**, 50 S.W.3d 23, 25–26 & n.1 (Tex.App.—Beaumont 2001, orig. proceeding) (contract to build Texas residence listing Wal-Mart as subcontractor involved interstate commerce); **Palm Harbor Homes, Inc. v. McCoy**, 944 S.W.2d 716, 720 (Tex.App.—Fort Worth 1997, orig. proceeding) (purchase of mobile home manufactured in Texas that included components purchased or manufactured in other states involved interstate commerce). The FAA does not require a substantial effect on interstate commerce; it requires only that commerce be involved or affected. **In re L&L Kempwood**, 9 S.W.3d at 126–27; **Royce Homes, L.P. v. Bates**, 315 S.W.3d 77, 85 (Tex.App.—Houston [1st Dist.] 2010, no pet.); **In re Big 8 Food Stores**, 166 S.W.3d 869, 879 (Tex.App.—El Paso 2005, orig. proceeding); *see also* **Service Corp. v. Lopez**, 162 S.W.3d 801, 807 (Tex.App.—Corpus Christi 2005, no pet.) (whether party anticipated substantial effect on interstate commerce is irrelevant). For example, interstate commerce can be involved or affected if (1) headquarters are located in another state, (2) materials are transported across state lines, (3) parts are manufactured in another state, (4) invoices are prepared in another state, or (5) interstate mail and phone calls support a contract. **In re Big 8**, 166 S.W.3d at 879; **Service Corp.**, 162 S.W.3d at 807; *see* **Royce Homes**, 315 S.W.3d at 85. However, the mere fact that the contract involves interstate commerce does not preclude enforcement under the TAA as well as the FAA. **Nafta Traders**, 339 S.W.3d at 98; **In re D. Wilson Constr.**, 196 S.W.3d at 780.

(3) Contract defenses. The agreement can withstand scrutiny under traditional state-law contract defenses. **Nafta Traders**, 339 S.W.3d at 98; **In re D. Wilson Constr.**, 196 S.W.3d at 780; **In re Nexion Health**, 173 S.W.3d at 69.

(4) Contrary Texas law. Texas law adversely affects the enforceability of the agreement. *See* **Nafta Traders**, 339 S.W.3d at 98; **In re Olshan Found.**, 328 S.W.3d at 891; **In re D. Wilson Constr.**, 196 S.W.3d at 780; **In re Nexion Health**, 173 S.W.3d at 69. For the FAA to preempt the TAA, an FAA-enforceable agreement must be unenforceable under Texas law because the TAA (1) expressly exempts the agreement from coverage or (2) imposes a requirement for enforceability not found in the FAA. **Nafta Traders**, 339 S.W.3d at 98; **In re D. Wilson Constr.**, 196 S.W.3d at 780; *see* **Ellis v. Schlimmer**, 337 S.W.3d 860, 862 (Tex.2011); *see, e.g.,* **In re Olshan Found.**, 328 S.W.3d at 888 (TAA affected enforceability by adding signature requirement to arbitration agreements in service contracts of $50,000 or less); **In re Nexion Health**, 173 S.W.3d at 69 (TAA affected enforceability by adding signature requirement to arbitration agreements in personal-injury cases).

Note

Similarly, the FAA may preempt Texas law—other than the TAA—if an FAA-enforceable agreement is unenforceable under Texas law because the Texas law imposes a requirement for enforceability not found in the FAA. See, e.g., ***Fredericksburg Care Co. v. Perez****, 461 S.W.3d 513, 518 (Tex.2015) (CPRC §74.451 affected enforceability because it required arbitration agreement for health-care-liability claim to include bold and conspicuous warning of patient's right to consult attorney);* ***Cleveland Constr., Inc. v. Levco Constr., Inc.****, 359 S.W.3d 843, 855–56 (Tex.App.—Houston [1st Dist.] 2012, pet. dism'd) (Bus. & Com. Code §272.001 affected enforceability because it voided choice of venue in arbitration agreement).*

2. What FAA preempts. When both acts apply, the FAA preempts the TAA only to the extent that the TAA would thwart the goals and policies of the FAA. *See* **In re D. Wilson Constr.**, 196 S.W.3d at 779; **Royce Homes**, 315 S.W.3d at 85. The FAA and the TAA are not mutually exclusive; the FAA preempts only contrary state law, not consonant state law. **In re D. Wilson Constr.**, 196 S.W.3d at 779. The FAA does not, however, preempt state law that allows parties to agree to a greater review of arbitration awards. **Nafta Traders**, 339 S.W.3d at 101. When the FAA preempts the TAA, the agreement does not necessarily have to be arbitrated exclusively under the FAA. *See* **In re D. Wilson Constr.**, 196 S.W.3d at 780. The agreement can still be arbitrated under the TAA, but TAA provisions inconsistent with the FAA are not enforceable. *See id.*

§5. Motion to compel contractual arbitration under FAA

The substantive law created under the FAA applies in both federal and state courts. **Nitro-Lift Techs. v. Howard**, 568 U.S. 17, 20 (2012).

Note

The FAA refers to an "application" to compel contractual arbitration, but "application to compel" and "motion to compel" seem to be used interchangeably by the courts. We use "motion to compel" throughout this subchapter.

§5.1 Who may compel or be compelled under FAA.

1. Signatory. Either party to a contract that contains an arbitration provision can compel the other party to participate in arbitration. The party may initiate the arbitration proceedings either before or after suit is filed. An assignee of a contract is in the same position as the original signatory to the contract. *See* **In re FirstMerit Bank**, 52 S.W.3d 749, 755–56 (Tex.2001).

Note

A party's name change after signing a contract does not convert the party into a nonsignatory. ***In re H&R Block Fin. Advisors, Inc.****, 235 S.W.3d 177, 178 (Tex.2007).*

2. Nonsignatory. A nonsignatory to an arbitration agreement can sometimes compel arbitration or be compelled to arbitrate. *See* **Bonsmara Nat. Beef Co. v. Hart of Tex. Cattle Feeders, LLC**, 603 S.W.3d 385, 400 (Tex.2020); **In re Labatt Food Serv.**, 279 S.W.3d 640, 643 (Tex.2009); **In re Weekley Homes, L.P.**, 180 S.W.3d 127, 131 (Tex.2005); *see, e.g.,* **In re Rubiola**, 334 S.W.3d 220, 224–25 (Tex.2011) (because arbitration agreement expressly provided that certain nonsignatories were considered parties, nonsignatories could compel arbitration). The determination of whether a nonsignatory can compel arbitration or be compelled to arbitrate goes to the validity of the arbitration clause and thus is for the court (not the arbitrators) to decide unless the parties clearly and unmistakably provide otherwise. *See* **Jody James Farms, JV v. Altman Grp.**, 547 S.W.3d 624, 629 (Tex.2018) (whether nonsignatory can compel); **In re Rubiola**, 334 S.W.3d at 224 (same); **In re Labatt Food**, 279 S.W.3d at 643 (whether nonsignatory can be compelled); **In re Weekley Homes**, 180

S.W.3d at 130 (same). See "Valid," ch. 4-C, §5.2.1(1)(b); "Agreement not valid," ch. 4-C, §7.2. When making this determination, courts apply Texas procedural rules. **In re Labatt Food**, 279 S.W.3d at 643; **In re Weekley Homes**, 180 S.W.3d at 130. A nonsignatory may be able to compel arbitration or be compelled to arbitrate if the terms of the arbitration agreement expressly cover disputes involving unspecified third parties or provide that certain nonsignatories are considered parties to the agreement. *See* **Jody James Farms**, 547 S.W.3d at 633; **In re Rubiola**, 334 S.W.3d at 224–25. See "Parties' agreement," ch. 4-C, §8.2.2(1)(b). Courts have also recognized several theories under which a nonsignatory may enforce or be bound by an arbitration agreement. See "Exception—party is not signatory," **O'Connor's Federal Rules * Civil Trials**, ch. 7-E, §2.1.4(1)(a)[2] (2021 ed.).

Note

The FAA does not specify whether state or federal substantive law applies to the determination of whether a nonsignatory can compel arbitration or be compelled to arbitrate. In ***Labatt****, the Texas Supreme Court stated that until the U.S. Supreme Court addresses this issue, it will apply state substantive law and attempt to keep it consistent with federal law.* ***In re Labatt Food****, 279 S.W.3d at 643.*

(1) Incorporation by reference. A nonsignatory can be compelled to arbitrate if the arbitration clause was incorporated by reference into the agreement that relates to the dispute. *See* **In re Kellogg Brown & Root, Inc.**, 166 S.W.3d 732, 739 (Tex.2005); **Kirby Highland Lakes Surgery Ctr., L.L.P. v. Kirby**, 183 S.W.3d 891, 902–03 (Tex.App.—Austin 2006, orig. proceeding).

(2) Assumption. A nonsignatory can be compelled to arbitrate under the theory of assumption. **In re Kellogg Brown & Root**, 166 S.W.3d at 739.

(3) Agency. A nonsignatory can compel arbitration or be compelled to arbitrate under the theory of agency. *See* **Jody James Farms**, 547 S.W.3d at 635; **In re Kaplan Higher Educ. Corp.**, 235 S.W.3d 206, 209 (Tex.2007); **In re Kellogg Brown & Root**, 166 S.W.3d at 739. To establish that there is an agency relationship between the signatory and the nonsignatory, a party must show that the nonsignatory was subject to the signatory's control and was authorized to act as its agent. **Jody James Farms**, 547 S.W.3d at 635. The party must also show that the agency relationship arose at the will of and through some act of the nonsignatory. *See, e.g.*, **Albertson's Holdings, LLC v. Kay**, 514 S.W.3d 878, 884 (Tex.App.—Tyler 2017, no pet.) (husband could not be compelled under theory of agency to arbitrate agreement signed by wife because marital relationship alone does not establish agency relationship).

(4) Alter ego. A nonsignatory can be compelled to arbitrate under the theory of alter ego. **In re Kellogg Brown & Root**, 166 S.W.3d at 739. Generally, a corporate relationship alone will not bind a nonsignatory to an arbitration agreement. **In re Merrill Lynch Trust Co.**, 235 S.W.3d 185, 191 (Tex.2007).

(5) Third-party beneficiary. Under Texas law, a nonsignatory who is a third-party beneficiary of the contract can compel arbitration or be compelled to arbitrate. **In re NEXT Fin. Grp.**, 271 S.W.3d 263, 267 (Tex.2008); **In re Kellogg Brown & Root**, 166 S.W.3d at 739; *e.g.*, **In re Labatt Food**, 279 S.W.3d at 645–46 (beneficiary bringing wrongful-death action was bound by arbitration agreement made by decedent because wrongful-death actions are derivative under Texas law); **Albertson's Holdings**, 514 S.W.3d at 884–85 (beneficiary bringing loss-of-consortium claim was not bound by spouse's arbitration agreement because loss-of-consortium claims are not entirely derivative under Texas law); *see* **Jody James Farms**, 547 S.W.3d at 635–36. For a discussion of the requirements to considered a third-party beneficiary of a contract, see "Third-party beneficiary," **O'Connor's Texas Causes of Action**, ch. 5-B, §2.2.4 (2021 ed.).

(6) Equitable estoppel. A nonsignatory can compel arbitration or be compelled to arbitrate under the theory of equitable estoppel. **Meyer v. WMCO-GP, LLC**, 211 S.W.3d 302, 305–06 (Tex.2006) (TAA); *see* **Jody James Farms**, 547 S.W.3d at 636; **In re Kellogg Brown & Root**, 166 S.W.3d at 739. There are two equitable-estoppel theories under which a nonsignatory can enforce or be bound by an arbitration clause:

(a) Direct-benefits estoppel. Under direct-benefits estoppel, a plaintiff is estopped from claiming benefits under a contract while seeking to avoid an arbitration agreement that is included in the contract. *See* **Bonsmara Nat. Beef**,

603 S.W.3d at 400; **Jody James Farms**, 547 S.W.3d at 637; **G.T. Leach Builders, LLC v. Sapphire V.P., LP**, 458 S.W.3d 502, 527 (Tex.2015) (TAA); **In re Kellogg Brown & Root**, 166 S.W.3d at 739. This doctrine can apply in a suit brought by a nonsignatory plaintiff against a signatory or in a suit brought by a signatory plaintiff against a nonsignatory. *See, e.g.*, **Meyer**, 211 S.W.3d at 305–06 (nonsignatory-Ds could compel signatory-P to arbitrate when P's right to recover damages depended on agreement containing arbitration clause); *see also* **Bonsmara Nat. Beef**, 603 S.W.3d at 401 (doctrine is meant to compel arbitration with nonsignatories). Direct-benefits estoppel applies if the plaintiff either pursues a claim "on the contract" or seeks and obtains substantial benefits that arise from the contract. *See* **In re Weekley Homes**, 180 S.W.3d at 132–33; **In re Kellogg Brown & Root**, 166 S.W.3d at 740. However, a plaintiff will not be compelled to arbitrate under a claim on the contract simply because its claim relates to the contract. **G.T. Leach Builders**, 458 S.W.3d at 527; **In re Kellogg Brown & Root**, 166 S.W.3d at 741. Arbitration will be compelled only if the plaintiff seeks, through its claim, to derive a direct benefit from the contract containing the arbitration agreement. **Jody James Farms**, 547 S.W.3d at 637; **G.T. Leach Builders**, 458 S.W.3d at 527; **In re Kellogg Brown & Root**, 166 S.W.3d at 741. Whether a plaintiff seeks a direct benefit from a contract containing an arbitration agreement turns on the substance of its claim. **In re Weekley Homes**, 180 S.W.3d at 131–32; *e.g.*, **Rocha v. Marks Transp.**, 512 S.W.3d 529, 538 (Tex.App.—Houston [1st Dist.] 2016, no pet.) (direct-benefits estoppel did not bind nonsignatory P to arbitration because her slip-and-fall claim alleged hazardous conditions on D's premises and did not involve duty or liability arising from her husband's purchase contract with D).

(b) Concerted-misconduct estoppel. Under concerted-misconduct estoppel, a nonsignatory can be compelled to arbitrate when a signatory to the contract alleges that the nonsignatory and one or more of the other signatories engaged in substantially interdependent and concerted misconduct. *See* **In re Merrill Lynch Trust**, 235 S.W.3d at 191. However, neither the U.S. Supreme Court nor the Texas Supreme Court has compelled arbitration based solely on the theory of concerted-misconduct estoppel. *See id.* at 191–92. Although concerted-misconduct estoppel has been recognized by the Fifth Circuit, the issue of whether it is a viable theory for compelling arbitration is not well settled in federal courts. *Id.* at 192. See "Equitable estoppel," **O'Connor's Federal Rules * Civil Trials**, ch. 7-E, §2.1.4(1)(a)[2][a] (2021 ed.).

Note

Some federal courts have recognized a third estoppel theory under which a nonsignatory can compel arbitration—the "intertwined-claims" or "alternative-estoppel" theory. ***Jody James Farms**, 547 S.W.3d at 639. Under this theory, a nonsignatory can compel arbitration if (1) the nonsignatory has a close relationship with a signatory to the contract and (2) the claims are "intimately" founded in and intertwined with the underlying contract obligations. Id. In **Jody James Farms**, the Texas Supreme Court declined to determine the validity of this theory under Texas law but acknowledged that, if the Court were to accept the theory, the nonsignatory in that case did not show its applicability. Id.; see also **Natgasoline LLC v. Refractory Constr. Servs., Co.**, 566 S.W.3d 871, 888–89 (Tex.App.—Houston [14th Dist.] 2018, pet. denied) (court noted that **Jody James Farms** declined to determine validity of intertwined-claims theory; court found that, even if valid, theory did not apply under facts of case).*

§5.2 Motion to compel arbitration under FAA. For the court to compel arbitration under the FAA, the party seeking to compel arbitration must show that there is a valid arbitration agreement and the claim falls within the scope of that agreement. **Bonsmara Nat. Beef Co. v. Hart of Tex. Cattle Feeders, LLC**, 603 S.W.3d 385, 397 (Tex.2020); **Jody James Farms, JV v. Altman Grp.**, 547 S.W.3d 624, 633 (Tex.2018); **In re Dillard Dept. Stores**, 186 S.W.3d 514, 515 (Tex.2006). The claim must also be arbitrable under federal law. *See* **In re American Homestar**, 50 S.W.3d 480, 485 (Tex.2001).

1. Valid agreement & claim within scope.

(1) Valid arbitration agreement. The party moving for arbitration must show that the claim is subject to a valid arbitration agreement. **Henry v. Cash Biz, LP**, 551 S.W.3d 111, 115 (Tex.2018); **In re Odyssey Healthcare, Inc.**, 310 S.W.3d 419, 422 (Tex.2010). Courts must resolve any doubts about an agreement to arbitrate in favor of arbitration. **Henry**, 551 S.W.3d at 115; **Cantella & Co. v. Goodwin**, 924 S.W.2d 943, 944 (Tex.1996). Generally, state law governs whether a party agreed to arbitrate. **In re Labatt Food Serv.**, 279 S.W.3d 640, 643 (Tex.2009); **In re Weekley Homes, L.P.**, 180 S.W.3d 127, 130 (Tex.2005).

(a) Written. The terms of the arbitration agreement must be in writing. *See* 9 U.S.C. §4; **Dean Witter Reynolds, Inc. v. Byrd**, 470 U.S. 213, 218 (1985). An arbitration agreement does not have to be in any particular form; however, the language of the agreement must clearly indicate the intent to arbitrate. **Forged Components, Inc. v. Guzman**, 409 S.W.3d 91, 100 (Tex.App.—Houston [1st Dist.] 2013, no pet.); *see also* **In re D. Wilson Constr. Co.**, 196 S.W.3d 774, 781 (Tex.2006) (valid agreement to arbitrate exists when signed contract incorporates by reference another document containing arbitration clause).

(b) Valid. There must be a valid arbitration agreement for the court to compel arbitration. **Jody James Farms**, 547 S.W.3d at 633; **In re 24R, Inc.**, 324 S.W.3d 564, 566 (Tex.2010); **In re Odyssey Healthcare**, 310 S.W.3d at 422. An agreement to arbitrate is valid if it meets the requirements of the general contract law of the state. **In re Rubiola**, 334 S.W.3d 220, 224 (Tex.2011); **In re Poly-Am., L.P.**, 262 S.W.3d 337, 347 (Tex.2008); **In re Dillard Dept. Stores**, 186 S.W.3d at 515; *see* 9 U.S.C. §2 (written agreement to arbitrate is considered valid unless it can be revoked under contract law); **Morgan v. Bronze Queen Mgmt. Co.**, 474 S.W.3d 701, 705–06 (Tex.App.—Houston [14th Dist.] 2014, no pet.) (arbitration agreement requires mutual assent to be enforceable; unilateral offer from one party does not create an agreement). Thus, the arbitration agreement must be based on valid consideration. **In re Palm Harbor Homes, Inc.**, 195 S.W.3d 672, 676 (Tex.2006); *see, e.g.*, **In re 24R**, 324 S.W.3d at 566–67 (mutual agreement to arbitrate in at-will employment situation provided sufficient consideration to support arbitration agreement). If one party to the agreement can avoid its promise to arbitrate by amending the provision or terminating it altogether, the agreement is illusory and not enforceable. **In re 24R**, 324 S.W.3d at 567. See "Illusory agreement," ch. 4-C, §7.2.4; "Proving an enforceable contract," **O'Connor's Texas Causes of Action**, ch. 5-A, §2 (2021 ed.).

Note

For an arbitration agreement to be valid in an at-will employment relationship, the employee must have received notice of the agreement and accepted it. ***In re Dallas Peterbilt, Ltd.****, 196 S.W.3d 161, 162 (Tex.2006); see, e.g.,* ***Doe v. Columbia N. Hills Hosp. Subsidiary, L.P.****, 521 S.W.3d 76, 81–82 (Tex.App.—Fort Worth 2017, pet. denied) (in at-will employment relationship, merely posting arbitration policy on employer's intranet website was insufficient to give employee notice of policy). The notice analysis is not limited to the underlying agreement; it includes all communications between the employer and the employee.* ***In re Dallas Peterbilt, Ltd.****, 196 S.W.3d at 162.*

(c) Signature not required. The FAA does not require that an agreement to arbitrate be signed by the parties. **In re Polymerica**, 296 S.W.3d 74, 76 (Tex.2009); **In re Macy's Tex., Inc.**, 291 S.W.3d 418, 419 (Tex.2009); **In re AdvancePCS Health L.P.**, 172 S.W.3d 603, 606 (Tex.2005); **SK Plymouth, LLC v. Simmons**, 605 S.W.3d 706, ___ (Tex.App.—Houston [1st Dist.] 2020, no pet.).

Note

Although the FAA does not require that an arbitration agreement be signed, the terms of the parties' agreement may require a signature as a condition precedent to enforceability. ***SK Plymouth****, 605 S.W.3d at ___. But a blank signature block in the agreement, without more, is insufficient to establish that a signature is a condition precedent to enforceability. Id. at ___.*

[1] Signed. If the parties signed an arbitration agreement, they are bound by its terms unless there is fraud, misrepresentation, or deceit. **In re McKinney**, 167 S.W.3d 833, 835 (Tex.2005); *see, e.g.*, **Momentis U.S. Corp. v. Weisfeld**, No. 05-13-01250-CV, 2014 WL 3700697 (Tex.App.—Dallas 2014, no pet.) (memo op.; 7-23-14) (Ps agreed to arbitration clause in online form when they electronically signed it by checking "I agree" button and clicking "Sign & Submit" button). This is true even if the parties did not read the agreement before they signed it or thought the agreement stated different terms. **In re McKinney**, 167 S.W.3d at 835; *see* **In re Merrill Lynch Trust Co.**, 235 S.W.3d 185, 190 (Tex.2007).

[2] Unsigned. If the parties did not sign the agreement, the party seeking to enforce arbitration must establish that the parties agreed to arbitrate the dispute. **In re Big 8 Food Stores**, 166 S.W.3d 869, 876 (Tex.App.—El Paso 2005, orig. proceeding); *see* **SK Plymouth**, 605 S.W.3d at ___.

(2) Claim within scope. The party moving for arbitration must show that the claim falls within the scope of the arbitration agreement. **Henry**, 551 S.W.3d at 115; **In re Rubiola**, 334 S.W.3d at 223; **In re Dallas Peterbilt, Ltd.**, 196 S.W.3d at 163; **In re Dillard Dept. Stores**, 186 S.W.3d at 515. To determine whether the claim is within the scope of the arbitration agreement, the court examines the terms of the agreement and the factual allegations of the plaintiff's claim. *See* **Henry**, 551 S.W.3d at 115; **In re Rubiola**, 334 S.W.3d at 225. Generally, federal law governs the scope of the arbitration agreement. **In re Labatt Food**, 279 S.W.3d at 643; **In re Weekley Homes**, 180 S.W.3d at 130.

(a) Terms of agreement. Many arbitration agreements provide that "any controversy or claim arising from or relating to" the contract is subject to arbitration. *E.g.*, **In re Kaplan Higher Educ. Corp.**, 235 S.W.3d 206, 208 & n.1 (Tex.2007); **In re Bank One**, 216 S.W.3d 825, 826 (Tex.2007). Under a broad arbitration clause, arbitration can be compelled even though the particular dispute is not specifically covered. *See* **In re D. Wilson Constr.**, 196 S.W.3d at 783. Such an arbitration clause may encompass different causes of action and claims for different types of damages. For example, an agreement to arbitrate all disputes arising from a contract may encompass some tort claims. **Merrill Lynch, Pierce, Fenner & Smith, Inc. v. Wilson**, 805 S.W.2d 38, 39 (Tex.App.—El Paso 1991, no writ). An arbitration agreement includes a tort claim if the tort is so interwoven with the contract that it could not stand alone. *Id.*

(b) Factual allegations. If the facts alleged in support of the claim have a "significant relationship" to or are "factually intertwined" with the contract that is subject to the arbitration agreement, the claim is within the scope of the agreement and is arbitrable. **Pennzoil Co. v. Arnold Oil Co.**, 30 S.W.3d 494, 498 (Tex.App.—San Antonio 2000, orig. proceeding); *see, e.g.*, **In re Dallas Peterbilt, Ltd.**, 196 S.W.3d at 163 (arbitration clause in employment contract covered race-discrimination claim); **In re Dillard Dept. Stores**, 186 S.W.3d at 515 (arbitration clause in employment contract covered defamation claim). However, if the facts alleged stand alone and are completely independent of the contract, the claim is not subject to arbitration. **Pennzoil Co.**, 30 S.W.3d at 498.

2. Arbitrable claim. For the court to compel arbitration under the FAA, the claim must be arbitrable and there must be no other legal constraint, such as a federal statute, that renders the claim nonarbitrable. *See* **In re American Homestar**, 50 S.W.3d at 485; *see, e.g.*, **In re FirstMerit Bank**, 52 S.W.3d 749, 755 (Tex.2001) (loan agreement's broad arbitration language covered all claims relating to purchase of home and bank's right to repossess).

(1) Conflicting federal statute. If a federal statute shows clear congressional intent to preclude application of the FAA, a claim cannot be submitted to arbitration. **In re American Homestar**, 50 S.W.3d at 485. To determine whether a federal statute overrides the FAA, courts look to (1) the statute's text, (2) the statute's legislative history, and (3) whether there is an inherent conflict between arbitration and the statute's underlying purpose. **Shearson/American Express, Inc. v. McMahon**, 482 U.S. 220, 226–27 (1987); **In re American Homestar**, 50 S.W.3d at 485; **In re David's Supermkts., Inc.**, 43 S.W.3d 94, 98 (Tex.App.—Waco 2001, orig. proceeding). See "Dispute is arbitrable," **O'Connor's Federal Rules * Civil Trials**, ch. 7-E, §2.1.4(2) (2021 ed.).

(2) Conflicting state statute. If a state statute precludes application of the FAA, the FAA controls over the conflicting state statute as long as the claim is subject to a valid arbitration clause. *See, e.g.*, **Nitro-Lift Techs. v. Howard**, 568 U.S. 17, 21–22 (2012) (parties entered into noncompetition agreement that contained valid arbitration clause; FAA controlled over state statute that limited enforceability of noncompetition agreements).

Note

If the court has determined that an arbitration agreement is valid and enforceable, questions about the validity of the remainder of the contract are for the arbitrator to decide. ***Nitro-Lift Techs.****, 568 U.S. at 20. See "Questions of arbitrability," ch. 4-C, §8.2.2.*

§6. Motion to compel contractual arbitration under TAA

The procedure to compel contractual arbitration under the Texas Arbitration Act (TAA) is outlined in CPRC §§171.021 to 171.026 and 171.096(d).

Note

The TAA refers to an "application" to compel contractual arbitration, but "application to compel" and "motion to compel" seem to be used interchangeably by the courts. We use "motion to compel" throughout this subchapter.

§6.1 Who may compel or be compelled under TAA.

1. Signatory. Either party to a contract that contains an arbitration provision may compel the other party to participate in arbitration. See "Signatory," ch. 4-C, §5.1.1.

2. Nonsignatory. A nonsignatory to an arbitration agreement can sometimes compel arbitration or be compelled to arbitrate. *E.g.*, **G.T. Leach Builders, LLC v. Sapphire V.P., LP**, 458 S.W.3d 502, 524 (Tex.2015) (nonsignatories could not compel arbitration when joinder provision in arbitration clause stated arbitration "may include" other parties; provision permitted signatories to consent to additional parties but did not require them to do so); *see* **Meyer v. WMCO-GP, LLC**, 211 S.W.3d 302, 305–06 (Tex.2006). The courts may rely on the same legal theories under both the TAA and the FAA to bind nonsignatories to arbitration agreements. *See, e.g.*, **Rachal v. Reitz**, 403 S.W.3d 840, 846–47 & n.5 (Tex.2013) (beneficiary of trust containing arbitration provision was bound under direct-benefits estoppel). See "Nonsignatory," ch. 4-C, §5.1.2.

§6.2 Motion to compel arbitration under TAA.

For the court to compel arbitration under the TAA, the party seeking arbitration must establish that there is a valid arbitration agreement and the claim falls within the scope of that agreement. **Rachal v. Reitz**, 403 S.W.3d 840, 843 (Tex.2013); *see* **Richmont Holdings, Inc. v. Superior Recharge Sys.**, 392 S.W.3d 633, 635 (Tex.2013); **Phillips v. ACS Mun. Brokers, Inc.**, 888 S.W.2d 872, 875 (Tex.App.—Dallas 1994, no writ). The claim must also be arbitrable. *See* Tex. Civ. Prac. & Rem. Code §171.002. Once these matters are proved, the court must order the parties to arbitrate. **Kilroy v. Kilroy**, 137 S.W.3d 780, 787 (Tex.App.—Houston [1st Dist.] 2004, orig. proceeding); **Phillips**, 888 S.W.2d at 875; *see* Tex. Civ. Prac. & Rem. Code §171.021(a).

1. Valid agreement & claim within scope.

(1) Valid arbitration agreement. The party moving for arbitration must show that the claim is subject to a valid arbitration agreement.

(a) Agreement. The TAA requires only that there be a written agreement to arbitrate; a formal contract is not required. *E.g.*, **Rachal**, 403 S.W.3d at 844–45 (trust was an agreement under TAA). Although the formal requirements of a contract are not necessary, the agreement must be supported by mutual assent of the parties. *Id.* at 845. Parties generally show mutual assent by signing an agreement; however, a nonsignatory-party can assent to an agreement by obtaining or seeking benefits under the agreement. *Id.* at 845–46. See "Who may compel or be compelled under TAA," ch. 4-C, §6.1; "Signature," ch. 4-C, §6.2.1(1)(d).

(b) Written. The TAA requires that the terms of the arbitration agreement be in writing. **Burlington N. R.R. v. Akpan**, 943 S.W.2d 48, 52 (Tex.App.—Fort Worth 1996, no writ); *see* Tex. Civ. Prac. & Rem. Code §171.001(a). An arbitration agreement does not have to be in any particular form; however, the language of the agreement must clearly indicate the intent to arbitrate. **Bates v. MTH Homes-Tex., L.P.**, 177 S.W.3d 419, 422 (Tex.App.—Houston [1st Dist.] 2005, orig. proceeding).

(c) Valid. The TAA requires that there be a valid arbitration agreement for the court to compel arbitration. **J.M. Davidson, Inc. v. Webster**, 128 S.W.3d 223, 227 (Tex.2003). A written agreement to arbitrate is valid if it provides for arbitration of an existing controversy or a controversy that arises between the parties after the date of the agreement. Tex. Civ. Prac. & Rem. Code §171.001(a). Arbitration agreements are generally interpreted under traditional contract principles. **J.M. Davidson**, 128 S.W.3d at 227; *see also* Tex. Civ. Prac. & Rem. Code §171.001(b) (arbitration agreement can be revoked based on legal or equitable ground for revoking a contract). See "Valid," ch. 4-C, §5.2.1(1)(b).

(d) Signature.

[1] Generally—not required. The TAA generally does not require that the agreement be signed by either party. **Akpan**, 943 S.W.2d at 52; *see* Tex. Civ. Prac. & Rem. Code §171.001. See "Who may compel or be compelled under TAA," ch. 4-C, §6.1.

[a] Signed. If the parties signed an arbitration agreement, they are bound by its terms unless there is fraud, misrepresentation, or deceit. **Royston, Rayzor, Vickery & Williams, LLP v. Lopez**, 467 S.W.3d 494, 500 (Tex.2015); *see* **EZ Pawn Corp. v. Mancias**, 934 S.W.2d 87, 90 (Tex.1996).

[b] Unsigned. If the parties did not sign the agreement, the party seeking to enforce arbitration must establish that the parties agreed to arbitrate the dispute. See "Agreement," ch. 4-C, §6.2.1(1)(a).

[2] Required by statute. An agreement to arbitrate must be signed when required by statute. However, the FAA preempts state contractual requirements that apply only to arbitration clauses. **In re Weekley Homes, L.P.**, 180 S.W.3d 127, 130 n.4 (Tex.2005). See "FAA preemption of TAA," ch. 4-C, §4.5. The following statutes require that the arbitration agreement be signed:

[a] The CPRC requires that an arbitration agreement be signed by the parties and their attorneys in two situations: (1) for contracts of $50,000 or less and (2) for personal-injury claims. *See* Tex. Civ. Prac. & Rem. Code §171.002(a)(2), (a)(3), (b)(2), (c)(2).

Note

Because a legal-malpractice suit is not a personal-injury claim, a mandatory arbitration clause in an attorney-client agreement is enforceable in a legal-malpractice case even if the agreement is not (1) signed by each party on the advice of counsel and (2) signed by each party's attorney, as required by CPRC §171.002(c). See ***In re Pham****, 314 S.W.3d 520, 525–26 (Tex.App.—Houston [14th Dist.] 2010, orig. proceeding);* ***Miller v. Brewer****, 118 S.W.3d 896, 898–99 (Tex.App.—Amarillo 2003, no pet.); see also* ***Dugger v. Arredondo****, 408 S.W.3d 825, 833 (Tex.2013) (implying but not directly deciding that legal-malpractice claim is not personal-injury claim). Contra* ***In re Godt****, 28 S.W.3d 732, 739 (Tex.App.—Corpus Christi 2000, orig. proceeding). See "TAA,"* ***O'Connor's Texas Causes of Action****, ch. 17, §6.4.1 (2021 ed.).*

---

[b] The Government Code requires that an arbitration clause in a contingent-fee agreement be signed by the attorney and the client. *See* Tex. Gov't Code §82.065(a); **In re Godt**, 28 S.W.3d at 738. A contingent-fee agreement that does not meet the statutory requirements is voidable by the client. **Tillery & Tillery v. Zurich Ins.**, 54 S.W.3d 356, 359 (Tex.App.—Dallas 2001, pet. denied).

(e) Type of arbitration.

[1] Binding. Arbitration is binding if the arbitration clause states that (1) it is binding or that any controversy or claim arising from or relating to the contract or a breach of the contract will be settled by arbitration and (2) any court having jurisdiction over the case may enter a judgment on the award. *See* **Porter & Clements, L.L.P. v. Stone**, 935 S.W.2d 217, 220–21 (Tex.App.—Houston [1st Dist.] 1996, no writ). Unless the contract to arbitrate specifically forecloses certain relief, the relief can be granted. *See, e.g.*, **J.J. Gregory Gourmet Servs. v. Antone's Import Co.**, 927 S.W.2d 31, 35–36 (Tex.App.—Houston [1st Dist.] 1995, no writ) (injunctive relief allowed because arbitration clause did not specifically prohibit it); *cf.* **Mastrobuono v. Shearson Lehman Hutton, Inc.**, 514 U.S. 52, 59–61 & n.7 (1995) (FAA; punitive damages allowed because arbitration clause made no express reference to them).

Note

An agreement that the arbitrator's decision is "final and binding" does not constitute a waiver of the right to appeal a judgment rendered on the arbitration award. ***Center Rose Partners v. Bailey****, 587 S.W.3d 514, 523 (Tex.App—Houston [14th Dist] 2019, no pet.).*

---

[2] Nonbinding. Arbitration is not binding if the arbitration clause specifically states that the arbitration is nonbinding. *See* **Porter & Clements**, 935 S.W.2d at 221–22. When a contract does not state whether arbitration is binding or nonbinding, the courts assume it is binding. *See id.*

(2) Claim within scope. The party moving for arbitration must show that the claim falls within the scope of the arbitration agreement. **Rachal**, 403 S.W.3d at 843; **J.M. Davidson**, 128 S.W.3d at 227. To determine whether the claim is within the scope of the arbitration agreement, the court examines the factual allegations of the plaintiff's claim. **Rachal**, 403 S.W.3d at 850. See "Factual allegations," ch. 4-C, §5.2.1(2)(b).

2. Arbitrable claim. For the court to compel arbitration under the TAA, the claim must be arbitrable and there must be no other legal constraint, such as a statutory restriction, that renders the claim nonarbitrable. *See* Tex. Civ. Prac. & Rem. Code §171.002. Although most disputes are arbitrable, a claim cannot be submitted to arbitration if a statute shows clear legislative intent to preclude application of the TAA. Under the TAA, the following matters cannot be submitted to arbitration:

(1) A contract subject to an agreement to arbitrate if the agreement is unconscionable when it is made. Tex. Civ. Prac. & Rem. Code §171.022.

(2) A collective-bargaining agreement between an employer and a labor union. Tex. Civ. Prac. & Rem. Code §171.002(a)(1); **Jefferson Cty. v. Jefferson Cty. Constables Ass'n**, 546 S.W.3d 661, 665 (Tex.2018).

(3) A contract for acquisition by an individual (not a corporation or other business entity) of property, services, money, or credit when the total consideration is $50,000 or less, unless the agreement is in writing and signed by both parties and their attorneys. *See* Tex. Civ. Prac. & Rem. Code §171.002(a)(2), (b).

(4) A claim for personal injury, unless each party, on the advice of counsel, agrees in writing to arbitrate and the agreement is signed by each party and its attorney. Tex. Civ. Prac. & Rem. Code §171.002(a)(3), (c).

(5) A claim for workers' compensation benefits. Tex. Civ. Prac. & Rem. Code §171.002(a)(4).

(6) An agreement made before January 1, 1966. Tex. Civ. Prac. & Rem. Code §171.002(a)(5).

§7. Objections to arbitration

Once a party seeking arbitration establishes the existence of a valid arbitration agreement, the burden shifts to the party opposing arbitration to raise an affirmative defense to the agreement's enforcement. **Bonsmara Nat. Beef Co. v. Hart of Tex. Cattle Feeders, LLC**, 603 S.W.3d 385, 397–98 (Tex.2020) (FAA); **Venture Cotton Coop. v. Freeman**, 435 S.W.3d 222, 227 (Tex.2014) (FAA); **J.M. Davidson, Inc. v. Webster**, 128 S.W.3d 223, 227 (Tex.2003) (TAA); *e.g.*, **Ellis v. Schlimmer**, 337 S.W.3d 860, 861–62 (Tex.2011) (although movants did not specifically invoke TAA in motion, their attorney specifically referred to it at hearing; thus, burden was on nonmovant to show agreement was unenforceable under TAA and preempted by FAA).

§7.1 No agreement. The party opposing arbitration may claim that there was never an agreement to arbitrate. The parties' agreement to arbitrate must be clear. **Trico Mar. Servs. v. Stewart & Stevenson Tech. Servs.**, 73 S.W.3d 545, 548 (Tex.App.—Houston [1st Dist.] 2002, orig. proceeding) (FAA). Whether there is an agreement to arbitrate is a threshold inquiry for the court. **In re Morgan Stanley & Co.**, 293 S.W.3d 182, 187 (Tex.2009) (FAA); **Southwinds Express Constr., LLC v. D.H. Griffin of Tex., Inc.**, 513 S.W.3d 66, 72 (Tex.App.—Houston [14th Dist.] 2016, no pet.) (TAA). See "Substantive arbitrability," ch. 4-C, §8.2.2(1). The party opposing arbitration has the burden to prove there is no agreement to arbitrate. **Cantella & Co. v. Goodwin**, 924 S.W.2d 943, 944 (Tex.1996) (FAA). To do so, the party can raise a contract-formation defense, which raises the issue of whether there was ever an agreement to arbitrate. *See, e.g.*, **In re Morgan Stanley & Co.**, 293 S.W.3d at 187 (FAA; lack of mental capacity is contract-formation defense). When a party files a response denying that there is an agreement to arbitrate, the court must summarily resolve that issue. Tex. Civ. Prac. & Rem. Code §171.021(b) (TAA); **Jack B. Anglin Co. v. Tipps**, 842 S.W.2d 266, 268–69 (Tex.1992) (FAA and TAA). For the requirements for the formation of an FAA agreement, see "Valid arbitration agreement," ch. 4-C, §5.2.1(1). For the requirements for the formation of a TAA agreement, see "Valid arbitration agreement," ch. 4-C, §6.2.1(1).

Note

Even when there is no dispute that the parties initially agreed to arbitration, if the parties enter into a later contract, the party opposing arbitration may claim that the original arbitration agreement has been revoked by the later contract or that the terms of the later contract are not governed by the original arbitration agreement. See, e.g., ***Southwinds Express****, 513 S.W.3d at 72 (TAA; D argued that some of P's claims were governed by later oral agreement and thus original arbitration agreement did not apply to those claims because oral agreement was independent of original contract; trial court held all claims were governed by original contract, regardless of whether oral agreement was independent of original contract or modified it);* ***Texas La Fiesta Auto Sales, LLC v. Belk****, 349 S.W.3d 872, 879–80 (Tex.App.—Houston [14th Dist.] 2011, no pet.) (FAA; D argued that arbitration clause in later contract superseded earlier contract's arbitration agreement and rendered it invalid and nonbinding). The issue of whether the original arbitration agreement no longer applies is for the court to decide.* ***Southwinds Express****, 513 S.W.3d at 72–73 (TAA);* ***Texas La Fiesta****, 349 S.W.3d at 880–81 (FAA). See "Substantive arbitrability," ch. 4-C, §8.2.2(1).*

§7.2 Agreement not valid. The party opposing arbitration may claim that the agreement to arbitrate is not valid. Validity defenses to arbitration that relate to the arbitration agreement itself, not to the contract as a whole, are generally determined by the court. **Nitro-Lift Techs. v. Howard**, 568 U.S. 17, 21 (2012) (FAA); **Perry Homes v. Cull**, 258 S.W.3d 580, 589 (Tex.2008) (FAA); *see* **In re Olshan Found. Repair Co.**, 328 S.W.3d 883, 891–92 (Tex.2010) (FAA and TAA); **In re Morgan Stanley & Co.**, 293 S.W.3d 182, 185 (Tex.2009) (FAA); **In re FirstMerit Bank**, 52 S.W.3d 749, 756 (Tex.2001) (FAA). But the parties can agree to submit questions of validity to an arbitrator as long as the evidence is clear and unmistakable that they agreed to do so. **IHS Acquisition No. 131, Inc. v. Iturralde**, 387 S.W.3d 785, 793 (Tex.App.—El Paso 2012, no pet.) (FAA). See "Questions of arbitrability," ch. 4-C, §8.2.2. A defensive claim relates to the arbitration agreement if it singles out the arbitration clause from other contractual provisions. *See* **In re RLS Legal Solutions, L.L.C.**, 221 S.W.3d 629, 630 (Tex.2007) (FAA). The following are some defenses the party can raise to prove the arbitration agreement is not valid:

1. Fraud. The party opposing arbitration may claim that the arbitration agreement was induced or procured by fraud. **Forest Oil Corp. v. McAllen**, 268 S.W.3d 51, 56 (Tex.2008) (TAA); **In re FirstMerit**, 52 S.W.3d at 756 (FAA); *see, e.g.,* **In re U.S. Home Corp.**, 236 S.W.3d 761, 764 (Tex.2007) (FAA; evidence that Ps did not read arbitration clause because it was on the back of a single-sheet contract was insufficient to show fraud); **In re Oakwood Mobile Homes, Inc.**, 987 S.W.2d 571, 573–74 (Tex.1999) (FAA; no fraud because P did not assert that D-seller made any false representations); **Henry v. Gonzalez**, 18 S.W.3d 684, 691 (Tex.App.—San Antonio 2000, pet. dism'd) (TAA; evidence that P did not know contract included arbitration agreement was insufficient to show fraud). See "Fraud," **O'Connor's Texas Causes of Action**, ch. 12-A, §1 et seq. (2021 ed.).

2. Unconscionability. The party opposing arbitration may claim that the arbitration agreement was unconscionable at the time it was made. Tex. Civ. Prac. & Rem. Code §171.022 (TAA); *see* **In re Odyssey Healthcare, Inc.**, 310 S.W.3d 419, 422–23 (Tex.2010) (FAA); **In re FirstMerit**, 52 S.W.3d at 756 (FAA). A party's claim of unconscionability can include procedural unconscionability or substantive unconscionability. *See* **Royston, Rayzor, Vickery & Williams, LLP v. Lopez**, 467 S.W.3d 494, 499 (Tex.2015) (TAA); **In re Olshan Found.**, 328 S.W.3d at 892 (FAA and TAA). See "Unconscionability," **O'Connor's Texas Causes of Action**, ch. 5-B, §5.1.17 (2021 ed.).

(1) Procedural unconscionability. Procedural unconscionability refers to the circumstances surrounding the actual making of the arbitration agreement. **Royston, Rayzor, Vickery & Williams, LLP**, 467 S.W.3d at 499 (TAA); **In re Palm Harbor Homes, Inc.**, 195 S.W.3d 672, 677 (Tex.2006) (FAA). Procedural unconscionability focuses on the facts surrounding the bargaining process. **LDF Constr., Inc. v. Texas Friends of Chabad Lubavitch, Inc.**, 459 S.W.3d 720, 731 (Tex.App.—Houston [14th Dist.] 2015, no pet.) (TAA). See "Procedural unconscionability," **O'Connor's Texas Causes of Action**, ch. 5-B, §5.1.17(1) (2021 ed.). Procedural unconscionability may be demonstrated by the following factors:

(a) A party's inability to bargain. **Whataburger Rests. LLC v. Cardwell**, 545 S.W.3d 73, 80 (Tex.App.—El Paso 2017, no pet.) (FAA). An inability to bargain may be shown if a party lacked the means to understand the agreement

and misrepresentations were made about what was being signed. *See* **In re AdvancePCS Health L.P.**, 172 S.W.3d 603, 608 (Tex.2005) (FAA); *see, e.g.*, **Delfingen US-Tex., L.P. v. Valenzuela**, 407 S.W.3d 791, 800–01 (Tex.App.—El Paso 2013, no pet.) (FAA; P, who was illiterate in English, attended orientation session for new employees during which D's representative translated documents to be signed; P's allegations that representative did not explain or translate arbitration agreement and misled P about its importance were sufficient to support trial court's finding of procedural unconscionability). But a gross disparity in bargaining power between the parties does not amount to procedural unconscionability. *See* **In re AdvancePCS**, 172 S.W.3d at 608 (FAA); **In re Halliburton Co.**, 80 S.W.3d 566, 572 (Tex.2002) (FAA). For example, the disparity in bargaining power between an employer and an at-will employee is not unconscionable. **In re Halliburton Co.**, 80 S.W.3d at 572 (FAA); *see* **Albertson's Holdings, LLC v. Kay**, 514 S.W.3d 878, 886 (Tex.App.—Tyler 2017, no pet.) (FAA). Similarly, a party's claim that she is unsophisticated or unable to understand the contract does not, by itself, establish procedural unconscionability. *See* **In re Palm Harbor Homes**, 195 S.W.3d at 679 (FAA).

(b) The lack of a viable alternative. *See* **Whataburger Rests.**, 545 S.W.3d at 80 (FAA). Claims of no viable alternative may be expressed in terms of an "adhesion contract," in which one party had absolutely no bargaining power or ability to change the contract terms. *See* **In re Oakwood Mobile Homes**, 987 S.W.2d at 574 (FAA); *see also* Adhesion Contract, *Black's Law Dictionary* (11th ed. 2019) (defined as standard-form contract in which one party has little choice about the terms). Adhesion contracts, however, are also not automatically unconscionable. **In re U.S. Home**, 236 S.W.3d at 764 (FAA); **In re AdvancePCS**, 172 S.W.3d at 608 (FAA).

(c) Whether the contract is illegal or against public policy. **Whataburger Rests.**, 545 S.W.3d at 80 (FAA).

(d) Whether the contract is oppressive or unreasonable or results in unfair surprise. *See* **In re Palm Harbor Homes**, 195 S.W.3d at 679 (FAA); **Whataburger Rests.**, 545 S.W.3d at 80 (FAA).

(2) Substantive unconscionability. Substantive unconscionability refers to the fairness of the terms and conditions of the arbitration agreement itself. **Royston, Rayzor, Vickery & Williams, LLP**, 467 S.W.3d at 499 (TAA); **In re Palm Harbor Homes**, 195 S.W.3d at 677 (FAA); **In re Halliburton Co.**, 80 S.W.3d at 571 (FAA); *see* **In re Odyssey Healthcare**, 310 S.W.3d at 422 (FAA; substantive unconscionability refers to whether arbitration agreement preserves party's substantive rights and remedies).

Note

A provision in an arbitration agreement that is deemed unconscionable can generally be severed from the agreement as long as the provision does not represent the essential purpose of the agreement. ***Venture Cotton Coop. v. Freeman****, 435 S.W.3d 222, 230 (Tex.2014) (FAA);* ***In re Poly-Am., L.P.****, 262 S.W.3d 337, 360 (Tex.2008) (FAA). To determine the arbitration agreement's essential purpose, courts look to whether the parties would have entered into the agreement without the unenforceable provision.* ***Venture Cotton****, 435 S.W.3d at 230 (FAA);* ***In re Poly-Am.****, 262 S.W.3d at 360 (FAA). If the provision is severable, the court can compel arbitration under the remainder of the agreement. See* ***Venture Cotton****, 435 S.W.3d at 230 (FAA);* ***In re Poly-Am.****, 262 S.W.3d at 360–61 (FAA).*

(a) Test. An agreement will generally be considered substantively unconscionable if it is grossly one-sided. **In re Poly-Am.**, 262 S.W.3d at 348 (FAA); *see* **In re Olshan Found.**, 328 S.W.3d at 892 (FAA and TAA). The test for substantive unconscionability is whether, given the parties' commercial backgrounds and the commercial demands of the particular trade or case, the arbitration agreement is so one-sided that it is unconscionable under the circumstances at the time the parties signed the contract. **In re Olshan Found.**, 328 S.W.3d at 892 (FAA and TAA); **In re FirstMerit**, 52 S.W.3d at 757 (FAA); *e.g.*, **In re Palm Harbor Homes**, 195 S.W.3d at 678 (FAA; binding only one party to arbitration was not unconscionable).

(b) Excessive costs. Although arbitration is intended to be a less expensive and more efficient alternative to litigation, when the costs imposed by an arbitration agreement are excessive and effectively prevent a party from asserting her rights in an arbitration proceeding, the arbitration agreement may be substantively unconscionable. **In re Olshan Found.**, 328 S.W.3d at 893 (FAA and TAA).

[1] Burden to prove excessive costs. The party opposing arbitration has the burden to show that the arbitration agreement is unconscionable because the costs of arbitration would be prohibitively expensive. **In re Olshan Found.**, 328 S.W.3d at 893 (FAA and TAA); *see* **In re Odyssey Healthcare**, 310 S.W.3d at 422 (FAA). The party opposing arbitration must submit specific evidence showing the likelihood of incurring excessive costs for her particular arbitration. **In re Olshan Found.**, 328 S.W.3d at 895 & n.5 (FAA and TAA); *see, e.g.*, **In re Odyssey Healthcare**, 310 S.W.3d at 422–23 (FAA; even if being forced to arbitrate in different city from where P lived would have caused her substantial expense, P did not prove that incurred costs would be likely). The party can submit invoices, expert testimony, cost estimates, or other comparable evidence. **In re Olshan Found.**, 328 S.W.3d at 895 (FAA and TAA). Evidence that other parties in similar cases have incurred excessive costs is not sufficient to show excessive costs for the party's particular arbitration. *Id.* Once the party has met her burden, the other party must show contradictory evidence that arbitration costs will not be excessive. *See id.*

[2] Factors that determine excessive costs. In determining whether costs are excessive, a court will generally use a case-by-case analysis that should focus on the following: (1) the party's ability to pay the arbitration fees and costs, (2) the actual amount of the fees compared to the amount of the underlying claim, (3) the expected cost differential between arbitration and litigation, and (4) whether that cost differential is so substantial that it would deter a party from bringing a claim. **In re Olshan Found.**, 328 S.W.3d at 893–94 (FAA and TAA); *see, e.g.*, **Olshan Found. Repair Co. v. Ayala**, 180 S.W.3d 212, 215–16 (Tex.App.—San Antonio 2005, pet. denied) (arbitration with American Arbitration Association; agreement was unconscionable when cost of arbitration was more than three times the amount of underlying claim). The key inquiry is what the total cost is to the party pursuing the claim, not where the cost goes. **In re Olshan Found.**, 328 S.W.3d at 893 (FAA and TAA).

(c) Waiver of statutory rights & remedies. An arbitration agreement covering statutory claims is valid as long as it does not waive substantive rights and remedies provided under the statute and the arbitration procedures are fair. **In re Poly-Am.**, 262 S.W.3d at 349 (FAA). But if a party is forced to give up substantive rights and remedies provided under a specific statute, the arbitration agreement is substantively unconscionable. *See, e.g., id.* at 349–50 (FAA; arbitration provision that substantively limited employer's liability for wrongful retaliation by eliminating key remedies under Workers' Compensation Act's antiretaliation provisions was unconscionable); *see also* **Venture Cotton**, 435 S.W.3d at 230 (FAA) (although statutory remedies under DTPA can be contractually waived, arbitration provision that prohibited recovery of attorney fees and enhanced damages under DTPA was unconscionable because provision did not comply with DTPA's specific requirements for waiver of statutory rights).

(d) Recovery of attorney fees. An arbitration agreement that allows for only one party to recover attorney fees is not, by itself, substantively unconscionable, although it may be relevant to a broader examination of unconscionability. **Venture Cotton**, 435 S.W.3d at 231 (FAA); *see also* **In re Fleetwood Homes**, 257 S.W.3d 692, 695 (Tex.2008) (FAA; allowing prevailing party to recover attorney fees and limiting discovery for both parties was not unconscionable).

(e) Attorney-client disputes under employment contract. An arbitration agreement covering disputes between an attorney and her client in an employment contract between them is not presumptively unconscionable. *See, e.g.*, **Royston, Rayzor, Vickery & Williams, LLP**, 467 S.W.3d at 500–01 (TAA; agreement was not unconscionable when it required binding arbitration of all attorney-client disputes except claims brought by law firm for recovery of fees). See "Mandatory arbitration," **O'Connor's Texas Causes of Action**, ch. 17, §6.4 (2021 ed.).

Note

An arbitration provision in an attorney-client employment contract is not rendered invalid even if an attorney does not explain the advantages and disadvantages of the arbitration provision before a prospective client signs the contract. See ***Royston, Rayzor, Vickery & Williams, LLP****, 467 S.W.3d at 504 (TAA). Although the Court in* ***Royston*** *stated that its opinion did not diminish any applicable ethical obligations an attorney may have, it declined to impose, as a matter of public policy, a legal requirement that attorneys explain to prospective clients the arbitration provisions in attorney-client employment contracts. Id. at 504–05; see also Tex. Cmte. on Prof'l Ethics, Op. 586 (2008) (to satisfy her*

ethical duty under Tex. Disciplinary R Prof'l Conduct 1.03(b), attorney should explain advantages and disadvantages of arbitration provision in attorney-client employment contract to extent she reasonably believes is necessary for client to make informed decision).

3. Duress. The party opposing arbitration may claim that it agreed to the arbitration clause under duress. **In re RLS Legal Solutions**, 221 S.W.3d at 630 (FAA). See "Duress," **O'Connor's Texas Causes of Action**, ch. 5-B, §5.1.10 (2021 ed.). However, proof that the party was under duress to execute the contract containing the arbitration clause is not sufficient; the party must prove it was under duress to agree to the arbitration clause apart from the other provisions in the contract. **In re RLS Legal Solutions**, 221 S.W.3d at 630 (FAA); *see, e.g.*, **In re FirstMerit**, 52 S.W.3d at 758 (FAA; no duress when sellers refused to sell home unless buyers signed arbitration addendum).

4. Illusory agreement. The party opposing arbitration may claim that the arbitration clause is illusory. *See* **In re 24R, Inc.**, 324 S.W.3d 564, 566–67 (Tex.2010) (FAA). An arbitration clause is illusory if it binds one party to arbitrate while allowing the other party to choose whether to arbitrate—that is, the clause provides one party with a unilateral and unrestricted right to amend or terminate the arbitration agreement and avoid its promise to arbitrate. **Royston, Rayzor, Vickery & Williams, LLP**, 467 S.W.3d at 505 (TAA); *see* **In re 24R**, 324 S.W.3d at 567; **J.M. Davidson, Inc. v. Webster**, 128 S.W.3d 223, 229–30 (Tex.2003) (TAA); **In re Halliburton Co.**, 80 S.W.3d at 569–70 (FAA); *see, e.g.*, **In re Odyssey Healthcare**, 310 S.W.3d at 424 (FAA; arbitration agreement was enforceable because both parties mutually promised to submit all employment disputes to arbitration and limitations were placed on D's right to amend or terminate agreement). The mere fact that an arbitration clause is one-sided does not make it illusory. *E.g.*, **Royston, Rayzor, Vickery & Williams, LLP**, 467 S.W.3d at 505–06 (TAA; arbitration clause providing for arbitration of all claims except one party's claims for fees and expenses was not illusory because it did not give that party the right to choose whether to arbitrate or litigate; both parties were still bound to arbitration of claims other than those specifically excluded); **Southwinds Express Constr., LLC v. D.H. Griffin of Tex., Inc.**, 513 S.W.3d 66, 79 (Tex.App.—Houston [14th Dist.] 2016, no pet.) (TAA; arbitration clause providing that parties would mediate all disputes before arbitration unless one party in its sole discretion believed that mediation would be useless was not illusory because clause did not allow party to avoid arbitration or unsatisfactory arbitration result).

5. Minority. The party opposing arbitration may claim that she, or the person on whose behalf the suit was filed, was a minor at the time the minor entered into the arbitration agreement and that the minor subsequently voided the agreement. *See* **PAK Foods Houston, LLC v. Garcia**, 433 S.W.3d 171, 176 (Tex.App.—Houston [14th Dist.] 2014, pet. dism'd) (FAA). The party opposing arbitration must specifically show that the minor chose to set aside the arbitration agreement. *See, e.g., id.* at 176–77 (P's filing of suit did not, by itself, void agreement but language in response to motion to compel was definitive statement that voided agreement). See "Minority," **O'Connor's Texas Causes of Action**, ch. 5-B, §5.1.5(2)(a) (2021 ed.).

§7.3 Claim outside scope of agreement. The party opposing arbitration may argue that the claim is outside the scope of the arbitration agreement. *See* **Henry v. Cash Biz, LP**, 551 S.W.3d 111, 115 (Tex.2018) (FAA) **In re Poly-Am., L.P.**, 262 S.W.3d 337, 348 (Tex.2008) (FAA); **In re FirstMerit Bank**, 52 S.W.3d 749, 754–55 (Tex.2001) (FAA). See "Claim within scope," ch. 4-C, §5.2.1(2). Any doubts about whether the claim falls within the scope of an arbitration agreement are resolved in favor of arbitration. **Henry**, 551 S.W.3d at 115 (FAA); **Rachal v. Reitz**, 403 S.W.3d 840, 850 (Tex.2013) (TAA); **In re Bank One**, 216 S.W.3d 825, 826 (Tex.2007) (FAA).

§7.4 Claim not arbitrable. The party opposing arbitration may argue that the claim is not arbitrable by law. *See* **In re American Homestar**, 50 S.W.3d 480, 485 (Tex.2001) (FAA; party opposing arbitration must show clear congressional intent to preclude application of FAA). See "Arbitrable claim," ch. 4-C, §5.2.2 (FAA); "Arbitrable claim," ch. 4-C, §6.2.2 (TAA); "Questions of arbitrability," ch. 4-C, §8.2.2.

§7.5 Waiver. The party opposing arbitration may claim that the party seeking arbitration waived its right to arbitrate. There is a strong presumption against the waiver of a contractual right to arbitrate. **Perry Homes v. Cull**, 258 S.W.3d 580, 584 (Tex.2008) (FAA); **In re Bank One**, 216 S.W.3d 825, 827 (Tex.2007) (FAA); **EZ Pawn Corp. v. Mancias**, 934 S.W.2d 87, 89 (Tex.1996) (FAA and TAA). Whether a party has waived its right to arbitration by its litigation conduct is a question of arbitrability for the court to decide. **G.T. Leach Builders, LLC v. Sapphire V.P., LP**, 458 S.W.3d 502, 520 (Tex.2015) (TAA); *see* **Perry Homes**, 258 S.W.3d at 588 (FAA).

1. Express waiver. A party may waive its right to arbitrate by expressly indicating that it wants to resolve the case in a judicial forum. *See* **In re Citigroup Global Mkts., Inc.**, 258 S.W.3d 623, 625–26 (Tex.2008) (FAA); *see, e.g.*, **G.T. Leach Builders**, 458 S.W.3d at 511 (TAA; requesting and agreeing to new trial date was not express waiver of right to arbitrate).

2. Implied waiver. A party may impliedly waive its right to arbitrate. To establish implied waiver of the right to arbitrate, the party opposing arbitration must show that (1) the other party (i.e., the movant filing the motion to compel) substantially invoked the judicial process and (2) this action was prejudicial to the party opposing arbitration. **G.T. Leach Builders**, 458 S.W.3d at 511–12 (TAA); *see* **Henry v. Cash Biz, LP**, 551 S.W.3d 111, 116 (Tex.2018) (FAA); **RSL Funding, LLC v. Pippins**, 499 S.W.3d 423, 430 (Tex.2016) (FAA); *see also* **LaLonde v. Gosnell**, 593 S.W.3d 212, 219–20 (Tex.2019) (case under CPRC ch. 150; universal test for implied waiver in any context is whether party's conduct clearly demonstrates intent to relinquish, abandon, or waive right at issue).

Note

In ***Bonsmara Nat. Beef****, the party seeking arbitration filed a motion to compel, which was denied by the trial court* ***Bonsmara Nat. Beef Co. v. Hart of Tex. Cattle Feeders, LLC****, 603 S.W.3d 385, 389 (Tex.2020). Instead of filing an interlocutory appeal, the party proceeded to trial and later filed an appeal after final judgment claiming the trial court erred in denying the motion to compel. Id. The dissenting justices in the Supreme Court argued that the party's failure to file an interlocutory appeal and its participation in the trial constituted implied waiver of its right to arbitrate. Id. at 407–08 (Green, Hecht, Devine, JJ., dissenting). The majority rejected this position and explained that the waiver doctrine looks at a party's conduct before moving for an order to compel arbitration—a party's actions after it unsuccessfully moves to compel are not relevant to the waiver analysis. Id. at 395–96 (majority op.). In holding that the party could challenge the interlocutory order on appeal after final judgment, the majority also explained that the waiver doctrine does not target appeals or impact a court's appellate jurisdiction. See id.*

(1) Substantially invoked judicial process. The party opposing arbitration must show that the other party substantially invoked the judicial process. **RSL Funding**, 499 S.W.3d at 430 (FAA); **G.T. Leach Builders**, 458 S.W.3d at 511–12 (TAA); **Kennedy Hodges, L.L.P. v. Gobellan**, 433 S.W.3d 542, 545 (Tex.2014) (TAA); **Perry Homes**, 258 S.W.3d at 589–90 (FAA).

(a) Test. The court will apply a totality-of-the-circumstances test to determine whether the judicial process was substantially invoked. **RSL Funding**, 499 S.W.3d at 430 (FAA); **Richmont Holdings, Inc. v. Superior Recharge Sys.**, 455 S.W.3d 573, 575 (Tex.2014) (TAA); **Perry Homes**, 258 S.W.3d at 590 (FAA). The court will determine the point at which an arbitrable dispute arose and then look at the movant's conduct after that point to determine whether the movant substantially invoked the judicial process. *See* **RSL Funding**, 499 S.W.3d at 430 (FAA). The conduct must go beyond merely filing suit or conducting initial discovery. **Henry**, 551 S.W.3d at 116 (FAA). In determining whether the judicial process was substantially invoked, courts can consider factors such as the following: (1) when the movant knew of the arbitration clause, (2) the length of and reason for any delay in moving to compel arbitration, (3) whether the movant asserted affirmative claims for relief, (4) how much discovery was conducted, (5) who initiated the discovery, (6) whether the discovery related to the merits, (7) how much the discovery would be useful for arbitration, (8) whether the movant asked the court to dispense of claims on the merits, (9) the time and expense already spent toward litigation, (10) whether actions in the court would be duplicated in arbitration, and (11) when the case is set for trial. *See* **RSL Funding**, 499 S.W.3d at 430 (FAA); **G.T. Leach Builders**, 458 S.W.3d at 512 (TAA); **Richmont Holdings**, 455 S.W.3d at 575 (TAA); **Perry Homes**, 258 S.W.3d at 591–92 (FAA).

(b) Waiver. The presumption against waiver is so strong that the Texas Supreme Court has only once held that a party waived arbitration by substantially invoking the judicial process. **Perry Homes**, 258 S.W.3d at 589–90 (FAA; P objected to arbitration, conducted extensive discovery, and then moved to compel arbitration just before trial). Some courts of appeals have found waiver in situations such as the following: • Defendant engaged in pretrial activity, including merits-

based discovery for 19 months and the filing of a joint motion for continuance two months before trial, before moving to compel arbitration immediately after plaintiff filed a second motion to compel production. **El Paso Healthcare Sys. v. Green**, 485 S.W.3d 227, 232–34 (Tex.App.—El Paso 2016, pet. granted, judgm't vacated w.r.m.) (FAA and TAA). • Plaintiff engaged in discovery, demanded a jury trial, and failed to comply with arbitration deadlines. *See* **CropMark Direct, LLC v. Urbanczyk**, 377 S.W.3d 761, 763–65 (Tex.App.—Amarillo 2012, pet. denied) (TAA). • Plaintiff engaged in extensive discovery during 13 months of aggressive litigation, sought injunctive relief, and brought in third parties. *See* **Adams v. StaxxRing, Inc.**, 344 S.W.3d 641, 649–50 (Tex.App.—Dallas 2011, pet. denied) (TAA).

(c) No waiver. A party does not substantially invoke the judicial process by doing any of the following: • Providing information to the district attorney that resulted in criminal charges against the plaintiffs. **Henry**, 551 S.W.3d at 118 (FAA). • Filing a declaratory-judgment action against certain parties with whom there was an arbitration agreement because it was procedurally necessary to include them under the Declaratory Judgments Act. *See* **RSL Funding**, 499 S.W.3d at 434 (FAA). • Filing a defensive motion (e.g., a motion to designate responsible third party, a motion to quash depositions, a motion for continuance). *See* **G.T. Leach Builders**, 458 S.W.3d at 513 (TAA). • Filing a separate suit against a plaintiff that filed an earlier suit against the party and moving to transfer venue of the earlier suit. *See* **Richmont Holdings**, 455 S.W.3d at 576 (TAA). • Filing suit against one party with whom there was no arbitration agreement while litigating a related but distinct claim against another party with whom there was an arbitration agreement. *See* **RSL Funding**, 499 S.W.3d at 426 (FAA); **Kennedy Hodges**, 433 S.W.3d at 545 (TAA); **In re Service Corp.**, 85 S.W.3d 171, 175 (Tex.2002) (FAA). • Filing suit against a party and moving for a no-answer default judgment before intervening in another existing suit involving that party and moving to compel arbitration. *See* **Kennedy Hodges**, 433 S.W.3d at 545–46 (TAA). • Moving between federal courts before filing an answer and a motion to compel in state court. **In re Citigroup**, 258 S.W.3d at 625 (FAA). • Filing a motion to set aside a default judgment. **In re Bank One**, 216 S.W.3d at 827 (FAA). • Filing an answer and conducting discovery. **In re Bruce Terminix Co.**, 988 S.W.2d 702, 704 (Tex.1998) (FAA); *see, e.g.*, **RSL Funding**, 499 S.W.3d at 434 (FAA; no waiver when P participated in discovery that was initiated by D and certain discovery was related to nonarbitrable claims). • Attempting to settle the claim. **Cooper Indus. v. Pepsi-Cola Metro. Bottling Co.**, 475 S.W.3d 436, 451 (Tex.App.—Houston [14th Dist.] 2015, no pet.) (FAA); **In re Certain Underwriters at Lloyd's**, 18 S.W.3d 867, 876 (Tex.App.—Beaumont 2000, orig. proceeding) (FAA).

(2) Prejudicial. The party opposing arbitration must show that it suffered actual prejudice as a result of the other party's inconsistent action. *See* **G.T. Leach Builders**, 458 S.W.3d at 511–12 (TAA); **Kennedy Hodges**, 433 S.W.3d at 545 (TAA); **Perry Homes**, 258 S.W.3d at 595 (FAA); **In re Fleetwood Homes**, 257 S.W.3d 692, 694 (Tex.2008) (FAA). "Prejudice" refers to the inherent unfairness (in terms of delay, expense, or damage to a party's legal position) that occurs when a party forces litigation of an issue and then seeks to compel arbitration of the same issue. **Kennedy Hodges**, 433 S.W.3d at 545 (TAA); **Perry Homes**, 258 S.W.3d at 597 (FAA); *see* **G.T. Leach Builders**, 458 S.W.3d at 515 (TAA). Mere delay in seeking arbitration does not demonstrate prejudice. **G.T. Leach Builders**, 458 S.W.3d at 515 (TAA); **In re Vesta Ins. Grp.**, 192 S.W.3d 759, 763 (Tex.2006) (FAA); **EZ Pawn**, 934 S.W.2d at 89–90 (FAA); *see* **El Paso Healthcare**, 485 S.W.3d at 235 (FAA and TAA; delay is not dispositive of prejudice but is one factor courts can consider).

§8. Trial court's order compelling or denying arbitration

§8.1 Hearing.

In deciding whether to compel arbitration, Texas courts follow Texas procedural rules when applying both the FAA and the TAA. *See* **Jack B. Anglin Co. v. Tipps**, 842 S.W.2d 266, 268–69 (Tex.1992) (FAA and TAA); **Cooper Indus. v. Pepsi-Cola Metro. Bottling Co.**, 475 S.W.3d 436, 441 (Tex.App.—Houston [14th Dist.] 2015, no pet.) (FAA).

1. Hearing on submission. If material facts are uncontroverted, the trial court may summarily decide whether to compel arbitration based on the affidavits, pleadings, discovery, and stipulations. *See* **Jack B. Anglin**, 842 S.W.2d at 269 (FAA and TAA); **APC Home Health Servs. v. Martinez**, 600 S.W.3d 381, 388–89 (Tex.App.—El Paso 2019, no pet) (FAA); **In re Estate of Guerrero**, 465 S.W.3d 693, 700 (Tex.App.—Houston [14th Dist.] 2015, pet. denied) (FAA).

2. Evidentiary hearing. If material facts are controverted by admissible evidence, the trial court must conduct an evidentiary hearing to resolve the disputed facts. **Jack B. Anglin**, 842 S.W.2d at 269 (FAA and TAA); **APC Home Health**, 600 S.W.3d at 389 (FAA); *see also* **In re Estate of Guerrero**, 465 S.W.3d at 704–05 (FAA; trial court did not abuse its discretion in denying motion to compel arbitration when D did not authenticate arbitration agreement and attached sales

documents; although facts were disputed, no evidence in record that D requested hearing or objected when trial court did not hold one). When the court holds a hearing to resolve fact questions, the parties should introduce evidence with all the formalities of a nonjury trial (i.e., with witnesses and a court reporter).

3. Pre-arbitration discovery.

(1) Court lacks information. Pre-arbitration discovery is permissible when the trial court cannot make a proper decision on the motion to compel because it lacks information. **In re Houston Pipe Line Co.**, 311 S.W.3d 449, 451 (Tex.2009) (FAA); **In re ReadyOne Indus.**, 400 S.W.3d 164, 168 (Tex.App.—El Paso 2013, orig. proceeding) (FAA).

(a) By application or in court's discretion.

[1] Application. A party seeking pre-arbitration discovery must file an application showing that the discovery sought is necessary and related to the issues raised in the application. *E.g.*, **In re DISH Network, L.L.C.**, 563 S.W.3d 433, 440 (Tex.App.—El Paso 2018, orig. proceeding) (TAA; party's assertion that she was entitled to discovery in objection to hearing on motion to compel was insufficient); *see* Tex. Civ. Prac. & Rem. Code §171.086(a)(4), (6) (TAA).

[2] Court's discretion. The court has discretion to order pre-arbitration discovery on its own motion if it determines that the discovery is necessary for it to make a proper decision on the motion to compel. *See* **In re DISH Network**, 563 S.W.3d at 441 (TAA).

(b) Scope. Discovery must be limited to gathering information about the scope of the arbitration agreement or a defense to it; discovery on the merits of the underlying controversy is not allowed. **In re Houston Pipe Line**, 311 S.W.3d at 451 (FAA); **In re ReadyOne**, 400 S.W.3d at 168 (FAA); *see* **In re Susan Newell Custom Home Builders, Inc.**, 420 S.W.3d 459, 460 (Tex.App.—Dallas 2014, orig. proceeding) (FAA; discovery must be related to questions of arbitrability). Discovery must be reasonably necessary; thus, a party opposing arbitration must show a colorable basis or reason to believe that the requested discovery is necessary to establish its defense. **In re VNA, Inc.**, 403 S.W.3d 483, 487–88 (Tex.App.—El Paso 2013, orig. proceeding); **In re ReadyOne**, 400 S.W.3d at 168–69 (FAA); *see, e.g.*, **In re Houston Pipe Line**, 311 S.W.3d at 451–52 (FAA; trial court abused discretion by ordering overbroad discovery that went beyond issues in motion to compel instead of ruling on legal issues in motion). If the trial court orders pre-arbitration discovery that is not reasonably necessary, the error cannot be cured on appeal, and mandamus is appropriate. *See* **In re ReadyOne**, 400 S.W.3d at 168 (FAA).

(2) Parties' agreement. Pre-arbitration discovery is permissible when the parties modify an arbitration agreement (e.g., through a Rule 11 agreement) to allow for certain discovery to take place before the hearing on the motion to compel. *See* **In re F.C. Holdings, Inc.**, 349 S.W.3d 811, 815 (Tex.App.—Tyler 2011, orig. proceeding).

4. Deferral of ruling on motion.

(1) No deferral—merits-based discovery. The trial court cannot defer ruling on a motion to compel arbitration until all merits-based discovery in the case is complete. *See* **In re Champion Techs.**, 173 S.W.3d 595, 599 (Tex.App.—Eastland 2005, orig. proceeding) (FAA); **In re MHI Prtshp.**, 7 S.W.3d 918, 923 (Tex.App.—Houston [1st Dist.] 1999, orig. proceeding) (TAA); *cf.* **In re Heritage Bldg. Sys.**, 185 S.W.3d 539, 542 (Tex.App.—Beaumont 2006, orig. proceeding) (FAA; court had no discretion to delay ruling on motion to compel arbitration until after court-ordered mediation).

(2) Not appealable. An order that defers a ruling on a motion to compel is not appealable regardless of whether the FAA or TAA applies; when a trial court defers ruling on a motion to compel, mandamus is the appropriate method for seeking review. **In re F.C. Holdings**, 349 S.W.3d at 815; *see* 9 U.S.C. §16 (FAA); Tex. Civ. Prac. & Rem. Code §51.016 (FAA), §171.098 (TAA). See "Other orders," ch. 4-C, §8.3.1(c); "Order deferring ruling on motion to compel," ch. 4-C, §8.3.1(2)(c)[2]; "Arbitration orders," **O'Connor's Texas Civil Appeals**, ch. 1-B, §2.4.3(1) (2020 ed.).

§8.2 Ruling.

1. Arbitration agreements favored. Public policy strongly favors resolving disputes through arbitration. **Jack B. Anglin Co. v. Tipps**, 842 S.W.2d 266, 268 (Tex.1992) (FAA and TAA); *see* **Nitro-Lift Techs. v. Howard**, 568 U.S. 17, 20 (2012) (FAA); **Howsam v. Dean Witter Reynolds, Inc.**, 537 U.S. 79, 83 (2002) (FAA). The court should resolve any doubts

about whether a claim falls within the scope of an agreement to arbitrate in favor of arbitration. **In re Rubiola**, 334 S.W.3d 220, 225 (Tex.2011) (FAA); **In re Kellogg Brown & Root, Inc.**, 166 S.W.3d 732, 737 (Tex.2005) (FAA); **Prudential Secs. Inc. v. Marshall**, 909 S.W.2d 896, 899 (Tex.1995) (FAA).

2. Questions of arbitrability. In ruling on a motion to compel arbitration, the court typically decides only certain issues about the arbitration, leaving other issues to be resolved by the arbitrator. In determining the types of issues to be decided by the court or the arbitrator, courts have made a distinction between questions of substantive arbitrability and questions of procedural arbitrability. **G.T. Leach Builders, LLC v. Sapphire V.P., LP**, 458 S.W.3d 502, 520 (Tex.2015) (TAA). Questions of substantive arbitrability are generally decided by the court, while questions of procedural arbitrability are generally decided by the arbitrator. *Id.*; *see* **BG Grp. v. Republic of Arg.**, 572 U.S. 25, 34 (2014) (FAA); **Howsam**, 537 U.S. at 84 (FAA).

(1) Substantive arbitrability.

(a) Generally. Questions of substantive arbitrability, which are generally decided by the court, relate to "gateway issues"—that is, the existence, enforceability, and scope of an arbitration agreement. *See* **Howsam**, 537 U.S. at 83–84 (FAA; court decides questions of whether parties to a dispute have agreed to submit it to arbitration); **G.T. Leach Builders**, 458 S.W.3d at 520–21 (TAA; court's role is to decide whether parties made valid and enforceable arbitration agreement and whether present dispute falls within scope of agreement); **In re Weekley Homes, L.P.**, 180 S.W.3d 127, 130 (Tex.2005) (FAA; court decides "gateway matters" such as whether valid arbitration agreement exists and whether nonsignatory can be bound). Questions of substantive arbitrability include the following:

[1] Whether a defense to formation of the agreement (e.g., lack of mental capacity) applies. **In re Morgan Stanley & Co.**, 293 S.W.3d 182, 189 (Tex.2009) (FAA).

[2] Whether the parties to the suit are bound by an arbitration clause in a contract. **Howsam**, 537 U.S. at 84 (FAA); *e.g.*, **In re Weekley Homes**, 180 S.W.3d at 130 (FAA; court determined nonsignatory could be compelled to arbitrate); *see* **Jody James Farms, JV v. Altman Grp.**, 547 S.W.3d 624, 629 (Tex.2018) (FAA; whether claim involving nonsignatory must be arbitrated is "gateway" issue for court to decide). See "Who may compel or be compelled under FAA," ch. 4-C, §5.1; "Who may compel or be compelled under TAA," ch. 4-C, §6.1.

[3] Whether an arbitration clause applies to a particular type of controversy. **Howsam**, 537 U.S. at 84 (FAA); *see* **G.T. Leach Builders**, 458 S.W.3d at 521 (TAA); **Perry Homes v. Cull**, 258 S.W.3d 580, 589 (Tex.2008) (FAA).

[4] Whether the arbitration clause itself (as opposed to the contract as a whole) is valid. *See* **Nitro-Lift Techs.**, 568 U.S. at 21 (FAA); **Perry Homes**, 258 S.W.3d at 589 (FAA); **In re Weekley Homes**, 180 S.W.3d at 130 (FAA). See "Procedural arbitrability," ch. 4-C, §8.2.2(2)(c).

[5] Whether a party has waived its right to arbitration based on its litigation conduct. **G.T. Leach Builders**, 458 S.W.3d at 520 (TAA); **Perry Homes**, 258 S.W.3d at 589 (FAA). See "Implied waiver," ch. 4-C, §7.5.2.

[6] Whether a party is immune from suit or has waived such immunity. *E.g.*, **San Antonio River Auth. v. Austin Bridge & Road, L.P.**, 601 S.W.3d 616, 626–27 (Tex.2020) (TAA; governmental immunity).

[7] Whether a clause in the arbitration agreement giving the arbitrator the power to decide issues of substantive arbitrability is valid. *See* **FirstLight Fed. Credit Un. v. Loya**, 478 S.W.3d 157, 164 (Tex.App.—El Paso 2015, no pet.) (FAA; if arbitration agreement has delegation clause, challenges to clause are decided by court and challenges to agreement as a whole are decided by arbitrator).

[8] Whether the parties have agreed to class arbitration. **Robinson v. Home Owners Mgmt. Enters.**, 590 S.W.3d 518, 529 (Tex.2019) (FAA).

Note

The court should find that the parties agreed to class arbitration only if the arbitration agreement specifically references class arbitration; class arbitration will not be inferred solely from the fact that

the parties agreed to arbitrate generally. ***Robinson****, 590 S.W.3d at 534 (FAA). Any ambiguity about whether the parties agreed to class arbitration will also preclude a determination of classwide arbitration. Id. at 533–34.*

(b) Parties' agreement. The parties can agree to submit most questions of substantive arbitrability to an arbitrator as long as the evidence is "clear and unmistakable" that they agreed to do so. *See* **Howsam**, 537 U.S. at 83 (FAA); **Robinson**, 590 S.W.3d at 532 (FAA); *see, e.g.*, **Jody James Farms**, 547 S.W.3d at 631–32 (FAA; mere incorporation of American Arbitration Association rules in parties' arbitration agreement is not clear and unmistakable evidence of intent to submit questions of arbitrability between signatory and nonsignatory to arbitrator); **FirstLight Fed. Credit Un.**, 478 S.W.3d at 164–65 (FAA; arbitration agreement specifically gave arbitrator power to decide disputes only about validity and enforceability; arbitrator did not have power to hear disputes about scope of arbitration agreement); **Saxa Inc. v. DFD Architecture Inc.**, 312 S.W.3d 224, 229–30 (Tex.App.—Dallas 2010, pet. denied) (TAA; broad arbitration clause covering "any" claim between parties and incorporating arbitration association's rules that gave arbitrator power to rule on her own jurisdiction was clear evidence that parties agreed to submit questions of substantive arbitrability to arbitrator). *But see* **Denar Rests., LLC v. King**, No. 02-13-00142-CV, 2014 WL 2430854 (Tex.App.—Fort Worth 2014, no pet.) (memo op.; 5-30-14) (FAA; although arbitration agreement gave arbitrator power to resolve "gateway" issue, question of whether arbitration agreement became effective by its terms was decided by court). The parties cannot, however, agree to submit questions of the court's jurisdiction to an arbitrator. *See, e.g.*, **San Antonio River Auth.**, 601 S.W.3d at 626–27 (question of governmental immunity could not be decided by arbitrator because it implicates court's subject-matter jurisdiction).

Note

Some federal appellate courts have applied a "wholly groundless" exception to questions of arbitrability under the FAA. ***Henry Schein, Inc. v. Archer & White Sales, Inc.****, __ U.S. __, 139 S.Ct. 524, 527–28 (2019). Under this exception, the court will decide questions of substantive arbitrability even when there is a clear and unmistakable intent to delegate these questions to an arbitrator if the court finds that the question of whether the arbitration agreement applies to a particular dispute is wholly groundless. See id. In* ***Henry Schein, Inc.****, however, the U.S. Supreme Court rejected this exception as being inconsistent with the FAA and held that, when an agreement between the parties delegates questions of arbitrability to the arbitrator, the court has no power to decide the arbitrability issue. Id. at 529.*

(2) Procedural arbitrability. Questions of procedural arbitrability, which are generally decided by the arbitrator, relate to the meaning and application of procedural prerequisites to an obligation to arbitrate. **BG Grp.**, 572 U.S. at 34 (FAA); **G.T. Leach Builders**, 458 S.W.3d at 520–21 (TAA); *see* **Perry Homes**, 258 S.W.3d at 589 (FAA; arbitrators decide matters that grow out of dispute and bear on its final disposition). Questions of procedural arbitrability include the following:

(a) Whether time limits, notice requirements, and other procedural conditions precedent to arbitration have been satisfied. **Howsam**, 537 U.S. at 85 (FAA); *e.g.*, **G.T. Leach Builders**, 458 S.W.3d at 521–22 (TAA; whether deadline set by parties' contract barred arbitration demand was question for arbitrator because deadline was procedural limit on parties' rights under arbitration agreement); *see* **Perry Homes**, 258 S.W.3d at 588–89 (FAA). Some courts, however, have recognized a narrow exception to the arbitrator's determination of these issues: when clearly established proof shows a strictly procedural requirement has not been met and that requirement precludes arbitration, the court can deny a motion to compel arbitration on that ground. **Southwinds Express Constr., LLC v. D.H. Griffin of Tex., Inc.**, 513 S.W.3d 66, 77–78 (Tex.App.—Houston [14th Dist.] 2016, no pet.) (TAA); **Amir v. International Bank of Commerce**, 419 S.W.3d 687, 692 (Tex.App.—Houston [1st Dist.] 2013, no pet.) (FAA); *e.g.*, **Seven Hills Commercial, LLC v. Mirabal Custom Homes, Inc.**, 442 S.W.3d 706, 722–23 (Tex.App.—Dallas 2014, pet. denied) (FAA; no clearly established proof that procedural requirement had not been met because parties disagreed about facts relevant to determination; thus, whether conditions precedent were met was question for arbitrator); **In re Pisces Foods, L.L.C.**, 228 S.W.3d 349, 352–53 (Tex.App.—Austin 2007, orig. proceeding) (FAA; clearly established proof that procedural requirement had not been met when parties did not allege they

requested mediation, which was a prerequisite to arbitration under parties' contract; thus, whether conditions precedent were met was question for court). This exception applies only when the issues are factually undisputed. **Seven Hills Commercial**, 442 S.W.3d at 722 (FAA); *see* **In re Pisces Foods**, 228 S.W.3d at 352 (FAA).

(b) Whether principles such as estoppel, laches, or waiver apply to the parties' claims. **Howsam**, 537 U.S. at 85 (FAA); **G.T. Leach Builders**, 458 S.W.3d at 520 (TAA); *see* **Perry Homes**, 258 S.W.3d at 588–89 (FAA; waiver of particular claim or defense and waiver related to limitations periods are issues for arbitrator; waiver by litigation conduct is issue for court).

(c) Whether the contract as a whole (as opposed to the arbitration clause) is valid. **Nitro-Lift Techs.**, 568 U.S. at 20–21 (FAA); **Perry Homes**, 258 S.W.3d at 589 (FAA); *e.g.*, **In re Labatt Food Serv.**, 279 S.W.3d 640, 648–49 (Tex.2009) (FAA; claim that one of contract's provisions was illegal related to entire contract and was question for arbitrator); **In re Merrill Lynch Trust Co.**, 235 S.W.3d 185, 190 (Tex.2007) (FAA; claim that contract was illusory related to entire contract and was question for arbitrator); *see also* **In re Olshan Found. Repair Co.**, 328 S.W.3d 883, 900 (Tex.2010) (Hecht & Medina, JJ., concurring) (FAA and TAA; if arbitrator determines contract is void, court can sanction party for filing groundless motion to compel arbitration).

(d) Whether a particular arbitral forum is available to hear the parties' claims. **Bonsmara Nat. Beef Co. v. Hart of Tex. Cattle Feeders, LLC**, 603 S.W.3d 385, 398 (Tex.2020) (FAA).

Note

Federal cases have recognized a narrow exception under which the court, as opposed to the arbitrator, can determine the availability of a particular arbitral forum. See ***Bonsmara Nat. Beef****, 603 S.W.3d at 399 (FAA). The court can make this determination if (1) the parties intended for a procedural provision to preclude arbitration and (2) there was a clear breach of that procedural provision. E.g., id. at 399–400 (FAA; Court recognized exception but determined it did not apply because there was no evidence that parties intended unavailability of arbitration before Texas Cattle Feeders Association to preclude arbitration altogether).*

---

3. Order.

(1) Granting motion. If the court grants the motion to compel arbitration, the court must do the following:

(a) Order arbitration. Order the parties to proceed to arbitration if (1) no objection is filed to the motion to compel arbitration or (2) an objection is filed but the court overrules the objection. *See* Tex. Civ. Prac. & Rem. Code §171.021 (TAA).

(b) Stay proceedings. Sign an order that stays the proceedings during the arbitration. Tex. Civ. Prac. & Rem. Code §171.021(c) (TAA), §171.025(a) (TAA); **In re Merrill Lynch Trust**, 235 S.W.3d at 195 (FAA); *see* 9 U.S.C. §3 (FAA; court must stay proceedings on application of party if action is arbitrable); **RSL Funding, LLC v. Pippins**, 499 S.W.3d 423, 429 (Tex.2016) (FAA; same); *see also* **In re Merrill Lynch & Co.**, 315 S.W.3d 888, 891–92 (Tex.2010) (FAA; litigation can be stayed even when arbitration is potentially pending). Arbitration should be given priority over litigation if it will likely resolve material issues in the suit. **In re Merrill Lynch & Co.**, 315 S.W.3d at 891 (FAA); **In re Merrill Lynch Trust**, 235 S.W.3d at 195 (FAA). Litigation involving claims related to both signatories and nonsignatories should be stayed. *See* **In re Merrill Lynch & Co.**, 315 S.W.3d at 891 (FAA); **In re Merrill Lynch Trust**, 235 S.W.3d at 195–96 (FAA). If the matter referred to arbitration is severable from the rest of the proceeding, the order must stay only the matter referred to arbitration. Tex. Civ. Prac. & Rem. Code §171.025(b) (TAA); **Cash Am. Int'l v. Exchange Servs.**, 83 S.W.3d 183, 186–87 (Tex.App.—Amarillo 2002, no pet.) (TAA).

(2) Denying motion. If the court sustains an objection to arbitration, the court must deny the motion to compel arbitration. Tex. Civ. Prac. & Rem. Code §171.021(b) (TAA). For a discussion of the review of the trial court's denial of a motion to compel, see "Order denying motion," ch. 4-C, §8.3.1(1)(a) (TAA), and "Order denying arbitration," ch. 4-C, §8.3.1(2)(a) (FAA).

§8.3 Appellate court's review of order.

1. Review after interlocutory order. Generally, interlocutory orders are not appealable unless made appealable by statute. The CPRC permits appeal of certain interlocutory orders regarding arbitration. *See* Tex. Civ. Prac. & Rem. Code §51.016 (FAA), §171.098 (TAA). See "Arbitration orders," **O'Connor's Texas Civil Appeals**, ch. 1-B, §2.4.3(1) (2020 ed.).

Caution

CPRC §51.016 allows for interlocutory appeals of FAA orders that would be appealable in a federal district court under 9 U.S.C. §16(a). See "FAA," ch. 4-C, §8.3.1(2). Because the FAA provisions in 9 U.S.C. §16(a) are similar but not identical to the TAA provisions in CPRC §171.098(a), parties seeking review of an order under both acts should make sure an interlocutory appeal is authorized. See "Arbitration orders," ***O'Connor's Texas Civil Appeals****, ch. 1-B, §2.4.3(1) (2020 ed.); "Other orders,"* ***O'Connor's Texas Civil Appeals****, ch. 10-B, §5.1.2(12)(b)[2] (2020 ed.).*

---

(1) TAA. Whether the party can file an interlocutory appeal or must seek relief by filing a petition for mandamus generally depends on whether the court granted or denied the motion to compel arbitration.

(a) Order denying motion. If the court denies a motion to compel arbitration made under CPRC §171.021, the party seeking arbitration may file an interlocutory appeal. Tex. Civ. Prac. & Rem. Code §171.098(a)(1); **Royston, Rayzor, Vickery & Williams, LLP v. Lopez**, 467 S.W.3d 494, 499 (Tex.2015); **Chambers v. O'Quinn**, 242 S.W.3d 30, 31 (Tex.2007); **Certain Underwriters at Lloyd's v. Celebrity, Inc.**, 988 S.W.2d 731, 732 (Tex.1998). Because of the permissive nature of CPRC §171.098, a party's decision not to pursue an interlocutory appeal does not affect its right to appeal the interlocutory order after final judgment. *See* **Bonsmara Nat. Beef Co. v. Hart of Tex. Cattle Feeders, LLC**, 603 S.W.3d 385, 390–91 & n.4 (Tex.2020) (FAA). For a discussion of similar CPRC provisions that have been found to allow for an appeal of an interlocutory order after final judgment, see "Note," **O'Connor's Texas Civil Appeals**, ch. 1-B, §2.4.1 (2020 ed.).

(b) Order granting motion. If the court grants a motion to compel arbitration, the party objecting to arbitration is not entitled to an interlocutory appeal of the order. **Human Biostar, Inc. v. Celltex Therapeutics Corp.**, 514 S.W.3d 844, 847 (Tex.App.—Houston [14th Dist.] 2017, pet. denied); **Mohamed v. Auto Nation USA Corp.**, 89 S.W.3d 830, 833 (Tex.App.—Houston [1st Dist.] 2002, no pet.); **Elm Creek Villas Homeowner Ass'n v. Beldon Roofing & Remodeling Co.**, 940 S.W.2d 150, 153 (Tex.App.—San Antonio 1996, no writ). The party may be able to seek review of the order by petition for writ of mandamus. **In re Wolff**, 231 S.W.3d 466, 467 (Tex.App.—Dallas 2007, orig. proceeding); **Mohamed**, 89 S.W.3d at 834. Mandamus relief is generally unavailable, however, because an order compelling arbitration is appealable from a final judgment, and therefore the party seeking mandamus will rarely be able to meet the requirement of no adequate remedy by appeal. *Cf.* **In re Gulf Expl., LLC**, 289 S.W.3d 836, 842 (Tex.2009) (FAA; any balancing of benefits and detriments of delaying arbitration in determining adequacy of appeal must "tilt strongly against mandamus review" because FAA and TAA both exclude immediate review of orders compelling arbitration).

(c) Other orders. Mandamus relief may be available for an interlocutory order that is not subject to immediate appeal if the order defers ruling on the motion to compel arbitration. *See, e.g.*, **In re MHI Prtshp.**, 7 S.W.3d 918, 920–21 (Tex.App.—Houston [1st Dist.] 1999, orig. proceeding) (court had no discretion to defer ruling on arbitration motion until after completion of discovery); *see also* **Bison Bldg. Materials, Ltd. v. Aldridge**, 422 S.W.3d 582, 586–87 (Tex.2012) (order directing rehearing of arbitration is not appealable if it defers a final ruling until arbitration is complete; when interlocutory appeal is not authorized, mandamus may be appropriate if trial court unreasonably delays proceedings by ordering re-arbitration for arbitrary or unsupported reasons).

(2) FAA. CPRC §51.016 allows an interlocutory appeal of an FAA order that would be appealable in federal court under 9 U.S.C. §16. *E.g.*, **CMH Homes v. Perez**, 340 S.W.3d 444, 451–52 (Tex.2011) (appeal of order appointing arbitrator was not permitted under 9 U.S.C. §16); *see also* **SSP Holdings L.P. v. Lopez**, 432 S.W.3d 487, 491–92 (Tex.App.—San Antonio 2014, pet. denied) (CPRC §51.016 is effective for interlocutory appeals filed on or after September 1, 2009; date suit was filed does not control). See "FAA," **O'Connor's Texas Civil Appeals**, ch. 1-B, §2.4.3(1)(a)[2] (2020 ed.). If an inter-

locutory appeal is unavailable, a party may be entitled to mandamus relief in limited circumstances. *See* **CMH Homes**, 340 S.W.3d at 452.

Practice Tip

If you are unsure whether the order is covered under 9 U.S.C. §16 and thus is immediately appealable under CPRC §51.016, you should file both an appeal and a petition for writ of mandamus or, at a minimum, ask in the alternative that the appellate court consider the appeal as a petition for mandamus. See ***CMH Homes****, 340 S.W.3d at 453–54;* ***Texas La Fiesta Auto Sales, LLC v. Belk****, 349 S.W.3d 872, 877–78 (Tex.App.—Houston [14th Dist] 2011, no pet.). If your appeal is dismissed for lack of jurisdiction, mandamus relief is then potentially available. See* ***CMH Homes****, 340 S.W.3d at 454;* ***Texas La Fiesta****, 349 S.W.3d at 879.*

(a) Order denying arbitration. If the court denies a motion to compel arbitration in a suit subject to the FAA, the party may file an interlocutory appeal. **Beldon Roofing Co. v. Sunchase IV Homeowners' Ass'n**, 494 S.W.3d 231, 236 (Tex.App.—Corpus Christi 2015, no pet.); **Big Bass Towing Co. v. Akin**, 409 S.W.3d 835, 838 (Tex.App.—Dallas 2013, no pet.); *see* 9 U.S.C. §16(a)(1)(B); Tex. Civ. Prac. & Rem. Code §51.016; **Albertson's Holdings, LLC v. Kay**, 514 S.W.3d 878, 882 (Tex.App.—Tyler 2017, no pet.). Because of the permissive nature of the CPRC §51.016, a party's decision not to pursue an interlocutory appeal does not affect its right to appeal the interlocutory order after final judgment. **Bonsmara Nat. Beef**, 603 S.W.3d at 390–91. For a discussion of similar CPRC provisions that have been found to allow for an appeal of an interlocutory order after final judgment, see "Note," **O'Connor's Texas Civil Appeals**, ch. 1-B, §2.4.1 (2020 ed.).

(b) Order granting arbitration. The FAA does not allow immediate appellate review of an interlocutory order compelling arbitration. 9 U.S.C. §16(b)(2), (b)(3); *see also* **In re Gulf Expl., LLC**, 289 S.W.3d at 839–40 (order compelling arbitration and staying underlying litigation is not immediately appealable, but order compelling arbitration and dismissing underlying litigation is appealable as final judgment). Mandamus relief is usually not available in such cases either because an order compelling arbitration is appealable from a final judgment, and therefore the party seeking mandamus will rarely be able to meet the requirement of no adequate remedy by appeal. **In re Gulf Expl., LLC**, 289 S.W.3d at 842. See "Review after final judgment," ch. 4-C, §8.3.2. In rare situations, however, mandamus relief may be available. For example, when there are conflicting statutory mandates, mandamus may be necessary to preserve important substantive and procedural rights. **In re Gulf Expl., LLC**, 289 S.W.3d at 843; *see* **In re Poly-Am., L.P.**, 262 S.W.3d 337, 352 (Tex.2008); **In re Prudential Ins.**, 148 S.W.3d 124, 136 (Tex.2004).

(c) Other orders.

[1] Order denying contracted-for arbitration rights. Mandamus relief may be available for an interlocutory order that is not subject to immediate appeal if the order denies a party its contracted-for arbitration rights. *See* **CMH Homes**, 340 S.W.3d at 452; *see, e.g.*, **In re Serv. Corp.**, 355 S.W.3d 655, 658 (Tex.2011) (mandamus relief was available because court abused its discretion by choosing arbitrator rather than complying with contract provision governing choice of arbitrator; party had no adequate remedy by appeal because FAA does not provide for review of this type of order in state court); **In re Louisiana Pac. Corp.**, 972 S.W.2d 63, 65 (Tex.1998) (same).

[2] Order deferring ruling on motion to compel. Mandamus relief may be available for an interlocutory order that is not subject to immediate appeal if the order defers ruling on the motion to compel arbitration. *See, e.g.*, **In re Heritage Bldg. Sys.**, 185 S.W.3d 539, 542 (Tex.App.—Beaumont 2006, orig. proceeding) (court had no discretion to delay ruling on motion to compel arbitration until after court-ordered mediation); **In re Champion Techs.**, 173 S.W.3d 595, 599 (Tex.App.—Eastland 2005, orig. proceeding) (court had no discretion to defer ruling on arbitration motion until after completion of discovery).

2. Review after final judgment. After final judgment, a party may appeal an order denying or compelling arbitration. *See* Tex. Civ. Prac. & Rem. Code §51.016 (FAA; appeal from judgment may be taken in same manner as permitted under 9 U.S.C. §16); **Green Tree Fin. Corp. v. Randolph**, 531 U.S. 79, 89 (2000) (FAA; order compelling arbitration); **Perry Homes v. Cull**, 258 S.W.3d 580, 587 (Tex.2008) (same); **Chambers**, 242 S.W.3d at 32 (TAA; order compelling arbitra-

tion); *see also* 9 U.S.C. §16(a)(3) (FAA; appeal can be taken from final decision on arbitration). See "Final order," **O'Connor's Federal Rules * Civil Trials**, ch. 7-E, §5.1.1 (2021 ed.). Resolution of the parties' dispute does not moot the right to arbitration. **Bonsmara Nat. Beef**, 603 S.W.3d at 396 (FAA).

Note

A party can file an appeal after final judgment of an order denying a motion to compel arbitration regardless of whether it pursued an interlocutory appeal. ***Bonsmara Nat. Beef****, 603 S.W.3d at 387 (FAA). See "Order denying arbitration," ch. 4-C, §8.3.1(2)(a).*

3. Standard of review. Generally, orders granting or denying arbitration under either the TAA or the FAA are reviewed under the abuse-of-discretion standard. *See* **Henry v. Cash Biz, LP**, 551 S.W.3d 111, 115 (Tex.2018) (FAA; order denying); **In re Labatt Food Serv.**, 279 S.W.3d 640, 642–43 (Tex.2009) (FAA; order denying); **Perry Homes**, 258 S.W.3d at 598 (FAA; order granting); **Chambers v. O'Quinn**, 305 S.W.3d 141, 146 (Tex.App.—Houston [1st Dist.] 2009, pet. denied) (TAA; order granting); **Stanford Dev. Corp. v. Stanford Condo. Owners Ass'n**, 285 S.W.3d 45, 48 (Tex.App.—Houston [1st Dist.] 2009, no pet.) (TAA; order denying); **Teel v. Beldon Roofing & Remodeling Co.**, 281 S.W.3d 446, 448 (Tex.App.—San Antonio 2007, pet. denied) (FAA; order granting). Under this standard, the appellate court defers to the trial court's factual findings if they are supported by evidence but reviews the trial court's legal determinations de novo. **Henry**, 551 S.W.3d at 115 (FAA); **In re Labatt Food**, 279 S.W.3d at 643 (FAA); **Albertson's Holdings**, 514 S.W.3d at 882 (FAA); **Stanford Dev.**, 285 S.W.3d at 48 (TAA); *see also* **Sidley Austin Brown & Wood, LLP v. J.A. Green Dev. Corp.**, 327 S.W.3d 859, 862–63 (Tex.App.—Dallas 2010, no pet.) (under TAA or FAA, appellate court applies no-evidence standard to trial court's factual findings and de novo review to legal determinations; standard is same as abuse-of-discretion standard). The following are examples of legal issues that are reviewed de novo: • Whether the arbitration agreement is valid. **In re D. Wilson Constr. Co.**, 196 S.W.3d 774, 781 (Tex.2006) (FAA); **J.M. Davidson, Inc. v. Webster**, 128 S.W.3d 223, 227 (Tex.2003) (TAA). • Whether an arbitration agreement is ambiguous. **In re D. Wilson Constr.**, 196 S.W.3d at 781 (FAA). • Whether an arbitration agreement is enforceable. **In re Labatt Food**, 279 S.W.3d at 643 (FAA). • Whether the claim falls within the scope of the agreement. **Henry**, 551 S.W.3d at 115 (FAA); **In re Stanford Grp.**, 273 S.W.3d 807, 813 (Tex.App.—Houston [14th Dist.] 2008, orig. proceeding) (FAA). • Whether a party waived its right to arbitrate. **RSL Funding, LLC v. Pippins**, 499 S.W.3d 423, 430 (Tex.2016) (FAA); **Perry Homes**, 258 S.W.3d at 598 (FAA); **Citizens Nat'l Bank v. Bryce**, 271 S.W.3d 347, 354 (Tex.App.—Tyler 2008, no pet.) (FAA and TAA).

§9. Arbitrator's award

§9.1 Written. The arbitrator's award must be in writing and signed by the arbitrators. Tex. Civ. Prac. & Rem. Code §171.053(a) (TAA).

§9.2 Attorney fees. An attorney representing a party in an arbitration proceeding may be entitled to attorney fees as part of the arbitration award. Tex. Civ. Prac. & Rem. Code §171.048(a), (c) (TAA). Attorney fees must be awarded if the fees are provided for in the arbitration agreement or by law. Tex. Civ. Prac. & Rem. Code §171.048(c) (TAA); *see* **Cooper v. Bushong**, 10 S.W.3d 20, 26 (Tex.App.—Austin 1999, pet. denied) (TAA); *see, e.g.*, **Monday v. Cox**, 881 S.W.2d 381, 384 (Tex.App.—San Antonio 1994, writ denied) (TAA; attorney fees awarded under DTPA, which provides for attorney fees for groundless suit).

Note

Once an arbitrator decides the issue of attorney fees, a reviewing court generally cannot modify the award to include appellate attorney fees. ***D.R. Horton-Tex., Ltd. v. Bernhard****, 423 S.W.3d 532, 536 (Tex.App.—Houston [14th Dist.] 2014, pet. denied) (TAA).*

§9.3 Deadline to issue award.

1. Generally. The arbitrator must issue the award within the time established by the parties' agreement, or if no time is specified, within the time as ordered by the court. Tex. Civ. Prac. & Rem. Code §171.053(c) (TAA); *e.g.*, **Sims v. Build-**

ing Tomorrow's Talent, LLC, No. 07-12-00170-CV, 2014 WL 1800839 (Tex.App.—Amarillo 2014, pet. denied) (memo op.; 4-30-14) (TAA; arbitrator's final judgment was not issued until over one year after trial court's deadline and two and a half years after parties' agreed deadline; trial court's order confirming award reversed).

2. Extension. The parties can extend the time for the arbitrator to issue the award if the extension is made in writing. Tex. Civ. Prac. & Rem. Code §171.053(d) (TAA). The extension can be made before or after the original deadline expires. *Id.*

3. Objection to missed deadline. A party can object if the arbitrator does not issue an award before the required deadline. Tex. Civ. Prac. & Rem. Code §171.053(e) (TAA); **Sims**, No. 07-12-00170-CV, 2014 WL 1800839 (memo op.) (TAA). The party must notify the arbitrator of the objection before the award is delivered to that party. Tex. Civ. Prac. & Rem. Code §171.053(e) (TAA); *e.g.*, **Sims**, No. 07-12-00170-CV, 2014 WL 1800839 (memo op.) (TAA; D's attorney sent several e-mails and letters to arbitrator objecting to late award). If the party objects after delivery of the award, the objection is waived. Tex. Civ. Prac. & Rem. Code §171.053(e) (TAA).

§9.4 Arbitrator's review of award. The parties may file an application asking the arbitrator to clarify, modify, or correct its award. Tex. Civ. Prac. & Rem. Code §171.054(a), (b) (TAA); *see, e.g.*, **Sydow v. Verner, Liipfert, Bernhard, McPherson & Hand**, 218 S.W.3d 162, 170 (Tex.App.—Houston [14th Dist.] 2007, no pet.) (TAA; arbitrator could correct award because he intended to include prejudgment interest on attorney fees but forgot to do so).

1. Deadline. The deadline to file an application with the arbitrator to modify, correct, or clarify an award is 20 days after the award is delivered to the party. Tex. Civ. Prac. & Rem. Code §171.054(a), (c) (TAA).

2. Notice. The applicant must give prompt written notice of the application. Tex. Civ. Prac. & Rem. Code §171.054(d) (TAA). The notice should instruct the opposing party to serve any objection within ten days of the notice. *Id.*

3. Grounds. To ask the arbitrator to modify or correct an award, the party must have proper grounds. *See* Tex. Civ. Prac. & Rem. Code §§171.054(a), 171.091(a) (TAA); **Sydow**, 218 S.W.3d at 167 (TAA); **Barsness v. Scott**, 126 S.W.3d 232, 240–41 (Tex.App.—San Antonio 2003, pet. denied) (TAA). See "Grounds," ch. 4-C, §9.5.2(2).

§9.5 Trial court's review of award. After the arbitrator's award is issued, a party can file a motion with the trial court to confirm, modify, or vacate the award. A party may instead file a motion for summary judgment to confirm, modify, or vacate the award; however, by filing a motion for summary judgment, the party assumes the additional burdens and procedural requirements of summary-judgment practice. **Baker Hughes Oilfield Opers., Inc. v. Hennig Prod. Co.**, 164 S.W.3d 438, 442–43 (Tex.App.—Houston [14th Dist.] 2005, no pet.) (TAA); **Crossmark, Inc. v. Hazar**, 124 S.W.3d 422, 430 (Tex.App.—Dallas 2004, pet. denied) (TAA); *see, e.g.*, **Mariner Fin. Grp. v. Bossley**, 79 S.W.3d 30, 35 (Tex.2002) (under National Association of Securities Dealers Code of Arbitration; although Ps had ultimate burden of proving arbitrator's partiality, Ds who moved for traditional summary judgment did not carry summary-judgment burden of establishing that there was no fact issue on arbitrator's partiality).

Note

A motion to modify or vacate the award is the exclusive remedy for attacking an arbitration award; that is, a party cannot collaterally attack the award if a motion to modify or vacate is unsuccessful. See, e.g., ***Blue Cross Blue Shield v. Juneau****, 114 S.W.3d 126, 135–36 (Tex.App.—Austin 2003, no pet.) (TAA; party could not file suit against individual arbitrator on evident-partiality grounds). Unless there is a statutory ground to modify or vacate an award, a court does not have jurisdiction to review other complaints about arbitration, including whether the evidence was sufficient to support the award.* ***Patten v. Johnson****, 429 S.W.3d 767, 779 (Tex.App.—Dallas 2014, pet. denied) (TAA);* ***Blue Cross****, 114 S.W.3d at 135 (TAA).*

1. Motion to confirm award. A party may file a motion with the court to confirm the arbitrator's award. 9 U.S.C. §9 (FAA); Tex. Civ. Prac. & Rem. Code §171.087 (TAA). Under the FAA, the motion must be filed within one year after the award is made; under the TAA, there is no specified deadline for filing the motion. *See* 9 U.S.C. §9 (FAA); Tex. Civ. Prac.

& Rem. Code §171.087 (TAA); **Davis v. Merriman**, No. 04-13-00518-CV, 2015 WL 1004357 (Tex.App.—San Antonio 2015, pet. denied) (memo op.; 3-4-15) (TAA; footnote 3). The court must confirm the award unless the other party offers grounds for modifying, correcting, or vacating it. 9 U.S.C. §9 (FAA); Tex. Civ. Prac. & Rem. Code §171.087 (TAA); **Callahan & Assocs. v. Orangefield ISD**, 92 S.W.3d 841, 844 (Tex.2002) (TAA).

2. Motion to modify or correct award. A party may file a motion with the court to modify or correct the arbitrator's award. *See* 9 U.S.C. §11 (FAA); Tex. Civ. Prac. & Rem. Code §171.091 (TAA). Under the TAA, a motion to modify or correct the award can be joined in the alternative with a motion to vacate the award. Tex. Civ. Prac. & Rem. Code §171.091(d). See "Motion to vacate award," ch. 4-C, §9.5.3.

(1) Deadlines.

(a) Under FAA. Under the FAA, the deadline to serve notice of a motion to modify or correct an arbitration award is three months after the award is filed or delivered. 9 U.S.C. §12.

(b) Under TAA. Under the TAA, the deadline to file a motion with the trial court to modify or correct an arbitration award is 90 days after the award is delivered to the party. Tex. Civ. Prac. & Rem. Code §171.091(b).

(2) Grounds.

(a) Under FAA. The exclusive grounds for modifying an arbitration award under the FAA are those listed in 9 U.S.C. §11. **Hall St. Assocs. v. Mattel, Inc.**, 552 U.S. 576, 584 (2008). A party may file a motion with the court to modify or correct the award on any of the following grounds:

[1] Evident miscalculation. The arbitrator's award contains an evident miscalculation of numbers or a mistake in the description of any person, thing, or property referred to in the award. 9 U.S.C. §11(a). "Miscalculation" implies inadvertence or an error caused by an oversight. *Cf.* **Crossmark**, 124 S.W.3d at 436 (TAA).

[2] Unsubmitted issue. The arbitrator's award resolves a matter that was not submitted to arbitration, unless the unsubmitted matter does not affect the merits of the decision on the matter that was submitted. 9 U.S.C. §11(b).

[3] Error in form. The arbitrator's award contains an error in the form of the award, on a matter not affecting the merits of the controversy. 9 U.S.C. §11(c).

(b) Under TAA. Under the TAA, a party may file a motion with the court to modify or correct an arbitration award on any of the following grounds:

[1] Evident miscalculation. The arbitrator's award contains an evident miscalculation of numbers or a mistake in the description of any person, thing, or property referred to in the award. Tex. Civ. Prac. & Rem. Code §171.091(a)(1). "Miscalculation" implies inadvertence or an error caused by an oversight. **Crossmark**, 124 S.W.3d at 436. By comparison, an arbitrator's "evident mistake" in failing to award damages is not a ground for modifying or correcting an award. **Callahan & Assocs.**, 92 S.W.3d at 844.

[2] Unsubmitted issue. The arbitrator's award resolves a matter that was not submitted to arbitration, and the award can be corrected without affecting any decision made on issues that were submitted. Tex. Civ. Prac. & Rem. Code §171.091(a)(2). The arbitrator is limited to deciding matters submitted to arbitration. **Sydow v. Verner, Liipfert, Bernhard, McPherson & Hand**, 218 S.W.3d 162, 168 (Tex.App.—Houston [14th Dist.] 2007, no pet.); **Baker Hughes**, 164 S.W.3d at 443.

[3] Error in form. The arbitrator's award contains an error in the form of the award, on a matter not affecting the merits of the controversy. Tex. Civ. Prac. & Rem. Code §171.091(a)(3).

3. Motion to vacate award. A party may file a motion with the court to vacate the arbitrator's award. *See* 9 U.S.C. §10 (FAA); Tex. Civ. Prac. & Rem. Code §171.088 (TAA).

(1) Deadlines.

(a) Under FAA. Under the FAA, the deadline to serve notice of a motion to vacate an arbitration award is three months after the award is filed or delivered. 9 U.S.C. §12; **Broemer v. Houston Lawyer Referral Serv.**, 407 S.W.3d 477, 480 (Tex.App.—Houston [14th Dist.] 2013, no pet.); **Eurocapital Grp. v. Goldman Sachs & Co.**, 17 S.W.3d 426, 430 (Tex.App.—Houston [1st Dist.] 2000, no pet.).

(b) Under TAA. Under the TAA, the deadline to file a motion to vacate an arbitration award is 90 days after the party receives a copy of the award. Tex. Civ. Prac. & Rem. Code §171.088(b); **Kreit v. Brewer & Pritchard, P.C.**, 530 S.W.3d 231, 237 (Tex.App.—Houston [14th Dist.] 2017, pet. denied). If the ground for the motion to vacate is corruption, fraud, or other undue means (see "Corruption," ch. 4-C, §9.5.3(2)(b)[1][a]), the deadline is 90 days after the party learned or should have learned of the ground. Tex. Civ. Prac. & Rem. Code §171.088(b); **Louisiana Nat. Gas Pipeline, Inc. v. Bludworth Bond Shipyard, Inc.**, 875 S.W.2d 458, 462 (Tex.App.—Houston [1st Dist.] 1994, writ denied); *see* **Kreit**, 530 S.W.3d at 237. A motion to vacate is waived if it is filed after the statutory deadline. **Telеometrics Int'l v. Hall**, 922 S.W.2d 189, 192 (Tex.App.—Houston [1st Dist.] 1995, writ denied). Although the statute provides a limitations period for filing the motion, the motion does not need to include every ground the party will raise for vacating the arbitration award. **Black v. Shor**, 443 S.W.3d 154, 163 (Tex.App.—Corpus Christi 2013, pet. denied). Thus, if a motion to vacate has been timely filed, the party can raise additional grounds for vacating the award after the 90-day deadline as long as the grounds are raised before the court confirms the award. *See id.* at 164. See "Motion to confirm award," ch. 4-C, §9.5.1.

Caution

The challenging party may not have a full 90 days to file a motion to vacate. ***Hamm v. Millennium Income Fund, L.L.C.****, 178 S.W.3d 256, 264 (Tex.App.—Houston [1st Dist.] 2005, pet. denied) (FAA and TAA). If the other party moves to confirm the award, the challenging party should immediately move to vacate. Id.; see* ***Human Biostar, Inc. v. Celltex Therapeutics Corp.****, 514 S.W.3d 844, 851 (Tex.App.—Houston [14th Dist.] 2017, pet. denied). Once an award has been confirmed, a party cannot file a motion to vacate. See* ***Human Biostar****, 514 S.W.3d at 851;* ***Black****, 443 S.W.3d at 163–64;* ***Hamm****, 178 S.W.3d at 269.*

(2) Grounds. The statutory grounds in 9 U.S.C. §10(a) and CPRC §171.088(a) are the exclusive grounds for vacating an arbitration award.

Note

One court has held that nothing in the FAA or TAA prevents parties from agreeing to narrow the review of an arbitration award to a specific subset of the statutory grounds for vacating an award. E.g., ***Denbury Onshore, LLC v. TexCal Energy S. Tex., L.P.****, 513 S.W.3d 511, 519 (Tex.App.—Houston [14th Dist.] 2016, no pet.) (parties agreed to restrict grounds for vacating award to fraud and corruption).*

(a) Under FAA. The exclusive grounds for vacating an arbitration award under the FAA are those listed in 9 U.S.C. §10(a). **Hall St.**, 552 U.S. at 584; *see* **Nafta Traders, Inc. v. Quinn**, 339 S.W.3d 84, 87 (Tex.2011). A party may file a motion with the court to vacate an arbitration award on any of the following grounds.

Note

The U.S. Supreme Court has determined that "manifest disregard of the law" is not an independent ground for vacating an arbitration award under the FAA. ***Hall St.****, 552 U.S. at 583–85. After* ***Hall Street****, federal courts have disagreed on what role that phrase continues to play in FAA cases. Compare* ***Doscher v. Sea Port Grp. Secs., LLC****, 832 F.3d 372, 375 n.3 (2d Cir.2016) (manifest disregard continues as "judicial gloss" on 9 U.S.C. §10),* ***Wachovia Secs., LLC v. Brand****, 671 F.3d 472, 483 (4th Cir.2012) (manifest disregard continues either as independent ground for review or as "judicial gloss" on 9 U.S.C. §10), and* ***Comedy Club, Inc. v. Improv W. Assocs.****, 553 F.3d 1277, 1290 (9th Cir.2009) (manifest disregard remains valid ground to vacate because it is part of, or shorthand for, 9 U.S.C. §10(a)(4)), with* ***Frazier v. CitiFinancial Corp.****, 604 F.3d 1313, 1323–24 (11th Cir.2010) (manifest disregard is not independent ground to vacate; arbitration awards under FAA can be vacated only for reasons in 9 U.S.C. §10), and* ***Citigroup Global Mkts., Inc. v. Bacon****, 562 F.3d 349, 353*

(5th Cir.2009) (same). In a later case, the Supreme Court refused to rule on this disagreement. See ***Stolt-Nielsen S.A. v. AnimalFeeds Int'l****, 559 U.S. 662, 672 n.3 (2010).*

[1] Corruption, fraud, or undue means. The award was procured by corruption, fraud, or other undue means. 9 U.S.C. §10(a)(1); **Perry Homes v. Cull**, 173 S.W.3d 565, 570 (Tex.App.—Fort Worth 2005), *rev'd on other grounds*, 258 S.W.3d 580 (Tex.2008); *see* **Roehrs v. FSI Holdings, Inc.**, 246 S.W.3d 796, 810 (Tex.App.—Dallas 2008, pet. denied). See "Corruption, fraud, or undue means," ch. 4-C, §9.5.3(2)(b)[1].

[2] Arbitrator's evident partiality or corruption. There was "evident partiality" or corruption of the arbitrator who was appointed as a neutral arbitrator. 9 U.S.C. §10(a)(2). A neutral arbitrator has a duty to disclose any dealings she is aware of that might create an impression of possible bias. **Commonwealth Coatings Corp. v. Continental Cas. Co.**, 393 U.S. 145, 149 (1968); **Tenaska Energy, Inc. v. Ponderosa Pine Energy, LLC**, 437 S.W.3d 518, 523 (Tex.2014). Familial relationships or other close social ties should be disclosed, but trivial relationships do not need to be. **Perry Homes**, 173 S.W.3d at 571; *see* **Tenaska Energy**, 437 S.W.3d at 526 & n.16 (when some but not all information about a relationship is disclosed, courts should compare disclosed information to undisclosed information to determine if undisclosed information is trivial). A party establishes an arbitrator's evident partiality by proving that the arbitrator did not disclose facts that might have created a reasonable impression of the arbitrator's partiality to an objective observer. *E.g.*, **Tenaska Energy**, 437 S.W.3d at 524–25 (evident partiality when arbitrator did not fully disclose extent of business contacts with P's law firm, which had recommended him as arbitrator); **Builders First Source-S.Tex., LP v. Ortiz**, 515 S.W.3d 451, 458 (Tex.App.—Houston [14th Dist.] 2017, pet. denied) (evident partiality when arbitrator waited until almost a year into arbitration to disclose that D's attorney had appeared before her in two previous arbitrations); **Henry v. Halliburton Energy Servs.**, 100 S.W.3d 505, 509 (Tex.App.—Dallas 2003, pet. denied) (no evident partiality when arbitrator did not disclose his move to law firm that had represented D more than six years before arbitration began). Evident partiality is exhibited by the nondisclosure itself, regardless of whether the undisclosed information establishes actual bias. **Tenaska Energy**, 437 S.W.3d at 524–25.

Note

A party does not waive an evident-partiality objection if the party proceeds to arbitration based on undisclosed facts—which must be more than trivial—showing the arbitrator's partiality before the arbitrator made the award. See ***Tenaska Energy****, 437 S.W.3d at 528. See "Note," ch. 4-C, §9.5.3(2)(b)[2]. Similarly, a party does not waive an evident-partiality challenge based on a waiver-of-conflicts provision that is conditioned on full disclosure if full disclosure of those conflicts is not made. See, e.g.,* ***Tenaska Energy****, 437 S.W.3d at 528–29 (because arbitrator did not fully disclose information on potential partiality, D did not waive partiality challenge). In* ***Tenaska Energy****, the Court expressed no opinion on whether parties could contractually waive the full-disclosure requirement. Id. at 529.*

[3] Procedural misconduct. The arbitrator refused to postpone the hearing after a sufficient showing of cause for the postponement, refused to hear pertinent and material evidence, or committed any other misbehavior that prejudiced the rights of the party. 9 U.S.C. §10(a)(3); **SSP Holdings L.P. v. Lopez**, 432 S.W.3d 487, 496–97 (Tex.App.—San Antonio 2014, pet. denied); **Perry Homes**, 173 S.W.3d at 570.

[4] Arbitrator exceeded powers. The arbitrator exceeded her powers, or so imperfectly executed them that a mutual, final, and definite award on the subject matter submitted was not made. 9 U.S.C. §10(a)(4); **Perry Homes**, 173 S.W.3d at 570–71.

[a] Award lacks connection to agreement. An arbitrator exceeds her powers by issuing an award that has no connection to the parties' agreement. *See* **Oxford Health Plans LLC v. Sutter**, 569 U.S. 564, 569 (2013). That is, an arbitrator exceeds her powers by deciding matters that are not part of the arbitration agreement and, in effect, by imparting her own ideas of justice. **Forged Components, Inc. v. Guzman**, 409 S.W.3d 91, 104 (Tex.App.—Houston [1st Dist.] 2013, no pet.). Thus, to vacate an award on this ground, the party must show more than an error, even a serious one, by the arbitrator; instead, the party must show that the arbitrator acted outside her authority by issuing an award that

simply reflects her view of public policy rather than the evident purpose and intent of the parties' agreement. *See* **Oxford Health Plans**, 569 U.S. at 569; *see, e.g.*, **Stolt-Nielsen S.A.**, 559 U.S. at 671–72 (award was vacated when arbitrators inferred from agreement that parties agreed to class-action arbitration even though agreement was silent on issue and parties had stipulated that they had never agreed to class arbitration). The question for the court is not whether the arbitrator construed the agreement correctly but whether she construed it at all, and if the arbitrator even arguably construed or applied the agreement, the award should not be vacated. **Oxford Health Plans**, 569 U.S. at 569.

[b] Selection of arbitrator violates agreement. If an arbitrator is appointed in violation of the terms of an arbitration agreement, the arbitration panel exceeds its powers by deciding the dispute. *See, e.g.*, **Americo Life, Inc. v. Myer**, 440 S.W.3d 18, 24–25 (Tex.2014) (in "tripartite arbitration," in which both parties appoint an arbitrator and those arbitrators select third member of panel, party's first-choice arbitrator was improperly disqualified on impartiality grounds because arbitration agreement did not require arbitrators to be impartial; panel thus exceeded its authority in issuing arbitration award because it was formed in violation of parties' agreement); **Guillen-Chavez v. ReadyOne Indus.**, 588 S.W.3d 281, 286 (Tex.App.—El Paso 2019, pet. denied) (arbitrator who was not selected from pool of local arbitrators as specified in parties' Rule 11 agreement did not have authority to render arbitration award); *see also* 9 U.S.C. §5 (arbitration agreement must be followed if it provides method for appointing arbitrator). In other words, if an arbitrator is selected in violation of an arbitration agreement, the panel does not have jurisdiction over the dispute. **Americo Life**, 440 S.W.3d at 21. If the arbitration agreement incorporates by reference outside rules governing the arbitration proceeding, those rules are incorporated only to the extent they do not conflict with the express terms of the agreement. *E.g., id.* at 24–25 (agreement provided for arbitrator that was knowledgeable and independent but did not specify impartial, and incorporated rules of American Arbitration Association (AAA); agreement controlled even though AAA's rules were later amended to require impartiality).

(b) Under TAA. The exclusive grounds for vacating an arbitration award under the TAA are those listed in CPRC §171.088(a). **Hoskins v. Hoskins**, 497 S.W.3d 490, 494–95 (Tex.2016). A party may file a motion with the court to vacate an arbitration award on any of the following statutory grounds.

Note

In 2016, the Supreme Court resolved a split among the courts of appeals and held that the statutory grounds in CPRC §171.088 are the exclusive grounds for vacating an arbitration award under the TAA—a party cannot rely on common-law grounds, such as manifest disregard of the law. ***Hoskins****, 497 S.W.3d at 494–95.*

[1] Corruption, fraud, or undue means. The award was procured by corruption, fraud, or other undue means. Tex. Civ. Prac. & Rem. Code §171.088(a)(1).

[a] Corruption. To vacate an arbitration award because of corruption, the party must show some dishonest practice, such as bribery. *See* **Las Palmas Med. Ctr. v. Moore**, 349 S.W.3d 57, 69 (Tex.App.—El Paso 2010, pet. denied); *see also* Corruption, *Black's Law Dictionary* (11th ed. 2019) (defined as depravity, perversion, or impairment of integrity).

[b] Fraud. To vacate an arbitration award because of fraud, the party must establish the following: (1) the elements of fraud by clear and convincing evidence, (2) that the fraud was not discoverable with due diligence either before or during the arbitration, and (3) that the fraud materially related to an issue in the arbitration. **Las Palmas**, 349 S.W.3d at 67. For the elements of fraud, see "Fraud," **O'Connor's Texas Causes of Action**, ch. 12-A, §1 et seq. (2021 ed.). Fraud can occur by the overt misrepresentation of facts or by nondisclosure when a party has a duty to disclose. *See* **Las Palmas**, 349 S.W.3d at 67–68.

[c] Undue means. To vacate an arbitration award because of undue means, the party must show immoral, illegal, or bad-faith conduct. **Las Palmas**, 349 S.W.3d at 69.

[2] Evident partiality. The party's rights were prejudiced by the "evident partiality" of the arbitrator who was appointed as a neutral arbitrator. Tex. Civ. Prac. & Rem. Code §171.088(a)(2)(A); **Forest Oil Corp. v. El Rucio**

Land & Cattle Co., 518 S.W.3d 422, 431 (Tex.2017); **Burlington N. R.R. v. TUCO Inc.**, 960 S.W.2d 629, 636 (Tex.1997); *cf.* **Tenaska Energy**, 437 S.W.3d at 523–24 & n.7 (evident partiality under FAA). A neutral arbitrator has a duty to disclose all information that might reasonably affect her impartiality, including a familial or close social relationship; however, disclosure of trivial relationships or connections is not required. **TUCO**, 960 S.W.2d at 637; *see* **Forest Oil**, 518 S.W.3d at 431; *see also* **Karlseng v. Cooke**, 346 S.W.3d 85, 97 (Tex.App.—Dallas 2011, no pet.) (arbitrator must make reasonable effort to determine if she has any interests, contacts, or relationships that are required to be disclosed). A party establishes an arbitrator's evident partiality by proving that the arbitrator did not disclose facts that might have created a reasonable impression of the arbitrator's partiality to an objective observer. **Forest Oil**, 518 S.W.3d at 431; *e.g.*, **TUCO**, 960 S.W.2d at 636–37 (nondisclosure of arbitrator's referral to represent co-arbitrator's law firm in federal lawsuit was evident partiality); **Karlseng**, 346 S.W.3d at 94 (nondisclosure of arbitrator's direct, personal, professional, social, and business relationship with P's attorney was evident partiality); **J.D. Edwards World Solutions Co. v. Estes, Inc.**, 91 S.W.3d 836, 840 (Tex.App.—Fort Worth 2002, pet. denied) (nondisclosure of arbitrator's ongoing representation of D was evident partiality). But the arbitrator's impartiality cannot be affected by information that she is completely unaware of. *E.g.*, **Forest Oil**, 518 S.W.3d at 431 (although P's earlier objection to using arbitrator as mediator in another case was not disclosed to D in present case, no evident partiality because nondisclosure was trivial and there was no evidence arbitrator knew about that mediation that never happened). Evident partiality is exhibited by the nondisclosure itself, regardless of whether the undisclosed information establishes actual bias. **TUCO**, 960 S.W.2d at 636; **Karlseng**, 346 S.W.3d at 95.

Note

A party seeking to vacate an arbitration award on evident-partiality grounds waives the objection if the party did not object to known facts showing the arbitrator's partiality before the arbitrator made the award. ***TUCO****, 960 S.W.2d at 637 n.9; e.g.,* ***Kendall Builders, Inc. v. Chesson****, 149 S.W.3d 796, 806 (Tex.App.—Austin 2004, pet. denied) (trial court erred in vacating arbitration award because P knew of arbitrator's partiality and waited to object until after unfavorable arbitration award was issued). The complaining party is presumed to have known of the arbitrator's partiality if the undisclosed relationship was open, obvious, or easy to discover. See* ***Mariner Fin.****, 79 S.W.3d at 33–34. For other issues of waiver under the FAA that may apply to the TAA, see "Note," ch. 4-C, §9.5.3(2)(a)[2].*

[3] Arbitrator's corruption or misconduct. The party's rights were prejudiced by the arbitrator's corruption, misconduct, or willful misbehavior. Tex. Civ. Prac. & Rem. Code §171.088(a)(2)(B), (a)(2)(C).

[4] Arbitrator exceeded powers. The arbitrator exceeded her powers. Tex. Civ. Prac. & Rem. Code §171.088(a)(3)(A).

[a] Generally. An arbitrator's authority derives from the arbitration agreement and is limited to a decision on the matters specified in the agreement, either expressly or by necessary implication. **City of Pasadena v. Smith**, 292 S.W.3d 14, 20 & n.41 (Tex.2009); **Humitech Dev. Corp. v. Perlman**, 424 S.W.3d 782, 792 (Tex.App.—Dallas 2014, no pet.), *overruled on other grounds*, **Hoskins v. Hoskins**, 497 S.W.3d 490 (Tex.2016). An arbitrator exceeds her authority if she decides a matter that the parties did not agree to submit to arbitration or if the arbitration award cannot be rationally inferred from the parties' agreement; she does not exceed her authority by making a mistake of fact or law in applying substantive law. **Humitech Dev.**, 424 S.W.3d at 792; *see* **D.R. Horton-Tex., Ltd. v. Bernhard**, 423 S.W.3d 532, 534 (Tex.App.—Houston [14th Dist.] 2014, pet. denied); **Pheng Invs. v. Rodriquez**, 196 S.W.3d 322, 329 (Tex.App.—Fort Worth 2006, no pet.), *overruled on other grounds*, **Hoskins v. Hoskins**, 497 S.W.3d 490 (Tex.2016). Thus, the question for the court is not whether the arbitrator decided an issue correctly, but whether she had the authority to decide the issue at all. **Forest Oil**, 518 S.W.3d at 431; **D.R. Horton-Tex.**, 423 S.W.3d at 534.

[b] Expanded scope of judicial review. Parties can contractually agree in their arbitration agreement to limit an arbitrator's power to that of a judge, thus allowing for judicial review of an arbitration award for reversible error. **Nafta Traders**, 339 S.W.3d at 95; *see* **Forest Oil**, 518 S.W.3d at 432. If the parties contractually limit the scope of the arbitrator's power and the arbitrator exceeds that power, the parties have contractually provided a means for vacating the award under CPRC 171.088(a)(3)(A). *See* **Nafta Traders**, 339 S.W.3d at 96. The FAA does not preempt state law permitting

such expanded judicial review. *Id.* at 101. See "FAA preemption of TAA," ch. 4-C, §4.5.

Practice Tip

Although the U.S. Supreme Court has held that an agreement expanding the scope of judicial review impermissibly enlarges the grounds for vacating an arbitration award under the FAA, the Texas Supreme Court has held that such an agreement is permissible under the TAA. See ***Nafta Traders****, 339 S.W.3d at 87; see also* ***Hoskins****, 497 S.W.3d at 494–95 & n.7 (Court's holding that CPRC §171.088(a) provides exclusive grounds for vacating arbitration award does not conflict with holding in* ***Nafta Traders****). Thus, when drafting an arbitration agreement, parties should (1) specify whether the TAA will apply and (2) add language to the agreement that limits the arbitrator's powers to allow for expanded judicial review of the arbitration award. See* ***Nafta Traders****, 339 S.W.3d at 101;* ***Denbury Onshore****, 513 S.W.3d at 518–19. By doing so, parties can get the benefits of arbitration while also retaining the right to have an adverse award reviewed by the courts. But if the parties contractually agree to expanded judicial review of the arbitration award, the arbitration should be conducted more like a trial. See* ***Nafta Traders****, 339 S.W.3d at 101. For example, a record of the proceedings must be kept, and all complaints must be preserved. Id. This may result in a loss of some of the potential time or money savings of arbitration. See id. at 101–02.*

---

[5] Procedural misconduct. The arbitrator refused to postpone the hearing after a showing of sufficient cause for the postponement, refused to hear material evidence, or otherwise conducted the hearing in a way that substantially prejudiced the rights of the party. Tex. Civ. Prac. & Rem. Code §171.088(a)(3)(B)–(a)(3)(D); **Hoskins**, 497 S.W.3d at 494; *see* **Las Palmas**, 349 S.W.3d at 72–73; *see, e.g.*, **Kosty v. South Shore Harbour Cmty. Ass'n**, 226 S.W.3d 459, 463–64 (Tex.App.—Houston [1st Dist.] 2006, pet. denied) (arbitrator did not err in excluding evidence that was immaterial to the arbitration).

[6] No arbitration agreement. There was no arbitration agreement, the issue was not adversely determined in proceedings to compel or stay arbitration, and the party did not participate in the arbitration hearing without raising the objection. Tex. Civ. Prac. & Rem. Code §171.088(a)(4); **Kreit**, 530 S.W.3d at 241; *see* **Pheng Invs.**, 196 S.W.3d at 329.

§9.6 Appellate court's review of trial court's order.

1. Procedure to challenge arbitration orders.

(1) Interlocutory appeal. Certain orders from the trial court's review of an arbitration award (e.g., an order vacating an award) are immediately appealable. For lists of those orders that can be immediately appealed under either the FAA or the TAA, see "Arbitration orders," **O'Connor's Texas Civil Appeals**, ch. 1-B, §2.4.3(1) (2020 ed.).

Note

In ***Bonsmara Nat. Beef****, the Supreme Court held that a party can file an appeal after final judgment of an order denying a motion to compel FAA arbitration even if the party did not file an earlier interlocutory appeal as permitted by CPRC §51.016.* ***Bonsmara Nat. Beef Co. v. Hart of Tex. Cattle Feeders, LLC****, 603 S.W.3d 385, 387 (Tex.2020) (FAA). The Court based its holding on the permissive nature of the statute, which states that a party "may" file an interlocutory appeal. See id. at 390–91. See "Review after interlocutory order," ch. 4-C, §8.3.1. Because CPRC §171.098 contains similar permissive language, the Court indicated that its holding would apply to the appeal of an order denying a motion to compel under the TAA as well. See id. at 390–91 & n.4. Sections 51.016 and 171.098 also allow a party to immediately appeal certain interlocutory orders from the trial court's review of an arbitration award; thus, a party would presumably be able to appeal rulings on those orders after final judgment regardless of whether an interlocutory appeal was filed.*

(2) Appeal after final judgment. A party can generally challenge a trial court's order on an arbitration award by appealing after final judgment. *See* **Bonsmara Nat. Beef**, 603 S.W.3d at 387; **Center Rose Partners v. Bailey**, 587 S.W.3d 514, 524 (Tex.App—Houston [14th Dist.] 2019, no pet.); *see also* Tex. Civ. Prac. & Rem. Code §171.098(b) (arbitration orders under TAA may be appealed in same manner and to same extent as order or judgment in any other civil action).

Note

In ***Center Rose****, the court held that an agreement between the parties stating that the "arbitrator's decision" was nonappealable did not constitute a waiver of the right to request that the arbitrator's award be vacated or the right to challenge the trial court's judgment rendered on the arbitration award on appeal after final judgment.* ***Center Rose****, 587 S.W.3d at 524. The court explained that to waive the right to appeal the trial court's judgment on the arbitration award, the agreement would need to expressly state that any judgment rendered on the decision—as opposed to the decision itself—was nonappealable. Id.*

2. Standards of review for arbitration orders. The review of arbitration awards is narrow, and the court must indulge every reasonable presumption in favor of the arbitration award. **Providian Bancorp Servs. v. Thomas**, 255 S.W.3d 411, 415 (Tex.App.—El Paso 2008, no pet.) (TAA); *see* **East Tex. Salt Water Disposal Co. v. Werline**, 307 S.W.3d 267, 271 (Tex.2010) (TAA); **International Bank of Commerce v. International Energy Dev. Corp.**, 981 S.W.2d 38, 42–43 (Tex.App.—Corpus Christi 1998, pet. denied) (FAA). The appropriate standard of review depends on the type of arbitration order issued by the trial court.

Note

If grounds for enforcing or vacating an arbitration award are sought in a motion for summary judgment, the appellate court will use the general summary-judgment standards of review. ***Las Palmas Med. Ctr. v. Moore****, 349 S.W.3d 57, 65 (Tex.App.—El Paso 2010, pet. denied) (TAA);* ***Crossmark, Inc. v. Hazar****, 124 S.W.3d 422, 430 (Tex.App.—Dallas 2004, pet. denied) (TAA). See "Review," ch. 7-B, §14.*

(1) Order confirming award. The trial court's order confirming the arbitration award is reviewed de novo. **Human Biostar, Inc. v. Celltex Therapeutics Corp.**, 514 S.W.3d 844, 849–50 (Tex.App.—Houston [14th Dist.] 2017, pet. denied) (TAA); **Providian Bancorp**, 255 S.W.3d at 414 (TAA); **American Rlty. Trust, Inc. v. JDN Real Estate—McKinney, L.P.**, 74 S.W.3d 527, 531 (Tex.App.—Dallas 2002, pet. denied) (FAA).

(2) Order vacating award. The trial court's order vacating the arbitration award is reviewed de novo. **SSP Holdings L.P. v. Lopez**, 432 S.W.3d 487, 492 (Tex.App.—San Antonio 2014, pet. denied) (FAA); **Humitech Dev. Corp. v. Perlman**, 424 S.W.3d 782, 790 (Tex.App.—Dallas 2014, no pet.) (TAA), *overruled on other grounds*, **Hoskins v. Hoskins**, 497 S.W.3d 490 (Tex.2016); *see* **Las Palmas**, 349 S.W.3d at 65–67 (TAA). *But see* **Koch v. Koch**, 27 S.W.3d 93, 95 (Tex.App.—San Antonio 2000, no pet.) (abuse-of-discretion standard). But if the trial court attempts to resolve factual disputes based on a claim of evident partiality or misconduct, the appellate court will review the trial court's factual findings for legal and factual sufficiency. **Las Palmas**, 349 S.W.3d at 66 (TAA); *see* **Kendall Builders, Inc. v. Chesson**, 149 S.W.3d 796, 802–03 (Tex.App.—Austin 2004, pet. denied) (TAA).

(3) SAPCR order. In a suit affecting the parent-child relationship (SAPCR), the standard of review to challenge a SAPCR order is whether the award is in the best interest of the child. *See* Tex. Fam. Code §153.0071(b); **Cooper v. Bushong**, 10 S.W.3d 20, 25–26 (Tex.App.—Austin 1999, pet. denied) (TAA).

D. Special Judge

§1. General

§1.1 Rules. None. See Tex. Civ. Prac. & Rem. Code ch. 151.

§1.2 Purpose. A trial by a special judge is a procedure by which the parties try all or part of their case to a retired or former judge (not a sitting judge) who is selected by the parties to hear the case. This type of ADR is sometimes called "rent a former judge" ADR or "private trial" and is functionally the same as a trial before the court. Compared to a trial by a sitting judge, a special-judge procedure is more predictable (no multiple trial settings), more economical for both attorneys and parties, and more effective for complex trials or trials involving secret or private matters (e.g., noncompete agreements, trade-secret cases, divorces). *See* Marshall, *Tex. Civ. Prac. & Rem. Code ch. 151—Special Judges: Special Judge & Special Setting*, Chapter 151: Real Trial and Real Appeal, State Bar of Texas CLE, p. 3 (2008). The special-judge procedure also provides the following advantages over arbitration: (1) the matter is heard by a former judge, rather than by an arbitrator who may not be an attorney, (2) the special judge's decision can be appealed, which is not possible with an arbitration decision, and (3) a trial by special judge is likely to be less expensive than arbitration. See "Arbitration," ch. 4-C, §1 et seq.

§1.3 Forms. **O'Connor's Texas Civil Forms**, FORMS 4D:1 et seq. (2020 ed.).

§1.4 Other references. Marshall, *Tex. Civ. Prac. & Rem. Code ch. 151—Special Judges: Special Judge & Special Setting*, Chapter 151: Real Trial and Real Appeal, State Bar of Texas CLE (2008); State Bar of Texas, *Chapter 151: Real Trial & Real Appeal*, Online CLE (2008), www.texasbarcle.com; **O'Connor's Texas Civil Appeals** (2020 ed.).

§2. Types of cases for referral to special judge

Any civil or family-law matter pending in a district court, a statutory probate court, or a statutory county court can be referred to a special judge by agreement of the parties. Tex. Civ. Prac. & Rem. Code §151.001. See **O'Connor's Texas Civil Forms**, FORM 4D:1 (2020 ed.).

§3. Special judge's qualifications & powers

§3.1 Qualifications. The special judge must be a retired or former judge who (1) served as a judge for at least four years in a district court, statutory county court, statutory probate court, or appellate court, (2) developed substantial experience in her area of specialty, (3) was not removed from office and did not resign while under investigation for discipline or removal, and (4) annually completes at least five days (i.e., 30 hours) of continuing legal education in courses approved by the State Bar of Texas or the Texas Supreme Court. Tex. Civ. Prac. & Rem. Code §151.003. In effect, the special judge must maintain a level of professional competence beyond that required of sitting judges.

§3.2 Powers. While trying the case, the special judge has the same powers as the referring judge, except the special judge cannot hold a person in contempt of court unless the person is a witness before the special judge. Tex. Civ. Prac. & Rem. Code §151.006(b); *e.g.*, **NCF, Inc. v. Harless**, 846 S.W.2d 79, 82–83 (Tex.App.—Dallas 1992, orig. proceeding) (special judge could not enforce turnover order by contempt).

§4. Agreed motion for trial by special judge

§4.1 Referral request. The motion must request a referral to a special judge. Tex. Civ. Prac. & Rem. Code §151.002(1). The case must be a "pending matter," which can include a case in arbitration; a referral cannot be requested before a suit is filed. *See* Tex. Civ. Prac. & Rem. Code §151.001. The parties may, however, be able to provide by contract that they agree to a referral to a special judge in the event of a lawsuit. *See* Marshall, *Tex. Civ. Prac. & Rem. Code ch. 151—Special Judges: Special Judge & Special Setting*, Chapter 151: Real Trial and Real Appeal, State Bar of Texas CLE, p. 5 (2008).

§4.2 Jury waiver. The motion must waive the parties' right to a jury trial. Tex. Civ. Prac. & Rem. Code §151.002(2).

§4.3 Issues to be referred. The motion must identify the issues to be referred to the special judge. Tex. Civ. Prac. & Rem. Code §151.002(3).

1. Trial issues. The motion can ask that the special judge hear any or all of the issues in the case, whether they are issues of law or fact. Tex. Civ. Prac. & Rem. Code §151.001. For example, the motion could ask for the special judge to

resolve all discovery disputes or a motion for summary judgment. *See* Marshall, *Tex. Civ. Prac. & Rem. Code ch. 151—Special Judges: Special Judge & Special Setting*, Chapter 151: Real Trial and Real Appeal, State Bar of Texas CLE, pp. 5–6 (2008).

2. Post-trial issues. The motion can ask that the special judge hear all postjudgment issues, including remand from the appellate court, collection of judgment, writ of attachment, and turnover orders. *See* State Bar of Texas, *Chapter 151: Real Trial & Real Appeal*, Online CLE (2008), www.texasbarcle.com.

§4.4 Place for trial. The motion must identify the time and place for the agreed trial. Tex. Civ. Prac. & Rem. Code §151.002(4). Chapter 151 places no restrictions on venue; thus, the trial can be held at the place most convenient for the parties and witnesses. See "Place for trial," ch. 4-D, §6.3.

§4.5 Special judge. The motion must identify the name of the special judge, state that the special judge has agreed to hear the case, and identify the fee the parties have agreed to pay the judge. Tex. Civ. Prac. & Rem. Code §151.002(5).

Practice Tip

One simple way to locate a special judge is to search the Internet for "private trials." State Bar of Texas, Chapter 151: Real Trial & Real Appeal, Online CLE (2008), www.texasbarcle.com. Then verify with the Texas Center for the Judiciary that the judge has fulfilled the CLE requirements for the calendar year. Id.

§5. Order of referral

§5.1 Discretionary. Whether to refer a case to a special judge is within the discretion of the referring judge. Tex. Civ. Prac. & Rem. Code §151.001 (judge "may" order referral). Some judges are reluctant to refer a case to a special judge.

§5.2 Contents of order. The order of referral must identify the issues referred and the name of the special judge. Tex. Civ. Prac. & Rem. Code §151.004. The order may designate the time and place for trial and the time for filing the special judge's report. *Id.* The court clerk will send the special judge a copy of the order. *Id.* See **O'Connor's Texas Civil Forms**, FORM 4D:2 (2020 ed.).

§5.3 Effect of referral. The referral will stay all proceedings until after the conclusion of the special trial. Tex. Civ. Prac. & Rem. Code §151.001. The stay prevents conflicting rulings if the special judge hears only part of the case and then returns it to the referring judge.

§6. Trial procedure

§6.1 Rules for special trial. The case will be conducted in the same manner as a nonjury trial under the TRCPs and the TREs. Tex. Civ. Prac. & Rem. Code §§151.005, 151.006(a). The parties have the right to be represented by an attorney. Tex. Civ. Prac. & Rem. Code §151.007.

§6.2 Court reporter. A court reporter is required for the trial. Tex. Civ. Prac. & Rem. Code §151.008. The court reporter must have the same qualifications required for a reporter in the referring judge's court. *Id.* The court reporter cannot be a public employee if the trial is held during regular work hours, unless the referring judge orders otherwise. Tex. Civ. Prac. & Rem. Code §151.010. Although the CPRC states "the special judge shall provide a court reporter," the attorneys should probably arrange for the court reporter. *See* Tex. Civ. Prac. & Rem. Code §151.008.

Practice Tip

In a relatively simple matter (e.g., proving up a divorce, the hearing for a summary judgment), the parties can ask the referring judge to allow the hearing before the special judge to be recorded by audio or video recording, to reduce the cost of the procedure.

§6.3 Place for trial.

1. Private location. The parties must agree on a place for the trial. *See* Tex. Civ. Prac. & Rem. Code §151.002(4) (motion must state place agreed on by parties). Typically, they agree to hold the trial in one of the attorneys' conference

rooms or to rent a conference room at a local hotel. The privacy of the special-judge proceeding is one of the reasons for its popularity, especially in family-law matters. *See* Marshall, *Tex. Civ. Prac. & Rem. Code ch. 151—Special Judges: Special Judge & Special Setting*, Chapter 151: Real Trial and Real Appeal, State Bar of Texas CLE, p. 3 (2008).

2. Not public courtroom. The trial cannot be held in a public courtroom, unless otherwise ordered by the referring judge. Tex. Civ. Prac. & Rem. Code §151.010.

§6.4 Special judge's file. The file of the case remains with the referring judge's clerk. The special judge can obtain copies of relevant documents from the referring judge's file, or the attorneys can provide the special judge with the copies. State Bar of Texas, *Chapter 151: Real Trial & Real Appeal*, Online CLE (2008), www.texasbarcle.com. Any additional pleadings filed with the special judge become part of the special judge's file.

§6.5 Costs & fees. The parties must pay "in equal shares" for the costs related to the trial—that is, the special judge's fee, the court reporter's fee, and other administrative costs. Tex. Civ. Prac. & Rem. Code §151.009(a). In multiparty cases, the costs are divided between the parties, not between the sides of the litigation. *See id.* ("the parties" shall pay the costs). Each party must pay the costs of its own witnesses and any other costs related only to its case. Tex. Civ. Prac. & Rem. Code §151.009(b). Neither the state nor the local government may pay any costs related to a trial by a special judge. Tex. Civ. Prac. & Rem. Code §151.009(c).

§6.6 Special judge's verdict. The verdict of the special judge must comply with the requirements for a verdict by the court in which the action was filed. Tex. Civ. Prac. & Rem. Code §151.011. The verdict will stand as a verdict of the referring judge's court. *Id.* The special judge must submit the verdict to the referring judge within 60 days after the date the trial adjourns, unless the order of referral specifies a different date. *Id.*

§6.7 Return of special judge's file. At the conclusion of the proceedings (i.e., when the verdict is signed and post-trial motions are resolved), the special judge must send all documents in the file to the referring court's clerk. *See* State Bar of Texas, *Chapter 151: Real Trial & Real Appeal*, Online CLE (2008), www.texasbarcle.com.

§7. Post-trial motions

§7.1 Motion for verdict. At the conclusion of the hearing, the parties can make a motion for the special judge to sign a verdict. *See* Tex. Civ. Prac. & Rem. Code §151.011.

§7.2 Motion to seal records. If the issues that were submitted to the special judge involved private or confidential matters, the parties should consider asking the special judge to seal the record. See "Motion to Seal Court Records," ch. 5-L, §1 et seq. The special judge's verdict, however, cannot be sealed. Tex. R. Civ. P. 76a(1). If one of the parties files an appeal, the record is automatically unsealed.

1. Agreed motion. The parties can make an agreed motion to seal the record. Whether an agreed motion to seal can bypass the requirements of TRCP 76a is an open question. The agreed motion should include a request that the sealing order permit unsealing only when both parties consent to unsealing or when an appeal is filed. *See* State Bar of Texas, *Chapter 151: Real Trial & Real Appeal*, Online CLE (2008), www.texasbarcle.com.

2. Opposed motion. A party can make a motion under TRCP 76a to seal the record. Before the special judge can sign an order sealing the record, the motion to seal must be posted for the public to read and the judge must hold a public hearing. See "Public notice," ch. 5-L, §4; "Hearing on motion to seal," ch. 5-L, §5.

Note

Documents filed in family-law cases, unfiled discovery in trade-secret cases, and some settlement agreements are not "court records" as defined by TRCP 76a; thus, they may be sealed only if permitted by another rule or statute. See, e.g., Tex. Civ. Prac. & Rem. Code §134A.006 (in action for misappropriation of trade secret, court can seal records to preserve secrecy of trade secret). See "Documents that are not court records," ch. 5-L, §2.3; "Protecting documents that are not court records," ch. 5-L, §8.

§7.3 Motion for new trial.

1. Filed with referring judge. If the special judge does not file a verdict within the time specified by CPRC §151.011, the referring court may grant a new trial on a party's motion after notice and a hearing. Tex. Civ. Prac. & Rem. Code §151.012. See **O'Connor's Texas Civil Forms**, FORM 4D:3 (2020 ed.). If the parties still want a special trial, the referring court can refer the case to a new special judge.

2. Filed with special judge. If one of the parties disagrees with the verdict, that party can file a motion for new trial with the special judge.

§8. Review

§8.1 Judgment. If the verdict results in a final judgment or an appealable order, the date the special judge signs the verdict begins the deadlines for the appeal. See "Appellate Deadlines," **O'Connor's Texas Civil Appeals**, ch. 1-C, §1 et seq. (2020 ed.).

§8.2 Right to appeal. The parties have a right to appeal. Tex. Civ. Prac. & Rem. Code §151.013. The case is appealed to the appellate courts, not to the referring court. *Id.* The right to appeal cannot be invoked until (1) the special judge submits a verdict to the trial court, (2) all claims are resolved, and (3) the trial court signs an order memorializing the finality of the case. **Baroid Equip., Inc. v. Odeco Drilling, Inc.**, 64 S.W.3d 504, 505 (Tex.App.—Houston [1st Dist.] 2001, pet. denied).

§8.3 Record on appeal. If the case is appealed, the record will consist of the following: (1) the relevant pleadings filed in the referring judge's court and those filed with the special judge and (2) the transcript of the testimony and the exhibits received by the special judge. See "Record on Appeal," **O'Connor's Texas Civil Appeals**, ch. 6-A, §1 et seq. (2020 ed.).

A. Pretrial Conference

§1. General

§1.1 Rule. Tex. R. Civ. P. 166. See Tex. Gov't Code §21.001(a) (courts have power to enforce their orders); Tex. R. Jud. Admin. 7(a)(6) (courts must "utilize methods to expedite the disposition of cases on the docket").

§1.2 Purpose. TRCP 166 gives trial judges the power to control pretrial matters and to assist in settling cases. *See* **Lindley v. Johnson**, 936 S.W.2d 53, 55 (Tex.App.—Tyler 1996, writ denied). The purpose of a pretrial conference is to assist in the disposition of the case without undue expense or burden to the parties. Tex. R. Civ. P. 166; **JPMorgan Chase Bank v. Orca Assets G.P., L.L.C.**, 546 S.W.3d 648, 653 (Tex.2018); **Walden v. Affiliated Computer Servs.**, 97 S.W.3d 303, 322 (Tex.App.—Houston [14th Dist.] 2003, pet. denied); *see* **Unitrust, Inc. v. Jet Fleet Corp.**, 673 S.W.2d 619, 622 n.1 (Tex.App.—Dallas 1984, no writ) (purpose is to simplify and shorten trials by limiting issues to be tried, if possible).

§1.3 Timetables & forms. Appendix IV, Timetable 8, Pretrial motions; Appendix IV, Timetable 9, Discovery schedule for Level 1; Appendix IV, Timetable 10, Discovery schedule for Level 2; **O'Connor's Texas Civil Forms**, FORM 5A:1 (2020 ed.).

§2. Procedure

§2.1 Automatic pretrial calendar. The court may establish a pretrial calendar "by rule." Tex. R. Civ. P. 166. Attorneys should always check the local rules to see if the rules create automatic deadlines for discovery, pleadings, motions, or any other matters.

§2.2 Initiating pretrial conference. The court can schedule a pretrial conference either on its own initiative or on the motion of a party. To request a pretrial conference, a party should file a motion stating the reasons for the conference. Whether the trial court conducts a pretrial conference is a matter within its discretion; a party cannot force the trial court to conduct one. **Taiwan Shrimp Farm Vill. Ass'n v. U.S.A. Shrimp Farm Dev., Inc.**, 915 S.W.2d 61, 69 (Tex.App.—Corpus Christi 1996, writ denied); **Ryland Grp. v. White**, 723 S.W.2d 160, 163 (Tex.App.—Houston [1st Dist.] 1986, orig. proceeding). Parties should move for a pretrial conference during the early stages of litigation if electronic information will likely be sought in discovery. See "Electronic discovery vs. conventional discovery," ch. 6-C, §2.3.

§3. Scope of pretrial conference

§3.1 Issues of law & fact. A court can resolve purely legal issues at a pretrial conference, including issues that are ordinarily fact questions but have become questions of law because reasonable minds cannot differ on the outcome. *See* **JPMorgan Chase Bank v. Orca Assets G.P., L.L.C.**, 546 S.W.3d 648, 653 (Tex.2018); **Audubon Indem. Co. v. Custom Site-Prep, Inc.**, 358 S.W.3d 309, 319 (Tex.App.—Houston [1st Dist.] 2011, pet. denied); **Walden v. Affiliated Computer Servs.**, 97 S.W.3d 303, 322 (Tex.App.—Houston [14th Dist.] 2003, pet. denied). But a court cannot resolve contested issues of fact. **Provident Life & Acc. Ins. v. Hazlitt**, 216 S.W.2d 805, 807 (Tex.1949); **McCreight v. City of Cleburne**, 940 S.W.2d 285, 288 (Tex.App.—Waco 1997, writ denied); *see* **Caldwell v. Barnes**, 154 S.W.3d 93, 97 (Tex.2004).

Note

Some courts have held that a court may render final judgment at a pretrial conference in the limited situation where determination of a legal issue is dispositive of the entire case. See ***Walden****, 97 S.W.3d at 322–23;* ***Martin v. Dosohs I, Ltd.****, 2 S.W.3d 350, 355 (Tex.App.—San Antonio 1999, pet. denied);* ***Para-Chem S., Inc. v. Sandstone Prods.****, No. 01-06-01073-CV, 2009 WL 276507 (Tex.App.—Houston [1st Dist.] 2009, pet. denied) (memo op.; 2-5-09); see also* ***Soefje v. Jones****, 270 S.W.3d 617, 625 (Tex.App.—San Antonio 2008, no pet.) (although summary judgment is preferred method to dispose of case before trial, judgment can be rendered at pretrial hearing in limited circumstances when only legal issues are decided). But due process requires that the defendant have notice that the court would convert the pretrial conference into a disposition hearing. See* ***Soefje****, 270 S.W.3d at 625;* ***Walden****, 97 S.W.3d at 323 & n.16;* ***Murphree v. Ziegelmair****, 937 S.W.2d 493, 495 (Tex.App.—Houston [1st Dist.]*

*1995, no writ); **Unitrust, Inc. v. Jet Fleet Corp.**, 673 S.W.2d 619, 622 (Tex.App.—Dallas 1984, no writ).*

§3.2 Matters that aid disposition. TRCP 166 contains a catch-all provision that allows the court to consider any matter that "may aid in the disposition of the action." Tex. R. Civ. P. 166(p); *see* **Williams v. Akzo Nobel Chems., Inc.**, 999 S.W.2d 836, 842 (Tex.App.—Tyler 1999, no pet.).

§3.3 Trial setting. Although not specifically listed in TRCP 166, setting the date for trial is commonly done by pretrial order. *See, e.g.,* **Loffland Bros. v. Downey**, 822 S.W.2d 249, 250–51 (Tex.App.—Houston [1st Dist.] 1991, orig. proceeding) (docket-control order set trial date and deadlines for discovery and amending pleadings). The trial court must give the parties 45 days' notice of the first trial setting. Tex. R. Civ. P. 245; **Smith v. Lippmann**, 826 S.W.2d 137, 138 n.1 (Tex.1992). See "Deadline begins—notice of trial," ch. 5-B, §4.1.1. However, if the case has been previously set for trial and the parties received 45 days' notice of the original trial setting, the court may reset the trial to a later date on any reasonable notice. Tex. R. Civ. P. 245; **Arkla, Inc. v. Harris**, 846 S.W.2d 623, 628 (Tex.App.—Houston [14th Dist.] 1993, orig. proceeding).

§3.4 Pleading deadlines. By a pretrial order, the court can set deadlines for amendments to pleadings that supersede the deadlines in TRCP 63. Tex. R. Civ. P. 166; *see* **Wilson v. Korthauer**, 21 S.W.3d 573, 577–78 (Tex.App.—Houston [14th Dist.] 2000, pet. denied); **Texas Commerce Bank Reagan v. Lebco Constructors, Inc.**, 865 S.W.2d 68, 79 (Tex.App.—Corpus Christi 1993, writ denied). After those deadlines have passed, parties must secure leave of court to amend their pleadings. **Texas Commerce Bank**, 865 S.W.2d at 79. See "After deadline in pretrial order," ch. 5-F, §3.2.1; "Motion for leave to amend," ch. 8-F, §2.

§3.5 Discovery deadlines. The pretrial conference is most often used to determine what discovery has been completed and what discovery has not yet begun. *See* Tex. R. Civ. P. 166(c) (court can consider discovery schedule at pretrial conference). Every case must be governed by a discovery-control plan, which sets the deadlines for discovery. Tex. R. Civ. P. 190.1. See "Discovery-control plans," ch. 6-A, §7; "Discovery periods," ch. 6-A, §8. The court can change the deadlines set by the discovery rules only for good cause. Tex. R. Civ. P. 191.1.

§3.6 Pending motions. At the pretrial conference, the trial court may require the parties to argue pending motions—dilatory pleas, motions, and exceptions. Tex. R. Civ. P. 166(a). A dilatory plea, most commonly a plea in abatement, asks the court to abate or dismiss the proceeding because of a fundamental defect in how the action was brought. The court can set an abbreviated discovery schedule to resolve pretrial motions. *See* **Montalvo v. Fourth Ct. of Appeals**, 917 S.W.2d 1, 2 (Tex.1995).

§3.7 Joint pretrial status report. The trial court has the authority to require the parties to confer and file a joint pretrial status report. *See* **Koslow's v. Mackie**, 796 S.W.2d 700, 703 (Tex.1990).

§3.8 Contentions & admissions of parties. The court may require the parties to confer and narrow the factual and legal issues of the trial. Tex. R. Civ. P. 166(d) to (g), (j); **Koslow's v. Mackie**, 796 S.W.2d 700, 703 (Tex.1990).

1. Facts. The court may require the parties to submit written statements of their contentions, to consider the contested issues of fact and simplification of the issues, and to discuss possible stipulations of fact. Tex. R. Civ. P. 166(d) to (f).

2. Law. The court may require the parties to identify the legal issues for the court and to agree to the application of the law and the contested issues of law. Tex. R. Civ. P. 166(g), (j).

§3.9 Trial witnesses & exhibits.

1. Identification of experts. The court may require the parties to appear for a pretrial conference to exchange information about experts—names, addresses, telephone numbers, and the subject of each expert's testimony. Tex. R. Civ. P. 166(i). The schedule for designating experts is determined with reference to the end of the discovery period and according to whether the party is seeking affirmative relief. *See* Tex. R. Civ. P. 195.2. When a court signs an order setting the deadline for the parties to identify experts, the order controls over the deadlines in TRCP 195.2(a) and (b). Tex. R. Civ. P. 195.2; *see* **State Farm Fire & Cas. Co. v. Price**, 845 S.W.2d 427, 434 (Tex.App.—Amarillo 1992, writ dism'd). The court cannot set an unreasonable deadline. *See, e.g.,* **Loffland Bros. v. Downey**, 822 S.W.2d 249, 252 (Tex.App.—Houston [1st Dist.] 1991, orig.

proceeding) (eight months before trial was unreasonable). If the court does not sign an order setting the deadline for designation of experts, the parties must designate experts according to the schedule in TRCP 195.2. See "Deadlines for securing discovery from experts," ch. 6-D, §6. When the court signs a pretrial order on the discovery of experts, it cannot disregard its own order at trial. *See, e.g.*, **Dennis v. Haden**, 867 S.W.2d 48, 51 (Tex.App.—Texarkana 1993, writ denied) (court should not have admitted testimony of expert whose report had not been provided).

2. Witness list. The court may require the parties to exchange information about the fact witnesses who will be called to testify at trial and the rebuttal and impeachment witnesses whose testimony can reasonably be anticipated before trial—names, addresses, telephone numbers, and the subject of each witness's testimony. Tex. R. Civ. P. 166(h).

2021 Rule Amendments

For cases filed on or after January 1, 2021, a party is required to disclose certain information about trial witnesses in pretrial disclosures under TRCP 194.4 without waiting for a discovery request from the other party. See Tex. R. Civ. P. 194.4(a)(1). See "Trial witnesses," ch. 6-B, §2.9; "Final pretrial disclosures," ch. 6-E, §3.5.

3. Exhibits. The court may require the parties to mark and exchange exhibits, stipulate to the exhibits' authenticity and admissibility, and make written objections. Tex. R. Civ. P. 166(*l*), (m); *see, e.g.*, **Owens-Corning Fiberglas Corp. v. Malone**, 916 S.W.2d 551, 556–57 (Tex.App.—Houston [1st Dist.] 1996) (court ordered D to file list of objections to P's exhibits), *aff'd*, 972 S.W.2d 35 (Tex.1998); **British Am. Ins. v. Howarton**, 877 S.W.2d 347, 350 (Tex.App.—Houston [1st Dist.] 1994, writ dism'd) (videotape not listed as exhibit was excluded at trial); *see also* Tex. R. Civ. P. 192.5(c)(2) (trial exhibits disclosed under TRCP 166 are not "work product").

Practice Tip

There are two reasons to request a pretrial exchange of trial exhibits. First, if a privileged document has been inadvertently produced, the producing party may use the snap-back provisions of TRCP 193.3(d) to assert a privilege. See Tex. R. Civ. P. 193 cmt. 4. See "Use snap-back provision," ch. 6-A, §18.2.4. Second, if a party produces a document in response to discovery, the producing party may prevent the self-authentication of the document by objecting to its authenticity. Tex. R. Civ. P. 193.7 & cmt. 7; see Tex. R. Civ. P. 176.6(c) (production by nonparties). See "Authenticity," ch. 8-C, §8.4.

§3.10 Jury questions. The court may require the parties to prepare proposed jury questions, instructions, and definitions or, for a nonjury trial, proposed findings of fact and conclusions of law. Tex. R. Civ. P. 166(k).

§3.11 Master or auditor. The court may consider the advisability of referring issues to a master or auditor for findings to be used as evidence in a jury trial. Tex. R. Civ. P. 166(n), 171. See "Master in Chancery," ch. 1-K, §1 et seq.

§3.12 Settlement. The court may encourage the parties to settle the case. Tex. R. Civ. P. 166(o). See "Alternative Dispute Resolution," ch. 4-A, §1 et seq.

§4. Hearing on pretrial conference

§4.1 Type of hearing. The pretrial conference may be held by telephone, by mail, in the judge's chambers, or in the courtroom. *See* Tex. R. Jud. Admin. 7(a)(6)(b); *see, e.g.*, **Koslow's v. Mackie**, 796 S.W.2d 700, 703 (Tex.1990) (court required written status report to be mailed).

§4.2 Attendance. The court can require the parties' attorneys, the parties themselves, or the parties' authorized agents to attend the pretrial conference. Tex. R. Civ. P. 166; *see, e.g.*, **Koslow's v. Mackie**, 796 S.W.2d 700, 703 (Tex.1990) (pleadings were struck after Ds did not submit status report or appear at hearing).

§4.3 Evidence. If a pending motion is one that must be supported by evidence (e.g., a motion to abate), the parties should be prepared to present evidence at the pretrial conference.

§4.4 Objections. Generally, objections at the pretrial conference about rulings that must be made at trial are premature and do not preserve error. *See* **Clark v. Trailways, Inc.**, 774 S.W.2d 644, 647 n.2 (Tex.1989) (dicta); *see, e.g.*, **Texas Commerce Bank Reagan v. Lebco Constructors, Inc.**, 865 S.W.2d 68, 78 (Tex.App.—Corpus Christi 1993, writ denied) (objection at pretrial conference to allocation of peremptory challenges did not preserve error); *see also* **Reveal v. West**, 764 S.W.2d 8, 10 (Tex.App.—Houston [1st Dist.] 1988, orig. proceeding) (pretrial ruling that document was privileged was merely a ruling similar to motion in limine). But under TRCP 166(m), the trial court has the authority to rule on objections to exhibits at a pretrial conference, and one court has held that those objections will preserve error. *See* **Owens-Corning Fiberglas Corp. v. Malone**, 916 S.W.2d 551, 557 (Tex.App.—Houston [1st Dist.] 1996), *aff'd*, 972 S.W.2d 35 (Tex.1998); *see also* **In re Marriage of Harrison**, 557 S.W.3d 99, 122–23, (Tex.App.—Houston [14th Dist.] 2018, pet. denied) (relying on **Owens-Corning**; court can make pretrial ruling on admissibility of evidence); **Huckaby v. A.G. Perry & Son, Inc.**, 20 S.W.3d 194, 203–04 (Tex.App.—Texarkana 2000, pet. denied) (same).

Caution

Do not rely on an objection made at a pretrial conference to preserve error. If the matter is one that will arise at trial (e.g., the introduction of evidence), make sure to object on the record during the trial.

---

§5. Pretrial order

§5.1 In writing. The pretrial order must be in writing. **Palacios v. Winters**, 26 S.W.3d 734, 735 (Tex.App.—Corpus Christi 2000, no pet.); **FDIC v. Finlay**, 832 S.W.2d 158, 160 (Tex.App.—Houston [1st Dist.] 1992, writ denied).

§5.2 Contents. The pretrial order must specify the actions taken and rulings made at the pretrial conference. Tex. R. Civ. P. 166; **FDIC v. Finlay**, 832 S.W.2d 158, 160 (Tex.App.—Houston [1st Dist.] 1992, writ denied). The pretrial order will control the suit unless it is modified at trial to prevent manifest injustice. Tex. R. Civ. P. 166. In most cases, the pretrial order includes the following: (1) the actions taken at the pretrial conference, (2) the pleadings that can be amended and the deadline to amend, (3) any agreements made by the parties, (4) the court's rulings on any pleas or motions, and (5) whether the case will be tried to the court or to a jury. *See id.* See "Scope of pretrial conference," ch. 5-A, §3.

Caution

To modify a statutorily mandated deadline, a pretrial order must explicitly reference that deadline and address any extensions; setting a general discovery deadline in the order itself does not extend a specific statutory deadlnie. See, e.g., ***Shinogle v. Whitlock****, 596 S.W.3d 772, 776 (Tex.2020) (scheduling order that set general deadline for providing export reports did not extend deadline for serving expert reports under CPRC §128.053);* ***Crosstex Energy Servs. v. Pro Plus, Inc.****, 430 S.W.3d 384, 395 (Tex.2014) (docket-control order that set general deadline for designating experts did not extend deadline for filing mandatory certificate of merit under CPRC §150.002);* ***Spectrum Healthcare Res. v. McDaniel****, 306 S.W.3d 249, 253–54 & n.5 (Tex.2010) (docket-control order that set general deadline for producing expert reports did not extend deadline for serving export reports under CPRC §74.351).*

---

§5.3 Notice. The parties are entitled to notice of pretrial orders. *See* **Loffland Bros. v. Downey**, 822 S.W.2d 249, 251 (Tex.App.—Houston [1st Dist.] 1991, orig. proceeding). The court must send the pretrial order to each party's attorney in charge. Tex. R. Civ. P. 8; **Loffland Bros.**, 822 S.W.2d at 251.

§5.4 Discretion to modify order. Under TRCP 166, the court can modify its pretrial order to prevent "manifest injustice." **Treviño v. Treviño**, 64 S.W.3d 166, 170 (Tex.App.—San Antonio 2001, no pet.); *see, e.g.*, **Griffin v. Wolfe**, 626 S.W.2d 895, 897 (Tex.App.—Fort Worth 1981, no writ) (court's refusal to permit amendment was not abuse of discretion). The modification does not have to be in writing; the court can implicitly overrule its pretrial order. *See* **In re Estate of Henry**, 250 S.W.3d 518, 527 (Tex.App.—Dallas 2008, no pet.); **Treviño**, 64 S.W.3d at 170; **Schoen v. Redwood Constr., Inc.**, No.

01-09-00371-CV, 2011 WL 478563 (Tex.App.—Houston [1st Dist.] 2011, no pet.) (memo op.; 1-31-11). *But see* **Susanoil, Inc. v. Continental Oil Co.**, 516 S.W.2d 260, 264 (Tex.App.—San Antonio 1973, no writ) (court should modify pretrial order by written order or oral statement on the record).

§6. Binding effect of pretrial order

§6.1 On procedure for trial. A pretrial order controls the procedure for the case. If the order changes the deadlines in the rules of procedure, the order prevails. **Lindley v. Johnson**, 936 S.W.2d 53, 55 (Tex.App.—Tyler 1996, writ denied); *see, e.g.*, **ForScan Corp. v. Dresser Indus.**, 789 S.W.2d 389, 393 (Tex.App.—Houston [14th Dist.] 1990, writ denied) (deadline for amending pleadings in pretrial order prevailed over deadline in TRCP 63).

§6.2 On procedure for SJ. A pretrial order controls the procedure for the case in a summary-judgment proceeding. For example, if a pretrial order requires the parties to designate experts by a certain date, a party generally cannot rely on the affidavit of an undesignated expert in a summary-judgment proceeding. **Fort Brown Villas III Condo. Ass'n v. Gillenwater**, 285 S.W.3d 879, 882 (Tex.2009); **Total Clean, LLC v. Cox Smith Matthews Inc.**, 330 S.W.3d 657, 663–64 (Tex.App.—San Antonio 2010, pet. denied); *see* Tex. R. Civ. P. 193.6(a). See "Timely," ch. 6-A, §16.3.

§6.3 On trial judge. The trial court cannot disregard its own pretrial order. **Mercedes-Benz Credit Corp. v. Rhyne**, 925 S.W.2d 664, 666 (Tex.1996). For example, if the trial court signed an order setting the case on the jury docket, the court cannot ignore that order on the eve of trial, even if no jury fee was paid. *Id.* The parties are entitled to rely on the trial court's pretrial order. **Dennis v. Haden**, 867 S.W.2d 48, 51 (Tex.App.—Texarkana 1993, writ denied). But this does not mean that the trial court is prohibited from modifying its pretrial order. *See, e.g.*, **Treviño v. Treviño**, 64 S.W.3d 166, 170 (Tex.App.—San Antonio 2001, no pet.) (court implicitly modified docket-control order by overruling Ps' motion to strike and by setting Ds' motion for summary judgment for submission). See "Discretion to modify order," ch. 5-A, §5.4.

§6.4 On parties. The parties must comply with the pretrial order. *See, e.g.*, **British Am. Ins. v. Howarton**, 877 S.W.2d 347, 350–51 (Tex.App.—Houston [1st Dist.] 1994, writ dism'd) (party could not introduce videotape because it was not listed as exhibit as required by pretrial order); **Dennis v. Haden**, 867 S.W.2d 48, 51 (Tex.App.—Texarkana 1993, writ denied) (party could not call expert to testify because expert's report was not produced as required by pretrial order); **ForScan Corp. v. Dresser Indus.**, 789 S.W.2d 389, 393 (Tex.App.—Houston [14th Dist.] 1990, writ denied) (party could not amend pleadings after deadline set in pretrial order).

§6.5 On rescheduled trial. A pretrial order setting discovery deadlines applies unless the trial is rescheduled for a date more than three months after the discovery period ends. *See* Tex. R. Civ. P. 190.5(b). But if the suit is an expedited action under TRCP 169, the discovery deadlines in the pretrial order apply, even if the trial is rescheduled. *See* Tex. R. Civ. P. 190.5 & cmt. (2013). See "Expedited Actions," ch. 2-C, §1 et seq.

§6.6 Not on retrial. The discovery deadlines in a pretrial order do not apply after a new trial is granted. *See, e.g.*, **State Dept. of Hwys. & Pub. Transp. v. Ross**, 718 S.W.2d 5, 11 (Tex.App.—Tyler 1986, orig. proceeding) (order closing discovery did not remain in effect after mistrial). After a new trial is ordered, a suit stands on the docket as if it had never been tried. *Id.*

§7. Sanctions

The trial court has the power to enforce its orders with sanctions. **In re Montelongo**, 586 S.W.3d 513, 519 (Tex.App.—Houston [14th Dist.] 2019, orig. proceeding); **In re Patton**, 47 S.W.3d 825, 827 (Tex.App.—Fort Worth 2001, orig. proceeding); *see* Tex. Gov't Code §21.001(a) (court has all powers necessary to enforce its orders); **Woodall v. Clark**, 802 S.W.2d 415, 418 (Tex.App.—Beaumont 1991, no writ) (Gov't Code §21.001(a) gives court power to dismiss suit for repeated refusal to comply with pretrial order). Courts may impose the sanctions listed in TRCP 215 for violations of pretrial orders. *E.g.*, **Koslow's v. Mackie**, 796 S.W.2d 700, 703–04 & n.1 (Tex.1990) (sanctions for not appearing at pretrial conference); *see* **In re Marriage of Harrison**, 557 S.W.3d 99, 123 (Tex.App.—Houston [14th Dist.] 2018, pet. denied); **Taylor v. Taylor**, 254 S.W.3d 527, 532 (Tex.App.—Houston [1st Dist.] 2008, no pet.). Any sanctions imposed for violation of a pretrial order must be just and appropriate. **Taylor**, 254 S.W.3d at 532; **In re Bledsoe**, 41 S.W.3d 807, 812 (Tex.App.—Fort Worth 2001, orig. proceeding); *e.g.*, **In re Montelongo**, 586 S.W.3d at 519 (court abused its discretion by removing case from jury docket as

sanction after attorney appeared on time at pretrial conference but was not present in courtroom when judge called case); *see* **Koslow's**, 796 S.W.2d at 703 n.1; *see, e.g.*, **Roberts v. Golden Crest Waters, Inc.**, 1 S.W.3d 291, 292–93 (Tex.App.—Corpus Christi 1999, no pet.) (court abused its discretion by imposing death-penalty sanctions for failure to file pretrial statement). See "Motion for Sanctions," ch. 5-K, §1 et seq.

§8. Review

§8.1 Standard of review. In most cases, the standard of review for a pretrial order is abuse of discretion. *See* **In re Estate of Henry**, 250 S.W.3d 518, 526 (Tex.App.—Dallas 2008, no pet.); *see, e.g.*, **TransAmerican Nat. Gas Corp. v. Powell**, 811 S.W.2d 913, 916–17 (Tex.1991) (pretrial order imposing discovery sanctions). However, if the trial court summarily disposes of a party's claim or defense, the court will review the pretrial order the same as it would an appeal of a summary judgment or directed verdict. **JPMorgan Chase Bank v. Orca Assets G.P., L.L.C.**, 546 S.W.3d 648, 653 (Tex.2018); *see* **Walden v. Affiliated Computer Servs.**, 97 S.W.3d 303, 324 (Tex.App.—Houston [14th Dist.] 2003, pet. denied) (review of pretrial order same as for directed verdict); *see, e.g.*, **McCreight v. City of Cleburne**, 940 S.W.2d 285, 287 (Tex.App.—Waco 1997, writ denied) (pretrial order that disposed of one of P's theories of liability was reviewed under same standard as for partial summary judgment entered in response to parties' cross-motions). See "Both parties move for SJ," ch. 7-B, §14.4.1; "Review," ch. 8-G, §8.

§8.2 Appeal. A pretrial order may be appealed after a final judgment is entered. *See* **FDIC v. Finlay**, 832 S.W.2d 158, 161 (Tex.App.—Houston [1st Dist.] 1992, writ denied).

§8.3 Mandamus. A pretrial order can be the subject of a petition for writ of mandamus if an appeal would not provide effective relief. *See, e.g.*, **Loffland Bros. v. Downey**, 822 S.W.2d 249, 251–52 (Tex.App.—Houston [1st Dist.] 1991, orig. proceeding) (party missed deadline for naming experts because it did not receive docket-control order).

B. Request for Jury Trial

§1. General

§1.1 Rules. Tex. R. Civ. P. 216 to 220, 245. See U.S. Const. amend. 7; Tex. Const. art. 1, §15, art. 5, §10; Tex. Est. Code §55.002 (contested issues tried by jury); Tex. Fam. Code §6.703 (right to jury in divorce action); Tex. Gov't Code §51.604 (jury fee).

§1.2 Purpose. A request for a jury trial invokes the party's right to a jury trial.

§1.3 Forms. **O'Connor's Texas Civil Forms**, FORMS 5B:1 et seq. (2020 ed.).

§2. Right to jury trial

The U.S. and Texas Constitutions guarantee the right to a jury trial. U.S. Const. amend. 7; Tex. Const. art. 1, §15. In civil matters, a party has the right to a jury trial for any action that is the same as or analogous to those actions that could have been submitted to a jury in 1876, the year the Texas Constitution was adopted. **Barshop v. Medina Cty. Underground Water Conserv. Dist.**, 925 S.W.2d 618, 636 (Tex.1996). To receive a jury trial, a party must have a right to a jury trial and must properly request a jury under TRCP 216(a). **Huddle v. Huddle**, 696 S.W.2d 895, 895 (Tex.1985); **In re J.N.F.**, 116 S.W.3d 426, 431 (Tex.App.—Houston [14th Dist.] 2003, no pet.). A summary judgment does not violate a party's constitutional right to a jury trial. **Willms v. Americas Tire Co.**, 190 S.W.3d 796, 810 (Tex.App.—Dallas 2006, pet. denied); *see also* **Ramirez v. Consolidated HGM Corp.**, 124 S.W.3d 914, 916 (Tex.App.—Amarillo 2004, no pet.) (party is not entitled to jury trial on fact issues arising from preliminary motions and pleas that do not involve merits or ultimate disposition of case).

§3. Requirements

To make a proper request for a jury trial, a party must do two things at least 30 days before the date the case is set for trial: (1) make a written request for a jury trial and (2) pay the jury fee or file an affidavit of inability to pay. Tex. R. Civ. P. 216 (request and jury fee), Tex. R. Civ. P. 217 (affidavit of inability); *see* **Huddle v. Huddle**, 696 S.W.2d 895, 895 (Tex.1985); **Universal Printing Co. v. Premier Victorian Homes, Inc.**, 73 S.W.3d 283, 289 (Tex.App.—Houston [1st Dist.] 2001, pet. denied). When one party requests a jury and pays a fee, all other parties in the suit acquire the right to a jury trial. **In re Marriage of Harrison**, 557 S.W.3d 99, 136 (Tex.App.—Houston [14th Dist.] 2018, pet. denied); **White Motor Co. v. Loden**, 373 S.W.2d 863, 865 (Tex.App.—Dallas 1963, no writ); *see* **Mercedes-Benz Credit Corp. v. Rhyne**, 925 S.W.2d 664, 666 (Tex.1996). Thus, any party in the suit can rely on any other party's proper jury request. **In re Marriage of Harrison**, 557 S.W.3d at 136; *see* **Mercedes-Benz**, 925 S.W.2d at 666; **White Motor**, 373 S.W.2d at 865.

§3.1 Request.

1. In writing. The request for a jury trial (also called a jury demand) must be in writing and must be filed with the clerk. Tex. R. Civ. P. 216(a); **In re T.H.**, 131 S.W.3d 598, 601 (Tex.App.—Texarkana 2004, pet. denied). The request may be included in the plaintiff's petition or the defendant's answer, or it can be filed as a separate document. *See, e.g.*, **ForScan Corp. v. Dresser Indus.**, 789 S.W.2d 389, 392 (Tex.App.—Houston [14th Dist.] 1990, writ denied) (cover letter to clerk that stated jury fee was enclosed but did not request jury was insufficient). Two courts have held that the request for a setting on the jury docket was a sufficient request for a jury trial under TRCP 216. *E.g.*, **Higginbotham v. Collateral Prot., Inc.**, 859 S.W.2d 487, 489 (Tex.App.—Houston [1st Dist.] 1993, writ denied); **Sheth v. White**, 722 S.W.2d 805, 805 (Tex.App.—Houston [14th Dist.] 1987, orig. proceeding).

2. Allegations.

(1) For timely request. In the request, the party should state that it wants a jury trial and that it is tendering the jury fee to the clerk. *See* Tex. R. Civ. P. 216. See **O'Connor's Texas Civil Forms**, FORM 5B:1 (2020 ed.).

(2) For untimely request. If the case is set for trial on the nonjury docket, the party should file a request for a jury trial and a motion to strike the nonjury setting. See **O'Connor's Texas Civil Forms**, FORMS 5B:1 to 5B:2 (2020 ed.). In the motion to strike the nonjury setting, the party should allege the following under oath (and attach affidavits if necessary):

(a) A jury is available. The attorney should contact the clerk to determine whether a jury is available. If a jury is not available, the party should file a motion for continuance so the case can be reset on the jury docket. *See* **McCrann v. Tandy Computer Leasing**, 737 S.W.2d 10, 11 (Tex.App.—Corpus Christi 1987, no writ).

(b) A jury trial can be had without any (1) additional delay, (2) interference with the trial court's docket, or (3) injury to the opposing party. **General Motors Corp. v. Gayle**, 951 S.W.2d 469, 476 (Tex.1997); **Monroe v. Alternatives in Motion**, 234 S.W.3d 56, 70 (Tex.App.—Houston [1st Dist.] 2007, no pet.).

(c) There is a disputed fact in the case, and an instructed verdict would not be proper. **Halsell v. Dehoyos**, 810 S.W.2d 371, 372 (Tex.1991); **In re V.R.W.**, 41 S.W.3d 183, 194 (Tex.App.—Houston [14th Dist.] 2001, no pet.), *disapproved on other grounds*, **In re J.F.C.**, 96 S.W.3d 256 (Tex.2002).

(d) The reason the jury request was not made earlier.

(e) The Texas Constitution guarantees a jury trial in this type of case. Tex. Const. art. 1, §15.

§3.2 Jury fee. To make a proper request for a jury trial, the party must not only file a request for a jury but also pay the jury fee or file an affidavit of inability to pay. **In re J.N.F.**, 116 S.W.3d 426, 431 (Tex.App.—Houston [14th Dist.] 2003, no pet.); *see* **Huddle v. Huddle**, 696 S.W.2d 895, 895 (Tex.1985); **Walton v. Canon, Short & Gaston, P.C.**, 23 S.W.3d 143, 149 (Tex.App.—El Paso 2000, no pet.).

1. Amount. The jury fee is $40 in district and county court. Tex. Gov't Code §51.604(a). This fee includes the amount required under TRCP 216. Tex. Gov't Code §51.604(c); *see* Tex. R. Civ. P. 216(b) (jury fee in district court is $10; jury fee in county court is $5).

Practice Tip

When paying the filing fees and the jury fee, give the clerk separate checks. If you give the clerk one check and it is not enough to cover both fees, the clerk will apply it to the filing fees and you will not have paid the jury fee. See, e.g., ***Universal Printing Co. v. Premier Victorian Homes, Inc.****, 73 S.W.3d 283, 289–90 (Tex.App.—Houston [1st Dist.] 2001, pet. denied) ($105 paid by Ds did not cover jury fee after filing costs were deducted).*

---

2. Indigent. An indigent is not required to pay a jury fee. Tex. R. Civ. P. 217. Instead, the indigent must file a jury request before the deadline in TRCP 217 and file an affidavit of inability to pay before the deadline for paying the fee. See "Deadline to pay jury fee," ch. 5-B, §4.2. In the affidavit, the indigent must swear that she cannot obtain the money necessary for the fee, by pledge of property or otherwise. Tex. R. Civ. P. 217. See "Suit by Indigent," ch. 2-J, §1 et seq.

§4. Deadlines

§4.1 Deadline to file jury request.

1. Deadline begins—notice of trial. A party's notice from the trial court that the case is set for trial triggers the party's deadline to request a jury trial. TRCP 245 requires the trial court to give the parties 45 days' notice of the first trial setting so that a party can make a timely request for a jury trial. *See* **In re J.C.**, 108 S.W.3d 914, 916–17 (Tex.App.—Texarkana 2003, no pet.); **Hardin v. Hardin**, 932 S.W.2d 566, 567 (Tex.App.—Tyler 1995, no writ). If the trial court notifies the parties that a case is set on the nonjury docket without giving the parties enough time to request a jury trial, the appellate court will consider a late request to have been timely. **In re J.C.**, 108 S.W.3d at 916–17; **In re V.R.W.**, 41 S.W.3d 183, 195 (Tex.App.—Houston [14th Dist.] 2001, no pet.), *disapproved on other grounds*, **In re J.F.C.**, 96 S.W.3d 256 (Tex.2002); *see, e.g.*, **Simpson v. Stem**, 822 S.W.2d 323, 324 (Tex.App.—Waco 1992, orig. proceeding) (court gave less than 30 days' notice of trial setting; party's request for jury trial was deemed timely); *see also* **Martin v. Black**, 909 S.W.2d 192, 197–98 (Tex.App.—Houston [14th Dist.] 1995, writ denied) (because case was not set for trial, request made as soon as P thought fact issue would be tried was timely).

2. Reasonable time before trial. The request for a jury trial should be made a "reasonable time before" the date the case is set for trial on the nonjury docket, but at least 30 days in advance. Tex. R. Civ. P. 216(a); **Mercedes-Benz**

Credit Corp. v. Rhyne, 925 S.W.2d 664, 666 (Tex.1996); **Halsell v. Dehoyos**, 810 S.W.2d 371, 371 (Tex.1991); *e.g.*, **In re T.H.**, 131 S.W.3d 598, 601–02 (Tex.App.—Texarkana 2004, pet. denied) (oral request for jury trial after trial began was not acceptable).

(1) 30 days—presumed reasonable. A request for a jury trial made at least 30 days before trial is presumed to have been made a reasonable time before the trial. **Halsell**, 810 S.W.2d at 371; **Southern Farm Bur. Cas. Ins. v. Penland**, 923 S.W.2d 758, 760 (Tex.App.—Corpus Christi 1996, no writ).

(2) Less than 30 days—no presumption. If the request is made less than 30 days before trial, there is no presumption the request is reasonable. In such a case, the decision to permit a jury trial is strictly within the trial court's discretion.

3. Reschedule trial after late request. If the case is reset, the 30-day deadline is based on the new trial date. **Halsell**, 810 S.W.2d at 371; **Whiteford v. Baugher**, 818 S.W.2d 423, 425 (Tex.App.—Houston [1st Dist.] 1991, writ denied). Thus, when a case is reset for trial, an untimely request can become timely. **Halsell**, 810 S.W.2d at 371; *see also* **Ricardo N., Inc. v. Turcios de Argueta**, 907 S.W.2d 423, 429 (Tex.1995) (untimely request for 1987 trial was timely for 1991 trial after remand from federal court).

4. Retrial after waiver. If a party waived a jury on the first trial but the case is reversed and remanded for another trial—even if the case is only partially remanded—either party may request a jury trial for the retrial. **In re Baker**, 495 S.W.3d 393, 396 (Tex.App.—Houston [14th Dist.] 2016, orig. proceeding); *see* **Gordon v. Gordon**, 704 S.W.2d 490, 492 (Tex.App.—Corpus Christi 1986, writ dism'd).

§4.2 Deadline to pay jury fee.

1. Deadline in TRCP 216. Under TRCP 216, the deadlines for paying the jury fee and filing the written jury request are the same—30 days before the date the case is set for trial. Tex. R. Civ. P. 216(a), (b); **Mercedes-Benz Credit Corp. v. Rhyne**, 925 S.W.2d 664, 666 & n.1 (Tex.1996). Even if a jury fee is not timely paid, the trial court has discretion to permit a jury trial if it will not interfere with the court's docket, delay the trial, or prejudice the opposing party. **General Motors Corp. v. Gayle**, 951 S.W.2d 469, 476 (Tex.1997); **In re D.R.**, 177 S.W.3d 574, 579–80 (Tex.App.—Houston [1st Dist.] 2005, pet. denied). See "Reasonable time before trial," ch. 5-B, §4.1.2.

2. Deadline in Gov't Code §51.604. Under Gov't Code §51.604, the deadline to pay the jury fee is "not later than the 10th day before the jury trial is scheduled to begin." Tex. Gov't Code §51.604(b); **Universal Printing Co. v. Premier Victorian Homes, Inc.**, 73 S.W.3d 283, 292 (Tex.App.—Houston [1st Dist.] 2001, pet. denied).

Caution

The jury fee paid under Gov't Code §51.604 includes the fee paid under TRCP 216. Tex. Gov't Code §51.604(c). Thus, the portion of the jury fee due under Rule 216—$10 in district court or $5 in county court—must be paid 30 days before trial, and the remainder of the jury fee due under §51.604—$30 in district court or $35 in county court—must be paid 10 days before trial. See ***In re I.M.B.***, *148 S.W.3d 653, 656 (Tex.App.—Beaumont 2004, no pet.) (applying former version of §51.604);* ***Universal Printing***, *73 S.W.3d at 292 (same). See "Amount," ch. 5-B, §3.2.1. To be safe, pay both fees at the same time you make your request, at least 30 days before the date the case is set for trial. See "Deadline in TRCP 216," ch. 5-B, §4.2.1.*

---

§5. Response

§5.1 Request filed at least 30 days before trial.

The trial court may deny a request for a jury trial filed at least 30 days before the trial date only if the party opposing it can rebut the presumption that the request was made a reasonable time before trial. **Halsell v. Dehoyos**, 810 S.W.2d 371, 371 (Tex.1991); **Southern Farm Bur. Cas. Ins. v. Penland**, 923 S.W.2d 758, 760 (Tex.App.—Corpus Christi 1996, no writ). To oppose a timely request for a jury trial, the party should file a response showing that a jury trial will (1) injure the party, (2) disrupt the court's docket, or (3) interfere with the ordinary

handling of the court's business. *See* **Halsell**, 810 S.W.2d at 371. Under certain circumstances, a request filed more than 30 days before trial may be considered untimely. *E.g.*, **Girdner v. Rose**, 213 S.W.3d 438, 443–44 (Tex.App.—Eastland 2006, no pet.) (although P's request was made 41 days before trial, it was untimely because it was made more than two years after suit was filed, multiple continuances had already been granted, and request was dilatory tactic that would delay trial and allow P to live in disputed property rent-free while suit was pending); *see, e.g.*, **Crittenden v. Crittenden**, 52 S.W.3d 768, 769–70 (Tex.App.—San Antonio 2001, pet. denied) (wife's timely request for jury was denied because husband's objection showed that wife had previously agreed to settlement, no jury was available for six months, and she had engaged in tactics to delay divorce). Because the right to a jury trial is guaranteed by the Texas Constitution, a court should seldom deny a party a jury trial if the request for a jury was timely. *See* Tex. Const. art. 1, §15.

§5.2 Request filed less than 30 days before trial. To oppose a request for a jury trial and a motion to strike the nonjury setting filed after the deadline, a party should allege the following:

1. The request was made too late. *See* **Monroe v. Alternatives in Motion**, 234 S.W.3d 56, 69 (Tex.App.—Houston [1st Dist.] 2007, no pet.) (denying untimely jury request is within trial court's discretion).

2. Granting the request would (1) delay the trial, (2) interfere with the court's docket, or (3) injure the opposing party. **General Motors Corp. v. Gayle**, 951 S.W.2d 469, 476 (Tex.1997); **Monroe**, 234 S.W.3d at 70.

§6. Order

§6.1 Clerk's duty. Generally, the court does not sign an order on a request for a jury trial. **Mercedes-Benz Credit Corp. v. Rhyne**, 925 S.W.2d 664, 666 (Tex.1996). The court clerk simply notes on the court's docket sheet that the jury fee was paid. Tex. Gov't Code §51.604(a); Tex. R. Civ. P. 216(b). When the court actually signs an order setting the case for a jury trial, it cannot disregard the order and withdraw the case from the jury docket just before trial, even if no jury fee was paid. **Mercedes-Benz**, 925 S.W.2d at 666.

§6.2 Request contested. The court will make a ruling on the request for a jury trial only if the request is contested.

Practice Tip

If the trial court denies you a jury trial, immediately file a verified motion for continuance, even if handwritten, asking that the case be continued so it may be reset on the jury docket. See "Motion for Continuance," ch. 5-D, §1 et seq.

§6.3 Withdrawing request for jury. A party may withdraw its request for a jury trial so the case may be heard by the court. If the party who requested the jury trial withdraws its request, the other party may prevent the withdrawal by either making a timely objection or filing its own request for a jury. **Lambert v. Coachmen Indus.**, 761 S.W.2d 82, 85 (Tex.App.—Houston [14th Dist.] 1988, writ denied); *see, e.g.*, **In re Marriage of Harrison**, 557 S.W.3d 99, 136–37 (Tex.App.—Houston [14th Dist.] 2018, pet. denied) (wife's objection to husband's request to withdraw case from jury docket was waived because objection was untimely). The trial court cannot withdraw a case from the jury docket over a party's timely objection, even if the objecting party did not request a jury or pay the fee. *See* Tex. R. Civ. P. 220; **In re J.N.F.**, 116 S.W.3d 426, 434 (Tex.App.—Houston [14th Dist.] 2003, no pet.). If the court permits withdrawal of the jury request, it can also permit withdrawal of the jury fee deposit. Tex. R. Civ. P. 220.

§6.4 No sua sponte withdrawal. A trial court cannot withdraw a case from the jury docket on its own initiative. **Bank of Houston v. White**, 737 S.W.2d 387, 388 (Tex.App.—Houston [14th Dist.] 1987, orig. proceeding). If the court signed an order setting the case for a jury trial—even if the order was signed by mistake—the court cannot disregard its own order and force the parties to try the case without a jury. **Mercedes-Benz Credit Corp. v. Rhyne**, 925 S.W.2d 664, 666 (Tex.1996); **Texas Valley Ins. Agency v. Sweezy Constr., Inc.**, 105 S.W.3d 217, 221 (Tex.App.—Corpus Christi 2003, no pet.).

§7. Waiver of jury

§7.1 Failure to appear at trial. A party will waive its request for a jury trial if it does not appear for a scheduled trial. Tex. R. Civ. P. 220; **Bradley Motors, Inc. v. Mackey**, 878 S.W.2d 140, 141 (Tex.1994); *see* **In re W.B.W.**, 2 S.W.3d 421,

422–23 (Tex.App.—San Antonio 1999, no pet.) (party, even if not personally present, appears for trial when attorney is present); *see also* **In re Montelongo**, 586 S.W.3d 513, 521 (Tex.App.—Houston [14th Dist.] 2019, orig. proceeding) (party's failure to appear at pretrial conference does not waive request for jury trial).

Note

Some courts have held that a failure by both a party and its attorney to appear at the designated time for jury selection can constitute a waiver of a jury trial. E.g., ***In re Marriage of Harrison****, 557 S.W.3d 99, 136–37 (Tex.App.—Houston [14th Dist.] 2018, pet. denied) (right to jury trial waived when pro se party arrived almost two hours after designated time for appearance and did not object to lack of jury trial until several hours after that);* ***Maldonado v. Puente****, 694 S.W.2d 86, 89 (Tex.App.—San Antonio 1985, no writ) (right to jury trial waived when parties and their attorney arrived 40 minutes after designated time for appearance);* ***In re T.K.****, No. 09-09-00472-CV, 2010 WL 890657 (Tex.App.—Beaumont 2010, no pet.) (memo op.; 3-11-10) (right to jury trial waived when party and her attorney of record arrived four hours after jury had been dismissed).*

§7.2 Failure to object to nonjury trial. A party will waive its request for a jury trial if it does not object when the trial court begins a nonjury trial. **In re D.R.**, 177 S.W.3d 574, 580 (Tex.App.—Houston [1st Dist.] 2005, pet. denied); **Sunwest Reliance Acquisitions Grp. v. Provident Nat'l Assur. Co.**, 875 S.W.2d 385, 387 (Tex.App.—Dallas 1993, no writ).

Note

Some courts have held that to avoid waiving its request for a jury trial, a party must simply obtain an adverse ruling on the jury request. ***E.E. v. TDFPS****, 598 S.W.3d 389, 398 (Tex.App.—Austin 2020, no pet.); see, e.g.,* ***Coleman v. Sadler****, 608 S.W.2d 344, 346–47 (Tex.App.—Amarillo 1980, no writ) (D did not waive request by announcing ready at nonjury trial because adverse ruling removed jury-trial alternative and left D with no choice between jury and nonjury trial).*

§7.3 Failure to object to discharge of jury. A party will waive its request for a jury trial if it does not object when the trial court dismisses the jury, resolves the case by summary disposition, and signs a judgment. **Rodriguez v. Texas Dept. of MHMR**, 942 S.W.2d 53, 55–56 (Tex.App.—Corpus Christi 1997, no writ).

§7.4 Waiver by contract. Parties may contractually agree to waive their right to a jury trial. **In re Prudential Ins.**, 148 S.W.3d 124, 132 (Tex.2004); *see* **In re Bank of Am.**, 278 S.W.3d 342, 344 (Tex.2009) (clarifying that **In re Prudential** does not impose a presumption against contractual jury waiver).

1. Conspicuous. A jury-waiver provision should be conspicuous. *See* **In re Bank of Am.**, 278 S.W.3d at 345. To be conspicuous, the jury-waiver provision should be in capital letters, bolded, and captioned as a waiver provision. *See, e.g., id.* (waiver provision was captioned "Waiver of Trial by Jury," was bolded, and had words "waiver" and "trial by jury" underlined); **In re General Elec. Capital Corp.**, 203 S.W.3d 314, 316 (Tex.2006) (waiver provision was in capital letters and bolded); *see also* Tex. Bus. & Com. Code §1.201(b)(10) (conspicuous term is one that is written or displayed in a manner that a reasonable person against whom the term would operate should have noticed it).

2. Knowingly & voluntarily made. A jury waiver must be knowingly and voluntarily made. **In re Prudential**, 148 S.W.3d at 132; *see* **In re Bank of Am.**, 278 S.W.3d at 344–45. Which party has the burden of proof on this issue depends on whether the jury-waiver provision is conspicuous and whether fraud or imposition is alleged.

(1) Burden on party opposing waiver. If a jury-waiver provision is conspicuous, it is presumed to have been knowingly and voluntarily made unless one of the parties alleges fraud or imposition connected to the execution of the waiver provision. **In re Bank of Am.**, 278 S.W.3d at 345; *see* **In re Frank Kent Motor Co.**, 361 S.W.3d 628, 629 (Tex.2012) (employer's threat to terminate at-will employee if jury-waiver agreement is not signed does not constitute coercion that

would invalidate agreement). Thus, if the jury-waiver provision is conspicuous and no fraud or imposition is alleged, the party opposing the waiver has the burden to rebut the presumption that the waiver was knowingly and voluntarily made. *See* **In re Bank of Am.**, 278 S.W.3d at 345.

(2) Burden on party seeking to enforce waiver.

(a) Fraud or imposition. If one of the parties alleges fraud or imposition connected to the execution of the jury-waiver provision, the party seeking to enforce the waiver provision—even if it is conspicuous—must prove that it was knowingly and voluntarily made. *See* **In re Bank of Am.**, 278 S.W.3d at 345.

(b) Inconspicuous provision. If a jury-waiver provision is not conspicuous, the party seeking to enforce the provision must prove that the waiver was knowingly and voluntarily made. *E.g.*, **In re Key Equip. Fin. Inc.**, 371 S.W.3d 296, 301–02 (Tex.App.—Houston [1st Dist.] 2012, orig. proceeding) (although not conspicuous, jury-waiver provision was enforced because provision was reasonably placed and in same typeface as other provisions, contract was between sophisticated parties that had history of signing similar agreements, and P's in-house counsel reviewed agreement).

3. Timely. A party should timely assert a contractual jury waiver or the waiver can be lost. *See, e.g.*, **In re General Elec.**, 203 S.W.3d at 314–15 (P retained right to assert contractual jury waiver, despite ten-month delay in filing motion to quash D's jury demand, because P never received notice of demand); **Rivercenter Assocs. v. Rivera**, 858 S.W.2d 366, 367 (Tex.1993) (P lost right to assert contractual jury waiver because it did not file motion to quash D's jury demand until more than four months after receiving notice of demand).

4. Nonsignatories. A nonsignatory agent can assert a valid jury waiver when it acts on behalf of a signatory. **In re Credit Suisse First Boston Mortg. Capital, L.L.C.**, 273 S.W.3d 843, 847 (Tex.App.—Houston [14th Dist.] 2008, orig. proceeding).

§8. Review

§8.1 Denial of jury trial. The denial of a jury trial is reviewed for abuse of discretion. **In re A.L.M.-F.**, 593 S.W.3d 271, 282 (Tex.2019); **Mercedes-Benz Credit Corp. v. Rhyne**, 925 S.W.2d 664, 666 (Tex.1996). The denial can be reviewable on appeal from a final judgment or by mandamus. **In re Reiter**, 404 S.W.3d 607, 611 (Tex.App.—Houston [1st Dist.] 2010, orig. proceeding); *see* **Halsell v. Dehoyos**, 810 S.W.2d 371, 372 (Tex.1991) (appeal); **In re Baker**, 495 S.W.3d 393, 397 (Tex.App.—Houston [14th Dist.] 2016, orig. proceeding) (mandamus).

1. Appeal. A party can challenge the wrongful denial of a jury trial by appeal from the final judgment. *See* **In re Reiter**, 404 S.W.3d at 611. Unless there are no material fact issues and the trial court could have granted an instructed verdict, the wrongful denial of a jury trial is always harmful error. *See* **Caldwell v. Barnes**, 154 S.W.3d 93, 98 (Tex.2004); **Halsell**, 810 S.W.2d at 372. If the party was entitled to a jury trial and there were material fact issues in the case, the appellate court must reverse and remand for a retrial. *See* **Caldwell**, 154 S.W.3d at 98; **Halsell**, 810 S.W.2d at 372.

2. Mandamus. Mandamus is available to a party whose right to a jury trial was wrongfully denied when the party can show that it has no adequate remedy by appeal. *See, e.g.*, **In re Baker**, 495 S.W.3d at 396–97 (appeal is particularly inadequate to review denial of jury trial in child-custody cases).

§8.2 Contractual jury waiver. A contractual jury waiver that is enforced by the trial court can be reviewed on appeal. **In re Prudential Ins.**, 148 S.W.3d 124, 138 (Tex.2004). But if the trial court refuses to enforce a contractual jury waiver, it is reviewable by mandamus. *See id.* at 139.

C. Motion to Challenge the Judge

§1. General

A judge may be removed from a case for one of three reasons: (1) she is subject to a statutory strike as an assigned judge, (2) she is constitutionally disqualified, or (3) she is subject to disqualification or recusal under rules promulgated by the Supreme Court. Tex Const. art. 5, §11 (constitutional disqualifications); Tex. Gov't Code §74.053(d) (statutory strike); Tex R Civ. P. 18a, 18b (disqualification and recusal rules promulgated by Court); **In re Union Pac. Res.**, 969 S.W.2d 427, 428 (Tex 1998).

§1.1 Rules. Tex R. Civ. P. 18a, 18b. See Tex Const. art. 5, §11 (disqualification); Tex. Civ. Prac. & Rem. Code §30.016 (tertiary motion to disqualify or recuse in district and statutory county courts); Tex Gov't Code §24.002 (assignment of judge or transfer of case on recusal), §25.00255 (motion to disqualify or recuse statutory probate judge), §25.00256 (tertiary motion to disqualify or recuse in statutory probate courts), §74.053 (objection to assigned judge); Tex. R. App. P. 16.2, 16.3 (recusal of appellate justice).

§1.2 Purpose. A motion to challenge the trial judge seeks to remove the judge from the case so another judge can be assigned to preside over the case.

§1.3 Forms. **O'Connor's Texas Civil Forms**, FORMS 5C:1 et seq. (2020 ed.).

§1.4 Other references. **O'Connor's Texas Civil Appeals** (2020 ed.).

§2. Types of motions

There are four types of challenges to the trial judge.

§2.1 Objection to assigned judge. An objection to an assigned judge is a peremptory challenge that, if timely made, results in the automatic removal of the assigned judge. Tex Gov't Code §74.053(b); **In re Perritt**, 992 S.W.2d 444, 446 (Tex 1999). Various code provisions refer to a judge assigned to serve as an "assigned" or a "visiting" judge. *See* Tex Gov't Code §§74.053 to 74.054 ("assigned judge"), §74.060(b) ("visiting judge"). See "Objection to assigned judge," ch. 5-C, §3.

§2.2 Motion to disqualify or recuse. A motion to disqualify seeks to prevent a judge from hearing a case for a constitutional reason or a reason under TRCP 18b(a), which is based on constitutional grounds. *See* **Tesco Am., Inc. v. Strong Indus.**, 221 S.W.3d 550, 553 (Tex 2006); **In re Union Pac. Res.**, 969 S.W.2d 427, 428 (Tex 1998). A motion to recuse seeks to prevent a judge from hearing a case for a nonconstitutional reason under TRCP 18b(b). See "Motion to disqualify or recuse," ch. 5-C, §4.

§2.3 Tertiary motion to disqualify or recuse. The third (or later) motion to disqualify or recuse a judge in the same case by the same party is called a "tertiary" motion. Tex Civ. Prac. & Rem. Code §30.016; Tex Gov't Code §25.00256. Although the substantive law is the same as for motions to disqualify or recuse, separate rules govern the procedure for tertiary motions. See "Tertiary motion to disqualify or recuse," ch. 5-C, §5.

5-1. Comparison of Disqualification, Recusal & Objection to Assigned Judge

		Disqualification	Recusal	Objection to assigned judge
1	Source of challenge	Constitution, statutes, and rules	Statutes and rules	Statute
2	Discretionary or mandatory	Mandatory	Mandatory, unless waived	Mandatory, if timely
3	Waivable	No	Yes	Yes
4	Parties may consent to judge	No	Yes	Yes
5	Effect if judge serves after valid challenge	Judgment void	Reversible error	Judgment void
6	Requires written motion	No	Yes	Yes
7	Judgment subject to collateral attack	Yes	No	No

§3. Objection to assigned judge

§3.1 Who may make assignment. Most assignments of judges are made by the presiding judge of the administrative region, who has the authority to assign judges residing within the region. Tex. Gov't Code §74.056(c); **Chandler v. Chandler**, 991 S.W.2d 367, 379 (Tex.App.—El Paso 1999, pet. denied), *disapproved on other grounds*, **Agar Corp. v. Electro Circuits Int'l**, 580 S.W.3d 136 (Tex.2019). However, assignments of judges can be made by the Chief Justice of the Texas Supreme Court when (1) the assigned judge does not reside within the administrative region to which she is assigned or (2) the presiding judge of the administrative region is incapacitated, dies, resigns, or is disqualified in the matter. Tex. Gov't Code §74.049 (situation 2), §74.057(a) (situation 1); **State v. Preslar**, 751 S.W.2d 477, 479 (Tex.1988) (situations 1 and 2).

§3.2 Who may be assigned. An assigned judge is assigned under Gov't Code chapter 74 to sit temporarily for the regular judge of the court. *See* Tex. Gov't Code §74.052 (assignment of judges generally), §74.053 (objection to assigned judges), §74.054 (judges who may be assigned). Judges assigned to hear a TRCP 18a motion (disqualification or recusal) are appointed under Gov't Code chapter 74—not under TRCP 18a—and are subject to challenge as an assigned judge. **In re Perritt**, 992 S.W.2d 444, 447 (Tex.1999). There are four types of judges who may be assigned as visiting judges, and the assignment order must state which type of judge is being assigned. Tex. Gov't Code §74.053(a)(1).

1. **Active judge.** An "active judge" is a current judicial officeholder. Tex. Gov't Code §74.041(4). The term includes the following judges: a district judge, a constitutional or statutory county-court judge, or an active appellate justice (Supreme Court, Court of Criminal Appeals, or court of appeals) who has had trial-court experience. Tex. Gov't Code §74.054(a)(1), (5); *see, e.g.*, **O.C.S., Inc. v. Pi Energy Corp.**, 24 S.W.3d 548, 551 (Tex.App.—Houston [1st Dist.] 2000, no pet.) (district judge was assigned to hear motion to recuse in another court).

2. **Retired judge.** A "retired judge" (1) is a retiree or (2) served as an active judge for at least eight years in a district, statutory probate, statutory county, or appellate court and was vested under the Texas County and District Retirement System when she left office. Tex. Gov't Code §§74.041(6), 74.055(c)(1); *see* Tex. Gov't Code §74.054(a)(3), (4); **Mitchell Energy Corp. v. Ashworth**, 943 S.W.2d 436, 440–41 (Tex.1997); **Chandler v. Chandler**, 991 S.W.2d 367, 380 (Tex.App.—El Paso 1999, pet. denied), *disapproved on other grounds*, **Agar Corp. v. Electro Circuits Int'l**, 580 S.W.3d 136 (Tex.2019). To be eligible for assignment, a retired judge must meet the qualifications listed in Gov't Code §74.055(c).

3. **Former judge.** A "former judge" is someone who served for at least eight years as an active judge in a district, statutory probate, statutory county, or appellate court but who is not a retired judge. Tex. Gov't Code §§74.041(5), 74.055(c)(1); *see* Tex. Gov't Code §74.054(a)(3), (4). To be eligible for assignment, a former judge must meet the qualifications listed in Gov't Code §74.055(c). A judge's status as a former judge is fixed when she leaves office. **Mitchell Energy**, 943 S.W.2d at 437.

4. **Senior judge.** A "senior judge" is a retired judge who has chosen to be a judicial officer. Tex. Gov't Code §74.041(7); *see* Tex. Gov't Code §§74.054(a)(2), 75.001.

§3.3 Notice of assignment. If time permits, and if it is practical, the presiding judge of the administrative region must give the parties notice of the assignment of a visiting judge. Tex. Gov't Code §74.053(a)(2); **In re Canales**, 52 S.W.3d 698, 701 (Tex.2001); **Tivoli Corp. v. Jewelers Mut. Ins.**, 932 S.W.2d 704, 709 (Tex.App.—San Antonio 1996, writ denied). Notice of assignment may be given by e-mail. Tex. Gov't Code §74.053(f).

§3.4 Deadline to object. An objection to an assigned judge must be filed before the date of the first hearing (including pretrial hearings) or trial over which the assigned judge is to preside, or within seven days after receiving actual notice of the assignment, whichever is earlier. Tex. Gov't Code §74.053(c); **In re Approximately $17,239.00**, 129 S.W.3d 167, 168 (Tex.App.—Houston [14th Dist.] 2003, orig. proceeding). The presiding judge may extend the deadline for good cause on a party's written motion. Tex. Gov't Code §74.053(c). If an assigned judge who heard part of the case is reassigned to hear an additional part of the case by a new order of assignment, the reassignment does not give the parties a new opportunity to object. **In re Canales**, 52 S.W.3d 698, 704 (Tex.2001). The requirement in TRCP 18a(b)(1)(B) that the motion to recuse be filed at least ten days before the hearing or trial does not apply to objections to assigned judges. *See* Tex. Gov't Code §74.053(c); Tex. R. Civ. P. 18a(b)(1)(B). See "Motion to recuse," ch. 5-C, §4.1.6(2).

Caution

The objection must be the first matter presented to the assigned judge for a ruling. ***Chandler v. Chandler****, 991 S.W.2d 367, 383 (Tex.App.—El Paso 1999, pet. denied), disapproved on other grounds,* ***Agar Corp. v. Electro Circuits Int'l****, 580 S.W.3d 136 (Tex.2019); see* ***In re Approximately $17,239.00****, 129 S.W.3d at 168–69. The objection is too late if it is filed after the assigned judge makes a ruling, even on a pretrial motion submitted without a hearing. See* ***In re S.N.Z.****, 421 S.W.3d 899, 907 (Tex.App.—Dallas 2014, pet. denied);* ***Tivoli Corp. v. Jewelers Mut. Ins.****, 932 S.W.2d 704, 709 (Tex.App.—San Antonio 1996, writ denied). An objection after ordinary docket call is timely.* ***Lee v. Bachus****, 900 S.W.2d 390, 392 (Tex.App.—Texarkana 1995, orig. proceeding).*

§3.5 Challenges.

1. Active judge—no challenge. A party cannot challenge an active judge. An active judge assigned under Gov't Code chapter 74 is not subject to a §74.053 objection. Tex. Gov't Code §74.053(e). See "Active judge," ch. 5-C, §3.2.1.

Practice Tip

If the presiding judge discusses possible appointments for an assigned judge and the parties voice an objection to one of the judges mentioned, the oral objection does not count as a formal objection to an assigned judge. ***Kellogg v. Martin****, 810 S.W.2d 302, 304–05 (Tex.App.—Texarkana 1991, orig. proceeding).*

2. Retired, former, or senior judge.

(1) Single challenge. Each party is entitled to make one challenge in a case to an assigned judge who is a retired, former, or senior judge appointed under Gov't Code §74.054. *See* Tex. Gov't Code §74.053(b); *see, e.g.*, **In re Perritt**, 992 S.W.2d 444, 446 n.2 (Tex.1999) (former judge); **Flores v. Banner**, 932 S.W.2d 500, 501 (Tex.1996) (retired judge). For definitions of retired, former, and senior judges, see "Who may be assigned," ch. 5-C, §3.2. Under Gov't Code §74.053, "party" includes multiple parties aligned in a case as determined by the presiding judge. Tex. Gov't Code §74.053(g).

(2) Unlimited challenges. Each party has unlimited challenges to an assigned judge who was defeated in the last primary or general election in which she was seeking reelection. *See* Tex. Gov't Code §74.053(b), (d).

§3.6 Automatic removal. A proper and timely objection to an assigned judge is a peremptory objection; the removal is mandatory and automatic. Tex. Gov't Code §74.053(b); **In re Canales**, 52 S.W.3d 698, 701 (Tex.2001); **Flores v. Banner**, 932 S.W.2d 500, 501 (Tex.1996).

§3.7 How to object to assigned judge.

1. In writing. The objection must be in writing and must be filed with the court. **Morris v. Short**, 902 S.W.2d 566, 569 (Tex.App.—Houston [1st Dist.] 1995, writ denied); *see* **Wolfe v. Wolfe**, 918 S.W.2d 533, 540–41 (Tex.App.—El Paso 1996, writ denied). See **O'Connor's Texas Civil Forms**, FORM 5C:1 (2020 ed.). Gov't Code §74.053(b) does not state that an objection must be in writing, but the use of the word "files" presupposes that it will be. **Morris**, 902 S.W.2d at 569; **Kellogg v. Martin**, 810 S.W.2d 302, 305 (Tex.App.—Texarkana 1991, orig. proceeding). The objection may be handwritten. **Morris**, 902 S.W.2d at 569. The objection may also be filed by e-mail. Tex. Gov't Code §74.053(f). If a party learns at docket call that a visiting judge was assigned to the case, the objection must still be in writing—an oral objection at the hearing is not enough. **Morris**, 902 S.W.2d at 569; *see* **Money v. Jones**, 766 S.W.2d 307, 308 (Tex.App.—Dallas 1989, writ denied).

2. Identify challenged judge. The objection should identify the assigned judge by name. *See, e.g.*, **Texas Empl. Comm'n v. Alvarez**, 915 S.W.2d 161, 164 (Tex.App.—Corpus Christi 1996, orig. proceeding) (because party did not name judge in objection and did not reurge objection when case was reset, judge was unaware of objection). However, if the challenged judge's identity can be determined from the objection, the lack of a name is not critical. *See, e.g.*, **Flores v. Banner**, 932 S.W.2d 500, 501–02 (Tex.1996) (because movant did not know name of judge to be assigned, she filed objection to "any" assigned judge; objection was effective).

3. Grounds.

(1) Standard objection. An objection under Gov't Code §74.053 to an assigned judge should state that the party objects to the judge's assignment. Because a §74.053 objection depends on the judge's status, the judge's status should be identified in the objection. A party does not need to provide a reason for the objection. **In re Perritt**, 992 S.W.2d 444, 446 (Tex.1999).

(2) Objections to procedural errors in assignment. A party must object to any procedural errors in the assignment or waive the error. *See, e.g.*, **In re General Elec. Capital Corp.**, 63 S.W.3d 568, 572 (Tex.App.—El Paso 2001, orig. proceeding) (waived objection that assigned judge did not take required oath); *cf.* **Lopez v. State**, 57 S.W.3d 625, 629 (Tex.App.—Corpus Christi 2001, pet. ref'd) (criminal case; waived objection that record did not contain copy of order of assignment).

(3) Disqualification or recusal challenges. When a party has exhausted its objections to assigned judges, the party can assert any available disqualification or recusal challenges. See "Motion to disqualify or recuse," ch. 5-C, §4.

4. Identify number of challenges. Although not required by statute, the party should state the number of objections to other assigned judges, if any, that it has made in the same case. *See* **Amateur Athletic Found. v. Hoffman**, 893 S.W.2d 602, 604 (Tex.App.—Dallas 1994, orig. proceeding) (Whittington, J., dissenting).

5. Verification.

(1) Standard objection. There is no statutory requirement that a standard objection to an assigned judge be verified. **O'Connor v. Lykos**, 960 S.W.2d 96, 99 & n.6 (Tex.App.—Houston [1st Dist.] 1997, orig. proceeding). The standard objection does not need to be verified because a party does not need to assert any facts in an objection to an assigned judge. *Id.* at 99. However, one court of appeals has stated in dicta that the objection must be verified. *See* **Hawkins v. Estate of Volkmann**, 898 S.W.2d 334, 343–44 (Tex.App.—San Antonio 1994, writ denied) (court overruled unverified challenge to assigned judge). Until the issue is resolved by the Supreme Court, parties should verify objections to assigned judges.

(2) Other challenges. If facts are necessary to support other challenges to the assigned judge (see "Objections to procedural errors in assignment," ch. 5-C, §3.7.3(2)), the motion should be verified. See "Verified," ch. 5-C, §4.1.2.

§3.8 No hearing. When a party files a timely objection to an assigned judge under Gov't Code §74.053(b), no hearing is necessary because the removal is automatic. The only fact issue that could arise is whether the objection was timely, and for that reason, the judge and the parties should make a record. If the assigned judge is challenged for other reasons ("Objections to procedural errors in assignment," ch. 5-C, §3.7.3(2)), a hearing is necessary. See "Hearing after referral," ch. 5-C, §4.6.

§3.9 Termination of assignment. The term for an assignment depends on the language in the order of assignment. **In re Republic Parking Sys.**, 60 S.W.3d 877, 879 (Tex.App.—Houston [14th Dist.] 2001, orig. proceeding). Generally, judges are assigned either for a period of time or for a particular case. *Id.* Typical orders of assignment contain the language that the assignment is to continue until the assigned judge completes the trial of any case begun during the period of assignment, passes on motions for new trial, and completes all other matters arising from any cause heard by the assigned judge. *See* **Davis v. Crist Indus.**, 98 S.W.3d 338, 341 (Tex.App.—Fort Worth 2003, pet. denied). The following is a representative sample of cases determining when an assignment ends: • Power expires on the date set in the order, if the judge does not begin the trial by that date. **In re Republic Parking Sys.**, 60 S.W.3d at 880. • Power expires when the court loses plenary power over the case. **Ex parte Eastland**, 811 S.W.2d 571, 572 (Tex.1991). • Power expires when the appeal is perfected. **Starnes v. Chapman**, 793 S.W.2d 104, 106 (Tex.App.—Dallas 1990, orig. proceeding). • Power expires when the assigned judge grants a new trial. **O'Connor v. Lykos**, 960 S.W.2d 96, 98 (Tex.App.—Houston [1st Dist.] 1997, orig. proceeding). • Power extends to postjudgment discovery after the trial court loses plenary power, unless limited by language in the assignment. **O'Connor v. Smith**, 815 S.W.2d 338, 346 (Tex.App.—Houston [1st Dist.] 1991, orig. proceeding).

§4. Motion to disqualify or recuse

A motion to disqualify seeks to prevent a judge from hearing a case for a constitutional reason or a reason under TRCP 18b(a). *See* **In re Union Pac. Res.**, 969 S.W.2d 427, 428 (Tex.1998). TRCP 18b(a) incorporates the grounds for disqualifica-

tion from the Texas Constitution. *See* Tex. Const. art. 5, §11; **Tesco Am., Inc. v. Strong Indus.**, 221 S.W.3d 550, 553 (Tex.2006). A motion to recuse, on the other hand, seeks to prevent a judge from hearing a case for a nonconstitutional reason. *See* Tex. R. Civ. P. 18b(b). Disqualification and recusal remove only the individually challenged judge—not the court as an entity—from participation in a case. *See* **Davis v. West**, 433 S.W.3d 101, 107 (Tex.App.—Houston [1st Dist.] 2014, pet. denied).

Note

In this section, we use the phrase "regional presiding judge" to refer to the presiding judge of the administrative judicial region in which the court considering the motion to disqualify or recuse is located. See Tex. R. Civ. P. 18a(e)(1).

§4.1 Motion. A party in a case can file a motion to disqualify or recuse a judge sitting in the case in any trial court, except a statutory probate court (which is governed by Gov't Code chapter 25), justice court (which is governed by TRCP 528), or municipal court (which is governed by Gov't Code chapter 29). *See* TRCP 18a(a) & cmt. See "Motion to disqualify or recuse," **O'Connor's Texas Civil Appeals**, ch. 3-I, §5.1 (2020 ed.).

1. Written.

(1) Motion to disqualify. A motion to disqualify should be in writing. *See* Tex. R. Civ. P. 18a(a) (party may seek to disqualify by "filing" motion). Because disqualification can be raised at any time, even on appeal or in a collateral attack on the judgment, an oral motion to disqualify may be permissible. *See* **Zarate v. Sun Oper. Ltd.**, 40 S.W.3d 617, 621 (Tex.App.—San Antonio 2001, pet. denied). See "Disqualification," ch. 5-C, §7.3.1.

(2) Motion to recuse. A motion to recuse should be in writing. *See* Tex. R. Civ. P. 18a(a); *see, e.g.*, **Barron v. State**, 108 S.W.3d 379, 383 (Tex.App.—Tyler 2003, no pet.) (oral motion to recuse improper). TRCP 18a(a) does not state that a motion to recuse must be in writing, but its use of the word "filing" presupposes that it will be.

2. Verified. Any motion to remove a judge from hearing the case must be verified. Tex. R. Civ. P. 18a(a)(1); *see* **Johnson v. Sepulveda**, 178 S.W.3d 117, 118–19 (Tex.App.—Houston [14th Dist.] 2005, no pet.) (unverified motion to recuse was ineffective).

3. Grounds. To conserve space in this book, a complete discussion of the grounds for disqualification and recusal is included in a companion book, **O'Connor's Texas Civil Appeals**. For the forms for disqualification and recusal, see **O'Connor's Texas Civil Forms**, FORMS 5C:3, 5C:5 (2020 ed.).

(1) Identify specific grounds. A motion to disqualify or recuse must identify the specific legal grounds for disqualification or recusal. Tex. R. Civ. P. 18a(a)(2).

(a) Disqualification. A trial judge may be disqualified under Texas Constitution art. 5, §11, or under TRCP 18b(a), which is based on constitutional grounds. *See* **Tesco Am., Inc. v. Strong Indus.**, 221 S.W.3d 550, 553 (Tex.2006).

[1] Texas Constitution. Under the Texas Constitution, a judge must be disqualified from hearing a case if (1) the judge served as an attorney in the case, (2) the judge "may be interested" in the outcome of the case, or (3) one of the parties is related to the judge. Tex. Const. art. 5, §11. See "Disqualification under Texas Constitution," **O'Connor's Texas Civil Appeals**, ch. 3-I, §3.1 (2020 ed.).

[2] TRCP 18b(a). Under TRCP 18b(a), a judge must be disqualified from hearing a case under any of the following circumstances:

[a] The judge served as an attorney in the case. Tex. R. Civ. P. 18b(a)(1); **In re O'Connor**, 92 S.W.3d 446, 448 (Tex.2002).

[b] An attorney with whom the judge previously practiced law served on the case while associated with the judge. Tex. R. Civ. P. 18b(a)(1); **In re O'Connor**, 92 S.W.3d at 448–49.

[c] The judge knows that she has an interest in the suit, either individually or as a fiduciary. Tex. R. Civ. P. 18b(a)(2). A disqualifying interest is generally either financial or personal. See "Disqualifying interests," **O'Connor's Texas Civil Appeals**, ch. 3-I, §3.1.2 (2020 ed.).

[d] The judge is related to a party by affinity or consanguinity within the third degree. Tex. R. Civ. P. 18b(a)(3). Government Code §§573.021 to 573.025 define the relationships that fall within and trigger this prohibition. See "Related to party," **O'Connor's Texas Civil Appeals**, ch. 3-I, §3.1.3 (2020 ed.).

(b) Recusal. A trial judge may be subject to recusal under TRCP 18b(b) or a statute that supports grounds for recusal. See "Grounds for recusal," **O'Connor's Texas Civil Appeals**, ch. 3-I, §4 (2020 ed.).

(2) Not based on judge's rulings. The motion must not be based only on the judge's rulings in the case. Tex. R. Civ. P. 18a(a)(3) & cmt. See "Challenged judge's rulings," ch. 5-C, §4.6.3(2).

(3) Waiver. The parties may waive a ground for recusal after it is fully disclosed on the record. Tex. R. Civ. P. 18b(e). Parties cannot waive a constitutionally based ground for disqualification. **Spigener v. Wallis**, 80 S.W.3d 174, 180 (Tex.App.—Waco 2002, no pet.); *see* Tex. R. Civ. P. 18a(b)(2), (g)(3)(B); **Freedom Comms. v. Coronado**, 372 S.W.3d 621, 624 (Tex.2012); **Buckholts ISD v. Glaser**, 632 S.W.2d 146, 148 (Tex.1982); **Jennings v. Garner**, 721 S.W.2d 445, 446 (Tex.App.—Tyler 1986, no writ); *see also* **Davis v. West**, 433 S.W.3d 101, 107 (Tex.App.—Houston [1st Dist.] 2014, pet. denied) (disqualification is a jurisdictional issue).

4. Facts. A motion to disqualify or recuse must state with particularity facts that would be admissible in evidence and support the challenge. *See* Tex. R. Civ. P. 18a(a)(4). Facts should be based on personal knowledge but may be stated on information and belief if the grounds supporting the belief are specifically stated. Tex. R. Civ. P. 18a(a)(4)(A).

5. Defects in motion.

(1) Motion to disqualify. A challenged judge cannot deny a motion to disqualify because of procedural defects; instead, she must either order the disqualification or refer the motion to the regional presiding judge. Tex. R. Civ. P. 18a(f)(1). See "Response by challenged judge," ch. 5-C, §4.3. The regional presiding judge cannot deny a motion to disqualify because it was not filed or served in compliance with TRCP 18a. Tex. R. Civ. P. 18a(g)(3)(B).

(2) Motion to recuse. A challenged judge cannot deny a motion to recuse because of procedural defects; instead, she must either order the recusal or refer the motion to the regional presiding judge. Tex. R. Civ. P. 18a(f)(1); *see, e.g.*, **In re Marshall**, 515 S.W.3d 420, 422 (Tex.App.—Houston [14th Dist.] 2017, orig. proceeding) (judge had duty to comply with TRCP 18a(f)(1) even though motion to recuse was handwritten). See "Response by challenged judge," ch. 5-C, §4.3. If the motion is referred, the regional presiding judge may then deny the motion to recuse if it does not comply with TRCP 18a. Tex. R. Civ. P. 18a(g)(3)(A). The regional presiding judge can deny the motion without an oral hearing, but the order must describe how the motion does not comply. *Id.* Even if the motion is amended to correct the procedural defect, the motion will count in determining whether a tertiary motion to recuse has been filed. *Id.* See "Tertiary motion to disqualify or recuse," ch. 5-C, §5.

6. Deadline to file.

(1) Motion to disqualify. A motion to disqualify should be filed as soon as practicable after the party learns of the reason for disqualification. Tex. R. Civ. P. 18a(b)(2). Disqualification cannot be waived, however, and thus can be raised at any time, even on appeal or in a collateral attack on the judgment. See "Waiver," ch. 5-C, §4.1.3(3); "Disqualification," ch. 5-C, §7.3.1.

(2) Motion to recuse. A motion to recuse must be filed (1) as soon as practicable after the party learns of the reason for recusal and (2) at least ten days before the date set for the trial or other hearing. Tex. R. Civ. P. 18a(b)(1). A motion to recuse may be filed after the ten-day deadline if the party did not know and should not have reasonably known (1) that the judge it seeks to recuse would preside at the trial or hearing or (2) of the reason for recusal until after that deadline. Tex. R. Civ. P. 18a(b)(1)(B).

Note

When a case is reversed for retrial, a party can file a motion to recuse after remand. See ***Winfield v. Daggett****, 846 S.W.2d 920, 922 (Tex.App.—Houston [1st Dist.] 1993, orig. proceeding) (under former TRCP 18a(a), now TRCP 18a(b)(1)(B); when new trial is granted, case stands on docket as if it had not been tried).*

7. Notice to other parties. The party filing the motion must serve on all other parties copies of the motion by the same method that was used for filing, if possible. Tex. R. Civ. P. 18a(d). TRCP 18a does not specify when to serve a motion to disqualify or recuse. Because the challenged judge must either grant the motion or refer it within three business days after it is filed, a party should serve the motion at the same time it is filed. See "When to serve," ch. 1-D, §5; "Deadline to grant motion or refer," ch. 5-C, §4.3.2.

8. Delivery by clerk. Once the motion to disqualify or recuse is filed, the clerk must immediately deliver a copy of the motion to the challenged judge and the regional presiding judge. Tex. R. Civ. P. 18a(e)(1).

§4.2 Response by other party. Any other party in the case can file a response to the motion. Tex. R. Civ. P. 18a(c)(1). See **O'Connor's Texas Civil Forms**, FORMS 5C:4, 5C:6 (2020 ed.).

1. Grounds.

(1) Refute grounds in motion. The party should refute the allegations made in the motion to disqualify or recuse. See "Grounds," ch. 5-C, §4.1.3.

(2) Request sanctions. If the motion to disqualify or recuse was (1) groundless and filed in bad faith or to harass or (2) clearly brought for the purpose of unnecessary delay and without sufficient cause, the party responding to the motion may ask for sanctions. Tex. R. Civ. P. 18a(h). See "Sanctions," ch. 5-C, §4.7.4.

2. Deadline to file. A response must be filed before the motion is heard. Tex. R. Civ. P. 18a(c)(1).

3. Notice to other parties. The party filing the response must serve on all other parties copies of the response by the same method that was used for filing, if possible. Tex. R. Civ. P. 18a(d). TRCP 18a does not specify when to serve a response to a motion to disqualify or recuse. Thus, a party should serve the response at the same time it is filed. See "When to serve," ch. 1-D, §5.

4. Delivery by clerk. Once the response to the motion is filed, the clerk must immediately deliver a copy of the response to the challenged judge and the regional presiding judge. Tex. R. Civ. P. 18a(e)(1).

§4.3 Response by challenged judge.

1. Judge's options. The challenged judge should not file a response to a motion to disqualify or recuse. Tex. R. Civ. P. 18a(c)(2). The judge has two options—either (1) grant the motion to disqualify or recuse or (2) refer the motion for a hearing before another judge. *See* Tex. R. Civ. P. 18a(f)(1).

Note

A challenged judge cannot overrule or refuse to rule on a motion that is procedurally or substantively defective; the judge must grant the motion or refer it. See ***In re Marshall****, 515 S.W.3d 420, 422 (Tex.App.—Houston [14th Dist.] 2017, orig. proceeding). If referred, another judge will determine the procedural adequacy and merits of the motion. See id. See "Defects in motion," ch. 5-C, §4.1.5; "Hearing after referral," ch. 5-C, §4.6.*

(1) Judge grants motion. When a challenged judge grants a motion to disqualify or recuse, she must sign and file an order to that effect and the regional presiding judge must transfer the case to another court or assign another judge to the case. *See* Tex. R. Civ. P. 18a(f)(1)(A), (g)(7); **Davis v. West**, 433 S.W.3d 101, 107 (Tex.App.—Houston [1st Dist.] 2014, pet. denied); *see also* Tex. Gov't Code §24.002 (voluntary recusal). See "Granting motion," ch. 5-C, §4.7.2.

(2) Judge refers motion. When a challenged judge declines to disqualify or recuse herself, she must sign and file an order referring the motion to the regional presiding judge. Tex. R. Civ. P. 18a(f)(1)(B); *see* Tex. Gov't Code §74.059(c)(3). The challenged judge cannot deny the motion; she must refer the motion to the presiding judge for a hearing. *See* Tex. R. Civ. P. 18a(f)(1)(B); **In re Perritt**, 992 S.W.2d 444, 447 (Tex.1999) (under former TRCP 18a(d), now TRCP 18a(f)(1)(B)).

2. Deadline to grant motion or refer. The challenged judge must either grant the motion to disqualify or recuse or refer the motion within three business days after the motion is filed. Tex. R. Civ. P. 18a(f)(1).

3. Delivery of order. The clerk must immediately deliver a copy of the order of disqualification, recusal, or referral to the regional presiding judge. Tex. R. Civ. P. 18a(e)(2).

4. Prohibited actions.

(1) Ignore or overrule. The challenged judge cannot ignore the motion or overrule it and proceed to trial. *See* Tex. R. Civ. P. 18a(f)(1); **Johnson v. Pumjani**, 56 S.W.3d 670, 672 (Tex.App.—Houston [14th Dist.] 2001, no pet.) (under former TRCP 18a(c), now TRCP 18a(f)(1)).

(2) Take any further action.

(a) Motion filed before evidence offered at trial. When a motion to disqualify or recuse has been filed before evidence has been offered at trial, the challenged judge cannot take any further action in the case until the motion to disqualify or recuse is resolved. Tex. R. Civ. P. 18a(f)(2)(A). Any order signed by the challenged judge while the motion is pending is void. **In re Rio Grande Valley Gas Co.**, 987 S.W.2d 167, 179 (Tex.App.—Corpus Christi 1999, orig. proceeding); *see* **In re Marshall**, 515 S.W.3d at 422; **Brosseau v. Ranzau**, 911 S.W.2d 890, 893 (Tex.App.—Beaumont 1995, no writ). There is one exception: a judge may sign an order while the motion is pending if "good cause" is identified in the order or on the record. *See* Tex. R. Civ. P. 18a(f)(2)(A). Good cause must relate to whether there is justification for the challenged judge to act at a specific time instead of waiting for the appropriate judge to act. **In re Marshall**, 515 S.W.3d at 422. The judge cannot just state that there is good cause to take further action in the case; she must include the basis for finding good cause. *See* **In re Stearman**, 252 S.W.3d 113, 116–17 (Tex.App.—Waco 2008, orig. proceeding) (under former TRCP 18a(d), now TRCP 18a(f)(2)(A)).

(b) Motion filed after evidence offered at trial. When a motion to disqualify or recuse is filed after evidence has been offered at trial, the challenged judge can proceed with the trial unless the regional presiding judge issues a stay. Tex. R. Civ. P. 18a(f)(2)(B).

5. Noncompliance. If the challenged judge does not comply with a duty under TRCP 18a, the movant can notify the regional presiding judge. Tex. R. Civ. P. 18a(f)(3).

§4.4 Duties of regional presiding judge & assigned judge.

1. After challenged judge's response.

(1) Order of disqualification or recusal. If the challenged judge orders herself disqualified or recused, the regional presiding judge must assign another judge to the case. *See* Tex. Gov't Code §74.059(c)(3).

(2) Order of referral. If the challenged judge refers the motion, the regional presiding judge must rule on the motion or assign a judge to rule on it. Tex. R. Civ. P. 18a(g)(1). If a party moves to disqualify or recuse the regional presiding judge, the judge can do either of the following:

(a) Assign a judge to rule on the original referred motion. *Id.*

(b) Sign and file with the clerk an order referring the motion that challenges the regional presiding judge to the Chief Justice. *Id.* The Chief Justice has authority to assign judges and issue orders as allowed under TRCP 18a or by statute. Tex. R. Civ. P. 18a(i).

Note

Either party may file an objection to the assigned judge. See Tex. Gov't Code §74.053(b). For the procedure for objecting to an assigned judge, see "Objection to assigned judge," ch. 5-C, §3.

2. Interim orders in pending case. The regional presiding judge or assigned judge may issue interim or ancillary orders in the pending case as justice may require. Tex. R. Civ. P. 18a(g)(4).

§4.5 Discovery. Discovery requests and subpoenas cannot be issued to the challenged judge unless ordered by the regional presiding judge or assigned judge. Tex. R. Civ. P. 18a(g)(5).

§4.6 Hearing after referral. The party that filed the motion to disqualify or recuse is entitled to a hearing on the motion. *See* Tex. R. Civ. P. 18a(g)(6). The motion must be heard by the regional presiding judge or assigned judge as soon as practicable and may be heard immediately after the motion is referred. Tex. R. Civ. P. 18a(g)(6)(A). The hearing gives the movant an opportunity to develop a record to support its motion. **In re Rio Grande Valley Gas Co.**, 987 S.W.2d 167, 179 (Tex.App.—Corpus Christi 1999, orig. proceeding) (under former TRCP 18a(d), now TRCP 18a(g)(6)).

1. Notice of hearing. All parties must receive notice of the hearing on a motion to disqualify or recuse. Tex. R. Civ. P. 18a(g)(6)(B).

2. By telephone. The hearing on a motion to disqualify or recuse can be conducted by telephone on the record. Tex. R. Civ. P. 18a(g)(6)(C). Evidence submitted by fax or e-mail may be considered as long as it is admissible under the TREs. *Id.*

3. Burden of proof. The party who filed the motion to disqualify or recuse has the burden of proof at the hearing on the motion. *See* **Drake v. Walker**, 529 S.W.3d 516, 528 (Tex.App.—Dallas 2017, no pet.); *see also* **Sparkman v. Peoples Nat'l Bank**, 553 S.W.2d 680, 681 (Tex.App.—Waco 1977, writ ref'd n.r.e.) (judge is presumed to be qualified until contrary evidence is shown).

(1) Evidence—generally. The movant must provide sworn evidence to support the allegations in its motion. *See* Tex. R. Civ. P. 18a(a)(4)(C); **Urdiales v. Concord Techs. Del., Inc.**, 120 S.W.3d 400, 403–04 (Tex.App.—Houston [14th Dist.] 2003, pet. denied).

(2) Challenged judge's rulings. Although a challenged judge's rulings cannot be the sole basis for a motion to disqualify or recuse, the judge hearing the motion can consider evidence of the challenged judge's rulings when one or more sufficient other grounds are raised. Tex. R. Civ. P. 18a cmt. Rulings do not include the judge's statements or remarks about a case. *Id.*

4. No participation by challenged judge. The challenged judge should not voluntarily participate in the recusal hearing or in a mandamus proceeding regarding the recusal. **Blanchard v. Krueger**, 916 S.W.2d 15, 19 n.9 (Tex.App.—Houston [1st Dist.] 1995, orig. proceeding). Active participation in the recusal proceedings, such as hiring an attorney or filing a response, can lead to the judge's recusal. *Id.*

§4.7 Order on motion to disqualify or recuse.

1. Written. The ruling must be by a written order. Tex. R. Civ. P. 18a(g)(2).

2. Granting motion.

(1) Motion to disqualify or recuse—generally. If the motion to disqualify or recuse is granted, the regional presiding judge must transfer the case to another court or assign another judge to hear the case. Tex. R. Civ. P. 18a(g)(7). The phrase "another judge" does not exclude the judge assigned to hear the motion to disqualify or recuse. **District Judges of Collin Cty. v. Commissioner's Ct. of Collin Cty.**, 677 S.W.2d 743, 745 (Tex.App.—Dallas 1984, writ ref'd n.r.e.) (under former TRCP 18a(f), now TRCP 18a(g)(7)).

(2) Motion to disqualify—constitutional grounds. If a district-court judge is disqualified on constitutional grounds, the parties may, by consent, appoint a proper person to try the case. Tex. Const. art. 5, §11. If they are unable to do so, a competent person may be appointed to try the case in the same county where it is pending. *Id.*

3. **Denying motion.** If the motion to disqualify or recuse is denied, the case will be returned to the challenged judge for a trial on the merits. *See* Tex. R. Civ. P. 18a(f)(2).

4. **Sanctions.** If a motion to disqualify or recuse was (1) groundless and filed in bad faith or to harass or (2) clearly brought for the purpose of unnecessary delay and without sufficient cause, the judge who heard the motion, after notice and a hearing, may order the party who filed the motion, her attorney, or both to pay the attorney fees and expenses of the other parties. Tex. R. Civ. P. 18a(h).

§5. Tertiary motion to disqualify or recuse

§5.1 Definition. A tertiary motion to disqualify or recuse is a party's third (or later) motion filed in the same case to disqualify or recuse a judge in a district court or statutory county court. Tex. Civ. Prac. & Rem. Code §30.016(a) (district and statutory county courts); Tex. Gov't Code §25.00256(a) (statutory probate courts). Under either CPRC §30.016(a) or Gov't Code §25.00256(a), a tertiary motion may be filed against a different judge than the judge against whom the previous motions for disqualification or recusal were filed. *See* **Gonzalez v. Guilbot**, 315 S.W.3d 533, 539–40 (Tex.2010).

§5.2 Differences in procedure. Except for the differences noted below, the procedure for a tertiary motion to disqualify or recuse a judge is the same as for other motions to disqualify or recuse. Tex. Civ. Prac. & Rem. Code §30.016(b).

1. **Judge declines to recuse.** When a judge declines to recuse herself after a tertiary motion, the judge must continue to (1) preside over the case, (2) sign orders in the case, and (3) move the case to final disposition as though a motion had not been filed. Tex. Civ. Prac. & Rem. Code §30.016(b); Tex. Gov't Code §25.00256(b); **Gonzalez v. Guilbot**, 315 S.W.3d 533, 539 (Tex.2010).

2. **Attorney fees & costs.** If the judge hearing the tertiary motion denies it, attorney fees and costs must be awarded to the party opposing the motion. Tex. Civ. Prac. & Rem. Code §30.016(c); Tex. Gov't Code §25.00256(c). The party making the motion and its attorney are jointly and severally liable for the attorney fees and costs. Tex. Civ. Prac. & Rem. Code §30.016(c); Tex. Gov't Code §25.00256(c). The fees and costs must be paid within 30 days after the order is rendered, unless the order is superseded. Tex. Civ. Prac. & Rem. Code §30.016(c); Tex. Gov't Code §25.00256(c).

3. **Review.** The denial of a tertiary disqualification or recusal motion is reviewable only on appeal from a final judgment. Tex. Civ. Prac. & Rem. Code §30.016(d); Tex. Gov't Code §25.00256(d).

4. **If denial reversed.** If a tertiary motion is ultimately sustained, the new judge for the case must vacate all orders signed by the sitting judge while the motion was pending. Tex. Civ. Prac. & Rem. Code §30.016(e); Tex. Gov't Code §25.00256(e).

§6. Voluntary disqualification or recusal

Even if a party has not filed a motion, a judge, on her own motion, should voluntarily disqualify or recuse herself in any proceeding in which one of the grounds listed in TRCP 18b is present (e.g., the judge's impartiality might reasonably be questioned). *See* Tex. Gov't Code §24.002; Tex. R. Civ. P. 18b; **Dunn v. County of Dallas**, 794 S.W.2d 560, 562 (Tex.App.—Dallas 1990, no writ); *see also* **Sao Paulo State v. American Tobacco Co.**, 535 U.S. 229, 230 (2002) (interpreting 28 U.S.C. §455(a)). The judge must sign an order of disqualification or recusal. *See, e.g.*, **Carmody v. State Farm Lloyds**, 184 S.W.3d 419, 423 (Tex.App.—Dallas 2006, no pet.) (notation on docket sheet satisfied requirement of order of recusal). Once the judge enters the order, the judge must (1) request that the regional presiding judge assign another judge to hear the case and (2) take no further action in the case unless there is good cause. Tex. Gov't Code §24.002. The judge should generally follow the same procedures as if a party had filed a motion to disqualify or recuse. See "Motion to disqualify or recuse," ch. 5-C, §4.

§7. Review

§7.1 Appeal.

1. **Record.** For a proper review of the trial court's decision, the party must present the appellate court with a record of the motion and proceedings. *See* **Ceballos v. El Paso Health Care Sys.**, 881 S.W.2d 439, 445 (Tex.App.—El Paso 1994, writ denied).

2. Motion to disqualify. A party can appeal an order granting or denying a motion to disqualify as allowed by other law. Tex. R. Civ. P. 18a(j)(2).

3. Motion to recuse.

(1) Denying motion. A party can challenge an order denying a motion to recuse by appeal from the final judgment. Tex. R. Civ. P. 18a(j)(1)(A); *see* **Thuesen v. Amerisure Ins.**, 487 S.W.3d 291, 294 (Tex.App.—Houston [14th Dist.] 2016, no pet.). The standard of review for an order denying a motion to recuse is abuse of discretion. Tex. R. Civ. P. 18a(j)(1)(A); **Drake v. Walker**, 529 S.W.3d 516, 528 (Tex.App.—Dallas 2017, no pet.); **Thuesen**, 487 S.W.3d at 305.

(2) Granting motion. A party cannot challenge an order granting a motion to recuse by appeal; the order cannot be reviewed by appeal, mandamus, or any other means. Tex. R. Civ. P. 18a(j)(1)(B).

§7.2 Mandamus.

1. Motion to disqualify. An order denying or granting a motion to disqualify can be reviewed by mandamus. Tex. R. Civ. P. 18a(j)(2).

2. Motion to recuse. An order denying or granting a motion to recuse cannot be reviewed by mandamus. *See* Tex. R. Civ. P. 18a(j)(1).

3. Objection to assigned judge. An order denying an objection to an assigned judge can be reviewed by mandamus. *See* **In re Canales**, 52 S.W.3d 698, 701 (Tex.2001); **Flores v. Banner**, 932 S.W.2d 500, 501 (Tex.1996).

§7.3 Effect of erroneous denial. The erroneous denial of a motion to disqualify, a motion to recuse, or an objection to an assigned judge may affect any rulings made by the challenged judge.

1. Disqualification. All the orders or judgments of a trial judge who was constitutionally disqualified from sitting are void. **Tesco Am., Inc. v. Strong Indus.**, 221 S.W.3d 550, 555 (Tex.2006); **In re Union Pac. Res.**, 969 S.W.2d 427, 428 (Tex.1998); *see, e.g.*, **Freedom Comms. v. Coronado**, 372 S.W.3d 621, 624 (Tex.2012) (trial judge who took bribe was disqualified, and his order denying D's summary-judgment motion was void). A court of appeals has no authority to consider the merits of an appeal from a void order. *See* **Freedom Comms.**, 372 S.W.3d at 624. An order or judgment that is void because of the judge's disqualification is subject to collateral attack. **Gulf Maritime Whs. Co. v. Towers**, 858 S.W.2d 556, 559 (Tex.App.—Beaumont 1993, writ denied).

2. Recusal. The orders of a judge who should have recused herself as a result of a valid motion to recuse are not void. **In re Union Pac. Res.**, 969 S.W.2d at 428. Even though a judgment rendered by a judge subject to a valid motion for recusal may be reversed on appeal, it is not fundamental error. *Id.*

3. Objection to assigned judge. The orders of an assigned judge who should have been removed after an objection under Gov't Code §74.053 are void. **In re Canales**, 52 S.W.3d 698, 701 (Tex.2001); **Dunn v. Street**, 938 S.W.2d 33, 34–35 (Tex.1997); **Flores v. Banner**, 932 S.W.2d 500, 501 (Tex.1996).

D. Motion for Continuance

§1. General

§1.1 Rules. Tex. R. Civ. P. 247, 251 to 254, 330(d).

§1.2 Purpose. A motion for continuance is a request to postpone or delay a case that has been set for a hearing or trial. By comparison, a motion to extend is a request for more time to file a document. *See* Tex. R. Civ. P. 5. See "Motion to extend time," ch. 1-C, §9.1.

§1.3 Forms. **O'Connor's Texas Civil Forms**, FORMS 5D:1 et seq., 7B:2 to 7B:8 (2020 ed.).

§2. Motion

If a motion for continuance does not comply with the rules, the appellate court will presume the trial court did not abuse its discretion in denying the motion. **Villegas v. Carter**, 711 S.W.2d 624, 626 (Tex.1986); **In re Marriage of Harrison**, 557 S.W.3d 99, 117 (Tex.App.—Houston [14th Dist.] 2018, pet. denied); *see* Tex. R. Civ. P. 251 to 254.

§2.1 Written. A motion for continuance must be in writing. *See* **Green v. TDPRS**, 25 S.W.3d 213, 218 (Tex.App.—El Paso 2000, no pet.); **Favaloro v. Commission for Lawyer Discipline**, 13 S.W.3d 831, 838 (Tex.App.—Dallas 2000, no pet.). An oral request for a continuance does not preserve error. **In re Marriage of Harrison**, 557 S.W.3d 99, 118 (Tex.App.—Houston [14th Dist.] 2018, pet. denied); *see* **Phifer v. Nacogdoches Cty. Cent. Appr. Dist.**, 45 S.W.3d 159, 173 (Tex.App.—Tyler 2000, pet. denied). In an emergency, a handwritten motion is sufficient. *See* **Higginbotham v. Collateral Prot., Inc.**, 859 S.W.2d 487, 489–90 (Tex.App.—Houston [1st Dist.] 1993, writ denied).

Practice Tip

If a party made only an oral motion for continuance during trial, on appeal, the party should attempt to circumvent the requirement for a written and verified motion by arguing that the attorney's unsworn statement should be considered as sworn evidence because the other party did not object. See ***Banda v. Garcia****, 955 S.W.2d 270, 272 (Tex.1997) (opponent of attorney's unsworn testimony can waive oath requirement by not objecting when she knows or should know objection is necessary). See "Verification & affidavits," ch. 5-D, §2.3.*

---

§2.2 Specific. The motion must state the specific facts that support it. *See* **Blake v. Lewis**, 886 S.W.2d 404, 409 (Tex.App.—Houston [1st Dist.] 1994, no writ). General allegations (e.g., that the attorney is busy with personal matters or other cases, or that the attorney has not had time to prepare for the trial or hearing) are not enough to support a motion. *Id.*

§2.3 Verification & affidavits. The facts in the motion must be verified or supported by affidavit. Tex. R. Civ. P. 251, 252; **Taherzadeh v. Ghaleh-Assadi**, 108 S.W.3d 927, 928 (Tex.App.—Dallas 2003, pet. denied); **Hawthorne v. Guenther**, 917 S.W.2d 924, 929 (Tex.App.—Beaumont 1996, writ denied). If the motion is not verified or supported by affidavit, the appellate courts presume the trial court did not abuse its discretion in denying the motion. **Serrano v. Ryan's Crossing Apts.**, 241 S.W.3d 560, 564 (Tex.App.—El Paso 2007, pet. denied); **Daugherty v. Jacobs**, 187 S.W.3d 607, 619 (Tex.App.—Houston [14th Dist.] 2006, no pet.). *But see* **Villegas v. Carter**, 711 S.W.2d 624, 626 (Tex.1986) (unrealistic to apply presumption to nonattorney movant whose counsel withdraws through no fault of movant). See "Verification," ch. 1-B, §3.2.15; "Affidavits," ch. 1-B, §3.2.16; **O'Connor's Texas Civil Forms**, FORM 5D:4 (2020 ed.).

Note

Although TRCP 251 requires the motion to be verified or supported by an affidavit, CPRC §132.001 allows for the use of an unsworn declaration instead of a verification or an affidavit. See Tex. Civ. Prac. & Rem. Code §132.001(a). For the requirements for using an unsworn declaration, see "Unsworn declaration," ch. 1-B, §3.2.17.

§2.4 Request hearing. A hearing is generally not required on a motion for continuance. Most motions for continuance—whether verified or supported by affidavits—are decided on written submission. See "Verification & affidavits," ch. 5-D, §2.3. However, a movant may want to request a hearing to bring live witnesses to support the allegations in the motion.

§3. Deadline

A motion for continuance may be filed at any time after the defendant files an answer. Tex. R. Civ. P. 251.

§3.1 Before announcement of ready. A party should file a continuance before making an unconditional announcement of ready for trial. **Reyna v. Reyna**, 738 S.W.2d 772, 775 (Tex.App.—Austin 1987, no writ); *see, e.g.*, **E.C. v. Graydon**, 28 S.W.3d 825, 828 (Tex.App.—Corpus Christi 2000, no pet.) (announcement of ready waived motion for continuance).

§3.2 During trial. A party may file a written motion for continuance during trial if an unforeseeable emergency arises through no fault of that party. *See* **Butcher v. Tinkle**, 183 S.W.2d 227, 230 (Tex.App.—Beaumont 1944, writ ref'd w.o.m.). A continuance sought during trial will rarely be granted, and the trial court's denial of the motion is difficult to reverse on appeal.

§4. Response

If the nonmovant disagrees with the request for continuance, it should file a response and, when necessary, attach affidavits to controvert the allegations in the motion for continuance. See **O'Connor's Texas Civil Forms**, FORM 5D:3 (2020 ed.). Uncontroverted statements in a sworn motion for continuance must be accepted as true. See "Uncontested motion," ch. 5-D, §5.3.

§5. Ruling

§5.1 Obtain a ruling. To preserve error when the trial court refuses to grant a motion for continuance, the party should ask the trial court to make a ruling, either on the record in open court or by a written order. **Direkly v. ARA Devcon, Inc.**, 866 S.W.2d 652, 656 (Tex.App.—Houston [1st Dist.] 1993, writ dism'd). See "Record of ruling," ch. 1-G, §3. When a motion for continuance is presented in open court, an oral ruling on the record is sufficient to preserve error. See "Express ruling," ch. 1-G, §2.2.1. If the record does not contain an express ruling on the motion but shows some other action by the court that implicitly overruled the motion, error is preserved. *See* Tex. R. App. P. 33.1(a)(2)(A). See "Implicit ruling," ch. 1-G, §2.2.2.

§5.2 Court's discretion. The trial court's ruling on most motions for continuance is a matter of discretion. **State v. Wood Oil Distrib.**, 751 S.W.2d 863, 865 (Tex.1988); **Villegas v. Carter**, 711 S.W.2d 624, 626 (Tex.1986). The court may grant a motion for continuance if the motion is supported by an affidavit and states sufficient cause. *See* Tex. R. Civ. P. 247, 251, 252. In certain circumstances, however, the court must grant a motion for continuance. See "Continuance—Attorney unavailable," ch. 5-D, §11; "Continuance for legislator," ch. 5-D, §12; "Continuance for religious holy day," ch. 5-D, §13.

§5.3 Uncontested motion. If a motion for continuance is in substantial compliance with the rule, is properly verified, and is not controverted, the trial court must accept the statements in the motion as true. **Verkin v. Southwest Ctr. One, Ltd.**, 784 S.W.2d 92, 94 (Tex.App.—Houston [1st Dist.] 1989, writ denied); **Garza v. Serrato**, 699 S.W.2d 275, 281 (Tex.App.—San Antonio 1985, writ ref'd n.r.e.). The trial court has no discretion to reject uncontroverted facts in a sworn motion for continuance. **Verkin**, 784 S.W.2d at 94.

§6. Continuance on agreed motion

The court should respect agreements to postpone or continue a case unless the delay would unreasonably interfere with other business of the court. Tex. R. Civ. P. 330(d). The parties should prepare a written agreement to pass or continue a case, have the attorneys for all parties sign it, and file it with the court on or before docket call. *See* Tex. R. Civ. P. 11, 247, 251. See "Agreements between attorneys—Rule 11," ch. 1-H, §9. A party may orally announce the agreement to pass a case at docket call, but it should also file a written agreement. An agreement to pass, postpone, or continue a case pending in a district court is not binding on the court when the case has reached trial on two or more occasions. Tex. R. Civ. P. 330(d).

§7. Continuance based on insufficient notice of trial

§7.1 Notice of trial. The trial court must give the parties reasonable notice of the first trial setting of "not less than 45 days." Tex. R. Civ. P. 245; **Smith v. Lippmann**, 826 S.W.2d 137, 138 n.1 (Tex.1992). The trial court violates due process if it

does not give a party reasonable notice of a trial setting. **In re K.M.L.**, 443 S.W.3d 101, 119 (Tex.2014) (parental-rights-termination case); **Hardin v. Hardin**, 932 S.W.2d 566, 567 (Tex.App.—Tyler 1995, no writ) (appeal from divorce). The language of TRCP 245 is mandatory. **Hardin**, 932 S.W.2d at 567.

§7.2 Motion. When a party seeks a continuance because of insufficient notice of trial, the motion must state that (1) the party received less than 45 days' notice of trial, (2) the notice given was not reasonable, (3) the notice was not adequate to permit the party to prepare for trial, (4) the lack of reasonable notice violated the party's right of due process, and (5) the lack of 45 days' notice violated TRCP 245. *See* **Hardin v. Hardin**, 932 S.W.2d 566, 567 (Tex.App.—Tyler 1995, no writ). The allegations must be supported by sworn proof. Tex. R. Civ. P. 251. See "Verification & affidavits," ch. 5-D, §2.3.

§8. Continuance for additional discovery

A party requesting additional time for discovery, whether to obtain evidence or testimony, must fulfill the requirements of TRCP 252 under oath. **Verkin v. Southwest Ctr. One, Ltd.**, 784 S.W.2d 92, 94 (Tex.App.—Houston [1st Dist.] 1989, writ denied). See **O'Connor's Texas Civil Forms**, FORM 5D:1 (2020 ed.).

Practice Tip

Every case has a discovery-control plan that sets limits for the discovery period, interrogatories, and depositions. See "Discovery-control plans," ch. 6-A, §7. TRCP 190 permits the court to extend the time for discovery. Tex. R. Civ. P. 190.5. See "Modification of discovery periods," ch. 6-A, §8.2. Thus, before you file a motion for continuance for additional discovery, check whether you also need to file a motion to modify the discovery-control plan. See "Modifying discovery procedures," ch. 6-A, §6.

---

§8.1 Contents of motion.

1. Description of discovery. The motion must describe the specific discovery sought. **Wal-Mart Stores Tex., LP v. Crosby**, 295 S.W.3d 346, 356 (Tex.App.—Dallas 2009, pet. denied); *see, e.g.*, **Martinez v. Flores**, 865 S.W.2d 194, 197–98 (Tex.App.—Corpus Christi 1993, writ denied) (request for more time "to complete discovery" was not sufficient).

(1) Procedure for discovery. The motion should describe the procedure the party intends to use to obtain the discovery and the person from whom the discovery will be sought. *See, e.g.*, **State v. Wood Oil Distrib.**, 751 S.W.2d 863, 865 (Tex.1988) (depositions); **Tri-Steel Structures, Inc. v. Baptist Found.**, 166 S.W.3d 443, 447 (Tex.App.—Fort Worth 2005, pet. denied) (same); **Verkin v. Southwest Ctr. One, Ltd.**, 784 S.W.2d 92, 94 (Tex.App.—Houston [1st Dist.] 1989, writ denied) (requests for production and interrogatories). If a continuance is sought to depose a witness, the motion must include the witness's name and address (street, county, and state of residence). Tex. R. Civ. P. 252.

(2) Substance of discovery. The motion should describe the evidence or testimony needed. *See* Tex. R. Civ. P. 252; **Wal-Mart Stores**, 295 S.W.3d at 356. If a continuance is sought to depose a witness, the motion must state what the party expects to prove from the witness's testimony. Tex. R. Civ. P. 252.

(3) Discovery period. The motion should state whether the discovery period has expired.

2. Materiality. The motion must state that the discovery sought is material and show why it is material. Tex. R. Civ. P. 252; **J.E.M. v. Fidelity & Cas. Co.**, 928 S.W.2d 668, 676 (Tex.App.—Houston [1st Dist.] 1996, no writ); *see, e.g.*, **Celotex Corp. v. Gracy Meadow Owners Ass'n**, 847 S.W.2d 384, 388 (Tex.App.—Austin 1993, writ denied) (appellate court decided deposition testimony was immaterial).

3. Diligence. The motion must show that the party used due diligence to obtain the discovery. Tex. R. Civ. P. 252; **Risner v. McDonald's Corp.**, 18 S.W.3d 903, 909 (Tex.App.—Beaumont 2000, pet. denied); **Rhima v. White**, 829 S.W.2d 909, 912 (Tex.App.—Fort Worth 1992, writ denied); *see* **Stierwalt v. FFE Transp. Servs.**, 499 S.W.3d 181, 192 (Tex.App.—El Paso 2016, no pet.) (motion for continuance of summary-judgment hearing). The motion must describe the party's previous attempts to obtain the discovery. *See* Tex. R. Civ. P. 252; **Stierwalt**, 499 S.W.3d at 192; *see, e.g.*, **J.E.M.**, 928 S.W.2d at 676 (diligence shown when Ps stated they noticed witness's deposition soon after need for deposition arose but D refused to produce witness); *see also* **Barron v. Vanier**, 190 S.W.3d 841, 851 (Tex.App.—Fort Worth 2006, no pet.) (failure to file motion to

compel or to otherwise attempt to obtain objected-to items may indicate lack of diligence). Conclusory statements about diligence do not satisfy the requirements of TRCP 252. **Gregg v. Cecil**, 844 S.W.2d 851, 853 (Tex.App.—Beaumont 1992, no writ); *e.g.*, **Rocha v. Faltys**, 69 S.W.3d 315, 319 (Tex.App.—Austin 2002, no pet.) (no showing of diligence when affidavit did not describe particular efforts made to locate witness for deposition); *see* **Stierwalt**, 499 S.W.3d at 192. If a party does not diligently use the discovery procedures, it can seldom claim reversible error when the trial court refuses the continuance. **Wood Oil Distrib.**, 751 S.W.2d at 865; *e.g.*, **Hatteberg v. Hatteberg**, 933 S.W.2d 522, 526–27 (Tex.App.—Houston [1st Dist.] 1994, no writ) (party did not diligently use discovery procedures when she waited until nine days before trial to attempt to serve witnesses).

4. Not obtainable earlier. The motion must explain why the party was unable to obtain the discovery earlier. *See* Tex. R. Civ. P. 252 (party must state "cause of failure, if known"); *see, e.g.*, **Risner**, 18 S.W.3d at 909 (party did not explain why affidavits could not have been timely obtained during 18 months between filing of suit and summary-judgment hearing).

5. Not for delay. The motion must include the statement, "The continuance is not sought for delay only, but so that justice may be done." Tex. R. Civ. P. 252.

6. Not otherwise available. In a second (or later) motion for continuance, the motion must state that the evidence or testimony sought cannot be obtained from any other source. *See* Tex. R. Civ. P. 252; **Verkin**, 784 S.W.2d at 95. This statement is not necessary in the first motion for continuance based on the need for additional discovery. Tex. R. Civ. P. 252; **Verkin**, 784 S.W.2d at 95.

§8.2 Attachments.

1. Affidavits. The party must attach affidavits to support all factual allegations. Tex. R. Civ. P. 251; *see, e.g.*, **Rhima v. White**, 829 S.W.2d 909, 912 (Tex.App.—Fort Worth 1992, writ denied) (party did not file affidavit describing diligence). See "Note," ch. 5-D, §2.3. The person with knowledge of the facts stated in the motion (either the party or the attorney) should make an affidavit stating the facts supporting the motion. See "Affidavits," ch. 1-B, §3.2.16; **O'Connor's Texas Civil Forms**, FORM 5D:4 (2020 ed.).

Practice Tip

An attorney should sign an affidavit only for facts exclusively within her personal knowledge (e.g., the continuance is being sought because of her scheduling conflicts). An attorney should avoid signing an affidavit in support of a client's request for a continuance when the purported basis for the request is outside the attorney's personal knowledge; in such a case, the client should sign the affidavit.

2. Exhibits. Although not required, the party should attach outstanding discovery requests as exhibits to the motion. *See* **Verkin v. Southwest Ctr. One, Ltd.**, 784 S.W.2d 92, 96 (Tex.App.—Houston [1st Dist.] 1989, writ denied) (parties are not required to attach copies of discovery requests). All attachments to the motion should be verified by affidavit. See "Exhibits," ch. 1-B, §4.1.11.

§9. Continuance in summary-judgment case

A party who needs additional time to respond to a motion for summary judgment must ask for it. **Tenneco Inc. v. Enterprise Prods.**, 925 S.W.2d 640, 647 (Tex.1996).

§9.1 Continuance by agreement.

The parties may change the summary-judgment deadlines by agreement. See "Continuance on agreed motion," ch. 5-D, §6; "By agreement," ch. 7-B, §6.2.

§9.2 Motion to reset SJ hearing for lack of 21 days' notice.

1. Generally. When requesting a resetting of the hearing on a motion for summary judgment because the movant did not provide the nonmovant with the required 21 days' notice, the nonmovant should rely on TRCP 166a(c). See "Summary-judgment deadlines," ch. 7-B, §6; **O'Connor's Texas Civil Forms**, FORM 7B:2 (2020 ed.). The nonmovant should object to the lack of the 21 days' notice, file a motion to reset or delay the hearing, present sworn proof, and make a

record. *See* **Nguyen v. Short, How, Frels & Heitz, P.C.**, 108 S.W.3d 558, 560 (Tex.App.—Dallas 2003, pet. denied); *see, e.g.*, **Roob v. Von Beregshasy**, 866 S.W.2d 765, 766 (Tex.App.—Houston [1st Dist.] 1993, writ denied) (nonmovant should have made and filed reporter's record in appellate court). The nonmovant must raise the complaint of untimely notice in writing before or at the hearing; if the nonmovant knows of the hearing date but does not object to the untimely notice, the objection is waived. **Nguyen**, 108 S.W.3d at 560; *see* **Veal v. Veterans Life Ins.**, 767 S.W.2d 892, 895 (Tex.App.—Texarkana 1989, no writ); *see also* **Schied v. Merritt**, No. 01-15-00466-CV, 2016 WL 3751619 (Tex.App.—Houston [1st Dist.] 2016, no pet.) (memo op.; 7-12-16) (if nonmovant receives no notice, as opposed to untimely notice, complaint can be raised in post-judgment motion).

2. Compliance with TRCP 166a(g). Some cases hold that a nonmovant must comply with the requirements of TRCP 166a(g) when the movant does not give 21 days' notice. *See, e.g.*, **Pankow v. Colonial Life Ins.**, 932 S.W.2d 271, 275 (Tex.App.—Amarillo 1996, writ denied) (court required motion for continuance to explain need for additional evidence even though nonmovant did not get required 21 days' notice). But a nonmovant should file a request for continuance under TRCP 166a(g) only when it needs more than 21 days to prepare for the hearing, not when it seeks the 21 days it is entitled to under TRCP 166a(c).

Practice Tip

A nonmovant should not file a motion for continuance under TRCP 166a(g) when it objects that it did not get the notice required by TRCP 166a(c) because the court has the discretion to deny a motion for continuance under TRCP 166a(g). But the court does not have the discretion to refuse a request to reset the hearing when the nonmovant received less than the 21 days' notice required by TRCP 166a(c). When the court improperly overrules an objection to inadequate notice, it commits an error of law, not an abuse of discretion.

---

3. Preserving error. To preserve error when the nonmovant does not get the required 21 days' notice, the nonmovant only needs to make an objection and offer proof of the lack of proper notice. *See, e.g.*, **Guinn v. Zarsky**, 893 S.W.2d 13, 17 (Tex.App.—Corpus Christi 1994, no writ) (because nonmovant received less than 21 days' notice, court reversed SJ without requiring nonmovant to show need for time to obtain affidavits or discovery).

§9.3 Motion to continue SJ hearing. A motion requesting a continuance for additional time to secure affidavits or discovery for a summary-judgment hearing should satisfy all the requirements of both TRCP 166a(g) and TRCP 252. **Tenneco Inc. v. Enterprise Prods.**, 925 S.W.2d 640, 647 (Tex.1996); *see, e.g.*, **Kahanek v. Rogers**, 900 S.W.2d 131, 134 (Tex.App.—San Antonio 1995, no writ) (court noted the motion complied with both TRCP 166a(g) and 251). See **O'Connor's Texas Civil Forms**, FORM 7B:5 (2020 ed.).

1. Grounds. The party should allege that it cannot present by affidavits the facts essential to justify its opposition to the motion for summary judgment and that it needs additional time to secure affidavits or conduct discovery. Tex. R. Civ. P. 166a(g); **Joe v. Two Thirty Nine Jt.V.**, 145 S.W.3d 150, 161 (Tex.2004); *see* **Elizondo v. Krist**, 415 S.W.3d 259, 267 (Tex.2013); **Ford Motor Co. v. Castillo**, 279 S.W.3d 656, 662 (Tex.2009).

2. Factors to cover in motion. The motion for continuance should cover the following:

(1) Discovery period. The motion should identify the end of the discovery period.

(a) Motion during discovery period. When a motion for summary judgment is filed during the discovery period, the motion for continuance should (1) state that the discovery period has not expired, (2) identify the date it expires, and (3) argue that the motion for summary judgment addresses complex fact issues that require full discovery. When a case is complex and the motion for summary judgment challenges the merits of the case, full discovery is probably necessary. *See* **McClure v. Attebury**, 20 S.W.3d 722, 729 (Tex.App.—Amarillo 1999, no pet.) (when threshold issue is question of law, discovery requirements are minimal).

(b) Motion after discovery period. When a motion for summary judgment is filed after the discovery period, the party seeking a continuance must also ask the court to enlarge the discovery period. *See* Tex. R. Civ. P. 190.5(a), 191.1. See "Modification of discovery periods," ch. 6-A, §8.2.

(2) Description of specific discovery or affidavits. See "Description of discovery," ch. 5-D, §8.1.1.

(3) Materiality. See "Materiality," ch. 5-D, §8.1.2.

(4) Diligence. See "Diligence," ch. 5-D, §8.1.3.

(5) Length of time suit has been on file. The motion for continuance should state how long the case has been on file.

(a) Fact issues. When a motion for summary judgment based on facts is filed shortly after the lawsuit is commenced, the trial court should generally grant a motion for continuance. *See, e.g.*, **Levinthal v. Kelsey-Seybold Clinic, P.A.**, 902 S.W.2d 508, 512 (Tex.App.—Houston [1st Dist.] 1994, no writ) (P's motion for continuance should have been granted because D filed for SJ three months after P filed lawsuit and before D responded to discovery); **Verkin v. Southwest Ctr. One, Ltd.**, 784 S.W.2d 92, 96 (Tex.App.—Houston [1st Dist.] 1989, writ denied) (D's motion for continuance should have been granted because P filed for SJ 50 days after filing lawsuit and before D responded to discovery); *see also* **Joe**, 145 S.W.3d at 162 (even though D filed for SJ two months after P filed lawsuit, P's motion for continuance was denied because discovery sought was not material and would not raise fact issue justifying P's opposition to D's SJ motion).

(b) Legal issues. When a motion for summary judgment is based on a legal issue and facts are unnecessary, the court can overrule a motion for continuance even if the motion for summary judgment was filed shortly after the suit was commenced. *See, e.g.*, **White v. Mellon Mortg. Co.**, 995 S.W.2d 795, 804 (Tex.App.—Tyler 1999, no pet.) (even though D filed for SJ three months after suit was filed, P's motion for continuance was denied because discovery was unnecessary and irrelevant to determination of legal issues); *see also* **National Un. Fire Ins. v. CBI Indus.**, 907 S.W.2d 517, 521–22 (Tex.1995) (additional time for discovery was unnecessary because contract was unambiguous); **J.E.M. v. Fidelity & Cas. Co.**, 928 S.W.2d 668, 676–77 (Tex.App.—Houston [1st Dist.] 1996, no writ) (no discovery was necessary on issue of duty to defend, which was controlled by contract); **Mayhew v. Town of Sunnyvale**, 774 S.W.2d 284, 298 (Tex.App.—Dallas 1989, writ denied) (no discovery was necessary to review legislation).

(6) Abuse of discovery. If the movant for summary judgment abused the discovery process by withholding key evidence, the nonmovant is entitled to a continuance to complete the discovery before the court considers the motion for summary judgment. *See* **TemPay, Inc. v. TNT Concrete & Constr., Inc.**, 37 S.W.3d 517, 522–23 (Tex.App.—Austin 2001, pet. denied).

(7) Not for delay. See "Not for delay," ch. 5-D, §8.1.5.

3. Affidavit. The grounds for the continuance must be supported by affidavit. Tex. R. Civ. P. 166a(g); *see* **Ford Motor**, 279 S.W.3d at 662. See "Affidavits," ch. 7-B, §9.4. The affidavit must be specific. The affidavit must show why the continuance is necessary; conclusory statements are not sufficient. **Lee v. Haynes & Boone, L.L.P.**, 129 S.W.3d 192, 198 (Tex.App.—Dallas 2004, pet. denied); **Carter v. MacFadyen**, 93 S.W.3d 307, 310 (Tex.App.—Houston [14th Dist.] 2002, pet. denied). See "Not legal conclusions," ch. 7-B, §9.4.5; "Not factual conclusions," ch. 7-B, §9.4.6.

4. Response to motion. The movant for summary judgment may either agree or disagree with the nonmovant's request for a continuance. By agreeing with the request for a continuance, the movant prevents the nonmovant from arguing on appeal that, if it had had more time, it would have been able to secure evidence to prove a fact issue. If the movant disagrees with the request for a continuance, it should attempt to negate the grounds in the request.

5. Order on motion. The court may grant the party additional time to secure affidavits or discovery, deny the motion for summary judgment, or "make such other order as is just." Tex. R. Civ. P. 166a(g). To preserve error, the party requesting a continuance must get a ruling on the record. See "Obtain a ruling," ch. 5-D, §5.1.

§10. Continuance—Party or witness unavailable for trial

If a party or witness is unavailable for trial and the party cannot proceed to trial without that person, the party should move for a continuance. *See* **Hawthorne v. Guenther**, 917 S.W.2d 924, 929 (Tex.App.—Beaumont 1996, writ denied) (same rules apply when continuance sought for unavailability of party or witness). A trial court is not required to grant a motion for continuance just because a party is unable to be present at trial. **Holmes v. GMAC, Inc.**, 458 S.W.3d 85, 92 (Tex.App.—El Paso

2014, no pet.); **Humphrey v. Ahlschlager**, 778 S.W.2d 480, 483 (Tex.App.—Dallas 1989, no writ). The motion for continuance must include the following information. See **O'Connor's Texas Civil Forms**, FORM 5D:2, ¶¶9 to 18 (2020 ed.).

§10.1 Name & address of party or witness. The movant must provide the unavailable party's or witness's name and residential address (street, county, and state), not her office address. *See* Tex. R. Civ. P. 252; *see, e.g.*, **Hatteberg v. Hatteberg**, 933 S.W.2d 522, 526 (Tex.App.—Houston [1st Dist.] 1994, no writ) (motion did not identify home address, only office); **Gabaldon v. General Motors Corp.**, 876 S.W.2d 367, 370 (Tex.App.—El Paso 1993, no writ) (motion did not identify witnesses to be deposed).

§10.2 Unavailable. The movant should explain why the unavailable party or witness is not available to testify at trial. Conflicting business plans of the party or witness usually do not constitute sufficient grounds for continuance. *See* **Echols v. Brewer**, 524 S.W.2d 731, 734 (Tex.App.—Houston [14th Dist.] 1975, no writ).

§10.3 Description of testimony. The movant must describe the unavailable party's or witness's testimony and what the testimony is expected to prove. *See* Tex. R. Civ. P. 252; *see, e.g.*, **Richards v. Schion**, 969 S.W.2d 131, 133 (Tex.App.—Houston [1st Dist.] 1998, no pet.) (motion did not describe testimony of party who could not attend trial); **Lynd v. Wesley**, 705 S.W.2d 759, 764 (Tex.App.—Houston [14th Dist.] 1986, no writ) (motion did not describe what movant expected to prove by testimony of witness who was unlikely to attend trial).

§10.4 Materiality. The movant must state that the unavailable party's or witness's testimony is material and show how it is material. Tex. R. Civ. P. 252; **Aguilar v. Alvarado**, 39 S.W.3d 244, 249 (Tex.App.—Waco 1999, pet. denied); *see* **Richards v. Schion**, 969 S.W.2d 131, 132–33 (Tex.App.—Houston [1st Dist.] 1998, no pet.). The movant must show that proceeding without the party or witness will prejudice the movant's case. **Richards**, 969 S.W.2d at 133.

§10.5 Diligence. The movant must describe its diligence in attempting to obtain the required testimony of the unavailable party or witness. Tex. R. Civ. P. 252; **Holmes v. GMAC, Inc.**, 458 S.W.3d 85, 92 (Tex.App.—El Paso 2014, no pet.); **Aguilar v. Alvarado**, 39 S.W.3d 244, 249 (Tex.App.—Waco 1999, pet. denied); **Humphrey v. Ahlschlager**, 778 S.W.2d 480, 483 (Tex.App.—Dallas 1989, no writ). Without this diligence, the inability of a material witness to attend trial is not a sufficient ground for a continuance. **City of Gatesville v. Truelove**, 546 S.W.2d 79, 83 (Tex.App.—Waco 1976, no writ).

1. Witness within 100-mile range.

(1) Deposition not necessary to show diligence. If the witness lives within 100 miles of the courthouse where the suit is pending, the movant can prove diligence for a continuance based on that witness's absence by showing that the movant subpoenaed the witness to attend trial but the witness did not appear. *See* Tex. R. Civ. P. 252. See "Subpoenas," ch. 1-L, §1 et seq. The movant does not need to have taken the witness's deposition. Tex. R. Civ. P. 252. A last-minute attempt at service of a subpoena does not constitute diligence. *E.g.*, **Hatteberg v. Hatteberg**, 933 S.W.2d 522, 526 (Tex.App.—Houston [1st Dist.] 1994, no writ) (attempted service nine days before trial did not show diligence).

(2) Deposition necessary to show diligence. The movant's failure to depose a witness who lives within 100 miles of the courthouse where the suit is pending shows a lack of diligence if (1) the movant could have anticipated the witness would not be able to attend the trial because of age, infirmity, sickness, or official duty, or (2) the witness is about to leave or has left the state or county of suit and will not be present for the trial. Tex. R. Civ. P. 252.

2. Witness outside 100-mile range. If the witness lives more than 100 miles from the courthouse where the suit is pending, the movant should take the witness's deposition and not rely on a promise to attend the trial. If the witness lives more than 100 miles from the courthouse, the witness's absence is not a ground for a continuance. *See* Tex. R. Civ. P. 252.

§10.6 Medical-excuse affidavit. If a party or witness is unavailable because of illness, the movant must attach to the motion the affidavit of a doctor for the party or witness. **Hawthorne v. Guenther**, 917 S.W.2d 924, 930 (Tex.App.—Beaumont 1996, writ denied); *see, e.g.*, **Burke v. Scott**, 410 S.W.2d 826, 827 (Tex.App.—Austin 1967, writ ref'd n.r.e.) (court should have granted continuance because two doctors' affidavits confirmed D and critical witness were too ill to attend trial). The doctor's affidavit should state the nature and severity of the illness, that the party or witness is too ill to attend the trial, that the party's or witness's health will be jeopardized if the party or witness is forced to attend the trial the prognosis for

recovery, and when or if the party or witness will be able to testify. *See* **Olivares v. State**, 693 S.W.2d 486, 490 (Tex.App.—San Antonio 1985, writ dism'd); *see, e.g.*, **Holmes v. GMAC, Inc.**, 458 S.W.3d 85, 92 (Tex.App.—El Paso 2014, no pet.) (court denied motion for continuance based on party's health problems because motion did not state when party would be able to attend trial or testify); **Humphrey v. Ahlschlager**, 778 S.W.2d 480, 484 (Tex.App.—Dallas 1989, no writ) (court denied fourth motion for continuance based on witness's health problems because movant did not attempt to depose witness and motion did not contain any prognosis of witness's recovery or ability to testify); *see also* **American Trendex Corp. v. Ultradyne Corp.**, 490 S.W.2d 205, 207 (Tex.App.—Austin 1973, writ ref'd n.r.e.) (court denied third motion for continuance when one of several parties was ill because record showed no efforts to depose party and motion did not show how party's testimony would help provide defense).

§10.7 Not for delay. See "Not for delay," ch. 5-D, §8.1.5.

§10.8 Verified. See "Verification & affidavits," ch. 5-D, §2.3.

§10.9 Testimony not available. In a second (or later) motion for continuance, the movant must state that the unavailable party's or witness's testimony cannot be procured from any other source. Tex. R. Civ. P. 252.

§11. Continuance—Attorney unavailable

§11.1 Attorney's vacation letter. When a local rule mandates that the lead attorney is entitled to a continuance when a case is set for trial within the period designated by the attorney in a vacation letter, the court must grant the continuance. **In re North Am. Refractories Co.**, 71 S.W.3d 391, 394 (Tex.App.—Beaumont 2001, orig. proceeding). The trial court has a ministerial duty to grant the continuance in compliance with the local rules of procedure, unless the other party proves a due-process exception. *Id.* But an attorney may waive her right to rely on a vacation letter by acting in a manner that is inconsistent with reliance on the letter. *See id.*; *see, e.g.*, **Siegler v. Williams**, 658 S.W.2d 236, 239 (Tex.App.—Houston [1st Dist.] 1983, no writ) (member of attorney's firm agreed to preferential trial setting to take place during week covered by attorney's vacation letter; attorney's right to rely on letter was waived); **Bennett v. Coghlan**, No. 01-04-00104-CV, 2007 WL 2332969 (Tex.App.—Houston [1st Dist.] 2007, pet. denied) (memo op.; 8-16-07) (three months after filing vacation letter, attorney agreed to preferential trial setting during week covered by letter; attorney waived right to rely on letter).

§11.2 Attorney not available. Absence of counsel is not a ground for a continuance except at the discretion of the trial court. Tex. R. Civ. P. 253; **In re Marriage of Ramsey**, 487 S.W.3d 762, 765 (Tex.App.—Waco 2016, pet. denied); **Rehabilitation Facility v. Cooper**, 962 S.W.2d 151, 155 (Tex.App.—Austin 1998, no pet.); **Rabe v. Guaranty Nat'l Ins.**, 787 S.W.2d 575, 578 (Tex.App.—Houston [1st Dist.] 1990, writ denied). When an attorney is unavailable for trial, the record must show good cause or that the judge had knowledge of good cause for the continuance. **Rabe**, 787 S.W.2d at 578. The motion for continuance should include the information described below. See **O'Connor's Texas Civil Forms**, FORM 5D:2, ¶¶22 to 26 (2020 ed.).

1. **Attorney is necessary.** The motion should state that the attorney's presence is necessary for the proper representation of the case and give the reasons why. *See* Tex. R. Civ. P. 253; *see, e.g.*, **Rabe**, 787 S.W.2d at 579 (continuance was denied because motion contained no explanation of what P's attorney could have accomplished at hearing after P did not file response to motion for summary judgment).

2. **Reason attorney unavailable.** The motion should state why the attorney is not available for trial. If the attorney is in trial in another case, the motion should state why that case has priority. *See, e.g.*, **Smith v. Babcock & Wilcox Constr. Co.**, 913 S.W.2d 467, 468 (Tex.1995) (attorney was in trial in another county); **Dancy v. Daggett**, 815 S.W.2d 548, 549 & n.1 (Tex.1991) (attorney had hearing on criminal case in federal court, and under local rules, criminal case had priority). The motion must show some attempt to avoid the conflict in settings. *See* **Smock v. Fischel**, 207 S.W.2d 891, 892 (Tex.1948).

3. **No substitute possible.** The motion should state why another attorney in the firm could not handle the case. For a trial, the motion should state that no other attorney could try the case; for a hearing, it should state that the hearing is important and involves difficult questions of law as applied to the facts of the case. If two attorneys signed the pleadings, the trial court can presume that either attorney can represent the party. *See, e.g.*, **Rehabilitation Facility**, 962 S.W.2d at 155–56 (continuance was denied because motion contained no explanation why attorney who signed pleadings could not

conduct trial); **Rabe**, 787 S.W.2d at 579 (continuance was denied because motion contained no explanation why another attorney at firm could not represent P at summary-judgment hearing); **Echols v. Brewer**, 524 S.W.2d 731, 734 (Tex.App.—Houston [14th Dist.] 1975, no writ) (continuance was denied because another attorney's name appeared on pleadings). If the attorney has no associates, the motion should state this fact.

4. **Not for delay.** See "Not for delay," ch. 5-D, §8.1.5.

§11.3 Party not represented. When a party discovers shortly before trial that it does not have an attorney (e.g., the attorney withdraws or is unresponsive), through no fault or negligence of its own, the court should grant a motion for continuance. *See, e.g.*, **Villegas v. Carter**, 711 S.W.2d 624, 626 (Tex.1986) (court granted attorney's motion to withdraw two days before trial and party had to proceed pro se; denial of continuance was abuse of discretion because party was not negligent or at fault for attorney's withdrawal); **State v. Crank**, 666 S.W.2d 91, 94 (Tex.1984) (party had advance notice of hearing but waited until morning of hearing to discharge attorney; denial of continuance was not abuse of discretion because party's lack of representation was due to party's fault or negligence); **Harrison v. Harrison**, 367 S.W.3d 822, 833–34 (Tex.App.—Houston [14th Dist.] 2012, pet. denied) (court granted attorney's motion to withdraw for nonpayment of fees 40 days before trial; denial of continuance was abuse of discretion because failure to seek interim fees under circumstances in case was not party's fault); **St. Gelais v. Jackson**, 769 S.W.2d 249, 253–54 (Tex.App.—Houston [14th Dist.] 1988, no writ) (court granted attorney's motion to withdraw one month before trial; denial of continuance was not abuse of discretion because withdrawal was party's fault). In determining whether to grant a continuance when an attorney withdraws, the court may consider the entire procedural history of the case. **In re Marriage of Harrison**, 557 S.W.3d 99, 119 (Tex.App.—Houston [14th Dist.] 2018, pet. denied). The court should ensure that the party has time to get another attorney and that the new attorney has time to investigate the case and prepare for trial. *See* **Villegas**, 711 S.W.2d at 626; **Kahanek v. Rogers**, 900 S.W.2d 131, 133–34 (Tex.App.—San Antonio 1995, no writ); *see, e.g.*, **Gillie v. Boulas**, 65 S.W.3d 219, 222 (Tex.App.—Dallas 2001, pet. denied) (denial of continuances was not abuse of discretion because court had already postponed trial setting for almost four months, which should have been sufficient to allow party to get new attorney and for attorney to investigate case and prepare for trial); *see also* **McAleer v. McAleer**, 394 S.W.3d 613, 618–20 (Tex.App.—Houston [1st Dist.] 2012, no pet.) (although party was able to get new attorney nearly one month before trial, denial of continuance was abuse of discretion because former attorney was unresponsive and had possession of party's documents, which prevented new attorney from properly preparing for trial).

§11.4 Verified. See "Verification & affidavits," ch. 5-D, §2.3.

§12. Continuance for legislator

A party is entitled to a legislative continuance while the Legislature is in session if either the party or the attorney is unavailable because the party or attorney is a member or member-elect of the Legislature. Tex. Civ. Prac. & Rem. Code §30.003(b); Tex. R. Civ. P. 254. When properly requested, a legislative continuance is mandatory, unless the continuance violates the other party's due-process rights. **In re Ford Motor Co.**, 165 S.W.3d 315, 319 (Tex.2005); **Waites v. Sondock**, 561 S.W.2d 772, 776 (Tex.1977); **In re Starr Produce Co.**, 988 S.W.2d 808, 811 (Tex.App.—San Antonio 1999, orig. proceeding); **First Interstate Bank v. Burns**, 951 S.W.2d 237, 240 (Tex.App.—Austin 1997, no writ). See **O'Connor's Texas Civil Forms**, FORM 5D:2, ¶¶30 to 35 (2020 ed.).

§12.1 Motion. To obtain a legislative continuance, the party must file a sworn motion for continuance supported by an affidavit. Tex. Civ. Prac. & Rem. Code §30.003(d); Tex. R. Civ. P. 251, 254. The motion must be filed during the legislative session or within 30 days of the date the Legislature is to be in session. Tex. Civ. Prac. & Rem. Code §30.003(b).

1. **Grounds.**

(1) **Status of attorney.** The motion and affidavit must state that the party or its attorney is a member or member-elect of the Legislature and is or will be in actual attendance at the legislative session. Tex. Civ. Prac. & Rem. Code §30.003(b); Tex. R. Civ. P. 254; **In re Ford Motor Co.**, 165 S.W.3d 315, 319 (Tex.2005).

(2) **Legislator statements.** If the continuance is based on the attorney's participation in the Legislature, the motion and affidavit must also make these statements:

(a) The attorney intends to actively participate in the preparation or presentation of the case. Tex. Civ. Prac. & Rem. Code §30.003(e); Tex. R. Civ. P. 254; **In re Ford Motor Co.**, 165 S.W.3d at 319; **In re I.E.F.**, 345 S.W.3d 637, 638–39 (Tex.App.—San Antonio 2011, orig. proceeding).

(b) The attorney did not take the case for the purpose of getting a continuance. Tex. Civ. Prac. & Rem. Code §30.003(e); **In re Ford Motor Co.**, 165 S.W.3d at 319; **In re I.E.F.**, 345 S.W.3d at 638–39.

(3) Trial date. The motion should identify the date the case is set for trial; the timing of the attorney's employment in relation to the trial date determines whether the court has discretion to deny the motion. See "Ruling," ch. 5-D, §12.4. The motion should state whether, based on the date, the court's ruling is mandatory or discretionary.

(a) Mandatory. If the attorney was employed more than 30 days before the trial date, the motion should state that it is a mandatory motion and the court must grant the continuance. Tex. Civ. Prac. & Rem. Code §30.003(c).

(b) Discretionary. If the attorney was employed within 30 days of the trial date, the motion should state that it is a discretionary motion and the court may grant the continuance. Tex. Civ. Prac. & Rem. Code §30.003(c).

(4) No TRO. The motion should state that the case is not set for a temporary restraining order (TRO). *See* Tex. Civ. Prac. & Rem. Code §30.003(a); Tex. R. Civ. P. 254.

2. File with Ethics Commission. If the attorney for a party seeking a continuance is a member or member-elect of the Legislature, the attorney must file a copy of the motion for continuance with the Texas Ethics Commission. Tex. Civ. Prac. & Rem. Code §30.003(g). The copy must be sent to the Commission within three business days after the date the motion is filed. *Id.*

§12.2 Response. To contest a legislative continuance, a party should file a sworn response supported by affidavits that challenge the allegations in the motion. See **O'Connor's Texas Civil Forms**, FORM 5D:3, ¶¶43 to 50 (2020 ed.). The response must state the following:

1. The movant's attorney was employed within 30 days of the trial and the court has the discretion to deny the motion for continuance. Tex. Civ. Prac. & Rem. Code §30.003(c); *see* **In re CNA Holdings, Inc.**, 102 S.W.3d 280, 281 (Tex.App.—Beaumont 2003, orig. proceeding) (applying ten-day rule in former version of CPRC §30.003(c)).

2. The movant's attorney was employed for the purpose of getting a continuance.

3. The movant's attorney has no intention of participating in the preparation or presentation of the case.

4. Irreparable injury and harm will occur if the continuance is granted. This is the due-process exception (or "Waites exception") to a legislative continuance. The open-courts provision of the Texas Constitution prohibits a continuance when a party can show irreparable harm by the delay. *See* **Waites v. Sondock**, 561 S.W.2d 772, 776 (Tex.1977); *see also* Tex. Const. art. 1, §13 (remedy by due course of law).

§12.3 Hearing. The party opposing the continuance should move for a hearing. When a party claims that a legislative continuance will result in the loss of a substantial existing right, the trial court must hold a hearing. **In re Ford Motor Co.**, 165 S.W.3d 315, 319 (Tex.2005); **Waites v. Sondock**, 561 S.W.2d 772, 776 (Tex.1977). At the hearing, the party opposing the continuance must present evidence. *See* **Amoco Prod. v. Salyer**, 814 S.W.2d 211, 213 (Tex.App.—Corpus Christi 1991, orig. proceeding).

§12.4 Ruling. Some rulings on a legislative continuance are mandatory, and some are discretionary.

1. Mandatory rulings. The trial court has a mandatory duty to grant or deny a motion in the following instances:

(1) Mandatory grant—more than 30 days. The trial court must grant a properly requested motion for a legislative continuance if the attorney was employed more than 30 days before the date the case is set for trial. Tex. Civ. Prac. & Rem. Code §30.003(c); **In re Ford Motor Co.**, 165 S.W.3d 315, 318 (Tex.2005); *see* **In re CNA Holdings, Inc.**, 102 S.W.3d 280, 281 (Tex.App.—Beaumont 2003, orig. proceeding) (applying ten-day rule in former version of CPRC §30.003(c)). If the trial court grants the motion for a legislative continuance, the court must continue the case until 30 days after the Legislature

adjourns. Tex. Civ. Prac. & Rem. Code §30.003(b); Tex. R. Civ. P. 254.

Note

TRCP 254 provides that the continuance is mandatory if the attorney was employed more than 10 days before trial; however, CPRC §30.003(c) overrides the rule. See Tex. Gov't Code §22.004(b) (rules adopted by Supreme Court remain in effect until disapproved by Legislature).

(2) Mandatory denial. The trial court must overrule the motion in the following instances:

(a) TRO hearing. If a party makes a motion to continue a hearing on a TRO on legislative-continuance grounds, the court has no discretion and must overrule it. Tex. Civ. Prac. & Rem. Code §30.003(a); Tex. R. Civ. P. 254.

(b) Due process. If the **Waites** exception to the mandatory-legislative-continuance rule applies, the court must overrule the motion and deny the continuance. *E.g.,* **Waites v. Sondock**, 561 S.W.2d 772, 776 (Tex.1977) (mother filed contempt motion for enforcement of child support, claiming to be unable to feed her children). The **Waites** exception applies only if the party opposing the motion proves it has a substantial existing right that will be irreparably harmed by the continuance. *See id.*; *see, e.g.,* **In re Ford Motor Co.**, 165 S.W.3d at 319 (party did not have substantial existing right); **Amoco Prod. v. Salyer**, 814 S.W.2d 211, 212–13 (Tex.App.—Corpus Christi 1991, orig. proceeding) (party did not prove irreparable harm); **Condovest Corp. v. John St. Builders, Inc.**, 662 S.W.2d 138, 141 (Tex.App.—Austin 1983, no writ) (party proved substantial existing right).

(c) Purpose of hiring legislator. If the attorney took the case for the purpose of getting a continuance or does not intend to participate in the case, the court must overrule the motion for continuance. *See* Tex. Civ. Prac. & Rem. Code §30.003(e); Tex. R. Civ. P. 254.

2. Discretionary rulings—less than 30 days. The trial court has the discretion to overrule the motion for a legislative continuance if the attorney was employed within 30 days of the date the case is set for trial. Tex. Civ. Prac. & Rem. Code §30.003(c); *see* **In re CNA Holdings**, 102 S.W.3d at 281 (applying ten-day rule in former version of CPRC §30.003(c)).

§13. Continuance for religious holy day

A party or attorney who wants a continuance for a religious holy day must file an affidavit stating (1) the grounds for continuance and (2) that the party or attorney holds religious beliefs that prohibit her from taking part in court proceedings on the day she is required to appear in court. Tex. Civ. Prac. & Rem. Code §30.005(c). See **O'Connor's Texas Civil Forms**, FORM 5D:2, ¶¶36 to 39 (2020 ed.). The affidavit is proof of the facts stated and does not need to be corroborated. Tex. Civ. Prac. & Rem. Code §30.005(d). When properly requested, a continuance for a religious holy day is mandatory. *See* Tex. Civ. Prac. & Rem. Code §30.005(b).

§14. Review

§14.1 Standard of review. The ruling on a motion for continuance is reviewed for abuse of discretion. **Villegas v. Carter**, 711 S.W.2d 624, 626 (Tex.1986); **State v. Crank**, 666 S.W.2d 91, 94 (Tex.1984).

§14.2 Record. If the trial court conducted a hearing on the motion for continuance, the appellate record consists of the reporter's record of the hearing and the clerk's record with the motion, affidavits, response, and order. *See* **Roob v. Von Beregshasy**, 866 S.W.2d 765, 766 (Tex.App.—Houston [1st Dist.] 1993, writ denied). If no hearing was held, the reporter's record is not required.

§14.3 Appeal. Generally, the trial court's ruling on a motion for continuance can be reviewed only after the case is tried and appealed.

1. First motion. The trial court does not have the discretion to reject uncontroverted facts established in a party's first motion for continuance. **Roob v. Von Beregshasy**, 866 S.W.2d 765, 766 (Tex.App.—Houston [1st Dist.] 1993, writ denied); **Garza v. Serrato**, 699 S.W.2d 275, 281 (Tex.App.—San Antonio 1985, writ ref'd n.r.e.).

2. Second motion. Appellate courts rarely reverse a trial court for overruling a second (or later) motion for continuance seeking additional time for discovery. *See* **Eckman v. Centennial Sav. Bank**, 757 S.W.2d 392, 395 (Tex.App.—Dallas 1988, writ denied); **Employers Mut. Cas. Co. v. Gifford**, 723 S.W.2d 811, 812–13 (Tex.App.—Fort Worth 1987, no writ). If a party states sufficient good cause, however, the trial court should grant a second motion for continuance. *See, e.g.*, **Garza**, 699 S.W.2d at 281 (D should have been given more time to find rebuttal evidence after P produced last-minute medical evidence different from earlier evidence).

§14.4 Mandamus. When a continuance is within the discretion of the trial court, mandamus is not generally available to review the trial court's ruling. *See* **General Motors Corp. v. Gayle**, 924 S.W.2d 222, 227 (Tex.App.—Houston [14th Dist.] 1996, orig. proceeding). When the trial court has no discretion, mandamus may be available. *See, e.g.*, **Amoco Prod. v. Salyer**, 814 S.W.2d 211, 213 (Tex.App.—Corpus Christi 1991, orig. proceeding) (legislative continuance).

E. Motion in Limine

§1. General

§1.1 Rules. None. See Tex. R. Evid. 103, 104.

§1.2 Purpose. A motion in limine is a procedural device that permits a party to identify, before trial, certain evidentiary rulings that the court may be asked to make. **Greenberg Traurig of N.Y., P.C. v. Moody**, 161 S.W.3d 56, 91 (Tex.App.—Houston [14th Dist.] 2004, no pet.); **Lohmann v. Lohmann**, 62 S.W.3d 875, 881 (Tex.App.—El Paso 2001, no pet.). The purpose of this procedure is to prevent the jury from being exposed to potentially prejudicial information before a ruling on admissibility can be obtained. **Wackenhut Corp. v. Gutierrez**, 453 S.W.3d 917, 920 n.3 (Tex.2015); **Hartford Acc. & Indem. Co. v. McCardell**, 369 S.W.2d 331, 335 (Tex.1963); **Greenberg Traurig**, 161 S.W.3d at 91. It avoids the injection of irrelevant, inadmissible, and prejudicial information into the trial. **Wilkins v. Royal Indem. Co.**, 592 S.W.2d 64, 66 (Tex.App.—Tyler 1979, no writ). A motion in limine is optional; it is not a required procedural step for objections to evidence and does not preserve error for appeal. *See* **Wackenhut Corp.**, 453 S.W.3d at 920 n.3; **Bridges v. City of Richardson**, 354 S.W.2d 366, 367–68 (Tex.1962).

Practice Tip

Do not file a motion in limine when you want a pretrial ruling that excludes evidence. Instead, file a motion to exclude evidence. For an example, see "Motion to Exclude Expert," ch. 5-N, §1 et seq.

§1.3 Forms. **O'Connor's Texas Civil Forms**, FORMS 5E:1 et seq. (2020 ed.).

§2. Motion

Because no rule or statute provides for a motion in limine, the procedures for such motions have developed through case law.

§2.1 Procedure. A motion in limine must be in writing, and copies must be served on all parties. *See* Tex. R. Civ. P. 21(a). The motion should state (1) exactly what evidence the party anticipates its opponent will attempt to introduce or the question the opponent will ask in front of the jury, and (2) why the evidence or question is inadmissible.

§2.2 Deadline. A motion in limine should be filed and presented for a ruling before voir dire. *See* **City of Houston v. Watson**, 376 S.W.2d 23, 33 (Tex.App.—Houston 1964, writ ref'd n.r.e.) (after parties announce ready). However, because error can be based only on a ruling on evidence during trial and not on the motion itself, the timing of the motion is not critical.

§2.3 Grounds. Before drafting a motion in limine, the attorney should review the rules of evidence that govern the exclusion of evidence: TRE 401 to 610. A motion in limine can address any evidence the rules classify as inadmissible. For a collection of grounds for motions in limine, see **O'Connor's Texas Civil Forms**, FORM 5E:1 (2020 ed.).

§3. Response

It is not generally necessary to file a response to a motion in limine, although the party may file a response to address the issue of the admissibility of the evidence.

§4. Hearing

If the court holds a hearing on a motion in limine, it is solely for argument of counsel, not for presentation of evidence. If the court schedules a pretrial conference, the party may ask the court to consider the motion at that time. *See* Tex. R. Civ. P. 166(g).

§5. Ruling on the motion

§5.1 Written order. The party should present a written order for the trial court's signature and file it with the court. *See* Tex. R. App. P. 33.1(a)(2); **Wilkins v. Royal Indem. Co.**, 592 S.W.2d 64, 67 (Tex.App.—Tyler 1979, no writ). See **O'Connor's Texas Civil Forms**, FORM 5E:2 (2020 ed.).

§5.2 Function of order. The trial court's ruling on a motion in limine is not a ruling that excludes or admits evidence. **Fort Worth Hotel L.P. v. Enserch Corp.**, 977 S.W.2d 746, 757 (Tex.App.—Fort Worth 1998, no pet.). It is merely a tentative ruling that prohibits a party from asking a certain question or offering certain evidence in front of the jury without first approaching the bench for a ruling. *Id.*; **Chavis v. Director, State Workers' Comp. Div.**, 924 S.W.2d 439, 446 (Tex.App.—Beaumont 1996, no writ). A limine order may also prevent parties from referring to matters during voir dire or the opening statement without first approaching the bench for a ruling. *See, e.g.*, **Babcock v. Northwest Mem'l Hosp.**, 767 S.W.2d 705, 708–09 (Tex.1989) (P could mention the "lawsuit crisis" or "liability-insurance crisis" in voir dire).

§6. Offer & objection at trial

§6.1 When motion denied. When a trial court denies a motion in limine, the court has refused to require the person who intends to offer the evidence to approach the bench before offering it.

1. Offer. At trial, the party seeking to introduce the evidence must offer the evidence. The denial of the motion in limine does not admit the evidence.

2. Objection. If the evidence is offered at trial, the party that wants to exclude it must object when the evidence is offered. **Hartford Acc. & Indem. Co. v. McCardell**, 369 S.W.2d 331, 335 (Tex.1963); **Sims v. State**, 816 S.W.2d 502, 504 (Tex.App.—Houston [1st Dist.] 1991, writ denied); *see* Tex. R. Evid. 103(a)(1). The denial of the motion in limine does not preserve error.

§6.2 When motion granted. When a trial court grants a motion in limine, the person offering the evidence must approach the bench for a ruling on the admissibility of the evidence before offering it in front of the jury.

1. Offer. When a motion in limine is granted, the party that wants to introduce the evidence must (1) approach the bench and ask for a ruling, (2) formally offer the evidence, and (3) obtain a ruling on the offer. *See* **Johnson v. Garza**, 884 S.W.2d 831, 834 (Tex.App.—Austin 1994, writ denied); **Tempo Tamers, Inc. v. Crow-Houston Four, Ltd.**, 715 S.W.2d 658, 662–63 (Tex.App.—Dallas 1986, writ ref'd n.r.e.). The court's ruling granting the motion in limine does not exclude the evidence. *See* **Johnson**, 884 S.W.2d at 834. If necessary, the party offering the evidence should ask the court to remove the jury for a hearing on the admissibility of the evidence. *See* Tex. R. Evid. 103(d). Whether the offer takes place at a bench conference or in a hearing outside the presence of the jury, the party should make sure the court reporter records the offer and the ruling.

2. Objection. If a party introduces evidence in violation of the ruling on the motion in limine (i.e., without first asking for a bench conference), the party that made the motion in limine must object. **Pool v. Ford Motor Co.**, 715 S.W.2d 629, 637 (Tex.1986). If the party does not object, the jury will consider the evidence, and the error in its admission is waived. *Id.*; *see* **In re Toyota Motor Sales, U.S.A., Inc.**, 407 S.W.3d 746, 760 (Tex.2013). The court's ruling granting the motion in limine does not preserve error. **In re Toyota Motor Sales**, 407 S.W.3d at 760; **Pool**, 715 S.W.2d at 637.

3. Bill of exception. If the trial court rules the evidence is not admissible, the party seeking to introduce the evidence must preserve it in a bill of exception (or offer of proof). **Johnson**, 884 S.W.2d at 834. See "Offer of Proof & Bill of Exception," ch. 8-E, §1 et seq.

§7. Ruling on the offer

Once the party offers the evidence and the opposing party makes an objection, both parties should ensure the court makes a ruling on the record to either admit or exclude the evidence. See "Court's ruling," ch. 1-G, §2.

§8. When limine order violated

§8.1 Pursue adverse ruling. If an order on a motion in limine is violated and prejudicial information is revealed to the jury, the party that wanted the evidence excluded must object immediately after the information is revealed or else it waives the error. *See* **In re Toyota Motor Sales, U.S.A., Inc.**, 407 S.W.3d 746, 760 (Tex.2013); **Weidner v. Sanchez**, 14 S.W.3d 353, 364–65 (Tex.App.—Houston [14th Dist.] 2000, no pet.). The party must make a series of objections, called "pursuing an adverse ruling." See "When jury hears inadmissible evidence," ch. 8-D, §6.7. By making the appropriate objections,

the party preserves the issue for appeal. *See, e.g.*, **In re Toyota Motor Sales**, 407 S.W.3d at 760 (party that requested limine order itself introduced evidence into record and did not object, ask for limiting instruction, or move for mistrial; any alleged error was waived); **Dove v. Director, State Empls. Workers' Comp. Div.**, 857 S.W.2d 577, 579 & n.2 (Tex.App.—Houston [1st Dist.] 1993, writ denied) (party made motion for mistrial; error preserved); **Cody v. Mustang Oil Tool Co.**, 595 S.W.2d 214, 216 (Tex.App.—Eastland 1980, writ ref'd n.r.e.) (same).

§8.2 Sanction. A court may strike pleadings as a sanction for a violation of a motion in limine if the circumstances warrant harsh sanctions. *See, e.g.*, **Lassiter v. Shavor**, 824 S.W.2d 667, 669–70 (Tex.App.—Dallas 1992, no writ) (sanction was abuse of discretion because there was no evidence of direct relationship between sanctions and offensive conduct). A court may impose a fine or hold a party or witness in contempt of court for violating an order on a motion in limine. *See* **Onstad v. Wright**, 54 S.W.3d 799, 802 (Tex.App.—Texarkana 2001, pet. denied) (attorney was fined $32,198); **Kidd v. Lance**, 794 S.W.2d 586, 588 (Tex.App.—Austin 1990, orig. proceeding) (attorney and party were held in contempt; fine limited to $500 by statute).

§9. Review

§9.1 Court's ruling on motion. The trial court's ruling on a motion in limine is never reversible error. **Hartford Acc. & Indem. Co. v. McCardell**, 369 S.W.2d 331, 335 (Tex.1963); *see also* **State v. Wood Oil Distrib.**, 751 S.W.2d 863, 866 (Tex.1988) (appellate complaint of ruling on motion in limine presents nothing for review). Even if the trial court makes an erroneous ruling on a motion in limine, there is no reversible error unless the court, during the trial, erroneously admits or excludes evidence over a proper objection. **Acord v. General Motors Corp.**, 669 S.W.2d 111, 116 (Tex.1984). The right to appeal an erroneous ruling on the admission or exclusion of evidence does not depend on a motion in limine. **Hartford Acc. & Indem.**, 369 S.W.2d at 335.

§9.2 Violation of order. The violation of an order on the motion in limine is reversible if the harm resulting from the violation is incurable. *See* **Lohmann v. Lohmann**, 62 S.W.3d 875, 881 (Tex.App.—El Paso 2001, no pet.); **Weidner v. Sanchez**, 14 S.W.3d 353, 363 (Tex.App.—Houston [14th Dist.] 2000, no pet.); *see, e.g.*, **National Un. Fire Ins. v. Kwiatkowski**, 915 S.W.2d 662, 664–65 (Tex.App.—Houston [14th Dist.] 1996, no writ) (reversed because jury argument violated motion in limine, even though appellant made no objection to some comments); **Kendrix v. Southern Pac. Transp.**, 907 S.W.2d 111, 112–14 (Tex.App.—Beaumont 1995, writ denied) (reversed because no instructions could cure improper impression the statement left in minds of jurors); **Dove v. Director, State Empls. Workers' Comp. Div.**, 857 S.W.2d 577, 580 (Tex.App.—Houston [1st Dist.] 1993, writ denied) (reversed because repeated violations of order to first approach the bench permitted jury to hear prejudicial matters not curable by instruction to disregard).

F. Motion to Amend Pleadings—Pretrial

§1. General

§1.1 Rules. Tex. R. Civ. P. 63 to 65. See Tex. R. Civ. P. 66 to 67 (trial amendments).

§1.2 Purpose. A party amends its pleadings to correct errors and defects in the pleadings.

§1.3 Forms. **O'Connor's Texas Civil Forms**, FORMS 5F:1 et seq. (2020 ed.).

§2. General rules for amending pleadings

Three sections in this book discuss amending pleadings: "Amending or supplementing pleadings," ch. 1-B, §3.6; this subchapter, "Motion to Amend Pleadings—Pretrial," ch. 5-F, §1 et seq.; and "Motion to Amend Pleadings—Trial & Post-trial," ch. 8-F, §1 et seq.

§3. Rules for amending pleadings before trial

TRCP 63 does not allow a party the unlimited right to amend its pleadings before trial. **Stevenson v. Koutzarov**, 795 S.W.2d 313, 321 (Tex.App.—Houston [1st Dist.] 1990, writ denied), *disapproved on other grounds*, **Agar Corp. v. Electro Circuits Int'l**, 580 S.W.3d 136 (Tex.2019).

§3.1 No leave to amend required. A party is not required to secure leave of court to amend its pleadings in the following instances:

1. Before deadline in pretrial order. When a pretrial order establishes deadlines to amend, a party must file amendments according to those deadlines. **Mackey v. U.P. Enters.**, 935 S.W.2d 446, 461 (Tex.App.—Tyler 1996, no writ); **ForScan Corp. v. Dresser Indus.**, 789 S.W.2d 389, 393 (Tex.App.—Houston [14th Dist.] 1990, writ denied). TRCP 166, the rule governing pretrial orders, prevails over TRCP 63, the rule governing pretrial amendments. **G.R.A.V.I.T.Y. Enters. v. Reece Sup.**, 177 S.W.3d 537, 542–43 (Tex.App.—Dallas 2005, no pet.); **ForScan Corp.**, 789 S.W.2d at 393.

2. Before deadline for expedited actions. A party can amend its pleadings to remove a suit from the expedited-actions process in TRCP 169 without filing a motion for leave if the party files the amendment no later than 30 days after the discovery period is closed or at least 30 days before trial, whichever is earlier. Tex. R. Civ. P. 169(c)(2). See "Expedited Actions," ch. 2-C, §1 et seq.

3. At least seven days before trial. When no pretrial order establishes deadlines to amend, the following rules govern amendments made at least seven days before trial:

(1) No surprise. A party has the right to amend pleadings at least seven days before trial, as long as the amendment does not operate as a surprise to the opposing party. Tex. R. Civ. P. 63; **Sosa v. Central Power & Light**, 909 S.W.2d 893, 895 (Tex.1995). The seven days are counted from the original trial date; that is, the date the case is set for trial, not the date the trial actually begins. **Taiwan Shrimp Farm Vill. Ass'n v. U.S.A. Shrimp Farm Dev., Inc.**, 915 S.W.2d 61, 69 (Tex.App.—Corpus Christi 1996, writ denied); **AmSav Grp. v. American S&L Ass'n**, 796 S.W.2d 482, 490 (Tex.App.—Houston [14th Dist.] 1990, writ denied). If the case actually goes to trial at a later date, the new setting does not enlarge the time to amend pleadings. *See* **Taiwan Shrimp**, 915 S.W.2d at 69–70; **AmSav Grp.**, 796 S.W.2d at 490.

(2) Surprise. The court has the discretion to strike an amendment filed seven days or more before trial if the party opposing the amendment shows the amendment was a surprise. *See, e.g.*, **Flo Trend Sys. v. Allwaste, Inc.**, 948 S.W.2d 4, 7 (Tex.App.—Houston [14th Dist.] 1997, no writ) (no abuse of discretion in striking amendment filed seven days before trial because it added new theory of liability); **Favor v. Hochheim Prairie Farm Mut. Ins.**, 939 S.W.2d 180, 181–82 (Tex.App.—San Antonio 1996, writ denied) (same); **Stevenson v. Koutzarov**, 795 S.W.2d 313, 321 (Tex.App.—Houston [1st Dist.] 1990, writ denied) (court abused discretion in refusing to strike amendment filed eight days before trial because it was a wholesale revision of lawsuit), *disapproved on other grounds*, **Agar Corp. v. Electro Circuits Int'l**, 580 S.W.3d 136 (Tex.2019). See "Surprise," ch. 5-F, §5.2.1.

§3.2 Leave to amend required. A party must secure leave of court to amend pleadings in the following instances:

1. **After deadline in pretrial order.** To amend its pleadings after the deadline in a pretrial order, the party must secure leave of court. **Hart v. Moore**, 952 S.W.2d 90, 95 (Tex.App.—Amarillo 1997, pet. denied); **Texas Commerce Bank Reagan v. Lebco Constructors, Inc.**, 865 S.W.2d 68, 78–79 (Tex.App.—Corpus Christi 1993, writ denied); *see, e.g.*, **Roskey v. Continental Cas. Co.**, 190 S.W.3d 875, 881 (Tex.App.—Dallas 2006, pet. denied) (court did not abuse discretion in refusing amendment six days after deadline in pretrial order because party could have amended pleading during 17 months that case was pending). The rules that govern late amendments, addressed in §§3.2.2 and 3.2.3, below, also control late amendments filed after the deadline in a pretrial order. **Texas Commerce Bank**, 865 S.W.2d at 79; *see, e.g.*, **Brown v. State**, 984 S.W.2d 348, 350 (Tex.App.—Fort Worth 1999, pet. denied) (court abused its discretion in permitting amendment that changed nature of case 18 days after deadline in pretrial order).

2. **After deadline for expedited actions.** If an amendment that removes a suit from the expedited-actions process in TRCP 169 is filed more than 30 days after the discovery period was closed or less than 30 days before trial, whichever is earlier, the party must file a motion for leave. Tex. R. Civ. P. 169(c)(2). See "Removal by pleading," ch. 2-C, §3.2. The motion must show that good cause for filing the pleading outweighs any prejudice to an opposing party. Tex. R. Civ. P. 169(c)(2). For the effect of a late amendment that removes a suit from the expedited-actions process, see "Expedited actions," ch. 5-F, §6.2.4(1).

3. **Less than seven days before trial.** All pleadings, responses, or pleas offered for filing less than seven days from the date of trial can be filed only with leave of court, which the court must grant unless the party resisting the amendment objects and shows surprise. Tex. R. Civ. P. 63; **Chapin & Chapin, Inc. v. Texas Sand & Gravel Co.**, 844 S.W.2d 664, 665 (Tex.1992); *see* **B.C. v. Steak N Shake Opers., Inc.**, 598 S.W.3d 256, 261 (Tex.2020); **Burrow v. Arce**, 997 S.W.2d 229, 246 (Tex.1999); **Guereque v. Thompson**, 953 S.W.2d 458, 463 (Tex.App.—El Paso 1997, pet. denied); *see also* **Nichols v. Bridges**, 163 S.W.3d 776, 782 (Tex.App.—Texarkana 2005, no pet.) (TRCP 63 applies to special-appearance and summary-judgment proceedings because they are considered "trials").

Note

If the amending party does not file a motion for leave, leave to file a late amendment may still be presumed as long as there is some affirmative indication in the record that the trial court considered the late filing. ***B.C.****, 598 S.W.3d at 259; see, e.g.,* ***Guereque****, 953 S.W.2d at 463–64 (leave to file not presumed when party did not file motion for leave and court's order explicitly stated it considered only pleadings filed at least seven days before hearing). See "Motion or indication in record," ch. 7-B, §6.8.3(2). Whether the late amendment operated as a surprise to the opposing party is a separate analysis from whether there is an affirmative indication in the record.* ***B.C.****, 598 S.W.3d at 261–61 & n.29.*

(1) Procedural change. If a change to the pleading is merely procedural and does not change any substantive issues in the trial, the court must permit the amendment unless there is a showing of surprise or prejudice. *See* Tex. R. Civ. P. 63; **Chapin & Chapin**, 844 S.W.2d at 665. For example, adding a verified denial to an answer is a procedural change. **Chapin & Chapin**, 844 S.W.2d at 665.

(2) Substantive change. If a change to the pleading is substantive and changes the nature of the trial, the trial judge has discretion to deny leave to amend. **Chapin & Chapin**, 844 S.W.2d at 665; *see, e.g.*, **Hardin v. Hardin**, 597 S.W.2d 347, 349–50 (Tex.1980) (court had discretion to deny amendment offered on day of trial to add affirmative defenses); **Bekins Moving & Storage Co. v. Williams**, 947 S.W.2d 568, 574 (Tex.App.—Texarkana 1997, no writ) (same). When a party offers an amendment that makes a substantive change, the burden is on the party opposing the amendment to object and show surprise. Tex. R. Civ. P. 63; **Burrow**, 997 S.W.2d at 246; **Chapin & Chapin**, 844 S.W.2d at 665.

§3.3 Service of amended pleadings. Amended pleadings do not need to be served on parties who have filed petitions or answers in the case; service of the amended pleading needs only to comply with the requirements of TRCP 21 and 21a. *See* **Burrow v. Arce**, 997 S.W.2d 229, 246 (Tex.1999). However, service of an amended petition on a nonanswering defendant must be by service of process if the petition includes more claims or more damages. See "Amending the petition," ch. 7-A, §3.2.1.

§4. Motion for leave to amend pleadings before trial

§4.1 Written motion for leave. When a motion for leave is required (see "Leave to amend required," ch. 5-F, §3.2), the motion should be in writing, unless it is made in open court and dictated into the record. **Pennington v. Gurkoff**, 899 S.W.2d 767, 771 (Tex.App.—Fort Worth 1995, writ denied). The better practice is to file a written motion, even when an oral motion was made on the record. In the motion for leave to amend, the party should state why the amendment is appropriate and necessary. See **O'Connor's Texas Civil Forms**, FORM 5F:1 (2020 ed.).

§4.2 Amended pleading. The amended pleading must be in writing and signed by the attorney or the party. **Pennington v. Gurkoff**, 899 S.W.2d 767, 771 (Tex.App.—Fort Worth 1995, writ denied); *see* Tex. R. Civ. P. 45, 57, 63; *see, e.g.*, **First Nat'l Indem. Co. v. First Bank & Trust**, 753 S.W.2d 405, 407 (Tex.App.—Beaumont 1988, no writ) (error was not preserved when amendment to pleadings was not reduced to writing). See "Signature block," ch. 1-B, §3.2.12. The amended pleading should be filed along with (but not attached to) the motion for leave to amend.

§5. Response to motion for pretrial amendment

§5.1 Motion to strike vs. response. To object to an amended pleading that is already on file, the party should file a motion to strike; to object to a motion for leave to file an amended pleading, the party should file a response with objections. See **O'Connor's Texas Civil Forms**, FORM 5F:2 (2020 ed.) (response), **O'Connor's Texas Civil Forms**, FORM 5F:3 (2020 ed.) (motion to strike).

§5.2 Objections. A motion to strike or a response should object to the amendment by alleging surprise and prejudice.

Practice Tip

*Although TRCP 63 does not require a showing of lack of diligence by the party offering the amendment, some courts of appeals have stated that a lack of diligence supports a denial of the amendment. See, e.g., **Taiwan Shrimp Farm Vill. Ass'n v. U.S.A. Shrimp Farm Dev., Inc.**, 915 S.W.2d 61, 70 (Tex.App.—Corpus Christi 1996, writ denied) (no error to refuse pretrial amendment filed three days before trial because defense was known earlier); **AmSav Grp. v. American S&L Ass'n**, 796 S.W.2d 482, 490 (Tex.App.—Houston [14th Dist.] 1990, writ denied) (same; 11 days after deadline). The Supreme Court, however, has never recognized lack of diligence as a factor in pretrial amendments, and one court of appeals has specifically held that it is not a proper factor to consider. **Zavala v. Trujillo**, 883 S.W.2d 242, 249 (Tex.App.—El Paso 1994, writ denied) (only factors are surprise or prejudice).*

1. Surprise. The party opposing the amendment must show surprise. Unless the party opposing the amendment shows surprise, the court must permit the amended pleading. Tex. R. Civ. P. 63; **Hardin v. Hardin**, 597 S.W.2d 347, 349 (Tex.1980). Courts must construe TRCP 63 liberally. **Goswami v. Metropolitan S&L Ass'n**, 751 S.W.2d 487, 490 (Tex.1988). Courts may consider the following factors:

(1) How long the suit had been on file before the amendment was filed. **Dunnagan v. Watson**, 204 S.W.3d 30, 38 (Tex.App.—Fort Worth 2006, pet. denied).

(2) How close to trial the amendment was filed. *Id.*

(3) Whether the amendment presents a new claim. *Id.*

(4) If the amendment presents a new claim, whether it is based on recently discovered matters. *Id.*

(5) Whether the opposing party alleged surprise and that it was not prepared to try the new claim. *Id.*

2. Prejudice. Although TRCP 63 does not require a showing of prejudice, the Supreme Court has discussed it as a factor in evaluating pretrial amendments. *See* **Hardin**, 597 S.W.2d at 349 (amended answer filed after filing deadline). Thus, the party opposing a pretrial amendment should attempt to convince the trial court that the amendment will prejudice its claim or defense on the merits. *See* **Halmos v. Bombardier Aerospace Corp.**, 314 S.W.3d 606, 622 & n.3 (Tex.App.—

Dallas 2010, no pet.); *cf.* Tex. R. Civ. P. 66 (prejudice for trial amendment). The party can prove prejudice or show prejudice on the face of the amendment. See "Show prejudice on its face," ch. 8-F, §3.2.2.

§6. Rulings on pretrial amendments

§6.1 Amendment denied. If the trial court denies the amendment and makes a record of its ruling, the party who wanted to amend has preserved error on the issue for appeal.

§6.2 Amendment permitted.

1. Express ruling. If the trial court permits the amendment and makes a record of its ruling, both parties have preserved error on the issue for appeal.

2. Presumed ruling. If the trial court does not make a ruling on whether the amendment is permitted (or if the trial court denies the amendment but the ruling does not appear in the record), the trial court is presumed to have granted leave to file the amended pleading. *E.g.*, **Lee v. Key W. Towers, Inc.**, 783 S.W.2d 586, 588 (Tex.1989) (trial court was presumed to have considered verified denial filed three days before trial); **Goswami v. Metropolitan S&L Ass'n**, 751 S.W.2d 487, 490 (Tex.1988) (trial court was presumed to have considered amendment filed four days before summary-judgment hearing). The presumption results from the liberal construction of TRCP 63 in favor of amendments. **Lee**, 783 S.W.2d at 588; **Goswami**, 751 S.W.2d at 490. The party opposing the amendment should ensure that the court makes a ruling on the record denying the filing of the amendment.

3. Motion for continuance. If the trial court permits a late amendment and the party opposing the amendment needs additional time to prepare for trial (e.g., time for additional discovery), that party can request a continuance. **Fletcher v. Edwards**, 26 S.W.3d 66, 74 (Tex.App.—Waco 2000, pet. denied); **Louisiana & Ark. Ry. v. Blakely**, 773 S.W.2d 595, 597 (Tex.App.—Texarkana 1989, writ denied); *see also* **Stevenson v. Koutzarov**, 795 S.W.2d 313, 321 (Tex.App.—Houston [1st Dist.] 1990, writ denied) (court abused its discretion in refusing to strike amended pleadings even though party opposing amendment did not move for continuance because amendments filed ten and eight days before trial were wholesale revision of lawsuit), *disapproved on other grounds*, **Agar Corp. v. Electro Circuits Int'l**, 580 S.W.3d 136 (Tex.2019). See "Motion for Continuance," ch. 5-D, §1 et seq.

(1) Cost of continuance. The court may order the party filing a late amendment that causes surprise to the other party to pay the cost of the continuance, including attorney fees. Tex. R. Civ. P. 70.

(2) Refusal of continuance = waiver. If the party opposing an amendment refuses the trial court's offer of continuance, that party waives its right to complain of the late amendment on appeal. **Kaufman Nw., Inc. v. Bi-Stone Fuel Co.**, 529 S.W.2d 281, 288 (Tex.App.—Tyler 1975, writ ref'd n.r.e.).

4. Motion to reopen discovery period. A party can file a motion to reopen the discovery period in the following situations:

(1) Expedited actions. If the trial court permits a late amendment that removes the suit from the expedited-actions process in TRCP 169—making the Level 1 discovery-control plan inapplicable—and discovery cannot be completed before the deadline under a Level 2 or 3 discovery-control plan, a party can file a motion to reopen the discovery period. *See* Tex. R. Civ. P. 169(c)(3), 190.2(a)(1), (c). See "Expedited Actions," ch. 2-C, §1 et seq.; "Period reopens," ch. 6-A, §8.1.1(2).

(2) Divorce actions. If the filing of a pleading makes a Level 1 discovery-control plan inapplicable to a suit for divorce and discovery cannot be completed before the deadline under a Level 2 or 3 discovery-control plan, a party can file a motion to reopen the discovery period. *See* Tex. R. Civ. P. 169(c)(3), 190.2(a)(2), (c). See "Period reopens," ch. 6-A, §8.1.1(2).

(3) Other actions. If the trial court permits a late amendment and the party opposing the amendment needs additional discovery, that party can file a motion to reopen the discovery period. *See* Tex. R. Civ. P. 190.5. See "Modification of discovery periods," ch. 6-A, §8.2.

§6.3 Sample rulings.

1. Amendments permitted. The following pretrial amendments were permitted: • In personal-injury suit, amendment of petition seven days before summary-judgment hearing to delete factual allegations on which motion for sum-

mary judgment was based and to add lack of discovery of injury. **Sosa v. Central Power & Light**, 909 S.W.2d 893, 894–95 (Tex.1995). • In suit on sworn account, amendment to add a verified denial of allegations of open account six days before trial. **Chapin & Chapin, Inc. v. Texas Sand & Gravel Co.**, 844 S.W.2d 664, 664–65 (Tex.1992).

2. Amendments denied. The following pretrial amendments were denied: • In suit for promissory note, amendment to add claims for duress, failure of consideration, fraud, illegality, and unjust enrichment on day of trial. **Hardin v. Hardin**, 597 S.W.2d 347, 348, 350 (Tex.1980). • In suit to recover delinquent taxes, amended answer raising new defense less than seven days before trial. **Phifer v. Nacogdoches Cty. Cent. Appr. Dist.**, 45 S.W.3d 159, 171 (Tex.App.—Tyler 2000, pet. denied). • In suit for damages arising from divorce action, amendments received seven days before trial that completely revised lawsuit. **Stevenson v. Koutzarov**, 795 S.W.2d 313, 321 (Tex.App.—Houston [1st Dist.] 1990, writ denied), *disapproved on other grounds*, **Agar Corp. v. Electro Circuits Int'l**, 580 S.W.3d 136 (Tex.2019).

§7. Costs

If the trial court allows a party to file a late-amended or supplemental pleading that causes surprise to the other party, the trial court may charge the cost of a continuance to the filing party. Tex. R. Civ. P. 70.

§8. Review

See "Appellate review of amended pleadings," ch. 1-B, §3.6.3.

G. Motion to Transfer to Multidistrict Litigation Pretrial Court

§1. General

§1.1 Rules. Tex. Gov't Code §§74.161 to 74.164; Tex. R. Jud. Admin. 11.7, 13.

§1.2 Purpose. Under Texas Rule of Judicial Administration (TRJA) 13, cases pending in different counties that involve the same material questions of fact may be consolidated for pretrial purposes, including summary judgment, and transferred to a multidistrict litigation (MDL) pretrial court. *See* Tex. Gov't Code §74.162; Tex. R. Jud. Admin. 13.3(a)(1), 13.6(b). Consolidation of related cases in a single pretrial court allows for more efficient resolution of recurring or related legal issues and more consistent rulings in those cases. **In re GlobalSantaFe Corp.**, 275 S.W.3d 477, 483 (Tex.2008) (consolidation of asbestos and silica cases); *see* **In re Champion Indus. Sales, LLC**, 398 S.W.3d 812, 819 (Tex.App.—Corpus Christi 2012, orig. proceeding) (goal of TRJA 13 is to eliminate duplicative discovery, minimize demands on witnesses, prevent inconsistent decisions on common issues, and lessen unnecessary travel).

§1.3 Forms. **O'Connor's Texas Civil Forms**, FORMS 5G:1 et seq. (2020 ed.).

§2. Applicability of TRJA 13

§2.1 Actions that can be transferred. TRJA 13 applies to civil actions involving one or more common questions of fact, including civil actions involving claims for asbestos-related or silica-related injuries, that are filed on or after September 1, 2003; to the extent permitted by CPRC chapter 90, the rule also applies to civil actions involving claims for asbestos-related or silica-related injuries that were filed before September 1, 2003. Tex. R. Jud. Admin. 13.1(b); *see* Tex. Gov't Code §74.162; Tex. R. Jud. Admin. 13.11(a); *see also* Tex. R. Jud. Admin. 13.1(c) (TRJA 11 applies to all other cases to which TRJA 13 does not apply). *See generally* Tex. Civ. Prac. & Rem. Code §90.010 (MDL rules for asbestos and silica claims).

§2.2 Prohibited transfers. For actions commenced on or after or pending on September 1, 2019, and for which the trial, or any new trial or retrial following a motion, appeal, or otherwise, begins on or after September 1, 2019, the following cannot be transferred to an MDL pretrial court: (1) actions brought under Business & Commerce Code chapter 17, subchapter E—except an action specifically authorized by Business & Commerce Code §17.50—and (2) actions brought under Human Resources Code chapter 36. Acts 2019, 86th Leg., R.S., ch. 397, §§2, 3, 4, eff. Sept. 1, 2019; *see* Tex. Gov't Code §74.1625(a); Tex. R. Jud. Admin. 13.1(d).

§3. Judicial panel on multidistrict litigation

§3.1 MDL Panel. The MDL procedure is governed by a judicial panel (MDL Panel) consisting of five members, who must be active court of appeals justices or administrative judges, designated by the Supreme Court Chief Justice. Tex. Gov't Code §74.161(a). The MDL Panel includes temporary members designated by the Supreme Court Chief Justice when regular members are unable to sit. Tex. R. Jud. Admin. 13.2(a). Any action taken by the panel must have a concurrence of three panel members. Tex. Gov't Code §74.161(b). The panel may prescribe any rules for conducting its business, as long as they are not inconsistent with the law or the rules adopted by the Supreme Court. Tex. Gov't Code §74.163(b).

§3.2 MDL Panel Clerk. The MDL Panel Clerk is the clerk of the Supreme Court. Tex. R. Jud. Admin. 13.2(c). The motion to transfer, the response, and any reply are filed with the MDL Panel Clerk, and the clerk is responsible for filing notice of a request for transfer filed by a judge. See "Notice," ch. 5-G, §4.4; "Filing & service," ch. 5-G, §6.

§4. Motion to transfer to pretrial court

§4.1 Who may file.

1. Party. A party in the case may file a motion to transfer the case and related cases to a pretrial court. Tex. R. Jud. Admin. 13.3(a).

2. Judge. A trial court judge or a presiding judge of an administrative judicial region may file a written request listing related cases to be transferred. Tex. R. Jud. Admin. 13.3(b).

§4.2 Motion.

1. In writing. The motion must be in writing and must conform to TRAP 9.4. Tex. R. Jud. Admin. 13.3(a), (e). Unless leave of the MDL Panel is requested, the portions of the motion required by TRJA 13.3(a)(1) and (a)(2) must not exceed 20 pages. Tex. R. Jud. Admin. 13.3(e).

2. Common issues. The motion must identify the common questions of fact involved in the cases. Tex. R. Jud. Admin. 13.3(a)(1).

3. Reasons to transfer. The motion must state why the transfer would be convenient for the parties and witnesses and would promote the just and efficient conduct of the action. Tex. R. Jud. Admin. 13.3(a)(2); *see* Tex. Gov't Code §74.163(a)(2); **In re GlobalSantaFe Corp.**, 275 S.W.3d 477, 483 (Tex.2008).

4. Agreement of parties. The motion must state whether all parties agree to the motion. Tex. R. Jud. Admin. 13.3(a)(3).

5. Appendix. The motion must contain an appendix that lists the following:

(1) Related cases. The cause number, style, and trial court of each related case for which transfer is sought. Tex. R. Jud. Admin. 13.3(a)(4)(A).

(2) Parties. A list of all parties in those cases, along with their attorneys' names, addresses, telephone and fax numbers, and e-mail addresses. Tex. R. Jud. Admin. 13.3(a)(4)(B).

§4.3 Brief. The MDL Panel may request additional briefing from any party. Tex. R. Jud. Admin. 13.3(e).

§4.4 Notice. A party must file a notice with the trial court that a motion to transfer has been filed. Tex. R. Jud. Admin. 13.3(i). If a judge files a request for transfer, the MDL Panel Clerk must file the notice with the trial court. *Id.*

§4.5 Stay. Filing a motion to transfer does not automatically limit the trial court's jurisdiction or suspend proceedings or orders in that court. Tex. R. Jud. Admin. 13.4(a). However, the trial court or MDL Panel may stay all or a part of any proceedings until the MDL Panel makes a ruling. Tex. R. Jud. Admin. 13.4(b).

§4.6 Retransfer. On a party's motion, at the request of the pretrial court, or on its own initiative, the MDL Panel may transfer cases from one pretrial court to another when the pretrial judge has died, resigned, been replaced, or been disqualified, or in any other situation when retransfer would promote the just and efficient conduct of the cases. Tex. R. Jud. Admin. 13.3(o).

§4.7 Show-cause order. The MDL Panel may, on its own initiative, issue an order to show cause why related cases should not be transferred to a pretrial court. Tex. R. Jud. Admin. 13.3(c).

§5. Response

§5.1 Who may respond. Any other party in the cases to be transferred may file the following:

1. A response to a motion or request for transfer within 20 days after service of the motion or request. Tex. R. Jud. Admin. 13.3(d)(1).

2. A response to an MDL Panel show-cause order within the time provided in the order. Tex. R. Jud. Admin. 13.3(d)(2). See "Show-cause order," ch. 5-G, §4.7.

3. A reply to a response within ten days after service of the response. Tex. R. Jud. Admin. 13.3(d)(3).

§5.2 Form of response. The response or reply must be in writing and must conform with TRAP 9.4. Tex. R. Jud. Admin. 13.3(e). Unless leave of the MDL Panel is requested, the response or reply must not exceed 20 pages. *Id.*

§5.3 Brief. The MDL Panel may request additional briefing from any party. Tex. R. Jud. Admin. 13.3(e).

§6. Filing & service

§6.1 Filing. A motion, request, response, or reply must be electronically filed (e-filed) with the MDL Panel Clerk. www.txcourts.gov/courts/overview/about-texas-courts/multi-district-litigation-panel.aspx; *see* Tex. R. Jud. Admin. 13.3(f).

Note

Although TRJA 13.3(f) states that the MDL Panel Clerk may require a document to be e-filed, all documents must be e-filed with the MDL Panel Clerk using the electronic-filing manager established by the Office of Court Administration. See Tex. R. App. P. 9.2(c)(2); www.txcourts.gov/courts/overview/about-texas-courts/multi-district-litigation-panel.aspx. Documents filed with the MDL Panel Clerk are governed by the e-filing rules for the Supreme Court. www.txcourts.gov/courts/overview/about-texas-courts/multi-district-litigation-panel.aspx. For the procedure to e-file a document in the Supreme Court, see "E-filing," ***O'Connor's Texas Civil Appeals****, ch. 1-E, §5.1 (2020 ed.), or go to the Supreme Court's website at www.txcourts.gov/supreme.*

§6.2 Service. All papers filed under TRJA 13.3 must be served on all parties to the cases to be transferred in accordance with TRAP 9.5. Tex. R. Jud. Admin. 13.3(h). The MDL Panel Clerk may designate a party to serve a request on all other parties. *Id.*

§6.3 Filing fees. The MDL Panel Clerk may set reasonable fees approved by the Supreme Court for filing and other services. Tex. R. Jud. Admin. 13.3(g). The fee for filing a motion to transfer to pretrial court is $275; the fee for filing any other motion or document, other than an appeal of a pretrial court order by motion for rehearing, is $50. Tex.Sup.Ct. Order, Misc. Docket No. 15-9158 (eff. Sept. 1, 2015).

§7. Hearing

§7.1 Hearing. The MDL Panel is not required to hold a hearing; it may decide the matter on the written submission. Tex. R. Jud. Admin. 13.3(k). The panel may hold an oral hearing at a time and place of its choosing, and the MDL Panel Clerk must give notice of the date of submission or the time and place of the hearing to all parties. Tex. R. Jud. Admin. 13.3(k), (n). The clerk may determine the manner in which notice is given, including whether notice should be given by e-mail or fax. Tex. R. Jud. Admin. 13.3(n).

§7.2 Evidence. A party may file evidence only with leave of the MDL Panel. Tex. R. Jud. Admin. 13.3(j). The panel will accept as true the facts stated in a motion, response, or reply, unless another party contradicts them. *Id.* If the panel decides to accept evidence, it may order the parties to submit affidavits or deposition evidence and to file documents, discovery, or stipulations from the related cases. *Id.*

§8. Order

The MDL Panel must issue a written order to transfer the case. Tex. R. Jud. Admin. 13.3(*l*). The written order must have a concurrence of at least three members of the panel and contain a finding that (1) the related cases involve one or more common questions of fact, and (2) the transfer will be for the convenience of the parties and will promote the just and efficient conduct of the related cases. *Id.* The order must be signed by either the MDL Panel chair or the clerk and must identify the members who concurred in the ruling. Tex. R. Jud. Admin. 13.3(m). If the panel refuses to rule, the movant may file an original mandamus proceeding in the Supreme Court. *See* Tex. R. Jud. Admin. 13.9(a).

§9. Transfer

§9.1 When effective. A case is deemed transferred when the transfer notice is filed with the trial and pretrial courts. Tex. R. Jud. Admin. 13.5(a); **In re Fluor Enters.**, 186 S.W.3d 639, 646 (Tex.App.—Austin 2006, orig. proceeding). After the notice is filed, the trial court cannot take any further action in the case except for good cause stated in the order and after conferring with the pretrial court. Tex. R. Jud. Admin. 13.5(b). Any service of process issued by the trial court may be completed and the return filed in the pretrial court. *Id.*

§9.2 Contents of notice. The transfer notice must include the following:

1. A list of all parties who have appeared and remain in the case, along with the names, addresses, telephone and bar numbers of their attorneys, or if a party is pro se, the party's name, address, and telephone number. Tex. R. Jud. Admin. 13.5(a)(1).

2. A list of the parties who have not yet appeared in the case. Tex. R. Jud. Admin. 13.5(a)(2).

3. A copy of the MDL transfer order. Tex. R. Jud. Admin. 13.5(a)(3). See "Order," ch. 5-G, §8.

§9.3 Transfer of files. If the trial and pretrial courts are in different counties, the trial-court clerk must transmit the case file to the pretrial-court clerk. Tex. R. Jud. Admin. 13.5(c). If the trial and pretrial courts are in the same county, the trial court must transfer the case file to the pretrial court according to the local rules of the courts of that county. *Id.* The pretrial court may direct the manner in which the pretrial documents are filed, including electronic filing. *Id.*

§9.4 Fees. The party moving for transfer must pay the costs of refiling the transferred cases in the pretrial court, including filing fees and other reasonable costs, unless the MDL Panel decides otherwise. Tex. R. Jud. Admin. 13.5(d).

§9.5 Tag-along cases. A tag-along case is one that is related to the transferred cases but is not subject to the transfer order. Tex. R. Jud. Admin. 13.2(g). Tag-along cases are deemed transferred when the transfer notice is filed in both the trial and pretrial courts. Tex. R. Jud. Admin. 13.5(e). Within 30 days after the transfer notice is served, a party to the tag-along case or any of the related cases may move for the pretrial court to remand on the ground that the case is not a tag-along case. *Id.* If the motion to remand is granted, the case must be returned to the trial court, and the pretrial court may assess costs, including attorney fees, in the remand order. *Id.* The remand order may be appealed to the MDL Panel by filing a motion for rehearing with the MDL Panel Clerk. *Id.*

Note

TRJA 13 does not state whether a pretrial court can allow a late-filed motion for remand on the ground that the case is not a tag-along case. One court, however, has assumed without deciding that the pretrial court has such discretion. ***In re Champion Indus. Sales, LLC****, 398 S.W.3d 812, 821 (Tex.App.—Corpus Christi 2012, orig. proceeding).*

---

§10. Pretrial proceedings

§10.1 Assignment of pretrial judge. The MDL Panel may assign as the pretrial judge any active district judge or any former or retired district or appellate judge approved by the Supreme Court Chief Justice. Tex. R. Jud. Admin. 13.6(a); *see* Tex. Gov't Code §74.164. For definitions of active, former, and retired judges, see "Who may be assigned," ch. 5-C, §3.2. The assigned judge has exclusive jurisdiction over each related case that is transferred unless a case is (1) retransferred by the MDL panel, (2) finally resolved, or (3) remanded to the trial court for trial. Tex. R. Jud. Admin. 13.6(a). A pretrial judge appointed under TRJA 13 is not subject to an objection to an assigned judge under Gov't Code §74.053. Tex. R. Jud. Admin. 13.6(a); *see* **In re Perritt**, 992 S.W.2d 444, 447 n.4 (Tex.1999) (TRJA 11).

§10.2 Authority of pretrial court. The pretrial court has the authority to decide all pretrial matters (e.g., jurisdiction, joinder, venue) in the related cases transferred to the court. Tex. R. Jud. Admin. 13.6(b). This includes disposition by means other than a trial on the merits (e.g., default judgment, summary judgment, settlement). *Id.*; *see* Tex. Gov't Code §§74.162, 74.163(a)(3). The pretrial court may set aside or modify any pretrial ruling made by the trial court before transfer over which the trial court would not have lost plenary power. Tex. R. Jud. Admin. 13.6(b). After transfer, the pretrial court should, at the earliest practical date, conduct a hearing and enter a case-management order. Tex. R. Jud. Admin. 13.6(c). The case-management order should address all matters pertinent to the conduct of the litigation. *Id.* For a list of these matters, see TRJA 13.6(c).

§10.3 Trial settings. The pretrial court must confer, or order the parties to confer, with the trial court regarding trial settings or matters regarding remand. Tex. R. Jud. Admin. 13.6(d). The pretrial court must defer appropriately to the trial court's docket. *Id.* The trial court must not continue or postpone a trial setting without the pretrial court's concurrence. *Id.*

§10.4 Remand. The pretrial court may order remand of cases or separable triable portions of cases when pretrial proceedings are sufficiently completed. Tex. R. Jud. Admin. 13.7(b). However, remand is required for a trial on the merits. Tex. Gov't Code §74.163(a)(3). The pretrial court will not remand a case in which it has rendered a final and appealable judgment. Tex. R. Jud. Admin. 13.7(a).

§10.5 Orders after remand.

1. Concurrence required. The trial court cannot, over an objection, vacate, set aside, or modify pretrial-court orders without the written concurrence of the pretrial court. Tex. R. Jud. Admin. 13.8(b). If the pretrial court is unavailable for any reason, the concurrence of the MDL Panel Chair must be obtained. Tex. R. Jud. Admin. 13.8(d).

2. Exception. The trial court does not need a written concurrence to vacate, set aside, or modify pretrial-court orders regarding the admissibility of evidence at trial (other than expert evidence) when the ruling is necessary because of changed circumstances, to correct an error of law, or to prevent manifest injustice. Tex. R. Jud. Admin. 13.8(c). The trial court must support its action with specific findings and conclusions in a written order or stated on the record. *Id.*

§11. Review

§11.1 MDL Panel order. An order of the MDL Panel, including an order granting or denying a motion to transfer, may be reviewed only by the Supreme Court in an original mandamus proceeding. Tex. R. Jud. Admin. 13.9(a); *see* Tex. Gov't Code §74.163(a)(4).

§11.2 Pretrial or trial-court order. An order or judgment of the pretrial or trial court may be reviewed by the appellate court that normally reviews orders of the court in which the case is pending, whether or not that court issued the order or judgment to be reviewed. Tex. R. Jud. Admin. 13.9(b); **In re Fluor Enters.**, 186 S.W.3d 639, 642 (Tex.App.—Austin 2006, orig. proceeding). A case under such a review cannot be transferred for docket equalization among the appellate courts. Tex. R. Jud. Admin. 13.9(b). The appellate court must expedite the review of an order or judgment in a case pending in a pretrial court regardless of whether review is sought by appeal, accelerated appeal, or mandamus. Tex. R. Jud. Admin. 13.9(c) & cmt.

H. Motion for Additional Resources

§1. General

§1.1 Rules. Tex. Gov't Code §§74.251 to 74.257; Tex. R. Jud. Admin. 16.

§1.2 Purpose. Gov't Code §§74.251 to 74.257 and Texas Rule of Judicial Administration (TRJA) 16 provide for the allocation of additional judicial resources to large or complex civil cases. *See* Tex. R. Jud. Admin. 16.1(a) & cmt.; House Cmte. on Judiciary & Civil Jurisprudence, Bill Analysis, Tex. H.B. 79, 82nd Leg., C.S. (2011). A motion for additional resources is designed to give courts the ability to get a variety of additional resources for cases that require special attention. *See* House Cmte. on Judiciary & Civil Jurisprudence, Bill Analysis, Tex. H.B. 79, 82nd Leg., C.S. (2011); Tex. R. Jud. Admin. 16 cmt.

§1.3 Forms. **O'Connor's Texas Civil Forms**, FORMS 5H:1 et seq. (2020 ed.).

§2. Judicial Committee for Additional Resources

The Judicial Committee for Additional Resources (JCAR) oversees the process of assigning additional resources to a case. *See* Tex. Gov't Code §74.254; Tex. R. Jud. Admin. 16.2(a).

§2.1 Members of JCAR. The JCAR consists of the Chief Justice of the Texas Supreme Court and the presiding judges of the administrative judicial regions, with the Chief Justice serving as the presiding officer. Tex. Gov't Code §74.254(a), (b); Tex. R. Jud. Admin. 16.2(a), (c).

Note

In this subchapter, "presiding judge" means the presiding judge of the administrative judicial region in which the case is filed.

§2.2 JCAR clerk. The Administrative Director of the Office of Court Administration (OCA) serves as the JCAR clerk. Tex. R. Jud. Admin. 16.2(b).

§2.3 OCA. The OCA, which operates under the direction and supervision of the Texas Supreme Court and the Chief Justice, must help the JCAR fulfill its duties. *See* Tex. Gov't Code §§72.011(a), 72.026; Tex. R. Jud. Admin. 16.3(a). See "Review of request by JCAR," ch. 5-H, §6.3.

§3. Scope of rule

§3.1 When applicable. The procedures for allocating additional resources to a case apply only to civil actions in a constitutional county court, county court at law, probate court, or district court. Tex. R. Jud. Admin. 16.1(b).

§3.2 When not applicable. The procedures for allocating additional resources to a case do not apply to the following:

1. Criminal matters. Tex. Gov't Code §74.251(1); Tex. R. Jud. Admin. 16.1(c)(1).

2. Grants for local court improvement under Gov't Code §72.029. Tex. R. Jud. Admin. 16.1(c)(2).

3. Cases in which judicial review of a state-agency decision in a contested case is sought under Gov't Code §§2001.171 to 2001.178. *See* Tex. Gov't Code §74.251(2); Tex. R. Jud. Admin. 16.1(c)(3).

4. Cases that have been transferred by the judicial panel on multidistrict litigation to a district court for consolidated pretrial proceedings under Gov't Code §§74.161 to 74.164. Tex. Gov't Code §74.251(3); Tex. R. Jud. Admin. 16.1(c)(4). See "Motion to Transfer to Multidistrict Litigation Pretrial Court," ch. 5-G, §1 et seq.

§4. Motion for additional resources

§4.1 By party. Any party to a case can file a motion for additional resources. Tex. Gov't Code §74.253(a); Tex. R. Jud. Admin. 16.6(a). See **O'Connor's Texas Civil Forms**, FORM 5H:1 (2020 ed.).

1. In writing. A party's motion for additional resources must be in writing. Tex R Jud. Admin. 16.6(a).

2. Grounds. The motion for additional resources must state the following:

(1) How the case involves or is likely to involve considerations that justify additional resources. Tex R Jud. Admin. 16.6(a)(1). See "Factors to consider," ch. 5-H, §6.1.1.

(2) What additional resources will promote the just and efficient conduct of the case. Tex R Jud. Admin. 16.6(a)(2). For the additional resources available, see "Available resources," ch. 5-H, §4.3.

(3) When the requested resources are needed. Tex R Jud. Admin. 16.6(a)(3).

(4) Whether all the parties to the case agree to the motion. Tex R Jud. Admin. 16.6(a)(4).

3. Deadline. TRJA 16.6(a) does not provide a deadline for filing a motion for additional resources. A party should, however, file the motion as soon as possible after learning that the case involves or is likely to involve considerations that justify additional resources. See "Factors to consider," ch. 5-H, §6.1.1.

§4.2 On court's initiative. The trial court, on its own initiative, can determine whether a case requires additional resources. Tex Gov't Code §74.253(a); Tex R Jud. Admin. 16.6(b); *see also* Tex R Jud. Admin. 16.2(d) ("trial court" means the judge of the court in which a case is filed or assigned). See "Trial-court action," ch. 5-H, §6.1. For the additional resources available, see "Available resources," ch. 5-H, §4.3.

§4.3 Available resources. The additional resources that can be made available are the following:

1. The assignment of an active or retired judge, subject to the consent of the trial court. Tex Gov't Code §74.254(d)(1); Tex R Jud. Admin. 16.5(a).

Note

Because the TRJA 16 procedures are not exclusive, judges can still be assigned under the general provisions of Gov't Code §§74.052 to 74.062. Tex. R. Jud. Admin. 16 cmt. However, a judge who was defeated in the last primary or general election in which she was seeking reelection cannot be assigned to a case under Gov't Code §74.254(d). See Tex. Gov't Code §74.254(e) (judge to whom Gov't Code §74.053(d) applies cannot be assigned); see also Tex. Gov't Code §74.053(d) (judge or justice defeated in last primary or general election in which she was seeking reelection cannot sit in case if either party objects). See "Objection to assigned judge," ch. 5-C, §3.

---

2. Legal, administrative, or clerical personnel. Tex Gov't Code §74.254(d)(2); Tex R Jud. Admin. 16.5(b).

3. Information and communication technology, including case-management software, video teleconferencing, and specially designed hardware or software to facilitate showing evidence to the judge or jury. Tex Gov't Code §74.254(d)(3); Tex R Jud. Admin. 16.5(c).

4. Specialized continuing legal education. Tex Gov't Code §74.254(d)(4); Tex R Jud. Admin. 16.5(d).

5. An associate judge. Tex Gov't Code §74.254(d)(5); Tex R Jud. Admin. 16.5(e). See "Associate Judge," ch. 1-J, §1 et seq.

6. Special accommodations or furnishings for the parties. Tex Gov't Code §74.254(d)(6); Tex R Jud. Admin. 16.5(f).

7. Other services or items necessary to try the case. Tex Gov't Code §74.254(d)(7); Tex R Jud. Admin. 16.5(g).

8. Any other appropriate resources. Tex Gov't Code §74.254(d)(8); Tex R Jud. Admin. 16.5(h).

§4.4 Effect of filing motion.

1. Jurisdiction. Filing a motion for additional resources does not deprive the trial court of jurisdiction or suspend any proceedings or orders of the court. Tex R Jud. Admin. 16.9(a).

2. No stay or continuance. Filing a motion for additional resources is not grounds for a stay or continuance of the proceedings while the motion or request is being considered by the trial court, the presiding judge, or the JCAR. Tex. Gov't Code §74.256; *see* Tex. R. Jud. Admin. 16.9(b).

§5. Response

A response is not required by TRJA 16, but if a party chooses to respond, it should refute the movant's arguments in its response. See "Grounds," ch. 5-H, §4.1.2.

§6. Determining whether additional resources are necessary

§6.1 Trial-court action. The trial court, on a party's motion or its own initiative, must determine whether a case requires additional resources. Tex. Gov't Code §74.253(a); Tex. R. Jud. Admin. 16.6(b).

1. Factors to consider. In determining whether a case requires additional resources, the trial court may consider whether the case involves or is likely to involve any of the following:

(1) A large number of parties separately represented by counsel. Tex. Gov't Code §74.252(b)(1); Tex. R. Jud. Admin. 16.4(a).

(2) Coordination with related actions pending in one or more courts in other Texas counties or in one or more U.S. district courts. Tex. Gov't Code §74.252(b)(2); Tex. R. Jud. Admin. 16.4(b).

(3) Numerous pretrial motions that present difficult or novel legal issues that will be time-consuming to resolve. Tex. Gov't Code §74.252(b)(3); Tex. R. Jud. Admin. 16.4(c).

(4) A large number of witnesses or substantial documentary evidence. Tex. Gov't Code §74.252(b)(4); Tex. R. Jud. Admin. 16.4(d).

(5) Substantial postjudgment supervision. Tex. Gov't Code §74.252(b)(5); Tex. R. Jud. Admin. 16.4(e).

(6) A trial that will last more than four weeks. Tex. Gov't Code §74.252(b)(6); Tex. R. Jud. Admin. 16.4(f).

(7) A substantial additional burden on the trial court's docket and the resources available to hear the case. Tex. Gov't Code §74.252(b)(7); Tex. R. Jud. Admin. 16.4(g).

2. Optional hearing. The trial court has discretion whether to conduct an evidentiary hearing to determine if additional resources are required. Tex. Gov't Code §74.253(a). The court may direct the parties to attend a conference to provide information to help the court make the determination. *Id.*

3. Order.

(1) Grants motion. If the trial court determines that additional resources are needed, it must do the following:

(a) Prepare request. The trial court must prepare a written request describing the case, what additional resources are needed, and why the resources are needed. Tex. R. Jud. Admin. 16.6(c)(1); *see* Tex. Gov't Code §74.253(b)(2). For the additional resources available, see "Available resources," ch. 5-H, §4.3.

(b) Submit request. The trial court must submit the request to the presiding judge of the administrative region in which the trial court is located. Tex. R. Jud. Admin. 16.6(c)(2); *see* Tex. Gov't Code §74.253(b)(1).

(c) Notify JCAR clerk. The trial court must mail or e-mail a copy of the request to the JCAR clerk. Tex. R. Jud. Admin. 16.6(c)(3); *see* Tex. R. Jud. Admin. 16.2(b). On receiving the request, the JCAR clerk must send a copy to the JCAR. Tex. R. Jud. Admin. 16.6(d); *see also* Tex. R. Jud. Admin. 16.3(b) (JCAR clerk must file any requests for additional resources).

(2) Denies motion. If the trial court determines that additional resources are not needed, the case continues as it is.

§6.2 Review of request by presiding judge. On receipt of the trial court's request for additional resources, the presiding judge must review the request. Tex. R. Jud. Admin. 16.7(a). In reviewing the request, the presiding judge can consider the same factors that the trial court considered in determining that additional resources were necessary. *See* Tex. R. Jud. Admin. 16.4. See "Factors to consider," ch. 5-H, §6.1.1. The presiding judge's options depend on whether she agrees with the trial court's determination.

1. Agrees with trial court. If the presiding judge agrees with the trial court that additional resources are necessary, she must do one of the following:

(1) Use existing resources. The presiding judge can use resources previously allotted to the presiding judge, if the resources are permitted for the requested purpose. Tex. R. Jud. Admin. 16.7(a)(1); *see* Tex. Gov't Code §74.253(c)(1).

(2) Submit request to JCAR. If there are not enough existing resources at the presiding judge's disposal or the previously allotted resources are not permitted to be used for the requested purpose, the presiding judge can submit a request to the JCAR for additional resources. *See* Tex. Gov't Code §74.253(c)(2); Tex. R. Jud. Admin. 16.7(a)(2); *see also* Tex. R. Jud. Admin. 16.3(b) (JCAR clerk must file any requests for additional resources). See "Review of request by JCAR," ch. 5-H, §6.3.

2. Does not agree with trial court. If the presiding judge does not agree with the trial court that additional resources are necessary, she can deny the request for additional resources. *See* Tex. Gov't Code §74.253(c); Tex. R. Jud. Admin. 16.7(a), (c).

§6.3 Review of request by JCAR. If the JCAR receives a request for additional resources from the presiding judge, it must determine whether the case requires additional resources. Tex. Gov't Code §74.254(c); Tex. R. Jud. Admin. 16.7(b). The OCA must provide the JCAR with staff, meeting facilities, or technology if necessary to help the JCAR determine whether additional resources are required. Tex. R. Jud. Admin. 16.3(a)(1); *see* Tex. Gov't Code §74.254(b). In reviewing the request, the JCAR can consider the same factors that the trial court and the presiding judge considered in determining that additional resources were necessary. *See* Tex. R. Jud. Admin. 16.4. See "Factors to consider," ch. 5-H, §6.1.1. The JCAR's options depend on whether it agrees with the presiding judge's determination.

1. Agrees with presiding judge. If the JCAR agrees with the presiding judge that additional resources are necessary, it can make available whatever resources it deems necessary or appropriate. Tex. Gov't Code §74.254(c); Tex. R. Jud. Admin. 16.7(b).

(1) Additional resources. For the additional resources that can be made available, see "Available resources," ch. 5-H, §4.3.

(2) Cost limitations. The JCAR cannot provide additional resources in an amount that exceeds the amount appropriated for that purpose. Tex. Gov't Code §74.254(f). Additional resources are subject to the availability of (1) appropriations made by the Legislature or through budget execution authority or other budget adjustment methods or (2) funds provided by grants or donations. Tex. R. Jud. Admin. 16.11(b); *see* Tex. Gov't Code §74.254(c). The OCA must request appropriations from the Legislature if necessary to help the JCAR provide additional resources. Tex. R. Jud. Admin. 16.3(a)(2).

2. Does not agree with presiding judge. If the JCAR does not agree with the presiding judge that additional resources are necessary, it can deny the request for additional resources. *See* Tex. Gov't Code §74.254(c); Tex. R. Jud. Admin. 16.7(b), (c).

§7. Notice of action taken on request for additional resources

§7.1 To trial court within 15 days after receiving request. Within 15 days after the presiding judge and the JCAR clerk receive the copy of the trial court's request for additional resources under TRJA 16.6(c), either the presiding judge or the JCAR clerk must notify the trial court of any action on the request, including the inability to take action. Tex. R. Jud. Admin. 16.6(d). See "Order," ch. 5-H, §6.1.3. That is, within 15 days after the presiding judge and the JCAR clerk receive the copy of the trial court's request, the trial court must receive notice of one of the following: (1) the presiding judge has approved or denied the request, (2) the presiding judge submitted the request to the JCAR and it has approved or denied

the request, (3) the presiding judge is still reviewing the request, (4) the presiding judge submitted the request to the JCAR and it is still reviewing the request, or (5) the presiding judge or the JCAR has been unable to take any action on the request. *See* Tex. R. Jud. Admin. 16.6(d), 16.7(a), (c).

§7.2 To JCAR clerk after approval or denial of request.

1. By presiding judge. The presiding judge must notify the JCAR clerk in writing once she approves or denies the request for additional resources under TRJA 16.7(a)(1). Tex. R. Jud. Admin. 16.7(c).

2. By JCAR. The JCAR must notify the JCAR clerk in writing once it approves or denies the request for additional resources submitted under TRJA 16.7(a)(2). Tex. R. Jud. Admin. 16.7(c).

§7.3 To trial court after approval or denial of request. After receiving notice from the presiding judge or the JCAR approving or denying the request for additional resources, the JCAR clerk must transmit a copy to the affected trial court. Tex. R. Jud. Admin. 16.7(c).

Note

The 15-day notice required under TRJA 16.6(d) and the notice required under TRJA 16.7(c) may overlap if the presiding judge or the JCAR makes a final decision before the 15-day deadline expires. That is, if the presiding judge or the JCAR has approved or denied the trial court's request within 15 days after receiving the request, the notice given to the trial court under TRJA 16.7(c) will likely satisfy the 15-day notice requirement under TRJA 16.6(d). But if the presiding judge or the JCAR takes longer than 15 days to reach a decision, the trial court must receive notice of both (1) the status of the request within 15 days under TRJA 16.6(d) and (2) the final decision under TRJA 16.7(c). Regardless of when a final decision is reached, within 15 days after the presiding judge and the JCAR clerk receive the copy of the trial court's request, the trial court must receive notice of the status of the request. See "To trial court within 15 days after receiving request," ch. 5-H, §7.1.

§8. Implementing decision on request for additional resources

§8.1 Filing approval or denial of request. The JCAR clerk must file any written determination by the presiding judge or the JCAR on the request for additional resources. Tex. R. Jud. Admin. 16.3(b).

§8.2 Filing cost report. If additional resources are allocated under TRJA 16.7, the OCA must prepare and file with the JCAR clerk a report stating the additional resources and their cost. Tex. R. Jud. Admin. 16.3(c).

Note

The costs for additional resources will be paid by the State and cannot be taxed against any party or against the county where the case is pending. Tex. Gov't Code §74.255; Tex. R. Jud. Admin. 16.11(a).

§8.3 Providing resources to trial court.

1. Determination by presiding judge. If the presiding judge determines that a case requires additional resources and the judge can use resources previously allotted to her, she must provide those approved additional resources to the trial court. *See* Tex. R. Jud. Admin. 16.7(a)(1).

2. Determination by JCAR. If the JCAR determines that a case requires additional resources, the presiding judge and the OCA must cooperate with the trial court or its designee in providing the approved additional resources. Tex. R. Jud. Admin. 16.8; *see* Tex. R. Jud. Admin. 16.3(a)(3) (OCA must help JCAR by providing additional resources approved by JCAR to trial court).

§9. Review

A determination made by a trial court, a presiding judge, or the JCAR of a motion or request for additional resources is not appealable or subject to review by mandamus. Tex. Gov't Code §74.257; Tex. R. Jud. Admin. 16.10.

I. Motions for Severance & Separate Trials

§1. General

§1.1 Rules. Tex. R. Civ. P. 41 (severance), Tex. R. Civ. P. 174(b) (separate trials). See Tex. Civ. Prac. & Rem. Code §41.009 (bifurcated trial for exemplary damages).

§1.2 Purpose. The rules permit a court to divide a lawsuit into separate lawsuits or separate parts.

§1.3 Forms. **O'Connor's Texas Civil Forms**, FORMS 5I:1 et seq. (2020 ed.).

§1.4 Other references. Cunningham & Hutchinson, *Bifurcated Trials: Creative Uses of the* Moriel *Decision*, 46 Baylor L.Rev. 807 (1994); **O'Connor's Texas Causes of Action** (2021 ed.); **O'Connor's Texas Civil Appeals** (2020 ed.).

§2. Distinction between severance & separate trials

§2.1 Severance. When a court grants a motion for severance, it divides a lawsuit into two or more independent lawsuits, each of which will terminate with a separate, final, enforceable, and appealable judgment. See "Motion for severance," ch. 5-I, §3.

§2.2 Separate trials—bifurcation. When the court orders separate trials under TRCP 174, the court divides the case into two or more parts, which are tried separately to the same jury and resolved by one final judgment. An order for a separate trial leaves the lawsuit intact but enables the court to determine some issues separately from others. See "Motion for separate (bifurcated) trial," ch. 5-I, §4. For a discussion of a separate trial for exemplary damages under CPRC chapter 41, see "Motion to bifurcate exemplary damages," ch. 5-I, §5.

Note

For the rules that govern joining and separating permissive claims, see "Permissive joinder of claims," ch. 2-F, §7.

§3. Motion for severance

A motion to sever asks the court to divide a lawsuit into independent suits that may be resolved separately. A severance splits a single suit into two or more independent lawsuits, with each resulting in a separate judgment. **Van Dyke v. Boswell, O'Toole, Davis & Pickering**, 697 S.W.2d 381, 383 (Tex.1985). Courts sever cases primarily to avoid prejudice, promote justice, and increase convenience. **In re State**, 355 S.W.3d 611, 613 (Tex.2011); **F.F.P. Oper. Partners v. Duenez**, 237 S.W.3d 680, 693 (Tex.2007); **Guaranty Fed. Sav. Bank v. Horseshoe Oper. Co.**, 793 S.W.2d 652, 658 (Tex.1990). See **O'Connor's Texas Civil Forms**, FORM 5I:1 (2020 ed.).

Practice Tip

In a motion to sever, you can ask the court, as an alternative, to grant a separate trial for the claim or issue that you want severed. Tex. R. Civ. P. 174(b). A severable cause of action can be tried separately under TRCP 174(b). ***Kansas Univ. Endowment Ass'n v. King****, 350 S.W.2d 11, 19 (Tex.1961). See "Motion for separate (bifurcated) trial," ch. 5-I, §4.*

§3.1 Motion. For allegations supporting severance, the movant should review **Liberty Nat'l Fire Ins. v. Akin**, 927 S.W.2d 627, 629 (Tex.1996), and **Guaranty Fed. Sav. Bank v. Horseshoe Oper. Co.**, 793 S.W.2d 652, 658 (Tex.1990). The motion should allege the following:

1. **More than one cause.** The controversy involves more than one cause of action. **State v. Morello**, 547 S.W.3d 881, 889 (Tex.2018); **In re State**, 355 S.W.3d 611, 614 (Tex.2011); **F.F.P. Oper. Partners v. Duenez**, 237 S.W.3d 680, 693 (Tex.2007); **Liberty Nat'l**, 927 S.W.2d at 629; **Guaranty Fed.**, 793 S.W.2d at 658; *e.g.*, **McGuire v. Commercial Un. Ins.**, 431 S.W.2d 347, 351 (Tex.1968) (one P's wrongful-death suit and other P's personal-injury suit); **Black v. Smith**, 956 S.W.2d

72, 75 (Tex.App.—Houston [14th Dist.] 1997, orig. proceeding) (personal-injury claims and claims against D's insurer for invasion of privacy); **U.S. Fire Ins. v. Millard**, 847 S.W.2d 668, 672 (Tex.App.—Houston [1st Dist.] 1993, orig. proceeding) (claims for uninsured-motorist benefits and bad-faith insurance claims).

2. Independent claim. The severed claim could be independently asserted in a separate lawsuit. **Morello**, 547 S.W.3d at 889; **In re State**, 355 S.W.3d at 614; **Duenez**, 237 S.W.3d at 693; **Liberty Nat'l**, 927 S.W.2d at 629; **Guaranty Fed.**, 793 S.W.2d at 658. To be severable, the causes must be capable of being brought as separate suits with separate, final judgments. **Martinez v. Humble Sand & Gravel, Inc.**, 875 S.W.2d 311, 312 (Tex.1994); *e.g.*, **H.E. Butt Grocery Co. v. Currier**, 885 S.W.2d 175, 177 (Tex.App.—Corpus Christi 1994, no writ) (discovery order could not be severed because it was not a claim).

3. Not interwoven. The severed claim is not so interwoven with the remaining action that it involves the same facts and issues. **Morello**, 547 S.W.3d at 889; **In re State**, 355 S.W.3d at 614; **Duenez**, 237 S.W.3d at 693; **Liberty Nat'l**, 927 S.W.2d at 629; **Guaranty Fed.**, 793 S.W.2d at 658; *e.g.*, **Pilgrim Enters. v. Maryland Cas. Co.**, 24 S.W.3d 488, 491–92 (Tex.App.—Houston [1st Dist.] 2000, no pet.) (severance of P's claims was proper because insurer's duties to defend and to indemnify are not inextricably interwoven).

§3.2 Objection. To object to a motion to sever, the party must make a specific and timely objection. **Shank, Irwin, Conant & Williamson v. Durant, Mankoff, Davis, Wolens & Francis**, 748 S.W.2d 494, 501 (Tex.App.—Dallas 1988, no writ); *see* Tex. R. App. P. 33.1(a)(1); *see also* **State v. Morello**, 547 S.W.3d 881, 888–89 (Tex.2018) (although party did not object to severance until appeal, his objection that improper severance deprived court of appeals of jurisdiction to consider his appeal was not waived because challenges to lack of subject-matter jurisdiction can be raised for first time on appeal).

§3.3 Hearing & evidence. It is unclear whether the trial court should receive and consider evidence in ruling on a severance. In **Jones v. Ray**, 886 S.W.2d 817, 820 (Tex.App.—Houston [1st Dist.] 1994, orig. proceeding), the court held that the trial court should look exclusively to the live pleadings on file and should not consider evidence. Other courts have made statements indicating that evidence should be considered. *See, e.g.*, **Allstate Ins. v. Hunter**, 865 S.W.2d 189, 194 (Tex.App.—Corpus Christi 1993, orig. proceeding) (D did not carry its burden of proof on motion to sever); **Progressive Cty. Mut. Ins. v. Parks**, 856 S.W.2d 776, 780 (Tex.App.—El Paso 1993, orig. proceeding) (pleadings alone are insufficient to require severance); **Geophysical Data Processing Ctr., Inc. v. Cruz**, 576 S.W.2d 666, 667 (Tex.App.—Beaumont 1978, no writ) (propriety of severance does not always depend on pleadings).

§3.4 Order on motion to sever. Under TRCP 41, the trial court has broad discretion to sever a lawsuit into separate suits. **State v. Morello**, 547 S.W.3d 881, 889 (Tex.2018); **Liberty Nat'l Fire Ins. v. Akin**, 927 S.W.2d 627, 629 (Tex.1996); **Guaranty Fed. Sav. Bank v. Horseshoe Oper. Co.**, 793 S.W.2d 652, 658 (Tex.1990). However, the trial court's discretion is not unlimited. **Womack v. Berry**, 291 S.W.2d 677, 683 (Tex.1956); *see, e.g.*, **In re Union Carbide Corp.**, 273 S.W.3d 152, 156 (Tex.2008) (court should not order severance before ruling on motion to strike intervention). The court must exercise "a sound and legal discretion within limits created by the circumstances of the particular case." *Cf.* **Womack**, 291 S.W.2d at 683 (separate trials under TRCP 174(b)).

1. Immediately effective. The order severing part of a lawsuit is effective when it is signed. **McRoberts v. Ryals**, 863 S.W.2d 450, 452–53 (Tex.1993). When a lawsuit is severed, the clerk assigns the severed cause a new cause number. If the clerk delays in assigning a cause number, it does not delay the effectiveness of the severance, but it can sometimes cause problems for the parties. *See id.* at 453 n.3. The trial court should assign a cause number to the severed action at the same time it signs the order of severance. *Id.* As an alternative, the trial court can condition the severance order's effectiveness on the clerk's assignment of a cause number and the party's payment of fees for the severance. *Id.*

2. Separate file. The clerk does not need to create a separate physical file for a severed cause of action. **McRoberts**, 863 S.W.2d at 453 n.4; *see* **Darden v. Kitz Corp.**, 997 S.W.2d 388, 392 (Tex.App.—Beaumont 1999, pet. denied).

§3.5 Deadline for motion to sever. The trial court cannot sever a case after the case has been submitted to the trier of fact. Tex. R. Civ. P. 41; **State Dept. of Hwys. & Pub. Transp. v. Cotner**, 845 S.W.2d 818, 819 (Tex.1993) (jury trial); **In re El Paso Cty. Hosp. Dist.**, 979 S.W.2d 10, 12 (Tex.App.—El Paso 1998, orig. proceeding) (nonjury trial on stipulated

facts). Despite the prohibition in TRCP 41 against postsubmission severances, the trial court may order a partial new trial. *See* Tex. R. Civ. P. 320. TRCP 320 is an exception to TRCP 41. **Cotner**, 845 S.W.2d at 819. See "Partial new trial," ch. 10-B, §8.3.

§3.6 Severance proper but not required.

1. Interlocutory summary judgment. The trial court may sever from the rest of the lawsuit a partial summary judgment granted on a claim or defense or granted to one of multiple parties, thus allowing the summary judgment to be appealed. *See, e.g.*, **Cherokee Water Co. v. Forderhause**, 641 S.W.2d 522, 525 (Tex.1982) (SJ on suit to declare rights under a deed could be severed from suit to reform deed); **Pilgrim Enters. v. Maryland Cas. Co.**, 24 S.W.3d 488, 491–92 (Tex.App.—Houston [1st Dist.] 2000, no pet.) (SJ on duty-to-defend claims severed from remaining claims); **Guidry v. National Freight, Inc.**, 944 S.W.2d 807, 812 (Tex.App.—Austin 1997, no writ) (SJ in favor of one D severed from claims against other Ds). The trial court cannot be forced to sever an interlocutory summary judgment. **Marshall v. Harris**, 764 S.W.2d 34, 35 (Tex.App.—Houston [1st Dist.] 1989, orig. proceeding).

Note

If a judgment being appealed is actually a partial summary judgment, the appellate court can abate the appeal so that the trial court can modify its order and make the judgment final. See Tex. R. App. P. 27.2, 27.3. See "Summary disposition," ch. 9-C, §6.3.2(2).

2. Attorney fees. The trial court should not sever a claim for attorney fees without distinguishing between a claim for attorney fees that is an independent lawsuit (e.g., an attorney's suit against the client for not paying fees) and a claim that is dependent on another claim (e.g., claim for attorney fees as part of a suit on a note). If the claim for attorney fees is an independent cause of action, it may be severed and resolved by a separate judgment. If the claim is dependent on another claim, it should not be severed because it cannot be resolved by a separate judgment. Trial courts, however, rarely make this distinction. Though it cannot be severed, a dependent claim for attorney fees can be bifurcated for a separate trial and all issues resolved by one judgment. See "Motion for separate (bifurcated) trial," ch. 5-I, §4.

3. Third-party action. The court may sever a third party's claims from the rest of the suit. *See, e.g.*, **Guaranty Fed. Sav. Bank v. Horseshoe Oper. Co.**, 793 S.W.2d 652, 658 (Tex.1990) (fraud severed from wrongful dishonor of check).

4. Counterclaim.

(1) Permissive counterclaim. The trial court may sever a permissive counterclaim. *See* Tex. R. Civ. P. 41 (any claim may be severed); *see, e.g.*, **Straughan v. Houston Citizens Bank & Trust Co.**, 580 S.W.2d 29, 33 (Tex.App.—Houston [1st Dist.] 1979, no writ) (trial court did not abuse discretion in severing permissive counterclaim). For the rules governing permissive counterclaims, see "Permissive joinder of claims," ch. 2-F, §7.

(2) Compulsory counterclaim. The Supreme Court has held—without determining whether the particular counterclaims at issue were in fact compulsory—that a trial court has the discretion to sever any claim as long as the court applies the criteria under TRCP 41. **McGuire v. Commercial Un. Ins.**, 431 S.W.2d 347, 351 (Tex.1968); *see* **Trebesch v. Morris**, 118 S.W.3d 822, 828–29 (Tex.App.—Fort Worth 2003, pet. denied). Some courts of appeals have held, however, that a court cannot sever a compulsory counterclaim and that doing so is an abuse of discretion. *E.g.*, **Rucker v. Bank One Tex.**, 36 S.W.3d 649, 651–52 (Tex.App.—Waco 2000, pet. denied) (in breach-of-contract suit, trial court abused its discretion by severing compulsory counterclaim for fraudulent inducement); **Fuentes v. McFadden**, 825 S.W.2d 772, 779–80 (Tex.App.—El Paso 1992, no writ) (in breach-of-contract suit, trial court abused its discretion by severing compulsory counterclaims for fraudulent inducement and DTPA violations); **Mathis v. Bill De La Garza & Assocs.**, 778 S.W.2d 105, 106 (Tex.App.—Texarkana 1989, no writ) (in suit for payment on a contract, trial court abused its discretion by severing compulsory counterclaim for breach of contract).

5. Separate cause of action. The trial court may, and in some cases must, sever a lawsuit involving two or more separate and distinct causes of action.

§3.7 **Severance required.** If the joint trial of multiple claims will prejudice one of the claims, the trial court must either sever the lawsuit into separate trials or bifurcate the trial (see "Motion for separate (bifurcated) trial," ch. 5-I, §4). This type of prejudice occurs when evidence is admissible on one claim but is prejudicial to the other claim. **Liberty Nat'l Fire Ins. v. Akin**, 927 S.W.2d 627, 630 (Tex.1996). For example, when a plaintiff sues an insurer for breach of contract and for bad faith, evidence of a settlement offer could prejudice the insurer's defense of the coverage dispute. *Id.*; **U.S. Fire Ins. v. Millard**, 847 S.W.2d 668, 672–73 (Tex.App.—Houston [1st Dist.] 1993, orig. proceeding); **State Farm Mut. Auto. Ins. v. Wilborn**, 835 S.W.2d 260, 261–62 (Tex.App.—Houston [14th Dist.] 1992, orig. proceeding); *see also* **Allstate Ins. v. Evins**, 894 S.W.2d 847, 850 (Tex.App.—Corpus Christi 1995, orig. proceeding) (decision whether to sever contract and bad-faith claims against insurer when evidence of settlement offer could prejudice insurer's defense should be left to trial court's discretion).

§3.8 **Severance not permitted.** When a party makes a proper objection, severance is not permitted in the following instances:

1. **Indivisible injury.** The court cannot sever claims against several defendants when the injury is indivisible. *See* **Landers v. East Tex. Salt Water Disposal Co.**, 248 S.W.2d 731, 734–35 (Tex.1952). *But see* **Morgan v. Compugraphic Corp.**, 675 S.W.2d 729, 733–34 (Tex.1984) (court did not abuse its discretion when it severed case against defaulting party that involved indivisible injury; any error in severing would have been harmless). When the torts of two or more parties cause an indivisible injury, the claims should be tried together. If not, each tortfeasor could make the "empty-chair" argument. **Jones v. Ray**, 886 S.W.2d 817, 821–22 (Tex.App.—Houston [1st Dist.] 1994, orig. proceeding).

2. **Dividing a cause of action.** The court cannot sever a single cause of action into multiple claims. *E.g.*, **Pierce v. Reynolds**, 329 S.W.2d 76, 78 & n.1 (Tex.1959) (court should not have divided one claim into two lawsuits based on dates the damages accrued); **Duncan v. Calhoun Cty. Nav. Dist.**, 28 S.W.3d 707, 711 (Tex.App.—Corpus Christi 2000, pet. denied) (in condemnation suit, issues of right-to-take and just compensation are components of one claim); **Ryland Grp. v. White**, 723 S.W.2d 160, 162 (Tex.App.—Houston [1st Dist.] 1986, orig. proceeding) (in personal-injury suit, negligence cannot be severed from contribution); **Garrison v. Texas Commerce Bank**, 560 S.W.2d 451, 453 (Tex.App.—Houston [1st Dist.] 1977, writ ref'd n.r.e.) (in divorce suit, property issues cannot be severed from divorce). However, an erroneous severance is waived if the party does not object. *See* **Pierce**, 329 S.W.2d at 78.

3. **Same liability.** The court cannot sever a cause of action against one defendant from a cause of action against another defendant when the defendants are alleged to have the same liability. *See, e.g.*, **McRoberts v. Tesoro S&L Ass'n**, 781 S.W.2d 705, 706 (Tex.App.—San Antonio 1989, writ denied) (court cannot sever cause of action against maker of note—the partnership—from cause of action against guarantors—the individual partners).

4. **Prejudice.** The court cannot sever a case if separate trials of the claims would prejudice one of the parties. *See, e.g.*, **In re State**, 355 S.W.3d 611, 614 (Tex.2011) (in suit for condemnation of tract of land, Ds split property into eight parcels; suit could not be severed into eight cases without causing great inconvenience and prejudice to P).

§4. Motion for separate (bifurcated) trial

The purpose of a motion for separate trials on issues or between the parties is to avoid prejudice, promote justice, and further convenience of the parties and the court. **In re Ethyl Corp.**, 975 S.W.2d 606, 610 (Tex.1998); **Womack v. Berry**, 291 S.W.2d 677, 683 (Tex.1956). A separate trial on issues leaves the lawsuit intact but bifurcates the case into two or more parts that are tried separately to the same jury. *See, e.g.*, **Transportation Ins. v. Moriel**, 879 S.W.2d 10, 30 (Tex.1994) (liability and damages should have been tried separately). See **O'Connor's Texas Civil Forms**, FORM 5I:4 (2020 ed.). Although TRCP 174(b) gives the trial court the power to conduct bifurcated trials, the courts generally should not try cases piecemeal. **Moriel**, 879 S.W.2d at 30 n.29.

§4.1 **Motion.** TRCP 174(b) permits the trial court to bifurcate the trial of any claim, cross-claim, counterclaim, third-party claim, or separate issue.

1. **Grounds in most cases.** The trial court may bifurcate the case for convenience or to avoid prejudice. Tex. R. Civ. P. 174(b); **Tarrant Reg'l Water Dist. v. Gragg**, 151 S.W.3d 546, 556 (Tex.2004). The following are some examples of

when bifurcation is proper: • In a suit against an insurance company in which there was a settlement offer, bifurcated trial on contractual and bad-faith claims. *See* **Liberty Nat'l Fire Ins. v. Akin**, 927 S.W.2d 627, 630 (Tex.1996). • Bifurcated exemplary damages from the issues of liability and actual damages. **Transportation Ins. v. Moriel**, 879 S.W.2d 10, 30 (Tex.1994); *see* Tex. Civ. Prac. & Rem. Code §41.009. See "Motion to bifurcate exemplary damages," ch. 5-I, §5. • Bifurcated trials on the issues of marriage and divorce. *See* **Winfield v. Renfro**, 821 S.W.2d 640, 652 (Tex.App.—Houston [1st Dist.] 1991, writ denied). • In a suit for recovery under the uninsured-motorist provision of a contract, bifurcated trial on the issue of whether the plaintiff released the insurance company. **Johnson v. State Farm Mut. Auto. Ins.**, 762 S.W.2d 267, 268–69 (Tex.App.—San Antonio 1988, writ denied). • Bifurcated trial on the defendant's issue of limitations from the plaintiff's personal-injury suit. **Phipps v. Miller**, 597 S.W.2d 458, 460 (Tex.App.—Dallas 1980, writ ref'd n.r.e.).

Note

In a personal-injury case, the trial court cannot bifurcate the trial on liability from the issue of actual damages. ***Iley v. Hughes****, 311 S.W.2d 648, 651 (Tex.1958).*

2. Grounds in mass torts. For mass-tort litigation (e.g., asbestos litigation), the Supreme Court expanded on the TRCP 174(b) grounds (convenience and prejudice) by adopting the "Maryland factors." *See* **In re Ethyl Corp.**, 975 S.W.2d 606, 610–11 (Tex.1998) (Maryland factors useful in determining whether to consolidate or order separate trials). The Maryland factors are: (1) common worksite, (2) similar occupation, (3) similar time of exposure, (4) type of disease, (5) whether plaintiffs were living or deceased, (6) status of discovery in each case, (7) whether all plaintiffs were represented by the same counsel, and (8) type of cancer alleged. *Id.* at 611.

§4.2 Response. If any party objects to a motion to bifurcate, the party must make a specific and timely objection or it waives error. *See* Tex. R. App. P. 33.1(a)(1); **Winkle v. Tullos**, 917 S.W.2d 304, 312–13 (Tex.App.—Houston [14th Dist.] 1995, writ denied). The party opposing a motion to bifurcate should file a response stating its objections. See **O'Connor's Texas Civil Forms**, FORM 5I:5 (2020 ed.). Some of the objections a party may assert are the following:

1. Bifurcating the trial will not be convenient. *See* **Kaiser Found. Health Plan v. Bridewell**, 946 S.W.2d 642, 645 (Tex.App.—Waco 1997, orig. proceeding).

2. Bifurcating the trial will not avoid prejudice. *See id.* at 645–46; **Greater Houston Transp. Co. v. Zrubeck**, 850 S.W.2d 579, 587 (Tex.App.—Corpus Christi 1993, writ denied).

3. The court should not try the case piecemeal. **Transportation Ins. v. Moriel**, 879 S.W.2d 10, 30 n.29 (Tex.1994).

4. Liability and damages are elements of an indivisible cause of action and cannot be tried separately. **Iley v. Hughes**, 311 S.W.2d 648, 651 (Tex.1958); **Waples-Platter Co. v. Commercial Std. Ins.**, 294 S.W.2d 375, 377 (Tex.1956).

§4.3 Hearing to bifurcate. Unless there is a reason to present evidence, a hearing for the receipt of evidence is not necessary. The motion can be resolved either by submission or at a hearing for argument only.

§4.4 One judgment. After one part of a bifurcated case is tried, any order the court signs is interlocutory and not appealable; the court cannot sign a final, appealable judgment until all parts of the case have been tried. **Hall v. City of Austin**, 450 S.W.2d 836, 838 (Tex.1970).

§5. Motion to bifurcate exemplary damages

§5.1 Defendant's motion. Only the defendant may move to bifurcate the issue of exemplary damages from the suit. Tex. Civ. Prac. & Rem. Code §41.009(a). When there are multiple defendants, any one of them may make the motion. Tex. Civ. Prac. & Rem. Code §41.009(b). See **O'Connor's Texas Civil Forms**, FORM 5I:6 (2020 ed.).

1. Deadline. The defendant must make a motion to bifurcate the trial before the voir dire examination of the jury or the time specified in a pretrial order. Tex. Civ. Prac. & Rem. Code §41.009(a).

2. Grounds. The motion should state that the defendant requests a bifurcated trial on exemplary damages, as provided by CPRC §41.009(c)(1).

§5.2 Plaintiff's response. If the defendant makes a timely request under CPRC §41.009, the trial court must grant the motion. The only ground for objecting is that the defendant's motion is untimely. *See* Tex. Civ. Prac. & Rem. Code §41.009(a).

§5.3 Trial procedure. For more information about the jury questions and the burdens of proof for the issues in an exemplary-damages case, see "Bifurcated trial on exemplary damages," **O'Connor's Texas Causes of Action**, ch. 42-B, §9 (2021 ed.).

1. Phase 1. In Phase 1, the jury will resolve the issues of liability for actual damages, the amount of actual damages, and liability for exemplary damages. Tex. Civ. Prac. & Rem. Code §41.009(c); **Transportation Ins. v. Moriel**, 879 S.W.2d 10, 30 (Tex.1994). The jury is presented with evidence and jury questions on all the issues except the amount of exemplary damages. **Moriel**, 879 S.W.2d at 30. Evidence that is relevant only to the amount of exemplary damages is not admissible during the first phase of a bifurcated trial. Tex. Civ. Prac. & Rem. Code §41.011(b).

2. Phase 2. If the jury found the defendant was liable for actual damages, awarded actual damages, and was unanimous in finding liability for exemplary damages, the jury will determine the amount of exemplary damages in Phase 2. *See* Tex. Civ. Prac. & Rem. Code §§41.003(d), 41.009(d); *see also* Tex. Civ. Prac. & Rem. Code §41.004(b) (claimant who elects to have recovery multiplied under another statute cannot be awarded exemplary damages). The jury should determine the amount of exemplary damages by considering the evidence presented during both parts of the trial. **Moriel**, 879 S.W.2d at 30. Several factors are relevant to the jury's determination. See "Proving aggravated conduct," **O'Connor's Texas Causes of Action**, ch. 42-B, §6 (2021 ed.).

(1) Section 41.011(a) factors. The jury must consider evidence relating to the following issues:

(a) The nature of the wrong. Tex. Civ. Prac. & Rem. Code §41.011(a)(1).

(b) The character of the conduct involved. Tex. Civ. Prac. & Rem. Code §41.011(a)(2).

(c) The degree of culpability of the wrongdoer. Tex. Civ. Prac. & Rem. Code §41.011(a)(3).

(d) The situation and sensibilities of the parties concerned. Tex. Civ. Prac. & Rem. Code §41.011(a)(4).

(e) The extent to which the conduct offends a public sense of justice and propriety. Tex. Civ. Prac. & Rem. Code §41.011(a)(5).

(f) The net worth of the defendant. Tex. Civ. Prac. & Rem. Code §41.011(a)(6); *see also* Tex. Civ. Prac. & Rem. Code §41.001(7-a) (net worth is person's total assets minus total liabilities on a date determined by trial court to be appropriate). The trial court must first authorize discovery of evidence of a defendant's net worth. *See* Tex. Civ. Prac. & Rem. Code §41.0115(a). The procedure for getting authorization is as follows:

[1] A party must file a motion requesting discovery of the defendant's net worth. Tex. Civ. Prac. & Rem. Code §41.0115(a). The parties may submit evidence in support of or in opposition to the motion in the form of an affidavit or a response to discovery. *Id.*; *see also* Tex. Civ. Prac. & Rem. Code §41.0115(c) (only evidence submitted under §41.0115(a) can be considered by court reviewing grant or denial of motion). All parties must be provided with notice and an opportunity to be heard on the motion. *See* Tex. Civ. Prac. & Rem. Code §41.0115(a).

Note

A party making a request under CPRC §41.0115(a) is presumed to have had adequate time for discovery of facts relating to exemplary damages to allow a defendant to file a no-evidence motion for summary judgment on the requesting party's exemplary-damages claim. Tex. Civ. Prac. & Rem. Code §41.0115(d); see Tex. R. Civ. P. 166a(i).

[2] After notice and a hearing, the court may grant the motion if it finds that the claimant (i.e., the party seeking recovery of damages) demonstrated a substantial likelihood of success on the merits of its claim for exemplary damages. Tex. Civ. Prac. & Rem. Code §41.0115(a); *see* Tex. Civ. Prac. & Rem. Code §41.001(1) (defining "claimant"). If discovery of a defendant's net worth is authorized, the court must issue a written order to that effect, and it must authorize use of the least burdensome method available for getting the evidence. *See* Tex. Civ. Prac. & Rem. Code §41.0115(a), (b).

(2) Other factors. Some courts have allowed evidence of other factors, not mentioned in CPRC §41.011(a), to be submitted to the jury, including (1) the frequency of the wrongs committed, (2) the plaintiff's attorney fees and other damages, and (3) the size of the award needed to deter similar wrongs in the future. See "Other factors," **O'Connor's Texas Causes of Action**, ch. 42-B, §6.2.2 (2021 ed.).

§5.4 Plaintiff's burden.

1. Preponderance of the evidence. The Phase 1 issues of liability for and the amount of actual damages must be decided by a preponderance of the evidence. See "Issues on actual damages," **O'Connor's Texas Causes of Action**, ch. 42-B, §9.2.1(1) (2021 ed.). "Preponderance of the evidence" means the greater weight and degree of credible evidence. **Upjohn Co. v. Freeman**, 847 S.W.2d 589, 591 (Tex.App.—Dallas 1992, no writ).

2. Clear & convincing evidence. The Phase 1 issue of liability for exemplary damages and the Phase 2 issue of the amount of exemplary damages must be decided by clear and convincing evidence. To decide liability, the plaintiff must prove in Phase 1 that the harm for which it seeks recovery of exemplary damages resulted from fraud, malice, or gross negligence. Tex. Civ. Prac. & Rem. Code §41.003(a); **Dillard Dept. Stores v. Silva**, 148 S.W.3d 370, 372–73 (Tex.2004); *see also* Tex. Const. art. 16, §26 (liability for exemplary damages when D causes death by willful act or omission or gross neglect). "Clear and convincing evidence" means the degree of proof that will produce in the fact-finder's mind a firm belief or conviction about the truth of the allegations. **State v. Addington**, 588 S.W.2d 569, 570 (Tex.1979). The burden of proof cannot be shifted to the defendant or be satisfied by evidence of ordinary negligence, bad faith, or deceptive trade practice. Tex. Civ. Prac. & Rem. Code §41.003(b).

§5.5 Actual, not nominal, damages. As a rule, the plaintiff must recover actual damages; nominal damages are not sufficient to support an award of exemplary damages. Tex. Civ. Prac. & Rem. Code §41.004(a). See "Actual damages required," **O'Connor's Texas Causes of Action**, ch. 42-B, §4.1 (2021 ed.). However, an award of actual damages is not required to recover exemplary damages in a wrongful-death suit brought under Labor Code §408.001 by an employee's surviving spouse or heirs for the death of the employee caused by the intentional act or omission or the gross negligence of the employer. *See* **Wright v. Gifford-Hill & Co.**, 725 S.W.2d 712, 714 (Tex.1987). In a wrongful-death suit brought under Labor Code §408.001, the plaintiff may still be required to present evidence of the amount of actual damages. See "Requirement of actual damages," **O'Connor's Texas Causes of Action**, ch. 7-B, §6.5.2(2) (2021 ed.).

§5.6 Unanimous jury. The jury must render a unanimous verdict on the issues of liability for and the amount of exemplary damages. Tex. Civ. Prac. & Rem. Code §41.003(d); Tex. R. Civ. P. 292(b). See "Exemplary-damages cases," ch. 8-K, §4.2. The jury may render a less-than-unanimous verdict on the issues of liability for and the amount of actual damages. See "Most trials," ch. 8-K, §4.1.

§5.7 One judgment. After a bifurcated trial under CPRC chapter 41, the trial court will enter one judgment that resolves all the issues.

§6. Review

§6.1 Motion to sever.

1. No interlocutory appeal. When the trial court grants or denies a motion for severance, the order cannot be appealed until after a final judgment is rendered in the case. *See* **Finder v. E.L. Cheeney Co.**, 368 S.W.2d 62, 64 (Tex.App.—Beaumont 1963, no writ).

2. Regular appeal. The appellate court will not reverse an order granting a severance unless the trial court abused its discretion. **F.F.P. Oper. Partners v. Duenez**, 237 S.W.3d 680, 693 (Tex.2007); **Guaranty Fed. Sav. Bank v. Horseshoe Oper. Co.**, 793 S.W.2d 652, 658 (Tex.1990); *see* **State v. Morello**, 547 S.W.3d 881, 889 (Tex.2018). If the trial court abused its discretion, the appellate court will reverse and remand. **Nicor Expl. Co. v. Florida Gas Transmission Co.**, 911 S.W.2d 479, 482–83 (Tex.App.—Corpus Christi 1995, writ denied).

3. Mandamus. When the trial court has a duty to either grant or deny severance, it has no discretion, and its order can be reviewed by mandamus. *See, e.g.,* **Lusk v. Puryear**, 896 S.W.2d 377, 380–81 (Tex.App.—Amarillo 1995, orig.

proceeding) (trial court improperly granted severance); **F.A. Richard & Assocs. v. Millard**, 856 S.W.2d 765, 767 (Tex.App.—Houston [1st Dist.] 1993, orig. proceeding) (trial court improperly denied severance). Mandamus is appropriate to review the issue of severance only when there is no adequate remedy by appeal. *E.g.*, **In re State**, 355 S.W.3d 611, 614–15 (Tex.2011) (mandamus conditionally granted); **Liberty Nat'l Fire Ins. v. Akin**, 927 S.W.2d 627, 629 (Tex.1996) (mandamus denied); **McLain v. Smith**, 899 S.W.2d 412, 414 (Tex.App.—Amarillo 1995, orig. proceeding) (same). See "Severance," **O'Connor's Texas Civil Appeals**, ch. 10-B, §5.1.2(16) (2020 ed.).

4. Severance on appeal. The rules that prohibit severance by the trial court of part of a cause of action do not apply to appellate courts. Under TRCP 320 and TRAP 44.1(b), an appellate court can grant a new trial on points that affect only a part of the case if that part is clearly separable without unfairness to the parties; however, an appellate court cannot grant a new trial on damages if liability was contested. A partial new trial may be ordered despite the prohibition in TRCP 41 against postsubmission severance. **State Dept. of Hwys. & Pub. Transp. v. Cotner**, 845 S.W.2d 818, 819 (Tex.1993). An appellate court may affirm part of a case and sever part for remand, even though the trial court could not have. *See* Tex. R. App. P. 43.2(a), (d); *see, e.g.*, **Collins v. Collins**, 904 S.W.2d 792, 795 (Tex.App.—Houston [1st Dist.] 1995) (appellate court can affirm divorce and remand property issues), *writ denied*, 923 S.W.2d 569 (Tex.1996). Appellate courts regularly sever and remand the issue of attorney fees from the rest of the case, even when the attorney fees are dependent on another claim. *See, e.g.*, **Woods Expl. & Prod'g Co. v. Arkla Equip. Co.**, 528 S.W.2d 568, 571 (Tex.1975) (claim for attorney fees for suit on a note was severed on appeal); **Permian Report v. Lacy**, 817 S.W.2d 175, 178 (Tex.App.—El Paso 1991, writ denied) (claim for attorney fees for declaratory-judgment action was severed on appeal).

§6.2 Motion to bifurcate. The trial court's decision on bifurcation is reviewed for abuse of discretion. **Johnson v. State Farm Mut. Auto. Ins.**, 762 S.W.2d 267, 269 (Tex.App.—San Antonio 1988, writ denied).

J. Joining Parties or Claims

§1. General

§1.1 Rules. Tex. R. Civ. P. 43 (interpleader), Tex. R. Civ. P. 60 to 61 (intervention), Tex. R. Civ. P. 174 (consolidation).

§1.2 Purpose. The rules of joinder permit additional parties and claims to be brought into a lawsuit. Joinder may be accomplished through intervention, interpleader, or consolidation.

§1.3 Forms. **O'Connor's Texas Civil Forms**, FORMS 5J:1 et seq. (2020 ed.).

§1.4 Other references. McDonald & Carlson, *Texas Civil Practice* §5:82 (2d ed.).

§2. Petition in intervention

The purpose of a petition in intervention is to join a lawsuit that is already in progress. The sufficiency of the petition in intervention is tested by the allegations of fact on which the right to intervene depends. **Serna v. Webster**, 908 S.W.2d 487, 492 (Tex.App.—San Antonio 1995, no writ), *overruled on other grounds*, **Ex parte E.H.**, 602 S.W.3d 486 (Tex.2020); **H. Tebbs, Inc. v. Silver Eagle Distribs.**, 797 S.W.2d 80, 84 (Tex.App.—Austin 1990, no writ).

§2.1 Filing the petition. The rules of pleading apply to intervenors just as they do to other parties. Tex. R. Civ. P. 61.

1. In writing. To intervene, a party must file a written pleading. **Diaz v. Attorney Gen.**, 827 S.W.2d 19, 22 (Tex.App.—Corpus Christi 1992, no writ). See **O'Connor's Texas Civil Forms**, FORM 5J:1 (2020 ed.).

2. No motion for leave. An intervenor is not required to get the court's permission to intervene. Tex. R. Civ. P. 60; **Nghiem v. Sajib**, 567 S.W.3d 718, 721 (Tex.2019); **In re Union Carbide Corp.**, 273 S.W.3d 152, 154–55 (Tex.2008); **Guaranty Fed. Sav. Bank v. Horseshoe Oper. Co.**, 793 S.W.2d 652, 657 (Tex.1990). A nonparty may intervene in a suit as a plaintiff or a defendant without leave of court. *See* Tex. R. Civ. P. 60.

3. Interest of intervenor.

(1) Legal or equitable. The interest the intervenor asserts in the lawsuit may be legal or equitable. **Guaranty Fed.**, 793 S.W.2d at 657; **Zeifman v. Michels**, 229 S.W.3d 460, 464 (Tex.App.—Austin 2007, no pet.); **Gracida v. Tagle**, 946 S.W.2d 504, 506 (Tex.App.—Corpus Christi 1997, orig. proceeding).

(2) Not contingent or remote. The interest must be more than a mere contingent or remote interest. **Zeifman**, 229 S.W.3d at 464; **Intermarque Auto. Prods. v. Feldman**, 21 S.W.3d 544, 549 (Tex.App.—Texarkana 2000, no pet.).

(3) Justiciable interest. The intervenor must have a justiciable interest in the suit. **In re Union Carbide**, 273 S.W.3d at 154–55; **Henderson Edwards Wilson, L.L.P. v. Toledo**, 244 S.W.3d 851, 853 (Tex.App.—Dallas 2008, no pet.). A party has a justiciable interest in the suit when its interests will be affected by the litigation. **Law Offices of Windle Turley, P.C. v. Ghiasinejad**, 109 S.W.3d 68, 70 (Tex.App.—Fort Worth 2003, no pet.); *see* **In re Union Carbide**, 273 S.W.3d at 155. That is, a party can intervene if it (1) could have brought all or part of the same suit in its own name or (2) would have been able to defeat all or part of the recovery if the suit had been filed against it. **Guaranty Fed.**, 793 S.W.2d at 657; *e.g.*, **Jenkins v. Entergy Corp.**, 187 S.W.3d 785, 796–97 (Tex.App.—Corpus Christi 2006, pet. denied) (subsidiary corporation accused of conspiring with parent corporation had justiciable interest in P's suit against parent corporation); **Feldman**, 21 S.W.3d at 549 (corporate policy owner could not intervene to claim right to defense costs paid by insurer to additional insured); *see, e.g.*, **Ghiasinejad**, 109 S.W.3d at 70–71 (attorney with contingent-fee contract had justiciable interest in P's suit); **Live Oak Resort, Inc. v. Texas Alcoholic Bev. Comm'n**, 920 S.W.2d 795, 798 (Tex.App.—Houston [1st Dist.] 1996, no writ) (protesters could not intervene in suit involving denial of TABC license because Alco. Bev. Code §11.67 provides that in such a suit TABC is the only D); **Beutel v. Dallas Cty. Flood Control Dist.**, 916 S.W.2d 685, 691–92 (Tex.App.—Waco 1996, writ denied) (lienholder who did not have interest in property at time of taking could not intervene in condemnation).

4. Proper venue or joinder. Each intervening plaintiff must, independently of every other plaintiff, establish proper venue or proper joinder. *See* Tex. Civ. Prac. & Rem. Code §15.003(a). See "Venue or joinder proper in multiple-plaintiff case," ch. 3-C, §2.6.4.

5. Subject-matter jurisdiction. The court must have subject-matter jurisdiction over any claims for relief asserted by the intervenor. *See* **Abdullatif v. Erpile, LLC**, 460 S.W.3d 685, 690–91 (Tex.App.—Houston [14th Dist.] 2015, no pet.). The petition in intervention should allege facts that demonstrate the court's subject-matter jurisdiction. *See id.* at 691. See "Subject-matter jurisdiction," ch. 2-B, §5.2.

6. For all purposes. Once a party intervenes, the intervenor becomes a party to the suit for all purposes. **In re J.D.**, 304 S.W.3d 522, 525 (Tex.App.—Waco 2009, no pet.); **In re D.D.M.**, 116 S.W.3d 224, 231 (Tex.App.—Tyler 2003, no pet.).

§2.2 Deadline to file.

1. Before judgment. Generally, a petition in intervention must be filed before judgment is rendered. *See* **State v. Naylor**, 466 S.W.3d 783, 788 (Tex.2015); **Texas Mut. Ins. v. Ledbetter**, 251 S.W.3d 31, 36 (Tex.2008); **First Alief Bank v. White**, 682 S.W.2d 251, 252 (Tex.1984). Although the petition can be filed anytime before judgment is rendered, the petition must still be timely filed. *See* **Texas Mut. Ins.**, 251 S.W.3d at 36–37; *see, e.g.*, **Armstrong v. Tidelands Life Ins.**, 466 S.W.2d 407, 412 (Tex.App.—Corpus Christi 1971, no writ) (petition in intervention untimely when intervenors filed it after suit had been on file for almost four years and after D filed motion for summary judgment). If the suit is stayed, an intervenor who was not a party to the suit when the stay was imposed can file a petition, but the petition will not be considered effective until the date the stay is eventually lifted. **In re Helena Chem. Co.**, 286 S.W.3d 492, 498 (Tex.App.—Corpus Christi 2009, orig. proceeding).

Note

A petition in intervention is not subject to the seven-day requirement in TRCP 63 concerning amendments and responses to pleadings. ***In re Estate of York****, 951 S.W.2d 122, 124–25 (Tex.App.—Corpus Christi 1997, no writ).*

2. After judgment.

(1) Generally. A petition in intervention is generally too late and will not be permitted if it is filed after judgment is rendered. **Texas Mut. Ins.**, 251 S.W.3d at 36; **First Alief Bank**, 682 S.W.2d at 252; **Gore v. Peck**, 191 S.W.3d 927, 928 (Tex.App.—Dallas 2006, no pet.); *e.g.*, **Naylor**, 466 S.W.3d at 788–89 (intervention filed after oral rendition of divorce was too late). Except in limited circumstances, an intervention filed after rendition of judgment may be considered only if the trial court sets aside the judgment. **Naylor**, 466 S.W.3d at 788; *see* **First Alief Bank**, 682 S.W.2d at 252.

Note

A person or entity not named as a party may attempt to intervene after judgment through the virtual-representation doctrine; however, to do so, the prospective intervenor must first show that it has standing under the virtual-representation doctrine and then meet certain equitable considerations. See ***Naylor****, 466 S.W.3d at 791;* ***In re Lumbermens Mut. Cas. Co.****, 184 S.W.3d 718, 722 (Tex.2006). For a discussion of the virtual-representation doctrine, see "Virtual party," ch. 2-B, §4.1.2. The equitable considerations a court will evaluate are (1) the length of time the intervenor knew of its interest in the case before attempting to intervene, (2) whether there would be any prejudice to the intervenor if intervention is denied, (3) whether there would be any prejudice to the existing parties as a result of the untimely intervention, and (4) whether there are any other circumstances that weigh in favor of or against the intervention. See* ***Naylor****, 466 S.W.3d at 791;* ***In re Lumbermens****, 184 S.W.3d at 726. Equitable considerations alone will not provide a basis for postjudgment intervention; the prospective intervenor must first establish its standing under the virtual-representation doctrine. See* ***Naylor****, 466 S.W.3d at 791–92.*

(2) Exceptions. A petition in intervention filed after judgment is rendered has been permitted when (1) the intervenor does not attack the existing judgment but instead seeks protection of property interests under CPRC §31.002

(turnover of property) or (2) the intervenor is a subrogee whose interest was at first adequately represented by someone else but was later abandoned. *See* **Texas Mut. Ins.**, 251 S.W.3d at 36 (exception #2); **Breazeale v. Casteel**, 4 S.W.3d 434, 436 (Tex.App.—Austin 1999, pet. denied) (exception #1).

§2.3 Notice of petition.

1. Citation not necessary. An intervenor may serve a petition in intervention on the parties in the suit under TRCP 21 and 21a. *See* **Baker v. Monsanto Co.**, 111 S.W.3d 158, 160 (Tex.2003); Tex. R. Civ. P. 60 cmt. The intervenor does not need to serve process on the parties that are before the court or on a defendant who makes a general appearance before the limitations period runs. **Baker**, 111 S.W.3d at 160; *see* **McWilliams v. Snap-Pac Corp.**, 476 S.W.2d 941, 949–50 (Tex.App.—Houston [1st Dist.] 1971, writ ref'd n.r.e.); McDonald & Carlson, *Texas Civil Practice* §5:82 (2d ed.). An intervenor's claim against a defendant served under TRCP 21 and 21a is barred if the limitations period runs before the defendant makes a general appearance. *See* **Baker**, 111 S.W.3d at 160–61.

2. Citation necessary. An intervenor must serve citation on (1) any defendant that has not made a general appearance and from whom the intervenor seeks affirmative relief, (2) any third party brought into the lawsuit by the intervenor, and (3) the plaintiff, if the intervenor's claim is against the plaintiff and the plaintiff makes no further appearance after the intervention. **Baker**, 111 S.W.3d at 160.

§2.4 Motion to strike. If any party in the suit opposes the intervention, that party must challenge it by filing a motion to strike the petition in intervention. Tex. R. Civ. P. 60; **Nghiem v. Sajib**, 567 S.W.3d 718, 721 (Tex.2019); **In re Union Carbide Corp.**, 273 S.W.3d 152, 154–55 (Tex.2008); **Guaranty Fed. Sav. Bank v. Horseshoe Oper. Co.**, 793 S.W.2d 652, 657 (Tex.1990). See **O'Connor's Texas Civil Forms**, FORM 5J:2 (2020 ed.). A court cannot strike an intervention on its own initiative. *See* **Guaranty Fed.**, 793 S.W.2d at 657; **Flores v. Melo-Palacios**, 921 S.W.2d 399, 404 (Tex.App.—Corpus Christi 1996, writ denied).

Note

A motion to strike is used to challenge whether an intervenor can properly be made a party to the suit, which is distinct from the question of whether the court has subject-matter jurisdiction over the intervenor's claims for relief. See ***Abdullatif v. Erpile, LLC**, 460 S.W.3d 685, 694 (Tex.App.—Houston [14th Dist.] 2015, no pet.). A challenge to the court's subject-matter jurisdiction over the intervenor's claims should be raised in a plea to the jurisdiction. See "Plea to the Jurisdiction—Challenging the Court," ch. 3-F, §1 et seq.*

1. Allegations. The motion to strike should allege the following:

(1) The intervenor does not have a justiciable interest in the suit—that is, the intervenor (1) could not have brought all or part of the same suit in its own name or (2) would not have been able to defeat all or part of the recovery if the suit had been filed against it. *See* **Guaranty Fed.**, 793 S.W.2d at 657; **Law Offices of Windle Turley, P.C. v. Ghiasinejad**, 109 S.W.3d 68, 70 (Tex.App.—Fort Worth 2003, no pet.).

(2) The intervention will complicate the case by an excessive multiplication of the issues. *See* **Guaranty Fed.**, 793 S.W.2d at 657; **Ghiasinejad**, 109 S.W.3d at 70.

(3) The intervention is not essential to protect the intervenor's interest. *See* **Guaranty Fed.**, 793 S.W.2d at 657; **Ghiasinejad**, 109 S.W.3d at 70.

2. Waiver. If the party opposing the intervention does not move to strike, that party waives any right to object. *See* **Ghidoni v. Stone Oak, Inc.**, 966 S.W.2d 573, 586–87 (Tex.App.—San Antonio 1998, pet. denied) (motions to abate or sever are not substitutes for motion to strike).

§2.5 Hearing on motion to strike.

1. Make a record. If the trial court conducts a hearing to receive evidence on the motion to strike, the parties should request a court reporter. Without a reporter's record of the hearing, an appellant cannot challenge the ruling on appeal. *See* **Saldana v. Saldana**, 791 S.W.2d 316, 320 (Tex.App.—Corpus Christi 1990, no writ).

2. Burden on intervenor. At the hearing, the burden is on the intervenor to show it has a justiciable interest in the lawsuit. **Nghiem v. Sajib**, 567 S.W.3d 718, 721 (Tex.2019); **Intermarque Auto. Prods. v. Feldman**, 21 S.W.3d 544, 549 (Tex.App.—Texarkana 2000, no pet.). The intervenor should be given the opportunity to respond to the motion, but the issue of whether it has a justiciable interest may be resolved by reference to the petition in intervention. **Potash Corp. v. Mancias**, 942 S.W.2d 61, 64 (Tex.App.—Corpus Christi 1997, orig. proceeding). To establish the right to intervene as a plaintiff, the intervenor must show that it could have brought all or part of the same action in its own name; to establish the right to intervene as a defendant, the intervenor must show it would be able to defeat all or part of the suit if the suit had been brought against it. **Guaranty Fed. Sav. Bank v. Horseshoe Oper. Co.**, 793 S.W.2d 652, 657 (Tex.1990); **Feldman**, 21 S.W.3d at 549.

§2.6 Order on motion to strike.

1. Trial-court standard. The trial court has broad discretion to rule on the motion to strike the petition in intervention. **Guaranty Fed. Sav. Bank v. Horseshoe Oper. Co.**, 793 S.W.2d 652, 657 (Tex.1990). The trial court may strike a petition in intervention if (1) the intervenor does not meet the test for intervention (see "Petition in intervention," ch. 5-J, §2), (2) the intervention will complicate the case by an excessive multiplication of the issues, or (3) the intervention is not essential to protect the intervenor's interest. *See* **Guaranty Fed.**, 793 S.W.2d at 657; *see, e.g.*, **Law Offices of Windle Turley, P.C. v. Ghiasinejad**, 109 S.W.3d 68, 71 (Tex.App.—Fort Worth 2003, no pet.) (intervention was struck because it would have injected new issues into already complicated case). To determine whether an intervention is appropriate, the trial court can consider the allegations of fact in both the plea in intervention and the motion to strike. **Intermarque Auto. Prods. v. Feldman**, 21 S.W.3d 544, 548 n.7 (Tex.App.—Texarkana 2000, no pet.).

2. Options. The trial court has a number of options regarding a petition in intervention. It may (1) try the intervention claim, (2) sever the intervention claim, (3) order a separate trial on the intervention claim, or (4) strike the petition in intervention for good cause. **Saldana v. Saldana**, 791 S.W.2d 316, 320 (Tex.App.—Corpus Christi 1990, no writ). However, the court must rule on the motion to strike before considering other matters. *E.g.*, **In re Union Carbide Corp.**, 273 S.W.3d 152, 156 (Tex.2008) (court must rule on motion to strike before considering severance).

§3. Interpleader suit

By filing an interpleader, a party may protect itself from multiple liability by interpleading the property that is subject to conflicting claims. Tex. R. Civ. P. 43; **Clayton v. MONY Life Ins.**, 284 S.W.3d 398, 401 (Tex.App.—Beaumont 2009, no pet.); *see* **Fort Worth Transp. Auth. v. Rodriguez**, 547 S.W.3d 830, 850 (Tex.2018); **Davis v. East Tex. S&L Ass'n**, 354 S.W.2d 926, 930 (Tex.1962). This procedure is useful when two or more persons claim insurance proceeds, escrow accounts, or trust funds that are in the hands of a disinterested party. *See, e.g.*, **Great Am. Reserve Ins. v. Sanders**, 525 S.W.2d 956, 958 (Tex.1975) (insurance proceeds claimed by widow and former wife). A suit filed as an interpleader is a suit in equity. **Northshore Bank v. Commercial Credit Corp.**, 668 S.W.2d 787, 790 (Tex.App.—Houston [14th Dist.] 1984, writ ref'd n.r.e.). See **O'Connor's Texas Civil Forms**, FORMS 5J:4 to 5J:6 (2020 ed.).

§3.1 Interpleader-party.

1. Plaintiff-stakeholder. A party that is subject to multiple liability because several claims have been or may be asserted against the same property may file an interpleader, joining the competing claimants to the lawsuit as defendants. Tex. R. Civ. P. 43.

2. Defendant-stakeholder. A defendant already in a suit may file an interpleader as a cross-claim or counterclaim. Tex. R. Civ. P. 43. When multiple claims are made for the same property, TRCP 43 authorizes a defendant to join all claimants in the lawsuit and tender the disputed property into the registry of the court. **Clayton v. MONY Life Ins.**, 284 S.W.3d 398, 402 (Tex.App.—Beaumont 2009, no pet.); **Olmos v. Pecan Grove MUD**, 857 S.W.2d 734, 741 (Tex.App.—Houston [14th Dist.] 1993, no writ).

3. Garnishee. A garnishee subject to conflicting claims may file an interpleader. **Northshore Bank v. Commercial Credit Corp.**, 668 S.W.2d 787, 789 (Tex.App.—Houston [14th Dist.] 1984, writ ref'd n.r.e.).

§3.2 Petition.

1. Deadline to file. The TRCPs do not provide a deadline for filing the petition in interpleader. *See* Tex. R. Civ. P. 43.

Note

Some courts of appeals have applied a timeliness requirement to interpleader suits. See ***Clements v. Minnesota Life Ins.****, 176 S.W.3d 258, 263 (Tex.App.—Houston [1st Dist.] 2004, no pet.);* ***Serna v. Webster****, 908 S.W.2d 487, 491 (Tex.App.—San Antonio 1995, no writ), overruled on other grounds,* ***Ex parte E.H.****, 602 S.W.3d 486 (Tex.2020);* ***Olmos v. Pecan Grove MUD****, 857 S.W.2d 734, 741 (Tex.App.—Houston [14th Dist.] 1993, no writ). Thus, if the stakeholder unreasonably delayed in filing the action for interpleader, the action was barred. In* ***Martinez****, the Supreme Court clarified that the only requirement for bringing an action for interpleader under the TRCPs is conflicting claims; thus, unreasonable delay does not make interpleader improper.* ***State Farm Life Ins. v. Martinez****, 216 S.W.3d 799, 807 (Tex.2007). But unreasonable delay may bar the stakeholder from recovering attorney fees or may subject the stakeholder to any applicable statutory penalties. Id. See "Attorney fees," ch. 5-J, §3.2.5.*

2. Rival claims. The stakeholder must show it is subject to (or has reasonable grounds to anticipate) rival claims to the same funds or property and there is a reasonable doubt in law or fact as to which claim is valid. **Tri-State Pipe & Equip., Inc. v. Southern Cty. Mut. Ins.**, 8 S.W.3d 394, 402 (Tex.App.—Texarkana 1999, no pet.); *see* **Fort Worth Transp. Auth. v. Rodriguez**, 547 S.W.3d 830, 850 (Tex.2018) (stakeholder must face rival claims); **Martinez**, 216 S.W.3d at 807 (only requirement for interpleader is conflicting claims); **Davis v. East Tex. S&L Ass'n**, 354 S.W.2d 926, 930 (Tex.1962) (claims must place stakeholder in some real doubt or hazard).

3. Unconditional tender. The stakeholder must show it unconditionally tendered the disputed funds or property into the court's registry. **Fort Worth Transp. Auth.**, 547 S.W.3d at 850–51; **Tri-State Pipe & Equip.**, 8 S.W.3d at 402; **Serna**, 908 S.W.2d at 491; *see* **Rapp v. Mandell & Wright, P.C.**, 127 S.W.3d 888, 895 (Tex.App.—Corpus Christi 2004, pet. denied). Only an unconditional tender is required, not an actual deposit of the funds into the court's registry. **Clayton v. MONY Life Ins.**, 284 S.W.3d 398, 404 (Tex.App.—Beaumont 2009, no pet.); **Heggy v. American Trading Empl. Ret. Account Plan**, 123 S.W.3d 770, 776 (Tex.App.—Houston [14th Dist.] 2003, pet. denied); *see also* **Young v. Gumfory**, 322 S.W.3d 731, 741 (Tex.App.—Dallas 2010, no pet.) (tender is unconditional offer by debtor to pay full amount of debt or obligation). The stakeholder must tender the funds or property so the court can allocate it among the parties as part of the judgment.

4. Discharge. The stakeholder should ask the court to sign an order of discharge.

5. Attorney fees. Generally, an innocent, disinterested stakeholder is entitled to recover attorney fees from tendered funds. **Fort Worth Transp. Auth.**, 547 S.W.3d at 851; *see* **U.S. v. Ray Thomas Gravel Co.**, 380 S.W.2d 576, 580 (Tex.1964) (disinterested stakeholder is entitled to attorney fees if it had reasonable doubts about which party was entitled to funds and it interpleaded claimants in good faith). See "Interested stakeholder," ch. 5-J, §3.3.3. But a stakeholder is not entitled to recover attorney fees if the stakeholder unreasonably delayed in filing the action for interpleader or is responsible for the conflicting claims. **Fort Worth Transp. Auth.**, 547 S.W.3d at 851 (responsible for conflicting claims); **Martinez**, 216 S.W.3d at 803 (unreasonable delay). The stakeholder must segregate claims for which attorney fees are recoverable (e.g., interpleader) from claims for which they are not. *See* **Tony Gullo Motors I, L.P. v. Chapa**, 212 S.W.3d 299, 311 (Tex.2006). See "Fees were segregated," ch. 1-H, §10.1.7.

Note

The Texas Supreme Court has not defined "innocent" within the context of interpleader. E.g., ***Fort Worth Transp. Auth.****, 547 S.W.3d at 852 & n.10 (because interpleading parties were not disinterested, Court did not reach issue of what "innocent" means in context of interpleader).*

§3.3 Response. The following are some of the allegations a party opposing the interpleader may assert:

1. No rival claims. The stakeholder is not subject to and has no reasonable grounds to anticipate rival claims to the same funds or property, and thus interpleader is improper. *See* **State Farm Life Ins. v. Martinez**, 216 S.W.3d 799, 803 (Tex.2007); **Davis v. East Tex. S&L Ass'n**, 354 S.W.2d 926, 930 (Tex.1962); **Olmos v. Pecan Grove MUD**, 857 S.W.2d 734, 741 (Tex.App.—Houston [14th Dist.] 1993, no writ).

2. No unconditional tender. The stakeholder has not unconditionally tendered the funds or property into the court's registry, and thus interpleader is improper. *See* **Fort Worth Transp. Auth. v. Rodriguez**, 547 S.W.3d 830, 850–51 (Tex.2018); **Tri-State Pipe & Equip., Inc. v. Southern Cty. Mut. Ins.**, 8 S.W.3d 394, 402–03 (Tex.App.—Texarkana 1999, no pet.); *see, e.g.*, **Rapp v. Mandell & Wright, P.C.**, 127 S.W.3d 888, 895–96 (Tex.App.—Corpus Christi 2004, pet. denied) (deposit was not unconditional because it was made without waiver of rights and there was no disinterested person to qualify as stakeholder).

3. Interested stakeholder. The stakeholder is an interested stakeholder because it asserts a claim to the interpleaded funds or property, and thus interpleader is improper. *See* **Fort Worth Transp. Auth.**, 547 S.W.3d at 852; **FinServ Cas. Corp. v. Transamerica Life Ins.**, 523 S.W.3d 129, 141 (Tex.App.—Houston [14th Dist.] 2016, pet. denied).

Note

In ***Fort Worth Transp. Auth.****, interpleaders who were alleged tortfeasors tendered $100,000 in anticipation of litigation, claiming that the cumulative liability of all defendants for all claims was limited to $100,000 by the damages cap under the Texas Tort Claims Act* ***Fort Worth Transp. Auth.****, 547 S.W.3d at 836. The interpleaders asserted that the claims against them were defensible and that they would put up a defense if the trial court did not accept their interpleader terms (i.e., did not cap their cumulative liability at $100,000 and dismiss all claims against them). Id. at 851–52. The Court held that the interpleaders' assertion, as well as their status as alleged tortfeasors, prevented them from being "disinterested stakeholders." Id. at 852.*

4. Unreasonable delay. The stakeholder has unreasonably delayed filing the action for interpleader and thus is not entitled to recover attorney fees. *See* **Martinez**, 216 S.W.3d at 807.

5. Stakeholder responsible. The stakeholder is responsible for the conflicting claims and thus is not entitled to recover attorney fees. **Fort Worth Transp. Auth.**, 547 S.W.3d at 851; *e.g.*, **Brown v. Getty Reserve Oil, Inc.**, 626 S.W.2d 810, 815 (Tex.App.—Amarillo 1981, writ dism'd) (stakeholder improperly created fund that became subject of conflicting claims).

§3.4 Hearing on interpleader. The court must conduct a hearing on the initial issue of whether interpleader is appropriate. *See* **Taliaferro v. Texas Commerce Bank**, 669 S.W.2d 172, 174 (Tex.App.—Fort Worth 1984, no writ). The stakeholder must introduce evidence to support the petition in interpleader and, if appropriate, attorney fees. *Id.*

§3.5 Order on interpleader.

1. Interpleader appropriate. If the court determines the suit is properly an interpleader action, it may do the following: (1) require the stakeholder to deposit the funds or property into the court's registry (if not already on deposit), (2) discharge the stakeholder from the suit, (3) grant costs and attorney fees to the stakeholder, and (4) continue the suit on the merits between the rival claimants to determine their respective rights to the money or property.

2. Interpleader not appropriate. If the suit is not properly brought as an interpleader action, the court will dismiss it and order the interpleaded funds, if still in the court registry, to be returned to the party or parties that deposited them. *See* **Fort Worth Transp. Auth. v. Rodriguez**, 547 S.W.3d 830, 852–53 (Tex.2018).

§3.6 Trial on the merits. During the trial on the merits, each claimant has the burden to prove its own claim to the funds; a claimant cannot merely disprove the other's right. **McBryde v. Curry**, 914 S.W.2d 616, 620 (Tex.App.—Texarkana 1995, writ denied); **Northshore Bank v. Commercial Credit Corp.**, 668 S.W.2d 787, 789 (Tex.App.—Houston [14th Dist.] 1984, writ ref'd n.r.e.).

§4. Motion to consolidate

The same legal principles apply in ordering consolidation under TRCP 174(a) as in ordering separate trials under TRCP 174(b). **Dal-Briar Corp. v. Baskette**, 833 S.W.2d 612, 615 (Tex.App.—El Paso 1992, orig. proceeding). See "Motion for separate (bifurcated) trial," ch. 5-I, §4.

§4.1 Motion. TRCP 174(a) gives the trial court broad discretion to consolidate cases with common issues of law or fact. **Owens-Corning Fiberglas Corp. v. Martin**, 942 S.W.2d 712, 716 (Tex.App.—Dallas 1997, no writ). See **O'Connor's Texas Civil Forms**, FORM 5J:7 (2020 ed.).

1. Standards to apply. Suits to be consolidated should relate to substantially the same subject matter, and the same evidence should be material, relevant, and admissible in both suits. **Owens-Corning**, 942 S.W.2d at 716; **Lone Star Ford, Inc. v. McCormick**, 838 S.W.2d 734, 737 (Tex.App.—Houston [1st Dist.] 1992, writ denied).

2. Pending before the court. A court may consolidate lawsuits pending in different district courts within the same county. **Starnes v. Holloway**, 779 S.W.2d 86, 96 (Tex.App.—Dallas 1989, writ denied). A court in one county cannot order a matter pending in another county to be transferred out of that county and into its court unless there is some specific statutory authority. **Flores v. Peschel**, 927 S.W.2d 209, 213 (Tex.App.—Corpus Christi 1996, orig. proceeding). See "Motion to Transfer to Multidistrict Litigation Pretrial Court," ch. 5-G, §1 et seq.

3. Filing of motion—local rules. Some local rules require that the motion to consolidate be filed in the court in which the first-filed case is pending. *E.g.*, **Starnes**, 779 S.W.2d at 96 (Dallas Cty. Loc. R. 1.1(e), now 1.04); *see also* **Santa Fe Drilling Co. v. O'Neill**, 774 S.W.2d 423, 424 (Tex.App.—Houston [14th Dist.] 1989, orig. proceeding) (Harris Cty. Loc. R. 3.2.3 (district courts) requires that motion to consolidate be heard in court where first-filed case is pending). However, a consolidation order based on a motion filed in the court of the later-filed case is not void. **Starnes**, 779 S.W.2d at 96.

§4.2 Objection. A party that objects to a motion to consolidate must make a specific and timely objection. Tex. R. App. P. 33.1(a)(1).

§4.3 Order. In deciding whether to consolidate, the trial court must weigh the judicial economy and convenience that may be gained by the consolidation against the risk of an unfair trial because of prejudice or jury confusion. **In re Ethyl Corp.**, 975 S.W.2d 606, 610 (Tex.1998); **Owens-Corning Fiberglas Corp. v. Martin**, 942 S.W.2d 712, 716 (Tex.App.—Dallas 1997, no writ). If consolidation would result in an unfair trial, the cases should not be joined. **In re Van Waters & Rogers, Inc.**, 145 S.W.3d 203, 207 (Tex.2004); *see* **In re Ethyl Corp.**, 975 S.W.2d at 610.

§5. Review

§5.1 Intervention.

1. No interlocutory appeal. The trial court's ruling on a petition in intervention generally cannot be appealed until after the court signs a final judgment in the case. *See* **Southwestern Bell Tel. Co. v. Public Util. Comm'n**, 615 S.W.2d 947, 952 (Tex.App.—Austin 1981), *writ ref'd n.r.e.*, 622 S.W.2d 82 (Tex.1981); *see, e.g.*, **Metromedia Long Distance, Inc. v. Hughes**, 810 S.W.2d 494, 499 (Tex.App.—San Antonio 1991, writ denied) (trial court struck plea in intervention); **Hart v. Hart**, 679 S.W.2d 80, 80 (Tex.App.—Texarkana 1984, no writ) (trial court granted intervention). But if venue is at issue, CPRC §15.003(b) allows an interlocutory appeal of an intervention decision. See "Exception—multiple plaintiffs," ch. 3-C, §5.2.2.

2. Mandamus. Mandamus relief may be appropriate when the trial court erroneously rules on a petition in intervention. *See, e.g.*, **In re Lewis**, 357 S.W.3d 396, 402–03 (Tex.App.—Fort Worth 2011, orig. proceeding) (in SAPCR suit, court denied motion to strike petition in intervention; mandamus granted because intervenors did not have standing under Fam. Code §102.004); **In re O'Quinn**, 355 S.W.3d 857, 866 (Tex.App.—Houston [1st Dist.] 2011, orig. proceeding) (court denied motion to strike petition in intervention; mandamus not appropriate because intervenors had standing to assert claims for declaratory relief); **In re Salverson**, No. 01-12-00343-CV, 2012 WL 1454549 (Tex.App.—Houston [1st Dist.] 2012, orig. proceeding) (memo op.; 4-23-12) (in SAPCR suit, court granted motion to strike petition in intervention; mandamus granted because intervenors' petition was considered under incorrect statute); *see also* **In re Union Carbide Corp.**, 273 S.W.3d 152, 156–57 (Tex.2008) (court did not rule on motion to strike petition in intervention and instead severed intervenors' claims into separate suit; mandamus granted because intervention resulted in violation of procedures for random assignment of cases in Galveston County).

3. Standard. The appellate court will review the trial court's ruling on intervention for abuse of discretion. **In re Lumbermens Mut. Cas. Co.**, 184 S.W.3d 718, 722 (Tex.2006); **Guaranty Fed. Sav. Bank v. Horseshoe Oper. Co.**, 793

S.W.2d 652, 657 (Tex.1990). The trial court abuses its discretion in denying an intervention if (1) the intervenor could have brought all or part of the same action in its own name, or if the action had been brought against it, the intervenor could have defeated all or part of the recovery, (2) the intervention would not complicate the case by an excessive multiplication of issues, and (3) the intervention was essential (or almost essential) to protect the intervenor's interest. **Guaranty Fed.**, 793 S.W.2d at 657; **Zeifman v. Michels**, 229 S.W.3d 460, 466 (Tex.App.—Austin 2007, no pet.) (list is not exclusive); **Jenkins v. Entergy Corp.**, 187 S.W.3d 785, 796–97 (Tex.App.—Corpus Christi 2006, pet. denied). If the appellate court finds the trial court's ruling was wrong, the court applies the harmless-error rule in TRAP 44.1 and 61.1.

§5.2 Interpleader. If the order granting interpleader disposes of all issues involving the interpleader, it is a final, appealable order. **K&S Interests, Inc. v. Texas Am. Bank/Dallas**, 749 S.W.2d 887, 889–90 (Tex.App.—Dallas 1988, writ denied); **Taliaferro v. Texas Commerce Bank**, 660 S.W.2d 151, 154–55 (Tex.App.—Fort Worth 1983, no writ). If the order is final, any party that wants to appeal must perfect its appeal from the date the court signs the order granting the interpleader.

§5.3 Consolidation.

1. No interlocutory appeal. When the trial court grants a motion to consolidate separate lawsuits, the order generally cannot be appealed until after a final judgment is rendered in the case. **Carter v. Sun City Towing & Recovery, L.P.**, 225 S.W.3d 161, 162 (Tex.App.—El Paso 2005, no pet.).

2. Mandamus. Mandamus relief may be appropriate when the trial court erroneously grants a motion to consolidate. *See, e.g.*, **In re Van Waters & Rogers, Inc.**, 145 S.W.3d 203, 211 (Tex.2004) (mandamus granted because consolidation of 20 toxic-tort claims was likely to create juror confusion, which could not be remedied by appeal); **In re Wal-Mart Stores**, No. 14-05-00137-CV, 2005 WL 2076644 (Tex.App.—Houston [14th Dist.] 2000, orig. proceeding) (memo op.; 8-30-05) (mandamus not appropriate when trial court consolidated claims of only three Ps and issues involved were not complex); *see also* **Hong Kong Dev., Inc. v. Nguyen**, 229 S.W.3d 415, 444–45 (Tex.App.—Houston [1st Dist.] 2007, no pet.) (dicta; although party's claims were mooted when final judgment was rendered, appellate court stated D could have sought mandamus relief before final judgment because consolidating forcible-detainer suit with tort claims deprived D of inexpensive, speedy, and summary ruling on right to immediate possession of property).

3. Standard. The appellate court will review the trial court's ruling on consolidation for abuse of discretion. **Allison v. Arkansas La. Gas Co.**, 624 S.W.2d 566, 568 (Tex.1981); **Hong Kong Dev.**, 229 S.W.3d at 439.

K. Motion for Sanctions

§1. General

§1.1 Rules. Tex. Civ. Prac. & Rem. Code §§9.011 to 9.014 (groundless pleadings), §§10.001 to 10.006 (frivolous pleadings); Tex. R. Civ. P. 13 (groundless pleadings), Tex. R. Civ. P. 21b (failure to serve copies), Tex. R. Civ. P. 215 (discovery abuse). See Tex. Civ. Prac. & Rem. Code ch. 105 (frivolous claim by state agency); Tex. Gov't Code §21.002 (officer of court can be held in contempt), Tex. Gov't Code §82.061 (attorney can be fined or imprisoned for misbehavior or contempt); Tex. R. Civ. P. 166a(h) (party can be ordered to pay reasonable expenses for filing affidavit in bad faith).

§1.2 Purpose. The purpose of sanctions is to secure the parties' compliance with the rules, punish those that violate the rules, and deter other litigants from violating the rules. **Chrysler Corp. v. Blackmon**, 841 S.W.2d 844, 849 (Tex.1992); **Bodnow Corp. v. City of Hondo**, 721 S.W.2d 839, 840 (Tex.1986); **Liles v. Contreras**, 547 S.W.3d 280, 287 (Tex.App.—San Antonio 2018, pet. denied); **Tidrow v. Roth**, 189 S.W.3d 408, 412 (Tex.App.—Dallas 2006, no pet.); *see* **Falk & Mayfield L.L.P. v. Molzan**, 974 S.W.2d 821, 827 (Tex.App.—Houston [14th Dist.] 1998, pet. denied) (purpose of sanctions for groundless pleadings under TRCP 13 is to prevent abuses in the pleading process). In most cases, the imposition of sanctions should not prevent a decision on the merits of the case. **Chrysler Corp.**, 841 S.W.2d at 850; **TransAmerican Nat. Gas Corp. v. Powell**, 811 S.W.2d 913, 918 (Tex.1991).

§1.3 Forms. **O'Connor's Texas Civil Forms**, FORMS 5K:1 et seq. (2020 ed.).

§1.4 Other references. **O'Connor's Texas Civil Appeals** (2020 ed.).

§2. Authority for sanctions

§2.1 Rule or statute. Most sanctions are imposed under the authority of a specific statute or rule that permits the court to order sanctions. *See* Tex. Civ. Prac. & Rem. Code §§9.012, 10.002, 10.004, 105.001 to 105.005; Tex. R. Civ. P. 13, 166a(h), 215.

Note

The rules and statutes discussed in this subchapter grant the authority to order sanctions to the court. See ***Aleman v. Texas Med. Bd.****, 573 S.W.3d 796, 807 (Tex.2019) (TRCP 13 and CPRC ch. 10 apply to courts, not administrative agencies). Depending on the situation, however, there may be another governing body with the authority to order sanctions in the case. See, e.g., id. (TRCP 13 and CPRC ch. 10 did not grant State Office of Administrative Hearings authority to impose sanctions, but Office did have authority to sanction under Administrative Procedure Act).*

§2.2 Inherent power. Sanctions may also be imposed under the court's inherent power. **In re Bennett**, 960 S.W.2d 35, 40 (Tex.1997); **Westview Drive Invs. v. Landmark Am. Ins.**, 522 S.W.3d 583, 613 (Tex.App.—Houston [14th Dist.] 2017, pet. denied); *see* **Brewer v. Lennox Hearth Prods.**, 601 S.W.3d 704, 708 (Tex.2020); **Altesse Healthcare Solutions, Inc. v. Wilson**, 540 S.W.3d 570, 574–75 (Tex.2018). A trial court has inherent power to impose sanctions for abuses of the judicial process not covered by rule or statute. **Brewer**, 601 S.W.3d at 718; **Liles v. Contreras**, 547 S.W.3d 280, 290 (Tex.App.—San Antonio 2018, pet. denied); **Kutch v. Del Mar Coll.**, 831 S.W.2d 506, 510 (Tex.App.—Corpus Christi 1992, no writ); *see* **Eichelberger v. Eichelberger**, 582 S.W.2d 395, 398 (Tex.1979) (court may call on its inherent powers to aid in exercise of jurisdiction, administration of justice, and preservation of its independence and integrity). The court has discretion to impose sanctions to the extent necessary to deter, alleviate, or counteract bad-faith abuse of the judicial process. **Brewer**, 601 S.W.3d at 718; **Liles**, 547 S.W.3d at 290; **Westview Drive**, 522 S.W.3d at 613; **Kutch**, 831 S.W.2d at 510. For the court to impose sanctions under its inherent power, there must be an explicit finding of bad faith. **Brewer**, 601 S.W.3d at 718. "Bad faith" includes the intent to engage in conduct for an impermissible reason, willful noncompliance, or willful ignorance of the facts; mere errors in judgment, lack of diligence, unreasonableness, negligence, or gross negligence, without more, will not constitute bad faith. *Id.* at 718–19. Direct or circumstantial evidence can support a finding of bad faith, but if there is no direct evidence, the record must reasonably support an inference of intent or willfulness. *E.g.*, *id.* at 719 (record

did not support reasonable inference of bad faith when there was no evidence attorney knew or had reason to believe that pretrial survey, which was used to gauge viewpoints toward D's legal position, would fail to exclude case-related individuals from survey database). The bad-faith requirement applies to any sanctions imposed under a court's inherent power; the requirement is not limited to particular types of sanctions, such as attorney fees. *See id.* at 720–22 & n.71.

Note

*In **Brewer**, the Texas Supreme Court clarified that a court cannot impose sanctions under its inherent power unless the conduct in question was committed in bad faith. **Brewer**, 601 S.W.3d at 718. Some courts of appeals have required that the conduct also significantly interfere with the court's legitimate exercise of one of its traditional core functions, which include hearing evidence, deciding issues of fact or questions of law, rendering final judgment, enforcing its judgment, managing its docket, and issuing and enforcing orders. See id. at 718 n.50; **Liles**, 547 S.W.3d at 290–91; see, e.g., **Kennedy v. Kennedy**, 125 S.W.3d 14, 19 (Tex.App.—Austin 2002, pet. denied); **McWhorter v. Sheller**, 993 S.W.2d 781, 789 (Tex.App.—Houston [14th Dist.] 1999, pet. denied); **Kutch**, 831 S.W.2d at 510. Because the Court in **Brewer** vacated the sanctions order based on a lack of bad faith, it declined to address whether significant interference with the legitimate exercise of one of a traditional core function is an additional requirement of a court's inherent power to sanction. **Brewer**, 601 S.W.3d at 717.*

§3. Standards for imposing sanctions

Sanctions must be "just." Tex. R. Civ. P. 215.2(b); **Altesse Healthcare Solutions, Inc. v. Wilson**, 540 S.W.3d 570, 575 (Tex.2018); **Horizon Health Corp. v. Acadia Healthcare Co.**, 520 S.W.3d 848, 884 (Tex.2017); **Paradigm Oil, Inc. v. Retamco Oper., Inc.**, 372 S.W.3d 177, 184 (Tex.2012); **Spohn Hosp. v. Mayer**, 104 S.W.3d 878, 882 (Tex.2003); **TransAmerican Nat. Gas Corp. v. Powell**, 811 S.W.2d 913, 917 (Tex.1991). In other words, the punishment should fit the crime. **Altesse Healthcare Solutions**, 540 S.W.3d at 572; **Paradigm Oil**, 372 S.W.3d at 187; **TransAmerican**, 811 S.W.2d at 917. The standards for imposing sanctions apply not only to charges of discovery abuse but also when there is pleadings abuse or when the court imposes sanctions under its inherent power. *See* **Altesse Healthcare Solutions**, 540 S.W.3d at 574–75 (sanctions under court's inherent power); **Nath v. Texas Children's Hosp.**, 446 S.W.3d 355, 364 (Tex.2014) (sanctions for pleadings abuse).

§3.1 Regular sanctions. Courts use a two-part test to determine whether sanctions are just:

1. Direct relationship. The sanction must be directly related to the offensive conduct. **Altesse Healthcare Solutions, Inc. v. Wilson**, 540 S.W.3d 570, 574 (Tex.2018); **Paradigm Oil, Inc. v. Retamco Oper., Inc.**, 372 S.W.3d 177, 184 (Tex.2012); **American Flood Research, Inc. v. Jones**, 192 S.W.3d 581, 583 (Tex.2006); **TransAmerican Nat. Gas Corp. v. Powell**, 811 S.W.2d 913, 917 (Tex.1991); *e.g.*, **Remington Arms Co. v. Caldwell**, 850 S.W.2d 167, 171 (Tex.1993) (no direct relationship between D's conduct and striking D's pleadings because D's failure to designate expert witness did not cause P prejudice); **In re J.D.N.**, 183 S.W.3d 128, 131–32 (Tex.App.—Dallas 2006, no pet.) (direct relationship between D's conduct and striking his answer because D refused to provide information about finances necessary for child-support determination); **Magnuson v. Mullen**, 65 S.W.3d 815, 826 (Tex.App.—Fort Worth 2002, pet. denied) (direct relationship between P's conduct and dismissal because P frustrated all attempts to define the cause of action and investigate defenses); *see* **Nath v. Texas Children's Hosp.**, 446 S.W.3d 355, 363 (Tex.2014) (**Nath I**) (must be "direct nexus" between offensive conduct, offender, and sanction award). A just sanction must be directed against the abuse and toward remedying the prejudice caused to the innocent party. **American Flood**, 192 S.W.3d at 583; **Spohn Hosp. v. Mayer**, 104 S.W.3d 878, 882 (Tex.2003); **TransAmerican**, 811 S.W.2d at 917.

2. Necessary severity. The sanction must not be excessive; it should be no more severe than necessary to satisfy its legitimate purposes. **Altesse Healthcare Solutions**, 540 S.W.3d at 574; **Nath I**, 446 S.W.3d at 363; **Paradigm Oil**, 372 S.W.3d at 187; **Spohn Hosp.**, 104 S.W.3d at 882; **TransAmerican**, 811 S.W.2d at 917; *see, e.g.*, **Jones v. American Flood Research, Inc.**, 218 S.W.3d 929, 932–33 (Tex.App.—Dallas 2007, no pet.) ($15,000 sanction against attorney for failure of his clients to appear for deposition was excessive); **Zappe v. Zappe**, 871 S.W.2d 910, 912–13 (Tex.App.—Corpus Christi

1994, no writ) (incomplete answers to discovery did not justify striking party's pleadings and other sanctions in child-custody suit). The courts should consider the least stringent sanction necessary to promote compliance. **Nath I**, 446 S.W.3d at 363; **American Flood**, 192 S.W.3d at 583; **Spohn Hosp.**, 104 S.W.3d at 882.

(1) Sanctions for discovery abuse. Sanctions for discovery abuse must not be excessive. **Spohn Hosp.**, 104 S.W.3d at 882. Discovery sanctions severe enough to inhibit presentation of the merits of a case should be reserved for a party's flagrant bad faith or an attorney's callous disregard for the discovery rules. *Id.* at 883; **TransAmerican**, 811 S.W.2d at 918; *see, e.g.*, **Paradigm Oil**, 372 S.W.3d at 186–87 (court properly struck Ds' answer and rendered default judgment, but sanction barring Ds from participating in post-default damages trial for unliquidated damages was excessive; sanction barring Ds from damages trial would more likely be justified if discovery abuse involved spoliation). See "Discovery abuse," ch. 5-K, §5.1; "Sanctions for discovery abuse," ch. 5-K, §7.1.

(2) Sanctions for pleadings abuse. Sanctions for pleadings abuse must not be excessive. *See* **Nath I**, 446 S.W.3d at 363. See "Groundless or frivolous pleadings, motions, or other papers," ch. 5-K, §5.2; "Types of sanctions," ch. 5-K, §7. If a court is imposing a monetary sanction for pleadings abuse, it should consider certain factors in assessing whether the amount of the sanction is excessive. *See* **Bennett v. Grant**, 525 S.W.3d 642, 654 (Tex.2017); **Nath I**, 446 S.W.3d at 371–72; **Low v. Henry**, 221 S.W.3d 609, 620–21 & n.5 (Tex.2007); *see also* **Nath v. Texas Children's Hosp.**, 576 S.W.3d 707, 709 (Tex.2019) (**Nath II**) (when court shifts attorney fees as a sanction, court should assess reasonableness of fee amount in determining whether sanction is excessive). The court does not need to consider all the factors but should consider the relevant ones. **Bennett**, 525 S.W.3d at 654; **Nath I**, 446 S.W.3d at 372; **Low**, 221 S.W.3d at 620–21. The following is a nonexclusive list of factors that a court should consider when assessing the amount of monetary sanctions:

(a) The offender's good or bad faith. **Nath I**, 446 S.W.3d at 371 n.29; **Low**, 221 S.W.3d at 620 n.5.

(b) The degree to which the misconduct involved willful, vindictive, negligent, or frivolous behavior. **Nath I**, 446 S.W.3d at 371 n.29; **Low**, 221 S.W.3d at 620 n.5.

(c) The offender's knowledge, experience, and expertise. **Nath I**, 446 S.W.3d at 371 n.29; **Low**, 221 S.W.3d at 620 n.5.

(d) Any history of sanctionable conduct by the offender. **Nath I**, 446 S.W.3d at 371 n.29; **Low**, 221 S.W.3d at 620 n.5.

(e) The reasonableness and necessity of the out-of-pocket expenses incurred by the party requesting sanctions that resulted from the misconduct. **Nath I**, 446 S.W.3d at 371 n.29; **Low**, 221 S.W.3d at 620 n.5.

(f) The nature and extent of any prejudice suffered by the party requesting sanctions that resulted from the misconduct. **Nath I**, 446 S.W.3d at 371 n.29; **Low**, 221 S.W.3d at 620 n.5.

(g) The client's and attorney's relative culpability and any potential effect on the attorney-client privilege. **Nath I**, 446 S.W.3d at 371 n.29; **Low**, 221 S.W.3d at 620 n.5.

(h) The risk of discouraging the specific type of litigation involved. **Nath I**, 446 S.W.3d at 371 n.29; **Low**, 221 S.W.3d at 620 n.5.

(i) The impact of the sanction on the offender, including her ability to pay. **Nath I**, 446 S.W.3d at 371 n.29; **Low**, 221 S.W.3d at 620 n.5.

(j) The impact of the sanction on the party requesting sanctions, including her need for compensation. **Nath I**, 446 S.W.3d at 371 n.29; **Low**, 221 S.W.3d at 620 n.5.

(k) The relative size of the sanction necessary to attain the sanction's objective. **Nath I**, 446 S.W.3d at 371 n.29; **Low**, 221 S.W.3d at 620 n.5.

(*l*) The burdens on the court resulting from the misconduct, including the court's time, juror fees, and other court costs. **Nath I**, 446 S.W.3d at 371 n.29; **Low**, 221 S.W.3d at 620 n.5.

(m) The degree to which the behavior of the party requesting sanctions contributed to the expenses incurred. **Low**, 221 S.W.3d at 620 n.5; *e.g.*, **Nath I**, 446 S.W.3d at 371–72 & n.29 (trial court should have considered extent to which

Ds were responsible for attorney fees and expenses incurred when P's pleadings were sanctionable when filed but Ds litigated merits issues for over four years before moving for summary judgment and seeking sanctions against P); *see* **Bennett**, 525 S.W.3d at 655.

(3) Sanctions under court's inherent power. Sanctions awarded by a court under its inherent power must not be excessive. **Brewer v. Lennox Hearth Prods.**, 601 S.W.3d 704, 718 (Tex.2020); *e.g.*, **Altesse Healthcare Solutions**, 540 S.W.3d at 574–75 (sanctions imposed by trial court under its inherent power against D for knowing violation of TRO amounted to double recovery for P and were excessive). The severity of the sanctions should be based on the degree of bad faith. **Brewer**, 601 S.W.3d at 720; *see* **Altesse Healthcare Solutions**, 540 S.W.3d at 575–76 (sanctions severe enough to prevent decision on merits are justified only in most severe cases of flagrant bad faith).

§3.2 Death-penalty sanctions. A death-penalty sanction is one that has the effect of adjudicating the dispute without regard to the merits. **TransAmerican Nat. Gas Corp. v. Powell**, 811 S.W.2d 913, 918 (Tex.1991); *see* **Altesse Healthcare Solutions, Inc. v. Wilson**, 540 S.W.3d 570, 575 (Tex.2018). Death-penalty sanctions should be imposed only in exceptional cases when they are clearly justified and it is apparent that no lesser sanctions would promote compliance with the rules. **Cire v. Cummings**, 134 S.W.3d 835, 840–41 (Tex.2004); **Spohn Hosp. v. Mayer**, 104 S.W.3d 878, 882 (Tex.2003); **GTE Comms. Sys. v. Tanner**, 856 S.W.2d 725, 729 (Tex.1993); *see* **Altesse Healthcare Solutions**, 540 S.W.3d at 575 (courts should avoid "trial by sanctions" whenever possible; sanctions so severe that they prevent decision on merits are not justified except in most extreme cases of flagrant bad faith). Death-penalty sanctions include dismissal, default judgment, excluding evidence, and jury instructions resolving fact issues in favor of one party. *See, e.g.*, **Paradigm Oil, Inc. v. Retamco Oper., Inc.**, 372 S.W.3d 177, 184 (Tex.2012) (default judgment); **Spohn Hosp.**, 104 S.W.3d at 883 (jury instructions); **Hernandez v. Mid-Loop, Inc.**, 170 S.W.3d 138, 144 (Tex.App.—San Antonio 2005, no pet.) (dismissal); **Adkins Servs. v. Tisdale Co.**, 56 S.W.3d 842, 845 (Tex.App.—Texarkana 2001, no pet.) (order excluding evidence). Courts use a four-part test to determine whether death-penalty sanctions are appropriate.

1. **Direct relationship.** See "Direct relationship," ch. 5-K, §3.1.1.

2. **Necessary severity.** See "Necessary severity," ch. 5-K, §3.1.2.

3. **Lesser sanction first.**

(1) Typical misconduct. Generally, the trial court must use a lesser sanction first to determine whether it is adequate to secure compliance, deterrence, and punishment of the offender. **Chrysler Corp. v. Blackmon**, 841 S.W.2d 844, 849 (Tex.1992); *see* **Cire**, 134 S.W.3d at 840–41. The trial court is not required to order every lesser sanction that could possibly be imposed before imposing death-penalty sanctions. **Cire**, 134 S.W.3d at 842. An order compelling discovery, by itself, is not a lesser sanction. **Paradigm Oil, Inc. v. Retamco Oper., Inc.**, 161 S.W.3d 531, 539 (Tex.App.—San Antonio 2004, pet. denied); **In re Western Star Trucks US, Inc.**, 112 S.W.3d 756, 766 (Tex.App.—Eastland 2003, orig. proceeding); **Andras v. Memorial Hosp. Sys.**, 888 S.W.2d 567, 572 (Tex.App.—Houston [1st Dist.] 1994, writ denied). The courts of appeals are split on whether an order to compel, joined with a statement that noncompliance will result in sanctions, constitutes a lesser sanction. *Compare* **Paradigm Oil**, 161 S.W.3d at 539 (order to compel under threat of dismissal met requirement of lesser sanction), **HRN, Inc. v. Shell Oil Co.**, 102 S.W.3d 205, 218 (Tex.App.—Houston [14th Dist.] 2003) (same), *rev'd on other grounds*, 144 S.W.3d 429 (Tex.2004), *and* **Andras**, 888 S.W.2d at 572 (same), *with* **In re Polaris Indus.**, 65 S.W.3d 746, 753 (Tex.App.—Beaumont 2001, orig. proceeding) (neither threat nor intent to sanction constitute sanctions), *and* **Williams v. Akzo Nobel Chems., Inc.**, 999 S.W.2d 836, 844 (Tex.App.—Tyler 1999, no pet.) (threat of dismissal for noncompliance is not lesser sanction).

(2) Egregious misconduct. In a case of egregious misconduct (e.g., a violation of earlier court orders, a blatant disregard for the discovery process), the court is not required to use a lesser sanction before imposing death-penalty sanctions as long as the record reflects that the court considered lesser sanctions and the party's conduct justifies the presumption that its claims or defenses lack merit. **Cire**, 134 S.W.3d at 842; *see* **Altesse Healthcare Solutions**, 540 S.W.3d at 576. See "No merit," ch. 5-K, §3.2.4. The court generally must give a reasoned explanation why lesser sanctions would have been ineffective and why the sanction imposed was appropriate. *See* **Cire**, 134 S.W.3d at 842; **GTE**, 856 S.W.2d at 729–30; *see, e.g.*, **Altesse Healthcare Solutions**, 540 S.W.3d at 576 (trial court's statement that no lesser sanction "would be adequate

punishment" was insufficient to show that court duly considered lesser sanctions first); *see also* **Gilbert v. Moseley**, 453 S.W.3d 480, 487–88 (Tex.App.—Texarkana 2014, no pet.) (when, under facts of case, there was no realistic lesser sanction trial judge could have imposed, absence of explicit language stating judge considered lesser sanctions and found them ineffective was not controlling). The order cannot simply say that the court "considered" a lesser sanction before imposing death-penalty sanctions. *See* **In re Adkins**, 70 S.W.3d 384, 391 (Tex.App.—Fort Worth 2002, orig. proceeding); *see also* **In re N.R.C.**, 94 S.W.3d 799, 812 (Tex.App.—Houston [14th Dist.] 2002, pet. denied) (silent record does not support conclusion that court considered lesser sanctions).

4. No merit. For death-penalty sanctions to be appropriate, the party's conduct must justify the presumption that its claims or defenses lack merit. **Paradigm Oil**, 372 S.W.3d at 184; **Hamill v. Level**, 917 S.W.2d 15, 16 (Tex.1996); **TransAmerican**, 811 S.W.2d at 918; *e.g.*, **Altesse Healthcare Solutions**, 540 S.W.3d at 572 (monetary recovery that went beyond ordinary death-penalty sanctions was not justified because D's noncompliance with TRO did not indicate its claims and defenses lacked merit; TRO was difficult to comply with and D did eventually comply while TRO was still in effect); **Cire**, 134 S.W.3d at 839 (death-penalty sanctions were justified when P deliberately destroyed audiotapes she refused to produce because they were unfavorable to her claims); **Knoderer v. State Farm Lloyds**, No. 06-13-00027-CV, 2014 WL 4699136 (Tex.App.—Texarkana 2014, no pet.) (memo op.; 9-19-14) (death-penalty sanctions not justified when P destroyed evidence indicating photographs used to impeach D's expert were fabricated; evidence did not go to ultimate issues); *see, e.g.*, **Andras**, 888 S.W.2d at 573 (lawsuit against hospital for overcharging was properly dismissed because P's attorney refused to produce canceled checks).

§4. Persons who may be sanctioned

The court should impose the sanctions against the offender. **Nath v. Texas Children's Hosp.**, 446 S.W.3d 355, 363 (Tex.2014); **Spohn Hosp. v. Mayer**, 104 S.W.3d 878, 882 (Tex.2003); **TransAmerican Nat. Gas Corp. v. Powell**, 811 S.W.2d 913, 917 (Tex.1991). Before imposing sanctions that severely inhibit the presentation of a party's claim, the court should make a record identifying who was responsible for the sanctionable conduct—the party, the attorney, or both. *See* **Nath**, 446 S.W.3d at 363; **Spohn Hosp.**, 104 S.W.3d at 882; **TransAmerican**, 811 S.W.2d at 917.

§4.1 Party. The court may impose sanctions on the party. *E.g.*, Tex. Civ. Prac. & Rem. Code §§9.012(c), 10.004(a); Tex. R. Civ. P. 13, 215.1(d), 215.2(b), 215.3; *see* **TransAmerican Nat. Gas Corp. v. Powell**, 811 S.W.2d 913, 917 (Tex.1991). A party must bear some responsibility for its counsel's sanctionable conduct when the party is or should be aware of counsel's conduct and any violation of the discovery rules. **TransAmerican**, 811 S.W.2d at 917; **Paradigm Oil, Inc. v. Retamco Oper., Inc.**, 161 S.W.3d 531, 537 (Tex.App.—San Antonio 2004, pet. denied). A party should not be punished for discovery abuse for which it is not responsible. **TransAmerican**, 811 S.W.2d at 917; *e.g.*, **Paradigm Oil**, 161 S.W.3d at 537 (sanctions on party were proper because party was responsible for discovery abuse); **In re Harvest Cmty.**, 88 S.W.3d 343, 348 (Tex.App.—San Antonio 2002, orig. proceeding) (no evidence party was guilty of anything but hiring offensive attorney); **Smith v. Nguyen**, 855 S.W.2d 263, 266–67 (Tex.App.—Houston [14th Dist.] 1993, writ denied) (nothing in record implicated party in late designation of witnesses); *see also* **In re Garza**, 544 S.W.3d 836, 841–42 (Tex.2018) (abuse of discretion for trial court to impose sanctions on party for lawful actions taken by nonparties). The trial court cannot impose a sanction that adversely affects parties who were not implicated in the abuse. **Arkla, Inc. v. Harris**, 846 S.W.2d 623, 628–29 (Tex.App.—Houston [14th Dist.] 1993, orig. proceeding); *see also* **Knoderer v. State Farm Lloyds**, 515 S.W.3d 21, 31–32 (Tex.App.—Texarkana 2017, pet. denied) (wife was not personally liable for husband's sanctionable conduct, but her community property was subject to liability for his conduct). Parties that can be sanctioned include the following:

1. An individual. *See, e.g.*, **Nath v. Texas Children's Hosp.**, 446 S.W.3d 355, 358 (Tex.2014) (sanctions against individual for filing groundless pleadings in bad faith and for improper purpose); **Cire v. Cummings**, 134 S.W.3d 835, 841 (Tex.2004) (death-penalty sanctions against individual for destruction of evidence); **Akinwamide v. Transportation Ins.**, 499 S.W.3d 511, 528–29 (Tex.App.—Houston [1st Dist.] 2016, pet. denied) (sanctions under CPRC ch. 10 against pro se party).

2. A corporation. *See, e.g.*, **Downer v. Aquamarine Operators, Inc.**, 701 S.W.2d 238, 242–43 (Tex.1985) (court struck D-corporation's answer after D's requested deponents did not appear at deposition when it had been rescheduled twice and D did not appear at hearing on motion for sanctions).

3. A state agency. *See* Tex. Civ. Prac. & Rem. Code §105.002. A state agency may be sanctioned for filing a claim—either originally or as a counterclaim or cross-claim—that is frivolous. Tex. Civ. Prac. & Rem. Code §105.002(1). CPRC

chapter 105 waives immunity for agencies with statewide jurisdiction. *See* Tex. Civ. Prac. & Rem. Code §105.001(3)(C). A state agency may also be sanctioned for a frivolous regulatory action taken on or after September 1, 2019. *See* Tex. Civ. Prac. & Rem. Code §105.005.

Note

Before the 2019 amendments, CPRC §105.002 permitted sanctions not only for claims that were frivolous but also for claims that were unreasonable or without foundation. See Tex. Civ. Prac. & Rem. Code §105.002(1) (pre-9-1-19 version). This standard still applies to claims filed before September 1, 2019. See Acts 2019, 86th Leg., R.S., ch. 504, §§7, 8, eff. Sept. 1, 2019.

§4.2 Attorney. If the attorney was responsible for the sanctionable conduct and the party was unaware of it, the court should sanction the attorney, not the party. *See* Tex. Civ. Prac. & Rem. Code §§9.012(c), 10.004(a); Tex. R. Civ. P. 13, 215.1(d), 215.2(b)(8); **American Flood Research, Inc. v. Jones**, 192 S.W.3d 581, 584 (Tex.2006); **TransAmerican Nat. Gas Corp. v. Powell**, 811 S.W.2d 913, 917 (Tex.1991); **In re Barnes**, 956 S.W.2d 746, 748 (Tex.App.—Corpus Christi 1997, orig. proceeding); *see, e.g.*, **Jones v. Andrews**, 873 S.W.2d 102, 106 (Tex.App.—Dallas 1994, no writ) (party should not be punished by death-penalty sanctions because attorney did not timely ask for extension). When multiple attorneys are involved in the sanctionable conduct, they can be held jointly and severally liable. *See, e.g.*, **Kugle v. DaimlerChrysler Corp.**, 88 S.W.3d 355, 364–65 (Tex.App.—San Antonio 2002, pet. denied) (three attorneys were jointly and severally liable for fraud in personal-injury suit). There is disagreement, however, on whether law firms are sanctionable. *Compare* **Yuen v. Gerson**, 342 S.W.3d 824, 828–29 (Tex.App.—Houston [14th Dist.] 2011, pet. denied) (law firms cannot be sanctioned), *with* **Finlay v. Olive**, 77 S.W.3d 520, 527 (Tex.App.—Houston [1st Dist.] 2002, no pet.) (law firm can be sanctioned for groundless pleadings filed on its behalf by attorney employed at firm).

§4.3 Both party & attorney. When both the party and the attorney are implicated in sanctionable conduct, the court may sanction both of them. *E.g.*, Tex. Civ. Prac. & Rem. Code §§9.012(c), 10.004(a); Tex. R. Civ. P. 13, 215.1(d); *see, e.g.*, **Kugle v. DaimlerChrysler Corp.**, 88 S.W.3d 355, 365–66 (Tex.App.—San Antonio 2002, pet. denied) (attorneys were liable for monetary sanctions and suit was dismissed); **In re Zenergy, Inc.**, 968 S.W.2d 1, 11 (Tex.App.—Corpus Christi 1997, orig. proceeding) (party and attorney were jointly and severally liable for monetary sanctions).

§4.4 Nonparty.

1. Discovery abuse. When a nonparty refuses to comply with a subpoena (to produce documents or to appear) or a court order (e.g., to appear for a deposition or to permit inspection of land), the court can treat the noncompliance as contempt. *See* Tex. R. Civ. P. 176.8(a), 196.7, 205.3(a), 215.2(a), (c); **City of Houston v. Chambers**, 899 S.W.2d 306, 309 (Tex.App.—Houston [14th Dist.] 1995, orig. proceeding) (addressed former TRCP 215(2)(a)). Neither TRCP 215.2(b) nor TRCP 215.3 authorizes other sanctions against a nonparty. **Pope v. Davidson**, 849 S.W.2d 916, 920 (Tex.App.—Houston [14th Dist.] 1993, orig. proceeding); *see, e.g.*, **Chambers**, 899 S.W.2d at 309 (because nonparty had not violated order in resisting discovery, court could not impose monetary sanctions); **Texas Atty. Gen. Office v. Adams**, 793 S.W.2d 771, 775 (Tex.App.—Fort Worth 1990, no writ) (court could not sanction nonparty by ordering it to pay attorney fees of $9,628 for refusing to comply with subpoena). When a person is found guilty of contempt, the court is limited to a monetary fine or incarceration. Tex. Gov't Code §21.002(b); **In re Acceptance Ins.**, 33 S.W.3d 443, 450 (Tex.App.—Fort Worth 2000, orig. proceeding); *see, e.g.*, **Pope**, 849 S.W.2d at 920 (court could not require nonparty to perform community service). See "Sanctions under Government Code," ch. 5-K, §7.6.

2. Pleadings abuse. A nonparty cannot be sanctioned for pleadings abuse under TRCP 13. **Chambers**, 899 S.W.2d at 309; *see also* Tex. Civ. Prac. & Rem. Code §9.012 (addresses pleading abuse by party). TRCP 13 applies only to parties and their attorneys. **Chambers**, 899 S.W.2d at 309; *see, e.g.*, **Jimenez v. Transwestern Prop. Co.**, 999 S.W.2d 125, 130 (Tex.App.—Houston [14th Dist.] 1999, no pet.) (paralegal could not be sanctioned under TRCP 13); **Adams**, 793 S.W.2d at 775 (nonparty's groundless claims of privilege could not be punished under TRCP 13).

§5. Conduct that justifies sanctions

§5.1 Discovery abuse.

1. No designation of witness. The court can impose sanctions on a corporation or other entity that does not designate a witness under TRCP 199.2(b)(1) or TRCP 200.1(b). Tex. R. Civ. P. 215.1(b)(1). See "When organization deposed," ch. 6-F, §4.6.3.

2. Oral discovery. The court can impose sanctions on a party, other deponent, or person designated to testify on behalf of a party or other deponent. See "Grounds for sanctions," ch. 6-F, §10.1.

3. Written discovery. The court can impose sanctions on a party for any of the following:

(1) Not serving answers or objections to interrogatories submitted under TRCP 197 after proper service of the interrogatories. Tex. R. Civ. P. 215.1(b)(3)(A); *see* **Swain v. Southwestern Bell Yellow Pages, Inc.**, 998 S.W.2d 731, 732–33 (Tex.App.—Fort Worth 1999, no pet.).

(2) Not answering an interrogatory submitted under TRCP 197. Tex. R. Civ. P. 215.1(b)(3)(B).

(3) Not serving a written response to a properly served request for inspection submitted under TRCP 196. Tex. R. Civ. P. 215.1(b)(3)(C).

(4) Not responding that discovery will be permitted as requested or not permitting discovery in response to a request for inspection submitted under TRCP 196. Tex. R. Civ. P. 215.1(b)(3)(D).

(5) Not providing disclosures under TRCP 194. *See* **Magnuson v. Mullen**, 65 S.W.3d 815, 828 (Tex.App.—Fort Worth 2002, pet. denied) (under pre-1-1-21 version of TRCP 194); *see also* **Liles v. Contreras**, 547 S.W.3d 280, 289–90 (Tex.App.—San Antonio 2018, pet. denied) (under pre-1-1-21 version of TRCP 194, party's response to request for disclosure asking for any settlement agreements described settlement agreement but did not disclose its contents; four-month delay in supplementing response to provide settlement agreement was sanctionable conduct).

2021 Rule Amendments

In 2020, the Supreme Court approved significant amendments to TRCP 194. See Tex.Sup.Ct. Order, Misc. Docket No. 20-9153 (eff. Jan. 1, 2021). Under the amendments, a party is now generally required to disclose certain information and material without waiting for a discovery request from the other party. See Tex. R. Civ. P. 194.1(a). See "Required disclosures—Cases filed on or after 1-1-21," ch. 6-E, §3. The amendments apply to cases filed on or after January 1, 2021, except those filed in justice court. Tex.Sup.Ct. Order, Misc. Docket No. 20-9153 (eff. Jan. 1, 2021).

---

4. Evasive or incomplete answer. For purposes of sanctions, an evasive or incomplete answer is treated as a failure to answer. Tex. R. Civ. P. 215.1(c).

5. Frivolous objections. The court can impose sanctions when an attorney files frivolous objections to discovery. *See, e.g.*, **Childs v. Argenbright**, 927 S.W.2d 647, 649 (Tex.App.—Tyler 1996, no writ) (attorney filed nine pages of objections to interrogatories without answering any of them).

6. False discovery certification. The court can impose sanctions available under CPRC chapter 10 on an attorney who signed a discovery disclosure, request, notice, response, or objection in violation of TRCP 191.3(b) or (c). Tex. R. Civ. P. 191.3(e). For the representations certified by the signer of discovery under TRCP 191.3, see "Certification by signature," ch. 6-A, §4.1. The sanction can be imposed on the person who made the certification, the party on whose behalf it was made, or both. Tex. R. Civ. P. 191.3(e). See "Sanctions under CPRC §10.004," ch. 5-K, §7.2.

7. False testimony. The court can impose sanctions when a party gives false testimony. *See* **In re Reece**, 341 S.W.3d 360, 368 (Tex.2011) (if party-deponent lies during deposition, court can impose sanctions that range from payment of attorney fees to default judgment); *see, e.g.*, **Schaver v. British Am. Ins.**, 795 S.W.2d 875, 878–79 (Tex.App.—Beaumont

1990, no writ) (because P did not disclose postinjury work history and falsified employment status, causing extra depositions of doctors, court imposed monetary sanctions; when P did not pay, court dismissed suit).

8. Improper discovery methods. The court can impose sanctions when an attorney engages in improper discovery procedures. *See, e.g.,* **Sanchez v. Brownsville Sports Ctr., Inc.**, 51 S.W.3d 643, 659 (Tex.App.—Corpus Christi 2001, pet. granted, judgm't vacated w.r.m.) (attorney went to D's store and pretended to be interested in buying vehicle).

9. Spoliation of evidence. The court can impose sanctions when a party destroys evidence it had a duty to preserve. **Brookshire Bros. v. Aldridge**, 438 S.W.3d 9, 21 (Tex.2014); *see* **Cire v. Cummings**, 134 S.W.3d 835, 841 (Tex.2004). Sanctions that are similar to death-penalty sanctions, such as dismissing a party's claims or defenses, can be imposed only if the spoliation is intentional or if negligent spoliation irreparably deprives a nonspoliating party of any meaningful ability to present a claim or defense. **Petroleum Solutions, Inc. v. Head**, 454 S.W.3d 482, 489 (Tex.2014). See "Sanctions," ch. 6-A, §24.2.2(3)(b)[1].

10. Pattern of abuse. The court can consider a pattern of discovery abuse to justify sanctions. *See* **Downer v. Aquamarine Operators, Inc.**, 701 S.W.2d 238, 242–43 (Tex.1985); *see, e.g.,* **Chasewood Oaks Condos. Homeowners Ass'n v. Amatek Holdings, Inc.**, 977 S.W.2d 840, 844–45 (Tex.App.—Fort Worth 1998, pet. denied) (P actively frustrated D's legitimate attempts to investigate potential defenses).

§5.2 Groundless or frivolous pleadings, motions, or other papers. When seeking sanctions for the signing of groundless or frivolous pleadings, motions, or other papers, the party can choose between CPRC §9.012 (pleadings and motions), CPRC §10.004 (same), and TRCP 13 (pleadings, motions, and other papers). Of the three, CPRC §10.004 is usually the best choice. First, CPRC §9.012 does not apply in any proceeding to which either CPRC §10.004 or TRCP 13 applies. Tex. Civ. Prac. & Rem. Code §9.012(h). Second, TRCP 13 is narrower in scope than CPRC §10.004 and imposes a greater burden of proof on the party seeking sanctions. TRCP 13 requires a showing that a pleading, motion, or other paper was both groundless and brought in bad faith, brought for the purpose of harassment, or false when made. **Nath v. Texas Children's Hosp.**, 446 S.W.3d 355, 362–63 (Tex.2014). By comparison, CPRC §10.004 allows sanctions when pleadings or motions are brought for an improper purpose, including harassment, delay, or increasing the cost of litigation, even if they are not groundless or frivolous. *See* Tex. Civ. Prac. & Rem. Code §§10.001, 10.004; **Nath**, 446 S.W.3d at 362; **Save Our Springs Alliance, Inc. v. Lazy Nine MUD**, 198 S.W.3d 300, 321 (Tex.App.—Texarkana 2006, pet. denied). CPRC §10.004 also allows sanctions for groundless pleadings or motions that are brought negligently or as a result of poor judgment. *See* Tex. Civ. Prac. & Rem. Code §10.001(2) to (4); **Low v. Henry**, 221 S.W.3d 609, 617 (Tex.2007); *see also* **Nath**, 446 S.W.3d at 369 (whether pleading or motion is groundless is assessed at time of filing). The advantage of TRCP 13, however, is that it permits death-penalty sanctions. See "Sanctions under TRCP 13," ch. 5-K, §7.3. When in doubt, a party should seek sanctions under both CPRC §10.004 and TRCP 13. *See* **Alexander v. Alexander**, 956 S.W.2d 712, 713 (Tex.App.—Houston [14th Dist.] 1997, pet. denied).

1. CPRC ch. 10. The court can impose sanctions on the attorney (or pro se party) who signed the pleading or motion, the party represented by the attorney, or both if the pleading or motion was signed in violation of CPRC §10.001. Tex. Civ. Prac. & Rem. Code §10.004(a); *see* **Low**, 221 S.W.3d at 617. See "Order under CPRC ch. 10," ch. 5-K, §11.2; **O'Connor's Texas Civil Forms**, FORM 5K:1, §B (2020 ed.). For the representations certified by the signer of the pleading or motion under CPRC §10.001, see "Under CPRC ch. 10," ch. 1-B, §3.2.12(3)(a).

2. TRCP 13. The court can impose sanctions on the attorney (or pro se party) who signed the pleading, motion, or other paper, the party represented by the attorney, or both if the pleading, motion, or other paper was signed in violation of TRCP 13. Tex. R. Civ. P. 13. See "Order under TRCP 13," ch. 5-K, §11.3; **O'Connor's Texas Civil Forms**, FORM 5K:1, §A (2020 ed.). For the representations certified by the signer of the pleading, motion, or other paper under TRCP 13, see "Under TRCP 13," ch. 1-B, §3.2.12(3)(b).

(1) Objective test—groundless. A groundless pleading, motion, or other paper is one that has no basis in law or fact and is not warranted by a good-faith argument for the extension, modification, or reversal of existing law. Tex. R. Civ. P. 13; **GTE Comms. Sys. v. Tanner**, 856 S.W.2d 725, 730 (Tex.1993). The standard is objective: Did the party and attorney make a "reasonable inquiry" into the legal and factual basis of the claim? **Lake Travis ISD v. Lovelace**, 243 S.W.3d

244, 254 (Tex.App.—Austin 2007, no pet.). To decide whether the investigation was reasonable, the court looks to the facts available to the litigant and the circumstances at the time the party filed the pleading, motion, or other paper. **Tarrant Cty. v. Chancey**, 942 S.W.2d 151, 155 (Tex.App.—Fort Worth 1997, no writ). In some cases, the court must also determine whether, at the time the pleading, motion, or other paper was filed, the legal arguments asserted in it were warranted by a good-faith argument for the extension of existing law. *See, e.g.*, **Lake Travis ISD**, 243 S.W.3d at 254–55 (sanction reversed; P offered arguable legal basis for extension of law); **McIntyre v. Wilson**, 50 S.W.3d 674, 687 (Tex.App.—Dallas 2001, pet. denied) (same); **Bradt v. Sebek**, 14 S.W.3d 756, 765–67 (Tex.App.—Houston [1st Dist.] 2000, pet. denied) (sanctions affirmed; P offered no arguable legal basis for extension of law).

(2) Subjective test—bad faith, harassment. A groundless pleading, motion, or other paper is not sanctionable unless it was also brought in bad faith, brought for the purpose of harassment, or false when made. Tex. R. Civ. P. 13; **Nath**, 446 S.W.3d at 362–63; *see* **GTE**, 856 S.W.2d at 731. Bad faith is more than mere bad judgment or negligence; it is motivated by dishonest, discriminatory, or malicious purposes. **Parker v. Walton**, 233 S.W.3d 535, 540 (Tex.App.—Houston [14th Dist.] 2007, no pet.); **Estate of Davis v. Cook**, 9 S.W.3d 288, 298 (Tex.App.—San Antonio 1999, no pet.). Thus, the party seeking sanctions must prove the pleading party's subjective state of mind.

3. CPRC ch. 9. The court can impose sanctions on the attorney (or pro se party) who signed the pleading or motion, the party represented by the attorney, or both if the pleading or motion was signed in violation of CPRC §9.011. Tex. Civ. Prac. & Rem. Code §9.012(c). See **O'Connor's Texas Civil Forms**, FORM 5K:1, §C (2020 ed.). For the representations certified by the signer of the pleading or motion under CPRC §9.011, see "Under CPRC ch. 9," ch. 1-B, §3.2.12(3)(c). Sanctions under CPRC §9.012 are not available in any proceeding in which sanctions are available under CPRC §10.004 or TRCP 13. Tex. Civ. Prac. & Rem. Code §9.012(h); *see also* **Nath**, 446 S.W.3d at 362 n.6 (CPRC chapter 9 has largely been supplanted by CPRC chapter 10). Under CPRC §9.011, the court may sanction a party for filing pleadings or motions that are (1) groundless and (2) brought in bad faith, to harass, or for any improper purpose (e.g., to cause delay or needless increase in cost of litigation). **Elkins v. Stotts-Brown**, 103 S.W.3d 664, 668 (Tex.App.—Dallas 2003, no pet.); **Herrmann & Andreas Ins. Agency, Inc. v. Appling**, 800 S.W.2d 312, 320 (Tex.App.—Corpus Christi 1990, no writ). CPRC §9.012(d) gives the party a 90-day grace period to withdraw, amend, or move to dismiss the offending pleading or motion.

4. CPRC ch. 105.

(1) Frivolous claims. The court can impose sanctions on a state agency for bringing a claim—either originally or as a counterclaim or cross-claim—if (1) the court finds the action was frivolous and (2) the action is dismissed or judgment is awarded to the party. Tex. Civ. Prac. & Rem. Code §105.002. Section 105.002 does not require the party to prevail before the party is entitled to sanctions. **State Office of Risk Mgmt. v. Herrera**, 288 S.W.3d 543, 550–51 (Tex.App.—Amarillo 2009, no pet.).

Note

Before the 2019 amendments to CPRC chapter 105, CPRC §105.002 permitted sanctions not only for claims that were frivolous but also for claims that were unreasonable or without foundation. See Tex. Civ. Prac. & Rem. Code §105.002(1) (pre-9-1-19 version). This standard still applies to claims filed before September 1, 2019. See Acts 2019, 86th Leg., R.S., ch. 504, §§7, 8, eff. Sept. 1, 2019.

(2) Frivolous regulatory actions. The court, when reviewing a decision in a contested case under Gov't Code chapter 2001, can impose sanctions on a state agency for a regulatory action taken on or after September 1, 2019, if (1) the party prevails on review and (2) there is final determination that the regulatory action is frivolous. *See* Tex. Civ. Prac. & Rem. Code §105.005.

5. TRCP 18a(h). A judge who hears a motion to disqualify or recuse can impose sanctions on the party who filed the motion, her attorney, or both if the motion was (1) groundless and filed in bad faith or to harass or (2) clearly brought for the purpose of unnecessary delay and without sufficient cause. Tex. R. Civ. P. 18a(h). See "Motion to disqualify or recuse," ch. 5-C, §4.

§5.3 Failure to serve—TRCP 21b. The court can impose sanctions on a party (or attorney advising it) that does not serve on or deliver to other parties copies of pleadings, motions, or other papers as required by TRCP 21 and 21a. Tex. R. Civ.

P. 21b; **Union City Body Co. v. Ramirez**, 911 S.W.2d 196, 200 (Tex.App.—San Antonio 1995, orig. proceeding); *see* Tex. R. Civ. P. 215.2(b). See **O'Connor's Texas Civil Forms**, FORM 5K:3 (2020 ed.).

§5.4 Contempt under Government Code. Under Gov't Code §21.002, a court can punish an attorney or other person for contempt of court; under Gov't Code §82.061, a court can punish an attorney for misbehavior or contempt of court. See "Sanctions under Government Code," ch. 5-K, §7.6.

§5.5 Affidavits made in bad faith—TRCP 166a(h). In a summary-judgment proceeding, if a party relies on an affidavit made in bad faith or for the purpose of delay, the court must order the party to pay the other party reasonable expenses caused by the affidavit, including reasonable attorney fees. Tex. R. Civ. P. 166a(h). See "Sanctions under TRCP 166a(h)," ch. 5-K, §7.8.

§5.6 Violation of limine order. The court may strike pleadings as a sanction for a violation of a motion in limine. See "Sanction," ch. 5-E, §8.2.

§5.7 Bad-faith abuse of judicial process. The court can impose sanctions on a party or attorney for bad-faith abuse of the judicial process under the court's inherent power. See "Inherent power," ch. 5-K, §2.2.

5-2. Summary of Sanctions

Sanctionable conduct		Authority	Who can be sanctioned	Available relief
1	Frivolous pleadings	Tex. Civ. Prac. & Rem. Code ch. 10	Attorney and party	Reasonable expenses (including attorney fees), penalty to be paid into court, and directive to perform or refrain from performing act.
2	Groundless pleadings	Tex. Civ. Prac. & Rem. Code §§9.011 to 9.014	Attorney and party	Striking of pleadings, dismissal of party and order to pay reasonable expenses (including attorney fees) incurred because of filing of pleadings.
3	Frivolous claim or regulatory action by state agency	Tex. Civ. Prac. & Rem. Code ch. 105	State agency	Fees, expenses, reasonable attorney fees, and all other costs allowed by law or rule.
4	Groundless pleadings brought in bad faith or for harassment	Tex. R. Civ. P. 13	Attorney and party	Sanctions under Tex. R. Civ. P. 215.2(b)—for list of sanctions under Tex. R. Civ. P. 215, see ch. 5-K, §7.1.
5	Groundless motion to disqualify or recuse	Tex. R. Civ. P. 18a(h)	Attorney and party	Reasonable attorney fees and expenses.
6	Failure to serve or deliver pleadings and motions	Tex. R. Civ. P. 21b	Attorney and party	Sanctions under Tex. R. Civ. P. 215.2(b)—for list of sanctions under Tex. R. Civ. P. 215, see ch. 5-K, §7.1.
7	Bad-faith affidavits in summary-judgment proceedings	Tex. R. Civ. P. 166a(h)	Attorney and party	Reasonable expenses, including attorney fees.
8	Discovery abuses	Tex. R. Civ. P. 191.3, 199.5(d), 215	Attorney and party	See ch. 5-K, §7.1.
9	Contempt of court	Tex. Gov't Code §21.002	Attorney and party	Fine or confinement. See ch. 5-K, §7.6.1.

5-2. Summary of Sanctions				
Sanctionable conduct		Authority	Who can be sanctioned	Available relief
10	Contempt of court or related misbehavior	Tex. Gov't Code §82.061	Attorney	Imprisonment or fine.
11	Any bad-faith conduct related to trial	Inherent power	Attorney and party	Sanction necessary to deter, alleviate, and counteract abuse.

§6. Conduct that does not justify sanctions

The rules do not permit sanctions in the following circumstances:

- A court cannot impose a sanction when there has been no conduct justifying sanctions in the matter before the court. *See, e.g.*, **Thompson v. Davis**, 901 S.W.2d 939, 940 (Tex.1995) (court could not extend sanction from earlier motion to modify child support to later motion to modify custody).
- A court cannot sanction a party for filing a motion for summary judgment claiming there is no fact issue about a disputed issue, unless the motion is groundless. **GTE Comms. Sys. v. Tanner**, 856 S.W.2d 725, 730 (Tex.1993).
- A court cannot sanction a party or its attorney for a groundless affidavit filed by the party but signed by a witness. *Id.*
- A court cannot impose sanctions under TRCP 13 for a plaintiff's failure to give the defendant the required notice of intention to file suit; the appropriate remedy is abatement, not dismissal. **Trimble v. Itz**, 898 S.W.2d 370, 374 (Tex.App.—San Antonio 1995), *writ denied*, 906 S.W.2d 481 (Tex.1995).
- A court cannot impose sanctions under TRCP 13 on a plaintiff for lacking sufficient proof of its claim. **Trimble**, 898 S.W.2d at 374.
- A court cannot strike all of a party's pleadings because the party filed an amended petition after the deadline in the pretrial order. **Granado v. Madsen**, 729 S.W.2d 866, 871 (Tex.App.—Houston [14th Dist.] 1987, writ ref'd n.r.e.).
- A court cannot impose sanctions under TRCP 13 for the continuation of a suit after it is shown to be baseless. **Karagounis v. Property Co. of Am.**, 970 S.W.2d 761, 765 (Tex.App.—Amarillo 1998, pet. denied).

§7. Types of sanctions

The choice of sanctions is within the discretion of the court. **Bodnow Corp. v. City of Hondo**, 721 S.W.2d 839, 840 (Tex.1986).

Note

The ultimate sanctions of dismissal or default are limited by constitutional considerations. When a trial court imposes the ultimate sanction, it is adjudicating the party's claims without regard to the merits. ***TransAmerican Nat. Gas Corp. v. Powell****, 811 S.W.2d 913, 918 (Tex.1991). A court may dismiss or default a party only when a party's actions justify the presumption that its claims or defenses lack merit Id.*

§7.1 Sanctions for discovery abuse.

1. Disallow discovery. The court may disallow further discovery of any kind or of a particular kind by the disobedient party. Tex. R. Civ. P. 215.2(b)(1).

2. Award costs & expenses. The court may charge all or part of the expenses of discovery, taxable court costs, or both, against the disobedient party or the party's attorney. Tex. R. Civ. P. 215.2(b)(2); *see* **Chrysler Corp. v. Blackmon**, 841 S.W.2d 844, 849 (Tex.1992); *see also* **Onstad v. Wright**, 54 S.W.3d 799, 804–05 (Tex.App.—Texarkana 2001, pet. denied) (P's attorney fined $32,198 to compensate D for mistrial due to violation of limine order). If the disobedient party is not able to pay, the trial court cannot enforce the sanctions by jailing the party until it pays. **Ex parte Dolenz** 893 S.W.2d 677, 680–81 (Tex.App.—Dallas 1995, orig. proceeding).

3. Establish facts. The court may order that the discovery matters the disobedient party did not produce will be deemed in favor of the other party. Tex. R. Civ. P. 215.2(b)(3); **Spohn Hosp. v. Mayer**, 104 S.W.3d 878, 881 n.2 (Tex.2003).

4. Limit or exclude evidence. The court may refuse to allow the disobedient party to support or oppose designated claims or defenses, or the court may prohibit the party from introducing designated matters into evidence. Tex. R. Civ. P. 215.2(b)(4). Whether the court should limit or exclude evidence that the disobedient party refused to produce or attempted to conceal depends on whether the evidence is beneficial or detrimental to the disobedient party's case. **CRSS, Inc. v. Montanari**, 902 S.W.2d 601, 610 (Tex.App.—Houston [1st Dist.] 1995, writ denied).

(1) Undisclosed evidence beneficial. When the evidence that the disobedient party did not disclose is beneficial to the disobedient party, the court may (1) prohibit the party from introducing it, (2) establish those facts against the party, and (3) prohibit the party from supporting or opposing designated claims or defenses. *See* Tex. R. Civ. P. 215.2(b)(3), (4); *see, e.g.*, **Adkins Servs. v. Tisdale Co.**, 56 S.W.3d 842, 843 (Tex.App.—Texarkana 2001, no pet.) (court excluded P's evidence because P did not answer interrogatories and requests for admissions); **CRSS**, 902 S.W.2d at 610 (court should have prevented disobedient party from offering witnesses and prohibited it from cross-examining opposing party's witnesses). See "Objecting to unidentified witness," ch. 6-E, §2.8.

(2) Undisclosed evidence detrimental. When the evidence that the disobedient party did not disclose is detrimental to the disobedient party, the court should permit the other party to introduce the evidence. As a sanction on the disobedient party, the court may prohibit it from supporting or opposing designated claims or defenses and may establish the facts in the concealed evidence against that party. Tex. R. Civ. P. 215.2(b)(3), (4); *see* **City of San Antonio v. Fulcher**, 749 S.W.2d 217, 220 (Tex.App.—San Antonio 1988, writ denied) (disobedient party should not be permitted to offer evidence that contradicts undisclosed evidence). See "Establish facts," ch. 5-K, §7.1.3.

5. Strike pleadings. The court may (1) strike all or part of the disobedient party's pleadings, (2) dismiss (with or without prejudice) all or part of the disobedient party's suit or proceedings, or (3) render a default judgment against the disobedient party. Tex. R. Civ. P. 215.2(b)(5). See "Death-penalty sanctions," ch. 5-K, §3.2.

6. Stay proceedings. The court may stay further proceedings until the order is obeyed. Tex. R. Civ. P. 215.2(b)(5).

7. Hold in contempt. Along with any of the sanctions in TRCP 215.2(b)(1) to (5), the court may treat a party's refusal to obey an order as contempt of court. Tex. R. Civ. P. 215.2(b)(6). However, the court cannot hold a party or person in contempt for refusing to submit to a physical or mental examination under TRCP 204. Tex. R. Civ. P. 215.2(b)(6).

8. Sanctions for refusal to comply with TRCP 204. When a party refuses to comply with an order under TRCP 204 requiring the party to appear or to produce another person for a physical or mental examination, the court may impose the sanctions listed in TRCP 215.2(b)(1) to (5) (see ch. 5-K, §7.1.1 through §7.1.6, above), unless the party shows that it was unable to appear or to produce the person for examination. Tex. R. Civ. P. 215.2(b)(7).

9. Attorney fees & reasonable expenses. Along with any of the sanctions in TRCP 215.2(b)(1) to (7), the court may require the offending party, the attorney advising the party, or both to pay reasonable expenses, including attorney fees, incurred because of the discovery abuse. Tex. R. Civ. P. 215.2(b)(8); *see* **CHRISTUS Health Gulf Coast v. Carswell**, 505 S.W.3d 528, 539–40 (Tex.2016); *see, e.g.*, **Porretto v. Texas Gen. Land Office**, 448 S.W.3d 393, 402–03 (Tex.2014) (no abuse of discretion to award attorney fees and expenses to P when D produced only some documents requested by P, D acknowledged that there were other responsive documents but that it would not search for them without further specification, and D did not respond to motion for sanctions). The party seeking attorney fees as sanctions must show some evidence that attorney fees were incurred and how those fees were caused by or resulted from the sanctionable conduct. **CHRISTUS**, 505 S.W.3d at 540; *cf.* **Nath v. Texas Children's Hosp.**, 576 S.W.3d 707, 709 (Tex.2019) (attorney fees as sanctions under CPRC ch. 10 and TRCP 13). See "Direct relationship," ch. 5-K, §3.1.1. The party must also show some evidence of the reasonableness of the fees. *Cf.* **Nath**, 576 S.W.3d at 709–10 (attorney fees as sanctions under CPRC ch. 10 and TRCP 13). See "Attorney fees from adverse party," ch. 1-H, §10; "Note," ch. 5-K, §7.2. The court should not impose sanctions under subsection (b)(8) if the court finds the noncompliance was substantially justified or if other circumstances make an award of expenses unjust. Tex. R. Civ. P. 215.2(b)(8).

10. Loss of privilege. When a party refuses to comply with discovery, the trial court may permit privileged information (noncore work product) to be produced as a sanction. **Occidental Chem. Corp. v. Banales**, 907 S.W.2d 488, 490 (Tex.1995).

11. Any sanctions under TRCP 215.2(b). If the court finds a party is abusing the discovery process in seeking, making, or resisting discovery, or if the court finds that any interrogatory or request for inspection or production is unreasonably frivolous, oppressive, or harassing or that a response or answer is unreasonably frivolous or made for the purpose of delay, then the court may, after notice and a hearing, impose any appropriate sanction authorized by TRCP 215.2(b)(1) to (5) and (b)(8). Tex. R. Civ. P. 215.3; *see* **Knoderer v. State Farm Lloyds**, 515 S.W.3d 21, 33 (Tex.App.—Texarkana 2017, pet. denied); *see, e.g.*, **Aguilar v. Trujillo**, 162 S.W.3d 839, 848 (Tex.App.—El Paso 2005, pet. denied) (sanctions striking Ps' experts were upheld because one P violated Tex. Disciplinary R. Prof'l Conduct 4.02(b) by contacting D's consulting expert without consent and by hiring him to be Ps' expert witness).

12. Deem admissions. For sanctions for failure to comply with a request for admissions, see "Challenging the response," ch. 6-H, §5.

13. Strike expert testimony. The trial court may strike the testimony of a disobedient party's expert witness. *See* **State Farm Fire & Cas. Co. v. Rodriguez**, 88 S.W.3d 313, 325–26 (Tex.App.—San Antonio 2002, pet. denied). As long as the exclusion of testimony impairs only the presentation of a party's case and does not prevent a trial on the merits, striking the testimony is within the court's discretion and is not a death-penalty sanction. *Id.* at 326.

14. Other sanctions that are "just." The trial court is not limited to the sanctions listed in TRCP 215.2(b). For example, even though TRCP 215.2(b) does not mention community service, the trial court can impose it as a sanction under the rule. *E.g.*, **Cap Rock Elec. Coop. v. Texas Utils. Elec. Co.**, 874 S.W.2d 92, 98 (Tex.App.—El Paso 1994, no writ) (court ordered corporate officers and directors who attempted to hide documents to perform 200 hours of community service); **Braden v. South Main Bank**, 837 S.W.2d 733, 742 (Tex.App.—Houston [14th Dist.] 1992, writ denied) (court ordered attorney who filed frivolous objections to interrogatories to perform ten hours of community service); *see* **Braden v. Downey**, 811 S.W.2d 922, 930 (Tex.1991) (order to perform community service must be deferred until it can be challenged on appeal); *see, e.g.*, **Hill & Griffith Co. v. Bryant**, 139 S.W.3d 688, 694 (Tex.App.—Tyler 2004, pet. denied) (court ordered attorney who attempted to hide documents to perform 50 hours of community service).

§7.2 Sanctions under CPRC §10.004. The following sanctions are available under CPRC §10.004: (1) ordering the party to perform or refrain from performing an act, (2) ordering a monetary penalty paid to the court, and (3) ordering the party to pay the other party the amount of reasonable expenses it incurred because of the filing of the frivolous pleading, including attorney fees. Tex. Civ. Prac. & Rem. Code §10.004(c). The party seeking attorney fees as sanctions must show some evidence that attorney fees were incurred and how those fees were caused by or resulted from the sanctionable conduct. **Nath v. Texas Children's Hosp.**, 576 S.W.3d 707, 709 (Tex.2019). The party must also show some evidence of the reasonableness of the fees. *E.g.*, *id.* at 709–10 (conclusory affidavits containing generalities about fees were insufficient to support sanctions award).

Note

The Texas Supreme Court has clarified the evidentiary requirements necessary to establish reasonable attorney fees in a fee-shifting situation. See ***Rohrmoos Venture v. UTSW DVA Healthcare, LLP***, *578 S.W.3d 469, 501–02 (Tex.2019). Although* ***Rohrmoos*** *did not involve sanctions, the evidentiary requirements established in that case apply in all fee-shifting situations. See* ***Nath***, *576 S.W.3d at 709–10. For further discussion of the requirements under* ***Rohrmoos***, *see "Attorney fees from adverse party," ch. 1-H, §10.*

§7.3 Sanctions under TRCP 13. Under TRCP 13, the court can impose any appropriate sanction in TRCP 215.2(b). **Bradt v. Sebek**, 14 S.W.3d 756, 762 (Tex.App.—Houston [1st Dist.] 2000, pet. denied). The rules leave the choice of sanctions to the trial court. See "Sanctions for discovery abuse," ch. 5-K, §7.1.

§7.4 Sanctions under CPRC §9.012. The following sanctions are available under CPRC §9.012: (1) striking the pleadings or the offending part of the pleadings, (2) dismissing the party, or (3) ordering the party to pay the other party the amount of reasonable expenses it incurred because of the filing of the pleading, including costs, reasonable attorney fees, witness fees, fees of experts, and deposition expenses. Tex. Civ. Prac. & Rem. Code §9.012(e).

§7.5 Sanctions under CPRC ch. 105.

1. Section 105.002. A court may award up to $1 million for fees, expenses, and reasonable attorney fees incurred by the party in defending a state agency's action, in addition to all other costs allowed by law or rule. Tex. Civ. Prac. & Rem. Code §105.002.

Note

Before the 2019 amendments to CPRC chapter 105, CPRC §105.002 did not include a cap on the sanctions award. See Tex. Civ. Prac. & Rem. Code §105.002 (pre-9-1-19 version). Thus, the $1 million limit on sanctions does not apply to claims filed before September 1, 2019. See Acts 2019, 86th Leg., R.S., ch. 504, §§7, 8, eff. Sept. 1, 2019.

2. Section 105.005. For regulatory actions taken on or after September 1, 2019, a court may award up to $1 million for reasonable attorney fees and costs incurred in defending against a frivolous regulatory action during a contested case under Gov't Code chapter 2001 and judicial review of the decision in the contested case, in addition to all other costs allowed by rule or law. Tex. Civ. Prac. & Rem. Code §105.005.

§7.6 Sanctions under Government Code. A court may impose fines and confinement or imprisonment as sanctions for a person held in contempt of court under Gov't Code §21.002 or §82.061. Contempt can be either civil or criminal; however, the distinction does not depend on whether the underlying case is civil or criminal but on the nature and purpose of the court's punishment. *See* **Ex parte Werblud**, 536 S.W.2d 542, 545–46 (Tex.1976) (civil contempt is to coerce person to obey court order; criminal contempt is to punish person for some act); **Cadle Co. v. Lobingier**, 50 S.W.3d 662, 667 (Tex.App.—Fort Worth 2001, pet. denied) (same). See "Types of contempt," **O'Connor's Texas Civil Appeals**, ch. 10-E, §2.1 (2020 ed.).

1. Section 21.002.

(1) Civil contempt. The court can fine a person or require a person to be confined in jail for civil contempt. See "Civil contempt," **O'Connor's Texas Civil Appeals**, ch. 10-E, §2.3.1 (2020 ed.).

(a) Fine. Gov't Code §21.002 does not limit the maximum fine a court can impose for civil contempt. **In re Reece**, 341 S.W.3d 360, 366 n.9 (Tex.2011); **Galtex Prop. Investors, Inc. v. City of Galveston**, 113 S.W.3d 922, 927 (Tex.App.—Houston [14th Dist.] 2003, no pet.); **Cadle Co.**, 50 S.W.3d at 667–68.

(b) Confinement. The court can require a person to be confined in jail for civil contempt until she complies with the court's order. Tex. Gov't Code §21.002(e). The maximum time a person can be confined for civil contempt is 18 months. Tex. Gov't Code §21.002(h)(2). The 18-month limit does not apply to contempt under Family Code chapter 157, when a person disobeys a court order to make child-support payments. Tex. Gov't Code §21.002(f).

(2) Criminal contempt. If the offensive conduct takes place in a county or district court, the court can impose a fine of up to $500 or order confinement for up to six months, or both. Tex. Gov't Code §21.002(b); **In re Long**, 984 S.W.2d 623, 625 (Tex.1999); **Cadle Co.**, 50 S.W.3d at 667–68; *see also* Tex. Gov't Code §21.002(c) (for contemptuous conduct in justice or municipal courts, the limit is $100 and three days' confinement). The maximum time a person can be confined for criminal contempt is 18 months, including three or more periods of confinement for contempt arising from the same matter that equal a total of 18 months. Tex. Gov't Code §21.002(h)(1). See "Criminal contempt," **O'Connor's Texas Civil Appeals**, ch. 10-E, §2.3.2 (2020 ed.).

2. Section 82.061. Gov't Code §82.061 does not provide limits for monetary fines or imprisonment for contempt. However, under Gov't Code §21.002, an attorney cannot be confined for contempt for longer than 18 months. *See* Tex. Gov't Code §21.002(h) ("notwithstanding any other law," person cannot be confined for contempt for more than 18 months).

§7.7 Sanctions under TRCP 18a(h). Under TRCP 18a(h), a judge who hears a motion to disqualify or recuse that is groundless or clearly brought for unnecessary delay can impose sanctions requiring the party who filed the motion, her attorney, or both to pay the attorney fees and expenses of the other parties. Tex. R. Civ. P. 18a(h).

§7.8 Sanctions under TRCP 166a(h). In a summary-judgment proceeding, the court can impose sanctions requiring a party to pay the other party's reasonable expenses, including reasonable attorney fees, caused by an affidavit made in bad faith or for the purpose of delay. Tex. R. Civ. P. 166a(h); **Ramirez v. Encore Wire Corp.**, 196 S.W.3d 469, 476 (Tex.App.—Dallas 2006, no pet.). The court can also find any offending party or attorney guilty of contempt. Tex. R. Civ. P. 166a(h); **Ramirez**, 196 S.W.3d at 476.

§7.9 Sanctions under TRCP 193.6. Under TRCP 193.6, a party who does not timely make, amend, or supplement a discovery response, including a required disclosure, or identify a witness cannot introduce the material into evidence or the testimony of the witness unless the court finds there was good cause for the failure and that admitting the material or testimony will not unfairly surprise or prejudice the other parties. Tex. R. Civ. P. 193.6(a). See "Timely," ch. 6-A, §16.3; "Exclude witness," ch. 6-E, §2.8.2. The sanction in Rule 193.6 is automatic; thus, no motion for sanctions or motion to compel is required to trigger it, and death-penalty sanctions are beyond its scope. *See* **In re M.J.M.**, 406 S.W.3d 292, 299 (Tex.App.—San Antonio 2013, no pet.); **White v. Perez**, No. 2-09-251-CV, 2010 WL 87469 (Tex.App.—Fort Worth 2010, pet. denied) (memo op.; 1-7-10); *see also* **Alvarado v. Farah Mfg. Co.**, 830 S.W.2d 911, 914 (Tex.1992) (sole sanction in rule is exclusion of evidence; applying former TRCP 215(5), now TRCP 193.6).

§7.10 Sanctions for violations of pretrial orders. A trial court can impose just and appropriate sanctions for violations of its pretrial orders. **Taylor v. Taylor**, 254 S.W.3d 527, 532 (Tex.App.—Houston [1st Dist.] 2008, no pet.); *see* **Koslow's v. Mackie**, 796 S.W.2d 700, 703–04 & n.1 (Tex.1990). See "Sanctions," ch. 5-A, §7.

§7.11 Improper sanctions. There are limits to the types of sanctions a trial court may impose, even when the conduct justifies sanctions.

1. Prohibit access to court. A trial court cannot sanction a party by prohibiting it from filing pleadings or motions. *See* **Glass v. Glass**, 826 S.W.2d 683, 686–87 (Tex.App.—Texarkana 1992, writ denied), *overruled on other grounds*, **Nath v. Texas Children's Hosp.**, 576 S.W.3d 707 (Tex.2019); **Kahn v. Garcia**, 816 S.W.2d 131, 133–34 (Tex.App.—Houston [1st Dist.] 1991, orig. proceeding); *see also* Tex. Const. art. 1, §13 (open-courts provision). *But cf.* Tex. Civ. Prac. & Rem. Code §11.101(a) (court may prohibit pro se litigant from filing suit without permission of local administrative judge if court determines, after notice and hearing, that the person is a vexatious litigant). Such a prohibition denies the party the means to communicate with the trial court. **Kahn**, 816 S.W.2d at 133.

2. Prevent review. A trial court cannot sanction a party by striking post-trial motions, thus foreclosing the appeal. **Lehtonen v. Clarke**, 784 S.W.2d 945, 946–47 (Tex.App.—Houston [14th Dist.] 1990, writ denied). TRAP 42.3 does not authorize an appellate court to dismiss a party's appeal as punishment. *See* **O'Connor v. Sam Houston Med. Hosp., Inc.**, 807 S.W.2d 574, 576 (Tex.1991) (applying former TRAP 60(a)).

3. Dismiss separate lawsuit. A trial court cannot dismiss a separate lawsuit as a discovery sanction. **McKellar Dev. Grp. v. Fairbank**, 827 S.W.2d 579, 581 (Tex.App.—San Antonio 1992, no writ).

4. Sanctions after special exceptions. A trial court cannot impose a monetary sanction for refusal to amend pleadings after special exceptions are sustained. **D.A. Buckner Constr., Inc. v. Hobson**, 793 S.W.2d 74, 75–76 (Tex.App.—Houston [14th Dist.] 1990, orig. proceeding). When special exceptions are sustained, the party can either amend the pleadings or refuse to amend and test the validity of the court's ruling. *Id.* at 75. See "Special Exceptions—Challenging the Pleadings," ch. 3-G, §1 et seq.

5. Security for costs. A trial court cannot require a party to post a specific amount of a bond as security for the suit as a sanction. **Johnson v. Smith**, 857 S.W.2d 612, 615–16 (Tex.App.—Houston [1st Dist.] 1993, orig. proceeding).

6. Charity work by nonparty. A trial court cannot require a nonparty to perform indigent medical care as a sanction. **Pope v. Davidson**, 849 S.W.2d 916, 920 (Tex.App.—Houston [14th Dist.] 1993, orig. proceeding). Contempt is the only sanction that a court may impose on a nonparty. See "Nonparty," ch. 5-K, §4.4.

7. Arbitrary fine under TRCP 215.3. Under TRCP 215.3, a trial court cannot impose an arbitrary monetary fine on a party for discovery abuse. *E.g.*, **Ford Motor Co. v. Tyson**, 943 S.W.2d 527, 532–33 (Tex.App.—Dallas 1997, orig. proceeding) (fine of $10 million set aside); **Owens-Corning Fiberglas Corp. v. Caldwell**, 807 S.W.2d 413, 415–16

(Tex.App.—Houston [1st Dist.] 1991, orig. proceeding) (fine of $2.3 million set aside). A sanction under TRCP 215.3 must be compensatory or remedial; an arbitrary fine cannot be imposed solely for punishment. **Ford Motor**, 943 S.W.2d at 533. Monetary sanctions under TRCP 215.3 must be related to the expenses caused by the abuse. **Clone Component Distribs. v. State**, 819 S.W.2d 593, 597 (Tex.App.—Dallas 1991, no writ) (reversed $50,000 fine). A fine for discovery abuse is arbitrary if it is unrestrained by law or statute and unrelated to any damages or expenses incurred by the injured party. **Ford Motor**, 943 S.W.2d at 534. Arbitrariness is a characteristic of a substantive due-process violation. *Id.*

8. Arbitrary amount for expenses. When a court awards expenses under TRCP 215.2(b)(2) or awards expenses and attorney fees under TRCP 215.2(b)(8), the amount awarded cannot be arbitrary; the amount must be related to the harm suffered by the other party. **Hanley v. Hanley**, 813 S.W.2d 511, 522 (Tex.App.—Dallas 1991, no writ); *see* **CHRISTUS Health Gulf Coast v. Carswell**, 505 S.W.3d 528, 540 (Tex.2016); *see, e.g.,* **Kugle v. DaimlerChrysler Corp.**, 88 S.W.3d 355, 364–65 (Tex.App.—San Antonio 2002, pet. denied) (monetary sanction of $865,000 assessed against P's attorneys was upheld as cost for defense of fraudulent personal-injury suit).

9. Discovery of attorney notes. The privilege for core work product, which relates to an attorney's thought processes, is absolute, and the trial court cannot order production of core work product as a sanction. **Occidental Chem. Corp. v. Banales**, 907 S.W.2d 488, 490 (Tex.1995). The court can order noncore work product to be produced as a sanction. *See id.*

10. Trial setting. An early trial setting is not an appropriate sanction for discovery abuse. **Arkla, Inc. v. Harris**, 846 S.W.2d 623, 629 (Tex.App.—Houston [14th Dist.] 1993, orig. proceeding).

11. Penalty paid to litigant. When a statute authorizes a monetary penalty as a sanction, the trial court cannot require a party to pay the penalty into the court registry for the other party's benefit. **Sterling v. Alexander**, 99 S.W.3d 793, 799–800 (Tex.App.—Houston [14th Dist.] 2003, pet. denied).

12. Death-penalty sanctions. Sanctions that terminate the lawsuit are proper only under certain conditions. See "Death-penalty sanctions," ch. 5-K, §3.2.

§8. Motion for sanctions

§8.1 On court's initiative. A court may impose sanctions under CPRC chapter 10, TRCP 13, or TRCP 191.3 on its own initiative without a motion. *See* Tex. Civ. Prac. & Rem. Code §10.002(b); Tex. R. Civ. P. 13, 191.3(e); **Koslow's v. Mackie**, 796 S.W.2d 700, 704 (Tex.1990). The sanctioned party is entitled to notice and a hearing. **Aldine ISD v. Baty**, 946 S.W.2d 851, 852 (Tex.App.—Houston [14th Dist.] 1997, no writ) (sanctions under TRCP 13); *see* Tex. Civ. Prac. & Rem. Code §10.002(b) (person to be sanctioned under §10.001 must receive show-cause hearing), §10.003 (court must provide notice and reasonable opportunity to respond). The trial court cannot impose monetary sanctions on its own initiative after a voluntary dismissal or settlement unless the court issued the show-cause order before the dismissal or settlement. Tex. Civ. Prac. & Rem. Code §10.004(e); **In re Bennett**, 960 S.W.2d 35, 40 n.5 (Tex.1997); **Scott & White Mem'l Hosp. v. Schexnider**, 940 S.W.2d 594, 596 n.1 (Tex.1996).

§8.2 By party.

1. Identify sanctionable conduct. The motion for sanctions must identify the specific conduct that deserves sanction. Because the trial court may consider other matters that have occurred in the litigation, the motion for sanctions may include other, earlier conduct that warrants sanctions. *See* **Downer v. Aquamarine Operators, Inc.**, 701 S.W.2d 238, 241 (Tex.1985); **Medical Prot. Co. v. Glanz**, 721 S.W.2d 382, 388 (Tex.App.—Corpus Christi 1986, writ ref'd).

2. Identify authority for sanction. The motion for sanctions must identify the specific statute, rule, or order the party violated. A court cannot grant sanctions under a statute or rule that is not identified in the motion. *E.g.,* **Ball v. Rao**, 48 S.W.3d 332, 338 (Tex.App.—Fort Worth 2001, pet. denied) (court could not grant sanctions under CPRC §9.011 because statute was not included as ground for sanctions in motion).

3. Request sanction. The movant should identify the sanction it wants the court to impose (e.g., monetary sanctions, default, dismissal) and argue that the sanction (1) has a direct relationship to the offensive conduct and (2) is not

excessive. A party should not ask for a death-penalty sanction in its first motion for sanctions unless it is apparent that a lesser sanction will not promote compliance. **GTE Comms. Sys. v. Tanner**, 856 S.W.2d 725, 729 (Tex.1993); **Sanchez v. Brownsville Sports Ctr., Inc.**, 51 S.W.3d 643, 659 (Tex.App.—Corpus Christi 2001, pet. granted, judgm't vacated w.r.m.). See "Standards for imposing sanctions," ch. 5-K, §3.

4. Be verified. If the motion for sanctions contains evidence that does not appear in the court's record, the motion should be verified and have affidavits attached as necessary. *See* Tex. R. Civ. P. 215.6.

5. Deadline to file.

(1) Pretrial conduct. To be entitled to sanctions based on pretrial conduct, the party must secure a pretrial hearing and ruling on that conduct, or it waives any claim for sanctions based on that conduct. **Remington Arms Co. v. Caldwell**, 850 S.W.2d 167, 170 (Tex.1993); **Finlay v. Olive**, 77 S.W.3d 520, 526 (Tex.App.—Houston [1st Dist.] 2002, no pet.). However, if the grounds for pretrial sanctions are not known until after the trial has begun, the claim for sanctions is not waived. **Remington Arms**, 850 S.W.2d at 170.

(2) Trial conduct. To be entitled to sanctions based on trial conduct, the party must file a motion for sanctions before the court loses plenary power over its judgment. **Scott & White Mem'l Hosp. v. Schexnider**, 940 S.W.2d 594, 596 (Tex.1996); *see* **Unifund CCR Partners v. Villa**, 299 S.W.3d 92, 95–96 (Tex.2009); **Crites v. Collins**, 284 S.W.3d 839, 843 (Tex.2009); *see also* **Wythe II Corp. v. Stone**, 342 S.W.3d 96, 109–10 (Tex.App.—Beaumont 2011, pet. denied) (party must file motion for sanctions under TRCP 166a(h) based on summary-judgment affidavit filed in bad faith or brought solely for delay before court loses plenary power). See "Postjudgment motions & finality," ch. 9-C, §6.4.1. Neither the filing of a nonsuit nor the removal of a case to federal court deprives the trial court of jurisdiction to impose sanctions for conduct before the nonsuit or removal. **In re Bennett**, 960 S.W.2d 35, 38–40 (Tex.1997); *see* **Crites**, 284 S.W.3d at 843 (court has power to impose sanctions after a nonsuit as long as motion is filed before court loses plenary power). But when sanctions are imposed after removal to federal court, the sanctions cannot affect the merits of the litigation pending in federal court. **In re Bennett**, 960 S.W.2d at 39–40.

§8.3 Proper court. Ordinarily, a motion for sanctions should be filed in the court where the action is pending. **Mantri v. Bergman**, 153 S.W.3d 715, 718 (Tex.App.—Dallas 2005, pet. denied) (sanctions under CPRC ch. 10). When sanctions are sought against a nonparty who refuses to answer questions at a deposition, the motion should be filed in the court in the district where the deposition is being taken. Tex. R. Civ. P. 215.1(a); **Latham v. Thornton**, 806 S.W.2d 347, 349–50 (Tex.App.—Fort Worth 1991, orig. proceeding).

§9. Response

When a party is notified that a motion for sanctions is pending against it, the party should take the following steps.

§9.1 File response. The party charged with sanctionable conduct should file a response to the motion for sanctions and inform the trial court, under oath, why sanctions should not be imposed. The response should make the following arguments, as appropriate: (1) no sanctionable conduct occurred, (2) there is no relationship between the offensive conduct and the sanction requested, (3) the sanction requested is excessive and, if death-penalty sanctions are requested, the court did not impose a lesser sanction first, and (4) the party's claims or defenses in the underlying suit are meritorious. See "Standards for imposing sanctions," ch. 5-K, §3; **O'Connor's Texas Civil Forms**, FORMS 5K:2, 5K:4 (2020 ed.). The party should attach as many affidavits as necessary.

§9.2 Ask for hearing. The party charged with sanctionable conduct should follow the procedure in the local rules for securing a hearing to present evidence.

§10. Hearing

§10.1 Necessity of hearing. CPRC §§9.012(c) and 10.003, TRCP 13, 21b, 215.2(b), and 215.3, and due process all require the court to hold a hearing before imposing sanctions. *See* **Horizon Health Corp. v. Acadia Healthcare Co.**, 520 S.W.3d 848, 884 (Tex.2017) (discovery sanctions); **R.M. Dudley Constr. Co. v. Dawson**, 258 S.W.3d 694, 709–10 (Tex.App.—Waco 2008, pet. denied) (sanctions under CPRC ch. 10). A court cannot strike a party's pleadings, render a default judgment,

or impose monetary sanctions without giving the party an opportunity to be heard. *See* **Sears, Roebuck & Co. v. Hollingsworth**, 293 S.W.2d 639, 642 (Tex.1956) (sanctions for disregarding subpoena were reversed because there was no notice or hearing); **Tidrow v. Roth**, 189 S.W.3d 408, 413 (Tex.App.—Dallas 2006, no pet.) (sanctions for discovery abuse were reversed because there was no notice or hearing).

1. Oral hearing. In most cases, the court should conduct an oral hearing to receive evidence on the allegation that sanctions are warranted. *See, e.g.,* **Bedding Component Manufactors, Ltd. v. Royal Sleep Prods.**, 108 S.W.3d 563, 564 (Tex.App.—Dallas 2003, no pet.) (sanctions under TRCP 13 were reversed because there was no hearing to present evidence); **Bisby v. Dow Chem. Co.**, 931 S.W.2d 18, 21 (Tex.App.—Houston [1st Dist.] 1996, no writ) (same). At an oral hearing, the trial court must permit the party to introduce evidence before imposing sanctions. **Davila v. World Car Five Star**, 75 S.W.3d 537, 544 (Tex.App.—San Antonio 2002, no pet.).

2. Hearing by submission. The court is not required to hold an oral hearing; sanctions can be resolved by a hearing on submission. *See, e.g.,* **Cire v. Cummings**, 134 S.W.3d 835, 843–44 (Tex.2004) (nothing in TRCP 215.3 requires an oral hearing).

§10.2 Necessity of adequate notice. Due process and various provisions in the CPRC and TRCPs require the court to give the party notice of the hearing on sanctions. *See* Tex. Civ. Prac. & Rem. Code §§9.012(c), 10.003; Tex. R. Civ. P. 13, 21b, 215.2(b), 215.3; **Horizon Health Corp. v. Acadia Healthcare Co.**, 520 S.W.3d 848, 884 (Tex.2017) (discovery sanctions); **Low v. Henry**, 221 S.W.3d 609, 618 (Tex.2007); **Cire v. Cummings**, 134 S.W.3d 835, 843 (Tex.2004). The notice of the hearing on sanctions must be adequate. **Plano S&L Ass'n v. Slavin**, 721 S.W.2d 282, 284 (Tex.1986). Oral notice is not adequate; the party must be given written notice of the hearing. **In re Acceptance Ins.**, 33 S.W.3d 443, 451 (Tex.App.—Fort Worth 2000, orig. proceeding). One day's notice of the hearing is not adequate. **Plano S&L**, 721 S.W.2d at 284. If the party does not receive adequate notice, the party should bring the lack of adequate notice to the trial court's attention at the hearing, object to the hearing going forward, and move for a continuance. **Low**, 221 S.W.3d at 618. If the party does not make a timely objection, it waives error. *See* **Low**, 221 S.W.3d at 618.

§10.3 Make a record. The party charged with sanctionable conduct should treat the hearing on sanctions as a hearing for evidence, not just for argument. The party should make sure the court reporter is present and transcribes the entire hearing, including arguments. Once the hearing starts, the attorneys and parties should be sworn and should formally offer evidence on the issue of sanctions.

§10.4 Burden.

1. On court's initiative. When the court sets a matter for sanctions on its own initiative, the party seeking to avoid sanctions must prove that sanctions should not be imposed. *See* Tex. Civ. Prac. & Rem. Code §10.002(b) (show-cause hearing).

2. On party's motion. At a hearing on sanctions, the party that filed the motion for sanctions must first prove the allegations in its motion. **GTE Comms. Sys. v. Tanner**, 856 S.W.2d 725, 729 (Tex.1993). Once the movant proves that the other party's conduct justifies sanctions, the other party must produce evidence demonstrating why sanctions should not be imposed.

Note

Under TRCP 13, the trial court begins with the presumption that all pleadings are filed in good faith. ***GTE****, 856 S.W.2d at 731;* ***Trimble v. Itz****, 898 S.W.2d 370, 373 (Tex.App.—San Antonio 1995), writ denied, 906 S.W.2d 481 (Tex.1995). Thus, the party seeking sanctions has the burden to overcome this presumption.* ***GTE****, 856 S.W.2d at 731. Although CPRC §10.001 does not have the same presumption, courts have extended the good-faith presumption found in TRCP 13 to §10.001 sanctions claims.* ***Thottumkal v. McDougal****, 251 S.W.3d 715, 718 (Tex.App.—Houston [14th Dist.] 2008, pet. denied); see* ***Low v. Henry****, 221 S.W.3d 609, 614 (Tex.2007);* ***Save Our Springs Alliance, Inc. v. Lazy Nine MUD****, 198 S.W.3d 300, 321 (Tex.App.—Texarkana 2006, pet. denied).*

3. Burden on party to be sanctioned. To avoid sanctions, the party or attorney charged with sanctionable conduct should prove the allegations in its response. See "File response," ch. 5-K, §9.1.

§10.5 Entire case. In imposing sanctions, the trial court may consider all matters that have occurred in the litigation; the court is not limited to considering the specific violation. **Downer v. Aquamarine Operators, Inc.**, 701 S.W.2d 238, 241 (Tex.1985); **Medical Prot. Co. v. Glanz**, 721 S.W.2d 382, 388 (Tex.App.—Corpus Christi 1986, writ ref'd).

§10.6 Violations by both parties. The trial court is justified in refusing to impose sanctions if both sides are equally guilty. *See* **Larson v. H.E. Butt Grocery Co.**, 769 S.W.2d 694, 695–96 (Tex.App.—Corpus Christi 1989, writ denied) (record showed lack of candor and attempts at gamesmanship on both sides).

§11. Order for sanctions

The court may impose sanctions on a person who abused the discovery process or signed a pleading in violation of CPRC §9.011, CPRC §10.001, or TRCP 13. The court's discretion is limited by a requirement that the sanction be "just." Tex. R. Civ. P. 215.2(b); **Spohn Hosp. v. Mayer**, 104 S.W.3d 878, 882 (Tex.2003); **TransAmerican Nat. Gas Corp. v. Powell**, 811 S.W.2d 913, 917 (Tex.1991). See **O'Connor's Texas Civil Forms**, FORM 5K:5 (2020 ed.).

§11.1 Order for discovery sanctions.

1. Sanctions. The court may impose sanctions on the party, the attorney, both the party and the attorney, or a nonparty. See "Persons who may be sanctioned," ch. 5-K, §4.

2. Attorney fees & costs. The court may award attorney fees and costs to the prevailing party. See "Attorney fees & reasonable expenses," ch. 5-K, §7.1.9.

3. Explanation. The court must explain the reason for imposing sanctions by stating the following: (1) a description of the sanctionable conduct, (2) the relationship between the conduct and the sanctions, and (3) the necessity for the severity of the sanctions. *See* **CHRISTUS Health Gulf Coast v. Carswell**, 505 S.W.3d 528, 540 (Tex.2016); **Spohn Hosp. v. Mayer**, 104 S.W.3d 878, 882 (Tex.2003). If death-penalty sanctions are imposed, the court must also (1) state that a lesser sanction was imposed without effect, or provide a reasoned explanation why a lesser sanction was not imposed and why the death-penalty sanction was appropriate, and (2) state that the party's conduct justifies the presumption that its claims or defenses lack merit. *See* **Cire v. Cummings**, 134 S.W.3d 835, 842 (Tex.2004); **GTE Comms. Sys. v. Tanner**, 856 S.W.2d 725, 729–30 (Tex.1993). See "Standards for imposing sanctions," ch. 5-K, §3. The court is not required to list each possible lesser sanction in its order and explain why each would be ineffective. **Cire**, 134 S.W.3d at 842.

4. Separate findings. When judgment is rendered as a sanction for discovery abuse, the court should file separate findings of fact. See "After hearing on sanctions under TRCP 215," ch. 10-E, §2.2.1.

§11.2 Order under CPRC ch. 10.

1. Sanctions. The court may impose sanctions on the attorney, the party, or both. Tex. Civ. Prac. & Rem. Code §10.004(a). The sanction is limited to an amount sufficient to deter repetition of the conduct by others. Tex. Civ. Prac. & Rem. Code §10.004(b); **University of Tex. at Arlington v. Bishop**, 997 S.W.2d 350, 357 (Tex.App.—Fort Worth 1999, pet. denied). When a party is represented by an attorney, the court cannot impose monetary sanctions on the party for violating CPRC §10.001(2) (pleadings not supported by existing law or argument to extend, modify, or reverse existing law). Tex. Civ. Prac. & Rem. Code §10.004(d); *see* **Nath v. Texas Children's Hosp.**, 446 S.W.3d 355, 362 (Tex.2014). If a party appears pro se, the court may impose sanctions on the party for violating CPRC §10.001(2). *See* Tex. Civ. Prac. & Rem. Code §10.004(d).

2. Attorney fees & costs. The court may award the prevailing party attorney fees and costs for inconvenience, harassment, and out-of-pocket expenses incurred by the party or caused by the litigation. Tex. Civ. Prac. & Rem. Code §§10.002(c), 10.004(c)(3). See "Sanctions under CPRC §10.004," ch. 5-K, §7.2.

3. Explanation. When the court imposes sanctions, it must include in the order a description of the conduct that violated CPRC §10.001 and an explanation of the basis for the sanctions imposed. Tex. Civ. Prac. & Rem. Code §10.005; **Bishop**, 997 S.W.2d at 355. When imposing a monetary penalty, the court should explain how it determined the amount of sanctions, particularly when those sanctions are severe. **Low v. Henry**, 221 S.W.3d 609, 620–21 (Tex.2007); *see* **Nath**, 446 S.W.3d at 372. See "Necessary severity," ch. 5-K, §3.1.2.

4. Not separate findings. The court should not file separate findings of fact to support sanctions under CPRC chapter 10. See "Groundless pleadings," ch. 10-E, §2.2.2(3).

Note

Some courts have held that, while it is error for the trial court to not describe the sanctionable conduct in the sanctions order, the error is harmless when the information can be supplied by the court's findings of fact. See ***State Office of Risk Mgmt. v. Foutz****, 279 S.W.3d 826, 836–37 (Tex.App.—Eastland 2009, no pet.);* ***Bishop****, 997 S.W.2d at 355–56. But cf.* ***Friedman & Assocs. v. Beltline Rd., Ltd.****, 861 S.W.2d 1, 2–3 (Tex.App.—Dallas 1993, writ dism'd) (court's failure to state particulars of good cause in sanctions order under TRCP 13 renders order unenforceable).*

§11.3 Order under TRCP 13.

1. Sanctions. The court may impose sanctions on the attorney, the party, or both. Tex. R. Civ. P. 13. The trial court has the discretion to determine the severity of the sanctions, but the rule requires the court to impose punishment for a violation. *See id.*

2. Attorney fees & costs. The court may award attorney fees and costs to the prevailing party. See "Attorney fees & reasonable expenses," ch. 5-K, §7.1.9.

3. Explanation. The order must specifically identify the sanctionable conduct and state good cause for imposing sanctions. *See* Tex. R. Civ. P. 13.

Practice Tip

Make an objection on the record if the order does not identify the sanctionable conduct or does not make a statement of good cause. See ***Jimenez v. Transwestern Prop. Co.****, 999 S.W.2d 125, 130–31 (Tex.App.—Houston [14th Dist.] 1999, no pet.). If no objection is made, the error is waived.* ***Appleton v. Appleton****, 76 S.W.3d 78, 87 (Tex.App.—Houston [14th Dist.] 2002, no pet.);* ***Texas-Ohio Gas, Inc. v. Mecom****, 28 S.W.3d 129, 135–36 (Tex.App.—Texarkana 2000, no pet.); see also* ***Thomas v. Thomas****, 917 S.W.2d 425, 433 (Tex.App.—Waco 1996, no writ) (D preserved error by raising sanctions issue in motion for new trial when D did not have opportunity to object before sanctions order).*

(1) Identify sanctionable conduct. The order must identify the specific acts or omissions on which the court based the sanctions. **Jimenez**, 999 S.W.2d at 130; **Luxenberg v. Marshall**, 835 S.W.2d 136, 140–41 (Tex.App.—Dallas 1992, orig. proceeding); *e.g.*, **Tarrant Cty. v. Chancey**, 942 S.W.2d 151, 155 (Tex.App.—Fort Worth 1997, no writ) (statement that pleading was filed to harass and cause unnecessary delays was too general). When imposing death-penalty sanctions, the court should explain why it imposed the sanction on the party and not just the attorney. *See* **TransAmerican Nat. Gas Corp. v. Powell**, 811 S.W.2d 913, 917 (Tex.1991).

(2) State good cause. Sanctions can be imposed only for good cause. Tex. R. Civ. P. 13; **Daniel v. Webb**, 110 S.W.3d 708, 711–12 (Tex.App.—Amarillo 2003, no pet.); **Murphy v. Friendswood Dev. Co.**, 965 S.W.2d 708, 709 (Tex.App.—Houston [1st Dist.] 1998, no pet.). Thus, the court must include a statement of good cause in the order to support the imposition of sanctions. Tex. R. Civ. P. 13; **Tarrant Restoration v. TX Arlington Oaks Apts., Ltd.**, 225 S.W.3d 721, 733 (Tex.App.—Dallas 2007, pet. dism'd); **Chancey**, 942 S.W.2d at 155; **Kahn v. Garcia**, 816 S.W.2d 131, 133 (Tex.App.—Houston [1st Dist.] 1991, orig. proceeding).

4. Not separate findings. The court should not file separate findings of fact to support sanctions under TRCP 13. See "Groundless pleadings," ch. 10-E, §2.2.2(3).

Note

Some courts have held that, while it is error for the trial court to not include the particulars of good cause (i.e., the specific acts or omissions on which the sanctions are based) in the sanctions order, the error is harmless when the information can be supplied by the court's findings of fact. See ***Keith v. Keith****, 221 S.W.3d 156, 165 (Tex.App.—Houston [1st Dist.] 2006, no pet.);* ***Office of the Atty. Gen. v. De Leon****, No. 04-13-00501-CV, 2014 WL 7441464 (Tex.App.—San Antonio 2014, no pet.) (memo op.; 12-31-14). But see* ***Friedman & Assocs. v. Beltline Rd., Ltd.****, 861 S.W.2d 1, 2–3 (Tex.App.—Dallas 1993, writ dism'd) (court's failure to state particulars of good cause in order renders order unenforceable).*

§11.4 Order under CPRC ch. 9.

1. Withdraw or amend. Before imposing sanctions, the court must give the attorney or party 90 days to withdraw or amend the offending pleadings. Tex. Civ. Prac. & Rem. Code §9.012(c), (d); **Elkins v. Stotts-Brown**, 103 S.W.3d 664, 668 (Tex.App.—Dallas 2003, no pet.).

2. Sanctions. The court may impose sanctions on the attorney, the party, or both. Tex. Civ. Prac. & Rem. Code §9.012(c). The court may strike the pleadings or dismiss the offending party. Tex. Civ. Prac. & Rem. Code §9.012(e)(1), (e)(2).

3. Attorney fees & costs. The court may award the objecting party reasonable expenses incurred because of the filing, including attorney fees, witness fees, expert fees, and deposition expenses. Tex. Civ. Prac. & Rem. Code §9.012(e)(3). If the objecting party has been sanctioned in the same matter, that party cannot be awarded costs and fees. Tex. Civ. Prac. & Rem. Code §9.012(f).

§12. Review

§12.1 Standard of review. Sanctions orders are reviewed for abuse of discretion. **Brewer v. Lennox Hearth Prods.**, 601 S.W.3d 704, 717 (Tex.2020); **Altesse Healthcare Solutions, Inc. v. Wilson**, 540 S.W.3d 570, 573 (Tex.2018); **In re National Lloyds Ins.**, 507 S.W.3d 219, 226 (Tex.2016); **Nath v. Texas Children's Hosp.**, 446 S.W.3d 355, 361 (Tex.2014); *see also* **Falk & Mayfield L.L.P. v. Molzan**, 974 S.W.2d 821, 827 (Tex.App.—Houston [14th Dist.] 1998, pet. denied) (degree of discretion for trial court is greater when sanctions are imposed for groundless pleadings rather than for discovery abuse). If the trial court made findings of fact to support the sanctions order, the appellate court should not treat the findings as findings of fact made under TRCP 296, which are reviewable under legal-sufficiency and factual-sufficiency standards. **IKB Indus. v. Pro-Line Corp.**, 938 S.W.2d 440, 442 (Tex.1997); **Chrysler Corp. v. Blackmon**, 841 S.W.2d 844, 852 (Tex.1992). The findings filed by the trial court after sanctions are merely to assist the appellate court in deciding whether the trial court abused its discretion. **Chrysler Corp.**, 841 S.W.2d at 852. The appellate court should not limit its review to the findings of fact; it must make an independent review of the entire record to determine whether the trial court abused its discretion. **American Flood Research, Inc. v. Jones**, 192 S.W.3d 581, 583 (Tex.2006).

§12.2 Method of review.

1. By appeal. A party is entitled to challenge the sanctions on appeal after a final judgment is rendered in the case. Tex. R. Civ. P. 215.1(d), 215.2(b)(8), 215.3. When a sanction can be appealed, mandamus is not appropriate. *See, e.g.*, **Street v. Second Ct. of Appeals**, 715 S.W.2d 638, 639 (Tex.1986) (sanction for attorney fees should be challenged on appeal); **Keller Indus. v. Blanton**, 804 S.W.2d 182, 186 (Tex.App.—Houston [14th Dist.] 1991, orig. proceeding) (sanctions for costs of out-of-state depositions should be challenged on appeal). Even when a case is settled or dismissed by a nonsuit, sanctions can be reviewed on appeal. *See* **Felderhoff v. Knauf**, 819 S.W.2d 110, 111 (Tex.1991) (appeal after nonsuit); **Braden v. South Main Bank**, 837 S.W.2d 733, 741 (Tex.App.—Houston [14th Dist.] 1992, writ denied) (appeal after settlement).

2. By mandamus. Ordinarily, sanctions are not reviewable by mandamus because the party has an adequate remedy by appeal. *See* **In re Casey**, 589 S.W.3d 850, 855 (Tex.2019); **Street**, 715 S.W.2d at 639. However, when the trial court imposes severe sanctions that effectively preclude a decision on the merits of a party's claims or have the effect of adjudicating all or a substantial part of the dispute, appellate review may be inadequate and mandamus review is

appropriate. **In re Garza**, 544 S.W.3d 836, 840 (Tex.2018); *see* **TransAmerican Nat. Gas Corp. v. Powell**, 811 S.W.2d 913, 920 (Tex.1991); *see, e.g.*, **In re Carnival Corp.**, 193 S.W.3d 229, 233 (Tex.App.—Houston [1st Dist.] 2006, orig. proceeding) (sanctions order precluded decision on merits because it entered judgment in favor of P on all liability issues; mandamus appropriate).

(1) Monetary sanction threatens litigation. When the trial court imposes monetary sanctions that threaten a party's ability or willingness to continue with the litigation so that an eventual appeal would not provide an adequate remedy, mandamus review is appropriate. *See* **Braden v. Downey**, 811 S.W.2d 922, 929 (Tex.1991); *see also* **In re Ford Motor Co.**, 988 S.W.2d 714, 723 (Tex.1998) (appeal is not adequate remedy when court imposes monetary penalty on a party's prospective exercise of its legal rights). In determining whether mandamus review is appropriate, the appellate court should focus on the effect of the monetary sanctions on the party's access to the courts and not on the intended purpose or specific amount of the sanctions. *See* **In re Casey**, 589 S.W.3d at 855–56; **In re Ford Motor Co.**, 988 S.W.2d at 722. In most situations, the trial court can prevent mandamus review by either (1) providing that the sanctions are payable only on a date that coincides with or follows the rendition of a final order terminating the litigation or (2) making express written findings after a prompt hearing on why the monetary sanctions do not have a preclusive effect. **In re Casey**, 589 S.W.3d at 855; **Braden**, 811 S.W.2d at 929; **Prime Grp. v. O'Neill**, 848 S.W.2d 376, 379 (Tex.App.—Houston [14th Dist.] 1993, orig. proceeding); **Susman Godfrey, L.L.P. v. Marshall**, 832 S.W.2d 105, 108 (Tex.App.—Dallas 1992, orig. proceeding).

(2) Community service before judgment. When the trial court orders a party or attorney to perform community service that must be completed before final judgment, mandamus review is appropriate. **Braden**, 811 S.W.2d at 930.

§12.3 Record. The record should include the order imposing sanctions, the motion for sanctions, the response, the findings of fact and conclusions of law (if filed), and a transcript of the hearing on the motion. If the trial court does not hear evidence and states that it bases its opinion on the papers on file and argument of counsel, the parties are not required to produce a reporter's record. **Otis Elevator Co. v. Parmelee**, 850 S.W.2d 179, 180–81 (Tex.1993).

§12.4 Lack of good-cause findings under TRCP 13. The courts of appeals disagree on the appropriate remedy when the sanctioned party objects to the lack of particularized findings of good cause that are required by TRCP 13. Some courts have reversed the sanctions order and rendered judgment that the order is unenforceable. *E.g.*, **Thomas v. Thomas**, 917 S.W.2d 425, 432–33 (Tex.App.—Waco 1996, no writ); **Friedman & Assocs. v. Beltline Rd., Ltd.**, 861 S.W.2d 1, 3 (Tex.App.—Dallas 1993, writ dism'd); *see, e.g.*, **Guerra v. L&F Distribs.**, 521 S.W.3d 878, 889 (Tex.App.—San Antonio 2017, no pet.). At least one court has held that it may abate the appeal and order the trial court to properly state the particulars of good cause. *E.g.*, **Campos v. Ysleta Gen. Hosp., Inc.**, 879 S.W.2d 67, 70–71 (Tex.App.—El Paso 1994, writ denied); *see also* **Murphy v. Friendswood Dev. Co.**, 965 S.W.2d 708, 710 (Tex.App.—Houston [1st Dist.] 1998, no pet.) (abatement was not practical because successor judge, who had not observed sanctions hearing, was not in position to state particulars of good cause; case was remanded for new hearing).

L. Motion to Seal Court Records

§1. General

§1.1 Rule. Tex. R. Civ. P. 76a.

§1.2 Purpose. In response to a legislative directive, the Supreme Court adopted TRCP 76a to establish a system to control the sealing of court records. Tex. Gov't Code §22.010 (legislative directive); **General Tire, Inc. v. Kepple**, 970 S.W.2d 520, 523 & n.8 (Tex.1998); **Boardman v. Elm Block Dev. L.P.**, 872 S.W.2d 297, 298–99 (Tex.App.—Eastland 1994, no writ). Because TRCP 76a recognizes the public's right to have access to judicial records, the rule provides strict requirements for securing an order to seal court records. *See* **Boardman**, 872 S.W.2d at 299.

§1.3 Forms. O'Connor's Texas Civil Forms, FORMS 5L:1 et seq., 6A:10 (2020 ed.).

§2. What documents are "court records"

§2.1 Presumption of openness. All court records are presumed to be open to the general public and can be sealed only after all the requirements set out in TRCP 76a are satisfied. **General Tire, Inc. v. Kepple**, 970 S.W.2d 520, 523 (Tex.1998); **Burlington N. R.R. v. Southwestern Elec. Power Co.**, 905 S.W.2d 683, 684 (Tex.App.—Texarkana 1995, no writ).

§2.2 Documents that are court records. All documents that relate to a lawsuit, with few exceptions, are considered court records.

1. Court orders & opinions. Court orders and opinions are court records and cannot be sealed under any circumstances. Tex. R. Civ. P. 76a(1); **Fox v. Anonymous**, 869 S.W.2d 499, 503 (Tex.App.—San Antonio 1993, writ denied).

2. Filed documents. Generally, all documents filed with the court in connection with any civil matter are court records. Tex. R. Civ. P. 76a(2)(a); *e.g.*, **Cortez v. Johnston**, 378 S.W.3d 468, 472–73 (Tex.App.—Texarkana 2012, pet. denied) (motion to compel and for sanctions, which had attached as exhibits P's deposition and D's complaint with Judicial Conduct Commission, was court record); **McAfee, Inc. v. Weiss**, 336 S.W.3d 840, 843–44 (Tex.App.—Dallas 2011, pet. denied) (arbitration award was court record). The exceptions are listed in "Documents that are not court records," ch. 5-L, §2.3.

3. Filed settlement agreements. Settlement agreements filed with the court are considered court records. Tex. R. Civ. P. 76a(2)(a). Unfiled settlement agreements are court records only if they seek to restrict disclosure of information concerning matters that have a probable adverse effect on the general public health or safety, the administration of public office, or the operation of government. Tex. R. Civ. P. 76a(2)(b).

4. Discovery products.

(1) Filed discovery. Filed discovery products are court records. Tex. R. Civ. P. 76a(2)(a).

(2) Unfiled discovery. TRCP 76a does not presume that unfiled discovery products are court records. **Eli Lilly & Co. v. Biffle**, 868 S.W.2d 806, 808 (Tex.App.—Dallas 1993, no writ). Unfiled discovery products are court records only if they concern matters that have a probable adverse effect on the general public health or safety, the administration of public office, or the operation of government. Tex. R. Civ. P. 76a(2)(c); **General Tire, Inc. v. Kepple**, 970 S.W.2d 520, 523 (Tex.1998); *e.g.*, **Cortez**, 378 S.W.3d at 475 (trial court did not abuse discretion in determining that documents, including responses to requests for disclosure, were court records; documents contained allegations that could affect reputations of four judges and questioned operations of certain district courts). If a court attempts to limit the disclosure or distribution of unfiled discovery (e.g., by a protective order), it must comply with TRCP 76a. *See* **Chandler v. Hyundai Motor Co.**, 829 S.W.2d 774, 774–75 (Tex.1992).

§2.3 Documents that are not court records. TRCP 76a does not apply to documents that are not court records as defined in TRCP 76a(2). *See* **General Tire, Inc. v. Kepple**, 970 S.W.2d 520, 524 (Tex.1998); **Wood v. James R. Moriarty, P.C.**, 940 S.W.2d 359, 361 (Tex.App.—Dallas 1997, no writ). Documents that are not court records under TRCP 76a may be sealed only if another rule or statute permits.

Practice Tip

If a party wants to limit dissemination of documents it believes are not court records, the party should file a motion for protective order under TRCP 192.6, not a motion to seal under TRCP 76a. See ***Kepple****, 970 S.W.2d at 525 (analyzing former TRCP 166b(5)(c), now TRCP 192.6(b)(5));* ***Roberts v. West****, 123 S.W.3d 436, 440 (Tex.App.—San Antonio 2003, pet. denied). See "Protecting documents that are not court records," ch. 5-L, §8.*

1. In camera discovery. Documents filed for in camera inspection, solely for the purpose of getting a ruling on their discoverability, are not court records. Tex. R. Civ. P. 76a(2)(a)(1); **Texans United Educ. Fund v. Texaco, Inc.**, 858 S.W.2d 38, 40 (Tex.App.—Houston [14th Dist.] 1993, writ denied); *see also* **U.S. Gov't v. Marks**, 949 S.W.2d 320, 324 (Tex.1997) (transcript of certain statements about grand-jury investigation made by federal prosecutor during ex parte hearing was not court record under TRCP 76a(2)(a)(2)).

2. Restricted by other law. Documents to which another law restricts access (e.g., certain employment records, financial information, medical records) are not court records. Tex. R. Civ. P. 76a(2)(a)(2).

3. Family Code cases. Documents filed in a suit that originally arose under the Family Code (e.g., divorce, adoption, termination of parental rights, paternity, juvenile-delinquency cases) are not court records. Tex. R. Civ. P. 76a(2)(a)(3); **P.I.A., Inc. v. Sullivan**, 837 S.W.2d 844, 845–46 (Tex.App.—Fort Worth 1992, orig. proceeding).

4. Unfiled discovery.

(1) Trade-secret suit. Unfiled discovery products in a case initiated to preserve bona fide trade secrets or other intangible property rights are not court records. Tex. R. Civ. P. 76a(2)(c); **Eli Lilly & Co. v. Marshall**, 829 S.W.2d 157, 158 (Tex.1992) (trade-secret interest can justify restricting access to documents). For the definition of a trade secret, see "What is a trade secret?," ch. 6-B, §2.24.1.

(2) No adverse effect on public. Unfiled discovery products are not court records if they do not have a probable adverse effect on the general public health or safety, the administration of public office, or the operation of government. Tex. R. Civ. P. 76a(2)(c). There is no presumption in TRCP 76a that unfiled discovery products are court records. **BP Prods. N. Am., Inc. v. Houston Chronicle Publ'g**, 263 S.W.3d 31, 34 (Tex.App.—Houston [1st Dist.] 2006, no pet.); **Eli Lilly & Co. v. Biffle**, 868 S.W.2d 806, 808 (Tex.App.—Dallas 1993, no writ); *see* **Kepple**, 970 S.W.2d at 523. For the procedure to limit the dissemination of unfiled discovery, see "Protecting documents that are not court records," ch. 5-L, §8.

5. Unfiled settlement agreements + no adverse effect on public. Unfiled settlement agreements are not court records if they do not seek to restrict disclosure of information concerning matters that have a probable adverse effect on the general public health or safety, the administration of public office, or the operation of government. Tex. R. Civ. P. 76a(2)(b).

§3. Sealing court records

§3.1 Motion to seal records under TRCP 76a.

1. In writing. The party or intervenor who wants court records sealed must file a written motion to seal. Tex. R. Civ. P. 76a(3); *see* Tex. R. Civ. P. 76a(7) (any person can intervene anytime before or after judgment to seal records). See **O'Connor's Texas Civil Forms**, FORM 5L:1 (2020 ed.). The motion itself must be open to public inspection. Tex. R. Civ. P. 76a(3).

2. Grounds. A party or an intervenor seeking to have documents protected from disclosure under TRCP 76a should allege the following:

(1) There is a serious, specific, and substantial interest in sealing the records that outweighs the presumption of openness and any probable adverse effect on the general public health or safety. Tex. R. Civ. P. 76a(1)(a); *e.g.*, **Fox v. Doe**, 869 S.W.2d 507, 512 (Tex.App.—San Antonio 1993, writ denied) (public health and safety would not be adversely affected by

nondisclosure of names in settlement agreement of minor's sexual-assault claim against employee of corporation); **Cortez v. Johnston**, No. 06-13-00120-CV, 2014 WL 1513306 (Tex.App.—Texarkana 2014, no pet.) (memo op.; 4-16-14) (P's interest in privacy did not outweigh presumption of openness).

(2) There are no other, less restrictive means that will adequately protect the specific interest asserted. Tex. R. Civ. P. 76a(1)(b); *e.g.*, **BP Prods. N. Am., Inc. v. Houston Chronicle Publ'g**, 263 S.W.3d 31, 35 (Tex.App.—Houston [1st Dist.] 2006, no pet.) (by producing redacted witness statements, D conceded less restrictive means to sealing witness statements was available); **Compaq Computer Corp. v. Lapray**, 75 S.W.3d 669, 674 (Tex.App.—Beaumont 2002, no pet.) (fact that documents contained trade secrets was insufficient to establish element of no other, less restrictive means).

3. Notice. The party or intervenor seeking to seal court records must post a public notice. Tex. R. Civ. P. 76a(3). See "Public notice," ch. 5-L, §4; **O'Connor's Texas Civil Forms**, FORM 5L:2 (2020 ed.).

4. Request to close courtroom. In addition to the request to seal court records, a party or an intervenor may request that the courtroom be closed to the public when the records are later presented in court. *See* **Volvo Car Corp. v. Marroquin**, No. 13-06-00070-CV, 2009 WL 3647348 (Tex.App.—Corpus Christi 2009, pet. denied) (memo op.; 11-5-09). A trial court may close its courtroom to protect the dissemination of certain sensitive information to the public. *See* **In re Samsung Telecomms.**, No. 05-99-01960-CV, 1999 WL 1081387 (Tex.App.—Dallas 1999, orig. proceeding) (no pub.; 12-2-99) (civil courtroom can be closed to protect trade secrets).

§3.2 Motion for temporary sealing order. A party or an intervenor can ask the court to immediately enter a temporary order sealing court records. Tex. R. Civ. P. 76a(5); *see* Tex. R. Civ. P. 76a(7) (any person can intervene anytime before or after judgment to seal records). See **O'Connor's Texas Civil Forms**, FORM 5L:1 (2020 ed.).

1. Grounds. The party or intervenor must show a compelling need for a temporary sealing order. Tex. R. Civ. P. 76a(5). Specifically, the party or intervenor must show that she will suffer an immediate and irreparable injury to a specific interest of hers before public notice can be posted and a hearing held. *Id.* See "Public notice," ch. 5-L, §4; "Hearing on motion to seal," ch. 5-L, §5.

2. By affidavit or verification. The party or intervenor must show a compelling need for a temporary sealing order through specific facts presented in an affidavit or verification. Tex. R. Civ. P. 76a(5).

3. Request final sealing order. If the court grants a temporary sealing order, it must set a time for the hearing, as required under TRCP 76a(4). Tex. R. Civ. P. 76a(5). See "Hearing on motion to seal," ch. 5-L, §5; "Contents," ch. 5-L, §6.1.2. At the hearing, the party or intervenor has the same burden of proof for sealing court records as if a temporary sealing order had not been requested. *See* Tex. R. Civ. P. 76a(5). Thus, in the motion for a temporary sealing order, the party or intervenor should request a final sealing order and show the required grounds. See "Grounds," ch. 5-L, §3.1.2.

4. Notice. The party or intervenor must give notice of the motion for a temporary sealing order under TRCP 21 and 21a to all parties that have filed an answer. Tex. R. Civ. P. 76a(5).

§3.3 Motion to modify or withdraw temporary sealing order. If a temporary sealing order is entered, any party or intervenor can file a motion to modify or withdraw the order. Tex. R. Civ. P. 76a(5). See "Temporary order," ch. 5-L, §6.1; **O'Connor's Texas Civil Forms**, FORM 5L:7 (2020 ed.). The party or intervenor can file a motion to withdraw the entire sealing order or to modify it by having certain documents removed from the order.

1. Grounds.

(1) Not court records. The party or intervenor can show that all or some of the documents under the temporary sealing order are not court records. *See* Tex. R. Civ. P. 76a(2). See "Documents that are not court records," ch. 5-L, §2.3.

(2) No compelling need. The party or intervenor can show that the adverse party did not show a compelling need to have all or some of the documents sealed under the temporary sealing order—that is, the adverse party did not show that she will suffer an immediate and irreparable injury to a specific interest of hers before public notice can be posted and a hearing held. *See* Tex. R. Civ. P. 76a(5).

2. **Notice.** The movant must give notice of the motion to all parties. *See* Tex. R. Civ. P. 76a(5).

3. **Hearing.** A hearing must be held on the motion as soon as practicable. Tex. R. Civ. P. 76a(5).

§3.4 Agreement not to disclose under TRCP 11. A TRCP 11 agreement not to disclose unfiled discovery cannot protect court documents from disclosure without the additional procedural requirements of a motion under TRCP 76a. *Cf.* **General Tire, Inc. v. Kepple**, 970 S.W.2d 520, 524 (Tex.1998) (before court can protect discovery from dissemination under TRCP 166b(5)(c), now TRCP 192.6(b)(5), it must observe the requirements of TRCP 76a). The Supreme Court obliquely addressed the issue of TRCP 11 agreements limiting disclosure of documents in **In re Dallas Morning News, Inc.**, 10 S.W.3d 298, 299 (Tex.1999), which dealt with appellate jurisdiction over a TRCP 11 order protecting documents from disclosure. In that case, the court reversed the mandamus granted by the court of appeals, presumably because an appeal was an adequate remedy to challenge the decision to hold a hearing on the TRCP 11 agreement long after the trial court's plenary power had expired. *See* **In re Dallas Morning News**, 10 S.W.3d at 299. If the TRCP 11 agreement had prevented disclosure of documents, appeal would not have been an adequate remedy and the Supreme Court could have decided the issue by mandamus.

§4. Public notice

Court records may be sealed only after public notice and a hearing. Tex. R. Civ. P. 76a(3), (4).

§4.1 Public notice. The party or intervenor seeking to seal court records must post a public notice wherever meetings of county governmental bodies are required to be posted. Tex. R. Civ. P. 76a(3); **General Tire, Inc. v. Kepple**, 970 S.W.2d 520, 523 (Tex.1998). The notice must state the following:

1. The hearing will be in open court. Tex. R. Civ. P. 76a(3). See "Hearing on motion to seal," ch. 5-L, §5.
2. Any person may intervene and be heard. Tex. R. Civ. P. 76a(3).
3. The specific time and place of the hearing. *Id.*
4. The style and number of the case. *Id.*
5. A brief description of the nature of the case and the records sought to be sealed. *Id.*; *e.g.*, **Fox v. Doe**, 869 S.W.2d 507, 510–11 (Tex.App.—San Antonio 1993, writ denied) (guardian ad litem's description of suit as one involving minor's claim of sexual abuse against employee of corporation was sufficient).
6. The identity of the movant. Tex. R. Civ. P. 76a(3); *e.g.*, **Fox v. Doe**, 869 S.W.2d at 510–11 (guardian ad litem's description of P as anonymous was sufficient).

§4.2 Filed with two clerks. Immediately after posting the notice, the movant must file a verified copy of the notice with the clerk of the trial court and the clerk of the Supreme Court. Tex. R. Civ. P. 76a(3).

§5. Hearing on motion to seal

Court records may be sealed only after a public hearing. Tex. R. Civ. P. 76a(4); **Chandler v. Hyundai Motor Co.**, 844 S.W.2d 882, 884–85 (Tex.App.—Houston [1st Dist.] 1992, no writ).

§5.1 Open court. A hearing to seal court records must be open to the public. Tex. R. Civ. P. 76a(4). At the hearing, the court may inspect documents in camera when necessary. *Id.*

§5.2 Deadline. A public hearing must be held as soon as practical, but not less than 14 days after a motion to seal is filed and public notice is posted. Tex. R. Civ. P. 76a(4).

§5.3 Participants. Both parties and any nonparty intervenor may participate in the hearing on a motion to seal court records. Tex. R. Civ. P. 76a(4).

§5.4 Burden. The movant seeking to seal the records has the burden of proof to establish the standards by a preponderance of the evidence. **Wood v. James R. Moriarty, P.C.**, 940 S.W.2d 359, 361 (Tex.App.—Dallas 1997, no writ); *see* Tex. R. Civ. P. 76a(1); **Roberts v. West**, 123 S.W.3d 436, 440 (Tex.App.—San Antonio 2003, pet. denied). The party with the burden

of proof must show (1) there is a specific, serious, and substantial interest that clearly outweighs both the presumption of openness and any probable adverse effect that sealing would have on the general public health or safety, and (2) there are no other, less restrictive means that will adequately protect the specific interest asserted. See "Grounds," ch. 5-L, §3.1.2.

§5.5 Procedure. TRCP 76a(4) provides that the same procedure as in TRCP 120a (special appearance) applies to motions to seal or unseal cases. **Fox v. Doe**, 869 S.W.2d 507, 512 (Tex.App.—San Antonio 1993, writ denied). TRCP 120a allows proof by way of pleadings, stipulations, discovery, affidavits, and oral testimony. Tex. R. Civ. P. 120a(3). See "Hearing," ch. 3-B, §9.

§6. Orders on motion to seal

§6.1 Temporary order. The trial court may enter a temporary sealing order after the motion is filed and notice is given to the parties. Tex. R. Civ. P. 76a(5). See "Motion for temporary sealing order," ch. 5-L, §3.2.

1. Written. The order must be in writing. Tex. R. Civ. P. 76a(6).

2. Contents. The temporary sealing order must identify the specific court records to be temporarily sealed, state the time for a hearing, and direct the movant to post the necessary public notice. *See* Tex. R. Civ. P. 76a(5). See **O'Connor's Texas Civil Forms**, FORM 5L:6 (2020 ed.).

§6.2 Sealing order.

1. Written. The order sealing court records must be in writing, separate from any other order and from the judgment in the case. Tex. R. Civ. P. 76a(6). A trial court cannot evade the requirements of TRCP 76a by closing the record with an unwritten order. **Davenport v. Garcia**, 834 S.W.2d 4, 24 (Tex.1992).

2. Contents. The sealing order must include (1) the style and number of the case, (2) the specific reasons for the court's findings and conclusions, (3) the specific portions of the records to be sealed, and (4) the time period for which the records are to be sealed. Tex. R. Civ. P. 76a(6). See **O'Connor's Texas Civil Forms**, FORM 5L:5 (2020 ed.).

§7. Continuing jurisdiction

§7.1 Intervenors. Any person has the right to intervene anytime before or after an order is entered to seal or unseal court records. Tex. R. Civ. P. 76a(7); **General Tire, Inc. v. Kepple**, 970 S.W.2d 520, 523 (Tex.1998); **Roberts v. West**, 123 S.W.3d 436, 443 (Tex.App.—San Antonio 2003, pet. denied).

§7.2 Jurisdiction. The trial court that issued the sealing order will maintain continuing jurisdiction to enforce, alter, or vacate the order sealing or unsealing court records. Tex. R. Civ. P. 76a(7); *see* **Boyles v. Kerr**, 815 S.W.2d 545, 545 (Tex.1991).

§7.3 Rehearing. No party or intervenor who had actual notice of the hearing preceding the sealing or unsealing order may ask the court to reconsider the order without first showing a change in circumstances that materially affects the order. Tex. R. Civ. P. 76a(7); *see also* **Public Citizen v. Insurance Servs. Office, Inc.**, 824 S.W.2d 811, 813 (Tex.App.—Austin 1992, no writ) (nonparty represented at TRCP 76a hearing is "a party with actual notice"). The changed circumstances do not need to relate to the case. Tex. R. Civ. P. 76a(7).

§7.4 Burden. The burden of proof under TRCP 76a(1) is always on the party seeking to seal records, even after an order sealing the records is signed. Tex. R. Civ. P. 76a(7).

§8. Protecting documents that are not court records

§8.1 Motion for protective order. A party who wants to restrict the dissemination of unfiled discovery documents or other documents that are not court records should file a motion for protective order under TRCP 192.6(a). **General Tire, Inc. v. Kepple**, 970 S.W.2d 520, 524–25 (Tex.1998) (analyzing former TRCP 166b(5)(c), now TRCP 192.6(b)(5)); **Roberts v. West**, 123 S.W.3d 436, 440 (Tex.App.—San Antonio 2003, pet. denied); *see also* Tex. Civ. Prac. & Rem. Code §134A.006(a) (in an action for misappropriation of trade secret, there is a presumption in favor of granting protective orders to preserve secrecy of trade secret). See "Motion for protective order," ch. 6-A, §20; **O'Connor's Texas Civil Forms**, FORM 6A:10 (2020

ed.). The party should not cite TRCP 76a in such a motion. If no person (another party, intervenor, or the court) claims that the unfiled discovery documents are court records, TRCP 76a does not apply. **Kepple**, 970 S.W.2d at 525.

§8.2 Response to motion for protective order. In response to the motion for protective order under TRCP 192.6(a), anyone who wants the documents to be accessible (the other party, an intervenor, or even the judge) must show that the documents are court records. **General Tire, Inc. v. Kepple**, 970 S.W.2d 520, 525 (Tex.1998) (analyzing former TRCP 166b(5)(c), now TRCP 192.6(b)(5)). The burden is on the person attempting to benefit from the presumption of openness in TRCP 76a to prove that the documents are court records. **Upjohn Co. v. Freeman**, 906 S.W.2d 92, 96 (Tex.App.—Dallas 1995, no writ).

§8.3 Decision on court-records allegations. Before the court addresses the issue of whether TRCP 76a prevents sealing, the court must decide whether the documents are court records. **General Tire, Inc. v. Kepple**, 970 S.W.2d 520, 525 (Tex.1998); *see* **Compaq Computer Corp. v. Lapray**, 75 S.W.3d 669, 673–74 (Tex.App.—Beaumont 2002, no pet.) (called a "**Kepple** inquiry"). For purposes of that decision, the trial court is not required to post a notice or hold a hearing. **Kepple**, 970 S.W.2d at 525. The court should not give an intervenor access to the records before deciding whether the records are court records. *Id.* at 524–25.

1. Not court records. If the court determines that the documents are not court records, dissemination can be restricted under TRCP 192.6(a) without reference to TRCP 76a. **Kepple**, 970 S.W.2d at 525 (analyzing former TRCP 166b(5)(c), now TRCP 192.6(b)(5)).

2. Court records. If the court determines that the documents are court records, the party seeking to restrict dissemination must comply with the requirements of TRCP 76a. **Kepple**, 970 S.W.2d at 525. For a discussion of these requirements, see "Sealing court records," ch. 5-L, §3; "Public notice," ch. 5-L, §4; and "Hearing on motion to seal," ch. 5-L, §5.

§9. Gag order

§9.1 Constitutional limitations. Any restraint on speech is presumptively unconstitutional, even if imposed by court order. *E.g.*, **Davenport v. Garcia**, 834 S.W.2d 4, 10 (Tex.1992) (trial court could not prevent guardian ad litem, who had been dismissed from case, from discussing case); **Low v. King**, 867 S.W.2d 141, 142 (Tex.App.—Beaumont 1993, orig. proceeding) (trial court could not prevent party from placing ad in newspaper seeking witnesses); *see also* **Star-Telegram, Inc. v. Walker**, 834 S.W.2d 54, 56–58 (Tex.1992) (trial court could not prevent newspaper from using rape victim's name, even though it had been expunged from court records). A gag order in a civil proceeding is valid only when (1) an imminent and irreparable harm to the judicial process will deprive litigants of a just resolution of their dispute, and (2) the judicial action represents the least restrictive means to prevent that harm. **Grigsby v. Coker**, 904 S.W.2d 619, 620 (Tex.1995); **Davenport**, 834 S.W.2d at 10; *cf.* **In re Houston Chronicle Publ'g**, 64 S.W.3d 103, 107–08 (Tex.App.—Houston [14th Dist.] 2001, orig. proceeding) (gag order in Yates criminal trial, which restricted parties and attorneys from making statements to press, did not violate constitutional rights of publisher).

§9.2 Motion. The party moving for a gag order should file a motion stating the specific reasons a gag order should be imposed and the limits of the gag order. *See* **Grigsby v. Coker**, 904 S.W.2d 619, 620–21 (Tex.1995). See **O'Connor's Texas Civil Forms**, FORM 5L:9 (2020 ed.).

§9.3 Notice & hearing. The court must hold a hearing to receive evidence. **Grigsby v. Coker**, 904 S.W.2d 619, 620–21 (Tex.1995).

§9.4 Findings. The court must make written findings supported by the evidence. **Grigsby v. Coker**, 904 S.W.2d 619, 620 (Tex.1995). The findings must state both of the following: (1) an imminent and irreparable harm to the judicial process will deprive litigants of a just resolution of their dispute and (2) the judicial action represents the least restrictive means to prevent that harm. *Id.*; **Davenport v. Garcia**, 834 S.W.2d 4, 10 (Tex.1992). See **O'Connor's Texas Civil Forms**, FORM 5L:11 (2020 ed.).

§10. Review

§10.1 Motion to seal.

1. Appeal. Any party or intervenor who participated in the hearing preceding the order may seek review by appeal because any order sealing or unsealing court records is deemed to be severed from the case and is a final judgment. Tex.

R. Civ. P. 76a(8); *see* **Eli Lilly & Co. v. Marshall**, 829 S.W.2d 157, 158 (Tex.1992); **Wood v. James R. Moriarty, P.C.**, 940 S.W.2d 359, 360–61 (Tex.App.—Dallas 1997, no writ). "Any order" refers to an order fully disposing of a motion under TRCP 76a—that is, a final determination on sealing. **In re Dallas Morning News, Inc.**, 10 S.W.3d 298, 305 (Tex.1999) (Gonzales, Phillips, Hecht, Owen, JJ., concurring); *see* **Oryon Techs. v. Marcus**, 429 S.W.3d 762, 765 (Tex.App.—Dallas 2014, no pet.); **Cortez v. Johnston**, No. 06-13-00120-CV, 2014 WL 1513306 (Tex.App.—Texarkana 2014, no pet.) (memo op.; 4-16-14).

(1) Standard of review. TRCP 76a decisions are reviewed for abuse of discretion. **General Tire, Inc. v. Kepple**, 970 S.W.2d 520, 526 (Tex.1998).

(2) Expedited. The appellate court may expedite the appeal of a TRCP 76a order. **Dallas Morning News, Inc. v. Fifth Ct. of Appeals**, 842 S.W.2d 655, 657 n.2 (Tex.1992).

(3) Abatement. The appellate court may abate the appeal and order the trial court to give further notice or to hold additional hearings. Tex. R. Civ. P. 76a(8); **Chandler v. Hyundai Motor Co.**, 829 S.W.2d 774, 775 n.1. (Tex.1992).

(4) Other orders. During the appeal of a TRCP 76a order sealing records, the court may limit access to the records subject to the order. **Dallas Morning News**, 842 S.W.2d at 657–58.

2. Mandamus.

(1) Generally not necessary. Mandamus is generally not necessary to challenge a TRCP 76a order because TRCP 76a(8) deems such an order severed and final. *See* Tex. R. Civ. P. 76a(8); **Chandler**, 829 S.W.2d at 775; **Marshall**, 829 S.W.2d at 158.

(2) Exceptions. Mandamus may be appropriate to challenge an interim order that causes harm that cannot be remedied by appeal. **In re Dallas Morning News**, 10 S.W.3d at 306 (Gonzales, Phillips, Hecht, Owen, JJ., concurring). Mandamus may also be appropriate when a trial court refuses to hold a hearing and render a decision on a motion under TRCP 76a. *See* **Marshall**, 829 S.W.2d at 158.

3. Record. For the appellate court to review an error in a sealing order, the appellant (or relator) must file a reporter's record from the hearing. *See* **Wood**, 940 S.W.2d at 362. Without the reporter's record, the appellate court must presume that sufficient evidence was produced at the trial-court level to support the order. *Id.* at 363.

§10.2 Gag order. A party may challenge a gag order by mandamus. **Grigsby v. Coker**, 904 S.W.2d 619, 621 (Tex.1995). For the appellate court to review an error in a gag order, the relator must file a reporter's record from the hearing. *See* Tex. R. App. P. 52.7(a). See "Record," ch. 5-L, §10.1.3.

M. Motion for Judicial Notice

This subchapter discusses judicial notice under TRE 201 to 204. For a discussion of a court's ability to take judicial notice of the reasonableness of attorney fees under CPRC chapter 38, see "Judicial notice," ch. 1-H, §10.1.4(1)(a)[2].

§1. General

§1.1 Rules. Tex. R. Evid. 201 to 204.

§1.2 Purpose. Judicial notice promotes judicial efficiency by avoiding the expenditure of time and effort involved in producing unnecessary evidence. Brown & Rondon, **Texas Rules of Evidence Handbook**, Rule 201 (2021 ed.) (n.2). It dispenses with formal proof of a fact that is either known throughout the jurisdiction or easily determined from reliable sources. *See* Brown & Rondon, **Texas Rules of Evidence Handbook**, Rule 201 (2021 ed.) (n.1).

§1.3 Forms. **O'Connor's Texas Civil Forms**, FORMS 5M:1 et seq. (2020 ed.).

§1.4 Other references. Wellborn, *Judicial Notice Under Article II of the Texas Rules of Evidence*, 19 St. Mary's L.J. 1 (1987); Brown & Rondon, **Texas Rules of Evidence Handbook** (2021 ed.).

§2. Types of judicial notice

Matters that can be judicially noticed are often divided into four categories: adjudicative facts, law, legislative facts, and reasoning facts. *See* Brown & Rondon, **Texas Rules of Evidence Handbook**, Rule 201 (2021 ed.) (nn.7–15). Different rules of proof and procedure apply to each.

§2.1 Adjudicative facts. A court can take judicial notice of certain adjudicative facts. *See* Tex. R. Evid. 201(a), (b). Adjudicative facts are facts that go to the jury and are proved by the introduction of evidence. Brown & Rondon, **Texas Rules of Evidence Handbook**, Rule 201 (2021 ed.) (nn.17–18). They relate to the parties, their activities, their properties, and their businesses. Brown & Rondon, **Texas Rules of Evidence Handbook**, Rule 201 (2021 ed.) (n.19). When an adjudicative fact is not subject to reasonable dispute, the fact can be judicially noticed under the procedural requirements of TRE 201. See "Adjudicative facts," ch. 5-M, §4.1.

§2.2 Law. A court can take judicial notice of the law of the forum and the law of the United States, sister states, and foreign countries. See Brown & Rondon, **Texas Rules of Evidence Handbook**, Rule 201 (2021 ed.) (§A.3).

1. Texas law. Generally, a Texas court is required to take judicial notice of Texas public statutes and case law. *See* **Kish v. Van Note**, 692 S.W.2d 463, 467 (Tex.1985); **Watts v. State**, 99 S.W.3d 604, 610 (Tex.Crim.App.2003). Judicial notice of such law is not governed by the TREs and is mandatory without the need for any formal motion or request. *See* **Kish**, 692 S.W.2d at 467; **Watts**, 99 S.W.3d at 610. When a statute is ambiguous, however, a party (1) may request that the court take judicial notice of pertinent legislative facts to support a particular construction of the statute and (2) must provide appropriate information and materials. Brown & Rondon, **Texas Rules of Evidence Handbook**, Rule 201 (2021 ed.) (n.25). See "Legislative facts," ch. 5-M, §2.3; "Texas statutes," ch. 5-M, §4.2. Judicial notice of the existence and content of Texas local ordinances, as well as the contents of the Texas Register and Administrative Code, is governed by the requirements and procedures under TRE 204. See "Texas city & county ordinances," ch. 5-M, §4.3; "Texas Register & Administrative Code," ch. 5-M, §4.4; **O'Connor's Texas Civil Forms**, FORM 5M:1 (2020 ed.).

2. Foreign law. Judicial notice of federal law, a sister state's law, or a foreign country's law is governed by the requirements and procedures under TRE 202 and 203. See "Laws of sister state," ch. 5-M, §4.5; "Federal laws," ch. 5-M, §4.6; "Foreign laws," ch. 5-M, §4.7; **O'Connor's Texas Civil Forms**, FORMS 5M:2 to 5M:3 (2020 ed.). Although the TREs require the court to take judicial notice of foreign law if properly requested, the court will not necessarily apply the law to the case. **Pittsburgh Corning Corp. v. Walters**, 1 S.W.3d 759, 769 (Tex.App.—Corpus Christi 1999, pet. denied). The court's power to take judicial notice of foreign law is distinct from a choice-of-law determination. *Id.* Thus, to have foreign law applied to a case, a party must file a preliminary motion requesting application of foreign law in addition to the request to take judicial notice. *Id.*

§2.3 Legislative facts. A court can take judicial notice of legislative facts. See Brown & Rondon, **Texas Rules of Evidence Handbook**, Rule 201 (2021 ed.) (§A.2).

1. Defined. Unlike adjudicative facts, legislative facts do not just concern the parties; they are general facts that help the court determine the content of law and policy and exercise its judgment or discretion in determining what judicial course of action to take. *See* Brown & Rondon, **Texas Rules of Evidence Handbook**, Rule 201 (2021 ed.) (n.21). Legislative facts typically include information on the impact of earlier and proposed law, legislative history of a statute, and the basis for the exercise of legislative power. *Id.*; *see, e.g.*, **In re Sigmar**, 270 S.W.3d 289, 302 (Tex.App.—Waco 2008, orig. proceeding) (legal practices and procedures of foreign country are legislative facts). Legislative facts are not limited, however, to materials developed by or for legislatures. Brown & Rondon, **Texas Rules of Evidence Handbook**, Rule 201 (2021 ed.) (n.26). Legislative facts have been broadly defined by the courts to include established truths, facts, or pronouncements that do not change from case to case. *Cf.* **U.S. v. Bowers**, 660 F.2d 527, 530–31 (5th Cir.1981) (interpreting FRE 201). For example, courts have judicially noticed the validity of certain well-established scientific principles and techniques as legislative facts. *E.g.*, **Emerson v. State**, 880 S.W.2d 759, 764 (Tex.Crim.App.1994) (HGN testing for sobriety); *see* Brown & Rondon, **Texas Rules of Evidence Handbook**, Rule 201 (2021 ed.) (nn.28–30).

2. Not governed by TREs. Because legislative facts are not adjudicative facts, they are not governed by the requirements or procedures under TRE 201. **In re Sigmar**, 270 S.W.3d at 301–02; *see* Brown & Rondon, **Texas Rules of Evidence Handbook**, Rule 201 (2021 ed.) (n.28). Thus, a party's right to be heard, the requirement of indisputability, and the court's duty to instruct the jury do not apply to legislative facts. *See* **In re Graves**, 217 S.W.3d 744, 751 n.6 (Tex.App.—Waco 2007, orig. proceeding); **Perkins v. Delaney**, 170 S.W.3d 136, 137 (Tex.App.—Eastland 2005, no pet.). See "Types of facts," ch. 5-M, §4.1.1; "Response," ch. 5-M, §5; "Jury instruction," ch. 5-M, §7.3.

3. Discretionary. Whether legislative facts will be judicially noticed is within the court's discretion; a formal motion will not make judicial notice mandatory. *See* **In re Graves**, 217 S.W.3d at 751 n.6; Brown & Rondon, **Texas Rules of Evidence Handbook**, Rule 201 (2021 ed.) (n.28).

§2.4 Reasoning facts. A court can take judicial notice of reasoning facts (also referred to as "nonadjudicative" or "nonevidence" facts). See Brown & Rondon, **Texas Rules of Evidence Handbook**, Rule 201 (2021 ed.) (§A.4).

1. Defined. Reasoning facts are not adjudicative facts, but are facts of general knowledge that an average fact-finder has about humankind, human affairs, and the environment. *See* Brown & Rondon, **Texas Rules of Evidence Handbook**, Rule 201 (2021 ed.) (n.45); *see, e.g.*, **El Chico Corp. v. Poole**, 732 S.W.2d 306, 311 (Tex.1987) (common knowledge that alcohol distorts perception, slows reaction, and impairs motor skills); **City of Austin v. Selter**, 415 S.W.2d 489, 501 (Tex.App.—Austin 1967, writ ref'd n.r.e.) (common knowledge that death by drowning is painful). Reasoning facts are used to draw inferences, evaluate evidence, judge the credibility of witnesses, and interpret what is seen and heard from the witness stand. Brown & Rondon, **Texas Rules of Evidence Handbook**, Rule 201 (2021 ed.) (n.45).

2. Not governed by TREs. Because reasoning facts are not adjudicative facts, they are not governed by the requirements or procedures under TRE 201. *See* Brown & Rondon, **Texas Rules of Evidence Handbook**, Rule 201 (2021 ed.) (nn.43–44). Thus, a party's right to be heard, the requirement of indisputability, and the court's duty to instruct the jury do not apply to reasoning facts. *See* Brown & Rondon, **Texas Rules of Evidence Handbook**, Rule 201 (2021 ed.) (n.14). See "Types of facts," ch. 5-M, §4.1.1; "Response," ch. 5-M, §5; "Jury instruction," ch. 5-M, §7.3.

3. Formalized notice unnecessary. Because reasoning facts are universally known and of such a fundamental nature, they are not introduced into evidence and are not appropriate subjects for formalized judicial notice. *See* Brown & Rondon, **Texas Rules of Evidence Handbook**, Rule 201 (2021 ed.) (n.47).

§3. Motion for judicial notice

§3.1 Court's motion. A court may take judicial notice on its own motion, without a request from the parties, under TRE 201(c)(1) (adjudicative facts), TRE 202(b)(1) (federal laws and laws of sister states), and TRE 204(b)(1) (Texas city and county ordinances, contents of Texas Register, and agency rules published in Administrative Code). *See, e.g.*, **In re Houston Chronicle Publ'g**, 64 S.W.3d 103, 105 (Tex.App.—Houston [14th Dist.] 2001, orig. proceeding) (on its own, trial court in Yates criminal trial judicially noticed that parties were discussing case with media and issued gag order); **International Ass'n of Firefighters v. City of San Antonio**, 822 S.W.2d 122, 127 (Tex.App.—San Antonio 1991, writ denied) (on its

own, appellate court judicially noticed city charter even though trial court was not asked to do so). It is unclear whether the court can inquire into the law of a foreign jurisdiction on its own initiative. Brown & Rondon, **Texas Rule of Evidence Handbook**, Rule 203 (2021 ed.) (n.235).

§3.2 Party's motion.

1. In writing. In most cases, when a formal request for judicial notice is required, the request should be in writing, although there is no such requirement in the TREs. During trial, a motion may be oral. *See, e.g.,* **Cutler v. Cutler**, 543 S.W.2d 1, 2 (Tex.App.—Dallas 1976, writ ref'd n.r.e.) (oral motion made on the record during trial); **Utica Mut. Ins. v. Bennett**, 492 S.W.2d 659, 663–64 (Tex.App.—Houston [1st Dist.] 1973, writ dism'd) (oral motion requesting notice of Mississippi law, along with copies of cases, was sufficient).

Practice Tip

When it is apparent that foreign law applies at the outset of a case, it is common to request judicial notice of the law in a pleading and not in a motion. See Tex. R. Evid. 203(a)(1). But the failure to plead foreign law does not prevent the court from judicially noticing the law in a later motion. ***Daugherty v. Southern Pac. Transp.****, 772 S.W.2d 81, 83 (Tex.1989).*

2. Type of information. The party should attach to the motion copies of the information that supports the request for judicial notice. The trial court has discretion to determine whether the party has complied with this requirement. **Daugherty**, 772 S.W.2d at 83. The type of information required depends on the type of judicial notice requested. For adjudicative facts, see "Necessary information for verifiable adjudicative facts," ch. 5-M, §4.1.2. For city or county ordinances, see "Texas city & county ordinances," ch. 5-M, §4.3. For Texas Register or codified rules of the agencies published in the Administrative Code, see "Texas Register & Administrative Code," ch. 5-M, §4.4. For laws of sister states, see "Laws of sister state," ch. 5-M, §4.5. For federal laws, see "Federal laws," ch. 5-M, §4.6.

3. Verification. Whenever the party furnishes the court with factual information outside the record and the information is not universally known, the information must be supported by an affidavit. For example, the movant should verify the laws of foreign jurisdictions and statements of experts on those laws. *See, e.g.,* **Holden v. Capri Lighting, Inc.**, 960 S.W.2d 831, 833 (Tex.App.—Amarillo 1997, no pet.) (copy of California case without affidavit from California attorney was insufficient). Although TRE 204 does not require it, some appellate courts require municipal ordinances to be verified. See "Texas city & county ordinances," ch. 5-M, §4.3.

§3.3 Notice. A party is entitled to notice of the request to take judicial notice. If the court takes judicial notice on its own initiative without notice to the parties, either party may request an opportunity to be heard after judicial notice has been taken. Tex. R. Evid. 201(e) (adjudicative facts), Tex. R. Evid. 202(c)(2) (federal laws and laws of sister states), Tex. R. Evid. 204(c)(2) (Texas city and county ordinances, contents of Texas Register, and agency rules published in Administrative Code).

§3.4 Deadlines. A court may take judicial notice of most matters at any stage of the proceeding. Tex. R. Evid. 201(d) (adjudicative facts), Tex. R. Evid. 202(d) (federal laws and laws of sister states); *see, e.g.,* **City of Dallas v. Moreau**, 718 S.W.2d 776, 781 (Tex.App.—Corpus Christi 1986, writ ref'd n.r.e.) (request for judicial notice of city charter at JNOV hearing was timely); *see also* **Office of Pub. Util. Counsel v. Public Util. Comm'n**, 878 S.W.2d 598, 600 (Tex.1994) (court may take judicial notice for first time during appeal). Judicial notice of a foreign country's law, however, must be made far enough in advance of trial to comply with the deadlines in TRE 203 and 1009. See "Foreign laws," ch. 5-M, §4.7.

Caution

Although TRE 202 and 203 give the court wide latitude in taking judicial notice of foreign law during a proceeding, this does not mean that choice-of-law issues can be raised at any point. ***Pittsburgh Corning Corp. v. Walters****, 1 S.W.3d 759, 769 (Tex.App.—Corpus Christi 1999, pet. denied). If a party is also requesting the application of foreign law, the party must make that request in a prelimi-*

nary motion, preferably at the same time the request for judicial notice is made. Id.

§4. Grounds for judicial notice

§4.1 Adjudicative facts.

1. Types of facts. For a court to take judicial notice of an adjudicative fact, the fact must not be subject to reasonable dispute because either (1) it is generally known within the court's territorial jurisdiction (a notorious fact) or (2) it can be accurately and readily determined from sources whose accuracy cannot be reasonably questioned (a verifiable fact). Tex. R. Evid. 201(b); **Freedom Comms. v. Coronado**, 372 S.W.3d 621, 623 (Tex.2012); **In re J.L.**, 163 S.W.3d 79, 84 (Tex.2005). See "Adjudicative facts," ch. 5-M, §2.1.

(1) Notorious fact. If a fact is generally known within the court's territorial jurisdiction, it is a notorious fact. *See* Tex. R. Evid. 201(b)(1); Brown & Rondon, **Texas Rules of Evidence Handbook**, Rule 201 (2021 ed.) (n.55). Notorious facts are facts that everyone of average intelligence and knowledge within the court's territorial jurisdiction can be presumed to know. *See* **City of Garland v. Louton**, 683 S.W.2d 725, 726 (Tex.App.—Dallas 1984), *rev'd on other grounds*, 691 S.W.2d 603 (Tex.1985); *see, e.g.*, **Choice Auto Brokers, Inc. v. Dawson**, 274 S.W.3d 172, 174 n.1 (Tex.App.—Houston [1st Dist.] 2008, no pet.) (judicial notice of eBay auction process). One of the most common types of notorious facts is geographic facts, such as the location of cities and counties, boundaries, dimensions, and distances. *See* **Barber v. Intercoast Jobbers & Brokers**, 417 S.W.2d 154, 157–58 (Tex.1967); *see, e.g.*, **Harper v. Killion**, 348 S.W.2d 521, 523 (Tex.1961) (Jacksonville is in Cherokee County); **Apostolic Ch. v. American Honda Motor Co.**, 833 S.W.2d 553, 555–56 (Tex.App.—Tyler 1992, writ denied) (Highway 96 is known as Tenaha Highway and is in Shelby County). A fact can be commonly known even though it has to be processed with commonly possessed mental skills. **Drake v. Holstead**, 757 S.W.2d 909, 910 (Tex.App.—Beaumont 1988, no writ). Because notorious facts are commonly known, it is not necessary to provide the court with any extrinsic documentation to support them. **Tranter v. Duemling**, 129 S.W.3d 257, 262 (Tex.App.—El Paso 2004, no pet.); **Drake**, 757 S.W.2d at 911. Facts known personally by the trial judge or known only to a specially informed group of people are not notorious. Brown & Rondon, **Texas Rules of Evidence Handbook**, Rule 201 (2021 ed.) (nn.66–67). See "Fact not generally known," ch. 5-M, §5.2.1.

(2) Verifiable fact. If a fact can be accurately and readily determined from a reliable source, it is a verifiable fact. Tex. R. Evid. 201(b)(2); *see, e.g.*, **Concord Oil Co. v. Pennzoil Expl. & Prod.**, 966 S.W.2d 451, 459 (Tex.1998) (standard royalty in oil and gas leases around 1937); **City of Houston v. Todd**, 41 S.W.3d 289, 301 (Tex.App.—Houston [1st Dist.] 2001, pet. denied) (railroads supplied transportation to all developed sections of Texas by 1900, determined by consulting history sources); **Texas DPS v. Ackerman**, 31 S.W.3d 672, 676 (Tex.App.—Waco 2000, pet. denied) (population, determined by consulting federal census); *see also* **D Mag. Partners v. Rosenthal**, 529 S.W.3d 429, 436–37 (Tex.2017) (although Wikipedia can be used as source of authority, concerns about its reliability can often preclude its use, particularly when it is sole source of authority on issue of any significance to case). See Brown & Rondon, **Texas Rules of Evidence Handbook**, Rule 201 (2021 ed.) (§B.2). Some common types of verifiable facts that courts have taken judicial notice of include the following:

(a) Court's records. A court can take judicial notice of its own records (e.g., pleadings, affidavits, orders, judgments) in a case involving the same subject matter and between the same, or practically the same, parties. *See, e.g.*, **In re S.M.R.**, 434 S.W.3d 576, 582 (Tex.2014) (in case terminating D's parental rights, trial court took judicial notice of its order granting temporary managing conservatorship of D's children to TDFPS); **In re Shell E&P, Inc.**, 179 S.W.3d 125, 130 (Tex.App.—San Antonio 2005, orig. proceeding) (trial judge could take judicial notice of his own order from related case between substantially same parties); *see also* **Texas Real Estate Comm'n v. Nagle**, 767 S.W.2d 691, 694 (Tex.1989) (use to which judicial notice of court's own files may be put is limited by doctrines of res judicata and collateral estoppel). Unlike other verifiable facts, because the court has access to its own records, it is not necessary to supply the court with a copy of the records to be judicially noticed. *See* **Estate of York**, 934 S.W.2d 848, 851 (Tex.App.—Corpus Christi 1996, no writ) (for purposes of judicial economy, party need not offer proof of what is contained in court's own file).

[1] Generally. In general, the facts that the court can take judicial notice of are whether a particular document has been filed with the court, the date on which the document was filed, and whether the document was before

the court at the time of a hearing or trial. **In re C.S.**, 208 S.W.3d 77, 81 (Tex.App.—Fort Worth 2006, pet. denied). The court cannot take judicial notice of the truth of the factual statements and allegations in the pleadings, affidavits, or other documents in the court's file. *E.g.*, **Guyton v. Monteau**, 332 S.W.3d 687, 693 (Tex.App.—Houston [14th Dist.] 2011, no pet.) (court cannot take judicial notice of testimony from earlier hearing or trial; for earlier testimony to be considered, it must be authenticated and entered into evidence).

[2] Orders & judgments. For a court's own orders and judgments, the court can take judicial notice of the truth of the results reached. *See, e.g.*, **In re H.M.P.**, No. 13-08-00643-CV, 2010 WL 40124 (Tex.App.—Corpus Christi 2010, no pet.) (memo op.; 1-7-10) (in determining whether party violated earlier court order, court took judicial notice of order's requirements); **Longhurst v. Clark**, No. 01-07-00226-CV, 2008 WL 3876175 (Tex.App.—Houston [1st Dist.] 2008, no pet.) (memo op.; 8-21-08) (in calculating amount of overdue child-support payments, court took judicial notice of amount awarded and interest charged in earlier order).

(b) Records of another court. A court can take judicial notice of another court's records if a party provides proof of the records. **Freedom Comms.**, 372 S.W.3d at 623; *see* **Brown v. Brown**, 145 S.W.3d 745, 750 (Tex.App.—Dallas 2004, pet. denied). See "Necessary information for verifiable adjudicative facts," ch. 5-M, §4.1.2. Proof can be shown by a verified copy of the record or a reference to where the record can be found if it has been made public. *See, e.g.*, **Freedom Comms.**, 372 S.W.3d at 623–24 (D provided copy of federal-court plea agreement; court took judicial notice); **MCI Sales & Serv. v. Hinton**, 329 S.W.3d 475, 497 n.21 (Tex.2010) (P provided copy of amicus brief filed in U.S. Supreme Court; court took judicial notice); **Ramey v. Bank of N.Y.**, No. 14-06-00824-CV, 2010 WL 2853887 (Tex.App.—Houston [14th Dist.] 2010, no pet.) (memo op.; 7-22-10) (P provided court with URL where published bankruptcy order could be found; court took judicial notice).

(c) Matters of public record. A court can take judicial notice of matters that are verified by a public record. **Besing v. Smith**, 843 S.W.2d 20, 21 (Tex.1992); **Langdale v. Villamil**, 813 S.W.2d 187, 190 (Tex.App.—Houston [14th Dist.] 1991, no writ); *see, e.g.*, **Office of Pub. Util. Counsel v. Public Util. Comm'n**, 878 S.W.2d 598, 600 (Tex.1994) (court erred in not taking judicial notice of order from Public Utility Commission (PUC); movant provided court with citation to volume and page number where published order could be located in PUC bulletin); **In re Caraway**, No. 2-05-359-CV, 2007 WL 1879768 (Tex.App.—Fort Worth 2007, no pet.) (memo op.; 6-28-07) (court took judicial notice that judge's oath or anti-bribery affidavit was not filed with Secretary of State or the appropriate judicial administrative region).

(d) Weather. A court can take judicial notice of the weather on a particular day when verified. *See* **J. Weingarten, Inc. v. Tripplett**, 530 S.W.2d 653, 656 (Tex.App.—Beaumont 1975, writ ref'd n.r.e.) (court may consult weather-bureau records to judicially notice weather for particular day).

(e) Dates & holidays. A court can take judicial notice of dates and holidays when verified. *See, e.g.*, **Higginbotham v. General Life & Acc. Ins.**, 796 S.W.2d 695, 696 (Tex.1990) (court could take judicial notice that 12:01 p.m. on March 18, 1986, was an early afternoon on Tuesday and not a statutory holiday); **Garcia v. Vera**, No. 01-05-01161-CV, 2006 WL 2865033 (Tex.App.—Houston [1st Dist.] 2006, no pet.) (memo op.; 10-5-06) (date courthouse was closed was verified by district clerk's office).

(f) Definitions. A court can take judicial notice of definitions of terms and phrases when verified. *See, e.g.*, **Burger v. Burger**, No. 2-05-170-CV, 2006 WL 495663 (Tex.App.—Fort Worth 2006, no pet.) (memo op.; 3-2-06) (footnote 24; court took judicial notice of dictionary definition of "Jocasta").

2. Necessary information for verifiable adjudicative facts. For judicial notice of "verifiable" adjudicative facts, a party is required to furnish the court with "necessary information." Tex R Evid. 201(c)(2); *see* **Freedom Comms.**, 372 S.W.3d at 623. Necessary information includes documentation that qualifies as a source whose accuracy cannot reasonably be questioned. **Public Util. Comm'n**, 878 S.W.2d at 600 (published PUC order); *see, e.g.*, **Magee v. Ulery**, 993 S.W.2d 332, 338–39 (Tex.App.—Houston [14th Dist.] 1999, no pet.) (court supplied with information from Medical Examiners Board should have taken judicial notice of physician's age and practice status); **Drake**, 757 S.W.2d at 911 (court supplied with computation should have taken judicial notice of the distance a car would travel at a given speed); **Wagner & Brown v. E.W. Moran Drilling Co.**, 702 S.W.2d 760, 772–73 (Tex.App.—Fort Worth 1986, no writ) (court supplied with appropriate Federal Reserve bulletins took judicial notice of the discount rate on 90-day commercial paper in effect at a Federal Reserve

bank); *see also* Brown & Rondon, **Texas Rules of Evidence Handbook**, Rule 201 (2021 ed.) (§C; industry source routinely used and relied on by those in same industry is sufficiently accurate for judicial notice). A movant should attach verified copies of the information to the motion. Once the court has been given the motion and necessary information, judicial notice of the adjudicative fact is mandatory. Tex. R. Evid. 201(c)(2); **Drake**, 757 S.W.2d at 910–11.

§4.2 Texas statutes. A party is not required to provide the court with information about Texas laws. Texas courts are required to take judicial notice of the public statutes of this state. **Kish v. Van Note**, 692 S.W.2d 463, 467 (Tex.1985).

1. Unambiguous statute. If a statute is clear and unambiguous, a party should not provide the court with legislative facts to explain its meaning. Instead, the court should give the statute its common meaning. **St. Luke's Episcopal Hosp. v. Agbor**, 952 S.W.2d 503, 505 (Tex.1997).

2. Ambiguous statute. When a statute is ambiguous, the party should provide the court with information about the following: (1) the object sought to be attained, (2) the circumstances under which the statute was enacted, (3) the legislative history, (4) the common law or former statutory provisions, (5) the consequences of a particular construction, (6) the administrative construction of the statute, and (7) the effect of the title (caption), preamble, and emergency provisions. Tex. Gov't Code §311.023. The court may take judicial notice of these sources. The party should argue that it seeks an interpretation (1) to obtain a just and reasonable result, as intended by the Legislature, (2) to make execution of the statute reasonably feasible, as intended by the Legislature, and (3) that favors the public interest over any private interest. *See* Tex. Gov't Code §311.021(3) to (5).

§4.3 Texas city & county ordinances. For judicial notice of Texas municipal and county ordinances, the party must furnish the court with "necessary information" to enable it to comply with the request. Tex. R. Evid. 204(b)(2). The movant must attach copies of the ordinance, which probably should be certified or verified even though TRE 204 does not specifically impose such a requirement. *See, e.g.*, **City of Houston v. Southwest Concrete Constr., Inc.**, 835 S.W.2d 728, 733 n.5 (Tex.App.—Houston [14th Dist.] 1992, writ denied) (court refused to take judicial notice because ordinance was not verified); **Hollingsworth v. King**, 810 S.W.2d 772, 774 (Tex.App.—Amarillo 1991) (court refused to take judicial notice of unauthenticated municipal ordinances), *writ denied*, 816 S.W.2d 340 (Tex.1991).

§4.4 Texas Register & Administrative Code. The provisions of TRE 204 that refer to taking judicial notice of the contents of the Texas Register and the Texas Administrative Code duplicate provisions in the Administrative Procedure and Texas Register Acts. **Metro Fuels, Inc. v. City of Austin**, 827 S.W.2d 531, 532 n.3 (Tex.App.—Austin 1992, no writ); *see* Tex. Gov't Code §2002.022(a) (contents of Texas Register are to be judicially noticed), §2002.054(1) (state-agency rules published in Administrative Code are to be judicially noticed). Because Gov't Code §2002.022(a) and §2002.054(1) require the court to take judicial notice, it is probably not necessary for the party to file a written motion or supply necessary information, as stated in TRE 204. However, for the convenience of a court that does not regularly deal with matters in the Texas Register or the Texas Administrative Code, the party should file a motion and provide copies of the information it wants the court to take notice of. As a source of law, agency regulations are like statutes or the decisions of a higher court to which a lower court owes obedience under the doctrine of stare decisis. **Eckmann v. Des Rosiers**, 940 S.W.2d 394, 399 (Tex.App.—Austin 1997, no writ).

§4.5 Laws of sister state. For judicial notice of the constitutions, public statutes, rules, regulations, ordinances, court decisions, and common law of any other state, territory, or jurisdiction of the United States, a party must furnish the court with "necessary information" before the court is required to take judicial notice. Tex. R. Evid. 202(b)(2); *see* **Pittsburgh Corning Corp. v. Walters**, 1 S.W.3d 759, 769 (Tex.App.—Corpus Christi 1999, pet. denied).

1. Necessary information. The party requesting notice should attach to its motion the information the court needs to determine the applicability of another state's law to the case. **Daugherty v. Southern Pac. Transp.**, 772 S.W.2d 81, 83 (Tex.1989); *see* **Knops v. Knops**, 763 S.W.2d 864, 867 (Tex.App.—San Antonio 1988, no writ) (broad request without any information is not sufficient); *see also* **Wickware v. Session**, 538 S.W.2d 466, 469 (Tex.App.—Tyler 1976, writ ref'd n.r.e.) (photocopy of statute and oral motion requesting notice of California probate code were sufficient). The movant should attach copies of the law to be judicially noticed and include citations to the law in its motion and notice. *See, e.g.*, **Burns v. Resolution Trust Corp.**, 880 S.W.2d 149, 151 (Tex.App.—Houston [14th Dist.] 1994, no writ) (copies of relevant Colorado

statutes were attached to request); **Cal Growers, Inc. v. Palmer Whs. & Transfer Co.**, 687 S.W.2d 384, 386 (Tex.App.—Houston [14th Dist.] 1985, no writ) (even though copy of California statute was not provided, court could take judicial notice because motion cited statute). In some instances, it might be helpful to supply the court with deposition testimony or an affidavit from a practicing attorney in the sister state to prove that the documentary evidence—such as a copy of the statute or case law—is still controlling law in that jurisdiction. Brown & Rondon, **Texas Rules of Evidence Handbook**, Rule 202 (2021 ed.) (n.204).

2. No request. If no one makes a request for judicial notice of the laws of another state, or if no one submits proper proof, a Texas court can presume that the laws of that state are the same as the laws of Texas. **Coca-Cola Co. v. Harmar Bottling Co.**, 218 S.W.3d 671, 684–85 (Tex.2006). However, the court cannot make this presumption if it is contrary to a policy directive in a Texas statute. *See id.* at 685. For example, the policy of the Texas Antitrust Act to promote competition in trade "within the state of Texas" is contrary to the presumption that antitrust statutes of Arkansas, Louisiana, and Oklahoma are the same as that of Texas. *Id.* The dissent in **Harmar** makes a compelling argument that the reasoning behind the exception is flawed. *See id.* at 695–96 (Brister, J., Jefferson, C.J., O'Neill, Medina, JJ., dissenting). See Brown & Rondon, **Texas Rules of Evidence Handbook**, Rule 202 (2021 ed.).

§4.6 Federal laws. For judicial notice of federal laws, a party should attach to its motion the information the court needs to determine the law's applicability to the case. *See* Tex. R. Evid. 202(b)(2). On a party's motion supported by the necessary information, a court must take judicial notice of federal laws. *Id.; see, e.g.*, **Daugherty v. Southern Pac. Transp.**, 772 S.W.2d 81, 83 (Tex.1989) (dicta; OSHA regulation). TRE 202 does not permit judicial notice of private orders. **Centex Corp. v. Dalton**, 810 S.W.2d 812, 824 (Tex.App.—San Antonio 1991), *rev'd on other grounds*, 840 S.W.2d 952 (Tex.1992).

§4.7 Foreign laws. The procedure for judicial notice of foreign laws is more complicated than that for other types of laws. TRE 203 is considered a "hybrid rule"; the presentation of the law to the court resembles the presentment of evidence, but it is ultimately decided as a question of law. **Long Distance Int'l v. Telefonos de Mexico, S.A. de C.V.**, 49 S.W.3d 347, 351 (Tex.2001); **PennWell Corp. v. Ken Assocs.**, 123 S.W.3d 756, 760 (Tex.App.—Houston [14th Dist.] 2003, pet. denied). For more detailed information about proving laws of foreign countries, see Brown & Rondon, **Texas Rules of Evidence Handbook**, Rule 203 (2021 ed.).

Note

TRCP 308b applies to the recognition or enforcement of a judgment or arbitration award based on foreign law in a suit involving a marriage relationship or a parent-child relationship under the Family Code. Tex. R. Civ. P. 308b(b)(1). The deadlines and procedures for raising a foreign-law issue under TRE 203(a) and (b) do not apply to actions to which Rule 308b applies. See Tex. R. Civ. P. 308b(c)(2); Tex. R. Evid. 203(e). Rule 308b provides its own deadlines and procedures for notice, pretrial conferences, hearings, and orders.

1. Pleading. To raise an issue about the laws of a foreign country, a party must plead the law in its petition, its answer, or a written motion. Tex. R. Evid. 203(a)(1).

2. Proof of foreign law—30 days before trial. The party must provide the proof of foreign law at least 30 days before the date of trial. Tex. R. Evid. 203(a)(2).

(1) Copies of law. The movant must provide copies of the foreign law on which it intends to rely. Tex. R. Evid. 203(a)(2).

(2) Expert opinion. TRE 203 permits the movant to provide proof from an expert in the form of affidavits or deposition testimony explaining the foreign law. *See, e.g.*, **Reading & Bates Constr. Co. v. Baker Energy Res.**, 976 S.W.2d 702, 707 (Tex.App.—Houston [1st Dist.] 1998, pet. denied) (parties provided affidavits of law professors explaining Canadian law); **Trailways, Inc. v. Clark**, 794 S.W.2d 479, 484 (Tex.App.—Corpus Christi 1990, writ denied) (D provided letter from Mexican attorney explaining Mexican law).

3. Translation of foreign law—45 days. If the foreign laws, the expert's opinion explaining the laws, or other sources of information are in a language other than English, the movant must provide the following information to the court

and other parties at least 45 days before trial: (1) a copy of the foreign-language text, (2) a copy of the English translation, and (3) an affidavit or unsworn declaration from a qualified translator that sets forth the translator's qualifications and certifies that the translation is accurate. *See* Tex. R. Evid. 203(b), 1009(a); **In re Estates of Garcia-Chapa**, 33 S.W.3d 859, 862 (Tex.App.—Corpus Christi 2000, no pet.); *see, e.g.*, **Trailways, Inc.**, 794 S.W.2d at 484 (D provided certified translation). The 45-day deadline can be enlarged or shortened on a motion showing good cause. Tex. R. Evid. 1009(f).

Note

*TRE 203(b) requires a party to provide a copy of the foreign-language text and an English translation at least 30 days before trial; however, TRE 1009(a) requires the party to provide the text and translation, along with the translator's affidavit or unsworn declaration, at least 45 days before trial for the translation to be admissible as evidence. Therefore, a party should comply with the deadline and procedures in TRE 1009(a) if it wants to dispense with the need for live testimony of the translation of the foreign-language document. See Tex. R. Evid. 1009(a), (e). See Brown & Rondon, **Texas Rules of Evidence Handbook**, Rule 203 (2021 ed.) (n.232).*

4. Challenging translation—15 days before trial.

(1) Objection. To challenge the accuracy of the translation of a foreign law, a party must serve objections to the translation at least 15 days before trial. Tex. R. Evid. 1009(b). The 15-day period can be altered on a motion showing good cause. Tex. R. Evid. 1009(f). The objection should identify specific inaccuracies of the translation and offer an accurate translation. Tex. R. Evid. 1009(b). See **O'Connor's Texas Civil Forms**, FORM 5M:7 (2020 ed.).

(2) Effect of objection. The trial court must determine whether there is a genuine issue, to be resolved by the trier of fact, about the accuracy of a material part of the translation. Tex. R. Evid. 1009(d). If necessary, the trial court may appoint a qualified translator to translate the foreign law. Tex. R. Evid. 1009(g). The reasonable value of the translator's services is taxed as court costs. *Id.*

(3) When no objection made. When no objection or conflicting translation is timely served, the trial court must admit a translation if it complies with TRE 1009(a) and the underlying foreign-language documents are otherwise admissible. Tex. R. Evid. 1009(c). A party who does not serve a conflicting translation or objections cannot attack the accuracy of the translation. *Id.*

5. Court's sources of proof. If the court considers sources other than those submitted by a party, the court must give all parties notice and a reasonable opportunity to comment on the sources and to submit additional materials to the court. Tex. R. Evid. 203(c); **Lawrenson v. Global Mar., Inc.**, 869 S.W.2d 519, 525 (Tex.App.—Texarkana 1993, writ denied); *see also* **Ossorio v. Leon**, 705 S.W.2d 219, 221–22 (Tex.App.—San Antonio 1985, no writ) (after introduction of foreign law in motion for summary judgment, court granted postponement to comply with requirements in TRE 203).

§5. Response

If timely requested, a party is entitled to an opportunity to be heard on the propriety of taking judicial notice and the nature of the matter to be noticed. Tex. R. Evid. 201(e) (adjudicative facts), Tex. R. Evid. 202(c)(2) (federal laws and laws of sister states), Tex. R. Evid. 204(c)(2) (Texas city and county ordinances, contents of Texas Register, and agency rules published in Administrative Code).

§5.1 Form. If the motion for judicial notice was in writing, the response should be in writing. See **O'Connor's Texas Civil Forms**, FORMS 5M:4 to 5M:6 (2020 ed.).

§5.2 Objections. Some of the objections a party can file in response to a motion for judicial notice include the following:

1. Fact not generally known. The adjudicative fact to be judicially noticed is not indisputable because it is not generally known within the court's territorial jurisdiction. *See* Tex. R. Evid. 201(b)(1). Some arguments that can be made to support this response include the following:

(1) Fact only personally known. The adjudicative fact to be judicially noticed is based on the personal knowledge of the other party or the trial judge, but it is disputed. *E.g.*, **Eagle Trucking Co. v. Texas Bitulithic Co.**, 612 S.W.2d 503, 506 (Tex.1981) (court could not take judicial notice that certain land was outside residential or business district); **1.70 Acres v. State**, 935 S.W.2d 480, 489 (Tex.App.—Beaumont 1996, no writ) (court could not take judicial notice of time to drive a certain 9.2 miles).

(2) Fact known by special class. The adjudicative fact to be judicially noticed is commonly known by only a specially informed class of persons. *See, e.g.*, **Soto v. Texas Indus.**, 820 S.W.2d 217, 220 (Tex.App.—Fort Worth 1991, no writ) (fact that concrete walls do not fall in the absence of negligence was not within general knowledge).

2. Fact not verifiable. The adjudicative fact to be judicially noticed is not indisputable because it cannot be easily and accurately determined from a reliable source. *See* Tex. R. Evid. 201(b)(2).

3. Lack of sufficient information. The movant did not present sufficient information for the court to take judicial notice. *See, e.g.*, **Pittsburgh Corning Corp. v. Walters**, 1 S.W.3d 759, 769–70 (Tex.App.—Corpus Christi 1999, pet. denied) (D's motion did not contain significant recitation of California law or note where such law could be located).

4. Foreign law. Some objections to a motion to take judicial notice of foreign laws include the following: (1) the movant did not provide a copy of the foreign-language text and an English translation at least 30 days before trial, as required by TRE 203(b), (2) the movant did not provide the proof of foreign law at least 30 days before trial, as required by TRE 203(a)(2), or (3) the movant's expert did not properly interpret the law of the foreign jurisdiction. When objecting to the interpretation, the nonmovant must provide its own expert testimony to counter the movant's expert's interpretation. See "Expert opinion," ch. 5-M, §4.7.2(2).

§6. Hearing

Most motions for judicial notice can be resolved without a formal hearing to receive evidence.

§7. Ruling

§7.1 Order. The court, not the jury, must determine whether the matter requested should be judicially noticed. *See* Tex. R. Evid. 201(b), 202(e), 203(d), 204(d). To preserve error, the party should make sure the court signs a written order. See **O'Connor's Texas Civil Forms**, FORMS 5M:8 to 5M:9 (2020 ed.).

1. When mandatory.

(1) Adjudicative facts.

(a) Notorious facts. Judicial notice of notorious facts is mandatory when properly requested by a party. *See* Tex. R. Evid. 201(c)(2). Notorious facts do not require extrinsic support. **Tranter v. Duemling**, 129 S.W.3d 257, 262 (Tex.App.—El Paso 2004, no pet.).

(b) Verifiable facts. Judicial notice of verifiable facts is mandatory when properly requested by a party and the court has been supplied with the necessary information. Tex. R. Evid. 201(c)(2); **Office of Pub. Util. Counsel v. Public Util. Comm'n**, 878 S.W.2d 598, 600 (Tex.1994).

(2) Law. Under TRE 202 and 204, judicial notice of Texas, federal, and sister-state law is mandatory when properly requested by a party and the court has been supplied with the necessary information. Tex. R. Evid. 202(b)(2) (federal laws and laws of sister states), Tex. R. Evid. 204(b)(2) (Texas city and county ordinances, contents of Texas Register, and agency rules published in Administrative Code). No similar mandate exists for judicial notice of a foreign country's law under TRE 203.

2. When discretionary. Judicial notice of adjudicative facts and law is discretionary when the court exercises its right to judicially notice facts and law on its own motion. Tex. R. Evid. 201(c)(1), 202(b)(1), 204(b)(1); *see* **Daugherty v. Southern Pac. Transp.**, 772 S.W.2d 81, 83 (Tex.1989).

§7.2 Established fact. Once the court has judicially noticed a fact, that fact is established as a matter of law. **Langdale v. Villamil**, 813 S.W.2d 187, 190 (Tex.App.—Houston [14th Dist.] 1991, no writ).

§7.3 Jury instruction. Once the court has judicially noticed an adjudicative fact, it must instruct the jury in a civil case to accept that fact as conclusive. Tex. R. Evid. 201(f); *see, e.g.*, **Hoechst Celanese Corp. v. Arthur Bros.**, 882 S.W.2d 917, 930 (Tex.App.—Corpus Christi 1994, writ denied) (dicta; trial court took judicial notice of and instructed jury on D's net worth); **Allied Gen. Agency, Inc. v. Moody**, 788 S.W.2d 601, 607 (Tex.App.—Dallas 1990, writ denied) (court took judicial notice of and instructed jury on definition of "promotion" from three dictionaries); *see also* **O'Connell v. State**, 17 S.W.3d 746, 749 (Tex.App.—Austin 2000, no pet.) (error for court to instruct jury on legislative fact, rather than adjudicative fact).

§8. Review

§8.1 Record. The appellate record must contain (1) the motion for judicial notice, (2) all supporting information, and (3) the court's ruling. *See* **Metro Fuels, Inc. v. City of Austin**, 827 S.W.2d 531, 532 (Tex.App.—Austin 1992, no writ) (court of appeals refused to take judicial notice of ordinance because it was not included in record).

§8.2 Standard of review. A court's decision to take or refuse to take judicial notice of adjudicative facts will be reviewed for an abuse of discretion. *See* **In re A.R.**, 236 S.W.3d 460, 477 (Tex.App.—Dallas 2007, no pet.); **In re Graves**, 217 S.W.3d 744, 752 (Tex.App.—Waco 2007, orig. proceeding). A court's decision to take or refuse to take judicial notice of law will be reviewed de novo. *See* Tex. R. Evid. 202(e) (question of law), Tex. R. Evid. 203(d) (same), Tex. R. Evid. 204(d) (same). When a court erroneously takes or refuses to take judicial notice of a matter, the error is reversible only if it probably caused the rendition of an improper judgment. Tex. R. App. P. 44.1(a)(1); **Daugherty v. Southern Pac. Transp.**, 772 S.W.2d 81, 83 (Tex.1989); **Magee v. Ulery**, 993 S.W.2d 332, 339 (Tex.App.—Houston [14th Dist.] 1999, no pet.).

N. Motion to Exclude Expert

§1. General

§1.1 Rules. Tex R Evid. 104, 401 to 403, 702 to 705.

§1.2 Purpose. Under TRE 702, the trial court must act as a "gatekeeper" to determine an expert's qualifications and whether the expert's opinion is admissible. **E.I. du Pont de Nemours & Co. v. Robinson**, 923 S.W.2d 549, 556 (Tex1995).

§1.3 Forms. **O'Connor's Texas Civil Forms**, FORMS 5N:1 et seq. (2020 ed.).

§1.4 Other references. Squires & Harrison, *Motions to Disqualify or Exclude Expert Witnesses*, Ultimate Motions Practice, State Bar of Texas CLE, ch. 10 (2013); Brown, *Eight Gates for Expert Witnesses*, 36 Hous.L.Rev. 743 (1999); Brown & Love, *Tips on Expert Witness Practice*, 33 The Advoc. (Texas) 34 (Winter 2005); Johnson, *Appellate Issues Regarding the Admission or Exclusion of Expert Testimony in Texas*, 52 S.Tex.L.Rev. 153 (2010); Temple & Hollabaugh, *Expert Witness Issues on Appeal in State & Federal Court: Securing the Record from Adverse Robinson/Havner Rulings & the Standards of Review*, 33 The Advoc. (Texas) 28 (Winter 2005); **O'Connor's Texas Causes of Action** (2021 ed.); Brown & Rondon, **Texas Rules of Evidence Handbook** (2021 ed.).

§2. *Daubert-Robinson* test for expert testimony

The language of TRE 702 and 705(c) suggests four distinct but interrelated tests for the admissibility of expert testimony: qualifications, knowledge, helpfulness, and foundation data. *See* **Whirlpool Corp. v. Camacho**, 298 S.W.3d 631, 637 (Tex2009).

§2.1 Qualifications test. The witness must be qualified to give an expert opinion "by knowledge, skill, experience, training, or education." Tex R Evid. 702. See Brown & Rondon, **Texas Rules of Evidence Handbook**, Rule 702 (2021 ed.) (nn.105–109). In deciding if a witness is qualified as an expert, trial courts must ensure that those who purport to be experts have expertise in the actual subject they are offering an opinion about. **Cooper Tire & Rubber Co. v. Mendez**, 204 S.W.3d 797, 800 (Tex2006); **Roberts v. Williamson**, 111 S.W.3d 113, 121 (Tex2003); **Broders v. Heise**, 924 S.W.2d 148, 153 (Tex1996). When a subject is substantially developed in more than one field, testimony can come from a qualified expert in any of those fields. **Broders**, 924 S.W.2d at 154.

1. Education or training. The first inquiry is whether the witness is qualified by education or training to give an expert opinion.

(1) Qualified. The following witnesses were qualified: • Pediatrician, who was not a neurologist but was certified in pediatric advanced life support and studied and advised parents of the effects of pediatric neurological injuries, was qualified to testify about a newborn child's neurological injuries. **Roberts**, 111 S.W.3d at 121–22. • Police officer with training and experience in investigating accidents was qualified to testify that the driver's inattention caused the accident. **Ter-Vartanyan v. R&R Freight, Inc.**, 111 S.W.3d 779, 781 (TexApp.—Dallas 2003, pet. denied). • Otolaryngologist was qualified to testify about facial plastic surgery. **Keo v. Vu**, 76 S.W.3d 725, 732–33 (TexApp.—Houston [1st Dist.] 2002, pet. denied). • Neurologist was qualified to testify on standard of care and treatment of strokes even though he admitted no knowledge of the standard of care applied to cardiologists. **Blan v. Ali**, 7 S.W.3d 741, 746 (TexApp.—Houston [14th Dist.] 1999, no pet.).

(2) Not qualified. The following witnesses were not qualified: • Witness with chemistry and engineering degrees was not qualified to testify about wax migration and contamination in tires and its effect on tire failure because he had no training or experience relating specifically to tire chemistry or design. **Cooper Tire**, 204 S.W.3d at 806–07. • Witness with bacteriology and public-health degrees was not qualified to testify about transmission of AIDS virus through blood transfusion because he had no medical training or experience relating to blood transfusions. **United Blood Servs. v. Longoria**, 938 S.W.2d 29, 30–31 (Tex1997). • Emergency-room doctor was not qualified to testify in death case about cause of brain injury. **Broders**, 924 S.W.2d at 153. • Psychiatrist was not qualified to give opinion about postoperative care following neurosurgery. **Tomasi v. Liao**, 63 S.W.3d 62, 66 (TexApp.—San Antonio 2001, no pet.).

2. Specialized knowledge, skill & experience. If a witness is not qualified by education or training to give an expert opinion, the second inquiry is whether the witness is qualified by specialized knowledge, skill, or experience. *See* **Guadalupe-Blanco River Auth. v. Kraft**, 77 S.W.3d 805, 807 (Tex2002) (appraisal expertise is a form of specialized knowledge).

(1) Qualified. The following witnesses were qualified: • Witness with 35 years of experience in construction damage and repair of residential and commercial property who was a licensed master plumber and property inspector and who consulted treatises and other works by engineers and people involved in construction was qualified to testify about damage to residences caused by construction-equipment vibrations even though he was not an engineer. **C.C. Carlton Indus. v. Blanchard**, 311 S.W.3d 654, 658 (Tex.App.—Austin 2010, no pet.). • Witness with experience in conducting grain-performance trials was qualified to testify about suitability of a particular seed to dry-land farming even though he was not a plant pathologist. **Helena Chem. Co. v. Wilkins**, 47 S.W.3d 486, 500 (Tex.2001). • Surgeon with 11 years of surgical practice was qualified to testify that foreign object he removed from patient was a surgical sponge. **Mitchell v. Baylor Univ. Med. Ctr.**, 109 S.W.3d 838, 842 (Tex.App.—Dallas 2003, no pet.). • Trooper with 16 years of experience in accident investigation was qualified to testify about highway design. **Huckaby v. A.G. Perry & Son, Inc.**, 20 S.W.3d 194, 208 (Tex.App.—Texarkana 2000, pet. denied). • Appraiser with 20 years of experience was qualified to testify that ranch could not be partitioned. **Egan v. Egan**, 8 S.W.3d 1, 4 (Tex.App.—San Antonio 1999, pet. denied).

(2) Not qualified. The following witnesses were not qualified: • Engineer who had experience in designing and testing fighter planes, but had no experience regarding cars, could not testify about design defects in cars. **Gammill v. Jack Williams Chevrolet, Inc.**, 972 S.W.2d 713, 719 (Tex.1998). • Coworker was not qualified to testify that lift belt would have prevented back injury. **Leitch v. Hornsby**, 935 S.W.2d 114, 119 (Tex.1996). • Railroad engineer was not qualified to testify about braking defects because nothing connected engineer's experience and training with the matter at issue. **Houghton v. Port Terminal R.R.**, 999 S.W.2d 39, 48–49 (Tex.App.—Houston [14th Dist.] 1999, no pet.).

3. License. A professional license is not a requirement for the qualification of a witness. **Cura-Cruz v. CenterPoint Energy Houston Elec., LLC**, 522 S.W.3d 565, 573 (Tex.App.—Houston [14th Dist.] 2017, pet. denied); **Harnett v. State**, 38 S.W.3d 650, 659 (Tex.App.—Austin 2000, pet. ref'd); **Southland Lloyd's Ins. v. Tomberlain**, 919 S.W.2d 822, 827 (Tex.App.—Texarkana 1996, writ denied); **Tidwell v. Terex Corp.**, No. 01-10-01119-CV 2012 WL 3776027 (Tex.App.—Houston [1st Dist.] 2012, no pet.) (memo op.; 8-30-12); *see* **Reid Rd. MUD v. Speedy Stop Food Stores**, 337 S.W.3d 846, 852 n.3 (Tex.2011) (TRCP 702 does not require witness to have any particular license to qualify as expert). *But see* **Prellwitz v. Cromwell, Truemper, Levy, Parker & Woodsmale, Inc.**, 802 S.W.2d 316, 317 (Tex.App.—Dallas 1990, no writ) (witness who is to give expert opinion about standard of care within particular licensed profession must be licensed in same profession). Before an expert can testify about the standard of care in a medical-malpractice suit, however, the expert must meet the requirements of CPRC §§74.401 to 74.403. See "Expert's qualifications," **O'Connor's Texas Causes of Action**, ch. 20-A, §8.3 (2021 ed.).

§2.2 Knowledge test. The subject of the testimony must be "scientific, technical, or other specialized knowledge." Tex. R. Evid. 702; **Helena Chem. Co. v. Wilkins**, 47 S.W.3d 486, 499 (Tex.2001). An expert cannot offer an opinion based on a discipline that itself lacks reliability (e.g., astrology). **Kumho Tire Co. v. Carmichael**, 526 U.S. 137, 151 (1999). Valid knowledge consists of facts, as well as conclusions or ideas inferred from facts "on good grounds." **Daubert v. Merrell Dow Pharms.**, 509 U.S. 579, 590 (1993); *e.g.*, **GTE Sw., Inc. v. Bruce**, 998 S.W.2d 605, 619–20 (Tex.1999) (in suit for emotional distress, expert could not testify that certain conduct was extreme and outrageous; issue did not involve specialized knowledge); **Warren v. Hartnett**, 561 S.W.2d 860, 863 (Tex.App.—Dallas 1977, writ ref'd n.r.e.) (in probate case, expert could not testify based on handwriting sample that testatrix lacked testamentary capacity).

§2.3 Helpfulness test. The knowledge must "help the trier of fact to understand the evidence or to determine a fact in issue." Tex. R. Evid. 702; *e.g.*, **K-Mart Corp. v. Honeycutt**, 24 S.W.3d 357, 360–61 (Tex.2000) (human-factors expert was excluded as not helpful to the jury; opinions were within the average juror's common knowledge). Under TRE 702, it is the court's duty to determine whether the expert's testimony is sufficiently reliable and relevant to help a jury. **Gammill v. Jack Williams Chevrolet, Inc.**, 972 S.W.2d 713, 725 (Tex.1998). See Brown & Rondon, **Texas Rules of Evidence Handbook**, Rule 702 (2021 ed.) (§B.2). Thus, there are two parts of the helpfulness test.

1. Reliability of opinion. Each material part of an expert's opinion must be reliable. **Gharda USA, Inc. v. Control Solutions, Inc.**, 464 S.W.3d 338, 349 (Tex.2015); **Whirlpool Corp. v. Camacho**, 298 S.W.3d 631, 637 (Tex.2009); *see* **E.I. du Pont de Nemours & Co. v. Robinson**, 923 S.W.2d 549, 557 (Tex.1995); *see also* **Gunn v. McCoy**, 554 S.W.3d 645, 662 (Tex.2018) (expert's opinion may be considered unreliable if it is based on assumed facts that vary materially from actual facts or if it is based on tests or data that do not support conclusions reached). All expert testimony—not just scientific

expert testimony—must be shown to be reliable before it is admitted. **Kumho Tire Co. v. Carmichael**, 526 U.S. 137, 147 (1999); **Gammill**, 972 S.W.2d at 726. To determine whether an expert's testimony is reliable, the court should consider (1) the factors set out in **Daubert-Robinson** and (2) the "analytical gap" analysis expressed in **Gammill**. *See* **Gharda USA**, 464 S.W.3d at 349; **Transcontinental Ins. v. Crump**, 330 S.W.3d 211, 219 (Tex.2010); *see also* **Whirlpool Corp.**, 298 S.W.3d at 638 (in few cases will evidence be such that reliability determination can be based only on factors in **Robinson** to the exclusion of qualified expert's experience, and vice versa).

(1) *Daubert-Robinson* factors. In the area of hard science, experts are qualified to give an opinion according to the rules of scientific discipline as provided in **Daubert-Robinson**. **Gammill**, 972 S.W.2d at 725–26; *see, e.g.*, **Helm v. Swan**, 61 S.W.3d 493, 496–97 (Tex.App.—San Antonio 2001, pet. denied) (experts' medical opinions on causation did not meet **Daubert-Robinson** criteria for scientific reliability). An expert's opinion is not admissible if it is based on flawed methodology and reasoning. **Seger v. Yorkshire Ins. Co.**, 503 S.W.3d 388, 410 n.23 (Tex.2016); **Merrell Dow Pharms. v. Havner**, 953 S.W.2d 706, 714 (Tex.1997); **Austin v. Kerr-McGee Ref. Corp.**, 25 S.W.3d 280, 288 (Tex.App.—Texarkana 2000, no pet.). Some of the relevant factors that can be considered when assessing the reliability of expert testimony are the following:

(a) The extent to which the theory has been or can be tested. **Daubert v. Merrell Dow Pharms.**, 509 U.S. 579, 593 (1993); **Cooper Tire & Rubber Co. v. Mendez**, 204 S.W.3d 797, 801 (Tex.2006); **Robinson**, 923 S.W.2d at 557; *e.g.*, **Texas Workers' Comp. Ins. Fund v. Lopez**, 21 S.W.3d 358, 364–65 (Tex.App.—San Antonio 2000, pet. denied) (P's expert introduced articles demonstrating that his theory had been subjected to reliable testing); **America W. Airlines, Inc. v. Tope**, 935 S.W.2d 908, 918–19 (Tex.App.—El Paso 1996, writ dism'd) (mental-health worker's opinion could not be tested).

(b) The extent to which the technique relies on the expert's subjective interpretation. **Robinson**, 923 S.W.2d at 557; *e.g.*, **Cooper Tire**, 204 S.W.3d at 802 (expert conducted no quantitative analysis of his theory); **Lopez**, 21 S.W.3d at 364–65 (expert's causation testimony was based on objective criteria); **America W. Airlines**, 935 S.W.2d at 918–19 (mental-health worker's opinion was entirely subjective).

(c) Whether the theory has been or could be subjected to peer review or publication. **Daubert**, 509 U.S. at 593; **Robinson**, 923 S.W.2d at 557; *e.g.*, **Cooper Tire**, 204 S.W.3d at 802 (expert's theory was never subjected to peer review, and the only publication supporting theory was his own); **America W. Airlines**, 935 S.W.2d at 918–19 (peer review of mental-health worker's opinion was limited, and she offered no examples of publication of her work). Publication and other peer review are significant indicators of the reliability of scientific evidence when the expert's testimony is in an area in which peer review or publication would not be uncommon. **Havner**, 953 S.W.2d at 726; *see, e.g.*, **Bostic v. Georgia-Pac. Corp.**, 439 S.W.3d 332, 357–59 (Tex.2014) (certain publications relied on by P's experts were not scientific studies, and other peer-reviewed scientific studies did not significantly link mesothelioma to occasional asbestos exposure similar to that of P; evidence not reliable). Publication in reputable, established scientific journals and other forms of peer review increase the likelihood that substantive flaws in methodology will be detected. **Havner**, 953 S.W.2d at 726–27. Publication is not a prerequisite for scientific reliability in every case. *Id.* at 727.

(d) The technique's potential rate of error. **Daubert**, 509 U.S. at 594; **Robinson**, 923 S.W.2d at 557; *e.g.*, **Cooper Tire**, 204 S.W.3d at 802 (rate of error was unknown because there was no testing of expert's theory); **Lopez**, 21 S.W.3d at 364–65 (confidence level in studies cited by P was 95%, within the acceptable range required under **Havner**); **America W. Airlines**, 935 S.W.2d at 918–19 (potential rate of error in mental-health worker's opinion was "wholly unexplored").

(e) Whether the underlying theory or technique has been generally accepted as valid by the relevant scientific community. **Daubert**, 509 U.S. at 594; **Robinson**, 923 S.W.2d at 557; *see, e.g.*, **Neal v. Dow Agrosciences, LLC**, 74 S.W.3d 468, 473–74 (Tex.App.—Dallas 2002, no pet.) (court struck causation testimony; scientific literature relied on by expert did not support expert's conclusion).

(f) The nonjudicial uses of the theory or technique. **Robinson**, 923 S.W.2d at 557; *e.g.*, **Lopez**, 21 S.W.3d at 364–66 (expert's theory had been used to develop better clothing to protect workers from lung disease); **Waring v. Wommack**, 945 S.W.2d 889, 892 (Tex.App.—Austin 1997, no writ) (test performed by accident-reconstruction engineer had nonjudicial uses).

(2) *Gammill* "analytical gap" analysis. The **Daubert-Robinson** rules of scientific discipline do not always help evaluate the reliability of opinions in areas not considered "hard science," such as fields based primarily on experience and training. **Gammill**, 972 S.W.2d at 726; *see* **Kumho Tire**, 526 U.S. at 150–51 (**Daubert-Robinson** factors can be helpful but are not definitive); **Mack Trucks, Inc. v. Tamez**, 206 S.W.3d 572, 579 (Tex.2006) (courts can apply **Daubert-Robinson** factors to determine reliability of nonscientific expert's opinion if doing so would be helpful). In the area of so-called "soft sciences," experts are qualified to give an opinion as long as the analytical gap between the expert's methodology and the opinion offered is not too great. *See* **Transcontinental Ins.**, 330 S.W.3d at 219; **Gammill**, 972 S.W.2d at 727. In assessing the gap, the court should consider the following:

(a) Is the expert's field of expertise legitimate? **In re J.R.**, 501 S.W.3d 738, 748 (Tex.App.—Waco 2016, pet. denied); **Coastal Tankships, U.S.A., Inc. v. Anderson**, 87 S.W.3d 591, 601 (Tex.App.—Houston [1st Dist.] 2002, pet. denied); *e.g.*, **In re A.J.L.**, 136 S.W.3d 293, 298–99 (Tex.App.—Fort Worth 2004, no pet.) (play therapy is a legitimate field of expertise).

(b) Is the subject matter of the expert's testimony within the scope of that field? **In re J.R.**, 501 S.W.3d at 748; **Coastal Tankships**, 87 S.W.3d at 601; *see, e.g.*, **Gammill**, 972 S.W.2d at 726 (beekeeper could testify that bees take off into the wind based on beekeeper's own observations); **JCPenney Life Ins. v. Baker**, 33 S.W.3d 417, 428 (Tex.App.—Fort Worth 2000, no pet.) (internist's opinion about cause of death, based on his experience and observation, was reliable even though he was not a pathologist).

(c) Does the expert's testimony properly rely on the principles involved in the expert's field of study? **In re J.R.**, 501 S.W.3d at 748; **Coastal Tankships**, 87 S.W.3d at 601; *see, e.g.*, **Transcontinental Ins.**, 330 S.W.3d at 220 (treating physician's opinion on cause of P's death based on differential diagnosis was reliable); *see also* **Gharda USA**, 464 S.W.3d at 349 (analytical gap may include situation in which expert unreliably applies otherwise sound principles).

(d) Did the expert show a connection between the data relied upon and the opinion offered? **Southwestern Energy Prod. v. Berry-Helfand**, 491 S.W.3d 699, 717 (Tex.2016); **Gharda USA**, 464 S.W.3d at 349; **Houston Unlimited, Inc. Metal Processing v. Mel Acres Ranch**, 443 S.W.3d 820, 835 (Tex.2014); **Volkswagen v. Ramirez**, 159 S.W.3d 897, 906 (Tex.2004). If the "analytical gap" between the expert's data and the expert's offered testimony is too great, the testimony is unreliable. **Gunn**, 554 S.W.3d at 663; **Southwestern Energy**, 491 S.W.3d at 717; **Houston Unlimited**, 443 S.W.3d at 835; **Kerr-McGee Corp. v. Helton**, 133 S.W.3d 245, 254 (Tex.2004); **Gammill**, 972 S.W.2d at 727; *see, e.g.*, **Kia Motors Corp. v. Ruiz**, 432 S.W.3d 865, 877–78 (Tex.2014) (expert's testimony on structural defects in air-bag system was specific enough that there was no analytical gap between data and opinion that those defects prevented air bag from deploying); **Halim v. Ramchandani**, 203 S.W.3d 482, 492 (Tex.App.—Houston [14th Dist.] 2006, no pet.) (expert's testimony based on experience and knowledge of relevant literature was reliable; analytical connection was sufficient); **Gross v. Burt**, 149 S.W.3d 213, 238 (Tex.App.—Fort Worth 2004, pet. denied) (expert's experience and review of scientific literature did not support opinion; testimony was therefore "no evidence" that D's medical negligence was proximate cause of Ps' harm).

2. Relevance of opinion. The expert's opinion must be relevant. **Daubert**, 509 U.S. at 597; **Robinson**, 923 S.W.2d at 555; *see* Tex. R. Evid. 702; *see also* Tex. R. Evid. 401 (definition of relevant evidence), Tex. R. Evid. 402 (admissibility of relevant evidence). To be relevant, the testimony must be "sufficiently tied to the facts of the case" so that it will assist the jury in resolving a factual dispute. **Innovative Block v. Valley Builders Sup.**, 603 S.W.3d 409, 422 (Tex.2020); **Gharda USA**, 464 S.W.3d at 348; **Robinson**, 923 S.W.2d at 556. Evidence that has no relationship to any of the issues in the case is irrelevant and does not satisfy TRE 702's requirement that the testimony help the jury. **Robinson**, 923 S.W.2d at 556; *see* **U.S. Rest. Props. Oper. L.P. v. Motel Enters.**, 104 S.W.3d 284, 292 (Tex.App.—Beaumont 2003, pet. denied). Thus, the testimony is inadmissible under TRE 702 as well as under TRE 401 and 402. **Robinson**, 923 S.W.2d at 556.

Note

An expert witness may offer an opinion on a mixed question of law and fact as long as the opinion is confined to the relevant issues and is based on proper legal concepts. ***Birchfield v. Texarkana Mem'l Hosp.***, *747 S.W.2d 361, 365 (Tex.1987). An expert cannot testify about an opinion on a pure question of law.* ***Greenberg Traurig of N.Y., P.C. v. Moody***, *161 S.W.3d 56, 94 (Tex.App.—Houston [14th*

*Dist] 2004, no pet.); **Upjohn Co. v. Rylander**, 38 S.W.3d 600, 611 (Tex.App.—Austin 2000, pet. denied).*

§2.4 Foundation test. The expert's opinion must be based on sufficient "underlying facts or data." Tex. R. Evid. 705(c); *see* Tex. R. Evid. 703 (basis of opinion testimony by expert); *see also* **Caffe Ribs, Inc. v. State**, 487 S.W.3d 137, 144 (Tex.2016) (facts on which expert's opinion is based do not need to be undisputed). An expert's opinion is not admissible if it is based on unreliable foundation evidence. **Innovative Block v. Valley Builders Sup.**, 603 S.W.3d 409, 422–23 (Tex.2020); **Merrell Dow Pharms. v. Havner**, 953 S.W.2d 706, 714 (Tex.1997); *see, e.g.*, **Gharda USA, Inc. v. Control Solutions, Inc.**, 464 S.W.3d 338, 352 (Tex.2015) (experts' theories on origin of fire were based on unreliable opinions of two other experts retained in case); **Marathon Corp. v. Pitzner**, 106 S.W.3d 724, 729 (Tex.2003) (expert opinion was speculation not based on evidence); *see also* **Houston Unlimited, Inc. Metal Processing v. Mel Acres Ranch**, 443 S.W.3d 820, 833 (Tex.2014) (if expert's material factual assumptions have no evidentiary support in the record or those assumptions are contrary to proven facts, expert's testimony based on those assumptions is not competent evidence). For example, an expert's opinion may be excluded for lack of a proper foundation when the expert does not rule out alternative causes of an incident. *See* **Bustamante v. Ponte**, 529 S.W.3d 447, 456–57 (Tex.2017) (expert must exclude all other plausible causes, not all potential causes); *see, e.g.*, **Wal-Mart Stores v. Merrell**, 313 S.W.3d 837, 839–40 (Tex.2010) (expert's testimony was conclusory because he did not adequately explain how he excluded other possible cause of fire); **E.I. du Pont de Nemours & Co. v. Robinson**, 923 S.W.2d 549, 558–59 (Tex.1995) (expert's testimony was not based on reliable foundation because he did not conduct test to exclude other possible causes); **Martinez v. City of San Antonio**, 40 S.W.3d 587, 594–95 (Tex.App.—San Antonio 2001, pet. denied) (expert's testimony was properly excluded; expert did not rule out other plausible causes of contamination); *see also* **JLG Trucking, LLC v. Garza**, 466 S.W.3d 157, 162–63 (Tex.2015) (error to exclude evidence of second accident P was involved in because exclusion meant P's expert did not have to negate alternative cause of injury; second accident was relevant to whether D's negligence in first accident caused P's injury).

§3. Gatekeeper hearing on qualifications & opinions of experts

If specialized knowledge will help the fact-finder understand the evidence or decide a fact issue, a witness who qualifies as an expert may testify in the form of an opinion "or otherwise." Tex. R. Evid. 702; *see* **Louder v. De Leon**, 754 S.W.2d 148, 149 (Tex.1988); *see, e.g.*, **GTE Sw., Inc. v. Bruce**, 998 S.W.2d 605, 620 (Tex.1999) (in suit for intentional infliction of emotional distress, expert could not testify that certain conduct was extreme and outrageous; issue involved only general knowledge and experience rather than expertise).

§3.1 Deadline to object to expert. Issues about the admissibility of the expert's opinion should be resolved as early as possible, preferably before trial. **Maritime Overseas Corp. v. Ellis**, 971 S.W.2d 402, 412–13 (Tex.1998) (Gonzalez, J., concurring). However, a deficiency in the expert's opinion may not emerge until after the trial begins. *E.g.*, **General Motors Corp. v. Iracheta**, 161 S.W.3d 462, 471 (Tex.2005) (objection after cross-examination of expert was not too late because unreliability of expert's testimony was not fully apparent until cross-examination); *see also* **North Dallas Diagnostic Ctr. v. Dewberry**, 900 S.W.2d 90, 96 (Tex.App.—Dallas 1995, writ denied) (expert was challenged on voir dire). For a discussion of when an objection is required to preserve error, see "Preserving error," ch. 5-N, §6.2.

Practice Tip

To avoid surprises at trial, the parties can consider including a specific date in the scheduling order for objections to be made and heard. See "Scope of pretrial conference," ch. 5-A, §3.

§3.2 Objection to expert. To object to an expert, the party should make a written pretrial objection to the admissibility of the expert's opinion under TRE 104(c). See the procedures used in **Merrell Dow Pharms. v. Havner**, 953 S.W.2d 706, 709 (Tex.1997), and **E.I. du Pont de Nemours & Co. v. Robinson**, 923 S.W.2d 549, 552 (Tex.1995). For more details on the procedures for making the motion, see **O'Connor's Texas Civil Forms**, FORMS 5N:1, 5N:3 (2020 ed.).

Practice Tip

Do not include an objection to an expert in a motion in limine. A ruling on a motion in limine does not preserve error for either party. See "Preserving error," ch. 5-N, §3.7.

1. Allegations. The party must specifically identify each expert and each expert's opinion and conclusion that the party seeks to exclude. The motion should challenge the expert on some or all of the following grounds:

(1) The expert is not qualified to give the opinion. See "Qualifications test," ch. 5-N, §2.1.

(2) The subject of the testimony is not specialized knowledge. See "Knowledge test," ch. 5-N, §2.2.

(3) The expert's opinion is not reliable. See "Reliability of opinion," ch. 5-N, §2.3.1.

(4) The expert's opinion is not relevant. See "Relevance of opinion," ch. 5-N, §2.3.2.

(5) The underlying facts of the expert's opinion do not provide a sufficient basis for the opinion. See "Foundation test," ch. 5-N, §2.4. An objection to an expert's qualifications does not preserve error regarding the foundation for the expert's opinion. **City of Paris v. McDowell**, 79 S.W.3d 601, 605 (Tex.App.—Texarkana 2002, no pet.).

(6) The probative value of the opinion is substantially outweighed by the danger of unfair prejudice, confusion, or delay. Tex. R. Evid. 403; **Robinson**, 923 S.W.2d at 557; **State v. Malone Serv.**, 829 S.W.2d 763, 767 (Tex.1992); **North Dallas Diagnostic Ctr. v. Dewberry**, 900 S.W.2d 90, 95–96 (Tex.App.—Dallas 1995, writ denied). Once the court finds that the expert's opinion is admissible, the court has the additional duty to weigh the expert's testimony against the danger of unfair prejudice, confusion of the issues, the possibility of misleading the jury, or undue delay. Tex. R. Evid. 403; *see* **Texas Workers' Comp. Ins. Fund v. Lopez**, 21 S.W.3d 358, 364 (Tex.App.—San Antonio 2000, pet. denied).

2. Challenger's evidence. Because the party challenging the expert initially bears no burden to undermine the expert or the expert's opinion, that party is not required to provide evidence to support its challenges.

3. Hearing. The party objecting to the expert should ask the court to set the objections for a hearing. Johnson, *Appellate Issues Regarding the Admission or Exclusion of Expert Testimony in Texas*, 52 S.Tex.L.Rev. 153, 185–86 (2010). See "TRE 104 hearing," ch. 5-N, §3.5.

§3.3 Sponsor's response to objection. Once a party objects to the expert's testimony, the party sponsoring the expert bears the burden of responding to each objection and showing that the testimony is admissible by a preponderance of the evidence. *See* **E.I. du Pont de Nemours & Co. v. Robinson**, 923 S.W.2d 549, 557 (Tex.1995); **Texas Mut. Ins. v. Lerma**, 143 S.W.3d 172, 175 (Tex.App.—San Antonio 2004, pet. denied); **Frias v. Atlantic Richfield Co.**, 104 S.W.3d 925, 927 (Tex.App.—Houston [14th Dist.] 2003, no pet.); **Purina Mills, Inc. v. Odell**, 948 S.W.2d 927, 933 (Tex.App.—Texarkana 1997, pet. denied); *see also* **Weiss v. Mechanical Associated Servs.**, 989 S.W.2d 120, 124 & n.6 (Tex.App.—San Antonio 1999, pet. denied) (in no-evidence summary-judgment proceeding, nonmovant had burden to bring forward competent evidence supporting admissibility of expert opinion); *cf.* **Daubert v. Merrell Dow Pharms.**, 509 U.S. 579, 592 n.10 (1993) (under FRE 104, admissibility of expert testimony must be established by "preponderance of proof"). See **O'Connor's Texas Civil Forms**, FORMS 5N:2, 5N:4 (2020 ed.).

1. Allegations. If the party challenging the expert made specific complaints about the expert's qualifications or the relevance or reliability of the opinion, the sponsor of the expert should respond only to those complaints. If, however, the movant made only a general complaint under **Robinson**, the sponsor of the expert should assume the full burden and allege the following:

(1) The expert is qualified. The party sponsoring the expert must show that the expert's knowledge, experience, skill, training, or education qualifies the expert to give an opinion on the specific issue before the court. See "Qualifications test," ch. 5-N, §2.1.

(2) The subject of the testimony is specialized knowledge that is appropriate for an expert's opinion. See "Knowledge test," ch. 5-N, §2.2.

(3) The expert's opinion is reliable. See "Reliability of opinion," ch. 5-N, §2.3.1.

(4) The expert's opinion is relevant. See "Relevance of opinion," ch. 5-N, §2.3.2.

(5) The underlying facts of the expert's opinion provide a sufficient basis for the expert's opinion. See "Foundation test," ch. 5-N, §2.4.

(6) The probative value of the opinion is not substantially outweighed by the danger of unfair prejudice, confusion, or delay. Tex. R. Evid. 403; **Robinson**, 923 S.W.2d at 557. See "Allegations," ch. 5-N, §3.2.1.

2. Sponsor's evidence. To meet its burden of showing that the opinion is admissible, the party sponsoring the expert should attach verified proof to the response, either by affidavit or by deposition testimony. The evidence should show the expert is qualified, the expert's opinion is relevant, and the expert's opinion is reliable. See "Allegations," ch. 5-N, §3.3.1. To bolster the expert's testimony, the party may also submit other evidence, including the affidavit or deposition of another expert and the published works of the challenged expert or other experts. *See* **Pink v. Goodyear Tire & Rubber Co.**, 324 S.W.3d 290, 301 & n.5 (Tex.App.—Beaumont 2010, pet. dism'd).

§3.4 Reply by party challenging expert. If the response of the expert's sponsor seems to meet its burden of showing that its expert's opinion is admissible, the party challenging the expert should probably file a reply with verified proof showing that (1) the expert is not qualified, (2) the expert's opinion is not relevant, or (3) the expert's opinion is not reliable. By filing evidence with its reply, the party will preserve its evidence in the event the trial court resolves the issue without a hearing.

§3.5 TRE 104 hearing. In making the determination of admissibility, the court is not bound by the rules of evidence except those that deal with privileges. Tex. R. Evid. 104(a). In most cases, the court should conduct a pretrial hearing to determine the admissibility of the expert's opinion. The court has discretion, however, to decide whether to even conduct an evidentiary hearing. **State v. Petropoulos**, 346 S.W.3d 525, 529 n.1 (Tex.2011); *see, e.g.*, **Piro v. Sarofim**, 80 S.W.3d 717, 720 (Tex.App.—Houston [1st Dist.] 2002, no pet.) (court's refusal to hold live gatekeeper hearing was not abuse of discretion). If a live hearing is held, it should be conducted with all the formalities of trial and should be recorded by the court reporter. Without a record from the hearing, the appellant will not be able to show harm. See "Record," ch. 5-N, §6.1.

1. Sponsor. To meet its burden of showing that the opinion is admissible, the expert's sponsor should offer the testimony of the challenged expert, either live or by deposition. To bolster the expert's testimony, qualifications, relevance, and reliability, the sponsor may offer other evidence, including the testimony of another expert and the published works of the challenged expert or other experts. *See* **Pink v. Goodyear Tire & Rubber Co.**, 324 S.W.3d 290, 301 & n.5 (Tex.App.—Beaumont 2010, pet. dism'd).

2. Challenger. If the sponsor meets its burden of showing that the opinion is admissible, the party challenging the expert should attempt to undermine the expert by providing the testimony of its own expert that challenges (1) the qualifications of the sponsor's expert and (2) the scientific validity of the opinion offered by the sponsor's expert. The challenger's expert should show why the sponsor's expert's opinion fails the **Daubert-Robinson** test.

§3.6 Ruling. After receiving evidence, the trial court must rule on each objection raised by the motion. If the sponsoring party does not meet its burden of proof, the trial court should exclude the expert. To exclude the expert witness, the order should state unequivocally that the expert and the expert's evidence are excluded.

Practice Tip

If the trial court excludes the expert testimony, the sponsoring party should make a separate offer of proof for every excluded opinion. See "Offer of Proof & Bill of Exception," ch. 8-E, §1 et seq.

---

§3.7 Preserving error. To preserve a complaint that an expert's testimony is unreliable and thus no evidence, a party must object to the testimony before trial or when the testimony is offered. See "Preserving error," ch. 5-N, §6.2. The court's order after a gatekeeper hearing should be considered a pretrial ruling on the admissibility of the expert's opinion, not a ruling on a motion in limine. A ruling on a motion in limine does not preserve error. See "Function of order," ch. 5-E, §5.2.

Whether the ruling after the gatekeeper hearing preserves error depends on the wording of the order. If the order unequivocally states that the expert's testimony will or will not be admitted at trial, the ruling is a pretrial ruling on the admissibility of the evidence and preserves error. *See* Tex. R. Evid. 103(a); **Huckaby v. A.G. Perry & Son, Inc.**, 20 S.W.3d 194, 205–06 (Tex.App.—Texarkana 2000, pet. denied). If the ruling is tentative and requires the parties to approach the bench or to reurge their objections at trial, the ruling is a motion-in-limine ruling and does not preserve error. See "Offer & objection at trial," ch. 5-E, §6.

§4. Motion to disqualify expert

The only Texas court to consider the issue of disqualifying a nonattorney expert because the expert switched sides is the Corpus Christi Court of Appeals in **Formosa Plastics Corp. v. Kajima Int'l**, 216 S.W.3d 436, 447 (Tex.App.—Corpus Christi 2006, pet. denied). In doing so, the court applied the **Koch** test. *Id.* at 448; *see* **Koch Ref. Co. v. Jennifer L. Boudreaux MV**, 85 F.3d 1178, 1181 (5th Cir.1996).

§4.1 Burden of proof. The party moving for disqualification has the burden to establish that disqualification is necessary. **Formosa Plastics Corp. v. Kajima Int'l**, 216 S.W.3d 436, 449 (Tex.App.—Corpus Christi 2006, pet. denied); **Koch Ref. Co. v. Jennifer L. Boudreaux MV**, 85 F.3d 1178, 1181 (5th Cir.1996). To disqualify an expert who switched sides, the first party to hire the expert must establish the two **Koch** factors and (perhaps) additional factors:

1. ***Koch* factor #1—confidential relationship.** It was objectively reasonable for the first party who claims to have retained the expert to conclude that it had a confidential relationship with the expert. **Formosa Plastics**, 216 S.W.3d at 449; **Koch Ref.**, 85 F.3d at 1181. In evaluating whether there was a confidential relationship, the **Formosa** court listed 11 factors to consider. **Formosa Plastics**, 216 S.W.3d at 449. A confidential relationship with one expert in a firm of experts is not imputed to the entire firm, as it is with the disqualification of attorneys. *Id.* at 451.

2. ***Koch* factor #2—confidential information.** The party who first retained the expert disclosed confidential or privileged information to the expert. **Formosa Plastics**, 216 S.W.3d at 448; **Koch Ref.**, 85 F.3d at 1181. Confidential information is information that either (1) is of particular significance or (2) can be identified as either attorney work product or within the scope of the attorney-client privilege. **Formosa Plastics**, 216 S.W.3d at 449. It can include the following: discussions of litigation strategy, the kinds of experts the party will employ, the role of each expert, the party's evaluation of the strengths and weaknesses of each side, and anticipated defenses. *Id.* at 450.

3. **Additional factors.** The **Formosa** court suggested—but did not apply—other factors: (1) whether the disqualification would be prejudicial, (2) whether the disqualification would promote the integrity of the judicial process, and (3) whether the disqualification would affect the public interest. **Formosa Plastics**, 216 S.W.3d at 448 (dicta); *see also* **Koch Ref.**, 85 F.3d at 1181 (dicta; factor #3).

§4.2 Trial-court order. The trial court has the inherent power to disqualify an expert who switched sides, which is derived from the necessity to protect privileges and to preserve public confidence in the judicial proceedings. **Formosa Plastics Corp. v. Kajima Int'l**, 216 S.W.3d 436, 488 (Tex.App.—Corpus Christi 2006, pet. denied) (Yañez, J., dissenting); *see* **Koch Ref. Co. v. Jennifer L. Boudreaux MV**, 85 F.3d 1178, 1181 (5th Cir.1996).

§5. Experts in medical-malpractice suits

Information about experts in medical-malpractice suits is covered in "Expert testimony," **O'Connor's Texas Causes of Action**, ch. 20-A, §8 (2021 ed.).

§6. Review

§6.1 Record. When appealing from a final judgment rendered in a trial in which the trial court ruled on a motion to exclude an expert at an evidentiary hearing, the appellant should include the record of the hearing in the appellate record. **Exxon Corp. v. Makofski**, 116 S.W.3d 176, 196 (Tex.App.—Houston [14th Dist.] 2003, pet. denied) (Seymore, J., dissenting). *But see id.* at 180 (majority op.) (D did not waive error by not submitting record of pretrial hearing because P waived complaint on appeal). For example, if the trial court excluded an expert in a gatekeeper hearing and later rendered a summary judgment, the appellant should request the reporter's record from the gatekeeper hearing and the clerk's record from the trial, which includes all the pleadings necessary to challenge the summary judgment and the court's ruling on the expert.

§6.2 Preserving error. A party should always object to deficiencies in the other party's expert evidence (e.g., the underlying methodology, technique, or foundation evidence used). However, when a party's expert evidence is deficient on its face, an objection may not be necessary.

1. Underlying methodology. An objection is required to challenge the underlying methodology, technique, or foundation evidence used by the expert. **Pike v. Texas EMC Mgmt.**, __ S.W.3d __, 2020 WL 3405812 (Tex.2020) (No. 17-0557; 6-19-20); **City of San Antonio v. Pollock**, 284 S.W.3d 809, 816–17 (Tex.2009); **Coastal Transp. Co. v. Crown Cent. Pet. Corp.**, 136 S.W.3d 227, 233 (Tex.2004). To preserve a complaint that scientific evidence is unreliable, a party must object to the evidence before trial or when the evidence is offered. **Pike**, __ S.W.3d at __, 2020 WL 3405812; **Guadalupe-Blanco River Auth. v. Kraft**, 77 S.W.3d 805, 807 (Tex.2002); **Maritime Overseas Corp. v. Ellis**, 971 S.W.2d 402, 409 (Tex.1998); *e.g.*, **Kerr-McGee Corp. v. Helton**, 133 S.W.3d 245, 251–52 (Tex.2004) (complaint was preserved when D objected to testimony immediately after cross-examination); *see* **Southwestern Energy Prod. v. Berry-Helfand**, 491 S.W.3d 699, 716 (Tex.2016). The objecting party cannot argue for the first time on appeal that the scientific evidence is unreliable and should be ignored. *See* **Maritime Overseas**, 971 S.W.2d at 409; *see also* **City of San Antonio**, 284 S.W.3d at 818 (when expert opinion is admitted without objection, it may be considered probative even if basis for opinion is unreliable). Without a timely objection, the offering party would not have a chance to cure the defect in the evidence and would be subject to trial and appeal by ambush. **Pike**, __ S.W.3d at __, 2020 WL 3405812; **City of San Antonio**, 284 S.W.3d at 817; **Kerr-McGee**, 133 S.W.3d at 252; **Maritime Overseas**, 971 S.W.2d at 409.

2. Conclusory evidence. An objection is not required to challenge the face of the record—for example, when expert testimony is speculative or conclusory on its face. **Pike**, __ S.W.3d at __, 2020 WL 3405812; **Windrum v. Kareh**, 581 S.W.3d 761, 770 (Tex.2019); **City of San Antonio**, 284 S.W.3d at 818; **Coastal Transp.**, 136 S.W.3d at 233; *see* **Bombardier Aerospace Corp. v. SPEP Aircraft Holdings, LLC**, 572 S.W.3d 213, 223 (Tex.2019). In such a case, the party may challenge the legal sufficiency of the evidence on appeal even when no objection was made to its admissibility. **Coastal Transp.**, 136 S.W.3d at 233; *see* **Pike**, __ S.W.3d at __, 2020 WL 3405812; **Windrum**, 581 S.W.3d at 770; **Bombardier Aerospace**, 572 S.W.3d at 223. For ways to preserve a legal-sufficiency challenge, see "Preserving legal-sufficiency point," ch. 10-B, §13.1.3.

§6.3 Standard of review. The trial court's decision to admit expert testimony is reviewed for abuse of discretion. **Innovative Block v. Valley Builders Sup.**, 603 S.W.3d 409, 423 (Tex.2020); **Southwestern Energy Prod. v. Berry-Helfand**, 491 S.W.3d 699, 716 (Tex.2016); **Gharda USA, Inc. v. Control Solutions, Inc.**, 464 S.W.3d 338, 347 (Tex.2015); **Whirlpool Corp. v. Camacho**, 298 S.W.3d 631, 638 (Tex.2009). When a party claims that the evidence or expert testimony is unreliable and thus legally insufficient to support a verdict, the appellate court will use a no-evidence review and consider whether the testimony would allow reasonable and fair-minded jurors to reach the verdict. **Whirlpool Corp.**, 298 S.W.3d at 638; *see* **Gharda USA**, 464 S.W.3d at 347–48. A no-evidence review encompasses the entire record, including any contrary evidence that may show the expert's opinion is unreliable. **Gharda USA**, 464 S.W.3d at 348; **Whirlpool Corp.**, 298 S.W.3d at 638.

§6.4 Render or remand. When expert testimony is admitted over objection and on appeal the expert's testimony is found to have been inadmissible, the appellate court should reverse and render judgment if the lower court's judgment cannot be sustained without the inadmissible expert testimony. *See* **Kerr-McGee Corp. v. Helton**, 133 S.W.3d 245, 258–60 (Tex.2004). However, if the appellate court overrules existing precedent that the losing party relied on at trial, the court should remand for a new trial. *See* **Bulanek v. WesTTex 66 Pipeline Co.**, 209 S.W.3d 98, 100 (Tex.2006).

Chapter 6. Discovery

A. General Rules for Discovery

§1. General

§1.1 Rules. Tex. R. Civ. P. 176, 190 to 205, 215.

§1.2 Purpose. The purpose of discovery is to allow the parties to obtain full knowledge of the issues and facts of the lawsuit before trial. **West v. Solito**, 563 S.W.2d 240, 243 (Tex.1978). The objective of the Texas discovery rules is to prevent trial by ambush. **Gutierrez v. Dallas ISD**, 729 S.W.2d 691, 693 (Tex.1987).

§1.3 Timetables & forms. Appendix IV, Timetable 9, Discovery schedule for Level 1; Appendix IV, Timetable 10, Discovery schedule for Level 2; **O'Connor's Texas Civil Forms**, FORMS 1B:12, 1H:13, 6A:1 et seq. (2020 ed.).

§1.4 Other references. Texas Pattern Jury Charges—General Negligence, Intentional Personal Torts & Workers' Compensation, PJC 1.13 (2018 ed.) (instruction on spoliation); Simmons, *The Dog Ate My Evidence: Spoliation Under the New Texas Framework*, Advanced Civil Trial Course, State Bar of Texas CLE, ch. 15 (2016); Hoffman, *The New Spoliation: How the Texas Supreme Court Clarified & Redefined the Law*, 78 Tex.B.J. 270 (Apr.2015); Downing et al., *"Be Careful What You Ask For, You May Get It": Common Sense Discovery Requests & Responses*, Advanced Family Law Course, State Bar of Texas CLE, ch. 15 (2006); Griesel, *The "New" Texas Discovery Rules: Three Years Later*, Advanced Evidence & Discovery Course, State Bar of Texas CLE, ch. 2 (2002); **O'Connor's Texas Civil Appeals** (2020 ed.); Brown & Rondon, **Texas Rules of Evidence Handbook** (2021 ed.).

Practice Tip

Before engaging in discovery, prepare a draft of the jury charge based on all the pleadings. Only when you know what questions the jury will be asked can you design an intelligent discovery plan.

§2. Terms & definitions

The following are definitions of several key terms used throughout this chapter.

§2.1 Discovery periods. Discovery periods determine how long the parties have to conduct discovery. See "Discovery periods," ch. 6-A, §8.

§2.2 Documents & tangible things. The phrase "documents and tangible things" includes papers, books, accounts, drawings, graphs, charts, photographs, electronic or videotape recordings, data, and data compilations. Tex. R. Civ. P. 192.3(b).

§2.3 Nonparty witness. The term "nonparty witness" means a witness who is not a party and is not retained by, employed by, or otherwise subject to the control of a party. *See* Tex. R. Civ. P. 199.3, 205.1; *see, e.g.*, **In re Carnival Corp.**, 193 S.W.3d 229, 235 (Tex.App.—Houston [1st Dist.] 2006, orig. proceeding) (D's independent contractor was not subject to D's control).

§2.4 Party witness. The term "party witness" includes the party and witnesses who are retained by, employed by, or otherwise subject to the control of the party. *See* Tex. R. Civ. P. 199.3.

§2.5 Possession. The phrase "possession, custody, or control" of an item means that the person either has physical possession of the item or has a right to possession that is equal or superior to that of the person who has physical possession. Tex. R. Civ. P. 192.7(b); **In re Kuntz**, 124 S.W.3d 179, 181 (Tex.2003); **GTE Comms. Sys. v. Tanner**, 856 S.W.2d 725, 729 (Tex.1993). Mere access to documents is not "physical possession" of the documents under TRCP 192.7(b). **In re Kuntz**, 124 S.W.3d at 184. The right to obtain possession is a legal right based on the relationship between the party responding to discovery and the person or entity that has actual possession. **GTE**, 856 S.W.2d at 729; *see, e.g.*, **State v. Lowry**, 802 S.W.2d 669, 673–74 (Tex.1991) (request to Attorney General was sufficient to require production of documents held by all divisions of office). A party is required to produce only those documents or tangible things in its possession, custody, or control. Tex. R. Civ. P. 192.3(b); **GTE**, 856 S.W.2d at 728–29; *see also* **In re U-Haul Int'l**, 87 S.W.3d 653, 656–57 (Tex.App.—San Antonio 2002, orig. proceeding) (P did not meet burden of proving that D had right to obtain possession of documents from D's related subsidiary).

§2.6 Privilege & confidentiality. Although the terms "privilege" and "confidentiality" are used interchangeably in many rules and statutes limiting the scope of discovery, they represent different legal concepts. An evidentiary privilege addresses what evidence is or is not discoverable for purposes of litigation (e.g., communications and records between a dentist and patient are privileged under Occupations Code §258.102). By comparison, confidentiality involves the legal and ethical responsibilities of a certain person or entity to certain other persons regarding particular information (e.g., HIV-test results are confidential under Health & Safety Code §81.103).

§2.7 Side. The term "side" refers to all the litigants with generally common interests in the litigation. Tex. R. Civ. P. 190.3(b)(2). The concept of "side" in TRCP 190.3(b)(2) was borrowed from TRCP 233, which governs the allocation of peremptory strikes, and from FRCP 30(a)(2). Tex. R. Civ. P. 190 cmt. 6 (1999); *see also* Tex. R. Civ. P. 169(d)(3)(A) (in expedited actions, "side" has same definition as that in TRCP 233). See "Peremptory challenges," ch. 8-A, §7. In most cases there are only two sides—plaintiffs and defendants. Tex. R. Civ. P. 190 cmt. 6 (1999). In complex cases, however, there may be more than two sides, such as when defendants have sued third parties not named by the plaintiffs or when defendants have sued each other. *Id.*

§2.8 Withholding statement. The term "withholding statement" means a statement in which a party claims that information responsive to written discovery is privileged. Tex. R. Civ. P. 193.3(a). A withholding statement may be included in the discovery response or filed separately. *Id.* The withholding statement must (1) state that information responsive to the written-discovery request or required disclosure is being withheld, (2) identify the request or required disclosure that the information or material relates to, and (3) identify the privilege asserted. *Id.*; *see* **In re Lumbermen's Underwriting Alliance**, 421 S.W.3d 289, 292 (Tex.App.—Texarkana 2014, orig. proceeding); **In re Monsanto Co.**, 998 S.W.2d 917, 924 (Tex.App.—Waco 1999, orig. proceeding).

2021 Rule Amendments

In 2020, the Supreme Court approved significant amendments to TRCP 194 and 195. See Tex.Sup.Ct. Order, Misc. Docket No. 20-9153 (eff. Jan. 1, 2021). Under the amendments, a party is now generally required to provide certain information and material without waiting for a discovery request from the other party. See Tex. R. Civ. P. 194.1(a). See "Required disclosures—Cases filed on or after 1-1-21," ch. 6-E, §3. The amendments apply to cases filed on or after January 1, 2021, except those filed in justice court. Tex.Sup.Ct. Order, Misc. Docket No. 20-9153 (eff. Jan. 1, 2021).

§2.9 Work product. The term "work product" includes (1) material prepared or mental impressions developed in anticipation of litigation or for trial, by or for a party or its representatives, including the party's attorneys, consultants, sureties, indemnitors, insurers, employees, or agents, or (2) communications made in anticipation of litigation or for trial between a party and its representatives or among a party's representatives, including the party's attorneys, consultants, sureties, indemnitors, insurers, employees, or agents. Tex. R. Civ. P. 192.5(a). The work-product discovery exemption replaced the "attorney work product" and "party communication" exemptions in former TRCP 166b. Tex. R. Civ. P. 192 cmt. 8.

1. Core work product. Core work product is the work product of an attorney or an attorney's representative containing that person's mental impressions, opinions, conclusions, or legal theories. Tex. R. Civ. P. 192.5(b)(1).

2. Noncore work product. Noncore work product, which is not specifically defined in the TRCPs, is all work product except that of an attorney or an attorney's representative containing that person's mental impressions, opinions, conclusions, or legal theories. *See* Tex. R. Civ. P. 192.5(b)(1). Noncore work product includes party communications. *See* Tex. R. Civ. P. 192.5(a)(2).

§2.10 Written discovery. The term "written discovery" includes (1) required disclosures, (2) requests for production and inspection of documents and tangible things, (3) requests for entry on property, (4) interrogatories, and (5) requests for admissions. Tex. R. Civ. P. 192.7(a). It does not include depositions on written questions. *See id.*

2021 Rule Amendments

In 2020, the Supreme Court approved significant amendments to TRCP 194 to require a party to disclose certain information without waiting for a discovery request from the other party. See Tex. R. Civ. P. 194.1(a); Tex.Sup.Ct. Order, Misc. Docket No. 20-9153 (eff. Jan. 1, 2021). For a discussion of these amendments, see "Required disclosures—Cases filed on or after 1-1-21," ch. 6-E, §3.

§3. Preservation of evidence

A party may have a common-law, statutory, regulatory, or ethical duty to preserve evidence. **Clements v. Conard**, 21 S.W.3d 514, 523 (Tex.App.—Amarillo 2000, pet. denied); **Trevino v. Ortega**, 969 S.W.2d 950, 955 (Tex.1998) (Baker, J., concurring).

§3.1 Common-law duty.

1. When duty arises. A party has a common-law duty to preserve evidence when it knows or reasonably should know that (1) there is a substantial chance that a claim will be filed and (2) evidence in its possession or control will be material and relevant to that claim. **Brookshire Bros. v. Aldridge**, 438 S.W.3d 9, 20 (Tex.2014); **Wal-Mart Stores v. Johnson**, 106 S.W.3d 718, 722 (Tex.2003). See "Possession," ch. 6-A, §2.5; "Duty to preserve," ch. 6-A, §24.2.1(1)(a).

2. Scope of duty. The common-law duty to preserve evidence does not require a party to keep every document or item in its possession. **Adobe Land Corp. v. Griffin, L.L.C.**, 236 S.W.3d 351, 357 (Tex.App.—Fort Worth 2007, pet. denied), *disapproved on other grounds*, **Brookshire Bros. v. Aldridge**, 438 S.W.3d 9 (Tex.2014). A party must, however, preserve evidence that it knows or reasonably should know is relevant to the claim, is likely to be requested in discovery, or is the subject of a discovery order. **Adobe Land**, 236 S.W.3d at 357–58; **Trevino v. Ortega**, 969 S.W.2d 950, 957 (Tex.1998) (Baker, J., concurring); *see* **Brookshire Bros.**, 438 S.W.3d at 20. Although a party does not have to take extraordinary measures, it must exercise reasonable care in preserving potentially relevant evidence. **Miner Dederick Constr., LLP v. Gulf Chem. & Metallurgical Corp.**, 403 S.W.3d 451, 466 (Tex.App.—Houston [1st Dist.] 2013), *pet. denied*, 455 S.W.3d 164 (Tex.2015); **Trevino**, 969 S.W.2d at 957 (Baker, J., concurring); *see* **Brookshire Bros.**, 438 S.W.3d at 20.

§3.2 Statutory, regulatory & ethical duties. A number of statutes, regulations, and canons of ethics require the preservation of records for certain periods of time. *See* **Trevino v. Ortega**, 969 S.W.2d 950, 955 (Tex.1998) (Baker, J., concurring); *see, e.g.*, Tex. Bus. & Com. Code §72.002 (three-year retention of business records required to be kept by state law unless another law provides otherwise); 29 C.F.R. §1602.40 (two-year retention of school-personnel or employment records).

§4. Discovery certificates

§4.1 Certification by signature. All written discovery—including disclosures, discovery requests, notices, objections, and responses—must be signed. Tex. R. Civ. P. 191.3(a). The signature must be the attorney's, unless the party is pro se. *Id.* TRCP 191.3(a) applies to documents used to satisfy a discovery request, response, or objection (e.g., a withholding statement). Tex. R. Civ. P. 191 cmt. 3. See "Who must sign," ch. 1-B, §3.2.12(1).

1. Effect of signature on disclosure. The signature of an attorney (or pro se party) on a disclosure made under TRCP 194 or 195 constitutes a certification that, to the best of the signer's knowledge, information, and belief, formed after a reasonable inquiry, the disclosure is complete and correct at the time it is made. *See* Tex. R. Civ. P. 191.3(b).

2. Effect of signature on other discovery. The signature of an attorney (or pro se party) on a discovery request, notice, response, or objection constitutes a certification that, to the best of the signer's knowledge, information, and belief, formed after a reasonable inquiry, the discovery (1) is consistent with the TRCPs or presents a good-faith argument for the extension, change, or reversal of existing law, (2) has a good-faith factual basis, (3) is not made for an improper purpose such as delay, harassment, or expense, and (4) is not unreasonable or unduly burdensome or expensive, given the needs of the case. Tex. R. Civ. P. 191.3(c); *see also* Tex. Civ. Prac. & Rem. Code §9.011 (signing of pleadings), §10.001 (signing of pleadings and motions).

3. Effect of no signature. If a discovery request, notice, response, or objection is not signed, it must be struck. Tex. R. Civ. P. 191.3(d). The omission of a signature can be remedied by providing one as soon as the omission is called to the party's attention. *Id.* A party who receives an unsigned request or notice is not required to take any action in response to it. *Id.*

4. Effect of false signature. The court can impose sanctions under CPRC chapter 10 on a person who signs a false certification on a discovery disclosure, request, notice, response, or objection. Tex. R. Civ. P. 191.3(e).

§4.2 Certificate of conference.

1. Under TRCP 191. Parties and their attorneys are expected to cooperate in discovery and to make any agreements that are reasonably necessary to efficiently dispose of the case. Tex. R. Civ. P. 191.2 & cmt. 2; **In re Alford Chevrolet-Geo**, 997 S.W.2d 173, 184 (Tex.1999). All discovery motions or requests for hearings relating to discovery must contain a certificate by the party filing the document stating that a reasonable effort was made to resolve the dispute without the need for court intervention and that the effort failed. Tex. R. Civ. P. 191.2; **United Servs. Auto. Ass'n v. Thomas**, 893 S.W.2d 628, 629 (Tex.App.—Corpus Christi 1994, writ denied). See **O'Connor's Texas Civil Forms**, FORM 1B:12 (2020 ed.). Because TRCP 191.2 is for the benefit of the trial court, the failure to include a certificate is not grounds for mandamus. **Groves v. Gabriel**, 874 S.W.2d 660, 661 n.3 (Tex.1994).

2. Under local rules. In some counties (e.g., Harris, Dallas, Tarrant), courts require a more detailed certificate. See the relevant county's local rules for the requirements. See **O'Connor's Texas Civil Forms**, FORM 1B:12 (2020 ed.).

§4.3 Certificate of written discovery. Some local rules require parties to file a certificate of written discovery with the court when serving discovery requests or responses. See **O'Connor's Texas Civil Forms**, FORM 6A:5 (2020 ed.). TRCP 191.4 contains no such requirement, so a certificate is necessary only if required by local rule.

§5. Forms of discovery

TRCP 192 provides the only permissible forms of discovery. *See* Tex. R. Civ. P. 192.1. When appropriate, a court may order, or the parties may agree to, discovery methods other than those provided in the discovery rules. Tex. R. Civ. P. 191.1 & cmt. 1. See "Modifying discovery procedures," ch. 6-A, §6. The permissible forms of discovery may be combined in the same document and may be taken in any sequence. Tex. R. Civ. P. 192.2(b).

§5.1 Required disclosures. A party is generally required to disclose to other parties the information and material described in TRCP 194.2, 194.3, and 194.4 without a discovery request. Tex. R. Civ. P. 194.1(a). The party cannot object or assert certain privileges to avoid disclosure. *See* Tex. R. Civ. P. 194.5 & cmt. 1 (1999). See "Disclosures," ch. 6-E, §1 et seq.

2021 Rule Amendments

In 2020, the Supreme Court approved significant amendments to TRCP 194 and 195. See Tex.Sup.Ct. Order, Misc. Docket No. 20-9153 (eff. Jan. 1, 2021). Under the amendments, a party is now generally required to provide certain information and material without waiting for a discovery request from the other party. See Tex. R. Civ. P. 194.1(a). The amendments apply to cases filed on or after January 1, 2021, except those filed in justice court. Tex.Sup.Ct. Order, Misc. Docket No. 20-9153 (eff. Jan. 1, 2021). For cases filed before this date, a party must still serve a request for disclosure to obtain the information. See Tex. R. Civ. P. 194.1 (pre-1-1-21 version).

§5.2 Deposition on oral examination. A deposition on oral examination allows a party to question a witness under oath before trial. Depositions can be used to acquire information from both parties and nonparties. *See* Tex. R. Civ. P. 199.1(a), 201.1(a), 202.1, 205.1(a). Because they are expensive and time-consuming, depositions should be used only after a party knows something about the case. See "Depositions," ch. 6-F, §1 et seq.

§5.3 Deposition on written questions. A deposition on written questions allows a party to submit written questions to a witness who answers them orally under oath. *See* Tex. R. Civ. P. 200.1(a), 200.4. Depositions on written questions can be used to acquire information from both parties and nonparties. Although they sound like depositions on oral examination, they are actually similar to interrogatories because they are written and are relatively inexpensive. Depositions on written questions are most often used to obtain records from a nonparty (e.g., a hospital) and, at the same time, to ask the custodian of records the necessary questions to prove up the records. See "Deposition on written questions," ch. 6-F, §15.

§5.4 Interrogatories. Interrogatories are written questions used to acquire information from another party. *See* Tex. R. Civ. P. 197.1. Most interrogatory answers are signed by the party under oath. See "Signed & verified by party," ch. 6-G,

§4.1.1(4). Interrogatories are a relatively inexpensive method of discovery, but they are slower than depositions. They should be used to narrow the issues and to identify the legal theories and factual bases of the parties' claims or defenses. The rule on discovery limitations specifies the number of interrogatories a party may submit. *See* Tex. R. Civ. P. 190. See "Interrogatories," ch. 6-G, §1 et seq.

§5.5 Request for admissions. A request for admissions is used to force another party to admit or deny specific facts, thus narrowing the fact issues for trial. *See* Tex. R. Civ. P. 198.1. Responses to requests for admissions are signed by the attorney. TRCP 198 does not limit the number of requests. See "Requests for Admissions," ch. 6-H, §1 et seq.

§5.6 Request for production & inspection. A request for production is used to obtain or inspect documents, records, and other tangible things in a party's possession. Tex. R. Civ. P. 196.1(a). To obtain or inspect documents or tangible things from a nonparty, a party must serve a notice of production and a subpoena, not a request. Tex. R. Civ. P. 205.3; *see* Tex. R. Civ. P. 176. See "Securing Documents & Tangible Things," ch. 6-I, §1 et seq.

§5.7 Request for medical records. A party may obtain the medical records of another party or of a nonparty through required disclosures under TRCP 194 or by a medical authorization. *See* Tex. R. Civ. P. 194.2(b)(10), (11), 196.1(c). See "Medical Records," ch. 6-J, §1 et seq.

2021 Rule Amendments

In 2020, the Supreme Court approved significant amendments to TRCP 194. See Tex.Sup.Ct. Order, Misc. Docket No. 20-9153 (eff. Jan. 1, 2021). Under the amendments, a party is now generally required to provide certain material, including relevant medical records, without waiting for a discovery request from the other party. See Tex. R. Civ. P. 194.1(a). The amendments apply to cases filed on or after January 1, 2021, except those filed in justice court. Tex.Sup.Ct. Order, Misc. Docket No. 20-9153 (eff. Jan. 1, 2021). For cases filed before this date, a party must still serve a request for disclosure or obtain a medical authorization to discover the information. See Tex. R. Civ. P. 194.1 (pre-1-1-21 version). See "Disclosures," ch. 6-E, §1 et seq.

---

§5.8 Motion for physical or mental examination. A motion for physical or mental examination may be used to obtain an examination of a party, someone in the party's custody, or someone under the party's legal control. Tex. R. Civ. P. 204.1(a), (c). See "Motion to examine the person," ch. 6-J, §5.

§5.9 Request for entry on land. A request to enter land may be used to gain entry on land owned by a party to inspect the land or anything on it. Tex. R. Civ. P. 196.7(a). To gain entry on the land of a nonparty, the party must ask for a hearing, file and serve a motion (not a request) and notice of hearing, and get a court order. Tex. R. Civ. P. 196.7(a)(2), (b). See "Entry on Land," ch. 6-K, §1 et seq.

§5.10 Subpoena. A subpoena may be used to secure documents from a party or nonparty. *See* Tex. R. Civ. P. 176, 205. In most cases, a subpoena is issued to compel a nonparty to attend a deposition and to produce documents. See "Securing things from a nonparty," ch. 6-I, §5.

§5.11 Expert's report. An expert's report includes the discoverable factual observations, tests, supporting data, calculations, photographs, and opinions of the expert. *See* Tex. R. Civ. P. 195.5(b). If a retained testifying expert has not reduced her report to tangible form, the court may order the expert to reduce it to tangible form and to produce it. *Id.* See "Expert's report," ch. 6-D, §7; **O'Connor's Texas Civil Forms**, FORM 6D:1 (2020 ed.).

§6. Modifying discovery procedures

§6.1 Modifying discovery by agreement. The discovery rules permit the parties to modify most discovery procedures. Tex. R. Civ. P. 191.1. For example, the parties can agree to use a form of discovery not provided for in the TRCPs. Tex. R. Civ. P. 191 cmt. 1. Agreements to modify discovery are subject to the following rules.

1. Rule 11. To be enforceable, the parties' agreement to modify a discovery rule must comply with TRCP 11 or, if it affects an oral deposition, must be made part of the record of the deposition. Tex. R. Civ. P. 191.1; **In re BP Prods. N. Am.,**

Inc., 244 S.W.3d 840, 845–46 (Tex.2008). An agreement that does not comply with TRCP 11 is not enforceable. *E.g.*, **London Mkt. Cos. v. Schattman**, 811 S.W.2d 550, 552 (Tex.1991) (oral agreement to extend time to respond to discovery was not enforceable because it did not meet requirements of TRCP 11). See "Agreements between attorneys—Rule 11," ch. 1-H, §9; **O'Connor's Texas Civil Forms**, FORM 1H:13 (2020 ed.) (Rule 11 agreement), **O'Connor's Texas Civil Forms**, FORM 6A:3 (2020 ed.) (agreement to extend time to respond to discovery).

2. Restrictions. The parties may modify a discovery rule unless the modification is specifically prohibited. Tex. R. Civ. P. 191.1; **In re BP Prods.**, 244 S.W.3d at 845. The court may set aside the parties' enforceable agreement, but it should give effect to the agreement whenever possible. **In re BP Prods.**, 244 S.W.3d at 846. Generally, the court should not ignore the parties' agreement without a showing of specific misrepresentation or good cause.

§6.2 Modifying discovery by court order. Certain discovery rules permit a court to modify discovery procedures in specific instances. *See, e.g.*, Tex. R. Civ. P. 190.4(a) (in Level 3 cases, court may set its own discovery-control plan "tailored to the circumstances of the specific suit"), Tex. R. Civ. P. 190.5 (court may modify discovery-control plan "at any time"). Other discovery procedures may be modified by the court only under the following conditions.

1. Good cause. The court may modify a discovery procedure if there is good cause. Tex. R. Civ. P. 191.1; **In re BP Prods. N. Am., Inc.**, 244 S.W.3d 840, 846 (Tex.2008); *see, e.g.*, **Alvarado v. Farah Mfg. Co.**, 830 S.W.2d 911, 914 (Tex.1992) (courts should not excuse parties from their failure to timely respond to discovery without a strict showing of good cause). Inadvertence of counsel (i.e., an attorney's inadvertent noncompliance with discovery rules) is not sufficient to establish good cause. **Alvarado**, 830 S.W.2d at 915. See **O'Connor's Texas Civil Forms**, FORM 6A:2 (2020 ed.) (motion to extend time to respond to discovery).

2. Restrictions. The court may modify a discovery procedure if the modification is not specifically prohibited. Tex. R. Civ. P. 191.1. For example, the court cannot simply opt out of the discovery rules by form orders or approve a discovery-control plan that does not contain the matters specified in TRCP 190.4. Tex. R. Civ. P. 191.1 cmt. 1. The court also cannot abate discovery in a way that prevents a party from obtaining basic information that goes to the heart of the litigation. *See* **In re Van Waters & Rogers, Inc.**, 62 S.W.3d 197, 200 (Tex.2001); **In re Colonial Pipeline Co.**, 968 S.W.2d 938, 941–42 (Tex.1998).

§6.3 Chart summary. Chart 6-1, below, summarizes the various types of enforceable agreements on discovery.

6-1. Enforceable Agreements on Discovery

	Type of agreement	Can agree under TRCP 11?	Can agree during deposition?	Need court order?	TRCP
1	To modify any court order	No	No	Yes	191 cmt. 1
2	To modify duty to disclose[1]	Yes	No	No	194.1(a)
3	To modify deadline to make initial disclosures[1]	Yes	No	No	194.2(a)
4	To extend discovery deadlines	Yes	Yes[2]	No	191 cmt. 1
5	To extend time to supplement	Yes	Yes[2]	No	191.1, 193.5(b)
6	To modify deposition procedure	Yes	Yes[2]	No	191 cmt. 1
7	To modify time to designate experts	Yes	No	No	191.1, 195.2
8	To adopt new method of discovery	Yes	Yes[2]	No	191 cmt. 1
9	To serve request less than 30 days before end of discovery period	Yes	No	No	190 cmt. 4 (1999)
10	To modify any discovery procedure not prohibited by TRCPs	Yes	Yes[2]	No	191.1
11	To produce documents or tangible things at a different time and place than stated in the request or response	Yes	Yes[2]	No	194.1(b), 196.3(a), 197.2(c)

6-1. Enforceable Agreements on Discovery					
	Type of agreement	Can agree under TRCP 11?	Can agree during deposition?	Need court order?	TRCP
12	To take deposition outside discovery period	Yes	Yes[2]	No	199.2(a), 200.1(a)
13	To be controlled by Level 3	No	No	Yes	190 cmt. 1 (1999)
14	In Level 1 (divorce only)—To agree to be controlled by Level 2	Yes	No	No	190.2(a)(2)
15	In Level 3—To modify discovery	No	No	Yes	190.4(a)

[1] For a discussion of the changes to the disclosure procedure under the 2021 amendments to TRCP 194, see "Disclosures," ch. 6-E, §1 et seq.
[2] Attorneys can make an enforceable agreement on the record during a deposition only as it affects the deposition. Tex R. Civ. P. 191.1.

§7. Discovery-control plans

The purpose of discovery-control plans is to promote the efficient resolution of cases by assigning each case to one of three levels, depending on the amount in controversy and the issues involved in the case.

§7.1 Discovery-control plan required. Every case must be governed by a discovery-control plan. Tex. R. Civ. P. 190.1. A plaintiff must allege in the first numbered paragraph of the original petition whether discovery is intended to be conducted under Level 1, 2, or 3 of TRCP 190. Tex. R. Civ. P. 190.1. See "Discovery-control plans," ch. 2-B, §2.

§7.2 Level 1. The Level 1 discovery-control plan governs expedited actions and certain suits for divorce. Tex. R. Civ. P. 190.2(a); *see* Tex. R. Civ. P. 169(d)(1), 190 cmt. (2013).

2021 Rule Amendments

In 2020, the Supreme Court approved significant amendments to TRCP 169 and 190 that modify the applicability of the expedited-actions process and several of the limitations under Level 1 discovery. See Tex.Sup.Ct. Order, Misc. Docket No. 20-9153 (eff. Jan. 1, 2021). The amendments apply to cases filed on or after January 1, 2021, except those filed in justice court. Id.

1. Application.

(1) Expedited actions.

(a) Generally. The Level 1 discovery-control plan governs an expedited action under TRCP 169. Tex. R. Civ. P. 190.2(a)(1). See "Expedited Actions," ch. 2-C, §1 et seq.

(b) Exceptions. The Level 1 discovery-control plan does not apply in the following instances.

[1] Suit for injunctive relief. When a party files a petition for injunctive relief. *See* Tex. R. Civ. P. 169(a), 190 cmt. 2 (1999).

[2] Suits brought under certain statutes. When a party files a claim that is exempt from Level 1 discovery by statute. *See* Tex. R. Civ. P. 169 cmt. (2021); *see, e.g.,* Tex. Est. Code §53.107 (Level 1 discovery does not apply to probate proceedings), Tex. Est. Code §1053.105 (Level 1 discovery does not apply to guardianship proceedings).

2021 Rule Amendments

Before the 2021 amendments to TRCP 169, claims governed by the Family Code, the Property Code, the Tax Code, and CPRC chapter 74 (the Medical Liability Act) were specifically exempt from the expedited-actions process and thus generally from Level 1 discovery; however, certain divorce suits, al-

though not expedited actions, were governed by Level 1 discovery (see ch. 6-A, §7.2.1(2)(a)[1]). See Tex. R. Civ. P. 169(a)(2) (pre-1-1-21 version). For cases filed on or after January 1, 2021, Level 1 discovery can apply to these actions if they meet the requirements of an expedited action under TRCP 169 and are not otherwise exempt. See Tex. R. Civ. P. 169 cmt. (2021).

[3] Suits brought in justice court. When a party files a claim in justice court. *See* Tex.Sup.Ct. Order, Misc. Docket No. 20-9153 (eff. Jan. 1, 2021); Tex.Sup.Ct. Order, Misc. Docket No. 13-9022 (eff. Mar. 1, 2013).

[4] Removal from expedited-actions process. When a party files a pleading or an amended or supplemental pleading that removes a suit from the expedited-actions process in TRCP 169. *See* Tex. R. Civ. P. 169(c)(1)(B), (c)(2), 190.2(a)(1), (c). See "Removal from TRCP 169 procedure," ch. 2-C, §3.

(2) Certain divorce suits.

(a) Generally.

[1] Before 1-1-21. For cases filed before January 1, 2021, the Level 1 discovery-control plan governs suits for divorce not involving children in which the party pleads that the value of the marital estate is more than zero but not more than $50,000. Tex. R. Civ. P. 190.2(a)(2) (pre-1-1-21 version); *see* Tex. R. Civ. P. 190 cmt. 2 (1999); Tex.Sup.Ct. Order, Misc. Docket No. 20-9153 (eff. Jan. 1, 2021).

[2] On or after 1-1-21. For cases filed on or after January 1, 2021, the Level 1 discovery-control plan governs suits for divorce not involving children in which a party pleads that the value of the marital estate is more than zero but not more than $250,000. Tex. R. Civ. P. 190.2(a)(2); *see* Tex. R. Civ. P. 190 cmt. 2 (1999); Tex.Sup.Ct. Order, Misc. Docket No. 20-9153 (eff. Jan. 1, 2021).

(b) Exceptions. The Level 1 discovery-control plan does not apply in the following instances:

[1] Parties agree. When the parties agree to be governed by the Level 2 discovery-control plan. Tex. R. Civ. P. 190.2(a)(2). See "Level 2," ch. 6-A, §7.3.

[2] Court order. When the trial court orders a Level 3 discovery-control plan. Tex. R. Civ. P. 190.2(a)(2). See "Level 3," ch. 6-A, §7.4.

2. Discovery limitations.

(1) Discovery period. See "Level 1," ch. 6-A, §8.1.1.

(2) Oral depositions. The number of hours allowed for examination depends on when the case was filed. The court may modify the deposition hours so that no party is given an unfair advantage. Tex. R. Civ. P. 190.2(b)(2). See "Depositions," ch. 6-F, §1 et seq.

(a) Before 1-1-21. For cases filed before January 1, 2021, each party may take no more than six hours to examine and cross-examine all witnesses in oral depositions. Tex. R. Civ. P. 190.2(b)(2) (pre-1-1-21 version). The parties may agree to extend this time, but they cannot extend it beyond ten hours without a court order. *Id.*

(b) On or after 1-1-21. For cases filed on or after January 1, 2021, each party may take no more than 20 hours to examine and cross-examine all witnesses in oral depositions. Tex. R. Civ. P. 190.2(b)(2).

(3) Written discovery. In Level 1 cases, written discovery is subject to certain limitations.

(a) Interrogatories.

[1] Number. A party may serve no more than 15 interrogatories on any other party. Tex. R. Civ. P. 190.2(b)(3). See "Number of interrogatories," ch. 6-G, §3.1.3.

[2] Discrete subparts. Each discrete subpart of an interrogatory is considered a separate interrogatory. Tex. R. Civ. P. 190.2(b)(3). But not every separate factual inquiry is a discrete subpart. Tex. R. Civ. P. 190 cmt. 3 (1999).

[3] Identification or authentication interrogatories—no limit. The limit on the number of interrogatories that can be served does not include interrogatories that ask a party to identify or authenticate specific documents. Tex. R. Civ. P. 190.2(b)(3).

[4] No deposition on written questions to avoid limits. Although depositions on written questions are allowed, they cannot be used to avoid the limits on the number of interrogatories served. *See* Tex. R. Civ. P. 190 cmt. 5 (1999).

(b) Requests for production. A party may serve no more than 15 written requests for production on any other party. Tex. R. Civ. P. 190.2(b)(4). Each discrete subpart of a request for production is considered a separate request for production. *Id.* See "Number of requests," ch. 6-I, §3.1.4.

(c) Requests for admissions. A party may serve no more than 15 written requests for admissions on any other party. Tex. R. Civ. P. 190.2(b)(5). Each discrete subpart of a request for admissions is considered a separate request for admissions. *Id.* See "Number of requests," ch. 6-H, §3.1.3.

(d) Disclosures.

[1] Before 1-1-21. For cases filed before January 1, 2021, a party may request disclosure of all documents, electronic information, and tangible items that the disclosing party has in its possession, custody, or control and that it may use to support its claims or defenses. Tex. R. Civ. P. 190.2(b)(6) (pre-1-1-21 version); *see* Tex.Sup.Ct. Order, Misc. Docket No. 20-9153 (eff. Jan. 1, 2021). See "Electronic Discovery," ch. 6-C, §1 et seq.; "Requests for disclosure—Cases filed before 1-1-21," ch. 6-E, §2. This request is in addition to the content subject to disclosure under TRCP 194.2. Tex. R. Civ. P. 190.2(b)(6) (pre-1-1-21 version). See "Content of request," ch. 6-E, §2.1.2. A request for disclosure made under TRCP 190.2(b)(6) is not considered a request for production. Tex. R. Civ. P. 190.2(b)(6) (pre-1-1-21 version).

[2] On or after 1-1-21. For cases filed on or after January 1, 2021, parties are required to disclose certain information and materials described in TRCP 194 and 195. *See* Tex. R. Civ. P. 194.1(a), 190 cmt. (2021); Tex.Sup.Ct. Order, Misc. Docket No. 20-9153 (eff. Jan. 1, 2021). The party seeking discovery does not have to serve a request for disclosure to trigger the opposing party's duty to produce the information. *See* Tex. R. Civ. P. 194.1(a). See "Required disclosures—Cases filed on or after 1-1-21," ch. 6-E, §3.

§7.3 Level 2. Level 2 discovery is generally the default discovery track when Level 1 discovery is not applicable. *See* Griesel, *The "New" Texas Discovery Rules: Three Years Later*, Advanced Evidence & Discovery Course, State Bar of Texas CLE, ch. 2, p. 4 (2002). If the plaintiff does not plead a discovery level in its original petition, the case is automatically a Level 2 case. Tex. R. Civ. P. 190 cmt. 1 (1999).

1. Application. Unless a suit is governed by Level 1 under TRCP 190.2 or Level 3 under TRCP 190.4, discovery will be governed by Level 2 under TRCP 190.3. Tex. R. Civ. P. 190.3(a).

2. Discovery limitations. In Level 2 cases, discovery is subject to the following limitations:

(1) Discovery period. See "Level 2," ch. 6-A, §8.1.2.

(2) Oral depositions. Each side is limited to 50 hours of oral depositions to examine and cross-examine parties on the opposing side, experts designated by those parties, and persons subject to those parties' control. Tex. R. Civ. P. 190.3(b)(2). See "Side," ch. 6-A, §2.7. TRCP 190.3(b)(2) does not limit the time for deposing witnesses who are not subject to either party's control (e.g., an eyewitness to an accident). In addition, each side is limited to six hours when examining or cross-examining an individual witness. Tex. R. Civ. P. 199.5(c). See "Time limits on oral depositions," ch. 6-F, §6.

(a) If one side designates more than two experts, the opposing side may have an additional six hours of total deposition time for each additional expert designated. Tex. R. Civ. P. 190.3(b)(2). The rule does not state whether the additional six hours must be used for the expert's deposition. In most cases, the additional six hours would likely be used for additional expert testimony, but a party could make a compelling argument that additional testimony from nonexperts is necessary to counter an expert's testimony.

(b) The court may modify the deposition hours and must do so when one side or party would otherwise have an unfair advantage. Tex. R. Civ. P. 190.3(b)(2).

(3) Interrogatories. A party may serve no more than 25 interrogatories on any other party. Tex. R. Civ. P. 190.3(b)(3). Each discrete subpart of an interrogatory is considered a separate interrogatory. *Id.* But not every separate factual inquiry is a discrete subpart. Tex. R. Civ. P. 190 cmt. 3 (1999). The limit of 25 does not include interrogatories that ask a party to identify or authenticate specific documents. Tex. R. Civ. P. 190.3(b)(3). See "Interrogatories," ch. 6-G, §1 et seq.

(4) Other written discovery. TRCP 190 does not limit other written discovery in Level 2 cases.

§7.4 Level 3. Level 3 discovery is court-managed discovery, similar to federal-court practice. Griesel, *The "New" Texas Discovery Rules: Three Years Later*, Advanced Evidence & Discovery Course, State Bar of Texas CLE, ch. 2, p. 4 (2002). Level 3 is designed for more complex cases that do not easily fit into the framework of Level 1 or 2. *Id.* Once a suit is designated as Level 3, all changes to the default provisions must be made by court order. *See* Tex. R. Civ. P. 191 cmt. 1; *see also* Griesel, *The "New" Texas Discovery Rules: Three Years Later*, Advanced Evidence & Discovery Course, State Bar of Texas CLE, ch. 2, p. 6 (2002) (court may modify any discovery procedure or limitation by order for good cause). Level 3 discovery cannot be changed by agreement of the parties without a court order.

Note

A court cannot order a Level 3 discovery-control plan for an expedited action; for a Level 1 case, the court can order a Level 3 discovery-control plan only for certain suits for divorce. See Tex. R. Civ. P. 190.2(a)(2), 169 cmt. 2 (2013). See "Expedited Actions," ch. 2-C, §1 et seq.; "Court order," ch. 6-A, §7.2.1(2)(b)[2].

1. Application. The court must on a party's motion, and may on its own initiative, order that discovery be conducted as a Level 3 case with a discovery-control plan tailored to the specific suit. Tex. R. Civ. P. 190.4(a). A case can be in Level 3 only by court order; a plaintiff's statement in the opening paragraph of its petition that the case is to be governed under Level 3 does not make Level 3 applicable. Tex. R. Civ. P. 190 cmt. 1 (1999). The court should act on a party's motion or agreed order as soon as reasonably possible. Tex. R. Civ. P. 190.4(a). See **O'Connor's Texas Civil Forms**, FORMS 6A:6 to 6A:7 (2020 ed.).

2. Discovery limitations. The court-ordered discovery-control plan may address any issue related to discovery or the matters listed in TRCP 166. Tex. R. Civ. P. 190.4(b). The court may simply adopt discovery limitations under Level 1, if applicable, or otherwise under Level 2, or it may change any limitations on the time for or amount of discovery set out in TRCP 190. *See* Tex. R. Civ. P. 190.4(b) & cmt. 1 (1999); *see also* **In re Alford Chevrolet-Geo**, 997 S.W.2d 173, 181 (Tex.1999) (trial court may limit discovery pending resolution of threshold issues like venue, jurisdiction, forum non conveniens, and official immunity). The plan must include the following information: (1) a date for trial or for a conference to determine a trial date, (2) a discovery period during which, for the entire case or an appropriate phase of it, all discovery must be conducted or all discovery requests must be sent, (3) appropriate limits on the amount of discovery, and (4) deadlines for joining additional parties, amending or supplementing pleadings, and designating expert witnesses. Tex. R. Civ. P. 190.4(b).

§8. Discovery periods

The purpose of discovery periods is to speed the resolution of cases. The party seeking discovery must serve requests for discovery early enough to allow the responding party to serve its response within the discovery period. Tex. R. Civ. P. 190 cmt. 4 (1999); **Pape v. Guadalupe-Blanco River Auth.**, 48 S.W.3d 908, 913 (Tex.App.—Austin 2001, pet. denied). The court may also set a deadline for sending discovery requests instead of or in addition to a deadline for completing discovery. Tex. R. Civ. P. 190 cmt. 4 (1999).

Note

If a party's pleading (in a suit other than one under the Family Code, in justice court, or for guardianship or probate proceedings) does not contain a specific statement of relief under TRCP 47(c), the party cannot conduct discovery until the pleading is amended to comply. See Tex. R. Civ. P. 47. See "Specific statement of relief," ch. 1-B, §3.2.8(2).

§8.1 Length of discovery periods. The length of a discovery period for a specific case depends on the applicable discovery-control plan. Every case must be assigned to one of three levels, depending on the amount in controversy and the issues involved. See "Discovery-control plans," ch. 6-A, §7.

2021 Rule Amendments

In 2020, the Supreme Court approved amendments to TRCP 190 that modify the discovery periods for Level 1 and Level 2 cases. See Tex.Sup.Ct. Order, Misc. Docket No. 20-9153 (eff. Jan. 1, 2021). The amendments apply to cases filed on or after January 1, 2021, except those filed in justice court. Id.

1. Level 1.

(1) Original period.

(a) Before 1-1-21. For cases filed before January 1, 2021, the discovery period in a Level 1 case begins when the suit is filed and continues until 180 days after the first discovery request is served on a party. Tex. R. Civ. P. 190.2(b)(1) (pre-1-1-21 version).

(b) On or after 1-1-21. For cases filed on or after January 1, 2021, the discovery period in a Level 1 case begins when the first initial disclosures under TRCP 194 are due and continues for 180 days. Tex. R. Civ. P. 190.2(b)(1). The first initial disclosures are generally due within 30 days after the filing of the first answer or general appearance. Tex. R. Civ. P. 194.2(a). See "Deadline," ch. 6-E, §3.3.1.

2021 Rule Amendments

In 2020, the Supreme Court approved significant amendments to TRCP 194. See Tex.Sup.Ct. Order, Misc. Docket No. 20-9153 (eff. Jan. 1, 2021). Under the amendments, a party is now generally required to make initial disclosures of certain information without waiting for a discovery request from the other party. See Tex. R. Civ. P. 194.2. For a detailed discussion of these amendments, see "Required disclosures—Cases filed on or after 1-1-21," ch. 6-E, §3.

(2) Period reopens.

(a) Deadline. The discovery period in a Level 1 case reopens if (1) a suit is removed from the expedited-actions process in TRCP 169 or (2) in a suit for divorce, the filing of a pleading makes TRCP 190.2 inapplicable (e.g., the pleading makes the amount in controversy more than $250,000). *See* Tex. R. Civ. P. 190.2(a)(2), (c). See "Removal from TRCP 169 procedure," ch. 2-C, §3; "Motion to reopen discovery period," ch. 5-F, §6.2.4. Discovery must then be completed within the limitations of TRCP 190.3 (Level 2) or TRCP 190.4 (Level 3), whichever applies. Tex. R. Civ. P. 190.2(c).

(b) Redeposing witness. Any person already deposed may be redeposed as long as the party has not already used its allotted deposition time. *See* Tex. R. Civ. P. 190.2(b)(2), (c). See "Oral depositions," ch. 6-A, §7.2.2(2).

(c) Continuing trial date. On any party's motion, the court should continue the trial date if necessary to permit the completion of discovery. Tex. R. Civ. P. 190.2(c).

2. Level 2.

(1) Most cases.

(a) Before 1-1-21. For cases filed before January 1, 2021, the discovery period in a Level 2 case begins when the suit is filed and continues until the earliest of the following: (1) 30 days before trial, (2) nine months after the date

of the first oral deposition, or (3) nine months after the due date of the first response to written discovery. Tex. R. Civ. P. 190.3(b)(1)(B) (pre-1-1-21 version); *see* **Ersek v. Davis & Davis, P.C.**, 69 S.W.3d 268, 273 (Tex.App.—Austin 2002, pet. denied); **Pape**, 48 S.W.3d at 913.

(b) On or after 1-1-21. For cases filed on or after January 1, 2021, the discovery period in a Level 2 case begins when the first initial disclosures under TRCP 194 are due and continues until the earlier of the following: (1) 30 days before trial or (2) nine months after the first initial disclosures under TRCP 194 are due. Tex. R. Civ. P. 190.3(b)(1)(B). The first initial disclosures are generally due within 30 days after the filing of the first answer or general appearance. Tex. R. Civ. P. 194.2(a). See "Deadline," ch. 6-E, §3.3.1.

2021 Rule Amendments

In 2020, the Supreme Court approved significant amendments to TRCP 194. See Tex.Sup.Ct. Order, Misc. Docket No. 20-9153 (eff. Jan. 1, 2021). Under the amendments, a party is now generally required to make initial disclosures of certain information without waiting for a discovery request from the other party. See Tex. R. Civ. P. 194.2. For a detailed discussion of these amendments, see "Required disclosures—Cases filed on or after 1-1-21," ch. 6-E, §3.

(2) Family Code cases.

(a) Before 1-1-21. For Family Code cases filed before January 1, 2021, the discovery period begins when the suit is filed and continues until 30 days before the date set for trial. Tex. R. Civ. P. 190.3(b)(1)(A) (pre-1-1-21 version).

(b) On or after 1-1-21. For Family Code cases filed on or after January 1, 2021, the discovery period begins when the first initial disclosures under TRCP 194 are due and continues until 30 days before the date set for trial. Tex. R. Civ. P. 190.3(b)(1)(A). The first initial disclosures are generally due within 30 days after the filing of the first answer or general appearance. Tex. R. Civ. P. 194.2(a). See "Deadline," ch. 6-E, §3.3.1.

2021 Rule Amendments

In 2020, the Supreme Court approved significant amendments to TRCP 194. See Tex.Sup.Ct. Order, Misc. Docket No. 20-9153 (eff. Jan. 1, 2021). Under the amendments, a party is now generally required to make initial disclosures of certain information without waiting for a discovery request from the other party. See Tex. R. Civ. P. 194.2. For a detailed discussion of these amendments, see "Required disclosures—Cases filed on or after 1-1-21," ch. 6-E, §3.

3. Level 3. Discovery in a Level 3 case must be conducted during the discovery period for Level 1 or Level 2, whichever applies, unless the court orders a different period. Tex. R. Civ. P. 190.4(b).

§8.2 Modification of discovery periods. The court may modify a discovery period at any time; it must do so when justice requires it. Tex. R. Civ. P. 190.5. See **O'Connor's Texas Civil Forms**, FORM 6A:8 (2020 ed.). Expedited actions are not subject to mandatory additional discovery, but the court may still allow additional discovery if the conditions of TRCP 190.5(a) are met. Tex. R. Civ. P. 190.5 & cmt. (2013). See "Expedited Actions," ch. 2-C, §1 et seq. If a suit is not governed by the expedited-actions process in TRCP 169, the court must allow additional discovery in the following circumstances.

1. Amended or supplemental pleadings. When pleadings are amended or supplemented, or when new information is disclosed in a discovery response, the court must allow additional related discovery if the movant shows both of the following:

(1) After deadline. The pleadings or responses were made after the discovery deadline or so close to the deadline that the movant did not have an adequate opportunity to conduct discovery related to the new matters. Tex. R. Civ. P. 190.5(a)(1).

(2) Unfair prejudice. The movant would be unfairly prejudiced without the additional discovery. Tex. R. Civ. P. 190.5(a)(2).

2. Material changes. The court must allow additional discovery on matters that have materially changed after the discovery deadline when there is more than a three-month gap between the end of the discovery period and the trial date. Tex. R. Civ. P. 190.5(b).

§8.3 Certain discovery excepted. The limitations on discovery under TRCP 190 do not apply to discovery conducted under TRCP 202 ("Depositions Before Suit or to Investigate Claims") or TRCP 621a ("Discovery and Enforcement of Judgment"). Tex. R. Civ. P. 190.6. But TRCP 202 cannot be used to avoid the limitations of TRCP 190. Tex. R. Civ. P. 190.6.

§9. Securing discovery

Chart 6-2, below, summarizes the rules for the various types of discovery.

6-2. Securing & Responding to Discovery

		Need motion & order?	Response signed by	Response verified?	Cross-reference
	A. Party discovery				
1	Required disclosures	No	Attorney	No	ch. 6-E, §1 et seq.
2	Deposition (oral or written questions)	No	Party	Yes	ch. 6-F, §1 et seq.
3	Interrogatories about fact and trial witnesses or legal contentions	No	Attorney	No	ch. 6-G, §4.1.1(4), (5)
4	Interrogatories about other matters	No	Attorney and party	Yes, by party	ch. 6-G, §4.1.1(4), (5)
5	Request for admissions	No	Attorney	No	ch. 6-H, §1 et seq.
6	Request to produce documents	No	Attorney	No	ch. 6-I, §1 et seq.
7	Authorization for medical records	No	Party	No	ch. 6-J, §1 et seq.
8	Physical or mental examination	Yes	Attorney	No	ch. 6-J, §5
9	Request to inspect land	No	Attorney	No	ch. 6-K, §1 et seq.
	B. Nonparty discovery				
10	Deposition (oral or written questions)	No, just notice and subpoena	Nonparty	Yes	ch. 6-F, §1 et seq.
11	Notice to produce documents	No, just notice and subpoena	Nonparty	No	ch. 6-I, §5
12	Deposition before suit	Yes	Nonparty	Yes	ch. 6-F, §16
13	Medical records	Yes	Nonparty	No	ch. 6-J, §4
14	Motion to inspect land	Yes	Nonparty	No	ch. 6-K, §4

§9.1 Securing discovery from parties.

1. By discovery procedures. All forms of discovery can be used to secure discovery from parties. See "Forms of discovery," ch. 6-A, §5.

2. By agreement. Parties are expected to cooperate in discovery. Tex. R. Civ. P. 191.2; *see* **In re Alford Chevrolet-Geo**, 997 S.W.2d 173, 184 (Tex.1999). To this end, parties may make any agreements that are reasonably necessary to efficiently dispose of the case. Tex. R. Civ. P. 191.2. See "Modifying discovery by agreement," ch. 6-A, §6.1.

§9.2 Securing discovery from nonparties. A party can use only the discovery procedures outlined in TRCP 205.1 to secure discovery from a nonparty. **In re Guzman**, 19 S.W.3d 522, 524 (Tex.App.—Corpus Christi 2000, orig. proceeding).

1. Court order. A party can obtain a court order for (1) entry on land under TRCP 196.7, (2) taking a deposition before suit under TRCP 202, or (3) a physical or mental examination under TRCP 204. Tex. R. Civ. P. 205.1.

2. Subpoena. A party can serve a subpoena on a nonparty to compel (1) an oral deposition, (2) a deposition on written questions, (3) the production of documents or tangible things, served with a notice of deposition on oral examination under TRCP 199.2(b)(5) or written questions under TRCP 200.1(b), or (4) the production of documents and tangible things under TRCP 205. Tex. R. Civ. P. 205.1.

§10. Pretrial conference

Generally, the trial court uses the pretrial conference to oversee discovery—to determine what discovery has been completed and what discovery remains to be done. See "Pretrial Conference," ch. 5-A, §1 et seq.

§11. Special master for discovery

A special master may be appointed only for good cause and only in exceptional cases involving discovery questions that require examination of highly technical and complex matters. **In re Harris**, 315 S.W.3d 685, 705 (Tex.App.—Houston [1st Dist.] 2010, orig. proceeding); *see* Tex. R. Civ. P. 171. See "Master in Chancery," ch. 1-K, §1 et seq.

§12. Filing & retaining discovery

§12.1 Filing discovery. Most discovery is not filed unless it is necessary. This rule was adopted to resolve storage problems encountered by the court clerks. Griesel, *The "New" Texas Discovery Rules: Three Years Later*, Advanced Evidence & Discovery Course, State Bar of Texas CLE, ch. 2, p. 6 (2002).

1. Discovery materials to be filed. The following discovery materials must be filed.

(1) Discovery requests, deposition notices, and subpoenas required to be served on nonparties. Tex. R. Civ. P. 191.4(b)(1). For rules on filing deposition materials, see "Filing deposition documents," ch. 6-F, §4.4.

(2) Motions and responses to motions relating to discovery matters. Tex. R. Civ. P. 191.4(b)(2).

(3) Agreements relating to discovery matters, to the extent necessary to comply with TRCP 11. Tex. R. Civ. P. 191.4(b)(3).

(4) Pretrial disclosures under TRCP 194. Tex. R. Civ. P. 194.4(a). See "Final pretrial disclosures," ch. 6-E, §3.5.

2. Discovery materials not to be filed. The following discovery materials must not be filed.

(1) Discovery requests, deposition notices, and subpoenas required to be served only on parties. Tex. R. Civ. P. 191.4(a)(1).

(2) Responses and objections to discovery requests and deposition notices from parties or nonparties. Tex. R. Civ. P. 191.4(a)(2).

(3) Documents and tangible things produced in discovery. Tex. R. Civ. P. 191.4(a)(3).

(4) Withholding statements prepared in compliance with TRCP 193.3(b) or (d). Tex. R. Civ. P. 191.4(a)(4).

3. Exceptions. TRCP 191.4(c) lists the exceptions to the do-not-file rule:

(1) The court may order that discovery materials be filed. Tex. R. Civ. P. 191.4(c)(1). This provision is an additional safeguard against destruction of discovery in cases in which it should be preserved, such as cases involving TRCP 76a (sealing court records). Griesel, *The "New" Texas Discovery Rules: Three Years Later*, Advanced Evidence & Discovery Course, State Bar of Texas CLE, ch. 2, p. 6 (2002).

(2) A person may file discovery materials in support of or in opposition to a motion or for other use in a court proceeding. Tex. R. Civ. P. 191.4(c)(2).

(3) A person may file discovery materials necessary for a proceeding in an appellate court. Tex. R. Civ. P. 191.4(c)(3).

§12.2 Retaining discovery during trial. When a person (whether a party or a nonparty) serves discovery materials that must not be filed under TRCP 191.4, the person must retain the original or a copy of the materials while the case is

pending, including any appeals begun within six months after the judgment is signed. Tex. R. Civ. P. 191.4(d); **National Family Care Life Ins. v. Fletcher**, 57 S.W.3d 662, 667 n.6 (Tex.App.—Beaumont 2001, pet. denied). The court may modify this requirement. Tex. R. Civ. P. 191.4(d).

§12.3 Retaining depositions after trial. Beginning one year after a case is finally resolved (either by a final judgment that is not appealed or by an appellate-court mandate), a party has 30 days to withdraw any depositions (transcripts or depositions on written questions) that it offered. Tex.Sup.Ct. Order, Misc. Docket No. 05-9025 (eff. June 1, 2005); *see also* Tex. R. Civ. P. 191.4(e) (trial-court clerk must retain and dispose of depositions as directed by Supreme Court). After the 30-day deadline, the trial-court clerk may dispose of the depositions unless otherwise directed by the court. Tex.Sup.Ct. Order, Misc. Docket No. 05-9025 (eff. June 1, 2005).

§13. Service of discovery materials

§13.1 Service on all parties. When a party serves discovery materials (disclosures, discovery requests, notices, responses, objections), it must serve a copy of those materials on all other parties of record. Tex. R. Civ. P. 191.5.

§13.2 Service with original pleadings. Whether the parties can serve discovery requests with their original pleadings depends on when the case is filed.

2021 Rule Amendments

In 2020, the Supreme Court approved significant amendments to TRCP 190 and 194. See Tex.Sup.Ct. Order, Misc. Docket No. 20-9153 (eff. Jan. 1, 2021). Under the amendments, a party is now generally required to disclose certain information and material without waiting for a discovery request from the other party and must do so within 30 days after the filing of the first answer or general appearance. See Tex. R. Civ. P. 194.1(a), 194.2(a); Tex.Sup.Ct. Order, Misc. Docket No. 20-9153 (eff. Jan. 1, 2021). See "Required disclosures—Cases filed on or after 1-1-21," ch. 6-E, §3. The amendments also changed the beginning of the discovery period from when suit is filed to when the first initial disclosures are due. See Tex. R. Civ. P. 190.2(b)(1), 190.3(b)(1). See "Discovery periods," ch. 6-A, §8. The amendments apply to cases filed on or after January 1, 2021, except those filed in justice court. Tex.Sup.Ct. Order, Misc. Docket No. 20-9153 (eff. Jan. 1, 2021).

---

1. Before 1-1-21. For cases filed before January 1, 2021, plaintiffs and defendants can serve discovery requests with their original pleadings. *See* Tex. R. Civ. P. 190.2(b)(1) (pre-1-1-21 version), 190.3(b)(1) (pre-1-1-21 version).

Practice Tip

Many plaintiffs include a request for disclosure as part of their original petition, changing the caption to "Plaintiff's Original Petition & Request for Disclosures" and noting the full name of the document on the citation. If the plaintiff serves discovery with the petition but in a separate document, the citation should identify the discovery as one of the documents being served on the defendant. See, e.g., ***Sosa v. Williams****, 936 S.W.2d 708, 710 (Tex.App.—Waco 1996, writ denied) (because citation did not state that requests for admissions were served, P, who sought to rely on deemed admissions for summary judgment, had burden to conclusively prove proper service; based on return and D's controverting affidavit, P did not prove proper service).*

---

2. On or after 1-1-21. For cases filed on or after January 1, 2021, parties generally cannot serve discovery requests with their original pleadings. *See* Tex. R. Civ. P. 192.2(a). A party cannot serve discovery on another party until after the other party's initial disclosures are due unless otherwise agreed to by the parties or ordered by the court. *Id.*

§14. Deadline to respond to discovery

For the general rules for computing deadlines, see "Computing response deadlines," ch. 1-D, §6.

§14.1 Deadline to serve response. The party responding to the discovery must serve its response (answers, objections, and assertions of privilege) on the other party before the deadline for discovery.

2021 Rule Amendments

In 2020, the Supreme Court approved significant amendments to TRCP 194. See Tex.Sup.Ct. Order, Misc. Docket No. 20-9153 (eff. Jan. 1, 2021). Under the amendments, a party is now generally required to disclose certain information to other parties within 30 days after the filing of the first answer or general appearance without waiting for a discovery request. See Tex. R. Civ. P. 194.1(a), 194.2(a). The amendments apply to cases filed on or after January 1, 2021, except those filed in justice court. Tex.Sup.Ct. Order, Misc. Docket No. 20-9153 (eff. Jan. 1, 2021). See "Required disclosures—Cases filed on or after 1-1-21," ch. 6-E, §3. For cases filed before January 1, 2021, the party should file its responses to requests for disclosure in accordance with the deadlines discussed in §§14.1.1 and 14.1.2(1), below.

---

1. Standard time to respond—30 days. When a party is served with a request for written discovery, the request generally must provide at least 30 days to respond. *E.g.*, Tex. R. Civ. P. 196.2(a) (request for production), Tex. R. Civ. P. 196.7(c)(1) (request for entry on land), Tex. R. Civ. P. 197.2(a) (interrogatories), Tex. R. Civ. P. 198.2(a) (request for admissions). A discovery request can provide more than 30 days to answer, but it cannot provide less than 30 days. For most methods of service (e.g., e-service, personal or commercial delivery), the deadline to respond to the discovery request is 30 days; however, when service is by mail or fax, the party has an additional 3 days (if mailed) or 1 day (if faxed after 5:00 p.m.) to respond. *See* Tex. R. Civ. P. 21a(b)(2), (c). See chart 6-3 under "Served before answer date—50 days," ch. 6-A, §14.1.2. For a discussion of the deadlines to respond for all methods of service, see "Computing response deadlines," ch. 1-D, §6.

2. Served before answer date.

(1) Before 1-1-21. For cases filed before January 1, 2021, a defendant can be served with requests for written discovery before its answer is due. In this situation, the defendant generally must serve its response within 50 days after the discovery request was served. *E.g.*, Tex. R. Civ. P. 196.2(a) (pre-1-1-21 version; request for production), Tex. R. Civ. P. 196.7(c)(1) (pre-1-1-21 version; request for entry on land), Tex. R. Civ. P. 197.2(a) (pre-1-1-21 version; interrogatories), Tex. R. Civ. P. 198.2(a) (pre-1-1-21 version; request for admissions). This is true regardless of when the defendant actually files its answer. For example, if a request for written discovery is filed with the petition, the defendant has 50 days to respond even if it files its answer before the due date. When service is by mail or fax, the defendant has an additional 3 days (if mailed) or 1 day (if faxed after 5:00 p.m.) to respond. *See* Tex. R. Civ. P. 21a(b)(2), (c). See chart 6-3, below. For a discussion of the deadlines to respond for all methods of service, see "Computing response deadlines," ch. 1-D, §6.

(2) On or after 1-1-21. For cases filed on or after January 1, 2021, the defendant cannot be served with discovery until after its initial disclosures under TRCP 194 are due. *See* Tex. R. Civ. P. 192.2(a). These disclosures are generally due within 30 days after the filing of the first answer or general appearance. Tex. R. Civ. P. 194.2(a). Because the defendant cannot be served with discovery before its answer date, it will generally have 30 days to respond to discovery requests. See "Standard time to respond—30 days," ch. 6-A, §14.1.1.

2021 Rule Amendments

In 2020, the Supreme Court approved amendments to TRCP 192.2 and 194. See Tex.Sup.Ct. Order, Misc. Docket No. 20-9153 (eff. Jan. 1, 2021). Under the amendments, a party generally cannot serve discovery requests on another party until after that party's initial disclosures now required under TRCP 194 are due. See Tex. R. Civ. P. 192.2(a). These initial disclosures are generally due within 30 days after the filing of the first answer or general appearance. Tex. R. Civ. P. 194.2(a). TRCP 196, 197, and 198, which provide the response deadlines for various forms of discovery, were amended accordingly to eliminate the scenario where a defendant was served with discovery before its answer was due and thus had 50 days to respond. See Tex. R. Civ. P. 196.2(a), 196.7(c)(1), 197.2(a), 198.2(a). For a

detailed discussion of required disclosures under the 2021 amendments, see "Required disclosures—Cases filed on or after 1-1-21," ch. 6-E, §3.

6-3. Deadlines to Respond to Discovery		
	Method of service	**Computing deadline**
1	E-service	Date of e-service + 30 days = 30 days
2	Service by U.S. mail	Date of mailing (generally, the postmark) + 3 days + 30 days = 33 days
3	Service by delivery (personal or commercial)	Date of delivery + 30 days = 30 days
4	Service by fax before 5:00 p.m.	Date of fax + 30 days = 30 days
5	Service by fax after 5:00 p.m.	Date of fax + 1 day + 30 days = 31 days
6	E-mail	Date of e-mail + 30 days = 30 days
7	Service on defendant before answer date—request for entry, interrogatories, request for admissions, request for production[1]	Date of service + 50 days = 50 to 53 days, depending on type of service. See rows 1-6, above.

[1] See "Served before answer date," ch. 6-A, §14.1.2.

3. Discovery deadline in pretrial orders. If the court signs a pretrial order governing discovery, the parties must comply with its terms. *See* **Werner v. Miller**, 579 S.W.2d 455, 456 (Tex.1979). But the trial court cannot arbitrarily shorten discovery deadlines by pretrial order. **General Elec. Co. v. Salinas**, 861 S.W.2d 20, 23 (Tex.App.—Corpus Christi 1993, orig. proceeding). See "Discovery deadlines," ch. 5-A, §3.5.

4. Discovery deadline when trial reset. When the date for trial is reset, the original discovery deadlines set in the docket-control order are generally not extended. *See* **In re Kings Ridge Homeowners Ass'n**, 303 S.W.3d 773, 779 n.6 (Tex.App.—Fort Worth 2009, orig. proceeding); *see also* **Fort Brown Villas III Condo. Ass'n v. Gillenwater**, 285 S.W.3d 879, 882 (Tex.2009) (pre-1999 discovery rules had fluid deadline for discovery disclosure; post-1999 discovery rules have specific date to complete discovery that depends on discovery-control plan, not trial date); *cf.* **Eaton Metal Prods. v. U.S. Denro Steels, Inc.**, No. 14-09-00757-CV, 2010 WL 3795192 (Tex.App.—Houston [14th Dist.] 2010, no pet.) (memo op.; 9-30-10) (resetting of trial did not extend discovery deadlines established in Rule 11 agreement). The "hard deadline" established by the discovery rules requires a party to comply with the discovery deadlines; otherwise, the evidence not timely disclosed may be excluded under TRCP 193.6. *See* **Fort Brown Villas**, 285 S.W.3d at 882. See "Timely," ch. 6-A, §16.3. To extend the discovery deadlines, the party should move to modify the discovery-control plan under TRCP 190.5, or the parties should file a Rule 11 agreement. *See* **In re Kings Ridge**, 303 S.W.3d at 782. See "Modifying discovery procedures," ch. 6-A, §6.

§14.2 Deadlines for expert discovery. See "Deadlines for securing discovery from experts," ch. 6-D, §6.

§15. Extending time to respond to discovery

To extend the time to respond to discovery, a party must secure either an agreement or a court order. Without an extension, all untimely objections to the discovery request are waived. *See* **Hobson v. Moore**, 734 S.W.2d 340, 341 (Tex.1987).

§15.1 Agreement to extend. See "Modifying discovery by agreement," ch. 6-A, §6.1; **O'Connor's Texas Civil Forms**, FORM 6A:3 (2020 ed.).

§15.2 Court order to extend. To secure additional time to respond to discovery, the party must file a motion to extend time showing good cause for the late response. *See* Tex. R. Civ. P. 191.1. See **O'Connor's Texas Civil Forms**, FORM 6A:2 (2020 ed.). Because TRCP 191.1 states that the court can modify discovery procedures (including the deadlines to respond) only on "good cause," the rule seems to conflict with TRCP 5. TRCP 5 requires only "cause shown" for a motion to extend that is filed before the deadline sought to be extended. See "Motion to extend time," ch. 1-C, §9.1. Until the courts clarify this, all motions to extend time in discovery matters—even if filed before the deadline to respond—should include a showing of good cause. See "Modifying discovery by court order," ch. 6-A, §6.2.

§16. Producing written discovery

§16.1 Form of response.

1. Written. The party must provide written responses to discovery requests. Tex. R. Civ. P. 193.1; *e.g.*, Tex. R. Civ. P. 196.2(a) (request for production), Tex. R. Civ. P. 197.2(a) (interrogatories), Tex. R. Civ. P. 198.2(a) (request for admissions). A party cannot answer written-discovery requests orally. *See* Tex. R. Civ. P. 193.1; *see, e.g.*, **Sharp v. Broadway Nat'l Bank**, 784 S.W.2d 669, 671 (Tex.1990) (oral identification of witness not proper). The responding party's answers, objections, and other responses must be preceded by the corresponding request or required disclosure. Tex. R. Civ. P. 193.1. See **O'Connor's Texas Civil Forms**, FORMS 6G:3, 6H:3, 6I:3 (2020 ed.).

2. Signed. The responses to written discovery must be signed by the attorney (or pro se party). Tex. R. Civ. P. 191.3(a). See "Certification by signature," ch. 6-A, §4.1; "Securing discovery," ch. 6-A, §9.

3. Verified. The only written responses to discovery that must be verified are answers to interrogatories. See "Securing discovery," ch. 6-A, §9; "Signed & verified by party," ch. 6-G, §4.1.1(4).

§16.2 Service on attorney in charge. Discovery responses must be served on the attorney in charge. *See* Tex. R. Civ. P. 8 (all communications about lawsuit must be sent to attorney in charge); *see, e.g.*, **Reichhold Chems., Inc. v. Puremco Mfg.**, 854 S.W.2d 240, 246 (Tex.App.—Waco 1993, writ denied) (response to discovery served on cocounsel, instead of attorney in charge, was not timely). See "Attorney in charge," ch. 1-H, §3.1.

§16.3 Timely. A party must timely respond to discovery requests. Tex. R. Civ. P. 193.1; **In re Dawson**, 550 S.W.3d 625, 629 (Tex.2018). Discovery responses must be served within the time permitted by the rules, ordered by the court, or agreed to by the parties. See "Deadline to serve response," ch. 6-A, §14.1. When a party does not produce discovery, including a required disclosure, or ignores the request, the evidence that was not timely disclosed will be excluded at trial unless there was good cause for not producing the discovery or unless the other parties will not be unfairly surprised or prejudiced. Tex. R. Civ. P. 193.6(a); *see* **Fort Brown Villas III Condo. Ass'n v. Gillenwater**, 285 S.W.3d 879, 881 (Tex.2009); **F&H Invs. v. State**, 55 S.W.3d 663, 670–71 (Tex.App.—Waco 2001, no pet.); *see also* **In re M.J.M.**, 406 S.W.3d 292, 298–99 (Tex.App.—San Antonio 2013, no pet.) (death-penalty sanctions that prohibit a party from presenting all evidence are beyond scope of TRCP 193.6(a)). The exclusion of evidence under TRCP 193.6 applies equally to trial proceedings and summary-judgment proceedings. **Fort Brown Villas**, 285 S.W.3d at 882. See "Objecting to unidentified witness," ch. 6-E, §2.8.

§16.4 What to produce.

1. Information requested. A party is required to produce all information requested unless the party serves timely objections or assertions of privilege. *See* Tex. R. Civ. P. 193.2, 193.3. See "Burden to partially comply," ch. 6-A, §18.10.

2. Information in possession. A party is required to produce all documents or things requested that are in its possession, custody, or control. Tex. R. Civ. P. 196.3(a). See "Possession," ch. 6-A, §2.5.

§16.5 What not to produce. A party who makes a proper and timely objection or assertion of privilege is not required to produce the following:

1. Evidence subject to objection or privilege. A party is not required to produce evidence that is subject to an objection or an assertion of privilege. See "Burden to partially comply," ch. 6-A, §18.10.

2. Information not reasonably available. A party is not required to produce information that is not reasonably available to the party or its attorney when the response is made. *See* Tex. R. Civ. P. 193.1.

3. Impeachment or rebuttal evidence. A party is not required to produce impeachment or rebuttal evidence in anticipation of the other party's case. *See* Tex. R. Civ. P. 192.3(d) (parties may obtain discovery of trial witnesses but not of rebuttal or impeachment witnesses if the need for their testimony cannot reasonably be anticipated before trial).

§16.6 Organization of discovery materials. The responding party must either produce the discovery materials as they are kept in the usual course of business or organize and label them to correspond with the categories of the request. Tex. R. Civ. P. 196.3(c); **Porretto v. Texas Gen. Land Office**, 448 S.W.3d 393, 403 (Tex.2014).

§16.7 Authenticity of produced documents. See "Offering documents," ch. 6-I, §8.1.

§17. Supplementing discovery responses

§17.1 When supplementation required. The burden to supplement written discovery responses is on the party responding to the discovery; the party requesting the discovery has no burden to request supplementation. *See* Tex. R. Civ. P. 193.5(a); *see, e.g.*, **In re Dawson**, 550 S.W.3d 625, 629–30 (Tex.2018) (D had duty to supplement discovery responses to identify responsible third party; P did not have duty to conduct independent investigation of third party's involvement). A party should always supplement (even when unsure whether it is necessary) because the court may exclude the information if it is not properly supplemented. *See* Tex. R. Civ. P. 193.6(a); **Alvarado v. Farah Mfg. Co.**, 830 S.W.2d 911, 913–14 (Tex.1992); **Boothe v. Hausler**, 766 S.W.2d 788, 789 (Tex.1989). See **O'Connor's Texas Civil Forms**, FORMS 6A:33 to 6A:34 (2020 ed.). A party must supplement a discovery response in the following instances.

2021 Rule Amendments

In 2020, the Supreme Court approved significant amendments to TRCP 194. See Tex.Sup.Ct. Order, Misc. Docket No. 20-9153 (eff. Jan. 1, 2021). Under the amendments, a party is now generally required to disclose certain information and material without waiting for a discovery request from the other party. See Tex. R. Civ. P. 194.1(a). The amendments apply to cases filed on or after January 1, 2021, except those filed in justice court. Tex.Sup.Ct. Order, Misc. Docket No. 20-9153 (eff. Jan. 1, 2021). As with other written discovery responses, the required disclosures must be timely amended and supplemented under TRCP 193.5. Tex. R. Civ. P. 194 cmt. (2021). For a detailed discussion of required disclosures, see "Required disclosures—Cases filed on or after 1-1-21," ch. 6-E, §3.

1. Discovery response incomplete when made. A party must supplement a discovery response when the party obtains information revealing that its response was incomplete or incorrect when made. Tex. R. Civ. P. 193.5(a).

2. Discovery response no longer complete. A party must supplement a discovery response when the party discovers that its response, though complete and correct when made, is no longer complete and correct. Tex. R. Civ. P. 193.5(a); *see* **Boothe**, 766 S.W.2d at 789; *see, e.g.*, **Alvarado**, 830 S.W.2d at 916 (P should have supplemented discovery response to include unlisted witness).

3. For summary-judgment witnesses. A party must timely supplement responses to written discovery requesting the designation of witnesses before submitting evidence in a summary-judgment procedure. *See* **Fort Brown Villas III Condo. Ass'n v. Gillenwater**, 285 S.W.3d 879, 882 (Tex.2009) (exclusion of witnesses not timely identified under TRCP 193.6 applies equally to trial and SJ proceedings); **F.W. Indus. v. McKeehan**, 198 S.W.3d 217, 221 (Tex.App.—Eastland 2005, no pet.) (timeliness of expert discovery is determined by discovery deadline in TRCP 195.2, even in SJ proceedings); **Cunningham v. Columbia/St. David's Healthcare Sys.**, 185 S.W.3d 7, 13 (Tex.App.—Austin 2005, no pet.) (nondesignated expert's affidavit cannot be considered as SJ evidence unless party shows good cause or lack of unfair surprise or prejudice).

§17.2 Extent of supplementation.

1. Written discovery.

(1) Identity of witnesses. A discovery request for the identification of persons with knowledge of relevant facts, trial witnesses, or expert witnesses must be supplemented in writing. Tex. R. Civ. P. 193.5(a)(1); *see, e.g.*, **Sharp v. Broadway Nat'l Bank**, 784 S.W.2d 669, 671 (Tex.1990) (although expert witness was deposed, he was not identified in written supplement to request for disclosure; witness should have been excluded); **Yeldell v. Holiday Hills Ret. & Nursing Ctr., Inc.**, 701 S.W.2d 243, 246–47 (Tex.1985) (party did not supplement identity of fact witness after learning she had knowledge of relevant facts; witness was properly excluded).

(2) Other information. A discovery request for information other than the identification of witnesses must be supplemented in writing unless the information was made known in writing, on the record at a deposition, or through other discovery responses. Tex. R. Civ. P. 193.5(a)(2).

2. Discovery from retained testifying expert. When a party's retained testifying expert changes or modifies her opinion, the party must supplement the expert's deposition testimony or written report with the expert's mental impressions or opinions and the basis for them. Tex. R. Civ. P. 195.6; **VingCard A.S. v. Merrimac Hospitality Sys.**, 59 S.W.3d 847, 856 (Tex.App.—Fort Worth 2001, pet. denied); *see, e.g.*, **Aluminum Co. of Am. v. Bullock**, 870 S.W.2d 2, 3–4 (Tex.1994) (Ps should have supplemented discovery responses to show material change in their expert's testimony; expert stated in deposition that D was not consciously indifferent but testified at trial that D was grossly negligent). See "Supplementing discovery of retained testifying expert," ch. 6-D, §5.1.

3. Order or agreement. Supplementation of discovery responses is required when the court orders it or the parties agree to it. *See* Tex. R. Civ. P. 191.1; *see, e.g.*, **Cole v. Huntsville Mem'l Hosp.**, 920 S.W.2d 364, 376 (Tex.App.—Houston [1st Dist.] 1996, writ denied) (failure to supplement as required by order contributed to imposition of death-penalty sanctions), *disapproved on other grounds*, **Brown v. De La Cruz**, 156 S.W.3d 560 (Tex.2004).

§17.3 When supplementation not required.

1. Deposition testimony of fact witness. A party is not required to supplement the deposition testimony of fact witnesses. See "Deposition of fact witnesses," ch. 6-F, §11.1.

2. Information provided by other means. A party is not required to supplement responses to written-discovery requests for most discovery matters if the additional or corrective information was made known to the other party in writing, on the record at a deposition, or through other discovery responses. Tex. R. Civ. P. 193.5(a)(2); **City of Paris v. McDowell**, 79 S.W.3d 601, 606 (Tex.App.—Texarkana 2002, no pet.). Supplementation by other means, as outlined in TRCP 193.5(a)(2), applies only to "other information" and does not apply to supplementation of witness information listed in TRCP 193.5(a)(1).

3. Lapse of request. A party is not required to supplement discovery if the requesting party does not maintain a valid request for information. *See, e.g.*, **Kawasaki Motors Corp., U.S.A. v. Thompson**, 872 S.W.2d 221, 224 (Tex.1994) (parties' agreement inadvertently eliminated question about experts).

§17.4 Deadline to supplement responses.

1. Under TRCPs.

(1) After discovering need to supplement. A party must supplement or amend its responses to written discovery "reasonably promptly" after the party discovers the need to do so. Tex. R. Civ. P. 193.5(b); **In re Dawson**, 550 S.W.3d 625, 630 (Tex.2018); **Wigfall v. TDCJ**, 137 S.W.3d 268, 273 (Tex.App.—Houston [1st Dist.] 2004, no pet.); *e.g.*, **Hooper v. Chittaluru**, 222 S.W.3d 103, 110 (Tex.App.—Houston [14th Dist.] 2006, pet. denied) (P's supplemental expert designation one day after deposition of D's expert was reasonably prompt because P could not have cross-designated D's expert until learning of his opinions at deposition). Although there is a presumption that a supplemented discovery response made less than 30 days before trial is not reasonably prompt (see "Less than 30 days before trial," ch. 6-A, §17.4.1(3)), the converse is not true—a supplemented discovery response made more than 30 days before trial is not necessarily reasonably prompt. **Snider v. Stanley**, 44 S.W.3d 713, 715 (Tex.App.—Beaumont 2001, pet. denied). The following supplementations were not reasonably prompt: • Disclosure of witness statements 41 days before trial, on last day for discovery, nine months after discovery request. **Matagorda Cty. Hosp. Dist. v. Burwell**, 94 S.W.3d 75, 81 (Tex.App.—Corpus Christi 2002), *rev'd on other grounds*, 189 S.W.3d 738 (Tex.2006). • Plaintiff's designation of expert eight months after request, after defendant filed motion for summary judgment. **Ersek v. Davis & Davis, P.C.**, 69 S.W.3d 268, 271 n.2 (Tex.App.—Austin 2002, pet. denied). • Defendants' designation of expert 30 days before trial. **Snider**, 44 S.W.3d at 715.

(2) At least 30 days before trial. A party may supplement its discovery responses as late as 30 days before trial. Tex. R. Civ. P. 193.5(b); *see* **Aluminum Co. of Am. v. Bullock**, 870 S.W.2d 2, 3–4 (Tex.1994) (designation of experts under former TRCP 166b(6)(b)). If a case is set for trial "for the week of" instead of on a certain date, the 30 days run from the actual date of trial, not the Monday of that week. *See* Tex. R. Civ. P. 193.5(b) (specifies "before trial," not "before the week set for trial").

(3) Less than 30 days before trial. To supplement discovery responses less than 30 days before trial, a party must show good cause for the late supplementation or show that it will not unfairly surprise or prejudice the other parties.

Tex. R. Civ. P. 193.6(a), (b); **Rutledge v. Staner**, 9 S.W.3d 469, 472 (Tex.App.—Tyler 1999, pet. denied); *see, e.g.*, **Forman v. Fina Oil & Chem. Co.**, 858 S.W.2d 373, 374 (Tex.1993) (good cause for late designation of expert because P designated same doctor as D did three days after receiving D's designation). There is a presumption that a supplemental or amended response made less than 30 days before trial is not made "reasonably promptly." Tex. R. Civ. P. 193.5(b). If the party does not carry its burden, the court may exclude the evidence or grant a continuance to allow the other parties to conduct discovery on new information disclosed in the supplementation. Tex. R. Civ. P. 193.6(a), (c).

2. By court order or agreement. A party must supplement its responses to written discovery according to the modified deadlines in any court order or agreement between the parties. *See* Tex. R. Civ. P. 191.1 (discovery procedures can be modified by court order or agreement); *see, e.g.*, **Mack v. Suzuki Motor Corp.**, 6 S.W.3d 732, 733–34 (Tex.App.—Houston [1st Dist.] 1999, no pet.) (expert report struck because P served it after deadline in agreed scheduling order).

§17.5 Not filed. Most supplemental or amended responses to written discovery are not filed with the court. See "Filing discovery," ch. 6-A, §12.1.

§17.6 Form of supplemental discovery. Supplemental or amended responses to written discovery should be made in the same form as the original responses. Tex. R. Civ. P. 193.5(b); **State Farm Fire & Cas. Co. v. Morua**, 979 S.W.2d 616, 618 (Tex.1998); *see, e.g.*, **Varner v. Howe**, 860 S.W.2d 458, 462–63 (Tex.App.—El Paso 1993, no writ) (witness identified by letter supplementing interrogatory answers should have been excluded because letter did not meet requirements for interrogatories). See **O'Connor's Texas Civil Forms**, FORM 6A:34 (2020 ed.).

1. Written. The party should provide the supplemental or amended response in writing. *See* Tex. R. Civ. P. 193.5(b). For exceptions, see "Information provided by other means," ch. 6-A, §17.3.2.

2. Verified. A supplemental or amended response must be verified by the party if the original response was required to be verified. Tex. R. Civ. P. 193.5(b). For a list of written discovery that must be verified, see "Securing discovery," ch. 6-A, §9.

3. Objections to form of response. A supplemental or amended response that is not in the correct form or that is not verified when required is not deemed untimely unless the party making the response refuses to correct the defect within a reasonable time after it is pointed out. Tex. R. Civ. P. 193.5(b).

§17.7 Review. If a party supplements discovery less than 30 days before trial and the trial court admits the untimely disclosed evidence over the opposing party's objection, the objecting party—to obtain a reversal on appeal—must show that the trial court's error probably caused the rendition of an improper judgment. **Bott v. Bott**, 962 S.W.2d 626, 628 (Tex.App.—Houston [14th Dist.] 1997, no pet.); *see* Tex. R. App. P. 44.1(a)(1).

§18. Resisting discovery

6-4. Burdens in Discovery Procedure

Burden		Discovery from party	Discovery from nonparty*
		Burden is on—	
1	To plead objection	Party resisting discovery, ch. 6-A, §18.1	
2	To assert privilege	Party resisting discovery, ch. 6-A, §18.2	
3	To request privilege log	Party seeking discovery, ch. 6-A, §18.2.2	
4	To secure hearing	Party seeking discovery, ch. 6-A, §18.6.1	Party resisting discovery, ch. 6-A, §18.4.1
5	To produce evidence at hearing	Party resisting discovery, ch. 6-A, §18.7	
6	To ask for in camera inspection	Party resisting discovery, ch. 6-A, §18.8.1	
7	To secure ruling	Party seeking discovery, ch. 6-A, §18.6.1	Party resisting discovery, ch. 6-A, §18.4.1

* Assumes that the nonparty does not object to producing discovery but one of the parties does

The discovery rules provide two procedures for resisting discovery: (1) making discovery objections and (2) asserting claims of privilege.

Note

Even though TRCP 196.2(b) seems to say that a party responding to discovery must make its objections and assert its privileges at the same time, the discovery rules permit a party to file its objections first and wait until after the court rules on the objections to file its assertions of privilege if an objection and a privilege apply to the same information. ***In re Lincoln Elec. Co.****, 91 S.W.3d 432, 436–37 (Tex.App.—Beaumont 2002, orig. proceeding).*

§18.1 Making objections. The party resisting discovery has the burden to plead its objections to discovery. **State v. Lowry**, 802 S.W.2d 669, 671 (Tex.1991). No matter how improper the discovery request, the resisting party must timely object, or else it waives its objections. *See* Tex. R. Civ. P. 193.2(a) (party must make "any" objection to written discovery in writing); **Young v. Ray**, 916 S.W.2d 1, 3 (Tex.App.—Houston [1st Dist.] 1995, orig. proceeding) (party must timely object or objection is waived). The only discovery request a party is not required to respond or object to is one that is not signed. See "Effect of no signature," ch. 6-A, §4.1.3.

1. Timely objection. The party resisting discovery must object at or before the time to respond to discovery. Tex. R. Civ. P. 193.2(a); **In re National Lloyds Ins.**, 507 S.W.3d 219, 223 (Tex.2016); *see* **Remington Arms Co. v. Canales**, 837 S.W.2d 624, 625 (Tex.1992); **Hobson v. Moore**, 734 S.W.2d 340, 341 (Tex.1987). Otherwise, the objection is waived unless the party (1) obtained an extension of time by agreement or by court order or (2) can show good cause for not timely objecting. *See* Tex. R. Civ. P. 191.1, 193.2(e). After the deadline to respond, a party can amend its objection or response only to include a ground that was initially inapplicable or that was unknown after reasonable inquiry. *See* Tex. R. Civ. P. 193.2(d), (e).

2. Specific objection. The party resisting discovery must make a specific objection for each item it wants to exclude from discovery. *See* Tex. R. Civ. P. 193.2(a); **In re National Lloyds**, 507 S.W.3d at 223; *see, e.g.*, **In re Alford Chevrolet-Geo**, 997 S.W.2d 173, 181 (Tex.1999) (party's conclusory objections alleging undue burden and harassment were unsuccessful); *see also* **National Un. Fire Ins. v. Hoffman**, 746 S.W.2d 305, 307 & n.3 (Tex.App.—Dallas 1988, orig. proceeding) (party made general objections by merely reciting particular privileges). Valid objections obscured by unfounded objections are automatically waived unless the party shows good cause. Tex. R. Civ. P. 193.2(e).

§18.2 Asserting privileges. To protect privileged information from written discovery, a party must timely "assert" a privilege under TRCP 193.3. **In re Shipmon**, 68 S.W.3d 815, 822 (Tex.App.—Amarillo 2001, orig. proceeding); **In re Monsanto Co.**, 998 S.W.2d 917, 924 (Tex.App.—Waco 1999, orig. proceeding); *see also* Tex. R. Civ. P. 176.6(c) (nonparty objecting to subpoena requesting documents must follow provisions of TRCP 193.3). A party should not "object" to discovery that asks for privileged information. Tex. R. Civ. P. 193.2(f); **In re Christus Health Se. Tex.**, 167 S.W.3d 596, 599 (Tex.App.—Beaumont 2005, orig. proceeding); **In re Anderson**, 163 S.W.3d 136, 140 (Tex.App.—San Antonio 2005, orig. proceeding); *see* **In re Shipmon**, 68 S.W.3d at 822. If a party mistakenly objects to a request for privileged information instead of asserting a privilege, the privilege is not waived, but the party must comply with TRCP 193.3 when the error is pointed out. Tex. R. Civ. P. 193.2(f); **In re University of Tex. Health Ctr.**, 33 S.W.3d 822, 826 (Tex.2000).

1. Make assertion. A privilege against written discovery must be asserted as follows:

(1) Withhold information. The party must withhold the privileged information from the discovery it produces. Tex. R. Civ. P. 193.3(a). The party can withhold only the information sought to be protected; it cannot withhold other information requested in the same discovery request. See "Burden to partially comply," ch. 6-A, §18.10.

(2) Withholding statement. The party must serve a withholding statement. Tex. R. Civ. P. 193.3(a). See "Withholding statement," ch. 6-A, §2.8; **O'Connor's Texas Civil Forms**, FORM 6A:19 (2020 ed.).

(3) Exemption for litigation materials. A party is not required to assert a privilege in the withholding statement for materials created by or for attorneys for the litigation. Tex. R. Civ. P. 193.3(c). These materials will presumably

be withheld on the grounds of attorney-client privilege or core work product. Tex. R. Civ. P. 193 cmt. 3. A party may withhold a privileged communication to or from an attorney or attorney's representative or a privileged document of an attorney or attorney's representative if (1) the communication was created when the party consulted an attorney to obtain professional legal services from the attorney in the prosecution or defense of a specific claim in the litigation in which discovery is requested or required and (2) the communication was about the litigation in which the discovery is requested or required. Tex. R. Civ. P. 193.3(c).

Note

TRCP 193.3(c) does not prohibit a party from specifically requesting information that may be subject to the attorney-client privilege or core-work-product exemption if the party has a good-faith basis for asserting that the information is discoverable. Tex. R. Civ. P. 193 cmt. 3. For example, a party can request information described by TRE 503(d)(1), the crime-fraud exception. See Tex. R. Civ. P. 193 cmt. 3.

2. Request privilege log. After receiving a withholding statement, a party seeking discovery may request in writing that the withholding party identify the information or material withheld. Tex. R. Civ. P. 193.3(b); **In re Christus Health**, 167 S.W.3d at 599; **In re Anderson**, 163 S.W.3d at 140; **In re Monsanto Co.**, 998 S.W.2d at 924. The document listing the information withheld from discovery is called a privilege log. See **O'Connor's Texas Civil Forms**, FORM 6A:20 (2020 ed.).

3. Serve privilege log. Within 15 days after service of the request for the privilege log, the withholding party must serve a response. Tex. R. Civ. P. 193.3(b); **In re Lumbermen's Underwriting Alliance**, 421 S.W.3d 289, 292 (Tex.App.—Texarkana 2014, orig. proceeding); **In re Anderson**, 163 S.W.3d at 140. See **O'Connor's Texas Civil Forms**, FORM 6A:21 (2020 ed.). The response must include the following information:

(1) Assert privilege. The party must assert a specific privilege for each item or group of items withheld. Tex. R. Civ. P. 193.3(b)(2); **In re Christus Health**, 167 S.W.3d at 599; **In re Anderson**, 163 S.W.3d at 140; **In re Monsanto Co.**, 998 S.W.2d at 924.

(2) Describe information or material withheld. The party must specify the nature of the information or material withheld without revealing the privileged information itself. Tex. R. Civ. P. 193.3(b)(1); **In re Lumbermen's Underwriting**, 421 S.W.3d at 292; **In re Christus Health**, 167 S.W.3d at 599; **In re Anderson**, 163 S.W.3d at 140. The withheld information or material must be described in a way that allows the party seeking discovery to assess the applicability of the privilege. Tex. R. Civ. P. 193.3(b)(1); **In re Christus Health**, 167 S.W.3d at 599; **In re Anderson**, 163 S.W.3d at 140–41; **In re Monsanto Co.**, 998 S.W.2d at 924. A description of a document should include the document number ("Bates number"), author or source, recipient, persons receiving copies, date, title, document type, number of pages, and any other relevant information. *See* **In re Monsanto Co.**, 998 S.W.2d at 925.

4. Use snap-back provision. An inadvertent production of privileged information is considered involuntary. *See* Tex. R. Civ. P. 193.3(d); **In re Living Ctrs.**, 175 S.W.3d 253, 260 (Tex.2005); **In re Certain Underwriters at Lloyd's London**, 294 S.W.3d 891, 906 (Tex.App.—Beaumont 2009, orig. proceeding); **In re Monsanto Co.**, 998 S.W.2d at 921 n.2. Parties and nonparties may rely on TRCP 193.3(d)—known as the "snap-back provision"—to assert a claim of privilege after inadvertent production of their own privileged documents. **In re Certain Underwriters**, 294 S.W.3d at 904–05; *see* **In re City of Dickinson**, 568 S.W.3d 642, 649 (Tex.2019).

(1) Purpose. The purpose of the snap-back provision in TRCP 193.3(d) is to reduce costs and risks in large document productions. Tex. R. Civ. P. 193 cmt. 4. The provision focuses on the intent to waive the privilege, not on the intent to produce the information or material. **In re Christus Spohn Hosp. Kleberg**, 222 S.W.3d 434, 439 (Tex.2007); **Warrantech Corp. v. Computer Adapters Servs.**, 134 S.W.3d 516, 524–25 (Tex.App.—Fort Worth 2004, no pet.); Tex. R. Civ. P. 193 cmt. 4. A party who does not diligently screen documents before producing them does not waive a claim of privilege. **In re Christus Spohn Hosp. Kleberg**, 222 S.W.3d at 439; **Warrantech Corp.**, 134 S.W.3d at 525; **In re AEP Tex. Cent. Co.**, 128 S.W.3d 687, 693 (Tex.App.—San Antonio 2003, orig. proceeding); Tex. R. Civ. P. 193 cmt. 4.

(2) Procedure. A party may claim a privilege on information that it inadvertently produced by following the snap-back provision in TRCP 193.3(d). *See* Tex. R. Civ. P. 193 cmt. 4 (snap-back provision in TRCP 193.3 overrules **Granada**

Corp. v. First Ct. of Appeals, 844 S.W.2d 223 (Tex.1992), on inadvertent production). In limited circumstances, a party who inadvertently produced privileged information to its own testifying expert (making the information discoverable to the opposing party) may be able to use the snap-back provision. See "Invoke snap-back provision," ch. 6-D, §4.1.1(6)(b)[2][a].

(a) Amend withholding statement. The party must serve on the other parties an amended withholding statement that (1) identifies the information produced, (2) identifies the privilege asserted for that information, and (3) requests that all copies of the privileged information be returned. *See* Tex. R. Civ. P. 193.3(d). See **O'Connor's Texas Civil Forms**, FORM 6A:22 (2020 ed.).

(b) Deadline. The party must amend its withholding statement within ten days after discovering the accidental production, unless the time is shortened by the court. Tex. R. Civ. P. 193.3(d). The ten-day period runs from the party's first awareness of the mistake, not from the production of the information. Tex. R. Civ. P. 193 cmt. 4.

(c) Return material. Once the party has complied with the snap-back provision, any party who obtained the information or material must promptly return or destroy it and all copies. *See* Tex. R. Civ. P. 193.3(d); *see, e.g.*, **In re City of Dickinson**, 568 S.W.3d at 649 (party requested for e-mails that were inadvertently e-filed to be destroyed by receiving party).

Practice Tip

To avoid complications at trial about inadvertently disclosed documents, ask the court to require all parties to make pretrial identification of documents that they intend to offer. Tex. R. Civ. P. 193 cmt. 4. This will trigger the obligation to assert any overlooked privileges under TRCP 193.3. Tex. R. Civ. P. 193 cmt. 4.

§18.3 Objecting to amended discovery requests. When a party receives an amended discovery request, the party is not required to restate its objections and reassert its privileges to the parts of the request that are the same as the original. *See, e.g.*, **In re University of Tex. Health Ctr.**, 33 S.W.3d 822, 826 (Tex.2000) (hospital was not required to reassert privileges when deposition was reset).

§18.4 Objections regarding discovery & nonparties.

1. Party information from nonparty. When discovery about a party is sought from a nonparty, the party should file a motion for protective order to prevent disclosure of the information. Only a protective order—not an objection—will prevent the nonparty from producing the discovery. *See* Tex. R. Civ. P. 192.6(b). When both the party and the nonparty object to the discovery, the party and the nonparty can coordinate their efforts, and the nonparty should withhold the requested information. When only the party objects and the nonparty is willing to produce the information, the party must quickly file a motion for protective order, set the motion for a hearing, and get a ruling before the nonparty produces the information. *See* Tex. R. Civ. P. 176.6(e) (party affected by subpoena may move for protective order before time to respond), Tex. R. Civ. P. 192.6(a) (party affected by discovery request may file motion for protective order within time to respond). But if the nonparty produces the information, the party may recover any privileged information. *See* Tex. R. Civ. P. 193.3(d). See "Use snap-back provision," ch. 6-A, §18.2.4.

2. Nonparty information from party. The discovery rules do not require notice to a nonparty when a party seeks information about it from another party. *See* **In re CI Host, Inc.**, 92 S.W.3d 514, 517 (Tex.2002). The party from whom the discovery is sought should inform the court when the information sought is the privileged information of a nonparty. The court should give serious consideration to the interest of a nonparty whose information is sought in discovery. *See id.*

§18.5 Burden to challenge objections. The party seeking discovery can put the other party's objections and claims of privilege at issue by making a global challenge. *See* **In re E.I. DuPont de Nemours & Co.**, 136 S.W.3d 218, 226–27 (Tex.2004). At the hearing, the court may ask the party seeking discovery to specifically challenge the other party's objections and claims of privilege. *Id.* at 227 & n.5.

§18.6 Burden to secure hearing & ruling. Either party may ask for a hearing on objections, claims of privilege, motions for protective orders, motions to quash, or motions to compel. *See* Tex. R. Civ. P. 176.6(d), (e), 192.6, 193.4.

1. **Most discovery.** If neither party asks for a hearing, the party who sent the request for discovery waives the requested discovery. **Roberts v. Whitfill**, 191 S.W.3d 348, 361 n.3 (Tex.App.—Waco 2006, no pet.); *cf.* **Remington Arms Co. v. Caldwell**, 850 S.W.2d 167, 170 (Tex.1993) (party who does not request pretrial ruling on discovery dispute waives sanctions claim for that issue). Thus, once objections or claims of privilege have been served, the party seeking discovery has the burden to secure a hearing to resolve the discovery dispute. *See* Tex. R. Civ. P. 193.4(a); **McKinney v. National Un. Fire Ins.**, 772 S.W.2d 72, 75 (Tex.1989).

2. **Discovery involving nonparty.** To block a nonparty from producing information about a party in response to a discovery request, the party should secure a hearing and a ruling before the nonparty produces the information. See "Party information from nonparty," ch. 6-A, §18.4.1.

§18.7 Burden to provide evidence. Once a hearing is set, the party resisting discovery must produce any evidence necessary to support a claim of privilege or an objection to discovery.

1. **When necessary.** Generally, when a party makes an objection or asserts a claim of privilege, that party has the burden to produce evidence to support its objection or claim of privilege. Tex. R. Civ. P. 193.4(a), 199.6; *e.g.*, **In re CI Host, Inc.**, 92 S.W.3d 514, 516–17 (Tex.2002) (evidence was necessary to support objection that information on computer tapes was protected); *see* **In re E.I. DuPont de Nemours & Co.**, 136 S.W.3d 218, 227 (Tex.2004); **Huie v. DeShazo**, 922 S.W.2d 920, 926 (Tex.1996); *see, e.g.*, **General Motors Corp. v. Tanner**, 892 S.W.2d 862, 863–64 (Tex.1995) (evidence was necessary to support objection that testing would destroy evidence). Merely listing a specific privilege or exemption from discovery in a privilege log is insufficient. **In re Crestcare Nursing & Rehab. Ctr.**, 222 S.W.3d 68, 73 (Tex.App.—Tyler 2006, orig. proceeding). When evidence is necessary, it must be produced at or before the hearing. Tex. R. Civ. P. 193.4(a). The evidence can include the following:

(1) **Affidavits.** When a party relies on affidavits, the affidavits must be served at least seven days before the hearing or, if the party is objecting to written discovery, at another reasonable time that the court permits. Tex. R. Civ. P. 193.4(a); **In re Monsanto Co.**, 998 S.W.2d 917, 924 (Tex.App.—Waco 1999, orig. proceeding); *see* Tex. R. Civ. P. 199.6. An affidavit must be based on the affiant's personal knowledge and must show that the facts in it are true. See "Personal knowledge," ch. 1-B, §3.2.16(3)(a). The affidavit must contain something more than global allegations that the documents are privileged or a mere recitation of facts ascertainable from the documents themselves. **Barnes v. Whittington**, 751 S.W.2d 493, 495 (Tex.1988). An affidavit that addresses groups of documents rather than each document individually may be sufficient to make a prima facie showing of a privilege. *See* **In re E.I. DuPont de Nemours**, 136 S.W.3d at 223; *see, e.g.*, **In re Monsanto Co.**, 998 S.W.2d at 927–28 (corporate attorney's affidavit that log of 117 documents involved confidential communications among counsel and work papers reflecting attorneys' mental processes was prima facie proof of attorney-client privilege). The affidavits should be offered into evidence at the hearing. *See, e.g.*, **In re Monsanto Co.**, 998 S.W.2d at 926 (trial court considered affidavits even though they were not offered; formal admission would have been better but was not necessary under circumstances).

(2) **Live testimony.** If a party intends to rely on live testimony at the hearing, it should proceed with all the formalities of trial—that is, make sure a court reporter is present, have the witnesses sworn, introduce exhibits, and make objections to the other party's evidence. *See* Tex. R. Civ. P. 193.4(a), 199.6. The witness should explain why specific documents are exempt from discovery. *See, e.g.*, **Conrad v. Wilson**, 873 S.W.2d 467, 469–70 (Tex.App.—Beaumont 1994, orig. proceeding) (testimony of hospital's general counsel that "some of the things asked for are protected" was not specific).

(3) **Documents for inspection.** When a party is resisting discovery on the grounds of privilege or relevance, the documents themselves may be the only adequate evidence to support the claim. **In re E.I. DuPont de Nemours**, 136 S.W.3d at 223; *see* **In re National Lloyds Ins.**, 532 S.W.3d 794, 804 (Tex.2017) (work-product privilege); **State v. Lowry**, 802 S.W.2d 669, 673 (Tex.1991) (investigative privilege); **Axelson, Inc. v. McIlhany**, 798 S.W.2d 550, 553 (Tex.1990) (relevance objection). A representative sample of documents, rather than each and every document, may be appropriate to establish the privilege. *See* **In re Living Ctrs.**, 175 S.W.3d 253, 261 (Tex.2005). See "In camera inspection," ch. 6-A, §18.8.

2. **When not necessary.** In some cases, an objection or claim of privilege does not need to be supported by evidence. *See, e.g.*, **In re Union Pac. Res.**, 22 S.W.3d 338, 341 (Tex.1999) (evidence was not necessary to support relevance

objection); **Loftin v. Martin**, 776 S.W.2d 145, 148 (Tex.1989) (request was so vague and overbroad that party did not know how to respond); **Garner, Lovell & Stein, P.C. v. Burnett**, 911 S.W.2d 108, 112–13 (Tex.App.—Amarillo 1995, orig. proceeding) (request for documents created after lawsuit filed was clearly not proper discovery); **Texas Tech Univ. Health Sci. Ctr. v. Schild**, 828 S.W.2d 502, 504 (Tex.App.—El Paso 1992, orig. proceeding) (request obviously asked for information that would reveal attorney's thought processes and trial strategy). When in doubt, a party should file an affidavit that explains the reasons for the objection or claim of privilege.

§18.8 In camera inspection. The court may require an in camera inspection. Tex. R. Civ. P. 193.4(a), 199.6; **In re Silver**, 540 S.W.3d 530, 539 (Tex.2018); **In re CI Host, Inc.**, 92 S.W.3d 514, 516 (Tex.2002). When an inspection is critical for evaluating a privilege claim, the court must examine the documents before ruling on the claim. **In re Silver**, 540 S.W.3d at 539; **In re Christus Santa Rosa Health Sys.**, 492 S.W.3d 276, 279 (Tex.2016); **In re Memorial Hermann Hosp. Sys.**, 464 S.W.3d 686, 698 (Tex.2015).

1. Make prima facie case. The party resisting discovery must first establish a prima facie case for its claim of privilege by producing evidence (i.e., affidavits or live testimony). **In re Christus Santa Rosa Health**, 492 S.W.3d at 279; **In re Living Ctrs.**, 175 S.W.3d 253, 261 (Tex.2005); *see, e.g.*, **In re Crestcare Nursing & Rehab. Ctr.**, 222 S.W.3d 68, 74 (Tex.App.—Tyler 2006, orig. proceeding) (conclusory affidavit stating that personnel files were "confidential" was insufficient for prima facie showing). See "Affidavits," ch. 6-A, §18.7.1(1); "Live testimony," ch. 6-A, §18.7.1(2). The prima facie standard requires only the minimum amount of evidence necessary to support a rational inference that the fact allegation is true. **In re Memorial Hermann**, 464 S.W.3d at 698; **In re E.I. DuPont de Nemours & Co.**, 136 S.W.3d 218, 223 (Tex.2004); **In re Crestcare Nursing**, 222 S.W.3d at 73.

2. Identify documents to be inspected. Once a party makes a prima facie case for its claim of privilege, the party seeking discovery should, based on the privilege log, identify the documents or groups of documents it believes the court should inspect in camera. **In re Monsanto Co.**, 998 S.W.2d 917, 925 (Tex.App.—Waco 1999, orig. proceeding).

3. Produce documents for inspection. The party resisting discovery should mark each document with the appropriate privilege and file the documents in a sealed wrapper with the court for an in camera inspection. *See* Tex. R. Civ. P. 193.4(a), 199.6; **Axelson, Inc. v. McIlhany**, 798 S.W.2d 550, 553 n.6 (Tex.1990).

4. Conduct inspection. Once the party makes a prima facie showing of privilege and tenders documents to the trial court, the court must conduct an in camera inspection before deciding whether to compel production. **In re Christus Santa Rosa Health**, 492 S.W.3d at 279; **In re E.I. DuPont de Nemours**, 136 S.W.3d at 223.

§18.9 Nonparty objections to discovery. Parties must follow the applicable rules of procedure for obtaining nonparty records. A nonparty (e.g., a witness subpoenaed for a deposition who is not subject to the control of a party) who objects to discovery must follow the same procedures as a party. Tex. R. Civ. P. 176.6(c) to (e); **In re Diversicare Gen. Partner, Inc.**, 41 S.W.3d 788, 794 (Tex.App.—Corpus Christi 2001, orig. proceeding), *overruled on other grounds*, **In re Arriola**, 159 S.W.3d 670 (Tex.App.—Corpus Christi 2004, orig. proceeding); *see, e.g.*, **State v. Walker**, 873 S.W.2d 379, 380 (Tex.1994) (DA's office, a nonparty, filed motion to quash and for protective order); **Olinger v. Curry**, 926 S.W.2d 832, 835 (Tex.App.—Fort Worth 1996, orig. proceeding) (nonparty objected at deposition). See "Objecting to trial & discovery subpoenas," ch. 1-L, §4; "Challenging nonparty discovery subpoena," ch. 6-I, §5.5.

§18.10 Burden to partially comply.

1. Partial compliance necessary. A party is required to comply with written discovery to the extent that it does not object. Tex. R. Civ. P. 192.6 (motion for protective order), Tex. R. Civ. P. 193.2(b) & cmt. 2 (objections to written discovery), Tex. R. Civ. P. 193.3(a) (assertions of privilege). For example, when a party objects to producing documents from a remote time period, it must produce documents from a more recent period. Tex. R. Civ. P. 193 cmt. 2.

2. No compliance necessary. A party is not required to partially comply if (1) complying before getting a ruling is unreasonable, (2) the production would be burdensome and duplicative if the objection were overruled, or (3) the request is overbroad and not in compliance with the rule requiring specific requests for documents (e.g., request for "all documents relevant to the lawsuit"). *See* Tex. R. Civ. P. 192.6, 193.2(b) & cmt. 2. See "Undue burden," ch. 6-A, §20.1.1; "Overbroad," ch. 6-A, §20.1.3.

§18.11 Ruling on objections & claims of privilege. To the extent the court sustains an objection or claim of privilege, the party has no further duty to respond to the request or required disclosure. Tex. R. Civ. P. 193.4(b). To the extent the court overrules an objection or claim of privilege, the party must produce the requested or required material or information within 30 days after the court's ruling or when ordered by the court. *Id.*

§19. Types of objections to discovery

§19.1 Valid objections to discovery requests. See **O'Connor's Texas Civil Forms**, FORM 6A:9 (2020 ed.). A party may object to a discovery request for the following reasons:

1. Not within scope of discovery. A party may object to a discovery request that asks for information outside the scope of discovery. A discovery request is outside the scope of discovery when it asks for information that (1) is not relevant, (2) is not proportional to the needs of the case, or (3) will not be admissible at trial and is not reasonably calculated to lead to the discovery of admissible evidence. *See* Tex. R. Civ. P. 192.3(a), 192.4(b); **In re North Cypress Med. Ctr. Oper. Co.**, 559 S.W.3d 128, 129 (Tex.2018); **In re State Farm Lloyds**, 520 S.W.3d 595, 599 (Tex.2017); **In re National Lloyds Ins.**, 449 S.W.3d 486, 488 (Tex.2014).

(1) Not relevant. Information that is not relevant to the suit is outside the scope of discovery. See "Relevant," ch. 6-B, §2.1.1(1).

Note

*For the form of objections based on relevance, see the charts produced by Ford in **Ford Motor Co. v. Ross**, 888 S.W.2d 879, 900–02 (Tex.App.—Tyler 1994, orig. proceeding).*

---

(2) Not proportional. Information that is not proportional to the needs of the case is outside the scope of discovery. See "Proportional," ch. 6-B, §2.1.1(2).

(3) Will not lead to admissible evidence. Information that will not be admissible at trial and is not reasonably calculated to lead to the discovery of admissible evidence is outside the scope of discovery. See "Reasonably calculated to lead to admissible evidence," ch. 6-B, §2.1.1(3).

2. Not permissible form of discovery. A party may object when a discovery request asks for a type of discovery that is not permitted by the rules of discovery. *See, e.g.*, Tex. R. Civ. P. 195.1 (discovery of information on testifying experts allowed through disclosures, depositions, and reports under TRCP 195), Tex. R. Civ. P. 197.1 (interrogatories not permitted for discovery of information covered by TRCP 195); **In re Guzman**, 19 S.W.3d 522, 524–25 (Tex.App.—Corpus Christi 2000, orig. proceeding) (court cannot require party to execute authorization for nonparty to produce information; nonparty discovery must comply with TRCP 205.1); *see also* Tex. R. Civ. P. 191 cmt. 1 (court may order, or parties may agree to, use of discovery methods other than those prescribed in TRCPs).

3. Not reasonably available. A party is not required to produce information that is not reasonably available to the party or its attorney when the response is made. Tex. R. Civ. P. 193.1. For a discussion of what a party must show when information is not available to answer a request for admissions, see "Lack of information," ch. 6-H, §4.2.4.

4. Request lacks specificity. A party may object when a request lacks specificity or is so vague and unclear that the party cannot identify the information requested. *See* **Davis v. Pate**, 915 S.W.2d 76, 79 n.2 (Tex.App.—Corpus Christi 1996, orig. proceeding) (distinguishing requests that are overbroad from those that lack specificity).

5. Improper procedure.

(1) Improper discovery request. When a party makes an improper request for discovery, the other party may file either an objection or a motion for protective order, whichever is appropriate, before the response is due, stating why the request is improper. Tex. R. Civ. P. 192.6, 193.2. For example, a party may object when the other party serves more than 25 written interrogatories in Level 2 discovery. *See* Tex. R. Civ. P. 190.3(b)(3). The responding party should answer 25 interrogatories and object to the others. *See* Tex. R. Civ. P. 193.2(b) & cmt. 2.

(2) No specific statement of relief. When a party who makes a discovery request did not include a specific statement of relief in its original pleading as required by TRCP 47(c), the other party may object to the discovery request. *See* **In re Greater McAllen Star Props., Inc.**, 444 S.W.3d 743, 750–51 (Tex.App.—Corpus Christi 2014, orig. proceeding). A party cannot conduct discovery until it has filed an amended pleading that complies with TRCP 47(c). *See* Tex. R. Civ. P. 47. A party is not required to reissue discovery requests after amending its pleadings to comply with TRCP 47(c). **In re Greater McAllen Star**, 444 S.W.3d at 751. The time to respond to the discovery requests begins to run on the date the amended pleading is filed. *Id.*

6. Same information already provided. A party may object if the information has already been provided in response to other discovery in another form. *See, e.g.*, **Sears, Roebuck & Co. v. Ramirez**, 824 S.W.2d 558, 559 (Tex.1992) (D not required to produce tax returns to prove net worth because it had produced audited, certified annual report).

7. Burdensome, harassing, or overbroad. A party may object when a discovery request is unduly burdensome, harassing, or overbroad. See "Grounds to limit scope of discovery," ch. 6-A, §20.1.

§19.2 Invalid objections to discovery requests. The following are some invalid objections to discovery requests: • The information requested is privileged. A party must follow the procedure for asserting a privilege under TRCP 193.3. See "Asserting privileges," ch. 6-A, §18.2. • The evidence will not be admissible at trial. As long as information appears reasonably calculated to lead to the discovery of admissible evidence, it is discoverable. Tex. R. Civ. P. 192.3(a). • The other party combined two forms of discovery. Different forms of discovery may be combined in the same document and may be taken in any order or sequence. Tex. R. Civ. P. 192.2(b).

§20. Motion for protective order

A party or nonparty resisting discovery may file a motion for protective order in response to a discovery request or a motion to compel. Tex. R. Civ. P. 192.6(a); *see* **In re Alford Chevrolet-Geo**, 997 S.W.2d 173, 180–81 (Tex.1999). See **O'Connor's Texas Civil Forms**, FORM 6A:10 (2020 ed.). The person from whom discovery is sought and any other person affected by the discovery request have independent rights to seek a protective order. *See* Tex. R. Civ. P. 192.6(a); *see, e.g.*, **In re Garza**, 544 S.W.3d 836, 841–42 (Tex.2018) (P and nonparty custodians of records had independent rights to seek protection from discovery subpoena). If a party moves for a protective order, the party seeking the discovery should file a motion to compel rather than a response to the motion for protective order. *See* **Pace v. Jordan**, 999 S.W.2d 615, 622 (Tex.App.—Houston [1st Dist.] 1999, pet. denied). See "After objection to discovery," ch. 6-A, §22.1.8; **O'Connor's Texas Civil Forms**, FORM 6A:24 (2020 ed.). A person should not seek a protective order when an objection or a claim of privilege is more appropriate. Tex. R. Civ. P. 192.6(a).

§20.1 Grounds to limit scope of discovery. Under TRCP 192.4, the trial court has the authority to limit the scope of discovery. Tex. R. Civ. P. 192 cmt. 7. A person may file a motion for protective order for the following reasons:

1. Undue burden. A person may ask for protection from a discovery request that is unduly burdensome, annoying to produce, or unnecessarily expensive. Tex. R. Civ. P. 176.7 (undue burden of subpoena), Tex. R. Civ. P. 192.4 (limitations on scope of discovery), Tex. R. Civ. P. 192.6(b) (order to protect movant from undue burden, expense, or annoyance); **In re Alford Chevrolet-Geo**, 997 S.W.2d 173, 181 (Tex.1999) (same). The person resisting discovery has the burden to plead and prove that the request will impose an undue burden. **ISK Biotech Corp. v. Lindsay**, 933 S.W.2d 565, 568–69 (Tex.App.—Houston [1st Dist.] 1996, orig. proceeding); **Tjernagel v. Roberts**, 928 S.W.2d 297, 302 (Tex.App.—Amarillo 1996, orig. proceeding). To prove undue burden, the person resisting discovery must do more than make conclusory allegations that the requested discovery is unduly burdensome. **In re Alford Chevrolet-Geo**, 997 S.W.2d at 181; *see, e.g.*, **In re Amaya**, 34 S.W.3d 354, 358–59 (Tex.App.—Waco 2001, orig. proceeding) (no evidence was produced to show undue burden). The person cannot rely on problems in retrieving documents caused by the way she filed them in her own records. **ISK Biotech**, 933 S.W.2d at 569. Once the person resisting discovery proves that the request for discovery is unduly burdensome, the person requesting discovery must show that it is not. **Forward v. Housing Auth.**, 864 S.W.2d 167, 169 (Tex.App.—Tyler 1993, no writ); *see also* Tex. R. Civ. P. 191.3(c)(4) (signature on discovery request is certification that request is not unduly burdensome). A request is unduly burdensome when the discovery is any of the following:

(1) Duplicative. The discovery is unreasonably cumulative or duplicative. Tex. R. Civ. P. 192.4(a); *see* **Walker v. Packer**, 827 S.W.2d 833, 843 (Tex.1992) (discovery that compels production of patently irrelevant or duplicative documents can constitute undue burden).

(2) Obtainable from alternative source. The discovery can be obtained from some other source that is more convenient, less burdensome, or less expensive. Tex. R. Civ. P. 192.4(a); **Brewer & Pritchard, P.C. v. Johnson**, 167 S.W.3d 460, 466 (Tex.App.—Houston [14th Dist.] 2005, pet. denied); *e.g.*, **In re Arras**, 24 S.W.3d 862, 864 (Tex.App.—El Paso 2000, orig. proceeding) (deposition of nonparty for addresses of other parties was inconvenient and burdensome).

(3) Not proportional. The discovery is not proportional to the needs of the case. *See* Tex. R. Civ. P. 192.4(b); **In re State Farm Lloyds**, 520 S.W.3d 595, 599 (Tex.2017). See "Proportional," ch. 6-B, §2.1.1(2).

2. Harassing. A person may ask for protection from a discovery request that is harassing. *See* Tex. R. Civ. P. 192.6. By signing discovery requests, attorneys certify that the discovery is not sought for the purpose of harassment. Tex. R. Civ. P. 191.3(c)(3); *see also* Tex. R. Civ. P. 199.5(h) (attorney cannot ask deposition questions solely to harass or mislead the witness), Tex. R. Civ. P. 215.3 (harassing discovery request is ground for sanctions).

3. Overbroad. A person may ask for protection from a discovery request that is overbroad. Generally, an overbroad request for documents is merely a "fishing expedition" into the other party's files, which is prohibited. **In re American Optical Corp.**, 988 S.W.2d 711, 713 (Tex.1998); **Dillard Dept. Stores v. Hall**, 909 S.W.2d 491, 492 (Tex.1995); **Loftin v. Martin**, 776 S.W.2d 145, 148 (Tex.1989); *see also* **Texaco, Inc. v. Dominguez**, 812 S.W.2d 451, 455–56 (Tex.App.—San Antonio 1991, orig. proceeding) (trial court cannot permit party to search through other party's records to make sure that party produced all requested documents). When a request asks for "all documents," the party may object to the request as overbroad and refuse to comply with it entirely, or the party may file a motion for protective order. *See* Tex. R. Civ. P. 192.6(a) (protective order), Tex. R. Civ. P. 193 cmt. 2 (object and refuse to comply). When an overbroad request asks for irrelevant information, the party is not required to detail its objections to the request; an overbroad request for irrelevant information is improper whether it is burdensome or not. **In re Allstate Cty. Mut. Ins.**, 227 S.W.3d 667, 670 (Tex.2007); *see* **In re National Lloyds Ins.**, 449 S.W.3d 486, 488 (Tex.2014).

(1) Overbroad request. The following are examples of overbroad requests: • Request for all e-mails and other correspondence related to reports covering insurance claims that were in different counties, occurred on different dates, and were for different causes of loss than the claims at issue. **In re National Lloyds Ins.**, 507 S.W.3d 219, 225–26 (Tex.2016). • Request for all claim files from the past year for storm-damaged properties of unrelated third parties involving the same adjusting firms that handled the plaintiff's claims. **In re National Lloyds**, 449 S.W.3d at 488–89. • Request to depose expert witnesses' corporate representatives on financial information for all cases their companies handled for defendant and other automobile manufacturers over a 12-year period. **In re Ford Motor Co.**, 427 S.W.3d 396, 397 (Tex.2014). • Request for approximately 20,000 pages of documents relating to defects in products that were not at issue in the case. **In re Graco Children's Prods.**, 210 S.W.3d 598, 600–01 (Tex.2006). • Request to identify all the defendant's safety employees over a 30-year period. **In re CSX Corp.**, 124 S.W.3d 149, 153 (Tex.2003). • Request for almost every document related to asbestos products that the defendant produced over a 50-year period. **In re American Optical**, 988 S.W.2d at 713. • Request for all information about criminal conduct at one store for seven years. **K Mart Corp. v. Sanderson**, 937 S.W.2d 429, 431 (Tex.1996).

(2) Limited request. A request for "any and all" documents is generally not overbroad if it is limited by time, location, or scope or if it is restricted to a type or class of documents. *See* **In re National Lloyds**, 507 S.W.3d at 225–26; **In re National Lloyds**, 449 S.W.3d at 489; **In re Allstate**, 227 S.W.3d at 669; **Texaco, Inc. v. Sanderson**, 898 S.W.2d 813, 815 (Tex.1995); **In re Patel**, 218 S.W.3d 911, 915 (Tex.App.—Corpus Christi 2007, orig. proceeding). The underlying information is not discoverable, however, merely because the request is limited. **In re National Lloyds**, 449 S.W.3d at 489–90. The request should be tailored to documents related to the litigated dispute. *See id.* at 488; **In re Allstate**, 227 S.W.3d at 670.

4. Invades protected rights. A person may ask for protection from a discovery request that is an invasion of personal, constitutional, or property rights. Tex. R. Civ. P. 192.6(b); *see* **Hoffman v. Fifth Ct. of Appeals**, 756 S.W.2d 723, 723 (Tex.1988).

5. Temporary protection. A person may ask for temporary protection from discovery pending the resolution of threshold issues like venue, jurisdiction, forum non conveniens, and official immunity. **In re Alford Chevrolet-Geo**, 997 S.W.2d at 181.

§20.2 Procedure for motion.

1. File timely. A motion for protective order should be filed as soon as the person realizes a protective order is necessary and before the deadline to produce the requested discovery. *See* Tex. R. Civ. P. 192.6(a); *see, e.g.*, **Bohmfalk v. Linwood**, 742 S.W.2d 518, 520 (Tex.App.—Dallas 1987, no writ) (party waived inadequate notice of deposition because party did not file motion for protective order to reschedule it). See "Timely objection," ch. 6-A, §18.1.1.

2. Withhold information. The person must withhold the information subject to the motion for protective order. In most cases, a party must partially comply with a written-discovery request. See "Burden to partially comply," ch. 6-A, §18.10.

3. Attach evidence. To support the motion, the person should attach affidavits, discovery pleadings, or other necessary documents. *See* Tex. R. Civ. P. 193.4(a), 199.6. See "Burden to provide evidence," ch. 6-A, §18.7; "In camera inspection," ch. 6-A, §18.8. The person "must show particular, specific and demonstrable injury by facts sufficient to justify a protective order." **Masinga v. Whittington**, 792 S.W.2d 940, 940 (Tex.1990); **In re Amaya**, 34 S.W.3d 354, 356–57 (Tex.App.—Waco 2001, orig. proceeding); *see also* **In re Collins**, 286 S.W.3d 911, 919 (Tex.2009) (health-care-liability claimants seeking protective order for information released under CPRC §74.052(c) have same burden as parties seeking protective order for ordinary discovery).

§20.3 Order. Generally, the person seeking discovery should secure a hearing and a ruling on an objection to discovery, but there are exceptions. See "Burden to secure hearing & ruling," ch. 6-A, §18.6. The trial court has broad discretion to protect a person with a protective order. *See* Tex. R. Civ. P. 192.6(b); **Axelson, Inc. v. McIlhany**, 798 S.W.2d 550, 553 (Tex.1990). The court may protect the person by ordering any of the relief listed in TRCP 192.6(b), but it is not limited by that list.

1. Limit scope of discovery. The protective order may provide that the requested discovery not be sought in whole or in part, or it may limit the extent or subject matter of discovery. Tex. R. Civ. P. 192.6(b)(1), (b)(2). For example, the court can strike certain subject areas from a notice of deposition if it determines that they are not relevant. *See* **Lindsey v. O'Neill**, 689 S.W.2d 400, 403 (Tex.1985). The court can also redact privileged or sensitive information from documents to be produced. **R.K. v. Ramirez**, 887 S.W.2d 836, 843 (Tex.1994); **M.A.W. v. Hall**, 921 S.W.2d 911, 916 (Tex.App.—Houston [14th Dist.] 1996, orig. proceeding).

2. Specify procedure for discovery. The protective order may provide that the discovery not be undertaken at the time or place specified. Tex. R. Civ. P. 192.6(b)(3). The protective order may specify the terms, conditions, methods, and time and place of the discovery. Tex. R. Civ. P. 192.6(b)(4).

3. Seal or limit distribution of discovery. The protective order may seal or limit the distribution of discovery to the parties. Tex. R. Civ. P. 192.6(b)(5); *see, e.g.*, **In re Ford Motor Co.**, 211 S.W.3d 295, 300–01 (Tex.2006) (protective order provided that certain documents would not be disclosed or distributed).

4. Limits of protective order.

(1) Sealing court records. A court cannot use a protective order to bypass the requirements of TRCP 76a. *See* Tex. R. Civ. P. 192.6(b)(5). An order sealing or limiting the distribution of documents must be made on a showing of good cause and in accordance with the provisions of TRCP 76a. *See* Tex. R. Civ. P. 192.6(b)(5); **Chandler v. Hyundai Motor Co.**, 829 S.W.2d 774, 774–75 (Tex.1992); *see also* **Stroud v. VBFSB Holding**, 917 S.W.2d 75, 83 (Tex.App.—San Antonio 1996, writ denied) (stipulation and protective order did not constitute sealing order), *disapproved on other grounds*, **Agar Corp. v. Electro Circuits Int'l**, 580 S.W.3d 136 (Tex.2019). The person requesting the order to seal or limit distribution has the burden of proving the elements of TRCP 76a(1). **BP Prods. N. Am., Inc. v. Houston Chronicle Publ'g**, 263 S.W.3d 31, 35 (Tex.App.—Houston [1st Dist.] 2006, no pet.). See "Motion to Seal Court Records," ch. 5-L, §1 et seq.

(2) Preventing shared discovery. A court cannot render a protective order so broad that it prevents the sharing of discovery products with other litigants in other lawsuits. *See* **Garcia v. Peeples**, 734 S.W.2d 343, 348 (Tex.1987). Under the doctrine of shared discovery, the products of discovery may be disseminated to other litigants and potential

litigants. **Eli Lilly & Co. v. Marshall**, 850 S.W.2d 155, 160 (Tex.1993); *see, e.g.*, **Garcia**, 734 S.W.2d at 346–47 (P sought to share discovery from car manufacturer with other litigants involved in similar suits against other manufacturers).

§21. Motion to quash or modify subpoena

See "Objecting to trial & discovery subpoenas," ch. 1-L, §4; "Challenging nonparty discovery subpoena," ch. 6-I, §5.5; **O'Connor's Texas Civil Forms**, FORM 6A:13 (2020 ed.).

§22. Motion to compel discovery

A party is entitled to secure discovery from another party without court intervention. When the other party refuses to comply with a proper discovery request, the party seeking discovery may file a motion to compel the other party to respond. Tex. R. Civ. P. 215.1(b). See **O'Connor's Texas Civil Forms**, FORM 6A:24 (2020 ed.).

§22.1 Grounds. A party may file a motion to compel discovery and request a hearing in the following instances:

1. **Inadequate disclosures.** See "Objecting to responses," ch. 6-E, §2.5; "Objections," ch. 6-E, §3.7.

2. **Refusal to answer or appear at deposition.** See "To compel attendance," ch. 6-F, §7.6; "Motion to compel answer," ch. 6-F, §9.4.

3. **Inadequate answers to interrogatories.** See "Objecting to answers," ch. 6-G, §8.

4. **Inadequate responses to request for admissions.** See "Challenging the response," ch. 6-H, §5.

5. **Inadequate responses to request for production.** See "Compelling production & sanctions," ch. 6-I, §6.

6. **Inadequate responses to request to produce electronic information.** See "Motion to compel," ch. 6-C, §8.1.

7. **Refusal to follow agreed schedule.** When a party does not comply with a TRCP 11 agreement setting deadlines for discovery, the other party should file a motion to compel compliance. *See* **Sullivan v. Bickel & Brewer**, 943 S.W.2d 477, 484 (Tex.App.—Dallas 1995, writ denied).

8. **After objection to discovery.** When a party serves objections or claims of privilege to a discovery request or required disclosure or files a motion to quash or a motion for protective order, the party seeking discovery can either move for a hearing on the objections or file a motion to compel production, or both. *See* Tex. R. Civ. P. 193.4(a), 215.1(b); **McKinney v. National Un. Fire Ins.**, 772 S.W.2d 72, 75 (Tex.1989); *see, e.g.*, **Pace v. Jordan**, 999 S.W.2d 615, 622 (Tex.App.—Houston [1st Dist.] 1999, pet. denied) (Ps waived deposition because they did not get ruling on Ds' motion for protective order and did not file motion to compel).

Practice Tip

The advantage of filing a motion to compel, instead of merely requesting a hearing on the other party's objections, is that a motion to compel can include requests for expenses and attorney fees. See Tex. R. Civ. P. 215.1(d).

---

§22.2 Request for sanctions. The court can impose sanctions against a party for refusing to comply with proper discovery requests, regardless of whether the party has disobeyed an order compelling discovery. *See* Tex. R. Civ. P. 215.1(b). Thus, the party seeking discovery can include a motion for sanctions in its first motion to compel discovery. **Lewis v. Illinois Employers Ins.**, 590 S.W.2d 119, 120 (Tex.1979). A party may pursue sanctions instead of filing a motion to compel. *See* Tex. R. Civ. P. 215.1(b)(3)(D); **Adkins Servs. v. Tisdale Co.**, 56 S.W.3d 842, 845 (Tex.App.—Texarkana 2001, no pet.). See "Motion for Sanctions," ch. 5-K, §1 et seq.

§22.3 Request for expenses. The party seeking discovery should include a request for expenses, including attorney fees, in its motion to compel. *See* Tex. R. Civ. P. 215.1(d).

§22.4 Response to motion to compel. The party against whom the motion to compel was filed should always file a response. See **O'Connor's Texas Civil Forms**, FORM 6A:25 (2020 ed.). Under some local rules, failure to file a response

permits the court to conclude that there is no opposition to the relief sought in the motion. **Cire v. Cummings**, 134 S.W.3d 835, 844 (Tex.2004); *e.g.*, Harris Cty. Loc. R. 3.3.2 (district courts).

§22.5 Ruling.

1. Order. The court may either deny the motion to compel or grant the motion and order the responding party to answer the discovery requests, produce discovery, or appear for a deposition. See **O'Connor's Texas Civil Forms**, FORM 6A:26 (2020 ed.). In certain circumstances, the court may both grant and deny the motion in part.

2. Award of expenses. The court's discretion to award expenses to either the moving party or the responding party depends on whether the motion to compel is granted or denied.

(1) Motion granted. If the court grants the motion, the court, after giving the parties an opportunity for a hearing, must award the movant reasonable expenses, including attorney fees, unless the court finds that the respondent's opposition to the motion was substantially justified or that other circumstances make an award of expenses unjust. Tex. R. Civ. P. 215.1(d); *see* **Hanley v. Hanley**, 813 S.W.2d 511, 522 (Tex.App.—Dallas 1991, no writ). Expenses may be charged against the party or deponent whose conduct made the motion necessary, the party or attorney advising such conduct, or both. Tex. R. Civ. P. 215.1(d).

(2) Motion denied. If the court denies the motion, the court, after giving the parties an opportunity for a hearing, may award the responding party reasonable expenses, including attorney fees, unless the court finds that the making of the motion was substantially justified or that other circumstances make an award of expenses unjust. Tex. R. Civ. P. 215.1(d); *see* **Hood v. Edward D. Jones & Co.**, 277 S.W.3d 498, 500 (Tex.App.—El Paso 2009, pet. denied). Expenses may be charged against the movant or the attorney advising the motion. Tex. R. Civ. P. 215.1(d).

(3) Motion granted in part, denied in part. If the court grants the motion in part and denies it in part, the court may apportion the reasonable expenses among the parties and persons in a just manner. Tex. R. Civ. P. 215.1(d).

§23. Motion for discovery sanctions

Sanctions for discovery abuse are imposed to (1) secure compliance with the discovery rules, (2) deter other litigants from violating the discovery rules, (3) punish parties that violate the discovery rules, and (4) promote settlements. *See* **Schein v. American Rest. Grp.**, 852 S.W.2d 496, 497 (Tex.1993); **Chrysler Corp. v. Blackmon**, 841 S.W.2d 844, 849 (Tex.1992). See "Motion for Sanctions," ch. 5-K, §1 et seq.; **O'Connor's Texas Civil Forms**, FORM 6A:27 (2020 ed.).

§23.1 Standard for sanctions. See "Standards for imposing sanctions," ch. 5-K, §3.

§23.2 Motion.

1. Grounds. See "Discovery abuse," ch. 5-K, §5.1.

2. Persons who may be sanctioned. See "Persons who may be sanctioned," ch. 5-K, §4.

3. Permissible discovery sanctions. See "Sanctions for discovery abuse," ch. 5-K, §7.1.

4. Impermissible sanctions. See "Improper sanctions," ch. 5-K, §7.11.

§23.3 Response. See **O'Connor's Texas Civil Forms**, FORM 6A:28 (2020 ed.).

§23.4 Hearing. A party must be given notice and an opportunity to be heard before sanctions are imposed. The hearing on sanctions may be before the court or by submission. See "Hearing," ch. 5-K, §10.

§23.5 Order for sanctions. See "Order for discovery sanctions," ch. 5-K, §11.1; **O'Connor's Texas Civil Forms**, FORM 6A:29 (2020 ed.).

§24. Spoliation

Spoliation is the improper loss or destruction of relevant evidence. *See* **Brookshire Bros. v. Aldridge**, 438 S.W.3d 9, 13 (Tex.2014); **Wal-Mart Stores v. Johnson**, 106 S.W.3d 718, 721 (Tex.2003); **Cresthaven Nursing Residence v. Freeman**,

134 S.W.3d 214, 225 (Tex.App.—Amarillo 2003, no pet.); *see also* **Miner Dederick Constr., LLP v. Gulf Chem. & Metallurgical Corp.**, 403 S.W.3d 451, 467 (Tex.App.—Houston [1st Dist.] 2013) (spoliation can include altering evidence), *pet. denied*, 455 S.W.3d 164 (Tex.2015). A party that does not reasonably preserve discoverable evidence can impair the opposing party's ability to present its claims or defenses. **Brookshire Bros.**, 438 S.W.3d at 16; *see* **Johnson**, 106 S.W.3d at 721.

§24.1 Court determines whether spoliation occurred. The trial court—not the jury—must determine whether a party spoliated evidence and what remedy is appropriate. **Wackenhut Corp. v. Gutierrez**, 453 S.W.3d 917, 921 (Tex.2015); **Brookshire Bros. v. Aldridge**, 438 S.W.3d 9, 20 (Tex.2014); *see* **Trevino v. Ortega**, 969 S.W.2d 950, 954 (Tex.1998) (Baker, J., concurring). Because spoliation is an evidentiary concept, rather than a separate cause of action, and because spoliation is basically a type of discovery abuse, it is a matter to be resolved by the trial court. **Brookshire Bros.**, 438 S.W.3d at 19–20; **Telesis/Parkwood Ret. I, Ltd. v. Anderson**, 462 S.W.3d 212, 253 (Tex.App.—El Paso 2015, no pet.). The court can hold an evidentiary hearing before making its spoliation findings, but it must be outside the presence of the jury. **Brookshire Bros.**, 438 S.W.3d at 20.

§24.2 Analyzing spoliation—two-step process. In analyzing a spoliation claim, the trial court must use a two-step process: (1) the court must determine as a question of law whether a party spoliated evidence and (2) if the party did so, the court must assess an appropriate remedy. **Brookshire Bros. v. Aldridge**, 438 S.W.3d 9, 14 (Tex.2014).

1. Determining whether party spoliated evidence. To determine that a party spoliated evidence, the court must find that (1) the party had a duty to preserve the evidence and (2) the party breached that duty by not preserving the evidence. **Brookshire Bros.**, 438 S.W.3d at 20. The party requesting the evidence (i.e., the party alleging spoliation) has the burden to establish both duty and breach. *Id.*

(1) Requesting party's burden.

(a) Duty to preserve. The requesting party must show that the producing party (i.e., the alleged spoliator) had a duty to preserve the evidence. **Brookshire Bros.**, 438 S.W.3d at 20; **Wal-Mart Stores v. Johnson**, 106 S.W.3d 718, 722 (Tex.2003). See "Preservation of evidence," ch. 6-A, §3. For a discussion of preserving electronically stored evidence, see "Preservation," ch. 6-C, §3.2. The duty to preserve arises when a party knows or reasonably should know the following:

[1] There is a substantial chance a claim will be filed. **Brookshire Bros.**, 438 S.W.3d at 20; **Johnson**, 106 S.W.3d at 722. A party can anticipate a claim will be filed and be under a duty to preserve without receiving actual notice of a suit. *See* **IQ Holdings, Inc. v. Stewart Title Guar. Co.**, 451 S.W.3d 861, 867 (Tex.App.—Houston [1st Dist.] 2014, no pet.). But for there to be a "substantial chance" of a claim being filed, there must be more than a mere possibility or unwarranted fear of litigation. **Brookshire Bros.**, 438 S.W.3d at 20; **National Tank Co. v. Brotherton**, 851 S.W.2d 193, 204 (Tex.1993); *see also* **IQ Holdings**, 451 S.W.3d at 867 (objective standard is used to determine whether there is substantial chance of claim being filed).

[2] Evidence in the party's possession or control will be material and relevant to the claim. **Brookshire Bros.**, 438 S.W.3d at 20; **Johnson**, 106 S.W.3d at 722.

(b) Breach of duty. The requesting party must show that the producing party breached the duty to preserve material and relevant evidence. **Brookshire Bros.**, 438 S.W.3d at 20. The producing party breaches its duty to preserve evidence if it does not exercise reasonable care. *Id.*; *see* **Miner Dederick Constr., LLP v. Gulf Chem. & Metallurgical Corp.**, 403 S.W.3d 451, 466–67 (Tex.App.—Houston [1st Dist.] 2013) (producing party must exercise reasonable care in preserving evidence, which includes duty to not alter evidence's condition; extraordinary measures to preserve evidence are not necessary), *pet. denied*, 455 S.W.3d 164 (Tex.2015). The producing party's breach can be either intentional or negligent. **Brookshire Bros.**, 438 S.W.3d at 20; **Trevino v. Ortega**, 969 S.W.2d 950, 957 (Tex.1998) (Baker, J., concurring). See "Assess culpability," ch. 6-A, §24.2.2(1).

(2) Producing party's rebuttal. To rebut the spoliation claim, the producing party can do the following:

(a) Challenge requesting party's allegations. The producing party can challenge the requesting party's allegations (e.g., the requesting party did not establish that there was a duty to preserve evidence). See "Requesting party's burden," ch. 6-A, §24.2.1(1).

(b) Provide reasonable explanation. The producing party can provide a reasonable explanation for the loss or destruction of the evidence. For example, the producing party can show the following:

[1] Loss or destruction beyond its control. The producing party can show that the loss or destruction of the evidence was beyond its control. **Trevino**, 969 S.W.2d at 957 (Baker, J., concurring); *see* **Brookshire Bros.**, 438 S.W.3d at 21 n.8 (no breach of duty to preserve evidence if it is lost or destroyed through no fault of producing party, such as by act of God); *see, e.g.*, **Walker v. Thomasson Lumber Co.**, 203 S.W.3d 470, 477 (Tex.App.—Houston [14th Dist.] 2006, no pet.) (nonparty had possession and control of allegedly defective utility pole and destroyed it in ordinary course of business).

[2] Destruction in ordinary course of business. The producing party can show that it destroyed or discarded the evidence in the ordinary course of business, such as in compliance with a corporate retention policy, and thus it did not violate the duty to preserve evidence. *See* **Trevino**, 969 S.W.2d at 957 (Baker, J., concurring); *see, e.g.*, **Brumfield v. Exxon Corp.**, 63 S.W.3d 912, 920 (Tex.App.—Houston [14th Dist.] 2002, pet. denied) (videotapes were routinely recorded over after 30 days); **Ordonez v. M.W. McCurdy & Co.**, 984 S.W.2d 264, 273–74 (Tex.App.—Houston [1st Dist.] 1998, no pet.) (log books were thrown away under D's normal business practice, not to conceal them from P). But when a party's duty to preserve evidence arises before it destroys evidence, the fact that it followed a corporate retention policy will not justify the destruction. *E.g.*, **Adobe Land Corp. v. Griffin, L.L.C.**, 236 S.W.3d 351, 360 (Tex.App.—Fort Worth 2007, pet. denied) (D's duty to preserve evidence arose before it destroyed herbicide sample), *disapproved on other grounds*, **Brookshire Bros. v. Aldridge**, 438 S.W.3d 9 (Tex.2014).

Note

In ***Brookshire Bros.***, *the Court suggested that a reasonable document (or other evidentiary) retention policy that is of limited duration may be a sufficient explanation for the destruction of evidence that would immunize a party from a spoliation finding. See* ***Brookshire Bros.***, *438 S.W.3d at 27 n.19; id. at 30–31 (Guzman, Devine, Brown, JJ., dissenting). The Court, however, did not address the reasonableness of the corporate defendant's retention policy because it was not challenged.* ***Brookshire Bros.***, *438 S.W.3d at 27 n.19. The dissent argued that the majority's spoliation framework will open the door to corporations shielding themselves from spoliation liability by establishing limited-duration corporate retention policies. Id. at 38 (Guzman, Devine, Brown, JJ., dissenting). To avoid potential spoliation issues, attorneys should review their clients' retention policies and make sure they can explain how those policies comply with the duty to preserve evidence. See "Preparing for electronic discovery," ch. 6-C, §3.*

---

2. Assessing appropriate remedy. If the court determines that a party has spoliated evidence, the court must assess and impose an appropriate remedy. **Brookshire Bros.**, 438 S.W.3d at 14. That is, the court must assess the culpability of the producing party, evaluate any prejudice suffered by the requesting party, and impose a remedy. *Id.*

(1) Assess culpability. Before imposing a remedy, the court must assess the culpability of the producing party. *See* **Brookshire Bros.**, 438 S.W.3d at 21. In assessing culpability, the court must determine whether the producing party acted intentionally or negligently. *See id.* at 21–22. This determination affects the type of remedy the court can impose. *See id.* at 21. See "Types of remedies," ch. 6-A, §24.2.2(3)(b).

(a) Intentional spoliation. Intentional spoliation, also referred to as bad-faith or willful spoliation, occurs when a party acts with a subjective purpose to conceal or destroy discoverable evidence. **Brookshire Bros.**, 438 S.W.3d at 24. Intentional spoliation includes "willful blindness," which occurs when a party allows for the destruction of relevant and discoverable evidence, although the party does not directly destroy the evidence. *Id.*

Note

Willful blindness can be difficult to assess in the context of automatic electronic deletion systems, especially when a potential party controls large volumes of electronic information and is trying to determine

before litigation what information may be discoverable. ***Brookshire Bros.****, 438 S.W.3d at 24 n.17. See "Note," ch. 6-A, §24.2.1(2)(b)[2]. For a discussion of electronic discovery, see "Electronic Discovery," ch. 6-C, §1 et seq.*

(b) Negligent spoliation. Negligent spoliation occurs when a party conceals or destroys discoverable evidence but does not deliberately do so. *See* **Brookshire Bros.**, 438 S.W.3d at 23. The party lacks the state of mind of a "wrongdoer." *Id.*

(2) Evaluate prejudice. Before imposing a remedy, the court must evaluate any prejudice suffered by the requesting party. *See* **Brookshire Bros.**, 438 S.W.3d at 21 & n.9. In assessing prejudice, the court must look at the following factors:

(a) Relevance & harm. The court must look at (1) the relevance of the missing evidence to key issues in the case and (2) whether the missing evidence was harmful to the producing party's case or whether it would have been helpful to the requesting party's case. **Brookshire Bros.**, 438 S.W.3d at 21; *see* **Trevino**, 969 S.W.2d at 958 (Baker, J., concurring). A party's intentional spoliation of evidence, without any contradictory evidence, may be sufficient to support a finding that the missing evidence is relevant and harmful to the producing party. **Brookshire Bros.**, 438 S.W.3d at 22. A party's negligent spoliation of evidence, however, cannot support those findings without some proof—which can be circumstantial—of what the missing evidence would show. *Id.* at 22 & n.12; *see* **Trevino**, 969 S.W.2d at 958 (Baker, J., concurring).

(b) Other evidence. The court must look at whether there is other competent evidence available to replace the missing evidence. **Brookshire Bros.**, 438 S.W.3d at 21–22; **Trevino**, 969 S.W.2d at 958 (Baker, J., concurring). This factor accounts for whether the missing evidence is cumulative of other competent evidence. **Brookshire Bros.**, 438 S.W.3d at 21–22. The court must be cautious when evaluating this factor because the mere presence of other evidence does not automatically mean there is no prejudice. *See id.* at 22. For example, the court could still find prejudice even though there is eyewitness testimony in addition to a destroyed videotape because the eyewitness may be biased or may not accurately remember the events as they occurred—issues that would not be present with the videotape. *Id.* Thus, the type and quality of the available evidence compared to the missing evidence is critical in analyzing prejudice. *Id.*

(3) Impose remedy. After assessing the culpability of the producing party and evaluating the prejudice to the requesting party, the court can impose an appropriate remedy. *See* **Brookshire Bros.**, 438 S.W.3d at 21.

(a) Standard. The remedy must be directly related to the spoliation and not be excessive. **Brookshire Bros.**, 438 S.W.3d at 21. That is, the remedy for spoliation must be proportionate to the culpability of the producing party and the prejudice to the requesting party. *Id.*; *see* **TransAmerican Nat. Gas Corp. v. Powell**, 811 S.W.2d 913, 917 (Tex.1991). See "Regular sanctions," ch. 5-K, §3.1.

(b) Types of remedies.

[1] Sanctions. The court can impose sanctions on the producing party. **Brookshire Bros.**, 438 S.W.3d at 21. Sanctions available for discovery abuse under TRCP 215.2 and 215.3 are available to a court when imposing a remedy for spoliation. **Brookshire Bros.**, 438 S.W.3d at 21. See "Sanctions for discovery abuse," ch. 5-K, §7.1. Sanctions can include an award of attorney fees and costs, the exclusion of evidence, striking a party's pleadings, or dismissing a party's claims. **Brookshire Bros.**, 438 S.W.3d at 21; *see* **Trevino**, 969 S.W.2d at 959–60 (Baker, J., concurring) (courts generally exclude evidence when producing party attempts to admit evidence or testimony related to destroyed evidence); *see, e.g.*, **Cire v. Cummings**, 134 S.W.3d 835, 843 (Tex.2004) (P's pleadings struck because she deliberately destroyed evidence after court ordered production); **Daniel v. Kelley Oil Corp.**, 981 S.W.2d 230, 235 (Tex.App.—Houston [1st Dist.] 1998, pet. denied) (P's pleadings struck because she intentionally fabricated false evidence by altering audiotapes). Sanctions that are similar to death-penalty sanctions, such as dismissing a party's claims or defenses, can be imposed only in the same manner as would a spoliation jury instruction—that is, only if the producing party acted intentionally or the requesting party was irreparably prevented from presenting a claim or defense. **Petroleum Solutions, Inc. v. Head**, 454 S.W.3d 482, 489 (Tex.2014).

[2] Spoliation jury instruction. The court can give a spoliation instruction for the jury to presume that the missing evidence is relevant and harmful to the producing party. *See* **Brookshire Bros.**, 438 S.W.3d at 22. A spolia-

tion instruction, which is inherently a sanction, can operate as a death-penalty sanction because it likely tilts a trial in favor of the requesting party by shifting the focus of the case from the merits to the improper conduct. **Petroleum Solutions**, 454 S.W.3d at 489; **Brookshire Bros.**, 438 S.W.3d at 22–23; *see* **Johnson**, 106 S.W.3d at 724. See "Death-penalty sanctions," ch. 5-K, §3.2. Thus, a spoliation instruction can be imposed only in certain circumstances and should be used cautiously. **Brookshire Bros.**, 438 S.W.3d at 23. Before imposing the spoliation instruction, the court must find that there is no lesser sanction that would be sufficient to minimize the prejudice caused by the producing party. *Id.* at 25. See "Necessary severity," ch. 5-K, §3.1.2; "Typical misconduct," ch. 5-K, §3.2.3(1).

Note

Although the Court in ***Brookshire Bros.*** *determined when a spoliation instruction may be given, it did not provide guidance on the specific language that the instruction should contain. Texas Pattern Jury Charges—General Negligence, Intentional Personal Torts & Workers' Compensation (2018), PJC 1.13 cmt.; Simmons, The Dog Ate My Evidence: Spoliation Under the New Texas Framework, Advanced Civil Trial Course, State Bar of Texas CLE, ch. 15, p. 8 (2016). The Texas Pattern Jury Charge, however, provides the following instruction: "{Name of spoliating party} {destroyed/failed to preserve/destroyed or failed to preserve} {describe evidence}. You {must/may} consider that this evidence would have been unfavorable to {name of spoliating party} on the issue of {describe issue(s) to which evidence would have been relevant}." PJC 1.13; see* ***Mercedes-Benz USA, LLC v. Carduco, Inc.****, 562 S.W.3d 451, 486 (Tex.App.—Corpus Christi 2016) (memo op.), rev'd on other grounds, 583 S.W.3d 553 (Tex.2019). Whether "must" or "may" is used should be based on the facts as applied to the spoliation standards set out in* ***Brookshire Bros.*** *PJC 1.13 cmt.*

[a] Generally—intentional spoliation. For a spoliation instruction to be an appropriate remedy, the court generally must find that the producing party intentionally spoliated evidence. *E.g.*, **Brookshire Bros.**, 438 S.W.3d at 23 (although D saved only eight minutes of video footage, it ran from when P entered store until after his fall; spoliation instruction improper because no evidence that D saved only that footage to intentionally conceal relevant evidence); *see* **Wackenhut Corp. v. Gutierrez**, 453 S.W.3d 917, 921 (Tex.2015); **Petroleum Solutions**, 454 S.W.3d at 489. For the meaning of intentional spoliation, see "Assess culpability," ch. 6-A, §24.2.2(1). Because the instruction is based on a presumption of wrongdoing, the court will not infer that a party who only negligently spoliated evidence did so because the evidence was unfavorable to its case; a spoliation instruction in such a case would not be just or proportionate. *See* **Brookshire Bros.**, 438 S.W.3d at 23–24.

[b] Exception—negligent spoliation & inability to present claim. In rare situations, a spoliation instruction can be an appropriate remedy when the producing party only negligently spoliated evidence. **Brookshire Bros.**, 438 S.W.3d at 25–26. For a spoliation instruction to be an appropriate remedy in this situation, the court must find that the negligent spoliation irreparably prevented the requesting party from presenting a claim or defense. **Wackenhut Corp.**, 453 S.W.3d at 921; **Petroleum Solutions**, 454 S.W.3d at 489; **Brookshire Bros.**, 438 S.W.3d at 25–26; *see* **Johnson**, 106 S.W.3d at 721. In such a case, a spoliation instruction is not excessive. **Brookshire Bros.**, 438 S.W.3d at 25–26.

[3] Other remedy. The court can impose any other remedy it deems appropriate based on the facts of the case. **Brookshire Bros.**, 438 S.W.3d at 21.

§24.3 Admitting spoliation evidence at trial.

1. Generally—not admissible. Evidence bearing on issues of whether a party spoliated evidence or how culpable a party is generally cannot be admitted at trial because such evidence has no effect on facts that are of consequence to determining the action—that is, the evidence is not relevant. *See* **Petroleum Solutions, Inc. v. Head**, 454 S.W.3d 482, 488 (Tex.2014); **Brookshire Bros. v. Aldridge**, 438 S.W.3d 9, 26 (Tex.2014). See Brown & Rondon, **Texas Rules of Evidence Handbook**, Rule 401 (2021 ed.) (§B.1). At trial, the jury does not need to hear evidence that focuses on the producing party's breach and culpability and that is unrelated to the merits. **Brookshire Bros.**, 438 S.W.3d at 26. Such evidence is critical to the court's spoliation findings but has no bearing on issues to be resolved by the jury. *Id.* at 26–27.

2. Exception. Evidence bearing on certain spoliation issues can be admitted at trial if it relates to the substance of the lawsuit. *See* **Brookshire Bros.**, 438 S.W.3d at 26. For example, a party could offer indirect evidence to prove the contents of missing evidence that is relevant to a claim or defense, as long as the offered evidence is permitted under the TREs. **Brookshire Bros.**, 438 S.W.3d at 26.

§24.4 Review.

1. Generally. See "Review of discovery orders," ch. 6-A, §26.

2. Standard of review. The standard of review for a trial court's imposition of a spoliation remedy, including a spoliation jury instruction, is abuse of discretion. **Wackenhut Corp. v. Gutierrez**, 453 S.W.3d 917, 921 (Tex.2015); **Brookshire Bros. v. Aldridge**, 438 S.W.3d 9, 27 (Tex.2014); *see* **Wal-Mart Stores v. Johnson**, 106 S.W.3d 718, 723 (Tex.2003). When a court erroneously admits spoliation evidence or erroneously submits a spoliation instruction, the error is reversible if it probably caused the rendition of an improper judgment. **Knoderer v. State Farm Lloyds**, 515 S.W.3d 21, 39 (Tex.App.—Texarkana 2017, pet. denied); *see* Tex. R. App. P. 44.1(a), 61.1; **Brookshire Bros.**, 438 S.W.3d at 29. When a spoliation instruction is erroneously submitted, the likelihood of harm is substantial, particularly in a closely contested case. *E.g.*, **Knoderer**, 515 S.W.3d at 40–41 (spoliation was peripheral issue in case; harmless error); *see, e.g.*, **Brookshire Bros.**, 438 S.W.3d at 29 (case was closely contested, with significant emphasis on spoliation issue; harmful error).

§25. Waiver of sanctions, discovery & objections

§25.1 Waiver of sanctions. If a party does not get a pretrial ruling on known discovery misconduct that occurred before the trial, the party waives any claim for sanctions based on that misconduct. **Meyer v. Cathey**, 167 S.W.3d 327, 333 (Tex.2005); **Remington Arms Co. v. Caldwell**, 850 S.W.2d 167, 170 (Tex.1993). But if the misconduct involves failure to disclose information requested in discovery, the court can impose suitable trial sanctions, such as excluding testimony about the undisclosed information. *See* **Remington Arms**, 850 S.W.2d at 170–71.

§25.2 Waiver of discovery.

1. Discovery proponent. If a party seeking discovery does not ask for a hearing on the other party's objections or motion for protective order or on its own motion to compel, it waives its right to the requested discovery. *See, e.g.*, **Pace v. Jordan**, 999 S.W.2d 615, 622 (Tex.App.—Houston [1st Dist.] 1999, pet. denied) (party did not get ruling on other party's objections and did not file motion to compel).

2. Discovery opponent. A party resisting discovery waives its right to use, at a hearing or trial, information it withheld from discovery under a claim of privilege unless it first amends or supplements its discovery responses. Tex. R. Civ. P. 193.4(c).

§25.3 Waiver of objections & privileges. There are several ways a party can waive its claims of privilege, other objections to discovery, and even the right to requested discovery.

1. Did not comply with procedures. If a party does not comply with the procedures for resisting discovery, the party can waive its claims of privilege and other objections to the discovery. *See* Tex. R. Civ. P. 193.2(e). But a party does not waive a privilege if it mistakenly objects to a request for privileged information instead of complying with TRCP 193.3. See "Asserting privileges," ch. 6-A, §18.2.

(1) Did not timely respond or object.

(a) To discovery requests.

[1] Waiver. If a party does not timely respond to a discovery request, the party waives its objections to the request and must produce the discovery. *See* Tex. R. Civ. P. 193.1, 193.2(e); **In re National Lloyds Ins.**, 507 S.W.3d 219, 223 (Tex.2016); *see, e.g.*, **Hobson v. Moore**, 734 S.W.2d 340, 341 (Tex.1987) (D waived law-enforcement privilege because he filed late objections to interrogatories); **Villarreal v. Dominguez**, 745 S.W.2d 570, 572 (Tex.App.—Corpus Christi 1988, orig. proceeding) (D waived its privileges from discovery by not objecting to request for production).

[2] Exceptions. There are four exceptions to the rule of mandatory waiver for not timely responding to a discovery request:

[a] The parties agree to an extension, and the agreement meets the requirements of TRCP 11. Tex. R. Civ. P. 191.1; **Young v. Ray**, 916 S.W.2d 1, 3 (Tex.App.—Houston [1st Dist.] 1995, orig. proceeding); *see* **Remington Arms Co. v. Canales**, 837 S.W.2d 624, 625 (Tex.1992).

[b] The parties agree to an extension that affects an oral deposition, and the agreement is made part of the record of the deposition. Tex. R. Civ. P. 191.1.

[c] The court signs an order extending the time to respond to discovery. *Id.*; **Remington Arms**, 837 S.W.2d at 625; **Young**, 916 S.W.2d at 3.

[d] The party proves that it had good cause for not timely objecting. Tex. R. Civ. P. 193.2(e); **Remington Arms**, 837 S.W.2d at 625; **Young**, 916 S.W.2d at 3.

(b) To inadequate responses. If a party does not object before trial to the other party's discovery responses that it knows are inadequate, it waives the objection. *E.g.*, **Interceramic, Inc. v. South Orient R.R.**, 999 S.W.2d 920, 930 (Tex.App.—Texarkana 1999, pet. denied) (inadequate supplemental responses to discovery).

(c) To motion to compel. Under some local rules, if a party does not file a response to a motion to compel, the court can conclude that the party does not oppose the relief sought in the motion. **Cire v. Cummings**, 134 S.W.3d 835, 844 (Tex.2004); *e.g.*, Harris Cty. Loc. R. 3.3.2 (district courts).

(2) Did not respond correctly. If a party does not prove the elements of a privilege, the party can waive its claim. *See, e.g.*, **Dunn Equip., Inc. v. Gayle**, 725 S.W.2d 372, 374–75 (Tex.App.—Houston [14th Dist.] 1987, orig. proceeding) (P, objecting to discovery of its insurance company's file, waived privilege because it did not support claim with any evidence). If a party obscures valid objections with unfounded objections, the party waives its valid objections unless it can show good cause. Tex. R. Civ. P. 193.2(e).

(3) Abused discovery. If a party abuses discovery, the court may find that the party waived its discovery privileges and objections. **Occidental Chem. Corp. v. Banales**, 907 S.W.2d 488, 490 (Tex.1995); *e.g.*, **In re LaVernia Nursing Facility, Inc.**, 12 S.W.3d 566, 571 (Tex.App.—San Antonio 1999, orig. proceeding) (court found that D waived privilege by concealing records).

(4) Did not obtain ruling. If the party seeking discovery does not obtain a ruling on the objections or assertions of privilege, the party waives the right to the discovery. *See* Tex. R. Civ. P. 193.4(b), 199.6. The party resisting discovery does not waive its objections if they are not resolved before trial. Tex. R. Civ. P. 199.6.

2. Deliberately waived privilege.

(1) Disclosure generally.

(a) Voluntary disclosure or consent to disclosure. If a party voluntarily and deliberately discloses or consents to disclosure of "any significant part" of the privileged matter, it waives the privilege unless the disclosure itself was privileged. Tex. R. Evid. 511(a)(1); *see* Brown & Rondon, **Texas Rules of Evidence Handbook**, Rule 511 (2021 ed.) (n.897). In determining waiver by disclosure, the court should consider whether the producing party intended to waive the particular privilege, not whether it intended to produce the information. *See* Tex. R. Civ. P. 193.3(d) & cmt. 4.

(b) Testimony about character or character trait. If a party calls a person to whom privileged communications have been made to testify about the party's character or character trait, it waives the privilege to the extent the communications are relevant to the party's character or character trait. Tex. R. Evid. 511(a)(2).

(2) Disclosure in federal or state proceedings—attorney-related privileges. If a party discloses a communication or information covered by the attorney-client privilege or work-product protection in a federal or state proceeding or to a federal or state agency or office, the disclosure can result in a "subject-matter waiver"—that is, waiver of privilege for both disclosed and undisclosed information. Tex. R. Evid. 511(b)(1). Subject-matter waiver of an attorney-related privilege oc-

curs only when (1) the waiver is intentional, (2) the disclosed and undisclosed privileged information concern the same subject matter, and (3) the disclosed and undisclosed privileged information should in fairness be considered together. *Id.*

Note

The 2015 amendments to TRE 511 were designed to align Texas law with federal law on waiver of privilege by voluntary disclosure, with TRE 511(a) stating the general rule and TRE 511(b) incorporating the provisions of FRE 502. TRE 511 cmt. See Brown & Rondon, ***Texas Rules of Evidence Handbook****, Rule 511 (2021 ed.). Thus, courts may look to federal law for guidance in interpreting the rule. Cf.* ***Prairie View A&M Univ. v. Chatha****, 381 S.W.3d 500, 507 (Tex.2012) (court may look to federal law for guidance only when relevant provisions of federal law are analogous; case involved employment-discrimination claims under Texas Commission on Human Rights Act). For a discussion of FRE 502, see "Disclosure of privileged or protected information—attorney-related privileges,"* ***O'Connor's Federal Rules * Civil Trials****, ch. 6-A, §9.3.2 (2021 ed.).*

---

(3) Limits on waiver.

(a) Inadvertent disclosure. The inadvertent disclosure of privileged material does not automatically waive a claim of privilege if the procedure under TRCP 193.3(d) is followed. Tex. R. Civ. P. 193.3(d) & cmt. 4; Tex. R. Evid. 511(b)(2); *see* **In re Living Ctrs.**, 175 S.W.3d 253, 260 (Tex.2005). By using the snap-back provision in TRCP 193.3(d), a party can preserve the privilege for documents inadvertently disclosed to the other party. See "Use snap-back provision," ch. 6-A, §18.2.4.

Note

The Supreme Court has held that, unlike a failure to follow the procedures outlined in TRCP 193.3(d), missing the statutory deadline in the Public Information Act for requesting a ruling from the Attorney General on an exception to disclosure does not waive the attorney-client privilege. ***Paxton v. City of Dallas****, 509 S.W.3d 247, 263–64 (Tex.2017); see Tex. Gov't Code §§552.301(b), 552.302. The Court reasoned that TRCP 193.3(d) contemplates inadvertent but actual disclosure followed by conduct that is inconsistent with claiming the privilege.* ***Paxton****, 509 S.W.3d at 263. In* ***Paxton****, on the other hand, there was no disclosure, and the party made efforts to maintain the confidentiality of the information. Id. at 263–64. See "Public Information Act," ch. 6-B, §3.27.*

(b) Compelled disclosure. The disclosure of privileged material that was either compelled erroneously or made without an opportunity to claim the privilege does not waive a claim of privilege. Tex. R. Evid. 512; *see* **In re Office of the Atty. Gen.**, No. 02-13-00455-CV, 2014 WL 491684 (Tex.App.—Fort Worth 2014, orig. proceeding) (memo op.; 2-6-14) (allowing court to compel waiver would render any privilege vulnerable to forced waiver).

(c) In camera disclosure. The disclosure of privileged material for an in camera inspection does not waive a claim of privilege. **M.A.W. v. Hall**, 921 S.W.2d 911, 916 (Tex.App.—Houston [14th Dist.] 1996, orig. proceeding); **Johnson v. Casseb**, 722 S.W.2d 253, 256 (Tex.App.—San Antonio 1986, orig. proceeding).

(d) Parties' agreement—attorney-related privileges. The parties can enter into an agreement to limit the effect of waiver by disclosure between them in any state proceeding. *See* Tex. R. Evid. 511(b)(4). See **O'Connor's Texas Civil Forms**, FORM 6A:23 (2020 ed.). The agreement applies only to communications or information covered by the attorney-client privilege or work-product protection and is binding only on the parties to the agreement unless it is incorporated into a court order. Tex. R. Evid. 511(b)(4).

(e) Court order—attorney-related privileges. A federal or state court order providing that a communication or information covered by the attorney-client privilege or work-product protection is not waived by a disclosure connected to the litigation pending before that court is also not a waiver of the privilege or protection in a Texas state proceeding. Tex. R. Evid. 511(b)(3).

3. Disclosed materials to testifying expert. If a party discloses privileged materials to its own testifying expert, either deliberately or inadvertently, it waives the privilege. *See* **In re Christus Spohn Hosp. Kleberg**, 222 S.W.3d 434, 440–41 (Tex.2007). If the disclosure was inadvertent, the party must generally choose between waiving the privilege or replacing its testifying expert. See "Materials inadvertently disclosed to expert," ch. 6-D, §4.1.1(6)(b)[2]. In very limited circumstances, the party may be able to use the snap-back provision to retrieve the material. See "Invoke snap-back provision," ch. 6-D, §4.1.1(6)(b)[2][a].

4. Used document to refresh recollection. If a party uses documents to refresh the recollection of a witness, the documents are discoverable under certain circumstances. See Brown & Rondon, **Texas Rules of Evidence Handbook**, Rule 612 (2021 ed.).

(1) Before testifying. If the witness uses a document before testifying, the court may require that the document be produced. Tex. R. Evid. 612(a)(2), (b); **Goode v. Shoukfeh**, 943 S.W.2d 441, 449 (Tex.1997); **Portland S&L Ass'n v. Bernstein**, 716 S.W.2d 532, 541 (Tex.App.—Corpus Christi 1985, writ ref'd n.r.e.), *overruled on other grounds*, **Dawson-Austin v. Austin**, 968 S.W.2d 319 (Tex.1998). The waiver applies to the parts of the document that relate to the witness's testimony. *See* Tex. R. Evid. 612(b).

(2) While testifying. If the witness uses a document while testifying, the adverse party has a right to see it. Tex. R. Evid. 612(a)(1), (b); *see* **Goode**, 943 S.W.2d at 449; **City of Denison v. Grisham**, 716 S.W.2d 121, 123 (Tex.App.—Dallas 1986, orig. proceeding).

5. Waived privilege by offensive use. Under the doctrine of waiver by offensive use, a party cannot "use one hand to seek affirmative relief and with the other lower an iron curtain of silence" around the facts of the case. *E.g.*, **Ginsberg v. Fifth Ct. of Appeals**, 686 S.W.2d 105, 107–08 (Tex.1985) (P could not claim psychotherapist-patient privilege to exclude information that would assist D).

(1) Offensive-use doctrine. The Supreme Court set out the test for the application of the offensive-use doctrine in **Republic Ins. v. Davis**, 856 S.W.2d 158, 163 (Tex.1993) (attorney-client privilege), and restated it in **Texas DPS Officers Ass'n v. Denton**, 897 S.W.2d 757, 761 (Tex.1995) (5th Amendment privilege). Before a party waives a privilege by offensive use, the court must determine that (1) the party is seeking affirmative relief, (2) the evidence the party refuses to produce is outcome-determinative, and (3) there is no alternative source for the evidence. *E.g.*, **Denton**, 897 S.W.2d at 761 (privilege waived because party seeking evidence met all three elements); **TransAmerican Nat. Gas Corp. v. Flores**, 870 S.W.2d 10, 11–12 (Tex.1994) (trial court should not have found waiver because party seeking evidence met only first element); **Republic Ins.**, 856 S.W.2d at 164 (privilege not waived because party seeking evidence did not meet first element since declaratory-judgment action is not request for affirmative relief); *see also* **In re M-I L.L.C.**, 505 S.W.3d 569, 579 (Tex.2016) (offensive-use doctrine not implicated when privilege holder conceded trade secrets were discoverable and simply wanted to prevent disclosure during temporary-injunction hearing). If the party seeking evidence proves all three elements, the party asserting the privilege must decide whether to continue to assert the privilege or to abandon it and produce the evidence. *See* **Denton**, 897 S.W.2d at 761.

(2) Remedial action. If the party continues to assert the privilege even after the party seeking the evidence proves all three elements of the test, the court must take some remedial action. For example, the court may limit the discovery inquiry, restrict the evidence the party asserting the privilege introduces on the subject, delay the trial (when the Fifth Amendment privilege is asserted), and ultimately, if the party asserting the privilege is the plaintiff, dismiss the suit. **Denton**, 897 S.W.2d at 763. The court must consider a number of factors before forcing the party resisting discovery to choose between its privilege and the suit. *Id.* For a list of factors affecting the choice of remedies, *see* **Denton**, 897 S.W.2d at 763.

§26. Review of discovery orders

§26.1 Review by appeal. Most orders relating to discovery disputes are reviewed on appeal after final judgment. *See* **Walker v. Packer**, 827 S.W.2d 833, 842 (Tex.1992); *see, e.g.*, **Vega v. Davila**, 31 S.W.3d 376, 378 (Tex.App.—Corpus Christi 2000, no pet.) (court had jurisdiction to hear appeal from order overruling motion to quash subpoena for deposition). The standard for review of a discovery order is abuse of discretion. **Ford Motor Co. v. Castillo**, 279 S.W.3d 656, 661 (Tex.2009). A trial court abuses its discretion when it reaches a result so arbitrary and unreasonable that it amounts to a clear and prejudicial error of law. **Ford Motor**, 279 S.W.3d at 661; **Walker**, 827 S.W.2d at 839.

§26.2 Review by mandamus. Most orders relating to discovery disputes cannot be reviewed by mandamus. The appellate courts will grant a petition for writ of mandamus only if the following conditions are met:

1. Abuse of discretion. The trial court clearly abused its discretion in making a discretionary ruling. **In re Prudential Ins.**, 148 S.W.3d 124, 135 (Tex.2004); *see* **In re National Lloyds Ins.**, 532 S.W.3d 794, 802–03 (Tex.2017) (abuse of discretion for trial court to compel production of irrelevant information or information that is relevant but privileged); **In re Rescue Concepts, Inc.**, 556 S.W.3d 331, 338 (Tex.App.—Houston [1st Dist.] 2017, orig. proceeding) (same). The party seeking mandamus must show that the trial court's discovery ruling was so arbitrary and unreasonable as to amount to a clear and prejudicial error of law. **In re Christus Santa Rosa Health Sys.**, 492 S.W.3d 276, 279 (Tex.2016); **Walker v. Packer**, 827 S.W.2d 833, 839 (Tex.1992). That is, the party must show the appellate court that the trial court acted without reference to any guiding rules and principles. **In re Colonial Pipeline Co.**, 968 S.W.2d 938, 941 (Tex.1998).

2. No adequate remedy by appeal. There is no adequate remedy by appeal. **In re Dana Corp.**, 138 S.W.3d 298, 301 (Tex.2004); **Walker**, 827 S.W.2d at 842; *e.g.*, **In re Deere & Co.**, 299 S.W.3d 819, 820 (Tex.2009) (mandamus was proper because discovery order requiring D to produce documents from an indefinite time period was overbroad); *see, e.g.*, **In re Weekley Homes, L.P.**, 295 S.W.3d 309, 322–23 (Tex.2009) (harm from ordering access to party's computer hard drive could not be remedied on appeal); **In re Bay Area Citizens Against Lawsuit Abuse**, 982 S.W.2d 371, 375 (Tex.1998) (no adequate remedy by appeal because discovery orders violated First Amendment rights). An appellate remedy is adequate when the detriments of mandamus review outweigh the benefits. **In re Prudential**, 148 S.W.3d at 136. Whether an appellate remedy is adequate depends on the circumstances. *Id.* at 137. In **Walker**, the Supreme Court identified three discovery situations where a party does not have an adequate appellate remedy for an erroneous ruling by the trial court. **Walker**, 827 S.W.2d at 843–44; *see also* **In re McAllen Med. Ctr., Inc.**, 275 S.W.3d 458, 468 (Tex.2008) (situations where appellate remedy is inadequate are not limited to those identified in **Walker**).

(1) When the appellate court cannot cure the trial court's discovery error. **In re Christus Santa Rosa Health**, 492 S.W.3d at 279; **Walker**, 827 S.W.2d at 843. This happens when the trial court erroneously orders the disclosure of privileged information that will materially affect the rights of the aggrieved party, such as attorney-client privileged information. **Walker**, 827 S.W.2d at 843; *see* **In re Christus Santa Rosa Health**, 492 S.W.3d at 279 (mandamus appropriate when trial court does not conduct adequate in camera inspection of allegedly privileged documents before compelling production when inspection is critical to evaluating privilege claim); *see also* **In re Perry**, 60 S.W.3d 857, 858 (Tex.2001) (mandamus appropriate to prevent disclosure of information protected by legislative immunity). This also happens when the discovery order imposes a burden on the producing party far out of proportion to any benefit to the requesting party. **Walker**, 827 S.W.2d at 843; *see* **In re Weekley Homes**, 295 S.W.3d at 322.

(2) When the party's ability to present a viable claim or defense at trial is severely compromised by the trial court's discovery error. **In re Allied Chem. Corp.**, 227 S.W.3d 652, 658 (Tex.2007); **Montalvo v. Fourth Ct. of Appeals**, 917 S.W.2d 1, 2 (Tex.1995); **Walker**, 827 S.W.2d at 843. The party seeking mandamus must show harm to prove lack of adequate remedy by appeal. **Montalvo**, 917 S.W.2d at 2. The delay, inconvenience, or expense of an appeal is not sufficient harm. **Walker**, 827 S.W.2d at 843. Denial of discovery that goes to the heart of the party's case may be sufficient harm. **In re Allied Chem.**, 227 S.W.3d at 658; **Walker**, 827 S.W.2d at 843; *see, e.g.*, **Peters v. Moore**, 835 S.W.2d 764, 768 (Tex.App.—Houston [14th Dist.] 1992, orig. proceeding) (mandamus available when court refused to permit experts to testify).

(3) When the trial court disallows discovery, the missing discovery cannot be made part of the appellate record, and the reviewing court is unable to evaluate the effect of the trial court's error. **Walker**, 827 S.W.2d at 843–44. If the procedures of TRCP 193.4 are followed, however, this situation should seldom arise. **Walker**, 827 S.W.2d at 844 (discussing former TRCP 166b(4)).

§26.3 Record. If evidence was received at the hearing on discovery, the party challenging the trial court's order must provide the appellate court with a reporter's record from the hearing. *See* Tex. R. App. P. 34.1, 34.6, 52.7(a)(2). For the record in an appeal, see "Record on Appeal," **O'Connor's Texas Civil Appeals**, ch. 6-A, §1 et seq. (2020 ed.); for the record in a mandamus proceeding, see "Record for petition for original writ," **O'Connor's Texas Civil Appeals**, ch. 10-A, §7 (2020 ed.). A reporter's record is not necessary if the trial court clearly based its order on the papers on file and the arguments of counsel. *See* **Otis Elevator Co. v. Parmelee**, 850 S.W.2d 179, 181 (Tex.1993). When a reporter's record is not necessary, the petitioner may file with the petition an affidavit attesting that no evidence was heard. See "Statement," **O'Connor's Texas Civil Appeals**, ch. 10-A, §7.1.2(2) (2020 ed.).

§26.4 Findings of fact. Findings of fact are helpful, but not required, when challenging the trial court's findings on discovery sanctions. See "Findings of fact are helpful," ch. 10-E, §2.2.

B. Scope of Discovery

§1. General

§1.1 Rule. Tex. R. Civ. P. 192.3.

§1.2 Purpose. The scope of discovery controls what information can and cannot be discovered. This subchapter discusses what is discoverable and what is not.

§1.3 Form. **O'Connor's Texas Civil Forms**, FORM 6B:1 (2020 ed.).

§1.4 Other references. Sedona Conference, *Sedona Conference Glossary: eDiscovery & Digital Information Management (Fifth Edition)*, 21 Sedona Conf.J. 263 (2020), thesedonaconference.org/publications; Browning, *Digging for the Digital Dirt: Discovery & Use of Evidence from Social Media Sites*, 14 SMU Sci. & Tech.L.Rev. 465 (2011); **O'Connor's Texas Causes of Action** (2021 ed.); **O'Connor's Texas Family Law Handbook** (2021 ed.); Brown & Rondon, **Texas Rules of Evidence Handbook** (2021 ed.).

§2. What is discoverable?

§2.1 Scope & limitations.

1. General rule. A party can seek discovery of unprivileged information that is relevant to the subject of the suit and proportional to the needs of the case. *See* Tex. R. Civ. P. 192.3(a), 192.4(b); **In re Turner**, 591 S.W.3d 121, 126 (Tex.2019); **In re North Cypress Med. Ctr. Oper. Co.**, 559 S.W.3d 128, 129 (Tex.2018); **In re National Lloyds Ins.**, 532 S.W.3d 794, 808 (Tex.2017); **In re State Farm Lloyds**, 520 S.W.3d 595, 599, 604 (Tex.2017); **In re CSX Corp.**, 124 S.W.3d 149, 152 (Tex.2003). Discovery can include evidence that may be inadmissible at trial as long as the information sought appears reasonably calculated to lead to the discovery of admissible evidence. Tex. R. Civ. P. 192.3(a); **In re Turner**, 591 S.W.3d at 126. While the scope of discovery is quite broad, it is confined by the subject matter of the case and the reasonable expectation of obtaining information that will help resolve the dispute. Tex. R. Civ. P. 192 cmt. 1; **In re CSX Corp.**, 124 S.W.3d at 152; *see* **In re American Optical Corp.**, 988 S.W.2d 711, 713 (Tex.1998) (court must impose reasonable discovery limits); **K Mart Corp. v. Sanderson**, 937 S.W.2d 429, 431 (Tex.1996) (discovery cannot be used to "fish" for evidence).

(1) Relevant. For information to be discoverable, it must be relevant to the suit. Tex. R. Civ. P. 192.3(a); *e.g.*, **In re North Cypress Med.**, 559 S.W.3d at 129 (information about hospital's negotiated reimbursement rates from private insurers and government programs was relevant to uninsured P's claim that rates hospital billed her for same services were unreasonable); **In re National Lloyds**, 532 S.W.3d at 808 (information in billing records of party opposing discovery was not, by itself, relevant to determining reasonableness of requesting party's attorney fees; information would be discoverable if opposing party relied on billing records to assess reasonableness of requesting party's fees or to recover its own attorney fees). Evidence is relevant if it has any tendency to make a fact of consequence more or less probable than it would be without the evidence. Tex. R. Evid. 401; **In re North Cypress Med.**, 559 S.W.3d at 131; **In re National Lloyds**, 532 S.W.3d at 808. A party must preserve evidence when it knows or reasonably should know that the evidence is relevant to litigation. See "Preservation of evidence," ch. 6-A, §3.

(2) Proportional. For information to be discoverable, the discovery request must be proportional to the needs of the case. *See* Tex. R. Civ. P. 192.4(b); **In re State Farm**, 520 S.W.3d at 599. A discovery request will be considered proportional if the burden or expense of the proposed discovery is justified when weighed against the following factors: (1) the likely benefit of the requested discovery, (2) the needs of the case, (3) the amount in controversy, (4) the parties' resources, (5) the importance of the issues at stake in the litigation, (6) the importance of the proposed discovery in resolving the litigation, (7) any other factor addressing jurisprudential concerns. **In re State Farm**, 520 S.W.3d at 608–11; *see* Tex. R. Civ. P. 192.4(b).

Note

In 2015, the FRCPs were amended to, among other things, move the proportionality considerations in former FRCP 26(b)(2)(C)(iii) to become part of the scope of discovery in FRCP 26(b)(1). See ***In re State Farm****, 520 S.W.3d at 614. The 2015 amendments did not change the existing responsibilities of the court and parties to consider proportionality; instead, the amendments highlighted the fact that, for information to be discoverable, there must be more than relevance—there must also be proportionality. See id. In line with the limitations on the scope of discovery found in TRCP 192.4, the Texas Supreme Court in* ***In re State Farm*** *provided for similar guiding principles, emphasizing that "proportionality is the polestar."* ***In re State Farm****, 520 S.W.3d at 615. Although the Court discussed the proportionality guidelines in the context of electronic-discovery disputes, it emphasized that all discovery is subject to proportionality considerations. See id. at 599. For a further discussion of the proportionality considerations in the electronic-discovery context, see "Factors," ch. 6-C, §6.1.2(2).*

(3) Reasonably calculated to lead to admissible evidence. For information to be discoverable, it must be admissible at trial or reasonably calculated to lead to the discovery of admissible evidence. *See* Tex. R. Civ. P. 192.3(a); **In re North Cypress Med.**, 559 S.W.3d at 129. For example, when a suit does not include a claim for exemplary damages, a defendant may object to a request for information about its net worth on the ground that the information is not within the scope of discovery because it is not calculated to lead to admissible evidence. *See* **Al Parker Buick Co. v. Touchy**, 788 S.W.2d 129, 130–31 (Tex.App.—Houston [1st Dist.] 1990, orig. proceeding).

2. Limitations on discovery. Even if a party seeks information that is relevant and proportional, there may be other limitations that affect whether the information is discoverable.

(1) Information is exempt. If the information is subject to a discovery exemption, it is not discoverable. See "What is not discoverable?," ch. 6-B, §3.

(2) Discovery procedure not permitted. If no discovery rule permits the type of discovery procedure involved, the information is not discoverable unless the court orders or the parties agree to the discovery procedure. *See* Tex. R. Civ. P. 191 & cmt. 1 (trial court may order or parties may agree to use discovery methods other than those prescribed in the rules). See "General Rules for Discovery," ch. 6-A, §1 et seq.

(3) Information is cumulative or obtainable from other source. If the requested information is cumulative or obtainable from a more convenient, less expensive, or less burdensome source, the court can limit discovery to prevent unwarranted delay and expense. Tex. R. Civ. P. 192.4(a) & cmt. 7. See "Grounds to limit scope of discovery," ch. 6-A, §20.1.

§2.2 Potential parties. The names, addresses, and telephone numbers of potential parties to the suit are discoverable. Tex. R. Civ. P. 192.3(i); *see* Tex. R. Civ. P. 192.5(c)(3), 194.2(b)(2); **Helfand v. Coane**, 12 S.W.3d 152, 157 n.3 (Tex.App.—Houston [1st Dist.] 2000, pet. denied).

§2.3 Party contentions. An opinion or contention relating to a fact or the application of the law to a fact is discoverable. Tex. R. Civ. P. 192.3(j); *see* Tex. R. Civ. P. 194.2(b)(3), 197.1. See "Contentions," ch. 6-E, §2.1.2(1)(c); "Contentions," ch. 6-E, §3.3.2(3); "Party contentions," ch. 6-G, §3.2.5.

§2.4 Party admissions. A party's statement of opinion, of fact, of the application of law to fact, or of the genuineness of a document described in the request (and attached or made available for inspection and copying) is discoverable through a request for admissions. Tex. R. Civ. P. 198.1. See "Requests for Admissions," ch. 6-H, §1 et seq.

§2.5 Party's statements. Some party statements are discoverable. Tex. R. Civ. P. 192.3(h). These statements, even if made or prepared in anticipation of litigation, are not protected by the work-product privilege. Tex. R. Civ. P. 192.5(c)(1).

1. Party as witness. A party's statements as a witness are discoverable. See "Witness statements," ch. 6-B, §2.6.

2. Party's statements from another suit. A party's statements contained in noncore work product in one suit may be discoverable in another suit. **Republic Ins. v. Davis**, 856 S.W.2d 158, 164–65 (Tex.1993). To be privileged, work product must be made in the same suit in which the privilege is being asserted. *Id.*; *see* Tex. R. Civ. P. 192.5(a)(2) (communication made in anticipation of litigation or trial).

§2.6 Witness statements. A witness statement is (1) a written statement signed, adopted, or approved in writing by the person making it, or (2) a stenographic, mechanical, electrical, or other type of recording of a witness's oral statement, or any substantially verbatim transcription of such a recording. Tex. R. Civ. P. 192.3(h). Notes taken by another person during a conversation or interview with a witness are not considered a witness statement. *Id.*

1. Discoverable. Witness statements, regardless of when they are made, are not protected from discovery by the work-product privilege. Tex. R. Civ. P. 192.5(c)(1); *see* **Spohn Hosp. v. Mayer**, 72 S.W.3d 52, 62 (Tex.App.—Corpus Christi 2001), *rev'd on other grounds*, 104 S.W.3d 878 (Tex.2003); **In re Team Transp.**, 996 S.W.2d 256, 259 (Tex.App.—Houston [14th Dist.] 1999, orig. proceeding). For example, a letter to a party's insurance carrier describing an accident, prepared by an employee who witnessed the accident, is discoverable. **In re Team Transp.**, 996 S.W.2d at 258–59; *see also* **In re Learjet Inc.**, 59 S.W.3d 842, 846 (Tex.App.—Texarkana 2001, orig. proceeding) (edited and unedited versions of videotaped witness statements, which were used in mediation, were discoverable). Most insurance companies call witnesses immediately after an accident and record their statements over the telephone. Those statements are discoverable. *See, e.g.*, **In re Jimenez**, 4 S.W.3d 894, 896 (Tex.App.—Houston [1st Dist.] 1999, orig. proceeding) (D's statement to carrier was discoverable); **In re W&G Trucking, Inc.**, 990 S.W.2d 473, 475 (Tex.App.—Beaumont 1999, orig. proceeding) (same); *see also* **In re Ford Motor Co.**, 988 S.W.2d 714, 719 (Tex.1998) (in case predating 1999 discovery rules, P's statement to insurance carrier was not protected from discovery because there was no attorney-client relationship between them). An insurance company cannot avoid producing these statements by hiring an attorney to conduct postaccident interviews. The work-product privilege does not permit an attorney to hide from discovery facts that were acquired by the attorney. **Owens-Corning Fiberglas Corp. v. Caldwell**, 818 S.W.2d 749, 750 n.2 (Tex.1991). The purpose of the work-product privilege is to shelter the mental processes of the attorney, not the facts about the case. *Id.* at 750 & n.2.

Practice Tip

When an attorney sends an investigator to talk to a witness, the attorney should instruct the investigator not to take a statement (recorded or signed) if the information is not favorable. When the information is not favorable, the investigator can simply prepare a memo stating the substance of the interview. That memo is not discoverable as a witness statement. Tex. R. Civ. P. 192.3(h).

2. Not discoverable. Witness statements are protected from discovery if they are shielded by some other objection or privilege (e.g., the attorney-client privilege). *See* Tex. R. Civ. P. 192 cmt. 9; **In re Fontenot**, 13 S.W.3d 111, 113 (Tex.App.—Fort Worth 2000, orig. proceeding). For example, a party's statement provided to its attorney is not discoverable because it is protected under TRE 503. *See, e.g.*, **In re Fontenot**, 13 S.W.3d at 114 (P's written narrative and confidential claim questionnaire, given by P to his attorneys, were not discoverable).

§2.7 Person's own statements. If a person (whether a party or a witness) made a statement about the subject matter of the litigation, that person is entitled to receive a copy of the statement from any party who has possession of it. Tex. R. Civ. P. 192.3(h). The person must make a written request for the copy. *Id.* See **O'Connor's Texas Civil Forms**, FORM 6B:1 (2020 ed.).

§2.8 Fact witnesses. A party may obtain discovery of the names, addresses, and telephone numbers of people with knowledge of relevant facts. Tex. R. Civ. P. 192.3(c); *see* **Smith v. Southwest Feed Yards**, 835 S.W.2d 89, 90 (Tex.1992). The reason for requiring the disclosure of the names, addresses, and telephone numbers is to allow the opposing party to locate, interview, and depose the witnesses. **$23,900 v. State**, 899 S.W.2d 314, 317 (Tex.App.—Houston [14th Dist.] 1995, no writ). The plain language of TRCP 192.3(c) and 192.5(c)(3) clearly indicates that information about the identity and location of people with knowledge of relevant facts can never be protected from discovery. **Giffin v. Smith**, 688 S.W.2d 112, 113 (Tex.1985) (under former TRCP 166b).

1. Who is a fact witness. A person has knowledge of relevant facts when that person has or may have knowledge of discoverable matters. Tex. R. Civ. P. 192.3(c); **Jamail v. Anchor Mortg. Servs.**, 809 S.W.2d 221, 223 (Tex.1991). The person does not need to have admissible information. Tex. R. Civ. P. 192.3(c); *see* **In re Team Transp.**, 996 S.W.2d 256, 259 (Tex.App.—Houston [14th Dist.] 1999, orig. proceeding). Personal knowledge is not required. Tex. R. Civ. P. 192.3(c); **In re Team Transp.**, 996 S.W.2d at 259. Fact witnesses include expert witnesses who have discoverable factual information. See "Types of experts," ch. 6-D, §2.

2. What is discoverable about fact witnesses. Information about fact witnesses is discoverable. Tex. R. Civ. P. 192.3(c) (scope of discovery), Tex. R. Civ. P. 192.5(c)(1) (exception to work-product privilege); *see* Tex. R. Civ. P. 194.2(b)(5) (disclosures). See "Disclosures," ch. 6-E, §1 et seq.

(1) Identity. A party is entitled to the name, address, and telephone number of any person with knowledge of relevant facts. Tex. R. Civ. P. 192.3(c), 194.2(b)(5); *see, e.g.*, **$23,900**, 899 S.W.2d at 316–17 (address of police headquarters was sufficient for officer, even though interrogatory also asked for residential address). See "Identify witness," ch. 6-E, §2.2.2(1)(e)[1]; "Fact witnesses," ch. 6-E, §3.3.2(5).

(2) Connection with case. A party is entitled to a brief description of the person's connection with the suit. Tex. R. Civ. P. 192.3(c), 194.2(b)(5). See "Identify connection with case," ch. 6-E, §2.2.2(1)(e)[2]; "Fact witnesses," ch. 6-E, §3.3.2(5).

(3) Witness statements. A party is entitled to any witness statements made by a fact witness. Tex. R. Civ. P. 192.3(h). See "Witness statements," ch. 6-B, §2.6.

(4) Matters not privileged. A party is entitled to any information in the possession of the witness that is not privileged and is relevant to the subject matter of the pending action, whether it relates to the claim or defense of the party seeking discovery or to the claim or defense of any other party. Tex. R. Civ. P. 192.3(a).

§2.9 Trial witnesses. A party is entitled to discovery of the name, address, and telephone number of any person who is expected to be called to testify at trial. Tex. R. Civ. P. 194.4(a)(1); *see* Tex. R. Civ. P. 192.3(d), 192.5(c)(1). A party is not entitled to secure information about rebuttal or impeaching witnesses unless the need for the testimony can reasonably be anticipated before trial. *See* Tex. R. Civ. P. 192.3(d), 194.4(a)(1).

2021 Rule Amendments

For cases filed on or after January 1, 2021, a party is required to disclose this information about trial witnesses in pretrial disclosures under TRCP 194.4 without waiting for a discovery request from the other party. Tex. R. Civ. P. 194.4(a)(1); Tex.Sup.Ct. Order, Misc. Docket No. 20-9153 (eff. Jan. 1, 2021). See "Final pretrial disclosures," ch. 6-E, §3.5.

§2.10 Experts. See "Information discoverable from experts," ch. 6-D, §4.

§2.11 Documents & tangible things. A party can discover the existence, description, nature, custody, condition, location, and contents of documents and tangible things that constitute or contain relevant information and are in the possession, custody, or control of the other party. Tex. R. Civ. P. 192.3(b); *see* Tex. R. Civ. P. 196 (request for production). See "Documents & tangible things," ch. 6-A, §2.2; "Possession," ch. 6-A, §2.5. To be discoverable, the document or thing must already exist. **Smith v. O'Neal**, 850 S.W.2d 797, 799 (Tex.App.—Houston [14th Dist.] 1993, no writ). A request for production does not require a party to create a document to satisfy the request. *Id.* See "Securing Documents & Tangible Things," ch. 6-I, §1 et seq. The following types of documents are discoverable:

1. Income-tax returns. Income-tax returns are discoverable if they are relevant and material. **Hall v. Lawlis**, 907 S.W.2d 493, 494 (Tex.1995). If part, but not all, of an income-tax return is discoverable, discovery must be limited to the relevant and material parts. *See* **Maresca v. Marks**, 362 S.W.2d 299, 301 (Tex.1962). Unlike with other discovery requests, when a party objects to a request for income-tax returns, the requesting party has the burden to show that all or part of the return is relevant and material to the case. **In re Williams**, 328 S.W.3d 103, 116 (Tex.App.—Corpus Christi 2010, orig. proceeding); **In re Brewer Leasing, Inc.**, 255 S.W.3d 708, 713–14 (Tex.App.—Houston [1st Dist.] 2008, orig. proceeding). The requesting party must also show that the relevant information cannot be obtained from another source. **In re Williams**, 328 S.W.3d at 116; **El Centro del Barrio, Inc. v. Barlow**, 894 S.W.2d 775, 780 (Tex.App.—San Antonio 1994, orig. proceeding); *see* **Wal-Mart Stores v. Alexander**, 868 S.W.2d 322, 331 (Tex.1993) (Gonzalez, J., concurring) (trial courts should not allow discovery of tax returns if there are other adequate methods to determine net worth); *see, e.g.*, **Sears, Roebuck & Co. v. Ramirez**, 824 S.W.2d 558, 559 (Tex.1992) (trial court should not have ordered production of tax returns because D had already produced audited, certified annual reports containing D's net worth; thus, tax returns were duplicative).

2. Financial statements. Financial statements reflecting the defendant's net worth may be discoverable when a plaintiff sues for exemplary damages. *See* Tex. Civ. Prac. & Rem. Code §41.0115(a). The trial court, however, must first authorize discovery of evidence of a defendant's net worth. *See id.* For the procedure for getting authorization, see "Section 41.011(a) factors," ch. 5-I, §5.3.2(1)(f). If the pleadings do not request exemplary damages, the defendant's net worth is outside the scope of discovery. **Al Parker Buick Co. v. Touchy**, 788 S.W.2d 129, 131 (Tex.App.—Houston [1st Dist.] 1990, orig. proceeding).

3. Photographs. "Photographs" are defined in the TREs to include a photographic image or its equivalent stored in any form. Tex. R. Evid. 1001(c). Photographs and other electronic images are discoverable. Tex. R. Civ. P. 192.3(b). Photographs are not "communications" exempt from discovery under TRCP 192.5(a) (work product). *See* Tex. R. Civ. P. 192.5(c)(4); *see also* **Terry v. Lawrence**, 700 S.W.2d 912, 913 (Tex.1985) (under former TRCP 166b; investigative privilege does not protect photos from discovery).

4. Insurance & indemnity agreements. Insurance policies and indemnity agreements are generally discoverable. Tex. R. Civ. P. 192.3(f). By being permitted to discover insurance and indemnity agreements, the plaintiff can determine the settlement value of the case. **Carroll Cable Co. v. Miller**, 501 S.W.2d 299, 299 (Tex.1973). Even though an insurance policy or indemnity agreement may be discoverable, it is not automatically admissible as evidence at trial. Tex. R. Civ. P. 192.3(f). TRCP 192.3(f) does not prohibit discovery of other insurance information as long as it is otherwise discoverable under TRCP 192.3(a). **In re Dana Corp.**, 138 S.W.3d 298, 302–03 (Tex.2004). See "Scope & limitations," ch. 6-B, §2.1.

5. Settlement agreements. The existence and contents of relevant portions of a settlement agreement are discoverable. Tex. R. Civ. P. 192.3(g); *see* Tex. R. Civ. P. 194.2(b)(8). Merely providing information about the settlement (e.g., party names, amount) is not enough—the responding party must provide the relevant parts of the written agreement so that the requesting party can examine the contents. *See* **Liles v. Contreras**, 547 S.W.3d 280, 289–90 (Tex.App.—San Antonio 2018, pet. denied). A settlement agreement made in another dispute may be discoverable if it is relevant to the pending litigation. **Ford Motor Co. v. Leggat**, 904 S.W.2d 643, 649 (Tex.1995); **In re Frank A. Smith Sales, Inc.**, 32 S.W.3d 871, 874 (Tex.App.—Corpus Christi 2000, orig. proceeding). In most cases, the dollar amount of the parties' settlement is not relevant. *See, e.g.*, **Leggat**, 904 S.W.2d at 649 (settlement amounts not relevant to determine D's net worth or motives); **Palo Duro Pipeline Co. v. Cochran**, 785 S.W.2d 455, 457 (Tex.App.—Houston [14th Dist.] 1990, orig. proceeding) (settlement amounts not relevant to issue of conspiracy). But the dollar amount may be relevant under some circumstances, such as when the case may involve a determination of settlement credits. *See* **In re GreCon, Inc.**, 542 S.W.3d 774, 782, 784 (Tex.App.—Houston [14th Dist.] 2018, orig. proceeding). Even though a settlement agreement may be discoverable, it is not automatically admissible as evidence at trial. Tex. R. Civ. P. 192.3(g); *see also* Tex. R. Evid. 408 (settlement agreements not admissible to prove validity or amount of disputed claim); **Leggat**, 904 S.W.2d at 649 (settlement agreements not admissible to prove liability).

6. Claim files.

(1) Claim file in same suit. The claim file of a party's insurance company is generally discoverable in the same suit. *See, e.g.*, **In re Ford Motor Co.**, 988 S.W.2d 714, 719 (Tex.1998) (D entitled to claim file from P's carrier); **Dunn Equip., Inc. v. Gayle**, 725 S.W.2d 372, 374–75 (Tex.App.—Houston [14th Dist.] 1987, orig. proceeding) (P entitled to claim file from D's carrier). But if the claim file is exempt from discovery under one cause of action, the party cannot get it for another cause of action in the same suit. **Maryland Am. Gen. Ins. v. Blackmon**, 639 S.W.2d 455, 457–58 (Tex.1982).

(2) Claim file in separate suit. The claim file of an insurance company is sometimes discoverable in another suit. *Compare* **Turbodyne Corp. v. Heard**, 720 S.W.2d 802, 804 (Tex.1986) (documents from claim file in main suit were discoverable in subrogation action), **Lewis v. Wittig**, 877 S.W.2d 52, 58 (Tex.App.—Houston [14th Dist.] 1994, orig. proceeding) (claim files of client companies were discoverable in malpractice suit against attorneys), *and* **Eddington v. Touchy**, 793 S.W.2d 335, 337 (Tex.App.—Houston [1st Dist.] 1990, orig. proceeding) (documents from claim file were discoverable by attorney who sued insurance company for settling with attorney's client without attorney's permission) *with* **Humphreys v. Caldwell**, 888 S.W.2d 469, 471 (Tex.1994) (after first suit, D in that suit sued P's carrier; claim file in first suit was not discoverable).

7. Investigative reports. Investigative reports are discoverable when they are not prepared in anticipation of litigation. *See, e.g.*, **Axelson, Inc. v. McIlhany**, 798 S.W.2d 550, 552–53 (Tex.1990) (internal kickback investigation, unre-

lated to the matter that gave rise to litigation, was discoverable); **In re Weeks Mar., Inc.**, 31 S.W.3d 389, 391 (Tex.App.—San Antonio 2000, orig. proceeding) (D's investigative report made after P hired attorney was not discoverable). See "Work-product privilege," ch. 6-B, §3.3.

8. Electronic information. Information stored or available electronically, either in a computer database or on some form of social media, may be discoverable.

(1) Computer database. If discoverable information is contained in a party's computer databases or files, it is discoverable upon a specific request. *See* Tex. R. Civ. P. 192.3(b) (any data compilations), Tex. R. Civ. P. 196.4 (electronic or magnetic data). Computer data can be requested in hard copy (printed version) or in electronic files. *See* Tex. R. Civ. P. 196.4. See "Electronic Discovery," ch. 6-C, §1 et seq.

(2) Social media. "Social media" refers to Internet applications that permit individuals to interactively share content and communicate. Sedona Conference, *Sedona Conference Glossary: eDiscovery & Digital Information Management (Fifth Edition)*, 21 Sedona Conf.J. 263, 372 (2020), thesedonaconference.org/publications. Information about these social interactions is discoverable and is most effectively obtained (1) through specific requests to the party or (2) by having the party execute a consent form or authorization that allows the discovering party to request the information directly from the social-networking site. *See* Browning, *Digging for the Digital Dirt: Discovery & Use of Evidence from Social Media Sites*, 14 SMU Sci. & Tech.L.Rev. 465, 473 (2011); *see, e.g.*, **In re Christus Health Se. Tex.**, 399 S.W.3d 343, 348 (Tex.App.—Beaumont 2013, orig. proceeding) (Ps' social-media posts about family member's death were within scope of discovery related to their mental-anguish claims, but D's request for production was overbroad because it was not limited to posts from certain time period).

9. Personnel files. When relevant, a party may discover the documents in the personnel file of a party or witness. *See* **In re Crestcare Nursing & Rehab. Ctr.**, 222 S.W.3d 68, 74 (Tex.App.—Tyler 2006, orig. proceeding); **In re LaVernia Nursing Facility, Inc.**, 12 S.W.3d 566, 570 (Tex.App.—San Antonio 1999, orig. proceeding). A personnel file includes all matters about the employee, even if filed separately under a different name. *E.g.*, **In re LaVernia Nursing**, 12 S.W.3d at 570 (personnel file included disciplinary actions filed separately).

§2.12 Entry on land. A party has a right of entry on land when it is relevant to the suit. The purpose of the entry must be to inspect, measure, survey, photograph, conduct nondestructive tests, or sample the land or a designated object or operation on the land. *See* Tex. R. Civ. P. 196.5, 196.7(a). See "Entry on Land," ch. 6-K, §1 et seq.

§2.13 Certain work product. Most work product is not discoverable. See "Work-product privilege," ch. 6-B, §3.3. But some work product is discoverable. For the definition of work product, see "Work product," ch. 6-A, §2.9.

1. Facts. Most facts about the case are discoverable. The work-product privilege does not permit the attorney to hide from discovery facts that were acquired by the attorney and are relevant and not exempt from discovery by some other privilege. **Owens-Corning Fiberglas Corp. v. Caldwell**, 818 S.W.2d 749, 750 n.2 (Tex.1991); *see* **In re Ford Motor Co.**, 988 S.W.2d 714, 719 (Tex.1998); *see also* **Hickman v. Taylor**, 329 U.S. 495, 511 (1947) (relevant and nonprivileged information in attorney's file may be discovered); **Leede Oil & Gas, Inc. v. McCorkle**, 789 S.W.2d 686, 687 (Tex.App.—Houston [1st Dist.] 1990, orig. proceeding) (neutral recitals of case facts in attorney's file were discoverable). An attorney cannot classify a document or certain information as work product simply by including it within protected documents. *See* **In re National Lloyds Ins.**, 532 S.W.3d 794, 807 (Tex.2017); **National Un. Fire Ins. v. Valdez**, 863 S.W.2d 458, 460 (Tex.1993); **Lewis v. Wittig**, 877 S.W.2d 52, 57–58 (Tex.App.—Houston [14th Dist.] 1994, orig. proceeding).

2. Need & hardship exception. A party may secure noncore work product under the need-and-hardship exception in TRCP 192.5(b)(2). **In re National Lloyds**, 532 S.W.3d at 804; **In re Maher**, 143 S.W.3d 907, 912 (Tex.App.—Fort Worth 2004, orig. proceeding); **In re Monsanto Co.**, 998 S.W.2d 917, 930 (Tex.App.—Waco 1999, orig. proceeding). If the court permits discovery of noncore work product under this exception, it must prevent the disclosure of mental impressions, opinions, conclusions, or legal theories, which are not discoverable. Tex. R. Civ. P. 192.5(b)(4); **In re National Lloyds**, 532 S.W.3d at 804. To meet the need-and-hardship exception, the party seeking discovery must show the following:

(1) Noncore work product. The information is not core work product. *See* Tex. R. Civ. P. 192.5(b)(1) (core work product is not discoverable); **In re National Lloyds**, 532 S.W.3d at 804 (need-and-hardship exception applies only to

"other work product"); **In re Team Transp.**, 996 S.W.2d 256, 259 (Tex.App.—Houston [14th Dist.] 1999, orig. proceeding) (same). For a definition, see "Noncore work product," ch. 6-A, §2.9.2.

(2) Substantial need. The party has a substantial need for the information to prepare its case. Tex. R. Civ. P. 192.5(b)(2); **In re National Lloyds**, 532 S.W.3d at 804; **In re Bexar Cty. Crim. Dist. Atty's Office**, 224 S.W.3d 182, 188 (Tex.2007); **Flores v. Fourth Ct. of Appeals**, 777 S.W.2d 38, 42 (Tex.1989), *modified on other grounds*, **National Tank Co. v. Brotherton**, 851 S.W.2d 193 (Tex.1993); *see, e.g.*, **State v. Lowry**, 802 S.W.2d 669, 673 (Tex.1991) (Ds had substantial need because State collected information during investigation that led to lawsuit and could provide evidence for defense); **Dillard Dept. Stores v. Sanderson**, 928 S.W.2d 319, 321–22 (Tex.App.—Beaumont 1996, orig. proceeding) (trial court did not abuse its discretion in finding issues of witness credibility and witness's failing memory were sufficient to show substantial need).

(3) Undue hardship. The party is unable, without undue hardship, to obtain the substantial equivalent of the information by other means. Tex. R. Civ. P. 192.5(b)(2); **In re National Lloyds**, 532 S.W.3d at 806; **In re Bexar Cty.**, 224 S.W.3d at 188; **Flores**, 777 S.W.2d at 42; *see, e.g.*, **Lowry**, 802 S.W.2d at 673 (Ds showed undue hardship because it would have been extremely difficult and costly to duplicate material that State had gathered).

3. Exceptions in TRCP 192.5(c). The following information is discoverable even if it was collected or prepared in anticipation of litigation:

(1) Witness information. Information discoverable under TRCP 192.3 (scope of discovery) concerning experts, trial witnesses, witness statements, and contentions. Tex. R. Civ. P. 192.5(c)(1); **In re National Lloyds**, 532 S.W.3d at 814. See "Witness statements," ch. 6-B, §2.6.

(2) Trial exhibits. Trial exhibits required to be disclosed by court order under TRCP 166 (pretrial order) or by TRCP 190.4 (Level 3 discovery-control plan). Tex. R. Civ. P. 192.5(c)(2).

(3) Party & fact witnesses. The name, address, and telephone number of any potential party or any person with knowledge of relevant facts. Tex. R. Civ. P. 192.5(c)(3).

(4) Photographs. Photographs and other electronic images that contain images of underlying facts (e.g., a photograph of an accident scene) or that the party intends to offer into evidence. Tex. R. Civ. P. 192.5(c)(4); *see also* Tex. R. Civ. P. 192.3(b) (scope of discovery). See "Photographs," ch. 6-B, §2.11.3.

(5) TRE 503(d) exceptions. Any work product created under circumstances within an exception to the attorney-client privilege in TRE 503(d) (crime-fraud and other exceptions). Tex. R. Civ. P. 192.5(c)(5); **Goode v. Shoukfeh**, 943 S.W.2d 441, 448 (Tex.1997). The same exceptions that apply to attorney-client communications apply to work product. Tex. R. Civ. P. 192.5(c)(5). See "TRE 503(d) exceptions," ch. 6-B, §2.14.1.

4. Waiver by offensive use. Information classified as work product may be discoverable under the offensive-use doctrine. *See* **Occidental Chem. Corp. v. Banales**, 907 S.W.2d 488, 490 (Tex.1995) (dicta; case involved sanctions). See "Waived privilege by offensive use," ch. 6-A, §25.3.5. For example, a party opposing discovery of its billing records may waive the work-product privilege by relying on its billing records to contest the reasonableness of the other party's attorney fees or to recover its own attorney fees. **In re National Lloyds**, 532 S.W.3d at 807. See "Core work product," ch. 6-B, §3.3.4(1).

§2.14 Certain attorney-client communications. Most communications between an attorney and a client are privileged and are not discoverable. See "Attorney-client privilege," ch. 6-B, §3.4. But the following communications between an attorney and a client are not privileged and are discoverable:

1. TRE 503(d) exceptions. If the communication falls within one of the five exceptions listed in TRE 503(d), it is discoverable.

(1) Crime or fraud. Communications made in furtherance of a crime or fraud are discoverable. Tex. R. Evid. 503(d)(1); Tex. R. Civ. P. 192.5(c)(5); *see* **Granada Corp. v. First Ct. of Appeals**, 844 S.W.2d 223, 227 (Tex.1992), *overruled on other grounds*, TRCP 193.3 & cmt. 4 (TRCP 193.3(d) overrules **Granada** to the extent that they conflict). The crime-fraud exception applies only if (1) the party seeking the information makes a prima facie case of contemplated crime or fraud and

(2) the information sought is related to the prima facie proof. **Granada**, 844 S.W.2d at 227; **In re JDN Real Estate-McKinney L.P.**, 211 S.W.3d 907, 924 (Tex.App.—Dallas 2006, orig. proceeding). To establish a prima facie case, the party seeking the information must establish the elements of the crime or fraud and that it was ongoing or about to be committed when the attorney-client communications were made. *See* **In re Park Cities Bank**, 409 S.W.3d 859, 869 (Tex.App.—Tyler 2013, orig. proceeding); **In re Small**, 346 S.W.3d 657, 666 (Tex.App.—El Paso 2009, orig. proceeding). The prima facie proof must show a violation serious enough to defeat the privilege. **In re Monsanto Co.**, 998 S.W.2d 917, 934 (Tex.App.—Waco 1999, orig. proceeding).

(2) Claimants through same deceased client. Communications that are relevant to an issue between parties who assert claims through the same deceased client are discoverable. Tex. R. Evid. 503(d)(2); Tex. R. Civ. P. 192.5(c)(5); **In re Texas A&M-Corpus Christi Found.**, 84 S.W.3d 358, 361 (Tex.App.—Corpus Christi 2002, orig. proceeding). Other than this narrow exception, communications between an attorney and client survive the client's death. *See* Tex. R. Evid. 503(c); **Swidler & Berlin v. U.S.**, 524 U.S. 399, 410 (1998).

(3) Breach of duty. Communications relevant to the breach of a duty either by an attorney to the client or by a client to the attorney are discoverable. Tex. R. Evid. 503(d)(3); Tex. R. Civ. P. 192.5(c)(5); **Scrivner v. Hobson**, 854 S.W.2d 148, 151 (Tex.App.—Houston [1st Dist.] 1993, orig. proceeding).

(4) Attestation by attorney. Communications relevant to an issue about a document to which the attorney was an attesting witness are discoverable. Tex. R. Evid. 503(d)(4); Tex. R. Civ. P. 192.5(c)(5).

(5) Joint clients. In a suit between clients who jointly consulted or retained an attorney, communications with the attorney that are common to the interests of both clients and are relevant to the dispute are discoverable. Tex. R. Evid. 503(d)(5); Tex. R. Civ. P. 192.5(c)(5); *see* **Scrivner**, 854 S.W.2d at 152.

2. Preexisting documents. Documents that preexisted the attorney-client relationship, delivered to the attorney by the client, are discoverable. **MortgageAmerica Corp. v. American Nat'l Bank**, 651 S.W.2d 851, 858 (Tex.App.—Austin 1983, writ ref'd n.r.e.).

3. Conditions of employment. Nonconfidential matters of employment, such as the terms, conditions, and purpose of the attorney's employment, are discoverable. **Allstate Tex. Lloyds v. Johnson**, 784 S.W.2d 100, 105 (Tex.App.—Waco 1989, orig. proceeding); **Borden, Inc. v. Valdez**, 773 S.W.2d 718, 720–21 (Tex.App.—Corpus Christi 1989, orig. proceeding).

4. Discussions with employees. Communications with the client's employees are discoverable unless the discussion falls within the provisions of TRE 503(a) (definition of client, representative, lawyer, and confidential communication) and TRE 503(b) (attorney-client privilege). See "Who is included," ch. 6-B, §3.4.1.

5. Identity of witnesses. The names and locations of the people with knowledge of relevant facts are discoverable. See "Fact witnesses," ch. 6-B, §2.8.

6. Offensive use. Information covered by the attorney-client privilege may be discoverable under the offensive-use doctrine. *E.g.*, **In re Tjia**, 50 S.W.3d 614, 617 (Tex.App.—Amarillo 2001, orig. proceeding) (in breach-of-contract suit, attorney's letter to P, his client, was discoverable by D when P said it relied on advice of counsel in making decision not to sublease). See "Waived privilege by offensive use," ch. 6-A, §25.3.5.

§2.15 Certain accountant-client communications. Communications between an accountant and a client are usually not discoverable. See "Accountant-client privilege," ch. 6-B, §3.7. Accountant-client communications are discoverable in the following instances:

1. When the client or its representative gives permission to disclose the information. Tex. Occ. Code §901.457(a).

2. When required by the professional standards for reporting on the examination of a financial statement. Tex. Occ. Code §901.457(b)(1).

3. To respond to a summons or subpoena under the provisions of the Internal Revenue Code, the 1933 Securities Act, the 1934 Securities Exchange Act, or the Securities Act (TRCS art. 581-1 et seq.). Tex. Occ. Code §901.457(b)(2).

Note

Effective January 1, 2022, the Securities Act, Texas Revised Civil Statutes article 581-1 et seq., will be repealed and recodified at Gov't Code title 12. See H.B. 4171, §§1.01, 3.01, 4.02, 86th Leg., R.S., eff. Jan. 1, 2022.

4. To respond to a court order signed by a judge if the order (1) is addressed to the accountant, (2) identifies the client's name, and (3) requests specific information about the client. Tex. Occ. Code §901.457(b)(3).

5. In an investigation conducted by the Texas State Board of Public Accountancy. Tex. Occ. Code §901.457(b)(4); *see also* Tex. Occ. Code §901.002(2) ("Board" defined as Texas State Board of Public Accountancy).

6. In an ethical investigation conducted by a professional organization of certified public accountants. Tex. Occ. Code §901.457(b)(5).

7. In the course of a peer-review proceeding under Occupations Code §901.159 or when required by the Public Company Accounting Oversight Board or its successor. Tex. Occ. Code §901.457(b)(6).

8. In the course of a practice review by another certified public accountant or certified public accountancy firm for a potential acquisition or merger of a firm with another, if the firms sign a nondisclosure agreement as to all client information they have shared. Tex. Occ. Code §901.457(b)(7).

§2.16 Certain marital communications. Most communications between spouses are not discoverable. *See* Tex. R. Evid. 504. See "Marital-communications privilege," ch. 6-B, §3.9. The marital-communications privilege does not protect the following information from disclosure:

1. Nonconfidential communications. There is no marital-communications privilege for communications made in the presence of a third person. **Fasken v. Fasken**, 260 S.W. 701, 702 (Tex.1924). These communications are not privileged and are discoverable. *See id.*; **Wiggins v. Tiller**, 230 S.W. 253, 254 (Tex.App.—San Antonio 1921, no writ); *cf.* **Bear v. State**, 612 S.W.2d 931, 931–32 (Tex.Crim.App.1981) (criminal case interpreting former Code of Crim. Proc. art. 38.11). If one spouse discusses the other spouse with a third person, that conversation is not privileged. *Cf.* **Gibbons v. State**, 794 S.W.2d 887, 892 (Tex.App.—Tyler 1990, no pet.) (interpreting former TRCrE 504).

2. Nonverbal communications. There is no marital-communications privilege for nonverbal communications. *See* **Pereira v. U.S.**, 347 U.S. 1, 6 (1954) (actions are not communications and thus are not privileged); *cf.* **Freeman v. State**, 786 S.W.2d 56, 59 (Tex.App.—Houston [1st Dist.] 1990, no pet.) (criminal case interpreting former TRCrE 504(2)(a)).

3. Crime or fraud. There is no marital-communications privilege for communications made in furtherance of a crime or fraud. Tex. R. Evid. 504(a)(4)(A). See "Crime or fraud," ch. 6-B, §2.14.1(1).

4. Suits between spouses. There is no marital-communications privilege in a civil suit between spouses or in a proceeding between a surviving spouse and a person who makes a claim through the deceased spouse. Tex. R. Evid. 504(a)(4)(B); *see, e.g.,* **Earthman's, Inc. v. Earthman**, 526 S.W.2d 192, 206 (Tex.App.—Houston [1st Dist.] 1975, no writ) (discussions between spouses were admissible in suit between them).

5. Crime against spouse or minor child. There is no marital-communications privilege in a proceeding in which the party is accused of a criminal act against the spouse, any member of either spouse's household, or any minor child. Tex. R. Evid. 504(a)(4)(C).

6. Commitment proceedings. There is no marital-communications privilege in a proceeding to commit either spouse or to place the property of one spouse under the control of the other because of a mental or physical condition. Tex. R. Evid. 504(a)(4)(D).

7. Competence hearings. There is no marital-communications privilege in a hearing brought by or on behalf of either spouse to establish competence. Tex. R. Evid. 504(a)(4)(E).

8. **Communications made before marriage.** There is no marital-communications privilege for communications made before marriage. *See* Tex. R. Evid. 504(a)(1) (communication is confidential if made to "person's spouse").

§2.17 Parent-child communications. There is no privilege for communications between parent and child. *Cf.* **Port v. Heard**, 764 F.2d 423, 428–30 (5th Cir.1985) (in criminal case, parent spent six months in jail for refusing to divulge communications by child accused of murder); **Diehl v. State**, 698 S.W.2d 712, 712–14 (Tex.App.—Houston [1st Dist.] 1985, pet. ref'd) (search warrant based on affidavit of D's 11-year-old child).

§2.18 Certain physician-patient information. Medical information about a patient is usually not discoverable, but TRE 509(e) and Occupations Code §§159.002 to 159.005 contain several exceptions to the physician-patient privilege. For a discussion of when medical information is not discoverable, see "Physician-patient privilege," ch. 6-B, §3.10.

Note

The 2015 restyling of the TREs deleted the reference to "confidentiality" and "administrative proceedings" in TRE 509(e) because the rule is only a privilege rule and the rules of evidence govern only proceedings in Texas courts. Tex. R. Evid. 509 cmt. (2015). Occupations Code §159.003 contains some exceptions similar to those found in TRE 509(e) that apply to the privilege of confidentiality in a court or administrative proceeding; however, reconciling the provisions in TRE 509 with those in the Occupations Code that address a physician-patient privilege applicable to court proceedings was beyond the scope of the restyling project. See Tex. R. Evid. 509 cmt. (2015). Occupations Code §159.004 also lists exceptions to a physician's duty to keep patient information confidential, but those exceptions apply in situations other than court and administrative proceedings. See Tex. Occ. Code §159.004; Tex. R. Evid. 509 cmt. (2015). The exceptions in Occupations Code §159.004 are not discussed here because they do not affect the discovery of medical information.

1. **TRE exceptions.**

(1) Patient vs. physician. Medical information is discoverable if the communication or record is relevant to a claim or defense in (1) a suit by the patient against the physician or (2) a license-revocation proceeding in which the patient is a complaining witness. Tex. R. Evid. 509(e)(1).

(2) Written consent. Medical information is discoverable if the patient or an agent consents in writing, as provided in TRE 509(f), to release privileged information. Tex. R. Evid. 509(e)(2). A patient's authorization for doctors to release information to an insurance company does not authorize the insurance company to release the information in a suit in which the patient is not a party. **Alpha Life Ins. v. Gayle**, 796 S.W.2d 834, 836 (Tex.App.—Houston [14th Dist.] 1990, orig. proceeding); *see* Tex. R. Evid. 509(f)(4).

(3) Suit to collect. Medical information is discoverable in a suit to collect a claim for medical services rendered to the patient. Tex. R. Evid. 509(e)(3).

(4) Relevant to claim or defense. Medical information is discoverable if (1) any party relies on the patient's physical, mental, or emotional condition as part of the party's claim or defense and (2) the communication or record is relevant to that condition. Tex. R. Evid. 509(e)(4); *see, e.g.*, **Rios v. Texas Dept. of MHMR**, 58 S.W.3d 167, 168–69 (Tex.App.—San Antonio 2001, no pet.) (in personal-injury suit, D could depose doctor that P consulted for second opinion). This exception applies even when the patient is not a party to the litigation. *See, e.g.*, **In re Whiteley**, 79 S.W.3d 729, 732 (Tex.App.—Corpus Christi 2002, orig. proceeding) (other patients' redacted medical records were discoverable because D relied on defense that same surgical procedure was successful on other patients). For a discussion of discoverable mental-health information relevant to a suit, see "Relevant to claim or defense," ch. 6-B, §2.19.5.

(5) Disciplinary investigation. Medical information is discoverable in the disciplinary investigation of a physician under the Medical Practice Act, Occupations Code §164.001 et seq., or of a registered nurse under Occupations Code §301.451 et seq. Tex. R. Evid. 509(e)(5). But the board conducting the investigation must protect the identity of any

patient whose medical records are examined unless the records would be subject to disclosure under TRE 509(e)(1) or the patient has consented to the disclosure as provided in TRE 509(f). Tex. R. Evid. 509(e)(5).

(6) Involuntary commitment. Medical information is discoverable in an involuntary-commitment proceeding, a proceeding for court-ordered treatment, or a probable-cause hearing under various statutes. *See* Tex. R. Evid. 509(e)(6).

(7) Institutional abuse or neglect. Medical information is discoverable in a suit for abuse or neglect of a resident in an "institution," as defined by Health & Safety Code §242.002. Tex. R. Evid. 509(e)(7); *e.g.*, **In re Arriola**, 159 S.W.3d 670, 674 (Tex.App.—Corpus Christi 2004, orig. proceeding) (medical information about nursing-facility resident was discoverable when P alleged he abused a fellow resident).

2. Occupations Code exceptions.

(1) Related to judicial proceeding. Medical information is discoverable if the communication or record is subpoenaed under the TRCPs, the Code of Criminal Procedure, or CPRC chapter 121 and the disclosure or release of the communication or record is related to a judicial proceeding in which the patient is a party. Tex. Occ. Code §159.002(f).

(2) Patient vs. physician. Medical information is discoverable in a proceeding brought by the patient against the physician, including (1) a malpractice proceeding or (2) a license-revocation proceeding in which the patient is a complaining witness and disclosure is relevant to the physician's claim or defense. Tex. Occ. Code §159.003(a)(1).

(3) Written consent. Medical information is discoverable if the patient or authorized representative consents in writing, as provided in Occupations Code §159.005, to release privileged information. Tex. Occ. Code §159.003(a)(2).

(4) Suit to collect. Medical information is discoverable in a suit to collect a claim for medical services provided to the patient. Tex. Occ. Code §159.003(a)(3).

(5) Suit for monetary damages. Medical information is discoverable in a proceeding brought by the patient or on the patient's behalf for the recovery of monetary damages for a physical or mental condition, including the patient's death. Tex. Occ. Code §159.003(a)(4).

(6) Disciplinary investigation. Medical information is discoverable in a disciplinary investigation of a physician under Occupations Code title 3, subtitle B, as long as the board conducting the investigation protects the identity of any patient whose billing or medical records are examined and to whom no other exception applies. *See* Tex. Occ. Code §159.003(a)(5).

(7) Involuntary commitment. Medical information is discoverable in an involuntary-commitment proceeding, a proceeding for court-ordered treatment, or a probable-cause hearing under various statutes. *See* Tex. Occ. Code §159.003(a)(7).

(8) Execution of will. Medical information is discoverable if the patient's physical or mental condition is relevant to the execution of a will. Tex. Occ. Code §159.003(a)(8).

(9) Relevant to proceeding for injunctive relief. Medical information is discoverable if it is relevant to a proceeding under Occupations Code §159.009 for injunctive relief based on the unauthorized release of a confidential communication. Tex. Occ. Code §159.003(a)(9).

(10) Records request. Medical information is discoverable if it satisfies a request for billing or medical records of a deceased or incompetent person under CPRC §74.051(e). Tex. Occ. Code §159.003(a)(11).

(11) Court order. Medical information is discoverable to a court or a party to an action under a court order. Tex. Occ. Code §159.003(a)(12).

§2.19 Certain mental-health information. Mental-health information about a patient is usually not discoverable. Tex. R. Evid. 510(b). See "Mental-health-information privilege," ch. 6-B, §3.11. There are six exceptions to the mental-health-information privilege that make mental-health information discoverable. Tex. R. Evid. 510(d).

1. Patient vs. professional. Mental-health information is discoverable if the information is relevant to a claim or defense in (1) a suit by the patient against the professional or (2) a license-revocation proceeding in which the patient is a complaining witness. Tex. R. Evid. 510(d)(1).

2. Written waiver. Mental-health information is discoverable if a patient waives the right to the privilege in writing. Tex. R. Evid. 510(d)(2).

3. Suit for debt. Mental-health information is discoverable if the professional sues to collect on a claim for mental-health or emotional-health services rendered to the patient. Tex. R. Evid. 510(d)(3).

4. Communication made during court-ordered examination. Mental-health information is discoverable if (1) the patient made a communication to a professional during a court-ordered examination, (2) the examination related to the patient's mental or emotional condition or disorder, (3) the patient was told the communication would not be privileged, (4) the communication is being offered to prove an issue involving the patient's mental or emotional health, and (5) the court imposes safeguards against unauthorized disclosure of the information. Tex. R. Evid. 510(d)(4); **Subia v. Texas Dept. of Human Servs.**, 750 S.W.2d 827, 830 (Tex.App.—El Paso 1988, no writ); **Dudley v. State**, 730 S.W.2d 51, 54 (Tex.App.—Houston [14th Dist.] 1987, no writ).

5. Relevant to claim or defense. Mental-health information is discoverable when any party relies on the patient's physical, mental, or emotional condition as part of its claim or defense, even when the patient is not a party to the litigation. Tex. R. Evid. 510(d)(5); *e.g.*, **R.K. v. Ramirez**, 887 S.W.2d 836, 842 (Tex.1994) (P claimed hospital was negligent because its doctor was physically and emotionally impaired); **Groves v. Gabriel**, 874 S.W.2d 660, 661 (Tex.1994) (P's allegation of severe emotional distress waived her privilege relating to her mental-health records); **M.A.W. v. Hall**, 921 S.W.2d 911, 914-15 (Tex.App.—Houston [14th Dist.] 1996, orig. proceeding) (Ps claimed doctor was impaired by drugs); **Easter v. McDonald**, 903 S.W.2d 887, 890-91 (Tex.App.—Waco 1995, orig. proceeding) (P claimed mental-health counselor was negligent in diagnosis of patient). The patient's condition becomes part of a claim or defense if the pleadings indicate that the jury must make a factual determination about the condition itself. **R.K.**, 887 S.W.2d at 843. Whether the patient's condition is part of a claim or defense is determined from the face of the pleadings. *Id.* at 843 n.7; *see* **Easter**, 903 S.W.2d at 891 n.1. See Brown & Rondon, **Texas Rules of Evidence Handbook**, Rule 510 (2021 ed.) (n.849).

6. Institutional abuse or neglect. Mental-health information is discoverable in a suit for abuse or neglect of a resident of an "institution," as defined by Health & Safety Code §242.002. Tex. R. Evid. 510(d)(6).

§2.20 Certain medical matters under TRCP 204. If the mental or physical condition of a party or a person under the party's control is in controversy, the person may be compelled on a motion showing good cause to submit to an examination. Tex. R. Civ. P. 204.1(a), (c); *see* **Coates v. Whittington**, 758 S.W.2d 749, 750-51 (Tex.1988) (mental exam); **In re Caballero**, 36 S.W.3d 143, 144 (Tex.App.—Corpus Christi 2000, orig. proceeding) (physical exam). See "Motion to examine the person," ch. 6-J, §5.

§2.21 Certain medical requests under Family Code. In a suit affecting the parent-child relationship under Family Code title 2 or 5, the court, on a party's motion or on its own initiative, may appoint (1) a psychiatrist or psychologist to examine a child who is the subject of a suit or any other party to the suit or (2) a nonphysician expert qualified to take blood and other samples to conduct a paternity test. Tex. R. Civ. P. 204.4; *see also* Tex. Fam. Code §§160.501 to 160.512 (genetic testing). See "Experts," **O'Connor's Texas Family Law Handbook**, ch. 4-D, §12.3.5 (2021 ed.).

§2.22 Certain medical records under HIPAA. Nonparty medical records are discoverable under the Health Information Portability & Accountability Act (HIPAA) in the following situations:

1. Court order. In response to a court order, if the covered entity (i.e., the health-care entity providing the records) discloses only the information expressly authorized by the order. 45 C.F.R. §164.512(e)(1)(i).

2. Subpoena. In response to a subpoena, if the covered entity receives satisfactory assurance from the party seeking the information that it has made reasonable efforts to (1) provide notice of the request to the nonparty patient whose records are sought or (2) obtain a qualified protective order. 45 C.F.R. §164.512(e)(1)(ii).

§2.23 Certain health-care information from hospital. Most health-care information in a hospital's possession is not discoverable. But a hospital and its agents or employees may release health-care information about a patient if (1) the patient or the patient's legally authorized representative makes the request, (2) a person presents a written authorization signed by the patient or the patient's legally authorized representative that meets the requirements of Health & Safety Code §241.152(b), or (3) the disclosure is authorized by Health & Safety Code §241.153. *See* Tex. Health & Safety Code §241.152(a), (b).

§2.24 Certain trade secrets. Generally, a person has a qualified privilege to refuse to disclose and to prevent other persons from disclosing a trade secret. Tex. R. Evid. 507(a). See "Trade-secret privilege," ch. 6-B, §3.14; Brown & Rondon, **Texas Rules of Evidence Handbook**, Rule 507 (2021 ed.). But in certain situations, trade secrets may be discoverable. A party's opinion that the information is a trade secret or a party's desire to avoid disclosing the information to others does not protect the information under the trade-secret privilege. *See* **In re Lowe's Cos.**, 134 S.W.3d 876, 878–79 (Tex.App.—Houston [14th Dist.] 2004, orig. proceeding). Any disclosure required by the court must be subject to an appropriate protective order. **In re Continental Gen. Tire, Inc.**, 979 S.W.2d 609, 613 (Tex.1998); **In re Leviton Mfg. Co.**, 1 S.W.3d 898, 902 (Tex.App.—Waco 1999, orig. proceeding); *see* Tex. R. Evid. 507(c); *see also* **In re M-I L.L.C.**, 505 S.W.3d 569, 579–80 (Tex.2016) (trial court had obligation to conduct in camera review of affidavit allegedly containing trade secrets to determine whether disclosure was necessary and what protective measures should be taken); *cf.* Tex. Civ. Prac. & Rem. Code §134A.006(a) (in action for misappropriation of trade secret, there is a presumption in favor of granting protective order to preserve secrecy of trade secret).

Note

CPRC chapter 134A, the Texas Uniform Trade Secrets Act (TUTSA), provides a uniform framework for actions involving trade-secret misappropriation. See Senate Cmte. on State Affairs, Bill Analysis, Tex. S.B. 953, 83rd Leg., R.S. (2013). For a discussion of trade-secret misappropriation, see "Trade-Secret Misappropriation," ***O'Connor's Texas Causes of Action****, ch. 28-A, §1 et seq. (2021 ed.).*

1. What is a trade secret? "Trade secret" means all forms and types of information, including business, scientific, technical, economic, or engineering information, and any formula, design, prototype, pattern, plan, compilation, program device, program, code, device, method, technique, process, procedure, financial data, or list of actual or potential customers or suppliers, if (1) the owner of the trade secret has taken reasonable measures under the circumstances to keep the information secret and (2) the information derives independent economic value from its secrecy (i.e., it is not generally known or readily ascertainable through proper means by another person who can obtain economic value from the information's disclosure or use). Tex. Civ. Prac. & Rem. Code §134A.002(6); Brown & Rondon, **Texas Rules of Evidence Handbook**, Rule 507 (2021 ed.) (nn.541–542); *see* **Computer Assocs. Int'l v. Altai, Inc.**, 918 S.W.2d 453, 455 (Tex.1996) (trade secret is formula, pattern, device, or compilation of information that is used in trade-secret holder's business and gives holder an advantage over competitors). Information can be considered a trade secret whether it is tangible or intangible and regardless of whether or how it is stored, compiled, or memorialized physically, electronically, graphically, photographically, or in writing. Tex. Civ. Prac. & Rem. Code §134A.002(6); Brown & Rondon, **Texas Rules of Evidence Handbook**, Rule 507 (2021 ed.) (n.543). For a more detailed discussion of the definition of a trade secret under both TUTSA and the common law, see "Plaintiff owned trade secret," **O'Connor's Texas Causes of Action**, ch. 28-A, §2.1 (2021 ed.); "Plaintiff owned trade secret," **O'Connor's Texas Causes of Action**, ch. 28-B, §2.1 (2021 ed.).

2. When is a trade secret discoverable? Once a trade secret has been established, the party requesting discovery has the burden to show that the trade secret should be disclosed. *See* **In re Continental Gen. Tire**, 979 S.W.2d at 613; **In re Leviton Mfg.**, 1 S.W.3d at 902. For the procedure for establishing a trade secret, see "Asserting privilege," ch. 6-B, §3.14.1. A trade secret should be disclosed only if doing so is necessary to prevent fraud or injustice; that is, disclosure is required only if the information is necessary for fair adjudication of a claim or defense. **In re Continental Gen. Tire**, 979 S.W.2d at 612; *see* Tex. R. Evid. 507(a); **In re Bass**, 113 S.W.3d 735, 737 (Tex.2003); **In re Leviton Mfg.**, 1 S.W.3d at 902 & n.1. For the information to be necessary, it must be both material and necessary to the litigation. **In re Bass**, 113 S.W.3d at 743.

(1) Material to claim or defense. The requesting party must show that the information to be disclosed is material to an existing claim or defense. **In re Bass**, 113 S.W.3d at 743; *see* **In re XTO Res. I, LP**, 248 S.W.3d 898, 904 (Tex.App.—Fort Worth 2008, orig. proceeding).

(2) Necessary for fair adjudication. The requesting party must show that the information to be disclosed is necessary for fair adjudication of a claim or defense and unavailable from any other source. **In re Continental Gen. Tire**, 979 S.W.2d at 615; *see* **In re Bridgestone/Firestone, Inc.**, 106 S.W.3d 730, 736 (Tex.2003) (O'Neill & Schneider, JJ., concurring) (disclosure of trade secret is generally proper if upholding privilege would "significantly impair" party from establishing or rebutting material element of claim or defense; party is significantly impaired when information is unavailable from any other source and there is no other adequate proof). To satisfy the test for necessity, the requesting party must show with specificity that the presentation of the case on the merits will suffer without the information, likely leading to an unjust result. **In re Union Pac. R.R.**, 294 S.W.3d 589, 592 (Tex.2009); **In re Bridgestone/Firestone**, 106 S.W.3d at 732–33; *see* **John Paul Mitchell Sys. v. Randalls Food Mkts., Inc.**, 17 S.W.3d 721, 739 (Tex.App.—Austin 2000, pet. denied) (requesting party must describe with particularity how disclosing trade secret is necessary, not just useful, for determining central issues); *see, e.g.*, **In re Continental Tire N. Am., Inc.**, 74 S.W.3d 884, 886 (Tex.App.—Eastland 2002, orig. proceeding) (P did not establish that she was entitled to discover trade secrets merely by making allegation that information was reasonably calculated to lead to admissible evidence). A court determines whether information is necessary by weighing the requesting party's need for the information against any potential harm to the resisting party. **In re Bridgestone/Firestone**, 106 S.W.3d at 732.

§2.25 Certain information about informant. The United States, Texas, and their political subdivisions have a privilege to not disclose the identity of a person who has provided information about an investigation of a possible violation of the law. Tex. R. Evid. 508(a); *see* **Roviaro v. U.S.**, 353 U.S. 53, 59–60 (1957). But information about an informant is discoverable in the following situations:

1. The informant's identity or interest in the subject matter of the communication was disclosed to those who would have cause to resent the communication, by the holder of the privilege or by the informant's own action. Tex. R. Evid. 508(c)(1)(A).

2. The informant appears as a witness for the public entity. Tex. R. Evid. 508(c)(1)(B).

3. The informant can testify about a material issue on the merits of a civil case. Tex. R. Evid. 508(c)(2)(B). The court must permit the entity with the privilege to present the matter for an in camera hearing, generally by affidavit, to determine whether the informant can supply the testimony. Tex. R. Evid. 508(c)(2)(C)(i).

4. The information from an informant is relied on to establish the legality of the means by which evidence was obtained, and the court does not believe that the evidence is reliable or credible. Tex. R. Evid. 508(c)(3)(A).

§2.26 Certain information in journalist's possession. Information obtained or prepared while acting as a journalist is usually not discoverable. *See* Tex. Civ. Prac. & Rem. Code §22.023. See "Journalist's privilege," ch. 6-B, §3.18. But in certain situations, any information, document, or item, or the source of any such information, document, or item, obtained or prepared while acting as a journalist may be discoverable. Tex. Civ. Prac. & Rem. Code §22.024.

1. When information is discoverable. The journalist's privilege does not apply when, after notice and a hearing, a party makes a clear and specific showing of the following:

(1) The party exhausted all reasonable efforts to get the information from other sources. Tex. Civ. Prac. & Rem. Code §22.024(1).

(2) The subpoena compelling the information is not overbroad, unreasonable, or oppressive and, when appropriate, is limited to verifying published information and any circumstances about the accuracy of the published information. Tex. Civ. Prac. & Rem. Code §22.024(2).

(3) The party gave reasonable and timely notice of the demand for the information. Tex. Civ. Prac. & Rem. Code §22.024(3).

(4) The interest of the requesting party outweighs the public interest in gathering and disseminating the news. Tex. Civ. Prac. & Rem. Code §22.024(4).

(5) The subpoena is not being used to obtain peripheral, nonessential, or speculative information. Tex. Civ. Prac. & Rem. Code §22.024(5).

(6) The information is relevant and material to the proceeding for which the information is sought and is essential for the requesting party's maintenance of a claim or defense. Tex. Civ. Prac. & Rem. Code §22.024(6).

2. Who may be compelled to disclose. A journalist, the journalist's employer, or an independent contractor of the journalist may be compelled to testify about the information or to produce or disclose it. Tex. Civ. Prac. & Rem. Code §22.024. For the definition of a journalist, see "Journalist," ch. 6-B, §3.18.1(1).

§2.27 Shared discovery. The doctrine of shared discovery allows litigants access to discovery in other lawsuits for use in their own suits. **Eli Lilly & Co. v. Marshall**, 850 S.W.2d 155, 160 (Tex.1993); *see* Tex. R. Civ. P. 192.3(a) ("any matter that is not privileged").

§2.28 Any matter subject to waiver. A party is entitled to discover anything it requested if the other party has waived its objections or claims of privilege. See "Waiver of sanctions, discovery & objections," ch. 6-A, §25.

§3. What is not discoverable?

To determine what is not discoverable, read TRCP 192, which outlines the scope of discovery and, by implication, the matters outside the scope of discovery. Also read TRE 501 to 513, which list the privileges from discovery.

§3.1 Outside scope of discovery. Information is not discoverable if it is not relevant to the subject matter of the pending action, is not proportional to the needs of the case because of undue burden or expense, or is not admissible at trial and is not reasonably calculated to lead to the discovery of admissible evidence. *See* Tex. R. Civ. P. 192.3(a), 192.4(b); *see also* Tex. R. Evid. 401 (defining relevant evidence). The scope of discovery is confined by the subject matter of the case and reasonable expectations of obtaining information that will help resolve the dispute. Tex. R. Civ. P. 192 cmt. 1.

§3.2 Limitation on scope of discovery. The court has the power to limit discovery if it determines that the discovery is unreasonably cumulative or duplicative or the discovery can be obtained from a more convenient, less burdensome, or less expensive source. Tex. R. Civ. P. 192.4(a); *see* **In re Colonial Pipeline Co.**, 968 S.W.2d 938, 941–42 (Tex.1998) (scope of discovery is largely within trial court's discretion).

§3.3 Work-product privilege. The work product of a party or its representatives—including the party's attorneys, consultants, sureties, indemnitors, insurers, employees, or agents—is exempt from discovery. Tex. R. Civ. P. 192.5(a), (b). For the definition of work product, see "Work product," ch. 6-A, §2.9. The work-product discovery exemption replaced the "attorney work product" and "party communication" exemptions from former TRCP 166b. Tex. R. Civ. P. 192 cmt. 8. The term "work product" applies only to materials prepared, mental impressions developed, or communications made in anticipation of litigation or for trial. Tex. R. Civ. P. 192.5(a); **In re National Lloyds Ins.**, 532 S.W.3d 794, 803 (Tex.2017); **Huie v. DeShazo**, 922 S.W.2d 920, 927 (Tex.1996); **National Tank Co. v. Brotherton**, 851 S.W.2d 193, 200 (Tex.1993). The primary purpose of the work-product privilege is to protect the mental processes, conclusions, and legal theories of the attorney and provide a privileged area so the attorney can analyze and prepare the case for trial. **In re National Lloyds**, 532 S.W.3d at 803; **In re Bexar Cty. Crim. Dist. Atty's Office**, 224 S.W.3d 182, 186 (Tex.2007); **Owens-Corning Fiberglas Corp. v. Caldwell**, 818 S.W.2d 749, 750 (Tex.1991); *see* Tex. R. Civ. P. 192.5(b)(1) (defining "core work product"); *see also* **National Tank**, 851 S.W.2d at 202–03 & n.11 (explanation of work-product privilege under former TRCP 166b(3)(a)). The work-product privilege is essential to the attorney-client relationship. **Occidental Chem. Corp. v. Banales**, 907 S.W.2d 488, 490 (Tex.1995). The work-product privilege promotes the adversary system by safeguarding the fruits of an attorney's trial preparations from the other party. **Wiley v. Williams**, 769 S.W.2d 715, 717 (Tex.App.—Austin 1989, orig. proceeding).

Note

The work-product privilege and the attorney-client privilege are often confused. They cover much of the same material, but with some important differences. The work-product privilege covers work relating to the preparation of the client's lawsuit; the attorney-client privilege covers communications with the client. See ***National Tank****, 851 S.W.2d at 200;* ***Owens-Corning****, 818 S.W.2d at 750. The work-product privilege depends on proof that the materials were prepared in anticipation of litigation or for trial; the attorney-client privilege does not.* ***National Tank****, 851 S.W.2d at 202;* ***Boring & Tunneling Co. v. Salazar****, 782 S.W.2d 284, 288 (Tex.App.—Houston [1st Dist.] 1989, orig. proceeding). See "Attorney-client privilege," ch. 6-B, §3.4.*

1. Date of occurrence. To qualify as work product, material must have been prepared or mental impressions developed in anticipation of litigation or for trial—that is, after the occurrence or transaction on which the suit is based. *See* Tex. R. Civ. P. 192.5(a). In most cases, the date of the occurrence is easy to determine—it is the date of the injury. Sometimes, however, it is more difficult. *See, e.g.,* **Jackson v. Downey**, 817 S.W.2d 858, 860 (Tex.App.—Houston [1st Dist.] 1991, orig. proceeding) (in suit against insurance company for refusal to pay medical claim, occurrence was date insurance company informed insured that coverage was denied, not date insurance company made internal decision to terminate benefits); **National Sur. Corp. v. Dominguez**, 715 S.W.2d 67, 68–69 (Tex.App.—Corpus Christi 1986, orig. proceeding) (in suit to recover on surety bond, occurrence was date surety denied bank coverage, not date bank was found liable to customer).

2. Anticipation of litigation. The materials must have been prepared or the mental impressions developed in anticipation of litigation or for trial. Tex. R. Civ. P. 192.5(a); **In re National Lloyds**, 532 S.W.3d at 803; **National Tank**, 851 S.W.2d at 202. Courts use a two-part test to determine whether the party asserting the privilege prepared the materials in anticipation of litigation:

(1) Objective test. First, the court must determine whether a reasonable person, based on the circumstances at the time of the investigation, would have anticipated litigation. **National Tank**, 851 S.W.2d at 203; *see* **In re Park Cities Bank**, 409 S.W.3d 859, 867 (Tex.App.—Tyler 2013, orig. proceeding). "Imminence" of litigation is not a factor. *See* **National Tank**, 851 S.W.2d at 203–04. This objective part of the test is satisfied when a reasonable person would conclude from the severity of the accident and other circumstances surrounding it that there is a substantial chance that litigation would follow. *Id.* at 204.

(2) Subjective test. Second, the court must make a subjective determination whether the party resisting discovery believed in good faith that there was a substantial chance that litigation would follow and conducted the investigation for the purpose of preparing for the litigation. **National Tank**, 851 S.W.2d at 204; *see* **In re Park Cities Bank**, 409 S.W.3d at 867. This subjective part of the test examines the potential defendant's reaction to circumstances surrounding the occurrence.

Note

Reports prepared in the ordinary course of business may be exempt from discovery under the anticipation-of-litigation exception. There is no specific rule that makes ordinary-course-of-business documents discoverable. ***National Tank****, 851 S.W.2d at 206. The court must consider the reasons that gave rise to the defendant's ordinary business practice. Id. This does not mean, however, that all the claim files of an insurance company are privileged. Id. at 206 n.13.*

3. Prepared by or for party. To qualify as work product, the materials assembled for litigation must have been prepared by or for a party or a party's representatives, including the party's attorneys, consultants, sureties, indemnitors, insurers, employees, or agents. Tex. R. Civ. P. 192.5(a)(1); *see* **In re National Lloyds**, 532 S.W.3d at 803; **Humphreys v. Caldwell**, 888 S.W.2d 469, 471 (Tex.1994); *see, e.g.,* **Marshall v. Hall**, 943 S.W.2d 180, 183 (Tex.App.—Houston [1st Dist.] 1997, orig. proceeding) (interview notes prepared by attorney's employee were protected); **Bearden v. Boone**, 693 S.W.2d

25, 28 (Tex.App.—Amarillo 1985, orig. proceeding) (investigator's work conducted for attorney was protected). In a criminal prosecution, the work-product privilege extends only to a litigation file that is still active. See "Law-enforcement privilege," ch. 6-B, §3.22.

4. Work product exempt from discovery.

(1) Core work product. Core work product—work product that contains the attorney's (or her representative's) mental impressions, opinions, conclusions, or legal theories—is not discoverable. Tex. R. Civ. P. 192.5(b)(1); **In re National Lloyds**, 532 S.W.3d at 803–04; **In re Bexar Cty.**, 224 S.W.3d at 187. The protection for the attorney's thought processes is absolute. **Occidental Chem.**, 907 S.W.2d at 490. An attorney's thought processes include strategy decisions and issue formulation. **In re National Lloyds**, 532 S.W.3d at 804; **Occidental Chem.**, 907 S.W.2d at 490. Even the mechanical compilation of information (e.g., billing records) can be considered core work product to the extent the compilation reveals the attorney's thought processes. **In re National Lloyds**, 532 S.W.3d at 804; *see* **Occidental Chem.**, 907 S.W.2d at 490. Specifically, the privilege protects the following: • The attorney's billing invoices, audits, documents showing flat rates, and payment logs, ledgers, and summaries. **In re National Lloyds**, 532 S.W.3d at 805–06. • The attorney's litigation file. **National Un. Fire Ins. v. Valdez**, 863 S.W.2d 458, 460 (Tex.1993). • Indexes, notes, and memos prepared by an attorney. **Garcia v. Peeples**, 734 S.W.2d 343, 348 (Tex.1987). • The attorney's notes and correspondence prepared in connection with the lawsuit. **Occidental Chem.**, 907 S.W.2d at 490; **Humphreys**, 888 S.W.2d at 471. • The attorney's notes made during trial. **Goode v. Shoukfeh**, 943 S.W.2d 441, 449 (Tex.1997). Core work product is not subject to the need-and-hardship exception in TRCP 192.5(b)(2). See "Need & hardship exception," ch. 6-B, §2.13.2.

Note

In ***In re National Lloyds****, the Court held that the party's request to produce all attorney billing records, which was analogous to the request made in* ***Valdez*** *for the attorney's entire litigation file, violated the work-product privilege.* ***In re National Lloyds****, 532 S.W.3d at 805–06. In* ***Valdez****, the Court held that a party cannot request an attorney's entire litigation file because it goes to the heart of the work-product privilege, and the attorney's selection and ordering of documents in anticipation of litigation is protected work product even if the individual documents are not privileged.* ***Valdez****, 863 S.W.2d at 460–61. Similarly, billing records reveal the attorney's thought processes, including when and where attorneys strategically deploy a client's resources, which issues were addressed by experienced attorneys, the subject-matter expertise of an attorney working on a particular part of the case, and information on the hiring of consultants.* ***In re National Lloyds****, 532 S.W.3d at 805. In response to the requesting party's argument that redaction of privileged material should be sufficient to allow for disclosure of the billing records, the Court held that redaction would be insufficient as a matter of law to mask the attorney's thought processes and strategies and thus is inadequate to protect the work-product nature of the total billing information. Id. at 805–06. But see id. at 823 (Johnson, Lehrmann, Boyd, JJ., dissenting) (trial court's order authorizing party to redact privileged information before producing documents was adequate to protect privileged information).*

(2) Noncore work product. Noncore work product—work product that does not reflect the attorney's thought processes—is generally exempt from discovery. *See* **In re National Lloyds**, 532 S.W.3d at 803–04. But if the party seeking discovery proves the need-and-hardship exception, noncore work product is discoverable. Tex. R. Civ. P. 192.5(b)(2); *see* **In re National Lloyds**, 532 S.W.3d at 804. See "Need & hardship exception," ch. 6-B, §2.13.2.

5. Duration. The work-product privilege is perpetual. **Occidental Chem.**, 907 S.W.2d at 490; **Owens-Corning**, 818 S.W.2d at 751–52. This means the attorney's mental impressions and opinions from one suit are not discoverable in another suit. **Humphreys**, 888 S.W.2d at 471; **Owens-Corning**, 818 S.W.2d at 751–52; **Cigna Corp. v. Spears**, 838 S.W.2d 561, 564 (Tex.App.—San Antonio 1992, orig. proceeding); *see* **In re Bexar Cty.**, 224 S.W.3d at 186 (privilege continues indefinitely beyond suit for which materials were originally prepared).

§3.4 Attorney-client privilege. The purpose of the attorney-client privilege is to foster the client's confidence in the attorney and to encourage free communication between them. *See* **In re National Lloyds Ins.**, 532 S.W.3d 794, 803

(Tex.2017); **Maryland Am. Gen. Ins. v. Blackmon**, 639 S.W.2d 455, 458 (Tex.1982); **West v. Solito**, 563 S.W.2d 240, 245 (Tex.1978). The attorney-client privilege, a creation of common law now codified in TRE 503(b), ensures that confidential communications between the attorney and the client made for the purpose of rendering legal services will not be disclosed. **In re Ford Motor Co.**, 988 S.W.2d 714, 718 (Tex.1998); **Huie v. DeShazo**, 922 S.W.2d 920, 922 (Tex.1996); **Republic Ins. v. Davis**, 856 S.W.2d 158, 160 (Tex.1993). The attorney-client privilege is the oldest of the privileges for confidential communications known to the common law. **In re XL Specialty Ins.**, 373 S.W.3d 46, 49 (Tex.2012); **In re City of Georgetown**, 53 S.W.3d 328, 332 (Tex.2001). For a discussion of attorney-client communications that are discoverable, see "Certain attorney-client communications," ch. 6-B, §2.14.

1. Who is included. The attorney-client privilege covers attorney-client communications between the following persons:

(1) Attorney. An attorney is a person who is authorized, or who the client reasonably believes is authorized, to practice law in any state or nation. Tex. R. Evid. 503(a)(3). Thus, there are two requirements for a person to qualify as an attorney under TRE 503(a)(3): (1) the person must be engaged in the practice of law and (2) the person must be authorized to practice law or the client must reasonably believe that the person is authorized. **In re Silver**, 540 S.W.3d 530, 535 (Tex.2018).

(a) Engaged in practice of law. An attorney is a person who is engaged in the practice of law. **In re Silver**, 540 S.W.3d at 535; *see* Tex. R. Evid. 503(a)(3). A person is engaged in the practice of law if she is "pursuing the legal profession"—that is, she is performing services such as conducting cases in court, preparing legal opinions on various points of law, and advising clients on legal questions. *E.g.*, **In re Silver**, 540 S.W.3d at 535–36 (registered patent agents engage in practice of law by preparing patent applications, representing clients in front of U.S. Patent and Trademark Office, and advising clients of alternative forms of protection); *see* Practice of Law, *Black's Law Dictionary* (11th ed. 2019) (practice of law encompasses broad range of services, including activities that few attorneys engage in but that require legal expertise). The person must provide legal services directly to the client. **In re Silver**, 540 S.W.3d at 536.

(b) Authorized. An attorney is a person who is authorized to practice law. Tex. R. Evid. 503(a)(3); **In re Silver**, 540 S.W.3d at 533. "Authorized" means to be sanctioned by authority or approved. *E.g.*, **In re Silver**, 540 S.W.3d at 537–38 (because registered patent agents are approved to practice law before U.S. Patent and Trademark Office and Office gets its authority to approve from Congress, agents are authorized under TRE 503); *see also* Authorize, *Black's Law Dictionary* (11th ed. 2019) (defined as to give legal authority or to empower). A license is not required for a person to be authorized and thus qualify as an attorney under TRE 503. **In re Silver**, 540 S.W.3d at 537. Even if a person is not actually authorized to practice law, the attorney-client privilege can still apply if the client reasonably believes the person is authorized. *See* Tex. R. Evid. 503(a)(3); **In re Silver**, 540 S.W.3d at 537.

(2) Attorney's representative. An attorney's representative includes a person employed by the attorney to assist in the rendition of professional legal services. Tex. R. Evid. 503(a)(4)(A); **National Tank Co. v. Brotherton**, 851 S.W.2d 193, 197 (Tex.1993). Secretaries, paralegals, accountants, and investigators are included in this definition. *See* **Bearden v. Boone**, 693 S.W.2d 25, 27–28 (Tex.App.—Amarillo 1985, orig. proceeding).

(3) Client. A client is a person, public officer, corporation, association, or other organization or entity, either public or private. Tex. R. Evid. 503(a)(1); *see, e.g.*, **Markowski v. City of Marlin**, 940 S.W.2d 720, 726–27 (Tex.App.—Waco 1997, writ denied) (city council's consultation with its attorney in closed session was protected by privilege).

(4) Client's representative. A client's representative includes (1) a person with the authority to obtain legal services or to act on legal advice rendered on the client's behalf or (2) any other person who, for the purpose of effectuating legal representation for the client, makes or receives a confidential communication while acting in the scope of employment for the client. Tex. R. Evid. 503(a)(2); **In re Monsanto Co.**, 998 S.W.2d 917, 929 (Tex.App.—Waco 1999, orig. proceeding). TRE 503(a)(2) was amended in 1998, by adding (a)(2)(B), to adopt the subject-matter test. Tex. R. Evid. 503 cmt.; **In re** ***Monsanto Co.***, *998 S.W.2d at 922. The subject-matter test covers more types of communications by more people at different* levels within a corporation than the old control-group test did. **Ford Motor Co. v. Leggat**, 904 S.W.2d 643, 646 (Tex.1995). For an in-depth discussion of these tests, see Brown & Rondon, **Texas Rules of Evidence Handbook**, Rule 503 (2021 ed.) (nn.103–134).

2. Professional relationship. For the attorney-client privilege to apply, there must be a professional relationship between the attorney and the client. **In re Rescue Concepts, Inc.**, 556 S.W.3d 331, 339 (Tex.App.—Houston [1st Dist.] 2017, orig. proceeding); *see, e.g.*, **Huie**, 922 S.W.2d at 925 (no attorney-client relationship between trustee's attorney and beneficiary); *see also* **Joe v. Two Thirty Nine Jt.V.**, 145 S.W.3d 150, 164 (Tex.2004) (conducting legal research for city-council vote did not create attorney-client relationship between D and city); **Parker v. Carnahan**, 772 S.W.2d 151, 156 (Tex.App.—Texarkana 1989, writ denied) (signing tax return in attorney's office did not create attorney-client relationship). The attorney-client relationship is contractual; the parties must demonstrate an intent to create the relationship either explicitly or through their conduct. **In re Rescue Concepts**, 556 S.W.3d at 339. Courts use an objective standard to determine if what the parties said and did shows a sufficient meeting of the minds or agreement to create an attorney-client relationship. *Id.*

3. Who may assert. The attorney-client privilege belongs to the client, not the attorney. **West**, 563 S.W.2d at 244 n.2. The attorney-client privilege may be asserted by the client, the client's guardian, the personal representative of a deceased client, or the successor, trustee, or similar representative of the client. Tex. R. Evid. 503(c). The attorney is presumed to have the authority to assert the privilege on the client's behalf. *Id.*; *e.g.*, **Cole v. Gabriel**, 822 S.W.2d 296, 296 (Tex.App.—Fort Worth 1991, orig. proceeding) (attorney had no standing to assert attorney-client privilege in his individual capacity).

4. Duration. The attorney-client privilege continues for as long as the client asserts it. **Bearden**, 693 S.W.2d at 27–28; *see* **Maryland Am.**, 639 S.W.2d at 458. It does not terminate at the conclusion of the employment or the end of the dispute for which the client hired the attorney. **Bearden**, 693 S.W.2d at 27–28. The privilege survives the client's death. **Swidler & Berlin v. U.S.**, 524 U.S. 399, 410 (1998); *see* Tex. R. Evid. 503(c).

5. What is protected. The attorney-client privilege will protect information when the communication is between the attorney and client, the communication is confidential, and the communication is made to facilitate the rendition of professional legal services. Tex. R. Evid. 503(b)(1).

Note

An attorney can simultaneously represent two or more clients on the same matter if the clients consent and there is no substantial risk that representation of one client will materially and adversely affect representation of the other client. ***In re XL Specialty****, 373 S.W.3d at 50; see also* ***Nester v. Textron, Inc.****, No. A-13-CA-920-LY, 2015 WL 1020673 (W.D.Tex.2015) (slip op.; 3-9-15) (under Texas law, attorney-client privilege applied to communications between parent company's in-house counsel and indirect subsidiary's management personnel because parent company and indirect subsidiary were jointly represented by same attorney). If the criteria discussed below are met, communications made in representing the joint clients are privileged except in a suit between the clients.* ***In re XL Specialty****, 373 S.W.3d at 50;* ***In re JDN Real Estate-McKinney L.P.****, 211 S.W.3d 907, 922 (Tex.App.—Dallas 2006, orig. proceeding). See "Joint clients," ch. 6-B, §2.14.1(5).*

---

(1) Attorney-client communication. There must be a communication between the attorney and the client. *See* Tex. R. Evid. 503(b)(1).

(a) Communication. The attorney-client privilege applies to the complete communication, including legal advice, opinions, mental analysis, and the specific facts these are based on. *See* **In re Rescue Concepts**, 556 S.W.3d at 345 (attorney-client privilege covers whole document, not just parts relating to legal advice, opinions, or mental analysis); **Pittsburgh Corning Corp. v. Caldwell**, 861 S.W.2d 423, 425 (Tex.App.—Houston [14th Dist.] 1993, orig. proceeding) (same). Not all statements and communications made between an attorney and a client are privileged. *See* **Borden, Inc. v. Valdez**, 773 S.W.2d 718, 720–21 (Tex.App.—Corpus Christi 1989, orig. proceeding) (attorney can be deposed but cannot be questioned about privileged matters). A communication made to an attorney after a person was told that no attorney-client relationship would be accepted is not a privileged communication. **McGrede v. Rembert Nat'l Bank**, 147 S.W.2d 580, 584 (Tex.App.—Texarkana 1941, writ dism'd).

(b) Between attorney & client. To be privileged, the communication must be made between some combination of the attorney, the attorney's representative, the client, and the client's representative. *See* Tex. R. Evid. 503(b)(1). See "Who is included," ch. 6-B, §3.4.1. Specifically, the communication must be made:

[1] Between the client or the client's representative and the attorney or the attorney's representative. Tex R Evid. 503(b)(1)(A).

[2] Between the attorney and the attorney's representative. Tex R Evid. 503(b)(1)(B).

[3] By the client, client's representative, client's attorney, or client's attorney's representative to an attorney representing another party in a pending suit or to the other party's attorney's representative, if the communication is about a matter of common interest in the pending suit. Tex R Evid. 503(b)(1)(C).

[4] Between the client's representatives or between the client and its representative. Tex R Evid. 503(b)(1)(D).

[5] Among the attorneys and their representatives representing the same client. Tex R Evid. 503(b)(1)(E).

(2) Confidential communication. The communication must be confidential. Tex R Evid. 503(b)(1). A communication is confidential if it is not intended to be disclosed to third persons. Tex R Evid. 503(a)(5); *see, e.g.*, **Huie**, 922 S.W.2d at 925 (trustee had expectation that communication to attorney would be confidential). If the communication between the client and the attorney is made in the presence of a third person who is not an agent or representative of the attorney, it is not privileged. **Ledisco Fin. Servs. v. Viracola**, 533 S.W.2d 951, 959 (Tex.App.—Texarkana 1976, no writ).

(3) Legal services. The communication must be made to facilitate the rendition of professional legal services. Tex R Evid. 503(b)(1); **Huie**, 922 S.W.2d at 923. The attorney-client privilege does not apply if the attorney is acting in a capacity other than that of an attorney. **In re Texas Farmers Ins. Exch.**, 990 S.W.2d 337, 340 (Tex.App.—Texarkana 1999, orig. proceeding); *see, e.g.*, **Clayton v. Canida**, 223 S.W.2d 264, 266 (Tex.App.—Texarkana 1949, no writ) (no privilege because attorney was acting as accountant). A person cannot cloak a material fact with the privilege merely by communicating it to an attorney. **Huie**, 922 S.W.2d at 923.

§3.5 Allied-litigant privilege. The allied-litigant privilege is an exception to the general rule that disclosure of privileged information to third parties waives the privilege. *See* **In re XL Specialty Ins.**, 373 S.W.3d 46, 49–50 (Tex.2012). To assert the allied-litigant privilege, the parties must be represented by different attorneys, be parties to a pending litigation, and share a common legal interest. *Id.* at 51–53. But the privilege only protects communications between a party, its attorney, or a representative of either to another party's attorney or its attorney's representative about a matter of common interest; it does not protect communications made to the other party. *See* Tex R Evid. 503(b)(1)(C); **In re XL Specialty**, 373 S.W.3d at 52–53. See Brown & Rondon, **Texas Rules of Evidence Handbook**, Rule 503 (2021 ed.) (nn.209–215).

Note

*In **In re XL Specialty**, 373 S.W.3d at 50, 52, the Supreme Court stated that although the privilege defined in TRE 503(b)(1)(C) has been called many things by the courts—the "joint-client privilege," the "joint-defense privilege," and the "common-interest privilege"—it is most accurately described as the "allied-litigant privilege." These privileges are distinct doctrines that serve different purposes, but only the allied-litigant privilege serves the purpose intended by TRE 503(b)(1)(C). **In re XL Specialty**, 373 S.W.3d at 50, 52. The joint-client privilege can be asserted by parties who are represented by the same attorney in the same matter, while TRE 503(b)(1)(C) requires the parties to have different attorneys. **In re XL Specialty**, 373 S.W.3d at 50, 53. The joint-defense privilege can be asserted only by defendants in pending litigation, but the TRE 503(b)(1)(C) privilege applies to both plaintiffs and defendants. **In re XL Specialty**, 373 S.W.3d at 51–52. The common-interest privilege can be asserted by both litigants and nonlitigants, but the TRE 503(b)(1)(C) privilege applies only to parties to pending litigation. **In re XL Specialty**, 373 S.W.3d at 51–52.*

§3.6 Confidential client information. A client's confidential information is protected from discovery because an attorney is prohibited from knowingly disclosing it. *See* Tex Disciplinary R Prof'l Conduct 1.05(b)(1); **Perez v. Kirk & Carrigan**, 822 S.W.2d 261, 265 n.5 (Tex.App.—Corpus Christi 1991, writ denied). Confidential information includes both privileged and unprivileged information. Tex Disciplinary R Prof'l Conduct 1.05(a). Rule 1.05 expands the privilege from

discovery in TRE 503 to include unprivileged information. An attorney may reveal confidential client information only as permitted under Rule 1.05(b), (c), and (d) and other rules. **Duncan v. Board of Disciplinary Appeals**, 898 S.W.2d 759, 761 (Tex.1995).

Note

Whether an attorney knowingly revealed confidential information in violation of Rule 1.05(b) by e-mailing the confidential information requires a case-by-case analysis. Cmte. on Prof'l Ethics, State Bar of Tex., Op. 648 (2015). Generally, an attorney may communicate confidential information by e-mail. Id. But in certain circumstances (e.g., when the e-mail contains highly sensitive information, when the e-mail is sent to a shared account or could be accessed by a third person, when the e-mail is sent from a borrowed computer), the attorney should consider whether the e-mail should be encrypted or another form of communication should be used to better protect the confidentiality of the information. Id.

§3.7 Accountant-client privilege. Generally, a communication made by a client to an accountant or to a partner, member, officer, shareholder, or employee of the accountant or the accountant's firm in connection with services provided to the client is confidential and not discoverable. Tex. Occ. Code §901.457(a). For information that is discoverable, see "Certain accountant-client communications," ch. 6-B, §2.15. No accountant-client privilege is recognized under federal law. **U.S. v. Arthur Young & Co.**, 465 U.S. 805, 817 (1984).

§3.8 Nondiscoverable consulting expert. Consulting experts are protected from discovery as part of the work-product privilege. *See* Tex. R. Civ. P. 195 cmt. 1 (1999). See "Consulting-only expert," ch. 6-D, §2.2.1.

§3.9 Marital-communications privilege. The purpose of the marital-communications privilege is to preserve the integrity of the marital relationship. Generally, communications between spouses are privileged and not discoverable. Tex. R. Evid. 504. See Brown & Rondon, **Texas Rules of Evidence Handbook**, Rule 504 (2021 ed.). For a list of discoverable matters between spouses, see "Certain marital communications," ch. 6-B, §2.16.

1. Existence of marriage. The person claiming the marital-communications privilege must prove a marriage. *Cf.* **Lara v. State**, 740 S.W.2d 823, 837 (Tex.App.—Houston [1st Dist.] 1987, pet. ref'd) (applying former TRCrE 504; held no common-law marriage).

2. Who may assert. The marital-communications privilege may be asserted by the person who made the statement, her guardian, her personal representative (if she is deceased), or her spouse on her behalf. Tex. R. Evid. 504(a)(3). There is a presumption that one spouse has the authority to assert the privilege on the other spouse's behalf. *Id.*

3. Duration. The marital-communications privilege survives a divorce or the death of one of the spouses. **Wiggins v. Tiller**, 230 S.W. 253, 254 (Tex.App.—San Antonio 1921, no writ).

4. What is protected. The privilege exempts from discovery any spousal communication made privately and not intended for disclosure. Tex. R. Evid. 504(a)(1).

§3.10 Physician-patient privilege. Generally, a confidential communication between a physician and a patient about the professional services rendered by the physician is privileged and not discoverable. Tex. Occ. Code §159.002(a); Tex. R. Evid. 509(c)(1); **Mutter v. Wood**, 744 S.W.2d 600, 600 (Tex.1988); **Kavanaugh v. Perkins**, 838 S.W.2d 616, 621 (Tex.App.—Dallas 1992, orig. proceeding); *see also* Tex. Health & Safety Code §241.152 (hospital must have written authorization to disclose patient's health-care information). For information that is discoverable, see "Certain physician-patient information," ch. 6-B, §2.18. There are two rationales for the physician-patient privilege: (1) to encourage the full communication necessary for effective treatment and (2) to prevent the unnecessary disclosure of a patient's highly personal information. **In re Collins**, 286 S.W.3d 911, 916 (Tex.2009); **R.K. v. Ramirez**, 887 S.W.2d 836, 840 (Tex.1994).

1. Physician. A physician is a person licensed, or who the patient reasonably believes is licensed, to practice medicine in any state or nation. Tex. R. Evid. 509(a)(2).

2. Patient. A patient is any person who consults or is seen by a physician for medical care. Tex. R. Evid. 509(a)(1); *e.g.*, **Tarrant Cty. Hosp. Dist. v. Hughes**, 734 S.W.2d 675, 677 (Tex.App.—Fort Worth 1987, orig. proceeding) (because blood donors were not patients, their identities were not protected by physician-patient privilege). Generally, the physician-patient relationship is voluntary and wholly contractual, created by an express or implied agreement. *E.g.*, **Garay v. County of Bexar**, 810 S.W.2d 760, 764 (Tex.App.—San Antonio 1991, writ denied) (even though person was unconscious, physician-patient relationship was established). But a physician may agree in advance to the creation of a physician-patient relationship, such as when a physician's agreement with a hospital requires the physician to treat all the hospital's patients. **Lection v. Dyll**, 65 S.W.3d 696, 704 (Tex.App.—Dallas 2001, pet. denied); *see* **Hand v. Tavera**, 864 S.W.2d 678, 680 (Tex.App.—San Antonio 1993, no writ) (when patient who is enrolled in prepaid medical plan goes to hospital emergency room and plan's designated doctor is consulted, there is physician-patient relationship).

3. Who may assert. The physician-patient privilege may be asserted by the patient, a representative of the patient, or the physician on the patient's behalf. Tex. R. Evid. 509(d); **Bristol-Myers Squibb Co. v. Hancock**, 921 S.W.2d 917, 920 (Tex.App.—Houston [14th Dist.] 1996, orig. proceeding). There is a presumption that the doctor has the authority to assert the privilege on the patient's behalf. Tex. R. Evid. 509(d).

4. What is protected. The privilege protects from discovery confidential communications made by the patient relating to or in connection with professional services that the physician rendered to the patient and records of the patient's identity, diagnosis, evaluation, or treatment that are created or maintained by a physician. *See* Tex. Occ. Code §159.002(a), (b); Tex. R. Evid. 509(c); *see, e.g.*, **In re Columbia Valley Reg'l Med. Ctr.**, 41 S.W.3d 797, 799 (Tex.App.—Corpus Christi 2001, orig. proceeding) (information about nurse's charting customs was privileged because it related to treatment of patient, and redaction of privileged portions of nonparty's medical records did not make records discoverable).

§3.11 Mental-health-information privilege. Generally, a confidential communication made to a mental-health professional is privileged and not discoverable. Tex. R. Evid. 510(b)(1)(A); **R.K. v. Ramirez**, 887 S.W.2d 836, 839-40 (Tex.1994). For information that is discoverable, see "Certain mental-health information," ch. 6-B, §2.19. There are two rationales for the mental-health-information privilege: (1) to encourage the full communication necessary for effective treatment and (2) to prevent the unnecessary disclosure of a patient's highly personal information. **R.K.**, 887 S.W.2d at 840.

1. Professional. A mental-health professional is (1) a person authorized to practice medicine in any state or nation, (2) a person licensed or certified by Texas in the diagnosis, evaluation, or treatment of mental or emotional disorders, (3) a person involved in the treatment or examination of drug abusers, or (4) a person the patient reasonably believes is in one of the above categories. Tex. R. Evid. 510(a)(1). The definition includes clinical psychologists.

2. Patient. A patient is any person who consults or is seen by a professional to receive diagnosis, evaluation, or treatment of any mental or emotional condition or disorder, including alcoholism and drug addiction, or who is being treated voluntarily for drug abuse. Tex. R. Evid. 510(a)(2).

3. Who may assert. The mental-health-information privilege may be asserted by the patient, a representative of the patient, or the professional on the patient's behalf. Tex. R. Evid. 510(c). There is a presumption that the professional has the authority to assert the privilege on the patient's behalf. *Id.*

4. Duration. The mental-health-information privilege applies regardless of when the professional's services were received. Brown & Rondon, **Texas Rules of Evidence Handbook**, Rule 510 (2021 ed.) (n.731). Confidentiality attaches and continues even if the professional therapeutic relationship has ended or the patient has died. *Id.*

5. What is protected. The privilege protects from discovery communications by the patient and records of the patient's identity, diagnosis, evaluation, and treatment. Tex. R. Evid. 510(b)(1).

§3.12 Other medical privileges. A number of other statutes protect a patient's medical records.

1. Chiropractor records. The communications and records of a chiropractor's patient are confidential and privileged. Tex. Occ. Code §201.402.

2. Podiatrist records. The communications and records of a podiatrist's patient are confidential and privileged. Tex. Occ. Code §202.402.

3. Dentist records. The communications and records of a dentist's patient are privileged. Tex. Occ. Code §258.102.

4. Results of HIV test. The results of a person's HIV test are confidential and cannot be disclosed except as permitted by Health & Safety Code §81.103(b). *See* Tex. Health & Safety Code §81.103(a); **J.K. & Susie L. Wadley Research Inst. & Blood Bank v. Whittington**, 843 S.W.2d 77, 85 (Tex.App.—Dallas 1992, orig. proceeding).

5. Blood-bank records. The medical and donor records of a blood bank are confidential and cannot be disclosed except as permitted under Health & Safety Code chapter 162. Tex. Health & Safety Code §162.003; *see, e.g.*, **Tarrant Cty. Hosp. Dist. v. Curry**, 907 S.W.2d 445, 445–46 (Tex.1995) (donor's birth date was confidential).

6. EMS-patient communications & records. The communications and records of a patient treated by emergency-medical-services personnel or by a physician providing medical supervision are confidential and privileged. Tex. Health & Safety Code §773.091.

7. Hospital patient's privilege. A hospital and its agents or employees cannot disclose health-care information about a patient except as provided in Health & Safety Code §§241.152 and 241.153. For the categories of information that are discoverable from a hospital, see "Certain health-care information from hospital," ch. 6-B, §2.23.

§3.13 Peer-review & medical-committee privileges. Occupations Code §160.007(e) (peer review) and Health & Safety Code §161.032 (medical committee) limit the discovery of documents from medical institutions. In analyzing these two statutory exemptions from discovery, attorneys should read the following Supreme Court cases: **In re Memorial Hermann Hosp. Sys.**, 464 S.W.3d 686, 716–19 (Tex.2015) (discovery requested by doctor); **In re University of Tex. Health Ctr.**, 33 S.W.3d 822, 824–27 (Tex.2000) (discovery requested by third party); **Brownwood Reg'l Hosp. v. Eleventh Ct. of Appeals**, 927 S.W.2d 24, 26–27 (Tex.1996) (same); **Irving Healthcare Sys. v. Brooks**, 927 S.W.2d 12, 16–17 (Tex.1996) (discovery requested by doctor); **Memorial Hosp. v. McCown**, 927 S.W.2d 1, 12 (Tex.1996) (discovery requested by third party).

1. Information exempt from discovery.

(1) Peer-review committee. Peer-review proceedings are confidential, and communications to a peer-review committee are privileged. Tex. Occ. Code §160.007(a). The peer-review privilege in the Occupations Code applies to professional-review actions or medical peer review conducted by a professional-review body or medical-peer-review committee. Tex. Occ. Code §160.001.

(a) Protected entities. The term "medical-peer-review committee" or "professional-review body" means a committee of a health-care entity, of the governing board of a health-care entity, or of the medical staff of a health-care entity that (1) operates under written bylaws approved by the policy-making body or the governing board of the health-care entity and (2) is authorized to evaluate the quality of medical and health-care services or the competence of physicians, including evaluation of the performance of the functions specified by Health & Safety Code §85.204. Tex. Occ. Code §151.002(a)(8); *see* **In re Christus Santa Rosa Health Sys.**, 492 S.W.3d 276, 280 (Tex.2016); **In re Memorial Hermann**, 464 S.W.3d at 698. The functions and activities of a particular committee determine whether it qualifies as a protected entity under Occupations Code §151.002(a)(8). *See* **In re Higby**, 414 S.W.3d 771, 780 (Tex.App.—Houston [1st Dist.] 2013, orig. proceeding). For a list of people and entities included under the term "medical-peer-review committee," see Occupations Code §151.002(a)(8).

(b) Scope of privilege. The peer-review privilege provides that, unless disclosure is required or authorized by law, medical-peer-review records (1) are not subject to subpoena or discovery and (2) are not admissible as evidence in any civil, judicial, or administrative proceeding without a written waiver of the privilege of confidentiality. Tex. Occ. Code §160.007(e); **In re University of Tex. Health Ctr.**, 33 S.W.3d at 827; **Memorial Hosp.**, 927 S.W.2d at 4; *see* **In re Memorial Hermann**, 464 S.W.3d at 699; **Irving Healthcare**, 927 S.W.2d at 16–17. Records, reports, evaluations, and recommendations received, maintained, or developed by a peer-review committee are privileged from discovery. Tex. Occ. Code §160.007(e); *e.g.*, **Brownwood Reg'l**, 927 S.W.2d at 27 (peer-review documents were privileged even though patient sued hospital for malpractice); **Irving Healthcare**, 927 S.W.2d at 16–17 (peer-review documents were privileged even though doctor sued other doctor for maliciously providing false information to peer-review committee); **Memorial Hosp.**, 927 S.W.2d at 4 (peer-review documents were privileged even though media D in libel case sought peer-review documents to

defend itself); *see* **In re Living Ctrs.**, 175 S.W.3d 253, 258 & n.4 (Tex.2005) (peer-review privilege protects the evaluative process, including discussions about future committee operating procedures).

(c) Waiver of privilege. The privilege may be waived in writing by the chair, vice chair, or secretary of the peer-review committee. Tex. Occ. Code §160.007(e); *see* **In re University of Tex. Health Ctr.**, 33 S.W.3d at 827; **Irving Healthcare**, 927 S.W.2d at 16–17.

(2) Medical committee.

(a) Protected entities. The term "medical committee" means any committee of a hospital, medical organization, university medical school or health-science center, HMO, extended-care facility, hospital district, or hospital authority, including ad hoc and joint committees. Tex. Health & Safety Code §161.031(a), (b); *see* **In re Memorial Hermann**, 464 S.W.3d at 716.

(b) Scope of privilege. The medical-committee privilege provides that records and proceedings of medical committees are confidential and are not subject to court subpoena. Tex. Health & Safety Code §161.032(a); **In re University of Tex. Health Ctr.**, 33 S.W.3d at 825; **Memorial Hosp.**, 927 S.W.2d at 8.

Note

Committees of certain entities may qualify as both a medical committee and a peer-review committee, and the records and proceedings of these committees are subject to the confidentiality provisions of both Health & Safety Code §161.032 and Occupations Code §160.007. See ***In re Memorial Hermann**, 464 S.W.3d at 717. A medical committee deemed to also be a medical peer-review committee cannot claim that its records and proceedings are governed only by the confidentiality provisions in Health & Safety Code §161.032 and that the disclosure provisions in Occupations Code §160.007 do not apply. See* ***In re Memorial Hermann**, 464 S.W.3d at 717 & n.162. In* ***In re Memorial Hermann**, the Court held that an exception to confidentiality in Occupations Code §160.007(b) applied to the committee in that case, which was both a medical committee and a medical peer-review committee, because Occupations Code §160.007 is both later-enacted and more specific about when records and proceedings are confidential.* ***In re Memorial Hermann**, 464 S.W.3d at 718–19.*

2. What is not exempt. Not all information reviewed by the committee is exempt from discovery.

(1) Disclosure required by law. Medical-peer-review records are discoverable and admissible into evidence when their disclosure is required or authorized by law. Tex. Occ. Code §160.007(e); **In re University of Tex. Health Ctr.**, 33 S.W.3d at 827; **Memorial Hosp.**, 927 S.W.2d at 4; *see* **Irving Healthcare**, 927 S.W.2d at 16–17. When disclosure is required by law and that disclosure is itself privileged, the privilege is not waived by the disclosure. *See* Tex. Occ. Code §160.007(d) to (g); **In re University of Tex. Health Ctr.**, 33 S.W.3d at 827. When a protected entity responds to discovery with privileged information, that limited waiver does not extend to other privileged information. *See* **In re University of Tex. Health Ctr.**, 33 S.W.3d at 827 (voluntary production of information about committee recommendations does not waive privilege protecting committee documents themselves). For a list of disclosures authorized by law, see Occupations Code §§160.002 and 160.007.

(2) Business records & other documents. The business records of a hospital, HMO, medical organization, university medical center or health-science center, hospital district, hospital authority, or extended-care facility are discoverable. Tex. Health & Safety Code §161.032(f); **Irving Healthcare**, 927 S.W.2d at 18; *see* **Memorial Hosp.**, 927 S.W.2d at 10–11 (business records must be treated the same under Health & Safety Code §161.032 and Occupations Code §160.007); *see, e.g.*, **In re Osteopathic Med. Ctr.**, 16 S.W.3d 881, 886 (Tex.App.—Fort Worth 2000, orig. proceeding) (incident report on slip-and-fall submitted to peer-review committee was discoverable); *see also* Tex. Health & Safety Code §161.032(g) (records from medical committee of university medical school or health-science center, including a joint committee, are discoverable if required by federal law as a condition of receiving federal money). For other exceptions, see chart 6-5, below.

3. Application of exemption. The extent of the exemption from discovery depends on whether the party seeking discovery from the committee is the doctor who was investigated by the committee or a third party, generally the plaintiff in a medical-malpractice suit. See chart 6-5, below.

6-5. Medical-Committee Privileges			
Information sought in discovery		**Is information discoverable by—**	
		Doctor who was investigated?	**Party who sued doctor?**
1	Committee's recommendation and final decision to censure, revoke, suspend, restrict, limit, or deny membership or privileges in health-care entity	Yes. Tex. Occ. Code §160.007(d); **In re Christus Santa Rosa Health**, 492 S.W.3d 276, 281 (Tex.2016); **Irving Healthcare**, 927 S.W.2d 12, 18 (Tex.1996).	No. *See* Tex. Occ. Code §160.007(d), (e); **Irving Healthcare**, 927 S.W.2d at 18.
2	Committee documents relating to peer review, other than those in row 1, above	No. *See* Tex. Occ. Code §160.007(a); Tex. Health & Safety Code §161.032(a); **Irving Healthcare**, 927 S.W.2d at 18.	No. *See* Tex. Occ. Code §160.007(a); Tex. Health & Safety Code §161.032(a); **Irving Healthcare**, 927 S.W.2d at 18.
3	Committee's initial credentialing of doctor	No. **Brownwood Reg'l**, 927 S.W.2d 24, 26–27 (Tex.1996); **Memorial Hosp.**, 927 S.W.2d 1, 11 (Tex.1996); *see* Tex. Health & Safety Code §161.032(a).	No. **Brownwood Reg'l**, 927 S.W.2d at 26–27; **Memorial Hosp.**, 927 S.W.2d at 11; *see* Tex. Health & Safety Code §161.032(a).
4	Committee's minutes of meetings	No. **Brownwood Reg'l**, 927 S.W.2d at 27; **Memorial Hosp.**, 927 S.W.2d at 10; *see* Tex. Health & Safety Code §161.032(a).	No. **Brownwood Reg'l**, 927 S.W.2d at 27; **Memorial Hosp.**, 927 S.W.2d at 10; *see* Tex. Health & Safety Code §161.032(a).
5	Documents created by or at request of committee to evaluate medical care	No. **In re UT Health**, 33 S.W.3d 822, 825 (Tex.2000); *see* **Brownwood Reg'l**, 927 S.W.2d at 27.	No. **In re UT Health**, 33 S.W.3d at 825; *see* **Brownwood Reg'l**, 927 S.W.2d at 27.
6	Documents provided by doctor to committee, including application	Yes. **Irving Healthcare**, 927 S.W.2d at 21.	No. **Irving Healthcare**, 927 S.W.2d at 21.
7	Doctor- or hospital-generated patient medical records in committee's possession	Yes.[1] **Irving Healthcare**, 927 S.W.2d at 18; *see* Tex. Health & Safety Code §161.032(c).	Yes.[1] **Irving Healthcare**, 927 S.W.2d at 18; *see* Tex. Health & Safety Code §161.032(c).
8	Health-care facility's business records in committee's possession	Yes.[2] Tex. Health & Safety Code §161.032(f); **Irving Healthcare**, 927 S.W.2d at 18; **Memorial Hosp.**, 927 S.W.2d at 9.	Yes.[2] Tex. Health & Safety Code §161.032(f); **Irving Healthcare**, 927 S.W.2d at 18; **Memorial Hosp.**, 927 S.W.2d at 9.
9	Documents in public domain reviewed by committee	Yes. **Irving Healthcare**, 927 S.W.2d at 18.	Yes. **Irving Healthcare**, 927 S.W.2d at 18.
10	Committee's documents when doctor waives privilege	No. *See* Tex. Occ. Code §160.007(e); **Irving Healthcare**, 927 S.W.2d at 16–17.	No. *See* Tex. Occ. Code §160.007(e); **Irving Healthcare**, 927 S.W.2d at 16–17.
11	Committee's documents when committee waives privilege in writing	Yes. Tex. Occ. Code §160.007(e); **Irving Healthcare**, 927 S.W.2d at 16–17.	Yes. Tex. Occ. Code §160.007(e); **Irving Healthcare**, 927 S.W.2d at 16–17.
12	Documents provided to committee shared with persons not covered by privilege	Yes.[2] **Irving Healthcare**, 927 S.W.2d at 18.	Yes.[2] **Irving Healthcare**, 927 S.W.2d at 18.
13	Committee's documents sought in anticompetitive actions or in civil-rights suits brought under 42 U.S.C. §1983	Yes. Tex. Occ. Code §160.007(b); **Irving Healthcare**, 927 S.W.2d at 16; *see* **In re Memorial Hermann**, 464 S.W.3d at 700.	Yes. Tex. Occ. Code §160.007(b); **Irving Healthcare**, 927 S.W.2d at 16; *see* **In re Memorial Hermann**, 464 S.W.3d at 700.
14	Bylaws, rules, and regulations of hospital's medical staff or board of trustees	Yes. **Brownwood Reg'l**, 927 S.W.2d at 27; *see* **In re Memorial Hermann**, 464 S.W.3d at 714.	Yes. **Brownwood Reg'l**, 927 S.W.2d at 27; *see* **In re Memorial Hermann**, 464 S.W.3d at 714.

6-5. Medical-Committee Privileges			
Information sought in discovery		Is information discoverable by—	
		Doctor who was investigated?	Party who sued doctor?
15	Deposition of committee member about committee deliberations	No. **Irving Healthcare**, 927 S.W.2d at 18.	No. **Irving Healthcare**, 927 S.W.2d at 18.

[1] The information is discoverable, unless subject to some other privilege (e.g., physician-patient), but must be obtained from some source other than the committee.

[2] The information is discoverable but must be obtained from some source other than the committee.

4. Other peer-review committees. There are a number of other peer-review discovery exemptions that protect records created by peer-review committees of nonphysicians. *E.g.*, Tex. Occ. Code §202.454 (podiatric peer review), §261.051 (dental peer review), §303.006 (nursing peer review).

§3.14 Trade-secret privilege. Generally, a person has a qualified privilege to refuse to disclose and to prevent other persons from disclosing a trade secret that the person owns. Tex. R. Evid. 507(a); **In re Continental Gen. Tire, Inc.**, 979 S.W.2d 609, 610 (Tex.1998); *see also* Tex. R. Civ. P. 76a(2)(c) (court records open to public do not include discovery in cases initiated to preserve bona fide trade secrets). See "Note," ch. 6-B, §2.24; Brown & Rondon, **Texas Rules of Evidence Handbook**, Rule 507 (2021 ed.). For the definition of a trade secret, see "What is a trade secret?," ch. 6-B, §2.24.1.

1. Asserting privilege. To assert the trade-secret privilege, the party resisting discovery must establish that the information is a trade secret. **In re Continental Gen. Tire**, 979 S.W.2d at 613; *e.g.*, **In re Waste Mgmt.**, 392 S.W.3d 861, 870 (Tex.App.—Texarkana 2013, orig. proceeding) (D never established that order compelling disclosure of certain internal business records would disclose trade secrets; merely claiming trade secrets are involved is insufficient). In determining whether information is a trade secret, courts generally consider the following nondispositive factors: (1) the extent to which the information is known outside the business, (2) the extent to which it is known by employees and others involved in the business, (3) the extent of the measures taken to guard the secrecy of the information, (4) the value of the information to the business and to its competitors, (5) the amount of effort or money expended in developing the information, and (6) the ease or difficulty with which the information could be properly acquired or duplicated by others. **In re Union Pac. R.R.**, 294 S.W.3d 589, 592 (Tex.2009); **In re Bass**, 113 S.W.3d 735, 739 (Tex.2003). Once the party resisting discovery has established that the information is a trade secret, the burden shifts to the requesting party to establish that the trade secret should be disclosed. See "When is a trade secret discoverable?," ch. 6-B, §2.24.2. If the requesting party does not meet this burden, the trade-secret privilege applies. *See* **In re Continental Gen. Tire**, 979 S.W.2d at 613; **In re Goodyear Tire & Rubber Co.**, 392 S.W.3d 687, 693 (Tex.App.—Dallas 2010, orig. proceeding).

2. No shielding discoverable documents. Discoverable documents cannot be shielded from discovery by placing them in a file with trade secrets. *See* **Chapa v. Garcia**, 848 S.W.2d 667, 668 (Tex.1992).

§3.15 Privilege against self-incrimination. A person cannot be compelled to give self-incriminating evidence in a criminal proceeding. U.S. Const. amend. 5; Tex. Const. art. 1, §10. A witness (whether a party or a nonparty) has the right to assert the Fifth Amendment privilege to avoid civil discovery if the witness has a reasonable fear that the answers might be incriminating. *See* **Texas DPS Officers Ass'n v. Denton**, 897 S.W.2d 757, 760 (Tex.1995); **Gebhardt v. Gallardo**, 891 S.W.2d 327, 330 (Tex.App.—San Antonio 1995, orig. proceeding). The Fifth Amendment privilege against self-incrimination also applies to document production, as long as the incriminating documents are personally connected to the witness. **In re Speer**, 965 S.W.2d 41, 47 (Tex.App.—Fort Worth 1998, orig. proceeding). That is, the documents must have been written by the witness or under the witness's immediate supervision. *Id.* The person asserting the Fifth Amendment privilege must raise it in response to each specific inquiry, or else the privilege is waived. **Gebhardt**, 891 S.W.2d at 330.

1. Remedial steps & sanctions. If a party refuses on Fifth Amendment grounds to comply with a discovery order, the court should consider remedial steps short of sanctions; if they are not effective, the court can impose graduated levels of sanctions, up to and including death-penalty sanctions. **Denton**, 897 S.W.2d at 759.

2. Adverse impact. There are a number of adverse consequences to invoking the Fifth Amendment in discovery. First, a deposition during which a witness invoked the Fifth Amendment can be read into evidence. **Smith v. Smith**, 720

S.W.2d 586, 594–95 (Tex.App.—Houston [1st Dist.] 1986, no writ). Second, in a civil trial, a party can be forced to invoke the Fifth Amendment in front of a jury. *See* Brown & Rondon, **Texas Rules of Evidence Handbook**, Rule 513 (2021 ed.) (n.986). Third, the jury can be asked to draw an inference against the party who invoked the Fifth Amendment. *See* Tex. R. Evid. 513(c); **Baxter v. Palmigiano**, 425 U.S. 308, 318 (1976); **Wilz v. Flournoy**, 228 S.W.3d 674, 677 (Tex.2007); **In re Edge Capital Grp.**, 161 S.W.3d 764, 769 (Tex.App.—Beaumont 2005, orig. proceeding). Fourth, the party's invocation of the Fifth Amendment may be the subject of comment by the other party. Tex. R. Evid. 513(c).

§3.16 Clergy privilege. Confidential communications are privileged if they are made to a clergy member in the clergy member's professional capacity as spiritual adviser. Tex. R. Evid. 505(b). See Brown & Rondon, **Texas Rules of Evidence Handbook**, Rule 505 (2021 ed.).

1. Clergy member. The term "clergy member" includes a minister, priest, rabbi, accredited Christian Science Practitioner, or other similar functionary of a religious organization, or an individual that a communicant reasonably believes is a clergy member. Tex. R. Evid. 505(a)(1).

2. Communicant. The term "communicant" means a person who consults a clergy member in the clergy member's professional capacity as a spiritual adviser. Tex. R. Evid. 505(a)(2).

3. Who may assert. The clergy privilege may be asserted by the communicant, her guardian or conservator, her personal representative (if she is deceased), or the clergy member on the communicant's behalf. Tex. R. Evid. 505(c). The clergy member to whom the communication was made is presumed to have authority to assert the privilege on the communicant's behalf. *Id.*

4. What is protected. The privilege protects confidential communications made privately and not intended for further disclosure except to other people present in furtherance of the purpose of the communication. Tex. R. Evid. 505(a)(3); *see, e.g.*, **Nicholson v. Wittig**, 832 S.W.2d 681, 685 (Tex.App.—Houston [1st Dist.] 1992, orig. proceeding) (clergy privilege includes all conversations with hospital chaplain, even secular ones conducted when other people are present). The clergy privilege may protect the identity of the communicant. **Simpson v. Tennant**, 871 S.W.2d 301, 306 (Tex.App.—Houston [14th Dist.] 1994, orig. proceeding).

§3.17 ADR privilege. Generally, any communication about the subject matter of a dispute made by any participant in an alternative-dispute-resolution procedure is confidential and not discoverable. See "Confidentiality," ch. 4-A, §7.

§3.18 Journalist's privilege. Generally, information obtained by a journalist is privileged and not discoverable. *See* Tex. Civ. Prac. & Rem. Code §22.023. The rationale for the journalist's privilege is to (1) increase the free flow of information, (2) preserve a free and active press, and (3) protect the public's right to effective law enforcement and the fair administration of justice. Tex. Civ. Prac. & Rem. Code §22.022. For a discussion of when information from a journalist is discoverable, see "Certain information in journalist's possession," ch. 6-B, §2.26.

1. Who is protected.

(1) Journalist. A journalist is protected from being compelled to disclose information. Tex. Civ. Prac. & Rem. Code §22.023(a). The term "journalist" is defined as the following:

(a) A person or a parent, subsidiary, division, or affiliate of a person who "gathers, compiles, prepares, collects, photographs, records, writes, edits, reports, investigates, processes, or publishes" information that is disseminated by a news medium (see "News medium," ch. 6-B, §3.18.1(2)(a)) or communication-service provider (see "Communication-service provider," ch. 6-B, §3.18.1(2)(b)) for a substantial portion of her livelihood or for substantial financial gain. Tex. Civ. Prac. & Rem. Code §22.021(2).

(b) A person who supervises or assists in gathering, preparing, and disseminating information. Tex. Civ. Prac. & Rem. Code §22.021(2)(A).

(c) A journalist, scholar, or researcher employed by an institution of higher education at the time she obtained or prepared the information. Tex. Civ. Prac. & Rem. Code §22.021(2)(B).

(d) A person who at the time she obtained or prepared the information (1) earned a significant portion of her livelihood by obtaining or preparing information for dissemination by a news medium or communication-service provider or (2) was an agent, assistant, employee, or supervisor of a news medium or communication-service provider. *Id.*

(2) News medium or communication-service provider. A news medium or communication-service provider is protected from being compelled to disclose information. Tex. Civ. Prac. & Rem. Code §22.023(b).

(a) News medium. A news medium is an entity that disseminates news or information to the public through print, television, radio, or photographic, mechanical, electronic, or other means that are accessible to the public. Tex. Civ. Prac. & Rem. Code §22.021(3). A news medium includes the following: (1) a newspaper, magazine, or periodical, (2) a book publisher, (3) a news agency, (4) a wire service, (5) a radio or television station or network, (6) a cable, satellite, or other transmission system, carrier, or channel, (7) a channel or programming service for a station, network, system, or carrier, (8) an audio or audiovisual production company, (9) an Internet company or provider, or (10) a parent, subsidiary, division, or affiliate of such an entity. *Id.*

(b) Communication-service provider. A communication-service provider is a person or a parent, subsidiary, division, or affiliate of a person who transmits information chosen by a customer through electronic means. Tex. Civ. Prac. & Rem. Code §22.021(1). A communication-service provider includes the following: (1) a telecommunications carrier, (2) an information-service provider, (3) an interactive-computer-service provider, and (4) an information-content provider. *Id.*; *see also* 47 U.S.C. §153 (defining telecommunications carrier and information-service provider), §230(f) (defining interactive-computer-service provider and information-content provider).

2. What is protected. The privilege protects (1) any information, document, or item—regardless of its confidentiality—obtained or prepared while acting as a journalist and (2) the source of any such information, document, or item. Tex. Civ. Prac. & Rem. Code §22.023.

3. When privilege applies. The privilege applies during an official proceeding before a public servant. *See* Tex. Civ. Prac. & Rem. Code §§22.021(4), 22.023(a).

(1) Official proceeding. An official proceeding is any administrative, executive, legislative, or judicial proceeding, including presuit depositions and arbitrations. *See* Tex. Civ. Prac. & Rem. Code §22.021(4), (5)(C).

(2) Public servant. A public servant is a person elected, selected, appointed, employed, or designated as one of the following, even if the person has not qualified for office or begun her duties: (1) a government officer, employee, or agent, (2) a juror, (3) an arbitrator, referee, or other person authorized by law or a written agreement to hear or decide a controversy, (4) an attorney or notary public performing a governmental function, or (5) a person performing a governmental function under a claim of right, although not legally qualified to do so. Tex. Civ. Prac. & Rem. Code §22.021(5).

4. No waiver. Publication or dissemination of the privileged information by a news medium or communication-service provider does not waive the journalist's privilege. Tex. Civ. Prac. & Rem. Code §22.026.

§3.19 Political vote. No person can be forced to disclose her vote in a political election conducted by secret ballot, unless the vote was cast illegally. Tex. R. Evid. 506. A person who casts an illegal vote does not have a privilege to refuse to disclose the vote; an illegal voter is not considered a "voter" for any purpose. **Oliphint v. Christy**, 299 S.W.2d 933, 939 (Tex.1957); **Simmons v. Jones**, 838 S.W.2d 298, 300 (Tex.App.—El Paso 1992, no writ).

§3.20 Reports required by law. Any person or entity required by law to make a report has a privilege to refuse to disclose the contents of the report if the law requiring the report permits the person to refuse to disclose it. Tex. R. Evid. 502(a). The purpose of this privilege is to enhance the government's ability to obtain self-reporting information. The rule protects reports "required by law to be made" if the law requiring the report to be made makes such a report privileged. *See, e.g.*, **Star-Telegram, Inc. v. Schattman**, 784 S.W.2d 109, 111 (Tex.App.—Fort Worth 1990, orig. proceeding) (because EEOC sexual-harassment guidelines in 29 C.F.R. §1604.11 do not require a report, internal investigation was not exempt from discovery under TRE 502).

§3.21 Social Security information. The Social Security Act provides that information obtained by the Secretary of Health and Human Services or the Secretary of Labor or any employee of either must not be disclosed, except as provided by

regulation. 42 U.S.C. §1306(a). The statute does not say who can assert the privilege or how it is waived. **Texas Empls. Ins. v. Jackson**, 719 S.W.2d 245, 247 (Tex.App.—El Paso 1986, writ ref'd n.r.e.).

§3.22 Law-enforcement privilege.

Note

In 2007, the Legislature enacted CPRC §30.006, which is similar to Gov't Code §552.108. The bill analysis for CPRC §30.006 does not mention the Government Code section or indicate which section should apply when the sections overlap. See Senate Cmte. on State Affairs, Bill Analysis, Tex. H.B. 1572, 80th Leg., R.S. (2007).

1. Under Government Code.

(1) Information about crime. Information about detection, investigation, or prosecution of a crime and records or notations maintained for internal use in matters relating to law enforcement or prosecution are not discoverable if the law-enforcement agency or prosecutor can show any of the following:

(a) The release of information would interfere with the detection, investigation, or prosecution of a crime, or the release of internal records or notations would interfere with law enforcement or prosecution. Tex. Gov't Code §552.108(a)(1) (release of information), §552.108(b)(1) (release of internal records or notations).

(b) The information relates only to an investigation that did not result in conviction or deferred adjudication. Tex. Gov't Code §552.108(a)(2), (b)(2).

(c) The information relates to a threat against a peace officer or detention officer that was collected or distributed under Gov't Code §411.048. Tex. Gov't Code §552.108(a)(3).

(d) The information was prepared by an attorney for the State in anticipation of or in the course of preparing for criminal litigation. Tex. Gov't Code §552.108(a)(4)(A), (b)(3)(A). In a criminal prosecution, the work-product privilege extends only to a litigation file that is still active. *See, e.g.*, **State v. Walker**, 873 S.W.2d 379, 380 n.1 (Tex.1994) (case still active when Ds received deferred adjudication and probation).

(e) The information reflects the mental impressions or legal reasoning of an attorney representing the State. Tex. Gov't Code §552.108(a)(4)(B), (b)(3)(B). See "Work-product privilege," ch. 6-B, §3.3.

(2) Exception. Basic information about an arrested person, an arrest, or a crime is considered public information and is discoverable. Tex. Gov't Code §552.108(c). Although "basic information" is not defined in the Government Code, courts have held that it includes the arrestee's name, alias, Social Security number, race, sex, age, occupation, physical condition, name of arresting officer, and the charge, as well as a detailed description of the offense. **Thomas v. Cornyn**, 71 S.W.3d 473, 479 (Tex.App.—Austin 2002, no pet.).

2. Under CPRC.

(1) Information about crime. Information, records, documents, evidentiary materials, and tangible things from a nonparty law-enforcement agency are not discoverable if both of the following are shown:

(a) The information, records, documents, evidentiary materials, or tangible things deal with (1) the detection, investigation, or prosecution of a crime or (2) an investigation by the nonparty law-enforcement agency that does not result in conviction or deferred adjudication. Tex. Civ. Prac. & Rem. Code §30.006(c)(1).

(b) The release of the information, records, documents, evidentiary materials, or tangible things would interfere with the detection, investigation, or prosecution of criminal acts. Tex. Civ. Prac. & Rem. Code §30.006(c)(2).

(2) Exceptions.

(a) By motion. On a party's motion, a court can order discovery of information, records, documents, evidentiary materials, or tangible things from a nonparty law-enforcement agency if the court determines, after an in camera inspection, that (1) the discovery sought is relevant and (2) there is a specific need for the discovery. Tex. Civ. Prac. & Rem. Code §30.006(d).

(b) By law. CPRC §30.006 does not apply to (1) actions in which a law-enforcement agency is a party, (2) a report of an accident under Transportation Code chapter 550, or (3) photographs, field measurements, scene drawings, and accident reconstruction done in conjunction with the investigation of the underlying accident. Tex. Civ. Prac. & Rem. Code §30.006(b), (e).

§3.23 Identity of informant. The United States, Texas, and their political subdivisions have the privilege to refuse to disclose the identity of a person who has provided information about an investigation of a possible violation of the law. Tex. R. Evid. 508(a); *see* **Roviaro v. U.S.**, 353 U.S. 53, 59–60 (1957); *see also* **State v. Lowry**, 802 S.W.2d 669, 673 (Tex.1991) (discussing informant and investigative privileges). For discoverable information about an informant, see "Certain information about informant," ch. 6-B, §2.25.

§3.24 Religious sermons. A written copy or audio or video recording of a sermon delivered by a religious leader during religious worship of a religious organization is privileged from discovery by a governmental entity in any civil or administrative proceeding in which the governmental entity is a party. Tex. Civ. Prac. & Rem. Code §150A.002.

§3.25 Disclosure of membership list. The First Amendment protects the right of association, which in turn protects from discovery the membership list of an organization engaged in the advocacy of particular beliefs. **NAACP v. Alabama**, 357 U.S. 449, 462–63 (1958); **Ex parte Lowe**, 887 S.W.2d 1, 2 (Tex.1994). Before a court can order disclosure of the membership list of an organization engaged in the advocacy of particular beliefs, the party seeking the list must show a compelling state interest. **Ex parte Lowe**, 887 S.W.2d at 3; **Tilton v. Moyé**, 869 S.W.2d 955, 956 (Tex.1994); *see* **Martin v. Khoury**, 843 S.W.2d 163, 167 (Tex.App.—Texarkana 1992, orig. proceeding).

§3.26 Environmental-audit privilege. The Texas Environmental, Health & Safety Audit Privilege Act creates a documentary privilege for environmental audits and assessments conducted at real-property operations and facilities in Texas. *See* Tex. Health & Safety Code §1101.101. The privilege can be waived only by the owner or operator of the land. *See* Tex. Health & Safety Code §1101.103(a). See the "Voluntary Environmental Self-Policing & Self-Disclosure Interim Policy Statement," Environmental Protection Agency's policy statement on audit privileges, "Voluntary Environmental Self-Policing & Self-Disclosure Interim Policy Statement," 60 Fed. Reg. 16875 (4-3-95).

§3.27 Public Information Act. If documents or other information are privileged or confidential under "other law," they are excepted from disclosure under the Public Information Act (formerly known as the Open Records Act). *See* Tex. Gov't Code §§552.022, 552.101; **Texas DPS v. Cox Tex. Newspapers, L.P.**, 343 S.W.3d 112, 114 & n.4 (Tex.2011); **In re City of Georgetown**, 53 S.W.3d 328, 331–32 (Tex.2001). "Other law" includes statutes other than Gov't Code chapter 552, judicial decisions, and rules promulgated by the judiciary (e.g., the TRCPs and TREs). **Texas DPS**, 343 S.W.3d at 114; **In re City of Georgetown**, 53 S.W.3d at 332.

Note

A governmental entity asserting an exception to disclosure under the Public Information Act must request a ruling from the Attorney General within ten business days after receiving a request for the information. Tex. Gov't Code §552.301(b); ***Paxton v. City of Dallas****, 509 S.W.3d 247, 252 (Tex.2017). If the governmental entity's request is untimely, the information must be released unless there is a compelling reason to withhold it. Tex. Gov't Code §552.302;* ***City of Houston v. Houston Mun. Empls. Pension Sys.****, 549 S.W.3d 566, 585 (Tex.2018);* ***Paxton****, 509 S.W.3d at 252. The attorney-client privilege is a compelling reason for withholding information, and missing the deadline in Gov't Code §552.301 does not, by itself, waive the attorney-client privilege.* ***Paxton****, 509 S.W.3d at 261, 264; see also* ***City of Dallas v. Abbott****, 304 S.W.3d 380, 381 (Tex.2010) (city's request to Attorney General for ruling affirming exception to public-disclosure requirement was timely under Gov't Code §552.301; attorney-client privilege protected documents from public disclosure).*

§3.28 Legislative privilege. People acting in a legislative capacity generally cannot be compelled to testify about their legislative activities. **In re Perry**, 60 S.W.3d 857, 860 (Tex.2001).

§3.29 Privileges of foreign jurisdictions. When the laws of a foreign jurisdiction protect relevant information from discovery, the court must balance the interest of the Texas court with that of the foreign nation. **Volkswagen, A.G. v. Valdez**, 909 S.W.2d 900, 902 (Tex.1995). The court must weigh the following factors: (1) the importance of the discovery request to the investigation or litigation, (2) the degree of specificity of the request, (3) whether the information originated in the United States, (4) the availability of alternative means of securing the information, and (5) the extent to which noncompliance with the request would undermine important interests of the United States, or the extent to which compliance would undermine important interests of the foreign jurisdiction where the information is located. *Id.*; *see* Restatement Fourth, Foreign Relations Law of the United States §426, comment a.

C. Electronic Discovery

§1. General

§1.1 Rules. Tex. R. Civ. P. 192.3(b), 196.4.

§1.2 Purpose. Electronic discovery (or e-discovery) involves the process of identifying, locating, preserving, collecting, preparing, reviewing, and producing discoverable information that is stored in electronic, magnetic, or digital form. *See* Sedona Conference, *Sedona Conference Glossary: eDiscovery & Digital Information Management (Fifth Edition)*, 21 Sedona Conf.J. 263, 303 (2020), thesedonaconference.org/publications. Electronic discovery requires, at the very least, an understanding of (1) the systems for creating, storing, and reading electronic data, (2) the methods for preserving electronic data, (3) the methods for searching, identifying, and producing relevant electronic data, and (4) the traditional discovery methods for obtaining and producing electronic data and the evidentiary implications of those methods. Unfortunately, the TRCPs and the CPRC do not provide a comprehensive scheme for electronic discovery. Although the 1999 amendments to TRCP 196.4 provided some guidelines on discovering and producing "electronic or magnetic data," the TRCPs remain silent on many (and often costly) issues involving electronic discovery and the means for resolving electronic-discovery disputes.

Note

The TRCPs were amended in 1999 and the FRCPs were amended in 2006 to include specific rules on electronic discovery. Federal cases construing the FRCPs provide some guidance on electronic-discovery issues, but the TRCPs and FRCPs differ in several substantive ways. For a discussion of federal electronic-discovery rules, see "Electronic Discovery," ***O'Connor's Federal Rules * Civil Trials****, ch. 6-C, §1 et seq. (2021 ed.). Although there are fewer reported Texas cases that address electronic discovery, the opinions in* ***In re State Farm Lloyds****, 520 S.W.3d 595 (Tex.2017), and* ***In re Weekley Homes, L.P.****, 295 S.W.3d 309 (Tex.2009), detail the scope of electronic discovery and set out an extensive procedure for requesting production of electronic information. See "Scope of electronic discovery," ch. 6-C, §6; "Requests for production," ch. 6-C, §7.1.5.*

---

§1.3 Forms. **O'Connor's Texas Civil Forms**, FORM 2A:1 (2020 ed.) (preservation letter), **O'Connor's Texas Civil Forms**, FORM 6A:1 (2020 ed.) (Rule 11 agreed preservation plan), **O'Connor's Texas Civil Forms**, FORM 6A:10 (2020 ed.) (motion for protection from discovery), **O'Connor's Texas Civil Forms**, FORM 6A:24 (2020 ed.) (motion to compel); **O'Connor's Federal Civil Forms**, FORM 6A:3 (2020 ed.) (stipulated preservation plan and order), **O'Connor's Texas Civil Forms**, FORM 6A:4 (2020 ed.) (stipulated discovery plan and order).

§1.4 Other references.

1. Sedona Conference.

- Sedona Conference, *Sedona Conference Glossary: eDiscovery & Digital Information Management (Fifth Edition)*, 21 Sedona Conf.J. 263 (2020), thesedonaconference.org/publications (referred to as Sedona Conference, *Sedona Conference Glossary*).

- Sedona Conference, *Sedona Conference Commentary on Legal Holds, Second Edition: The Trigger & the Process*, 20 Sedona Conf.J. 341 (2019), thesedonaconference.org/publications (referred to as Sedona Conference, *Commentary on Legal Holds*).

- Sedona Conference, *Sedona Conference Principles, Third Edition: Best Practices, Recommendations & Principles for Addressing Electronic Document Production*, 19 Sedona Conf.J. 1 (2018), thesedonaconference.org/publications (referred to as Sedona Conference, *Sedona Principles, Third Edition*).

- Sedona Conference, *Sedona Conference Guidance for the Selection of Electronic Discovery Providers*, 18 Sedona Conf.J. 55 (2017), thesedonaconference.org/publications (referred to as Sedona Conference, *Selection of Electronic Discovery Providers*).

• Sedona Conference, *Sedona Conference TAR Case Law Primer*, 18 Sedona Conf.J. 1 (2017), thesedonaconference.org/publications (referred to as Sedona Conference, *TAR Case Law Primer*).

• Sedona Conference, *Sedona Conference "Jumpstart Outline": Questions to Ask Your Client & Your Adversary to Prepare for Preservation, Rule 26 Obligations, Court Conferences & Requests for Production* (2016), thesedonaconference.org/publications (referred to as Sedona Conference, *Jumpstart Outline*).

• Sedona Conference, *Sedona Conference Best Practices Commentary on the Use of Search & Information Retrieval Methods in E-Discovery*, 15 Sedona Conf.J. 217 (2014), thesedonaconference.org/publications (referred to as Sedona Conference, *Commentary on Search & Retrieval*).

2. Standards & guidelines.

• Hedges et al., *Managing Discovery of Electronic Information*, Federal Judicial Center (3d ed. 2017), www.fjc.gov/publications.

• Lau & Lee, *Technology-Assisted Review for Discovery Requests: A Pocket Guide for Judges* (2017), Federal Judicial Center, www.fjc.gov/publications (referred to as Lau & Lee, *Technology-Assisted Review for Discovery Requests*).

• National Conference of Commissioners on Uniform State Laws, *Uniform Rules Relating to the Discovery of Electronically Stored Information* (2007), uniformlaws.org/home (referred to as NCCUSL, *Uniform Rules*).

• Conference of Chief Justices, *Guidelines for State Trial Courts Regarding Discovery of Electronically-Stored Information* (2006), ncsc.contentdm.oclc.org/digital/collection/civil/id/56 (referred to as Conference of Chief Justices, *Guidelines for State Trial Courts*).

3. Additional references.

• Facciola & Favro, *Safeguarding the Seed Set: Why Seed Set Documents May Be Entitled to Work Product Protection*, Fed.Cts.L.Rev. (2015), www.fclr.org (referred to as Facciola & Favro, *Safeguarding the Seed Set*).

• Frazier, *4 Strategies to Reduce eDiscovery Review Costs*, Tex. Lawyer (8-12-15).

• Auttonberry, Comment, *Predictive Coding: Taking the Devil out of the Details*, 74 La.L.Rev. 613 (2014), digitalcommons.law.lsu.edu/lalrev/vol74/iss2/13.

• Hampton, *Predictive Coding: It's Here to Stay* (2014), www.skadden.com/insights/publications/2014/06/predictive-coding-its-here-to-stay.

• Browning, *Burn After Reading: Preservation & Spoliation of Evidence in the Age of Facebook*, 16 SMU Sci. & Tech.L.Rev. 273 (2013) (referred to as Browning, *Preservation & Spoliation*).

• Grossman & Cormack, *Grossman-Cormack Glossary of Technology-Assisted Review*, Fed.Cts.L.Rev. (2013), www.fclr.org (referred to as Grossman & Cormack, *Grossman-Cormack Glossary*).

• Fuchs & Wolinsky, *Understand Predictive Coding Options*, Tex. Lawyer (9-3-12).

• Equivio, *Top 10 Best Practices in Predictive Coding* (2012), www.equivio.com (search by article title) (referred to as Equivio, *Top 10 Best Practices*).

• Shah, *Use of "Predictive Coding" to Limit Cost & Improve Efficiency in Healthcare E-discovery: The Light Is Green, but Proceed with Caution* (2012), www.ebglaw.com/content/uploads/2014/06/48548_Shah-AHLA-Use-of-Predictive-Coding-1-2012.pdf (referred to as Shah, *Use of "Predictive Coding" to Limit Cost & Improve Efficiency*).

• Peck, *Search, Forward: Will Manual Document Review & Keyword Searches Be Replaced by Computer-Assisted Coding?* (2011), law.duke.edu/sites/default/files/centers/judicialstudies/TAR_conference/Panel_1-Background_Paper.pdf (referred to as Peck, *Search, Forward*).

- Ball, *E-Discovery: A Special Master's Perspective*, 51 The Advoc. (Texas) 42 (Summer 2010) (referred to as Ball, *A Special Master's Perspective*).
- Hecht, *Taking Point on E-Discovery: Texas Rule of Civil Procedure 196.4*, 51 The Advoc. (Texas) 18 (Summer 2010) (referred to as Hecht, *Taking Point on E-Discovery*).
- Raymond, *Tackling E-Discovery on a Budget*, 51 The Advoc. (Texas) 50 (Summer 2010).
- Ball, *The Perfect Preservation Letter* (2006), www.craigball.com/perfect%20preservation%20letter.pdf.

4. ***O'Connor's* books.** **O'Connor's Federal Rules * Civil Trials** (2021 ed.).

§2. Understanding electronic discovery

§2.1 Electronic information. Electronic information is any type of information that is created, stored, or retrieved and processed in electronic, magnetic, or digital form. *See* Conference of Chief Justices, *Guidelines for State Trial Courts*, at 1. It is distinct from information stored only on paper, film, or other nonelectronic media. *See* NCCUSL, *Uniform Rules*, Rule 1 cmt. Electronic information is subject to discovery just like conventional documents and tangible things. *See* Tex. R. Civ. P. 192 cmt. 2 (things relevant to the subject matter of the suit are within the scope of discovery regardless of their form); *see also* Tex. R. Civ. P. 196.4 (to discover information that is in electronic or magnetic form, party must specifically request production of electronic or magnetic data and specify form of production).

Note

The TRCPs use the term "electronic or magnetic data." Tex. R. Civ. P. 196.4. The FRCPs use the term "electronically stored information," typically referred to as "ESI." See, e.g., Fed. R. Civ. P. 26(b)(2)(B). There is no substantive difference between the terms. In this subchapter, the terms "electronic data," "electronic information," and "electronically stored information" are used interchangeably.

---

1. **Types of information.** Electronic information includes the following: (1) databases, (2) data files, (3) program files, (4) image files (e.g., JPEG, TIFF), (5) e-mail messages and files, (6) voicemail messages and files, (7) text messages, (8) temporary files, (9) system-history files, (10) deleted files, programs, or e-mails, (11) backup files and archival tapes, (12) website files, (13) website information stored in textual, graphical, or audio format, (14) cache files, and (15) cookies. *See* **In re Weekley Homes, L.P.**, 295 S.W.3d 309, 314 (Tex.2009); **Super Film v. UCB Films, Inc.**, 219 F.R.D. 649, 657 (D.Kan.2004); **Thompson v. U.S. Dept. of Hous. & Urban Dev.**, 219 F.R.D. 93, 96 (D.Md.2003). See "What is ESI?," **O'Connor's Federal Rules * Civil Trials**, ch. 6-C, §2 (2021 ed.).

2. **Sources of information.** Electronic information can be located in many places, including the following: (1) mainframe computers, (2) network servers, (3) Internet ("web") servers, (4) desktop and laptop computers, (5) hard drives, (6) flash drives, which include "thumb" drives, secure digital cards, and other flash memory cards, (7) e-mail servers, (8) handheld devices like personal digital assistants (PDAs) and portable media players (PMPs) (e.g., MP4 players, Internet tablets like iPads), (9) cell phones and smart phones (e.g., iPhones, BlackBerrys, Android devices), (10) smart watches, (11) event recorders in cars, trucks, and trains, (12) medical devices, (13) global positioning system (GPS) devices, and (14) the "cloud." *See* **In re Seroquel Prods. Liab. Litig.**, 244 F.R.D. 650, 654 (M.D.Fla.2007); Sedona Conference, *Commentary on Search & Retrieval*, 15 Sedona Conf.J. at 226; Conference of Chief Justices, *Guidelines for State Trial Courts*, at v.

§2.2 Definitions. To understand electronic discovery, a party must become familiar with the terminology. The definitions provided here are important for a basic understanding of electronic discovery, but the list is not intended to be comprehensive. For more electronic-discovery terms, see Sedona Conference, *Sedona Conference Glossary*.

1. **Active data.** "Active data" is data that is currently being created, received, or processed or that needs to be accessed frequently and quickly. Hedges, *Managing Discovery of Electronic Information*, at 21. Active data is usually immediately accessible and does not have to be restored or reconstructed. Sedona Conference, *Sedona Conference Glossary*, 21 Sedona Conf.J. at 266.

2. Archival data. "Archival data" is data maintained for long-term storage and record-keeping purposes. Sedona Conference, *Sedona Conference Glossary*, 21 Sedona Conf.J. at 269. Archival data may not be immediately accessible. *Id.*

3. Backup data. "Backup data" is a copy of electronically stored information that serves as a source for the recovery of the data in the event of a system problem or other computer disaster. Sedona Conference, *Sedona Conference Glossary*, 21 Sedona Conf.J. at 272. Backup data is often stored on magnetic backup tapes or removable disk drives. Hedges, *Managing Discovery of Electronic Information*, at 49–50; *see* Sedona Conference, *Sedona Conference Glossary*, 21 Sedona Conf.J. at 272 ("backup tape" entry). Because information found on backup tapes must be restored, recovery can involve substantial expense. *See* Hedges, *Managing Discovery of Electronic Information*, at 5.

4. Backup-tape recycling. "Backup-tape recycling" (also called "backup-tape rotation") is the process by which backup tapes are overwritten with new data, usually on a fixed schedule. Sedona Conference, *Sedona Conference Glossary*, 21 Sedona Conf.J. at 272.

5. Deleted data. "Deleted data" is data that once existed on a computer as active data but has been deleted by the computer system or a user. Hedges, *Managing Discovery of Electronic Information*, at 51; *see* Sedona Conference, *Sedona Conference Glossary*, 21 Sedona Conf.J. at 294. Generally, deletion does not actually erase the data from the computer; rather, deletion makes the data inaccessible with normal software but leaves it on the computer. *See* Sedona Conference, *Sedona Conference Glossary*, 21 Sedona Conf.J. at 294; Hedges, *Managing Discovery of Electronic Information*, at 5. Deleted data can remain on the computer until it is overwritten or "wiped." Sedona Conference, *Sedona Conference Glossary*, 21 Sedona Conf.J. at 294. Recovery of deleted data is difficult, expensive, and sometimes incomplete.

6. Forensic copy. A "forensic copy" (also known as a forensic duplicate, forensic image, mirror image, or bit-by-bit duplicate) is an exact copy of the entire physical storage media. *See* Sedona Conference, *Sedona Conference Glossary*, 21 Sedona Conf.J. at 312.

7. Forensics. "Forensics" is the scientific examination and analysis of data stored on or retrieved from a computer in such a way that the information can be used as evidence in court. Sedona Conference, *Sedona Conference Glossary*, 21 Sedona Conf.J. at 312. Forensics may involve recreating deleted or missing files from hard drives, validating dates and logged-in editors of documents, and certifying key elements of documents or hardware for legal purposes. *Id.*

8. Form of production. "Form of production" is the manner in which requested electronic information is produced. *See* Sedona Conference, *Sedona Conference Glossary*, 21 Sedona Conf.J. at 313. Electronic information can be produced in a variety of forms and formats. Hedges, *Managing Discovery of Electronic Information*, at 31. See "Format," ch. 6-C, §2.3.3. The form of production determines whether the information can be electronically searched, whether relevant information is obscured, and whether confidential or privileged information is disclosed, and how the information can be used in later stages of the litigation. Hedges, *Managing Discovery of Electronic Information*, at 31–32.

9. Hard drive. "Hard drive" is a computer's storage device that has components on which data can be written and erased magnetically. Sedona Conference, *Sedona Conference Glossary*, 21 Sedona Conf.J. at 316.

10. Information governance. "Information governance" (IG) is an organization's coordinated, inter-disciplinary approach to satisfying information compliance requirements and managing information risks while optimizing value. Sedona Conference, *Sedona Principles, Third Edition*, 19 Sedona Conf.J. at 59. Among other things, IG encompasses and seeks to reconcile retention, privacy, and preservation requirements. *Id.* at 59–60. An organization is not required to maintain an IG program, but having a comprehensive IG program allows an organization to more efficiently search for, identify, and produce information. *Id.* at 60–61.

11. Legacy data. "Legacy data" is data that was created and stored with software or hardware that has become obsolete or has been replaced. Hedges, *Managing Discovery of Electronic Information*, at 53. Legacy data may be expensive to recover and produce. *Id.*; *see* Sedona Conference, *Sedona Conference Glossary*, 21 Sedona Conf.J. at 330.

12. Metadata. "Metadata" is information describing the history, tracking, or management of an electronic file. **In re Weekley Homes, L.P.**, 295 S.W.3d 309, 320 n.9 (Tex.2009); **In re Honza**, 242 S.W.3d 578, 580 n.4 (Tex.App.—Waco 2008, orig. proceeding); *see* Sedona Conference, *Sedona Conference Glossary*, 21 Sedona Conf.J. at 337 (metadata is structural

information of file rather than content of file). It is commonly described as "data about data" and it can describe how, when, and by whom the electronic information was collected, created, assessed, or modified and how it was formatted. *See* **In re State Farm Lloyds**, 520 S.W.3d 595, 601 (Tex.2017); Hedges, *Managing Discovery of Electronic Information*, at 53. Some metadata can be seen by users, while other metadata is hidden or embedded and not visible. Hedges, *Managing Discovery of Electronic Information*, at 53; *see* **In re State Farm**, 520 S.W.3d at 601 (metadata does not normally appear on the printed page); Sedona Conference, *Sedona Principles, Third Edition*, 19 Sedona Conf.J. at 169 (metadata can include formatting codes, formulas, and other information associated with file). Examples of metadata include a file's name, author, and creation date, its edit history, and comments. Sedona Conference, *Sedona Principles, Third Edition*, 19 Sedona Conf.J. at 210 App. B. Metadata can be not only important to the usability and searchability of electronic information but also relevant to the merits of the case. *See id.* at 169–70. Depending on the facts and needs of a case, a particular piece of metadata may be critical or completely irrelevant. *Id.* at 170. See "Metadata," ch. 6-C, §7.1.5(1)(a)[4]. There are various types of metadata; two in particular are embedded and file-system metadata.

(1) Embedded metadata. "Embedded metadata" (also called "application metadata") includes commands that control or manipulate data, such as computational formulas in spreadsheets or formatting commands in a word-processing document. Hedges, *Managing Discovery of Electronic Information*, at 51 ("embedded data" entry); *see* Sedona Conference, *Sedona Principles, Third Edition*, 19 Sedona Conf.J. at 169–70, 210 App. B. This type of metadata is embedded in the file it describes and moves with the file when the file is copied or moved. Sedona Conference, *Sedona Principles, Third Edition*, 19 Sedona Conf.J. at 170, 211 App. B. Embedded metadata instructs the computer how to display the document (e.g., fonts, spacing, sizing, color) and reflects modifications such as prior edits or editorial comments. *Id.* at 170, 210 App. B; *see* Hedges, *Managing Discovery of Electronic Information*, at 51.

(2) File-system metadata. "File-system metadata" (also called "system-generated metadata" or "system metadata") is information about a file that is created and applied by a computer process or application or by the file's user (e.g., a file's title, location, creation date, and modification dates). *See* Sedona Conference, *Sedona Principles, Third Edition*, 19 Sedona Conf.J. at 170; Sedona Conference, *Sedona Conference Glossary*, 21 Sedona Conf.J. at 377, 385 ("system-generated metadata" and "user created metadata" entries). File-system metadata is typically stored externally on a party's information-management system; it is not embedded in the file. Sedona Conference, *Sedona Principles, Third Edition*, 19 Sedona Conf.J. at 170, 211 App. B.

13. Mirror imaging. "Mirror imaging" (also known as forensic imaging, forensic copying, forensic duplication, or bit-by-bit duplication) is the creation of an exact copy of a computer hard drive or other physical storage media. *See* Sedona Conference, *Sedona Conference Glossary*, 21 Sedona Conf.J. at 312, 339 ("forensic copy" and "mirror image" entries).

14. Native format. "Native format" is the form in which electronic information is originally created and normally used (e.g., Microsoft Excel produces native files with a .xls extension; older versions of Microsoft Word produce native files with a .doc extension). *See* **In re State Farm**, 520 S.W.3d at 601; Sedona Conference, *Sedona Conference Glossary*, 21 Sedona Conf.J. at 340; Hedges, *Managing Discovery of Electronic Information*, at 32. Information in native format may contain "user-created data" that may not be apparent on the face of the document when printed, such as formulas and comments in spreadsheets, speaker notes in presentation files, or tracked changes in word-processing files. Sedona Conference, *Sedona Principles, Third Edition*, 19 Sedona Conf.J. at 170–71. This data may be stored in a variety of ways within a native file format. *Id.* at 171.

15. Near-line data. "Near-line data" is electronic information that is not actively available but is available through an automated system that retrieves removable storage media or tapes. Sedona Conference, *Sedona Conference Glossary*, 21 Sedona Conf.J. at 342 ("near-line data storage" entry).

16. Offline storage. "Offline storage" is removable-disk or magnetic-tape media that can be labeled and stored on a shelf. **Zubulake v. UBS Warburg LLC**, 217 F.R.D. 309, 319 (S.D.N.Y.2003). Offline storage is generally used to make disaster-recovery copies of electronic records. *Id.* Access to offline storage requires manual action and takes longer than active or near-line data. *Id.*

17. Optical character recognition. "Optical character recognition" (OCR) is a technology process that captures text from an image to create a parallel text file that can be associated with the image and searched in a database. Sedona Conference, *Sedona Conference Glossary*, 21 Sedona Conf.J. at 346. OCR software evaluates scanned data for shapes it recognizes as letters or numerals. *Id.*

18. Static format. "Static format" (also called "imaged format") is a format used to retain an image of an electronic document as it would appear in its original program or application. Sedona Conference, *Sedona Conference Glossary*, 21 Sedona Conf.J. at 340 ("native format" entry). In static format, the information cannot be manipulated and metadata cannot be viewed. *Id.*; *see* **In re State Farm**, 520 S.W.3d at 601. Static format may be searchable to a limited extent, however, using OCR. **In re State Farm**, 520 S.W.3d at 601. See "Optical character recognition," ch. 6-C, §2.2.17. Examples of static formats include PDF, TIFF, and JPEG. **In re State Farm**, 520 S.W.3d at 601.

(1) PDF. PDF (portable document format) is a file format that preserves formatting information (e.g., margins, spacing, fonts) from the original software program so that the information can be viewed and printed as it was intended to be seen, regardless of whether the viewer has access to the software used to create it. *See* Sedona Conference, *Sedona Conference Glossary*, 21 Sedona Conf.J. at 353; Hedges, *Managing Discovery of Electronic Information*, at 54.

(2) TIFF. TIFF (tagged image file format) is a file format for storing images, including photographs. *See* Sedona Conference, *Sedona Conference Glossary*, 21 Sedona Conf.J. at 377. The images can be black-and-white, grayscale, or color. *Id.*

(3) JPEG. JPEG (joint photographic experts group) is a file format for storing images, usually high-quality digital photographs. *See* Sedona Conference, *Sedona Conference Glossary*, 21 Sedona Conf.J. at 328.

19. Systems data. "Systems data" is a computer's records about its use, such as when users logged on or off a computer or network, what passwords they used, what websites they visited, and what documents they printed or faxed. Conference of Chief Justices, *Guidelines for State Trial Courts*, at vi; *see* Hedges, *Managing Discovery of Electronic Information*, at 21. Systems data may be more remote and more costly to produce than active data. Hedges, *Managing Discovery of Electronic Information*, at 21.

§2.3 Electronic discovery vs. conventional discovery. Although electronic discovery and conventional discovery involve the same procedural methods (e.g., requests for production), the process of electronic discovery is much more complicated. For example, in conventional discovery, an attorney does not have to worry about what type of filing system the other party uses (e.g., a filing cabinet), but in electronic discovery, she does. Significant differences between electronic and conventional information affect how discovery is conducted, but the general discovery rules in the TRCPs apply to electronic information when not otherwise specified.

1. Volume. Most information today is stored in some sort of digital or electronic format, and the volume of electronic information that is created and distributed within and among organizations is growing exponentially. *See* Sedona Conference, *Sedona Principles, Third Edition*, 19 Sedona Conf.J. at 59. In fact, electronic information is now so pervasive that in most cases its volume dwarfs that of any paper-based information. *Id.* at 56; *see* Hedges, *Managing Discovery of Electronic Information*, at 3.

2. Locations. Electronic information can be stored in many different locations. See "Sources of information," ch. 6-C, §2.1.2. For example, one draft of an electronic document may be located on the drafter's, reviewer's, and recipient's hard drives, on the company's and other network servers, on a laptop or home computer, and on backup tapes. Hedges, *Managing Discovery of Electronic Information*, at 3.

3. Format. The format in which electronic information is created, stored, and produced differs from that of conventional information in the following ways:

(1) Some digital transactions create no permanent documents in any form and are stored in databases that do not allow for any corresponding hard-copy materials. *See* Hedges, *Managing Discovery of Electronic Information*, at 4; Conference of Chief Justices, *Guidelines for State Trial Courts*, at vi.

(2) Some electronic information depends on the system that created it and is incomprehensible and unusable when separated from the system. Sedona Conference, *Sedona Principles, Third Edition*, 19 Sedona Conf.J. at 212 App. B; Hedges, *Managing Discovery of Electronic Information*, at 4.

(3) Electronic information can be produced for discovery in a variety of forms and formats, including the following:

(a) Static format (e.g., a TIFF or PDF file—essentially a photograph of a document). *See* Sedona Conference, *Sedona Conference Glossary*, 21 Sedona Conf.J. at 353, 377; Hedges, *Managing Discovery of Electronic Information*, at 32. See "Static format," ch. 6-C, §2.2.18; "Static format," ch. 6-C, §7.1.5(1)(a)[2].

(b) Native format—the form in which it was created and used in the normal course of business. Hedges, *Managing Discovery of Electronic Information*, at 32; *see* Sedona Conference, *Sedona Conference Glossary*, 21 Sedona Conf.J. at 340. See "Native format," ch. 6-C, §2.2.14; "Native format," ch. 6-C, §7.1.5(1)(a)[1].

(c) "TIFF, Text, and Load Files" (TIFF+)—a combination of a static electronic image (e.g., a TIFF file), a text file containing extracted text from the document, and one or more separate load files containing selected metadata. Sedona Conference, *Sedona Principles, Third Edition*, 19 Sedona Conf.J. at 172. See "TIFF+ format," ch. 6-C, §7.1.5(1)(a)[3].

4. Complexity. Electronic information is complex in the way it is created, maintained, and stored. *See* Sedona Conference, *Commentary on Search & Retrieval*, 15 Sedona Conf.J. at 226. For example, even routine discovery requests can require searches of and retrieval from numerous storage devices, such as servers, networked workstations, desktop computers, laptops, home computers, removable media, handheld devices, and the "cloud." *Id.* Electronic discovery is further complicated by the fact that electronic information almost always flows through a "network" in which it has likely been replicated, distributed, modified, linked, attached, accessed, backed up, overwritten, deleted, undeleted, fragmented, defragmented, morphed, and multiplied. *Id.*

5. Indestructibility. Deletion of electronic information does not necessarily get rid of the information (as shredding a paper document does). Hedges, *Managing Discovery of Electronic Information*, at 5. See "Deleted data," ch. 6-C, §2.2.5.

6. Dynamic nature. Information stored in a static medium like paper does not change. Electronic data, however, is dynamic; it changes every time a user saves a file, loads new software, turns off a computer, or performs other everyday functions. *See* Sedona Conference, *Sedona Principles, Third Edition*, 19 Sedona Conf.J. at 209 App. B. Thus, as part of ordinary computer operations, electronic information is routinely altered, overwritten, or erased. *See* Sedona Conference, *Commentary on Search & Retrieval*, 15 Sedona Conf.J. at 226. As a result, normal computer use creates a risk that a party may unintentionally lose potentially discoverable information. *See* 2006 Adv. Cmte. Notes to Fed. R. Civ. P. 37 at ¶1, **O'Connor's Federal Rules * Civil Trials**, Appendix V (2021 ed.).

7. Costs. The cost to a responding party of locating, reviewing, and preparing electronic information for production is generally much greater than it is for conventional discovery. Conference of Chief Justices, *Guidelines for State Trial Courts*, at vi. *See generally* Raymond, *Tackling E-Discovery on a Budget* (explaining how to lower the high costs of e-discovery). The cost of restoring backup tapes, for example, is much higher than the cost of making documents available for the requesting party to review. *See* Conference of Chief Justices, *Guidelines for State Trial Courts*, at vi. Recovery or retrieval of electronic information may also require the added cost of outside experts or forensic examiners. *Id.*

8. Preservation. Because electronic information is easily altered or destroyed in ways that conventional information is not, electronic information presents unique problems when there is a duty to preserve evidence. See "Preservation," ch. 6-C, §3.2.

§3. Preparing for electronic discovery

A party should prepare for electronic discovery even before litigation begins. *See* Sedona Conference, *Sedona Principles, Third Edition*, 19 Sedona Conf.J. at 98-99. Once suit has been filed, the attorney must plan for how electronic information will be discovered and produced. *See* Hedges, *Managing Discovery of Electronic Information*, at 5-6 (judge should encourage parties to identify potential problems with discovery of electronic information in earliest stages of litigation).

§3.1 Learn about parties' systems. In preparing for electronic discovery, an attorney should learn about the types of systems the parties use to create, store, and retrieve electronic information. *See* **In re Weekley Homes, L.P.**, 295 S.W.3d 309, 321–22 (Tex.2009); Conference of Chief Justices, *Guidelines for State Trial Courts*, at 1. The attorney must be familiar with how the parties regularly use computers and must understand what information is available, how routine computer operations may change it, and what is involved in producing it. This knowledge will allow the attorney to instruct the client

about specific preservation and production responsibilities and to properly structure discovery requests tailored to the opposing party's electronic systems. *See* Sedona Conference, *Jumpstart Outline*, at 2. The attorney should consider gathering information on the following when preparing for electronic discovery:

1. Any document-retention policies. *See id.* at 5-6; Ball, *A Special Master's Perspective*, 51 The Advoc. (Texas) at 44.

2. Any people with potentially relevant information about the client's computer or e-mail systems. *See* Sedona Conference, *Jumpstart Outline*, at 8. The attorney should identify the people who know the most about the client's computer systems and meet with them well before the pretrial conference. Hedges, *Managing Discovery of Electronic Information*, at 13. It may also be helpful to have those people present at the conference. *Id.* See "Schedule pretrial meeting or conference," ch. 6-C, §4.

3. Any current or former databases, e-mail systems, and file servers on the parties' networks that store or have stored electronic information, as well as any information stored outside the parties' own networks (e.g., web-based e-mail). *See* Sedona Conference, *Jumpstart Outline*, at 8–10; Ball, *A Special Master's Perspective*, 51 The Advoc (Texas) at 43–44. The attorney should focus on whether (1) the system backs up information and allows for selective restoration of files and (2) content is regularly overwritten, reformatted, or otherwise destroyed. *See* Sedona Conference, *Jumpstart Outline*, at 12–13; Ball, *A Special Master's Perspective*, 51 The Advoc. (Texas) at 44.

4. Any hard drives in company and noncompany desktop or laptop computers. *See* Sedona Conference, *Jumpstart Outline*, at 10–11. The attorney should focus on the parties' policies for (1) backing up the hard drives, (2) erasing or reformatting the hard drives, and (3) saving files and e-mails to the hard drives. *See id.* at 10–13.

§3.2 Preservation. In preparing for electronic discovery, a party should give all other potential parties notice to keep them from altering or destroying relevant evidence. See "Spoliation," ch. 6-A, §24. Preservation of electronically stored evidence is particularly challenging because information stored on computer systems is dynamic by nature. See "Dynamic nature," ch. 6-C, §2.3.6. To ensure that relevant evidence, including not only electronic information but also documents and tangible things, is preserved, a party should take certain steps. The preservation steps should be reasonable and proportional to the needs of the case. Hedges, *Managing Discovery of Electronic Information*, at 40; *see* Sedona Conference, *Commentary on Legal Holds*, 20 Sedona Conf.J. at 355. See "Proportional," ch. 6-C, §6.1.2.

1. Identify source of duty to preserve. A party should identify sources that impose a duty to preserve evidence. Although the TRCPs themselves do not impose this duty, it can arise from many other sources, including the common law, statutes and regulations, and a court order or the parties' agreement. The source of the duty to preserve evidence should be cited in any request to preserve that evidence.

(1) Common law.

(a) When duty arises. A party's duty to preserve electronic evidence under common law arises when suit is brought or when litigation is reasonably foreseeable—that is, when there is a reasonable anticipation of or an investigation into litigation. Sedona Conference, *Sedona Principles, Third Edition*, 19 Sedona Conf.J. at 93. See "When duty arises," ch. 6-A, §3.1.1. When a duty to preserve arises can often be ambiguous, however, and may depend on the specific circumstances of the case. *See* Sedona Conference, *Commentary on Legal Holds*, 20 Sedona Conf.J. at 354–55, 381–82 (guidance for determining "trigger" date of duty to preserve).

(b) What information must be preserved. A party's duty to preserve electronic evidence is similar to that for traditional paper-based evidence—namely, parties have a duty to preserve information they know is relevant to potential or ongoing litigation. *See* **Brookshire Bros. v. Aldridge**, 438 S.W.3d 9, 20 (Tex.2014); **Wal-Mart Stores v. Johnson**, 106 S.W.3d 718, 722 (Tex.2003). See "Scope of duty," ch. 6-A, §3.1.2; "Scope of electronic discovery," ch. 6-C, §6. But a party needs to preserve only unique instances of relevant electronic information, not multiple or duplicative copies of the same information. Sedona Conference, *Sedona Principles, Third Edition*, 19 Sedona Conf.J. at 94.

(2) Independent requirement. A party may be required to preserve evidence based on an independent requirement, which can come from many sources, including statutes, administrative regulations, an order in another case,

or a party's own electronic-information retention protocols. See "Statutory, regulatory & ethical duties," ch. 6-A, §3.2; "Independent requirement," **O'Connor's Federal Rules * Civil Trials**, ch. 6-C, §4.2.1(2) (2021 ed.).

(3) Court order or parties' agreement. A party may be required to preserve evidence based on a court order or the parties' agreement. See "Agreements & stipulations," ch. 6-C, §4.2; "Court order or parties' agreement," **O'Connor's Federal Rules * Civil Trials**, ch. 6-C, §4.2.1(3) (2021 ed.).

2. Communicate duty.

(1) Persons to receive notice.

(a) Parties. Once a duty to preserve evidence arises, all parties should be given notice of the need to preserve information that is relevant to the claims and defenses and proportional to the needs of the case. Sedona Conference, *Sedona Principles, Third Edition*, 19 Sedona Conf.J. at 104; *see* **Zubulake v. UBS Warburg LLC**, 220 F.R.D. 212, 216 (S.D.N.Y.2003). See "Spoliation," ch. 6-A, §24; "Scope of electronic discovery," ch. 6-C, §6. Without some form of notice, the court is unlikely to be sympathetic to a party's complaint about the destruction of evidence by its adversary. *See, e.g.*, **Chidichimo v. University of Chi. Press**, 681 N.E.2d 107, 110 (Ill.App.Ct.1997) (because P did not take reasonable steps to give notice of suit and ensure preservation and protection against routine destruction of data, court found no duty to preserve relevant computer records; reasonable person in D's position would not have foreseen that data would be material to potential suit).

(b) Nonparties. A party may need to give notice to nonparties, such as cloud service providers, data-processing contractors, and vendors. Sedona Conference, *Sedona Principles, Third Edition*, 19 Sedona Conf.J. at 143; *see* Hedges, *Managing Discovery of Electronic Information*, at 29–30. These nonparties may not be aware of the suit or of any potential obligation they may have to preserve electronic information associated with the suit. Sedona Conference, *Sedona Principles, Third Edition*, 19 Sedona Conf.J. at 143.

(2) Preservation letter. To ensure that all appropriate persons have notice and are aware of electronic-discovery intentions, a letter should be sent to each of them outlining the type of information to be preserved. *See* **Cache La Poudre Feeds, LLC v. Land O'Lakes, Inc.**, 244 F.R.D. 614, 623 (D.Colo.2007) (because of dynamic nature of electronic information, attorneys should address preservation issues in demand letters sent to potential adverse parties); *see also* Browning, *Preservation & Spoliation*, 16 SMU Sci. & Tech.L.Rev. at 278 (parties can address preservation of social media through preservation letters sent before or with formal discovery requests). A preservation letter usually (1) describes the potential litigation and the parties involved, (2) asks the recipient to suspend any document-destruction policy, (3) reminds the recipient of the duty to preserve all information relevant to the suit, (4) identifies the specific documents, electronic information, and tangible things that should be preserved, and (5) provides instructions on how to preserve those items. *See* Ball, *The Perfect Preservation Letter*, at 6–8. See **O'Connor's Texas Civil Forms**, FORM 2A:1 (2020 ed.). This initial preservation letter is vital, not only to protect relevant data but also to enable the court to impose sanctions on parties who destroy or modify electronic information after receiving notice of its relevance. See "Spoliation," ch. 6-A, §24; "Sanctions for lost ESI," **O'Connor's Federal Rules * Civil Trials**, ch. 6-C, §12 (2021 ed.).

Practice Tip

When requesting that an opposing party preserve electronic information, follow up on the preservation letter by having opposing counsel agree to the preservation in writing. See "Agreements & stipulations," ch. 6-C, §4.2; ***O'Connor's Texas Civil Forms**, FORM 6A:1 (2020 ed.).*

---

3. Preserve own evidence—litigation hold. Once a duty to preserve evidence arises, a party should suspend its document-retention policy and put a "litigation hold" (also called a "legal hold") in place to ensure that relevant electronic information is preserved. **Zubulake**, 220 F.R.D. at 218; *see* Hedges, *Managing Discovery of Electronic Information*, at 5 (dynamic nature of electronically stored information makes it vital that litigant or potential litigant institute litigation hold whenever litigation is reasonably anticipated). A litigation hold suspends the normal disposition or processing of records. Sedona Conference, *Sedona Conference Glossary*, 21 Sedona Conf.J. at 330 ("legal hold" entry). An effective litigation hold

requires a party to (1) identify and preserve relevant electronic information, (2) give written notice of the hold to the employees most likely to have relevant information, clearly identifying the information that must be preserved and specifying how it must be kept, (3) review and amend the litigation hold as necessary, and (4) monitor compliance with the litigation hold. *See* Sedona Conference, *Sedona Principles, Third Edition*, 19 Sedona Conf.J. at 105–06; Sedona Conference, *Commentary on Legal Holds*, 20 Sedona Conf.J. at 355–58. A party should consider making a mirror image of its computer system at the time the duty to preserve arises. **Zubulake**, 220 F.R.D. at 218.

Note

In an influential opinion, a federal court imposed specific responsibilities on attorneys representing parties who are under a duty to preserve electronic information. ***Zubulake v. UBS Warburg LLC***, *229 F.R.D. 422, 433–34 (S.D.N.Y.2004). Under* ***Zubulake***, *an attorney should (1) understand the client's document-retention policies and related computer systems, (2) issue a litigation hold and reissue it periodically, (3) monitor compliance with the litigation hold, (4) speak directly to "key players" about the preservation duty, (5) tell all employees to produce electronic copies of their relevant active electronic files, and (6) identify all backup media that must be preserved and make sure it is safely stored. Id. at 432–34; see also* ***Chin v. Port Auth. of N.Y. & N.J.***, *685 F.3d 135, 162 (2d Cir.2012) (failure to adopt sound preservation policies is factor courts can consider when determining whether discovery sanctions are appropriate). See "Zubulake steps,"* ***O'Connor's Federal Rules * Civil Trials***, *ch. 6-C, §4.2.3(1) (2021 ed.). No Texas court has specifically addressed these same duties of parties or attorneys to preserve electronic information.*

§3.3 Electronic-discovery provider. In preparing for electronic discovery, a party—and anyone else who has a vested interest in the process and outcome—should evaluate and define the need for an electronic-discovery provider. *See* Sedona Conference, *Selection of Electronic Discovery Providers*, 18 Sedona Conf.J. at 67–68. An electronic-discovery provider includes but is not limited to an organization that offers services, software, solutions, or a combination of these things. *Id.* at 60 n.1. An electronic-discovery provider may be necessary to assess a technological solution (e.g., licensing or acquiring an appropriate software solution or e-discovery tool), to assist with transactional needs (e.g., preserving, collecting, recovering, or producing electronic data, performing complex searching and tagging), or both. *Id.* at 67–68. Issues to consider when evaluating and selecting an electronic-discovery provider include the volume of electronic information, the type of matter involved (e.g., investigation, litigation, third-party subpoena), the type and source of the electronic information, proportionality-analysis considerations, any potential international-discovery considerations, and time constraints. *Id.* at 62–63. For a detailed discussion of finding and selecting an appropriate electronic-discovery provider, see Sedona Conference, *Selection of Electronic Discovery Providers*. Generally, once the need for an electronic-discovery provider has been defined, a party should do the following:

1. Scope the project. To successfully match the right services to the party's business needs, the party must thoroughly "scope" the business requirements of the project—that is, clearly define the parameters of the work for which the party is seeking a solution. Sedona Conference, *Selection of Electronic Discovery Providers*, 18 Sedona Conf.J. at 74.

2. Collect information about providers. To collect information about potential providers, the party should seek out referrals, attend and participate in associations and conferences, and make use of publicly available resources such as industry websites, blogs, magazines, and surveys. Sedona Conference, *Selection of Electronic Discovery Providers*, 18 Sedona Conf.J. at 79–80.

3. Develop short list of providers. To develop a short list of potential providers—that is, a smaller group of strong candidates to focus attention on—the party should request specific information from each provider that helps the party determine such aspects as the provider's stability, quality, infrastructure, process, and security, as well as the quality and experience of the provider's personnel. *See* Sedona Conference, *Selection of Electronic Discovery Providers*, 18 Sedona Conf.J. at 82.

4. Draft information request & evaluate responses. To help in selecting a provider from the short list of potential providers, the party should draft a final, case-specific information request that includes assumptions all potential

providers should use and provide a form response in a spreadsheet. *See* Sedona Conference, *Selection of Electronic Discovery Providers*, 18 Sedona Conf.J. at 66, 106. The party should then evaluate the responses by using a scoring sheet or decision matrix where each item in the information request is assigned a level of importance specific to the project and then each provider response is given a grade or number that assesses the sufficiency of the response. *Id.* at 115.

5. Communicate selection & contract with selected provider. To secure the selected provider, the party should communicate that selection to the provider and enter into a contract with the provider that contains provisions like liability, indemnity, confidentiality, and insurance, among other terms. Sedona Conference, *Selection of Electronic Discovery Providers*, 18 Sedona Conf.J. at 116–17.

§3.4 Inadvertent disclosure of privileged information. In preparing for electronic discovery, a party should develop a plan to reduce the risks of inadvertently disclosing privileged electronic information. Because of the volume of information that may be subject to a discovery request and the time necessary to screen it, discovery of electronic information carries an increased risk of inadvertent disclosure of privileged information. NCCUSL, *Uniform Rules*, Rule 9 cmt. There is, however, a general presumption against waiver. *See* Tex. R. Civ. P. 193.3(d). A party who produces information without intending to waive a claim of privilege does not waive that claim if, within ten days (or a shorter time ordered by the court) after learning of the inadvertent production, the party amends its response, identifying the information produced and stating the privilege asserted. *Id.* See "Use snap-back provision," ch. 6-A, §18.2.4.

§3.5 Costs. In preparing for electronic discovery, a party should consider the costs of electronic discovery and any potential for sharing or shifting those costs. Electronic data is voluminous and can be stored in many locations, some of which are difficult to access. Thus, the cost of locating requested electronic information, screening it, and preparing it for production can be much higher than the cost of conventional discovery. *See* Hedges, *Managing Discovery of Electronic Information*, at 26. See "Costs," ch. 6-I, §3.3.4.

1. Responding party's burden. Generally, the responding party bears the cost of producing electronic discovery. Tex. R. Civ. P. 196.6. If the trial court orders the responding party to comply with a request over the party's objection that it cannot, through reasonable efforts, retrieve or produce the information requested, the court must order the requesting party to pay the reasonable expenses of any extraordinary steps required to retrieve and produce the information. Tex. R. Civ. P. 196.4; *see* **In re Weekley Homes, L.P.**, 295 S.W.3d 309, 316 (Tex.2009). See "Response," ch. 6-C, §7.1.5(2).

2. Requesting party's burden. The requesting party must bear the cost of inspecting, sampling, testing, photographing, or copying electronic data. Tex. R. Civ. P. 196.6.

§4. Schedule pretrial meeting or conference

If an attorney anticipates that electronic discovery will be an issue in the case, she should consider requesting a Rule 11 agreement or a pretrial conference to discuss the issues and develop an electronic-discovery plan. *See* Tex. R. Civ. P. 11 (agreements between attorneys), Tex. R. Civ. P. 166(p) (at pretrial conference, court can consider any matter that will aid in disposition of suit); **In re Weekley Homes, L.P.**, 295 S.W.3d 309, 321 (Tex.2009) (before requesting electronic information, parties should share information and try to agree on protocols for electronic discovery); Sedona Conference, *Sedona Principles, Third Edition*, 19 Sedona Conf.J. at 71 (as soon as practicable, parties should confer and seek to reach agreement about preservation and production of electronic information); Hedges, *Managing Discovery of Electronic Information*, at 9 (parties should meet and confer in earliest stages of suit and try to agree on electronic-discovery issues); *see, e.g.*, **MRT, Inc. v. Vounckx**, 299 S.W.3d 500, 508 (Tex.App.—Dallas 2009, no pet.) (parties did not discuss their electronic-information systems and had different expectations about what the discovery requests meant, resulting in multiple discovery motions); *cf.* Fed. R. Civ. P. 26(f)(3)(C) (parties must meet early in litigation process, confer on issues about disclosure or discovery of electronically stored information, and develop a discovery plan). See "Agreements between attorneys—Rule 11," ch. 1-H, §9; "Initiating pretrial conference," ch. 5-A, §2.2.

Practice Tip

Although there is no requirement under Texas law that parties meet to discuss electronic-discovery matters, the parties should still meet informally to formulate a specific request for electronic information and to resolve any discovery disputes. See ***In re State Farm Lloyds****, 520 S.W.3d 595, 606 (Tex.2017);* ***In re Weekley Homes****, 295 S.W.3d at 322; Hecht, Taking Point on E-Discovery, 51 The Advoc. (Texas) at 19. Because the party requesting electronic information may have to pay the reasonable expense of any extraordinary steps that the responding party must take to retrieve and produce the information, the requesting party should meet and collaborate with the responding party to address all possible methods of production and to avoid any unnecessary expenses. See* ***In re State Farm****, 520 S.W.3d at 608 & n.44. See "Costs," ch. 6-C, §3.5; "Extraordinary steps," ch. 6-C, §7.1.5(1)(c). If more information is needed after the informal meeting, a party should obtain it through discovery or a pretrial conference with the court. Hecht, Taking Point on E-Discovery, 51 The Advoc. (Texas) at 19. A party should not wait until a hearing on a motion to compel to make a specific request. Id.*

§4.1 Issues to discuss. The parties should consider discussing the following issues:

1. The scope of relevance as defined by the claims and defenses. Sedona Conference, *Sedona Principles, Third Edition*, 19 Sedona Conf.J. at 72. See "Types of information," ch. 6-C, §2.1.1.

2. The sources and locations of electronic information that will be subject to preservation and discovery. *See* Sedona Conference, *Sedona Principles, Third Edition*, 19 Sedona Conf.J. at 72; Hedges, *Managing Discovery of Electronic Information*, at 11; Conference of Chief Justices, *Guidelines for State Trial Courts*, at 2–3. See "Sources of information," ch. 6-C, §2.1.2. The parties should also consider how to conduct searches for relevant electronic information in those sources. See "Search techniques for electronic information," ch. 6-C, §5.

3. The relevant time period for producing the electronic information. *See* Sedona Conference, *Sedona Principles, Third Edition*, 19 Sedona Conf.J. at 72.

4. The identities of people who know about the parties' computer systems and custodians of electronic information. *See id.*; Hedges, *Managing Discovery of Electronic Information*, at 12; Conference of Chief Justices, *Guidelines for State Trial Courts*, at 2. See "Disclosures," ch. 6-C, §7.1.1.

5. The form or forms of preservation and production of electronic information and the associated costs. *See* Sedona Conference, *Sedona Principles, Third Edition*, 19 Sedona Conf.J. at 72; Hedges, *Managing Discovery of Electronic Information*, at 12; Conference of Chief Justices, *Guidelines for State Trial Courts*, at 3. See "Costs," ch. 6-C, §3.5; "Form of production," ch. 6-C, §7.1.5(1)(a).

6. The types of metadata to be preserved and possibly produced. Sedona Conference, *Sedona Principles, Third Edition*, 19 Sedona Conf.J. at 72. See "Metadata," ch. 6-C, §2.2.12; "Metadata," ch. 6-C, §7.1.5(1)(a)[4].

7. The identification of any sources of information that are not reasonably available because of undue burden or cost. Sedona Conference, *Sedona Principles, Third Edition*, 19 Sedona Conf.J. at 72. See "Is electronic information reasonably available?," ch. 6-C, §6.2.

8. The potential use of search technology and other methods of reducing the volume of electronic information to be preserved or produced. Sedona Conference, *Sedona Principles, Third Edition*, 19 Sedona Conf.J. at 72. See "Search techniques for electronic information," ch. 6-C, §5.

9. Issues related to assertions of privilege and inadvertent production of privileged documents. Sedona Conference, *Sedona Principles, Third Edition*, 19 Sedona Conf.J. at 72. See "Inadvertent disclosure of privileged information," ch. 6-C, §3.4.

10. Issues related to confidential or private information that may require special treatment or protection during or after production. Sedona Conference, *Sedona Principles, Third Edition*, 19 Sedona Conf.J. at 72

§4.2 Agreements & stipulations. Parties and their attorneys are expected to cooperate in discovery and to make any agreements that are reasonably necessary for the efficient disposition of the case. Tex. R. Civ. P. 191.2; **In re Weekley Homes, L.P.**, 295 S.W.3d 309, 321 (Tex.2009); **In re BP Prods. N. Am., Inc.**, 244 S.W.3d 840, 847–48 (Tex.2008). An agreement of the parties is enforceable if it complies with TRCP 11. Tex. R. Civ. P. 191.1; **In re BP Prods.**, 244 S.W.3d at 845. If the parties meet informally, they should incorporate their discovery plan into a Rule 11 agreement. See "Agreements between attorneys—Rule 11," ch. 1-H, §9; "Rule 11," ch. 6-A, §6.1.1; **O'Connor's Federal Civil Forms**, FORM 6A:4 (2020 ed.).

§5. Search techniques for electronic information

The parties should consider how to conduct searches to locate electronic information within sources identified as likely to contain relevant material (e.g., an e-mail database). *See* Hedges, *Managing Discovery of Electronic Information*, at 34. Aside from traditional manual review of electronic information, the parties can consider several different search techniques. *See id.* at 35.

Practice Tip

If the parties intend to use a new or complex search technique, they should consider having a representative from the electronic-discovery vendor that will perform the searches attend any conferences or hearings that address the search technique. See, e.g., ***Da Silva Moore v. Publicis Groupe****, 287 F.R.D. 182, 193 (S.D.N.Y.2012) (court stated that it was "very helpful" when vendors were present and spoke at hearing about protocol involving predictive coding), adopted by No. 11 Civ. 1279 (ALC) (AJP), 2012 WL 1446534 (S.D.N.Y.2012) (slip op.; 4-26-12).*

---

§5.1 Keyword searches. The parties can consider keyword searches to locate relevant electronic information. *See* **Victor Stanley, Inc. v. Creative Pipe, Inc.**, 250 F.R.D. 251, 260 (D.Md.2008); Lau & Lee, *Technology-Assisted Review for Discovery Requests*, at 2–3. A keyword search involves a specified word or combination of words. *See* Sedona Conference, *Sedona Conference Glossary*, 21 Sedona Conf.J. at 329 ("keyword" entry). Keyword searches are currently the most common search technique used to cull an entire set of electronic information. Sedona Conference, *Commentary on Search & Retrieval*, 15 Sedona Conf.J. at 231; *see* **Da Silva Moore v. Publicis Groupe**, 287 F.R.D. 182, 190 (S.D.N.Y.2012), *adopted by* No. 11 Civ. 1279 (ALC) (AJP), 2012 WL 1446534 (S.D.N.Y.2012) (slip op.; 4-26-12).

1. Process. The process of using keyword searches usually includes the following steps: (1) attorneys develop a list of keywords, (2) the list of keywords is applied to all the electronic information, and (3) the parties manually review only the electronic information that contains the keywords. *See* **Da Silva Moore**, 287 F.R.D. at 190–91. Especially in cases involving a high volume of electronic information, keyword searches may be necessary to narrow the amount of electronic information because traditional manual review of all the electronic information is virtually impossible. *See id.* at 190; Sedona Conference, *Commentary on Search & Retrieval*, 15 Sedona Conf.J. at 232. To improve the effectiveness of keyword searches, the parties can consider seeking expert assistance to create an effective list of keywords. *See* **Victor Stanley, Inc.**, 250 F.R.D. at 262. See "Electronic-discovery provider," ch. 6-C, §3.3. To enhance keyword searches, the parties can use more advanced search techniques such as Boolean connectors, elimination of duplicate documents, grouping of "near duplicates," and threading e-mail chains. *See* Peck, *Search, Forward*, at 26.

Note

Generally, a trial court should not be involved in managing how a party performs keyword searches of its electronic information for documents responsive to a discovery request. ***In re Master Flo Valve Inc.****, 485 S.W.3d 207, 220 (Tex.App.—Houston [14th Dist.] 2016, orig. proceeding). In* ***In re Master Flo Valve****, the court analogized an order requiring the defendant to conduct certain keyword searches to the inspection of a defendant's computer hard drive ordered in* ***In re Weekley Homes, L.P.****, 295 S.W.3d 309 (Tex.2009), because both orders intruded on the producing party's right to develop its own means of searching for responsive documents.* ***In re Master Flo Valve****, 485 S.W.3d at 219–20. The*

court used the test from ***In re Weekley Homes*** *as guidance and held that a trial court should not issue an order directing a party to conduct certain keyword searches unless the party has failed to adequately search for responsive documents.* ***In re Master Flo Valve,*** *485 S.W.3d at 219–20. See "Accessing hard drive," ch. 6-C, §8.1.2.*

2. Limitations. Courts have become increasingly critical of keyword searches. *See* **Victor Stanley, Inc.**, 250 F.R.D. at 260–62; Sedona Conference, *Commentary on Search & Retrieval,* 15 Sedona Conf.J. at 234. Keyword searches are limited because the people who originally created the electronic information may describe the same concept using different words, may misspell words, or may use abbreviations for certain terms. *See* Sedona Conference, *Commentary on Search & Retrieval,* 15 Sedona Conf.J. at 233; Lau & Lee, *Technology-Assisted Review for Discovery Requests,* at 3; Peck, *Search, Forward,* at 26. Without cooperation from all the parties, the attorneys who develop the list of keywords are essentially guessing what words will produce relevant information; thus, the list of keywords is often overinclusive, resulting in a high return of irrelevant information. *See* **Da Silva Moore**, 287 F.R.D. at 190–91; Peck, *Search, Forward,* at 26.

§5.2 Technology-assisted review. The parties can consider technology-assisted review (TAR) to locate relevant electronic information. *See* **Da Silva Moore v. Publicis Groupe**, 287 F.R.D. 182, 193 (S.D.N.Y.2012), *adopted by* No. 11 Civ. 1279 (ALC) (AJP), 2012 WL 1446534 (S.D.N.Y.2012) (slip op.; 4-25-12); Lau & Lee, *Technology-Assisted Review for Discovery Requests,* at 1; *see also* 2015 Adv. Cmte. Notes to Fed. R. Civ. P. 26 at ¶16, **O'Connor's Federal Rules * Civil Trials**, Appendix V (2021 ed.) (computer-based methods of searching electronic information continue to develop and should be considered by courts and parties in attempt to reduce burden or expense of electronic discovery). TAR is a software tool that predicts the relevance of electronic information to a discovery request. *See* **Dynamo Holdings L.P. v. Commissioner of Internal Revenue**, 143 T.C. 183, 190 (U.S. Tax Ct.2014) (slip op.); **Progressive Cas. Ins. v. Delaney**, No. 2:11-cv-00678-LRH-PAL, 2014 WL 3563467 (D.Nev.2014) (slip op.; 7-18-14); Sedona Conference, *Sedona Conference Glossary,* 21 Sedona Conf.J. at 379; Sedona Conference, *Commentary on Search & Retrieval,* 15 Sedona Conf.J. at 242; *see also* **Rio Tinto PLC v. Vale S.A.**, 306 F.R.D. 125, 126 (S.D.N.Y.2015) (TAR is also referred to as predictive coding or computer-assisted review). To determine whether TAR is an appropriate search technique, courts may consider the following: (1) the parties' agreement, (2) the volume of electronic information, (3) the reasonableness of TAR compared to other available search techniques, (4) any factors for limiting discovery, such as that the discovery request is unreasonably cumulative or duplicative or is outside the scope of discovery, and (5) the transparency of the discovery process. *See* **Da Silva Moore**, 287 F.R.D. at 192; Sedona Conference, *TAR Case Law Primer,* 18 Sedona Conf.J. at 14. For a discussion of case law on the subject of TAR, see Sedona Conference, *TAR Case Law Primer.*

1. Process. Although the specific TAR process can differ depending on the parties' agreement and the software used, the process often includes the following steps:

(1) Select software vendor & expert. The producing party selects a TAR software vendor and the expert who will train the software. *See* Equivio, *Top 10 Best Practices,* at 2 (due consideration should be given to selection of expert). The expert is typically a senior attorney or group of attorneys but can also include an expert from the software vendor. *See id.* at 3 ("collaborative training approach" involves team of two or three experts who participate together in training); *see, e.g.*, **Da Silva Moore**, 287 F.R.D. at 202 (producing party's attorneys worked with TAR vendor's expert to review and code seed set). The parties can also agree to share the selection of the experts, who will then participate together in training the software. *See, e.g.*, **In re Actos (Pioglitazone) Prods. Liab. Litig.**, No. 6:11-md-2299, 2012 WL 7861249 (W.D.La.2012) (case mgmt. order; 7-27-12) (parties each chose three experts to work together to train software).

(2) Generate control set. The expert may generate a control set that is made up of a random, statistically representative sample of documents from the universe of potentially responsive documents and is kept separate from the seed set. *See* **Rio Tinto**, 306 F.R.D. at 132; **Edwards v. National Milk Producers Fed'n**, No. 3:11-CV-04766-JSW, 2013 WL 12415224 (N.D.Cal.2013) (joint stip. & order; 4-16-13); Grossman & Cormack, *Grossman-Cormack Glossary,* at 13. The expert reviews and codes the sample for relevancy, and the control set is then used to measure how well the TAR software has been trained. *See* **Rio Tinto**, 306 F.R.D. at 132; Grossman & Cormack, *Grossman-Cormack Glossary,* at 13.

(3) Code seed set. The expert reviews and codes a relatively small sample of documents—known as a "seed set"—to use in training the TAR software. *See* **Da Silva Moore**, 287 F.R.D. at 184; **Dynamo Holdings**, 143 T.C. at 191 (slip

op.).

Note

Some courts have stressed the need for cooperation and transparency between parties during the TAR process, particularly in the development of the seed set. See ***Da Silva Moore****, 287 F.R.D. at 192;* ***Bridgestone Am., Inc. v. International Bus. Machs. Corp.****, No. 3:13-1196, 2014 WL 4923014 (M.D.Tenn.2014) (order; 7-22-14); Sedona Conference, TAR Case Law Primer, 18 Sedona Conf.J. at 30. Parties may voluntarily share seed-set documents or methodologies and may even work together to code the seed set. See Facciola & Favro, Safeguarding the Seed Set, at 17–18; see, e.g.,* ***Rio Tinto****, 306 F.R.D. at 132 (parties agreed that producing party would provide requesting party with description of size of seed set and methodology used to identify it);* ***Da Silva Moore****, 287 F.R.D. at 186–87 (producing party agreed to provide requesting parties with all nonprivileged seed documents, as well as expert's document-coding designations). But it is unclear how cooperative and transparent the parties should be when privilege issues are implicated in developing the seed set. See* ***Rio Tinto****, 306 F.R.D. at 128; Lau & Lee, Technology-Assisted Review for Discovery Requests, at 10; Facciola & Favro, Safeguarding the Seed Set, at 6–7.*

(4) Train software. The software applies the principles it learns from the seed set to predict how the expert would code the documents outside the seed set. **Da Silva Moore**, 287 F.R.D. at 184; *see* Lau & Lee, *Technology-Assisted Review for Discovery Requests*, at 4. The coding and predicting continues (i.e., iterative review) until the software is able to accurately predict how the expert would code the documents, at which point the software codes the remaining electronic information. *See* **Da Silva Moore**, 287 F.R.D. at 184. When the software completes the coding, it selects a random sample of the coded documents for quality control. Shah, *Use of "Predictive Coding" to Limit Cost & Improve Efficiency*, at 9. The expert assesses the sample of coded documents for both the percentage of relevant documents identified (called "completeness" or "recall") and the percentage of the identified documents that are actually relevant (called "accuracy" or "precision"). *Id.*; *see* **Da Silva Moore**, 287 F.R.D. at 184; Lau & Lee, *Technology-Assisted Review for Discovery Requests*, at 5. If the expert finds errors, additional seed-set documents are chosen, reviewed, and coded until the software reaches acceptable levels of completeness and accuracy. Shah, *Use of "Predictive Coding" to Limit Cost & Improve Efficiency*, at 9.

(5) Validate results. The expert validates the results by reviewing a random sample of the documents that the software has identified as likely to be nonresponsive to the discovery request. *See* **Rio Tinto**, 306 F.R.D. at 133; **Edwards**, No. 3:11-CV-04766-JSW, 2013 WL 12415224 (joint stip. & order); Equivio, *Top 10 Best Practices*, at 6. This process of "testing the rest" is a quality-assurance measure that verifies that the documents identified as nonresponsive do in fact contain a very low number of relevant documents. Equivio, *Top 10 Best Practices*, at 6; *see* Auttonberry, Comment, *Predictive Coding: Taking the Devil out of the Details*, 74 La.L.Rev. at 638. But, like other aspects of TAR, experts disagree about the reliability of quality-control sampling in general. Auttonberry, Comment, *Predictive Coding: Taking the Devil out of the Details*, 74 La.L.Rev. at 639.

Note

During the TAR process, other procedural issues that may arise and need to be addressed include (1) what an acceptable measure of completeness might be, (2) whether a party using TAR must respond to subsequent rounds of document requests that require the party to retrain the TAR tool, and (3) whether the party using TAR can manually review documents that TAR has identified as likely responsive before producing them. Sedona Conference, Sedona Conference TAR Case Law Primer, 18 Sedona Conf.J. at 37.

2. Benefits.

(1) Lower costs. TAR may offer the potential for lower costs, particularly in larger cases, because it requires fewer attorneys and fewer review hours. *See* Lau & Lee, *Technology-Assisted Review for Discovery Requests*, at 5; Fuchs & Wolinsky, *Understand Predictive Coding Options*; Shah, *Use of "Predictive Coding" to Limit Cost & Improve Efficiency*, at 10.

(2) Greater accuracy. TAR can potentially provide greater accuracy than keyword searches because it does not rely on attorneys to develop the list of keywords and it is not based on particular keywords or Boolean operators. *See* **Da Silva Moore**, 287 F.R.D. at 190–91; **Progressive**, No. 2:11-cv-00678-LRH-PAL, 2014 WL 3563467 (slip op.); Fuchs & Wolinsky, *Understand Predictive Coding Options*.

3. **Drawbacks.**

(1) Garbage in, garbage out. TAR output depends on the quality and consistency of the input it receives from the expert during training. Sedona Conference, *Commentary on Search & Retrieval*, 15 Sedona Conf.J. at 242. It is essential that there is active project management from the beginning of the TAR process. *See* Fuchs & Wolinsky, *Understand Predictive Coding Options*. Careful selection of the expert or group of experts, allocation of sufficient resources to the software-training process, proper front-end planning, and development of a control set can all contribute to achieving greater accuracy from the TAR process. *See* Auttonberry, Comment, *Predictive Coding: Taking the Devil out of the Details*, 74 La.L.Rev. at 643; Equivio, *Top 10 Best Practices*, at 2.

(2) Potential privilege issues. Because of its relative newness, it is unclear to what extent TAR can handle privilege issues. *See* Lau & Lee, *Technology-Assisted Review for Discovery Requests*, at 10; Facciola & Favro, *Safeguarding the Seed Set*, at 6–7; Shah, *Use of "Predictive Coding" to Limit Cost & Improve Efficiency*, at 10.

§5.3 Targeted searches. The parties can consider targeted searches to locate relevant electronic information. *See* **Oracle Corp. v. SAP AG**, 566 F.Supp.2d 1010, 1014 (N.D.Cal.2008).

§5.4 Testing & sampling. The parties can consider testing or sampling to locate relevant electronic information contained in sources identified as not reasonably available. *See* Hedges, *Managing Discovery of Electronic Information*, at 22. See "Information not reasonably available," ch. 6-C, §6.2.2. Sampling can help refine the search parameters and determine the benefits and burdens of a more complete search. *See* Hedges, *Managing Discovery of Electronic Information*, at 22. See "Testing or sampling," ch. 6-C, §7.1.5(1)(b).

§5.5 Other restrictions. The parties can consider other restrictions on searches for electronic information, such as limiting the time period for discovery or the amount of hours the producing party must spend searching, compiling, and reviewing electronic information.

§6. Scope of electronic discovery

A party may secure the production of unprivileged electronic information that is both relevant to the subject of the suit, which includes inadmissible evidence if the information requested is reasonably calculated to lead to the discovery of admissible evidence, and proportional to the needs of the case. *See* Tex. R. Civ. P. 192.3(a), 192.4, 196.4; **In re State Farm Lloyds**, 520 S.W.3d 595, 604, 607 (Tex.2017). In addition to considering relevance and proportionality, a party should consider whether the electronic information is reasonably available. *See* Tex. R. Civ. P. 196.4. Courts should determine on a case-by-case basis whether a discovery request for electronic information is proportional to the needs of the case and whether the requested information is reasonably available. *See* **In re State Farm**, 520 S.W.3d at 599; **In re Weekley Homes, L.P.**, 295 S.W.3d 309, 315 (Tex.2009).

§6.1 Is electronic information relevant & proportional?

1. **Relevant.** For information to be discoverable, it must be relevant to the claims and defenses asserted in the suit. *See* Tex. R. Civ. P. 192.3(a), 196.4; **In re State Farm Lloyds**, 520 S.W.3d 595, 604 (Tex.2017). See "Scope & limitations," ch. 6-B, §2.1.

2. **Proportional.** For information to be discoverable, the discovery request must be proportional to the needs of the case. *See* Tex. R. Civ. P. 192.4(b); **In re State Farm**, 520 S.W.3d at 599.

Note

In 2015, the FRCPs were amended to, among other things, move the proportionality considerations in former FRCP 26(b)(2)(C)(iii) to become part of the scope of discovery in FRCP 26(b)(1). See **In re State**

Farm, *520 S.W.3d at 614. The 2015 amendments did not change the existing responsibilities of the court and parties to consider proportionality; instead, the amendments highlighted the fact that, for information to be discoverable, there must be more than relevance—there must also be proportionality. See id. In line with the limitations on the scope of discovery found in TRCP 192.4, the Texas Supreme Court in* ***In re State Farm*** *provided for similar guiding principles, emphasizing that "proportionality is the polestar."* ***In re State Farm***, *520 S.W.3d at 615. Although the proportionality factors set out in* ***In re State Farm*** *differ from the proportionality factors in FRCP 26(b)(1), the Court stated that its proportionality analysis aligns with electronic-discovery practice under the FRCPs. See* ***In re State Farm***, *520 S.W.3d at 612.*

(1) Applicability. Proportionality should be considered and applied by the parties and the court in all aspects of the discovery and production of electronic information, including issues of preservation, searches, and forms of production. Sedona Conference, *Sedona Principles, Third Edition*, 19 Sedona Conf.J. at 67; *see, e.g.*, **In re State Farm**, 520 S.W.3d at 607 (applying proportionality inquiry to discovery dispute based on form of production requested).

(2) Factors. A discovery request will be considered proportional if the burden or expense of the proposed discovery is justified when weighed against the following factors:

(a) The likely benefit of the requested discovery. **In re State Farm**, 520 S.W.3d at 608; *see* Tex. R. Civ. P. 192.4(b). For example, if the benefits of a requested form of production are minimal or speculative, any additional effort or expense to produce the information will likely lead to the denial of the requested information. **In re State Farm**, 520 S.W.3d at 608. On the other hand, if there is a particularized need for the information, it will more likely be discoverable, but—depending on other proportionality factors—cost-shifting may be warranted based on any "extraordinary steps" taken by the producing party. **In re State Farm**, 520 S.W.3d at 608. See "Costs," ch. 6-C, §3.5; "Extraordinary steps," ch. 6-C, §7.1.5(1)(c).

(b) The needs of the case. **In re State Farm**, 520 S.W.3d at 608; *see* Tex. R. Civ. P. 192.4(b). For example, metadata may be necessary to the litigation in a wrongful-termination case when the timing of events before and after termination or the authorship of case-critical documents is a central issue. **In re State Farm**, 520 S.W.3d at 609. See "Metadata," ch. 6-C, §7.1.5(1)(a)[4].

(c) The amount in controversy. **In re State Farm**, 520 S.W.3d at 610; *see* Tex. R. Civ. P. 192.4(b). Because the relative inaccessibility of some electronic information can contribute to increased costs and burdens to produce it, the amount in controversy is pivotal in determining whether production is warranted. **In re State Farm**, 520 S.W.3d at 610.

(d) The parties' resources. **In re State Farm**, 520 S.W.3d at 610; *see* Tex. R. Civ. P. 192.4(b). This factor encompasses both whether a party has the financial resources to produce electronic information in a given form and whether a party has the technological resources to properly use electronic information in a given form. **In re State Farm**, 520 S.W.3d at 610–11. Although the parties' financial resources are a valid consideration, a party seeking discovery is not prohibited from making requests to an indigent party or justified in making unlimited requests to a wealthy party. *Id.*

(e) The importance of the issues at stake in the litigation. **In re State Farm**, 520 S.W.3d at 611; *see* Tex. R. Civ. P. 192.4(b).

(f) The importance of the proposed discovery in resolving the litigation. **In re State Farm**, 520 S.W.3d at 611; *see* Tex. R. Civ. P. 192.4(b).

(g) Any other factor bearing on proportionality. **In re State Farm**, 520 S.W.3d at 611. The proportionality factors are not exclusive; thus, because technology is constantly evolving, courts can evaluate any other factor that addresses jurisprudential concerns. *Id.* at 611–12.

§6.2 Is electronic information reasonably available? In response to a discovery request, the responding party must produce electronic information that is reasonably available to it in the ordinary course of business. Tex. R. Civ. P. 196.4; *see* **In re State Farm Lloyds**, 520 S.W.3d 595, 600 (Tex.2017); **In re Weekley Homes, L.P.**, 295 S.W.3d 309, 315 (Tex.2009); **In re Methodist Primary Care Grp.**, 553 S.W.3d 709, 715 (Tex.App.—Houston [14th Dist.] 2018, orig. proceeding). See "Response," ch. 6-C, §7.1.5(2).

Note

Under TRCP 196.4, the responding party must produce electronic information that is "reasonably available"; FRCP 26(b)(2)(B), on the other hand, requires the information to be "reasonably accessible." In the Third Edition of the Sedona Principles, the scope of discovery is discussed in terms of preserving and producing electronic information from sources that are "readily accessible." Sedona Conference, Sedona Principles, Third Edition, 19 Sedona Conf.J. at 134. Under that framework, potential sources of discoverable information exist along a continuum that (1) starts with electronic information that is readily accessible, (2) continues through a variety of sources that are less accessible because of increasing burden or cost or that are largely duplicative of more accessible sources, and (3) ends with sources that clearly are not readily accessible and for which the cost of preservation and production is not proportional to the needs of the case. Id. at 134–35. This framework is intended to cover concerns about proportionality under FRCP 26(b)(1) and analyzing data sources that are claimed to be not reasonably accessible under FRCP 26(b)(2). Sedona Conference, Sedona Principles, Third Edition, 19 Sedona Conf.J. at 135 n.112. Whether a similar framework will evolve for discovery of electronic information in Texas is unclear.

1. Information reasonably available. Whether electronic information is reasonably available will largely depend on how it is stored—information will generally be considered reasonably available if it is stored in a readily usable format. *See* **Zubulake v. UBS Warburg LLC**, 217 F.R.D. 309, 318 (S.D.N.Y.2003). Reasonably available data may include (1) active data that is available to the responding party in the ordinary course of business, (2) near-line data, and (3) offline storage. *See id.* at 318–19; Hedges, *Managing Discovery of Electronic Information*, at 21. See "Definitions," ch. 6-C, §2.2. Although TRCP 196.4 does not comprehensively define the term "reasonable," it naturally raises the jurisprudential considerations in TRCP 192.4. *See* **In re State Farm**, 520 S.W.3d at 607. Thus, if retrieval and production of the information is not unduly burdensome or expensive, the information is reasonably available. *See* **In re Weekley Homes**, 295 S.W.3d at 315. See "Grounds to limit scope of discovery," ch. 6-A, §20.1; "Proportional," ch. 6-C, §6.1.2.

2. Information not reasonably available.

(1) Generally. If the responding party cannot retrieve the electronic information or produce it through reasonable efforts, the party should object that the information is not reasonably available. *See* Tex. R. Civ. P. 196.4. See "Object," ch. 6-C, §7.1.5(2)(b). The responding party may, however, have to produce electronic information that is not reasonably available if ordered to do so by the court. **In re State Farm**, 520 S.W.3d at 600; **In re Weekley Homes**, 295 S.W.3d at 315; Tex. R. Civ. P. 196 cmt. 3. If, in complying with the order, the responding party must take extraordinary steps to retrieve and produce the electronic information, the court must require the requesting party to pay the responding party's reasonable expenses. Tex. R. Civ. P. 196.4. See "Extraordinary steps," ch. 6-C, §7.1.5(1)(c).

(2) Examples. Information that is not reasonably available may include (1) information stored on backup tapes, (2) erased, fragmented, or damaged data, and (3) legacy data. *See* **Zubulake**, 217 F.R.D. at 319–20; Hedges, *Managing Discovery of Electronic Information*, at 24. See "Definitions," ch. 6-C, §2.2. These types of data are removed from the ordinary course of business and may involve substantial costs, time, and active intervention of computer specialists to produce. *See* Hedges, *Managing Discovery of Electronic Information*, at 21–22. Systems data, which includes such information as when people logged on or off a computer or network, what applications and passwords they used, and what websites they visited, may also be more remote than active data and more costly to produce. *Id.* at 21.

§7. Discovering & producing electronic information

§7.1 Discovery from parties.

1. Disclosures. A party must disclose the identities of people who have knowledge of the party's electronic-information systems and each person's connection with the case. *See* Tex. R. Civ. P. 194.2(b)(5). The party must also disclose certain information about any expert it plans to call as a witness. *See* Tex. R. Civ. P. 194.3, 195.5(a). See "Select forensic expert," ch. 6-C, §8.1.2(4); "Testifying experts," ch. 6-E, §2.2.2(1)(f); "Expert disclosures," ch. 6-E, §3.4.

2. Depositions. A party seeking information about an organization's sources of electronic information should consider deposing an information-technology employee or other person who knows about the organization's electronic-information system. *See* Tex. R. Civ. P. 195.1, 199.2(b)(1); **In re Weekley Homes, L.P.**, 295 S.W.3d 309, 315 (Tex.2009). See "Unknown corporate witness," ch. 6-F, §4.5.1(2)(c); "When organization deposed," ch. 6-F, §4.6.3.

3. Interrogatories. A party may use interrogatories to request information about the opposing party's electronic information. *See* Tex. R. Civ. P. 197.1. Interrogatories can be useful in determining the extent of the opposing party's discoverable electronic information (e.g., ask for identity of opposing party's computer-network specialist, ask about document-retention or destruction policies) or the opposing party's compliance with its preservation duty (e.g., ask for dates and actions taken to preserve electronic information, ask about recipients of any litigation holds). See "Interrogatories," ch. 6-G, §1 et seq.

4. Requests for admissions. A party may request that the opposing party admit the truth of matters relating to electronic information. *See* Tex. R. Civ. P. 198.1. A party may respond by admitting, denying, or stating why it cannot truthfully admit or deny each matter. Tex. R. Civ. P. 198.2(b). See "Requests for Admissions," ch. 6-H, §1 et seq.

5. Requests for production.

(1) Request. To obtain electronic information, a party must specifically request it. Tex. R. Civ. P. 196.4 & cmt. 3; **In re Weekley Homes**, 295 S.W.3d at 314; *see* **In re Waste Mgmt.**, 392 S.W.3d 861, 874 (Tex.App.—Texarkana 2013, orig. proceeding) (party must specify subject matter being requested, such as deleted e-mails); Sedona Conference, *Sedona Principles, Third Edition*, 19 Sedona Conf.J. at 87 (to extent possible, party should clearly and specifically identify each item or category of electronic information it seeks). A request for "all documents" does not include electronic information. *See, e.g.*, **In re Lowe's Cos.**, 134 S.W.3d 876, 880 n.7 (Tex.App.—Houston [14th Dist.] 2004, orig. proceeding) (dicta; although Ps claimed that database was within request for all documents concerning claims against D, Ps did not specifically request electronic information); *cf.* **County of Dallas v. Harrison**, 759 S.W.2d 530, 531 (Tex.App.—Dallas 1988, no writ) (because "photographs" and "videotape recordings" are two different categories of documents under former TRCP 166b(2)(b), now TRCP 192.3(b), D's request for photographs did not apply to videotapes). If the party does not make a specific request for electronic information, the responding party generally cannot be compelled to produce it and cannot be sanctioned for not producing it. *See* **In re Harris**, 315 S.W.3d 685, 700–02 (Tex.App.—Houston [1st Dist.] 2010, orig. proceeding); **MRT, Inc. v. Vounckx**, 299 S.W.3d 500, 508–09 (Tex.App.—Dallas 2009, no pet.); **In re Lowe's Cos.**, 134 S.W.3d at 880 n.7 (dicta). But if the responding party understands the scope of the discovery sought before the court intervenes, the request will be considered reasonably specific. *See* **In re Shipman**, 540 S.W.3d 562, 567 (Tex.2018); *see, e.g.*, **In re Weekley Homes**, 295 S.W.3d at 314–15 (although P should have specifically requested production of deleted e-mails, purpose of TRCP 196.4 was met because request was made clear during course of discovery and before hearing on motion to compel); **In re Methodist Primary Care Grp.**, 553 S.W.3d 709, 715–16 (Tex.App.—Houston [14th Dist.] 2018, orig. proceeding) (although requests did not reference TRCP 196.4, they defined "document" as including "all other electronic information . . . produced in their native format," and motion to compel clearly sought production of electronic data).

Practice Tip

To properly draft a request for electronic information, you should first familiarize yourself with the opposing party's systems and applications, including how information is stored and retrieved. See "Learn about parties' systems," ch. 6-C, §3.1. You may not know the details of the opposing party's systems and applications before making the request, but to the extent you know of the specific electronic information you seek, you should request that information. Sedona Conference, Sedona Principles, Third Edition, 19 Sedona Conf.J. at 87.

(a) Form of production. A party's request for production must specify the form or forms in which the party wants the electronic information to be produced. Tex. R. Civ. P. 196.4 & cmt. 3; *e.g.*, **In re State Farm Lloyds**, 520 S.W.3d 595, 606 (Tex.2017) (parties requested that electronic information be produced in native or near native format). *But see* **In re Waste Mgmt.**, 392 S.W.3d at 873–74 (request does not have to specify exact file format; request that electronic in-

formation be produced in reasonable manner or in reasonably usable form is sufficient). Generally, when determining what form or forms to specify, the requesting party should consider (1) the forms most likely to provide the information needed to establish the relevant facts of the case, (2) the need to receive electronic information in particular formats to functionally access, cull, analyze, search, and display the information produced, (3) whether the electronic information sought is reasonably available in the forms requested, (4) the relative value and potential challenges created by responding with electronic information in the requested format, and (5) the requesting party's own ability to effectively manage, reasonably use, and protect the electronic information in the forms requested. Sedona Conference, *Sedona Principles, Third Edition*, 19 Sedona Conf.J. at 173–74. Different types or categories of information may be stored in different forms; thus, a party may need to request the production of one set of data in a particular form and request production of a different set of data in a different form. *Id.* at 88. Although the necessary form or forms of production will depend on the facts of the case, the requesting party will generally need to address whether electronic information should be produced in native or static format and whether metadata should be included.

Note

In ***In re State Farm****, the responding party objected that it could not retrieve the electronic information in the form requested—native format—through reasonable efforts and asserted that a reasonably usable form—static format—was readily available in the ordinary course of business. See* ***In re State Farm****, 520 S.W.3d at 600–01. The Court rejected the notion that the form requested controls and concluded that, when a reasonably usable form other than the one requested is readily available in the ordinary course of business, the trial court must assess whether any enhanced burden or expense associated with the requested form is justified when weighed against the proportional needs of the case. Id. at 607. See "Proportional," ch. 6-C, §6.1.2.*

[1] Native format. The request may specify that electronic information be produced in its native format. *See* **In re Methodist Primary Care**, 553 S.W.3d at 715. See "Native format," ch. 6-C, §2.2.14. Depending on the circumstances of a particular case, it may be appropriate for a party to request that certain types of electronic information—such as word-processing documents, electronic spreadsheet files, portable database files, text-messaging logs, image files, and sound files—be produced in their native format. *See* Sedona Conference, *Sedona Principles, Third Edition*, 19 Sedona Conf.J. at 177–78. A file in native format contains metadata that itself needs to be preserved and may be requested. *See id.* at 180. See "Metadata," below.

Note

There can be certain technological challenges associated with producing electronic information in its native format. Sedona Conference, Sedona Principles, Third Edition, 19 Sedona Conf.J. at 178. For example, it may be difficult to effectively redact information, there may be issues with Bates numbering, and the requesting party may not have access to or the equipment or expertise required to use suitable applications for accessing, searching, and displaying native format. Id. Even if a request for production of electronic information in its native format is warranted under the circumstances of the case, the requesting party should consider these technological challenges before making its request. See id.

[2] Static format. The request may specify that electronic information be produced as static images. See "Static format," ch. 6-C, §2.2.18. For example, the requesting party may want to specify that certain types of electronic information—such as e-mail kept on the Internet through services like Google or Yahoo—be converted to a reasonably usable format (e.g., downloaded and saved as PDF files). *See* Sedona Conference, *Sedona Principles, Third Edition*, 19 Sedona Conf.J. at 176.

[3] TIFF+ format. The request may specify that the electronic information be produced as "TIFF, Text, and Load Files" (TIFF+). *See* Sedona Conference, *Sedona Principles, Third Edition*, 19 Sedona Conf.J. at 172. TIFF+ is currently the most common way to produce electronic information. *Id.* This format consists of a combination of a static electronic

image (e.g., TIFF file), a text file containing extracted text from the document, and one or more separate load files containing selected metadata. *Id.* A requesting party can reassemble the components in a way that is compatible with a chosen review platform so that the information can be text-searched and sorted or filtered based on available metadata fields. *Id.* at 172–73.

[4] Metadata. The request may specify that electronic information be produced with all metadata intact. See "Metadata," ch. 6-C, §2.2.12. Before requesting metadata, a party should consider (1) the data types that are relevant to the claims or defenses, (2) what metadata associated with those data types may be relevant or may play a functional role in the use of relevant electronic information, and (3) whether that metadata should be preserved, requested, or produced. Sedona Conference, *Sedona Principles, Third Edition,* 19 Sedona Conf.J. at 170; *see* **In re State Farm**, 520 S.W.3d at 609 (metadata's relevance must be obvious or linked to a claim or defense; metadata must not be of merely hypothetical value). The relevance of metadata and the relative significance to a suit must be determined on a case-by-case basis. **In re State Farm**, 520 S.W.3d at 609. Generally, metadata may be necessary when the who, what, where, when, and why regarding creation of the electronic information is an actual issue in the suit. *Id.* See "Factors," ch. 6-C, §6.1.2(2)(b).

Note

One problem with requesting metadata is the danger that information recorded by the computer as embedded metadata may be inaccurate. See Sedona Conference, Sedona Principles, Third Edition, 19 Sedona Conf.J. at 171. See "Embedded metadata," ch. 6-C, §2.2.12(1). For example, when a new employee uses a word-processing program to create a memorandum by using a template created by a former employee, the metadata for the new memorandum may incorrectly identify the former employee as the author. See Sedona Conference, Sedona Principles, Third Edition, 19 Sedona Conf.J. at 171.

(b) Testing or sampling. A party's request for production may ask that sources of electronic information be tested or sampled to see if they contain any relevant evidence. *See* Tex. R. Civ. P. 196.1(b); **In re Weekley Homes**, 295 S.W.3d at 315; Sedona Conference, *Sedona Principles, Third Edition,* 19 Sedona Conf.J. at 115. See "Items to be tested," ch. 6-I, §3.2.2. For example, if a requesting party is unsure whether relevant and otherwise unavailable electronic information is located on backup tapes, the party can request that the tapes be sampled so the parties can better understand the nature and relevance of any electronic information the tapes may contain. Sedona Conference, *Sedona Principles, Third Edition,* 19 Sedona Conf.J. at 115. Depending on the circumstances, sampling may establish that there is no need for the tapes to be preserved or that it is reasonable to preserve and restore only certain parts of the available tapes. *Id.*

(c) Extraordinary steps. A party's request for production must specify any extraordinary steps the producing party must take to retrieve, translate, and produce the electronic information. Tex. R. Civ. P. 196.4 & cmt. 3; *see* **In re State Farm**, 520 S.W.3d at 608 & n.44. See "Generally," ch. 6-C, §6.2.2(1).

Note

No Texas appellate court has specifically addressed what would constitute "extraordinary steps." See, e.g., ***In re Waste Mgmt.****, 392 S.W.3d at 877 (court did not determine whether a "do-over" of producing records in native format with metadata after records were produced in PDF was an "extraordinary step"). The requesting party should consider whether the burden or expense of the proposed discovery outweighs its likely benefits when evaluating any extraordinary steps necessary to produce the requested information. See Tex. R. Civ. P. 192.4(b);* ***In re State Farm****, 520 S.W.3d at 607;* ***In re Weekley Homes****, 295 S.W.3d at 315. See "Factors," ch. 6-C, §6.1.2(2)(a).*

(d) Access to hard drive. A party may request access to an opposing party's computer hard drive or other electronic storage device. *See* **In re Honza**, 242 S.W.3d 578, 581–82 (Tex.App.—Waco 2008, orig. proceeding). The request must demonstrate (1) the particular characteristics of the electronic storage devices involved, (2) the familiarity of the requesting party's experts with those characteristics, and (3) a reasonable likelihood that the proposed search methodology will yield the information sought. *See* **In re Weekley Homes**, 295 S.W.3d at 311; **In re VERP Inv.**, 457 S.W.3d 255, 263

(Tex.App.—Dallas 2015, orig. proceeding); *see, e.g.*, **In re Jordan**, 364 S.W.3d 425, 426 (Tex.App.—Dallas 2012, orig. proceeding) (requests merely asking for computer hard drives without specifying exact information sought were insufficient). If the responding party does not adequately produce the requested data, the requesting party can file a motion to compel. See "Accessing hard drive," ch. 6-C, §8.1.2.

(2) Response. The responding party must, for each item or category requested, either produce the information or object to its production. *See* Sedona Conference, *Sedona Principles, Third Edition*, 19 Sedona Conf.J. at 89.

(a) Produce. The responding party must produce electronic information that is responsive to the request, reasonably available to the responding party in the ordinary course of business, and in a reasonably usable form. Tex. R. Civ. P. 196.4 & cmt. 3; **In re Weekley Homes**, 295 S.W.3d at 322. See "Scope of electronic discovery," ch. 6-C, §6; "Form of production," ch. 6-C, §7.1.5(1)(a).

Practice Tip

If the producing party believes the request is too ambiguous as to the form of production, she should contact the requesting party to discuss the preferred form to ensure that production of the electronic information meets the requirements of TRCP 196.4. See, e.g., **In re Waste Mgmt.**, *392 S.W.3d at 874–75 (request that electronic information be produced in a "reasonable manner" was appropriate under TRCP 196.4; nothing in record indicated that production of information in PDF files, rather than native format with metadata, would suffice). See "Schedule pretrial meeting or conference," ch. 6-C, §4.*

(b) Object. If the responding party cannot, through reasonable efforts, retrieve the requested electronic information or produce it in the form requested, that party must object. Tex. R. Civ. P. 193.2, 196.4; **In re Weekley Homes**, 295 S.W.3d at 322. See "Contents of response," ch. 6-I, §3.4. If the responding party is able to produce some but not all of the requested electronic information, it must object to the information it cannot retrieve or produce. *See* Tex. R. Civ. P. 193.2(b); Sedona Conference, *Sedona Principles, Third Edition*, 19 Sedona Conf.J. at 89; Hecht, *Taking Point on E-Discovery*, 51 The Advoc. (Texas) at 20. The responding party must specifically state the reason for its objection. Tex. R. Civ. P. 193.2(a); Sedona Conference, *Sedona Principles, Third Edition*, 19 Sedona Conf.J. at 89. The responding party has the burden to produce evidence to support its objection. *E.g.*, **In re CI Host, Inc.**, 92 S.W.3d 514, 516–17 (Tex.2002) (evidence was necessary to support objection that information on computer tapes was protected); *see* Tex. R. Civ. P. 193.4.

[1] Information itself not reasonably available. The responding party can object that the requested information is not reasonably available because it is not stored in a readily usable format. See "Is electronic information reasonably available?," ch. 6-C, §6.2.

[2] Requested form not reasonably available. The responding party can object that the information is not reasonably available in the form specified by the requesting party and that the responding party should instead be allowed to produce the information in another reasonably usable form. *See* Tex. R. Civ. P. 192.4, 196.4; **In re State Farm**, 520 S.W.3d at 607. See "Form of production," ch. 6-C, §7.1.5(1)(a).

(3) Hearing. Either party may request a hearing on the responding party's objection. Tex. R. Civ. P. 193.4(a); **In re Weekley Homes**, 295 S.W.3d at 322. In ruling on the objection, the court will weigh the proportional needs of the case against any burden or expense associated with production. *See* **In re State Farm**, 520 S.W.3d at 607; **In re Weekley Homes**, 295 S.W.3d at 322. See "Proportional," ch. 6-C, §6.1.2. Thus, the responding party should support its objection by presenting evidence that the burden or expense of the requested discovery is not justified based on the proportional needs of the case, relying on the factors in TRCP 192.4(b). *See* Tex. R. Civ. P. 192.4(b); **In re State Farm**, 520 S.W.3d at 607; **In re Weekley Homes**, 295 S.W.3d at 322. The requesting party should reply by presenting evidence showing that the proportional needs of the case outweigh any burden or expense incurred by the responding party in producing the information. *See* Tex. R. Civ. P. 192.4(b); **In re State Farm**, 520 S.W.3d at 607; **In re Weekley Homes**, 295 S.W.3d at 322. In making its determination, the court may order the responding party to sample or inspect the sources that potentially contain the requested information. **In re Weekley Homes**, 295 S.W.3d at 315. The court may also order the deposition of witnesses who are knowledgeable about the responding party's information systems. *Id.*

Practice Tip

A responding party should inform the court if production of requested electronic information affects the privacy rights of nonparties. E.g., ***In re CI Host****, 92 S.W.3d at 517 (requested backup tapes contained some nonparty information protected from disclosure under federal law). See "Nonparty information," ch. 6-I, §4.1. The responding party should also consider notifying the nonparty about the request so that the nonparty can raise its own objections to the production of the information.*

(4) Order. The court will issue an order sustaining or overruling the responding party's objections. *See* Tex. R Civ. P. 193.4(b). In ruling on the objections, the court should attempt to protect sensitive information and choose the least intrusive means of retrieval if it orders the responding party to produce. **In re Weekley Homes**, 295 S.W.3d at 322; **In re VERP**, 457 S.W.3d at 261; *e.g.*, **In re Clark**, 345 S.W.3d 209, 212–13 (Tex.App.—Beaumont 2011, orig. proceeding) (order requiring that surnames of party's attorneys, as well as the words "attorney" and "lawyer," be excluded from hard-drive search was not sufficient attempt to protect sensitive information). If a forensic expert is necessary, the court can protect the information in several ways. See "Select forensic expert," ch. 6-C, §8.1.2(4).

(a) Request is not proportional. If the court determines that the burden or expense associated with production of the requested information outweighs the proportional needs of the case, it can do one of the following:

[1] Sustain the objection and order that the responding party is not required to produce the requested information. *See* Tex. R. Civ. P. 196.4.

[2] Sustain the objection and order the responding party to produce the information in the form offered by the responding party. **In re State Farm**, 520 S.W.3d at 607.

[3] Sustain the objection and order the responding party to produce the information in a form that the court determines is proportional to the needs of the case. *Id.*

[4] Overrule the objection and order the responding party to produce the requested information in the form requested if there is a particularized need. *See* Tex. R. Civ. P. 196.4; **In re State Farm**, 520 S.W.3d at 607; **In re Weekley Homes**, 295 S.W.3d at 322. If the court orders production, it must also order the requesting party to pay the reasonable expenses of any extraordinary steps required to retrieve and produce the information. Tex. R. Civ. P. 196.4; **In re State Farm**, 520 S.W.3d at 607. See "Extraordinary steps," ch. 6-C, §7.1.5(1)(c).

(b) Request is proportional. If the court determines that the proportional needs of the case outweigh the burden or expense associated with production of the requested information, it will overrule the objection and order the responding party to comply with the request for production. *See* **In re Weekley Homes**, 295 S.W.3d at 315. If the court orders production, it may also order the requesting party to pay the reasonable expenses of any extraordinary steps required to retrieve and produce the information. *See* Tex. R. Civ. P. 196.4; **In re State Farm**, 520 S.W.3d at 607. See "Extraordinary steps," ch. 6-C, §7.1.5(1)(c).

§7.2 Discovery from nonparties. A party may request production of electronic information from a nonparty. *See* Tex. R. Civ. P. 196 cmt. 6, 205.3(a). Because of the considerable costs involved with nonparty discovery of electronic information, requests to nonparties should be narrowly focused to avoid any undue burden or expense. See "Securing things from a nonparty," ch. 6-I, §5.

§8. Resolving electronic-discovery disputes

When an electronic-discovery dispute arises, the requesting party can file a motion to compel. If the responding party had a duty to preserve electronically stored information but lost the information, the requesting party can also ask for sanctions. See "Sanctions for lost ESI," **O'Connor's Federal Rules * Civil Trials**, ch. 6-C, §12 (2021 ed.). If the responding party disputes the request for electronically stored information, the party can file a motion for protective order.

§8.1 Motion to compel.

1. Generally. If the responding party does not produce the requested electronic information, the requesting party can file a motion to compel. *See* Tex. R. Civ. P. 215.1 (motion for order compelling discovery). See "Motion to compel discovery,"

ch. 6-A, §22. For a discussion of specific grounds for compelling discovery of electronic information, see "Motion to compel," **O'Connor's Federal Rules * Civil Trials**, ch. 6-C, §11.2 (2021 ed.).

2. Accessing hard drive. If a party requested access to an opposing party's computer hard drive and the opposing party did not adequately produce the requested data, the requesting party can file a motion to compel. *See* **In re Weekley Homes, L.P.**, 295 S.W.3d 309, 312 (Tex.2009); **In re Clark**, 345 S.W.3d 209, 211 (Tex.App.—Beaumont 2011, orig. proceeding). The requesting party must produce evidence showing that its motion to compel should be granted. *See* **In re VERP Inv.**, 457 S.W.3d 255, 262–63 (Tex.App.—Dallas 2015, orig. proceeding). To avoid undue intrusion, examination of a party's computer hard drive is generally discouraged; thus, access will normally be granted only if that party's conduct suggests that it may be withholding, concealing, or destroying discoverable electronic information. *See* **In re Shipman**, 540 S.W.3d 562, 569 (Tex.2018); **In re Weekley Homes**, 295 S.W.3d at 317; **In re Methodist Primary Care Grp.**, 553 S.W.3d 709, 720–21 (Tex.App.—Houston [14th Dist.] 2018, orig. proceeding). See "ESI withheld, concealed, or destroyed," **O'Connor's Federal Rules * Civil Trials**, ch. 6-C, §11.2.2(2)(a)[3] (2021 ed.). Mere skepticism that the responding party has not produced the requested information does not justify access to the party's hard drive. *E.g.*, **In re Shipman**, 540 S.W.3d at 567–68 (requesting party's suspicion that there was unrecovered data on responding party's hard drive was, by itself, insufficient to warrant hard-drive access); *see* **In re Methodist Primary Care**, 553 S.W.3d at 718. Thus, to justify access to an opposing party's computer hard drive, the requesting party must do the following in its motion to compel.

Note

Although this analysis is typically applied when a party requests access to an opposing party's hard drive, it is not limited to these situations. See ***In re Methodist Primary Care****, 553 S.W.3d at 718. Courts may apply it to other highly intrusive forms of discovery that involve direct access to a party's data by the opposing party or the opposing party's expert. E.g., id. (analysis applied when party requested that expert be permitted to search medical practice's cloud-based practice-management system).*

(1) Show inadequate production. As a threshold matter, the requesting party must show that the responding party has defaulted on its discovery obligations to search its records and adequately produce the requested data. **In re Shipman**, 540 S.W.3d at 567; **In re Weekley Homes**, 295 S.W.3d at 317; **In re Methodist Primary Care**, 553 S.W.3d at 718; **In re VERP**, 457 S.W.3d at 262; **In re Pinnacle Eng'g**, 405 S.W.3d 835, 843 (Tex.App.—Houston [1st Dist.] 2013, orig. proceeding); *see* **In re Clark**, 345 S.W.3d at 212. Even if this threshold requirement is shown, direct access to the responding party's computer hard drive is not automatic. **In re VERP**, 457 S.W.3d at 263; *see* **In re Weekley Homes**, 295 S.W.3d at 318; **In re Pinnacle Eng'g**, 405 S.W.3d at 844. The requesting party should also show that a search of the responding party's computer hard drive may recover deleted material. **In re Weekley Homes**, 295 S.W.3d at 317; *see* **In re Methodist Primary Care**, 553 S.W.3d at 718; **In re VERP**, 457 S.W.3d at 262; **In re Pinnacle Eng'g**, 405 S.W.3d at 844–45. A conclusory statement that deleted material "must exist" is not sufficient. *See* **In re Weekley Homes**, 295 S.W.3d at 320; **In re Harris**, 315 S.W.3d 685, 700 (Tex.App.—Houston [1st Dist.] 2010, orig. proceeding).

(2) Show that retrieval of data is feasible. The requesting party must show that retrieval of the requested data is feasible. **In re Weekley Homes**, 295 S.W.3d at 318; **In re Pinnacle Eng'g**, 405 S.W.3d at 844; *e.g.*, **In re VERP**, 457 S.W.3d at 263 (P did not provide any evidence that court order requiring "bit-level review" of computer and all files could retrieve the kind of information he sought); **In re Stern**, 321 S.W.3d 828, 846 (Tex.App.—Houston [1st Dist.] 2010, orig. proceeding) (D stated that e-mail was stored on web-based Internet service and could not be found on hard drive; P did not show that e-mails were saved to hard drive, so hard drive should not be produced). The requesting party should show that the particular electronic storage device will allow retrieval of deleted or overwritten material and what that retrieval will involve. **In re Weekley Homes**, 295 S.W.3d at 320. Thus, to show feasibility, the requesting party must have some knowledge of the responding party's electronic storage devices. *Id.* at 318. See "Learn about parties' systems," ch. 6-C, §3.1.

(3) Show relationship between hard drive & claim. The requesting party must show that there is some direct relationship between the computer hard drive and the claim itself. *See* **In re Weekley Homes**, 295 S.W.3d at 319; **In re Pinnacle Eng'g**, 405 S.W.3d at 847.

(4) Select forensic expert. The requesting party must select a forensic expert to make a mirror image of the computer hard drive. **In re Honza**, 242 S.W.3d 578, 582 (Tex.App.—Waco 2008, orig. proceeding); *see* **In re Weekley Homes**, 295 S.W.3d at 319; **In re VERP**, 457 S.W.3d at 263. See "Mirror imaging," ch. 6-C, §2.2.13. A forensic expert is a computer expert who creates forensic images of a particular electronic storage device and then searches the images for specified documents using a predetermined list of terms. **In re Harris**, 315 S.W.3d at 704; *see* **In re Weekley Homes**, 295 S.W.3d at 321.

(a) Qualifications. The party must show (1) how the expert is qualified to perform the search, (2) that the expert is familiar with the particularities of the hard drive at issue, and (3) any methodologies used by the expert to allow for retrieval of deleted data. *See* **In re Weekley Homes**, 295 S.W.3d at 321; **In re VERP**, 457 S.W.3d at 263; **In re Pinnacle Eng'g**, 405 S.W.3d at 845.

(b) Limited access. The expert must be given limited access to the documents on the electronic storage device; unrestricted authorization to search the electronic storage device would be an impermissible "fishing expedition." **In re Weekley Homes**, 295 S.W.3d at 318; *see, e.g.*, **In re Stern**, 321 S.W.3d at 845–46 (court abused discretion by allowing expert to have unrestricted access to all documents on D's hard drive and freedom to use or modify search terms); **In re Honza**, 242 S.W.3d at 582–83 (discovery order was not overbroad when expert was limited to searching for two specific documents).

(c) Copies to opposing party. After creating the mirror image and analyzing it for relevant documents, the expert must compile the documents obtained and provide copies to the opposing party. **In re Honza**, 242 S.W.3d at 582. The opposing party must be allowed to review the documents, produce documents responsive to the request for production, and create a privilege log for any withheld documents. *Id.*

Note

The requesting party should ask the trial court to conduct an in camera review if there are any disputes over the privilege log. See ***In re Honza****, 242 S.W.3d at 582.*

(d) Protective order. The expert must be subject to a protective order that prohibits her from disclosing confidential or privileged information other than what is allowed by the discovery order. *E.g.*, **In re Honza**, 242 S.W.3d at 582–83 (expert was prohibited from disclosing confidential information observed during imaging process, and expert and P's representatives were subject to contempt for violating order); *see, e.g.*, **In re Pinnacle Eng'g**, 405 S.W.3d at 846 (nothing in order compelling production of hard drives provided guidelines for how expert would protect Ds' privacy interests or handle privileged matters; trial court abused discretion in compelling production).

§8.2 Motion for protective order. A responding party who resists discovery may file a motion for protective order in response to a discovery request or to a motion to compel. Tex. R. Civ. P. 192.6(a). See "Motion for protective order," ch. 6-A, §20. For a discussion of specific grounds for protecting the disclosure of electronic information, see "Motion for protective order," **O'Connor's Federal Rules * Civil Trials**, ch. 6-C, §11.1 (2021 ed.).

D. Securing Discovery from Experts

§1. General

§1.1 Rules. Tex. R. Civ. P. 192.3, 192.7, 194.3, 195. See Tex. R. Civ. P. 197.1 (interrogatories cannot be used to secure information covered by TRCP 195).

§1.2 Purpose. This section discusses discovery about and from expert witnesses.

§1.3 Forms. **O'Connor's Texas Civil Forms**, FORMS 6D:1 et seq. (2020 ed.).

§1.4 Other references. Gold, *"Questioning God": Issues & Tactics When a Party Is Designated as a Testifying Expert*, Litigation Strategies Course, State Bar of Texas CLE, ch. 2 (2011); Gold, *"So, Who Died & Made You King?": How & When to Ask the Right Questions About Experts Under Texas' New Discovery Rules*, Advanced Expert Witness Course, State Bar of Texas CLE, ch. 14.1 (2004); Griesel, *The "New" Texas Discovery Rules: Three Years Later*, Advanced Evidence & Discovery Course, State Bar of Texas CLE, ch. 2, §IX (2002); **O'Connor's Texas Causes of Action** (2021 ed.); Brown & Rondon, **Texas Rules of Evidence Handbook** (2021 ed.).

§2. Types of experts

An expert witness is a person with specialized knowledge who is consulted in anticipation of litigation or in preparation for trial and who renders opinions about the matters at issue. *See* Tex. R. Civ. P. 192.3(e); Tex. R. Evid. 702 to 704. TRCP 192.3(e) recognizes two categories of experts: (1) testifying experts, which can be subdivided into retained and nonretained, and (2) consulting experts, which can be subdivided into consulting-only experts, consulting experts whose work was reviewed by a testifying expert, and consulting experts who obtain factual knowledge about the case.

§2.1 Testifying experts. A testifying expert is an expert who may be called to testify as an expert witness at trial. Tex. R. Civ. P. 192.7(c).

1. Making designation. Testifying experts are either retained or nonretained, and different discovery rules apply to each.

(1) Retained testifying expert. A retained testifying expert is an expert who is retained by, employed by, or otherwise subject to the control of the party. *See* Tex. R. Civ. P. 195.5(a)(4). Examples include a physician employed to give an opinion in a breast-implant case and an accident reconstructionist retained in a car-accident case. Certain information about retained testifying experts is generally discoverable. See "Discovery about retained expert," ch. 6-D, §3.1.1.

Practice Tip

In medical-malpractice cases, plaintiff's and defense attorneys are sure to argue about the phrase "retained by, employed by." Does it include an emergency-room physician that the plaintiff did not choose and perhaps did not even pay? Probably not. Whether it includes treating physicians, who are seldom under a party's control and are often hostile to being called as witnesses, is an open question. Until this phrase is clarified by the courts, a party should probably designate as retained experts only those physicians employed for litigation or subject to a party's control.

---

(2) Nonretained testifying expert. A nonretained expert is an expert who is not retained by, employed by, or otherwise subject to the party's control. *See* Tex. R. Civ. P. 195.5(a)(3). Examples include an emergency-room physician, an accident investigator for the DPS, and the other party's expert whom the party intends to call to testify. Certain information about nonretained testifying experts is discoverable. See "Discovery about nonretained expert," ch. 6-D, §3.1.2.

2. Changing designation. Under certain circumstances, a witness who is originally designated as a testifying expert may be dedesignated and redesignated as a consulting-only expert. *See* **Castellanos v. Littlejohn**, 945 S.W.2d 236, 240 (Tex.App.—San Antonio 1997, orig. proceeding); *see also* **In re Christus Spohn Hosp. Kleberg**, 222 S.W.3d 434, 445 (Tex.2007) (attorney who discovers privileged documents were inadvertently provided to testifying expert may presumably

withdraw expert's designation to avoid discovery of documents). See "Consulting-only expert," ch. 6-D, §2.2.1. To be permissible, the dedesignation must not be part of a bargain between the parties to suppress testimony or be done for some other improper purpose. *E.g.*, **In re State Farm Mut. Auto. Ins.**, 100 S.W.3d 338, 340–41 (Tex.App.—San Antonio 2002, orig. proceeding) (dedesignation improper when D waited to dedesignate until after trial court had ruled certain documents were discoverable; timing of dedesignation suggested D was trying to conceal evidence); **Castellanos**, 945 S.W.2d at 240 (dedesignation proper when evidence showed designation as testifying expert was result of clerical error); *see, e.g.*, **Tom L. Scott, Inc. v. McIlhany**, 798 S.W.2d 556, 559–60 (Tex.1990) (dedesignation improper when parties bargained for "rights" to experts during settlement negotiations and made settlement contingent on experts not being required to give testimony); *see also* **Harnischfeger Corp. v. Stone**, 814 S.W.2d 263, 265 (Tex.App.—Houston [14th Dist.] 1991, orig. proceeding) (improper for trial court to deny D2 discovery from witness that P designated as consulting expert in suit against D2 when D1 had designated witness as testifying expert in earlier companion case that involved same accident and negligence claims; D2 was entitled to depose witness based on his designation as testifying expert in companion case).

§2.2 Consulting experts. A consulting expert is an expert who has been consulted, retained, or specially employed by a party in anticipation of litigation or in preparation for trial, but who is not a testifying expert. Tex. R. Civ. P. 192.7(d).

1. Consulting-only expert. A consulting-only expert is an expert (1) who is hired as a trial consultant only, (2) who is not expected to testify, (3) who has no firsthand factual knowledge about the case and no secondhand factual knowledge except for knowledge acquired through the consultation, and (4) whose work product, opinions, or mental impressions are not reviewed by the testifying expert. Tex. R. Civ. P. 192.3(e), 192.7(d); *see* Tex. R. Civ. P. 192.3(c); **In re Ford Motor Co.**, 988 S.W.2d 714, 719 (Tex.1998); **Lindsey v. O'Neill**, 689 S.W.2d 400, 402 (Tex.1985). The consulting-only expert privilege grants the party and its attorney a sphere of protection and privacy in which to develop their case. **General Motors Corp. v. Gayle**, 951 S.W.2d 469, 474 (Tex.1997). A party's employee can be a consulting-only expert if she was not employed in the area that is the subject of litigation, has no firsthand knowledge of facts, and was reassigned to that area specifically to assist her employer in anticipation of litigation or in preparation for trial. *See* Tex. R. Civ. P. 192.7(d); **Axelson, Inc. v. McIlhany**, 798 S.W.2d 550, 555 (Tex.1990). Information about consulting-only experts is not discoverable. *See* **Axelson, Inc.**, 798 S.W.2d at 554 & n.8; *see, e.g.*, **Castellanos v. Littlejohn**, 945 S.W.2d 236, 239 (Tex.App.—San Antonio 1997, orig. proceeding) (because P's attorney hired doctor to examine P, not to treat P or to testify, doctor was not discoverable). See "No discovery about consulting-only expert," ch. 6-D, §3.2.1.

Practice Tip

Initially treating an expert as a consulting-only expert and assuring that the expert does not obtain factual knowledge of the case may allow the attorney to explore the consulting expert's opinions before designating her as a testifying expert and exposing those opinions to discovery. To protect an expert's status as just a consulting-only expert, do not let the consulting expert view the site of the accident or examine or test the physical evidence in the case, do not let the consulting expert's work be reviewed by the testifying expert, and do not let the consulting expert interact with the testifying expert. Keep separate, segregated files for each expert, and keep a log of all documents reviewed by each expert.

2. Consulting expert + work reviewed = testifying expert. A consulting expert whose mental impressions and opinions were reviewed by a testifying expert is considered to be, and is treated just like, a testifying expert. Tex. R. Civ. P. 192.3(e); **In re Ford Motor Co.**, 988 S.W.2d at 719; **Martin v. Boles**, 843 S.W.2d 90, 92 (Tex.App.—Texarkana 1992, orig. proceeding). A consulting expert whose work was reviewed by the testifying expert is discoverable to the same extent as a testifying expert. **Beam v. A.H. Chaney, Inc.**, 56 S.W.3d 920, 925 (Tex.App.—Fort Worth 2001, pet. denied). Because employees of the testifying expert are not considered consulting experts if they did not form an opinion reviewed by the testifying expert, their disclosure is not required. *See, e.g.*, *id.* at 925–26 (testifying expert's employee who did not form opinions or mental impressions in case and simply functioned as assistant was not consulting expert). See "Discovery about consulting expert + work reviewed," ch. 6-D, §3.2.2.

3. Consulting expert + obtained facts = dual-capacity witness. A consulting expert who obtained knowledge about the case either firsthand or in some way other than in consultation about the case is considered a "dual-capacity

witness" and is discoverable as a fact witness. *See* Tex. R. Civ. P. 192.3(c). For example, when a consulting expert visits an accident site to measure skid marks, the expert acquires firsthand information about the case; thus, the expert's identity and factual knowledge must be disclosed, just as with other fact witnesses. *See, e.g.*, **Axelson, Inc.**, 798 S.W.2d at 555 (consultants hired after accident to examine wellhead equipment were discoverable as fact witnesses; employee could not be a consulting-only expert because he was employed in area that became subject of litigation). By comparison, when a consulting expert examines a photograph of the accident site, the expert does not become discoverable as a fact witness. See "Discovery about consulting expert + obtained facts," ch. 6-D, §3.2.3.

§3. Available discovery procedures

6-6. Procedures for Securing Discovery About & from Experts

	Type of discovery	Testifying expert who is—		Consulting expert—	
		Retained	Nonretained	Whose work was reviewed	With facts
1	Disclosures. Tex. R. Civ. P. 192.1(a), 194.3.	Yes. Tex. R. Civ. P. 195.1, 195.5(a).	Yes. Tex. R. Civ. P. 195.5(a).	No.	Yes. Tex. R. Civ. P. 194.2(b)(5).
2	Oral deposition. Tex. R. Civ. P. 192.1(f), 199.	Yes. Tex. R. Civ. P. 195.4.	Yes. Tex. R. Civ. P. 205.1(a).	Yes. Tex. R. Civ. P. 205.1(a).	Yes. Tex. R. Civ. P. 205.1(a).
3	Court-ordered expert report. Tex. R. Civ. P. 195.5(b).	Yes.	No.	No.	No.
4	Request for documents, separate from deposition. Tex. R. Civ. P. 176, 192.1(b).	No.	Yes. Tex. R. Civ. P. 195 cmt. 2 (1999).	Yes.	Yes.
5	Deposition on written questions. Tex. R. Civ. P. 192.1(f), 200, 205.1(b).	No.	Yes.	Yes.	Yes.
6	Interrogatories. Tex. R. Civ. P. 192.1(d), 197.1.	No.	No.	Yes.	Yes.
7	Request for admissions. Tex. R. Civ. P. 192.1(e), 198.1.	No.	No.	Yes.	Yes.

§3.1 Testifying experts. TRCP 195 is the main rule governing discovery from testifying experts.

2021 Rule Amendments

In 2020, the Supreme Court approved significant amendments to TRCP 194 and 195. See Tex.Sup.Ct. Order, Misc. Docket No. 20-9153 (eff. Jan. 1, 2021). Under the amendments, a party is now required to disclose the expert-witness information outlined in TRCP 195.5(a) without waiting for a discovery request from the other party. See Tex. R. Civ. P. 194.3, 195.5(a). The amendments apply to cases filed on or after January 1, 2021, except those filed in justice court. Tex.Sup.Ct. Order, Misc. Docket No. 20-9153 (eff. Jan. 1, 2021). For cases filed before January 1, 2021, a party must still use requests for disclosure or other permissible discovery procedures to obtain the information. See "Disclosures," ch. 6-E, §1 et seq.

1. Discovery about retained expert. There are four discovery procedures that can be used to secure information about or from a retained testifying expert: (1) required disclosures, (2) an expert report, (3) an oral deposition, and (4) a request for production with oral deposition. *See* Tex. R. Civ. P. 194.3, 195.1, 195.4, 195.5. A party cannot seek information about a retained testifying expert through depositions on written questions, interrogatories, or other forms of discovery not listed in TRCP 195.1. *See, e.g.*, **In re National Lloyds Ins.**, 532 S.W.3d 794, 814 (Tex.2017) (Ps sought discovery of attorney-billing information from expert using interrogatories and requests for production, which are not permissible methods for

obtaining expert discovery under TRCP 195.1). For the types of discoverable information about retained testifying experts, see "Information about retained testifying experts," ch. 6-D, §4.1.1; for the types of discoverable information about retained nontestifying experts, see "Consulting experts," ch. 6-D, §4.2.

2. Discovery about nonretained expert. There are four discovery procedures that can be used to secure information about or from a nonretained testifying expert: (1) required disclosures, (2) an oral deposition, (3) a deposition on written questions, and (4) a subpoena. *See* Tex. R. Civ. P. 176, 194.3, 195.5(a)(1) to (3), 205.1. For example, a DPS officer who investigated an accident can be deposed on written questions or subpoenaed to attend an oral deposition, and information about the officer can be secured from a party through disclosures. TRCP 195.1 lists the permissible discovery tools for testifying experts, but Comment 2 to the rule states that TRCP 195 does not address depositions of nonretained testifying experts or the production from them of the materials listed in TRCP 192.3(e)(5) (witness bias) and TRCP 192.3(e)(6) (documents provided to or reviewed by the expert). Tex. R. Civ. P. 195 cmt. 2 (1999). For the scope of discovery from nonretained experts, see "Information about nonretained experts," ch. 6-D, §4.1.2.

(1) Discovery from party. Under TRCP 195.5, a party—without waiting for a discovery request—is required to disclose a nonretained testifying expert's name, address, and telephone number, the subject matter the expert will testify about, and documents reflecting the general substance of the expert's mental impressions and opinions and a brief summary of the basis for them. TRCP 195.5(a)(1) to (3). See "2021 Rule Amendments," ch. 6-D, §3.1. To secure additional information about a nonretained testifying expert, the party seeking discovery can use other available discovery procedures (e.g., an oral deposition of the other party).

(2) Discovery from nonretained expert. To secure information from a nonretained testifying expert, a party can use a subpoena and deposition (oral or written) to secure the following: (1) detailed information about those matters listed in TRCP 195.5(a)(2) and (3) (the subject of testimony and substance of opinion) and (2) any other discoverable information outlined in TRCP 192.3(e) (scope of discovery). For example, to secure information about a nonretained testifying expert's bias, the party may depose the expert or subpoena records from her.

(3) Discovery from treating doctors. Medical information is protected from disclosure by a number of federal and state rules and statutes. See "Physician-patient privilege," ch. 6-B, §3.10; "Mental-health-information privilege," ch. 6-B, §3.11; "Other medical privileges," ch. 6-B, §3.12.

(a) Ex parte communications not prohibited. Ex parte communications between an attorney and the treating doctor of a party-patient are not specifically prohibited by any rule or statute. **Durst v. Hill Country Mem'l Hosp.**, 70 S.W.3d 233, 237–38 (Tex.App.—San Antonio 2001, no pet.); *see, e.g.*, **Hogue v. Kroger Store**, 875 S.W.2d 477, 480–81 (Tex.App.—Houston [1st Dist.] 1994, writ denied) (trial court's finding that ex parte communications that did not involve disclosure of privileged information were not improper was reasonable; court refused to permit P to cross-examine P's treating doctor about propriety of ex parte communications with D's attorney). But ex parte communications are limited by the physician-patient privilege, which generally prohibits the disclosure of confidential communications between a physician and patient. *See* **In re Collins**, 286 S.W.3d 911, 916 (Tex.2009). See "Physician-patient privilege," ch. 6-B, §3.10. In most cases, a treating doctor will not speak to an attorney ex parte without a signed medical authorization. See "Disclosure from other health-care provider or entity," ch. 6-J, §3.2.2. The Supreme Court has suggested that the statutory authorization forms given in medical-malpractice suits under CPRC §74.052 actually authorize ex parte communications. *See* **In re Collins**, 286 S.W.3d at 916–18 (CPRC §74.052 contemplates that ex parte communications are necessary to allow Ds to evaluate claims and settle those with merit early in litigation). For a discussion of the CPRC §74.052 authorization form for release of protected health-care information, see "Authorization form," **O'Connor's Texas Causes of Action**, ch. 20-A, §7.1.5 (2021 ed.).

Note

*In **In re Collins**, the Supreme Court clarified its opinion in **Mutter v. Wood**, 744 S.W.2d 600 (Tex.1988), which held that the trial court abused its discretion by requiring the plaintiff to sign an authorization form allowing the defendant's attorney to discuss the plaintiff's medical information with treating physicians. See **In re Collins**, 286 S.W.3d at 918. In **Collins**, the Supreme Court made clear*

*that the **Mutter** holding was not because the authorization form allowed for ex parte communications, but because it allowed access to information that was not relevant to the underlying suit, which was a clear violation of the physician-patient privilege. Id.*

(b) Preventing ex parte communications. To prevent ex parte communications with a treating doctor, the attorney should take the following steps:

[1] Notify the treating doctor in writing that the doctor's patient (the attorney's client) does not authorize the doctor to discuss the patient's treatment or condition outside the presence of the patient's attorney, and that divulging any confidential information is a violation of the physician-patient privilege.

[2] Draft the medical authorization to expressly prohibit any ex parte communications. See "No ex parte discovery," ch. 6-J, §3.2.3.

[3] Move for a protective order at the outset of the case to prevent ex parte communications with any of the patient's doctors. *See* **In re Collins**, 286 S.W.3d at 914; **In re Trostel**, No. 05-00-02059-CV, 2001 WL 670490 (Tex.App.—Dallas 2001, orig. proceeding) (no pub.; 6-15-01). The motion should include the following arguments: (1) the patient's treating doctor has information that is not relevant to the suit, (2) the irrelevant information is privileged, and (3) prohibiting ex parte communications with the doctor is necessary to protect the patient's privileged information. *See* **In re Collins**, 286 S.W.3d at 914. See "Motion for protective order," ch. 6-A, §20.

§3.2 Consulting experts.

1. No discovery about consulting-only expert. Consulting-only experts are protected from discovery as part of the work-product privilege. *See* Tex. R. Civ. P. 195 cmt. 1 (1999). Because no information about a consulting-only expert is discoverable, there are no discovery tools that can be used to secure information about them or from them.

2. Discovery about consulting expert + work reviewed. A party cannot use TRCP 195 (discovery from testifying experts) to secure information about a consulting expert whose work was reviewed by the testifying expert. See chart 6-6 under "Available discovery procedures," ch. 6-D, §3. But a party can use any other discovery rule to secure this information. *See* Tex. R. Civ. P. 195 cmt. 1 (1999) (methods of securing discovery about consulting expert whose work was reviewed by testifying expert are not limited by TRCP 195). Thus, a party can use interrogatories, requests for admissions, requests for production, and any other type of discovery.

3. Discovery about consulting expert + obtained facts. The discovery procedures available to secure information about a consulting expert who has firsthand knowledge about the facts or secondhand knowledge gained outside the consultation are the same as those for securing information about fact witnesses. *See* Tex. R. Civ. P. 192.3(c). Thus, to secure information about these consulting experts, a party can use required disclosures in TRCP 194.2(b)(5) (for fact witnesses), interrogatories, requests for admissions, and any other type of discovery. See "2021 Rule Amendments," ch. 6-D, §3.1.

§4. Information discoverable from experts

6-7. Scope of Discovery from Experts

	Information to be discovered	Testifying expert who is—		Consulting expert—	
		Retained	Nonretained	Whose work was reviewed	With facts
1	Identity of expert. Tex. R. Civ. P. 192.3(e)(1).	Yes	Yes	Yes	Yes
2	Subject matter of testimony. Tex. R. Civ. P. 192.3(e)(2).	Yes	Yes	Yes	N/A
3	Facts learned through consultation. Tex. R. Civ. P. 192.3(e)(3).	Yes	Yes	Yes	No
4	Firsthand facts acquired directly from evidence. Tex. R. Civ. P. 192.3(e)(3).	Yes	Yes	Yes	Yes

6-7. Scope of Discovery from Experts					
Information to be discovered		Testifying expert who is—		Consulting expert—	
		Retained	Nonretained	Whose work was reviewed	With facts
5	Secondhand facts learned outside consultation. Tex. R. Civ. P. 192.3(e)(3).	Yes	Yes	Yes	Yes
6	Mental impressions, opinions and methods used to derive opinions. Tex. R. Civ. P. 192.3(e)(4).	Yes	Yes	Yes	No
7	Bias of witness. Tex. R. Civ. P. 192.3(e)(5).	Yes	Yes	Yes	Maybe[1]
8	Materials and documents created or used by expert. Tex. R. Civ. P. 192.3(e)(6).	Yes	Yes	Yes	No
9	Written report. Tex. R. Civ. P. 192.3(e)(6).	Yes	Maybe[2]	Yes	N/A
10	Résumé and bibliography. Tex. R. Civ. P. 192.3(e)(7).	Yes	Yes	Yes	No

[1] When a party is entitled to bias information about a consulting expert with facts, it cannot obtain that information under TRCP 192.3(e), which outlines the scope of discovery for consulting and testifying experts.

[2] If the nonretained expert did not create a written report, a party cannot force the expert to prepare one.

§4.1 Testifying experts. The information a party can discover about a testifying expert depends on whether the expert is retained.

2021 Rule Amendments

In 2020, the Supreme Court approved significant amendments to TRCP 194 and 195. See Tex.Sup.Ct Order, Misc. Docket No. 20-9153 (eff. Jan. 1, 2021). Under the amendments, a party is now generally required to disclose the expert-witness information outlined in TRCP 195.5 without waiting for a discovery request from the other party. See Tex. R. Civ. P. 194.3, 195.5. See "Required disclosures—Cases filed on or after 1-1-21," ch. 6-E, §3. Communications between the party's attorney and any testifying expert, however, are generally protected from discovery. Tex. R. Civ. P. 195.5(c). See "Protected communications," ch. 6-E, §3.4.3. These amendments apply to cases filed on or after January 1, 2021, except those filed in justice court. Tex.Sup.Ct. Order, Misc. Docket No. 20-9153 (eff. Jan. 1, 2021).

1. Information about retained testifying experts. Parties are entitled to full discovery of each other's retained testifying experts. *See* Tex. R. Civ. P. 192.3(e), 192.5(c)(1), 195.5(a); **Aluminum Co. of Am. v. Bullock**, 870 S.W.2d 2, 4 (Tex.1994); **Collins v. Collins**, 904 S.W.2d 792, 800 (Tex.App.—Houston [1st Dist.] 1995), *writ denied*, 923 S.W.2d 569 (Tex.1996). The following is a list of the discoverable information about retained testifying experts:

(1) Identity. A party is entitled to the names, addresses, and telephone numbers of the retained testifying expert witnesses. Tex. R. Civ. P. 192.3(e)(1); *see* **Morrow v. H.E.B., Inc.**, 714 S.W.2d 297, 297 (Tex.1986) (duty to supplement if witness acquires new address). For cases filed on or after January 1, 2021, TRCP 195.5 requires automatic disclosure of this information; no discovery request is necessary. Tex. R. Civ. P. 195.5(a)(1).

(2) Subject of testimony. A party is entitled to discover the subject matter on which the retained testifying expert will testify. Tex. R. Civ. P. 192.3(e)(2); *see* **Aluminum Co.**, 870 S.W.2d at 4. For cases filed on or after January 1, 2021, TRCP 195.5 requires automatic disclosure of this information; no discovery request is necessary. Tex. R. Civ. P. 195.5(a)(2). More detailed information can be secured through an oral deposition or an expert's report. *See* Tex. R. Civ. P. 195.1, 195.4, 195.5(b).

(3) Facts. A party is entitled to discover the facts known by the retained testifying expert that relate to or form the basis of the expert's mental impressions and opinions formed or made in connection with the case, regardless of when and how the factual information was acquired. Tex. R. Civ. P. 192.3(e)(3). For cases filed on or after January 1, 2021, TRCP 195.5 requires automatic disclosure of this information; no discovery request is necessary. *See* Tex. R. Civ. P. 195.5(a)(3). More detailed information can be secured through an oral deposition or an expert's report. *See* Tex. R. Civ. P. 195.1, 195.4, 195.5(b).

(4) Opinions. A party is entitled to discover the mental impressions and opinions of the retained testifying expert and any methods used to derive them. Tex. R. Civ. P. 192.3(e)(4); **Yarborough v. Tarrant Appr. Dist.**, 846 S.W.2d 552, 553 (Tex.App.—Fort Worth 1993, no writ). Any information about the testifying expert's mental impressions or opinions is discoverable. Tex. R. Civ. P. 192.3(e)(3), (e)(4); *e.g.*, **In re Family Hospice, Ltd.**, 62 S.W.3d 313, 316 (Tex.App.—El Paso 2001, orig. proceeding) (expert's notes made while reviewing interrogatories were discoverable). For cases filed on or after January 1, 2021, TRCP 195.5 requires automatic disclosure of the general substance of the retained testifying expert's mental impressions and opinions and a brief summary of the basis for them; no discovery request is necessary. Tex. R. Civ. P. 195.5(a)(3). More detailed information can be secured through an oral deposition or an expert's report. *See* Tex. R. Civ. P. 195.1, 195.4, 195.5(b).

Practice Tip

TRCP 192.3(e)(4) permits discovery of the expert's method in arriving at an opinion. But TRCP 195.5(a)(3) does not include this among the matters that must be provided in the required disclosures. A responding party should include the expert's methodology, even though it is not required by TRCP 195.5(a)(3), because that party will have the burden to show the expert's methodology is sound if the expert's opinion is challenged as inadmissible under TRE 702. See ***Merrell Dow Pharms. v. Havner****, 953 S.W.2d 706, 714 (Tex.1997) (expert's opinion is not admissible if based on flawed methodology). See "Motion to Exclude Expert," ch. 5-N, §1 et seq.*

---

(5) Evidence of bias. A party is entitled to discover information about the retained testifying expert's potential bias. Tex. R. Civ. P. 192.3(e)(5); **In re Ford Motor Co.**, 427 S.W.3d 396, 397 (Tex.2014); **In re Doctors' Hosp.**, 2 S.W.3d 504, 507 (Tex.App.—San Antonio 1999, orig. proceeding); *see also* Tex. R. Evid. 613(b) (admissibility of evidence of witness's bias). See Brown & Rondon, **Texas Rules of Evidence Handbook**, Rule 613 (2021 ed.) (§B). Information about a retained testifying expert's bias can be obtained through required disclosures, the expert's report, or an oral deposition of the expert. *See* Tex. R. Civ. P. 195.1, 195.4, 195.5; **In re Ford Motor**, 427 S.W.3d at 397.

(a) List of expert's other cases. For cases filed on or after January 1, 2021, a party is specifically entitled to a list of all other cases in which the expert testified as an expert at trial or by deposition within the last four years, except when the expert is the disclosing party's attorney and is testifying about attorney fees. Tex. R. Civ. P. 195.5(a)(4)(D). TRCP 195.5 requires automatic disclosure of this information; no discovery request is necessary. Tex. R. Civ. P. 195.5(a)(4)(D). More detailed information can be secured through an oral deposition. *See* Tex. R. Civ. P. 195.1, 195.4.

Note

For cases filed before January 1, 2021, this information can be secured through a targeted request for disclosure asking for the information as part of the expert's résumé, by deposition, or as part of a court-ordered report. See Tex. R. Civ. P. 195.1 (pre-1-1-21 version).

(b) Discovery beyond expert's own deposition to impeach. Discovery of evidence beyond the expert's own deposition, such as personal financial records, appointment books, or other information not directly related to the suit, is generally not discoverable to impeach a nonparty witness with evidence of bias. *See* **In re Ford Motor**, 427 S.W.3d at 397; **Russell v. Young**, 452 S.W.2d 434, 435 (Tex.1970); **In re Makris**, 217 S.W.3d 521, 524 (Tex.App.—San Antonio 2006, orig. proceeding). Whether a party can obtain this type of discovery to impeach a nonparty expert depends on whether the expert's credibility is at issue.

[1] Credibility not at issue. If the expert's credibility is not at issue, the party must show the possibility that the expert is biased before it is entitled to the additional discovery to impeach the expert. *See* **In re Ford Motor**, 427 S.W.3d at 398; *see, e.g.*, **In re Makris**, 217 S.W.3d at 524–26 (no evidence presented to show expert was biased); **In re Wharton**, 226 S.W.3d 452, 457–58 (Tex.App.—Waco 2005, orig. proceeding) (same).

[2] Credibility at issue. If the party can show that the expert's credibility is at issue, the party may be entitled to the additional discovery to impeach the expert. *See, e.g.*, **Walker v. Packer**, 827 S.W.2d 833, 838–39 (Tex.1992) (because expert's credibility was put at issue when colleague contradicted his testimony, Ps could depose expert's employer's representative and request certain employment records to explore expert's potential bias).

Note

In ***Walker***, *the Texas Supreme Court held that discovery beyond the expert's deposition—specifically, the deposition of the expert's employer's representative—should have been allowed to explore the expert's possible bias when extrinsic evidence had been discovered to put the expert's credibility in doubt. See* ***Walker***, *827 S.W.2d at 838–39. But the Court later held that after deposing two experts, a plaintiff could not depose their corporate representatives about detailed financial and business information to show the experts' bias.* ***In re Ford Motor***, *427 S.W.3d at 397. The Court distinguished* ***Walker*** *because in* ***In re Ford***, *neither expert's credibility was at issue and the plaintiff had not shown any other reason for deposing the representatives. Id. at 398. The Court in* ***In re Ford*** *also raised the question whether the specific holding in* ***Walker***—*that deposing the expert's employer's representative was justified—would still apply because the case was decided before TRCP 195 was adopted.* ***In re Ford Motor***, *427 S.W.3d at 398. TRCP 195 provides only for expert disclosures, expert reports, and experts' oral depositions as the permissible methods for seeking information about an expert's potential bias. See Tex. R. Civ. P. 195.1;* ***In re Ford Motor***, *427 S.W.3d at 398. See "Available discovery procedures," ch. 6-D, §3.*

(6) Materials used by expert.

(a) Expert materials = generally discoverable. A party is entitled to all documents, tangible things, models, reports, or compilations of data that have been provided to, reviewed by, or prepared by or for the retained testifying expert in anticipation of the expert's testimony. *See* Tex. R. Civ. P. 192.3(e)(6); **In re City of Dickinson**, 568 S.W.3d 642, 646 (Tex.2019); **In re National Lloyds Ins.**, 532 S.W.3d 794, 813–14 & n.92 (Tex.2017); **In re Christus Spohn Hosp. Kleberg**, 222 S.W.3d 434, 437–38 (Tex.2007). These materials are discoverable if they are provided to a testifying expert, regardless of whether they were actually read by or prepared for the expert. *See* Tex. R. Civ. P. 192.3(e)(6); **In re Christus Spohn Hosp. Kleberg**, 222 S.W.3d at 444–45. Everything provided to, reviewed by, or prepared by or for the retained testifying expert in preparation of the expert's testimony, including the expert's file, communications with the parties and their attorneys, and drafts of reports prepared by the expert, may be discoverable. *See* Tex. R. Civ. P. 195.5(a)(4)(A). For cases filed on or after January 1, 2021, TRCP 195.5 requires automatic disclosure of this information; no discovery request is necessary. Tex. R. Civ. P. 195.5(a)(4)(A). A party can also obtain this information through an oral deposition with a request for documents. *See* Tex. R. Civ. P. 195.1, 195.4.

Practice Tip

Do not rely on cases that apply old TRCP 166b to decide what documents used by retained testifying experts are discoverable. TRCP 192.3(e)(6), which was adopted in 1999 to replace TRCP 166b, expanded the list of the discoverable documents used by an expert to form an opinion. TRCP 192.3(e)(6) includes documents that were "provided to" or "reviewed by" an expert. ***In re Christus Spohn Hosp. Kleberg***, *222 S.W.3d at 438. The change was made to avoid disputes about what documents the expert may have relied on to reach an opinion. Id.*

(b) Application of privilege to expert materials.

[1] Party testifies as expert. When a party or a party's employee testifies as an expert witness in the party's own case, testifying-expert materials are not discoverable if protected by the attorney-client privilege. *See* **In re City**

of Dickinson, 568 S.W.3d at 646. Discovery of testifying-expert materials is merely permissible and not required under TRCP 192.3, and the rule does not specifically prohibit using the attorney-client privilege to withhold testifying-expert materials; thus, the materials can be withheld if the attorney-client privilege applies. **In re City of Dickinson**, 568 S.W.3d at 646; *see* Tex. R. Civ. P. 192.3(a), (e)(6).

[2] Materials inadvertently disclosed to expert. When a party inadvertently discloses privileged materials to its own testifying expert, those materials become discoverable and generally cannot be retrieved by the party under the snap-back provision. **In re Christus Spohn Hosp. Kleberg**, 222 S.W.3d at 440–41. The policy concerns underlying the expert-disclosure rule mandate that the rules requiring discovery of the materials provided to an expert, TRCP 192.3(e)(6) and TRCP 192.5(c)(1), prevail over the snap-back provision in TRCP 193.3(d). Once privileged materials are inadvertently disclosed, the party has two options to avoid waiving the privilege.

Practice Tip

One way to avoid inadvertent disclosure of privileged information to a testifying expert is to keep a detailed log of all documents provided and to make sure all documents provided contain an identifying Bates number.

[a] Invoke snap-back provision. Although the snap-back provision generally does not apply to privileged documents inadvertently disclosed to an expert, the party may be able to make a persuasive argument that the disclosed materials could not, by their nature, have influenced the expert's opinion. **In re Christus Spohn Hosp. Kleberg**, 222 S.W.3d at 441. See "Use snap-back provision," ch. 6-A, §18.2.4. The party seeking snap-back under this argument bears a heavy burden, considering the underlying purpose of the expert-disclosure rule. **In re Christus Spohn Hosp. Kleberg**, 222 S.W.3d at 441.

[b] Request replacement expert. As an alternative to snap-back, the party can withdraw the expert's designation and name a new expert. **In re Christus Spohn Hosp. Kleberg**, 222 S.W.3d at 445. If the deadline for designating experts has passed, the party should file a motion for leave to designate a replacement. *See id.* The court should carefully weigh a request for leave to designate a replacement expert against the possibility of imposing what may amount to death-penalty sanctions against the party. *Id.*

(7) Expert's report. A party is entitled to copies of reports prepared by or for the retained testifying expert in anticipation of the expert's testimony. Tex. R. Civ. P. 192.3(e)(6). For cases filed on or after January 1, 2021, TRCP 195.5 requires automatic disclosure of this information; no discovery request is necessary. Tex. R. Civ. P. 195.5(a)(4)(A). But a draft expert report is protected from discovery, regardless of the form in which it is recorded. Tex. R. Civ. P. 195.5(d). When a retained testifying expert has not prepared a written report, the court may order that a report be put in writing or other tangible form and be produced. Tex. R. Civ. P. 195.5(b); **Loftin v. Martin**, 776 S.W.2d 145, 147 (Tex.1989); *see, e.g.*, **Dennis v. Haden**, 867 S.W.2d 48, 51–52 (Tex.App.—Texarkana 1993, writ denied) (because party did not provide expert's report as required by pretrial order, expert should have been excluded). See "Expert's report," ch. 6-D, §7; **O'Connor's Texas Civil Forms**, FORM 6D:1 (2020 ed.).

(8) Résumé & bibliography. A party is entitled to the current résumé and bibliography of retained testifying experts. Tex. R. Civ. P. 192.3(e)(7). For cases filed on or after January 1, 2021, TRCP 195.5 requires automatic disclosure of this information; no discovery request is necessary. Tex. R. Civ. P. 195.5(a)(4)(B). If the facts on the résumé change before trial, the party who retained the expert has a duty to supplement. *See, e.g.*, **City of Paris v. McDowell**, 79 S.W.3d 601, 606 (Tex.App.—Texarkana 2002, no pet.) (expert earned a master's degree between initial disclosure and trial, which was not reflected on résumé).

(9) Qualifications. For cases filed on or after January 1, 2021, a party is specifically entitled to information about the expert's qualifications, including a list of all publications the expert authored in the last ten years. Tex. R. Civ. P. 195.5(a)(4)(C). TRCP 195.5 requires automatic disclosure of this information; no discovery request is necessary. Tex. R. Civ. P. 195.5(a)(4)(C).

(10) Statement of compensation. For cases filed on or after January 1, 2021, a party is specifically entitled to a statement of the compensation that will be paid for the expert's study and testimony in the case. Tex. R. Civ. P. 195.5(a)(4)(E). TRCP 195.5 requires automatic disclosure of this information; no discovery request is necessary. Tex. R. Civ. P. 195.5(a)(4)(E).

2. Information about nonretained experts. The following is a list of the information discoverable about and from nonretained testifying experts:

(1) Identity. A party is entitled to the name, address, and telephone number of the nonretained testifying expert witnesses. Tex. R. Civ. P. 192.3(e)(1). For cases filed on or after January 1, 2021, TRCP 195.5 requires automatic disclosure of this information; no discovery request is necessary. Tex. R. Civ. P. 195.5(a)(1).

(2) Subject of testimony. A party is entitled to discover the subject matter of the nonretained testifying expert's testimony. Tex. R. Civ. P. 192.3(e)(2). For cases filed on or after January 1, 2021, TRCP 195.5 requires automatic disclosure of this information; no discovery request is necessary. Tex. R. Civ. P. 195.5(a)(2). A more detailed form of the information may be obtained from the nonretained expert through an oral deposition, a deposition on written questions, or a subpoena. *See* Tex. R. Civ. P. 176, 205; Tex. R. Civ. P. 195 cmt. 2 (1999).

(3) Facts. A party is entitled to discover the facts known by the nonretained testifying expert that relate to or form the basis of the expert's mental impressions and opinions. Tex. R. Civ. P. 192.3(e)(3). For cases filed on or after January 1, 2021, TRCP 195.5 requires automatic disclosure of this information; no discovery request is necessary. *See* Tex. R. Civ. P. 195.5(a)(3). A more detailed form of this information may be obtained from the nonretained expert through an oral deposition, a deposition on written questions, or a subpoena. *See* Tex. R. Civ. P. 176, 205; Tex. R. Civ. P. 195 cmt. 2 (1999).

(4) Opinions. A party is entitled to discover the general substance of the nonretained testifying expert's mental impressions and opinions and the basis for them. Tex. R. Civ. P. 192.3(e)(4). For cases filed on or after January 1, 2021, TRCP 195.5 requires automatic disclosure of documents reflecting this information; no discovery request is necessary. Tex. R. Civ. P. 195.5(a)(3). A more detailed form of this information may be obtained from the nonretained expert through an oral deposition, a deposition on written questions, or a subpoena. *See* Tex. R. Civ. P. 176, 205; Tex. R. Civ. P. 195 cmt. 2 (1999).

(5) Evidence of bias. A party is entitled to discover information about the nonretained testifying expert's potential bias. Tex. R. Civ. P. 192.3(e)(5). This information can be secured from the nonretained expert through an oral deposition, a deposition on written questions, or a subpoena. *See* Tex. R. Civ. P. 176, 205; Tex. R. Civ. P. 195 cmt. 2 (1999). Bias evidence about a nonretained testifying expert cannot be secured through TRCP 195. *See* Tex. R. Civ. P. 195 cmt. 2 (1999).

(6) Materials used by expert. A party is entitled to all documents, tangible things, physical models, reports, compilations of data, or other materials provided to, reviewed by, or prepared by or for the nonretained testifying expert in anticipation of the expert's testimony. Tex. R. Civ. P. 192.3(e)(6). This information can be secured from the nonretained expert through an oral deposition, a deposition on written questions, or a subpoena. *See* Tex. R. Civ. P. 176, 205; Tex. R. Civ. P. 195 cmt. 2 (1999). Materials used by a nontestifying expert cannot be secured through TRCP 195. *See* Tex. R. Civ. P. 195 cmt. 2 (1999).

(7) Expert's report. A report prepared by the nonretained testifying expert can be secured from the expert through TRCP 176 or TRCP 205. A nonretained expert's report cannot be secured through TRCP 195. Tex. R. Civ. P. 195 cmt. 2 (1999). See "Expert's report," ch. 6-D, §7.

(8) Résumé & bibliography. A party is entitled to the current résumé and bibliography of the nonretained testifying expert. Tex. R. Civ. P. 192.3(e)(7). The nonretained expert's résumé and bibliography can be secured from the nonretained expert through an oral deposition, a deposition on written questions, or a subpoena. *See* Tex. R. Civ. P. 176, 205; Tex. R. Civ. P. 195 cmt. 2 (1999).

§4.2 Consulting experts.

1. Consulting-only expert—no discovery. Consulting-only experts are protected from discovery as part of the work-product privilege. *See* Tex. R. Civ. P. 195 cmt. 1 (1999). No information about a consulting-only expert is discoverable—

not the expert's identity, mental impressions, opinions, or work product. Tex. R. Civ. P. 192.3(e); **In re City of Georgetown**, 53 S.W.3d 328, 334 (Tex.2001); **In re Ford Motor Co.**, 988 S.W.2d 714, 719 (Tex.1998); *see also* **Aguilar v. Trujillo**, 162 S.W.3d 839, 848 (Tex.App.—El Paso 2005, pet. denied) (P abused discovery process when he contacted D's consulting expert without D's consent and hired him to be Ps' expert witness). Tests conducted by a consulting expert are protected from discovery as long as the tests are not conducted on the physical evidence in the case and the results are not reviewed by a testifying expert. *See* Tex. R. Civ. P. 192.3(e); *see, e.g.*, **General Motors Corp. v. Gayle**, 951 S.W.2d 469, 474–75 (Tex.1997) (order allowing P's representative to attend crash testing was abuse of discretion because it prevented D from consulting privately with expert before deciding whether to designate him as witness). Materials protected by the privilege for the nondiscoverable consulting-only expert cannot be discovered, and the privilege is not subject to the need-and-hardship exception in TRCP 192.5(b)(2). *See* Tex. R. Civ. P. 192.3(e); Tex. R. Civ. P. 195 cmt. 1 (1999).

2. Information about consulting expert + work reviewed. A party is entitled to obtain the same information about a consulting expert whose work was reviewed by a testifying expert as it can obtain about the testifying expert. Tex. R. Civ. P. 192.3(e); **Vela v. Wagner & Brown, Ltd.**, 203 S.W.3d 37, 58 (Tex.App.—San Antonio 2006, no pet.). See "Information about retained testifying experts," ch. 6-D, §4.1.1.

Practice Tip

Although TRCP 195 limits the procedures for securing discovery about testifying experts, it does not limit the procedures for securing discovery about discoverable consulting experts. Tex. R. Civ. P. 195 cmt. 1 (1999). Discovery about discoverable consulting experts can be obtained through any means permitted by the TRCPs (interrogatories, requests for production, depositions, etc.).

3. Information about consulting expert + obtained facts. A consulting expert with facts about the case is discoverable as a fact witness. See "Consulting expert + obtained facts = dual-capacity witness," ch. 6-D, §2.2.3. A party can obtain the same information about a consulting expert who has knowledge of facts as it can obtain about a fact witness. *See* Tex. R. Civ. P. 192.3(c) (scope of discovery), Tex. R. Civ. P. 192.5(c)(1) (exception to work product), Tex. R. Civ. P. 194.2(b)(5) (required disclosures). A party may obtain this discovery through TRCP 194.2(b)(5) and any other discovery rule except TRCP 195. The information discoverable about a consulting expert with facts includes the following:

(1) Identity. A party is entitled to the name, address, and telephone number of an expert who has firsthand knowledge of facts or secondhand knowledge of facts obtained outside the consultation. *See* Tex. R. Civ. P. 192.3(c) (scope of discovery), Tex. R. Civ. P. 194.2(b)(5) (required disclosures about fact witnesses).

(2) Connection with case. A party is entitled to obtain a brief description of the consulting expert's connection with the case. Tex. R. Civ. P. 192.3(c), 194.2(b)(5). This does not mean the party must provide a narrative statement of the facts the expert knows. Tex. R. Civ. P. 192 cmt. 3. For example, the description could be "examined wellhead after accident." *See id.*

(3) Facts known by consultant. A party is entitled to obtain the following information known by the consultant:

(a) Firsthand facts. The consultant's firsthand knowledge about information in the case. *See* Tex. R. Civ. P. 192.3(c).

(b) Secondhand facts. The consultant's secondhand knowledge (i.e., hearsay) about facts in the case learned in some way other than in consultation about the case (i.e., not in anticipation of litigation or in preparation for trial). *See* Tex. R. Civ. P. 192.3(c).

(4) Witness statements. A party is entitled to obtain a witness statement given by a consulting expert who has knowledge of the facts. Tex. R. Civ. P. 192.3(h).

§5. Supplementing expert discovery

A party has a duty to amend and supplement discovery about its testifying experts. Tex. R. Civ. P. 195.6. See **O'Connor's Texas Civil Forms**, FORMS 6D:2 to 6D:3 (2020 ed.).

§5.1 Supplementing discovery of retained testifying expert. An expert cannot give an opinion at trial that was not provided in response to discovery, unless there is good cause to permit it or the opinion would not unfairly surprise or prejudice the other parties. Tex. R. Civ. P. 193.6(a); *see* **Moore v. Memorial Hermann Hosp. Sys.**, 140 S.W.3d 870, 874 (Tex.App.—Houston [14th Dist.] 2004, no pet.); *see, e.g.*, **VingCard A.S. v. Merrimac Hospitality Sys.**, 59 S.W.3d 847, 856–57 (Tex.App.—Fort Worth 2001, pet. denied) (court did not find good cause but found admission of expert's opinion harmless error); *see also* **Ersek v. Davis & Davis, P.C.**, 69 S.W.3d 268, 271 (Tex.App.—Austin 2002, pet. denied) (court did not find good cause for designating expert after deadline, more than a year after filing suit).

1. Written discovery responses. A party's duty to amend and supplement written discovery about a retained testifying expert is governed by TRCP 193.5. Tex. R. Civ. P. 195.6; **VingCard A.S.**, 59 S.W.3d at 855. See "Supplementing discovery responses," ch. 6-A, §17.

2. Deposition testimony.

(1) Supplementation required. To the extent a party's retained testifying expert changes or modifies her opinion, the party must amend and supplement the expert's deposition testimony about the expert's mental impressions or opinions and the basis for them. Tex. R. Civ. P. 195.6; *see* **Collins v. Collins**, 923 S.W.2d 569, 569 (Tex.1996); *see, e.g.*, **Farm Servs. v. Gonzales**, 756 S.W.2d 747, 750 (Tex.App.—Corpus Christi 1988, writ denied) (testimony of expert who changed her opinion after deposition should have been excluded); *see also* **Titus Cty. Hosp. Dist. v. Lucas**, 988 S.W.2d 740, 740 (Tex.1998) (acknowledging narrow duty to supplement certain expert testimony); **Collins v. Collins**, 904 S.W.2d 792, 801 (Tex.App.—Houston [1st Dist.] 1995) (in divorce proceeding, husband could not testify about value of business because he did not identify himself as expert and said in deposition that he would not testify as expert), *writ denied*, 923 S.W.2d 569 (Tex.1996).

(2) Supplementation not required. An expert can modify her testimony based on refinements in her calculations made shortly before trial without triggering the need to supplement. **Exxon Corp. v. West Tex. Gathering Co.**, 868 S.W.2d 299, 304 (Tex.1993); *see, e.g.*, **Koko Motel, Inc. v. Mayo**, 91 S.W.3d 41, 51 (Tex.App.—Amarillo 2002, pet. denied) (change in opinion was merely a refinement because data and formula were already in record). An expert can also modify her testimony without supplementation if the opinion expands on a subject that has already been disclosed. **Norfolk S. Ry. v. Bailey**, 92 S.W.3d 577, 581 (Tex.App.—Austin 2002, no pet.); *see* **Navistar Int'l Transp. v. Crim Truck & Tractor Co.**, 883 S.W.2d 687, 691 (Tex.App.—Texarkana 1994, writ denied). The testimony of an expert should not be barred because a change in some minor detail of the person's work was not disclosed a month before trial. **Exxon Corp.**, 868 S.W.2d at 304.

3. Expert's report. A party has a duty to amend and supplement the report of the retained testifying expert on the expert's mental impressions or opinions and the basis for them. Tex. R. Civ. P. 195.6.

§5.2 Supplementing discovery of nonretained testifying expert. A party has a duty to amend and supplement discovery about a nonretained testifying expert as set out in TRCP 193.5. Under that rule, a party has a duty to supplement its written responses to discovery relating to a nonretained expert. See "When supplementation required," ch. 6-A, §17.1. A party has no burden to supplement the deposition testimony of a nonretained testifying expert. *See* Tex. R. Civ. P. 193.5(a) (duty to supplement written discovery, not oral discovery). The nonretained testifying expert has no burden to supplement her own responses to discovery. *See* Tex. R. Civ. P. 205 (discovery from nonparties).

Practice Tip

Instruct your experts to promptly inform you of any changes in their responses (oral or written) so you can timely supplement or amend your discovery responses. Whether or not you think the changes are material, supplement or amend your discovery responses to ensure the expert's changed testimony is not excluded.

§6. Deadlines for securing discovery from experts

The deadline for securing discovery from experts depends on the designation of the experts.

§6.1 Deadlines to designate testifying experts. The designation of testifying experts is accomplished by providing the information about the experts required under TRCP 195.5(a). Tex. R. Civ. P. 195.2. TRCP 195.2 establishes a schedule for

providing the required expert disclosures. The schedule may be modified by court order (for good cause) or by agreement of the parties. Tex. R. Civ. P. 191.1; *see* Tex. R. Civ. P. 195.2 & cmt. 3 (1999); *see also* Griesel, *The "New" Texas Discovery Rules: Three Years Later*, Advanced Evidence & Discovery Course, State Bar of Texas CLE, ch. 2, p. 22 (2002) (court can modify schedule if contested issue requiring expert testimony is raised by affirmative defense rather than by primary liability claim). The deadlines for designating testifying experts and providing the information required by TRCP 195.5(a) are determined based on whether the expert is testifying for a party seeking affirmative relief. *See* Tex. R. Civ. P. 195.2.

2021 Rule Amendments

In 2020, the Supreme Court approved significant amendments to TRCP 195 that modify the procedure and deadline for designating expert witnesses. See Tex.Sup.Ct. Order, Misc. Docket No. 20-9153 (eff. Jan. 1, 2021). A party is now generally required to disclose certain information about expert witnesses without waiting for a discovery request from the other party. See Tex. R. Civ. P. 194.3, 195.5(a). Designation of an expert is accomplished by making these required disclosures. Tex. R. Civ. P. 195.2. The amendments apply to cases filed on or after January 1, 2021, except for those filed in justice courts. Tex.Sup.Ct. Order, Misc. Docket No. 20-9153 (eff. Jan. 1, 2021). For cases filed before January 1, 2021, designation is accomplished by responding to requests for disclosure. See Tex. R. Civ. P. 195.2 (pre-1-1-21 version).

1. Plaintiff's expert.

(1) Before 1-1-21. For cases filed before January 1, 2021, a party seeking affirmative relief (generally the plaintiff) must designate its testifying experts within 30 days after service of the request for disclosures or 90 days before the end of the discovery period, whichever is later. Tex. R. Civ. P. 195.2(a) (pre-1-1-21 version); *see* **Ersek v. Davis & Davis, P.C.**, 69 S.W.3d 268, 270 (Tex.App.—Austin 2002, pet. denied); **Snider v. Stanley**, 44 S.W.3d 713, 715 (Tex.App.—Beaumont 2001, pet. denied). See "Discovery periods," ch. 6-A, §8.

Note

The Austin Court of Appeals has held that if a party responded to a request for disclosure of experts with "no experts at this time," the party cannot designate an expert for the first time after the deadline in TRCP 195.2. See ***Ersek****, 69 S.W.3d at 270–71.*

(2) On or after 1-1-21. For cases filed on or after January 1, 2021, a party seeking affirmative relief (generally the plaintiff) must designate its testifying experts at least 90 days before the end of the discovery period. Tex. R. Civ. P. 195.2(a). See "Discovery periods," ch. 6-A, §8.

2. Defendant's expert.

(1) Before 1-1-21. For cases filed before January 1, 2021, a party who is not seeking affirmative relief (generally the defendant) must designate its testifying experts within 30 days after service of the request for disclosures or 60 days before the end of the discovery period, whichever is later. *See* Tex. R. Civ. P. 195.2(b) (pre-1-1-21 version); **Wigfall v. TDCJ**, 137 S.W.3d 268, 272 (Tex.App.—Houston [1st Dist.] 2004, no pet.). See "Discovery periods," ch. 6-A, §8.

(2) On or after 1-1-21. For cases filed on or after January 1, 2021, a party who is not seeking affirmative relief (generally the defendant) must designate its testifying experts 60 days before the end of the discovery period. *See* Tex. R. Civ. P. 195.2(b). See "Discovery periods," ch. 6-A, §8.

§6.2 Deadlines to depose testifying experts.

1. Deposing retained testifying experts. TRCP 195.3 establishes a schedule for deposing testifying experts retained by, employed by, or otherwise subject to the control of a party.

(1) Plaintiff did not provide report. If the party seeking affirmative relief (generally, the plaintiff) did not provide a report when it designated its retained testifying expert, it must tender the expert for deposition reasonably promptly

after designation and before the other party is required to designate its experts. Tex. R. Civ. P. 195.3(a)(1) & cmt. 3 (1999); **Vaughn v. Ford Motor Co.**, 91 S.W.3d 387, 389 (Tex.App.—Eastland 2002, pet. denied). When, because of the plaintiff's actions, the deposition cannot be concluded more than 15 days before the deadline for designating other experts, the deadline must be extended for other experts testifying on the same subject. Tex. R. Civ. P. 195.3(a)(1); *see also* Gold, *"So, Who Died & Made You King?": How & When to Ask the Right Questions About Experts Under Texas' New Discovery Rules*, Advanced Expert Witness Course, State Bar of Texas CLE, ch. 14.1, p. 11 (2004) (under TRCP 195.3, deadline should arguably not be extended if P attempted in good faith to schedule expert's deposition before deadline expired).

(2) Plaintiff provided report. If the party seeking affirmative relief (generally the plaintiff) provided a report when it designated its retained testifying expert, the burden shifts to the other party to designate its experts testifying on the same subject before the plaintiff is required to tender its expert for deposition. Tex. R. Civ. P. 195.3(a)(2) & cmt. 3 (1999). This provision is a compromise designed to allow defendants to obtain sufficient information from plaintiffs to enable them to obtain appropriate experts, yet prevent plaintiffs from being unfairly surprised or "sandbagged." Griesel, *The "New" Texas Discovery Rules: Three Years Later*, Advanced Evidence & Discovery Course, State Bar of Texas CLE, ch. 2, p. 22 (2002).

(3) Defendant's experts. A party not seeking affirmative relief (generally the defendant) must tender its expert for deposition "reasonably promptly" after it designates its expert and after the plaintiff's experts have been deposed on the same subject. Tex. R. Civ. P. 195.3(b).

2. Deposing nonretained testifying experts. A party is not required to tender a nonretained testifying expert for a deposition. *See* Tex. R. Civ. P. 195 cmt. 2 (1999) (TRCP 195 does not address depositions of nonretained testifying experts). The deposition of a nonretained testifying expert may be taken according to the same rules as for deposing nonparties. *See* Tex. R. Civ. P. 199 (oral depositions), Tex. R. Civ. P. 205 (discovery from nonparties). See "Procedure for standard oral deposition," ch. 6-F, §4.

§6.3 Deadlines to supplement. See "Deadline to supplement responses," ch. 6-A, §17.4.

§6.4 Discovery deadline after trial reset. See "Discovery deadline when trial reset," ch. 6-A, §14.1.4.

§7. Expert's report

§7.1 Contents of expert's report. An expert's report includes the discoverable factual observations, tests, supporting data, calculations, photographs, and opinions of the expert. *See* Tex. R. Civ. P. 195.5(b). The report must provide the expert's opinion and the basis for it. *See* **Mauzey v. Sutliff**, 125 S.W.3d 71, 84 (Tex.App.—Austin 2003, pet. denied) (trial courts must ensure that expert report fully discloses substance of and basis for expert's mental impressions). For example, a report in a medical-malpractice suit might contain a medical history, a diagnosis, a prognosis, opinions, impressions, and causation. **Tibbetts v. Gagliardi**, 2 S.W.3d 659, 663 n.1 (Tex.App.—Houston [14th Dist.] 1999, pet. denied); *see* Tex. Civ. Prac. & Rem. Code §74.351(j), (r)(6).

§7.2 Securing report from retained testifying expert. A retained expert's report can be secured through a disclosure or by court order.

1. By disclosure. Depending on when the case was filed, a retained testifying expert's report can be secured through a request for disclosure or by required disclosures.

2021 Rule Amendments

In 2020, the Supreme Court approved significant amendments to TRCP 194 and 195. See Tex.Sup.Ct. Order, Misc. Docket No. 20-9153 (eff. Jan. 1, 2021). Under the amendments, a party is now generally required to disclose the expert-witness information outlined in TRCP 195.5(a) without waiting for a discovery request from the other party. See Tex. R. Civ. P. 194.3, 195.5(a). See "Required disclosures—Cases filed on or after 1-1-21," ch. 6-E, §3. The amendments apply to cases filed on or after January 1, 2021, except those filed in justice court. Tex.Sup.Ct. Order, Misc. Docket No. 20-9153 (eff. Jan. 1, 2021).

(1) Before 1-1-21. For cases filed before January 1, 2021, a party can ask for a report from the other party's retained testifying expert in a request for disclosure. Tex. R. Civ. P. 194.2(f)(4)(A) (pre-1-1-21 version). If the expert has not produced a tangible report, the responding party can either (1) ask its retained expert to produce a report or (2) if the party does not want to incur the expense of producing a report, tender its retained expert for deposition. *See* Tex. R. Civ. P. 195.3 & cmt. 3 (1999). The production of the report will trigger the other party's burden to designate its experts. *See* Tex. R. Civ. P. 195 cmt. 3 (1999).

(2) On or after 1-1-21. For cases filed on or after January 1, 2021, TRCP 195.5 requires a party to automatically disclose any report prepared by the retained testifying expert without waiting for a discovery request from the other party. Tex. R. Civ. P. 195.5(a)(4)(A). But a party is not required to disclose a draft expert report, regardless of the form in which it is recorded. Tex. R. Civ. P. 195.5(d). If the expert has not created a tangible report, the disclosing party can either (1) ask its retained expert to produce a report or (2) if the party does not want to incur the expense of creating a report, tender its retained expert for deposition. *See* Tex. R. Civ. P. 195.3 & cmt. 3 (1999). The production of the report will trigger the other party's burden to designate its experts. *See* Tex. R. Civ. P. 195 cmt. 3 (1999).

Note

FRCP 26(a), which the amendments to TRCP 194 are based on, specifically requires a party's expert disclosures to be accompanied by a written report if the expert is a retained testifying expert. See Fed. R. Civ. P. 26(a)(2)(B); Tex. R. Civ. P. 194 cmt. (2021). See "Report or disclosure," ***O'Connor's Federal Rules * Civil Trials****, ch. 6-E, §5.2.2 (2021 ed.). Although TRCP 195.5(a) does not explicitly state the same requirements as the federal rule for who must provide a written report, any report prepared by the expert in anticipation of the expert's testimony must be included as part of the expert's disclosures under TRCP 195.5(a)(4)(A). See "Expert disclosures," ch. 6-E, §3.4.*

2. By court order. A party can file a motion asking for a court order requiring the other party to produce an expert report from its retained testifying experts. *See* Tex. R. Civ. P. 195.5(b). See **O'Connor's Texas Civil Forms**, FORM 6D:1 (2020 ed.). The court can order that a retained expert's report that has not been recorded or put in tangible form be reduced to a tangible form and produced. Tex. R. Civ. P. 195.5(b). The court can order a report from a testifying expert in addition to a deposition. *Id.*

§7.3 Securing report from nonretained expert. A nonretained expert's report cannot be secured through TRCP 195.5(b). *See* Tex. R. Civ. P. 195 cmt. 2 (1999).

1. From nonretained expert.

(1) By deposition & subpoena. If the nonretained expert prepared a report, a copy can be secured from the expert through a discovery subpoena to appear and produce at a deposition or simply to produce. *See* Tex. R. Civ. P. 176.2, 205.1, 205.3. See "Securing things from a nonparty," ch. 6-I, §5.

(2) By payment. A party may offer to pay a nonretained expert to prepare a report. But if the nonretained expert had a privileged relationship with the other party (e.g., doctor-patient), a party cannot offer to pay the nonretained expert to prepare a report without the other party's consent.

2. From other party.

(1) By disclosures. Depending on when the case was filed, a nonretained expert's report can be secured from the other party through a request for disclosure or by required disclosures. See "2021 Rule Amendments," ch. 6-D, §7.2.1.

(a) Before 1-1-21. For cases filed before January 1, 2021, if the nonretained expert's report was provided to, reviewed by, or prepared for the retained testifying expert, the party can secure it as part of the request for information about the retained expert. *See* Tex. R. Civ. P. 194.2(f)(4)(A) (pre-1-1-21 version).

(b) On or after 1-1-21. For cases filed on or after January 1, 2021, if the nonretained expert's report was provided to, reviewed by, or prepared for the retained testifying expert, the party is required to disclose the report under TRCP 195.5 without waiting for a discovery request from the other party. *See* Tex. R. Civ. P. 195.5(a)(4)(A).

(2) By production of medical records. In a suit alleging physical or mental injury, the injured party is required to produce medical records or provide an authorization permitting disclosure of medical records. Tex. R. Civ. P. 194.2(b)(10). See "Disclosure of party's medical records or authorization," ch. 6-J, §3.

(3) By request for production. If a party has a copy of a nontestifying expert's report that was not provided to its retained testifying expert, other parties can secure a copy of it by a request for production. *See* Tex. R. Civ. P. 196.1(a).

(4) By request for witness statement. If a party has a copy of a witness statement made by the nonretained testifying expert, other parties are entitled to obtain a copy of it. Tex. R. Civ. P. 192.3(h).

3. Under Public Information Act. If the nonretained expert is a police officer or other public official, a party may be able to secure a copy of the officer's report under the Public Information Act. *See* Tex. Gov't Code §§552.021, 552.022.

§8. Paying the expert

§8.1 Expert fees for most discovery. As a rule, a party pays the fees charged by its own expert. The amount of the fees is established by the contract between the party and the expert.

§8.2 Expert fees for depositions.

1. Retained expert of opposing party. When a party takes the oral deposition of an expert witness retained by the opposing party, all reasonable fees charged by the expert for time spent in preparing for, giving, reviewing, and correcting the deposition must be paid by the party who retained the expert. Tex. R. Civ. P. 195.7. If the party who retained the expert suspects the other side is purposefully running up the costs and abusing TRCP 195.7, that party can seek relief under TRCP 191.1 (court has the power to modify discovery procedures and limitations) and TRCP 192.6 (party can seek protective order). TRCP 191.1 permits a court, for good cause, to modify the allocation of fees and expenses. *See* Tex. R. Civ. P. 191.1 & cmt. 1. See "Modifying discovery by court order," ch. 6-A, §6.2.

2021 Rule Amendments

For cases filed on or after January 1, 2021, a party must provide a statement of the compensation to be paid for its expert's study and testimony in the case as part of the party's required expert disclosures. Tex. R. Civ. P. 195.5(a)(4)(E). See "Expert disclosures," ch. 6-E, §3.4.

2. Nonretained expert. The TRCPs do not address the issue of who pays for the deposition of a nonretained expert. *See* Tex. R. Civ. P. 195 cmt. 2 (1999). The nonretained expert's fees for the deposition should probably be paid by the party who notices the deposition. For example, if the defendant notices the deposition of an emergency-room doctor who treated the plaintiff after an accident, the defendant should pay for the expert's fees.

E. Disclosures

§1. General

§1.1 Rules. TRCP 194, 195.

§1.2 Purpose. Disclosures are designed to produce basic discovery of specific categories of information. Tex. R. Civ. P. 194 cmt. 1 (1999). Unlike interrogatories, disclosures are not verified, and no objections are permitted. *See* Tex. R. Civ. P. 194.5.

§1.3 Forms. See **O'Connor's Texas Civil Forms**, FORMS 6E:1 et seq. (2020 ed.).

§1.4 Other references. Griesel, *The "New" Texas Discovery Rules: Three Years Later*, Advanced Evidence & Discovery Course, State Bar of Texas CLE, ch. 2 (2002); Pemberton, *The First Year Under the New Discovery Rules: The Big Issues Thus Far*, Advanced Evidence & Discovery Course, State Bar of Texas CLE (1999).

§2. Requests for disclosure—Cases filed before 1-1-21

For cases filed before January 1, 2021, a party can obtain the information outlined in TRCP 194.2 from another party by serving that party with a request for disclosure. Tex. R. Civ. P. 194.1 (pre-1-1-21 version).

2021 Rule Amendments

In 2020, the Supreme Court approved significant amendments to TRCP 194 and 195. See Tex.Sup.Ct. Order, Misc. Docket No. 20-9153 (eff. Jan. 1, 2021). Under the amendments, a party is now generally required to disclose certain information without waiting for a discovery request from the other party. See Tex. R. Civ. P. 194.2, 195.5(a). The amendments apply to cases filed on or after January 1, 2021, except those filed in justice court. Tex.Sup.Ct. Order, Misc. Docket No. 20-9153 (eff. Jan. 1, 2021). In this section, citations to these rules reference the pre-1-1-21 version, and citations to the rule comments reference the comments to the 1999 amendments.

---

§2.1 Making requests for disclosure.

1. Procedure.

(1) Format. The request for disclosure should be typed on letter-size paper. Some attorneys include the request in their first pleading—either the original petition or the original answer. See "Request for disclosure," ch. 2-B, §14; "Request for disclosure," ch. 3-E, §8.

(2) Served on party. A request for disclosure can be served only on another party. Tex. R. Civ. P. 194.1. It cannot be served on a nonparty. *See id.*

(3) Time to serve request for disclosure.

(a) How early. A request for disclosure may be served anytime after suit is filed. *See* Tex. R. Civ. P. 190.2(b)(1), 190.3(b)(1). The rules provide that a plaintiff may serve the initial set of discovery with its original petition.

[1] With or as part of P's original petition. The plaintiff should consider serving the request for disclosure along with or as part of the original petition. If the plaintiff includes the request in the petition, the plaintiff should change the title of the instrument to "Plaintiff's Original Petition and Request for Disclosure." If the plaintiff serves a request for disclosure as a separate document but with the original petition, the plaintiff must list the request as one of the documents served in both the citation and the return for the citation.

[2] Along with D's answer. Generally, a defendant who wants to serve a request for disclosure early will serve it with the answer, even though a defendant may serve its request anytime after suit is filed.

(b) How late. For most methods of service (e.g., e-service, personal or commercial delivery), the deadline to serve the request is 30 days before the end of the discovery period. *See* Tex. R. Civ. P. 194.1. See "Discovery periods," ch. 6-A,

§8. But when service is by mail or fax, the request should be served at least 33 days (if mailed) or 31 days (if faxed after 5:00 p.m.) before the end of the discovery period. *See* Tex. R. Civ. P. 21a(b)(2), (c). See "Deadline to serve response," ch. 6-A, §14.1.

(4) Specify time to answer. The person serving the request for disclosure should specify when the answers are due, but must allow at least 30 days after service of the request. *See* Tex. R. Civ. P. 194.1, 194.3.

(a) For most disclosures. In most cases, a party will ask the other party to answer a request for disclosure within the shortest time permitted by TRCP 194.1—that is, "within 30 days of service." When the plaintiff serves a request for disclosure on the defendant before the defendant's answer is due, the defendant generally has 50 days after the date of service of the request to respond. Tex. R. Civ. P. 194.3(a). For most methods of service (e.g., e-service, personal or commercial delivery), the deadline to respond to the request for disclosure is 30 or 50 days; however, when service is by mail or fax, the answering party has an additional 3 days (if mailed) or 1 day (if faxed after 5:00 p.m.) to respond. *See* Tex. R. Civ. P. 21a(b)(2), (c). See "Deadline to serve response," ch. 6-A, §14.1.

(b) For testifying experts. The time to respond to a request asking for disclosure of the other party's testifying experts is governed by TRCP 195.2. See "Deadlines to designate testifying experts," ch. 6-D, §6.1.

(c) By agreement or court order. The parties may modify the deadlines in TRCP 194.3 by agreement or with a court order. Tex. R. Civ. P. 191.1. See "Modifying discovery procedures," ch. 6-A, §6.

2. Content of request.

(1) Standard requests. A party may make the request in the language suggested by TRCP 194.1 by stating the following: "Pursuant to Rule 194, you are requested to disclose, within [*30 or 50*] days of the service of this request, the information or material described in Rule [*identify rule, e.g., 194.2; 194.2(a), (c), and (f); 194.2(d)-(g)*]." See **O'Connor's Texas Civil Forms**, FORM 6E:1 (2020 ed.). Or, a party may make requests for the individual items in the subparts of TRCP 194.2.

Practice Tip

The problem with the request provided in TRCP 194.1 and the more specific requests below is that the party receiving the request might not be aware that a consulting expert with knowledge of facts is discoverable as a fact witness. Thus, you should use targeted requests to ask for information about experts. See "Targeted request," ch. 6-E, §2.1.2(2).

TRCP 194.2 permits a party to ask for the following information:

(a) Correct party names. A party may ask for the correct names of the parties to the lawsuit. Tex. R. Civ. P. 194.2(a).

(b) Potential parties. A party may ask for the name, address, and telephone number of any potential party. Tex. R. Civ. P. 194.2(b). Potential parties can be a good source of information, just like fact witnesses.

(c) Contentions. A party may ask for the legal theories and, in general, the factual bases of the responding party's claims or defenses. Tex. R. Civ. P. 192.3(j), 194.2(c). These requests are similar to so-called "contention interrogatories" and may be used for the same purpose. Tex. R. Civ. P. 194 cmt. 2.

(d) Damages. A party may ask for the amount and any method of calculating economic damages. Tex. R. Civ. P. 194.2(d).

(e) Fact witnesses. A party may ask for the name, address, and telephone number of any person with knowledge of relevant facts, and a brief statement of each identified person's connection with the case. Tex. R. Civ. P. 194.2(e). See "Fact witnesses," ch. 6-B, §2.8.

(f) Retained testifying experts. See "Information about retained testifying experts," ch. 6-D, §4.1.1. A party may ask for the following information about a retained testifying expert:

[1] The expert's name, address, and telephone number. Tex. R. Civ. P. 194.2(f)(1).

[2] The subject matter on which the expert will testify. Tex. R. Civ. P. 194.2(f)(2).

[3] The general substance of the expert's mental impressions and opinions and a brief summary of the basis for them. Tex. R. Civ. P. 194.2(f)(3).

[4] All documents, tangible things, reports, models, or data compilations that have been provided to, reviewed by, or prepared by or for the expert in anticipation of the expert's testimony. Tex. R. Civ. P. 194.2(f)(4)(A); **VingCard A.S. v. Merrimac Hospitality Sys.**, 59 S.W.3d 847, 855 (Tex.App.—Fort Worth 2001, pet. denied).

Note

When a party or a party's employee testifies as an expert in the party's own case, the testifying-expert materials described in TRCP 194.2(f)(4)(A) are not discoverable if protected by the attorney-client privilege. See ***In re City of Dickinson****, 568 S.W.3d 642, 646–47 (Tex.2019). TRCP 194.2 merely permits a party to request disclosure but does not require disclosure.* ***In re City of Dickinson****, 568 S.W.3d at 646. Requests for disclosure under TRCP 194.2 are subject to the attorney-client privilege as are the provisions of TRCP 192, which outline permissible discovery.* ***In re City of Dickinson****, 568 S.W.3d at 647; see Tex. R. Civ. P. 194 cmt. 1. See "Party testifies as expert," ch. 6-D, §4.1.1(6)(b)[1].*

[5] The expert's current résumé and bibliography. Tex. R. Civ. P. 194.2(f)(4)(B). The request should ask that the expert produce, as part of her résumé, a list of all other cases in which she has testified as an expert at trial or by deposition within the past four years. See "List of expert's other cases," ch. 6-D, §4.1.1(5)(a).

(g) Nonretained testifying experts. See "Information about nonretained experts," ch. 6-D, §4.1.2. A party may ask for the following information about a nonretained testifying expert:

[1] The expert's name, address, and telephone number. Tex. R. Civ. P. 194.2(f)(1).

[2] The subject matter on which the expert will testify. Tex. R. Civ. P. 194.2(f)(2).

[3] Either (1) the general substance of the expert's mental impressions and opinions and a brief summary of the basis for them or (2) documents reflecting this information. Tex. R. Civ. P. 194.2(f)(3).

(h) Documents. A party may ask for the following documents:

[1] Discoverable indemnity and insuring agreements. Tex. R. Civ. P. 194.2(g). See "Insurance & indemnity agreements," ch. 6-B, §2.11.4.

[2] Discoverable settlement agreements. Tex. R. Civ. P. 194.2(h). See "Settlement agreements," ch. 6-B, §2.11.5.

[3] Discoverable witness statements. Tex. R. Civ. P. 194.2(i). See "Discoverable," ch. 6-B, §2.6.1.

(i) Medical records. See "Medical Records," ch. 6-J, §1 et seq. In a suit alleging physical or mental injury and damages from the occurrence that is the subject of the suit, a party may ask for medical records as follows:

[1] From the party who alleges injury, (1) all medical records and bills that are reasonably related to the injuries or damages asserted, or (2) as an alternative, an authorization permitting the disclosure of those medical records and bills. Tex. R. Civ. P. 194.2(j); **In re Shipmon**, 68 S.W.3d 815, 820 (Tex.App.—Amarillo 2001, orig. proceeding).

[2] From the party who obtained the injured party's medical records with an authorization furnished by the injured party, a copy of all the records it obtained. Tex. R. Civ. P. 194.2(k).

(j) Responsible third party. A party may ask for the name, address, and telephone number of any person who may be designated as a responsible third party. Tex. R. Civ. P. 194.2(*l*).

(2) Targeted request. To secure specific information, the party should consider using a "targeted" request that identifies, in a separate sentence, the discoverable information sought under TRCP 194.2. For example, if a party wants a business entity to name others who may be potential parties because of their ownership interest in the entity, the request could state, "You are requested to disclose the information or material described in Rule 194.2(b). Please answer to the full extent authorized by the rules, which should include the names of all individuals and entities with an ownership interest in the business." For other targeted requests, see **O'Connor's Texas Civil Forms**, FORM 6E:2 (2020 ed.). Although nothing prevents a party from focusing its request by targeting an issue, a party may not expand the scope of its request beyond TRCP 194.2.

(3) Additional requests—Level 1 discovery. In addition to the standard requests for disclosure under TRCP 194.2, a party under a Level 1 discovery-control plan can request disclosure of all documents, electronic information, and tangible items that the disclosing party has in its possession, custody, or control and that it may use to support its claims or defenses. Tex. R. Civ. P. 190.2(b)(6). See "Level 1," ch. 6-A, §7.2.

§2.2 Responding to requests for disclosure.

1. Procedure.

(1) Time to respond.

(a) For most disclosures. Generally, a party has 30 days after the date of service to respond to a request for disclosure. Tex. R. Civ. P. 194.3. When a request for disclosure is served on a defendant before the defendant's answer is due, the defendant generally has 50 days after service of the request to respond. Tex. R. Civ. P. 194.3(a). For most methods of service (e.g., e-service, personal or commercial delivery), the deadline to respond to the request for disclosure is 30 or 50 days; however, when service is by mail or fax, the answering party has an additional 3 days (if mailed) or 1 day (if faxed after 5:00 p.m.) to respond. *See* Tex. R. Civ. P. 21a(b)(2), (c). See "Deadline to serve response," ch. 6-A, §14.1. For a discussion of extending the time to respond, see "Extending time to respond to discovery," ch. 6-A, §15.

(b) For testifying experts. TRCP 195.2 establishes the schedule for furnishing information about testifying experts. Tex. R. Civ. P. 195.2; *see also* Tex. R. Civ. P. 194.2(f) (information party may request), Tex. R. Civ. P. 194.3(b) (response to 194.2(f) request controlled by Tex. R. Civ. P. 195). See "Deadlines for securing discovery from experts," ch. 6-D, §6.

(2) Not filed. The responding party's disclosures are not filed with the court. Tex. R. Civ. P. 191.4(a)(2); **National Family Care Life Ins. v. Fletcher**, 57 S.W.3d 662, 667 n.6 (Tex.App.—Beaumont 2001, pet. denied). For exceptions, see "Exceptions," ch. 6-A, §12.1.3.

(3) Form of responses. To properly respond to requests for disclosure, the answers, objections, and other responses must be made in the form required by the rules. See **O'Connor's Texas Civil Forms**, FORM 6E:3 (2020 ed.).

(a) In writing. The response must be in writing. Tex. R. Civ. P. 193.1, 194.3; **VingCard A.S. v. Merrimac Hospitality Sys.**, 59 S.W.3d 847, 855 (Tex.App.—Fort Worth 2001, pet. denied). Each answer must follow the question it responds to. Tex. R. Civ. P. 193.1.

(b) Signed. The response must be signed by an attorney (or a pro se party). Tex. R. Civ. P. 191.3(a).

(c) Not verified. The response should not be verified.

(d) Separate answers. The response must provide separate answers for each request.

(e) Separate set of answers. In most cases, each set of requests for disclosure should be answered separately. In a multiparty case, a party responding to the same disclosures from different opposing parties may file one response that is sufficient to answer all sets. *Cf.* **Ward v. O'Connor**, 816 S.W.2d 446, 446 (Tex.App.—San Antonio 1991, no writ) (Ps filed one list of fact and expert witnesses in response to interrogatories from two Ds).

(f) Documents & tangible things. The responding party must serve copies of documents and other tangible items with the response, unless the responsive items are voluminous, in which case the response must state a reasonable time and place for producing the documents. Tex. R. Civ. P. 194.4. The responding party must produce the documents

at the time and place stated in the request, unless otherwise agreed to by the parties or ordered by the court. *Id.* The requesting party must have a reasonable opportunity to inspect the documents or other items. *Id.*

2. Content of response. A party must provide a complete response, based on all information reasonably available to the responding party or its attorney at the time the response is made. Tex. R. Civ. P. 193.1. When asked, a party must produce the following information:

(1) Responses to standard requests.

(a) Correct party name. A party must provide its correct name. Tex. R. Civ. P. 194.2(a); *see* **Bailey v. Vanscot Concrete Co.**, 894 S.W.2d 757, 761 n.3 (Tex.1995), *disapproved on other grounds*, **Chilkewitz v. Hyson**, 22 S.W.3d 825 (Tex.1999).

(b) Potential parties. A party must identify any potential parties and provide their names, addresses, and telephone numbers. Tex. R. Civ. P. 194.2(b); *see* **Helfand v. Coane**, 12 S.W.3d 152, 157 n.3 (Tex.App.—Houston [1st Dist.] 2000, pet. denied).

(c) Contentions. A party must disclose its legal theories and, in general, the factual bases of its claims or defenses. Tex. R. Civ. P. 194.2(c). The party is not required to marshal all evidence that may be offered at trial or to brief legal issues. Tex. R. Civ. P. 194.2(c) & cmt. 2. For example, a plaintiff would be required to disclose that it claimed damages suffered in a car accident caused by the defendant's negligence in speeding but would not be required to state the speed at which the defendant was driving; a defendant in the same suit would be required to disclose its denial of the speeding allegation. Tex. R. Civ. P. 194 cmt. 2. TRCP 194.2(c) is intended to require disclosure of a party's basic assertions made in prosecution or defense of claims. Tex. R. Civ. P. 194 cmt. 2. A defendant cannot respond to a request for contentions by reurging its general denial. Pemberton, *The First Year Under the New Discovery Rules: The Big Issues Thus Far*, Advanced Evidence & Discovery Course, State Bar of Texas CLE, §II.I.2 (1999).

Practice Tip

When responding to a contention request, the parties should review their pleadings and include all of their legal theories and the factual bases for them. If a legal theory or factual basis is omitted, the court may limit the subject matter on which the party can present evidence. See, e.g., ***National Family Care Life Ins. v. Fletcher****, 57 S.W.3d 662, 668 (Tex.App.—Beaumont 2001, pet. denied) (in limiting evidence, trial court was too restrictive in interpreting D's response).*

(d) Damages. A party must disclose the amount of economic damages and any method of calculating them. Tex. R. Civ. P. 194.2(d). For example, a plaintiff would be required to state how loss of past earnings and future earning capacity was calculated, and a defendant in the same suit would be required to disclose any grounds for contesting the damages calculations. Tex. R. Civ. P. 194 cmt. 2. If a plaintiff cannot demonstrate its method of calculation, the court may limit the damages the plaintiff can recover. *See* **Butan Valley, N.V. v. Smith**, 921 S.W.2d 822, 832 (Tex.App.—Houston [14th Dist.] 1996, no writ). A party is not required to state a method of calculating noneconomic damages, such as for mental anguish. Tex. R. Civ. P. 194 cmt. 2.

(e) Fact witnesses. A party must identify persons who have knowledge of relevant facts and provide a brief statement of each person's connection with the case. Tex. R. Civ. P. 194.2(e). See "Fact witnesses," ch. 6-B, §2.8.

[1] Identify witness. A party must identify all persons (other than herself) who have knowledge of relevant facts by name, address, and telephone number. Tex. R. Civ. P. 194.2(e); *see, e.g.*, **Apresa v. Montfort Ins.**, 932 S.W.2d 246, 248 (Tex.App.—El Paso 1996, no writ) (witnesses excluded at trial because answers did not provide addresses and telephone numbers). Even when a party answering the request for disclosure has little or no use for a witness's testimony, the party must still identify the witness as a source of relevant facts. *See* **Walsh v. Mullane**, 725 S.W.2d 263, 265 (Tex.App.—Houston [1st Dist.] 1986, writ ref'd n.r.e.). The other party may have an important use for that witness's testimony. **Stevenson v. Koutzarov**, 795 S.W.2d 313, 318 (Tex.App.—Houston [1st Dist.] 1990, writ denied), *disapproved on other grounds*, **Agar Corp. v. Electro Circuits Int'l**, 580 S.W.3d 136 (Tex.2019). Fact witnesses typically include eyewitnesses; parties and their

spouses, employers, and coworkers; treating doctors; other medical personnel; attorneys (for attorney fees); nonretained experts (e.g., police officers); and experts who have firsthand knowledge of the facts of the case or secondhand knowledge obtained outside the consultation. See "Consulting expert + obtained facts = dual-capacity witness," ch. 6-D, §2.2.3.

[2] Identify connection with case. A party must provide a brief description of the person's connection with the suit. Tex. R. Civ. P. 192.3(c), 194.2(e); **Beam v. A.H. Chaney, Inc.**, 56 S.W.3d 920, 922 (Tex.App.—Fort Worth 2001, pet. denied). This does not mean the party must provide a narrative statement of the facts the person knows. Tex. R. Civ. P. 192 cmt. 3. The description could be "treating physician," "eyewitness," "chief financial officer," or "plaintiff's mother and eyewitness to accident." *Id.*

(f) Testifying experts. A party must provide information about the experts it plans to call as witnesses. *See* Tex. R. Civ. P. 194.2(f). The requirement to identify experts does not depend on whether the expert is compensated for her time as a witness. **Baylor Med. Plaza Servs. v. Kidd**, 834 S.W.2d 69, 73 (Tex.App.—Texarkana 1992, writ denied).

[1] Retained testifying experts. For retained testifying experts, a party must provide (1) the identity and location, including the name, address, and telephone number, of its expert witness, (2) the subject matter of the expert's testimony, (3) the expert's mental impressions and opinions and a brief summary of the basis for them, (4) all documents, reports, or compilations provided to, reviewed by, or prepared by or for the expert in anticipation of the expert's testimony, and (5) the expert's current résumé and bibliography. Tex. R. Civ. P. 194.2(f); *see* **Mares v. Ford Motor Co.**, 53 S.W.3d 416, 418–19 (Tex.App.—San Antonio 2001, no pet.). A list of specific facts known by the expert is not required; a general description of the categories of facts known is sufficient. *See* **J.G. v. Murray**, 915 S.W.2d 548, 550–51 (Tex.App.—Corpus Christi 1995, orig. proceeding). For the definition of retained experts, see "Retained testifying expert," ch. 6-D, §2.1.1(1).

[a] Name of retained experts. A party should list the names of all experts it has retained to testify on its behalf and the experts subject to the party's control. For example, the party should list a doctor who was hired to give an opinion in a medical-malpractice case or an accident reconstructionist who was hired to give an opinion in a car-accident case.

[b] Parties. A party should always list the name of any party who might testify as an expert witness. *See, e.g.*, **Collins v. Collins**, 904 S.W.2d 792, 799–800 (Tex.App.—Houston [1st Dist.] 1995) (in divorce suit, husband could not testify about value of business because he was not identified as expert witness), *writ denied*, 923 S.W.2d 569 (Tex.1996); **Tinkle v. Henderson**, 777 S.W.2d 537, 539 (Tex.App.—Tyler 1989, writ denied) (because D-doctors did not list themselves as experts, they could not testify as expert witnesses).

Note

When a party or a party's employee testifies as an expert in the party's own case, the testifying-expert materials described in TRCP 194.2(f)(4)(A) are not discoverable if protected by the attorney-client privilege. See ***In re City of Dickinson****, 568 S.W.3d 642, 646–47 (Tex.2019). See "Note," ch. 6-E, §2.1.2(1)(f)[4].*

[c] Attorney. If there is a claim for attorney fees, the party should list the attorney as an expert to testify about attorney fees. *See, e.g.*, **E.F. Hutton & Co. v. Youngblood**, 741 S.W.2d 363, 364 (Tex.1987) (because attorney was not listed as expert, he could not testify about attorney fees); **Campos v. State Farm Gen. Ins.**, 943 S.W.2d 52, 54–55 (Tex.App.—San Antonio 1997, writ denied) (same); *see also* **Northwestern Nat'l Cty. Mut. Ins. v. Rodriguez**, 18 S.W.3d 718, 721–22 (Tex.App.—San Antonio 2000, pet. denied) (good cause permitted undesignated attorney to testify about fees because he was identified as fact witness on damages). The answer should state that the attorney will testify about attorney fees for trial and for appeal.

[2] Nonretained testifying experts. For nonretained testifying experts, a party must provide (1) the identity and location, including the name, address, and telephone number of its expert, (2) the subject matter of the expert's testimony, and (3) either (a) the general substance of the expert's mental impressions and opinions and a brief summary of the basis for them, or (b) documents reflecting this information. Tex. R. Civ. P. 194.2(f). A list of specific facts known by the

expert is not required; a general description of the categories of facts known is sufficient. For the definition of nonretained experts, see "Changing designation," ch. 6-D, §2.1.2. The list of nonretained testifying experts could include the following:

[a] Treating doctor. A party should list the treating doctor as a nonretained testifying expert if the party intends to call the doctor to testify and the doctor is not retained by, employed by, or otherwise subject to the control of the party. For example, if the party was treated by an emergency-room doctor, the doctor is a nonretained expert as long as the doctor is not paid for her expert opinion and is not otherwise subject to the party's control. Not all treating doctors are nonretained. For example, if the attorney referred the party to a doctor for purposes of treatment and litigation, the doctor would be a retained doctor.

[b] Accident investigator. A party should list an accident investigator who is employed by a local police department or some state agency (e.g., the DPS) as a nonretained testifying expert if the party intends to call the person to testify as an expert.

(g) Documents. A party must produce the following documents in response to a request for disclosure:

[1] Discoverable indemnity and insuring agreements. Tex. R. Civ. P. 194.2(g). See "Insurance & indemnity agreements," ch. 6-B, §2.11.4.

[2] Discoverable settlement agreements. Tex. R. Civ. P. 194.2(h). See "Settlement agreements," ch. 6-B, §2.11.5.

[3] Discoverable witness statements. Tex. R. Civ. P. 194.2(i). See "Discoverable," ch. 6-B, §2.6.1.

(h) Medical records. In a suit alleging physical or mental injury, the parties must produce the following medical records:

[1] The party alleging injury must produce medical records and bills reasonably related to the injuries or damages asserted, or an authorization permitting disclosure of those medical records and bills. Tex. R. Civ. P. 194.2(j). For medical authorization under Health & Safety Code §241.152, see "Medical authorization," ch. 6-J, §3.2.

[2] The other party must produce medical records and bills that it obtained through an authorization furnished by the party alleging injury. Tex. R. Civ. P. 194.2(k).

(i) Responsible third party. A party must provide the name, address, and telephone number of any person who may be designated as a responsible third party. Tex. R. Civ. P. 194.2(*l*); *see, e.g.*, **In re Dawson**, 550 S.W.3d 625, 629–30 (Tex.2018) (D's supplemental response that included only name and phone number of third party was not sufficient).

(2) Responses to additional requests—Level 1 discovery. A party must provide all documents, electronic information, and tangible items that the party has in its possession, custody, or control and that it may use to support its claims or defenses if the requesting party is under a Level 1 discovery-control plan and served these requests for disclosure in addition to the standard requests under TRCP 194.2. Tex. R. Civ. P. 190.2(b)(6). See "Additional requests—Level 1 discovery," ch. 6-E, §2.1.2(3).

§2.3 Objecting to requests. A party abuses the discovery process if it does not respond fully to a request for disclosure. Tex. R. Civ. P. 194 cmt. 1.

1. No objections. No objections are permitted to requests for disclosure. Tex. R. Civ. P. 194 5. The procedure for requests for disclosure is designed to afford parties basic discovery without objection. Tex. R. Civ. P. 194 cmt. 1; *see* Tex. R. Civ. P. 194.5.

2. Asserting privileges.

(1) Most privileges. A party may assert privileges to protect information sought in a request for disclosure (other than work product). Tex. R. Civ. P. 194 cmt. 1; *see, e.g.*, **In re City of Dickinson**, 568 S.W.3d 642, 646–47 (Tex.2019) (when party's corporate representative testified as expert in party's own case, party asserted attorney-client privilege in response to request for disclosure of testifying-expert materials). See "Asserting privileges," ch. 6-A, §18.2

(2) Work product. A party cannot assert work-product privilege in response to a request for disclosure. Tex. R. Civ. P. 194.5 & cmt. 1; *see, e.g.*, **In re Jimenez**, 4 S.W.3d 894, 895–96 (Tex.App.—Houston [1st Dist.] 1999, orig. proceeding) (D's statement to his insurer was not protected as work product).

3. Moving for protection. Only in rare cases will a party be able to protect information requested in disclosures. For example, a party could file a motion for protective order to prevent disclosure of a person's residential address if the disclosure might result in harm to that person. Tex. R. Civ. P. 194 cmt. 1. See "Motion for protective order," ch. 6-A, §20; **O'Connor's Texas Civil Forms**, FORM 6A:10 (2020 ed.).

§2.4 Supplementing or amending disclosures.

1. Deadline to supplement answers. See "Deadline to supplement responses," ch. 6-A, §17.4.

2. Supplementing expert disclosures. See "Supplementing expert discovery," ch. 6-D, §5.

3. Substance of supplemental response. For the substance of what additional information must be provided, see "Extent of supplementation," ch. 6-A, §17.2.

§2.5 Objecting to responses.

1. Technical errors. If a party makes a technical error in responding to requests for disclosure (e.g., the response is not signed), the requesting party must raise the issue as soon as possible. *See* Tex. R. Civ. P. 191.3(d) (unsigned discovery response will be struck unless signed after party is made aware of omission); *cf.* **State Farm Fire & Cas. Co. v. Morua**, 979 S.W.2d 616, 617 (Tex.1998) (verification of interrogatories under former TRCP 168); **Kramer v. Lewisville Mem'l Hosp.**, 858 S.W.2d 397, 407 (Tex.1993) (same). A party waives any technical error it does not raise before trial. *Cf.* **Morua**, 979 S.W.2d at 619 (party waived error in interrogatory responses).

2. Procedure. The procedure for objecting to answers filed in response to requests for disclosure is similar to that for objecting to answers to interrogatories. See "Objecting to answers," ch. 6-G, §8.

§2.6 Using disclosures as evidence.

1. Similar to interrogatories. The procedures for using disclosures as evidence is similar to that for using answers to interrogatories. See "Using interrogatories as evidence," ch. 6-G, §9.

2. Superseded responses. A response to a request for disclosure under TRCP 194.2(c) (legal theories) or TRCP 194.2(d) (damages) that has been changed by an amended or supplemental response is not admissible and cannot be used for impeachment. Tex. R. Civ. P. 194.6. The purpose of this provision is to encourage parties to disclose and discuss their basic legal and factual assertions early in the case. Griesel, *The "New" Texas Discovery Rules: Three Years Later*, Advanced Evidence & Discovery Course, State Bar of Texas CLE, ch. 2, p. 19 (2002).

§2.7 Objecting to late or partial disclosures.

1. Late disclosure. When a party's response to the requests is late, the trial court can exclude the information or testimony that was not timely disclosed. Tex. R. Civ. P. 193.6(a); *see, e.g.*, **Ersek v. Davis & Davis, P.C.**, 69 S.W.3d 268, 273 (Tex.App.—Austin 2002, pet. denied) (expert witness's testimony was excluded because expert was not timely designated). If a party serves a late response to the requests, the trial court can also look to TRCP 215.3 for sanctions—that is, postpone the trial and impose appropriate sanctions to compensate the nonoffending party for any wasted expenses in preparing for trial. *See* Tex. R. Civ. P. 215.3; *see also* Tex. R. Civ. P. 193.6(c) (court may grant a continuance to allow party to respond and opposing party to conduct discovery). At a hearing on a motion for sanctions, the party objecting to an untimely designated expert witness has the burden to produce evidence showing that the designation was not timely. *See* **Mentis v. Barnard**, 870 S.W.2d 14, 16 (Tex.1994); **Sims v. Brackett**, 885 S.W.2d 450, 454 (Tex.App.—Corpus Christi 1994, writ denied).

2. Partial disclosure. When a party's response to the requests does not furnish all the information required by TRCP 194, the trial court must exclude the testimony on the omitted information unless there is a showing of good cause, lack of surprise, or lack of prejudice. *See, e.g.*, **VingCard A.S. v. Merrimac Hospitality Sys.**, 59 S.W.3d 847, 855–56 (Tex.App.—Fort Worth 2001, pet. denied) (although P identified its expert, it did not provide mental impressions and opinions; thus, court should have excluded expert's opinion).

§2.8 Objecting to unidentified witness. To exclude the testimony of a witness not identified in disclosures, a party must make a timely objection. The objection should be made either in a pretrial motion to exclude or when the witness is offered at trial. *See* **Clark v. Trailways, Inc.**, 774 S.W.2d 644, 647 (Tex.1989). Once an objection is made, the exclusion is automatic unless the other party proves good cause or lack of unfair surprise or prejudice.

1. Form of objection. The party should object that the witness should not be permitted to testify because the witness was not disclosed in response to a request asking for the identity of fact or expert witnesses.

2. Exclude witness. On objection, the court must exclude a witness (other than a named party) from testifying if the witness was not listed in response to the requests, unless the court finds (1) there was good cause for the failure to timely respond, or (2) the failure to timely respond will not unfairly surprise or prejudice the other parties. Tex. R. Civ. P. 193.6(a); **Fort Brown Villas III Condo. Ass'n v. Gillenwater**, 285 S.W.3d 879, 881 (Tex.2009); **Snider v. Stanley**, 44 S.W.3d 713, 715 (Tex.App.—Beaumont 2001, pet. denied); *see* **Alvarado v. Farah Mfg. Co.**, 830 S.W.2d 911, 914 (Tex.1992); *see also* **In re M.J.M.**, 406 S.W.3d 292, 298–99 (Tex.App.—San Antonio 2013, no pet.) (death-penalty sanctions that prohibit party from calling all witnesses are beyond scope of TRCP 193.6(a)). The purpose of the exclusion rule is to require complete responses to discovery, promote responsible assessment of settlement, and prevent trial by ambush. **Alvarado**, 830 S.W.2d at 914.

3. Continuance. If the party offering the witness cannot prove good cause, lack of unfair surprise, or lack of unfair prejudice, the party should ask for a continuance. The court may grant a continuance to allow the party to make, amend, or supplement the response and to allow discovery on any new information presented. Tex. R. Civ. P. 193.6(c); *see* **Henderson v. Wellmann**, 43 S.W.3d 591, 598 (Tex.App.—Houston [1st Dist.] 2001, no pet.).

4. Appropriate sanctions. See "Sanctions for discovery abuse," ch. 5-K, §7.1.

5. Preserving error when witness excluded.

(1) Hearing on exclusion. If an objection is made to an unidentified witness, the party offering the witness should ask the court to conduct a hearing on its failure to identify the witness. The burden is on the party offering an unidentified witness to prove good cause, lack of unfair surprise, or lack of unfair prejudice. Tex. R. Civ. P. 193.6(b); *see* **Sharp v. Broadway Nat'l Bank**, 784 S.W.2d 669, 671 (Tex.1990); **Morrow v. H.E.B., Inc.**, 714 S.W.2d 297, 298 (Tex.1986). The court should permit the witness to testify if the party offering the witness can show either (1) good cause for not timely identifying the witness or (2) no unfair surprise or prejudice to the other party. Tex. R. Civ. P. 193.6(a), (b); *see* **Gee v. Liberty Mut. Fire Ins.**, 765 S.W.2d 394, 395–96 (Tex.1989) (court found no good cause under former TRCP 215(5)); **Northwestern Nat'l Cty. Mut. Ins. v. Rodriguez**, 18 S.W.3d 718, 722–23 & n.1 (Tex.App.—San Antonio 2000, pet. denied) (court found no unfair surprise under TRCP 193.6(a)). The trial court has discretion to determine whether there is good cause to permit the witness to testify or whether there is no surprise or prejudice. *See* **Morrow**, 714 S.W.2d at 298. The trial court's findings must be supported by the record. Tex. R. Civ. P. 193.6(b); *see* **Northwestern Nat'l**, 18 S.W.3d at 722 n.1. The hearing must be conducted outside the presence of the jury.

(a) Unidentified witness permitted to testify. The following are examples of when an unidentified witness was or should have been permitted to testify: • D's experts permitted to give same opinions given in earlier trial, even though D did not disclose the experts' opinions in response to request for disclosure. **Mares v. Ford Motor Co.**, 53 S.W.3d 416, 419 (Tex.App.—San Antonio 2001, no pet.). • P's unidentified witness should have been permitted to testify because she was P's employee and was a substitute for another of P's employees who had been identified as witness but had left P's employment. **Best Indus. Unif. Sup. Co. v. Gulf Coast Alloy Welding, Inc.**, 41 S.W.3d 145, 148–49 (Tex.App.—Amarillo 2000, pet. denied).

Note

Under the discovery rules, a named party cannot be excluded as a fact witness because the party was not listed as a fact witness in response to a request for disclosure. See Tex. R. Civ. P. 193.6(a) (party cannot offer the testimony of a witness "other than a named party" who was not listed). Even though an unlisted party may testify as a fact witness, nothing in the rules or case law permits a party not designated as a testifying expert to testify as an expert. ***Collins v. Collins****, 904 S.W.2d 792, 801*

(Tex.App.—Houston [1st Dist.] 1995), writ denied, 923 S.W.2d 569 (Tex.1996).

(b) Unidentified witness excluded. The following are examples of when the unidentified witness was not or should not have been permitted to testify: • P's expert's affidavit should have been excluded when P disclosed expert in response to no-evidence motion for summary judgment five months after expert-designation deadline. **Fort Brown Villas III Condo. Ass'n v. Gillenwater**, 285 S.W.3d 879, 881–82 (Tex.2009). • P's expert should have been excluded, even though deposed, because he was not identified in response to interrogatories. **Sharp**, 784 S.W.2d at 670–72. • P's expert should have been excluded because he was not identified in response to interrogatories, and counsel's inadvertence was not good cause. *Id.*; **E.F. Hutton & Co. v. Youngblood**, 741 S.W.2d 363, 364 (Tex.1987). • P's witnesses should have been excluded even though D's attorney already had the special knowledge necessary to cross-examine the witnesses at trial. **E.F. Hutton**, 741 S.W.2d at 364. • State's witnesses should have been excluded because State did not file a response to the request for disclosures and did not prove good cause. **F&H Invs. v. State**, 55 S.W.3d 663, 669–71 (Tex.App.—Waco 2001, no pet.). • Witness who had been a party to the suit but had settled before trial and who had identified himself as expert witness could not testify as expert for another party who had not identified him as expert. **Codner v. Arellano**, 40 S.W.3d 666, 675–76 (Tex.App.—Austin 2001, no pet.). • Witness should have been excluded because party's expectation that case would settle was not good cause for not identifying witness. **Rainbo Baking Co. v. Stafford**, 787 S.W.2d 41, 41 (Tex.1990); **Cruz v. Furniture Technicians**, 949 S.W.2d 34, 36 (Tex.App.—San Antonio 1997, pet. denied). • Designated fact witness should have been excluded as expert witness. **Collins**, 904 S.W.2d at 801–02 (party); **Baylor Med. Plaza Servs. v. Kidd**, 834 S.W.2d 69, 73–74 (Tex.App.—Texarkana 1992, writ denied) (witness).

(2) Present evidence. A party offering an unidentified witness must present sworn testimony to explain why the witness was not listed. The court reporter should transcribe the proceeding. To prove good cause or lack of unfair surprise or prejudice for not listing the unidentified witness, the party should establish the following:

(a) The party made a good-faith effort to locate the witness. *See* **Clark v. Trailways, Inc.**, 774 S.W.2d 644, 647 (Tex.1989) (inability to locate witness despite good-faith efforts might support finding of good cause).

(b) The party did not know of the existence of the witness or did not know the witness had knowledge about the case. To prove this, both the attorney and the party should testify at the hearing that they did not know of the witness. If either the party or the attorney had the information, it should have been disclosed. **Yeldell v. Holiday Hills Ret. & Nursing Ctr., Inc.**, 701 S.W.2d 243, 246 (Tex.1985) (attorney knew of witness); **Williams v. Union Carbide Corp.**, 734 S.W.2d 699, 701 (Tex.App.—Houston [1st Dist.] 1987, writ ref'd n.r.e.) (party knew of witness).

(c) The other parties were aware of the unidentified witness and her testimony. To prove this, the party should demonstrate that the identity of the witness was certain and her personal knowledge of relevant facts was communicated to all other parties through a timely response to other written discovery or deposition. Tex. R. Civ. P. 193.5(a)(2); *see* **Northwestern Nat'l**, 18 S.W.3d at 722–23.

(3) Get ruling on record. The party attempting to overcome the automatic exclusion of the witness should ask the court to (1) state on the record whether good cause, lack of unfair surprise, or lack of unfair prejudice was proved, and (2) identify the particulars of its ruling.

(4) Make offer of proof. If the court excludes any evidence, the party must make an offer of proof to preserve the testimony of the witness so the appellate courts can determine whether the erroneous exclusion was harmful. *See* Tex. R. Evid. 103(a)(2). If a party presents the witness's testimony as part of the hearing on exclusion, and the court reporter transcribes it, the court reporter's record will include the evidence. If the witness's testimony is not presented at the hearing, the party should ask the court for permission to make an offer of proof during the trial. If for some reason the court does not permit the party to make an offer of proof, the evidence may be preserved in a formal bill of exception. *See* Tex. R. App. P. 33.2. See "Offer of Proof & Bill of Exception," ch. 8-E, §1 et seq.; **O'Connor's Texas Civil Forms**, FORMS 8E:1 et seq. (2020 ed.).

6. Offering witness for impeachment or rebuttal. A party may ask the trial court for permission to offer an undesignated witness for impeachment or rebuttal. See "Impeachment & rebuttal evidence not produced in discovery," ch. 8-C, §5.3.

§2.9 Review. For the rules and forms for prosecuting or responding to an appeal or original proceeding, see **O'Connor's Texas Civil Appeals** (2020 ed.).

1. Appeal or mandamus? See "Review of discovery orders," ch. 6-A, §26.

2. Unidentified witness. On appeal, the party objecting to the exclusion or admission of the testimony of an unidentified witness must show that the court abused its discretion. *See* **Mentis v. Barnard**, 870 S.W.2d 14, 16 (Tex.1994) (objection to exclusion under former TRCP 166b); **Henry S. Miller Co. v. Bynum**, 836 S.W.2d 160, 162 (Tex.1992) (objection to admission). Obtaining a reversal on the admission or exclusion of an unidentified witness is a two-step process: the party must show (1) it proved good cause or lack of unfair surprise or prejudice (or the other party did not prove good cause or lack of unfair surprise or prejudice), and (2) the trial court's erroneous ruling was harmful. *See* **Mentis**, 870 S.W.2d at 16 (testimony excluded at trial); **Alvarado v. Farah Mfg. Co.**, 830 S.W.2d 911, 916–17 (Tex.1992) (testimony admitted at trial). Once error in the trial court's ruling is demonstrated, the appellate court must review the entire record to determine the harm. To determine whether the erroneous admission or exclusion of the testimony of an unidentified witness was harmful, the appellate court must determine whether the error probably caused the rendition of an improper judgment. Tex. R. App. P. 44.1(a)(1).

(1) Unidentified witness permitted to testify. If the court admitted the testimony of an unidentified witness, to challenge that ruling on appeal, the appellant must show that the admitted testimony (1) disputed a material allegation in the case and (2) was not cumulative. **Boothe v. Hausler**, 766 S.W.2d 788, 789 (Tex.1989). If the testimony of the unidentified witness was cumulative of other evidence, the courts will hold that it was harmless error to admit it. *Id.*; **Beam v. A.H. Chaney, Inc.**, 56 S.W.3d 920, 924 (Tex.App.—Fort Worth 2001, pet. denied). The test of whether the evidence was cumulative is whether other similar evidence was offered at trial, not whether other similar evidence was available in discovery. **Jamail v. Anchor Mortg. Servs.**, 809 S.W.2d 221, 223 (Tex.1991).

(2) Unidentified witness excluded. If the court excluded the testimony of an unidentified witness, to challenge that ruling on appeal, the appellant must show that the excluded testimony (1) was preserved by an offer of proof or a formal bill of exception, (2) was controlling on a material issue in the case, and (3) was not cumulative. **Williams Distrib. Co. v. Franklin**, 898 S.W.2d 816, 817 (Tex.1995) (elements 2 and 3); **Mentis**, 870 S.W.2d at 16 (elements 2 and 3); **McInnes v. Yamaha Motor Corp.**, 673 S.W.2d 185, 187 (Tex.1984) (element 1). To prove the "controlling" element, it is not necessary for the party to show that no other controlling evidence could have been introduced through another witness. **Williams Distrib.**, 898 S.W.2d at 817.

§3. Required disclosures—Cases filed on or after 1-1-21

For cases filed on or after January 1, 2021, TRCP 194 requires a party to automatically disclose basic discovery without waiting for a discovery request from the other party. *See* Tex. R. Civ. P. 194.1(a) & cmt. (2021). The party must provide complete disclosures based on all information reasonably available to the party or its attorney at the time the disclosures are made. Tex. R. Civ. P. 193.1; *see* Tex. R. Civ. P. 194 cmt. (2021). The party must disclose the required information even if (1) it has not fully investigated the case, (2) another party's disclosures are insufficient, or (3) another party has not made its disclosures. Tex. R. Civ. P. 194 cmt. (2021). The duty to disclose is mandatory unless (1) otherwise agreed by the parties or ordered by the court or (2) a specific exemption applies. Tex. R. Civ. P. 194.1(a). See "Exempt proceedings," ch. 6-E, §3.3.3.

2021 Rule Amendments

In 2020, the Supreme Court approved significant amendments to TRCP 194 and 195 that are based on FRCP 26(a). See Tex. R. Civ. P. 194 cmt. (2021); Tex.Sup.Ct. Order, Misc. Docket No. 20-9153 (eff. Jan. 1, 2021). Under the amendments, a party is now generally required to disclose certain information without waiting for a discovery request from the other party. See Tex. R. Civ. P. 194.2, 195.5(a). The amendments apply to cases filed on or after January 1, 2021, except those filed in justice court. Tex.Sup.Ct. Order, Misc. Docket No. 20-9153 (eff. Jan. 1, 2021).

§3.1 Stages of disclosure. Disclosures must be made in three distinct stages.

1. Initial disclosures. Initial disclosures require the parties to exchange information about potential witnesses, documentary evidence, damages, and insurance early in the case. *See* Tex. R. Civ. P. 194.2. See "Initial disclosures," ch. 6-E, §3.3.

2. Expert disclosures. Expert disclosures identify expert witnesses and provide information about their qualifications and the subject matter and general substance of their expected testimony. *See* Tex. R. Civ. P. 194.3, 195.5(a). See "Expert disclosures," ch. 6-E, §3.4.

3. Final pretrial disclosures. Final pretrial disclosures, which are made as the trial date approaches, identify the particular evidence that may be offered at trial. *See* Tex. R. Civ. P. 194.4. See "Final pretrial disclosures," ch. 6-E, §3.5.

§3.2 Form of disclosures. Disclosures must meet the same general discovery requirements as all other written discovery responses. *See* Tex. R. Civ. P. 194 cmt. (2021).

1. In writing & served. All discovery disclosures must be in writing and served on all parties of record. *See* Tex. R. Civ. P. 191.5, 194 cmt. (2021).

2. Signed. All discovery disclosures must be signed by an attorney of record or the party if pro se. *See* Tex. R. Civ. P. 191.3(a), 194 cmt. (2021).

3. Filing. TRCP 194 does not require initial and expert disclosures to be filed, but filing may be required by court order or the parties may file the disclosures for use in a court proceeding. *See* Tex. R. Civ. P. 191.4(a), (c). See "Filing & retaining discovery," ch. 6-A, §12. All final pretrial disclosures, however, must be filed in the court. Tex. R. Civ. P. 194.4(a).

4. Not verified. The disclosures do not need be verified. *See* Tex. R. Civ. P. 194.

5. Documents, ESI & tangible things. A party should produce copies of all responsive documents, electronically stored information, and tangible things with its disclosures. *See* Tex. R. Civ. P. 194.1(b). If the party does not produce the documents or other items, it must state in its disclosures a reasonable time and method for their production. *Id.* The disclosing party must produce the documents or other items at the time and in the method stated, unless otherwise agreed to by the parties or ordered by the court. *Id.* The opposing party must have a reasonable opportunity to inspect the documents or other items. *Id.*

§3.3 Initial disclosures.

1. Deadline. The initial disclosures must generally be made within 30 days after the filing of the first answer or general appearance. Tex. R. Civ. P. 194.2(a). See "Deadline to answer," ch. 3-E, §2. If a party is first served or otherwise joined after the filing of the first answer or general appearance, she must make the initial disclosures within 30 days after being served or joined. Tex. R. Civ. P. 194.2(a). These deadlines can be modified by the parties' agreement or court order. *Id.*

2. Contents. A party must provide certain specified information in its initial disclosures. *See* Tex. R. Civ. P. 194.2(b).

Note

In certain suits under the Family Code, parties must make the disclosures specified in TRCP 194.2(c) in addition to those listed below.

(1) Correct party name. A party must provide its correct name. Tex. R. Civ. P. 194.2(b)(1).

(2) Potential parties. A party must provide the names, addresses, and telephone numbers of any potential parties. Tex. R. Civ. P. 194.2(b)(2).

(3) Contentions. A party must disclose its legal theories and, in general, the factual bases of its claims or defenses. Tex. R. Civ. P. 194.2(b)(3). The party is not required to marshal all evidence that may be offered at trial. *Id.* See "Contentions," ch. 6-E, §2.2.2(1)(c).

(4) Damages. A party must disclose the amount and any method of calculating economic damages. Tex. R. Civ. P. 194.2(b)(4).

(5) Fact witnesses. A party must provide the names, addresses, and telephone numbers of persons having knowledge of relevant facts and a brief statement of each identified person's connection to the case. Tex. R. Civ. P. 194.2(b)(5). See "Fact witnesses," ch. 6-E, §2.2.2(1)(e).

(6) Information in support of claims or defenses. A party must provide all documents, electronically stored information, and tangible things that it has in its possession, custody, or control that may be used to support its claims or defenses, unless the documents or information would be used solely for impeachment purposes. Tex. R. Civ. P. 194.2(b)(6). The party can disclose the information either by providing copies of the discovery or by describing the discovery by category and location. *Id.*

(7) Documents. A party must provide discoverable indemnity and insuring agreements, settlement agreements, and witness statements. *See* Tex. R. Civ. P. 194.2(b)(7) to (9). See "Witness statements," ch. 6-B, §2.6; "Insurance & indemnity agreements," ch. 6-B, §2.11.4; "Settlement agreements," ch. 6-B, §2.11.5.

(8) Medical records. In a suit alleging physical or mental injury, the parties must produce certain medical records or provide an authorization permitting disclosure of the records. Tex. R. Civ. P. 194.2(b)(10), (11). See "Medical records," ch. 6-E, §2.2.2(1)(h).

(9) Responsible third party. A party must provide the name, address, and telephone number of any person who may be designated as a responsible third party. Tex. R. Civ. P. 194.2(b)(12).

3. Exempt proceedings. Unless otherwise ordered by the court, the following proceedings are exempt from the initial-disclosure requirement: (1) actions for review on an administrative record, (2) forfeiture actions arising from a state statute, (3) petitions for habeas corpus, (4) actions under the Family Code filed by or against the Title IV-D agency in a Title IV-D case, (5) child-protection actions under Family Code title 5, subtitle E, (6) protective-order actions under Family Code title 4, (7) other actions involving domestic violence, and (8) actions on appeal from a justice court. Tex. R. Civ. P. 194.2(d).

§3.4 Expert disclosures. A party must provide certain information about the experts that it plans to call as witnesses. *See* Tex. R. Civ. P. 195.5. Draft expert disclosures, however, are protected from discovery, regardless of the form in which they are recorded. Tex. R. Civ. P. 195.5(d). For a discussion of expert reports, see "Expert's report," ch. 6-D, §7.

1. Deadline. The deadline for providing expert disclosures depends on whether the expert is testifying for a party seeking affirmative relief. *See* Tex. R. Civ. P. 195.2.

(1) Plaintiff's expert. A party seeking affirmative relief (generally the plaintiff) must provide expert disclosures at least 90 days before the end of the discovery period. Tex. R. Civ. P. 195.2(a).

(2) Defendant's expert. A party who is not seeking affirmative relief (generally the defendant) must provide expert disclosures at least 60 days before the end of the discovery period. Tex. R. Civ. P. 195.2(b).

2. Contents. The specific information that a party is required to disclose depends on whether the testifying expert is retained or nonretained. See "Testifying experts," ch. 6-E, §2.2.2(1)(f). For the definitions of these terms, see "Making designation," ch. 6-D, §2.1.1. For more information on what can be discovered from testifying experts and the methods for discovery, see "Testifying experts," ch. 6-D, §4.1.

(1) Retained testifying experts. A party must provide the following information about its retained testifying experts as part of its required disclosures under TRCP 195.5:

(a) The expert's name, address, and telephone number. Tex. R. Civ. P. 195.5(a)(1).

(b) The subject matter on which the expert will testify. Tex. R. Civ. P. 195.5(a)(2).

(c) The general substance of the expert's mental impressions and opinions and a brief summary of the basis for them. Tex. R. Civ. P. 195.5(a)(3).

(d) All documents, tangible things, reports, models, or data compilations that have been provided to, reviewed by, or prepared by or for the expert in anticipation of the expert's testimony. Tex. R. Civ. P. 195.5(a)(4)(A).

(e) The expert's current résumé and bibliography. Tex. R. Civ. P. 195.5(a)(4)(B)

(f) The expert's qualifications, including a list of all publications the expert authored in the last ten years. Tex. R. Civ. P. 195.5(a)(4)(C).

(g) A list of all other cases in which the expert testified as an expert at trial or by deposition within the last four years, except when the expert is the disclosing party's attorney and is testifying about attorney fees. Tex. R. Civ. P. 195.5(a)(4)(D).

(h) A statement of the compensation that will be paid for the expert's study and testimony in the case. Tex. R. Civ. P. 195.5(a)(4)(E).

(2) Nonretained testifying experts. A party must provide the following information about its nonretained testifying experts as part of its required disclosures under TRCP 195.5:

(a) The expert's name, address, and telephone number. Tex. R. Civ. P. 195.5(a)(1).

(b) The subject matter on which the expert will testify. Tex. R. Civ. P. 195.5(a)(2).

(c) Either (1) the general substance of the expert's mental impressions and opinions and a brief summary of the basis for them or (2) documents reflecting this information. Tex. R. Civ. P. 195.5(a)(3).

(3) Protected communications. Communications between any testifying expert and the disclosing party's attorney are protected from discovery, regardless of their form, except to the extent that they (1) relate to compensation for the expert's study or testimony or (2) identify facts, data, or assumptions that the attorney provided and that the expert considered or relied on in forming her opinions. Tex. R. Civ. P. 195.5(c).

§3.5 Final pretrial disclosures.

1. Deadline. Unless the court orders otherwise, the parties must make their final pretrial disclosures at least 30 days before trial. Tex. R. Civ. P. 194.4(b).

2. Contents. A party is required to disclose the following information, unless the evidence will be used solely for impeachment purposes. Tex. R. Civ. P. 194.4(a).

(1) Witness identity. The party must disclose the name, and if not previously provided, the address and telephone number of (1) each person the party expects to call as a witness and (2) each person the party might call as a witness if the need arises. Tex. R. Civ. P. 194.4(a)(1).

(2) Document identity. The party must disclose an identification of each document or other exhibit, including summaries of other evidence, that (1) the party expects to offer as evidence and (2) the party might offer as evidence if the need arises. Tex. R. Civ. P. 194.4(a)(2).

(3) Exempt proceedings. Unless otherwise ordered by the court, actions arising under the Family Code filed by or against the Title IV-D agency in a Title IV-D case are exempt from the final-pretrial-disclosure requirement. Tex. R. Civ. P. 194.4(c).

§3.6 Supplementing or amending disclosures. As with other written discovery, disclosures must be timely amended or supplemented under TRCP 193.5. Tex. R. Civ. P. 194 cmt. (2021).

1. Deadline to supplement disclosures. See "Deadline to supplement responses," ch. 6-A, §17.4.

2. Supplementing expert discovery. See "Supplementing expert discovery," ch. 6-D, §5.

3. Substance of supplemental response. For the substance of what additional information must be provided, see "Extent of supplementation," ch. 6-A, §17.2.

§3.7 Objections.

1. No objections or assertion of work product. The party making the disclosures cannot object or assert work-product privilege to avoid providing the required information. Tex. R. Civ. P. 194.5. See "Certain work product," ch. 6-B, §2.13.

2. Technical errors. If the disclosing party makes a technical error in providing the information, the other party must raise the issue as soon as possible; a party waives any technical error it does not raise before trial. See "Technical errors," ch. 6-E, §2.5.1.

§3.8 Using disclosures as evidence.

1. Similar to interrogatories. The procedure for using disclosures as evidence is similar to that for using answers to interrogatories. See "Using interrogatories as evidence" ch. 6-G, §9.

2. Superseded disclosures. A disclosure under TRCP 194.2(b)(3) (legal theories) or TRCP 194.2(b)(4) (damages) that has been changed by an amended or supplemental response is not admissible and cannot be used for impeachment. Tex. R. Civ. P. 194.6.

§3.9 Late or partial disclosures.

1. Late disclosure. When a party's disclosure is late, the trial court can exclude the information or testimony that was not timely disclosed. *See* Tex. R. Civ. P. 193.6(a). See "Late disclosure," ch. 6-E, §2.7.1.

2. Partial disclosure. When a party's disclosures do not furnish all the information required by TRCP 194 or 195, the trial court may exclude the testimony on the omitted information unless there is a showing of good cause, lack of surprise, or lack of prejudice. See "Partial disclosure," ch. 6-E, §2.7.2.

§3.10 Objecting to unidentified witness. To exclude the testimony of a witness not identified in disclosures, a party must make a timely objection. See "Objecting to unidentified witness," ch. 6-E, §2.8.

§3.11 Review. See "Review," ch. 6-E, §2.9.

F. Depositions

§1. General

§1.1 Rules. Tex. R. Civ. P. 176, 199 to 203, 205, 215.5. See Tex. Civ. Prac. & Rem. Code §7.011 (attorney's liability for costs), §20.001 (persons who may take depositions), §20.002 (depositions in Texas for use in foreign jurisdiction); Tex. Gov't Code §52.059 (charges for depositions).

§1.2 Purpose. The purpose of depositions is to elicit and preserve sworn testimony for use in trial.

§1.3 Forms. See **O'Connor's Texas Civil Forms**, FORMS 6F:1 et seq. (2020 ed.).

§1.4 Other references. Gold, *Rooting for Acorns, Discovery in Texas,* Advanced Personal Injury Course, State Bar of Texas CLE, ch. 14.2 (2017); Graham, *Depositions: Procedure*, Advanced Evidence & Discovery Course, State Bar of Texas CLE, ch. 7 (2011); Court Reporters Certification Board, *Uniform Format Manual for Texas Reporters' Records* (2010), txcourts.gov/jbcc/court-reporters-certification/statutes-rules-and-resources-for-court-reporters-firms; Hoffman, *Depositions*, Spring Training: Winning Before Trial, State Bar of Texas CLE, ch. 5 (2010); Fineberg & Shore, *Discovery Update*, Advanced Civil Trial Course, State Bar of Texas CLE, ch. 1 (2001); Fineberg & Shore, *New Investigative Discovery: Depositions, How Do You Investigate Your Claim, Preparation, Rule 202, Deposition in Anticipation of Filing*, Advanced Civil Trial Course, State Bar of Texas CLE, Tab A (1999); Bishop, *International Litigation in Texas: Obtaining Evidence in Foreign Countries*, 19 Hous.L.Rev. 361 (1982); Brown & Rondon, **Texas Rules of Evidence Handbook** (2021 ed.).

§2. Scope

The scope of discovery for depositions is governed by TRCP 192. See "Scope of Discovery," ch. 6-B, §1 et seq.

§3. Deposition officer

The deposition officer is a person who is authorized by law to administer an oath and who is in charge of the stenographic or nonstenographic recording of the deposition. *See* Tex. R. Civ. P. 199.1. The deposition officer is responsible for the amount of time each party or side uses during the deposition. For the definition of "side," see "Side," ch. 6-A, §2.7.

§3.1 Stenographic depositions. Stenographic oral depositions taken in Texas generally must be recorded by a certified shorthand reporter. Tex. Gov't Code §154.101(f).

Note

Effective September 1, 2019, a person certified as an apprentice court reporter or a provisional court reporter under Gov't Code §154.1011 may engage in shorthand reporting, subject to the terms of the person's certification. See Acts 2019, 86th Leg., R.S., ch. 606, §§7.08, 16.01, eff. Sept. 1, 2019. Before the 2019 amendments to Gov't Code ch. 154, a person could not engage in shorthand reporting unless she was certified by the Texas Supreme Court under Gov't Code §154.101.

§3.2 Nonstenographic depositions. Audio or video depositions may be recorded by any person who is qualified to administer an oath. *See* Tex. R. Civ. P. 199.1(c); *see also* Tex. Gov't Code §602.002 (list of persons who are qualified to administer oath, including notaries public). A court reporter or any person authorized to administer oaths may act as the deposition officer at a nonstenographic deposition. See "Alternative means for conducting deposition," ch. 6-F, §4.5.4.

§3.3 Deposition on written questions. Depositions on written questions may be taken by (1) a clerk of the district court, (2) a judge or clerk of the county court, (3) a court reporter, or (4) a notary public. Tex. Civ. Prac. & Rem. Code §20.001(a) (persons 1, 2, and 4).

§4. Procedure for standard oral deposition

The most common type of deposition is the oral deposition recorded stenographically by a court reporter or by a mechanical recording device operated by a notary public. The deposition consists of a series of questions by one attorney, answers by the deponent, and objections and cross-examination by the other attorneys.

§4.1 Agreements for scheduling deposition. Most depositions are taken by agreement. TRCP 191.1 permits the parties to modify the deposition procedure by agreement and to take the deposition before any person, at any time or place and on any notice. If the parties make an agreement about the taking of the deposition, it should be recorded in the deposition transcript. Tex. R. Civ. P. 191.1. To be enforceable when not recorded in the transcript, the agreement must comply with TRCP 11. Tex. R. Civ. P. 191.1. See "Agreement recorded in deposition," ch. 1-H, §9.1.3; "Modifying discovery by agreement," ch. 6-A, §6.1; **O'Connor's Texas Civil Forms**, FORM 6F:1 (2020 ed.).

§4.2 Scheduling expert's deposition. TRCP 195.3 establishes a schedule for depositions of testifying experts retained by, employed by, or otherwise subject to the control of a party. See "Deadlines to depose testifying experts," ch. 6-D, §6.2. Depositions of experts who are not retained by a party are controlled by TRCP 176 and 205, and the deposition rules. Tex. R. Civ. P. 195 cmt. 2 (1999).

§4.3 Deadline to take deposition. An oral deposition must be taken during the discovery period unless the parties agree otherwise or a party obtains leave of court. Tex. R. Civ. P. 199.2(a). See "Discovery periods," ch. 6-A, §8; **O'Connor's Texas Civil Forms**, FORM 6F:7 (2020 ed.). For expert depositions, see "Deadlines to depose testifying experts," ch. 6-D, §6.2.

§4.4 Filing deposition documents. Chart 6-8, below, summarizes the filing requirements for deposition documents.

6-8. Filing Deposition Documents

	Document	File?	TRCP
1	Notice of deposition and subpoena required to be served only on a party	No	191.4(a)(1)
2	Notice of deposition and subpoena required to be served on a nonparty	Yes	191.4(b)(1)
3	Motions for protection and to quash	Yes	191.4(b)(2)
4	Agreements about depositions	Yes	11, 191.4(b)(3)
5	The deposition	No	191.4(a)(3)
6	The responses and objections to deposition notices	No	191.4(a)(2)
7	Any document the trial court orders to be filed	Yes	191.4(c)(1)
8	Any document necessary to support or oppose a motion or other matter in the trial or appellate court	Yes	191.4(c)(2), (c)(3)

§4.5 Notice of oral deposition. See **O'Connor's Texas Civil Forms**, FORM 6F:1 (2020 ed.).

1. Contents of notice. The notice of intent to take a deposition must be in writing. *See* Tex. R. Civ. P. 199.2(a).

(1) Service. The notice of deposition must be served on the deponent and the other parties in the lawsuit. Tex. R. Civ. P. 199.2(a).

(2) Identity of deponent. The notice of deposition must identify the witness to be deposed. Tex. R. Civ. P. 199.2(b)(1).

(a) Party witness. When the deponent is a party or is retained by, employed by, or subject to the control of a party, the notice of deposition served on the party's attorney has the same effect as a subpoena served on the deponent. Tex. R. Civ. P. 199.3.

(b) Nonparty witness. When the deponent is not a party, the notice should include the deponent's address so the officer or court reporter who issues the subpoena can locate the witness. *See* Tex. R. Civ. P. 176.5. See "Subpoenas," ch. 1-L, §1 et seq.; "Challenging nonparty discovery subpoena," ch. 6-I, §5.5.

(c) Unknown corporate witness. When the deposition notice is sent to a corporation or other entity and the identity of a person in the organization with knowledge of a certain subject is unknown, the notice can require the organization to identify a witness to be deposed. *See* Tex. R. Civ. P. 199.2(b)(1); **Allstate Tex. Lloyds v. Johnson**, 784 S.W.2d 100, 104 (Tex.App.—Waco 1989, orig. proceeding). The notice must describe the subjects about which testimony is requested and direct the organization to designate the person who will testify on its behalf. *See* Tex. R. Civ. P. 199.2(b)(1); **Lindsey v. O'Neill**, 689 S.W.2d 400, 402 (Tex.1985). This procedure does not limit a party's right to depose other employees of the entity. **Hospital Corp. v. Farrar**, 733 S.W.2d 393, 395 (Tex.App.—Fort Worth 1987, orig. proceeding).

2. Date for oral deposition. The notice of deposition must state the day and time for the oral deposition. Tex. R. Civ. P. 199.2(b)(2); *cf.* **St. Luke's Episcopal Hosp. v. Garcia**, 928 S.W.2d 307, 312 (Tex.App.—Houston [14th Dist.] 1996, orig. proceeding) (because subpoena did not identify date for deposition on written questions, nonparty did not waive its objections). After stating the date, the notice should include the phrase, "and continuing from day to day until the deposition is completed." The date for the deposition depends on how much notice a party must give the other party and the deponent, which in turn depends on whether the deponent is a party or nonparty and whether the deponent is required to bring documents or other things to the deposition. See chart 6-9 under "Certificate of service," ch. 6-F, §4.5.8.

(1) For deposition with documents.

(a) Party deposition with documents.

[1] Initial setting. For a deposition of a party when production of documents or tangible things is requested, the notice of deposition must be served on the witness at least 30 days before the deposition. *See* Tex. R. Civ. P. 199 cmt. 1. TRCP 199.2(b)(5) incorporates into deposition procedures the requirements for requests for production under TRCP 196, including the 30-day deadline for responses. Tex. R. Civ. P. 199 cmt. 1; *see* Tex. R. Civ. P. 196.2(a) (response to request for production must be served within 30 days). See "Time to respond," ch. 6-I, §3.3.2. The date for the deposition should probably be set at least 40 days after the date the notice is served, so the party noticing the deposition can reschedule it if the witness files a response on the last day refusing to produce.

[2] Rescheduled setting. When rescheduling the deposition of a party with documents or tangible things, the party noticing the deposition is not required to provide an additional 30 days' notice as long as no additional documents or things are requested. Because it is the request for documents that triggers the 30 days' notice requirement, the purpose of the 30 days' notice—to provide the deponent time to file a response to the request for documents—is satisfied by the first notice. *See* Tex. R. Civ. P. 199.2(b)(5).

(b) Nonparty deposition with documents. For a deposition of a nonparty when production of documents or tangible things is requested, the notice of deposition must be served on the nonparty a reasonable time before the date for compliance. *See* Tex. R. Civ. P. 199.2(a). The party must also serve a subpoena to appear and produce with or after the notice of deposition. Tex. R. Civ. P. 205.2. Although a document request to a party requires a 30-day response period, there is no similar requirement for a document request to a nonparty. *See* Tex. R. Civ. P. 176.6(c), 199.2(b)(5), 205.3.

(2) For deposition without documents.

(a) Party deposition without documents. To take a deposition of a party without a request for production of documents or tangible things, the notice of deposition must be served a reasonable time before the date of the deposition. Tex. R. Civ. P. 199.2(a); *see* Tex. R. Civ. P. 199.2(b)(2). Neither TRCP 199.2(a) nor TRCP 199.2(b)(2) states how much notice is reasonable. As a general rule, ten days' notice should be reasonable, but depending on the circumstances, a shorter time might also be reasonable. *Compare* **Gutierrez v. Walsh**, 748 S.W.2d 27, 28 (Tex.App.—Corpus Christi 1988, no writ) (six days was reasonable), *and* **Bohmfalk v. Linwood**, 742 S.W.2d 518, 520 (Tex.App.—Dallas 1987, no writ) (four days was reasonable), *with* **Hycarbex, Inc. v. Anglo-Suisse, Inc.**, 927 S.W.2d 103, 111–12 (Tex.App.—Houston [14th Dist.] 1996, no writ) (four days was unreasonable), **Bloyed v. General Motors Corp.**, 881 S.W.2d 422, 437 (Tex.App.—Texarkana 1994) (Thursday notice of Monday deposition was unreasonable), *aff'd*, 916 S.W.2d 949 (Tex.1996), *and* **Hogan v. Beckel**, 783 S.W.2d 307, 309 (Tex.App.—San Antonio 1989, writ denied) (same).

(b) Nonparty deposition without documents. To take a deposition of a nonparty without a request for documents or tangible things, the party must serve the notice and the subpoena a reasonable time before the date for the deposition. *See* Tex. R. Civ. P. 199.2(a), 205.2. However, the notice must be served before or at the same time as the subpoena; the subpoena cannot be served before the notice. Tex. R. Civ. P. 205.2.

3. Place for deposition. The notice of deposition must identify a reasonable location for the deposition. Tex. R. Civ. P. 199.2(b)(2). Where the deposition may be taken depends on a number of factors. *See id.*

(1) Deposition of most witnesses. The deposition of most witnesses may be taken in the following places: (1) the county of the witness's residence, (2) the county where the witness is employed or regularly transacts business in

person, or (3) any convenient place, as directed by the court in which the case is pending. Tex. R. Civ. P. 199.2(b)(2)(A), (b)(2)(B), (b)(2)(E); **Grass v. Golden**, 153 S.W.3d 659, 662 (Tex.App.—Tyler 2004, orig. proceeding); *see* **First State Bank v. Chappell & Handy, P.C.**, 729 S.W.2d 917, 922 (Tex.App.—Corpus Christi 1987, writ ref'd n.r.e.) (court can order deposition in county other than one provided for in rule when deponent is being difficult about scheduling deposition); *see, e.g.*, **In re Rogers**, 43 S.W.3d 20, 29 (Tex.App.—Amarillo 2001, orig. proceeding) (court could not order depositions in Dallas when nothing in record showed Dallas to be reasonable or convenient for any of the witnesses).

(2) Deposition of party & representative. The deposition of a party, or a person designated by a party under TRCP 199.2(b)(1), may also be taken in the county of suit. Tex. R. Civ. P. 199.2(b)(2)(C); **Grass**, 153 S.W.3d at 662; **Davis v. Ruffino**, 881 S.W.2d 186, 187 (Tex.App.—Houston [1st Dist.] 1994, orig. proceeding); *see also* **Wal-Mart Stores v. Street**, 754 S.W.2d 153, 155 (Tex.1988) (when deponent was associated with party but was not designated representative, his deposition could not be taken in county of suit over his objection); **Borden, Inc. v. Valdez**, 773 S.W.2d 718, 721 (Tex.App.—Corpus Christi 1989, orig. proceeding) (same).

(3) Deposition of nonresident or transient. The deposition of a person who is either a nonresident of Texas or a transient may be taken (1) in the county where the witness was served with the subpoena, (2) within 150 miles of the place of service, or (3) in any convenient place, as directed by the court in which the case is pending. Tex. R. Civ. P. 199.2(b)(2)(D), (b)(2)(E); **Grass**, 153 S.W.3d at 662; *see, e.g.*, **Street**, 754 S.W.2d at 155 (chairman of the board, who was not a designated witness, had to be deposed in the county for Bentonville, Arkansas, his county of residence); **Butan Valley, N.V. v. Smith**, 921 S.W.2d 822, 829 (Tex.App.—Houston [14th Dist.] 1996, no writ) (corporate director, who was not a designated witness, had to be deposed in his country of residence, Saudi Arabia). "Convenience" is determined from the perspective of the witness. **Grass**, 153 S.W.3d at 662.

4. Alternative means for conducting deposition. If the deposition is to be taken by telephone, other remote electronic means, or by a nonstenographic recording (audio or video recording), the notice must identify the means for conducting the deposition. *See* Tex. R. Civ. P. 199.1(c), 199.2(b)(3). To take a deposition by alternative means, the party must observe additional notice requirements.

(1) For telephonic deposition. For a deposition by telephone, the notice must be served a reasonable time before the deposition. Tex. R. Civ. P. 199.1(b). See "Deposition by telephone," ch. 6-F, §14.

(2) For electronically recorded deposition. For a deposition by nonstenographic means, the notice must be served at least five days before the deposition. Tex. R. Civ. P. 199.1(c). See "Deposition by nonstenographic recording device," ch. 6-F, §13.

5. Additional attendee. The notice of deposition, or a separate notice, must identify any person who will attend the deposition who is not listed in TRCP 199.5(a)(3)—that is, any person who is not the deponent, one of the parties, the spouse of one of the parties, an attorney, an employee of one of the attorneys, or the officer taking the deposition. Tex. R. Civ. P. 199.2(b)(4), 199.5(a)(3); *see, e.g.*, **Burrhus v. M&S Sup.**, 933 S.W.2d 635, 640–41 (Tex.App.—San Antonio 1996, writ denied) (party attending deposition required to give notice before bringing an expert to deposition of other party's expert). If a party other than the party who set the deposition intends to bring to the deposition a person not listed in TRCP 199.5(a)(3), that party must give the other parties reasonable notice. *See* Tex. R. Civ. P. 199.5(a)(3); **Burrhus**, 933 S.W.2d at 641. To exclude a person from the deposition, a party must secure a protective order. **Burrhus**, 933 S.W.2d at 641

6. Request for documents. The notice of deposition may include a request that the witness produce at the deposition documents or tangible things within the scope of discovery and within the witness's possession, custody, or control. Tex. R. Civ. P. 199.2(b)(5).

(1) Documents from parties. A notice of deposition to a party or its agents that includes a request for documents or tangible things has the same effect as a subpoena. *See* Tex. R. Civ. P. 199.3.

(2) Documents from nonparties. To be compelled to bring documents or tangible things to a deposition, a nonparty must be served with the notice of deposition and a subpoena. *See* Tex. R. Civ. P. 199.2(b)(5), 205.1(c). The subpoena and the notice of deposition must include the list of documents or things to be produced at the deposition. *See* Tex. R. Civ. P.

176.2(b) (subpoena must command person to produce "designated" documents), Tex. R. Civ. P. 199.2(b)(5) (list of materials to be produced by nonparty that are identified in subpoena must be attached to or included in deposition notice), Tex. R. Civ. P. 200.1(b) (same).

7. Signed. The notice of deposition must be signed by the attorney (or party when pro se). Tex. R. Civ. P. 191.3(a). See "Certification by signature," ch. 6-A, §4.1.

Practice Tip

Before the adoption of the 1999 discovery rules, court reporters issued subpoenas and notices of depositions with their own signatures. Now, because discovery must be signed by the attorney, court reporters are sending subpoenas and notices to the attorneys for their signatures, which is burdensome. To simplify this process, the attorneys can agree that all deposition subpoenas and notices may be signed by the court reporter as the attorney's agent. See "Modifying discovery by agreement," ch. 6-A, §6.1.

8. Certificate of service. The notice of deposition must contain a certificate of service stating that it was served on all parties. *See* Tex. R. Civ. P. 21(d), 199.2(a). If notice is not served on all parties, the deposition cannot be used at trial. **Shenandoah Assocs. v. J&K Props., Inc.**, 741 S.W.2d 470, 492 (Tex.App.—Dallas 1987, writ denied). See "Certificate of service," ch. 1-B, §3.2.13.

6-9. Deadlines to Serve Notice & Subpoena

Purpose of discovery	Type of discovery	Party or nonparty		Time for notice	Time for subpoena	Cross-reference
To secure testimony	Oral deposition	1	Party	Reasonable time. Tex. R. Civ. P. 199.2(a).		ch. 6-F, §4.5.2(2)(a)
		2	Nonparty	Reasonable time. Tex. R. Civ. P. 199.2(a).	With or after notice. Tex. R. Civ. P. 205.2.	ch. 6-F, §4.5.2(2)(b)
	Deposition on written questions	3	Party	20 days. Tex. R. Civ. P. 200.1(a).		ch. 6-F, §15.3.3
		4	Nonparty	20 days. Tex. R. Civ. P. 200.1(a).	With or after notice. Tex. R. Civ. P. 205.2.	ch. 6-F, §15.3.3

6-9. Deadlines to Serve Notice & Subpoena

Purpose of discovery	Type of discovery	Party or nonparty		Time for notice	Time for subpoena	Cross-reference
To secure testimony and tangible things	Oral deposition and request for documents	5	Party	30 days. Tex. R. Civ. P. 196.2(a), 199.2(b)(5) & cmt. 1.		ch. 6-F, §4.5.2(1)(a)
		6	Nonparty	Reasonable time. Tex. R. Civ. P. 199.2(a), (b)(5), 205.2.	With or after notice. Tex. R. Civ. P. 205.2.	ch. 6-F, §4.5.2(1)(b)
	Deposition on written questions and request for documents	7	Party	30 days. Tex. R. Civ. P. 196.2(a), 199.2(b)(5), 200.1(b).		ch. 6-F, §15.3.3
		8	Nonparty	20 days. Tex. R. Civ. P. 199.2(b)(5), 200.1(a).	With or after notice. Tex. R. Civ. P. 205.2.	ch. 6-F, §15.3.3
To secure tangible things (not testimony)	Request for production	9	Party	30 days.[1] Tex. R. Civ. P. 196.2(a).		ch. 6-I, §3.1.3
	Subpoena for production	10	Nonparty	Reasonable time. Tex. R. Civ. P. 205.3(a).	10 days after notice. Tex. R. Civ. P. 205.2.	ch. 6-I, §5.3.1

[1] For cases filed before January 1, 2021, when request is served before answer is due, defendant has 50 days after service to respond to request. See "Served before answer date," ch. 6-A, §14.1.2.

§4.6 Responding to notice of deposition.

1. When no documents requested. When no documents are requested, no response is necessary unless the party objects to the time, place, or other conditions of the deposition. See "Objecting before oral deposition," ch. 6-F, §7.

2. When documents requested. For the procedure to object to production of documents, see "Making objections," ch. 6-A, §18.1. For the procedure to assert privileges, see "Asserting privileges," ch. 6-A, §18.2. To object to the time, place, or other conditions of the deposition, see "Objecting before oral deposition," ch. 6-F, §7.

(1) Party's response. When a party, or a witness subject to its control, is served with a deposition notice that requests the production of documents or tangible things, the party's response, objections, and privilege claims are governed by the request-for-production rule TRCP 196), as well as the procedures and duties imposed by TRCP 193. Tex. R. Civ. P. 199.2(b)(5) & cmt. 1. When a party is requested to produce documents at a deposition, it must file a response to the request, just as if it had been served with a request for production of documents. For parties and witnesses subject to the party's control, TRCP 199.2(b)(5) incorporates the procedures for responding to requests for production under TRCP 196. Tex. R. Civ. P. 199 cmt. 1. See "Procedure to respond," ch. 6-I, §3.3.

(2) Nonparty's response. When a nonparty is served with a notice and subpoena to appear at a deposition and produce documents or tangible things, the nonparty's response, objections, motion for protective order, and privilege claims are governed by TRCP 176 (subpoena rule), as well as TRCP 205 (rule governing discovery from nonparties). Tex. R. Civ. P. 199.2(b)(5); *see also* Tex. R. Civ. P. 176.6(c) (production of documents), Tex. R. Civ. P. 193.3 (asserting a privilege). See "Subpoenas," ch. 1-L, §1 et seq.; "Challenging nonparty discovery subpoena," ch. 6-I, §5.5. When a nonparty objects to a

subpoena to produce documents at a deposition, it must make its objections and assertions of privilege in writing before the time specified for compliance in the subpoena. Tex. R. Civ. P. 176.6(d). If the nonparty contends that the subpoenaed documents are privileged, it must comply with TRCP 193.3 and file a withholding statement. *See* Tex. R. Civ. P. 176.6(c). See "Making objections," ch. 6-A, §18.1; "Asserting privileges," ch. 6-A, §18.2. The nonparty must comply with the subpoena to the extent that it does not object or assert privileges to the documents. Tex. R. Civ. P. 176.6(a), (c), (d).

3. When organization deposed. When a deposition notice directs a corporation or other entity to identify a person with knowledge of a certain subject, the organization must (1) designate the persons who will testify on behalf of the organization and (2) identify the matters each person will testify about. Tex. R. Civ. P. 199.2(b)(1); *see also* Tex. R. Civ. P. 176.6(b) (when subpoena directed to an organization). The organization's response must be served on the other party a "reasonable time before the deposition." Tex. R. Civ. P. 199.2(b)(1).

§4.7 Oath. Before beginning the deposition, the deponent must be sworn. Tex. R. Civ. P. 199.5(b); Tex. R. Evid. 603. The oath must be administered by the deposition officer. Tex. R. Civ. P. 203.2(a). See "Deposition officer," ch. 6-F, §3. When a deposition is taken outside Texas, the oath can be administered by a person who has the authority to do so under the laws of that jurisdiction. Tex. R. Civ. P. 201.1(b); *see also* Tex. Civ. Prac. & Rem. Code §20.001(b), (c) (persons who may take depositions).

§4.8 Interrogation. The scope of the examination is governed by TRCP 192. See "Scope of Discovery," ch. 6-B, §1 et seq.; "To cancel or limit because of privilege," ch. 6-F, §7.2.

1. First question. No matter who noticed the deponent to appear, the attorney who asks the first question at the deposition is the attorney who (1) will get the deposition from the court reporter and (2) is personally responsible, along with her firm, for the cost of taking the deposition. Tex. R. Civ. P. 203.3(a)(1) (get deposition); Tex. Gov't Code §52.059(a), (d)(2)(C) (personally responsible). See "Paying for deposition," ch. 6-F, §4.13.

2. Oral examination. The attorney who noticed the deponent to appear will most often begin the interrogation. If the deponent was called as an adverse witness, the deposition will begin with cross-examination. That attorney should finish all questions before any other attorney attempts to question the deponent. After the examination by the attorney who noticed the deposition, the other attorneys, one at a time, have the opportunity to examine the deponent.

3. Written questions. A party may, instead of participating in the examination, serve written questions in a sealed envelope on the party noticing the oral deposition. The noticing party must then deliver them to the deposition officer, who must open the envelope and propound the questions to the witness at the deposition. Tex. R. Civ. P. 199.5(b).

4. Documents. When required to bring documents, the deponent may provide copies of the documents if the originals are made available for inspection. Tex. R. Civ. P. 203.4. If the deponent brings the originals, the court reporter will make copies, attach them to the deposition, and return the originals to the deponent. *Id.* The originals must be available for production for a hearing or for the trial on seven days' notice from any party. *Id.*

Practice Tip

When a witness provides documents as part of a deposition, and the witness is not going to appear in person at trial, you must "prove up" the documents during the deposition. Documents are not admissible simply because they were produced during a deposition. See ***James v. Hudgins****, 876 S.W.2d 418, 422 (Tex.App.—El Paso 1994, writ denied).*

---

§4.9 Signing deposition. Once the deposition is prepared, the deponent must review it and sign it under oath, unless the parties and the deponent agree to waive the signature. Tex. R. Civ. P. 203.1. The court reporter usually handles the signature in one of the following ways:

1. Represented deponent. If the deponent is represented by an attorney at the deposition, the court reporter will send the original deposition to the attorney, along with a sheet to note corrections. Tex. R. Civ. P. 203.1(a). The attorney will arrange for the deponent to review the deposition, sign the signature page under oath, and return the deposition to the court reporter. Tex. R. Civ. P. 203.1(b).

2. Unrepresented deponent. If the deponent is not represented by an attorney at the deposition, the court reporter will send the deposition (usually a copy) and a correction sheet directly to the deponent to be reviewed, signed, notarized, and returned. *See* Tex. R. Civ. P. 203.1.

§4.10 Changing answers. The deponent may submit changes to the deposition and the reasons for the changes—in writing and under oath—to the court reporter within 20 days after the submission of the deposition to the deponent or counsel. Tex. R. Civ. P. 203.1(b). If the deponent does not return the deposition to the court reporter within 20 days after receiving it, the deponent waives the right to make changes. *Id.* The changes should be noted on a form provided for changes; they are not made in the deposition itself. *See id.* The court reporter will attach the deponent's changes to the deposition; the original transcription is not retyped.

§4.11 Refusing to sign deposition. When a party files a motion to suppress the deposition under TRCP 203.5 because the deponent refused to sign the deposition, the court must determine whether the reason the witness refused to sign impugns the reliability of the deposition. **Hill v. Rich**, 522 S.W.2d 597, 600 (Tex.App.—Austin 1975, writ ref'd n.r.e.). Suppression is not justified by the mere lack of a signature. **Smith v. Smith**, 720 S.W.2d 586, 599 (Tex.App.—Houston [1st Dist.] 1986, no writ). Unless the deposition is suppressed, it may be used at trial. *See* Tex. R. Civ. P. 203.5, 203.6.

§4.12 Not filed. Depositions are not filed with the court; they are kept by the custodial attorney. *See* Tex. R. Civ. P. 203.3(a). After the court reporter receives the signed deposition, the court reporter must (1) attach any corrections, (2) send the deposition to the attorney who asked the first question (unless the parties agreed otherwise) with notice to the other attorneys, and (3) file with the trial court a sworn certificate that meets the requirements of TRCP 203.2. Tex. R. Civ. P. 203.1(b), 203.2, 203.3. If the deposition is taken by nonstenographic means, the original record of the deposition is sent to the party who requested the nonstenographic recording, not the party who asked the first question. *See* Tex. R. Civ. P. 203.3(a).

§4.13 Paying for deposition.

1. Cost of original. The attorney who takes the deposition and that attorney's firm are jointly and severally liable for the court reporter's charges for reporting the deposition, for transcribing it, and for providing the copies of it requested by that attorney. Tex. Gov't Code §52.059(a). An attorney "takes" a deposition if the attorney secures the deponent's appearance through formal or informal means or asks the first question. Tex. Gov't Code §52.059(d)(2); *see* Tex. R. Civ. P. 203.3(a) (original deposition transcript is delivered to the attorney "who asked the first question"). The attorney (and the attorney's firm) who asks for a copy of the deposition is personally responsible for the court reporter's charges for that copy. Tex. Gov't Code §52.059(b); *cf.* Tex. Civ. Prac. & Rem. Code §7.011 (attorney who is not a party is not liable for the costs of the proceedings). If the attorney refuses to be bound by the provisions of Gov't Code §52.059(a) and (b), the attorney must state on the record who will pay the cost of the deposition. Tex. Gov't Code §52.059(c).

2. Cost of copy. The custodial attorney must make the original deposition available to other parties for copying. Tex. R. Civ. P. 203.3(c). It is not necessary for the parties to pay the court reporter for more than the original transcript of the deposition; the court reporter's charge for a copy of a deposition is much higher than the photocopy cost. The parties can agree to split the cost of the original deposition and the cost of the photocopy.

§5. Subpoenas for deposition

See "Subpoenas," ch. 1-L, §1 et seq.; "Securing things from a nonparty," ch. 6-I, §5.

§6. Time limits on oral depositions

§6.1 Limits under discovery-control plans. A party's or side's total deposition time depends on the discovery limitations for the case. For the definition of "side," see "Side," ch. 6-A, §2.7. For discovery limitations for the case, see "Discovery limitations," ch. 6-A, §7.2.2; "Discovery limitations," ch. 6-A, §7.3.2; "Discovery limitations," ch. 6-A, §7.4.2.

§6.2 Limits on witness deposition. No side may examine or cross-examine a witness for more than six hours, excluding breaks. Tex. R. Civ. P. 199.5(c). For purposes of this rule, each person designated by an organization under TRCP 199.2(b)(1) is a separate witness. Tex. R. Civ. P. 199 cmt. 2. The time credited to a party includes ordinary pauses by the interrogator or the witness but not off-the-record discussion or protracted lapses (e.g., when a witness is reviewing a stack of documents).

Court Reporters Certification Board, *Uniform Format Manual for Texas Reporters' Records*, §3.4 cmt., ¶3 (2010), txcourts.gov/jbcc/court-reporters-certification/statutes-rules-and-resources-for-court-reporters-firms.

Practice Tip

Because each side can depose a witness for only six hours, a party should prepare for depositions by conducting its written discovery first. The party should not waste valuable deposition time by covering subjects that can be asked about in written discovery.

§6.3 Breaks. Breaks do not count against the time limits. Tex. R. Civ. P. 199.5(c). Even though private conferences between the witness and the witness's attorney during the actual taking of the deposition are improper (except for determining whether a privilege should be asserted), during agreed recesses and adjournments, the witness may confer privately with the witness's attorney. Tex. R. Civ. P. 199.5(d).

§6.4 Timekeeper. The deposition officer, generally the court reporter, is the timekeeper for purposes of the time limits on discovery. *See* Tex. R. Civ. P. 203.2(e). When a deposition is recorded without a court reporter, the person administering the oath to the witness, generally a notary public, must act as the timekeeper. *See* Tex. R. Civ. P. 199.1(c), 203.2(e); *see also* Tex. Gov't Code §602.002(5) (notary public may administer oaths). The deposition officer can use a time-stamping machine, a stopwatch, or another time-keeping device. Court Reporters Certification Board, *Uniform Format Manual for Texas Reporters' Records*, §3.4 cmt., ¶3 (2010), txcourts.gov/jbcc/court-reporters-certification/statutes-rules-and-resources-for-court-reporters-firms. The sworn certificate filed with the court must state the amount of time used by each party at the deposition. Tex. R. Civ. P. 203.2(e).

§7. Objecting before oral deposition

To object to the time, place, manner of proceeding, or scope of a deposition, the party should file one of the following: (1) a written objection to the deposition, (2) a motion to quash the deposition, or (3) a motion for protective order. Tex. R. Civ. P. 192.6, 199.4. See "Objecting to trial & discovery subpoenas," ch. 1-L, §4; "Motion for protective order," ch. 6-A, §20; **O'Connor's Texas Civil Forms**, FORMS 6A:13, 6F:2 (2020 ed.). The objection or motion should be filed as soon as possible—certainly before the date of the deposition, unless filing the motion earlier is not feasible. **Bohmfalk v. Linwood**, 742 S.W.2d 518, 520 (Tex.App.—Dallas 1987, no writ); *see, e.g.*, **Siegel v. Smith**, 836 S.W.2d 193, 194–95 (Tex.App.—San Antonio 1992, writ denied) (P filed motion on day of deposition with evidence of medical reason for inability to attend; abuse of discretion for trial court to deny motion).

§7.1 To object to time or place. To object to the time or place designated for an oral deposition, the party or witness must file a motion for protective order or a motion to quash the notice of deposition. Tex. R. Civ. P. 192.6(a), 199.4; *see, e.g.*, **Bohmfalk v. Linwood**, 742 S.W.2d 518, 520 (Tex.App.—Dallas 1987, no writ) (party waived argument about inadequate notice of deposition because he did not file motion for protective order to reschedule). The motion must identify a reasonable time and place for the deposition with which the party or witness will comply. Tex. R. Civ. P. 192.6(a); **Grass v. Golden**, 153 S.W.3d 659, 662 (Tex.App.—Tyler 2004, orig. proceeding). See "Date for oral deposition," ch. 6-F, §4.5.2; "Place for deposition," ch. 6-F, §4.5.3. If the motion is filed within three business days after service of the notice of deposition, the deposition is automatically stayed until the motion can be determined. Tex. R. Civ. P. 199.4. A TRCP 199.4 objection does not delay the time for compliance with a document request served with a deposition notice; it only delays the time of the deposition itself.

§7.2 To cancel or limit because of privilege. To prevent a deposition or limit the scope of the interrogation because of a particular privilege, the objecting party should file either a motion for protective order or a motion to quash the subpoena, with affidavits that prove it is entitled to the privilege. See "What is not discoverable?," ch. 6-B, §3. For example, if a consulting-only expert is noticed for deposition, the party seeking to prevent the deposition should file a motion for protective order or a motion to quash the subpoena and attach an affidavit swearing that the expert was hired in anticipation of litigation, the expert will not testify, and the expert's work has not been reviewed by a testifying expert. *See* **Essex Crane Rental Corp. v. Kitzman**, 723 S.W.2d 241, 242–43 (Tex.App.—Houston [1st Dist.] 1986, orig. proceeding).

§7.3 To prevent apex deposition. An apex deposition is the deposition of a corporate president or other high-level corporate official. **In re Alcatel USA, Inc.**, 11 S.W.3d 173, 175 (Tex.2000); **Crown Cent. Pet. Corp. v. Garcia**, 904 S.W.2d

125, 127 (Tex.1995). The "apex doctrine" allows corporate officials to potentially avoid unduly burdensome depositions based on their position in the company. *See* **In re Miscavige**, 436 S.W.3d 430, 435 (Tex.App.—Austin 2014, orig. proceeding).

1. Application.

(1) Official not named as party. If a corporate official is not named as a party in the suit, the apex doctrine applies only when the corporate official's position is related to the information sought by the deposing party. *See* **In re TMX Fin.**, 472 S.W.3d 864, 873 (Tex.App.—Houston [1st Dist.] 2015, orig. proceeding); **In re Miscavige**, 436 S.W.3d at 437; **Simon v. Bridewell**, 950 S.W.2d 439, 442 (Tex.App.—Waco 1997, orig. proceeding) (memo op.). For example, if a party seeks to depose the CEO of General Motors on an alleged defect in a car's design, the deposition relates to the official's status as CEO and the opposing party can seek to prevent the deposition based on the apex doctrine. **In re Miscavige**, 436 S.W.3d at 437; *see* **In re TMX Fin.**, 472 S.W.3d at 873–74. But if a party seeks to depose the CEO of General Motors because she witnessed a car accident, the deposition is unrelated to the official's status as CEO and she can be deposed like any other witness. **In re Miscavige**, 436 S.W.3d at 437; *see* **Simon**, 950 S.W.2d at 442.

(2) Official named as party. If a corporate official is a named party in the suit, the apex doctrine does not apply to protect her from being deposed if the dispute in the case is unrelated to the party's status as a corporate official. **In re Miscavige**, 436 S.W.3d at 437; *see* **In re Titus Cty.**, 412 S.W.3d 28, 35–36 (Tex.App.—Texarkana 2013, orig. proceeding); **Simon**, 950 S.W.2d at 442–43. That is, if a corporate official is sued based on some tort, contract dispute, or other theory of liability that does not arise from actions she took in her official capacity, she can be deposed like any other individual. **In re Miscavige**, 436 S.W.3d at 438. But when a corporate official is named as a defendant based on her official capacity, it is unclear whether the apex doctrine applies to protect her from being deposed. *Compare* **In re Titus Cty.** 412 S.W.3d at 35 (apex doctrine does not apply to protect named parties from being deposed), *and* **Simon**, 950 S.W.2d at 443 (same), *with* **In re Miscavige**, 436 S.W.3d at 438 (if corporate official is named as defendant based on her official capacity, apex doctrine applies).

2. Procedure.

(1) Party opposing deposition moves for protection or to quash. To prevent an apex deposition, the corporation must file a motion for protective order or a motion to quash accompanied by the official's affidavit denying any personal knowledge of relevant facts. *See* **In re Alcatel USA**, 11 S.W.3d at 175; **Crown Cent.**, 904 S.W.2d at 128; **In re Continental Airlines, Inc.**, 305 S.W.3d 849, 852 (Tex.App.—Houston [14th Dist.] 2010, orig. proceeding). See **O'Connor's Texas Civil Forms**, FORMS 6A:10, 6A:13, 6A:18, 6F:2 (2020 ed.).

(2) Party seeking deposition opposes motion. Once the corporation's motion and affidavit are filed, the party seeking the apex deposition must show that the official has unique or superior personal knowledge of discoverable information. **In re BP Prods. N. Am., Inc.**, 244 S.W.3d 840, 842 n.2 (Tex.2008); **In re TMX Fin.**, 472 S.W.3d at 872. A mere showing that a corporate official has some knowledge of discoverable information or that the official knew about the complained-of activity is insufficient to warrant the apex deposition. *See* **In re Alcatel USA**, 11 S.W.3d at 179; **In re Miscavige**, 436 S.W.3d at 436; *see, e.g.*, **AMR Corp. v. Enlow**, 926 S.W.2d 640, 644 (Tex.App.—Fort Worth 1996, orig. proceeding) (highest-ranking officer could not be deposed simply because he had ultimate responsibility); *see also* **In re TMX Fin.**, 472 S.W.3d at 875 (even though official was sole member, employee, and manager of corporation, apex doctrine could still apply).

(3) Court's ruling. The court must determine whether the party seeking the deposition has shown that the official has any unique or superior personal knowledge of discoverable information. **In re Alcatel USA**, 11 S.W.3d at 175–76; **Crown Cent.**, 904 S.W.2d at 128.

(a) Denies motion. If the party seeking the deposition establishes that the official has any unique or superior personal knowledge, the court should deny the motion and allow the apex deposition. *See* **In re Alcatel USA**, 11 S.W.3d at 176; **Crown Cent.**, 904 S.W.2d at 128.

(b) Grants motion. If the party seeking the deposition does not establish that the official has any unique or superior personal knowledge, the court should grant the motion and require the party to attempt to obtain the discovery

through less intrusive methods. **In re Alcatel USA**, 11 S.W.3d at 176; **Crown Cent.**, 904 S.W.2d at 128. After making a good-faith effort at less intrusive discovery, the party seeking the deposition may attempt to show that (1) there is a reasonable indication that the official's deposition will lead to the discovery of admissible evidence and (2) the less intrusive discovery was unsatisfactory, insufficient, or inadequate. **In re BP Prods.**, 244 S.W.3d at 842 n.2; **In re Alcatel USA**, 11 S.W.3d at 176; **Crown Cent.**, 904 S.W.2d at 128; *see* **In re Daisy Mfg. Co.**, 17 S.W.3d 654, 657–58 (Tex.2000) (merely completing some less intrusive discovery does not trigger automatic right to depose apex official).

Note

This same balancing of interests used to determine whether an apex deposition is warranted also applies if an apex deposition is sought under the limited discovery allowed in a special appearance under TRCP 120a. See ***In re Miscavige***, *436 S.W.3d at 439–40. See "Discovery," ch. 3-B, §7. If a plaintiff is seeking an apex deposition in a special appearance, the defendant can invoke the apex doctrine and prevent the deposition unless the plaintiff can show that (1) the official has some unique or superior personal knowledge relevant to personal jurisdiction or (2) there is a reasonable indication that the official's deposition will lead to the discovery of admissible evidence about personal jurisdiction, and less intrusive discovery was unsatisfactory, insufficient, or inadequate.* ***In re Miscavige***, *436 S.W.3d at 440.*

§7.4 To exclude extra person. To object to the attendance of an extra person who was identified under TRCP 199.5(a)(3), the party should file an objection before the deposition and ask the court to exclude that person.

§7.5 To object to overbroad request. To object to a notice of a deposition that is overbroad or unlikely to produce relevant information, the party or witness should file a motion for protective order or a motion to quash the notice of deposition. *See* **In re Univar USA Inc.**, 311 S.W.3d 186, 189 (Tex.App.—Beaumont 2010, orig. proceeding). See "Motion for protective order," ch. 6-A, §20; "Motion to quash or modify subpoena," ch. 6-A, §21.

§7.6 To compel attendance.

1. Party witness. If a party (or a person retained by, employed by, or subject to the control of the party) refused to appear for a deposition, the party who noticed the deposition should file a motion to compel the party to attend the deposition and a motion for sanctions. *See* Tex. R. Civ. P. 215.1(b)(2)(A); *see also* Tex. R. Civ. P. 181 (party witness is subject to same process to compel as any other witness). See "Refusal to attend deposition," ch. 6-F, §10.1.1.

2. Nonparty witness. If a nonparty witness refused to appear for a deposition, the party who subpoenaed the witness for deposition should file a motion to compel the witness to appear for the deposition and a motion to hold the witness in contempt of court. *See* Tex. R. Civ. P. 176.8(a). A witness who refuses to comply with a subpoena without an adequate excuse may be deemed in contempt of court. *Id.* See "Discovery abuse," ch. 5-K, §5.1; "By nonparty witness-deponent," ch. 6-F, §10.1.1(3).

§7.7 Other objections. See "Valid objections to discovery requests," ch. 6-A, §19.1.

§8. Conduct during oral deposition

If the attorneys and witnesses do not comply with TRCP 199.5(d), the court may allow into evidence at trial the statements, objections, discussions, and other occurrences during the oral deposition that reflect on the credibility of the witness or the testimony. Tex. R. Civ. P. 199.5(d).

§8.1 Conduct of attorneys. Attorneys should cooperate with and be courteous to each other and the witness. Tex. R. Civ. P. 199.5(d). The oral deposition must be conducted in the same manner as if the testimony were being elicited in open court. *Id.* An attorney must not ask a question at an oral deposition solely to harass or mislead the witness, for any other improper purpose, or without a good-faith legal basis. Tex. R. Civ. P. 199.5(h). An attorney must not object to a question at an oral deposition, instruct the witness not to answer a question, or suspend the deposition unless there is a good-faith factual and legal basis to do so. *Id.*

§8.2 Conduct of witness. The witness should not be evasive and should not unduly delay the examination. Tex. R. Civ. P. 199.5(d).

§8.3 Conferring with witness. Private conferences between the witness and the witness's attorney during the actual taking of the deposition are improper except for determining whether a privilege should be asserted. Tex. R. Civ. P. 199.5(d). Private conferences may be held during agreed recesses and adjournments. *Id.*

§8.4 Conduct of court reporter. The court reporter or other officer taking the oral deposition does not rule on objections, but records them for a ruling by the court. Tex. R. Civ. P. 199.5(e). The officer taking the oral deposition cannot stop recording the testimony when an objection has been made. *Id.*

§9. Objecting during oral deposition

§9.1 Procedure to object. Objections are made and recorded in the deposition and reserved for a ruling by the trial court. *See* Tex. R. Civ. P. 199.5(e).

1. Permissible objections. TRCP 199.5(e) governs the types of objections and limits the exact words that may be used in an objection. The only objections the parties can make during the deposition are (1) "Objection, leading," (2) "Objection, form," and (3) "Objection, nonresponsive." Tex. R. Civ. P. 199.5(e). If these objections are not stated as phrased in TRCP 199.5(e), they are waived. *Id.* All other objections should be made at trial, unless the parties agree to another method. *Id.*; *see* Tex. R. Civ. P. 191.1. The parties can agree to a running objection to repeated offers of the same evidence. See "Running objection," ch. 8-D, §6.4. The parties can also agree to reserve all objections, including those stated in TRCP 199.5(e), until the time of trial. Tex. R. Civ. P. 191.1.

Practice Tip

If the witness's testimony is to be presented at trial by deposition, the parties should agree to make all objections on the record during the deposition.

(1) Objection to leading question. Leading questions are those that suggest the desired answer. **GAB Bus. Servs. v. Moore**, 829 S.W.2d 345, 351 (Tex.App.—Texarkana 1992, no writ). See Brown & Rondon, **Texas Rules of Evidence Handbook**, Rule 611 (2021 ed.) (§C).

(2) Objection to form of question. Objections to the form of the question include the following: (1) the question assumes facts that are in dispute or are not in evidence, (2) the question is argumentative, (3) the question misquotes the deponent, (4) the question calls for speculation, (5) the question is vague, ambiguous, or confusing, (6) the question is compound, (7) the question is too general, (8) the question calls for a narrative answer, (9) the question has been asked and answered, (10) the question is harassing and oppressive, and (11) the question is an incomplete hypothetical. *See* Tex. R. Civ. P. 199 cmt. 4; **St. Luke's Episcopal Hosp. v. Garcia**, 928 S.W.2d 307, 309 (Tex.App.—Houston [14th Dist.] 1996, orig. proceeding).

(3) Objection to nonresponsiveness of answer. If the deponent's response addresses issues not raised by the question or states more than is strictly required to answer the question, the attorney must object or else any complaint is waived. *See* Tex. R. Civ. P. 199.5(e).

2. Request for explanation of objections. If requested by the party interrogating the deponent, the objecting party must give a clear and concise explanation of its objection, or the objection is waived. Tex. R. Civ. P. 199.5(e).

3. Sanctionable objections. Argumentative or suggestive objections or explanations waive the objection and may be grounds for terminating the oral deposition or assessing costs or other sanctions. Tex. R. Civ. P. 199.5(e).

§9.2 Instructions not to answer. There are very few instances when it is proper for an attorney to instruct the deponent not to answer. When requested by the opposing party, the attorney who instructed the witness not to answer must give a concise, nonargumentative, and nonsuggestive explanation of the grounds for the instruction. Tex. R. Civ. P. 199.5(f). After giving the requested explanation, if the attorney who asked the question insists that it is a proper line of inquiry, the

objecting attorney may suspend the deposition to get a court ruling. See "Suspending deposition," ch. 6-F, §9.3. If the objecting attorney does not suspend the deposition but refuses to permit the deponent to answer, the attorney who asked the question may suspend the deposition and file a motion to compel the deponent to answer (referred to as "certifying the question"). *See generally* **Huie v. DeShazo**, 922 S.W.2d 920, 922 (Tex.1996) (Supreme Court stayed deposition while considering writ of mandamus on motion to compel testimony over assertion of attorney-client privilege). See "Motion to compel answer," ch. 6-F, §9.4. An attorney may object and instruct a witness not to answer a question during an oral deposition only for one of the following reasons:

1. Preserve privileges. To prevent the discovery of privileged information, the attorney may object and instruct the witness not to answer. Tex. R. Civ. P. 199.5(f). If the witness answers and discloses privileged information, the privilege may be waived. *See, e.g.,* **Delaporte v. Preston Square, Inc.**, 680 S.W.2d 561, 564 (Tex.App.—Dallas 1984, writ ref'd n.r.e.) (party who answered question about privileged matter in deposition waived privilege; however, trial court sustained objection to question about same matter at trial). If necessary for an in camera review, the deposition questions can be answered in front of the court reporter in the absence of the party seeking discovery and then be submitted to the court in camera. *See* Tex. R. Civ. P. 199.6.

2. Comply with court order or TRCPs. An attorney may instruct a witness not to answer a question if answering would violate a court order or the TRCPs. Tex. R. Civ. P. 199.5(f); **In re Lowe's Cos.**, 134 S.W.3d 876, 878 (Tex.App.—Houston [14th Dist.] 2004, orig. proceeding). For example, if a deponent is asked for net-worth information in a suit that involves only actual damages, the deponent should be instructed not to answer because the information is not relevant under the TRCPs. If the deponent is asked for information the court has already ruled is not discoverable, the deponent should be instructed not to answer. *See* Tex. R. Civ. P. 199.5(f).

3. Protect a witness. An attorney may instruct a witness not to answer if one of the parties asks the witness questions that are abusive or for which any answer would be misleading. Tex. R. Civ. P. 199.5(f). For example, an attorney could instruct a witness not to answer when the question incorporates such unfair assumptions or is so worded that any answer would necessarily be misleading—the "when did you stop beating your spouse" sort of question. Tex. R. Civ. P. 199 cmt. 4. Abusive questions include questions that inquire into matters clearly beyond the scope of discovery or that are argumentative, repetitious, or harassing. *Id.*

4. Stopwatch objection. When a party exceeds the deposition time limits, the other party should object and suspend the deposition to obtain a court ruling. Tex. R. Civ. P. 199.5(f), (g).

§9.3 Suspending deposition. A party or witness may suspend the deposition for the time necessary to obtain a court ruling if the time limitations for the deposition have expired or the deposition is being conducted or defended in violation of the rules. Tex. R. Civ. P. 199.5(g); *e.g.,* **Wilson v. Shamoun & Norman, LLP**, 523 S.W.3d 222, 229–30 (Tex.App.—Dallas 2017, pet. denied) (party could not rely on TRCP 199.5(g) to suspend deposition before it started based on argument that trial court did not have jurisdiction); *see, e.g.,* **Flores v. Garcia**, No. 13-15-00047-CV, 2015 WL 5895087 (Tex.App.—Corpus Christi 2015, no pet.) (memo op.; 10-8-15) (party could rely on TRCP 199.5(g) to suspend deposition so court could rule on motion requesting instruction that opposing counsel not ask harassing and misleading questions).

§9.4 Motion to compel answer. When a witness refuses to answer a question at a deposition, the party asking the question may file a motion to compel along with a copy of the deposition (or the certified question) and request a hearing. Tex. R. Civ. P. 199.6, 215.1(b)(2)(B); *see, e.g.,* **Huie v. DeShazo**, 922 S.W.2d 920, 922 (Tex.1996) (after witness refused to answer questions based on privilege, P filed motion to compel with certified questions); **Koepp v. Utica Mut. Ins.**, 833 S.W.2d 514, 514 (Tex.1992) (after P refused to answer questions about drug use, D filed motion to compel). The certified question is an excerpt from the deposition prepared by the court reporter to be used when a party intends to ask for an immediate court ruling. See "Motion to compel discovery," ch. 6-A, §22.

§9.5 Motion to suppress. To object to errors or irregularities in the taking of a deposition—how the deposition was prepared, transcribed, signed, certified, sealed, endorsed, or delivered—the party must file a written motion to suppress and serve it on all other parties. Tex. R. Civ. P. 203.5; *see* Tex. R. Civ. P. 202.3(b)(2). The motion to suppress must be served before the trial commences if the deposition officer delivered the deposition at least one entire day before the day of trial. Tex. R. Civ.

P. 203.5; **SAVA gumarska in kemijska industria d.d. v. Advanced Polymer Sci., Inc.**, 128 S.W.3d 304, 316 (Tex.App.—Dallas 2004, no pet.); **Klorer v. Block**, 717 S.W.2d 754, 759 (Tex.App.—San Antonio 1986, writ ref'd n.r.e.). See **O'Connor's Texas Civil Forms**, FORM 6F:3 (2020 ed.).

§10. Deposition sanctions

§10.1 Grounds for sanctions. A party or a deponent can be sanctioned for violating deposition procedures. For the standards for imposing sanctions, see "Motion for Sanctions," ch. 5-K, §1 et seq.

1. Refusal to attend deposition.

(1) By party-deponent. If the party to be deposed does not attend a noticed or court-ordered deposition, the trial court can impose sanctions, including the ultimate sanction of dismissal or default. Tex. R. Civ. P. 215.2(b); *e.g.*, **Petitt v. Laware**, 715 S.W.2d 688, 691–92 (Tex.App.—Houston [1st Dist.] 1986, writ ref'd n.r.e.) (P refused to attend court-ordered deposition; case dismissed); *see, e.g.*, **Greater Houston Transp. v. Wilson**, 725 S.W.2d 427, 431 (Tex.App.—Houston [14th Dist.] 1987, writ ref'd n.r.e.) (D did not attend deposition; default judgment entered). But sanctions that inhibit the presentation of the merits, such as dismissal or default, should be reserved for a party's flagrant bad faith or repeated discovery abuses. *See* **TransAmerican Nat. Gas Corp. v. Powell**, 811 S.W.2d 913, 918 (Tex.1991); *see, e.g.*, **Hogan v. Beckel**, 783 S.W.2d 307, 309–10 (Tex.App.—San Antonio 1989, writ denied) (dismissal was improper when P did not appear for one noticed deposition that she tried to reschedule). See "Necessary severity," ch. 5-K, §3.1.2; "Types of sanctions," ch. 5-K, §7. There is no requirement that the failure to attend be willful. **Meek v. Bishop, Peterson & Sharp**, 919 S.W.2d 805, 809 (Tex.App.—Houston [14th Dist.] 1996, writ denied); *see* Tex. R. Civ. P. 215.1(b)(2)(A). In addition to or instead of a sanctions order, the court can hold the party in contempt. Tex. R. Civ. P. 215.2(a), (b)(6).

(2) By party who noticed deposition. If the party giving notice of the deposition does not attend the deposition, and if another party or that party's attorney does attend, the court may award the attending party reasonable expenses, including attorney fees. Tex. R. Civ. P. 215.5(a); *see* **Hlavinka v. Griffin**, 721 S.W.2d 521, 523–24 (Tex.App.—Corpus Christi 1986, no writ).

(3) By nonparty witness-deponent.

(a) If the witness does not attend a deposition, and the fault lies with the party giving notice, the court may order that party to pay reasonable expenses, including attorney fees, to any party that does attend. Tex. R. Civ. P. 215.5(b).

(b) If a nonparty witness refuses to attend a deposition after being subpoenaed by a party or ordered by the trial court, the court may hold the nonparty witness in contempt. Tex. R. Civ. P. 176.8(a), 215.2(a).

2. Refusal to answer questions. If a deponent refuses to answer a proper question asked in a deposition, the trial court can impose sanctions. Tex. R. Civ. P. 215.1(b)(2)(B). A deponent's evasive or incomplete answer can be treated as a refusal to answer a question. Tex. R. Civ. P. 215.1(c). When a trial court orders a deponent to answer a question and the deponent refuses, the court can impose sanctions.

(1) Contempt. The court can hold the deponent (party or nonparty) in contempt and punish the deponent with a fine or confinement. Tex. R. Civ. P. 176.8(a), 215.2(a), (b)(2).

(2) Strike pleadings. The court can strike a party's pleadings. Tex. R. Civ. P. 215.2(b)(5); *see, e.g.*, **First State Bank v. Chappell & Handy, P.C.**, 729 S.W.2d 917, 921 (Tex.App.—Corpus Christi 1987, writ ref'd n.r.e.) (court struck D-corporation's counterclaim and defensive pleadings because D's officer refused to answer questions after being ordered to answer).

(3) Award expenses. The court can require a party whose conduct necessitated the motion for sanctions, the attorney advising such conduct, or both to pay the moving party's reasonable expenses, including attorney fees. Tex. R. Civ. P. 215.2(b)(8); *see also* Tex. R. Civ. P. 215.3 (sanctions may be imposed for abusing discovery process). The court cannot order a nonparty deponent whose conduct necessitated the motion to pay the moving party's expenses. **In re White**, 227 S.W.3d 234, 237 (Tex.App.—San Antonio 2007, orig. proceeding).

3. Lying during deposition. If a party-deponent lies (i.e., perjures herself) during a deposition, the trial court can impose sanctions ranging from the payment of expenses and attorney fees to a default judgment. *See* Tex. R. Civ. P. 215.2(b); **In re Reece**, 341 S.W.3d 360, 368 (Tex.2011). The court cannot, however, hold the party in contempt for lying during a deposition unless, by lying, the party has obstructed the court in the performance of its duties. **In re Reece**, 341 S.W.3d at 367.

§10.2 Appropriate court to hear objections & motions. TRCP 215.1(a) determines the appropriate court to hear and determine objections and motions about a deposition.

1. Party deponent. The court where the suit is filed should hear and determine objections made about a deposition of a party. *See* Tex. R. Civ. P. 215.1(a). Any district court in the district where a party's deposition is being taken may also hear a motion relating to the taking of a deposition. *Id.*

2. Nonparty deponent. A district court in the district where the deposition is being taken should hear and determine the objections made about the deposition of a nonparty. *See* Tex. R. Civ. P. 215.1(a); **Latham v. Thornton**, 806 S.W.2d 347, 349 (Tex.App.—Fort Worth 1991, orig. proceeding).

§11. Supplementing deposition testimony

§11.1 Deposition of fact witnesses. A party does not have a general duty to supplement the deposition testimony of fact witnesses who change their minds about facts disclosed in a deposition. Tex. R. Civ. P. 193 cmt. 5; **Titus Cty. Hosp. Dist. v. Lucas**, 988 S.W.2d 740, 740 (Tex.1998); *see* **Collins v. Collins**, 923 S.W.2d 569, 569 (Tex.1996).

Practice Tip

To avoid the surprise at trial that the other party's witnesses have changed their minds about the facts of the case, the parties can enter into a Rule 11 agreement to supplement the deposition testimony of fact witnesses who are aligned with each party.

§11.2 Deposition testimony of retained expert. See "Supplementing discovery of retained testifying expert," ch. 6-D, §5.1.

§11.3 Deposition testimony of nonretained expert. See "Supplementing discovery of nonretained testifying expert," ch. 6-D, §5.2.

§12. Using deposition at trial

§12.1 Admissibility. A deposition is admissible at trial according to the rules of evidence. Tex. R. Civ. P. 203.6(b), (c); *see* **Jones v. Colley**, 820 S.W.2d 863, 866 (Tex.App.—Texarkana 1991, writ denied) (party is entitled to offer deposition testimony into evidence in most effective manner, provided it does not convey false impression).

1. Deposition taken in same proceeding. A deposition taken in the same proceeding as the trial is not hearsay, and the deponent does not need to be unavailable for the deposition to be used as evidence. Tex. R. Civ. P. 203.6(b)(1); Tex. R. Evid. 801(e)(3). The deposition can be used instead of or in addition to live testimony. "Same proceeding" includes any other suit involving the same subject matter between the same parties or their representatives or successors in interest. Tex. R. Civ. P. 203.6(b); *see* Tex. R. Evid. 801(e)(3).

(1) Party not present at deposition. Depositions taken in the absence of a party may be used at trial if the party received notice but chose not to attend. *See* **Bohmfalk v. Linwood**, 742 S.W.2d 518, 520–21 (Tex.App.—Dallas 1987, no writ).

(2) Not party at time of deposition. A deposition may not be used against a party that was joined after the deposition was taken unless the late party had a reasonable opportunity to redepose the deponent after being joined and did not exercise that opportunity. Tex. R. Civ. P. 203.6(b)(2); *see* **Stevenson v. Koutzarov**, 795 S.W.2d 313, 317 (Tex.App.—Houston [1st Dist.] 1990, writ denied), *disapproved on other grounds*, **Agar Corp. v. Electro Circuits Int'l**, 580 S.W.3d 136

(Tex.2019). See "Restricted use," ch. 6-F, §16.9.2. If a deposition was taken before a party was joined, it can be used at trial if the late party has an interest similar to any party already in the suit when the deposition was taken.

Practice Tip

If you took a deposition before a party was added, and if the late party does not have similar interests with any other party, you should redepose the witness to give the late party the opportunity for cross-examination. See ***Elizondo v. Tavarez****, 596 S.W.2d 667, 671 (Tex.App.—Corpus Christi 1980, writ ref'd n.r.e.). You can satisfy the requirement to redepose the witness by deposing the witness with written questions. If you represent a late party, and one of the parties sends a deposition on written questions to a witness who was deposed before your client was added, you should file objections to the deposition on written questions, and notice the witness to appear for an oral deposition. See* ***Stevenson****, 795 S.W.2d at 316 n.1.*

2. Deposition from other proceeding. Depositions from other proceedings can be used if they are admissible under the rules of evidence. Tex. R. Civ. P. 203.6(c); *see, e.g.*, **Dillee v. Sisters of Charity**, 912 S.W.2d 307, 310 & n.6 (Tex.App.—Houston [14th Dist.] 1995, no writ) (deposition from another case was admissible under TRE 801 as admission by a party-opponent).

(1) Party deposition. The deposition of an opposing party taken in another proceeding is admissible as a party-admission or as former testimony. *See* Tex. R. Evid. 801(e)(2), 804(b)(1)(A); *see, e.g.*, **Worley v. Butler**, 809 S.W.2d 242, 245 (Tex.App.—Corpus Christi 1990, no writ) (client's testimony at first trial about employment contract with his attorney was admissible against him in later lawsuit over attorney fees); *see also* Tex. R. Evid. 801(e)(1) (prior statement by witness).

Note

The Supreme Court's 2015 amendment to TRE 801(e)(2) deleted the reference to the term "admissions" in the title of the rule because not all statements under that subdivision necessarily admit anything. TRE 801 cmt. The amendment is meant to be only stylistic without any change to the application of the hearsay exclusion. See id.

(2) Nonparty deposition. The deposition of a nonparty taken in another proceeding is admissible as former testimony if the deponent is unavailable to testify. Tex. R. Evid. 804(b)(1)(A); **Smith v. Smith**, 720 S.W.2d 586, 599 (Tex.App.—Houston [1st Dist.] 1986, no writ); *see* Tex. R. Civ. P. 203.6(c); *see, e.g.*, **Celotex Corp. v. Tate**, 797 S.W.2d 197, 205 (Tex.App.—Corpus Christi 1990, writ dism'd) (deposition of claimant in workers' compensation case, who died, was admissible in another case). Unavailability of a witness is defined as (1) a claim of privilege, (2) a refusal to testify, (3) a lack of memory, (4) a death or physical or mental illness or infirmity, or (5) an absence from the hearing and inability of the proponent to procure attendance or testimony by reasonable means. Tex. R. Evid. 804(a); *see, e.g.*, **Keene Corp. v. Rogers**, 863 S.W.2d 168, 177–78 (Tex.App.—Texarkana 1993, writ filed, bankruptcy stay granted 3-30-94) (because party did not prove unavailability, court should have excluded expert's deposition from another case). The party against whom the deposition is offered, or a person with a similar interest, must have had an opportunity and similar motive to develop the former testimony by direct examination, cross-examination, or redirect examination. Tex. R. Evid. 804(b)(1)(A)(ii).

§12.2 Procedure. Deposition testimony is introduced at trial as follows:

1. Read into evidence. The party offering deposition testimony must read a transcribed deposition (or play a videotape deposition) before the jury. *See* Tex. R. Civ. P. 203.6(b). When introducing a written deposition, one attorney reads the questions and another attorney, sitting in the witness stand, reads the answers given by the deponent.

Caution

When you read a deposition into evidence or play a videotape deposition, insist that the court reporter transcribe the testimony as the jury hears it. If the court reporter does not transcribe the deposition

testimony as it is presented at trial, the appellate record will not contain the deposition testimony of the witness. If you do not object on the record during the trial, you will waive the issue of an incomplete record on appeal. E.g., ***Lascurain v. Crowley****, 917 S.W.2d 341, 344–45 (Tex.App.—El Paso 1996, no writ) (court reporter left courtroom during deposition testimony with permission of parties). If the court reporter appeared to be transcribing the testimony but was not, you may be able to reconstruct the record.* ***State Farm Fire & Cas. Ins. v. Vandiver****, 941 S.W.2d 343, 347–48 (Tex.App.—Waco 1997, no writ).*

2. Submit deposition as offer of proof. If the court rules a deposition inadmissible, the party may submit the deposition as an offer of proof, have it marked as an exhibit, identify the portions offered by line and page number, and file it with the court reporter. *See* Tex. R. Evid. 103(a)(2); **Hooper v. Chittaluru**, 222 S.W.3d 103, 107–08 (Tex.App.—Houston [14th Dist.] 2006, pet. denied). The offer of proof should be made before the charge is read to the jury. Tex. R. Evid. 103(c); **Fletcher v. Minnesota Mining & Mfg.**, 57 S.W.3d 602, 607 (Tex.App.—Houston [1st Dist.] 2001, pet. denied). If, for some reason, the deposition is not immediately offered as an offer of proof, it may be filed as a formal bill of exception after the trial. Tex. R. App. P. 33.2. See "Offer of Proof & Bill of Exception," ch. 8-E, §1 et seq.

§12.3 Trial objections to deposition testimony. At trial, unless the parties made a different agreement on objections, a party may urge (1) those objections to leading, form, and nonresponsiveness that were made during the deposition and (2) all other objections. Tex. R. Civ. P. 199.5(e). See "Procedure to object," ch. 6-F, §9.1.

§12.4 Objection to trial testimony. A party may object to the trial testimony of a witness if it is materially different from the witness's deposition testimony. See "Impeaching by earlier inconsistent statement," ch. 8-C, §6.2.

§12.5 Use in summary-judgment cases. When a deposition is used as summary-judgment evidence, it is not necessary for the deposition to be authenticated by an affidavit that certifies the truthfulness and correctness of the copied material. *See* Tex. R. Civ. P. 166a(d); Tex. R. Evid. 901(a); **McConathy v. McConathy**, 869 S.W.2d 341, 342 (Tex.1994).

§13. Deposition by nonstenographic recording device

A party may take a deposition by videotape or other recording device. Tex. R. Civ. P. 199.1(c). A video deposition has a more powerful effect on the jury than a deposition that is read to the jury. **Ochs v. Martinez**, 789 S.W.2d 949, 956 (Tex.App.—San Antonio 1990, writ denied).

§13.1 Deposition officer. When a deposition is to be recorded by video or audio recording without a simultaneous stenographic recording by a court reporter, the party noticing the deposition is responsible for obtaining a person authorized by law to act as the deposition officer and administer the oath. Tex. R. Civ. P. 199.1(c), 203.2.

§13.2 Notice. To take a videotape deposition, the party must give the witness and the other parties at least five days' notice in writing. Tex. R. Civ. P. 199.1(c). The notice must state that the deposition (1) will be recorded by nonstenographic means, (2) will be recorded by videotape or audiotape (or by some other means), and (3) will or will not also be recorded stenographically. *Id.* The notice may be included in the deposition notice or served separately. *Id.* See "Notice of oral deposition," ch. 6-F, §4.5; **O'Connor's Texas Civil Forms**, FORM 6F:1, ¶3 (2020 ed.).

§13.3 Response. After a party gives notice of its intent to take a nonstenographic deposition, any other party may serve written notice designating an additional method of recording (usually stenographic) at its own expense. Tex. R. Civ. P. 199.1(c); *see also* Tex. R. Civ. P. 203.6(a) (court may require nonstenographic recording be reduced to writing by certified court reporter). Unless one of the parties elects to pay for a court reporter to transcribe the testimony, or the court orders that the deposition be transcribed for trial, no stenographic transcript is necessary. Tex. R. Civ. P. 199.1(c), 203.6(a).

§13.4 Recording. The party taking the deposition is responsible for ensuring that the recording is intelligible, accurate, and trustworthy. Tex. R. Civ. P. 199.1(c).

§13.5 Copies. The original video recording must be available for inspection on reasonable request. Tex. R. Civ. P. 203.3(c). Any party and the witness may obtain a duplicate copy at their own expense. *Id.*

§13.6 Use at trial. A party may play a recording of a nonstenographic deposition at trial instead of reading the deposition. Tex. R. Civ. P. 203.6(a). A party may use a written transcription of a nonstenographic deposition to the same

extent as one taken by stenographic means. *Id.*; **Wrenn v. G.A.T.X. Logistics, Inc.**, 73 S.W.3d 489, 499 (Tex.App.—Fort Worth 2002, no pet.). The court, on a motion showing good cause, may order the party to provide a transcript of the deposition. Tex. R. Civ. P. 203.6(a).

Note

If a party objects to the introduction of a videotape deposition at trial, the court does not need to view the videotape before ruling unless the objection is specific to a visual aspect of the deposition. ***Diamond Offshore Servs. v. Williams****, 542 S.W.3d 539, 546 (Tex.2018); see* ***Gunn v. McCoy****, 554 S.W.3d 645, 666 n.10 (Tex.2018). Generally, a trial court must view other video evidence before ruling on admissibility when the contents of the video are at issue.* ***Diamond Offshore****, 542 S.W.3d at 546.*

§14. Deposition by telephone

A deposition by telephone is useful when the deponent is far away and the parties need only limited information.

§14.1 Notice. A written notice to take a deposition by telephone or other remote electronic means must be served on the witness and all parties a reasonable time before the deposition is to be taken. Tex. R. Civ. P. 199.1(b). See "Notice of oral deposition," ch. 6-F, §4.5; **O'Connor's Texas Civil Forms**, FORM 6F:1, ¶5 (2020 ed.). For a discussion of taking a telephone deposition without a request for documents, see "For deposition without documents," ch. 6-F, §4.5.2(2). For a discussion of taking a telephone deposition that requests the production of documents, see "For deposition with documents," ch. 6-F, §4.5.2(1).

§14.2 Location of witness. A deposition by telephone is considered to have been taken "in the district and at the place where the witness is located when answering the questions." Tex. R. Civ. P. 199.1(b). The person administering the oath to the witness must have the power to administer an oath in the jurisdiction where the witness is located. *Id.*; *see* Tex. Civ. Prac. & Rem. Code §20.001(b), (c).

§14.3 Location of deposition officer. The deposition officer may be located with the party who noticed the deposition or with the witness. Tex. R. Civ. P. 199.1(b); *see* **Clone Component Distribs. v. State**, 819 S.W.2d 593, 598 (Tex.App.—Dallas 1991, no writ).

§14.4 Exhibits. If it is necessary to question the witness about exhibits and the deposition officer is not physically in the same room as the witness, the parties should send premarked exhibits to the witness before the deposition. Another option is to use a fax machine to transfer copies of exhibits during the deposition. *See* **Clone Component Distribs. v. State**, 819 S.W.2d 593, 599–600 (Tex.App.—Dallas 1991, no writ).

§15. Deposition on written questions

Depositions on written questions are useful for securing testimony from a deponent with limited relevant information—for example, a custodian of business records. A deposition on written questions is relatively inexpensive compared to an oral deposition. Depositions on written questions are similar to interrogatories in that the questions are drafted in advance. They are unlike interrogatories in other ways—depositions on written questions can be served on nonparties (interrogatories can be served only on parties), and depositions on written questions are not limited in number (interrogatories are limited). Depositions on written questions cannot be used to circumvent the limits on interrogatories. Tex. R. Civ. P. 190 cmt. 5 (1999).

§15.1 Procedure. A deposition on written questions proceeds much like the standard oral deposition that is transcribed by a court reporter. For most of the requirements, see "Procedure for standard oral deposition," ch. 6-F, §4. This section will focus on the differences between the two procedures.

§15.2 Deposition officer. The only persons who can take a deposition on written questions are (1) a clerk of the district court, (2) a judge or clerk of the county court, (3) a court reporter, or (4) a notary public. Tex. Civ. Prac. & Rem. Code §20.001(a) (persons 1, 2, and 4).

§15.3 Notice of deposition on written questions. The notice to take a deposition on written questions must comply with the following rules on oral depositions: TRCP 199.1(b), 199.2(b), and 199.5(a)(3). Tex. R. Civ. P. 200.1(b).

1. Name of deponent. The notice must state the deponent's name (if known) and the deponent's address for service. *See* Tex. R. Civ. P. 199.2(b)(1) (contents of notice), Tex. R. Civ. P. 200.1(a) (notice must be served on witness). The name of the deponent might not be known if the deponent is a custodian of records or if the party has asked an organization to provide a deponent to give testimony about a certain subject. *See* Tex. R. Civ. P. 199.2(b)(1), 200.1(b). The notice of a deposition on written questions to a nonparty business association or business entity can require the nonparty to designate a deponent to testify on a particular subject. *See* Tex. R. Civ. P. 199.2(b)(1), 200.1(b).

2. Place for deposition. The notice must state the place for the deposition, which must be reasonable. Tex. R. Civ. P. 199.2(b)(2), 200.1(b). See "Place for deposition," ch. 6-F, §4.5.3.

3. Date for deposition. The notice must state the time for the deposition, which must be reasonable. Tex. R. Civ. P. 199.2(b)(2), 200.1(b). The notice must be served on the witness and all parties at least 20 days before the deposition is to be taken. Tex. R. Civ. P. 200.1(a). When a notice requests that a party (not a nonparty) produce documents, the notice must be served at least 30 days before the deposition. See "Party deposition with documents," ch. 6-F, §4.5.2(1)(a); chart 6-9 under "Certificate of service," ch. 6-F, §4.5.8; **O'Connor's Texas Civil Forms**, FORM 6F:4 (2020 ed.).

4. Designation of documents. The notice must identify the documents and other items the deponent is required to produce. *See* Tex. R. Civ. P. 200.1(b).

5. Extra persons in attendance. The notice must identify any person not listed in TRCP 199.5(a)(3) who will attend the deposition. *See* Tex. R. Civ. P. 199.5(a)(3), 200.1(b). See "Additional attendee," ch. 6-F, §4.5.5.

6. Signed. The notice must be signed by the attorney (or party when pro se). Tex. R. Civ. P. 191.3(a). See "Certification by signature," ch. 6-A, §4.1.

7. Subpoena. When the deponent is a nonparty, a subpoena must be issued. Tex. R. Civ. P. 200.2, 205.1(b); **St. Luke's Episcopal Hosp. v. Garcia**, 928 S.W.2d 307, 311 (Tex.App.—Houston [14th Dist.] 1996, orig. proceeding). If the nonparty deponent is required to produce documents, the subpoena must meet the requirements of TRCP 176. Tex. R. Civ. P. 176, 199.2(b)(5), 200.1(b). See "Subpoenas," ch. 1-L, §1 et seq.; "Securing things from a nonparty," ch. 6-I, §5.

8. Direct questions. The questions the deponent is required to answer must be attached to the notice. Tex. R. Civ. P. 200.3(a). See **O'Connor's Texas Civil Forms**, FORM 6F:5 (2020 ed.) (deposition on written questions for custodian of records).

9. Provide to deposition officer. The party that noticed the deposition must send a copy of the notice and copies of all questions to the officer designated to take the deposition, generally the court reporter. Tex. R. Civ. P. 200.1(a). If the deponent is a nonparty, the court reporter will issue a subpoena.

§15.4 Cross-questions. Any other party in the suit may object to the direct questions and serve cross-questions within ten days after the notice and the direct questions are served. Tex. R. Civ. P. 200.3(b). See **O'Connor's Texas Civil Forms**, FORM 6F:6 (2020 ed.).

§15.5 Redirect questions. Any party may object to the cross-questions and serve redirect questions within five days after being served cross-questions. Tex. R. Civ. P. 200.3(b).

§15.6 Recross questions. Any party may object to the redirect questions and serve recross questions within three days after being served redirect questions. Tex. R. Civ. P. 200.3(b).

§15.7 Objections to questions.

1. Deadline for objections.

(1) To direct questions. Objections to direct questions must be served on the party propounding them within the time allowed for serving the succeeding cross-questions. See "Cross-questions," ch. 6-F, §15.4.

(2) To cross-questions. Objections to cross-questions must be served on the party propounding them within the time allowed for serving the succeeding redirect questions. See "Redirect questions," ch. 6-F, §15.5.

(3) To redirect questions. Objections to redirect questions must be served on the party propounding them within the time allowed for serving the succeeding recross questions. See "Recross questions," ch. 6-F, §15.6.

(4) To recross questions. Objections to recross questions must be served within five days after redirect questions are served or the time of the deposition on written questions, whichever is earlier. Tex. R. Civ. P. 200.3(b).

2. Objections to form only. The deadline for objections applies only to objections to form, not objections to substantive issues or privileges. **St. Luke's Episcopal Hosp. v. Garcia**, 928 S.W.2d 307, 310 (Tex.App.—Houston [14th Dist.] 1996, orig. proceeding). Objections to the form of the question are waived unless asserted in accordance with TRCP 200.3(b). Tex. R. Civ. P. 200.3(c). Examples of objections to form include the following: (1) assumes facts in dispute or not in evidence, (2) is argumentative, (3) misquotes a deponent, (4) is leading, (5) calls for speculation, (6) is ambiguous or unintelligible, (7) is compound, (8) is too general, (9) calls for a narrative answer, and (10) has been asked and answered. **St. Luke's**, 928 S.W.2d at 309.

§15.8 Objections to assertions of privileges. To lodge objections to assertions of privilege, the deponent or a party should file a motion to quash or a motion for protective order. If the deponent is a nonparty, the movant should press for a hearing before the date of the deposition. See "Objecting before oral deposition," ch. 6-F, §7.

§15.9 Taking deposition. At the time of the deposition, the deposition officer administers the oath, asks the questions, receives any documents produced, and transcribes the deponent's testimony. *See* Tex. R. Civ. P. 200.4; *see also* **In re Toyota Motor Corp.**, 191 S.W.3d 498, 503 (Tex.App.—Waco 2006, orig. proceeding) (attorneys are not permitted to answer written deposition questions for clients). The officer then prepares the questions and answers and certifies and delivers them to the deponent for examination and signature. Tex. R. Civ. P. 200.4. When necessary, the officer has authority to summon and administer an oath to an interpreter. *Id.*

§15.10 Filing deposition. Nonparty deposition notices and subpoenas must be filed with the court. Tex. R. Civ. P. 191.4(b)(1). No other deposition documents should be filed. Tex. R. Civ. P. 191.4(a)(1). For exceptions to the do-not-file rule, see "Exceptions," ch. 6-A, §12.1.3.

§16. Deposition before suit

A deposition before suit or to investigate a claim is an examination by oral or written questions taken by court order before a lawsuit is filed. Tex. R. Civ. P. 202.1. The proceeding is not, in itself, a separate lawsuit but is incident to and in anticipation of a suit. **Office Empls. Int'l Un. Local 277 v. Southwestern Drug Corp.**, 391 S.W.2d 404, 406 (Tex.1965) (applying former TRCP 187); **Lee v. GST Transp. Sys.**, 334 S.W.3d 16, 19 (Tex.App.—Dallas 2008, pet. denied). **In re Jorden**, 249 S.W.3d 416, 419 (Tex.2008). TRCP 202 applies to all discovery before suit covered by the former rules governing depositions to perpetuate testimony (former TRCP 187) and bills of discovery (former TRCP 737). Tex. R. Civ. P. 202 cmt. 1.

Note

Courts must strictly limit and carefully supervise presuit discovery to prevent abuse of TRCP 202. ***In re Wolfe****, 341 S.W.3d 932, 933 (Tex.2011). A party cannot obtain relief through a TRCP 202 proceeding that would be denied in the anticipated action or potential claim.* ***In re DePinho****, 505 S.W.3d 621, 623 (Tex.2016);* ***In re City of Dallas****, 501 S.W.3d 71, 73 (Tex.2016);* ***In re Wolfe****, 341 S.W.3d at 933. Thus, to prevent a party from circumventing discovery limitations that would govern the anticipated suit or potential claim, the scope of discovery in presuit depositions is the same as if the anticipated suit or potential claim had already been filed.* ***In re Wolfe****, 341 S.W.3d at 933; see Tex. R. Civ. P. 202.5.*

§16.1 Petition. The requirements for the petition are stated in TRCP 202.2.

1. Form. The petition must be in the name of the petitioner and must be verified. Tex. R. Civ. P. 202.2(a), (c). See **O'Connor's Texas Civil Forms**, FORM 6F:8 (2020 ed.).

2. Grounds. The petition must state one of two possible grounds for a deposition before suit: (1) to perpetuate or obtain testimony for use in an anticipated suit or (2) to investigate a potential claim. Tex. R. Civ. P. 202.1, 202.2(d); **In re City of Tatum**, 567 S.W.3d 800, 804 (Tex.App.—Tyler 2018, orig. proceeding); **In re PrairieSmarts LLC**, 421 S.W.3d 296, 305 (Tex.App.—Fort Worth 2014, orig. proceeding).

(1) Anticipation of suit. A petition for a TRCP 202 deposition may be filed in anticipation of a suit. Tex. R. Civ. P. 202.1(a), 202.2(d)(1). Such a petition must include the statement: "The petitioner anticipates the institution of a suit in which the petitioner may be a party." Tex. R. Civ. P. 202.2(d)(1). In addition, the petition must do the following:

(a) Identify subject matter. The petition must identify the subject matter of the anticipated action and the petitioner's interest in it. Tex. R. Civ. P. 202.2(e). The petitioner is not required to plead a specific cause of action. **In re East**, 476 S.W.3d 61, 66 (Tex.App.—Corpus Christi 2014, orig. proceeding); **City of Houston v. U.S. Filter Wastewater Grp.**, 190 S.W.3d 242, 245 n.2 (Tex.App.—Houston [1st Dist.] 2006, no pet.).

(b) Identify adverse persons. The petition must either (1) include the names, addresses, and telephone numbers of the persons whom the petitioner expects to have interests adverse to the petitioner's in the anticipated suit, or (2) state that the information cannot be ascertained through diligent inquiry and describe those persons. Tex. R. Civ. P. 202.2(f); *see* **U.S. Gov't v. Marks**, 949 S.W.2d 320, 322 (Tex.1997) (former TRCP 187).

(2) Investigate claim. A petition for a TRCP 202 deposition may be filed to investigate a claim. Tex. R. Civ. P. 202.1(b), 202.2(d)(2). Such a petition must include the statement: "The petitioner seeks to investigate a potential claim by or against the petitioner." Tex. R. Civ. P. 202.2(d)(2). Under TRCP 202.2(d)(2), there is no expectation of a suit. This ground can help plaintiffs comply with TRCP 13 and CPRC §9.011, which require plaintiffs to make a good-faith inquiry before deciding whether to file suit.

Note

A TRCP 202 deposition cannot be used to investigate a claim for which the statute of limitations has run. See ***Glassdoor, Inc. v. Andra Grp.****, 575 S.W.3d 523, 527 (Tex.2019). Once the statute of limitations on the potential claim has run, the TRCP 202 proceeding to investigate that claim is rendered moot. Id. at 527 & n.3.*

(a) Adverse persons. When investigating a claim, unlike in a deposition in anticipation of suit, the petitioner is not required to identify those who may have an adverse interest. *See* Tex. R. Civ. P. 202.2(f); Fineberg & Shore, *Discovery Update*, Advanced Civil Trial Course, State Bar of Texas CLE, ch. 1, p. 3 (2001).

(b) Limitations.

[1] Health-care claim. A presuit deposition under TRCP 202 cannot be taken to investigate a potential claim against a health-care provider until after an expert report is served. **In re Jorden**, 249 S.W.3d 416, 418 (Tex.2008); *see* Tex. Civ. Prac. & Rem. Code §74.351(s); **In re Turner**, 591 S.W.3d 121, 125–26 (Tex.2019). The filing of a petition for a TRCP 202 deposition, however, does not trigger the 120-day deadline for serving an expert report. **Drake v. Walker**, 529 S.W.3d 516, 518 (Tex.App.—Dallas 2017, no pet.); *see* Tex. Civ. Prac. & Rem. Code §74.351(a) (expert report must be served within 120 days after D's original answer is filed). That is, because a TRCP 202 proceeding is not a separate, independent lawsuit, the filing of the TRCP 202 petition does not trigger the deadline for filing an original answer or the subsequent 120-day deadline for serving the expert report. *See* Tex. Civ. Prac. & Rem. Code §74.351(a); **Drake**, 529 S.W.3d at 526.

[2] Trade secret. A presuit deposition under TRCP 202 generally cannot be taken to discover trade-secret information to determine if the petitioner has a potential claim. *See* **In re Rockafellow**, __ S.W.3d __ & n.3, 2011 WL 2848638 (Tex.App.—Amarillo 2011, orig. proceeding) (No. 07-11-00066-CV; 7-19-11) (undesignated op.); **In re Hewlett Packard**, 212 S.W.3d 356, 363–64 (Tex.App.—Austin 2006, orig. proceeding); *see also* **In re PrairieSmarts**, 421 S.W.3d at 308 n.11 (court declined to hold that trade-secret information can never be obtained under TRCP 202 simply because suit has not been filed). For a petitioner to take a presuit deposition to discover trade-secret information, the petitioner must satisfy the requirements of both TRE 507 and TRCP 202.4(a)(2). **In re PrairieSmarts**, 421 S.W.3d at 305–06. See "When is a trade secret discoverable?," ch. 6-B, §2.24.2; "Proof," ch. 6-F, §16.6.2.

3. Deponent information. The petition must identify (1) the persons to be deposed by name, address, and telephone number, (2) the substance of the testimony the petitioner expects to elicit from each, and (3) the petitioner's reasons for desiring to obtain the testimony of each. Tex. R. Civ. P. 202.2(g). If documents need to be produced at the deposi-

tion, the petition should also identify the documents the persons will be requested to bring. See "Request for documents," ch. 6-F, §4.5.6. The person sought to be deposed does not need to be a potentially liable defendant in the claim under investigation. **U.S. Filter**, 190 S.W.3d at 245.

4. Prayer. The petition must request an order authorizing the petitioner to take the depositions of the persons named in the petition. Tex. R. Civ. P. 202.2(h).

§16.2 Where to file. A petition under TRCP 202 must be filed in a proper court of any county where venue of the anticipated suit may lie, if suit is anticipated, or where the witness resides, if no suit is anticipated. Tex. R. Civ. P. 202.2(b); **In re Akzo Nobel Chem., Inc.**, 24 S.W.3d 919, 920 (Tex.App.—Beaumont 2000, orig. proceeding).

§16.3 Court's jurisdiction. The court in which the petition is filed must have both subject-matter jurisdiction over the action and personal jurisdiction over the potential defendant. **In re Doe**, 444 S.W.3d 603, 608 (Tex.2014).

1. Subject-matter jurisdiction. The court must have subject-matter jurisdiction over the anticipated suit or potential claim. **In re DePinho**, 505 S.W.3d 621, 623 (Tex.2016); *see* **In re Doe**, 444 S.W.3d at 608. For a general discussion of when a defendant can dismiss a cause of action for lack of subject-matter jurisdiction, see "Plea to the Jurisdiction—Challenging the Court," ch. 3-F, §1 et seq. Because the court must have subject-matter jurisdiction, a petitioner cannot seek a TRCP 202 deposition in certain situations, including the following:

(1) A petitioner cannot seek a TRCP 202 deposition to investigate a potential federal antitrust suit. *See* **In re Doe**, 444 S.W.3d at 608.

(2) A petitioner cannot seek a TRCP 202 deposition to investigate a claim that is not ripe. **In re DePinho**, 505 S.W.3d at 624. See "Not ripe," ch. 3-F, §3.3. For a claim to be ripe, the facts must be sufficiently developed to show an injury has occurred or is likely to occur, rather than being contingent or remote. *E.g.*, **In re DePinho**, 505 S.W.3d at 624–25 (claim for tortious interference with patent application was not ripe because application had not been filed; TRCP 202 deposition was improper). See "Ripeness," **O'Connor's Texas Causes of Action**, ch. 52, §3.4 (2021 ed.).

(3) A petitioner cannot seek a TRCP 202 deposition to investigate a claim that does not meet the trial court's amount-in-controversy requirement. *See, e.g.*, **In re City of Dallas**, 501 S.W.3d 71, 73–74 (Tex.2016) (because petitioner did not specify amount of damages it would seek for anticipated tortious-interference claim, trial court could not have determined whether it had subject-matter jurisdiction; thus, granting TRCP 202 deposition was improper).

2. Personal jurisdiction. The court must have personal jurisdiction over the potential defendant. **In re Doe**, 444 S.W.3d at 608. That is, the potential defendant must have sufficient minimum contacts with Texas for the court to exercise personal jurisdiction over her. *See id.* at 610. For a discussion of minimum contacts in challenging personal jurisdiction, see "No minimum contacts," ch. 3-B, §2.4.2. The petitioner has the burden to plead sufficient allegations to establish the court's personal jurisdiction. **In re Doe**, 444 S.W.3d at 610.

Note

In ***In re Doe****, the petitioner filed a TRCP 202 petition to discover the identity of an anonymous Internet blogger who allegedly defamed the petitioner. See* ***In re Doe****, 444 S.W.3d at 604–05. The petitioner sought to depose Google, the blog's host, to get the information in anticipation of suit against the blogger for libel and business disparagement. Id. at 605. The trial court ordered the deposition, but the Supreme Court held that because the trial court did not have personal jurisdiction over the blogger, the deposition should have been denied. Id. at 604–05. Although a petitioner's burden to establish personal jurisdiction over a potential defendant may be heavy, particularly when the potential defendant's identity is unknown or cannot be obtained, TRCP 202 does not provide every petitioner with access to information that it may need.* ***In re Doe****, 444 S.W.3d at 610. Because the question of personal jurisdiction may be impossible to answer in cases with an anonymous potential defendant, a petitioner's only recourse to determine the defendant's identity may be to file an expensive and cumbersome suit. See id. at 613 (Lehrmann, Johnson, Boyd, Devine, JJ., dissenting).*

§16.4 Notice & service.

1. Persons named in petition. At least 15 days before the hearing, the petition and the notice of the hearing must be served on the deponent and any potential adverse party named in the petition. Tex. R. Civ. P. 202.3(a); **U.S. Gov't v. Marks**, 949 S.W.2d 320, 322 (Tex.1997) (former TRCP 187). See **O'Connor's Texas Civil Forms**, FORMS 6F:9 to 6F:10 (2020 ed.). The petitioner may request a shorter period of notice if "justice or necessity" requires that the deposition be taken on shorter notice. Tex. R. Civ. P. 202.3(d). TRCP 202.3(a) provides that service can be accomplished under TRCP 21a. However, to secure the attendance of the witness at the hearing, the witness must be served with a subpoena.

Note

The procedures and limitations set out in the discovery rules may be modified in any suit by agreement of the parties. Tex. R. Civ. P. 191.1. See "Modifying discovery procedures," ch. 6-A, §6. Although parties can modify discovery procedures by agreement, some parties cannot agree to modifications of TRCP 202 procedures at the expense of other parties. See, e.g., ***In re Does 1&2****, 337 S.W.3d 862, 864–65 (Tex.2011) (P and D1 could not agree that D1 would produce documents under subpoena duces tecum, rather than through TRCP 202 deposition, without also agreeing with D2 and D3, who were potentially adverse parties). Thus, parties who want to agree to modifications of discovery procedures that may affect a party's rights under TRCP 202 should make sure to include all potentially adverse parties in the agreement to avoid circumventing TRCP 202's procedural protections.*

2. Persons not named in petition. Unnamed persons who are described in the petition and who the petitioner expects will have interests adverse to the petitioner may be served by publication. Tex. R. Civ. P. 202.3(b)(1). The notice must state the place for the hearing and the time it will be held, which must be more than 14 days after the first publication of the notice. *Id.* The petition and notice must be published once each week for two consecutive weeks in the newspaper of broadest circulation in the county in which the petition is filed, or if no such newspaper exists, in the newspaper of broadest circulation in the nearest county where a newspaper is published. *Id.* Any interested party may move, in the proceeding or by bill of review, to suppress any deposition, in whole or in part, taken on notice by publication, and may also attack or oppose the deposition by any other means available. Tex. R. Civ. P. 202.3(b)(2).

3. In probate cases. A petition to take a deposition in anticipation of an application for probate of a will, and a notice of the hearing on the petition, may be served by posting as prescribed by Estates Code §51.053. Tex. R. Civ. P. 202.3(c). The notice and petition must be directed to all parties interested in the testator's estate and must comply with the requirements of Estates Code §§51.002 and 51.003 to the extent that they apply. Tex. R. Civ. P. 202.3(c).

§16.5 Response.

1. Objecting to petition. The deponent or any potential adverse party can file objections to the petition if it does not meet the requirements under TRCP 202. *See, e.g.,* **In re East**, 476 S.W.3d 61, 63–64 (Tex.App.—Corpus Christi 2014, orig. proceeding) (deponent filed answer and general denial in response to TRCP 202 petition); **In re Reassure Am. Life Ins.**, 421 S.W.3d 165, 169 (Tex.App.—Corpus Christi 2013, orig. proceeding) (deponent filed objections to TRCP 202 petition on grounds that it did not identify substance of testimony or reason for seeking testimony). A merits-based defense to the potential lawsuit is not a valid objection to a presuit deposition. **In re East**, 476 S.W.3d at 67.

Note

If the deponent or any potential adverse party objects to the taking of the deposition after the deposition has been ordered, it should file a motion to vacate the order for the deposition and ask for a hearing. See ***U.S. Gov't v. Marks****, 949 S.W.2d 320, 322 (Tex.1997) (former TRCP 187). If a potential adverse party did not receive notice of the order and wants to object to the deposition, it should file a motion to intervene as an interested party. Id. at 322–23.*

2. Not removable to federal court. A TRCP 202 proceeding is not removable to federal court. *See* **Texas v. Real Parties in Interest**, 259 F.3d 387, 394 (5th Cir.2001) (when TRCP 202 is used as investigatory tool for potential claims, claim is not subject to removal); **McCrary v. Kansas City S. R.R.**, 121 F.Supp.2d 566, 569 (E.D.Tex.2000) (TRCP 202 proceeding is not a "civil action" under 28 U.S.C. §1441(b) because it does not assert a claim on which relief can be granted); **Mayfield-George v. Texas Rehab. Comm'n**, 197 F.R.D. 280, 283 (N.D.Tex.2000) (same). The All Writs Act, 28 U.S.C. §1651(a), does not provide an independent ground to remove a TRCP 202 claim from state court. **Real Parties**, 259 F.3d at 392. For a TRCP 202 proceeding to be enjoined under the All Writs Act, it must develop into a claim that threatens an earlier federal-court judgment. **Real Parties**, 259 F.3d at 395. For a detailed discussion of the use of the All Writs Act to support removal, see Hoffman, *Removal Jurisdiction & the All Writs Act*, 148 U.Pa.L.Rev. 401 (1999).

§16.6 Hearing.

1. Subpoena witness. The petitioner should issue and serve a subpoena on the witness to appear at the hearing.

2. Proof. The petitioner should show (1) that allowing the deposition may prevent a failure or delay of justice in an anticipated suit or (2) that the likely benefits of allowing the deposition to investigate a potential claim outweigh the burden or expense of the procedure. Tex. R. Civ. P. 202.4(a); **In re East**, 476 S.W.3d 61, 68 (Tex.App.—Corpus Christi 2014, orig. proceeding); **In re PrairieSmarts LLC**, 421 S.W.3d 296, 306 (Tex.App.—Fort Worth 2014, orig. proceeding); *see, e.g.*, **In re Hewlett Packard**, 212 S.W.3d 356, 361–62 (Tex.App.—Austin 2006, orig. proceeding) (petitioner did not show that benefit of potentially avoiding lawsuit outweighed burden of disclosure of trade secrets). The petitioner should include facts explaining the necessity of a presuit deposition; a petition that merely tracks the language of TRCP 202 is insufficient. **In re East**, 476 S.W.3d at 69; *see* **In re Does 1&2**, 337 S.W.3d 862, 865 (Tex.2011); **DeAngelis v. Protective Parents Coalition**, 556 S.W.3d 836, 856 (Tex.App.—Fort Worth 2018, no pet.); *see also* **In re Dallas Cty. Hosp. Dist.**, No. 05-14-00249-CV, 2014 WL 1407415 (Tex.App.—Dallas 2014, orig. proceeding) (memo op.; 4-1-14) (neither verified pleadings nor argument of counsel are competent evidence to prove basis for granting TRCP 202 deposition).

§16.7 Order. See **O'Connor's Texas Civil Forms**, FORM 6F:11 (2020 ed.).

1. Required findings. The order must contain one of the following findings: (1) allowing the deposition may prevent a failure or delay of justice in an anticipated suit, or (2) the likely benefits of allowing the deposition to investigate a potential claim outweigh the burden or expense of the procedure. Tex. R. Civ. P. 202.4(a); **In re City of Tatum**, 567 S.W.3d 800, 804 (Tex.App.—Tyler 2018, orig. proceeding); **In re Emergency Consultants, Inc.**, 292 S.W.3d 78, 79 (Tex.App.—Houston [14th Dist.] 2007, orig. proceeding); *see* **In re East**, 476 S.W.3d 61, 66 (Tex.App.—Corpus Christi 2014, orig. proceeding). The required findings cannot be implied from support in the record. **In re Does 1&2**, 337 S.W.3d 862, 865 (Tex.2011); **In re City of Tatum**, 567 S.W.3d at 804; **In re East**, 476 S.W.3d at 66.

2. Discovery permitted.

(1) Deposition. The order must state the type of deposition (oral or written) to be conducted and may also state the time and place for the deposition. Tex. R. Civ. P. 202.4(b). The time and place may be stated in the notice of deposition instead of in the order. *Id.* Depositions are the only form of discovery that may be ordered under TRCP 202. **In re Akzo Nobel Chem., Inc.**, 24 S.W.3d 919, 921 (Tex.App.—Beaumont 2000, orig. proceeding).

Note

A court cannot order a TRCP 202 deposition before ruling on a motion to dismiss under the Texas Citizens Participation Act (TCPA). ***In re Elliott****, 504 S.W.3d 455, 457–58 (Tex.App.—Austin 2016, orig. proceeding). The filing of a TCPA motion stays all discovery proceedings until the court has ruled on the motion. Tex. Civ. Prac. & Rem. Code §27.003(c);* ***In re Elliott****, 504 S.W.3d at 457. See "Note," ch. 3-K, §2.1.1(1); "Effect of motion on discovery," ch. 3-K, §3.5.*

---

(2) Subpoena for documents. As part of the deposition, the court may permit the issuance of a subpoena to produce documents at the deposition. *See* Tex. R. Civ. P. 199.2(b)(5), 200.1(b), 202.5, 205.1(c); **In re City of Tatum**, 567 S.W.3d at 808 (dicta); **In re Anand**, No. 01-12-01106-CV, 2013 WL 1316436 (Tex.App.—Houston [1st Dist.] 2013, orig.

proceeding) (memo op.; 4-2-13); Fineberg & Shore, *Discovery Update*, Advanced Civil Trial Course, State Bar of Texas CLE, ch. 1, p. 4 (2001).

Caution

At least two courts of appeals have held that a court cannot order production of documents in conjunction with a TRCP 202 deposition. E.g., ***DeAngelis v. Protective Parents Coalition****, 556 S.W.3d 836, 858 (Tex.App.—Fort Worth 2018, no pet);* ***In re Pickrell****, No. 10-17-00091-CV, 2017 WL 1452851 (Tex.App.—Waco 2017, orig. proceeding) (memo op.; 4-19-17). But this holding seems to contradict TRCP 202, which states that presuit depositions are governed by the rules applicable to depositions of nonparties. See Tex. R. Civ. P. 202.5;* ***In re City of Tatum****, 567 S.W.3d at 808 & n.7 (dicta); Gold, Rooting for Acorns, Discovery in Texas, Advanced Personal Injury Course, State Bar of Texas CLE, ch. 14.2, pp. 39–40 (2017). TRCP 205, which governs discovery from nonparties, allows a request for production to be served with a notice of deposition. Tex. R. Civ. P. 205.1(c).*

3. Protection for others. The order must also contain any provisions the court deems necessary to protect the witness or any other person who might be affected by the deposition. Tex. R. Civ. P. 202.4(b); *e.g.*, **Valley Baptist Med. Ctr. v. Gonzalez**, 18 S.W.3d 673, 678 (Tex.App.—Corpus Christi 1999) (suggested court could order bond to protect D from costs), *vacated as moot*, 33 S.W.3d 821 (Tex.2000); **In re Fernandez**, No. 04-99-00841-CV, 1999 WL 1327603 (Tex.App.—San Antonio 1999, orig. proceeding) (no pub.; 12-30-99) (ordered counsel to consult doctor before deposing ill party).

§16.8 Taking deposition. The same rules apply in taking presuit depositions as in other depositions. Tex. R. Civ. P. 202.5. See "Procedure for standard oral deposition," ch. 6-F, §4.

§16.9 Use at trial.

1. Impeachment. Testimony from a presuit deposition is admissible to impeach a witness, even if the other parties were not notified of the deposition. Fineberg & Shore, *Discovery Update*, Advanced Civil Trial Course, State Bar of Texas CLE, ch. 1, p. 4 (2001).

2. Restricted use. The court may restrict or prohibit the use of a deposition taken under TRCP 202 in a later lawsuit to protect a person who was not served with notice of the deposition from unfair prejudice. Tex. R. Civ. P. 202.5. If a party objects to the use of a TRCP 202 deposition, the party must show that it (1) did not receive notice of the deposition and (2) will be unfairly prejudiced by the use of the deposition. To show unfair prejudice, the party would probably have to prove the deponent gave false testimony. *See* Fineberg & Shore, *New Investigative Discovery: Depositions, How Do You Investigate Your Claim, Preparation, Rule 202, Deposition in Anticipation of Filing*, Advanced Civil Trial Course, State Bar of Texas CLE, Tab A, §II.C (1999).

§16.10 Appellate review.

1. Appeal. A TRCP 202 order allowing or denying presuit discovery from a third party against whom suit is not contemplated is a final, appealable order. **In re Jorden**, 249 S.W.3d 416, 419 (Tex.2008); **Ross Stores v. Redken Labs.**, 810 S.W.2d 741, 742 (Tex.1991); **IFS Sec. Grp. v. American Equity Ins.**, 175 S.W.3d 560, 563 (Tex.App.—Dallas 2005, no pet.).

2. Mandamus. A TRCP 202 order allowing or denying presuit discovery from a party against whom suit is contemplated is not a final, appealable order. **In re Jorden**, 249 S.W.3d at 419; **In re Elliott**, 504 S.W.3d 455, 459 (Tex.App.—Austin 2016, orig. proceeding); **In re East**, 476 S.W.3d 61, 65 n.5 (Tex.App.—Corpus Christi 2014, orig. proceeding); **IFS Sec. Grp.**, 175 S.W.3d at 563. Thus, a party should challenge such a TRCP 202 order by filing a petition for writ of mandamus. *See* **In re City of Dallas**, 501 S.W.3d 71, 73 (Tex.2016); **In re Wolfe**, 341 S.W.3d 932, 933 (Tex.2011); **In re PrairieSmarts LLC**, 421 S.W.3d 296, 304 (Tex.App.—Fort Worth 2014, orig. proceeding). See "Review by mandamus," ch. 6-A, §26.2.

§17. Deposition in another state

§17.1 Deposition officer. A deposition may be taken before a person authorized by state law to administer oaths in the place where the deposition is being taken. Tex. R. Civ. P. 201.1(b).

§17.2 Procedure. A deposition in another state may be taken by notice, letter rogatory, letter of request, agreement of the parties, or court order. Tex. R. Civ. P. 201.1(a). Parties may also take the deposition of a witness in another state by telephone or video conference while the parties and their attorneys are in Texas. Tex. R. Civ. P. 199.1(b), 201.1(g); *see* **Clone Component Distribs. v. State**, 819 S.W.2d 593, 598 (Tex.App.—Dallas 1991, no writ). See "Deposition by telephone," ch. 6-F, §14.

Practice Tip

The easiest way to arrange for a deposition in another state is to contact an attorney or court reporter in the other state and make arrangements through that person.

§18. Deposition in foreign country

Obtaining discovery in foreign countries is extremely complicated. Most foreign countries are hostile to the American form of pretrial discovery.

Practice Tip

Before taking a deposition in a foreign country, refer to the website of the U.S. Department of State, Bureau of Consular Affairs, at travel.state.gov/content/travel/en/legal.html.

§18.1 Procedure. The procedure for foreign discovery is outlined in TRCP 201. *See* **Smith v. Smith**, 720 S.W.2d 586, 598–99 (Tex.App.—Houston [1st Dist.] 1986, no writ) (substantial compliance with former TRCP 188, now TRCP 201, is sufficient). A deposition in a foreign jurisdiction may be taken by notice, letter rogatory, letter of request, agreement of the parties, or court order. Tex. R. Civ. P. 201.1(a). A deposition may also be taken by any other means under the terms of any applicable treaty or convention. Tex. R. Civ. P. 201.1(d). The Hague Evidence Convention is the most well-known treaty for obtaining evidence abroad.

1. Notice. Parties may take by notice the deposition of a witness in a foreign jurisdiction before a person authorized to administer oaths, either under the law of the place where the examination is held or under Texas law. Tex. R. Civ. P. 201.1(b). There are two serious drawbacks to taking depositions by notice in foreign countries: (1) the parties have no power to compel the attendance of a witness, and (2) taking testimony in some countries violates local laws and, in some cases, results in criminal penalties. *See* Bishop, *International Litigation in Texas: Obtaining Evidence in Foreign Countries*, 19 Hous.L.Rev. 361, 364–65 (1982).

2. Letter of request. Generally, if the foreign country subscribes to the Hague Evidence Convention, the method to obtain discovery is by letter of request under the Convention. Bishop, *International Litigation in Texas: Obtaining Evidence in Foreign Countries*, 19 Hous.L.Rev. 361, 371 (1982). The Hague Evidence Convention supplements, but does not replace, other means of obtaining evidence located abroad. **Societe Nationale Industrielle Aerospatiale v. U.S. Dist. Ct.**, 482 U.S. 522, 534–39 (1987); **Sandsend Fin. Consultants, Ltd. v. Wood**, 743 S.W.2d 364, 365–66 (Tex.App.—Houston [1st Dist.] 1988, orig. proceeding). The procedure for discovery under the Hague Evidence Convention can be found in 28 U.S.C. chapter 117.

3. Letter rogatory. If the foreign country does not subscribe to the Hague Evidence Convention, a party must use a letter rogatory to take the deposition in that country. *See* Bureau of Consular Affairs, *Preparation of Letters Rogatory*, travel.state.gov/content/travel/en/legal/travel-legal-considerations/internl-judicial-asst/obtaining-evidence/Preparation-Letters-Rogatory.html. A letter rogatory is a judicial request addressed to a foreign authority asking it to use its coercive powers to require a person within its territory to be deposed. *See* Bishop, *International Litigation in Texas: Obtaining Evidence in Foreign Countries*, 19 Hous.L.Rev. 361, 383 (1982). In some countries, only the judicial officer can ask the witness questions, not the attorneys. *See id.* at 384. The letter rogatory must be addressed to the appropriate authority in the jurisdiction. Tex. R. Civ. P. 201.1(c)(1).

§18.2 Officer to conduct deposition. A deposition may be taken in a foreign country by one of the following:

1. A U.S. minister, commissioner, or chargé d'affaires who is a resident of and is accredited in the country where the deposition is taken. Tex. Civ. Prac. & Rem. Code §20.001(c)(1).

2. A U.S. consul general, consul, vice-consul, commercial agent, vice-commercial agent, deputy consul, or consular agent who is a resident of and is accredited in the country where the deposition is taken. Tex. Civ. Prac. & Rem. Code §20.001(c)(2).

3. Any notary public. Tex. Civ. Prac. & Rem. Code §20.001(c)(3); *e.g.*, **Kugle v. DaimlerChrysler Corp.**, 88 S.W.3d 355, 362 (Tex.App.—San Antonio 2002, pet. denied) (deponent in Mexico permitted to be sworn by Texas notary); *see also* Tex. R. Civ. P. 201.1(b) (deposition officer may be a person authorized to administer oaths in place where deposition taken).

4. If the deponent is a witness who is a member of the U.S. Armed Forces or Auxiliary or a civilian employed by such forces or auxiliary outside the United States, the deposition may be taken by a commissioned officer in the Armed Forces or Auxiliary or Reserve. Tex. Civ. Prac. & Rem. Code §20.001(d).

§18.3 Depositions in Texas for use in foreign jurisdictions. If a court of record of any other state or foreign jurisdiction issues an order that requires a witness's oral or written deposition testimony in Texas, the witness may be compelled to appear and testify in the same manner and by the same process used for taking testimony in a proceeding pending in Texas. Tex. R. Civ. P. 201.2.

G. Interrogatories

§1. General

§1.1 Rules. Tex. R. Civ. P. 197.

§1.2 Purpose. Interrogatories are written questions served on a party that require the party to file written answers, generally under oath. Interrogatories are used to narrow the issues.

§1.3 Forms. See **O'Connor's Texas Civil Forms**, FORMS 6G:1 et seq. (2020 ed.).

§1.4 Other references. Downing et al., *"Be Careful What You Ask For, You May Get It": Common Sense Discovery Requests & Responses*, Advanced Family Law Course, State Bar of Texas CLE, ch. 15, §III.B (2006); Griesel, *The "New" Texas Discovery Rules: Three Years Later*, Advanced Evidence & Discovery Course, State Bar of Texas CLE, ch. 2, §XI (2002).

§2. Scope

The scope of discovery for interrogatories is governed by TRCP 192 and 197. See "Scope of Discovery," ch. 6-B, §1 et seq. Interrogatories are used to find out the specific legal and factual contentions supporting the other party's claims or defenses.

§2.1 Party contentions. An interrogatory may ask whether the party makes specific legal or factual contentions and may ask the party to state its legal theories and to describe, in general, the factual bases for the party's claims or defenses. Tex. R. Civ. P. 197.1. See "Party contentions," ch. 6-G, §3.2.5.

§2.2 Trial witnesses. An interrogatory may ask the other party to provide a list of its trial witnesses. See "Trial witnesses," ch. 6-G, §3.2.3. Formerly, a party could secure a list of trial witnesses only by court order.

§2.3 Limits of interrogatories.

1. Not for testifying-expert information. An interrogatory cannot be used to request information about another party's testifying expert witnesses. *See* Tex. R. Civ. P. 195.1 (party may obtain information about testifying expert witnesses only through disclosures, depositions, and reports allowed under TRCP 195); Tex. R. Civ. P. 197.1 (interrogatories cannot be used to secure information covered by TRCP 195).

2. No fishing. An interrogatory cannot be used to fish for information or to require the responding party to provide a statement of all its available proof. Tex. R. Civ. P. 197.1 & cmt. 1; **K Mart Corp. v. Sanderson**, 937 S.W.2d 429, 431 (Tex.1996).

§3. Serving interrogatories

§3.1 Procedure. The interrogatories must be in writing. Tex. R. Civ. P. 197.1. See **O'Connor's Texas Civil Forms**, FORMS 6G:1 to 6G:2 (2020 ed.).

Practice Tip

Ask the other party to agree to e-mail a copy of any request for written discovery. It will make responding to interrogatories and other discovery much simpler.

---

1. Serve on party. Interrogatories can be served only on another party. Tex. R. Civ. P. 197.1. They cannot be served on nonparty witnesses. *See* Tex. R. Civ. P. 205.1.

2. Time to serve interrogatories. For cases filed on or after January 1, 2021, interrogatories cannot be served on a party until after that party's initial disclosures under TRCP 194 are due. *See* Tex. R. Civ. P. 190.2(b)(1), 190.3(b)(1), 192.2(a). See "Deadline," ch. 6-E, §3.3.1. For most methods of service (e.g., e-service, personal or commercial delivery), the deadline to serve interrogatories is 30 days before the end of the discovery period. *See* Tex. R. Civ. P. 197.1. See "Discovery periods," ch. 6-A, §8. But when service is by mail or fax, interrogatories should be served at least 33 days (if mailed) or 31

days (if faxed after 5:00 p.m.) before the end of the discovery period. *See* Tex. R. Civ. P. 21a(b)(2), (c). See "Deadline to serve response," ch. 6-A, §14.1.

2021 Rule Amendments

In 2020, the Supreme Court approved significant amendments to TRCP 190, 192.2, and 194. See Tex.Sup.Ct. Order, Misc. Docket No. 20-9153 (eff. Jan. 1, 2021). Under the amendments, a party generally cannot serve discovery requests on another party until after that party's initial disclosures now required under TRCP 194 are due. Tex. R. Civ. P. 192.2(a). See "Required disclosures—Cases filed on or after 1-1-21," ch. 6-E, §3. Initial disclosures are generally due within 30 days after the filing of the first answer or general appearance. Tex. R. Civ. P. 194.2(a). But if a party is served or otherwise joined after the filing of the first answer or general appearance, its initial disclosures are generally due within 30 days after being served or joined. Id. The amendments apply to cases filed on or after January 1, 2021, except those filed in justice court. Tex.Sup.Ct. Order, Misc. Docket No. 20-9153 (eff. Jan. 1, 2021). For cases filed before January 1, 2021, a party can serve interrogatories anytime after suit is filed. See id. See "Discovery periods," ch. 6-A, §8; "Service with original pleadings," ch. 6-A, §13.2.

3. Number of interrogatories.

(1) Limited interrogatories. The number of interrogatories each party is permitted to serve (other than those about identifying or authenticating documents) is governed by the discovery-control plan in effect. See "Discovery-control plans," ch. 6-A, §7. Parties in a Level 1 case are limited to 15 interrogatories, parties in a Level 2 case are limited to 25 interrogatories, and parties in a Level 3 case are limited to either 15 interrogatories (if Level 1 limitations apply) or 25 interrogatories (if Level 2 limitations apply) unless expressly changed by court order. *See* Tex. R. Civ. P. 190.2(b)(3), 190.3(b)(3), 190.4(b). Each discrete subpart of an interrogatory is considered a separate interrogatory. Tex. R. Civ. P. 190.2(b)(3), 190.3(b)(3). A discrete subpart asks for information not logically or factually related to the primary interrogatory. Tex. R. Civ. P. 190 cmt. 3 (1999); **In re SWEPI L.P.**, 103 S.W.3d 578, 589 (Tex.App.—San Antonio 2003, orig. proceeding). Not every separate factual inquiry is a discrete subpart. Tex. R. Civ. P. 190 cmt. 3 (1999). If a party needs more than the allotted number of interrogatories, it must get an agreement with the other party or file a motion to modify the discovery-control plan and ask for a court order. Tex. R. Civ. P. 190.5, 191.1. See "Modifying discovery procedures," ch. 6-A, §6.

(2) Unlimited interrogatories. There is no limit to the number of interrogatories a party may serve asking for the identification or authentication of specific documents. Tex. R. Civ. P. 190.2(b)(3), 190.3(b)(3).

(3) Unlimited sets. Although the number of interrogatories is limited, the number of sets of interrogatories that can be sent is unlimited. *See* Tex. R. Civ. P. 190 cmt. 3 (1999).

4. Specify time to answer. The interrogatories should specify when the answers are due, generally 30 days after service of the interrogatories. *See* Tex. R. Civ. P. 197.2(a). When service is by mail or fax, the answering party has an additional 3 days (if mailed) or 1 day (if faxed after 5:00 p.m.) to respond. *See* Tex. R. Civ. P. 21a(b)(2), (c). See "Deadline to serve response," ch. 6-A, §14.1.

2021 Rule Amendments

In 2020, the Supreme Court approved significant amendments to TRCP 192.2 and 194. See Tex.Sup.Ct. Order, Misc. Docket No. 20-9153 (eff. Jan. 1, 2021). Under the amendments, a party generally cannot serve discovery requests on another party until after that party's initial disclosures now required under TRCP 194 are due. See Tex. R. Civ. P. 192.2(a). These initial disclosures are generally due within 30 days after the filing of the first answer or general appearance. Tex. R. Civ. P. 194.2(a). Because discovery must now be served after the first answer or general appearance, TRCP 197 was amended to eliminate the scenario where a defendant was served with interrogatories before its answer was due and thus had 50 days to respond. See Tex. R. Civ. P. 197.2(a). The amendments apply to cases filed on or after

January 1, 2021, except those filed in justice court. Tex.Sup.Ct. Order, Misc. Docket No. 20-9153 (eff. Jan. 1, 2021). For a detailed discussion of required disclosures under the 2021 amendments, see "Required disclosures—Cases filed on or after 1-1-21," ch. 6-E, §3.

5. Combine with request for production. The discovery rules permit a party to combine different forms of discovery requests in the same document. Tex. R. Civ. P. 192.2(b). Thus, if an interrogatory asks for the identification of documents, it can be followed by a request to produce those documents.

§3.2 Standard interrogatories. The following are interrogatories that seek information not subject to disclosure under TRCP 194. See **O'Connor's Texas Civil Forms**, FORM 6G:2 (2020 ed.).

1. Documents.

(1) Existence & location. An interrogatory may ask about the existence, description, nature, custody, condition, location, and contents of documents that are relevant or will lead to relevant evidence. Tex. R. Civ. P. 192.3(b). See "Possession," ch. 6-A, §2.5; **O'Connor's Texas Civil Forms**, FORM 6G:2 (2020 ed.). An interrogatory that asks for information about documents can be followed by a request to produce those documents. *See* Tex. R. Civ. P. 192.2(b).

(2) Authentication. An interrogatory may ask for the authentication of specific documents. Tex. R. Civ. P. 190.2(b)(3), 190.3(b)(3).

2. Person answering. An interrogatory may ask the other party to identify the persons answering the interrogatories, supplying information, or in any way assisting with the preparation of the answers. A party may want to depose anyone who provided information for the answers. See **O'Connor's Texas Civil Forms**, FORM 6G:2 (2020 ed.).

3. Trial witnesses. An interrogatory may ask the other party to identify its trial witnesses (fact and expert). *See* Tex. R. Civ. P. 192.3(d). Because the only information that is authorized by TRCP 192.3(d) is the identity of trial witnesses, it should not conflict with the limitations in TRCP 195.1 and 197.1, which limit the discovery tools a party can use to seek information about the testifying experts. See "Trial witnesses," ch. 6-B, §2.9; **O'Connor's Texas Civil Forms**, FORM 6G:2 (2020 ed.).

4. Discoverable consulting experts. An interrogatory may ask for information about discoverable consulting expert witnesses.

(1) Consultant's work reviewed. When the consulting expert's opinions, mental impressions, or work product were reviewed by a testifying expert, a party is entitled to discover the same information about the consulting expert as about the testifying expert. Tex. R. Civ. P. 192.3(e). See "Discovery about consulting expert + work reviewed," ch. 6-D, §3.2.2; **O'Connor's Texas Civil Forms**, FORM 6G:2 (2020 ed.).

(2) Consultant with facts. When a consulting expert has firsthand knowledge about the case or secondhand knowledge gained outside the consultation, a party is entitled to discover the same information about the consulting expert as about other fact witnesses. See "Discovery about consulting expert + obtained facts," ch. 6-D, §3.2.3; **O'Connor's Texas Civil Forms**, FORM 6G:2 (2020 ed.).

5. Party contentions. An interrogatory may ask whether the party makes specific legal or factual contentions and may ask the party to state its legal theories and to describe, in general, the factual bases for the party's claims or defenses. Tex. R. Civ. P. 197.1. For example, an interrogatory may ask whether the party claims a breach of implied warranty, or when the party contends that limitations began to run. Tex. R. Civ. P. 197 cmt. 1. However, an interrogatory cannot ask the party to state all its legal and factual assertions or to marshal all its proof or the proof the party intends to offer at trial. Tex. R. Civ. P. 197.1 & cmt. 1. See **O'Connor's Texas Civil Forms**, FORM 6G:2 (2020 ed.).

6. Impeachment & rebuttal evidence. The party should consider asking for the other party's rebuttal and impeachment evidence and witnesses. Tex. R. Civ. P. 192.3(d); *see* Tex. R. Civ. P. 166(h). Rebuttal and impeachment evidence is discoverable only if the party responding to the request has enough information to anticipate its use at trial. Tex. R. Civ. P. 192.3(d). Unless specifically asked, a party is not required to anticipate the other party's case and identify witnesses to be

used for impeachment or rebuttal. *See* Tex. R. Civ. P. 192.3(d) (party cannot obtain discovery of rebuttal or impeaching witnesses whose testimony cannot reasonably be anticipated before trial). See "Impeachment & rebuttal evidence not produced in discovery," ch. 8-C, §5.3; **O'Connor's Texas Civil Forms**, FORM 6G:2 (2020 ed.).

7. Elements of claim or defense. An interrogatory may ask for information based on the elements of the claim or defense. See **O'Connor's Texas Civil Forms**, FORMS 6G:1 et seq. (2020 ed.) for interrogatories in the following types of lawsuits: breach of contract (**O'Connor's Texas Civil Forms**, FORMS 6G:4 to 6G:5 (2020 ed.)), suit on a sworn account (**O'Connor's Texas Civil Forms**, FORMS 6G:6 to 6G:7 (2020 ed.)), automobile accident (**O'Connor's Texas Civil Forms**, FORMS 6G:8 to 6G:9 (2020 ed.)), slip-and-fall (**O'Connor's Texas Civil Forms**, FORMS 6G:10 to 6G:11 (2020 ed.)), and suit under the DTPA (**O'Connor's Texas Civil Forms**, FORMS 6G:12 to 6G:13 (2020 ed.)).

§4. Responding to interrogatories

§4.1 Procedure.

1. Form of answers. The answers to interrogatories must be made in the form required by TRCP 197.2. See **O'Connor's Texas Civil Forms**, FORM 6G:3 (2020 ed.).

(1) In writing. The party must respond to interrogatories in writing. Tex. R. Civ. P. 197.2(a). Oral information is not a substitute for written answers. *See, e.g.*, **Sharp v. Broadway Nat'l Bank**, 784 S.W.2d 669, 671 (Tex.1990) (oral identification of witness was not sufficient). Each answer, objection, or other response must follow the question it applies to. Tex. R. Civ. P. 193.1.

(2) Separate answers. Each interrogatory must be answered separately. **Orkin Exterminating Co. v. Williamson**, 785 S.W.2d 905, 910 (Tex.App.—Austin 1990, writ denied); *see* Tex. R. Civ. P. 197.2(b). If an interrogatory asks a question already answered in response to another interrogatory, the answer to the later interrogatory may refer to the earlier answer.

(3) Separate answer set. In most cases, a party should file a separate set of answers for each set of interrogatories. In a multiparty case, a party responding to the same interrogatories from different opposing parties may file one response that is sufficient to answer all sets. *See, e.g.*, **Ward v. O'Connor**, 816 S.W.2d 446, 447 (Tex.App.—San Antonio 1991, no writ) (Ps filed one list of fact and expert witnesses in response to requests from two Ds).

(4) Signed & verified by party. The party must sign most answers to interrogatories under oath. Tex. R. Civ. P. 197.2(d). An affidavit verifying the answers to interrogatories must be unqualified and cannot be made "to the best of my knowledge." *See* **Ebeling v. Gawlik**, 487 S.W.2d 187, 189 (Tex.App.—Houston [1st Dist.] 1972, no writ). There are two exceptions to the rule that requires a party to sign and verify its answers under oath: (1) a party is not required to verify its answer when the answer states that it is based on information obtained from other persons, and (2) a party is not required to sign or verify its answer to an interrogatory that asks about persons with knowledge of relevant facts, trial witnesses, and legal contentions. Tex. R. Civ. P. 197.2(d).

(5) Signed by attorney. The party's attorney must sign the answers to interrogatories. Tex. R. Civ. P. 191.3(a)(1); Tex. R. Civ. P. 197 cmt. 2. An attorney is not required to verify the answers. Tex. R. Civ. P. 197.2(d).

2. Time to respond. Generally, a party has 30 days after the date of service of the interrogatories to respond. Tex. R. Civ. P. 197.2(a). When service is by mail or fax, the answering party has an additional 3 days (if mailed) or 1 day (if faxed after 5:00 p.m.) to respond. *See* Tex. R. Civ. P. 21a(b)(2), (c). See "Deadline to serve response," ch. 6-A, §14.1. To extend the time to respond, see "Extending time to respond to discovery," ch. 6-A, §15.

2021 Rule Amendments

In 2020, the Supreme Court approved significant amendments to TRCP 192.2 and 194. See Tex.Sup.Ct. Order, Misc. Docket No. 20-9153 (eff. Jan. 1, 2021). Under the amendments, a party generally cannot serve discovery requests on another party until after that party's initial disclosures now required under TRCP 194 are due. See Tex. R. Civ. P. 192.2(a). These initial disclosures are generally due within 30

days after the filing of the first answer or general appearance. Tex. R. Civ. P. 194.2(a). Because discovery must now be served after the first answer or general appearance, TRCP 197 was amended to eliminate the scenario where a defendant was served with interrogatories before its answer was due and thus had 50 days to respond. See Tex. R. Civ. P. 197.2(a). The amendments apply to cases filed on or after January 1, 2021, except those filed in justice court. Tex.Sup.Ct. Order, Misc. Docket No. 20-9153 (eff. Jan. 1, 2021). For a detailed discussion of required disclosures under the 2021 amendments, see "Required disclosures—Cases filed on or after 1-1-21," ch. 6-E, §3.

3. Not filed. The answers to interrogatories are not filed with the court. Tex. R. Civ. P. 191.4(a). See "Filing discovery," ch. 6-A, §12.1.

§4.2 Answers. Each interrogatory must be answered fully. The party must make a complete response, based on all information reasonably available to the responding party or its attorney when the response is made. Tex. R. Civ. P. 193.1. The sufficiency of the answers to any set of interrogatories must be decided on a case-by-case basis. **Alexander v. Barlow**, 671 S.W.2d 531, 533 (Tex.App.—Houston [1st Dist.] 1983, writ ref'd n.r.e.). The court will treat an evasive or incomplete answer as a failure to answer. Tex. R. Civ. P. 215.1(c). When the interrogatory asks for information permitted by the rules of discovery, the information must be disclosed. When the interrogatory asks for more information than the rules permit, the party must file an objection.

1. Existence & location of documents. When asked in an interrogatory, a party is required to supply information about the existence, description, nature, custody, condition, location, and contents of documents that are relevant or will lead to relevant evidence. Tex. R. Civ. P. 192.3(b). See "Possession," ch. 6-A, §2.5.

2. Evidence equally available. When an interrogatory asks for information that is available from public records, from the business records of the responding party, or from a compilation, abstract, or summary of the responding party's business records, the responding party is not obligated to give a narrative answer to the interrogatory if the burden of ascertaining the answer is substantially the same for both parties. Tex. R. Civ. P. 197.2(c). In such a case, the responding party may answer the interrogatory by specifying and, when applicable, producing the records or a compilation, abstract, or summary of the records. *Id.*; *see* **Clear Lake City Water Auth. v. Winograd**, 695 S.W.2d 632, 641 (Tex.App.—Houston [1st Dist.] 1985, writ ref'd n.r.e.). The records must be specified in sufficient detail to permit the requesting party to locate and identify them as readily as the responding party can. Tex. R. Civ. P. 197.2(c). If the responding party has specified business records, it must state a reasonable time and place for examination of the documents. *Id.* The responding party must produce the documents at the time and place stated and must provide the requesting party a reasonable opportunity to inspect them. *Id.* The rule requires a balancing test of the relative burden imposed on the two parties. *E.g.*, **State Farm Mut. Auto. Ins. v. Engelke**, 824 S.W.2d 747, 752 (Tex.App.—Houston [1st Dist.] 1992, orig. proceeding) (because responding party's witness testified information was available from its computer, it was less burdensome for responding party to produce information).

3. Witnesses. When asked in an interrogatory, a party is required to identify the following witnesses:

(1) Person answering. The party must identify any person answering the interrogatories, supplying information, or assisting with the preparation of the answers.

(2) Trial witnesses. The party must list all persons the party plans to call as witnesses at trial, no matter what they will testify about. *See* Tex. R. Civ. P. 192.3(d); *see, e.g.*, **Jamail v. Anchor Mortg. Servs.**, 809 S.W.2d 221, 223 (Tex.1991) (witness who was called to testify about lending regulations of mortgage company should have been listed as fact witness, even though witness did not know facts of case); *see also* **Baylor Med. Plaza Servs. v. Kidd**, 834 S.W.2d 69, 73 (Tex.App.—Texarkana 1992, writ denied) (designation of witness by one party does not relieve other party from designating its own witnesses). The response should list the following persons as trial witnesses:

(a) Fact witnesses. The party must list all persons who have knowledge of relevant facts that it might call as witnesses at trial. See "Fact witnesses," ch. 6-B, §2.8. Along with its own witnesses, the party should consider including the following: (1) any person who was deposed, (2) the other party, (3) the other party's fact witnesses, (4) the other party's

consulting expert with knowledge of facts, and (5) character witnesses. *See* **Clayton v. First State Bank**, 777 S.W.2d 577, 580 (Tex.App.—Fort Worth 1989, writ denied) (character witnesses). Parties should err on the side of inclusion. At trial, the court will not permit a party to call a witness that the party did not specifically identify.

Practice Tip

If a named party is not listed in response to an interrogatory asking for trial witnesses, the unlisted party can still testify. See Tex. R. Civ. P. 193.6(a).

(b) Expert witnesses. The party should list all experts that it intends to call to testify, which could include the following: (1) retained testifying experts, (2) nonretained testifying experts, (3) the party (if the party intends to testify as an expert), (4) the party's attorney (for attorney fees), (5) the opposing party's testifying experts (if the party intends to call them), and (6) the opposing party's consulting experts who lost their consulting-only status. *See, e.g.*, **Baylor Med. Plaza**, 834 S.W.2d at 73 (witness listed as fact witness by both P and D could not be called as expert by P). The party should compare this list to the list of testifying experts it produced under TRCP 195. See "Expert disclosures," ch. 6-E, §3.4. If any of the experts listed in response to an interrogatory asking for trial witnesses are not listed in the party's TRCP 195 disclosures, the party should amend its disclosures.

(c) Impeachment & rebuttal witnesses. When an interrogatory asks for impeachment and rebuttal information, and the responding party knows it will impeach or rebut the other party's witness or evidence, the responding party must list that evidence. See "Impeachment & rebuttal evidence," ch. 6-G, §3.2.6; "Impeachment & rebuttal evidence not produced in discovery," ch. 8-C, §5.3.

4. Discoverable consulting experts. When asked in an interrogatory, a party is required to identify the following expert witnesses:

(1) Consultant's work reviewed. If any opinions, mental impressions, or work product of an informally consulted expert were reviewed by a testifying expert, the other party is entitled to obtain the same information about the consulting expert as about the testifying expert. Tex. R. Civ. P. 192.3(e). See "Discovery about consulting expert + work reviewed," ch. 6-D, §3.2.2; "Information discoverable from experts," ch. 6-D, §4.

(2) Consultant with facts. A consulting expert who obtained knowledge about the case either firsthand or in some way other than in consultation about the case is discoverable as a fact witness. Tex. R. Civ. P. 192.3(c). When a consulting expert has firsthand knowledge of facts or secondhand knowledge acquired in some way other than in consultation about the case, the other party is entitled to obtain the same information about the expert as about other fact witnesses. See "Discovery about consulting expert + obtained facts," ch. 6-D, §3.2.3.

5. Contentions. When asked in an interrogatory, a party is required to provide information about specific factual or legal assertions. *See* Tex. R. Civ. P. 197.1 & cmt. 1. See "Party contentions," ch. 6-G, §3.2.5. The use of the answers to these "contention interrogatories" is limited, just like the use of similar disclosures under TRCP 194.6. Tex. R. Civ. P. 197 cmt. 1.

§5. Supplementing or amending answers to interrogatories

§5.1 What to supplement. When a party discovers additional information after responding to discovery, the party must supplement or amend its response. Tex. R. Civ. P. 193.5(a) (duty to supplement), Tex. R. Civ. P. 193.6 (effect of failure to supplement). For the substance of what additional information to provide, see "Supplementing discovery responses," ch. 6-A, §17.

§5.2 Deadline to supplement. A party must serve supplemental or amended answers to interrogatories reasonably promptly after the party discovers the need for such a response, but no later than 30 days before trial. Tex. R. Civ. P. 193.5(b). See "Deadline to supplement responses," ch. 6-A, §17.4.

§5.3 Form of supplement. Supplemental or amended answers to interrogatories must be made in the same form as the original answers. Tex. R. Civ. P. 193.5(b). See "Form of supplemental discovery," ch. 6-A, §17.6. For the exceptions, see "Information provided by other means," ch. 6-A, §17.3.2.

§5.4 No continuing duty to supplement. If the party that served the interrogatory is dismissed from the suit, the party that answered the interrogatory no longer has a duty to supplement its answers to the dismissed party's interrogatories. **Austin Ranch Enters. v. Wells**, 760 S.W.2d 703, 710 (Tex.App.—Fort Worth 1988, writ denied). Thus, the remaining parties cannot object to the responding party's failure to supplement answers to interrogatories propounded by the dismissed party. *Id.*

§6. Objecting to questions

§6.1 Procedure to object. See "Making objections," ch. 6-A, §18.1.

1. When to serve. Objections to interrogatories must be served on the other party on or before the date the answers to the interrogatories are due. Tex. R. Civ. P. 193.2(a). See "Timely objection," ch. 6-A, §18.1.1.

2. Objection defers answer. When a party objects to an interrogatory, the answer to that interrogatory is deferred until the court rules on the objection. *See* Tex. R. Civ. P. 193.2(b). The party must answer all other interrogatories by the answer deadline. *Id.*

3. Form of objections. In the response or in a separate document, the party should state the specific objection to the interrogatory. Tex. R. Civ. P. 193.2(a).

4. Partial compliance. The party must comply with each part of the request to which the party has not objected or has not asserted a privilege. See "Burden to partially comply," ch. 6-A, §18.10. Any material subject to an objection or assertion of privilege should be withheld from the information the party produces. Tex. R. Civ. P. 192.3(a), 193.3(a).

5. Not filed. The objections to interrogatories are not filed with the court. Tex. R. Civ. P. 191.4(a). See "Filing discovery," ch. 6-A, §12.1.

§6.2 Valid objections. For a list of objections, see "Types of objections to discovery," ch. 6-A, §19. See **O'Connor's Texas Civil Forms**, FORM 6G:3 (2020 ed.). The following are some additional objections that are specific to interrogatories:

1. Number of questions. "The interrogatories ask more than [15 or 25] questions." *See* Tex. R. Civ. P. 190.2(b)(3), 190.3(b)(3), 190.4(b). See "Number of interrogatories," ch. 6-G, §3.1.3. When a party asks more than the maximum number of questions, the responding party cannot merely object and refuse to answer any of them. The party's options are (1) to answer the interrogatories in order up to the maximum number and object to the rest of them, or (2) to file objections and a motion for protective order to stay the deadline to answer until the set of interrogatories is redrafted to comply with the rules. *See* Tex. R. Civ. P. 192.6, 193.2(b) & cmt. 2; **Owens v. Wallace**, 821 S.W.2d 746, 749 (Tex.App.—Tyler 1992, orig. proceeding) (citing former TRCP 168, which allowed 30 questions).

2. Improper request. "The interrogatory requests information about testifying experts, which is obtainable only through disclosures under TRCP 195 or through depositions." *See* Tex. R. Civ. P. 197.1. See "Disclosures," ch. 6-E, §1 et seq.

3. Premature request. "The interrogatory is premature because it requests information that will not be known until after additional discovery is completed. This interrogatory will be answered promptly once additional discovery is completed." *See* Tex. R. Civ. P. 193.1 (responding party must make complete response based on information available).

4. Duplicative. "The interrogatory duplicates matters already produced in disclosures under TRCP 194.2."

§6.3 Invalid objections. See "Invalid objections to discovery requests," ch. 6-A, §19.2.

§6.4 Waiver of objections. A party waives any error in the form or substance of the interrogatories if it does not object within the time provided to answer. Tex. R. Civ. P. 193.2(e). When a party answers an interrogatory without making an objection, the party must answer fully, even if the interrogatory is objectionable. *See* **In re Striegler**, 915 S.W.2d 629, 641 (Tex.App.—Amarillo 1996, writ denied).

§7. Asserting a privilege

A party cannot object to an interrogatory on the grounds that it calls for privileged information. Instead, the party must assert a privilege under TRCP 193.3. See "Asserting privileges," ch. 6-A, §18.2.

§8. Objecting to answers

§8.1 Move to compel answers. A party may file a motion to compel answers when the interrogatories are not answered, when they are not answered properly, or when objections are served. Tex. R. Civ. P. 215.1(b), 215.2(b), 215.3. See "Motion to compel discovery," ch. 6-A, §22.

§8.2 Object to formal defects. A party must object to formal (i.e., technical) defects in the answer so that the responding party has the opportunity to correct them before trial. *See* **State Farm Fire & Cas. Co. v. Morua**, 979 S.W.2d 616, 620 (Tex.1998) (court should not exclude witness based on technical defect in answer when no objection was made before trial); **$23,900 v. State**, 899 S.W.2d 314, 317 (Tex.App.—Houston [14th Dist.] 1995, no writ) (party should file pretrial objections or motion to compel compliance with rules). Formal defects do not impair the integrity of the answers unless the party refuses to cure the defect after it is identified by the other party. *See* Tex. R. Civ. P. 197 cmt. 2; *see also* Tex. R. Civ. P. 193.5(b) (failure to properly supplement discovery does not make response untimely unless party refuses to correct defect).

§8.3 Challenge privileges after withholding statement. After receiving a withholding statement indicating that information is being withheld on grounds of privilege, the party seeking discovery should ask the withholding party to provide a privilege log. Tex. R. Civ. P. 193.3(b). See "Request privilege log," ch. 6-A, §18.2.2.

§8.4 Move for sanctions. See "Motion for discovery sanctions," ch. 6-A, §23.

1. Late or inadequate answer. When an answer to an interrogatory is inadequate, the party seeking discovery can ask the court to impose reasonable sanctions. *See, e.g.*, **Hamill v. Level**, 917 S.W.2d 15, 16 (Tex.1996) (even though P was repeatedly late in answering interrogatories, dismissal was not warranted because it was more severe than necessary); **Clark Equip. Co. v. Pitner**, 923 S.W.2d 117, 121–22 (Tex.App.—Houston [14th Dist.] 1996, writ denied) (because P's answer to D1's interrogatory provided everything but substance of expert's testimony, D2 could have asked to limit testimony, not exclude expert); **Orkin Exterminating Co. v. Williamson**, 785 S.W.2d 905, 910–11 (Tex.App.—Austin 1990, writ denied) (because D's answer was not sufficient to identify witness, witness not permitted to testify). If an answer is evasive or incomplete, the court will treat it as a failure to answer. Tex. R. Civ. P. 215.1(c).

2. No answers. When a party refuses to provide answers to interrogatories, the party seeking discovery may ask the court to dismiss the suit, render a default judgment, exclude evidence, or impose other sanctions. *See* Tex. R. Civ. P. 215.1(b)(3)(A) (failure to serve response), Tex. R. Civ. P. 215.1(b)(3)(B) (failure to answer particular interrogatory); *see, e.g.*, **Swain v. Southwestern Bell Yellow Pages, Inc.**, 998 S.W.2d 731, 732–33 (Tex.App.—Fort Worth 1999, no pet.) (P not permitted to testify about damages because he refused to respond to interrogatory about damages); **Fears v. Mechanical & Indus. Technicians, Inc.**, 654 S.W.2d 524, 529 (Tex.App.—Tyler 1983, writ ref'd n.r.e.) (default rendered because D did not file answers to interrogatories). When a party completely fails to answer, the party seeking discovery is not required to file a motion to compel before filing a motion for sanctions. *See* **Swain**, 998 S.W.2d at 733.

§8.5 Request hearing. The party seeking discovery must request a hearing on the objection or on the motion to compel, or it will waive its objections to the answers to the interrogatories. *See* Tex. R. Civ. P. 193.4; **McKinney v. National Un. Fire Ins.**, 772 S.W.2d 72, 75 (Tex.1989). See "Burden to secure hearing & ruling," ch. 6-A, §18.6.

§9. Using interrogatories as evidence

§9.1 By whom, against whom.

1. Against answering party. Generally, the answers to interrogatories cannot be used as evidence by the party that answered them. Tex. R. Civ. P. 197.3; **Morgan v. Anthony**, 27 S.W.3d 928, 929 (Tex.2000); **Yates v. Fisher**, 988 S.W.2d 730, 731 (Tex.1998). However, when a party is questioned under oath about an answer, is subject to cross-examination, and affirms that everything contained in the answer is true, the interrogatory answer becomes competent evidence. *See* **Morgan**, 27 S.W.3d at 929; **Price Pfister, Inc. v. Moore & Kimmey, Inc.**, 48 S.W.3d 341, 348–49 (Tex.App.—Houston [14th Dist.] 2001, pet. denied).

2. By any other party. Even if the parties in a multiparty case do not have common causes of action, all parties can rely on the answers to interrogatories by any other party. *E.g.*, **Ticor Title Ins. v. Lacy**, 803 S.W.2d 265, 265–66 (Tex.1991) (in case predating request for disclosures, nonsettling D was entitled to rely on P's failure to designate witnesses in response to settling D's interrogatories).

§9.2 Using answers in trial. Interrogatories are considered evidence once they are admitted into evidence by a ruling of the court. *See* **Cornell v. Cornell**, 570 S.W.2d 22, 23 (Tex.App.—San Antonio 1978, no writ). A party's answers to interrogatories are not hearsay. *See* Tex. R. Evid. 801(e)(1)(A)(i), (e)(2). There are three steps to introducing the answers to interrogatories.

1. Identify. The interrogatories and answers must be identified. The best procedure is to mark the interrogatories with an exhibit number.

2. Offer. The interrogatories and answers must be formally offered into evidence.

3. Admit. The court must admit the interrogatories and answers into evidence. Interrogatories that are not admitted into evidence cannot be considered in support of the judgment. **Sammons Enters. v. Manley**, 540 S.W.2d 751, 757 (Tex.App.—Texarkana 1976, writ ref'd n.r.e.); *see* **Cornell**, 570 S.W.2d at 23; *see also* **Eubanks v. Eubanks**, 892 S.W.2d 181, 181–82 (Tex.App.—Houston [14th Dist.] 1994, no writ) (interrogatories read into record, but not admitted into evidence, became testimonial evidence).

§9.3 Using supplanted answers. Supplanted answers to interrogatories are not valid answers and cannot be used as evidence. They can, in some cases, be used to impeach the new answers. *See* **Thomas v. International Ins.**, 527 S.W.2d 813, 820 (Tex.App.—Waco 1975, writ ref'd n.r.e.). However, supplanted answers that inquire about either a party's legal theories or damages cannot be used for impeachment. Tex. R. Civ. P. 197.3.

§9.4 Using answers in summary judgment. Interrogatory answers can be used in a summary-judgment proceeding. **Judwin Props., Inc. v. Griggs & Harrison**, 911 S.W.2d 498, 503–04 (Tex.App.—Houston [1st Dist.] 1995, no writ). Because answers can be used only against the party answering them, a party cannot rely on its own answers to raise a fact issue. *See* Tex. R. Civ. P. 197.3; **Yates v. Fisher**, 988 S.W.2d 730, 731 (Tex.1998); *see also* **Buck v. Blum**, 130 S.W.3d 285, 290 (Tex.App.—Houston [14th Dist.] 2004, no pet.) (answers cannot be used against another party, even a codefendant); **Garcia v. National Eligibility Express, Inc.**, 4 S.W.3d 887, 890 (Tex.App.—Houston [1st Dist.] 1999, no pet.) (answers cannot be used in favor of answering party even if other party puts them in evidence and does not timely challenge them on appeal).

§10. Objecting to unidentified trial witness

See "Objecting to unidentified witness," ch. 6-E, §2.8.

§11. Review

See "Review of discovery orders," ch. 6-A, §26.

H. Requests for Admissions

§1. General

§1.1 Rule. Tex. R. Civ. P. 198.

§1.2 Purpose. Requests for admissions are narrowly drawn questions that call for the responding party to either admit or deny a specific fact. They seldom lead to the discovery of additional evidence. Their primary function is to simplify trials by eliminating matters that there is no real controversy about but that may be difficult or expensive to prove. **Medina v. Zuniga**, 593 S.W.3d 238, 244 (Tex.2019); **Stelly v. Papania**, 927 S.W.2d 620, 622 (Tex.1996); **Boulet v. State**, 189 S.W.3d 833, 838 (Tex.App.—Houston [1st Dist.] 2006, no pet.).

§1.3 Forms. See **O'Connor's Texas Civil Forms**, FORMS 6H:1 et seq. (2020 ed.).

§1.4 Other references. Griesel, *The "New" Texas Discovery Rules: Three Years Later*, Advanced Evidence & Discovery Course, State Bar of Texas CLE, ch. 2, §XII (2002).

§2. Scope

The scope of discovery by requests for admissions is governed principally by TRCP 192. See "Scope of Discovery," ch. 6-B, §1 et seq. Requests for admissions are often used to prove the genuineness of documents and may be used to ask a party to admit an opinion or fact or the application of law to facts. Tex. R. Civ. P. 198.1. However, requests for admissions cannot be used to ask a party to admit a conclusion of law. **Boulet v. State,** 189 S.W.3d 833, 838 (Tex.App.—Houston [1st Dist.] 2006, no pet.).

§3. Requests for admissions

Before drafting requests for admissions, the attorney should examine the live pleadings of both parties. The requests for admissions should be used to affirm evidence of incidental but important issues in the pleadings (e.g., the identity of the property owner, the validity of the signatures on the contract, that notice was timely).

§3.1 Procedure. Requests for admissions must be in writing. Tex. R. Civ. P. 198.1. See **O'Connor's Texas Civil Forms,** FORMS 6H:1 to 6H:2 (2020 ed.).

1. Serve on party. Requests for admissions may be served only on other parties. Tex. R. Civ. P. 198.1. A party's duty to respond to requests for admissions depends on receipt of the requests. **Approximately $14,980.00 v. State**, 261 S.W.3d 182, 186 (Tex.App.—Houston [14th Dist.] 2008, no pet.); **Payton v. Ashton**, 29 S.W.3d 896, 898 (Tex.App.—Amarillo 2000, no pet.); *see* Tex. R. Civ. P. 21a.

2. Time to serve requests for admissions. For cases filed on or after January 1, 2021, requests for admissions cannot be served on a party until after that party's initial disclosures under TRCP 194 are due. *See* Tex. R. Civ. P. 190.2(b)(1), 190.3(b)(1), 192.2(a). See "Deadline," ch. 6-E, §3.3.1. For most methods of service (e.g., e-service, personal or commercial delivery), the deadline to serve requests for admissions is 30 days before the end of the discovery period. *See* Tex. R. Civ. P. 198.1. See "Discovery periods," ch. 6-A, §8. But when service is by mail or fax, the requests should be served at least 33 days (if mailed) or 31 days (if faxed after 5:00 p.m.) before the end of the discovery period. *See* Tex. R. Civ. P. 21a(b)(2), (c). See "Deadline to serve response," ch. 6-A, §14.1.

2021 Rule Amendments

In 2020, the Supreme Court approved significant amendments to TRCP 190, 192.2, and 194. See Tex.Sup.Ct. Order, Misc. Docket No. 20-9153 (eff. Jan. 1, 2021). Under the amendments, a party generally cannot serve discovery requests on another party until after that party's initial disclosures now required under TRCP 194 are due. Tex. R. Civ. P. 192.2(a). See "Required disclosures—Cases filed on or after 1-1-21," ch. 6-E, §3. Initial disclosures are generally due within 30 days after the filing of the first answer or general appearance. Tex. R. Civ. P. 194.2(a). But if a party is served or otherwise joined after the filing of the first answer or general appearance, its initial disclosures are generally due within

30 days after being served or joined. Id. The amendments apply to cases filed on or after January 1, 2021, except those filed in justice court. Tex.Sup.Ct. Order, Misc. Docket No. 20-9153 (eff. Jan. 1, 2021). For cases filed before January 1, 2021, a party can serve requests for admissions anytime after suit is filed. See id. See "Discovery periods," ch. 6-A, §8; "Service with original pleadings," ch. 6-A, §13.2.

3. Number of requests. Parties in a Level 1 case are limited to 15 written requests for admissions. Tex. R. Civ. P. 190.2(b)(5). Each discrete subpart of a request for admissions is considered a separate request for admissions. *Id.* There is no limit specified in the TRCPs on the number of requests for admissions or the number of sets of requests a party may serve in a Level 2 or 3 case. *See* Tex. R. Civ. P. 190.3(b), 190.4(b), 198. However, in a Level 3 case, the discovery limitations of Level 1 or 2 apply—depending on the damages sought and issues involved—unless expressly changed by court order. *See* Tex. R. Civ. P. 190.4(b). Thus, a party in a Level 3 case may also be limited to 15 written requests for admissions.

4. Specify time to answer. The requests for admissions should specify the time to answer, generally 30 days after service of the requests. *See* Tex. R. Civ. P. 198.2(a). When service is by mail or fax, the answering party has an additional 3 days (if mailed) or 1 day (if faxed after 5:00 p.m.) to respond. *See* Tex. R. Civ. P. 21a(b)(2), (c). See "Deadline to serve response," ch. 6-A, §14.1.

2021 Rule Amendments

In 2020, the Supreme Court approved significant amendments to TRCP 192.2 and 194. See Tex.Sup.Ct. Order, Misc. Docket No. 20-9153 (eff. Jan. 1, 2021). Under the amendments, a party generally cannot serve discovery requests on another party until after that party's initial disclosures now required under TRCP 194 are due. See Tex. R. Civ. P. 192.2(a). These initial disclosures are generally due within 30 days after the filing of the first answer or general appearance. Tex. R. Civ. P. 194.2(a). Because discovery must now be served after the first answer or general appearance, TRCP 198 was amended to eliminate the scenario where a defendant was served with requests for admissions before its answer was due and thus had 50 days to respond. See Tex. R. Civ. P. 198.2(a). The amendments apply to cases filed on or after January 1, 2021, except those filed in justice court. Tex.Sup.Ct. Order, Misc. Docket No. 20-9153 (eff. Jan. 1, 2021). For a detailed discussion of required disclosures under the 2021 amendments, see "Required disclosures—Cases filed on or after 1-1-21," ch. 6-E, §3.

§3.2 Typical requests. The requests for admissions should begin with a request that the party "admit the truth of the following statements." *See* Tex. R. Civ. P. 198.1. The requests should be made in short, simple, declarative sentences. For example, "Admit or deny the following: The promissory note, a copy of which is attached to this request and marked Exhibit A, is a genuine copy of the note that is the subject of this litigation." A party should not pair a request with its mirror opposite; if both admissions are deemed admitted, the admissions establish both the positive and negative of the proposition, thus creating a fact issue. *E.g.*, **CEBI Metal v. Garcia**, 108 S.W.3d 464, 466–67 (Tex.App.—Houston [14th Dist.] 2003, no pet.) (deemed admissions of requests paired with exact opposites could not support summary judgment); **Noons v. Arabghani**, No. 13-03-628-CV, 2005 WL 2037985 (Tex.App.—Corpus Christi 2005, pet. denied) (memo op.; 8-25-05) (same). See **O'Connor's Texas Civil Forms**, FORMS 6H:1 et seq. (2020 ed.) for requests for admissions in the following types of lawsuits: breach of contract (**O'Connor's Texas Civil Forms**, FORMS 6H:4 to 6H:5 (2020 ed.)), suit on a sworn account (**O'Connor's Texas Civil Forms**, FORMS 6H:6 to 6H:7 (2020 ed.)), automobile accident (**O'Connor's Texas Civil Forms**, FORMS 6H:8 to 6H:9 (2020 ed.)), slip-and-fall (**O'Connor's Texas Civil Forms**, FORMS 6H:10 to 6H:11 (2020 ed.)), and suit under the DTPA (**O'Connor's Texas Civil Forms**, FORMS 6H:12 to 6H:13 (2020 ed.)).

§4. Responding to requests for admissions

§4.1 Procedure.

1. Form of answers. The answers to requests for admissions must be made in the form required by Tex. R. Civ. P. 198.2. See **O'Connor's Texas Civil Forms**, FORM 6H:3 (2020 ed.).

(1) In writing. The party must respond to requests for admissions in writing. Tex. R. Civ. P. 198.2(a). Each answer, objection, or other response must be preceded by the request it applies to. Tex. R. Civ. P. 193.1.

(2) Signed. The response to the requests for admissions must be signed by the attorney (or party when pro se). Tex. R. Civ. P. 191.3(a); *see, e.g.*, **In re Estate of Herring**, 970 S.W.2d 583, 588–89 (Tex.App.—Corpus Christi 1998, no pet.) (unsigned responses treated as failure to respond; requests were deemed admitted); *see also* Tex. R. Civ. P. 191.3(d) (unsigned response must be struck unless failure to sign is corrected).

(3) Not verified. The answers to the requests for admissions do not need to be verified. **Guzman v. Carnevale**, 964 S.W.2d 311, 313–14 (Tex.App.—Corpus Christi 1998, no pet.).

2. Time to respond. Generally, a party has 30 days after the date of service of the requests for admissions to serve a response. Tex. R. Civ. P. 198.2(a). When service is by mail or fax, the answering party has an additional 3 days (if mailed) or 1 day (if faxed after 5:00 p.m.) to respond. *See* Tex. R. Civ. P. 21a(b)(2), (c).

2021 Rule Amendments

In 2020, the Supreme Court approved significant amendments to TRCP 192.2 and 194. See Tex.Sup.Ct. Order, Misc. Docket No. 20-9153 (eff. Jan. 1, 2021). Under the amendments, a party generally cannot serve discovery requests on another party until after that party's initial disclosures now required under TRCP 194 are due. See Tex. R. Civ. P. 192.2(a). These initial disclosures are generally due within 30 days after the filing of the first answer or general appearance. Tex. R. Civ. P. 194.2(a). Because discovery must now be served after the first answer or general appearance, TRCP 198 was amended to eliminate the scenario where a defendant was served with requests for admissions before its answer was due and thus had 50 days to respond. See Tex. R. Civ. P. 198.2(a). The amendments apply to cases filed on or after January 1, 2021, except those filed in justice court. Tex.Sup.Ct. Order, Misc. Docket No. 20-9153 (eff. Jan. 1, 2021). For a detailed discussion of required disclosures under the 2021 amendments, see "Required disclosures—Cases filed on or after 1-1-21," ch. 6-E, §3.

---

3. Extending time to respond.

(1) By Rule 11 agreement. A party may ask opposing counsel for a Rule 11 agreement extending the time to respond to requests for admissions. See "Agreements between attorneys—Rule 11," ch. 1-H, §9.

(2) By motion. A party may ask the court to extend the time to respond to requests for admissions only if the motion is made before the date to answer. See "Extending time to respond to discovery," ch. 6-A, §15. Once the time to respond expires, it is too late to ask the court for more time to serve answers to requests for admissions. **Cherry v. North Am. Lloyds**, 770 S.W.2d 4, 5 (Tex.App.—Houston [1st Dist.] 1989, writ denied). The answers are automatically deemed admitted against the defaulting party the day after the answers are due. *Id.* To avoid the effect of the deemed answers, the defaulting party must file a motion to strike, withdraw, or amend the deemed admissions. *Id.* See "Avoiding deemed admissions," ch. 6-H, §7.

§4.2 Response. The response to a request for admissions must (1) admit, (2) specifically deny, (3) set out in detail the reasons why the answering party cannot truthfully admit or deny the matter, (4) object, (5) assert a privilege, or (6) move for a protective order. Tex. R. Civ. P. 198.2(b) (responses 1-5); *see* **Reynolds v. Murphy**, 188 S.W.3d 252, 260–61 (Tex.App.—Fort Worth 2006, pet. denied) (response 6). If the court determines that a response does not comply with the requirements of TRCP 198, it may (1) deem the matter admitted or (2) require an amended answer. Tex. R. Civ. P. 215.4(a).

1. Admissions. To admit, the party simply states that it admits the request. *See* Tex. R. Civ. P. 198.2(b). Evasive or incomplete answers are treated as a failure to answer, and the request is deemed admitted. Tex. R. Civ. P. 215.4(a).

2. Denials. To deny, the party simply states that it denies the request. *See* Tex. R. Civ. P. 198.2(b). A denial must "fairly meet the substance of the request." *Id.* A party may qualify an answer or deny part of a request only when good faith requires. *Id.*

3. Cannot admit or deny. If the party claims it cannot admit or deny the request, it must explain in detail the reasons why it cannot admit or deny. Tex. R. Civ. P. 198.2(b).

4. Lack of information. A party can refuse to admit or deny the request on the ground that it lacks information or knowledge to admit or deny only if the party states (1) it made a reasonable inquiry, and (2) the information known or easily obtained by the party is insufficient to enable the party to admit or deny. Tex. R. Civ. P. 198.2(b); *see* **Montes v. Lazzara Shipyard**, 657 S.W.2d 886, 888–89 (Tex.App.—Corpus Christi 1983, no writ). Once the party acquires information responsive to the answer, it must supplement its answer.

5. Objections & privileges. The party must make its objections and assert its privileges before the time to serve the answers expires. Tex. R. Civ. P. 193.2, 193.3, 198.2. Objections and privileges served after the deadline are waived, and the requests are deemed admitted. See "Answer deemed admitted," ch. 6-H, §6.1.

(1) Objections. Objections must be specific. To object to only part of the matter in a request, the party must identify the specific part and admit or deny the remainder. Tex. R. Civ. P. 193.2, 198.2(b).

(a) Valid objections. Examples of valid objections to requests for admissions include the following: • The party in a Level 1 case served more than 15 requests for admissions. *See* Tex. R. Civ. P. 190.2(b)(5). See "Number of requests," ch. 6-H, §3.1.3. • The request asks the party to admit a proposition of law. **Cedyco Corp. v. Whitehead**, 253 S.W.3d 877, 880–81 (Tex.App.—Beaumont 2008, pet. denied); **Esparza v. Diaz**, 802 S.W.2d 772, 775 (Tex.App.—Houston [14th Dist.] 1990, no writ). Answers that constitute admissions of law are not binding on a court and do not prevent a party from proving fact issues. **Esparza**, 802 S.W.2d at 775. • The request asks the party to admit matters that are hearsay. *E.g.*, **Gaynier v. Ginsberg**, 715 S.W.2d 749, 759 (Tex.App.—Dallas 1986, writ ref'd n.r.e.) (improper to ask whether certain documents were those of treating doctor, now deceased). • The request is premature because the party will not know the answer until discovery is completed. *See* Tex. R. Civ. P. 193.1. • The party cannot admit or deny the genuineness of the document attached to the request because the copy is illegible. The party must be able to inspect the original before responding. *See* Tex. R. Civ. P. 198.2(b). • When the State is a party, it may object before trial that the requests for admissions will prejudice the rights of the State under the provisions of Gov't Code §402.004. *See* **Lowe v. Texas Tech Univ.**, 540 S.W.2d 297, 300–01 (Tex.1976); **Carrasco v. Texas Transp.**, 908 S.W.2d 575, 578–79 (Tex.App.—Waco 1995, no writ); *see also* **Employees Ret. Sys. v. Bass**, 840 S.W.2d 710, 713–14 (Tex.App.—Eastland 1992, no writ) (Gov't Code §402.004 prevents deemed admissions against State).

(b) Invalid objections. Examples of invalid objections to requests for admissions include the following: • The request relates to statements of opinion or of fact. Tex. R. Civ. P. 198.1. • The request relates to the application of law to fact, or to mixed questions of law and fact. *Id.*; **Laycox v. Jaroma, Inc.**, 709 S.W.2d 2, 4 (Tex.App.—Corpus Christi 1986, writ ref'd n.r.e.). • The request relates to a document that will not be admissible at trial. Tex. R. Civ. P. 192.3(a). The general rule is that as long as information appears reasonably calculated to lead to the discovery of admissible evidence, it is discoverable. *Id.* • The request presents a genuine issue for trial. Tex. R. Civ. P. 198.2(b).

(2) Privileges. A party must assert its privileges in a withholding statement. Tex. R. Civ. P. 193.3(a). See "Asserting privileges," ch. 6-A, §18.2.

6. Protective order. A party may file a motion for protective order within the time period for answering requests for admissions. *See* Tex. R. Civ. P. 192.6(a). See "Motion for protective order," ch. 6-A, §20. If a party objects that a set of requests for admissions is unduly burdensome and harassing, the party does not need to file a more specific objection to each request to prevent the requests from being deemed. *E.g.*, **Reynolds**, 188 S.W.3d at 260 (Ds' motion objecting that P's 996 requests for admissions were unduly burdensome and harassing prevented deemed admissions). Even if the trial court does not rule on the motion for protective order, a timely motion prevents the requests from being deemed admitted. *See id.* at 261.

§4.3 Amending or withdrawing answers. The court has the authority to permit a party to amend or withdraw its admissions. **Marshall v. Vise**, 767 S.W.2d 699, 700 (Tex.1989). The court may permit amendment or withdrawal when the moving party shows (1) good cause, (2) that the party relying on the responses will not be unduly prejudiced, and (3) that the withdrawal will serve the purpose of legitimate discovery and the merits of the case. Tex. R. Civ. P. 198.3; **Stelly v. Papania**, 927 S.W.2d 620, 622 (Tex.1996); *e.g.*, **Texas Capital Secs., Inc. v. Sandefer**, 58 S.W.3d 760, 770–71 (Tex.App.—Houston [1st Dist.] 2001, pet. denied) (motion to withdraw did not show good cause).

§5. Challenging the response

§5.1 Challenging response to requests. The requesting party can move to determine the sufficiency of the responding party's answers or objections. Tex. R. Civ. P. 215.4(a).

1. Challenging answers. If the court decides an answer does not comply with TRCP 198, the court may deem the request admitted or order that an amended answer be served. Tex. R. Civ. P. 215.4(a); **Taylor v. Taylor**, 747 S.W.2d 940, 945 (Tex.App.—Amarillo 1988, writ denied). See **O'Connor's Texas Civil Forms**, FORM 6H:16 (2020 ed.).

(1) Evasive answer. The party who served the requests should challenge answers that do not specifically deny or affirm the requests. *See* Tex. R. Civ. P. 198.2(b). The court may treat an evasive answer as a failure to answer and deem the request admitted. Tex. R. Civ. P. 215.4(a); **State v. Carrillo**, 885 S.W.2d 212, 216 (Tex.App.—San Antonio 1994, no writ).

(2) Quibbling. The party who served the requests should challenge answers that quibble over the meaning of simple words. If an answer quibbles over the meaning of a word, the court may hold that the answer is evasive and deem the request admitted. *See* **McPeak v. Texas DPS**, 346 S.W.2d 138, 140 (Tex.App.—Dallas 1961, no writ).

(3) Refusal to answer. The party who served the requests should challenge a refusal to answer made on the ground that the responding party did not have sufficient information. The refusal to answer is not valid unless the party also states that it made a reasonable effort to ascertain the requested matters. **U.S. Fire Ins. v. Maness**, 775 S.W.2d 748, 749 (Tex.App.—Houston [1st Dist.] 1989, writ ref'd); **Stewart v. Vaughn**, 504 S.W.2d 600, 602 (Tex.App.—Houston [14th Dist.] 1974, no writ).

2. Challenging objections. If the court determines that an objection is not justified, it may order the request to be answered or deem it admitted. For example, a party should challenge an objection made on the ground that the request was confusing if it was not. *See, e.g.*, **Gray v. Armstrong**, 364 S.W.2d 485, 488 (Tex.App.—Dallas 1962, no writ) (because request was not confusing, court deemed it admitted).

3. Challenging privileges. After receiving a withholding statement in response to a request for admissions indicating that information has been withheld on grounds of privilege, a party seeking the discovery may ask the withholding party to provide a privilege log. Tex. R. Civ. P. 193.3(b). See "Request privilege log," ch. 6-A, §18.2.2.

§5.2 Expenses for failure to admit. If the responding party refuses to admit the truth of a matter asked or the genuineness of a document, and the party who served the request later proves the matter to be true or the document genuine, the requesting party may be entitled to reasonable expenses incurred in making that proof, including reasonable attorney fees. Tex. R. Civ. P. 215.4(b); **Medina v. Zuniga**, 593 S.W.3d 238, 243 (Tex.2019); **Peralta v. Durham**, 133 S.W.3d 339, 341 (Tex.App.—Dallas 2004, no pet.). The award of costs is mandatory unless the court finds one of the following: (1) the request was objectionable, (2) the admission sought was of no substantial importance, (3) the responding party had a reasonable ground to believe that it would prevail on the matter, or (4) there was another good reason for the refusal to admit. Tex. R. Civ. P. 215.4(b); **Peralta**, 133 S.W.3d at 341. If the responding party is served with a request for merits-preclusive admissions, the very nature of such a request provides the responding party with good reason for the refusal to admit. **Medina**, 593 S.W.3d at 245; *see* Tex. R. Civ. P. 215.4(b)(4). In this situation, due process is implicated, and the responding party cannot be required to pay expenses for refusing to admit the truth of the merits-preclusive matters. *See* **Medina**, 593 S.W.3d at 245 (same due-process concerns that arise in context of deemed admissions also arise when court sanctions party under TRCP 215.4 for denying merits-preclusive requests for admissions). For what constitutes a merits-preclusive request for admissions, see "Merits-preclusive effect," ch. 6-H, §7.2.2(1)(b)[1].

§6. Deemed admissions

§6.1 Answer deemed admitted. Requests are automatically deemed admitted as a matter of law on the day after the answers are due if no answers, objections, or assertions of privilege are served. *See* Tex. R. Civ. P. 198.2(c); **Marino v. King**, 355 S.W.3d 629, 633 (Tex.2011); **Marshall v. Vise**, 767 S.W.2d 699, 700 (Tex.1989); **Payton v. Ashton**, 29 S.W.3d 896, 897–98 (Tex.App.—Amarillo 2000, no pet.). The trial court does not have the discretion to refuse to deem the requests admitted. **Barker v. Harrison**, 752 S.W.2d 154, 155 (Tex.App.—Houston [1st Dist.] 1988, writ dism'd).

§6.2 Motion to deem.

1. Not necessary. Once the answers are overdue and no response has been served, it is not necessary for the requesting party to file a motion to ask the court to deem unanswered requests for admissions admitted. Tex. R. Civ. P. 198.2(c); *see* **Marshall v. Vise**, 767 S.W.2d 699, 700 (Tex.1989).

2. Necessary. When a party responding to requests for admissions serves timely but evasive answers or invalid objections, the party who sent the requests should file a motion asking the court to deem the requests admitted. Tex. R. Civ. P. 215.4(a); *see* **State v. Carrillo**, 885 S.W.2d 212, 216 (Tex.App.—San Antonio 1994, no writ); **Taylor v. Taylor**, 747 S.W.2d 940, 945 (Tex.App.—Amarillo 1988, writ denied). See **O'Connor's Texas Civil Forms**, FORM 6H 14 (2020 ed.).

§6.3 Response to motion to deem. When a party files a motion to deem answers admitted, the other party should file a response that challenges the grounds in the motion or asks the court for permission to amend its answers. *See* Tex. R. Civ. P. 215.4(a). See **O'Connor's Texas Civil Forms**, FORM 6H:15 (2020 ed.).

§7. Avoiding deemed admissions

§7.1 Take a nonsuit. If the statute of limitations has not run, a plaintiff can avoid the effect of deemed admissions by taking a nonsuit and refiling the case. Deemed admissions in one suit are not effective in another. Tex. R. Civ. P. 198.3; **Osteen v. Glynn Dodson, Inc.**, 875 S.W.2d 429, 431 (Tex.App.—Waco 1994, writ denied). See **O'Connor's Texas Civil Forms**, FORM 7F:1 (2020 ed.).

§7.2 Strike deemed admissions. A party may move to withdraw or amend the admissions deemed against it. In many cases, a party first realizes the requests for admissions were deemed admitted when the propounding party files a motion for summary judgment based on deemed admissions. *See* **Wheeler v. Green**, 157 S.W.3d 439, 441–42 (Tex.2005). When this occurs, the party should follow the procedure outlined here:

1. Motion for continuance. If a motion for summary judgment (or any other motion that depends on the deemed admissions) is pending, the party against whom the admissions were deemed should file a motion to continue the summary-judgment hearing. The party attempting to challenge the deemed findings will need more time than permitted under TRCP 166a to respond to the motion for summary judgment. See "Motion for Continuance," ch. 5-D, §1 et seq.; **O'Connor's Texas Civil Forms**, FORMS 5D:1 to 5D:2, 7B:5 (2020 ed.). If the party does not realize the admissions were deemed until the hearing and the motion for summary judgment is granted, the party can file a motion for new trial. *See* **Wheeler**, 157 S.W.3d at 441-42. See "No opportunity to file response," ch. 10-B, §11.1.2(2).

2. Motion to strike deemed admissions. The party against whom the admissions were deemed should file a motion to strike the deemed admissions. See **O'Connor's Texas Civil Forms**, FORM 6H:17 (2020 ed.). TRCP 198.3 permits the court to allow a party to withdraw or amend its admissions based on certain grounds.

(1) Good cause.

(a) Generally. The party must state good cause, explaining why it did not timely serve its answers to the requests for admissions. Tex. R. Civ. P. 198.3(a); **Wheeler**, 157 S.W.3d at 442; **Wal-Mart Stores v. Deggs**, 968 S.W.2d 354, 356 (Tex.1998). Good cause can be an accident or a mistake, as long as it was not intentional or the result of conscious indifference. **Marino v. King**, 355 S.W.3d 629, 633 (Tex.2011); **Wheeler**, 157 S.W.3d at 442; **In re Sewell**, 472 S.W.3d 449, 455 (Tex.App.—Texarkana 2015, orig. proceeding), *disapproved on other grounds*, **In re Bayview Loan Servicing, LLC**, 532 S.W.3d 510 (Tex.App.—Texarkana 2017, orig. proceeding); *e.g.*, **Boulet v. State**, 189 S.W.3d 833, 837 (Tex.App.—Houston [1st Dist.] 2006, no pet.) (mistake in calendar entry was sufficient to establish good cause). Even a slight excuse can be enough to establish good cause. **Boulet**, 189 S.W.3d at 836; **In re Kellogg-Brown & Root, Inc.**, 45 S.W.3d 772, 775 (Tex.App.—Tyler 2001, orig. proceeding).

(b) Merits-preclusive deemed admissions. When a party attempts to use requests for admissions to compromise the other party's right to present the merits of its case (i.e., essentially asking the party to admit it has no cause of action or ground of defense), due process is implicated and the burden shifts to the party opposing the motion to strike to demonstrate that the moving party acted in flagrant bad faith or with callous disregard for the rules of civil procedure. *See*

Marino, 355 S.W.3d at 634; **Wheeler**, 157 S.W.3d at 443–44; **In re Sewell**, 472 S.W.3d at 455–56; **Time Warner, Inc. v. Gonzalez**, 441 S.W.3d 661, 665–66 (Tex.App.—San Antonio 2014, pet. denied).

[1] Merits-preclusive effect. Requests for admissions are improper when used to establish controverted issues that make up the fundamental legal issues of a case. **Time Warner**, 441 S.W.3d at 668. For example, asking a party to admit the invalidity of her claims or concede her defenses is an improper use of requests for admissions. *See* **Medina v. Zuniga**, 593 S.W.3d 238, 244 (Tex.2019); *see, e.g.*, **Ramirez v. Noble Energy, Inc.**, 521 S.W.3d 851, 857–58 (Tex.App.—Houston [1st Dist.] 2017, no pet.) (deemed admission that D was not proper D in suit was merits-preclusive). Because merits-preclusive admissions implicate due-process concerns, courts must presume that requests for admissions are merits-preclusive unless the record affirmatively establishes that they are not. **Ramirez**, 521 S.W.3d at 858; **In re Sewell**, 472 S.W.3d at 461. For an opposing party to establish that the deemed admissions are not merits-preclusive, the record must show either that the requests for admissions seek to authenticate or prove the admissibility of documents or that they involve uncontroverted facts. **Ramirez**, 521 S.W.3d at 858; **In re Sewell**, 472 S.W.3d at 461.

[2] Bad faith or callous disregard. When a party moves to strike deemed admissions that have a merits-preclusive effect, the party opposing the motion to strike must demonstrate that the moving party acted in flagrant bad faith or with callous disregard for the rules of civil procedure. *See* **Marino**, 355 S.W.3d at 634; **Wheeler**, 157 S.W.3d at 443; **In re Sewell**, 472 S.W.3d at 456; **Time Warner**, 441 S.W.3d at 665. See "Bad faith," ch. 6-H, §7.2.4(2)(a). If the opposing party cannot demonstrate bad faith or callous disregard, the party moving to strike the deemed admissions is presumed to have established good cause under TRCP 198.3. *See* **Medina v. Raven**, 492 S.W.3d 53, 62 (Tex.App.—Houston [1st Dist.] 2016, no pet.); **In re Sewell**, 472 S.W.3d at 456; **Time Warner**, 441 S.W.3d at 665.

(2) No undue prejudice. The party must state that the other party will not be unduly prejudiced by the striking of the deemed admissions. Tex. R. Civ. P. 198.3(b); **Wheeler**, 157 S.W.3d at 442. Undue prejudice depends on whether withdrawing admissions will delay the trial or significantly hamper the other party's ability to prepare for it. *E.g.*, **Marino**, 355 S.W.3d at 633 (trial court should have permitted withdrawal of deemed admissions; P's filing of responses to admissions one day late but several months before summary-judgment hearing would not hamper D in preparing for trial); **Wheeler**, 157 S.W.3d at 443 (trial court should have permitted withdrawal of deemed admissions; P's filing of responses to admissions two days late but six months before summary judgment hearing did not hamper D in preparing for trial); *see, e.g.*, **Deggs**, 968 S.W.2d at 357 (trial court should have permitted withdrawal of deemed admissions; P did not depend on admissions to develop case); **Morgan v. Timmers Chevrolet, Inc.**, 1 S.W.3d 803, 806–07 (Tex.App.—Houston [1st Dist.] 1999, pet. denied) (trial court should not have permitted withdrawal of deemed admissions in middle of trial; Ps were unduly prejudiced because they had relied on admissions to limit discovery).

Note

When merits-preclusive admissions are deemed admitted, it is unclear whether the party moving to strike the deemed admissions has the burden of proving no undue prejudice or the opposing party has the burden of proving undue prejudice. See ***In re Sewell**, 472 S.W.3d at 456 n.3 (Supreme Court has not decided whether movant must show that striking merits-preclusive deemed admissions will not unduly prejudice nonmovant or whether nonmovant must show that it will be unduly prejudiced if admissions are struck); see, e.g.,* ***Ramirez**, 521 S.W.3d at 861–62 (motion to withdraw deemed admissions should have been granted when nonmovant did not prove bad faith or callous disregard and presented no evidence that withdrawal would cause it undue prejudice);* ***Time Warner**, 441 S.W.3d at 667 (nonmovant argued that striking admissions would cause him undue prejudice). Until the issue of who has the burden is decided, both parties should address undue prejudice.*

(3) Presentation of merits will suffer if motion denied. The party should state that if the admissions are not struck, presentation of the merits will suffer because the case would be decided on deemed—but possibly untrue—facts. **Wheeler**, 157 S.W.3d at 443 n.2; **Boulet**, 189 S.W.3d at 836–37; *see* Tex. R. Civ. P. 198.3(b) (must show that "presentation of the merits of the action will be subserved" by allowing withdrawal); *see, e.g.*, **In re Kellogg-Brown & Root, Inc.**, 45 S.W.3d at 777 (trial court's denial of motion to withdraw deemed admissions precluded D from presenting any viable defense at trial).

3. Attachments to motion to strike. The party against whom the admissions were deemed should attach the following to the motion to strike:

(1) Affidavits. In affidavits, the party should state detailed facts that support the excuses and explanations for all three elements: good cause, no prejudice, and presentation of merits. *See, e.g.*, **Ramsey v. Criswell**, 850 S.W.2d 258, 259–60 (Tex.App.—Texarkana 1993, no writ) (trial court properly denied motion because it was unverified and party had not attached or offered affidavits or other proof).

(2) Answers. The party should attach the answers it would have served in response to the requests for admissions if it had not missed the deadline.

4. Response to motion to strike.

(1) Generally. When a party files a motion to strike the deemed admissions, the party requesting the admissions should file a response that challenges the grounds in the motion. See **O'Connor's Texas Civil Forms**, FORM 6H:18 (2020 ed.).

(2) Merits-preclusive deemed admissions.

(a) Bad faith. When merits-preclusive admissions are deemed against a party, the party opposing the motion to strike has the burden to demonstrate that the moving party acted in flagrant bad faith or with callous disregard for the rules of civil procedure. *See* **Marino**, 355 S.W.3d at 634; **Wheeler**, 157 S.W.3d at 443–44; **Ramirez**, 521 S.W.3d at 861; **Time Warner**, 441 S.W.3d at 666. Bad faith is not simply bad judgment or negligence; it is conscious wrongdoing for a dishonest, discriminatory, or malicious purpose. **Ramirez**, 521 S.W.3d at 857; **Time Warner**, 441 S.W.3d at 666. A determination of bad faith or callous disregard for the rules is reserved for cases in which a party knew of pending deadlines and either consciously or flagrantly did not comply with them. **Ramirez**, 521 S.W.3d at 860. If the party cannot demonstrate bad faith or callous disregard, the party moving to strike the deemed admissions is presumed to have established the first and third elements of TRCP 198.3 (i.e., that there is good cause for granting the motion to strike the deemed admissions and that presentation of the merits will not suffer). *See* **In re Sewell**, 472 S.W.3d at 456. See "Merits-preclusive deemed admissions," ch. 6-H, §7.2.2(1)(b); "Presentation of merits will suffer if motion denied," ch. 6-H, §7.2.2(3).

(b) Undue prejudice. It is unclear which party has the burden of proving undue prejudice when merits-preclusive admissions are deemed against a party. See "Note," ch. 6-H, §7.2.2(2).

5. Hearing.

(1) Request hearing. The party who filed the motion to strike the deemed admissions should request a hearing on the motion.

(2) Present evidence. The party who filed the motion to strike the deemed admissions should present the testimony of as many witnesses as are necessary to convince the trial court to permit withdrawal of the admissions. The hearing should be treated as a full trial on the issues of good cause and no prejudice.

(3) Record hearing. The party should make sure the court reporter transcribes the hearing. Without a record of the hearing, it is impossible to prove good cause and lack of prejudice on appeal. *See* **Ruiz v. Nicolas Trevino Forwarding Agency, Inc.**, 888 S.W.2d 86, 89 (Tex.App.—San Antonio 1994, no writ).

6. Secure ruling. The party attempting to set aside the deemed admissions must make sure the court rules on its motion to strike. **Laycox v. Jaroma, Inc.**, 709 S.W.2d 2, 3 (Tex.App.—Corpus Christi 1986, writ ref'd n.r.e.).

(1) Deemed admissions set aside. The courts have set aside deemed admissions in the following instances: • When the party rebuts the presumption of service. *See, e.g.*, **Approximately $14,980.00 v. State**, 261 S.W.3d 182, 189 (Tex.App.—Houston [14th Dist.] 2008, no pet.) (notice sent by certified mail was returned "unclaimed," and return receipt showed two unsuccessful delivery attempts). • When the requests were not answered because of some confusion caused by the party serving the request. *See, e.g.*, **City of Houston v. Riner**, 896 S.W.2d 317, 319–20 (Tex.App.—Houston [1st Dist.] 1995, writ denied) (P left requests with building guard, who was not a representative of D, and D never received them);

Birdo v. Holbrook, 775 S.W.2d 411, 413 (Tex.App.—Fort Worth 1989, writ denied) (pro se P sent multiple requests for same information). • When the party shows diligence in attempting to resolve the problem as soon as it was discovered. *See, e.g.*, **In re Kellogg-Brown & Root, Inc.**, 45 S.W.3d at 776 (attorney immediately prepared and delivered responses after she realized she never received requests and could not find them in her office); **Esparza v. Diaz**, 802 S.W.2d 772, 776 (Tex.App.—Houston [14th Dist.] 1990, no writ) (D filed answers six months before trial, P was not injured, and trial was not delayed); **Employers Ins. of Wausau v. Halton**, 792 S.W.2d 462, 467 (Tex.App.—Dallas 1990, writ denied) (attorney drafted answers immediately after receiving requests for admissions, but they were not typed and served; attorney filed motion to set aside deemed answers as soon as he discovered the problem); **Boone v. Texas Empls. Ins.**, 790 S.W.2d 683, 688–89 (Tex.App.—Tyler 1990, no writ) (attorney immediately filed motion to withdraw deemed admissions). • When the error is clerical. *See, e.g.*, **Burden v. John Watson Landscape Illumination**, 896 S.W.2d 253, 255–56 (Tex.App.—Eastland 1995, writ denied) (attorney did not see letter from court shortening time to respond to 14 days); **Cudd v. Hydrostatic Transmission, Inc.**, 867 S.W.2d 101, 104–05 (Tex.App.—Corpus Christi 1993, no writ) (mistake in counting days to answer); **North River Ins. v. Greene**, 824 S.W.2d 697, 701 (Tex.App.—El Paso 1992, writ denied) (incorrect diary entry for date answers were due).

(2) Deemed admissions not set aside. The courts have refused to set aside deemed admissions in the following instances: • The party's failure to respond to requests for admissions was the result of a disputed oral agreement to extend time. **Hoffman v. Texas Commerce Bank**, 846 S.W.2d 336, 339–40 (Tex.App.—Houston [14th Dist.] 1992, writ denied). • The party did not attach affidavits to unverified motion to withdraw deemed admissions or offer other evidence to support its allegations that he was sick and his attorney was out of town on the day of filing. **Ramsey**, 850 S.W.2d at 259–60.

§8. Admissions as evidence

§8.1 Admissions as evidence.

1. Only in same suit. Answers to requests for admissions are admissible only in the same suit. Tex. R. Civ. P. 198.3; **Osteen v. Glynn Dodson, Inc.**, 875 S.W.2d 429, 431 (Tex.App.—Waco 1994, writ denied).

2. Only against party addressed. Answers to requests for admissions and deemed admissions are admissible only against the party to whom the requests for admissions were addressed. Tex. R. Civ. P. 198.3; **Thalman v. Martin**, 635 S.W.2d 411, 414 (Tex.1982); **Hartman v. Trio Transp.**, 937 S.W.2d 575, 578 (Tex.App.—Texarkana 1996, writ denied). A statement by an agent or employee is admissible against the principal only if (1) the statement concerns a matter within the scope of the agency or employment, and (2) it was made during the existence of that relationship. Tex. R. Evid. 801(e)(2)(D); **Hartman**, 937 S.W.2d at 579–80.

Note

The Supreme Court's 2015 amendment to TRE 801(e)(2) deleted the reference to the term "admissions" in the title of the rule because not all statements under that subdivision necessarily admit anything. Tex. R. Evid. 801 cmt. The amendment is meant to be only stylistic without any change to the application of the hearsay exclusion. See id.

3. Not against other parties. Admissions of a party are not admissible against a third party and do not bind coparties. *See* **Wal-Mart Stores v. Deggs**, 968 S.W.2d 354, 357 (Tex.1998) (allowing party to fall into trap produced by another party's failure to respond is contrary to intent of rules); **Bleeker v. Villarreal**, 941 S.W.2d 163, 168–69 (Tex.App.—Corpus Christi 1996, writ dism'd); **USX Corp. v. Salinas**, 818 S.W.2d 473, 479 (Tex.App.—San Antonio 1991, writ denied).

4. Not by addressed party. The party to whom the requests were addressed cannot use its own self-serving answers. **Sympson v. Mor-Win Prods.**, 501 S.W.2d 362, 364 (Tex.App.—Fort Worth 1973, no writ); *see* Tex. R. Evid. 801(e)(2).

5. Not the denial. A party cannot introduce into evidence a party's denial or refusal to admit a fact. *See* **Americana Motel, Inc. v. Johnson**, 610 S.W.2d 143, 143 (Tex.1980) (denial of request for admissions cannot be used as summary-judgment evidence). When a party denies or refuses to make an admission of fact, it is nothing more than a refusal to admit a fact; it is not evidence of any fact except the fact of refusal. **Newman v. Utica Nat'l Ins.**, 868 S.W.2d 5, 8 (Tex.App.—Houston [1st Dist.] 1993, writ denied).

§8.2 Using admissions at trial. When a party intends to use the other party's responses to requests for admissions at trial, that party should file them with the clerk. *See* Tex. R. Civ. P. 191.4(c)(2). Admissions made by parties in response to requests for admissions that are on file with the court do not need to be introduced into evidence to be properly before the trial and appellate courts. **Red Ball Motor Freight, Inc. v. Dean**, 549 S.W.2d 41, 43 (Tex.App.—Tyler 1977, writ dism'd). If the trier of fact returns findings that contradict a request that has been admitted or deemed, the admission must be accepted as controlling. **Beutel v. Dallas Cty. Flood Control Dist.**, 916 S.W.2d 685, 694 (Tex.App.—Waco 1996, writ denied).

Practice Tip

*For dramatic effect, a party may introduce the admissions into evidence by formally reading the specific admissions to the jury. See **Wal-Mart Stores v. Deggs**, 968 S.W.2d 354, 356 (Tex.1998); **Parkway Hosp., Inc. v. Lee**, 946 S.W.2d 580, 587 (Tex.App.—Houston [14th Dist.] 1997, writ denied), disapproved on other grounds, **Roberts v. Williamson**, 111 S.W.3d 113 (Tex.2003).*

1. No contradictory proof. A request for admissions, once admitted or deemed, is a judicial admission, and a party cannot introduce conflicting testimony over an objection. **Marshall v. Vise**, 767 S.W.2d 699, 700 (Tex.1989); **Beutel**, 916 S.W.2d at 694; **Bay Area Thoracic & Cardiovascular Surgical Ass'n v. Nathanson**, 908 S.W.2d 10, 11 (Tex.App.—Houston [1st Dist.] 1995, no writ).

2. Waiver of admissions. A party can waive its right to rely on the other party's admissions. When the admitting party attempts to offer evidence that contradicts the admissions, the party relying on the admissions must object, or it will waive its right to rely on the binding effect of the admissions. **Marshall**, 767 S.W.2d at 700; *see, e.g.*, **Acevedo v. Commission for Lawyer Discipline**, 131 S.W.3d 99, 104–05 (Tex.App.—San Antonio 2004, pet. denied) (no obligation to object because no controverting evidence offered until after trial). If controverting evidence is introduced without objection, the admissions are no longer conclusive, but they are still evidence. **Parkway Hosp.**, 946 S.W.2d at 587–88.

§8.3 Using admissions in summary judgment. The same rules apply when relying on admissions in a summary-judgment procedure as at trial—answers to requests for admissions and deemed admissions are admissible only against the party to whom the requests for admissions were addressed. *See* **Americana Motel, Inc. v. Johnson**, 610 S.W.2d 143, 143 (Tex.1980) (cannot use denials to request for admissions); **Schulz v. State Farm Mut. Auto. Ins.**, 930 S.W.2d 872, 876 (Tex.App.—Houston [1st Dist.] 1996, no writ) (cannot use own answers to admissions). The trial court cannot consider affidavits to contradict deemed admissions. **Beasley v. Burns**, 7 S.W.3d 768, 770 (Tex.App.—Texarkana 1999, pet. denied). See "Using admissions at trial," ch. 6-H, §8.2.

§9. Review

§9.1 Standard on appeal. The trial court has broad discretion to grant or refuse a party leave to withdraw deemed admissions. **Stelly v. Papania**, 927 S.W.2d 620, 622 (Tex.1996); **Approximately $14,980.00 v. State**, 261 S.W.3d 182, 185 (Tex.App.—Houston [14th Dist.] 2008, no pet.); **In re Kellogg-Brown & Root, Inc.**, 45 S.W.3d 772, 775 (Tex.App.—Tyler 2001, orig. proceeding). The trial court's decision will be set aside on appeal only on a showing of a clear abuse of discretion. **Stelly**, 927 S.W.2d at 622.

§9.2 Appeal or mandamus? Generally, mandamus relief is not available to review a trial court's action relating to deemed admissions. *See* **Sutherland v. Moore**, 716 S.W.2d 119, 121 (Tex.App.—El Paso 1986, orig. proceeding) (mandamus not available to review trial court's withdrawal of deemed admissions). See "Review of discovery orders," ch. 6-A, §26.

I. Securing Documents & Tangible Things

§1. General

§1.1 Rules. Tex. R. Civ. P. 176, 196, 205.

§1.2 Purpose. TRCP 196 provides the discovery procedure for obtaining documents and other tangible things from a party, and TRCP 176 provides the procedure for obtaining documents and other tangible things from a nonparty.

§1.3 Forms. See **O'Connor's Texas Civil Forms**, FORMS 6I:1 et seq. (2020 ed.).

§1.4 Other references. Griesel, *The "New" Texas Discovery Rules: Three Years Later*, Advanced Evidence & Discovery Course, State Bar of Texas CLE, ch. 2, §X (2002).

§2. Scope

A party may secure the production of any document, tangible item, or information in electronic or magnetic form that is not privileged and is relevant to the subject matter of the suit and proportional to the needs of the case. *See* Tex. R. Civ. P. 192.3(a), 192.4(b). See "Scope & limitations," ch. 6-B, §2.1; "Documents & tangible things," ch. 6-B, §2.11. A party may also request the production of an item for inspection, sampling, testing, photographing, and copying. Tex. R. Civ. P. 196.1(a); *see, e.g.*, **General Motors Corp. v. Tanner**, 892 S.W.2d 862, 863 (Tex.1995) (party wanted to examine item under microscope); **General Elec. Co. v. Salinas**, 861 S.W.2d 20, 23 (Tex.App.—Corpus Christi 1993, orig. proceeding) (party wanted to test materials involved in residential fire).

§3. Securing things from a party

To obtain documents and other tangible things from another party, a party serves a request for production. Tex. R. Civ. P. 196.1(a). No motion is necessary.

§3.1 Procedure.

1. Form of request. The request for production must be in writing. Tex. R. Civ. P. 192.7(a); *see* **City of San Antonio v. Vela**, 762 S.W.2d 314, 319 (Tex.App.—San Antonio 1988, writ denied). See **O'Connor's Texas Civil Forms**, FORMS 6I:1 to 6I:2 (2020 ed.).

2. Time to serve. For cases filed on or after January 1, 2021, requests for production cannot be served on a party until after that party's initial disclosures under TRCP 194 are due. *See* Tex. R. Civ. P. 190.2(b)(1), 190.3(b)(1), 192.2(a). See "Deadline," ch. 6-E, §3.3.1. For most methods of service (e.g., e-service, personal or commercial delivery), the deadline for serving a request is 30 days before the end of the discovery period. *See* Tex. R. Civ. P. 196.1(a). See "Discovery periods," ch. 6-A, §8. But when service is by mail or fax, the request should be served at least 33 days (if mailed) or 31 days (if faxed after 5:00 p.m.) before the end of the discovery period. *See* Tex. R. Civ. P. 21a(b)(2), (c). See "Deadline to serve response," ch. 6-A, §14.1.

2021 Rule Amendments

In 2020, the Supreme Court approved significant amendments to TRCP 190, 192.2, and 194. See Tex.Sup.Ct. Order, Misc. Docket No. 20-9153 (eff. Jan. 1, 2021). Under the amendments, a party generally cannot serve discovery requests on another party until after that party's initial disclosures now required under TRCP 194 are due. Tex. R. Civ. P. 192.2(a). See "Required disclosures—Cases filed on or after 1-1-21," ch. 6-E, §3. Initial disclosures are generally due within 30 days after the filing of the first answer or general appearance. Tex. R. Civ. P. 194.2(a). But if a party is served or otherwise joined after the filing of the first answer or general appearance, its initial disclosures are generally due within 30 days after being served or joined. Id. The amendments apply to cases filed on or after January 1, 2021, except those filed in justice court. Tex.Sup.Ct. Order, Misc. Docket No. 20-9153 (eff. Jan. 1, 2021). For cases filed before January 1, 2021, a party can serve requests for production anytime after suit is filed. See id. See "Discovery periods," ch. 6-A, §8; "Service with original pleadings," ch. 6-A, §13.2.

3. Specify time & place to respond. The request must state the time and place for production. Tex. R. Civ. P. 196.1(b). The date to respond to the request is generally 30 days after the date the request was served. Tex. R. Civ. P. 196.2(a). When service is by mail or fax, the answering party has an additional 3 days (if mailed) or 1 day (if faxed after 5:00 p.m.) to respond. *See* Tex. R. Civ. P. 21a(b)(2), (c). See "Deadline to serve response," ch. 6-A, §14.1.

2021 Rule Amendments

In 2020, the Supreme Court approved significant amendments to TRCP 192.2 and 194. See Tex.Sup.Ct. Order, Misc. Docket No. 20-9153 (eff. Jan. 1, 2021). Under the amendments, a party generally cannot serve discovery requests on another party until after that party's initial disclosures now required under TRCP 194 are due. See Tex. R. Civ. P. 192.2(a). These initial disclosures are generally due within 30 days after the filing of the first answer or general appearance. Tex. R. Civ. P. 194.2(a). Because discovery must now be served after the first answer or general appearance, TRCP 196 was amended to eliminate the scenario where a defendant was served with requests for production before its answer was due and thus had 50 days to respond. See Tex. R. Civ. P. 196.2(a). The amendments apply to cases filed on or after January 1, 2021, except those filed in justice court. Tex.Sup.Ct. Order, Misc. Docket No. 20-9153 (eff. Jan. 1, 2021). For a detailed discussion of required disclosures under the 2021 amendments, see "Required disclosures—Cases filed on or after 1-1-21," ch. 6-E, §3.

4. Number of requests. Parties in a Level 1 case are limited to 15 written requests for production. Tex. R. Civ. P. 190.2(b)(4). Each discrete subpart of a request for production is considered a separate request for production. *Id.* There is no limit specified in the TRCPs on the number of items a party can ask to have produced or the number of sets of requests it can serve in a Level 2 or 3 case. *See* Tex. R. Civ. P. 190.3(b), 190.4(b), 196. However, in a Level 3 case, the discovery limitations of Level 1 or 2 apply—depending on the damages sought and issues involved—unless expressly changed by court order. *See* Tex. R. Civ. P. 190.4(b). Thus, a party in a Level 3 case may also be limited to 15 written requests for production.

5. Not filed. The request for production is not filed with the court. Tex. R. Civ. P. 191.4(a)(1). See "Filing discovery," ch. 6-A, §12.1.

§3.2 Request. A request for documents or things must be reasonably tailored to request only matters relevant to the case. **In re National Lloyds Ins.**, 507 S.W.3d 219, 223–24 (Tex.2016); **Texaco, Inc. v. Sanderson**, 898 S.W.2d 813, 815 (Tex.1995).

1. Items to produce. The request for production must identify items, either individually or by category, and describe each item and category with reasonable particularity. Tex. R. Civ. P. 196.1(b); *see, e.g.*, **Texaco** 898 S.W.2d at 815 (request for all documents generally too broad); **County of Dallas v. Harrison**, 759 S.W.2d 530, 531 (Tex.App.—Dallas 1988, no writ) (request for photographs did not include videotape). A request for production cannot be used as a fishing expedition for information. **In re American Optical Corp.**, 988 S.W.2d 711, 713 (Tex.1998); **Dillard Dept. Stores v. Hall**, 909 S.W.2d 491, 492 (Tex.1995). See "Overbroad," ch. 6-A, §20.1.3.

(1) Electronic information. To obtain discovery of magnetic or electronic information, the requesting party must (1) specifically request the data, (2) specify the form in which the data should be produced, and (3) specify any extraordinary steps necessary for retrieval and translation. Tex. R. Civ. P. 196.4 & cmt. 3. See "Requests for production," ch. 6-C, §7.1.5.

(2) Other things. The request for production should ask for documents and other things based on the elements of the claim or defense. See **O'Connor's Texas Civil Forms**, FORMS 6I:1 et seq. (2020 ed.), for suggested requests for production in the following types of lawsuits: breach of contract (**O'Connor's Texas Civil Forms**, FORM 6I:4 (2020 ed.)), suit on a sworn account (**O'Connor's Texas Civil Forms**, FORM 6I:5 (2020 ed.)), automobile accident (**O'Connor's Texas Civil Forms**, FORMS 6I:6 to 6I:7 (2020 ed.)), slip-and-fall (**O'Connor's Texas Civil Forms**, FORMS 6I:8 to 6I:9 (2020 ed.)), and suit under the DTPA (**O'Connor's Texas Civil Forms**, FORMS 6I:10 to 6I:11 (2020 ed.)).

2. Items to be tested. If the requesting party intends to test or sample the requested item, the party must describe with specificity the means, manner, and procedure for testing or sampling. Tex. R. Civ. P. 196.1(b). The requesting

party should identify to what extent, if any, the testing or sampling will destroy or alter the item. If the testing will destroy or materially alter the item, the requesting party must secure a court order before conducting the test. *See* Tex. R. Civ. P. 196.5.

3. Particulars for compliance. The request for production should state the particulars for compliance: the deadline (generally 30 days after service of the request), the place to produce documents (generally the office of the attorney), and the way to produce the documents (organized as they are kept in the ordinary course of business or organized and labeled to correspond with each particular request). Tex. R. Civ. P. 196.1(b), 196.3(c). See "Deadline to serve response," ch. 6-A, §14.1.

4. Appropriate requests. The following requests were held proper: • Request for all documents relating to incident in which plaintiff was injured, excluding work product. **K Mart Corp. v. Sanderson**, 937 S.W.2d 429, 430–31 (Tex.1996). • Request for personnel file. **Tri-State Wholesale Associated Grocers, Inc. v. Barrera**, 917 S.W.2d 391, 399 (Tex.App.—El Paso 1996, writ dism'd). See "Personnel files," ch. 6-B, §2.11.9. • Request for "any and all" lease agreements between the parties since 1974. **Chamberlain v. Cherry**, 818 S.W.2d 201, 204 (Tex.App.—Amarillo 1991, orig. proceeding).

Practice Tip

If you believe the other party is going to hide documents, skip the request for production. Instead, as early as possible in the lawsuit, subpoena for an oral deposition the lowest-level employee of the party who keeps the documents and request a list of documents as part of the deposition notice. You have a better chance of getting the documents if a layperson (not an attorney) is subpoenaed (not noticed) for deposition and swears under oath (not just states in response to a request for production) that the documents produced are all the documents that were requested.

5. Inappropriate requests.

(1) Trial exhibits. A party should not ask for copies of the other party's trial exhibits in a request for production. **Texas Tech Univ. Health Sci. Ctr. v. Schild**, 828 S.W.2d 502, 504 (Tex.App.—El Paso 1992, orig. proceeding). Trial exhibits may be secured before trial if a pretrial or discovery-control order requires their production. Tex. R. Civ. P. 166(*l*), 190.4. See "Exhibits," ch. 5-A, §3.9.3.

(2) To create a document. A party should not ask the other party to create a document. **In re Colonial Pipeline Co.**, 968 S.W.2d 938, 942 (Tex.1998); **McKinney v. National Un. Fire Ins.**, 772 S.W.2d 72, 73 n.2 (Tex.1989); *see also* **In re Guzman**, 19 S.W.3d 522, 525 (Tex.App.—Corpus Christi 2000, orig. proceeding) (court cannot require nonparty to create document). To be subject to discovery, the thing or document must be in the custody, control, or possession of a party on whom the request is served. **In re Colonial**, 968 S.W.2d at 942; **Smith v. O'Neal**, 850 S.W.2d 797, 799 (Tex.App.—Houston [14th Dist.] 1993, no writ).

§3.3 Procedure to respond.

1. Form of response. See **O'Connor's Texas Civil Forms**, FORM 6I:3 (2020 ed.).

(1) In writing. The party responding to a request for production must serve a written response on the requesting party. Tex. R. Civ. P. 196.2(a); *see* **Cellular Mktg., Inc. v. Houston Cellular Tel. Co.**, 838 S.W.2d 331, 333 n.2 (Tex.App.—Houston [14th Dist.] 1992, writ denied). Each answer, objection, or other response must be preceded by the request it applies to. Tex. R. Civ. P. 193.1.

(2) Not verified. The response does not need to be verified. *See* Tex. R. Civ. P. 191.3(a).

(3) Signed. The response must be signed by the attorney (or party when pro se). Tex. R. Civ. P. 191.3(a).

2. Time to respond. Generally, a party has 30 days after the date of service of the request for documents to respond. Tex. R. Civ. P. 196.2(a); *see* **Schein v. American Rest. Grp.**, 852 S.W.2d 496, 497 n.2 (Tex.1993). When service is by mail or fax, the answering party has an additional 3 days (if mailed) or 1 day (if faxed after 5:00 p.m.) to respond. *See* Tex. R.

Civ. P. 21a(b)(2), (c). See "Deadline to serve response," ch. 6-A, §14.1. The party must file its answers and objections and assert its privileges by the deadline; if not, the party waives its objections and privileges. See "Waiver of objections & privileges," ch. 6-A, §25.3. Once a party's objections and privileges are waived, the party must produce the requested documents. To extend the time to respond, see "Extending time to respond to discovery," ch. 6-A, §15.

2021 Rule Amendments

In 2020, the Supreme Court approved significant amendments to TRCP 192.2 and 194. See Tex.Sup.Ct. Order, Misc. Docket No. 20-9153 (eff. Jan. 1, 2021). Under the amendments, a party generally cannot serve discovery requests on another party until after that party's initial disclosures now required under TRCP 194 are due. See Tex. R. Civ. P. 192.2(a). These initial disclosures are generally due within 30 days after the filing of the first answer or general appearance. Tex. R. Civ. P. 194.2(a). Because discovery must now be served after the first answer or general appearance, TRCP 196 was amended to eliminate the scenario where a defendant was served with requests for production before its answer was due and thus had 50 days to respond. See Tex. R. Civ. P. 196.2(a). The amendments apply to cases filed on or after January 1, 2021, except those filed in justice court. Tex.Sup.Ct. Order, Misc. Docket No. 20-9153 (eff. Jan. 1, 2021). For a detailed discussion of required disclosures under the 2021 amendments, see "Required disclosures—Cases filed on or after 1-1-21," ch. 6-E, §3.

3. Not filed. The written response and the documents produced in response to the request are not filed with the court. Tex. R. Civ. P. 191.4(a). The documents should be kept by the party that requested their production. Other parties should be provided with copies of the documents.

4. Costs. The cost of producing materials is the responsibility of the responding party. Tex. R. Civ. P. 196.6. The cost of inspecting, sampling, testing, photographing, or copying materials is the responsibility of the requesting party. *Id.*; **Limas v. De Delgado**, 770 S.W.2d 953, 954 (Tex.App.—El Paso 1989, no writ). For good cause, the court can order that costs be apportioned differently than provided for in TRCP 196.6. Tex. R. Civ. P. 196.6.

§3.4 Contents of response. See **O'Connor's Texas Civil Forms**, FORM 6I:3 (2020 ed.). For each item or category of items, the responding party must make one of the following responses:

1. Party will comply. When complying with the request, the party should state that the production, inspection, or other requested action will be permitted as requested. Tex. R. Civ. P. 196.2(b)(1).

(1) Production of things. A party must produce all the documents and things that are requested, discoverable, in its possession (actual or constructive), and not subject to an objection. Tex. R. Civ. P. 196.3(a). See "Possession," ch. 6-A, §2.5.

(2) Organization of documents. Documents must be (1) produced as they are kept in the ordinary course of business or (2) organized and labeled to correspond to each particular request. Tex. R. Civ. P. 196.3(c); **Porretto v. Texas Gen. Land Office**, 448 S.W.3d 393, 403 (Tex.2014); *e.g.*, **Steenbergen v. Ford Motor Co.**, 814 S.W.2d 755, 758–59 (Tex.App.—Dallas 1991, writ denied) (D could produce documents as kept in course of business because P's request did not seek to organize or label according to categories). A party producing documents cannot collect the requested documents and shuffle them before turning them over to the requesting party.

(3) Electronic or magnetic data. When a request for production asks for electronic or magnetic information, the responding party must produce the data responsive to the request. Tex. R. Civ. P. 196.4. If the responding party cannot reasonably retrieve the requested information or produce it in the form requested, the responding party must object to the request. *Id.*; *see* Tex. R. Civ. P. 193.2(b).

2. Party objects to procedure to respond. When a party intends to comply with the request but objects to the time, place, or method identified in the request for compliance, the response should state both the objection and the solution.

(1) Objection to time & place. When a party objects to the time or place of production or inspection, the response should state that it would be more reasonable to produce or inspect the documents at a different time or place and de-

scribe the suggested terms (e.g., at the corporate office instead of the attorney's office, or produce all copies instead of permitting inspection first). Tex. R. Civ. P. 193.2(b), 196.2(b)(3). The responding party must then comply with that time and place without further request or order. Tex. R. Civ. P. 193.2(b).

(2) Objection to method of compliance. When a party objects to a request for production because it asks the party to produce a large number of documents, the responding party may notify the requesting party in its response that the documents are available in its office for inspection and copying. *See* **Overall v. Southwestern Bell Yellow Pages, Inc.**, 869 S.W.2d 629, 631 (Tex.App.—Houston [14th Dist.] 1994, no writ). When a request for production asks for a manageable number of documents, the responding party should attach them to the response. *See, e.g., id.* (documents excluded from trial for failure to provide copies with response).

3. Party objects to number of requests. A party can object when another party serves more than 15 written requests for production in a Level 1 case. *See* Tex. R. Civ. P. 190.2(b)(4). See "Number of requests," ch. 6-I, §3.1.4.

4. Party objects to production. When objecting to the production of documents and things, the objection must be in writing, must be contained either in the response or in a separate document, and must provide specific reasons why the discovery should not be permitted. Tex. R. Civ. P. 193.2(a). A party's objections must be supported by a good-faith factual or legal basis. Tex. R. Civ. P. 193.2(c). A party must comply with the requests to which it does not object. Tex. R. Civ. P. 193.2(b) & cmt. 2. See "Burden to partially comply," ch. 6-A, §18.10.

(1) Overbroad. A party can object when a request asks for "all documents" without limiting the request in time, place, or subject matter, can refuse to comply with it entirely, or can file a motion for protective order. *See* Tex. R. Civ. P. 192.6(a), 193 cmt. 2. See "Overbroad," ch. 6-A, §20.1.3; **O'Connor's Texas Civil Forms**, FORMS 6A:9 to 6A:10 (2020 ed.).

(2) Destruction by testing. A party can object when testing or sampling the thing to be produced will destroy or materially alter the condition of it. *See* Tex. R. Civ. P. 196.5; **General Motors Corp. v. Tanner**, 892 S.W.2d 862, 863–64 (Tex.1995) (applying former TRCP 167(1)(g); must support objection with evidence).

(3) Other objections. For other objections, see "Valid objections to discovery requests," ch. 6-A, §19.1; "Grounds to limit scope of discovery," ch. 6-A, §20.1.

5. Party asserts privileges. When asserting privileges in response to the request, the party must file a withholding statement to comply with TRCP 193.3. Tex. R. Civ. P. 193.2(f); *see* Tex. R. Civ. P. 196.2(b). See "Asserting privileges," ch. 6-A, §18.2. A party must comply with the requests to which it does not assert a privilege. Tex. R. Civ. P. 193.2(b) & cmt. 2. See "Burden to partially comply," ch. 6-A, §18.10.

6. Party unable to locate things. If a party is unable to locate documents or things responsive to the request, it must state that after a diligent search no items were identified that are responsive to the request. Tex. R. Civ. P. 196.2(b)(4).

§3.5 Hearing on objections & privileges. Generally, the burden to secure a hearing and a ruling on objections or assertions of privileges is on the party seeking discovery. See "Burden to secure hearing & ruling," ch. 6-A, §18.6. The burden to produce evidence is on the party objecting to discovery. See "Burden to provide evidence," ch. 6-A, §18.7.

§3.6 Supplementing or amending responses. When a party discovers additional information after responding to discovery, the party must supplement or amend its response. Tex. R. Civ. P. 193.5 (duty to supplement), Tex. R. Civ. P. 193.6 (sanctions for failure to supplement). For the substance of what additional information to provide, see "Supplementing discovery responses," ch. 6-A, §17.

1. Time to serve supplemental or amended response. A party should serve a supplemental or amended response to requests for production reasonably promptly after the party discovers the need for such a response. Tex. R. Civ. P. 193.5(b).

2. Form of response. Supplemental or amended responses must be made in the same form as the original responses. Tex. R. Civ. P. 193.5(b).

§4. Securing things from a party about a nonparty

§4.1 Nonparty information. When a party seeks information from another party about a nonparty, the production can affect the privacy interests of the nonparty. **In re Temple-Inland, Inc.**, 8 S.W.3d 459, 462–63 (Tex.App.—Beaumont

2000, orig. proceeding). The court can restrict the dissemination of discoverable information about nonparties, even when no privilege is involved. *See, e.g., id.* (court limited dissemination of list of former employees that ascribed criminal and other embarrassing conduct to them). For a nonparty's medical records in the possession of a party, see "Request to party for nonparty's medical records," ch. 6-J, §4.

§4.2 Who can object. Any person affected by the discovery request can object to it—including other parties and nonparties. Tex. R. Civ. P. 192.6(a).

§5. Securing things from a nonparty

To secure documents and other tangible things from a nonparty, the party serves a notice to produce or appear and a discovery subpoena. Tex. R. Civ. P. 205.3(a); *see* Tex. R. Civ. P. 196 cmt. 6. A party is not required to file a motion for production to obtain documents from a nonparty in an ongoing suit. Tex. R. Civ. P. 205 cmt. By comparison, a party is required to file a motion and secure a court order to depose a nonparty before suit under TRCP 202, to secure a physical or mental examination of a nonparty under TRCP 204, and to secure entry on a nonparty's land under TRCP 196.7. Tex. R. Civ. P. 205.1.

§5.1 Notice.

1. Contents of notice.

(1) For documents only. When a nonparty is required to produce documents or things without appearing for a deposition, the notice of production must provide: (1) the name of the person from whom production is sought, (2) a reasonable time and place for production, (3) a description of the items to be produced, and (4) if testing or sampling is requested, information about the means, manner, and procedure. Tex. R. Civ. P. 205.3(b).

(2) For documents at deposition. When a nonparty is required to produce documents at an oral deposition, the notice for the deposition must comply with TRCP 199.2. Tex. R. Civ. P. 205.1(c). See "Contents of notice," ch. 6-F, §4.5.1.

2. Filing. Discovery notices served on nonparties must be filed with the clerk. Tex. R. Civ. P. 191.4(b)(1).

§5.2 Discovery subpoena. The subpoena is the instrument that compels a nonparty to comply with a notice for discovery. *See* **St. Luke's Episcopal Hosp. v. Garcia**, 928 S.W.2d 307, 312 (Tex.App.—Houston [14th Dist.] 1996, orig. proceeding). For general information about subpoenas, see "Subpoenas," ch. 1-L, §1 et seq. The scope of production of a discovery subpoena is governed by TRCP 192.3. *See* **Martin v. Khoury**, 843 S.W.2d 163, 166 (Tex.App.—Texarkana 1992, orig. proceeding) (under former TRCP 166b). A subpoena cannot be used to secure information that is not discoverable by other forms of discovery requests. *See* Tex. R. Civ. P. 176.3(b) (subpoena cannot be used to circumvent discovery rules); **Prestige Ford Co. v. Gilmore**, 56 S.W.3d 73, 80 (Tex.App.—Houston [14th Dist.] 2001, pet. denied) (same).

1. Types of discovery subpoenas. There are three types of discovery subpoenas.

(1) To produce. A nonparty may be subpoenaed to produce documents or things without being required to appear for a deposition. Tex. R. Civ. P. 176.6(c), 205.3(a). When the subpoena commands a witness to produce documents or other things but not to give testimony, the witness does not need to appear in person at the time and place of production. Tex. R. Civ. P. 176.6(c).

(2) To appear. A nonparty may be subpoenaed to appear for a deposition without producing any documents. Tex. R. Civ. P. 205.1(a), (b). The discovery subpoena should direct the witness to appear for deposition at the time and place stated in the notice of deposition. Tex. R. Civ. P. 176.1(e), 176.2.

(3) To appear & produce. A nonparty may be subpoenaed to appear for a deposition and produce documents or other things. Tex. R. Civ. P. 205.1(c); *see, e.g.,* **In re Amaya**, 34 S.W.3d 354, 356–57 (Tex.App.—Waco 2001, orig. proceeding) (nonparty could not refuse to appear and produce documents); *see also* Tex. R. Civ. P. 205.3(a) (production of documents and things without deposition). See "Documents from nonparties," ch. 6-F, §4.5.6(2).

2. Filing. Subpoenas required to be served on nonparties must be filed with the clerk. Tex. R. Civ. P. 191.4(b)(1).

§5.3 Time to serve notice & subpoena. The notice (of either intent to take the nonparty's deposition or intent to compel the nonparty to produce documents and things, or both) and the subpoena compelling the nonparty to comply must be served on the nonparty and the other parties. Tex. R. Civ. P. 205.2. See chart 6-9 under "Certificate of service," ch. 6-F, §4.5.8.

1. Nonparty documents without deposition. To compel the production of documents from a nonparty without requiring the nonparty to appear for an oral deposition, the notice to produce and the subpoena must be served a reasonable time before the response is due. Tex. R. Civ. P. 205.3(a). The notice to produce must be served at least ten days before service of the subpoena. Tex. R. Civ. P. 205.2. The ten-day gap between service of the notice and the subpoena gives anyone (party or nonparty) who objects to the production of the documents time to move for a protective order before the nonparty produces the documents.

2. Nonparty deposition with documents. To compel the production of documents from a nonparty at a deposition, the notice of deposition and the subpoena must be served a reasonable time before the deposition. See "Nonparty deposition with documents," ch. 6-F, §4.5.2(1)(b).

3. Nonparty deposition without documents. To compel the appearance of a nonparty at a deposition without requiring the production of documents, the notice of deposition and the subpoena must be served a reasonable time before the deposition; the subpoena cannot be served before the notice. See "Nonparty deposition without documents," ch. 6-F, §4.5.2(2)(b).

§5.4 Nonparty's response to discovery subpoena. A nonparty must respond to the discovery subpoena and notice as required by TRCP 176.6. Tex. R. Civ. P. 205.3(d). The rules governing a nonparty's response to a notice and subpoena to produce documents are similar to the rules governing a party's response to a request for production. See "Procedure to respond," ch. 6-I, §3.3.

1. No appearance necessary. A nonparty requested to produce documents or other things is not required to appear in person at the time and place of production unless the person is also subpoenaed to attend and give testimony. Tex. R. Civ. P. 176.6(c).

2. Organization of documents. A nonparty must produce the documents either (1) as they are kept in the ordinary course of business, or (2) organized and labeled to correspond to each request. Tex. R. Civ. P. 176.6(c). See "Organization of documents," ch. 6-I, §3.4.1(2).

§5.5 Challenging nonparty discovery subpoena. See "Objecting to trial & discovery subpoenas," ch. 1-L, §4; **O'Connor's Texas Civil Forms**, FORMS 6A:13 to 6A:14 (2020 ed.).

1. Who can challenge. The subpoena can be challenged by the person subpoenaed, a party to the suit, or any person affected by the subpoena. *See* Tex. R. Civ. P. 176.6(d), (e).

2. Deadline to challenge. Any challenge to the subpoena must be made before the time specified for compliance in the subpoena. Tex. R. Civ. P. 176.6(d), (e).

3. How to challenge subpoena.

(1) Objections & privileges. A person who has been subpoenaed may make written objections to production or assert privileges by withholding documents under TRCP 193.3. *See* Tex. R. Civ. P. 176.6(c), (d). See "Types of challenges," ch. 1-L, §4.3; "Asserting privileges," ch. 6-A, §18.2.

(2) Motion for protective order. A person who has been subpoenaed, a party, or any person affected by the discovery subpoena may file a motion for protective order under TRCP 192.6. Tex. R. Civ. P. 176.6(e). The person subpoenaed, the parties, and persons affected by the subpoena all have an independent right to challenge the subpoena by a motion for protective order—that is, one person's challenge to the subpoena will not affect another person's right to bring her own challenge. *See, e.g.*, **In re Garza**, 544 S.W.3d 836, 841–42 (Tex.2018) (nonparty custodians of records were permitted to seek protection from discovery subpoena even though P had already sought and been denied protection from same request). See "Filing motion for protective order or objection," ch. 1-L, §4.3.1; "Motion for protective order," ch. 6-A, §20.

4. Effect of challenge to discovery.

(1) Objection to time & place. When a nonparty or party objects to the time or place of a nonparty's oral deposition by filing a motion for protection or a motion to quash within three business days after service of the notice of deposition, the motion stays the deposition until the motion can be decided by the court. Tex. R. Civ. P. 199.4.

(2) Other objections by nonparty. When the nonparty challenges the subpoena by filing objections, assertions of privileges, or a motion for protection, the nonparty should produce all requested information not subject to its challenges. *See* Tex. R. Civ. P. 192.6(a), (b).

(3) Other objections by parties & third persons. When a party or a third person affected by the discovery challenges the discovery sought from a nonparty by filing a motion for protection or a motion to quash, the motion does not prevent the nonparty from producing the discovery. *See* Tex. R. Civ. P. 176.6(e) (although subpoenaed witness "need not" produce documents for which protection is sought, rule does not prohibit production). The party or affected person must secure a court order staying production of the discovery, or the nonparty may produce it. See "On objections by other persons," ch. 6-I, §5.5.5(2).

5. Burden to get ruling.

(1) On objection by nonparty. The burden to get a ruling on a nonparty's objections is on the party that issued the subpoena. Although TRCP 176.6(d) and (e) require the subpoenaed person to object to a discovery subpoena or seek a protective order before the time specified for compliance, they do not require the witness to get a ruling before the time for compliance. *See* **Olinger v. Curry**, 926 S.W.2d 832, 835 (Tex.App.—Fort Worth 1996, orig. proceeding). The party who issued the subpoena may move for an order anytime after an objection is made or a motion for protection is filed. Tex. R. Civ. P. 176.6(d), (e).

(2) On objections by other persons. The burden to get a ruling on objections filed by a party or third person affected by the subpoena is on the party or third person that filed the motion objecting to production. The reason the burden is on the party or third person is that, unless prevented by a court order, a nonparty may produce documents even when a motion for protection was filed. *See* Tex. R. Civ. P. 176.6(e) (rule does not prohibit subpoenaed witness from producing after objection filed).

6. Ruling on objections. The court may sustain objections, grant a protective order, or impose reasonable conditions on compliance with a subpoena, including compensation to the nonparty for undue hardship. *See* Tex. R. Civ. P. 176.7.

§5.6 Cost of document production. The party who issues the subpoena requiring production of documents or other things must reimburse the nonparty for the reasonable costs of production. Tex. R. Civ. P. 205.3(f); **Wichita Cty. v. Environmental Eng'g & Geotechnics, Inc.**, 576 S.W.3d 851, 859 (Tex.App.—Austin 2019, no pet.). The nonparty should present sufficient evidence supporting the amount and reasonableness of the costs it incurred. *See* **Wichita Cty.**, 576 S.W.3d at 861.

§5.7 Copies for other parties. The party who issued the subpoena must make the produced materials available to the other parties for inspection on reasonable notice. Tex. R. Civ. P. 205.3(e). At their own expense, the other parties may obtain copies of the documents from the party who issued the subpoena. *Id.*

§6. Compelling production & sanctions

§6.1 Motion to compel & for sanctions. If the party or nonparty responding to the request for or notice of production refuses to produce documents, the party requesting documents can move to compel production and move for sanctions or an order of contempt. *See* Tex. R. Civ. P. 215.2. See "Motion to compel discovery," ch. 6-A, §22; "Motion for discovery sanctions," ch. 6-A, §23.

1. Sanctions against party. When a party refuses to produce a properly requested document, the court can exclude the document, limit the testimony about the document or the issue, or impose any other sanction listed in TRCP 215.2(b). *See, e.g.*, **Porretto v. Texas Gen. Land Office**, 448 S.W.3d 393, 402–03 (Tex.2014) (no abuse of discretion to award attorney fees and expenses to P when D produced only some documents requested by P, D acknowledged that there were other responsive documents but stated that it would not search for them without further specification, and D did not respond to motion for sanctions). See "Sanctions for discovery abuse," ch. 5-K, §7.1.

2. Sanctions against nonparty. Contempt is the only sanction the court may impose on a nonparty for not complying with an order under TRCP 205.3. *See* Tex. R. Civ. P. 176.8(a), 215.2(a), (c). See "Discovery abuse," ch. 5-K, §4.4.1.

§6.2 Other remedies. When the party requesting documents believes the responding party has overlooked or ignored relevant documents in responding to the request, the requesting party can (1) ask the court to appoint a master, (2) take depositions, or (3) send written interrogatories. *See* **Texaco, Inc. v. Dominguez**, 812 S.W.2d 451, 456 (Tex.App.—San Antonio 1991, orig. proceeding). The party cannot ask the court for permission to go through the other party's files. *Id.* at 455–56.

§7. Securing documents from a financial institution

§7.1 Exclusive discovery procedure. To secure a customer's records from a bank or other financial institution, a party must comply with Finance Code §59.006, which is the exclusive method to compel discovery of a customer's records. Tex. Fin. Code §59.006(a); *see* Tex. Civ. Prac. & Rem. Code §30.007; **Enviro Prot., Inc. v. National Bank**, 989 S.W.2d 454, 455 (Tex.App.—El Paso 1999, no pet.) (applying provisions from former CPRC §30.007).

§7.2 Definitions under Finance Code §59.001.

1. Financial institution. A "financial institution" is defined as any of the following, but does not include an entity organized under the laws of another state or under federal law that has its main office in another state and does not maintain a branch or other office in Texas. Tex. Fin. Code §59.001(5).

(1) A bank, whether chartered under the laws of Texas, another state, the United States, or another country. Tex. Fin. Code §201.101(1)(A).

(2) A savings-and-loan association chartered under Finance Code chapter 62 or similar laws of another state. Tex. Fin. Code §201.101(1)(B).

(3) A federal savings-and-loan association, federal savings bank, federal credit union, or credit union chartered under Finance Code chapter 122 or similar laws of another state. Tex. Fin. Code §201.101(1)(C), (1)(D).

(4) A trust company chartered under the laws of Texas or another state. Tex. Fin. Code §201.101(1)(E).

2. Record. "Record" means financial or other customer information maintained by a financial institution. Tex. Fin. Code §59.001(7).

3. Record request. "Record request" means a valid and enforceable subpoena, request for production, or other instrument issued under authority of a tribunal that compels production of a customer record. Tex. Fin. Code §59.001(8).

4. Tribunal. "Tribunal" means a court or other adjudicatory tribunal with jurisdiction to issue a request for records, including a government agency exercising adjudicatory functions and an alternative-dispute-resolution mechanism, voluntary or required, under which a party may compel the production of records. Tex. Fin. Code §59.001(10).

§7.3 Procedure to secure party-customer records.

1. Requesting records. The party requesting records from a financial institution about one of its customers who is a party to the suit must do the following:

(1) Serve the bank with a record request that gives the financial institution at least 24 days to comply with the request. Tex. Fin. Code §59.006(b)(1); *see, e.g.*, **Enviro Prot., Inc. v. National Bank**, 989 S.W.2d 454, 456 (Tex.App.—El Paso 1999, no pet.) (subpoena to produce records from bank not valid because it was not issued with 24 days' notice).

(2) Pay the financial institution's reasonable costs of complying with the record request or post a cost bond in an amount estimated by the financial institution to cover the costs before the financial institution complies with the record request. Tex. Fin. Code §59.006(b)(2). Costs include costs of reproduction, postage, research, delivery, and attorney fees. *Id.* If the requesting party has not paid the institution's costs or posted a cost bond, the court cannot order a financial institution to produce the requested record or find the financial institution in contempt of court for not producing the record. Tex. Fin. Code §59.006(b-1).

2. Objecting to request. The bank's customer has the burden of preventing or limiting the financial institution's compliance with a record request by seeking an appropriate remedy, including filing a motion to quash the record request or

a motion for protective order. Tex. Fin. Code §59.006(e); *see, e.g.*, **In re Estate of Gaines**, 262 S.W.3d 50, 54 (Tex.App.—Houston [14th Dist.] 2008, no pet.) (bank-account holder filed motion to quash subpoena). Any motion must be served on the financial institution and the requesting party before the date that compliance with the request is required. Tex. Fin. Code §59.006(e).

§7.4 Procedure to secure nonparty-customer records.

1. Requesting records. When the financial institution's customer is not a party to the proceeding in which the request was issued, the requesting party must do the following:

(1) Serve the financial institution with a record request. See "Requesting records," ch. 6-I, §7 3.1.

(2) Pay the financial institution's reasonable costs. See "Requesting records," ch. 6-I, §7.3.1.

(3) Give notice to the nonparty-customer stating the customer's rights under Finance Code §59.006(e), and serve a copy of the request on the customer under TRCP 21a. Tex. Fin. Code §59.006(c)(1).

(4) File with the tribunal and the financial institution a certificate of service indicating that the nonparty-customer was mailed or served with the notice and a copy of the record request. Tex. Fin. Code §59.006(c)(2).

(5) Request the nonparty-customer's written consent authorizing the financial institution to comply with the request. Tex. Fin. Code §59.006(c)(3).

2. Objecting to request. The nonparty-customer's procedure to object is to withhold written consent authorizing the financial institution to comply with the request. *See* Tex. Fin. Code §59.006(d) (sole means of obtaining access to records of nonparty is to file motion seeking in camera inspection).

3. Procedure to compel disclosure for nonparty-customer records.

(1) File motion for in camera review. When a nonparty-customer refuses to give consent or does not respond to the request under Finance Code §59.006(c)(3) by the date for compliance, the sole means of obtaining access to the requested record is for the requesting party to file a written motion seeking an in camera inspection of the requested record by the court. Tex. Fin. Code §59.006(d).

(2) Court inspection. In response to a motion for in camera inspection, the court may inspect the requested record to determine its relevance to the matter before the tribunal. Tex. Fin. Code §59.006(d). The tribunal may order redaction of parts of the record that it determines should not be produced. *Id.* The court must sign a protective order preventing the record from being disclosed to a person who is not a party to the proceeding and from being used for any purpose other than resolving the dispute before the court. *Id.*

§7.5 Deadline to produce.

1. Party-customer. The financial institution must produce the records of a party within 24 days after receiving the record request, as provided by Finance Code §59.006(b), unless the requesting party has not paid the financial institution's costs or posted a cost bond. *See* Tex. Fin. Code §59.006(b-1), (f)(1).

2. Nonparty-customer. The financial institution must produce the records of a nonparty before the later of the following:

(1) The 15th day after receiving a customer consent to disclose a record. Tex. Fin. Code §59.006(f)(2).

(2) If the nonparty-customer did not sign a consent on or before the date for compliance with the request, the 15th day after the date a court ordered production of the records. Tex. Fin. Code §59.006(f)(3).

§7.6 No interlocutory appeal. By statute, an order to quash or for protection or other remedy granted or denied by the tribunal under Finance Code §59.006(d) or (e) is not a final order and is not subject to an interlocutory appeal. Tex. Fin. Code §59.006(g).

§7.7 Exemptions. Finance Code §59.006 does not create a right of privacy in a customer record. Tex. Fin. Code §59.006(a); **Martin v. Darnell**, 960 S.W.2d 838, 843 (Tex.App.—Amarillo 1997, orig. proceeding) (citing statutory language from former CPRC §30.007(b)). Section 59.006 does not apply to and does not require or authorize a financial institution to give a customer notice of the following:

1. A demand or inquiry from a state or federal government agency authorized by law to conduct an examination of the financial institution. Tex. Fin. Code §59.006(a)(1).

2. A record request from a state or federal government agency or instrumentality under statutory or administrative authority that provides for, or is accompanied by, a specific mechanism for discovery and protection of a financial institution's customer record, including a record request from a federal agency subject to the Right to Financial Privacy Act of 1978, 12 U.S.C. §3401 et seq., as amended, or from the IRS under §1205, Internal Revenue Code of 1986. Tex. Fin. Code §59.006(a)(2).

3. A record request from or report to a government agency arising from (1) the investigation or prosecution of a criminal offense, (2) the investigation of alleged abuse, neglect, or exploitation of an elderly or person with a disability in accordance with Human Resources Code chapter 48, or (3) the assessment for or provision of guardianship services under Human Resources Code chapter 161, subchapter E. Tex. Fin. Code §59.006(a)(3).

4. A record request in connection with a garnishment proceeding in which the financial institution is the garnishee and the customer is the debtor. Tex. Fin. Code §59.006(a)(4).

5. A record request by a duly appointed receiver for the customer. Tex. Fin. Code §59.006(a)(5).

6. An investigative demand or inquiry from a state legislative investigating committee. Tex. Fin. Code §59.006(a)(6).

7. An investigative demand or inquiry from the Texas Attorney General as authorized by law other than the procedural law governing discovery in civil cases. Tex. Fin. Code §59.006(a)(7).

8. The voluntary use or disclosure of a record by a financial institution subject to other applicable state or federal law. Tex. Fin. Code §59.006(a)(8).

9. A record request in connection with an investigation conducted under Estates Code §§1054.151, 1054.152, or 1102.001. Tex. Fin. Code §59.006(a)(9).

§8. Using requested documents

§8.1 Offering documents. To use a document produced in response to a request for or notice of production, the party offering the document must prove its authenticity and its admissibility.

1. Self-authenticating. A party's production of a document in response to written discovery authenticates the document for use against that party in any pretrial proceeding or at trial, unless the producing party timely objects to the document's authenticity. Tex. R. Civ. P. 193.7. See "Objection to authenticity," ch. 6-I, §8.3.1. Authentication, however, does not establish admissibility. Tex. R. Civ. P. 193 cmt. 7; *see* Tex. R. Evid. 901(a).

2. Admissibility. To use a document produced in response to a request for or notice of production, the party offering the document must prove it is admissible, lay the proper predicate for its admission, offer it into evidence, and get the court to rule on its admissibility. *See* Tex. R. Evid. 104, 105, 402. See "Introducing Evidence," ch. 8-C, §1 et seq. Just because a document was produced by the other party in discovery does not mean the document is admissible. For example, although an insurance policy is discoverable, it is generally not admissible. *See* Tex. R. Evid. 411.

§8.2 Using the response. When relevant to the suit, a party may read into evidence the other party's response to the request for documents. *See, e.g.,* **Wal-Mart Stores v. Cordova**, 856 S.W.2d 768, 772 (Tex.App.—El Paso 1993, writ denied) (on rebuttal, P read into evidence D's response that D had no safety manual at the time of the accident).

§8.3 Objections to documents.

1. Objection to authenticity. A party may object, either in writing or on the record, to the authenticity of all or part of a document it produced in discovery. Tex. R. Civ. P. 193.7. The objection must be made within ten days after the party

had actual notice the document would be used. *Id.* In appropriate circumstances, the court can alter the ten-day period. Tex R. Civ. P. 193 cmt. 7. The objection to authenticity must specify the basis for the objection and must have a good-faith factual and legal basis. Tex R. Civ. P. 193.7. An objection made to the authenticity of part of a document does not affect the authenticity of the remainder. *Id.* Once an objection is made, the court must permit the party attempting to use the document a reasonable opportunity to establish its authenticity. *Id.*

Practice Tip

To avoid complications about authenticity at trial, a party should ask the court to require in its pretrial order that the parties identify all the documents they intend to offer at trial. This will trigger the obligation to object to authenticity and the ability to "snap back" an inadvertently produced privileged document. Tex. R. Civ. P. 193 cmt. 7; see Tex. R. Civ. P. 193.3(d). See "Exhibits," ch. 5-A, §3.9.3.

2. Other objections to documents. To object to a document produced in response to a request for or notice of production, see "Objecting to Evidence," ch. 8-D, §1 et seq.

§9. Review

§9.1 Record. If the court rules that documents presented for an in camera inspection under seal are not discoverable, the party that was denied discovery of the documents must make sure the documents are transferred under seal to the appellate court to permit the appellate court to evaluate them. **Pope v. Stephenson**, 787 S.W.2d 953, 954 (Tex.1990).

§9.2 Appeal or mandamus? See "Review of discovery orders," ch. 6-A, §26.

J. Medical Records

§1. General

§1.1 Rules. Tex. R. Civ. P. 194.2(b)(10), (11), 204; Tex. R. Evid. 509(e)(4), 510(d)(5). See Tex. Occ. Code §159.002(b); Tex. Health & Safety Code §§241.151(2), 241.152.

§1.2 Purpose. The discovery rules provide two procedures specific to the discovery of medical records: required disclosures and a motion to examine the person. The parties may also use all the other traditional methods of discovery: a request for production, a notice of deposition with a notice to the party to bring the medical records, and a deposition on written questions of a records custodian.

§1.3 Forms. See **O'Connor's Texas Civil Forms**, FORMS 6J:1 et seq. (2020 ed.).

§1.4 Other references. Griesel, *The "New" Texas Discovery Rules: Three Years Later*, Advanced Evidence & Discovery Course, State Bar of Texas CLE, ch. 2, §XVIII (2002); Fineberg & Shore, *Discovery Update*, Advanced Civil Trial Course, State Bar of Texas CLE, ch. 1, §IV.A.2 (2001).

§2. Scope

A party is entitled to discover the medical records of any person who is claiming physical or mental injury arising from the event that is the subject of the suit. Tex. R. Civ. P. 194.2(b)(10). See "Certain physician-patient information," ch. 6-B, §2.18; "Certain mental-health information," ch. 6-B, §2.19; "Certain medical matters under TRCP 204," ch. 6-B, §2.20; "Certain medical requests under Family Code," ch. 6-B, §2.21; "Certain medical records under HIPAA," ch. 6-B, §2.22; "Certain health-care information from hospital," ch. 6-B, §2.23.

§3. Disclosure of party's medical records or authorization

§3.1 Disclosure of medical records or for authorization. In a suit alleging physical or mental injury and damages, the injured party is required to either produce all relevant medical records and bills or furnish an authorization permitting the disclosure of those medical records. Tex. R. Civ. P. 194.2(b)(10). See "Medical records," ch. 6-E, §2.2.2(1)(h). For cases filed on or after January 1, 2021, TRCP 194 requires automatic disclosure of this information without a discovery request from the other party. Tex. R. Civ. P. 194.2(b)(10). See "Medical records," ch. 6-E, §3.3.2(8).

2021 Rule Amendments

In 2020, the Supreme Court approved significant amendments to TRCP 194. See Tex.Sup.Ct. Order, Misc. Docket No. 20-9153 (eff. Jan. 1, 2021). Under the amendments, a party is now required to disclose certain information, including medical records, without a discovery request from the other party. See Tex. R. Civ. P. 194.2(b). The amendments apply to cases filed on or after January 1, 2021, except those filed in justice court. Tex.Sup.Ct. Order, Misc. Docket No. 20-9153 (eff. Jan. 1, 2021). For cases filed before January 1, 2021, a party may still ask for this information using a request for disclosure. See Tex. R. Civ. P. 194.2(j), (k) (pre-1-1-21 version). See "Disclosures," ch. 6-E, §1 et seq.

---

§3.2 Medical authorization.

1. Disclosure from hospital. A party may serve a written request for the injured party to sign a medical authorization permitting a hospital to disclose the party's medical records. *See* Tex. Health & Safety Code §241.152. A medical authorization is valid for 180 days after the date it is signed, unless it provides otherwise or is revoked. Tex. Health & Safety Code §241.152(c), (d).

(1) Requirements. An authorization must (1) be in writing, (2) be dated and signed by the patient or legal representative, (3) identify the information to be disclosed, (4) describe the purpose of the requested disclosure, (5) identify the person or entity authorized to make the requested disclosure, (6) identify the person or entity to whom the information is to be disclosed, (7) include the expiration date or expiration event of the authorization, and (8) be contained in a separate

document from the one that contains the consent to medical treatment obtained from the patient. *See* 45 C.F.R §164.508(b), (c) (authorizations generally); Tex. Health & Safety Code §241.152(b) (authorization for hospital to disclose information).

Note

Federal law requires that all medical authorizations contain statements that place the patient or legal representative on notice of (1) her right to revoke the authorization in writing, (2) the ability or inability to condition treatment, payment, enrollment, or eligibility for benefits on the authorization, and (3) the potential for the disclosed information to be redisclosed and no longer protected. 45 C.F.R §164.508(c)(2). These notice statements are designed to cover authorizations requested for a variety of reasons, not just for the disclosure of medical records. Although they are not applicable to every situation, they should be included in all authorizations nonetheless.

(2) Providing records. The hospital or its agent must provide copies of the medical records within 15 days after the request and payment for reasonable fees are received. Tex. Health & Safety Code §241.154(a). The hospital or its agent is permitted to charge fees as set out in Health & Safety Code §241.154(b).

2. Disclosure from other health-care provider or entity. A party may serve a written request for the injured party to sign a medical authorization permitting a health-care provider or entity other than a hospital to disclose the party's medical records. *See* 45 C.F.R §164.508(a). The authorization must (1) be dated and signed by the patient or legal representative, and if signed by a representative, describe the representative's authority to act for the patient, (2) identify the information to be disclosed, (3) describe the purpose of the requested disclosure, (4) identify the person or entity authorized to make the requested disclosure, (5) identify the person or entity to whom the information is to be disclosed, and (6) include the expiration date or expiration event of the authorization. 45 C.F.R §164.508(c)(1). The authorization must also contain certain notice statements. See "Note," ch. 6-J, §3.2.1(1).

3. No ex parte discovery. A party should consider adding to a medical authorization a statement that the patient does not authorize any health-care professional to discuss the patient's treatment with anyone outside the presence of the patient's attorney. *See* **In re Trostel**, No. 05-00-02059-CV, 2001 WL 670490 (Tex.App.—Dallas 2001, orig. proceeding) (no pub.; 6-15-01). See "Discovery from treating doctors," ch. 6-D, §3.1.2(3).

§3.3 Health-care-liability claim. In a suit asserting a health-care-liability claim, the parties are entitled to obtain copies of the claimant's medical records from any other party in possession of the records within 45 days after receiving a written request for the records. Tex. Civ. Prac. & Rem. Code §74.051(d).

§3.4 Order compelling production. An order compelling the release of medical records must be restricted to maintain the confidentiality of records not relevant to the underlying suit. **Groves v. Gabriel**, 874 S.W.2d 660, 661 (Tex.1994); *see* Tex. R. Civ. P. 196.1(c)(3). The order must meet the standard set out in **Mutter v. Wood**, 744 S.W.2d 600, 601 (Tex.1988). Depending on the circumstances, **Mutter** may require a time limitation on disclosure. **Groves**, 874 S.W.2d at 661.

§4. Request to party for nonparty's medical records

§4.1 Service on nonparty. When a party requests that another party produce a nonparty's medical records, the requesting party must serve the nonparty with the request for production under TRCP 21a unless (1) the nonparty signed a release that is effective for the requesting party, (2) the identity of the nonparty will not be disclosed, either directly or indirectly, by production of the records, or (3) the court orders that service is not required based on good cause. Tex. R. Civ. P. 196.1(c)(1), (c)(2), 205.3(c); *see also* **In re Columbia Valley Reg'l Med. Ctr.**, 41 S.W.3d 797, 800–02 (Tex.App.—Corpus Christi 2001, orig. proceeding) (redaction of information does not defeat medical privilege).

§4.2 Confidentiality. Production of a nonparty's medical records under TRCP 196.1(c) is subject to the laws concerning confidentiality of medical and mental-health records. Tex. R. Civ. P. 196.1(c)(3); **In re Columbia Valley Reg'l Med. Ctr.**, 41 S.W.3d 797, 800 (Tex.App.—Corpus Christi 2001, orig. proceeding). See "Certain medical records under HIPAA," ch. 6-B, §2.22. TRCP 196.1(c) does not expand the scope of discovery of a nonparty's medical records. Tex. R. Civ. P. 196 cmt. 8; **In re Columbia Valley**, 41 S.W.3d at 800. See "Certain physician-patient information," ch. 6-B, §2.18; "Physician-patient privilege," ch. 6-B, §3.10.

§5. Motion to examine the person

§5.1 Motion. To request a mental or physical examination under TRCP 204.1, the movant must file a motion for an order compelling the examination of the person. See **O'Connor's Texas Civil Forms**, FORM 6J:2 (2020 ed.). The examination under TRCP 204.1 is limited to a party or a person in the custody or conservatorship or under the legal control of a party. Tex. R. Civ. P. 204.1(a).

1. Elements. The court may issue an order for examination only when (1) the movant shows good cause, and (2) either (a) the mental or physical condition of a party, or of a person under the legal control of a party, is in controversy, or (b) the party responding to the motion designated a psychologist as a testifying expert or disclosed a psychologist's records for possible use at trial. Tex. R. Civ. P. 204.1(c); **In re Transwestern Publ'g Co.**, 96 S.W.3d 501, 504–05 (Tex.App.—Fort Worth 2002, orig. proceeding).

(1) Good cause. There must be good cause for the examination. Tex. R. Civ. P. 204.1(c); **In re H.E.B. Grocery Co.**, 492 S.W.3d 300, 303 (Tex.2016); **Coates v. Whittington**, 758 S.W.2d 749, 753 (Tex.1988). "Good cause" requires a showing of each of the following components:

(a) The examination is relevant to the issues in controversy. **In re H.E.B. Grocery**, 492 S.W.3d at 303; **Coates**, 758 S.W.2d at 753. The movant must show that the examination will produce or is likely to lead to evidence relevant to the case. **In re H.E.B. Grocery**, 492 S.W.3d at 303; **Coates**, 758 S.W.2d at 753; *see, e.g.*, **In re Caballero**, 36 S.W.3d 143, 145 (Tex.App.—Corpus Christi 2000, orig. proceeding) (mandamus to compel physical examination denied because Ds were unable to articulate why examination would shed any light on P's condition before hysterectomy).

(b) There is a reasonable connection between the condition in controversy and the examination sought. **In re H.E.B. Grocery**, 492 S.W.3d at 303; **Coates**, 758 S.W.2d at 753.

(c) It is not possible to obtain the information sought through some other, less intrusive means. **In re H.E.B. Grocery**, 492 S.W.3d at 303; **Coates**, 758 S.W.2d at 753; *e.g.*, **In re Caballero**, 36 S.W.3d at 145 (mandamus denied because Ds did not show information was not available through less intrusive means).

(2) In controversy. The movant may show that the mental or physical condition (including the blood type) of a party, or of a person in the custody or conservatorship or under the legal control of a party, is in controversy. Tex. R. Civ. P. 204.1(c)(1); **In re Transwestern**, 96 S.W.3d at 504–05; *see* **In re H.E.B. Grocery**, 492 S.W.3d at 303; **Coates**, 758 S.W.2d at 750–51. The requirement for showing a condition is "in controversy" may be satisfied by a party's pleadings or by proof.

(a) Pleading "in controversy."

[1] Objecting party's pleadings. A condition may be in controversy if the party objecting to the examination made it an issue by pleading the condition in support of or in defense of its position. *See* **In re H.E.B. Grocery**, 492 S.W.3d at 304; *see, e.g.*, **Laub v. Millard**, 925 S.W.2d 363, 364–65 (Tex.App.—Houston [1st Dist.] 1996, orig. proceeding) (in suit to set aside gifts, P put her mental condition in controversy by pleading that statute of limitations was tolled because she was incompetent); **Crouch v. Gleason**, 875 S.W.2d 738, 740 (Tex.App.—Amarillo 1994, orig. proceeding) (in contract dispute, P put his mental condition in controversy by alleging that D exploited P's mental weakness); **Beamon v. O'Neill**, 865 S.W.2d 583, 586 (Tex.App.—Houston [14th Dist.] 1993, orig. proceeding) (in PI suit, P put his physical condition in controversy); **Exxon Corp. v. Starr**, 790 S.W.2d 883, 887 (Tex.App.—Tyler 1990, orig. proceeding) (P put his mental condition in controversy by claiming severe mental injury and designating psychological experts). A party's mental condition is not in controversy just because the party makes a routine request for damages for mental anguish or emotional distress. **Coates**, 758 S.W.2d at 753; *see, e.g.*, **In re Doe**, 22 S.W.3d 601, 607–08 (Tex.App.—Austin 2000, orig. proceeding) (court abused discretion in ordering mental examination in PI suit alleging sexual assault). A party's state of mind is not equivalent to a mental condition. *E.g.*, **Amis v. Ashworth**, 802 S.W.2d 374, 378 (Tex.App.—Tyler 1990, orig. proceeding) (mental-health professional not permitted to examine party based on pleadings of self-defense).

[2] Movant's pleadings. The condition may be in controversy if the movant put it in controversy by pleading the condition in support of or in defense of its position. *See, e.g.*, **Coates**, 758 S.W.2d at 752 (D's allegations of contributory negligence did not justify examination of P); **Spear v. Gayle**, 857 S.W.2d 122, 125 (Tex.App.—Houston [1st Dist.] 1993, orig. proceeding) (P's allegations that D was negligent in failing to seek help to cure psychosexual disorder did not put D's mental health in controversy).

(b) Proof of "in controversy." If the parties' pleadings did not put a party's mental or physical condition in controversy, the movant must provide evidence showing it is in controversy. *E.g.*, **Walsh v. Ferguson**, 712 S.W.2d 885, 887 (Tex.App.—Austin 1986, orig. proceeding) (examination not permitted in divorce because husband did not assert his mental or physical condition in support or in defense of his position, and wife did not offer any proof at hearing).

(3) Other party's psychologist. Instead of showing the condition is "in controversy," a movant may show the other party identified a psychologist as a testifying expert or disclosed a psychologist's records for possible use at trial. Tex. R. Civ. P. 204.1(c)(2). The movant must still demonstrate good cause. Tex. R. Civ. P. 204.1(c); **In re Transwestern**, 96 S.W.3d at 504–05. This provision does not apply in cases under Family Code title 2 or 5. Tex. R. Civ. P. 204.1(c)(2). See "In Family Code matters," ch. 6-J, §5.5.1(2).

2. Physician. The motion should suggest a physician or psychologist who will conduct the examination. *See* Tex. R. Civ. P. 204.1(d) (order must identify person to perform examination); **Employers Mut. Cas. Co. v. Street**, 702 S.W.2d 779, 780–81 (Tex.App.—Fort Worth 1986, orig. proceeding) (moving party does not have absolute right to choose examining physician; trial court has discretion to choose neutral physician to conduct examination).

3. Time to serve motion for examination. For cases filed on or after January 1, 2021, a motion requesting a physical or mental examination cannot be served on a party until after that party's initial disclosures under TRCP 194 are due. *See* Tex. R. Civ. P. 190.2(b)(1), 190.3(b)(1), 192.2(a). See "Deadline," ch. 6-E, §3.3.1. For most methods of service (e.g., e-service, personal or commercial delivery), the deadline to serve the motion is 30 days before the end of the discovery period. *See* Tex. R. Civ. P. 204.1(a). See "Discovery periods," ch. 6-A, §8. But when service is by mail or fax, the motion should be served at least 33 days (if mailed) or 31 days (if faxed after 5:00 p.m.) before the end of the discovery period. *See* Tex. R. Civ. P. 21a(b)(2), (c). See "Deadline to serve response," ch. 6-A, §14.1.

2021 Rule Amendments

In 2020, the Supreme Court approved significant amendments to TRCP 190, 192.2, and 194. See Tex.Sup.Ct. Order, Misc. Docket No. 20-9153 (eff. Jan. 1, 2021). Under the amendments, a party generally cannot serve discovery requests on another party until after that party's initial disclosures now required under TRCP 194 are due. Tex. R. Civ. P. 192.2(a). See "Required disclosures—Cases filed on or after 1-1-21," ch. 6-E, §3. Initial disclosures are generally due within 30 days after the filing of the first answer or general appearance. Tex. R. Civ. P. 194.2(a). But if a party is served or otherwise joined after the filing of the first answer or general appearance, its initial disclosures are generally due within 30 days after being served or joined. Id. The amendments apply to cases filed on or after January 1, 2021, except those filed in justice court. Tex.Sup.Ct. Order, Misc. Docket No. 20-9153 (eff. Jan. 1, 2021). For cases filed before January 1, 2021, a party can serve a motion requesting a physical or mental examination anytime after suit is filed. See id. See "Discovery periods," ch. 6-A, §8; "Service with original pleadings," ch. 6-A, §13.2.

---

4. Notice. The party seeking the examination must give notice to all parties and to the person to be examined. Tex. R. Civ. P. 204.1(b).

5. Hearing request. The party seeking discovery must ask for and secure a hearing on the motion. *See* Tex. R. Civ. P. 204.1. If there is no hearing, the request for examination is waived.

§5.2 Response. A response is not required by TRCP 204; however, if a party chooses to respond, it should refute the movant's arguments and file the response before the hearing. See **O'Connor's Texas Civil Forms**, FORM 6J:3 (2020 ed.).

§5.3 Hearing. The court must conduct a hearing on a motion made under TRCP 204. At the hearing, the movant must present evidence. **Walsh v. Ferguson**, 712 S.W.2d 885, 887 (Tex.App.—Austin 1986, orig. proceeding). If the court grants the motion without receiving evidence at the hearing, the appellate court will find that the trial court abused its discretion and will reverse. *See id.*

§5.4 Order. The order must (1) be in writing, (2) identify the person to be examined, (3) specify the time, place, manner, conditions, and scope of the examination, and (4) identify the person or persons to make the examination. *See* Tex. R. Civ. P. 204.1(d). See **O'Connor's Texas Civil Forms**, FORM 6J:4 (2020 ed.).

§5.5 Examination.

1. Medical professional.

(1) In most cases. A qualified physician may conduct a mental or physical examination. Tex. R. Civ. P. 204.1(a)(1). A psychologist may conduct a mental examination if the party responding to the motion identified a psychologist as a testifying expert or disclosed a psychologist's records for possible use at trial. Tex. R. Civ. P. 204.1(c)(2). A vocational rehabilitation specialist is not a physician or a psychologist and cannot conduct an examination. *See* Tex. R. Civ. P. 204.5; **Moore v. Wood**, 809 S.W.2d 621, 624 (Tex.App.—Houston [1st Dist.] 1991, orig. proceeding) (construing former TRCP 167a(a)); *see also* Tex. R. Civ. P. 191 cmt. 1 (trial court may order, or parties may agree to, discovery methods other than those prescribed in the rules).

(2) In Family Code matters. In cases arising under title 2 or 5 of the Family Code, TRCP 204.4 provides that the court on a party's motion or on its own initiative may appoint the following:

(a) A psychiatrist or psychologist to make mental examinations of any children who are the subject of the suit, or of any other parties. Tex. R. Civ. P. 204.4(a).

(b) A nonphysician expert qualified in paternity testing to take blood and other bodily fluids to conduct tests in paternity disputes. Tex. R. Civ. P. 204.4(b); *see also* Tex. Fam. Code §§160.501 to 160.512 (genetic testing).

2. Attendance of attorney. The trial court has the discretion to permit or prohibit a party's attorney from attending the person's examination. **Simmons v. Thompson**, 900 S.W.2d 403, 404 (Tex.App.—Texarkana 1995, orig. proceeding) (physical examination). Because the medical professional conducting the examination is chosen by the adverse party, the party's attorney should probably be permitted to attend. *See id.* (Grant, J., dissenting).

§6. Using medical records

§6.1 Medical records. Medical records may be introduced into evidence by a custodian who testifies by affidavit or in person that the records are kept in the course of regularly conducted business activity. Tex. R. Evid. 803(6), (7), 902(10). See "Business record," ch. 8-C, §8.4.3(7); "Business records by affidavit," ch. 8-C, §8.4.4(1). To introduce an affidavit to prove past medical expenses, see "Affidavit for past expenses," ch. 8-C, §8.4.4(2).

§6.2 Physical or mental examination. If a physical or mental examination was ordered under TRCP 204, the parties may introduce the testimony of the doctor or medical professional who conducted the examination, either by deposition or as a live witness. *See* Tex. R. Civ. P. 204.2(b). For a discussion of the discoverability of mental-health information, see "Communication made during court-ordered examination," ch. 6-B, §2.19.4.

§6.3 Refusal to make a report. If a physician or psychologist does not make a report required by court order, the court may exclude the testimony if offered at trial. Tex. R. Civ. P. 204.2(a).

§6.4 Effect of no examination. If no examination is sought under TRCP 204, the party whose condition is in controversy cannot comment to the fact-finder that she was willing to submit to an examination or that the other party did not seek an examination. Tex. R. Civ. P. 204.3. The primary purpose of TRCP 204.3 is to ensure that the defendant is not penalized for not seeking a physical examination. **Parkway Hosp., Inc. v. Lee**, 946 S.W.2d 580, 585 (Tex.App.—Houston [14th Dist.] 1997, writ denied) (interpreting former TRCP 167a(c)), *disapproved on other grounds*, **Roberts v. Williamson**, 111 S.W.3d 113 (Tex.2003).

§7. Review

See "Review of discovery orders," ch. 6-A, §26.

K. Entry on Land

§1. General

§1.1 Rule. Tex. R. Civ. P. 196.7.

§1.2 Purpose. A request or motion for entry on land allows a party to gain entry to land to inspect, measure, survey, photograph, test, and sample the property or any designated object or operation on the property. Tex. R. Civ. P. 196.7(a).

§1.3 Forms. See **O'Connor's Texas Civil Forms**, FORMS 6K:1 et seq. (2020 ed.).

§1.4 Other references. Griesel, *The "New" Texas Discovery Rules: Three Years Later*, Advanced Evidence & Discovery Course, State Bar of Texas CLE, ch. 2, §X (2002).

§2. Scope

The scope of discovery for entry on land is governed by TRCP 196.7. The rules of discovery do not entitle a party to gain entry to another's property to reenact an event that is the basis of the suit. **Amis v. Ashworth**, 802 S.W.2d 374, 377 (Tex.App.—Tyler 1990, orig. proceeding); *see* **In re Goodyear Tire & Rubber Co.**, 437 S.W.3d 923, 929 (Tex.App.—Dallas 2014, orig. proceeding) (TRCP 196.7 does not allow for entry on property to create new evidence for demonstrative purposes). See "Scope of Discovery," ch. 6-B, §1 et seq.

§3. Request to enter land of a party

A party may gain entry on the land of another party by serving a request on all parties; a motion to the court is not required. Tex. R. Civ. P. 196.7(a)(1). A party is not entitled to trespass on another party's property to conduct an investigation or inspection without first serving a request under TRCP 196.7(a). **Schenck v. Ebby Halliday Real Estate, Inc.**, 803 S.W.2d 361, 372 (Tex.App.—Fort Worth 1990, no writ).

§3.1 Request. To gain entry on land of another party, the party must serve a request, which should include the following: (1) the identification of the land or other property in the possession or control of the party, (2) the particulars about the inspection—the time, place, manner, condition, and scope of the inspection, (3) a specific description of the desired means, manner, and procedure for testing or sampling (i.e., to inspect, measure, survey, photograph, test, or sample property), and (4) the identity of the person or persons who are to conduct the inspection, testing, or sampling. Tex. R. Civ. P. 196.7(a), (b). The test cannot materially alter or destroy the thing to be examined. Tex. R. Civ. P. 196.5; *see* **General Motors Corp. v. Tanner**, 892 S.W.2d 862, 863–64 (Tex.1995). See **O'Connor's Texas Civil Forms**, FORM 6K:1 (2020 ed.).

§3.2 Time to serve. For cases filed on or after January 1, 2021, a request for entry on land cannot be served on a party until after that party's initial disclosures under TRCP 194 are due. *See* Tex. R. Civ. P. 190.2(b)(1), 190.3(b)(1), 192.2(a). See "Deadline," ch. 6-E, §3.3.1. For most methods of service (e.g., e-service, personal or commercial delivery), the deadline to serve the request is 30 days before the end of the discovery period. *See* Tex. R. Civ. P. 196.7(a)(1). See "Discovery periods," ch. 6-A, §8. But when service is by mail or fax, the request should be served at least 33 days (if mailed) or 31 days (if faxed after 5:00 p.m.) before the end of the discovery period. *See* Tex. R. Civ. P. 21a(b)(2), (c). See "Deadline to serve response," ch. 6-A, §14.1.

2021 Rule Amendments

In 2020, the Supreme Court approved significant amendments to TRCP 190, 192.2, and 194. See Tex.Sup.Ct. Order, Misc. Docket No. 20-9153 (eff. Jan. 1, 2021). Under the amendments, a party generally cannot serve discovery requests on another party until after that party's initial disclosures now required under TRCP 194 are due. Tex. R. Civ. P. 192.2(a). See "Required disclosures—Cases filed on or after 1-1-21," ch. 6-E, §3. Initial disclosures are generally due within 30 days after the filing of the first answer or general appearance. Tex. R. Civ. P. 194.2(a). But if a party is served or otherwise joined after the filing of the first answer or general appearance, its initial disclosures are generally due within 30 days after being served or joined. Id. The amendments apply to cases filed on or after January 1,

2021, except those filed in justice court. Tex.Sup.Ct. Order, Misc. Docket No. 20-9153 (eff. Jan. 1, 2021). For cases filed before January 1, 2021, a party can serve a request for entry on land anytime after suit is filed. See id. See "Discovery periods," ch. 6-A, §8; "Service with original pleadings," ch. 6-A, §13.2

§3.3 Response.

1. Time to respond. Generally, a party has 30 days after the date of service of a request to enter land to respond to the request. Tex. R. Civ. P. 196.7(c)(1). When service is by mail or fax, the answering party has an additional 3 days (if mailed) or 1 day (if faxed after 5:00 p.m.) to respond. *See* Tex. R. Civ. P. 21a(b)(2), (c). See "Deadline to serve response," ch. 6-A, §14.1. To extend the time to respond, see "Extending time to respond to discovery," ch. 6-A, §15.

2021 Rule Amendments

In 2020, the Supreme Court approved significant amendments to TRCP 192.2 and 194. See Tex.Sup.Ct. Order, Misc. Docket No. 20-9153 (eff. Jan. 1, 2021). Under the amendments, a party generally cannot serve discovery requests on another party until after that party's initial disclosures now required under TRCP 194 are due. See Tex. R. Civ. P. 192.2(a). These initial disclosures are generally due within 30 days after the filing of the first answer or general appearance. Tex. R. Civ. P. 194.2(a). Because discovery must now be served after the first answer or general appearance, TRCP 196 was amended to eliminate the scenario where a defendant was served with a request to enter land before its answer was due and thus had 50 days to respond. See Tex. R. Civ. P. 196.7(c)(1). The amendments apply to cases filed on or after January 1, 2021, except those filed in justice court. Tex.Sup.Ct. Order, Misc. Docket No. 20-9153 (eff. Jan. 1, 2021). For a detailed discussion of required disclosures under the 2021 amendments, see "Required disclosures—Cases filed on or after 1-1-21," ch. 6-E, §3.

2. Contents of response. In response to a request for entry on land, a party must assert its objections and claims of privilege and then state one of the following: (1) entry will be permitted as requested, (2) entry will be permitted with certain conditions or limitations, (3) entry will be permitted at a different time or place, as specified in the response, or (4) entry will not be permitted. *See* Tex. R. Civ. P. 196.7(c)(2). If entry will not be permitted, the party must state its reasons in the response. Tex. R. Civ. P. 196.7(c)(2)(C). See **O'Connor's Texas Civil Forms**, FORM 6K:2 (2020 ed.).

§4. Motion to enter land of a nonparty

A party may gain entry on the land of a nonparty by filing a motion, requesting a hearing, and obtaining an order. Tex. R. Civ. P. 196.7(a)(2), (b).

§4.1 Motion. To gain entry on the land of a nonparty, the party must file a motion. See **O'Connor's Texas Civil Forms**, FORM 6K:3 (2020 ed.). The motion should include the following:

1. An explanation of good cause and relevance. Tex. R. Civ. P. 196.7(d); **In re Sun City Gun Exch., Inc.**, 545 S.W.3d 1, 7 (Tex.App.—El Paso 2017, orig. proceeding); **In re SWEPI L.P.**, 103 S.W.3d 578, 583 (Tex.App.—San Antonio 2003, orig. proceeding). Good cause is generally shown when (1) the information sought will in some way aid the movant in preparation or defense of the case (i.e., the discovery sought is relevant and material) and (2) the substantial equivalent of the information cannot be obtained through other means. **In re Sun City Gun Exch.**, 545 S.W.3d at 7; **In re SWEPI**, 103 S.W.3d at 584.

2. The scope of the inspection. Tex. R. Civ. P. 196.7(b).

3. The desired means, manner, and procedure for testing or sampling. *Id.*

4. The identity of the person or persons who will conduct the inspection, testing, or sampling. *Id.*

5. A request for a hearing. *See* Tex. R. Civ. P. 196.7(a)(2).

§4.2 Time to serve. For most methods of service (e.g., e-service, personal or commercial delivery), the deadline to serve a motion for entry on the land of a nonparty is 30 days before the end of the discovery period. *See* Tex. R. Civ. P. 196.7(a)(2);

In re SWEPI L.P., 103 S.W.3d 578, 583 (Tex.App.—San Antonio 2003, orig. proceeding). See "Discovery periods," ch. 6-A, §8. But when service is by mail or fax, the request should be served at least 33 days (if mailed) or 31 days (if faxed after 5:00 p.m.) before the end of the discovery period. *See* Tex. R. Civ. P. 21a(b)(2), (c). See "Deadline to serve response," ch. 6-A, §14.1.

§4.3 Service of motion & notice. The party seeking entry on the land of a nonparty must serve the motion and notice of the hearing on the nonparty and all the parties. Tex. R. Civ. P. 196.7(a)(2).

§4.4 Response. The nonparty has the following options:

1. **Comply.** The nonparty may inform the party requesting entry that it has no objection to the motion.

2. **Object.** The nonparty may inform the party requesting entry that it objects to the motion requesting entry. See **O'Connor's Texas Civil Forms**, FORM 6K:4 (2020 ed.).

3. **Move for protective order.** The nonparty may file a motion for protective order under TRCP 192.6 to protect itself from undue burden, unnecessary expense, harassment, annoyance, or invasion of personal, constitutional, or property rights. See "Motion for protective order," ch. 6-A, §20.

§4.5 Hearing. The court cannot sign an order requiring inspection of the property of a nonparty without a hearing. Tex. R. Civ. P. 196.7(a)(2). At the hearing, the parties and the nonparty may assert objections. *See* Tex. R. Civ. P. 196.7(c)(2).

§4.6 Order. The order for entry on a nonparty's property should include the following: (1) identification of the property and its owner, (2) good cause, (3) a statement that the land or property or an object on it is relevant to the subject matter of the action, (4) the time, place, manner, conditions, and scope of the inspection, (5) a description of any desired means, manner, and procedure for testing or sampling, and (6) a list of the persons performing the inspection, testing, or sampling. *See* Tex. R. Civ. P. 196.7(b), (d). See **O'Connor's Texas Civil Forms**, FORM 6K:5 (2020 ed.).

§5. Using evidence at trial

To introduce the inspection, measurement, survey, photograph, results of a test, or samples of the land, the party offering the evidence must prove that it is admissible, lay the proper predicate for its admission, offer it into evidence, and get the court to rule on its admissibility. *See* Tex. R. Evid. 104, 105, 402. Just because information was gained in response to a request or motion for entry on land does not mean it is admissible.

Note

If a party attempts to introduce evidence about property gained by trespass, the court should exclude it. See, e.g., ***Schenck v. Ebby Halliday Real Estate, Inc.****, 803 S.W.2d 361, 372–73 (Tex.App.—Fort Worth 1990, no writ) (testimony of appraiser);* ***Day & Zimmermann, Inc. v. Strickland****, 483 S.W.2d 541, 546–47 (Tex.App.—Texarkana 1972, writ ref'd n.r.e.) (testimony of architect).*

§6. Review

See "Review of discovery orders," ch. 6-A, §26.

Chapter 7. Disposition Without Trial

A. Default Judgment

§1. General

§1.1 Rules. Tex. R. Civ. P. 99, 106, 107, 124, 239 to 241, 243, 245, 252, 306, 320, 321, 329. See Tex. R. App. P. 26.1, 30.

§1.2 Purpose. A default judgment permits the trial court to render judgment for the plaintiff without a traditional trial. Only a plaintiff is entitled to a default judgment; a default judgment cannot be rendered for a defendant on the merits of its answer. **Freeman v. Freeman**, 327 S.W.2d 428, 431 (Tex.1959), *disapproved on other grounds*, **Mapco, Inc. v. Forrest**, 795 S.W.2d 700 (Tex.1990); **State v. Herrera**, 25 S.W.3d 326, 327–28 (Tex.App.—Austin 2000, no pet.). When a plaintiff does not appear at trial, the proper remedy is dismissal of the suit for want of prosecution, not a default judgment. **Smock v. Fischel**, 207 S.W.2d 891, 892 (Tex.1948); **Leeper v. Haynsworth**, 179 S.W.3d 742, 745 (Tex.App.—El Paso 2005, no pet.). See "Involuntary Dismissal," ch. 7-G, §1 et seq.

§1.3 Timetables & forms. Appendix IV, Timetable 8, Pretrial motions; Appendix IV, Timetable 11, No-answer default judgment; **O'Connor's Texas Civil Forms**, FORMS 7A:1 et seq., 9C:2 to 9C:3 (2020 ed.).

§1.4 Other references. Dyer, *A Practical Guide to the Equitable Bill of Review*, 10 J. Consumer & Commercial L. 104 (2007); Pendery et al., *Dealing with Default Judgments*, 35 St. Mary's L.J. 1 (2003); **O'Connor's Texas Causes of Action** (2021 ed.); **O'Connor's Texas Civil Appeals** (2020 ed.).

§2. Types of default judgments

§2.1 Generally—no-answer & post-answer default. Default judgments can generally be divided into two types—those rendered before the defendant appears or files an answer to the lawsuit (no-answer default) and those rendered after the defendant files an answer (post-answer default). The major distinction between these judgments is that in a no-answer default case, the defendant admits all of the plaintiff's allegations except unliquidated damages. In contrast, in a post-answer default case, the defendant denies the allegations in the plaintiff's petition and the plaintiff must prove all the elements of its claims. See "No-answer default," ch. 7-A, §3; "Post-answer default," ch. 7-A, §4.

7-1. Comparison of No-Answer and Post-Answer Default Judgments

	No-answer default	Post-answer default
1	Court can grant default judgment without a hearing, except for unliquidated damages.	Court cannot grant default judgment without a hearing.
2	Default constitutes admission by D of allegations in P's pleadings, except for unliquidated damages.	Default does not constitute admission by D of P's claims or abandonment of D's defenses.
3	P must prove unliquidated damages and causal nexus.	P must prove all elements of cause of action and damages, as in a trial on the merits.
4	D does not waive pleading defects.	D waives pleading defects unless D filed special exceptions.
5	D has no right to notice of hearing unless D files answer before final judgment rendered.	D has right to notice of hearing or trial.
6	D has no right to participate unless D files answer or makes appearance before hearing on unliquidated damages.	D has right to participate if D makes appearance.
7	If D files answer requesting jury after default judgment is rendered but before hearing on damages, D is entitled to jury trial on damages alone; if D does not make appearance, D waives right to jury.	If jury trial was requested before default, D has right to jury if D makes appearance; if D does not make appearance, D waives right to jury.
8	P must file certificate of last known address and servicemembers' affidavit.	P is not required to file certificate of last known address or servicemembers' affidavit.
9	Sufficiency of service of process on D is an issue; default judgment will be set aside if service is defective.	Sufficiency of service is not an issue because D has answered.

§2.2 Other variations. Although default judgments are generally divided into no-answer and post-answer defaults, there are variations that do not fit into either category. *See* **Paradigm Oil, Inc. v. Retamco Oper., Inc.**, 372 S.W.3d 177, 184 (Tex.2012); **Sedona Pac. Hous. Prtshp. v. Ventura**, 408 S.W.3d 507, 511 (Tex.App.—El Paso 2013, no pet.).

1. Post-appearance default. A post-appearance default can be taken when a defendant makes an appearance in the case but does not file an answer. *See, e.g.*, **LBL Oil Co. v. International Power Servs.**, 777 S.W.2d 390, 390–91 (Tex.1989) (D, who was owner of "Oklahoma dba" and was not served, filed motion to dismiss, alleging that P mistakenly sued Texas corporation with similar name); **Sedona Pac. Hous.**, 408 S.W.3d at 512–13 (Rule 11 agreement outside context of special appearance). When the defendant makes an appearance, the plaintiff must—as a matter of due process—give the defendant notice of the trial or dispositive default-judgment hearing before the court can render the default judgment. *See* **LBL Oil**, 777 S.W.2d at 390–91; **Sedona Pac. Hous.**, 408 S.W.3d at 512; **Yuen v. Fisher**, 227 S.W.3d 193, 198–99 (Tex.App.—Houston [1st Dist.] 2007, no pet.). As a general rule, the plaintiff can prove notice by filing an affidavit with the certificate of service from the notice of hearing sent to the defendant. See **O'Connor's Texas Civil Forms**, FORM 7A:5 (2020 ed.).

2. Judgment nihil dicit. A judgment nihil dicit (Latin for "he says nothing") can be taken when a defendant either (1) did not answer but filed a dilatory plea that does not put the merits of the case at issue or (2) filed an answer but later withdrew it. **Paradigm Oil**, 372 S.W.3d at 184 n.8; **Sedona Pac. Hous.**, 408 S.W.3d at 512; *see, e.g.*, **Texas Quarries, Inc. v. Pierce**, 244 S.W.2d 571, 572 (Tex.App.—San Antonio 1951, no writ) (D filed plea of privilege, which was sustained, for venue to be in another county and filed motion for continuance on date of trial but never filed answer). A judgment nihil dicit and a no-answer default judgment are so similar that the same rules apply as to the judgment's effect and validity. **Stoner v. Thompson**, 578 S.W.2d 679, 682 (Tex.1979). In both, the defendant has admitted to the plaintiff's allegations, but the judgment nihil dicit acts as a stronger confession. *Id.* That is, a judgment nihil dicit acts as a waiver of all objections to service and an abandonment of all defenses. *See* **Sharif v. Par Tech, Inc.**, 135 S.W.3d 869, 872 (Tex.App.—Houston [1st Dist.] 2004, no pet.); **Peerless Pump-FMC Corp. v. Gunter**, 470 S.W.2d 299, 301 (Tex.App.—Eastland 1971, no writ).

3. Default judgment as discovery sanction. A default judgment as a discovery sanction can be entered by the trial court (e.g., when the court strikes the defendant's answer). **Paradigm Oil**, 372 S.W.3d at 184. See "Strike pleadings," ch. 5-K, §7.1.5; "Note," ch. 7-A, §3.13.3(3).

§3. No-answer default

A no-answer default judgment can be rendered when the defendant does not appear in some manner or file an answer. Before taking a default judgment, the plaintiff should confirm that the petition, the citation, the service, and the return are adequate to support a default judgment. If the plaintiff amends its petition, it may need to re-serve the defendant before taking a default.

§3.1 Effect of defendant's failure to appear or answer. The court may render a default judgment on the pleadings against a defendant who has not appeared or filed an answer. Tex. R. Civ. P. 239; **Sedona Pac. Hous. Prtshp. v. Ventura**, 408 S.W.3d 507, 511–12 (Tex.App.—El Paso 2013, no pet.). When a defendant does not file an answer, all allegations of facts—including those establishing liability—in the plaintiff's petition are deemed admitted except for the amount of unliquidated damages. **Paradigm Oil, Inc. v. Retamco Oper., Inc.**, 372 S.W.3d 177, 183 (Tex.2012); **Jackson v. Biotectronics, Inc.**, 937 S.W.2d 38, 41 (Tex.App.—Houston [14th Dist.] 1996, no writ); *see* **Dolgencorp of Tex., Inc. v. Lerma**, 288 S.W.3d 922, 930 (Tex.2009); **Argyle Mech., Inc. v. Unigus Steel, Inc.**, 156 S.W.3d 685, 687 (Tex.App.—Dallas 2005, no pet.). After a no-answer default, the only claim the plaintiff is required to prove is its claim for unliquidated damages. **Dolgencorp of Tex.**, 288 S.W.3d at 930; *see* Tex. R. Civ. P. 243; **Paradigm Oil**, 372 S.W.3d at 183.

§3.2 Sufficiency of plaintiff's petition. The plaintiff's petition will support a default judgment if the petition (1) states a cause of action within the court's jurisdiction, (2) gives fair notice to the defendant of the claim asserted, and (3) does not affirmatively disclose the invalidity of the claim on its face. **Jackson v. Biotectronics, Inc.**, 937 S.W.2d 38, 42 (Tex.App.—Houston [14th Dist.] 1996, no writ); *see* **Paramount Pipe & Sup. Co. v. Muhr**, 749 S.W.2d 491, 494 (Tex.1988).

1. Amending the petition.

(1) Adding claims or damages—service required. When, after service of the original petition, the plaintiff amends to ask for a more onerous judgment by adding claims, adding new elements of damages, or increasing the amount of

damages, the plaintiff must serve the defendant with the amended petition before taking a default judgment. *See* **In re E.A.**, 287 S.W.3d 1, 6 (Tex.2009); **AAMCO Transmissions, Inc. v. Bova**, 484 S.W.3d 520, 523 (Tex.App.—Houston [1st Dist.] 2016, no pet.). The plaintiff does not need to serve the defendant with a new citation. **In re E.A.**, 287 S.W.3d at 6.

Note

Service of a new citation is not required when serving a more onerous amended petition on a nonanswering defendant. ***In re E.A.****, 287 S.W.3d at 6. The Supreme Court held that TRCP 21a, which applies to all pleadings required to be served under TRCP 21 other than the original petition, does not require the plaintiff to serve a new citation for amended petitions.* ***In re E.A.****, 287 S.W.3d at 4.*

(2) No additional claims or damages—no service required. If the amended petition does not add claims or increase damages, it does not need to be re-served. *E.g.*, **AAMCO Transmissions**, 484 S.W.3d at 523 (amended petition omitted two potentially jointly liable Ds); **Palomin v. Zarsky Lumber Co.**, 26 S.W.3d 690, 694 (Tex.App.—Corpus Christi 2000, pet. denied) (amended petition made minor change in D's name); **Halligan v. First Heights, F.S.A.**, 850 S.W.2d 801, 802–03 (Tex.App.—Houston [14th Dist.] 1993, no writ) (amended petition in intervention did not assert new claims or seek additional damages).

2. Variance between pleadings & judgment. A default judgment must be based on the pleadings. The judgment, therefore, cannot rely on causes of action that are not adequately pleaded or award damages in excess of the damages specifically pleaded. *See* **Capitol Brick, Inc. v. Fleming Mfg. Co.**, 722 S.W.2d 399, 401 (Tex.1986); **Gulf States Pet. Corp. v. General Elec. Capital Auto Lease**, 134 S.W.3d 504, 511 (Tex.App.—Eastland 2004, no pet.); **Simon v. BancTexas Quorum**, 754 S.W.2d 283, 286 (Tex.App.—Dallas 1988, writ denied).

§3.3 Sufficiency of citation. The citation must strictly comply with TRCP 99. See "Requirements for the citation," ch. 2-I, §2.

§3.4 Sufficiency of service. The face of the record must show strict compliance with the type of service used, but the court is not required to review the entire record to determine proper service. **All Commercial Floors, Inc. v. Barton & Rasor**, 97 S.W.3d 723, 726 (Tex.App.—Fort Worth 2003, no pet.). See "Serving the Defendant with Suit," ch. 2-I, §1 et seq. A default judgment cannot withstand a direct attack by a defendant who was not served in strict compliance with the appropriate service rules. **Wood v. Brown**, 819 S.W.2d 799, 800 (Tex.1991); *see* **Uvalde Country Club v. Martin Linen Sup. Co.**, 690 S.W.2d 884, 885 (Tex.1985). See "Direct attacks on default judgment," ch. 7-A, §7.1. Actual notice of suit is not a substitute for proper service. **Wilson v. Dunn**, 800 S.W.2d 833, 836 (Tex.1990). A default judgment is void unless the defendant (1) was served with process in strict compliance with the law, (2) accepted or waived service, or (3) made an appearance. Tex. R. Civ. P. 124; **Min v. Avila**, 991 S.W.2d 495, 500 (Tex.App.—Houston [1st Dist.] 1999, no pet.); *see, e.g.*, **All Commercial Floors**, 97 S.W.3d at 727 (return not signed by person designated to receive service for corporation; default judgment void); **Ackerly v. Ackerly**, 13 S.W.3d 454, 457–58 (Tex.App.—Corpus Christi 2000, no pet.) (docket sheet did not show issue, service, or return of citation; default judgment void).

§3.5 Sufficiency of return. For the requirements for the return, see "Proof of service—The return," ch. 2-I, §9.

§3.6 Amending the citation & return. The court can permit an amendment to the citation and the return. Tex. R. Civ. P. 118. See "Amending the citation & return," ch. 2-I, §10.2.

§3.7 Sufficiency of defendant's answer. An answer, even if defective, places the merits of the plaintiff's case at issue and will prevent a no-answer default judgment if it is filed before the rendition (i.e., the announcement) of judgment. When an answer is defective, the plaintiff's remedy is to file special exceptions. See "Special Exceptions—Challenging the Pleadings," ch. 3-G, §1 et seq.

1. Filing constituted answer. In the following cases, the court found the defendant's filing sufficient to constitute an answer: • Pauper's affidavit. **Hughes v. Habitat Apts.**, 860 S.W.2d 872, 873 (Tex.1993). • Letter from pro se defendant to district clerk in which defendant confirmed he received the citation and provided his current address. **Smith v. Lippmann**, 826 S.W.2d 137, 138 (Tex.1992). • Motion to dismiss from pro se defendant that contained the proper style of the case, includ-

ing the names of the parties and the trial court. **Rhojo Enters. v. Stevens**, 540 S.W.3d 621, 624–25 (Tex.App.—Beaumont 2018, no pet.). • Letter to court acknowledging acceptance of citation and responding to P's allegations. **Guadalupe Econ. Servs. v. DeHoyos**, 183 S.W.3d 712, 716–17 (Tex.App.—Austin 2005, no pet.). • Answer for corporation signed by a nonattorney. **Custom-Crete, Inc. v. K-Bar Servs.**, 82 S.W.3d 655, 657–58 (Tex.App.—San Antonio 2002, no pet.); **Handy Andy, Inc. v. Ruiz**, 900 S.W.2d 739, 741 (Tex.App.—Corpus Christi 1994, writ denied). • Plea in abatement. **Alcala v. Williams**, 908 S.W.2d 54, 56 (Tex.App.—San Antonio 1995, no writ); **Schulz v. Schulz**, 726 S.W.2d 256, 258 (Tex.App.—Austin 1987, no writ). • Letter to court from secretary-treasurer of corporation that contained defendant's address, admitted debt, and made counterclaim. **Santex Roofing & Sheet Metal, Inc. v. Venture Steel, Inc.**, 737 S.W.2d 55, 56–57 (Tex.App.—San Antonio 1987, no writ). • Answer not signed by either the party or the attorney. **Frank v. Corbett**, 682 S.W.2d 587, 588 (Tex.App.—Waco 1984, no writ).

2. Filing did not constitute an answer. In the following cases, the court did not find the defendant's filing sufficient to constitute an answer: • Letter from pro se defendant to plaintiff's attorney that did not have a case heading or certificate of service. **Cotton v. Cotton**, 57 S.W.3d 506, 511–12 (Tex.App.—Waco 2001, no pet.). • Motion for new trial. **First State Bldg. & Loan Ass'n v. B.L. Nelson & Assocs.**, 735 S.W.2d 287, 289 (Tex.App.—Dallas 1987, no writ); **Gonzalez v. Regalado**, 542 S.W.2d 689, 691 (Tex.App.—Waco 1976, writ ref'd n.r.e.). • Motion to transfer venue. **Duplantis v. Noble Toyota, Inc.**, 720 S.W.2d 863, 866 (Tex.App.—Beaumont 1986, no writ).

§3.8 Timeliness of defendant's answer.

1. Before deadline. If the defendant filed an answer before the deadline to answer, the plaintiff cannot obtain a default judgment. *See* Tex. R. Civ. P. 239. The deadline to file an answer is 10:00 a.m. on the first Monday after 20 days have passed from the date the defendant was served with citation. Tex. R. Civ. P. 99(b). See "Deadline to answer," ch. 3-E, §2.

2. After deadline. If the defendant filed an answer after the deadline but before the court rendered a default judgment, the court cannot render a default judgment. *E.g.*, **Davis v. Jefferies**, 764 S.W.2d 559, 560 (Tex.1989) (answer filed one day after deadline, but more than two hours before default judgment was rendered); **Dowell Schlumberger, Inc. v. Jackson**, 730 S.W.2d 818, 819–20 (Tex.App.—El Paso 1987, writ ref'd n.r.e.) (answer filed during default hearing but before court rendered judgment); *see* Tex. R. Civ. P. 239. See "Rendition," ch. 9-C, §3.1. If an answer is mailed to the clerk before a default judgment is announced, it is considered filed before the judgment is rendered, even if it is not received until after the judgment is signed. **Milam v. Miller**, 891 S.W.2d 1, 2 (Tex.App.—Amarillo 1994, writ ref'd); **Thomas v. Gelber Grp.**, 905 S.W.2d 786, 788–89 (Tex.App.—Houston [14th Dist.] 1995, no writ). See "Mail," ch. 1-C, §4.1.2(1).

§3.9 Moving for no-answer default judgment. Most default judgments are granted on a motion. However, it is not necessary to file a motion for default judgment to obtain a default judgment. The plaintiff is entitled to have the judge or clerk call the case on appearance day and to ask the court to grant a default judgment. *See* Tex. R. Civ. P. 238, 239. When the case is called, the court can grant a default judgment if no answer is on file and the citation has been on file with the clerk for at least ten days, not counting the day the citation was filed and the day of the default judgment. Tex. R. Civ. P. 107(h); *see* Tex. R. Civ. P. 239. See "Filing date," ch. 2-I, §9.4.9; "Deadline to answer," ch. 3-E, §2; **O'Connor's Texas Civil Forms**, FORM 7A:1 (2020 ed.).

1. When to move for default.

(1) In most cases. The plaintiff may move for a default judgment when the defendant's deadline to file an answer has expired and the citation and proof of service have been on file with the clerk at least ten days, not counting the day of filing and the day of the judgment. *See* Tex. R. Civ. P. 107(h), 239; **Union Pac. Corp. v. Legg**, 49 S.W.3d 72, 78 (Tex.App.—Austin 2001, no pet.); *see, e.g.*, **AAMCO Transmissions, Inc. v. Bova**, 484 S.W.3d 520, 526 (Tex.App.—Houston [1st Dist.] 2016, no pet.) (default judgment entered before deadline to answer amended petition, but four months after D was served with original petition, was not void). See "Filing date," ch. 2-I, §9.4.9; "Deadline to answer," ch. 3-E, §2. The plaintiff should move for default as soon as it can because the defendant can prevent a default judgment by filing an answer even if the deadline has passed. See "After deadline," ch. 7-A, §3.8.2.

Caution

If a plaintiff obtains a no-answer default judgment against a defendant who is covered by insurance but the defendant has not notified its carrier according to the notice-of-suit provision in the insurance policy, the carrier may not be liable for the judgment against the defendant. See ***Liberty Mut. Ins. v. Cruz****, 883 S.W.2d 164, 165–66 (Tex.1993). Compliance with the notice provision is a condition precedent to the carrier's liability.* ***Harwell v. State Farm Mut. Auto. Ins.****, 896 S.W.2d 170, 173–74 (Tex.1995); see also* ***Liberty Mut. Ins.****, 883 S.W.2d at 166 (if insurer knows of suit, it might choose to answer for insured-D and litigate merits of suit). If the carrier is not notified about the suit until after a judgment becomes final and nonappealable, the carrier is prejudiced as a matter of law and is not bound by the judgment against the defendant.* ***Harwell****, 896 S.W.2d at 174–75.*

(2) After motion to quash granted. If the court grants a motion to quash, the plaintiff may move for a default judgment if the defendant does not file an answer by 10:00 a.m. on the first Monday after 20 days from the date the service or citation was quashed. Tex. R. Civ. P. 122; **Wells v. Southern States Lumber & Sup.**, 720 S.W.2d 227, 228 (Tex.App.—Houston [14th Dist.] 1986, no writ). See "Motion to Quash—Challenging the Service," ch. 3-J, §1 et seq.

(3) After Secretary of State served. If the Secretary of State was served as the defendant's agent, the period for filing the answer runs from the date the Secretary of State was served, not from the date the Secretary of State forwarded the process to the defendant. **Bonewitz v. Bonewitz**, 726 S.W.2d 227, 230 (Tex.App.—Austin 1987, writ ref'd n.r.e.). The Secretary of State is considered the agent of the defendant for service of process, and service on the Secretary of State is constructive service on the defendant. *Id.* Before taking a default, the plaintiff must obtain a certificate (referred to as a "**Whitney** certificate") from the Secretary of State certifying compliance with the statute that authorizes substituted service—that is, certifying that the process was forwarded to the defendant by certified mail, return receipt requested. *See* **Whitney v. L&L Rlty. Corp.**, 500 S.W.2d 94, 96 (Tex.1973). The defendant is considered served even if the process is returned to the Secretary of State with a notation that it was refused or unclaimed. See "Proof of service," ch. 2-I, §5.2.

(4) After notice to Attorney General. In some suits against the State, the plaintiff must send a notice of intent to take a default to the Attorney General by certified mail, return receipt requested, at least ten days before the entry of the default judgment. Tex. Civ. Prac. & Rem. Code §§30.004(b), 39.001. Before taking a default judgment against the State, any state agency, or any state official or employee, the plaintiff should check the list of persons and entities in CPRC chapter 104 that must be represented by the Attorney General. If the plaintiff does not give the Attorney General notice, the default judgment will be set aside without costs. Tex. Civ. Prac. & Rem. Code §§30.004(d), 39.002. Whether a plaintiff must give the Attorney General ten days' notice before taking a post-answer default judgment against the State has not been decided. *See* **Director, State Empls. Workers' Comp. Div. v. Evans**, 889 S.W.2d 266, 267 n.1 (Tex.1994).

(5) No default after service by publication. There is no procedure in Texas for a default judgment when service is by publication. **McCarthy v. Jesperson**, 527 S.W.2d 825, 826 (Tex.App.—El Paso 1975, no writ). Instead, the plaintiff must follow the unique trial procedure outlined in TRCP 244. See "Trial," ch. 10-B, §10.1.

2. Documents to file.

(1) Instrument to prove damages. The court can award damages based on affidavits, live testimony, or documents. *See* **Ingram Indus. v. U.S. Bolt Mfg.**, 121 S.W.3d 31, 37 (Tex.App.—Houston [1st Dist.] 2003, no pet.); **Aavid Thermal Techs. v. Irving ISD**, 68 S.W.3d 707, 711–12 (Tex.App.—Dallas 2001, no pet.); **Pentes Design, Inc. v. Perez**, 840 S.W.2d 75, 80 (Tex.App.—Corpus Christi 1992, writ denied). If the claim is for liquidated damages, the plaintiff should attach a written instrument to prove these damages so that a hearing and receipt of other evidence is not required. *See* Tex. R. Civ. P. 241. See "Liquidated damages—hearing not required," ch. 7-A, §3.13.1. If the claim is for unliquidated damages, the plaintiff can prove damages by affidavits or live testimony; however, the evidence must establish a "causal nexus" between the event sued on and the plaintiff's injuries. See "Offer proof of damages," ch. 7-A, §3.13.2(2); "Establish causal nexus," ch. 7-A, §3.13.2(3); **O'Connor's Texas Civil Forms**, FORM 7A:4 (2020 ed.).

(2) Certificate of last known address. At the time or immediately before a default judgment is rendered, the plaintiff must certify to the clerk in writing the last known mailing address of the defendant. Tex. R. Civ. P. 239a; *see*

Katy Venture, Ltd. v. Cremona Bistro Corp., 469 S.W.3d 160, 162 (Tex.2015). See **O'Connor's Texas Civil Forms**, FORM 7A:2 (2020 ed.). The certificate must be filed in the papers of the court. Tex. R. Civ. P. 239a. Immediately after the default judgment is signed, the clerk must mail written notice to the defaulting party at the address given. *Id.*; **John v. State**, 826 S.W.2d 138, 139 n.1 (Tex.1992). See "Notice after no-answer default," ch. 7-A, §6.1. Failure to comply with this requirement does not affect the finality of the judgment. Tex. R. Civ. P. 239a; **Katy Venture**, 469 S.W.3d at 163. However, failure to comply with TRCP 239a can be grounds for setting aside a default judgment in a bill-of-review proceeding but is not grounds for reversing the judgment in a restricted appeal. **Jordan v. Jordan**, 36 S.W.3d 259, 264 (Tex.App.—Beaumont 2001, pet. denied); *see* **Katy Venture**, 469 S.W.3d at 163. See "Restricted appeal," ch. 7-A, §7.1.2; "Bill of review," ch. 7-A, §7.1.3.

(3) Servicemembers' affidavit. If the defendant is a member of the armed services, the plaintiff must file an affidavit setting forth facts that show that (1) the defendant is not currently in the military, (2) the defendant is currently in the military, or (3) the plaintiff is unable to determine whether the defendant is in the military. 50 U.S.C. §3931(b)(1); **Hawkins v. Hawkins**, 999 S.W.2d 171, 174 (Tex.App.—Austin 1999, no pet.) (under former 50 U.S.C. app. §520). See **O'Connor's Texas Civil Forms**, FORM 7A:3 (2020 ed.). If the defendant is not in the military, the court can render a default judgment. If the defendant is in the military, the court must appoint an attorney to represent the defendant. 50 U.S.C. §3931(b)(2). If the court is unable to determine whether the defendant is in the military, the plaintiff may be required to file a bond. 50 U.S.C. §3931(b)(3).

(4) Motion for severance. If a plaintiff is taking a default judgment against one defendant in a case with multiple defendants, the plaintiff should consider filing a motion to sever its claims against that defendant so the default judgment can become final and the judgment can be executed. **Castano v. Foremost Cty. Mut. Ins.**, 31 S.W.3d 387, 388 (Tex.App.—San Antonio 2000, no pet.). See "No-answer default," ch. 7-A, §5.3.1.

(5) Proposed default judgment. The plaintiff should always file a proposed default judgment, either final or partial. See **O'Connor's Texas Civil Forms**, FORM 9C:2 (2020 ed.).

(a) Liquidated damages. If damages are liquidated and proved by a written instrument attached to the petition, the plaintiff can file a proposed final default judgment. See "Liquidated damages—hearing not required," ch. 7-A, §3.13.1.

(b) Unliquidated damages. If damages are unliquidated, the plaintiff can file a proposed partial default judgment on liability and ask for a hearing to determine the amount of unliquidated damages. See "Unliquidated damages—hearing required," ch. 7-A, §3.13.2. The advantage of getting the court to sign a partial default judgment as soon as possible is that if the defendant files an answer after the court renders a judgment on liability but before the hearing on damages, the judgment on liability will not be set aside. If the plaintiff can prove the unliquidated-damages claim before the court renders the default judgment on liability, the plaintiff should file a final default judgment.

§3.10 Response to motion for default—the answer. If the defendant gets notice that a motion for no-answer default is pending, it should immediately file an answer. The clerk should note on the answer the date and the exact minute it was filed. If the answer is filed after the deadline to answer but before the trial court renders judgment, the court cannot render a default judgment. See "After deadline," ch. 7-A, §3.8.2.

§3.11 Hearing on liability. A hearing on liability for a no-answer default judgment can be conducted through an oral hearing or simply through submission of the motion for default judgment. See "Hearing on motion," ch. 1-E, §4.

Note

Some courts may prefer that the motion for a no-answer default judgment be set for submission rather than for an oral hearing. Because a nonanswering defendant admits all factual allegations in the plaintiff's petition, including those establishing liability, a hearing on submission is generally appropriate. See ***Paradigm Oil, Inc. v. Retamco Oper., Inc.***, *372 S.W.3d 177, 183 (Tex.2012). See "Effect of defendant's failure to appear or answer," ch. 7-A, §3.1. Check with the court clerk to see what*

the judge prefers.

1. Notice not required. If the defendant does not make an appearance or file an answer, the plaintiff is not required to give the defendant notice of the hearing before the court renders the default judgment. **Long v. McDermott**, 813 S.W.2d 622, 624 (Tex.App.—Houston [1st Dist.] 1991, no writ); **Olivares v. Cauthorn**, 717 S.W.2d 431, 434 (Tex.App.—San Antonio 1986, writ dism'd); *see* **Novosad v. Brian K. Cunningham, P.C.**, 38 S.W.3d 767, 772–73 (Tex.App.—Houston [14th Dist.] 2001, no pet.). The defendant received all the notice it was entitled to when it was served with process. **Continental Carbon Co. v. Sea-Land Serv.**, 27 S.W.3d 184, 189 (Tex.App.—Dallas 2000, pet. denied).

2. Right to answer. If the defendant appears at the hearing on liability, it should immediately file an answer, even if handwritten. A late answer will prevent a default judgment from being rendered as long as the court has not already rendered a judgment. See "After deadline," ch. 7-A, §3.8.2.

§3.12 Rendition of default judgment. The court renders a no-answer default judgment either by announcing in open court that it renders judgment or by signing a judgment to that effect. See "Rendition," ch. 9-C, §3.1.

§3.13 Hearing on damages. Once the court renders a no-answer default judgment, whether a hearing on damages is necessary depends on the type of damages the plaintiff requested in its petition.

1. Liquidated damages—hearing not required. "Liquidated damages" are damages that can be accurately calculated from (1) the factual (as opposed to conclusory) allegations in the petition and (2) a written instrument attached to the petition. Tex. R. Civ. P. 241; **Aavid Thermal Techs. v. Irving ISD**, 68 S.W.3d 707, 711 (Tex.App.—Dallas 2001, no pet.); **Novosad v. Brian K. Cunningham, P.C.**, 38 S.W.3d 767, 773 (Tex.App.—Houston [14th Dist.] 2001, no pet.); **Abcon Paving, Inc. v. Crissup**, 820 S.W.2d 951, 953 (Tex.App.—Fort Worth 1991, no writ). When damages are liquidated and the written instrument proves the amount of damages, it is not necessary to hold a hearing, unless the defendant is entitled to and demands a jury trial. *See* Tex. R. Civ. P. 241; **Aavid Thermal**, 68 S.W.3d at 711. The trial court can award liquidated damages that are proved by the written instrument. Tex. R. Civ. P. 241; *e.g.*, **Aavid Thermal**, 68 S.W.3d at 711 (amount of ad valorem taxes calculated from petition and attached documents); **Novosad**, 38 S.W.3d at 773 (amount for professional services and attorney fees proved by original invoices).

Note

If a claim for liquidated damages is inadequately described in the plaintiff's petition, or if the claim is not supported by a written instrument attached to the petition, the damages are considered unliquidated. See, e.g., ***Atwood v. B&R Sup. & Equip. Co.****, 52 S.W.3d 265, 268 (Tex.App.—Corpus Christi 2001, no pet.) (because written instrument was not submitted, claim was unliquidated);* ***Kelley v. Southwestern Bell Media, Inc.****, 745 S.W.2d 447, 448–49 (Tex.App.—Houston [1st Dist] 1988, no writ) (because petition did not allege date of default, claim was unliquidated).*

2. Unliquidated damages—hearing required. "Unliquidated damages" are damages that cannot be accurately calculated from (1) the factual allegations in the petition and (2) the written instruments attached to the petition. **Atwood**, 52 S.W.3d at 268. Unliquidated damages are disputed or uncertain. *See* **Paradigm Oil, Inc. v. Retamco Oper., Inc.**, 372 S.W.3d 177, 186 (Tex.2012) (unliquidated damages cannot be calculated exactly and involve range of possible answers); *see, e.g.*, **Fogel v. White**, 745 S.W.2d 444, 446 (Tex.App.—Houston [14th Dist.] 1988, orig. proceeding) (because outcome of tort claim is uncertain, damages are unliquidated). When damages are unliquidated, the court must hold a hearing and receive evidence on damages before it can render a final default judgment. Tex. R. Civ. P. 243; **Holt Atherton Indus. v. Heine**, 835 S.W.2d 80, 83 (Tex.1992); **Argyle Mech., Inc. v. Unigus Steel, Inc.**, 156 S.W.3d 685, 688 (Tex.App.—Dallas 2005, no pet.). If the defendant appears at the hearing on damages, it has the right to participate at the hearing. **Paradigm Oil**, 372 S.W.3d at 183. See "Right to participate," ch. 7-A, §3.13.3(3). On appeal, if the appellate court finds the plaintiff did not present legally sufficient evidence at the hearing, the court will remand for a new trial on damages. **Dolgencorp of Tex., Inc. v. Lerma**, 288 S.W.3d 922, 929 (Tex.2009); **Holt Atherton**, 835 S.W.2d at 86.

Note

Although a petition can include unliquidated damages, a party must specify the range of monetary relief sought. See Tex. R Civ. P. 47(c). See "Specific statement of relief," ch. 1-B, §3.2.8(2).

(1) Ask for court reporter. When the defendant is not present for the no-answer default hearing on damages and evidence is introduced, the plaintiff should make sure the court reporter transcribes the hearing. Generally, when a defendant, through no fault of its own, is unable to procure a record of the evidence presented, it may be entitled to a new trial. **Smith v. Smith**, 544 S.W.2d 121, 123 (Tex.1976); **Alvarado v. Reif**, 783 S.W.2d 303, 305 (Tex.App.—Eastland 1989, no writ).

(2) Offer proof of damages. At the hearing, the plaintiff must present evidence of its damages. For example, in a personal-injury case, the plaintiff must present evidence of pain, suffering, lost wages, medical expenses, and the reasonableness and necessity of the medical expenses. **Transport Concepts, Inc. v. Reeves**, 748 S.W.2d 302, 305 (Tex.App.—Dallas 1988, no writ). TRCP 243 does not specify either the type of hearing or the type of evidence required. **Arenivar v. Providian Nat'l Bank**, 23 S.W.3d 496, 498 (Tex.App.—Amarillo 2000, no pet.). Thus, the court can award unliquidated damages based on affidavits or live testimony. *See, e.g.*, **Ingram Indus. v. U.S. Bolt Mfg.**, 121 S.W.3d 31, 37 (Tex.App.—Houston [1st Dist.] 2003, no pet.) (affidavit testimony satisfied TRCP 243's evidentiary-hearing requirement); **Pentes Design, Inc. v. Perez**, 840 S.W.2d 75, 80 (Tex.App.—Corpus Christi 1992, writ denied) (witness testimony at default hearing supported claims for unliquidated damages); *see also* **Texas Commerce Bank v. New**, 3 S.W.3d 515, 517 (Tex.1999) (unobjected-to hearsay evidence in affidavit can support award of damages).

(3) Establish causal nexus. When damages are unliquidated, the plaintiff must present evidence of the "causal nexus" between the event sued on and the plaintiff's injuries. **Morgan v. Compugraphic Corp.**, 675 S.W.2d 729, 732 (Tex.1984). By its default, the defendant admits only that it caused the event that led to the suit, not that there is a connection between the event and the damages. *Id.* Thus, the plaintiff must offer proof of its damages and connect the damages to the defendant's conduct. *Id.* Types of suits in which courts have required plaintiffs to prove a causal nexus include the following: • Breach of warranty and violation of the DTPA. **Capitol Brick, Inc. v. Fleming Mfg. Co.**, 722 S.W.2d 399, 402 (Tex.1986). • Personal injury. **Morgan**, 675 S.W.2d at 732; **Transport Concepts**, 748 S.W.2d at 304–05. • Breach of warranty of title to real estate. **Gibraltar Sav. Ass'n v. Kilpatrick**, 770 S.W.2d 14, 18 (Tex.App.—Texarkana 1989, writ denied).

(4) Prove attorney fees.

(a) Evidence. A demand for reasonable attorney fees is a claim for unliquidated damages, and the award must be based on evidence. **Higgins v. Smith**, 722 S.W.2d 825, 827–28 (Tex.App.—Houston [14th Dist.] 1987, no writ); **Nettles v. Del Lingco**, 638 S.W.2d 633, 636 (Tex.App.—El Paso 1982, no writ). Attorney fees can be proved by affidavit. See "Evidence," ch. 1-H, §10.2.2. The court should not consider the unsworn testimony of the plaintiff's attorney to support an award of attorney fees. **Bloom v. Bloom**, 767 S.W.2d 463, 471 (Tex.App.—San Antonio 1989, writ denied). However, if the court awards attorney fees based on unsworn testimony at a hearing at which the defendant was present but did not object, the defendant waives that issue on appeal. See "Attorney's appearance before court," ch. 1-H, §5.2.

(b) No judicial notice. Attorney fees in a default-judgment case cannot be established by the judicial-notice provision in CPRC §38.004. That provision permits judicial notice of attorney fees only when a case is tried on the merits. See "Judicial notice," ch. 1-H, §10.1.4(1)(a)[2].

3. Defendant's rights in a no-answer default.

(1) Right to notice. Ordinarily, a defendant against whom a no-answer default judgment was rendered does not have a right to notice of a hearing on unliquidated damages. **Long v. McDermott**, 813 S.W.2d 622, 624 (Tex.App.—Houston [1st Dist.] 1991, no writ). But when a defendant makes an appearance or files an answer after default judgment was rendered but before the hearing on damages, the defendant is entitled to notice of all later hearings. *See* **Bradford v. Bradford**, 971 S.W.2d 595, 597 (Tex.App.—Dallas 1998, no pet.).

(2) Right to jury. If the defendant filed an answer requesting a jury after the court rendered a default judgment on liability but before the hearing on damages, the defendant is entitled to a jury trial on damages. Tex. R. Civ. P. 241,

243. TRCP 243 calls this limited jury trial on damages a "writ of inquiry." **Marr v. Marr**, 905 S.W.2d 331, 334 (Tex.App.—Waco 1995, no writ); **Maywald Trailer Co. v. Perry**, 238 S.W.2d 826, 827 (Tex.App.—Galveston 1951, writ ref'd n.r.e.).

(3) Right to participate. If the defendant appears at the hearing on damages, it has the right to cross-examine witnesses and to present evidence on unliquidated damages only. **Northeast Wholesale Lumber, Inc. v. Leader Lumber, Inc.**, 785 S.W.2d 402, 407 (Tex.App.—Dallas 1989, no writ); **Bass v. Duffey**, 620 S.W.2d 847, 849–50 (Tex.App.—Houston [14th Dist.] 1981, no writ); **Maywald Trailer**, 238 S.W.2d at 827. See "Unliquidated damages—hearing required," ch. 7-A, §3.13.2. The defendant may introduce evidence to mitigate the plaintiff's unliquidated damages and evidence to negate the causal nexus. *See* **Morgan**, 675 S.W.2d at 732; **Fiduciary Mortg. Co. v. City Nat'l Bank**, 762 S.W.2d 196, 199 (Tex.App.—Dallas 1988, writ denied); **Maywald Trailer**, 238 S.W.2d at 827. Once the court renders a default judgment on liability, the defendant cannot offer evidence to support its defenses or call witnesses to disprove liability. *See, e.g.*, **Downer v. Aquamarine Operators, Inc.**, 701 S.W.2d 238, 243 (Tex.1985) (once its answer was struck and default judgment was rendered on liability, D was not entitled to introduce evidence of contributory negligence).

Note

When a trial court strikes a defendant's answer as a discovery sanction, the resulting default—which is technically post-answer but is similar to a no-answer default judgment—must be evaluated under both the general rules for default judgments and those for discovery abuse. ***Paradigm Oil**, 372 S.W.3d at 184. Thus, even though a sanctions order striking an answer may prevent the defendant from contesting liability, the order generally cannot prevent the defendant from participating in a post-default hearing on unliquidated damages. See, e.g., id. at 186–87 (sanction of default judgment rendered against D on liability was appropriate, but sanction preventing D from participating in post-default trial on damages and attorney fees, both of which were unliquidated, was excessive). A sanction barring a defendant from participating in the hearing on unliquidated damages might be justified, however, if the defendant was responsible for destruction of evidence (i.e., spoliation) that directly and significantly impaired a party's ability to prove damages. Id. at 186; see* ***In re Dynamic Health, Inc.**, 32 S.W.3d 876, 885 (Tex.App.—Texarkana 2000, orig. proceeding).*

§3.14 Findings of fact. When the trial court awards unliquidated damages after a default, the defendant should ask the court to file findings of fact and conclusions of law. *See* **IKB Indus. v. Pro-Line Corp.**, 938 S.W.2d 440, 443 (Tex.1997). See "Requesting findings of fact," ch. 10-E, §3. A request for findings of fact and conclusions of law accomplishes two things. First, it extends the time for the trial court to consider the basis for its judgment. **IKB Indus.**, 938 S.W.2d at 442–43. Second, it extends the time for perfecting the appeal. Tex. R. App. P. 26.1(a)(4). See "Effect on appellate timetable," ch. 10-E, §6.1. Findings of fact and conclusions of law are not appropriate for a default judgment based on liquidated damages. **IKB Indus.**, 938 S.W.2d at 443.

§3.15 Waiver. The plaintiff waives the right to default if it proceeds to trial as though the defendant had filed an answer. **Artripe v. Hughes**, 857 S.W.2d 82, 87 (Tex.App.—Corpus Christi 1993, writ denied). Once the parties announce ready for trial and the jury has been selected, it is too late to ask for a default judgment. **Dodson v. Citizens State Bank**, 701 S.W.2d 89, 94 (Tex.App.—Amarillo 1986, writ ref'd n.r.e.).

§4. Post-answer default

A post-answer default occurs when a defendant who filed an answer does not appear at trial or a dispositive hearing. **Dolgencorp of Tex., Inc. v. Lerma**, 288 S.W.3d 922, 925 (Tex.2009); **Stoner v. Thompson**, 578 S.W.2d 679, 682 (Tex.1979).

§4.1 Effect of defendant's answer. By filing an answer, the defendant prevents the court from rendering a default judgment without a hearing. *See* **Dolgencorp of Tex., Inc. v. Lerma**, 288 S.W.3d 922, 930 (Tex.2009). Even if the defendant does not appear at trial, a filed answer serves as a denial of the plaintiff's allegations. **Frymire Eng'g Co. v. Grantham**, 524 S.W.2d 680, 681 (Tex.1975); **Flores v. Brimex L.P.**, 5 S.W.3d 816, 820 (Tex.App.—San Antonio 1999, no pet.). Thus, the plaintiff must offer evidence and prove its case as in a trial on the merits. **Dolgencorp of Tex.**, 288 S.W.3d at 930. See "Trial," ch. 7-A, §4.5.

§4.2 Sufficiency of plaintiff's pleadings. A post-answer default, like a no-answer default, must be supported by the plaintiff's petition. *See* **Stoner v. Thompson**, 578 S.W.2d 679, 684 (Tex.1979). See "Sufficiency of plaintiff's petition," ch. 7-A, §3.2.

§4.3 Notice of trial or dispositive hearing. A post-answer default is valid only if the defendant received notice of the setting for trial or other dispositive hearing at which the default was rendered. **$429.30 v. State**, 896 S.W.2d 363, 366 (Tex.App.—Houston [1st Dist.] 1995, no writ); **Matsushita Elec. Corp. v. McAllen Copy Data, Inc.**, 815 S.W.2d 850, 853 (Tex.App.—Corpus Christi 1991, writ denied); *see* Tex. R. Civ. P. 21(b), 245. A court can render a default judgment for failure to appear only if the hearing is a dispositive hearing. *See* **Masterson v. Cox**, 886 S.W.2d 436, 437–38 (Tex.App.—Houston [1st Dist.] 1994, no writ). Before rendering a default judgment against a defendant who answered but did not appear for trial or a dispositive hearing, the trial court should determine whether the defendant received proper notice. *See, e.g.*, **Cliff v. Huggins**, 724 S.W.2d 778, 779 (Tex.1987) (reversed; D did not receive notice of trial setting); **Murphree v. Ziegelmair**, 937 S.W.2d 493, 495 (Tex.App.—Houston [1st Dist.] 1995, no writ) (reversed; Ds did not have notice that failure to attend pretrial conference could result in immediate disposition).

1. Due process. A defendant who filed an answer has a constitutional right to notice of all hearings. *See* **Smith v. Holmes**, 53 S.W.3d 815, 817 (Tex.App.—Austin 2001, no pet.); *cf.* **LBL Oil Co. v. International Power Servs.**, 777 S.W.2d 390, 390–91 (Tex.1989) (post-appearance default judgment; once D makes appearance, notice of hearing is required as matter of due process). A party's right to be heard in a contested case is fundamental. *See* **LBL Oil**, 777 S.W.2d at 390–91; **Bloom v. Bloom**, 767 S.W.2d 463, 472 (Tex.App.—San Antonio 1989, writ denied).

2. TRCP 245. A defendant who filed an answer (or appeared in the case) must be given 45 days' notice of a setting that results in a post-answer default judgment. *See* Tex. R. Civ. P. 245; **Pessel v. Jenkins**, 125 S.W.3d 807, 808–09 (Tex.App.—Texarkana 2004, no pet.); **Burress v. Richardson**, 97 S.W.3d 806, 807 (Tex.App.—Dallas 2003, no pet.); **Custom-Crete, Inc. v. K-Bar Servs.**, 82 S.W.3d 655, 659 (Tex.App.—San Antonio 2002, no pet.). The defendant is entitled to 45 days' notice of the first trial setting; if the trial date is reset, the defendant is entitled to "reasonable" notice of the second or later setting. Tex. R. Civ. P. 245. Because the notice is mandatory and involves constitutional rights, a post-answer default must be set aside when the court's notice is returned as undeliverable. *See* **Burress**, 97 S.W.3d at 807; **Transoceanic Shipping Co. v. General Univ'l Sys.**, 961 S.W.2d 418, 419–20 & n.2 (Tex.App.—Houston [1st Dist.] 1997, no writ). *But see* **Withrow v. Schou**, 13 S.W.3d 37, 41–42 (Tex.App.—Houston [14th Dist.] 1999, pet. denied) (trial court is not required to find D's attorney and send another notice of trial setting after first notice was returned as undeliverable).

§4.4 Motion. A motion for post-answer default is not always necessary. Generally, when a defendant does not appear for trial or a dispositive hearing, the court decides to go forward with a post-answer default hearing on its own initiative. For the form for a motion for post-answer default, see **O'Connor's Texas Civil Forms**, FORM 7A:7 (2020 ed.).

§4.5 Trial. If the defendant does not appear at a scheduled trial, the court can conduct the trial without the defendant and grant a default judgment if the plaintiff proves all aspects of its case with evidence. **Bradley Motors, Inc. v. Mackey**, 878 S.W.2d 140, 141 (Tex.1994).

1. Right to jury. When the defendant does not appear for a scheduled trial, the case can be tried by the court, even if the defendant requested a jury. When the defendant does not appear at trial, it waives its right to a jury trial. **Bradley Motors**, 878 S.W.2d at 141; **Hanners v. State Bar**, 860 S.W.2d 903, 911 (Tex.App.—Dallas 1993, no writ). If the defendant requested a jury trial before its answer was struck and then appears for trial, it is entitled to a jury trial. *See, e.g.*, **Brantley v. Etter**, 662 S.W.2d 752, 756 (Tex.App.—San Antonio 1983) (D was still entitled to jury trial on damages after D's answer was struck as a sanction), *writ ref'd n.r.e.*, 677 S.W.2d 503 (Tex.1984); *see also* **Otis Elevator Co. v. Parmelee**, 850 S.W.2d 179, 181 (Tex.1993) (trial court could not award unliquidated damages without a hearing after imposing sanction equivalent to default judgment).

2. Ask for court reporter. The plaintiff should ask the court reporter to record the hearing. If the defendant cannot get the court reporter to prepare a record because the reporter did not transcribe the hearing, the defendant is entitled to a new trial in most cases. **Smith v. Smith**, 544 S.W.2d 121, 123 (Tex.1976); **Carstar Collision, Inc. v. Mercury Fin. Co.**, 23 S.W.3d 368, 370 (Tex.App.—Houston [1st Dist.] 1999, pet. denied); *see, e.g.*, **Sharif v. Par Tech, Inc.**, 135

S.W.3d 869, 873 (Tex.App.—Houston [1st Dist.] 2004, no pet.) (default judgment reversed because there was no reporter's record). See "Post-answer default judgment," **O'Connor's Texas Civil Appeals**, ch. 6-C, §3.1.6 (2020 ed.).

3. Prove liability & damages. At trial, the plaintiff must carry its burden to prove all the elements of its cause of action; the defendant has admitted nothing by its default. **Stoner v. Thompson**, 578 S.W.2d 679, 682 (Tex.1979); **Flores v. Brimex L.P.**, 5 S.W.3d 816, 820 (Tex.App.—San Antonio 1999, no pet.); **Onwuteaka v. Gill**, 908 S.W.2d 276, 281 (Tex.App.—Houston [1st Dist.] 1995, no writ); **Holberg v. Short**, 731 S.W.2d 584, 587 (Tex.App.—Houston [14th Dist.] 1987, no writ). The plaintiff's evidence must be sufficient to support both the liability finding and the damages award. *See* **Stone Res. v. Barnett**, 661 S.W.2d 148, 151 (Tex.App.—Houston [1st Dist.] 1983, no writ). On appeal, if the appellate court finds the plaintiff did not present legally sufficient evidence to support the post-answer default, the court will remand for a new trial. **Dolgencorp of Tex., Inc. v. Lerma**, 288 S.W.3d 922, 930 (Tex.2009).

§5. Drafting default judgment

For a no-answer default judgment, see **O'Connor's Texas Civil Forms**, FORM 9C:2 (2020 ed.); for a post-answer default judgment, see **O'Connor's Texas Civil Forms**, FORM 9C:3 (2020 ed.).

§5.1 General terms. The default judgment, like any judgment, should identify the parties and the relief granted. See "Judgment," ch. 9-C, §1 et seq.

§5.2 Service & jurisdiction. The no-answer default judgment should recite all the jurisdictional requisites: (1) the citation was duly served with process, (2) the return of service was on file for ten days before the default was rendered, and (3) the defendant failed to answer and appear. For documents that may need to be attached to the judgment, see "Documents to file," ch. 7-A, §3.9.2.

§5.3 Final judgment.

1. No-answer default. To be final and appealable, a no-answer default judgment must dispose of all issues and parties in the plaintiff's petition. **Houston Health Clubs, Inc. v. First Ct. of Appeals**, 722 S.W.2d 692, 693 (Tex.1986); *see* **Castano v. Foremost Cty. Mut. Ins.**, 31 S.W.3d 387, 388 (Tex.App.—San Antonio 2000, no pet.) (default judgment against one D was not final because order to sever other Ds was not signed). There is no presumed disposition of issues in a no-answer default-judgment case. **Houston Health Clubs**, 722 S.W.2d at 693. See "Summary disposition," ch. 9-C, §6.3.2(2).

Practice Tip

If you are suing multiple defendants, some of whom have answered and some of whom have not, and you are seeking a default judgment against only one, do not draft the default judgment to say that the judgment disposes of all parties and all claims and is therefore final. See ***In re Daredia****, 317 S.W.3d 247, 248–49 (Tex.2010). Otherwise, you may lose your right to obtain a judgment against the remaining defendants because they have been unequivocally, even though inadvertently, dismissed from the case. See id. See "Statement of finality," ch. 9-C, §4.3.*

2. Post-answer default. Courts of appeals disagree on whether a post-answer default judgment is presumed to dispose of all issues to make the judgment final and appealable. *Compare* **Shoreline, Inc. v. Hisel**, 115 S.W.3d 21, 24 (Tex.App.—Corpus Christi 2003, pet. denied) (because post-answer default judgment does not follow conventional trial on merits, presumption of finality does not apply), *and* **New Braunfels Transmission, Inc. v. Clarke**, No. 03-09-00414-CV, 2010 WL 2698769 (Tex.App.—Austin 2010, no pet.) (memo op.; 7-7-10) (same), *with* **Thomas v. DuBovy-Longo**, 786 S.W.2d 506, 507 (Tex.App.—Dallas 1990, writ denied) (because case is set for conventional trial on merits and P has to prove case at trial setting, presumption of finality applies).

§6. Notice of default judgment

§6.1 Notice after no-answer default. The clerk of the trial court is required to send to the defendant, at the last known mailing address certified by the plaintiff, written notice that a no-answer default judgment has been rendered against

it. Tex. R. Civ. P. 239a. The clerk must note on the docket that she mailed the notice to the defendant immediately after the default judgment was signed. *Id.* The purpose of TRCP 239a is to give the defendant an opportunity to file a motion for new trial after a no-answer default judgment. **Bloom v. Bloom**, 767 S.W.2d 463, 468 (Tex.App.—San Antonio 1989, writ denied). Once notice is properly sent, a rebuttable presumption arises that the defendant received the notice. **Continental Cas. Co. v. Davilla**, 139 S.W.3d 374, 383 (Tex.App.—Fort Worth 2004, pet. denied) (Gardner, J., concurring); *see* Tex. R. Civ. P. 21a(e). The clerk's failure to give notice does not affect the finality of the judgment. Tex. R. Civ. P. 239a; **Garza v. Attorney Gen.**, 166 S.W.3d 799, 815 (Tex.App.—Corpus Christi 2005, no pet.); *see* **Campbell v. Fincher**, 72 S.W.3d 723, 724–25 (Tex.App.—Waco 2002, no pet.) (failure to give notice is not reversible error).

§6.2 Notice after post-answer default. Notice of a post-answer default judgment is governed by the rule that governs notice of judgments. See "TRCP 306a," ch. 9-C, §5.2.1.

§7. Attacking default judgment

A default judgment may be attacked either directly or collaterally, depending on whether it is void or voidable. *See* **PNS Stores v. Rivera**, 379 S.W.3d 267, 271–72 (Tex.2012) (void judgment can be attacked directly or collaterally, but voidable judgment can be attacked only directly). A direct attack attempts to vacate the judgment and must be brought within a definite time period after the judgment is signed. *See id.* at 271 & n.7. A collateral attack, which can be brought at any time, seeks to avoid the binding effect of the judgment in a proceeding to obtain specific relief that is barred by the judgment. *See id.* at 272; **Henderson v. Chambers**, 208 S.W.3d 546, 550 (Tex.App.—Austin 2006, no pet.).

§7.1 Direct attacks on default judgment. A defendant can directly attack a default judgment by a motion for new trial, a restricted appeal, or a bill of review. *See* **PNS Stores v. Rivera**, 379 S.W.3d 267, 271 (Tex.2012); *see, e.g.*, **Fidelity & Guar. Ins. v. Drewery Constr. Co.**, 186 S.W.3d 571, 573 (Tex.2006) (motion for new trial); **Primate Constr., Inc. v. Silver**, 884 S.W.2d 151, 152 (Tex.1994) (restricted appeal); **Min v. Avila**, 991 S.W.2d 495, 499–500 (Tex.App.—Houston [1st Dist.] 1999, no pet.) (bill of review). When a no-answer default judgment is challenged by a direct attack, the record must show strict compliance with the manner and mode of service; otherwise, the service is invalid and the default judgment is void. **Primate Constr.**, 884 S.W.2d at 152; **Min**, 991 S.W.2d at 500; *see* **Insurance Co. of Pa. v. Lejeune**, 297 S.W.3d 254, 256 (Tex.2009).

Caution

Although a defendant can attack a default judgment by filing an ordinary appeal (if it received notice of the judgment in time to file the appeal), it generally should not do so. See ***Barrett v. Westover Park Cmty. Ass'n****, No. 01-10-01112-CV, 2012 WL 682342 (Tex.App.—Houston [1st Dist.] 2012, no pet.) (memo op.; 3-1-12). See "Deadline to file notice of appeal,"* ***O'Connor's Texas Civil Appeals****, ch. 5-A, §5 (2020 ed.). The better practice is to file a motion for new trial first. The defendant—by filing an appeal rather than a motion for new trial—will not have developed any evidence necessary to contradict a claim of effective service. See* ***Barrett****, No. 01-10-01112-CV, 2012 WL 682342 (memo op.). The defendant will also not be able to cure those deficiencies in the record by submitting evidence after the appeal is filed; that evidence is not part of the appellate record and cannot be considered. See, e.g.,* ***Barrett****, No. 01-10-01112-CV, 2012 WL 682342 (memo op.) (affidavits not considered).*

1. Motion for new trial. A defendant who suffered a default judgment may ask the trial court to overturn the default by granting a motion for new trial. *See* Tex. R. Civ. P. 320. A motion for new trial gives the defendant the first opportunity to attack a default judgment. **Barrett**, No. 01-10-01112-CV, 2012 WL 682342 (memo op.). See "MNT after default judgment," ch. 10-B, §9.

(1) Deadline. A motion for new trial must be filed within 30 days after the judgment was signed. See "Deadlines for MNT," ch. 10-B, §5.

(2) Record. In a motion for new trial (and a bill of review), the record is not limited as it is in a restricted appeal; the parties can present evidence (e.g., affidavits, depositions, testimony) to develop the record and explain what

happened. **Fidelity & Guar.**, 186 S.W.3d at 573–74 (motion for new trial); *see* **Sutherland v. Spencer**, 376 S.W.3d 752, 754–55 (Tex.2012) (motion for new trial); **Ginn v. Forrester**, 282 S.W.3d 430, 432 (Tex.2009) (restricted appeal); **Gold v. Gold**, 145 S.W.3d 212, 214 (Tex.2004) (bill of review); *see also* **Marrot Comms. v. Town & Country Prtshp.**, 227 S.W.3d 372, 379 (Tex.App.—Houston [1st Dist.] 2007, pet. denied) (motion for new trial; because extrinsic evidence is allowed, parties can address **Craddock** factors for motion for new trial or elements of bill of review). See "Verification," ch. 10-B, §9.2. For the limits on the record in a restricted appeal, see "Error is apparent from face of record," ch. 7-A, §7.1.2(2)(e). Because the record is not limited in a motion for new trial, the court can examine the critical question of why the defendant did not appear. **Sutherland**, 376 S.W.3d at 755; **Fidelity & Guar.**, 186 S.W.3d at 574.

(3) Grounds. A defendant can file a motion for new trial if (1) the defendant was not properly served with notice of the suit, the trial, or the hearing, or (2) after receiving proper notice, the defendant did not appear because of a mistake or accident. See "Sworn motion," ch. 10-B, §9.1.

(4) Review. For the methods of review when the trial court denies or grants a motion for new trial, see "Review," ch. 10-B, §17.

2. Restricted appeal. A defendant who did not participate in the trial of the case or the hearing that resulted in the judgment being appealed may obtain review of the judgment by a restricted appeal. *See* Tex. R. App. P. 30; **Quaestor Invs. v. State of Chiapas**, 997 S.W.2d 226, 227 & n.1 (Tex.1999); **Norman Comms. v. Texas Eastman Co.**, 955 S.W.2d 269, 270 (Tex.1997).

Note

Some statutes and older cases refer to the restricted appeal by its old name, "writ of error." E.g., Tex. Civ. Prac. & Rem. Code §51.013; ***Primate Constr.****, 884 S.W.2d at 152; see* ***Quaestor Invs.****, 997 S.W.2d at 227 n.1 (writ of error is from former TRAP 45, now TRAP 30).*

(1) Deadline. A restricted appeal must be filed within six months after the judgment was signed. Tex. R. App. P. 26.1(c); **Hubicki v. Festina**, 226 S.W.3d 405, 407 (Tex.2007); **Quaestor Invs.**, 997 S.W.2d at 227.

(2) Allegations. To obtain review by restricted appeal, the defendant must show that the following requirements are satisfied.

Note

In a non-default-judgment case, the Supreme Court recently held that the first four requirements below are jurisdictional but the fifth one is not and instead goes to the merits of the appeal. See ***Ex parte E.H.****, 602 S.W.3d 486, 497 (Tex.2020) (restricted appeal from order granting petition for expunction). Thus, the defendant must satisfy the first four requirements to establish the court's authority to hear the restricted appeal and then must satisfy the fifth requirement to prevail. Id.*

(a) Appeal was timely filed. The restricted appeal was filed within six months after the judgment. Tex. Civ. Prac. & Rem. Code §51.013; Tex. R. App. P. 26.1(c); **Ex parte E.H.**, 602 S.W.3d at 495; **Norman Comms.**, 955 S.W.2d at 270; *see also* **Quaestor Invs.**, 997 S.W.2d at 229 (removal suspends six-month timetable; time clock restarts when federal court executes remand order and mails certified copy to state court).

(b) Defendant was party. The defendant was a party in the suit being challenged. **Ex parte E.H.**, 602 S.W.3d at 495; **Norman Comms.**, 955 S.W.2d at 270. A restricted appeal is also available to (1) a person whose privity of estate, title, or interest is apparent from the record in the trial court, or (2) a person who is a party under the doctrine of virtual representation. **Gunn v. Cavanaugh**, 391 S.W.2d 723, 725 (Tex.1965). See "Virtual party," ch. 2-B, §4.1.2.

(c) Defendant did not participate at trial or hearing. The defendant did not participate, either in person or through counsel, in the actual trial of the case or the hearing that resulted in the judgment being appealed. *See*

Tex. R. App. P. 30; **Ex parte E.H.**, 602 S.W.3d at 495; **Pike-Grant v. Grant**, 447 S.W.3d 884, 886 (Tex.2014); **Norman Comms.**, 955 S.W.2d at 270. If the record shows the defendant participated in the "decision-making event" that produced the final judgment adjudicating the defendant's rights, the defendant cannot proceed by restricted appeal. **Texaco, Inc. v. Central Power & Light Co.**, 925 S.W.2d 586, 589 (Tex.1996). "Participation" means taking part in a hearing in open court that leads to the rendition of judgment on questions of law (if the case was disposed of on the questions of law) or on questions of fact (if the final judgment was rendered on the facts). **Withem v. Underwood**, 922 S.W.2d 956, 957 (Tex.1996); *see* **Pike-Grant**, 447 S.W.3d at 887; *see also* **Stubbs v. Stubbs**, 685 S.W.2d 643, 645 (Tex.1985) (party who signed waiver of citation could still appeal by writ of error). The policy behind the nonparticipation requirement is to deny restricted appeal to those who should have pursued a quicker, ordinary appeal. **Texaco, Inc.**, 925 S.W.2d at 590.

(d) Defendant did not file postjudgment motion or notice of appeal. The defendant did not file a postjudgment motion, a request for findings of fact, or a notice of appeal within the time permitted by TRAP 26.1(a). Tex. R. App. P. 30; **Aviation Composite Techs. v. CLB Corp.**, 131 S.W.3d 181, 184 (Tex.App.—Fort Worth 2004, no pet.); *e.g.*, **Aero at Sp. z.o.o. v. Gartman**, 469 S.W.3d 314, 315 (Tex.App.—Fort Worth 2015, no pet.) (D's special appearance that implicitly asked trial court to vacate default judgment qualified as postjudgment motion; thus, restricted appeal was not permitted); *see* **Ex parte E.H.**, 602 S.W.3d at 495.

(e) Error is apparent from face of record. The trial court erred, and the error is apparent from the face of the record. **Norman Comms.**, 955 S.W.2d at 270; **General Elec. Co. v. Falcon Ridge Apts., Jt.V.**, 811 S.W.2d 942, 943 (Tex.1991); *e.g.*, **Pike-Grant**, 447 S.W.3d at 886–87 (although recital on face of judgment indicated that wife attended divorce hearing in November, other references in record conclusively established that hearing occurred in September without wife's participation; trial court erred in dismissing restricted appeal); *see* **Ex parte E.H.**, 602 S.W.3d at 495. A restricted appeal requires error to be apparent from the face of the record, not inferred from the record. **Gold**, 145 S.W.3d at 213; *e.g.*, **Ginn**, 282 S.W.3d at 431 (no reversible error when record was silent on whether notice was sent); **Alexander v. Lynda's Boutique**, 134 S.W.3d 845, 849–50 (Tex.2004) (same).

[1] Documents included. The "face of the record" includes the reporter's record, if any, and the clerk's record. *See* **Pike-Grant**, 447 S.W.3d at 886–87; **Norman Comms.**, 955 S.W.2d at 270. Only documents on file with the court at the time of the judgment determine the face of the record. **Laas v. Williamson**, 156 S.W.3d 854, 857 (Tex.App.—Beaumont 2005, no pet.).

[2] No extrinsic evidence. The appellate court cannot consider evidence outside the record. **General Elec.**, 811 S.W.2d at 944; *see* **Ginn**, 282 S.W.3d at 432.

[3] No presumption of proper service. The judgment's recitals in a restricted appeal do not raise a presumption of proper service because such a presumption cannot be confirmed or rebutted by evidence outside the record. **Fidelity & Guar.**, 186 S.W.3d at 573 (motion for new trial); *see* **Primate Constr.**, 884 S.W.2d at 152. Thus, if the petition, citation, or return of service is inadequate on its face to support a no-answer default judgment, the court of appeals will reverse the default judgment. *See* **Hubicki**, 226 S.W.3d at 407–08; *see, e.g.*, **Bank of N.Y. Mellon v. Redbud 115 Land Trust**, 452 S.W.3d 868, 871 (Tex.App.—Dallas 2014, pet. denied) (invalid service on D-bank because P did not comply with rules for serving financial institution); **Autozone, Inc. v. Duenes**, 108 S.W.3d 917, 920–21 (Tex.App.—Corpus Christi 2003, no pet.) (invalid service on foreign corporation).

3. Bill of review. A defendant may attack a default judgment by a bill of review, which is generally an equitable action brought after it is too late either to appeal or to file a motion for new trial. **Mabon Ltd. v. Afri-Carib Enters.**, 369 S.W.3d 809, 812 (Tex.2012); **Caldwell v. Barnes**, 154 S.W.3d 93, 96 (Tex.2004) (**Caldwell II**); **King Ranch, Inc. v. Chapman**, 118 S.W.3d 742, 751 (Tex.2003); **Wembley Inv. v. Herrera**, 11 S.W.3d 924, 926–27 (Tex.1999); **Caldwell v. Barnes**, 975 S.W.2d 535, 537 (Tex.1998) (**Caldwell I**); **State v. 1985 Chevrolet Pickup Truck**, 778 S.W.2d 463, 464 (Tex.1989); *see* Tex. R. Civ. P. 329b(f). In certain types of proceedings, a statutory bill of review is available. *See* **Valdez v. Hollenbeck**, 465 S.W.3d 217, 221 (Tex.2015). See "Statutory bill of review," ch. 7-A, §7.1.3(2). Although a bill of review attacks a default judgment from a particular case, the bill of review is an independent suit filed under a different cause number. **In re J.J.**, 394 S.W.3d 76, 81 (Tex.App.—El Paso 2012, no pet.). The bill of review must, however, be brought in the court that rendered the original judgment. **Valdez**, 465 S.W.3d at 226; **Frost Nat'l Bank v. Fernandez**, 315 S.W.3d 494, 504 (Tex.2010); *see also* **In**

re J.J., 394 S.W.3d at 81–82 (once jurisdiction attaches to proper court, bill of review may be transferred to different court).

Note

In this bill-of-review section, the defendant in the earlier suit (now the petitioner for the bill of review) is referred to as the defendant-petitioner; the plaintiff in the earlier suit (now the respondent for the bill of review) is referred to as the plaintiff-respondent.

(1) Equitable bill of review.

(a) Deadline.

[1] Generally. A petition for an equitable bill of review must be filed after the trial court's plenary power expires but within the residual four-year statute of limitations. *See* Tex. Civ. Prac. & Rem. Code §16.051 (residual limitations period); Tex. R. Civ. P. 329b(f) (plenary power); **PNS Stores**, 379 S.W.3d at 275 (within four years after rendition of judgment); **Caldwell I**, 975 S.W.2d at 538 (residual four-year limitations period applies to bill of review).

[2] Extrinsic fraud. If the defendant-petitioner can show extrinsic fraud, the four-year statute of limitations is tolled. **PNS Stores**, 379 S.W.3d at 275; *see* **Temple v. Archambo**, 161 S.W.3d 217, 223–24 (Tex.App.—Corpus Christi 2005, no pet.); **Law v. Law**, 792 S.W.2d 150, 153 (Tex.App.—Houston [1st Dist.] 1990, writ denied). Extrinsic fraud is wrongful conduct outside the trial—such as keeping a party away from court or making false promises of compromise—that prevents a losing party from fully litigating rights or defenses and prevents a real trial on the issues involved. **Temple**, 161 S.W.3d at 224; *see, e.g.*, **PNS Stores**, 379 S.W.3d at 275–76 (some evidence of extrinsic fraud shown when P's attorney did not comply with TRCP 239a; he provided clerk with address of D's registered agent rather than D's last known address, which he knew); *see also* **Alexander v. Hagedorn**, 226 S.W.2d 996, 1002 (Tex.1950) (bill of review not proper because false testimony on element of cause of action was intrinsic fraud). Although evidence of extrinsic fraud tolls the four-year statute of limitations, it does not do so indefinitely—the limitations period begins to run when the defendant-petitioner knew or should have known about the default judgment. **PNS Stores**, 379 S.W.3d at 277 n.16.

(b) Record. In an equitable bill of review (and a motion for new trial), the record is not limited as it is in a restricted appeal; the parties can present evidence (e.g., affidavits, depositions, testimony) to develop the record and explain what happened. **Fidelity & Guar.**, 186 S.W.3d at 573–74 (motion for new trial); *see* **Ginn**, 282 S.W.3d at 432 (restricted appeal); **Gold**, 145 S.W.3d at 214 (bill of review); **Min**, 991 S.W.2d at 499–500 (bill of review); *see also* **Marrot Comms.**, 227 S.W.3d at 379 (motion for new trial; because extrinsic evidence is allowed, parties can address **Craddock** factors for motion for new trial or elements of bill of review). For the limits on the record in a restricted appeal, see "Error is apparent from face of record," ch. 7-A, §7.1.2(2)(e). Because the record is not limited in a bill of review, the court can examine the critical question of why the defendant did not appear. **Fidelity & Guar.**, 186 S.W.3d at 574.

(c) Sufficient cause. The defendant-petitioner must show sufficient cause for the court to grant the bill of review. *See* Tex. R. Civ. P. 329b(f). To do so, the defendant-petitioner must file a petition alleging certain grounds for the bill of review. *See* **1985 Chevrolet**, 778 S.W.2d at 464; **Beck v. Beck**, 771 S.W.2d 141, 141 (Tex.1989); **Baker v. Goldsmith**, 582 S.W.2d 404, 408 (Tex.1979). The grounds the defendant-petitioner must allege depend on whether the defendant-petitioner claims a due-process violation (i.e., no service of process or no notice of trial setting or dispositive hearing) in the bill of review.

[1] No due-process violation. To establish sufficient cause when there is no due-process violation claimed, the defendant-petitioner must demonstrate the following:

[a] Meritorious defense. The defendant-petitioner must allege sworn facts sufficient to constitute a meritorious defense to the action. **1985 Chevrolet**, 778 S.W.2d at 464; **Baker**, 582 S.W.2d at 408; *see* **Mabon Ltd.**, 369 S.W.3d at 812; **Caldwell II**, 154 S.W.3d at 96. It must also present prima facie proof, generally at a preliminary hearing, in support of the allegation. *See* **Beck**, 771 S.W.2d at 142; **Baker**, 582 S.W.2d at 408.

• **Prima facie proof.** The defendant-petitioner must make a prima facie showing of the defense as a preliminary matter. *See* **Caldwell II**, 154 S.W.3d at 97; **1985 Chevrolet**, 778 S.W.2d at 464; **Beck**, 771 S.W.2d at 142;

Baker, 582 S.W.2d at 408. To make a prima facie showing, the defendant-petitioner must prove that (1) its defense is not barred as a matter of law and (2) it will be entitled to judgment on retrial if no contrary evidence is offered. **Baker**, 582 S.W.2d at 408–09; **Ortmann v. Ortmann**, 999 S.W.2d 85, 88 (Tex.App.—Houston [14th Dist.] 1999, pet. denied). Prima facie proof can consist of answers to interrogatories, admissions, affidavits on file, and other documents or evidence that the court, in its discretion, may receive. **Baker**, 582 S.W.2d at 409; **Temple**, 161 S.W.3d at 223. If the defendant-petitioner makes a prima facie showing, the court will conduct a trial on the remaining bill-of-review grounds. **Beck**, 771 S.W.2d at 142; **Baker**, 582 S.W.2d at 409. See "No due-process violation," ch. 7-A, §7.1.3(1)(e)[1]. If no prima facie showing is made, the court will deny the bill-of-review petition. **Beck**, 771 S.W.2d at 142; **Baker**, 582 S.W.2d at 409.

- **Pretrial hearing.** In determining whether the defendant-petitioner has met its burden, the court may conduct a pretrial hearing, sometimes referred to as a "**Baker** hearing." *See* **Beck**, 771 S.W.2d at 142; **Baker**, 582 S.W.2d at 408; **Maree v. Zuniga**, 502 S.W.3d 359, 362 (Tex.App.—Houston [14th Dist.] 2016, no pet.). Some courts have held that a **Baker** hearing is not required, and thus the bill-of-review grounds can be tried together without a separate hearing on the meritorious defense. *See* **Ramsey v. State**, 249 S.W.3d 568, 576 (Tex.App.—Waco 2008, no pet.); **Thompson v. Ballard**, 149 S.W.3d 161, 165 (Tex.App.—Tyler 2004, no pet.); **Ortmann**, 999 S.W.2d at 88. If a **Baker** hearing is held, the court can consider only whether the defendant-petitioner has presented a prima facie meritorious defense; consideration of the other grounds—without notice and an opportunity to be heard as to a trial on the merits of the bill-of-review petition—is improper. *See* **Beck**, 771 S.W.2d at 142; **Baker**, 582 S.W.2d at 408–09; *see, e.g.*, **Maree**, 502 S.W.3d at 365–66 (error for court to dismiss bill-of-review petition at **Baker** hearing based on D-petitioner's failure to prove lack of fault or negligence when court gave notice only of **Baker** hearing, not trial on merits of bill-of-review petition).

[b] Justification for failure to assert defense. The defendant-petitioner must justify its failure to present a defense by alleging fraud, accident, wrongful act by the plaintiff, or official mistake. **Mabon Ltd.**, 369 S.W.3d at 812; **Caldwell II**, 154 S.W.3d at 96; **Wembley Inv.**, 11 S.W.3d at 927; **Caldwell I**, 975 S.W.2d at 537; **1985 Chevrolet**, 778 S.W.2d at 464; *see, e.g.*, **Baker**, 582 S.W.2d at 407 (letter that constituted answer was misplaced at courthouse).

[c] No fault or negligence. The defendant-petitioner must show the default judgment was not rendered as a result of its own fault or negligence. **Mabon Ltd.**, 369 S.W.3d at 812; **Caldwell II**, 154 S.W.3d at 96; **Caldwell I**, 975 S.W.2d at 537; **Texas Mach. & Equip. Co. v. Gordon Knox Oil & Expl. Co.**, 442 S.W.2d 315, 317–18 (Tex.1969); *see* **King Ranch**, 118 S.W.3d at 752 (allegations of fraud or negligence by party's own attorney are insufficient to support bill of review); *see, e.g.*, **Campus Invs. v. Cullever**, 144 S.W.3d 464, 466 (Tex.2004) (although D was properly served through Secretary of State, D did not receive service of process because it was negligent in not updating addresses for registered agent and registered office with Secretary of State; trial court's denial of bill of review was proper). To establish a lack of fault or negligence, the defendant-petitioner must also show that it diligently pursued all legal remedies as to any motions (e.g., motion for new trial, motion to reinstate) that could have been filed in the underlying proceeding. **Mabon Ltd.**, 369 S.W.3d at 813; **Gold**, 145 S.W.3d at 214. But the defendant-petitioner is not required to show that it diligently monitored the case status. **Mabon Ltd.**, 369 S.W.3d at 813.

[2] Due-process violation. To establish sufficient cause when there is a due-process violation claimed, a defendant-petitioner is not required to prove the first two grounds set out above. **Katy Venture, Ltd. v. Cremona Bistro Corp.**, 469 S.W.3d 160, 164 (Tex.2015); **Mabon Ltd.**, 369 S.W.3d at 812; **Caldwell II**, 154 S.W.3d at 96–97; *see* **Peralta v. Heights Med. Ctr., Inc.**, 485 U.S. 80, 86–87 (1988) (judgment rendered without service violates due process). Thus, when a defendant-petitioner claims it was not served with process or it did not receive notice of the trial or default judgment, it must prove only the third ground (i.e., no fault or negligence in allowing a default judgment to be rendered). **Katy Venture**, 469 S.W.3d at 164; *see* **Mabon Ltd.**, 369 S.W.3d at 812 (third ground is conclusively established if D-petitioner proves it was not served); **Caldwell II**, 154 S.W.3d at 97 (same). See "Due-process violation," ch. 7-A, §7.1.3(1)(e)[2]. A defendant who was not served with process or who did not receive notice cannot be at fault or negligent in allowing a default judgment to be rendered. **Caldwell II**, 154 S.W.3d at 97; *see* **Cash v. Beaumont Dealers Auto Auction, Inc.**, 275 S.W.3d 915, 918 (Tex.App.—Beaumont 2009, no pet.).

Note

*In **Katy Venture**, the defendants did not receive notice of process that was properly served on the Secretary of State because they had not provided an updated registered address to the Secretary of State. See **Katy Venture**, 469 S.W.3d at 162. See "Service on Secretary of State," ch. 2-I, §5. However, after obtaining a default judgment, the plaintiff certified an outdated address as the defendants' "last known mailing address" for serving notice of a default judgment under TRCP 239a. **Katy Venture**, 469 S.W.3d at 162. See "Notice after no-answer default," ch. 7-A, §6.1. The defendants filed a bill of review asserting a due-process violation for failure to receive notice of the default judgment, but the trial court denied their bill of review and granted the plaintiff's motion for summary judgment. **Katy Venture**, 469 S.W.3d at 162–63. The Supreme Court held, however, that the trial court should not have granted summary judgment because the defendants raised a genuine issue of material fact about their lack of fault or negligence in failing to receive notice of the default judgment. See id. at 164 (Ds offered some evidence that P provided out-of-date address despite knowing Ds' correct, current address; although Ds' negligence in not updating registered address contributed to lack of actual service of process, there was fact issue about whether Ds' negligence or P's action was the reason Ds did not receive notice of default judgment). Thus, although a defendant may be negligent in fulfilling a particular requirement that affects service of process, it is not necessarily precluded from challenging a default judgment if it did not receive notice of the default judgment because the specific notice requirements of TRCP 239a were not met.*

(d) Defenses. The plaintiff-respondent can raise a number of defenses to the petition for an equitable bill of review.

[1] Untimeliness. The defendant-petitioner is generally not entitled to relief by bill of review unless it files the petition within the residual four-year statute of limitations. See "Deadline," ch. 7-A, §7.1.3(1)(a).

[2] Failure to exhaust other remedies. The defendant-petitioner is not entitled to relief by bill of review unless it exhausted all other remedies available under Texas law at the time it filed the bill of review. **Wembley Inv.**, 11 S.W.3d at 927; **Caldwell I**, 975 S.W.2d at 537–38. For example, a defendant-petitioner is not entitled to relief by way of bill of review if it could have, but did not, file a motion to reinstate, a motion for new trial, or a direct appeal. *See* **Gold**, 145 S.W.3d at 214; *see also* **In re Estrada**, 492 S.W.3d 42, 50–51 (Tex.App.—Corpus Christi 2016, orig. proceeding) (D-petitioners failed to exhaust remedies by not using procedures under TRCP 306a to extend time to file postjudgment motions). By comparison, a defendant-petitioner is not required to file a restricted appeal in order to have "exhausted all other remedies." **Gold**, 145 S.W.3d at 214.

[3] Laches. Because a bill of review is an equitable remedy, laches may be raised as a defense. **Caldwell I**, 975 S.W.2d at 538. The two elements of laches are (1) unreasonable delay by one with legal or equitable rights in asserting them, and (2) a good-faith change of position by another to its own detriment because of the delay. *Id.*; **Rogers v. Ricane Enters.**, 772 S.W.2d 76, 80 (Tex.1989). Generally, laches will not bar a suit before the limitations period expires unless some extraordinary circumstance rendered it inequitable to permit the defendant-petitioner to assert its rights. *E.g.*, **Caldwell I**, 975 S.W.2d at 538–39 (laches did not bar bill of review filed almost two years after petitioner first learned of judgment). See "Laches," **O'Connor's Texas Causes of Action**, ch. 52, §3.2 (2021 ed.).

(e) Trial. The defendant-petitioner's burden at trial depends on whether the defendant-petitioner claimed a due-process violation.

[1] No due-process violation. If the defendant-petitioner did not claim a due-process violation and met its burden to present a prima facie meritorious defense, the court will conduct a separate trial in which the defendant-petitioner must prove the two remaining bill-of-review grounds by a preponderance of the evidence. *See* **1985 Chevrolet**, 778 S.W.2d at 464–65; **Beck**, 771 S.W.2d at 142; **Baker**, 582 S.W.2d at 409. If the defendant-petitioner does so, the court will permit the parties to revert to their original status as plaintiff and defendant with the burden on the original plaintiff to prove the underlying cause of action. *See* **1985 Chevrolet**, 778 S.W.2d at 465; **Baker**, 582 S.W.2d at 409. Once the trial is finished, the court will render a new final judgment. *See* **1985 Chevrolet**, 778 S.W.2d at 465; **Baker**, 582 S.W.2d at 409.

[2] Due-process violation. If the defendant-petitioner claimed a due-process violation, the court will conduct a trial in which the defendant-petitioner must prove only that it was not served with process. **Caldwell II**, 154 S.W.3d at 97. Proving process was not served conclusively establishes that the default judgment was not rendered as a result of the defendant-petitioner's own fault or negligence. *Id.* at 97–98. If the defendant-petitioner proves that it was not served with process, the court will permit the parties to revert to their original status as plaintiff and defendant with the burden on the original plaintiff to prove the underlying cause of action. *Id.* Once the trial is finished, the court will render a new final judgment. *See* **1985 Chevrolet**, 778 S.W.2d at 465.

(2) Statutory bill of review. A statutory bill of review, which is rare, generally occurs in probate and guardianship proceedings. **Valdez**, 465 S.W.3d at 226; *see, e.g.,* **Ablon v. Campbell**, 457 S.W.3d 604, 609 (Tex.App.—Dallas 2015, pet. denied) (guardianship proceeding under former Prob. Code §657, now Tex. Est. Code §1056.101); **Buck v. Estate of Buck**, 291 S.W.3d 46, 52–53 (Tex.App.—Corpus Christi 2009, no pet.) (probate proceeding under former Prob. Code §31, now Tex. Est. Code §55.251). A statutory bill of review is not subject to the limitations or requirements of an equitable bill of review. **In re Cunningham**, 454 S.W.3d 139, 144 & n.3 (Tex.App.—Texarkana 2014, orig. proceeding); **Buck**, 291 S.W.3d at 53; **Chavez v. Chavez**, No. 01-13-00727-CV, 2014 WL 5343231 (Tex.App.—Houston [1st Dist.] 2014, no pet.) (memo op.; 10-21-14); *see* **Westchester Fire Ins. v. Nuckols**, 666 S.W.2d 372, 375 (Tex.App.—Eastland 1984, writ ref'd n.r.e.). If a statute imposes a specific limitations period for filing a bill of review, that statutory period controls over the residual four-year limitations period for an equitable bill of review. *E.g.,* **Valdez**, 465 S.W.3d at 227–28 (two-year statute of limitations for bill of review under former Prob. Code §31, now Tex. Est. Code §55.251, controlled); *see* Tex. Civ. Prac. & Rem. Code §16.051 (residual limitations period).

§7.2 Collateral attacks on default judgment. If a defendant is unable to attack a default judgment directly by one of the above methods, it may be able to attack the judgment collaterally to avoid the effect of the judgment. *See* **PNS Stores v. Rivera**, 379 S.W.3d 267, 272–73 (Tex.2012). But there is no set procedure and no statute of limitations for bringing a collateral attack. **Texas DOT v. T. Brown Constructors, Inc.**, 947 S.W.2d 655, 659 (Tex.App.—Austin 1997, pet. denied).

1. When to use. A defendant can collaterally attack only a void judgment. *See* **PNS Stores**, 379 S.W.3d at 271–72 (void judgment can be attacked directly or collaterally, but voidable judgment can be attacked only directly). If a judgment of a court of general jurisdiction is void, it can be collaterally attacked in another court of equal jurisdiction. **Browning v. Placke**, 698 S.W.2d 362, 363 (Tex.1985); **Armentor v. Kern**, 178 S.W.3d 147, 149 (Tex.App.—Houston [1st Dist.] 2005, no pet.). Certain jurisdictional defects render a judgment void; all other defects render the judgment voidable, and those judgments can be attacked only directly. **Browning**, 698 S.W.2d at 363; *see* **PNS Stores**, 379 S.W.3d at 272–73. See "Direct attacks on default judgment," ch. 7-A, §7.1.

(1) Defects in jurisdiction—generally. A judgment is void and can be collaterally attacked if the court rendering the judgment had no jurisdiction over the parties or property, no jurisdiction over the subject matter, no jurisdiction to enter that particular judgment, or no capacity to act as a court. **PNS Stores**, 379 S.W.3d at 272; **Browning**, 698 S.W.2d at 363; *cf.* **Browning v. Prostok**, 165 S.W.3d 336, 346 (Tex.2005) (attack on bankruptcy order).

(2) Defects in personal jurisdiction—no due process. A judgment is void and can be collaterally attacked when the record identifies substantial defects in personal jurisdiction that violate due process. **PNS Stores**, 379 S.W.3d at 273; *see* **In re E.R.**, 385 S.W.3d 552, 566 (Tex.2012). For defects in personal jurisdiction to violate due process, there must be a complete failure or lack of service rather than merely technical defects in service. **PNS Stores**, 379 S.W.3d at 274.

2. Review of record. In a collateral attack, the judgment is presumed to be valid. **PNS Stores**, 379 S.W.3d at 273; **Stewart v. USA Custom Paint & Body Shop, Inc.**, 870 S.W.2d 18, 20 (Tex.1994). Although the judgment is presumed valid, the court may look beyond the face of the judgment to determine whether the record demonstrates that the court lacked jurisdiction. **PNS Stores**, 379 S.W.3d at 273. The presumption disappears if the record establishes a jurisdictional defect sufficient to void the judgment. *Id.*; *see* **Alfonso v. Skadden**, 251 S.W.3d 52, 55 (Tex.2008); **Wagner v. D'Lorm**, 315 S.W.3d 188, 194 n.2 (Tex.App.—Austin 2010, no pet.).

§7.3 Mandamus. Mandamus is not an appropriate means of reviewing a final default judgment if the trial court had jurisdiction when it rendered the default judgment. **In re Barber**, 982 S.W.2d 364, 368 (Tex.1998); *see* **Thursby v. Stovall**,

647 S.W.2d 953, 954 (Tex.1983). In certain unique circumstances, however, mandamus relief may be appropriate. *See, e.g.*, **In re Barber**, 982 S.W.2d at 368 (mandamus appropriate when trial court did not acknowledge validity of its own order setting aside default).

B. Motion for Summary Judgment—General Rules

§1. General

§1.1 Rule. Tex. R. Civ. P. 166a.

§1.2 Purpose. The purpose of summary-judgment procedure is to allow courts to summarily end a case when only a question of law is involved and there is no genuine issue of fact. **G&H Towing Co. v. Magee**, 347 S.W.3d 293, 296–97 (Tex.2011); *see* **City of Houston v. Clear Creek Basin Auth.**, 589 S.W.2d 671, 678 n.5 (Tex.1979) (SJ procedure allows trial court to promptly dispose of cases that involve unmeritorious claims or untenable defenses). Summary-judgment procedure should not deprive litigants of their right to a trial by jury or to try a case by affidavit and deposition testimony. *See* **Clear Creek**, 589 S.W.2d at 678 n.5; **Collins v. County of El Paso**, 954 S.W.2d 137, 145 (Tex.App.—El Paso 1997, pet. denied).

§1.3 Timetable & forms. Appendix IV, Timetable 12, Motion for summary judgment; **O'Connor's Texas Civil Forms**, FORMS 7B:1 et seq., 7C:1 et seq., 9C:4, 10B:6 (2020 ed.).

§1.4 Other references. McDonald & Carlson, *Texas Civil Practice* §18.19 (2d ed.); **O'Connor's Texas Causes of Action** (2021 ed.); **O'Connor's Texas Civil Appeals** (2020 ed.); Brown & Rondon, **Texas Rules of Evidence Handbook** (2021 ed.).

§2. Types of motions for summary judgment

There are three types of motion for summary judgment.

§2.1 Traditional motion. The first type of motion for summary judgment is the traditional motion, which depends on summary-judgment evidence. *See* Tex. R. Civ. P. 166a(c). See "Traditional Motion for Summary Judgment," ch. 7-C, §1 et seq.

§2.2 No-evidence motion. The second type of motion for summary judgment is the no-evidence motion, which is usually made without summary-judgment evidence. *See* Tex. R. Civ. P. 166a(i). See "No-Evidence Motion for Summary Judgment," ch. 7-D, §1 et seq.

§2.3 Hybrid motion. The third type of motion for summary judgment is the hybrid motion, which combines a traditional motion with a no-evidence motion. *See* **Neely v. Wilson**, 418 S.W.3d 52, 59 (Tex.2013); **Buck v. Palmer**, 381 S.W.3d 525, 527 n.2 (Tex.2012); **Young Ref. Corp. v. Pennzoil Co.**, 46 S.W.3d 380, 385 (Tex.App.—Houston [1st Dist.] 2001, pet. denied). In a hybrid motion, the movant presents grounds appropriate for both traditional summary judgment and no-evidence summary judgment in a single motion. **Binur v. Jacobo**, 135 S.W.3d 646, 650–51 (Tex.2004); *see* **B.C. v. Steak N Shake Opers., Inc.**, 598 S.W.3d 256, 257 n.1 (Tex.2020). The movant should clearly set forth the standards on which the summary judgment is sought. *See, e.g.*, **Waite v. Woodard, Hall & Primm, P.C.**, 137 S.W.3d 277, 281 (Tex.App.—Houston [1st Dist.] 2004, no pet.) (hybrid motion that did not cite to or make argument under TRCP 166a(c) did not give "fair notice" of attempt to obtain traditional SJ). When presented with both traditional and no-evidence grounds for summary judgment, a court will typically, but is not required to, consider the no-evidence grounds first. **B.C.**, 598 S.W.3d at 260–61; *see* **Community Health Sys. Prof'l Servs. v. Hansen**, 525 S.W.3d 671, 680 (Tex.2017); **Merriman v. XTO Energy, Inc.**, 407 S.W.3d 244, 248 (Tex.2013).

Practice Tip

Although not required by TRCP 166a, a movant should use separate headings to clearly distinguish the grounds for traditional summary judgment from the grounds for no-evidence summary judgment. ***Binur****, 135 S.W.3d at 651; see* ***Galindo v. Snoddy****, 415 S.W.3d 905, 907 n.4 (Tex.App.—Texarkana 2013, no pet.).*

---

§2.4 Comparison of summary-judgment procedures. Chart 7-2, below, shows a comparison of the procedures in a traditional summary judgment and a no-evidence summary judgment.

7-2. Comparison of Summary-Judgment Procedures			
		Traditional MSJ—Tex. R. Civ. P. 166a(a), (b)	**No-evidence MSJ—Tex. R. Civ. P. 166a(i)**
1	Initial assumption	Nonmovant has a supportable claim or defense.	Nonmovant does not have a supportable claim or defense.
2	Movant's burden	Movant must prove its claim or defense or disprove an element of nonmovant's claim or defense as a matter of law.	Movant must allege there is no evidence to prove a specific element of nonmovant's claim or defense.
3	Nonmovant's burden	Nonmovant does not have burden until movant offers proof it is entitled to SJ as a matter of law.	Nonmovant has the burden to raise fact issue on its claim or defense.
4	Shifting of burden to nonmovant	Burden shifts to nonmovant when movant produces SJ evidence proving that it is entitled to SJ.	Burden shifts to nonmovant when movant alleges nonmovant has no evidence.
5	Earliest time to file	Anytime after suit is filed.	After adequate time for discovery.

§3. Summary judgment or special exceptions

Defects in the other party's petition, counterclaim, or cross-claim can be challenged by special exceptions (which can lead to an order of dismissal or the striking of the claim) or by a motion for summary judgment (which can lead to a judgment). To determine whether a party should challenge defects in the other party's pleadings by special exceptions rather than by a motion for summary judgment, see "Special exceptions & summary judgments," ch. 3-G, §10.

§4. Motion for summary judgment

For the requirements of and burden of proof for a motion for summary judgment, see "Traditional Motion for Summary Judgment," ch. 7-C, §1 et seq., and "No-Evidence Motion for Summary Judgment," ch. 7-D, §1 et seq.

§5. Special exceptions in summary-judgment procedure

The purpose of special exceptions in the summary-judgment procedure is to ensure that the parties and the trial court are focused on the same grounds. **McConnell v. Southside ISD**, 858 S.W.2d 337, 342–43 (Tex.1993); *see* **Harwell v. State Farm Mut. Auto. Ins.**, 896 S.W.2d 170, 175 (Tex.1995). See **O'Connor's Texas Civil Forms**, FORM 7B:1 (2020 ed.).

§5.1 When necessary. If the motion or response states grounds that are unclear or ambiguous, it is "prudent trial practice" to file special exceptions. **McConnell v. Southside ISD**, 858 S.W.2d 337, 342–43 (Tex.1993); *see* **Nall v. Plunkett**, 404 S.W.3d 552, 555 (Tex.2013); **Pettitte v. SCI Corp.**, 893 S.W.2d 746, 748 (Tex.App.—Houston [1st Dist.] 1995, no writ).

§5.2 When not necessary. It is not necessary to file special exceptions in the following situations: (1) when the grounds for the motion or response are stated only in a brief or other document but not in the motion or response, (2) when the motion or response presents no grounds, or (3) when the motion or response clearly presents some grounds but not others. **McConnell v. Southside ISD**, 858 S.W.2d 337, 340–42 (Tex.1993).

§5.3 In writing. The special exceptions must be in writing. **McConnell v. Southside ISD**, 858 S.W.2d 337, 343 n.7 (Tex.1993).

§5.4 Ruling. The party who files special exceptions in a summary-judgment proceeding should ask the trial court to sign a written order overruling or sustaining the special exceptions at or before the hearing on the motion for summary judgment. *See* **McConnell v. Southside ISD**, 858 S.W.2d 337, 343 n.7 (Tex.1993). Only if the trial court abuses its discretion will its ruling on the special exceptions be disturbed. **Alejandro v. Bell**, 84 S.W.3d 383, 389 (Tex.App.—Corpus Christi 2002, no pet.). See "Standard of review," ch. 3-G, §12.1.2. The ruling on the special exceptions can be included in the summary judgment. The courts disagree on the effect of a trial court's failure or refusal to rule on the nonmovant's special exceptions.

1. Express ruling required. Some courts require the nonmovant to secure an express ruling on its special exceptions to avoid waiving them as a ground for error on appeal. These courts hold that the failure or refusal to rule on

special exceptions, coupled with the granting of a summary judgment, does not amount to a ruling on the special exceptions. *See* **Franco v. Slavonic Mut. Fire Ins.**, 154 S.W.3d 777, 785 (Tex.App.—Houston [14th Dist.] 2004, no pet.) (appellate court cannot infer from granting of D's SJ motion that trial court overruled P's special exceptions); **Rosas v. Hatz**, 147 S.W.3d 560, 563 (Tex.App.—Waco 2004, no pet.) (same); **Winfield v. Pietsch**, No. 07-09-0261-CV, 2011 WL 336131 (Tex.App.—Amarillo 2011, no pet.) (memo op.; 2-3-11) (same). These courts maintain the requirement for an express ruling even if the nonmovant requested a ruling and the court refused to rule. *See, e.g.*, **Franco**, 154 S.W.3d at 784 (appellant presented order for overruling special exceptions, but court refused to sign it).

2. Implicit ruling sufficient. Some courts hold that a court's failure or refusal to rule on the nonmovant's special exceptions, coupled with the granting of a summary judgment, implicitly overrules the special exceptions and preserves error for the appeal. *See* **Slagle v. Prickett**, 345 S.W.3d 693, 702 (Tex.App.—El Paso 2011, no pet.); **Fieldtech Avionics & Instrs., Inc. v. Component Control.Com, Inc.**, 262 S.W.3d 813, 824 n.3 (Tex.App.—Fort Worth 2008, no pet.); **Alejandro**, 84 S.W.3d at 389; **Lesikar v. Moon**, No. 01-12-00406-CV, 2014 WL 4374117 (Tex.App.—Houston [1st Dist.] 2014, pet. denied) (memo op.; 9-4-14).

Caution

The Supreme Court has held that a party must obtain an express ruling from the trial court on its objections to summary-judgment evidence to preserve error on appeal; the Court suggested that an implicit ruling may be sufficient to preserve error on appeal only when the implication is "clear" from the record. ***Seim v. Allstate Tex. Lloyds**, 551 S.W.3d 161, 165–66 (Tex.2018). Although the Court did not address rulings on special exceptions, special exceptions are a type of objection, so the same rules should apply to their overruling. See "Secure ruling on objections," ch. 7-B, §10.2. Thus, the best practice is for a party to obtain an express ruling on any special exceptions to avoid waiver.*

§5.5 Deadlines for special exceptions. See "For special exceptions," ch. 7-B, §6.6.

§6. Summary-judgment deadlines

§6.1 By rule—21 days before hearing.

1. Filing & serving motion & notice. The nonmovant is entitled to at least 21 days' notice of the date set for the hearing or submission of the motion. Tex. R. Civ. P. 166a(c); **Lewis v. Blake**, 876 S.W.2d 314, 316 (Tex.1994). That is, the movant must file and serve the motion and notice of hearing at least 21 days before the hearing. Tex. R. Civ. P. 166a(c); *see also* **Jones v. Illinois Empls. Ins.**, 136 S.W.3d 728, 734–35 (Tex.App.—Texarkana 2004, no pet.) (cross-motion for SJ embodied in response to motion for SJ not timely when filed 7 days before hearing; 21 days' notice required). The nonmovant is entitled to 21 days' notice of each motion. Tex. R. Civ. P. 166a(c); *see* **Luna v. Estate of Rodriguez**, 906 S.W.2d 576, 582 (Tex.App.—Austin 1995, no writ). However, reconsideration of the court's ruling on the motion does not require another 21 days' notice. **Winn v. Martin Homebuilders, Inc.**, 153 S.W.3d 553, 556 (Tex.App.—Amarillo 2004, pet. denied).

(1) Deadlines affected by type of service. Depending on the type of service, the movant may be required to serve the motion and notice of hearing more than 21 days before the hearing.

(a) By e-service—21 days. When the motion and notice of hearing are served electronically (e-served), they must be served at least 21 days before the hearing. *See* Tex. R. Civ. P. 21a(a)(1), 166a(c). See "Generally—e-service," ch. 1-D, §4.2.1(1); "E-service," ch. 1-D, §6.1.

(b) By delivery—21 days. When the motion and notice of hearing are served by delivery, they must be served at least 21 days before the hearing. *See* Tex. R. Civ. P. 21a(a)(2), 166a(c); **Lewis**, 876 S.W.2d at 316. See "Delivery," ch. 1-D, §4.2.2(2).

(c) By mail—24 days. When the motion and notice of hearing are served by mail, they must be mailed at least 24 days before the hearing because TRCP 21a extends the minimum notice by 3 days. **Lewis**, 876 S.W.2d at 315; **Chadderdon v. Blaschke**, 988 S.W.2d 387, 388 (Tex.App.—Houston [1st Dist.] 1999, no pet.); *see* Tex. R. Civ. P. 21a(c), 166a(c). See "Mail," ch. 1-D, §4.2.2(1).

(d) By fax.

[1] Generally—21 days. When the motion and notice of hearing are served by fax, they generally must be faxed at least 21 days before the hearing. *See* Tex. R. Civ. P. 21a(a)(2), 166a(c).

[2] After 5:00 p.m.—22 days. When the motion and notice of hearing are served by fax and received after 5:00 p.m. local time of the recipient, the documents are deemed served on the next day rather than the day they are faxed. *See* Tex. R. Civ. P. 21a(b)(2). See "Fax," ch. 1-D, §6.4. In this situation, the motion and notice of hearing must be faxed at least 22 days before the hearing. See chart 1-2 under "E-mail," ch. 1-D, §6.5.

(e) By e-mail—21 days. When the motion and notice of hearing are served by e-mail, they must be served at least 21 days before the hearing. *See* Tex. R. Civ. P. 21a(a)(2), 166a(c). See "E-mail," ch. 1-D, §4.2.2(4).

(2) Computing days. The 21 (or 24) days' notice of the hearing must be calculated from the date of service of the motion and notice of hearing. *See* **Lewis**, 876 S.W.2d at 316. In computing the number of days, the day the motion and notice of hearing are served is not counted (it is "day 0"), but the day of the hearing is counted (it is "day 21" or "day 24"). *Id.*; *see* Tex. R. Civ. P. 4, 166a(c). If the motion is filed and served before the hearing date is set and the notice of the hearing is filed and served later, the 21 (or 24) days' notice of the hearing must be calculated from the date of service of the notice, not the motion. **Chadderdon**, 988 S.W.2d at 388. For a detailed discussion of computing deadlines, see "Computing time limits—days," ch. 1-C, §7.1; "Computing response deadlines," ch. 1-D, §6; chart 1-2 under "E-mail," ch. 1-D, §6.5.

2. Form for notice of hearing. If the date for the hearing is known before the motion for summary judgment is served, the notice of the hearing can be included in the motion itself or served as a separate document from the motion with its own certificate of service. If the date for the hearing is not known at the time the motion for summary judgment is served, the notice of the hearing must be served as a separate document with its own certificate of service. See "Included in SJ motion," ch. 7-B, §7.3; "Separate notice," ch. 7-B, §7.4.

§6.2 By agreement. The parties may change the deadlines by agreement. If the agreement meets the requirements of TRCP 11, the court should enforce it. *See, e.g.*, **EZ Pawn Corp. v. Mancias**, 934 S.W.2d 87, 91 (Tex.1996) (because parties made Rule 11 agreement to permit nonmovant to file response a week before the hearing, trial court should have disregarded response filed after that deadline). See "Agreements between attorneys—Rule 11," ch. 1-H, §9.

§6.3 For response—7 days before hearing. The nonmovant must file and serve its response and affidavits at least seven days before the hearing. Tex. R. Civ. P. 166a(c); **Carpenter v. Cimarron Hydrocarbons Corp.**, 98 S.W.3d 682, 686 (Tex.2002); *see* **B.C. v. Steak N Shake Opers., Inc.**, 598 S.W.3d 256, 259 (Tex.2020); *see also* **Alford v. Thornburg**, 113 S.W.3d 575, 586 (Tex.App.—Texarkana 2003, no pet.) (affidavit that was timely filed but served late was not considered by court because nonmovant did not ask to serve affidavit late or request continuance); **Hammonds v. Thomas**, 770 S.W.2d 1, 2 (Tex.App.—Texarkana 1989, no writ) (court should have considered nonmovant's affidavits filed six days before hearing because seventh day before hearing was July 4, a national holiday). See "Computing time limits—days," ch. 1-C, §7.1. If the nonmovant is allowed to file documents in paper form by mailing, the nonmovant can file the response by mailing it on the day it is due, and it is timely filed even if it reaches the court less than seven days before the hearing, as long as it is received by the clerk no more than ten days after the due date. *See* Tex. R. Civ. P. 5; **Geiselman v. Cramer Fin. Grp.**, 965 S.W.2d 532, 535 (Tex.App.—Houston [14th Dist.] 1997, no writ). See "How to file," ch. 1-C, §4. The three-day rule for mailing in TRCP 21a does not require the nonmovant to mail the response ten days before the hearing because the movant is not required to act after receiving the response. **Holmes v. Ottawa Truck, Inc.**, 960 S.W.2d 866, 869 (Tex.App.—El Paso 1997, pet. denied). The 7-day deadline gives the nonmovant at least 14 days to obtain and file summary-judgment evidence. *See* **Extended Servs. Program, Inc. v. First Extended Serv.**, 601 S.W.2d 469, 470 (Tex.App.—Dallas 1980, writ ref'd n.r.e.) (21 days' notice of hearing minus 7-day deadline to file response before hearing = 14 days to file response and SJ evidence).

§6.4 For SJ evidence. The deadline to file affidavits, unfiled discovery, and other summary-judgment evidence is the same deadline that applies to the motion or response. Tex. R. Civ. P. 166a(c), (d). No evidence can be filed after the court rules on the motion, even if the motion was a partial motion. *See* Tex. R. Civ. P. 166a(c); **Valores Corporativos, S.A. de C.V. v. McLane Co.**, 945 S.W.2d 160, 162 (Tex.App.—San Antonio 1997, writ denied). See "Filing late evidence," ch. 7-B, §6.8.4.

§6.5 For movant's reply to response. If the nonmovant filed a response to the motion for summary judgment, the movant may want to reply to the response. There is no deadline in TRCP 166a for a movant's reply to a response. **Cal-**

laghan Ranch, Ltd. v. Killam, 53 S.W.3d 1, 4 (Tex.App.—San Antonio 2000, pet. denied); **Knapp v. Eppright**, 783 S.W.2d 293, 296 (Tex.App.—Houston [14th Dist.] 1989, no writ); *see, e.g.*, **Reynolds v. Murphy**, 188 S.W.3d 252, 259 (Tex.App.—Fort Worth 2006, pet. denied) (movant's objections to nonmovant's response filed the day of hearing were not untimely). However, the local rules of some courts set time limits for responsive pleadings. *See, e.g.*, Harris Cty. Loc. R. 3.3.3 (in district courts, responses must be filed at least two working days before submission). If the movant needs time to cure defects in its motion, pleadings, or summary-judgment evidence, it should request a continuance of the hearing.

§6.6 For special exceptions.

1. For nonmovant. If the nonmovant challenges the motion for summary judgment by special exceptions, it must file and serve them at least seven days before the hearing. **McConnell v. Southside ISD**, 858 S.W.2d 337, 343 n.7 (Tex.1993).

2. For movant. If the movant challenges the response to the motion for summary judgment by special exceptions, it must file and serve them at least three days before the hearing. **McConnell**, 858 S.W.2d at 343 n.7.

§6.7 For filing an amendment to pleadings. The filing deadlines for amendments to the pleadings (petition and answer) are different from the filing deadlines for amendments to the summary-judgment motion and response. See "Procedure to amend," ch. 7-B, §8.1.

§6.8 Late filing.

1. Filing a late motion. To file a motion for summary judgment with less than 21 days' notice, the movant must obtain leave of court. Tex. R. Civ. P. 166a(c); *see, e.g.*, **Hall v. Stephenson**, 919 S.W.2d 454, 461 (Tex.App.—Fort Worth 1996, writ denied) (court granted leave for party to file MSJ 17 days before hearing). *But see* **Stephens v. Turtle Creek Apts., Ltd.**, 875 S.W.2d 25, 26–27 (Tex.App.—Houston [14th Dist.] 1994, no writ) (notice provisions in TRCP 166a(c) must be strictly construed; 6 days' notice of MSJ hearing was insufficient). The nonmovant must be given notice if leave is granted. Tex. R. Civ. P. 166a(c). If the movant does not obtain leave of court, the nonmovant must object to the late motion or else the error is waived. **Ajibade v. Edinburg Gen. Hosp.**, 22 S.W.3d 37, 40 (Tex.App.—Corpus Christi 2000, no pet.); **Luna v. Estate of Rodriguez**, 906 S.W.2d 576, 582 (Tex.App.—Austin 1995, no writ).

2. Filing an amended motion after the hearing. To file an amendment or supplement to add an additional ground to the motion for summary judgment after the hearing, the movant must give the nonmovant another 21 days to respond. *See, e.g.*, **Sams v. N.L. Indus.**, 735 S.W.2d 486, 488 (Tex.App.—Houston [1st Dist.] 1987, no writ) (movant's post-hearing "reply" that added new grounds for SJ required 21 days' notice).

3. Filing a late response. To file a response (or an amendment to a response) less than seven days before the summary-judgment hearing, the nonmovant must obtain leave of court. Tex. R. Civ. P. 166a(c).

(1) Standard. Leave to file a late response is proper if there is (1) good cause and (2) no undue prejudice. **Wheeler v. Green**, 157 S.W.3d 439, 442 (Tex.2005); *see also* **Carpenter v. Cimarron Hydrocarbons Corp.**, 98 S.W.3d 682, 687–88 (Tex.2002) (standard for allowing late SJ response is same as standard for withdrawing deemed admissions). Good cause is established by sworn proof that the nonmovant's failure to timely respond was not intentional or the result of conscious indifference but was the result of an accident or mistake. *See* **Wheeler**, 157 S.W.3d at 442. The lack of undue prejudice is established by showing that the late response will not unduly delay or otherwise injure the movant. *Id.* at 443.

(2) Motion or indication in record. To obtain leave of court, the nonmovant should file and obtain a ruling on a motion for leave to file a late summary-judgment response that establishes good cause and no undue prejudice. *See* **Wheeler**, 157 S.W.3d at 442. If the nonmovant does not file a motion for leave, the record must contain an affirmative indication that the trial court considered the late response; otherwise, the nonmovant waives the issues raised in the late response. *See* **B.C. v. Steak N Shake Opers., Inc.**, 598 S.W.3d 256, 259 (Tex.2020); **INA v. Bryant**, 686 S.W.2d 614, 615 (Tex.1985); **K-Six TV, Inc. v. Santiago**, 75 S.W.3d 91, 96 (Tex.App.—San Antonio 2002, no pet.). The indication can be found in a separate order, a recital in the summary judgment itself, or an oral ruling made at the summary-judgment hearing and contained in the reporter's record. *E.g.*, **B.C.**, 598 S.W.3d at 259–60 (recital that court considered "pleadings, evidence, and arguments of counsel" without limitation was affirmative indication that court considered late response). A silent

record supports a presumption that the court did not consider the late response. *Id.* at 260.

Note

In its motion for leave, the nonmovant can ask the court to continue the hearing to a later date as an alternative. See "Motion to continue hearing," ch. 7-B, §6.9.1.

4. Filing late evidence. To file late summary-judgment evidence, the party (movant or nonmovant) must obtain leave of court. Tex. R. Civ. P. 166a(c); **Benchmark Bank v. Crowder**, 919 S.W.2d 657, 663 (Tex.1996). The record must contain a ruling on a motion for leave or some other affirmative indication that the trial court considered the late summary-judgment evidence. *See* **B.C.**, 598 S.W.3d at 259; **Mathis v. RKL Design/Build**, 189 S.W.3d 839, 842–43 (Tex.App.—Houston [1st Dist.] 2006, no pet.). If a party files late summary-judgment evidence or a late amendment to the evidence and nothing appears in the record to indicate that the late filing was accepted, the evidence will not be considered as being before the trial court when it ruled on the motion for summary judgment. *See* **B.C.**, 598 S.W.3d at 260; **Benchmark Bank**, 919 S.W.2d at 663; **Mathis**, 189 S.W.3d at 843; *see, e.g.,* **Mello v. A.M.F., Inc.**, 7 S.W.3d 329, 332 (Tex.App.—Beaumont 1999, pet. denied) (no ruling permitting filing of supplemental evidence by nonmovants on day of SJ hearing); **Basin Credit Consultants, Inc. v. Obregon**, 2 S.W.3d 372, 374 (Tex.App.—San Antonio 1999, pet. denied) (same, for affidavits filed by nonmovant after SJ hearing); **Luna**, 906 S.W.2d at 582 & n.6 (same, for evidence filed by both parties on day of hearing); **Texas Airfinance Corp. v. Lesikar**, 777 S.W.2d 559, 561–62 (Tex.App.—Houston [14th Dist.] 1989, no writ) (same, for affidavit filed by movant 12 days before hearing).

§6.9 Motions for more time.

1. Motion to continue hearing. When a nonmovant needs additional time to secure affidavits or discovery or to amend its pleading, it should file a motion for continuance. *See* Tex. R. Civ. P. 166a(g). See "Motion to continue SJ hearing," ch. 5-D, §9.3; **O'Connor's Texas Civil Forms**, FORM 7B:5 (2020 ed.). The trial court has the discretion to deny a motion for continuance under TRCP 251. A motion for continuance is not the correct motion to file when the nonmovant did not get the required 21 days' notice; the nonmovant should instead file a motion to reset the hearing date.

2. Motion to reset SJ hearing. When a nonmovant did not get 21 days' notice of the hearing, it should file a motion to reset the hearing date. The trial court does not have the discretion to deny a motion to reset the hearing when the nonmovant was not given the full 21 days' notice required by TRCP 166a(c). See "Motion to reset SJ hearing for lack of 21 days' notice," ch. 5-D, §9.2; **O'Connor's Texas Civil Forms**, FORM 7B:2 (2020 ed.).

§6.10 Summary chart for SJ deadlines. Chart 7-3, below, summarizes the filing deadlines in summary-judgment cases, including whether leave is required for a late filing, whether an objection to a late filing is necessary, and whether error is waived if no objection is made. Service deadlines may vary if service is accomplished by a method other than personal delivery. See "Computing response deadlines," ch. 1-D, §6.

7-3. Filing Deadlines in Summary-Judgment Cases

	Document	Deadline to file before hearing	Ask for leave to file late	Objection necessary if late	If no objection, is complaint waived?
	Movant				
1	Motion for SJ	21 days	Yes	Yes	Yes
2	SJ evidence to support motion	21 days	Yes	No	No
3	Amended motion with new ground	21 days	Yes	Yes	Yes
4	Amended pleading (e.g., answer)	7 days	No	Yes	Yes
5	Special exceptions to the response	3 days	Yes	?	?

7-3. Filing Deadlines in Summary-Judgment Cases					
	Document	Deadline to file before hearing	Ask for leave to file late	Objection necessary if late	If no objection, is complaint waived?
		Nonmovant			
6	Response to motion for SJ	7 days	Yes	No	No
7	SJ evidence to support response	7 days	Yes	No	No
8	Amended response	7 days	Yes	No	No
9	Amended pleading (e.g., petition)	7 days	No	Yes	Yes
10	Special exceptions to the motion	7 days	Yes	?	?

§7. Notice

§7.1 Notice of SJ hearing. The nonmovant is entitled to receive sufficient notice of the hearing or submission (collectively "the hearing") date on the summary-judgment motion so it knows when its response is due. **Martin v. Martin, Martin & Richards, Inc.**, 989 S.W.2d 357, 359 (Tex1998); **Rorie v. Goodwin**, 171 S.W.3d 579, 583 (TexApp.—Tyler 2005, no pet.); **Aguirre v. Phillips Props., Inc.**, 111 S.W.3d 328, 332 (TexApp.—Corpus Christi 2003, pet. denied); *e.g.*, **Ready v. Alpha Bldg. Corp.**, 467 S.W.3d 580, 585 (TexApp.—Houston [1st Dist.] 2015, no pet.) (notice stating only that motion would be submitted "after" certain date, without specific submission date, was insufficient to inform P when response was due). See "For response—7 days before hearing," ch. 7-B, §6.3. If the movant does not provide timely notice, the summary judgment will be reversed. **Etheredge v. Hidden Valley Airpark Ass'n**, 169 S.W.3d 378, 383 (TexApp.—Fort Worth 2005, pet. denied); **Guinn v. Zarsky**, 893 S.W.2d 13, 17 (TexApp.—Corpus Christi 1994, no writ).

Practice Tip

The movant's attorney should contact the attorneys for the other parties and discuss mutually agreeable dates before calling the court clerk to set the summary-judgment hearing.

1. First setting. The movant is required to give the nonmovant 21 days' notice of the hearing on a summary-judgment motion. Tex. R. Civ. P. 166a(c); **Lewis v. Blake**, 876 S.W.2d 314, 316 (Tex1994). To compute the deadline for serving the notice, which may vary based on the method of service, see "By rule—21 days before hearing," ch. 7-B, §6.1.

2. Resetting the hearing. Once a nonmovant is given 21 days' notice of the hearing, if the hearing date is reset, the nonmovant is not entitled to another 21 days' notice of the new date. **Birdwell v. Texins Credit Un.**, 843 S.W.2d 246, 250 (TexApp.—Texarkana 1992, no writ). The nonmovant is entitled only to reasonable notice of the resetting. **Skelton v. Commission for Lawyer Discipline**, 56 S.W.3d 687, 691 (TexApp.—Houston [14th Dist.] 2001, no pet.). Reasonable notice generally means at least seven days before the hearing. *Id.* But in certain circumstances, less than seven days may be considered reasonable notice. *See, e.g.*, **Brown v. Capital Bank**, 703 S.W.2d 231, 233–34 (TexApp.—Houston [14th Dist.] 1985, writ ref'd n.r.e.) (nonmovant, who had more than 21 days' notice of original setting, never filed response to MSJ even though case had been reset twice and first resetting occurred only 4 days before hearing; 3 days' notice of second resetting was sufficient).

§7.2 In writing. The movant must give the nonmovant written notice of the hearing on the motion for summary judgment. *See* Tex. R. Civ. P. 21a(a) ("[e]very notice required by these rules . . . may be served by delivering . . . ."), Tex. R. Civ. P. 166a(c) (does not specify written notice). The notice must include the fact that a hearing has been set, and it must give the date and time for the hearing. **Mosser v. Plano Three Venture**, 893 S.W.2d 8, 11 (TexApp.—Dallas 1994, no writ).

§7.3 Included in SJ motion. The notice of the date and time for the hearing may be attached to the motion for summary judgment. The notice must state the actual date and time for the hearing; a movant's written request for a certain hearing date is not notice of the date of the hearing. **Veal v. Veterans Life Ins.**, 767 S.W.2d 892, 895 (TexApp.—Texarkana 1989, no writ).

§7.4 Separate notice. If the notice of the hearing is a separate document from the motion for summary judgment, the notice must contain its own certificate of service. **Tanksley v. CitiCapital Commercial Corp.**, 145 S.W.3d 760, 763 (Tex.App.—Dallas 2004, pet. denied); *see* Tex. R. Civ. P. 21(b), (d), 21a(a); *see, e.g.*, **Guinn v. Zarsky**, 893 S.W.2d 13, 17 (Tex.App.—Corpus Christi 1994, no writ) (notice of hearing, which was on a separate sheet in same envelope as SJ motion, was not sufficient because it was not certified). If the motion is filed and served before the hearing date is set and the notice of the hearing is filed and served later, the movant must give the nonmovant 21 days' notice of the hearing, counting from the date of service of the notice, not the motion. **Chadderdon v. Blaschke**, 988 S.W.2d 387, 388 (Tex.App.—Houston [1st Dist.] 1999, no pet.). Regardless of how long the motion is on file, the movant must give the nonmovant 21 days' notice of the hearing date when it sets the motion for a hearing. *Id.* See "Filing & serving motion & notice," ch. 7-B, §6.1.1.

§8. Amending the petition or answer

The filing requirements and deadlines for amending the pleadings (petition and answer) are different from the filing requirements and deadlines for amending the motion for summary judgment and response. By understanding the differences, a nonmovant may be able to avoid a final summary judgment.

§8.1 Procedure to amend. The trial court must render a summary judgment on the pleadings on file at the time of the hearing. Tex. R. Civ. P. 166a(c). A party may file an amended pleading after it files its motion or response. *See, e.g.*, **Cluett v. Medical Prot. Co.**, 829 S.W.2d 822, 825–26 (Tex.App.—Dallas 1992, writ denied) (movant filed amended petition after SJ motion but four months before hearing).

1. Amending pleadings before hearing. A party should file an amended petition or answer as soon as it becomes aware it is necessary, but no later than seven days before the hearing. *See* Tex. R. Civ. P. 63; **B.C. v. Steak N Shake Opers., Inc.**, 598 S.W.3d 256, 261 (Tex.2020); **Sosa v. Central Power & Light**, 909 S.W.2d 893, 895 (Tex.1995). In computing the seven-day period, the day the party files the amended pleading is not counted, but the day of the hearing on the motion for summary judgment is counted. **Sosa**, 909 S.W.2d at 895. If the party decides to amend after the seven-day deadline (e.g., six days before the hearing), it should file its amended pleading before the hearing even if a motion for leave to amend has not been filed. *See* **Goswami v. Metropolitan S&L Ass'n**, 751 S.W.2d 487, 490 (Tex.1988) (nonmovant filed amended petition four days before hearing). Unless the record shows that the trial court denied leave to file, the appellate court will assume the trial court considered the amended pleading. *See* **B.C.**, 598 S.W.3d at 261; **Goswami**, 751 S.W.2d at 490; *see, e.g.*, **Honea v. Morgan Drive Away, Inc.**, 997 S.W.2d 705, 707 (Tex.App.—Eastland 1999, no pet.) (when order said trial court considered all "timely" pleadings, court presumably denied leave to file and did not consider late-amended pleadings). Leave to file within seven days before the hearing is presumed granted when (1) the summary judgment states that all pleadings were considered, (2) the record does not show that an amended pleading was not considered, and (3) the opposing party does not show surprise. **B.C.**, 598 S.W.3d at 261; *e.g.*, **Continental Airlines, Inc. v. Kiefer**, 920 S.W.2d 274, 276 (Tex.1996) (leave presumed granted when amended pleading was filed five days before hearing and judgment stated court granted SJ "after examining the pleadings"); *see* **Goswami**, 751 S.W.2d at 490. If the late amendment creates a fact issue, the appellate courts will reverse the summary judgment. *See* **Goswami**, 751 S.W.2d at 490–91.

2. Amending pleadings after hearing. Once the hearing date for the motion for summary judgment has passed, a party may file an amended pleading before the court signs a judgment if the party secures a written order granting leave to file. *See* Tex. R. Civ. P. 166a(c); *see, e.g.*, **Cherry v. McCall**, 138 S.W.3d 35, 42–43 (Tex.App.—San Antonio 2004, pet. denied) (nonmovant did not obtain leave to file amended petition almost three weeks after hearing); **Hussong v. Schwan's Sales Enters.**, 896 S.W.2d 320, 323 (Tex.App.—Houston [1st Dist.] 1995, no writ) (nonmovant did not obtain leave to file amended petition one month after hearing and before court granted SJ). Unless the record shows that the court granted leave to file, the appellate courts will assume leave was denied. **Leinen v. Buffington's Bayou City Serv.**, 824 S.W.2d 682, 685 (Tex.App.—Houston [14th Dist.] 1992, no writ).

§8.2 Objecting to amendment.

1. Amendment filed before hearing. Under TRCP 63, the party opposing the amendment has the burden to show surprise. If a party objects to a late amendment, it should make sure the record reflects its objection and the court's ruling. Unless the record shows that the court denied leave to file the late amendment, the appellate courts will assume it was granted. **Goswami v. Metropolitan S&L Ass'n**, 751 S.W.2d 487, 490 (Tex.1988).

2. Amendment filed after hearing. The party opposing an amendment filed after the hearing has no burden to object unless the party filing the amendment asks for leave to file.

§9. Summary-judgment evidence

§9.1 Generally.

1. Admissible. Summary-judgment evidence must be admissible under the rules of evidence. **United Blood Servs. v. Longoria**, 938 S.W.2d 29, 30 (Tex.1997); *see* Tex. R. Civ. P. 166a(f) (affidavits must set forth facts that would be admissible in evidence). That is, facts must be proved by the same type of evidence that would be admissible at trial, except that facts are proved by affidavits, depositions, interrogatories, and other discovery rather than by oral testimony. *See* Tex. R. Civ. P. 166a(c); **Jensen Constr. Co. v. Dallas Cty.**, 920 S.W.2d 761, 768 (Tex.App.—Dallas 1996, writ denied), *disapproved on other grounds*, **Travis Cty. v. Pelzel & Assocs.**, 77 S.W.3d 246 (Tex.2002). Evidentiary exclusions also apply to summary-judgment proceedings as they would at trial. **Fort Brown Villas III Condo. Ass'n v. Gillenwater**, 285 S.W.3d 879, 882 (Tex.2009); *see* Tex. R. Civ. P. 193.6 (party cannot introduce into evidence information not timely disclosed or offer testimony of witness not timely identified). See "Timely," ch. 6-A, §16.3.

2. On file. Summary-judgment evidence must generally be on file at the time of the hearing to be considered by the court. *See* Tex. R. Civ. P. 166a(c); **Lance v. Robinson**, 543 S.W.3d 723, 732 (Tex.2018). "On file" means the evidence was offered and admitted; the fact that evidence may be omitted from the record does not mean that it is not on file with the court. *See, e.g.*, **Lance**, 543 S.W.3d at 732–33 (court considered deeds on file from earlier temporary-injunction hearing as evidence at SJ hearing; Ps expressly referenced injunction-hearing transcript in SJ motion and were not required to refile deeds as attachments); *see also* Tex. R. App. P. 34.5(c) (appellate record can be supplemented to include previously omitted evidence). To rely on evidence not on file at the time of the hearing, a party must obtain the court's permission to file the evidence and then do so before judgment. *See* Tex. R. Civ. P. 166a(c).

Note

If certain requirements are met, a party may also be able to rely on discovery that is not on file with the clerk. ***Lance****, 543 S.W.3d at 732 n.7. See "Unfiled discovery," ch. 7-B, §9.5.2.*

3. Attached. A party can attach affidavits or other documents to the motion or the response. Either party can rely on the attached evidence—that is, the movant can rely on evidence filed by the nonmovant and vice versa. *See* **Wilson v. Burford**, 904 S.W.2d 628, 629 (Tex.1995); *see, e.g.*, **Schlumberger Tech. v. Pasko**, 544 S.W.3d 830, 835 (Tex.2018) (movant could rely on evidence attached to nonmovant's response; movant was not required to refile evidence 21 days before SJ hearing). The motion or response should contain a section called "Summary-Judgment Evidence" identifying the attached documents. The motion or response must specifically identify the portions of the evidence that the party wants the court to consider. **Gonzales v. Shing Wai Brass & Metal Wares Factory, Ltd.**, 190 S.W.3d 742, 746 (Tex.App.—San Antonio 2005, no pet.). When an entire document (e.g., a deposition) is attached to a motion or response and is referred to only generally, that reference does not satisfy the requirement for specificity. **Gonzales**, 190 S.W.3d at 746; *see, e.g.*, **Upchurch v. Albear**, 5 S.W.3d 274, 284–85 (Tex.App.—Amarillo 1999, pet. denied) (3,000-page attachment to motion was not proper SJ evidence because it was not indexed and motion did not cite specific parts of it). If the party is going to rely on an assortment of evidence, it should organize the evidence in an appendix. *See* Tex. R. Civ. P. 166a(d). If all the summary-judgment proof is presented in an appendix, the following items should be included:

(1) A table of contents with references to the tabs where the different items are located.

(2) A statement that all the summary-judgment proof in the appendix is incorporated by reference into the motion or response. The same statement should be included in the motion or response.

(3) A verification for all evidence that is required to be verified. See "Verification," ch. 1-B, §3.2.15; "Affidavits," ch. 1-B, §3.2.16. For the requirements for using an unsworn declaration in place of a verification or an affidavit, see "Unsworn declaration," ch. 1-B, §3.2.17. It is not necessary to separately authenticate each piece of documentary evidence. **Llopa, Inc. v. Nagel**, 956 S.W.2d 82, 87 (Tex.App.—San Antonio 1997, pet. denied).

§9.2 Pleadings as proof.

1. General rule. As a general rule, pleadings are not summary-judgment evidence. **Laidlaw Waste Sys. v. City of Wilmer**, 904 S.W.2d 656, 660 (Tex.1995); **Hidalgo v. Surety S&L Ass'n**, 462 S.W.2d 540, 545 (Tex.1971).

(1) Petition or answer. A party cannot rely on factual statements contained in its own petition or answer as summary-judgment proof. **Hidalgo**, 462 S.W.2d at 545; **Flameout Design & Fabrication, Inc. v. Pennzoil Caspian Corp.**, 994 S.W.2d 830, 838 (Tex.App.—Houston [1st Dist.] 1999, no pet.).

(2) Motion or response. A party cannot rely on factual statements contained in its own motion for summary judgment or response as summary-judgment proof, even if the motion or response is verified. **Quanaim v. Frasco Rest. & Catering**, 17 S.W.3d 30, 42 (Tex.App.—Houston [14th Dist.] 2000, pet. denied) (response); **Barrow v. Jack's Catfish Inn**, 641 S.W.2d 624, 625 (Tex.App.—Corpus Christi 1982, no writ) (motion).

(3) Pleadings as exhibits. A party cannot rely on other pleadings attached as exhibits to its own motion or response as summary-judgment evidence, even if the pleadings are verified. *See, e.g.*, **Laidlaw Waste**, 904 S.W.2d at 660–61 (P could not rely on its own verified petition attached as an exhibit to its response).

2. Exceptions.

(1) Other party's pleadings. When a party's pleadings contain statements admitting facts or conclusions that directly contradict the party's own theory of recovery or defense, the pleadings may constitute summary-judgment proof for the other party. *E.g.*, **H2O Solutions, Ltd. v. PM Rlty. Grp.**, 438 S.W.3d 606, 616–17 (Tex.App.—Houston [1st Dist.] 2014, pet. denied) (SJ for D on breach-of-contract claim proper when P's earlier pleadings contained judicial admissions that established there was no valid contract between P and D); *see* **Lyons v. Lindsey Morden Claims Mgmt.**, 985 S.W.2d 86, 92 (Tex.App.—El Paso 1998, no pet.) (SJ may be granted on other party's pleadings that contain judicial admissions); *see also* **Perry v. Houston ISD**, 902 S.W.2d 544, 547–48 (Tex.App.—Houston [1st Dist.] 1995, writ dism'd) (nonmovant can use movant's exhibit against movant to create fact issues). Although pleadings are not "evidence," when the motion for summary judgment is based on the nonmovant's pleadings, the court assumes the facts in the nonmovant's pleadings are true. See "Moving on the pleadings," ch. 7-C, §2.5.2.

(2) Suit on sworn account. When the underlying claim is a suit on a sworn account, the plaintiff's pleadings establish a prima facie case if the defendant does not file a verified denial. **Powers v. Adams**, 2 S.W.3d 496, 498 (Tex.App.—Houston [14th Dist.] 1999, no pet.).

§9.3 Types of witnesses.

1. Disinterested witness. The best summary-judgment proof may be the uncontradicted testimony of a disinterested witness. *See, e.g.*, **Hunsucker v. Omega Indus.**, 659 S.W.2d 692, 696 (Tex.App.—Dallas 1983, no writ) (testimony of disinterested witnesses, who identified truck that left accident scene as belonging to D, raised fact issue of whether driver was within scope of employment).

2. Interested witness. To establish facts, an interested witness's testimony must be clear, positive, direct, credible, free from contradiction, and uncontroverted even though it could have been readily controverted. Tex. R. Civ. P. 166a(c); **McIntyre v. Ramirez**, 109 S.W.3d 741, 749 (Tex.2003); **Trico Techs. v. Montiel**, 949 S.W.2d 308, 310 (Tex.1997). If the testimony does not meet these requirements, it will not support a summary judgment. *See* **Casso v. Brand**, 776 S.W.2d 551, 558 (Tex.1989). The phrase "could have been readily controverted" in TRCP 166a(c) does not simply mean the party's summary-judgment proof could have been easily and conveniently rebutted; instead, it means the testimony is of a nature that can be effectively countered by opposing evidence. **Trico Techs.**, 949 S.W.2d at 310; **Casso**, 776 S.W.2d at 558. If the credibility of the affiant is likely to be a dispositive factor in the resolution of the case, summary judgment is not appropriate. **Casso**, 776 S.W.2d at 558; **CEBI Metal v. Garcia**, 108 S.W.3d 464, 465 (Tex.App.—Houston [14th Dist.] 2003, no pet.).

3. Expert witness. An expert's opinion testimony can establish or defeat a claim as a matter of law. *See* **Burrow v. Arce**, 997 S.W.2d 229, 235 (Tex.1999). For purposes of summary-judgment proof, experts are considered interested witnesses. *See* Tex. R. Civ. P. 166a(c) (last sentence). An expert's testimony (fact or opinion) must be clear, positive, direct,

credible, free from contradiction, and uncontroverted even though it could have been readily controverted by another expert. *Id.*; **Wadewitz v. Montgomery**, 951 S.W.2d 464, 466 (Tex.1997); **Anderson v. Snider**, 808 S.W.2d 54, 55 (Tex.1991). The expert's opinion must meet the test for expert testimony. See "*Daubert-Robinson* test for expert testimony," ch. 5-N, §2. The testimony of an expert should include (1) the expert's qualifications, (2) the opinion, (3) the facts on which the opinion is based, and (4) the reasoning on which the opinion is based. *See* **United Blood Servs. v. Longoria**, 938 S.W.2d 29, 30 (Tex.1997) (qualifications of expert); **Anderson**, 808 S.W.2d at 55 (expert's reasoning). Expert testimony that merely states unsubstantiated legal conclusions is not proper summary-judgment evidence. **Burrow**, 997 S.W.2d at 235; **Wadewitz**, 951 S.W.2d at 466; **Anderson**, 808 S.W.2d at 55; **Barraza v. Eureka Co.**, 25 S.W.3d 225, 230 (Tex.App.—El Paso 2000, pet. denied). See "Not legal conclusions," ch. 7-B, §9.4.5. If an expert's testimony meets the test under TRE 702 and the requirements of TRCP 166a(c) and (f), it will support a summary judgment even when the expert is a party to the suit. *See* **Anderson**, 808 S.W.2d at 55; **Shook v. Herman**, 759 S.W.2d 743, 746 (Tex.App.—Dallas 1988, writ denied). If the expert's opinion is based on records, the records should be attached to the affidavit or included with the other summary-judgment evidence. *See* Tex. R. Civ. P. 166a(f); **Ceballos v. El Paso Health Care Sys.**, 881 S.W.2d 439, 444 (Tex.App.—El Paso 1994, writ denied). See "Failure to attach exhibit," ch. 7-B, §10.1.1(1)(b).

Caution

If you use an expert's affidavit in a summary-judgment hearing, you cannot later claim consulting-only status for that expert. See ***Hardesty v. Douglas****, 894 S.W.2d 548, 551 (Tex.App.—Waco 1995, orig. proceeding). That expert's opinion will be subject to discovery. See id.*

(1) Attorney expert. If unchallenged, the movant's affidavit by an attorney as an expert on attorney fees is sufficient to support a summary judgment for fees. If the nonmovant believes the amount of attorney fees the movant claims is unreasonable, the nonmovant should challenge the attorney fees in the response and file a controverting affidavit by an attorney as an expert on attorney fees. *See* **Guity v. C.C.I. Enter.**, 54 S.W.3d 526, 528 (Tex.App.—Houston [1st Dist.] 2001, no pet.). If the movant's affidavit is controverted, the court cannot award attorney fees without holding a hearing. *See id.* See "Evidence," ch. 1-H, §10.2.2.

(2) Medical expert. CPRC chapter 74 limits the persons who can testify as experts in a medical-malpractice case against doctors and other health-care providers. *See* Tex. Civ. Prac. & Rem. Code §§74.401 to 74.403. See "Expert's qualifications," **O'Connor's Texas Causes of Action**, ch. 20-A, §8.3 (2021 ed.).

§9.4 Affidavits. The most common form of summary-judgment evidence is the affidavit. The affidavit must meet certain requirements; a defective affidavit cannot support a summary judgment. See "Objections to summary-judgment evidence," ch. 7-B, §10.

1. Sworn. The minimum requirement for an affidavit is that it must be sworn; however, a jurat is not specifically required. *See* **Mansions in the Forest, L.P. v. Montgomery Cty.**, 365 S.W.3d 314, 316–17 (Tex.2012). See "Jurat," ch. 1-B, §3.2.16(1)(e). An unsworn statement that purports to be an affidavit will not support a summary judgment. *See* **Mansions in the Forest**, 365 S.W.3d at 316; **Perkins v. Crittenden**, 462 S.W.2d 565, 568 (Tex.1970).

2. Admissible evidence. The affidavit must contain facts that would be admissible in evidence at a conventional trial on the merits. Tex. R. Civ. P. 166a(f); **United Blood Servs. v. Longoria**, 938 S.W.2d 29, 30 (Tex.1997); *see, e.g.*, **Rabe v. Dillard's, Inc.**, 214 S.W.3d 767, 769 (Tex.App.—Dallas 2007, no pet.) (confidential ADR communications described in SJ affidavit were inadmissible and should have been excluded); **Powell v. Vavro, McDonald & Assocs.**, 136 S.W.3d 762, 765 (Tex.App.—Dallas 2004, no pet.) (hearsay statements in SJ affidavits were inadmissible and should have been excluded); **Beasley v. Burns**, 7 S.W.3d 768, 770 (Tex.App.—Texarkana 1999, pet. denied) (party cannot offer affidavit that contradicts deemed admissions).

3. Competent witness. The affidavit must affirmatively show that the witness is competent to testify about the matters in the affidavit. Tex. R. Civ. P. 166a(f). See "Competency of witness," ch. 1-B, §3.2.16(2); "Lack of competence," ch. 7-B, §10.1.1(2).

Note

Courts often treat a witness's competence and personal knowledge as the same issue, but they are not. Competence, a TRE 601 issue, is whether the witness has the ability to testify—is the witness too young, too old, or too mentally unstable to testify—and it is evaluated under TRE 104(a) without considering the admissibility of specific testimony. See Brown & Rondon, ***Texas Rules of Evidence Handbook****, Rule 601 (2021 ed.) (nn.22–27). Personal knowledge, a TRE 602 issue, is whether the witness knows enough about the subject to testify, and it is evaluated under TRE 104(b). See Brown & Rondon,* ***Texas Rules of Evidence Handbook*** *Rule 602 (2021 ed.) (nn.102–103).*

4. Personal knowledge. A summary-judgment affidavit must state that it is based on the affiant's personal knowledge and that the facts in it are true. *See* Tex. R. Civ. P. 166a(f); **Kerlin v. Arias**, 274 S.W.3d 666, 668 (Tex.2008); **Ryland Grp. v. Hood**, 924 S.W.2d 120, 122 (Tex.1996). But a statement, by itself, that the affidavit is based on personal knowledge is insufficient; the affidavit must affirmatively show a basis for the personal knowledge. **Kerlin**, 274 S.W.3d at 668; **Pipkin v. Kroger Tex., L.P.**, 383 S.W.3d 655, 669 (Tex.App.—Houston [14th Dist.] 2012, pet. denied); *see, e.g.*, **Spradlin v. State**, 100 S.W.3d 372, 381 (Tex.App.—Houston [1st Dist.] 2002, no pet.) (affidavit not proper SJ evidence because affiant's personal knowledge was explained only by her marital status). Statements based merely on the affiant's "best knowledge" are not sufficient to raise a fact issue and are improper summary-judgment evidence. **Price v. American Nat'l Ins.**, 113 S.W.3d 424, 429–30 (Tex.App.—Houston [1st Dist.] 2003, no pet.); **Geiselman v. Cramer Fin. Grp.**, 965 S.W.2d 532, 537 (Tex.App.—Houston [14th Dist.] 1997, no writ); *see* **Flanagan v. Martin**, 880 S.W.2d 863, 866 (Tex.App.—Waco 1994, writ dism'd) (best knowledge and belief). See "Personal knowledge," ch. 1-B, §3.2.16(3)(a); "Lack of personal knowledge," ch. 7-B, §10.1.1(3).

Note

Although a summary-judgment affidavit must state that it is based on the affiant's personal knowledge, some courts have held the personal-knowledge requirement is satisfied even if the affidavit includes no such recitation, as long as it clearly shows the affiant is speaking from personal knowledge. See, e.g., ***Pipkin****, 383 S.W.3d at 669 (because affiant was "personally acquainted" with facts and was present and shopping with P when P slipped and fell, affidavit was sufficient to show that affiant was testifying from personal knowledge);* ***Closs v. Goose Creek Consol. ISD****, 874 S.W.2d 859, 868 (Tex.App.—Texarkana 1994, no writ) (although there was no specific recitation that affidavit was based on personal knowledge, because affiant was custodian of school-district records, affidavit satisfied TRCP 166a(f)). To avoid the exclusion of an affidavit as improper summary-judgment evidence, a party should include a recitation that the facts stated in the affidavit are within the affiant's personal knowledge and are true. See* ***O'Connor's Texas Civil Forms****, FORM 1B:8 (2020 ed.).*

5. Not legal conclusions. The affidavit must state facts and cannot merely recite legal conclusions. **Brownlee v. Brownlee**, 665 S.W.2d 111, 112 (Tex.1984). Legal conclusions not supported by facts will not support a summary judgment. *See* **Anderson v. Snider**, 808 S.W.2d 54, 55 (Tex.1991). Legal conclusions in affidavits have no probative force. **801 Nolana, Inc. v. RTC Mortg. Trust**, 944 S.W.2d 751, 754 (Tex.App.—Corpus Christi 1997, writ denied); *see* **Life Ins. Co. of Va. v. Gar-Dal, Inc.**, 570 S.W.2d 378, 381–82 (Tex.1978). The following are examples of legal conclusions for which no underlying facts were stated: • The assault had nothing to do with work; it occurred for reasons personal to the physician. **Walls Reg'l Hosp. v. Bomar**, 9 S.W.3d 805, 807 (Tex.1999). • The defendant did not commit legal malpractice, was not negligent, and did not breach the contract. **Anderson**, 808 S.W.2d at 55. • The indebtedness was renewed and extended. **Mercer v. Daoran Corp.**, 676 S.W.2d 580, 583 (Tex.1984). • The parties modified the contractual obligations. **Brownlee**, 665 S.W.2d at 112. • The party held adverse possession to the property. **Ellis v. Jansing**, 620 S.W.2d 569, 571 (Tex.1981). • Not all offsets and payments were credited. **Gar-Dal**, 570 S.W.2d at 381–82. • The note was purchased for valuable consideration, in good faith, and without notice of default or dishonor. **Hidalgo v. Surety S&L Ass'n**, 487 S.W.2d 702, 703 (Tex.1972).

6. Not factual conclusions. The affidavit must be based on facts and cannot merely recite factual conclusions. Conclusory statements that are not supported by facts are not proper summary-judgment proof. *See* **Elizondo v. Krist**, 415

S.W.3d 259, 264 (Tex.2013); **McIntyre v. Ramirez**, 109 S.W.3d 741, 749–50 (Tex.2003); **Ryland Grp.**, 924 S.W.2d at 122. Unsupported conclusory statements are not credible and are not susceptible to being readily controverted. **Ryland Grp.**, 924 S.W.2d at 122; *see* Tex. R. Civ. P. 166a(c).

(1) By expert witness. Unsupported conclusory statements by an expert witness will not support a summary judgment. **Rogers v. Zanetti**, 518 S.W.3d 394, 405 (Tex.2017); **IHS Cedars Treatment Ctr. v. Mason**, 143 S.W.3d 794, 803 (Tex.2004); **McIntyre**, 109 S.W.3d at 749–50; *see, e.g.*, **Elizondo**, 415 S.W.3d at 264–65 (statement that settlement value of case was $2-3 million rather than the $50,000 received in settlement was conclusory when there was no connection of settlement amounts to specific injuries and no comparison of settlement amounts to similar claims); **Ryland Grp.**, 924 S.W.2d at 122 (statement that D's failure to notify anyone of use of untreated wood on P's deck violated industry practice was conclusory); **Karen Corp. v. Burlington N. & Santa Fe Ry.**, 107 S.W.3d 118, 126 (Tex.App.—Fort Worth 2003, pet. denied) (statement that attorney fees were excessive was conclusory). The expert's statements must explain the link between the facts that she relied on and the opinion that she reached. **Starwood Mgmt. v. Swaim**, 530 S.W.3d 673, 679 (Tex.2017). Opinion testimony cannot be based on the assumption of an unproven fact. **Sipes v. General Motors Corp.**, 946 S.W.2d 143, 148 (Tex.App.—Texarkana 1997, writ denied); *see* **Rogers**, 518 S.W.3d at 405.

(2) By lay witness. Unsupported conclusory statements by a lay witness will not support a summary judgment. *See, e.g.*, **Purcell v. Bellinger**, 940 S.W.2d 599, 601–02 (Tex.1997) (mother's statement about child's interest in pursuing paternity suit was conclusory); **Laidlaw Waste Sys. v. City of Wilmer**, 904 S.W.2d 656, 661 (Tex.1995) (statements that area exceeded statutory minimum size and that boundary did not close were conclusory); **Continental Casing Corp. v. Samedan Oil Corp.**, 751 S.W.2d 499, 501 (Tex.1988) (statement about offset was conclusory because it did not expressly state whether it was taken before or after bankruptcy).

7. Papers referenced in affidavits. Copies of all papers referenced in the affidavit must be attached to or served with the affidavit. *See* Tex. R. Civ. P. 166a(f). The copies must be sworn or certified. *See id.*

8. Filing the affidavits.

(1) Attach to motion or response. The affidavits should be incorporated by reference in and filed with the motion or response. Affidavits attached to the original petition or the answer but not included as part of the motion or response are not competent summary-judgment proof. *E.g.*, **Speck v. First Evangelical Lutheran Ch.**, 235 S.W.3d 811, 816 (Tex.App.—Houston [1st Dist.] 2007, no pet.) (affidavit attached to pleadings but not to SJ response was not competent SJ proof); **Boeker v. Syptak**, 916 S.W.2d 59, 61–62 (Tex.App.—Houston [1st Dist.] 1996, no writ) (copy of petition and its affidavits attached to SJ motion was competent SJ proof); **Sugarland Bus. Ctr., Ltd. v. Norman**, 624 S.W.2d 639, 642 (Tex.App.—Houston [14th Dist.] 1981, no writ) (affidavit attached to pleadings but not to SJ motion was not competent SJ proof).

(2) Affidavit & amended motion or response. An amended motion or response should expressly incorporate by reference the affidavits attached to the earlier motion or response, but failure to do so is not fatal. **Vaughn v. Burroughs Corp.**, 705 S.W.2d 246, 248 (Tex.App.—Houston [14th Dist.] 1986, no writ); *see* **R.I.O. Sys. v. Union Carbide Corp.**, 780 S.W.2d 489, 492 (Tex.App.—Corpus Christi 1989, writ denied) (SJ proof attached to earlier motion was proper proof for later motion). *But see* **Corpus Christi Mun. Gas Corp. v. Tuloso-Midway ISD**, 595 S.W.2d 203, 204 (Tex.App.—Eastland 1980, writ ref'd n.r.e.) (evidence attached to earlier motion could not support SJ).

9. Affidavits made in bad faith. If a party relies on an affidavit made in bad faith or solely for the purpose of delay, the court must award the other party reasonable expenses caused by the affidavit, including reasonable attorney fees. Tex. R. Civ. P. 166a(h); **Ramirez v. Encore Wire Corp.**, 196 S.W.3d 469, 476 (Tex.App.—Dallas 2006, no pet.). Any offending party or attorney may be found guilty of contempt. Tex. R. Civ. P. 166a(h); **Ramirez**, 196 S.W.3d at 476.

10. Sham affidavit. The affidavit must not be a "sham" affidavit. *See* **Lujan v. Navistar, Inc.**, 555 S.W.3d 79, 86 (Tex.2018); **Farroux v. Denny's Rests., Inc.**, 962 S.W.2d 108, 111 (Tex.App.—Houston [1st Dist.] 1997, no pet.). A sham affidavit is one that contradicts an affiant's earlier sworn testimony for the purpose of creating a fact issue to avoid summary judgment. **Farroux**, 962 S.W.2d at 111; *see* **Lujan**, 555 S.W.3d at 87. To determine whether an affidavit is a sham, the court should conduct a case-specific inquiry and examine the nature and extent of the differences between the asserted facts; a

finding of bad faith is not required. **Lujan**, 555 S.W.3d at 88–89; *see* **E-Learning LLC v. AT&T Corp.**, 517 S.W.3d 849, 855 (Tex.App.—San Antonio 2017, no pet.). If the affidavit and the earlier testimony are consistent in the major allegations but contain some differences in the details, the affidavit will not be considered a sham, and the fact issue can defeat a summary-judgment motion. *See* **Lujan**, 555 S.W.3d at 88; **E-Learning**, 517 S.W.3d at 855. But if the affidavit clearly contradicts the earlier testimony on material points and the affiant cannot offer a sufficient explanation for the contradiction, the sham-affidavit rule applies and the court should disregard the affidavit when determining whether the responding party has raised a genuine fact issue to defeat summary judgment. *See* **Lujan**, 555 S.W.3d at 88; **E-Learning**, 517 S.W.3d at 855; **Farroux**, 962 S.W.2d at 111. Examples of a sufficient explanation may include that the affiant was confused about what she was being asked at an earlier deposition or that additional relevant materials were discovered after the testimony was given. **Lujan**, 555 S.W.3d at 85–86; **Farroux**, 962 S.W.2d at 111 & n.1.

Note

Before the Court's decision in ***Lujan****, the courts of appeals disagreed on whether the sham-affidavit rule applied under Texas law. See* ***Lujan****, 555 S.W.3d at 86. The Court agreed with the majority view that a court's authority under TRCP 166a(c) to distinguish between genuine and nongenuine fact issues includes the authority to apply the sham-affidavit rule.* ***Lujan****, 555 S.W.3d at 86 & n.1.*

§9.5 Discovery products. Discovery products used to support a summary-judgment motion or a response can be filed separately or attached to the motion or response. *See* **Enterprise Leasing Co. v. Barrios**, 156 S.W.3d 547, 549 (Tex.2004); **McConathy v. McConathy**, 869 S.W.2d 341, 342 n.2 (Tex.1994).

Note

Two types of discovery products cannot be used as summary-judgment evidence: a party's own answers to interrogatories and a party's own answers in response to requests for admissions. See "Using answers in summary judgment," ch. 6-G, §9.4; "Using admissions in summary judgment," ch. 6-H, §8.3.

1. Discovery on file. The court will consider the discovery on file at the time of the hearing. *See* Tex. R. Civ. P. 166a(c); **Lance v. Robinson**, 543 S.W.3d 723, 732 (Tex.2018). See "On file," ch. 7-B, §9.1.2. For a party to rely on discovery on file with the court, the motion or response must specifically refer to it. *See* Tex. R. Civ. P. 166a(c); **Lance**, 543 S.W.3d at 732; *see, e.g.*, **Steinkamp v. Caremark**, 3 S.W.3d 191, 194–95 (Tex.App.—El Paso 1999, pet. denied) (party made court aware of the particular evidence she was relying on by referring to portions of it and stating that it was already before the court); *see also* **Ramirez v. Colonial Freight Whs. Co.**, 434 S.W.3d 244, 252 (Tex.App.—Houston [1st Dist.] 2014, pet. denied) (to incorporate by reference, party does not need to use "magic language" but instead must make court aware that previously filed documents are being relied on).

2. Unfiled discovery. TRCP 166a(d) permits discovery not on file with the clerk to be used as summary-judgment evidence. The following items must be served on all parties and filed with the court in advance of the summary-judgment hearing. *See* Tex. R. Civ. P. 166a(d) & cmt. (1990); **Gomez v. Tri City Cmty. Hosp., Ltd.**, 4 S.W.3d 281, 283–84 (Tex.App.—San Antonio 1999, no pet.).

(1) Statement of intent. In the motion or response, the party should include a statement of intent to use unfiled discovery products as summary-judgment proof. Tex. R. Civ. P. 166a(d); **McConathy**, 869 S.W.2d at 342 n.2. The statement of intent can be included in or attached to the motion or response. *See, e.g.*, **Garcia v. Andrews**, 867 S.W.2d 409, 411–12 (Tex.App.—Corpus Christi 1993, no writ) (statement of intent in motion for SJ satisfied requirement). Even if no specific statement of intent is made, the requirement in TRCP 166a(d) is satisfied if the party clearly relies on evidence attached to its motion or response. **McConathy**, 869 S.W.2d at 342 n.2; *see, e.g.*, **Mathis v. RKL Design/Build**, 189 S.W.3d 839, 842 (Tex.App.—Houston [1st Dist.] 2006, no pet.) (response listing exhibits and identifying deposition excerpts by page number served as statement of intent).

(2) Unfiled discovery products.

(a) Attached to motion or response. The party should attach one of the following to the motion or response: (1) copies of the unfiled discovery, (2) appendixes containing the unfiled discovery, or (3) a notice containing specific

references to the unfiled discovery. Tex. R. Civ. P. 166a(d); *e.g.*, **E.B. Smith Co. v. U.S. Fid. & Guar. Co.**, 850 S.W.2d 621, 623–24 (Tex.App.—Corpus Christi 1993, writ denied) (broad statements about unfiled depositions in statement of intent were not sufficient; depositions themselves or notice with quotations from depositions were necessary). When attaching copies of or appendixes containing unfiled discovery, a party should also include in the motion or response specific references to the portions of the unfiled discovery relied on. *See, e.g.*, **Barraza v. Eureka Co.**, 25 S.W.3d 225, 228–29 (Tex.App.—El Paso 2000, pet. denied) (attaching portions of unfiled discovery and making specific reference to some of it in SJ response was sufficient); **Guthrie v. Suiter**, 934 S.W.2d 820, 826 (Tex.App.—Houston [1st Dist.] 1996, no writ) (attaching 300-page deposition to motion was not sufficient; party should have identified what evidence in the deposition it relied on); *see also* **Rogers v. Ricane Enters.**, 772 S.W.2d 76, 81 (Tex.1989) (general references to voluminous record were insufficient to support SJ). A general reference to the unfiled discovery may be sufficient, however, when the attached discovery is not voluminous. *See, e.g.*, **Ramirez**, 434 S.W.3d at 251 (general reference to P's own deposition was sufficient because referenced testimony was less than 50 pages and issues raised in deposition were not complex).

(b) Waiver of objections. Objections to unfiled discovery are waived if they are not made before the court rules on the motion for summary judgment. **Grainger v. Western Cas. Life Ins.**, 930 S.W.2d 609, 613–14 (Tex.App.—Houston [1st Dist.] 1996, writ denied); *see* **Fred Loya Ins. Agency, Inc. v. Cohen**, 446 S.W.3d 913, 926 (Tex.App.—El Paso 2014, pet. denied).

3. Unverified discovery. It is not necessary to verify by affidavit the authenticity of most discovery products.

(1) Discovery responses.

(a) Other party's discovery responses. When relying on another party's discovery responses (e.g., documents that are not self-authenticating, answers to interrogatories), a party does not need to authenticate them unless the producing party filed timely objections to their authenticity. Tex. R. Civ. P. 193.7; **Blanche v. First Nationwide Mortg. Corp.**, 74 S.W.3d 444, 451 (Tex.App.—Dallas 2002, no pet.).

(b) Party's own discovery responses. A party relying on its own discovery responses must authenticate them. **Blanche**, 74 S.W.3d at 451–52; *see, e.g.*, **Banowsky v. State Farm Mut. Auto. Ins.**, 876 S.W.2d 509, 513 (Tex.App.—Amarillo 1994, no writ) (D should have authenticated release from its file). The affidavit authenticating a party's own documents must be made by a person with knowledge of the documents' authenticity. *See* **In re G.F.O.**, 874 S.W.2d 729, 731 (Tex.App.—Houston [1st Dist.] 1994, no writ). See "Authenticity," ch. 8-C, §8.4.

(2) Deposition excerpts. When relying on deposition excerpts, it is not necessary to authenticate them. **McConathy**, 869 S.W.2d at 341. To prevent any objections to verification, the party should include in the photocopied excerpts a copy of the verification page signed by the court reporter.

§9.6 Stipulations. A party may rely on the parties' stipulations in a summary-judgment motion or response. Tex. R. Civ. P. 166a(c)(ii). The stipulations should be in writing, signed by both parties, and filed with the court. Tex. R. Civ. P. 11. See "Agreements between attorneys—Rule 11," ch. 1-H, §9. Typical stipulations in summary-judgment proceedings include the terms of a contract in dispute, the agreed facts, and the legal issues in dispute. *See* **Francis v. International Serv. Ins.**, 546 S.W.2d 57, 58–59 (Tex.1976).

§9.7 Reporter's record.

1. From another hearing in same suit. If the trial court conducts another hearing in the same case before the hearing on the motion for summary judgment, the reporter's record from that hearing may be used as summary-judgment proof. On appeal, the record must reflect that the reporter's record was considered at the summary-judgment hearing. *E.g.*, **Munoz v. Gulf Oil Co.**, 693 S.W.2d 372, 373 (Tex.1984) (reporter's record from hearing, which did not bear a file mark, could not be considered on appeal); **Munoz v. Gulf Oil Co.**, 732 S.W.2d 62, 64 (Tex.App.—Houston [14th Dist.] 1987, writ ref'd n.r.e.) (reporter's record from hearing, which bore a file mark, could be considered on appeal).

2. From another case. Sworn testimony from another case between the same parties may be used as summary-judgment proof. **Austin Bldg. Co. v. National Un. Fire Ins.**, 432 S.W.2d 697, 698–99 (Tex.1968); *see also* **Murillo v. Valley Coca-Cola Bottling Co.**, 895 S.W.2d 758, 761–62 (Tex.App.—Corpus Christi 1995, no writ) (reporter's record from another trial was admissible because D was sued for same incident by another P). See "Deposition from other proceeding," ch. 6-F, §12.1.2.

§9.8 Public records. A party may rely on public records as summary-judgment evidence. *See* Tex. R. Civ. P. 166a(c); **Fleming v. Wilson**, __ S.W.3d __, 2020 WL 5985187 (Tex.2020) (No. 19-0230; 10-9-20). The records must be properly authenticated or certified to qualify as competent summary-judgment evidence. *See* Tex. R. Civ. P. 166a(c); **Fleming**, __ S.W.3d at __, 2020 WL 5985187. See "Authenticity," ch. 8-C, §8.4.

§9.9 Conflicts in SJ proof. Conflicting statements in summary-judgment evidence made by the same witness may raise a fact issue. **Gaines v. Hamman**, 358 S.W.2d 557, 562 (Tex.1962) (conflict between affidavit and deposition); **Waldmiller v. Continental Express, Inc.**, 74 S.W.3d 116, 125 (Tex.App.—Texarkana 2002, no pet.) (conflict between affidavits); *see* Tex. R. Civ. P. 166a(c) ("free from contradictions"). But when a party submits an affidavit that conflicts with the party's earlier sworn testimony, a fact issue is raised only if the affidavit is not considered to be a sham. See "Sham affidavit," ch. 7-B, §9.4.10.

§9.10 No oral testimony. No oral testimony may be considered in support of a motion for summary judgment or response. Tex. R. Civ. P. 166a(c). See "On objections to expert—*Daubert-Robinson* hearing," ch. 7-B, §11.2.

§10. Objections to summary-judgment evidence

§10.1 Generally. If a party's affidavits (or other summary-judgment proof) contain evidence that would not be admissible at trial, the opposing party should object and move to strike the inadmissible evidence. *See* Tex. R. Civ. P. 166a(f) ("affidavits . . . shall set forth such facts as would be admissible in evidence"). A party generally must object in writing (in a response, a reply, special exceptions, separate objections, or a motion to strike) to formal deficiencies in the summary-judgment proof, or it waives the objection. *See* **Seim v. Allstate Tex. Lloyds**, 551 S.W.3d 161, 166 (Tex.2018); **City of Houston v. Clear Creek Basin Auth.**, 589 S.W.2d 671, 677 (Tex.1979). But if the defect is one of substance, no objection is necessary to preserve the error and the defect may be raised for the first time on appeal. **Seim**, 551 S.W.3d at 166; **Brown v. Brown**, 145 S.W.3d 745, 751 (Tex.App.—Dallas 2004, pet. denied); *see* **Clear Creek**, 589 S.W.2d at 677. A defect is formal (and the objection to it is waivable) if the summary-judgment proof is competent but inadmissible; a defect is substantive (and the objection to it is not waivable) if the summary-judgment proof is incompetent. **Mathis v. Bocell**, 982 S.W.2d 52, 60 (Tex.App.—Houston [1st Dist.] 1998, no pet.). While objections to formal defects in the evidence are objections to its admissibility that can be cured before judgment, objections to substantive defects in the evidence are never waived because incompetent evidence cannot support a judgment under any circumstances. *Id.*

Caution

Courts of appeals often disagree about whether a particular defect is one of form or one of substance. See, e.g., ***Brown****, 145 S.W.3d at 752 & n.1 (split of authority on failure to attach referenced document to affidavit or motion);* ***Dailey v. Albertson's, Inc.****, 83 S.W.3d 222, 226 (Tex.App.—El Paso 2002, no pet.) (whether lack of personal knowledge is defect of form or substance is subject of some confusion); see also* ***Trusty v. Strayhorn****, 87 S.W.3d 756, 762–63 (Tex.App.—Texarkana 2002, no pet.) (courts disagree about whether objections to defects in form under TRCP 166a(f) must be made by parties seeking reversal or affirmance on appeal or only when reversal is sought). See "Failure to attach exhibit," ch. 7-B, §10.1.1(1)(b); "Lack of personal knowledge," ch. 7-B, §10.1.1(3); "Failure to attach exhibit," ch. 7-B, §10.1.2(1); "Lack of personal knowledge," ch. 7-B, §10.1.2(6). Thus, to avoid waiver, parties should always object in writing to all defects in the evidence and obtain rulings on the objections. See* ***O'Connor's Texas Civil Forms****, FORMS 7C:3 to 7C:6, 7C:9, 7C:11 (2020 ed.).*

1. Waivable objections to evidence. TRCP 166a(f) requires a party to object to formal defects in the affidavits or their attachments (i.e., other evidence). Formal defects are not grounds for reversal unless the objecting party specifically objected and the other party was given the opportunity to amend but refused. Tex. R. Civ. P. 166a(f); **Seim**, 551 S.W.3d at 164; **Bauer v. Jasso**, 946 S.W.2d 552, 556–57 (Tex.App.—Corpus Christi 1997, no writ). Some courts of appeals have held that both movants and nonmovants must object to formal defects in order to preserve error for appeal—the appellee cannot assert a formal defect to justify affirmance of a summary judgment in its favor unless it made the objection in writing. *See* **Trusty**, 87 S.W.3d at 762–63 (TRCP 166a(f) applies to defects in form asserted as grounds for affirmance); **Martin v. Durden**,

965 S.W.2d 562, 565 (Tex.App.—Houston [14th Dist.] 1997, pet. denied) (same). *But see* **Ceballos v. El Paso Health Care Sys.**, 881 S.W.2d 439, 444 (Tex.App.—El Paso 1994, writ denied) (dicta; Rule 166a(f) requires objection to formal defect only when defect is urged as grounds for reversal, and not for affirmance, of SJ); **Williams v. Conroe ISD**, 809 S.W.2d 954, 958 (Tex.App.—Beaumont 1991, no pet.) (same). The following are some of the objections to evidence that a party must specifically make to avoid waiver:

(1) Formal defects in affidavit.

(a) Defective content of affidavit. If the movant's affidavit meets the minimum requirements for a valid affidavit, formal defects in the affidavit are not grounds for reversal unless the nonmovant specifically objected and the movant was given the opportunity to amend but did not. Tex. R. Civ. P. 166a(f). The party objecting to the content of an affidavit must identify the specific statements that are objectionable and state why they are objectionable. *See, e.g.*, **Haynes v. Haynes**, 178 S.W.3d 350, 355 (Tex.App.—Houston [14th Dist.] 2005, pet. denied) (court of appeals overruled challenge to SJ because P did not identify the part of affidavit that contained hearsay). An entire affidavit cannot be excluded if only part of it is inadmissible. *See, e.g.*, **Spradlin v. State**, 100 S.W.3d 372, 381 (Tex.App.—Houston [1st Dist.] 2002, no pet.) (specific statements in affidavit not based on personal knowledge excluded from SJ evidence). When the trial court sustains an objection to an entire affidavit, the party offering the affidavit should either ask to amend it or ask that only the objectionable part be struck. See "Request for partial admission of evidence," ch. 8-D, §7.1.3(2).

(b) Failure to attach exhibit. Some courts of appeals have held that the failure to attach a document referenced in an affidavit is a defect of form and thus will be waived if no objection is made. *See, e.g.*, **Sunsinger v. Perez**, 16 S.W.3d 496, 500–01 (Tex.App.—Beaumont 2000, pet. denied); **Martin**, 965 S.W.2d at 565; **Jones v. WKB Value Partners**, No. 04-07-00865-CV, 2008 WL 2261192 (Tex.App.—San Antonio 2008, no pet.) (memo op.; 6-4-08). Some courts determine whether the failure to attach documents is a defect of form or substance by analyzing whether the failure goes to the admissibility of the evidence or to its competence. *See, e.g.*, **Mathis**, 982 S.W.2d at 60 (lack of exhibits made affidavit inadmissible, not incompetent); *see also* **Brown**, 145 S.W.3d at 752 (lack of exhibits made affidavit conclusory). If an affidavit relies on facts contained in a missing exhibit but the same information is supplied elsewhere in the summary-judgment evidence, the missing exhibit is merely a formal defect and the error is waivable. *See* **Watts v. Hermann Hosp.**, 962 S.W.2d 102, 105 (Tex.App.—Houston [1st Dist.] 1997, no pet.). For a discussion of cases holding that the failure to attach an exhibit is a defect of substance, see "Failure to attach exhibit," ch. 7-B, §10.1.2(1).

(c) Absence of jurat. When a purported affidavit lacks a jurat and the offering party does not provide extrinsic evidence to show that it was sworn to before an authorized officer, the opposing party must object, or the objection is waived. **Mansions in the Forest, L.P. v. Montgomery Cty.**, 365 S.W.3d 314, 317 (Tex.2012). See "Sworn," ch. 7-B, §9.4.1.

(d) Defect in jurat. The objection that a jurat is defective must be made, or else it is waived. *See* **Ford Motor Co. v. Leggat**, 904 S.W.2d 643, 645–46 (Tex.1995); *see, e.g.*, **Wasserberg v. 84 Lumber Co.**, No. 14-10-00136-CV, 2011 WL 3447493 (Tex.App.—Houston [14th Dist.] 2011, no pet.) (memo op.; 8-9-11) (error in date of jurat was defect in form).

(2) Lack of competence. The objection that an affidavit was made by an incompetent witness must be made, or else it is waived. **Rizkallah v. Conner**, 952 S.W.2d 580, 586 (Tex.App.—Houston [1st Dist.] 1997, no writ); *see* **Woods Expl. & Prod'g Co. v. Arkla Equip. Co.**, 528 S.W.2d 568, 570–71 (Tex.1975). TRCP 166a(f) states that the affidavit must show affirmatively that the witness is competent. See "Competency of witness," ch. 1-B, §3.2.16(2).

Note

Courts often treat a witness's competence and personal knowledge as the same issue, but they are not. See "Note," ch. 7-B, §9.4.3.

---

(3) Lack of personal knowledge. The Supreme Court has issued inconsistent opinions on whether the objection that an affidavit is not based on personal knowledge is a defect of form or of substance. *Compare* **Grand Prairie**

ISD v. Vaughan, 792 S.W.2d 944, 945 (Tex.1990) (lack of personal knowledge is defect of form), *with* **Laidlaw Waste Sys. v. City of Wilmer**, 904 S.W.2d 656, 661 (Tex.1995) (reaching the opposite result without specifically affirming lower court's statement that lack of personal knowledge is defect of substance). Relying on **Vaughan**, some courts of appeals have held that an affidavit not based on personal knowledge is a defect of form and thus will be waived if no objection is made. *E.g.*, **Washington DC Party Shuttle, LLC v. IGuide Tours, LLC**, 406 S.W.3d 723, 736 (Tex.App.—Houston [14th Dist.] 2013, pet. denied); **Wolfe v. Devon Energy Prod. Co.**, 382 S.W.3d 434, 452 (Tex.App.—Waco 2012, pet. denied); **Rizkallah**, 952 S.W.2d at 585; *see* **Stewart v. Sanmina Tex. L.P.**, 156 S.W.3d 198, 207 (Tex.App.—Dallas 2005, no pet.); **Youngblood v. U.S. Silica Co.**, 130 S.W.3d 461, 468–69 (Tex.App.—Texarkana 2004, pet. denied). For a discussion of cases holding that lack of personal knowledge is a defect of substance that can be raised for the first time on appeal, see "Lack of personal knowledge," ch. 7-B, §10.1.2(6). See also "Personal knowledge," ch. 1-B, §3.2.16(3)(a).

(4) Not readily controvertible. The objection that an affidavit contains declarations that are not easily controverted must be made, or else it is waived. *See* **Patterson v. Mobiloil Fed. Credit Un.**, 890 S.W.2d 551, 554 (Tex.App.—Beaumont 1994, no writ). See "Interested witness," ch. 7-B, §9.3.2.

(5) Hearsay evidence. The objection that testimony contains hearsay must be made, or else it is waived. **Harrell v. Patel**, 225 S.W.3d 1, 6 (Tex.App.—El Paso 2005, pet. denied). Unless a party objects to hearsay evidence, the evidence will support a summary judgment. *See* Tex. R. Evid. 103(a)(1), 802; **Harrell**, 225 S.W.3d at 6; *see, e.g.*, **Southland Corp. v. Lewis**, 940 S.W.2d 83, 85 (Tex.1997) (hearsay excluded because party objected); **Fortis Benefits v. Cantu**, 170 S.W.3d 755, 759 (Tex.App.—Waco 2005) (unobjected-to hearsay considered in support of SJ), *rev'd in part on other grounds*, 234 S.W.3d 642 (Tex.2007); **Columbia Rio Grande Reg'l Hosp. v. Stover**, 17 S.W.3d 387, 396 (Tex.App.—Corpus Christi 2000, no pet.) (hearsay objections waived because not specific enough).

(6) Failure to lay predicate. The objection that an affidavit does not lay the proper predicate for admissibility must be made, or else it is waived. **Life Ins. Co. of Va. v. Gar-Dal, Inc.**, 570 S.W.2d 378, 380–81 (Tex.1978); **Seidner v. Citibank**, 201 S.W.3d 332, 334–35 (Tex.App.—Houston [14th Dist.] 2006, pet. denied); **Cottrell v. Carrillon Assocs.**, 646 S.W.2d 491, 494 (Tex.App.—Houston [1st Dist.] 1982, writ ref'd n.r.e.).

(7) Not best evidence. The objection that the copy of a document offered is not the "best evidence" of the contents of the document must be made, or else it is waived. *See* Tex. R. Evid. 1002 (an original writing is required to prove its contents unless admissible under another TRE or by law). A copy of a document is not admissible if the original document is not produced, its content is disputed, and its absence is not explained. *See, e.g.*, **Mercer v. Daoran Corp.**, 676 S.W.2d 580, 584 (Tex.1984) (court should have sustained objection to unsigned copy of promissory note). The best-evidence rule applies only when a party seeks to prove the contents of a disputed document not in evidence. *See* **Osuna v. Quintana**, 993 S.W.2d 201, 206 (Tex.App.—Corpus Christi 1999, no pet.); **White v. Bath**, 825 S.W.2d 227, 231 (Tex.App.—Houston [14th Dist.] 1992, writ denied).

(8) Underlying methodology to expert opinion. The objection that expert testimony is not admissible under TRE 702 (testimony by experts) or TRCP 193.6(a) (exclusion of evidence for not timely responding to discovery) must be made, or else it is waived. *See, e.g.*, **Harris Cty. Appraisal Dist. v. Riverway Holdings, L.P.**, No. 14-09-00786-CV, 2011 WL 529466 (Tex.App.—Houston [14th Dist.] 2011, pet. denied) (memo op.; 2-15-11) (challenge to expert's methodology, raised for first time in motion for new trial, could not be considered on appeal); *see also* **Pink v. Goodyear Tire & Rubber Co.**, 324 S.W.3d 290, 301 (Tex.App.—Beaumont 2010, pet. dism'd) (express ruling required to preserve objection to methodology, technique, or foundational data on which expert opinion is based). See "*Daubert-Robinson* test for expert testimony," ch. 5-N, §2; "Underlying methodology," ch. 5-N, §6.2.1.

2. Nonwaivable objections to evidence. Substantive errors in the summary-judgment evidence are not waivable. **Brown**, 145 S.W.3d at 751. But a party should still object to all errors in the summary-judgment evidence, even nonwaivable errors. If a party did not object in the summary-judgment proceeding, the following are objections to defects of substance that can be made for the first time on appeal:

(1) Failure to attach exhibit. Several courts of appeals have held that the failure to attach a document referenced in an affidavit is a defect of substance, and no objection is necessary to preserve error. *See, e.g.*, **Galindo v. Dean**,

69 S.W.3d 623, 627 (Tex.App.—Eastland 2002, no pet.) (medical records); **Natural Gas Clearinghouse v. Midgard Energy Co.**, 23 S.W.3d 372, 378–79 (Tex.App.—Amarillo 1999, pet. denied) (consultant's records supporting opinion on damages); **Mincron SBC Corp. v. Worldcom, Inc.**, 994 S.W.2d 785, 795–96 (Tex.App.—Houston [1st Dist.] 1999, no pet.) (invoices supporting disputed damages); **Gorrell v. Texas Utils. Elec. Co.**, 915 S.W.2d 55, 60 (Tex.App.—Fort Worth 1995, writ denied) (sworn or certified copies of exhibits); **Ceballos**, 881 S.W.2d at 445 (medical records supporting nontreating doctor's and nurse's opinions); *see also* **Sorrells v. Giberson**, 780 S.W.2d 936, 938 (Tex.App.—Austin 1989, writ denied) (in suit on a note, failure to attach note was reversible error because affidavit did not prove elements of suit). For a discussion of cases holding that the failure to attach an exhibit is merely a defect of form, see "Failure to attach exhibit," ch. 7-B, §10.1.1(1)(b).

(2) Unsubstantiated legal conclusion. Legal conclusions unsupported by evidence are defects of substance, and no objection is necessary to preserve error. **Hou-Tex, Inc. v. Landmark Graphics**, 26 S.W.3d 103, 112 (Tex.App.—Houston [14th Dist.] 2000, no pet.); **Rizkallah**, 952 S.W.2d at 587. See "Not legal conclusions," ch. 7-B, §9.4.5.

(3) Unsubstantiated factual conclusion. Factual conclusions, opinions, and subjective beliefs unsupported by evidence are defects of substance, and no objection is necessary to preserve error. **Harley-Davidson Motor Co. v. Young**, 720 S.W.2d 211, 213 (Tex.App.—Houston [14th Dist.] 1986, no writ); *see* **Denco CS Corp. v. Body Bar, LLC**, 445 S.W.3d 863, 873 & n.17 (Tex.App.—Texarkana 2014, no pet.). Bare conclusions are not evidence and are not probative of any facts. *See* **Bavishi v. Sterling Air Conditioning, Inc.**, No. 01-10-00610-CV, 2011 WL 3525417 (Tex.App.—Houston [1st Dist.] 2011, no pet.) (memo op.; 8-11-11). See "Not factual conclusions," ch. 7-B, §9.4.6.

(4) Conflict in movant's SJ proof. If the movant's affidavit testimony or other evidence contains conflicting statements that raise a fact issue, the evidence will not support a summary judgment even if no objection is made. *See* Tex. R. Civ. P. 166a(c); **Dillard v. NCNB Tex. Nat'l Bank**, 815 S.W.2d 356, 360–61 (Tex.App.—Austin 1991, no writ), *disapproved on other grounds*, **Amberboy v. Societe de Banque Privee**, 831 S.W.2d 793 (Tex.1992).

(5) Conclusory expert opinion. If an expert's opinion is speculative or conclusory, no objection is necessary to preserve error. See "Conclusory evidence," ch. 5-N, §6.2.2.

(6) Lack of personal knowledge. Some courts have held that if an affiant's testimony reflects a lack of personal knowledge, the defect is one of substance, and no objection is necessary to preserve error. *E.g.*, **Stone v. Midland Multifamily Equity REIT**, 334 S.W.3d 371, 375 (Tex.App.—Dallas 2011, no pet.); **Dailey**, 83 S.W.3d at 226; **Fernandez v. Peters**, No. 03-09-00687-CV, 2010 WL 4137491 (Tex.App.—Austin 2010, no pet.) (memo op.; 10-19-10). For a discussion of cases holding that lack of personal knowledge is merely a defect of form, see "Lack of personal knowledge," ch. 7-B, §10.1.1(3).

(7) Lack of authentication. If the summary-judgment evidence completely lacks authentication, the defect is one of substance, and no objection is necessary to preserve error. *See, e.g.*, **Blanche v. First Nationwide Mortg. Corp.**, 74 S.W.3d 444, 451 (Tex.App.—Dallas 2002, no pet.) (Ps submitted over 300 pages of documents in response to MSJ but included only one affidavit that did not identify, reference, or attempt to authenticate documents; defect was substantive and could be raised for first time on appeal); *see also* **Perkins v. Crittenden**, 462 S.W.2d 565, 566–67 (Tex.1970) (unsworn statement and unverified copy of promissory note could not support SJ in suit to recover on note; objection was preserved when raised for first time on appeal); *cf.* **In re Estate of Guerrero**, 465 S.W.3d 693, 706–07 (Tex.App.—Houston [14th Dist.] 2015, pet. denied) (in motion to compel arbitration, absence of affidavit verifying copy of arbitration agreement and other contract documents as proof of execution was substantive defect).

§10.2 Secure ruling on objections. A party should ask the court to make written rulings on its objections to the summary-judgment evidence. *See* **Seim v. Allstate Tex. Lloyds**, 551 S.W.3d 161, 165–66 (Tex.2018); **Exxon Mobil Corp. v. Rincones**, 520 S.W.3d 572, 583 (Tex.2017); **Jones v. Ray Ins. Agency**, 59 S.W.3d 739, 753 (Tex.App.—Corpus Christi 2001), *pet. denied*, 92 S.W.3d 530 (Tex.2002). The failure to secure a written ruling on an objection will cause problems only when the objection is waivable; thus, if no objection is necessary to preserve error, no ruling is required. For the summary-judgment objections that are preserved without an objection, see "Nonwaivable objections to evidence," ch. 7-B, §10.1.2.

Practice Tip

To preserve error when a court refuses to overrule your objections to the motion for summary judgment, file a motion for new trial within 30 days after the judgment, reurge the objections, and include an objection to the court's refusal to rule. See ***Alejandro v. Bell****, 84 S.W.3d 383, 388 (Tex.App.—Corpus Christi 2002, no pet.). When the motion for new trial is overruled, either by order or by operation of law, your objections are preserved for appeal. See "Refusal to rule + objection," ch. 1-G, §2.2.3.*

1. Express ruling. A party should obtain an express ruling from the trial court on its objections to the summary-judgment evidence. **Seim**, 551 S.W.3d at 165–66; *see* **Parkway Dental Assocs. v. Ho & Huang Props., L.P.**, 391 S.W.3d 596, 603–04 (Tex.App.—Houston [14th Dist.] 2012, no pet.); **Rodriguez v. Wal-Mart Stores**, 52 S.W.3d 814, 823 (Tex.App.—San Antonio 2001), *rev'd in part on other grounds*, 92 S.W.3d 502 (Tex.2002). This practice ensures that error is preserved for appeal. *See* **Seim**, 551 S.W.3d at 165–66.

2. Implicit ruling. The Supreme Court has suggested that an implicit ruling on a party's objections to the summary-judgment evidence may be sufficient to preserve error on appeal when the implication is "clear" from the record. **Seim**, 551 S.W.3d at 166. The Court did not, however, explain what constitutes a clearly implied ruling by the trial court. *See id.*

Caution

Before the Court's ruling in ***Seim****, the courts of appeals were split on whether a trial court's implicit ruling on objections to summary-judgment evidence was sufficient to preserve error.* ***Seim****, 551 S.W.3d at 165–66. Although the Court suggested that an implicit ruling might be sufficient under certain circumstances, it rejected the view that a ruling on the summary-judgment motion alone constitutes an implicit ruling on the objections. See id. The Court similarly rejected the idea that error is preserved as long as the record indicates "in some way" that the trial court ruled on the objections. See, e.g., id. (SJ order stating that court considered motions, briefs, and all competent SJ evidence was not sufficient to show implicit ruling on objections). Until the Court defines what constitutes a clearly implied ruling, a party should obtain an express ruling on any objections in order to avoid waiving error.*

§11. Hearing

§11.1 On SJ motion.

1. Notice. The nonmovant is entitled to receive sufficient notice of a hearing date on the motion so that it knows when its response is due. See "Notice," ch. 7-B, §7.

2. On submission. The hearing for summary judgment is for argument only; no oral testimony may be presented. Tex. R. Civ. P. 166a(c); **Jack B. Anglin Co. v. Tipps**, 842 S.W.2d 266, 269 n.4 (Tex.1992); **Martin v. Cohen**, 804 S.W.2d 201, 203 (Tex.App.—Houston [14th Dist.] 1991, no writ). A party is not entitled to a hearing to present argument for a motion for summary judgment. **In re American Media Consol.**, 121 S.W.3d 70, 74 (Tex.App.—San Antonio 2003, orig. proceeding). The court can decide the motion for summary judgment on submission, without an appearance by the attorneys before the court. *See* **Martin v. Martin, Martin & Richards, Inc.**, 989 S.W.2d 357, 359 (Tex.1998).

3. Evidence on file. In ruling on the motion for summary judgment, the court will consider all of the evidence on file at the time of the hearing. **Lance v. Robinson**, 543 S.W.3d 723, 732 (Tex.2018). See "On file," ch. 7-B, §9.1.2.

§11.2 On objections to expert—*Daubert-Robinson* hearing. If a movant files a motion for summary judgment that includes objections to the nonmovant's expert, the court should hold a **Daubert-Robinson** hearing separate from the hearing on the motion for summary judgment, although it is not required to do so. *See* **Rayon v. Energy Specialties, Inc.**, 121 S.W.3d 7, 19–20 (Tex.App.—Fort Worth 2002, no pet.); *see, e.g.*, **Weiss v. Mechanical Associated Servs.**, 989 S.W.2d 120, 124 & n.6 (Tex.App.—San Antonio 1999, pet. denied) (when trial court granted motion for SJ that included objection to

nonmovant's expert, appellate court assumed that trial court found expert's opinion inadmissible); *cf.* **Heller v. Shaw Indus.**, 167 F.3d 146, 151 (3d Cir.1999) (before considering motion for SJ, court held **Daubert** hearing to determine admissibility of expert's opinion). The **Daubert-Robinson** ("DR") and summary-judgment ("SJ") hearings should be held separately for the following reasons: (1) the purposes of the hearings are different (DR—for testimony; SJ—for argument), (2) the trial burdens are different (DR—preponderance of the evidence; SJ—as a matter of law), (3) the appellate standards are different (DR—abuse of discretion; SJ—de novo), and (4) the appellate records are different (DR—reporter's record required; SJ—no reporter's record required). See "Motion to Exclude Expert," ch. 5-N, §1 et seq.

§12. Summary judgment

§12.1 Not sua sponte. The trial court does not have the authority to grant summary judgment on its own initiative. **Daniels v. Daniels**, 45 S.W.3d 278, 282 (Tex.App.—Corpus Christi 2001, no pet.). When granting a summary judgment, the court is limited to the grounds stated in the motion for summary judgment. See "Stated in motion," ch. 7-C, §2.4.1.

§12.2 Judgment or order?

Practice Tip

Whether the proposed order or judgment should be attached to the motion or brought to the hearing depends on a court's local rules. A party should attempt to reach an agreement on the wording of the order or judgment ("approved as to form") with opposing counsel before submitting it to the court. Some judges, however, prefer to draft their own orders and judgments.

---

1. Judgment. If the trial court grants the motion for summary judgment and no other issues remain, the court should sign a final judgment.

2. Order. See **O'Connor's Texas Civil Forms**, FORM 7C:12 (2020 ed.).

(1) Denies SJ. If the trial court denies the motion for summary judgment, the court should sign an order denying the motion.

(2) Grants partial SJ. If the trial court grants the motion for summary judgment but other issues remain pending, the court should sign an order granting the partial summary judgment.

(a) Nonsuit or severance. If the case is not fully adjudicated on the motion, the court may nonsuit or sever the unadjudicated part of the case, in which case the order granting the summary judgment becomes final. If, after granting a partial summary judgment, the court signs an order of nonsuit or severance that disposes of or severs all remaining claims, the appellate deadlines for the summary judgment begin to run on the date the court signs the order of nonsuit or severance. *See* **Park Place Hosp. v. Estate of Milo**, 909 S.W.2d 508, 510 (Tex.1995). See "Motion for severance," ch. 5-I, §3; "Voluntary Dismissal—Nonsuit," ch. 7-F, §1 et seq.

(b) Unadjudicated issues. Claims not adjudicated by the motion for summary judgment are preserved for disposition by the trial court after resolution of the motion. Tex. R. Civ. P. 166a(e); *see* **McNally v. Guevara**, 52 S.W.3d 195, 196 (Tex.2001) (no presumption that SJ motion addresses all of movant's claims).

§12.3 Drafting SJ. See **O'Connor's Texas Civil Forms**, FORM 9C:4 (2020 ed.).

1. Identify grounds. Although it is helpful on appeal for the summary judgment to include the grounds on which it was granted, it is not necessary. On appeal, the court will consider all grounds for summary judgment included in the motion for summary judgment. See "Grounds for review," ch. 7-B, §14.3.1. The appellate court will not affirm a summary judgment on a ground not presented to the trial court in the motion. See "Stated in motion," ch. 7-C, §2.4.1.

2. State whether final or partial. The judgment should state whether it is intended to be a final or partial summary judgment.

(1) Final SJ. If the parties intend the summary judgment to be a final, appealable judgment, the judgment should (1) actually dispose of all claims and parties, or (2) state with unmistakable clarity that it is a final judgment for all

claims and all parties. **Lehmann v. Har-Con Corp.**, 39 S.W.3d 191, 192–93 (Tex.2001). A "Mother Hubbard" clause stating that "all relief not expressly granted herein is denied" is ambiguous and does not by itself indicate that a summary judgment is final for purposes of appeal. *See* **Farm Bur. Cty. Mut. Ins. v. Rogers**, 455 S.W.3d 161, 164 (Tex.2015); **Lehmann**, 39 S.W.3d at 192–93. See "Statement of finality," ch. 9-C, §4.3; "What judgments are final," ch. 9-C, §6.3.

Note

An order granting a motion for partial summary judgment that contains an unequivocal statement of finality is considered final for purposes of appeal, even if the party moving for summary judgment did not move for summary judgment on all claims and did not intend the summary judgment to be final. See ***Lehmann****, 39 S.W.3d at 204. See "Judgment includes statement of finality," ch. 9-C, §6.3.1(2)(a)[1].*

(2) Partial SJ. If the parties intend the summary judgment to be a partial judgment, the judgment should say so. A summary judgment is a partial, interlocutory order if it does not dispose of all claims and all parties. **Lehmann**, 39 S.W.3d at 205. The following orders are not final orders:

(a) An order that adjudicates the plaintiff's claims but not a counterclaim, cross-claim, or third-party claim. *Id.* Or the converse, an order that adjudicates a counterclaim, cross-claim, or third-party claim but not the plaintiff's claims. *Id.*

(b) An order that disposes of the claims by only one of multiple plaintiffs. *Id.*; **Liu v. Yang**, 69 S.W.3d 225, 228 (Tex.App.—Corpus Christi 2001, no pet.). Or the converse, an order that disposes of the claims against only one of multiple defendants. **Lehmann**, 39 S.W.3d at 205.

(c) An order that resolves the issue of liability in favor of the movant but leaves the issue of damages for a later hearing. *See* Tex. R. Civ. P. 166a(a) (SJ may be rendered on issue of liability alone, although there is a genuine issue as to amount of damages).

3. Resolve issues on the merits. A summary judgment should not state that the case is dismissed. **Martinez v. Southern Pac. Transp.**, 951 S.W.2d 824, 830 (Tex.App.—San Antonio 1997, no writ); **Heibel v. Bermann**, 407 S.W.2d 945, 947 (Tex.App.—Houston 1966, no writ). A summary judgment should dispose of claims on the merits, not by dismissal. *See, e.g.*, **Martinez**, 951 S.W.2d at 830 (appellate court reformed judgment to delete "dismissal with prejudice" language, leaving "take nothing" language).

4. Overrule objections. The nonmovant should make sure the summary judgment includes a statement that all of its objections and any special exceptions were overruled. See "Ruling," ch. 7-B, §5.4; "Secure ruling on objections," ch. 7-B, §10.2. If the court refuses to rule, the nonmovant should object to the refusal in writing. By objecting to the court's refusal to rule, the nonmovant will preserve error on the objection. Tex. R. App. P. 33.1(a)(2)(B). See "Refusal to rule + objection," ch. 1-G, §2.2.3.

§12.4 Making partial SJ final. To convert a partial summary judgment into a final one, the unadjudicated claims can be resolved on the merits by another summary judgment or at trial, or resolved procedurally by a nonsuit or a severance. See "What judgments are final," ch. 9-C, §6.3.

Note

If a judgment being appealed is actually a partial summary judgment, the appellate court can abate the appeal so that the trial court can modify its order and make the judgment final. See Tex. R. App. P. 27.2, 27.3. See "Note," ch. 9-C, §6.3.2(2).

§13. Motion for reconsideration

A party may file a motion to reconsider the court's summary-judgment ruling. When a party files a motion requesting a reconsideration of a motion for summary judgment that was granted, the motion is effectively a motion for new trial. See

"MNT after summary judgment," ch. 10-B, §11; **O'Connor's Texas Civil Forms**, FORM 10B:6 (2020 ed.). When a party files a motion requesting a reconsideration of a motion for summary judgment that was denied, the party should reurge all the grounds raised in the original motion for summary judgment and summarize any objections to the other party's motion or response. *See, e.g.*, **State Farm Lloyds v. Page**, 315 S.W.3d 525, 531–32 (Tex.2010) (because motion for reconsideration was limited to grounds in traditional MSJ and did not reurge no-evidence MSJ grounds, D's no-evidence MSJ arguments were not preserved). A party may also refile the motion for summary judgment.

§14. Review

§14.1 Appellate record. The appellate record for summary judgment is limited to the clerk's record. As a rule, no reporter's record is necessary because no oral testimony can be received at the hearing. *See* Tex. R. Civ. P. 166a(c); **McConnell v. Southside ISD**, 858 S.W.2d 337, 343 n.7 (Tex.1993). However, a reporter's record may be necessary if the court made rulings about the summary judgment that are reflected only in the reporter's record. *See, e.g.*, **Aguilar v. LVDVD, L.C.**, 70 S.W.3d 915, 917 (Tex.App.—El Paso 2002, pet. denied) (proper to include reporter's record in appellate record because hearing preserved ruling on written objections). See "Summary judgment," **O'Connor's Texas Civil Appeals**, ch. 6-C, §3.2.2 (2020 ed.).

§14.2 Final SJ. As a general rule, only final summary judgments can be appealed. See "Final judgment," ch. 9-C, §6. If a summary judgment leaves some claims unresolved, it is an interlocutory order and cannot be appealed until after the rendition of a final judgment. *See* **Farm Bur. Cty. Mut. Ins. v. Rogers**, 455 S.W.3d 161, 164 (Tex.2015); **Lehmann v. Har-Con Corp.**, 39 S.W.3d 191, 205 (Tex.2001). If the summary judgment grants more relief than requested in the motion but contains unequivocal language that it disposes of all claims and parties, the summary judgment is final for purposes of appeal. *See* **Ritzell v. Espeche**, 87 S.W.3d 536, 538 (Tex.2002); **Lehmann**, 39 S.W.3d at 205–07. See "Judgment includes statement of finality," ch. 9-C, §6.3.1(2)(a)[1].

§14.3 Appeal when SJ granted. A summary judgment becomes final and appealable when the trial court disposes of all the parties and issues in the lawsuit. **Park Place Hosp. v. Estate of Milo**, 909 S.W.2d 508, 510 (Tex.1995). Once the trial court grants a final summary judgment, the nonmovant may appeal.

1. Grounds for review.

(1) Expressly presented to trial court. The appellate court may review any ground the movant presented to the trial court in its motion for summary judgment, regardless of whether the trial court identified the ground relied on to grant the summary judgment. **Cincinnati Life Ins. v. Cates**, 927 S.W.2d 623, 625 (Tex.1996). Any issues not expressly presented to the trial court by motion or a response cannot be considered by the appellate court as grounds for reversing a summary-judgment ruling. Tex. R. Civ. P. 166a(c); **ExxonMobil Corp. v. Lazy R Ranch, LP**, 511 S.W.3d 538, 545 (Tex.2017); **Wells Fargo Bank v. Murphy**, 458 S.W.3d 912, 916 (Tex.2015); *see, e.g.*, **McAllen Hosps., L.P. v. State Farm Cty. Mut. Ins.**, 433 S.W.3d 535, 541–42 (Tex.2014) (appellate court could not resolve question of whether P had separate cause of action against third party to enforce lien because issue was not raised in D's MSJ). Similarly, the appellate court cannot infer from the pleadings other grounds for granting the summary judgment that were not expressly before the trial court. **Nall v. Plunkett**, 404 S.W.3d 552, 555 (Tex.2013). The appellate court commits reversible error if it sua sponte addresses grounds to reverse a summary judgment that have not been preserved in the trial court or raised during the appeal. *See, e.g.*, **Wells Fargo**, 458 S.W.3d at 916 (appellate court erred by sua sponte recharacterizing Ps' claims as not falling under the Declaratory Judgments Act and reversing SJ award of attorney fees).

(2) When not identified in judgment. When the summary judgment does not state the grounds on which it was granted, the nonmovant must show that each ground alleged in the motion is insufficient to support the judgment. **Jones v. Hyman**, 107 S.W.3d 830, 832 (Tex.App.—Dallas 2003, no pet.). Otherwise, the summary judgment may be affirmed on any one meritorious ground alleged. **Community Health Sys. Prof'l Servs. v. Hansen**, 525 S.W.3d 671, 680 (Tex.2017); **Merriman v. XTO Energy, Inc.**, 407 S.W.3d 244, 248 (Tex.2013); **Dow Chem. Co. v. Francis**, 46 S.W.3d 237, 242 (Tex.2001).

(3) From earlier SJ motions. The appellate court may review grounds in earlier summary-judgment motions, even though they were denied. **Baker Hughes, Inc. v. Keco R. & D., Inc.**, 12 S.W.3d 1, 5 (Tex.1999).

2. SJ grants more relief than requested. A summary judgment on a claim not addressed in the motion is generally reversible error. **G&H Towing Co. v. Magee**, 347 S.W.3d 293, 297 (Tex.2011). When a summary judgment disposes of more claims than the motion requested, the appellate court should affirm the grounds on which the judgment was properly granted and reverse only those portions that are erroneous. *Id.* at 298; **Page v. Geller**, 941 S.W.2d 101, 102 (Tex.1997); *e.g.*, **Bandera Elec. Coop. v. Gilchrist**, 946 S.W.2d 336, 337 (Tex.1997) (P's motion for SJ did not address counterclaim). The appellate court should not reverse the entire case. *See* **Bandera Elec.**, 946 S.W.2d at 337; **Page**, 941 S.W.2d at 102.

3. SJ erroneously granted. When a trial court erroneously grants a summary judgment, the appellate court should affirm the summary judgment if later events in the trial court made the erroneous decision harmless. **Progressive Cty. Mut. Ins. v. Boyd**, 177 S.W.3d 919, 921 (Tex.2005); *see, e.g.*, **Martin v. Martin, Martin & Richards, Inc.**, 989 S.W.2d 357, 359 (Tex.1998) (harmless error to grant D's motion for SJ without notice to P because trial court considered P's response after SJ and reconfirmed its ruling).

4. Interlocutory appeal. A trial court, on its own initiative or on a party's motion, can allow an appeal from an order that is not otherwise appealable if the following conditions are met: (1) the order to be appealed involves a controlling question of law about which there is a substantial ground for difference of opinion and (2) an immediate appeal from the order may materially advance the ultimate termination of the litigation. Tex. Civ. Prac. & Rem. Code §51.014(d); Tex. R. Civ. P. 168. Permission must be stated in the order being appealed rather than in a separate order. Tex. R. Civ. P. 168 & cmt. Although the trial court can grant permission to appeal, the court of appeals has discretion to accept or refuse to hear the appeal. *See* Tex. Civ. Prac. & Rem. Code §51.014(f). See "Interlocutory appeal by permission," **O'Connor's Texas Civil Appeals**, ch. 3-P, §2.1 (2020 ed.).

§14.4 Appeal when SJ denied. In most cases, an order denying a motion for summary judgment is not a final judgment and thus is not appealable. *See* **Ackermann v. Vordenbaum**, 403 S.W.2d 362, 365 (Tex.1966). There are exceptions:

1. Both parties move for SJ. When both parties move for a final summary judgment and the trial court grants one motion but denies the other, the party that did not prevail may appeal both on the summary judgment granted against it and on its motion for summary judgment that was denied. **Holmes v. Morales**, 924 S.W.2d 920, 922 (Tex.1996); *see* **Gilbert Tex. Constr., L.P. v. Underwriters at Lloyd's London**, 327 S.W.3d 118, 124 (Tex.2010); **Commissioners Ct. v. Agan**, 940 S.W.2d 77, 81 (Tex.1997); **Jones v. Strauss**, 745 S.W.2d 898, 900 (Tex.1988). If the appellate court finds that the summary judgment was erroneously granted, the court will review the ruling on the opposing motion and grant summary judgment based on that motion if it finds that the trial court should have granted it. *See* **Texas Mut. Ins. v. PHI Air Med., LLC**, ___ S.W.3d ___, 2020 WL 3477002 (Tex.2020) (No. 18-0216; 6-26-20); **SeaBright Ins. v. Lopez**, 465 S.W.3d 637, 641–42 (Tex.2015); **Southwestern Bell Tel., L.P. v. Emmett**, 459 S.W.3d 578, 583 (Tex.2015); **Southern Crushed Concrete, LLC v. City of Houston**, 398 S.W.3d 676, 678 (Tex.2013). The reviewing court should review the summary-judgment evidence presented by both sides and determine all questions presented. **Texas Mut.**, ___ S.W.3d at ___, 2020 WL 3477002; **SeaBright Ins.**, 465 S.W.3d at 641; **Southwestern Bell**, 459 S.W.3d at 583; **Valence Oper. Co. v. Dorsett**, 164 S.W.3d 656, 661 (Tex.2005); **Agan**, 940 S.W.2d at 81. For the appellate court to reverse and render for the other party, that party must be entitled to a final—not partial—summary judgment as a matter of law. **CU Lloyd's v. Feldman**, 977 S.W.2d 568, 569 (Tex.1998); **Bowman v. Lumberton ISD**, 801 S.W.2d 883, 889 (Tex.1990); *see* **Strauss**, 745 S.W.2d at 900. If the appellate court finds that neither party met its summary-judgment burden, the court will remand the case for further proceedings. **Barbara Techs. v. State Farm Lloyds**, 589 S.W.3d 806, 828 (Tex.2019). See "When both parties move for SJ," ch. 7-C, §4.8.

Caution

Although the denial of a motion for summary judgment is generally not appealable unless there is a competing cross-motion, in ***Farm Bur. Cty. Mut. Ins. v. Rogers****, 455 S.W.3d 161, 163 (Tex.2015), the Supreme Court held that the lack of a competing cross-motion was not what made the order denying a motion for summary judgment unappealable; instead, the order was unappealable because it did not contain language of finality and there was no evidence in the record showing that the trial court meant to dispose of a claim for attorney fees. The Court explained that, as in* ***Lehmann v. Har-Con Corp.****,*

39 S.W.3d 191, 200 (Tex.2001), the trial court's intent to dispose of all claims must be clear from the order; that is, there must be express language disposing of all claims. ***Farm Bur.****, 455 S.W.3d at 163. But in* ***Farm Bur.****, there was no indication of finality; a Mother Hubbard clause did not implicitly dispose of the attorney-fees claim, nor did the order's language taxing costs. Id. at 163–64. Had the order expressly disposed of the attorney-fees claim, presumably it would have been final and appealable despite the lack of a competing cross-motion for summary judgment. See "Judgment includes statement of finality," ch. 9-C, §6.3.1(2)(a)[1].*

2. Denial of earlier SJ. In the appeal of a summary judgment, the appellate court may review grounds in earlier summary-judgment motions that the trial court denied. **Baker Hughes, Inc. v. Keco R. & D., Inc.**, 12 S.W.3d 1, 5 (Tex.1999).

3. Denial of official-immunity SJ.

(1) Appeal. Under CPRC §51.014(a)(5), a party may appeal an order denying a motion for summary judgment based on an assertion of immunity by an officer or employee of the State or a political subdivision of the State. See "Denial of official-immunity summary judgment," **O'Connor's Texas Civil Appeals**, ch. 1-B, §2.4.1(4) (2020 ed.); "Summary judgment," **O'Connor's Texas Causes of Action**, ch. 24-A, §4.1.1(2) (2021 ed.).

(2) Stay. The interlocutory appeal of an order denying a summary judgment based on an assertion of immunity does not automatically stay the commencement of trial during the appeal. Tex. Civ. Prac. & Rem. Code §51.014(c). To determine whether a defendant is entitled to a stay after the denial of a summary judgment based on an assertion of immunity, see "Orders resulting in automatic stay after motion denied & deadlines met," **O'Connor's Texas Civil Appeals**, ch. 3-P, §3.1.2 (2020 ed.).

4. Denial of free-speech SJ. Under CPRC §51.014(a)(6), a defendant in a defamation case may appeal an order denying a motion for summary judgment to the court of appeals if (1) the defendant is a member of the electronic or print media or a person whose communication was published by the electronic or print media and (2) the motion for summary judgment was based in whole or in part on a claim or defense involving free speech or free press under the First Amendment to the U.S. Constitution, Texas Constitution article 1, §8, or CPRC chapter 73 (libel). *See* **Scripps NP Oper., LLC v. Carter**, 573 S.W.3d 781, 788 (Tex.2019); **Dallas Symphony Ass'n v. Reyes**, 571 S.W.3d 753, 756–57 (Tex.2019). See "Denial of free-speech summary judgment," **O'Connor's Texas Civil Appeals**, ch. 1-B, §2.4.1(5) (2020 ed.); "Interlocutory appeal," **O'Connor's Texas Causes of Action**, ch. 18-A, §6.6 (2021 ed.).

Note

In ***Dallas Symphony****, the Court resolved a split among the courts of appeals about whether interlocutory review under CPRC §51.014(a)(6) was limited to the denial of summary judgment only on claims or defenses implicating constitutional grounds of free speech or free press. See* ***Dallas Symphony****, 571 S.W.3d at 760–61. The Court clarified that, under CPRC §51.014(a)(6), a party can appeal the denial of a motion for summary judgment if at least one ground in the motion is based on a free-speech or free-press claim or defense; if so, all issues raised in the motion for summary judgment—including nonconstitutional grounds—can be reviewed on appeal.* ***Dallas Symphony****, 571 S.W.3d at 759–60. In that case, the party's motion for summary judgment included defenses based on free speech and free press, but the party appealed based on the court's denial of its motion on tortious-interference grounds. Id. at 756–57. The Court held that, because the tortious-interference claims were included in a motion that was based in part on a claim or defense involving free speech or free press, review of the denial of summary judgment was proper. See id. at 759–60.*

5. Denial of electric-utility-liability SJ. Under CPRC §51.014(a)(13), an electric utility may appeal the denial of a motion for summary judgment based on liability in a suit under CPRC §75.0022.

§14.5 Mandamus.

1. Refusal to rule. Mandamus is appropriate when the trial court refuses to rule on a timely submitted motion for summary judgment, thereby preventing the movant from perfecting a statutory interlocutory appeal. *See* **In re Ameri-**

can Media Consol., 121 S.W.3d 70, 73 (Tex.App.—San Antonio 2003, orig. proceeding) (mandamus denied); **Grant v. Wood**, 916 S.W.2d 42, 45 (Tex.App.—Houston [1st Dist.] 1995, orig. proceeding) (mandamus granted). If the record does not reflect a refusal to rule but shows only a failure to rule, mandamus is not appropriate. *See* **In re American Media**, 121 S.W.3d at 73.

2. Denial of SJ. Mandamus is generally not available when the trial court denies a motion for summary judgment, no matter how meritorious the motion. **In re United Servs. Auto. Ass'n**, 307 S.W.3d 299, 314 (Tex.2010). But in certain extraordinary situations, mandamus relief may be granted. *E.g., id.* (court granted mandamus because D had already been through one trial in forum that lacked jurisdiction, had subsequently appealed to both the court of appeals and the Supreme Court, and was facing another trial on claim that had since been barred by limitations).

C. Traditional Motion for Summary Judgment

§1. General

§1.1 Rule. Tex. R. Civ. P. 166a(c).

§1.2 Purpose. The purpose of the summary-judgment procedure is to permit the trial court to promptly dispose of cases that involve unmeritorious claims or untenable defenses. **City of Houston v. Clear Creek Basin Auth.**, 589 S.W.2d 671, 678 n.5 (Tex.1979).

§1.3 Timetable & forms. Appendix IV, Timetable 12, Motion for summary judgment; **O'Connor's Texas Civil Forms**, FORMS 7B:1 et seq., 7C:1 et seq. (2020 ed.).

§1.4 Other references. **O'Connor's Texas Causes of Action** (2021 ed.); **O'Connor's Texas Civil Practice & Remedies Code Plus** (2020–21 ed.).

§2. Traditional motion for summary judgment

§2.1 When to file. A plaintiff may move for a traditional summary judgment anytime after the defendant answers the lawsuit. Tex. R. Civ. P. 166a(a). A defendant may move for a traditional summary judgment at any time. Tex. R. Civ. P. 166a(b).

§2.2 In writing. The motion for summary judgment must be in writing. **City of Houston v. Clear Creek Basin Auth.**, 589 S.W.2d 671, 677 (Tex.1979).

§2.3 Unverified. The motion for summary judgment should not be verified. A factual statement in a verified motion for summary judgment is not summary-judgment proof. **Hidalgo v. Surety S&L Ass'n**, 462 S.W.2d 540, 545 (Tex.1971). If a party needs sworn evidence to support its motion for summary judgment, it must attach affidavits or other sworn evidence.

§2.4 Grounds.

1. Stated in motion.

(1) Generally. The motion for summary judgment must state the grounds on which it is made. Tex. R. Civ. P. 166a(c); **KCM Fin. LLC v. Bradshaw**, 457 S.W.3d 70, 79 (Tex.2015); **Nall v. Plunkett**, 404 S.W.3d 552, 555 (Tex.2013); **McConnell v. Southside ISD**, 858 S.W.2d 337, 341 (Tex.1993). The trial court cannot grant a summary judgment on grounds not presented in the motion; doing so is generally reversible error. **G&H Towing Co. v. Magee**, 347 S.W.3d 293, 297 (Tex.2011); *see* **Ineos USA, LLC v. Elmgren**, 505 S.W.3d 555, 566 (Tex.2016); **Johnson v. Brewer & Pritchard, P.C.**, 73 S.W.3d 193, 204 (Tex.2002); *see, e.g.*, **Science Spectrum, Inc. v. Martinez**, 941 S.W.2d 910, 912 (Tex.1997) (D's motion for SJ did not raise issue that D had created dangerous condition); **Sysco Food Servs. v. Trapnell**, 890 S.W.2d 796, 805 (Tex.1994) (D waived issue of collateral estoppel because it raised issue only in its brief); *see also* **Teer v. Duddlesten**, 664 S.W.2d 702, 703–04 (Tex.1984) (court could not grant SJ for party that did not file motion for SJ). There is, however, a limited exception to this rule. The error is harmless if the ground not presented in the motion is precluded as a matter of law by other grounds raised in the case. *E.g.*, **G&H Towing**, 347 S.W.3d at 297–98 (in case involving D's vicarious liability for agent's negligent entrustment, D's SJ motion was granted even though vicarious-liability issue was omitted; error was harmless because court determined agent had not negligently entrusted vehicle and thus D could not be vicariously liable). If a ground that may support a summary judgment is not stated in the motion, the ground cannot be supplied by a prayer for general relief. **Golden Triangle Energy v. Wickes Lumber**, 725 S.W.2d 439, 441 (Tex.App.—Beaumont 1987, no writ).

Practice Tip

Never file a trial brief to support a motion for summary judgment; instead, include in the motion all arguments supporting the grounds. See ***McConnell***, *858 S.W.2d at 339–40. Begin each ground for summary judgment by incorporating by reference all the facts from other parts of the motion that are necessary to that ground. See* ***Johnson***, *73 S.W.3d at 204.*

---

(2) Incorporation by reference from coparty's motion. Some courts have held that a party's motion for summary judgment may adopt and incorporate by reference grounds from a coparty's motion for summary judgment. *E.g.*,

Lockett v. HB Zachry Co., 285 S.W.3d 63, 72–73 (Tex.App.—Houston [1st Dist.] 2009, no pet.) (when Ds shared common interests and identical defenses, D1 could adopt and incorporate by reference D2's MSJ, which was sufficient to apprise P of D1's grounds for SJ); **Chapman v. King Ranch, Inc.**, 41 S.W.3d 693, 699–700 (Tex.App.—Corpus Christi 2001) (same), *rev'd on other grounds,* 118 S.W.3d 742 (Tex.2003). But other courts, relying on **McConnell**, reject such incorporation by reference and hold that a motion for summary judgment must itself assert the grounds relied on. *E.g.*, **Camden Mach. & Tool v. Cascade Co.**, 870 S.W.2d 304, 310 (Tex.App.—Fort Worth 1993, no writ); **Rentfro v. Cavazos**, No. 04-10-00617-CV, 2012 WL 566364 (Tex.App.—San Antonio 2012, pet. denied) (memo op.; 2-15-12).

2. Specificity = fair notice. The grounds in the motion are sufficiently specific if they give "fair notice" to the nonmovant. **Seaway Prods. Pipeline Co. v. Hanley**, 153 S.W.3d 643, 649 (Tex.App.—Fort Worth 2004, no pet.); **Thomas v. Cisneros**, 596 S.W.2d 313, 316 (Tex.App.—Austin 1980, writ ref'd n.r.e.); *see, e.g.,* **Upchurch v. Albear**, 5 S.W.3d 274, 284–85 (Tex.App.—Amarillo 1999, pet. denied) (general reference to voluminous record, which did not direct attention to evidence relied on, did not satisfy fair-notice requirement). If the grounds are vague, the nonmovant should file special exceptions. See "Special exceptions in summary-judgment procedure," ch. 7-B, §5; **O'Connor's Texas Civil Forms**, FORM 7B:1 (2020 ed.).

3. Contained in pleadings. The grounds presented in the motion for summary judgment should be contained in the movant's pleadings. The movant should amend its pleadings if the grounds are not contained in the pleadings. See "Amending the petition or answer," ch. 7-B, §8. If a party asserts a ground for summary judgment that is not contained in its pleadings (e.g., an affirmative defense), the nonmovant can defeat the motion for summary judgment by objecting to the lack of pleadings. See "Challenge movant's pleadings," ch. 7-C, §3.6.2.

§2.5 SJ based on facts or pleadings.

1. Moving on the facts. When a movant files a motion for summary judgment based on the summary-judgment evidence, the court can grant the motion only when the movant's evidence, as a matter of law, either proves all the elements of the movant's claim or defense or disproves the facts of at least one element of the nonmovant's claim or defense. *See, e.g.,* **Park Place Hosp. v. Estate of Milo**, 909 S.W.2d 508, 511 (Tex.1995) (causation disproved as a matter of law); **Lear Siegler, Inc. v. Perez**, 819 S.W.2d 470, 471–72 (Tex.1991) (same). When evaluating a motion for summary judgment based on summary-judgment proof, the trial court must do the following:

(1) Assume all the nonmovant's proof is true. **Little v. TDCJ**, 148 S.W.3d 374, 381 (Tex.2004); **M.D. Anderson Hosp. & Tumor Inst. v. Willrich**, 28 S.W.3d 22, 23 (Tex.2000); **Nixon v. Mr. Prop. Mgmt.**, 690 S.W.2d 546, 548–49 (Tex.1985).

(2) Make every reasonable inference in favor of the nonmovant. **Little**, 148 S.W.3d at 381; **M.D. Anderson**, 28 S.W.3d at 23; **Nixon**, 690 S.W.2d at 548–49.

(3) Resolve doubts about the existence of a genuine issue of a material fact against the movant. *See* **Little**, 148 S.W.3d at 381; **M.D. Anderson**, 28 S.W.3d at 23; **Nixon**, 690 S.W.2d at 548–49.

2. Moving on the pleadings. The movant may file a motion for summary judgment that shows the nonmovant has no viable cause of action or defense based on the nonmovant's pleadings. *See, e.g.,* **National Un. Fire Ins. v. Merchants Fast Motor Lines, Inc.**, 939 S.W.2d 139, 141 (Tex.1997) (no duty to defend insurance claim based on allegations in pleadings and terms of policy); **Trinity River Auth. v. URS Consultants, Inc.**, 889 S.W.2d 259, 261 (Tex.1994) (petition showed statute of repose had run); **Helena Labs. v. Snyder**, 886 S.W.2d 767, 768–69 (Tex.1994) (no cause of action for negligent interference with family relationship); **City of Houston v. Clear Creek Basin Auth.**, 589 S.W.2d 671, 680 (Tex.1979) (under the Water Code, P-city had no cause of action against D for discharging polluted waste outside P's boundaries). In some cases when the motion is based on the pleadings, the parties may include summary-judgment proof. *See, e.g.,* **St. John v. Pope**, 901 S.W.2d 420, 424 (Tex.1995) (facts in affidavit proved no doctor-patient relationship, and thus there was no duty). When evaluating a motion for summary judgment based on the nonmovant's pleadings, the trial court must do the following:

(1) Assume all allegations and facts in the nonmovant's pleading are true. **Natividad v. Alexsis, Inc.**, 875 S.W.2d 695, 699 (Tex.1994); **Valles v. Texas Comm'n on Jail Standards**, 845 S.W.2d 284, 286 (Tex.App.—Austin 1992,

writ denied); *see also* **American Tobacco Co. v. Grinnell**, 951 S.W.2d 420, 434 (Tex.1997) (not incumbent on nonmovant-P to produce evidence supporting allegations made in her pleadings).

(2) Make all inferences in the nonmovant's pleadings in the light most favorable to the nonmovant. **Medina v. Herrera**, 927 S.W.2d 597, 602 (Tex.1996); **Natividad**, 875 S.W.2d at 699; **Valles**, 845 S.W.2d at 286.

(3) Ensure that any defects in the pleadings cannot be cured by amendment. **In re B.I.V.**, 870 S.W.2d 12, 13 (Tex.1994).

Practice Tip

In most cases, before the court grants a "no cause of action" summary judgment, it must give the nonmovant adequate opportunity to amend to plead a viable cause of action. See ***Perry v. S.N.****, 973 S.W.2d 301, 303 (Tex.1998). Thus, the movant should first file special exceptions to the pleading. See "P has no viable cause of action—Dismissal or SJ," ch. 3-G, §10.1.1; "P pleads cause of action defectively—Special exceptions," ch. 3-G, §10.1.2. If the nonmovant refuses to cure defects in its pleadings after the defects are identified by special exceptions, a summary judgment for the movant is proper.* ***Natividad****, 875 S.W.2d at 699; see* ***Texas Dept. of Corr. v. Herring****, 513 S.W.2d 6, 10 (Tex.1974). If the nonmovant's pleadings affirmatively demonstrate that no cause of action exists or that the nonmovant's recovery is barred, the court can grant summary judgment without first giving the nonmovant an opportunity to amend its pleadings. See* ***Peek v. Equipment Serv.****, 779 S.W.2d 802, 805 (Tex.1989).*

§2.6 Request for final SJ. If the movant intends for the summary judgment to be final, it must ask the court to dispose of all issues and all parties. **Continental Airlines, Inc. v. Kiefer**, 920 S.W.2d 274, 276–77 (Tex.1996); **Teer v. Duddlesten**, 664 S.W.2d 702, 703 (Tex.1984). If the motion does not dispose of everything, the judgment will not be final.

1. All parties. The motion should ask for relief for and against all parties in the suit and name all the parties. *See* **Continental Airlines**, 920 S.W.2d at 276–77.

2. All issues. The motion should ask the court to dispose of all the issues (claims, counterclaims, cross-claims, third-party claims), all theories of damages (actual, exemplary), and all other claims (attorney fees, costs, interest). The motion should identify all the issues on which it seeks summary judgment. *See* **Continental Airlines**, 920 S.W.2d at 276 (motion "on all claims" did not encompass issues outside motion). If the movant accidentally does not include one of its claims in its motion for summary judgment, it cannot contend on appeal that it intended to abandon that claim; the unadjudicated claim makes what was intended to be a final judgment interlocutory. *See, e.g.,* **McNally v. Guevara**, 52 S.W.3d 195, 196 (Tex.2001) (when Ds' motion for SJ did not include their claim for attorney fees, judgment was not appealable because it did not appear final on its face and did not dispose of Ds' attorney-fees claim).

3. Request for final SJ. The motion should ask the court to render a final, appealable judgment. See "Statement of finality," ch. 9-C, §4.3.

4. Sever or dismiss other claims. A summary judgment on some of the claims can be transformed into a final judgment by severing or dismissing the remaining claims. *See* **Lightning Oil Co. v. Anadarko E&P Onshore, LLC**, 520 S.W.3d 39, 44 (Tex.2017).

§2.7 Request for partial SJ. A party may file a motion for partial summary judgment asking the court to dispose of some but not all of the issues or parties in the case.

1. Parties & claims. The motion should identify the parties against whom, and the claims on which, the movant seeks a partial summary judgment. *See* Tex. R. Civ. P. 166a(a), (b).

2. Request partial judgment. The motion should ask the court to grant a partial summary judgment. The order granting a partial summary judgment is interlocutory and cannot be appealed until a final judgment is rendered. To convert a partial summary judgment into a final judgment, see "Making partial SJ final," ch. 7-B, §12.4.

§2.8 Supporting evidence. Most motions for summary judgment require supporting evidence. The summary-judgment proof should be incorporated by reference in and attached to the motion or the response. See "Summary-judgment evidence," ch. 7-B, §9. Attaching evidence to a traditional motion for summary judgment does not preclude a party from asserting that there is no evidence on a particular element of a claim or defense. **Binur v. Jacobo**, 135 S.W.3d 646, 651 (Tex.2004). See "No-evidence motion for summary judgment," ch. 7-D, §2.

§2.9 Attorney fees. If the movant is entitled to attorney fees, it should include a request for attorney fees in its original pleading and in the motion for summary judgment. See **O'Connor's Texas Civil Forms**, FORM 7C:1, ¶24 (2020 ed.).

1. Proof of attorney fees. The movant should support the request for attorney fees with an affidavit by an attorney proving the amount, the necessity, and the reasonableness of the fees. *See* **Roberts v. Roper**, 373 S.W.3d 227, 233 (Tex.App.—Dallas 2012, no pet.). See "Attorney fees from adverse party," ch. 1-H, §10; "Attorney Fees," **O'Connor's Texas Causes of Action**, ch. 45-A, §1 et seq. (2021 ed.); **O'Connor's Texas Civil Forms**, FORM 1H:14 (2020 ed.).

2. No judicial notice. Attorney fees in a summary-judgment case cannot be established using the judicial-notice provision in CPRC §38.004. That provision permits judicial notice of attorney fees only when a case is tried on the merits. See "Judicial notice," ch. 1-H, §10.1.4(1)(a)[2].

§2.10 Notice. The movant must give the nonmovant written notice of the hearing on the motion. See "Notice," ch. 7-B, §7.

§2.11 Successive motions. TRCP 166a does not limit the number of motions for summary judgment that may be filed. **Cameron Cty. v. Carrillo**, 7 S.W.3d 706, 709 (Tex.App.—Corpus Christi 1999, no pet.).

§3. Nonmovant's response to traditional motion for summary judgment

The response to the motion for summary judgment serves two functions: (1) it identifies defects in the motion, and (2) it presents reasons the summary judgment should not be granted. The only defect that does not need to be specifically raised in the response is an attack on the legal sufficiency of the grounds for the judgment. See "Objections to SJ motion," ch. 7-C, §3.6. All other defects must be raised in the response.

§3.1 In writing. The response to the motion for summary judgment must be in writing. **City of Houston v. Clear Creek Basin Auth.**, 589 S.W.2d 671, 677 (Tex.1979).

§3.2 Unverified. The response should not be verified; a verified response does not present summary-judgment evidence. *See* **Quanaim v. Frasco Rest. & Catering**, 17 S.W.3d 30, 42 (Tex.App.—Houston [14th Dist.] 2000, pet. denied); **Webster v. Allstate Ins.**, 833 S.W.2d 747, 749 (Tex.App.—Houston [1st Dist.] 1992, no writ).

§3.3 Deadline. The response must be filed and served at least seven days before the hearing. See "For response—7 days before hearing," ch. 7-B, §6.3.

§3.4 Grounds to defeat SJ.

1. Defeating SJ on facts. To defeat a motion for summary judgment on the facts, the nonmovant can show any of the following:

(1) Movant's SJ burden not met. The movant did not prove as a matter of law all the elements of its cause of action or defense. *See* **City of Houston v. Clear Creek Basin Auth.**, 589 S.W.2d 671, 678 (Tex.1979); **Rizkallah v. Conner**, 952 S.W.2d 580, 582 (Tex.App.—Houston [1st Dist.] 1997, no writ).

(2) Fact issue. The summary-judgment evidence raises a genuine issue of material fact. *See, e.g.,* **Dillard's, Inc. v. Newman**, 299 S.W.3d 144, 148 (Tex.App.—Amarillo 2008, pet. denied) (fact issue raised about D-movant's affirmative defense). The evidence that raises a fact issue can be either the movant's summary-judgment evidence or evidence produced by the nonmovant in response to the motion. See "Nonmovant's SJ evidence," ch. 7-C, §3.5.

(3) Court barred. The court is barred by rules of law or evidence from giving weight to the movant's evidence offered to prove a vital fact. See "Objections to summary-judgment evidence," ch. 7-B, §10.

(4) Nonmovant's affirmative defense. The nonmovant has an affirmative defense to the movant's cause of action or defense. *See* **Ingersoll-Rand Co. v. Valero Energy Corp.**, 997 S.W.2d 203, 210–11 (Tex.1999), *overruled on other grounds*, **In re J.B. Hunt Transp.**, 492 S.W.3d 287 (Tex.2016). For the nonmovant to assert an affirmative defense to defeat a motion for summary judgment, it must assert the defense in its response and provide sufficient summary-judgment evidence to create a fact issue on each element of the defense. *See* **Via Net v. TIG Ins.**, 211 S.W.3d 310, 313 (Tex.2006); **Bassett v. American Nat'l Bank**, 145 S.W.3d 692, 696 (Tex.App.—Fort Worth 2004, no pet.); *see, e.g.*, **Keenan v. Gibraltar Sav. Ass'n**, 754 S.W.2d 392, 393–94 (Tex.App.—Houston [14th Dist.] 1988, no writ) (nonmovant's defense that movant did not credit offsets did not preclude SJ because nonmovant did not present proof). If the defense relied on is not also asserted in the nonmovant's pleadings, the nonmovant should amend its pleadings. *See* **Via Net**, 211 S.W.3d at 313 (when nonmovant raises unpleaded defense for first time in SJ response, movant can object that defense has not been properly pleaded). The nonmovant is not required to prove the affirmative defense by a preponderance of the evidence or as a matter of law; raising a fact issue is enough to defeat the summary judgment. *See* **American Petrofina, Inc. v. Allen**, 887 S.W.2d 829, 830 (Tex.1994); **Brownlee v. Brownlee**, 665 S.W.2d 111, 112 (Tex.1984). See "Burden on nonmovant," ch. 7-C, §4.2.

2. Defeating SJ on pleadings. To defeat a motion for summary judgment on the pleadings, the nonmovant can show that the facts are undisputed and the motion for summary judgment presents a question of law that must be resolved in the nonmovant's favor. *See, e.g.*, **Zurich Am. Ins. v. McVey**, 339 S.W.3d 724, 734 (Tex.App.—Austin 2011, pet. denied) (undisputed facts established application of legal issue). When material facts are undisputed, a nonmovant may defeat a motion for summary judgment by establishing that the movant's legal position is unsound. **Pagosa Oil & Gas, L.L.C. v. Marrs & Smith Prtshp.**, 323 S.W.3d 203, 215 (Tex.App.—El Paso 2010, pet. denied).

§3.5 Nonmovant's SJ evidence. In most cases, the nonmovant should file summary-judgment evidence to raise a fact issue. See "Summary-judgment evidence," ch. 7-B, §9. If the movant's summary-judgment evidence includes affidavits, the nonmovant should file counteraffidavits to raise fact issues. For example, if a movant files an affidavit alleging the reasonableness of attorney fees, the nonmovant must file a controverting affidavit if it wants to raise a fact issue. *See* **American 10-Minute Oil Change, Inc. v. Metropolitan Nat'l Bank-Farmers Branch**, 783 S.W.2d 598, 602 (Tex.App.—Dallas 1989, no pet.). See "Moving on the facts," ch. 7-C, §2.5.1.

§3.6 Objections to SJ motion. In the response to the motion for summary judgment, the nonmovant must object to any defect in the form or substance of the motion, pleadings, or evidence. If the nonmovant does not make any objections in its response, its objections are waived, and on appeal it can argue only that the grounds for summary judgment presented to the trial court are insufficient as a matter of law. **City of Houston v. Clear Creek Basin Auth.**, 589 S.W.2d 671, 678 (Tex.1979); *see* **Scown v. Neie**, 225 S.W.3d 303, 307 (Tex.App.—El Paso 2006, pet. denied); **French v. Gill**, 206 S.W.3d 737, 743 (Tex.App.—Texarkana 2006, no pet.); **Roadside Stations, Inc. v. 7HBF, Ltd.**, 904 S.W.2d 927, 932 (Tex.App.—Fort Worth 1995, no writ).

1. Challenge movant's SJ evidence. The nonmovant should object to any defects in the movant's affidavits or other summary-judgment evidence. See "Objections to summary-judgment evidence," ch. 7-B, §10.

2. Challenge movant's pleadings. If the movant's pleadings do not support the motion for summary judgment, the nonmovant must object, or it waives the error.

(1) Defective pleadings. A motion for summary judgment should not be based on a pleading deficiency that could be cured by an amendment. **In re B.I.V.**, 870 S.W.2d 12, 13 (Tex.1994). See "P pleads cause of action defectively—Special exceptions," ch. 3-G, §10.1.2. Thus, the nonmovant can object to the movant's motion for summary judgment on the ground that the motion is an attempt to circumvent the special-exceptions practice and request additional time to amend. *See* **Kassen v. Hatley**, 887 S.W.2d 4, 13 n.10 (Tex.1994); **Texas Dept. of Corr. v. Herring**, 513 S.W.2d 6, 10 (Tex.1974).

(2) Inadequate pleadings. An unpleaded claim or defense included in the motion for summary judgment is tried by consent if the nonmovant does not object in its response. *See* **Godoy v. Wells Fargo Bank**, 575 S.W.3d 531, 537 (Tex.2019); **D.R. Horton-Tex., Ltd. v. Markel Int'l Ins. Co.**, 300 S.W.3d 740, 743 (Tex.2009); *see, e.g.*, **Roark v. Stallworth Oil & Gas, Inc.**, 813 S.W.2d 492, 495 (Tex.1991) (P-nonmovant waived objection to Ds' unpleaded defense raised in Ds' motion but not in their answer); **Roadside Stations**, 904 S.W.2d at 930 (D-nonmovant waived objection to P's unpleaded claim

raised in P's motion but not in its petition). When a nonmovant objects to the variance between the movant's motion for summary judgment and the movant's pleadings, the movant should immediately file an amended pleading that conforms the pleadings to the motion. See "Amending the petition or answer," ch. 7-B, §8.

3. Challenge movant's motion. The nonmovant should challenge all legal and procedural shortcomings in the motion for summary judgment. See "Motion for Summary Judgment—General Rules," ch. 7-B, §1 et seq. For example, if the movant sought summary judgment on a theory not included in its pleadings, the nonmovant should object that the pleadings do not support the motion.

4. Challenge movant's notice. If the movant did not timely file and serve the motion, the evidence, and the notice of hearing, the nonmovant must object to the lack of 21 days' notice in writing. *See* Tex. R. Civ. P. 166a(c). The 21-day notice requirement for the motion is waived if the nonmovant does not object in writing and under oath before or at the hearing. **Nguyen v. Short, How, Frels & Heitz, P.C.**, 108 S.W.3d 558, 560 (Tex.App.—Dallas 2003, pet. denied); **Veal v. Veterans Life Ins.**, 767 S.W.2d 892, 895 (Tex.App.—Texarkana 1989, no writ). The nonmovant should file a motion to reset the date of the hearing, along with an affidavit that identifies the date it received the motion and notice of hearing and a request that the hearing on the motion be reset to allow the full 21 days' notice. See "Summary-judgment deadlines," ch. 7-B, §6; "Motion to reset SJ hearing," ch. 7-B, §6.9.2; **O'Connor's Texas Civil Forms**, FORM 7B:2 (2020 ed.).

5. File special exceptions. If the motion is unclear or ambiguous, the nonmovant should challenge it by special exceptions. See "Special exceptions in summary-judgment procedure," ch. 7-B, §5.

§3.7 Waiver. The nonmovant should assert all of its challenges to the summary judgment in its response. On appeal, the appellate courts will not consider any issues as grounds for reversal that were not presented to the trial court by written response. Tex. R. Civ. P. 166a(c); **Lopez v. Muñoz, Hockema & Reed, L.L.P.**, 22 S.W.3d 857, 862 (Tex.2000); **City of Houston v. Clear Creek Basin Auth.**, 589 S.W.2d 671, 679 (Tex.1979).

§3.8 Consider amending pleadings. Amending the pleadings to add new issues or to delete factual admissions can sometimes be the easiest and most effective way to avoid a final summary judgment. *See* **Strather v. Dolgencorp, Inc.**, 96 S.W.3d 420, 423 (Tex.App.—Texarkana 2002, no pet.). See "Amending the petition or answer," ch. 7-B, §8. Once the pleadings are amended to add or delete issues, the movant may respond by amending its motion for summary judgment. **Smith v. Atlantic Richfield Co.**, 927 S.W.2d 85, 88 (Tex.App.—Houston [1st Dist.] 1996, writ denied). If the movant does not amend its motion for summary judgment to address an amended petition adding new claims, only a partial summary judgment can be granted. See "Partial SJ," ch. 7-B, §12.3.2(2).

§3.9 Consider nonsuit. If the statute of limitations has not run, a plaintiff may avoid a summary judgment by taking a nonsuit. The plaintiff can take a nonsuit after the defendant files a motion for summary judgment, but the nonsuit must be filed before the court rules on the motion for summary judgment. See "Before SJ," ch. 7-F, §3.2.

§4. Burden of proof

§4.1 Burden on movant. The movant for summary judgment must show (1) there is no genuine issue of material fact and (2) the movant is entitled to judgment as a matter of law. Tex. R. Civ. P. 166a(c); **Hillis v. McCall**, ___ S.W.3d ___, 2020 WL 1233348 (Tex.2020) (No. 18-1065; 3-13-20); **KMS Retail Rowlett, LP v. City of Rowlett**, ___ S.W.3d ___, 2019 WL 2147205 (Tex.2019) (No. 17-0850; 5-17-19); **ConocoPhillips Co. v. Koopmann**, 547 S.W.3d 858, 865 (Tex.2018); **Helix Energy Solutions Grp. v. Gold**, 522 S.W.3d 427, 431 (Tex.2017); *see also* **Rayon v. Energy Specialties, Inc.**, 121 S.W.3d 7, 11–12 (Tex.App.—Fort Worth 2002, no pet.) (fact is "material" only if it affects outcome of suit under governing law; material fact issue is "genuine" only if evidence is such that reasonable jury could find fact in favor of nonmovant). Even if the nonmovant does not file a response and the motion for summary judgment is uncontroverted, the movant must still carry the burden of proof. **City of Houston v. Clear Creek Basin Auth.**, 589 S.W.2d 671, 678 (Tex.1979).

§4.2 Burden on nonmovant. When the movant does not meet its burden of proof, the burden does not shift to the nonmovant. **Chavez v. Kansas City S. Ry.**, 520 S.W.3d 898, 900 (Tex.2017); **Amedisys, Inc. v. Kingwood Home Health Care, LLC**, 437 S.W.3d 507, 511 (Tex.2014); **M.D. Anderson Hosp. & Tumor Inst. v. Willrich**, 28 S.W.3d 22, 23 (Tex.2000). The burden shifts to the nonmovant only after the movant has established that it is entitled to summary judgment as a mat-

ter of law. **Chavez**, 520 S.W.3d at 900; **Amedisys, Inc**, 437 S.W.3d at 511; **State v. $90,235**, 390 S.W.3d 289, 292 (Tex.2013). The movant cannot rely on a legal presumption to shift the burden of proof to the nonmovant. **Chavez**, 520 S.W.3d at 900; *see* **Missouri-Kan.-Tex. R.R. v. City of Dallas**, 623 S.W.2d 296, 298 (Tex.1981). Once the movant has established that it is entitled to summary judgment as a matter of law, the nonmovant must produce summary-judgment evidence to raise a fact issue. **Amedisys, Inc**, 437 S.W.3d at 511.

§4.3 When plaintiff moves for SJ on its cause of action.

7-4. P Moves for Summary Judgment on its Cause of Action

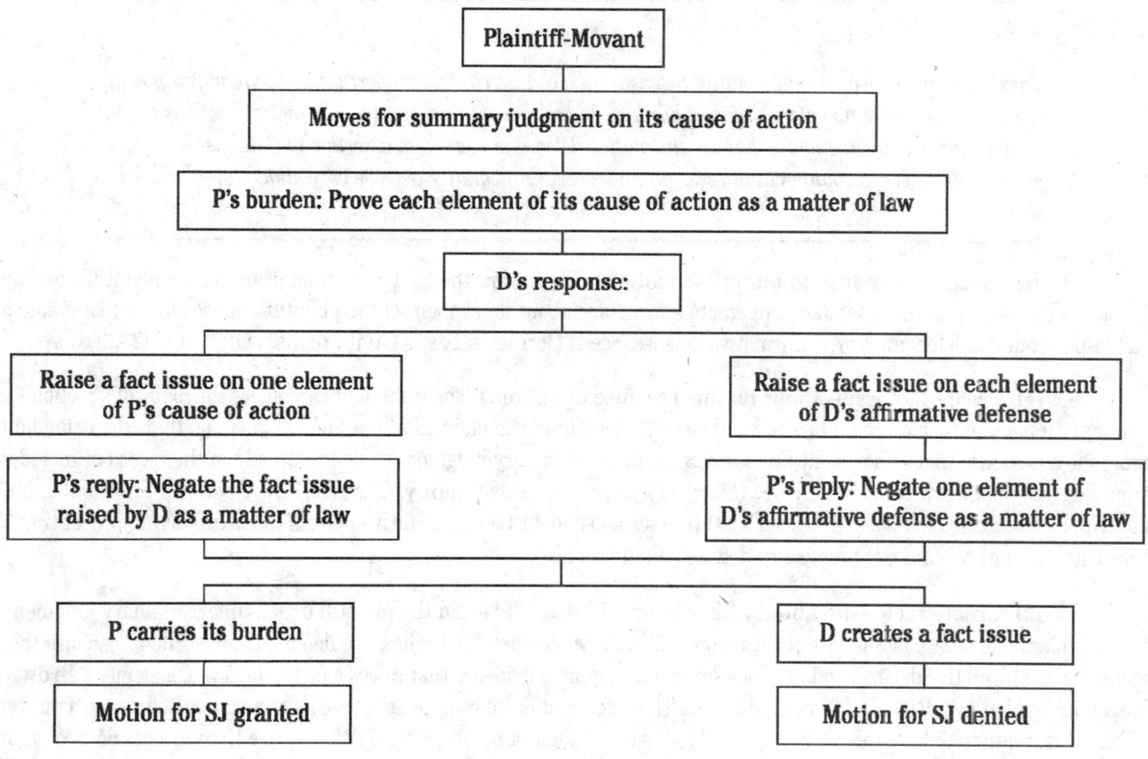

1. Plaintiff's motion. See **O'Connor's Texas Civil Forms**, FORM 7C:1 (2020 ed.).

(1) Prove plaintiff's cause of action. When the plaintiff moves for summary judgment on its own cause of action, it must prove it is entitled to summary judgment by establishing each element of its claim as a matter of law. **MMP, Ltd. v. Jones**, 710 S.W.2d 59, 60 (Tex.1986); **Fry v. Commission for Lawyer Discipline**, 979 S.W.2d 331, 334 (Tex.App.—Houston [14th Dist.] 1998, pet. denied). If the plaintiff does not conclusively establish all the elements necessary to its cause of action, summary judgment is improper. *See, e.g.*, **Wesson v. Jefferson S&L Ass'n**, 641 S.W.2d 903, 906 (Tex.1982) (because P did not prove it was D's duty to procure insurance, an essential element, SJ was improper).

(a) Liquidated damages. The plaintiff must prove its liquidated damages as a matter of law. See "Damages," ch. 2-B, §9; "General Concepts," **O'Connor's Texas Causes of Action**, ch. 41-A, §1 et seq. (2021 ed.).

(b) Unliquidated damages. When the damages are unliquidated, the court may grant an interlocutory summary judgment on liability and hold a hearing on damages. Tex. R. Civ. P. 166a(a); *see* **Pinnacle Anesthesia Consultants, P.A. v. Fisher**, 309 S.W.3d 93, 100 (Tex.App.—Dallas 2009, pet. denied); **Beck v. West Houston Airport Corp.**, No. 14-09-00471-CV, 2010 WL 3168394 (Tex.App.—Houston [14th Dist.] 2010, no pet.) (memo op.; 8-12-10).

(2) Ignore defendant's affirmative defense. When a defendant pleads an affirmative defense in its original answer, the plaintiff may ignore it in the motion for summary judgment. *See* **Bauer v. Jasso**, 946 S.W.2d 552, 555–56 (Tex.App.—Corpus Christi 1997, no writ). The defendant's affirmative defense will not, without summary-judgment evidence, defeat the plaintiff's motion for summary judgment. **Brownlee v. Brownlee**, 665 S.W.2d 111, 112 (Tex.1984); **Brown v. Aztec Rig Equip., Inc.**, 921 S.W.2d 835, 845 (Tex.App.—Houston [14th Dist.] 1996, writ denied). If the plaintiff wants to force the defendant to prove its affirmative defense, the plaintiff may move for a no-evidence summary judgment under TRCP 166a(i). See "No-evidence motion for summary judgment," ch. 7-D, §2.

Note

The distinction between an affirmative defense and a counterclaim is important in summary-judgment practice because the two place different burdens on the movant and provide different protections to the nonmovant. The distinction is that an affirmative defense is merely an assertion of a defense and does not seek damages; a counterclaim seeks damages. See "Affirmative defense vs. counterclaim," ch. 3-E, §5.1.

2. Defendant's response to plaintiff's motion. To prevent the trial court from granting the plaintiff's motion for summary judgment, the defendant can create a fact issue about an element of the plaintiff's cause of action or create a fact issue about the defendant's own affirmative defense. See **O'Connor's Texas Civil Forms**, FORM 7C:3 (2020 ed.).

(1) Create fact issue about plaintiff's cause of action. The defendant can defeat the plaintiff's motion for summary judgment by creating a fact issue about one element of the plaintiff's cause of action. To do that, the defendant must file a response that either identifies a fact issue in the summary-judgment evidence already in the record or includes summary-judgment evidence that creates a fact issue. *See, e.g.*, **Geiselman v. Cramer Fin. Grp.**, 965 S.W.2d 532, 537 (Tex.App.—Houston [14th Dist.] 1997, no writ) (D's response identified substantive defects in P's affidavits, preventing P from establishing ownership of promissory note as a matter of law).

(2) Create fact issue about affirmative defense. To avoid the plaintiff's motion for summary judgment, the defendant can create fact issues about its own affirmative defense. To do that, the defendant must file a response that identifies its affirmative defense and provides summary-judgment evidence that raises a fact issue on each element. **Brownlee**, 665 S.W.2d at 112; **Brown**, 921 S.W.2d at 845. The defendant is not required to prove its affirmative defense as a matter of law; it is required only to raise a fact issue about each element of its affirmative defense. *See* **Brownlee**, 665 S.W.2d at 112. If the defendant did not plead an affirmative defense in its answer, it can still assert one in its response if the plaintiff does not object. If the plaintiff objects, the defendant can then move to amend its pleadings. See "Procedure to amend," ch. 7-B, §8.1. If the plaintiff moved for summary judgment under TRCP 166a(i) on the defendant's affirmative defense, the defendant is required to produce evidence to support its affirmative defense. See "Nonmovant's response to no-evidence motion for summary judgment," ch. 7-D, §3.

3. Plaintiff's reply to defendant's response. If the defendant, by its response and summary-judgment evidence, challenges the plaintiff's right to summary judgment, the plaintiff should file a reply to assure the court that summary judgment in its favor is still warranted.

(1) Negate fact issues about plaintiff's cause of action. If the defendant identifies or raises fact issues about the plaintiff's right to a summary judgment on its cause of action, the plaintiff may salvage its right to a summary judgment by showing as a matter of law that there are no fact issues.

(2) Negate fact issues about affirmative defenses. If the defendant raises fact issues to support its affirmative defense, the plaintiff may salvage its right to a summary judgment by negating as a matter of law the existence of at least one element of the affirmative defense.

§4.4 When plaintiff moves for SJ on defendant's counterclaim.

7-5. P Moves for Summary Judgment on D's Counterclaim

Plaintiff-Movant

Moves for summary judgment on D's counterclaim

P's burden: Disprove one element of D's counterclaim as a matter of law

D's response: Raise a fact issue on challenged element of D's counterclaim

P's reply: Negate the fact issues raised by D as a matter of law

P carries its burden and negates D's fact issues	D raises a fact issue on each element of D's counterclaim
Motion for SJ granted	Motion for SJ denied

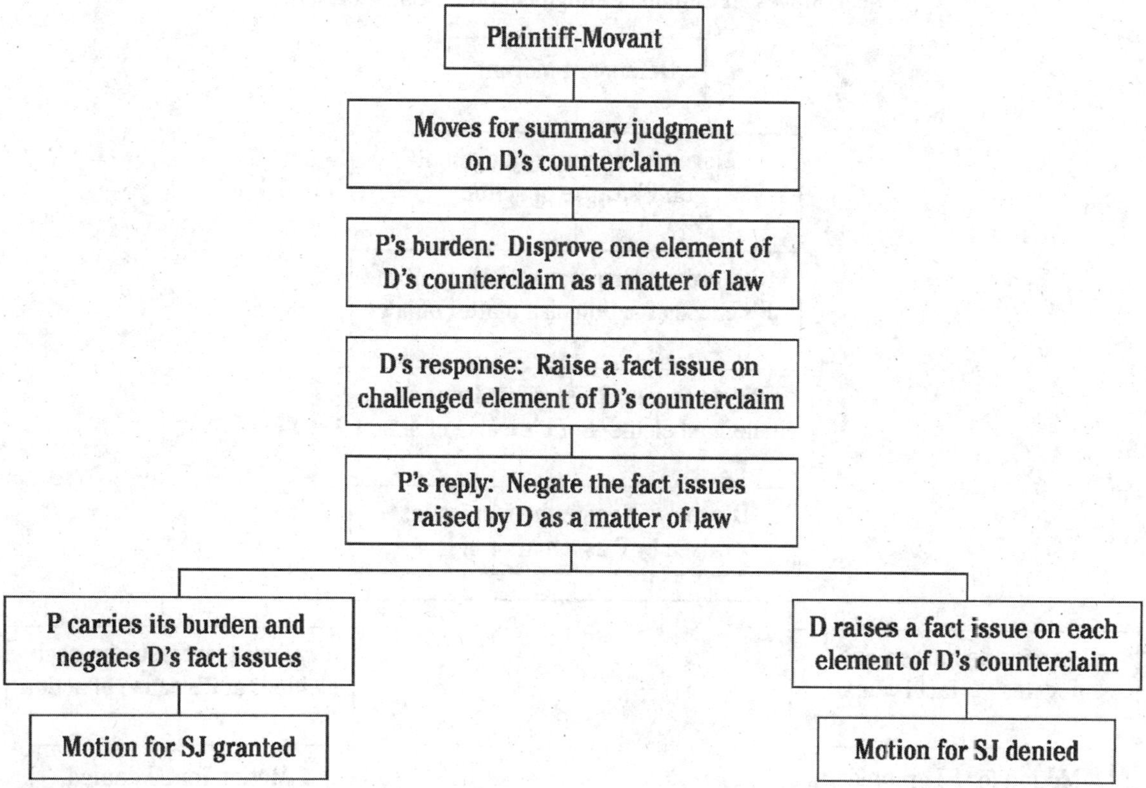

1. Plaintiff's motion. When the defendant asserts a counterclaim in its original answer, for the plaintiff to be entitled to a final summary judgment under TRCP 166a(c), the plaintiff must prove as a matter of law all the elements of its cause of action and must negate as a matter of law at least one element of the defendant's counterclaim. *See* **Taylor v. GWR Oper. Co.**, 820 S.W.2d 908, 910 (Tex.App.—Houston [1st Dist.] 1991, writ denied). The plaintiff can also seek a no-evidence summary judgment on the counterclaim under TRCP 166a(i). See "No-evidence motion for summary judgment," ch. 7-D, §2. The two motions can be combined in one motion for summary judgment, but they should each be argued separately in the motion.

2. Defendant's response to plaintiff's motion. If the plaintiff disproves as a matter of law one or more essential elements of the defendant's counterclaim, the plaintiff is entitled to a summary judgment unless the defendant can either (1) *identify* a fact issue in the elements the plaintiff negated or (2) *create* a fact issue by producing controverting evidence that raises a fact issue on one of the elements the plaintiff negated.

3. Plaintiff's reply to defendant's response. If the defendant produces controverting evidence that raises a fact issue on the elements of its counterclaim negated by the plaintiff, the plaintiff must eliminate the fact issue or the summary judgment will be denied.

§4.5 When defendant moves for SJ on plaintiff's cause of action. The defendant can move for a traditional summary judgment on the plaintiff's cause of action under TRCP 166a(b)—that is, by proving conclusively that the plaintiff has no cause of action. *See* **Randall's Food Mkts., Inc. v. Johnson**, 891 S.W.2d 640, 644 (Tex.1995). See **O'Connor's Texas**

Civil Forms, FORM 7C:2 (2020 ed.). The defendant can also force the plaintiff to provide evidence supporting its cause of action under TRCP 166a(i). See "No-Evidence Motion for Summary Judgment," ch. 7-D, §1 et seq.

7-6. D Moves for Summary Judgment on P's Cause of Action

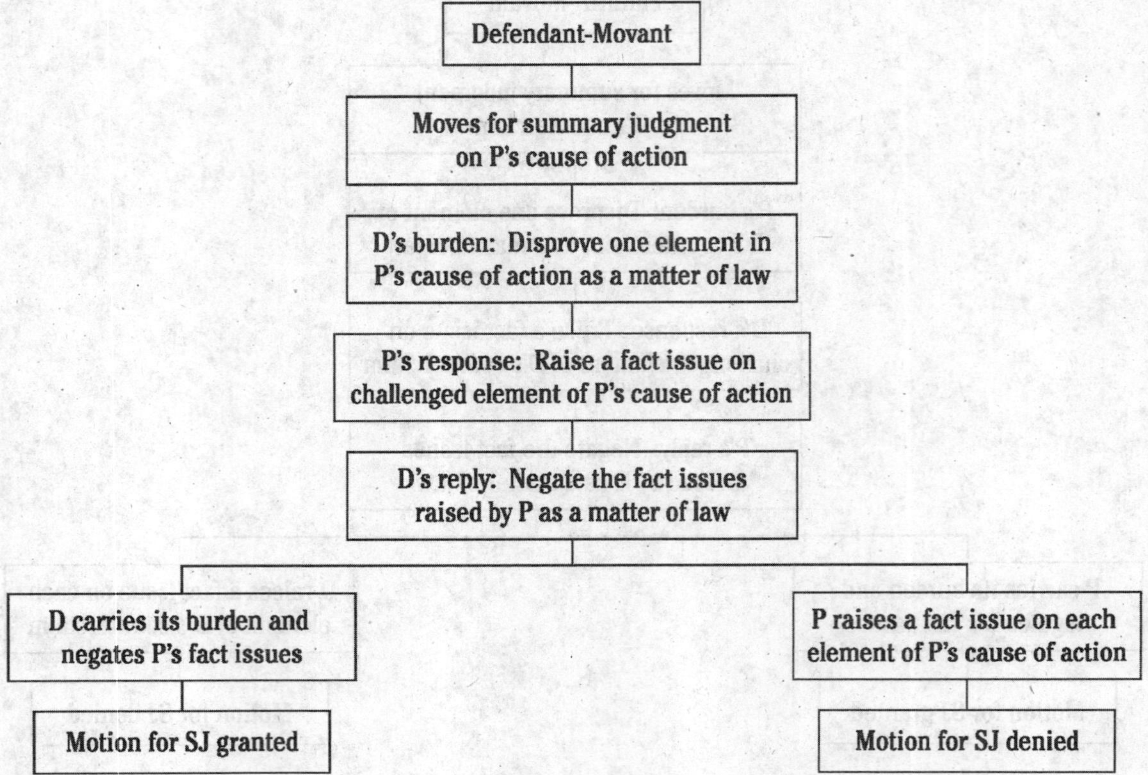

1. Defendant's motion. A defendant moving for summary judgment on the plaintiff's cause of action assumes the burden of showing as a matter of law that the plaintiff has no cause of action. *See* **Lear Siegler, Inc. v. Perez**, 819 S.W.2d 470, 471 (Tex.1991); **Griffin v. Rowden**, 654 S.W.2d 435, 436 (Tex.1983). The defendant does not need to disprove all the elements of the plaintiff's cause of action; it must disprove only one. *See* **Murphy Expl. & Prod. v. Adams**, 560 S.W.3d 105, 108 (Tex.2018); **Stanfield v. Neubaum**, 494 S.W.3d 90, 96 (Tex.2016); **Nall v. Plunkett**, 404 S.W.3d 552, 555 (Tex.2013); *see, e.g.*, **Walker v. Harris**, 924 S.W.2d 375, 378 (Tex.1996) (D negated duty); **Doe v. Boys Clubs of Greater Dallas, Inc.**, 907 S.W.2d 472, 481–82 (Tex.1995) (D disproved causation). The defendant must disprove the plaintiff's cause of action as pleaded. **GNG Gas Sys. v. Dean**, 921 S.W.2d 421, 426 (Tex.App.—Amarillo 1996, writ denied). If the defendant cannot meet that burden, it is not entitled to a summary judgment. *See* **Griffin**, 654 S.W.2d at 436.

2. Plaintiff's response to defendant's motion. If the defendant disproves as a matter of law one or more essential elements of the plaintiff's cause of action, the defendant is entitled to a summary judgment unless the plaintiff can either (1) *identify* a fact issue in the elements the defendant negated or (2) *create* a fact issue by producing controverting evidence that raises a fact issue on one of the elements the defendant negated. *See* **Stanfield**, 494 S.W.3d at 97; **Centeq Rlty., Inc. v. Siegler**, 899 S.W.2d 195, 197 (Tex.1995); **Prescott v. CSPH, Inc.**, 878 S.W.2d 692, 693–94 (Tex.App.—Amarillo 1994, writ denied); *see also* **Gammill v. Jack Williams Chevrolet, Inc.**, 875 S.W.2d 27, 28–29 (Tex.App.—Fort Worth 1994, writ denied) (Ps filed affidavits stating that tests showed vehicle was defective after Ds filed affidavits stating that it was not).

3. Defendant's reply to plaintiff's response. If the plaintiff produces controverting evidence that raises a fact issue on the elements of its cause of action negated by the defendant, the defendant must eliminate the fact issue or the summary judgment will be denied.

§4.6 When defendant moves for SJ on its affirmative defense.

7-7. D Moves for Summary Judgment on its Affirmative Defense

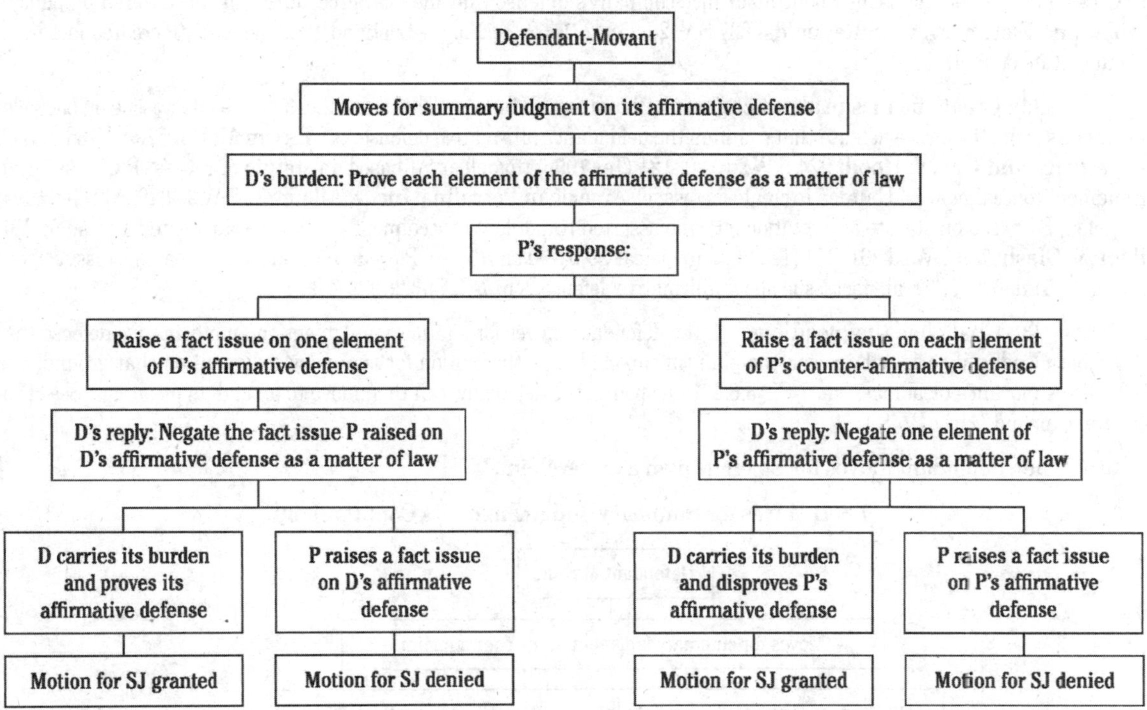

1. Defendant's motion. The defendant can move for summary judgment on its affirmative defense. *See* **Dallas Morning News, Inc. v. Tatum**, 554 S.W.3d 614, 625 (Tex.2018); **Exxon Mobil Corp. v. Rincones**, 520 S.W.3d 572, 593 (Tex.2017); **Randall's Food Mkts., Inc. v. Johnson**, 891 S.W.2d 640, 644 (Tex.1995). A defendant who relies on an affirmative defense should plead the defense in its answer to the suit. *See* **Roark v. Stallworth Oil & Gas, Inc.**, 813 S.W.2d 492, 494 (Tex.1991). But an unpleaded affirmative defense can also serve as a basis for summary judgment when it is raised in a motion for summary judgment and the opposing party does not object in response to the motion or before the rendition of judgment. *Id.*; *see* **Godoy v. Wells Fargo Bank**, 575 S.W.3d 531, 537 (Tex.2019). When a defendant moves for summary judgment on its affirmative defense, it must prove each element of its defense as a matter of law, leaving no issues of material fact. **Johnson & Johnson Med., Inc. v. Sanchez**, 924 S.W.2d 925, 927 (Tex.1996); *see* **Exxon Mobil**, 520 S.W.3d at 593; **KCM Fin. LLC v. Bradshaw**, 457 S.W.3d 70, 79 (Tex.2015); **FDIC v. Lenk**, 361 S.W.3d 602, 609 (Tex.2012). For example, when a defendant moves for summary judgment on a statute-of-limitations defense, the defendant must (1) conclusively prove when the cause of action accrued, and (2) if the plaintiff pleaded a tolling provision, conclusively negate its application as a matter of law. *See* **Rhône-Poulenc, Inc. v. Steel**, 997 S.W.2d 217, 224 (Tex.1999); **Velsicol Chem. Corp. v. Winograd**, 956 S.W.2d 529, 530 (Tex.1997); **Jennings v. Burgess**, 917 S.W.2d 790, 793 (Tex.1996); *see, e.g.*, **In re Estate of Matejek**, 960 S.W.2d 650, 651 (Tex.1997) (when P does not raise discovery rule in pleadings, D is not required to negate it in motion for SJ). See **O'Connor's Texas Civil Forms**, FORM 7C:2 (2020 ed.).

2. Plaintiff's response. The plaintiff, as the nonmovant, does not have any burden of proof unless the defendant conclusively proves all the elements of its affirmative defense. See **O'Connor's Texas Civil Forms**, FORM 7C:4 (2020 ed.). If the defendant establishes its right to an affirmative defense as a matter of law, it is entitled to summary judgment unless the plaintiff can do one of the following:

(1) Create fact issue. The plaintiff can create a fact issue by producing controverting evidence on one of the elements of the defendant's affirmative defense. *See, e.g.*, **McFadden v. American United Life Ins.**, 658 S.W.2d 147, 148 (Tex.1983) (P created fact issue about insurance company's defense that medical procedure was not covered by policy); **Woodbine Elec. Serv. v. McReynolds**, 837 S.W.2d 258, 261–62 (Tex.App.—Eastland 1992, no writ) (P created fact issue about statute of limitations).

(2) Create fact issue about counter-affirmative defense. The plaintiff can create a fact issue on each element of its own affirmative defense that counters the defendant's affirmative defense. *See* **Exxon Mobil**, 520 S.W.3d at 593; *see, e.g.*, **Ryland Grp. v. Hood**, 924 S.W.2d 120, 121 (Tex.1996) (to defeat SJ based on statute of repose, P who asserted fraudulent concealment had burden to create fact issue); **American Petrofina, Inc. v. Allen**, 887 S.W.2d 829, 830 (Tex.1994) (to defeat SJ based on statute of limitations, P who asserted fraudulent concealment had burden to create fact issue); **Williams v. Glash**, 789 S.W.2d 261, 264 (Tex.1990) (to defeat SJ based on release, P produced evidence to create fact issue about mutual mistake). See "Create fact issue about affirmative defense," ch. 7-C, §4.3.2(2).

(3) Challenge the pleadings. If the defendant moves for summary judgment on an affirmative defense that it did not plead in its original answer, the plaintiff can challenge the motion for summary judgment on that ground. See "Challenge movant's pleadings," ch. 7-C, §3.6.2. In response, the defendant can then move to amend its pleadings. See "Procedure to amend," ch. 7-B, §8.1.

§4.7 When defendant moves for SJ on its own counterclaim.

7-8. D Moves for Summary Judgment on its Counterclaim

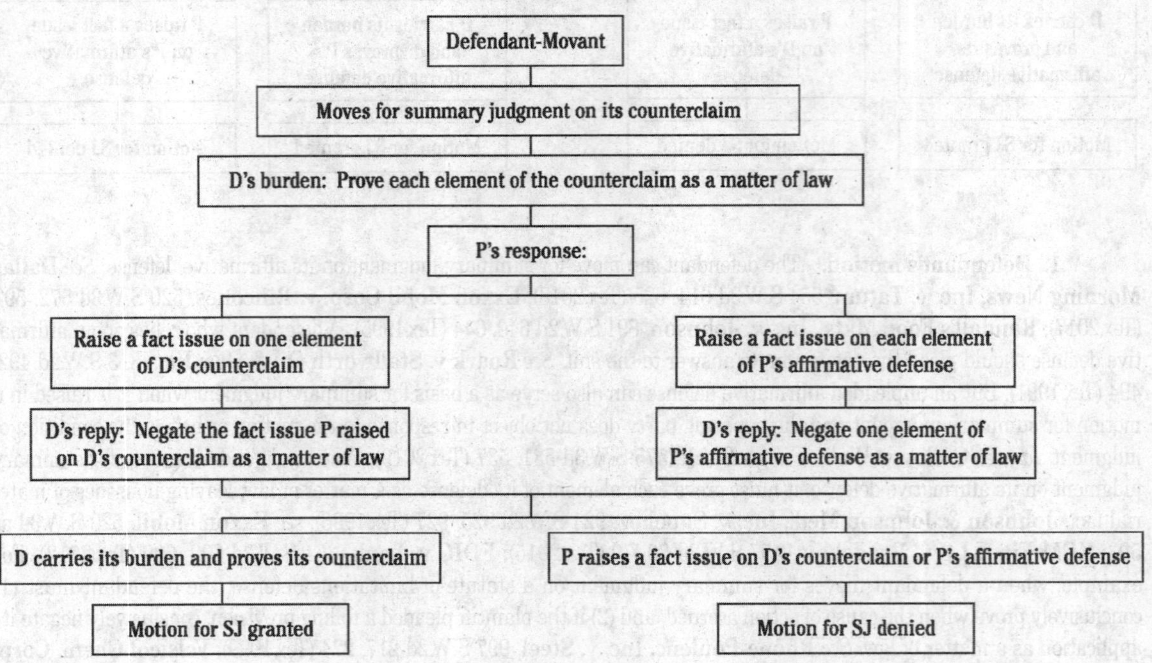

1. Defendant's motion. When the defendant moves for summary judgment on its counterclaim, the defendant's burden is the same as for a plaintiff moving for summary judgment on its cause of action—the defendant must prove each el-

ement of its counterclaim as a matter of law. **Texas Commerce Bank v. Correa**, 28 S.W.3d 723, 726 (Tex.App.—Corpus Christi 2000, pet. denied). See "Plaintiff's motion," ch. 7-C, §4.3.1; **O'Connor's Texas Civil Forms**, FORM 7C:2 (2020 ed.).

2. Plaintiff's response. If the defendant establishes its right to summary judgment on its counterclaim as a matter of law, to defeat the summary judgment, the plaintiff must either (1) create a fact issue about at least one element of the counterclaim or (2) create a fact issue on each element of the plaintiff's own affirmative defense to the defendant's counterclaim. See "Defendant's response to plaintiff's motion," ch. 7-C, §4.3.2; **O'Connor's Texas Civil Forms**, FORM 7C:4 (2020 ed.).

§4.8 When both parties move for SJ.

1. Burdens. When both parties move for summary judgment, each party must carry its own burden as the movant and, in response to the other party's motion, as the nonmovant. *See* **ConocoPhillips Co. v. Koopmann**, 547 S.W.3d 858, 865 (Tex.2018); **Moayedi v. Interstate 35/Chisam Rd., L.P.**, 438 S.W.3d 1, 3–4 (Tex.2014); **Martin v. Harris Cty. Appr. Dist.**, 44 S.W.3d 190, 193 (Tex.App.—Houston [14th Dist.] 2001, pet. denied).

2. Evidence. When both motions are before the court, the court may consider all the summary-judgment evidence in deciding whether to grant either motion. **Barbara Techs. v. State Farm Lloyds**, 589 S.W.3d 806, 811 (Tex.2019); **Martin**, 44 S.W.3d at 193; **Rose v. Baker & Botts**, 816 S.W.2d 805, 810 (Tex.App.—Houston [1st Dist.] 1991, writ denied). The court can rely on one party's evidence to supply missing evidence in the other party's motion. **Seaman v. Seaman**, 686 S.W.2d 206, 210 (Tex.App.—Houston [1st Dist.] 1984, writ ref'd n.r.e.).

3. SJ not automatic. Simply because both parties move for summary judgment does not mean the litigation can be resolved as a matter of law. *See* **Calhoun v. Killian**, 888 S.W.2d 51, 54 (Tex.App.—Tyler 1994, writ denied). There may be fact issues that must be tried on the merits.

§5. Hearing

See "Hearing," ch. 7-B, §11.

§6. Judgment

See "Summary judgment," ch. 7-B, §12.

§7. Review

The appellate court reviews a traditional motion for summary judgment de novo. **Hillis v. McCall**, 602 S.W.3d 436, 439 (Tex.2020); **KMS Retail Rowlett, LP v. City of Rowlett**, 593 S.W.3d 175, 181 (Tex.2019); **City of Richardson v. Oncor Elec. Delivery Co.**, 539 S.W.3d 252, 258 (Tex.2018); **Helix Energy Solutions Grp. v. Gold**, 522 S.W.3d 427, 431 (Tex.2017). On review, the appellate court will assume all evidence favorable to the nonmovant is true and will make every reasonable inference and resolve any doubts in the nonmovant's favor. **Hillis**, 602 S.W.3d at 440; **Community Health Sys. Prof'l Servs. v. Hansen**, 525 S.W.3d 671, 680 (Tex.2017); **Kachina Pipeline Co. v. Lillis**, 471 S.W.3d 445, 449 (Tex.2015). For a discussion of the review of summary judgments generally, see "Review," ch. 7-B, §14.

D. No-Evidence Motion for Summary Judgment

The no-evidence summary-judgment motion is a procedural device designed to help the party who does not have the burden of proof at trial, generally the defendant. A party cannot file a no-evidence summary-judgment motion on a claim or defense on which it has the burden of proof. **Thomas v. Omar Invs.**, 156 S.W.3d 681, 684 (Tex.App.—Dallas 2005, no pet.); **Waite v. Woodard, Hall & Primm, P.C.**, 137 S.W.3d 277, 280 (Tex.App.—Houston [1st Dist.] 2004, no pet.); *see* **Nowak v. DAS Inv.**, 110 S.W.3d 677, 680 (Tex.App.—Houston [14th Dist.] 2003, no pet.). The only instance in which a no-evidence motion can help the plaintiff is when the burden of proof is on the defendant (e.g., to challenge a defendant's affirmative defense or counterclaim).

§1. General

§1.1 Rule. Tex. R. Civ. P. 166a(i).

§1.2 Purpose. The purpose of the no-evidence summary-judgment procedure, which is modeled after federal summary-judgment practice, is to "pierce the pleadings" and evaluate the evidence to see if a trial is necessary. **Benitz v. Gould Grp.**, 27 S.W.3d 109, 112 (Tex.App.—San Antonio 2000, no pet.). To accomplish this, the no-evidence summary-judgment procedure is designed to isolate and dispose of claims or defenses not supported by facts. *Cf.* **Celotex Corp. v. Catrett**, 477 U.S. 317, 323–24 (1986) (purpose of FRCP 56(e) is to dispose of unsupported claims). A no-evidence summary judgment does not violate the right to a jury trial. **Springer v. American Zurich Ins.**, 115 S.W.3d 582, 585 (Tex.App.—Waco 2003, pet. denied).

§1.3 Timetable & forms. Appendix IV, Timetable 12, Motion for summary judgment; **O'Connor's Texas Civil Forms**, FORMS 7B:1 et seq., 7C:1 et seq. (2020 ed.).

§2. No-evidence motion for summary judgment

§2.1 When to file. The no-evidence motion for summary judgment cannot be filed until after the nonmovant has had "an adequate time for discovery." Tex. R. Civ. P. 166a(i); **Agar Corp. v. Electro Circuits Int'l**, 580 S.W.3d 136, 148 (Tex.2019); **Fort Brown Villas III Condo. Ass'n v. Gillenwater**, 285 S.W.3d 879, 882 (Tex.2009). But TRCP 166a(i) does not require that discovery be completed. **Dishner v. Huitt-Zollars, Inc.**, 162 S.W.3d 370, 376 (Tex.App.—Dallas 2005, no pet.); **Specialty Retailers, Inc. v. Fuqua**, 29 S.W.3d 140, 145 (Tex.App.—Houston [14th Dist.] 2000, pet. denied).

1. After discovery period. When a no-evidence motion for summary judgment is filed after the discovery period for the case, the motion is presumed timely. *See* Notes & Comments to Tex. R. Civ. P. 166a(i) (discovery period set by pretrial order should be adequate opportunity for discovery unless there is a contrary showing).

2. During discovery period. When a no-evidence motion for summary judgment is filed before the end of the discovery period, it is considered timely as long as the nonmovant had adequate time for discovery. *See* Tex. R. Civ. P. 166a(i); **McInnis v. Mallia**, 261 S.W.3d 197, 200 (Tex.App.—Houston [14th Dist.] 2008, no pet.). Although a trial court has broad discretion to deny a request for continuance, a no-evidence summary judgment can be reversed on the ground that the nonmovant did not have adequate time for discovery. *See* **Brewer & Pritchard, P.C. v. Johnson**, 167 S.W.3d 460, 468 (Tex.App.—Houston [14th Dist.] 2005, pet. denied); **TemPay, Inc. v. TNT Concrete & Constr., Inc.**, 37 S.W.3d 517, 522–23 (Tex.App.—Austin 2001, pet. denied). See "Challenge timing of motion," ch. 7-D, §3.3.2.

(1) Adequate time—factors. The amount of time necessary to be considered "adequate time" depends on the facts and circumstances of each case. *See* **McInnis**, 261 S.W.3d at 201. The courts examine the following factors when determining whether the nonmovant had adequate time for discovery: (1) the nature of the claim, (2) the evidence necessary to controvert the motion, (3) the length of time the case was on file, (4) the length of time the no-evidence motion was on file, (5) whether the movant requested stricter deadlines for discovery, (6) the amount of discovery already conducted, and (7) whether the discovery deadlines in place were specific or vague. **McInnis**, 261 S.W.3d at 201; **Community Initiatives, Inc. v. Chase Bank**, 153 S.W.3d 270, 278 (Tex.App.—El Paso 2004, no pet.). On appeal, the factors showing inadequate time for discovery must be specifically addressed in the appellant's brief, or the brief presents nothing for review. *See* **Robertson v. Southwestern Bell Yellow Pages, Inc.**, 190 S.W.3d 899, 903 (Tex.App.—Dallas 2006, no pet.).

(2) Adequate time—examples. The following are examples of when time for discovery was considered adequate: • Three-year-old case in which discovery had been pursued for a year and a half and the most important witness

had been deposed. **Community Initiatives**, 153 S.W.3d at 278–79. • Twenty-eight-month-old case in which the plaintiff had had one year to develop its case outside of a bankruptcy stay and had already received a continuance. **McMahan v. Greenwood**, 108 S.W.3d 467, 498 (Tex.App.—Houston [14th Dist.] 2003, pet. denied). • Seven-month-old case in which the plaintiff, who needed minimal evidence to controvert the defendant's motion, did not initiate or respond to discovery requests. **Restaurant Teams Int'l v. MG Secs. Corp.**, 95 S.W.3d 336, 339–41 (Tex.App.—Dallas 2002, no pet.). • Five-year-old case in which the plaintiff did not comply with the scheduling order it requested. **Martinez v. City of San Antonio**, 40 S.W.3d 587, 591–92 (Tex.App.—San Antonio 2001, pet. denied).

§2.2 Form of motion. The motion for no-evidence summary judgment must follow the general summary-judgment rules. That is, it must be in writing and should not be verified. See "In writing," ch. 7-C, §2.2; "Unverified," ch. 7-C, §2.3; **O'Connor's Texas Civil Forms**, FORMS 7C:1 to 7C:2 (2020 ed.).

§2.3 Allegations. The no-evidence motion for summary judgment should be organized as follows:

1. Discovery statement. The motion should state that an adequate time for discovery has passed. See "When to file," ch. 7-D, §2.1. The movant should identify the date the suit was filed and describe the discovery completed and any pending discovery.

2. Nonmovant's claim. The motion should identify and list the elements of the nonmovant's claims or defenses on which the movant requests a no-evidence summary judgment. *See* **Holloway v. Texas Elec. Util. Constr., Ltd.**, 282 S.W.3d 207, 213 (Tex.App.—Tyler 2009, no pet.).

3. Specific element challenged. The motion must state that there is no evidence to support one or more specific elements of a claim or defense on which the nonmovant has the burden of proof at trial. Tex. R. Civ. P. 166a(i); **KCM Fin. LLC v. Bradshaw**, 457 S.W.3d 70, 79 (Tex.2015); **Boerjan v. Rodriguez**, 436 S.W.3d 307, 310 (Tex.2014); **Timpte Indus. v. Gish**, 286 S.W.3d 306, 310 (Tex.2009). The motion cannot be conclusory or generally allege that there is no evidence to support the nonmovant's claim or defense. **Timpte Indus.**, 286 S.W.3d at 310; **Holloway**, 282 S.W.3d at 213; **Ortiz v. Collins**, 203 S.W.3d 414, 425 (Tex.App.—Houston [14th Dist.] 2006, pet. denied); Notes & Comments to Tex. R. Civ. P. 166a(i); *see* **Community Health Sys. Prof'l Servs. v. Hansen**, 525 S.W.3d 671, 695–96 (Tex.2017) (motion that states there is no evidence for "one or more" or "any of" elements of plaintiff's claim is not sufficient). The purpose of this specificity requirement is to provide the other parties with fair notice (i.e., provide adequate information for opposing the motion and define the issues). **Timpte Indus.**, 286 S.W.3d at 311. When a no-evidence motion for summary judgment does not challenge specific elements, it should be treated as a traditional motion for summary judgment under TRCP 166a(c), which imposes the burden of proof on the movant, not as a motion under TRCP 166a(i), which imposes the burden on the nonmovant. *See* **Michael v. Dyke**, 41 S.W.3d 746, 751–52 (Tex.App.—Corpus Christi 2001, no pet.); **Amouri v. Southwest Toyota, Inc.**, 20 S.W.3d 165, 168 (Tex.App.—Texarkana 2000, pet. denied); **Weaver v. Highlands Ins.**, 4 S.W.3d 826, 829 n.2 (Tex.App.—Houston [1st Dist.] 1999, no pet.); *see also* **Hamlett v. Holcomb**, 69 S.W.3d 816, 819 (Tex.App.—Corpus Christi 2002, no pet.) (when motion was ambiguous about whether it was no-evidence or traditional motion, court presumed it was filed as traditional motion under TRCP 166a(c)).

§2.4 Relief. The motion should include a prayer for relief requesting either final or partial summary judgment. See "Request for final SJ," ch. 7-C, §2.6; "Request for partial SJ," ch. 7-C, §2.7.

§2.5 No supporting evidence. A no-evidence motion for summary judgment does not require supporting evidence. **Town of Dish v. Atmos Energy Corp.**, 519 S.W.3d 605, 608 n.3 (Tex.2017); **Williams v. Bank One** 15 S.W.3d 110, 116 (Tex.App.—Waco 1999, no pet.); *see* **McClure v. Attebury**, 20 S.W.3d 722, 727 (Tex.App.—Amarillo 1999, no pet.). But the fact that evidence is attached to a no-evidence motion does not mean the court can disregard the motion or treat it as a traditional summary-judgment motion. **Binur v. Jacobo**, 135 S.W.3d 646, 651 (Tex.2004).

§2.6 Attorney fees. If the movant is entitled to attorney fees, the movant should include a request for attorney fees in the motion. Because the movant has the burden of proof on its attorney fees, the movant must support its claim for attorney fees with summary-judgment evidence. See "Attorney fees," ch. 7-C, §2.9.

§2.7 Notice. The movant must give the nonmovant written notice of the hearing on the motion. See "Notice," ch. 7-B, §7.

§3. Nonmovant's response to no-evidence motion for summary judgment

The nonmovant's response to a no-evidence motion for summary judgment serves three functions: (1) it supplies evidence to raise a fact issue on the challenged element, (2) it identifies any procedural defect in the motion, and (3) it presents any other reasons why the summary judgment should not be granted. Because TRCP 166a(i) requires the trial court to grant the no-evidence motion for summary judgment if the nonmovant does not produce evidence that raises a genuine issue of material fact, the court may grant a no-evidence summary judgment by default if the nonmovant does not file a response and the motion states sufficient grounds for a final summary judgment. **Roventini v. Ocular Sci., Inc.**, 111 S.W.3d 719, 722 (Tex.App.—Houston [1st Dist.] 2003, no pet.); *see* **Town of Dish v. Atmos Energy Corp.**, 519 S.W.3d 605, 608 (Tex.2017). See "Mandatory," ch. 7-D, §7.1.

§3.1 Form of response. The response to the no-evidence motion for summary judgment must follow the general summary-judgment rules. That is, it must be in writing and should not be verified. See "In writing," ch. 7-C, §3.1; "Unverified," ch. 7-C, §3.2.

§3.2 Deadline. The response and any evidence opposing the motion must be filed and served at least seven days before the hearing. *See* **B.C. v. Steak N Shake Opers., Inc.**, 598 S.W.3d 256, 259 (Tex.2020). See "For response—7 days before hearing," ch. 7-B, §6.3.

§3.3 Objections. In the response to the motion for summary judgment, the nonmovant should object to any defect in the form or substance of the motion or pleadings. The nonmovant will waive most objections to the summary judgment not included in its response. *See* **Fletcher v. Edwards**, 26 S.W.3d 66, 72 n.5 (Tex.App.—Waco 2000, pet. denied). See "Waiver," ch. 7-C, §3.7. To preserve error on appeal, the nonmovant should ensure that the record includes written rulings on the objections. See "Secure ruling on objections," ch. 7-B, §10.2; **O'Connor's Texas Civil Forms**, FORMS 7C:3 to 7C:6, 7C:9, 7C:11 (2020 ed.).

1. Challenge notice. If the movant did not file and serve the motion, the notice of hearing, and the evidence at least 21 days before the hearing, the nonmovant must object. *See* Tex. R. Civ. P. 166a(d). See "Summary-judgment deadlines," ch. 7-B, §6; "Challenge movant's notice," ch. 7-C, §3.6.4; **O'Connor's Texas Civil Forms**, FORM 7B:2 (2020 ed.).

2. Challenge timing of motion. If the no-evidence motion was filed before the end of the discovery period, the nonmovant may allege that the motion was premature because the nonmovant did not have adequate time for discovery. See "During discovery period," ch. 7-D, §2.1.2. The nonmovant must file either an affidavit explaining the need for further discovery or a verified motion for continuance. **Tenneco Inc. v. Enterprise Prods.**, 925 S.W.2d 640, 647 (Tex.1996); **Brown v. Brown**, 145 S.W.3d 745, 749 (Tex.App.—Dallas 2004, pet. denied). See "Motion to continue SJ hearing," ch. 5-D, §9.3; **O'Connor's Texas Civil Forms**, FORM 7B:5 (2020 ed.).

3. Challenge motion. The nonmovant should challenge all legal and procedural shortcomings in the motion.

(1) Lacks specificity. When a no-evidence motion globally challenges the nonmovant's claim or defense, the nonmovant should object. *See* Notes & Comments to Tex. R. Civ. P. 166a(i) ("paragraph (i) does not authorize conclusory motions or general no-evidence challenges"). However, most courts hold that the failure to object does not waive the error. *E.g.*, **Garcia v. State Farm Lloyds**, 287 S.W.3d 809, 818 (Tex.App.—Corpus Christi 2009, pet. denied); **Bean v. Reynolds Rlty. Grp.**, 192 S.W.3d 856, 859 (Tex.App.—Texarkana 2006, no pet.); **In re Estate of Swanson**, 130 S.W.3d 144, 147 (Tex.App.—El Paso 2003, no pet.); **Crocker v. Paulyne's Nursing Home, Inc.**, 95 S.W.3d 416, 419 (Tex.App.—Dallas 2002, no pet.); **Cuyler v. Minns**, 60 S.W.3d 209, 213 (Tex.App.—Houston [14th Dist.] 2001, pet. denied); **Callaghan Ranch, Ltd. v. Killam**, 53 S.W.3d 1, 3 (Tex.App.—San Antonio 2000, pet. denied). *But see* **Williams v. Bank One**, 15 S.W.3d 110, 117 (Tex.App.—Waco 1999, no pet.) (error was not preserved when nonmovant did not object to lack of specificity); **Roth v. FFP Oper. Partners**, 994 S.W.2d 190, 195 (Tex.App.—Amarillo 1999, pet. denied) (Ps could not challenge sufficiency of no-evidence motion on appeal because no objection was presented to trial court). When a no-evidence motion for summary judgment does not challenge specific elements, it should be treated as a traditional motion for summary judgment under TRCP 166a(c), which imposes the burden of proof on the movant. See "Specific element challenged," ch. 7-D, §2.3.3.

(2) Movant's burden. When a no-evidence motion challenges the evidence to support an element on which the movant—not the nonmovant—has the burden of proof at trial, the nonmovant should object. **Texas Mut. Ins. v. Sara Care Child Care Ctr., Inc.**, 324 S.W.3d 305, 318 (Tex.App.—El Paso 2010, pet. denied).

(3) Other challenges. See "Motion for Summary Judgment—General Rules," ch. 7-B, §1 et seq.

4. Challenge use of SJ. If the motion for summary judgment is based on a pleading defect in the nonmovant's petition or answer, the nonmovant should (1) object on the ground that the movant is required to challenge pleadings by special exceptions and (2) move to correct the defect. See "Special exceptions & summary judgments," ch. 3-G, §10; "Defective pleadings," ch. 7-C, §3.6.2(1).

5. Challenge SJ evidence. If the movant has included evidence with its no-evidence motion or has filed a hybrid motion supported by evidence, the nonmovant should challenge the evidence. See "Objections to summary-judgment evidence," ch. 7-B, §10.

§3.4 Burden of proof. The nonmovant has the entire burden of proof once the movant files a no-evidence motion. *See* Tex. R. Civ. P. 166a(i); *see, e.g.*, **Town of Dish v. Atmos Energy Corp.**, 519 S.W.3d 605, 608 (Tex.2017) (SJ was proper when nonmovant did not respond to no-evidence motion). The burden of proof in a summary-judgment proceeding is on the same party who would have the burden of proof at trial. **Marsaglia v. UTEP**, 22 S.W.3d 1, 3 (Tex.App.—El Paso 1999, pet. denied); **Esco Oil & Gas, Inc. v. Sooner Pipe & Sup.**, 962 S.W.2d 193, 197 n.3 (Tex.App.—Houston [1st Dist.] 1998, pet. denied). The burden on the nonmovant is to raise a genuine issue of material fact about the element challenged by the motion for summary judgment. Tex. R. Civ. P. 166a(i); **First United Pentecostal Ch. v. Parker**, 514 S.W.3d 214, 220 (Tex.2017); **KCM Fin. LLC v. Bradshaw**, 457 S.W.3d 70, 79 (Tex.2015); **Merriman v. XTO Energy, Inc.**, 407 S.W.3d 244, 248 (Tex.2013); *see* **Rayon v. Energy Specialties, Inc.**, 121 S.W.3d 7, 11–12 (Tex.App.—Fort Worth 2002, no pet.) (fact is "material" only if it affects outcome of suit under governing law; material fact issue is "genuine" only if evidence is such that reasonable jury could find fact in favor of nonmovant). The trial court must resolve all reasonable doubts about the facts in favor of the nonmovant. **Lehrer v. Zwernemann**, 14 S.W.3d 775, 777 (Tex.App.—Houston [1st Dist.] 2000, pet. denied); *see* **Painter v. Amerimex Drilling I, Ltd.**, 561 S.W.3d 125, 130 (Tex.2018).

7-9. No-Evidence Motion for Summary Judgment under TRCP 166a(i)

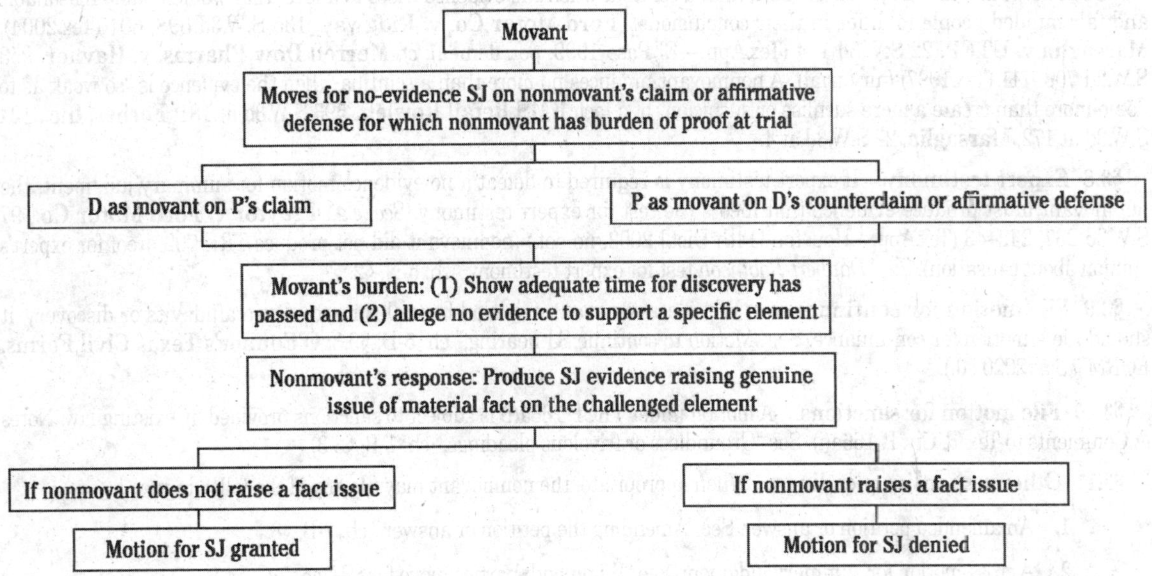

§3.5 Grounds for response. To defeat a no-evidence motion for summary judgment, the nonmovant must prove there is a genuine issue of material fact on the elements challenged by the movant. *See* Tex. R. Civ. P. 166a(i); **KMS Retail Rowlett, LP v. City of Rowlett**, 593 S.W.3d 175, 181 (Tex.2019); **Boerjan v. Rodriguez**, 436 S.W.3d 307, 310 (Tex.2014). The response should include a heading for each challenged element and under that heading a discussion of the evidence that creates a fact issue for that element. If the nonmovant discusses all the facts under one general heading called "Facts," the

nonmovant may forget to address one of the elements. *Cf.* **Johnson v. Brewer & Pritchard, P.C.**, 73 S.W.3d 193, 204 (Tex.2002) (although movant addressed issue of fiduciary relationship, it did not address issue of breach).

Practice Tip

When a no-evidence motion challenges all the elements of the cause of action, the nonmovant should remember to support its damages with evidence. The court will grant a no-evidence motion for summary judgment when a nonmovant does not support a challenged damages element with evidence. ***Dow Chem. Co. v. Francis****, 46 S.W.3d 237, 242 (Tex.2001).*

§3.6 Presenting SJ evidence under TRCP 166a(i). The Notes & Comments to TRCP 166a(i) state that to defeat a no-evidence motion, the nonmovant "is not required to marshal its proof; its response need only point out evidence that raises a fact issue on the challenged elements." **Saenz v. Southern Un. Gas Co.**, 999 S.W.2d 490, 493 (Tex.App.—El Paso 1999, pet. denied). The nonmovant should present summary-judgment evidence in the same form that would be admissible at trial. See "Summary-judgment evidence," ch. 7-B, §9.

§3.7 Sufficiency of evidence. TRCP 166a(i) states that the court must grant the motion unless the nonmovant presents summary-judgment evidence that raises a genuine issue of material fact on each element challenged. **In re Mohawk Rubber Co.**, 982 S.W.2d 494, 498 (Tex.App.—Texarkana 1998, orig. proceeding). A no-evidence motion is essentially a motion for a pretrial directed verdict. **Thomas v. Omar Invs.**, 156 S.W.3d 681, 684 (Tex.App.—Dallas 2005, no pet.); **Ridgway v. Ford Motor Co.**, 82 S.W.3d 26, 29 (Tex.App.—San Antonio 2002), *rev'd on other grounds*, 135 S.W.3d 598 (Tex.2004); *see* **Painter v. Amerimex Drilling I, Ltd.**, 561 S.W.3d 125, 130 (Tex.2018). To defeat a no-evidence motion for summary judgment, the nonmovant must produce more than a scintilla of evidence to raise a genuine issue of material fact on the challenged elements. Tex. R. Civ. P. 166a(i); **KMS Retail Rowlett, LP v. City of Rowlett**, 593 S.W.3d 175, 181 (Tex.2019); **Painter**, 561 S.W.3d at 130; **Forbes, Inc. v. Granada Biosciences, Inc.**, 124 S.W.3d 167, 172 (Tex.2003). If the nonmovant presents more than a scintilla of evidence on the challenged elements, it is entitled to a trial on the merits. **Ridgway**, 82 S.W.3d at 29. A nonmovant produces more than a scintilla when the evidence "rises to a level that would enable reasonable and fair-minded people to differ in their conclusions." **Ford Motor Co. v. Ridgway**, 135 S.W.3d 598, 601 (Tex.2004); **Marsaglia v. UTEP**, 22 S.W.3d 1, 4 (Tex.App.—El Paso 1999, pet. denied); *cf.* **Merrell Dow Pharms. v. Havner**, 953 S.W.2d 706, 711 (Tex.1997) (jury trial). A nonmovant produces no more than a scintilla when the evidence is "so weak as to do no more than create a mere surmise or suspicion" of a fact. **KMS Retail Rowlett**, 593 S.W.3d at 181; **Forbes, Inc.**, 124 S.W.3d at 172; **Marsaglia**, 22 S.W.3d at 4.

§3.8 Expert testimony. If expert testimony is required to defeat a no-evidence motion for summary judgment, the nonmovant must produce evidence that meets the test for expert testimony. *See, e.g.*, **Praytor v. Ford Motor Co.**, 97 S.W.3d 237, 242–43 (Tex.App.—Houston [14th Dist.] 2002, no pet.) (nonmovant did not produce TRE 702 proof for expert's opinion about causation). See "*Daubert-Robinson* test for expert testimony," ch. 5-N, §2.

§3.9 File motion for continuance. When a nonmovant needs additional time to secure affidavits or discovery, it should file a motion for continuance. See "Motion to continue SJ hearing," ch. 5-D, §9.3; **O'Connor's Texas Civil Forms**, FORM 7B:5 (2020 ed.).

§3.10 File motion for sanctions. A motion under TRCP 166a(i) is subject to sanctions provided by existing law. Notes & Comments to Tex. R. Civ. P. 166a(i). See "Groundless or frivolous pleadings," ch. 1-B, §3.3.

§3.11 Other responsive pleadings. When appropriate, the nonmovant may file any of the following:

1. An amended petition or answer. See "Amending the petition or answer," ch. 7-B, §8.
2. A cross-motion for summary judgment. See "When both parties move for SJ," ch. 7-C, §4.8.
3. A nonsuit. See "Consider nonsuit," ch. 7-C, §3.9.

§4. Movant's reply to nonmovant's response

§4.1 Deadline. There is no deadline in TRCP 166a for a movant to file a reply to the nonmovant's response. **Callaghan Ranch, Ltd. v. Killam**, 53 S.W.3d 1, 4 (Tex.App.—San Antonio 2000, pet. denied). See "For movant's reply to response," ch. 7-B, §6.5.

§4.2 Negate nonmovant's evidence. In the reply, the movant can attempt to negate the nonmovant's claim that there is evidence of a triable fact regarding its claims or defenses. *Cf.* **Irby v. Bittick**, 44 F.3d 949, 953 (11th Cir.1995) (under FRCP 56(e), nonmovant must do more than assert there is some doubt about the material facts).

§4.3 Object to nonmovant's SJ evidence. The movant should object to any of the nonmovant's summary-judgment evidence that would not be admissible at trial. *See* Tex. R. Civ. P. 166a(f). See "Objections to summary-judgment evidence," ch. 7-B, §10.

§4.4 Produce SJ evidence. When a nonmovant produces summary-judgment evidence supporting the challenged element of its claim or defense, the movant can produce summary-judgment evidence to attempt to disprove or discredit the nonmovant's evidence. See "Summary-judgment evidence," ch. 7-B, §9.

§4.5 Respond to motion for continuance. See "Response to motion," ch. 5-D, §9.3.4.

§4.6 File special exceptions. If the claims in the response are vague, unintelligible, unclear, or ambiguous, the movant can challenge them by special exceptions. See "Special exceptions & summary judgments," ch. 3-G, §10; "Special exceptions in summary-judgment procedure," ch. 7-B, §5.

§4.7 No additional grounds. In its reply, the movant cannot add new challenges to the nonmovant's claims or defenses. *See* **Community Initiatives, Inc. v. Chase Bank**, 153 S.W.3d 270, 280 (Tex.App.—El Paso 2004, no pet.) (movant may not use reply to meet specificity requirements of TRCP 166a(i) or to assert new grounds for SJ); *see, e.g.*, **Specialty Retailers, Inc. v. Fuqua**, 29 S.W.3d 140, 148 (Tex.App.—Houston [14th Dist.] 2000, pet. denied) (nonmovant had no burden to present evidence to support claims challenged for the first time in reply).

§5. Nonmovant's time to cure

The court should give the nonmovant the opportunity to cure any defects in its summary-judgment evidence identified by the movant in its reply. *See* Tex. R. Civ. P. 166a(f) (party should be given opportunity to cure defects in form of affidavits and attachments); *see also* Tex. R. Civ. P. 166a(g) (court may deny SJ or grant continuance to allow nonmovant to obtain affidavit or deposition testimony necessary to support its claims).

§5.1 Deadline to cure. Nothing in TRCP 166a provides a deadline to cure defects in a party's evidence once objections have been filed. Under the TRCP 166a(a) and (b) summary-judgment procedure, the time to cure is built in because an adverse ruling is not fatal to the party with the summary-judgment burden of proof. Under TRCP 166a(a) and (b), if the trial court rules adversely to the movant (the party with the summary-judgment burden of proof) based on defects in its evidence, the court merely denies the motion, which is in effect an opportunity to cure because the movant can file another motion. By comparison, in a no-evidence summary judgment under TRCP 166a(i), if the trial court rules adversely to the nonmovant (the party with the burden of proof) based on defects in the response or the evidence, the court grants the motion for summary judgment, which is fatal to the nonmovant's case. The opportunity to cure in TRCP 166a(f) should apply to both the movant and nonmovant in both types of summary judgments. *See, e.g.*, **Webster v. Allstate Ins.**, 833 S.W.2d 747, 750 (Tex.App.—Houston [1st Dist.] 1992, no writ) (trial court should not have sustained objections to party's evidence on day of hearing without giving party chance to amend).

§5.2 Motion for continuance. If the movant identified defects in the nonmovant's pleading, response, or evidence, the nonmovant should file a motion for continuance asking the court for time to cure the defects. *See* **Peerenboom v. HSP Foods, Inc.**, 910 S.W.2d 156, 160 (Tex.App.—Waco 1995, no writ); **Webster v. Allstate Ins.**, 833 S.W.2d 747, 750 (Tex.App.—Houston [1st Dist.] 1992, no writ). See "Motion to continue SJ hearing," ch. 5-D, §9.3. The nonmovant will need additional time because the movant's reply, if filed by the three-day deadline recommended for the movant's special exceptions in **McConnell v. Southside ISD**, 858 S.W.2d 337, 343 n.7 (Tex.1993), will not provide the nonmovant with sufficient time to cure the defect. The nonmovant should ask the court to state a deadline to cure the defects and a date for the hearing. *See, e.g.*, **Peerenboom**, 910 S.W.2d at 160 (appellate court did not consider evidence because party did not file it at least seven days before new hearing date).

§6. Hearing

See "Hearing," ch. 7-B, §11.

§7. Trial court's ruling under TRCP 166a(i)

§7.1 Mandatory. TRCP 166a(i) requires the trial court to grant the motion for no-evidence summary judgment if the nonmovant does not produce summary-judgment evidence that raises a genuine issue of material fact. **Dolcefino v. Randolph**, 19 S.W.3d 906, 917 (Tex.App.—Houston [14th Dist.] 2000, pet. denied); **Saenz v. Southern Un. Gas Co.**, 999 S.W.2d 490, 493 (Tex.App.—El Paso 1999, pet. denied).

§7.2 Judgment. See "Summary judgment," ch. 7-B, §12.

§8. Review

In reviewing a no-evidence summary judgment, the appellate court must consider all the evidence in the light most favorable to the party against whom the summary judgment was rendered, crediting evidence favorable to that party if reasonable jurors could and disregarding contrary evidence unless reasonable jurors could not. **Gonzalez v. Ramirez**, 463 S.W.3d 499, 504 (Tex.2015); **Boerjan v. Rodriguez**, 436 S.W.3d 307, 311–12 (Tex.2014); **Timpte Indus. v. Gish**, 286 S.W.3d 306, 310 (Tex.2009); *see* **City of Keller v. Wilson**, 168 S.W.3d 802, 827 (Tex.2005). The appellate court will affirm a no-evidence summary judgment if the record shows one of the following: (1) there is no evidence on the challenged element, (2) the evidence offered to prove the challenged element is no more than a scintilla, (3) the evidence establishes the opposite of the challenged element, or (4) the court is barred by law or the rules of evidence from considering the only evidence offered to prove the challenged element. **Southwestern Bell Tel., L.P. v. Emmett**, 459 S.W.3d 578, 589 (Tex.2015); **Merriman v. XTO Energy, Inc.**, 407 S.W.3d 244, 248 (Tex.2013); **City of Keller**, 168 S.W.3d at 810. Generally, the review of judgments granted under TRCP 166a(i) is the same as under TRCP 166a(a) and (b). See "Review," ch. 7-B, §14.

E. Motion for Judgment on Agreed Statement of Facts

§1. General

§1.1 Rules. Tex. R. Civ. P. 263. See Tex. R. Civ. P. 11.

§1.2 Purpose. The purpose of a motion for judgment on an agreed statement of facts under TRCP 263 is to ask the trial court to render a decision on the law when the facts are not in controversy. **State Bar v. Faubion**, 821 S.W.2d 203, 205 (Tex.App.—Houston [14th Dist.] 1991, writ denied). TRCP 263 requires the parties to agree on all facts essential for the determination of the lawsuit, leaving to the court the function of deciding questions of law.

§1.3 Forms. **O'Connor's Texas Civil Forms**, FORMS 7E:1 et seq., 9C:5 (2020 ed.).

§2. Distinction between agreed statement & stipulations

§2.1 Differences. An agreed case under TRCP 263 is not the same thing as a case tried on stipulated facts. *See* **Perry v. Aetna Life Ins.**, 380 S.W.2d 868, 875 (Tex.App.—Tyler 1964, writ ref'd n.r.e.). Parties may stipulate to some undisputed facts without submitting the case as an agreed case. *See id.* The ordinary stipulation permits the trial court to make any findings and inferences supported by the evidence. **Farah v. First Nat'l Bank**, 624 S.W.2d 341, 345 (Tex.App.—Fort Worth 1981, writ ref'd n.r.e.); **Parsons v. Watley**, 492 S.W.2d 61, 63 (Tex.App.—Eastland 1973, no writ); **Perry**, 380 S.W.2d at 874. Submitting a case on an agreed statement of facts does not permit the court to make inferences from the facts, unless the parties so stipulate. **Alma Grp. v. Palmer**, 143 S.W.3d 840, 843 (Tex.App.—Corpus Christi 2004, pet. denied); **Perry**, 380 S.W.2d at 874; *see* **Cummins & Walker Oil Co. v. Smith**, 814 S.W.2d 884, 886 (Tex.App.—San Antonio 1991, no writ).

§2.2 Test for agreed case. To determine whether a stipulation of facts is an agreed statement of facts under TRCP 263, answer the following questions. If the answers are mostly yes, the case probably falls under TRCP 263. • Does the instrument denote itself as an agreed statement of facts and refer to TRCP 263? *See* **Abbott v. Blue Cross & Blue Shield**, 113 S.W.3d 753, 759 (Tex.App.—Austin 2003, pet. denied). • Does it purport to contain all the facts necessary to decide the case? If it is clear from the record that the trial court considered other facts outside the stipulation, the case was not an agreed case under Tex. R. Civ. P. 263. **Peterson v. NCNB Tex. Nat'l Bank**, 838 S.W.2d 263, 265 (Tex.App.—Dallas 1992, no writ); **Farah v. First Nat'l Bank**, 624 S.W.2d 341, 345 (Tex.App.—Fort Worth 1981, writ ref'd n.r.e.); *see* **Parsons v. Watley**, 492 S.W.2d 61, 63 (Tex.App.—Eastland 1973, no writ). • Did the judge certify and approve the agreed statement of facts? *See* Tex. R. Civ. P. 263; **Peterson**, 838 S.W.2d at 265; **Parsons**, 492 S.W.2d at 63. • Does the instrument place the ultimate facts that are essential to determination of the case beyond the need for adjudication? *See* **Texas Farm Bur. Mut. Ins. v. Sturrock**, 146 S.W.3d 123, 125 n.2 (Tex.2004). • Does the judgment show the case was tried as an agreed case? *See* **Tarrant Appr. Dist. v. Gateway Ctr. Assocs.**, 34 S.W.3d 712, 713 (Tex.App.—Fort Worth 2000, no pet.).

§3. Motion

§3.1 In writing. The motion for judgment on an agreed statement of facts must be in writing. *See* Tex. R. Civ. P. 11, 263; *see, e.g.*, **Beddall v. Reader's Wholesale Distribs.**, 408 S.W.2d 237, 238 (Tex.App.—Houston 1966, no writ) (oral stipulation in open court was not an agreed statement of facts under TRCP 263). *But see* **Lambda Constr. Co. v. Chamberlin Waterproofing & Roofing Sys.**, 784 S.W.2d 122, 125 (Tex.App.—Austin 1990, writ denied) (telephone conference was considered an agreed statement of facts under TRCP 263). See **O'Connor's Texas Civil Forms**, FORM 7E:1 (2020 ed.).

§3.2 Identify all necessary facts. The motion for judgment must state specific facts that the parties agree on and seek a judgment on. *See* **Cummins & Walker Oil Co. v. Smith**, 814 S.W.2d 884, 886 (Tex.App.—San Antonio 1991, no writ) (presumption that all facts are included in the agreed statement). The motion should expressly state that the case is to be tried on the agreed facts and that those are all the facts of the case. *See id.* Parties can agree only to the facts and cannot stipulate to the law. See **O'Connor's Texas Civil Forms**, FORM 7E:2 (2020 ed.).

§3.3 Request for judgment. The agreed statement should ask the court to resolve the controversy on the agreed statement of facts.

§3.4 Signatures of parties. The parties or their attorneys must sign the agreed statement of facts. *See* Tex. R. Civ. P. 11, 263.

§3.5 Certificate for judge. The agreed statement should contain a certificate for the court to sign, certifying and approving the agreed facts. Tex R Civ. P. 263; **Davis v. State**, 904 S.W.2d 946, 949 n.3 (Tex.App.—Austin 1995, no writ). The certification shows the appellate court the facts on which the trial court based its judgment. **State Farm Lloyds v. Kessler**, 932 S.W.2d 732, 735 (Tex.App.—Fort Worth 1996, writ denied). See **O'Connor's Texas Civil Forms**, FORM 7E:2 (2020 ed.).

§3.6 Proposed judgment. The parties should submit a proposed judgment for the court to sign, and they should file it with the agreed statement. The judgment can be a simple, one-sentence judgment: "On the agreed statement of facts, judgment is rendered for . . . ."

§3.7 Filed with court. The agreed statement must be filed with the court. Tex R Civ. P. 263.

§3.8 Strict compliance not required. When parties stipulate to all the facts in a case, the stipulation may be treated as a submission of an agreed statement even if it does not strictly comply with TRCP 263. **Addison Urban Dev. Partners v. Alan Ritchey Materials Co.**, 437 S.W.3d 597, 601 (Tex.App.—Dallas 2014, no pet.); **City of Galveston v. Giles**, 902 S.W.2d 167, 169 n.1 (Tex.App.—Houston [1st Dist.] 1995, no writ); **Reed v. Valley Fed. S&L Co.**, 655 S.W.2d 259, 264 (Tex.App.—Corpus Christi 1983, writ ref'd n.r.e.). Even if the parties did not meet the technical requirements of TRCP 263, if the final judgment appears to be the product of a TRCP 263 agreed case, the appellate court will treat it as one. *E.g.*, **Addison Urban Dev.**, 437 S.W.3d at 601 (court did not sign or certify agreed statement); **Giles**, 902 S.W.2d at 169 n.1 (same); **Lambda Constr. Co. v. Chamberlin Waterproofing & Roofing Sys.**, 784 S.W.2d 122, 125 (Tex.App.—Austin 1990, writ denied) (although no statement of facts was prepared, telephone conference in which parties stipulated to all material facts was considered a submission on agreed statement of facts under TRCP 263).

§4. Hearing

§4.1 Argument only. The hearing under TRCP 263 is not for evidence; all material evidence must be included in the agreed statement. If the court holds a hearing, it is for argument only.

§4.2 Presumption of all facts. All facts necessary to the presentation of the case are conclusively presumed to have been brought before the court. **Jim Sowell Constr. Co. v. Dallas Cent. Appr. Dist.**, 900 S.W.2d 82, 84 (Tex.App.—Dallas 1995, writ denied). The court cannot draw any inference or find any facts not included in the agreement. *See* **Diamond Shamrock Ref. & Mktg. Co. v. Nueces Cty. Appr. Dist.**, 876 S.W.2d 298, 301 n.2 (Tex.1994); **Lawler v. Lomas & Nettleton Mortg. Investors**, 691 S.W.2d 593, 595 (Tex.1985); **Jim Sowell Constr.**, 900 S.W.2d at 84. But an inference of facts beyond the agreed statement of facts may be compelled by the facts as a matter of law. **Lawler**, 691 S.W.2d at 595; **Davis v. State**, 904 S.W.2d 946, 950 (Tex.App.—Austin 1995, no writ).

§4.3 Binding effect. The court is bound by the agreed statement of facts. **Tarrant Appr. Rev. Bd. v. Martinez Bros. Invs.**, 946 S.W.2d 914, 917 (Tex.App.—Fort Worth 1997, no writ); **Crow-Southland Jt.V. v. North Fort Worth Bank**, 838 S.W.2d 720, 723 (Tex.App.—Dallas 1992, writ denied).

§5. Judgment

§5.1 Court certification. Once a case is submitted on an agreed statement, the court must sign and certify the statement as correct. Tex R Civ. P. 263; **Perry v. Aetna Life Ins.**, 380 S.W.2d 868, 874 (Tex.App.—Tyler 1964, writ ref'd n.r.e.). If the court does not sign or certify the statement as required by TRCP 263, the appellate court will consider it as a TRCP 263 case only if it is clear that the case was tried on agreed facts. **Crow-Southland Jt.V. v. North Fort Worth Bank**, 838 S.W.2d 720, 723 (Tex.App.—Dallas 1992, writ denied); *see* **Abbott v. Blue Cross & Blue Shield**, 113 S.W.3d 753, 758–59 (Tex.App.—Austin 2003, pet. denied) (court refused to certify stipulations and considered evidence outside stipulations).

§5.2 Judgment. The court should sign a judgment declaring its interpretation of the law that applies to the agreed statement of facts. Tex R Civ. P. 263. The court's judgment must declare only the law necessarily arising from the agreed facts. **Harris Cty. Appr. Dist v. Transamerica Container Leasing Inc.**, 920 S.W.2d 678, 680 (Tex.App.—Houston [1st Dist.] 1995, writ denied); **State Bar v. Faubion**, 821 S.W.2d 203, 205 (Tex.App.—Houston [14th Dist.] 1991, writ denied). See **O'Connor's Texas Civil Forms**, FORM 9C:5 (2020 ed.).

§5.3 No findings of fact. The court cannot make findings of fact besides those agreed to by the parties. **Crow-Southland Jt.V. v. North Fort Worth Bank**, 838 S.W.2d 720, 725 (Tex.App.—Dallas 1992, writ denied). Findings of fact are not appropriate in the trial of an agreed case. **International Un. v. General Motors Corp.**, 104 S.W.3d 126, 129 (Tex.App.—Fort Worth 2003, no pet.); **Port Arthur ISD v. Port Arthur Teachers Ass'n**, 990 S.W.2d 955, 957 (Tex.App.—Beaumont 1999, pet. denied); **City of Galveston v. Giles**, 902 S.W.2d 167, 170 n.2 (Tex.App.—Houston [1st Dist.] 1995, no writ).

§5.4 Object to judgment. If the trial court interprets a statement by the parties as an agreement to submit the issue on agreed facts, a party not intending such an agreement must object to preserve error. **Lambda Constr. Co. v. Chamberlin Waterproofing & Roofing Sys.**, 784 S.W.2d 122, 125 (Tex.App.—Austin 1990, writ denied).

§6. Review

§6.1 Record. The agreed statement signed and certified by the court, along with the court's judgment, is the record of the case for the appeal. Tex. R. Civ. P. 263; **Texas Farm Bur. Mut. Ins. v. Sturrock**, 146 S.W.3d 123, 125 n.2 (Tex.2004).

§6.2 No presumptions. On appeal, the courts make no presumed findings in favor of the judgment. **Patterson-UTI Drilling Co. v. Webb Cty. Appr. Dist.**, 182 S.W.3d 14, 17 (Tex.App.—San Antonio 2005, no pet.); **State Farm Lloyds v. Kessler**, 932 S.W.2d 732, 735 (Tex.App.—Fort Worth 1996, writ denied).

§6.3 Limited scope. The appeal is limited to the single issue of whether the law as applied to the agreed facts is correct. **TPCIGA v. Morrison**, 212 S.W.3d 349, 353 (Tex.App.—Austin 2006, pet. denied); **Roberts v. Squyres**, 4 S.W.3d 485, 488 (Tex.App.—Beaumont 1999, pet. denied); **Tarrant Appr. Rev. Bd. v. Martinez Bros. Invs.**, 946 S.W.2d 914, 917 (Tex.App.—Fort Worth 1997, no writ); **Crow-Southland Jt.V. v. North Fort Worth Bank**, 838 S.W.2d 720, 723 (Tex.App.—Dallas 1992, writ denied). The review is de novo. **Patterson-UTI Drilling Co. v. Webb Cty. Appr. Dist.**, 182 S.W.3d 14, 17 (Tex.App.—San Antonio 2005, no pet.); **Orange Cty. Appr. Dist. v. Agape Neighborhood Imprv., Inc.**, 57 S.W.3d 597, 601 (Tex.App.—Beaumont 2001, pet. denied). The appellate court does not review the legal or factual sufficiency of the evidence. **City of Harlingen v. Avila**, 942 S.W.2d 49, 51 (Tex.App.—Corpus Christi 1997, writ denied); **Crow-Southland**, 838 S.W.2d at 723.

§6.4 Render or remand. If the appellate court determines that the trial court erred, in most cases it should render the judgment the trial court should have rendered. If, however, the appellate court decides there are factual issues unresolved by the agreed statement that prevent a judgment, the court should remand the case to the trial court. *See, e.g.*, **Cameron Cty. Appr. Rev. Bd. v. Creditbanc Sav. Ass'n**, 763 S.W.2d 577, 580–81 (Tex.App.—Corpus Christi 1988, writ denied) (valuation of property improvements unresolved by agreed statement).

F. Voluntary Dismissal—Nonsuit

§1. General

§1.1 Rules. Tex. R. Civ. P. 96, 162, 163.

§1.2 Purpose. A nonsuit is a voluntary dismissal of the moving party's claims.

§1.3 Forms. **O'Connor's Texas Civil Forms**, FORMS 7F:1 et seq. (2020 ed.).

§1.4 Other references. **O'Connor's Texas Causes of Action** (2021 ed.).

§2. Motion

A plaintiff has a right to a nonsuit the moment it makes a timely oral or written request for nonsuit. **Travelers Ins. v. Joachim**, 315 S.W.3d 860, 862 (Tex.2010); **In re Greater Houston Orthopaedic Specialists, Inc.**, 295 S.W.3d 323, 325 (Tex.2009); **Greenberg v. Brookshire**, 640 S.W.2d 870, 872 (Tex.1982); *see* **Morath v. Lewis**, 601 S.W.3d 785, 787 (Tex.2020). A nonsuit nullifies the controversy and renders certain interlocutory orders in the case moot. **In re Bennett**, 960 S.W.2d 35, 38 (Tex.1997); *see* **Morath**, 601 S.W.3d at 788; **City of Dallas v. Albert**, 354 S.W.3d 368, 375 (Tex.2011). However, the plaintiff's nonsuit will not affect any pending claims for relief made by the defendant. See "Effect on defendant's claims," ch. 7-F, §6.3. Once the plaintiff requests a nonsuit, she cannot withdraw the request. **Trigg v. Moore**, 335 S.W.3d 243, 245 (Tex.App.—Amarillo 2010, pet. denied).

§2.1 Oral or written. To take a nonsuit, the party can either file a written motion for nonsuit (sometimes called a notice of nonsuit) or make an oral announcement of the nonsuit in open court. **Greenberg v. Brookshire**, 640 S.W.2d 870, 872 (Tex.1982). See **O'Connor's Texas Civil Forms**, FORM 7F:1 (2020 ed.). In this section, "motion for nonsuit" refers to both an oral request and a written motion for nonsuit.

§2.2 Grounds. There are no formal requirements for the motion for nonsuit. **Greenberg v. Brookshire**, 640 S.W.2d 870, 872 (Tex.1982). The motion does not need to state a reason for taking the nonsuit. *See id.*

§2.3 With or without prejudice. The motion should state whether the party requests a dismissal with or without prejudice. If the case is dismissed with prejudice, the order is a final adjudication on the merits and the lawsuit cannot be refiled. See "With prejudice," ch. 7-F, §5.4. If the case is dismissed without prejudice, the order is not a final adjudication on the merits and the parties are merely placed in the positions they would have been if the suit had not been brought. See "Without prejudice," ch. 7-F, §5.3.

§2.4 Movant.

1. Plaintiff. In most cases, the party taking a nonsuit is the plaintiff.

2. Defendant. A defendant may nonsuit its counterclaims. *See* **City of Dallas v. Albert**, 354 S.W.3d 368, 375 (Tex.2011); **Mackie v. McKenzie**, 890 S.W.2d 807, 808 (Tex.1994); **Mossler v. Shields**, 818 S.W.2d 752, 753 (Tex.1991).

§2.5 Partial nonsuit.

1. Parties. The plaintiff can nonsuit some parties without nonsuiting others, as long as doing so will not prejudice another party. *See* Tex. R. Civ. P. 162, 163; **C/S Solutions, Inc. v. Energy Maint. Servs. Grp.**, 274 S.W.3d 299, 306 (Tex.App.—Houston [1st Dist.] 2008, no pet.).

2. Claims. The plaintiff cannot nonsuit only some of the claims against a party, but instead must nonsuit the entire case. *See* Tex. R. Civ. P. 162, 163; **C/S Solutions**, 274 S.W.3d at 306.

Note

Although a plaintiff cannot nonsuit only some of her claims, she can voluntarily dismiss certain claims either by filing an amended pleading that omits a claim under TRCP 63 or by abandoning a claim under TRCP 165. ***C/S Solutions****, 274 S.W.3d at 306. See "Alternatives to nonsuit," ch. 7-F, §2.8. If a*

plaintiff files a written "nonsuit" that abandons certain claims, it is actually an amended pleading voluntarily dismissing the claims and will be treated as such, despite the fact that the word "nonsuit" appears. ***C/S Solutions**, 274 S.W.3d at 306–07. The distinction between a nonsuit under TRCP 162 and an amended pleading that voluntarily dismisses some claims has no practical effect unless the "nonsuit" violates the timing requirements of TRCP 63.* ***C/S Solutions**, 274 S.W.3d at 306 & n.6.*

§2.6 Service of notice. TRCP 162 requires the movant to serve notice of the nonsuit in accordance with TRCP 21a on any party that has answered or has been served with process. **Novosad v. Brian K. Cunningham, P.C.**, 38 S.W.3d 767, 772 (Tex.App.—Houston [14th Dist.] 2001, no pet.). A certificate of service creates a presumption that the notice of nonsuit was received; the presumption vanishes when opposing evidence is introduced. **Wembley Inv. v. Herrera**, 11 S.W.3d 924, 927 (Tex.1999). But the lack of a certificate of service on a notice of nonsuit does not affect the finality of the judgment. **McGrew v. Heard**, 779 S.W.2d 455, 458 (Tex.App.—Houston [1st Dist.] 1989, orig. proceeding).

§2.7 Costs. The clerk must tax the court costs of the nonsuit against the party moving for dismissal, unless the court orders otherwise. Tex. R. Civ. P. 162; **Leon Springs Gas Co. v. Restaurant Equip. Leasing Co.**, 961 S.W.2d 574, 579 (Tex.App.—San Antonio 1997, no pet.).

§2.8 Alternatives to nonsuit. There are other ways to eliminate parties or claims from the suit.

1. Nonsuit by amendment. Because an amended pleading supersedes and supplants all previous pleadings, an amendment of the pleading can effectively work as a nonsuit of parties and claims. **Randolph v. Jackson Walker L.L.P.**, 29 S.W.3d 271, 274 (Tex.App.—Houston [14th Dist.] 2000, pet. denied); *see* Tex. R. Civ. P. 65 (substituted instrument is no longer regarded as part of the pleadings). See "Amended pleadings," ch. 1-B, §3.6.1(1).

(1) Generally—omission results in nonsuit.

(a) Omitted parties. As a general rule, omitting a party from an amended petition effectively nonsuits that party. **American Petrofina, Inc. v. Allen**, 887 S.W.2d 829, 831 (Tex.1994) (omitted Ps); **Webb v. Jorns**, 488 S.W.2d 407, 409 (Tex.1972) (omitted D); **Randolph**, 29 S.W.3d at 274 (omitted Ds). But if a petition omits a party by mistake and the party is renamed in a later petition, the omission does not operate as a nonsuit. **American Petrofina**, 887 S.W.2d at 831; **Woodruff v. Wright**, 51 S.W.3d 727, 733 (Tex.App.—Texarkana 2001, pet. denied). In such a case, the party seeking to exclude the temporarily dismissed party has the burden to show that it was prejudiced when the omitted party was later renamed. **American Petrofina**, 887 S.W.2d at 831. By including the generic term "et al." in the style of the case of an amended petition, a party negates the intent to nonsuit any of the parties named in the earlier petition. *See id.*; **Abramcik v. U.S. Home Corp.**, 792 S.W.2d 822, 824 (Tex.App.—Houston [14th Dist.] 1990, writ denied).

(b) Omitted claims. As a general rule, omitting a claim from an amended petition effectively nonsuits that claim. **FKM Prtshp. v. Board of Regents**, 255 S.W.3d 619, 633 (Tex.2008); *see, e.g.*, **Dolenz v. All Saints Episcopal Hosp.**, 638 S.W.2d 141, 142 (Tex.App.—Fort Worth 1982, writ ref'd n.r.e.) (P abandoned claim because he went to trial on amended petition that did not contain the claim).

(2) Exception—party's intent. A party may be able to argue that certain circumstances indicate that it did not actually intend to nonsuit the party or claim in question. *See* **FKM Prtshp.**, 255 S.W.3d at 633; *see, e.g.*, **Spellmann v. Love**, 534 S.W.3d 685, 690–91 (Tex.App.—Corpus Christi 2017, pet. denied) (although P's fourth amended petition removed all claims against certain Ds, those Ds were still included in style of case, Ds were listed in "Parties" section of petition, petition prayed for judgment against Ds, and order of nonsuit stated it did not release any claims P could assert against Ds; those Ds were not nonsuited); **Ortiz v. Collins**, 203 S.W.3d 414, 421 n.4 (Tex.App.—Houston [14th Dist.] 2006, pet. denied) (P's amended petition stated that it did not waive right to pursue claims not repleaded in amended petition; claims were not nonsuited); **Cox v. Union Oil Co.**, 917 S.W.2d 524, 527 (Tex.App.—Beaumont 1996, no writ) (D was omitted from preamble of petition but named in body of petition; D was not nonsuited); *see also* **Green v. Vidlak**, 76 S.W.3d 117, 119–20 (Tex.App.—Amarillo 2002, no pet.) (even though D was listed in style of amended petition, omission of D's name from text of amended petition resulted in nonsuit; P did not raise argument that omission of D's name was inadvertent).

2. **TRCP 165—abandonment.** A party may abandon any part of its claim and have that fact noted on the record. Tex. R. Civ. P. 165; *see also* **Jones v. Nightingale**, 900 S.W.2d 87, 90 (Tex.App.—San Antonio 1995, writ ref'd) (claims abandoned under TRCP 165 barred from relitigation by compulsory-counterclaim rule).

§3. Deadlines for nonsuit

§3.1 Before resting. A nonsuit in a trial must be taken before the plaintiff introduces all of its evidence other than rebuttal evidence (i.e., before it rests). Tex. R. Civ. P. 162; **Morath v. Lewis**, 601 S.W.3d 785, 787 (Tex.2020); **Epps v. Fowler**, 351 S.W.3d 862, 868 (Tex.2011); **In re Team Rocket, L.P.**, 256 S.W.3d 257, 259 (Tex.2008); **Villafani v. Trejo**, 251 S.W.3d 466, 468–69 (Tex.2008). As long as the plaintiff has not rested its case, the plaintiff is not limited to filing a motion for nonsuit in the trial court. *See* **Morath**, 601 S.W.3d at 787–88 (when trial-court proceedings are stayed pending interlocutory appeal, nonsuit can be filed directly in Supreme Court); **Houston Mun. Empls. Pension Sys. v. Ferrell**, 248 S.W.3d 151, 157 (Tex.2007) (same); *see, e.g.*, **UTMB v. Estate of Blackmon**, 195 S.W.3d 98, 100 (Tex.2006) (P had right to nonsuit during interlocutory appeal to court of appeals).

Note

*Although the Court in **Morath** stated that a nonsuit could be filed directly in the Supreme Court when all trial-court proceedings are stayed pending interlocutory appeal, the Court did not address whether a nonsuit could be filed in the trial court during such a stay. See **Morath**, 601 S.W.3d at 787–88.*

§3.2 Before SJ. A nonsuit in a summary-judgment proceeding must be taken before the court grants ("renders") a summary judgment. **Pace Concerts, Ltd. v. Resendez**, 72 S.W.3d 700, 702 (Tex.App.—San Antonio 2002, pet. denied); **Taliaferro v. Smith**, 804 S.W.2d 548, 550 (Tex.App.—Houston [14th Dist.] 1991, no writ). See "Rendition," ch. 9-C, §3.1.

§4. Objections to nonsuit

There are only a few legitimate objections a party can make to a nonsuit. See **O'Connor's Texas Civil Forms**, FORM 7F:2 (2020 ed.).

§4.1 Request too late. A defendant should object when the request for nonsuit is too late—that is, when (1) the plaintiff asks for a nonsuit after it introduced all of its evidence other than rebuttal evidence (see "Before resting," ch. 7-F, §3.1), or (2) the plaintiff asks for a nonsuit on a claim already resolved by summary judgment. *See* **Hyundai Motor Co. v. Alvarado**, 892 S.W.2d 853, 855 (Tex.1995) (once summary judgment is granted, P cannot take nonsuit on any claim resolved by summary judgment).

§4.2 Order too inclusive. A party must object when the order of nonsuit dismisses more claims or parties than requested in the nonsuit. *See* **Shadowbrook Apts. v. Abu-Ahmad**, 783 S.W.2d 210, 211 (Tex.1990).

§5. Order of nonsuit

§5.1 Court's authority. A court cannot nonsuit parties without a motion for nonsuit of those parties. **Shadowbrook Apts. v. Abu-Ahmad**, 783 S.W.2d 210, 211 (Tex.1990). When properly requested, the court generally does not have the authority to deny a nonsuit. **Travelers Ins. v. Joachim**, 315 S.W.3d 860, 862 (Tex.2010); **Zimmerman v. Ottis**, 941 S.W.2d 259, 261 (Tex.App.—Corpus Christi 1996, orig. proceeding); **Baldwin v. Klanke**, 877 S.W.2d 879, 881 (Tex.App.—Houston [1st Dist.] 1994, no writ). However, the court can deny a nonsuit in limited circumstances. *See, e.g.*, Tex. Fam. Code §161.203 (in suit seeking termination of parental rights, nonsuit cannot be taken unless court approves it); **Oryx Capital Int'l v. Sage Apts., L.L.C.**, 167 S.W.3d 432, 438 (Tex.App.—San Antonio 2005, no pet.) (trial court cannot sign nonsuit in violation of stay issued by court of appeals).

Note

*Even though a court generally does not have the authority to deny a nonsuit, the court may be able to sanction a movant who files the motion for nonsuit for an improper purpose. See **Liles v. Contreras**,*

547 S.W.3d 280, 295–96 (Tex.App.—San Antonio 2018, pet. denied). See "Motion for Sanctions," ch. 5-K, §1 et seq.

§5.2 Written order. A written order is not required. Tex. R. Civ. P. 162; **Epps v. Fowler**, 351 S.W.3d 862, 868 (Tex.2011). When the court signs an order granting a nonsuit, it is simply a ministerial act. **Klein v. Hernandez,** 315 S.W.3d 1, 4 (Tex.2010); **Greenberg v. Brookshire**, 640 S.W.2d 870, 872 (Tex.1982). A written order, however, is important for establishing finality for appeal. See "Effect on finality of judgment," ch. 7-F, §6.9.

1. Most cases. Once a nonsuit is requested in open court or in writing, the court should sign an order granting the dismissal. The signing of the order of dismissal—not the filing of the nonsuit—triggers the appellate deadlines. **In re Bennett**, 960 S.W.2d 35, 38 (Tex.1997); **Park Place Hosp. v. Estate of Milo**, 909 S.W.2d 508, 510 (Tex.1995); **Farmer v. Ben E. Keith Co.**, 907 S.W.2d 495, 496 (Tex.1995); *see, e.g.*, **Coastal Banc SSB v. Helle**, 48 S.W.3d 796, 800 (Tex.App.—Corpus Christi 2001, pet. denied) (oral rendition of nonsuit did not begin appellate timetable); **Iacono v. Lyons**, 6 S.W.3d 715, 716 (Tex.App.—Houston [1st Dist.] 1999, order) (docket notation that nonsuit was "entered" did not begin appellate timetable).

2. After conventional trial on merits. A separate order on the nonsuit is not necessary when the nonsuit is filed before the court signs a judgment after a conventional trial on the merits (i.e., a jury or nonjury trial). After a conventional trial on the merits, the judgment is presumed to be final and dispositive. See "After conventional trial," ch. 9-C, §6.3.1(1). A default judgment, summary judgment, or judgment of dismissal is not a conventional trial on the merits for purposes of transforming a nonsuit into a final judgment. *See* **In re Bro Bro Props., Inc.**, 50 S.W.3d 528, 530 (Tex.App.—San Antonio 2000, orig. proceeding) (nonsuit announced before default judgment did not become effective by rendition of default judgment).

Practice Tip

To avoid problems about the finality of the judgment, insist that the court sign an order of nonsuit or memorialize the nonsuit in the final judgment.

§5.3 Without prejudice. In most cases, the court should sign an order dismissing the nonsuited claims without prejudice to their refiling. *See* Tex. R. Civ. P. 162.

1. To plaintiff. The dismissal after a nonsuit is not an adjudication of the plaintiff's rights; the nonsuit merely places the plaintiff in the position it was in before filing the lawsuit. **McGowen v. Huang**, 120 S.W.3d 452, 462 (Tex.App.—Texarkana 2003, pet. denied); **KT Bolt Mfg. v. Texas Elec. Cooperatives**, 837 S.W.2d 273, 275 (Tex.App.—Beaumont 1992, writ denied).

2. To defendant. If, at the time the plaintiff files a nonsuit, the defendant has already filed a counterclaim, motion for sanctions, or any other request for affirmative relief, the nonsuit does not prevent the court from considering the defendant's request. Tex. R. Civ. P. 96, 162. See "Effect on defendant's claims," ch. 7-F, §6.3.

§5.4 With prejudice. A dismissal with prejudice is an adjudication on the merits. **Mossler v. Shields**, 818 S.W.2d 752, 754 (Tex.1991). Generally, if the court signs an order dismissing the suit with prejudice, res judicata applies and the plaintiff cannot relitigate the same claims against the same defendant. **Epps v. Fowler**, 351 S.W.3d 862, 868–69 (Tex.2011); **Travelers Ins. v. Joachim**, 315 S.W.3d 860, 862 (Tex.2010); *see, e.g.*, **Galvan v. America's Favorite Chicken Co.**, 934 S.W.2d 409, 410 (Tex.App.—San Antonio 1996, writ denied) (when party mistakenly filed for nonsuit with prejudice, res judicata barred later suit). See "Res Judicata—Claim preclusion," ch. 9-D, §3.

Caution

Check the order before the time expires to challenge it. If the order states that the dismissal is with prejudice when it should be without prejudice, you must attack the order directly—through a timely motion for new trial or a bill of review—or the order will be final and the underlying claim will be barred by res judicata. See ***Travelers Ins.****, 315 S.W.3d at 866.*

§6. Effect of nonsuit

§6.1 Effect on plaintiff's suit. A nonsuit renders the merits of the case moot and extinguishes the court's jurisdiction to decide the controversy. **Morath v. Lewis**, 601 S.W.3d 785, 788 (Tex.2020). It is effective as soon as the plaintiff files a motion for nonsuit or asks for one in open court. **Epps v. Fowler**, 351 S.W.3d 862, 868 (Tex.2011); **Travelers Ins. v. Joachim**, 315 S.W.3d 860, 862 (Tex.2010); **Greenberg v. Brookshire**, 640 S.W.2d 870, 872 (Tex.1982). However, the court may defer signing an order of dismissal to hear matters that are collateral to the merits of the underlying case (i.e., costs, attorney fees, sanctions). **UTMB v. Estate of Blackmon**, 195 S.W.3d 98, 100–01 (Tex.2006); *see* Tex. R. Civ. P. 162; **Travelers Ins.**, 315 S.W.3d at 863; **In re Bennett**, 960 S.W.2d 35, 38 (Tex.1997). Although the court may hold a hearing on these matters, the nonsuit still renders the merits of the case moot. *E.g.*, **Estate of Blackmon**, 195 S.W.3d at 101 (court could sign order on costs requested by D in plea to the jurisdiction, but P's nonsuit deprived court of jurisdiction over D's appeal); **Mobley v. Mobley**, 506 S.W.3d 87, 90–91 (Tex.App.—Texarkana 2016, no pet.) (nonsuit that was filed after trial court granted motion for partial summary judgment rendered appeal of merits of summary judgment moot); *see* **City of Dallas v. Albert**, 354 S.W.3d 368, 375 (Tex.2011); **Travelers Ins.**, 315 S.W.3d at 862. Pleadings filed by the defendant after the nonsuit will not continue the suit. *See* **Ault v. Mulanax**, 724 S.W.2d 824, 828 (Tex.App.—Texarkana 1986, orig. proceeding).

§6.2 Effect on refiling suit.

1. Rule. In most cases, when the court signs an order on the plaintiff's nonsuit dismissing the suit without prejudice, the plaintiff can refile the same suit. **Epps v. Fowler**, 351 S.W.3d 862, 869 (Tex.2011); **In re Team Rocket, L.P.**, 256 S.W.3d 257, 259 (Tex.2008); **Aetna Cas. & Sur. Co. v. Specia**, 849 S.W.2d 805, 806 (Tex.1993).

2. Exceptions.

(1) After statute of limitations. An attempt to litigate a claim that was earlier dismissed on a nonsuit (or a compulsory counterclaim to the nonsuited claim) is barred if the statute of limitations has run on the claim by the time the second suit is filed. *See* **Weiman v. Addicks-Fairbanks Rd. Sand Co.**, 846 S.W.2d 414, 421 (Tex.App.—Houston [14th Dist.] 1992, writ denied) (compulsory counterclaim); **Guaranty Cty. Mut. Ins. v. Reyna**, 700 S.W.2d 325, 327 (Tex.App.—San Antonio 1985) (nonsuit), *writ ref'd n.r.e.*, 709 S.W.2d 647 (Tex.1986); *see, e.g.*, **Bailey v. Gardner**, 154 S.W.3d 917, 920 (Tex.App.—Dallas 2005, no pet.) (statute of limitations not tolled when P made tactical decision to nonsuit claim because expert was unavailable; refiling of suit barred by statute of limitations).

(2) After summary judgment. A plaintiff cannot escape the effect of a summary judgment on a claim by taking a nonsuit. **Hyundai Motor Co. v. Alvarado**, 892 S.W.2d 853, 854–55 (Tex.1995). When a plaintiff takes a nonsuit on a claim that was resolved by a partial summary judgment, the claim is considered dismissed with prejudice. *Id.* at 855; *see* **Mobley v. Mobley**, 506 S.W.3d 87, 91–92 (Tex.App.—Texarkana 2016, no pet.). After the court grants a partial summary judgment, the plaintiff may take a nonsuit only on the unadjudicated claims. *See* **Hyundai Motor**, 892 S.W.2d at 855.

§6.3 Effect on defendant's claims. When the court signs an order on the plaintiff's nonsuit, the dismissal does not prevent the defendant or intervenor from being heard on its own claims for affirmative relief. Tex. R. Civ. P. 96, 162; **City of Dallas v. Albert**, 354 S.W.3d 368, 375 (Tex.2011); **Epps v. Fowler**, 351 S.W.3d 862, 868 (Tex.2011); **In re Greater Houston Orthopaedic Specialists, Inc.**, 295 S.W.3d 323, 324 (Tex.2009); **Villafani v. Trejo**, 251 S.W.3d 466, 469 (Tex.2008); **BHP Pet. Co. v. Millard**, 800 S.W.2d 838, 840–41 (Tex.1990); *see* **Austin State Hosp. v. Graham**, 347 S.W.3d 298, 301 (Tex.2011); *see also* **Klein v. Dooley**, 949 S.W.2d 307, 308 (Tex.1997) (nonsuit does not affect D's derivative DTPA claim for costs and attorney fees). Not all claims are claims for affirmative relief under TRCP 162.

1. Independent of P's claim. For a claim to qualify as a claim for affirmative relief under TRCP 162, it must allege the defendant has a cause of action on which it can recover independent of the plaintiff's claim, even if the plaintiff abandons or is unable to establish its claims. **UTMB v. Estate of Blackmon**, 195 S.W.3d 98, 101 (Tex.2006); **General Land Office v. OXY U.S.A., Inc.**, 789 S.W.2d 569, 570 (Tex.1990); *see, e.g.*, **Ulloa v. Davila**, 860 S.W.2d 202, 204 (Tex.App.—San Antonio 1993, no writ) (counterclaim did more than resist Ps' suit). The following are examples of independent claims: • An intervening insurance carrier's subrogation claim. **Texas Mut. Ins. v. Ledbetter**, 251 S.W.3d 31, 38 (Tex.2008). • A defendant's request for a declaratory judgment if it seeks resolution of continuing issues. **BHP Pet.**, 800 S.W.2d at 842. • A defendant's motion to dismiss under the Texas Citizens Participation Act seeking dismissal with prejudice, attorney fees,

and sanctions. **Gaskamp v. WSP USA, Inc.**, 596 S.W.3d 457, 468–69 (Tex.App.—Houston [1st Dist.] 2020, pet. filed 5-5-20); **Rauhauser v. McGibney**, 508 S.W.3d 377, 381–82 (Tex.App.—Fort Worth 2014, no pet.), *overruled on other grounds*, **Sullivan v. Abraham**, 488 S.W.3d 294 (Tex.2016); *see* **Walker v. Hartman**, 516 S.W.3d 71, 80 (Tex.App.—Beaumont 2017, pet. denied). • A request for attorney fees if the defendant pleads a claim for which damages and attorney fees are recoverable. *See* **Leon Springs Gas Co. v. Restaurant Equip. Leasing Co.**, 961 S.W.2d 574, 578 (Tex.App.—San Antonio 1997, no pet.). • A request to compel arbitration. **Quanto Int'l Co. v. Lloyd**, 897 S.W.2d 482, 487 (Tex.App.—Houston [1st Dist.] 1995, orig. proceeding); *see* **Joe Williamson Constr. Co. v. Raymondville ISD**, 251 S.W.3d 800, 805–06 (Tex.App.—Corpus Christi 2008, no pet.). *Contra* **In re Riggs**, 315 S.W.3d 613, 615 & n.2 (Tex.App.—Fort Worth 2010, orig. proceeding).

2. Derivative of P's claim. A claim that mirrors the controlling issues in a case is not an independent claim for affirmative relief. **In re Estate of Kidd**, 812 S.W.2d 356, 359 (Tex.App.—Amarillo 1991, writ denied). The following are examples of derivative claims: • A defendant's request for a declaratory judgment that seeks a finding of no liability. **BHP Pet.**, 800 S.W.2d at 841. • A request for attorney fees when a defendant claims them solely for the defense of the plaintiff's suit. **Polansky v. Berenji**, 393 S.W.3d 362, 367 (Tex.App.—Austin 2012, no pet.); **Smith v. Texas Farmers Ins.**, 82 S.W.3d 580, 588–89 (Tex.App.—San Antonio 2002, pet. denied). *Contra* **In re C.A.S.**, 128 S.W.3d 681, 686 (Tex.App.—Dallas 2003, no pet.); **In re Frost Nat'l Bank**, 103 S.W.3d 647, 650 (Tex.App.—Corpus Christi 2003, orig. proceeding). • A counterclaim that asks for indemnity, contribution, or costs. **Pleasants v. Emmons**, 871 S.W.2d 296, 298 (Tex.App.—Eastland 1994, no writ).

§6.4 Effect on venue. Whether a motion to transfer venue fixes venue in the county of the defendant's choice when the plaintiff's case is dismissed on a nonsuit depends on the state of the record at the time the nonsuit was filed. **GeoChem Tech v. Verseckes**, 962 S.W.2d 541, 543 (Tex.1998). The venue facts in the plaintiff's petition, the motion to transfer venue, and any response must be examined to determine whether the defendant established a prima facie case of venue. *See id.*

1. Before D files venue motion. If the plaintiff takes a nonsuit before the defendant files a motion to transfer venue, the dismissal does not fix venue in the county where the plaintiff first filed suit unless the plaintiff's petition alleged facts invoking a mandatory-venue provision. *See* **Peysen v. Dawson**, 974 S.W.2d 377, 380 (Tex.App.—San Antonio 1998, no pet.) (because only venue fact in P's petition was that one of Ds lived in Bexar County, it was a county of permissive venue, not mandatory venue). Venue is not fixed merely by filing suit. **Hyman Farm Serv. v. Earth Oil & Gas Co.**, 920 S.W.2d 452, 456 (Tex.App.—Amarillo 1996, no writ).

2. Before court rules on D's motion. If the plaintiff takes a nonsuit after the defendant files a motion to transfer venue but before the court rules on the motion, the motion to transfer fixes venue in the county of the defendant's choice if the uncontradicted venue facts compel venue in that county. *See* **GeoChem Tech**, 962 S.W.2d at 543–44 (venue facts in Ds' motions permitted P to refile in either of two counties of mandatory venue).

3. After court rules on D's motion. If the plaintiff takes a nonsuit after the trial court grants the defendant's motion to transfer venue, the ruling fixes venue if the suit is later refiled. **In re Team Rocket, L.P.**, 256 S.W.3d 257, 260 (Tex.2008); **Le v. Kilpatrick**, 112 S.W.3d 631, 633 (Tex.App.—Tyler 2003, no pet.); **Hendrick Med. Ctr. v. Howell**, 690 S.W.2d 42, 44 (Tex.App.—Dallas 1985, orig. proceeding).

§6.5 Effect on injunction. When the underlying suit is dismissed by a nonsuit, any temporary injunction is automatically dissolved and any appeal becomes moot. **General Land Office v. OXY U.S.A., Inc.**, 789 S.W.2d 569, 571 (Tex.1990).

§6.6 Effect on motion to dismiss baseless cause of action. When a plaintiff files a nonsuit after a defendant has filed a motion to dismiss the plaintiff's cause of action on the ground that it has no basis in law or fact, the court cannot rule on the motion to dismiss if the nonsuit is filed at least three days before the hearing date. Tex. R. Civ. P. 91a.5(a); *see* Tex. R. Civ. P. 91a.5(c) & cmt. That is, a timely filed nonsuit precludes the court from ruling on the motion. *See* Tex. R. Civ. P. 91a.5(a), (c). See "Motion to Dismiss—Baseless Cause of Action," ch. 3-H, §1 et seq.

§6.7 Effect on attorney fees. When the plaintiff takes a nonsuit, the defendant, as a prevailing party, may be entitled to attorney fees as provided by an attorney-fees provision in a written contract. *See* **Epps v. Fowler**, 351 S.W.3d 862, 865 (Tex.2011). See "Attorney Fees Under Written Contract," **O'Connor's Texas Causes of Action**, ch. 45-C, §1 et seq. (2021 ed.). If the contract does not define who is a prevailing party, the defendant's right to recover attorney fees is determined by whether the nonsuit was ordered with or without prejudice.

1. With prejudice. When the plaintiff takes a nonsuit with prejudice, the defendant is the prevailing party and is entitled to attorney fees. **Epps**, 351 S.W.3d at 868. Under res judicata, a nonsuit with prejudice makes a permanent and inalterable change in the parties' legal relationship because the plaintiff cannot sue the defendant again for a claim arising from the same subject matter. *Id.* at 868–69.

2. Without prejudice.

(1) Generally. When the plaintiff takes a nonsuit without prejudice, the defendant is generally not a prevailing party because the parties' legal relationship has not changed; the plaintiff can seek the same relief by refiling the same claims. **Epps**, 351 S.W.3d at 869.

Note

*The mere possibility that limitations would bar future suits does not make a defendant a prevailing party. **Epps**, 351 S.W.3d at 869 n.8. There is no material change in the parties' legal relationship unless the defendant has secured a favorable ruling on a res judicata defense. Id.*

(2) Plaintiff avoided unfavorable ruling. When the plaintiff takes a nonsuit without prejudice, a defendant is a prevailing party and is entitled to attorney fees if the court finds that the plaintiff took the nonsuit to avoid an unfavorable ruling on the merits. **Epps**, 351 S.W.3d at 870.

(a) Defendant's motion. The defendant must ask the court to find that the plaintiff took the nonsuit to avoid an unfavorable ruling on the merits. **Epps**, 351 S.W.3d at 870. Factors that may support the defendant's motion include the following:

[1] The plaintiff nonsuited after a motion for summary judgment was filed. *Id.* at 871; *e.g.*, **Referente v. City View Courtyard, L.P.**, 477 S.W.3d 882, 886–87 (Tex.App.—Houston [1st Dist.] 2015, no pet.) (Ps nonsuited one year after summary-judgment motion was filed and six days before motion's submission date).

[2] The plaintiff's failure to respond to requests for admissions or other discovery that could support entry of an adverse judgment was unexcused. **Epps**, 351 S.W.3d at 871. The defendant's motion will not be successful, however, if the plaintiff shows that later discovery revealed flaws in the plaintiff's claims that were not present when the claims were filed. *Id.*; *see, e.g.*, **Referente**, 477 S.W.3d at 887–88 (Ps offered no evidence of postfiling change in law or discovery of unknown flaws in their claims that caused them to nonsuit; nonsuit was to avoid unfavorable ruling on merits).

[3] The plaintiff did not timely identify experts or other critical witnesses. **Epps**, 351 S.W.3d at 871.

[4] There are procedural obstacles to receiving a favorable ruling, such as the plaintiff's inability to join necessary parties. *Id.*

(b) Evidence. To determine if the plaintiff took the nonsuit to avoid an unfavorable ruling, the court should rely on the record and affidavits as much as possible and should take live testimony only in rare instances. **Epps**, 351 S.W.3d at 870.

§6.8 Effect on sanctions.

1. Timing of motion. A party can bring a motion for sanctions before or after the nonsuit, as long as the motion is filed while the court retains plenary power. **Crites v. Collins**, 284 S.W.3d 839, 843 (Tex.2009); *see* **In re Bennett**, 960 S.W.2d 35, 38 (Tex.1997); **Scott & White Mem'l Hosp. v. Schexnider**, 940 S.W.2d 594, 596 (Tex.1996). Once the court's plenary power expires, the court can no longer impose sanctions. **Crites**, 284 S.W.3d at 843; **Schexnider**, 940 S.W.2d at 596.

2. Order for sanctions. Whether a particular order for sanctions survives a nonsuit and can later be enforced or appealed depends on the purpose of the sanction. **Villafani v. Trejo**, 251 S.W.3d 466, 470 (Tex.2008).

(1) Sanction does not survive nonsuit. If a sanction serves no purpose beyond the specific proceeding, the sanctions order does not survive the nonsuit. **Villafani**, 251 S.W.3d at 470. For example, an order excluding a witness as a

discovery sanction does not survive a nonsuit because the reason for the sanction—to ensure a party is afforded a fair trial—no longer matters. *Id.* Similarly, an order excluding evidence as a discovery sanction usually does not survive the dismissal and refiling of the same suit. *See, e.g.*, **Schein v. American Rest. Grp.**, 852 S.W.2d 496, 497 (Tex.1993) (sanction for failure to respond to interrogatories and request for production); **Aetna Cas. & Sur. Co. v. Specia**, 849 S.W.2d 805, 807 (Tex.1993) (sanction for failure to supplement discovery).

(2) Sanction survives nonsuit. If the sanction may serve a purpose beyond the specific proceeding, the sanctions order survives the nonsuit. **Villafani**, 251 S.W.3d at 470; *see* **Crites**, 284 S.W.3d at 842. For example, monetary sanctions survive a nonsuit because they may serve compensatory and punitive purposes. **Villafani**, 251 S.W.3d at 470. Similarly, dismissal with prejudice as a sanction survives a nonsuit because the sanction serves to deter meritless claims. *E.g.*, **CTL/Thompson Tex., LLC v. Starwood Homeowner's Ass'n**, 390 S.W.3d 299, 300–01 (Tex.2013) (motion to dismiss claim for damages from services provided by architect, engineer, or surveyor under CPRC §150.002); **Villafani**, 251 S.W.3d at 470–71 (motion to dismiss health-care-liability claim); *see, e.g.*, **Rauhauser v. McGibney**, 508 S.W.3d 377, 381–82 (Tex.App.—Fort Worth 2014, no pet.) (motion to dismiss claim based on exercise of free speech under Texas Citizens Participation Act), *overruled on other grounds*, **Sullivan v. Abraham**, 488 S.W.3d 294 (Tex.2016). Thus, when a sanctions order would survive a nonsuit, the sanctions or the denial of those sanctions can still be appealed. *See* **CTL/Thompson**, 390 S.W.3d at 300–01; **Villafani**, 251 S.W.3d at 470.

§6.9 Effect on finality of judgment. If the nonsuit specifically disposes of the last remaining claim in the suit, the order on the nonsuit is a final, appealable judgment. *See* **Unifund CCR Partners v. Villa**, 299 S.W.3d 92, 96–97 (Tex.2009); **Crites v. Collins**, 284 S.W.3d 839, 840–41 (Tex.2009); **Coastal Banc SSB v. Helle**, 48 S.W.3d 796, 799–800 (Tex.App.—Corpus Christi 2001, pet. denied). See "Judgment actually disposes of all parties & claims," ch. 9-C, §6.3.1(2)(a)[2]. If the nonsuit disposes of some claims but other, unadjudicated claims remain, the order on the nonsuit is interlocutory. *See* **Crites**, 284 S.W.3d at 840 (order of nonsuit does not necessarily dispose of any cross-actions, such as motion for sanctions, unless they are specifically disposed of in the order); *see, e.g.*, **Law Offices of Windle Turley, P.C. v. French**, 109 S.W.3d 599, 601 (Tex.App.—Dallas 2003, no pet.) (nonsuit order that did not specifically state it was a final judgment or dispose of all claims was interlocutory); **In re Romero**, 956 S.W.2d 659, 662 (Tex.App.—San Antonio 1997, orig. proceeding) (because nonsuit order dismissing P's claim against D did not dispose of the insurer's subrogation claim, it was interlocutory). For a discussion of when an interlocutory judgment becomes final, see "Interlocutory judgments—merger or severance," ch. 9-C, §6.3.1(2)(b).

§7. Reinstatement of nonsuited case

The nonsuit does not divest the trial court of jurisdiction. **Quanto Int'l Co. v. Lloyd**, 897 S.W.2d 482, 485 (Tex.App.—Houston [1st Dist.] 1995, orig. proceeding); *see* **Missouri Pac. R.R. v. Whitaker**, 815 S.W.2d 348, 349 n.2 (Tex.App.—Tyler 1991, orig. proceeding). Thus, at any time while the trial court has plenary power over its judgment, a party may ask the court to set aside the nonsuit and reinstate the case. **Trimble v. Financial Freedom Senior Funding Corp.**, __ S.W.3d __, 2016 WL 7368059 (Tex.App.—Houston [1st Dist.] 2016, no pet.) (No. 01-15-00851-CV; 12-20-16); **Missouri Pac. R.R.**, 815 S.W.2d at 349 n.2. The parties may also file an agreed motion to reinstate the case. *See* **McClendon v. State Farm Mut. Auto. Ins.**, 796 S.W.2d 229, 233 (Tex.App.—El Paso 1990, writ denied). The motion to set aside a nonsuited case can be labeled a motion to reinstate after nonsuit, a motion to set aside the nonsuit, a motion to withdraw the nonsuit, or even a motion for new trial. *See, e.g.*, **Osborne v. St. Luke's Episcopal Hosp.**, 915 S.W.2d 906, 909 (Tex.App.—Houston [1st Dist.] 1996, writ denied) (motion to set aside nonsuit); **Quanto Int'l**, 897 S.W.2d at 484 (motion to reinstate); **Golodetz Trading Corp. v. Curland**, 886 S.W.2d 503, 504 (Tex.App.—Houston [1st Dist.] 1994, no writ) (motion to withdraw nonsuit). See **O'Connor's Texas Civil Forms**, FORM 7F:3 (2020 ed.).

Note

A motion to reinstate a nonsuited case is not a motion to reinstate under TRCP 165a, which governs reinstatement of cases dismissed for want of prosecution. See ***In re Simon Prop. Grp.***, *985 S.W.2d 212, 214 (Tex.App.—Corpus Christi 1999, orig. proceeding).*

§8. Review

§8.1 Appeal.

1. Plaintiff's right to appeal. Taking a nonsuit does not prevent the plaintiff from challenging any action of the trial court before the nonsuit was taken. *E.g.*, **Felderhoff v. Knauf**, 819 S.W.2d 110, 111 (Tex.1991) (after nonsuit, P appealed sanctions imposed by trial court before nonsuit).

2. Defendant's right to appeal.

(1) No claim for affirmative relief. If a plaintiff takes a nonsuit against a defendant who has no outstanding claims for affirmative relief, the defendant is no longer a party to the suit and does not have standing to appeal. *See, e.g.*, **United Oil & Minerals, Inc. v. Costilla Energy, Inc.**, 1 S.W.3d 840, 844 (Tex.App.—Corpus Christi 1999, pet. dism'd) (party nonsuited by amended petition had no standing to appeal final judgment); **Preston v. American Eagle Ins.**, 948 S.W.2d 18, 21 (Tex.App.—Dallas 1997, no writ) (persons nonsuited before summary judgment had no standing to appeal judgment). When the plaintiff nonsuits its claims, there is no longer a case or controversy, and the court of appeals has no jurisdiction over the suit. *See, e.g.*, **UTMB v. Estate of Blackmon**, 195 S.W.3d 98, 101 (Tex.2006) (after P nonsuited case, court had no jurisdiction to issue order on D's interlocutory appeal from its plea to the jurisdiction).

(2) Claim for affirmative relief. If the plaintiff takes a nonsuit against a defendant who has an affirmative claim for relief, the nonsuit does not prevent the defendant from appealing the trial court's ruling on that claim even if the ruling occurred before the nonsuit. **Villafani v. Trejo**, 251 S.W.3d 466, 470 (Tex.2008); *see* **Hernandez v. Ebrom**, 289 S.W.3d 316, 317 (Tex.2009).

3. Appellate deadlines. The appellate timetable runs from the signing date of whatever order makes a judgment final and appealable—that is, the order that disposes of any parties or issues remaining in the case after the nonsuit. **Martinez v. Humble Sand & Gravel, Inc.**, 875 S.W.2d 311, 313 (Tex.1994); *see* **Crites v. Collins**, 284 S.W.3d 839, 840–41 (Tex.2009); **Builders First Source-S.Tex., LP v. Ortiz**, 515 S.W.3d 451, 457 (Tex.App.—Houston [14th Dist.] 2017, pet. denied). If no other claims remain in the case after a nonsuit, the appellate deadlines run from the date the court signed the order of nonsuit. **In re Bennett**, 960 S.W.2d 35, 38 (Tex.1997); **Farmer v. Ben E. Keith Co.**, 907 S.W.2d 495, 496 (Tex.1995). If other claims remain in the case after a nonsuit, the appellate deadlines run from the date the court signed the final judgment or the date the court severed the claim from the rest of the case. See "What judgments are final," ch. 9-C, §6.3. The period within which a party must perfect an appeal is calculated from the date the order or judgment was signed, not from the filing of the notice of nonsuit. **Farmer**, 907 S.W.2d at 496.

4. Plenary power. The court retains plenary power over an order of dismissal for 30 days after the date it signs the order. **America's Favorite Chicken Co. v. Galvan**, 897 S.W.2d 874, 876 (Tex.App.—San Antonio 1995, writ denied); **Harris Cty. Appr. Dist. v. Wittig**, 881 S.W.2d 193, 194 (Tex.App.—Houston [1st Dist.] 1994, orig. proceeding). If certain post-trial motions are filed, the court retains plenary power for as long as 105 days after the judgment is signed. See "Effect of PPE motions," ch. 9-C, §6.4.2.

§8.2 Mandamus. If a trial court refuses to grant a plaintiff's timely motion for nonsuit and there are no other pending claims, the plaintiff may seek mandamus relief. **In re Greater Houston Orthopaedic Specialists, Inc.**, 295 S.W.3d 323, 326 (Tex.2009); **Hooks v. Fourth Ct. of Appeals**, 808 S.W.2d 56, 59 (Tex.1991); *see* **Greenberg v. Brookshire**, 640 S.W.2d 870, 872 (Tex.1982). If a trial court reinstates a nonsuited case over the plaintiff's objection, the plaintiff may seek mandamus relief. **Johnson v. Harless**, 651 S.W.2d 259, 260 (Tex.1983); **Quanto Int'l Co. v. Lloyd**, 897 S.W.2d 482, 485 (Tex.App.—Houston [1st Dist.] 1995, orig. proceeding).

G. Involuntary Dismissal

§1. General

§1.1 Rule. Tex. R. Civ. P. 165a.

§1.2 Purpose. The purpose of a dismissal is to dispose of the case without a trial.

§1.3 Timetables & forms. Appeal After Late Notice of Judgment, **O'Connor's Texas Civil Appeals**, Appendix IV, Timetable 3 (2020 ed.); Appeal of Dismissal for Want of Prosecution, **O'Connor's Texas Civil Appeals**, Appendix IV, Timetable 7 (2020 ed.); **O'Connor's Texas Civil Forms**, FORM 7G:1 (2020 ed.).

§1.4 Other references. **O'Connor's Texas Causes of Action** (2021 ed.).

§2. Grounds for dismissal

To be entitled to a dismissal in a Texas court, the defendant must make some complaint about the plaintiff's lawsuit or conduct that, if not cured, entitles the defendant to move for a dismissal.

§2.1 Bar to suit. Most requests to dismiss are made as part of another motion alleging that the plaintiff cannot maintain the suit as filed. The defendant must prove there is a bar to the plaintiff's suit or a defect in the pleadings, the court, the parties, or the claim for liability that cannot be cured by amendment. The following are some of the grounds that bar a suit:

1. The trial court does not have jurisdiction over the defendant or its property. See "Special Appearance—Challenging Personal Jurisdiction," ch. 3-B, §1 et seq.

2. A Texas court is not the appropriate forum for the lawsuit. See "Forum Non Conveniens—Challenging the Texas Forum," ch. 3-D, §1 et seq. If the court sustains a motion to dismiss on the ground of forum non conveniens, it may either dismiss or stay the suit.

3. The trial court does not have subject-matter jurisdiction. See "Plea to the Jurisdiction—Challenging the Court," ch. 3-F, §1 et seq.

4. The case is moot. See "Mootness," ch. 3-F, §3.4.

5. The plaintiff's petition does not state a cause of action against the defendant. See "Special Exceptions—Challenging the Pleadings," ch. 3-G, §1 et seq.; "Motion to Abate—Challenging the Suit," ch. 3-I, §1 et seq.

6. The cause of action has no basis in law or fact. See "Motion to Dismiss—Baseless Cause of Action," ch. 3-H, §1 et seq.

7. The legal action is based on, related to, or in response to the defendant's exercise of its right to free speech, right to petition, or right of association. See "Motion to Dismiss—Anti-SLAPP Motion," ch. 3-K, §1 et seq.

§2.2 Failure to prosecute. An unreasonable delay in the prosecution of a case raises a presumption that the plaintiff has abandoned the case, thus justifying dismissal if the plaintiff does not sufficiently explain the delay after the defendant has moved for dismissal. *E.g.*, **In re Conner**, 458 S.W.3d 532, 534-35 (Tex.2015) (when Ps did not provide good cause for almost ten-year delay, trial court abused its discretion in disregarding conclusive presumption of abandonment and not dismissing case). For a discussion of how a plaintiff can reinstate a case after it is dismissed for want of prosecution, see "Motion to reinstate," ch. 10-F, §3. The trial court's authority to dismiss for want of prosecution comes from two sources: TRCP 165a and the court's inherent power. **In re Conner**, 458 S.W.3d at 534; **Villarreal v. San Antonio Truck & Equip.**, 994 S.W.2d 628, 630 (Tex.1999).

1. TRCP 165a. A trial court may dismiss a suit under TRCP 165a for failure of a party to (1) appear at trial or a hearing after receiving notice or (2) dispose of the case within the time standards. **In re Conner**, 458 S.W.3d at 535; **Villarreal**, 994 S.W.2d at 630. See **O'Connor's Texas Civil Forms**, FORM 7G:1 (2020 ed.).

(1) Failure to appear. The court has the authority under TRCP 165a(1) to dismiss a suit when a party seeking affirmative relief (generally the plaintiff) does not appear at trial or another hearing after receiving notice of the setting.

Tex. R. Civ. P. 165a(1); **Alexander v. Lynda's Boutique**, 134 S.W.3d 845, 851 (Tex.2004); *see, e.g.*, **Degen v. General Coatings, Inc.**, 705 S.W.2d 734, 735 (Tex.App.—Houston [14th Dist.] 1986, no writ) (docket call was not hearing or trial; court could not dismiss suit under TRCP 165a for failure to appear at docket call). Before dismissing the suit, the court must give the plaintiff notice of its intent to dismiss and a date and time for the dismissal hearing. Tex. R. Civ. P. 165a(1). See "Notice of intent to dismiss," ch. 7-G, §3. A separate notice of intent to dismiss is not required, however, if the court specifies in the notice of trial or hearing that a party's failure to appear may result in dismissal. *E.g.*, **Alexander**, 134 S.W.3d at 851–52 (pretrial-conference order stated failure to appear could result in dismissal); *see, e.g.*, **Bridwell v. Mulder**, 315 S.W.3d 657, 659 (Tex.App.—Dallas 2010, no pet.) (notice of trial setting stated failure to appear would result in dismissal). See "Dismissal for failure to appear," ch. 10-F, §3.4.1.

(2) Failure to comply with time standards. The court has the authority under TRCP 165a(2) to dismiss a suit that was not disposed of within the time limits in the Rules of Judicial Administration. **In re Conner**, 458 S.W.3d at 535; **Polk v. Southwest Crossing Homeowners Ass'n**, 165 S.W.3d 89, 96 (Tex.App.—Houston [14th Dist.] 2005, pet. denied); **Johnson-Snodgrass v. KTAO, Inc.**, 75 S.W.3d 84, 87 (Tex.App.—Fort Worth 2002, pet. dism'd). Rule 6 of the Rules of Judicial Administration provides that civil jury cases (other than family-law cases) should be brought to trial or final disposition within 18 months after the appearance date, and civil nonjury cases (other than family-law cases) within 12 months after the appearance date. Tex. R. Jud. Admin. 6.1(a); *see* **In re Conner**, 458 S.W.3d at 535 (civil jury cases). Contested family-law cases should be disposed of within six months and uncontested family-law cases within three months. Tex. R. Jud. Admin. 6.1(b). See "Failure to comply with time standards," ch. 10-F, §3.4.2(2).

2. Inherent power. Under the common law, the trial court has the inherent power to dismiss—independent of its authority under TRCP 165a—when a plaintiff does not prosecute its case with diligence. **Villarreal**, 994 S.W.2d at 630; **Binner v. Limestone Cty.**, 129 S.W.3d 710, 712 (Tex.App.—Waco 2004, pet. denied); *see* **Rizk v. Mayad**, 603 S.W.2d 773, 776 (Tex.1980); **Veterans' Land Bd. v. Williams**, 543 S.W.2d 89, 90 (Tex.1976). Factors the court may consider when deciding whether to dismiss under its inherent power include (1) the length of time the case was on file, (2) the extent of activity in the case, (3) whether a trial setting was requested, and (4) whether there were any reasonable excuses for the delay. **Texas Mut. Ins. v. Olivas**, 323 S.W.3d 266, 274 (Tex.App.—El Paso 2010, no pet.); **Maida v. Fire Ins. Exch.**, 990 S.W.2d 836, 842 (Tex.App.—Fort Worth 1999, no pet.). See "Inherent power," ch. 10-F, §3.4.2(3).

§2.3 Sanctions. Some rules and code provisions permit the trial court to strike pleadings or dismiss a suit as a sanction. *See, e.g.*, Tex. Civ. Prac. & Rem. Code §9.012(e) (groundless suit); Tex. R. Civ. P. 13 (frivolous pleadings), Tex. R. Civ. P. 215.2(b)(5) (discovery abuse). See "Groundless or frivolous pleadings," ch. 1-B, §3.3; "Conduct that justifies sanctions," ch. 5-K, §5; "Motion for discovery sanctions," ch. 6-A, §23.

§2.4 Frivolous indigent suit. The trial court has the authority to dismiss a suit filed by an indigent if the trial court finds that (1) the allegation of poverty in the affidavit is false or (2) the action is frivolous or malicious. See "Summary dismissal," ch. 2-J, §6.

§2.5 Medical-malpractice suit—no expert report. When a plaintiff in a medical-malpractice suit does not comply with the provisions for filing an expert report under CPRC §74.351(a), the defendant may move to dismiss under CPRC §74.351(b)(2). See "Expert report," **O'Connor's Texas Causes of Action**, ch. 20-A, §7.2 (2021 ed.).

§2.6 Improper grounds for dismissal.

1. Conflict in trial settings. The trial court cannot dismiss a suit if the party informs the court that its attorney is in another trial. *See, e.g.*, **Dancy v. Daggett**, 815 S.W.2d 548, 549 (Tex.1991) (attorney in criminal trial in federal court); **Seigle v. Hollech**, 892 S.W.2d 201, 203–04 (Tex.App.—Houston [14th Dist.] 1994, no writ) (attorney in criminal trial in state court). *But see* **Burton v. Hoffman**, 959 S.W.2d 351, 352–53 (Tex.App.—Austin 1998, no pet.) (dismissal upheld when attorney knew of conflicting trial settings but waited until Friday before Monday setting to seek continuance and sent associate to argue motion who then refused to put on evidence when given opportunity).

2. Special exceptions. A court cannot dismiss a party's suit after sustaining special exceptions without giving the party the opportunity to amend its pleadings to cure the defect. See "Court sustains special exceptions," ch. 3-G, §9.2.2.

3. Summary judgment. A summary judgment should not state that the case is dismissed. See "Resolve issues on the merits," ch. 7-B, §12.3.3.

§3. Notice of intent to dismiss

A trial court generally cannot dismiss a suit without giving the plaintiff notice of its intent to dismiss. **Alexander v. Lynda's Boutique**, 134 S.W.3d 845, 852 (Tex.2004); **Villarreal v. San Antonio Truck & Equip.**, 994 S.W.2d 628, 630 (Tex.1999); **Creel v. District Atty.**, 818 S.W.2d 45, 46 (Tex.1991). A dismissal without notice violates the party's due-process rights and must be reversed. **Villarreal**, 994 S.W.2d at 630; **Saldana v. Hinojosa**, 517 S.W.3d 239, 241 (Tex.App.—San Antonio 2017, no pet.); **Smith v. McKee**, 145 S.W.3d 299, 302 (Tex.App.—Fort Worth 2004, no pet.); **Hubert v. Illinois State Assistance Comm'n**, 867 S.W.2d 160, 163 (Tex.App.—Houston [14th Dist.] 1993, no writ). For the exception, see "Dismissal without notice," ch. 7-G, §3.2.

§3.1 Requirements.

1. Identify grounds for dismissal. The notice to dismiss must state whether the dismissal is under TRCP 165a(1) for failure to appear, under TRCP 165a(2) for failure to comply with the Supreme Court's time standards, or under the court's inherent power for failure to diligently prosecute the suit. *See* **Alexander v. Lynda's Boutique**, 134 S.W.3d 845, 850 (Tex.2004); **Villarreal v. San Antonio Truck & Equip.**, 994 S.W.2d 628, 630–31 & n.4 (Tex.1999); **Saldana v. Hinojosa**, 517 S.W.3d 239, 243 (Tex.App.—San Antonio 2017, no pet.). The trial court cannot dismiss on a ground that is not stated in the notice of dismissal. *See* **Villarreal**, 994 S.W.2d at 631–32 (notice under TRCP 165a(1) does not support dismissal under TRCP 165a(2) or inherent power); **Johnson-Snodgrass v. KTAO, Inc.**, 75 S.W.3d 84, 88 (Tex.App.—Fort Worth 2002, pet. dism'd) (notice under TRCP 165a does not support dismissal under inherent power); **Lopez v. Harding**, 68 S.W.3d 78, 81 (Tex.App.—Dallas 2001, no pet.) (same). *But see* **Steward v. Colonial Cas. Ins.**, 143 S.W.3d 161, 164 (Tex.App.—Waco 2004, no pet.) (notice under TRCP 165a is sufficient without specific reference to subsection (1) or (2)).

2. Sent to party or attorney. TRCP 165a(1) requires the clerk of the trial court to mail a notice of the court's intention to dismiss the suit to either the attorneys of record or the parties (if pro se). See "Sent to attorney or pro se party," ch. 1-H, §6.1.

(1) Notice to attorneys. TRCP 165a(1) requires the clerk to send a notice of the court's intent to dismiss to "each attorney of record." **Ginn v. Forrester**, 282 S.W.3d 430, 432 (Tex.2009); **Alexander**, 134 S.W.3d at 851; *e.g.*, **Cannon v. ICO Tubular Servs.**, 905 S.W.2d 380, 388 (Tex.App.—Houston [1st Dist.] 1995, no writ) (dismissal reversed because notices not sent to all attorneys of record), *overruled on other grounds*, **Lane Bank Equip. Co. v. Smith S. Equip., Inc.**, 10 S.W.3d 308 (Tex.2000); *see also* **Kenley v. Quintana Pet. Corp.**, 931 S.W.2d 318, 320–21 (Tex.App.—San Antonio 1996, writ denied) (dismissal reversed because notice sent to attorney of record but not attorney in charge).

Note

The TRCPs do not state how the clerk should determine the attorney's current address. Some courts have interpreted TRCP 165a(1) as requiring that notices of intent to dismiss be sent to the attorney's address shown on the docket or the papers on file with the court. E.g., ***Perdue v. Patten Corp.****, 142 S.W.3d 596, 605 (Tex.App.—Austin 2004, no pet.);* ***Ewton v. Gayken****, 130 S.W.3d 382, 384 (Tex.App.—Beaumont 2004, pet. denied);* ***Osterloh v. Ohio Decorative Prods.****, 881 S.W.2d 580, 581–82 (Tex.App.—Houston [1st Dist.] 1994, no writ); see also* ***Dickerson v. Sonat Expl. Co.****, 975 S.W.2d 339, 341–42 (Tex.App.—Tyler 1998, pet. denied) (when notices are returned as undeliverable, court should reexamine file to determine whether there is evidence of more recent address). In other courts, clerks may use administrative tools such as attorney registers to help determine the address for notice. E.g.,* ***Marathon Pet. Co. v. Cherry Moving Co.****, 550 S.W.3d 791, 803–04 (Tex.App.—Houston [14th Dist.] 2018, no pet.).*

(2) Notice to pro se party. When a party is not represented by counsel, the notice must be sent to the party. Tex. R. Civ. P. 165a(1); **General Elec. Co. v. Falcon Ridge Apts., Jt.V.**, 811 S.W.2d 942, 943 (Tex.1991).

3. State when & where. The notice of intent to dismiss must identify the date and place of the dismissal hearing. Tex. R. Civ. P. 165a(1); **Ginn**, 282 S.W.3d at 433; **Alexander**, 134 S.W.3d at 851; **Brown v. Brookshires Grocery Store**, 10 S.W.3d 351, 353 (Tex.App.—Dallas 1999, pet. denied); **Rohus v. Licona**, 942 S.W.2d 111, 112 (Tex.App.—Houston [1st Dist.] 1997, no writ). The notice cannot merely state that the case will be dismissed if a timely motion to retain is not filed. **Cannon**, 905 S.W.2d at 388.

§3.2 Dismissal without notice. When an indigent's claim has "no arguable basis in law," neither CPRC §13.001 nor §14.003 requires the court to give the indigent notice of its intent to dismiss. See "No notice," ch. 2-J, §6.5.

§4. Response to threat of dismissal

§4.1 Motion to retain. When a case is set on the court's dismissal docket for want of prosecution, the plaintiff should file a verified motion to retain. *See* Tex. R. Civ. P. 165a(1). See **O'Connor's Texas Civil Forms**, FORM 7G:2 (2020 ed.). The motion to retain informs the court why the case should not be dismissed.

1. Grounds. The motion should show good cause for keeping the case on the docket and comply with any requirements stated in the notice of dismissal. *See* Tex. R. Civ. P. 165a(1); *see, e.g.*, **Villarreal v. San Antonio Truck & Equip.**, 994 S.W.2d 628, 632 (Tex.1999) (notice of dismissal only required D to appear and announce ready for trial; D did not have to show good cause); **Douglas v. American Title Co.**, No. 14-08-00676-CV, 2009 WL 3851674 (Tex.App.—Houston [14th Dist.] 2009, no pet.) (memo op.; 11-19-09) (dismissal without hearing was proper because P did not comply with requirements in notice that he file a verified motion to retain showing of good cause); **Nabelek v. Aldrich**, No. 14-04-00886-CV, 2006 WL 8451661 (Tex.App.—Houston [14th Dist.] 2006, no pet.) (memo op.; 6-22-06) (if court wanted D to argue good cause in motion to retain, court needed to state so in notice of dismissal).

2. Ruling. If the court retains the case, it must assign a trial date, and any continuances must be by court order. Tex. R. Civ. P. 165a(1). If the court dismisses the case, the plaintiff should file a motion to reinstate to inform the court why the dismissal was wrong. See "Motion to Reinstate After Dismissal for Want of Prosecution," ch. 10-F, §1 et seq.; **O'Connor's Texas Civil Forms**, FORM 10F:1 (2020 ed.).

§4.2 Response to motion to dismiss. When the dismissal is based on the defendant's motion to dismiss, the plaintiff should file a response to the motion challenging the grounds for dismissal; if the defendant's motion was verified and included affidavits, so should the plaintiff's response.

§5. Hearing

If the trial court dismisses a lawsuit without a hearing, the lack of a hearing raises due-process concerns. *See* **Creel v. District Atty.**, 818 S.W.2d 45, 46 (Tex.1991) (no notice or hearing). In a few situations, however, a motion to dismiss may be submitted for the trial court's ruling without a hearing.

§5.1 Bar to suit. If the trial court sustains a challenge to the continuation of the suit by a motion to abate, special exceptions, or some other motion, and the plaintiff fails to correct the problem, the case is ripe for dismissal. See "Move to dismiss," ch. 3-G, §9.4.1(1). In some cases, the hearing on the initial motion satisfies the requirements of due process (e.g., the hearing on a motion to abate). In other cases, another hearing is necessary to determine whether the plaintiff's attempt to correct the problem was sufficient to satisfy the court's order (e.g., if the plaintiff amends after special exceptions).

§5.2 DWOP. Before dismissing a case for want of prosecution, the court should conduct an oral hearing and give the plaintiff the opportunity to present evidence. *See* Tex. R. Civ. P. 165a(1) (court must send notice of intention to dismiss and date and place of dismissal); **Alexander v. Lynda's Boutique**, 134 S.W.3d 845, 852 (Tex.2004) (court must give party opportunity to be heard before dismissing); **Villarreal v. San Antonio Truck & Equip.**, 994 S.W.2d 628, 630 (Tex.1999) (same). If the court provided notice that failure to attend a hearing might result in dismissal for want of prosecution, the court may decide at that hearing to dismiss the case if the party seeking relief does not attend. **Alexander**, 134 S.W.3d at 852. The court is not required to hold a separate dismissal hearing to allow the party to explain its reasons for not appearing. *See id.*

§5.3 Sanctions. The court must hold a hearing before dismissing a case as a sanction. See "Hearing," ch. 5-K, §10.

§5.4 Frivolous indigent suit. To determine whether a hearing is necessary before the court can dismiss a suit filed by a party claiming indigency under TRCP 145, see "Hearing," ch. 2-J, §6.3.

§6. Order of dismissal

§6.1 Language of dismissal. When a court dismisses a case, the order should be drafted to dismiss the suit and nothing else. If the order purports to make any decision on the merits, it is reversible error. **Garcia-Marroquin v. Nueces Cty. Bail Bond Bd.**, 1 S.W.3d 366, 379 n.8 (Tex.App.—Corpus Christi 1999, no pet.); **Alvarado v. Magic Valley Elec. Co-op, Inc.**, 784 S.W.2d 729, 733 (Tex.App.—San Antonio 1990, writ denied). For example, the statement "plaintiff take nothing" constitutes a decision on the merits. **Garcia-Marroquin**, 1 S.W.3d at 379 n.8; **De La Garza v. Express-News Corp.**, 722 S.W.2d 251, 253 (Tex.App.—San Antonio 1986, no writ). It is unclear, however, whether the statement "all other relief is expressly denied" constitutes a decision on the merits. *Compare* **Alvarado**, 784 S.W.2d at 733 (statement is decision on merits), *and* **Patterson v. Herb Easley Motors, Inc.**, No. 2-04-351-CV, 2005 WL 2044671 (Tex.App.—Fort Worth 2005, no pet.) (memo op.; 8-25-05) (same), *with* **Christensen v. Chase Bank USA**, 304 S.W.3d 548, 553–54 (Tex.App.—Dallas 2009, pet. denied) (statement is not decision on merits).

§6.2 Type of dismissal. There are two types of dismissals: with and without prejudice. If the order of dismissal does not state that the case is dismissed with prejudice, the case is presumed to be dismissed without prejudice. **Greenwood v. Tillamook Country Smoker, Inc.**, 857 S.W.2d 654, 656 (Tex.App.—Houston [1st Dist.] 1993, no writ).

1. Without prejudice. In most cases, the trial court can dismiss only without prejudice.

(1) Failure to prosecute. The trial court should dismiss without prejudice for a failure to appear or prosecute under TRCP 165a or under the court's inherent power. *See* **Attorney Gen. v. Rideaux**, 838 S.W.2d 340, 342 (Tex.App.—Houston [1st Dist.] 1992, no writ) (failure to prosecute or to appear does not support dismissal with prejudice). Because a dismissal for want of prosecution is not a trial on the merits, a take-nothing judgment, which is the equivalent of a dismissal with prejudice, is inappropriate. **Attorney Gen. v. Abbs**, 812 S.W.2d 605, 608 (Tex.App.—Dallas 1991, no writ); *see* **Dick Poe Motors, Inc. v. DaimlerChrysler Corp.**, 169 S.W.3d 478, 484–85 (Tex.App.—El Paso 2005, no pet.); **Maldonado v. Puente**, 694 S.W.2d 86, 92 (Tex.App.—San Antonio 1985, no writ).

(2) No jurisdiction. In most cases, the trial court should dismiss without prejudice after it sustains a plea to the jurisdiction. See "Without prejudice—most pleas," ch. 3-F, §6.1.2(1).

(3) Special exceptions. In most cases, if a party refuses to amend after the court sustains special exceptions, the court should dismiss the objectionable claims without prejudice. See "Dismissal without prejudice," ch. 3-G, §9.5.3(2)(a).

(4) Case moot. A dismissal for mootness is not a ruling on the merits; thus, a case dismissed for mootness should be dismissed without prejudice. **Ritchey v. Vasquez**, 986 S.W.2d 611, 612 (Tex.1999).

2. With prejudice. In some cases, the trial court may dismiss all or part of a plaintiff's suit with prejudice.

(1) Sanctions. For groundless pleadings, the TRCPs permit a court to dismiss a suit or strike pleadings as a sanction. *See* Tex. R. Civ. P. 13, 215.2(b)(5); *see also* Tex. Civ. Prac. & Rem. Code §9.012(e) (permits court to dismiss a party or strike pleadings for groundless suit). For frivolous pleadings, CPRC §10.004 does not list dismissal as one of the sanctions available. When a case is dismissed as a sanction, the sanction is referred to as a "death-penalty" sanction. See "Motion for Sanctions," ch. 5-K, §1 et seq.

(2) Special exceptions. If a party refuses to amend after the court sustains special exceptions and the defect cannot be cured by amendment, the court can dismiss with prejudice. See "Dismissal with prejudice," ch. 3-G, §9.5.3(2)(b).

§6.3 Effect of dismissal.

1. Dismissal with prejudice. A dismissal with prejudice to refiling is a final determination on the merits. **Mossler v. Shields**, 818 S.W.2d 752, 754 (Tex.1991); *see* **Garcia-Marroquin v. Nueces Cty. Bail Bond Bd.**, 1 S.W.3d 366, 379 n.8 (Tex.App.—Corpus Christi 1999, no pet.) (take-nothing judgment is equivalent to decision on merits). Such a dismissal has full res judicata and collateral-estoppel effect, barring relitigation of the same cause of action or issues between

the same parties. **Williams v. TDCJ-Inst. Div.**, 176 S.W.3d 590, 594 (Tex.App.—Tyler 2005, pet. denied); *see* **Barr v. Resolution Trust Corp.**, 837 S.W.2d 627, 630–31 (Tex.1992); *see, e.g.*, **Hammonds v. Holmes**, 559 S.W.2d 345, 346–47 (Tex.1977) (P argued that second suit was brought in different capacity). The plaintiff can appeal the dismissal but cannot refile the lawsuit unless the dismissal is reversed on appeal. *See* **Mossler**, 818 S.W.2d at 754.

Note

The notation "with prejudice to refiling" is not appropriate when the trial court dismisses a motion, as opposed to a lawsuit. ***Republic Royalty Co. v. Evins****, 931 S.W.2d 338, 344 (Tex.App.—Corpus Christi 1996, orig. proceeding). Such a notation does not prevent the party from refiling the motion. Id. At most, it is an indication that the trial court will not look favorably on another motion asking for the same relief. Id.*

2. Dismissal without prejudice. A dismissal without prejudice to refiling is not a final determination on the merits. Thus, if the statute of limitations has not run, the case may be refiled without appealing the order of dismissal. *See* **Webb v. Jorns**, 488 S.W.2d 407, 409 (Tex.1972); **Denton v. Texas DPS Officers Ass'n**, 862 S.W.2d 785, 787 (Tex.App.—Austin 1993), *aff'd*, 897 S.W.2d 757 (Tex.1995); **Palmer v. Cantrell**, 747 S.W.2d 39, 40 (Tex.App.—Houston [1st Dist.] 1988, no writ).

§6.4 Preservation of error. If the trial court's order dismissed a suit with prejudice when only a dismissal without prejudice was appropriate, the notation "with prejudice" must be challenged in some postjudgment motion (e.g., a motion for new trial, a motion to modify the judgment, or as part of a motion to reinstate); otherwise, the error is waived and the suit cannot be refiled. **El Paso Pipe & Sup. v. Mountain States Leasing, Inc.**, 617 S.W.2d 189, 190 (Tex.1981). See "Inappropriate order of dismissal," ch. 10-B, §12.2.2.

§7. Request for findings of fact

If the trial court holds a hearing and receives evidence before dismissing the case, the plaintiff should ask the court to file findings of fact and conclusions of law. To determine when findings should be requested, see "After dismissal hearings," ch. 10-E, §2.2.2.

§8. Notice of dismissal order

§8.1 Notice of order. The clerk must send notice that the court signed an order of dismissal by first-class mail; certified mail is not required. Tex. R. Civ. P. 165a(1), 306a(3). See "Notice of judgment," ch. 9-C, §5. However, the clerk is not required to affirmatively show in the record that such notice was mailed. **Ginn v. Forrester**, 282 S.W.3d 430, 433 (Tex.2009); **Alexander v. Lynda's Boutique**, 134 S.W.3d 845, 849 (Tex.2004); **General Elec. Co. v. Falcon Ridge Apts., Jt.V.**, 811 S.W.2d 942, 943 (Tex.1991). The clerk is not required to send a copy of the dismissal order; a postcard notice of the dismissal is sufficient. If the clerk does not send the notice, the postjudgment periods listed in TRCP 306a(1) are not affected, except as provided by TRCP 306a(4). Tex. R. Civ. P. 165a(1). If a party receives late notice of the judgment, TRCP 306a(4) permits the party to file a motion that effectively extends the time for post-trial motions. See "Motion to Extend Postjudgment Deadlines," ch. 10-G, §1 et seq.

§8.2 Notice to attorneys. The clerk must send notice of the dismissal to the "attorneys of record," which includes all attorneys of record for the parties. Tex. R. Civ. P. 165a(1), 306a(3); **Cannon v. ICO Tubular Servs.**, 905 S.W.2d 380, 388 (Tex.App.—Houston [1st Dist.] 1995, no writ), *overruled on other grounds*, **Lane Bank Equip. Co. v. Smith S. Equip., Inc.**, 10 S.W.3d 308 (Tex.2000); *cf.* Tex. R. Civ. P. 8 ("attorney in charge" includes only one attorney for each party). See "Attorney," ch. 1-H, §6.1.1.

§8.3 Notice to pro se party. The clerk must send notice of the dismissal to any party who is not represented by counsel. Tex. R. Civ. P. 165a(1), 306a(3); **General Elec. Co. v. Falcon Ridge Apts., Jt.V.**, 811 S.W.2d 942, 943 (Tex.1991).

§9. Reinstatement

§9.1 Appealing DWOP. See "Motion to Reinstate After Dismissal for Want of Prosecution," ch. 10-F, §1 et seq.

§9.2 Appealing other dismissals. See "Motion for New Trial," ch. 10-B, §1 et seq.

§9.3 Appealing late notice of dismissal order. See "Motion to Extend Postjudgment Deadlines," ch. 10-G, §1 et seq.

§10. Review

The order dismissing a case is a final, appealable order. *See* **Stewart v. USA Custom Paint & Body Shop, Inc.**, 870 S.W.2d 18, 20 (Tex.1994) (properly executed order of dismissal is a judgment). Because an order refusing to dismiss for want of prosecution cannot effectively be challenged by appeal, a defendant may seek review by mandamus. **In re Conner**, 458 S.W.3d 532, 535 (Tex.2015).

H. Offer of Settlement

§1. General

§1.1 Rule. Tex. R. Civ. P. 167. See Tex. Civ. Prac. & Rem. Code ch. 42.

§1.2 Purpose. The purpose of the offer-of-settlement procedure is to encourage early settlements by shifting litigation costs to the party that rejected a fair settlement offer. *See* Tex. R. Civ. P. 167.1; *cf.* Fed. R. Civ. P. 68(d) (postoffer costs can be shifted to party who rejects settlement offer).

Note

TRCP 167 and CPRC chapter 42 govern the requirements for the recovery of litigation costs; they do not govern the requirements for enforcing a settlement agreement itself. See, e.g., ***Amedisys, Inc. v. Kingwood Home Health Care, LLC****, 437 S.W.3d 507, 512–13 (Tex.2014) (because P sought to recover for breach of settlement agreement, not to recover litigation costs, P had to establish valid contract under common law, including elements of offer and acceptance; TRCP 167 and CPRC ch. 42 did not govern validity of settlement agreement).*

§1.3 Timetable & forms. Appendix IV, Timetable 13, Offer of settlement; **O'Connor's Texas Civil Forms**, FORMS 7H:1 et seq. (2020 ed.).

§1.4 Other references. Harrison, *Texas Hold 'Em: Offer of Settlement Under Rule 167*, 70 Tex.B.J. 936 (Dec.2007); **O'Connor's Texas Causes of Action** (2021 ed.).

§2. Availability & election of settlement procedure

§2.1 Availability.

1. Available. The offer-of-settlement procedure can be used only for claims seeking monetary damages. *See* Tex. Civ. Prac. & Rem. Code §42.002(a); Tex. R. Civ. P. 167.1, 167.2(d); *see also* Tex. Civ. Prac. & Rem. Code §42.001(1) (definition of "claim").

2. Not available. The offer-of-settlement procedure cannot be used in the following cases:

(1) Class actions. Tex. Civ. Prac. & Rem. Code §42.002(b)(1); Tex. R. Civ. P. 167.1(a).

Note

Neither CPRC chapter 42 nor TRCP 167 makes it clear whether "class action" includes all cases filed as class actions or only those cases certified as class actions.

(2) Shareholder derivative actions. Tex. Civ. Prac. & Rem. Code §42.002(b)(2); Tex. R. Civ. P. 167.1(b).

(3) Actions by or against a governmental unit. Tex. Civ. Prac. & Rem. Code §42.002(b)(3); Tex. R. Civ. P. 167.1(c); *see also* Tex. Civ. Prac. & Rem. Code §42.001(4) (definition of "governmental unit").

(4) Family Code actions. Tex. Civ. Prac. & Rem. Code §42.002(b)(4); Tex. R. Civ. P. 167.1(d).

(5) Workers' compensation actions. Tex. Civ. Prac. & Rem. Code §42.002(b)(5); Tex. R. Civ. P. 167.1(e).

(6) Actions filed in a justice-of-the-peace court or small-claims court. Tex. Civ. Prac. & Rem. Code §42.002(b)(6); Tex. R. Civ. P. 167.1(f).

Note

Small-claims courts have been abolished; now small-claims proceedings must be conducted by justice courts. See Tex. Gov't Code §27.060(a).

(7) Mediation, arbitration, or other ADR proceedings. Tex. R. Civ. P. 167.7.

(8) Suits seeking equitable relief only. *See* Tex. Civ. Prac. & Rem. Code §42.001(1) ("claim" is limited to suit for monetary relief); Tex. R. Civ. P. 167.1 (same).

(9) Cases filed before January 1, 2004. Acts 2003, 78th Leg., R.S., ch. 204, §2.02, eff. Sept. 1, 2003.

§2.2 Other settlement offers.

1. No restriction on making other offers. Neither TRCP 167 nor CPRC chapter 42 affects or limits a party's right to make a settlement offer (1) that does not comply with the requirements of TRCP 167 or CPRC §42.003 or (2) in a case to which TRCP 167 or CPRC chapter 42 does not apply. *See* Tex. Civ. Prac. & Rem. Code §42.002(d); Tex. R. Civ. P. 167.7.

2. No basis for litigation costs. A settlement offer cannot be the basis for awarding litigation costs to any party if the offer (1) does not comply with TRCP 167 or CPRC §42.003, (2) is not made under TRCP 167, or (3) is made in a case to which TRCP 167 or CPRC chapter 42 does not apply. *See* Tex. Civ. Prac. & Rem. Code §42.002(e); Tex. R. Civ. P. 167.7. See "Litigation costs," ch. 7-H, §6.

§3. Defendant's declaration

The offer-of-settlement procedure is not automatically available. Before either party (plaintiff or defendant) can make a settlement offer under TRCP 167, the defendant must file a declaration invoking the rule. Tex. Civ. Prac. & Rem. Code §42.002(c); Tex. R. Civ. P. 167.2(a). Only a defendant can invoke the offer-of-settlement procedure. Tex. Civ. Prac. & Rem. Code §42.002(c); Tex. R. Civ. P. 167.2(a).

Caution

When filing a counterclaim or a TRCP 167 declaration, the defendant may end up paying the plaintiff's litigation costs. Therefore, a defendant should carefully consider whether to file a counterclaim or declaration.

§3.1 Definition of defendant. A defendant is a person from whom a party seeks monetary damages, including a counterdefendant (i.e., a plaintiff subject to monetary damages in a counterclaim), cross-defendant, or third-party defendant. Tex. Civ. Prac. & Rem. Code §42.001(3); *see* Tex. R. Civ. P. 167.1, 167.2(a).

§3.2 Multiple defendants. In a case with multiple defendants, the procedure applies only to the defendant filing the declaration. *See* Tex. Civ. Prac. & Rem. Code §42.002(c); Tex. R. Civ. P. 167.2(a).

§3.3 Deadline. The defendant must file a TRCP 167 declaration at least 45 days before trial. Tex. R. Civ. P. 167.2(a). On a motion based on good cause, the court may sign a pretrial order modifying this time limit. Tex. R. Civ. P. 167.5(a).

§3.4 No withdrawal. TRCP 167 does not provide for the withdrawal or revocation of a declaration once it has been filed. Harrison, *Texas Hold 'Em: Offer of Settlement Under Rule 167*, 70 Tex.B.J. 936, 937 (Dec. 2007).

§4. Settlement offer

Once the defendant has invoked TRCP 167 by filing a declaration, either party may make a settlement offer under the offer-of-settlement procedure.

§4.1 In writing. A settlement offer must be in writing and must state that it is made under CPRC chapter 42 and TRCP 167. Tex. Civ. Prac. & Rem. Code §42.003(a)(1), (a)(2); Tex. R. Civ. P. 167.2(b)(1), (b)(2); *see* Tex. Civ. Prac. & Rem. Code §42.001(6).

§4.2 Parties. A settlement offer must identify the party or parties making the offer and the party or parties to whom the offer is made. Tex. R. Civ. P. 167.2(b)(3). In multiparty cases, the court will look to the plain language of an offer to determine whether the offer is a single offer to multiple parties or a series of offers made to each party individually. *See, e.g.*, **Grocers Sup. v. Cabello**, 390 S.W.3d 707, 732 (Tex.App.—Dallas 2012, no pet.) (although offer allocated total award among Ps, it was consistently described as one offer made to the Ps generally and said nothing as to whether or how it could be accepted by only one P; offer was single offer to multiple parties).

§4.3 Terms.

1. Claims by and against defendant. A settlement offer can be made only for claims brought by and against the defendant who filed the declaration invoking the offer-of-settlement procedure. Tex. R. Civ. P. 167.2(a); **Note Inv. Grp. v. Associates First Capital Corp.**, 476 S.W.3d 463, 475 (Tex.App.—Beaumont 2015, no pet.). A claim does not have to be formally pleaded when a settlement offer is made to be covered by the offer. **Note Inv.**, 476 S.W.3d at 478.

2. Monetary claims. A settlement offer must state the amount for which the monetary claims—including attorney fees, interest, and costs—between the parties may be settled. Tex. R. Civ. P. 167.2(b)(4); *see* Tex. Civ. Prac. & Rem. Code §42.003(a)(3).

3. No nonmonetary claims. A settlement offer must not include nonmonetary claims or other claims that fall outside TRCP 167. Tex. R. Civ. P. 167.2(d); *see also* Tex. R. Civ. P. 167.1 (listing claims that fall outside TRCP 167).

4. Other conditions. A settlement offer may require the offeree to meet other reasonable conditions, including executing releases, indemnities, or other documents. Tex. R. Civ. P. 167.2(c). A condition is presumed reasonable unless an offeree objects in writing to the condition before the deadline for acceptance. *Id.* If an offeree objects to an offer's condition, that offer cannot be the basis for cost-shifting unless the trial court determines that the condition was reasonable. *Id.*

§4.4 Deadlines.

1. Making the offer. A settlement offer must be made as follows:

(1) After the defendant files a TRCP 167 declaration. Tex. R. Civ. P. 167.2(e)(1). See "Defendant's declaration," ch. 7-H, §3.

(2) More than 60 days after both the plaintiff and defendant have appeared in the case. Tex. R. Civ. P. 167.2(e)(2).

(3) More than 14 days before the case is set for a conventional trial on the merits (not summary judgment), unless the settlement offer answers an earlier offer and is made within 7 days after the earlier offer. Tex. R. Civ. P. 167.2(e)(3).

2. Accepting the offer. The settlement offer must state an acceptance deadline. Tex. Civ. Prac. & Rem. Code §42.003(a)(4); Tex. R. Civ. P. 167.2(b)(5). The acceptance deadline must be at least 14 days after the offer is served. Tex. R. Civ. P. 167.2(b)(5).

3. Modifying the deadlines. On a motion based on good cause, the court may sign a pretrial order modifying the time limits for making an offer. Tex. R. Civ. P. 167.5(a).

§4.5 Service. A settlement offer must be served on all parties to whom it is made. Tex. Civ. Prac. & Rem. Code §42.003(a)(5); Tex. R. Civ. P. 167.2(b)(6); *see* Tex. R. Civ. P. 21a(a).

§4.6 Filing. A settlement offer does not need to be filed with the court. Tex. Civ. Prac. & Rem. Code §42.003(b).

§4.7 Designating or joining additional party. An offeror may designate a responsible third party or join another party after making a TRCP 167 offer. *See* Tex. R. Civ. P. 167.3(d). See "Third-party petitions," ch. 3-E, §7.3; "RTP," ch. 3-E, §7.4. The offer cannot be the basis for awarding litigation costs if the offeree files a timely objection after service of the pleading or designation. See "To additional parties," ch. 7-H, §5.2.2.

§5. Withdrawal, acceptance, objections & rejection

§5.1 Withdrawing the offer. Before a settlement offer is accepted, an offeror may withdraw it by serving written notice of the withdrawal on the offeree. Tex. R. Civ. P. 167.3(a). The withdrawal takes effect when the notice is served. *Id.*; *see* Tex. R. Civ. P. 21a(a). Once the offer is withdrawn, it cannot be accepted and cannot be the basis for cost-shifting. Tex. R. Civ. P. 167.3(a).

§5.2 Objecting to the offer.

1. To the conditions. An offeree may object to a settlement offer's conditions by serving written notice on the offeror before the acceptance deadline. Tex. R. Civ. P. 167.2(c). If the offeree objects to the offer on this ground, the offer cannot be the basis for cost-shifting unless the court finds that the conditions were reasonable. *Id.*

2. To additional parties. If an offeror joins another party or designates a responsible third party after making an offer, the offeree may file an objection to the offer within 15 days after service of the pleading or designation. Tex. R. Civ. P. 167.3(d). If the offeree objects to the offer on this ground, the offer cannot be the basis for cost-shifting. *Id.*

§5.3 Accepting the offer. An offeree may accept a settlement offer by serving written notice on the offeror on or before the offer's acceptance deadline and before the offer is withdrawn. Tex. R. Civ. P. 167.3(b). When the offer is accepted, either party may file the offer and acceptance and ask the court to enforce the settlement. *Id.* See "Consent judgment," ch. 7-I, §3.2.1.

§5.4 Rejecting the offer. An offeree may reject a settlement offer by serving written notice on the offeror on or before the acceptance deadline. Tex. R. Civ. P. 167.3(c). An offer that is not withdrawn or accepted on or before the acceptance deadline is deemed rejected. *Id.*

§5.5 Making successive offers. A party may make another offer after having made or rejected an earlier offer. Tex. R. Civ. P. 167.2(f). Rejection of a later offer can be the basis for cost-shifting only if the offer was more favorable to the offeree than any other offer. *Id.*

§6. Litigation costs

Litigation costs are defined as the money spent and the obligations incurred that directly relate to the action in a settlement offer. Tex. Civ. Prac. & Rem. Code §42.001(5); Tex. R. Civ. P. 167.4(c). Litigation costs include (1) court costs, (2) reasonable deposition costs, (3) reasonable fees for no more than two testifying expert witnesses, and (4) reasonable attorney fees. Tex. Civ. Prac. & Rem. Code §42.001(5); Tex. R. Civ. P. 167.4(c). See "Court Costs," **O'Connor's Texas Causes of Action**, ch. 44, §1 et seq. (2021 ed.); "Attorney Fees," **O'Connor's Texas Causes of Action**, ch. 45-A, §1 et seq. (2021 ed.). An offeror can recover litigation costs from a rejecting offeree if the judgment awarded is significantly less favorable to the offeree than the rejected offer. Tex. Civ. Prac. & Rem. Code §42.004(a); Tex. R. Civ. P. 167.4(a); **Grocers Sup. v. Cabello**, 390 S.W.3d 707, 730 (Tex.App.—Dallas 2012, no pet.). For a discussion of the practical effects of and strategies for making or rejecting a settlement offer, see Harrison, *Texas Hold 'Em: Offer of Settlement Under Rule 167*, 70 Tex.B.J. 936, 938–40 (Dec.2007).

Note

One court has held that, under TRCP 167, judgment means the damages awarded by the fact-finder, rather than the final judgment rendered by the court. ***Bobo v. Varughese****, 507 S.W.3d 817, 828 (Tex.App.—Texarkana 2016, no pet.). Thus, prejudgment interest is not included in the judgment amount. Id.*

§6.1 Significantly less favorable. A judgment is significantly less favorable in either of the following situations:

1. Plaintiff rejected offer. The judgment is significantly less favorable to the plaintiff if the plaintiff rejected the defendant's offer and the award is less than 80% of the rejected offer. Tex. Civ. Prac. & Rem. Code §42.004(b)(1); Tex. R. Civ. P. 167.4(b)(1); *see* **Grocers Sup. v. Cabello**, 390 S.W.3d 707, 730 (Tex.App.—Dallas 2012, no pet.).

2. Defendant rejected offer. The judgment is significantly less favorable to the defendant if the defendant rejected the plaintiff's offer and the award is more than 120% of the rejected offer. Tex. Civ. Prac. & Rem. Code §42.004(b)(2);

Tex. R. Civ. P. 167.4(b)(2).

Example

Assume that the jury awards the plaintiff $120,000 in damages. If the plaintiff rejected a settlement offer from the defendant that was over $150,000 (80% of $150,000 = $120,000), the verdict is "significantly less favorable" to the plaintiff than the defendant's settlement offer, and the plaintiff must pay the defendant's litigation costs. On the other hand, if the defendant rejected a settlement offer from the plaintiff that was under $100,000 (120% of $100,000 = $120,000), the verdict is "significantly less favorable" to the defendant than the plaintiff's settlement offer, and the defendant must pay the plaintiff's litigation costs.

§6.2 Calculating costs.

1. After rejection. The offeror may recover only those litigation costs it incurred between the date of rejection and the date of judgment. Tex. Civ. Prac. & Rem. Code §42.004(c); Tex. R. Civ. P. 167.4(a).

2. Cap on costs. The judgment damages limit the recoverable litigation costs. Recoverable litigation costs cannot exceed the total amount the plaintiff recovers or would recover before (1) adding an award of litigation costs under CPRC chapter 42 or TRCP 167 in favor of the plaintiff or (2) subtracting as an offset an award of litigation costs under CPRC chapter 42 or TRCP 167 in favor of the defendant. Tex. Civ. Prac. & Rem. Code §42.004(d); Tex. R. Civ. P. 167.4(d)(2). Thus, the plaintiff could have to pay its entire award as recoverable litigation costs to the defendant; similarly, the defendant could have to pay litigation costs up to the amount of the plaintiff's verdict.

Example

Assume the defendant makes a $200,000 settlement offer, which the plaintiff rejects. The plaintiff then receives a verdict for $120,000 in damages. This verdict is significantly less favorable to the plaintiff than the settlement offer ($120,000 is less than $160,000, which is 80% of $200,000). The defendant may therefore recover up to $120,000 in litigation costs. If the defendant had at least $120,000 in litigation costs, the plaintiff's total recovery would be $0 ($120,000 less a $120,000 offset).

3. Defendant's costs awarded as offset. If the defendant recovers litigation costs, those costs are awarded in the judgment as an offset against the plaintiff's recovery. Tex. Civ. Prac. & Rem. Code §42.004(g); Tex. R. Civ. P. 167.4(g).

4. No double recovery. An offeror that recovers litigation costs under another law (e.g., CPRC chapter 38) cannot recover the same litigation costs under TRCP 167. Tex. Civ. Prac. & Rem. Code §42.004(e); Tex. R. Civ. P. 167.4(e).

5. No costs to rejecting party. If a party is entitled to litigation costs under another law (e.g., CPRC chapter 38) but that party rejects a TRCP 167 settlement offer and litigation costs are imposed against it, the party cannot recover under the other law the litigation costs it incurred after rejecting the offer. Tex. Civ. Prac. & Rem. Code §42.004(f); Tex. R. Civ. P. 167.4(f). In other words, a party that rejects a fair settlement offer may lose some of its own litigation costs as well as having to pay those of the other side.

§6.3 Awarding costs. The court will award TRCP 167 litigation costs by incorporating them with the jury's verdict into the final judgment. *See* Tex. R. Civ. P. 167.4(a).

1. Post-trial hearing. The court should hold a post-trial hearing on the amount and reasonableness of the litigation costs and on the reasonableness of any conditions in the rejected offer.

(1) Amount & reasonableness of litigation costs. On request, the court must hold a post-trial hearing for evidence before awarding litigation costs. Tex. R. Civ. P. 167.5(c). The court should determine the amount of litigation costs to be awarded and should consider any challenge to their reasonableness. *See* Tex. R. Civ. P. 167.4, 167.5. If the reasonableness of the litigation costs is challenged and the court finds the costs to be reasonable, the court must award an additional amount

to cover any attorney fees and expenses incurred in responding to post-trial discovery on reasonableness. Tex. R. Civ. P. 167.5(b). For a discussion of determining the reasonableness of attorney fees, which are part of the litigation costs awarded under TRCP 167, see "Attorney fees from adverse party," ch. 1-H, §10.

(2) Reasonableness of conditions. When an offeree properly objected to an offer's condition (e.g., that the offeree execute a release, indemnity, or other document as part of the settlement), no award of litigation costs can be based on that offer unless the court determines that the condition was reasonable. Tex. R. Civ. P. 167.2(c). Thus, before the court awards litigation costs based on an offer with conditions that the offeree properly objected to, the court must conduct a hearing for evidence to determine the reasonableness of the conditions. *See id.* See "To the conditions," ch. 7-H, §5.2.1.

2. Post-trial discovery. On a motion based on good cause, the rejecting party may conduct post-trial discovery on the reasonableness of the offeror's costs. Tex. R. Civ. P. 167.5(b).

3. Admissibility of evidence. Evidence relating to a settlement offer is admissible only as needed to enforce the settlement agreement or to obtain litigation costs. Tex. R. Civ. P. 167.6; *see* Tex. R. Evid. 408(b). The provisions of TRCP 167 cannot be made known to the jury. Tex. R. Civ. P. 167.6.

4. Award mandatory. Normally, to recover attorney fees, a party must plead for their recovery in a petition or answer. *See* **Swate v. Medina Cmty. Hosp.**, 966 S.W.2d 693, 701 (Tex.App.—San Antonio 1998, pet. denied) (unless mandatory statute says otherwise, court's jurisdiction to render judgment for attorney fees must be invoked by pleadings). But TRCP 167's award of attorney fees (and other litigation costs) is mandatory once TRCP 167 is properly invoked. Thus, even when a party's petition or answer does not ask for attorney fees or other litigation costs, the court must award litigation costs against the party that rejected a TRCP 167 offer. *See* Tex. R. Civ. P. 167.4(a).

I. Settlement of the Suit

§1. General

§1.1 Rules. Tex R Civ. P. 11, 76a, 97(a). See Tex. Civ. Prac. & Rem. Code §§32.001 to 32.003.

§1.2 Purpose. When parties settle a lawsuit, they resolve the dispute according to the terms of a private contract. *See* **Montanaro v. Montanaro**, 946 S.W.2d 428, 431 (Tex.App.—Corpus Christi 1997, no writ). The settlement brings the lawsuit to a conclusion, avoids the expense and uncertainty of litigation, and gives the parties the opportunity to construct remedies that give both parties something and let both parties avoid the possibility of total loss. *See* **Transport Ins. v. Faircloth**, 898 S.W.2d 269, 280 (Tex.1995). Public policy favors the amicable settlement of controversies. *Id.*

§1.3 Forms. **O'Connor's Texas Civil Forms**, FORMS 7H:1 et seq., 7I:1 et seq. (2020 ed.).

§1.4 Other references. **O'Connor's Texas Causes of Action** (2021 ed.).

§2. Provisions in settlement agreement

Settlement agreements are governed by the law of contracts. **Schlumberger Tech. v. Swanson**, 959 S.W.2d 171, 178 (Tex.1997); **Williams v. Glash**, 789 S.W.2d 261, 264 (Tex.1990).

§2.1 Release. A release is a contractual surrender by one party of its cause of action against the other party. **Lloyd v. Ray**, 606 S.W.2d 545, 547 (Tex.App.—San Antonio 1980, writ ref'd n.r.e.). A release extinguishes a claim or cause of action, the same way a judgment would. **Dresser Indus. v. Page Pet., Inc.**, 853 S.W.2d 505, 508 (Tex.1993); **Derr Constr. Co. v. City of Houston**, 846 S.W.2d 854, 858 (Tex.App.—Houston [14th Dist.] 1992, no writ). In certain circumstances, a release must meet the fair-notice requirements—that is, it must be specific and conspicuous. *See* **Dresser Indus.**, 853 S.W.2d at 509 (fair-notice requirements are limited to releases that relieve party in advance of liability for its own negligence); *see, e.g.*, **National Prop. Holdings, L.P. v. Westergren**, 453 S.W.3d 419, 424 (Tex.2015) (title of release was bolded, capitalized, and underlined, as were keywords in text).

Caution

The settlement agreement and release can state that, in executing the agreement, the releasing party relies on her own judgment and understanding of the agreement and not on any statement or representation of the other party or her agent. See ***Italian Cowboy Partners v. Prudential Ins.***, *341 S.W.3d 323, 336 (Tex.2011) (provision in lease agreement). See* ***O'Connor's Texas Civil Forms***, *FORM 7I:1, ¶10 (2020 ed.). That is, a releasing party must make sure to review the release herself and not rely on the other party's statements and representations about it. If the releasing party chooses not to review the release after being given a reasonable opportunity to do so, her reliance on the other party's representations to her detriment will not negate the validity of the release. See, e.g.,* ***National Prop. Holdings***, *453 S.W.3d at 425–26 (P's decision to not read release because he did not have his glasses and was "in a hurry" and to instead rely on D's representations was not justifiable and did not support fraudulent-inducement claim).*

1. Identity of parties. To be effective, a release must identify the parties to the release.

(1) Releasing party. A release binds only the person or entity specifically identified or named in the release as the releasing party. Both parties and nonparties may release claims by settlement agreements. For example, spouses and other family members may relinquish possible causes of action that have not been asserted. When a minor releases rights, if there is a conflict of interest on the part of the child's parents or guardians, the minor must be represented by a guardian ad litem, who determines and advises the court whether the settlement is in the minor's best interests. See "Appointing a guardian ad litem under TRCP 173," ch. 1-I, §3.

Practice Tip

The settlement agreement should always provide that both parties release each other, instead of just providing that the plaintiff releases the defendant. See Tex. R. Civ. P. 97(a) (agreed judgment between some parties before final disposition on the merits of other claims does not bar the claims of any other party if there is no written consent that the judgment will act as a bar).

(2) Released party. A release discharges only the person or entity specifically identified or named in the release. *E.g.*, **Angus Chem. Co. v. IMC Fertilizer, Inc.**, 939 S.W.2d 138, 139 (Tex.1997) (release of tortfeasor did not release tortfeasor's insurer); **McMillen v. Klingensmith**, 467 S.W.2d 193, 196 (Tex.1971) (release of one doctor did not release other doctors); *see also* **Knutson v. Morton Foods, Inc.**, 603 S.W.2d 805, 806 (Tex.1980) (release of employee did not release principal under doctrine of respondeat superior). A person is specifically identified when the language is sufficiently particular so that a stranger to the release could readily identify the released party even though the party's name is missing. *E.g.*, **Duncan v. Cessna Aircraft Co.**, 665 S.W.2d 414, 419–20 (Tex.1984) (release of "any other corporations . . . responsible" in settlement with pilot did not release manufacturer of aircraft); **Frazer v. Texas Farm Bur. Mut. Ins.**, 4 S.W.3d 819, 823–24 (Tex.App.—Houston [1st Dist.] 1999, no pet.) (release of insurer "and its affiliated companies" sufficiently identified insurer's underwriters); **Lloyd**, 606 S.W.2d at 546–47 & n.1 (release of one doctor and "all other persons, firms and corporations" did not release a second, unnamed doctor). In a few situations, a release also releases entities not specifically named. *See, e.g.*, **Winkler v. Kirkwood Atrium Office Park**, 816 S.W.2d 111, 113–14 (Tex.App.—Houston [14th Dist.] 1991, writ denied) (release of health club from any injuries suffered while participating in its programs released all individuals and entities involved in its operation, maintenance, and administration).

(3) Attorneys. Attorneys representing parties in a consent judgment are bound by that judgment. **Newman v. Link**, 889 S.W.2d 288, 289 (Tex.1994). If the attorneys have complaints about attorney fees and ad litem costs, they must object before the judgment becomes final. *See id.*

(4) Insurer. If the parties intend to release the defendant's insurer, the insurer should be named as a released party in the settlement papers. In Texas, if the injured party cannot sue the tortfeasor, it cannot sue the tortfeasor's insurer. **Angus Chem.**, 939 S.W.2d at 138. Thus, when an injured party releases the tortfeasor, it can no longer sue the tortfeasor's insurer in Texas. *Id.* However, the release of the tortfeasor does not prevent the injured party from suing the tortfeasor's insurer in another jurisdiction. *E.g., id.* at 138–39 (Louisiana law permits direct suits against insurers).

2. Description of dispute & released claims. The release should describe the dispute and the extent to which the release is intended to settle it. A release discharges only the claims specifically mentioned in the release. **Keck, Mahin & Cate v. National Un. Fire Ins.**, 20 S.W.3d 692, 698 (Tex.2000); **Memorial Med. Ctr. v. Keszler**, 943 S.W.2d 433, 434–35 (Tex.1997); **Victoria Bank & Trust Co. v. Brady**, 811 S.W.2d 931, 938 (Tex.1991); *see* **Baty v. Protech Ins. Agency**, 63 S.W.3d 841, 854–55 (Tex.App.—Houston [14th Dist.] 2001, pet. denied) (release that does not list one of the claims "strongly suggests" parties did not intend to release that claim). If the claim is not clearly within the subject matter of the release, it is not discharged. **Brady**, 811 S.W.2d at 938. The release does not have to specifically describe each potential cause of action to be released. **Keck, Mahin & Cate**, 20 S.W.3d at 698; **Kalyanaram v. Burck**, 225 S.W.3d 291, 299 (Tex.App.—El Paso 2006, no pet.); *see* **Memorial Med. Ctr.**, 943 S.W.2d at 434–35. The release may be broad (releasing all claims, known or unknown) or narrow (releasing only the particular claims asserted in the lawsuit). *See, e.g.*, **Keck, Mahin & Cate**, 20 S.W.3d at 698 (all claims for malpractice attributable to legal services); **Memorial Med. Ctr.**, 943 S.W.2d at 435 (all present and future claims relating to doctor's relationship with hospital); **Brady**, 811 S.W.2d at 938 (claims attributable to specific loan transaction between bank and customer); **Kalyanaram**, 225 S.W.3d at 299–300 (all known and unknown claims arising from employment relationship).

Practice Tip

If the release is a separate instrument from the settlement agreement, make sure the description of the released claims is stated in identical language in both the release and the settlement agreement. In ***Memorial Med. Ctr.****, 943 S.W.2d at 434, the terms were much broader in the release than in the settle-*

ment agreement, and the court held that the defendant was released according to the terms stated in the release, not those stated in the settlement agreement.

3. Consideration. The release should state the supporting consideration. *See* **Torchia v. Aetna Cas. & Sur. Co.**, 804 S.W.2d 219, 222–23 (Tex.App.—El Paso 1991, writ denied) (release stated consideration and identified claims released). Inadequacy of the consideration is not a sufficient reason to set aside a release. *Id.* at 223. Although in most cases the consideration is the payment of money damages, the settlement of a contested lawsuit may itself be sufficient consideration to support a release. *See* **Schuh v. Schuh**, 453 S.W.2d 203, 204 (Tex.App.—Dallas 1970, no writ); *see also* **Adams v. Petrade Int'l**, 754 S.W.2d 696, 723 (Tex.App.—Houston [1st Dist.] 1988, writ denied) (release is surrender of cause of action, which may be given for inadequate or no consideration).

4. Covenant not to sue. A release is not a covenant not to sue and does not bar future suits. *See* **National Prop. Holdings**, 453 S.W.3d at 428–29. If the parties want the settlement agreement to include a contractual obligation not to sue in the future such that any suit by one party would entitle the other party to damages for breach of the agreement, the agreement or the release must specifically include language to that effect. *See id.* at 428. Although a release may include language that constitutes an affirmative defense to a future suit, the release is not a covenant not to sue unless it includes specific language barring a future suit. *See id.* at 428–29; *see also* Tex. R. Civ. P. 94 (release must be pleaded as affirmative defense).

§2.2 Other provisions.

1. Assignment of causes of action. If the identity of persons to be released is unknown, the plaintiff may assign any unreleased claims to the released parties. Such an assignment prevents the plaintiff from later suing any other persons without authority from the owner of the claim. **Duke v. Brookshire Grocery Co.**, 568 S.W.2d 470, 472 (Tex.App.—Texarkana 1978, no writ). A settling defendant who is jointly responsible for the plaintiff's personal injuries cannot preserve contribution rights against codefendants by purchasing the plaintiff's claim. **Beech Aircraft Corp. v. Jinkins**, 739 S.W.2d 19, 22 (Tex.1987); *see* **International Proteins Corp. v. Ralston-Purina Co.**, 744 S.W.2d 932, 934 (Tex.1988); **Filter Fab, Inc. v. Delauder**, 2 S.W.3d 614, 617 (Tex.App.—Houston [14th Dist.] 1999, no pet.).

2. Indemnity. A settlement agreement may contain provisions by which the plaintiff agrees to indemnify the defendant. An indemnity agreement is a promise by the indemnitor to safeguard or hold the indemnitee harmless against existing or future loss or liability, or both. **Dresser Indus. v. Page Pet., Inc.**, 853 S.W.2d 505, 508 (Tex.1993); **Wallerstein v. Spirt**, 8 S.W.3d 774, 779 (Tex.App.—Austin 1999, no pet.). Unlike a release, which bars a cause of action, an indemnity provision creates a potential cause of action between the indemnitee and the indemnitor. **Wallerstein**, 8 S.W.3d at 779. By the agreement, the plaintiff accepts liability for any claims that third parties may assert against the settling defendant arising from the matter being settled. Thus, the indemnity protects that defendant against liability on cross-claims and other claims. The agreement creates a circular pattern of indemnity that extinguishes the plaintiff's cause of action. For example, in **Bonniwell v. Beech Aircraft Corp.**, 663 S.W.2d 816, 819 (Tex.1984), the plaintiffs settled with defendant-operator and agreed to indemnify it from any further liability. As the court explained, any judgment the plaintiffs obtained against the defendant-manufacturer would be collected from defendant-operator, which would be reimbursed by the plaintiffs. **Bonniwell**, 663 S.W.2d at 819; *see also* **Phillips Pipe Line Co. v. McKown**, 580 S.W.2d 435, 440 (Tex.App.—Tyler 1979, writ ref'd n.r.e.) (when landowner released contractor, he also released pipeline owner because contractor had a duty to indemnify pipeline owner). A defendant who is a party to a settlement agreement cannot then seek indemnity from its codefendants. **Trussway, Inc. v. Wetzel**, 928 S.W.2d 174, 176 (Tex.App.—Beaumont 1996, writ denied).

3. Covenants not to execute. A settlement agreement may contain covenants not to execute on the judgment against the settling defendant. Covenants not to execute are often made between a plaintiff and a defendant when the defendant's insurer has refused to provide a defense. These covenants are usually given in exchange for an assignment to the plaintiff of the defendant's rights against its insurer. Covenants not to execute are invalid if (1) they are made before the plaintiff's claim is adjudicated in a full adversarial trial, (2) the defendant's insurer tendered a defense, and (3) the insurer has either accepted coverage or made a good-faith effort to adjudicate coverage issues before adjudication of the plaintiff's claim. **State Farm Fire & Cas. Co. v. Gandy**, 925 S.W.2d 696, 714 (Tex.1996).

4. Confidentiality. A settlement agreement may contain confidentiality provisions. These agreements, however, are subject to the restrictions in TRCP 76a(2)(b). Under TRCP 76a(2)(b), the parties cannot by their settlement agreements,

without notice and hearing, seal information relating to matters that may adversely affect the general public health or safety, the administration of public office, or the operation of government. See "Motion to Seal Court Records," ch. 5-L, §1 et seq.

5. Structured payment. A settlement agreement may contain a provision for structured payment of damages by which the plaintiff receives deferred payments rather than one lump sum. The benefit to the plaintiff is the assurance of support for a number of years; the benefit to the defendant is the reduced cost of settlement because of delayed payments. CPRC chapter 139 covers structured settlements in personal-injury cases.

(1) Offer must be in writing. If a plaintiff is either incapacitated, as defined by Estates Code §1002.017, or substantially disabled as a result of the personal injury, an offer of structured settlement must be in writing and presented to the plaintiff's attorney. *See* Tex. Civ. Prac. & Rem. Code §§139.002, 139.101.

(2) Offer must be explained. Before the offer expires, the plaintiff's attorney must explain to the plaintiff or the plaintiff's representative the terms, conditions, and other attributes of the settlement agreement and the appropriateness of the settlement under the circumstances. Tex. Civ. Prac. & Rem. Code §139.102(b).

6. Agreement to vacate judgment. A settlement agreement may contain an agreement to vacate the judgments of the trial court and the court of appeals in the case. *See* **Houston Cable TV, Inc. v. Inwood W. Civic Ass'n**, 860 S.W.2d 72, 73 (Tex.1993). A settlement agreement does not automatically require an appellate court to vacate its opinion. **Crown Life Ins. v. Casteel**, 22 S.W.3d 378, 392 (Tex.2000). In most cases, only the judgment will be vacated. **Houston Cable**, 860 S.W.2d at 73. A private agreement between litigants does not operate to vacate a court's writing on matters of public importance. *Id.*

7. Reservation of right to appeal. A settlement agreement may contain a reservation of the right to appeal some issues. *See* **Coble v. City of Mansfield**, 134 S.W.3d 449, 453 (Tex.App.—Fort Worth 2004, no pet.). An opinion issued in an appeal from a judgment rendered on a settlement agreement does not constitute an advisory opinion.

8. Reservation of other claims. A settlement agreement may contain a reservation of the right to pursue other claims. *See, e.g.*, **Transportation Ins. v. Moriel**, 879 S.W.2d 10, 15–16 (Tex.1994) (settlement release preserved right to sue for bad faith and punitive damages); **Indiana Lumbermen's Mut. Ins. v. State**, 1 S.W.3d 264, 268 (Tex.App.—Fort Worth 1999, pet. denied) (party reserved its right to defend against another lawsuit by the State).

9. Agreed judgment or dismissal order. A settlement agreement can state that the parties will ask the court to render an agreed judgment or dismiss the case. *See* Tex. Civ. Prac. & Rem. Code §154.071; **Compania Financiara Libano, S.A. v. Simmons**, 53 S.W.3d 365, 368 (Tex.2001). If the parties agree to memorialize the settlement by an agreed judgment, the judgment should accurately state the terms of the settlement. **Vickrey v. American Youth Camps, Inc.**, 532 S.W.2d 292, 292 (Tex.1976). However, it is not necessary for the judgment to incorporate all the terms of the settlement agreement; even unincorporated terms can be enforced. **Compania Financiara**, 53 S.W.3d at 368.

§2.3 Relationship between settling parties. Once a settlement agreement is executed, it extinguishes any duty of good faith and fair dealing that existed between the parties before settlement. *See, e.g.*, **Stewart Title Guar. Co. v. Aiello**, 941 S.W.2d 68, 71–72 (Tex.1997) (insurer no longer had duties to insured after settlement). The parties become the judgment creditor and judgment debtor, with all the remedies for enforcing the judgment. *See id.*

§3. Enforceable settlement agreements

§3.1 Agreement to settle.

1. Presuit settlement agreement. An oral agreement to settle a dispute before a lawsuit is filed is not governed by TRCP 11. *See* **Estate of Pollack v. McMurrey**, 858 S.W.2d 388, 393 (Tex.1993) (TRCP 11 applies only to agreements in pending suits). An oral agreement to settle before suit is filed is governed by the law of contracts and by Business & Commerce Code §26.01, the statute of frauds. *See* **Carter v. Allstate Ins.**, 962 S.W.2d 268, 270–71 (Tex.App.—Houston [1st Dist.] 1998, pet. denied) (agreement by insurer to settle before suit was enforceable); *see also* **Banda v. Garcia**, 955 S.W.2d 270, 272 (Tex.1997) (court assumed without discussion that oral pretrial settlement agreement was enforceable).

2. Settlement agreement after suit filed. To be enforceable, a settlement agreement must comply with TRCP 11. **Padilla v. LaFrance**, 907 S.W.2d 454, 460 (Tex1995); **Roeglin v. Daves**, 83 S.W.3d 326, 330 (TexApp.—Austin 2002, pet. denied); *see also* **Kennedy v. Hyde**, 682 S.W.2d 525, 529 (Tex1984) (Supreme Court does not require "slavish adherence" to literal requirements of TRCP 11). The agreement must be in writing, signed, and filed with the papers as part of the record, or it must be made in open court and entered of record. **Padilla**, 907 S.W.2d at 459; **Neasbitt v. Warren**, 105 S.W.3d 113, 116 (TexApp.—Fort Worth 2003, no pet.); **Ronin v. Lerner**, 7 S.W.3d 883, 886 (TexApp.—Houston [1st Dist.] 1999, no pet.). The agreement must contain all essential terms of the settlement (e.g., amount of compensation, liability to be released). **Disney v. Gollan**, 233 S.W.3d 591, 595 (TexApp.—Dallas 2007, no pet.); *see* **Padilla**, 907 S.W.2d at 460. See "Agreements between attorneys—Rule 11," ch. 1-H, §9.

(1) Written agreement. A written settlement agreement must be signed by the parties and be filed with the papers as part of the record of the case. *See* **Padilla**, 907 S.W.2d at 461. It is not necessary for the entire agreement to be contained in one document. *E.g., id.* at 460 (series of faxes). The agreement may be filed with the court even after one of the parties withdraws consent to the settlement; however, it must be filed before one of the parties attempts to enforce it. *Id.* at 461.

(2) Oral agreement. An oral settlement agreement is enforceable if it is made in open court and entered of record, satisfying the requirements of TRCP 11. **Padilla**, 907 S.W.2d at 459; **Neasbitt**, 105 S.W.3d at 116; **Ronin**, 7 S.W.3d at 886. The TRCP 11 requirement "entered of record" is satisfied if the agreement is noted in the judgment or in an order of the court. **City of Houston v. Clear Creek Basin Auth.**, 589 S.W.2d 671, 677 (Tex1979).

§3.2 Enforcing settlement agreement.

1. Consent judgment. When the parties reach a settlement agreement in pending litigation, the court may render a judgment based on the agreement as long as no party has withdrawn consent. **Padilla v. LaFrance**, 907 S.W.2d 454, 461 (Tex1995); **Staley v. Herblin**, 188 S.W.3d 334, 337 (TexApp.—Dallas 2006, pet. denied); *e.g.*, **S&A Rest. Corp. v. Leal**, 892 S.W.2d 855, 857–58 (Tex1995) (party withdrew consent to settlement agreement dictated into record before court rendered judgment; judgment reversed); **Kelley v. Pirtle**, 826 S.W.2d 653, 654 (TexApp.—Texarkana 1992, writ denied) (court orally rendered judgment in open court before party withdrew consent; judgment affirmed); *see also* **Chisholm v. Chisholm**, 209 S.W.3d 96, 98 (Tex2006) (party never gave consent because she said she did not understand agreement before judgment was signed). This consent judgment can be enforced like any other judgment rendered by the court; that is, it can be enforced even after the court's plenary power expires. See "Power to enforce judgment," ch. 9-C, §8. A court's approval of a settlement agreement in open court is not a rendition of judgment. **In re Vaishangi, Inc.**, 442 S.W.3d 256, 259 (Tex2014); **S&A Rest.**, 892 S.W.2d at 858. See "Rendition," ch. 9-C, §3.1.

Practice Tip

Once you reach a settlement, immediately ask the court to render judgment on the settlement agreement to prevent the other party from revoking the agreement and to ensure the agreement is enforceable as a consent judgment. See ***In re Vaishangi****, 442 S.W.3d at 259. If the agreement is dictated into the record, ask the judge to state on the record, "I now render judgment on the agreement."* ***Galerie D'Tile, Inc. v. Shinn****, 792 S.W.2d 792, 794 (Tex.App.—Houston [14th Dist] 1990, no writ); see* ***In re Vaishangi****, 442 S.W.3d at 259. Make sure the judge uses the present tense and not the future tense. See, e.g.,* ***Tinney v. Willingham****, 897 S.W.2d 543, 545 n.2 (Tex.App.—Fort Worth 1995, no writ) (because court said "I will" approve, it did not render judgment). The judge can sign the written judgment later.*

---

2. Suit to enforce as contract. If the court cannot render judgment on a settlement agreement because a party withdrew consent, the settlement agreement may be enforced as a contract if the agreement complies with TRCP 11. **Ford Motor Co. v. Castillo**, 279 S.W.3d 656, 663 (Tex2009); **Padilla**, 907 S.W.2d at 461; *see also* **Lane-Valente Indus. (Nat'l), Inc. v. J.P. Morgan Chase**, 468 S.W.3d 200, 204 (TexApp.—Houston [14th Dist.] 2015, no pet.) (contract law governs enforcement of settlement agreement). A settlement agreement is enforceable as a contract even if its terms are not

incorporated into a judgment. **Compania Financiara Libano, S.A. v. Simmons**, 53 S.W.3d 365, 368 (Tex.2001); **Padilla**, 907 S.W.2d at 461; *see also* Tex. Civ. Prac. & Rem. Code §154.071(a) (settlement agreements reached in ADR are enforceable like other contracts). If the suit that gave rise to the settlement agreement is still pending in the trial court, a party seeking to enforce the agreement may amend its pleadings in the suit to add a claim for breach of contract or file a counterclaim asserting breach of contract. *See* **Mantas v. Fifth Ct. of Appeals**, 925 S.W.2d 656, 658 (Tex.1996); *see, e.g.*, **Amedisys, Inc. v. Kingwood Home Health Care, LLC**, 437 S.W.3d 507, 510 (Tex.2014) (amended pleading); **Padilla**, 907 S.W.2d at 462 (counterclaim); *see also* **Ford Motor**, 279 S.W.3d at 663 (party withdrawing consent can conduct discovery to prepare defense against breach-of-contract claim). A party may also assert its claim in a motion to enforce. *See* **Kanan v. Plantation Homeowner's Ass'n**, 407 S.W.3d 320, 334 (Tex.App.—Corpus Christi 2013, no pet.); **Neasbitt v. Warren**, 105 S.W.3d 113, 117–18 (Tex.App.—Fort Worth 2003, no pet.); *see also* **In re Vaishangi**, 442 S.W.3d at 260 (party cannot file motion to enforce after trial court's plenary power has expired). If the suit is not pending in the trial court, a party seeking to enforce the settlement agreement must file a separate breach-of-contract suit under a new cause number. **Mantas**, 925 S.W.2d at 658–59; *see* **In re Vaishangi**, 442 S.W.3d at 260; **Ford Motor**, 279 S.W.3d at 663.

§4. Settlement credits under proportionate responsibility

The Texas proportionate-responsibility statute provides rules for apportioning liability for damages among the plaintiff and multiple defendants. *See* Tex. Civ. Prac. & Rem. Code ch. 33. For a detailed discussion of proportionate responsibility and contribution, see "Proportionate Responsibility & Contribution," **O'Connor's Texas Causes of Action**, ch. 51, §1 et seq. (2021 ed.).

§4.1 Settlement credits. The proportionate-responsibility statute provides rules for applying a settlement "credit" (or a reduction of damages) based on a plaintiff's settlement with one of the defendants in a lawsuit. That is, if the plaintiff settled with a defendant, the court must reduce the amount the plaintiff can recover from a nonsettling defendant. For a detailed discussion of settlement credits, see "Settlement credit," **O'Connor's Texas Causes of Action**, ch. 51, §5.2 (2021 ed.).

§4.2 One-satisfaction rule. The one-satisfaction rule provides that a party is entitled to recover damages only once for a single injury. **Sky View at Las Palmas, LLC v. Mendez**, 555 S.W.3d 101, 106–07 (Tex.2018); **Crown Life Ins. v. Casteel**, 22 S.W.3d 378, 390 (Tex.2000). The rule prevents a party from recovering more than the amount required for the full satisfaction of its damages. **First Title Co. v. Garrett**, 860 S.W.2d 74, 78 (Tex.1993); *see* **Waite Hill Servs. v. World Class Metal Works, Inc.**, 959 S.W.2d 182, 184 (Tex.1998). The one-satisfaction rule applies whether the defendants committed joint or separate acts that resulted in the injury. **Sky View**, 555 S.W.3d at 107; **Casteel**, 22 S.W.3d at 390. See "One-satisfaction rule," **O'Connor's Texas Causes of Action**, ch. 41-A, §5 (2021 ed.).

Chapter 8. The Trial

A. Jury Selection

§1. General

§1.1 Rules. Tex. R. Civ. P. 221 to 236, 281, 284. See Tex. Gov't Code ch. 62 (petit juries).

§1.2 Purpose. The purpose of jury selection is to seat a fair and impartial jury. **Hallett v. Houston Nw. Med. Ctr.**, 689 S.W.2d 888, 889 (Tex.1985). The right to a fair and impartial trial is codified in Tex. Gov't Code §62.105. **Babcock v. Northwest Mem'l Hosp.**, 767 S.W.2d 705, 708 (Tex.1989).

§1.3 Forms. **O'Connor's Texas Civil Forms**, FORMS 8A:1 et seq. (2020 ed.).

§1.4 Other references. Babcock & Gilman, *Use of Social Media in Voir Dire*, 60 The Advoc. (Texas) 44 (Fall 2012); Enoch & Johnson, *Narrowing the Ability to Strike Jurors: The Texas Supreme Court Addresses Important Voir Dire Issues*, 39 Tex. Tech L.Rev. 229 (2006–07); **O'Connor's Federal Rules * Civil Trials** (2021 ed.); **O'Connor's Texas Civil Practice & Remedies Code Plus** (2020–21 ed.).

§2. Number of jurors

§2.1 District court. A jury in district court is composed of 12 persons. Tex. Const. art. 5, §13; Tex. Gov't Code §62.201; **McDaniel v. Yarbrough**, 898 S.W.2d 251, 252 (Tex.1995); *see also* Tex. R. Civ. P. 292(a) (when as many as three jurors die or become disabled from sitting, the remaining jurors can render and return a verdict). However, the parties may agree to try a case with fewer than 12 jurors. Tex. Gov't Code §62.201. See "Verdict by fewer than 12 jurors," ch. 8-K, §3.

§2.2 County court or justice court. A jury in constitutional county court, county court at law, or justice court is composed of six persons. *See* Tex. Const. art. 5, §17; Tex. Gov't Code §§25.0007, 62.301; Tex. R. Civ. P. 504.2(f).

Note

For cases filed in a county court at law on or after September 1, 2020, if the amount in controversy exceeds $250,000, the jury must be composed of 12 persons unless all the parties agree to a smaller jury. See Acts 2019, 86th Leg., R.S., ch. 696, §§3, 33, 36, 37, eff. Sept. 1, 2020 (amending Gov't Code §25.0007 and §62.301).

---

§2.3 Statutory probate court. Generally, a jury in statutory probate court is composed of six persons. *See* Tex. Gov't Code §§25.0027, 62.301. In cases involving matters in which the statutory probate court has concurrent jurisdiction with the district court, however, the jury is composed of 12 persons. *See* Tex. Gov't Code §§25.0027, 62.201.

§2.4 Alternate jurors. Alternate jurors replace jurors who, before the jury retires to deliberate its verdict, become or are found to be unable to perform their duties or disqualified from jury service. Tex. Gov't Code §62.020(d); *see* **In re M.G.N.**, 441 S.W.3d 246, 248 (Tex.2014). Alternate jurors are drawn and selected just as regular jurors are. Tex. Gov't Code §62.020(c); **In re M.G.N.**, 441 S.W.3d at 248. The number of alternate jurors depends on the impaneling court.

1. **District court.** In district court, up to four alternate jurors may be impaneled. Tex. Gov't Code §62.020(a).

2. **County court.** In county court, up to two alternate jurors may be impaneled. Tex. Gov't Code §62.020(b).

§3. Qualifications & exemptions of jurors

§3.1 General qualifications. All individuals are considered competent jurors unless disqualified by statute. Tex. Gov't Code §62.101. To be qualified to serve as a juror, a person must:

1. Be at least 18 years of age. Tex. Gov't Code §62.102(1).

2. Be a citizen of the United States. Tex. Gov't Code §62.102(2).

3. Be a resident of Texas and the county where she is to serve. Tex. Gov't Code §62.102(3).

4. Be qualified to vote in the county where she is to serve. Tex. Gov't Code §62.102(4). A person who is not registered to vote is not disqualified from serving as a juror. Tex. Gov't Code §62.1031.

5. Be of sound mind and good moral character. Tex. Gov't Code §62.102(5).

6. Be able to read and write. Tex. Gov't Code §62.102(6); **Jenkins v. Chapman**, 636 S.W.2d 238, 240 (Tex.App.—Texarkana 1982, writ dism'd). The trial court may suspend this requirement if there are not enough jurors in the county who can read and write. Tex. Gov't Code §62.103(a).

7. Have not served as a juror for six or more days during the preceding three months in the county court or during the preceding six months in the district court. Tex. Gov't Code §62.102(7). The court may suspend this restriction if the county's sparse population makes it seriously inconvenient to enforce. Tex. Gov't Code §62.103(b).

8. Have not been convicted of misdemeanor theft or a felony. Tex. Gov't Code §62.102(8); *see also* **Volkswagen v. Ramirez**, 79 S.W.3d 113, 119–21 (Tex.App.—Corpus Christi 2002) (dismissal of felony conviction after community supervision restored felon's right to serve on jury), *rev'd on other grounds*, 159 S.W.3d 897 (Tex.2004).

9. Not be under indictment or other legal accusation for misdemeanor theft or a felony. Tex. Gov't Code §62.102(9); *see* **Palmer Well Servs. v. Mack Trucks, Inc.**, 776 S.W.2d 575, 576 (Tex.1989). The parties may waive the error by agreeing to continue with a juror who is under indictment. **Mendoza v. Varon**, 563 S.W.2d 646, 648 (Tex.App.—Dallas 1978, writ ref'd n.r.e.). If a juror's indictment is discovered after the verdict is rendered and that juror's vote is required for a verdict of ten jurors, the judgment must be reversed. **Palmer Well Servs.**, 776 S.W.2d at 577.

Note

Even though a person convicted of or under indictment or other legal accusation for misdemeanor theft or a felony cannot serve on a jury, TRCP 230 prohibits asking a panelist if she has been convicted of or charged with such an offense.

§3.2 Physical qualifications. A blind or deaf person is not disqualified solely because of the disability, unless the disability renders the person unfit in that particular case. Tex. Gov't Code §62.104(a), (b) (blindness), §62.1041(a), (b) (deafness); *cf.* **Galloway v. Superior Court**, 816 F.Supp. 12, 18–19 (D.D.C.1993) (Americans with Disabilities Act prohibited automatic disqualification of person based on blindness). The court is required to provide an interpreter for a deaf juror during the trial and the deliberations. Tex. Civ. Prac. & Rem. Code §§21.002(a), 21.009; *cf.* **Saunders v. State**, 49 S.W.3d 536, 539–40 (Tex.App.—Eastland 2001, pet. ref'd) (criminal case; juror entitled to interpreter during deliberations).

§3.3 Statutory disqualifications. If a person is disqualified by statute, the court must excuse that person from service. **Compton v. Henrie**, 364 S.W.2d 179, 182 (Tex.1963). Under Gov't Code §62.105, a panelist is disqualified from serving as a juror on a particular case in the following instances:

1. Witness. The person is a witness in the case. Tex. Gov't Code §62.105(1).

2. Interest. The person has a direct or indirect interest in the case. Tex. Gov't Code §62.105(2). The trial court must make a factual determination whether a panelist is interested in the case. *Cf.* **Malone v. Foster**, 977 S.W.2d 562, 564 (Tex.1998) (court must make factual determination of bias or prejudice under Gov't Code §62.105(4)); **Pharo v. Chambers Cty.**, 922 S.W.2d 945, 949 (Tex.1996) (court must make factual determination whether person is interested in case under former TRCP 226a, §II(1), now TRCP 226a, §II(2)).

(1) Examples of disqualifying interests. • The employee of a party. **Preston v. Ohio Oil Co.**, 121 S.W.2d 1039, 1041–42 (Tex.App.—Eastland 1938, writ ref'd). *But see* **Pharo**, 922 S.W.2d at 949 & n.4 (employee of governmental-entity party is not automatically disqualified). • Stockholders of a party corporation. **Texas Power & Light Co. v. Adams**, 404 S.W.2d 930, 943 (Tex.App.—Tyler 1966, no writ). • Insureds of a party insurer. **Texas Empls. Ins. v. Lane**, 251 S.W.2d 181, 181–82 (Tex.App.—Fort Worth 1952, writ ref'd n.r.e.).

(2) Examples of interests too remote to disqualify. • Social relationship with employee of governmental-entity party. *E.g.*, **Pharo**, 922 S.W.2d at 947–49 (juror dating a deputy sheriff in suit against county for negligence of sheriff).

• Members of a cooperative buying club that is a party. *E.g.*, **Guerra v. Wal-Mart Stores**, 943 S.W.2d 56, 59 (Tex.App.—San Antonio 1997, writ denied) (panelists were members of Sam's Shopping Club, and its parent company was sued in negligence case). • Taxpayer residents of a city-party. **City of Hawkins v. E.B. Germany & Sons**, 425 S.W.2d 23, 26 (Tex.App.—Tyler 1968, writ ref'd n.r.e.). • A casual friend who had former business relationship with one of the parties. *E.g.*, **Gant v. Dumas Glass & Mirror, Inc.**, 935 S.W.2d 202, 208–09 (Tex.App.—Amarillo 1996, no writ) (panelist rented property from D eight years earlier and became friendly with him).

3. Relative. The person is related by consanguinity or affinity within the third degree to a party in the case. Tex. Gov't Code §62.105(3). Degrees of relationship are determined according to the civil-law method. Tex. Gov't Code §573.021; *see* Tex. Gov't Code §§573.022 to 573.025. See "Relatives Within the Third Degree of Person," **O'Connor's Texas Civil Practice & Remedies Code Plus**, chart 7 (2020–21 ed.), showing which relatives are within the third degree.

4. Same case. The person has served as a juror in an earlier trial of the same case or in another case involving the same questions of fact. Tex. Gov't Code §62.105(5).

5. Bias or prejudice. The person has a bias or prejudice in favor of or against a party in the case. Tex. Gov't Code §62.105(4). A bias is an inclination toward one side of an issue over the other. **Hyundai Motor Co. v. Vasquez**, 189 S.W.3d 743, 751 (Tex.2006); **Goode v. Shoukfeh**, 943 S.W.2d 441, 453 (Tex.1997); **Compton**, 364 S.W.2d at 182. Prejudice is the prejudgment of an issue. **Hyundai Motor**, 189 S.W.3d at 751; **Compton**, 364 S.W.2d at 182. Prejudice includes bias. **Hyundai Motor**, 189 S.W.3d at 751; **Goode**, 943 S.W.2d at 453; **Compton**, 364 S.W.2d at 182. A panelist who is biased or prejudiced in favor of or against a party or the type of lawsuit should be disqualified. **Murff v. Pass**, 249 S.W.3d 407, 411 (Tex.2008). For a panelist to be disqualified on the basis of bias, the panelist's state of mind must lead to the inference that she cannot or will not act with impartiality. **Cortez v. HCCI-San Antonio, Inc.**, 159 S.W.3d 87, 94 (Tex.2005); **Compton**, 364 S.W.2d at 182. A panelist does not have a disqualifying bias if she states that she has a "better understanding" of or an initial "leaning" toward one party if the statement is based on skepticism or an opinion about the evidence rather than an ultimate conclusion. **Cortez**, 159 S.W.3d at 93–94; *see* **El Hafi v. Baker**, 164 S.W.3d 383, 385 (Tex.2005) (perspective based on knowledge and experience does not make panelist biased). A statement that is more of a preview of a panelist's opinion rather than an expression of actual bias is not a ground for disqualification. **Cortez**, 159 S.W.3d at 94. Disqualification for bias or prejudice does not depend on a few "magic words" but on the record as a whole. *Id.* at 93. If bias or prejudice is established as a matter of law, the prospective juror is automatically disqualified. **Goode**, 943 S.W.2d at 452–53; **Compton**, 364 S.W.2d at 182. If bias or prejudice is not established as a matter of law, the trial court must make a factual determination whether the panelist's bias or prejudice merits disqualification. **Malone**, 977 S.W.2d at 564; **Swap Shop v. Fortune**, 365 S.W.2d 151, 154 (Tex.1963); *see* **Cortez**, 159 S.W.3d at 93.

(1) Rehabilitation. When a panelist makes a statement that appears to show bias or prejudice, additional questioning may help clarify the statement and "rehabilitate" the panelist. **Cortez**, 159 S.W.3d at 92–93. Voir dire does not stop the moment a panelist gives an answer that might be disqualifying. *Id.* at 91–92. Because the appearance of partiality may result from inappropriate leading questions, confusion, misunderstanding, or ignorance of the law, the trial court should allow examination to continue to inquire into the panelist's apparent bias. *E.g., id.* at 92–93 (insurance adjuster who initially said "I would feel bias" was permitted to explain that he was biased against lawsuit abuse, not P's case); *see, e.g.*, **McMillin v. State Farm Lloyds**, 180 S.W.3d 183, 196–97 (Tex.App.—Austin 2005, pet. denied) (panelists who admitted they were initially biased were not disqualified because they later stated they could award the full amount of damages if proved). The trial court also has the discretion to stop the line of questioning to clarify the panelist's response. **Murff**, 249 S.W.3d at 411.

(2) No recantation. When the record as a whole shows a panelist is materially biased or prejudiced, the panelist's ultimate recantation or denial of bias will not prevent disqualification. **Cortez**, 159 S.W.3d at 92. For example, a panelist's statement that she can be "fair and impartial" does not rehabilitate the panelist if the record as a whole shows she is biased. *Id.* at 93.

(3) Examples of bias or prejudice. • Panelist stated he could not be fair to defendant because of results of his father's medical treatment. **Shepherd v. Ledford**, 962 S.W.2d 28, 34 (Tex.1998). • Panelists stated they would award damages to plaintiff even if he did not prove his case. **Silsbee Hosp., Inc. v. George**, 163 S.W.3d 284, 295–96 (Tex.App.—Beaumont 2005, pet. denied). • Juror placed higher burden on juvenile than required by law. **W.D.A. v. State**, 835 S.W.2d

227, 229 (Tex.App.—Waco 1992, no writ). • Juror was prejudiced against drinking and said it would affect her judgment. **Flowers v. Flowers**, 397 S.W.2d 121, 123–24 (Tex.App.—Amarillo 1965, no writ).

(4) Examples of no bias or prejudice. • Panelist, confused about the definition of "preponderance of the evidence," stated he would hold plaintiff to a clear-and-convincing standard of proof but later agreed he would follow instructions given by the court. **Murff**, 249 S.W.3d at 411. • Panelist admitted that being a personal-injury defense attorney would influence how he viewed the evidence. **El Hafi**, 164 S.W.3d at 385. • Panelist admitted he had preconceived notions about the case because he worked as an insurance adjuster, but on further questioning stated he would listen to the evidence. **Cortez**, 159 S.W.3d at 93. • Panelist stated he did not know if he could award plaintiffs loss-of-consortium damages. **Malone**, 977 S.W.2d at 564.

§3.4 Exemptions from jury service. A person qualified to be a juror may claim an exemption from jury service by filing a statement of exemption before the date on which she is required to appear. *See* Tex. Gov't Code §62 107(a). After that date, the person must present sworn evidence before the court.

1. Statutorily defined exemptions.

(1) Specific exemptions. Gov't Code §62.106 allows the following persons to claim exemptions from jury service: (1) a person over 70, (2) a person with legal custody of a child younger than 12, if jury service would require leaving the child without adequate supervision, (3) a student in secondary school or a person enrolled and in actual attendance at an institution of higher education, (4) an officer or employee of the legislative branch of state government, (5) the primary caretaker of a person who is unable to care for herself, (6) in a county with a population of at least 200,000, a person who has served as a juror during the preceding 24-month period, (7) in a county with a population of at least 250,000, a person who has served as a juror during the preceding three-year period, or (8) a member of the U.S. military serving on active duty and deployed to a location away from her home station and outside her county of residence. Tex. Gov't Code §62.106(a).

(2) Reasonable excuse. Outside of Gov't Code §62.106, the court may grant an exemption for any "reasonable sworn excuse" and release the person from jury service. Tex. Gov't Code §62.110(a). The commissioners court may approve a plan permitting the court's designee to hear any reasonable excuse and release the person from jury service if (1) the excuse is considered sufficient and (2) the juror provides the court's designee with a statement of the grounds for the exemption, lack of qualification, or other excuse. Tex. Gov't Code §62.110(b). Neither the court nor the court's designee may release a person from service for economic reasons under §62.110(a) or (b) unless each party of record is present and approves the release. Tex. Gov't Code §62.110(c).

2. Permanent exemptions. A person who is older than 70, has a physical or mental impairment, or is unable to comprehend or communicate in English may establish a permanent exemption from jury service. *See* Tex. Gov't Code §§62.108(a), 62.109(a).

§4. Assembling prospective jurors

§4.1 Jury source. The Secretary of State compiles a list of prospective jurors by combining the lists furnished by the voter registrar of each county and the Department of Public Safety containing the names of (1) licensed drivers, (2) registered voters, and (3) holders of a personal identification card or certificate issued by the Department of Public Safety. *See* Tex. Gov't Code §62.001(a), (c) to (g). The Secretary of State sends each county its list of prospective jurors before the end of each year. Tex. Gov't Code §62.001(g).

§4.2 Counties with interchangeable jury panels. The laws for interchangeable jury panels govern (1) counties with at least three district courts and (2) counties with a single district court and a single county court at law that has concurrent jurisdiction with the district court on any matter. *See* Tex. Gov't Code §§62.016, 62.0175. In addition, district judges in counties with two district courts can elect to be governed by the laws for interchangeable jury panels. *See* Tex. Gov't Code §62.017(j) (adoption of this method is discretionary). The judges of a county governed by the laws for interchangeable jury panels determine the approximate number of prospective jurors necessary for each week of the year for the general panel. Tex. Gov't Code §§62.016(a), 62.017(a), 62.0175(a). The names are drawn from the jury wheel or selected using an electronic or mechanical device. *See* Tex. Gov't Code §§62.004(a), 62.011(a), 62.016(b), 62.017(b), 62.0175(b). When impaneled,

the prospective jurors can constitute a general panel for service in most courts of the county. *See* Tex. Gov't Code §62.016(e) (prospective jurors must be used interchangeably in all justice, county, and district courts in the county), §62.017(e) (if district judges have adopted interchangeable-jury methods, prospective jurors are used interchangeably in both district courts and, on approval of both district judges, can be used interchangeably in all justice, county, and district courts in the county), §62.0175(e) (prospective jurors are used interchangeably in both district court and county court at law with concurrent jurisdiction and, on the approval of both judges, can be used interchangeably in all justice courts, county courts, county courts at law, and district courts in the county). The district judge who impanels the jury for the week inquires into the prospective jurors' general qualifications for jury duty. *See* **Benavides v. Soto**, 893 S.W.2d 69, 70–71 (Tex.App.—Corpus Christi 1994, no writ).

Practice Tip

If the attorneys in the case believe additional prospective jurors will be necessary because they anticipate the case will result in a number of challenges for cause, they can ask the trial judge to request a larger panel.

§4.3 Other counties. In counties not governed by the laws providing for interchangeable jury panels, the clerk assembles a panel for a particular court by randomly drawing slips of paper with names on them from a container and listing them in the order selected. Tex. R. Civ. P. 224. In those counties, the clerk is authorized to select 24 panelists for the district court and 12 for the county court. *Id.*

§4.4 Objection to prospective jurors. There are two ways to object to the selection of prospective jurors.

1. Challenge the array. A party may challenge the array. Tex. R. Civ. P. 221; **Martinez v. City of Austin**, 852 S.W.2d 71, 73 (Tex.App.—Austin 1993, writ denied). This objection challenges the procedure for selecting and summoning prospective jurors or asserts a violation of the jury-wheel statute. **Martinez**, 852 S.W.2d at 73; *see* Tex. Gov't Code §§62.001 to 62.021. The challenge must be by written motion, supported by affidavit and filed with the particular judge in charge of the local jury system. *See* Tex. R. Civ. P. 221; **State v. Smith**, 671 S.W.2d 32, 36 (Tex.1984); **Texas Empls. Ins. v. Burge**, 610 S.W.2d 524, 525 (Tex.App.—Beaumont 1980, writ ref'd n.r.e.). Noncompliance with TRCP 221 waives any objection to the array, unless there was fundamental error. *See* **Mann v. Ramirez**, 905 S.W.2d 275, 278 (Tex.App.—San Antonio 1995, writ denied) (procedural errors do not rise to level of fundamental error). An objection to the array may be made to the trial judge only if the party had no opportunity to object at the time the impaneling judge assembled the array. *E.g.*, **Mendoza v. Ranger Ins.**, 753 S.W.2d 779, 780–81 (Tex.App.—Fort Worth 1988, writ denied) (lack of randomness of panel did not become apparent until voir dire). If the movant successfully challenges the array, the entire array is dismissed, and a new one is summoned. **Martinez**, 852 S.W.2d at 73.

2. Request jury shuffle. In counties governed by the laws on interchangeable jury panels, after the panel is assigned to a court and before voir dire, a party may request a jury shuffle. Tex. R. Civ. P. 223; *see* **BNSF Ry. v. Wipff**, 408 S.W.3d 662, 666 (Tex.App.—Fort Worth 2013, no pet.); **Martinez**, 852 S.W.2d at 73. The order in which the panelists are listed on the jury list is important because the first 12 (or 6 in county court) unchallenged panelists will sit on the jury.

(1) Before voir dire. A party must make a request for a jury shuffle before voir dire. Tex. R. Civ. P. 223. When a detailed, case-specific juror questionnaire is used, the phrase "before voir dire" has been construed to mean before the responses to the questionnaire are examined by the parties. *See, e.g.*, **Carr v. Smith**, 22 S.W.3d 128, 133–34 (Tex.App.—Fort Worth 2000, pet. denied) (distinguishing between standard juror questionnaire and 13-page form with 63 specially tailored questions). But even if the responses have been examined, the request for a jury shuffle may be considered timely (i.e., "before voir dire") as long as the attorney has not viewed the panel and the court has not given the panel its approved instructions under TRCP 226a. *See* **BNSF Ry.**, 408 S.W.3d at 667.

(2) Procedure for jury shuffle. When requested, the names of the members of the panel must be placed in a receptacle, shuffled, drawn, and transcribed on the jury list in the order drawn. Tex. R. Civ. P. 223; *see, e.g.*, **Whiteside v. Watson**, 12 S.W.3d 614, 617–18 (Tex.App.—Eastland 2000, pet. granted, judgm't vacated w.r.m.) (shuffle of jury cards did not comply with rule). It is not necessary for the judge to draw the names from the receptacle; the bailiff can perform that task. **Whiteside**, 12 S.W.3d at 618 n.1.

(3) One jury shuffle. Only one jury shuffle is allowed in each case. Tex. R. Civ. P. 223; **Martinez**, 852 S.W.2d at 73. *But see* **Whiteside**, 12 S.W.3d at 618–19 (second shuffle was proper after first shuffle did not comply with TRCP 223; any error in second shuffle was harmless because underlying purpose of TRCP 223 was substantially complied with).

§5. Voir dire examination

§5.1 Purpose. During voir dire, each party has the opportunity to examine the members of the panel to determine whether any of them are disqualified or should not serve on the case. *See* **Implement Dealers Mut. Ins. v. Castleberry**, 368 S.W.2d 249, 254 (Tex.App.—Beaumont 1963, writ ref'd n.r.e.). The right to conduct a proper voir dire is linked to the constitutional right to a fair trial. **Babcock v. Northwest Mem'l Hosp.**, 767 S.W.2d 705, 709 (Tex.1989) Voir dire protects the right to an impartial jury by exposing possible juror biases. **Hyundai Motor Co. v. Vasquez**, 189 S.W.3d 743, 749 (Tex.2006); *see also* **In re Commitment of Hill**, 334 S.W.3d 226, 228 (Tex.2011) (parties have right to question panelists to discover biases and to properly use peremptory challenges).

§5.2 Right to initiate voir dire. Except for good cause shown on the record, the party with the burden of proof on the whole case should be allowed to initiate voir dire. *See* Tex. R. Civ. P. 265, 266; **Ocean Transp. v. Greycas, Inc.**, 878 S.W.2d 256, 268–69 (Tex.App.—Corpus Christi 1994, writ denied).

§5.3 Control of voir dire. The trial court has broad discretion in conducting voir dire. **Cortez v. HCCI-San Antonio, Inc.**, 159 S.W.3d 87, 92 (Tex.2005). This discretion includes whether to permit questions about the weight a panelist would give (or not give) to a particular fact or set of facts. **Hyundai Motor Co. v. Vasquez**, 189 S.W.3d 743, 753 (Tex.2006).

1. Scope of examination. A party is entitled to inquire into matters reasonably related to the kinds of issues presented by the case. *See* **Babcock v. Northwest Mem'l Hosp.**, 767 S.W.2d 705, 709 (Tex.1989); **Texas Empls. Ins. v. Loesch**, 538 S.W.2d 435, 440 (Tex.App.—Waco 1976, writ ref'd n.r.e.). The trial court is more likely to be reversed on appeal if it prevents a party from asking a question that may reveal an external bias or prejudice than if it allows the question. *See* **Babcock**, 767 S.W.2d at 708–09. The court should give the attorneys broad latitude during the examination of the jury panel. *Id.*; **Loesch**, 538 S.W.2d at 440. The examination must probe for a panelist's bias or prejudice against a party or claim. However, after the recitation of facts, the examination cannot be used to gauge the potential impact of evidence on the panelist's verdict. **Hyundai Motor**, 189 S.W.3d at 756–57. Thus, if the question is directed at finding out the weight a panelist would place on certain evidence, the trial court has the discretion to prohibit the question. *Id.* at 755; **In re Commitment of Barbee**, 192 S.W.3d 835, 846 (Tex.App.—Beaumont 2006, no pet.). The substance of a question, not its form, determines whether it probes for prejudices or previews a potential verdict. **Hyundai Motor**, 189 S.W.3d at 757–58. If the trial court prohibits a question, the attorney should propose a different question or specify the area of inquiry to preserve error. *Id.* at 758.

(1) Proper questions & comments. The following matters have been found to be proper on voir dire: • The panelist's ability to have a party prove both required elements of a statute before deciding the verdict. **In re Commitment of Hill**, 334 S.W.3d 226, 229–30 (Tex.2011). • The panelist's relationship to a party. *See* Tex. Gov't Code §§62.105(3), 573.022 to 573.025. • The panelist's bias or prejudice caused by media coverage of the "lawsuit crisis" and the "insurance crisis." **Babcock**, 767 S.W.2d at 708–09; *see* **National Cty. Mut. Fire Ins. v. Howard**, 749 S.W.2d 618, 621 (Tex.App.—Fort Worth 1988, writ denied). • The panelist's bias or prejudice against the type of lawsuit. *See* **Compton v. Henrie**, 364 S.W.2d 179, 180 (Tex.1963). • The panelist's bias in favor of or against a party because of nationality, wealth, or status. **Haryanto v. Saeed**, 860 S.W.2d 913, 918 (Tex.App.—Houston [14th Dist.] 1993, writ denied). • Informing the panel of the party's own insurance coverage. **University of Tex. at Austin v. Hinton**, 822 S.W.2d 197, 201 (Tex.App.—Austin 1991, no writ). • The panelist's bias or prejudice in favor of or against a party in the case. **American Cyanamid Co. v. Frankson**, 732 S.W.2d 648, 653 (Tex.App.—Corpus Christi 1987, writ ref'd n.r.e.); *see* Tex. Gov't Code §62.105(4). • The panelist's ability to award a certain sum of money if warranted by the evidence. *See* **Cavnar v. Quality Control Parking, Inc.**, 678 S.W.2d 548, 555 (Tex.App.—Houston [14th Dist.] 1984), *rev'd in part on other grounds*, 696 S.W.2d 549 (Tex.1985). • The panelist's acquaintance with potential witnesses. **Employers Mut. Liab. Ins. v. Butler**, 511 S.W.2d 323, 325–26 (Tex.App.—Texarkana 1974, writ ref'd n.r.e.). • The panelist's relationship with an organization that the other attorney belongs to. **Lopez v. Allee**, 493 S.W.2d 330, 335 (Tex.App.—San Antonio 1973, writ ref'd n.r.e.). • The panelist's bias against the use of intoxicants. **Flowers v. Flowers**, 397 S.W.2d 121, 122–23 (Tex.App.—Amarillo 1965, no writ). • The panelist's representation by one of the

attorneys. **Implement Dealers Mut. Ins. v. Castleberry**, 368 S.W.2d 249, 254 (Tex.App.—Beaumont 1963, writ ref'd n.r.e.). • The panelist's financial interest in the litigation. **Carey v. Planters' State Bank**, 280 S.W. 251, 252 (Tex.App.—San Antonio 1926, writ dism'd); *see* Tex. Gov't Code §62.105(2). • The panelist's relationship with the other attorney. **Anderson v. Owen**, 269 S.W. 454, 455 (Tex.App.—Galveston 1924, no writ).

Practice Tip

In exemplary-damages cases, attorneys cannot question panelists about exemplary damages based on a preponderance of the evidence because the burden for exemplary damages is clear and convincing evidence. See Tex. Civ. Prac. & Rem. Code §41.003(a). See "Motion to bifurcate exemplary damages," ch. 5-I, §5.

(2) Improper questions & comments. The following matters have been found to be improper on voir dire: • Isolating one specific fact of the case and asking whether the panelist could be fair, regardless of the other evidence, based on that specific fact. **Hyundai Motor**, 189 S.W.3d at 756–57; *see, e.g.*, **In re Commitment of Barbee**, 192 S.W.3d at 846 (improper to ask if panelist could be fair to party who was previously convicted for crimes against children). • Asking the panelist if one party is starting out ahead after the panelist heard a summary of the facts of the case. **Cortez**, 159 S.W.3d at 94. • For a plaintiff, telling the panel that the defendant has insurance or the plaintiff has no insurance; for a defendant, telling the panel that the plaintiff has insurance. **Ford v. Carpenter**, 216 S.W.2d 558, 559 (Tex.1949). • Asking a question for which the prejudicial effect outweighs the probative value. *See* **Gulf States Utils. Co. v. Reed**, 659 S.W.2d 849, 855–56 (Tex.App.—Houston [14th Dist.] 1983, writ ref'd n.r.e.). • Advising the panel of the effect of their answers. **Robinson v. Lovell**, 238 S.W.2d 294, 298 (Tex.App.—Galveston 1951, writ ref'd n.r.e.). • Discussing evidence that will be inadmissible at trial. *See, e.g.*, **Travelers Ins. v. DeLeon**, 456 S.W.2d 544, 545 (Tex.App.—Amarillo 1970, writ ref'd n.r.e.) (in workers' compensation case, weekly compensation benefits); **Christie v. Brewer**, 374 S.W.2d 908, 911–12 (Tex.App.—Austin 1964, writ ref'd n.r.e.) (in suit to rescind stock purchases, other party's indictment for matters relating to same transaction).

2. Time for examination. The trial court has the right to reasonably limit the time for questioning the panelists. **Greer v. Seales**, No. 09-05-001-CV, 2006 WL 439109 (Tex.App.—Beaumont 2006, no pet.) (memo op.; 2-23-06); *see* **McCoy v. Wal-Mart Stores**, 59 S.W.3d 793, 797 (Tex.App.—Texarkana 2001, no pet.); *cf.* **McCarter v. State**, 837 S.W.2d 117, 119 (Tex.Crim.App.1992) (criminal case; judge can impose reasonable restrictions on voir dire). To preserve error when the trial court limits the time for voir dire, the objecting party must show all of the following: (1) the party did not attempt to prolong voir dire, (2) the party was prevented from asking proper and relevant voir dire questions because the court imposed unreasonable time limitations, and (3) the party was not permitted to examine prospective jurors who actually served on the jury. **McCoy**, 59 S.W.3d at 797; **Greer**, No. 09-05-001-CV, 2006 WL 439109 (memo op.). The party must identify the specific questions it was not permitted to ask. *See, e.g.*, **Greer**, No. 09-05-001-CV, 2006 WL 439109 (memo op.) (identifying general topics of questions did not preserve error); *cf.* **Clemments v. State**, 940 S.W.2d 207, 209–10 (Tex.App.—San Antonio 1996, pet. ref'd) (criminal case; identifying specific questions preserved error). The specific questions must be identified to the court before the jury is selected. *See* **S.D.G. v. State**, 936 S.W.2d 371, 380–81 (Tex.App.—Houston [14th Dist.] 1996, writ denied).

3. Objections to judge's bias. A party may object to improper comments made by a trial judge during voir dire that showed the judge's bias to the jury. *See* **In re Commitment of Barbee**, 192 S.W.3d at 847; *see also* **Metzger v. Sebek**, 892 S.W.2d 20, 37–38 (Tex.App.—Houston [1st Dist.] 1994, writ denied) (objection to comments made by judge during trial). Generally, the court does not show bias when it (1) discusses how to phrase a particular question, (2) speculates on reasons for an attorney's question, or (3) criticizes the attorney. *See* **Dow Chem. Co. v. Francis**, 46 S.W.3d 237, 240 (Tex.2001) (judicial remarks during trial that are critical of, disapproving of, or hostile to counsel, parties, or their cases ordinarily do not constitute bias); *see, e.g.*, **In re Commitment of Barbee**, 192 S.W.3d at 847–48 (judge's remark that counsel was trying to "bust" entire panel and that he wanted counsel to be honest did not constitute bias). Although the judge can have these discussions with the attorney in the panel's presence, she should avoid doing so. *See* **In re Commitment of Barbee**, 192 S.W.3d at 847–48. To preserve error, the attorney must object to the judge's comments at the time they are made and request an instruction to cure any error. **Dow Chem.**, 46 S.W.3d at 241; **In re Commitment of Barbee**, 192 S.W.3d at 847.

§5.4 Error.

1. Types of errors. The following are types of errors that can be made during voir dire examination.

(1) By court—refusal to allow questions. The trial court refuses to allow a permissible line of questioning. **In re Commitment of Hill**, 334 S.W.3d 226, 228–29 (Tex.2011); **Babcock v. Northwest Mem'l Hosp.**, 767 S.W.2d 705, 708–09 (Tex.1989). This type of error may be a ground for a new trial. *See* **In re Commitment of Hill**, 334 S.W.3d at 230; **Babcock**, 767 S.W.2d at 709. See "Abuse of discretion," ch. 8-A, §11.2; "Motion for New Trial," ch. 10-B, §1 et seq.

(2) By attorney—improper question or statement. An attorney asks an improper question or makes an improper statement. *See, e.g.*, **Texas Empls. Ins. v. Loesch**, 538 S.W.2d 435, 440–41 (Tex.App.—Waco 1976, writ ref'd n.r.e.) (P's attorney attacked D and its attorneys by indicating that D did not want to comply with provisions of its insurance policy, was attempting to avoid liability by deception, and engaged in conspiracy by concealing P's true condition). If the question or statement is curable, the other attorney must object and, if the objection is sustained, ask for an instruction to disregard the question or statement. See "Object to improper question or statement & pursue adverse ruling," ch. 8-A, §5.4.2(3).

(3) By panelist.

(a) Erroneous answer. A panelist makes an erroneous or incorrect material answer to a question. Tex. R. Civ. P. 327(a). This type of error may be a ground for a new trial. See "Erroneous juror answer during voir dire," ch. 10-B, §14.1.1(1)(d).

(b) Prejudicial statement. A panelist makes a spontaneous, prejudicial statement. *See* **Brentwood Fin. Corp. v. Lamprecht**, 736 S.W.2d 836, 840 (Tex.App.—San Antonio 1987, writ ref'd n.r.e.). If the statement is curable, the party must object and, if the objection is sustained, ask for an instruction to disregard the statement. See "Object to improper question or statement & pursue adverse ruling," ch. 8-A, §5.4.2(3). If the statement poisons the panel, the party should move to strike the entire panel. *See, e.g.*, **Reviea v. Marine Drilling Co.**, 800 S.W.2d 252, 256 (Tex.App.—Corpus Christi 1990, writ denied) (panelist's spontaneous remark about excessive insurance rates did not require trial court to strike panel). In most cases, the party moving to strike the entire panel must ask the panel follow-up questions to establish that the panel was affected by the statement. *See* **Brentwood Fin.**, 736 S.W.2d at 840.

(c) No response. A panelist does not respond to a question. But the courts generally find the lack of a response not to be juror misconduct and hold that there is no harm to the complainant. *See* **Kiefer v. Continental Airlines, Inc.**, 10 S.W.3d 34, 40 (Tex.App.—Houston [14th Dist.] 1999, pet. denied); **Durbin v. Dal-Briar Corp.**, 871 S.W.2d 263, 272–73 (Tex.App.—El Paso 1994, writ denied), *disapproved on other grounds*, **Golden Eagle Archery Inc. v. Jackson**, 24 S.W.3d 362 (Tex.2000); **Missouri Pac. R.R. v. Cunningham**, 515 S.W.2d 678, 685 (Tex.App.—San Antonio 1974, writ dism'd).

2. Preserving error. To preserve error during voir dire, the attorney should take the following steps:

(1) Make a record. The attorney should always ask the court reporter to record the complete voir dire, including bench conferences. *See* Tex. R. App. P. 13.1(a) (duties of court reporter include making a full record of proceedings); *see, e.g.*, **Soto v. Texas Indus.**, 820 S.W.2d 217, 219 (Tex.App.—Fort Worth 1991, no writ) (court of appeals could not consider **Batson** objection because no record was made of voir dire); **Loesch**, 538 S.W.2d at 441 (court of appeals could not determine whether D's voir dire cured any error in P's voir dire because record did not include D's voir dire). *But see* **McCoy v. Wal-Mart Stores**, 59 S.W.3d 793, 796 (Tex.App.—Texarkana 2001, no pet.) (court of appeals permitted case to be abated for determination on what transpired at unrecorded bench conferences during voir dire). See "Duties of court reporter," ch. 1-E, §3. The record must contain the question the party wanted to ask and the court's ruling that prevented the question. *See* **In re Commitment of Hill**, 334 S.W.3d at 229; **Babcock**, 767 S.W.2d at 708. If the nature of the question is apparent from the context, it is not necessary to state the specific question on the record. *E.g.*, **Babcock**, 767 S.W.2d at 708 (language in motions in limine and recorded voir dire made it obvious what questions Ps wanted to ask).

(2) Conduct complete voir dire. The attorney must conduct a complete voir dire. Without a complete voir dire, the party waives the right to complain of prejudice. **City of San Antonio v. Willinger**, 345 S.W.2d 577, 578 (Tex.App.—San Antonio 1961, no writ). A complete voir dire includes the following:

(a) An inquiry about the subject on voir dire. *Id.* at 578–79.

(b) Specific rather than general questions. *Id.* Because individual panelists are often reluctant to respond to general questions, general questions are not a good predicate for complaints of concealment of information, incorrect answers, or a failure to answer. *See, e.g.*, **Durbin**, 871 S.W.2d at 273 (question whether anyone had a problem with large jury verdicts); **Soliz v. Saenz**, 779 S.W.2d 929, 933 (Tex.App.—Corpus Christi 1989, writ denied) (question whether panelists could follow the law); **Barron v. State**, 378 S.W.2d 144, 145–46 (Tex.App.—San Antonio 1964, no writ) (question whether any person knew the State's witnesses).

(c) Questions that are clear and unambiguous. **Willinger**, 345 S.W.2d at 578–79. The attorney must ensure that the members of the jury panel hear the questions and understand them. *E.g.*, **Barron**, 378 S.W.2d at 145–46 (panelist did not pay attention to questions); *see, e.g.*, **Burton v. R.E. Hable Co.**, 852 S.W.2d 745, 746 (Tex.App.—Tyler 1993, no writ) (panelist did not understand question).

(d) The pursuit of inquiries suggested by the answers of the panelists. **Willinger**, 345 S.W.2d at 578–79.

(3) Object to improper question or statement & pursue adverse ruling. When an attorney asks an objectionable question or makes an objectionable statement that is curable or a panelist makes a prejudicial statement that is curable, the attorney opposing the question or statement must object; if the objection is sustained, the attorney must request an instruction to disregard the question or statement. *See, e.g.*, **Brentwood Fin.**, 736 S.W.2d at 840 (instruction was sufficient to cure adverse effect of panelist's statement); **Loesch**, 538 S.W.2d at 441 (D's attorney objected but did not ask for instruction to disregard P's attorney's improper statements). If the court sustains the objection and instructs the jury to disregard, the attorney must then ask for a mistrial to preserve error for appeal. See "Motion for mistrial," ch. 8-D, §6.7.4. This is called "pursuing an adverse ruling." If the attorney does not pursue the objection to an adverse ruling, the error is waived. See "When jury hears inadmissible evidence," ch. 8-D, §6.7.

§6. Challenges for cause

§6.1 Purpose. A challenge for cause is an objection to a panelist, alleging some fact that by law disqualifies the person from serving as a juror or renders the person unfit to sit on the jury. Tex. R. Civ. P. 228; **Wooten v. Southern Pac. Transp.**, 928 S.W.2d 76, 80 (Tex.App.—Houston [14th Dist.] 1995, no writ). The challenge for cause permits the parties to eliminate panelists who are disqualified from serving on the jury (e.g., for bias or prejudice). As soon as it becomes apparent that a panelist may be disqualified, the attorney should ask the panelist to approach the bench for questioning outside the hearing of the rest of the panel.

§6.2 Grounds for challenges for cause.

1. General qualifications. See "General qualifications," ch. 8-A, §3.1.

2. Statutory disqualification. See "Statutory disqualifications," ch. 8-A, §3.3.

3. Other grounds for disqualification. The court may exercise its discretion and excuse a panelist for cause even when there is no statutory ground for disqualification. *See* Tex. R. Civ. P. 228 ("or which in the opinion of the court, renders him an unfit person to sit on the jury").

§6.3 Preserving error. To complain about error when the trial court refuses to permit a challenge for cause, the attorney must follow the procedure set out in **Cortez v. HCCI-San Antonio, Inc.**, 159 S.W.3d 87 (Tex.2005), and **Hallett v. Houston Nw. Med. Ctr.**, 689 S.W.2d 888 (Tex.1985). To preserve error, the attorney must take the following steps:

1. Challenge for cause. During voir dire, the attorney must challenge a panelist for cause (the "for-cause panelist"). The record must reflect that the court overruled the challenge for cause. If there is a discussion with the for-cause panelist at the bench, the attorney must make sure the court reporter records it.

2. Object to exhaustion. The timing of the objection to the exhaustion of the peremptory strikes is critical. The record must show that the attorney objected to the exhaustion of peremptory strikes before or at the same time the attorney submitted its peremptory-strike list to the clerk. See "Turn in strike list," ch. 8-A, §6.3.3. To properly object, the party must do all of the following:

(1) Notice of exhaustion. Inform the court that, as a result of the court's refusal to strike the for-cause panelist, the party will exhaust its peremptory challenges before it can strike an objectionable panelist on the list. *See* **Cortez**, 159 S.W.3d at 90–91; **Hallett**, 689 S.W.2d at 890. The latest this notice can be given is before the party learns of the other party's peremptory strikes and of the composition of the jury. *See* **Cortez**, 159 S.W.3d at 91. Once a jury is chosen, it is too late to notify the court that an objectionable panelist is on the jury. *See id.*

(2) Identification of objectionable panelist. Identify an objectionable panelist who will remain on the jury list once the party uses its last peremptory strike. **Cortez**, 159 S.W.3d at 90–91; *see* **Hallett**, 689 S.W.2d at 890.

(a) The objectionable panelist may be either the panelist who should have been struck for cause or another objectionable panelist. *See, e.g.*, **Cortez**, 159 S.W.3d at 90 (panelist other than for-cause panelist left on list); **Shepherd v. Ledford**, 962 S.W.2d 28, 34 (Tex.1998) (for-cause panelist left on list); **Hallett**, 689 S.W.2d at 889–90 (same). In most appeals, the error is waived because the party did not identify the objectionable panelist who remained on the panel. *See, e.g.*, **Pharo v. Chambers Cty.**, 893 S.W.2d 264, 268 (Tex.App.—Houston [1st Dist.] 1995) (statement that "I object to this juror" did not identify panelist), *aff'd*, 922 S.W.2d 945 (Tex.1996). The party does not need to state why the panelist is objectionable. **Cortez**, 159 S.W.3d at 91.

(b) The objectionable panelist must actually serve on the jury. To determine if a panelist will probably remain on the panel, the attorney should count 12 panelists, skipping the party's own peremptory strikes and any strikes the attorney believes the other party will make. The attorney should identify someone within those 12 panelists as the objectionable panelist. The rationale for identifying someone who could remain on the panel is the harmless-error rule—the objectionable panelist might be struck by the other party or might be so far down the list that the panelist could not have been picked for the jury. *See* **Carpenter v. Wyatt Constr. Co.**, 501 S.W.2d 748, 750–51 (Tex.App.—Houston [14th Dist.] 1973, writ ref'd n.r.e.), *disapproved on other grounds*, **Cortez v. HCCI-San Antonio, Inc.**, 159 S.W.3d 87 (Tex.2005).

Practice Tip

It is probably not necessary to take the additional step of specifying the relief you want—either a reversal of the for-cause ruling or an additional peremptory strike. See ***Sullemon v. U.S. Fid. & Guar. Co.***, *734 S.W.2d 10, 13–14 (Tex.App.—Dallas 1987, no writ). However, until the Supreme Court specifically addresses the issue, a party should always identify the relief it wants.*

---

3. Turn in strike list. After notifying the court that an objectionable juror will remain on the jury list, the attorney should turn in the strike list. *See* **Cortez**, 159 S.W.3d at 90–91.

Practice Tip

To preserve error, the attorney should state on the record, "Because the court refused to remove Mr. Smith for cause, the {party} will have no peremptory strikes left to challenge an objectionable panelist, {identify either Mr. Smith or another objectionable panelist on the jury list}. To cure the error, the {party} asks the court to strike Mr. Smith for cause or, in the alternative, grant the {party} an additional peremptory strike." If the request is denied, the attorney should state, "Having stated my objection on the record, I now hand my list of peremptory challenges to the clerk." After the jury is selected, the attorney should ask the court reporter to take possession of the juror information sheets and the strike lists so they can be included in the record.

---

§7. Peremptory challenges

Peremptory challenges, commonly referred to as "peremptory strikes," are made after the panel has been interviewed by both sides and all challenges for cause have been resolved.

§7.1 Purpose. A peremptory strike is a challenge to a panelist without assigning a reason. Tex. R. Civ. P. 232; **Hyundai Motor Co. v. Vasquez**, 189 S.W.3d 743, 749–50 (Tex.2006); **Patterson Dental Co. v. Dunn**, 592 S.W.2d 914, 917 (Tex.1979).

Peremptory strikes permit the parties to reject certain panelists who may be unsympathetic to their position; the strikes do not permit the parties to select the members for the jury. **Hyundai Motor**, 189 S.W.3d at 750; **Patterson Dental**, 592 S.W.2d at 919.

§7.2 Allocation of strikes.

1. Two-party case. In a two-party case, each side is entitled to six peremptory strikes in district court or three in county court. Tex. R. Civ. P. 233; *see* **Perkins v. Freeman**, 518 S.W.2d 532, 533 (Tex.1974).

2. Multiparty case. In a case in which there are multiple parties on the same side, the number of peremptory strikes allocated to each party depends on (1) how the parties are aligned and (2) whether the parties aligned on the same side are antagonistic to each other. *See* Tex. R. Civ. P. 233; **Scurlock Oil Co. v. Smithwick**, 724 S.W.2d 1, 5 (Tex.1986); **Garcia v. Central Power & Light Co.**, 704 S.W.2d 734, 736 (Tex.1986).

(1) Are parties properly aligned? In most multiparty cases, the alignment of the parties is not at issue. When there are multiple parties, all plaintiffs and all defendants are aligned as if they were simply one plaintiff and one defendant. *See* **Patterson Dental Co. v. Dunn**, 592 S.W.2d 914, 917 (Tex.1979) (litigants on same side of docket are deemed to be one "party" under TRCP 233). This alignment presumes that the designation of each party as a "plaintiff" or "defendant" correctly identifies which side of the docket the party belongs on. But this presumption may not be true in all cases. The term "side" is defined as litigants with a common interest in an issue to be submitted to the jury, and thus is not synonymous with terms such as "party," "litigant," or "person." Tex. R. Civ. P. 233; **"Y" Propane Serv. v. Garcia**, 61 S.W.3d 559, 569 (Tex.App.—San Antonio 2001, no pet.). If there is an issue on which a party has a common interest with an opposing party such that they may no longer be considered adversaries, the two may be considered on the same side. *See, e.g.*, **Moore v. Altra Energy Techs.**, 321 S.W.3d 727, 747 (Tex.App.—Houston [14th Dist.] 2010, pet. denied) (trial court should have aligned co-D with P and given each side same number of strikes); **American Cyanamid Co. v. Frankson**, 732 S.W.2d 648, 651 (Tex.App.—Corpus Christi 1987, writ ref'd n.r.e.) (co-Ds expected to settle with P were aligned with P and received no jury strikes). To overcome the presumption of sides, a party must make a motion to realign the parties before the exercise of peremptory strikes and show which parties share a common interest on the jury issues. *See* Tex. R. Civ. P. 233; **Pojar v. Cifre**, 199 S.W.3d 317, 326 (Tex.App.—Corpus Christi 2006, pet. denied). See **O'Connor's Texas Civil Forms**, FORM 8A:1 (2020 ed.).

(2) Are aligned parties antagonistic to each other? When there are multiple parties, the trial court must determine whether the parties on the same side of the suit—not opposing parties—are antagonistic to each other before the court can allocate peremptory strikes. **Central Power**, 704 S.W.2d at 736; **Patterson Dental**, 592 S.W.2d at 918. The antagonism must relate to an issue of fact that the jury will decide, not a matter that constitutes a pure question of law. **Patterson Dental**, 592 S.W.2d at 918; *see, e.g.*, **"Y" Propane**, 61 S.W.3d at 570 (antagonism in possible future contribution suit did not establish antagonism in primary suit). For example, defendants are considered antagonistic to each other when each contends the other is solely responsible for the plaintiff's injuries. **Patterson Dental**, 592 S.W.2d at 918. When determining whether parties are antagonistic to each other, the court can consider the pleadings, pretrial discovery, statements made during voir dire examination, and any other information brought to its attention. **Central Power**, 704 S.W.2d at 737; *see* **Scurlock Oil**, 724 S.W.2d at 5. The court's finding must be made after voir dire but before the parties exercise their peremptory strikes. *E.g.*, **Central Power**, 704 S.W.2d at 737 (statements made during voir dire established there was no antagonism); *see* Tex. R. Civ. P. 233; **Patterson Dental**, 592 S.W.2d at 919.

(3) How should strikes be allocated?

(a) No antagonism. If the court decides the parties on the same side are not antagonistic to each other, each side must receive the same number of strikes—that is, six strikes for district court or three strikes for county court. *See* Tex. R. Civ. P. 233; **Central Power**, 704 S.W.2d at 736.

(b) Antagonism. If the court decides the parties on the same side are antagonistic to each other, each party gets its own set of strikes. *See* **Patterson Dental**, 592 S.W.2d at 918 (error to require antagonistic parties on same side to share six strikes); *see, e.g.*, **Van Allen v. Blackledge**, 35 S.W.3d 61, 64 (Tex.App.—Houston [14th Dist.] 2000, pet. denied) (antagonistic Ds each received 6 strikes for total of 12 strikes on their side). If antagonistic parties are given ad-

ditional strikes, they should not be permitted to coordinate on how to exercise the strikes. *See* **In re M.N.G.**, 147 S.W.3d 521, 532 (Tex.App.—Fort Worth 2004, pet. denied); **Van Allen**, 35 S.W.3d at 65.

(c) Motion to equalize. If the allocation of strikes would result in one party or side gaining an unfair advantage, a party can—before the exercise of strikes—make a motion to equalize the peremptory strikes. Tex. R. Civ. P. 233; *see, e.g.*, **Patterson Dental**, 592 S.W.2d at 920 (four-to-one ratio of strikes between sides was erroneous; generally, two-to-one ratio is maximum disparity allowed). The motion should be made orally after voir dire. *See, e.g.*, **Patterson Dental**, 592 S.W.2d at 917 (party objected to court's allocation of strikes and made oral motion to equalize); **Texas Commerce Bank Reagan v. Lebco Constructors, Inc.**, 865 S.W.2d 68, 77–78 (Tex.App.—Corpus Christi 1993, writ denied) (pretrial motion to equalize did not preserve error when no objection to court's allocation of strikes was made after voir dire); **Diamond Shamrock Corp. v. Wendt**, 718 S.W.2d 766, 768 (Tex.App.—Corpus Christi 1986, writ ref'd n.r.e.) (party objected to court's allocation of strikes and made oral motion to equalize). Equalization, for purposes of allocating strikes, does not mean that each side or party gets the same number of peremptory strikes. *E.g.*, **Patterson Dental**, 592 S.W.2d at 920 (two-to-one ratio of strikes between sides is generally not considered abuse of discretion); **Pojar**, 199 S.W.3d at 330 (when P received six strikes, co-Ds were not entitled to six strikes each just because they were antagonistic to each other). When the court equalizes strikes, it can do so by increasing the strikes allocated to a single party on one side, decreasing the strikes allocated to multiple parties on the other side, or both. **Patterson Dental**, 592 S.W.2d at 920; *see, e.g.*, **Diamond Shamrock**, 718 S.W.2d at 770 (error to give two antagonistic Ds each 6 strikes and increase P's strikes to 12 when one D's interests were closely identified with those of P); **Williams v. Texas City Ref., Inc.**, 617 S.W.2d 823, 826–27 (Tex.App.—Houston [14th Dist.] 1981, writ ref'd n.r.e.) (because of antagonism to D and settlement agreement with P, third-party D was given one strike).

3. Objections. When the court errs in allocating peremptory strikes, to preserve error, the party must object to the allocation of strikes after voir dire and before the exercise of the strikes. **In re M.N.G.**, 147 S.W.3d at 532; **Van Allen**, 35 S.W.3d at 65; *see* **In re T.E.T.**, 603 S.W.2d 793, 798 (Tex.1980). The party must be specific about whether it is objecting to the allocation of the strikes or the alignment of the parties. *See, e.g.*, **Pojar**, 199 S.W.3d at 327–28 (error not preserved on allocation-of-strikes issue because D only argued for realignment of sides at trial).

4. Alternate jurors. When the trial court impanels alternate jurors under Gov't Code §62.020, the sides must be given additional peremptory strikes. **Temple EasTex, Inc. v. Old Orchard Creek Partners**, 848 S.W.2d 724, 738 (Tex.App.—Dallas 1992, writ denied). See "Alternate jurors," ch. 8-A, §2.4. If the trial court impanels one or two alternate jurors, the sides are each entitled to one additional peremptory strike. Tex. Gov't Code §62.020(e). If the trial court impanels three or four alternate jurors, the sides are each entitled to two additional peremptory strikes. *Id.*

§7.3 *Batson* limitations on peremptory strikes. The objection that a panelist was excluded because of some protected classification is called a **Batson** challenge, after the first criminal case that held racially based challenges were unconstitutional. *See* **Batson v. Kentucky**, 476 U.S. 79, 96 (1986); *see also* **Goode v. Shoukfeh**, 943 S.W.2d 441, 450 (Tex.1997) (calling it **Edmonson** challenge in civil context and **Batson** challenge in criminal context only). A party in a civil case has standing to assert the equal-protection rights of a panelist who was excluded from the jury because of a protected classification. **Edmonson v. Leesville Concrete Co.**, 500 U.S. 614, 629–30 (1991); *see* **Powers v. Palacios**, 813 S.W.2d 489, 490–91 (Tex.1991). It is not necessary for the struck panelist and the party challenging the strike to be members of the same cognizable group. **Powers v. Ohio**, 499 U.S. 400, 402 (1991); **Davis v. Fisk Elec. Co.**, 268 S.W.3d 508, 516 n.5 (Tex.2008); *see* **Flowers v. Mississippi**, __ U.S. __, 139 S.Ct. 2228, 2243 (2019). A party may challenge any peremptory strike that violates a panelist's equal-protection rights. **Ohio**, 499 U.S. at 415–16. The TRCPs have not been amended to incorporate the **Batson** holding. **Goode**, 943 S.W.2d at 450. Therefore, the courts often look to criminal cases for guidance. *Id.*

1. Protected classifications. Litigants cannot exercise peremptory strikes to exclude panelists based solely on the following characteristics:

(1) Race. **Flowers**, __ U.S. at __, 139 S.Ct. at 2234; **Foster v. Chatman**, __ U.S. __, 136 S.Ct. 1737, 1747 (2016); **Batson**, 476 U.S. at 96; **Davis**, 268 S.W.3d at 510; *e.g.*, **Palacios**, 813 S.W.2d at 490 & n.1 (only black panelist struck and race "figured into" strike).

(2) Ethnicity. **Hernandez v. New York**, 500 U.S. 352, 355 (1991) (Hispanic); **Benavides v. American Chrome & Chems., Inc.**, 893 S.W.2d 624, 626–27 (Tex.App.—Corpus Christi 1994) (same), *writ denied*, 907 S.W.2d 516 (Tex.1995).

(3) Gender. **J.E.B. v. Alabama**, 511 U.S. 127, 143 (1994); **Davis**, 268 S.W.3d at 510. Strikes based on characteristics that are disproportionately associated with one gender are not necessarily prohibited. *E.g.*, **J.E.B.**, 511 U.S. at 143 & n.16 (challenge to all nurses would not be gender-based even though it would disproportionately affect women).

2. Others may be protected. Other "cognizable" groups under **Batson** may include the following:

(1) Native Americans. *See* **U.S. v. Childs**, 5 F.3d 1328, 1337 (9th Cir.1993); **U.S. v. Iron Moccasin**, 878 F.2d 226, 229 (8th Cir.1989); **U.S. v. Chalan**, 812 F.2d 1302, 1313–14 (10th Cir.1987).

(2) Italian-Americans. *See* **U.S. v. Biaggi**, 853 F.2d 89, 95–96 (2d Cir.1988). *But see* **U.S. v. Bucci**, 839 F.2d 825, 832–33 (1st Cir.1988) (whether Italian-Americans are a cognizable group is a question of fact). A list of cases involving **Batson** challenges to Italian-Americans can be found in **U.S. v. Campione**, 942 F.2d 429, 432–33 (7th Cir.1991).

(3) Asian-Americans. *See* **U.S. v. Sneed**, 34 F.3d 1570, 1578–79 (10th Cir.1994).

(4) Disabled persons. Protections similar to **Batson** may prevent litigants from striking disabled persons from the jury panel solely because of their disability. The Americans with Disabilities Act (ADA) and the Texas Government Code prohibit the automatic exclusion of a person on the grounds of disability. *See* 42 U.S.C. §12132 (any disability); Tex. Gov't Code §62.104(a) (blindness), §62.1041(a) (deafness). The ADA applies to everything the State does, including acts of the judiciary. *E.g.*, **Galloway v. Superior Court**, 816 F.Supp. 12, 18–19 (D.D.C.1993) (ADA prevented federal court from automatically excluding blind persons from juries).

(5) Persons of a particular religious affiliation. No Texas civil court has addressed this issue. The Court of Criminal Appeals has held that **Batson** does not prohibit strikes based on religion. **Casarez v. State**, 913 S.W.2d 468, 495–96 (Tex.Crim.App.1995). The Fifth Circuit has similarly stated that no precedent clearly dictates that **Batson** should be extended to religion. **Fisher v. Texas**, 169 F.3d 295, 305 (5th Cir.1999); *see also* **U.S. v. Heron**, 721 F.3d 896, 902 (7th Cir.2013) (after P did not raise religion-based **Batson** claim in district court, appellate court held that striking juror based on her or her mother's religious devotion, i.e., "religiosity," was not plain error). *But see* **U.S. v. Brown**, 352 F.3d 654, 668–69 (2d Cir.2003) (extending **Batson**'s protection to strikes based on religious affiliation). See "Religion," **O'Connor's Federal Rules * Civil Trials**, ch. 8-A, §7.3.1(4) (2021 ed.).

3. Unprotected classifications. Litigants may exercise peremptory strikes to exclude panelists based on the following:

(1) Appearance. **Purkett v. Elem**, 514 U.S. 765, 769 (1995) (long, unkempt hair, mustache, and beard); **Mayr v. Lott**, 943 S.W.2d 553, 556–57 (Tex.App.—Waco 1997, no writ) (large gold hat).

(2) Age. **Dominguez v. State Farm Ins.**, 905 S.W.2d 713, 716–17 (Tex.App.—El Paso 1995, writ dism'd).

(3) Occupation or employment status. *See* **Brumfield v. Exxon Corp.**, 63 S.W.3d 912, 916 (Tex.App.—Houston [14th Dist.] 2002, pet. denied); **Dominguez**, 905 S.W.2d at 717.

(4) Medical treatment received by panelist. **Mayr**, 943 S.W.2d at 556.

4. Procedure for *Batson* challenge. After voir dire, if one party (**Batson** movant) believes the other party (**Batson** respondent) used its peremptory strikes in a discriminatory manner, the **Batson** movant should follow the three-step procedure adopted in **Goode**, 943 S.W.2d at 445–46.

(1) Step 1—Movant makes prima facie case. The **Batson** movant must make a prima facie case of discriminatory use of peremptory strikes by the **Batson** respondent. **Goode**, 943 S.W.2d at 445. A prima facie case is established by a suspect pattern of strikes against members of a protected class. **Dominguez**, 905 S.W.2d at 715. A reasonable inference is sufficient to establish a prima facie case. **Johnson v. California**, 545 U.S. 162, 167–68 & n.3 (2005). To make a **Batson** challenge, the movant must show (1) the **Batson** respondent exercised a peremptory strike to remove a

panelist of a protected class, and (2) that peremptory strike, along with other circumstances, raises an inference that the **Batson** respondent excluded the panelist because of her status. *See* **Lott v. City of Fort Worth**, 840 S.W.2d 146, 150 (Tex.App.—Fort Worth 1992, no writ). A prima facie case requires a party to come forward with facts, not just numbers. *See, e.g.,* **Brown v. Kinney Shoe Corp.**, 237 F.3d 556, 562–63 (5th Cir.2001) (standing alone, fact that P used four peremptory strikes to remove white jurors did not make a prima facie case). If the **Batson** movant makes a prima facie case, it creates a rebuttable presumption of discriminatory use of strikes by the **Batson** respondent. **Lott**, 840 S.W.2d at 150.

(2) Step 2—Respondent offers neutral explanation. After the **Batson** movant makes a prima facie case, the burden shifts to the **Batson** respondent to offer a neutral explanation for the strike. **Flowers**, __ U.S. at __, 139 S.Ct. at 2243; **Goode**, 943 S.W.2d at 445. The issue at this stage is the facial validity of the explanation. **Goode**, 943 S.W.2d at 445; **Jackson v. Stroud**, 539 S.W.3d 502, 507 (Tex.App.—Houston [1st Dist.] 2017, no pet.).

(a) Neutral explanation. To rebut the movant's prima facie case, the **Batson** respondent should offer a neutral explanation for each strike challenged by the **Batson** movant. **Jackson**, 539 S.W.3d at 507; **In re A.D.E.**, 880 S.W.2d 241, 243 (Tex.App.—Corpus Christi 1994, no writ), *disapproved on other grounds*, **In re J.F.C.**, 96 S.W.3d 256 (Tex.2002). A neutral explanation is one based on something other than the race, gender, or other discriminatory characteristic of the panelist. *See* **Goode**, 943 S.W.2d at 445. A neutral explanation may be the attorney's hunch, the panelist's failure to make eye contact, inattentiveness, appearance, or employment status. *See, e.g.,* **TXI Transp. v. Hughes**, 224 S.W.3d 870, 892–93 (Tex.App.—Fort Worth 2007) (occupation and length of residence in community were sufficient reasons to strike panelist), *rev'd on other grounds*, 306 S.W.3d 230 (Tex.2010); **Mayr**, 943 S.W.2d at 556–57 (large gold hat was sufficient reason to strike panelist). The explanation must be clear and reasonably specific. **Jackson**, 539 S.W.3d at 507. But it does not need to be plausible. **Purkett**, 514 U.S. at 768; **Jackson**, 539 S.W.3d at 507; **Molina v. Pigott**, 929 S.W.2d 538, 545 (Tex.App.—Corpus Christi 1996, writ denied). When a peremptory strike is based on a panelist's nonverbal conduct, the **Batson** respondent must specifically describe that conduct. **Davis**, 268 S.W.3d at 518; **Price v. Short**, 931 S.W.2d 677, 682 (Tex.App.—Dallas 1996, no writ). The **Batson** respondent must do more than just assert that the nonverbal conduct happened; the conduct must be proved and reflected in the record. **Davis**, 268 S.W.3d at 518.

(b) Interpretation of explanation. At step two, the court will consider the reason offered as neutral unless a discriminatory intent is inherent in the explanation. **Goode**, 943 S.W.2d at 445; **Jackson**, 539 S.W.3d at 507. Even if the respondent offers a "silly or superstitious" explanation for the strike, the trial court must assume that the reasons given are true. **Goode**, 943 S.W.2d at 445. The persuasiveness of the explanation becomes an issue only at step three. *Id.* If the **Batson** respondent admits the discriminatory characteristic played any role in making its strike, the peremptory strike is constitutionally defective. **Benavides**, 893 S.W.2d at 626–27.

(3) Step 3—Court analyzes arguments. The **Batson** movant has the right to rebut the respondent's explanations and cross-examine the respondent's attorney regarding the motivation for the strikes. **Goode**, 943 S.W.2d at 451–52; *see* **Davis**, 268 S.W.3d at 514–15. After both parties present their positions, the court must determine whether the **Batson** respondent's explanations were neutral or if they were merely a pretext for purposeful discrimination. **Purkett**, 514 U.S. at 768; **Lott**, 840 S.W.2d at 150; *see* **Goode**, 943 S.W.2d at 445–46 (step three is stage in which court makes its determination). The courts must look at "all relevant circumstances" when considering a **Batson** challenge. **Flowers**, __ U.S. at __, 139 S.Ct. at 2243; **Davis**, 268 S.W.3d at 525; *see* **Miller-El v. Dretke**, 545 U.S. 231, 240 (2005). Courts have identified several factors that can be used in making a determination on a **Batson** challenge, including:

(a) Whether an analysis of the statistical data on the peremptory strikes indicates a disparity too great to be mere happenstance. **Miller-El**, 545 U.S. at 240–41; *e.g.,* **Davis**, 268 S.W.3d at 516 (D struck 83% of black panelists and 5.5% of nonblack panelists; court called the statistics "remarkable"); *see* **Flowers**, __ U.S. at __, 139 S.Ct. at 2246; **Jackson**, 539 S.W.3d at 508.

(b) Whether there was any questioning directed to the challenged juror and whether the questions asked were meaningful. **Lott**, 840 S.W.2d at 151; *see* **Short**, 931 S.W.2d at 685 (unless panelist was questioned, court may assume the attorney's explanation for a strike is a pretext for a racially discriminatory strike).

(c) Whether there was disparate treatment (i.e., the **Batson** respondent did not strike persons with characteristics the same as or similar to the challenged juror). **Jackson**, 539 S.W.3d at 508; **Lott**, 840 S.W.2d at 151; *see* **Da-**

vis, 268 S.W.3d at 512 (referred to as "comparative juror analysis"); *see, e.g.*, **Flowers**, __ U.S. at __, 139 S.Ct. at 2248–49 (prosecutors stated that they struck black panelist because she was connected with several people involved in the case, but they did not strike white jurors with similar connections).

(d) Whether there was a disparate examination of panelists. **Lott**, 840 S.W.2d at 151; *see* **Davis**, 268 S.W.3d at 513–14; *see, e.g.*, **Flowers**, __ U.S. at __, 139 S.Ct. at 2246–47 (on average, prosecutors asked each black panelist 29 questions and each white panelist 1 question); **Miller-El**, 545 U.S. at 255 (prosecutors gave black panelists a graphic account of the death penalty and nonblack panelists a bland description before asking about a panelist's feelings on the subject).

(e) Whether the **Batson** respondent offered an explanation based on a group bias when the group trait was not shown to apply to the challenged juror. **Lott**, 840 S.W.2d at 151.

(f) Whether the reasons the **Batson** respondent gave for the peremptory strike were related to the facts of the case. **Lott**, 840 S.W.2d at 151; *see, e.g.*, **Mayr**, 943 S.W.2d at 556 (in PI case, striking a juror because she had undergone chiropractic treatment was related to case).

(g) Whether the use of the jury shuffle indicates the respondent's decisions were probably based on race. *See, e.g.*, **Miller-El**, 545 U.S. at 253–54 (prosecution sought jury shuffle when predominant number of black panelists were seated in the front of the panel and delayed making formal objection to D's shuffle until after racial composition was revealed, raising suspicion that prosecution sought to exclude black panelists from jury).

(h) Whether there is a history of systematically excluding members of a protected classification from juries. *See, e.g.*, **Flowers**, __ U.S. at __, 139 S.Ct. at 2244–45 (history of prosecutors' peremptory strikes in D's first four trials supported finding that use of strikes in sixth trial was motivated by discriminatory intent); **Miller-El**, 545 U.S. at 263–64 (D.A.'s office had adopted formal policy to exclude minorities from jury service).

5. Deadline for *Batson* challenge. A **Batson** movant must make a **Batson** challenge before the court impanels the jury and dismisses the excluded panelists. Tex. Code Crim. Proc. art. 35.261(a); *see* **In re K.M.B.**, 91 S.W.3d 18, 27 (Tex.App.—Fort Worth 2002, no pet.); **Pierson v. Noon**, 814 S.W.2d 506, 508 (Tex.App.—Houston [14th Dist.] 1991, writ denied). If the **Batson** movant makes an objection for the first time in a motion for new trial, it is too late. *See* **Jones v. Martin K. Eby Constr. Co.**, 841 S.W.2d 426, 430 (Tex.App.—Dallas 1992, writ denied).

6. *Batson* record. The **Batson** movant must make a record to illustrate on appeal that the trial court abused its discretion. *See* **Goode**, 943 S.W.2d at 446; **In re A.D.E.**, 880 S.W.2d at 245. There are two parts of the record for a **Batson** objection. First, the **Batson** movant should introduce into evidence the information cards provided by the panelists. *See* **Goode**, 943 S.W.2d at 451; **In re A.D.E.**, 880 S.W.2d at 245. Although the cards do not contain information about the races of the panelists, they can be used to show the pretext of the strike. Second, the **Batson** movant should (1) ask the court to take judicial notice of the racial composition of the panel, (2) state the composition on the record, and (3) identify the panelists who were excluded by name, race, or other status, and their position on the panel. For example, the **Batson** movant should state the panel was composed of 24 persons, including 16 white, 5 African-American, and 3 Mexican-American; identify the panel number of each minority member; and list those who were excluded—panelist number three, Mrs. Smith, who is an African-American, etc.

7. *Batson* hearing. A **Batson** hearing must be held in open court. **Goode**, 943 S.W.2d at 451. The **Batson** respondent's attorney does not need to be put under oath; unsworn statements may be offered to explain peremptory strikes. *Id.* The **Batson** movant has the right to cross-examine the **Batson** respondent's attorney. *Id.* at 452. For making a **Batson** record, see "*Batson* record," ch. 8-A, §7.3.6. For introducing other evidence, the TRCPs and TREs apply. **Goode**, 943 S.W.2d at 451.

Practice Tip

*If the **Batson** respondent's attorney uses voir dire notes to refresh her recollection while giving testimony during the hearing, the **Batson** movant's attorney is entitled to examine the notes. **Goode**, 943 S.W.2d at 449; see Tex. R. Evid. 612(a)(1), (b); see also **Brooks v. Armco, Inc.**, 194 S.W.3d 661, 666 (Tex.App.—Texarkana 2006, pet. denied) (court found D's attorney cited notes only to confirm truth of testimony,*

*not to refresh memory; P's attorney not entitled to review notes). If the **Batson** respondent's attorney uses voir dire notes only before the hearing, the issue of whether to require the production of the notes is within the trial court's discretion. **Goode**, 943 S.W.2d at 449; see Tex. R. Evid. 612(a)(2), (b).*

8. **Court's ruling.** If the court determines the explanation was merely pretext, the misused strikes will not be restored to the party because doing so would reward the party for attempting discriminatory strikes. **Peetz v. State**, 180 S.W.3d 755, 760–61 (Tex.App.—Houston [14th Dist.] 2005, no pet.).

9. **Trial remedies.** The civil courts often look to criminal cases to determine remedies for a **Batson** violation. *See* **Texas Tech Univ. Health Sci. Ctr. v. Apodaca**, 876 S.W.2d 402, 406 (Tex.App.—El Paso 1994, writ denied). If the trial court decides a panelist was improperly excluded, the court may reinstate the challenged panelist to the panel or may dismiss the panel and call a new one. *See* **Batson**, 476 U.S. at 99 n.24; *see, e.g.*, **Short**, 931 S.W.2d at 681 (trial court reinstated four panelists).

§8. Jury panel

§8.1 After challenges for cause. After the parties make their challenges for cause, at least 24 persons must remain on the panel in district court (12 in county court). *See* Tex. R. Civ. P. 231. If the jury panel has fewer than those numbers, the trial court must direct the clerk to call other panelists to complete the panel. *Id.*; *e.g.*, **McRae v. Echols**, 8 S.W.3d 797, 798–99 (Tex.App.—Waco 2000, pet. denied) (error to begin voir dire with 23 jurors, but error did not cause rendition of improper judgment). The burden is on the trial court, not the parties, to summon additional panelists. *See* Tex. R. Civ. P. 231.

§8.2 After peremptory strikes. After the parties deliver their peremptory strikes to the clerk, the clerk calls the names of the panelists who have not been struck by either party, and those persons make up the jury panel. Tex. R. Civ. P. 234. If the jury is left incomplete after the parties have exercised their peremptory strikes, the court must direct the clerk to draw or summon other jurors to complete the jury. Tex. R. Civ. P. 235; **Thomas v. City of O'Donnell**, 811 S.W.2d 757, 759 (Tex.App.—Amarillo 1991, no writ). The burden is on the trial court, not the parties, to summon additional jurors. *See* Tex. R. Civ. P. 235; **Thomas**, 811 S.W.2d at 759. Once the jury is called, the court cannot add or subtract jurors. **Dunlap v. Excel Corp.**, 30 S.W.3d 427, 433 (Tex.App.—Amarillo 2000, no pet.).

1. **District court.** In a district court, the first 12 persons not struck make up the jury panel. Tex. R. Civ. P. 234; **Dunlap**, 30 S.W.3d at 433; *see* Tex. Const. art. 5, §13; Tex. Gov't Code §62.201.

2. **County court.** In a county court, the first six persons not struck make up the jury panel. Tex. R. Civ. P. 234; *see* Tex. Const. art. 5, §17; Tex. Gov't Code §62.301.

Note

For cases filed in a county court at law on or after September 1, 2020, if the amount in controversy exceeds $250,000, the jury must be composed of 12 persons unless all the parties agree to a smaller jury. See Acts 2019, 86th Leg., R.S., ch. 696, §§3, 33, 36, 37, eff. Sept. 1, 2020 (amending Tex. Gov't Code §25.0007 and §62.301).

§9. Juror communication

Immediately after jurors are selected for a case, the court must instruct them about limitations on their outside communication during the case. *See* Tex. R. Civ. P. 226a, §II, 284.

§9.1 No electronic devices. Jurors must turn off their phones and other electronic devices and may not communicate with anyone through any electronic device while in the courtroom or while deliberating. Tex. R. Civ. P. 226a, §II(1), 284.

§9.2 No posting or searching for information about case. Jurors cannot post any information about the case on the Internet or search for information about the case on the Internet or elsewhere. Tex. R. Civ. P. 284; *see* Tex. R. Civ. P. 226a, §II(1), (6).

§9.3 No communication about case. When jurors are allowed to separate, either during trial or after the case is submitted to them, they may not communicate with, or permit themselves to be addressed by, anyone about anything related to the case. Tex. R. Civ. P. 284. Jurors cannot communicate about the case either in person or by any other means (e.g., by phone, text message, e-mail, chat room, blog, or social-networking website). Tex. R. Civ. P. 226a, §II(4).

§9.4 No communication with person in case. Jurors should not talk to lawyers, witnesses, parties, or anyone else involved in the case other than to exchange casual greetings like "hello" and "good morning." Tex. R. Civ. P. 226a, §II(2). If a juror has a question or needs to communicate with the court, the presiding juror will tell the officer in charge of the jury, who will inform the court. Tex. R. Civ. P. 285. See "Jury's questions to trial court," ch. 8-I, §8.1.

§10. Juror note-taking

The TRCPs allow jurors to take notes in civil cases. *See* Tex. R. Civ. P. 226a, §II(10), 281; *cf.* **Price v. State**, 887 S.W.2d 949, 954 (Tex.Crim.App.1994) (juror note-taking approved in criminal cases). Jurors may take notes during a civil trial if it will help focus their attention on the evidence; the notes themselves, however, are not evidence. Tex. R. Civ. P. 226a, §II(10). Jurors must use only the materials provided by the court and cannot use a personal electronic device. *Id.* Jurors are admonished not to take notes if it will distract them from the evidence. *Id.*

§10.1 Consulting notes. The court can permit jurors to consult their notes during deliberations. Tex. R. Civ. P. 226a, §II(10), 281. Jurors cannot share their notes with anyone, however, including with other jurors. Tex. R. Civ. P. 226a, §II(10).

§10.2 Location of notes. Jurors must leave their notes in the jury room or with the bailiff during trial. Tex. R. Civ. P. 226a, §II(10). If the court allows the jurors to consult their notes during deliberations the bailiff will collect the notes and give them to the court when the jurors are not deliberating. *Id.* After deliberations, the bailiff will collect the notes and will destroy them when the jurors are released. *Id.*

§11. Review

§11.1 Appellate record. To create a record for challenging most errors in selecting the jury (e.g., **Batson** challenge, strike for cause), the party should ask the court reporter to take possession of the juror information sheets and the strike lists and request that they be included in the appellate record. *Cf.* **Whitsey v. State**, 796 S.W.2d 707, 714–15 (Tex.Crim.App.1990) (prosecutor noted which potential jurors were black by writing "B" on their juror information sheets).

§11.2 Abuse of discretion. The test for abuse of discretion is whether the trial court acted without reference to any guiding rules and principles or whether the act was arbitrary and unreasonable. Abuse of discretion is the standard used to review complaints such as the following:

1. Voir dire ruling. **In re Commitment of Hill**, 334 S.W.3d 226, 229 (Tex.2011); *see, e.g.*, **Hyundai Motor Co. v. Vasquez**, 189 S.W.3d 743, 760 (Tex.2006) (trial court did not abuse discretion in denying line of questions); **Babcock v. Northwest Mem'l Hosp.**, 767 S.W.2d 705, 709 (Tex.1989) (trial court abused discretion by denying line of questions). For example, a court abuses its discretion when it denies a party's right to ask a proper question and that denial prevents the determination of whether there are grounds to challenge for cause or denies intelligent use of peremptory challenges. **Babcock**, 767 S.W.2d at 709.

2. Ruling on challenge for cause. *E.g.*, **Cortez v. HCCI-San Antonio, Inc.**, 159 S.W.3d 87, 93 (Tex.2005) (because veniremember was not biased as matter of law, trial court was within its discretion to not strike him for cause).

3. Substituting alternate juror. *See* **In re M.G.N.**, 441 S.W.3d 246, 249 (Tex.2014).

4. Proceeding with fewer than 12 jurors. *See id.*; **McDaniel v. Yarbrough**, 898 S.W.2d 251, 253 (Tex.1995).

5. **Batson** ruling. **Davis v. Fisk Elec. Co.**, 268 S.W.3d 508, 515 (Tex.2008); **Goode v. Shoukfeh**, 943 S.W.2d 441, 446 (Tex.1997). If the court abuses its discretion on a **Batson** ruling, the case must be reversed and remanded for a new trial. *See* **Jackson v. Stroud**, 539 S.W.3d 502, 508–09 (Tex.App.—Houston [1st Dist.] 2017, no pet.). In federal courts and in Texas criminal courts, the standard for reviewing a **Batson** ruling is "clearly erroneous." **Whitsey v. State**, 796 S.W.2d 707, 726 (Tex.Crim.App.1990); *see* **Hernandez v. New York**, 500 U.S. 352, 365–66 (1991).

Note

If the appellate court finds the trial court abused its discretion, it will generally conduct a harm analysis to determine if there is reversible error. See ch. 8-A, §11.3, below. In some cases, however, the finding of an abuse of discretion is dispositive; that is, reversal is warranted by the abuse itself. For example, in ***Batson*** *cases, if the appellate court finds the trial court abused its discretion by improperly excluding a potential juror, the error requires reversal and remand because the improper exclusion of even one juror based on a protected classification is a constitutional violation. See* ***Haynes v. Union Pac. RR,*** *395 S.W.3d 192, 197 (Tex.App.—Houston [1st Dist.] 2012, pet. denied).*

§11.3 Harmless error. The test for harmless error is whether the error probably caused the rendition of an improper judgment or probably prevented the appellant from properly presenting its case to the appellate court. Tex. R. App. P. 44.1(a). The harmless-error standard is used to review procedural errors in impaneling a jury, such as the following:

1. Ruling on request for jury shuffle. *See* **Jackson v. Williams Bros. Constr. Co.**, 364 S.W.3d 317, 321 (Tex.App.—Houston [1st Dist.] 2011, pet. denied); **Whiteside v. Watson**, 12 S.W.3d 614, 620 (Tex.App.—Eastland 2000, pet. granted, judgm't vacated w.r.m.); *see, e.g.*, **Rivas v. Liberty Mut. Ins.**, 480 S.W.2d 610, 612 (Tex.1972) (although trial court refused to shuffle jury panel after proper request, court substantially complied with underlying purpose of random selection of jurors under TRCP 223; no improper judgment). At least one court has used the presumed-harm standard to review the denial of a jury shuffle. See "Presumed harm," ch. 8-A, §11.5.2.

2. Clerk's mistake in calling jurors. *E.g.*, **Wells v. Barrow**, 153 S.W.3d 514, 517–18 (Tex.App.—Amarillo 2004, no pet.) (clerk omitted panelist's name when calling names for jury, and unselected panelist served instead; no improper judgment because unselected panelist was qualified).

§11.4 Relaxed harmless error. The test for the "relaxed" harmless-error rule is whether the trial was materially unfair. **Lopez v. Foremost Paving, Inc.**, 709 S.W.2d 643, 644 (Tex.1986). The party challenging the error does not need to show injury. *See* **Patterson Dental Co. v. Dunn**, 592 S.W.2d 914, 921 (Tex.1979); *cf.* **Compton v. Henrie**, 364 S.W.2d 179, 182 (Tex.1963) (no need to establish probable injury in juror-disqualification cases; decided before adoption of relaxed harmless-error rule). To show the trial was materially unfair, the movant must show the evidence was conflicting and hotly contested. **Lopez**, 709 S.W.2d at 644. The existence of antagonism between the parties is a question of law reviewable de novo. **Pojar v. Cifre**, 199 S.W.3d 317, 324 (Tex.App.—Corpus Christi 2006, pet. denied); *see* **Garcia v. Central Power & Light Co.**, 704 S.W.2d 734, 736 (Tex.1986); **Patterson Dental**, 592 S.W.2d at 919. The relaxed harmless-error standard has been used to review the following types of error:

1. Allocation of strikes. *E.g.*, **Lopez**, 709 S.W.2d at 644 (error in awarding twice as many strikes to Ds as to Ps). *But see* **Torrington Co. v. Stutzman**, 46 S.W.3d 829, 851 (Tex.2000) (dicta; party must show erroneous allocation probably caused rendition of improper judgment).

2. Error in selecting jury. *E.g.*, **Carr v. Smith**, 22 S.W.3d 128, 135–36 (Tex.App.—Fort Worth 2000, pet. denied) (error in granting shuffle after voir dire began); **Mann v. Ramirez**, 905 S.W.2d 275, 281 (Tex.App.—San Antonio 1995, writ denied) (error in excusing panelist for nonstatutory reasons).

§11.5 Presumed harm. In some circumstances, an appellate court can presume harm if, in reviewing a trial court's erroneous jury-selection ruling, it cannot determine whether the error affected the jury's verdict. *See* **Cortez v. HCCI-San Antonio, Inc.**, 159 S.W.3d 87, 91 (Tex.2005); **BNSF Ry. v. Wipff**, 408 S.W.3d 662, 668 (Tex.App.—Fort Worth 2013, no pet.). The standard is similar to **Casteel** error in broad-form jury-charge submissions—that is, when a trial court submits a broad-form question with multiple theories of liability, some of which are invalid, harm is presumed, and a new trial may be required if the appellate court cannot determine whether the improperly submitted theories formed the sole basis for the jury's verdict. See "Presumed harm," ch. 8-I, §9.1.4(2). The presumed-harm standard has been used to review procedural rulings, such as the following:

1. Denial of challenge for cause. *See* **Cortez**, 159 S.W.3d at 91 (harm presumed if trial court's refusal to dismiss veniremember for bias results in challenger using peremptory strike against that veniremember and challenger is prevented from striking other objectionable jurors).

2. Improper denial of jury shuffle. *See, e.g.*, **BNSF Ry.**, 408 S.W.3d at 668–69 (court presumed harm because D complained about participation of two objectionable jurors that it would have struck but could not and D had no other way to show harm; participation of those jurors resulted from improper denial of jury shuffle); *cf.* **Mendoza v. Ranger Ins.**, 753 S.W.2d 779, 781 (Tex.App.—Fort Worth 1988, writ denied) (harm presumed when jury was not randomly selected cross-section of community). Most courts, however, have used the harmless-error standard to review rulings on a request for a jury shuffle. See "Harmless error," ch. 8-A, §11.3.1.

B. Opening Statement

§1. General

§1.1 Rules. Tex. R. Civ. P. 265(a), 266. See Tex. R. Civ. P. 269 (closing argument).

§1.2 Purpose. Immediately after the jury is impaneled, the parties make opening statements in which they briefly tell the jury the nature of their claims or defenses, the relief sought, and what they expect to prove. Tex. R. Civ. P. 265(a). Assertions made during opening argument are not evidence and are not judicial admissions. **Weslaco Fed'n of Teachers v. Texas Educ. Agency**, 27 S.W.3d 258, 263 (Tex.App.—Austin 2000, no pet.) (not judicial admissions); **Carrasco v. Texas Transp.**, 908 S.W.2d 575, 580 (Tex.App.—Waco 1995, no writ) (not evidence).

§1.3 Forms. **O'Connor's Texas Civil Forms**, FORMS 8B:1 et seq. (2020 ed.).

§2. Right to make first opening statement

The right to make the first opening statement is an important advantage—the party that makes the first opening statement gets to summarize its case to the jury before its opponent. *See* Tex. R. Civ. P. 265(a). The right to make the first opening statement is related to the right to initiate voir dire, the right to open and close the evidence, and the right to open and close the final argument. See "Right to initiate voir dire," ch. 8-A, §5.2; "Right to open evidence," ch. 8-C, §2; "Right to open & close final argument," ch. 8-J, §2.

§2.1 Rule—P goes first. The party with the burden of proof on the whole case has the right to make the first opening statement to the jury (and introduce evidence first). Tex. R. Civ. P. 265(a), (b). Most often, that party is the plaintiff.

§2.2 Exceptions—D goes first. There are exceptions to the rule that the plaintiff has the right to make the first opening statement.

1. Burden of proof. A defendant has the right to make the first opening statement and introduce evidence first if it has the burden of proof for the entire case under the pleadings. Tex. R. Civ. P. 265(a), (b). To determine who has the burden of proof on the whole case, ask which party would lose the case if no evidence were introduced. If the defendant would lose, then the defendant has the burden of proof. **Union City Transfer v. Adams**, 248 S.W.2d 256, 260 (Tex.App.—Fort Worth 1952, writ ref'd n.r.e.); *see, e.g.*, **Ocean Transp. v. Greycas, Inc.**, 878 S.W.2d 256, 269 (Tex.App.—Corpus Christi 1994, writ denied) (in suit on a note, D did not have right to make first opening statement because P had burden to prove deficiency and attorney fees).

2. Admission under TRCP 266. A defendant has the right to make the first opening statement (and introduce evidence first) if, before the trial begins, the defendant admits the plaintiff is entitled to recover, subject to proof of defensive allegations in the answer. Tex. R. Civ. P. 266; *cf.* **First State Bank v. Fatheree**, 847 S.W.2d 391, 397 (Tex.App.—Amarillo 1993, writ denied) (D stipulated to liability on promissory notes subject to findings on her affirmative defenses; D had right to open and close final argument). The admission must relieve the plaintiff from the necessity of offering any evidence to support its case. *E.g.*, **Trice v. Stamford Builders Sup.**, 248 S.W.2d 213, 215 (Tex.App.—Eastland 1952, no writ) (D stipulated P held title to property unless D could prove title through plea of limitation; D had right to open and close final argument). A defendant cannot secure the right to open merely by voluntarily assuming the burden of proof; the defendant must unequivocally admit liability and damages or establish them as a matter of law and remove them as issues from the case. *See, e.g.*, **Seigler v. Seigler**, 391 S.W.2d 403, 404 (Tex.1965) (contestants of will could not voluntarily assume burden; they had to remove issue of testamentary capacity from case); **4M Linen & Unif. Sup. Co. v. W.P. Ballard & Co.**, 793 S.W.2d 320, 324–25 (Tex.App.—Houston [1st Dist.] 1990, writ denied) (even though D stipulated liability, P had burden on attorney fees; P had right to open and close final argument).

§3. Order of opening statements

§3.1 First opening statement. The party who the court decided has the right to make the first opening statement will make its statement after the jury is impaneled and before any evidence is introduced. *See* Tex. R. Civ. P. 265(a).

§3.2 Other opening statements.

1. Two-party case. The party adverse to the party who made the first statement may make a statement of the case either (1) after the other party's opening statement and before any evidence is introduced or (2) before the adverse party introduces its own evidence. *See* Tex. R. Civ. P. 265(a), (c).

2. Multiparty case. In a multiparty case, the court will determine the order for other parties to make their statements. Tex. R. Civ. P. 265(a). The trial court may require all the parties on one side to make their opening statements together, either after the first opening statement or before introducing their own evidence. *E.g.*, **Fibreboard Corp. v. Pool**, 813 S.W.2d 658, 691 (Tex.App.—Texarkana 1991, writ denied) (all Ds must make opening statements at same time).

§4. Limits of opening statement

The trial court has broad discretion to limit opening statements. **Tacon Mech. Contractors, Inc. v. Grant Sheet Metal, Inc.**, 889 S.W.2d 666, 675 (Tex.App.—Houston [14th Dist.] 1994, writ denied).

§4.1 Rules for opening statements. The opening statements must observe the following rules:

1. Brief. The parties must briefly state to the jury the nature of their claims or defenses, what they expect to prove, and the relief they seek. Tex. R. Civ. P. 265(a).

2. No details. The parties may not detail the evidence by naming witnesses they intend to call and outlining the substance of their expected testimony. *E.g.*, **Ranger Ins. v. Rogers**, 530 S.W.2d 162, 170 (Tex.App.—Austin 1975, writ ref'd n.r.e.) (party improperly identified witnesses and summarized expected testimony); *see* **Guerrero v. Smith**, 864 S.W.2d 797, 799 (Tex.App.—Houston [14th Dist.] 1993, no writ).

3. No display. The parties may not read from, describe, or display documents or photographs to the jury. *E.g.*, **Guerrero**, 864 S.W.2d at 799 (party displayed photograph during opening statement); *see* **Ranger Ins.**, 530 S.W.2d at 170.

§4.2 Improper argument by both parties. If both parties make improper comments in their opening statements, the error in one cancels the other and on appeal will be considered harmless error. *See* **Wells v. HCA Health Servs.**, 806 S.W.2d 850, 855 (Tex.App.—Fort Worth 1990, writ denied); **Ranger Ins. v. Rogers**, 530 S.W.2d 162, 170–71 (Tex.App.—Austin 1975, writ ref'd n.r.e.). If one party discusses a particular issue, that party cannot object if the other party also discusses it. *See, e.g.*, **Smith v. Smith**, 720 S.W.2d 586, 593 (Tex.App.—Houston [1st Dist.] 1986, no writ) (P's attorney referred to criminal proceedings after D's attorney referred to them).

§5. Objecting & preserving error

§5.1 Timely. A complaint about an improper comment during the opening statement is waived unless an objection is timely made, which means the objection must be made at the earliest practical moment. **City of Corsicana v. Herod**, 768 S.W.2d 805, 816 (Tex.App.—Waco 1989, no writ). If the party does not object to the first reference, it waives any error. *See id.* To preserve error, the party must distinctly point out the error and state the grounds of the objection. *Id.*

§5.2 Incurable error. Although the rule is that a party must object to improper opening statements, if the cumulative effect of the improper statements is so prejudicial that an instruction to disregard would not remove the prejudice produced, the error is not waived. **Mapco, Inc. v. Jenkins**, 476 S.W.2d 55, 61–62 (Tex.App.—Amarillo 1971, writ ref'd n.r.e.). The same rules regarding incurable error in the final argument apply to the opening statement. See "Incurable argument," ch. 8-J, §5.2.

C. Introducing Evidence

§1. General

§1.1 Rules. Tex. R. Civ. P. 265 to 267; Tex. R. Evid. 103, 403, 614, 701 to 705, 1008; Tex. R. App. P. 33.1.

§1.2 Purpose. The parties prove their case for the jury (or the judge in a nonjury trial) by introducing evidence. Most evidence is introduced in the form of the testimony of witnesses who, under oath, relate facts within their knowledge. **Goudeau v. Marquez**, 830 S.W.2d 681, 683 (Tex.App.—Houston [1st Dist.] 1992, no writ); **Bloom v. Bloom**, 767 S.W.2d 463, 470–71 (Tex.App.—San Antonio 1989, writ denied). The decision to admit evidence—as opposed to the task of evaluating it—is within the exclusive authority of the trial court. **City of Brownsville v. Alvarado**, 897 S.W.2d 750, 753 (Tex.1995).

§1.3 Timetable & forms. Appendix IV, Timetable 14, Offer of proof & bill of exception; **O'Connor's Texas Civil Forms**, FORMS 8C:1 et seq. (2020 ed.).

§1.4 Other references. Morales, *Social Media Evidence: "What You Post or Tweet Can & Will Be Used Against You in a Court of Law"*, 60 The Advoc. (Texas) 32 (Fall 2012); Wilson, *Admissibility of Web-Based Data*, 52 The Advoc. (Texas) 31 (Fall 2010); **O'Connor's Texas Causes of Action** (2021 ed.); Brown & Rondon, **Texas Rules of Evidence Handbook** (2021 ed.).

§2. Right to open evidence

The party with the burden of proof on the entire case has the right to present its evidence first. Tex. R. Civ. P. 265(b), 266; **Amis v. Ashworth**, 802 S.W.2d 379, 384 (Tex.App.—Tyler 1990, orig. proceeding). In most cases, the opening party is the plaintiff, not because the plaintiff filed the suit, but because the plaintiff is usually the party asking for relief. **Pace Corp. v. Jackson**, 284 S.W.2d 340, 350 (Tex.1955). See "Right to make first opening statement," ch. 8-B, §2.

§3. Invoking "the Rule"

To exclude witnesses from the courtroom during the trial, a party should invoke "the Rule" at the beginning of the trial. TRCP 267(a) and TRE 614 require the trial court, at the request of either party, to administer the oath to the witnesses and remove them from the courtroom so they cannot hear the testimony given by other witnesses. **Drilex Sys. v. Flores**, 1 S.W.3d 112, 116–17 (Tex.1999).

§3.1 Court's instructions. The court must instruct the witnesses that they are not to converse about the case with each other or with any person other than the attorneys in the case (except by permission of the court) and that they are not to read any reports of or comments on the testimony in the case while under the Rule. Tex. R. Civ. P. 267(d); *see* Tex. R. Evid. 614; **Drilex Sys. v. Flores**, 1 S.W.3d 112, 117 (Tex.1999). The parties are obligated to ensure that their witnesses comply with the Rule unless they are exempted from it. *See* **Drilex Sys.**, 1 S.W.3d at 120.

§3.2 Persons not excluded. The following persons should not be excluded from the courtroom during trial: (1) a party who is a natural person or the spouse of that party, (2) an officer or employee of a party that is not a natural person and who is designated as its representative by its attorney, or (3) a person whose presence is shown by a party to be essential to the presentation of the case. Tex. R. Civ. P. 267(b); Tex. R. Evid. 614; **Drilex Sys. v. Flores**, 1 S.W.3d 112, 116–17 (Tex.1999); *e.g.*, **Century 21 Real Estate Corp. v. Hometown Real Estate Co.**, 890 S.W.2d 118, 129–30 (Tex.App.—Texarkana 1994, writ denied) (although trial court erred by not requiring corporation to name representative and not excluding its other officers, error was not reversible because officers' working relationship and affiliation with suit indicated that allowing them to hear each other's testimony was not so prejudicial as to cause rendition of improper judgment); *see also* **In re M-I L.L.C.**, 505 S.W.3d 569, 578 (Tex.2016) (Rule's exemption for designated representatives does not apply to in camera hearings under Texas Uniform Trade Secrets Act).

§3.3 Exemption. Once the Rule is invoked, the parties should ask the court to exempt any witnesses whose presence in the courtroom is essential to the presentation of the case. Tex. R. Civ. P. 267(b)(3); Tex. R. Evid. 614(c); **Drilex Sys. v. Flores**, 1 S.W.3d 112, 117 (Tex.1999). Witnesses whom the trial court exempts are not placed under the Rule. **Drilex Sys.**, 1 S.W.3d at 117. To exempt an expert from the Rule, the party must show that the expert needs to be present in the courtroom to form an opinion based on more accurate factual assumptions. *See* Tex. R. Evid. 703; **Drilex Sys.**, 1 S.W.3d at 119.

§3.4 Violation of the Rule. A nonexempt witness violates the Rule by remaining in the courtroom during the testimony of another witness, by learning about another's trial testimony through discussions with persons other than the attorneys, or by reading comments about the testimony. **Drilex Sys. v. Flores**, 1 S.W.3d 112, 117 (Tex.1999). When a witness who was placed under the Rule violates the Rule, the trial court can allow or exclude all or part of the witness's testimony or hold the witness in contempt. Tex. R. Civ. P. 267(e); **Drilex Sys.**, 1 S.W.3d at 117; **In re K.M.B.**, 91 S.W.3d 18, 28 (Tex.App.—Fort Worth 2002, no pet.). When a witness who was not placed under the Rule violates the restrictions of the Rule, the court can exclude the witness's testimony but cannot hold the witness in contempt. *See* **Drilex Sys.**, 1 S.W.3d at 120.

§4. Scope of examination

§4.1 Direct examination. The scope of direct examination is limited by the pleadings. When evidence is not relevant under the pleadings, it should not be admitted. Tex. R. Evid. 402. The court should admit all relevant evidence unless some rule or principle requires its exclusion. **Stokes v. Puckett**, 972 S.W.2d 921, 926 (Tex.App.—Beaumont 1998, pet. denied). See Brown & Rondon, **Texas Rules of Evidence Handbook**, Rule 401 (2021 ed.). When evidence is relevant but its probative value is substantially outweighed by its prejudicial effect, the evidence should be excluded. Tex. R. Evid. 403. See Brown & Rondon, **Texas Rules of Evidence Handbook**, Rule 403 (2021 ed.).

§4.2 Cross-examination. A witness may be cross-examined on any relevant matter, including credibility. Tex. R. Evid. 611(b); *see* Tex. R. Evid. 405(a)(1) (cross-examination allowed on relevant specific instances of conduct); **Continental Cas. Co. v. Thomas**, 463 S.W.2d 501, 506–07 (Tex.App.—Beaumont 1971, no writ) (cross-examination allowed on all phases of case). See Brown & Rondon, **Texas Rules of Evidence Handbook**, Rule 611 (2021 ed.). Due process requires that a party be given the opportunity to confront and cross-examine adverse witnesses. **Davidson v. Great Nat'l Life Ins.**, 737 S.W.2d 312, 314 (Tex.1987); **State Office of Risk Mgmt. v. Escalante**, 162 S.W.3d 619, 628 (Tex.App.—El Paso 2005, pet. dism'd). Texas does not limit a litigant's cross-examination to the matters covered by direct examination. **CPS Int'l v. Harris & Westmoreland**, 784 S.W.2d 538, 543 (Tex.App.—Texarkana 1990, no writ). See Brown & Rondon, **Texas Rules of Evidence Handbook**, Rule 611 (2021 ed.) (§B).

§4.3 Redirect examination. On redirect examination, the party may ask the witness to explain answers given on cross-examination, including material elicited for the first time. **Sims v. Brackett**, 885 S.W.2d 450, 455 (Tex.App.—Corpus Christi 1994, writ denied). The purpose of redirect is to prevent the jury from being left with a false and incomplete picture created by cross-examination. *Id.* The TREs do not address the scope of redirect examination. *See* Brown & Rondon, **Texas Rules of Evidence Handbook**, Rule 611 (2021 ed.) (n.514). A trial court cannot deny the parties the right to conduct redirect examination. **Sims**, 885 S.W.2d at 455.

§4.4 Recross examination. On recross examination, the party may ask the witness to explain answers given on redirect examination and to expand on new material elicited for the first time. *See* Tex. R. Evid. 611(b); **Jarvis v. K&E Re One, LLC**, 390 S.W.3d 631, 644 (Tex.App.—Dallas 2012, no pet.).

§4.5 Rebuttal evidence. Once the plaintiff or the defendant rests, the other party may introduce evidence to rebut the last round of evidence. On rebuttal, a party is limited to evidence that directly answers or disproves the last round of the other party's evidence. **In re Bledsoe**, 41 S.W.3d 807, 813 (Tex.App.—Fort Worth 2001, orig. proceeding); **Gendke v. Travelers Ins.**, 368 S.W.2d 3, 5 (Tex.App.—Waco 1963, no writ).

§4.6 Questions by jurors. It is unclear whether the trial court in a civil case can permit jurors to ask questions of the witnesses. *Compare* **Hudson v. Markum**, 948 S.W.2d 1, 3 (Tex.App.—Dallas 1997, writ denied) (generally permissible for jurors to ask questions of witnesses if procedural safeguards are followed; any error must be preserved by objection or is otherwise waived), *and* **Fazzino v. Guido**, 836 S.W.2d 271, 275–76 (Tex.App.—Houston [1st Dist.] 1992, writ denied) (same), *with* **Morrison v. State**, 845 S.W.2d 882, 889 (Tex.Crim.App.1992) (error to allow jurors to ask questions of witnesses in criminal case because it compromises fair trial by modifying jury's role as neutral fact-finder), *and* **In re J.T.**, 592 S.W.3d 782, 783–84 (Tex.App.—Waco 2019, no pet.) (error to allow jurors to ask questions of witnesses; court agreed with rationale in **Morrison** and found no legal distinction on this issue between civil and criminal jury trials).

§5. Introducing testimony

§5.1 Discovery products. See "Using disclosures as evidence," ch. 6-E, §2.6; "Using disclosures as evidence," ch. 6-E, §3.8; "Using deposition at trial," ch. 6-F, §12; "Using interrogatories as evidence," ch. 6-G, §9; "Admissions as evidence," ch. 6-H, §8; "Using requested documents," ch. 6-I, §8; "Using medical records," ch. 6-J, §6; "Using evidence at trial," ch. 6-K, §5.

§5.2 Over closed-circuit TV. If a witness was deposed before trial, the parties may file an agreed motion asking the court to permit the witness to be examined over closed-circuit television or other two-way electronic communication that is capable of visually and audibly recording the proceedings. Tex. Civ. Prac. & Rem. Code §30.012(a), (b).

§5.3 Impeachment & rebuttal evidence not produced in discovery. A party may introduce rebuttal or impeachment evidence, even though it was not produced in discovery, if (1) the evidence is solely for impeachment or rebuttal, (2) its use could not have been anticipated, and (3) the evidence is not responsive to a direct discovery request. *See e.g.*, **Aluminum Co. of Am. v. Bullock**, 870 S.W.2d 2, 4 (Tex.1994) (party should have been permitted to use undesignated expert to rebut unexpected change in material testimony of the other party's expert); **Emery v. Rollins**, 880 S.W.2d 237, 239–40 (Tex.App.—Houston [14th Dist.] 1994, writ denied) (documents could be used as rebuttal evidence because their need was unanticipated); **Dennis v. Haden**, 867 S.W.2d 48, 51–52 (Tex.App.—Texarkana 1993, writ denied) (when D did not supply expert's report as required, P should have been permitted to use deposition of undesignated witness on rebuttal); **Munoz v. Missouri Pac. R.R.**, 823 S.W.2d 766, 769 (Tex.App.—Corpus Christi 1992, no writ) (D's rebuttal testimony was admitted when D did not learn of impeachment witness until trial-time deposition of another witness); **Tinkle v. Henderson**, 777 S.W.2d 537, 540 (Tex.App.—Tyler 1989, writ denied) (court properly admitted testimony of fact witness offered to rebut matter that arose during trial); **Ellsworth v. Bishop Jewelry & Loan Co.**, 742 S.W.2d 533, 534 (Tex.App.—Dallas 1987, writ denied) (party had good cause to use undisclosed medical expert to rebut the testimony of a medical expert who testified beyond the subject matter identified in the interrogatory); *see also* Tex. R. Civ. P. 166(h) (exchange of list of fact witnesses at pretrial conference does not include rebuttal or impeaching witnesses the necessity of whose testimony cannot be anticipated before trial).

§5.4 Testimony of a fact witness. The testimony of a fact witness is limited to the facts within the witness's personal knowledge. **United Way v. Helping Hands Lifeline Found.**, 949 S.W.2d 707, 713 (Tex.App.—San Antonio 1997, writ denied).

1. Lay witness. A lay witness (i.e., a nonexpert witness) may testify in the form of an opinion only if the opinion is (1) rationally based on the witness's perception and (2) helpful to clearly understanding the witness's testimony or to determining a fact in issue. Tex. R. Evid. 701 & cmt. See Brown & Rondon, **Texas Rules of Evidence Handbook**, Rule 701 (2021 ed.).

2. Access to notes when used to refresh memory. If a witness refers to notes while on the stand, TRE 612(a)(1) grants the adverse party access to the notes; if a witness uses notes to refresh her recollection before taking the stand, TRE 612(a)(2) gives the trial court discretion to allow the adverse party access to the notes. **Goode v. Shoukfeh**, 943 S.W.2d 441, 449 (Tex.1997). See Brown & Rondon, **Texas Rules of Evidence Handbook**, Rule 612 (2021 ed.).

§5.5 Testimony from expert. If specialized knowledge will help the fact-finder understand the evidence or decide a fact issue, a witness who qualifies as an expert may testify in the form of an opinion. Tex. R. Evid. 702; **Broders v. Heise**, 924 S.W.2d 148, 152 (Tex.1996). See "*Daubert-Robinson* test for expert testimony," ch. 5-N, §2; Brown & Rondon, **Texas Rules of Evidence Handbook**, Rule 702 (2021 ed.). Opinion testimony from an expert "can rise no higher than the facts upon which it is based." **Sipes v. General Motors Corp.**, 946 S.W.2d 143, 148 (Tex.App.—Texarkana 1997, writ denied). Once an expert is challenged, the party offering the expert has the burden to respond to each objection and show the testimony is admissible by a preponderance of the evidence. *See* **E.I. du Pont de Nemours & Co. v. Robinson**, 923 S.W.2d 549, 557 (Tex.1995); *cf.* **Daubert v. Merrell Dow Pharms.**, 509 U.S. 579, 592 n.10 (1993) (under FRE 104, admissibility of expert testimony must be established by "preponderance of proof"). That party must prove the reliability of the underlying tests on which the expert's opinion is based. **Merrell Dow Pharms. v. Havner**, 953 S.W.2d 706, 712–14 (Tex.1997). For the allegations a party should make to prove admissibility, see "Sponsor's response to objection," ch. 5-N, §3.3. For the qualifications of and objections to an expert who testifies in a medical-liability suit against a physician or other health-care provider, see "Expert testimony," **O'Connor's Texas Causes of Action**, ch. 20-A, §8 (2021 ed.).

§5.6 Testimony from expert about learned treatise. To use a "learned treatise" on direct examination, a party must take the following steps: (1) prove the treatise was published, (2) prove the expert relied on it as authority (by admission or judicial notice) before trial to corroborate her opinion, and then (3) read the statement in the treatise to the jury. *See* Tex. R. Evid. 803(18). To use a "learned treatise" on cross-examination, a party must take the following steps: (1) prove the treatise was published, (2) prove the treatise is authoritative, and (3) read the statement in the treatise to the jury. *See id.*

Statements from a learned treatise are admissible only when used in the direct or cross-examination of an expert. **Owens-Corning Fiberglas Corp. v. Malone**, 916 S.W.2d 551, 559 (Tex.App.—Houston [1st Dist.] 1996), *aff'd*, 972 S.W.2d 35 (Tex.1998). The treatise itself cannot be introduced into evidence as an exhibit or taken by the jury to the jury room. Tex. R. Evid. 803(18); *e.g.*, **Kahanek v. Rogers**, 12 S.W.3d 501, 504 (Tex.App.—San Antonio 1999, pet. denied) (because physician's desk reference was learned treatise, it could not be taken into jury room). See Brown & Rondon, **Texas Rules of Evidence Handbook**, Rule 803 (2021 ed.) (§B.14).

§5.7 Dying declaration. To introduce a dying declaration, a party must prove the following: (1) the declarant made a statement when she believed death was imminent, (2) the statement was about the cause or circumstances of what the declarant believed to be her impending death, (3) the declarant was physically and mentally able to recollect and accurately narrate the cause or circumstances, and (4) the declarant is unavailable at the time of trial. *See* Tex. R. Evid. 804(b)(2). See Brown & Rondon, **Texas Rules of Evidence Handbook**, Rule 804 (2021 ed.) (§B.2).

§5.8 Audio or video recording. If a recording is a fair representation of a transaction, conversation, or occurrence, it is admissible. **Seymour v. Gillespie**, 608 S.W.2d 897, 898 (Tex.1980); *see also* **Diamond Offshore Servs. v. Williams**, 542 S.W.3d 539, 546–47 (Tex.2018) (before ruling on admissibility, trial court should view video evidence when contents of video are at issue; trial court abused its discretion in excluding surveillance video without viewing it when probative value of video substantially outweighed TRE 403 factors of cumulativeness and unfair prejudice). To introduce a recording, a party must establish the following: (1) the recording machine can accurately record and reproduce sounds or images, (2) the operator was experienced and qualified to operate the recording machine, (3) the recording is authentic or correct—the witness heard (or saw) what was being recorded, (4) no changes, additions, or deletions were made to the recording, (5) the recording was preserved in a proper manner, (6) the witness recognizes and can identify the voices heard (and the locations and persons seen) on the recording, and (7) if the subject of the recording is a conversation, the testimony elicited was made voluntarily without any kind of inducement. **Seymour**, 608 S.W.2d at 898. Some of these elements may be inferred from the evidence and are not required to be proved. *Id.*

Practice Tip

When introducing orally recorded testimony (video, tape, or digitally recorded), make sure the court reporter stays in the courtroom and transcribes the testimony as it is heard by the jury. Court reporters often take a break while taped testimony is played and simply type into the record "The tape was played for the jury." Thus, that part of the evidence is not included in the appellate record. If you do not object to the court reporter's absence, you will waive the issue of an incomplete record. E.g., ***Lascurain v. Crowley****, 917 S.W.2d 341, 344–45 (Tex.App.—El Paso 1996, no writ) (court reporter left courtroom during deposition testimony with permission of parties). If the court reporter appeared to be transcribing the testimony but was not, you may be able to reconstruct the record.* ***State Farm Fire & Cas. Ins. v. Vandiver****, 941 S.W.2d 343, 347–49 (Tex.App.—Waco 1997, no writ).*

§5.9 Results of experiment. To introduce the results of an experiment that the other party was not invited to attend, the offering party must prove the following: (1) the party conducted an out-of-court experiment and (2) the circumstances surrounding the experiment were substantially similar to the conditions that gave rise to the litigation. **Fort Worth & Denver Ry. v. Williams**, 375 S.W.2d 279, 281–82 (Tex.1964); **Horn v. Hefner**, 115 S.W.3d 255, 256 (Tex.App.—Texarkana 2003, no pet.); *see, e.g.*, **Ford Motor Co. v. Miles**, 967 S.W.2d 377, 388–89 (Tex.1998) (because party never contended tests were conducted under similar conditions, videotapes of tests should have been excluded); **Alice Leasing Corp. v. Castillo**, 53 S.W.3d 433, 446 (Tex.App.—San Antonio 2001, pet. denied) (because videotaped demonstration was substantially similar to conditions of accident, it was admissible). It is not necessary that the conditions be identical. **Williams**, 375 S.W.2d at 282; **Horn**, 115 S.W.3d at 256; *see* **Mottu v. Navistar Int'l Transp.**, 804 S.W.2d 144, 148 (Tex.App.—Houston [14th Dist.] 1990, writ denied) (if major dissimilarities in conditions are present, videotapes of tests are excluded).

§5.10 Similar accidents. To introduce evidence of earlier, similar accidents, the party must show with specificity that the earlier accidents occurred in a similar manner and could be attributed to a similar cause. *See* **Huckaby v. A.G. Perry & Son, Inc.**, 20 S.W.3d 194, 202 (Tex.App.—Texarkana 2000, pet. denied); *see also* **Nissan Motor Co. v. Armstrong**, 145

S.W.3d 131, 138 (Tex.2004) (in products-liability case, court analyzed criteria for admitting evidence of similar accidents to show product is unreasonably dangerous). See Brown & Rondon, **Texas Rules of Evidence Handbook**, Rules 401 to 403 (2021 ed.) (§A.6). If the party does not establish one of the factors listed below, evidence of similar accidents is neither relevant nor material and is prejudicial. **Huckaby**, 20 S.W.3d at 202.

1. The conditions surrounding the earlier accidents were reasonably similar. *Id.*; **Henry v. Mrs. Baird's Bakeries, Inc.**, 475 S.W.2d 288, 294 (Tex.App.—Fort Worth 1971, writ ref'd n.r.e.); *see* **Kia Motors Corp. v. Ruiz**, 432 S.W.3d 865, 881 (Tex.2014); **Nissan Motor**, 145 S.W.3d at 138.

2. The conditions of the earlier accidents and the party's accident were connected in some special way. **Huckaby**, 20 S.W.3d at 202; **Henry**, 475 S.W.2d at 294; *see, e.g.*, **Dallas Ry. & Terminal Co. v. Farnsworth**, 227 S.W.2d 1017, 1019–20 (Tex.1950) (evidence street-car operator started car too quickly at each of three stops before P got off was closely related to issue of whether operator gave P enough time to get off car before starting it).

3. The earlier accidents were attributable to the same condition that caused the party's accident. *See* **Huckaby**, 20 S.W.3d at 202; **Henry**, 475 S.W.2d at 294; *see, e.g.*, **Bell v. Buddies Super-Mkt.**, 516 S.W.2d 447, 450–51 (Tex.App.—Tyler 1974, writ ref'd n.r.e.) (earlier "near-falls" were caused by ramp's rough concrete and were not attributable to ramp's steep slope, which caused P's fall).

§6. Impeaching a witness

The credibility of a witness may be attacked by any party, including the party calling the witness. Tex. R. Evid. 607; *e.g.*, **Owens-Corning Fiberglas Corp. v. Malone**, 916 S.W.2d 551, 567 (Tex.App.—Houston [1st Dist.] 1996) (court permitted Ps to call D's expert in their case-in-chief and impeach him), *aff'd*, 972 S.W.2d 35 (Tex.1998). See Brown & Rondon, **Texas Rules of Evidence Handbook**, Rule 607 (2021 ed.).

§6.1 Impeaching by reputation for truthfulness. There are two questions to ask a witness about the reputation of another witness: (1) Does the witness know the general character or reputation for truthfulness of the witness intended to be impeached? (2) If so, what is the character of the witness, good or bad? **International Sec. Life Ins. v. Melancon**, 463 S.W.2d 762, 767 (Tex.App.—Beaumont 1971, writ ref'd n.r.e.); *see* Tex. R. Evid. 404(a)(4), 608. Once the court determines the impeaching witness is qualified to speak on the general reputation of the other witness, the other party has the right to cross-examine the impeaching witness about her means of knowledge before she answers the question about the other witness's reputation for truthfulness. *See* **Melancon**, 463 S.W.2d at 767. See Brown & Rondon, **Texas Rules of Evidence Handbook**, Rule 608 (2021 ed.).

§6.2 Impeaching by earlier inconsistent statement. To impeach a witness with an earlier statement (whether oral or written) that is inconsistent with the witness's trial statement, the attorney must tell the witness about the contents of the earlier statement and when, where, and to whom it was made. Tex. R. Evid. 613(a)(1). The attorney is not required to interrupt her examination of the witness to give the witness an opportunity to explain or deny the earlier statement. *See* Tex. R. Evid. 613 cmt. However, the witness must be given the opportunity to do so at some point during the proceedings. Tex. R. Evid. 613(a)(3); *see* Tex. R. Evid. 613 cmt. (witness may have to wait until redirect to explain statement); *see also* Meeting of the Sup. Ct. Advisory Cmte. at pp. 26667–26689 (Oct. 18, 2013), www.txcourts.gov/scac/meetings/2011-2020 (discussing effect of proposed rule on timing of when witness must be given opportunity to explain or deny). If the statement is in writing, it does not need to be shown to the witness, but it must be shown to opposing counsel on request. Tex. R. Evid. 613(a)(2). Only if the witness unequivocally admits to having made the statement is extrinsic evidence of the earlier statement not admissible. Tex. R. Evid. 613(a)(4) & cmt.; *see* **Downen v. Texas Gulf Shrimp Co.**, 846 S.W.2d 506, 512 (Tex.App.—Corpus Christi 1993, writ denied). TRE 613(a) does not apply to an opposing party's statement under TRE 801(e)(2). Tex. R. Evid. 613(a)(5). See Brown & Rondon, **Texas Rules of Evidence Handbook**, Rule 613 (2021 ed.) (§A).

§6.3 Impeaching by bias. To impeach a witness by proof of circumstances or statements showing bias or interest, the attorney must tell the witness about the circumstances supporting the claim of bias or the details of the statement, including the contents and when, where, and to whom it was made. Tex. R. Evid. 613(b)(1). The attorney is not required to interrupt her examination of the witness to give the witness an opportunity to explain or deny the circumstances or statement. *See* Tex. R. Evid. 613 cmt. However, the witness must be given the opportunity to do so at some point during the proceedings. Tex.

R. Evid. 613(b)(3); *see* Tex. R. Evid. 613 cmt. (witness may have to wait until redirect to explain circumstances or statement); *see also* Meeting of the Sup. Ct. Advisory Cmte. at pp. 26667–26689 (Oct. 18, 2013), www.txcourts.gov/scac/meetings/2011-2020 (discussing effect of proposed rule on timing of when witness must be given opportunity to explain or deny). If the statement is in writing, it does not need to be shown to the witness, but it must be shown to opposing counsel on request. Tex. R. Evid. 613(b)(2). Only if the witness unequivocally admits to the bias or interest is extrinsic evidence of the earlier statement not admissible. Tex. R. Evid. 613(b)(4) & cmt.; *see* **Walker v. Packer**, 827 S.W.2d 833, 839 n.5 (Tex.1992). See Brown & Rondon, **Texas Rules of Evidence Handbook**, Rule 613 (2021 ed.) (§B).

§6.4 Impeaching by conviction. Before attempting to attack the credibility of a witness by introducing a conviction, the party must give the other party advance written notice (if the other party timely requested it) of the intent to use the conviction. Tex. R. Evid. 609(f). The credibility of a witness may be attacked on the ground that the witness was convicted of a crime if (1) the witness admits the conviction on the stand or the conviction is of public record, (2) the crime was a felony or involved moral turpitude, and (3) the court determines the probative value of admitting the evidence outweighs its prejudicial effect. Tex. R. Evid. 609(a); *see* **Porter v. Nemir**, 900 S.W.2d 376, 382 (Tex.App.—Austin 1995, no writ). To impeach by conviction, a party must prove the following: (1) the witness was convicted of a felony or a crime that involved moral turpitude, (2) the conviction is not over ten years old, (3) the witness has not been pardoned, the conviction has not been annulled, and a certificate of rehabilitation has not been issued, (4) the conviction was not the result of a juvenile adjudication, and (5) no appeal is pending on the conviction. Tex. R. Evid. 609; *see* **In re G.M.P.**, 909 S.W.2d 198, 209 (Tex.App.—Houston [14th Dist.] 1995, no writ); *see, e.g.*, **Reviea v. Marine Drilling Co.**, 800 S.W.2d 252, 258 (Tex.App.—Corpus Christi 1990, writ denied) (20-year-old conviction too remote to impeach). See Brown & Rondon, **Texas Rules of Evidence Handbook**, Rule 609 (2021 ed.).

§7. Rehabilitating a witness

§7.1 Proving truthfulness. In most civil cases, supporting evidence of a party's good character is not admissible. **Commonwealth Lloyd's Ins. v. Thomas**, 678 S.W.2d 278, 294 (Tex.App.—Fort Worth 1984, writ ref'd n.r.e.); *see* Tex. R. Evid. 608(a); **Rose v. Intercontinental Bank**, 705 S.W.2d 752, 757 (Tex.App.—Houston [1st Dist.] 1986, writ ref'd n.r.e.). Testimony of a witness's good character for truth or honesty, however, is admissible when the character of the witness is directly at issue, after a witness is impeached, or when one party (in its pleadings or by the evidence) charges the other party with a crime of moral turpitude. **Thomas**, 678 S.W.2d at 294; *see, e.g.*, **State Bar v. Evans**, 774 S.W.2d 656, 658 (Tex.1989) (attorney charged with conduct involving moral turpitude was permitted to offer evidence of pertinent character trait). To rehabilitate a witness's character for truth, the party must introduce evidence through another witness as follows: (1) prove the rehabilitating witness has knowledge of the character of the witness who was attacked (i.e., establish facts that show how the witness knows of the character of the person), (2) prove the witness has an opinion about that person's character for truthfulness, and (3) have the witness state her opinion regarding that person's character for truthfulness. *See* Tex. R. Evid. 404(a)(4), 608(a). See Brown & Rondon, **Texas Rules of Evidence Handbook**, Rule 608 (2021 ed.) (nn.329–343).

§7.2 Rebutting charge of recent fabrication or improper influence. When a witness who testified at a trial or hearing is accused of recent fabrication or improper influence during cross-examination, a party may introduce an earlier consistent statement to prove through a second witness that (1) the first witness made an out-of-court statement consistent with testimony before testifying and (2) the statement was made before a reason to fabricate arose. *See* Tex. R. Evid. 801(e)(1)(B); **Skillern & Sons, Inc. v. Rosen**, 359 S.W.2d 298, 301–02 (Tex.1962); **Reviea v. Marine Drilling Co.**, 800 S.W.2d 252, 257 (Tex.App.—Corpus Christi 1990, writ denied); *cf.* **Tome v. U.S.**, 513 U.S. 150, 156–58 (1995) (criminal case interpreting FRE 801(d)). See Brown & Rondon, **Texas Rules of Evidence Handbook**, Rule 801 (2021 ed.) (§B.1(2)).

§8. Introducing documents

Every exhibit must meet certain threshold requirements before it can be admitted into evidence: (1) the qualifying witness must be competent, (2) the witness must have personal knowledge sufficient to authenticate the exhibit, (3) the exhibit must be relevant to the trial, and (4) the exhibit must be authenticated. *See* Tex. R. Evid. 401 (relevance), Tex. R. Evid. 601 (competence), Tex. R. Evid. 602 (personal knowledge), Tex. R. Evid. 901(a) (authentication). However, just because an exhibit is relevant and authentic does not mean it is admissible; the exhibit may be excluded on other grounds (e.g., hearsay). *See* **Director, State Empls. Workers' Comp. Div. v. Lara**, 901 S.W.2d 635, 638 (Tex.App.—El Paso 1995, writ denied).

§8.1 Competence. The witness must be competent to testify, which means the witness must be able to accurately perceive, recall, and recount. *See* Tex. R. Evid. 601(a). See "Competency of witness," ch. 1-B, §3.2.16(2); Brown & Rondon, **Texas Rules of Evidence Handbook**, Rule 601 (2021 ed.) (§A). Courts often confuse competence with personal knowledge. *See, e.g.*, **Davidson v. Great Nat'l Life Ins.**, 737 S.W.2d 312, 314–15 (Tex.1987) (although court said witness was competent to authenticate photographs, court discussed personal knowledge).

§8.2 Personal knowledge. The witness must have personal knowledge on which to base the authentication. *See* Tex. R. Evid. 602; *see, e.g.*, **City of Dallas v. GTE Sw., Inc.**, 980 S.W.2d 928, 935 (Tex.App.—Fort Worth 1998, pet. denied) (witness did not have personal knowledge about exhibit); **Savage v. Psychiatric Inst.**, 965 S.W.2d 745, 753–54 (Tex.App.—Fort Worth 1998, pet. denied) (attorney's affidavit did not establish his personal knowledge about documents). See "Personal knowledge," ch. 1-B, §3.2.16(3)(a); Brown & Rondon, **Texas Rules of Evidence Handbook**, Rule 602 (2021 ed.).

§8.3 Relevance. To be relevant, the exhibit must tend to make the existence of a material fact more or less probable than it would otherwise have been. Tex. R. Evid. 401; **Edwards v. TEC**, 936 S.W.2d 462, 466–67 (Tex.App.—Fort Worth 1996, no writ); *see* **Diamond Offshore Servs. v. Williams**, 542 S.W.3d 539, 544 (Tex.2018); *see, e.g.*, **Prestige Ford Co. v. Gilmore**, 56 S.W.3d 73, 80 (Tex.App.—Houston [14th Dist.] 2001, pet. denied) (report made existence of material fact less probable). See Brown & Rondon, **Texas Rules of Evidence Handbook**, Rule 401 (2021 ed.) (§B).

§8.4 Authenticity. Authentication is a prerequisite to admissibility. **In re G.F.O.**, 874 S.W.2d 729, 731 (Tex.App.—Houston [1st Dist.] 1994, no writ); *see* Tex. R. Evid. 901(a). See Brown & Rondon, **Texas Rules of Evidence Handbook**, Rule 901 (2021 ed.).

1. Proof of authenticity. Authentication is established by evidence that the matter in question is what its proponent claims it to be. Tex. R. Evid. 901(a); **In re G.F.O.**, 874 S.W.2d at 731. Under TRE 901(b), the proponent can provide extrinsic evidence of authenticity, which is generally done through a sponsoring witness, or can rely on evidence within the document itself to prove authenticity. *See, e.g.*, **Fleming v. Wilson**, __ S.W.3d __, 2020 WL 5985187 (Tex.2020) (No. 19-0230; 10-9-20) (trial court did not abuse discretion by finding that watermark from district clerk's office, stamp and signature confirming filing, and judge's signature were sufficient proof of authenticity of judgment and verdict from another trial; documents were authentic under either TRE 901(b)(4) or TRE 901(b)(7)); *see also* Tex. R. Evid. 901(b)(1) to (10) (examples of evidence that proponent can use to satisfy authenticity requirement). See Brown & Rondon, **Texas Rules of Evidence Handbook**, Rule 901 (2021 ed.) (§B). The proponent can also show that the document meets the requirements for self-authentication. *See* Tex. R. Evid. 902. See "Documents that are self-authenticating," ch. 8-C, §8.4.4.

2. Presumption of authenticity for certain discovery documents. Documents produced in response to written discovery are presumed authentic and may be used in a pretrial proceeding or at trial against the producing party or nonparty. Tex. R. Civ. P. 176.6(c), 193.7; *see also* Tex. R. Evid. 901(b)(10) (any method of authentication provided by statute or other rule meets requirements of TRE 901(a)). See "Using requested documents," ch. 6-I, §8; "Other party's discovery responses," ch. 7-B, §9.5.3(1)(a). To use a discovery document against someone other than the producing party, a witness must vouch for the document's authenticity, or the document must satisfy the requirements for self-authentication. *See* **In re G.F.O.**, 874 S.W.2d at 731. See ch. 8-C, §8.4.3, below; "Documents that are self-authenticating," ch. 8-C, §8.4.4.

3. Documents authenticated by witness. The following are examples of documents that can be authenticated through a sponsoring witness.

(1) Signed instrument. To introduce a signed document, a party can do any of the following: (1) call the signing person (as an adverse witness, if necessary) to identify the signature as her own, (2) call a witness who saw the person sign the document, (3) call a witness who is familiar with the person's signature and can identify it, or (4) call a handwriting expert who can testify that, based on handwriting comparisons, the signature was made by the person. *See* Tex. R. Evid. 901(b). See Brown & Rondon, **Texas Rules of Evidence Handbook**, Rule 901 (2021 ed.) (§B).

(2) Copy of document. A duplicate is admissible as an original unless a question is raised about the authenticity of the original or it would be unfair to introduce the duplicate. Tex. R. Evid. 1003; **ESIS, Inc. v. Johnson**, 908 S.W.2d 554, 561 (Tex.App.—Fort Worth 1995, writ denied); *see also* **Owens-Corning Fiberglas Corp. v. Malone**, 916 S.W.2d 551, 558 (Tex.App.—Houston [1st Dist.] 1996) (copy admissible despite extraneous markings), *aff'd*, 972 S.W.2d 35 (Tex.1998). See

Brown & Rondon, **Texas Rules of Evidence Handbook**, Rule 1003 (2021 ed.). If a question is raised regarding the authenticity of the original, to introduce a copy, the party must prove the following: (1) the original was lost or destroyed, is not obtainable, is outside Texas, or is in the possession of the opponent, (2) a copy of the original was made, and (3) the offered document is a true and accurate copy of the original. *See* Tex. R. Evid. 1003, 1004.

Practice Tip

Do not object to a witness discussing the contents of a document in evidence with the "best-evidence" objection. The best-evidence rule comes into play only when a witness is asked to discuss the contents of a disputed document that is not in evidence. See ***White v. Bath****, 825 S.W.2d 227, 231 (Tex.App.—Houston [14th Dist] 1992, writ denied). Once the document is introduced, a witness may discuss it or read from it.*

(3) Summary. To introduce a summary, a party must prove the following: (1) the chart, summary, or calculation is a summary of other records, (2) the other records are voluminous writings, recordings, or photographs that are admissible, (3) the other records cannot be conveniently examined in court, and (4) the other records were made available to the other party for inspection and copying. Tex. R. Evid. 1006; *see, e.g.*, **Aquamarine Assocs. v. Burton Shipyard, Inc.**, 659 S.W.2d 820, 821–22 (Tex.1983) (because underlying business records were not shown to be admissible, summary was not admissible); **Duncan Dev., Inc. v. Haney**, 634 S.W.2d 811, 812–13 (Tex.1982) (summary of invoices received from subcontractors was admissible as summary of business records of contractor). The court may order that the other records be produced in court. Tex. R. Evid. 1006. See Brown & Rondon, **Texas Rules of Evidence Handbook**, Rule 1006 (2021 ed.).

(4) Websites. To introduce a printout from a website, a party must prove that the printout accurately reflects the content of the website and the image of the page on the computer from which the printout was made. Wilson, *Admissibility of Web-Based Data*, 52 The Advoc. (Texas) 31, 32 (Fall 2010). Authentication of a website printout is generally proved through affidavit testimony. *Id.*; *see* Tex. R. Evid. 901(b)(1). Courts disagree on whether an affidavit can simply state that the printout is a true and correct copy of a web page. *Compare* **Burnett Ranches, Ltd. v. Cano Pet., Inc.**, 289 S.W.3d 862, 871 (Tex.App.—Amarillo 2009, pet. denied) (P's attorney's affidavit stating document was true and correct copy of "Environmental Overview" printed from D's website was not properly authenticated because affidavit did not establish that website from which he obtained the document was D's), *with* **Daimler-Benz A.G. v. Olson**, 21 S.W.3d 707, 717 (Tex.App.—Austin 2000, pet. dism'd) (P's attorney's affidavit that attachments containing information from D's websites were within his personal knowledge and were accurate copies of original was proper to authenticate attachments). To avoid these problems with the sufficiency of affidavit testimony, a party should consider using discovery methods such as requests for admissions (e.g., ask the party to admit that Exhibit A came from its website) or deposition testimony (e.g., ask the witness if a specific web address is the employer's website). Wilson, *Admissibility of Web-Based Data*, 52 The Advoc. (Texas) 31, 32 (Fall 2010). The printout of a website may also be authenticated by its appearance, contents, substance, internal patterns, or other distinctive characteristics. *See* Tex. R. Evid. 901(b)(4). For a more detailed discussion of the authenticity of electronic information such as websites, e-mail, and instant messages, see Brown & Rondon, **Texas Rules of Evidence Handbook**, Rule 901 (2021 ed.) (nn.76–85, 155–179).

(5) Photograph. To introduce a photograph, a party must prove the following: (1) the witness saw the subject of the photograph at or near the time of the event in issue, (2) the witness recognizes the exhibit as a representation of the subject seen, and (3) the exhibit is a true and accurate representation of the subject as it appeared at the relevant time. *See* **State v. City of Greenville**, 726 S.W.2d 162, 168 (Tex.App.—Dallas 1986, writ ref'd n.r.e.). An original of a photograph includes the negative or any print made from it. Tex. R. Evid. 1001(d). If a verbal description of the matter is admissible, a photograph of it is generally also admissible. **City of Greenville**, 726 S.W.2d at 168. A court should exclude a photograph if its probative value is substantially outweighed by the danger of unfair prejudice. Tex. R. Evid. 403; **Castro v. Sebesta**, 808 S.W.2d 189, 193 (Tex.App.—Houston [1st Dist.] 1991, no writ); *see also* **Fibreboard Corp. v. Pool**, 813 S.W.2d 658, 671 (Tex.App.—Texarkana 1991, writ denied) (if relevant, photograph can be admissible, even if gruesome). See Brown & Rondon, **Texas Rules of Evidence Handbook**, Rule 1001 (2021 ed.) (§D.1).

(6) Public record. To introduce a public record or statement of a public office, the record must show on its face (or it must be proved by a witness) that it contains reports of (1) the office's activities, (2) matters observed under a legal

duty to report, or (3) factual findings from a legally authorized investigation. Tex. R. Evid. 803(8)(A); *see* Tex. R. Evid. 901(b)(7); **Commission for Lawyer Discipline v. Cantu**, 587 S.W.3d 779, 786 (Tex.2019); **State v. Foltin**, 930 S.W.2d 270, 272 (Tex.App.—Houston [14th Dist.] 1996, writ denied). The court should admit records that meet these requirements unless the opposing party demonstrates that the source of information or other circumstances indicate a lack of trustworthiness. *See* Tex. R. Evid. 803(8)(B); **Commission for Lawyer Discipline**, 587 S.W.3d at 786 n.4. Conclusions and opinions contained in an investigatory report admissible under TRE 803(8)(A)(iii) are admissible if they are based on the factual investigation and satisfy TRE 803's requirement of trustworthiness. *See* **Ter-Vartanyan v. R&R Freight, Inc.**, 111 S.W.3d 779, 784 (Tex.App.—Dallas 2003, pet. denied) (police accident report admissible); **McRae v. Echols**, 8 S.W.3d 797, 800 (Tex.App.—Waco 2000, pet. denied) (same). Not everything in an official record is exempt from the hearsay rule. For example, a statement of an eyewitness included in a police report is not admissible under TRE 803(8). **Kratz v. Exxon Corp.**, 890 S.W.2d 899, 905 (Tex.App.—El Paso 1994, no writ). See Brown & Rondon, **Texas Rules of Evidence Handbook**, Rule 803 (2021 ed.) (§B.4).

(7) Business record.

(a) Generally. To introduce a business record through a witness, a party must prove the following: (1) the record is a memorandum, report, or other compilation of data, (2) the witness is the custodian or another qualified witness, (3) the record was made from information transmitted by a person with knowledge of the facts, (4) the record was made at or near the time of the acts, events, conditions, opinions, or diagnoses appearing on it, (5) the record was made as part of the regular practice of that business activity, and (6) the record was kept in the course of a regularly conducted business activity. *See* Tex. R. Evid. 101(h)(4), 803(6)(A)-(6)(D); *see, e.g.*, **Freeman v. American Motorists Ins.**, 53 S.W.3d 710, 715 (Tex.App.—Houston [1st Dist.] 2001, no pet.) (letter from doctor to P's attorney about P's condition was inadmissible as business record because it did not qualify as routine entry); **Brooks v. Housing Auth.**, 926 S.W.2d 316, 322 (Tex.App.—El Paso 1996, no writ) (records of security guard were admissible as business records); **Connor v. Wright**, 737 S.W.2d 42, 44–45 (Tex.App.—San Antonio 1987, no writ) (business records of attorney were admissible to prove attorney fees). The court should admit records that meet these requirements unless the opposing party demonstrates that the source of information or the method or circumstances of preparation indicate a lack of trustworthiness. Tex. R. Evid. 803(6)(E). See Brown & Rondon, **Texas Rules of Evidence Handbook**, Rule 803 (2021 ed.) (§B.2).

(b) Third-party record. Under certain circumstances, a business record created by a third-party entity may be admissible under TRE 803(6) as another party's own business records. *See* **National Health Res. v. TBF Fin., LLC**, 429 S.W.3d 125, 130 (Tex.App.—Dallas 2014, no pet.); **Dodeka, L.L.C. v. Campos**, 377 S.W.3d 726, 732 (Tex.App.—San Antonio 2012, no pet.); **Simien v. Unifund CCR Partners**, 321 S.W.3d 235, 240–41 (Tex.App.—Houston [1st Dist.] 2010, no pet.). A party can establish the admissibility of a third-party entity's business records if a sponsoring witness can testify to the following: (1) the records were incorporated and kept in the course of the party's business, (2) the business typically relies on the accuracy of the contents of the records, and (3) the circumstances otherwise indicate the trustworthiness of the records. **Rogers v. RREF II CB Acquisitions, LLC**, 533 S.W.3d 419, 432 (Tex.App.—Corpus Christi 2016, no pet.); **Ortega v. CACH, LLC**, 396 S.W.3d 622, 629 (Tex.App.—Houston [14th Dist.] 2013, no pet.); **Dodeka, L.L.C.**, 377 S.W.3d at 732; **Simien**, 321 S.W.3d at 240–41; *see* **National Health**, 429 S.W.3d at 130; *see also* **Duncan Dev.**, 634 S.W.2d at 813–14 (under former TRCS art. 3137e, now TRE 803(6), proof that party used reliable method to verify accuracy of third-party entities' business records was sufficient to establish admissibility). For further discussion of admitting a third party's business records as another party's own records, see Brown & Rondon, **Texas Rules of Evidence Handbook**, Rule 803 (2021 ed.) (nn.640–643).

4. Documents that are self-authenticating. If a document can overcome the hearsay objection, it can be admitted into evidence without a sponsoring witness or other extrinsic evidence as long as it is self-authenticating. Tex. R. Evid. 902; *see* **Fleming**, ___ S.W.3d at ___, 2020 WL 5985187; **Larson v. Family Violence & Sexual Assault Prevention Ctr.**, 64 S.W.3d 506, 511 (Tex.App.—Corpus Christi 2001, pet. denied). See Brown & Rondon, **Texas Rules of Evidence Handbook**, Rule 902 (2021 ed.). A self-authenticating document under TRE 902 must satisfy the requirements of TRE 901. Brown & Rondon, **Texas Rules of Evidence Handbook**, Rule 902 (2021 ed.) (n.279). A party can object to a self-authenticating document on grounds other than authentication, such as relevance, hearsay, or unfair prejudice. Brown & Rondon, **Texas Rules of Evidence Handbook**, Rule 902 (2021 ed.) (n.285).

(1) Business records by affidavit. A party can prove specific information from business records with an affidavit from the custodian of the records. *See* Tex. R. Evid. 803(6)(D), 902(10); *see, e.g.*, **Fullick v. City of Baytown**, 820 S.W.2d 943, 945–46 (Tex.App.—Houston [1st Dist.] 1991, no writ) (tax statements from school districts, supported by affidavit, were admissible); **March v. Victoria Lloyds Ins.**, 773 S.W.2d 785, 789 (Tex.App.—Fort Worth 1989, writ denied) (report of blood alcohol level, supported by affidavit, was admissible); **National Std. Ins. v. Gayton**, 773 S.W.2d 75, 76 (Tex.App.—Amarillo 1989, no writ) (doctor's records with factual observations and diagnosis, supported by affidavit, were admissible). To introduce business records by affidavit of a custodian or other qualified witness, a party must show that the following prerequisites have been met:

(a) Records are admissible. The records must be admissible under TRE 803(6) or 803(7). Tex. R. Evid. 902(10).

(b) Records are attached to affidavit. The records must be attached to an affidavit that complies with TRE 902(10)(B) and any other requirements of law. Tex. R. Evid. 902(10). An affidavit under TRE 902(10) includes an unsworn declaration made under penalty of perjury. Tex. R. Evid. 902(10)(B) & cmt. (2014); *see* Tex. Civ. Prac. & Rem. Code §132.001. See "Unsworn declaration," ch. 1-B, §3.2.17.

[1] Form under TRE 902(10)(B). An affidavit that follows the sample form provided in TRE 902(10)(B) is sufficient, but the sample form is not exclusive. Tex. R. Evid. 902(10)(B). See **O'Connor's Texas Civil Forms**, FORM 8C:2 (2020 ed.).

[2] Any other requirements of law. The affidavit under TRE 902(10)(B) must comply with any other requirements of law. Tex. R. Evid. 902(10). The phrase "any other requirements of law" incorporates the requirements of CPRC §§18.001 and 18.002 for affidavits offered as proof of the cost or necessity of services or medical expenses. Tex. R. Evid. 902 cmt. (2014). See "Affidavit for past expenses," ch. 8-C, §8.4.4(2).

(c) Records & affidavit are served. The records and affidavit must be served on each party at least 14 days before trial. Tex. R. Evid. 902(10)(A). A party is not required to file the records and affidavit with the court. *See* Tex. R. Evid. 902 cmt. (2014); *see also* Tex.Sup.Ct. Order, Misc. Docket No. 14-9174 (eff. Sept. 1, 2014) (filing requirement eliminated for cases filed on or after Sept. 1, 2014). The records and affidavit can be served by any method permitted under TRCP 21a. Tex. R. Evid. 902(10)(A). See "Methods of service," ch. 1-D, §4.2. Even if the service requirements of TRE 902(10)(A) are not met, the court may order that a business record be treated as presumptively authentic if good cause is shown. Tex. R. Evid. 902(10).

(2) Affidavit for past expenses. CPRC §18.001 permits a party to prove by affidavit the necessity of a service and the reasonableness of the amount charged for that service. *See* Tex. Civ. Prac. & Rem. Code §18.001(b); **Gunn v. McCoy**, 554 S.W.3d 645, 672 (Tex.2018); *see also* **Beauchamp v. Hambrick**, 901 S.W.2d 747, 749 (Tex.App.—Eastland 1995, no writ) (CPRC §18.001 allows for admissibility by affidavit of evidence of reasonableness and necessity of charges, which would otherwise be inadmissible hearsay). The affidavit is not conclusive proof, however, and can be controverted. **Gunn**, 554 S.W.3d at 672. See "Counteraffidavit," ch. 8-C, §8.4.4(2)(e).

Note

In 2019, the Legislature approved significant amendments to CPRC §18.001. See H.B. 1693, §1, 86th Leg., R.S., eff. Sept. 1, 2019. These amendments apply to actions commenced on or after September 1, 2019; actions commenced before that date are governed by the former law. H.B. 1693, §§2, 3, 86th Leg., R.S., eff. Sept. 1, 2019. Where appropriate, this section addresses both the new and former law.

(a) Form. The affidavit must (1) be taken before an officer with authority to administer oaths, (2) be made by the person who provided the services or the person in charge of the records that show the services provided and the charges made, (3) state that the services were necessary and were provided at a cost reasonable at the time and place of service, and (4) include an itemized statement of the services and charges. *See* Tex. Civ. Prac. & Rem. Code §§18.001(b), (c), 18.002; **Walker v. Ricks**, 101 S.W.3d 740, 747–48 (Tex.App.—Corpus Christi 2003, no pet.). An affidavit that substantially

complies with CPRC §18.001 will satisfy the requirements of authentication. *See* Tex. Civ. Prac. & Rem. Code §18.002(c). The form of an affidavit provided under CPRC §18.002 is not exclusive. Tex. Civ. Prac. & Rem. Code §18.002(c). See "Affidavit for past expenses," **O'Connor's Texas Causes of Action**, ch. 41-B, §6.3.1(1)(b) (2021 ed.).

[1] By provider. A party can prove the necessity of services and the reasonableness of the cost of the services with an affidavit from the provider of the services. *See* Tex. Civ. Prac. & Rem. Code §18.001(c)(2)(A). An affidavit that follows the sample form provided in CPRC §18.002(a) is sufficient. See **O'Connor's Texas Civil Forms**, FORM 8C:3 (2020 ed.).

[2] By custodian. A party can prove the necessity of services and the reasonableness of the cost of the services with an affidavit from the custodian of the billing records. *See* Tex. Civ. Prac. & Rem. Code §18.001(c)(2)(B). An affidavit that follows the sample form provided in CPRC §18.002(b) is sufficient. See **O'Connor's Texas Civil Forms**, FORM 8C:4 (2020 ed.).

[3] For medical expenses. A party can prove the necessity of past medical services and the reasonableness of the expenses for those services with an affidavit from the provider of the services or a custodian of the records that show the services provided and the charges incurred. *See* Tex. Civ. Prac. & Rem. Code §18.001(c)(2); **Gunn**, 554 S.W.3d at 672. If the affiant is a custodian of records, the custodian does not have to be the custodian for the medical provider who performed the services. *E.g.*, **Gunn**, 554 S.W.3d at 674 (affidavits from subrogation agents for health-insurance carriers that paid P's medical expenses were sufficient evidence). *But see id.* at 687 (Johnson & Boyd, JJ., dissenting) (person with no medical training and no connection with medical services is not proper affiant for necessity of services provided). The only requirement is that the custodian be in a position to testify about the necessity of the services and reasonableness of the expenses. *See* **Gunn**, 554 S.W.3d at 673. An affidavit that substantially complies with the sample form provided in CPRC §18.002(b-1) is sufficient. See **O'Connor's Texas Civil Forms**, FORM 8C:5 (2020 ed.).

Note

The affidavit should state the amount actually paid or incurred for the services, which is not necessarily the same as the amount billed. See Tex. Civ. Prac. & Rem. Code §41.0105; ***Gunn****, 554 S.W.3d at 672.*

(b) Deadline to serve.

[1] Before 9-1-19. For actions commenced before September 1, 2019, the affidavit must be served on each party at least 30 days before the first day that evidence is presented at trial. Tex. Civ. Prac. & Rem. Code §18.001(d) (pre-9-1-19 version).

[2] On or after 9-1-19. For actions commenced on or after September 1, 2019, the affidavit must generally be served on each party by the earliest of (1) 90 days after the date when the defendant files its answer, (2) the date when the offering party must designate any expert witness under a court order, or (3) the date when the offering party must designate any expert witness as required by the TRCPs. Tex. Civ. Prac. & Rem. Code §18.001(d). But if a party offers an affidavit for services that are provided for the first time by a provider after the defendant files its answer, that affidavit must be served on each party by the earlier of the date when the offering party must designate any expert witness (1) under a court order or (2) as required by the TRCPs. Tex. Civ. Prac. & Rem. Code §18.001(d-1). The deadline for serving an affidavit can be modified by agreement of the parties or with leave of court. Tex. Civ. Prac. & Rem. Code §18.001(i).

(c) Notice. For actions commenced on or after September 1, 2019, the party offering the affidavit must file notice with the clerk stating that it served a copy of the affidavit on the other parties as required by CPRC §18.001. Tex. Civ. Prac. & Rem. Code §18.001(d-2). Except as provided by the TREs, the party is not required to file the affidavit itself with the clerk before the trial commences. *Id.*

(d) Attached records.

[1] Not filed. Except as provided by the TREs, records attached to the affidavit do not need to be filed with the court clerk before the trial begins. *See* Tex. Civ. Prac. & Rem. Code §18.001(d-2).

Note

Before the 2019 amendments, CPRC §18.001 explicitly stated that the records attached to the affidavit did not need to be filed with the court clerk. See Tex. Civ. Prac. & Rem. Code §18.001(d) (pre-9-1-19 version). Although the amended statute deleted the reference to the attached records and now states only that the affidavit does not need to be filed, the records attached to the affidavit would presumably still not need to be filed either. See Tex. Civ. Prac. & Rem. Code §18.001(d-2); see also Tex. R Evid. 902 cmt. (2014) (requirement that business records be filed with court was removed by 2014 amendments).

[2] Admissibility standards—medical expenses. Evidence of medical expenses is allowed only if the expenses have been paid or will be paid after any necessary credits or adjustments. *See* Tex. Civ. Prac. & Rem. Code §41.0105; **Haygood v. De Escabedo**, 356 S.W.3d 390, 398 (Tex.2011). If a medical bill or other itemized statement attached to an affidavit for past medical expenses reflects a charge that is unrecoverable, the reference to that charge is not admissible at trial. Tex. Civ. Prac. & Rem. Code §18.002(b-2).

Note

In certain cases, a plaintiff may assign to her medical provider the plaintiff's interest in any proceeds that may be recovered in a pending suit; in turn, the medical provider may sell a plaintiff's accounts receivable to a third-party company at a discounted rate (a practice known as "factoring"). See ***Amigos Meat Distribs. v. Guzman****, 526 S.W.3d 511, 524 (Tex.App.—Houston [1st Dist.] 2017, pet. denied);* ***Katy Springs & Mfg. v. Favalora****, 476 S.W.3d 579, 600–01 & n.4 (Tex.App.—Houston [14th Dist.] 2015, pet. denied). But if the record shows that the plaintiff remains liable for the full amount originally billed by the medical provider, then evidence of that full amount—not just the discounted amount the provider received—is admissible. See* ***Amigos Meat****, 526 S.W.3d at 525;* ***Katy Springs****, 476 S.W.3d at 604.*

(e) Counteraffidavit. If an opposing party wants to controvert the affidavit on the cost and necessity of services, it must do so by serving a counteraffidavit. *See* Tex. Civ. Prac. & Rem. Code §18.001(e); **Gunn**, 554 S.W.3d at 672. See **O'Connor's Texas Civil Forms**, FORM 8C:6 (2020 ed.). The counteraffidavit must be taken before a person authorized to administer oaths and must show (1) the affiant is qualified as an expert to contravene the particular service and charge involved and (2) the specific reason why the service was not necessary or the charge was unreasonable. *See* Tex. Civ. Prac. & Rem. Code §18.001(f); **Turner v. Peril**, 50 S.W.3d 742, 747 (Tex.App.—Dallas 2001, pet. denied). If a proper counteraffidavit is served, the original affidavit is no longer sufficient to prove the necessity of the services and the reasonableness of the cost of the services, and expert testimony may then be necessary. **McGibney v. Rauhauser**, 549 S.W.3d 816, 826 (Tex.App.—Fort Worth 2018, pet. denied).

[1] Deadline to serve.

[a] Before 9-1-19. For actions commenced before September 1, 2019, the counteraffidavit must generally be served on each party or each party's attorney no later than 30 days after the opposing party receives a copy of the affidavit on the cost and necessity of services and at least 14 days before the first day evidence is presented at trial. Tex. Civ. Prac. & Rem. Code §18.001(e) (pre-9-1-19 version). If the court grants permission, however, the counteraffidavit can be served anytime before the commencement of trial. *Id.*

[b] On or after 9-1-19. For actions commenced on or after September 1, 2019, the counteraffidavit must generally be served on each party or each party's attorney by the earliest of (1) 120 days after the date when the defendant files its answer, (2) the date when the party offering the counteraffidavit must designate expert witnesses under a court order, or (3) the date when the party offering the counteraffidavit must designate any expert witness as required by the TRCPs. Tex. Civ. Prac. & Rem. Code §18.001(e). But if a party offers an affidavit for services that are provided for the first time by a provider after the defendant files its answer, the counteraffidavit must be served on each party by the latest of (1) 30 days after service of the affidavit on the party offering the counteraffidavit, (2) the date when the party offering the

counteraffidavit must designate any expert witness under a court order, or (3) the date when the party offering the counteraffidavit must designate any expert witness as required by the TRCPs. *See* Tex. Civ. Prac. & Rem. Code §18.001(e-1). The deadline for serving a counteraffidavit can be modified by agreement of the parties or with leave of court. Tex. Civ. Prac. & Rem. Code §18.001(i).

[2] Notice. For actions commenced on or after September 1, 2019, the party offering the counteraffidavit must file notice with the clerk stating that it served a copy of the counteraffidavit on the other parties or their attorneys as required by CPRC §18.001. Tex. Civ. Prac. & Rem. Code §18.001(g).

(f) Supplemental affidavit. For actions commenced on or after September 1, 2019, if continuing services are provided after the deadline for serving an affidavit or a counteraffidavit, the offering party can supplement the affidavit. *See* Tex. Civ. Prac. & Rem. Code §18.001(h).

[1] Affidavit. A party can supplement an affidavit served under CPRC §18.001(d) or (d-1) no later than 60 days before the date when the trial commences. Tex. Civ. Prac. & Rem. Code §18.001(h)(1). This deadline can be modified by agreement of the parties or with leave of court. Tex. Civ. Prac. & Rem. Code §18.001(i).

[2] Counteraffidavit. A party can supplement a counteraffidavit served under CPRC §18.001(e) or (e-1) no later than 30 days before the date when the trial commences. Tex. Civ. Prac. & Rem. Code §18.001(h)(2). This deadline can be modified by agreement of the parties or with leave of court. Tex. Civ. Prac. & Rem. Code §18.001(i).

(g) Not evidence of causation. For actions commenced on or after September 1, 2019, the Legislature clarified that an affidavit for past expenses is not evidence of and cannot support a finding of the causation element of the cause of action that is the basis of the suit. Tex. Civ. Prac. & Rem. Code §18.001(b). Similarly, the counteraffidavit cannot be used to controvert the causation element of the underlying cause of action. Tex. Civ. Prac. & Rem. Code §18.001(f).

(3) Domestic public record under seal. To introduce a domestic record under seal, a party must show the following: (1) the document bears a seal of the United States, a state, or any other political subdivision listed in TRE 902(1)(A), and (2) the document bears a signature purporting to be an execution or attestation. Tex. R. Evid. 902(1); *see* Tex. R. Evid. 1005. The document must also meet the requirements of TRE 803(8)(A). See "Public record," ch. 8-C, §8.4.3(6).

(4) Domestic public record not under seal. To introduce a public record that is not under seal, a party must show the following: (1) the document bears the signature in the official capacity of an officer or employee of an entity listed in TRE 902(1)(A), and (2) a public officer having a seal and having official duties in the district or political subdivision of the officer or employee certifies that the signer of the document has the official capacity and that the person's signature is genuine. Tex. R. Evid. 902(2); *see* Tex. R. Evid. 1005; **Al-Nayem Int'l Trading, Inc. v. Irving ISD**, 159 S.W.3d 762, 764 (Tex.App.—Dallas 2005, no pet.) (tax statements, not certified); **Shaw v. Kennedy, Ltd.**, 879 S.W.2d 240, 246 (Tex.App.—Amarillo 1994, no writ) (copies of application for and order accepting the closing of bankruptcy proceedings, certified by bankruptcy court).

(5) Foreign public documents. For a discussion of how to introduce public documents from other countries, see TRE 902(3) and Brown & Rondon, **Texas Rules of Evidence Handbook**, Rule 902 (2021 ed.) (§C).

(6) Excerpt from commercial publication. To introduce an excerpt from a commercial publication, a party must show the following: (1) the document is the original or a photocopy of a market quotation, list, directory, or other compilation, and (2) the publication is generally used and relied on by the public or by persons in particular occupations. Tex. R. Evid. 803(17) (market reports and commercial publications); *see* Tex. R. Evid. 902(6) (newspapers and periodicals); **Lewis v. Southmore Sav. Ass'n**, 480 S.W.2d 180, 186 (Tex.1972) (market reports); *see, e.g.*, **Curran v. Unis**, 711 S.W.2d 290, 296–97 (Tex.App.—Dallas 1986, no writ) (photocopies of pages from business-reporting service regarding ownership of a partnership were admissible).

D. Objecting to Evidence

§1. General

§1.1 Rules. Tex R Civ. P. 166(m), 267; Tex R Evid. 103 to 106, 403, 614; Tex R App. P. 33.1, 44.1.

§1.2 Purpose. The primary reason to object to evidence is to prevent it from being introduced in the trial and heard by the jury. A secondary reason to object is to preserve the issue for appellate review. *See* Tex R Evid. 103(a); Tex R App. P. 33.1(a).

§1.3 Forms. **O'Connor's Texas Civil Forms**, FORMS 5E:1 et seq. (2020 ed.).

§1.4 Other references. *McCormick on Evidence* §52 (8th ed.); **O'Connor's Texas Civil Appeals** (2020 ed.); Brown & Rondon, **Texas Rules of Evidence Handbook** (2021 ed.).

§2. Time to make objections

§2.1 Pretrial objections.

1. Motion in limine. A party can object to evidence before trial in a motion in limine. A ruling on a motion in limine is not a ruling on the admissibility of the evidence and does not preserve error on appeal; it merely prevents the attorneys from referring to the subject matter of the motion in front of a jury without first obtaining a ruling. When the evidence is offered at trial, the party must object to preserve error. See "Motion in Limine," ch. 5-E, §1 et seq.

2. Motion to exclude. A party can object to evidence before trial in a motion to exclude. *See* **Owens-Corning Fiberglas Corp. v. Malone**, 916 S.W.2d 551, 557 (Tex.App.—Houston [1st Dist.] 1996), *aff'd*, 972 S.W.2d 35 (Tex.1998). At trial, the court may reconsider its pretrial rulings on the admissibility of evidence. **Reveal v. West**, 764 S.W.2d 8, 11 (Tex.App.—Houston [1st Dist.] 1988, orig. proceeding). Unlike rulings on motions in limine, rulings on motions to exclude evidence preserve error on appeal. *See* **Owens-Corning**, 916 S.W.2d at 557. However, despite a pretrial ruling, if a party affirmatively states at trial that it has no objection to the admission of evidence, the party waives any error in the admission of the evidence. **Pojar v. Cifre**, 199 S.W.3d 317, 341 (Tex.App.—Corpus Christi 2006, pet. denied).

3. Objections to exhibits. A trial court may require parties to submit written pretrial objections to tendered exhibits. Tex R Civ. P. 166(m); *see* Tex R Civ. P. 193 cmt. 7.

§2.2 Trial objections. When objectionable evidence is offered at trial, the party that believes the evidence is not admissible must object. **Clark v. Trailways, Inc.**, 774 S.W.2d 644, 647 (Tex.1989). If a party does not object to the evidence, it waives any error in its admission. Tex R Evid. 103(a)(1); Tex R App. P. 33.1(a); *see* **Service Corp. v. Guerra**, 348 S.W.3d 221, 234 (Tex.2011). To preserve error, the party must state the substance of the objection on the record. Tex R App. P. 33.1(a)(1)(A). If the objection is apparent from the context, however, the objection alone will preserve error. *Id.*; **Ramirez v. Volkswagen**, 788 S.W.2d 700, 705 (Tex.App.—Corpus Christi 1990, writ denied).

Note

If a party timely objects to evidence offered at trial and that same evidence was addressed by the opposing attorney during voir dire of the jury panel without objection, the objection at trial is not waived. ***Service Corp.****, 348 S.W.3d at 234. Error is not waived because statements made by attorneys during the jury-selection process are not evidence. Id. See "Voir dire examination," ch. 8-A, §5; "Waiver," ch. 8-D, §6.8.*

---

§2.3 Timing of objections. An objection to evidence during trial must be made as soon as the reason for the objection becomes apparent. Tex R Evid. 103(a)(1)(A); **Wolfe v. East Tex. Seed Co.**, 583 S.W.2d 481, 482 (Tex.App.—Houston [1st Dist.] 1979, writ dism'd).

1. Too early. If an objection is premature, it does not preserve error. *See* **Correa v. General Motors Corp.**, 948 S.W.2d 515, 518 (Tex.App.—Corpus Christi 1997, no writ) (general objection to anticipated evidence does not preserve error); *see, e.g.*, **Bushell v. Dean**, 803 S.W.2d 711, 711–12 (Tex.1991) (error not preserved because D objected before witness testified and did not reurge objection during testimony).

2. On time. Generally, the objection must be made at the time the evidence is offered. **MBank Dallas v. Sunbelt Mfg.**, 710 S.W.2d 633, 638 (Tex.App.—Dallas 1986, writ ref'd n.r.e.). For testimonial evidence, the objection must be made after the question is asked and before the witness answers. An objection made after the witness answers is timely in some situations, such as when the witness makes an objectionable answer to a proper question, the witness answers an objectionable question too quickly for the objection to be made, or the witness volunteers an objectionable statement. *See* Brown & Rondon, **Texas Rules of Evidence Handbook**, Rule 103 (2021 ed.) (nn.133–139); *see, e.g.*, **Beall v. Ditmore**, 867 S.W.2d 791, 794 (Tex.App.—El Paso 1993, writ denied) (in response to D's question, P mentioned insurance). In these instances, the party must also make other objections. See "When jury hears inadmissible evidence," ch. 8-D, §6.7.

3. Too late. An objection is not timely if it is not made as soon as the question is asked or shortly thereafter. *See, e.g.*, **Miles v. Ford Motor Co.**, 922 S.W.2d 572, 591 (Tex.App.—Texarkana 1996) (objection to expert's testimony regarding previously undisclosed theory of recovery was untimely when made after theory was completely introduced), *rev'd in part on other grounds*, 967 S.W.2d 377 (Tex.1998); **Seneca Res. v. Marsh & McLennan, Inc.**, 911 S.W.2d 144, 152 (Tex.App.—Houston [1st Dist.] 1995, no writ) (objection made after lengthy testimony in violation of motion in limine was untimely). An objection is not timely if it is made the second time the evidence is offered. *See* **In re A.V.**, 849 S.W.2d 393, 396 (Tex.App.—Fort Worth 1993, writ denied).

§3. Specific vs. general objections

§3.1 Specific objections. An objection must be specific. Tex. R. Evid. 103(a)(1)(B); Tex. R. App. P. 33.1(a)(1)(A); **Service Corp. v. Guerra**, 348 S.W.3d 221, 234 (Tex.2011). There are at least three reasons the courts require a specific objection. A specific objection (1) enables the court to understand the challenge, (2) permits the court to make an informed ruling, and (3) gives the party offering the evidence the opportunity to remedy the defect and offer it again in admissible form. **McKinney v. National Un. Fire Ins.**, 772 S.W.2d 72, 74 (Tex.1989).

1. How to make specific objections. There are two parts to an objection. First, the objection must identify the exact part of the question or the evidence that is objectionable. **Speier v. Webster Coll.**, 616 S.W.2d 617, 619 (Tex.1981). Second, the objection must identify the legal principle the court will violate if it admits the evidence (if it is not apparent from the context). **United Cab Co. v. Mason**, 775 S.W.2d 783, 785 (Tex.App.—Houston [1st Dist.] 1989, writ denied); *see* Tex. R. Evid. 103(a)(1)(B).

2. Rulings on specific objections on appeal.

(1) Untenable specific objection sustained. If the trial court sustains an untenable specific objection and excludes the evidence, the appellate court should uphold the ruling if there was any valid ground for excluding the evidence. **State Bar v. Evans**, 774 S.W.2d 656, 658 n.5 (Tex.1989). Thus, if a party made the wrong objection and the court sustained it, on appeal, the ruling is not reversible error if it is supported by the record. *See* Brown & Rondon, **Texas Rules of Evidence Handbook**, Rule 103 (2021 ed.) (nn.114–115).

(2) Untenable specific objection overruled. If the trial court overrules an untenable specific objection and admits the evidence, the appellate court will uphold the ruling even if the party could have made valid objections to the evidence. **Wilkerson v. PIC Rlty. Corp.**, 590 S.W.2d 780, 782 (Tex.App.—Houston [14th Dist.] 1979, no writ); *see, e.g.*, **Smith v. Levine**, 911 S.W.2d 427, 436 (Tex.App.—San Antonio 1995, writ denied) (overruling of relevance objection to photos upheld even though party could have objected that photos were not produced in discovery); **Richard Gill Co. v. Jackson's Landing Owners' Ass'n**, 758 S.W.2d 921, 927–28 (Tex.App.—Corpus Christi 1988, writ denied) (overruling of objection to designation of expert upheld even though party could have objected to subject matter of testimony).

§3.2 General objections. A general objection is one that merely challenges the admissibility of the evidence or objects to evidence for vague or inexact reasons. *See* **Sciarrilla v. Osborne**, 946 S.W.2d 919, 924 (Tex.App.—Beaumont 1997, pet. denied); **Mayfield v. Employers Reinsurance Corp.**, 539 S.W.2d 398, 400 (Tex.App.—Tyler 1976, writ ref'd n.r.e.); *see, e.g.*, **Lege v. Jones**, 919 S.W.2d 870, 874 (Tex.App.—Houston [14th Dist.] 1996, no writ) (objection that evidence is "immaterial and irrelevant" is a general objection); **Ramirez v. Johnson**, 601 S.W.2d 149, 151 (Tex.App.—San Antonio 1980, writ ref'd n.r.e.) ("note our exception" does not preserve objection).

1. Reason to avoid general objections. A general objection is no objection at all. **Murphy v. Waldrip**, 692 S.W.2d 584, 591 (Tex.App.—Fort Worth 1985, writ ref'd n.r.e.).

2. Rulings on general objections on appeal.

(1) General objection sustained. When the trial court sustains a general objection and excludes the evidence, the appellate court will uphold the objection if there was a valid ground for excluding the evidence and the proponent of the evidence did not request a more specific objection. *McCormick on Evidence* §52 (8th ed.). The appellate court will assume the valid ground for the objection was apparent to the trial court when neither the trial court nor the proponent of the evidence asked for a more specific objection. *See* **General Acc. Fire & Life Assur. Corp. v. Camp**, 348 S.W.2d 782, 784 (Tex.App.—Houston [1st Dist.] 1961, no writ); *see, e.g.*, **Hannum v. General Life & Acc. Ins.**, 745 S.W.2d 500, 502 (Tex.App.—Corpus Christi 1988, no writ) (because document was not properly authenticated, no error to exclude it on a general objection).

(2) General objection overruled. When the trial court overrules a general objection and admits the evidence, the appellate court will hold that the general objection did not preserve error. **Speier v. Webster Coll.**, 616 S.W.2d 617, 619 (Tex.1981); **Lege**, 919 S.W.2d at 874. Normally, a party cannot complain on appeal that the trial court erred in overruling a general objection by raising a ground it did not raise with the trial court. *See* **Pfeffer v. Southern Tex. Laborers' Pension Trust Fund**, 679 S.W.2d 691, 693 (Tex.App.—Houston [1st Dist.] 1984, writ ref'd n.r.e.) (appellant may not enlarge ground for error with objection not asserted at trial). There are two exceptions: (1) if the ground for exclusion is so obvious that it is indicated by a general phrase and (2) if the evidence was not admissible for any purpose. **Ramirez**, 601 S.W.2d at 151 (#1); **Mueller v. Central Power & Light Co.**, 403 S.W.2d 901, 904 (Tex.App.—Corpus Christi 1966, no writ) (#2); *see* Tex. R. Evid. 103(a)(1)(B) (#1).

§4. Objecting to a witness

§4.1 Taking witness on voir dire. If a party believes a witness is not qualified to testify because of lack of knowledge, the party should object; if the objection is overruled, the party should ask to take the witness on voir dire before the witness testifies. *See* **Marling v. Maillard**, 826 S.W.2d 735, 739 (Tex.App.—Houston [14th Dist.] 1992, no writ). This technique is essentially a cross-examination of the witness on the limited issue of knowledge before the proponent's direct examination.

1. No right to voir dire. The party does not have an absolute right to conduct a voir dire examination. *See* Tex. R. Evid. 705(b) (party may be able to voir dire expert about underlying facts or data). The court has the discretion to permit or deny voir dire. **In re Estate of Trawick**, 170 S.W.3d 871, 875 (Tex.App.—Texarkana 2005, no pet.); *see* Tex. R. Evid. 705(b). If the court permits voir dire, it must be conducted outside the presence of the jury. Tex. R. Evid. 705(b); *see* **Exxon Corp. v. Makofski**, 116 S.W.3d 176, 192–93 (Tex.App.—Houston [14th Dist.] 2003, pet. denied). See Brown & Rondon, **Texas Rules of Evidence Handbook**, Rule 705 (2021 ed.) (§B).

2. Repeat objection after voir dire. After completing the voir dire of the witness, the party should repeat its objection to the testimony. When the party does not object after voir dire, the court will assume the party decided not to challenge the witness. **Marling**, 826 S.W.2d at 739.

3. Scope of examination. The purpose of a voir dire examination is to test the personal knowledge of a witness. *See* **Celotex Corp. v. Tate**, 797 S.W.2d 197, 206 (Tex.App.—Corpus Christi 1990, writ dism'd) (either cross-examination or voir dire can be used to challenge knowledge of witness).

§4.2 Objection to opinion of expert. To object to the opinion of an expert, the party should object that the expert is not qualified, the opinion is not relevant or reliable, or the probative value of the opinion is substantially outweighed by the danger of unfair prejudice, confusion, or delay. **E.I. du Pont de Nemours & Co. v. Robinson**, 923 S.W.2d 549, 556–57 (Tex.1995); *see* Tex. R. Evid. 104(a), 401 to 403, 702, 703, 705. See "Motion to Exclude Expert," ch. 5-N, §1 et seq.

§4.3 Objection to witness who violated "the Rule." If a witness violates "the Rule," the trial court must determine whether it will permit the witness to testify. *See, e.g.*, **Drilex Sys. v. Flores**, 1 S.W.3d 112, 117–18 (Tex.1999) (court struck

expert for violating the Rule); **In re D.T.C.**, 30 S.W.3d 43, 49–50 (Tex.App.—Houston [14th Dist.] 2000, no pet.) (court struck three witnesses for violating the Rule); **Guerrero v. Smith**, 864 S.W.2d 797, 800–01 (Tex.App.—Houston [14th Dist.] 1993, no writ) (witness who heard D's testimony was permitted to testify). See "Invoking 'the Rule'," ch. 8-C, §3.

§4.4 Failing to supplement discovery. If a party attempts to introduce evidence that was not disclosed even though a pretrial order or a discovery request required disclosure, the other party should object. *See* Tex. R. Civ. P. 193.6(a). See "Pretrial Conference," ch. 5-A, §1 et seq.; "Objecting to unidentified witness," ch. 6-E, §2.8.

§4.5 Preserving error. When evidence is excluded, the party must make an offer of proof (or, after trial, a bill of exception) to preserve the testimony of the witness so the appellate courts can determine whether the erroneous exclusion was harmful. See "Offer of Proof & Bill of Exception," ch. 8-E, §1 et seq.

§5. Objecting to a question

Generally, an improper question that is not answered by the witness does not constitute reversible error. *See* **Luna v. North Star Dodge Sales, Inc.**, 667 S.W.2d 115, 119–20 (Tex.1984). In most cases, the error in asking a prejudicial question can be cured by an instruction to the jury to disregard the question. When the trial court sustains the objection, to preserve error, the party should "pursue an adverse ruling." See "When jury hears inadmissible evidence," ch. 8-D, §6.7. Whether the error is reversible is judged by the same standard as for improper jury argument, set out in **Standard Fire Ins. v. Reese**, 584 S.W.2d 835, 839–40 (Tex.1979). **Luna**, 667 S.W.2d at 120. See "Test for reversible jury argument," ch. 8-J, §5.2.

§6. Objecting to the evidence

§6.1 Outside presence of jury. Objections to evidence made during the trial but outside the presence of the jury do not need to be repeated in front of the jury to preserve error. Tex. R. Evid. 103(b); **Kia Motors Corp. v. Ruiz**, 432 S.W.3d 865, 880 (Tex.2014); *see* **Austin v. Weems**, 337 S.W.3d 415, 421–22 (Tex.App.—Houston [1st Dist.] 2011, no pet.) (pretrial motion to exclude eliminates need to repeat objection); **Huckaby v. A.G. Perry & Son, Inc.**, 20 S.W.3d 194, 204 (Tex.App.—Texarkana 2000, pet. denied) (same); *see also* Tex. R. App. P. 33.1(c) (no formal exception or separate order is required to preserve complaint for appeal).

§6.2 Multiple parties. In a multiparty case, each party has the obligation and the right to make its own objections to the admission and exclusion of evidence. **Bohls v. Oakes**, 75 S.W.3d 473, 477 (Tex.App.—San Antonio 2002, pet. denied); **Wolfe v. East Tex. Seed Co.**, 583 S.W.2d 481, 482 (Tex.App.—Houston [1st Dist.] 1979, writ dism'd). One party's objection does not preserve error for any other party. *E.g.*, **Beutel v. Dallas Cty. Flood Control Dist.**, 916 S.W.2d 685, 694 (Tex.App.—Waco 1996, writ denied) (offer of proof by one D did not preserve error for other D); **Howard v. Phillips**, 728 S.W.2d 448, 451 (Tex.App.—Fort Worth 1987, no writ) (offer of proof by one D did not preserve error for other D); **Wolfe**, 583 S.W.2d at 482 (objection to evidence by one D did not preserve error for other D). There is an exception to this rule—one party's objection may preserve error for another party if the trial court has ruled that objections made by one party preserve error for the other parties on the same side. **Owens-Corning Fiberglas Corp. v. Malone**, 916 S.W.2d 551, 556–57 (Tex.App.—Houston [1st Dist.] 1996), *aff'd*, 972 S.W.2d 35 (Tex.1998); **Celotex Corp. v. Tate**, 797 S.W.2d 197, 201–02 (Tex.App.—Corpus Christi 1990, writ dism'd).

§6.3 Repeating the objection. A party should object every time inadmissible evidence is offered. If a party objects to certain evidence but later does not object when the same evidence is introduced, the party waives its objection. **Richardson v. Green**, 677 S.W.2d 497, 501 (Tex.1984); **Marling v. Maillard**, 826 S.W.2d 735, 739 (Tex.App.—Houston [14th Dist.] 1992, no writ). For a limited exception to this rule, see ch. 8-D, §6.4, below.

§6.4 Running objection. A party can preserve error for repeated offers of the same evidence through a running objection. **Volkswagen v. Ramirez**, 159 S.W.3d 897, 907 (Tex.2004). By making a running objection, a party avoids annoying the jury by repeatedly making the same objection. However, a running objection must be specific and unambiguous. *Id.*; *see* **Low v. Henry**, 221 S.W.3d 609, 619 (Tex.2007). Unless a party has explicitly obtained a running objection from the trial court, a party could waive its objection on appeal by not continuing to object to the same or similar evidence each time it is mentioned. Brown & Rondon, **Texas Rules of Evidence Handbook**, Rule 103 (2021 ed.) (n.155). In a jury trial, the safest procedure is to object each time objectionable evidence is offered. *See id.* Some of the types of waiver that can result from a running objection include:

1. **Different evidence.** A running objection does not preserve error against evidence that is similar to but slightly different from the evidence subject to the running objection. *See, e.g.*, **Pojar v. Cifre**, 199 S.W.3d 317, 339 & n.8 (Tex.App.—Corpus Christi 2006, pet. denied) (dicta; running objection to any mention of D's marijuana use may not have applied to testimony about bumper stickers on D's car that advocated legalizing marijuana); *cf.* **Richardson v. Green**, 677 S.W.2d 497, 501 (Tex.1984) (party's objection to testimony about first interview of child did not apply to videotaped recording of second interview of child because, despite being on same topic, interviews were distinct).

2. **Different witness.** In a jury trial, a running objection does not apply to similar evidence from other witnesses. **Davis v. Fisk Elec. Co.**, 187 S.W.3d 570, 587 (Tex.App.—Houston [14th Dist.] 2006), *rev'd in part on other grounds*, 268 S.W.3d 508 (Tex.2008). However, if the trial court grants a specific request that a running objection apply to similar evidence from all witnesses, the objection will be effective for all. **Huckaby v. A.G. Perry & Son, Inc.**, 20 S.W.3d 194, 203 (Tex.App.—Texarkana 2000, pet. denied). In a nonjury trial, a clearly made running objection is effective for all evidence from all witnesses. **Commerce, Crowdus & Canton, Ltd. v. DKS Constr., Inc.**, 776 S.W.2d 615, 620 (Tex.App.—Dallas 1989, no writ).

3. **Other waivers.** The following are examples of other ways a party may waive error despite a running objection: • Running objection was waived when objecting party introduced same evidence. **Halim v. Ramchandani**, 203 S.W.3d 482, 492 (Tex.App.—Houston [14th Dist.] 2006, no pet.). • Running objection to the questioning of a witness did not apply to jury argument. **Davis v. Stallones**, 750 S.W.2d 235, 238 (Tex.App.—Houston [1st Dist.] 1987, no writ).

§6.5 Hearsay. A party should object if the opposing party introduces evidence that is hearsay. *See* Tex. R. Evid. 802; **De La Garza v. Salazar**, 851 S.W.2d 380, 383 (Tex.App.—San Antonio 1993, no writ); *see, e.g.*, **Austin v. Weems**, 337 S.W.3d 415, 425 (Tex.App.—Houston [1st Dist.] 2011, no pet.) (hearsay objection to officer's testimony was waived when P stated she had no objection). If a party is unsure whether the testimony meets the definition of hearsay, the party should also object under TRE 801. Brown & Rondon, **Texas Rules of Evidence Handbook**, Rule 802 (2021 ed.) (n.452). Inadmissible hearsay admitted without objection can still have probative value. Tex. R. Evid. 802; **Texas Commerce Bank v. New**, 3 S.W.3d 515, 517 (Tex.1999); *see* **Lee v. Dykes**, 312 S.W.3d 191, 198 (Tex.App.—Houston [14th Dist.] 2010, no pet.) (although inadmissible evidence can be probative when admitted without objection, it is not necessarily probative because it is uncontroverted or admitted without objection). For a complete discussion of hearsay, see *Article III: Hearsay*, Brown & Rondon, **Texas Rules of Evidence Handbook**, Rule 801 (2021 ed.).

§6.6 Rule of optional completeness. A party may object on the ground of optional completeness when the other party attempts to introduce part of a document or written statement. *See* Tex. R. Evid. 106, 107; **Jones v. Colley**, 820 S.W.2d 863, 866 (Tex.App.—Texarkana 1991, writ denied). To rely on TRE 106 or 107 to introduce omitted parts of a document, the party offering the remainder of the document must show that (1) the other party introduced only part of a document or written statement, and (2) the remainder of the document or written statement should be admitted so that in fairness it can be considered contemporaneously with the original part introduced. *See* Tex. R. Evid. 106, 107. TRE 106 and 107 also apply to depositions. *See* **Jones**, 820 S.W.2d at 866.

§6.7 When jury hears inadmissible evidence. Occasionally, evidence is presented to a jury before the party can object; for example, when a witness blurts out an answer or gives an answer that is not responsive to the question. To preserve error after the jury hears inadmissible evidence, the party must make a number of objections in the proper order until the court makes an adverse ruling. **One Call Sys. v. Houston Lighting & Power**, 936 S.W.2d 673, 677 (Tex.App.—Houston [14th Dist.] 1996, writ denied); **Hur v. City of Mesquite**, 893 S.W.2d 227, 231 (Tex.App.—Amarillo 1995, writ denied). This procedure is called "pursuing an adverse ruling." The order of making the objections is as follows:

1. **Make objection.** The party must make a proper and specific objection.

• If the court overrules the objection, the error is preserved. *See* **Lone Star Ford, Inc. v. Carter**, 848 S.W.2d 850, 854 (Tex.App.—Houston [14th Dist.] 1993, no writ) (improper jury argument). When a court overrules an objection, the party has secured an adverse ruling, and it is not necessary to request an instruction to disregard or move for a mistrial.

• If the court sustains the objection, to preserve error the party must pursue an adverse ruling by making the objections listed in ch. 8-D, §6.7.2, below. **One Call**, 936 S.W.2d at 677. If the party stops before receiving an adverse ruling,

the error is not preserved. **Hur**, 893 S.W.2d at 231; **Ortiz v. Ford Motor Credit Co.**, 859 S.W.2d 73, 77–78 (Tex.App.—Corpus Christi 1993, writ denied). A party cannot complain on appeal after it received all the relief it requested from the trial court. **Cook v. Caterpillar, Inc.**, 849 S.W.2d 434, 442 (Tex.App.—Amarillo 1993, writ denied). Therefore, to preserve error once the objection is sustained, the party must continue with the following steps:

2. Request instruction. The party must ask the court to instruct the jury to disregard the evidence. **State Bar v. Evans**, 774 S.W.2d 656, 658 n.6 (Tex.1989); **Peshak v. Greer**, 13 S.W.3d 421, 425 (Tex.App.—Corpus Christi 2000, no pet.); **Chavis v. Director, State Workers' Comp. Div.**, 924 S.W.2d 439, 447 (Tex.App.—Beaumont 1996, no writ). If the party makes no other objection or skips the request for an instruction to disregard and asks for a mistrial, the party waives any objection to curable error. *See* **Evans**, 774 S.W.2d at 658 n.6; **Peshak**, 13 S.W.3d at 424–25. The party must press the court to instruct the jury to disregard or to deny the request. If the court instructs the jury, the party must continue with the steps described in ch. 8-D, §6.7.3, below, to preserve error.

Practice Tip

If the error is incurable by an instruction to disregard, it is not necessary to request an instruction. See ***Evans****, 774 S.W.2d at 658 n.6. However, do not assume the error is incurable. Ask for an instruction even if you think the error is incurable.*

---

3. Motion to strike. It is unclear whether a motion to strike the evidence must be made along with the other objections. TRE 103(a)(1)(A) refers to an objection or a motion to strike. *See* **Ortiz**, 859 S.W.2d at 77 (opinion did not list motion to strike as one of necessary objections). Most courts use the two terms interchangeably. *See* **Smith Motor Sales, Inc. v. Texas Motor Vehicle Comm'n**, 809 S.W.2d 268, 272 (Tex.App.—Austin 1991, writ denied) (to challenge evidence on appeal, party must make timely objection or motion to strike). However, two courts have said a motion to strike is necessary along with the other objections. *See* **Parallax Corp. v. City of El Paso**, 910 S.W.2d 86, 90 (Tex.App.—El Paso 1995, writ denied) (party waived error because it did not make motion to strike); **Hur**, 893 S.W.2d at 231 (mentions motion to strike as one of the necessary objections). If the court grants a motion to strike, the ruling purports to, but does not, strike the information from the court reporter's record. If the court grants the motion, the party must continue with the step described in ch. 8-D, §6.7.4, below, to preserve error.

4. Motion for mistrial. If the court sustains the objections and instructs the jury to disregard, the party should make a motion for mistrial to preserve error. *See* **Hur**, 893 S.W.2d at 231–32; **Ortiz**, 859 S.W.2d at 77. *But see* **Condra Funeral Home v. Rollin**, 314 S.W.2d 277, 279–80 (Tex.1958) (not necessary for P to move for mistrial after trial court sustained objection and instructed jury to disregard); **Hur v. City of Mesquite**, 916 S.W.2d 510, 511–12 (Tex.App.—Amarillo 1995, no writ) (on motion for rehearing, court reviewed evidence of error, seeming to shift from position that motion for mistrial is necessary to preserve error).

8-1. Pursuing an Adverse Ruling

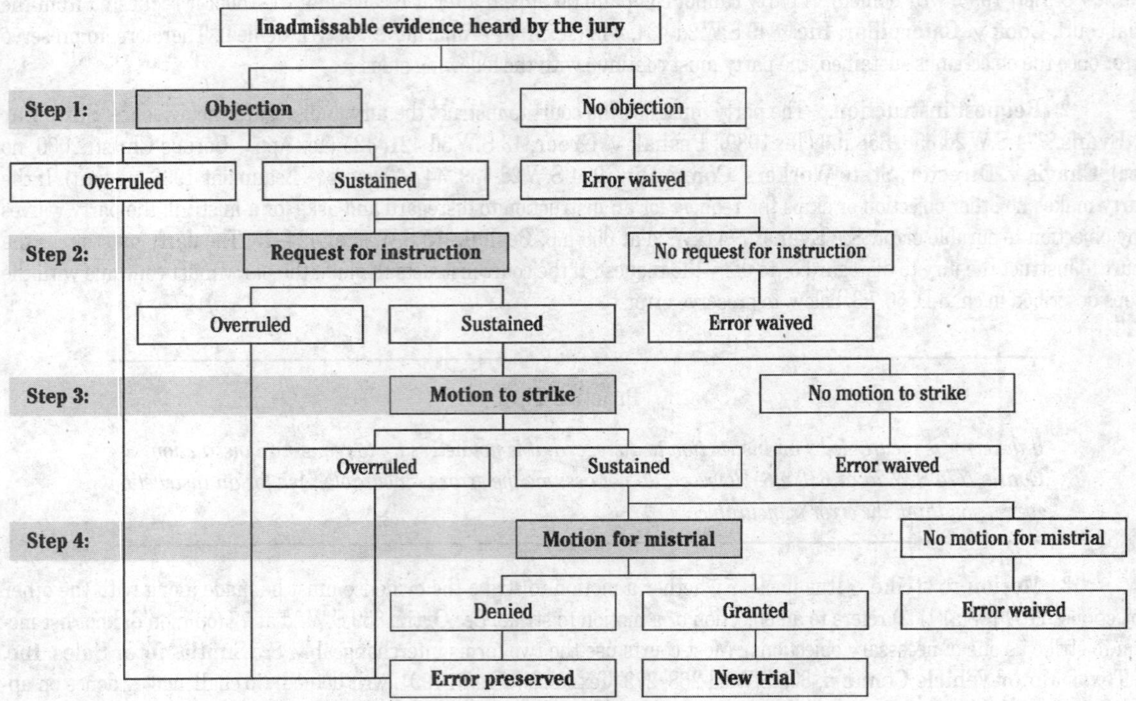

§6.8 Waiver.

1. No objection. Most complaints about evidence are waived if no objection is made. *See* **Bay Area Healthcare Grp. v. McShane**, 239 S.W.3d 231, 235 (Tex.2007); **Austin v. Weems**, 337 S.W.3d 415, 421 (Tex.App.—Houston [1st Dist.] 2011, no pet.); *see also* Tex. R. Evid. 802 (inadmissible hearsay admitted without objection can be probative).

2. Different forms of same evidence. An objection to evidence is waived if the same evidence was previously admitted without objection, even though the evidence is in a different form. *See* **Sauceda v. Kerlin**, 164 S.W.3d 892, 919 (Tex.App.—Corpus Christi 2005), *rev'd on other grounds*, 263 S.W.3d 920 (Tex.2008); *see, e.g.*, **Texaco, Inc. v. Pennzoil Co.**, 729 S.W.2d 768, 842 (Tex.App.—Houston [1st Dist.] 1987, writ ref'd n.r.e.) (no error in admitting magazine article over objection because same evidence was admitted through author's testimony).

3. Withdrawn objection. If an objection is withdrawn, it does not preserve error. *See* **Beken v. Elstner**, 503 S.W.2d 408, 410 (Tex.App.—Houston [14th Dist.] 1973, no writ); *see also* **Austin**, 337 S.W.3d at 425 (affirmatively stating "no objection" at trial withdraws objection otherwise preserving error as to that evidence).

4. No adverse ruling. If the jury hears objectionable evidence, the error is waived if the party does not pursue an adverse ruling through an objection, a motion to instruct the jury to disregard, a motion to strike, and a motion for mistrial. *See* **Hur v. City of Mesquite**, 893 S.W.2d 227, 231 (Tex.App.—Amarillo 1995, writ denied). See "When jury hears inadmissible evidence," ch. 8-D, §6.7.

5. After conditional admissibility. When a proponent's evidence is subject to the objection of relevance (and therefore admissibility), the trial court may admit the evidence subject to the condition that the proponent later "prove up" the relevance. *See* **Owens-Corning Fiberglas Corp. v. Keeton**, 922 S.W.2d 658, 661 (Tex.App.—Austin 1996, writ denied).

If the proponent does not prove up the relevance before it closes, the opposing party must repeat the objection and pursue an adverse ruling (i.e., objection, instruction, request to strike, and motion for mistrial). *See, e.g., id.* at 661–62 (opposing party waived error because it made only a motion for mistrial).

§7. Ruling on objection

The trial court has the discretion to admit or exclude evidence; the appellate courts will reverse only for an abuse of discretion. *See* **Fleming v. Wilson**, __ S.W.3d __, 2020 WL 5985187 (Tex.2020) (No. 19-0230; 10-9-20); **National Liab. & Fire Ins. v. Allen**, 15 S.W.3d 525, 527–28 (Tex.2000); **City of Brownsville v. Alvarado**, 897 S.W.2d 750, 753 (Tex.1995); *see also* **Diamond Offshore Servs. v. Williams**, 542 S.W.3d 539, 545–46 (Tex.2018) (generally, courts should view video evidence before ruling on admissibility when contents of video are at issue; failure to view evidence is abuse of discretion).

§7.1 Ruling.

1. **Sustains objection.** If the trial court sustains the objection, it will not admit the evidence. The party who offered the evidence still has other options that it must exercise, or it waives the error. See ch. 8-D, §7.1.3, below.

2. **Overrules objection.** If the trial court overrules the objection, it will admit the evidence. The party whose objection was overruled still has other options that it must exercise, or it waives the error. See ch. 8-D, §7.1.3, below.

3. **Next objection & request.**

(1) Request for limited admissibility. After the trial court rules on the admissibility of evidence, whichever party received an adverse ruling—either the party offering it or the party objecting to it—may ask the court to limit the admissibility of the evidence by instructing the jury to consider it only for a certain purpose. *See* **Larson v. Cactus Util. Co.**, 730 S.W.2d 640, 642 (Tex.1987). If the court ruled the evidence was inadmissible, the party that offered it should offer the evidence again by asking the court to admit it for limited purposes. *See* Tex. R. Evid. 105(b)(2); **Bean v. Baxter Healthcare Corp.**, 965 S.W.2d 656, 660 (Tex.App.—Houston [14th Dist.] 1998, no pet.). If the court ruled the evidence was admissible, the party that objected to it should ask the court to limit the purpose for which the evidence may be considered. *See* Tex. R. Evid. 105(a); **Horizon/CMS Healthcare Corp. v. Auld**, 34 S.W.3d 887, 906 (Tex.2000); **In re K.S.**, 76 S.W.3d 36, 40 (Tex.App.—Amarillo 2002, no pet.); **City of Austin v. Houston Lighting & Power Co.**, 844 S.W.2d 773, 793 (Tex.App.—Dallas 1992, writ denied). Unless a party requests that the court instruct the jury to consider the evidence only for a limited purpose, the party waives a complaint on the general admission of the evidence. **Horizon**, 34 S.W.3d at 906; **Birchfield v. Texarkana Mem'l Hosp.**, 747 S.W.2d 361, 365 (Tex.1987); **In re K.S.**, 76 S.W.3d at 40.

(2) Request for partial admission of evidence. If the trial court ruled the evidence was inadmissible, the party offering it can offer the evidence again with the objectionable part excised. The party that offers the evidence that is admitted subject to the deletion of specifically identified information has a duty to redact or sanitize the document before submitting the evidence to the jury. **American Gen. Fire & Cas. Co. v. McInnis Book Store**, 860 S.W.2d 484, 488 (Tex.App.—Corpus Christi 1993, no writ); *see also* **Olson v. Bayland Publ'g**, 781 S.W.2d 659, 665 (Tex.App.—Houston [1st Dist.] 1989, writ denied) (court did not abuse discretion by excluding evidence that offering party did not attempt to redact), *overruled on other grounds*, **Sage St. Assocs. v. Northdale Constr. Co.**, 863 S.W.2d 438 (Tex.1993).

§7.2 Types of rulings. Under TRAP 33.1(a)(2), error is preserved by an express ruling, an implicit ruling, or a refusal to rule when a proper objection is made. See "Types of rulings," ch. 1-G, §2.2.

Practice Tip

When a court avoids making a ruling by saying "move on" or "handle that on cross," it is not an implicit ruling and does not preserve error. To preserve error, you must ask the court for an actual ruling; if the court refuses, then you have preserved error. Do not count on preserving error by an implicit ruling.

---

§8. Review

§8.1 Admissibility. In making the preliminary decision on the admissibility of evidence, the trial court is not bound by the TREs, except those relating to privileges. Tex. R. Evid. 104(a). Thus, the review of an erroneous decision on privilege is

probably a review of a legal error, not abuse of discretion. Other decisions on admissibility are reviewed for abuse of discretion. *See* **Diamond Offshore Servs. v. Williams**, 542 S.W.3d 539, 545 (Tex.2018); *see, e.g.*, **Crescendo Invs. v. Brice**, 61 S.W.3d 465, 477–78 (Tex.App.—San Antonio 2001, pet. denied) (compensation information); **Southwestern Bell Tel. Co. v. Sims**, 615 S.W.2d 858, 862 (Tex.App.—Houston [1st Dist.] 1981, no writ) (qualifications of experts).

§8.2 Record on appeal. To successfully challenge a ruling on the admissibility of evidence, the appellant must request the court reporter's record. See "Rulings on evidence," **O'Connor's Texas Civil Appeals**, ch. 6-C, §3.1.3 (2020 ed.); "Requesting reporter's record," **O'Connor's Texas Civil Appeals**, ch. 6-C, §6 (2020 ed.). If evidence was excluded, the record must contain an offer of proof or a bill of exception. See "Offer of Proof & Bill of Exception," ch. 8-E, §1 et seq.

§8.3 Evidence rulings & harmless-error rule. If evidence is erroneously admitted or excluded, the appellate courts will apply the harmless-error review in TRAP 44.1(a) to determine whether the error is reversible. *See* **Owens-Corning Fiberglas Corp. v. Malone**, 972 S.W.2d 35, 43 (Tex.1998); *see also* **Dow Chem. Co. v. Francis**, 46 S.W.3d 237, 241 (Tex.2001) (remanded because court of appeals did not conduct harm analysis under TRAP 44.1(a)).

1. Standard under TRAP 44. To obtain a reversal based on the erroneous admission or exclusion of evidence, the appellant must establish that the error probably caused the rendition of an improper judgment. *See* Tex. R. App. P. 44.1(a)(1); **Diamond Offshore Servs. v. Williams**, 542 S.W.3d 539, 551 (Tex.2018) (erroneous exclusion); **Caffe Ribs, Inc. v. State**, 487 S.W.3d 137, 144–45 (Tex.2016) (erroneous exclusion); **State v. Central Expressway Sign Assocs.**, 302 S.W.3d 866, 870 (Tex.2009) (erroneous exclusion); **Reliance Steel & Aluminum Co. v. Sevcik**, 267 S.W.3d 867, 871 (Tex.2008) (erroneous admission); **Nissan Motor Co. v. Armstrong**, 145 S.W.3d 131, 144 (Tex.2004) (erroneous admission); *see also* **JBS Carriers, Inc. v. Washington**, 564 S.W.3d 830, 836 (Tex.2018) (appellant is not required to show that, "but for" exclusion of evidence, judgment would have been different).

2. Harmless-error review. The erroneous admission or exclusion of evidence is likely harmful, and thus probably caused the rendition of an improper judgment, if the evidence was crucial to a key issue. **Diamond Offshore**, 542 S.W.3d at 551; **Caffe Ribs**, 487 S.W.3d at 145; **Reliance Steel**, 267 S.W.3d at 873; *e.g.*, **JBS Carriers**, 564 S.W.3d at 840 (in negligence action involving pedestrian-truck collision, exclusion of evidence of decedent's mental illness and intoxication was harmful because evidence was crucial to key issue of what her state of mind was and whether her actions met standard of reasonable care). But such error is not conclusively or per se harmful. **Gunn v. McCoy**, 554 S.W.3d 645, 668 (Tex.2018). On the other hand, the error is likely harmless if the evidence was cumulative or if the rest of the evidence was so one-sided that the error likely made no difference in the judgment. **JBS Carriers**, 564 S.W.3d at 840; **Morale v. State**, 557 S.W.3d 569, 576 (Tex.2018); **Gunn**, 554 S.W.3d at 668; **Central Expressway Sign**, 302 S.W.3d at 870. When determining whether an erroneous admission of evidence was harmful error, the appellate court may also consider the amount of emphasis placed on the erroneous evidence and whether the admission was calculated or inadvertent. **Reliance Steel**, 267 S.W.3d at 873–74; **Nissan Motor**, 145 S.W.3d at 144.

Note

There is no specific test for harmless-error review; it is a matter of judgment based on the appellate court's evaluation of the entire case, considering the state of the evidence, the strength of the case, and the verdict. ***Reliance Steel****, 267 S.W.3d at 871; see* ***Caffe Ribs****, 487 S.W.3d at 145;* ***Central Expressway Sign****, 302 S.W.3d at 870.*

§8.4 Reversing judgment. If the appellate court sets aside a verdict because of an erroneous ruling excluding evidence, the court cannot render a judgment contrary to the verdict. **Transport Ins. v. Faircloth**, 898 S.W.2d 269, 275 (Tex.1995); *see* **Hyundai Motor Co. v. Chandler**, 882 S.W.2d 606, 620 (Tex.App.—Corpus Christi 1994, writ denied). Instead, the court must remand for a new trial to give the opposing party an opportunity to impeach the evidence or to respond with rebuttal evidence. **Transport Ins.**, 898 S.W.2d at 275. If, however, the court can exclude the improperly admitted evidence, the record may be sufficient to support a rendition. *See, e.g.*, **McElroy v. Fitts**, 876 S.W.2d 190, 199 (Tex.App.—El Paso 1994, writ dism'd) (court subtracted amounts attributable to evidence that should have been excluded and, as modified, affirmed that part of the judgment).

E. Offer of Proof & Bill of Exception

§1. General

§1.1 Rules. Tex. R. Evid. 103(a)(2) (offer of proof); Tex. R. App. P. 33.2 (bill of exception). See Tex. R. Civ. P. 75a (exhibits tendered on bill of exception).

§1.2 Purpose. The primary purpose of an offer of proof and a bill of exception is to include excluded evidence in the record so the appellate court can determine whether the trial court erred in excluding it. **Mack Trucks, Inc. v. Tamez**, 206 S.W.3d 572, 577 (Tex.2006); **Ludlow v. DeBerry**, 959 S.W.2d 265, 269–70 (Tex.App.—Houston [14th Dist.] 1997, no writ); **Sullivan v. Bickel & Brewer**, 943 S.W.2d 477, 484 (Tex.App.—Dallas 1995, writ denied); *see* Tex. R. Evid. 103(a)(2), (c); Tex. R. App. P. 33.1, 33.2. Another purpose is to permit the trial court to reconsider its ruling in light of the actual evidence. **Ludlow**, 959 S.W.2d at 270.

§1.3 Timetable & forms. Appendix IV, Timetable 14, Offer of proof & bill of exception; **O'Connor's Texas Civil Forms**, FORMS 8E:1 et seq. (2020 ed.).

§1.4 Other references. Brown & Rondon, **Texas Rules of Evidence Handbook** (2021 ed.).

§2. Difference between offer & bill

To preserve error when the trial court excludes evidence, a party must comply with TRE 103(a)(2), which states that error cannot be predicated on the exclusion of evidence unless the substance of the evidence was made known to the court by an offer. **Ludlow v. DeBerry**, 959 S.W.2d 265, 269–70 (Tex.App.—Houston [14th Dist.] 1997, no writ). There are two types of offers, one made during trial (an offer of proof) and one made after trial (a formal bill of exception). *See* **Clone Component Distribs. v. State**, 819 S.W.2d 593, 596 (Tex.App.—Dallas 1991, no writ).

§2.1 Offer of proof. An offer of proof (formerly called an informal bill of exception) is a trial-time offer of evidence the court excluded. *See* Tex. R. Evid. 103(a)(2); Tex. R. App. P. 33.1(a)(1)(A). A party makes an offer of proof by presenting the excluded evidence in the form of a summary or in question-and-answer form and, in a jury trial, outside the presence of the jury. *See* Tex. R. Evid. 103(c).

§2.2 Formal bill of exception. A formal bill of exception is a post-trial offer of evidence in written form. *See* Tex. R. App. P. 33.2; **Clone Component Distribs. v. State**, 819 S.W.2d 593, 596–97 (Tex.App.—Dallas 1991, no writ). A formal bill is necessary only when the complaint or evidence is not preserved in an offer of proof. *See* Tex. R. App. P. 33.2.

§3. Offer of proof

When the trial court rules evidence is not admissible and excludes it, the party who offered the evidence should make an offer of proof to get the evidence into the record for the appeal. *See* Tex. R. Evid. 103(a)(2); **Gunn v. McCoy**, 554 S.W.3d 645, 666 (Tex.2018); **Akin v. Santa Clara Land Co.**, 34 S.W.3d 334, 339 (Tex.App.—San Antonio 2000, pet. denied); **Wade v. Commission for Lawyer Discipline**, 961 S.W.2d 366, 374 (Tex.App.—Houston [1st Dist.] 1997, no writ). See Brown & Rondon, **Texas Rules of Evidence Handbook**, Rule 103 (2021 ed.) (§A.2). If the substance of the evidence is apparent from the record, an offer of proof is not necessary. Tex. R. Evid. 103(a)(2); **Marathon Corp. v. Pitzner**, 55 S.W.3d 114, 143 (Tex.App.—Corpus Christi 2001), *rev'd on other grounds*, 106 S.W.3d 724 (Tex.2003); *see* **Chance v. Chance**, 911 S.W.2d 40, 52 (Tex.App.—Beaumont 1995, writ denied). A party should preserve excluded evidence in an offer of proof instead of a formal bill of exception. An offer of proof is easier to make than a formal bill.

§3.1 Offer evidence. Before a party is entitled to make an offer of proof, it must offer the evidence at trial. **Ulogo v. Villanueva**, 177 S.W.3d 496, 501 (Tex.App.—Houston [1st Dist.] 2005, no pet.); **Estate of Veale v. Teledyne Indus.**, 899 S.W.2d 239, 242 (Tex.App.—Houston [14th Dist.] 1995, writ denied). The party cannot rely on a motion-in-limine ruling. **Ulogo**, 177 S.W.3d at 500–01. *But see* **Durbin v. Dal-Briar Corp.**, 871 S.W.2d 263, 270 (Tex.App.—El Paso 1994, writ denied) (formal offer was not necessary because D stipulated that P could submit depositions as bill of exception), *disapproved on other grounds*, **Golden Eagle Archery, Inc. v. Jackson**, 24 S.W.3d 362 (Tex.2000).

§3.2 Specify purpose of evidence. When an objection is lodged, the party offering the evidence should specify the purpose for which the evidence is offered and the reason it is admissible. **Ulogo v. Villanueva**, 177 S.W.3d 496, 501–02 (Tex.App.—Houston [1st Dist.] 2005, no pet.); **Estate of Veale v. Teledyne Indus.**, 899 S.W.2d 239, 242 (Tex.App.—Houston [14th Dist.] 1995, writ denied).

§3.3 Get a ruling excluding evidence. Before a party is entitled to make an offer of proof, the court must make a ruling that the evidence is inadmissible. Tex. R. App. P. 33.1(a)(2); **Ulogo v. Villanueva**, 177 S.W.3d 496, 502 (Tex.App.—Houston [1st Dist.] 2005, no pet.); *see* **Estate of Veale v. Teledyne Indus.**, 899 S.W.2d 239, 242 (Tex.App.—Houston [14th Dist.] 1995, writ denied).

§3.4 Make an offer. Once the court rules the evidence is inadmissible, the party must make an offer of proof. *See* **Gunn v. McCoy**, 554 S.W.3d 645, 666 (Tex.2018); **Estate of Veale v. Teledyne Indus.**, 899 S.W.2d 239, 242–43 (Tex.App.—Houston [14th Dist.] 1995, writ denied). To preserve error, the offer of proof must show the nature of the excluded evidence with sufficient specificity to allow the reviewing court to determine its admissibility. **In re N.R.C.**, 94 S.W.3d 799, 806 (Tex.App.—Houston [14th Dist.] 2002, pet. denied); *e.g.*, **Chapman v. Olbrich**, 217 S.W.3d 482, 494–95 (Tex.App.—Houston [14th Dist.] 2006, no pet.) (error not preserved because offer of proof did not include excluded exhibit). Formal proof is not required, and courts prefer a concise statement over a lengthy presentation. **In re N.R.C.**, 94 S.W.3d at 806.

1. Oral testimony. To preserve testimonial evidence, the party offering it must make an offer of proof in the presence of the judge, the court reporter, and opposing counsel but, in a jury trial, outside the presence of the jury. *See* Tex. R. Evid. 103(c). The offer of proof is conducted outside the presence of the jury to prevent the jury from hearing inadmissible evidence. *See* Tex. R. Evid. 103(d). When making an offer of proof, the attorney should make a concise statement of what testimony would be elicited from the witness. **In re N.R.C.**, 94 S.W.3d at 806. At the request of either party, the court must permit the offer to be made in question-and-answer form. Tex. R. Evid. 103(c). The court may add a comment to the offer to show the character of the evidence, the form in which it was offered, the objection, and the ruling. *Id.*

2. Documents & things. To preserve documentary evidence, the party should, at the time the document is excluded, say, "I make an offer of proof of this document and ask that it be filed with the record." An offer of proof to preserve an excluded document may be made in the presence of the jury because the jury is not prejudiced by evidence in an excluded document that it cannot see. The court reporter should mark the document as an offer of proof and identify it with an exhibit number. The document will be filed with the court clerk so it will be included with the exhibits in the reporter's record. Tex. R. Civ. P. 75a; *see* **Owens-Ill., Inc. v. Chatham**, 899 S.W.2d 722, 731 (Tex.App.—Houston [14th Dist.] 1995, writ dism'd).

(1) Filed discovery. Even when a document is already on file with the court—for example, a deposition—if the court refuses to permit it to be introduced into evidence, the party should submit it as an offer of proof and get the court to rule on the offer. *See, e.g.*, **McInnes v. Yamaha Motor Corp.**, 673 S.W.2d 185, 187 (Tex.1984) (excluded deposition that was not offered as bill did not preserve error); **Malone v. Foster**, 956 S.W.2d 573, 577 (Tex.App.—Dallas 1997) (same), *aff'd*, 977 S.W.2d 562 (Tex.1998).

(2) Taped evidence. To preserve tape-recorded evidence ruled inadmissible by the trial court, the party should, at the time the tape is excluded, say, "I make an offer of proof of this tape and ask that it be filed with the record." As part of the offer, the party must describe the excluded evidence on the tape and specify the purpose of the evidence. *See, e.g.*, **Gunn**, 554 S.W.3d at 666 (offer of proof for excluded video deposition showed that video contained adequate testimony about expert's qualifications); **Chubb Lloyds Ins. v. Kizer**, 943 S.W.2d 946, 949 (Tex.App.—Fort Worth 1997, writ denied) (error waived because party did not make bill to preserve audio portion of tape when court permitted only the video portion). If a transcript of the tape is available, the party should file it as part of the offer; if not, the party should ask permission to file a transcript as part of the offer of proof as soon as one can be made.

§3.5 Obtain a ruling. Error is preserved by the court's explicit ruling that the evidence in the offer of proof is not admissible during trial. *See, e.g.*, **Greenstein, Logan & Co. v. Burgess Mktg., Inc.**, 744 S.W.2d 170, 181 (Tex.App.—Waco 1987, writ denied) (error was not preserved because reporter's record did not show what was refused). However, under TRAP 33, error can also be preserved if the trial court implicitly overrules the offer or if the court refuses to rule on the offer and the complaining party objects to the refusal. Tex. R. App. P. 33.1(a)(2). See "Types of rulings," ch. 1-G, §2.2.

§3.6 Deadline. An offer of proof must be made as soon as practicable; in a jury trial, the offer must be made before the court reads the charge to the jury. Tex. R. Evid. 103(c). Making the offer before the charge is read to the jury gives the trial court the opportunity to correct the error. Although nothing in TRAP 33 states a deadline for making an offer of proof, under TRAP 33.1(a)(1)(B), the record must show that the parties complied with the TREs.

§4. Formal bill of exception

The formal bill of exception is a procedure to preserve error about matters outside the record. *See* Tex. R. App. P. 33.2. The formal bill is an archaic leftover from a different era of trial practice. Because the requirements for a formal bill are so strict, it can be a trap. On the other hand, a formal bill may be the last chance, and sometimes the only chance, to preserve some kinds of error.

§4.1 In writing. The formal bill of exception must be in writing. *See* Tex. R. App. P. 33.2(a). It should state the party's objection and the trial court's ruling or action, together with the circumstances or evidence needed to explain the situation. *See* Tex. R. App. P. 33.2. All factual statements contained in the bill must be verified by affidavit.

§4.2 Presented to judge. The formal bill must be presented to the trial judge for a ruling. Tex. R. App. P. 33.2(c)(1).

1. Parties agree. If the parties agree on the contents of the bill, the judge must sign the bill and file it with the clerk. Tex. R. App. P. 33.2(c)(2). The bill is then complete.

2. Parties do not agree. If the parties do not agree on the contents of the bill, the judge, after providing notice and a hearing, must do one of the following:

(1) Judge signs bill. If the judge finds that the bill is correct, she should sign the bill and file it with the clerk. Tex. R. App. P. 33.2(c)(2)(A). The bill is then complete.

(2) Judge suggests corrections. If the judge finds that the bill is incorrect, the judge may suggest a correction or amendment to accurately reflect the trial-court proceedings. Tex. R. App. P. 33.2(c)(2)(B). If the complaining party agrees with the suggested corrections, the changes can be made, and the judge will sign the amended bill and file it with the trial-court clerk. *Id.* The bill is then complete.

(3) Judge refuses to sign bill. If the judge finds that the bill is incorrect and the complaining party rejects the suggested corrections, the judge should endorse the bill "refused" and return it to the party. Tex. R. App. P. 33.2(c)(2)(C).

(a) Judge's bill. The judge should prepare and sign a bill that, in the judge's opinion, correctly reflects what was said or what happened in the trial court. Tex. R. App. P. 33.2(c)(2)(C); *see* **Houston Lighting & Power Co. v. Russo Props., Inc.**, 710 S.W.2d 711, 717 (Tex.App.—Houston [1st Dist.] 1986, no writ). In most instances, the other party in the case will prepare a proposed judge's bill for the judge's signature.

(b) Party files refused bill. If the complaining party disagrees with the judge's bill, the party can file the refused bill with the trial-court clerk. Tex. R. App. P. 33.2(c)(3).

Note

When the judge disagrees with the party's bill, TRAP 33.2(c)(2)(C) contemplates that two bills will be filed, one by the party and one by the judge. See ***Houston Lighting & Power****, 710 S.W.2d at 717.*

(c) Bystanders' bill. The party filing the refused bill must also file a "bystanders' bill," in which at least three bystanders, who are not interested in the outcome of the case, state they were present and observed the matter that the bill addresses. *See* Tex. R. App. P. 33.2(c)(3); *see also* **Smith v. United Gas Pipe Line Co.**, 228 S.W.2d 139, 143 (Tex.1950) (attorneys in the case cannot submit bystanders' affidavits); **Circle Y v. Blevins**, 826 S.W.2d 753, 755 (Tex.App.—Texarkana 1992, writ denied) (same). Filing the bystanders' affidavits without the bill of exception does not preserve error. **Citizens Law Inst. v. State**, 559 S.W.2d 381, 383 (Tex.App.—Dallas 1977, no writ). Filing the refused bill without the bystanders' affidavits does not preserve error. **Boddy v. Canteau**, 441 S.W.2d 906, 914 (Tex.App.—San Antonio 1969, writ ref'd n.r.e.).

§4.3 Additional affidavits. Any party may file affidavits to controvert or maintain the judge's or party's bill of exception within ten days after the bill was filed. Tex. R. App. P. 33.2(c)(3).

§4.4 Objections to bill. The other parties in the case must be given the opportunity to review the bill, make objections, and file controverting affidavits. *See* Tex. R. App. P. 33.2(c)(3). Additional affidavits must be filed within ten days. *Id.*

§4.5 Deadline. The deadline for filing the complete formal bill of exception is 30 days after the party's notice of appeal is filed. Tex. R. App. P. 33.2(e)(1). The court of appeals may extend the time to file a formal bill if, within 15 days after the date the bill is due, the party files a motion to extend time that complies with TRAP 10.5(b). Tex. R. App. P. 33.2(e)(3).

§5. Refusal to permit offer or bill

It is reversible error for the trial court to refuse to permit a party to make a timely offer of proof or bill of exception. **State v. Biggers**, 360 S.W.2d 516, 517 (Tex 1962); **In re Marriage of Goodwin**, 562 S.W.2d 532, 533 (Tex.App.—Texarkana 1978, no writ). However, if the appellate court can determine from the record what evidence would have been preserved, the trial court's refusal to permit a party to make a bill is not reversible error. **Pennington v. Brock**, 841 S.W.2d 127, 131 (Tex.App.—Houston [14th Dist.] 1992, no writ); *see* **Ledisco Fin. Servs. v. Viracola**, 533 S.W.2d 951, 959 (Tex.App.—Texarkana 1976, no writ). If the evidence the party attempted to preserve in a bill was immaterial to the outcome of the suit, the court's refusal to permit the party to make a bill is not reversible error. **4M Linen & Unif. Sup. Co. v. W.P. Ballard & Co.**, 793 S.W.2d 320, 328 (Tex.App.—Houston [1st Dist.] 1990, writ denied); **Dorn v. Cartwright**, 392 S.W.2d 181, 186 (Tex.App.—Dallas 1965, writ ref'd n.r.e.).

§6. Review

An appellate court cannot reach the question of whether evidence was erroneously excluded unless the excluded evidence is included in the record for its review. **McInnes v. Yamaha Motor Corp.**, 673 S.W.2d 185, 187 (Tex 1984); **Hartford Ins. v. Jiminez**, 814 S.W.2d 551, 552–53 (Tex.App.—Houston [1st Dist.] 1991, no writ).

§6.1 Record. Testimonial and documentary evidence in an offer of proof will be included in the reporter's record. *See* **Owens-Ill., Inc. v. Chatham**, 899 S.W.2d 722, 726 (Tex.App.—Houston [14th Dist.] 1995, writ dism'd). Testimonial and documentary evidence included in a formal bill of exception will be included in the clerk's record. *See* Tex. R. App. P. 33.2(f).

§6.2 Standard of review. To challenge evidence erroneously excluded, see "Evidence rulings & harmless-error rule," ch. 8-D, §8.3.

§6.3 Conflict between record & bill. On appeal, if the appellate court finds a conflict between the provisions of a bill of exception and the reporter's record, the bill will control. Tex. R. App. P. 33.2(d); **Mea v. Mea**, 464 S.W.2d 201, 204 (Tex.App.—Tyler 1971, no writ).

§6.4 Another party's bill. A party cannot rely on another party's bill of exception unless the party specifically adopts the other party's bill or joins in making it. **Howard v. Phillips**, 728 S.W.2d 448, 451 (Tex.App.—Fort Worth 1987, no writ).

F. Motion to Amend Pleadings—Trial & Post-trial

Three sections in this book discuss amending pleadings. See "Amending or supplementing pleadings," ch. 1-B, §3.6; "Motion to Amend Pleadings—Pretrial," ch. 5-F, §1 et seq.; and this subchapter.

§1. General

§1.1 Rules. Tex. R. Civ. P. 62 to 67.

§1.2 Purpose. A trial or post-trial amendment allows a party to amend its pleadings to (1) correct errors and defects, (2) add or delete claims or defenses, or (3) conform the pleadings to the evidence. Tex. R. Civ. P. 66, 67.

§1.3 Forms. **O'Connor's Texas Civil Forms**, FORMS 8F:1 et seq. (2020 ed.).

§2. Motion for leave to amend

A party may amend its pleadings during trial or after the verdict but before the court renders judgment. *See* Tex. R. Civ. P. 63, 66; **Greenhalgh v. Service Lloyds Ins.**, 787 S.W.2d 938, 940 (Tex.1990).

§2.1 When motion required.

1. During trial. A party should seek leave to amend its pleadings during trial whenever it introduces evidence that is unsupported by its pleadings or is notified—usually by an opposing party's objection—of a defect, fault, or omission in its pleadings. *See* Tex. R. Civ. P. 63, 66; *see, e.g.*, **Ritchie v. Rupe**, 339 S.W.3d 275, 306 (Tex.App.—Dallas 2011) (after Ds moved for directed verdict asserting they were not liable in their individual capacities, P sought leave to amend to allege Ds were liable in their representative capacities), *rev'd on other grounds*, 443 S.W.3d 856 (Tex.2014); **THI of Tex. v. Perea**, 329 S.W.3d 548, 570–71 (Tex.App.—Amarillo 2010, pet. denied) (Ps sought leave to amend to add claim after introducing evidence during their case-in-chief); **Deutsch v. Hoover, Bax & Slovacek, L.L.P.**, 97 S.W.3d 179, 185 (Tex.App.—Houston [14th Dist.] 2002, no pet.) (counter-D moved for directed verdict asserting statute of limitations and sought leave to amend after counter-P objected that limitations had not been pleaded).

2. Before submission of jury charge. A party should seek leave to amend its pleadings before the charge is submitted to the jury to conform the pleadings to the evidence. *See* Tex. R. Civ. P. 63, 66, 67; **State Bar v. Kilpatrick**, 874 S.W.2d 656, 657–58 (Tex.1994); **Matthews v. General Acc. Fire & Life Assur. Corp.**, 343 S.W.2d 251, 254–55 (Tex.1961); *see, e.g.*, **Texas Indus. v. Vaughan**, 919 S.W.2d 798, 803–04 (Tex.App.—Houston [14th Dist.] 1996, writ denied) (court should have allowed amendment to add claim for mental anguish offered after objection at jury-charge conference).

3. Post-trial. A party should seek leave to amend its pleadings after the verdict has been returned to conform the pleadings to the verdict and the evidence when it recognizes or is notified—usually by an opposing party's objection—that the verdict is unsupported by the pleadings. *See* Tex. R. Civ. P. 63, 66; *see, e.g.*, **Greenhalgh v. Service Lloyds Ins.**, 787 S.W.2d 938, 939–40 (Tex.1990) (P sought leave to amend pleadings to conform amount of damages to verdict; amendment should have been allowed); **Allstate Prop. & Cas. Ins. v. Gutierrez**, 281 S.W.3d 535, 538–39 (Tex.App.—El Paso 2008, no pet.) (D sought leave to amend to add affirmative defense after verdict; amendment should have been allowed); *see also* Tex. R. Civ. P. 301 (judgment must conform to pleadings, evidence, and verdict); **Hampden Corp. v. Remark, Inc.**, 331 S.W.3d 489, 495 (Tex.App.—Dallas 2010, pet. denied) (nonjury trial; post-trial amendment made after closing argument but before court rendered judgment). See "Amendments after judgment," ch. 8-F, §4.

Caution

A party who prosecutes a suit as an expedited action cannot recover a judgment greater than the amount specified in TRCP 169(b). Tex. R. Civ. P. 169(b). If the jury awards damages greater than this amount, the party cannot move to amend the pleadings to conform to a higher damages award. See Tex. R. Civ. P. 169 cmt. 4 (2013). In such a case, the rule in **Greenhalgh** *does not apply. See Tex. R. Civ. P. 169 cmt. 4 (2013). See "Expedited Actions," ch. 2-C, §1 et seq.; "Amendments conforming pleadings to damages award," ch. 8-F, §3.2.1(1).*

§2.2 **When motion not required.** When an unpleaded issue is tried by consent, the issue is treated as if it had been raised by the pleadings. Tex. R. Civ. P. 67; **Roark v. Stallworth Oil & Gas, Inc.**, 813 S.W.2d 492, 495 (Tex.1991). Thus, the proponent of an issue tried by consent is not required to seek leave to amend its pleadings. *See* Tex. R. Civ. P. 66, 67; **Hartford Fire Ins. v. C. Springs 300, Ltd.**, 287 S.W.3d 771, 779–80 (Tex.App.—Houston [1st Dist.] 2009, pet. denied); **Ranger Ins. v. Robertson**, 707 S.W.2d 135, 142 (Tex.App.—Austin 1986, writ ref'd n.r.e.). However, if the party can make a motion to amend its pleadings before judgment is rendered, it should probably do so. *See, e.g.*, **Bell v. Meeks**, 725 S.W.2d 179, 179–80 (Tex.1987) (Ps permitted to add DTPA misrepresentation claim after verdict); **Campbell v. Salazar**, 960 S.W.2d 719, 731 (Tex.App.—El Paso 1997, pet. denied) (in addition to TRCP 63 and 66, TRCP 67 supported trial amendment to conform pleadings to evidence submitted to jury without objection); **Centroplex Ford, Inc. v. Kirby**, 736 S.W.2d 261, 265 (Tex.App.—Austin 1987, no writ) (no error in permitting post-verdict amendment when motion to amend was intended to conform pleadings to verdict). See "TRCP 67," ch. 8-F, §2.4.2.

§2.3 **Procedure.**

1. Seek leave. A party must seek leave from the court to amend its pleadings. Tex. R. Civ. P. 63, 67; *see* Tex. R. Civ. P. 66. The motion for leave to amend may be made orally or in writing. *See* **Smith Detective Agency & Nightwatch Serv. v. Stanley Smith Sec., Inc.**, 938 S.W.2d 743, 746 (Tex.App.—Dallas 1996, writ denied).

2. Offer written amendment. A party must offer its proposed amendment to the pleadings. *See* **Hunt v. Baldwin**, 68 S.W.3d 117, 134–35 (Tex.App.—Houston [14th Dist.] 2001, no pet.); **Smith Detective Agency**, 938 S.W.2d at 748. The amended pleadings must be in writing. **City of Fort Worth v. Zimlich**, 29 S.W.3d 62, 73 (Tex.2000); *see* **Hunt**, 68 S.W.3d at 134–35 (record must reflect that written trial amendment was offered). The amended pleadings should be signed by the attorney or the party and tendered to the court for filing. *See* Tex. R. Civ. P. 45, 57, 63; **Smith Detective Agency**, 938 S.W.2d at 748. See "Signature block," ch. 1-B, §3.2.12. If a party makes an oral amendment and the opposing party does not object, the error is waived. **Zimlich**, 29 S.W.3d at 73.

§2.4 **Grounds.** A party's right to amend its pleadings is subject only to the opposing party's right to show surprise or prejudice. **Greenhalgh v. Service Lloyds Ins.**, 787 S.W.2d 938, 939–40 (Tex.1990); *see* Tex. R. Civ. P. 63, 66. See "Prove surprise or prejudice," ch. 8-F, §3.2. But when making the motion for leave to amend, the party should state why the amendment is appropriate and necessary.

1. TRCP 63 & 66. A party may amend its pleadings to correct errors and defects, to add or delete claims or defenses, or to conform the pleadings to the evidence or the verdict. Tex. R. Civ. P. 63, 66. See "When motion required," ch. 8-F, §2.1. If the opposing party does not show surprise or prejudice, amendments must be freely permitted when they serve the presentation of the merits of the case. *See* Tex. R. Civ. P. 63, 66. Amendments that correct formal, procedural defects and do not change the substantive issues should almost always be granted. *See* **Chapin & Chapin, Inc. v. Texas Sand & Gravel Co.**, 844 S.W.2d 664, 665 (Tex.1992); **Francis v. Coastal Oil & Gas Corp.**, 130 S.W.3d 76, 91 (Tex.App.—Houston [1st Dist.] 2003, no pet.).

2. TRCP 67. Although no amendment of the pleadings is necessary when an issue is tried by consent, a party may amend its pleadings when an unpleaded issue was fully developed at trial without objection. *See* Tex. R. Civ. P. 67; **Allstate Prop. & Cas. Ins. v. Gutierrez**, 281 S.W.3d 535, 540 (Tex.App.—El Paso 2008, no pet.). See "When motion not required," ch. 8-F, §2.2. If an issue is tried by consent, an amendment would merely conform the pleadings to the evidence and should be granted unless the opposing party shows surprise or prejudice. *See* **Chapin & Chapin**, 844 S.W.2d at 665; **Allstate Prop. & Cas.**, 281 S.W.3d at 539–40.

(1) Issue tried by consent. An issue is tried by consent when (1) a party introduces evidence to support an unpleaded issue and (2) the opposing party does not object to the admission of that evidence or to the submission of a jury question on that issue. *See* Tex. R. Civ. P. 66, 67; **Ingram v. Deere**, 288 S.W.3d 886, 893 (Tex.2009); **Pine Trail Shores Owners' Ass'n v. Aiken**, 160 S.W.3d 139, 146 (Tex.App.—Tyler 2005, no pet.). This rule applies only in exceptional cases in which the record clearly shows the parties tried an unpleaded issue by consent. **Mastin v. Mastin**, 70 S.W.3d 148, 154 (Tex.App.—San Antonio 2001, no pet.); **In re Walters**, 39 S.W.3d 280, 289 (Tex.App.—Texarkana 2001, no pet.); *see* **Bos v. Smith**, 556 S.W.3d 293, 306–07 (Tex.2018) (court examines record not for evidence of the issue but instead for evidence of

trial of the issue). A party who allows an issue to be tried by consent and then does not challenge the lack of a pleading before submission of the case to the jury cannot assert the pleading deficiency for the first time on appeal. **Roark v. Stallworth Oil & Gas, Inc.**, 813 S.W.2d 492, 495 (Tex.1991); **National Convenience Stores v. Erevia**, 73 S.W.3d 518, 522 (Tex.App.—Houston [1st Dist.] 2002, pet. denied).

(2) Issue not tried by consent.

(a) Opposing party objects. When the opposing party objects to either the introduction of evidence or the submission of a jury question on the ground that the evidence or question is not supported by the pleadings, the issue is not tried by consent. **Hirsch v. Hirsch**, 770 S.W.2d 924, 926 (Tex.App.—El Paso 1989, no writ) (objection to jury question); *see* **Bedgood v. Madalin**, 600 S.W.2d 773, 775–76 (Tex.1980) (objection to evidence and jury question); **Texas Indus. v. Vaughan**, 919 S.W.2d 798, 803 (Tex.App.—Houston [14th Dist.] 1996, writ denied) (objection to jury question).

(b) Issue not developed. When a party introduces some evidence on an unpleaded issue but does not develop it, the issue is not tried by consent. *See* **Whatley v. City of Dallas**, 758 S.W.2d 301, 306–07 (Tex.App.—Dallas 1988, writ denied); **Realtex Corp. v. Tyler**, 627 S.W.2d 441, 443–44 (Tex.App.—Houston [1st Dist.] 1981, no writ).

(c) Evidence relevant to pleaded issue. When a party introduces evidence that is relevant to both pleaded and unpleaded issues, the unpleaded issue is not tried by consent. *See* **Bos**, 556 S.W.3d at 307; **Boyles v. Kerr**, 855 S.W.2d 593, 601 (Tex.1993); **Marrs & Smith Prtshp. v. D.K. Boyd Oil & Gas Co.**, 223 S.W.3d 1, 18–19 (Tex.App.—El Paso 2005, pet. denied).

§3. Response to motion for leave to amend

§3.1 Object. The party opposing the amendment must object to the motion for leave to amend.

1. To form.

(1) No leave sought. The opposing party must object if the amending party did not seek leave to amend its pleadings. See "Seek leave," ch. 8-F, §2.3.1. If the opposing party does not object and the court and the parties act as if leave had been granted, on appeal, the court will presume leave was granted. **Diesel Fuel Injection Serv. v. Gabourel**, 893 S.W.2d 610, 611 (Tex.App.—Corpus Christi 1994, no writ).

(2) No written amendment filed. The opposing party must object if the amending party did not file written amended pleadings. If the court accepts an oral amendment and the opposing party does not object, the error is waived. *See* Tex. R. App. P. 33.1; **City of Fort Worth v. Zimlich**, 29 S.W.3d 62, 73 (Tex.2000); **Kreighbaum v. Lester**, No. 05-06-01333-CV, 2007 WL 1829729 (Tex.App.—Dallas 2007, no pet.) (memo op.; 6-27-07). See "Offer written amendment," ch. 8-F, §2.3.2.

2. To substance. The opposing party must object to the amendment on the ground that it either causes surprise or prejudice or asserts a new cause of action or defense and thus is prejudicial on its face. **Greenhalgh v. Service Lloyds Ins.**, 787 S.W.2d 938, 939 (Tex.1990); **Smith Detective Agency & Nightwatch Serv. v. Stanley Smith Sec., Inc.**, 938 S.W.2d 743, 748–49 (Tex.App.—Dallas 1996, writ denied); *see* Tex. R. Civ. P. 63, 66. If the party does not object, the court must grant the trial amendment. **Greenhalgh**, 787 S.W.2d at 939; *e.g.*, **Varel Mfg. v. Acetylene Oxygen Co.**, 990 S.W.2d 486, 493 (Tex.App.—Corpus Christi 1999, no pet.) (D did not object to motion for leave to amend, so court had no basis to deny motion).

§3.2 Prove surprise or prejudice. The party opposing the amendment on substantive grounds must prove the amendment either (1) causes surprise or prejudice or (2) asserts a new cause of action or defense and thus is prejudicial on its face.

1. Show surprise or prejudice. The opposing party must present evidence of surprise or prejudice. **Greenhalgh v. Service Lloyds Ins.**, 787 S.W.2d 938, 939 (Tex.1990); *see* Tex. R. Civ. P. 63, 66. For example, the party may show that its pretrial preparation was made in reliance on the pleadings on file or that it decided not to pursue other avenues of pretrial investigation that it would have pursued under the proposed amended pleading. *See* **Whole Foods Mkt. Sw., L.P. v. Tijerina**, 979 S.W.2d 768, 777 (Tex.App.—Houston [14th Dist.] 1998, pet. denied); *see, e.g.*, **Krishnan v. Ramirez**, 42 S.W.3d 205, 225 (Tex.App.—Corpus Christi 2001, pet. denied) (no surprise or prejudice when opposing party did not make

any showing that her settlement strategy or trial posture would have changed); **Miller v. Wal-Mart Stores**, 918 S.W.2d 658, 666 (Tex.App.—Amarillo 1996, writ denied) (D proved surprise or prejudice by showing that trial strategy would have been different because amendment would have introduced new substantive matter reshaping P's theory of recovery). The party must show more than bare allegations of surprise or prejudice. *See* **Parkway Hosp., Inc. v. Lee**, 946 S.W.2d 580, 590 (Tex.App.—Houston [14th Dist.] 1997, writ denied), *disapproved on other grounds*, **Roberts v. Williamson**, 111 S.W.3d 113 (Tex.2003). If the party does not show surprise or prejudice, the court must grant the amendment. **Greenhalgh**, 787 S.W.2d at 939; *e.g.*, **Texas Indus. v. Vaughan**, 919 S.W.2d 798, 803–04 (Tex.App.—Houston [14th Dist.] 1996, writ denied) (trial court erred by not allowing trial amendment when opposing party did not present evidence of surprise or prejudice); *see* Tex. R. Civ. P. 63, 66.

(1) Amendments conforming pleadings to damages award. An amendment seeking to conform the pleadings to a higher damages award does not automatically constitute surprise to the opposing party. **Greenhalgh**, 787 S.W.2d at 940. See "Caution," ch. 8-F, §2.1.3. The opposing party must be able to show the increase resulted in surprise. **Greenhalgh**, 787 S.W.2d at 940; *e.g.*, **Weidner v. Sanchez**, 14 S.W.3d 353, 376–77 (Tex.App.—Houston [14th Dist.] 2000, no pet.) (P pleaded for $210,000 in actual damages and was awarded $275,000; opposing party should not have been surprised or prejudiced by increase because total amount of damages sought in pleadings was $360,000); *see, e.g.*, **Minnesota Life Ins. v. Vasquez**, 133 S.W.3d 320, 331 (Tex.App.—Corpus Christi 2004) (no evidence of surprise or prejudice because opposing party acknowledged that amount in dispute was greater than what was pleaded for and because increase was not enough to require different trial strategy), *rev'd on other grounds*, 192 S.W.3d 774 (Tex.2006); **Benefit Trust Life Ins. v. Littles**, 869 S.W.2d 453, 478 (Tex.App.—San Antonio 1993) (court found surprise and denied post-trial amendment when verdict increased punitive damages by 8,000%), *writ granted w.r.m.*, 873 S.W.2d 704 (Tex.1994).

(2) Amendments adding prejudgment interest. An amendment seeking to add a claim for prejudgment interest cannot cause surprise or prejudice to the opposing party because prejudgment interest requires no evidentiary proof at trial. **Benavidez v. Isles Constr. Co.**, 726 S.W.2d 23, 26 (Tex.1987); **Firefighters' & Police Officers' Civil Serv. Comm'n v. Herrera**, 981 S.W.2d 728, 734–35 (Tex.App.—Houston [1st Dist.] 1998, pet. denied).

2. Show prejudice on its face. The opposing party must show the amendment asserts a new cause of action or defense and thus is prejudicial on its face. **Greenhalgh**, 787 S.W.2d at 939; **Dallas City Limits Prop. Co. v. Austin Jockey Club, Ltd.**, 376 S.W.3d 792, 797 (Tex.App.—Dallas 2012, pet. denied); *see* Tex. R. Civ. P. 66. However, not all amendments that add a new cause of action or defense are prejudicial as a matter of law. **Hampden Corp. v. Remark, Inc.**, 331 S.W.3d 489, 498 (Tex.App.—Dallas 2010, pet. denied); **Stephenson v. LeBoeuf**, 16 S.W.3d 829, 839 (Tex.App.—Houston [14th Dist.] 2000, pet. denied); *e.g.*, **Allstate Prop. & Cas. Ins. v. Gutierrez**, 281 S.W.3d 535, 539–40 (Tex.App.—El Paso 2008, no pet.) (D amended pleading to include affirmative defense already tried by consent); *see* **State Bar v. Kilpatrick**, 874 S.W.2d 656, 658 (Tex.1994). A pleading that asserts a new cause of action or defense is prejudicial on its face if all of the following are met:

(1) Reshapes lawsuit. The pleading asserts a new substantive matter that reshapes the nature of the lawsuit. **Dallas City Limits**, 376 S.W.3d at 797; **Apodaca v. Rios**, 163 S.W.3d 297, 301 (Tex.App.—El Paso 2005, no pet.); *see also* **Chapin & Chapin, Inc. v. Texas Sand & Gravel Co.**, 844 S.W.2d 664, 665 (Tex.1992) (whether trial court should deny leave to amend depends on whether amendment is substantive or merely procedural).

(2) Not anticipated. The new matter could not have been anticipated by the opposing party in light of the development of the case. **Dallas City Limits**, 376 S.W.3d at 797; **Apodaca**, 163 S.W.3d at 301.

(3) Detrimental. If the amendment is permitted, the opposing party's presentation of the case will be detrimentally affected. **Dallas City Limits**, 376 S.W.3d at 797; **Apodaca**, 163 S.W.3d at 301.

§3.3 Show issue not tried by consent. The opposing party should argue that the issue was not tried by consent. *See, e.g.*, **Hampden Corp. v. Remark, Inc.**, 331 S.W.3d 489, 495 (Tex.App.—Dallas 2010, pet. denied) (Ds argued that issue was not tried by consent, in addition to arguing surprise or prejudice). See "TRCP 67," ch. 8-F, §2.4.2.

§3.4 Motion for continuance. If the court grants the motion for leave to amend, the opposing party may ask for a continuance. *See* Tex. R. Civ. P. 66 (court may grant postponement to enable opposing party to make trial amendment);

Deutsch v. Hoover, Bax & Slovacek, L.L.P., 97 S.W.3d 179, 185 (Tex.App.—Houston [14th Dist.] 2002, no pet.) (postponement may cure prejudice resulting from trial amendment). See "Motion for Continuance," ch. 5-D, §1 et seq.

§3.5 Motion for additional discovery. If the court grants the motion for leave to amend, the opposing party may be entitled to ask for additional discovery on the unpleaded issue. *See* Tex. R. Civ. P. 66.

§3.6 Sworn proof. In most cases, the response to an oral motion to amend is also made orally. *See* **Smith Detective Agency & Nightwatch Serv. v. Stanley Smith Sec., Inc.**, 938 S.W.2d 743, 748 (Tex.App.—Dallas 1996, writ denied). If the response is oral and the attorney states facts outside the record, the attorney should ask to be sworn; if the response is written and includes facts outside the record, it should be verified by affidavit. See "Attorney's appearance before court," ch. 1-H, §5.2.

§4. Amendments after judgment

§4.1 No new claims. After the trial court renders judgment, it is too late to seek leave to amend the pleadings to add new parties or claims. **Mitchell v. LaFlamme**, 60 S.W.3d 123, 132 (Tex.App.—Houston [14th Dist.] 2000, no pet.); **Cantu v. Martin**, 934 S.W.2d 859, 860–61 (Tex.App.—Corpus Christi 1996, no writ). See "Rendering, signing & entering judgment," ch. 9-C, §3.

§4.2 Conform pleadings to evidence. After the court renders judgment, it may be possible to amend the pleadings to conform them to the evidence as long as the court still has plenary power. *See* **Cantu v. Martin**, 934 S.W.2d 859, 861 (Tex.App.—Corpus Christi 1996, no writ) (dicta). To determine whether the court has plenary power, see chart 9-1 under "PPE motion withdrawn," ch. 9-C, §6.4.2(4).

§5. Review

See "Appellate review of amended pleadings," ch. 1-B, §3.6.3.

G. Motion for Directed Verdict

§1. General

§1.1 Rules. Tex R Civ. P. 268; Tex R App. P. 33.1.

§1.2 Purpose. The motion for directed verdict is a procedural device to ask the court to render judgment without submitting the charge to the jury because there is nothing for the jury to decide. **C.B. v. TDFPS**, 440 S.W.3d 756, 769 (Tex.App.—El Paso 2013, no pet.). A directed verdict is also called an instructed verdict; compare the title of TRCP 268, which calls it a motion for instructed verdict, with the body of the rule, which calls it a motion for directed verdict. A motion for directed verdict may be made in a nonjury trial, even though the name of the motion is technically incorrect because there is no jury to "direct." *See* **Carrasco v. Texas Transp.**, 908 S.W.2d 575, 576 (Tex.App.—Waco 1995, no writ). In a nonjury trial, the correct procedure is to make a "motion for judgment." *See* **McKinley Iron Works v. TEC**, 917 S.W.2d 468, 470 (Tex.App.—Fort Worth 1996, no writ).

§1.3 Forms. **O'Connor's Texas Civil Forms**, FORMS 8G:1 et seq. (2020 ed.).

§1.4 Other references. **O'Connor's Federal Rules * Civil Trials** (2021 ed.).

§2. Who can make the motion & when

There are several times during a trial when the parties can move for a directed verdict.

§2.1 After plaintiff rests. After the plaintiff rests (i.e., completes the presentation of its evidence), the defendant may make a motion for directed verdict. *See* **Wedgeworth v. Kirskey**, 985 S.W.2d 115, 116 (Tex.App.—San Antonio 1998, pet. denied) (court cannot render directed verdict before P rests); **Nassar v. Hughes**, 882 S.W.2d 36, 38 (Tex.App.—Houston [1st Dist.] 1994, writ denied) (same); **Buckner v. Buckner**, 815 S.W.2d 877, 878 (Tex.App.—Tyler 1991, no writ) (directed verdict before trial is premature); *see also* **Tana Oil & Gas Corp. v. McCall**, 104 S.W.3d 80, 82 (Tex.2003) (no error for court to grant directed verdict before Ps rested because directed verdict was not based on lack of evidence but rather on fact that Ps limited their claim to damages they could not recover as a matter of law). If the court grants a motion before the plaintiff rests, on appeal the appellant must show it was harmed because it was not able to present its evidence. *See* **Tana Oil**, 104 S.W.3d at 82.

§2.2 After defendant rests. After the defendant rests, either party may make a motion for directed verdict. *See, e.g.,* **Cecil Pond Constr. Co. v. Ed Bell Invs.**, 864 S.W.2d 211, 214 (Tex.App.—Tyler 1993, no writ) (P's motion for directed verdict, made before D presented evidence, was premature).

§2.3 After both sides close. After both sides close (i.e., offer their rebuttal testimony), either party may make a motion for directed verdict. To preserve error in the overruling of an earlier motion for directed verdict, the party must reurge the motion at the close of the evidence. See "Reurging motion at end of evidence," ch. 8-G, §6.

§2.4 If jury unable to reach verdict. If the trial court discharges the jury because it is unable to reach a verdict but does not grant a mistrial, the court may reconsider one of the party's motions for directed verdict. **Encina Prtshp. v. COREnergy, L.L.C.**, 50 S.W.3d 66, 69 (Tex.App.—Corpus Christi 2001, pet. denied); **Nelson v. Data Terminal Sys.**, 762 S.W.2d 744, 748–49 (Tex.App.—San Antonio 1988, writ denied).

§2.5 On court's motion. The court may grant a motion for directed verdict on its own initiative. **Valero Eastex Pipeline Co. v. Jarvis**, 926 S.W.2d 789, 792 (Tex.App.—Tyler 1996, writ denied); *see* **Adams v. Houston Nat'l Bank**, 1 S.W.2d 878, 879 (Tex.Comm'n App.1928, holding approved). Before granting a motion on its own initiative, the court must give the parties notice that it intends to consider granting a directed verdict sua sponte. The party against whom the motion may be granted should be given the opportunity to amend its pleadings or introduce additional evidence before the court grants a motion sua sponte. See "Motion to Amend Pleadings—Trial & Post-trial," ch. 8-F, §1 et seq.; "Motion to Reopen for Additional Evidence," ch. 8-H, §1 et seq.

§3. Motion

§3.1 Oral or written. A motion for directed verdict may be in writing or may be made orally. **Dillard v. Broyles**, 633 S.W.2d 636, 645 (Tex.App.—Corpus Christi 1982, writ ref'd n.r.e.); *see also* Tex. R. Civ. P. 268 ("shall state the specific grounds"). If the motion is made orally, it must be recorded by the court reporter and included in the reporter's record to preserve the grounds.

§3.2 Partial directed verdict. Although a partial directed verdict is not expressly contemplated by TRCP 268, the device can be used to remove certain parts of a case from the fact-finder. *E.g.*, **Johnson v. Swain**, 787 S.W.2d 36, 36 & n.1 (Tex.1989) (court granted partial directed verdict, holding D liable for damages caused by vicious animal).

§3.3 Specific reasons. The motion for directed verdict should state the specific reasons for the motion. Tex. R. Civ. P. 268. If, however, the court grants a directed verdict on a ground that is not specified in the motion, and there are no fact issues for the jury to resolve, it is not reversible error. **Texas Empls. Ins. v. Page**, 553 S.W.2d 98, 102 (Tex.1977); **Deutsch v. Hoover, Bax & Slovacek, L.L.P.**, 97 S.W.3d 179, 195 (Tex.App.—Houston [14th Dist.] 2002, no pet.); **Crescendo Invs. v. Brice**, 61 S.W.3d 465, 472 (Tex.App.—San Antonio 2001, pet. denied).

§4. Grounds for directed verdict

A party is entitled to a directed verdict in the following instances:

§4.1 No evidence. When the evidence does not raise a fact issue on a material issue in the suit. **Prudential Ins. v. Financial Rev. Servs.**, 29 S.W.3d 74, 77 (Tex.2000); **Double Ace, Inc. v. Pope**, 190 S.W.3d 18, 26 (Tex.App.—Amarillo 2005, no pet.); **Cherqui v. Westheimer St. Festival Corp.**, 116 S.W.3d 337, 343 (Tex.App.—Houston [14th Dist.] 2003, no pet.). The evidence must be evaluated in the light most favorable to the nonmovant. **Prudential Ins.**, 29 S.W.3d at 82.

Practice Tip

To avoid a directed verdict based on failure to prove part of the cause of action or defense, the party should prepare a draft of the charge before trial. During the trial, the party should use the draft of the charge as a checklist of the elements that must be supported with evidence.

---

§4.2 Conclusive evidence. When the evidence conclusively proves a fact that establishes the movant's right to judgment or that negates the nonmovant's right. **Westchester Fire Ins. v. Admiral Ins.**, 152 S.W.3d 172, 191 (Tex.App.—Fort Worth 2004, pet. denied); **Rowland v. City of Corpus Christi**, 620 S.W.2d 930, 932 (Tex.App.—Corpus Christi 1981, writ ref'd n.r.e.); *see* **Environmental Processing Sys. v. FPL Farming Ltd.**, 457 S.W.3d 414, 425–26 (Tex.2015); **Prudential Ins. v. Financial Rev. Servs.**, 29 S.W.3d 74, 77 (Tex.2000). That is, the court should direct a verdict when reasonable minds can draw only one conclusion from the evidence. **Vance v. My Apt. Steak House**, 677 S.W.2d 480, 483 (Tex.1984); **Collora v. Navarro**, 574 S.W.2d 65, 68 (Tex.1978); *see, e.g.*, **Shelton v. Swift Motors, Inc.**, 674 S.W.2d 337, 341 (Tex.App.—San Antonio 1984, writ ref'd n.r.e.) (evidence showed P sued wrong party; D was not liable to P). If there is any conflicting probative evidence, the trial court must submit the issue to the jury. **Air Conditioning, Inc. v. Harrison-Wilson-Pearson**, 253 S.W.2d 422, 425 (Tex.1952); **Facciolla v. Linbeck Constr. Corp.**, 968 S.W.2d 435, 440 (Tex.App.—Texarkana 1998, no pet.); **Nelson v. American Nat'l Bank**, 921 S.W.2d 411, 415 (Tex.App.—Corpus Christi 1996, no writ).

§4.3 Defect in pleadings. When the nonmovant's pleadings contain a specific defect that makes them incapable of supporting a judgment for the nonmovant. **Double Ace, Inc. v. Pope**, 190 S.W.3d 18, 26 (Tex.App.—Amarillo 2005, no pet.); **Sherman v. Elkowitz**, 130 S.W.3d 316, 319 (Tex.App.—Houston [14th Dist.] 2004, no pet.). For example, a motion for directed verdict should be granted when the substantive law does not permit the plaintiff to recover on its cause of action or does not permit the defendant to assert its defense. *See, e.g.*, **Dietrich v. Goodman**, 123 S.W.3d 413, 417 (Tex.App.—Houston [14th Dist.] 2003, no pet.) (court directed verdict because, under Water Code, flood water did not qualify as "surface water"); **Arguelles v. UT Fam. Med. Ctr.**, 941 S.W.2d 255, 258 (Tex.App.—Corpus Christi 1996, no writ) (court directed verdict because Texas does not recognize "lost chance of survival" doctrine in medical-malpractice suits); **Anderson v. Vinson Expl., Inc.**, 832 S.W.2d 657, 665 (Tex.App.—El Paso 1992, writ denied) (court directed verdict because under DTPA, an investor is not a "consumer").

§5. Response

§5.1 Objections. Generally, the party opposing the motion should respond to the motion and state the converse of the movant's allegations: (1) a fact issue was raised on all material issues in the case, (2) the evidence does not conclusively prove anything, and (3) no legal theory precludes a judgment. The party should argue that all the issues should be submitted to the jury.

§5.2 Leave to amend. If the motion for directed verdict is based on a defect in the pleadings that is curable by amendment, the nonmovant should ask for permission to amend the pleadings. See "Motion to Amend Pleadings—Trial & Post-trial," ch. 8-F, §1 et seq.

§5.3 Motion to reopen. If the motion for directed verdict is based on a lack of evidence of an essential element, the nonmovant should ask to reopen the evidence. *See* **MCI Telecomms. v. Tarrant Cty. Appr. Dist.**, 723 S.W.2d 350, 353 (Tex.App.—Fort Worth 1987, no writ). See "Motion to Reopen for Additional Evidence," ch. 8-H, §1 et seq.

§6. Reurging motion at end of evidence

§6.1 Rule. If the court overrules a motion for directed verdict during the trial, the movant has two options: (1) stand on the motion and test the ruling on appeal or (2) introduce additional evidence. If the movant chooses to introduce more evidence, the movant must make a second motion at the close of all the evidence; if it does not, it waives the grounds stated in the first motion. **1986 Dodge 150 Pickup v. State**, 129 S.W.3d 180, 183 (Tex.App.—Texarkana 2004, no pet.); **Horton v. Horton**, 965 S.W.2d 78, 86 (Tex.App.—Fort Worth 1998, no pet.); **Cliffs Drilling Co. v. Burrows**, 930 S.W.2d 709, 712 (Tex.App.—Houston [1st Dist.] 1996, no writ). This rule applies in both jury and nonjury trials. *See* **Horton**, 965 S.W.2d at 86 (jury); **Wenk v. City Nat'l Bank**, 613 S.W.2d 345, 348 (Tex.App.—Tyler 1981, no writ) (nonjury). In deciding the second motion, the trial court must consider the evidence introduced before the first motion and the evidence introduced before the second motion. To preserve error, all grounds in the first motion must be restated in the second motion, along with any additional grounds.

§6.2 Criticism & exceptions. The application of the rule requiring the motion to be reurged after the introduction of additional evidence has been criticized. *See* **Sipco Servs. Mar., Inc. v. Wyatt Field Serv.**, 857 S.W.2d 602, 608–10 (Tex.App.—Houston [1st Dist.] 1993, no writ) (Cohen, J., concurring). Before FRCP 50 was amended in 2006, federal courts operated under the same rule requiring the motion to be reurged at the close of the evidence. Now a party is only required to reurge the motion after a verdict has been reached. See "Renewing motion," **O'Connor's Federal Rules * Civil Trials**, ch. 8-G, §6 (2021 ed.).

§7. Order

The order sustaining or overruling the motion for directed verdict can be made in writing and filed with the clerk or made orally on the record. *See* Tex. R. App. P. 33.1(c) (signed order not required to preserve complaint for appeal).

§8. Review

§8.1 Record on appeal. To successfully challenge the granting or denial of a directed verdict, the appellant must file a complete reporter's record in the appellate court. **McDonald v. State**, 936 S.W.2d 734, 737 (Tex.App.—Waco 1997, no writ).

§8.2 Directed verdict denied. In reviewing the denial of a directed verdict, the appellate court is limited to the specific grounds stated in the motion. **Cooper v. Lyon Fin. Servs.**, 65 S.W.3d 197, 207 (Tex.App.—Houston [14th Dist.] 2001, no pet.); **American Petrofina Co. v. Panhandle Pet. Prods.**, 646 S.W.2d 590, 593 (Tex.App.—Amarillo 1983, no writ). An appeal from the denial of a directed verdict is a challenge to the legal sufficiency of the evidence. **Haynes & Boone, L.L.P. v. Chason**, 81 S.W.3d 307, 309 (Tex.App.—Tyler 2001, pet. denied); **Lochinvar Corp. v. Meyers**, 930 S.W.2d 182, 187 (Tex.App.—Dallas 1996, no writ); *see* **City of Keller v. Wilson**, 168 S.W.3d 802, 827–28 (Tex.2005) (explaining application of legal-sufficiency standard). The denial of a motion for directed verdict lays the foundation for challenging the evidence on appeal by issues or points of error contending there was "no evidence" of a certain fact or that a fact was established "as a matter of law." *See* **Weidner v. Sanchez**, 14 S.W.3d 353, 366 (Tex.App.—Houston [14th Dist.] 2000, no pet.) (no evidence); **White v. Liberty Eylau ISD**, 920 S.W.2d 809, 813 (Tex.App.—Texarkana 1996, writ denied) (as a mat-

ter of law); *see also* **Environmental Processing Sys. v. FPL Farming Ltd.**, 457 S.W.3d 414, 425–26 (Tex.2015) (although P improperly based motion on no-evidence grounds, Supreme Court considered whether P conclusively established, as a matter of law, lack of consent; trial court properly denied motion).

§8.3 Directed verdict granted. In reviewing the granting of a directed verdict, the appellate court can consider any reason the directed verdict should have been granted, even one that is not stated in the court's order or the party's motion. *See* **Double Ace, Inc. v. Pope**, 190 S.W.3d 18, 26 (Tex.App.—Amarillo 2005, no pet.); **Reyna v. First Nat'l Bank**, 55 S.W.3d 58, 69 (Tex.App.—Corpus Christi 2001, no pet.); **Gonzales v. Willis**, 995 S.W.2d 729, 740 (Tex.App.—San Antonio 1999, no pet.). The appellate court must consider all the evidence in the light most favorable to the party against whom the verdict was directed, crediting favorable evidence if reasonable jurors could and disregarding contrary evidence if reasonable jurors could not. **Robertson v. Odom**, 296 S.W.3d 151, 155 (Tex.App.—Houston [14th Dist.] 2009, no pet.); *see* **City of Keller v. Wilson**, 168 S.W.3d 802, 827 (Tex.2005). The appellate court must determine whether there is any probative evidence to raise a fact issue. **Porterfield v. Brinegar**, 719 S.W.2d 558, 559 (Tex.1986). If the record contains any probative and conflicting evidence on a material issue, the issue should have been resolved by the jury, and the appellate court must reverse. *See* **White v. Southwestern Bell Tel. Co.**, 651 S.W.2d 260, 262 (Tex.1983); **Rente Co. v. Truckers Express, Inc.**, 116 S.W.3d 326, 330 (Tex.App.—Houston [14th Dist.] 2003, no pet.); **Mills v. Angel**, 995 S.W.2d 262, 267 (Tex.App.—Texarkana 1999, no pet.).

§8.4 Nonjury trial. In reviewing the trial court's granting of a motion for judgment in a nonjury case, the appellate court examines the record as if the trial court had granted a motion for judgment based on all the facts and does not just rule on whether there was no evidence or whether a proposition was established as a matter of law. *See* **Qantel Bus. Sys. v. Custom Controls Co.**, 761 S.W.2d 302, 303–04 (Tex.1988).

H. Motion to Reopen for Additional Evidence

§1. General

§1.1 Rule. Tex. R. Civ. P. 270.

§1.2 Purpose. A party should move to reopen the evidence when it is necessary to include additional evidence in the record. When a party finishes presenting its evidence, it announces that it "rests." When all parties have rested, the parties proceed to offer their rebuttal evidence. After a party offers its rebuttal testimony, the party announces that it "closes." When all parties have closed, the evidence part of the trial is over, unless the court reopens the case for more evidence.

§1.3 Form. ***O'Connor's Texas Civil Forms***, FORM 8H:1 (2020 ed.).

§2. Motion to reopen

Reopening is particularly important when the trial court excluded evidence the party attempted to introduce, and after the party closed, the other party introduced evidence making the excluded evidence relevant. Reopening is also important when the trial court announces it intends to grant a directed verdict for lack of evidence. *See* **MCI Telecomms. v. Tarrant Cty. Appr. Dist.**, 723 S.W.2d 350, 353 (Tex.App.—Fort Worth 1987, no writ).

§2.1 Form. An oral motion to reopen is sufficient, but if the party has the opportunity, it should file a written motion. *See* Tex. R. Civ. P. 270. Most of the time, however, motions to reopen are made orally in open court when the party suddenly realizes it should offer additional testimony.

§2.2 Grounds. When asking the court to reopen, the party should show all of the following:

1. **Diligence.** The party was diligent in obtaining evidence. **Moore v. Jet Stream Invs.**, 315 S.W.3d 195, 201 (Tex.App.—Texarkana 2010, pet. denied); **Hernandez v. Lautensack**, 201 S.W.3d 771, 779 (Tex.App.—Fort Worth 2006, pet. denied); **Lopez v. Lopez**, 55 S.W.3d 194, 201 (Tex.App.—Corpus Christi 2001, no pet.); **In re A.F.**, 895 S.W.2d 481, 484 (Tex.App.—Austin 1995, no writ).

2. **Decisive evidence.** The additional evidence is decisive. **Moore**, 315 S.W.3d at 201; **Hernandez**, 201 S.W.3d at 779; **Lopez**, 55 S.W.3d at 201; **In re A.F.**, 895 S.W.2d at 484.

3. **No undue delay.** The receipt of additional evidence will not cause undue delay. **Moore**, 315 S.W.3d at 201; **Hernandez**, 201 S.W.3d at 779; **Lopez**, 55 S.W.3d at 201; **In re A.F.**, 895 S.W.2d at 484.

4. **No injustice.** The receipt of additional evidence will not cause an injustice. **Moore**, 315 S.W.3d at 201; **Hernandez**, 201 S.W.3d at 779; **Lopez**, 55 S.W.3d at 201; **In re A.F.**, 895 S.W.2d at 484.

§2.3 Verification. Although the motion to reopen is not required by TRCP 270 to be in writing, when the motion is in writing, it should be verified if it contains factual allegations outside the record.

§3. Response

A party must object to the other party's motion to reopen, or it waives error in the reopening. **MCI Telecomms. v. Tarrant Cty. Appr. Dist.**, 723 S.W.2d 350, 353 (Tex.App.—Fort Worth 1987, no writ).

§4. Standard

§4.1 Sound discretion. A trial court should permit a party to reopen the evidence when it clearly appears necessary to the administration of justice. Tex. R. Civ. P. 270. The decision to reopen is within the trial court's sound discretion. **Poag v. Flories**, 317 S.W.3d 820, 828 (Tex.App.—Fort Worth 2010, pet. denied); **Lopez v. Lopez**, 55 S.W.3d 194, 201 (Tex.App.—Corpus Christi 2001, no pet.); **In re Hawk**, 5 S.W.3d 874, 876–77 (Tex.App.—Houston [14th Dist.] 1999, no pet.). The trial court should liberally exercise its discretion to permit both sides to fully develop the case. **Lopez**, 55 S.W.3d at 201.

§4.2 Duty to reopen. The court may have the duty to reopen the evidence when the party moving to reopen has been diligent, the receipt of additional evidence would not cause undue delay or injustice, and the evidence would be decisive. **In**

re H.W., 85 S.W.3d 348, 357–58 (Tex.App.—Tyler 2002, no pet.); **Word of Faith World Outreach Ctr. Ch., Inc. v. Oechsner**, 669 S.W.2d 364, 367 (Tex.App.—Dallas 1984, no writ); *see* **Alkas v. United Sav. Ass'n**, 672 S.W.2d 852, 860 (Tex.App.—Corpus Christi 1984, writ ref'd n.r.e.); *see also* **Hill v. Melton**, 311 S.W.2d 496, 500 (Tex.App.—Dallas 1958, writ dism'd) (because party had right to reopen, abuse of discretion was not the correct standard of review).

§5. Deadline

The court can allow a party to offer additional evidence at any time. Tex. R. Civ. P. 270. But in a jury trial, the court cannot admit evidence on a controversial matter after the jury returns the verdict. *Id.*

§5.1 Party permitted to reopen. In the following cases, the trial court permitted or should have permitted the party to reopen: • Before the court rendered judgment more than two years after the trial (delay caused by an appeal), the court should have permitted the party to reopen. **Greater Fort Worth & Tarrant Cty. Cmty. Action Agency v. Mims**, 627 S.W.2d 149, 151 (Tex.1982). • After the case was submitted to the jury, the court permitted the party to reopen to establish standing. **Krishnan v. Ramirez**, 42 S.W.3d 205, 223 (Tex.App.—Corpus Christi 2001, pet. denied). • Before judgment, the court should have permitted the party to reopen to test the correctness of a plat prepared after trial that the court wanted attached to the judgment. **Templeton v. Dreiss**, 961 S.W.2d 645, 663–65 (Tex.App.—San Antonio 1998, pet. denied). • After the jury began considering the evidence, the court permitted the introduction of an invoice that was part of a series of invoices introduced during the trial. **Turner v. Lone Star Indus.**, 733 S.W.2d 242, 244–45 (Tex.App.—Houston [1st Dist.] 1987, writ ref'd n.r.e.). • After the defendant's motion for directed verdict, the court permitted the plaintiff to reopen to call another witness. **MCI Telecomms. v. Tarrant Cty. Appr. Dist.**, 723 S.W.2d 350, 353 (Tex.App.—Fort Worth 1987, no writ). • When the plaintiff submitted a brief that raised a new fact issue after the parties had rested and submitted the case on stipulated evidence, the court should have permitted the defendant to reopen. **Word of Faith World Outreach Ctr. Ch., Inc. v. Oechsner**, 669 S.W.2d 364, 368 (Tex.App.—Dallas 1984, no writ). • After the plaintiff had rested, the court permitted the plaintiff to reopen to introduce testimony on damages to her mobile home that her attorney had inadvertently omitted during direct examination. **Lifestyle Mobile Homes v. Ricks**, 653 S.W.2d 602, 604 (Tex.App.—Beaumont 1983, writ ref'd n.r.e.). • The court should have reopened evidence when, just after the close of evidence, the plaintiffs realized they had not proved damages. **Hill v. Melton**, 311 S.W.2d 496, 499–500 (Tex.App.—Dallas 1958, writ dism'd).

§5.2 Party not permitted to reopen. In the following cases, the trial court did not permit the party to reopen: • After the court granted other party's motion for summary judgment. **Poag v. Flories**, 317 S.W.3d 820, 824, 828 (Tex.App.—Fort Worth 2010, pet. denied) (movant did not show diligence in timely presenting additional evidence). • After resting, the plaintiff was not permitted to reopen to prove notice, which the defendant had denied by verified plea. **Apresa v. Montfort Ins.**, 932 S.W.2d 246, 250 (Tex.App.—El Paso 1996, no writ). • To ask for attorney fees under the Open Records Act, now the Public Information Act, after the close of the hearing. **McNamara v. Fulks**, 855 S.W.2d 782, 784 (Tex.App.—El Paso 1993, no writ). • Several months after closing and after the court announced its judgment. **Fisher v. Kerr Cty.**, 739 S.W.2d 434, 437 (Tex.App.—San Antonio 1987, no writ) (movant did not show diligence in presenting evidence at trial). • After the jury sent out a question about the evidence. **Walton Neon Co. v. Travel-Tex Corp.**, 482 S.W.2d 934, 936–37 (Tex.App.—Corpus Christi 1972, writ ref'd n.r.e.).

§6. Review

§6.1 Record. When a party is prevented from reopening, the party should make an offer of proof setting out the evidence the party tried to introduce. *See, e.g.*, **Word of Faith World Outreach Ctr. Ch., Inc. v. Oechsner**, 669 S.W.2d 364, 366 (Tex.App.—Dallas 1984, no writ) (error preserved by bill of exception); **Walton Neon Co. v. Travel-Tex Corp.**, 482 S.W.2d 934, 937 (Tex.App.—Corpus Christi 1972, writ ref'd n.r.e.) (error not preserved because no bill of exception). See "Offer of Proof & Bill of Exception," ch. 8-E, §1 et seq.

§6.2 Standard of review. The trial court's ruling on a motion to reopen the evidence should not be disturbed unless it clearly appears that the court abused its discretion. **In re H.W.**, 85 S.W.3d 348, 358 (Tex.App.—Tyler 2002, no pet.); **In re T.V.**, 27 S.W.3d 622, 624 (Tex.App.—Waco 2000, no pet.); **Word of Faith World Outreach Ctr. Ch., Inc. v. Oechsner**, 669 S.W.2d 364, 366 (Tex.App.—Dallas 1984, no writ). The error is reversible only if it probably caused the rendition of an improper judgment—that is, if the evidence could have produced a different result than that reached by the trial court in its judgment. *See* Tex. R. App. P. 44.1(a)(1); **Word of Faith**, 669 S.W.2d at 368.

I. Jury Charge

§1. General

§1.1 Rules. Tex. R. Civ. P. 271 to 279, 285 to 289.

§1.2 Purpose. The jury charge is the collection of questions, instructions, and definitions the court submits to the jury to resolve the factual disputes in the case. It is the trial court's responsibility to submit a proper charge. **Spencer v. Eagle Star Ins.**, 876 S.W.2d 154, 158 (Tex.1994).

§1.3 Forms. **O'Connor's Texas Civil Forms**, FORMS 8I:1 et seq. (2020 ed.).

§1.4 Other references. Texas Pattern Jury Charges—Business, Consumer, Insurance & Employment (2018), Family & Probate (2020), General Negligence, Intentional Personal Torts & Workers' Compensation (2018), Malpractice, Premises & Products (2018), Oil & Gas (2018); Arnot & Johnson, *Current Trends in Texas Charge Practice: Preservation of Error and Broad-Form Use*, 38 St. Mary's L.J. 371 (2007).

§2. Preparing draft of charge

Each party should have prepared a complete version of the charge—including its opponent's jury questions, instructions, and definitions—before engaging in discovery. The charge is each party's road map to the evidence it needs to develop or rebut. Just before trial, each party should review and revise the proposed charge. After the introduction of evidence is completed and before the informal charge conference, the parties should again review and revise their proposed charge.

§2.1 Broad-form questions.

1. Broad form required. The trial court must use broad-form submissions whenever feasible. Tex. R. Civ. P. 277; **Thota v. Young**, 366 S.W.3d 678, 689 (Tex.2012); **Columbia Rio Grande Healthcare, L.P. v. Hawley**, 284 S.W.3d 851, 855 (Tex.2009); **Hyundai Motor Co. v. Rodriguez**, 995 S.W.2d 661, 663–64 (Tex.1999); *see* **W&T Offshore, Inc. v. Fredieu**, __ S.W.3d __, 2020 WL 3240869 (Tex.2020) (No. 18-1134; 6-5-20). A broad-form submission should include all elements of proof within a single question with accompanying instructions. *See* **Diamond Offshore Mgmt. v. Guidry**, 171 S.W.3d 840, 844 (Tex.2005); **Keetch v. Kroger Co.**, 845 S.W.2d 262, 267 (Tex.1992) (Hecht, J., concurring).

2. Broad form not required. A broad-form submission may not be feasible when (1) there are alternative theories of liability and the law is unsettled or the court is not sure whether to submit a particular theory of liability or (2) there is doubt about the legal sufficiency of the evidence to support one or more elements of damages. *E.g.*, **Harris Cty. v. Smith**, 96 S.W.3d 230, 235–36 (Tex.2002) (broad-form damages question included element not supported by evidence); *see* **Romero v. KPH Consol., Inc.**, 166 S.W.3d 212, 215 (Tex.2005) (broad-form submission cannot be used to put before the jury issues that have no basis in law or evidence); *see, e.g.*, **Crown Life Ins. v. Casteel**, 22 S.W.3d 378, 389–90 (Tex.2000) (broad-form question included valid and invalid theories of liability).

3. Preserve error. To preserve complaints of error in a broad-form submission, the party opposing the submission must make timely and specific objections. **Thota**, 366 S.W.3d at 691; *see* **Bombardier Aerospace Corp. v. SPEP Aircraft Holdings, LLC**, 572 S.W.3d 213, 228 n.17 (Tex.2019); **Smith**, 96 S.W.3d at 236; **Casteel**, 22 S.W.3d at 389. See "Making formal objections," ch. 8-I, §4.3; "Review," ch. 8-I, §9.

§2.2 Proper tender of requests. Each party should reexamine the live pleadings and the evidence before preparing the draft charge.

1. Controlling & disputed fact issues. The litigants are entitled to have controlling and disputed fact issues submitted to the jury. *See* **Bel-Ton Elec. Serv. v. Pickle**, 915 S.W.2d 480, 481 (Tex.1996); **Aero Energy, Inc. v. Circle C Drilling Co.**, 699 S.W.2d 821, 823 (Tex.1985). A controlling issue is one that requires a factual determination to render judgment in the case. **Lehmann v. Wieghat**, 917 S.W.2d 379, 382 (Tex.App.—Houston [14th Dist.] 1996, writ denied). A fact issue that is established with uncontroverted evidence and is not in dispute should not be submitted to the jury. **T.O. Stanley Boot Co. v. Bank of El Paso**, 847 S.W.2d 218, 223 (Tex.1992).

2. Supported by pleadings & evidence. The litigants are entitled to have controlling issues submitted to the jury if they are properly pleaded and supported by the evidence. Tex. R. Civ. P. 278; **Union Pac. R.R. v. Williams**, 85 S.W.3d

162, 166 (Tex.2002); **Triplex Comms. v. Riley**, 900 S.W.2d 716, 718 (Tex.1995); *see* **Samedan Oil Corp. v. Intrastate Gas Gathering, Inc.**, 78 S.W.3d 425, 445 (Tex.App.—Tyler 2001, pet. granted, judgm't vacated w.r.m.). For evidence to support the submission, see "Questions," ch. 8-I, §6.1.

3. Form of requests. The draft of the charge must be in writing. Tex. R. Civ. P. 272; **Woods v. Crane Carrier Co.**, 693 S.W.2d 377, 379 (Tex.1985). The written request must be separate from the oral objections. Tex. R. Civ. P. 273; **Alaniz v. Jones & Neuse, Inc.**, 907 S.W.2d 450, 451 (Tex.1995).

§2.3 Cluster of related requests. The parties should submit the proposed charge in "clusters" of related requests. *See, e.g.*, **Lester v. Logan**, 907 S.W.2d 452, 453 (Tex.1995) (disapproving of court of appeals' opinion that held request on one piece of paper that included five related matters—one question, two instructions, and two definitions—was improper); **Aetna Cas. & Sur. Co. v. Moore**, 361 S.W.2d 183, 187 (Tex.1962) (request for question as part of series of nine related questions was proper and did not mislead or confuse trial court). Each cluster should include the name of the party submitting the request and a space for the judge's ruling and signature and the date. A single request with a large number of questions, instructions, and definitions is as weak as its most vulnerable part; when a request includes an objectionable question, instruction, or definition, the court can deny the entire request. *See, e.g.*, **Tempo Tamers, Inc. v. Crow-Houston Four, Ltd.**, 715 S.W.2d 658, 666–67 (Tex.App.—Dallas 1986, writ ref'd n.r.e.) (20 questions in a single request); **Hoover v. Barker**, 507 S.W.2d 299, 305 (Tex.App.—Austin 1974, writ ref'd n.r.e.) (54 questions in a single request). By organizing the requests in clusters of related questions, instructions, and definitions, the party will not necessarily preserve error if the trial court does not submit all or part of the request to the jury; the party must specifically object to the omission and obtain a ruling. *See* **Cruz v. Andrews Restoration, Inc.**, 364 S.W.3d 817, 830–31 (Tex.2012). See "Formal charge conference," ch. 8-I, §4.

1. Each cluster must be complete. All the elements—questions, instructions, and definitions—necessary for each cluster must be included in that cluster. *See, e.g.*, **Owens-Corning Fiberglas Corp. v. Keeton**, 922 S.W.2d 658, 662 (Tex.App.—Austin 1996, writ denied) (failure to submit proper instructions with broad-form question waived error); *see also* Tex. R. Civ. P. 279 (omissions from the charge). When a request contains a word or phrase that requires an instruction or definition, the appropriate instruction or definition must be included as part of the request. *See, e.g.*, **Select Ins. v. Boucher**, 561 S.W.2d 474, 479–80 (Tex.1978) (requested instruction on partial incapacity did not include definition of earning capacity); **Griffin v. Eakin**, 656 S.W.2d 187, 189–90 (Tex.App.—Austin 1983, writ ref'd n.r.e.) (request contained reference to "negligence, as that term is defined herein," but did not include definition of negligence). A party cannot complain on appeal if the trial court did not submit an instruction or definition with one cluster when it was not requested as part of that cluster but only as part of another cluster. *See* **Universal Servs. Co. v. Ung**, 904 S.W.2d 638, 640 (Tex.1995).

2. Each request in cluster must be correct. The party must tender the requests in "substantially correct wording." Tex. R. Civ. P. 278; **Railroad Comm'n v. Gulf Energy Expl. Corp.**, 482 S.W.3d 559, 571 (Tex.2016); **Willis v. Maverick**, 760 S.W.2d 642, 647 (Tex.1988). If any part of the cluster is defective, the entire cluster is not substantially correct. The trial court may refuse the whole request if it finds any part of the request defective. **Greenstein, Logan & Co. v. Burgess Mktg., Inc.**, 744 S.W.2d 170, 182 (Tex.App.—Waco 1987, writ denied). There is no clear-cut rule to determine when a request meets the "substantially correct" standard. As long as a request falls somewhere between absolutely correct and not affirmatively incorrect, it should be sufficient. *See, e.g.*, **Southwestern Bell Tel. Co. v. John Carlo Tex., Inc.**, 843 S.W.2d 470, 472 (Tex.1992) (although definition was not exactly correct, it was substantially correct); **Exxon Corp. v. Perez**, 842 S.W.2d 629, 630 n.1 (Tex.1992) (question was not affirmatively incorrect); **Placencio v. Allied Indus. Int'l**, 724 S.W.2d 20, 21–22 (Tex.1987) (question was affirmatively incorrect because it was not conditioned on the affirmative answer to another question).

§2.4 Proper burden of persuasion. The party must tender each question with the proper placement of the burden of persuasion. *See* **Texas Empls. Ins. v. Olivarez**, 694 S.W.2d 92, 93–94 (Tex.App.—San Antonio 1985, no writ). Generally, to place the burden of persuasion properly, the question should be asked so the party with the burden will benefit from an affirmative answer. **Turk v. Robles**, 810 S.W.2d 755, 759 (Tex.App.—Houston [1st Dist.] 1991, writ denied). In cases in which a party must prove a negative, it is sometimes difficult to determine who has the burden of persuasion and how to word the question so as not to confuse the jury. *See id.* (instruction on testamentary capacity to revoke will). If there is doubt about who has the burden of persuasion on a question, the instruction should ask the jury to answer the question with a complete statement, not just a yes or no. *See* **Walker v. Eason**, 643 S.W.2d 390, 391 (Tex.1982). For example, when a jury is required

to fill in the blank with either "She did have sufficient mental capacity" or "She did not have sufficient mental capacity," any error in misplacing the burden is harmless. *See id.* In cases submitted with broad-form questions, it is sometimes impossible to determine which party has the burden for each part of the charge. **State Dept. of Hwys. & Pub. Transp. v. Payne**, 838 S.W.2d 235, 240 (Tex.1992).

§2.5 Proper condition. When the answer to a follow-up question is conditioned on the jury's answer to an earlier question, the follow-up question must be preceded by an instruction telling the jury to answer the next question only if it responds in a certain way to the earlier question (e.g., "If you have answered 'Yes' to Question 3, then answer Question 4; otherwise, do not answer Question 4."). A request for a jury question is not correct if it conditions a question on the wrong question. If a party does not object to an erroneous conditional submission, the party waives the error. *See* **Wilgus v. Bond**, 730 S.W.2d 670, 672 (Tex.1987); **Matthews v. Candlewood Builders, Inc.**, 685 S.W.2d 649, 650 (Tex.1985). If an erroneous conditional submission deprives a party of the submission of an issue raised by the pleadings and evidence, it constitutes reversible error. **Varme v. Gordon**, 881 S.W.2d 877, 881 (Tex.App.—Houston [14th Dist.] 1994, writ denied); *see, e.g.*, **Washington v. Reliable Life Ins.**, 581 S.W.2d 153, 160 (Tex.1979) (remanded for new trial because improperly conditioned question was not reached); **Byrne v. Harris Adacom Network Servs.**, 11 S.W.3d 244, 248–49 (Tex.App.—Texarkana 1999, pet. denied) (improper conditioning was harmless error); **Owens-Corning Fiberglas Corp. v. Martin**, 942 S.W.2d 712, 723 (Tex.App.—Dallas 1997, no writ) (same). The submission of a conditional damages question is expressly permitted by TRCP 277, even though it incidentally informs the jury of the legal effect of its answers. **H.E. Butt Grocery Co. v. Bilotto**, 985 S.W.2d 22, 24 (Tex.1998).

§2.6 Proper damages questions. The damages questions must be submitted so they reflect the following:

1. **Proper measure.** The party must tender a damages question that asks the jury to consider the correct legal measure of damages. **Jackson v. Fontaine's Clinics, Inc.**, 499 S.W.2d 87, 90 (Tex.1973). A jury question that does not guide the jury to a finding on any proper legal measure of damages is fatally defective. *Id.*; **Samedan Oil Corp. v. Intrastate Gas Gathering, Inc.**, 78 S.W.3d 425, 452 (Tex.App.—Tyler 2001, pet. granted, judgm't vacated w.r.m.); **Browning Oil Co. v. Luecke**, 38 S.W.3d 625, 643 (Tex.App.—Austin 2000, pet. denied).

2. **Proper segregation.** The party must tender damages questions that properly segregate the damages due to each plaintiff, due from each defendant, and due on each individual claim. *See, e.g.*, **Minnesota Mining & Mfg. v. Nishika Ltd.**, 953 S.W.2d 733, 739 (Tex.1997) (damages were not segregated between Ps); **Green Int'l v. Solis**, 951 S.W.2d 384, 389 (Tex.1997) (attorney fees were not segregated according to claims); **Wingate v. Hajdik**, 795 S.W.2d 717, 719–20 (Tex.1990) (damages were not segregated between those due to corporation and those due to stockholder). However, the party does not have to tender damages questions that segregate the damages between multiple parties if the injury is indivisible. *See* **Stewart & Stevenson Servs. v. Serv-Tech, Inc.**, 879 S.W.2d 89, 101 (Tex.App.—Houston [14th Dist.] 1994, writ denied).

3. **Proper condition.** The party must tender a damages question that is properly conditioned on an affirmative answer to the corresponding liability question. *See* **Wilgus v. Bond**, 730 S.W.2d 670, 672 (Tex.1987).

4. **Alternative theories of liability.** A party is entitled to seek damages on alternative theories of liability. **Waite Hill Servs. v. World Class Metal Works, Inc.**, 959 S.W.2d 182, 184 (Tex.1998). Once the jury's verdict is in, the plaintiff should elect its remedy to avoid application of the "one satisfaction" rule. *See id.* at 184–85; **Birchfield v. Texarkana Mem'l Hosp.**, 747 S.W.2d 361, 367 (Tex.1987); **Household Credit Servs. v. Driscol**, 989 S.W.2d 72, 82 (Tex.App.—El Paso 1998, pet. denied).

§3. Informal charge conference

The informal charge conference is held whenever the local rules provide or the judge prefers. Normally, the judge calls a recess after both sides close, and the attorneys meet with the judge in chambers to assemble the charge.

§3.1 Deadline for requests. Each party must submit its requested questions, instructions, and definitions to the court by whatever deadline the court imposes. Under TRCP 166(k), the court can require the parties to submit the requests at or before the pretrial conference. Local rules often require the attorneys to submit their requests before trial.

§3.2 Proposed charge. The court compiles the proposed charge during the informal charge conference by assembling questions, instructions, and definitions from those the attorneys provide and making any changes it believes necessary. The court then gives the proposed charge to the attorneys to examine.

§3.3 Time to examine. The trial court must allow the parties a reasonable amount of time to examine the proposed charge and object to it. Tex. R. Civ. P. 272; **King Fisher Mar. Serv. v. Tamez**, 443 S.W.3d 838, 843 (Tex.2014). The court has the discretion to determine how much time to give the parties to examine the charge. *E.g.*, **Bekins Moving & Storage Co. v. Williams**, 947 S.W.2d 568, 575 (Tex.App.—Texarkana 1997, no writ) (32 minutes to review 51-page charge was reasonable; charge was largely in same form as before charge conference). If the trial court refuses to allow reasonable time to examine the charge, a party must make an objection on the record to preserve error. The objection must state the following: (1) that the party was not given adequate time to examine the charge, (2) how much time was given, (3) how much time was necessary, (4) that the charge was too complex and lengthy to examine in the amount of time given, and (5) that the lack of adequate time to examine the charge caused harm because the party was not able to make a proper record for appeal. *See, e.g.*, **Dillard v. Dillard**, 341 S.W.2d 668, 675 (Tex.App.—Austin 1960, writ ref'd n.r.e.) (although 15 minutes might not have been adequate amount of time to examine charge, appellant did not show harm). The evidence of the harm can be included in a bill of exception if any error is discovered later, after a closer examination of the charge. See "Offer of Proof & Bill of Exception," ch. 8-E, §1 et seq.

§4. Formal charge conference

After the informal charge conference, the trial court will hold a formal charge conference with a court reporter present to record the parties' comments on the charge. The parties must make all their objections to the charge, present any requests for additional questions and instructions, and get rulings on all objections and requests.

Caution

At the formal charge conference, you must make a record of all the objections and requests for questions, instructions, and definitions that you have for the proposed charge, even if you discussed the same requests at the informal charge conference. See ***Cruz v. Andrews Restoration, Inc.****, 364 S.W.3d 817, 830–31 (Tex.2012). To ensure that the objections and requests you made during the informal charge conference are preserved, restate the objections on the record, have the court overrule them orally, and ask the court to mark your written requests "refused" and sign them. See id.;* ***Alaniz v. Jones & Neuse, Inc.****, 907 S.W.2d 450, 451 (Tex.1995). See "Written rulings," ch. 8-I, §5.2.2.*

§4.1 Challenging charge. To preserve error in the charge, the party must make objections to defective submissions in the court's charge or submit written requests for additional questions, instructions, or definitions that are omitted from the charge. *See* Tex. R. Civ. P. 273, 274; **Railroad Comm'n v. Gulf Energy Expl. Corp.**, 482 S.W.3d 559, 571 (Tex.2016). Under the rules relating to the charge, objections and requests are not interchangeable. *See* Tex. R. Civ. P. 273. An objection to the charge can be made orally or in writing and must be specific. A request is a written question, instruction, or definition, submitted in substantially correct form.

For years, the Supreme Court strictly applied the rules for challenging the charge. However, in **State Dept. of Hwys. & Pub. Transp. v. Payne**, 838 S.W.2d 235, 241 (Tex.1992), the Court liberalized the procedure for objecting to the charge. The Court said there should be only one test to determine whether a party has preserved error in the jury charge: Did the party make the trial court "aware of the complaint, timely and plainly," and obtain a ruling? **Payne**, 838 S.W.2d at 241; *e.g.*, **Wackenhut Corp. v. Gutierrez**, 453 S.W.3d 917, 919–20 (Tex.2015) (error preserved when party stated specific reasons for opposing spoliation instruction in response to pretrial motion for sanctions and trial court ruled that instruction would be submitted to jury over party's objection); **Thota v. Young**, 366 S.W.3d 678, 689–91 (Tex.2012) (error preserved when party made specific and timely no-evidence objection to charge and submitted proposed charge that omitted the objected-to instructions); **Cruz v. Andrews Restoration, Inc.**, 364 S.W.3d 817, 829 (Tex.2012) (error not preserved because party did not timely or plainly make trial court aware of its charge complaint or obtain a ruling); *see also* **Galveston Cty. Fair & Rodeo, Inc. v. Glover**, 940 S.W.2d 585, 586–87 (Tex.1996) (complaint preserved even though party did not separately request in writing any definitions or instructions); **Alaniz v. Jones & Neuse, Inc.**, 907 S.W.2d 450, 451 (Tex.1995) (complaint preserved even though request was not separate from completed charge).

Practice Tip

When you are making your objections and requests, follow the rules set out below. On appeal, if you are worried you did not preserve error for appeal, cite **Payne** *and show that you timely made the trial court aware of your complaint and got a ruling.*

1. When to object—defect in charge. Object, no matter who has the burden of proof, when the court submits an erroneous or defective question, instruction, or definition. *See* **Equistar Chems., L.P. v. Dresser-Rand Co.**, 240 S.W.3d 864, 868 (Tex.2007) (erroneous instruction); **St. Joseph Hosp. v. Wolff**, 94 S.W.3d 513, 525 (Tex.2002) (erroneous definition); **Spencer v. Eagle Star Ins.**, 876 S.W.2d 154, 157 (Tex.1994) (defective instruction); **Religious of the Sacred Heart v. City of Houston**, 836 S.W.2d 606, 613–14 (Tex.1992) (defective question); *see also* **Seger v. Yorkshire Ins.**, 503 S.W.3d 388, 407–08 (Tex.2016) (when party preserves error by objecting to erroneous definition, appellate court measures legal sufficiency of evidence against definition that should have been used). *But see* **Payne**, 838 S.W.2d at 239–40 (request for a question preserved error in defective instruction); **Matthiessen v. Schaefer**, 900 S.W.2d 792, 797 (Tex.App.—San Antonio 1995, writ denied) (request for a question preserved error in defective question).

2. When to request—omission in charge.

(1) Question omitted. A party must submit a request when it has the burden of proof and the court omits a question. *See* **W.O. Bankston Nissan, Inc. v. Walters**, 754 S.W.2d 127, 128 (Tex.1988); **Wright Way Constr. Co. v. Harlingen Mall Co.**, 799 S.W.2d 415, 419 (Tex.App.—Corpus Christi 1990, writ denied); *see also* **United Scaffolding, Inc. v. Levine**, 537 S.W.3d 463, 481 (Tex.2017) (D has no obligation to object to P's omission of theory of recovery). When a party submits a written request before trial, if the court omits part of it from the charge but was aware of the request and refused it, the party can preserve error by objecting and identifying the portion of its written request that the court omitted. *See* **Cruz**, 364 S.W.3d at 830–31; **Alaniz**, 907 S.W.2d at 451. The party should probably locate its copy of the written request and ask the court to include it in the charge or write "refused" on it. See "Written rulings," ch. 8-I, §5.2.2.

(2) Instruction or definition omitted. A party must make a written request, no matter who has the burden of proof, when the court omits an instruction or definition. Tex. R. Civ. P. 278; **Gerdes v. Kennamer**, 155 S.W.3d 523, 534 (Tex.App.—Corpus Christi 2004, pet. denied); *see* Tex. R. Civ. P. 273; **TDFPS v. Parra**, 503 S.W.3d 646, 663 (Tex.App.—El Paso 2016, pet. denied). A party cannot dictate a requested instruction into the record. **Fairfield Estates L.P. v. Griffin**, 986 S.W.2d 719, 724 (Tex.App.—Eastland 1999, no pet.); **Jarrin v. Sam White Oldsmobile Co.**, 929 S.W.2d 21, 25 (Tex.App.—Houston [1st Dist.] 1996, writ denied); **Hartnett v. Hampton Inns, Inc.**, 870 S.W.2d 162, 165 (Tex.App.—San Antonio 1993, writ denied).

3. When to either object or request.

(1) Opponent's question omitted. A party may object or submit a request when its opponent has the burden of proof and the court omits part of the opponent's cause of action or defense. *See* **Brady v. Klentzman**, 515 S.W.3d 878, 885 (Tex.2017); **Religious of the Sacred Heart**, 836 S.W.2d at 614; *see, e.g.*, **Payne**, 838 S.W.2d at 239 (State preserved error by submitting the missing element of a question, even though it did not have the burden of proof); **Ramos v. Frito-Lay, Inc.**, 784 S.W.2d 667, 668 (Tex.1990) (D should have objected when court did not submit element of P's cause of action).

Practice Tip

It may seem odd to object to errors made by the other party in its jury questions, but if you do not, you may be bound by adverse express or deemed findings. See "Incomplete claim or defense submitted," ch. 8-I, §7.2.

(2) Erroneous burden of persuasion. A party may object to a question or submit a request when the court improperly places the burden of persuasion. *See* **Morris v. Holt**, 714 S.W.2d 311, 312–13 (Tex.1986) (preserved by request); **Turk v. Robles**, 810 S.W.2d 755, 759 (Tex.App.—Houston [1st Dist.] 1991, writ denied) (preserved by objection).

4. Rule to challenge charge. Challenging the charge can be confusing. When there is doubt about whether to object or request, a party should always object. If a party has the burden of proof on a question, it should also (not instead) submit a request. If a definition or instruction is omitted, the party should object and make a request, no matter who has the burden. Finally, the party should analyze its objections and requests in light of **Payne**: Did the party make the trial court "aware of the complaint, timely and plainly," and obtain a ruling? **Payne**, 838 S.W.2d at 241.

§4.2 Deadline to object & request.

1. Charge.

(1) General rule. At a minimum, the parties must make all objections to the charge before the court reads the charge to the jury. Tex. R. Civ. P. 272; **King Fisher Mar. Serv. v. Tamez**, 443 S.W.3d 838, 843 (Tex.2014); **Cruz v. Andrews Restoration, Inc.**, 364 S.W.3d 817, 830 (Tex.2012). But TRCP 272 allows the court to set a deadline for the parties to object to the charge that expires before the charge is read to the jury as long as the parties had a reasonable time to examine and object to the charge. *E.g.*, **King Fisher**, 443 S.W.3d at 845–46 (court did not abuse discretion by refusing to consider D's objection made right before charge was read to jury; D had reasonable time to examine and object to charge and at formal charge conference on previous day, court warned parties to make all objections to charge before conference ended). See "Time to examine," ch. 8-I, §3.3. The parties waive any objections to errors in the charge that are made after the charge is read to the jury. Tex. R. Civ. P. 272; **Missouri Pac. R.R. v. Cross**, 501 S.W.2d 868, 872 (Tex.1973); *e.g.*, **Mitchell v. Bank of Am.**, 156 S.W.3d 622, 627–28 (Tex.App.—Dallas 2004, pet. denied) (objections to charge in motion for new trial were untimely); *see also* **Wackenhut Corp. v. Gutierrez**, 453 S.W.3d 917, 919–20 & n.3 (Tex.2015) (no waiver when D objected to submission of spoliation instruction after charge was read to jury because same objection had been preserved in D's response to pretrial motion for sanctions; objection to particular wording of instruction after charge was read, rather than objection to submission itself, would have been untimely). A party cannot preserve error by a late objection, even if the court permits it and the other party agrees. **Cross**, 501 S.W.2d at 873; **Sudderth v. Howard**, 560 S.W.2d 511, 516 (Tex.App.—Amarillo 1977, writ ref'd n.r.e.).

Caution

*Although the Supreme Court held in **King Fisher** that trial courts have discretion to set a deadline for parties to object to the charge that expires before the charge is read to the jury, the Court stated that trial courts should consider good-faith charge objections that are brought after the formal charge conference ends but before the charge is read to the jury. **King Fisher**, 443 S.W.3d at 847. In **King Fisher**, however, even though there was no evidence that the defendant's last-minute objection was made in bad faith and the trial court could likely have reviewed the objection with minimal delay, the Supreme Court—noting that the trial court had provided the parties a reasonable amount of time to examine and object to the charge—held that the trial court did not abuse its discretion in refusing to consider the last-minute objection. Id. The Supreme Court refused to create a rule that would limit the trial court's discretion to set a deadline for making charge objections. Id. Thus, a party should make every attempt to lodge objections to the charge before any deadline set by the trial court. If the trial court refuses to consider a good-faith objection made after the deadline but before the charge is read to the jury, the party will at least have preserved the complaint for appeal, although the appellate court may ultimately hold that the trial court had discretion to refuse to consider the objection. See id. at 845.*

(2) Exceptions.

(a) Legal sufficiency. It is not necessary to challenge the legal sufficiency of the evidence before the charge is submitted to the jury. *See* Tex. R. Civ. P. 279; *see also* **Musallam v. Ali**, 560 S.W.3d 636, 639 (Tex.2018) (legal-sufficiency challenge could be raised by P for first time after verdict even though P requested submission of question). A legal-sufficiency challenge can be made for the first time in a motion for JNOV or in a motion for new trial. *See* **Musallam**, 560 S.W.3d at 639. See "Preserving legal-sufficiency point," ch. 10-B, §13.1.3.

(b) Recovery precluded. It is not necessary to object that a certain legal theory precludes recovery before the charge is submitted to the jury. *See, e.g.,* **USAA Tex. Lloyds Co. v. Menchaca**, 545 S.W.3d 479, 487 n.8 (Tex.2018) (D asserted that jury's failure to find contractual breach precluded P's recovery of insurance policy benefits; D preserved error by raising argument in motion for judgment on the verdict); **Holland v. Wal-Mart Stores**, 1 S.W.3d 91, 94 (Tex.1999) (statute did not permit attorney fees; D raised issue in motion for JNOV).

(c) Immaterial question. It is not necessary to object to an immaterial jury question before the charge is submitted to the jury. **BP Am. Prod. v. Red Deer Res.**, 526 S.W.3d 389, 402 (Tex.2017); *see* **United Scaffolding, Inc. v. Levine**, 537 S.W.3d 463, 481–82 (Tex.2017). Immateriality can be raised for the first time in a postverdict motion, such as a motion for JNOV or a motion for new trial. See "Immaterial jury finding," ch. 9-B, §3.4; "Immaterial jury finding," ch. 10-B, §13.4.

2. Supplemental instructions. If, after the jury retires to deliberate, the trial court decides to give the jury additional instructions, the parties must make any objections or requests before the court reads the supplemental charge to the jury. See "Supplemental instructions to jury," ch. 8-I, §8.2.

3. Presumption of timeliness. On appeal, the court will presume the parties timely objected unless the record shows otherwise. Tex. R. Civ. P. 272; **Acord v. General Motors Corp.**, 669 S.W.2d 111, 114 (Tex.1984). If the record shows that a party did not timely object, the party waives the error. **Ruff v. Christian Servs.**, 627 S.W.2d 799, 802 (Tex.App.—Tyler 1982, no writ); *see* **Morales v. Morales**, 98 S.W.3d 343, 346 (Tex.App.—Corpus Christi 2003, pet. denied).

§4.3 Making formal objections.

1. Orally or in writing. A party may object to the charge either orally, by dictating objections to the court reporter, or in writing. Tex. R. Civ. P. 272. At the formal charge conference, the parties will probably dictate the objections to the court reporter. Oral objections must be made in the presence of the trial judge, opposing counsel, and the court reporter. *Id.*; *see* **Brantley v. Sprague**, 636 S.W.2d 224, 225 (Tex.App.—Texarkana 1982, writ ref'd n.r.e.). If the trial judge is not present, the objections are waived. **Brantley**, 636 S.W.2d at 225.

2. Specific. A party must make timely and specific objections to the charge. **Burbage v. Burbage**, 447 S.W.3d 249, 256 (Tex.2014); **Thota v. Young**, 366 S.W.3d 678, 689 (Tex.2012); *see* Tex. R. Civ. P. 274; Tex. R. App. P. 33.1(a)(1)(A). The objection must clearly identify the error and explain the grounds for the complaint. Tex. R. Civ. P. 274; **BP Am. Prod. v. Red Deer Res.**, 526 S.W.3d 389, 401 (Tex.2017); **Burbage**, 447 S.W.3d at 256; **Texas Comm'n on Human Rights v. Morrison**, 381 S.W.3d 533, 536 (Tex.2012). If the objection does not meet both of these requirements, it will not preserve error. **Castleberry v. Branscum**, 721 S.W.2d 270, 276 (Tex.1986); *see* Tex. R. Civ. P. 274; **Burbage**, 447 S.W.3d at 256; **Morrison**, 381 S.W.3d at 536. A specific objection enables the trial court to understand the precise grounds and make an informed ruling. **McKinney v. National Un. Fire Ins.**, 772 S.W.2d 72, 74 (Tex.1989). It also affords the trial court an opportunity to remedy the defect. **Burbage**, 447 S.W.3d at 256; **Castleberry**, 721 S.W.2d at 276. If a general objection is paired with a written request that clearly reflects the error, the objection will be preserved. *See* **Universal Underwriters Ins. v. Pierce**, 795 S.W.2d 771, 773 (Tex.App.—Houston [1st Dist.] 1990, writ denied).

Caution

In cases involving allegations of ***Casteel*** *error—that is, when valid and invalid theories of liability or damages have been submitted in a broad-form question—the Supreme Court has declined to address whether a party must specifically object to both the inclusion of invalid theories of liability or damages and the form of the submission to preserve error. See* ***Burbage****, 447 S.W.3d at 256;* ***Romero v. KPH Consol., Inc.****, 166 S.W.3d 212, 229 (Tex.2005). See "Presumed harm," ch. 8-I, §9.1.4(2). Some courts of appeals have held that an objection to form is not necessary as long as a party has objected to the inclusion of invalid theories of liability or damages in the charge.* ***McFarland v. Boisseau****, 365 S.W.3d 449, 454–55 (Tex.App.—Houston [1st Dist.] 2011, no pet.); see* ***Schrock v. Sisco****, 229 S.W.3d 392, 395–96 (Tex.App.—Eastland 2007, no pet.);* ***Missouri Pac. R.R. v. Limmer****, 180 S.W.3d 803, 822–23 (Tex.App.—Houston [14th Dist.] 2005), rev'd on other grounds, 299 S.W.3d 78 (Tex.2009). Until the*

Supreme Court specifically addresses the issue, a party should object to both the inclusion of invalid theories of liability or damages and the form of the submission.

3. Not obscured by other objections. A party should not obscure a correct objection among voluminous, unfounded, and "stock" objections. Tex. R. Civ. P. 274; **Monsanto Co. v. Milam**, 494 S.W.2d 534, 536 (Tex.1973). See "Bad objections," ch. 8-I, §4.3.5(2) (objection (a)). There is no rule of thumb for when an objection has been "obscured." Generally, it is not the number of objections, but the use of repetitious or stock objections, that obscures a valid complaint. *See, e.g.*, **Monsanto Co.**, 494 S.W.2d at 536–37 (42 pages of stock objections on grounds of "no pleadings" and "insufficient pleadings" concealed valid objection); **Hinote v. Oil, Chem. & Atomic Workers Int'l Un.**, 777 S.W.2d 134, 143–45 (Tex.App.—Houston [14th Dist.] 1989, writ denied) (30 pages of invalid and stock objections on grounds of "factual insufficiency" and "against the great weight and preponderance of the evidence" concealed valid objection); **Baker Material Handling Corp. v. Cummings**, 692 S.W.2d 142, 145–46 (Tex.App.—Dallas 1985), *writ dism'd*, 713 S.W.2d 96 (Tex.1986) (17 objections did not obscure valid objection because there were no stock objections).

4. No adoption by reference. A party cannot adopt an objection from one question or instruction and apply it by reference to other questions or objections. Tex. R. Civ. P. 274; **C.T.W. v. B.C.G.**, 809 S.W.2d 788, 793 (Tex.App.—Beaumont 1991, no writ); **Washburn v. Krenek**, 684 S.W.2d 187, 190 (Tex.App.—Houston [14th Dist.] 1984, writ ref'd n.r.e.). A party cannot adopt another party's objections; each party must state its own objections to the charge. *See* **C.M. Asfahl Agency v. Tensor, Inc.**, 135 S.W.3d 768, 795–96 (Tex.App.—Houston [1st Dist.] 2004, no pet.); **Wright Way Constr. Co. v. Harlingen Mall Co.**, 799 S.W.2d 415, 420–21 (Tex.App.—Corpus Christi 1990, writ denied). However, the trial court at its discretion may permit joint objections to save time. *See* **Owens-Corning Fiberglas Corp. v. Malone**, 916 S.W.2d 551, 556 (Tex.App.—Houston [1st Dist.] 1996), *aff'd*, 972 S.W.2d 35 (Tex.1998).

5. Examples.

(1) Good objections. A valid objection is one that is appropriate to the charge in the case. The following are some good objections, if relevant to the case. Each of the statements below should be preceded with the statement "[Name of party] objects because."

Practice Tip

When you object, (1) identify the defect, (2) specify how the question, instruction, or definition is defective, (3) state why it is defective, and (4) state the exact correction you want the court to make.

(a) The charge submits an issue established as a matter of law. It is not necessary to submit *{identify issue}* to the jury because it was judicially admitted in the other party's pleadings. Once a fact is conclusively established by judicial admission, a jury question concerning the fact should not be submitted. **Horizon/CMS Healthcare Corp. v. Auld**, 34 S.W.3d 887, 905 (Tex.2000).

(b) Question number __ asks the jury to decide a question of law. **Grohman v. Kahlig**, 318 S.W.3d 882, 887 (Tex.2010); *see* **Gilbert Wheeler, Inc. v. Enbridge Pipelines (E. Tex.), L.P.**, 449 S.W.3d 474, 484 (Tex.2014); **Bank of Am. v. Jeff Taylor LLC**, 358 S.W.3d 848, 864 (Tex.App.—Tyler 2012, no pet.).

Note

The error in asking the jury to decide a question of law is considered harmless if the jury answers the question correctly or, if answered incorrectly, the trial court deems the question immaterial and disregards it. ***Grohman**, 318 S.W.3d at 887;* ***Bank of Am.**, 358 S.W.3d at 865.*

(c) The charge omits an element from the *{cause of action/defense}*, in that the element of *{identify the missing element}* is required to be submitted. *{Submit a written request for the missing element}*

(d) There is no evidence to support the submission of question number __, and that question should not be submitted to the jury.

(e) There is no evidence to support the submission of *{identify element in broad-form submission that has no support}*; the court should either submit individual questions for each element in the broad-form question or delete that element from the broad-form question. *See* **Harris Cty. v. Smith**, 96 S.W.3d 230, 235–36 (Tex.2002). See "Broad form not required," ch. 8-I, §2.1.2.

(f) Question number __, which inquires about *{identify cause of action}*, is improper because it is a broad-form question that includes an invalid theory of liability. *See* **Crown Life Ins. v. Casteel**, 22 S.W.3d 378, 387–88 (Tex.2000); **Schrock**, 229 S.W.3d at 394–95.

(g) The only evidence to support the submission of question number __ is circumstantial evidence, and because the evidence is equally consistent with either of two facts, neither fact can be inferred and the issue cannot be submitted to the jury. See "Circumstantial evidence," ch. 8-I, §6.1.2.

(h) Question number __, which inquires about *{identify cause of action}*, is improper because there are no pleadings to support its submission, and the issue was not tried by consent. *See* **Recognition Comms. v. American Auto. Ass'n**, 154 S.W.3d 878, 885–86 (Tex.App.—Dallas 2005, pet. denied). *{Identify the variance between the pleadings and the proof.}* See "Issue not tried by consent," ch. 8-F, §2.4.2(2).

(i) Question number __ *{is not conditioned/is improperly conditioned}* on an affirmative answer to question number __.

(j) Question number __ should not be submitted to the jury because it is not a controlling question. *{State reason.}*

(k) Question number __ is immaterial to the outcome of the case. *See* **BP Am.**, 526 S.W.3d at 402 (immateriality can be raised for first time in postverdict motion).

(l) The charge does not contain an *{instruction/definition}* necessary to the submission of the question of __, which is *{state the instruction or definition}*. *{Submit a written request for the omitted instruction or definition.}*

(m) Question number __ duplicates question number __.

(n) Question number __ does not properly place the burden of persuasion because *{state the reason}*.

(o) The following language in *{question/instruction/definition number __}*, *{quote the language}*, is a comment on the weight of the evidence because it suggests the trial court's opinion that *{state exactly why it is a comment on the evidence}*. Tex. R. Civ. P. 277; **Alvarez v. Missouri-Kan.-Tex. R.R.**, 683 S.W.2d 375, 377 (Tex.1984); **Garza v. Southland Corp.**, 836 S.W.2d 214, 220 (Tex.App.—Houston [14th Dist.] 1992, no writ).

(p) Question number __ presents an inferential-rebuttal defense. Tex. R. Civ. P. 277. An inferential-rebuttal issue is permitted only as an instruction. *Id.* *{Submit the inferential-rebuttal instruction.}*

(q) The instruction regarding __ should not be included because (1) the other party did not plead it, (2) the case was not tried on that theory, and (3) the jury questions do not rely on it. *See* **Texas Workers' Comp. Ins. Fund v. Mandlbauer**, 34 S.W.3d 909, 912 (Tex.2000).

(r) The instruction regarding __ is defective because *{state why}*.

(s) Definition number __ is an improper statement of the law in that *{state why}*. *See* **St. Joseph Hosp. v. Wolff**, 94 S.W.3d 513, 529 (Tex.2002).

(t) The instruction regarding __ is unnecessary, and even though it is a correct statement of the law, it amounts to a comment on the weight of the evidence that tilts or nudges the jury by *{state exactly how it nudges the jury}*. **Wal-Mart Stores v. Johnson**, 106 S.W.3d 718, 723–24 (Tex.2003); **Lone Star Gas Co. v. Lemond**, 897 S.W.2d 755, 756 (Tex.1995); **Lemos v. Montez**, 680 S.W.2d 798, 801 (Tex.1984). The more closely contested the case, the greater the chance that a superfluous instruction is error. **Johnson**, 106 S.W.3d at 724; *see* **Timberwalk Apts., Partners v. Cain**, 972 S.W.2d 749, 755 (Tex.1998); **Ford Motor Co. v. Miles**, 967 S.W.2d 377, 387 (Tex.1998).

(u) The charge, which is based on a statutory cause of action, does not track the language of the statute. *See* **Borneman v. Steak & Ale**, 22 S.W.3d 411, 413 (Tex.2000).

(v) The damages question is not properly related to the cause of action on which it must be conditioned. Question number __ must be conditioned on an affirmative answer to question number __. *See* **Wilgus v. Bond**, 730 S.W.2d 670, 672 (Tex.1987).

(w) *{The causes of action have different types of damages/The damages are owed to different plaintiffs}*, and the damages must be segregated. Question number __ must be conditioned on an affirmative answer to question number __, and question number __ must be conditioned on an affirmative answer to question number __.

(x) The instruction on the exemplary-damages question does not limit the jury's consideration to the harm caused to the plaintiff because it seeks to punish the defendant for harm caused to nonparties. *See* **Philip Morris USA v. Williams**, 549 U.S. 346, 353–55 (2007).

(y) Question number __ on attorney fees does not segregate the reasonable and necessary attorney fees incurred for prosecuting the causes of action on which attorney fees are recoverable from the causes of action on which no attorney fees may be recovered. Or, the question does not segregate the reasonable and necessary attorney fees incurred for prosecuting the cause of action against this party from the other parties. See "Proper segregation," ch. 8-I, §2.6.2.

(2) Bad objections. The following objections should not be made in any case.

(a) There is factually insufficient evidence to support the submission of question number __; or, question number __ is against the great weight of the evidence. An attorney should never object that the question should not be submitted because the evidence is "factually insufficient" or "against the great weight and preponderance" of the evidence. Such complaints are without merit at the charge conference. **Long Island Owner's Ass'n v. Davidson**, 965 S.W.2d 674, 680 (Tex.App.—Corpus Christi 1998, pet. denied); **Hinote**, 777 S.W.2d at 143. The trial court determines whether to submit a question to the jury on legal-sufficiency grounds, not on factual-sufficiency grounds. The court has a duty to submit the question if there is any probative evidence to support it. **American Home Assur. Co. v. Brandt**, 778 S.W.2d 141, 144 (Tex.App.—Texarkana 1989, writ denied). When a party makes factual-sufficiency objections to the charge, it undermines the party's valid objections to the charge and the attorney's credibility with the court. *See* **Hinote**, 777 S.W.2d at 143.

(b) With regard to question number __, there is a variance between the pleadings and the proof. This statement alone is not sufficient. If there is a variance between the pleadings and the proof, the party must identify the specific variance or defect in its objection. **Brown v. American Transfer & Storage Co.**, 601 S.W.2d 931, 938 (Tex.1980); **Ron Craft Chevrolet, Inc. v. Davis**, 836 S.W.2d 672, 675 (Tex.App.—El Paso 1992, writ denied).

(c) Question number __ "should read" a particular way. This objection alone is improper because it does not identify the error. **Garza**, 836 S.W.2d at 218.

(d) Question number __ could not form "a basis of liability" or "the basis of any judgment." To be proper, such objections must be more specific and must call the court's attention to the failure of the charge to submit a proper question. **Anderson v. Broome**, 233 S.W.2d 901, 904 (Tex.App.—El Paso 1950, writ ref'd n.r.e.).

(e) The instruction on __ may "confuse the jury" or "prejudice the defendant." Such complaints are too general because they do not explain how the instruction would confuse the jury or how it would prejudice the defendant. **Castleberry**, 721 S.W.2d at 277.

(f) The charge contains two (or more) theories of damages and will give the plaintiff a double recovery. Because a party is entitled to seek damages on alternative theories, this is not a valid objection. See "Alternative theories of liability," ch. 8-I, §2.6.4.

§4.4 Making formal request for additions to charge.

1. In writing. Once the court submits the proposed charge to the parties at the formal charge conference, if either party wants the court to include any additional questions, instructions, or definitions the party must tender the ad-

ditional request in writing or object to the omission of a written request that was made at the informal charge conference. *See* Tex. R. Civ. P. 273; *see, e.g.*, **Alaniz v. Jones & Neuse, Inc.**, 907 S.W.2d 450, 451 (Tex.1995) (objection at formal charge conference to exclusion of requested charge that was offered before informal charge conference preserved error).

2. Separate from objections. A party must tender the request separately from any objections. Tex. R. Civ. P. 273; **Woods v. Crane Carrier Co.**, 693 S.W.2d 377, 379 (Tex.1985); **Texas Empls. Ins. v. Eskue**, 574 S.W.2d 814, 818 (Tex.App.—El Paso 1978, no writ).

§5. Court's rulings on requests & objections

§5.1 Deadline for rulings. The court should announce its ruling on the requests and objections before it reads the charge to the jury. Tex. R. Civ. P. 272. The trial court's rulings on the objections should appear in the record. *See* **Reliance Ins. v. Dahlstrom Corp.**, 568 S.W.2d 733, 734 (Tex.App.—Eastland 1978, writ ref'd n.r.e.). However, if the court submits proposed questions or instructions over objections without an express ruling, the court implicitly overrules the objections. **Acord v. General Motors Corp.**, 669 S.W.2d 111, 114 (Tex.1984); *see also* Tex. R. App. P. 33.1(a)(2)(A) (trial court can make ruling on request or objection either expressly or implicitly).

Practice Tip

If the court overruled your requested questions, instructions, or definitions at the charge conference, but the record from the charge conference does not clearly show it, while the trial court still has plenary power, you should ask the court to sign an order reflecting its rulings and stating they were made before the charge was submitted to the jury.

§5.2 Method of ruling.

1. Oral rulings. If the objections are dictated into the record, the court should state its ruling on the objections immediately after each party makes its objections. *See* Tex. R. Civ. P. 272. On appeal, the trial court's ruling can be inferred from the record. For example, if a party makes an objection and the trial court makes no change to the charge, the objection is overruled. **Acord v. General Motors Corp.**, 669 S.W.2d 111, 114 (Tex.1984); *see* Tex. R. App. P. 33.1(a)(2)(A). If a commonsense interpretation of the objection and the court's ruling shows that the trial court necessarily overruled the objection, the appellate courts will hold that the objection was overruled. **Betty Leavell Rlty. Co. v. Raggio**, 669 S.W.2d 102, 104 (Tex.1984).

2. Written rulings. When the court refuses or modifies a request, it should endorse the request as either "refused" or "modified" and sign it. Tex. R. Civ. P. 276. When the court endorses "modified" on a request, the court should also state how the request has been modified. *Id.* However, even if the court did not endorse the refused instruction as required by TRCP 276, if the record clearly shows that the trial court was aware of the request and refused it, error is preserved. *See* Tex. R. App. P. 33.1(a)(2)(A); **Cruz v. Andrews Restoration, Inc.**, 364 S.W.3d 817, 830 (Tex.2012); **Dallas Mkt. Ctr. Dev. Co. v. Liedeker**, 958 S.W.2d 382, 387 (Tex.1997), *overruled on other grounds*, **Torrington Co. v. Stutzman**, 46 S.W.3d 829 (Tex.2000); **Chemical Express Carriers, Inc. v. Pina**, 819 S.W.2d 585, 589 (Tex.App.—El Paso 1991, writ denied). When there are several pages of requests, the court can endorse and sign the requests either separately or as a group. *See* **Greenstein, Logan & Co. v. Burgess Mktg., Inc.**, 744 S.W.2d 170, 181 (Tex.App.—Waco 1987, writ denied).

§6. Charge submitted to jury

The trial court is required to read the charge to the jury before the attorneys make their final arguments. Tex. R. Civ. P. 275.

§6.1 Questions. TRCP 278 requires the trial court to submit a requested question to the jury if the pleadings and any evidence support it. **Elbaor v. Smith**, 845 S.W.2d 240, 243 (Tex.1992); **Komet v. Graves**, 40 S.W.3d 596, 603 (Tex.App.—San Antonio 2001, no pet.); *see* **United Scaffolding, Inc. v. Levine**, 537 S.W.3d 463, 469 (Tex.2017). The trial court has broad discretion in submitting questions to the jury as long as the questions submitted control the disposition of the case and properly present the disputed issues for the jury's determination. **Moore v. Kitsmiller**, 201 S.W.3d 147, 153 (Tex.App.—Tyler 2006, pet. denied). The court can refuse to submit a question if (1) there is no evidence to support it, (2) there are no

pleadings to support it and the issue was not tried by consent, or (3) the issue is uncontroverted. *See* **Alaniz v. Jones & Neuse, Inc.**, 907 S.W.2d 450, 452 (Tex.1995) (no pleadings or evidence for lost future profits); **T.O. Stanley Boot Co. v. Bank of El Paso**, 847 S.W.2d 218, 222–23 (Tex.1992) (uncontroverted evidence on amount of notes).

Note

In 2020, TRCP 277 was amended to require certain jury questions in suits affecting the parent-child relationship (SAPCRs). See Tex. R. Civ. P. 277; Tex.Sup.Ct. Order, Misc. Docket No. 20-9056 (eff. May 1, 2020). For a discussion of jury instructions in SAPCRs, see "Jury issues & instructions," ***O'Connor's Texas Family Law Handbook****, ch. 4-H, §14.5 (2021 ed.).*

1. Direct evidence. When a material fact is supported by direct evidence, the issue must be submitted to the jury. *See* **Farley v. M M Cattle Co.**, 529 S.W.2d 751, 753–54 (Tex.1975).

2. Circumstantial evidence. When a material fact is supported by circumstantial evidence, the issue may be submitted to the jury if the material fact can reasonably be inferred from the facts proved. *See* **Hammerly Oaks, Inc. v. Edwards**, 958 S.W.2d 387, 392 (Tex.1997); **Russell v. Russell**, 865 S.W.2d 929, 933 (Tex.1993). Under the equal-inference rule, the jury cannot infer an ultimate fact from minimal circumstantial evidence that could give rise to several different inferences, none of which is more probable than another. **Hancock v. Variyam**, 400 S.W.3d 59, 70–71 (Tex.2013); *see* **Suarez v. City of Tex. City**, 465 S.W.3d 623, 634 (Tex.2015). Properly applied, the equal-inference rule is a type of "no-evidence" rule; when circumstantial evidence is so slight that any plausible inference is purely a guess, it is in effect no evidence. **Lozano v. Lozano**, 52 S.W.3d 141, 148 (Tex.2001) (Phillips, C.J., Enoch, Hankinson, Baker, Abbott, JJ., concurring & dissenting). But when circumstantial evidence supports more than one reasonable inference, the jury must decide which inference is more reasonable, subject to judicial review only to ensure the evidence is factually sufficient. *Id.* That is, the jury has the power to choose between competing reasonable inferences. *Id.*

§6.2 Instructions. The instructions to the jury include the general instructions given in all jury trials and the instructions that are specific to the case.

1. General. The trial court must give the jury the general instructions prescribed by Section III of TRCP 226a.

2. Specific. The trial court must give the jury the special instructions for the case. The court must submit any explanatory instructions necessary to enable the jury to reach a verdict. Tex. R. Civ. P. 277; **Wichita Cty. v. Hart**, 917 S.W.2d 779, 783–84 (Tex.1996). For an instruction to be proper, it must (1) assist the jury in its deliberations, (2) accurately state the law, and (3) be supported by the pleadings and evidence. **Gunn v. McCoy**, 554 S.W.3d 645, 675 (Tex.2018); **Seger v. Yorkshire Ins. Co.**, 503 S.W.3d 388, 408 (Tex.2016); **Thota v. Young**, 366 S.W.3d 678, 687 (Tex.2012). The court has considerable discretion in deciding what instructions are necessary. **Gunn**, 554 S.W.3d at 675; **Seger**, 503 S.W.3d at 408; **Thota**, 366 S.W.3d at 687.

(1) Inferential-rebuttal instructions. If the defendant introduced evidence that raised an inferential rebuttal, the inferential-rebuttal issue is submitted to the jury as an instruction, not as a question. Tex. R. Civ. P. 277; **Bed, Bath & Beyond, Inc. v. Urista**, 211 S.W.3d 753, 757 (Tex.2006). The purpose of the instruction is to tell the jury it is not required to find the defendant responsible for the accident if the true cause was something else. **Dew v. Crown Derrick Erectors, Inc.**, 208 S.W.3d 448, 450 (Tex.2006) (plurality op.). Jurors do not need to agree on who or what caused the accident, only that it was not the defendant. **Dillard v. Texas Elec. Coop.**, 157 S.W.3d 429, 434 (Tex.2005).

(2) Exemplary-damages instructions. For cases involving exemplary damages, the court—before closing arguments—must provide a written charge that informs the jury that its answer to the question regarding the amount of exemplary damages must be unanimous. Tex. Civ. Prac. & Rem. Code §41.003(e); *see* Tex. R. Civ. P. 226a, §III. See "Exemplary-damages cases," ch. 8-K, §4.2.

3. Erroneous.

(1) Misstatement of law. An instruction that misstates the law as applied to the facts of the case is reversible error. **Wakefield v. Bevly**, 704 S.W.2d 339, 350 (Tex.App.—Corpus Christi 1985, no writ).

(2) Improper burden of proof. An instruction that imposes a greater burden than the law requires is reversible error. *See* **American Home Assur. Co. v. Brandt**, 778 S.W.2d 141, 143–44 (Tex.App.—Texarkana 1989, writ denied).

§6.3 Definitions. A definition defines a term used in the charge. The purpose of a definition is to enable jurors to understand legal words or phrases so that they can properly answer the jury questions. **Oadra v. Stegall**, 871 S.W.2d 882, 890 (Tex.App.—Houston [14th Dist.] 1994, no writ). The trial court must submit any definitions necessary to enable the jury to reach a verdict. Tex. R. Civ. P. 277; **St. James Transp. Co. v. Porter**, 840 S.W.2d 658, 664 (Tex.App.—Houston [1st Dist.] 1992, writ denied); **Lumbermens Mut. Cas. Co. v. Garcia**, 758 S.W.2d 893, 894 (Tex.App.—Corpus Christi 1988, writ denied). The trial court has wide discretion in determining whether a definition is necessary, but legal or technical terms must be defined. **Seger v. Yorkshire Ins. Co.**, 503 S.W.3d 388, 408 (Tex.2016); *see, e.g.*, **Whiteside v. Watson**, 12 S.W.3d 614, 623–24 (Tex.App.—Eastland 2000, pet. granted, judgm't vacated w.r.m.) ("earning capacity" and "physical impairment" have specific legal definitions); **Allen v. Allen**, 966 S.W.2d 658, 659–60 (Tex.App.—San Antonio 1998, pet. denied) ("cohabitation" did not need to be defined); **Turner v. Roadway Express, Inc.**, 911 S.W.2d 224, 227 (Tex.App.—Fort Worth 1995, writ denied) ("recklessly" did not need to be defined); *see also* **Railroad Comm'n v. Gulf Energy Expl. Corp.**, 482 S.W.3d 559, 571 (Tex.2016) (when party's question generally tracked statutory language, party was not required to submit accompanying definition of statutory term because no case law provided guidance on what proper definition should be). The sufficiency of the definitions is left to the discretion of the trial court. **Porter**, 840 S.W.2d at 664. If a term is used more than once in the charge and the term requires a definition, the definition should follow the general instructions. **Woods v. Crane Carrier Co.**, 693 S.W.2d 377, 379 (Tex.1985).

§7. Waiver of omitted grounds & elements

§7.1 Entire claim or defense omitted. A party waives an entire theory of recovery or defense by not objecting to its omission from the charge. **Gulf States Utils. Co. v. Low**, 79 S.W.3d 561, 565 (Tex.2002); **Harmes v. Arklatex Corp.**, 615 S.W.2d 177, 179 (Tex.1981); *see* Tex. R. Civ. P. 279; *see, e.g.*, **United Scaffolding, Inc. v. Levine**, 537 S.W.3d 463, 481 (Tex.2017) (D did not waive argument that claim was submitted under improper theory of recovery by not objecting to charge; P had burden to request proper question); **Railroad Comm'n v. Gulf Energy Expl. Corp.**, 482 S.W.3d 559, 571 (Tex.2016) (no waiver when party objected to omission of statutory defense from charge even though party did not include accompanying definition of statutory term because no case law provided guidance on what proper definition should be); **Southwestern Bell Tel. Co. v. DeLanney**, 809 S.W.2d 493, 495 (Tex.1991) (P waived breach-of-contract claim). If, however, the complete theory of recovery or defense was proved as a matter of law, there is no waiver because a jury question is not required. *See* **Brown v. Bank of Galveston**, 963 S.W.2d 511, 515 (Tex.1998), *overruled on other grounds*, **Ford Motor Co. v. Ledesma**, 242 S.W.3d 32 (Tex.2007).

§7.2 Incomplete claim or defense submitted. TRCP 279 describes the procedure when an element of a ground of recovery or defense is omitted from the jury charge. **In re J.F.C.**, 96 S.W.3d 256, 262–63 (Tex.2002); *see* **Service Corp. v. Guerra**, 348 S.W.3d 221, 228–29 (Tex.2011); **Chon Tri v. J.T.T.**, 162 S.W.3d 552, 557 (Tex.2005).

1. Neither party objected. The trial court may make an express finding in support of the judgment when the charge was submitted with an element missing from a claim or defense and (1) the party with the burden of proof on the incomplete claim or defense did not request the missing element, (2) the opposing party did not object to the missing element, (3) the claim or defense consisted of more than one element, (4) the missing element is "necessarily referable" to the claim or defense, and (5) there is factually sufficient evidence to support a finding on the missing element. Tex. R. Civ. P. 279; **Gulf States Utils. Co. v. Low**, 79 S.W.3d 561, 564 (Tex.2002); *see* **Clayton W. Williams, Jr., Inc. v. Olivo**, 952 S.W.2d 523, 529 (Tex.1997); **Ramos v. Frito-Lay, Inc.**, 784 S.W.2d 667, 668 (Tex.1990); **Wal-Mart Stores v. Renteria**, 52 S.W.3d 848, 850 (Tex.App.—San Antonio 2001, pet. denied). By not objecting, the parties waive a jury trial on the omitted element and agree to submit the issue to the trial court. **Gulf States**, 79 S.W.3d at 565. If the trial court does not make an express finding on the omitted element before rendering judgment, the appellate court will deem a finding on the omitted element that supports the trial court's judgment. Tex. R. Civ. P. 279; **Service Corp.**, 348 S.W.3d at 228–29; **Chon Tri**, 162 S.W.3d at 557–58; *see, e.g.*, **Ramos**, 784 S.W.2d at 668 (Supreme Court deemed findings in support of trial court's judgment); **Cielo Dorado Dev., Inc. v. Certainteed Corp.**, 744 S.W.2d 10, 11 (Tex.1988) (same). The deemed finding must be supported by legally sufficient evidence from the trial. *See* **Longview Energy Co. v. Huff Energy Fund LP**, 533 S.W.3d 866, 875 (Tex.2017); **Service Corp.**, 348 S.W.3d at 229.

2. **Opposing party objected.** The trial court must render judgment against the party who had the burden of proof on a missing element when (1) the opposing party objected to the missing element, (2) an affirmative finding on the missing element is essential to the claim or defense, and (3) the missing element is not established as a matter of law in favor of the party with the burden of proof. *See* **McKinley v. Stripling**, 763 S.W.2d 407, 410 (Tex.1989); **Physicians & Surgeons Gen. Hosp. v. Koblizek**, 752 S.W.2d 657, 660 (Tex.App.—Corpus Christi 1988, writ denied). When the opposing party objects to a missing element, a court cannot deem the missing element in favor of the party with the burden of proof on that element. *See* **Physicians & Surgeons**, 752 S.W.2d at 660. In such a case, the party with the burden of proof did not secure a finding on the omitted element, which forecloses that claim or defense. *See* **Dallas Cty. Med. Soc'y v. Ubiñas-Brache**, 68 S.W.3d 31, 40 (Tex.App.—Dallas 2001, pet. denied).

§7.3 How trial court makes express findings. The trial court may make an express finding anytime before it renders the judgment. Tex. R. Civ. P. 279.

1. The party who will benefit from an express finding should ask the court to make an express, written finding. The trial court cannot make an express finding without a request from one of the parties. *Id.*

2. The other parties must be given notice of the request. *Id.*

3. The court must conduct a hearing on the request. *Id.*

4. The court must make an express finding in writing before rendering judgment. *Id.* When the court makes an express finding, it will render a judgment on the complete verdict. For example, assume that in a simple-negligence case no proximate-cause question was submitted, and the jury found the defendant negligent. If the court makes an express finding that the negligence was a proximate cause of the plaintiff's injury, the court will render judgment for the plaintiff. However, if the court makes an express finding that the negligence was not a proximate cause of the plaintiff's injury, the court will render judgment for the defendant.

§7.4 How appellate courts make deemed findings. The appellate courts may make a deemed finding only in the following circumstances:

1. The trial court did not make an express finding in writing before rendering judgment. Tex. R. Civ. P. 279; **In re J.F.C.**, 96 S.W.3d 256, 262–63 (Tex.2002).

2. The appellate court makes a finding to support the trial court's judgment. Tex. R. Civ. P. 279; **Gulf States Utils. Co. v. Low**, 79 S.W.3d 561, 564 (Tex.2002); *see* **In re J.F.C.**, 96 S.W.3d at 262–63. The appellate court cannot deem a finding that requires a different judgment than the one rendered by the trial court. **Gulf States**, 79 S.W.3d at 564; *see also* **Logan v. Mullis**, 686 S.W.2d 605, 609 (Tex.1985) (court of appeals erred by deeming a finding in support of verdict instead of final judgment).

§8. Supplemental instructions to jury

§8.1 Jury's questions to trial court. If the jury has a question or needs to communicate with the court, the presiding juror will tell the officer in charge of the jury, who will inform the trial court. Tex. R. Civ. P. 285; **Ross v. Texas Empls. Ins.**, 267 S.W.2d 541, 542 (Tex.1954). The trial court should assemble the jury and the attorneys in the courtroom, where the presiding juror will communicate with the court, either orally or in writing. Tex. R. Civ. P. 285, 286; **Mid-South Bottling Co. v. Cigainero**, 799 S.W.2d 385, 387 n.1 (Tex.App.—Texarkana 1990, writ denied). If the jury asks for additional instructions on the law, its request must be in writing. Tex. R. Civ. P. 286.

§8.2 Supplemental instructions to jury. After the jury retires, the trial court may—at the request of the jury, on the court's own initiative, or on the motion of a party—give the jury additional instructions on any matter of law. *See, e.g.*, **Lochinvar Corp. v. Meyers**, 930 S.W.2d 182, 187 (Tex.App.—Dallas 1996, no writ) (party made late objection to error in charge, which court corrected by supplemental instruction). When the jury is assembled for a supplemental charge, the court must give the instruction in writing. Tex. R. Civ. P. 286. The court must give the attorneys an opportunity to object to the supplemental instructions before it reads them to the jury. **Scroggs v. Morgan**, 130 S.W.2d 283, 285 (Tex.1939). The trial court may allow additional argument at its discretion. *See* **Geesbreght v. Geesbreght**, 570 S.W.2d 427, 433 (Tex.App.—Fort Worth 1978, writ dism'd).

§8.3 Verdict-urging instructions. TRCP 289 permits the trial court to discharge a jury without a verdict when (1) the jurors cannot agree and the parties consent to their discharge, (2) the jurors have been kept together for such time as to render it altogether improbable that they can agree, or (3) a calamity or accident occurs that, in the opinion of the court, requires discharge. **Shaw v. Greater Houston Transp.**, 791 S.W.2d 204, 205 (Tex.App.—Corpus Christi 1990, no writ). To determine whether the jurors will be able to reach a verdict, the trial court can ask them and in some circumstances can instruct them, to resume deliberations and attempt to reach a verdict. The supplemental charge is sometimes called an "**Allen**" charge, after **Allen v. U.S.**, 164 U.S. 492 (1896), or the "dynamite charge," because it is used to "blast" a jury out of deadlock to reach a verdict. **Stevens v. Travelers Ins.**, 563 S.W.2d 223, 226 (Tex.1978). The trial court cannot keep the jurors captive once they have announced they cannot reach a verdict. *See, e.g.*, **Shaw**, 791 S.W.2d at 209–10 (court's refusal to release jury was coercive and reversible).

1. Propriety of supplemental charge. There are two questions to consider when a jury has been unable to reach a verdict: (1) what kind of supplemental charge is permissible, and (2) how long should the jury be held?

(1) Supplemental charge. A supplemental charge should not be coercive. *See* **In re Commitment of Jones**, __ S.W.3d __ n.3, 2020 WL 3393468 (Tex.2020) (No. 19-0260; 6-19-20). To determine whether a particular charge is coercive, it must be broken down into its parts and analyzed for possible coercive statements. **Stevens**, 563 S.W.2d at 229; *see* **Firestone Tire & Rubber Co. v. Battle**, 745 S.W.2d 909, 916–17 (Tex.App.—Houston [1st Dist.] 1988, writ denied). A potentially coercive statement will not invalidate the charge unless it retains its coercive nature when read as a whole and all the circumstances surrounding its rendition are considered. **Stevens**, 563 S.W.2d at 229; *e.g.*, **Souris v. Robinson**, 725 S.W.2d 339, 343 (Tex.App.—Houston [14th Dist.] 1987, no writ) (supplemental charge that asked jury to return a verdict "today" was not coercive); *see* **In re Commitment of Jones**, __ S.W.3d at __ n.8, 2020 WL 3393468; **Golden v. First City Nat'l Bank**, 751 S.W.2d 639, 642 (Tex.App.—Dallas 1988, no writ). The supplemental charge should be addressed to all the jurors, not just those who do not agree with the majority. *See* **In re Commitment of Jones**, __ S.W.3d at __ n.8, 2020 WL 3393468; **Stevens**, 563 S.W.2d at 228. The supplemental charge must not suggest that the court will confine the jury until it reaches a verdict. **Stevens**, 563 S.W.2d at 232; **Shaw**, 791 S.W.2d at 209. The supplemental charge must not tell the jury that it will breach its responsibility by not reaching a verdict. *See* **Shaw**, 791 S.W.2d at 209.

(2) Length of deliberation. The length of time the jury is held in an effort to secure a verdict is left to the discretion of the trial court. **Conrey v. McGehee**, 473 S.W.2d 617, 620 (Tex.App.—Houston [14th Dist.] 1971, writ ref'd n.r.e.). Once it becomes clear the jury is deadlocked, either by their notes or by the passage of time, the trial court must release them. For example, the trial judge in **Shaw** should have released the jury after three days of deliberation when the jury repeatedly said it was deadlocked and even said it was unable to abide by the instruction. **Shaw**, 791 S.W.2d at 209–10; *see also* **Conrey**, 473 S.W.2d at 620 (holding jury for seven hours was not error).

2. Preserve error. To preserve error in the supplemental charge, the party must object.

(1) To supplemental charge. The party must object to the supplemental charge and identify each statement in the supplemental charge that is coercive and state why. The objection must be made before the court submits the supplemental charge to the jury. *E.g.*, **Golden**, 751 S.W.2d at 642 (D waived error by not objecting at the time the court submitted verdict-urging instruction to jury).

(2) To continuation of deliberations. The party should also object to the continued confinement of the jury by making a motion for mistrial. *See* **Shaw**, 791 S.W.2d at 206–07.

§9. Review

§9.1 Standard of review.

1. Legal correctness of jury charge. Whether a challenged part of the jury charge is legally correct or misstates the law is a legal question reviewed de novo. *See* **Seger v. Yorkshire Ins. Co.**, 503 S.W.3d 388, 408 (Tex.2016); **Transcontinental Ins. v. Crump**, 330 S.W.3d 211, 221 (Tex.2010); **St. Joseph Hosp. v. Wolff**, 94 S.W.3d 513, 525 (Tex.2002).

2. Rejection or submission of instruction, definition, or question. Whether a trial court should have rejected or submitted a particular instruction, definition, or question is reviewed for abuse of discretion. *See* **King Fisher Mar. Serv. v. Tamez**, 443 S.W.3d 838, 842 (Tex.2014); **Thota v. Young**, 366 S.W.3d 678, 687 (Tex.2012).

3. Submission of controlling issues—theories of recovery or defense. Whether a jury charge submits the controlling issues in the case—in terms of theories of recovery or defenses—is a legal question reviewed de novo. **Hamid v. Lexus**, 369 S.W.3d 291, 295 (Tex.App.—Houston [1st Dist.] 2011, no pet.); *see* **Shelby Distribs. v. Reta**, 441 S.W.3d 715, 722 n.4 (Tex.App.—El Paso 2014, no pet.). Similarly, whether there is legally sufficient evidence to support the submission of a particular theory of recovery or defense is also a legal question reviewed de novo. *See* **Elbaor v. Smith**, 845 S.W.2d 240, 243 (Tex.1992); **C.M. Asfahl Agency v. Tensor, Inc.**, 135 S.W.3d 768, 780 (Tex.App.—Houston [1st Dist.] 2004, no pet.).

4. Harmful error. To obtain reversal for a charge error, in certain situations an appellant must show harmful error; in other situations, error is presumed harmful.

(1) Show error caused harm. For the appellate court to reverse certain jury-charge errors, the appellant must show harmful error. **Boatland of Houston, Inc. v. Bailey**, 609 S.W.2d 743, 749–50 (Tex.1980); *see* **In re Commitment of Jones**, __ S.W.3d __, 2020 WL 3393468 (Tex.2020) (No. 19-0260; 6-19-20). Error in the jury charge is reversible only if it probably caused the rendition of an improper judgment or probably prevented the appellant from properly presenting the case on appeal. Tex. R. App. P. 44.1(a); **In re Commitment of Jones**, __ S.W.3d at __, 2020 WL 3393468; **Thota**, 366 S.W.3d at 687; **Columbia Rio Grande Healthcare, L.P. v. Hawley**, 284 S.W.3d 851, 856 (Tex.2009); *see* **United Scaffolding, Inc. v. Levine**, 537 S.W.3d 463, 469 (Tex.2017). See "Reversible error," **O'Connor's Texas Civil Appeals**, ch. 1-G, §7.1 (2021 ed.). A misunderstanding of the court's charge by the jury is not grounds for reversible error. **Holiday Inns, Inc. v. State**, 931 S.W.2d 614, 621 (Tex.App.—Amarillo 1996, writ denied); *see* **Stephens Cty. Museum, Inc. v. Swenson**, 517 S.W.2d 257, 260 (Tex.1974). Jury-charge error is generally considered harmful if it relates to a contested, critical issue. **Railroad Comm'n v. Gulf Energy Expl. Corp.**, 482 S.W.3d 559, 571 (Tex.2016); **Thota**, 366 S.W.3d at 687; **Columbia Rio Grande Healthcare**, 284 S.W.3d at 856. To determine harm, the appellate court must consider the entire record—the pleadings, the evidence, and the charge. **Timberwalk Apts., Partners v. Cain**, 972 S.W.2d 749, 756 (Tex.1998); **Reinhart v. Young**, 906 S.W.2d 471, 473 (Tex.1995); **Island Recreational Dev. Corp. v. Republic of Tex. Sav. Ass'n**, 710 S.W.2d 551, 555 (Tex.1986).

(a) Submitted question, instruction, or definition. The erroneous submission of a jury question, instruction, or definition is generally reversible error if it relates to a contested issue in the case. *See, e.g.*, **Transcontinental Ins.**, 330 S.W.3d at 224–25 (in workers' compensation case, submission of legally incorrect definition of "producing cause" was reversible error); **Quantum Chem. Corp. v. Toennies**, 47 S.W.3d 473, 480 (Tex.2001) (in age-discrimination case, erroneous instruction on causation was reversible error); **Timberwalk Apts.**, 972 S.W.2d at 755–56 (in premises-liability case, unnecessary instruction on tenant's requirement to give written request for repairs was reversible error). But the erroneous submission of a question, instruction, or definition is generally harmless if the jury's findings on other issues support the judgment. **Boatland of Houston**, 609 S.W.2d at 750; *see* **Gilbert Wheeler, Inc. v. Enbridge Pipelines (E. Tex.), L.P.**, 449 S.W.3d 474, 486 (Tex.2014) (submission of improper jury question may be harmless if jury's verdict was based on valid theory of liability); **Thota**, 366 S.W.3d at 693–94 (same); *see, e.g.*, **Reinhart**, 906 S.W.2d at 473–74 (in negligence case, erroneous submission of unavoidable-accident instruction was harmless because P did not object to similar sudden-emergency instruction); **City of Brownsville v. Alvarado**, 897 S.W.2d 750, 752 (Tex.1995) (submission of contributory-negligence question was harmless because jury's answer to first question finding no negligence rendered it immaterial); *see also* **Grohman v. Kahlig**, 318 S.W.3d 882, 889 (Tex.2010) (submission of question of law was harmless error because jury answered question as trial court should have). Even if other jury findings support the judgment, the erroneous submission of a question, instruction, or definition can be reversible error if the erroneously submitted issue confused or misled the jury. **Boatland of Houston**, 609 S.W.2d at 750.

(b) Refused question, instruction, or definition. The refusal to submit a jury question, instruction, or definition is reversible error if the question, instruction, or definition was reasonably necessary to enable the jury to render a proper verdict. *See* Tex. R. Civ. P. 277, 278; **Gunn v. McCoy**, 554 S.W.3d 645, 675 (Tex.2018); *see, e.g.*, **Railroad Comm'n**, 482 S.W.3d at 571–72 (failure to include question on good-faith defense was reversible error); **Columbia Rio Grande Healthcare**, 284 S.W.3d at 862 (failure to include instructions on independent-contractor status of doctor and lost chance of survival in health-care-liability case was reversible error); **Texas Workers' Comp. Ins. Fund v. Mandlbauer**, 34 S.W.3d 909, 912 (Tex.2000) (failure to include definition of term not used in charge was not error); **Southwestern Bell Tel. Co. v. John Carlo Tex., Inc.**, 843 S.W.2d 470, 472 (Tex.1992) (failure to define "justification," a defensive issue, was reversible er-

ror); **Wilen v. Falkenstein**, 191 S.W.3d 791, 804 (Tex.App.—Fort Worth 2006, pet. denied) (failure to include "knowingly" in definition of trespass was not error); **Vinson & Elkins v. Moran**, 946 S.W.2d 381, 405–06 (Tex.App.—Houston [14th Dist.] 1997, writ dism'd) (failure to define "agreed" in contract case was not reversible error).

(2) Presumed harm.

(a) Multiple theories of liability.

[1] Valid & invalid theories—applicable. When a trial court submits a broad-form question with multiple theories of liability, some of which are invalid, the error is presumed to be harmful, and a new trial is required when the appellate court cannot determine whether the improperly submitted theories formed the sole basis for the jury's finding. **Crown Life Ins. v. Casteel**, 22 S.W.3d 378, 388 (Tex.2000); *see, e.g.*, **Romero v. KPH Consol., Inc.**, 166 S.W.3d 212, 226 (Tex.2005) (applied **Casteel**'s presumed-harm analysis to broad-form question that included factually unsupported claim); *see also* Tex. R. App. P. 44.1(a)(2) (reversal if error probably prevented appellant from presenting case to appellate court); **Ford Motor Co. v. Castillo**, 444 S.W.3d 616, 621 (Tex.2014) (**Casteel** issues do not arise in every situation in which jury has more than one legal theory to choose from when answering a single question; for **Casteel** issue to arise, at least one choice must be legally invalid). This type of error is often referred to as **Casteel** error. *See* **Thota**, 366 S.W.3d at 686. If the appellate court is reasonably certain that the jury was not significantly influenced by the improperly submitted theory, however, error is not necessarily reversible. **Romero**, 166 S.W.3d at 227–28.

Note

*A party does not have to specifically cite or reference **Casteel** to preserve an appellate court's right to apply the presumed-harm analysis, if applicable, to the disputed charge issues. **Thota**, 366 S.W.3d at 691. Instead, error is preserved by making timely and specific objections to the charge. Id. See "Specific," ch. 8-I, §4.3.2.*

---

[2] Defenses & inferential-rebuttal instructions—not applicable. Defenses and inferential-rebuttal instructions are not theories of liability; thus, **Casteel** does not apply to cases involving a single theory of liability in which improper defenses or inferential-rebuttal instructions have also been submitted. *See* **Thota**, 366 S.W.3d at 692–93; **Bed, Bath & Beyond, Inc. v. Urista**, 211 S.W.3d 753, 756–57 (Tex.2006). Instead, the court must apply a traditional harm analysis. **Thota**, 366 S.W.3d at 693; **Urista**, 211 S.W.3d at 757. See "Legal correctness of jury charge," ch. 8-I, §9.1.1.

(b) Single theory of liability but multiple claims in evidence. **Casteel**'s presumed-harm analysis also applies when there is a single theory of liability but the trial court submits a question that allows a finding of liability based on evidence that cannot support recovery. *E.g.*, **Benge v. Williams**, 548 S.W.3d 466, 475–76 (Tex.2018) (based on expert testimony, jury could have found that D was negligent for failing to disclose medical resident's involvement in surgery; **Casteel** applied because P did not assert claim for recovery based on nondisclosure); *see, e.g.*, **Texas Comm'n on Human Rights v. Morrison**, 381 S.W.3d 533, 536–37 (Tex.2012) (based on information discussed by attorneys and witnesses at trial, jury could have found that D retaliated against P by denying P a promotion; **Casteel** applied because claim based on denied promotion was jurisdictionally barred); **Columbia Rio Grande Healthcare**, 284 S.W.3d at 864–65 (based on evidence presented at trial, jury could have found hospital liable for negligence based on acts of pathologist; **Casteel** applied because pathologist was independent contractor for whom hospital could not be liable). In such a case, error is presumed to be harmful, and a new trial is required when the appellate court cannot determine whether the improper evidentiary claim formed the sole basis for the jury's finding. *See* **Benge**, 548 S.W.3d at 476; **Morrison**, 381 S.W.3d at 538.

Note

*To avoid a potential **Casteel** error, the trial court should allow a limiting instruction if requested by the defendant. See **Benge**, 548 S.W.3d at 476.*

(c) Multiple elements of damages. **Casteel**'s presumed-harm analysis also applies when a trial court submits a broad-form question that commingles valid elements of damages and invalid elements of damages for which there

was no evidence. *See* **Harris Cty. v. Smith**, 96 S.W.3d 230, 234 (Tex.2002). In such a case, the error is presumed to be harmful, and a new trial is required when the appellate court cannot determine whether the improperly submitted elements of damages formed the sole basis for the jury's finding. *See id.*

§9.2 Challenge findings on omitted elements. A party should treat the court's findings on omitted elements—either the trial court's express findings or the court of appeals' deemed findings—as jury findings. The findings, express or deemed, should be challenged with factual-sufficiency and legal-sufficiency points of error in both the motion for new trial and the brief on appeal. The court of appeals will review deemed findings by the factual-sufficiency test and the legal-sufficiency test. *See* **Crosbyton Seed Co. v. Mechura Farms**, 875 S.W.2d 353, 364 (Tex.App.—Corpus Christi 1994, no writ). The Supreme Court can review deemed findings only by the legal-sufficiency test. *See* **American Nat'l Pet. Co. v. Transcontinental Gas Pipe Line Corp.**, 798 S.W.2d 274, 278–79 (Tex.1990); **Crosbyton Seed**, 875 S.W.2d at 364 n.9.

§9.3 Jury notations. On appeal, the courts will not consider the jury's margin notations on the verdict regarding its findings. **Thomas v. Oldham**, 895 S.W.2d 352, 359 (Tex.1995). The jury's notes are not the jury's verdict. *Id.* at 360; **Wal-Mart Stores v. Alexander**, 868 S.W.2d 322, 328 (Tex.1993).

§9.4 Remedy for error. Depending on the error in the submission of the jury charge, if the party complaining of the judgment objected to the erroneous submission, the appropriate remedy for harmful charge error is remand for a new trial or rendition of judgment. If neither party objected to the erroneous submission, the party in whose favor the court rendered judgment is entitled to an affirmance; the other party has waived the opportunity to have the case submitted under the correct substantive law. *See* **State Farm Life Ins. v. Beaston**, 907 S.W.2d 430, 436–37 (Tex.1995); **Allen v. American Nat'l Ins.**, 380 S.W.2d 604, 609 (Tex.1964); *see, e.g.*, **Green Int'l v. Solis**, 951 S.W.2d 384, 389–90 (Tex.1997) (parties failed to object to jury question that did not segregate attorney fees). See "Neither party objected," ch. 8-I, §7.2.1.

1. Defective submission.

(1) Objection—remand. If a defective question, instruction, or definition was submitted over the objection of the party without the burden of proof and the jury returns a verdict in favor of the party with the burden of proof, the party who objected is entitled to a new trial (not rendition of judgment) if there is any evidence supporting the defective question. *See* **Glenn v. Leal**, 596 S.W.3d 769, 772 (Tex.2020); *see, e.g.*, **Transcontinental Ins. v. Crump**, 330 S.W.3d 211, 226–27 (Tex.2010) (remanding because of defective definition); **Ford Motor Co. v. Ledesma**, 242 S.W.3d 32, 43–44 (Tex.2007) (same); **Borneman v. Steak & Ale**, 22 S.W.3d 411, 413 (Tex.2000) (remanding because of defective question); **Minnesota Mining & Mfg. v. Nishika Ltd.**, 953 S.W.2d 733, 739 (Tex.1997) (remanding because damages question did not segregate between Ps); **Spencer v. Eagle Star Ins.**, 876 S.W.2d 154, 157 (Tex.1994) (remanding because of defective instruction). In some cases, the court does not mention whether the party objected to the defective charge. *E.g.*, **Arthur Andersen & Co. v. Perry Equip. Corp.**, 945 S.W.2d 812, 817 (Tex.1997) (remanding because of defective instruction).

Note

The Texas Pattern Jury Charge is not always correct. See, e.g., ***Ledesma****, 242 S.W.3d at 41 (erroneous definitions of "manufacturing defect" and "producing cause");* ***State v. Williams****, 940 S.W.2d 583, 584 (Tex.1996) (erroneous premises-liability charge). When a case is submitted on an erroneous charge from the PJC, the appellate court should reverse and remand, not render judgment.* ***Ledesma****, 242 S.W.3d at 45;* ***City of San Antonio v. Rodriguez****, 931 S.W.2d 535, 536 (Tex.1996).*

(2) No objection—affirm. If neither party objected to the submission of a defective question, the party in whose favor the verdict was returned is entitled to an affirmance. The other party waived the opportunity to have the case submitted under the correct substantive law. *E.g.*, **Green Int'l**, 951 S.W.2d at 389–90 (parties failed to object to question that did not segregate attorney fees); **Allen**, 380 S.W.2d at 609 (jury found against P under erroneous submission); *see* **Casteel-Diebolt v. Diebolt**, 912 S.W.2d 302, 304 (Tex.App.—Houston [14th Dist.] 1995, no writ) (when party agrees to charge as submitted, it cannot complain about contents of charge on appeal).

2. Incomplete submission.

(1) Objection—render. If an incomplete question was submitted over the objection of the party without the burden of proof and the jury returned a verdict for the party with the burden of proof, the party who objected is entitled to a rendition. *See* **State Dept. of Hwys. & Pub. Transp. v. Payne**, 838 S.W.2d 235, 241 (Tex.1992).

(2) No objection—affirm. If an incomplete question was submitted and neither party objected, the party in whose favor the court rendered judgment is entitled to an affirmance. *See* **State Farm**, 907 S.W.2d at 436–37; **Ramos v. Frito-Lay, Inc.**, 784 S.W.2d 667, 668 (Tex.1990).

J. Final Argument

§1. General

§1.1 Rules. Tex. R. Civ. P. 266, 269.

§1.2 Purpose. After all the evidence is introduced, the attorneys summarize their case to the jury and argue the effect of the evidence.

§1.3 Forms. **O'Connor's Texas Civil Forms**, FORMS 8J:1 et seq. (2020 ed.).

§1.4 Other references. Townsend, *Improper Jury Argument and Professionalism: Rethinking Standard Fire v. Reese*, 67 Tex.B.J. 448 (2004); Brown & Rondon, **Texas Rules of Evidence Handbook** (2021 ed.).

§2. Right to open & close final argument

§2.1 Plaintiff opens & closes. As a general rule, the plaintiff has the right to open and close the final argument. Tex. R. Civ. P. 266.

§2.2 Defendant opens & closes. There are two exceptions to the general rule that the plaintiff has the right to open and close the final argument.

1. **Burden of proof.** A defendant has the right to open and close the final argument if it had the burden of proof for the whole case. Tex. R. Civ. P. 269(a). To determine who has the burden of proof, see "Burden of proof," ch. 8-B, §2.2.1.

2. **Burden in the charge.** A defendant has the right to open and close the final argument if it has the burden on all matters submitted to the jury in the court's charge. Tex. R. Civ. P. 269(a); *see* **First State Bank v. Fatheree**, 847 S.W.2d 391, 397 (Tex.App.—Amarillo 1993, writ denied); **Horton v. Dental Capital Leasing Corp.**, 649 S.W.2d 655, 657 (Tex.App.—Texarkana 1983, no writ). Because TRCP 269 does not become applicable until after the evidence is closed and the charge is read to the jury, it does not affect the right to make the opening statement or introduce evidence. *See* **Amis v. Ashworth**, 802 S.W.2d 379, 383 (Tex.App.—Tyler 1990, orig. proceeding).

§2.3 Other considerations. When there are several parties that have separate claims or defenses, the court must determine the order of the argument. Tex. R. Civ. P. 269(a). The court must assign an intervenor a position in the argument according to the nature of its claim. Tex. R. Civ. P. 269(c).

§3. Management of argument

§3.1 Court's authority. The trial court has the duty to supervise the scope of jury argument and to limit arguments to the evidence. **City of Dallas v. Andrews**, 236 S.W.2d 609, 611 (Tex.1951); *see* **National Un. Fire Ins. v. Soto**, 819 S.W.2d 619, 624 (Tex.App.—El Paso 1991, writ denied). The court should control the argument, even without an objection by opposing counsel. Tex. R. Civ. P. 269(g); **Texas Empls. Ins. v. Guerrero**, 800 S.W.2d 859, 867–68 (Tex.App.—San Antonio 1990, writ denied).

§3.2 Time to argue. The court has discretion in allotting time for the arguments. **Aultman v. Dallas Ry. & Terminal Co.**, 260 S.W.2d 596, 600 (Tex.1953). To complain on appeal that the court did not permit sufficient time for argument, the party must show the following: (1) it objected, (2) it requested additional time, (3) the court denied the request, and (4) the error probably caused the rendition of an improper judgment. *See* Tex. R. App. P. 44.1(a)(1); **Aetna Cas. & Sur. Co. v. Shiflett**, 593 S.W.2d 768, 772 (Tex.App.—Texarkana 1979, writ ref'd n.r.e.).

§3.3 Nonjury trial. In a nonjury trial, the court has discretion in deciding whether it will hear oral arguments. **City of Corpus Christi v. Krause**, 584 S.W.2d 325, 330 (Tex.App.—Corpus Christi 1979, no writ).

§4. Limits of final argument

§4.1 Order of argument. See "Right to make first opening statement," ch. 8-B, §2.

1. **Concluding argument.** The party with the burden on the case or on all matters submitted to the jury (generally the plaintiff) is entitled to make the concluding argument. Tex. R. Civ. P. 269(a). The plaintiff should present its entire case in the concluding argument. Tex. R. Civ. P. 269(b).

2. Responsive argument. The other party (generally the defendant) is entitled to present its case to the jury.

3. Rebuttal argument. The plaintiff's rebuttal is limited to matters in reply to the defendant's argument. Tex. R. Civ. P. 269(b).

§4.2 What attorneys may argue. Attorneys have great latitude to indulge in "flights of oratory." **Southwestern Greyhound Lines, Inc. v. Dickson**, 236 S.W.2d 115, 119 (Tex.1951).

1. Questions of fact. Attorneys should argue the facts to the jury. Tex. R. Civ. P. 269(e); *see* **Circle Y v. Blevins**, 826 S.W.2d 753, 758 (Tex.App.—Texarkana 1992, writ denied). Attorneys should discuss the reasonableness of the evidence and its probative effect or lack of probative effect. **Texas Sand Co. v. Shield**, 381 S.W.2d 48, 57–58 (Tex.1964). Based on the evidence, attorneys may suggest the correct answer to the jury questions.

2. Inferences from facts. Attorneys may argue reasonable deductions and inferences from the facts. **Anderson v. Vinson Expl., Inc.**, 832 S.W.2d 657, 667 (Tex.App.—El Paso 1992, writ denied). The argument that the jury should "send a message" is permissible when it is based on the facts. **Schindler Elevator Corp. v. Anderson**, 78 S.W.3d 392, 405 (Tex.App.—Houston [14th Dist.] 2001, pet. granted, judgm't vacated w.r.m.), *disapproved on other grounds*, **Roberts v. Williamson**, 111 S.W.3d 113 (Tex.2003).

3. Fair criticism. Attorneys may make fair and reasonable criticism of a witness's testimony, may comment on bias or interest of parties and witnesses, and may discuss the reasonableness or unreasonableness of the evidence. **Dyer v. Hardin**, 323 S.W.2d 119, 127 (Tex.App.—Amarillo 1959, writ ref'd n.r.e.).

4. Effect of answer under evidence. Attorneys may argue the legal effect of the jury's answer only if the attorney qualifies it with a request to make the finding "under the evidence." *See* **Cavnar v. Quality Control Parking, Inc.**, 678 S.W.2d 548, 554–55 (Tex.App.—Houston [14th Dist.] 1984), *rev'd in part on other grounds*, 696 S.W.2d 549 (Tex.1985). But see "Legal effect of answer," ch. 8-J, §4.3.2.

5. Concluding argument. In the concluding argument, attorneys are permitted to reply only to the argument of the opposing party. Tex. R. Civ. P. 269(b).

§4.3 What attorneys may not argue. There are limits to an attorney's jury arguments. **Southwestern Greyhound Lines, Inc. v. Dickson**, 236 S.W.2d 115, 119 (Tex.1951).

1. Questions of law. Attorneys cannot argue questions of law to the jury. *See* Tex. R. Civ. P. 269(d). They must address arguments on the law to the court. *Id.* They cannot embellish or mischaracterize the charge given by the court. *See* **Timberwalk Apts., Partners v. Cain**, 972 S.W.2d 749, 755 (Tex.1998).

2. Legal effect of answer. Attorneys should not tell the jury the legal effect of its answers. **Magic Chef, Inc. v. Sibley**, 546 S.W.2d 851, 857 (Tex.App.—San Antonio 1977, writ ref'd n.r.e.); *see also* **Louisiana & Ark. Ry. v. Capps**, 766 S.W.2d 291, 295–96 (Tex.App.—Texarkana 1989, writ denied) (no reversible error if jury can determine effect of answers through exercise of ordinary intelligence). For an exception, see "Effect of answer under evidence," ch. 8-J, §4.2.4.

3. Outside the record. Attorneys must stay within the evidence presented at trial. Tex. R. Civ. P. 269(e); **In re Toyota Motor Sales, U.S.A., Inc.**, 407 S.W.3d 746, 761 (Tex.2013); *e.g.*, **Texas Sand Co. v. Shield**, 381 S.W.2d 48, 57–58 (Tex.1964) (P's attorney should not have argued that D's attorney also represented infamous criminal who was not a party to the suit); **Lone Star Ford, Inc. v. Carter**, 848 S.W.2d 850, 853 (Tex.App.—Houston [14th Dist.] 1993, no writ) (in suit for contract damages related to purchase of vehicle, attorney should not have argued about persons killed in unrelated car accidents).

4. Matters covered by order in limine. Attorneys should not comment on matters in violation of a court's order in limine. *See* **National Un. Fire Ins. v. Kwiatkowski**, 915 S.W.2d 662, 664 (Tex.App.—Houston [14th Dist.] 1996, no writ). See "Motion in Limine," ch. 5-E, §1 et seq.

5. Improper viewpoint. Even though attorneys may argue the "Golden Rule," they cannot ask the jury to consider the case from an improper viewpoint. *E.g.*, **World Wide Tire Co. v. Brown**, 644 S.W.2d 144, 145–46 (Tex.App.—Houston [14th Dist.] 1982, writ ref'd n.r.e.) (argument asked jury to award what would satisfy them as Ps, instead of basing award on the evidence).

6. Sidebar remarks. Attorneys cannot engage in sidebar remarks while the other attorney is making jury argument (or examining a witness). *See* **Davis v. Southern Pac. Transp.**, 585 S.W.2d 801, 803 (Tex.App.—Houston [1st Dist.] 1979, no writ). TRCP 269(f) requires the trial court to repress sidebar remarks. **Wal-Mart Stores v. Reece**, 32 S.W.3d 339, 347 (Tex.App.—Waco 2000), *rev'd on other grounds*, 81 S.W.3d 812 (Tex.2002).

7. Personal criticism. Attorneys should not criticize each other during jury argument. Tex. R. Civ. P. 269(e); **Living Ctrs. v. Peñalver**, 256 S.W.3d 678, 681 (Tex.2008); *see, e.g.*, **Circle Y v. Blevins**, 826 S.W.2d 753, 758–59 (Tex.App.—Texarkana 1992, writ denied) (improper to argue attorney manufactured evidence); **Beavers v. Northrop Worldwide Aircraft Servs.**, 821 S.W.2d 669, 680 (Tex.App.—Amarillo 1991, writ denied) (improper to argue attorney misrepresented facts); **American Petrofina, Inc. v. PPG Indus.**, 679 S.W.2d 740, 755 (Tex.App.—Fort Worth 1984, writ dism'd) (improper to attack attorney's integrity); *see also* **Amelia's Auto., Inc. v. Rodriguez**, 921 S.W.2d 767, 772–73 (Tex.App.—San Antonio 1996, no writ) (reversible error for P's attorney to mention during examination of witness that D's trial attorney had been disbarred for five years for filing frivolous lawsuit); **Byas v. State**, 906 S.W.2d 86, 87–88 (Tex.App.—Fort Worth 1995, pet. ref'd) (reversible error in criminal case for prosecutor to refer to defense counsel as "very slick attorney").

8. Passion or prejudice. Attorneys cannot make arguments that appeal to the jury's racial, religious, or other passions or prejudices. *See* **Dickson**, 236 S.W.2d at 119; *see, e.g.*, **Living Ctrs.**, 256 S.W.3d at 679 (reversed because P compared D's attorney's attempts to limit damages in suit against nursing home to Germany's WWII T-Four project, in which the elderly and infirm were experimented on and killed); **Texas Empls. Ins. v. Haywood**, 266 S.W.2d 856, 858 (Tex.1954) (reversed because D argued that P's witnesses were not as believable as white people); **Texas Empls. Ins. v. Jones**, 361 S.W.2d 725, 726–27 (Tex.App.—Waco 1962, writ ref'd n.r.e.) (reversed because, among other things, P referred to religion of D's witness in derogatory fashion).

9. Credibility of witness. Attorneys cannot argue that, in their opinion, a witness is credible or not. Tex. Disciplinary R. Prof'l Conduct 3.04(c)(3); *cf.* **Menefee v. State**, 614 S.W.2d 167, 168 (Tex.Crim.App.1981) (criminal case reversed because attorney argued "I don't believe I have ever seen anybody that I thought was any more honest than [witness] is.").

10. Invocation of privilege. Generally, attorneys cannot comment on the other party's invocation of a privilege. Tex. R. Evid. 513(a). See Brown & Rondon, **Texas Rules of Evidence Handbook**, Rule 513 (2021 ed.) (§A). For exceptions, see TRE 504(b)(2) and 513(c).

11. Failure to seek medical exam. When the defendant does not seek a medical examination of the plaintiff under TRCP 204, the plaintiff's attorney cannot comment that (1) the plaintiff was willing to submit to a medical examination, (2) the defendant had the right to such an examination, or (3) the defendant did not seek an examination. Tex. R. Civ. P. 204.3. See "Effect of no examination," ch. 6-J, §6.4.

§5. Types of error in argument

There are two types of error in jury argument—curable and incurable. **Otis Elevator Co. v. Wood**, 436 S.W.2d 324, 333 (Tex.1968); **Gannett Outdoor Co. v. Kubeczka**, 710 S.W.2d 79, 86 (Tex.App.—Houston [14th Dist.] 1986, no writ).

§5.1 Curable argument.

Most improper jury arguments can be cured of their harmful effects by an objection and the court's instruction to the jury to disregard what it has just heard. **Otis Elevator Co. v. Wood**, 436 S.W.2d 324, 333 (Tex.1968).

1. Preserving error. If an improper argument is curable, the party must object promptly. **Otis Elevator**, 436 S.W.2d at 333; *see* **Standard Fire Ins. v. Reese**, 584 S.W.2d 835, 840–41 (Tex.1979); **Isern v. Watson**, 942 S.W.2d 186, 198 (Tex.App.—Beaumont 1997, pet. denied). The party must make sure the trial court rules on the objection, either sustaining or overruling it. Tex. R. App. P. 33.1(a)(2). Without a ruling on the objection, no error is preserved. *See* **Marling v. Maillard**, 826 S.W.2d 735, 741 (Tex.App.—Houston [14th Dist.] 1992, no writ); *see, e.g.*, **Phillips v. Bramlett**, 288 S.W.3d 876, 883 (Tex.2009) (error waived because party did not request or obtain ruling on objection). When the trial court sustains the objection, to preserve error, the party should pursue an adverse ruling through a request to instruct the jury to disregard, a motion to strike, and a motion for mistrial. See "When jury hears inadmissible evidence," ch. 8-D, §6.7.

2. Examples of curable jury argument. The errors in the following arguments were not so egregious that they were preserved without an objection: • Suggesting fraud by arguing a close connection between the plaintiff's attorney and

the doctor who treated the plaintiff. **Standard Fire**, 584 S.W.2d at 840–41. • In medical-malpractice case, suggesting the jury needed to "send a message" to doctors in the county where the court was located by awarding a large sum of money. **Phillips**, 288 S.W.3d at 882–83. • Remarking that opposing counsel had been suspended. **Double Ace, Inc. v. Pope**, 190 S.W.3d 18, 30 (Tex.App.—Amarillo 2005, no pet.). • In products-liability case, referencing unrelated litigation such as Ford Pintos, asbestos, and Dalkon shields. **Schindler Elevator Corp. v. Anderson**, 78 S.W.3d 392, 406 (Tex.App.—Houston [14th Dist.] 2001, pet. granted, judgm't vacated w.r.m.), *disapproved on other grounds*, **Roberts v. Williamson**, 111 S.W.3d 113 (Tex.2003). • Mentioning insurance. **Isern**, 942 S.W.2d at 198. • Mentioning collateral benefits in personal-injury action. **Macias v. Ramos**, 917 S.W.2d 371, 375 (Tex.App.—San Antonio 1996, no writ). • Asking the jury to place itself in the shoes of the party. **Goswami v. Thetford**, 829 S.W.2d 317, 320–21 (Tex.App.—El Paso 1992, writ denied).

§5.2 Incurable argument. An incurable argument is an argument so prejudicial or inflammatory that an instruction to the jury to disregard it cannot eliminate its harm. **Otis Elevator Co. v. Wood**, 436 S.W.2d 324, 333 (Tex.1968); **Melendez v. Exxon Corp.**, 998 S.W.2d 266, 280 (Tex.App.—Houston [14th Dist.] 1999, no pet.); *see* **Phillips v. Bramlett**, 288 S.W.3d 876, 883 (Tex.2009) (argument must be so extreme that it could have persuaded juror of ordinary intelligence to agree to verdict contrary to what she otherwise would have agreed); **Living Ctrs. v. Peñalver**, 256 S.W.3d 678, 680–81 (Tex.2008) (argument by its nature, degree, and extent must be such error that instruction from court or retraction of argument could not remove its effects).

1. Preserving error. When the harmful effects of an incurable jury argument cannot be cured by an instruction to disregard, the failure to object at trial does not waive the error for appeal. **Otis Elevator**, 436 S.W.2d at 333; **Texas Empls. Ins. v. Guerrero**, 800 S.W.2d 859, 863 (Tex.App.—San Antonio 1990, writ denied); **Mapco, Inc. v. Jenkins**, 476 S.W.2d 55, 61–62 (Tex.App.—Amarillo 1971, writ ref'd n.r.e.). If the attorney did not object to the argument during trial, to preserve error the attorney must complain about the argument in a motion for new trial. Tex. R. Civ. P. 324(b)(5); **Clark v. Bres**, 217 S.W.3d 501, 509 & n.1 (Tex.App.—Houston [14th Dist.] 2006, pet. denied); **Austin v. Shampine**, 948 S.W.2d 900, 906 (Tex.App.—Texarkana 1997, no writ); *see* **Phillips**, 288 S.W.3d at 883.

Practice Tip

Always object to an improper jury argument. Never assume a jury argument is so prejudicial that no objection is necessary. If you do not object and the appellate court decides the error was curable, you will have waived the error.

---

2. Examples of incurable jury argument. The errors in the following arguments were so egregious that no objection was necessary to preserve them, and even when an objection was made and the court instructed the jury to disregard, the error was not cured: • In wrongful-death suit against nursing home, argument by plaintiff's attorney comparing defendant's attempts to limit damages to Germany's World War II T-Four project, in which the elderly and infirm were experimented on and killed. **Living Ctrs.**, 256 S.W.3d at 679. • Personal address by party to jury, without court's permission, thanking them in Spanish. **General Motors Corp. v. Iracheta**, 161 S.W.3d 462, 472 (Tex.2005) (D's attorney objected after argument). • Appeals to racial prejudice. *E.g.*, **Texas Empls. Ins. v. Haywood**, 266 S.W.2d 856, 858 (Tex.1954) (D argued that P's witnesses were not as believable as white people). • Argument by plaintiff's attorney that defendant's counsel had characterized plaintiff as a liar, fraud, cheat, and impostor. **Southwestern Greyhound Lines, Inc. v. Dickson**, 236 S.W.2d 115, 118–19 (Tex.1951). *But see* **Clark**, 217 S.W.3d at 510–11 (characterization of P as liar, fraud, thief, and cheat is not incurable argument when supported by facts or invited by P). • Charges that opposing counsel manufactured evidence. **Circle Y v. Blevins**, 826 S.W.2d 753, 758–59 (Tex.App.—Texarkana 1992, writ denied) (there was an objection). *But see* **Checker Bag Co. v. Washington**, 27 S.W.3d 625, 643–44 (Tex.App.—Waco 2000, pet. denied) (no error when P's attorney commented that D's attorney tampered with evidence; comment was quickly withdrawn and D's attorney should have asked for instruction to disregard). • Appeals to ethnic solidarity. **Guerrero**, 800 S.W.2d at 866. • Personal attacks on opposing counsel. **American Petrofina, Inc. v. PPG Indus.**, 679 S.W.2d 740, 755 (Tex.App.—Fort Worth 1984, writ dism'd) (party objected). • Appeals to religious prejudice. **Texas Empls. Ins. v. Jones**, 361 S.W.2d 725, 727 (Tex.App.—Waco 1962, writ ref'd n.r.e.).

§6. Review

§6.1 Record of argument. To show error in improper argument, the appellant must prove the improper argument was not invited or provoked. **Living Ctrs. v. Peñalver**, 256 S.W.3d 678, 680 (Tex.2008); **Standard Fire Ins. v. Reese**, 584

S.W.2d 835, 839 (Tex.1979); **Amigos Meat Distribs. v. Guzman**, 526 S.W.3d 511, 525 (Tex.App.—Houston [1st Dist.] 2017, pet. denied). To establish this, the appellant must provide the appellate court with the entire record—the jury's voir dire, the opening statements, the evidence, and the final argument. *See* **Phillips v. Bramlett**, 258 S.W.3d 158, 170 (Tex.App.—Amarillo 2007), *rev'd on other grounds*, 288 S.W.3d 876 (Tex.2009); **Central Nat'l Gulfbank v. Comdata Network, Inc.**, 773 S.W.2d 626, 628 (Tex.App.—Corpus Christi 1989, no writ); *see also* **General Motors Corp. v. Iracheta**, 90 S.W.3d 725, 744 (Tex.App.—San Antonio 2002) (although P's statement to jury in Spanish during closing argument was not transcribed, judge noted content of statement on record, and copy of interpretation was filed with court; court could review impropriety of statement), *rev'd on other grounds*, 161 S.W.3d 462 (Tex.2005).

§6.2 Test for reversible jury argument. In **Standard Fire Ins. v. Reese**, 584 S.W.2d 835 (Tex.1979), the Supreme Court outlined the elements of improper, reversible jury argument:

1. The attorney made an improper argument. **Standard Fire**, 584 S.W.2d at 839.

2. The improper argument was not invited or provoked. *Id.*

3. The error was preserved by proper trial predicate (objection, motion to instruct, motion to strike, motion for mistrial). *See id.*

4. The error was not curable by instruction, prompt withdrawal of the statement, or reprimand by the court. *Id.* An appellant is required to show the error was incurable only if the trial court gave a curative instruction or the appellant did not ask for one. An appellant is not required to show the error was incurable if the appellant's objection to the argument was overruled or its request for a curative instruction was denied. *See* **Lone Star Ford, Inc. v. Carter**, 848 S.W.2d 850, 854 (Tex.App.—Houston [14th Dist.] 1993, no writ).

5. The argument, by its nature, degree, and extent, constituted reversible error. **Standard Fire**, 584 S.W.2d at 839. Relevant factors include the duration of the argument, whether it was repeated or abandoned, and whether such errors were cumulative. *Id.* at 839–40; *see, e.g.*, **Clark Equip. Co. v. Pitner**, 923 S.W.2d 117, 125 (Tex.App.—Houston [14th Dist.] 1996, writ denied) (counsel's comment about other lawsuits was not harmful error because it was a single sentence and was not repeated); **Brown v. Hopkins**, 921 S.W.2d 306, 319 (Tex.App.—Corpus Christi 1996, no writ) (improper comments were isolated and were later corrected); **National Un. Fire Ins. v. Kwiatkowski**, 915 S.W.2d 662, 665 (Tex.App.—Houston [14th Dist.] 1996, no writ) (based on the trial's short duration and the number of prejudicial remarks, error was harmful).

6. The court must review the entire record to determine whether the argument had a probable effect on a material finding. **Standard Fire**, 584 S.W.2d at 840. The court reviews the evidence to determine whether the verdict was based on the evidence or the improper argument. **Texas Sand Co. v. Shield**, 381 S.W.2d 48, 58–59 (Tex.1964); **Wooten v. Southern Pac. Transp.**, 928 S.W.2d 76, 80 (Tex.App.—Houston [14th Dist.] 1995, no writ). If a juror of ordinary intelligence could have been persuaded by the improper argument to agree to a verdict contrary to what she would have agreed to without the argument, the error was harmful. **Wells v. HCA Health Servs.**, 806 S.W.2d 850, 854 (Tex.App.—Fort Worth 1990, writ denied); **Gannett Outdoor Co. v. Kubeczka**, 710 S.W.2d 79, 86–87 (Tex.App.—Houston [14th Dist.] 1986, no writ). To obtain a reversal for abuse of discretion, a complaining party must make an affirmative showing of injury. **Aetna Cas. & Sur. Co. v. Shiflett**, 593 S.W.2d 768, 772 (Tex.App.—Texarkana 1979, writ ref'd n.r.e.).

K. Verdict

§1. General

§1.1 Rules. Tex. R. Civ. P. 290 to 295.

§1.2 Forms. None.

§1.3 Other references. **O'Connor's Federal Rules * Civil Trials** (2021 ed.); **O'Connor's Texas Causes of Action** (2021 ed.).

§2. Jury deliberations

Jury deliberations begin when the jury retires to deliberate on the jury charge and end when the jury is discharged from its duties. *See* **Golden Eagle Archery, Inc. v. Jackson**, 24 S.W.3d 362, 371 (Tex.2000) (deliberations begin when jury retires to weigh evidence); **Archer Daniels Midland Co. v. Bohall**, 114 S.W.3d 42, 46 (Tex.App.—Eastland 2003, no pet.) (deliberations cannot continue when jury is discharged); **Durkay v. Madco Oil Co.**, 862 S.W.2d 14, 23 n.2 (Tex.App.—Corpus Christi 1993, writ denied) (same).

§2.1 Kept together. When the jury retires for deliberation, the jurors must be kept together under the charge of an officer until they agree on a verdict or are discharged by the court. Tex. R. Civ. P. 282. The court may permit the jurors to separate for the night, for meals, and for other proper purposes. *Id.*

§2.2 No recording. No person may use a device to produce or make any recording (audio, visual, still photograph) of a jury while it is deliberating. Tex. Civ. Prac. & Rem. Code §24.001 (civil jury); Tex. Code Crim. Proc. art. 36.215 (criminal jury).

§3. Verdict by fewer than 12 jurors

In district court, a jury consists of 12 persons. Tex. Const. art. 5, §13; Tex. R. Civ. P. 234. See "Jury panel," ch. 8-A, §8. A trial cannot proceed with fewer than 12 jurors unless a juror dies, a juror is constitutionally "disabled," or the parties agree. *See* Tex. Gov't Code §62.201 (parties can agree); **In re M.G.N.**, 441 S.W.3d 246, 248 (Tex.2014) (court can proceed with fewer than 12 jurors if juror is disabled, not if juror is disqualified; if court proceeds with fewer than 12 jurors and learns dismissed juror was not disabled, court must declare mistrial); *see, e.g.*, **Dempsey v. Beaumont Hosp., Inc.**, 38 S.W.3d 287, 289 (Tex.App.—Beaumont 2001, pet. dism'd) (discovery during deliberations that juror was ineligible to serve because of felony conviction required mistrial).

§3.1 Juror disabled.

1. Definition of disabled. The term "disabled," as used in Texas Constitution article 5, §13, encompasses physical or mental incapacity, and any other condition or circumstance rendering a person incapable of fulfilling the function of a juror. **McDaniel v. Yarbrough**, 898 S.W.2d 251, 252–53 (Tex.1995). The juror must become mentally incompetent or sick or suffer some other physical or mental incapacity to be considered disabled. *Id.*; *see* **Fiore v. Fiore**, 946 S.W.2d 436, 438 (Tex.App.—Fort Worth 1997, writ denied) (juror's prejudice against party does not render juror disabled, even if prejudice causes physical reaction); **City of Jersey Village v. Campbell**, 920 S.W.2d 694, 698 (Tex.App.—Houston [1st Dist.] 1996, writ denied) (juror's bias or prejudice is not the same as loss of mental faculties). If the death or serious illness of a family member renders a juror unable to discharge her responsibilities, the trial may proceed with fewer than 12 jurors. **Yanes v. Sowards**, 996 S.W.2d 849, 852 (Tex.1999); **Summit Mach. Tool Mfg. v. Great N. Ins.**, 997 S.W.2d 840, 852 (Tex.App.—Austin 1999, no pet.). Temporary detention due to inclement weather does not rise to the level of constitutional disability. **McDaniel**, 898 S.W.2d at 251–52.

2. Effect of disability. A 12-person jury may continue to deliberate even if as many as 3 jurors die or become disabled. Tex. Const. art. 5, §13; Tex. R. Civ. P. 292(a); *see* **In re M.G.N.**, 441 S.W.3d 246, 248 (Tex.2014); **Yanes**, 996 S.W.2d at 850. If only 9 of the original 12 remain, those remaining must render a unanimous verdict. *See* Tex. Const. art. 5, §13; Tex. R. Civ. P. 292(a). If 4 or more persons die or become disabled, the court must declare a mistrial unless the parties agree to continue.

§3.2 Agreement. The parties may agree to proceed with a jury composed of fewer than 12 jurors. Tex. Gov't Code §62.201.

§4. Jury verdict

§4.1 Most trials. A verdict may be rendered by the concurrence, on each answer made, of the same 10 or more members of a 12-person jury (or 5 or more members of a 6-person jury). Tex. R. Civ. P. 292(a); *see* Tex. R. Civ. P. 226a, §III, ¶11; **In re Commitment of Jones**, ___ S.W.3d ___, 2020 WL 3393468 (Tex.2020) (No. 19-0260; 6-19-20); **Palmer Well Servs. v. Mack Trucks, Inc.**, 776 S.W.2d 575, 576 n.2 (Tex.1989). If the same 10 jurors do not agree on all the answers, the court may require the jury to continue its deliberations. *See* **Gonzalez v. Gutierrez**, 694 S.W.2d 384, 390 (Tex.App.—San Antonio 1985, no writ). The plaintiff must prove most issues by a preponderance of the evidence, which means the greater weight and degree of credible evidence. **Upjohn Co. v. Freeman**, 847 S.W.2d 589, 591 (Tex.App.—Dallas 1992, no writ).

§4.2 Exemplary-damages cases. For exemplary-damages cases, all 12 jurors must agree on both Phase 1 issues (liability and actual damages) and Phase 2 issues (amount of exemplary damages). *See* Tex. Civ. Prac. & Rem. Code §41.003(d); Tex. R. Civ. P. 292(b). Thus, all jurors must unanimously find the following: (1) liability on at least one claim for actual damages that will support an award of exemplary damages, (2) any additional conduct, such as fraud, malice, or gross negligence, required for an award of exemplary damages, and (3) the amount of exemplary damages. Tex. R. Civ. P. 226a, §III; *see* Tex. Civ. Prac. & Rem. Code §41.003(a); Tex. R. Civ. P. 292(b). The jury is not required to be unanimous in finding the amount of actual damages. Tex. R. Civ. P. 226a, §III. For the trial procedure and burden of proof for the Phase 1 and Phase 2 issues, see "Trial procedure," ch. 5-I, §5.3; "Plaintiff's burden," ch. 5-I, §5.4; "Trial procedure," **O'Connor's Texas Causes of Action**, ch. 42-B, §9.2 (2021 ed.).

§5. Objections to verdict

§5.1 Incomplete or unresponsive verdict. If the jury's verdict is incomplete or unresponsive to questions in the charge, the party who would benefit from responses to the unanswered questions must object before the court discharges the jury; otherwise, error is waived. *See* **Fleet v. Fleet**, 711 S.W.2d 1, 3 (Tex.1986). The trial court can order the jury to deliberate further and reform the verdict. Tex. R. Civ. P. 295. If the court orders further deliberations, it must inform the jury in writing in open court of the nature of the incompleteness or unresponsiveness and give the jury additional instructions as necessary. *Id.* If the jury cannot agree on answers and deliver a complete verdict, the court should declare a mistrial; it cannot render a judgment containing unanswered questions unless the questions are immaterial. **Fleet**, 711 S.W.2d at 2–3; *see* **In re Commitment of Jones**, ___ S.W.3d ___, 2020 WL 3393468 (Tex.2020) (No. 19-0260; 6-19-20). See "Immaterial jury finding," ch. 9-B, §3.4.

§5.2 Conflict in jury's answers. If the jury's answers conflict, the parties should object to the conflict before the court discharges the jury. **USAA Tex. Lloyds Co. v. Menchaca**, 545 S.W.3d 479, 526 (Tex.2018) (plurality op., Green, Hecht, Guzman, Brown, JJ.). To resolve the conflict, the trial court can order the jury to deliberate further and reform the verdict. Tex. R. Civ. P. 295; *see* **Menchaca**, 545 S.W.3d at 527 (plurality op., Green, Hecht, Guzman, Brown, JJ.). If the court orders further deliberations, it must inform the jury in writing in open court of the nature of the conflict and give the jury additional instructions as necessary. Tex. R. Civ. P. 295; **Menchaca**, 545 S.W.3d at 527. If there is no objection, the parties maintain that there is no conflict, and the plaintiff submitted its claims in a way that cannot support recovery in light of the jury's answers, the court can enter judgment for the defendant without ordering reformation. *See* **Menchaca**, 545 S.W.3d at 527. Even if a party does not object to the conflict before the jury is discharged, it can still preserve error by raising the issue in a postverdict motion, such as a motion to disregard, a motion for JNOV, or a motion for new trial. *Id.* at 530–31 (plurality op., Green, Hecht, Guzman, Brown, JJ.).

Note

*In **Menchaca**, the Supreme Court issued a plurality opinion holding that, under the particular circumstances of the case, the parties' failure to object to conflicting jury answers did not preclude the appellate court from considering the conflict and determining whether the verdict supported the trial court's judgment. See **Menchaca**, 545 S.W.3d at 531 (plurality op., Green, Hecht, Guzman, Brown, JJ.). See "Fatal conflict in jury answers," ch. 8-K, §9.3. Neither party objected in the trial court because they both believed they were entitled to judgment in their favor based on the jury's answers. **Menchaca**,*

545 S.W.3d at 531. Three justices disagreed with the plurality, extending the rule for incomplete verdicts and concluding that a party must always object to conflicting jury answers before the jury is discharged or else the error is not preserved for appellate review. ***Menchaca****, 545 S.W.3d at 519–20; see also* ***Columbia Med. Ctr. v. Bush****, 122 S.W.3d 835, 861 (Tex.App.—Fort Worth 2003, pet. denied) (conflict in jury answers waived because party did not object before jury was discharged);* ***Norwest Mortg. v. Salinas****, 999 S.W.2d 846, 865 (Tex.App.—Corpus Christi 1999, pet. denied) (same).*

§6. Request to poll jury

§6.1 Request. As soon as the verdict is returned, the parties should examine it for clerical and other errors and promptly ask the court to poll the jury before it is discharged. **Pate v. Texline Feed Mills, Inc.**, 689 S.W.2d 238, 243 (Tex.App.—Amarillo 1985, writ ref'd n.r.e.); *see also* Tex. R. Civ. P. 293 (if verdict is in proper form, no juror objects to its accuracy, and neither party requests poll, verdict shall be entered in court's minutes). The parties should always ask for a poll when the jury returns less than a unanimous verdict to determine whether the same jurors agreed on their answers to each question. *See* **Gonzalez v. Gutierrez**, 694 S.W.2d 384, 390–91 (Tex.App.—San Antonio 1985, no writ). Any party has the right to poll the jury. Tex. R. Civ. P. 294. The right to poll the jury can be waived and must be requested to be invoked. **Suggs v. Fitch**, 64 S.W.3d 658, 660 (Tex.App.—Texarkana 2001, no pet.). To preserve error, the party must secure a ruling refusing to poll. *E.g.*, **Greater Houston Transp. Co. v. Zrubeck**, 850 S.W.2d 579, 585 (Tex.App.—Corpus Christi 1993, writ denied) (error waived when court never ruled it would not poll and party did not object or request ruling).

§6.2 Procedure. To poll the jury, the court should read each question and the corresponding answer, call the name of each juror, and ask if that is the verdict of that juror. Tex. R. Civ. P. 294; *see also* **J.D. Abrams, Inc. v. McIver**, 966 S.W.2d 87, 95–96 (Tex.App.—Houston [1st Dist.] 1998, pet. denied) (judge did not read questions and answers, only asked "whether this was his/her answer to the questions"; error waived because party did not object).

§7. Discharging jury

Once the court receives the jury verdict, the court will discharge the jury. Once it discharges the jury, it cannot recall the jury for additional deliberations. **Archer Daniels Midland Co. v. Bohall**, 114 S.W.3d 42, 46–47 (Tex.App.—Eastland 2003, no pet.); **Branham v. Brown**, 925 S.W.2d 365, 368 (Tex.App.—Houston [1st Dist.] 1996, no writ). After the court discharges the jury, the bailiff will promptly destroy all juror notes. Tex. R. Civ. P. 226a, §II(10).

Note

The U.S. Supreme Court has held that, in certain circumstances, a court can rescind a jury-discharge order and recall the jury for further deliberations to correct an error in the jury's verdict. ***Dietz v. Bouldin****, __ U.S. __, 136 S.Ct. 1885, 1890 (2016). Rescinding a discharge order does not violate any federal rule or statute. Id. at __, 136 S.Ct. at 1893. See "Recall jury after discharge,"* ***O'Connor's Federal Rules * Civil Trials****, ch. 8-I, §9 (2021 ed.).*

§8. Postverdict contact with jurors

Communication between parties, counsel, and discharged jurors can be a valuable experience for all concerned. **Commission for Lawyer Discipline v. Benton**, 980 S.W.2d 425, 433 (Tex.1998). In particular, an attorney who has lost the case may ask the jurors why they were not persuaded and thus learn something that will help her in the future. *Id.* An attorney's postverdict contact with jurors is limited by the Texas Disciplinary Rules of Professional Conduct. Rule 3.06(d) prohibits attorneys connected with the case from asking "questions of or mak[ing] comments to a member of that jury that are calculated merely to harass or embarrass the juror or to influence his actions in future jury service." Tex. Disciplinary R. Prof'l Conduct 3.06(d). The Supreme Court has limited Rule 3.06(d) by striking the term "embarrass" and narrowing the term "harass" by defining it to include four elements: (1) a course of conduct, (2) directed at a specific person or persons, (3) causing or tending to cause substantial distress, and (4) having no legitimate purpose. **Benton**, 980 S.W.2d at 439–40.

§9. Review

§9.1 Disregard jury findings. For a discussion of how to ask the court to disregard some or all of the jury findings, see "Motion for JNOV," ch. 9-B, §1 et seq.

§9.2 Juror misconduct. For a discussion of how to ask the court for a new trial based on jury misconduct, see "MNT based on jury or bailiff misconduct," ch. 10-B, §14.

§9.3 Fatal conflict in jury answers. A party can argue on appeal that the jury's answers fatally conflict and thus that the verdict should be reversed. *See* **Arvizu v. Estate of Puckett**, 364 S.W.3d 273, 275 (Tex.2012). In reviewing the jury's answers for fatal conflict, the court must first determine whether the jury's findings create a conflict about the same material fact. **USAA Tex. Lloyds Co. v. Menchaca**, 545 S.W.3d 479, 508 (Tex.2018) (plurality op., Boyd, Hecht, Lehrmann, Devine, JJ.); **Arvizu**, 364 S.W.3d at 275. The court must reconcile any conflict in the jury's answers if reasonably possible to do so in light of the pleadings and evidence, the manner of submission, and other findings. **Menchaca**, 545 S.W.3d at 509 (plurality op., Boyd, Hecht, Lehrmann, Devine, JJ.); **Felton v. Lovett**, 388 S.W.3d 656, 663 (Tex.2012); *see* **Arvizu**, 364 S.W.3d at 276. If the court cannot reconcile the jury's answers, it must determine whether the conflict is fatal to the entry of judgment. **Arvizu**, 364 S.W.3d at 276. To determine whether the conflict is fatal, the court must consider the jury's answers by disregarding each conflicting answer one at a time while taking into consideration the rest of the verdict. *Id.* If, when considered in this way, one of the conflicting findings requires entry of a judgment that is different from that which the court has entered (e.g., one of conflicting answers would require judgment for the plaintiff and the other would require judgment for the defendant), then the answers fatally conflict. *E.g., id.* at 276–77 (conflict was not fatal because D would lose no matter which conflicting answer was disregarded); *see* **Menchaca**, 545 S.W.3d at 509.

Chapter 9. The Judgment

A. Motion for Judgment

§1. General

§1.1 Rules. Tex. R. Civ. P. 300 to 316.

§1.2 Purpose. The motion for judgment is a request for the court to sign the draft of the judgment prepared by the movant.

§1.3 Forms. **O'Connor's Texas Civil Forms**, FORMS 9A:1 et seq. (2020 ed.).

§1.4 Other references. **O'Connor's Texas Causes of Action** (2021 ed.).

§2. Motion

§2.1 Motion for judgment on the verdict. A motion for judgment should include a proposed judgment for the court to sign.

1. Winner. A party who won the case and wants a judgment on the jury's verdict (or in a nonjury trial, on the decision announced by the court) should file a motion for judgment. See **O'Connor's Texas Civil Forms**, FORM 9A:1 (2020 ed.). If the party files a motion for judgment and the court enters the judgment, the party cannot later attack the judgment unless it has reserved the right to do so. *See* **Hooks v. Samson Lone Star, L.P.**, 457 S.W.3d 52, 67 (Tex.2015); **Casu v. Marathon Ref. Co.**, 896 S.W.2d 388, 391–92 (Tex.App.—Houston [1st Dist.] 1995, writ denied); **Ashley v. North Houston Pole Line, L.P.**, No. 14-17-00870-CV, 2019 WL 6606391 (Tex.App.—Houston [14th Dist.] 2019, no pet.) (memo op.; 12-5-19). See "On the verdict," ch. 9-A, §2.1.2(1).

(1) Damages & interest. If the fact-finder found that one of the parties is entitled to damages, the motion should request damages and interest (prejudgment and postjudgment). See "Damages," ch. 9-C, §4.4; "Prejudgment interest," ch. 9-C, §4.5; "Postjudgment interest," ch. 9-C, §4.6.

(2) Attorney fees. The motion should request attorney fees when appropriate. See "Attorney fees from adverse party," ch. 1-H, §10.

(3) Costs. The motion should make a general request for costs. Itemization is not necessary. The court clerk will prepare a bill of costs. See "Costs," ch. 9-C, §4.9.

(4) Other relief. The motion should request any other relief appropriate to the case.

2. Loser. A party who lost the case often wants the court to sign a judgment so it can begin the appeal process. See **O'Connor's Texas Civil Forms**, FORM 9A:2 (2020 ed.).

(1) On the verdict. The losing party can ask the court to render a judgment on the verdict (or, in a nonjury trial, on the decision announced by the court) without losing the right to challenge the judgment on appeal. To preserve the right to appeal, the motion for judgment should state that the party (1) disagrees with the content and result of the proposed judgment, (2) agrees only to the form of the proposed judgment, and (3) plans to challenge the judgment on appeal. *See* **First Nat'l Bank v. Fojtik**, 775 S.W.2d 632, 633 (Tex.1989); **Casu**, 896 S.W.2d at 390. If the losing party asks the court to render a judgment without reserving the right to appeal, the party cannot complain about the judgment on appeal. **Casu**, 896 S.W.2d at 389–90; *see also* **Hardy v. Mann Frankfort Stein & Lipp Advisors, Inc.**, 263 S.W.3d 232, 252 (Tex.App.—Houston [1st Dist.] 2007) (presenting draft J requesting that trial court enter written J that conforms to its earlier oral decision does not waive right to complain about judgment on appeal), *rev'd on other grounds sub nom.* **Mann Frankfort Stein & Lipp Advisors, Inc. v. Fielding**, 289 S.W.3d 844 (Tex.2009). *But see* **Harry v. University of Tex. Sys.**, 878 S.W.2d 342, 344 (Tex.App.—El Paso 1994, no writ) (party moving for J on the verdict waives its right to complain about sufficiency of evidence on appeal but does not waive other complaints such as jury-charge error). If the losing party asks the court to render judgment and reserves the right to appeal, the party cannot take a position on appeal that is inconsistent with that judgment. *See* **Hooks**, 457 S.W.3d at 67; **Casu**, 896 S.W.2d at 391; *see, e.g.*, **Litton Indus. Prods. v. Gammage**, 668 S.W.2d 319, 321–22 (Tex.1984) (D moved for J on amount of actual damages; on appeal, D could attack trebling of damages under DTPA

but could not attack sufficiency of evidence supporting actual damages).

Note

The best practice is for the movant to include the reservation of the right to appeal in the motion for judgment. See ***Fojtik****, 775 S.W.2d at 633. In one case, however, the movant was able to reserve its right to appeal by raising an objection before the motion for judgment was filed. See, e.g.,* ***Chappell Hill Bank v. Lane Bank Equip. Co.****, 38 S.W.3d 237, 247 (Tex.App.—Texarkana 2001, pet. denied) (objection made in oral argument before motion for J was filed preserved right to appeal).*

(2) To limit damages. If the defendant is entitled to limit damages, the motion should state this. Damages are limited under a number of statutes. *See, e.g.*, Tex. Bus. & Com. Code §17.50(a), (b)(1) (in DTPA suits, P is limited to economic damages unless D acted knowingly or intentionally); Tex. Civ. Prac. & Rem. Code §41.008(b) (limit on exemplary-damages awards). See "Remedies," **O'Connor's Texas Causes of Action**, ch. 8, §3 (2021 ed.); "Damages Act cap," **O'Connor's Texas Causes of Action**, ch. 42-B, §7.1 (2021 ed.).

(3) To force election of remedies. When a plaintiff prevails on two theories of recovery for the same injury, the defendant should ask the trial court to require the plaintiff to elect damages because the plaintiff is not entitled to a double recovery. *E.g.*, **Waite Hill Servs. v. World Class Metal Works, Inc.**, 959 S.W.2d 182, 184 (Tex.1998) (before rendition of J, D requested that trial court require P to elect its remedy).

§2.2 Motion for judgment contrary to verdict. A party who seeks a judgment contrary to the jury's verdict should prepare a motion for judgment notwithstanding the verdict. See "Motion for JNOV," ch. 9-B, §1 et seq.

§2.3 Motion for judgment on agreement. A party who wants the court to sign a judgment on a settlement agreement should file a motion for judgment on the agreement and attach a verified copy of the agreement. See "Agreements between attorneys—Rule 11," ch. 1-H, §9. A judgment rendered on the parties' agreement cures all nonjurisdictional defects. **Mailhot v. Mailhot**, 124 S.W.3d 775, 777 (Tex.App.—Houston [1st Dist.] 2003, no pet.).

§3. Draft of judgment

The trial court will often ask the attorneys to prepare the judgment to reflect its decision, and it will sign the judgment at a later date. In most cases, the prevailing party will prepare a draft of the judgment for the trial court's signature and send copies to the other parties. Any party, however, may prepare a draft of the judgment. Tex. R. Civ. P. 305.

§4. Motion to sever, dismiss, or nonsuit

If the court renders a judgment on only part of the lawsuit, a party may file a motion to sever, dismiss, or nonsuit the remaining claims, making the judgment final and appealable. See "What judgments are final," ch. 9-C, §6.3.

§5. Response

Filing a response to a motion for judgment is generally not necessary. However, if the motion asks for relief to which the party is not entitled, the other party should file a response objecting to the relief. *See, e.g.*, **Wal-Mart Stores v. McKenzie**, 997 S.W.2d 278, 279–80 (Tex.1999) (D preserved error by objecting in its response to damages sought in motion for J). See **O'Connor's Texas Civil Forms**, FORM 9A:3 (2020 ed.).

§6. Hearing

A hearing on the motion for judgment is not necessary. If a party wants a hearing, it should request one in writing.

§7. Preservation of error

The motion for judgment preserves error in case the trial court modifies or rejects the proposed judgment. *See, e.g.*, **Emerson v. Tunnell**, 793 S.W.2d 947, 947–48 (Tex.1990) (P's motion for J on verdict for $238,000 preserved error when trial court signed J for only $208,284); **Texas Commerce Bank Reagan v. Lebco Constructors, Inc.**, 865 S.W.2d 68, 81 (Tex.App.—Corpus Christi 1993, writ denied) (Ps' proposed final J that included another party as jointly entitled to J preserved error

when trial court did not include that party in J). The trial court does not need to overrule a motion for judgment; the motion is overruled if the trial court enters a judgment different from the one proposed by the motion. *See, e.g.*, **Salinas v. Rafati**, 948 S.W.2d 286, 288 (Tex.1997) (when court granted motion to disregard jury findings, it automatically overruled motion for J on findings, thus preserving error); *see also* Tex. R. App. P. 33.1(a)(2)(A) (trial court may rule on motion expressly or implicitly).

B. Motion for JNOV

§1. General

§1.1 Rule. Tex. R. Civ. P. 301.

§1.2 Purpose. A motion for judgment notwithstanding the verdict (JNOV) and a motion to disregard a jury finding both ask the trial court to disregard all or some of the jury's findings on the jury questions and to render judgment for the movant. The only distinction between the two motions is that the motion for JNOV asks the trial court to disregard all the jury findings and sign a judgment contrary to those findings; the motion to disregard asks the trial court to disregard only some of the jury findings and sign a judgment on the remaining ones. *See* **Teston v. Miller**, 349 S.W.2d 296, 299 (Tex.App.—Beaumont 1961, writ ref'd n.r.e.). Motions for JNOV and motions to disregard preserve the "no evidence" and "as a matter of law" points for appeal. In this subchapter, both motions will be referred to as a motion for JNOV.

§1.3 Forms. O'Connor's Texas Civil Forms, FORMS 9B:1 et seq. (2020 ed.).

§1.4 Other references. O'Connor's Texas Civil Appeals (2020 ed.).

§2. Motion

§2.1 Written motion. The trial court cannot disregard a material jury finding on its own initiative—it can do so only on written motion. Tex. R. Civ. P. 301; **Law Offices of Windle Turley, P.C. v. French**, 140 S.W.3d 407, 414 (Tex.App.—Fort Worth 2004, no pet.); **Rush v. Barrios**, 56 S.W.3d 88, 93 (Tex.App.—Houston [14th Dist.] 2001, pet. denied); **Lamb v. Franklin**, 976 S.W.2d 339, 343 (Tex.App.—Amarillo 1998, no pet.). See **O'Connor's Texas Civil Forms**, FORMS 9B:1, 9B:3 (2020 ed.).

§2.2 Specific reasons. The motion must specifically identify the findings to be disregarded, present the reasons and authority for disregarding them, and request that the court sign either a judgment on the remaining findings or, if all the findings are to be disregarded, a judgment contrary to all the findings. **Dupree v. Piggly Wiggly Shop Rite Foods, Inc.**, 542 S.W.2d 882, 892 (Tex.App.—Corpus Christi 1976, writ ref'd n.r.e.), *disapproved on other grounds*, **Fifth Club, Inc. v. Ramirez**, 196 S.W.3d 788 (Tex.2006). At least two courts have held that once a party files a motion for JNOV, the court can grant a JNOV on a ground not included in the motion. *See* **$281,420.00 in U.S. Currency v. State**, 312 S.W.3d 586, 596 (Tex.App.—Corpus Christi 2008) (memo op.), *rev'd on other grounds*, 312 S.W.3d 547 (Tex.2010); *see, e.g.*, **McDade v. Texas Commerce Bank**, 822 S.W.2d 713, 717–18 (Tex.App.—Houston [1st Dist.] 1991, writ denied) (D's motion asserted there was no evidence to support two jury answers; court granted JNOV on statute of limitations).

§2.3 Attach proposed judgment. The party should attach a draft of the proposed judgment to the motion for JNOV. See **O'Connor's Texas Civil Forms**, FORM 9C:1 (2020 ed.).

§2.4 Effect of motion on plenary power & appellate deadlines. See "Motion for JNOV," ch. 9-C, §6.4.1(1)(c)[3]; "Changing judgment during plenary power," ch. 9-C, §7.1.

§3. Grounds for JNOV

A JNOV is proper only when a directed verdict would have been proper. Tex. R. Civ. P. 301; **Fort Bend Cty. Drainage Dist. v. Sbrusch**, 818 S.W.2d 392, 394 (Tex.1991); **Wal-Mart Stores v. Bolado**, 54 S.W.3d 837, 841 (Tex.App.—Corpus Christi 2001, no pet.). See "Grounds for directed verdict," ch. 8-G, §4. A motion for JNOV is proper in the following situations:

§3.1 No evidence. The court should grant a motion for JNOV if there is no evidence to support one or more of the jury findings on issues necessary to liability. **Tiller v. McLure**, 121 S.W.3d 709, 713 (Tex.2003); **Brown v. Bank of Galveston**, 963 S.W.2d 511, 513 (Tex.1998), *overruled on other grounds*, **Ford Motor Co. v. Ledesma**, 242 S.W.3d 32 (Tex.2007); *see* **Wal-Mart Stores v. Miller**, 102 S.W.3d 706, 709 (Tex.2003); **Lesikar v. Rappeport**, 33 S.W.3d 282, 308 (Tex.App.—Texarkana 2000, pet. denied). When the evidence is no more than a scintilla, it is no evidence. **Tabrizi v. Daz-Rez Corp.**, 153 S.W.3d 63, 66 (Tex.App.—San Antonio 2004, no pet.); **Rush v. Barrios**, 56 S.W.3d 88, 94–95 (Tex.App.—Houston [14th Dist.] 2001, pet. denied); *see also* **Ford Motor Co. v. Ridgway**, 135 S.W.3d 598, 601 (Tex.2004) (evidence is only a scintilla if it creates no more than a surmise or suspicion of its existence).

§3.2 Conclusive evidence. The court should grant a motion for JNOV if the evidence is conclusive and one party is entitled to recover as a matter of law. *E.g.*, **TRT Dev. Co.-KC v. Meyers**, 15 S.W.3d 281, 285 (Tex.App.—Corpus Christi 2000, no pet.) (JNOV was proper because allegedly slanderous statements were protected by qualified privilege); **Gallas v. Car Biz, Inc.**, 914 S.W.2d 592, 593 (Tex.App.—Dallas 1995, writ denied) (JNOV was proper in suit for declaration of ownership and conversion because underlying sale was void); **John Masek Corp. v. Davis**, 848 S.W.2d 170, 173–74 (Tex.App.—Houston [1st Dist.] 1992, writ denied) (JNOV was proper because D had right to unilaterally liquidate business and Ps could not sue for liquidation). That is, a motion for JNOV is proper if the evidence established an issue as a matter of law and the jury was not free to make contrary findings. **Gallas**, 914 S.W.2d at 593; **John Masek Corp.**, 848 S.W.2d at 173.

Practice Tip

In a motion for JNOV, never argue that the evidence was factually insufficient. A motion for JNOV will not preserve a complaint that the evidence was factually insufficient. ***Kratz v. Exxon Corp.****, 890 S.W.2d 899, 902 (Tex.App.—El Paso 1994, no writ). To preserve a complaint that the evidence was factually insufficient, the party must file a motion for new trial. See "MNT to challenge the evidence," ch. 10-B, §13.*

§3.3 Legal bar. The court should grant a motion for JNOV when a legal principle prevents a party from prevailing on its claim or defense even if that party proves all the allegations in its pleadings. **United Parcel Serv. v. Tasdemiroglu**, 25 S.W.3d 914, 916 n.4 (Tex.App.—Houston [14th Dist.] 2000, pet. denied); **John Masek Corp. v. Davis**, 848 S.W.2d 170, 173 (Tex.App.—Houston [1st Dist.] 1992, writ denied); *see, e.g.*, **Rush v. Barrios**, 56 S.W.3d 88, 94 (Tex.App.—Houston [14th Dist.] 2001, pet. denied) (JNOV was proper, based on equity, to reduce fee of discharged attorney); **Franklin Nat'l Bank v. Boser**, 972 S.W.2d 98, 106 (Tex.App.—Texarkana 1998, pet. denied) (JNOV should have been granted because D had a perfected security interest); **Farias v. Laredo Nat'l Bank**, 985 S.W.2d 465, 473–74 (Tex.App.—San Antonio 1997, pet. denied) (JNOV should have been granted because limitations expired).

§3.4 Immaterial jury finding. The trial court may, without a motion, disregard the finding on an immaterial jury question. *See* **W&T Offshore, Inc. v. Fredieu**, ___ S.W.3d ___, 2020 WL 3240869 (Tex.2020) (No. 18-1134; 6-5-20); **Hall v. Hubco, Inc.**, 292 S.W.3d 22, 27 (Tex.App.—Houston [14th Dist.] 2006, pet. denied); **Lesikar v. Rappeport**, 33 S.W.3d 282, 318 (Tex.App.—Texarkana 2000, pet. denied); **Farias v. Laredo Nat'l Bank**, 985 S.W.2d 465, 470 (Tex.App.—San Antonio 1997, pet. denied). A jury finding is immaterial if (1) the question should not have been submitted, (2) the question was properly submitted but was made immaterial by other findings, (3) the finding can be found elsewhere in the verdict, or (4) the finding cannot change the verdict's effect. **USAA Tex. Lloyds Co. v. Menchaca**, 545 S.W.3d 479, 506 (Tex.2018) (#1, 2); **BP Am. Prod. v. Red Deer Res.**, 526 S.W.3d 389, 402 (Tex.2017) (#3, 4); **City of Brownsville v. Alvarado**, 897 S.W.2d 750, 752 (Tex.1995) (#3, 4); **Spencer v. Eagle Star Ins.**, 876 S.W.2d 154, 157 (Tex.1994) (#1, 2); *see* **Quick v. City of Austin**, 7 S.W.3d 109, 116 (Tex.1998) (court may disregard as immaterial a jury's finding on a question of law). But a defective jury question does not make the jury's answer immaterial. **Menchaca**, 545 S.W.3d at 506; *see* **Spencer**, 876 S.W.2d at 157. Although a party is not required to challenge an immaterial jury finding, it should bring the error to the court's attention in some postverdict motion (i.e., a motion for JNOV, a motion to disregard immaterial finding, or a motion for new trial). *See* **BP Am.**, 526 S.W.3d at 402; *see, e.g.*, **United Scaffolding, Inc. v. Levine**, 537 S.W.3d 463, 481–82 (Tex.2017) (D preserved error by arguing for first time in its motion for JNOV that trial court improperly submitted general-negligence question); **City of Dallas v. Moreau**, 718 S.W.2d 776, 779 (Tex.App.—Corpus Christi 1986, writ ref'd n.r.e.) (court should have granted motion for JNOV because governmental immunity made jury's answers immaterial). If the court disregards an immaterial jury finding and signs a judgment based on the remaining findings, the judgment is not considered a JNOV. **Anderson, Greenwood & Co. v. Martin**, 44 S.W.3d 200, 216 (Tex.App.—Houston [14th Dist.] 2001, pet. denied).

§4. Deadlines

§4.1 To file motion. TRCP 301 does not state a filing deadline for a motion for JNOV. **Kirschberg v. Lowe**, 974 S.W.2d 844, 846 (Tex.App.—San Antonio 1998, no pet.). For years, courts of appeals have disagreed about the deadline for a motion for JNOV. *Compare* **BCY Water Sup. v. Residential Invs.**, 170 S.W.3d 596, 604–05 (Tex.App.—Tyler 2005, pet. denied) (motion for JNOV can be filed as long as trial court has jurisdiction over case), *and* **Needville ISD v. S.P.J.S.T.**

Rest Home, 566 S.W.2d 40, 42 (Tex.App.—Beaumont 1978, no writ) (motion for JNOV can be filed after J is entered but before J is final), *with* **Commonwealth Lloyd's Ins. v. Thomas**, 825 S.W.2d 135, 141 (Tex.App.—Dallas 1992) (motion for JNOV must be filed within 30 days after signing of J), *writ granted w.r.m.*, 843 S.W.2d 486 (Tex.1993). Despite the courts' disagreement, the motion for JNOV should be filed within the same time period as a motion for new trial—30 days after the date the trial court signed the judgment—to extend the appellate deadlines. See "Motion for JNOV," ch. 9-C, §6.4.1(1)(c)[3]; "Deadlines for MNT," ch. 10-B, §5.

Practice Tip

Until the Supreme Court settles the disagreement, file your motion for JNOV before the deadline for a motion for new trial and ask the trial court to rule on the motion no later than 75 days after it signed the judgment.

§4.2 For ruling. TRCP 301 does not state a deadline for the trial court to sign an order on the motion for JNOV. If no motion for new trial has been filed, the best practice is for the movant to request that the court sign a written order on the motion for JNOV within 30 days after the court signs the judgment because it is unclear whether a motion for JNOV extends the trial court's plenary power. See "Motion for JNOV," ch. 9-C, §6.4.1(1)(c)[3]; "No PPE motion filed," ch. 9-C, §6.4.2(1). If a motion for new trial is filed in conjunction with the motion for JNOV, the movant should request that the court sign a written order on the motion for JNOV before any action is taken on the motion for new trial—that is, before the motion for new trial is overruled by written order or the motion is overruled by operation of law 75 days after the court signed the judgment. *See* **Spiller v. Lyons**, 737 S.W.2d 29, 29 (Tex.App.—Houston [14th Dist.] 1987, no writ); **Needville ISD v. S.P.J.S.T. Rest Home**, 566 S.W.2d 40, 42 (Tex.App.—Beaumont 1978, no writ); **Commercial Std. Ins. v. Southern Farm Bur. Cas. Ins.**, 509 S.W.2d 387, 392 (Tex.App.—Corpus Christi 1974, writ ref'd n.r.e.). See "PPE motion overruled," ch. 9-C, §6.4.2(2); "Generally," ch. 10-B, §8.4.1.

§5. Response

If there is any chance the trial court might seriously consider the movant's motion for JNOV, the nonmovant should file a response explaining why a JNOV would be improper. See **O'Connor's Texas Civil Forms**, FORMS 9B:2, 9B:4 (2020 ed.).

§6. Order

§6.1 Hearing. The hearing on a motion for JNOV is for argument only; no oral testimony may be presented. The court can decide the motion on submission, without an appearance by the attorneys before the court. See "Hearing on motion," ch. 1-E, §4.

§6.2 Written order. The order granting or denying the motion for JNOV should be in writing. However, an oral ruling made on the record or an implicit ruling will also preserve error. See "Types of rulings," ch. 1-G, §2.2.

§6.3 Order or judgment. If the trial court grants the motion for JNOV, it should sign a final judgment. If the trial court denies the motion for JNOV, it should sign an order denying the motion. For the form of the judgment, see **O'Connor's Texas Civil Forms**, FORMS 9C:1 et seq. (2020 ed.).

§7. Review

§7.1 Standard of review. To determine whether the trial court erred in granting or denying a motion for JNOV based on the legal insufficiency of the evidence ("no evidence" or "conclusive evidence"), the appellate court must credit evidence favoring the verdict if reasonable jurors could do so and disregard contrary evidence unless reasonable jurors could not. *See* **Hill v. Shamoun & Norman, LLP**, 544 S.W.3d 724, 736 (Tex.2018); **Gharda USA, Inc. v. Control Solutions, Inc.**, 464 S.W.3d 338, 347 (Tex.2015); **National Prop. Holdings, L.P. v. Westergren**, 453 S.W.3d 419, 421 (Tex.2015); **Tanner v. Nationwide Mut. Fire Ins.**, 289 S.W.3d 828, 830 (Tex.2009); **City of Keller v. Wilson**, 168 S.W.3d 802, 827 (Tex.2005). See "Challenging sufficiency of evidence," ch. 10-B, §13.1; "Legal sufficiency," **O'Connor's Texas Civil Appeals**, ch. 1-G, §6.3.1 (2020 ed.).

§7.2 Challenging a JNOV.

1. Parties' arguments. On appeal, the parties should take the following positions:

(1) Appellant. The appellant's arguments on appeal are the standard ones: the trial court erred in its ruling on the motion for JNOV when it either granted or denied the motion. If the motion for JNOV contained multiple grounds and the trial court granted the JNOV but did not specify the basis for its ruling, the appellant must discredit each ground in the appellee's motion. **Fort Bend Cty. Drainage Dist. v. Sbrusch**, 818 S.W.2d 392, 394 (Tex.1991); **Requena v. Otis Elevator Co.**, 305 S.W.3d 156, 162 (Tex.App.—Houston [1st Dist.] 2009, no pet.); **Gallas v. Car Biz, Inc.**, 914 S.W.2d 592, 593 (Tex.App.—Dallas 1995, writ denied).

(2) Appellee. The appellee's argument as the successful movant for JNOV (i.e., the appellee received an adverse jury verdict but the trial court granted a JNOV in the appellee's favor) is that the trial court correctly granted its motion for JNOV. If there are additional reasons the court should affirm the judgment, the appellee must raise those issues as cross-points, or it will waive those arguments. *See* Tex. R. App. P. 38.2(b)(1); Tex. R. Civ. P. 324(c); **Dudley Constr., Ltd. v. ACT Pipe & Sup.**, 545 S.W.3d 532, 537–38 (Tex.2018). Issues that must be raised by cross-point include (1) insufficient evidence to support the verdict, (2) improper jury argument, and (3) any other reason that would vitiate the verdict or preclude affirming a judgment if the trial court had rendered judgment on the verdict. Tex. R. App. P. 38.2(b)(1); Tex. R. Civ. P. 324(c); **Dudley Constr.**, 545 S.W.3d at 537. The cross-points can include grounds not raised in the motion for JNOV. **Ingram v. Deere**, 288 S.W.3d 886, 893 (Tex.2009). For a more detailed discussion of the appellee's cross-points, see "Appeal in JNOV case," **O'Connor's Texas Civil Appeals**, ch. 7-C, §6.7.3(1) (2020 ed.).

Note

An appellee is not required to label its argument "cross-points" to avoid waiver; as long as the appellee makes a substantive argument that would vitiate the verdict or preclude affirming a judgment if the trial court had rendered judgment on the verdict, it has presented a sufficient cross-point. ***Dudley Constr.****, 545 S.W.3d at 538; see Tex. R. App. P. 38.2(b)(1); Tex. R. Civ. P. 324(c).*

2. Relief.

(1) No error in JNOV ruling. If the appellate court agrees with the appellee that the trial court correctly overruled or granted the motion for JNOV, it will affirm the judgment.

(2) Error in denying JNOV. If the appellate court agrees with the appellant that the trial court erred in denying the motion for JNOV, it will generally reverse and render a judgment for the appellant, unless it is necessary to remand for further proceedings or for a new trial in the interest of justice. Tex. R. App. P. 43.3; *see, e.g.*, **Jones & Gonzalez, P.C. v. Trinh**, 340 S.W.3d 830, 838 (Tex.App.—San Antonio 2011, no pet.) (appellate court reversed and rendered on liability issues and entitlement to attorney fees, but remanded solely to determine amount of attorney fees); **Prestige Ford Garland L.P. v. Morales**, 336 S.W.3d 833, 839 (Tex.App.—Dallas 2011, no pet.) (appellate court reversed and rendered judgment that appellee take nothing because suit was barred by statute of limitations); *cf.* **Scott v. Liebman**, 404 S.W.2d 288, 294 (Tex.1966) (court found error in granting JNOV and remanded in interest of justice because law on which case was originally tried had changed between time of trial and time of appeal), *overruled on other grounds*, **Parker v. Highland Park, Inc.**, 565 S.W.2d 512 (Tex.1978). An appellate court may remand for a new trial in the interest of justice only under unusual circumstances, and the record must reflect that the court had a sufficient reason for doing so. *Cf.* **Jackson v. Ewton**, 411 S.W.2d 715, 718 (Tex.1967) (error in granting JNOV).

(3) Error in granting JNOV. If the appellate court agrees with the appellant that the trial court erred in granting the motion for JNOV, it should reverse the judgment and render judgment in harmony with the verdict, unless (1) the appellee raises viable cross-points, including factual-sufficiency challenges, that would either vitiate the verdict or preclude affirming a judgment if the trial court had rendered judgment on the verdict, (2) a remand is necessary for further proceedings, or (3) the interest of justice requires that the case be remanded for a new trial. *See* Tex. R. App. P. 38.2(b), 43.3, 44.1(b); Tex. R. Civ. P. 324(c); **Miller v. Bock Laundry Mach. Co.**, 568 S.W.2d 648, 652 (Tex.1977); **Jackson**, 411 S.W.2d at

717; **Downing v. Burns**, 348 S.W.3d 415, 427–28 (Tex.App.—Houston [14th Dist.] 2011, no pet.); *see, e.g.*, **Dudley Constr.**, 545 S.W.3d at 537–38 (remanded for further proceedings to determine appropriate amount of recovery after appellee raised sufficient cross-points that vitiated jury's verdict of zero damages); **Scott**, 404 S.W.2d at 294 (remanded for new trial in interest of justice because law on which case was originally tried had changed between time of trial and time of appeal).

Note

In ***Dudley Constr.****, the Court clarified that a remand for further proceedings is not limited to situations where new evidence must be taken.* ***Dudley Constr.****, 545 S.W.3d at 540. Although the Court affirmed a remand to the trial court, it did not determine the scope of the remand, leaving the trial court to decide whether it could alter the judgment considering the evidence already in the record or whether a new trial was necessary. Id.*

C. Judgment

§1. General

§1.1 Rules. Tex R Civ. P. 300 to 316.

§1.2 Purpose. The judgment is the official announcement of the resolution of the issues in the lawsuit. **State v. Naylor**, 466 S.W.3d 783, 788 (Tex.2015); **Comet Aluminum Co. v. Dibrell**, 450 S.W.2d 56, 58–59 (Tex.1970). The judgment grants the prevailing party the relief it earned by its victory. **Jones v. Springs Ranch Co.**, 642 S.W.2d 551, 553 (Tex.App.—Amarillo 1982, no writ). The purpose of a signed judgment under TRCP 306a is to conclude the controversy between the parties and to fix a certain date from which appellate deadlines can be determined. **Burrell v. Cornelius**, 570 S.W.2d 382, 383 (Tex.1978) (fix date for appellate deadlines); **U.S. Denro Steels, Inc. v. Lieck**, 342 S.W.3d 677, 684 (Tex.App.—Houston [14th Dist.] 2011, pet. denied) (conclude controversy).

§1.3 Timetables & forms. Appendix IV, Timetable 17, Motion to extend postjudgment deadlines; Appendix IV, Timetable 18, Appeal to the court of appeals; **O'Connor's Texas Civil Forms**, FORMS 9C:1 et seq. (2020 ed.).

§1.4 Other references. Busby & Johnson, *Top 10 Trial Judgment Traps*, Advanced Civil Appellate Practice Course, State Bar of Texas CLE, ch. 4 (2013); **O'Connor's Texas Causes of Action** (2021 ed.); **O'Connor's Texas Civil Appeals** (2020 ed.).

§2. Essentials of valid judgment

§2.1 Conforms to pleadings or agreement. The judgment must conform to the pleadings or a settlement agreement.

1. Pleadings & proof. When a case is resolved by a fact-finder, the judgment must conform to the pleadings and proof. Tex. R. Civ. P. 301; **Latch v. Gratty, Inc.**, 107 S.W.3d 543, 546 (Tex.2003); **Mapco, Inc. v. Carter**, 817 S.W.2d 686, 688 (Tex.1991). See **O'Connor's Texas Civil Forms**, FORM 9C:1 (2020 ed.).

2. Agreement. When a case is resolved by a settlement agreement, the judgment must strictly or literally comply with that agreement. **Highland Homes Ltd. v. State**, 448 S.W.3d 403, 408 n.17 (Tex.2014); **Vickrey v. American Youth Camps, Inc.**, 532 S.W.2d 292, 292 (Tex.1976); *see, e.g.*, **Chisholm v. Chisholm**, 209 S.W.3d 96, 98 (Tex.2006) (judgment that improperly removed and added material terms did not strictly or literally comply with agreement and was set aside).

§2.2 Definite & certain. The judgment must be sufficiently definite and certain to define and protect the rights of the litigants. **Stewart v. USA Custom Paint & Body Shop, Inc.**, 870 S.W.2d 18, 20 (Tex.1994). If a judgment is not definite, it must provide a means of determining rights so the ministerial officers can execute on the judgment. *Id.*; **Olympia Marble & Granite v. Mayes**, 17 S.W.3d 437, 440 (Tex.App.—Houston [1st Dist.] 2000, no pet.). If a judgment is not definite and its meaning cannot be determined, it is not a final judgment. *See, e.g.*, **Hatton v. Burgess**, 167 S.W.2d 260, 262–63 (Tex.App.—Beaumont 1942, writ ref'd w.o.m.) (J was void because it did not provide sufficient information to identify land awarded to prevailing party).

§2.3 Jurisdiction. The judgment is void unless the court has jurisdiction.

1. Parties. The trial court must have jurisdiction over the parties. **State v. Owens**, 907 S.W.2d 484, 485 (Tex.1995); **Browning v. Placke**, 698 S.W.2d 362, 363 (Tex.1985).

2. Subject matter. The trial court must have jurisdiction over the subject matter of the suit. **Owens**, 907 S.W.2d at 485; **Browning**, 698 S.W.2d at 363; *see* **Carroll v. Carroll**, 304 S.W.3d 366, 368 (Tex.2010); **Dubai Pet. Co. v. Kazi**, 12 S.W.3d 71, 74–75 (Tex.2000).

3. Case. The trial court must have jurisdiction to render a judgment in the case. **Owens**, 907 S.W.2d at 485; *see, e.g.*, **Texas Prop. & Cas. Ins. Guar. Ass'n v. De Los Santos**, 47 S.W.3d 584, 588 (Tex.App.—Corpus Christi 2001, no pet.) (court did not have jurisdiction to sign second J 54 days after signing first J when no MNT was filed).

Note

When the Supreme Court reverses and remands a case to the trial court, the trial court's jurisdiction to preside over the case and enter a new judgment is not limited, but its authority to exercise jurisdiction is—it cannot take any action that is inconsistent with the Supreme Court's judgment. See ***Phillips v. Bramlett****, 407 S.W.3d 229, 234 (Tex.2013).*

4. Judge. The trial judge must be qualified by law to sit in the court. *See* **Tesco Am., Inc. v. Strong Indus.**, 221 S.W.3d 550, 555 (Tex.2006) (any orders or judgments rendered by constitutionally disqualified trial judge are void); **Owens**, 907 S.W.2d at 485 (court must have capacity to act as a court).

§3. Rendering, signing & entering judgment

A judgment routinely goes through three stages: rendition, signing, and entry. **Araujo v. Araujo**, 493 S.W.3d 232, 235 (Tex.App.—San Antonio 2016, no pet.); **General Elec. Capital Auto Fin. Leasing Servs. v. Stanfield**, 71 S.W.3d 351, 354 (Tex.App.—Tyler 2001, pet. denied). The judgment becomes effective once it is "rendered." **General Elec. Capital**, 71 S.W.3d at 354. The timetables for the appeal begin to run once the judgment is signed by the court. *Id.* When the judgment is "entered," it is noted in the court's records by the court clerk. **Araujo**, 493 S.W.3d at 235. The entry of the judgment has no legal significance for the parties or for the appellate timetable. *See* **General Elec. Capital**, 71 S.W.3d at 354.

§3.1 Rendition. Rendition is a present act that resolves the issues on which the ruling is made. **In re Vaishangi, Inc.**, 442 S.W.3d 256, 259 (Tex.2014); **Reese v. Piperi**, 534 S.W.2d 329, 330 (Tex.1976). A judgment is rendered when the court officially announces its decision orally in open court, by written memorandum filed with the clerk, or through some other public announcement. **Garza v. Texas Alcoholic Bev. Comm'n**, 89 S.W.3d 1, 6 (Tex.2002); **Genesis Prod'g Co. v. Smith Big Oil Corp.**, 454 S.W.3d 655, 659 (Tex.App.—Houston [14th Dist.] 2014, no pet.); *see* **S&A Rest. Corp. v. Leal**, 892 S.W.2d 855, 857 (Tex.1995). The rendition of a judgment is the critical moment when the judgment becomes effective. **Araujo v. Araujo**, 493 S.W.3d 232, 235 (Tex.App.—San Antonio 2016, no pet.); *see* **Verret v. Verret**, 570 S.W.2d 138, 140 (Tex.App.—Houston [1st Dist.] 1978, no writ).

1. Methods of rendition.

(1) Written. A written judgment is the preferred method of announcing or rendering a judgment. Some letters or e-mails from the trial court announcing the ruling can be the equivalent of a rendition of judgment. See "Rendition of judgment," ch. 1-G, §3.4.2. If possible, the parties should prepare a written judgment before the hearing at which the judgment will be announced. For example, the party filing a motion for summary judgment should prepare a summary judgment to submit along with its motion.

(2) Oral. When it is not possible to prepare a written judgment before the hearing, the alternative method of rendering the judgment is to have the court announce it in open court on the record. *See, e.g.,* **State v. Naylor**, 466 S.W.3d 783, 788 (Tex.2015) (oral announcement of divorce). The judge must announce the rendition as a present act, not as an intention to perform a future act. *Id.*; **S&A Rest.**, 892 S.W.2d at 858; *e.g.,* **Able Cabling Servs. v. Aaron-Carter Elec., Inc.**, 16 S.W.3d 98, 100–01 (Tex.App.—Houston [1st Dist.] 2000, pet. denied) (court's statement that "judgment *will be* rendered in accordance with the terms dictated into the record" did not indicate a present intent to render J); *see* **Alexander Dubose Jefferson & Townsend LLP v. Chevron Phillips Chem. Co.**, 540 S.W.3d 577, 582–83 (Tex.2018).

Practice Tip

The prevailing party should make sure the trial judge makes an effective oral rendition of the judgment on the record. On the record, the judge should say "I now render the following judgment: (state the result)." If the judge uses the future tense ("I plan to sign a judgment that will provide . . . ."), ask her to restate the rendition as a present act, not a future one.

2. Not rendition.

(1) Docket entry. Docket-sheet entries are inherently unreliable and are generally not specific enough to satisfy the requirements for a rendition. See "Docket entries," ch. 1-G, §3.3.

(2) Approval of settlement. A statement by the trial court that it understands the parties have agreed to settle or that it approves the settlement is not the rendition of an agreed judgment—the court's language must clearly indicate an intent to render judgment at that time. *See* **In re Vaishangi**, 442 S.W.3d at 259; **S&A Rest.**, 892 S.W.2d at 857–58; **Formby's KOA v. BHP Water Sup.**, 730 S.W.2d 428, 430 (Tex.App.—Dallas 1987, no writ). For a discussion of enforcing settlement agreements, see "Enforceable settlement agreements," ch. 7-I, §3.

(3) Order granting motion for judgment. An order that merely grants a motion for judgment is not a rendition of judgment; it adjudicates nothing. *E.g.*, **Naaman v. Grider**, 126 S.W.3d 73, 74 (Tex.2003) (appellate deadlines began when final J was signed, not one month later when motion for J was granted).

§3.2 Signing. When the trial judge signs a judgment without first making an oral announcement in open court, the act of signing the judgment is the official act of rendering the judgment. **Wittau v. Storie**, 145 S.W.3d 732, 735 (Tex.App.—Fort Worth 2004, no pet.). When the trial judge makes an oral announcement of the judgment in open court, the act of signing the judgment is only a ministerial act. **Dunn v. Dunn**, 439 S.W.2d 830, 832 (Tex.1969); **In re Bland**, 960 S.W.2d 123, 124 (Tex.App.—Houston [1st Dist.] 1997, orig. proceeding) (O'Connor, J., dissenting). The signature may be made by the judge personally or by someone authorized by the judge. See "Signature," ch. 1-G, §3.1.2. The signing of the judgment is significant because the deadlines for filing postjudgment motions and for perfecting an appeal start on the date the trial court signs the judgment or final order disposing of the case. *See* Tex. R. Civ. P. 306a(1); **In re Bennett**, 960 S.W.2d 35, 38 (Tex.1997); **Farmer v. Ben E. Keith Co.**, 907 S.W.2d 495, 496 (Tex.1995); **Martinez v. Humble Sand & Gravel, Inc.**, 875 S.W.2d 311, 313 (Tex.1994); *see also* Tex. R. Civ. P. 329b(a), (b) & (g) (time for filing motions); **Newsom v. Ballinger ISD**, 213 S.W.3d 375, 379 (Tex.App.—Austin 2006, no pet.) (deadlines start on date trial court signs J, even if J is void). The appellate deadlines begin when the judgment is signed, even if it is merely a ministerial act. **Harris Cty. Appr. Dist. v. Wittig**, 881 S.W.2d 193, 194 (Tex.App.—Houston [1st Dist.] 1994, orig. proceeding). The period of the court's plenary power to change the judgment is calculated from the date the final judgment is signed. *See* Tex. R. Civ. P. 329b(d).

§3.3 Entry. A judgment is entered when the court clerk performs the ministerial act of entering the judgment in the minutes of the court. **Araujo v. Araujo**, 493 S.W.3d 232, 235 (Tex.App.—San Antonio 2016, no pet.); **Oak Creek Homes, Inc. v. Jones**, 758 S.W.2d 288, 290 (Tex.App.—Waco 1988, no writ); *see* **Dunn v. Dunn**, 439 S.W.2d 830, 832 (Tex.1969); *see also* **Keim v. Anderson**, 943 S.W.2d 938, 942 (Tex.App.—El Paso 1997, no writ) (distinguishing entry of J from rendition of J). Once the judgment is signed by the trial court, it should be given to the clerk to file with the other documents of the case, and the clerk should make an entry in the minutes of the court. A signed judgment is valid whether or not it is filed or entered in the record. *See* **In re Barber**, 982 S.W.2d 364, 367 (Tex.1998) (date of signing, not date of entry, controls); *see, e.g.*, **Prinz v. Dutschmann**, 678 S.W.2d 256, 258 (Tex.App.—Corpus Christi 1984, no writ) (divorce decree was rendered when signed, not when entered in the record).

§4. Form of judgment

§4.1 Parties. The judgment must contain the full names of the parties as stated in the pleadings. Tex. R. Civ. P. 306; **City of Austin v. Castillo**, 25 S.W.3d 309, 314 (Tex.App.—Austin 2000, pet. denied); **Crystal City ISD v. Wagner**, 605 S.W.2d 743, 747 (Tex.App.—San Antonio 1980, writ ref'd n.r.e.). The judgment must identify the parties in their correct capacities, that is, the same capacities in which the plaintiff brought suit and the defendant was sued. *See, e.g.*, **Werner v. Colwell**, 909 S.W.2d 866, 869–70 (Tex.1995) (court could not render J against D as trustee when D was sued only as individual).

§4.2 Declaration of legal effects.

1. Resolution of issues. The judgment should determine the rights of all the parties and dispose of all the issues. The judgment must state for whom and against whom it is rendered. Tex. R. Civ. P. 306.

2. Appealability. The judgment should state whether the parties intend for the judgment to be appealable. *See* **In re Daredia**, 317 S.W.3d 247, 248 (Tex.2010); **Lehmann v. Har-Con Corp.**, 39 S.W.3d 191, 206 (Tex.2001). See "Final," ch. 9-C, §4.3.1(1). Whether a judgment is appealable depends on the type of judgment rendered.

(1) Final judgment. A judgment that is final is appealable. See "Final judgment," ch. 9-C, §6.

(2) Interlocutory judgment. Generally, an interlocutory judgment is not final and appealable; however, it can be converted into a final judgment by merger or severance. See "Interlocutory judgments—merger or severance," ch. 9-C, §6.3.1(2)(b). An interlocutory judgment can also be made appealable by statute or rule. See "Appeals from interlocutory orders," **O'Connor's Texas Civil Appeals**, ch. 1-B, §2.4 (2020 ed.).

(3) Agreed judgment. An agreed (or consent) judgment is one rendered on the agreement of the parties, and it constitutes a contract between them. *See* **Chang v. Nguyen**, 81 S.W.3d 314, 316 n.1 (Tex.App.—Houston [14th Dist.] 2001, no pet.); **Baw v. Baw**, 949 S.W.2d 764, 766–67 (Tex.App.—Dallas 1997, no writ). For an agreed judgment to be valid, each party must have explicitly and unmistakably consented to it. **Perez v. Williams**, 474 S.W.3d 408, 414 n.2 (Tex.App.—Houston [1st Dist.] 2015, no pet.); **Baw**, 949 S.W.2d at 766. A regular judgment does not necessarily transform into an agreed judgment just because the judgment's caption contains the word "agreed" or "consent" or the attorneys sign under the phrase "approved as to form and substance." *See* **Perez**, 474 S.W.3d at 414 n.2; **DeClaris Assocs. v. McCoy Workplace Solutions, L.P.**, 331 S.W.3d 556, 560 (Tex.App.—Houston [14th Dist.] 2011, no pet.); **In re D.C.**, 180 S.W.3d 647, 649–50 (Tex.App.—Waco 2005, no pet.); **Baw**, 949 S.W.2d at 766–67. *But see* **Cisneros v. Cisneros**, 787 S.W.2d 550, 552 (Tex.App.—El Paso 1990, no writ) (approval of substance of judgment is, in effect, agreement by signing party that judgment fulfills all essential requirements). See "Signature line for attorneys," ch. 9-C, §4.13. The appellate courts will look to the circumstances surrounding the judgment to determine whether the parties intended to enter into an agreed judgment. *See* **Chang**, 81 S.W.3d at 316 n.1; **First Am. Title Ins. v. Adams**, 829 S.W.2d 356, 364 (Tex.App.—Corpus Christi 1992, writ denied); **Hill v. Bellville Gen. Hosp.**, 735 S.W.2d 675, 678 (Tex.App.—Houston [1st Dist.] 1987, no writ).

(a) Generally—judgment not appealable. Generally, an agreed judgment is not appealable. *See* **In re A.M.S.**, 277 S.W.3d 92, 99 (Tex.App.—Texarkana 2009, no pet.); **Chang**, 81 S.W.3d at 316 n.1; **Baw**, 949 S.W.2d at 766.

Note

A motion for judgment, filed to begin appellate deadlines, does not result in an agreed judgment and does not prevent an appeal if the movant notes that it disagrees with the content and result of the judgment that will be entered or with the findings that the judgment will be based on. See ***First Nat'l Bank v. Fojtik****, 775 S.W.2d 632, 633 (Tex.1989);* ***Casu v. Marathon Ref. Co.****, 896 S.W.2d 388, 390 (Tex.App.—Houston [1st Dist.] 1995, writ denied). See "Motion for Judgment," ch. 9-A, §1 et seq.*

(b) Exceptions. An agreed judgment is appealable in the following situations:

[1] No jurisdiction. An agreed judgment is appealable if the trial court had no jurisdiction when it rendered the judgment. **In re A.M.S.**, 277 S.W.3d at 99; **Chang**, 81 S.W.3d at 316 n.1; **Baw**, 949 S.W.2d at 766.

[2] Fraud, collusion, or misrepresentation. An agreed judgment is appealable if it was the result of fraud, collusion, or misrepresentation. **In re A.M.S.**, 277 S.W.3d at 99; **Chang**, 81 S.W.3d at 316 n.1; **Baw**, 949 S.W.2d at 766. If there is an allegation of fraud, collusion, or misrepresentation and the allegation is not supported by the record, the party attacking the agreed judgment generally must file a motion for new trial and then appeal the denial of the motion. *See* Tex. R. Civ. P. 324(b); **In re O.A.G.**, No. 04-09-00222-CV, 2010 WL 1491647 (Tex.App.—San Antonio 2010, no pet.) (memo op.; 4-14-10). See "Motion for New Trial," ch. 10-B, §1 et seq.

§4.3 Statement of finality.

1. Final. The judgment should state whether it is intended to be a final or partial judgment. See "What judgments are final," ch. 9-C, §6.3. A statement that the plaintiff takes nothing or that the case is dismissed makes the judgment final as long as there are no other claims by other parties. **Lehmann v. Har-Con Corp.**, 39 S.W.3d 191, 205 (Tex.2001). But language about dismissal should not be used in a proceeding that resolves the case on the merits (e.g., a summary judgment); it should be used only in cases in which dismissal is appropriate. See "Resolve issues on the merits," ch. 7-B, §12.3.3; "Grounds for dismissal," ch. 7-G, §2. The following statements will indicate that the judgment is intended to be final:

(1) "This judgment finally disposes of all parties and all claims and is appealable." **In re Daredia**, 317 S.W.3d 247, 248 (Tex.2010); **Lehmann**, 39 S.W.3d at 206; *see* **Bella Palma, LLC v. Young**, 601 S.W.3d 799, 801 (Tex.2020); **In re**

R.R.K., 590 S.W.3d 535, 543 (Tex.2019); **In re Elizondo**, 544 S.W.3d 824, 825–26 (Tex.2018). This is the preferred statement to include in any judgment intended to be final. *See* **In re Daredia**, 317 S.W.3d at 248.

(2) "This judgment disposes of all parties and all claims in this cause of action and is therefore final." *E.g., id.* at 248–49 (although use of the word "final" is slightly less clear than "appealable," court held it was clear enough to constitute statement of finality).

Practice Tip

In a conventional trial on the merits, the judgment does not need to include a statement of finality because such judgments are presumed to be final. ***Moritz v. Preiss****, 121 S.W.3d 715, 718–19 (Tex.2003);* ***John v. Marshall Health Servs.****, 58 S.W.3d 738, 740 (Tex.2001);* ***North E. ISD v. Aldridge****, 400 S.W.2d 893, 897–98 (Tex.1966). See "After conventional trial," ch. 9-C, §6.3.1(1). However, if any of the claims were disposed of outside a conventional trial on the merits (e.g., by summary judgment, default judgment, or dismissal), the inclusion of a statement of finality will ensure that the judgment is final and appealable.*

2. Not final. A judgment is not final just because it is captioned a "final judgment," because the word "final" appears somewhere in the order, because it awards costs, or because it says it is appealable. **Lehmann**, 39 S.W.3d at 205; *see* **Farm Bur. Cty. Mut. Ins. v. Rogers**, 455 S.W.3d 161, 163 (Tex.2015).

§4.4 Damages. A money judgment should either state with certainty the amount to be recovered or furnish a means for determining the amount. **Beam v. Southwestern Bell Tel. Co.**, 164 S.W.2d 412, 416 (Tex.App.—Waco 1942, writ ref'd w.o.m.); *see* **In re Blankenhagen**, 513 S.W.3d 97, 100 (Tex.App.—Houston [14th Dist.] 2016, orig. proceeding). If the amount of money awarded is uncertain, the judgment will be considered interlocutory. *E.g.*, **In re Blankenhagen**, 513 S.W.3d at 100–01 (although default J contained statement of finality, it was not final because amount of damages had not yet been determined and could not be ascertained from J); **Olympia Marble & Granite v. Mayes**, 17 S.W.3d 437, 440 (Tex.App.—Houston [1st Dist.] 2000, no pet.) (J was not final because questions remained about date when prejudgment interest would begin to accrue); **H.E. Butt Grocery Co. v. Bay, Inc.**, 808 S.W.2d 678, 680–81 (Tex.App.—Corpus Christi 1991, writ denied) (default J was not final because it did not specify which interest rate applied for prejudgment interest); **Jones v. Liberty Mut. Ins.**, 733 S.W.2d 240, 242 (Tex.App.—El Paso 1987, no writ) (subrogation J was not final because medical payments for which insurance company was to be reimbursed had no termination date). See "General Concepts," **O'Connor's Texas Causes of Action**, ch. 41-A, §1 et seq. (2021 ed.).

1. Proportionate responsibility. In tort cases, the percentage of damages each party to a lawsuit must pay is determined using the proportionate-responsibility method. *See* Tex. Civ. Prac. & Rem. Code ch. 33. If a plaintiff is partially responsible for its own damages, the plaintiff's recovery is reduced or barred by the percentage of those damages attributed to the plaintiff. See "Proportionate Responsibility & Contribution," **O'Connor's Texas Causes of Action**, ch. 51, §1 et seq. (2021 ed.).

2. Alternative theories of recovery & defense.

(1) Alternative recoveries. When a plaintiff's petition contains alternative theories of recovery for the same injury, the court cannot render a judgment awarding relief on all the theories. **Waite Hill Servs. v. World Class Metal Works, Inc.**, 959 S.W.2d 182, 184 (Tex.1998); **Southern Cty. Mut. Ins. v. First Bank & Trust**, 750 S.W.2d 170, 173–74 (Tex.1988). A judgment on multiple theories would result in an impermissible double recovery for the same injury. *See* **Waite Hill**, 959 S.W.2d at 184; **Southern Cty.**, 750 S.W.2d at 173–74. When the jury returns favorable findings on alternative theories, the plaintiff is entitled to recover on the theory that results in the largest or most favorable recovery. **Parkway Co. v. Woodruff**, 901 S.W.2d 434, 441 (Tex.1995); **Boyce Iron Works, Inc. v. Southwestern Bell Tel. Co.**, 747 S.W.2d 785, 787 (Tex.1988); **Woodlands Land Dev. Co. v. Jenkins**, 48 S.W.3d 415, 419 (Tex.App.—Beaumont 2001, no pet.). If the plaintiff does not make an election, the trial court should render a judgment allowing the greatest recovery. **Birchfield v. Texarkana Mem'l Hosp.**, 747 S.W.2d 361, 367 (Tex.1987); **Hill v. Heritage Res.**, 964 S.W.2d 89, 128 (Tex.App.—El Paso 1997, pet. denied). See "Applied to theories of liability," **O'Connor's Texas Causes of Action**, ch. 41-A, §5.2.1 (2021 ed.).

(2) Alternative defenses. A court can render a judgment sustaining all the defendant's alternative defenses. By rendering a judgment for the defendant on all its defensive theories, the trial court can avoid a remand if one of the grounds is reversed on appeal. *See* **Oak Park Townhouses v. Brazosport Bank**, 851 S.W.2d 189, 190 (Tex.1993).

§4.5 Prejudgment interest. Prejudgment interest is compensation for the lost use of money owed as damages, computed from the accrual of the plaintiff's claim to the day before the judgment. **Ventling v. Johnson**, 466 S.W.3d 143, 153 (Tex.2015); **Phillips v. Bramlett**, 407 S.W.3d 229, 238 (Tex.2013); **Johnson & Higgins v. Kenneco Energy, Inc.**, 962 S.W.2d 507, 528 (Tex.1998). The award of prejudgment interest is meant to encourage settlements and to discourage delays in litigation. *See* **Johnson & Higgins**, 962 S.W.2d at 529. Prejudgment interest can be recovered by statute or under general principles of equity. *Id.* at 528. See "When recoverable," **O'Connor's Texas Causes of Action**, ch. 43, §2.1.1 (2021 ed.). When prejudgment interest is allowed, the judgment should include the exact amount of prejudgment interest due; if the calculation is not available, the judgment must include the appropriate interest rate and date of accrual. See **O'Connor's Texas Civil Forms**, FORM 9C:1 (2020 ed.).

1. Pleading prejudgment interest. A party does not need to plead for prejudgment interest when the party is entitled to it by statute or, in a breach-of-contract suit, when the contract provides for it. *See* **Benavidez v. Isles Constr. Co.**, 726 S.W.2d 23, 25 (Tex.1987); *see, e.g.*, Tex. Fin. Code §304.102 (prejudgment-interest award mandated in cases for wrongful death, personal injury, or property damage). A party must, however, plead for prejudgment interest in all other common-law cases when sought as an element of damages. *See* **DeGroot v. DeGroot**, 369 S.W.3d 918, 926 (Tex.App.—Dallas 2012, no pet.). See "Pleading prejudgment interest," **O'Connor's Texas Causes of Action**, ch. 43, §2.2 (2021 ed.).

2. Calculating prejudgment interest. Prejudgment interest is computed as simple interest—that is, it does not compound. Tex. Fin. Code §304.104; **Ventling**, 466 S.W.3d at 149; **Johnson & Higgins**, 962 S.W.2d at 532. Simple interest is calculated on the principal amount only, not on previously accumulated interest. Interest, *Black's Law Dictionary* (11th ed. 2019). Simple interest is computed by multiplying the amount of principal by the interest rate by the time of accrual (I = P × R × T). The following are the rules for computing principal, rate, and time of accrual under the Finance Code.

(1) Principal. For the purpose of computing prejudgment interest, principal is the amount of damages found by the trier of fact minus any amounts on which prejudgment interest is prohibited by statute or case law (e.g., exemplary damages, future damages, attorney fees, court costs). See "Prejudgment interest not permitted," ch. 9-C, §4.5.3.

(2) Rate. The rate for prejudgment interest is the same as for postjudgment interest. Tex. Fin. Code §304.103; **Johnson & Higgins**, 962 S.W.2d at 532. See "Rate," ch. 9-C, §4.6.2(2). Although Finance Code §304.103 sets the rate for prejudgment interest only for cases involving wrongful death, personal injury, and property damage, the Supreme Court has adopted the same rules for calculating prejudgment interest in all other cases. **Johnson & Higgins**, 962 S.W.2d at 530–31.

Note

Before the Legislature amended Finance Code §302.002 in 1999, that section provided for an interest rate of 6% per year in suits based on "all contracts ascertaining the amount payable" in which no interest rate was specified in the contract. The post-1999 version (1) provides an interest rate of 6% at which a creditor can charge an obligor "legal interest," (2) is located in the subchapter of the Finance Code titled "Usurious Interest," and (3) says nothing about applying to "all contracts ascertaining the amount payable." See Tex. Fin. Code §302.002. It is unclear whether, after the amendment, §302.002 still applies to prejudgment-interest awards in all contract suits in which no interest rate was specified in the contract. Compare ***Mobil Prod'g Tex. & N.M., Inc. v. Cantor****, 93 S.W.3d 916, 920 (Tex.App.—Corpus Christi 2002, no pet.) (court discussed §302.002 without mentioning 1999 amendment),* ***Roach v. Dickenson****, 50 S.W.3d 709, 714 n.2 (Tex.App.—Eastland 2001, no pet.) (court applied §302.002 without discussing 1999 amendment),* ***Academy Corp. v. Interior Buildout & Turnkey Constr., Inc.****, 21 S.W.3d 732, 744 (Tex.App.—Houston [14th Dist.] 2000, no pet.) (same), and* ***Vela v. Vela****, No. 14-12-00822-CV, 2013 WL 6700270 (Tex.App.—Houston [14th Dist.] 2013, no pet.) (memo op.; 9-24-13) (footnote 6; court cited §302.002 and* ***Academy Corp.****, in dicta, for the proposition that when the sum payable is ascertainable and the contract does not specify a rate of interest, prejudgment interest may be*

calculated at a rate of 6%), with ***GuideOne Lloyds Ins. v. First Baptist Ch.****, 268 S.W.3d 822, 835–36 (Tex.App.—Fort Worth 2008, no pet.) (court refused to apply §302.002),* ***Bufkin v. Bufkin****, 259 S.W.3d 343, 357 (Tex.App.—Dallas 2008, pet. denied) (court held that §302.002 does not apply in contract cases not involving extensions of credit),* ***Natural Gas Clearinghouse v. Midgard Energy Co.****, 113 S.W.3d 400, 413 (Tex.App.—Amarillo 2003, pet. denied) (court refused to apply §302.002), and* ***Walden v. Affiliated Computer Servs.****, 97 S.W.3d 303, 329–30 (Tex.App.—Houston [14th Dist.] 2003, pet. denied) (court declined to follow its previous opinion in* ***Academy Corp.*** *and held that §302.002 does not apply to award of prejudgment interest).*

(3) Accrual.

(a) Accrual begins.

[1] Generally. Generally, prejudgment interest begins to accrue on either (1) the 180th day after the defendant receives written notice of the plaintiff's claim or (2) the day suit is filed, whichever is earlier. Tex. Fin. Code §304.104; **Ventling**, 466 S.W.3d at 149; **State Farm Mut. Auto. Ins. v. Norris**, 216 S.W.3d 819, 822 (Tex.2006); **Johnson & Higgins**, 962 S.W.2d at 531; *see also* **Citizens Nat'l Bank v. Allen Rae Invs.**, 142 S.W.3d 459, 487–88 (Tex.App.—Fort Worth 2004, no pet.) (prejudgment interest began to accrue against D2 and D3 on day separate suit against them was filed, not on day suit was first filed against D1, even though suits were later consolidated).

[2] Amended petition. Some courts have held that, when a plaintiff amends its petition to add a claim on which it is ultimately entitled to prejudgment interest or to add a defendant against which it ultimately prevails, prejudgment interest does not begin to accrue until the date of the amended petition. *See* **Tex Star Motors, Inc. v. Regal Fin. Co.**, 401 S.W.3d 190, 204 (Tex.App.—Houston [14th Dist.] 2012, no pet.); **Qwest Comms. Int'l v. AT&T Corp.**, 114 S.W.3d 15, 39–40 (Tex.App.—Austin 2003), *rev'd in part on other grounds*, 167 S.W.3d 324 (Tex.2005); *see, e.g.*, **Christus Health Gulf Coast v. Carswell**, 433 S.W.3d 585, 611–12 (Tex.App.—Houston [1st Dist.] 2013) (prejudgment interest began to accrue on day P filed third amended petition because P prevailed only on claim first asserted in that petition), *rev'd in part on other grounds*, 505 S.W.3d 528 (Tex.2016). *But see* **Brownsville Pediatric Ass'n v. Reyes**, 68 S.W.3d 184, 196–97 (Tex.App.—Corpus Christi 2002, no pet.) (prejudgment interest against later-added D is calculated from day suit is first filed; calculating prejudgment interest from day D is added as party is contrary to plain language of Fin. Code §304.104).

(b) Accrual ends. Prejudgment interest stops accruing the day before the judgment is rendered. *See* Tex. Fin. Code §304.104; **Ventling**, 466 S.W.3d at 149.

(c) Tolling. In some situations, the accrual of prejudgment interest can be tolled. See "Tolling," **O'Connor's Texas Causes of Action**, ch. 43, §2.3.3(4) (2021 ed.).

3. Prejudgment interest not permitted. Examples of when a party is not entitled to prejudgment interest include the following:

(1) Future damages. Tex. Fin. Code §304.1045; **Finley v. P.G.**, 428 S.W.3d 229, 239 (Tex.App.—Houston [1st Dist.] 2014, no pet.).

(2) Exemplary damages. Tex. Civ. Prac. & Rem. Code §41.007; **C&H Nationwide, Inc. v. Thompson**, 903 S.W.2d 315, 325 (Tex.1994); **Ellis Cty. State Bank v. Keever**, 888 S.W.2d 790, 797 (Tex.1994).

(3) Attorney fees. **C&H Nationwide**, 903 S.W.2d at 325–26. See "Attorney fees," **O'Connor's Texas Causes of Action**, ch. 43, §2.1.2(2)(a) (2021 ed.).

(4) Costs. **C&H Nationwide**, 903 S.W.2d at 325–26. But if costs are part of the damages award, prejudgment interest may be proper. *See, e.g.*, **K-2, Inc. v. Fresh Coat, Inc.**, 253 S.W.3d 386, 399 (Tex.App.—Beaumont 2008) (prejudgment interest on costs was proper because they were part of P's loss under products-liability statute and were awarded as part of damages), *rev'd in part on other grounds*, 318 S.W.3d 893 (Tex.2010).

(5) Prejudgment interest itself. *See* **Ellis Cty.**, 888 S.W.2d at 797 n.13 (dicta).

(6) DTPA treble damages. Tex. Bus. & Com. Code §17.50(e), (f)(2); **Vail v. Texas Farm Bur. Mut. Ins.**, 754 S.W.2d 129, 137 (Tex.1988).

(7) Interpleaded funds. *See* **State Farm Life Ins. v. Martinez**, 216 S.W.3d 799, 808 (Tex.2007).

(8) Double recovery. Prejudgment interest cannot be awarded under both a statute and the common law because such an award would be impermissible double recovery. *See* **AMX Enters. v. Master Rlty. Corp.**, 283 S.W.3d 506, 513–14 (Tex.App.—Fort Worth 2009, no pet.).

§4.6 Postjudgment interest. Postjudgment interest is compensation for the lost use of money owed as damages, computed from the date the judgment was signed until the date of satisfaction. **Long v. Castle Tex. Prod.**, 426 S.W.3d 73, 77 (Tex.2014); **Phillips v. Bramlett**, 407 S.W.3d 229, 238 (Tex.2013); *see* Tex. Fin. Code §304.005(a). Postjudgment interest can be recovered on any state-court money judgment. *See* Tex. Fin. Code §304.001. All money judgments must specify the applicable postjudgment interest rate. *Id.* But because postjudgment interest is mandated by statute, it can be recovered even if the judgment does not mention it. **RAJ Partners v. Darco Constr. Corp.**, 217 S.W.3d 638, 653 (Tex.App.—Amarillo 2006, no pet.); **Jarrin v. Sam White Oldsmobile Co.**, 929 S.W.2d 21, 25 (Tex.App.—Houston [1st Dist.] 1996, writ denied); **Staff Indus. v. Hallmark Contracting, Inc.**, 846 S.W.2d 542, 551 (Tex.App.—Corpus Christi 1993, no writ).

1. Pleading postjudgment interest. Postjudgment interest is considered general damages and does not need to be specifically pleaded. *See* **Federal Pac. Elec. Co. v. Woodend**, 735 S.W.2d 887, 896 (Tex.App.—Fort Worth 1987, no writ) (general prayer for interest on judgment to be compounded annually is considered request for postjudgment interest); **Desoto v. Matthews**, 714 S.W.2d 133, 134 (Tex.App.—Houston [1st Dist.] 1986), *writ ref'd n.r.e.*, 721 S.W.2d 286 (Tex.1986) (general prayer for interest on judgment at legal rate is considered request for postjudgment interest).

2. Calculating postjudgment interest. Postjudgment interest is compounded annually. Tex. Fin. Code §304.006. Compound interest is calculated on both the principal amount and the previously accumulated interest. Interest, *Black's Law Dictionary* (11th ed. 2019); *see* **Ventling v. Johnson**, 466 S.W.3d 143, 149 (Tex.2015); **Debo Homes, LLC v. Miller**, No. 14-18-00546-CV, 2020 WL 1026413 (Tex.App.—Houston [14th Dist.] 2020, pet. denied) (memo op.; 3-3-20).

(1) Principal. For the purpose of computing postjudgment interest, principal is the amount of the judgment, including prejudgment interest and court costs. *See* Tex. Fin. Code §304.003(a); **Sisters of Charity of the Incarnate Word v. Dunsmoor**, 832 S.W.2d 112, 119 (Tex.App.—Austin 1992, writ denied).

(2) Rate. The interest rate for postjudgment interest is set either by contract or by statute.

(a) Most cases. Finance Code §304.003 controls the postjudgment interest rate in most cases. The postjudgment interest rate is the prime rate as published by the Board of Governors of the Federal Reserve System on the date of computation. Tex. Fin. Code §304.003(c)(1); **Hooks v. Samson Lone Star, L.P.**, 457 S.W.3d 52, 69 (Tex.2015). If the prime rate is less than 5%, the postjudgment interest rate is 5% per year; if the prime rate is more than 15%, the postjudgment interest rate is 15% per year. Tex. Fin. Code §304.003(c)(2), (c)(3). The daily prime rate is available on the Board of Governors of the Federal Reserve System website at www.federalreserve.gov/data.htm.

Note

The Consumer Credit Commissioner of Texas publishes the current "judgment rate" in a weekly Texas Credit Letter, located at occc.texas.gov/publications/interest-rates. To determine the current judgment rate, the Commissioner uses the prime rate published by the Board of Governors of the Federal Reserve System and the calculation method described in Finance Code §304.003.

(b) Some contract cases. If the judgment is on a contract that provides for interest or a time-price differential, the postjudgment interest rate is either the rate specified in the contract, which may be a variable rate, or 18% per year, whichever is less. Tex. Fin. Code §304.002; **Hooks**, 457 S.W.3d at 69; *see, e.g.*, **Cook Composites, Inc. v. Westlake Styrene Corp.**, 15 S.W.3d 124, 141 (Tex.App.—Houston [14th Dist.] 2000, pet. dism'd) (because contract rate of 1.5%, compounded monthly, would amount to more than 18% annually, proper interest rate was 18%); **AU Pharm. v. Boston**,

986 S.W.2d 331, 336 (Tex.App.—Texarkana 1999, no pet.) (because contract provided for postjudgment interest rate of zero, no postjudgment interest could be awarded); *see also* Tex. Fin. Code §301.002(16) (time-price differential is amount added to sales-contract price for buyer's privilege of paying late). If the contract does not provide the interest rate, however, then the rate is determined under Finance Code §304.003. *E.g.*, **Hooks**, 457 S.W.3d at 69–70 (because contract imposed maximum interest rate allowed by law only for past-due royalties, P was entitled to 18% interest rate for recovery of royalties but only 5% under Fin. Code §304.003 for other recoveries).

(3) Accrual. A judgment must be final to accrue postjudgment interest. **Ventling**, 466 S.W.3d at 149; *see* **Long**, 426 S.W.3d at 78–79. Like being final for purposes of appeal, to be final for purposes of accruing postjudgment interest, a judgment must dispose of all parties and claims. **Long**, 426 S.W.3d at 78–79; *see* **Ventling**, 466 S.W.3d at 151 (interlocutory order is not "judgment" that can accrue postjudgment interest). See "What judgments are final," ch. 9-C, §6.3. Postjudgment interest begins to accrue on the day the judgment is rendered (i.e., the day the final judgment is signed) and stops accruing on the day the judgment is satisfied. Tex. Fin. Code §304.005(a); **Ventling**, 466 S.W.3d at 149; **Long**, 426 S.W.3d at 78; **Phillips**, 407 S.W.3d at 239; *see also* **Debo Homes**, No. 14-18-00546-CV, 2020 WL 1026413 (memo op.) (unconditional payment interrupts running of postjudgment interest; postjudgment-interest calculation should have excluded amount that was deposited into court's registry). The Finance Code does not define "judgment" or differentiate between a trial court's original judgment and a judgment on remand or appeal. **Phillips**, 407 S.W.3d at 239. Thus, if an appellate court reverses a trial court's judgment and either renders the judgment that the trial court should have rendered or remands for further proceedings, the date postjudgment interest begins to accrue may be affected. *See* **Long**, 426 S.W.3d at 79.

(a) Appellate court reverses & renders judgment—date of original trial-court judgment. When an appellate court reverses a trial court's judgment and renders the judgment that the trial court should have rendered, "judgment is rendered" on the date the trial court signed the original, erroneous judgment, not the date of the appellate court's judgment; thus, postjudgment interest begins to accrue and is calculated from the date of the trial court's original judgment. **Long**, 426 S.W.3d at 80; **Phillips**, 407 S.W.3d at 239; *see also* **Danziger v. San Jacinto Sav. Ass'n**, 732 S.W.2d 300, 304–05 (Tex.1987) (court severed and remanded one claim from other claims on which court rendered judgment; postjudgment interest on rendered claims would accrue from date of trial court's original judgment).

(b) Appellate court reverses & remands.

[1] No new or additional evidence—date of original trial-court judgment. When an appellate court reverses and remands a case to the trial court for rendition of judgment consistent with the appellate court's opinion, and the trial court has a sufficient record to render a correct judgment so that it does not have to reopen the record to admit new or additional evidence, "judgment is rendered" on the date the trial court signed the original judgment; thus, postjudgment interest begins to accrue and is calculated from that date. **Ventling**, 466 S.W.3d at 150; **Phillips**, 407 S.W.3d at 239; *see* **Long**, 426 S.W.3d at 80–81.

[2] New or additional evidence required—date of later trial-court judgment. When an appellate court reverses and remands a case to the trial court and (1) the trial court did not have a sufficient record to render a correct judgment and must reopen the record to admit new or additional evidence, or (2) the record is reopened because the case is being retried, "judgment is rendered" on the date the trial court signs the later judgment, not the date of the original, erroneous judgment; thus, postjudgment interest begins to accrue and is calculated from the date of the trial court's later judgment. **Long**, 426 S.W.3d at 80–81; *see* **Ventling**, 466 S.W.3d at 150. The trial court should make the determination whether to reopen the record based on the claims and record as of the time of the remand. **Long**, 426 S.W.3d at 81–82. A party can challenge whether the trial court abused its discretion in determining whether the record should be reopened on appeal from the later judgment. *Id.* at 81 n.14.

Note

If claims are severed on remand and only some of the claims require reopening the record to admit new or additional evidence, postjudgment interest on those claims will accrue from the date of the trial court's later judgment; postjudgment interest on the remanded claims that do not require reopening the record will accrue from the date the trial court signed the original judgment. See, e.g., ***Ventling***,

466 S.W.3d at 152 (because court of appeals remanded P's claims for attorney fees and costs sepcrately from alimony claim, effectively severing those claims, and because additional testimony on remand pertained only to attorney fees and costs, postjudgment interest on attorney fees and costs accrued from date of later judgment on those claims, while postjudgment interest on alimony award accrued from date of original judgment).

§4.7 Attorney fees. When appropriate, the judgment should include a provision awarding attorney fees. See "Attorney fees from adverse party," ch. 1-H, §10; "Attorney Fees," **O'Connor's Texas Causes of Action**, ch. 45-A, §1 et seq. (2021 ed.). A claim for additional attorney fees incurred for enforcement and collection of the judgment does not make the judgment interlocutory. **Pillitteri v. Brown**, 165 S.W.3d 715, 718 (Tex.App.—Dallas 2004, no pet.). See "Is the language of the judgment definite?," **O'Connor's Texas Civil Appeals**, ch. 1-B, §2.1.4 (2020 ed.).

Note

A party can be awarded conditional appellate attorney fees, which become final when the appeal is concluded and the last appellate court to review the case issues its final judgment. ***Sky View at Las Palmas, LLC v. Mendez****, 555 S.W.3d 101, 116 (Tex.2018); see* ***Ventling v. Johnson****, 466 S.W.3d 143, 156 (Tex.2015). For a discussion of proving the reasonableness of attorney fees, see "Proving reasonableness & necessity of attorney fees," ch. 1-H, §10.2. The party can recover postjudgment interest on these appellate attorney fees, accruing from the date the appellate award is made final.* ***Ventling****, 466 S.W.3d at 156.*

§4.8 Guardian ad litem fees. See "Taxed as costs," ch. 1-I, §6.4.

§4.9 Costs. The judgment should state that costs are awarded against a certain party, not the amount of the costs awarded. After the judgment is signed, the clerk will send a cost bill to the party taxed with the costs. A trial court, however, is not required to assess costs for its judgment to be final. **City of Marshall v. Gonzales**, 107 S.W.3d 799, 803 (Tex.App.—Texarkana 2003, no pet.); **Thompson v. Beyer**, 91 S.W.3d 902, 905 (Tex.App.—Dallas 2002, no pet.). See "What judgments are final," ch. 9-C, §6.3; "Court Costs," **O'Connor's Texas Causes of Action**, ch. 44, §1 et seq. (2021 ed.).

1. Who is entitled to costs.

(1) Successful party. The successful party to a suit is entitled to recover from the other party all taxable court costs it incurred. Tex. R. Civ. P. 131; **Roberts v. Williamson**, 111 S.W.3d 113, 124 (Tex.2003); **Furr's Supermkts., Inc. v. Bethune**, 53 S.W.3d 375, 378 (Tex.2001); **Rogers v. Walmart Stores**, 686 S.W.2d 599, 601 (Tex.1985). Taxing costs against the successful party is contrary to TRCP 131. **Martinez v. Pierce**, 759 S.W.2d 114, 114 (Tex.1988). A "successful party" is one who obtains a judgment of a competent court vindicating a civil claim of right. **Prize Energy Res. v. Cliff Hoskins, Inc.**, 345 S.W.3d 537, 587 (Tex.App.—San Antonio 2011, no pet.), *overruled on other grounds*, **Nath v. Texas Children's Hosp.**, 576 S.W.3d 707 (Tex.2019). See "Successful party," **O'Connor's Texas Causes of Action**, ch. 44, §2.2.1(1) (2021 ed.). Whether a party is successful must be based on success on the merits, not on whether damages were awarded. **Mag Instr., Inc. v. G.T. Sales Inc.**, 294 S.W.3d 800, 808 (Tex.App.—Dallas 2009, pet. denied); **Nicholson v. Tashiro**, 140 S.W.3d 445, 447 (Tex.App.—Corpus Christi 2004, no pet.). In some cases, both parties can be considered successful or unsuccessful under TRCP 131. *See, e.g.*, **Prize Energy**, 345 S.W.3d at 587 (both parties partially successful); **Mobil Prod'g Tex. & N.M., Inc. v. Cantor**, 93 S.W.3d 916, 920 (Tex.App.—Corpus Christi 2002, no pet.) (both parties unsuccessful); **Building Concepts, Inc. v. Duncan**, 667 S.W.2d 897, 905–06 (Tex.App.—Houston [14th Dist.] 1984, writ ref'd n.r.e.) (both parties successful). In these cases, the courts of appeals are split on whether it is within the court's discretion to apportion costs between the parties or whether the party receiving the larger award is entitled to recover costs. *Compare* **Henry v. Masson**, 453 S.W.3d 43, 51 n.2 (Tex.App.—Houston [1st Dist.] 2014, no pet.) (court has discretion to apportion costs), **Bayer Corp. v. DX Terminals, Ltd.**, 214 S.W.3d 586, 612 (Tex.App.—Houston [14th Dist.] 2006, pet. denied) (same), **Mobil Prod'g**, 93 S.W.3d at 920 (court has discretion to apportion costs; no abuse of discretion in apportioning when neither party is wholly successful because one party expected to receive more and other party expected to pay less), *and* **Niemeyer v. Tana Oil & Gas Corp.**, 39 S.W.3d 380, 390 (Tex.App.—Austin 2001, pet. denied) (court has discretion to apportion costs), *with* **Chilton**

Ins. Co. v. Pate & Pate Enters., 930 S.W.2d 877, 895 (Tex.App.—San Antonio 1996, writ denied) (party receiving larger award is entitled to recover costs), *and* **Brender v. Sanders Plumbing, Inc.**, No. 02-05-067-CV, 2006 WL 2034244 (Tex.App.—Fort Worth 2006, pet. denied) (memo op.; 7-20-06) (same).

(2) Unsuccessful party. For the court to award costs to the unsuccessful party, the court must find good cause and state the reasons on the record. Tex. R. Civ. P. 141; **Roberts**, 111 S.W.3d at 124; **Furr's**, 53 S.W.3d at 378; **Rogers**, 686 S.W.2d at 601; *see, e.g.*, **Marshall Investigation & Sec. Agency v. Whitaker**, 962 S.W.2d 62, 62–63 (Tex.App.—Houston [1st Dist.] 1997, no pet.) (case remanded for trial court to state good cause). See " 'Good cause' exception," **O'Connor's Texas Causes of Action**, ch. 44, §2.2.2 (2021 ed.). As a matter of law, potential harm to the unsuccessful party's emotional state is not good cause to tax costs against the successful party. **Furr's**, 53 S.W.3d at 378.

2. Taxable court costs. Each party to a suit is responsible for accurately recording all costs and fees incurred during the lawsuit if the judgment provides for adjudication of such costs. Tex. Civ. Prac. & Rem. Code §31.007(a). For a list of costs taxable as court costs, see "Taxable costs," **O'Connor's Texas Causes of Action**, ch. 44, §2.3.1 (2021 ed.). For a list of costs not taxable as court costs, see "Nontaxable costs," **O'Connor's Texas Causes of Action**, ch. 44, §2.3.2 (2021 ed.).

§4.10 No findings of fact. The judgment in a nonjury case should not contain findings of fact. The findings of fact must be filed separately and should not be recited in the judgment. Tex. R. Civ. P. 299a. See "Not in judgment," ch. 10-E, §5.2.2.

§4.11 Date signed. The judgment should have a line, immediately above the trial judge's signature line, that reads: "Signed on ________, 20." **Burrell v. Cornelius**, 570 S.W.2d 382, 384 (Tex.1978). The date the judgment is signed is important because it starts the appellate timetable. **Farmer v. Ben E. Keith Co.**, 907 S.W.2d 495, 496 (Tex.1995); **Reese v. Piperi**, 534 S.W.2d 329, 331 (Tex.1976); *see* **Coinmach, Inc. v. Aspenwood Apt. Corp.**, 98 S.W.3d 377, 382 (Tex.App.—Houston [1st Dist.] 2003, no pet.) (date judgment was signed, not date it was filed, is relevant for determining appellate deadlines). The absence of a date on the judgment does not invalidate the judgment. Tex. R. Civ. P. 306a(2); **Hammett v. Lee**, 730 S.W.2d 350, 351 (Tex.App.—Dallas 1987, writ dism'd). If the date is omitted and it is an issue on appeal, the appellate court can ask the trial court to certify the date the judgment was signed. *See* **Hammett**, 730 S.W.2d at 351.

§4.12 Signature line for judge. The judgment must contain a signature line for the trial judge.

§4.13 Signature line for attorneys. Traditionally, the judgment contains signature lines for the attorneys to approve the form of the judgment. To ensure the judgment is not construed as an agreed (or consent) judgment, which is generally not appealable, the attorneys representing the losing party should sign under the statement "approved as to form only," not "approved as to form and substance." *See* **Chang v. Nguyen**, 81 S.W.3d 314, 316 n.1 (Tex.App.—Houston [14th Dist.] 2001, no pet.); **Transmission Exch. Inc. v. Long**, 821 S.W.2d 265, 275 (Tex.App.—Houston [1st Dist.] 1991, writ denied). However, even when an attorney signs under the statement "approved as to form and substance," the judgment does not necessarily transform into an agreed judgment. **Chang**, 81 S.W.3d at 316 n.1. See "Agreed judgment," ch. 9-C, §4.2.2(3).

§5. Notice of judgment

§5.1 Clerk's duty to give notice. The clerk must give the parties immediate notice, by first-class mail, that the court signed a judgment or an appealable order. Tex. R. Civ. P. 306a(3); *see* **Board of Trs. of Bastrop ISD v. Toungate**, 958 S.W.2d 365, 367 (Tex.1997); **Hubert v. Illinois State Assistance Comm'n**, 867 S.W.2d 160, 163 (Tex.App.—Houston [14th Dist.] 1993, no writ). The clerk must provide notice of the signing of the judgment and the date it was signed. **Winkins v. Frank Winther Invs.**, 881 S.W.2d 557, 558 (Tex.App.—Houston [1st Dist.] 1994, no writ). If the clerk does not give notice of the judgment, the party's right to due process—not merely a rule of procedure—is violated because the party is deprived of its right to be heard by the court. **Hubert**, 867 S.W.2d at 163. However, the lack of notice does not affect the beginning of the time periods listed in TRCP 306a(1) (except as provided by TRCP 306a(4) and TRAP 4.2) and does not constitute reversible error. *See* Tex. R. Civ. P. 306a(3); *cf.* **Campbell v. Fincher**, 72 S.W.3d 723, 724 (Tex.App.—Waco 2002, no pet.) (failure to give notice of default judgment under TRCP 239a does not constitute reversible error).

Note

*In **Lehmann v. Har-Con Corp.**, 39 S.W.3d 191, 206 (Tex.2001), the Supreme Court seemed to suggest that the court clerk is required to send the parties a copy of the judgment, citing TRCP 306a(3). However, by its very language, TRCP 306a(3) only requires the clerk to give notice that a judgment or an appealable order was signed. See Tex. R. Civ. P. 306a(3); see also Tex. R. Civ. P. 165a(1) (notice of signing, not copy of order), Tex. R. Civ. P. 239a (notice of judgment, not copy of judgment).*

§5.2 Rules requiring notice. There are three rules requiring the clerk to notify the parties that the court signed a judgment or appealable order: TRCP 165a(1), 239a, and 306a(3). These rules are for the administrative convenience of the parties. *See* **Campbell v. Fincher**, 72 S.W.3d 723, 724 (Tex.App.—Waco 2002, no pet.) (TRCP 239a).

1. TRCP 306a. Under TRCP 306a(3), the clerk of the trial court must give the parties or their attorneys of record immediate notice by first-class mail that the court signed a judgment or an appealable order. **John v. Marshall Health Servs.**, 58 S.W.3d 738, 739 n.3 (Tex.2001). The notice must be sent to all attorneys of record, not just lead counsel. Tex. R. Civ. P. 306a(3); **Cannon v. ICO Tubular Servs.**, 905 S.W.2d 380, 388 (Tex.App.—Houston [1st Dist.] 1995, no writ), *overruled on other grounds*, **Lane Bank Equip. Co. v. Smith S. Equip., Inc.**, 10 S.W.3d 308 (Tex.2000).

2. TRCP 165a. Under TRCP 165a(1), the clerk must give the parties notice that the court signed an order of dismissal. See "Notice of dismissal order," ch. 7-G, §8.

3. TRCP 239a. Under TRCP 239a, the clerk must give the defendant notice that the court signed a no-answer default judgment. See "Notice after no-answer default," ch. 7-A, §6.1.

§5.3 Late notice. The time periods for the court's plenary power and for filing postjudgment motions are calculated from the date the judgment is signed. See "Signing," ch. 9-C, §3.2. When a party receives late notice of the judgment and files a motion to extend postjudgment deadlines, the time periods are calculated from the date of actual notice. *See* Tex. R. Civ. P. 306a(4), (5). See "Motion to Extend Postjudgment Deadlines," ch. 10-G, §1 et seq.

§6. Final judgment

Whether a judgment is final has important implications for both parties. An appeal can be prosecuted only from a final judgment (with certain statutory exceptions). *See* Tex. Civ. Prac. & Rem. Code §§51.012, 51.014. The date the judgment or final order disposing of the case is signed starts the deadlines for filing postjudgment motions and for perfecting an appeal. Tex. R. Civ. P. 306a(1); **In re Bennett**, 960 S.W.2d 35, 38 (Tex.1997); **Farmer v. Ben E. Keith Co.**, 907 S.W.2d 495, 496 (Tex.1995); **Martinez v. Humble Sand & Gravel, Inc.**, 875 S.W.2d 311, 313 (Tex.1994); *see* Tex. R. Civ. P. 329b(a), (b), (g). The period of the court's plenary power to change the judgment is also calculated from the date the final judgment is signed. *See* Tex. R. Civ. P. 329b(e). See "Changing judgment during plenary power," ch. 9-C, §7.1. Even a void judgment can be final and can start the period for calculating deadlines. *See* **Newsom v. Ballinger ISD**, 213 S.W.3d 375, 379 (Tex.App.—Austin 2006, no pet.) (trial court's plenary power is not contingent on validity of J). *But see* **Metropolitan Transit Auth. v. Jackson**, 212 S.W.3d 797, 802–03 (Tex.App.—Houston [1st Dist.] 2006, pet. denied) (void J does not cause trial court's plenary power to expire). Only a final judgment is given preclusive effect in later suits. Most importantly, only a final judgment can be enforced. *See* Tex. R. Civ. P. 622; **In re Burlington Coat Factory Whs.**, 167 S.W.3d 827, 831 (Tex.2005). For more extensive treatment of issues relating to finality of judgments, see "Types of appeals," **O'Connor's Texas Civil Appeals**, ch. 1-B, §2 (2020 ed.).

Practice Tip

*If a party is uncertain whether the judgment is final, it should still appeal rather than risk losing the right to do so. **Lehmann v. Har-Con Corp.**, 39 S.W.3d 191, 196 (Tex.2001); see **In re Elizondo**, 544 S.W.3d 824, 827 (Tex.2018).*

§6.1 One-final-judgment rule.

1. Rule. Generally, only one final judgment can be rendered in a lawsuit. Tex. R. Civ. P. 301; **Long v. Castle Tex. Prod.**, 426 S.W.3d 73, 78 (Tex.2014); **Logan v. Mullis**, 686 S.W.2d 605, 609 (Tex.1985); *see* **In re Vaishangi, Inc.**, 442 S.W.3d 256, 260 (Tex.2014). By limiting the number of judgments to one per case, the one-final-judgment rule also limits the number of appeals to one per case.

2. Exceptions. There are a number of exceptions to the rule that only one final, appealable judgment can be rendered in each case. The most common types of proceedings that have multiple final judgments are probate, receivership, and partition cases. *See* **Lehmann v. Har-Con Corp.**, 39 S.W.3d 191, 195 (Tex.2001). See "Appeals from 'multiple final judgment' cases," **O'Connor's Texas Civil Appeals**, ch. 1-B, §2.2 (2020 ed.).

§6.2 Replacement judgment. When the court signs a judgment within its plenary power that is intended to replace an earlier judgment, it should specifically state that the first judgment is vacated. *See* **Mullins v. Thomas**, 150 S.W.2d 83, 84 (Tex.1941); **Hammett v. Lee**, 730 S.W.2d 350, 351 (Tex.App.—Dallas 1987, writ dism'd). If the second judgment does not expressly vacate the first judgment, however, many courts will presume that the first judgment is vacated unless the record indicates a contrary intent. *See, e.g.*, **SLT Dealer Grp. v. Americredit Fin. Servs.**, 336 S.W.3d 822, 832 (Tex.App.—Houston [1st Dist.] 2011, no pet.); **Lavender v. Lavender**, 291 S.W.3d 19, 22 (Tex.App.—Texarkana 2009, no pet.); **Abercia v. Kingvision Pay-Per-View, Ltd.**, 217 S.W.3d 688, 706 (Tex.App.—El Paso 2007, pet. denied); **Price Constr., Inc. v. Castillo**, 147 S.W.3d 431, 441 (Tex.App.—San Antonio 2004, pet. denied); **Quanaim v. Frasco Rest. & Catering**, 17 S.W.3d 30, 39–40 (Tex.App.—Houston [14th Dist.] 2000, pet. denied); **Owens-Corning Fiberglas Corp. v. Wasiak**, 883 S.W.2d 402, 411 (Tex.App.—Austin 1994, order). See "Second-judgment problems," ch. 10-B, §5.6; "Second-judgment problems," **O'Connor's Texas Civil Appeals**, ch. 5-A, §8.1 (2020 ed.).

§6.3 What judgments are final.

1. Judgments that are final.

(1) After conventional trial. A judgment signed following a conventional trial on the merits is presumed to be a final judgment disposing of all parties and claims. **Vaughn v. Drennon**, 324 S.W.3d 560, 562–63 (Tex.2010); **Moritz v. Preiss**, 121 S.W.3d 715, 718–19 (Tex.2003); **North E. ISD v. Aldridge**, 400 S.W.2d 893, 897–98 (Tex.1966); *see* **In re R.R.K.**, 590 S.W.3d 535, 541 (Tex.2019). A judgment after a conventional trial on the merits does not need to expressly dispose of all parties and claims to be final. **Vaughn**, 324 S.W.3d at 562; *see, e.g.*, **John v. Marshall Health Servs.**, 58 S.W.3d 738, 740 (Tex.2001) (even though J did not expressly dispose of P's claims against Ds with whom P was negotiating settlement, finality presumption was appropriate). But if the judgment is somehow ambiguous about finality, the presumption is overcome and an appellate court will examine the record to determine whether the judgment was intended to be final. **In re R.R.K.**, 590 S.W.3d at 541; *see* **Vaughn**, 324 S.W.3d at 563.

Note

*A "Mother Hubbard" provision ("all relief not granted is denied") in a judgment following a conventional trial on the merits indicates that the trial court intended the judgment to be final. See **In re R.R.K.**, 590 S.W.3d at 541; **Lehmann v. Har-Con Corp.**, 39 S.W.3d 191, 203–04 (Tex.2001). But such a provision does not, by itself, conclusively indicate that the judgment is final if other aspects of the judgment make the meaning of the provision uncertain. See, e.g., **In re R.R.K.**, 590 S.W.3d at 541–42 (memorandum order modifying child support was ambiguous about finality when it lacked required statutory elements under Tex. Fam. Code §105.006 and did not resolve possession and support issues; Mother Hubbard provision could not resolve ambiguity because it did not state that order was final, disposed of all claims and parties, and was appealable).*

---

(2) No conventional trial. There is no presumption of finality when a judgment is rendered at any time other than after a conventional trial on the merits (e.g., summary judgment, default judgment, order of dismissal). *See* **Crites v. Collins**, 284 S.W.3d 839, 840 (Tex.2009); **In re Burlington Coat Factory Whs.**, 167 S.W.3d 827, 829 (Tex.2005); **Lehmann**, 39 S.W.3d at 199–200; **North E. ISD**, 400 S.W.2d at 897. But a judgment rendered without a conventional trial will be considered final under certain circumstances.

(a) Judgments—generally. A judgment is final if it (1) unequivocally states that it disposes of all parties and claims or (2) actually disposes of all parties and claims. **Bella Palma, LLC v. Young**, 601 S.W.3d 799, 801 (Tex.2020); **Lehmann**, 39 S.W.3d at 200; *see* **In re Elizondo**, 544 S.W.3d 824, 825–26 (Tex.2018). These "tests" for determining finality apply to both orders and judgments and are not limited to situations involving summary judgments and default judgments. *E.g.*, **In re Elizondo**, 544 S.W.3d at 828–29 (statement-of-finality test applied to order on summary motion to remove lien).

[1] Judgment includes statement of finality. If the judgment unequivocally states that it disposes of all parties and claims, the judgment is final for purposes of appeal even if it leaves some claims unresolved. *See* **In re Elizondo**, 544 S.W.3d at 826–27; **Farm Bur. Cty. Mut. Ins. v. Rogers**, 455 S.W.3d 161, 163 (Tex.2015); **In re Burlington Coat Factory**, 167 S.W.3d at 830; **Ritzell v. Espeche**, 87 S.W.3d 536, 538 (Tex.2002); **Lehmann**, 39 S.W.3d at 200; *see also* **M.O. Dental Lab v. Rape**, 139 S.W.3d 671, 674–75 (Tex.2004) (SJ was final even though it did not dispose of claims against unserved D). Even if the parties do not intend for the judgment to dispose of all parties and issues but the judgment erroneously says it does, the judgment begins the appellate deadlines. *See* **Lehmann**, 39 S.W.3d at 204. For example, if a defendant moves for summary judgment on only one of the plaintiff's claims but the trial court signs a judgment that the plaintiff take nothing on all claims asserted, the judgment is erroneous but final as long as there are no other claims by other parties. **Jacobs v. Satterwhite**, 65 S.W.3d 653, 655 (Tex.2001); **Lehmann**, 39 S.W.3d at 200; *see* **Ritzell**, 87 S.W.3d at 538; *see also* **Ford v. Exxon Mobil Chem. Co.**, 235 S.W.3d 615, 617 (Tex.2007) (order disposing of all claims that does not itemize each element of damages pleaded may be erroneous but is final). A judgment granting more relief than a party is entitled to is not, for that reason alone, interlocutory. **Lehmann**, 39 S.W.3d at 200. If the judgment includes a clear and unequivocal statement of finality, the appellate court must take the judgment at face value and rule that it is final without reviewing the record in the case, even if the record would undermine finality. *See* **Bella Palma**, 601 S.W.3d at 801; **In re Elizondo**, 544 S.W.3d at 828. The record should be reviewed to determine finality only if the judgment does not include a clear and unequivocal statement of finality. **In re R.R.K.**, 590 S.W.3d at 540; **In re Elizondo**, 544 S.W.3d at 827–28.

Note

There is no "magic language" required for finality, but a judgment stating that it is final, that it disposes of all claims and parties, and that it is appealable will be considered a final judgment. ***Bella Palma****, 601 S.W.3d at 801; see* ***In re Daredia****, 317 S.W.3d 247, 248–49 (Tex.2010);* ***In re Burlington Coat Factory****, 167 S.W.3d at 830;* ***Lehmann****, 39 S.W.3d at 206. See "Final," ch. 9-C, §4.3.1. A "Mother Hubbard" provision ("all relief not granted is denied") in a summary-disposition order does not, by itself, conclusively indicate that the judgment is final.* ***Farm Bur.****, 455 S.W.3d at 163;* ***Lehmann****, 39 S.W.3d at 203–04. Similarly, a judgment is not final merely because it includes the word "final."* ***Lehmann****, 39 S.W.3d at 205;* ***Duke v. American W. Steel, LLC****, 526 S.W.3d 814, 817 (Tex.App.—Houston [1st Dist.] 2017, no pet.).*

[2] Judgment actually disposes of all parties & claims. A judgment is final for purposes of appeal if it actually disposes of all parties and claims in the lawsuit. **Bella Palma**, 601 S.W.3d at 801; **Farm Bur.**, 455 S.W.3d at 163; **Ford**, 235 S.W.3d at 617; **Lehmann**, 39 S.W.3d at 200; *see* **In re Elizondo**, 544 S.W.3d at 826–27. If the judgment resolves all claims, it is final even if it says it is not final. **Lehmann**, 39 S.W.3d at 200; *see* **McFadin v. Broadway Coffeehouse, LLC**, 539 S.W.3d 278, 283–84 (Tex.2018); **In re Burlington Coat Factory**, 167 S.W.3d at 830; *see also* **Newsom v. Ballinger ISD**, 213 S.W.3d 375, 379 (Tex.App.—Austin 2006, no pet.) (if judgment resolves all claims, it is final even if it is void). The judgment must either sufficiently define and protect the rights of all litigants or provide a definite means of determining those rights. **Hinde v. Hinde**, 701 S.W.2d 637, 639 (Tex.1985). In determining whether the judgment actually disposes of all parties and claims and thus is final, the appellate court can review the record in the case. *See* **In re Elizondo**, 544 S.W.3d at 827–28; **M.O. Dental Lab**, 139 S.W.3d at 674; **Jacobs**, 65 S.W.3d at 655; **Lehmann**, 39 S.W.3d at 205–06; *see, e.g.*, **Taub v. Dedman**, 56 S.W.3d 83, 87 (Tex.App.—Houston [14th Dist.] 2001, pet. denied) (specific enumeration of some Ds in SJ order indicated court did not intend to dispose of all parties).

(b) Interlocutory judgments—merger or severance. Generally, an interlocutory judgment is not final and not appealable. See "Appeals from interlocutory orders," **O'Connor's Texas Civil Appeals**, ch. 1-B, §2.4 (2020 ed.). An

interlocutory judgment can be converted into a final judgment by merger or severance. *See* **Bonsmara Nat. Beef Co. v. Hart of Tex. Cattle Feeders, LLC**, 603 S.W.3d 385, 390 (Tex.2020); **City of Beaumont v. Guillory**, 751 S.W.2d 491, 492 (Tex.1988); **Teer v. Duddlesten**, 664 S.W.2d 702, 704 (Tex.1984). A judgment becomes final on the date the judgment or order disposing of the last claim is signed or on the date the last unadjudicated claim is severed from the adjudicated claims. *See* **Farmer v. Ben E. Keith Co.**, 907 S.W.2d 495, 496 (Tex.1995).

[1] Last claim resolved—merger. An interlocutory judgment is merged into a final judgment when all the remaining claims are resolved, either on the merits or by dismissal. *See, e.g.*, **Parking Co. v. Wilson**, 58 S.W.3d 742, 742 (Tex.2001) (J signed after trial of last claim made earlier partial SJ final); **John**, 58 S.W.3d at 740 (J signed after directed verdict made earlier nonsuit and partial SJ final); **Clark v. Pimienta**, 47 S.W.3d 485, 486 (Tex.2001) (last partial SJ made earlier partial SJs final); **Wembley Inv. v. Herrera**, 11 S.W.3d 924, 926 (Tex.1999) (order nonsuiting last Ds made earlier default J as to other Ds final); **Webb v. Jorns**, 488 S.W.2d 407, 408–09 (Tex.1972) (order dismissing hospital as D became final when it was merged into final J); **Texas Sting, Ltd. v. R.B. Foods, Inc.**, 82 S.W.3d 644, 648 n.4 (Tex.App.—San Antonio 2002, pet. denied) (post-answer default made earlier dismissal final); **Campbell v. Kosarek**, 44 S.W.3d 647, 649 (Tex.App.—Dallas 2001, pet. denied) (J disposing of remaining Ds made earlier dismissal order against other Ds final). Under the merger doctrine, interlocutory judgments and orders are merged into the final judgment, even when they are not recorded in the judgment. **Webb**, 488 S.W.2d at 408–09; **Radelow-Gittens Real Prop. Mgmt. v. Pamex Foods**, 735 S.W.2d 558, 560 (Tex.App.—Dallas 1987, writ ref'd n.r.e.).

[2] Unresolved claim severed. An interlocutory judgment becomes final when the trial court severs the interlocutory judgment from the unadjudicated claims. *See* Tex. R. Civ. P. 41; *see, e.g.*, **Harris Cty. Flood Control Dist. v. Adam**, 66 S.W.3d 265, 266 (Tex.2001) (when order of severance was signed, SJ for two Ds became final); **Cherokee Water Co. v. Ross**, 698 S.W.2d 363, 365–66 (Tex.1985) (when order severing P's SJ from D's counterclaim was signed, SJ became final); **Castano v. Foremost Cty. Mut. Ins.**, 31 S.W.3d 387, 388 (Tex.App.—San Antonio 2000, no pet.) (because no-answer default J against one D was not severed, it was not final). If the interlocutory judgment disposes of only a subset of the claims between the same parties, severance will not make the judgment final. *E.g.*, **Duke**, 526 S.W.3d at 816 (severance of partial SJ dismissing Construction Trust Funds Act claims did not result in final judgment because other claims between same parties were still pending and SJ did not unequivocally state that it finally disposed of all claims). A severance order is effective immediately, and the judgment is final and appealable even if there is no separate physical file created or different cause number assigned to the order. **McRoberts v. Ryals**, 863 S.W.2d 450, 452–53 & n.4 (Tex.1993); **McWherter v. Agua Frio Ranch**, 224 S.W.3d 285, 290 (Tex.App.—El Paso 2005, no pet.). To be severable, a claim must be capable of becoming a separate suit with a separate, final judgment. **Martinez v. Humble Sand & Gravel, Inc.**, 875 S.W.2d 311, 312 (Tex.1994). See "Motion for severance," ch. 5-I, §3.

Caution

Courts sometimes condition the severance on a future act or event, but conditional language in a severance order should be avoided because it may cause confusion about when the severance becomes effective and when the severed interlocutory judgment becomes final. See, e.g., ***Doe v. Pilgrim Rest Baptist Ch.****, 218 S.W.3d 81, 82 (Tex.2007) (severance order conditioned on compliance with procedure did not become final until P paid filing fee);* ***Diversified Fin. Sys. v. Hill, Heard, O'Neal, Gilstrap & Goetz, P.C.****, 63 S.W.3d 795, 795 (Tex.2001) (partial SJ was not final at severance because order said partial SJ was to "proceed as such to final judgment");* ***Martinez****, 875 S.W.2d at 313–14 (partial SJ was not final at severance because order allowed for other Ds to be added).*

(c) Cases with multiple final judgments. There are some proceedings in which more than one "final" judgment can be signed in the same case. See "Exceptions," ch. 9-C, §6.1.2. In those cases, the resolution of certain discrete claims is considered a final judgment.

2. Judgments that are not final.

(1) Conventional trial + separate claims. When a trial court separates (but does not sever) an issue for later disposition, the judgment or order signed after the first trial is not a final judgment. **Hall v. City of Austin**, 450 S.W.2d 836, 838 (Tex.1970).

(2) Summary disposition. There is no presumption that a judgment signed after a summary disposition (e.g., summary judgment, no-answer default judgment) resolves all claims and is final. *See* **Crites**, 284 S.W.3d at 840; **Ford**, 235 S.W.3d at 617; **In re Burlington Coat Factory**, 167 S.W.3d at 829; **Lehmann**, 39 S.W.3d at 199–200; *see, e.g.*, **McNally v. Guevara**, 52 S.W.3d 195, 196 (Tex.2001) (SJ was not final because there was no presumption Ds abandoned claims not included in their SJ motion). When a trial court resolves some claims by summary disposition but leaves other claims unresolved, the judgment is not final. *See* **Farm Bur.**, 455 S.W.3d at 163; **Lehmann**, 39 S.W.3d at 199–200; *see, e.g.*, **In re Burlington Coat Factory**, 167 S.W.3d at 831 (default judgment was interlocutory because it did not dispose of all claims); **Nash v. Harris Cty.**, 63 S.W.3d 415, 416 (Tex.2001) (SJ was interlocutory because it did not dispose of all Ds); **Parking Co.**, 58 S.W.3d at 742 (SJ was interlocutory because it did not dispose of all claims); **Bobbitt v. Stran**, 52 S.W.3d 734, 735 (Tex.2001) (SJ was interlocutory because it did not dispose of all parties and claims); **McNally**, 52 S.W.3d at 196 (SJ was interlocutory because it did not dispose of claim for attorney fees); **Guajardo v. Conwell**, 46 S.W.3d 862, 864 (Tex.2001) (SJ was interlocutory because it did not dispose of claims by and against intervenor). However, an otherwise interlocutory judgment is final for purposes of appeal if it clearly and unequivocally states that it finally disposes of all claims, even if it does not actually resolve all claims. See "Judgment includes statement of finality," ch. 9-C, §6.3.1(2)(a)[1].

Note

If a judgment being appealed is actually a partial summary judgment, the appellate court can either dismiss the appeal or abate and remand to the trial court for it to decide whether it can modify its order and make the judgment final. See Tex. R. App. P. 27.2 (appellate court may permit interlocutory order to be modified to make it final); ***Lehmann****, 39 S.W.3d at 206 (if appellate court is uncertain about whether trial court intended for order to be final or interlocutory, it can abate appeal to allow trial court to clarify finality); see, e.g.,* ***McNally****, 52 S.W.3d at 196 (Supreme Court remanded to court of appeals to determine whether to abate appeal to allow trial court to sign final judgment or whether to dismiss appeal for lack of jurisdiction);* ***Mendoza v. Louisiana Stone, L.L.C.****, __ S.W.3d __, 2015 WL 6285563 (Tex.App.—Amarillo 2015, order) (No. 07-15-00133-CV; 10-20-15) (appeal abated so trial court could modify order that did not indicate whether parties were granted or denied recovery in whole or in part);* ***Iacono v. Lyons****, 6 S.W.3d 715, 717 (Tex.App.—Houston [1st Dist.] 1999, order) (appeal abated so trial court could sign order of nonsuit).*

---

(3) Bill of review. A bill of review that does not dispose of all the issues in the underlying case on the merits is interlocutory and not a final, appealable order. **Kiefer v. Touris**, 197 S.W.3d 300, 302 (Tex.2006); **Tesoro Pet. v. Smith**, 796 S.W.2d 705, 705 (Tex.1990); **In re S.D.E.**, 170 S.W.3d 642, 643 (Tex.App.—El Paso 2005, no pet.); **In re J.B.A.**, 127 S.W.3d 850, 851 (Tex.App.—Fort Worth 2004, no pet.); **Shahbaz v. Feizy Imp. & Exp. Co.**, 827 S.W.2d 63, 64–65 (Tex.App.—Houston [1st Dist.] 1992, no writ). To be a final judgment, the bill of review should either (1) deny any relief to the petitioner or (2) set aside the former judgment and substitute a new judgment that properly adjudicates all the issues of the case on the merits. **In re S.D.E.**, 170 S.W.3d at 643; **In re J.B.A.**, 127 S.W.3d at 851; **Shahbaz**, 827 S.W.2d at 64; *see, e.g.*, **Kiefer**, 197 S.W.3d at 302 (bill of review that set aside former parentage adjudication but did not substitute a new one was not final and appealable).

§6.4 Finality for purposes of changing the judgment. A judgment becomes final for purposes of changing it when the trial court loses plenary power. *See* Tex. R. Civ. P. 306a(1); **In re Panchakarla**, 602 S.W.3d 536, 539 (Tex.2020). See "Power to change judgment," ch. 9-C, §7. The date the court loses plenary power depends on the date the judgment was signed, whether one of the postjudgment motions extending the court's plenary power was filed, and if filed, whether the motion was overruled or granted. If no postjudgment motions are filed, the trial court loses plenary power and the judgment becomes final 30 days after it was signed. **Lane Bank Equip. Co. v. Smith S. Equip., Inc.**, 10 S.W.3d 308, 310 (Tex.2000).

1. Postjudgment motions & finality. Any postjudgment motion—no matter what it is called—will extend plenary power if it (1) seeks a substantive change in the judgment and (2) is filed within the time limits for a motion for new trial. *See* **Lane Bank**, 10 S.W.3d at 314; **In re Gillespie**, 124 S.W.3d 699, 703 (Tex.App.—Houston [14th Dist.] 2003, orig. proceeding).

Note

For a comparison of the effect of these motions on the court's plenary power and the appellate deadlines, see chart 5-2 under "Comparing the appellate timetable & plenary power," ***O'Connor's Texas Civil Appeals****, ch. 5-A, §6.3 (2020 ed.).*

(1) Motions that extend plenary power. The following motions extend the court's plenary power over the judgment:

(a) MNT. A motion for new trial. Tex. R. Civ. P. 329b(a), (e); **Lane Bank**, 10 S.W.3d at 310. See "Motion for New Trial," ch. 10-B, §1 et seq.

(b) Motion to reinstate. A verified motion to reinstate after dismissal for want of prosecution. Tex. R. Civ. P. 165a(3); *see* **Silguero v. State**, 287 S.W.3d 146, 149–50 (Tex.App.—Corpus Christi 2009, orig. proceeding) (affidavit or other sufficient evidence in record can substitute for verification and extend court's plenary power); *see, e.g.*, **3V, Inc. v. JTS Enters.**, 40 S.W.3d 533, 538–39 (Tex.App.—Houston [14th Dist.] 2000, no pet.) (affidavits were sufficient to verify motion to reinstate). See "Motion to Reinstate After Dismissal for Want of Prosecution," ch. 10-F, §1 et seq.

(c) Motion to modify judgment. A motion to modify, correct, or reform the judgment. Tex. R. Civ. P. 329b(g); **Lane Bank**, 10 S.W.3d at 310; *see* **Padilla v. LaFrance**, 907 S.W.2d 454, 458 (Tex.1995); *see, e.g.*, **Crotts v. Cole**, 480 S.W.3d 99, 102 (Tex.App.—Houston [14th Dist.] 2015, no pet.) (motion to reinstate based on trial court's final dismissal order under TRCP 91a was motion to modify J that extended court's plenary power). See "Motion to Modify the Judgment," ch. 10-D, §1 et seq.

[1] Motion for sanctions. A motion for sanctions to be incorporated in the judgment extends the court's plenary power. **Lane Bank**, 10 S.W.3d at 309–10; **Alpert v. Crain, Caton & James, P.C.**, 178 S.W.3d 398, 409–10 (Tex.App.—Houston [1st Dist.] 2005, pet. denied); **Estate of Davis v. Cook**, 9 S.W.3d 288, 296 (Tex.App.—San Antonio 1999, no pet.). See "Motion for Sanctions," ch. 5-K, §1 et seq.

[2] Motion for remittitur. No court has considered whether a motion for remittitur filed separately from a motion for new trial extends the court's plenary power, but under **Lane Bank** such a motion should because it seeks a substantive change in the judgment. A request for remittitur can be made in a motion for new trial, but it should extend the court's plenary power when filed separately. *Cf.* **Arkoma Basin Expl. Co. v. FMF Assocs. 1990-A, Ltd.**, 249 S.W.3d 380, 391 (Tex.2008) (signed order suggesting remittitur restarts appellate deadlines). See "Motion for Remittitur," ch. 10-C, §1 et seq.

[3] Motion for JNOV. No court has considered whether a motion for JNOV extends the court's plenary power, but under **Lane Bank** such a motion should because it seeks a substantive change in the judgment. By comparison, a motion for JNOV will extend the appellate deadlines if it is filed within the time limit for a motion for new trial and if it "assails" the trial court's judgment. *See* **Ryland Enter. v. Weatherspoon**, 355 S.W.3d 664, 666 (Tex.2011); **Kirschberg v. Lowe**, 974 S.W.2d 844, 847–48 (Tex.App.—San Antonio 1998, no pet.). See "Deadlines," ch. 9-B, §4; "Postjudgment motions that extend the appellate timetable," **O'Connor's Texas Civil Appeals**, ch. 5-A, §6 (2020 ed.).

(2) Motions that do not extend plenary power. The following postjudgment motions do not extend the court's plenary power.

(a) Request for findings of fact. A proper request for findings of fact does not extend the court's plenary power. **In re Gillespie**, 124 S.W.3d at 703; **Pursley v. Ussery**, 982 S.W.2d 596, 599 (Tex.App.—San Antonio 1998, pet. denied). A request for findings of fact does not seek a substantive change in the judgment. **In re Gillespie**, 124 S.W.3d at 703. By comparison, TRAP 26.1(a)(4) specifically states that a request for findings of fact extends appellate deadlines. See "Effect on appellate timetable," ch. 10-E, §6.1.

(b) Unverified motion to reinstate. Generally, an unverified motion to reinstate does not extend the court's plenary power. **Silguero**, 287 S.W.3d at 149; **3V, Inc.**, 40 S.W.3d at 538. But courts are generous in allowing alterna-

tive methods of verification. *See* **Silguero**, 287 S.W.3d at 149–50 (affidavit or other sufficient evidence in record can substitute for verification and extend court's plenary power); *see, e.g.*, **In re Dobbins**, 247 S.W.3d 394, 396–97 (Tex.App.—Dallas 2008, orig. proceeding) (evidentiary hearing and court master's recommendation of approval, made within 30 days, was sufficient substitute for verification and extended court's plenary power).

(c) Motion to enforce judgment. A motion for sanctions for failure to comply with the judgment does not extend the court's plenary power. **Guajardo v. Conwell**, 30 S.W.3d 15, 16 (Tex.App.—Houston [14th Dist.] 2000), *aff'd*, 46 S.W.3d 862 (Tex.2001).

(d) Other motions for nonsubstantive change in judgment. Generally, any other postjudgment motion asking for a nonsubstantive change in the judgment does not affect the trial court's plenary power over its judgment. *E.g.*, **Lane Bank**, 10 S.W.3d at 313–14 & n.4 (motion for judgment nunc pro tunc filed after court loses plenary power does not extend trial court's plenary power). However, if the trial court modifies the judgment while it still has plenary power, even if the change is nonsubstantive, the court's plenary power is extended. *See id.* at 313. See "Restarts appellate timetable," ch. 10-D, §6.2.1.

2. Effect of PPE motions. The effect of a plenary-power-extending motion (PPE motion) on the court's power to change the judgment is as follows:

(1) No PPE motion filed. If no PPE motion was filed, the trial court has plenary power to change its judgment for 30 days after it signs the judgment. Tex. R. Civ. P. 329b(d); **Lane Bank**, 10 S.W.3d at 310; **Board of Trs. of Bastrop ISD v. Toungate**, 958 S.W.2d 365, 367 (Tex.1997); **Sadeghian v. Shaw**, 76 S.W.3d 229, 231 (Tex.App.—Texarkana 2002, no pet.).

(2) PPE motion overruled. When a party timely files a PPE motion that is overruled, the trial court's plenary power over its judgment is extended until 30 days after the motion is overruled, either by written order or by operation of law, whichever occurs first. Tex. R. Civ. P. 329b(e), (g); **Faulkner v. Culver**, 851 S.W.2d 187, 188 (Tex.1993); *e.g.*, **In re Timberlake**, 501 S.W.3d 105, 111 (Tex.App.—Houston [14th Dist.] 2015, orig. proceeding) (court granted MNT during its additional 30 days of plenary power after MNT was overruled by operation of law); *see* Tex. R. App. P. 4.3(a); **Lane Bank**, 10 S.W.3d at 310. Such motions are overruled by operation of law on the 76th day after the judgment is signed, if not overruled earlier by a written order. *See* Tex. R. Civ. P. 329b(c); **In re Hidalgo**, 279 S.W.3d 456, 460 (Tex.App.—Dallas 2009), *rev'd on other grounds sub nom.* **Hidalgo v. Hidalgo**, 310 S.W.3d 887 (Tex.2010). When a PPE motion is overruled by operation of law on the 76th day after judgment, the trial court has plenary power over the judgment for 105 days, counting from the date it signed the judgment. *See* **L.M. Healthcare, Inc. v. Childs**, 929 S.W.2d 442, 444 (Tex.1996); **In re Hidalgo**, 279 S.W.3d at 460. If the trial court overrules a motion for new trial, an amended motion for new trial does not extend plenary power; the court has only 30 days from the date the first motion for new trial was overruled to rule on the amended motion. **In re Brookshire Grocery Co.**, 250 S.W.3d 66, 69–70 (Tex.2008). If, however, a party timely files a PPE motion other than an amended motion for new trial (e.g., a motion to modify the judgment) after the trial court overrules a motion for new trial, that PPE motion will extend the trial court's plenary power over its judgment. *Id.* at 72; *see* Tex. R. Civ. P 329b(e), (g); **L.M. Healthcare**, 929 S.W.2d at 444.

(3) PPE motion granted.

(a) MNT.

[1] MNT granted + new-trial judgment. When a trial court grants a motion for new trial, the original judgment is set aside and the case is reinstated on the trial court's docket. **Wilkins v. Methodist Health Care Sys.**, 160 S.W.3d 559, 563 (Tex.2005). The trial court retains ongoing plenary power until it signs another final judgment. *See* **In re Baylor Med. Ctr.**, 280 S.W.3d 227, 230–31 (Tex.2008). The trial court's plenary power is extended until 30 days after the new judgment is signed, unless one of the parties files a new PPE motion based on that judgment. *See* Tex. R. Civ. P. 329b(d). If a new PPE motion is filed, the date the trial court loses plenary power depends on whether the motion is overruled, granted, or withdrawn. See "Finality for purposes of changing the judgment," ch. 9-C, §6.4.

[2] MNT granted + order "ungranted." When a trial court grants a motion for new trial, it retains ongoing plenary power over the case and can set aside the new trial order anytime before it signs another final judgment.

Hidalgo v. Hidalgo, 310 S.W.3d 887, 889 (Tex.2010); **In re Baylor Med.**, 280 S.W.3d at 230–31. If the trial court "ungrants" the new-trial order and reinstates the original judgment, the trial court's plenary power is extended until 30 days after the date the judgment was reinstated, unless one of the parties files a new PPE motion. *Cf.* **In re Baylor Med.**, 280 S.W.3d at 231 (trial court's withdrawal of modification of judgment is itself a modification that restarts appellate timetable). The order ungranting a new trial does not automatically reinstate the original judgment; the trial court must enter a new judgment. **In re Department of Family & Prot. Servs.**, 273 S.W.3d 637, 644 (Tex.2009). If a new PPE motion is filed, the date the trial court loses plenary power depends on whether the motion is overruled, granted, or withdrawn. See "Finality for purposes of changing the judgment," ch. 9-C, §6.4.

(b) Other PPE motions. When a trial court grants a PPE motion (other than a motion for new trial) and modifies the judgment or signs a new judgment, the trial court's plenary power is extended until 30 days after the modified or new judgment is signed, unless one of the parties files a new PPE motion based on that modified or new judgment. *See* Tex. R. Civ. P. 329b(d); *see also* **Crotts**, 480 S.W.3d at 103 & n.5 (trial court's order granting P's motion to reinstate dismissed claims modified earlier final order, so there was no longer a final J and thus no timetable for expiration of court's plenary power). If a new PPE motion is filed, the date the trial court loses plenary power depends on whether the motion is overruled, granted, or withdrawn. See "Finality for purposes of changing the judgment," ch. 9-C, §6.4.

(4) PPE motion withdrawn. If the party who filed a PPE motion withdraws it, the limit of the trial court's plenary power reverts to 30 days after the judgment was signed. **In re Dilley ISD**, 23 S.W.3d 189, 191 (Tex.App.—San Antonio 2000, orig. proceeding); *see* **Rogers v. Clinton**, 794 S.W.2d 9, 11 (Tex.1990). The withdrawal of a PPE motion is treated like a notice of nonsuit—it is effective immediately. *See* **Rogers**, 794 S.W.2d at 11. If the party withdraws the motion more than 30 days after the judgment is signed, the trial court no longer has jurisdiction to change the judgment because its plenary power has already expired. **In re P.G.M.**, 405 S.W.3d 406, 414 (Tex.App.—Texarkana 2013, no pet.); **In re Dilley ISD**, 23 S.W.3d at 191–92.

Practice Tip

To ensure appellate review, every party should file a motion for new trial even when another party has already filed a PPE motion. Without filing its own motion for new trial, the party could miss the appellate deadlines if the other party withdraws its PPE motion.

9-1. Plenary-Power Deadlines

	Situation	Last day trial court has plenary power	Cross-reference
1	No PPE motion filed	Date judgment signed + 30 days	ch. 9-C, §6.4.2(1)
2	PPE motion overruled by court order	Date order overruling PPE motion signed + 30 days, but no later than 105 days after date judgment signed	ch. 9-C, §6.4.2(2)
3	PPE motion overruled by operation of law	Date judgment signed + 75 days + 30 days = 105 days	ch. 9-C, §6.4.2(2)
4	PPE motion granted by court order	Date new or modified judgment signed + 30 days, unless new PPE motion filed	ch. 9-C, §6.4.2(3)
5	PPE motion withdrawn by party	Date judgment signed + 30 days	ch. 9-C, §6.4.2(4)

§7. Power to change judgment

§7.1 Changing judgment during plenary power. The trial court has the power to change its judgment as long as it has plenary power over the judgment. *See* **In re Panchakarla**, 602 S.W.3d 536, 539 (Tex.2020). See chart 9-1 under "PPE motion withdrawn," ch. 9-C, §6.4.2(4). If the trial court changes the judgment by signing a modified judgment while it still has plenary power over the judgment, the timetables for postjudgment motions and appellate documents start over. Tex. R. Civ. P. 329b(h); Tex. R. App. P. 4.3(a); *see* Tex. R. App. P. 27.3. See "Modified judgment & postjudgment deadlines," ch. 10-D, §6.2.

§7.2 Changing judgment after plenary power. The court generally cannot change its judgment once it loses plenary power. There are two exceptions:

1. Correcting clerical errors. The trial court can correct clerical errors in the judgment. Only in a few cases are the appellate timetables extended if the court changes the judgment after it loses plenary power. See "Correction made after losing plenary power—judgment nunc pro tunc," ch. 10-H, §7.2.2.

2. Retaxing costs. The trial court can retax costs (i.e., correct errors in the clerk's tabulation of costs) after it loses plenary power. **Operation Rescue-Nat'l v. Planned Parenthood**, 937 S.W.2d 60, 87 (Tex.App.—Houston [14th Dist.] 1996), *aff'd as modified*, 975 S.W.2d 546 (Tex.1998). Taxing costs, as distinguished from adjudicating costs, is merely a ministerial duty of the clerk. **Wood v. Wood**, 320 S.W.2d 807, 813 (Tex.1959); **Operation Rescue**, 937 S.W.2d at 87; *see* Tex. R. Civ. P. 149, 622; **Campbell v. Wilder**, 487 S.W.3d 146, 152 (Tex.2016). The court must retax costs before the mandate in the case is issued and costs are paid. **Operation Rescue**, 937 S.W.2d at 87; *see* **Hartzell Propeller, Inc. v. Alexander**, 517 S.W.2d 455, 456 (Tex.App.—Texarkana 1974, no writ). *But see* **County of El Paso v. Dorado**, 180 S.W.3d 854, 873 (Tex.App.—El Paso 2005, pet. denied) (party can file motion to retax costs if it believes the bill of costs attached to the mandate is erroneous).

§8. Power to enforce judgment

The trial court has the power to enforce its orders after its plenary power expires. **Allen v. Allen**, 717 S.W.2d 311, 312 (Tex.1986); **Kenseth v. Dallas Cty.**, 126 S.W.3d 584, 600 (Tex.App.—Dallas 2004, pet. denied); *see* **Alexander Dubose Jefferson & Townsend LLP v. Chevron Phillips Chem. Co.**, 540 S.W.3d 577, 581 (Tex.2018). Enforcement orders cannot be inconsistent with the original judgment and cannot materially change a part of the judgment that was substantially adjudicated. **Cook v. Stallcup**, 170 S.W.3d 916, 920 (Tex.App.—Dallas 2005, no pet.); **Matz v. Bennion**, 961 S.W.2d 445, 452 (Tex.App.—Houston [1st Dist.] 1997, pet. denied).

§9. Review

§9.1 Calculating appellate deadlines. Appellate deadlines are calculated from the date the court signs a final judgment or appealable order and depend on whether either party filed a motion extending the appellate deadlines. Motions extending the appellate deadlines include (1) a motion for new trial, (2) a motion to modify the judgment, (3) a motion to reinstate under TRCP 165a, (4) a request for findings of fact when findings either are required by the TRCPs or could properly be considered by the appellate court, and (5) any motion that seeks a substantive change in the judgment. Tex. R. App. P. 26.1(a) (#1–4); **Lane Bank Equip. Co. v. Smith S. Equip., Inc.**, 10 S.W.3d 308, 314 (Tex.2000) (#5). See "Postjudgment motions that extend the appellate timetable," **O'Connor's Texas Civil Appeals**, ch. 5-A, §6 (2020 ed.).

9-2. Appellate Deadlines

		Appeal from final judgment		Appeal from interlocutory order	
		Notice of appeal	Appellate record	Notice of appeal	Appellate record
1	When no ADE motion* filed	30 days from judgment. Tex. R. App. P. 26.1.	60 days from judgment. Tex. R. App. P. 35.1.	20 days from order. *See* Tex. R. App. P. 26.1(b), 28.1(a).	10 days from notice of appeal. Tex. R. App. P. 35.1(b).
2	When ADE motion* filed	90 days from judgment. Tex. R. App. P. 26.1(a).	120 days from judgment. Tex. R. App. P. 35.1(a).	20 days from order. *See* Tex. R. App. P. 26.1(b), 28.1(a).	10 days from notice of appeal. Tex. R. App. P. 35.1(b).

* ADE motion = a timely filed appellate-deadline-extending motion.

§9.2 Acceptance of judgment. A party cannot treat a judgment as both right and wrong. **Kramer v. Kastleman**, 508 S.W.3d 211, 213 (Tex.2017); **Texas State Bank v. Amaro**, 87 S.W.3d 538, 544 (Tex.2002); **Carle v. Carle**, 234 S.W.2d 1002, 1004 (Tex.1950). Thus, under certain circumstances, a party may be estopped from appealing the judgment.

1. Acceptance-of-benefits doctrine. Generally, the acceptance-of-benefits doctrine prevents a party from appealing a judgment after voluntarily accepting the judgment's benefits. **Kramer**, 508 S.W.3d at 217; **Yazdani-Beioky v.**

Sharifan, 550 S.W.3d 808, 820 (Tex.App.—Houston [14th Dist.] 2018, pet. denied); *see* **Carle**, 234 S.W.2d at 1004. The doctrine can be applied only if the nonappealing party (i.e., the party asserting the doctrine) proves that the appealing party clearly intended to acquiesce in the judgment's validity and the nonappealing party was prejudiced as a result. *See* **Kramer**, 508 S.W.3d at 217; **Carle**, 234 S.W.2d at 1004; **Yazdani-Beioky**, 550 S.W.3d at 820. The acceptance-of-benefits doctrine is an estoppel-based doctrine that requires a court to make a fact-dependent inquiry. **Kramer**, 508 S.W.3d at 228. When making this inquiry, a court may consider several nonexclusive factors, one or more of which may be dispositive. *Id.* at 228–29.

Note

The acceptance-of-benefits doctrine applies to all appeals, but these issues most frequently arise in marital-dissolution cases. ***Kramer****, 508 S.W.3d at 219–20.*

(1) The court may consider whether acceptance of the benefits was voluntary or was the product of financial duress. *Id.* at 228. If the appealing party accepts benefits because of financial duress—which may occur when the party would otherwise not have enough money for the necessities of life—or other similar economic circumstances, her acceptance is not voluntary, and the party may appeal even though she accepted the benefits. *See id.* at 224; *see, e.g.*, **Cooper v. Bushong**, 10 S.W.3d 20, 23–24 (Tex.App.—Austin 1999, pet. denied) (no voluntary acceptance when P filed for bankruptcy and used benefits to pay for family necessities); **Smith v. Texas Commerce Bank**, 822 S.W.2d 812, 814 (Tex.App.—Corpus Christi 1992, writ denied) (acceptance of benefits to pay property taxes was not evidence of financial duress). Similarly, if the party is deceived into accepting the benefits of the judgment, her acceptance is not voluntary, and the party may appeal even though she accepted the benefits. *See* **Kramer**, 508 S.W.3d at 224.

(2) The court may consider whether the right to possession and control of the assets preceded the judgment on appeal or exists only by virtue of the judgment. *Id.* at 228.

(3) The court may consider whether the assets have been so dissipated, wasted, or converted as to prevent their recovery if the judgment is reversed or modified. *Id.* at 228–29.

(4) The court may consider whether the appealing party is entitled to the benefit as a matter of right or by the opposing party's concession. *Id.* at 229. If the reversal of the judgment could not possibly affect the party's right to the benefits she accepted under the judgment, the party may appeal even though she accepted those benefits. *Id.* at 218; **Carle**, 234 S.W.2d at 1004; *see* **Amaro**, 87 S.W.3d at 544. A reversal of a judgment does not affect the party's right to the benefits she accepted under the judgment if she accepted only the benefits she was entitled to (i.e., benefits the opposing party does not deny the appealing party has a right to retain) and the appeal involves only the party's right to further recovery (i.e., the benefits accepted are not at issue on appeal). *See* **Kramer**, 508 S.W.3d at 218; *see, e.g.*, **Briargrove Park Prop. Owners, Inc. v. Riner**, 867 S.W.2d 58, 60–61 (Tex.App.—Texarkana 1993, writ denied) (acceptance of past-due amounts awarded in J did not estop appeal of attorney fees).

(5) The court may consider whether the appeal, if successful, may result in a more favorable judgment but there is no risk of a less favorable one. **Kramer**, 508 S.W.3d at 229.

(6) If a less favorable judgment is possible, the court may consider whether there is no risk the appealing party could receive an award less than the value of the assets dissipated, wasted, or converted. *Id.*

(7) The court may consider whether the appealing party affirmatively sought enforcement of rights or obligations that exist only because of the judgment. *Id.*

(8) The court may consider whether the issue on appeal is severable from the benefits accepted. *Id.* When a judgment is severable, if the appealing party accepts benefits that the opposing party concedes the appealing party is entitled to, that part of the judgment can be severed from other issues that can then be appealed to determine the appealing party's further right to recovery without prejudice to the opposing party. *See id.* at 224–25; **Lipshy v. Lipshy**, 525 S.W.2d 222, 223–24 (Tex.App.—Dallas 1975, writ dism'd).

(9) The court may consider whether actual or reasonably certain prejudice is present. **Kramer**, 508 S.W.3d at 229. For example, in a divorce suit, if the appealing party voluntarily accepts cash that can be restored or otherwise taken

into consideration in redividing the marital estate, the use of that cash does not prejudice the opposing party, and the party challenging the judgment may appeal even though she accepted the benefits. *See id.* at 224.

(10) The court may consider whether any prejudice is curable. *Id.* at 229.

2. Release of judgment. A party who signs a release of judgment is estopped from challenging the judgment by appeal. **Rapp v. Mandell & Wright, P.C.**, 123 S.W.3d 431, 434 (Tex.App.—Houston [14th Dist.] 2003, pet. denied). A release of judgment is itself a complete relinquishment by the party of all its rights in the judgment. *Id.* When a party accepts money in complete satisfaction and release of judgment, the judgment has no further force or authority. *Id.*; *see* **Reames v. Logue**, 712 S.W.2d 802, 804–05 (Tex.App.—Dallas 1986, writ ref'd n.r.e.).

3. Voluntary-payment rule. A party waives its right to appeal and the controversy becomes moot if the party (1) voluntarily pays the judgment and (2) clearly misleads the party receiving payment about her intent to pursue an appeal. **Kramer**, 508 S.W.3d at 227–28; *see* **Hays St. Bridge Restoration Grp. v. City of San Antonio**, 570 S.W.3d 697, 702 (Tex.2019); **Miga v. Jensen**, 299 S.W.3d 98, 103 (Tex.2009); **Marshall v. Housing Auth.**, 198 S.W.3d 782, 787 (Tex.2006). Payment of a judgment will not make the appeal moot if it is the result of fraud, duress, or compulsion. *See* **Miga**, 299 S.W.3d at 103; *see, e.g.*, **Highland Ch. of Christ v. Powell**, 640 S.W.2d 235, 236–37 (Tex.1982) (party did not waive appeal when it paid to avoid execution of J because payment was made under "implied duress").

D. Res Judicata & Collateral Estoppel

§1. General

§1.1 Rules. None.

§1.2 Purpose. Res judicata is sometimes used as a generic term for a group of related concepts about the conclusive effects of final judgments. **Barr v. Resolution Trust Corp.**, 837 S.W.2d 627, 628 (Tex.1992); **Better Bus. Bur. v. John Moore Servs.**, 500 S.W.3d 26, 40 (Tex.App.—Houston [1st Dist.] 2016, pet. denied); **City of San Antonio v. Cortes**, 468 S.W.3d 580, 585 (Tex.App.—San Antonio 2015, pet. denied). Res judicata is designed to promote judicial efficiency and protect litigants from multiple lawsuits. **Citizens Ins. v. Daccach**, 217 S.W.3d 430, 449 (Tex.2007); *see* **Engelman Irrigation Dist. v. Shields Bros.**, 514 S.W.3d 746, 750 (Tex.2017) (policies behind res judicata "reflect the need to bring litigation to an end, prevent vexatious litigation, maintain stability of court decisions, promote judicial economy, and prevent double recovery").

§1.3 Forms. O'Connor's Texas Civil Forms, FORM 3E:11 (2020 ed.) (affirmative defenses), **O'Connor's Texas Civil Forms**, FORM 7C:2 (2020 ed.) (defendant's motion for summary judgment based on counterclaim or affirmative defense).

§1.4 Other references. Restatement Second, Judgments; Ratliff, *Offensive Collateral Estoppel & the Option Effect*, 67 Tex.L.Rev. 63 (1988).

§2. Res judicata & collateral estoppel

§2.1 Comparison. Within the general doctrine of res judicata, there are two principal categories: (1) claim preclusion (also known as res judicata) and (2) issue preclusion (also known as collateral estoppel). **Barr v. Resolution Trust Corp.**, 837 S.W.2d 627, 628 (Tex.1992). Both res judicata and collateral estoppel are affirmative defenses. *See* Tex. R. Civ. P. 94. See "Affirmative defenses in TRCP 94," ch. 3-E, §5.2. In this book, res judicata refers only to claim preclusion and is not used as the generic term covering both categories.

1. Res judicata—claim preclusion. Res judicata bars the litigation of claims actually litigated as well as those arising from the same transaction that could have been litigated. **Engelman Irrigation Dist. v. Shields Bros.**, 514 S.W.3d 746, 750 (Tex.2017); **Igal v. Brightstar Info. Tech. Grp.**, 250 S.W.3d 78, 86 (Tex.2008); **Compania Financiara Libano, S.A. v. Simmons**, 53 S.W.3d 365, 367 (Tex.2001); **Barr**, 837 S.W.2d at 630. Thus, res judicata focuses on what could have been litigated. **Van Dyke v. Boswell, O'Toole, Davis & Pickering**, 697 S.W.2d 381, 384 (Tex.1985). Res judicata requires mutuality of interests—the party invoking it and the party to be bound must have been parties in the earlier suit. See "Same parties," ch. 9-D, §3.2.2. Res judicata is broader than collateral estoppel. **Van Dyke**, 697 S.W.2d at 384.

2. Collateral estoppel—issue preclusion. Collateral estoppel bars the litigation of specific issues already decided in an earlier case; it does not bar an entire cause of action or defense. Thus, collateral estoppel focuses on what was actually litigated and essential to the judgment. **Van Dyke**, 697 S.W.2d at 384. Collateral estoppel does not require mutuality of interests—only the party against whom it is asserted or a person in privity with that party must have been a party in the earlier suit. See "Cast as adversaries," ch. 9-D, §4.2.3.

§2.2 Preclusive effect. The policies behind res judicata and collateral estoppel reflect the need to bring litigation to an end, prevent vexatious litigation, maintain the stability of court decisions, promote judicial economy, and prevent double recovery. **Barr v. Resolution Trust Corp.**, 837 S.W.2d 627, 629 (Tex.1992). When a lawsuit is divided into separate parts, neither res judicata nor collateral estoppel prevents the litigation of the second part of the lawsuit after the first part is litigated. *E.g.*, **Van Dyke v. Boswell, O'Toole, Davis & Pickering**, 697 S.W.2d 381, 384 (Tex.1985) (favorable resolution of claim for attorney fees did not preclude claim for legal malpractice because trial court severed the issues); *see also* **Finger v. Southern Refrigeration Servs.**, 881 S.W.2d 890, 895–96 (Tex.App.—Houston [1st Dist.] 1994, writ denied) (after directed verdict against P1 was reversed on appeal, the unfavorable resolution of the rest of the suit did not preclude retrial by P2 who had been directed out of suit); **Chandler v. Hendrick Mem'l Hosp., Inc.**, 317 S.W.2d 248, 251 (Tex.App.—Eastland 1958, writ ref'd n.r.e.) (judgment stated it did not resolve issue of hospital fees). An interlocutory order on matters incidental

to the main suit does not operate as res judicata or collateral estoppel. *E.g.*, **Texacadian Energy, Inc. v. Lone Star Energy Storage, Inc.**, 829 S.W.2d 369, 373 (Tex.App.—Corpus Christi 1992, writ denied) (denial of motion to perpetuate testimony did not resolve merits of fraud claim).

Note

Under CPRC §31.004(a), if a plaintiff brings suit in a district court after filing suit in a lower trial court (i.e., a justice-of-the-peace court, county court, or statutory county court), only those claims that were actually litigated in the lower trial court are barred by res judicata or collateral estoppel. ***C/S Solutions, Inc. v. Energy Maint. Servs. Grp.****, 274 S.W.3d 299, 310 & n.11 (Tex.App.—Houston [1st Dist.] 2008, no pet.); see, e.g.,* ***Kizer v. Meyer, Lytton, Alen & Whitaker, Inc.****, 228 S.W.3d 384, 391–92 (Tex.App.—Austin 2007, no pet.) (although breach-of-warranty claim in county court at law and breach-of-contract claim in district court were based on same conduct and likely sought same damages, claims were different and required proof of different elements; thus, breach-of-contract claim was not litigated in county court at law and could be brought in district court); see also Tex. Civ. Prac. & Rem. Code §31.004(c) (defining "lower trial court"). Thus, if a claim could have been litigated in the lower trial court but was not, it is not barred.* ***C/S Solutions****, 274 S.W.3d at 310;* ***Kizer****, 228 S.W.3d at 391. Similarly, under CPRC §31.005, if a plaintiff brings suit in a county court or statutory county court after filing suit in a justice-of-the-peace court, only the claims that were actually litigated are barred.* ***Wren v. Gusnowski****, 919 S.W.2d 847, 848–49 (Tex.App.—Austin 1996, no writ).*

§2.3 Which jurisdiction's law. The preclusive effect of a judgment must be determined according to the law of the jurisdiction that issued the initial judgment. *See, e.g.*, **Geary v. Texas Commerce Bank**, 967 S.W.2d 836, 839 (Tex.1998) (court applied federal res judicata to determine preclusive effect of bankruptcy judgment); **Purcell v. Bellinger**, 940 S.W.2d 599, 601 (Tex.1997) (court applied New York res judicata to determine preclusive effect of New York judgment).

§3. Res judicata—Claim preclusion

§3.1 Purpose. Res judicata, or claim preclusion, prevents the relitigation of a claim or cause of action that was adjudicated and resolved by a final judgment, as well as related matters that with the use of diligence should have been litigated in the earlier suit. **Citizens Ins. v. Daccach**, 217 S.W.3d 430, 449 (Tex.2007); **State & Cty. Mut. Fire Ins. v. Miller**, 52 S.W.3d 693, 696 (Tex.2001); **Amstadt v. U.S. Brass Corp.**, 919 S.W.2d 644, 652 (Tex.1996); *see* **Amedisys, Inc. v. Kingwood Home Health Care, LLC**, 437 S.W.3d 507, 516 (Tex.2014) (res judicata after settlement between parties). Claim preclusion prevents splitting a cause of action. **Barr v. Resolution Trust Corp.**, 837 S.W.2d 627, 629 (Tex.1992); **Jeanes v. Henderson**, 688 S.W.2d 100, 103 (Tex.1985); *see* **Ingersoll-Rand Co. v. Valero Energy Corp.**, 997 S.W.2d 203, 206–07 (Tex.1999), *overruled on other grounds*, **In re J.B. Hunt Transp.**, 492 S.W.3d 287 (Tex.2016). Texas courts apply the transactional test from the Restatement Second, Judgments to determine whether two claims involve the same cause of action for res judicata purposes. *See* **Citizens Ins.**, 217 S.W.3d at 449; **Barr**, 837 S.W.2d at 631; **Better Bus. Bur. v. John Moore Servs.**, 500 S.W.3d 26, 40 (Tex.App.—Houston [1st Dist.] 2016, pet. denied); **Hill v. Tx-An Anesthesia Mgmt.**, 443 S.W.3d 416, 424 (Tex.App.—Dallas 2014, no pet.); Restatement Second, Judgments §24. Under that test, the critical issue is whether the two claims arise from the same transaction and are based on the same "nucleus of operative facts." *See* **Better Bus. Bur.**, 500 S.W.3d at 40; **Pinebrook Props., Ltd. v. Brookhaven Lake Prop. Owners Ass'n**, 77 S.W.3d 487, 496 (Tex.App.—Texarkana 2002, pet. denied). A transaction is determined pragmatically, "giving weight to such considerations as whether the facts are related in time, space, origin, or motivation, whether they form a convenient trial unit, and whether their treatment as a trial unit conforms with the parties' expectations or business understanding or usage." **Citizens Ins.**, 217 S.W.3d at 449; **Hill**, 443 S.W.3d at 425; Restatement Second, Judgments §24(2); *e.g.*, **Barr**, 837 S.W.2d at 631 (partnership note and guarantee were part of single transaction); *see, e.g.*, **Southern Cty. Mut. Ins. v. Ochoa**, 19 S.W.3d 452, 466–67 (Tex.App.—Corpus Christi 2000, no pet.) (claim for breach of insurance contract should have been brought in **Stowers** suit).

Note

Res judicata can bar re-arbitration or litigation of matters that have already been arbitrated, as well as related matters that, through the use of diligence, should have been brought before the arbitrator. See ***W. Dow Hamm III Corp. v. Millennium Income Fund, L.L.C.****, 237 S.W.3d 745, 754 (Tex.App.—Houston [1st Dist.] 2007, orig. proceeding) (re-arbitration can be barred by res judicata); see, e.g.,* ***Bencor, Inc. v. Variable Annuity Life Ins.****, No. 01-09-00094-CV, 2011 WL 1330818 (Tex.App.—Houston [1st Dist.] 2011, pet. denied) (memo op.; 4-7-11) (suit was barred by res judicata because claims were sufficiently related to those in arbitration order and award). If res judicata is brought as a defense to the re-arbitration of a matter that has already been arbitrated, the issue is for the arbitrator to decide.* ***W. Dow Hamm III Corp.****, 237 S.W.3d at 755;* ***Aspri Invs. v. Afeef****, No. 04-10-00573-CV, 2011 WL 3849487 (Tex.App.—San Antonio 2011, pet. dism'd) (memo op.; 8-31-11), overruled on other grounds,* ***Hoskins v. Hoskins****, 497 S.W.3d 490 (Tex.2016). If, however, the party seeks to prevent either the arbitration of an issue that was previously decided by a court, or the litigation of an issue that was previously arbitrated, the court must decide whether res judicata applies. See* ***W. Dow Hamm III Corp.****, 237 S.W.3d at 755-56 (under prior-court-judgment exception, court determines whether res judicata bars later arbitration unless court's earlier action was only to confirm arbitration award);* ***Aspri Invs.****, No. 04-10-00573-CV, 2011 WL 3849487 (memo op.) (same); see, e.g.,* ***Bencor, Inc.****, No. 01-09-00094-CV, 2011 WL 1330818 (memo op.) (court decided whether res judicata barred litigation of previously arbitrated claims).*

§3.2 Elements of res judicata. A claim of res judicata requires proof of the following elements:

1. Final judgment. A court of competent jurisdiction signed a final judgment on the merits in the first suit. **Engelman Irrigation Dist. v. Shields Bros.**, 514 S.W.3d 746, 750 (Tex.2017); **Citizens Ins. v. Daccach**, 217 S.W.3d 430, 449 (Tex.2007); **Amstadt v. U.S. Brass Corp.**, 919 S.W.2d 644, 652 (Tex.1996); *e.g.*, **Igal v. Brightstar Info. Tech. Grp.**, 250 S.W.3d 78, 86–87 (Tex.2008) (administrative agency's final judgment on P's claims barred P's later-filed common-law action on same claims); *see, e.g.*, **Travelers Ins. v. Joachim**, 315 S.W.3d 860, 866 (Tex.2010) (order of dismissal with prejudice after nonsuit, although erroneous, was merely voidable and thus was final determination on the merits because P did not directly attack order; P's refiling of same cause of action was barred by res judicata); **Martin v. Martin, Martin & Richards, Inc.**, 989 S.W.2d 357, 358–59 (Tex.1998) (dismissal with prejudice of declaratory-judgment action did not resolve issue of validity of contract); *see also* **Glazer's Wholesale Distribs. v. Heineken USA, Inc.**, 95 S.W.3d 286, 301–02 (Tex.App.—Dallas 2001, pet. granted, judgm't vacated w.r.m.) (res judicata applies to arbitration awards reduced to final judgment). Res judicata does not apply if the court in the first suit lacked subject-matter jurisdiction; a judgment rendered without subject-matter jurisdiction is void and subject to collateral attack. *E.g.*, **Engelman Irrigation Dist.**, 514 S.W.3d at 750 (although sovereign immunity implicates subject-matter jurisdiction, it does not deprive courts of subject-matter jurisdiction; thus, judgment involving sovereign immunity was final and could not be collaterally attacked in later proceeding). See "Governmental immunity from suit," ch. 3-F, §3.7.

2. Same parties. The parties in the second suit are the same as those in the first suit or are in privity with them. **Igal**, 250 S.W.3d at 86; **Citizens Ins.**, 217 S.W.3d at 449; **Amstadt**, 919 S.W.2d at 652–53; *e.g.*, **State Farm Lloyds v. C.M.W.**, 53 S.W.3d 877, 886 (Tex.App.—Dallas 2001, pet. denied) (doctrine did not apply; insurer and insured were not in privity in underlying liability suit in which insurer reserved its rights to contest coverage); **Southwest Guar. Trust Co. v. Providence Trust Co.**, 970 S.W.2d 777, 784 (Tex.App.—Austin 1998, pet. denied) (doctrine did not apply because parties were not the same). Due process requires that res judicata operate only against persons who have already had their day in court, either as a party in the earlier suit or as a person in privity with a party. **Benson v. Wanda Pet. Co.**, 468 S.W.2d 361, 363 (Tex.1971).

(1) Privity. A party is in privity when it is so connected with a party to the first judgment that the parties share the same legal right that is the subject of the suit. **Amstadt**, 919 S.W.2d at 653; **Better Bus. Bur. v. John Moore Servs.**, 500 S.W.3d 26, 41 (Tex.App.—Houston [1st Dist.] 2016, pet. denied); **Hill v. Tx-An Anesthesia Mgmt.**, 443 S.W.3d 416, 425 (Tex.App.—Dallas 2014, no pet.). A party can be in privity when (1) it can control an action even if it is not a party to

the action, (2) its interests can be represented by a party to the action, or (3) it is a successor in interest to the other party and derives its claims through the other party. **Amstadt**, 919 S.W.2d at 653; **Hill**, 443 S.W.3d at 424–25; *e.g.*, **Better Bus. Bur.**, 500 S.W.3d at 41 (facts demonstrated there was identity of interest between corporation named in first suit and its officers and directors named in second suit).

(2) Coparties. When the parties are coparties rather than opposing parties, res judicata acts as a bar to a coparty's claim in a later suit only if one coparty filed a cross-action against another coparty in the earlier suit. **Getty Oil Co. v. Insurance Co. of N. Am.**, 845 S.W.2d 794, 800 (Tex.1992); *see* **Smith v. Baker**, 380 S.W.2d 725, 726 (Tex.App.—Waco 1964), *writ ref'd n.r.e.*, 383 S.W.2d 570 (Tex.1964).

3. Same or related claims. The second suit is based on the same claims that were raised or that could have been raised in the first suit. **Igal**, 250 S.W.3d at 86; **Citizens Ins.**, 217 S.W.3d at 449; **Compania Financiara Libano, S.A. v. Simmons**, 53 S.W.3d 365, 367 (Tex.2001); *e.g.*, **Robinson v. Garcia**, 5 S.W.3d 348, 351–52 (Tex.App.—Corpus Christi 1999, pet. denied) (P's claims in both tax suit and fee suit arose from attorney's representation of him in earlier lawsuit; tax suit was barred by fee suit). The claim must have existed at the time the original suit was filed; res judicata does not bar a claim that accrued after the original judgment. **Hernandez v. Del Ray Chem. Int'l**, 56 S.W.3d 112, 116 (Tex.App.—Houston [14th Dist.] 2001, no pet.); *see, e.g.*, **Compania Financiara**, 53 S.W.3d at 367 (res judicata did not bar P's suit to compel performance of settlement agreement after D breached agreement). When there is a legal relationship (e.g., under a lease, contract, or marriage) all claims resulting from the relationship will arise from the same subject matter and will be subject to res judicata. **Genecov Grp. v. Roosth Prod.**, 144 S.W.3d 546, 552 (Tex.App.—Tyler 2003, pet. denied); **Pinebrook Props., Ltd. v. Brookhaven Lake Prop. Owners Ass'n**, 77 S.W.3d 487, 497 (Tex.App.—Texarkana 2002, pet. denied). The same principles apply to compulsory counterclaims—a defendant must bring as a counterclaim any claim arising from the transaction that is the subject of the plaintiff's suit. **State & Cty. Mut. Fire Ins. v. Miller**, 52 S.W.3d 693, 696 (Tex.2001); **Barr v. Resolution Trust Corp.**, 837 S.W.2d 627, 630 (Tex.1992). Res judicata applies to (1) the cause of action filed by the plaintiff, (2) any counterclaims filed by the defendant, and (3) all compulsory counterclaims the defendant should have filed but did not. *See* **Musgrave v. Owen**, 67 S.W.3d 513, 519 (Tex.App.—Texarkana 2002, no pet.); Restatement Second, Judgments §§18, 21 to 23. See "Compulsory-counterclaim rule," ch. 2-F, §6.1.

§4. Collateral estoppel—Issue preclusion

§4.1 Purpose. Collateral estoppel, or issue preclusion, prevents a party from relitigating a particular fact issue that the party already litigated and lost in an earlier suit. **State & Cty. Mut. Fire Ins. v. Miller**, 52 S.W.3d 693, 696 (Tex.2001); **Quinney Elec., Inc. v. Kondos Entm't, Inc.**, 988 S.W.2d 212, 213 (Tex.1999); **Barr v. Resolution Trust Corp.**, 837 S.W.2d 627, 628 (Tex.1992); **City of San Antonio v. Cortes**, 468 S.W.3d 580, 586 (Tex.App.—San Antonio 2015, pet. denied). To invoke collateral estoppel, a party must establish (1) the same facts sought to be litigated in the second suit were fully litigated in the first suit, (2) those facts were essential to the judgment in the first suit, and (3) the parties were cast as adversaries in the first suit. **Sysco Food Servs. v. Trapnell**, 890 S.W.2d 796, 801 (Tex.1994); **Eagle Props., Ltd. v. Scharbauer**, 807 S.W.2d 714, 721 (Tex.1990); **Better Bus. Bur. v. John Moore Servs.**, 500 S.W.3d 26, 44 (Tex.App.—Houston [1st Dist.] 2016, pet. denied).

Note

Courts can apply principles of collateral estoppel to an arbitration award. ***Zea v. Valley Feed & Sup.****, 354 S.W.3d 873, 877 (Tex.App.—El Paso 2011, pet. dism'd);* ***Continental Holdings, Ltd. v. Leahy****, 132 S.W.3d 471, 474 (Tex.App.—Eastland 2003, no pet.); e.g.,* ***Casa del Mar Ass'n v. Gossen Livingston Assocs.****, 434 S.W.3d 211, 219 (Tex.App.—Houston [1st Dist.] 2014, pet. denied) (to prevail on collateral-estoppel defense in its motion for summary judgment, D had to establish that ultimate fact issues relied on were fully and fairly litigated in arbitration proceeding, were identical to relevant issues in current suit, and were essential to arbitration panel's award). Collateral estoppel does not bar litigation of an issue in a later suit if the issue was not actually decided in the earlier arbitration proceeding or if resolving the issue was not necessary to the arbitration award.* ***Zea****, 354 S.W.3d at 877;* ***Continental Holdings****, 132 S.W.3d at 474–75.*

§4.2 Elements of collateral estoppel. The claim of collateral estoppel requires proof of the following elements:

1. Issues litigated.

(1) Same issue actually litigated. Collateral estoppel applies only if the issue was actually litigated in an earlier proceeding. *E.g.*, **Texas DPS v. Petta**, 44 S.W.3d 575, 579 (Tex.2001) (issue of whether P reasonably believed she faced imminent harm was litigated in her criminal trial); **Johnson & Higgins v. Kenneco Energy, Inc.**, 962 S.W.2d 507, 521–22 (Tex.1998) (issue of contingency insurance was not litigated in federal court); **Housing Auth. v. Massey**, 878 S.W.2d 624, 626–27 (Tex.App.—Corpus Christi 1994, no writ) (collateral estoppel did not bar litigation of issues arising after first suit). "Actually litigated" means that an issue was raised by the pleadings or otherwise submitted for determination and was determined by the fact-finder. **Rexrode v. Bazar**, 937 S.W.2d 614, 617 (Tex.App.—Amarillo 1997, no writ). The issue decided in the first suit must be identical to the issue in the pending suit. **State & Cty. Mut. Fire Ins. v. Miller**, 52 S.W.3d 693, 696 (Tex.2001); **Petta**, 44 S.W.3d at 579. Collateral estoppel may bar relitigation of issues even if the later suit is based on a different cause of action. **Johnson & Higgins**, 962 S.W.2d at 521.

(2) Issue fully & fairly litigated. Collateral estoppel applies only if the issue was fully and fairly litigated in the first suit. **Miller**, 52 S.W.3d at 696; **Petta**, 44 S.W.3d at 579; **Sysco Food Servs. v. Trapnell**, 890 S.W.2d 796, 801 (Tex.1994); *e.g.*, **City of San Antonio v. Cortes**, 468 S.W.3d 580, 586 (Tex.App.—San Antonio 2015, pet. denied) (in first suit, court held that union's claims fell within scope of arbitration agreement and should be arbitrated; union member then filed suit based on same facts and issues as in first suit and, even though he added slightly different claim, collateral estoppel applied); **Rexrode**, 937 S.W.2d at 617 (P who sued D and D's insurer nonsuited D during trial; when insurer was granted directed verdict, P could not sue D again); **Phillips v. Allums**, 882 S.W.2d 71, 74–75 (Tex.App.—Houston [14th Dist.] 1994, writ denied) (D did not have full and fair opportunity to litigate issue of wrongful foreclosure in summary-judgment action); **Robbins v. HNG Oil Co.**, 878 S.W.2d 351, 357–58 (Tex.App.—Beaumont 1994, writ dism'd) (in first suit, 200 heirs sued Ds in federal court based on interpretation of deed, which was resolved against heirs; second suit, in which another heir sued based on same deed, was precluded by collateral estoppel). To determine whether the facts were fully and fairly litigated in the first suit, courts consider whether (1) the parties were fully heard, (2) the court supported its decision with a reasoned opinion, and (3) the decision was subject to appeal or was in fact reviewed on appeal. **Mower v. Boyer**, 811 S.W.2d 560, 562 (Tex.1991); **BP Auto. LP v. RML Waxahachie Dodge, LLC**, 517 S.W.3d 186, 200 (Tex.App.—Texarkana 2017, no pet.); **Better Bus. Bur. v. John Moore Servs.**, 500 S.W.3d 26, 45 (Tex.App.—Houston [1st Dist.] 2016, pet. denied).

2. Essential to judgment. Collateral estoppel applies only if the factual issues were essential to the first judgment. **Miller**, 52 S.W.3d at 696; **Sysco Food**, 890 S.W.2d at 801. To determine whether the same facts were essential to the first judgment, an attorney should remove those facts from the first judgment to see whether their absence changes the judgment. If it does, the facts were essential; if it does not, the facts were not essential. If the first judgment is based on the determination of two issues, either of which is sufficient to support the judgment, the judgment is not conclusive on either issue standing alone. **Eagle Props., Ltd. v. Scharbauer**, 807 S.W.2d 714, 722 (Tex.1990); Restatement Second, Judgments §27, cmt. i; *see* **Parker v. State Farm Mut. Auto. Ins.**, 83 S.W.3d 179, 182 (Tex.App.—San Antonio 2002, no pet.) (when jury refuses to find D negligent, its damages findings are not essential to outcome of suit; thus, collateral estoppel does not bar relitigation of same damages in another suit). In other words, there generally cannot be collateral estoppel by alternative holdings in a trial court's judgment. **Johnson & Higgins**, 962 S.W.2d at 522. The rationale is that when a judgment is based on alternative findings, each finding may not have been as rigorously considered as it would have been if only one had been necessary for the result, and the losing party might have been dissuaded from appealing one issue because the other one might uphold the judgment. **Eagle Props.**, 807 S.W.2d at 722. There is an exception to this rule: if the judgment based on alternative holdings was appealed and affirmed on both grounds, the judgment is conclusive on both. **Johnson & Higgins**, 962 S.W.2d at 522; Restatement Second, Judgments §27, cmt. o.

3. Cast as adversaries. Collateral estoppel bars a party from relitigating an issue resolved in an earlier suit against that same party, someone in privity with that party, or someone whose interest was actually and adequately represented in the earlier trial. **Benson v. Wanda Pet. Co.**, 468 S.W.2d 361, 363 (Tex.1971); *see* **Sysco Food**, 890 S.W.2d at 802–03; *see, e.g.*, **City of San Antonio**, 468 S.W.3d at 587 (union members are in privity with their union for purposes of collateral estoppel). Strict mutuality of parties is not required. **Petta**, 44 S.W.3d at 579; **Sysco Food**, 890 S.W.2d at 801. The

party asserting collateral estoppel does not need to have been a party or in privity with a party to the earlier litigation; only the party against whom the plea is being asserted must have been a party or in privity with a party. **Eagle Props.**, 807 S.W.2d at 721; **Logan v. McDaniel**, 21 S.W.3d 683, 687–88 (Tex.App.—Austin 2000, pet. denied).

(1) Defensive collateral estoppel. A defendant uses defensive collateral estoppel to prevent a plaintiff from relitigating issues the plaintiff lost against another defendant. **Johnson & Higgins**, 962 S.W.2d at 519; **Texas Gen. Indem. Co. v. Texas Workers' Comp. Comm'n**, 36 S.W.3d 635, 638 (Tex.App.—Austin 2000, no pet.); *see, e.g.*, **Hardy v. Fleming**, 553 S.W.2d 790, 791–92 (Tex.App.—El Paso 1977, writ ref'd n.r.e.) (in first suit, P sued employer under workers' compensation for an on-the-job heart attack, but jury found he did not have heart attack; in second suit, because P sued doctor for malpractice for advising him he could return to work just before alleged heart attack, doctor used defense of collateral estoppel to prevent relitigation of whether P had heart attack).

(2) Offensive collateral estoppel. Generally, a plaintiff can use offensive collateral estoppel to assert liability against a defendant who previously litigated and lost a fact issue in a suit involving another party. **Yarbrough's Dirt Pit, Inc. v. Turner**, 65 S.W.3d 210, 216 (Tex.App.—Beaumont 2001, no pet.); **Johnston v. American Med. Int'l**, 36 S.W.3d 572, 577 (Tex.App.—Tyler 2000, pet. denied); **Logan**, 21 S.W.3d at 687. A plaintiff cannot use offensive collateral estoppel, however, if the plaintiff could have easily joined in the earlier suit or if the application of offensive collateral estoppel would be unfair to the defendant. **Fletcher v. National Bank of Commerce**, 825 S.W.2d 176, 179 (Tex.App.—Amarillo 1992, no writ); *see* **Scurlock Oil Co. v. Smithwick**, 724 S.W.2d 1, 7 (Tex.1986); **Yarbrough's Dirt Pit**, 65 S.W.3d at 216–17. When deciding whether to apply offensive collateral estoppel, courts should consider the following factors discussed by the U.S. Supreme Court in **Parklane Hosiery Co. v. Shore**, 439 U.S. 322, 330–31 (1979): (1) whether use of collateral estoppel will reward the plaintiff who could have joined in the previous suit but chose a "wait and see" approach in case the first suit by another plaintiff would result in a favorable judgment, (2) whether the defendant in the first suit had the incentive to fully and vigorously litigate that suit, (3) whether the second suit gives the defendant procedural opportunities that were unavailable to the defendant in the first suit and that could result in a different outcome, and (4) whether the judgment in the first suit is inconsistent with any previous decision that was decided in the defendant's favor. **Fletcher**, 825 S.W.2d at 178–79; **Scurlock Oil Co. v. Smithwick**, 787 S.W.2d 560, 563 (Tex.App.—Corpus Christi 1990, no writ); *see* **Goldstein v. Commission for Lawyer Discipline**, 109 S.W.3d 810, 813 (Tex.App.—Dallas 2003, pet. denied).

§4.3 Exceptions to collateral estoppel.

1. Unfairness. The trial court has discretion to refuse to apply collateral estoppel when it is unfair to do so. *See* **Sysco Food Servs. v. Trapnell**, 890 S.W.2d 796, 804 (Tex.1994); **Scurlock Oil Co. v. Smithwick**, 724 S.W.2d 1, 7 (Tex.1986); **Tankersley v. Durish**, 855 S.W.2d 241, 245 (Tex.App.—Austin 1993, writ denied). For specific fairness issues related to offensive collateral estoppel, see "Offensive collateral estoppel," ch. 9-D, §4.2.3(2).

2. Restatement exceptions. The exceptions to the general rule of collateral estoppel listed in Restatement Second, Judgments §28 are the following:

(1) The party against whom preclusion is sought could not, as a matter of law, have obtained review of the judgment in the initial action.

(2) The issue is one of law, and either (1) the two actions involve substantially unrelated claims, or (2) a new determination is warranted to take account of an intervening change in the applicable legal context or otherwise to avoid inequitable administration of the laws. *See, e.g.*, **Sysco Food**, 890 S.W.2d at 804 (P was prevented by law from suing all Ds in federal court; collateral estoppel did not apply, giving P opportunity to bring claims against those Ds in state court); *see also* **Marino v. State Farm Fire & Cas. Ins.**, 787 S.W.2d 948, 949–50 (Tex.1990) (cause of action for bad faith was not barred by res judicata because it was based on rights acquired after first lawsuit and was not part of that cause of action).

(3) A new determination of the issue is warranted by differences in the quality or extensiveness of the procedures followed in the two courts or by factors relating to the allocation of jurisdiction between them.

(4) The party against whom preclusion is sought had a significantly heavier burden of persuasion on the issue in the first action than it had in the second action, the burden has shifted to its adversary, or the adversary has a significantly heavier burden than it had in the first action.

(5) There is a clear and convincing need for a new determination of the issue because of one of the following: (1) the determination could have an adverse impact on the public interest or the interests of persons who were not parties in the initial action, (2) it was not sufficiently foreseeable at the time of the first action that the issue would arise in the context of another action, or (3) the party against whom preclusion is sought, as a result of the conduct of its adversary or other special circumstances, did not have an adequate opportunity or incentive to obtain a full and fair adjudication in the initial action. *See, e.g.*, **Finger v. Southern Refrigeration Servs.**, 881 S.W.2d 890, 895–96 (Tex.App.—Houston [1st Dist.] 1994, writ denied) (suit was not barred because P, whom D sought to preclude, was improperly excluded from trial by D's motion for directed verdict on grounds that P had no damages; D argued to jury not to consider any damages to P who was excluded).

§5. Effect of pending appeal

A trial court's judgment is final for purposes of the preclusive effect of res judicata or collateral estoppel, even while the case is on appeal. **Amedisys, Inc. v. Kingwood Home Health Care, LLC**, 437 S.W.3d 507, 516 n.7 (Tex.2014); **Scurlock Oil Co. v. Smithwick**, 724 S.W.2d 1, 6 (Tex.1986); *see* Restatement Second, Judgments §13, cmt. b. This rule does not apply if the appeal is a trial de novo. **Scurlock Oil**, 724 S.W.2d at 6.

Chapter 10. Postjudgment Motions

A. Introduction

§1. Preservation generally

To preserve a complaint for appeal, a party must make an objection or present a motion to the trial court and obtain a ruling. TRAP 33 requires that most appellate complaints be presented first to the trial court. See "Preserving error," ch. 1-F, §4.

§2. Attorney responsibility

Immediately after trial, the attorney should mentally review the record and ask: Did the trial court do anything or refuse to do anything that the party wants to complain about on appeal? The attorney should make a list and check it against the record to see if, on each matter, there was a request, an objection, or a motion and either a ruling or a refusal to rule. If the attorney did not make a request, make an objection, make a motion, or get a ruling, the attorney may be able to preserve the complaint in a post-trial motion. As long as the trial court has plenary power over the case, a party may ask the trial court to make a written ruling on an issue raised during the trial.

Note

Some complaints can be made for the first time only in a post-trial motion. Postjudgment motions are thus the absolute last chance to preserve error for appeal.

B. Motion for New Trial

§1. General

§1.1 Rules. Tex. R. Civ. P. 306c, 320 to 329b; Tex. R. App. P. 33.1. See Tex. Gov't Code §51.317(b)(2) ($15 filing fee).

§1.2 Purpose. In a motion for new trial, a party asks the trial court to reconsider and correct trial error—the court's rulings or the jury's findings—by granting a new trial. **Smith v. Brock**, 514 S.W.2d 140, 142 (Tex.App.—Texarkana 1974, no writ); *see* **Barry v. Barry**, 193 S.W.3d 72, 74 (Tex.App.—Houston [1st Dist.] 2006, no pet.) (MNT must, by its very nature, seek to set aside existing judgment and request relitigation of issues). There are at least three reasons to file a motion for new trial: (1) to give the trial court one last chance to correct what the appellant will claim on appeal is reversible error, (2) to preserve that error for appeal, and (3) to extend the appellate deadlines. A party has the right to file a motion for new trial merely to extend the timetables for the appeal, even if there are no reasonable grounds for a new trial. **Old Republic Ins. v. Scott**, 846 S.W.2d 832, 833 (Tex.1993).

§1.3 Timetable & forms. Appendix IV, Timetable 18, Appeal to the court of appeals; **O'Connor's Texas Civil Forms**, FORMS 10B:1 et seq. (2020 ed.).

§1.4 Other references. O'Connor, *Appealing Jury Findings*, 12 Hous.L.Rev. 65 (1974); **O'Connor's Texas Civil Appeals** (2020 ed.); Brown & Rondon, **Texas Rules of Evidence Handbook** (2021 ed.).

§2. Motion

§2.1 When MNT necessary. TRCP 324(b) lists most of the complaints that must be urged in a motion for new trial to preserve error for appeal. In the appeal of a jury trial, the party must file a motion for new trial in the following instances.

Note

A motion for new trial is not necessary to preserve most errors in a nonjury trial. See "MNT after nonjury trial," ch. 10-B, §15.

---

1. To preserve post-trial complaints on which evidence must be heard—for example: • Jury misconduct. Tex. R. Civ. P. 324(b)(1). • Newly discovered evidence. *Id.* • Failure to set aside a default judgment. *Id.* • Lack of consent to an agreed judgment. **Hensley v. Salinas**, 583 S.W.2d 617, 618 (Tex.1979); **Sohocki v. Sohocki**, 897 S.W.2d 422, 424 (Tex.App.—Corpus Christi 1995, no writ). • Allegations that an agreed judgment was the result of fraud, collusion, or misrepresentation. *See* **In re O.A.G.**, No. 04-09-00222-CV, 2010 WL 1491647 (Tex.App.—San Antonio 2010, no pet.) (memo op.; 4-14-10). • Challenge to an award of guardian ad litem fees. **Navistar Int'l v. Valles**, 740 S.W.2d 4, 6 (Tex.App.—El Paso 1987, no writ).

2. To preserve the complaint that the evidence is factually insufficient to support a jury finding or, conversely, that the jury finding is against the overwhelming weight of the evidence. Tex. R. Civ. P. 324(b)(2), (b)(3); **Fredonia State Bank v. General Am. Life Ins.**, 881 S.W.2d 279, 281 (Tex.1994); **Cecil v. Smith**, 804 S.W.2d 509, 512 (Tex.1991). See "MNT to challenge the evidence," ch. 10-B, §13.

3. To preserve the complaint that the jury's damages are inadequate or excessive. Tex. R. Civ. P. 324(b)(4); **Hawthorne v. Guenther**, 917 S.W.2d 924, 937 (Tex.App.—Beaumont 1996, writ denied).

4. To preserve the complaint of incurable jury argument if the trial court did not already rule on it. Tex. R. Civ. P. 324(b)(5); **Warrantech Corp. v. Computer Adapters Servs.**, 134 S.W.3d 516, 531 n.10 (Tex.App.—Fort Worth 2004, no pet.).

5. To preserve complaints not brought to the trial court's attention during the trial or included in some other post-trial motion. *See* Tex. R. Civ. P. 324(a), (b) (listing complaints that require MNT to preserve error); *see, e.g.*, **Luna v. Southern Pac. Transp.**, 724 S.W.2d 383, 384 (Tex.1987) (complaint about apportionment of damages was waived because it was not preserved in MNT or earlier); *see also* Tex. R. App. P. 33.1(a) (party preserves complaint for appellate review by presenting it to trial court and obtaining ruling).

§2.2 In writing. The motion for new trial must be in writing and signed by the attorney or the party. Tex. R. Civ. P. 320.

§2.3 Points of error. The motion for new trial must list the complaints in the points of error. Tex. R. Civ. P. 321. The complaints in the points must be specific. Tex. R. Civ. P. 322. The party should state what happened and why it was error. The points should cover the "who," "what," and "why" of the complaint. For example:

> *The trial court (who) erred in overruling the defendant's objections that jury question number 4 contained a comment on the evidence (what) because the question assumed as true that the defendant was negligent (why).*

On appeal, these points can be used as the statement of the issues presented in the brief. *See* Tex. R. App. P. 38.1(f) (in appellate briefs, parties must "state concisely all issues or points presented for review"); **Gerdes v. Kennamer**, 155 S.W.3d 523, 532 (Tex.App.—Corpus Christi 2004, pet. denied) (issues raised on appeal must correspond with motion made to trial court).

§2.4 Prayer. The motion for new trial must include a request to relitigate the case. **Barry v. Barry**, 193 S.W.3d 72, 74 (Tex.App.—Houston [1st Dist.] 2006, no pet.); **Mercer v. Band**, 454 S.W.2d 833, 836 (Tex.App.—Houston [14th Dist.] 1970, no writ); *see, e.g.*, **Finley v. J.C. Pace Ltd.**, 4 S.W.3d 319, 320 (Tex.App.—Houston [1st Dist.] 1999, order) (although motion requested rehearing, it was MNT because it sought to set aside judgment for the purpose of litigating the issues). If the motion asks for other relief (e.g., to enter a different judgment), it is not a motion for new trial. **Mercer**, 454 S.W.2d at 836.

§2.5 Effect of MNT.

1. On plenary power. The timely filing of a motion for new trial extends the trial court's plenary power over the judgment. If the motion is denied, plenary power is extended until 30 days after the motion is denied, either by written order or by operation of law, whichever occurs first; however, plenary power cannot be extended more than 105 days after the date the judgment was signed. **Lane Bank Equip. Co. v. Smith S. Equip., Inc.**, 10 S.W.3d 308, 310 (Tex.2000). If the motion is granted, the case is reinstated on the trial court's docket and the court retains ongoing plenary power until it signs another final judgment. *See* **In re Baylor Med. Ctr.**, 280 S.W.3d 227, 230–31 (Tex.2008). See "Effect of PPE motions," ch. 9-C, §6.4.2; chart 9-1 under "PPE motion withdrawn," ch. 9-C, §6.4.2(4).

2. On appellate deadlines. See "Calculating appellate deadlines," ch. 9-C, §9.1.

§3. Verification & affidavits

It is usually not necessary to verify motions for new trial or to attach affidavits. For example, sworn proof is not necessary to challenge the sufficiency of the evidence.

§3.1 When verification required. It is necessary to verify a motion for new trial and include affidavits when the motion is based on the grounds listed in TRCP 324(b)(1) (jury misconduct, newly discovered evidence, failure to set aside a default judgment) or on any other ground that requires the presentation of evidence at a hearing. *See* **Zuniga v. Zuniga**, 13 S.W.3d 798, 803 n.4 (Tex.App.—San Antonio 1999, no pet.), *disapproved on other grounds*, **In re Z.L.T.**, 124 S.W.3d 163 (Tex.2003). See "Verification," ch. 1-B, §3.2.15; "Affidavits," ch. 1-B, §3.2.16; **O'Connor's Texas Civil Forms**, FORMS 1B:7 to 1B:8 (2020 ed.). When in doubt, parties should verify the motion. For the requirements for using an unsworn declaration instead of a verification or an affidavit, see "Unsworn declaration," ch. 1-B, §3.2.17; **O'Connor's Texas Civil Forms**, FORM 1B:9 (2020 ed.).

§3.2 Controverting affidavits. When the movant files a motion for new trial with affidavits, the nonmovant should consider filing controverting affidavits. On appeal, if there is no recorded hearing and no controverting affidavits, the appellate court will assume the movant's affidavit is true. *See* **Director, State Empls. Workers' Comp. Div. v. Evans**, 889 S.W.2d 266, 268–69 (Tex.1994); **Onyeanu v. Rivertree Apts. & Guaranteed Builders, Inc.**, 920 S.W.2d 397, 398 (Tex.App.—Houston [1st Dist.] 1996, no writ).

§4. Filing fee for MNT

§4.1 Amount & timing of fee. A $15 filing fee must be paid at the time a motion for new trial is filed. Tex. Gov't Code §51.317(b)(2). Before filing, the attorney should check with the court clerk to see if the county has other fees. There will be an additional fee, not more than $10, for court-records archiving. Tex. Gov't Code §51.317(b)(5).

§4.2 MNT timely but fee late. If a motion for new trial is filed without payment of the fee, the document is considered "conditionally filed" on the date it was tendered to the clerk. **Jamar v. Patterson**, 868 S.W.2d 318, 319 (Tex.1993). When the filing fee is paid, the document is deemed filed on the date it was originally tendered. *See id.* Case law distinguishes between the effect of late payment on the appellate deadlines and on the preservation of error of the issues in the motion for new trial.

1. Late fee & appellate deadlines. The payment of the filing fee has no effect on the appellate deadlines; the appellate deadlines are extended even when the filing fee for a motion for new trial is never paid. *E.g.*, **Garza v. Garcia**, 137 S.W.3d 36, 37–38 (Tex.2004) (fee not paid); **Tate v. E.I. DuPont de Nemours & Co.**, 934 S.W.2d 83, 84 (Tex.1996) (fee paid late).

2. Late fee & preservation of error.

(1) Paid before loss of plenary power.

(a) Before MNT overruled. When the filing fee for a motion for new trial is paid before the trial court loses plenary power and before the motion is overruled, the motion probably preserves error for appeal. *See* **Jamar**, 868 S.W.2d at 319 n.3 (trial court should not consider MNT before fee is paid).

(b) After MNT overruled. When the filing fee for a motion for new trial is paid before the trial court loses plenary power but after the motion is overruled, it is uncertain whether the motion preserves error for appeal. *See* **Tate**, 934 S.W.2d at 84 n.1 (Supreme Court did not express opinion on issue).

(2) Paid after loss of plenary power. When the filing fee for a motion for new trial is paid after the trial court loses plenary power, the motion does not preserve error for those issues that must be preserved in a motion for new trial. *See, e.g.*, **Garza**, 137 S.W.3d at 37–38 (factual-sufficiency complaint in MNT was not preserved because fee was never paid); **Marathon Corp. v. Pitzner**, 55 S.W.3d 114, 125 (Tex.App.—Corpus Christi 2001) (factual-sufficiency complaints in MNT were not preserved because fee was paid after trial court lost plenary power), *rev'd on other grounds*, 106 S.W.3d 724 (Tex.2003).

§5. Deadlines for MNT

§5.1 Original MNT. A motion for new trial must be filed within 30 days after the date the judgment was signed. Tex. R. Civ. P. 329b(a); **Padilla v. LaFrance**, 907 S.W.2d 454, 458 (Tex.1995); **Jamar v. Patterson**, 868 S.W.2d 318, 319 (Tex.1993); *see, e.g.*, **Williams v. Flores**, 88 S.W.3d 631, 632 (Tex.2002) (MNT timely filed on 32nd day after judgment because 30th day was Sunday and 31st day was legal holiday). A motion for new trial filed more than 30 days after the judgment was signed is void and cannot be considered by the trial court. *See* **Equinox Enters. v. Associated Media Inc.**, 730 S.W.2d 872, 875 (Tex.App.—Dallas 1987, no writ).

§5.2 No extensions. TRCP 5 prohibits the trial court from extending the time period "for taking any action under the rules relating to new trials." **Moritz v. Preiss**, 121 S.W.3d 715, 720 (Tex.2003); **Lind v. Gresham**, 672 S.W.2d 20, 22 (Tex.App.—Houston [14th Dist.] 1984, no writ). Thus, the trial court cannot grant an extension of time to file the motion for new trial. **Moritz**, 121 S.W.3d at 720; **Lind**, 672 S.W.2d at 22. If the court signs a modified judgment within its plenary power, however, the modified judgment acts as a new judgment that gives the parties another 30 days to file a motion for new trial. *See* **Check v. Mitchell**, 758 S.W.2d 755, 756 (Tex.1988); *see also* Tex. R. Civ. P. 329b(h) (if judgment is modified "in any respect, the time for appeal shall run" from date of modified judgment). See "Motion to Modify the Judgment," ch. 10-D, §1 et seq.

§5.3 Late MNT + plenary power. Even though the trial court cannot extend the time to file the motion for new trial, it can grant a new trial on the grounds stated in a late motion if the motion is filed before the court loses plenary power. **Moritz v. Preiss**, 121 S.W.3d 715, 720 (Tex.2003); *see* Tex. R. Civ. P. 320. The court is not actually granting the late motion; it is granting a new trial on its own initiative. *See* **Moritz**, 121 S.W.3d at 720. The late motion is meaningless for preserving error for appeal, but the grounds stated in the motion may convince the trial court that a new trial is necessary. *See id.*; **Kalteyer v. Sneed**, 837 S.W.2d 848, 851 (Tex.App.—Austin 1992, no writ).

§5.4 Premature MNT. A premature motion for new trial, filed before the judgment is signed, is deemed filed on the day of, but immediately after, the signing of the judgment. Tex. R. Civ. P. 306c; **Ryland Enter. v. Weatherspoon**, 355 S.W.3d 664, 665–66 (Tex.2011); **Padilla v. LaFrance**, 907 S.W.2d 454, 458 (Tex.1995).

Note

Two courts have held that a prematurely filed motion for new trial was not denied by a final judgment that contained a Mother Hubbard clause (i.e., a statement that all relief requested that is not expressly granted in the order is denied), but the courts did not address the premature motion for new trial. See, e.g., ***In re Piatt Servs. Int'l****, 493 S.W.3d 276, 282–83 (Tex.App.—Austin 2016, orig. proceeding) (final judgment containing Mother Hubbard clause could not be construed as denying prematurely filed MNT because it would have overruled MNT assailing the very judgment being created);* ***In re Timberlake****, 501 S.W.3d 105, 110 (Tex.App.—Houston [14th Dist.] 2015, orig. proceeding) (because prematurely filed MNT is deemed filed after final judgment is signed, trial court could not have denied MNT in its final judgment because MNT was not yet considered filed). Thus, the trial courts in those cases each retained plenary power to consider a timely, later-filed second motion for new trial when the prematurely filed motion had not been overruled. See* ***In re Piatt Servs.****, 493 S.W.3d at 283;* ***In re Timberlake****, 501 S.W.3d at 109–10. See "Amended MNT," ch. 10-B, §5.5. In* ***In re Piatt Servs.****, the court's holding was based on the specific language of the judgment in that case; the court did not rule out the possibility that a final judgment could be drafted in a way that would also overrule a prematurely filed motion for new trial. See* ***In re Piatt Servs.****, 493 S.W.3d at 283.*

§5.5 Amended MNT. An amended or supplemental motion for new trial is timely and may be filed without leave of court if it is filed within 30 days of the judgment and the trial court has not overruled the earlier motion for new trial. **In re Brookshire Grocery Co.**, 250 S.W.3d 66, 69–70 (Tex.2008). Even if filed with leave of court, an amended motion for new trial is not timely for purposes of extending plenary power if it is filed after an earlier motion for new trial was overruled. *Id.* at 71. A timely amended or supplemental motion for new trial preserves complaints for appeal. *See* **Moritz v. Preiss**, 121 S.W.3d 715, 721 (Tex.2003) (untimely amended MNT does not preserve issues for appellate review, even if they arose after court overruled earlier MNT).

Note

A trial court has discretion to consider an untimely amended motion for new trial as long as it has plenary power. ***In re Brookshire Grocery****, 250 S.W.3d at 71–72 & n.8. But an untimely amended motion for new trial can only provide the court with guidance in the exercise of its inherent authority.* ***Moritz****, 121 S.W.3d at 720. Because an untimely amended motion for new trial does not preserve complaints for appeal, a party should wait as long as possible to file an original motion for new trial to reduce the risk that it will waive issues on appeal.* ***In re Brookshire Grocery****, 250 S.W.3d at 75 (Hecht, J., dissenting).*

§5.6 Second-judgment problems.

1. Preservation of error. When the trial court corrects the judgment by signing a second judgment, a motion for new trial filed to challenge the first judgment is effective for the second judgment if the substance of the motion challenges the second judgment. **Fredonia State Bank v. General Am. Life Ins.**, 881 S.W.2d 279, 281 (Tex.1994); *see* Tex. R. App. P. 27.3.

2. Extending appellate deadlines. A motion for new trial filed after the first judgment, but not granted, is a prematurely filed motion as to a second judgment, and it extends the appellate timetable from the signing of the second judgment if the grounds in the motion "assail" the second judgment. **Wilkins v. Methodist Health Care Sys.**, 160 S.W.3d 559, 562 (Tex.2005); *see* Tex. R. Civ. P. 306c; Tex. R. App. P. 27.2; *see also* **Padilla v. LaFrance**, 907 S.W.2d 454, 458–59 (Tex.1995) (motion for reconsideration of summary judgment, filed before court signed severance order making judgment

final, extended appellate deadlines). However, a motion for new trial that is granted after the first judgment does not assail the second judgment for purposes of determining the appellate timetable. **Wilkins**, 160 S.W.3d at 564. In such a case, the motion for new trial is not prematurely filed as to the second judgment, and thus the appellate deadlines are not extended. *E.g., id.* (because MNT was granted before second judgment, notice of appeal was due 30 days after second judgment, not 90 days after).

§5.7 Late notice of judgment. If a party receives notice of the judgment 21 to 90 days after the judgment was signed, the deadline for filing a motion for new trial is counted from the date the party actually learned of or received notice of the judgment, rather than the date the judgment was signed. *See* Tex. R. Civ. P. 306a(4). See "Motion to Extend Postjudgment Deadlines," ch. 10-G, §1 et seq.

§5.8 MNT after citation by publication. The defendant may file a motion for new trial within two years after the court signs a judgment after citation by publication. Tex. R. Civ. P. 329(a); **Montgomery v. R.E.C. Interests, Inc.**, 130 S.W.3d 444, 445 n.1 (Tex.App.—Texarkana 2004, no pet.). The same is true if a judgment was signed after the citation was posted on the courthouse door. **Gray v. PHI Res.**, 710 S.W.2d 566, 568 (Tex.1986). See "MNT after service by publication," ch. 10-B, §10.

§5.9 After domesticated foreign judgment. Under the Uniform Enforcement of Foreign Judgments Act (UEFJA), CPRC ch. 35, a plaintiff's filing of an authenticated copy of a foreign judgment in a Texas court constitutes both the plaintiff's original petition and a final Texas judgment. **Walnut Equip. Leasing Co. v. Wen Lung Wu**, 920 S.W.2d 285, 286 (Tex.1996). The defendant must file a motion for new trial within 30 days after the foreign judgment is filed. **Moncrief v. Harvey**, 805 S.W.2d 20, 23 (Tex.App.—Dallas 1991, no writ); *see* **Walnut Equip.**, 920 S.W.2d at 286. Any motion to contest the enforcement of a foreign judgment under the UEFJA operates as a motion for new trial. **Moncrief**, 805 S.W.2d at 23; *e.g.*, **Wolf v. Andreas**, 276 S.W.3d 23, 26 (Tex.App.—El Paso 2008, no pet.) (counterclaim for declaratory judgment and injunctive relief was considered postjudgment motion).

§6. Response

When the movant files an unsworn motion for new trial, the nonmovant probably does not need to file a response. However, because some local rules infer acquiescence when the nonmovant does not file a response, the nonmovant's attorney should always check the local rules. *See, e.g.*, Harris Cty. Loc. R. 3.3.2 (district courts; not filing response can be considered representation of no opposition). When the movant files a sworn motion for new trial, the nonmovant should file a sworn response. See **O'Connor's Texas Civil Forms**, FORM 10B:7 (2020 ed.).

§7. Hearing

§7.1 Unsworn MNT—no hearing. Most motions for new trial do not require a hearing. The hearing on an unsworn motion is for argument only, and no evidence may be presented.

§7.2 Sworn MNT—hearing. If a motion for new trial requires sworn evidence to support it, it also requires a hearing to receive evidence. If the motion and affidavits are in proper form and timely filed, the motion alleges specific facts that, if true, would entitle the movant to a new trial, and a hearing is properly requested, the court must hold a hearing. *See* **Cecil v. Smith**, 804 S.W.2d 509, 511 n.5 (Tex.1991); **Hensley v. Salinas**, 583 S.W.2d 617, 618 (Tex.1979); **Neyland v. Raymond**, 324 S.W.3d 646, 652–53 (Tex.App.—Fort Worth 2010, no pet.); *see, e.g.*, **State Farm Lloyds v. Nicolau**, 951 S.W.2d 444, 452 (Tex.1997) (D was not entitled to MNT hearing because there was no showing that new evidence would likely result in different verdict). The types of motions for new trial that require a hearing include those based on jury misconduct, newly discovered evidence, failure to set aside a default judgment, and any other motion that must be supported by evidence. *See, e.g.*, **Hensley**, 583 S.W.2d at 618 (hearing required for MNT challenging agreed judgment); **Navistar Int'l v. Valles**, 740 S.W.2d 4, 6–7 (Tex.App.—El Paso 1987, no writ) (hearing required for MNT challenging guardian ad litem fees).

1. Setting. When a motion for new trial requires a hearing, the movant must ask the court for a setting and not allow its motion to be overruled by operation of law. *See* **Felt v. Comerica Bank**, 401 S.W.3d 802, 808 (Tex.App.—Houston [14th Dist.] 2013, no pet.); **Shamrock Roofing Sup. v. Mercantile Nat'l Bank**, 703 S.W.2d 356, 357–58 (Tex.App.—Dallas 1985, no writ). *But see* **Limestone Constr., Inc. v. Summit Commercial Indus. Props., Inc.**, 143 S.W.3d 538, 546 (Tex.App.—Austin 2004, no pet.) (because movant's affidavit established right to new trial, nonmovant had burden to request hearing).

2. Affidavits. When affidavits are filed as part of a motion for new trial, the proponent of the affidavits is not required to introduce them into evidence at the hearing on the motion. **Director, State Empls. Workers' Comp. Div. v. Evans**, 889 S.W.2d 266, 268 (Tex.1994). It is sufficient that the affidavits are attached to the motion for new trial and made part of the record. *Id.*

§8. Order

§8.1 In writing. The trial court's order on a motion for new trial must be in writing and signed by the trial court. Tex R. Civ. P. 329b(c); **In re Lovito-Nelson**, 278 S.W.3d 773, 775 (Tex.2009); **In re Barber**, 982 S.W.2d 364, 366 (Tex.1998). See "In writing," ch. 1-G, §3.1; **O'Connor's Texas Civil Forms**, FORM 10B:8 (2020 ed.). The trial court's oral pronouncement and docket entry are not a substitute for a written order. **In re Lovito-Nelson**, 278 S.W.3d at 775; **Faulkner v. Culver**, 851 S.W.2d 187, 188 (Tex.1993); *see also* **Estate of Townes v. Wood**, 934 S.W.2d 806, 807 (Tex.App.—Houston [1st Dist.] 1996, orig. proceeding) (written, signed order setting case for trial is not substitute for written, signed order granting MNT). See "Not an order," ch. 1-G, §3.3.1.

§8.2 Grounds. The trial court has broad discretion in granting a new trial. **In re Columbia Med. Ctr.**, 290 S.W.3d 204, 210 (Tex.2009). A new trial may be granted "for good cause, on motion or on the court's own motion." Tex. R. Civ. P. 320; **In re Columbia Med. Ctr.**, 290 S.W.3d at 210. The court must clearly identify its specific reasons for granting a new trial. **In re Columbia Med. Ctr.**, 290 S.W.3d at 212.

Caution

Broad reasons like "in the interest of justice" are not adequate for granting a new trial. ***In re Columbia Med. Ctr.****, 290 S.W.3d at 215. The court's stated reasons for granting a new trial must be legally appropriate and reasonably specific.* ***In re Toyota Motor Sales, U.S.A., Inc.****, 407 S.W.3d 746, 757 (Tex.2013);* ***In re United Scaffolding, Inc.****, 377 S.W.3d 685, 688–89 (Tex.2012). They must also be substantively valid. See* ***In re Toyota Motor Sales****, 407 S.W.3d at 758. See "Order granting new trial," ch. 10-B, §17.5.*

§8.3 Partial new trial. TRCP 320 permits the trial court to grant a new trial on part of the case under the following conditions:

1. Separable. The matter is clearly separable. Tex. R. Civ. P. 320; **State Dept. of Hwys. & Pub. Transp. v. Cotner**, 845 S.W.2d 818, 819 (Tex.1993); *see also* **Satellite Earth Stations E., Inc. v. Davis**, 756 S.W.2d 385, 387 (Tex.App.—Eastland 1988, writ denied) (when attorney fees are mandatory, they are clearly separable). To determine what is separable, consult TRCP 41 and 174(b). A partial new trial may be ordered despite the prohibition in TRCP 41 against postsubmission severances; thus, TRCP 320 is an exception to TRCP 41. **Cotner**, 845 S.W.2d at 819.

2. Not unfair. The matter is separable without unfairness to the parties. Tex R. Civ. P. 320; *e.g.*, **Cotner**, 845 S.W.2d at 819 (in personal-injury suit, court could not grant partial new trial to one P and affirm for other P).

3. Liquidated damages. The damages are liquidated, or the damages are unliquidated and liability is not contested. *See* Tex. R. Civ. P. 320. The court cannot grant a partial new trial on unliquidated damages if liability is contested. *Id.*; *see* **Redman Homes, Inc. v. Ivy**, 920 S.W.2d 664, 669 (Tex.1996).

§8.4 Deadline to sign order on MNT.

1. Generally. The court should sign an order granting or denying the motion within 75 days after the date the judgment was signed; if the court does not sign an order, the motion is overruled by operation of law on the 76th day after the date the judgment was signed. *See* Tex. R. Civ. P. 329b(c) ("overruled by operation of law on expiration of" 75 days); **In re Dickason**, 987 S.W.2d 570, 571 (Tex.1998) (court has plenary power to act on motion for 75 days after judgment was signed); **Thomas v. Oldham**, 895 S.W.2d 352, 356 (Tex.1995) (court may grant MNT within 75 days after judgment was signed). On two separate occasions, the Supreme Court has mistakenly said that a motion for new trial is overruled by operation of law on the 75th day, instead of "on expiration of" 75 days. *See, e.g.*, **Faulkner v. Culver**, 851 S.W.2d 187, 188 (Tex.1993) (MNT was overruled by operation of law 75 days after judgment was signed); **Clark & Co. v. Giles**, 639 S.W.2d 449, 450 (Tex.1982) (MNT was overruled by operation of law on 75th day).

2. Quo warranto proceeding. In an appeal in a quo warranto proceeding, the trial court can grant a timely filed motion for new trial until 50 days after the judgment was signed. Tex. R. App. P. 28.1(d). If the motion for new trial is not determined within the 50-day period, it is overruled by operation of law. *Id.*

§8.5 Deadline to change order on MNT. The court can change its order on the motion for new trial as long as it has plenary power over the judgment. To determine when plenary power expires, see chart 9-1 under "PPE motion withdrawn," ch. 9-C, §6.4.2(4).

1. When MNT granted. When a trial court grants a motion for new trial, it retains ongoing plenary power over the case and can set aside the new-trial order anytime before it signs another final judgment. See "MNT granted + order 'ungranted'," ch. 9-C, §6.4.2(3)(a)[2].

2. When MNT overruled. When the motion for new trial is overruled (either by written order or by operation of law), the court has the power to grant a new trial as long as it has plenary power over the judgment—that is, 30 days after the date the motion was overruled, but not later than 105 days after the date the judgment was signed. *See* Tex. R. Civ. P. 329b(c), (e); **L.M. Healthcare, Inc. v. Childs**, 929 S.W.2d 442, 444 (Tex.1996). See "PPE motion overruled," ch. 9-C, §6.4.2(2).

§9. MNT after default judgment

Most default judgments are granted because a defendant does not file an answer (no-answer default) or does not appear for trial or another dispositive hearing (post-answer default).

§9.1 Sworn motion. Before filing a motion for new trial to challenge a default judgment, the party should determine how and when the default judgment was rendered. Was the judgment rendered before or after the defendant answered? Was service on the defendant defective? Did the defendant have notice of the trial? How much time has passed since the judgment was rendered? The critical question is why the defendant did not appear. **Sutherland v. Spencer**, 376 S.W.3d 752, 755 (Tex.2012); **Fidelity & Guar. Ins. v. Drewery Constr. Co.**, 186 S.W.3d 571, 574 (Tex.2006). For ways to challenge a default judgment other than by a motion for new trial, see "Attacking default judgment," ch. 7-A, §7.

1. Improper service + no-answer default.

(1) Defects in service of process & plaintiff's petition. To challenge a no-answer default judgment rendered after improper service of process, the motion for new trial should object to any defects in the service documents and the plaintiff's petition.

(a) Defects in citation. The defendant should challenge defects in the citation. The citation must meet all the requirements of TRCP 15 and 99. See "Requirements for the citation," ch. 2-I, §2; **O'Connor's Texas Civil Forms**, FORM 10B:3, §A (2020 ed.).

(b) Defects in service. The defendant should challenge defects in the service of process. See "Sufficiency of service," ch. 7-A, §3.4; **O'Connor's Texas Civil Forms**, FORM 10B:3, §B (2020 ed.).

(c) Defects in return. The defendant should challenge defects in the return of service. The return must meet all the requirements of TRCP 107. See "Proof of service—The return," ch. 2-I, §9; **O'Connor's Texas Civil Forms**, FORM 10B:3, §F (2020 ed.).

(d) Defects in plaintiff's petition. The defendant should challenge defects in the plaintiff's petition. See **O'Connor's Texas Civil Forms**, FORM 10B:3, §H (2020 ed.). A plaintiff's petition will support a default judgment if it (1) attempts to state a cause of action within the court's jurisdiction against a defendant who is amenable to process, (2) gives fair notice to the defendant of its claim, and (3) does not affirmatively disclose the invalidity of its claim. *See* **Paramount Pipe & Sup. Co. v. Muhr**, 749 S.W.2d 491, 494 (Tex.1988); **Stoner v. Thompson**, 578 S.W.2d 679, 684–85 (Tex.1979). For a discussion of the sufficiency of the plaintiff's petition, see "Plaintiff's Original Petition," ch. 2-B, §1 et seq.; "Sufficiency of plaintiff's petition," ch. 7-A, §3.2.

(2) *Craddock* factors. If the defendant asserts that it did not file an answer because of improper service and proves that service was improper, the defendant does not need to establish the factors from **Craddock v. Sunshine Bus**

Lines, Inc., 133 S.W.2d 124 (Tex.1939), to be entitled to a new trial. *See* **Sutherland**, 376 S.W.3d at 755; **Fidelity & Guar.**, 186 S.W.3d at 574; **Kaminetzky v. Newman**, No. 01-10-01113-CV, 2011 WL 6938536 (Tex.App.—Houston [1st Dist.] 2011, no pet.) (memo op.; 12-29-11); *cf.* **Peralta v. Heights Med. Ctr., Inc.**, 485 U.S. 80, 86 (1988) (bill of review; when no-answer default is rendered against D after improper service and D had no notice of judgment, D is not required to prove meritorious defense to be entitled to new trial). Even if the defendant has actual notice of the lawsuit, without proper service, the defendant has no duty to act; thus, the court cannot render a default judgment. **Wilson v. Dunn**, 800 S.W.2d 833, 837 (Tex.1990); *see* **Fidelity & Guar.**, 186 S.W.3d at 574 n.1 (receiving suit papers or actual notice through procedure not authorized for service is treated the same as never receiving them). If the defendant is uncertain whether the court will sustain its argument that it did not receive proper service or notice, the defendant should allege and prove the three **Craddock** factors as an alternative ground for reversal. See "Failure to answer or appear after proper notice," ch. 10-B, §9.1.3.

2. No notice of trial + post-answer default.

(1) Allege no notice. When a post-answer default is rendered without proper notice, the motion should allege and prove that the defendant did not receive notice of the trial or dispositive hearing. See "Notice of trial or dispositive hearing," ch. 7-A, §4.3. Proof of lack of notice satisfies the first **Craddock** factor because, without notice, a defendant cannot intentionally or with conscious indifference fail to appear. *See* **Texas Sting, Ltd. v. R.B. Foods, Inc.**, 82 S.W.3d 644, 651–52 (Tex.App.—San Antonio 2002, pet. denied). See "Failure to answer or appear after proper notice," ch. 10-B, §9.1.3; **O'Connor's Texas Civil Forms**, FORM 10B:4, §A (2020 ed.).

(2) Other *Craddock* factors unnecessary. If a defendant is able to prove lack of notice of the trial or dispositive hearing, the defendant does not need to establish the remaining **Craddock** factors to be entitled to a new trial. *See* **Mathis v. Lockwood**, 166 S.W.3d 743, 744 (Tex.2005) (if first **Craddock** factor is established, D does not have to prove meritorious defense); **Lopez v. Lopez**, 757 S.W.2d 721, 723 (Tex.1988) (same); **Mahand v. Delaney**, 60 S.W.3d 371, 375 (Tex.App.—Houston [1st Dist.] 2001, no pet.) (if first **Craddock** factor is established, D does not have to prove meritorious defense or no delay or injury to P). See "Failure to answer or appear after proper notice," ch. 10-B, §9.1.3. Once a defendant makes an appearance, it is entitled to notice of the trial setting as a matter of due process under the 14th Amendment to the U.S. Constitution. **LBL Oil Co. v. International Power Servs.**, 777 S.W.2d 390, 390–91 (Tex.1989).

(3) Allege *Craddock* factors in alternative. If the defendant is uncertain whether the court will sustain its argument that it did not receive proper notice, the defendant should allege and prove the three **Craddock** factors as an alternative ground for reversal. See ch. 10-B, §9.1.3, below; **O'Connor's Texas Civil Forms**, FORM 10B:4, §B (2020 ed.).

3. Failure to answer or appear after proper notice. When a default judgment is rendered against a defendant who had notice of the suit, trial, or hearing but did not file an answer to the suit or did not appear at a trial or hearing, the motion for new trial should allege the three elements from **Craddock** listed below. *See* **Sutherland**, 376 S.W.3d at 755; **Fidelity & Guar.**, 186 S.W.3d at 574. When the defendant has notice of the trial and its attorney appears but the defendant does not, the defendant is not entitled to argue the **Craddock** factors. *See* **In re K.C.**, 88 S.W.3d 277, 279 (Tex.App.—San Antonio 2002, pet. denied). When a defendant establishes the **Craddock** factors, the trial court must set aside the default judgment. **Director, State Empls. Workers' Comp. Div. v. Evans**, 889 S.W.2d 266, 268 (Tex.1994). See **O'Connor's Texas Civil Forms**, FORMS 10B:3, §I (2020 ed.), **O'Connor's Texas Civil Forms**, FORMS 10B:4, §B (2020 ed.).

(1) Not intentional but accidental. The defendant must show that its failure to file an answer or appear at a hearing was not intentional or the result of conscious indifference but was due to a mistake or accident. **Sutherland**, 376 S.W.3d at 754; **Dolgencorp of Tex., Inc. v. Lerma**, 288 S.W.3d 922, 925 (Tex.2009); **In re R.R.**, 209 S.W.3d 112, 114 (Tex.2006); **Craddock**, 133 S.W.2d at 126. A mistake of law may satisfy this requirement. **Bank One v. Moody**, 830 S.W.2d 81, 84 (Tex.1992). However, not every mistake of law is sufficient. *Id.* "Not intentional" and "mistake or accident" are only one element, not two. *Id.* at 82–83. If the factual allegations in the defendant's motion and affidavits negate conscious indifference and the plaintiff does not controvert these allegations, the court must find that the defendant's failure to answer was the result of a mistake or accident. *See* **Milestone Oper., Inc. v. ExxonMobil Corp.**, 388 S.W.3d 307, 309–10 (Tex.2012); **Sutherland**, 376 S.W.3d at 755; **Fidelity & Guar.**, 186 S.W.3d at 575–76; **Old Republic Ins. v. Scott**, 873 S.W.2d 381, 382 (Tex.1994). See "Uncontroverted motion," ch. 10-B, §9.5.2. The **Craddock** standard is that the defendant knew it was sued but did not care. **Sutherland**, 376 S.W.3d at 755; **Fidelity & Guar.**, 186 S.W.3d at 575–76; *e.g.*, **Levine v.**

Shackelford, Melton & McKinley, L.L.P., 248 S.W.3d 166, 168–69 (Tex.2008) (pattern of ignoring deadlines and warnings from opposing party amounted to conscious indifference). Even a bad excuse can be sufficient to disprove conscious indifference. **Milestone Oper.**, 388 S.W.3d at 310; **Sutherland**, 376 S.W.3d at 755; **In re R.R.**, 209 S.W.3d at 115; **Fidelity & Guar.**, 186 S.W.3d at 576.

(a) Failure to answer or appear = accident. Default judgments in the following cases were reversed because the defendant pleaded and proved its failure to answer or appear was accidental. • Defendant's agent testified that he did not remember being served and had not turned over any suit papers to the defendant's attorney, which was his normal procedure for responding to service of suit papers; the plaintiff did not controvert the testimony. **Milestone Oper.**, 388 S.W.3d at 310. • The citation was left in a stack of papers on a desk and forgotten because the defendants spent limited time at the office due to weather conditions over a nearly three-week period during the Christmas holiday season. **Sutherland**, 376 S.W.3d at 755. • Attorney informed the court of a conflicting preferential trial setting in another county before trial and reasonably believed the court would delay the trial. **Dolgencorp of Tex.**, 288 S.W.3d at 927. • Defendant's registered agent received the petition and citation but could not verify that the documents were ever forwarded to the defendant; affidavits detailing procedures for handling service documents negated conscious indifference. **Fidelity & Guar.**, 186 S.W.3d at 575–76. • Because the executors were unaware of the suit when the Secretary of State was served on their behalf, their failure to answer was not intentional. **Estate of Pollack v. McMurrey**, 858 S.W.2d 388, 391 (Tex.1993). • In a writ-of-garnishment proceeding, the bank president testified the bank did not file an answer because he thought the bank had complied with procedures. **Bank One**, 830 S.W.2d at 84–85. • Defendant's office staff misplaced the citation it was supposed to send to defendant's attorney. **Strackbein v. Prewitt**, 671 S.W.2d 37, 39 (Tex.1984); *see also* **In re A.P.P.**, 74 S.W.3d 570, 574 (Tex.App.—Corpus Christi 2002, no pet.) (D's coworker delivered notice and petition to attorney's office, where notice was inadvertently misfiled). • Defendant searched his house after receiving an inquiry about the lawsuit, found the citation, and took it to the insurance company the next day. **Ward v. Nava**, 488 S.W.2d 736, 737–38 (Tex.1972). • Defendant's attorney thought only one suit was filed and assumed additional petitions e-mailed to him were duplicates of the original. **Titan Indem. Co. v. Old S. Ins. Grp.**, 221 S.W.3d 703, 711 (Tex.App.—San Antonio 2006, no pet.). • Attorney did not inform the defendant that, because of a conflict of interest, he could no longer represent him. **Hahn v. Whiting Pet. Corp.**, 171 S.W.3d 307, 310 (Tex.App.—Corpus Christi 2005, no pet.). • Husband's letter to the court administrator requesting clarification of the trial setting on his belief that he would get 45 days' notice negated conscious indifference. **In re Parker**, 20 S.W.3d 812, 819 (Tex.App.—Texarkana 2000, no pet.). • The citation was lost in the mail when it was sent by the defendant's office in Michigan to a claims office in Texas for handling. **K-Mart Corp. v. Armstrong**, 944 S.W.2d 59, 60 (Tex.App.—Amarillo 1997, writ denied). • Attorney's secretary made a mistake in getting a new trial setting, and the attorney was in another trial. **Aero Mayflower Transit Co. v. Spoljaric**, 669 S.W.2d 158, 160 (Tex.App.—Fort Worth 1984, writ dism'd). • Party changed attorneys; the new attorney believed a bankruptcy stay was in effect. **Martin v. Allman**, 668 S.W.2d 795, 799 (Tex.App.—Dallas 1984, no writ). • Corporate officer was served with two citations, one for each corporation; the officer thought the citations were copies, and only one corporation filed an answer. **National Rigging, Inc. v. City of San Antonio**, 657 S.W.2d 171, 172–73 (Tex.App.—San Antonio 1983, writ ref'd n.r.e.).

(b) Failure to answer or appear = conscious indifference. Default judgments in the following cases were affirmed because the defendant did not plead and prove it was not consciously indifferent. • Reliance on an agent, such as an insurance carrier, to file an answer did not satisfy the test because there was no proof the agent was not guilty of conscious indifference. **Holt Atherton Indus. v. Heine**, 835 S.W.2d 80, 83 (Tex.1992); **Memorial Hosp. Sys. v. Fisher Ins. Agency, Inc.**, 835 S.W.2d 645, 652 (Tex.App.—Houston [14th Dist.] 1992, no writ), *disapproved on other grounds*, **Michiana Easy Livin' Country, Inc. v. Holten**, 168 S.W.3d 777 (Tex.2005). • Experienced out-of-state attorney's claims that he lacked contacts in Texas who could file the answer and that he was occupied by other matters—including a breach of security caused by hackers breaking into his e-mail and leaking confidential records—did not disprove his conscious indifference because he knew of the lawsuit three weeks before the answer deadline, he did not seek Texas attorneys before the default judgment, and he did not explain the timing involved with the hacking incident. **Dodd v. Savino**, 426 S.W.3d 275, 288–90 (Tex.App.—Houston [14th Dist.] 2014, no pet.). • Pro se defendant refused to retrieve a certified letter after notice by the post office. **Osborn v. Osborn**, 961 S.W.2d 408, 412–13 (Tex.App.—Houston [1st Dist.] 1997, pet. denied). • Defendant's affidavit containing only general statements without dates and other verifying information did not disprove its conscious indifference. **Liberty Mut. Fire Ins. v. Ybarra**, 751 S.W.2d 615, 617–18 (Tex.App.—El Paso 1988, no writ); *see also* **Sheraton Homes,**

Inc. v. Shipley, 137 S.W.3d 379, 382 (Tex.App.—Dallas 2004, no pet.) (affidavits contained conclusory allegations that P's failure to answer was because P intended to retain attorney who was no longer in private practice; no explanations of mistake were provided). • Mistaken belief about bankruptcy was not a reason to reverse a default judgment. **Novosad v. Brian K. Cunningham, P.C.**, 38 S.W.3d 767, 771 (Tex.App.—Houston [14th Dist.] 2001, no pet.); **Dupnik v. Aransas Cty. Nav. Dist.**, 732 S.W.2d 780, 782 (Tex.App.—Corpus Christi 1987, no writ). • Defendant misunderstood the citation and thought he would get a notice of trial, but he did not ask or seek advice about the papers he had received. **Johnson v. Edmonds**, 712 S.W.2d 651, 652–53 (Tex.App.—Fort Worth 1986, no writ).

(2) Meritorious defense. The defendant must "set up" a meritorious defense. **Dolgencorp of Tex.**, 288 S.W.3d at 927; **In re R.R.**, 209 S.W.3d at 114; **Ivy v. Carrell**, 407 S.W.2d 212, 214 (Tex.1966); **Craddock**, 133 S.W.2d at 126. The defendant is not, however, required to prove the meritorious defense. **Titan Indem.**, 221 S.W.3d at 711; **In re A.P.P.**, 74 S.W.3d at 575; *see* **Evans**, 889 S.W.2d at 270. A meritorious defense is one that, if proved, would cause a different result on retrial, although not necessarily the opposite result. **Liepelt v. Oliveira**, 818 S.W.2d 75, 77 (Tex.App.—Corpus Christi 1991, no writ). To set up a meritorious defense, the defendant must allege facts, supported by affidavits or other evidence, that would constitute a defense to the plaintiff's cause of action. **Dolgencorp of Tex.**, 288 S.W.3d at 928; **Estate of Pollack**, 858 S.W.2d at 392; **Ivy**, 407 S.W.2d at 214; *e.g.*, **Lara v. Rosales**, 159 S.W.3d 121, 124 (Tex.App.—Corpus Christi 2004, pet. denied) (in personal-injury case, Ds' allegation that P's own negligence caused auto accident because P stopped suddenly in intersection set up meritorious defense); *see, e.g.*, **Angelo v. Champion Rest. Equip. Co.**, 713 S.W.2d 96, 97 (Tex.1986) (in suit on open account, allegation that payment had been made, supported by canceled checks and affidavit, set up meritorious defense); **Continental Carbon Co. v. Sea-Land Serv.**, 27 S.W.3d 184, 191 (Tex.App.—Dallas 2000, pet. denied) (in suit on sworn account, D's allegation that it did not owe debt was insufficient to set up meritorious defense). The trial court cannot consider controverting affidavits on the issue of a meritorious defense. **Dolgencorp of Tex.**, 288 S.W.3d at 928; **Estate of Pollack**, 858 S.W.2d at 392; *see* **Gotcher v. Barnett**, 757 S.W.2d 398, 403 (Tex.App.—Houston [14th Dist.] 1988, no writ) (P can establish lack of legal sufficiency of D's defenses but cannot controvert or negate those defenses).

(3) No delay or injury. The defendant must state that a new trial will not cause the plaintiff any delay or injury. **Dolgencorp of Tex.**, 288 S.W.3d at 925; **In re R.R.**, 209 S.W.3d at 114–15; **Craddock**, 133 S.W.2d at 126. The defendant should state it is ready for trial and willing to reimburse the plaintiff for all reasonable expenses incurred in getting the default. **Evans**, 889 S.W.2d at 270 n.3; **Titan Indem.**, 221 S.W.3d at 712; **In re A.P.P.**, 74 S.W.3d at 575; *see* **Tanknology/NDE Corp. v. Bowyer**, 80 S.W.3d 97, 103 (Tex.App.—Eastland 2002, pet. denied). Failure to offer reimbursement does not necessarily preclude a new trial. **Angelo**, 713 S.W.2d at 98; **General Elec. Capital Auto Fin. Leasing Servs. v. Stanfield**, 71 S.W.3d 351, 356 (Tex.App.—Tyler 2001, pet. denied). Once the defendant alleges that granting the motion will not cause delay or prejudice, the burden shifts to the plaintiff to prove injury. **Dolgencorp of Tex.**, 288 S.W.3d at 929; **In re R.R.**, 209 S.W.3d at 116; **Evans**, 889 S.W.2d at 270; **Estate of Pollack**, 858 S.W.2d at 393. The purpose of this element is to protect the plaintiff against the sort of delay that would cause it to be disadvantaged in the trial of its case (e.g., the loss of witnesses or other valuable evidence). **Dolgencorp of Tex.**, 288 S.W.3d at 929; **Evans**, 889 S.W.2d at 270.

§9.2 Verification. The defaulting party must attach affidavits to support the factual allegations in the motion. See "Affidavits," ch. 1-B, §3.2.16. For the requirements for using an unsworn declaration instead of an affidavit, see "Unsworn declaration," ch. 1-B, §3.2.17. If the factual allegations in the affidavits are not controverted, the trial court must accept them as true. **Director, State Empls. Workers' Comp. Div. v. Evans**, 889 S.W.2d 266, 269 (Tex.1994); **Old Republic Ins. v. Scott**, 873 S.W.2d 381, 382 (Tex.1994); **Litchfield v. Litchfield**, 794 S.W.2d 105, 106 (Tex.App.—Houston [1st Dist.] 1990, no writ). Not all of the allegations in the motion for new trial must be supported by affidavits. The defendant is not required to file sworn proof to support its allegation of no delay or injury. See "No delay or injury," ch. 10-B, §9.1.3(3).

1. No-answer default. The factual allegations that must be supported by affidavits when challenging a no-answer default judgment include (1) facts regarding any defects in the service, citation, or return of service, or (2) facts supporting the defendant's allegation that its failure to file an answer was not intentional or the result of conscious indifference but was due to a mistake or accident.

2. Post-answer default. The factual allegations that must be supported by affidavits when challenging a post-answer default judgment include (1) facts regarding lack of notice of the hearing or trial, or (2) facts supporting the defendant's allegations that its failure to appear was not intentional or the result of conscious indifference but was due to a mistake or accident.

§9.3 Request hearing. In its motion for new trial, the defendant should request a hearing and attach sworn affidavits to support the allegations in the motion. See "When verification required," ch. 10-B, §3.1. If the defendant requests a hearing but does not get one, the trial court must accept all statements in the sworn pleadings and affidavits as true. **Thermex Energy Corp. v. Rantec Corp.**, 766 S.W.2d 402, 406 (Tex.App.—Dallas 1989, writ denied); **Van Der Veken v. Joffrion**, 740 S.W.2d 28, 31 (Tex.App.—Texarkana 1987, no writ); *see, e.g.*, **Ward v. Nava**, 488 S.W.2d 736, 737 (Tex.1972) (in reversing denial of MNT, court relied solely on movant's affidavit when no evidentiary hearing was held).

§9.4 Sworn response. In most cases, the plaintiff should file a response and object to the motion for new trial. When appropriate, the plaintiff should also file a controverting affidavit to prevent the court from assuming the facts stated in the defendant's motion are true. If the defendant's sworn facts support the **Craddock** factors, and if those facts are not controverted by the plaintiff, the defendant will prevail. **McClure v. Landis**, 959 S.W.2d 679, 681 (Tex.App.—Austin 1997, pet. denied). See "Uncontroverted motion," ch. 10-B, §9.5.2.

§9.5 Hearing. When the court holds a hearing on the motion for new trial and controverting evidence is introduced, the issues in the affidavits become fact questions for the court to resolve. **Jackson v. Mares**, 802 S.W.2d 48, 50 (Tex.App.—Corpus Christi 1990, writ denied); *see* **Young v. Kirsch**, 814 S.W.2d 77, 80 (Tex.App.—San Antonio 1991, no writ). At the hearing, it is not necessary to introduce the affidavits into evidence; it is sufficient that the affidavits are attached to the motion and are part of the record. **Director, State Empls. Workers' Comp. Div. v. Evans**, 889 S.W.2d 266, 268 (Tex.1994). The affidavits are considered for purposes of the **Craddock** test even if they are not introduced into evidence. **Evans**, 889 S.W.2d at 268; **McClure v. Landis**, 959 S.W.2d 679, 681 (Tex.App.—Austin 1997, pet. denied).

1. Controverted motion. A hearing is necessary if any of the facts in the motion that support the **Craddock** factors are controverted. **Estate of Pollack v. McMurrey**, 858 S.W.2d 388, 392 (Tex.1993); **Puri v. Mansukhani**, 973 S.W.2d 701, 715 (Tex.App.—Houston [14th Dist.] 1998, no pet.). Thus, if the plaintiff controverts the facts in the motion, the defendant must request an evidentiary hearing; otherwise, the motion may be overruled and the defendant will not be able to show an abuse of discretion on appeal. **Puri**, 973 S.W.2d at 715; *see* **Evans**, 889 S.W.2d at 268; **Cocke v. Saks**, 776 S.W.2d 788, 789–90 (Tex.App.—Corpus Christi 1989, writ denied); *see, e.g.*, **Liberty Mut. Fire Ins. v. Ybarra**, 751 S.W.2d 615, 617–18 (Tex.App.—El Paso 1988, no writ) (trial court overruled MNT based on P's controverting affidavit).

2. Uncontroverted motion. A hearing is not necessary on an uncontroverted motion. The trial court must accept as true the defendant's uncontroverted affidavits. **Averitt v. Bruton Paint & Floor Co.**, 773 S.W.2d 574, 576 (Tex.App.—Dallas 1989, no writ). If the factual allegations in the defendant's affidavit support the **Craddock** factors, the court should grant a new trial. *See* **Holt Atherton Indus. v. Heine**, 835 S.W.2d 80, 82 (Tex.1992); **Strackbein v. Prewitt**, 671 S.W.2d 37, 38–39 (Tex.1984).

§10. MNT after service by publication

Service by publication is the method of notice that is least likely to bring the defendant's attention to the lawsuit. **Mullane v. Central Hanover Bank & Trust Co.**, 339 U.S. 306, 315 (1950); *see* **Gray v. PHI Res.**, 710 S.W.2d 566, 567–68 (Tex.1986) (posting petition on courthouse door is analogous to citation by publication). When the plaintiff serves the defendant by publication, special rules control the trial and the motion for new trial.

§10.1 Trial. When the plaintiff moves for judgment against a defendant who was served by publication and has not answered or appeared, the trial court must appoint an attorney ad litem to defend the case. Tex. R. Civ. P. 244; **Cahill v. Lyda**, 826 S.W.2d 932, 933 (Tex.1992); **Isaac v. Westheimer Colony Ass'n**, 933 S.W.2d 588, 590–91 (Tex.App.—Houston [1st Dist.] 1996, writ denied). The attorney must be paid a reasonable fee, which is taxed as part of the costs, for the attorney's services for the trial and appeal. **J.D. Abrams, Inc. v. McIver**, 966 S.W.2d 87, 97 (Tex.App.—Houston [1st Dist.] 1998, pet. denied). After judgment is rendered, the court must approve and sign a statement of the evidence. Tex. R. Civ. P. 244. A signed and approved statement of the evidence is separate from the court reporter's record. **Montgomery v. R.E.C. Interests, Inc.**, 130 S.W.3d 444, 446 (Tex.App.—Texarkana 2004, no pet.).

§10.2 Sworn MNT. A motion for new trial after service by publication is equivalent to an equitable bill of review. **Stock v. Stock**, 702 S.W.2d 713, 714 (Tex.App.—San Antonio 1985, no writ); *see* **Hunsinger v. Boyd**, 26 S.W.2d 905, 907 (Tex.1930). The motion must be verified by an affidavit and, if based on a ground other than invalid service, must show good

cause for granting a new trial. *See* Tex. R. Civ. P. 329(a). If the motion is based on invalid service, the party does not have to show good cause. **In re E.R.**, 385 S.W.3d 552, 563 (Tex.2012); **Velasco v. Ayala**, 312 S.W.3d 783, 792 (Tex.App.—Houston [1st Dist.] 2009, no pet.); *see* **Wiebusch v. Wiebusch**, 636 S.W.2d 540, 542 (Tex.App.—San Antonio 1982, no writ). See **O'Connor's Texas Civil Forms**, FORM 10B:5 (2020 ed.).

1. Service valid. The following are some of the allegations the defendant can make in a motion for new trial even if service was valid.

(1) The trial court did not appoint an attorney as required by TRCP 244. **Isaac v. Westheimer Colony Ass'n**, 933 S.W.2d 588, 591 (Tex.App.—Houston [1st Dist.] 1996, writ denied).

(2) The trial court did not approve and sign the statement of evidence as required by TRCP 244.

(3) There was insufficient evidence presented at the hearing to support the trial court's judgment.

(4) The court made an error in applying the law to the facts.

2. Service invalid. The following are some of the allegations the defendant can make in a motion for new trial to indicate that service was invalid.

(1) The plaintiff served citation by publication without conducting a diligent search for the defendant. **In re E.R.**, 385 S.W.3d at 564. See "Diligent search," ch. 2-I, §4.3.2(1)(a)[2].

(2) The citation by publication was defective. For example, the citation did not contain a brief statement of the nature of the suit as required by TRCP 114. **Wiebusch**, 636 S.W.2d at 542.

(3) The plaintiff procured the service by fraud. *See, e.g.,* **Morris v. Morris**, 759 S.W.2d 707, 709 (Tex.App.—San Antonio 1988, writ denied) (wife committed fraud in procuring divorce after citation by publication because she knew where husband was and could have served him with citation).

§10.3 Notice. The defendant must give notice of the motion for new trial to all parties to the trial court's judgment. *See* Tex. R. Civ. P. 329(a).

§10.4 Deadline. A defendant who was served by publication has two years after a judgment is rendered and signed to file a motion for new trial. Tex. R. Civ. P. 329(a); **In re E.R.**, 385 S.W.3d 552, 563 (Tex.2012); **Montgomery v. R.E.C. Interests, Inc.**, 130 S.W.3d 444, 445 n.1 (Tex.App.—Texarkana 2004, no pet.). If the motion for new trial is filed more than 30 days after the judgment was rendered and signed, the time period for the trial court's plenary power will be computed as if the judgment had been signed on the date the motion was filed. Tex. R. Civ. P. 306a(7), 329(d); *see* **Montgomery**, 130 S.W.3d at 446.

§10.5 Execution. The defendant can suspend the execution of the judgment during the pendency of the motion for new trial by filing a bond. Tex. R. Civ. P. 329(b). The amount for the bond is determined the same way supersedeas bonds are determined. *Id.*; *see also* Tex. R. App. P. 24.2 (supersedeas bonds). See "Superseding the Judgment," **O'Connor's Texas Civil Appeals**, ch. 4-B, §1 et seq. (2020 ed.).

§10.6 Property sold. If property is sold under execution of the judgment before the defendant posts the bond, the defendant will not be able to recover the property. If the court grants a new trial, the defendant will be able to get a judgment equal to the proceeds of the sale. Tex. R. Civ. P. 329(c).

§10.7 Hearing. A hearing on the motion for new trial does not seem to be necessary. *See* Tex. R. Civ. P. 329(a) (court may grant new trial upon petition supported by affidavits). If the plaintiff controverts any of the defendant's facts by filing an affidavit, the defendant should ask for a hearing. At the hearing, the defendant should introduce evidence to support all the facts in its motion for new trial.

§11. MNT after summary judgment

§11.1 Not generally necessary. An appellant does not need to file a motion for new trial to preserve most errors in a summary judgment. *See* Tex. R. Civ. P. 324(a); Tex. R. App. P. 33.1(a). The appellant can file a motion for new trial just to

extend the appellate deadlines. *See* **Thomley v. Southwood-Driftwood Apts., Ltd.**, 961 S.W.2d 6, 8 (Tex.App.—Amarillo 1996, order). See **O'Connor's Texas Civil Forms**, FORM 10B:6 (2020 ed.).

1. Not required. A motion for new trial is generally not required to preserve error about the merits of the summary judgment. **Lee v. Braeburn Valley W. Civic Ass'n**, 786 S.W.2d 262, 263 (Tex.1990). In most cases, the objections to the motion for summary judgment are made in the response to the motion, in a motion requesting more time for discovery, or in a motion to file a late response. As long as the objections to the motion for summary judgment are preserved for appeal in some prejudgment motion or objection, a motion for new trial is not necessary. For example, if the nonmovant filed a motion for permission to file a late response and the court overruled the motion, the nonmovant is not required to file a motion for new trial; its motion to file a late response preserved the error. See "Secure ruling on objections," ch. 7-B, §10.2.

2. Required.

(1) Newly discovered evidence. A party should file a motion for new trial to assert newly discovered evidence or any other matter on which evidence must be heard. Tex. R. Civ. P. 324(b)(1). See "When MNT necessary," ch. 10-B, §2.1.

(2) No opportunity to file response. When the nonmovant did not have an opportunity to file a summary-judgment response or to seek a continuance or permission to file a late response before summary judgment was rendered, the nonmovant should file a sworn motion for new trial, probably relying on the factors from **Craddock v. Sunshine Bus Lines, Inc.**, 133 S.W.2d 124 (Tex.1939). *See* **Ayele v. Jani-King**, 516 S.W.3d 630, 632–33 (Tex.App.—Houston [1st Dist.] 2017, no pet.); *see, e.g.*, **Weech v. Baptist Health Sys.**, 392 S.W.3d 821, 825–26 (Tex.App.—San Antonio 2012, no pet.) (in no-evidence summary judgment, court modified second prong of **Craddock** test and required party filing MNT to present evidence raising issue of material fact); *see also* **Limestone Constr., Inc. v. Summit Commercial Indus. Props., Inc.**, 143 S.W.3d 538, 542–44 (Tex.App.—Austin 2004, no pet.) (unclear whether **Craddock** applies in default summary-judgment context, but if nonmovant establishes lack of notice of no-evidence summary-judgment hearing, it does not need to prove anything else to prevail on MNT). In rare situations when, after summary judgment is rendered, a nonmovant discovers a procedural mistake that it should have included in a response, the nonmovant can raise the issue in a motion for new trial. *See, e.g.*, **Marino v. King**, 355 S.W.3d 629, 633–34 (Tex.2011) (pro se party could request in MNT to withdraw deemed admissions because she did not know that her responses to requests for admissions had been served untimely, that she should have moved to withdraw deemed admissions, or that she needed to file response to summary-judgment motion); **Wheeler v. Green**, 157 S.W.3d 439, 442 (Tex.2005) (same); *see also* **Imkie v. Methodist Hosp.**, 326 S.W.3d 339, 345 (Tex.App.—Houston [1st Dist.] 2010, no pet.) (**Wheeler** extended **Craddock** to summary judgments in rare circumstances when pro se party appeared at summary-judgment hearing but mistakenly did not file response to summary-judgment motion). The motion for new trial should include the grounds the nonmovant would have included in a timely response. For a discussion of the **Craddock** factors, see "Failure to answer or appear after proper notice," ch. 10-B, §9.1.3.

Caution

Do not confuse (1) a motion for new trial filed after the nonmovant did not have an opportunity to file a response with (2) a motion for new trial filed after the nonmovant had an opportunity to file a motion for leave to file a late response or a motion to continue the summary-judgment hearing. In ***Carpenter v. Cimarron Hydrocarbons Corp.****, 98 S.W.3d 682, 686 (Tex.2002), the Supreme Court held that a motion for new trial establishing the* ***Craddock*** *factors is not appropriate to challenge the trial court's denial of permission to file a late response to a motion for summary judgment. Instead, the nonmovant must base its appeal on the trial court's abuse of discretion in denying the motion for permission to file a late response. See* ***Carpenter****, 98 S.W.3d at 686. See "Filing a late response," ch. 7-B, §6.8.3.*

(3) Other matters. A party should file a motion for new trial to complain about any matter to which the party has not already objected or on which the court has not ruled. For example, if the trial court refused to rule on the nonmovant's objections to a motion for summary judgment, the nonmovant should file a motion for new trial reurging those objections and objecting to the court's earlier refusal to rule. When the motion for new trial is overruled, either by written order or by operation of law, the objections will be preserved for appeal. See "Refusal to rule + objection," ch. 1-G, §2.2.3.

§11.2 Verification. See "When verification required," ch. 10-B, §3.1.

§12. MNT after dismissal

The type of motion (verified vs. unverified) and the grounds to challenge a dismissal order depend on the underlying reason for the dismissal.

§12.1 Dismissal for failure to prosecute. If the trial court dismissed the suit for failure to prosecute or failure to appear at trial, the party should follow the procedures for a verified motion outlined in "Motion to Reinstate After Dismissal for Want of Prosecution," ch. 10-F, §1 et seq.

§12.2 Other dismissals. To determine the grounds for a motion for new trial following other dismissals, check the grounds on which the dismissal was based (e.g., for a motion for new trial following special exceptions, see "Special Exceptions—Challenging the Pleadings," ch. 3-G, §1 et seq.).

1. Verified vs. unverified motion. If both the dismissal order and the motion for new trial are based on the pleadings, verification of the motion is generally not necessary; if either the dismissal order or the motion for new trial is based on evidence, verification is necessary. See "When verification required," ch. 10-B, §3.1.

2. Inappropriate order of dismissal. If the trial court's order dismissed the suit with prejudice when the order should have dismissed without prejudice, the dismissal with prejudice must be challenged in a motion for new trial or a motion to reinstate; otherwise, the error is waived for appeal and the suit cannot be refiled. *See* **El Paso Pipe & Sup. v. Mountain States Leasing, Inc.**, 617 S.W.2d 189, 190 (Tex.1981).

§13. MNT to challenge the evidence

§13.1 Challenging sufficiency of evidence. Most motions for new trial following a jury trial are filed to challenge the sufficiency of the evidence. Because challenges to jury findings are some of the most important challenges a party can assert on appeal, it is important to preserve them in the motion for new trial. For a more detailed analysis on appealing jury findings and for additional flowcharts about the process, see O'Connor, *Appealing Jury Findings*, 12 Hous.L.Rev. 65 (1974).

1. Legal & factual sufficiency. Each jury finding is susceptible to two challenges—legal sufficiency and factual sufficiency. Chart 10-1, below, shows how each adverse jury finding may be challenged.

10-1. Grounds for Challenging Adverse Jury Findings

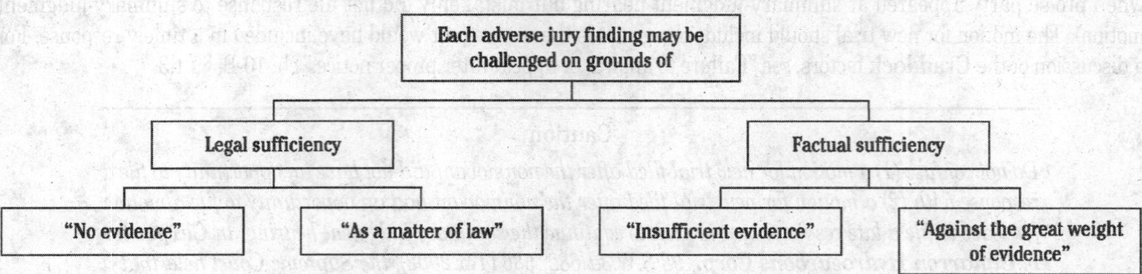

Choosing the proper terms for challenging a jury finding depends on who had the burden of proof on the issue at trial. If the movant had the burden of proof and the jury returned an adverse finding, the movant challenges the jury finding by saying that (1) the movant proved its issue as a matter of law or (2) the jury's answer is against the great weight and preponderance of the evidence. If the movant did not have the burden of proof, it challenges an adverse finding by saying that (1) there is no evidence to support the jury answer or (2) there is insufficient evidence to support the jury answer.

2. Preserving factual-sufficiency point. The only way to preserve factual-sufficiency challenges after a jury trial is in a motion for new trial. Tex. R. Civ. P. 324(b)(2); **Cecil v. Smith**, 804 S.W.2d 509, 510 (Tex.1991).

3. **Preserving legal-sufficiency point.** There are four ways to preserve legal-sufficiency challenges: (1) in a motion for directed verdict, (2) in an objection to the submission of a jury question, (3) in a motion for JNOV (or motion to disregard), and (4) in a motion for new trial. **Cecil**, 804 S.W.2d at 510–11; **Steves Sash & Door Co. v. Ceco Corp.**, 751 S.W.2d 473, 477 (Tex.1988); *see* **Musallam v. Ali**, 560 S.W.3d 636, 639 (Tex.2018) (objection to jury question and motion for JNOV); **Hill v. Shamoun & Norman, LLP**, 544 S.W.3d 724, 737 n.7 (Tex.2018) (motion for directed verdict). If the party properly preserves error in a motion for directed verdict, an objection to the charge, or a motion for JNOV, and if the appellate court sustains the challenge, the party may be entitled to rendition of judgment. *See* **Musallam**, 560 S.W.3d at 640. However, if a party makes a legal-sufficiency challenge for the first and only time in a motion for new trial, the party will not be entitled to rendition on appeal, only remand. **Horrocks v. Texas DOT**, 852 S.W.2d 498, 499 (Tex.1993); **Cecil**, 804 S.W.2d at 512; **ANA, Inc. v. Lowry**, 31 S.W.3d 765, 772 (Tex.App.—Houston [1st Dist.] 2000, no pet.).

4. **Standard challenges.** The following are models for challenging jury findings on the evidence:

(1) When movant has burden of proof on jury question.

- The evidence proves conclusively as a matter of law that [*state what the evidence proves*]. The jury's answer to question number __ is wrong, and the court erred in overruling [*the objections to the charge, the motion for directed verdict, or the motion for JNOV*].

- The jury's answer to question number __ is against the great weight and preponderance of the evidence and is manifestly unjust.

(2) When movant does not have burden of proof.

- There is no evidence to support the jury's answer to question number __, and the court erred in overruling [*the objections to the charge, the motion for directed verdict, or the motion for JNOV*].

- The evidence is insufficient to support the jury's answer to question number __.

§13.2 Challenging broad-form jury question. The Supreme Court requires that trial courts submit jury questions in broad form whenever feasible. **Thota v. Young**, 366 S.W.3d 678, 689 (Tex.2012); **Columbia Rio Grande Healthcare, L.P. v. Hawley**, 284 S.W.3d 851, 855 (Tex.2009). The submission of a broad-form jury question makes it more difficult for the losing party to successfully challenge the evidence on appeal. To challenge a verdict when the charge asked separate questions for each element of a cause of action, the appellant can focus on each adverse finding. To challenge a verdict when the charge asked only a broad-form question, the appellant must assume the jury found against it on all the elements of the cause of action and thus must challenge all the elements. *See, e.g.*, **Prudential Ins. v. Jefferson Assocs.**, 896 S.W.2d 156, 160 (Tex.1995) (charge included one question for multiple theories of liability); **GreenPoint Credit Corp. v. Perez**, 75 S.W.3d 40, 45–46 (Tex.App.—San Antonio 2002, pet. granted, judgm't vacated w.r.m.) (charge included one question for multiple theories of damages).

§13.3 Remittitur. The party may ask for a remittitur in either the motion for new trial or a separate motion. See "Motion for Remittitur," ch. 10-C, §1 et seq.

§13.4 Immaterial jury finding. An immaterial jury finding should be challenged in the motion for new trial or in some other postverdict motion. *See* **Musallam v. Ali**, 560 S.W.3d 636, 639–40 (Tex.2018); **BP Am. Prod. v. Red Deer Res.**, 526 S.W.3d 389, 402 (Tex.2017). See "Immaterial jury finding," ch. 9-B, §3.4. However, the trial court may disregard the finding on an immaterial jury question on its own initiative. **Clear Lake City Water Auth. v. Winograd**, 695 S.W.2d 632, 639 (Tex.App.—Houston [1st Dist.] 1985, writ ref'd n.r.e.). A jury finding is immaterial if the question was one that should not have been submitted or, even though properly submitted, was rendered immaterial by other findings. **Spencer v. Eagle Star Ins.**, 876 S.W.2d 154, 157 (Tex.1994). A jury's findings on a question of law may be deemed immaterial. **Quick v. City of Austin**, 7 S.W.3d 109, 116 (Tex.1998); **Spencer**, 876 S.W.2d at 157.

§14. MNT based on jury or bailiff misconduct

A new trial can be based on misconduct by the jury or the officer in charge of the jury (i.e., the bailiff). *See* Tex. R. Civ. P. 327(a); *see also* Tex. R. Civ. P. 226a (general instructions to jury), Tex. R. Civ. P. 283 (bailiff's duties), Tex. R. Civ. P. 285 (jury's communication with court through bailiff), Tex. R. Civ. P. 327(b) (prohibited testimony by jurors); Tex. R. Evid. 606(b)(1) (same).

§14.1 Sworn motion.

1. Allegations in MNT. To obtain a new trial based on misconduct, the movant must allege and prove (1) there was jury or bailiff misconduct, (2) the misconduct was material, and (3) based on the entire record, the misconduct probably resulted in injury to the movant. Tex. R. Civ. P. 327(a); **In re Health Care Unlimited, Inc.**, 429 S.W.3d 600, 602 (Tex.2014); **In re Whataburger Rests. LP**, 429 S.W.3d 597, 598 (Tex.2014); **Golden Eagle Archery, Inc. v. Jackson**, 24 S.W.3d 362, 372 (Tex.2000); **Redinger v. Living, Inc.**, 689 S.W.2d 415, 419 (Tex.1985). Determining whether misconduct occurred and caused injury are questions of fact. **In re Health Care Unlimited**, 429 S.W.3d at 602; **In re Whataburger**, 429 S.W.3d at 599; **Golden Eagle**, 24 S.W.3d at 372. The allegations in the motion for new trial must be based on knowledge of misconduct, not just suspicion. **American Home Assur. Co. v. Guevara**, 717 S.W.2d 381, 384–85 (Tex.App.—San Antonio 1986, no writ).

(1) Misconduct occurred. The movant must allege and prove misconduct occurred. Tex. R. Civ. P. 327(a). Misconduct is generally classified into four categories: jury misconduct during deliberations, bailiff misconduct, unauthorized contact or communication with a juror, and an erroneous juror answer on voir dire. *See id.*

(a) Jury misconduct during deliberations. Because of the restrictions on a juror's testimony in TRCP 327(b) and TRE 606(b)(1), proving jury misconduct during deliberations is very difficult. *See* **Golden Eagle**, 24 S.W.3d at 375. For a discussion of what constitutes deliberations, see "Juror testimony," ch. 10-B, §14.2.1. Jury misconduct during deliberations can be shown only when an outside influence has been improperly brought to bear on a juror. **Fillinger v. Fuller**, 746 S.W.2d 506, 509 (Tex.App.—Texarkana 1988, no writ); *see* **Golden Eagle**, 24 S.W.3d at 370; *see also* **Losier v. Ravi**, 362 S.W.3d 639, 646 (Tex.App.—Houston [14th Dist.] 2009, no pet.) ("jury misconduct" includes outside influence on jurors). Generally, a juror cannot testify about statements made or matters that occurred during the jury's deliberations or about anything affecting a juror's vote; however, a juror may testify about whether any outside influence was improperly brought to bear during deliberations. Tex. R. Civ. P. 327(b); Tex. R. Evid. 606(b)(1), (b)(2)(A); *see* **Ford Motor Co. v. Castillo**, 279 S.W.3d 656, 666 (Tex.2009); **Golden Eagle**, 24 S.W.3d at 370; **Soliz v. Saenz**, 779 S.W.2d 929, 931 (Tex.App.—Corpus Christi 1989, writ denied); *cf.* **Peña-Rodriguez v. Colorado**, __ U.S. __, 137 S.Ct. 855, 869 (2017) (Supreme Court recognized exception to prohibition against juror testimony about matters that occurred during deliberations when juror has shown she relied on racial bias to convict criminal D).

[1] Outside influence. An "outside influence" must have come from a source outside the jury and the formal deliberative process. *See* **Golden Eagle**, 24 S.W.3d at 370; **Editorial Caballero, S.A. de C.V. v. Playboy Enters.**, 359 S.W.3d 318, 324 (Tex.App.—Corpus Christi 2012, pet. denied); **Hutton v. AER Mfg. II, Inc.**, 224 S.W.3d 459, 463 (Tex.App.—Dallas 2007, pet. denied). For example, when an allegation of outside influence involves information not in evidence, that information must come from a nonjuror to be considered an outside influence. **Medicus Ins. v. Todd**, 400 S.W.3d 670, 683 (Tex.App.—Dallas 2013, no pet.); *see* **Editorial Caballero**, 359 S.W.3d at 324. Other examples of outside influence could include tampering with evidence or threats to a juror. *See* **Clancy v. Zale Corp.**, 705 S.W.2d 820, 829 (Tex.App.—Dallas 1986, writ ref'd n.r.e.).

Note

The Court of Criminal Appeals broadened the definition of "outside influence" by stating that information does not have to come from a nonjuror to be considered an outside influence. ***McQuarrie v. State****, 380 S.W.3d 145, 151, 154 (Tex.Crim.App.2012). In* ***McQuarrie****, the Court held that Internet research conducted by a juror while outside the jury room was an outside influence because it was "something originating from a source outside of the jury room and other than from the jurors themselves." Id. at 154. The dissenting judges disagreed with such a broad interpretation, stating that the term "outside*

influence" does not encompass information-gathering by a juror that does not involve communicating with a person outside the jury. Id. at 160–61 (Keller, P.J., Cochran, J., dissenting); see id. at 166–67 (Cochran, Keller, Price, Womack, JJ., dissenting). It is unclear if the holding in ***McQuarrie*** *will affect civil cases, particularly those involving Internet research. See, e.g.,* ***Editorial Caballero****, 359 S.W.3d at 325–26 (trial court did not abuse its discretion by finding no outside influence when juror conducted Internet research and read appellate decision from first trial of the case). For further discussion of* ***McQuarrie****, see Brown & Rondon,* ***Texas Rules of Evidence Handbook****, Rule 606 (2021 ed.) (nn.215–232).*

[2] Not outside influence. Broadly speaking, nothing that occurs during jury deliberations is an outside influence. *See* **Golden Eagle**, 24 S.W.3d at 370. Comments and statements made by a juror to the other jurors during deliberations are not outside influences. **Kendall v. Whataburger, Inc.**, 759 S.W.2d 751, 756 (Tex.App.—Houston [1st Dist.] 1988, no writ); *see* Tex. R. Civ. P. 327(b); **Golden Eagle**, 24 S.W.3d at 370; **Editorial Caballero**, 359 S.W.3d at 324. Likewise, personal pressures felt by jurors to wrap up deliberations (e.g., family pressure to leave for vacation, pressure from an employer to return to work, a death in the family) are not outside influences. *E.g.*, **Editorial Caballero**, 359 S.W.3d at 325 (death in family); *see, e.g.*, **Perry v. Safeco Ins.**, 821 S.W.2d 279, 280–81 (Tex.App.—Houston [1st Dist.] 1991, writ denied) (family's desire to go to amusement park); **Kirby Forest Indus. v. Kirkland**, 772 S.W.2d 226, 234 (Tex.App.—Houston [14th Dist.] 1989, writ denied) (pressure from employer to return to work); **Greco v. Greco**, No. 04-07-00748-CV, 2008 WL 4056328 (Tex.App.—San Antonio 2008, no pet.) (memo op.; 8-29-08) (jurors' desire to be home in time to watch basketball game). The following are some specific matters that were not considered outside influences.

[a] Jury charge & instructions. • The jurors' trading votes on two issues, in violation of court instructions. **Golden Eagle**, 24 S.W.3d at 370. • The jurors' misunderstanding or misinterpretation of the court's charge. **Compton v. Henrie**, 364 S.W.2d 179, 184 (Tex.1963); **Cortez v. Medical Prot. Co.**, 560 S.W.2d 132, 137 (Tex.App.—Corpus Christi 1977, writ ref'd n.r.e.). • The jury's response to a verdict-urging "dynamite" charge (i.e., an "**Allen**" charge). **Shaw v. Greater Houston Transp.**, 791 S.W.2d 204, 210 (Tex.App.—Corpus Christi 1990, no writ); **Golden v. First City Nat'l Bank**, 751 S.W.2d 639, 643–44 (Tex.App.—Dallas 1988, no writ); *see also* **Rosell v. Central W. Motor Stages, Inc.**, 89 S.W.3d 643, 661 (Tex.App.—Dallas 2002, pet. denied) (after jury deadlocked, bailiff told them that court would require them to deliberate another day, motivating jury to trade votes to reach verdict). • The jurors' discussion about their impressions of the scene, in violation of court instructions. **Soliz**, 779 S.W.2d at 932.

[b] Evidence not in record. • The jurors' speculation that the plaintiff had used alcohol and had received a settlement. **Golden Eagle**, 24 S.W.3d at 370. • A juror's belief that the plaintiff had filed a workers' compensation claim to get someone to pay his medical bills. **Weaver v. Westchester Fire Ins.**, 739 S.W.2d 23, 24 (Tex.1987). • A juror who used a dictionary to look up the word "negligence" and shared the definition with her fellow jurors. **Cooper Tire & Rubber Co. v. Mendez**, 155 S.W.3d 382, 413 (Tex.App.—El Paso 2004), *rev'd on other grounds*, 204 S.W.3d 797 (Tex.2006). • A juror who had worked in the construction industry and gave his opinion on the cost of home repairs. **Dietrich v. Goodman**, 123 S.W.3d 413, 422 (Tex.App.—Houston [14th Dist.] 2003, no pet.). • The jury's use of a discount formula from a juror's college textbook. **Crowson v. Kansas City S. Ry.**, 11 S.W.3d 300, 304–05 (Tex.App.—Eastland 1999, no pet.). • The jurors' discussion about the effect the plaintiff's victory would have on the talc mine and their fear that similar suits might close it down, leaving many without jobs. **Durbin v. Dal-Briar Corp.**, 871 S.W.2d 263, 272 (Tex.App.—El Paso 1994, writ denied), *disapproved on other grounds*, **Golden Eagle Archery, Inc. v. Jackson**, 24 S.W.3d 362 (Tex.2000). • A juror's discussion of personal experiences, insurance-liability questions, and a newspaper article not in evidence. **King v. Bauer**, 767 S.W.2d 197, 198 (Tex.App.—Corpus Christi 1989, writ denied); **Moon v. Firestone Tire & Rubber Co.**, 742 S.W.2d 792, 792–93 (Tex.App.—Houston [14th Dist.] 1987, writ denied). • A juror's statement that the plaintiff would still recover if the jury answered "no" to the negligence and proximate-cause questions. **Kendall**, 759 S.W.2d at 755–56.

(b) Bailiff misconduct. A bailiff's communication with the jury, except when inquiring as to whether the jury has agreed on a verdict or when making a communication as ordered by the court, can constitute misconduct. *See* Tex. R. Civ. P. 283, 327(a); **Pharo v. Chambers Cty.**, 922 S.W.2d 945, 950 (Tex.1996); *see, e.g.*, **Logan v. Grady**, 482 S.W.2d 313, 322 (Tex.App.—Fort Worth 1972, no writ) (reversible error for bailiff to tell jury, when it asked to rehear evidence, that it already had all it needed to answer jury question).

(c) Improper contact or communication with juror. Improper contact or communication between a juror and any of the attorneys, parties, witnesses, or anyone who might be connected with the case can constitute misconduct. *See* Tex. R. Civ. P. 226a, §II(2) (jurors should generally not talk to anyone involved in the case), Tex. R. Civ. P. 226a, §II(3) (jurors should not accept favors from anyone involved in the case), Tex. R. Civ. P. 327(a) (MNT can be based on communication with juror); *see, e.g.*, **In re Health Care Unlimited**, 429 S.W.3d at 602 (communication between juror and D's employee was misconduct); *see also* Tex. R. Civ. P. 226a, §II(5) (jurors should not discuss case with other jurors during trial). See "Juror communication," ch. 8-A, §9. In some instances, a showing of improper contact or communication with a juror, by itself, is prima facie proof of injury. See "Exception—overt act directed at juror," ch. 10-B, §14.1.1(3)(b).

(d) Erroneous juror answer during voir dire. A juror's untruthful, erroneous, or incomplete answer to a question during voir dire can constitute misconduct. *See* Tex. R. Civ. P. 327(a); *see, e.g.*, **Doucet v. Owens-Corning Fiberglas Corp.**, 966 S.W.2d 161, 162–63 (Tex.App.—Beaumont 1998, pet. denied) (juror did not disclose that he had been litigant in previous asbestos suit when panel was asked whether anyone had made a claim for asbestos-related injuries). See "Misconduct during voir dire," ch. 10-B, §14.2.1(3). A false answer during voir dire may entitle a party to a new trial only if the juror's concealment was in response to a specific and direct question calling for disclosure. **In re Zimmer, Inc.**, 451 S.W.3d 893, 903 (Tex.App.—Dallas 2014, orig. proceeding); **Wooten v. Southern Pac. Transp.**, 928 S.W.2d 76, 79 (Tex.App.—Houston [14th Dist.] 1995, no writ).

(2) Misconduct was material. The movant must allege and prove the misconduct was material. Tex. R. Civ. P. 327(a); *e.g.*, **Doucet**, 966 S.W.2d at 163–64 (in suit based on asbestos exposure, juror did not disclose that he had been litigant in previous asbestos-related suit and did not answer questions about working with products containing asbestos; misconduct was material but did not cause injury). Misconduct is material when it is reasonably calculated to prejudice the rights of the complaining party. **Sharpless v. Sim**, 209 S.W.3d 825, 829 (Tex.App.—Dallas 2006, pet. denied). If a juror gives erroneous or incomplete information on voir dire and that information would cause the juror to be disqualified from service, the misconduct is per se material. **In re Whataburger**, 429 S.W.3d at 599 n.1; **Burton v. R.E. Hable Co.**, 852 S.W.2d 745, 747 (Tex.App.—Tyler 1993, no writ). See "Misconduct during voir dire," ch. 10-B, §14.2.1(3); "Qualifications & exemptions of jurors," ch. 8-A, §3. If the misconduct is not per se material, the court must review the record and look at the context of the misconduct to determine if it is material. **In re Whataburger**, 429 S.W.3d at 599 n.1; *see* **Burton**, 852 S.W.2d at 747.

(3) Misconduct resulted in injury.

(a) Most cases. In most cases, the movant must allege and prove that, based on the entire record, the misconduct probably resulted in injury to the movant. Tex. R. Civ. P. 327(a). To show probable injury, the record must indicate the misconduct "most likely" caused a juror to vote differently on one or more issues vital to the judgment. **Redinger**, 689 S.W.2d at 419; *e.g.*, **In re Health Care Unlimited**, 429 S.W.3d at 603 (although juror's communication with D's employee was misconduct, no probable injury because communication, which began before trial, was about upcoming church retreat and did not affect outcome of trial); **In re Whataburger**, 429 S.W.3d at 599–600 (in premises-liability suit, no probable injury when juror did not disclose that she had been a D in previous credit-card collection suits; four other potential jurors, including one seated on jury, stated they were each a D in previous suits and P's attorney did not question or challenge them); **Pharo**, 922 S.W.2d at 950 (in damages suit against county, no probable injury when bailiff made reference to "raising taxes" because comment was made casually and was perceived as joke by jury). The record must show more than merely an appearance of impropriety. *See* **In re Health Care Unlimited**, 429 S.W.3d at 604.

(b) Exception—overt act directed at juror. Some acts are so prejudicial to fairness that the movant must show simply that the improper act occurred; by doing so, prima facie proof of injury is met. **Texas Empls. Ins. v. McCaslin**, 317 S.W.2d 916, 921 (Tex.1958); **Mercado v. Warner-Lambert Co.**, 106 S.W.3d 393, 396 (Tex.App.—Houston [1st Dist.] 2003, pet. denied). For example, a favor requested by a party or given to a juror is generally presumed to be harmful even without proof that it influenced the juror. *See, e.g.*, **McCaslin**, 317 S.W.2d at 921 (party went to juror's office and asked her to do all she could for her); **Texas Milk Prods. v. Birtcher**, 157 S.W.2d 633, 635–36 (Tex.1941) (party purchased soft drink for juror); **Texas Empls. Ins. v. Brooks**, 414 S.W.2d 945, 945–46 (Tex.App.—Beaumont 1967, no writ) (juror requested and received rides from P and P's brother-in-law); **Occidental Life Ins. v. Duncan**, 404 S.W.2d 52, 53–54 (Tex.App.—San Antonio 1966, writ ref'd n.r.e.) (party asked juror for aspirin). The presumption of harm is rebuttable. **Sharpless**, 209 S.W.3d at 828; *e.g.*, **Mercado**, 106 S.W.3d at 397 (harm not presumed when D's shadow juror requested cigarette and quarter from actual juror; court reasoned conduct did not rise to level of impropriety found in **McCaslin**).

2. Affidavits. The motion must be supported by affidavits confirming the claim of misconduct. Tex. R. Civ. P. 327(a); **Weaver**, 739 S.W.2d at 24. See "Affidavits," ch. 1-B, §3.2.16. The movant must attach one of the following types of affidavits:

(1) An affidavit by a juror describing the misconduct that occurred. *See* **In re Zimmer**, 451 S.W.3d at 901. If the misconduct occurred during deliberations, it must amount to an outside influence on the jury. *See* Tex. R. Evid. 606(b)(2)(A); **Golden Eagle**, 24 S.W.3d at 369. See "Jury misconduct during deliberations," ch. 10-B, §14.1.1(1)(a); "Juror testimony," ch. 10-B, §14.2.1.

(2) An affidavit by a nonjuror describing the misconduct. See "Nonjuror testimony," ch. 10-B, §14.2.2.

(3) An affidavit by an attorney or other person explaining why affidavits are not available and describing the diligence used in attempting to procure affidavits. **Roy Jones Lumber Co. v. Murphy**, 163 S.W.2d 644, 646 (Tex.1942); *see, e.g.*, **Ramsey v. Lucky Stores**, 853 S.W.2d 623, 636 (Tex.App.—Houston [1st Dist.] 1993, writ denied) (statement describing improper contacts with jurors did not explain lack of affidavit by juror); **American Home**, 717 S.W.2d at 384–85 (statement that jurors refused to sign affidavits was not enough to show diligence).

Note

Although TRCP 327(a) requires that the motion be supported by an affidavit, CPRC §132.001 provides for the use of an unsworn declaration instead of an affidavit. See Tex. Civ. Prac. & Rem. Code §132.001(a). For the procedure for using an unsworn declaration, see "Unsworn declaration," ch. 1-B, §3.2.17.

3. Request evidentiary hearing. In the motion for new trial, the movant should request a hearing to introduce evidence to prove the misconduct. *See* **In re Zimmer**, 451 S.W.3d at 902. The attorney should check the provisions of the local rules on securing a hearing for the receipt of evidence. See "Hearing," ch. 10-B, §14.3.

§14.2 Testimony. Live testimony from either a juror or a nonjuror is necessary to prove misconduct. *See* **In re Zimmer, Inc.**, 451 S.W.3d 893, 901–02 (Tex.App.—Dallas 2014, orig. proceeding). See "Hearing," ch. 10-B, §14.3.

1. Juror testimony. Whether a juror can testify about any misconduct generally depends on when the misconduct occurred or when the juror learned of the misconduct.

(1) Misconduct during deliberations. A juror can testify about an outside influence improperly brought to bear on a juror during deliberations. Tex. R. Civ. P. 327(b); Tex. R. Evid. 606(b)(2)(A); **Golden Eagle Archery, Inc. v. Jackson**, 24 S.W.3d 362, 370 (Tex.2000); *see* **Weaver v. Westchester Fire Ins.**, 739 S.W.2d 23, 24 (Tex.1987). Deliberations begin when the jury retires to deliberate on the jury charge and end when the jury is discharged from its duties. *See* **Golden Eagle**, 24 S.W.3d at 371 (deliberations begin when jury retires to weigh evidence); **Archer Daniels Midland Co. v. Bohall**, 114 S.W.3d 42, 46 (Tex.App.—Eastland 2003, no pet.) (deliberations cannot continue when jury is discharged). Generally, a juror cannot testify about any matter or statement that occurred during the jury's deliberations or about the effect of anything on a juror's vote. Tex. R. Civ. P. 327(b); Tex. R. Evid. 606(b)(1); **Golden Eagle**, 24 S.W.3d at 368; *see* **Chavarria v. Valley Transit Co.**, 75 S.W.3d 107, 110–11 (Tex.App.—San Antonio 2002, no pet.) (jurors' discussion of case during breaks in deliberations is the same as discussion during deliberations themselves). See "Jury misconduct during deliberations," ch. 10-B, §14.1.1(1)(a).

(2) Misconduct outside of deliberations. A juror can testify about any misconduct (her own, another juror's, or a nonjuror's) if it occurred outside of deliberations—that is, between voir dire and the beginning of deliberations. *See, e.g.*, **Golden Eagle**, 24 S.W.3d at 370 (incidental conversation between jurors during a trial break was not part of deliberations). A juror's testimony about conduct that occurred outside of deliberations is restricted by the general rules of evidence, but not by TRCP 327(b) or TRE 606(b). **Golden Eagle**, 24 S.W.3d at 370. Some of the matters a juror can testify about include the following: improper contacts with nonjurors; a conversation with another juror during a trial break; that another juror improperly viewed the scene of the event involved in the suit; and information showing that another juror is disqualified as a juror, if the information was not acquired during deliberations. *Id.*

(3) Misconduct during voir dire. A juror can testify about misconduct that occurred during voir dire. **Golden Eagle**, 24 S.W.3d at 372; *see, e.g.*, **Kiefer v. Continental Airlines, Inc.**, 10 S.W.3d 34, 40 (Tex.App.—Houston [14th Dist.] 1999, pet. denied) (at MNT hearing, juror testified she may have seen in public one of the witnesses introduced by P's attorney at voir dire); **Burton v. R.E. Hable Co.**, 852 S.W.2d 745, 746 (Tex.App.—Tyler 1993, no writ) (juror testified he misunderstood voir dire question). However, a juror cannot testify that another juror's voir dire response was untruthful if she learned of the untruthfulness during jury deliberations. *See* **Golden Eagle**, 24 S.W.3d at 372; *cf.* **Warger v. Shauers**, 574 U.S. 40, __ (2014) (under FRE 606(b), juror cannot testify about statements made during deliberations to prove another juror's dishonesty during voir dire).

2. Nonjuror testimony. A nonjuror can testify about any misconduct (her own, another nonjuror's, or a juror's), whether it occurred during or outside of deliberations. **Golden Eagle**, 24 S.W.3d at 369. A nonjuror's testimony is restricted by the general rules of evidence, but not by TRCP 327(b) or TRE 606(b). **Golden Eagle**, 24 S.W.3d at 369. For example, although a nonjuror can testify about what she saw happen at trial, she cannot testify about the jury's deliberations because the information would be hearsay. *See id.*; *see, e.g.*, **Mitchell v. Southern Pac. Transp.**, 955 S.W.2d 300, 323 (Tex.App.—San Antonio 1997, no writ) (conversation with daughter-in-law of alternate juror about what happened in jury's deliberation was hearsay), *disapproved on other grounds*, **Golden Eagle Archery, Inc. v. Jackson**, 24 S.W.3d 362 (Tex.2000).

§14.3 Hearing. The trial court must conduct a hearing if the movant (1) attached affidavits to the motion that described the misconduct or (2) stated a reasonable excuse for not filing affidavits alleging misconduct. *See* Tex. R. Civ. P. 327(a); **Golden Eagle Archery, Inc. v. Jackson**, 24 S.W.3d 362, 369 (Tex.2000); **Roy Jones Lumber Co. v. Murphy**, 163 S.W.2d 644, 646 (Tex.1942); **In re Zimmer, Inc.**, 451 S.W.3d 893, 901 (Tex.App.—Dallas 2014, orig. proceeding); *see, e.g.*, **Hatton v. Highlands Ins.**, 631 S.W.2d 787, 789 (Tex.App.—Tyler 1982, no writ) (affidavit attached to MNT based on jury misconduct specified acts of misconduct and names of jurors who committed misconduct; trial court should have granted movant's request for hearing). The affidavits themselves, however, are not evidence of the facts stated in them or a substitute for live testimony proving misconduct; the affidavits show only that there is sufficient evidence of misconduct to warrant an evidentiary hearing. *E.g.*, **In re Zimmer**, 451 S.W.3d at 901–02 (trial court abused its discretion in granting MNT when movant provided affidavits but did not offer testimony or other admissible evidence at hearing). If the movant does not attach affidavits alleging misconduct and does not state why it could not attach affidavits alleging misconduct, the court has discretion to grant a hearing. **Roy Jones Lumber**, 163 S.W.2d at 646; *see* **American Home Assur. Co. v. Guevara**, 717 S.W.2d 381, 384–85 (Tex.App.—San Antonio 1986, no writ). The movant should ask for a court reporter to transcribe the hearing.

§15. MNT after nonjury trial

§15.1 Not generally necessary. A party does not need to file a motion for new trial to preserve most errors in a nonjury trial. Tex. R. Civ. P. 324(a); **Park v. Essa Tex. Corp.**, 311 S.W.2d 228, 229 (Tex.1958); *see* Tex. R. App. P. 33.1(a). Parties often file a motion for new trial in a nonjury case just to extend the appellate deadlines.

1. Not required. In a nonjury trial, there is no need to complain in a motion for new trial about factual insufficiency of the evidence ("insufficient evidence" or "against the great weight"), about legal insufficiency of the evidence ("no evidence" or "as a matter of law"), or that damages are too large or too small. *See* Tex. R. Civ. P. 324(b)(2), (b)(4); **In re Parker**, 20 S.W.3d 812, 816 (Tex.App.—Texarkana 2000, no pet.); **Strickland v. Coleman**, 824 S.W.2d 188, 191 (Tex.App.—Houston [1st Dist.] 1991, no writ). These issues can be raised for the first time on appeal without a motion for new trial. *See* Tex. R. App. P. 33.1(d).

2. Required. If the complaint was not presented to the trial court during trial or in some other postjudgment motion, or if the complaint is one on which evidence must be presented, the complaining party must file a motion for new trial to preserve error. Tex. R. Civ. P. 324(b); *see* Tex. R. App. P. 33.1(a). Thus, the party must file a motion for new trial to complain about newly discovered evidence and any other matter on which evidence must be heard or about which the party has not already objected. Tex. R. Civ. P. 324(b)(1). See "When MNT necessary," ch. 10-B, §2.1.

§15.2 Verification. See "When verification required," ch. 10-B, §3.1.

§16. MNT based on newly discovered evidence

Whether the court grants a motion for new trial based on newly discovered evidence is a matter within its discretion. **Jackson v. Van Winkle**, 660 S.W.2d 807, 809 (Tex.1983), *overruled on other grounds*, **Moritz v. Preiss**, 121 S.W.3d 715 (Tex.2003); **In re A.G.C.**, 279 S.W.3d 441, 454 (Tex.App.—Houston [14th Dist.] 2009, no pet.); **Hooper v. Smallwood**, 270 S.W.3d 234, 245 & n.6 (Tex.App.—Texarkana 2008, pet. denied).

§16.1 Motion. To make a claim for a new trial because of newly discovered evidence, the movant must allege the following:

1. The movant discovered admissible and competent evidence after the trial. *See* **Jackson v. Van Winkle**, 660 S.W.2d 807, 809 (Tex.1983), *overruled on other grounds*, **Moritz v. Preiss**, 121 S.W.3d 715 (Tex.2003); *see, e.g.*, **Waffle House, Inc. v. Williams**, 313 S.W.3d 796, 813 (Tex.2010) (movant did not establish that evidence would have been admissible). The knowledge of both the party and the attorney is relevant. *See, e.g.*, **Dankowski v. Dankowski**, 922 S.W.2d 298, 305 (Tex.App.—Fort Worth 1996, writ denied) (evidence was not new).

2. The late discovery of the new evidence was not due to a lack of diligence. **Waffle House**, 313 S.W.3d at 813; **Jackson**, 660 S.W.2d at 809; **Dankowski**, 922 S.W.2d at 305. To establish this element, the movant generally must show the evidence could not have been discovered sooner because (1) the movant had no notice before trial that the evidence existed and (2) the movant used due diligence before trial to discover all available evidence. *See, e.g.*, **Alvarez v. Anesthesiology Assocs.**, 967 S.W.2d 871, 882–83 (Tex.App.—Corpus Christi 1998, no pet.) (even though Ds requested documents, Ds did not file a motion to compel when P refused; MNT denied).

3. The evidence is not merely cumulative of other evidence. **Waffle House**, 313 S.W.3d at 813; **Jackson**, 660 S.W.2d at 809. Evidence is cumulative when it is of the same kind and tends to prove the same point as other evidence. **New Amsterdam Cas. Co. v. Jordan**, 359 S.W.2d 864, 866 (Tex.1962); **In re Yarbrough**, 719 S.W.2d 412, 415 (Tex.App.—Amarillo 1986, no writ); *see, e.g.*, **Mitchell v. Bank of Am.**, 156 S.W.3d 622, 629 (Tex.App.—Dallas 2004, pet. denied) (documents from bank showing new address were cumulative of bank statement showing new address).

4. The evidence is not merely for impeachment. **New Amsterdam**, 359 S.W.2d at 866. When the only purpose of the new evidence is to impeach a witness, a new trial should not be granted. **Eckert v. Smith**, 589 S.W.2d 533, 538 (Tex.App.—Amarillo 1979, writ ref'd n.r.e.).

5. The evidence is so material that it would probably produce a different result at a new trial. **Waffle House**, 313 S.W.3d at 813; **Jackson**, 660 S.W.2d at 809. The new evidence must bring to light a new and independent truth so decisive that it demonstrates justice was not obtained. **New Amsterdam**, 359 S.W.2d at 867–68; *see, e.g.*, **State Farm Lloyds v. Nicolau**, 951 S.W.2d 444, 452 (Tex.1997) (new evidence would not have resulted in different verdict).

§16.2 Sworn motion. The motion must be verified and should include affidavits supporting each element listed above. *See* **Brown v. Hopkins**, 921 S.W.2d 306, 310–11 (Tex.App.—Corpus Christi 1996, no writ) (elements must be established by affidavit). See "Verification & affidavits," ch. 10-B, §3.

§16.3 Hearing. The movant should request an evidentiary hearing and ask for a court reporter to transcribe it. *See, e.g.*, **National Med. Fin. Servs. v. Irving ISD**, 150 S.W.3d 901, 905 (Tex.App.—Dallas 2004, no pet.) (section labeled "Notice of Hearing" at end of MNT was not a request to the court for a hearing). At the hearing, the movant must introduce evidence to prove each allegation in the motion. **Bell v. Showa Denko K.K.**, 899 S.W.2d 749, 757 (Tex.App.—Amarillo 1995, writ denied). See "Sworn MNT—hearing," ch. 10-B, §7.2.

§17. Review

§17.1 Appellate deadlines. A timely motion for new trial extends the appellate deadlines. Tex. R. App. P. 26.1(a)(1). See "Calculating appellate deadlines," ch. 9-C, §9.1.

§17.2 Standard of review. The standard of review for the trial court's ruling on a motion for new trial is abuse of discretion. **Director, State Empls. Workers' Comp. Div. v. Evans**, 889 S.W.2d 266, 268 (Tex.1994); **Cliff v. Huggins**, 724 S.W.2d 778, 778–79 (Tex.1987); *see* **In re Toyota Motor Sales, U.S.A., Inc.**, 407 S.W.3d 746, 749 (Tex.2013).

Note

The Supreme Court has clarified that it did not create a new standard of review in ***In re Toyota Motor Sales*** *when it granted courts the authority to conduct a merits review of new-trial orders in mandamus proceedings—the abuse-of-discretion standard applies to merits review, as it does in all mandamus proceedings.* ***In re Bent****, 487 S.W.3d 170, 177–78 (Tex.2016). See "Clear abuse of discretion,"* ***O'Connor's Texas Civil Appeals****, ch. 10-B, §4.2.1 (2020 ed.). "Merits review" simply refers to the court of appeals' authority to consider whether the record supports the trial court's reasons for granting a new trial.* ***In re Bent****, 487 S.W.3d at 178. See "Reasons stated in order not substantively valid or correct," ch. 10-B, §17.5.2(3).*

§17.3 Appellate record. If the movant filed a verified motion for new trial and the trial court conducted a hearing and received evidence, to appeal the court's denial of the motion, the movant must ask the court reporter to transcribe the hearing and include it in the reporter's record. *See* **American Paging v. El Paso Paging, Inc.**, 9 S.W.3d 237, 240 (Tex.App.—El Paso 1999, pet. denied). If no hearing was conducted on the motion, the appellate court can review a ruling based on the affidavits attached to a verified motion for new trial following a default judgment. **Ward v. Nava**, 488 S.W.2d 736, 737 (Tex.1972).

§17.4 Order denying new trial. The order denying a new trial is appealable as part of the appeal from the final judgment. *See* **Pine v. deBlieux**, 405 S.W.3d 140, 145 (Tex.App.—Houston [1st Dist.] 2013, no pet.); **Tactical Air Def. Servs. v. Searock**, 398 S.W.3d 341, 344 (Tex.App.—Dallas 2013, no pet.); **Westridge Apts. v. Gomez**, No. 07-09-0256-CV, 2009 WL 2601610 (Tex.App.—Amarillo 2009, no pet.) (memo op.; 8-25-09). However, an order denying an untimely motion for new trial does not preserve issues for appellate review, even if the trial court acts within its plenary-power period. **Moritz v. Preiss**, 121 S.W.3d 715, 720 (Tex.2003).

§17.5 Order granting new trial. The order granting a new trial can be reviewed by mandamus or, in some situations, may be reviewable on appeal to determine if the reasons stated in the order are facially or substantively valid. Some courts have held that mandamus relief is not available, however, for new-trial orders that do not set aside a jury verdict. *See, e.g.*, **In re Rathod**, No. 05-15-01354-CV, 2015 WL 6940134 (Tex.App.—Dallas 2015, orig. proceeding) (memo op.; 11-10-15) (mandamus not available for new-trial order issued after bench trial); **In re Cort**, No. 14-14-00646-CV, 2014 WL 4416074 (Tex.App.—Houston [14th Dist.] 2014, orig. proceeding) (memo op.; 9-9-14) (mandamus not available for new-trial order issued after post-answer default judgment); **In re Procesos Especializados en Metal, S.A. de C.V.**, No. 04-14-00543-CV, 2014 WL 4347724 (Tex.App.—San Antonio 2014, orig. proceeding) (memo op.; 9-3-14) (mandamus not available for new-trial order issued after no-answer default judgment); *see also* **In re Toyota Motor Sales, U.S.A., Inc.**, 407 S.W.3d 746, 762–63 (Tex.2013) (Lehrmann & Devine, JJ., concurring) (mandamus should not be available for new-trial orders that do not set aside jury verdicts because concern that court will substitute its judgment for jury's is not present).

1. Facial review—stated reasons not legally appropriate or specific. The trial court's order is reviewable by mandamus when the court's stated reasons for granting the new trial are not facially valid—that is, they are not legally appropriate or reasonably specific. **In re United Scaffolding, Inc.**, 377 S.W.3d 685, 688–89 (Tex.2012); *see* **In re Bent**, 487 S.W.3d 170, 176 (Tex.2016); **In re Whataburger Rests. LP**, 429 S.W.3d 597, 598 (Tex.2014).

(1) Reasons not legally appropriate. The trial court's order is reviewable by mandamus to determine if the court's stated reasons for granting a new trial, whether specific or not, are not legally appropriate (e.g., not based on a well-defined legal standard). *See* **In re Bent**, 487 S.W.3d at 176; **In re Toyota Motor Sales**, 407 S.W.3d at 756–57 & n.6; **In re United Scaffolding**, 377 S.W.3d at 688–89.

(a) Examples of legally appropriate reasons. The following are examples of legally appropriate reasons for granting a new trial:

[1] A violation of a limine order. *E.g.*, **In re Bent**, 487 S.W.3d at 181–82 (violation of limine order would have been appropriate ground for granting new trial, but record showed order was not violated).

[2] Juror misconduct. **In re Zimmer, Inc.**, 451 S.W.3d 893, 898 (Tex.App.—Dallas 2014, orig. proceeding).

[3] Factual sufficiency of the evidence. *Id.*

(b) Examples of legally inappropriate reasons. The following are examples of legally inappropriate reasons for granting a new trial:

[1] The court's reasons plainly state that the court merely substituted its own judgment for the jury's. **In re United Scaffolding**, 377 S.W.3d at 689.

[2] The court's reasons show a dislike for one party's lawyer. *Id.*

[3] The court's reasons were based on invidious discrimination. *Id.*

[4] The court's reasons were that the jury failed to award attorney fees under a mandatory-fee statute, but the court did not refer to any evidence offered to establish that the requested fees were reasonable and necessary. **In re Bent**, 487 S.W.3d at 184.

[5] The court's reasons were contrary to Texas law. *E.g.*, **In re Orren**, 533 S.W.3d 926, 930–31 (Tex.App.—Tyler 2017, orig. proceeding) (in personal-injury case arising from auto accident, court erred in granting new trial on basis that Texas law required jury to award at least some noneconomic damages for pain and suffering, mental anguish, and physical impairment; Texas law does not require such an award).

(2) Reasons not specific. The trial court's order is reviewable by mandamus to determine if the court did not specifically state its reasons for granting the new trial—that is, if the order provides little or no insight into the judge's reasoning. *See* **In re Bent**, 487 S.W.3d at 176; **In re United Scaffolding**, 377 S.W.3d at 689; **In re Columbia Med. Ctr.**, 290 S.W.3d 204, 213, 215 (Tex.2009).

(a) Explanation of court's reasoning. The court must provide a cogent and reasonably specific explanation of its reasoning for granting a new trial—simply restating a pro forma template is not sufficient. **In re Bent**, 487 S.W.3d at 176; **In re Toyota Motor Sales**, 407 S.W.3d at 756–57; **In re United Scaffolding**, 377 S.W.3d at 688–89; *see* **In re Columbia Med. Ctr.**, 290 S.W.3d at 213 (must be more than vague explanation); *see also* **In re Cook**, 356 S.W.3d 493, 495 (Tex.2011) (successor judge's order stating that original order granting MNT should remain unchanged was not sufficient under **In re Columbia Med. Ctr.**; successor judge must issue her own statement of specific reasons for granting MNT). The order must indicate that the court considered the specific facts and circumstances of the case and must explain how the evidence, or lack of evidence, undermines the jury's findings; in doing so, however, the court does not need to provide a detailed catalog of the evidence. **In re United Scaffolding**, 377 S.W.3d at 688–89; *e.g.*, **In re Bent**, 487 S.W.3d at 176 (trial court's conclusory statement that amount of jury's award "seems arbitrary," without reference to any evidence to support its conclusion, was not reasonably specific).

(b) Examples of reasons that are not specific.

[1] Interest of justice. A broad statement like "in the interest of justice" is not a sufficiently specific reason for granting a new trial. **In re Columbia Med. Ctr.**, 290 S.W.3d at 213; *e.g.*, **In re United Scaffolding**, 377 S.W.3d at 689–90 (mandamus appropriate because although court stated several reasons for granting new trial, its last reason was "in the interest of justice and fairness," and court used "and/or" between its reasons in order, which left open the possibility that "in the interest of justice and fairness" was its sole reason).

[2] Recitation of legal standard. The mere recitation of a legal standard is not a sufficiently specific reason for granting a new trial. *E.g.*, **In re United Scaffolding**, 377 S.W.3d at 689 (mere statement that finding is against great weight and preponderance of evidence was not sufficient).

2. Substantive review—based on merits. The trial court's order is subject to a merits-based review in the following situations:

(1) Void order. The trial court's order is reviewable by mandamus or on appeal when it is wholly void. *See* **In re Davenport**, 522 S.W.3d 452, 456 (Tex.2017); **In re Toyota Motor Sales**, 407 S.W.3d at 758; **In re Columbia Med. Ctr.**, 290 S.W.3d at 209; *see, e.g.*, **In re Dickason**, 987 S.W.2d 570, 571 (Tex.1998) (mandamus was granted to set aside void order granting MNT, which was signed after court lost plenary power); **In re Dilley ISD**, 23 S.W.3d 189, 191–92 (Tex.App.—San Antonio 2000, orig. proceeding) (same).

(2) **Jury answers not in conflict.** The trial court's order is reviewable by mandamus or on appeal when the order wrongly states that the answers to jury questions are in fatal conflict. *See* **In re Davenport**, 522 S.W.3d at 456; **In re Toyota Motor Sales**, 407 S.W.3d at 758; **In re Columbia Med. Ctr.**, 290 S.W.3d at 209. The appellate court can compare the jury charge against the jury's answers to determine whether the trial court was correct in concluding that there was a fatal conflict. **In re Toyota Motor Sales**, 407 S.W.3d at 758.

(3) **Reasons stated in order not substantively valid or correct.** The trial court's order is reviewable by mandamus to determine if the court's stated reasons for granting the new trial—even if legally appropriate and specific—are not substantively valid or correct (i.e., not supported by the record). **In re Toyota Motor Sales**, 407 S.W.3d at 758; *e.g.*, **In re Bent**, 487 S.W.3d at 176–77 (trial court abused discretion in granting MNT based on violation of limine order when record clearly established no violation); **In re Health Care Unlimited, Inc.**, 429 S.W.3d 600, 602 (Tex.2014) (trial court abused discretion in granting MNT based on jury misconduct when record showed only appearance of impropriety; TRCP 327 requires finding of misconduct, materiality, and probable injury); *see* **In re Davenport**, 522 S.W.3d at 456. If the court's stated reasons are not substantively valid or correct, the appellate court must order the trial court to vacate the new-trial order and enter judgment on the verdict. *See* **In re Davenport**, 522 S.W.3d at 459; **In re Bent**, 487 S.W.3d at 184; **In re Toyota Motor Sales**, 407 S.W.3d at 762.

Note

One court of appeals has held that a party must file a petition for writ of mandamus to seek review of a new-trial order on the basis that the trial court's stated reasons for granting the new trial are not substantively valid or correct. See ***United Scaffolding, Inc. v. Levine****, 520 S.W.3d 631, 636 (Tex.App.—Corpus Christi 2015) (memo op.), rev'd on other grounds, 537 S.W.3d 463 (Tex.2017). The court acknowledged that* ***In re Toyota Motor Sales*** *expanded the scope of mandamus relief to allow for review on such grounds but held that the expanded review does not allow for an appeal after completion of the new trial and entry of a final judgment in the case.* ***United Scaffolding****, 520 S.W.3d at 636 (memo op.). In reversing the court of appeals on other grounds, the Supreme Court declined to reach this issue.* ***United Scaffolding, Inc. v. Levine****, 537 S.W.3d 463, 483 (Tex.2017).*

C. Motion for Remittitur

§1. General

§1.1 Rules. Tex. R. Civ. P. 315, 320; Tex. R. App. P. 46.

§1.2 Purpose. A request for remittitur asks the court to reduce the damages because they are excessive. Remittitur procedure is designed to discourage the expense and delay of appeals. Both trial courts and courts of appeals may suggest remittitur. Tex. R. App. P. 46.1, 46.3. The trial court's power to suggest a remittitur is derived from its power to grant a new trial. *See* Tex. R. Civ. P. 320. The court does not have the power to increase the amount of damages by additur. *See* **Ponce v. Sandoval**, 68 S.W.3d 799, 805 (Tex.App.—Amarillo 2001, no pet.) (TRCPs do not provide for "additur" by the courts).

§1.3 Forms. **O'Connor's Texas Civil Forms**, FORMS 10C:1 et seq. (2020 ed.).

§1.4 Other references. **O'Connor's Texas Causes of Action** (2021 ed.).

§2. Request

§2.1 Form. The request for remittitur is usually included in a motion for new trial, although it may be made in a separate motion. *See* **C.M. Asfahl Agency v. Tensor, Inc.**, 135 S.W.3d 768, 796 (Tex.App.—Houston [1st Dist.] 2004, no pet.); *see, e.g.*, **Landmark Am. Ins. v. Pulse Ambulance Serv.**, 813 S.W.2d 497, 498 (Tex.1991) (party filed "motion for new trial, or in the alternative, for remittitur"); **Brookshire Bros. v. Wagnon**, 979 S.W.2d 343, 354 (Tex.App.—Tyler 1998, pet. denied) (party filed "motion for remittitur"). See "Motion for New Trial," ch. 10-B, §1 et seq.; **O'Connor's Texas Civil Forms**, FORM 10C:1 (2020 ed.). If a party does not ask for a remittitur in a postjudgment motion, it waives the complaint. *See* **Hawthorne v. Guenther**, 917 S.W.2d 924, 937 (Tex.App.—Beaumont 1996, writ denied).

§2.2 Suggest amount. In the motion, the movant should suggest the amount by which the judgment should be reduced. **Tidy Didy Wash, Inc. v. Barnett**, 246 S.W.2d 303, 306 (Tex.App.—Galveston 1952, writ ref'd n.r.e.); *see also* **Marathon Oil Co. v. Sterner**, 777 S.W.2d 128, 132 (Tex.App.—Houston [14th Dist.] 1989, no writ) (because D proposed reduction to $5,000 in motion for new trial, it could not argue on appeal for reduction to $10,000).

§3. Deadline

Whether the request for remittitur is filed as part of the motion for new trial or separately, it must be filed within the time limits for a motion for new trial. *See* Tex. R. Civ. P. 320. See "Deadlines for MNT," ch. 10-B, §5. If filed as a separate document, the request must be filed before the motion for new trial is overruled and within 30 days after the date the judgment was signed. *See* Tex. R. Civ. P. 329b(b).

§4. Response to request

A party may respond to a request for remittitur and explain why there is sufficient evidence to support the damages award in the judgment. See **O'Connor's Texas Civil Forms**, FORM 10C:2 (2020 ed.).

§5. Order

§5.1 Standard. The standard the trial court applies to a request for remittitur is the factual sufficiency of the evidence. **Rose v. Doctors Hosp.**, 801 S.W.2d 841, 847 (Tex.1990); **Larson v. Cactus Util. Co.**, 730 S.W.2d 640, 641 (Tex.1987). The court must examine all the evidence to determine whether there is sufficient evidence to support the damages award, remitting only the portion that is so factually insufficient (or against the great weight and preponderance of the evidence) as to be manifestly unjust. **Pope v. Moore**, 711 S.W.2d 622, 624 (Tex.1986); **Gray v. Allen**, 41 S.W.3d 330, 332 (Tex.App.—Fort Worth 2001, no pet.); **Gainsco Cty. Mut. Ins. v. Martinez**, 27 S.W.3d 97, 108 (Tex.App.—San Antonio 2000, pet. granted, judgm't vacated w.r.m.).

Note

When damages are challenged on appeal with a no-evidence point and the court of appeals finds no evidence to support them, the court should render a take-nothing judgment, not suggest a remittitur. ***Larson****, 730 S.W.2d at 641.*

§5.2 Must condition on new trial. The trial court cannot "order" a remittitur; it can only "suggest" a remittitur as an alternative to a new trial. **Arkoma Basin Expl. Co. v. FMF Assocs. 1990-A, Ltd.**, 249 S.W.3d 380, 390 (Tex.2008). The trial court cannot reduce the damages unless it gives the plaintiff the choice between remitting part of the damages or trying the case again. *See id.* See **O'Connor's Texas Civil Forms**, FORM 10C:3 (2020 ed.).

§6. Response to suggestion of remittitur

§6.1 Acceptance. A party who is awarded damages, generally the plaintiff, may remit any part of the judgment in open court or may execute and file with the court clerk a written remittitur signed and acknowledged by the party or the party's attorney. Tex. R. Civ. P. 315. See **O'Connor's Texas Civil Forms**, FORM 10C:4 (2020 ed.). If the party files a remittitur, the court will reform the judgment and affirm it in accordance with the remittitur. **Rose v. Doctors Hosp.**, 801 S.W.2d 841, 847 (Tex.1990).

§6.2 Rejection. If the party rejects the suggestion of remittitur, the court will grant a new trial. *See* **Rose v. Doctors Hosp.**, 801 S.W.2d 841, 847 (Tex.1990). The party cannot appeal the order granting a new trial. **Kolfeldt v. Thoma**, 822 S.W.2d 366, 368–69 (Tex.App.—Houston [14th Dist.] 1992, orig. proceeding).

§7. Review

§7.1 Appellate timetable begins. The appellate timetable begins to run on the date the trial court signs the order suggesting the remittitur. **Arkoma Basin Expl. Co. v. FMF Assocs. 1990-A, Ltd.**, 249 S.W.3d 380, 391 (Tex.2008). The order suggesting the remittitur acts as a modified judgment for purposes of the appellate timetable. *Id.* If the court later withdraws its order suggesting the remittitur, the judgment is considered to have been modified again. *See id.* (trial court that modifies judgment and then withdraws modification has modified judgment twice rather than never).

§7.2 Right to appeal. If the defendant ("the party benefiting from the remittitur") files an appeal, the plaintiff ("the remitting party") may perfect its own appeal to challenge the propriety of the remittitur. Tex. R. App. P. 46.2; *see* **J. Wigglesworth Co. v. Peeples**, 985 S.W.2d 659, 665 (Tex.App.—Fort Worth 1999, pet. denied).

§7.3 Exemplary-damages award. When an exemplary-damages award is challenged on appeal, the court of appeals must describe in detail the evidence supporting the award. **Leonard & Harral Packing Co. v. Ward**, 937 S.W.2d 425, 425 (Tex.1996); **Transportation Ins. v. Moriel**, 879 S.W.2d 10, 31 (Tex.1994); **Gray v. Allen**, 41 S.W.3d 330, 332 (Tex.App.—Fort Worth 2001, no pet.). Whether an award of exemplary damages is impermissibly excessive involves a Fourteenth Amendment due-process analysis. *See* **BMW v. Gore**, 517 U.S. 559, 568 (1996). See "Due-process cap," **O'Connor's Texas Causes of Action**, ch. 42-B, §7.2 (2021 ed.).

§7.4 Remittitur in court of appeals.

1. Standards.

(1) To review damages. The standard the court of appeals applies to review an issue of remittitur is the factual sufficiency of the evidence. **Transportation Ins. v. Moriel**, 879 S.W.2d 10, 30 (Tex.1994); **Pope v. Moore**, 711 S.W.2d 622, 624 (Tex.1986); **Gray v. Allen**, 41 S.W.3d 330, 332 (Tex.App.—Fort Worth 2001, no pet.). The court of appeals applies the same standard when it reviews a trial court's suggestion of remittitur as when it reviews a request for remittitur made on appeal. **Moriel**, 879 S.W.2d at 30; *see, e.g.*, **Pope**, 711 S.W.2d at 623 (review of suggestion of remittitur by court of appeals); **Gray**, 41 S.W.3d at 332 (review of suggestion of remittitur by trial court). A court of appeals will uphold the trial court's order suggesting remittitur (or make its own suggestion of remittitur) only if the evidence supporting the damages is so factually insufficient or so against the great weight and preponderance of the evidence as to be manifestly unjust. **Moriel**, 879 S.W.2d at 30; **Gray**, 41 S.W.3d at 332; *see, e.g.*, **Durham Transp. v. Beettner**, 201 S.W.3d 859, 876 (Tex.App.—Waco

2006, pet. denied) (court suggested remittitur to reduce damages for past medical expenses by $5,604); **Johnson v. J. Hiram Moore, Ltd.**, 763 S.W.2d 496, 502–03 (Tex.App.—Austin 1988, writ denied) (court suggested reduction of exemplary damages from $463,202 to $134,649). Abuse of discretion is not the correct standard. **Larson v. Cactus Util. Co.**, 730 S.W.2d 640, 641 (Tex.1987).

(2) To review attorney fees. If the court of appeals suggests a remittitur for damages on a claim for which the jury also awarded attorney fees (e.g., DTPA), the court can remand the case for a new trial on attorney fees if it believes the jury was influenced by the damages it awarded. **Bossier Chrysler-Dodge II, Inc. v. Rauschenberg**, 238 S.W.3d 376, 376 (Tex.2007); **Young v. Qualls**, 223 S.W.3d 312, 314 (Tex.2007); **Barker v. Eckman**, 213 S.W.3d 306, 313–15 (Tex.2006). The proper standard of review for this issue is whether the court is "reasonably certain" the jury was "significantly influenced" by the erroneous amount of damages it awarded. **Barker**, 213 S.W.3d at 313–14.

2. Review of trial-court remittitur. If the court of appeals sustains the plaintiff's contention on appeal that the trial court should not have suggested remittitur, the court of appeals must render the judgment that the trial court should have rendered. Tex. R. App. P. 46.2.

3. Suggestion of remittitur by CA. If the court of appeals suggests a remittitur, the court will affirm the trial court's judgment on the condition that the plaintiff accepts the court of appeals' suggestion.

(1) Plaintiff accepts. If the plaintiff files a remittitur in compliance with the court of appeals' suggestion, the court will reform the trial court's judgment and affirm it. **Rose v. Doctors Hosp.**, 801 S.W.2d 841, 847 (Tex.1990). After the court of appeals renders its opinion, the plaintiff may appeal the remittitur issue to the Supreme Court. *See id.* at 847–48. Remittitur is not a "take-it-or-leave-it" offer that bars an appeal to the Supreme Court. *See id.*

(2) Plaintiff rejects. If the plaintiff refuses to file or does not timely file a remittitur, the court of appeals will reverse the trial court's judgment and remand for a new trial. Tex. R. App. P. 46.3; **Rose**, 801 S.W.2d at 847; *see* **Missouri Pac. R.R. v. Alderete**, 945 S.W.2d 148, 153 (Tex.App.—San Antonio 1996, no writ).

§7.5 Voluntary remittitur. If the court of appeals reverses the trial court's judgment because of a legal error affecting only a portion of the damages awarded, the affected party may, within 15 days after the court of appeals' judgment, voluntarily remit the amount it believes will cure the reversible error. Tex. R. App. P. 46.5. If the court of appeals determines that remittitur is appropriate but that the voluntary remittitur is not sufficient to cure the error, the court must suggest an appropriate remittitur. See "Standards," ch. 10-C, §7.4.1. If the court of appeals determines that the voluntary remittitur cures the error, the court of appeals must accept the remittitur and reform and affirm the trial court's judgment in accordance with the remittitur. Tex. R. App. P. 46.5.

§7.6 Review by Supreme Court.

1. Permissible.

(1) Standard of review. The Supreme Court can review the standard the court of appeals applied in its review of a remittitur point. **Redman Homes, Inc. v. Ivy**, 920 S.W.2d 664, 669 (Tex.1996); **Pope v. Moore**, 711 S.W.2d 622, 623 (Tex.1986).

(2) Constitutionality of damages. The Supreme Court can remand cases for a determination of an appropriate remittitur if the damages awarded are unconstitutional. **Tony Gullo Motors I, L.P. v. Chapa**, 212 S.W.3d 299, 310 (Tex.2006); *see* **Bennett v. Grant**, 525 S.W.3d 642, 653 (Tex.2017); **Horizon Health Corp. v. Acadia Healthcare Co.**, 520 S.W.3d 848, 871 (Tex.2017).

2. Impermissible.

(1) Challenges to remittitur. Because the Supreme Court has no authority to review challenges to the factual sufficiency of the evidence, it cannot review challenges to remittitur. **Maritime Overseas Corp. v. Ellis**, 971 S.W.2d 402, 407 (Tex.1998); *see* **Tony Gullo Motors**, 212 S.W.3d at 310; **Redman Homes**, 920 S.W.2d at 669.

(2) Accepting remittitur. TRAP 46 does not authorize the Supreme Court to accept remittiturs. *See* **Tony Gullo Motors**, 212 S.W.3d at 310 & n.59; **Formosa Plastics Corp. USA v. Presidio Eng'rs & Contractors, Inc.**, 960

S.W.2d 41, 51 (Tex1998); **Redman Homes**, 920 S.W.2d at 669. However, in the past, the Court has accepted remittiturs when they cured an error in a portion of the jury's verdict that was (1) tainted by misconduct or impropriety and (2) definitely and accurately ascertainable. **Moore v. Grantham**, 599 S.W.2d 287, 292 (Tex1980); **Texas Empls. Ins. v. Lightfoot**, 162 S.W.2d 929, 931 (Tex1942).

D. Motion to Modify the Judgment

§1. General

§1.1 Rules. Tex. R. Civ. P. 329b; Tex. R. App. P. 26.1(a)(2).

§1.2 Purpose. A motion to modify the judgment is the procedure for asking the trial court to change the judgment.

§1.3 Form. **O'Connor's Texas Civil Forms**, FORM 10D:1 (2020 ed.).

§1.4 Other references. **O'Connor's Texas Causes of Action** (2021 ed.).

§2. Motion

§2.1 Grounds. If the judgment did not award a party all the relief it was entitled to, or awarded the other party more relief than it was entitled to, the complaint must be brought to the trial court's attention in a written motion. *See* Tex. R. Civ. P. 329b(g). The following are some examples of when a party should file a motion to modify the judgment.

1. Prejudgment interest. A party should file a motion to modify the judgment when the court does not award the correct amount of prejudgment interest. If a party does not bring the issue to the trial court's attention in a motion to modify the judgment or make some other objection on the record, the party cannot raise the issue on appeal. **Larrumbide v. Doctors Health Facilities**, 734 S.W.2d 685, 693 (Tex.App.—Dallas 1987, writ denied); *see* **Allright, Inc. v. Pearson**, 735 S.W.2d 240, 240 (Tex.1987); **Bulgerin v. Bulgerin**, 724 S.W.2d 943, 946 (Tex.App.—San Antonio 1987, no writ), *overruled on other grounds*, **Trinity Univ'l Ins. v. Cowan**, 945 S.W.2d 819 (Tex.1997). But in one case, without addressing the issue of waiver, the Supreme Court reversed the court of appeals' judgment and modified the date from which prejudgment interest was to accrue, even though no motion to modify the judgment had been filed. *See* **C&H Nationwide, Inc. v. Thompson**, 903 S.W.2d 315, 327–28 (Tex.1994), *overruled on other grounds*, **Carl J. Battaglia, M.D., P.A. v. Alexander**, 177 S.W.3d 893 (Tex.2005). The court of appeals had held that the plaintiffs waived error in the calculation of interest because they did not file a motion to modify the judgment. *See* **C&H Nationwide, Inc. v. Thompson**, 810 S.W.2d 259, 276 (Tex.App.—Houston [1st Dist.] 1991), *rev'd*, 903 S.W.2d 315 (Tex.1994). See "Prejudgment interest," ch. 9-C, §4.5.

2. Attorney fees. A party should file a motion to modify the judgment when the court does not award attorney fees or does not award the correct amount of fees. *See* **Texas Educ. Agency v. Maxwell**, 937 S.W.2d 621, 623 (Tex.App.—Eastland 1997, writ denied); **American Bank v. Waco Airmotive, Inc.**, 818 S.W.2d 163, 178 (Tex.App.—Waco 1991, writ denied). See "Attorney Fees," **O'Connor's Texas Causes of Action**, ch. 45-A, §1 et seq. (2021 ed.).

3. Costs. A party should file a motion to modify the judgment when the court does not award costs, awards costs to the wrong party, or does not award the correct amount of costs. *See* **Portland S&L Ass'n v. Bernstein**, 716 S.W.2d 532, 541 (Tex.App.—Corpus Christi 1985, writ ref'd n.r.e.), *overruled on other grounds*, **Dawson-Austin v. Austin**, 968 S.W.2d 319 (Tex.1998). To challenge the clerk's tabulation of the costs, the party should file a motion to retax costs. *See* **Campbell v. Wilder**, 487 S.W.3d 146, 152 (Tex.2016). See "Retaxing costs," ch. 9-C, §7.2.2; "Court Costs," **O'Connor's Texas Causes of Action**, ch. 44, §1 et seq. (2021 ed.).

4. Any other error or omission in judgment. A party should file a motion to modify the judgment when there is any other error in the judgment. *See, e.g.*, **L.M. Healthcare, Inc. v. Childs**, 929 S.W.2d 442, 443 (Tex.1996) (to change dismissal from "with prejudice" to "without prejudice"); **Heard v. Houston Post Co.**, 684 S.W.2d 210, 211–12 (Tex.App.—Houston [1st Dist.] 1984, writ ref'd n.r.e.) (after court ordered sheriff to turn over all information about criminal investigation except complainant's name, newspaper filed motion to modify J to require disclosure of name).

§2.2 Not verified. A motion to modify the judgment should not be verified or supported with affidavits unless it presents facts not in the record.

§3. Deadlines

The same rules apply to motions to modify judgments as to motions for new trial. See "Deadlines for MNT," ch. 10-B, §5.

§3.1 Original or amended motion. The deadline to file a motion to modify, correct, or reform an error in the judgment is the same as for a motion for new trial—within 30 days after the date the judgment was signed. Tex. R. Civ. P. 329b(a),

(g); **L.M. Healthcare, Inc. v. Childs**, 929 S.W.2d 442, 443 (Tex.1996); **Padilla v. LaFrance**, 907 S.W.2d 454, 458 (Tex.1995). An amended motion to modify may be filed within 30 days after the date the judgment was signed, as long as the original motion to modify has not been overruled by order of the trial court.

§3.2 After MNT overruled but within 30 days. A party can file a motion to modify the judgment even after the court has overruled a motion for new trial, as long as the motion to modify is filed within 30 days after the date the judgment was signed. **In re Brookshire Grocery Co.**, 250 S.W.3d 66, 72 (Tex.2008); **L.M. Healthcare, Inc. v. Childs**, 929 S.W.2d 442, 444 (Tex.1996); *see* **Dal-Chrome Co. v. Brenntag Sw., Inc.**, 183 S.W.3d 133, 146 (Tex.App.—Dallas 2006, no pet.).

§3.3 Premature motion. A premature motion to modify the judgment, filed before the judgment is signed, is deemed filed on the day of, but immediately after, the signing of the judgment. *See* Tex. R. Civ. P. 306c, 329b(g); *see, e.g.*, **Padilla v. LaFrance**, 907 S.W.2d 454, 458 (Tex.1995) (premature motion to reconsider is treated like premature motion to modify); *see also* Tex. R. App. P. 27.2 (premature proceeding relating to an appeal is not ineffective); **Ryland Enter. v. Weatherspoon**, 355 S.W.3d 664, 666 (Tex.2011) (premature-filing rules apply equally to motion for new trial and motion to modify judgment).

§3.4 Late motion. If a party discovers an error in the judgment more than 30 days after the judgment was signed, it should still file a motion to modify the judgment. Although a late motion to modify will not preserve error or extend the appellate deadlines, the court has the authority to correct the error on its own initiative if it still has plenary power over the judgment, even without a motion. See "Power to change judgment," ch. 9-C, §7. If the court has lost plenary power, the party should title the motion as a "Motion for Judgment Nunc Pro Tunc" and argue that the error is clerical and can be corrected even after the court loses plenary power. See "Motion for Judgment Nunc Pro Tunc," ch. 10-H, §1 et seq.

§4. Hearing

The hearing on a motion to modify the judgment is for argument only, not evidence. However, if a party files a motion to modify that for some reason must be supported by evidence, the party should ask for a court reporter and present evidence at the hearing.

§5. Order

§5.1 In writing. The court's order granting a motion to modify the judgment must be in writing and signed by the trial court, just like an order granting a motion for new trial. *See* Tex. R. Civ. P. 329b(c). See "In writing," ch. 10-B, §8.1.

§5.2 Deadlines. The deadlines to grant or overrule a motion to modify the judgment are the same as those for an order on a motion for new trial. See "Deadline to sign order on MNT," ch. 10-B, §8.4.

1. Grant motion. The trial court must sign an order granting a motion to modify within 75 days after the date the judgment was signed. Tex. R. Civ. P. 329b(c); *see, e.g.*, **L.M. Healthcare, Inc. v. Childs**, 929 S.W.2d 442, 443–44 (Tex.1996) (motion to modify granted on 75th day after J was signed).

2. Overrule motion. The trial court may overrule a motion to modify by written order; if it does not, the motion is overruled by operation of law on the 76th day after the judgment was signed, just like a motion for new trial. *See* Tex. R. Civ. P. 329b(c); *cf.* **Health Care Ctrs. v. Nolen**, 62 S.W.3d 813, 816 (Tex.App.—Waco 2001, no pet.) (MNT).

§6. Review

§6.1 Motion to modify & postjudgment deadlines.

1. Finality of judgment. A motion to modify the judgment delays the date the judgment becomes final, just like a motion for new trial does. *See* Tex. R. Civ. P. 329b(g); **Lane Bank Equip. Co. v. Smith S. Equip., Inc.**, 10 S.W.3d 308, 313 (Tex.2000); **Mackie v. McKenzie**, 890 S.W.2d 807, 808 (Tex.1994); **Home Owners Funding Corp. v. Scheppler**, 815 S.W.2d 884, 886 (Tex.App.—Corpus Christi 1991, no writ). See "Finality for purposes of changing the judgment," ch. 9-C, §6.4.

2. Appellate deadlines. The filing of a timely motion to substantively modify the judgment extends the appellate deadlines in the same way as a motion for new trial. Tex. R. Civ. P. 329b(g); **Ryland Enter. v. Weatherspoon**, 355

S.W.3d 664, 666 (Tex.2011); **Lane Bank**, 10 S.W.3d at 313; *see* **L.M. Healthcare, Inc. v. Childs**, 929 S.W.2d 442, 444 (Tex.1996). A motion to modify the judgment extends the appellate deadlines even if the motion is denied. See "Calculating appellate deadlines," ch. 9-C, §9.1.

§6.2 Modified judgment & postjudgment deadlines.

1. Restarts appellate timetable. Any modification of the judgment, whether material or not, made while the trial court has plenary power restarts the appellate timetable. Tex. R. Civ. P. 329b(h); Tex. R. App. P. 4.3(a), 27.3; **Lane Bank Equip. Co. v. Smith S. Equip., Inc.**, 10 S.W.3d 308, 313 (Tex.2000). Even clerical changes to the judgment made while the court has plenary power will restart the appellate timetable. **Lane Bank**, 10 S.W.3d at 313.

(1) Substantive & clerical changes. Some examples of changes to the judgment that restarted the appellate timetable include: • Revising docket number to reflect severance, correcting attorney's misspelled name, and stating that court and jury made findings required for termination. **In re J.L.**, 163 S.W.3d 79, 82–83 (Tex.2005). • Adding "Mother Hubbard" clause ("all relief not granted is denied"). **Mackie v. McKenzie**, 890 S.W.2d 807, 808 (Tex.1994). • Reinstating a default judgment. **Old Republic Ins. v. Scott**, 846 S.W.2d 832, 833 (Tex.1993). • Reducing damages. **Abercia v. Kingvision Pay-Per-View, Ltd.**, 217 S.W.3d 688, 706 (Tex.App.—El Paso 2007, pet. denied). • Identifying different grounds for summary judgment. **Quanaim v. Frasco Rest. & Catering**, 17 S.W.3d 30, 39–40 (Tex.App.—Houston [14th Dist.] 2000, pet. denied). • Changing the signature date. **Owens-Corning Fiberglas Corp. v. Wasiak**, 883 S.W.2d 402, 405 (Tex.App.—Austin 1994, order).

(2) Exception. The only exception to the rule that any modification of the judgment—even an immaterial one—restarts the appellate deadlines is if the face of the record shows that the trial court signed the modified judgment for the sole purpose of restarting the deadlines. **Mackie**, 890 S.W.2d at 808; **Abercia**, 217 S.W.3d at 706; *e.g.*, **Wang v. Hsu**, 899 S.W.2d 409, 411–12 (Tex.App.—Houston [14th Dist.] 1995, writ denied) (no evidence on face of record indicating court used second J to extend appellate deadlines; plenary power extended by second J that had different date from first J).

Note

Any change—whether substantive or clerical—the court makes to its judgment while it has plenary power will restart the appellate timetable under TRCP 329b(h). By comparison, only a motion that seeks a substantive change to the judgment will extend the appellate deadlines and the court's plenary power under TRCP 329b(g). ***Lane Bank**, 10 S.W.3d at 313. See "Finality for purposes of changing the judgment," ch. 9-C, §6.4.*

2. Extending appellate deadlines for second judgment. When the trial court modifies the judgment by signing a second judgment, the appellate deadlines can be extended in two ways.

(1) Motion to modify after first judgment. Generally, a motion to modify a judgment filed after the first judgment does not extend the appellate deadlines for the second judgment. *See* **Trans-Cont'l Props., Ltd. v. Taylor**, 717 S.W.2d 890, 890–91 (Tex.1986). However, if the complaint in the motion filed after the first judgment was not corrected by the second judgment and the substance of the motion is still a viable complaint about the second judgment, the motion extends the appellate deadlines for the second judgment. **Brighton v. Koss**, 415 S.W.3d 864, 865 (Tex.2013); *see* **Maddox v. Cosper**, 25 S.W.3d 767, 770 n.3 (Tex.App.—Waco 2000, no pet.); **Clark v. McFerrin**, 760 S.W.2d 822, 825 (Tex.App.—Corpus Christi 1988, writ denied). See "Second-judgment problems," ch. 10-B, §5.6.

(2) Motion to modify after second judgment. If the party files a motion to modify or another plenary-power-extending motion after the second judgment is signed, the motion extends the appellate deadlines for the second judgment. See "Motions that extend plenary power," ch. 9-C, §6.4.1(1).

E. Request for Findings of Fact & Conclusions of Law

§1. General

§1.1 Rules. Tex. R. Civ. P. 296 to 299a, 306c; Tex. R. App. P. 26.1(a)(4).

§1.2 Purpose. Findings of fact in a nonjury trial serve the same function as the jury's answers to jury questions—they resolve the factual disputes in the case. Conclusions of law are the court's statements of the legal principles it applied to the facts to resolve the case. Findings of fact are more important on appeal than conclusions of law because appellate courts review findings of fact for sufficiency of the evidence but review conclusions of law de novo. *See* **Hegar v. American Multi-Cinema, Inc.**, 605 S.W.3d 35, 40 (Tex.2020). See "Review of conclusions of law," ch. 10-E, §6.3.

Note

Throughout ch. 10-E, §2, below, findings of fact and conclusions of law will be referred to collectively as findings of fact.

§1.3 Timetables & forms. Appendix IV, Timetable 15, Request for findings of fact & conclusions of law; Appendix IV, Timetable 18, Appeal to the court of appeals; **O'Connor's Texas Civil Forms**, FORMS 10E:1 et seq. (2020 ed.).

§1.4 Other references. **O'Connor's Texas Civil Appeals** (2020 ed.); **O'Connor's Texas Family Law Handbook** (2021 ed.).

§2. Availability of findings of fact

§2.1 Findings of fact are necessary. In the following instances, parties should always ask the court to file findings of fact.

1. After nonjury trial of facts. Findings of fact may be requested in "any case tried in the district or county court without a jury." Tex. R. Civ. P. 296. A case is "tried" when there is a hearing before the court on conflicting evidence. **Besing v. Moffitt**, 882 S.W.2d 79, 81 (Tex.App.—Amarillo 1994, no writ). Litigants are entitled to findings of fact only on the merits of the case. See "Only on controlling issues," ch. 10-E, §5.2.3.

2. After motion for judgment in nonjury trial. Findings of fact should be requested in a nonjury case resolved by a judgment after the plaintiff rests. **Qantel Bus. Sys. v. Custom Controls Co.**, 761 S.W.2d 302, 304 (Tex.1988).

3. After mandamus initiated in trial court. Findings of fact should be requested in an original mandamus proceeding in the trial court, which is considered a civil action subject to the TRCPs. *See* **Anderson v. City of Seven Points**, 806 S.W.2d 791, 792 n.1 (Tex.1991); **City of Beaumont v. Spivey**, 1 S.W.3d 385, 389 (Tex.App.—Beaumont 1999, pet. denied).

4. To supply omitted elements of an issue. When only some elements of an issue are submitted to a jury, the party should request findings of fact on the omitted elements. *See* Tex. R. Civ. P. 299; *see also* **Insurance Co. of St. Louis v. Bellah**, 373 S.W.2d 691, 692 (Tex.App.—Fort Worth 1963, no writ) (courts are required to file findings of fact when certain issues are omitted from jury charge). See "Incomplete claim or defense submitted," ch. 8-I, §7.2.

5. When part of case is decided by court. When part of a case is tried to a jury and part is decided by the court, findings of fact should be requested on the court-decided issues. **Toles v. Toles**, 45 S.W.3d 252, 264 n.5 (Tex.App.—Dallas 2001, pet. denied); *see* **IKB Indus. v. Pro-Line Corp.**, 938 S.W.2d 440, 443 (Tex.1997); *see, e.g.*, **Heafner & Assocs. v. Koecher**, 851 S.W.2d 309, 312–13 (Tex.App.—Houston [1st Dist.] 1992, order) (divorce proceeding was tried to jury, but issue of attorney fees was tried to court).

6. To supply specific damages findings in nonjury trial. Findings of fact should be requested when the trial court makes a broad-form finding of actual damages and one of the damages elements is not supported by the evidence. *See* **Tagle v. Galvan**, 155 S.W.3d 510, 516 (Tex.App.—San Antonio 2004, no pet.).

§2.2 Findings of fact are helpful. Findings of fact are appropriate when (1) the trial court conducts an evidentiary hearing and (2) the findings could properly be considered by the appellate court. *See* **IKB Indus. v. Pro-Line Corp.**, 938 S.W.2d 440, 442–43 (Tex.1997). Findings in these instances are not given the same weight on appeal as findings made under TRCP 296 and 297. *See* **IKB Indus.**, 938 S.W.2d at 442. See "Review of findings of fact," ch. 10-E, §6.2.

1. After hearing on sanctions under TRCP 215. When a judgment is rendered as a sanction for discovery abuse, findings of fact supporting the sanctions are helpful. **IKB Indus.**, 938 S.W.2d at 442; **Chrysler Corp. v. Blackmon**, 841 S.W.2d 844, 852 (Tex.1992); **TransAmerican Nat. Gas Corp. v. Powell**, 811 S.W.2d 913, 919 n.9 (Tex.1991). The findings should be specifically tied to the appropriate legal standard. **Chrysler Corp.**, 841 S.W.2d at 853.

2. After dismissal hearings.

(1) Failure to prosecute. Findings of fact after a hearing on a motion to dismiss for failure to prosecute can help the appellate court understand the reasons why the trial court refused to reinstate. See "Motion to Reinstate After Dismissal for Want of Prosecution," ch. 10-F, §1 et seq.

Practice Tip

If you decide to file a request for findings of fact after a case is dismissed for want of prosecution, remember that the request is due before the motion to reinstate. Compare Tex. R. Civ. P. 296 (20 days) with Tex. R. Civ. P. 165a(3) (30 days).

(2) Jurisdictional challenge. Findings of fact can be helpful when the court rules on jurisdictional challenges after receiving evidence (e.g., when the trial court rules on a special appearance challenging personal jurisdiction or on a plea to the jurisdiction challenging subject-matter jurisdiction). *See* **Goodenbour v. Goodenbour**, 64 S.W.3d 69, 75 (Tex.App.—Austin 2001, pet. denied) (special appearance); **Hernandez v. Texas Dept. of Ins.**, 923 S.W.2d 192, 194 (Tex.App.—Austin 1996, no writ) (plea to the jurisdiction).

(3) Groundless pleadings. It is not necessary to ask for separate findings of fact when sanctions are imposed under TRCP 13 and CPRC §10.001; the court is required to include findings in the sanctions order. For sanctions under CPRC §9.012, separately filed findings of fact are helpful.

(4) Late report. In a medical-malpractice case, findings of fact are helpful when the court dismisses a plaintiff's suit for filing a late expert report. *See* **Mocega v. Urquhart**, 79 S.W.3d 61, 63–64 (Tex.App.—Houston [14th Dist.] 2002, pet. denied) (former TRCS art. 4590i, §13.01, now CPRC §74.351); *see also* Tex. Civ. Prac. & Rem. Code §74.351(a) (expert report must be served on D within 120 days after D's original answer was filed).

3. After hearing on venue. Findings of fact can be helpful to review a venue ruling. *See* **Coke v. Coke**, 802 S.W.2d 270, 278 (Tex.App.—Dallas 1990, writ denied); **Gaston v. Chaney**, 734 S.W.2d 735, 737 (Tex.App.—Eastland 1987, no writ).

4. After judgment with exemplary damages. When the trial court awards exemplary damages, findings of fact stating the court's reasons for refusing to disturb the jury's exemplary-damages award will "facilitate meaningful post-verdict review." **Transportation Ins. v. Moriel**, 879 S.W.2d 10, 33 (Tex.1994). Although it is optional for the trial court to make these findings, the courts of appeals are required to make them, whether they uphold, reduce, or eliminate the award. *See* Tex. Civ. Prac. & Rem. Code §41.013(a).

5. After hearing on remittitur. Findings of fact stating the trial court's reasons for suggesting remittitur are helpful for appellate courts. **Landon v. Jean-Paul Budinger, Inc.**, 724 S.W.2d 931, 940 (Tex.App.—Austin 1987, no writ).

6. After hearing to reinstate. Findings of fact are helpful after a hearing on a motion to reinstate a case that was dismissed for want of prosecution. *Cf.* **Phillips v. Beavers**, 938 S.W.2d 446, 446–47 (Tex.1997) (after dismissal for want of prosecution). See "Motion to Reinstate After Dismissal for Want of Prosecution," ch. 10-F, §1 et seq.

7. After hearing on MNT. Findings of fact are helpful after a hearing on a motion for new trial at which evidence was received. *See, e.g.,* **Higginbotham v. General Life & Acc. Ins.**, 796 S.W.2d 695, 695 (Tex.1990) (MNT after no-answer default judgment).

8. After default judgment on unliquidated damages. Findings of fact are helpful when the court renders a default judgment on unliquidated damages. *See* **IKB Indus.**, 938 S.W.2d at 443.

§2.3 Findings of fact are permitted after appealable orders. Specific rules permit the trial court to file findings of fact in the appeal of interlocutory orders. The request for findings of fact in an appeal of an interlocutory order does not extend the time to perfect the appeal. Tex. R. App. P. 28.1(b). See "Findings of fact & conclusions of law," **O'Connor's Texas Civil Appeals**, ch. 1-B, §2.6.3 (2020 ed.); "Motion for Interlocutory Appeal & Stay Pending Appeal," **O'Connor's Texas Civil Appeals**, ch. 3-P, §1 et seq. (2020 ed.).

1. After TRO or temporary injunction. TRCP 683 requires that each order granting a TRO or temporary injunction include the reasons for its issuance. **Transport Co. v. Robertson Transps.**, 261 S.W.2d 549, 553 (Tex.1953). The trial court can, but is not required to, file separate findings of fact. *See id.*; **Operation Rescue-Nat'l v. Planned Parenthood**, 937 S.W.2d 60, 82 (Tex.App.—Houston [14th Dist.] 1996), *aff'd as modified*, 975 S.W.2d 546 (Tex.1998).

2. After class-action certification. Implicit in TRCP 42(b)(3) is the requirement that the trial court make findings about the application of TRCP 42 to the facts of the case. TRCP 42 does not state whether the findings should be incorporated into the certification order or filed separately as findings of fact. *See, e.g.*, **General Motors Corp. v. Bloyed**, 916 S.W.2d 949, 955–56 (Tex.1996) (trial court filed findings of fact); **Texas Dept. of MHMR v. Petty**, 778 S.W.2d 156, 160 (Tex.App.—Austin 1989, writ dism'd) (trial court's findings were part of certification order). To award attorney fees in a class-action certification, the trial court must state its findings in writing or orally on the record. Tex. R. Civ. P. 42(h)(3).

3. After other appealable orders. TRAP 28.1(c) permits, but does not require, the trial court to file findings of fact after rendering an interlocutory order. *See, e.g.*, **Mueller v. Beamalloy, Inc.**, 994 S.W.2d 855, 858 (Tex.App.—Houston [1st Dist.] 1999, no pet.) (appointment of receiver).

4. To review supersedeas bonds. TRAP 24.4(d) permits the appellate court to remand the issue of the sufficiency of a supersedeas bond to the trial court to take evidence and file findings of fact. *See* **TransAmerican Nat. Gas Corp. v. Finkelstein**, 911 S.W.2d 153, 155 (Tex.App.—San Antonio 1995, order). See "Superseding the Judgment," **O'Connor's Texas Civil Appeals**, ch. 4-B, §1 et seq. (2020 ed.).

§2.4 Findings of fact are not appropriate. Findings of fact are not appropriate when they have no purpose. **IKB Indus. v. Pro-Line Corp.**, 938 S.W.2d 440, 443 (Tex.1997). In such cases, findings should not be requested, made, or considered on appeal. *Id.* When findings of fact are not appropriate, a request for findings does not extend the time to perfect an appeal, as it does when they are appropriate. *Id.*; *see* **Linwood v. NCNB Tex.**, 885 S.W.2d 102, 103 (Tex.1994).

1. After jury trial. Findings of fact are not appropriate on issues tried to a jury. **Favaloro v. Commission for Lawyer Discipline**, 13 S.W.3d 831, 840 (Tex.App.—Dallas 2000, no pet.).

2. After summary judgment. Findings of fact are not appropriate after the court renders a summary judgment. **IKB Indus.**, 938 S.W.2d at 441–42; **Linwood**, 885 S.W.2d at 103; **Willms v. Americas Tire Co.**, 190 S.W.3d 796, 810 (Tex.App.—Dallas 2006, pet. denied).

3. After directed verdict. Findings of fact are not appropriate in a case resolved by a directed verdict. **IKB Indus.**, 938 S.W.2d at 443; *see* **Ditto v. Ditto Inv.**, 309 S.W.2d 219, 220 (Tex.1958).

4. After JNOV. Findings of fact are not appropriate after the court renders a judgment notwithstanding the verdict. **IKB Indus.**, 938 S.W.2d at 443; **Fancher v. Cadwell**, 314 S.W.2d 820, 822 (Tex.1958).

5. After trial of agreed case. Findings of fact are not appropriate after the court renders a judgment on an agreed statement of facts under TRCP 263. See "No findings of fact," ch. 7-E, §5.3.

6. After default judgment on liquidated damages. Findings of fact are not appropriate after the court renders a default judgment based on liquidated damages. **IKB Indus.**, 938 S.W.2d at 443.

7. After dismissal on pleadings without evidence. Findings of fact are not appropriate after the court (1) dismisses a case for want of prosecution without a hearing to receive evidence, (2) dismisses for lack of subject-matter juris-

diction without sworn proof, (3) dismisses after refusal to amend following an order on special exceptions, or (4) renders any judgment without an evidentiary hearing. *See* **IKB Indus.**, 938 S.W.2d at 443 (listing inappropriate cases for findings of fact); *see, e.g.*, **Awde v. Dabeit**, 938 S.W.2d 31, 33 (Tex.1997) (based on pleadings, suit dismissed for lack of subject-matter jurisdiction); **F-Star Socorro, L.P. v. El Paso Cent. Appr. Dist.**, 324 S.W.3d 172, 174–75 (Tex.App.—El Paso 2010, no pet.) (after hearing parties' legal arguments, court dismissed suit for lack of subject-matter jurisdiction); **CMS Partners v. Plumrose USA, Inc.**, 101 S.W.3d 730, 736–37 (Tex.App.—Texarkana 2003, no pet.) (suit dismissed under forum-selection clause).

8. On undisputed issues. See "Only on controlling issues," ch. 10-E, §5.2.3.

§3. Requesting findings of fact

Either party may request that the court file findings of fact under TRCP 296. In cases governed by TRCP 296, the party who loses should always request findings of fact; otherwise, all findings are deemed in favor of the judgment. **Worford v. Stamper**, 801 S.W.2d 108, 109 (Tex.1990); **Roberson v. Robinson**, 768 S.W.2d 280, 281 (Tex.1989). Although the prevailing party probably does not want to ask for findings of fact, once the losing party makes a proper request for findings, the prevailing party should make sure they are filed. The rules provide for three requests for findings of fact.

§3.1 First request. The original request must be entitled "Request for Findings of Fact and Conclusions of Law." Tex. R. Civ. P. 296. See **O'Connor's Texas Civil Forms**, FORM 10E:1 (2020 ed.).

1. Deadline. The first request must be filed within 20 days after the date the judgment was signed. Tex. R. Civ. P. 296; **Willms v. Americas Tire Co.**, 190 S.W.3d 796, 801 (Tex.App.—Dallas 2006, pet. denied); **Ohio Cas. Grp. v. Risinger**, 960 S.W.2d 708, 712 (Tex.App.—Tyler 1997, writ denied); *see* **AD Villarai, LLC v. Chan Il Pak**, 519 S.W.3d 132, 135 (Tex.2017). If the request for findings is filed before the judgment is signed, it is considered a premature request and is deemed filed on the day of, but immediately after, the signing of the judgment. Tex. R. Civ. P. 306c; **Vargas v. TDPRS**, 973 S.W.2d 423, 426 (Tex.App.—Austin 1998, pet. granted, judgm't vacated w.r.m.); **Bello v. Bello**, No. 01-11-00594-CV, 2013 WL 4507876 (Tex.App.—Houston [1st Dist.] 2013, no pet.) (memo op.; 8-22-13); *see* Tex. R. App. P. 27.2; **Pursley v. Ussery**, 982 S.W.2d 596, 599 (Tex.App.—San Antonio 1998, pet. denied). The party requesting findings of fact must send a copy of the request to the other party. *See* Tex. R. Civ. P. 21a(a).

2. Clerk's duty. The court clerk must immediately call the request to the attention of the judge who tried the case. Tex. R. Civ. P. 296.

§3.2 Court's deadline to file findings. The trial court should file findings of fact within 20 days after the date the party requested findings. Tex. R. Civ. P. 297. The court must mail a copy of the findings of fact to all the parties. *Id.* Therefore, the party requesting findings should receive a copy in the mail. If it does not receive the findings, the party should file a second request.

§3.3 Second request. If the trial court does not file findings of fact within 20 days after the first request is filed, the party who asked for findings has 30 days after the date it filed its original request to file a "Notice of Past Due Findings of Fact and Conclusions of Law." Tex. R. Civ. P. 297. A party that does not file a notice of past-due findings of fact waives the right to complain that the trial court did not file findings. **AD Villarai, LLC v. Chan Il Pak**, 519 S.W.3d 132, 137 (Tex.2017); **Gnerer v. Johnson**, 227 S.W.3d 385, 389 (Tex.App.—Texarkana 2007, no pet.). In the notice of past-due findings of fact, the party must state the date the original request was filed and the date the findings of fact were due. Tex. R. Civ. P. 297; **Curtis v. Commission for Lawyer Discipline**, 20 S.W.3d 227, 232 (Tex.App.—Houston [14th Dist.] 2000, no pet.). See **O'Connor's Texas Civil Forms**, FORM 10E:3 (2020 ed.).

Practice Tip

Although all courts agree that a premature first request for findings is considered timely, several courts have held that a premature notice of past-due findings is not timely. See, e.g., ***Estate of Gorski v. Welch****, 993 S.W.2d 298, 301 (Tex.App.—San Antonio 1999, pet. denied);* ***Echols v. Echols****, 900 S.W.2d 160, 161–62 (Tex.App.—Beaumont 1995, writ denied);* ***Nisby v. Dentsply Int'l****, No. 05-14-00814-CV,*

2015 WL 2196627 (Tex.App.—Dallas 2015, no pet.) (memo op.; 5-11-15); ***Joseph v. Joseph****, No. 01-11-01096-CV, 2012 WL 1564318 (Tex.App.—Houston [1st Dist.] 2012, no pet.) (memo op.; 5-3-12). These courts held that TRCP 306c ("No . . . request for findings of fact . . . shall be held ineffective because prematurely filed . . . .") does not apply to notices of past-due findings.* ***Estate of Gorski****, 993 S.W.2d at 301;* ***Echols****, 900 S.W.2d at 161–62;* ***Nisby****, No. 05-14-00814-CV, 2015 WL 2196627 (memo op.);* ***Joseph****, No. 01-11-01096-CV, 2012 WL 1564318 (memo op.).*

§3.4 Court files findings. Once a second request is filed, the trial court has 40 days after the date the first request was filed to file findings of fact. Tex. R. Civ. P. 297.

1. Not in judgment. The requirement for filing findings under TRCP 296 to 298 cannot be satisfied by findings of fact in the judgment. TRCP 299a prohibits the trial court from reciting findings of fact in the judgment; they must be in a separate document. See "Not in judgment," ch. 10-E, §5.2.2.

2. Send findings to parties. Once the court makes findings of fact, it must mail a copy of the findings to each party. Tex. R. Civ. P. 297. This gives the parties time to meet the deadline in TRCP 298 for requesting additional or amended findings within ten days after the original findings are filed.

§3.5 Third request—for additional or amended findings. Once the trial court files findings of fact, either party may ask the trial court to make additional or amended findings.

1. Deadline to request. The request for additional or amended findings of fact must be filed within ten days after the trial court's original findings are filed. Tex. R. Civ. P. 298; **SMI/USA, Inc. v. Profile Techs.**, 38 S.W.3d 205, 209 (Tex.App.—Waco 2001, no pet.).

Note

Although TRCP 306c states that no prematurely filed request for findings of fact "shall be held ineffective," one court has held that a request for additional findings is ineffective if made before the trial court issues its original findings. See ***Mohnke v. Greenwood****, 915 S.W.2d 585, 590 (Tex.App.—Houston [14th Dist.] 1996, no writ).*

2. Proposed findings. The party must submit specific proposed findings of fact; a broad request for additional or amended findings is not sufficient. **Alvarez v. Espinoza**, 844 S.W.2d 238, 241–42 (Tex.App.—San Antonio 1992, writ dism'd). If the court omitted a finding on a material element, the party should ask the court to make the omitted finding; if the court made an error in a finding, the party should ask the court to amend the finding. See **O'Connor's Texas Civil Forms**, FORM 10E:4 (2020 ed.).

(1) By prevailing party. The prevailing party should request additional or amended findings of fact that support the judgment in its favor.

(2) By losing party. The losing party's request for additional or amended findings of fact is difficult to make because a request for findings inconsistent with the judgment will be denied, and a request for findings consistent with the judgment might be considered a waiver. *See* **In re Marriage of Grossnickle**, 115 S.W.3d 238, 254 (Tex.App.—Texarkana 2003, no pet.) (trial court is not required to make additional or amended findings contrary to other findings); **ASAI v. Vanco Insulation Abatement, Inc.**, 932 S.W.2d 118, 122 (Tex.App.—El Paso 1996, no writ) (same). In its request for additional findings, the losing party should (1) inform the trial court that a material issue disputed during the trial was not addressed in any of the findings, (2) request specific, additional findings on that issue that are consistent with the judgment, (3) inform the trial court that the party does not agree with the additional findings it requests, and (4) state that the findings are necessary so that, on appeal, the party may challenge either the findings or, if the additional findings are not entered, the lack of those findings. *See, e.g.*, **Vickery v. Commission for Lawyer Discipline**, 5 S.W.3d 241, 254 (Tex.App.—Houston [14th Dist.] 1999, pet. denied) (appellant's request did not inform trial court that it had omitted two essential elements in its original findings).

§3.6 Court's deadline to file additional findings. The trial court must file any additional or amended findings of fact no later than ten days after the date the request for additional findings is filed. Tex. R. Civ. P. 298. If the court refuses to make additional findings of fact requested by the losing party, the prevailing party cannot argue on appeal that findings should be deemed in support of the judgment. Tex. R. Civ. P. 299; **Boy Scouts v. Responsive Terminal Sys.**, 790 S.W.2d 738, 742–43 (Tex.App.—Dallas 1990, writ denied). Thus, the prevailing party should encourage the court to make additional findings when they are necessary.

§3.7 Findings in child-support cases. In a child-support case, Family Code §154.130 requires the court to file findings of fact when properly requested, "without regard to [TRCP] 296 through 299." The request for findings of fact under Family Code §154.130(a) may be made either orally during the hearing or in writing, filed before the final order is signed and no later than 20 days after the court has rendered the order. If the request is oral, it must be made on the record. *See* Tex. Fam. Code §154.130(a)(2). Family Code §154.130(b) lists the specific findings the court must make, but there is no deadline for the court to comply with a request for findings. *See* Tex. Fam. Code §154.130. See "Findings," **O'Connor's Texas Family Law Handbook**, ch. 4-F, §19.3.8 (2021 ed.).

§4. Response

The prevailing party should draft findings of fact when it receives notice that the other party has requested findings of fact. See **O'Connor's Texas Civil Forms**, FORM 10E:2 (2020 ed.). In drafting the findings of fact, the party should include a finding on each element of the cause of action and each defense. For the elements of various causes of action and defenses, see **O'Connor's Texas Causes of Action** (2021 ed.).

§5. Court's findings of fact & conclusions of law

§5.1 Who can file.

1. Generally. In most situations, findings of fact should be filed by the judge who tried the case. *See* Tex. R. Civ. P. 296.

2. When judge's term expires. The judge who tried the case may still have the authority to file findings of fact after her term of office has expired. *See* Tex. Civ. Prac. & Rem. Code §30.002(a).

(1) Term expires during period for filing findings. If the judge's term expires during the time period prescribed for filing findings of fact, she continues to have the authority to file findings in the case even after her term expires. *See* Tex. Civ. Prac. & Rem. Code §30.002(a); *see, e.g.*, **AD Villarai, LLC v. Chan Il Pak**, 519 S.W.3d 132, 140 (Tex.2017) (deadline for filing findings of fact was January 12; because judge's term expired December 31, which was during time for filing findings, judge had authority to file findings after term expired). The judge's successor does not have the authority to file findings of fact in such a case. *See* **AD Villarai**, 519 S.W.3d at 139 (simply because CPRC §30.002(a) provides that predecessor judge "may" file findings does not imply similar grant of authority to successor).

(2) Term expires before or after period for filing findings. If the judge's term expires before or after the time period prescribed for filing findings of fact, she no longer has the authority to file findings in the case once her term expires. *See* Tex. Civ. Prac. & Rem. Code §30.002(a); **AD Villarai**, 519 S.W.3d at 142. There is no rule permitting the judge's successor to file findings of fact in the case; thus, there would be no judge with the authority to file findings in this situation. **AD Villarai**, 519 S.W.3d at 142; *see* **Larry F. Smith, Inc. v. Weber Co.**, 110 S.W.3d 611, 616 (Tex.App.—Dallas 2003, pet. denied).

3. When judge resigns. Some courts have held that, if the judge who tried the case resigns before filing findings of fact, the judge's successor may file findings in the case under TRCP 18. *See, e.g.*, **2900 Smith, Ltd. v. Constellation NewEnergy, Inc.**, 301 S.W.3d 741, 744 n.6 (Tex.App.—Houston [14th Dist.] 2009, no pet.); **Fidelity & Guar. Life Ins. v. Pina**, 165 S.W.3d 416, 421 (Tex.App.—Corpus Christi 2005, no pet.); **Larry F. Smith, Inc.**, 110 S.W.3d at 616 (dicta).

Note

TRCP 18 addresses situations in which a judge dies, resigns, or is unable to hold court. Although some courts have applied Rule 18 to findings of fact, the Supreme Court has not decided the issue. See ***AD Villarai****, 519 S.W.3d at 138. Even if Rule 18 applies to findings of fact, "unable to hold court" refers to disability, not a judge's lack of authority to hold court (e.g., when she loses an election).* ***AD Villarai****, 519 S.W.3d at 138.*

4. When judge dies. If the judge dies before filing findings of fact in a pending case, the judge's successor may file findings of fact in the case. Tex. Civ. Prac. & Rem. Code §30.002(b).

§5.2 Form & content. The findings of fact and conclusions of law are generally prepared by the prevailing party. **Vickery v. Commission for Lawyer Discipline**, 5 S.W.3d 241, 253 (Tex.App.—Houston [14th Dist.] 1999, pet. denied); **Grossnickle v. Grossnickle**, 935 S.W.2d 830, 837 n.1 (Tex.App.—Texarkana 1996, writ denied). The findings must be made in writing, not orally. *See* **Larry F. Smith, Inc. v. Weber Co.**, 110 S.W.3d 611, 615 (Tex.App.—Dallas 2003, pet. denied).

1. Same document, separate headings. The findings and conclusions should be in the same document, but they should be stated under separate headings. When a finding of fact is mislabeled as a conclusion of law, the appellate court can treat it as a finding of fact. **Texas Outfitters Ltd. v. Nicholson**, 572 S.W.3d 647, 653 n.7 (Tex.2019); **Ray v. Farmers' State Bank**, 576 S.W.2d 607, 608 n.1 (Tex.1979).

2. Not in judgment. TRCP 299a requires the trial court to file findings of fact in a document separate from the judgment. Tex. R. Civ. P. 299a; **Guridi v. Waller**, 98 S.W.3d 315, 316–17 (Tex.App.—Houston [1st Dist.] 2003, no pet.); *see* **Salinas v. Beaudrie**, 960 S.W.2d 314, 317 (Tex.App.—Corpus Christi 1997, no pet.). When factual findings in the judgment conflict with those in the findings of fact, the separately filed findings of fact will control. Tex. R. Civ. P. 299a. Some courts hold that an appellate court cannot consider findings contained in the judgment. *E.g.*, **Sherer v. Sherer**, 393 S.W.3d 480, 484 n.7 (Tex.App.—Texarkana 2013, pet. denied); *see, e.g.*, **Casino Magic Corp. v. King**, 43 S.W.3d 14, 19 n.6 (Tex.App.—Dallas 2001, pet. denied); *see also* **Salinas**, 960 S.W.2d at 317 & n.5 (although court followed its precedent and held that findings in judgment could not be considered on appeal, court examined findings anyway and found them supported by evidence in record). Other courts, however, have determined that findings contained in the judgment can be considered on appeal if no one complains or requests findings and there is no conflict with separately filed findings. *E.g.*, **In re Estate of Jones**, 197 S.W.3d 894, 899–900 & n.4 (Tex.App.—Beaumont 2006, pet. denied); *see* **James J. Flanagan Shipping Corp. v. Del Monte Fresh Produce**, 403 S.W.3d 360, 364–65 (Tex.App.—Houston [1st Dist.] 2013, no pet.) (on appeal, findings contained in judgment have probative value unless they conflict with separately filed findings); **In re C.A.B.**, 289 S.W.3d 874, 880–81 (Tex.App.—Houston [14th Dist.] 2009, no pet.) (same); **In re Sigmar**, 270 S.W.3d 289, 295 n.2 (Tex.App.—Waco 2008, orig. proceeding) (same); **Hill v. Hill**, 971 S.W.2d 153, 157 (Tex.App.—Amarillo 1998, no pet.) (same).

Note

In some cases, the judge will issue a letter ruling with details about the decision. Generally, a letter ruling issued before judgment does not constitute findings of fact as contemplated by TRCP 296 to 299. See ***Cherokee Water Co. v. Gregg Cty. Appr. Dist.****, 801 S.W.2d 872, 878 (Tex.1990). Parties may, however, be able to rely on the findings of fact in the trial court's letter ruling if the court expresses its intent to have them do so. See, e.g.,* ***Moore v. Jet Stream Invs.****, 315 S.W.3d 195, 208–09 (Tex.App.—Texarkana 2010, pet. denied) (letter ruling could serve as findings of fact if letter were filed with clerk, but parties in this case could not rely on letter ruling when court did not specifically state that it intended to set forth findings of fact in letter);* ***Kendrick v. Garcia****, 171 S.W.3d 698, 701–02 (Tex.App.—Eastland 2005, pet. denied) (parties could rely on letter ruling when court did not enter formal findings and stated that it intended for parties to rely on letter ruling). Despite these opinions, the best practice is for parties to request formal findings of fact rather than rely on a letter ruling. See "Requesting findings of fact," ch. 10-E, §3.*

3. Only on controlling issues. The trial court is required to make findings of fact and conclusions of law only on controlling factual issues. **ASAI v. Vanco Insulation Abatement, Inc.**, 932 S.W.2d 118, 122 (Tex.App.—El Paso 1996, no writ); **Rafferty v. Finstad**, 903 S.W.2d 374, 376 (Tex.App.—Houston [1st Dist.] 1995, writ denied). An issue is controlling when it will support a judgment for one of the parties. **Taylor v. Texas DPS**, 754 S.W.2d 464, 468 (Tex.App.—Fort Worth 1988, writ denied). The trial court is not required to make findings on undisputed issues. **AD Villarai, LLC v. Chan Il Pak**, 519 S.W.3d 132, 135 (Tex.2017); **Barker v. Eckman**, 213 S.W.3d 306, 310 (Tex.2006).

§5.3 Late findings of fact & conclusions of law. The trial court can file findings of fact and conclusions of law after the deadline to file them has expired. **AD Villarai, LLC v. Chan Il Pak**, 519 S.W.3d 132, 141 & n.7 (Tex.2017); **Robles v. Robles**, 965 S.W.2d 605, 610 (Tex.App.—Houston [1st Dist.] 1998, pet. denied); **Morrison v. Morrison**, 713 S.W.2d 377, 380 (Tex.App.—Dallas 1986, writ dism'd). The trial court can file late findings and conclusions even after it loses plenary power. **AD Villarai**, 519 S.W.3d at 141; **In re Gillespie**, 124 S.W.3d 699, 703 (Tex.App.—Houston [14th Dist.] 2003, orig. proceeding). Because findings of fact and conclusions of law do not change the judgment, the court's loss of plenary power does not matter. **In re Gillespie**, 124 S.W.3d at 703.

§6. Review

§6.1 Effect on appellate timetable. A timely request for findings of fact and conclusions of law extends the time to perfect the appeal when (1) the findings and conclusions are required by TRCP 296 or (2) the trial court conducts an evidentiary hearing and the findings and conclusions can properly be considered by the appellate court. *See* Tex. R. App. P. 26.1(a)(4); **IKB Indus. v. Pro-Line Corp.**, 938 S.W.2d 440, 443 (Tex.1997); **Awde v. Dabeit**, 938 S.W.2d 31, 33 (Tex.1997). See "Request for findings of fact & conclusions of law," **O'Connor's Texas Civil Appeals**, ch. 5-A, §6.1.2 (2020 ed.).

1. Time extended. When a timely request for findings of fact is made in a case in which findings are required (see "Findings of fact are necessary," ch. 10-E, §2.1) or findings are helpful but not required (see "Findings of fact are helpful," ch. 10-E, §2.2), the request extends the time to perfect an appeal. **IKB Indus.**, 938 S.W.2d at 443; *see* **Gene Duke Builders, Inc. v. Abilene Hous. Auth.**, 138 S.W.3d 907, 908 (Tex.2004).

2. Time not extended. A request for findings of fact does not extend the time to perfect an appeal in the appeal of interlocutory orders (see "Findings of fact are permitted after appealable orders," ch. 10-E, §2.3) or when findings are not appropriate (see "Findings of fact are not appropriate," ch. 10-E, §2.4). See "Generally," **O'Connor's Texas Civil Appeals**, ch. 5-A, §5.2.2(1) (2020 ed.); "Filing deadlines not extended," **O'Connor's Texas Civil Appeals**, ch. 5-A, §6.2.4 (2020 ed.).

§6.2 Review of findings of fact.

1. When all necessary findings are filed. An appellant should treat the findings of fact as if they were jury findings and challenge all findings for legal and factual sufficiency. **Catalina v. Blasdel**, 881 S.W.2d 295, 297 (Tex.1994); **Las Colinas Obstetrics-Gynecology-Infertility Ass'n v. Villalba**, 324 S.W.3d 634, 638 (Tex.App.—Dallas 2010, no pet.); *see* **Texas Outfitters Ltd. v. Nicholson**, 572 S.W.3d 647, 653 (Tex.2019). When a reporter's record is part of the appellate record, findings of fact are not conclusive on appeal, even if unchallenged. **Zac Smith & Co. v. Otis Elevator Co.**, 734 S.W.2d 662, 666 (Tex.1987); *see* **Las Colinas**, 324 S.W.3d at 638; **City of Beaumont v. Spivey**, 1 S.W.3d 385, 392 (Tex.App.—Beaumont 1999, pet. denied). Before reversing on a factual-sufficiency point of error, the court of appeals must clearly state why the finding of fact is not supported by the evidence. **Ortiz v. Jones**, 917 S.W.2d 770, 772 (Tex.1996).

2. When some findings are omitted. When a party requests findings of fact and the court files them, the court of appeals can presume that omitted findings support the judgment only when (1) an element of the ground of recovery was included in the findings of fact, (2) the omitted element was not properly requested, and (3) the omitted finding is supported by the evidence. Tex. R. Civ. P. 299; **In re S.M.R.**, 434 S.W.3d 576, 580 (Tex.2014); **American Nat'l Ins. v. Paul**, 927 S.W.2d 239, 245 (Tex.App.—Austin 1996, writ denied); *see* **Seger v. Yorkshire Ins. Co.**, 503 S.W.3d 388, 401 (Tex.2016); *see, e.g.*, **Tarrant Cty. Water Control & Imprv. Dist. v. Haupt, Inc.**, 854 S.W.2d 909, 913 (Tex.1993) (because record contained some evidence of reasonableness, issue was deemed to support trial court's judgment). When a party does not request (and the trial court does not make) findings on an entire ground of recovery or defense, the appellate court cannot presume that specific ground of recovery or defense supports the judgment. Tex. R. Civ. P. 299; **F.R. Hernandez Constr. & Sup. Co. v.**

National Bank of Commerce, 578 S.W.2d 675, 678–79 (Tex.1979); **Nguyen v. Nguyen**, 355 S.W.3d 82, 92 (Tex.App.—Houston [1st Dist.] 2011, pet. denied). When findings are not requested or made on an entire claim or defense, the party waives its claim or defense just as if, in a jury trial, the party did not request a jury question on a claim or defense.

3. When findings are in conflict. If the trial court issues amended or additional findings of fact that conflict with the original findings, the later findings control. **Jefferson Cty. Drainage Dist. v. Lower Neches Valley Auth.**, 876 S.W.2d 940, 960 (Tex.App.—Beaumont 1994, writ denied).

4. When findings are filed late. If the trial court files late findings of fact, the only issue is whether the appellant was harmed. **In re E.A.C.**, 162 S.W.3d 438, 443 (Tex.App.—Dallas 2005, no pet.); *see* **Jardon v. Pfister**, 593 S.W.3d 810, 823 (Tex.App.—El Paso 2019, no pet.); **Robles v. Robles**, 965 S.W.2d 605, 610 (Tex.App.—Houston [1st Dist.] 1998, pet. denied). The appellant may be harmed because she (1) was unable to request additional findings or (2) was prevented from properly presenting her appeal. **Jardon**, 593 S.W.3d at 823; **In re E.A.C.**, 162 S.W.3d at 443; **Robles**, 965 S.W.2d at 610. If harm is shown, the appellate court may abate the appeal to give the appellant an opportunity to request additional or amended findings. **Jardon**, 593 S.W.3d at 823; **Robles**, 965 S.W.2d at 610; **Jefferson Cty. Drainage Dist.**, 876 S.W.2d at 960; **Morrison v. Morrison**, 713 S.W.2d 377, 380–81 (Tex.App.—Dallas 1986, writ dism'd).

5. When no additional findings are requested. If the appellant did not ask for additional findings, it cannot challenge the lack of findings on appeal. **Smith v. Smith**, 22 S.W.3d 140, 149 (Tex.App.—Houston [14th Dist.] 2000, no pet.); **Robles**, 965 S.W.2d at 611.

6. When findings are not required but helpful.

(1) General rule. When findings of fact are not required by TRCP 296 or some other rule or statute but are helpful to the appellate court, they are not reviewed for legal and factual sufficiency of the evidence as they are under TRCP 296. *See* **Chrysler Corp. v. Blackmon**, 841 S.W.2d 844, 852 (Tex.1992). When findings of fact are not required but are helpful, they do not have the same weight on appeal as findings made under TRCP 296 and are not binding on the appellate court. **IKB Indus. v. Pro-Line Corp.**, 938 S.W.2d 440, 442 (Tex.1997).

(2) Exception—special appearance. Even though findings of fact are not required by TRCP 296 or any other rule after a special appearance, when the trial court files findings after it denies a special appearance, those findings are reviewed for legal and factual sufficiency of the evidence. **BMC Software Belg., N.V. v. Marchand**, 83 S.W.3d 789, 794 (Tex.2002).

7. When findings are requested but not filed. When properly requested, the trial court has a mandatory duty to file findings of fact. **Cherne Indus. v. Magallanes**, 763 S.W.2d 768, 772 (Tex.1989); **In re Davis**, 30 S.W.3d 609, 613 (Tex.App.—Texarkana 2000, no pet.). See "Findings of fact are necessary," ch. 10-E, §2.1.

(1) Harmful error. If the trial court does not file findings of fact, it is presumed harmful error unless the record affirmatively shows the appellant suffered no harm. **AD Villarai, LLC v. Chan Il Pak**, 519 S.W.3d 132, 135 (Tex.2017); **Tenery v. Tenery**, 932 S.W.2d 29, 30 (Tex.1996); **Cherne Indus.**, 763 S.W.2d at 772. Error is harmful if it prevents a party from properly presenting its case to the appellate court. Tex. R. App. P. 44.1(a)(2); **Tenery**, 932 S.W.2d at 30. Generally, an appellant is harmed if the circumstances of the particular case require the appellant to guess at the reasons for the trial court's decision. **Liberty Mut. Fire Ins. v. Laca**, 243 S.W.3d 791, 794 (Tex.App.—El Paso 2007, no pet.); **Goggins v. Leo**, 849 S.W.2d 373, 379 (Tex.App.—Houston [14th Dist.] 1993, no writ); *see* **Larry F. Smith, Inc. v. Weber Co.**, 110 S.W.3d 611, 614 (Tex.App.—Dallas 2003, pet. denied) (when there is one ground of recovery or one defense, appellant usually does not have to guess reasons for judgment; when there is more than one, appellant must guess reasons for judgment unless findings are provided). In a complicated case with disputed facts or two or more grounds for recovery or defenses, the inference of harm cannot be overcome. **Randall v. Jennings**, 788 S.W.2d 931, 932 (Tex.App.—Houston [14th Dist.] 1990, no writ); *see* **Liberty Mut.**, 243 S.W.3d at 794. Oral statements made on the record are not a substitute for written findings. **In re W.E.R.**, 669 S.W.2d 716, 716 (Tex.1984); **Larry F. Smith, Inc.**, 110 S.W.3d at 615; *see* **Lopez v. Lopez**, 271 S.W.3d 780, 787 n.4 (Tex.App.—Waco 2008, no pet.).

Note

Although oral statements made on the record are not a substitute for written findings, some courts hold that if a ruling announced in open court gives the parties the reasons for the ruling and the parties do not have to guess the basis for it, there is no harm from the lack of written filed findings. E.g., ***Culver v. Culver****, 360 S.W.3d 526, 538 (Tex.App.—Texarkana 2011, no pet.); see, e.g.,* ***Sagemont Plaza Shopping v. Harris Cty. Appr. Dist.****, 30 S.W.3d 425, 427 (Tex.App.—Corpus Christi 2000, pet. denied);* ***Texas Workers' Comp. Ins. Fund v. Ashy****, 972 S.W.2d 208, 211–12 (Tex.App.—Beaumont 1998, pet. denied);* ***Elizondo v. Gomez****, 957 S.W.2d 862, 865 (Tex.App.—San Antonio 1997, pet. denied). See "Harmless error," ch. 10-E, §6.2.7(2).*

(a) Curable. If the error is curable, the appellate court may abate the appeal and remand the case to the trial court to make findings of fact. *See* Tex. R. App. P. 44.4(a)(2) (no reversal if trial court can correct failure to act); **AD Villarai**, 519 S.W.3d at 136 (preferred remedy is to direct trial court to file missing findings); *see, e.g.*, **Cherne Indus.**, 763 S.W.2d at 773 (trial judge was still on bench and could correct error); **Brooks v. Housing Auth.**, 926 S.W.2d 316, 319 (Tex.App.—El Paso 1996, no writ) (appeal was abated and trial judge was given 30 days to file findings).

(b) Not curable. If the error is not curable, the appellate court will reverse and remand the case for a new trial. *See, e.g.*, **Liberty Mut.**, 243 S.W.3d at 796 (reversed and remanded because judge who handled case was replaced as result of election); **Larry F. Smith, Inc.**, 110 S.W.3d at 616 (same).

(2) Harmless error. If the trial court does not file findings of fact, and the lack of findings is harmless error, the appellate court will affirm. *See* Tex. R. App. P. 44.1(a). The lack of findings is harmless if the record affirmatively shows that the complaining party suffered no injury. **Tenery**, 932 S.W.2d at 30; **Cherne Indus.**, 763 S.W.2d at 772; *see, e.g.*, **Graham Cent. Station, Inc. v. Peña**, 442 S.W.3d 261, 263 (Tex.2014) (lack of findings was harmless because it did not prevent D from properly presenting its case). For example, when the facts are undisputed and the only matters presented on appeal are legal issues to be reviewed de novo, the lack of findings of fact is harmless error. **Rollins v. American Express Travel Related Servs. Co.**, 219 S.W.3d 1, 5 (Tex.App.—Houston [1st Dist.] 2006, no pet.).

8. When findings are not requested or filed. When no findings of fact are requested or filed, the trial court's judgment implies all findings of fact necessary to support it. **Shields L.P. v. Bradberry**, 526 S.W.3d 471, 480 (Tex.2017); **Sixth RMA Partners v. Sibley**, 111 S.W.3d 46, 52 (Tex.2003); **BMC Software**, 83 S.W.3d at 795; **Worford v. Stamper**, 801 S.W.2d 108, 109 (Tex.1990); *see* **Chicago Title Ins. v. Cochran Invs.**, 602 S.W.3d 895, 899 n.2 (Tex.2020). When a reporter's record is filed, the implied findings are not conclusive, and an appellant may challenge them for both legal and factual sufficiency. **Shields L.P.**, 526 S.W.3d at 480; **Sibley**, 111 S.W.3d at 52; **BMC Software**, 83 S.W.3d at 795; **Roberson v. Robinson**, 768 S.W.2d 280, 281 (Tex.1989).

§6.3 Review of conclusions of law. The standard the court of appeals applies to review conclusions of law is de novo. **Hegar v. American Multi-Cinema, Inc.**, 605 S.W.3d 35, 40 (Tex.2020); **Southwestern Elec. Power Co. v. Lynch**, 595 S.W.3d 678, 683 (Tex.2020); **Bos v. Smith**, 556 S.W.3d 293, 299 (Tex.2018). The legal conclusions of the trial court are not binding on an appellate court; appellate courts are free to draw their own legal conclusions. *See* **Pegasus Energy Grp. v. Cheyenne Pet. Co.**, 3 S.W.3d 112, 121 (Tex.App.—Corpus Christi 1999, pet. denied); **Austin Hardwoods, Inc. v. Vanden Berghe**, 917 S.W.2d 320, 322 (Tex.App.—El Paso 1995, writ denied). An appellate court may uphold the trial court's conclusions of law if the judgment is supported by the evidence under any correct legal theory. **City of Houston v. Cotton**, 171 S.W.3d 541, 546 (Tex.App.—Houston [14th Dist.] 2005, pet. denied). Thus, an erroneous conclusion of law does not require reversal if the trial court ultimately rendered the proper judgment. **Bos**, 556 S.W.3d at 299; **BMC Software Belg., N.V. v. Marchand**, 83 S.W.3d 789, 794 (Tex.2002).

F. Motion to Reinstate After Dismissal for Want of Prosecution

§1. General

§1.1 Rules. Tex. R. Civ. P. 165a; Tex. R. App. P. 26.1(a)(3).

§1.2 Purpose. TRCP 165a permits a plaintiff to ask the court to reinstate a case after it was dismissed for want of prosecution.

§1.3 Timetable & forms. Appendix IV, Timetable 16, Motion to reinstate after dismissal for want of prosecution; **O'Connor's Texas Civil Forms**, FORMS 10F:1 et seq. (2020 ed.).

§2. Before dismissal

The trial court's authority to dismiss for want of prosecution comes from two sources: TRCP 165a and the court's inherent power. See "Failure to prosecute," ch. 7-G, §2.2.

§2.1 Notice case is on dismissal docket. A trial court cannot dismiss a suit without giving the plaintiff notice of its intent to dismiss. See "Notice of intent to dismiss," ch. 7-G, §3.

§2.2 Motion to retain. A plaintiff should file a motion to retain after it receives notice of the court's intent to dismiss and before the actual dismissal. See "Motion to retain," ch. 7-G, §4.1.

§3. Motion to reinstate

§3.1 Court's initiative. A trial court can reinstate the case on its own initiative without a motion within 30 days after dismissal. **Neese v. Wray**, 893 S.W.2d 169, 170 (Tex.App.—Houston [1st Dist.] 1995, no writ); *see* **Texas DPS v. Deck**, 954 S.W.2d 108, 111–12 (Tex.App.—San Antonio 1997, no writ).

§3.2 Plaintiff's motion. A motion to reinstate is not a prerequisite to appeal a dismissal for want of prosecution (DWOP). **Maida v. Fire Ins. Exch.**, 990 S.W.2d 836, 838 n.1 (Tex.App.—Fort Worth 1999, no pet.); **Hosey v. County of Victoria**, 832 S.W.2d 701, 703 (Tex.App.—Corpus Christi 1992, no writ). However, the motion to reinstate gives the plaintiff one last chance to convince the trial court to restore the case to the docket, permits the plaintiff to make a record for appeal, and extends the court's plenary power and the appellate deadlines. *See* Tex. R. Civ. P. 165a(3) (timely filed motion to reinstate extends court's plenary power to reinstate case until 30 days after motion is overruled).

§3.3 Verified. The plaintiff or its attorney must verify the motion to reinstate and, when necessary, attach affidavits. *See* Tex. R. Civ. P. 165a(3); **McConnell v. May**, 800 S.W.2d 194, 194 (Tex.1990); **Kenley v. Quintana Pet. Corp.**, 931 S.W.2d 318, 321 (Tex.App.—San Antonio 1996, writ denied). See "Verification," ch. 1-B, §3.2.15; "Affidavits," ch. 1-B, §3.2.16. An affidavit by the plaintiff's attorney can act as a substitute for verification. **Andrews v. Stanton**, 198 S.W.3d 4, 8–9 (Tex.App.—El Paso 2006, no pet.); *see* **3V, Inc. v. JTS Enters.**, 40 S.W.3d 533, 538–39 (Tex.App.—Houston [14th Dist.] 2000, no pet.); *see, e.g.*, **Guest v. Dixon**, 195 S.W.3d 687, 688–89 (Tex.2006) (affidavit of P's former attorney who had represented P for majority of time that case was pending was sufficient verification). In addition, the plaintiff can use an unsworn declaration instead of a verification. See "Unsworn declaration," ch. 1-B, §3.2.17. An unverified motion does not extend the trial court's plenary power or the deadlines for perfecting an appeal. *See* **Guest**, 195 S.W.3d at 688; **McConnell**, 800 S.W.2d at 194. The trial court can grant an unverified motion to reinstate, however, if it signs a written order within 30 days after the order of dismissal. **Dardari v. Texas Commerce Bank**, 961 S.W.2d 466, 469 (Tex.App.—Houston [1st Dist.] 1997, no pet.). The court cannot grant an unverified motion to reinstate more than 30 days after the order of dismissal because it no longer has plenary power. **In re Garcia**, 94 S.W.3d 832, 833–34 (Tex.App.—Corpus Christi 2002, orig. proceeding).

§3.4 Grounds to reinstate. The motion to reinstate must address the grounds for dismissal stated in the trial court's order. **Shook v. Gilmore & Tatge Mfg. Co.**, 951 S.W.2d 294, 296 (Tex.App.—Waco 1997, pet. denied). When the dismissal order does not identify the grounds for dismissal, the motion must address and negate all possible grounds. **Henderson v. Blalock**, 465 S.W.3d 318, 323 (Tex.App.—Houston [14th Dist.] 2015, no pet.); **Nichols v. Sedalco Constr. Servs.**, 228 S.W.3d 341, 342–43 (Tex.App.—Waco 2007, pet. denied); **Manning v. North**, 82 S.W.3d 706, 713 (Tex.App.—Amarillo 2002, no pet.). See **O'Connor's Texas Civil Forms**, FORM 10F:1 (2020 ed.).

1. Dismissal for failure to appear. When a court dismisses a suit for the plaintiff's failure to appear at the trial or other dispositive hearing under TRCP 165a(1), the plaintiff must establish by a verified motion that (1) it had no notice of the trial or hearing, (2) it had no notice of the court's intent to dismiss, or (3) although it had notice, its failure to appear was due to a mistake or accident.

(1) No notice of trial or hearing. If the plaintiff had no notice of the trial or hearing, the verified motion to reinstate should state that the plaintiff did not appear at the trial or hearing because it had no notice. The trial court cannot dismiss a suit for failure to appear unless the plaintiff was given proper notice of a trial or hearing. Tex. R. Civ. P. 165a(1).

(2) No notice of intent to dismiss. If the plaintiff had no notice of the court's intent to dismiss the suit or of the date and place of the dismissal hearing, the motion should state that the court could not dismiss the suit due to this lack of notice. The trial court cannot dismiss a suit for failure to appear without giving notice and an opportunity to be heard. See "Failure to appear," ch. 7-G, §2.2.1(1).

(3) Mistake or accident. If the plaintiff received notice of the trial or hearing and notice that failure to appear could result in dismissal, the verified motion should state that the plaintiff's failure to appear was not intentional or the result of conscious indifference, but was the result of a mistake or accident or is otherwise reasonably explained. *See* Tex. R. Civ. P. 165a(3); **Smith v. Babcock & Wilcox Constr. Co.**, 913 S.W.2d 467, 468 (Tex.1995). When the plaintiff received notice of the trial or hearing but did not appear, the standard of review is essentially the same as the **Craddock** standard for setting aside a default judgment. **Smith**, 913 S.W.2d at 468; *see* **Craddock v. Sunshine Bus Lines, Inc.**, 133 S.W.2d 124, 126 (Tex.1939). See "Failure to answer or appear after proper notice," ch. 10-B, §9.1.3. The failure to appear is not intentional or due to conscious indifference within the meaning of TRCP 165a(3) merely because it is deliberate; it must also be without adequate justification. **Smith**, 913 S.W.2d at 468. Conscious indifference means more than just negligence. *E.g., id.* (attorney, in trial in one county, mistakenly thought a continuance would be granted in case in another county; no conscious indifference); *see, e.g.*, **Quita, Inc. v. Haney**, 810 S.W.2d 469, 470 (Tex.App.—Eastland 1991, no writ) (attorney, in trial in one county, thought trial in other county would not be reached; no conscious indifference). Proof of justification (i.e., accident, mistake, or other reasonable explanation) negates intent or conscious indifference. **Smith**, 913 S.W.2d at 468; *see, e.g.*, **Henderson**, 465 S.W.3d at 323–24 (justification that P's attorney "overlooked the trial setting" without any contextual information or evidentiary explanation was inadequate to negate intent or conscious indifference). A mistake of law may satisfy this requirement. **Bank One v. Moody**, 830 S.W.2d 81, 85 (Tex.1992).

2. Dismissal for failure to prosecute. A motion to reinstate a case dismissed for failure to diligently prosecute gives the plaintiff the opportunity to ask the court to reconsider the dismissal. **Ellmossallamy v. Huntsman**, 830 S.W.2d 299, 302 (Tex.App.—Houston [14th Dist.] 1992, no writ).

(1) No notice of intent to dismiss. If the court dismissed the suit for failure to diligently prosecute without giving the plaintiff notice of its intent to dismiss, the plaintiff should file a verified motion to reinstate (1) proving lack of proper notice and (2) refuting the grounds for failure to prosecute. See "Notice of intent to dismiss," ch. 7-G, §3. The court can overrule the motion if the plaintiff merely proves lack of notice and does not address the failure to prosecute. *See* **Texas Sting, Ltd. v. R.B. Foods, Inc.**, 82 S.W.3d 644, 649 (Tex.App.—San Antonio 2002, pet. denied).

(2) Failure to comply with time standards. When a court dismisses a suit under TRCP 165a(2) for failure to comply with the Supreme Court's time standards, the plaintiff should file a verified motion to reinstate showing one of the following: (1) the suit was dismissed before the expiration of the appropriate time standard or (2) the plaintiff has a reasonable excuse for failing to prosecute the case within the time limits. *See, e.g.*, **Polk v. Southwest Crossing Homeowners Ass'n**, 165 S.W.3d 89, 96 (Tex.App.—Houston [14th Dist.] 2005, pet. denied) (dismissal affirmed; P did not bring case to trial or disposition for almost five years after D's appearance dates); **Johnson-Snodgrass v. KTAO, Inc.**, 75 S.W.3d 84, 87 (Tex.App.—Fort Worth 2002, pet. dism'd) (dismissal reversed; case was dismissed before it was 18 months old). See "Failure to comply with time standards," ch. 7-G, §2.2.1(2). The courts are split on whether the standard under TRCP 165a(3) applies to a dismissal for noncompliance with the Supreme Court's time standards. See "Caution," ch. 10-F, §3.4.2(3).

(3) Inherent power. When a court dismisses a suit under its inherent power for failure to prosecute, the plaintiff should file a verified motion to reinstate addressing the following issues: (1) the length of time the case was on file,

(2) the extent of activity in the case (i.e., showing plaintiff's diligence), (3) whether a trial setting was requested, and (4) a reasonable explanation for the delay. *See* **Henderson**, 465 S.W.3d at 321; **Maida v. Fire Ins. Exch.**, 990 S.W.2d 836, 842 (Tex.App.—Fort Worth 1999, no pet.). The purpose of the motion is to show that the plaintiff was "reasonably diligent" in prosecuting the suit. *See* **MacGregor v. Rich**, 941 S.W.2d 74, 75 (Tex.1997); *see also* **Veterans' Land Bd. v. Williams**, 543 S.W.2d 89, 90 (Tex.1976) ("due diligence"). A plaintiff is "reasonably diligent" if it acted as an ordinary, prudent person would have under the same or similar circumstances. **Manning**, 82 S.W.3d at 713. The motion must prove the plaintiff took the steps necessary to prepare for trial. *See, e.g.*, **Ellmossallamy**, 830 S.W.2d at 302 (P diligently pursued discovery, complied with D's requests, and was ready to proceed to trial).

Caution

The courts are split on whether the conscious-indifference standard of TRCP 165a(3) applies only to dismissal for failure to appear (see ch. 10-F, §3.4.1, above) or whether it also applies when the case is dismissed for noncompliance with the Supreme Court's time standards (see ch. 10-F, §3.4.2(2), above) or when the court exercises its inherent power to dismiss for lack of diligence. Compare ***Steward v. Colonial Cas. Ins.****, 143 S.W.3d 161, 164–65 (Tex.App.—Waco 2004, no pet.) (conscious-indifference standard applies only to cases dismissed for failure to appear),* ***Maida****, 990 S.W.2d at 840–41 (same),* ***Burton v. Hoffman****, 959 S.W.2d 351, 353–54 (Tex.App.—Austin 1998, no pet.) (same), and* ***Velvin Oil Co. v. R&S Trucking****, 578 S.W.3d 160, 163 (Tex.App.—Tyler 2019, no pet.) (memo op.; 4-10-19) (same), with* ***Zarychta v. Montgomery Cty. Dist. Atty.****, 398 S.W.3d 260, 264–65 (Tex.App.—Corpus Christi 2011, pet. dism'd) (conscious-indifference standard applies to all three grounds),* ***Cappetta v. Hermes****, 222 S.W.3d 160, 166–67 (Tex.App.—San Antonio 2006, no pet.) (same), and* ***Beames v. Hooks****, No. 01-14-00103-CV, 2015 WL 162226 (Tex.App.—Houston [1st Dist.] 2015, no pet.) (memo op.; 1-13-15) (same).*

§3.5 Challenging language of dismissal order. If the trial court's order mistakenly dismissed the suit "with prejudice" or stated that the plaintiff "take nothing," that statement must be challenged in the motion to reinstate or in a motion for new trial; otherwise, the error is waived and the suit cannot be refiled. *See* **El Paso Pipe & Sup. v. Mountain States Leasing, Inc.**, 617 S.W.2d 189, 190 (Tex.1981). See "Order of dismissal," ch. 7-G, §6. The wrong notation regarding dismissal does not require reinstatement of the case, just a correction of the order.

§3.6 Requesting hearing. Although a hearing on a motion to reinstate is mandatory, the plaintiff should still include a request for a hearing in its motion. *See* Tex. R. Civ. P. 165a(3); **Thordson v. City of Houston**, 815 S.W.2d 550, 550 (Tex.1991). See **O'Connor's Texas Civil Forms**, FORM 10F:1, ¶24 (2020 ed.). Even when a plaintiff does not ask for a hearing, the trial court must conduct one unless the plaintiff actually waives it. *See* **Parker v. Cain**, 505 S.W.3d 119, 122–23 (Tex.App.—Amarillo 2016, no pet.); **Enriquez v. Livingston**, 400 S.W.3d 610, 618–19 (Tex.App.—Austin 2013, pet. denied); **Matheson v. American Carbonics**, 867 S.W.2d 146, 147–48 & n.2 (Tex.App.—Texarkana 1993, no writ); *see, e.g.*, **Kelly v. Cunningham**, 848 S.W.2d 370, 371 (Tex.App.—Houston [1st Dist.] 1993, no writ) (Ps waived right to oral hearing by setting motion to reinstate on court's submission docket). However, some courts have held that the burden is on the plaintiff to request a hearing on the motion. *See, e.g.*, **Johnson v. Sepulveda**, 178 S.W.3d 117, 119 (Tex.App.—Houston [14th Dist.] 2005, no pet.) (relying on precedent that based its reasoning on cases predating 1983 version of TRCP 165a, court held P was required to alert court of need for hearing); **Rainbow Home Health, Inc. v. Schmidt**, 76 S.W.3d 53, 57 (Tex.App.—San Antonio 2002, pet. denied) (same). See "Hearing," ch. 10-F, §7.

Practice Tip

Always ask for a hearing on the motion to reinstate, attempt to get a setting for a hearing, and complain in writing if you do not get one.

§3.7 Amending the motion. The plaintiff must file an amended motion to reinstate within 30 days after the date the dismissal order was signed. *See, e.g.*, **Mandujano v. Oliva**, 755 S.W.2d 512, 514 (Tex.App.—San Antonio 1988, writ denied)

(P amended its motion to add verification before 30 days expired). If the court has already overruled the original motion, the plaintiff must seek leave of court to file an amended motion. Tex. R. Civ. P. 329b(b); *see also* **Mandujano**, 755 S.W.2d at 513 (amended motion was filed before trial court signed order overruling original motion).

§4. Deadline

The deadline for filing a motion to reinstate depends on whether the plaintiff received timely notice of the dismissal. See "Notice of dismissal order," ch. 7-G, §8; "Notice of judgment," ch. 9-C, §5.

§4.1 Timely notice of dismissal. If the plaintiff received timely notice of the dismissal of the suit, the plaintiff must file a motion to reinstate within 30 days after the trial court signed the order of dismissal. **Memorial Hosp. v. Gillis**, 741 S.W.2d 364, 365 (Tex.1987); **In re Montemayor**, 2 S.W.3d 542, 545 (Tex.App.—San Antonio 1999, orig. proceeding). Timely notice of dismissal is notice within 20 days after the dismissal. **Danforth Mem'l Hosp. v. Harris**, 573 S.W.2d 762, 763 (Tex.1978); *see* Tex. R. Civ. P. 306a(4); **In re Montemayor**, 2 S.W.3d at 545.

§4.2 Late notice of dismissal. If the plaintiff received notice of the dismissal of the suit 21 to 90 days after the date the judgment was signed, the plaintiff must file a motion to reinstate within 30 days after receiving notice of the dismissal and must include the allegations required for a motion to extend postjudgment deadlines. Tex. R. Civ. P. 306a(4), (5); Tex. R. App. P. 4.2(a)(1); *see* **Danforth Mem'l Hosp. v. Harris**, 573 S.W.2d 762, 763 (Tex.1978). See "Motion to Extend Postjudgment Deadlines," ch. 10-G, §1 et seq.

§4.3 Premature motion. If a plaintiff filed a motion to reinstate after dismissal but before the judgment was signed, the premature motion should be treated as timely. **In re Bokeloh**, 21 S.W.3d 784, 787–88 (Tex.App.—Houston [14th Dist.] 2000, orig. proceeding); *see* Tex. R. App. P. 27.2 (premature motion is considered effective); **Perez v. Texas Empls. Ins.**, 926 S.W.2d 425, 427 (Tex.App.—Austin 1996, order) (premature motion extends appellate timetable). *But see* **Brim Laundry Mach. Co. v. Washex Mach. Corp.**, 854 S.W.2d 297, 301 (Tex.App.—Fort Worth 1993, writ denied) (court applied TRCP 306c, which lists items that premature-filing rule applies to, in determining that prematurely filed motion to reinstate was ineffective). A motion to retain cannot be treated as a prematurely filed motion to reinstate. *See* **In re Bokeloh**, 21 S.W.3d at 790–91.

§5. Duty of court

§5.1 Clerk. The court clerk must deliver a copy of the motion to reinstate to the trial court. Tex. R. Civ. P. 165a(3); **Bush v. Ward**, 747 S.W.2d 43, 45 (Tex.App.—Beaumont 1988, no writ).

§5.2 Setting for hearing. When a timely motion to reinstate is filed, the trial court must set it for a hearing. See "Hearing mandatory," ch. 10-F, §7.1. The hearing must be held as soon as practicable. Tex. R. Civ. P. 165a(3).

§5.3 Notice of hearing. The court must notify all parties of the date, time, and place of the hearing. Tex. R. Civ. P. 165a(3).

§6. Response

The defendant should file a response to a motion to reinstate and challenge the grounds in the motion, verifying any factual allegations in the response with affidavits. See **O'Connor's Texas Civil Forms**, FORM 10F:2 (2020 ed.).

§7. Hearing

The hearing on the motion to reinstate remedies any violations of the plaintiff's due-process rights (e.g., lack of notice of the hearing or the dismissal) that occurred before the dismissal. **Dueitt v. Arrowhead Lakes Prop. Owners, Inc.**, 180 S.W.3d 733, 741 (Tex.App.—Waco 2005, pet. denied); **Manning v. North**, 82 S.W.3d 706, 715 (Tex.App.—Amarillo 2002, no pet.); **Texas Sting, Ltd. v. R.B. Foods, Inc.**, 82 S.W.3d 644, 648–49 (Tex.App.—San Antonio 2002, pet. denied). See "Notice of intent to dismiss," ch. 7-G, §3.

§7.1 Hearing mandatory. An oral hearing to receive evidence on a timely motion to reinstate is mandatory. **Thordson v. City of Houston**, 815 S.W.2d 550, 550 (Tex.1991); **Gulf Coast Inv. v. NASA 1 Bus. Ctr.**, 754 S.W.2d 152, 153 (Tex.1988); **Dueitt v. Arrowhead Lakes Prop. Owners, Inc.**, 180 S.W.3d 733, 740 (Tex.App.—Waco 2005, pet. denied); **Matheson v.**

American Carbonics, 867 S.W.2d 146, 148 (Tex.App.—Texarkana 1993, no writ). However, some courts have held that the burden is on the plaintiff to request a hearing on the motion. See "Requesting hearing," ch. 10-F, §3.6. If the trial court rules on the motion to reinstate without first conducting a hearing, the effect of the trial court's order depends on whether the motion is being granted or denied.

1. No hearing—motion granted. If the court grants the motion and reinstates the case without first conducting a hearing, the order is valid. *See* **Eagle Signal Corp. v. Wittig**, 766 S.W.2d 390, 392–93 (Tex.App.—Houston [1st Dist.] 1989, orig. proceeding).

2. No hearing—motion denied. If the court denies the motion to reinstate without first conducting a hearing, it may be reversible error. *See* **Bush v. Ward**, 747 S.W.2d 43, 45 (Tex.App.—Beaumont 1988, no writ). But any error in failing to conduct a hearing on the motion to reinstate may be harmless if (1) the plaintiff had notice and an opportunity to respond at the hearing on the motion to dismiss and (2) the motion to reinstate does not include any new arguments or additional or newly discovered evidence. *See* **Curnutt v. ConocoPhillips Co.**, 508 S.W.3d 641, 645 (Tex.App.—El Paso 2016, no pet.); **Dueitt**, 180 S.W.3d at 741; **Preslar v. Garcia**, No. 03-13-00449-CV, 2014 WL 824201 (Tex.App.—Austin 2014, no pet.) (memo op.; 2-26-14).

§7.2 Evidence. The plaintiff must present all necessary evidence at the hearing in support of each element of the grounds to reinstate. *See* **Bard v. Frank B. Hall & Co.**, 767 S.W.2d 839, 845 (Tex.App.—San Antonio 1989, writ denied). See "Grounds to reinstate," ch. 10-F, §3.4. Both the plaintiff and its attorney should formally present testimony about the reason for the dismissal, good cause to reinstate, and when necessary, the late notice of the dismissal. If no evidence is presented at the hearing, the dismissal will be affirmed on appeal. *See* **MacGregor v. Rich**, 941 S.W.2d 74, 76 (Tex.1997); **Balla v. Northeast Lincoln Mercury**, 717 S.W.2d 183, 184–85 (Tex.App.—Fort Worth 1986, no writ). The plaintiff should offer into evidence the affidavits attached to the motion, but it is not required to do so. *Cf.* **Director, State Empls. Workers' Comp. Div. v. Evans**, 889 S.W.2d 266, 268 (Tex.1994) (motion for new trial challenging post-answer default judgment).

§8. Request for findings of fact

If the trial court denied the motion to reinstate after receiving evidence, the plaintiff should ask the court to file findings of fact and conclusions of law. *See* **Burns v. Drew Woods, Inc.**, 900 S.W.2d 128, 129–30 (Tex.App.—Waco 1995, writ denied) (in appeal from denial of motion to reinstate, court focuses on trial court's role in fact-finding process).

§9. Order

§9.1 In writing. An order granting a motion to reinstate must be in writing and signed by the trial court. **Emerald Oaks Hotel/Conf. Ctr., Inc. v. Zardenetta**, 776 S.W.2d 577, 578 (Tex.1989); **Walker v. Harrison**, 597 S.W.2d 913, 915 (Tex.1980); **In re Wal-Mart Stores**, 20 S.W.3d 734, 740 (Tex.App.—El Paso 2000, orig. proceeding). An oral order and docket entry are ineffective to reinstate, and the motion will be deemed overruled by operation of law. **Emerald Oaks**, 776 S.W.2d at 578; **In re Wal-Mart**, 20 S.W.3d at 740.

§9.2 Deadline to reinstate.

1. Timely notice of dismissal. If the plaintiff filed a proper, timely, and verified motion to reinstate, the court must sign an order on the motion within 75 days after the date the judgment was signed, or the motion will be overruled by operation of law on the 76th day. *See* Tex. R. Civ. P. 165a(3); **Emerald Oaks Hotel/Conf. Ctr., Inc. v. Zardenetta**, 776 S.W.2d 577, 578 (Tex.1989). Once the motion is overruled, the trial court retains plenary power to change its ruling for 30 more days. Tex. R. Civ. P. 165a(3); *see* **Nealy v. Home Indem. Co.**, 770 S.W.2d 592, 594 (Tex.App.—Houston [14th Dist.] 1989, no writ). See chart 9-1 under "PPE motion withdrawn," ch. 9-C, §6.4.2(4).

2. Late notice of dismissal. If the plaintiff received late notice that the case was dismissed, the provisions of TRCP 306a(4) and (5) apply to determine when the motion to reinstate must be filed and when the trial court must sign the order on the motion. If the trial court determines the plaintiff received notice of the dismissal within the 21- to 90-day window in TRCP 306a(4) and TRAP 4.2(a)(1), the reinstatement order must be signed no later than 75 days after the date of actual notice, or the motion will be overruled by operation of law. See "Motion to Extend Postjudgment Deadlines," ch. 10-G, §1 et seq.

§10. Review

§10.1 Effect of motion to reinstate. Filing a proper motion to reinstate has the same effect on the appellate deadlines and the court's plenary power as the filing of a motion for new trial. **Butts v. Capitol City Nursing Home, Inc.**, 705 S.W.2d 696, 697 (Tex.1986). See "Effect of MNT," ch. 10-B, §2.5. If a motion is not verified or is not timely, it does not extend the deadlines or the court's plenary power. *See* **McConnell v. May**, 800 S.W.2d 194, 194 (Tex.1990); **Butts**, 705 S.W.2d at 697. If a motion to reinstate seeks more than reinstatement (e.g., it challenges the order that the case was dismissed "with prejudice"), it can be classified as a motion for new trial, and even an unverified motion will extend the appellate deadlines. *See* **State v. Martini**, 902 S.W.2d 138, 140–41 (Tex.App.—Houston [1st Dist.] 1995, no writ). If the plaintiff files a motion for new trial after dismissal for want of prosecution, the motion will be treated as a motion to reinstate, and it must be verified to extend the appellate deadlines. **City of McAllen v. Ramirez**, 875 S.W.2d 702, 704–05 (Tex.App.—Corpus Christi 1994, orig. proceeding). See "Verified," ch. 10-F, §3.3.

§10.2 Grounds for review. On appeal, the plaintiff may make either or both of the following arguments: (1) the trial court erred when it dismissed the case and (2) the trial court erred when it refused to reinstate the case. **Maida v. Fire Ins. Exch.**, 990 S.W.2d 836, 838 (Tex.App.—Fort Worth 1999, no pet.).

§10.3 Reporter's record. To appeal an order denying reinstatement, the plaintiff must file the reporter's record with the evidence from the hearing.

§10.4 Standard of review. To reverse a judgment of dismissal, the appellant must prove the trial court abused its discretion. *See* **MacGregor v. Rich**, 941 S.W.2d 74, 75 (Tex.1997) (dismissal for failure to prosecute); **State v. Rotello**, 671 S.W.2d 507, 509 (Tex.1984) (dismissal under local rule and court's inherent power for failure to prosecute); **Johnson-Snodgrass v. KTAO, Inc.**, 75 S.W.3d 84, 87 (Tex.App.—Fort Worth 2002, pet. dism'd) (dismissal under TRCP 165a). The standard of review for a motion to reinstate after failure to appear is whether the trial court abused its discretion in finding that the appellant's failure to appear was intentional or the result of conscious indifference—essentially the same standard used for setting aside a default judgment. *See* **Smith v. Babcock & Wilcox Constr. Co.**, 913 S.W.2d 467, 468 (Tex.1995).

§10.5 Mandamus. If the trial court erroneously reinstated a case after it lost plenary power, the reinstatement order can be challenged by mandamus. **Estate of Howley v. Haberman**, 878 S.W.2d 139, 140 (Tex.1994); **In re Garcia**, 94 S.W.3d 832, 833 (Tex.App.—Corpus Christi 2002, orig. proceeding); **In re Bokeloh**, 21 S.W.3d 784, 793 (Tex.App.—Houston [14th Dist.] 2000, orig. proceeding); *e.g.*, **City of McAllen v. Ramirez**, 875 S.W.2d 702, 704–05 (Tex.App.—Corpus Christi 1994, orig. proceeding) (trial court erroneously granted unverified motion for reinstatement and new trial).

G. Motion to Extend Postjudgment Deadlines

§1. General

§1.1 Rules. Tex. R. Civ. P. 306a(4), (5); Tex. R. App. P. 4.2.

§1.2 Purpose. A motion to extend postjudgment deadlines is the procedure used to ask the court to designate a new deadline for making motions on the judgment because the party did not receive timely notice of the judgment. A motion under TRCP 306a(5) extends the trial court's plenary power to consider postjudgment motions.

Note

*TRCP 306a(4), TRCP 306a(5), and TRAP 4.2 describe the procedure for this motion without assigning it a name. In this subchapter, we use the name from the Supreme Court's opinion in **John v. Marshall Health Servs.**, 58 S.W.3d 738, 739 (Tex.2001)—"motion to extend postjudgment deadlines."*

§1.3 Timetable & forms. Appendix IV, Timetable 17, Motion to extend postjudgment deadlines; **O'Connor's Texas Civil Forms**, FORMS 10G:1 et seq. (2020 ed.).

§1.4 Other references. **O'Connor's Texas Civil Appeals** (2020 ed.) (**O'Connor's Texas Appeals**).

§2. Notice of judgment

There are three rules requiring the court clerk to notify the parties about the judgment: TRCP 165a(1) (notice of signing order of dismissal for failure to prosecute), TRCP 239a (notice of no-answer default judgment), and TRCP 306a(3) (notice of judgment). See "Notice after no-answer default," ch. 7-A, §6.1; "Notice of intent to dismiss," ch. 7-G, §3; "Notice of judgment," ch. 9-C, §5. The clerk's failure to give the parties notice of the judgment as required by the rules does not affect the beginning of the time periods listed in TRCP 306a(1), except as provided by TRCP 306a(4). Tex. R. Civ. P. 306a(3).

§3. Motion

When a party does not receive notice or acquire actual knowledge of a judgment within 20 days after the judgment is signed, TRCP 306a(4) provides a limited time to request an extension before the judgment becomes final and the trial court loses plenary power. *See* Tex. R. App. P. 4.2(a)(1); **John v. State**, 826 S.W.2d 138, 140 n.2 (Tex.1992).

§3.1 Form. A motion to extend postjudgment deadlines (MEPD) may be made as part of a motion for new trial or a motion to reinstate, or it may be filed as a separate motion. *See* **In re Lynd Co.**, 195 S.W.3d 682, 686 (Tex.2006); **John v. Marshall Health Servs.**, 58 S.W.3d 738, 739–40 (Tex.2001); *see also* **In re J.Z.P.**, 484 S.W.3d 924, 925 (Tex.2016) (motion to reopen and vacate modification order was treated as MEPD when motion requested relief on grounds that party was not served with citation of modification hearing and did not know of order until a few days before motion was filed). See "Motion for New Trial," ch. 10-B, §1 et seq.; "Motion to Reinstate After Dismissal for Want of Prosecution," ch. 10-F, §1 et seq. An MEPD, however it is made, will extend the time to file post-trial motions, the trial court's plenary power, and the appellate deadlines. *See, e.g.*, **In re Wal-Mart Stores**, 20 S.W.3d 734, 739 n.6 (Tex.App.—El Paso 2000, orig. proceeding) (court's plenary power could have been extended by either motion to reinstate or MEPD); **University of Tex. v. Joki**, 735 S.W.2d 505, 506–07 (Tex.App.—Austin 1987, writ denied) (MNT extended time to perfect appeal); *see also* **Butts v. Capitol City Nursing Home, Inc.**, 705 S.W.2d 696, 697 (Tex.1986) (motion to reinstate extends time to perfect appeal, just like MNT).

§3.2 Allegations. The MEPD should cover the following issues:

1. Date of notice or actual knowledge. The motion must state that (1) the movant or its attorney received notice or acquired actual knowledge of the judgment on a specific date and (2) the date was more than 20 days but no more than 90 days after the judgment was signed. Tex. R. Civ. P. 306a(4), (5); *see* Tex. R. App. P. 4.2(a)(1); **Levit v. Adams**, 850 S.W.2d 469, 469–70 (Tex.1993); *see, e.g.*, **Gem Vending, Inc. v. Walker**, 918 S.W.2d 656, 657–58 (Tex.App.—Fort Worth 1996, orig. proceeding) (because party's attorney received notice within 20 days after judgment, tolling provisions of TRCP 306a(4) did not apply).

Note

A party is charged with notice or actual knowledge of the judgment when her attorney receives notice or acquires actual knowledge. ***Womack-Humphreys Architects, Inc. v. Barrasso****, 886 S.W.2d 809, 815 (Tex.App.—Dallas 1994, writ denied), disapproved on other grounds,* ***John v. Marshall Health Servs.****, 58 S.W.3d 738 (Tex.2001); see* ***Gem Vending****, 918 S.W.2d at 658. Similarly, notice to the attorney's law firm is notice to the attorney herself. See* ***A. Copeland Enters. v. Tindall****, 683 S.W.2d 596, 599 (Tex.App.—Fort Worth 1985, writ ref'd n.r.e.).*

2. Description of notice or actual knowledge. The motion must describe (1) who gave notice or how actual knowledge was acquired, (2) who received notice or acquired actual knowledge, and (3) any other relevant information. *See* Tex. R. Civ. P. 306a(4), (5); *see, e.g.*, **LDF Constr., Inc. v. Texas Friends of Chabad Lubavitch, Inc.**, 459 S.W.3d 720, 724–25 (Tex.App.—Houston [14th Dist.] 2015, no pet.) (movant attached copy of Judicial Information Management System entry showing that notice was mailed to incorrect floor in attorney's office building). The motion must identify the specific date that notice was received or actual knowledge was acquired. *E.g.*, **Womack-Humphreys**, 886 S.W.2d at 814–15 (statement in motion and affidavit that notice was received "after December 25" was not sufficient); *see, e.g.*, **Nathan A. Watson Co. v. Employers Mut. Cas. Co.**, 218 S.W.3d 797, 801–02 (Tex.App.—Fort Worth 2007, no pet.) (attorney's affidavit identifying date he first received notice was sufficient).

3. No earlier actual knowledge. The motion must state that neither the movant nor its attorney had actual knowledge of the judgment within 20 days after the judgment was signed. Tex. R. Civ. P. 306a(5); *see* **Nathan A. Watson Co.**, 218 S.W.3d at 801–02; **Womack-Humphreys**, 886 S.W.2d at 815; *see, e.g.*, **In re J.Z.P.**, 484 S.W.3d 924, 925 (Tex.2016) (party's affidavit and motion stated date she knew of modification order and that her attorney had not been given notice; court records also showed that notice had been sent only to adverse party and his attorney); **LDF Constr.**, 459 S.W.3d at 725 (attorney who was told by clerk that trial court had reached decision, but who did not receive clerk's mailed notice, did not have actual knowledge of signed judgment; party does not have obligation to inquire whether judgment was signed); **St. Louis Fed. S&L Ass'n v. Summerhouse Jt.V.**, 739 S.W.2d 441, 442 (Tex.App.—Corpus Christi 1987, no writ) (parties who were told by clerk that judgment was signed had actual knowledge).

4. No earlier notice from clerk. The motion must state that neither the movant nor its attorney received from the clerk any notice of the judgment within 20 days after the judgment was signed. Tex. R. Civ. P. 306a(5); *see* **Womack-Humphreys**, 886 S.W.2d at 815. TRCP 306a(5) requires the movant to negate timely receipt of the clerk's notice. **Womack-Humphreys**, 886 S.W.2d at 814–15.

§3.3 Request hearing. The movant should request a hearing on the motion and comply with the requirements of the local rules for securing a hearing. *See* **Xu v. Davis**, 884 S.W.2d 916, 917–18 (Tex.App.—Waco 1994, orig. proceeding). The trial court must hold a hearing before ruling on the motion. See "Hearing required," ch. 10-G, §6.1.

§3.4 Sworn motion. TRCP 306a(5) requires the movant to file a "sworn motion." The sworn motion establishes a prima facie case that the party did not receive timely notice and extends the court's plenary power to conduct a hearing to determine the exact date of notice or actual knowledge. **In re Lynd Co.**, 195 S.W.3d 682, 685 (Tex.2006). See "Plenary-power limits," ch. 10-G, §4.1. An unverified motion with attached affidavits satisfies TRCP 306a(5) if the affidavits verify the facts in the motion. *See* **City of Laredo v. Schuble**, 943 S.W.2d 124, 126 (Tex.App.—San Antonio 1997, orig. proceeding); **Womack-Humphreys Architects, Inc. v. Barrasso**, 886 S.W.2d 809, 814 n.4 (Tex.App.—Dallas 1994, writ denied), *disapproved on other grounds*, **John v. Marshall Health Servs.**, 58 S.W.3d 738 (Tex.2001).

Note

Generally, an unsworn declaration can be used instead of a verification or an affidavit. See Tex. Civ. Prac. & Rem. Code §132.001(a). For the procedure for using an unsworn declaration, see "Unsworn declaration," ch. 1-B, §3.2.17.

1. Verification. The verification (or affidavit) should directly and unequivocally state that the facts in the motion are true and within the affiant's personal knowledge. **Schuble**, 943 S.W.2d at 126 n.2. See "Verification," ch. 1-B, §3.2.15.

2. Affidavits. The motion should include the affidavits of the people who should have learned about the judgment but did not—the attorney and the party. *See, e.g.*, **Grondona v. Sutton**, 991 S.W.2d 90, 92 (Tex.App.—Austin 1998, pet. denied) (improper for trial court to rule on MEPD when attorney did not timely file affidavit, even though party's affidavit was timely filed). The affidavits must be based on personal knowledge. See "Affidavits," ch. 1-B, §3.2.16.

(1) Attorney. The attorney should (1) swear she did not receive timely notice of the judgment, (2) state the exact date the notice was received or actual knowledge was acquired, (3) describe the notice received or the actual knowledge acquired, and (4) state that no earlier notice was received from the clerk and that the attorney did not otherwise have actual knowledge of the judgment at an earlier time. *See* **Nathan A. Watson Co. v. Employers Mut. Cas. Co.**, 218 S.W.3d 797, 801 (Tex.App.—Fort Worth 2007, no pet.); **Womack-Humphreys**, 886 S.W.2d at 814–15. The attorney might also describe the office procedure for processing notices from the court and state that a review of the procedure revealed that no notice was received before that date. See **O'Connor's Texas Civil Forms**, FORM 10G:3 (2020 ed.).

(2) Party. The party should (1) swear it did not receive timely notice of the judgment, (2) state the exact date the notice was received or actual knowledge was acquired, (3) describe the notice received or the actual knowledge acquired, and (4) state that no earlier notice was received from the clerk and that the party did not otherwise have actual knowledge of the judgment at an earlier time. *See, e.g.*, **In re J.Z.P.**, 484 S.W.3d 924, 924–25 (Tex.2016) (party's affidavit stated she had never lived at address where citation for modification of divorce decree was posted and provided date she learned of contents of modification order); **In re Simpson**, 932 S.W.2d 674, 678 (Tex.App.—Amarillo 1996, no writ) (motion stated that party's attorney did not have notice or knowledge within 20 days but did not negate possibility that party received notice within 20 days). When the party is a corporation or other legal entity, an employee or agent may file the affidavit on behalf of the entity. *See, e.g.*, **Federal Ins. v. Ticor Title Ins.**, 774 S.W.2d 103, 104–05 (Tex.App.—Beaumont 1989, no writ) (affidavit filed by party's bond-claim attorney was sufficient). See **O'Connor's Texas Civil Forms**, FORM 10G:2 (2020 ed.).

(3) Clerk. If the court clerk has information about the late notice, the attorney should prepare an affidavit for the clerk to execute. *See* **In re Simpson**, 932 S.W.2d at 676–77.

§3.5 File notice of appeal. The party should file the notice of appeal with the trial court as soon as possible after learning of the judgment. Even if the notice of appeal is early, it will perfect the appeal. *See* Tex. R. App. P. 27.1(a) (premature notice of appeal is effective). See "Notice of Appeal," **O'Connor's Texas Civil Appeals**, ch. 5-A, §1 et seq. (2020 ed.).

Practice Tip

File a notice of appeal promptly to ensure that the notice is timely whether the MEPD is granted or overruled.

§4. Deadlines for movant

§4.1 Plenary-power limits. A motion to extend the time to file postjudgment motions under TRCP 306a(5) can be filed only while the trial court has plenary power. **John v. Marshall Health Servs.**, 58 S.W.3d 738, 741 (Tex.2001). The regular plenary-power timetable begins when the trial court signs the judgment (or order disposing of the case) and ends 30 days later if no motion for new trial or other plenary-power-extending (PPE) motion is filed. Tex. R. Civ. P. 306a(1) (beginning), Tex. R. Civ. P. 329b(d) (end). The extended plenary-power timetable, invoked by a proper MEPD, begins on the date of notice of the judgment (not the date the judgment was signed) and ends 30 days later if no motion for new trial or other PPE motion is filed. *See* **John**, 58 S.W.3d at 740–41; **Grondona v. Sutton**, 991 S.W.2d 90, 92 (Tex.App.—Austin 1998, pet. denied). A PPE motion is one that seeks a substantive change in the judgment. **Lane Bank Equip. Co. v. Smith S. Equip., Inc.**, 10 S.W.3d 308, 313 (Tex.2000). For a list of PPE motions, see "Motions that extend plenary power," ch. 9-C, §6.4.1(1). For the effect of PPE motions on the deadline to file an MEPD, see chart 9-1 under "PPE motion withdrawn," ch. 9-C, §6.4.2(4).

§4.2 TRCP 306a(4) limits.

1. Notice or actual knowledge of judgment. A party that receives notice or acquires actual knowledge of the judgment between 21 and 90 days after the judgment is signed may file an MEPD. *See* Tex. R. Civ. P. 306a(4); Tex. R. App. P. 4.2(a)(1).

(1) Earliest notice or knowledge. Notice received or actual knowledge acquired 21 days after the judgment is signed is the earliest notice or knowledge that entitles a party to file an MEPD. *See* Tex. R. Civ. P. 306a(4); Tex. R. App. P. 4.2(a)(1). When a party receives notice or acquires actual knowledge of a judgment within 20 days after the judgment is signed, the party cannot file an MEPD. *See, e.g.,* **In re Parker**, 117 S.W.3d 484, 487 (Tex.App.—Texarkana 2003, orig. proceeding) (party received notice 11 days after judgment); **In re Montemayor**, 2 S.W.3d 542, 545 (Tex.App.—San Antonio 1999, orig. proceeding) (party acquired actual knowledge 14 days after judgment). Notice of intent to enter judgment is not notice of the signing of the judgment. *See* **Western Imp. Motors, Inc. v. Mechinus**, 739 S.W.2d 125, 126 (Tex.App.—San Antonio 1987, writ denied).

(2) Latest notice or knowledge. TRCP 306a does not address the deadline for receiving late notice or acquiring actual knowledge of the judgment. The courts have interpreted the statement in TRCP 306a(4) that "in no event shall such periods [in TRCP 306a(1)] begin more than 90 days after" the judgment as preventing an MEPD when notice is received or actual knowledge is acquired more than 90 days after the judgment is signed. *See, e.g.,* **Estate of Howley v. Haberman**, 878 S.W.2d 139, 140 (Tex.1994) (too late to file MEPD because P learned of DWOP more than 90 days after dismissal); **Levit v. Adams**, 850 S.W.2d 469, 470 (Tex.1993) (same, because P learned of DWOP 91 days after dismissal).

2. Deadline for motion. TRCP 306a does not address the deadline for filing an MEPD. **John v. Marshall Health Servs.**, 58 S.W.3d 738, 741 (Tex.2001). A party may file an MEPD anytime within the trial court's plenary power, measured from the date determined under TRCP 306a(4). *E.g.,* **John**, 58 S.W.3d at 741 (MEPD filed 71 days after notice, which was 93 days after judgment was signed). See chart 9-1 under "PPE motion withdrawn," ch. 9-C, §6.4.2(4); Appendix IV, Timetable 17, Motion to extend postjudgment deadlines.

(1) Short plenary-power period. When no PPE motions (e.g., motion for new trial) are filed, the court's plenary power expires 30 days after the party received late notice or acquired actual knowledge of the judgment. In these cases, the deadline to file an MEPD is 30 days after the date of notice or knowledge. *E.g.,* **Green v. Guidry**, 34 S.W.3d 669, 670–71 (Tex.App.—Waco 2000, no pet.) (because no PPE motion was filed, deadline to file MEPD was 30 days after notice of judgment); *see* **John**, 58 S.W.3d at 741.

(2) Long plenary-power period. When a PPE motion (e.g., motion for new trial) is filed within 30 days after the late notice or actual knowledge of the judgment, the court's plenary power expires 30 days after that motion is overruled by written order or by operation of law, but no more than 105 days after the notice of the judgment. *See* **Green**, 34 S.W.3d at 670 & n.1. When a PPE motion is filed within 30 days after the late notice of the judgment, that motion extends the time to file an MEPD, which can be filed as long as the court has plenary power. *See, e.g.,* **John**, 58 S.W.3d at 741 (MNT filed 13 days after notice of judgment; MEPD filed 71 days after notice, within plenary power); **Grondona v. Sutton**, 991 S.W.2d 90, 92 (Tex.App.—Austin 1998, pet. denied) (MNT filed two days after notice of judgment; MEPD filed 84 days after notice of judgment, within plenary power); **Vineyard Bay Dev. Co. v. Vineyard on Lake Travis**, 864 S.W.2d 170, 172 (Tex.App.—Austin 1993, writ denied) (joint MNT and MEPD filed 24 days after notice of judgment, within plenary power). When a PPE motion is overruled by operation of law, the absolute last day to file an MEPD is 105 days after the party received notice of the judgment. **Green**, 34 S.W.3d at 670 & n.1.

Example

Assume the judgment was signed on day 0, P received notice of the judgment on day 50, and P filed an MNT on day 60. The MNT will extend the time P has to file an MEPD because it was filed within 30 days after the notice of the judgment. The time to file the MEPD is 30 days after the date the MNT is overruled, either by written order or by operation of law. Thus, the deadline to file an MEPD depends on whether the MNT is overruled by written order or by operation of law. If the court overrules the MNT by written order on day 70, P has until the end of day 100 to file the MEPD (70 + 30 = 100). If the court does not sign an order overruling the MNT, the MNT is overruled by operation of law on the expiration of day 125 (50 + 75 = 125); P has until the end of day 155 to file an MEPD (125 + 30 = 155). If no MNT is filed, P has until the end of day 80 to file an MEPD (50 + 30 = 80).

§5. Response

If the nonmovant objects to the allegations in the MEPD, the nonmovant should file a response challenging the motion. If the response contains factual recitations, it should be supported by affidavits. See **O'Connor's Texas Civil Forms**, FORM 10G:4 (2020 ed.).

§6. Hearing

§6.1 Hearing required. The trial court is required to hold a hearing on an MEPD. **Cantu v. Longoria**, 878 S.W.2d 131, 132 (Tex.1994); **In re Bokeloh**, 21 S.W.3d 784, 792 (Tex.App.—Houston [14th Dist.] 2000, orig. proceeding); **Xu v. Davis**, 884 S.W.2d 916, 918 (Tex.App.—Waco 1994, orig. proceeding); *see* Tex. R. Civ. P. 306a(5); Tex. R. App. P. 4.2(c). As a result of the Supreme Court's holding in **John v. Marshall Health Servs.**, 58 S.W.3d 738 (Tex.2001), an MEPD could conceivably be filed on the last day of the trial court's plenary power, which might preclude a hearing.

1. No hearing.

(1) Effect on evidence. If the trial court does not hold a hearing, it must accept the movant's affidavits as true. **Womack-Humphreys Architects, Inc. v. Barrasso**, 886 S.W.2d 809, 816 n.9 (Tex.App.—Dallas 1994, writ denied), *disapproved on other grounds*, **John v. Marshall Health Servs.**, 58 S.W.3d 738 (Tex.2001); *cf.* **Limestone Constr., Inc. v. Summit Commercial Indus. Props., Inc.**, 143 S.W.3d 538, 546 (Tex.App.—Austin 2004, no pet.) (no hearing on MNT).

(2) Effect on appeal. If the trial court does not hold a hearing, the movant may file a mandamus proceeding in the appellate court to require the trial court to conduct a hearing. *See* **Cantu**, 878 S.W.2d at 132; **In re Bokeloh**, 21 S.W.3d at 792.

2. Hearing. If the trial court holds a hearing, the court can consider evidence controverting the movant's proof. *See, e.g.*, **Xu**, 884 S.W.2d at 917 (nonmovant's contentions that movant received timely notice of judgment should be considered at a hearing).

§6.2 Burden. At the hearing, the movant must prove (1) the date it received the official notice of the judgment or acquired actual knowledge of the signing of the judgment, (2) that the date was more than 20 days after the judgment was signed, and (3) that the date was within 90 days after the judgment was signed. Tex. R. Civ. P. 306a(5) (elements 1 and 2); *see* Tex. R. App. P. 4.2(b); **In re Lynd Co.**, 195 S.W.3d 682, 686 (Tex.2006); **Estate of Howley v. Haberman**, 878 S.W.2d 139, 140 (Tex.1994).

§6.3 Deadline for hearing & ruling. TRCP 306a does not set a deadline for the court to conduct the hearing or make a ruling on the motion. The trial court should conduct a hearing and rule on the motion before its plenary power expires.

§6.4 Record. The movant should make sure the court reporter records the hearing on the motion so the movant can challenge an adverse ruling on appeal. If the court reporter does not record the evidence received at the hearing, the movant cannot offer proof of the late notice of the judgment in the appellate court. *See* **Corro v. Southwestern Bell Media, Inc.**, 784 S.W.2d 471, 474 (Tex.App.—Corpus Christi 1989, no writ).

§7. Order

§7.1 Written finding. The appellate rule, TRAP 4.2(c), requires the trial court to sign an order and to make a finding of the date of notice or actual knowledge of the judgment. **In re Bokeloh**, 21 S.W.3d 784, 792 (Tex.App.—Houston [14th Dist.] 2000, orig. proceeding); *see* **Sharm Inc. v. Martinez**, 885 S.W.2d 165, 166–67 (Tex.App.—Corpus Christi 1993, no writ) (former TRAP 5(b)(5)). By comparison, the trial rule, TRCP 306a, does not require the trial court to sign an order with such a finding. **In re Lynd Co.**, 195 S.W.3d 682, 686 (Tex.2006). If the trial court grants the motion but does not identify the date of notice or actual knowledge, the date may be implied from the court's order granting the motion, unless there is no evidence to support the implied finding or the party establishes an alternate date as a matter of law. *See id.*

Practice Tip

Even though TRCP 306a does not require the trial court to issue a written finding designating the actual date the party received notice or acquired actual knowledge of the judgment, TRAP 4.2(c) does; thus, the party should request one. See ***In re Lynd Co.****, 195 S.W.3d at 686. See* ***O'Connor's Texas Civil Forms****, FORM 10G:5 (2020 ed.).*

§7.2 Court grants motion. If the trial court grants the MEPD, it must designate a new date for the time periods in TRCP 306a(1) to begin running based on the date the movant received notice or acquired actual knowledge of the judgment. *See* Tex. R. Civ. P. 306a(4); Tex. R. App. P. 4.2(c); **In re Lynd Co.**, 195 S.W.3d 682, 686 (Tex.2006); **Levit v. Adams**, 850 S.W.2d 469, 469–70 (Tex.1993); *see, e.g.*, **Western Imp. Motors, Inc. v. Mechinus**, 739 S.W.2d 125, 126 (Tex.App.—San Antonio 1987, writ denied) (because movants learned of judgment on 59th day after it was signed, deadlines began to run on that date). Once the trial court establishes the new date for the judgment, the motion for new trial and notice of appeal will be considered timely if they are already filed. TRCP 306a(4) limits the reopening of the appellate time periods for the party who received late notice. The period cannot begin later than 90 days after the date the judgment or order was signed. Tex. R. Civ. P. 306a(4); Tex. R. App. P. 4.2(a)(1); **Levit**, 850 S.W.2d at 470.

§7.3 Court denies motion. If the trial court denies the MEPD, the time periods in TRCP 306a(1) will run from the date the judgment was signed. Even if the court denies the MEPD, it should make a written finding of the date of notice or actual knowledge of the judgment. Tex. R. App. P. 4.2(c).

§8. Review

§8.1 Appeal. The issue of late notice of the judgment cannot be raised for the first time on appeal. *See* **In re Estate of Padilla**, 103 S.W.3d 563, 567 (Tex.App.—San Antonio 2003, no pet.).

1. Court denies motion. If the trial court denies the MEPD, the movant may challenge the ruling by appeal. *See* **Hot Shot Messenger Serv. v. State**, 798 S.W.2d 413, 414–15 (Tex.App.—Austin 1990, writ denied); **Jimmy Swaggart Ministries v. City of Arlington**, 718 S.W.2d 83, 84–85 (Tex.App.—Fort Worth 1986, no writ).

2. Standard of review. The trial court's ruling is reviewed on appeal for legal and factual sufficiency of the evidence. **Nathan A. Watson Co. v. Employers Mut. Cas. Co.**, 218 S.W.3d 797, 800–01 (Tex.App.—Fort Worth 2007, no pet.); **Hot Shot**, 798 S.W.2d at 414.

3. When MEPD not available. When a party received notice or acquired actual knowledge of the judgment too late for an MEPD, the party may be able to challenge the judgment by a restricted appeal or a bill of review. *See* **Levit v. Adams**, 850 S.W.2d 469, 470 (Tex.1993). See "Attacking default judgment," ch. 7-A, §7.

§8.2 Mandamus.

1. Available.

(1) Court refuses hearing. If the trial court refuses to hold a hearing on the MEPD, the refusal can be challenged by mandamus. **Cantu v. Longoria**, 878 S.W.2d 131, 132 (Tex.1994); *see* **In re Bokeloh**, 21 S.W.3d 784, 792 (Tex.App.—Houston [14th Dist.] 2000, orig. proceeding).

(2) Court grants late motion. If the trial court grants a motion filed after 90 days, the order can be challenged by mandamus. **Estate of Howley v. Haberman**, 878 S.W.2d 139, 140 (Tex.1994).

2. Not available. When the party received notice or acquired actual knowledge of the judgment after the 90-day period, it is too late to file an MEPD, and the party cannot challenge the judgment by mandamus.

H. Motion for Judgment Nunc Pro Tunc

§1. General

§1.1 Rules. Tex. R. Civ. P. 306a(6), 316, 329b; Tex. R. App. P. 4.3(b).

§1.2 Purpose. The purpose of a judgment nunc pro tunc is to correct a clerical error in the judgment after the court's plenary power has expired. **Jenkins v. Jenkins**, 16 S.W.3d 473, 482 (Tex.App.—El Paso 2000, no pet.); **Ferguson v. Naylor**, 860 S.W.2d 123, 126 (Tex.App.—Amarillo 1993, writ denied); **West Tex. State Bank v. General Res. Mgmt.**, 723 S.W.2d 304, 306 (Tex.App.—Austin 1987, writ ref'd n.r.e.).

§1.3 Forms. **O'Connor's Texas Civil Forms**, FORMS 10H:1 et seq. (2020 ed.).

§2. Motion

§2.1 Ground. The only ground for a motion for judgment nunc pro tunc is to correct a clerical error made in entering the judgment. **Escobar v. Escobar**, 711 S.W.2d 230, 231 (Tex.1986). The inquiry in a proceeding for a judgment nunc pro tunc is what judgment was rendered, not what judgment should or might have been rendered. *Id.*; **In re A.M.R.**, 528 S.W.3d 119, 123 (Tex.App.—El Paso 2017, no pet.); **Hernandez v. Lopez**, 288 S.W.3d 180, 185 (Tex.App.—Houston [1st Dist.] 2009, no pet.). The court cannot correct a judicial error by signing a judgment nunc pro tunc after the expiration of its plenary power. See "Incorrect judgment nunc pro tunc," ch. 10-H, §6.2. When the error is judicial, a party must file a timely motion to modify the judgment. See "Motion to Modify the Judgment," ch. 10-D, §1 et seq.

1. Test to determine type of error. To determine whether an error was clerical or judicial, the attorney should ask the following: Was the error the result of judicial reasoning and determination? *See* **Gonzalez v. Doctors Hosp.**, 814 S.W.2d 536, 537 (Tex.App.—Houston [1st Dist.] 1991, no writ). If the answer is no, the error was clerical, and the trial court can correct the error, even though the judgment is final, by signing a judgment nunc pro tunc. *See* **Texas DOT v. A.P.I. Pipe & Sup.**, 397 S.W.3d 162, 167 (Tex.2013). If the answer is yes, the error was a judicial error, and it cannot be corrected by the trial court after the court loses plenary power. *See* **Finlay v. Jones**, 435 S.W.2d 136, 138–39 (Tex.1968).

2. Difference between clerical & judicial errors.

(1) Clerical error.

(a) Defined. A clerical error is a discrepancy between the entry of a judgment in the official record and the judgment as it was actually rendered. **Universal Underwriters Ins. v. Ferguson**, 471 S.W.2d 28, 29–30 (Tex.1971); **Morris v. O'Neal**, 464 S.W.3d 801, 810 (Tex.App.—Houston [14th Dist.] 2015, no pet.); *see* **Texas DOT**, 397 S.W.3d at 167 (if signed judgment inaccurately reflects court's true decision, error is clerical). A clerical error does not result from judicial reasoning or determination. **Texas DOT**, 397 S.W.3d at 167; **Andrews v. Koch**, 702 S.W.2d 584, 585 (Tex.1986). It is an error in entering or recording the court's decision. *See* **Escobar**, 711 S.W.2d at 231. Although a significant alteration to the judgment may be required to correct a clerical error, correction of a clerical error is not a substantive change in the judgment. *See* **Texas DOT**, 397 S.W.3d at 167; **In re Marriage of Ward**, 137 S.W.3d 910, 913 (Tex.App.—Texarkana 2004, no pet.); **Dickens v. Willis**, 957 S.W.2d 657, 659 (Tex.App.—Austin 1997, no pet.).

(b) Examples. The following are examples of clerical errors (which can be corrected by a judgment nunc pro tunc): • A discrepancy in the acreage description of land. *See* **Escobar**, 711 S.W.2d at 232. • An unintended judgment of dismissal caused by the clerk. **Knox v. Long**, 257 S.W.2d 289, 292–93 (Tex.1953), *overruled on other grounds*, **Jackson v. Hernandez**, 285 S.W.2d 184 (Tex.1955). • An error in the date of signing of the judgment. **Claxton v. (Upper) Lake Fork Water Control & Imprv. Dist.**, 220 S.W.3d 537, 543 (Tex.App.—Texarkana 2007, no pet.). • A discrepancy between the judgment signed and the judgment the court intended to sign. *E.g.*, **Andrews**, 702 S.W.2d at 586 (probate order to sell was different from order confirming sale); **Delaup v. Delaup**, 917 S.W.2d 411, 413 (Tex.App.—Houston [14th Dist.] 1996, no writ) (judgment did not reflect settlement agreement made in open court). • A judgment that granted a nonsuit with prejudice when the moving party requested a nonsuit without prejudice. **Thompson v. Texas Dept. of Human Res.**, 859 S.W.2d 482, 485 (Tex.App.—San Antonio 1993, no writ). • A mathematical error in the amount of damages. *See* **Travelers Cos. v. Wolfe**, 838 S.W.2d 708, 710 & n.2 (Tex.App.—Amarillo 1992, no writ). • A mistake in the party designations. *See,*

e.g., **Dickens**, 957 S.W.2d at 659–60 (clarification order changed "respondent" to "petitioner"). • A mistake in a party's name in the judgment. *E.g.*, **Gonzalez**, 814 S.W.2d at 537 (changed P's name from John to Juan). • A discrepancy between the body of the judgment actually rendered and the title of the document. *See, e.g.*, **Butler v. Continental Airlines, Inc.**, 31 S.W.3d 642, 647–48 (Tex.App.—Houston [1st Dist.] 2000, pet. denied) (only reference to motion for sanctions was in title of order).

(2) Judicial error.

(a) Defined. A judicial error occurs when the court considers an issue and makes an erroneous decision. *See* **Comet Aluminum Co. v. Dibrell**, 450 S.W.2d 56, 58–59 (Tex.1970). It is an error in rendering the judgment. **In re Daredia**, 317 S.W.3d 247, 249 (Tex.2010); **Escobar**, 711 S.W.2d at 231; **Claxton**, 220 S.W.3d at 543.

(b) Examples. The following are examples of judicial errors (which cannot be corrected by a judgment nunc pro tunc): • An order mistakenly containing language of finality. **In re Elizondo**, 544 S.W.3d 824, 829 (Tex.2018). • A judgment that changed a party's outright ownership of land into a mere easement. **Texas DOT**, 397 S.W.3d at 167. • A mistake in the award of prejudgment interest. **Comet Aluminum**, 450 S.W.2d at 59. • Erroneous recital that supported default judgment. *E.g.*, **Lone Star Cement Corp. v. Fair**, 467 S.W.2d 402, 405–06 (Tex.1971) (recital that D failed to appear and answer); **Finlay**, 435 S.W.2d at 138–39 (recital that D was served but did not answer). • An unintended judgment of dismissal. **In re Daredia**, 317 S.W.3d at 249–50; **Love v. State Bank & Trust Co.**, 90 S.W.2d 819, 820–21 (Tex.1936). • A judgment on arrears that incorrectly stated the date as a year later, creating another payment obligation. **Hernandez**, 288 S.W.3d at 188. • A judgment that granted a nonsuit with prejudice instead of without prejudice. *E.g.*, **In re Fuselier**, 56 S.W.3d 265, 268 (Tex.App.—Houston [1st Dist.] 2001, orig. proceeding) (drafting error made by attorney).

§2.2 Notice. The movant must give all interested parties notice of a motion for judgment nunc pro tunc. Tex. R. Civ. P. 316. If an interested party does not receive notice, the corrected judgment is a nullity. **West Tex. State Bank v. General Res. Mgmt.**, 723 S.W.2d 304, 307 (Tex.App.—Austin 1987, writ ref'd n.r.e.); *see* Tex. R. Civ. P. 316.

§3. Deadline

Attorneys often confuse the purpose, deadline, and effect of motions to modify the judgment with those of motions for judgment nunc pro tunc. The motion's purpose—whether it is to correct a judicial error or a clerical error—determines its deadline.

§3.1 For motion to modify the judgment. The deadline to file a motion to modify, correct, or reform an error in the judgment is the same as that for a motion for new trial—30 days after the trial court signs the judgment. Tex. R. Civ. P. 329b(a), (g). See "Deadlines for MNT," ch. 10-B, §5. The motion to modify the judgment can correct both types of error, judicial and clerical. **Riner v. Briargrove Park Prop. Owners, Inc.**, 976 S.W.2d 680, 682 n.1 (Tex.App.—Houston [1st Dist.] 1997, no writ); *see* **Lane Bank Equip. Co. v. Smith S. Equip., Inc.**, 10 S.W.3d 308, 313 (Tex.2000).

§3.2 For a motion for judgment nunc pro tunc. There is no deadline for filing a motion for judgment nunc pro tunc. *See* Tex. R. Civ. P. 316. The earliest a motion for judgment nunc pro tunc can be filed is the day after the court loses plenary power over the judgment. *See* **Riner v. Briargrove Park Prop. Owners, Inc.**, 976 S.W.2d 680, 682 (Tex.App.—Houston [1st Dist.] 1997, no writ) (judgment nunc pro tunc can be rendered only after court loses plenary power).

§4. Response

The party opposing the motion for judgment nunc pro tunc is not required to file a response. If a party believes the error was a judicial error and not a clerical one, it should file a motion citing authority to support its allegation that the error in the judgment was not clerical and cannot be changed because the court no longer has plenary power. *See* **In re A.M.R.**, 528 S.W.3d 119, 122 (Tex.App.—El Paso 2017, no pet.).

§5. Hearing

§5.1 Standard. At the hearing on a motion for judgment nunc pro tunc, the court must first determine (1) whether it previously rendered a judgment and (2) the contents of that judgment. **Escobar v. Escobar**, 711 S.W.2d 230, 232 (Tex.1986); **In re A.M.C.**, 491 S.W.3d 62, 67 (Tex.App.—Houston [14th Dist.] 2016, no pet.); *see* **Thompson v. Texas Dept. of Human Res.**, 859 S.W.2d 482, 484 (Tex.App.—San Antonio 1993, no writ). Whether a judgment was previously rendered and the

contents of that judgment are questions of fact. **Escobar**, 711 S.W.2d at 232; *see* **In re A.M.C.**, 491 S.W.3d at 67. Once the court makes that factual determination, the decision whether the error was clerical or judicial becomes a question of law. **Escobar**, 711 S.W.2d at 232; **In re A.M.C.**, 491 S.W.3d at 67; **Thompson**, 859 S.W.2d at 484.

§5.2 Movant's burden. The movant must present clear and convincing evidence that the error was clerical. **In re A.M.R.**, 528 S.W.3d 119, 122 (Tex.App.—El Paso 2017, no pet.); *see* **Claxton v. (Upper) Lake Fork Water Control & Imprv. Dist.**, 220 S.W.3d 537, 544–45 (Tex.App.—Texarkana 2007, no pet.); **Thompson v. Texas Dept. of Human Res.**, 859 S.W.2d 482, 485 (Tex.App.—San Antonio 1993, no writ). *But see* **In re A.M.C.**, 491 S.W.3d 62, 67 & n.7 (Tex.App.—Houston [14th Dist.] 2016, no pet.) (in earlier opinion, Fourteenth Court of Appeals incorrectly held that standard was clear and convincing evidence based on **Escobar**; instead, appellate court must defer to trial court if there is some probative evidence supporting trial court's determination). Evidence can consist of oral testimony of witnesses, written documents, the court's docket, and the judge's personal recollection. **In re A.M.R.**, 528 S.W.3d at 123; **In re A.M.C.**, 491 S.W.3d at 67. If the same trial judge who rendered the judgment grants the judgment nunc pro tunc, there is a presumption that her personal recollection supports the finding of a clerical error. **In re A.M.R.**, 528 S.W.3d at 123; **In re A.M.C.**, 491 S.W.3d at 67.

§6. Ruling

§6.1 Misnomer of judgment. If the court signs a corrected judgment while it still has plenary power, it is a modified judgment, not a judgment nunc pro tunc. *See* **Alford v. Whaley**, 794 S.W.2d 920, 922 (Tex.App.—Houston [1st Dist.] 1990, no writ). Even if the court mistakenly titles the judgment a "judgment nunc pro tunc," the judgment is not a judgment nunc pro tunc. *See* **Mathes v. Kelton**, 569 S.W.2d 876, 878 (Tex.1978); **Go Leasing, Inc. v. Groos Nat'l Bank**, 628 S.W.2d 143, 144–45 (Tex.App.—San Antonio 1982, no writ).

§6.2 Incorrect judgment nunc pro tunc. If the court attempts to correct a judicial error by signing a judgment nunc pro tunc after its plenary power expires, the judgment is void. **In re A.M.R.**, 528 S.W.3d 119, 123 (Tex.App.—El Paso 2017, no pet.); **Morris v. O'Neal**, 464 S.W.3d 801, 808 (Tex.App.—Houston [14th Dist.] 2015, no pet.); *see* **In re Elizondo**, 544 S.W.3d 824, 829 (Tex.2018); **Dikeman v. Snell**, 490 S.W.2d 183, 186 (Tex.1973). After the court's plenary power expires, the court cannot change the judgment by calling the correction of a judicial error a "judgment nunc pro tunc." *See* **Dikeman**, 490 S.W.2d at 186.

Note

As long as the trial court has plenary power over the judgment, it can correct any error, clerical or judicial, and a motion to correct the judgment should be titled "Motion to Modify (or Correct or Reform) the Judgment Under TRCP 329b." A TRCP 329b motion eliminates the argument whether the error in the judgment was clerical or judicial. After the court loses plenary power over the judgment, a motion to correct a clerical mistake in the judgment should be titled "Motion for Judgment Nunc Pro Tunc Under TRCP 316."

§7. Review

§7.1 Standard of review. Whether an error was judicial or clerical is a question of law that is reviewed de novo. **In re A.M.C.**, 491 S.W.3d 62, 67 (Tex.App.—Houston [14th Dist.] 2016, no pet.); *see* **Escobar v. Escobar**, 711 S.W.2d 230, 232 (Tex.1986).

§7.2 Appeal from granting motion. If the trial court corrects a clerical error in the judgment, the time to appeal depends on whether the court still had plenary power over the judgment.

1. Correction made before losing plenary power—modified judgment. Any change made to the judgment before the trial court loses plenary power, even a clerical change, will restart the deadlines for the appeal. **Lane Bank Equip. Co. v. Smith S. Equip., Inc.**, 10 S.W.3d 308, 313 (Tex.2000). See "Modified judgment & postjudgment deadlines," ch. 10-D, §6.2.

2. Correction made after losing plenary power—judgment nunc pro tunc. If, after it has lost plenary power, the court signs a judgment nunc pro tunc that corrects a clerical error, the deadline to challenge the correction begins to run when the trial court signs the judgment nunc pro tunc. *See* Tex. R. Civ. P. 306a(6); Tex. R. App. P. 4.3(b).

(1) Does not extend appellate deadlines. A judgment nunc pro tunc does not extend the appellate deadlines for any complaint about the original judgment. Tex. R. Civ. P. 306a(6); *e.g.*, **Gonzalez v. Doctors Hosp.**, 814 S.W.2d 536, 537 (Tex.App.—Houston [1st Dist.] 1991, no writ) (correction of P's name from John to Juan six months after judgment was signed did not extend appellate deadlines); **Cavalier Corp. v. Store Enters.**, 742 S.W.2d 785, 787 (Tex.App.—Dallas 1987, writ denied) (correction of corporate P's name after plenary power expired did not extend appellate deadlines).

(2) Does extend appellate deadlines. A judgment nunc pro tunc extends the appellate deadlines for any complaint about a matter not in the original judgment. TRAP 4.3(b) states that if the trial court corrects or reforms a judgment under TRCP 316 after the court's plenary power expires, all periods run from the date of the corrected judgment, but only for complaints that would not apply to the original judgment. TRCP 329b(h) states that if the trial court signs a corrected judgment after it loses plenary power over the judgment, no complaint will be heard on appeal that could have been presented in an appeal from the original judgment. Thus, if the trial court corrected a clerical error after it lost plenary power over the judgment, and that clerical correction requires some complaint not available before the trial court signed the judgment nunc pro tunc, the deadlines to complain about that issue are extended.

§7.3 No appeal from denial of motion. The movant cannot appeal from the order denying a motion for judgment nunc pro tunc because the order is not a final, appealable judgment. **Shadowbrook Apts. v. Abu-Ahmad**, 783 S.W.2d 210, 211 (Tex.1990).

§7.4 Mandamus. If the trial court denies a motion for judgment nunc pro tunc, the denial may be reviewable by mandamus. *See* **In re Bridges**, 28 S.W.3d 191, 195–96 (Tex.App.—Fort Worth 2000, orig. proceeding) (court reasoned that, because Supreme Court held in **Shadowbrook Apts.** that a party cannot appeal denial of a motion for judgment nunc pro tunc, P lacked an adequate remedy at law; thus, mandamus relief was appropriate).

Appendix I. Texas Rules of Civil Procedure

TABLE OF CONTENTS

TRCP 124	No judgment without service

Section 6. Costs and Security Therefor

TRCP 125	Parties responsible
TRCP 126	Fee for service of process in a county other than in the county of suit
TRCP 127	Parties liable for other costs
TRCP 129	How costs collected
TRCP 130	Officer to levy
TRCP 131	Successful party to recover
TRCP 133	Costs of motion
TRCP 136	Demand reduced by payments
TRCP 137	In assault and battery, etc.
TRCP 138	Cost of new trials
TRCP 139	On appeal and certiorari
TRCP 140	No fee for copy
TRCP 141	Court may otherwise adjudge costs
TRCP 142	Security for costs
TRCP 143	Rule for costs
TRCP 143a	Costs on appeal to county court
TRCP 144	Judgment on cost bond
TRCP 145	Payment of costs not required
TRCP 146	Deposit for costs
TRCP 147	Applies to any party
TRCP 148	Secured by other bond
TRCP 149	Execution for costs

Section 7. Abatement and Discontinuance of Suit

TRCP 150	Death of party
TRCP 151	Death of plaintiff
TRCP 152	Death of defendant
TRCP 153	When executor, etc., dies
TRCP 154	Requisites of scire facias
TRCP 155	Surviving parties
TRCP 156	Death after verdict or close of evidence
TRCP 158	Suit for the use of another
TRCP 159	Suit for injuries resulting in death
TRCP 160	Dissolution of corporation
TRCP 161	Where some defendants not served
TRCP 162	Dismissal or non-suit
TRCP 163	Dismissal as to parties served, etc
TRCP 165	Abandonment
TRCP 165a	Dismissal for want of prosecution

Section 8. Pre-trial Procedure

TRCP 166	Pre-trial conference
TRCP 166a	Summary judgment
TRCP 167	Offer of settlement; award of litigation costs
TRCP 168	Permission to appeal
TRCP 169	Expedited actions
TRCP 171	Master in chancery
TRCP 172	Audit
TRCP 173	Guardian ad litem
TRCP 174	Consolidation; separate trials
TRCP 175	Issue of law and dilatory pleas

Section 9. Evidence and Discovery

A. Evidence

TRCP 176	Subpoenas
TRCP 180	Refusal to testify
TRCP 181	Party as witness
TRCP 183	Interpreters
TRCP 185	Suit on account

B. Discovery

TRCP 190	Discovery limitations
TRCP 191	Modifying discovery procedures and limitations; conference requirement; signing disclosures, discovery requests, responses, and objections; filing requirements
TRCP 192	Permissible discovery: forms and scope; work product; protective orders; definitions
TRCP 193	Written discovery: response; objection; assertion of privilege; supplementation and amendment; failure to timely respond; presumption of authenticity
TRCP 194	Required disclosures
TRCP 195	Discovery regarding testifying expert witnesses
TRCP 196	Requests for production and inspection to parties; requests and motions for entry upon property
TRCP 197	Interrogatories to parties
TRCP 198	Requests for admissions
TRCP 199	Depositions upon oral examination
TRCP 200	Depositions upon written questions

TRCP 201	Depositions in foreign jurisdictions for use in Texas proceedings; depositions in texas for use in foreign proceedings
TRCP 202	Depositions before suit or to investigate claims
TRCP 203	Signing, certification and use of oral and written depositions
TRCP 204	Physical and mental examination
TRCP 205	Discovery from nonparties
TRCP 215	Abuse of discovery; sanctions

Section 10. The Jury in Court

TRCP 216	Request and fee for jury trial
TRCP 217	Oath of inability
TRCP 218	Jury docket
TRCP 219	Jury trial day
TRCP 220	Withdrawing cause from jury docket
TRCP 221	Challenge to the array
TRCP 222	When challenge is sustained
TRCP 223	Jury list in certain counties
TRCP 224	Preparing jury list
TRCP 225	Summoning talesman
TRCP 226	Oath to jury panel
TRCP 226a	Instructions to jury panel and jury
TRCP 227	Challenge to juror
TRCP 228	"Challenge for cause" defined
TRCP 229	Challenge for cause
TRCP 230	Certain questions not to be asked
TRCP 231	Number reduced by challenges
TRCP 232	Making peremptory challenges
TRCP 233	Number of peremptory challenges
TRCP 234	Lists returned to the clerk
TRCP 235	If jury is incomplete
TRCP 236	Oath to jury

Section 11. Trial of Causes

A. Appearance and Procedure

TRCP 237	Appearance day
TRCP 237a	Cases remanded from Federal Court
TRCP 238	Call of appearance docket
TRCP 239	Judgment by default
TRCP 239a	Notice of default judgment
TRCP 240	Where only some answer
TRCP 241	Assessing damages on liquidated demands
TRCP 243	Unliquidated demands
TRCP 244	On service by publication
TRCP 245	Assignment of cases for trial
TRCP 246	Clerk to give notice of settings
TRCP 247	Tried when set
TRCP 248	Jury cases
TRCP 249	Call of non-jury docket

B. Continuance and Change of Venue

TRCP 251	Continuance
TRCP 252	Application for continuance
TRCP 253	Absence of counsel as ground for continuance
TRCP 254	Attendance on legislature
TRCP 255	Change of venue by consent
TRCP 257	Granted on motion
TRCP 258	Shall be granted
TRCP 259	To what county
TRCP 261	Transcript on change

C. The Trial

TRCP 262	Trial by the court
TRCP 263	Agreed case
TRCP 264	Videotape trial
TRCP 265	Order of proceedings on trial by jury
TRCP 266	Open and close—admission
TRCP 267	Witnesses placed under rule
TRCP 268	Motion for instructed verdict
TRCP 269	Argument
TRCP 270	Additional testimony

D. Charge to the Jury

TRCP 271	Charge to the jury
TRCP 272	Requisites
TRCP 273	Jury submissions
TRCP 274	Objections and requests
TRCP 275	Charge read before argument
TRCP 276	Refusal or modification
TRCP 277	Submission to the jury
TRCP 278	Submission of questions, definitions, and instructions
TRCP 279	Omissions from the charge

E. Case to the Jury

TRCP 280	Presiding juror of jury

TRCP 281	Papers taken to jury room
TRCP 282	Jury kept together
TRCP 283	Duty of officer attending jury
TRCP 284	Judge to caution jury
TRCP 285	Jury may communicate with court
TRCP 286	Jury may receive further instructions
TRCP 287	Disagreement as to evidence
TRCP 288	Court open for jury
TRCP 289	Discharge of jury

F. Verdict

TRCP 290	Definition and substance
TRCP 291	Form of verdict
TRCP 292	Verdict by portion of original jury
TRCP 293	When the jury agree
TRCP 294	Polling the jury
TRCP 295	Correction of verdict

G. Findings by the Court

TRCP 296	Requests for findings of facts and conclusions of law
TRCP 297	Time to file findings of fact and conclusions of law
TRCP 298	Additional or amended findings of fact and conclusions of law
TRCP 299	Omitted findings
TRCP 299a	Findings of fact to be separately filed and not recited in a judgment

H. Judgments

TRCP 300	Court to render judgment
TRCP 301	Judgments
TRCP 302	On counterclaim
TRCP 303	On counterclaim for costs
TRCP 304	Judgment upon record
TRCP 305	Proposed judgment
TRCP 306	Recitation of judgment
TRCP 306a	Periods to run from signing of judgment
TRCP 306c	Prematurely filed documents
TRCP 307	Exceptions, etc., transcript
TRCP 308	Court shall enforce its decrees
TRCP 308a	In suits affecting the parent-child relationship
TRCP 308b	Determining the enforceability of a judgment or arbitration award based on foreign law in certain suits under the Family Code
TRCP 309	In foreclosure proceedings
TRCP 310	Writ of possession
TRCP 311	On appeal from probate court
TRCP 312	On appeal from justice court
TRCP 313	Against executors, etc.
TRCP 314	Confession of judgment

I. Remittitur and Correction

TRCP 315	Remittitur
TRCP 316	Correction of clerical mistakes in judgment record

J. New Trials

TRCP 320	Motion and action of court thereon
TRCP 321	Form
TRCP 322	Generality to be avoided
TRCP 324	Prerequisites of appeal
TRCP 326	Not more than two
TRCP 327	For jury misconduct
TRCP 329	Motion for new trial on judgment following citation by publication
TRCP 329a	County court cases
TRCP 329b	Time for filing motions

K. Certain District Courts

TRCP 330	Rules of practice and procedure in certain district courts

Part V. Rules of Practice in Justice Courts

TRCP 500	General rules
TRCP 501	Citation and service
TRCP 502	Institution of suit
TRCP 503	Default judgment; pre-trial matters; trial
TRCP 504	Jury
TRCP 505	Judgment; new trial
TRCP 506	Appeal
TRCP 507	Administrative rules for judges and court personnel
TRCP 508	Debt claim cases
TRCP 509	Repair and remedy cases
TRCP 510	Eviction cases

Part VI. Rules Relating to Ancillary Proceedings

Section 1. Attachment

TRCP 592	Application for writ of attachment and order
TRCP 592a	Bond for attachment
TRCP 592b	Form of attachment bond
TRCP 593	Requisites for writ
TRCP 594	Form of writ
TRCP 595	Several writs
TRCP 596	Delivery of writ
TRCP 597	Duty of officer
TRCP 598	Levy, how made
TRCP 598a	Service of writ on defendant
TRCP 599	Defendant may replevy
TRCP 600	Sale of perishable property
TRCP 601	To protect interests
TRCP 602	Bond of applicant for sale
TRCP 603	Procedure for sale
TRCP 604	Return of sale
TRCP 605	Judge may make necessary orders
TRCP 606	Return of writ
TRCP 607	Report of disposition of property
TRCP 608	Dissolution or modification of writ of attachment
TRCP 609	Amendment

Section 2. Distress Warrant

TRCP 610	Application for distress warrant and order
TRCP 611	Bond for distress warrant
TRCP 612	Requisites for warrant
TRCP 613	Service of warrant on defendant
TRCP 614	Defendant may replevy
TRCP 614a	Dissolution or modification of distress warrant
TRCP 615	Sale of perishable property
TRCP 616	To protect interests
TRCP 617	Procedure for sale
TRCP 618	Return of sale
TRCP 619	Citation for defendant
TRCP 620	Petition

Section 3. Executions

TRCP 621	Enforcement of judgment
TRCP 621a	Discovery and enforcement of judgment
TRCP 622	Execution
TRCP 623	On death of executor
TRCP 624	On death of nominal plaintiff
TRCP 625	On money of deceased
TRCP 626	On property of deceased
TRCP 627	Time for issuance
TRCP 628	Execution within thirty days
TRCP 629	Requisites of execution
TRCP 630	Execution on judgment for money
TRCP 631	Execution for sale of particular property
TRCP 632	Execution for delivery of certain property
TRCP 633	Execution for possession or value of personal property
TRCP 634	Execution superseded
TRCP 635	Stay of execution in justice court
TRCP 636	Indorsements by officer
TRCP 637	Levy of execution
TRCP 638	Property not to be designated
TRCP 639	Levy
TRCP 640	Levy on stock running at large
TRCP 641	Levy on shares of stock
TRCP 643	Levy on goods pledged or mortgaged
TRCP 644	May give delivery bond
TRCP 645	Property may be sold by defendant
TRCP 646	Forfeited delivery bond
TRCP 646a	Sale of real property
TRCP 647	Notice of sale of real estate
TRCP 648	"Courthouse door" defined
TRCP 649	Sale of personal property
TRCP 650	Notice of sale of personal property
TRCP 651	When execution not satisfied
TRCP 652	Purchaser failing to comply
TRCP 653	Resale of property
TRCP 654	Return of execution
TRCP 655	Return of execution by mail
TRCP 656	Execution docket

Section 4. Garnishment

TRCP 657	Judgment final for garnishment
TRCP 658	Application for writ of garnishment and order
TRCP 658a	Bond for garnishment

Part I. General Rules

TRCP 1. OBJECTIVE OF RULES

The proper objective of rules of civil procedure is to obtain a just, fair, equitable and impartial adjudication of the rights of litigants under established principles of substantive law. To the end that this objective may be attained with as great expedition and dispatch and at the least expense both to the litigants and to the state as may be practicable, these rules shall be given a liberal construction.

Oct. 29, 1940, eff. Sept. 1, 1941.

See also **O'Connor's Texas Rules**, "Introduction to the Texas Rules," ch. 1-A, §1 et seq.

TRCP 2. SCOPE OF RULES

These rules shall govern the procedure in the justice, county, and district courts of the State of Texas in all actions of a civil nature, with such exceptions as may be hereinafter stated. Where any statute in effect immediately prior to September 1, 1941, prescribed a rule of procedure in lunacy, guardianship, or estates of decedents, or any other probate proceedings in the county court differing from these Rules, and not included in the "List of Repealed Statutes," such statute shall apply; and where any statute in effect immediately prior to September 1, 1941, and not included in the "List of Repealed Statutes," prescribed a rule of procedure in any special statutory proceeding differing from these rules, such statute shall apply. All statutes in effect immediately prior to September 1, 1941, prescribing rules of procedure in bond or recognizance forfeitures in criminal cases are hereby continued in effect as rules of procedure governing such cases, but where such statutes prescribed no rules of procedure in such cases, these rules shall apply. All statutes in effect immediately prior to September 1, 1941, prescribing rules of procedure in tax suits are hereby continued in effect as rules of procedure governing such cases, but where such statutes prescribed no rules of procedure in such cases, these rules shall apply; provided, however, that Rule 117a shall control with respect to citation in tax suits.

Oct. 29, 1940, eff. Sept. 1, 1941. Amended by orders of Sept. 20, 1941, eff. Dec. 31, 1941; June 16, 1943, eff. Dec. 31, 1943; Aug. 18, 1947, eff. Dec. 31, 1947; April 10, 1986, eff. Sept. 1, 1986.

Source: FRCP 1 (adapted).

See also **O'Connor's Texas Rules**, "Introduction to the Texas Rules," ch. 1-A, §1 et seq.

TRCP 3. CONSTRUCTION OF RULES

Unless otherwise expressly provided, the past, present or future tense shall each include the other; the masculine, feminine, or neuter gender shall each include the other; and the singular and plural number shall each include the other.

Oct. 29, 1940, eff. Sept. 1, 1941.

See also Gov't Code §312.003.

TRCP 3a. LOCAL RULES

Each administrative judicial region, district court, county court, county court at law, and probate court may make and amend local rules governing practice before such courts, provided:

(1) that any proposed rule or amendment shall not be inconsistent with these rules or with any rule of the administrative judicial region in which the court is located;

(2) no time period provided by these rules may be altered by local rules;

(3) any proposed local rule or amendment shall not become effective until it is submitted and approved by the Supreme Court of Texas;

(4) any proposed local rule or amendment shall not become effective until at least thirty days after its publication in a manner reasonably calculated to bring it to the attention of attorneys practicing before the court or courts for which it is made;

(5) all local rules or amendments adopted and approved in accordance herewith are made available upon request to the members of the bar;

(6) no local rule, order, or practice of any court, other than local rules and amendments which fully comply with all requirements of this Rule 3a, shall ever be applied to determine the merits of any matter.

Oct. 29, 1940, eff. Sept. 1, 1941. Amended by order of June 10, 1980, eff. Jan. 1, 1981; renumbered from former Rule 817 and amended by order of Dec. 5, 1983, eff. April 1, 1984; amended by orders of April 10, 1986, eff. Sept. 1, 1986; July 15, 1987, eff. Jan. 1, 1988; April 24, 1990, eff. Sept. 1, 1990.

Comment—1990

To make Texas Rules of Civil Procedure timetables mandatory and to preclude use of unpublished local rules or other "standing" orders or local practices to determine issues of substantive merit.

See also TRJA 10; **O'Connor's Texas Rules**, "Local rules," ch. 1-A, §4.

ANNOTATIONS

Approximately $1,589.00 v. State, 230 S.W.3d 871, 874 (Tex.App.—Houston [14th Dist.] 2007, no pet.). "Rule 3a(2) absolutely prohibits application of a local rule that alters a time period set forth in the [TRCPs]. Rule 3a(2) does not distinguish a local rule that shortens a time period from a local rule that lengthens a time period."

TRCP 4. COMPUTATION OF TIME

In computing any period of time prescribed or allowed by these rules, by order of court, or by any applicable statute, the day of the act, event, or default after which the designated period of time begins to run is not to be included. The last day of the period so computed is to be included, unless it is a Saturday, Sunday, or legal holiday, in which event the period runs until the end of the next day which is not a Saturday, Sunday, or legal holiday. Saturdays, Sundays, and legal holidays shall not be counted for any purpose in any time period of five days or less in these rules, except that Saturdays, Sundays, and legal holidays shall be counted for purpose of the three-day periods in Rules 21 and 21a, extending other periods by three days when service is made by mail.

Oct. 29, 1940, eff. Sept. 1, 1941. Amended by orders of July 26, 1960, eff. Jan. 1, 1961; April 24, 1990, eff. Sept. 1, 1990; Dec. 11, 2013, eff. Jan. 1, 2014.

Comment—1990

Amended to omit counting Saturdays, Sundays and legal holidays in all periods of less than five days with certain exceptions.

See also Gov't Code §311.014; **O'Connor's Texas Rules**, "Rules for Filing Documents," ch. 1-C, §1 et seq.; **O'Connor's Texas Rules**, "Rules for Serving Documents," ch. 1-D, §1 et seq.; **O'Connor's Texas Rules**, "Motion for Summary Judgment—General Rules," ch. 7-B, §1 et seq.

ANNOTATIONS

Sosa v. Central Power & Light, 909 S.W.2d 893, 895 (Tex.1995). Ps filed their amended petition seven days before the hearing on the motion for summary judgment. "When Rule 4 is applied, the day on which [Ps] filed their amendment is not counted but the seventh day after it was filed is counted. . . . As we held in **Lewis** [below], the last day counted from the date of the filing may be the date of the hearing. Therefore, [Ps] timely filed their second amended original petition."

Lewis v. Blake, 876 S.W.2d 314, 316 (Tex.1994). TRCP 4 "applies to *any* period of time prescribed by the [TRCPs]. Applying Rule 4 to [TRCP] 166a(c), the . . . hearing on a motion for summary judgment may be set as early as the 21st day after the motion is served, or the 24th day if the motion is served by mail."

Peacock v. Humble, 933 S.W.2d 341, 342-43 (Tex.App.—Austin 1996, orig. proceeding). "The Code Construction Act [Gov't Code ch. 311] and [TRCP] 4 . . . are not consistent in the manner in which they address Saturdays, Sundays, and legal holidays when computing time periods of five days or less. [¶] When a rule of procedure conflicts with a statute, the rule yields to the legislative enactment. . . . Because the three-day filing period in the present case is statutory, the Code Construction Act's method for computing time applies rather than the method contained in Rule 4."

TRCP 5. ENLARGEMENT OF TIME

When by these rules or by a notice given thereunder or by order of court an act is required or allowed to be done at or within a specified time, the court for cause shown may, at any time in its discretion (a) with or without motion or notice, order the period enlarged if application therefor is made before the expiration of the period originally prescribed or as extended by a previous order; or (b) upon motion permit the act to be done after the expiration of the specified period where good cause is shown for the failure to act. The court may not enlarge the period for taking any action under the rules relating to new trials except as stated in these rules.

If any document is sent to the proper clerk by first-class United States mail in an envelope or wrapper properly addressed and stamped and is deposited in the mail on or before the last day for filing same, the same, if received by the clerk not more than ten days tardily, shall be filed by the clerk and be deemed filed in time. A legible postmark affixed by the United States Postal Service shall be prima facie evidence of the date of mailing.

Oct. 29, 1940, eff. Sept. 1, 1941. Amended by orders of Oct. 12, 1949, eff. March 1, 1950; July 21, 1970, eff. Jan. 1, 1971; Oct. 3, 1972, eff. Feb. 1, 1973; July 22, 1975, eff. Jan. 1, 1976; April 10, 1986, eff. Sept. 1, 1986; April 24, 1990, eff. Sept. 1, 1990.

Comment—1990

To make the last date for mailing under Rule 5 coincide with the last date for filing.

Source: FRCP 6(b), with changes: Second clause in federal rule requires a showing that failure to act "was the result of excusable neglect." Also, specific reference is made in this rule to time limitations relating to motions for new trial and for rehearings and to appeals and writs of error, while in the federal rule, cross-reference to such subjects is by rule number.

See also TRAP 4; **O'Connor's Texas Rules**, "Rules for Filing Documents," ch. 1-C, §1 et seq.; **O'Connor's Texas Rules**, "Motion for Continuance," ch. 5-D, §1 et seq.; **O'Connor's Texas Rules**, "General Rules for Discovery," ch. 6-A, §1 et seq.; **O'Connor's Texas Rules**, "Motion for New Trial," ch. 10-B, §1 et seq.

ANNOTATIONS

Morris v. Aguilar, 369 S.W.3d 168, 171 (Tex.2012). "By its own terms, Rule 5 only applies to deadlines in the [TRCPs]." *See also* **Chau v. Select Med. Corp.**, under this rule.

In re Brookshire Grocery Co., 250 S.W.3d 66, 73 (Tex.2008). "Rule 5 provides that a trial court 'may not enlarge the period for taking any action under the rules relating to new trial except as stated in these rules.' The [TRCPs] place no such limitation on motions relating to modifying, correcting, or reforming the judgment; treating such a motion as a motion for new trial—thereby extending the trial court's otherwise expired plenary power—would permit an end run around Rule 5's prohibition."

Ramos v. Richardson, 228 S.W.3d 671, 673 (Tex.2007). "The respondents argue that, for purposes of [TRCP 5,] the 'mailbox rule,' placing the notices of appeal into the outgoing prison mailbox is not the equivalent of placing them into the U.S. mail. But . . . an inmate who does everything necessary to satisfy timeliness requirements must not be penalized if the document is ultimately filed tardily because of an error on the part of officials over whom the inmate has no control."

Stokes v. Aberdeen Ins., 917 S.W.2d 267, 268 (Tex.1996). "[W]e hold that mailing the document to the proper court address is *conditionally effective* as mailing it to the proper court clerk's address. [¶] The clerk still must receive the document within ten days to perfect the filing."

Lofton v. Allstate Ins., 895 S.W.2d 693, 693-94 (Tex.1995). "While a postmark is *prima facie* evidence of mailing, no postmark is available in this case. In the absence of a proper postmark or certificate of mailing, an attorney's uncontroverted affidavit may be evidence of the date of mailing." *See also* **Landers v. State Farm Lloyds**, 257 S.W.3d 740, 745 (Tex.App.—Houston [1st Dist.] 2008, no pet.); **Arnold v. Shuck**, 24 S.W.3d 470, 472 (Tex.App.—Texarkana 2000, pet. denied).

Miller Brewing Co. v. Villarreal, 829 S.W.2d 770, 771-72 (Tex.1992). "[A] party who finds the courthouse closed on the last day that a document must be filed . . . may mail the document that day, and if it is received by the clerk not more than ten days later it is timely filed. He may also locate the clerk or judge of the court and file the document with them. In some circumstances a party may also move for an enlargement of time." *See also* **Garcia v. State Farm Lloyds**, 287 S.W.3d 809, 815 (Tex.App.—Corpus Christi 2009, pet. denied) ("not more than ten days tardily" requirement in Rule 5 refers to ten days past filing deadline).

Chau v. Select Med. Corp., 582 S.W.3d 413, 417-18 (Tex.App.—Eastland 2018, pet. denied). "The second paragraph of [TRCP] 5 contains the mailbox rule. According to its express terms, the second paragraph applies to any document. This includes original pleadings. . . . The first paragraph provides for when a judge may allow documents to be filed after the time limits set by the rules, but the second paragraph determines the legal effect of action taken *before* the last day to file. Each paragraph has a different scope: The first paragraph applies to deadlines established by these rules or by a notice given thereunder or by order of court, whereas the second paragraph applies to any document. [¶] Because the mailbox rule does not extend the substantive limitations period but instead defines what constitutes 'bringing suit,' there is no conflict that prevents the application of Rule 5 to a statutory deadline for bringing suit. [D] argues that Rule 5 only applies to the [TRCPs] and not a specific statutory deadline as provided in [Lab. Code] §21.254. [¶] In [**Morris v. Aguilar**, 369 S.W.3d 168 (Tex.2012)], the Texas Supreme Court quoted only the first paragraph of Rule 5 and made the following observation: By its own terms, Rule 5 only applies to deadlines in the [TRCPs]. . . . **Morris** appears to have used 'Rule 5' as a shorthand for the first paragraph, which concerns a court's power to extend a deadline for good cause. . . . As a result, we read the statement in **Morris** about Rule 5 as a reference only to good-cause extensions in the first paragraph of the rule." (Internal quotes omitted.) *See also* **Morris v. Aguilar**, under this rule.

Pediatrix Med. Servs. v. De La O, 368 S.W.3d 34, 38-39 (Tex.App.—El Paso 2012, no pet.). "Rule 5 does not enlarge the time in which to file a pleading, but instead defines when it is 'deemed filed in time.' Therefore, the U.S. Post Office acts as a branch of the court clerk's office for purposes of filing pleadings only when the provisions of Rule 5 are satisfied. The rule applies to filings that contemplate a filing deadline. Indeed, if the language of Rule 5 is construed under its plain meaning, it requires a pleading to be considered filed when it is deposited in the mail only if the pleading has to be filed on or before the last day for filing. [¶] [The] second amended petition was mailed on December 30, 2009 and it was received and filed by the court clerk on January 4, 2010. Because there was no preset deadline to file the second amended petition, the provisions of Rule 5 do not apply. Therefore, [the] second amended petition was filed on January 4, 2010, the date the court clerk actually received and filed it. . . ." *See also* **FP Asset Grp. v. Providence Bank**, No. 05-12-01728-CV, 2014 WL 3605770 (Tex.App.—Dallas 2014, no pet.) (memo op.; 7-22-14).

TRCP 6. SUITS COMMENCED ON SUNDAY

No civil suit shall be commenced nor process issued or served on Sunday, except in cases of injunction, attachment, garnishment, sequestration, or distress proceedings; provided that citation by publication published on Sunday shall be valid.

Oct. 29, 1940, eff. Sept. 1, 1941. Amended by order of Oct. 3, 1972, eff. Feb. 1, 1973.

See also **O'Connor's Texas Rules**, "Serving the Defendant with Suit," ch. 2-I, §1 et seq.

TRCP 7. MAY APPEAR BY ATTORNEY

Any party to a suit may appear and prosecute or defend his rights therein, either in person or by an attorney of the court.

Oct. 29, 1940, eff. Sept. 1, 1941.

Source: TRCS art. 1993 (repealed).

See also **O'Connor's Texas Rules**, "Rules for Serving Documents," ch. 1-D, §1 et seq.; **O'Connor's Texas Rules**, "The Attorney," ch. 1-H, §1 et seq.

ANNOTATIONS

Kunstoplast of Am., Inc. v. Formosa Plastics Corp., USA, 937 S.W.2d 455, 456 (Tex.1996). "Generally a corporation may be represented only by a licensed attorney. . . . We hold, however, that . . . a nonlawyer [is not precluded] from performing the specific ministerial task of [perfecting the appeal]."

Ayres v. Canales, 790 S.W.2d 554, 557 (Tex.1990). "Ordering a party to be represented by an attorney violates Rule 7." *See also* **Assignees of Best Buy v. Combs**, 395 S.W.3d 847, 862 (Tex.App.—Austin 2013, pet. denied) (trial court does not have power to appoint attorney without statutory or procedural authorization).

Kaminetzky v. Newman, No. 01-10-01113-CV, 2011 WL 6938536 (Tex.App.—Houston [1st Dist.] 2011, no pet.) (memo op.; 12-29-11). The right to represent oneself pro se "only applies . . . when the person is litigating his rights on his own behalf, instead of litigating certain rights in a representative capacity." *See also* **In re Gerstner**, No. 02-15-00315-CV, 2015 WL 6444797 (Tex.App.—Fort Worth 2015, orig. proceeding) (memo op.; 10-23-15) (sole proprietorship may appear pro se through its sole proprietor).

TRCP 8. ATTORNEY IN CHARGE

On the occasion of a party's first appearance through counsel, the attorney whose signature first appears on the initial pleadings for any party shall be the attorney in charge, unless another attorney is specifically designated therein. Thereafter, until such designation is changed by written notice to the court and all other parties in accordance with Rule 21a, said attorney in charge shall be responsible for the suit as to such party.

All communications from the court or other counsel with respect to a suit shall be sent to the attorney in charge.

Oct. 29, 1940, eff. Sept. 1, 1941. Amended by order of July 15, 1987, eff. Jan. 1, 1988.

See also **O'Connor's Texas Rules**, "The Attorney," ch. 1-H, §1 et seq.; **O'Connor's Texas Forms**, FORM 1H:1.

ANNOTATIONS

City of Tyler v. Beck, 196 S.W.3d 784, 787 (Tex.2006). "[N]othing in [TRCP 8] indicates that a motion filed by an attorney other than the designated attorney in charge is void or that other attorneys are not authorized to act on behalf of the party." *See also* **Sunbeam Envtl. Servs. v. Texas Workers' Comp. Ins. Facility**, 71 S.W.3d 846, 851 (Tex.App.—Austin 2002, no pet.).

Gem Vending, Inc. v. Walker, 918 S.W.2d 656, 658 (Tex.App.—Fort Worth 1996, orig. proceeding). "Notice to an attorney is notice to a party. [O]nce an attorney has entered an appearance in a case, all communications *must* be sent to that attorney."

Palmer v. Cantrell, 747 S.W.2d 39, 41 (Tex.App.—Houston [1st Dist.] 1988, no writ). "Where a single adverse party is represented by two attorneys who are not associated in a firm, we believe that it is sufficient to serve the attorney who is designated as lead counsel because he has 'control in the management of the cause. . . .'"

TRCP 9. NUMBER OF COUNSEL HEARD

Not more than two counsel on each side shall be heard on any question or on the trial, except in important cases, and upon special leave of the court.

Oct. 29, 1940, eff. Sept. 1, 1941.

See also **O'Connor's Texas Rules**, "The Attorney," ch. 1-H, §1 et seq.

TRCP 10. WITHDRAWAL OF ATTORNEY

An attorney may withdraw from representing a party only upon written motion for good cause shown. If another attorney is to be substituted as attorney for the party, the motion shall state: the name, address, telephone number, telecopier number, if any, and State Bar of Texas identification number of the substitute attorney; that the party approves the substitution; and that the withdrawal is not sought for delay only. If another attorney is not to be substituted as attorney for the party, the motion shall state: that a copy of the motion has been delivered to the party; that the party has been notified in writing of his right to object to the motion; whether the party consents to the motion; the party's last known address and all pending settings and deadlines. If the motion is granted, the withdrawing attorney shall immediately notify the party in writing of any additional settings or deadlines of which the attorney has knowledge at the time of the withdrawal and has not already notified the party. The Court may impose further conditions upon granting leave to withdraw. Notice or delivery to a party shall be either made to the party in person or mailed to the party's last known address by both certified and regular first class mail. If the attorney in charge withdraws and another attorney remains or becomes substituted, another attorney in charge must be designated of record with notice to all other parties in accordance with Rule 21a.

Oct. 29, 1940, eff. Sept. 1, 1941. Amended by orders of July 15, 1987, eff. Jan. 1, 1988; April 24, 1990, eff. Sept. 1, 1990.

Comment—1990

The amendment repeals the present rule and clarifies the requirements for withdrawal.

Comment—1988

The amendment repeals the present rule and makes provision for withdrawal of counsel, setting forth the requirements for withdrawal and withdrawal with substitution of counsel. The amendment also carries forward the requirements of amended Rule 8 regarding designation of attorney in charge.

Source: Tex Rules for Dist. & Cty. Cts. 46.

See also **O'Connor's Texas Rules**, "The Attorney," ch. 1-H, §1 et seq.; **O'Connor's Texas Forms**, FORMS 1H:6, 1H:7.

ANNOTATIONS

Rogers v. Clinton, 794 S.W.2d 9, 10 n.1 (Tex.1990). "Although a client may discharge his attorney at any time even without cause, an attorney may withdraw from representation of a client only if he satisfies the requirements of [TRCP] 10." *See also* **Sims v. Fitzpatrick**, 288 S.W.3d 93, 100 (Tex.App.—Houston [1st Dist.] 2009, no pet.) (granting motion to withdraw that does not comply with TRCP 10 may be harmless error if court allows time for party to secure new counsel and time for new counsel to investigate case and prepare for trial).

Jackson v. Jackson, 556 S.W.3d 461, 471 (Tex.App.—Houston [1st Dist.] 2018, no pet.). Attorney "had an independent duty under [Tex. Disciplinary R. Prof'l Conduct] 1.15(d), upon termination of her representation of [client], to 'take reasonable steps to the extent reasonably practicable to protect a client's interests, such as giving reasonable notice to the client [and] allowing time for employment of other counsel.' Moreover, the trial court, before allowing an attorney to withdraw, 'should see that the attorney has complied with the Code of Professional Responsibility.' [¶] We hold that, under the circumstances presented in this case, the trial court erred by granting [attorney's] motion to withdraw—a motion filed the morning trial was scheduled to begin that did not state whether [client] consented to the motion, that did not seek a continuance on [client's] behalf, and that did not take into account the foreseeable material adverse effects of self-representation on [client's] interests—without ascertaining the substantive basis of the dispute between [client] and [attorney] and, therefore, without determining whether [attorney] had good cause to withdraw, and without providing adequate time for [client] to secure other representation and for her new counsel to investigate the case and prepare for trial."

In re Marriage of Harrison, 557 S.W.3d 99, 115-16 (Tex.App.—Houston [14th Dist.] 2018, pet. denied). "An attorney may withdraw from representing a party only upon written motion for good cause shown. [TRCP 10] does not define good cause, but courts generally view the Texas Disciplinary Rules of Professional Conduct as articulating guidelines relevant to a 'good cause' determination supporting a Rule 10 motion to withdraw. [¶] Under the Disciplinary Rules of Professional Conduct, a lawyer must withdraw from representing a client if 'the representation will result in a violation of . . . applicable rules of professional conduct or other law.' . . . Further, because attorney-client confidentiality considerations may prevent a lawyer from revealing a detailed factual explanation in support of a motion to withdraw, a 'lawyer's statement that professional considerations require termination of the representation ordinarily should be accepted as sufficient.' [¶] At the hearings on her motion to withdraw, [attorney] asserted that she was required to withdraw due to [client's] actions, which had created what [attorney] described as an 'egregious' conflict. [Attorney] stated that, due to [client's] actions, [attorney] could not place [client's] interests above her own. . . . [¶] [Client], on the other hand, opposed [attorney's] withdrawal, telling the court she had 'not done anything to cause [attorney] to withdraw.' [¶] Based on our record, [client] has not shown that the trial court abused its discretion in accepting [attorney's] statement of the grounds for her motion to withdraw. [Attorney] explained that her continued representation of [client] would have caused [attorney] to violate the disciplinary rules by compromising her fiduciary duties to [client]. Under such circumstances, [attorney] was required to withdraw as [client's] counsel. . . . Although it would have been preferable to have obtained a more detailed explanation through an in camera conference or other means that would have preserved attorney-client privilege, [attorney's] explanation was sufficient to support good cause to withdraw."

Harrison v. Harrison, 367 S.W.3d 822, 827 (Tex.App.—Houston [14th Dist.] 2012, pet. denied). TRCP 10 "does not define 'good cause.' However, the Texas Disciplinary Rules of Professional Conduct articulate considerations relevant to the consideration of Rule 10 motions. [¶] [The Disciplinary Rules] provide[ ], among other things, that a lawyer shall not withdraw from representing a client 'unless withdrawal can be accomplished without material adverse effect on the interests of the client'; the client 'fails substantially to fulfill an obligation to the lawyer regarding the lawyer's services, including an obligation to pay the lawyer's fee as agreed, and has been given reasonable warning that the lawyer will withdraw unless the obligation is fulfilled'; and the representation 'will result in an unreasonable financial burden on the lawyer or has been rendered unreasonably difficult by the client.'"

TRCP 11. AGREEMENTS TO BE IN WRITING

Unless otherwise provided in these rules, no agreement between attorneys or parties touching any suit pending will be enforced unless it be in writing, signed and filed with the papers as part of the record, or unless it be made in open court and entered of record.

Oct. 29, 1940, eff. Sept. 1, 1941. Amended by order of July 15, 1987, eff. Jan. 1, 1988.

Comment—1988

The amendment makes it clear that Rule 11 is subject to modification by any other rule of Civil Procedure.

See also TRCP 191.1 (agreements modifying discovery); **O'Connor's Texas Rules**, "Agreements between attorneys—Rule 11," ch. 1-H, §9; **O'Connor's Texas Rules**, "Settlement of the Suit," ch. 7-I, §1 et seq.; **O'Connor's Texas Forms**, FORM 1H:13.

ANNOTATIONS

In re Vaishangi, Inc., 442 S.W.3d 256, 259 (Tex.2014). "We have generally treated Rule 11 agreements as separate and distinct from agreed judgments entered thereon. But nothing in the [TRCPs] prohibits a Rule 11 agreement from being, itself, an agreed judgment, so long as the agreement meets the requirements for a final judgment. *At 260:* Although fact issues about the scope and terms of the Rule 11 agreement may remain, those issues do not prevent the Court from determining as a matter of law whether the Rule 11 agreement constitutes an agreed judgment."

Exito Elecs. Co. v. Trejo, 142 S.W.3d 302, 305 (Tex.2004). "A Rule 11 Agreement between the parties, in and of itself, is not a plea, pleading, or motion. *At 306:* [W]hile filing a Rule 11 Agreement with the trial court is a requirement for enforcement, it is not in and of itself a request for enforcement or any other affirmative action by the trial court."

Compania Financiara Libano, S.A. v. Simmons, 53 S.W.3d 365, 368 (Tex.2001). A settlement agreement is enforceable as a contract even if its terms are not incorporated into the judgment.

Padilla v. LaFrance, 907 S.W.2d 454, 461 (Tex.1995). "The . . . filing requirement [in TRCP 11] is satisfied so long as the agreement is filed before it is sought to be enforced."

Coale v. Scott, 331 S.W.3d 829, 831-32 (Tex.App.—Amarillo 2011, no pet.). "[T]he trial court's authority to approve a Rule 11 agreement does not depend upon whether it has [plenary] jurisdiction. It may enforce a Rule 11 agreement touching upon the suit executed after the cause was tried and finally resolved via judgment. [A] settlement agreement . . . executed while the parties were attempting to sway the trial court to enforce its judgment logically falls within the scope of 'any suit pending' for purposes of Rule 11. [¶] [Party argued] that the Rule 11 agreement was unenforceable because they allegedly withdrew their consent to it before the trial court ordered its enforcement. We disagree. [¶] Rule 11 requires that the agreement be filed of record before the court may enforce it. If the accord is in writing, signed by the parties or their attorneys, and filed of record, it does not matter whether a party no longer agrees to it when the trial court is finally asked to enforce it. This is so because the agreement becomes a contract when executed, not when the trial court attempts to enforce it." *See also* **Lane-Valente Indus. (Nat'l), Inc. v. J.P. Morgan Chase**, 468 S.W.3d 200, 204 (Tex.App.—Houston [14th Dist.] 2015, no pet.) (Rule 11 agreement can be enforced as contract if one party withdraws consent before judgment is rendered, but party seeking enforcement must pursue separate breach-of-contract claim subject to normal rules of pleading and proof).

ExxonMobil Corp. v. Valence Oper. Co., 174 S.W.3d 303, 309 (Tex.App.—Houston [1st Dist.] 2005, pet. denied). "A trial court has a ministerial duty to enforce a valid Rule 11 agreement. [¶] However, it is not sufficient that a party's consent to a Rule 11 agreement may have been given at one time; consent must exist at the time that judgment is rendered." *See also* **Baylor Coll. of Med. v. Camberg**, 247 S.W.3d 342, 346 (Tex.App.—Houston [14th Dist.] 2008, pet. denied).

TRCP 12. ATTORNEY TO SHOW AUTHORITY

A party in a suit or proceeding pending in a court of this state may, by sworn written motion stating that he believes the suit or proceeding is being prosecuted or defended without authority, cause the attorney to be cited to appear before the court and show his authority to act. The notice of the motion shall be served upon the challenged attorney at least ten days before the hearing on the motion. At the hearing on the motion, the burden of proof shall be upon the challenged attorney to show sufficient authority to prosecute or defend the suit on behalf of the other party. Upon his failure to show such authority, the court shall refuse to permit the attorney to appear in the cause, and shall strike the pleadings if no person who is authorized to prosecute or defend appears. The motion may be heard and determined at any time before the parties have announced ready for trial, but the trial shall not be unnecessarily continued or delayed for the hearing.

Oct. 29, 1940, eff. Sept. 1, 1941. Amended by order of June 10, 1980, eff. Jan. 1, 1981.

Source: TRCS art. 320 (repealed), minor textual changes and added requirement that notice be served at least ten days before hearing on the motion.

See also **O'Connor's Texas Rules**, "The Attorney," ch. 1-H, §1 et seq.; **O'Connor's Texas Forms**, FORMS 1H:8, 1H:9, 1H:10.

ANNOTATIONS

In re Users Sys. Servs., 22 S.W.3d 331, 335 (Tex.1999). "[T]he procedure prescribed by Rule 12 for requiring an attorney to show his authority to act for a party presupposes the possibility that an attorney can be counsel of record for a party he is not authorized to represent. The [TRCPs] contemplate that authorization may not have existed or may cease before the attorney has withdrawn from the case."

Nolana Open MRI Ctr., Inc. v. Pechero, No. 13-13-00552-CV, 2015 WL 601916 (Tex.App.—Corpus Christi 2015, no pet.) (memo op.; 2-12-15). "Typically, a challenged attorney satisfies his burden [under TRCP 12] if he produces an affidavit or testimony from his client indicating the attorney was retained to provide representation in the case."

Air Park-Dallas Zoning Cmte. v. Crow-Billingsley Airpark, Ltd., 109 S.W.3d 900, 906 (Tex.App.—Dallas

2003, no pet.). "[A] Rule 12 motion may be properly brought when a new and different attorney attempts to appear as attorney of record purporting to advance a motion for new trial after the trial has concluded."

TRCP 13. EFFECT OF SIGNING OF PLEADINGS, MOTIONS AND OTHER PAPERS; SANCTIONS

The signatures of attorneys or parties constitute a certificate by them that they have read the pleading, motion, or other paper; that to the best of their knowledge, information, and belief formed after reasonable inquiry the instrument is not groundless and brought in bad faith or groundless and brought for the purpose of harassment. Attorneys or parties who shall bring a fictitious suit as an experiment to get an opinion of the court, or who shall file any fictitious pleading in a cause for such a purpose, or shall make statements in pleading which they know to be groundless and false, for the purpose of securing a delay of the trial of the cause, shall be held guilty of a contempt. If a pleading, motion or other paper is signed in violation of this rule, the court, upon motion or upon its own initiative, after notice and hearing, shall impose an appropriate sanction available under Rule 215,[1] upon the person who signed it, a represented party, or both.

Courts shall presume that pleadings, motions, and other papers are filed in good faith. No sanctions under this rule may be imposed except for good cause, the particulars of which must be stated in the sanction order. "Groundless" for purposes of this rule means no basis in law or fact and not warranted by good faith argument for the extension, modification, or reversal of existing law. A general denial does not constitute a violation of this rule. The amount requested for damages does not constitute a violation of this rule.

Oct. 29, 1940, eff. Sept. 1, 1941. Amended by orders of July 15, 1987, eff. Jan. 1, 1988; April 24, 1990, eff. Sept. 1, 1990.

Comment—1990

To require notice and hearing before a court determines to impose sanctions, to specify that any sanction imposed be appropriate, and to eliminate the 90-day "grace" period provided in the former version of the rule.

Source: Tex. Rules for Dist. & Cty. Cts. 51.

[1]Probably Vernon's Ann.Rules Civ.Proc., rule 215.2(b).

See also CPRC chs. 9, 10; **O'Connor's Texas Rules**, "Groundless or frivolous pleadings," ch. 1-B, §3.3; **O'Connor's Texas Rules**, "Motion for Sanctions," ch. 5-K, §1 et seq.; **O'Connor's Texas Forms**, FORMS 5K:1, 5K:2, 5K:5.

ANNOTATIONS

GTE Comms. Sys. v. Tanner, 856 S.W.2d 725, 731 (Tex.1993). TRCP 13 "prescribes that courts presume that papers are filed in good faith. Thus, the burden is on the party moving for sanctions to overcome this presumption. [¶] Rule 13 requires that sanctions imposed be 'appropriate,' which is the equivalent of 'just' under [TRCP] 215." *See also* **Olibas v. Gomez**, 242 S.W.3d 527, 534 (Tex.App.—El Paso 2007, pet. denied), *overruled on other grounds*, **Nath v. Texas Children's Hosp.**, 576 S.W.3d 707 (Tex.2019).

Gomer v. Davis, 419 S.W.3d 470, 477 (Tex.App.—Houston [1st Dist.] 2013, no pet.). "The party seeking to impose sanctions pursuant to Rule 13 must demonstrate first that the opposing party's pleadings are groundless, and then the party must demonstrate that the groundless pleadings were either filed in bad faith or filed for the purpose of harassment. *At 478:* When imposing Rule 13 sanctions, the trial court is required to state the particulars of good cause justifying the sanctions. The trial court abuses its discretion if it fails to comply with this requirement. However, if, as here, the party against whom sanctions are imposed does not object to the form of the sanctions order, that party waives any objection to the absence of a bad faith or harassment finding. In that circumstance, we consider whether the record contains any evidence to support an implied finding that the plaintiff brought her claim in bad faith or for the purpose of harassment."

Parker v. Walton, 233 S.W.3d 535, 539-40 (Tex.App.—Houston [14th Dist.] 2007, no pet.). "When determining whether Rule 13 sanctions are proper, the trial court must examine the facts available to the litigant and the circumstances existing when the litigant filed the pleading. Rule 13 requires sanctions based on the acts or omissions of the represented party or counsel and not merely on the legal merit of the pleading. The trial court must provide notice and hold an evidentiary hearing 'to make the necessary factual determinations about the motives and credibility of the person signing the groundless petition.' . . . Bad faith is not simply bad judgment or negligence; rather, it is the conscious doing of a wrong for dishonest, discriminatory, or malicious purposes. Improper motive is an essential element of bad faith. Harassment means that the pleading was intended to annoy, alarm, and abuse another person." *See also* **Zeifman v. Michels**, No. 03-12-00114-CV, 2013 WL 4516082 (Tex.App.—Austin 2013, no pet.) (memo op.; 8-22-13) (party acts in bad faith if she has been put on notice that her understanding of facts may be incorrect but does not make reasonable inquiry before further pursuing her claim); **Thielemann v. Kethan**, 371 S.W.3d 286, 294 (Tex.App.—Houston [1st Dist.] 2012, pet. denied) (party moving for sanctions must prove pleading party's subjective state of mind).

Loeffler v. Lytle ISD, 211 S.W.3d 331, 349-50 (Tex.App.—San Antonio 2006, pet. denied). "At the time these pleadings and motions were filed, [P] at the most provided the factual basis for these claims. The decision of what legal claims, objections, and motions to file was part and parcel of [P's] legal representation and was entrusted to . . . her attorney. Because a party should not be punished

for their attorney's conduct unless the party is implicated apart from having entrusted its legal representation, we conclude the trial court abused its discretion in imposing sanctions against [P] under . . . Rule 13." *See also* **Metzger v. Sebek**, 892 S.W.2d 20, 52-53 (Tex.App.—Houston [1st Dist.] 1994, writ denied) (party should be fined smaller amount because he was responsible only for affidavit with false information, not for pleadings).

TRCP 14. AFFIDAVIT BY AGENT

Whenever it may be necessary or proper for any party to a civil suit or proceeding to make an affidavit, it may be made by either the party or his agent or his attorney.

Oct. 29, 1940, eff. Sept. 1, 1941.

See also TRCP 197.2(d); **O'Connor's Texas Rules**, "Affidavits," ch. 1-B, §3.2.16; **O'Connor's Texas Forms**, FORM 1B:8.

ANNOTATIONS

Cantu v. Holiday Inns, Inc., 910 S.W.2d 113, 116 (Tex.App.—Corpus Christi 1995, writ denied). "A party's attorney may verify the pleading where he has knowledge of the facts, but does not have authority to verify based merely on his status as counsel. Here, counsel does not show any basis in the pleading or in her affidavit for her personal knowledge of relevant facts."

TRCP 14a. REPEALED BY ORDER OF APRIL 10, 1986, EFF. SEPT. 1, 1986

TRCP 14b. RETURN OR OTHER DISPOSITION OF EXHIBITS

The clerk of the court in which the exhibits are filed shall retain and dispose of the same as directed by the Supreme Court.

Jan. 1, 1967, eff. Jan. 1, 1967. Amended by order of July 15, 1987, eff. Jan. 1, 1988.

See also TRCP 75b.

Order Relating to Retention & Disposition of Exhibits in Civil Cases

In compliance with the provisions of Rule 14b, the Supreme Court hereby directs that exhibits offered or admitted into evidence shall be retained and disposed of by the clerk of the court in which the exhibits are filed upon the following basis.

This order shall apply only to: (1) those cases in which judgment has been rendered on service of process by publication and in which no motion for new trial was filed within two years after judgment was signed; and, (2) all other cases in which judgment has been signed for one year and in which no appeal was perfected or in which a perfected appeal was dismissed or concluded by a final judgement as to all parties and the issuance of the appellate court's mandate such that the case is no longer pending on appeal or in the trial court.

The party who offered an exhibit may withdraw it from the clerk's office within thirty days of the later of (1) a case becoming subject to this order, or (2) the effective date of this order. The clerk, unless otherwise directed by the court, may dispose of any exhibits remaining after such time period.

July 15, 1987, eff. Jan. 1, 1988. Amended by order of Jan. 27, 2005, eff. June 1, 2005.

TRCP 14c. DEPOSIT IN LIEU OF SURETY BOND

Wherever these rules provide for the filing of a surety bond, the party may in lieu of filing the bond deposit cash or other negotiable obligation of the government of the United States of America or any agency thereof, or with leave of court, deposit a negotiable obligation of any bank or savings and loan association chartered by the government of the United States of America or any state thereof that is insured by the government of the United States of America or any agency thereof, in the amount fixed for the surety bond, conditioned in the same manner as would be a surety bond for the protection of other parties. Any interest thereon shall constitute a part of the deposit.

June 10, 1980, eff. Jan. 1, 1981.

Part II. Rules of Practice in District and County Courts

SECTION 1. GENERAL RULES

TRCP 15. WRITS AND PROCESS

The style of all writs and process shall be "The State of Texas"; and unless otherwise specially provided by law or these rules every such writ and process shall be directed to any sheriff or any constable within the State of Texas, shall be made returnable on the Monday next after expiration of twenty days from the date of service thereof, and shall be dated and attested by the clerk with the seal of the court impressed thereon; and the date of issuance shall be noted thereon.

Oct. 29, 1940, eff. Sept. 1, 1941.

See also Loc. Gov't Code §86.021; **O'Connor's Texas Rules**, "Serving the Defendant with Suit," ch. 2-I, §1 et seq.; **O'Connor's Texas Rules**, "Default Judgment," ch. 7-A, §1 et seq.; **O'Connor's Texas Forms**, FORMS 2I:2, 2I:3.

ANNOTATIONS

Williams v. Williams, 150 S.W.3d 436, 445 (Tex.App.—Austin 2004, pet. denied). "[W]e . . . hold that citations *must* be expressly directed to the defendant under [TRCP] 99 and *may* also be addressed to the sheriff or constable under [TRCP] 15, but failure to include the sheriff or constable on the form of the citation will not render it void." *See also* **Barker CATV Constr., Inc. v. Ampro, Inc.**, 989 S.W.2d 789, 792 (Tex.App.—Houston [1st Dist.] 1999, no pet.).

TRCP 16. SHALL ENDORSE ALL PROCESS

Every officer or authorized person shall endorse on all process and precepts coming to his hand the day and hour

on which he received them, the manner in which he executed them, and the time and place the process was served and shall sign the returns officially.

Oct. 29, 1940, eff. Sept. 1, 1941. Amended by order of July 15, 1987, eff. Jan. 1, 1988.

Comment—1988

Article 3926a, effective September 1, 1981, authorizes the commissioner's court of each county to set a "reasonable" fee for service of process; mileage is no longer an authorized expense for serving process.

See also Loc. Gov't Code §§85.021, 86.021; TRCP 107; **O'Connor's Texas Rules**, "Serving the Defendant with Suit," ch. 2-I, §1 et seq.; **O'Connor's Texas Rules**, "Default Judgment," ch. 7-A, §1 et seq.

ANNOTATIONS

Deutsche Bank Trust Co. v. Hall, 400 S.W.3d 668, 670 (Tex.App.—Texarkana 2013, pet. denied). "[T]he . . . clerk employed the attachment of a green card (which bears the clerk's stamp that incorporates a date and time) in lieu of fully completing the return. [A] 'filed for record' stamp [does not] constitute[ ] an endorsement."

TRCP 17. OFFICER TO EXECUTE PROCESS

Except where otherwise expressly provided by law or these rules, the officer receiving any process to be executed shall not be entitled in any case to demand his fee for executing the same in advance of such execution, but his fee shall be taxed and collected as other costs in the case.

Oct. 29, 1940, eff. Sept. 1, 1941.

See also **O'Connor's Texas Rules**, "Serving the Defendant with Suit," ch. 2-I, §1 et seq.; **O'Connor's Texas Rules**, "Default Judgment," ch. 7-A, §1 et seq.

TRCP 18. WHEN JUDGE DIES DURING TERM, RESIGNS OR IS DISABLED

If the judge dies, resigns, or becomes unable to hold court during the session of court duly convened for the term, and the time provided by law for the holding of said court has not expired, such death, resignation, or inability on the part of the judge shall not operate to adjourn said court for the term, but such court shall be deemed to continue in session. If a successor to such judge shall qualify and assume office during the term, or if a judge be transferred to said district from some other judicial district, he may continue to hold said court for the term provided, and all motions undisposed of shall be heard and determined by him, and statements of facts and bills of exception shall be approved by him. If the time for holding such court expires before a successor shall qualify, and before a judge can be transferred to said district from some other judicial district, then all motions pending, including those for new trial, shall stand as continued in force until such successor has qualified and assumed office, or a judge has been transferred to said district who can hold said court, and thereupon such judge shall have power to act thereon at the succeeding term, or on an earlier day in vacation, on notice to all parties to the motion, and such orders shall have the same effect as if rendered in term time. The time for allowing statement of facts and bills of exception from such orders shall date from the time the motion was decided.

Oct. 29, 1940, eff. Sept. 1, 1941. Amended by order of June 16, 1943, eff. Dec. 31, 1943.

Source: TRCS art. 2288 (repealed).

ANNOTATIONS

2900 Smith, Ltd. v. Constellation NewEnergy, Inc., 301 S.W.3d 741, 744 n.6 (Tex.App.—Houston [14th Dist.] 2009, no pet.). TRCP 18 "'allows successor judges to dispose of unresolved matters and enter various orders so long as the successor judge does not render judgment without hearing evidence.'" *See also* **W.C. Banks, Inc. v. Team, Inc.**, 783 S.W.2d 783, 786 (Tex.App.—Houston [1st Dist.] 1990, no writ).

TRCP 18a. RECUSAL AND DISQUALIFICATION OF JUDGES

(a) ***Motion; Form and Contents.*** A party in a case in any trial court other than a statutory probate court or justice court may seek to recuse or disqualify a judge who is sitting in the case by filing a motion with the clerk of the court in which the case is pending. The motion:

(1) must be verified;

(2) must assert one or more of the grounds listed in Rule 18b;

(3) must not be based solely on the judge's rulings in the case; and

(4) must state with detail and particularity facts that:

(A) are within the affiant's personal knowledge, except that facts may be stated on information and belief if the basis for that belief is specifically stated;

(B) would be admissible in evidence; and

(C) if proven, would be sufficient to justify recusal or disqualification.

(b) ***Time for Filing Motion.***

(1) *Motion to Recuse.* A motion to recuse:

(A) must be filed as soon as practicable after the movant knows of the ground stated in the motion; and

(B) must not be filed after the tenth day before

the date set for trial or other hearing unless, before that day, the movant neither knew nor reasonably should have known:

(i) that the judge whose recusal is sought would preside at the trial or hearing; or

(ii) that the ground stated in the motion existed.

(2) *Motion to Disqualify.* A motion to disqualify should be filed as soon as practicable after the movant knows of the ground stated in the motion.

(c) ***Response to Motion.***

(1) *By Another Party.* Any other party in the case may, but need not, file a response to the motion. Any response must be filed before the motion is heard.

(2) *By the Respondent Judge.* The judge whose recusal or disqualification is sought should not file a response to the motion.

(d) ***Service of Motion or Response.*** A party who files a motion or response must serve a copy on every other party. The method of service must be the same as the method of filing, if possible.

(e) ***Duty of the Clerk.***

(1) *Delivery of a Motion or Response.* When a motion or response is filed, the clerk of the court must immediately deliver a copy to the respondent judge and to the presiding judge of the administrative judicial region in which the court is located ("the regional presiding judge").

(2) *Delivery of Order of Recusal or Referral.* When a respondent judge signs and files an order of recusal or referral, the clerk of the court must immediately deliver a copy to the regional presiding judge.

(f) ***Duties of the Respondent Judge; Failure to Comply.***

(1) *Responding to the Motion.* Regardless of whether the motion complies with this rule, the respondent judge, within three business days after the motion is filed, must either:

(A) sign and file with the clerk an order of recusal or disqualification; or

(B) sign and file with the clerk an order referring the motion to the regional presiding judge.

(2) *Restrictions on Further Action.*

(A) *Motion Filed Before Evidence Offered at Trial.* If a motion is filed before evidence has been offered at trial, the respondent judge must take no further action in the case until the motion has been decided, except for good cause stated in writing or on the record.

(B) *Motion Filed After Evidence Offered at Trial.* If a motion is filed after evidence has been offered at trial, the respondent judge may proceed, subject to stay by the regional presiding judge.

(3) *Failure to Comply.* If the respondent judge fails to comply with a duty imposed by this rule, the movant may notify the regional presiding judge.

(g) ***Duties of Regional Presiding Judge.***

(1) *Motion.* The regional presiding judge must rule on a referred motion or assign a judge to rule. If a party files a motion to recuse or disqualify the regional presiding judge, the regional presiding judge may still assign a judge to rule on the original, referred motion. Alternatively, the regional presiding judge may sign and file with the clerk an order referring the second motion to the Chief Justice for consideration.

(2) *Order.* The ruling must be by written order.

(3) *Summary Denial for Noncompliance.*

(A) *Motion to Recuse.* A motion to recuse that does not comply with this rule may be denied without an oral hearing. The order must state the nature of the noncompliance. Even if the motion is amended to correct the stated noncompliance, the motion will count for purposes of determining whether a tertiary recusal motion has been filed under the Civil Practice and Remedies Code.

(B) *Motion to Disqualify.* A motion to disqualify may not be denied on the ground that it was not filed or served in compliance with this rule.

(4) *Interim Orders.* The regional presiding judge or judge assigned to decide the motion may issue interim or ancillary orders in the pending case as justice may require.

(5) *Discovery.* Except by order of the regional presiding judge or the judge assigned to decide the motion, a subpoena or discovery request may not issue to the respondent judge and may be disregarded unless accompanied by the order.

(6) *Hearing.*

(A) *Time.* The motion must be heard as soon as practicable and may be heard immediately after it is referred to the regional presiding judge or an assigned judge.

(B) *Notice.* Notice of the hearing must be given to all parties in the case.

(C) *By Telephone.* The hearing may be conducted by telephone on the record. Documents submitted by facsimile or email, otherwise admissible under the rules of evidence, may be considered.

(7) *Reassignment of Case if Motion Granted.* If the

motion is granted, the regional presiding judge must transfer the case to another court or assign another judge to the case.

(h) ***Sanctions.*** After notice and hearing, the judge who hears the motion may order the party or attorney who filed the motion, or both, to pay the reasonable attorney fees and expenses incurred by other parties if the judge determines that the motion was:

(1) groundless and filed in bad faith or for the purpose of harassment, or

(2) clearly brought for unnecessary delay and without sufficient cause.

(i) ***Chief Justice.*** The Chief Justice of the Supreme Court of Texas may assign judges and issue any orders permitted by this rule or pursuant to statute.

(j) ***Appellate Review.***

(1) *Order on Motion to Recuse.*

(A) *Denying Motion.* An order denying a motion to recuse may be reviewed only for abuse of discretion on appeal from the final judgment.

(B) *Granting Motion.* An order granting a motion to recuse is final and cannot be reviewed by appeal, mandamus, or otherwise.

(2) *Order on Motion to Disqualify.* An order granting or denying a motion to disqualify may be reviewed by mandamus and may be appealed in accordance with other law.

June 10, 1980, eff. Jan. 1, 1981. Amended by orders of Dec. 15, 1983, eff. April 1, 1984; April 10, 1986, eff. Sept. 1, 1986; July 15, 1987, eff. Jan. 1, 1988; April 24, 1990, eff. Sept. 1, 1990; July 5, 2011, and July 22, 2011, eff. Aug. 1, 2011.

Comment—2011

Rule 18a governs the procedure for recusing or disqualifying a judge sitting in any trial court other than a statutory probate court, justice court, or municipal court. Chapter 25 of the Government Code governs statutory probate courts, Rule 528 governs justice courts, and Chapter 29 of the Government Code governs municipal courts. Under Rule 18a, a judge's rulings may not be the sole basis for a motion to recuse or disqualify the judge. But when one or more sufficient other bases are raised, the judge hearing the motion may consider evidence of rulings when considering whether to grant the motion. For purposes of this rule, the term "rulings" is not meant to encompass a judge's statements or remarks about a case.

Source: New rule.

See also Gov't Code §§74.053, 74.059(c)(3); TRAP 16; **O'Connor's Texas Rules**, "Motion to Challenge the Judge," ch. 5-C, §1 et seq.; **O'Connor's Texas Forms**, FORMS 5C.

ANNOTATIONS

In re Perritt, 992 S.W.2d 444, 445 (Tex.1999). "[A] judge designated by the presiding judge of the administrative judicial district to hear a recusal motion under [TRCP] 18a is also an assigned judge subject to objection and mandatory disqualification under [Gov't Code] §74.053(b). . . ."

In re Union Pac. Res., 969 S.W.2d 427, 428 (Tex.1998). Mandamus is not available to review the denial of a motion to recuse made under the TRCPs. TRCP 18a(f), now TRCP 18a(j)(1)(a), "expressly provide[s] for appellate review from a final judgment after denial of a recusal motion. If the appellate court determines . . . the trial judge should have been recused, the appellate court can reverse the trial court's judgment and remand for a new trial before a different judge."

In re Beddingfield, No. 10-15-00280-CV, 2015 WL 4985191 (Tex.App.—Waco 2015, orig. proceeding) (memo op.; 8-20-15). "There is no prohibition against the parties to a proceeding requesting and the trial court personnel setting matters for submission while a motion to recuse the particular trial court judge is pending pursuant to Rule 18a. Not all procedures are required to stop in a trial court just because such a motion has been filed. The only thing that cannot occur once a motion to recuse a trial court judge is filed is that the trial court judge that is the target of the motion cannot conduct any hearings or render any orders or judgments until the motion to recuse is resolved."

McElwee v. McElwee, 911 S.W.2d 182, 186 (Tex.App.—Houston [1st Dist.] 1995, writ denied). "Unlike recusal, disqualification cannot be waived. . . . Disqualification may be raised at any time." *See also* **Sparkman v. Microsoft Corp.**, No. 12-13-00175-CV, 2015 WL 1244538 (Tex.App.—Tyler 2015, pet. denied) (memo op.; 3-18-15) (recusal may be waived if not raised by proper motion).

TRCP 18b. GROUNDS FOR RECUSAL AND DISQUALIFICATION OF JUDGES

(a) ***Grounds for Disqualification.*** A judge must disqualify in any proceeding in which:

(1) the judge has served as a lawyer in the matter in controversy, or a lawyer with whom the judge previously practiced law served during such association as a lawyer concerning the matter;

(2) the judge knows that, individually or as a fiduciary, the judge has an interest in the subject matter in controversy; or

(3) either of the parties may be related to the judge by affinity or consanguinity within the third degree.

(b) ***Grounds for Recusal.*** A judge must recuse in any proceeding in which:

(1) the judge's impartiality might reasonably be questioned;

(2) the judge has a personal bias or prejudice concerning the subject matter or a party;

(3) the judge has personal knowledge of disputed evidentiary facts concerning the proceeding;

(4) the judge or a lawyer with whom the judge previously practiced law has been a material witness concerning the proceeding;

(5) the judge participated as counsel, adviser, or material witness in the matter in controversy, or expressed an opinion concerning the merits of it, while acting as an attorney in government service;

(6) the judge knows that the judge, individually or as a fiduciary, or the judge's spouse or minor child residing in the judge's household, has a financial interest in the subject matter in controversy or in a party to the proceeding, or any other interest that could be substantially affected by the outcome of the proceeding;

(7) the judge or the judge's spouse, or a person within the third degree of relationship to either of them, or the spouse of such a person:

(A) is a party to the proceeding or an officer, director, or trustee of a party;

(B) is known by the judge to have an interest that could be substantially affected by the outcome of the proceeding; or

(C) is to the judge's knowledge likely to be a material witness in the proceeding.

(8) the judge or the judge's spouse, or a person within the first degree of relationship to either of them, or the spouse of such a person, is acting as a lawyer in the proceeding.

(c) ***Financial Interests.*** A judge should inform himself or herself about personal and fiduciary financial interests, and make a reasonable effort to inform himself or herself about the personal financial interests of his or her spouse and minor children residing in the household.

(d) ***Terminology and Standards.*** In this rule:

(1) "proceeding" includes pretrial, trial, or other stages of litigation;

(2) the degree of relationship is calculated according to the civil law system;

(3) "fiduciary" includes such relationships as executor, administrator, trustee, and guardian;

(4) "financial interest" means ownership of a legal or equitable interest, however small, or a relationship as director, adviser, or other active participant in the affairs of a party, except that:

(A) ownership in a mutual or common investment fund that holds securities is not a "financial interest" in such securities unless the judge participates in the management of the fund;

(B) an office in an educational, religious, charitable, fraternal, or civic organization is not a "financial interest" in securities held by the organization;

(C) the proprietary interest of a policyholder in a mutual insurance company, of a depositor in a mutual savings association, or a similar proprietary interest, is a "financial interest" in the organization only if the outcome of the proceeding could substantially affect the value of the interest;

(D) ownership of government securities is a "financial interest" in the issuer only if the outcome of the proceeding could substantially affect the value of the securities;

(E) an interest as a taxpayer or utility ratepayer, or any similar interest, is not a "financial interest" unless the outcome of the proceeding could substantially affect the liability of the judge or a person related to him within the third degree more than other judges.

(e) ***Waiving a Ground for Recusal.*** The parties to a proceeding may waive any ground for recusal after it is fully disclosed on the record.

(f) ***Discovery and Divestiture.*** If a judge does not discover that the judge is recused under subparagraphs (b)(6) or (b)(7)(B) until after the judge has devoted substantial time to the matter, the judge is not required to recuse himself or herself if the judge or the person related to the judge divests himself or herself of the interest that would otherwise require recusal.

July 15, 1987, eff. Jan. 1, 1988. Amended by orders of April 24, 1990, eff. Sept. 1, 1990; July 5, 2011, and July 22, 2011, eff. Aug. 1, 2011.

Comment—2011

The amendments to Rule 18b are not intended to be substantive.

Comment—1990

The grounds for a judge's mandatory recusal have been expanded from those in prior Rule 18b(2).

Source: New rule. Former TRCP 18b repealed eff. Sept. 1, 1986, by order of Apr. 10, 1986 (705-06 S.W.2d [Tex.Cases] xxxiv).

See also Tex. Const. art. 5, §11; Gov't Code §§21.005, 74.053, 74.059(c)(3), 573.022–573.025; TRAP 16; **O'Connor's Texas Rules**, "Motion to Challenge the Judge," ch. 5-C, §1 et seq.; **O'Connor's Texas Forms**, FORMS 5C.

ANNOTATIONS

In re O'Connor, 92 S.W.3d 446, 449 (Tex.2002). Rule 18b(1)(a), now 18b(a)(1), "recognizes that a judge is vicariously disqualified under the [Texas] Constitution as having 'been counsel in the case' if a lawyer with whom the judge previously practiced law served as counsel to a party concerning the matter during their association." *See also*

Tesco Am., Inc. v. Strong Indus., 221 S.W.3d 550, 553 (Tex.2006) (disqualification of appellate judges); **Pena v. Pena**, 986 S.W.2d 696, 700 (Tex.App.—Corpus Christi 1998), *pet. denied*, 8 S.W.3d 639 (Tex.1999) (trial judge's attorney-client relationship with opposing counsel did not amount to constitutional disqualification).

Drake v. Walker, 529 S.W.3d 516, 528 (Tex.App.—Dallas 2017, no pet.). "The movant bears the burden of proving recusal is warranted, and the burden is met only through a showing of bias or impartiality to such an extent that the movant was deprived of a fair trial. The test for recusal is 'whether a reasonable member of the public at large, knowing all the facts in the public domain concerning the judge's conduct, would have a reasonable doubt that the judge is actually impartial.'" *See also* **In re Commitment of Winkle**, 434 S.W.3d 300, 311 (Tex.App.—Beaumont 2014, pet. denied).

Kennedy v. Wortham, 314 S.W.3d 34, 36 (Tex.App.—Texarkana 2010, pet. denied). "The interest that disqualifies a judge is an interest, however small, which rests on a direct pecuniary or personal interest in the result of the case. *At 37:* [P's] petition did not seek money damages; therefore, [trial judge] has no pecuniary interest in this case. Instead, [P] sought injunctive relief prohibiting 'all judges from discriminating.' [¶] Even if [P] obtained a judgment prohibiting all judges . . . from discriminating, it would not add one additional burden or duty that [trial judge] does not already have imposed by law. [¶] [Trial judge] did not have a direct interest in the case that would require her disqualification."

Ludlow v. DeBerry, 959 S.W.2d 265, 271 (Tex.App.—Houston [14th Dist.] 1997, no writ). "[O]pinions formed by the judge on the basis of facts introduced or events occurring during proceedings do not constitute a basis for a recusal motion unless they display a deep-seated favoritism or antagonism that would make fair judgment impossible. [J]udicial remarks during the course of a trial that are critical or disapproving or even hostile to counsel, parties, or their cases, ordinarily do not support recusal. Such remarks *may* do so if they reveal an opinion deriving from an extrajudicial source and such remarks *will* do so if they reveal such a high degree of favoritism or antagonism as to make fair judgment impossible." *See also* **Hansen v. JP Morgan Chase Bank**, 346 S.W.3d 769, 776 (Tex.App.—Dallas 2011, no pet.).

TRCP 18c. RECORDING AND BROADCASTING OF COURT PROCEEDINGS

A trial court may permit broadcasting, televising, recording, or photographing of proceedings in the courtroom only in the following circumstances:

(a) in accordance with guidelines promulgated by the Supreme Court for civil cases, or

(b) when broadcasting, televising, recording, or photographing will not unduly distract participants or impair the dignity of the proceedings and the parties have consented, and consent to being depicted or recorded is obtained from each witness whose testimony will be broadcast, televised, or photographed, or

(c) the broadcasting, televising, recording, or photographing of investiture, or ceremonial proceedings.

April 24, 1990, eff. Sept. 1, 1990.

Comment—1990

New rule. To provide for guidelines for broadcasting, televising, recording, and photographing court proceedings.

TRCP 19. NON-ADJOURNMENT OF TERM

Every term of court shall commence and convene by operation of law at the time fixed by statute without any act, order, or formal opening by a judge or other official thereof, and shall continue to be open at all times until and including the last day of the term unless sooner adjourned by the judge thereof.

Oct. 29, 1940, eff. Sept. 1, 1941. Amended by order of June 16, 1943, eff. Dec. 31, 1943.

TRCP 20. MINUTES READ AND SIGNED

On the last day of the session, the minutes shall be read, corrected and signed in open court by the judge. Each special judge shall sign the minutes of such proceedings as were had by him.

Oct. 29, 1940, eff. Sept. 1, 1941.

TRCP 21. FILING AND SERVING PLEADINGS AND MOTIONS

(a) ***Filing and Service Required.*** Every pleading, plea, motion, or application to the court for an order, whether in the form of a motion, plea or other form of request, unless presented during a hearing or trial, must be filed with the clerk of the court in writing, must state the grounds therefor, must set forth the relief or order sought, and at the same time a true copy must be served on all other parties, and must be noted on the docket.

(b) ***Service of Notice of Hearing.*** An application to the court for an order and notice of any hearing thereon, not presented during a hearing or trial, must be served upon all other parties not less than three days before the time specified for the hearing, unless otherwise provided by these rules or shortened by the court.

(c) ***Multiple Parties.*** If there is more than one other party represented by different attorneys, one copy of each pleading must be served on each attorney in charge.

(d) ***Certificate of Service.*** The party or attorney of record, must certify to the court compliance with this rule in writing over signature on the filed pleading, plea, motion, or application.

(e) *Additional Copies.* After one copy is served on a party, that party may obtain another copy of the same pleading upon tendering reasonable payment for copying and delivering.

(f) *Electronic Filing.*

(1) *Requirement.* Except in juvenile cases under Title 3 of the Family Code and truancy cases under Title 3A of the Family Code, attorneys must electronically file documents in courts where electronic filing has been mandated. Attorneys practicing in courts where electronic filing is available but not mandated and unrepresented parties may electronically file documents, but it is not required.

(2) *Email Address.* The email address of an attorney or unrepresented party who electronically files a document must be included on the document.

(3) *Mechanism.* Electronic filing must be done through the electronic filing manager established by the Office of Court Administration and an electronic filing service provider certified by the Office of Court Administration.

(4) *Exceptions.*

(A) Wills are not required to be filed electronically.

(B) The following documents must not be filed electronically:

(i) documents filed under seal or presented to the court in camera; and

(ii) documents to which access is otherwise restricted by law or court order.

(C) For good cause, a court may permit a party to file other documents in paper form in a particular case.

(5) *Timely Filing.* Unless a document must be filed by a certain time of day, a document is considered timely filed if it is electronically filed at any time before midnight (in the court's time zone) on the filing deadline. An electronically filed document is deemed filed when transmitted to the filing party's electronic filing service provider, except:

(A) if a document is transmitted on a Saturday, Sunday, or legal holiday, it is deemed filed on the next day that is not a Saturday, Sunday, or legal holiday; and

(B) if a document requires a motion and an order allowing its filing, the document is deemed filed on the date that the motion is granted.

(6) *Technical Failure.* If a document is untimely due to a technical failure or a system outage, the filing party may seek appropriate relief from the court. If the missed deadline is one imposed by these rules, the filing party must be given a reasonable extension of time to complete the filing.

(7) *Electronic Signatures.* A document that is electronically served, filed, or issued by a court or clerk is considered signed if the document includes:

(A) a "/s/" and name typed in the space where the signature would otherwise appear, unless the document is notarized or sworn; or

(B) an electronic image or scanned image of the signature.

(8) *Format.* An electronically filed document must:

(A) be in text-searchable portable document format (PDF);

(B) be directly converted to PDF rather than scanned, if possible;

(C) not be locked; and

(D) otherwise comply with the Technology Standards set by the Judicial Committee on Information Technology and approved by the Supreme Court.

(9) *Paper Copies.* Unless required by local rule, a party need not file a paper copy of an electronically filed document.

(10) *Electronic Notices From the Court.* The clerk may send notices, orders, or other communications about the case to the party electronically. A court seal may be electronic.

(11) *Non-Conforming Documents.* The clerk may not refuse to file a document that fails to conform with this rule. But the clerk may identify the error to be corrected and state a deadline for the party to resubmit the document in a conforming format.

(12) *Original Wills.* When a party electronically files an application to probate a document as an original will, the original will must be filed with the clerk within three business days after the application is filed.

(13) *Official Record.* The clerk may designate an electronically filed document or a scanned paper document as the official court record. The clerk is not required to keep both paper and electronic versions of the same document unless otherwise required by local rule. But the clerk must retain an original will filed for probate in a numbered file folder.

Oct. 29, 1940, eff. Sept. 1, 1941. Amended by orders of Sept. 20, 1941, eff. Dec. 31, 1941; Aug. 18, 1947, eff. Dec. 31, 1947; July 11, 1977, eff. Jan. 1, 1978; June 10, 1980, eff. Jan. 1, 1981; April 24, 1990, eff. Sept. 1, 1990; Dec. 11, 2013, eff. Jan. 1, 2014; Aug. 28, 2015, eff. Sept. 1, 2015.

Comment—2013

Rule 21 is revised to incorporate rules for electronic filing, in accordance with the Supreme Court's order—Misc. Docket No. 12-9206, amended by Misc. Docket Nos. 13-9092 and 13-9164—mandating electronic filing in civil cases beginning on January 1, 2014. The mandate will be implemented according to the schedule in the order and will be completed by July 1, 2016. The revisions reflect the fact that the mandate will only apply to a subset of Texas courts until that date.

Comment—1990

To require filing and service of all pleadings and motions on all parties and to consolidate notice and service Rules 21, 72 and 73.

Source: TRCS art. 2291 (repealed).

See also **O'Connor's Texas Rules**, "Rules of Pleading," ch. 1-B, §1 et seq.; **O'Connor's Texas Rules**, "Rules for Filing Documents," ch. 1-C, §1 et seq.; **O'Connor's Texas Rules**, "Rules for Serving Documents," ch. 1-D, §1 et seq.; **O'Connor's Texas Rules**, "Pretrial Motions," ch. 5, §1 et seq.

ANNOTATIONS

Jamar v. Patterson, 868 S.W.2d 318, 319 (Tex.1993). "[T]he date of filing is when the document is first tendered to the clerk [even if no filing fee is paid]. The filing [of the motion for new trial] was completed . . . when [D] paid the filing fee. *At 319 n.3:* The filing is not completed until the fee is paid, and absent emergency or other rare circumstances, the court should not consider it before then." *See also* **Tate v. E.I. DuPont de Nemours & Co.**, 934 S.W.2d 83, 84 (Tex.1996).

High Rev Power, L.L.C. v. Freeport Logistics, Inc., No. 05-13-01360-CV, 2016 WL 6462392 (Tex.App.—Dallas 2016, no pet.) (memo op.; 10-31-16). "Under rule 21(f)(5), . . . an electronically filed document is deemed filed when it is transmitted to the filing party's electronic service provider. Although [D's] motion for new trial was never forwarded to the county clerk's office, it was deemed filed . . . when it was successfully transmitted to [D's] electronic service provider." *See also* **Cummings v. Billman**, __ S.W.3d __, 2020 WL 938172 (Tex.App.—Fort Worth 2020, n.p.h.) (No. 02-20-00034-CV; 2-27-20) (document is deemed filed when transmitted; cancellation of transmittal before clerk processed and file-stamped document did not negate filing).

Perkins v. City of San Antonio, 293 S.W.3d 650, 654-55 (Tex.App.—San Antonio 2009, no pet.). TRCP 21 "is inapplicable to a trial setting. [When] the trial court's hearing [is] dispositive of the merits of [the] underlying case, the hearing [is] effectively a trial setting [and should be governed by TRCP 245]."

Approximately $1,589.00 v. State, 230 S.W.3d 871, 873-74 (Tex.App.—Houston [14th Dist.] 2007, no pet.). "Rule 21 does not expressly require that a motion and notice of hearing be *filed* at least three days before hearing. However, Rule 21 expressly requires that a motion and notice of hearing be *served* on opposing parties at the time of filing. Therefore, Rule 21 effectively requires that a motion and notice of hearing be *filed* at least three days before hearing, unless otherwise provided by the [TRCPs] or shortened by the court."

TRCP 21a. METHODS OF SERVICE

(a) ***Methods of Service.*** Every notice required by these rules, and every pleading, plea, motion, or other form of request required to be served under Rule 21, other than the citation to be served upon the filing of a cause of action and except as otherwise expressly provided in these rules, may be served by delivering a copy to the party to be served, or the party's duly authorized agent or attorney of record in the manner specified below:

(1) *Documents Filed Electronically.* A document filed electronically under Rule 21 must be served electronically through the electronic filing manager if the email address of the party or attorney to be served is on file with the electronic filing manager. If the email address of the party or attorney to be served is not on file with the electronic filing manager, the document may be served on that party or attorney under subparagraph (2).

(2) *Documents Not Filed Electronically.* A document not filed electronically may be served in person, mail, by commercial delivery service, by fax, by email, or by such other manner as the court in its discretion may direct.

(b) ***When Complete.***

(1) Service by mail or commercial delivery service shall be complete upon deposit of the document, postpaid and properly addressed, in the mail or with a commercial delivery service.

(2) Service by fax is complete on receipt. Service completed after 5:00 p.m. local time of the recipient shall be deemed served on the following day.

(3) Electronic service is complete on transmission of the document to the serving party's electronic filing service provider. The electronic filing manager will send confirmation of service to the serving party.

(c) ***Time for Action After Service.*** Whenever a party has the right or is required to do some act within a prescribed period after the service of a notice or other paper upon him and the notice or paper is served upon him by mail, three days shall be added to the prescribed period.

(d) ***Who May Serve.*** Notice may be served by a party to the suit, an attorney of record, a sheriff or constable, or by any other person competent to testify.

(e) ***Proof of Service.*** The party or attorney of record shall certify to the court compliance with this rule in writing over signature and on the filed instrument. A certificate by a party or an attorney of record, or the return of the officer, or the affidavit of any other person showing service of a notice shall be prima facie evidence of the fact of service. Nothing herein shall preclude any party from offering proof that the document was not received, or, if service was by mail, that the document was not received within three days from the date that it was deposited in the mail, and upon

so finding, the court may extend the time for taking the action required of such party or grant such other relief as it deems just.

(f) ***Procedures Cumulative.*** These provisions are cumulative of all other methods of service prescribed by these rules.

Aug. 18, 1947, eff. Dec. 31, 1947. Amended by orders of July 21, 1970, eff. Jan. 1, 1971; Oct. 3, 1972, eff. Feb. 1, 1973; July 11, 1977, eff. Jan. 1, 1978; June 10, 1980, eff. Jan. 1, 1981; Dec. 5, 1983, eff. April 1, 1984; April 24, 1990, eff. Sept. 1, 1990; Dec. 11, 2013, eff. Jan. 1, 2014.

Comment—2013

Rule 21a is revised to incorporate rules for electronic service in accordance with the Supreme Court's order—Misc. Docket No. 12-9206, amended by Misc. Docket Nos. 13-9092 and 13-9164—mandating electronic filing in civil cases beginning on January 1, 2014.

Comment—1990

To allow for service by current delivery means and technologies.

Source: New rule.

See also **O'Connor's Texas Rules**, "Rules of Pleading," ch. 1-B, §1 et seq.; **O'Connor's Texas Rules**, "Rules for Filing Documents," ch. 1-C, §1 et seq.; **O'Connor's Texas Rules**, "Rules for Serving Documents," ch. 1-D, §1 et seq.; **O'Connor's Texas Forms**, FORM 1B:13.

ANNOTATIONS

In re E.A., 287 S.W.3d 1, 4 (Tex.2009). "Nothing in the rules requires a plaintiff to serve a nonanswering defendant with new citation for a more onerous amended petition. While a nonanswering defendant must be served with a more onerous amended petition in order for a default judgment to stand, . . . Rule 21a service satisfies that requirement. *At 6:* Service of new citation is no longer required."

Mathis v. Lockwood, 166 S.W.3d 743, 745 (Tex.2005). "[N]otice properly sent pursuant to Rule 21a raises a presumption that notice was received. But we cannot presume that notice was properly sent; when that is challenged, it must be proved according to the rule. [¶] [T]he record contains no certificate of service, no return receipt from certified or registered mail, and no affidavit certifying service. Instead, the only evidence of service in the record was the oral assurance of counsel. As the rule's requirements are neither vague nor onerous, we decline to expand them this far." *See also* **Thomas v. Ray**, 889 S.W.2d 237, 238-39 (Tex.1994); **L'Arte de la Mode, Inc. v. Neiman Marcus Grp.**, 395 S.W.3d 291, 295 (Tex.App.—Dallas 2013, no pet.).

Lewis v. Blake, 876 S.W.2d 314, 315 (Tex.1994). "Rule 21a extends [the] minimum notice [of a hearing on a motion for summary judgment] by three days when the motion is served by mail. *At 316:* [The] hearing . . . may be set as early as the 21st day after the motion is served, or the 24th day if the motion is served by mail."

Brown v. Ogbolu, 331 S.W.3d 530, 534 (Tex.App.—Dallas 2011, no pet.). "[P] argues the record shows the counterclaim was not served on him because [D] did not complete the blank for the day on the certificate of service. We disagree. [¶] [D] served the counterclaim under rule 21a and included a certificate of service. While it is normal—and better practice—to include the date and manner of service in the certificate of service, the text of the rule does not require either. We conclude the certificate of service on [D's] counterclaim sufficiently complied with the certification requirement to raise the presumption of service." *See also* **Approximately $14,980.00 v. State**, 261 S.W.3d 182, 187 (Tex.App.—Houston [14th Dist.] 2008, no pet.).

Etheredge v. Hidden Valley Airpark Ass'n, 169 S.W.3d 378, 382 (Tex.App.—Fort Worth 2005, pet. denied). "[W]hen a party does not receive actual notice, if the serving party has complied with the requirements of Rule 21a, 'constructive notice' may be established if the serving party presents evidence that the intended recipient engaged in instances of selective acceptance or refusal of certified mail relating to the case, . . . or that the intended recipient refused all deliveries of certified mail." *See also* **Jacobs v. Jacobs**, 448 S.W.3d 626, 632 (Tex.App.—Houston [14th Dist.] 2014, no pet.).

TRCP 21b. SANCTIONS FOR FAILURE TO SERVE OR DELIVER COPY OF PLEADINGS AND MOTIONS

If any party fails to serve on or deliver to the other parties a copy of any pleading, plea, motion, or other application to the court for an order in accordance with Rules 21 and 21a, the court may in its discretion, after notice and hearing, impose an appropriate sanction available under Rule 215-2b.[1]

April 24, 1990, eff. Sept. 1, 1990.

Comment—1990

New rule. Repealed provisions of Rule 73, to the extent same are to remain operative, are moved to this new Rule 21b to provide sanctions for the failure to serve any filed documents on all parties.

[1] Probably Vernon's Ann.Rules Civ.Proc., rule 215.2(b).

See also **O'Connor's Texas Rules**, "Rules of Pleading," ch. 1-B, §1 et seq.; **O'Connor's Texas Rules**, "Rules for Filing Documents," ch. 1-C, §1 et seq.; **O'Connor's Texas Rules**, "Rules for Serving Documents," ch. 1-D, §1 et seq.; **O'Connor's Texas Rules**, "Motion for Sanctions," ch. 5-K, §1 et seq.; **O'Connor's Texas Forms**, FORMS 5K:3, 5K:4, 5K:5.

TRCP 21c. PRIVACY PROTECTION FOR FILED DOCUMENTS

(a) ***Sensitive Data Defined.*** Sensitive data consists of:

(1) a driver's license number, passport number, social security number, tax identification number, or similar government-issued personal identification number;

(2) a bank account number, credit card number, or other financial account number; and

(3) a birth date, home address, and the name of any person who was a minor when the underlying suit was filed.

(b) ***Filing of Documents Containing Sensitive Data Prohibited.*** Unless the inclusion of sensitive data is specifically required by a statute, court rule, or administrative regulation, an electronic or paper document, except for wills and documents filed under seal, containing sensitive data may not be filed with a court unless the sensitive data is redacted.

(c) ***Redaction of Sensitive Data: Retention Requirement.*** Sensitive data must be redacted by using the letter "X" in place of each omitted digit or character or by removing the sensitive data in a manner indicating that the data has been redacted. The filing party must retain an unredacted version of the filed document during the pendency of the case and any related appellate proceedings filed within six months of the date the judgment is signed.

(d) ***Notice to Clerk.*** If a document must contain sensitive data, the filing party must notify the clerk by:

(1) designating the document as containing sensitive data when the document is electronically filed; or

(2) if the document is not electronically filed, by including, on the upper left-hand side of the first page, the phrase: "NOTICE: THIS DOCUMENT CONTAINS SENSITIVE DATA."

(e) ***Non-Conforming Documents.*** The clerk may not refuse to file a document that contains sensitive data in violation of this rule. But the clerk may identify the error to be corrected and state a deadline for the party to resubmit a redacted, substitute document.

(f) ***Restriction on Remote Access.*** Documents that contain sensitive data in violation of this rule must not be posted on the Internet.

Added by order of Dec. 11, 2013, eff. Jan. 1, 2014.

Comment—2013

Rule 21c is added to provide privacy protection for documents filed in civil cases.

See also **O'Connor's Texas Rules**, "Documents with sensitive data—privacy protection," ch. 1-C, §4.2.

SECTION 2. INSTITUTION OF SUIT

TRCP 22. COMMENCED BY PETITION

A civil suit in the district or county court shall be commenced by a petition filed in the office of the clerk.

Oct. 29, 1940, eff. Sept. 1, 1941.

See also **O'Connor's Texas Rules**, "Rules for Filing Documents," ch. 1-C, §1 et seq.; **O'Connor's Texas Rules**, "Plaintiff's Original Petition," ch. 2-B, §1 et seq.; **O'Connor's Texas Rules**, "Serving the Defendant with Suit," ch. 2-I, §1 et seq.; **O'Connor's Texas Forms**, FORMS 2B.

TRCP 23. SUITS TO BE NUMBERED CONSECUTIVELY

It shall be the duty of the clerk to designate the suits by regular consecutive numbers, called file numbers, and he shall mark on each paper in every case the file number of the cause.

Oct. 29, 1940, eff. Sept. 1, 1941.

See also **O'Connor's Texas Rules**, "Rules for Filing Documents," ch. 1-C, §1 et seq.

TRCP 24. DUTY OF CLERK

When a petition is filed with the clerk he shall indorse thereon the file number, the day on which it was filed and the time of filing, and sign his name officially thereto.

Oct. 29, 1940, eff. Sept. 1, 1941.

See also TRCP 74; **O'Connor's Texas Rules**, "Rules for Filing Documents," ch. 1-C, §1 et seq.

ANNOTATIONS

Biffle v. Morton Rubber Indus., 785 S.W.2d 143, 144 (Tex.1990). "An instrument is deemed in law filed at the time it is delivered to the clerk, regardless of whether the instrument is filemarked."

TRCP 25. CLERK'S FILE DOCKET

Each clerk shall keep a file docket which shall show in convenient form the number of the suit, the names of the attorneys, the names of the parties to the suit, and the nature thereof, and, in brief form, the officer's return on the process, and all subsequent proceedings had in the case with the dates thereof.

Oct. 29, 1940, eff. Sept. 1, 1941.

See also **O'Connor's Texas Rules**, "Rules for Filing Documents," ch. 1-C, §1 et seq.

TRCP 26. CLERK'S COURT DOCKET

Each clerk shall also keep a court docket in a permanent record that shall include the number of the case and the names of parties, the names of the attorneys, the nature of the action, the pleas, the motions, and the ruling of the court as made.

Oct. 29, 1940, eff. Sept. 1, 1941. Amended by order of April 24, 1990, eff. Sept. 1, 1990.

See also **O'Connor's Texas Rules**, "Rules for Filing Documents," ch. 1-C, §1 et seq.

TRCP 27. ORDER OF CASES

The cases shall be placed on the docket as they are filed.

Oct. 29, 1940, eff. Sept. 1, 1941.

See also **O'Connor's Texas Rules**, "Rules for Filing Documents," ch. 1-C, §1 et seq.

SECTION 3. PARTIES TO SUITS

TRCP 28. SUITS IN ASSUMED NAME

Any partnership, unincorporated association, private corporation, or individual doing business under an assumed name may sue or be sued in its partnership, assumed or common name for the purpose of enforcing for or against it a substantive right, but on a motion by any party or on the court's own motion the true name may be substituted.

Editor's Note: Unincorporated nonprofit associations are legal entities liable for their contracts and torts, and their members are relieved from individual liability. Bus. Orgs. Code §252.006(a), (b).

Oct. 29, 1940, eff. Sept. 1, 1941. Amended by order of July 21, 1970, eff. Jan. 1, 1971.

Source: Part of FRCP 17(b).

See also **O'Connor's Texas Rules**, "Parties," ch. 2-B, §4; **O'Connor's Texas Forms**, FORMS 2B:9, 2B:10, 2B:11, 2B:12, 2B:13, 2B:14, 2B:15, 2B:16, 2B:17, 2B:18.

ANNOTATIONS

Sixth RMA Partners v. Sibley, 111 S.W.3d 46, 53 (Tex.2003). "Rule 28 requires that the correct legal name be substituted, but it does not mandate the procedural method by which substitution may be accomplished. . . . Under Rule 28, the 'true name' may be substituted 'on a motion by any party or on the court's own motion.' Therefore, the correct legal name may be substituted by filing either a motion requesting substitution or a pleading that substitutes the correct legal name for the assumed name." *See also* **CA Partners v. Spears**, 274 S.W.3d 51, 69 (Tex.App.—Houston [14th Dist.] 2008, pet. denied); **Holberg & Co. v. Citizens Nat'l Assur. Co.**, 856 S.W.2d 515, 518 (Tex.App.—Houston [1st Dist.] 1993, no writ).

Chilkewitz v. Hyson, 22 S.W.3d 825, 830 (Tex.1999). "Rule 28 is not a tolling provision when a party is sued in the name under which it conducts business and that party has actual notice of the suit. Rule 28 allows suit directly against the correct party in its assumed name. To the extent that [earlier opinions] indicate that Rule 28 is a tolling provision, we disapprove of them." *See also* **University of Tex. Health Sci. Ctr. v. Bailey**, 332 S.W.3d 395, 399-400 (Tex.2011); **Ibrahim v. Young**, 253 S.W.3d 790, 799-800 (Tex.App.—Eastland 2008, pet. denied).

Broemer v. Houston Lawyer Referral Serv., 407 S.W.3d 477, 482 n.16 (Tex.App.—Houston [14th Dist.] 2013, no pet.). "[A] party may not avoid liability under an assumed name merely because it did not file an assumed name certificate when there is evidence that the party did business under that name."

KM-Timbercreek, LLC v. Harris Cty. Appr. Dist., 312 S.W.3d 722, 730 (Tex.App.—Houston [1st Dist.] 2009, no pet.). "For a party to take advantage of Rule 28 and sue in its common name, 'there must be a showing that the named entity is in fact *doing business under* that common name.' For example, although others may commonly and informally use the name of the premises location to refer to a particular entity, this does not mean that the entity is 'doing business under' the premises name as an assumed or common name. Whether an entity does business under an assumed or common name is a question of fact for the trial court." *See also* **Seidler v. Morgan**, 277 S.W.3d 549, 553 (Tex.App.—Texarkana 2009, pet. denied).

TRCP 29. SUIT ON CLAIM AGAINST DISSOLVED CORPORATION

When no receiver has been appointed for a corporation which has dissolved, suit may be instituted on any claim against said corporation as though the same had not been dissolved, and service of process may be obtained on the president, directors, general manager, trustee, assignee, or other person in charge of the affairs of the corporation at the time it was dissolved, and judgment may be rendered as though the corporation had not been dissolved.

Oct. 29, 1940, eff. Sept. 1, 1941.

See also BOC §11.356; TRCP 160.

TRCP 30. PARTIES TO SUITS

Assignors, endorsers and other parties not primarily liable upon any instruments named in the chapter of the Business and Commerce Code, dealing with commercial paper, may be jointly sued with their principal obligors, or may be sued alone in the cases provided for by statute.

Oct. 29, 1940, eff. Sept. 1, 1941. Amended by order of July 15, 1987, eff. Jan. 1, 1988.

Source: TRCS art. 572 (repealed).

See also **O'Connor's Texas Rules**, "Parties," ch. 2-B, §4; **O'Connor's Texas Forms**, FORMS 2B:9, 2B:10, 2B:11, 2B:12, 2B:13, 2B:14, 2B:15, 2B:16, 2B:17, 2B:18.

ANNOTATIONS

Reed v. Buck, 370 S.W.2d 867, 872 (Tex.1963). "We hold that when a party signs a note in the capacity of a maker, the payee (or one standing in the shoes of a payee) may sue such maker singly and proceed to judgment upon the note without joining in the suit another or others who may also appear upon the note as co-makers."

TRCP 31. SURETY NOT TO BE SUED ALONE

No surety shall be sued unless his principal is joined with him, or unless a judgment has previously been rendered against his principal, except in cases otherwise provided for in the law and these rules.

Oct. 29, 1940, eff. Sept. 1, 1941.

Source: TRCS art. 6251 (repealed).

See also CPRC §17.001; **O'Connor's Texas Rules**, "Secondary parties," ch. 2-F, §6.2.1(2).

ANNOTATIONS

In re Red Dot Bldg. Sys., 504 S.W.3d 320, 323-24 (Tex.2016). "While, absent special circumstances, a surety cannot be sued without also suing its principal, [D] points to no authority for the reverse proposition. . . . [CPRC] §17.001(a) is to the contrary, providing that 'a principal obligor on a contract may be sued alone.'"

Hart v. First Fed. S&L Ass'n, 727 S.W.2d 723, 726 (Tex.App.—Austin 1987, no writ). "[T]he necessity of joining the principal debtor in the creditor's suit against the guarantor is subject to an exception for cases where the debtor is 'hopelessly insolvent.' *At 726 n.1:* [TRCP] 31 incorporates, in effect, the provisions of [CPRC] §17.001."

TRCP 32. MAY HAVE QUESTION OF SURETYSHIP TRIED

When any suit is brought against two or more defendants upon any contract, any one or more of the defendants being surety for the other, the surety may cause the question of suretyship to be tried and determined upon the issue made for the parties defendant at the trial of the cause, or at any time before or after the trial or at a subsequent term. Such proceedings shall not delay the suit of the plaintiff.

Oct. 29, 1940, eff. Sept. 1, 1941.

TRCP 33. SUITS BY OR AGAINST COUNTIES

Suits by or against a county or incorporated city, town or village shall be in its corporate name.

Oct. 29, 1940, eff. Sept. 1, 1941.

Source: TRCS art. 1980 (repealed).

See also **O'Connor's Texas Rules**, "Parties," ch. 2-B, §4; **O'Connor's Texas Forms**, FORM 2B:19.

ANNOTATIONS

Scott v. Graham, 292 S.W.2d 324, 327 (Tex.1956). "A county is not made a party to a suit by joining the commissioners and other officials of the county as parties."

TRCP 34. AGAINST SHERIFF, ETC.

Whenever a sheriff, constable, or a deputy or either has been sued for damages for any act done in his official character, and has taken an indemnifying bond for the acts upon which the suit is based, he may make the principal and surety on such bond parties defendant in such suit, and the cause may be continued to obtain service on such parties.

Oct. 29, 1940, eff. Sept. 1, 1941.

TRCP 35. ON OFFICIAL BONDS

In suits brought by the State or any county, city, independent school district, irrigation district, or other political subdivision of the State, against any officer who has held an office for more than one term, or against any depository which has been such depository for more than one term, or has given more than one official bond, the sureties on each and all such bonds may be joined as defendants in the same suit whenever it is difficult to determine when the default sued for occurred and which set of sureties on such bonds is liable therefor.

Oct. 29, 1940, eff. Sept. 1, 1941. Amended by order of June 16, 1943, eff. Dec. 13, 1943.

Source: TRCS art. 1989 (repealed).

TRCP 36. DIFFERENT OFFICIALS AND BONDSMEN

In suits by the State upon the official bond of a State officer, any subordinate officer who has given bond, payable either to the State or such superior officer, to cover all or part of the default sued for, together with the sureties on his official bond, may be joined as defendants with such superior officer and his bondsmen whenever it is alleged in the petition that both of such officers are liable for the money sued for.

Oct. 29, 1940, eff. Sept. 1, 1941.

TRCP 37. ADDITIONAL PARTIES

Before a case is called for trial, additional parties necessary or proper parties to the suit, may be brought in, either by the plaintiff or the defendant, upon such terms as the court may prescribe; but not at a time nor in a manner to unreasonably delay the trial of the case.

Oct. 29, 1940, eff. Sept. 1, 1941.

See also **O'Connor's Texas Rules**, "Parties & Claims," ch. 2-F, §1 et seq.

TRCP 38. THIRD-PARTY PRACTICE

(a) When defendant may bring in third party. At any time after commencement of the action a defending party, as a third-party plaintiff, may cause a citation and petition to be served upon a person not a party to the action who is or may be liable to him or to the plaintiff for all or part of the plaintiff's claim against him. The third-party plaintiff need not obtain leave to make the service if he files the third-party petition not later than thirty (30) days after he serves his original answer. Otherwise, he must obtain leave on motion upon notice to all parties to the action. The person served, hereinafter called the third-party defendant, shall make his defenses to the third-party plaintiff's claim under the rules applicable to the defendant, and his counterclaims against the third-party plaintiff and cross-claims

against other third-party defendants as provided in Rule 97. The third-party defendant may assert against the plaintiff any defenses which the third-party plaintiff has to the plaintiff's claim. The third-party defendant may also assert any claim against the plaintiff arising out of the transaction or occurrence that is the subject matter of the plaintiff's claim against the third-party plaintiff. The plaintiff may assert any claim against the third-party defendant arising out of the transaction or occurrence that is the subject matter of the plaintiff's claim against the third-party plaintiff, and the third-party defendant thereupon shall assert his defenses and his counterclaims and cross-claims. Any party may move to strike the third-party claim, or for its severance or separate trial. A third-party defendant may proceed under this rule against any person not a party to the action who is or who may be liable to him or to the third-party plaintiff for all or part of the claim made in the action against the third-party defendant.

(b) When plaintiff may bring in third party. When a counterclaim is asserted against a plaintiff, he may cause a third party to be brought in under circumstances which under this rule would entitle a defendant to do so.

(c) This rule shall not be applied, in tort cases, so as to permit the joinder of a liability or indemnity insurance company, unless such company is by statute or contract liable to the person injured or damaged.

(d) This rule shall not be applied so as to violate any venue statute, as venue would exist absent this rule.

Oct. 29, 1940, eff. Sept. 1, 1941. Amended by orders of March 31, 1941, eff. Sept. 1, 1941; Dec. 5, 1983, eff. April 1, 1984.

Source: FRCP 14.

See also CPRC §33.004 (responsible third parties); **O'Connor's Texas Rules**, "Parties & Claims," ch. 2-F, §1 et seq.; **O'Connor's Texas Rules**, "The Answer—Denying Liability," ch. 3-E, §1 et seq.

ANNOTATIONS

In re Essex Ins., 507 S.W.3d 418, 421-22 (Tex.App.—Houston [1st Dist.] 2016, orig. proceeding). "[T]he general rule is that an injured party may not sue the tortfeasor's insurer directly, unless the tortfeasor's liability has been finally determined. Thus, a suit brought by a third-party directly against an insurer before liability has been determined is subject to abatement or dismissal until liability is determined. [¶] [P] and [D] observe that the trial court in this case ordered separate trials. . . . Given that [TRCP] 38 and 51 prohibit the joinder that they seek, however, the denial of the severance is not ameliorated by the trial court's order of separate trials."

Goose Creek Consol. ISD v. Jarrar's Plumbing, Inc., 74 S.W.3d 486, 492 (Tex.App.—Texarkana 2002, pet. denied). "A third-party action is not an independent cause of action, but is derivative of the plaintiff's claim against the responsible third party. As such, an action for indemnification or contribution does not accrue for limitations purposes until a plaintiff recovers damages or settles its suit against a defendant."

TRCP 39. JOINDER OF PERSONS NEEDED FOR JUST ADJUDICATION

(a) Persons to be Joined if Feasible. A person who is subject to service of process shall be joined as a party in the action if (1) in his absence complete relief cannot be accorded among those already parties, or (2) he claims an interest relating to the subject of the action and is so situated that the disposition of the action in his absence may (i) as a practical matter impair or impede his ability to protect that interest or (ii) leave any of the persons already parties subject to a substantial risk of incurring double, multiple, or otherwise inconsistent obligations by reason of his claimed interest. If he has not been so joined, the court shall order that he be made a party. If he should join as a plaintiff but refuses to do so, he may be made a defendant, or, in a proper case, an involuntary plaintiff.

(b) Determination by Court Whenever Joinder Not Feasible. If a person as described in subdivision (a)(1)–(2) hereof cannot be made a party, the court shall determine whether in equity and good conscience the action should proceed among the parties before it, or should be dismissed, the absent person being thus regarded as indispensable. The factors to be considered by the court include: first, to what extent a judgment rendered in the person's absence might be prejudicial to him or those already parties; second, the extent to which, by protective provisions in the judgment, by the shaping of relief, or other measures, the prejudice can be lessened or avoided; third, whether a judgment rendered in the person's absence will be adequate; fourth, whether the plaintiff will have an adequate remedy if the action is dismissed for non-joinder.

(c) Pleading Reasons for Nonjoinder. A pleading asserting a claim for relief shall state the names, if known to the pleader, of any persons as described in subdivision (a)(1)–(2) hereof who are not joined, and the reasons why they are not joined.

(d) Exception of Class Actions. This rule is subject to the provisions of Rule 42.

Oct. 29, 1940, eff. Sept. 1, 1941. Amended by order of July 21, 1970, eff. Jan. 1, 1971.

Source: FRCP 19.

See also TRCP 40, 41, 51, 174; **O'Connor's Texas Rules**, "Plaintiff's Original Petition," ch. 2-B, §1 et seq.; **O'Connor's Texas Rules**, "Parties & Claims," ch. 2-F, §1 et seq.; **O'Connor's Texas Rules**, "The Answer—Denying Liability," ch. 3-E, §1 et seq.; **O'Connor's Texas Rules**, "Motion to Abate—Challenging the Suit," ch. 3-I, §1 et seq.; **O'Connor's Texas Rules**, "Motions for Severance & Separate Trials," ch. 5-I, §1 et seq.

ANNOTATIONS

Crawford v. XTO Energy, Inc., 509 S.W.3d 906, 913 (Tex.2017). "[O]nly [D] has actually claimed that the [potential parties to be joined] have . . . an interest; the [potential parties] themselves have not, either directly or indirectly. [T]he [potential parties] did not need to actually 'c[o]me to court to assert an interest' in order to claim an interest under Rule 39. But they needed to do *something*, and the [potential parties] have done nothing."

Brooks v. Northglen Ass'n, 141 S.W.3d 158, 162 (Tex.2004). "Rule 39 determines whether a trial court has authority to proceed without joining a person whose presence in the litigation is made mandatory by the Declaratory Judgment[s] Act. [¶] [N]othing in the rule precluded the trial court from rendering complete relief among [parties] who had sued for a declaration of rights. Although the parties continue to litigate its correctness, the trial court's judgment represents a final and complete adjudication of the dispute for the parties who were before the court."

Cooper v. Texas Gulf Indus., 513 S.W.2d 200, 204 (Tex.1974). "Under the provisions of our present Rule 39 it would be rare indeed if there were a person whose presence was so indispensable in the sense that his absence deprives the court of jurisdiction to adjudicate between the parties already joined." *See also* **Henry v. Cox**, 520 S.W.3d 28, 35-36 (Tex.2017) (Commissioners Court was indispensable); **State Office of Risk Mgmt. v. Herrera**, 288 S.W.3d 543, 549 (Tex.App.—Amarillo 2009, no pet.) (City was indispensable).

Longoria v. Exxon Mobil Corp., 255 S.W.3d 174, 180 (Tex.App.—San Antonio 2008, pet. denied). "Although [TRCP 39] provides for joinder in mandatory terms, 'there is no arbitrary standard or precise formula for determining whether a particular person falls within its provision.' If the trial court determines an absent person falls within the provisions of the rule, the court has a duty to effect the person's joinder. If a person required to be joined under Rule 39(a) cannot be joined, the trial court must decide 'whether in equity and in good conscience the action should proceed among the parties before it, or should be dismissed' by considering the factors listed in Rule 39(b). [¶] The joinder provisions of Rule 39 apply to both trespass to try title and declaratory judgment claims." *See also* **Pierce v. Blalack**, 535 S.W.3d 35, 40-41 (Tex.App.—Texarkana 2017, no pet.).

Gilmer ISD v. Dorfman, 156 S.W.3d 586, 588 (Tex.App.—Tyler 2003, no pet.). "A state official primarily responsible for enforcement of a statute must be joined in any suit affecting the constitutionality of that statute. Failure to add a necessary and indispensable party to the constitutional challenge of a statute leaves the trial court without jurisdiction."

TRCP 40. PERMISSIVE JOINDER OF PARTIES

(a) Permissive Joinder. All persons may join in one action as plaintiffs if they assert any right to relief jointly, severally, or in the alternative in respect of or arising out of the same transaction, occurrence, or series of transactions or occurrences and if any question of law or fact common to all of them will arise in the action. All persons may be joined in one action as defendants if there is asserted against them jointly, severally, or in the alternative any right to relief in respect of or arising out of the same transaction, occurrence, or series of transactions or occurrences and if any question of law or fact common to all of them will arise in the action. A plaintiff or defendant need not be interested in obtaining or defending against all the relief demanded. Judgment may be given for one or more of the plaintiffs according to their respective rights to relief, and against one or more defendants according to their respective liabilities.

(b) Separate Trials. The court may make such orders as will prevent a party from being embarrassed, delayed, or put to expense by the inclusion of a party against whom he asserts no claim and who asserts no claim against him, and may order separate trials or make other orders to prevent delay or prejudice.

Oct. 29, 1940, eff. Sept. 1, 1941.

See also TRCP 39, 41, 51, 174; **O'Connor's Texas Rules**, "Plaintiff's Original Petition," ch. 2-B, §1 et seq.; **O'Connor's Texas Rules**, "Parties & Claims," ch. 2-F, §1 et seq.; **O'Connor's Texas Rules**, "The Answer—Denying Liability," ch. 3-E, §1 et seq.; **O'Connor's Texas Rules**, "Motion to Abate—Challenging the Suit," ch. 3-I, §1 et seq.; **O'Connor's Texas Rules**, "Motions for Severance & Separate Trials," ch. 5-I, §1 et seq.

ANNOTATIONS

Landers v. East Tex. Salt Water Disposal Co., 248 S.W.2d 731, 734 (Tex.1952). "Where the tortious acts of two or more wrongdoers join to produce an indivisible injury, . . . all of the wrongdoers will be held jointly and severally liable for the entire damages and the injured party may proceed to judgment against any one separately or against all in one suit. If fewer than the whole number of wrongdoers are joined as defendants . . ., those joined may by proper cross action . . . bring in those omitted."

TRCP 41. MISJOINDER AND NON-JOINDER OF PARTIES

Misjoinder of parties is not ground for dismissal of an action. Parties may be dropped or added, or suits filed separately may be consolidated, or actions which have been improperly joined may be severed and each ground of recovery improperly joined may be docketed as a separate suit between the same parties, by order of the court on motion of any party or on its own initiative at any stage of the action, before the time of submission to the jury or to the court if trial is without a jury, on such terms as are just. Any claim against a party may be severed and proceeded with separately.

Oct. 29, 1940, eff. Sept. 1, 1941. Amended by order of March 31, 1941, eff. Sept. 1, 1941.

Source: FRCP 21.

See also TRCP 39, 40, 51, 174; **O'Connor's Texas Rules**, "Parties & Claims," ch. 2-F, §1 et seq.; **O'Connor's Texas Rules**, "The Answer—Denying Liability," ch. 3-E, §1 et seq.

ANNOTATIONS

F.F.P. Oper. Partners v. Duenez, 237 S.W.3d 680, 693 (Tex.2007). "'A claim is properly severable if (1) the controversy involves more than one cause of action, (2) the severed claim is one that would be the proper subject of a lawsuit if independently asserted, and (3) the severed claim is not so interwoven with the remaining action that they involve the same facts and issues.' [A]voiding prejudice, doing justice, and increasing convenience are the controlling reasons to allow a severance." *See also* **State v. Morello**, 547 S.W.3d 881, 889 (Tex.2018); **Guaranty Fed. Sav. Bank v. Horseshoe Oper. Co.**, 793 S.W.2d 652, 658 (Tex.1990); **In re A.C.**, No. 2-08-407-CV, 2009 WL 1815658 (Tex.App.—Fort Worth 2009, no pet.) (memo op.; 6-25-09).

Liberty Nat'l Fire Ins. v. Akin, 927 S.W.2d 627, 630 (Tex.1996). "A severance may . . . be necessary in some bad faith [and contract] cases. A trial court will . . . confront instances in which evidence admissible only on the bad faith claim would prejudice the insurer to such an extent that a fair trial on the contract claim would become unlikely. One example would be when the insurer has made a settlement offer on the disputed contract claim."

State Dept. of Hwys. & Pub. Transp. v. Cotner, 845 S.W.2d 818, 819 (Tex.1993). TRCP 41 "does not 'permit a trial court to sever a case after it has been submitted to the trier of fact.' [¶] A partial new trial may be ordered notwithstanding the prohibition in Rule 41 against post-submission severances. [TRCP] 320 is thus an exception to Rule 41."

Nichols v. Nichols, 331 S.W.3d 800, 804 (Tex.App.—Fort Worth 2010, no pet.). "In contrast to [TRCP] 329b, [TRCP] 41 [does not require] that a severance be determined 'by *written* order.' Furthermore, unlike Rule 329b, which requires a motion for new trial to be granted in writing before the relevant time period expires, nothing in Rule 41 requires a severance order to be in writing and signed before the remaining case is submitted to the trier of fact. [¶] [S]ubmission of the remaining cause to the trier of fact does not prevent a severance because a properly severable cause of action, if not tried, may still be tried separately. There is no justification for treating a properly severable cause of action differently. [T]he controlling reason for severance is to do justice, avoid prejudice, and promote convenience, not to prevent the trial of potentially viable claims."

TRCP 42. CLASS ACTIONS

(a) Prerequisites to a Class Action. One or more members of a class may sue or be sued as representative parties on behalf of all only if (1) the class is so numerous that joinder of all members is impracticable, (2) there are questions of law, or fact common to the class, (3) the claims or defenses of the representative parties are typical of the claims or defenses of the class, and (4) the representative parties will fairly and adequately protect the interests of the class.

(b) Class Actions Maintainable. An action may be maintained as a class action if the prerequisites of subdivision (a) are satisfied, and in addition:

(1) the prosecution of separate actions by or against individual members of the class would create a risk of

(A) inconsistent or varying adjudications with respect to individual members of the class which would establish incompatible standards of conduct for the party opposing the class, or

(B) adjudications with respect to individual members of the class which would as a practical matter be dispositive of the interests of the other members not parties to the adjudications or substantially impair or impede their ability to protect their interests; or

(2) the party opposing the class has acted or refused to act on grounds generally applicable to the class, thereby making appropriate final injunctive relief or corresponding declaratory relief with respect to the class as a whole; or

(3) the questions of law or fact common to the members of the class predominate over any questions affecting only individual members, and a class action is superior to other available methods for the fair and efficient adjudication of the controversy. The matters pertinent to these issues include:

(A) the interest of members of the class in individually controlling the prosecution or defense of separate actions;

(B) the extent and nature of any litigation concerning the controversy already commenced by or against members of the class;

(C) the desirability or undesirability of concentrating the litigation of the claims in the particular forum; and

(D) the difficulties likely to be encountered in the management of a class action.

(c) Determining by Order Whether to Certify a Class Action; Notice and Membership in Class.

(1) (A) When a person sues or is sued as a representative of a class, the court must—at an early practicable time—determine by order whether to certify the action as a class action.

(B) An order certifying a class action must define the class and the class claims, issues, or defenses, and must appoint class counsel under Rule 42(g).

(C) An order under Rule 42(c)(1) may be altered or amended before final judgment. The court may order the naming of additional parties in order to insure the adequacy of representation.

(D) An order granting or denying certification under Rule 42(b)(3) must state:

(i) the elements of each claim or defense asserted in the pleadings;

(ii) any issues of law or fact common to the class members;

(iii) any issues of law or fact affecting only individual class members;

(iv) the issues that will be the object of most of the efforts of the litigants and the court;

(v) other available methods of adjudication that exist for the controversy;

(vi) why the issues common to the members of the class do or do not predominate over individual issues;

(vii) why a class action is or is not superior to other available methods for the fair and efficient adjudication of the controversy; and

(viii) if a class is certified, how the class claims and any issues affecting only individual members, raised by the claims or defenses asserted in the pleadings, will be tried in a manageable, time efficient manner.

(2) (A) For any class certified under Rule 42(b)(1) or (2), the court may direct appropriate notice to the class.

(B) For any class certified under Rule 42(b)(3), the court must direct to class members the best notice practicable under the circumstances, including individual notice to all members who can be identified through reasonable effort. The notice must concisely and clearly state in plain, easily understood language:

(i) the nature of the action;

(ii) the definition of the class certified;

(iii) the class claims, issues, or defenses;

(iv) that a class member may enter an appearance through counsel if the member so desires;

(v) that the court will exclude from the class any member who requests exclusion, stating when and how members may elect to be excluded; and

(vi) the binding effect of a class judgment on class members under Rule 42(c)(3).

(3) The judgment in an action maintained as a class action under subdivision (b)(1) or (b)(2), whether or not favorable to the class, shall include and describe those whom the court finds to be members of the class. The judgment in an action maintained as a class action under subdivision (b)(3), whether or not favorable to the class, shall include and specify or describe those to whom the notice provided in subdivision (c)(2) was directed, and who have not requested exclusion, and whom the court finds to be members of the class.

(d) Actions Conducted Partially as Class Actions; Multiple Classes and Subclasses. When appropriate (1) an action may be brought or maintained as a class action with respect to particular issues, or (2) a class may be divided into subclasses and each subclass treated as a class, and the provisions of this rule shall then be construed and applied accordingly.

(e) Settlement, Dismissal or Compromise.

(1) (A) The court must approve any settlement, dismissal, or compromise of the claims, issues, or defenses of a certified class.

(B) Notice of the material terms of the proposed settlement, dismissal or compromise, together with an explanation of when and how the members may elect to be excluded from the class, shall be given to all members in such manner as the court directs.

(C) The court may approve a settlement, dismissal, or compromise that would bind class members only after a hearing and on finding that the settlement, dismissal, or compromise is fair, reasonable, and adequate.

(2) The parties seeking approval of a settlement, dismissal, or compromise under Rule 42(e)(1) must file a statement identifying any agreement made in connection with the proposed settlement, dismissal, or compromise.

(3) In an action previously certified as a class action under Rule 42(b)(3), the court may not approve a settlement unless it affords a new opportunity to request exclusion to individual class members who had an earlier opportunity to request exclusion but did not do so.

(4) (A) Any class member may object to a proposed settlement, dismissal, or compromise that requires court approval under Rule 42(e)(1)(A).

(B) An objection made under Rule 42(e)(4)(A) may be withdrawn only with the court's approval.

(f) Discovery. Unnamed members of a class action are not to be considered as parties for purposes of discovery.

(g) Class Counsel.

(1) *Appointing Class Counsel.*

(A) Unless a statute provides otherwise, a court that certifies a class must appoint class counsel.

(B) An attorney appointed to serve as class counsel must fairly and adequately represent the interests of the class.

(C) In appointing class counsel, the court

(i) must consider:

• the work counsel has done in identifying or investigating potential claims in the action;

• counsel's experience in handling class actions, other complex litigation, and claims of the type asserted in the action;

• counsel's knowledge of the applicable law; and

• the resources counsel will commit to representing the class;

(ii) may consider any other matter pertinent to counsel's ability to fairly and adequately represent the interests of the class;

(iii) may direct potential class counsel to provide information on any subject pertinent to the appointment and to propose terms for attorney fees and nontaxable costs; and

(iv) may make further orders in connection with the appointment.

(2) *Appointment Procedure.*

(A) The court may designate interim counsel to act on behalf of the putative class before determining whether to certify the action as a class action.

(B) When there is one applicant for appointment as class counsel, the court may appoint that applicant only if the applicant is adequate under Rule 42(g)(1)(B) and (C). If more than one adequate applicant seeks appointment as class counsel, the court must appoint the applicant or applicants best able to represent the interests of the class.

(C) The order appointing class counsel may include provisions about the award of attorney fees or nontaxable costs under Rule 42(h) and (i).

(h) Procedure for Determining Attorney Fees Award. In an action certified as a class action, the court may award attorney fees in accordance with subdivision (i) and nontaxable costs authorized by law or by agreement of the parties as follows:

(1) *Motion for Award of Attorney Fees.* A claim for an award of attorney fees and nontaxable costs must be made by motion, subject to the provisions of this subdivision, at a time set by the court. Notice of the motion must be served on all parties and, for motions by class counsel, directed to class members in a reasonable manner.

(2) *Objections to Motion.* A class member, or a party from whom payment is sought, may object to the motion.

(3) *Hearing and Findings.* The court must hold a hearing in open court and must find the facts and state its conclusions of law on the motion. The court must state its findings and conclusions in writing or orally on the record.

(i) Attorney's Fees Award.

(1) In awarding attorney fees, the court must first determine a lodestar figure by multiplying the number of hours reasonably worked times a reasonable hourly rate. The attorney fees award must be in the range of 25% to 400% of the lodestar figure. In making these determinations, the court must consider the factors specified in Rule 1.04(b), Tex. Disciplinary R. Prof. Conduct.

(2) If any portion of the benefits recovered for the class are in the form of coupons or other noncash common benefits, the attorney fees awarded in the action must be in cash and noncash amounts in the same proportion as the recovery for the class.

(j) Effective Date. Rule 42(i) applies only in actions filed after September 1, 2003.

Oct. 29, 1940, eff. Sept. 1, 1941. Amended by orders of Sept. 20, 1941, eff. Dec. 31, 1941; May 9, 1977, eff. Sept. 1, 1977; Dec. 5, 1983, eff. April 1, 1984; Oct. 9, 2003, eff. Jan. 1, 2004.

Comment—2003

The second paragraph of subdivision (a) regarding derivative suits has been deleted because it is redundant of Article 5.14 of the Business Corporation Act, which sets forth detailed procedures for derivative suits.

Subparagraph (b)(3) is omitted as unnecessary.

The requirement that certification be decided "at an early practicable time" is a change from the previous Texas rule 42(c)(1) and federal rule 23(c)(1), which required the trial court to decide the certification issue "as soon as practicable after the commencement of [the suit]." The amended language is not intended to permit undue delay or permit excessive discovery unrelated to certification, but is designed to encourage good practices in making certification decisions only after receiving the information necessary to decide whether certification should be granted or denied and how to define the class if certification is granted.

Source: FRCP 23, with change: In (b) deleted requirement that the action is not collusive.

See also CPRC §51.014(a)(3); **O'Connor's Texas Civil Appeals**, "Class certification," ch. 1-B, §2.4.1(2).

ANNOTATIONS

Generally

Citizens Ins. v. Daccach, 217 S.W.3d 430, 449 (Tex2007). TRCP 42 "is a form of joinder, a procedural mechanism established to increase judicial economy and efficiency for suits with parties too numerous for conventional joinder. *At 450:* Basic principles of res judicata apply to class actions just as they do to any other form of litigation. *At*

455: [W]hile we agree that Rule 42(d) allows a trial court to consider certifying a class whose representative has abandoned or split claims, we decline to take the further step of excepting a final judgment in such a class action from the principles of res judicata. *At 457:* We hold, therefore, that [TRCP] 42 requires the trial court . . . to consider the risk that a judgment in the class action may preclude subsequent litigation of claims not alleged, abandoned, or split from the class action. The trial court abuses its discretion if it fails to consider the preclusive effect of a judgment on abandoned claims, as res judicata could undermine the adequacy of representation requirement." *See also* **Phillips Pet. Co. v. Yarbrough**, 405 S.W.3d 70, 81-82 (Tex.2013); **Bowden v. Phillips Pet. Co.**, 247 S.W.3d 690, 697-98 (Tex.2008).

State Farm Mut. Auto. Ins. v. Lopez, 156 S.W.3d 550, 556 (Tex.2004). "[A] trial plan is required in every certification order to allow reviewing courts to assure that *all* requirements for certification under Rule 42 have been satisfied. The formulation of a trial plan assures that a trial court has fulfilled its obligation to rigorously analyze all certification prerequisites, and understands the claims, defenses, relevant facts, and applicable substantive law in order to make a meaningful determination of the certification issues." (Internal quotes omitted.) *See also* **BMG Direct Mktg., Inc. v. Peake**, 178 S.W.3d 763, 778 (Tex.2005); **North Am. Mortg. Co. v. O'Hara**, 153 S.W.3d 43, 44-45 (Tex.2004).

Intratex Gas Co. v. Beeson, 22 S.W.3d 398, 403-04 (Tex.2000). "For a class to be sufficiently defined, it must be precise: the class members must be presently ascertainable by reference to objective criteria. This means that the class should not be defined by criteria that are subjective or that require an analysis of the merits of the case. [H]owever, . . . a class definition will not fail merely because every potential class member cannot be identified at the suit's commencement."

Assignees of Best Buy v. Combs, 395 S.W.3d 847, 865 (Tex.App.—Austin 2013, pet. denied). "[W]hen the court appoints class counsel, it appoints class counsel to serve the interests of the class, as that class and its claims, issues, or defenses are defined in the certification order. *At 867:* We cannot conclude from Rule 42's express grant of power to appoint class counsel that the trial courts had the implied authority to appoint class counsel to act as individual counsel to individual class members in separate actions outside the class actions suing a different defendant and seeking a different type of relief. The plain language of Rule 42 limits the relief that the trial courts could provide to the settlement classes to the confines of their class claim for assignments. *At 868:* [TRCP 42's] express language contemplates only class representation, and neither the judicial-economy purpose of class actions nor the fiduciary duties owed by class counsel to the class support an implication of any additional power."

Standing

Heckman v. Williamson Cty., 369 S.W.3d 137, 151 (Tex.2012). "A plaintiff who brings a class action, rather than just suing on his own behalf, must still prove that he individually had standing to sue. The court must consider this threshold question even before reaching the separate issue of whether it can certify the putative class. Just as it must dismiss a case where the plaintiff lacks standing to bring any of his claims, a court must dismiss a class action for want of jurisdiction if the named plaintiff entirely lacked *individual* standing at the time he sued. [¶] We see no reason why a plaintiff who seeks to represent a class, but lacks standing on some of the purported class's claims, completely lacks standing to bring *any* claims. *At 152-53:* Whether considering the standing of one plaintiff or many, the court must analyze the standing of each individual plaintiff to bring each individual claim he or she alleges when that issue is before the court. . . . Thus, . . . the court must assess standing plaintiff by plaintiff, claim by claim. *At 154:* [W]here plaintiffs seek to represent a class, a plaintiff need not have standing on each and every one of the class's claims in order to satisfy the standing requirement. So long as an individual plaintiff has standing on *some* claim, he has standing to pursue class certification as to that claim." *See also* **DaimlerChrysler Corp. v. Inman**, 252 S.W.3d 299, 307 (Tex.2008).

Southwestern Bell Tel. Co. v. Marketing on Hold Inc., 308 S.W.3d 909, 918-19 (Tex.2010). "[T]he valid assignment of claims to a party is not invalidated by the party's designation as the representative in a class suit. Nothing unique to the class action context or to this case dictates that we take the extraordinary step of invalidating otherwise contractually valid assignments on . . . public policy grounds. [¶] [Assignee] is a member of the class that the trial court certified. [¶] If we were to hold, as [D] contends we should, that [assignee's] assignments are void on public policy grounds, we would abrogate [assignee's] individual standing to bring its claims as either a member of the putative class as defined by the trial court or in an individual lawsuit. [Assignee's] individual standing does not change based on whether it asserts that standing as a class member, in support of its bid to serve as the class representative, or as an individual litigant. The standing requirements remain the same because each class member and the class representative is an individual claimant seeking a personal recovery."

Mootness Exception

Heckman v. Williamson Cty., 369 S.W.3d 137, 162 (Tex.2012). "In a typical civil action, where a solo plaintiff brings a claim on his own behalf, the mootness analysis is usually straightforward: If the plaintiff's individual interest becomes moot, the entire suit ordinarily becomes moot. In a class action, however, the plaintiff brings a claim not just on his own behalf, but on behalf of an entire class of similarly-injured individuals. There, the named plaintiff's individual interest can become moot without necessarily af-

fecting the class's interest in how the suit turns out. *At 163:* Should a class action lawsuit survive when the individual claim of the named plaintiff becomes moot? [¶] Where, as here, the individual claims of the named plaintiffs become moot before the trial court decides whether to certify the class, the class action may still survive so long as it fits [some] limited exception[ ]. [¶] One such exception applies to 'inherently transitory' claims. This exception is premised on the idea that some claims, by their nature, are so short-lived that it may be impossible for the trial court to decide on certification before the named plaintiff's individual claims become moot. At the same time, . . . there continues to exist a population of individuals who suffer from the same alleged harms and therefore have the same inherently transitory claims against the same defendant. Such a claim, therefore, would apply to many people, yet simultaneously would never be subject to judicial review because it would continuously become moot before a judge could certify the putative class. *At 164-65:* [T]o qualify for the exception for 'inherently transitory' claims, the named plaintiff must show . . . that the claim is one of short duration, and . . . that there likely exists a continuing class of persons suffering the same alleged harm as the named plaintiff."

Growden v. Good Shepherd Health Sys., 550 S.W.3d 716, 724 (Tex.App.—Texarkana 2018, no pet.). "We have not found any case in which the Texas Supreme Court or a Texas court of appeals has recognized the picking-off exception to the mootness doctrine. However, because 'federal courts have extensively explored mootness in the class action context and have developed a body of exceptions,' we look to 'their decisions for guidance.' *At 726:* [T]he Fifth Circuit and other federal courts have recognized, at least in some instances, a picking-off exception to the mootness doctrine when the defendant satisfies the named plaintiff's individual claim as a part of its litigation strategy. To determine whether the record supports an inference that the satisfaction of the named plaintiff's claim is a litigation strategy employed by the defendant, the courts have considered a couple of factors. These factors include (1) when the defendant satisfied the named plaintiff's claim and (2) whether the satisfaction resulted from the standard operating procedure of the defendant, rather than a new ad hoc procedure. [¶] Additionally, . . . the Fifth Circuit [has] indicated the application of the picking-off exception would apply to those cases in which, at the time of the mooting of the named plaintiff's individual claim, 'there is pending before the district court a timely filed and diligently pursued motion for class certification.' *At 727:* In this case, [P's] timely filed motion to certify was pending before the trial court when [D satisfied her claim]. Although there is no indication in the record that a hearing on the motion to certify had been set, [D satisfied P's claim] only after [P] had sought discovery from it regarding her class claims and had filed a motion to compel [D] to fully answer her discovery requests. [¶] Based on this record, and following well-established federal law, we find that the picking-off exception to the mootness doctrine applies in this case and that the trial court erred in dismissing [P's] class-action claims."

Typicality

Southwestern Bell Tel. Co. v. Marketing on Hold Inc., 308 S.W.3d 909, 920 (Tex.2010). "'A claim is typical if it arises from the same event or practice or course of conduct that gives rise to the claims of other class members, and if his or her claims are based on the same legal theory.' [¶] We have not previously had an opportunity to address the typicality of an assignee-class representative's claims. Other courts considering this issue have focused on the legal theories behind the claims asserted, not the characteristics of the assignee, unless a defense unique to the assignee will 'skew the focus of the litigation and create a danger that absent class members will suffer if their representative is preoccupied with defenses unique to it.' [¶] Because [assignee] is the assignee of the customer-assignors, [assignee] steps into the customers' shoes and may assert a claim for the injury shared by the assignor and all members of the class. By definition, [assignee's] claims against [D] are the same as the class members. . . . We therefore conclude that [assignee] has satisfied the typicality requirement."

Predominance

Stonebridge Life Ins. v. Pitts, 236 S.W.3d 201, 206-07 (Tex.2007). "Equitable defenses raise important substantive issues that may have a significant effect on class-action litigation. [¶] In **Bernal**, we rejected the 'certify now and worry later' approach, holding it is improper to certify a class when it cannot be determined from the outset that individual issues can be considered in a manageable, time-efficient, and fair manner. [¶] Just as fairness and manageability concerns made **Bernal** inappropriate for class certification, the important and diverse individual issues involved in evaluating the class members' money-had-and-received claim compel the same result. [¶] At least one court has concluded that equitable claims for 'money had and received' are uncertifiable for this very reason: In order to prevail on money had and received, the plaintiffs will have to establish that they paid money to the defendants, either by mistake or fraud, that, in equity or good conscience, should be returned to the plaintiffs. This theory of recovery, therefore, requires individualized inquiry into the state of mind of each plaintiff. [¶] [T]he class representatives in this case failed to prove at the outset that individual issues can be considered in a fair, manageable, and time-efficient manner on a class-wide basis. Accordingly, Rule 42(b)(3)'s predominance requirement is not satisfied. . . ." (Internal quotes omitted.) *See also* **Best Buy Co. v. Barrera**, 248 S.W.3d 160, 162 (Tex.2007).

Southwestern Ref. Co. v. Bernal, 22 S.W.3d 425, 434 (Tex.2000). "Courts determine if common issues predominate by identifying the substantive issues of the case that will control the outcome of the litigation, assessing which issues will predominate, and determining if the predominating issues are, in fact, those common to the class. The test

for predominance is not whether common issues outnumber uncommon issues but . . . 'whether common or individual issues will be the object of most of the efforts of the litigants and the court.' If, after common issues are resolved, presenting and resolving individual issues is likely to be an overwhelming or unmanageable task for a single jury, then common issues do not predominate." *See also* **Southwestern Bell Tel. Co. v. Marketing on Hold Inc.**, 308 S.W.3d 909, 920-21 (Tex.2010); **Snyder Comms. v. Magaña**, 142 S.W.3d 295, 299-300 (Tex.2004); **Henry Schein, Inc. v. Stromboe**, 102 S.W.3d 675, 688 (Tex.2002).

Adequacy

Riemer v. State, 392 S.W.3d 635, 639 (Tex.2013). "Rule 42(a)(4)'s adequacy-of-representation prerequisite requires the proponent of class certification to establish that the class representative will fairly and adequately protect the interests of the class. '[A] class representative whose interests conflict with the interests of other class members may not adequately represent a class.' The existence of minor conflicts standing alone, however, will not prevent a class representative from adequately representing a class. For a conflict of interest to prevent class certification under Rule 42(a)(4), the conflict must be fundamental and go to the heart of the litigation. A conflict that is merely speculative or hypothetical will not defeat the adequacy-of-representation requirement."

Southwestern Bell Tel. Co. v. Marketing on Hold Inc., 308 S.W.3d 909, 925 (Tex.2010). "An assignee's interests are not 'necessarily antagonistic' solely because it is an assignee, but the perils of permitting an assignee to represent the class raise important concerns under rule 42. We believe courts should scrutinize carefully the motivating interests and incentives of parties that agree at an apparent financial loss to obtain the right to serve as the class representative. Rule 42's adequacy requirement raises these considerations, which include but are not limited to: (1) the assignee's connection to the classwide injury; (2) the benefits the assignee receives under the assignments; and (3) the assignee's motivation in asserting claims on behalf of the assignor(s). These considerations, in addition to other concerns that may be raised by the facts of each case, aim to ensure that the assignee's interests are aligned with the interests of the unnamed class members. *At 927:* [Assignee's] lack of any claim of its own makes it unique among the members of the class. Its only knowledge of the claims it holds must be obtained from its assignors. . . . While we recognize that class counsel's control over class litigation is often greater than it is in non-class litigation, the class action rule contemplates that the class representative is 'not simply lending [its] name[ ] to a suit controlled entirely by the class attorney.' In this case, [assignee's] interest in the litigation by assignment removes it and its counsel one step further from the class members, enhancing the risk of conflicts."

Enron Oil & Gas Co. v. Joffrion, 116 S.W.3d 215, 219 (Tex.App.—Tyler 2003, no pet.). The "factors to consider in determining if the adequacy of representation element is satisfied [include]: (1) adequacy of counsel; (2) potential for conflicts of interest; (3) personal integrity of the plaintiffs; (4) whether the class is unmanageable because of geographic limitations; (5) whether the representative plaintiffs can afford to finance the class action; and (6) the representative plaintiffs' familiarity with the litigation and his or her belief in the legitimacy of the action." *See also* **Supportkids, Inc. v. Morris**, 167 S.W.3d 422, 425-26 (Tex.App.—Houston [14th Dist.] 2005, pet. dism'd).

Numerosity

Rainbow Grp. v. Johnson, 990 S.W.2d 351, 357 (Tex.App.—Austin 1999, pet. dism'd). "Numerosity is not based on numbers alone. Rather, the test is whether joinder of all members is practicable in view of the size of the class and includes such factors as judicial economy, the nature of the action, geographical location of class members, and the likelihood that class members would be unable to prosecute individual lawsuits. Additionally, since class certification is not based on the merits of members' claims, proponents are not required to establish a prima facie case for class certification. Numerosity can therefore be established by the number of *potential* class members, not those proven to have been affected." *See also* **Lon Smith & Assocs. v. Key**, 527 S.W.3d 604, 625 (Tex.App.—Fort Worth 2017, pet. denied); **Life Partners v. McDermott**, No. 05-12-01623-CV, 2014 WL 2810472 (Tex.App.—Dallas 2014, no pet.) (memo op.; 6-23-14).

Discovery

In re SCI Tex. Funeral Servs., 236 S.W.3d 759, 760 (Tex.2007). The Supreme Court has "rejected a blanket rule that all class-wide discovery should be abated until after certification. But we also rejected the opposite rule (full class-wide discovery before certification), noting the special risk in class actions that one party might seek to improve its bargaining position by heaping massive discovery on the other. Instead, . . . trial courts [should] limit pre-certification discovery to the particular issues governing certification in each case, considering factors such as the importance, benefit, burden, expense, and time needed to produce the proposed discovery. *At 761:* The discovery orders here do not comply with this rule. . . . While [Ps] could have made a strong case for discovery related to the size of the class and representative samples of how [D] did business (necessary to establish numerosity, typicality, and so on), these issues did not justify the burden and expense of producing every [Ps'] contract and every . . . invoice [of D's]—discovery perhaps necessary to prove the ultimate issues but not tailored to the certification question before the court. [T]he trial court abused its discretion by compelling discovery that was not narrowly tailored to the relevant dispute."

Appellate Review

Phillips Pet. Co. v. Yarbrough, 405 S.W.3d 70, 76-77 (Tex.2013). "Generally, modifications of certification orders,

such as those modifying the size of a class or a class definition, are not appealable. However, in **De Los Santos [v. Occidental Chem. Corp.**, 933 S.W.2d 493 (Tex.1996),] we held that an order changing a class action from opt-out to mandatory 'alters the fundamental nature of the class' and that an interlocutory appeal of such an order is authorized [under CPRC §51.014(a)(3)]. [¶] The ruling in **De Los Santos** is narrow, reached in accordance with legislative intent 'that §51.014 be strictly construed as a narrow exception to the general rule that only final judgments and orders are appealable.'. . . Thus, . . . an order that changes the class in such a way as to raise significant concerns about whether certification remains proper alters the fundamental nature of the class and is therefore appealable."

Exxon Mobil Corp. v. Gill, 299 S.W.3d 124, 129 (Tex.2009). "When a class has been certified based on a significant misunderstanding of the law, we have concluded that 'remand to the trial court is appropriate so that it may determine the effect . . . on the requirements for class certification.'"

Stonebridge Life Ins. v. Pitts, 236 S.W.3d 201, 204-05 (Tex.2007). The Supreme Court "reviews a trial court's decision to certify a class under an abuse of discretion standard, but does so without indulging every presumption in favor of the trial court's decision. Actual conformance with Rule 42 is indispensable, and compliance with the rule must be demonstrated, not presumed." *See also* **National W. Life Ins. v. Rowe**, 164 S.W.3d 389, 392 (Tex.2005).

Ford Motor Co. v. Sheldon, 22 S.W.3d 444, 449 (Tex.2000). Unless the Supreme Court has specific statutory authority, it cannot review most interlocutory orders on class certification.

Deloitte & Touche LLP v. Fourteenth Ct. of Appeals, 951 S.W.2d 394, 396 (Tex.1997). The Supreme Court has mandamus jurisdiction to review an interlocutory class certification order over which it has no appellate jurisdiction.

Settlement

McAllen Med. Ctr., Inc. v. Cortez, 66 S.W.3d 227, 233 (Tex.2001). "Rule 42's typicality and adequacy-of-representation criteria . . . demand heightened scrutiny when a settlement occurs. . . . And when a settlement occurs, the potential for class representatives and counsel to ignore differences among class members, or even collude with defendants at absent class members' expense, mandates that the trial court rigorously scrutinize Rule 42's typicality and adequacy-of-representation criteria."

Attorney Fees

Kazman v. Frontier Oil Corp., 398 S.W.3d 377, 387 (Tex.App.—Houston [14th Dist.] 2013, no pet.). "Rule 42(i)(2) does not restrict 'benefits' to pecuniary benefits or tangible 'instruments' like coupons. . . . Thus, we conclude that 'benefits' may include any advantage, gain, or interest recovered by the class, including injunctive relief in the form of additional disclosures. [¶] [P] argues that because the class in this case recovered only the 'noncash common benefit' of additional disclosures and no cash, Rule 42(i)(2) precludes an award of attorney's fees in cash to class counsel. This application of the rule is consistent with the legislature's intent to promote the fair and efficient resolution of class actions and to curb abuses of the class-action procedure."

TRCP 43. INTERPLEADER

Persons having claims against the plaintiff may be joined as defendants and required to interplead when their claims are such that the plaintiff is or may be exposed to double or multiple liability. It is not ground for objection to the joinder that the claims of the several claimants or the titles on which their claims depend do not have a common origin or are not identical but are adverse to and independent of one another, or that the plaintiff avers that he is not liable in whole or in part to any or all of the claimants. A defendant exposed to similar liability may obtain such interpleader by way of cross-claim or counterclaim. The provisions of this rule supplement and do not in any way limit the joinder of parties permitted in any other rules.

Oct. 29, 1940, eff. Sept. 1, 1941.

Source: FRCP 22(1).

See also **O'Connor's Texas Rules**, "Joining Parties or Claims," ch. 5-J, §1 et seq.; **O'Connor's Texas Forms**, FORMS 5J:4, 5J:5, 5J:6.

ANNOTATIONS

Fort Worth Transp. Auth. v. Rodriguez, 547 S.W.3d 830, 850 (Tex.2018). "The Texas rule is that the innocent stakeholder in an interpleader is entitled to attorney's fees to be paid out of the interpleaded funds. *At 851:* When the interpleading party is responsible for the conflicting claims to the funds or property, that party is not entitled to attorney's fees incurred in interpleading the claimants. *At 852:* Under the unambiguous meaning of [the] term 'disinterested stakeholder,' a party who asserts a claim to the interpleaded funds is not a disinterested stakeholder. [¶] [Ds'] position as the alleged tortfeasors prevents them from being a 'disinterested stakeholder.' Texas courts have held, for example, that interpleader is proper to protect an insurance company facing competing claims over benefits. Similarly, interpleader is proper to protect a bank when multiple claimants assert claims to funds in an account. But we find no precedent to support extending the protection of interpleader—and the accompanying attorney's fees—to an alleged tortfeasor/defendant." (Internal quotes omitted.)

State Farm Life Ins. v. Martinez, 216 S.W.3d 799, 807 (Tex.2007). "[I]nterpleader is not improper merely because it is delayed; while some courts have listed prompt filing as an interpleader requirement, the rules of procedure require

only conflicting claims. When rival claims exist, courts must decide who gets the proceeds no matter how tardy the deposit; we cannot simply 'toss the money back out the clerk's window,' or return it to a stakeholder who makes no claim to it."

Great Am. Reserve Ins. v. Sanders, 525 S.W.2d 956, 958 (Tex.1975). Insurance company "was entitled to maintain an interpleader suit if there existed a reasonable doubt, either of fact or law, as to which of the rival claimants was entitled to the proceeds of the policy."

Clayton v. MONY Life Ins., 284 S.W.3d 398, 404 (Tex.App.—Beaumont 2009, no pet.). "Rule 43 requires only conflicting claims. [I]nterpleader is not precluded merely because one of the rival claimants alleges the stakeholder is also independently liable to that claimant, and the stakeholder denies that independent liability, but makes no claim to the stake. *At 405:* While independent liability does not necessarily and automatically preclude interpleader under Rule 43, liability for the independent pre-interpleader claims is not necessarily and automatically discharged by the tender."

TRCP 44. MAY APPEAR BY NEXT FRIEND

Minors, lunatics, idiots, or persons non compos mentis who have no legal guardian may sue and be represented by "next friend" under the following rules:

(1) Such next friend shall have the same rights concerning such suits as guardians have, but shall give security for costs, or affidavits in lieu thereof, when required.

(2) Such next friend or his attorney of record may with the approval of the court compromise suits and agree to judgments, and such judgments, agreements and compromises, when approved by the court, shall be forever binding and conclusive upon the party plaintiff in such suit.

Oct. 29, 1940, eff. Sept. 1, 1941.

Source: TRCS art. 1994, now Prop. Code §142.002.

See also TRCP 173; **O'Connor's Texas Rules**, "Guardian Ad Litem Under TRCP 173," ch. 1-I, §1 et seq.; **O'Connor's Texas Forms**, FORMS 1I:1, 1I:2, 1I:3.

ANNOTATIONS

In re Bridgestone Americas Tire Opers., LLC, 459 S.W.3d 565, 570 (Tex.2015). "The significance of a minor's having a legal guardian in the context of Rule 44 is that, when a minor already has a guardian who may sue on his behalf, the minor does not need next-friend representation in order to litigate his claims. For Rule 44 to make sense, it must be construed to enable minors to prosecute their claims—through a next friend—when they otherwise could not through a legal guardian. It follows that, if a legal guardian has been appointed or recognized in another jurisdiction, but that guardian lacks authority to sue on the minor's behalf in Texas and has no legal basis for obtaining such authority, the minor may sue by next friend under Rule 44. *At 572:* [A] nonresident guardian of a nonresident ward with no connection to Texas beyond a possible lawsuit simply has no authority to sue on behalf of the ward in Texas in his capacity as guardian. [¶] Accordingly, in this case, although the children's grandparents are recognized as the children's guardians under the law of Nuevo Leon where they reside, they have no authority to sue in that capacity on the children's behalf in Texas. To avoid depriving the children of the ability to pursue their claims before they turn 18, Rule 44 allows them to do so by next friend."

American Gen. Fire & Cas. Co. v. Vandewater, 907 S.W.2d 491, 492-93 (Tex.1995). "[A]n appellate court should evaluate whether the minor's interests have been properly protected and whether a deficiency in notice or due process has been shown to determine whether a trial court has obtained personal jurisdiction over a minor. In this case, the answer of [mother] in her capacity as [minor's] next friend was sufficient indication that [minor's] legal representative knew about the proceedings and could therefore defend against them." *See also* **Doe v. Texas Ass'n of Sch. Bds., Inc.**, 283 S.W.3d 451, 463 (Tex.App.—Fort Worth 2009, pet. denied).

In re KC Greenhouse Patio Apts., LP, 445 S.W.3d 168, 172 (Tex.App.—Houston [1st Dist.] 2012, orig. proceeding). TRCP 44 "does not authorize a trial court to transfer [the right to represent a minor] from a minor's parent to a third party by unilaterally replacing the parent as the minor's 'next friend' when a conflict of interest arises. [¶] [TRCP] 173—not rule 44—is the rule that grants a trial court authority to address conflicts of interest, and it does so through the appointment of a guardian ad litem, not the replacement of the next friend. Neither rule 44 nor rule 173 permits another person to sue as next friend for a minor who has a legal guardian or permits a court to replace a legal guardian with another person to act as next friend for purposes of pursuing a lawsuit on behalf of a minor."

SECTION 4. PLEADING

A. General

TRCP 45. DEFINITION AND SYSTEM

Pleadings in the district and county courts shall

(a) be by petition and answer;

(b) consist of a statement in plain and concise language of the plaintiff's cause of action or the defendant's grounds of defense. That an allegation be evidentiary or be of legal conclusion shall not be grounds for an objection when fair notice to the opponent is given by the allegations as a whole; and

(c) contain any other matter which may be required by any law or rule authorizing or regulating any particular action or defense.

Pleadings that are not filed electronically must be in writing, on paper measuring approximately 8½ inches by 11 inches, and signed by the party or his attorney. The use of recycled paper is strongly encouraged.

All pleadings shall be construed so as to do substantial justice.

Oct. 29, 1940, eff. Sept. 1, 1941. Amended by orders of July 15, 1987, eff. Jan. 1, 1988; April 24, 1990, eff. Sept. 1, 1990; Sept. 4, 1990; Dec. 11, 2013, eff. Jan. 1, 2014.

Comment—1990

To provide for filing of pleadings having either original or copies of signatures and verifications including documents telephonically transferred.

See also **O'Connor's Texas Rules**, "Rules of Pleading," ch. 1-B, §1 et seq.; **O'Connor's Texas Rules**, "Rules for Filing Documents," ch. 1-C, §1 et seq.; **O'Connor's Texas Rules**, "Plaintiff's Original Petition," ch. 2-B, §1 et seq.; **O'Connor's Texas Rules**, "Special Exceptions—Challenging the Pleadings," ch. 3-G, §1 et seq.; **O'Connor's Texas Rules**, "Default Judgment," ch. 7-A, §1 et seq.

ANNOTATIONS

Paramount Pipe & Sup. Co. v. Muhr, 749 S.W.2d 491, 494-95 (Tex.1988). "The purpose of the fair notice requirement is to provide the opposing party with sufficient information to enable him to prepare a defense. [¶] Rule 45 does not require that the plaintiff set out in his pleadings the evidence upon which he relies to establish his asserted cause of action." *See also* **Perez v. Briercroft Serv.**, 809 S.W.2d 216, 218 (Tex.1991); **Roark v. Allen**, 633 S.W.2d 804, 810 (Tex.1982).

Coffey v. Johnson, 142 S.W.3d 414, 417 (Tex.App.—Eastland 2004, no pet.). TRCP 45 "requires that a petition give fair notice of the plaintiff's claims. The test of fair notice is whether an opposing attorney of reasonable competence, with the pleadings before him, can determine the nature of the controversy and the testimony that would probably be relevant. A court must be able, from an examination of the plaintiff's pleadings alone, to ascertain with reasonable certainty the elements of a cause of action and the relief sought with sufficient particularity. . . ." *See also* **Taylor v. Taylor**, 337 S.W.3d 398, 401 (Tex.App.—Fort Worth 2011, no pet.).

TRCP 46. PETITION AND ANSWER; EACH ONE INSTRUMENT OF WRITING

The original petition, first supplemental petition, second supplemental petition, and every other, shall each be contained in one instrument of writing, and so with the original answer and each of the supplemental answers.

Oct. 29, 1940, eff. Sept. 1, 1941.

TRCP 47. CLAIMS FOR RELIEF

An original pleading which sets forth a claim for relief, whether an original petition, counterclaim, cross-claim, or third party claim, shall contain:

(a) a short statement of the cause of action sufficient to give fair notice of the claim involved;

(b) a statement that the damages sought are within the jurisdictional limits of the court;

Text of subsec. (c) effective for cases filed before January 1, 2021.

(c) except in suits governed by the Family Code, a statement that the party seeks:

(1) only monetary relief of $100,000 or less, including damages of any kind, penalties, costs, expenses, pre-judgment interest, and attorney fees; or

(2) monetary relief of $100,000 or less and non-monetary relief; or

(3) monetary relief over $100,000 but not more than $250,000; or

(4) monetary relief over $250,000 but not more than $1,000,000; or

(5) monetary relief over $1,000,000; and

Text of subsec. (c) effective for cases filed on or after January 1, 2021.

(c) except in suits governed by the Family Code, a statement that the party seeks:

(1) only monetary relief of $250,000 or less, excluding interest, statutory or punitive damages and penalties, and attorney fees and costs;

(2) monetary relief of $250,000 or less and non-monetary relief;

(3) monetary relief over $250,000 but not more than $1,000,000;

(4) monetary relief over $1,000,000; or

(5) only non-monetary relief; and

(d) a demand for judgment for all the other relief to which the party deems himself entitled.

Relief in the alternative or of several different types may be demanded; provided, further, that upon special exception the court shall require the pleader to amend so as to specify the maximum amount claimed. A party that fails to comply with (c) may not conduct discovery until the party's pleading is amended to comply.

Oct. 29, 1940, eff. Sept. 1, 1941. Amended by order of July 11, 1977, eff. Jan. 1, 1978; April 24, 1990, eff. Sept. 1, 1990; Feb. 12, 2013, eff. March 1, 2013; May 26, 2020, eff. Sept. 1, 2020; Dec. 23, 2020, eff. Jan. 1, 2021.

Comment—2021

Rule 47 is amended to implement section 22.004(h-1) of the Texas Government Code. A suit in which the original petition contains the statement in paragraph (c)(1) is governed by the expedited actions process in Rule 169.

Comment—2013

Rule 47 is amended to require a more specific statement of the relief sought by a party. The amendment requires parties to plead into or out of the expedited actions process governed by Rule 169, added to implement section 22.004(h) of the Texas Government Code. Except in a suit governed by the Family Code, the Property Code, the Tax Code, or Chapter 74 of the Civil Practice & Remedies Code, a suit in which the original petition contains the statement in paragraph (c)(1) is governed by the expedited actions process. The further specificity in paragraphs (c)(2)–(5) is to provide information regarding the nature of cases filed and does not affect a party's substantive rights.

Source: FRCP 8(a).

See also **O'Connor's Texas Rules**, "Rules of Pleading," ch. 1-B, §1 et seq.; **O'Connor's Texas Rules**, "Plaintiff's Original Petition," ch. 2-B, §1 et seq.; **O'Connor's Texas Rules**, "Special Exceptions—Challenging the Pleadings," ch. 3-G, §1 et seq.; **O'Connor's Texas Rules**, "Default Judgment," ch. 7-A, §1 et seq.; **O'Connor's Texas Forms**, FORMS 2B:1, 2B:2, 2B:3, 2B:4, 2B:5, 2B:6, 2B:7, 2B:8.

ANNOTATIONS

DeRoeck v. DHM Ventures, LLC, 556 S.W.3d 831, 833 (Tex.2018). "The court of appeals held that a cause of action for acknowledgment of a debt must be 'specifically and clearly' pleaded in 'plain and emphatic terms.' Because this holding conflicts with Rule 47(a)[,] we reverse and remand. . . . *At 835:* 'A petition is sufficient if it gives fair and adequate notice of the facts upon which the pleader bases his claim.' The key inquiry is whether the opposing party 'can ascertain from the pleading the nature and basic issue of the controversy and what testimony will be relevant.' *At 836:* [P's] amended petition was fair notice to [Ds] of its claim on their acknowledgement and thus satisfied Rule 47. The court of appeals erred in requiring a higher standard."

Boyles v. Kerr, 855 S.W.2d 593, 601 (Tex.1993). "A court should uphold the petition as to a cause of action that may be reasonably inferred from what is specifically stated, even if an element of the cause of action is not specifically alleged." *See also* **Lone Star Air Sys. v. Powers**, 401 S.W.3d 855, 861 (Tex.App.—Houston [14th Dist.] 2013, no pet.); **In re P.D.D.**, 256 S.W.3d 834, 839 (Tex.App.—Texarkana 2008, no pet.).

TRCP 48. ALTERNATIVE CLAIMS FOR RELIEF

A party may set forth two or more statements of a claim or defense alternatively or hypothetically, either in one count or defense or in separate counts or defenses. When two or more statements are made in the alternative and one of them if made independently would be sufficient, the pleading is not made insufficient by the insufficiency of one or more of the alternative statements. A party may also state as many separate claims or defenses as he has regardless of consistency and whether based upon legal or equitable grounds or both.

Oct. 29, 1940, eff. Sept. 1, 1941.

See **O'Connor's Texas Rules**, "Alternative claims or defenses," ch. 1-B, §3.2.9.

ANNOTATIONS

Birchfield v. Texarkana Mem'l Hosp., 747 S.W.2d 361, 367 (Tex.1987). "[W]here the prevailing party fails to elect between alternative measures of damages, the court should utilize the findings affording the greater recovery and render judgment accordingly."

Horizon Offshore Contractors, Inc. v. Aon Risk Servs., 283 S.W.3d 53, 59-60 (Tex.App.—Houston [14th Dist.] 2009, pet. denied). "[A] party may assert inconsistent facts or remedies simultaneously against different defendants, settle with one defendant, and still recover judgment against the other defendant even though the facts or remedies alleged against the second defendant are inconsistent with the facts or remedies alleged against the settling defendant. However, if a party successfully pursues one remedy against one defendant based on one set of alleged facts and then files a subsequent action against another defendant, the election of remedies will bar the second suit if the alleged facts or remedies in that suit are sufficiently inconsistent with the alleged facts or remedy sought in the first suit."

Household Credit Servs. v. Driscol, 989 S.W.2d 72, 80 (Tex.App.—El Paso 1998, pet. denied). "If a plaintiff pleads alternate theories of liability under Rule 48, a judgment that awards damages based upon more than one theory does not amount to a double recovery if the theories of liability arise from two separate and distinct injuries, and there has been a separate and distinct finding of damages on both theories of liability."

TRCP 49. WHERE SEVERAL COUNTS

Where there are several counts in the petition, and entire damages are given, the verdict or judgment, as the case may be, shall be good, notwithstanding one or more of such counts may be defective.

Oct. 29, 1940, eff. Sept. 1, 1941.

TRCP 50. PARAGRAPHS, SEPARATE STATEMENTS

All averments of claim or defense shall be made in numbered paragraphs, the contents of each of which shall be limited as far as practicable to a statement of a single set of circumstances; and a paragraph may be referred to by number in all succeeding pleadings, so long as the pleading containing such paragraph has not been superseded by an amendment as provided by Rule 65. Each claim founded upon a separate transaction or occurrence and each defense other than denials shall be stated in a separate count or defense whenever a separation facilitates the clear presentation of the matters set forth.

Oct. 29, 1940, eff. Sept. 1, 1941.

See also **O'Connor's Texas Rules**, "Rules of Pleading," ch. 1-B, §1 et seq.; **O'Connor's Texas Rules**, "Plaintiff's Original Petition," ch. 2-B, §1 et seq.

TRCP 51. JOINDER OF CLAIMS AND REMEDIES

(a) Joinder of Claims. The plaintiff in his petition or in a reply setting forth a counterclaim and the defendant in an answer setting forth a counterclaim may join either as independent or as alternate claims as many claims either legal or equitable or both as he may have against an opposing party. There may be a like joinder of claims when there are multiple parties if the requirements of Rules 39, 40, and 43 are satisfied. There may be a like joinder of cross claims or third-party claims if the requirements of Rules 38 and 97, respectively, are satisfied.

(b) Joinder of Remedies. Whenever a claim is one heretofore cognizable only after another claim has been prosecuted to a conclusion, the two claims may be joined in a single action; but the court shall grant relief in that action only in accordance with the relative substantive rights of the parties. This rule shall not be applied in tort cases so as to permit the joinder of a liability or indemnity insurance company, unless such company is by statute or contract directly liable to the person injured or damaged.

Oct. 29, 1940, eff. Sept. 1, 1941. Amended by orders of Sept. 20, 1941, eff. Dec. 31, 1941; July 26, 1960, eff. Jan. 1, 1961.

See also TRCP 39 to 41, 174; **O'Connor's Texas Family Law Handbook**, "Filing SAPCR with dissolution suit," ch. 4-A, §3.3.

TRCP 52. ALLEGING A CORPORATION

An allegation that a corporation is incorporated shall be taken as true, unless denied by the affidavit of the adverse party, his agent or attorney, whether such corporation is a public or private corporation and however created.

Oct. 29, 1940, eff. Sept. 1, 1941.

See also TRCP 93(6); **O'Connor's Texas Rules**, "The Answer—Denying Liability," ch. 3-E, §1 et seq.; **O'Connor's Texas Rules**, "Motion to Abate—Challenging the Suit," ch. 3-I, §1 et seq.

TRCP 53. SPECIAL ACT OR LAW

A pleading founded wholly or in part on any private or special act or law of this State or of the Republic of Texas need only recite the title thereof, the date of its approval, and set out in substance so much of such act or laws as may be pertinent to the cause of action or defense.

Oct. 29, 1940, eff. Sept. 1, 1941.

TRCP 54. CONDITIONS PRECEDENT

In pleading the performance or occurrence of conditions precedent, it shall be sufficient to aver generally that all conditions precedent have been performed or have occurred. When such performances or occurrences have been so plead, the party so pleading same shall be required to prove only such of them as are specifically denied by the opposite party.

Oct. 29, 1940, eff. Sept. 1, 1941. Amended by order of March 31, 1941, eff. Sept. 1, 1941.

See also **O'Connor's Texas Rules**, "Conditions precedent," ch. 2-B, §12; **O'Connor's Texas Rules**, "Denial of conditions precedent," ch. 3-E, §6.1; **O'Connor's Texas Forms**, FORMS 2B:1, 2B:2, 2B:3, 2B:4, 2B:5, 2B:6, 2B:7, 2B:8, 3E:1, 3E:2, 3E:3, 3E:4, 3E:5, 3E:6, 3E:7, 3E:8, 3E:9, 3E:10, 3E:11.

ANNOTATIONS

Associated Indem. Corp. v. CAT Contracting, Inc., 964 S.W.2d 276, 283 n.6 (Tex.1998). "Where a party avers generally that all conditions precedent have been performed or have occurred, he or she need only prove those that are specifically denied by the opposite party. This pleading rule, however, does not shift the burden of proof on those conditions which the opposite party denies." *See also* **Greathouse v. Charter Nat'l Bank-Sw.**, 851 S.W.2d 173, 177 (Tex.1992).

TRCP 55. JUDGMENT

In pleading a judgment or decision of a domestic or foreign court, judicial or quasi-judicial tribunal, or of a board or officer, it shall be sufficient to aver the judgment or decision without setting forth matter showing jurisdiction to render it.

Oct. 29, 1940, eff. Sept. 1, 1941.

See also CPRC ch. 36A.

TRCP 56. SPECIAL DAMAGE

When items of special damage are claimed, they shall be specifically stated.

Oct. 29, 1940, eff. Sept. 1, 1941.

See also **O'Connor's Texas Rules**, "Special damages," ch. 2-B, §9.2.1(2).

ANNOTATIONS

Arthur Andersen & Co. v. Perry Equip. Corp., 945 S.W.2d 812, 816 (Tex.1997). Special damages are also known as consequential damages. "Consequential damages . . . result naturally, but not necessarily, from the defendant's wrongful acts." *See also* **Archer v. DDK Holdings LLC**, 463 S.W.3d 597, 608-09 (Tex.App.—Houston [14th Dist.] 2015, no pet.).

TRCP 57. SIGNING OF PLEADINGS

Every pleading of a party represented by an attorney shall be signed by at least one attorney of record in his individual name, with his State Bar of Texas identification

number, address, telephone number, email address, and if available, fax number. A party not represented by an attorney shall sign his pleadings, state his address, telephone number, email address, and, if available, fax number.

Oct. 29, 1940, eff. Sept. 1, 1941. Amended by orders of June 10, 1980, eff. Jan. 1, 1981; April 24, 1990, eff. Sept. 1, 1990; Dec. 11, 2013, eff. Jan. 1, 2014.

Comment—1990

To supply attorney telecopier information with other identifying information on pleadings. Documents telephonically transferred are permitted to be filed under changes in Rule 45.

See also **O'Connor's Texas Rules**, "Rules of Pleading," ch. 1-B, §1 et seq.; **O'Connor's Texas Rules**, "Plaintiff's Original Petition," ch. 2-B, §1 et seq.; **O'Connor's Texas Forms**, FORM 1B:3.

ANNOTATIONS

W.C. Turnbow Pet. Co. v. Fulton, 194 S.W.2d 256, 257 (Tex.1946). "Counsel should sign their names to motions and pleadings 'to make themselves responsible for what is stated in them, and so as to leave no doubt as to the parties for whom they appear.' But . . . the signature to a pleading is a formal requisite and . . . failure to comply with the requirement is not fatal to the pleading."

TRCP 58. ADOPTION BY REFERENCE

Statements in a pleading may be adopted by reference in a different part of the same pleading or in another pleading or in any motion, so long as the pleading containing such statements has not been superseded by an amendment as provided by Rule 65.

Oct. 29, 1940, eff. Sept. 1, 1941.

See also **O'Connor's Texas Rules**, "Rules of Pleading," ch. 1-B, §1 et seq.

ANNOTATIONS

Fawcett v. Grosu, 498 S.W.3d 650, 659 (Tex.App.—Houston [14th Dist.] 2016, pet. denied). "[P] filed a second amended petition; hence, his original petition and exhibits A-E attached thereto[ ] were superseded. In his second amended petition, however, [P] incorporates by reference exhibits A-E of his original petition. This was improper under [TRCP] 58. . . . [Ds], however, did not file special exceptions, as is required by [TRCP] 90, to [P's] pleading defect. While we agree that the incorporation by reference was improper, we cannot agree that it precluded consideration of exhibits attached to the original petition and incorporated without objection into the second petition. [Ds'] failure to specifically except to [P's] pleading defects in writing waived such defect. We therefore consider the exhibits as part of our analysis."

TRCP 59. EXHIBITS AND PLEADING

Notes, accounts, bonds, mortgages, records, and all other written instruments, constituting, in whole or in part, the claim sued on, or the matter set up in defense, may be made a part of the pleadings by copies thereof, or the originals, being attached or filed and referred to as such, or by copying the same in the body of the pleading in aid and explanation of the allegations in the petition or answer made in reference to said instruments and shall be deemed a part thereof for all purposes. Such pleadings shall not be deemed defective because of the lack of any allegations which can be supplied from said exhibit. No other instrument of writing shall be made an exhibit in the pleading.

Oct. 29, 1940, eff. Sept. 1, 1941.

Source: Tex. Rules for Dist. & Cty. Cts. 19.

ANNOTATIONS

City of Abilene v. Carter, 530 S.W.3d 268, 276-77 (Tex.App.—Eastland 2017, no pet.). "[D] contends that documents attached to pleadings must be formally incorporated by reference in order for them to be considered as part of the pleadings under Rule 59. However, [D] has not cited any authority that Rule 59 requires specific language formally incorporating attached documents as a part of the pleadings. To the contrary, courts have held that the attachment of documents to pleadings and a simple reference to them in the pleadings makes them a part of the pleadings for all purposes under Rule 59."

TRCP 60. INTERVENOR'S PLEADINGS

Any party may intervene by filing a pleading, subject to being stricken out by the court for sufficient cause on the motion of any party.

Oct. 29, 1940, eff. Sept. 1, 1941. Amended by order of April 24, 1990, eff. Sept. 1, 1990.

Comment—1990

Rules 21 and 21a control notice and service of pleadings of intervenors.

Source: TRCS art. 1998 (repealed).

See also **O'Connor's Texas Rules**, "Joining Parties or Claims," ch. 5-J, §1 et seq.; **O'Connor's Texas Forms**, FORMS 5J:1, 5J:2, 5J:3.

ANNOTATIONS

In re Union Carbide Corp., 273 S.W.3d 152, 154-55 (Tex.2008). "Because intervention is allowed as a matter of right, the 'justiciable interest' requirement is of paramount importance: it defines the category of non-parties who may, without consultation with or permission from the original parties or the court, interject their interests into a pending suit to which the intervenors have not been invited. . . . If

any party to the pending suit moves to strike the intervention, the intervenors have the burden to show a justiciable interest in the pending suit. [¶] To constitute a justiciable interest, '[t]he intervenor's interest must be such that if the original action had never been commenced, and he had first brought it as the sole plaintiff, he would have been entitled to recover in his own name to the extent at least of a part of the relief sought' in the original suit."

Texas Mut. Ins. v. Ledbetter, 251 S.W.3d 31, 36 (Tex.2008). "There is no deadline for intervention in the [TRCPs]. Generally one cannot intervene after final judgment. But when a subrogee's interest has been adequately represented and then suddenly abandoned by someone else, it can intervene even after judgment or on appeal so long as there is neither unnecessary delay nor prejudice to the existing parties." *See also* **State v. Naylor**, 466 S.W.3d 783, 788 (Tex.2015) (petition in intervention filed after judgment may not be considered until judgment is set aside).

Baker v. Monsanto Co., 111 S.W.3d 158, 160 (Tex.2003). "Typically, an intervention involves a claim against persons who have already appeared. Under these circumstances, the plea in intervention is properly served by any of the methods provided in [TRCP] 21a. However, absent a subsequent appearance, service of citation is necessary against an original defendant when the intervenor seeks affirmative relief against a defendant who has not appeared at the time the intervention was filed. [¶] [I]ntervenors are required to serve citation on a defendant when that defendant fails to appear and answer the plaintiff's petition. [A]n intervenor must serve citation on any third-party defendant it seeks to bring into the suit. And if the intervenor's claim is against the plaintiff, it must serve citation on the plaintiff, if the plaintiff does not make any further appearance in the case after the intervention."

Guaranty Fed. Sav. Bank v. Horseshoe Oper. Co., 793 S.W.2d 652, 657 (Tex.1990). "An intervenor is not required to secure the court's permission to intervene; the party who opposed the intervention has the burden to challenge it by a motion to strike. [¶] [I]t is an abuse of discretion to strike a plea in intervention if (1) the intervenor [could have brought some or all of the same action in its own name, or, if the action had been brought against it, it could defeat some or all of the recovery], (2) the intervention will not complicate the case by an excessive multiplication of the issues, and (3) the intervention is almost essential to effectively protect the intervenor's interest." *See also* **Williamson v. Howard**, 554 S.W.3d 59, 66 (Tex.App.—El Paso 2018, no pet.).

Muller v. Stewart Title Guar. Co., 525 S.W.3d 859, 874 (Tex.App.—Houston [14th Dist.] 2017, no pet.). "Significant delay in filing a petition in intervention . . . may qualify as 'sufficient cause' to strike an intervention. . . . [¶] [P and intervenor argue] that because . . . intervention occurred before final judgment, the intervention was timely. However, 'untimely' with respect to a petition in intervention can refer to a petition filed so late that it would delay the proceeding or unjustifiably complicate it."

TRCP 61. TRIAL: INTERVENORS: RULES APPLY TO ALL PARTIES

These rules of pleading shall apply equally, so far as it may be practicable to intervenors and to parties, when more than one, who may plead separately.

Oct. 29, 1940, eff. Sept. 1, 1941.

TRCP 62. AMENDMENT DEFINED

The object of an amendment, as contra-distinguished from a supplemental petition or answer, is to add something to, or withdraw something from, that which has been previously pleaded so as to perfect that which is or may be deficient, or to correct that which has been incorrectly stated by the party making the amendment, or to plead new matter, additional to that formerly pleaded by the amending party, which constitutes an additional claim or defense permissible to the suit.

Oct. 29, 1940, eff. Sept. 1, 1941.

TRCP 63. AMENDMENTS AND RESPONSIVE PLEADINGS

Parties may amend their pleadings, respond to pleadings on file of other parties, file suggestions of death and make representative parties, and file such other pleas as they may desire by filing such pleas with the clerk at such time as not to operate as a surprise to the opposite party; provided, that any pleadings, responses or pleas offered for filing within seven days of the date of trial or thereafter, or after such time as may be ordered by the judge under Rule 166, shall be filed only after leave of the judge is obtained, which leave shall be granted by the judge unless there is a showing that such filing will operate as a surprise to the opposite party.

Oct. 29, 1940, eff. Sept. 1, 1941. Amended by orders of July 26, 1960, eff. Jan. 1, 1961; April 24, 1990, eff. Sept. 1, 1990.

Comment—1990

To require that all trial pleadings of all parties, except those permitted by Rule 66, be on file at least seven days before trial unless leave of court permits later filing.

See also **O'Connor's Texas Rules**, "Motion to Amend Pleadings—Pretrial," ch. 5-F, §1 et seq.; **O'Connor's Texas Rules**, "Motion to Amend Pleadings—Trial & Post-trial," ch. 8-F, §1 et seq.; **O'Connor's Texas Forms**, FORMS 5F, 8F.

ANNOTATIONS

Chapin & Chapin, Inc. v. Texas Sand & Gravel Co., 844 S.W.2d 664, 665 (Tex.1992). Under TRCP 63 and 66, " 'a trial court has no discretion to refuse an amendment unless: (1) the opposing party presents evidence of surprise or prej-

udice . . .; or (2) the amendment asserts a new cause of action or defense, and thus is prejudicial on its face. . . .' [¶] [W]e conclude that the trial court's refusal to allow [D] to verify its denial [less than seven days before trial] was an abuse of discretion." *See also* **Greenhalgh v. Service Lloyds Ins.**, 787 S.W.2d 938, 940 (Tex.1990).

Goswami v. Metropolitan S&L Ass'n, 751 S.W.2d 487, 490 (Tex.1988). "[I]n the absence of a sufficient showing of surprise by the opposing party, the failure to obtain leave of court when filing a late pleading may be cured by the trial court's action in considering the amended pleading. [¶] A summary judgment proceeding is a trial within the meaning of Rule 63." *See also* **John C. Flood of DC, Inc. v. SuperMedia, L.L.C.**, 408 S.W.3d 645, 653-54 (Tex.App.—Dallas 2013, pet. denied).

AAMCO Transmissions, Inc. v. Bova, 484 S.W.3d 520, 523 (Tex.App.—Houston [1st Dist.] 2016, no pet.). "Service of an amended petition on a party that has not appeared is necessary only when a plaintiff seeks a more onerous judgment than prayed for in the original pleading. [¶] A judgment is more onerous if it exposes the defendant to increased liability. Increases in potential liability may result, for example, from the addition of new causes of action, inclusion of new elements of damages, or an increase in the amount of damages previously pleaded." (Internal quotes omitted.)

Halmos v. Bombardier Aerospace Corp., 314 S.W.3d 606, 623 (Tex.App.—Dallas 2010, no pet.). "An amendment that is prejudicial on its face has three defining characteristics: (1) it asserts a new substantive matter that reshapes the nature of trial itself; (2) the opposing party could not have anticipated the new matter in light of the development of the case up to the time the amendment was requested; and (3) the amendment would detrimentally affect the opposing party's presentation of its case." *See also* **Thomas v. Graham Mortg. Corp.**, 408 S.W.3d 581, 593 (Tex.App.—Austin 2013, pet. denied).

TRCP 64. AMENDED INSTRUMENT

The party amending shall point out the instrument amended, as "original petition," or "plaintiff's first supplemental petition," or as "original answer," or "defendant's first supplemental answer" or other instrument filed by the party and shall amend by filing a substitute therefor, entire and complete in itself, indorsed "amended original petition," or "amended first supplemental petition," or "amended original answer," or "amended first supplemental answer," accordingly as said instruments of pleading are designated.

Oct. 29, 1940, eff. Sept. 1, 1941.

TRCP 65. SUBSTITUTED INSTRUMENT TAKES PLACE OF ORIGINAL

Unless the substituted instrument shall be set aside on exceptions, the instrument for which it is substituted shall no longer be regarded as a part of the pleading in the record of the cause, unless some error of the court in deciding upon the necessity of the amendment, or otherwise in superseding it, be complained of, and exception be taken to the action of the court, or unless it be necessary to look to the superseded pleading upon a question of limitation.

Oct. 29, 1940, eff. Sept. 1, 1941.

Source: Tex. Rules for Dist. & Cty. Cts. 14.

See also **O'Connor's Texas Rules**, "Amended pleadings," ch. 1-B, §3.6.1(1); **O'Connor's Texas Rules**, "Nonsuit by amendment," ch. 7-F, §2.8.1.

ANNOTATIONS

FKM Prtshp. v. Board of Regents, 255 S.W.3d 619, 633 (Tex.2008). "[A]mended pleadings and their contents take the place of prior pleadings. So, causes of action not contained in amended pleadings are effectively dismissed at the time the amended pleading is filed. . . ." *See also* **Deadmon v. DART**, 347 S.W.3d 442, 444 (Tex.App.—Dallas 2011, no pet.) (omitting parties' names from amended pleading dismisses them as effectively as entry of formal order of dismissal); **Kothmann v. F. Vosburg Hall & Marylou Hall Children's Crisis Found.**, No. 03-09-00081-CV, 2010 WL 2789805 (Tex.App.—Austin 2010, no pet.) (memo op.; 7-15-10) (footnote 3) (omitted claims are withdrawn even if summary judgment was already granted on those claims).

TRCP 66. TRIAL AMENDMENT

If evidence is objected to at the trial on the ground that it is not within the issues made by the pleading, or if during the trial any defect, fault or omission in a pleading, either of form or substance, is called to the attention of the court, the court may allow the pleadings to be amended and shall do so freely when the presentation of the merits of the action will be subserved thereby and the objecting party fails to satisfy the court that the allowance of such amendment would prejudice him in maintaining his action or defense upon the merits. The court may grant a postponement to enable the objecting party to meet such evidence.

Oct. 29, 1940, eff. Sept. 1, 1941. Amended by order of March 31, 1941, eff. Sept. 1, 1941.

See also **O'Connor's Texas Rules**, "Motion to Amend Pleadings—Trial & Post-trial," ch. 8-F, §1 et seq.; **O'Connor's Texas Forms**, FORMS 8F.

ANNOTATIONS

City of Fort Worth v. Zimlich, 29 S.W.3d 62, 73 (Tex.2000). "A trial amendment must be filed as a written pleading; an oral statement at trial is insufficient to modify

the pleadings. However, a party waives its complaint of any defect, omission, or fault in the pleadings if the party fails to specifically object before the submission of the charge to the jury."

State Bar v. Kilpatrick, 874 S.W.2d 656, 658 (Tex.1994). "A court may not refuse a trial amendment unless (1) the opposing party presents evidence of surprise or prejudice, or (2) the amendment asserts a new cause of action or defense, and thus is prejudicial on its face. The burden of showing surprise or prejudice rests on the party resisting the amendment." *See also* **Greenhalgh v. Service Lloyds Ins.**, 787 S.W.2d 938, 941 (Tex.1990); **Tony's Barbeque & Steakhouse, Inc. v. Three Points Invs.**, 527 S.W.3d 686, 691-92 (Tex.App.—Houston [14th Dist.] 2017, no pet.).

Zarate v. Rodriguez, 542 S.W.3d 26, 37-38 (Tex.App.—Houston [14th Dist.] 2017, pet. denied). "A trial amendment is prejudicial on its face if (1) the amendment asserts a new substantive matter that reshapes the nature of the trial itself; (2) the new matter is of such a nature that the opposing party could not have anticipated it in light of the development of the case up to the time the amendment was requested; and (3) the opposing party's presentation of its case would be detrimentally affected by the amendment. [¶] A trial court also has discretion to deny a trial amendment adding a new cause of action if the opposing party objects and 'it appears that the new matter was known to the party seeking to file the amendment, or by reasonable diligence it could have been known by the party.' Under this test, a discretionary trial amendment should not be rejected simply because it alleges a new cause of action. Instead, . . . we must examine the three factors listed above in the context of the entire case."

Deutsch v. Hoover, Bax & Slovacek, L.L.P., 97 S.W.3d 179, 185-86 (Tex.App.—Houston [14th Dist.] 2002, no pet.). TRCP 66 "suggests a postponement may cure any prejudice from a trial amendment. [N]othing in the rule [suggests] an offer of a mistrial does so, especially when the trial is virtually completed. A party seeking leave to amend its pleadings after the trial has commenced should not be rewarded by forcing the judge, jury, and opposing party to either acquiesce in the tardy amendment or start over. [T]he mistrial was the trial court's suggestion. . . . [D's] decision to refuse the trial court's offer . . . did not amount to a relinquishment of his objection [to the trial amendment]."

TRCP 67. AMENDMENTS TO CONFORM TO ISSUES TRIED WITHOUT OBJECTION

When issues not raised by the pleadings are tried by express or implied consent of the parties, they shall be treated in all respects as if they had been raised in the pleadings. In such case such amendment of the pleadings as may be necessary to cause them to conform to the evidence and to raise these issues may be made by leave of court upon motion of any party at any time up to the submission of the case to the Court or jury, but failure so to amend shall not affect the result of the trial of these issues; provided that written pleadings, before the time of submission, shall be necessary to the submission of questions, as is provided in Rules 277 and 279.

Oct. 29, 1940, eff. Sept. 1, 1941. Amended by orders of March 31, 1941, eff. Sept. 1, 1941; April 24, 1990, eff. Sept. 1, 1990.

See also **O'Connor's Texas Rules**, "TRCP 67," ch. 8-F, §2.4.2.

ANNOTATIONS

Bedgood v. Madalin, 600 S.W.2d 773, 775-76 (Tex.1980). "Rule 67 . . . requires that written pleadings, before the time of submission, shall be necessary to the submission of special issues even where issues are tried by implied consent. Since there were no proper pleadings, the trial court erred in overruling [Ds'] objections to the introduction of evidence and the submission of special issues. . . ."

Oil Field Haulers Ass'n v. Railroad Comm'n, 381 S.W.2d 183, 191 (Tex.1964). "[A] plaintiff may not sustain a favorable judgment on an unpleaded cause of action[ ] in the absence of trial by consent. . . ." *See also* **Huff Energy Fund, L.P. v. Longview Energy Co.**, 482 S.W.3d 184, 194 (Tex.App.—San Antonio 2015) (objection to submission of jury question on unpleaded issue prevents trial of that issue by implied consent), *aff'd*, 533 S.W.3d 866 (Tex.2017).

Case Corp. v. Hi-Class Bus. Sys., 184 S.W.3d 760, 771 (Tex.App.—Dallas 2005, pet. denied). "To determine whether an issue was tried by consent, the trial court examines the record not for evidence of the issue, but rather for evidence of trial of the issue. A party's unpleaded issue may be deemed tried by consent when evidence on the issue is developed under circumstances indicating both parties understood the issue was in the case, and the other party failed to make an appropriate complaint. On the other hand, trial by consent is inapplicable when evidence relevant to an unpleaded matter is also relevant to a pleaded issue; in that case admission of the evidence would not be calculated to elicit an objection . . ., and its admission ordinarily would not demonstrate a 'clear intent' on the part of all parties to try the unpleaded issue." *See also* **Bos v. Smith**, 556 S.W.3d 293, 306-07 (Tex.2018).

TRCP 68. COURT MAY ORDER REPLEADER

The court, when deemed necessary in any case, may order a repleader on the part of one or both of the parties, in order to make their pleadings substantially conform to the rules.

Oct. 29, 1940, eff. Sept. 1, 1941.

ANNOTATIONS

Miller v. Kossey, 802 S.W.2d 873, 877 (Tex.App.—Amarillo 1991, writ denied). "[W]hen [P] failed to comply

with the court's . . . order to send a new notice establishing a necessary element of her cause of action, the court was authorized to dismiss her DTPA action. Consequently, the court did not err in dismissing the action."

TRCP 69. SUPPLEMENTAL PETITION OR ANSWER

Each supplemental petition or answer, made by either party, shall be a response to the last preceding pleading by the other party, and shall not repeat allegations formerly pleaded further than is necessary as an introduction to that which is stated in the pleading then being drawn up. These instruments, to wit, the original petition and its several supplements, and the original answer and its several supplements, shall respectively, constitute separate and distinct parts of the pleadings of each party; and the position and identity, by number and name, with the indorsement of each instrument, shall be preserved throughout the pleadings of either party.

Oct. 29, 1940, eff. Sept. 1, 1941.

TRCP 70. PLEADING: SURPRISE: COST

When either a supplemental or amended pleading is of such character and is presented at such time as to take the opposite party by surprise, the court may charge the continuance of the cause, if granted, to the party causing the surprise if the other party satisfactorily shows that he is not ready for trial because of the allowance of the filing of such supplemental or amended pleading, and the court may, in such event, in its discretion require the party filing such pleading to pay to the surprised party the amount of reasonable costs and expenses incurred by the other party as a result of the continuance, including attorney fees, or make such other order with respect thereto as may be just.

Oct. 29, 1940, eff. Sept. 1, 1941. Amended by order of June 10, 1980, eff. Jan. 1, 1981.

See also **O'Connor's Texas Rules**, "Motion for Continuance," ch. 5-D, §1 et seq.; **O'Connor's Texas Rules**, "Motion to Amend Pleadings—Pretrial," ch. 5-F, §1 et seq.; **O'Connor's Texas Rules**, "Motion to Amend Pleadings—Trial & Post-trial," ch. 8-F, §1 et seq.; **O'Connor's Texas Forms**, FORMS 5F, 8F.

TRCP 71. MISNOMER OF PLEADING

When a party has mistakenly designated any plea or pleading, the court, if justice so requires, shall treat the plea or pleading as if it had been properly designated. Pleadings shall be docketed as originally designated and shall remain identified as designated, unless the court orders redesignation. Upon court order filed with the clerk, the clerk shall modify the docket and all other clerk records to reflect redesignation.

Oct. 29, 1940, eff. Sept. 1, 1941. Amended by order of July 15, 1987, eff. Jan. 1, 1988.

Source: FRCP 8(c), last sentence. See TRCP 94 for rest of FRCP 8.

See also **O'Connor's Texas Rules**, "Misnomer," ch. 2-B, §4.3.1(2)(a).

ANNOTATIONS

State Bar v. Heard, 603 S.W.2d 829, 833 (Tex.1980). "We look to the substance of a plea for relief to determine the nature of the pleading, not merely at the form of title given to it." *See also* **In re J.Z.P.**, 484 S.W.3d 924, 924-25 (Tex.2016) (party's motion was captioned as "Motion to Re-open and to Vacate Order" and not as motion under TRCP 306a; Court looked to substance of motion and treated it as extending postjudgment deadlines despite caption); **Riner v. City of Hunters Creek**, 403 S.W.3d 919, 921-22 (Tex.App.—Houston [14th Dist.] 2013, no pet.) (D specially excepted to P's petition on ground that it failed to establish subject-matter jurisdiction; court disregarded misnomer and treated challenge as plea to the jurisdiction instead of special exception).

TRCP 72. REPEALED BY ORDER OF APRIL 24, 1990, EFF. SEPT. 1, 1990

TRCP 73. REPEALED BY ORDER OF APRIL 24, 1990, EFF. SEPT. 1, 1990

TRCP 74. FILING WITH THE COURT DEFINED

The filing of pleadings, other papers and exhibits as required by these rules shall be made by filing them with the clerk of the court, except that the judge may permit the papers to be filed with him, in which event he shall note thereon the filing date and time and forthwith transmit them to the office of the clerk.

Oct. 29, 1940, eff. Sept. 1, 1941. Amended by order of July 20, 1966, eff. Jan. 1, 1967.

See also TRCP 24; **O'Connor's Texas Rules**, "Rules for Filing Documents," ch. 1-C, §1 et seq.

ANNOTATIONS

Miller Brewing Co. v. Villarreal, 829 S.W.2d 770, 771 (Tex.1992). "Under our current rules, a party who finds the courthouse closed on the last day that a document must be filed . . . may also locate the clerk or judge of the court and file the document with them."

Standard Fire Ins. v. LaCoke, 585 S.W.2d 678, 680 (Tex.1979). "The rule is traditionally stated to be that an instrument is deemed in law filed at the time it is left with the clerk, regardless of whether or not a file mark is placed on the instrument and regardless of whether the file mark gives some other date of filing." *See also* **Pipkin v. Kroger Tex., L.P.**, 383 S.W.3d 655, 663-64 (Tex.App.—Houston [14th Dist.] 2012, pet. denied) (despite court order making

e-filing mandatory, hard copy of affidavit was filed when left with clerk because court cannot contradict Texas law on when document is deemed filed).

TRCP 75. FILED PLEADINGS; WITHDRAWAL

All filed pleadings shall remain at all times in the clerk's office or in the court or in custody of the clerk, except that the court may by order entered on the minutes allow a filed pleading to be withdrawn for a limited time whenever necessary, on leaving a certified copy on file. The party withdrawing such pleading shall pay the costs of such order and certified copy.

Oct. 29, 1940, eff. Sept. 1, 1941.

ANNOTATIONS

Trinity Indus. v. Rivera, 745 S.W.2d 525, 526 (Tex.App.—Corpus Christi 1988, no writ). A party cannot terminate a suit by withdrawing its pleadings. "Under [the TRCPs], a final order terminating a lawsuit may be accomplished by a judgment on the merits, a dismissal or a non-suit."

TRCP 75a. FILING EXHIBITS: COURT REPORTER TO FILE WITH CLERK

The court reporter or stenographer shall file with the clerk of the court all exhibits which were admitted in evidence or tendered on bill of exception during the course of any hearing, proceeding, or trial.

July 20, 1966, eff. Jan. 1, 1967.

See also TRAP 13.1(b), (c).

TRCP 75b. FILED EXHIBITS: WITHDRAWAL

All filed exhibits admitted in evidence or tendered on bill of exception shall, until returned or otherwise disposed of as authorized by Rule 14b, remain at all times in the clerk's office or in the court or in the custody of the clerk except as follows:

(a) The court may by order entered on the minutes allow a filed exhibit to be withdrawn by any party only upon such party's leaving on file a certified, photo, or other reproduced copy of such exhibit. The party withdrawing such exhibit shall pay the costs of such order and copy.

(b) The court reporter or stenographer of the court conducting the hearing, proceedings, or trial in which exhibits are admitted or offered in evidence, shall have the right to withdraw filed exhibits, upon giving the clerk proper receipt therefor, whenever necessary for the court reporter or stenographer to transmit such original exhibits to an appellate court under the provisions of Rule 379 or to otherwise discharge the duties imposed by law upon said court reporter or stenographer.

July 20, 1966, eff. Jan. 1, 1967.

ANNOTATIONS

Perez v. Bagous, 833 S.W.2d 671, 674 (Tex.App.—Corpus Christi 1992, no writ). "Once a party has admitted an exhibit into evidence at trial, the exhibit may not be retrieved and used to create another during a jury recess without notifying opposing counsel or the court. It is wholly outside the scope of the rule to then enter this newly created exhibit into evidence without informing opposing counsel of the use of the entered exhibit."

TRCP 76. MAY INSPECT PAPERS

Each attorney at law practicing in any court shall be allowed at all reasonable times to inspect the papers and records relating to any suit or other matter in which he may be interested.

Oct. 29, 1940, eff. Sept. 1, 1941.

ANNOTATIONS

U.S. Gov't v. Marks, 949 S.W.2d 320, 326 (Tex.1997). P argues that sealing the transcript of the ex parte hearing between the judge and federal prosecutor violated TRCP 76. "This general rule is not absolute. Although not stated in the rule, there are exceptions, such as documents submitted *in camera* under a claim of privilege, documents subject to a protective order, or materials sealed under [TRCP] 76a. Rule 76 does not give [P] an absolute right to the transcript of the *in camera* hearing. *At 327:* However, the district court's order was overly broad in sealing the entire record rather than those portions that pertained to the grand jury proceeding."

Davenport v. Garcia, 834 S.W.2d 4, 24 (Tex.1992). Access to court records "is separately guaranteed to '[e]ach attorney at law practicing in any court . . . at all reasonable times to inspect.' . . . A court may not escape the strict obligations of [TRCP 76 and 76a] by tacitly closing the record through an unwritten order."

TRCP 76a. SEALING COURT RECORDS

1. Standard for Sealing Court Records. Court records may not be removed from court files except as permitted by statute or rule. No court order or opinion issued in the adjudication of a case may be sealed. Other court records, as defined in this rule, are presumed to be open to the general public and may be sealed only upon a showing of all of the following:

(a) a specific, serious and substantial interest which clearly outweighs:

(1) this presumption of openness;

(2) any probable adverse effect that sealing will have upon the general public health or safety;

(b) no less restrictive means than sealing records will adequately and effectively protect the specific interest asserted.

2. Court Records. For purposes of this rule, court records means:

(a) all documents of any nature filed in connection with any matter before any civil court, except:

(1) documents filed with a court in camera, solely for the purpose of obtaining a ruling on the discoverability of such documents;

(2) documents in court files to which access is otherwise restricted by law;

(3) documents filed in an action originally arising under the Family Code.

(b) settlement agreements not filed of record, excluding all reference to any monetary consideration, that seek to restrict disclosure of information concerning matters that have a probable adverse effect upon the general public health or safety, or the administration of public office, or the operation of government.

(c) discovery, not filed of record, concerning matters that have a probable adverse effect upon the general public health or safety, or the administration of public office, or the operation of government, except discovery in cases originally initiated to preserve bona fide trade secrets or other intangible property rights.

3. Notice. Court records may be sealed only upon a party's written motion, which shall be open to public inspection. The movant shall post a public notice at the place where notices for meetings of county governmental bodies are required to be posted, stating: that a hearing will be held in open court on a motion to seal court records in the specific case; that any person may intervene and be heard concerning the sealing of court records; the specific time and place of the hearing; the style and number of the case; a brief but specific description of both the nature of the case and the records which are sought to be sealed; and the identity of the movant. Immediately after posting such notice, the movant shall file a verified copy of the posted notice with the clerk of the court in which the case is pending and with the Clerk of the Supreme Court of Texas.

4. Hearing. A hearing, open to the public, on a motion to seal court records shall be held in open court as soon as practicable, but not less than fourteen days after the motion is filed and notice is posted. Any party may participate in the hearing. Non-parties may intervene as a matter of right for the limited purpose of participating in the proceedings, upon payment of the fee required for filing a plea in intervention. The court may inspect records in camera when necessary. The court may determine a motion relating to sealing or unsealing court records in accordance with the procedures prescribed by Rule 120a.

5. Temporary Sealing Order. A temporary sealing order may issue upon motion and notice to any parties who have answered in the case pursuant to Rules 21 and 21a upon a showing of compelling need from specific facts shown by affidavit or by verified petition that immediate and irreparable injury will result to a specific interest of the applicant before notice can be posted and a hearing held as otherwise provided herein. The temporary order shall set the time for the hearing required by paragraph 4 and shall direct that the movant immediately give the public notice required by paragraph 3. The court may modify or withdraw any temporary order upon motion by any party or intervenor, notice to the parties, and hearing conducted as soon as practicable. Issuance of a temporary order shall not reduce in any way the burden of proof of a party requesting sealing at the hearing required by paragraph 4.

6. Order on Motion to Seal Court Records. A motion relating to sealing or unsealing court records shall be decided by written order, open to the public, which shall state: the style and number of the case; the specific reasons for finding and concluding whether the showing required by paragraph 1, has been made; the specific portions of court records which are to be sealed; and the time period for which the sealed portions of the court records are to be sealed. The order shall not be included in any judgment or other order but shall be a separate document in the case; however, the failure to comply with this requirement shall not affect its appealability.

7. Continuing Jurisdiction. Any person may intervene as a matter of right at any time before or after judgment to seal or unseal court records. A court that issues a sealing order retains continuing jurisdiction to enforce, alter, or vacate that order. An order sealing or unsealing court records shall not be reconsidered on motion of any party or intervenor who had actual notice of the hearing preceding issuance of the order, without first showing changed circumstances materially affecting the order. Such circumstances need not be related to the case in which the order was issued. However, the burden of making the showing required by paragraph 1, shall always be on the party seeking to seal records.

8. Appeal. Any order (or portion of an order or judgment) relating to sealing or unsealing court records shall

be deemed to be severed from the case and a final judgment which may be appealed by any party or intervenor who participated in the hearing preceding issuance of such order. The appellate court may abate the appeal and order the trial court to direct that further public notice be given, or to hold further hearings, or to make additional findings.

9. Application. Access to documents in court files not defined as court records by this rule remains governed by existing law. This rule does not apply to any court records sealed in an action in which a final judgment has been entered before its effective date. This rule applies to cases already pending on its effective date only with regard to:

(a) all court records filed or exchanged after the effective date;

(b) any motion to alter or vacate an order restricting access to court records, issued before the effective date.

April 24, 1990, eff. Sept. 1, 1990.

Comment—1990

New rule to establish guidelines for sealing certain court records in compliance with Government Code §22.010.

Source: New rule.

See also CPRC §134A.002(6) (definition of "trade secret"); **O'Connor's Texas Rules**, "Motion to Seal Court Records," ch. 5-L, §1 et seq.; **O'Connor's Texas Rules**, "Scope of Discovery," ch. 6-B, §1 et seq.; **O'Connor's Texas Forms**, FORMS 5L:1, 5L:2, 5L:3, 5L:4, 5L:5, 5L:6, 5L:7, 5L:8.

ANNOTATIONS

In re M-I L.L.C., 505 S.W.3d 569, 579 (Tex.2016). Third-party D "asserts that exclusion of its designated representative [from the temporary-injunction hearing] would be inconsistent with [TRCP] 76a. By its express terms, however, Rule 76a only governs the sealing of 'court records.' It does not implicate oral testimony. . . ."

In re Continental Gen. Tire, Inc., 979 S.W.2d 609, 614 (Tex.1998). "[E]ven if a trade secret produced under a protective order is later determined to be a court record, this does not necessarily mean that the information must be made public. Rule 76a allows the information to remain sealed upon a showing that it meets the criteria specified in Rule 76a(1). That a document contains trade secret information is a factor to be considered in applying this sealing standard."

General Tire, Inc. v. Kepple, 970 S.W.2d 520, 525 (Tex.1998). "[W]e hold that when a party seeks a protective order under [TRCP] 166b(5)(c) [now TRCP 192.6] to restrict the dissemination of *unfiled* discovery, and no party or intervenor contends that the discovery is a 'court record,' a trial court need not conduct a hearing or render any findings on that issue. If a party or intervenor opposing a protective order claims that the discovery is a 'court record,' the court must make a threshold determination on that issue. However, public notice and a [TRCP] 76a hearing are mandated only if the court finds that the documents are court records."

In re Coastal Bend Coll., 276 S.W.3d 83, 86 (Tex.App.—San Antonio 2008, no pet.). " 'It is the burden of the party claiming the documents are open to the public to prove by a preponderance of the evidence that the documents are court records as defined by Rule 76a'. . . . *At 87:* [A] party must be allowed to tender a document in camera when necessary without converting the document to a 'court record.' 'Were it otherwise, trial courts could not review the documents themselves in determining how to apply Rule 76a without requiring [the party] to relinquish the very relief sought under the rule.' [¶] [In addition, inclusion of the words 'court records' in the title of the] pleading, absent a clear, deliberate and unequivocal statement within the pleading itself that the documents were 'court records' as defined by Rule 76a(2), is not a judicial admission."

Compaq Computer Corp. v. Lapray, 75 S.W.3d 669, 673 (Tex.App.—Beaumont 2002, no pet.). "Rule 76a contains no requirement that the trial court determine the discoverability of **court records** prior to determining whether to seal or unseal those records. Only under the 76a(2)(a)(1) exception—for documents filed in camera 'solely for the purpose of obtaining a ruling on the discoverability of such documents'—must the issue of discoverability be decided before the documents may become court records."

TRCP 77. LOST RECORDS AND PAPERS

When any papers or records are lost or destroyed during the pendency of a suit, the parties may, with the approval of the judge, agree in writing on a brief statement of the matters contained therein; or either party may supply such lost records or papers as follows:

a. After three days' notice to the adverse party or his attorney, make written sworn motion before the court stating the loss or destruction of such record or papers, accompanied by certified copies of the originals if obtainable, or by substantial copies thereof.

b. If, upon hearing, the court be satisfied that they are substantial copies of the original, an order shall be made substituting such copies or brief statement for the originals.

c. Such substituted copies or brief statement shall be filed with the clerk, constitute a part of the cause, and have the force and effect of the originals.

Oct. 29, 1940, eff. Sept. 1, 1941. Amended by order of June 16, 1943, eff. Dec. 31, 1943.

See also TRAP 34.5(e), 34.6(f); TRE 1003, 1004; **O'Connor's Texas Rules**, "Lost pleadings," ch. 1-C, §10.4.

ANNOTATIONS

Coke v. Coke, 802 S.W.2d 270, 275 (Tex.App.—Dallas 1990, writ denied). The court overruled the party's objection to the trial court's reconstruction of the lost file from the adverse party's documents. The party "testified that as far as he could tell, the copies were true duplicates of the originals."

B. Pleadings of Plaintiff

TRCP 78. PETITION; ORIGINAL AND SUPPLEMENTAL; INDORSEMENT

The pleading of plaintiff shall consist of an original petition, and such supplemental petitions as may be necessary in the course of pleading by the parties to the suit. The original petition and the supplemental petitions shall be indorsed, so as to show their respective positions in the process of pleading, as "original petition," "plaintiff's first supplemental petition," "plaintiff's second supplemental petition," and so on, to be successively numbered, named, and indorsed.

Oct. 29, 1940, eff. Sept. 1, 1941.

TRCP 78a. REPEALED BY ORDER OF DEC. 11, 2018, EFF. DEC. 11, 2018

TRCP 79. THE PETITION

The petition shall state the names of the parties and their residences, if known, together with the contents prescribed in Rule 47 above.

Oct. 29, 1940, eff. Sept. 1, 1941.

Source: New rule.

See also **O'Connor's Texas Rules**, "Plaintiff's Original Petition," ch. 2-B, §1 et seq.; **O'Connor's Texas Forms**, FORMS 2B.

ANNOTATIONS

Enserch Corp. v. Parker, 794 S.W.2d 2, 4-5 (Tex.1990). "If the plaintiff merely misnames the correct defendant (misnomer), limitations is tolled and a subsequent amendment . . . relates back to the date of the original petition. If, however, the plaintiff is mistaken as to which of two defendants is the correct one and there is . . . a corporation with the name of the erroneously named defendant (misidentification), then the plaintiff has sued the wrong party and limitations is not tolled."

TRCP 80. PLAINTIFF'S SUPPLEMENTAL PETITION

The plaintiff's supplemental petitions may contain special exceptions, general denials, and the allegations of new matter not before alleged by him, in reply to those which have been alleged by the defendant.

Oct. 29, 1940, eff. Sept. 1, 1941.

ANNOTATIONS

Moody-Rambin Interests v. Moore, 722 S.W.2d 790, 792 (Tex.App.—Houston [14th Dist.] 1987, no writ). " 'The proper way to bring new parties into a suit is by an amended pleading, and not by a supplemental pleading.' An exception to this rule exists if the necessity for adding a new party arises from facts pled in the defendant's answer."

TRCP 81. DEFENSIVE MATTERS

When the defendant sets up a counter claim, the plaintiff may plead thereto under rules prescribed for pleadings of defensive matter by the defendant, so far as applicable. Whenever the defendant is required to plead any matter of defense under oath, the plaintiff shall be required to plead such matters under oath when relied on by him.

Oct. 29, 1940, eff. Sept. 1, 1941.

ANNOTATIONS

Greater Fort Worth & Tarrant Cty. Cmty. Action Agency v. Mims, 627 S.W.2d 149, 152 (Tex.1982). "If the plaintiff contesting the counterclaim does not intend to urge any defensive theory which must be verified or any affirmative defense under [TRCP] 94, he is not required to answer the defendant's counterclaim."

TRCP 82. SPECIAL DEFENSES

The plaintiff need not deny any special matter of defense pleaded by the defendant, but the same shall be regarded as denied unless expressly admitted.

Oct. 29, 1940, eff. Sept. 1, 1941.

C. Pleadings of Defendant

TRCP 83. ANSWER; ORIGINAL AND SUPPLEMENTAL; INDORSEMENT

The answer of defendant shall consist of an original answer, and such supplemental answers as may be necessary, in the course of pleading by the parties to the suit. The original answer and the supplemental answers shall be indorsed, so as to show their respective positions in the process of pleading, as "original answer," "defendant's first supplemental answer," "defendant's second supplemental answer," and so on, to be successively numbered, named and indorsed.

Oct. 29, 1940, eff. Sept. 1, 1941.

Source: Tex. Rules for Dist. & Cty. Cts. 6.

See also **O'Connor's Texas Rules**, "Defendant's Pleadings," ch. 3-A, §1 et seq.

ANNOTATIONS

Smith v. Lippmann, 826 S.W.2d 137, 138 (Tex.1992). "[A] defendant, who timely files a pro se answer by a signed letter that identifies the parties, the case, and the defendant's current address, has sufficiently appeared by answer and deserves notice of any subsequent proceedings in the case."

TRCP 84. ANSWER MAY INCLUDE SEVERAL MATTERS

The defendant in his answer may plead as many several matters, whether of law or fact, as he may think necessary for his defense, and which may be pertinent to the cause, and such matters shall be heard in such order as may be directed by the court, special appearance and motion to transfer venue, and the practice thereunder being excepted herefrom.

Oct. 29, 1940, eff. Sept. 1, 1941. Amended by orders of Oct. 12, 1949, eff. March 1, 1950; April 12, 1962, eff. Sept. 1, 1962; June 15, 1983, eff. Sept. 1, 1983.

See also **O'Connor's Texas Rules**, "Defendant's Pleadings," ch. 3-A, §1 et seq.

TRCP 85. ORIGINAL ANSWER; CONTENTS

The original answer may consist of motions to transfer venue, pleas to the jurisdiction, in abatement, or any other dilatory pleas; of special exceptions, of general denial, and any defense by way of avoidance or estoppel, and it may present a cross-action, which to that extent will place defendant in the attitude of a plaintiff. Matters in avoidance and estoppel may be stated together, or in several special pleas, each presenting a distinct defense, and numbered so as to admit of separate issues to be formed on them.

Oct. 29, 1940, eff. Sept. 1, 1941. Amended by order of June 15, 1983, eff. Sept. 1, 1983.

See also **O'Connor's Texas Rules**, "Defendant's Response & Pleadings," ch. 3, §1 et seq.; **O'Connor's Texas Forms**, FORMS 3E:1, 3E:2, 3E:3, 3E:4, 3E:5, 3E:6, 3E:7, 3E:8, 3E:9, 3E:10, 3E:11.

TRCP 86. MOTION TO TRANSFER VENUE

1. Time to File. An objection to improper venue is waived if not made by written motion filed prior to or concurrently with any other plea, pleading or motion except a special appearance motion provided for in Rule 120a. A written consent of the parties to transfer the case to another county may be filed with the clerk of the court at any time. A motion to transfer venue because an impartial trial cannot be had in the county where the action is pending is governed by the provisions of Rule 257.

2. How to File. The motion objecting to improper venue may be contained in a separate instrument filed concurrently with or prior to the filing of a movant's first responsive pleading or the motion may be combined with other objections and defenses and included in the movant's first responsive pleading.

3. Requisites of Motion. The motion, and any amendments to it, shall state that the action should be transferred to another specified county of proper venue because:

(a) The county where the action is pending is not a proper county; or

(b) Mandatory venue of the action in another county is prescribed by one or more specific statutory provisions which shall be clearly designated or indicated.

The motion shall state the legal and factual basis for the transfer of the action and request transfer of the action to a specific county of mandatory or proper venue. Verification of the motion is not required. The motion may be accompanied by supporting affidavits as provided in Rule 87.

4. Response and Reply. Except as provided in paragraph 3(a) of Rule 87, a response to the motion to transfer is not required. Verification of a response is not required.

5. Service. A copy of any instrument filed pursuant to Rule 86 shall be served in accordance with Rule 21a.

Oct. 29, 1940, eff. Sept. 1, 1941. Amended by orders of March 31, 1941, eff. Sept. 1, 1941; June 16, 1943, eff. Dec. 31, 1943; July 20, 1954, eff. Jan. 1, 1955; April 12, 1962, eff. Sept. 1, 1962; June 15, 1983, eff. Sept. 1, 1983.

Source: TRCS art. 2007 (repealed). Changes: Requires the plea of privilege to state post-office address of defendant or attorney; increased time for filing a controverting affidavit to ten days.

See also CPRC ch. 15; **O'Connor's Texas Rules**, "Motion to Transfer—Challenging Venue," ch. 3-C, §1 et seq.; **O'Connor's Texas Forms**, FORMS 3C.

ANNOTATIONS

Wichita Cty. v. Hart, 917 S.W.2d 779, 781 (Tex.1996). "A defendant raises the question of proper venue by objecting to a plaintiff's venue choice through a motion to transfer venue. The fact that mandatory venue lies in another county provides one ground for a motion to transfer venue. If the plaintiff's chosen venue rests on a permissive venue statute and the defendant files a meritorious motion to transfer based on a mandatory venue provision, the trial court must grant the motion. A trial court's erroneous denial of a motion to transfer venue requires reversal of the judgment and remand for a new trial."

Toliver v. Dallas Fort Worth Hosp. Council, 198 S.W.3d 444, 446-47 (Tex.App.—Dallas 2006, no pet.). "A

party may expressly waive venue rights by clear, overt acts evidencing an intent to waive, or impliedly, by taking some action inconsistent with an intent to pursue the venue motion. . . . But filing a notice of removal to federal court before filing a motion to transfer in state court does not waive the motion." *See also* **Duran v. Entrust, Inc.**, No. 01-08-00589-CV, 2010 WL 1241093 (Tex.App.—Houston [1st Dist.] 2010, pet. denied) (memo op.; 3-25-10) (D waived motion to transfer venue by waiting four years to seek setting on the venue motion and by filing two summary-judgment motions during that time).

TRCP 87. DETERMINATION OF MOTION TO TRANSFER

1. Consideration of Motion. The determination of a motion to transfer venue shall be made promptly by the court and such determination must be made in a reasonable time prior to commencement of the trial on the merits. The movant has the duty to request a setting on the motion to transfer. Except on leave of court each party is entitled to at least 45 days notice of a hearing on the motion to transfer.

Except on leave of court, any response or opposing affidavits shall be filed at least 30 days prior to the hearing of the motion to transfer. The movant is not required to file a reply to the response but any reply and any additional affidavits supporting the motion to transfer must, except on leave of court, be filed not later than 7 days prior to the hearing date.

2. Burden of Establishing Venue.

(a) *In General.* A party who seeks to maintain venue of the action in a particular county in reliance upon Section 15.001 (General Rule), Sections 15.011–15.017 (Mandatory Venue), Sections 15.031–15.040 (Permissive Venue), or Sections 15.061 and 15.062 (Multiple Claims), Civil Practice and Remedies Code, has the burden to make proof, as provided in paragraph 3 of this rule, that venue is maintainable in the county of suit. A party who seeks to transfer venue of the action to another specified county under Section 15.001 (General Rule), Sections 15.011–15.017 (Mandatory Venue), Sections 15.031–15.040 (Permissive Venue), or Sections 15.061 and 15.062 (Multiple Claims), Civil Practice and Remedies Code, has the burden to make proof, as provided in paragraph 3 of this rule, that venue is maintainable in the county to which transfer is sought. A party who seeks to transfer venue of the action to another specified county under Sections 15.011–15.017, Civil Practice and Remedies Code on the basis that a mandatory venue provision is applicable and controlling has the burden to make proof, as provided in paragraph 3 of this rule, that venue is maintainable in the county to which transfer is sought by virtue of one or more mandatory venue exceptions.

(b) *Cause of Action.* It shall not be necessary for a claimant to prove the merits of a cause of action, but the existence of a cause of action, when pleaded properly, shall be taken as established as alleged by the pleadings. When the defendant specifically denies the venue allegations, the claimant is required, by prima facie proof as provided in paragraph 3 of this rule, to support such pleading that the cause of action taken as established by the pleadings, or a part of such cause of action, accrued in the county of suit. If a defendant seeks transfer to a county where the cause of action or a part thereof accrued, it shall be sufficient for the defendant to plead that if a cause of action exists, then the cause of action or part thereof accrued in the specific county to which transfer is sought, and such allegation shall not constitute an admission that a cause of action in fact exists. But the defendant shall be required to support his pleading by prima facie proof as provided in paragraph 3 of this rule, that, if a cause of action exists, it or a part thereof accrued in the county to which transfer is sought.

(c) *Other Rules.* A motion to transfer venue based on the written consent of the parties shall be determined in accordance with Rule 255. A motion to transfer venue on the basis that an impartial trial cannot be had in the county where the action is pending shall be determined in accordance with Rules 258 and 259.

3. Proof.

(a) *Affidavits and Attachments.* All venue facts, when properly pleaded, shall be taken as true unless specifically denied by the adverse party. When a venue fact is specifically denied, the party pleading the venue fact must make prima facie proof of that venue fact; provided, however, that no party shall ever be required for venue purposes to support by prima facie proof the existence of a cause of action or part thereof, and at the hearing the pleadings of the parties shall be taken as conclusive on the issues of existence of a cause of action. Prima facie proof is made when the venue facts are properly pleaded and an affidavit, and any duly proved attachments to the affidavit, are filed fully and specifically setting forth the facts supporting such pleading. Affidavits shall be made on personal knowledge, shall set forth specific facts as would be admissible in evidence, and shall show affirmatively that the affiant is competent to testify.

(b) *The Hearing.* The court shall determine the motion to transfer venue on the basis of the pleadings, any stipulations made by and between the parties and such affidavits and attachments as may be filed by the parties in accordance with the preceding subdivision of this paragraph 3 or of Rule 88.

(c) If a claimant has adequately pleaded and made prima facie proof that venue is proper in the county of suit as provided in subdivision (a) of paragraph 3, then the cause shall not be transferred but shall be retained in the county of suit, unless the motion to transfer is based on the grounds that an impartial trial cannot be had in the county where the action is pending as provided in Rules 257–259 or on an established ground of mandatory venue. A ground of mandatory venue is established when the party relying upon a mandatory exception to the general rule makes prima facie proof as provided in subdivision (a) of paragraph 3 of this rule.

(d) In the event that the parties shall fail to make prima facie proof that the county of suit or the specific county to which transfer is sought is a county of proper venue, then the court may direct the parties to make further proof.

4. No Jury. All venue challenges shall be determined by the court without the aid of a jury.

5. Motion for Rehearing. If venue has been sustained as against a motion to transfer, or if an action has been transferred to a proper county in response to a motion to transfer, then no further motions to transfer shall be considered regardless of whether the movant was a party to the prior proceedings or was added as a party subsequent to the venue proceedings, unless the motion to transfer is based on the grounds that an impartial trial cannot be had under Rules 257–259 or on the ground of mandatory venue, provided that such claim was not available to the other movant or movants.

Parties who are added subsequently to an action and are precluded by this rule from having a motion to transfer considered may raise the propriety of venue on appeal, provided that the party has timely filed a motion to transfer.

6. There shall be no interlocutory appeals from such determination.

Oct. 29, 1940, eff. Sept. 1, 1941. Amended by orders of Sept. 20, 1941, eff. Dec. 31, 1941; June 16, 1943, eff. Dec. 31, 1943; Aug. 18, 1947, eff. Dec. 13, 1947; June 15, 1983, eff. Sept. 1, 1983; July 15, 1987, eff. Jan. 1, 1988; April 24, 1990, eff. Sept. 1, 1990.

Comment—1990

To clarify that no proof of any kind is required of any party to establish any element of a cause of action or part thereof; proof is restricted to place, if any, and the pleadings establish all other elements and may not be controverted for venue purposes as to the existence of a cause of action or part thereof.

Source: TRCS art. 2008 (repealed in part by TRCPs). Change: Substituted service of notice of the controverting affidavit by registered mail for service by officer. Provisions for interlocutory appeals from orders sustaining or overruling pleas of privilege are included in art. 2008, which is deemed jurisdictional.

Editor's Note: CPRC §15.001, as referenced in TRCP 87(2)(a), is now CPRC §15.002.

See also CPRC ch. 15; **O'Connor's Texas Rules**, "Choosing the Court—Venue," ch. 2-H, §1 et seq.; **O'Connor's Texas Rules**, "Motion to Transfer—Challenging Venue," ch. 3-C, §1 et seq.; **O'Connor's Texas Forms**, FORMS 3C; **O'Connor's Texas Family Law Handbook**, "Challenging the Court," ch. 4-B, §1 et seq.

ANNOTATIONS

In re Team Rocket, L.P., 256 S.W.3d 257, 259-60 (Tex.2008). "[O]nly one venue determination may be made in a proceeding and [TRCP] 87 specifically prohibits changes in venue after the initial venue ruling. . . . Although a trial court's ruling transferring venue is interlocutory for the parties, and thus not subject to immediate appeal, the order is final for the transferring court as long as it is not altered within the court's 30-day plenary jurisdiction. . . . Just as a decision on the merits cannot be circumvented by nonsuiting and refiling the case, a final determination fixing venue in a particular county must likewise be protected from relitigation. [¶] Reading [CPRC] §15.064 . . . and Rule 87 together, we conclude that once a venue determination has been made, that determination is conclusive as to those parties and claims. Because venue is then fixed in any suit involving the same parties and claims, it cannot be overcome by a nonsuit and subsequent refiling in another county. [¶] To interpret the provisions otherwise would allow forum shopping, a practice we have repeatedly prohibited." *See also* **In re Lowe's Home Ctrs., L.L.C.**, 531 S.W.3d 861, 871-72 (Tex.App.—Corpus Christi 2017, orig. proceeding) (after initial venue determination, P could not nonsuit and refile in another county despite P's argument that venue was improper in first county).

HCA Health Servs. v. Salinas, 838 S.W.2d 246, 247-48 (Tex.1992). "[I]t is an abuse of discretion, correctable by mandamus, for a trial court to rule on a motion to transfer venue without giving the parties the notice required by [TRCP 87(1)]."

Ford Motor Co. v. Johnson, 473 S.W.3d 925, 928 (Tex.App.—Dallas 2015, pet. denied). "[P]rima facie proof [that venue is proper in the county of suit] is not subject to rebuttal, cross-examination, impeachment, or disproof. But, if the plaintiff fails to discharge its burden, the right to choose a proper venue passes to the defendant, who must then prove that venue is proper in the defendant's chosen county." *See also* **In re Harding**, 563 S.W.3d 366, 370 (Tex.App.—Texarkana 2018, orig. proceeding).

Rodriguez v. Printone Color Corp., 982 S.W.2d 69, 71 (Tex.App.—Houston [1st Dist.] 1998, pet. denied). "[S]tatements such as 'Defendant specifically denies those venue facts pleaded in Plaintiff's Petition' do not constitute a 'specific denial' as required by [TRCP] 87."

TRCP 88. DISCOVERY AND VENUE

Discovery shall not be abated or otherwise affected by pendency of a motion to transfer venue. Issuing process for

witnesses and taking depositions shall not constitute a waiver of a motion to transfer venue, but depositions taken in such case may be read in evidence in any subsequent suit between the same parties concerning the same subject matter in like manner as if taken in such subsequent suit. Deposition transcripts, responses to requests for admission, answers to interrogatories and other discovery products containing information relevant to a determination of proper venue may be considered by the court in making the venue determination when they are attached to, or incorporated by reference in, an affidavit of a party, a witness or an attorney who has knowledge of such discovery.

Oct. 29, 1940, eff. Sept. 1, 1941. Amended by orders of June 15, 1983, eff. Sept. 1, 1983; July 15, 1987, eff. Jan. 1, 1988.

See also **O'Connor's Texas Rules**, "Motion to Transfer—Challenging Venue," ch. 3-C, §1 et seq.

ANNOTATIONS

Montalvo v. Fourth Ct. of Appeals, 917 S.W.2d 1, 2 (Tex.1995). "[T]he trial court set a shortened schedule for completing discovery related to venue, filing [Ps'] response to the motions to transfer, and the hearing. [Ps] offered no argument or evidence that the limitation on discovery or the abbreviated schedule deprived them of any ability to develop evidence pertinent to the venue issue. Without a showing of such harm, the record is wholly insufficient to establish that [Ps] lacked an adequate remedy by appeal."

Double Diamond-Del., Inc. v. Alfonso, 487 S.W.3d 265, 272-73 (Tex.App.—Corpus Christi 2016, no pet.). "[Ds] objected to [Ps'] use of their own discovery responses as venue evidence. . . . [Ds] cited [TRCP] 197.3, which provides that '[a]nswers to interrogatories may be used only against the responding party.' [TRCP] 88 does not provide any such limitation when it stipulates that discovery . . . can be considered by the trial court in making its venue determination. [W]e conclude that the specific provisions in rule 88 allow a party to use its own discovery responses in the context of a venue determination."

TRCP 89. TRANSFERRED IF MOTION IS SUSTAINED

If a motion to transfer venue is sustained, the cause shall not be dismissed, but the court shall transfer said cause to the proper court; and the costs incurred prior to the time such suit is filed in the court to which said cause is transferred shall be taxed against the plaintiff. The clerk shall make up a transcript of all the orders made in said cause, certifying thereto officially under the seal of the court, and send it with the original papers in the cause to the clerk of the court to which the venue has been changed. Provided, however, if the cause be severable as to parties defendant and shall be ordered transferred as to one or more defendants but not as to all, the clerk, instead of sending the original papers, shall make certified copies of such filed papers as directed by the court and forward the same to the clerk of the court to which the venue has been changed. After the cause has been transferred, as above provided for the clerk of the court to which the cause has been transferred shall mail notification to the plaintiff or his attorney that transfer of the cause has been completed, that the filing fee in the proper court is due and payable within thirty days from the mailing of such notification, and that the case may be dismissed if the filing fee is not timely paid; and if such filing fee is timely paid, the cause will be subject to trial at the expiration of thirty days after the mailing of notification to the parties or their attorneys by the clerk that the papers have been filed in the court to which the cause has been transferred; and if the filing fee is not timely paid, any court of the transferee county to which the case might have been assigned, upon its own motion or the motion of a party, may dismiss the cause without prejudice to the refiling of same.

Oct. 29, 1940, eff. Sept. 1, 1941. Amended by orders of June 16, 1943, eff. Dec. 31, 1943; June 15, 1983, eff. Sept. 1, 1983.

See also **O'Connor's Texas Rules**, "Motion to Transfer—Challenging Venue," ch. 3-C, §1 et seq.

ANNOTATIONS

WTFO, Inc. v. Braithwaite, 899 S.W.2d 709, 718 (Tex.App.—Dallas 1995, no writ). "Where a cause of action is against several defendants jointly and severally, the trial court shall transfer the action as to those defendants whose motions are sustained. Comakers on a note are jointly and severally liable. Accordingly, because venue was proper in Dallas County, the trial court did not abuse its discretion in severing [D's] cause of action and transferring it to Dallas County."

TRCP 90. WAIVER OF DEFECTS IN PLEADING

General demurrers shall not be used. Every defect, omission or fault in a pleading either of form or of substance, which is not specifically pointed out by exception in writing and brought to the attention of the judge in the trial court before the instruction or charge to the jury or, in a non-jury case, before the judgment is signed, shall be deemed to have been waived by the party seeking reversal on such account; provided that this rule shall not apply as to any party against whom default judgment is rendered.

Oct. 29, 1940, eff. Sept. 1, 1941. Amended by order of June 10, 1980, eff. Jan. 1, 1981.

Source: New rule.

See also **O'Connor's Texas Rules**, "Special Exceptions—Challenging the Pleadings," ch. 3-G, §1 et seq.

ANNOTATIONS

Crosstex Energy Servs. v. Pro Plus, Inc., 430 S.W.3d 384, 395 (Tex.2014). "If a defect in the pleadings is incurable by amendment, a special exception is unnecessary."

TRCP 91. SPECIAL EXCEPTIONS

A special exception shall not only point out the particular pleading excepted to, but it shall also point out intelligibly and with particularity the defect, omission, obscurity, duplicity, generality, or other insufficiency in the allegations in the pleading excepted to.

Oct. 29, 1940, eff. Sept. 1, 1941. Amended by order of March 31, 1941, eff. Sept. 1, 1941.

See also **O'Connor's Texas Rules**, "Special Exceptions—Challenging the Pleadings," ch. 3-G, §1 et seq.; **O'Connor's Texas Forms**, FORMS 3G.

ANNOTATIONS

Parker v. Barefield, 206 S.W.3d 119, 120 (Tex.2006). If the trial court does not allow the party an opportunity to amend its pleadings, "the aggrieved party must prove that the opportunity to replead was requested and denied to preserve the error for review."

Friesenhahn v. Ryan, 960 S.W.2d 656, 658 (Tex.1998). "Special exceptions may be used to challenge the sufficiency of a pleading. When the trial court sustains special exceptions, it must give the pleader an opportunity to amend the pleading. If a party refuses to amend, or the amended pleading fails to state a cause of action, then summary judgment may be granted. Summary judgment may also be proper if a pleading deficiency is of the type that could not be cured by an amendment." *See also* **James v. Underwood**, 438 S.W.3d 704, 715-16 (Tex.App.—Houston [1st Dist.] 2014, no pet.).

Peek v. Equipment Serv., 779 S.W.2d 802, 805 (Tex.1989). "[T]he omission of any allegation regarding the amount in controversy from [P's] petition did not deprive the court of jurisdiction, but was instead a defect in pleading subject to special exception and amendment."

Gallien v. Washington Mut. Home Loans, Inc., 209 S.W.3d 856, 862-63 (Tex.App.—Texarkana 2006, no pet.). "[A]s a general rule, the trial court cannot dismiss a suit with prejudice when the plaintiff does not cure the objections made by special exceptions. More specifically, a trial court cannot dismiss a plaintiff's entire case with prejudice if the pleadings state a valid cause of action, but are vague, overbroad, or otherwise susceptible to valid special exceptions."

TRCP 91a. DISMISSAL OF BASELESS CAUSES OF ACTION

91a.1. Motion and Grounds. Except in a case brought under the Family Code or a case governed by Chapter 14 of the Texas Civil Practice and Remedies Code, a party may move to dismiss a cause of action on the grounds that it has no basis in law or fact. A cause of action has no basis in law if the allegations, taken as true, together with inferences reasonably drawn from them, do not entitle the claimant to the relief sought. A cause of action has no basis in fact if no reasonable person could believe the facts pleaded.

91a.2. Contents of Motion. A motion to dismiss must state that it is made pursuant to this rule, must identify each cause of action to which it is addressed, and must state specifically the reasons the cause of action has no basis in law, no basis in fact, or both.

91a.3. Time for Motion and Ruling. A motion to dismiss must be:

(a) filed within 60 days after the first pleading containing the challenged cause of action is served on the movant;

(b) filed at least 21 days before the motion is heard; and

(c) granted or denied within 45 days after the motion is filed.

91a.4. Time for Response. Any response to the motion must be filed no later than 7 days before the date of the hearing.

91a.5. Effect of Nonsuit or Amendment; Withdrawal of Motion.

(a) The court may not rule on a motion to dismiss if, at least 3 days before the date of the hearing, the respondent files a nonsuit of the challenged cause of action, or the movant files a withdrawal of the motion.

(b) If the respondent amends the challenged cause of action at least 3 days before the date of the hearing, the movant may, before the date of the hearing, file a withdrawal of the motion or an amended motion directed to the amended cause of action.

(c) Except by agreement of the parties, the court must rule on a motion unless it has been withdrawn or the cause of action has been nonsuited in accordance with (a) or (b). In ruling on the motion, the court must not consider a nonsuit or amendment not filed as permitted by paragraphs (a) or (b).

(d) An amended motion filed in accordance with (b) restarts the time periods in this rule.

91a.6. Hearing; No Evidence Considered. Each

party is entitled to at least 14 days' notice of the hearing on the motion to dismiss. The court may, but is not required to, conduct an oral hearing on the motion. Except as required by 91a.7, the court may not consider evidence in ruling on the motion and must decide the motion based solely on the pleading of the cause of action, together with any pleading exhibits permitted by Rule 59.

91a.7. Award of Costs and Attorney Fees. Except in an action by or against a governmental entity or a public official acting in his or her official capacity or under color of law, the court may award the prevailing party on the motion all costs and reasonable and necessary attorney fees incurred with respect to the challenged cause of action in the trial court. Any award of costs or fees must be based on evidence.

91a.8. Effect on Venue and Personal Jurisdiction. This rule is not an exception to the pleading requirements of Rules 86 and 120a, but a party does not, by filing a motion to dismiss pursuant to this rule or obtaining a ruling on it, waive a special appearance or a motion to transfer venue. By filing a motion to dismiss, a party submits to the court's jurisdiction only in proceedings on the motion and is bound by the court's ruling, including an award of attorney fees and costs against the party.

91a.9. Dismissal Procedure Cumulative. This rule is in addition to, and does not supersede or affect, other procedures that authorize dismissal.

Adopted by order of Feb. 12, 2013, eff. March 1, 2013. Amended by order of July 11, 2019, eff. Sept. 1, 2019.

Comment—2019

Rule 91a.7 is amended to implement changes to section 30.021 of the Texas Civil Practice and Remedies Code. The amendments to Rule 91a.7 apply only to civil actions commenced on or after September 1, 2019. A civil action commenced before September 1, 2019 is governed by the rule as adopted in Misc. Docket No. 13-9022.

Comment—2013

Rule 91a is a new rule implementing section 22.004(g) of the Texas Government Code, which was added in 2011 and calls for rules to provide for the dismissal of causes of action that have no basis in law or fact on motion and without evidence. A motion to dismiss filed under this rule must be ruled on by the court within 45 days unless the motion, pleading, or cause of action is withdrawn, amended, or nonsuited as specified in 91a.5. If an amended motion is filed in response to an amended cause of action in accordance with 91a.5(b), the court must rule on the motion within 45 days of the filing of the amended motion and the respondent must be given an opportunity to respond to the amended motion. The term "hearing" in the rule includes both submission and an oral hearing. Attorney fees awarded under 91a.7 are limited to those associated with challenged cause of action, including fees for preparing or responding to the motion to dismiss.

Editor's note: Rule 91a applies to all suits, except those brought under the Family Code or governed by CPRC chapter 14 (inmate litigation). TRCP 91a.1. *See* Tex.Sup.Ct. Order, Misc. Docket No. 13-9022 (eff. Mar. 1, 2013).

See also **O'Connor's Texas Rules**, "Motion to Dismiss—Baseless Cause of Action," ch. 3-H, §1 et seq.

ANNOTATIONS

Bethel v. Quilling, Selander, Lownds, Winslett & Moser, P.C., 595 S.W.3d 651, 654 (Tex.2020). "[P] reasons that affirmative defenses are generally waived unless they are raised in the defendant's pleading. Thus, [P] contends, a court must look to the defendant's pleading to determine whether an affirmative defense is properly before the court. However, Rule 91a.6 expressly limits the court's consideration to 'the pleading of the cause of action,' together with a narrow class of exhibits. Because only a plaintiff's pleading is a 'pleading of a cause of action,' [P] argues that courts may not consider a defendant's pleading in making a Rule 91a determination. [P] therefore concludes that an affirmative defense can never be the basis of a Rule 91a motion. [¶] We disagree. *At 655:* [P] urges us to focus on the rule's requirement that the court 'must decide the motion based *solely* on the pleading of the cause of action.' As [P] sees it, this provision prohibits a court deciding a Rule 91a motion from considering *anything* other than the plaintiff's pleading. Of course, it is not possible to 'decide the motion' without considering the motion itself, in addition to the plaintiff's pleading. Additionally, the rule provides that the court may hold a hearing on the motion. Thus, the rule contemplates that a court may consider at least the substance of the Rule 91a motion and arguments at the hearing, in addition to the plaintiff's pleadings, in deciding the motion. *At 656:* Rule 91a limits a court's factual inquiry to the plaintiff's pleadings but does not so limit the court's legal inquiry. In deciding a Rule 91a motion, a court may consider the defendant's pleadings if doing so is necessary to make the legal determination of whether an affirmative defense is properly before the court. We therefore conclude that Rule 91a permits motions to dismiss based on affirmative defenses 'if the allegations, taken as true, together with inferences reasonably drawn from them, do not entitle the claimant to the relief sought.' Of course, some affirmative defenses will not be conclusively established by the facts in a plaintiff's petition. Because Rule 91a does not allow consideration of evidence, such defenses are not a proper basis for a motion to dismiss."

ConocoPhillips Co. v. Koopmann, 547 S.W.3d 858, 880 (Tex.2018). "[D's] argument that it is the 'prevailing party' under Rule 91a because it later won on summary judgment as to [the] claims [in question] is unpersuasive. Rule 91a provides that a party who files a motion to dismiss is due attorney's fees when it prevails 'on the motion'—not on a later summary judgment motion asserting there is no genuine issue as to any material fact. Further, it is irrelevant that the arguments [D] made in its motion for summary judgment were the same as those it asserted in its motion to dismiss because a motion to dismiss is decided on the *plaintiff's* pleadings. [¶] We note that [D] could have challenged the trial court's denial of its motion to dismiss at the time it was denied. It chose not to. We reject [D's]

argument that it is entitled to recover attorney's fees as the prevailing party on the motion under Rule 91a when [D] received an adverse ruling on that motion, did not challenge the ruling at that time, and later prevailed on its motion for summary judgment. . . ."

Reynolds v. Quantlab Trading Partners US, LP, 608 S.W.3d 549, __ (Tex.App.—Houston [14th Dist.] 2020, n.p.h.). "Generally, our court may take judicial notice of its opinions and records in related proceedings involving the same parties. But Rule 91a.6 expressly prohibits the consideration of evidence and requires that the motion be decided based solely on the pleading of the cause of action. A party may not rely on judicial notice in a Rule 91a proceeding because judicial notice is 'a matter of evidence.'"

Reaves v. City of Corpus Christi, 518 S.W.3d 594, 601 (Tex.App.—Corpus Christi 2017, no pet.). "Rule 91a declares that the trial court 'must' grant or deny the motion within 45 days after it is filed. . . . When used in a statute, the terms 'must' and 'shall' are generally recognized as mandatory, creating a duty or obligation. [R]ule 91a's use of the word 'must' creates a mandatory duty. [¶] However, even if a statutory requirement is mandatory, this does not mean that compliance is necessarily jurisdictional. When attached to a deadline, words like 'must' and 'shall' are plainly mandatory in the sense that the non-movant has recourse if the trial court misses the deadline for ruling on the motion, but are not necessarily jurisdictional in the sense that missing the deadline will forever strip the trial court of the power to act. Rather, to determine whether the Legislature intended for a deadline to be jurisdictional, we look to . . . three factors . . .: 'the presence or absence of specific consequences for noncompliance,' the implications 'that result from each possible interpretation,' and the 'overall statutory objective' to be achieved. *At 603:* In view of [these] factors, . . . rule 91a's deadline for ruling on a motion to dismiss is not jurisdictional." *See also* **MedFin Manager, LLC v. Stone**, __ S.W.3d __, 2020 WL 5027201 (Tex.App.—San Antonio 2020, n.p.h.) (No. 04-19-00662-CV; 8-26-20).

In re Butt, 495 S.W.3d 455, 461-62 (Tex.App.—Corpus Christi 2016, orig. proceeding). "Though [TRCP] 91a is not identical to [FRCP] 12(b)(6), several Texas Courts of Appeals have interpreted Rule 91a as essentially calling for a Rule 12(b)(6)-type analysis and have relied on case law interpreting Rule 12(b)(6) in applying Rule 91a. We note, however that the [FRCPs] are based on a more stringent pleading standard than the [TRCPs], and Rule 91a did not revoke Texas's established 'fair notice' pleading standard. In short, 'Texas is a notice pleading jurisdiction, and a petition is sufficient if it gives fair and adequate notice of the facts upon which the pleader bases his claim.' Accordingly, in conducting our review [under Rule 91a], we apply the fair notice pleading standard whereby we must construe the pleadings liberally in favor of the plaintiff, look to the pleader's intent, and accept as true the factual allegations in the pleadings to determine if the cause of action has a basis in law or fact." *See also* **Thomas v. 462 Thomas Family Props., LP**, 559 S.W.3d 634, 639-40 (Tex.App.—Dallas 2018, pet. denied); **Aguilar v. Morales**, 545 S.W.3d 670, 677 (Tex.App.—El Paso 2017, pet. denied); **Auzenne v. Great Lakes Reinsurance, PLC**, 497 S.W.3d 35, 37 (Tex.App.—Houston [14th Dist.] 2016, no pet.). *But see* **GoDaddy.com, LLC v. Toups**, under this rule.

Walker v. Owens, 492 S.W.3d 787, 790-91 (Tex.App.—Houston [1st Dist.] 2016, no pet.). "[P] contends that the trial court erred in granting the motion [to dismiss] because it failed to comply with Rule 91a.3(c), which states that '[a] motion to dismiss must be . . . granted or denied within 45 days after the motion is filed.' Here, . . . the trial court granted the motion . . . more than 45 days after the motion was filed. [¶] [T]he trial court did not comply with the 45 day deadline, and its failure to do so was error. Rule 91a, however, does not contain any sanction for non-compliance with the 45 day deadline, and we have not identified any Texas authority addressing the effect of a trial court's failure to comply. In any case, the court's non-compliance with the mandatory language of the rule will not result in reversal if the error is found to be harmless. [P] has not identified any prejudice to him resulting from the trial court's error in failing to comply with [the] deadline. For example, he does not contend that the parties engaged in any discovery or other furtherance of the litigation process after the deadline passed. The motion simply remained pending during that period. The court's failure to dismiss the claim within 45 days, while error, was not harmful. . . ."

Thuesen v. Amerisure Ins., 487 S.W.3d 291, 294 (Tex.App.—Houston [14th Dist.] 2016, no pet.). "At issue is whether a trial court may consider a Rule 91a movant a 'prevailing party' entitled to attorney's fees under the rule if the trial court determines the respondent nonsuited the claims to avoid an adverse ruling on the 91a motion. We conclude that a trial court may not do so. *At 301:* Under the unambiguous language of Rule 91a, a claimant, up until three days before the hearing date on the motion to dismiss . . ., may nonsuit the claims challenged in the Rule 91a motion. If a claimant does so, the trial court cannot rule on the Rule 91a motion, and thus the movant cannot recover costs and attorney's fees. . . ."

Weizhong Zheng v. Vacation Network, Inc., 468 S.W.3d 180, 187 (Tex.App.—Houston [14th Dist.] 2015, pet. denied). "[A]ppellees assert that a prevailing party on a Rule 91a motion is entitled to recover only the attorney's fees incurred in the trial court. . . . We disagree. *At 188:* There is no limitation in the rule on the fees and costs the prevailing party is entitled to recover relative to the cause of action challenged in the trial court. Specifically, there is nothing to suggest that 'all costs and reasonable and necessary attorney fees' excludes appellate costs and fees which are generally recoverable when attorney's fees are authorized. Rather the word 'all' entails just that—'all' fees—which would include appellate fees, because they are part of the fees incurred to ultimately prevail, if the ruling is appealed."

Gaskill v. VHS San Antonio Partners, 456 S.W.3d 234, 239 (Tex.App.—San Antonio 2014, pet. denied). "[W]e hold that formal notice of a Rule 91a hearing must be provided to the parties, regardless of whether the trial court will hold an oral hearing. We further hold that Rule 91a does not contain implied notice of a hearing on the 45th day after the motion is filed that triggers the other deadlines in the rule."

GoDaddy.com, LLC v. Toups, 429 S.W.3d 752, 754-55 (Tex.App.—Beaumont 2014, pet. denied). "While not identical, [TRCP] 91a is analogous to [FRCP] 12(b)(6); therefore, we find case law interpreting Rule 12(b)(6) instructive. [¶] For a complaint to survive a Rule 12(b)(6) motion to dismiss, it must contain 'enough facts to state a claim to relief that is plausible on its face.' Facial plausibility requires facts that allow the court 'to draw the reasonable inference that the defendant is liable for the misconduct alleged.' [I]n determining whether the trial court erred in denying a defendant's motion to dismiss, we take all plaintiff's allegations as true and consider whether a plaintiff's petition contains 'enough facts to state a claim to relief that is plausible on its face.' Rule 12(b)(6) dismissal is appropriate if the court determines beyond doubt that the plaintiff can prove no set of facts to support a claim that would entitle him to relief. Just as a motion to dismiss for failure to state a claim under Rule 12(b)(6) is a proper vehicle to assert a claim of immunity under the federal rules, a motion to dismiss under Rule 91a is a proper vehicle to assert an affirmative defense of immunity . . . in the state court." *But see* **In re Butt**, under this rule.

TRCP 92. GENERAL DENIAL

A general denial of matters pleaded by the adverse party which are not required to be denied under oath, shall be sufficient to put the same in issue. When the defendant has pleaded a general denial, and the plaintiff shall afterward amend his pleading, such original denial shall be presumed to extend to all matters subsequently set up by the plaintiff.

When a counterclaim or cross-claim is served upon a party who has made an appearance in the action, the party so served, in the absence of a responsive pleading, shall be deemed to have pleaded a general denial of the counterclaim or cross-claim, but the party shall not be deemed to have waived any special appearance or motion to transfer venue. In all other respects the rules prescribed for pleadings of defensive matter are applicable to answers to counterclaims and cross-claims.

Oct. 29, 1940, eff. Sept. 1, 1941. Amended by orders of Dec. 5, 1983, eff. April 1, 1984; Dec. 19, 1984, eff. April 1, 1985.

Source: TRCS arts. 2006, 2012 (repealed). See TRCP 84 for rest of art. 2006.

See also **O'Connor's Texas Rules**, "The Answer—Denying Liability," ch. 3-E, §1 et seq.

ANNOTATIONS

Shell Chem. Co. v. Lamb, 493 S.W.2d 742, 744 (Tex.1973). "[A] general denial puts [P] on proof of every fact essential to his case and issue is joined on all material facts asserted by [P] except those which are required to be denied under oath."

TRCP 93. CERTAIN PLEAS TO BE VERIFIED

A pleading setting up any of the following matters, unless the truth of such matters appear of record, shall be verified by affidavit.

1. That the plaintiff has not legal capacity to sue or that the defendant has not legal capacity to be sued.

2. That the plaintiff is not entitled to recover in the capacity in which he sues, or that the defendant is not liable in the capacity in which he is sued.

3. That there is another suit pending in this State between the same parties involving the same claim.

4. That there is a defect of parties, plaintiff or defendant.

5. A denial of partnership as alleged in any pleading as to any party to the suit.

6. That any party alleged in any pleading to be a corporation is not incorporated as alleged.

7. Denial of the execution by himself or by his authority of any instrument in writing, upon which any pleading is founded, in whole or in part and charged to have been executed by him or by his authority, and not alleged to be lost or destroyed. Where such instrument in writing is charged to have been executed by a person then deceased, the affidavit shall be sufficient if it states that the affiant has reason to believe and does believe that such instrument was not executed by the decedent or by his authority. In the absence of such a sworn plea, the instrument shall be received in evidence as fully proved.

8. A denial of the genuineness of the indorsement or assignment of a written instrument upon which suit is brought by an indorsee or assignee and in the absence of such a sworn plea, the indorsement or assignment thereof shall be held as fully proved. The denial required by this subdivision of the rule may be made upon information and belief.

9. That a written instrument upon which a pleading is founded is without consideration, or that the consideration of the same has failed in whole or in part.

10. A denial of an account which is the foundation of the plaintiff's action, and supported by affidavit.

11. That a contract sued upon is usurious. Unless such plea is filed, no evidence of usurious interest as a defense shall be received.

12. That notice and proof of loss or claim for damage has not been given as alleged. Unless such plea is filed such notice and proof shall be presumed and no evidence to the contrary shall be admitted. A denial of such notice or such proof shall be made specifically and with particularity.

13. In the trial of any case appealed to the court from the Industrial Accident Board[1] the following, if pleaded, shall be presumed to be true as pleaded and have been done and filed in legal time and manner, unless denied by verified pleadings:

(a) Notice of injury.

(b) Claim for compensation.

(c) Award of the Board.

(d) Notice of intention not to abide by the award of the Board.

(e) Filing of suit to set aside the award.

(f) That the insurance company alleged to have been the carrier of the workers' compensation insurance at the time of the alleged injury was in fact the carrier thereof.

(g) That there was good cause for not filing claim with the Industrial Accident Board[1] within the one year period provided by statute.

(h) Wage rate.

A denial of any of the matters set forth in subdivisions (a) or (g) of paragraph 13 may be made on information and belief.

Any such denial may be made in original or amended pleadings; but if in amended pleadings the same must be filed not less than seven days before the case proceeds to trial. In case of such denial the things so denied shall not be presumed to be true, and if essential to the case of the party alleging them, must be proved.

14. That a party plaintiff or defendant is not doing business under an assumed name or trade name as alleged.

15. In the trial of any case brought against an automobile insurance company by an insured under the provisions of an insurance policy in force providing protection against uninsured motorists, an allegation that the insured has complied with all the terms of the policy as a condition precedent to bringing the suit shall be presumed to be true unless denied by verified pleadings which may be upon information and belief.

16. Any other matter required by statute to be pleaded under oath.

Oct. 29, 1940, eff. Sept. 1, 1941. Amended by orders of March 31, 1941, eff. Sept. 1, 1941; Sept. 20, 1941, eff. Dec. 31, 1941; June 16, 1943, eff. Dec. 31, 1943; Oct. 12, 1949, eff. March 1, 1950; July 21, 1970, eff. Jan. 1, 1971; July 22, 1975, eff. Jan. 1, 1976; June 15, 1983, eff. Sept. 1, 1983; Dec. 5, 1983, eff. April 1, 1984.

Source: TRCS arts. 573, 1999, 2010, 3734, 5074 (repealed), with changes: Basic statute relating to sworn pleadings, art. 2010, was combined with provisions from a number of other statutes which required sworn pleas. No change of meaning was intended by the combination. The scope of sworn denials, however, was broadened. Subdiv. (b) includes the plea that "the defendant has not legal capacity to be sued." Subdiv. (c) was extended to include a denial of defendant's liability in the capacity in which he is sued. In subdiv. (d) the term "cause of action" was replaced by the word "claim." Subdivs. (f) and (g) apply to allegations in any pleading, not merely to the petition as formerly stated in art. 2010.

[1] The name of the Industrial Accident Board was changed to the Texas Workers' Compensation Commission pursuant to Acts 1989, 71st Leg., 2nd C.S., ch. 1, §17.01. The Texas Workers' Compensation Commission was abolished and the Workers' Compensation Division of the Texas Department of Insurance was established pursuant to Acts 2005, 79th Leg., ch. 265, §1.003.

See also **O'Connor's Texas Rules**, "Verified pleas," ch. 3-E, §4; **O'Connor's Texas Forms**, FORM 3E:10.

ANNOTATIONS

Sixth RMA Partners v. Sibley, 111 S.W.3d 46, 56 (Tex.2003). "When capacity is contested, [TRCP 93(1)] requires that a verified plea be filed unless the truth of the matter appears of record. [¶] An argument that an opposing party does not have the capacity to participate in a suit can be waived by [the] failure to properly raise the issue in the trial court. [D] never raised [P's] failure to file an assumed name certificate . . . in the trial court. Therefore, [D] waived the complaint." *See also* **Nootsie, Ltd. v. Williamson Cty. Appr. Dist.**, 925 S.W.2d 659, 662 (Tex.1996); **Werner v. Colwell**, 909 S.W.2d 866, 870 (Tex.1995).

Pledger v. Schoellkopf, 762 S.W.2d 145, 146 (Tex.1988). "When capacity [to sue] is contested, Rule 93(2) requires that a verified plea be filed anytime the record does not affirmatively demonstrate the plaintiff's or defendant's right to bring suit or be sued in *whatever* capacity he is suing." *See also* **Pike v. Texas EMC Mgmt.**, ___ S.W.3d ___, 2020 WL 3405812 (Tex.2020) (No. 17-0557; 6-19-20).

Alphaville Ventures, Inc. v. First Bank, 429 S.W.3d 150, 153-54 (Tex.App.—Houston [14th Dist.] 2014, no pet.), *disapproved on other grounds,* **B.C. v. Steak N Shake Opers., Inc.**, 598 S.W.3d 256 (Tex.2020). "Rule 93(4) includes the following as a matter on which the defendant must file a verified denial: 'That there is a defect of parties, plaintiff or defendant.' Generally, a 'defect of parties' refers to joinder problems involving necessary or indispensable parties."

TRCP 94. AFFIRMATIVE DEFENSES

In pleading to a preceding pleading, a party shall set forth affirmatively accord and satisfaction, arbitration and

award, assumption of risk, contributory negligence, discharge in bankruptcy, duress, estoppel, failure of consideration, fraud, illegality, injury by fellow servant, laches, license, payment, release, res judicata, statute of frauds, statute of limitations, waiver, and any other matter constituting an avoidance or affirmative defense. Where the suit is on an insurance contract which insures against certain general hazards, but contains other provisions limiting such general liability, the party suing on such contract shall never be required to allege that the loss was not due to a risk or cause coming within any of the exceptions specified in the contract, nor shall the insurer be allowed to raise such issue unless it shall specifically allege that the loss was due to a risk or cause coming within a particular exception to the general liability; provided that nothing herein shall be construed to change the burden of proof on such issue as it now exists.

Oct. 29, 1940, eff. Sept. 1, 1941. Amended by order of March 31, 1941, eff. Sept. 1, 1941.

Source: Part of FRCP 8(c).

See also **O'Connor's Texas Rules**, "Affirmative defenses," ch. 3-E, §5; **O'Connor's Texas Forms**, FORM 3E:11; **O'Connor's Texas Family Law Handbook**, "Affirmative defenses," ch. 3-A, §9.3.3(7) (suit for divorce); **O'Connor's Texas Family Law Handbook**, "Affirmative defense," ch. 4-F, §7.2.3(6)(c) (suit for child support); **O'Connor's Texas Family Law Handbook**, "Affirmative defenses," ch. 4-H, §6.2.3(6)(c) (suit for termination).

ANNOTATIONS

Zorrilla v. Aypco Constr. II, LLC, 469 S.W.3d 143, 146 (Tex.2015). "[T]he paramount issue on appeal is whether the statutory cap on exemplary damages [under CPRC §41.008(b)] is waived if not pleaded as an affirmative defense or avoidance. Our courts of appeals are split on the issue. . . . We hold the exemplary damages cap is not a 'matter constituting an avoidance or affirmative defense' and need not be affirmatively pleaded because it applies automatically when invoked and does not require proof of additional facts."

State v. Lueck, 290 S.W.3d 876, 880 (Tex.2009). "[A]n affirmative defense . . . cannot be raised by a plea to the jurisdiction."

Quantum Chem. Corp. v. Toennies, 47 S.W.3d 473, 481 (Tex.2001). "It is the defendant's burden to plead and request instructions on an affirmative defense." *See also* **Superior Broad. Prods. v. Doud Media Grp.**, 392 S.W.3d 198, 205 (Tex.App.—Eastland 2012, no pet.); **Rio Grande Reg'l Hosp., Inc. v. Villarreal**, 329 S.W.3d 594, 621 (Tex.App.—Corpus Christi 2010, pet. granted, judgm't vacated w.r.m.).

Kinnear v. Texas Comm'n on Human Rights, 14 S.W.3d 299, 300 (Tex.2000). "Because the [Texas Commission on Human Rights] never pleaded sovereign immunity from liability as an affirmative defense to the requested attorney fees, it waived the defense, and the court of appeals erred in overturning the attorney fees award on sovereign immunity grounds." *See also* **Land Title Co. v. F.M. Stigler, Inc.**, 609 S.W.2d 754, 756 (Tex.1980) (ratification is affirmative defense that is waived unless affirmatively pleaded).

Texas Beef Cattle Co. v. Green, 921 S.W.2d 203, 212 (Tex.1996). "[A]n affirmative defense . . . is one of confession and avoidance. An affirmative defense does not seek to defend by merely denying the plaintiff's claims, but rather seeks to establish 'an independent reason why the plaintiff should not recover.'" *See also* **Moncrief Oil Int'l v. OAO Gazprom**, 332 S.W.3d 1, 15 (Tex.App.—Fort Worth 2010), *rev'd in part on other grounds*, 414 S.W.3d 142 (Tex.2013); **In re P.D.D.**, 256 S.W.3d 834, 839 (Tex.App.—Texarkana 2008, no pet.).

Shoemake v. Fogel, Ltd., 826 S.W.2d 933, 937 (Tex.1992). "Rule 94's requirement of pleading is not absolute. [¶] [T]he defense of [parental] immunity . . . is not waived by the failure to specifically plead it if it is apparent on the face of the petition and established as a matter of law." *See also* **Texas Tax Solutions, LLC v. City of El Paso**, 593 S.W.3d 903, 909-10 (Tex.App.—El Paso 2019, no pet.).

Casa Palmira, LP v. Taylor Child Care, LP, ___ S.W.3d ___, 2020 WL 2630701 (Tex.App.—El Paso 2020, no pet.) (No. 08-18-00009-CV; 5-22-20). "Rule 94 . . . requires that in pleading to a preceding pleading, a party shall set forth affirmatively waiver[ ] and any other matter constituting an avoidance or affirmative defense. This is true regardless of the alignment of the parties. Thus, in order for a plaintiff to rely on an affirmative defense, or 'matter of avoidance,' to defeat a defendant's affirmative defense, the plaintiff must allege it in a petition or supplemental petition." (Internal quotes omitted.)

Waggoner v. Sims, 401 S.W.3d 402, 404 n.1 (Tex.App.—Texarkana 2013, no pet.). "[P] suggests that because the limitations claim was not raised in the first responsive pleading to suit, it has been waived. Although [TRCP] 94 requires the claim to be pled, the Rule does not require the claim to be brought in the first responsive pleading on penalty of waiver."

Yanez v. Ducasson, No. 01-12-00173-CV, 2012 WL 6645011 (Tex.App.—Houston [1st Dist.] 2012, no pet.) (memo op.; 12-20-12). "While [TRCP 94] identifies 'failure of consideration' as an affirmative defense, it does not include lack of consideration. Failure of consideration is a legal principle distinct from lack of consideration. Moreover, the presence of consideration is a fundamental element to establish the existence of a contract. Accordingly, it is an element of the plaintiff's burden of proof in a breach of contract claim, not an affirmative defense or plea in avoidance." *See also* **Construction Fin. Servs. v. Chicago Title Ins.**, No.

04-12-00375-CV, 2013 WL 1846613 (Tex.App.—San Antonio 2013, pet. denied) (memo op.; 5-1-13) (footnote 8) (lack of consideration is not affirmative defense because it does not provide independent cause of action; rather, it goes directly to P's cause of action).

TRCP 95. PLEAS OF PAYMENT

When a defendant shall desire to prove payment, he shall file with his plea an account stating distinctly the nature of such payment, and the several items thereof; failing to do so, he shall not be allowed to prove the same, unless it be so plainly and particularly described in the plea as to give the plaintiff full notice of the character thereof.

Oct. 29, 1940, eff. Sept. 1, 1941.

See also **O'Connor's Texas Rules**, "The Answer—Denying Liability," ch. 3-E, §1 et seq.

ANNOTATIONS

Texas Mut. Ins. v. Ledbetter, 251 S.W.3d 31, 37 (Tex.2008). "Rule 95 . . . governs payment as an affirmative *defense*, not payment as an affirmative *claim*." *See also* **Southwestern Fire & Cas. Co. v. Larue**, 367 S.W.2d 162, 163 (Tex.1963).

Imperial Lofts, Ltd. v. Imperial Woodworks, Inc., 245 S.W.3d 1, 5 (Tex.App.—Waco 2007, pet. denied). "Payment is an affirmative defense to a claim on a debt, such as a promissory note, where typically the defendant alleges that it has paid the alleged debt. But the Rule 95 cases cited by [P] concern alleged payments made by the defendant to the plaintiff, not by third parties such as insurers. We thus reject [P's] application of Rule 95 to [D's] pleading of settlement payments, credits, and offsets [paid to P by insurance companies]. Accordingly, [D] was not barred by Rule 95 from presenting evidence of those payments, credits, and offsets."

TRCP 96. NO DISCONTINUANCE

Where the defendant has filed a counterclaim seeking affirmative relief, the plaintiff shall not be permitted by a discontinuance of his suit, to prejudice the right of the defendant to be heard on such counterclaim.

Oct. 29, 1940, eff. Sept. 1, 1941.

Source: TRCS art. 2016 (repealed).

See also TRCP 162; **O'Connor's Texas Rules**, "Effect on defendant's claims," ch. 7-F, §6.3.

TRCP 97. COUNTERCLAIM AND CROSS-CLAIM

(a) Compulsory Counterclaims. A pleading shall state as a counterclaim any claim within the jurisdiction of the court, not the subject of a pending action, which at the time of filing the pleading the pleader has against any opposing party, if it arises out of the transaction or occurrence that is the subject matter of the opposing party's claim and does not require for its adjudication the presence of third parties of whom the court cannot acquire jurisdiction; provided, however, that a judgment based upon a settlement or compromise of a claim of one party to the transaction or occurrence prior to a disposition on the merits shall not operate as a bar to the continuation or assertion of the claims of any other party to the transaction or occurrence unless the latter has consented in writing that said judgment shall operate as a bar.

(b) Permissive Counterclaims. A pleading may state as a counterclaim any claim against an opposing party whether or not arising out of the transaction or occurrence that is the subject matter of the opposing party's claim.

(c) Counterclaim Exceeding Opposing Claim. A counterclaim may or may not diminish or defeat the recovery sought by the opposing party. It may claim relief exceeding in amount or different in kind from that sought in the pleading of the opposing party, so long as the subject matter is within the jurisdiction of the court.

(d) Counterclaim Maturing or Acquired After Pleading. A claim which either matured or was acquired by the pleader after filing his pleading may be presented as a counterclaim by amended pleading.

(e) Cross-Claim Against Co-Party. A pleading may state as a cross-claim any claim by one party against a co-party arising out of the transaction or occurrence that is the subject matter either of the original action or of a counterclaim therein. Such cross-claim may include a claim that the party against whom it is asserted is or may be liable to the cross-claimant for all or part of a claim asserted in the action again the cross-claimant.

(f) Additional Parties. Persons other than those made parties to the original action may be made parties to a third party action, counterclaim or cross-claim in accordance with the provisions of Rules 38, 39 and 40.

(g) Tort shall not be the subject of set-off or counterclaim against a contractual demand nor a contractual demand against tort unless it arises out of or is incident to or is connected with same.

(h) Separate Trials; Separate Judgments. If the court orders separate trials as provided in Rule 174, judgment on a counterclaim or cross-claim may be rendered when the court has jurisdiction so to do, even if the claims of the opposing party have been dismissed or otherwise disposed of.

Oct. 29, 1940, eff. Sept. 1, 1941. Amended by orders of March 31, 1941, eff. Sept. 1, 1941; July 21, 1970, eff. Jan. 1, 1971; Dec. 5, 1983, eff. April 1, 1984.

See also CPRC §33.004 (responsible third parties); **O'Connor's Texas Rules**, "Parties & Claims," ch. 2-F, §1 et seq.; **O'Connor's Texas Rules**, "The Answer—Denying Liability," ch. 3-E, §1 et seq.; **O'Connor's Texas Forms**, FORMS 3E.

ANNOTATIONS

In re J.B. Hunt Transp., 492 S.W.3d 287, 292-93 (Tex.2016). In **Wyatt v. Shaw Plumbing Co.**, 760 S.W.2d 245 (Tex.1988), "we said that a counterclaim is compulsory if, among other things, 'it is not at the time of filing the answer the subject of a pending action.' [¶] There are two mistakes in that rendition of the compulsory-counterclaim rule. One problem is that the compulsory-counterclaim rule, located in [TRCP] 97(a), refers to 'the time of filing the *pleading*,' not 'the time of filing the *answer*' as we suggested. We therefore clarify that Rule 97 refers to *pleadings*, not *answers*. [¶] But the second . . . issue is that we erroneously conflated two distinct requirements in Rule 97(a). The first three clauses of Rule 97(a) read as follows: 'A pleading shall state as a counterclaim any claim within the jurisdiction of the court, not the subject of a pending action, which at the time of filing the pleading the pleader has against any opposing party[.]' Our decision in **Wyatt** combined 'at the time of filing the pleading . . .' with 'not the subject of a pending action,' creating the phrase '[the claim] is not at the time of filing the [pleading] the subject of a pending action.' But the third clause plainly does not modify the second clause. . . . Instead, the third clause must modify the word 'claim' in the first clause. [¶] This means that the second clause—'not the subject of a pending action'—is a standalone, unmodified phrase that modifies 'claim' in the first clause as well. [T]he claim must not have been the subject of a pending action *when the original suit was commenced*. If courts were to look at any subsequent snapshot in time, a wily litigant could avoid the compulsory-counterclaim rule by filing a second suit before that point in time to ensure that the litigant's claims are 'the subject of a pending action.' [A] counterclaim is compulsory if, in addition to Rule 97(a)'s other requirements, it was not the subject of a pending action when the original suit was commenced."

State & Cty. Mut. Fire Ins. v. Miller, 52 S.W.3d 693, 696 (Tex.2001). "[W]hen the parties are co-parties rather than opposing parties, the compulsory counterclaim rule and res judicata only act as a bar to a co-party's claim in a subsequent action if the co-parties had 'issues drawn between them' in the first action. For the purposes of res judicata, co-parties have issues drawn between them and become adverse when one co-party files a cross-action against a second co-party." *See also* **Getty Oil Co. v. Insurance Co. of N. Am.**, 845 S.W.2d 794, 800 (Tex.1992).

TRCP 98. SUPPLEMENTAL ANSWERS

The defendant's supplemental answers may contain special exceptions, general denial, and the allegations of new matter not before alleged by him, in reply to that which has been alleged by the plaintiff.

Oct. 29, 1940, eff. Sept. 1, 1941. Amended by order of March 31, 1941, eff. Sept. 1, 1941.

ANNOTATIONS

State v. Texas Mun. Power Agency, 565 S.W.2d 258, 277 (Tex.App.—Houston [1st Dist.] 1978, writ dism'd). "A supplemental answer is properly filed in response to any pleading of the plaintiff, regardless of whether it is an amended petition or a supplemental petition."

SECTION 5. CITATION

TRCP 99. ISSUANCE AND FORM OF CITATION

a. Issuance. Upon the filing of the petition, the clerk, when requested, shall forthwith issue a citation and deliver the citation as directed by the requesting party. The party requesting citation shall be responsible for obtaining service of the citation and a copy of the petition. Upon request, separate or additional citations shall be issued by the clerk. The clerk must retain a copy of the citation in the court's file.

Text of subsec. b effective for cases filed before January 1, 2021.

b. Form. The citation shall (1) be styled "The State of Texas," (2) be signed by the clerk under seal of court, (3) contain name and location of the court, (4) show date of filing of the petition, (5) show date of issuance of citation, (6) show file number, (7) show names of parties, (8) be directed to the defendant, (9) show the name and address of attorney for plaintiff, otherwise the address of plaintiff, (10) contain the time within which these rules require the defendant to file a written answer with the clerk who issued citation, (11) contain address of the clerk, and (12) shall notify the defendant that in case of failure of defendant to file an answer, judgment by default may be rendered for the relief demanded in the petition. The citation shall direct the defendant to file a written answer to the plaintiff's petition on or before 10:00 a.m. on the Monday next after the expiration of twenty days after the date of service thereof. The requirement of subsections 10 and 12 of this section shall be in the form set forth in section c of this rule.

Text of subsec. b effective for cases filed on or after January 1, 2021.

b. Form. The citation shall (1) be styled "The State of Texas," (2) be signed by the clerk under seal of court, (3) contain name and location of the court, (4) show date of filing of the petition, (5) show date of issuance of citation, (6) show file number, (7) show names of parties, (8) be directed to the defendant, (9) show the name and address of attorney for plaintiff, otherwise the address of plaintiff, (10) contain the time within which these rules require the defendant to file a written answer with the clerk who issued citation, (11)

contain address of the clerk, (12) notify the defendant that in case of failure of defendant to file and answer, judgment by default may be rendered for the relief demanded in the petition, and (13) notify the defendant that the defendant may be required to make initial disclosures. The citation shall direct the defendant to file a written answer to the plaintiff's petition on or before 10:00 a.m. on the Monday next after the expiration of twenty days after the date of service thereof. The requirement of subsections 10, 12, and 13 of this section shall be in the form set forth in section c of this rule.

Text of subsec. c effective for cases filed before January 1, 2021.

c. Notice. The citation shall include the following notice to the defendant: "You have been sued. You may employ an attorney. If you or your attorney do not file a written answer with the clerk who issued this citation by 10:00 a.m. on the Monday next following the expiration of twenty days after you were served this citation and petition, a default judgment may be taken against you."

Text of subsec. c effective for cases filed on or after January 1, 2021.

c. Notice. The citation shall include the following notice to the defendant: "You have been sued. You may employ an attorney. If you or your attorney do not file a written answer with the clerk who issued this citation by 10:00 a.m. on the Monday next following the expiration of twenty days after you were served this citation and petition, a default judgment may be taken against you. In addition to filing a written answer with the clerk, you may be required to make initial disclosures to the other parties of this suit. These disclosures generally must be made no later than 30 days after you file your answer with the clerk. Find out more at TexasLawHelp.org."

d. Copies. The party filing any pleading upon which citation is to be issued and served shall furnish the clerk with a sufficient number of copies thereof for use in serving the parties to be served, and when copies are so furnished the clerk shall make no charge for the copies.

Oct. 29, 1940, eff. Sept. 1, 1941. Amended by orders of Oct. 10, 1945, eff. Feb. 1, 1946; July 15, 1987, eff. Jan. 1, 1988; Dec. 12, 2011, eff. Jan. 1, 2012; Dec. 23, 2020, eff. Jan. 1, 2021.

See also **O'Connor's Texas Rules**, "Serving the Defendant with Suit," ch. 2-I, §1 et seq.; **O'Connor's Texas Rules**, "Default Judgment," ch. 7-A, §1 et seq.; **O'Connor's Texas Forms**, FORMS 2I.

ANNOTATIONS

Primate Constr., Inc. v. Silver, 884 S.W.2d 151, 153 (Tex.1994). "It is the responsibility of the one requesting service, not the process server, to see that service is properly accomplished. This responsibility extends to seeing that service is properly reflected in the record." *See also* **In re Buggs**, 166 S.W.3d 506, 508 (Tex.App.—Texarkana 2005, orig. proceeding).

Midstate Envtl. Servs. v. Peterson, 435 S.W.3d 287, 290 (Tex.App.—Waco 2014, no pet.). "One of the most glaring defects as to the citation [in this case] is the lack of a seal. While language in the citation recites that it was 'issued and given under my hand *and seal of said court* . . . ,' there is no seal visible on the copy of the original citation in the clerk's record. . . . Because we cannot presume a seal exists on the citation, the absence of a seal renders the original citation invalid. Accordingly, we join those courts that have held the absence of a seal is a defect in service that would make a default judgment improper."

Williams v. Williams, 150 S.W.3d 436, 445 (Tex.App.—Austin 2004, pet. denied). See annotation under TRCP 15.

Roberts v. Padre Island Brewing Co., 28 S.W.3d 618, 621-22 (Tex.App.—Corpus Christi 2000, pet. denied). "Reliance on the process server does not constitute due diligence in attempting service of process. A reasonable person . . . would have employed an alternate process server, a constable, or would have attempted service through other alternative court approved methods such as service through a court appointed third party. . . . Although the existence of diligence is usually a question of fact, a lack of diligence exists as a matter of law because it is clear that [P] did not exhaust all of the alternatives available to achieve proper service." *See also* **Holmes v. Texas Mut. Ins.**, 335 S.W.3d 738, 742 (Tex.App.—El Paso 2011, pet. denied); **Boyattia v. Hinojosa**, 18 S.W.3d 729, 734 (Tex.App.—Dallas 2000, pet. denied).

TRCP 100 to 102. REPEALED BY ORDER OF JULY 15, 1987, EFF. JAN. 1, 1988

TRCP 103. WHO MAY SERVE

Process—including citation and other notices, writs, orders, and other papers issued by the court—may be served anywhere by (1) any sheriff or constable or other person authorized by law, (2) any person authorized by law or by written order of the court who is not less than eighteen years of age, or (3) any person certified under order of the Supreme Court. Service by registered or certified mail and citation by publication must, if requested, be made by the clerk of the court in which the case is pending. But no person who is a party to or interested in the outcome of a suit may serve any process in that suit, and, unless otherwise authorized by a written court order, only a sheriff or constable may serve a citation in an action of forcible entry and detainer, a writ that requires the actual taking of possession of a person, property or thing, or process requiring that an enforcement action be physically enforced by the

person delivering the process. The order authorizing a person to serve process may be made without written motion and no fee may be imposed for issuance of such order.

Oct. 29, 1940, eff. Sept. 1, 1941. Amended by orders of June 10, 1980, eff. Jan. 1, 1981; July 15, 1987, eff. Jan. 1, 1988; June 29, 2005, eff. July 1, 2005.

Comment—2005

The rule is amended to include among the persons authorized to effect service those who meet certification requirements promulgated by the Supreme Court and to prohibit private individuals from serving certain types of process unless, in rare circumstances, a court authorizes an individual to do so.

Comment—1988

The amendment makes clear that the courts are permitted to authorize persons other than Sheriffs or Constables to serve Citation. Further, Sheriffs or Constables are not restricted to service in their county. The last sentence is added to avoid the necessity of motions and fees.

Source: New rule.

See also **O'Connor's Texas Rules**, "Serving the Defendant with Suit," ch. 2-I, §1 et seq.; **O'Connor's Texas Rules**, "Default Judgment," ch. 7-A, §1 et seq.

ANNOTATIONS

Garcia v. Tester, No. 13-15-00498-CV, 2016 WL 4578405 (Tex.App.—Corpus Christi 2016, no pet.) (memo op.; 9-1-16). "[D] argues that [process server's] affidavit is insufficient because it stated merely that [process server] was authorized by a written order of 'a court in this county' rather than by 'a written order of *the* court' as required by [TRCP 103]. [D] contends that, according to the plain language of [TRCP 103], a private process server in a given case must be authorized by a written order of the particular court in which that case is pending. [¶] We disagree with [D's] assertion. . . . [Process server's] averment that he is authorized 'to serve citations and other notices' is sufficient to show that he was, in fact, authorized under Rule 103 to serve process in this case." *See also* **Mayfield v. Dean Witter Fin. Servs.**, 894 S.W.2d 502, 505-06 (Tex.App.—Austin 1995, writ denied).

TRCP 104. REPEALED BY ORDER OF JULY 15, 1987, EFF. JAN. 1, 1988

TRCP 105. DUTY OF OFFICER OR PERSON RECEIVING

The officer or authorized person to whom process is delivered shall endorse thereon the day and hour on which he received it, and shall execute and return the same without delay.

Oct. 29, 1940, eff. Sept. 1, 1941. Amended by orders of July 11, 1978, eff. Jan. 1, 1978; July 15, 1987, eff. Jan. 1, 1988.

Source: TRCS art. 2025 (repealed).

See also **O'Connor's Texas Rules**, "Serving the Defendant with Suit," ch. 2-I, §1 et seq.; **O'Connor's Texas Rules**, "Default Judgment," ch. 7-A, §1 et seq.

ANNOTATIONS

Insurance Co. of Pa. v. Lejeune, 297 S.W.3d 254, 256 (Tex.2009). "Strict compliance with the rules governing service of citation is mandatory if a default judgment is to withstand an attack on appeal. Failure to comply with these rules constitutes error on the face of the record. Here, although [P] served [D] by certified mail, the record shows that the return of citation lacks the required notation showing the hour of receipt of citation. [P's] default judgment, therefore, cannot stand." *See also* **Business Staffing, Inc. v. Gonzalez**, 331 S.W.3d 791, 792 (Tex.App.—Eastland 2010, no pet.).

TRCP 106. METHOD OF SERVICE

(a) Unless the citation or court order otherwise directs, the citation must be served by:

(1) delivering to the defendant, in person, a copy of the citation, showing the delivery date, and of the petition; or

(2) mailing to the defendant by registered or certified mail, return receipt requested, a copy of the citation and of the petition.

(b) Upon motion supported by a statement—sworn to before a notary or made under penalty of perjury—listing any location where the defendant can probably be found and stating specifically the facts showing that service has been attempted under (a)(1) or (a)(2) at the location named in the statement but has not been successful, the court may authorize service:

(1) by leaving a copy of the citation and of the petition with anyone older than sixteen at the location specified in the statement; or

(2) in any other manner, including electronically by social media, email, or other technology that the statement or other evidence shows will be reasonably effective to give the defendant notice of the suit.

Oct. 29, 1940, eff. Sept. 1, 1941. Amended by orders of Aug. 18, 1947, eff. Dec. 31, 1947; July 22, 1975, eff. Jan. 1, 1976; July 11, 1977, eff. Jan. 1, 1978; June 10, 1980, eff. Jan. 1, 1981; July 15, 1987, eff. Jan. 1, 1988; April 24, 1990, eff. Sept. 1, 1990; Aug. 21, 2020, eff. Dec. 31, 2020; Dec. 18, 2020, eff. Dec. 31, 2020.

Comment—2020

Rule 106 is revised in response to section 17.033 of the Civil Practice and Remedies Code, which calls for rules to provide for substituted service of citation by social media. Amended Rule 106(b)(2) clarifies that a court may, in proper circumstances, permit service of citation electronically by social media, email, or other technology. In determining whether to permit electronic service of process, a court should consider whether the technology actually belongs to the defendant and whether the defendant regularly uses or recently used the technology. Other clarifying and stylistic changes have been made.

Comment—1988

Conforms to amendment to Rule 103.

Source: TRCS art. 2026 (repealed).

See also **O'Connor's Texas Rules**, "Serving the Defendant with Suit," ch. 2-I, §1 et seq.; **O'Connor's Texas Rules**, "Default Judgment," ch. 7-A, §1 et seq.; **O'Connor's Texas Forms**, FORMS 2I:4, 2I:5, 2I:6; **O'Connor's Texas Family Law Handbook**, "Service of process," ch. 3-A, §8 (suit for divorce); **O'Connor's Texas Family Law Handbook**, "Service of process," ch. 4-D, §5 (suit to dissolve marriage with children).

ANNOTATIONS

Zanchi v. Lane, 408 S.W.3d 373, 380 (Tex.2013). "[D] argues that in order to 'serve' an expert report on a defendant who has not yet been served with process, the claimant must comply with the service-of-citation requirements under [TRCP] 106. We disagree. Rule 106 by its terms applies solely to service of citation. If the Legislature had intended to require a claimant to serve an expert report in accordance with Rule 106, it clearly knew how to do so."

State Farm Fire & Cas. Co. v. Costley, 868 S.W.2d 298, 298-99 (Tex.1993). "Under Rule 106(b) a court may authorize substituted service only after a plaintiff has unsuccessfully tried to effect personal service or service by certified mail, return receipt requested, as required by Rule 106(a). . . . Thus, to require proof of actual notice upon substituted service would frustrate Rule 106(b)'s purpose of providing alternate methods [of service]." *See also* **Singh v. Trinity Mktg. & Distrib. Co.**, 397 S.W.3d 257, 263-64 (Tex.App.—El Paso 2013, no pet.).

Uvalde Country Club v. Martin Linen Sup. Co., 690 S.W.2d 884, 885 (Tex.1985). "There are no presumptions in favor of valid issuance, service, and return of citation in the face of a writ of error [now a restricted appeal] attack on a default judgment. Moreover, failure to affirmatively show strict compliance with the [TRCPs] renders the attempted service of process invalid and of no effect." *See also* **Steinke v. Mann**, 276 S.W.3d 608, 609-10 (Tex.App.—Waco 2008, no pet.) (court must expressly authorize service in accordance with either Rule 106(b)(1) or (b)(2)).

Creaven v. Creaven, 551 S.W.3d 865, 870 (Tex.App.—Houston [14th Dist.] 2018, no pet.). "When a trial court orders substituted service under [TRCP] 106, the only authority for the substituted service is the order itself. As a result, any deviation from the trial court's order necessitates a reversal of the default judgment based on service. *At 871:* [P] served [D] via substituted service under Rule 106, and thus she was required to follow the trial court's instructions precisely. The trial court required the citation and petition to be left . . . at an address located on the street named 'Cambrian Park' in Sugar Land, Texas. In the Affidavit of Service, the process server states that he served the citation and petition by *affixing* the documents to the front door at an address located on the street named 'Cambrian Court' in Sugar Land. *At 873-74:* [I]f [P] actually complied with the substituted service order—because Cambrian Park and Cambrian Court are indeed the same street or for any other reason—it was her responsibility to correct any errors in the return of service. This responsibility extends to seeing that service is properly reflected in the record. [¶] [P] had the ability to amend the return of service. [TRCP] 118 allows for liberal amendment of the return of service to show the facts of service. And if the facts as recited in the process server's return are incorrect and do not show proper service, the one requesting service must amend the return prior to judgment. [¶] [P] did not seek to amend the Affidavit of Service to show that service was completed at the address ordered by the trial court. Because of this failure, there remains an obvious defect on the face of the record based on inconsistencies between the Affidavit of Service and the substituted service order. [¶] We conclude that in failing to submit a return of service that shows [D] was served at the address referenced in the substituted service order, [P] failed to show she strictly complied with the order."

Luby v. Wood, No. 03-12-00179-CV, 2014 WL 1365736 (Tex.App.—Austin 2014, no pet.) (memo op.; 4-2-14). "[W]e have been unable to find any case supporting the proposition that a single attempt at service at a post office box is enough to warrant substituted service of process. [¶] Similarly, we have been unable to find any case standing for the proposition that mailing by regular mail a copy of the citation and the petition to a post office box under these circumstances can qualify as effective substituted service of process establishing jurisdiction over an individual. [Here], although the process server swore that the post office box was 'in current use,' the server's affidavit does not clarify whether that meant that [D] was regularly checking his mail there or simply that rental period for the box had not yet expired. Accordingly, the statement in the process server's affidavit [did not satisfy the requirements of Rule 106(b)]."

James v. Commission for Lawyer Discipline, 310 S.W.3d 586, 591 (Tex.App.—Dallas 2010, no pet.). "Rule 106 does not require that personal service be attempted at multiple locations before the trial court may authorize substituted service. . . ."

Coronado v. Norman, 111 S.W.3d 838, 842 (Tex.App.—Eastland 2003, pet. denied). The process server's "affidavit does not contain sufficient facts to satisfy Rule 106(b). While the . . . inclusion of the dates and times of attempted service [is not specifically required,] the specific dates and times of attempted service are important to establish sufficient facts to uphold a default judgment under Rule 106(b). Every attempt at personal service in this case may have been while [D] was at work. When told that [D] 'was not there,' the process server apparently did not try to find out where [D] could be located or when he would return."

TRCP 107. RETURN OF SERVICE

(a) The officer or authorized person executing the citation must complete a return of service. The return may, but need not, be endorsed on or attached to the citation.

(b) The return, together with any document to which it is attached, must include the following information:

(1) the cause number and case name;

(2) the court in which the case is filed;

(3) a description of what was served;

(4) the date and time the process was received for service;

(5) the person or entity served;

(6) the address served;

(7) the date of service or attempted service;

(8) the manner of delivery of service or attempted service;

(9) the name of the person who served or attempted to serve the process;

(10) if the person named in (9) is a process server certified under order of the Supreme Court, his or her identification number and the expiration date of his or her certification; and

(11) any other information required by rule or law.

(c) When the citation was served by registered or certified mail as authorized by Rule 106, the return by the officer or authorized person must also contain the return receipt with the addressee's signature.

(d) When the officer or authorized person has not served the citation, the return shall show the diligence used by the officer or authorized person to execute the same and the cause of failure to execute it, and where the defendant is to be found, if ascertainable.

(e) The officer or authorized person who serves or attempts to serve a citation must sign the return. If the return is signed by a person other than a sheriff, constable, or the clerk of the court, the return must either be verified or be signed under penalty of perjury. A return signed under penalty of perjury must contain the statement below in substantially the following form:

"My name is ______ (First) ______ (Middle) ______ (Last), my date of birth is ______, and my address is ______ (Street), ______ (City), ______ (State), ______ (Zip Code), and ______ (Country). I declare under penalty of perjury that the foregoing is true and correct.

Executed in ______ County, State of ______, on the ______ day of ______ (Month), ______ (Year).

______
Declarant"

(f) Where citation is executed by an alternative method as authorized by Rule 106, proof of service shall be made in the manner ordered by the court.

(g) The return and any document to which it is attached must be filed with the court and may be filed electronically or by facsimile, if those methods of filing are available.

(h) No default judgment shall be granted in any cause until proof of service as provided by this rule or by Rules 108 or 108a, or as ordered by the court in the event citation is executed by an alternative method under Rule 106, shall have been on file with the clerk of the court ten days, exclusive of the day of filing and the day of judgment.

Oct. 29, 1940, eff. Sept. 1, 1941. Amended by orders of July 11, 1977, eff. Jan. 1, 1978; June 10, 1980, eff. Jan. 1, 1981; July 15, 1987, eff. Jan. 1, 1988; April 24, 1990, eff. Sept. 1, 1990; Dec. 12, 2011, eff. Jan. 1, 2012.

Comment—1990

To state more directly that a default judgment can be obtained when the defendant has been served with process in a foreign country pursuant to the provisions of Rules 108 or 108a.

Comment—1988

Amendments are made to conform to changes in Rule 103.

Source: TRCS arts. 2034, 2036 (repealed).

See also TRCP 16; **O'Connor's Texas Rules**, "Proof of service—The return," ch. 2-I, §9; **O'Connor's Texas Rules**, "Default Judgment," ch. 7-A, §1 et seq.

ANNOTATIONS

Campus Invs. v. Cullever, 144 S.W.3d 464, 466 (Tex.2004). "When substituted service on a statutory agent is allowed, the designee is not an agent for *serving* but for *receiving* process on the defendant's behalf. A certificate . . . from the Secretary of State *conclusively* establishes that process was served. As the purpose of Rule 107 is to establish whether there has been proper citation and service, the Secretary's certificate fulfills that purpose." *See also* **El Paisano Nw. Hwy., Inc. v. Arzate**, No. 05-12-01457-CV, 2014 WL 1477701 (Tex.App.—Dallas 2014, no pet.) (memo op.; 4-14-14) (P who strictly complies with rules for substituted service on Secretary of State is not required to also strictly comply with TRCP 106 and 107).

Primate Constr., Inc. v. Silver, 884 S.W.2d 151, 152-53 (Tex.1994). "The return of service is not a trivial, formulaic document. It has long been considered prima facie evidence of the facts recited therein. [¶] The officer's return does not cease to be prima facie evidence of the facts of service simply because the facts are recited in a form rather than filled in by the officer. . . . If the facts as recited in the sheriff's return, pre-printed or otherwise, are incorrect and do not show proper service, the one requesting service must

amend the return prior to judgment." *See also* **Redwood Corp. v. Louiseau**, 113 S.W.3d 866, 869 (Tex.App.—Austin 2003, no pet.) (return is not prima facie evidence of anything about which it is silent).

Camoco, LLC v. Terrazas, 569 S.W.3d 270, 273-74 (Tex.App.—El Paso 2018, no pet.). TRCP 107 "requires the return to include, among other things, 'the manner of delivery of service or attempted service.' [¶] [A] long line of authority in this state holds that the manner of delivery of service or attempted service is not satisfied by merely stating that a person 'was served' or that citation was delivered 'by serving' a particular person. [¶] But here the return does not use the conclusory 'by serving' language; it states service was accomplished *by delivering*. [D] contends that 'by serving' and 'by delivering' are semantically identical in that both are stating the legal conclusion that service was made but fail to state the manner of delivery of service. We disagree. As several of our sister courts have concluded, the term 'by delivering' denotes personal service. Here, the return states service was accomplished 'by delivering to [D] . . . by delivering to its registered agent . . . by delivering to [the] designated person to accept service . . . .' Accordingly, the return contains a statement specifying the manner of service as personal service and references a party capable of receiving it."

Rhodes v. Kelly, No. 05-16-00888-CV, 2017 WL 2774452 (Tex.App.—Dallas 2017, pet. denied) (memo op.; 6-27-17). "Service of citation must be in strict compliance with the [TRCPs] to establish jurisdiction over a defendant and support a default judgment. If strict compliance is not shown, the service of process is invalid and of no effect. [¶] However, strict compliance with the rules does not require obeisance to the minutest detail. . . . As long as the record as a whole, including the petition, citation, and return, shows that the citation was served on the defendant in the suit, service of process will not be invalidated." (Internal quotes omitted.)

Yazdchi v. Wells Fargo, No. 01-15-00381-CV, 2016 WL 6212998 (Tex.App.—Houston [1st Dist.] 2016, no pet.) (memo op.; 10-25-16). "The return must show service of the correct pleading, and omitting the type of document served to the defendant does not show service of any pleading. [I]n this case an officer used a pre-printed form to document return of service, but left blank the spot to show what pleading, if any, was served on [D]. Thus, the face of the record indicates service was defective. . . ."

James v. Commission for Lawyer Discipline, 310 S.W.3d 586, 591 (Tex.App.—Dallas 2010, no pet.). "The trial court's order for substituted service did not prescribe a manner for the proof of service, and [D] argues that omission rendered the order for substituted service void. We disagree. '[I]n the absence of a specification in the trial court's [TRCP] 106 order of a *different* manner of proving service, proof of service in the normal manner authorized by [TRCP] 107 is sufficient.' "

Myan Mgmt. Grp. v. Adam Sparks Family Revocable Trust, 292 S.W.3d 750, 753-54 (Tex.App.—Dallas 2009, no pet.). "Service is invalid if the name on the return alters the identity of the defendant, but a minor change in the name does not render the return defective. [¶] Examples of name differences held not to invalidate service include the removal of a middle initial on the return, the omission of the corporate designation 'Inc.,' the lack of an accent mark on a corporate name, and the substitution of '@' for 'at.' [¶] [Here, r]emoving periods from 'L.L.C.' is a variation as minor as the lack of an accent mark on a corporate name. . . . Similarly, dropping 'Group, L.L.C.' from the entity name is like dropping 'Inc.' from the entity name. . . . Neither omission suggests that a different entity was served than the one listed in the petition."

All Commercial Floors, Inc. v. Barton & Rasor, 97 S.W.3d 723, 727 (Tex.App.—Fort Worth 2003, no pet.). "[A] corporation is not a person capable of accepting process, and it must be served through its agents. Therefore, because the record shows on its face that the return was not signed by the addressee or registered agent and [D] is not capable of receiving service, [P] has failed to strictly comply with Rule 107."

Union Pac. Corp. v. Legg, 49 S.W.3d 72, 78 (Tex.App.—Austin 2001, no pet.). "The clerk's return of the citation directed to [D] and the accompanying certified-mail receipt do not bear a file mark or other indication that they were in fact filed with the clerk on a particular day, or that they were, indeed, filed at all. Consequently, they do not show they were 'on file' for the requisite ten days before default judgment was granted. We hold this violates the strict-compliance requirement. *At 79:* Rule 107 also requires that the return receipt bear 'the addressee's signature' when service is by certified mail. The return receipt in this instance bears only a stamp rather than a handwritten signature. . . . We believe the return receipt does not bear the requisite addressee's signature. A stamped signature may be sufficient if shown to be authorized by proof in the record, but no such proof appears here. We hold the return fatally defective. . . ."

TRCP 108. SERVICE IN ANOTHER STATE

Where the defendant is absent from the State, or is a nonresident of the State, the form of notice to such defendant of the institution of the suit shall be the same as prescribed for citation to a resident defendant; and such notice may be served by any disinterested person who is not less than eighteen years of age, in the same manner as provided in Rule 106 hereof. The return of service in such cases shall be completed in accordance with Rule 107. A defendant served with such notice shall be required to appear and answer in the same manner and time and under the same penalties as if he had been personally served with a citation within this State to the full extent that he may be required to appear and answer under the Constitution of the United States in an action either in rem or in personam.

Oct. 29, 1940, eff. Sept. 1, 1941. Amended by order of July 22, 1975, eff. Jan. 1, 1976; Dec. 12, 2011, eff. Jan. 1, 2012.

See also **O'Connor's Texas Rules**, "Serving the Defendant with Suit," ch. 2-I, §1 et seq.

ANNOTATIONS

Paramount Pipe & Sup. Co. v. Muhr, 749 S.W.2d 491, 495-96 (Tex.1988). TRCP 108 "is a valid procedural alternative to service under the long-arm statute. . . . So long as the allegations confronting [D] were sufficient to satisfy due process requirements, the trial court had jurisdiction to render judgment by default against him. The only question . . . is whether the jurisdictional allegations in the petitions were sufficient, under the [U.S.] Constitution . . ., to require [D] to answer."

TRCP 108a. SERVICE OF PROCESS IN FOREIGN COUNTRIES

(a) *Method.* Service of process may be effected on a party in a foreign country if the citation and petition is served:

(1) as prescribed by the foreign country's law for service in that country in an action in its courts of general jurisdiction;

(2) as the foreign authority directs in response to a letter rogatory or letter of request;

(3) as provided by Rule 106(a);

(4) pursuant to the terms and provisions of any applicable international agreement;

(5) by diplomatic or consular officials when authorized by the United States Department of State; or

(6) by other means not prohibited by international agreement or the foreign country's law, as the court orders.

The method for service of process in a foreign country must be reasonably calculated, under all of the circumstances, to give actual notice of the proceedings to the defendant in time to answer and defend. A defendant served with process under this rule must appear and answer in the same manner and time and under the same penalties as if the defendant had been personally served with citation within this state to the full extent that the defendant may be required to appear and answer under the Constitution of the United States or under any applicable international agreement in an action either in rem or in personam.

(b) *Return.* Proof of service may be made as prescribed by the foreign country's law, by court order, by Rule 107, or by a method provided in any applicable international agreement.

Dec. 5, 1983, eff. April 1, 1984. Amended by order of Aug. 21, 2020, eff. Dec. 31, 2020; Dec. 18, 2020, eff. Dec. 31, 2020.

Comment—2020

Rule 108a is revised to provide that "other means" of service ordered under (a)(6) must not be prohibited by international agreement. Other clarifying and stylistic changes have been made.

See also CPRC §§17.044, 17.045; **O'Connor's Texas Rules**, "Service outside the United States," ch. 2-I, §11.

ANNOTATIONS

Commission of Contracts v. Arriba, Ltd., 882 S.W.2d 576, 584 (Tex.App.—Houston [1st Dist.] 1994, no writ). "[Ps] argue that service on a resident of a foreign country under the long-arm statute is improper, and that a resident of a foreign country can only be served according to the methods of service prescribed in [TRCP] 108a. *At 585:* We find a party in a foreign country may be served under the long-arm statute."

TRCP 109. CITATION BY PUBLICATION

When a party to a suit, his agent or attorney, shall make oath that the residence of any party defendant is unknown to affiant, and to such party when the affidavit is made by his agent or attorney, or that such defendant is a transient person, and that after due diligence such party and the affiant have been unable to locate the whereabouts of such defendant, or that such defendant is absent from or is a nonresident of the State, and that the party applying for the citation has attempted to obtain personal service of nonresident notice as provided for in Rule 108, but has been unable to do so, the clerk shall issue citation for such defendant for service by publication. In such cases it shall be the duty of the court trying the case to inquire into the sufficiency of the diligence exercised in attempting to ascertain the residence or whereabouts of the defendant or to obtain service of nonresident notice, as the case may be, before granting any judgment on such service.

Oct. 29, 1940, eff. Sept. 1, 1941. Amended by orders of Oct. 10, 1945, eff. Feb. 1, 1946; July 22, 1975, eff. Jan. 1, 1976; Dec. 5, 1983, eff. April 1, 1984.

Source: TRCS art. 2039 (repealed), first sentence.

See also **O'Connor's Texas Rules**, "Serving the Defendant with Suit," ch. 2-I, §1 et seq.; **O'Connor's Texas Rules**, "Default Judgment," ch. 7-A, §1 et seq.; **O'Connor's Texas Rules**, "MNT after service by publication," ch. 10-B, §10; **O'Connor's Texas Forms**, FORMS 2I:4, 2I:5, 2I:6; **O'Connor's Texas Family Law Handbook**, "Service by publication," ch. 3-A, §8.2.4 (suit for divorce); **O'Connor's Texas Family Law Handbook**, "Service by publication," ch. 4-D, §5.2.4 (suit to dissolve marriage with children).

ANNOTATIONS

In re E.R., 385 S.W.3d 552, 564 (Tex.2012). " '[I]f personal service can be effected by the exercise of reasonable dili-

gence, substituted service is not to be resorted to.' *At 565:* A diligent search must include inquiries that someone who really wants to find the defendant would make, and diligence is measured not by the quantity of the search but by its quality."

TRCP 109a. OTHER SUBSTITUTED SERVICE

Whenever citation by publication is authorized, the court may, on motion, prescribe a different method of substituted service, if the court finds, and so recites in its order, that the method so prescribed would be as likely as publication to give defendant actual notice. When such method of substituted service is authorized, the return of the officer executing the citation shall state particularly the manner in which service is accomplished, and shall attach any return receipt, returned mail, or other evidence showing the result of such service. Failure of defendant to respond to such citation shall not render the service invalid. When such substituted service has been obtained and the defendant has not appeared, the provisions of Rules 244 and 329 shall apply as if citation had been served by publication.

July 22, 1975, eff. Jan. 1, 1976.

See also **O'Connor's Texas Rules**, "Serving the Defendant with Suit," ch. 2-I, §1 et seq.; **O'Connor's Texas Forms**, FORMS 2I:4, 2I:5, 2I:6; **O'Connor's Texas Family Law Handbook**, "Substituted service—courthouse posting," ch. 4-D, §5.2.4(3)(b).

ANNOTATIONS

In re E.D., 553 S.W.3d 101, 105 (Tex.App.—Fort Worth 2018, no pet.). "A [TRCP] 109a order authorizing a method of substituted service other than publication could authorize service by the very same method as a [TRCP] 106 order authorizing substituted service. [T]he question of whether substituted service was ordered under rule 106(b) or rule 109a is generally of no practical concern. . . . *At 106-07:* But here, whether substituted service was ordered under rule 106 or 109a is a critical question. Jurisdiction turns on the answer, because when substituted service is ordered under rule 109a, the deadline for filing a motion for new trial is extended from 30 days to two years [under TRCP 329]. And here, [respondent's] motion to set aside the default judgment and for a new trial was filed 66 days after the judgment nunc pro tunc was signed. Thus, it was timely—subject to a two-year, rather than 30-day, deadline—only if the trial court ordered substituted service under rule 109a. [¶] Substituted service under rule 109a cannot be ordered unless citation by publication was authorized under [TRCP] 109. Thus, we face two questions: whether service by publication was authorized under rule 109 and, if so, whether the trial court's order authorized substituted service under 109a. [¶] As to the first question, to trigger the two-year deadline, service by publication must be 'authorized.' Rule 109 sets forth the requisites for authorization of service of citation by publication. . . . [Petitioner's] motion for substituted service did not comply with the requisites of this rule. It was not verified, nor did [petitioner] or his attorney sign an affidavit in support of the motion. [¶] As to the second question, any order granting substituted service under rule 109a must recite that the substituted method of service 'would be as likely as publication to give defendant actual notice.' The order here contained no such recitation. [¶] Because the order of substituted service was not authorized by rule 109 and it did not comply with rule 109a, we hold that the two-year period for filing a motion for new trial under rule 329 was never triggered."

TRCP 110. EFFECT OF RULES ON OTHER STATUTES

Where by statute or these rules citation by publication is authorized and the statute or rules do not specify the requisites of such citation or the method of service thereof, or where they direct that such citation be issued or served as in other civil actions, the provisions of these rules shall govern. Where, however, the statute authorizing citation by publication provides expressly for requisites of such citation or service thereof, or both, differing from the provisions of Rules 114, 115, and 116, these rules shall not govern, but the special statutory procedure shall continue in force; provided, however, that Rule 117a shall control with respect to citation in tax suits.

Oct. 29, 1940, eff. Sept. 1, 1941. Amended by order of Aug. 18, 1947, eff. Dec. 31, 1947.

TRCP 111. CITATION BY PUBLICATION IN ACTION AGAINST UNKNOWN HEIRS OR STOCKHOLDERS OF DEFUNCT CORPORATIONS

If the plaintiff, his agent, or attorney, shall make oath that the names of the heirs or stockholders against whom an action is authorized by Section 17.004, Civil Practice and Remedies Code, are unknown to the affiant, the clerk shall issue a citation for service by publication. Such citation shall be addressed to the defendants by a concise description of their classification, as "the Unknown Heirs of A.B., deceased," or "Unknown Stockholders of ________ Corporation," as the case may be, and shall contain the other requisites prescribed in Rules 114 and 115 and shall be served as provided by Rule 116.

Oct. 29, 1940, eff. Sept. 1, 1941. Amended by order of July 15, 1987, eff. Jan. 1, 1988.

See also **O'Connor's Texas Rules**, "Serving the Defendant with Suit," ch. 2-I, §1 et seq.; **O'Connor's Texas Rules**, "MNT after service by publication," ch. 10-B, §10.

TRCP 112. PARTIES TO ACTIONS AGAINST UNKNOWN OWNERS OR CLAIMANTS OF INTEREST IN LAND

In suits authorized by Section 17.005, Civil Practice and Remedies Code, all persons claiming under such convey-

ance whose names are known to plaintiff shall be made parties by name and cited to appear, in the manner now provided by law as in other suits; all other persons claiming any interest in such land under such conveyance may be made parties to the suit and cited by publication under the designation "all persons claiming any title or interest in land under deed heretofore given to _______ of _______________ as grantee" (inserting in the blanks the name and residence of grantee as given in such conveyance). It shall be permissible to join in one suit all persons claiming under two or more conveyances affecting title to the same tract of land.

Oct. 29, 1940, eff. Sept. 1, 1941. Amended by order of July 15, 1987, eff. Jan. 1, 1988.

See also CPRC §17.005; TRCP 113; **O'Connor's Texas Rules**, "Serving the Defendant with Suit," ch. 2-I, §1 et seq.; **O'Connor's Texas Rules**, "MNT after service by publication," ch. 10-B, §10.

TRCP 113. CITATION BY PUBLICATION IN ACTIONS AGAINST UNKNOWN OWNERS OR CLAIMANTS OF INTEREST IN LAND

In suits authorized by Section 17.005, Civil Practice and Remedies Code, plaintiff, his agent or attorney shall make and file with the clerk of the court an affidavit, stating

(a) the name of the grantee as set out in the conveyance constituting source of title of defendants, and

(b) stating that affiant does not know the names of any persons claiming title or interest under such conveyance other than as stated in plaintiff's petition and

(c) if the conveyance is to a company or association name as grantee, further stating whether grantee is incorporated or unincorporated, if such fact is known, and if such fact is unknown, so stating.

Said clerk shall thereupon issue a citation for service upon all persons claiming any title or interest in such land under such conveyance. The citation in such cases shall contain the requisites and be served in the manner provided by Rules 114, 115 and 116.

Oct. 29, 1940, eff. Sept. 1, 1941. Amended by orders of July 20, 1954, eff. Jan. 1, 1955; July 15, 1987, eff. Jan. 1, 1988; April 24, 1990, eff. Sept. 1, 1990.

See also CPRC §17.005; TRCP 112; **O'Connor's Texas Rules**, "Serving the Defendant with Suit," ch. 2-I, §1 et seq.; **O'Connor's Texas Rules**, "MNT after service by publication," ch. 10-B, §10.

ANNOTATIONS

Quarles v. Champion Int'l, 760 S.W.2d 792, 794 (Tex.App.—Beaumont 1988, writ denied). Service of citation by publication on a known party is improper, and "this notice requirement to a known party is of due process dimension."

TRCP 114. CITATION BY PUBLICATION; REQUISITES

Where citation by publication is authorized by these rules, the citation shall contain the requisites prescribed by Rules 15 and 99, in so far as they are not inconsistent herewith, provided that no copy of the plaintiff's petition shall accompany this citation, and the citation shall be styled "The State of Texas" and shall be directed to the defendant or defendants by name, if their names are known, or to the defendant or defendants as designated in the petition, if unknown, or such other classification as may be fixed by any statute or by these rules. Where there are two or more defendants or classes of defendants to be served by publication, the citation may be directed to all of them by name and classification, so that service may be completed by publication of the one citation for the required number of times. The citation shall contain the names of the parties, a brief statement of the nature of the suit (which need not contain the details and particulars of the claim) a description of any property involved and of the interest of the named or unknown defendant or defendants, and, where the suit involves land, the requisites of Rule 115. If issued from the district or county court, the citation shall command such parties to appear and answer at or before 10 o'clock a.m. of the first Monday after the expiration of 42 days from the date of issuance thereof, specifying the day of the week, the day of the month, and the time of day the defendant is required to answer. If issued from the justice of the peace court, such citation shall command such parties to appear and answer on or before the first day of the first term of court which convenes after the expiration of 42 days from the date of issue thereof, specifying the day of the week, and the day of the month, that such term will meet.

Oct. 29, 1940, eff. Sept. 1, 1941. Amended by orders of Sept. 20, 1941, eff. Dec. 31, 1941; Dec. 16, 1987, eff. Jan. 1, 1988.

See also **O'Connor's Texas Family Law Handbook**, "Suit for Divorce," ch. 3-A, §1 et seq.; **O'Connor's Texas Family Law Handbook**, "Suit to Dissolve Marriage with Children," ch. 4-D, §1 et seq.

TRCP 115. FORM OF PUBLISHED CITATION IN ACTIONS INVOLVING LAND

In citations by publication involving land, it shall be sufficient in making the brief statement of the claim in such citation to state the kind of suit, the number of acres of land involved in the suit, or the number of the lot and block, or any other plat description that may be of record if the land is situated in a city or town, the survey on which and the county in which the land is situated, and any special pleas

which are relied upon in such suit.

Oct. 29, 1940, eff. Sept. 1, 1941.

TRCP 116. SERVICE OF CITATION BY PUBLICATION

(a) *Public Information Internet Website Defined.* "Public Information Internet Website" means the website developed and maintained under section 72.034 of the Government Code.

(b) *Where to Publish.*

(1) Generally. Except as otherwise provided in (2), the citation must be served by publication in a newspaper under (c) and on the Public Information Internet Website under (d).

(2) When Newspaper Publication Not Required. The citation need not be published in a newspaper if:

(A) the party requesting citation files a Statement of Inability to Afford Payment of Court Costs under Rule 145;

(B) the total cost of the required publication exceeds $200 each week or an amount set by the Supreme Court, whichever is greater; or

(C) the county in which the publication is required does not have any newspaper published, printed, or generally circulated in the county.

(c) *Newspaper Publication.*

(1) Who Must Serve. The citation must be served by any sheriff or constable or by the clerk of the court in which the case is pending.

(2) Time for Publication. The citation must be published once each week for 4 consecutive weeks, and the first publication must be at least 28 days before the return is filed.

(3) Suits Not Involving Land Title or Real Estate Partition. In all suits that do not involve the title to land or the partition of real estate, the citation must be published in a newspaper in the county where the suit is pending.

(4) Suits Involving Land Title or Real Estate Partition. In all suits that involve the title to land or partition of real estate, the citation must be published in a newspaper in the county where the land, or a portion thereof, is situated.

(d) *Public Information Internet Website Publication.*

(1) Who Must Serve. The citation must be served by the clerk of the court in which the case is pending.

(2) Time for Publication. The citation must be published for at least 28 days before the return is filed.

(3) Other Guidelines. The citation must be published in accordance with any other guidelines established by the Office of Court Administration.

Oct. 29, 1940, eff. Sept. 1, 1941. Amended by order of Dec. 5, 1983, eff. April 1, 1984; orders of Jan. 14, 2020, and May 26, 2020, approved June 30, 2020, eff. July 1, 2020.

Comment—2020

Rule 116 is amended to implement section 72.034(d) of the Government Code.

See also **O'Connor's Texas Rules**, "Substituted service," ch. 2-I, §4.3.

TRCP 117. RETURN OF CITATION BY PUBLICATION

(a) *Return of Citation by Newspaper Publication.* If the citation was served by newspaper publication, the return must state how the citation was published, specify the dates of publication, be signed by the officer who served the citation, and be accompanied by an image of the publication.

(b) *Return of Citation by Public Information Internet Website Publication.* If the citation was served by publication on the Public Information Internet Website, the return must specify the dates of publication and be generated by the Office of Court Administration.

Oct. 29, 1940, eff. Sept. 1, 1941. Amended by order of Dec. 12, 2011, eff. Jan. 1, 2012; orders of Jan. 14, 2020, and May 26, 2020, approved June 30, 2020, eff. July 1, 2020.

Source: TRCS art. 2043, unchanged (repealed).

TRCP 117a. CITATION IN SUITS FOR DELINQUENT AD VALOREM TAXES

In all suits for collection of delinquent ad valorem taxes, the rules of civil procedure governing issuance and service of citation shall control the issuance and service of citation therein, except as herein otherwise specially provided.

1. Personal Service: Owner and Residence Known, Within State: Where any defendant in a tax suit is a resident of the State of Texas and is not subject to citation by publication under subdivision 3 below, the process shall conform substantially to the form hereinafter set out for personal service and shall contain the essential elements and be served and returned and otherwise regulated by the provisions of Rules 99 to 107, inclusive.

2. Personal Service: Owner and Residence Known, Out of State: Where any such defendant is absent from the State or is a non-resident of the State and is not subject to citation by publication under subdivision 3 below, the process shall conform substantially to the form hereinafter set out for personal service and shall contain the essential elements and be served and returned and otherwise regulated by the provisions of Rule 108.

**3. Service by Publication: Nonresident, Absent from State, Transient, Name Unknown, Residence

Unknown, Owner Unknown, Heirs Unknown, Corporate Officers, Trustees, Receivers or Stockholders Unknown, Any Other Unknown Persons Owing or Claiming or Having an Interest: Where any defendant in a tax suit is a nonresident of the State, or is absent from the State, or is a transient person, or the name or the residence of any owner of any interest in any property upon which a tax lien is sought to be foreclosed, is unknown to the attorney requesting the issuance of process or filing the suit for the taxing unit, and such attorney shall make affidavit that such defendant is a nonresident of the State, or is absent from the State, or is a transient person, or that the name or residence of such owner is unknown and cannot be ascertained after diligent inquiry, each such person in every such class above mentioned, together with any and all other persons, including adverse claimants, owning or claiming or having any legal or equitable interest in or lien upon such property, may be cited by publication. All unknown owners of any interest in any property upon which any taxing unit seeks to foreclose a lien for taxes, including stockholders of corporations—defunct or otherwise—their successors, heirs, and assigns, may be joined in such suit under the designation of "unknown owners" and citation be had upon them as such; provided, however, that record owners of such property or of any apparent interest therein, including, without limitation, record lien holders, shall not be included in the designation of "unknown owners"; and provided further that where any record owner has rendered the property involved within five years before the tax suit is filed, citation on such record owner may not be had by publication or posting unless citation for personal service has been issued as to such record owner, with a notation thereon setting forth the same address as is contained on the rendition sheet made within such five years, and the sheriff or other person to whom citation has been delivered makes his return thereon that he is unable to locate the defendant. Where any attorney filing a tax suit for a taxing unit, or requesting the issuance of process in such suit, shall make affidavit that a corporation is the record owner of any interest in any property upon which a tax lien is sought to be foreclosed, and that he does not know, and after diligent inquiry has been unable to ascertain, the location of the place of business, if any, of such corporation, or the name or place of residence of any officer of such corporation upon whom personal service may be had, such corporation may be cited by publication as herein provided. All defendants of the classes enumerated above may be joined in the same citation by publication.

An affidavit which complies with the foregoing requirements therefor shall be sufficient basis for the citation above mentioned in connection with it but shall be held to be made upon the criminal responsibility of affiant.

Such citation by publication shall be directed to the defendants by names or by designation as hereinabove provided, and shall be issued and signed by the clerk of the court in which such tax suit is pending. It shall be sufficient if it states the file number and style of the case, the date of the filing of the petition, the names of all parties by name or by designation as hereinabove provided, and the court in which the suit is pending; shall command such parties to appear and defend such suit at or before 10 o'clock a.m. of the first Monday after the expiration of forty-two days from the date of the issuance thereof, specifying such date when such parties are required to answer; shall state the place of holding the court, the nature of the suit, and the date of the issuance of the citation; and shall be signed and sealed by the clerk.

The citation shall be published in the English language one time a week for two weeks in some newspaper published in the county in which the property is located, which newspaper must have been in general circulation for at least one year immediately prior to the first publication and shall in every respect answer the requirements of the law applicable to newspapers which are employed for such a purpose, the first publication to be not less than twenty-eight days prior to the return day fixed in the citation; and the affidavit of the editor or publisher of the newspaper giving the date of publication, together with a printed copy of the citation as published, shall constitute sufficient proof of due publication when returned and filed in court. If there is no newspaper published in the county, then the publication may be made in a newspaper in an adjoining county, which newspaper shall in every respect answer the requirements of the law applicable to newspapers which are employed for such a purpose. The maximum fee for publishing the citation shall be the lowest published word or line rate of that newspaper for classified advertising. If the publication of the citation cannot be had for this fee, chargeable as costs and payable upon sale of the property, as provided by law, and this fact is supported by the affidavit of the attorney for the plaintiff or the attorney requesting the issuance of the process, then service of the citation may be made by posting a copy at the courthouse door of the county in which the suit is pending, the citation to be posted at least twenty-eight days prior to the return day fixed in the citation. Proof of the posting of the citation shall be made by affidavit of the attorney for the plaintiff, or of the person posting it. When citation is served as here provided it shall be sufficient, and no other form of citation or notice to the named defendants therein shall be necessary.

4. Citation in Tax Suits: General Provisions:

Any process authorized by this rule may issue jointly in behalf of all taxing units who are plaintiffs or intervenors in any tax suit. The statement of the nature of the suit, to be set out in the citation, shall be sufficient if it contains a brief general description of the property upon which the taxes are due and the amount of such taxes, exclusive of interest, penalties, and costs, and shall state, in substance, that in such suit the plaintiff and all other taxing units who may set up their claims therein seek recovery of the delinquent ad valorem taxes due on said property, and the (establishment and foreclosure) of liens, if any, securing the payment of same, as provided by law; that in addition to the taxes all interest, penalties, and costs allowed by law up to and including the day of judgment are included in the suit; and that all parties to the suit, including plaintiff, defendants, and intervenors, shall take notice that claims for any taxes on said property becoming delinquent subsequent to the filing of the suit and up to the day of judgment, together with all interest, penalties, and costs allowed by law thereon, may, upon requests therefore, be recovered therein without further citation or notice to any parties thereto. Such citation need not be accompanied by a copy of plaintiff's petition and no such copy need be served. Such citation shall also show the names of all taxing units which assess and collect taxes on said property not made parties to such suit, and shall contain, in substance, a recitation that each party to such suit shall take notice of, and plead and answer to, all claims and pleadings then on file or thereafter filed in said cause by all other parties therein, or who may intervene therein and set up their respective tax claims against said property. After citation or notice has been given on behalf of any plaintiff or intervenor taxing unit, the court shall have jurisdiction to hear and determine the tax claims of all taxing units who are parties plaintiff, intervenor or defendant at the time such process is issued and of all taxing units intervening after such process is issued, not only for the taxes, interest, penalties, and costs which may be due on said property at the time the suit is filed, but those becoming delinquent thereon at any time thereafter up to and including the day of judgment, without the necessity of further citation or notice to any party to said suit; and any taxing unit having a tax claim against said property may, by answer or intervention, set up and have determined its tax claim without the necessity of further citation or notice to any parties to such suit.

5. Form of Citation by Publication or Posting: The form of citation by publication or posting shall be sufficient if it is in substantially the following form, with proper changes to make the same applicable to personal property, where necessary, and if the suit includes or is for the recovery of taxes assessed on personal property, a general description of such personal property shall be sufficient:

THE STATE OF TEXAS §

COUNTY OF ______ §

In the name and by the authority of the State of Texas

Notice is hereby given as follows:

To ____________________

____

and any and all other persons, including adverse claimants, owning or having or claiming any legal or equitable interest in or lien upon the following described property delinquent to Plaintiff herein, for taxes, to-wit: ____________

____

Which said property is delinquent to Plaintiff for taxes in the following amounts:

$____, exclusive of interest, penalties, and costs, and there is included in this suit in addition to the taxes all said interest, penalties, and costs thereon, allowed by law up to and including the day of judgment herein.

You are hereby notified that suit has been brought by ____ as Plaintiffs, against ______ as Defendants, by petition filed on the ____ day of ______, 20__, in a certain suit styled ______ v. ______ for collection of the taxes on said property and that said suit is now pending in the District Court of ____ County, Texas, ______ Judicial District, and the file number of said suit is ______, that the names of all taxing units which assess and collect taxes on the property hereinabove described, not made parties to this suit, are ____________.

Plaintiff and all other taxing units who may set up their tax claims herein seek recovery of delinquent ad valorem taxes on the property hereinabove described, and in addition to the taxes all interest, penalties, and costs allowed by law thereon up to and including the day of judgment herein, and the establishment and foreclosure of liens, if any, securing the payment of same, as provided by law.

All parties to this suit, including plaintiff, defendants, and intervenors, shall take notice that claims

not only for any taxes which were delinquent on said property at the time this suit was filed but all taxes becoming delinquent thereon at any time thereafter up to the day of judgment, including all interest, penalties, and costs allowed by law thereon, may, upon request therefore, be recovered herein without further citation or notice to any parties herein, and all said parties shall take notice of and plead and answer to all claims and pleadings now on file and which may hereafter be filed in said cause by all other parties herein, and all of those taxing units above named who may intervene herein and set up their respective tax claims against said property.

You are hereby commanded to appear and defend such suit on the first Monday after the expiration of forty-two (42) days from and after the date of issuance hereof, the same being the ____ day of _______, A.D., 20__ (which is the return day of such citation), before the honorable District Court of _______ County, Texas, to be held at the courthouse thereof, then and there to show cause why judgment shall not be rendered for such taxes, penalties, interest, and costs, and condemning said property and ordering foreclosure of the constitutional and statutory tax liens thereon for taxes due the plaintiff and the taxing units parties hereto, and those who may intervene herein, together with all interest, penalties, and costs allowed by law up to and including the day of judgment herein, and all costs of this suit.

Issued and given under my hand and seal of said court in the City of _______, _______ County, Texas, this ____ day of _______, A.D., 20__.

____
Clerk of the District Court.
_______ County, Texas,
_______ Judicial District.

6. Form of Citation by Personal Service in or out of State: The form of citation for personal service shall be sufficient if it is in substantially the following form, with proper changes to make the same applicable to personal property, where necessary, and if the suit includes or is for the recovery of taxes assessed on personal property, a general description of such personal property shall be sufficient:

THE STATE OF TEXAS

To _______, Defendant _______,

GREETING:

YOU ARE HEREBY COMMANDED to appear and answer before the Honorable District Court, _______ Judicial District, _______ County, Texas, at the Courthouse of said county in _______, Texas, at or before 10 o'clock a.m. of the Monday next after the expiration of 20 days from the date of service of this citation, then and there to answer the petition of _______, Plaintiff, filed in said Court on the ____ day of _______, A.D., 20__, against _______, Defendant _______, said suit being number _______ on the docket of said Court, the nature of which demand is a suit to collect delinquent ad valorem taxes on the property hereinafter described.

The amount of taxes due Plaintiff, exclusive of interest, penalties, and costs, is the sum of $_______, said property being described as follows, to-wit: _____
____

The names of all taxing units which assess and collect taxes on said property, not made parties to this suit, are: _______________________________

Plaintiff and all other taxing units who may set up their tax claims herein seek recovery of delinquent ad valorem taxes on the property hereinabove described, and in addition to the taxes all interest, penalties, and costs allowed by law thereon up to and including the day of judgment herein, and the establishment and foreclosure of liens securing the payment of same, as provided by law.

All parties to this suit, including plaintiff, defendants, and intervenors, shall take notice that claims not only for any taxes which were delinquent on said property at the time this suit was filed but all taxes becoming delinquent thereon at any time thereafter up to the day of judgment, including all interest, penalties, and costs allowed by law thereon, may, upon request therefore, be recovered herein without further citation or notice to any parties herein, and all said parties shall take notice of and plead and answer to all claims and pleadings now on file and which may hereafter be filed in this cause by all other parties hereto, and by all of those taxing units above named, who may intervene herein and set up their respective tax claims against said property.

If this citation is not served within 90 days after the date of its issuance, it shall be returned unserved.

The officer executing this return shall promptly serve the same according to the requirements of law and the mandates hereof and make due return as the law directs.

Issued and given under my hand and seal of said Court at ____, Texas this the ____ day of ______, A.D., 20__.

____
Clerk of the District Court of
____ County, Texas.
By ______, Deputy.

Aug. 18, 1947, eff. Dec. 31, 1947. Amended by orders of May 4, 1948, eff. Oct. 1, 1948; July 17, 1950, eff. Dec. 1, 1950; July 15, 1987, eff. Jan. 1, 1988.

Comment—1988

This amendment updates the fee schedule for service of citation of publications to an acceptable fee level for both litigants and the publications.

Source: New rule.

See also **O'Connor's Texas Rules**, "Serving the Defendant with Suit," ch. 2-I, §1 et seq.

ANNOTATIONS

Mandel v. Lewisville ISD, 499 S.W.3d 65, 74 (Tex.App.—Fort Worth 2016, pet. denied). "[T]he question . . . is whether [TRCP] 21a . . . required service of the amended pleading or the intervention petitions upon [Ds] or whether, instead, [TRCP] 117a negated that requirement. [¶] The plain language of rule 117a signifies that in a suit for delinquent taxes, once a citation complying with the rule has been properly served, the party serving the citation along with intervening parties who do not serve citation may obtain a judgment for all taxes becoming delinquent before the rendition of the judgment 'without further . . . notice' to any defendant. In other words, the rule contemplates that after a citation is served, the party serving the citation and other parties may plead new claims and seek more onerous relief without further notice. *At 75:* Thus, the [TRCPs], which generally require the service of notice and pleadings, and rule 117a, which expressly negates the requirement of serving notice or pleadings in tax suits following the service of the citation, conflict. We conclude that rule 117a, which is the more specific rule, prevails in tax suits to the extent of the conflict."

Conseco Fin. Servicing Corp. v. Klein ISD, 78 S.W.3d 666, 675 (Tex.App.—Houston [14th Dist.] 2002, no pet.). "The permissive language in Rule 117a(4) indicates an intent to give *all other taxing* units the discretion to join the suit, rather than giving the taxing unit instituting the suit discretion to exclude other taxing units, or cause them to have to obtain issuance of their own citations. . . . Rule 117a does not require other taxing units to join a tax suit, but it clearly permits them to intervene without further service."

TRCP 118. AMENDMENT

At any time in its discretion and upon such notice and on such terms as it deems just, the court may allow any process or proof of service thereof to be amended, unless it clearly appears that material prejudice would result to the substantial rights of the party against whom the process issued.

Oct. 29, 1940, eff. Sept. 1, 1941.

See also **O'Connor's Texas Rules**, "Serving the Defendant with Suit," ch. 2-I, §1 et seq.

ANNOTATIONS

Higginbotham v. General Life & Acc. Ins., 796 S.W.2d 695, 697 (Tex.1990). Because a trial court's order holding that service was proper was "tantamount to formal amendment of the return of citation, the record was sufficient to show valid service."

LEJ Dev. Corp. v. Southwest Bank, 407 S.W.3d 863, 867-68 (Tex.App.—Fort Worth 2013, no pet.). "[T]he trial court may enter a postjudgment order granting amendment of a return of citation pursuant to rule 118 while the trial court retains plenary power. [¶] '[W]hen a return is amended under Rule 118, the amended return relates back and is regarded as filed when the original return was filed.' [This] satisfies the requirement that a return of service be on file for at least ten days before entry of judgment." *See also* **Gonzalez v. Tapia**, 287 S.W.3d 805, 808 (Tex.App.—Corpus Christi 2009, pet. denied) (trial court can amend proof of service after default judgment has become final and plenary power has expired).

TRCP 119. ACCEPTANCE OF SERVICE

The defendant may accept service of process, or waive the issuance or service thereof by a written memorandum signed by him, or by his duly authorized agent or attorney, after suit is brought, sworn to before a proper officer other than an attorney in the case, and filed among the papers of the cause, and such waiver or acceptance shall have the same force and effect as if the citation had been issued and served as provided by law. The party signing such memorandum shall be delivered a copy of plaintiff's petition, and the receipt of the same shall be acknowledged in such memorandum. In every divorce action such memorandum shall also include the defendant's mailing address.

Oct. 29, 1940, eff. Sept. 1, 1941. Amended by orders of Sept. 20, 1941, eff. Dec. 31, 1941; July 20, 1954, eff. Jan. 1, 1955; July 26, 1960, eff. Jan. 1, 1961.

Source: TRCS art. 2045 (repealed). Added requirement that the waiver of service be sworn to before an officer authorized to administer oaths.

See also CPRC §30.001; **O'Connor's Texas Rules**, "Serving the Defendant with Suit," ch. 2-I, §1 et seq.; **O'Connor's Texas Forms**, FORM 2I:1.

ANNOTATIONS

Deen v. Kirk, 508 S.W.2d 70, 71 (Tex.1974). "Under the provisions of [TRCP 119], a defendant may waive the issuance and service of citation by filing among the papers of the cause a verified written memorandum 'signed by him, or by his duly authorized agent or attorney, after suit is brought.' [TRCS] art. 2224 [now CPRC §30.001] prohibits the waiver of process by an instrument executed prior to institution of suit."

Approximately $58,641.00 v. State, 331 S.W.3d 579, 583 (Tex.App.—Houston [14th Dist.] 2011, no pet.). "A written recitation that the acceptance of service meets all requirements of Rule 119 satisfies the requirement of a written memorandum."

TRCP 119a. COPY OF DECREE

The district clerk shall forthwith mail a certified copy of the final divorce decree or order of dismissal to the party signing a memorandum waiving issuance or service of process. Such divorce decree or order of dismissal shall be mailed to the signer of the memorandum at the address stated in such memorandum or to the office of his attorney of record.

July 20, 1954, eff. Jan. 1, 1955.

TRCP 120. ENTERING APPEARANCE

The defendant may, in person, or by attorney, or by his duly authorized agent, enter an appearance in open court. Such appearance shall be noted by the judge upon his docket and entered in the minutes, and shall have the same force and effect as if the citation had been duly issued and served as provided by law.

Oct. 29, 1940, eff. Sept. 1, 1941.

Source: TRCS art. 2046 (repealed).

See also **O'Connor's Texas Rules**, "The Attorney," ch. 1-H, §1 et seq.; **O'Connor's Texas Rules**, "Special Appearance—Challenging Personal Jurisdiction," ch. 3-B, §1 et seq.

ANNOTATIONS

Mays v. Perkins, 927 S.W.2d 222, 225 (Tex.App.—Houston [1st Dist.] 1996, no writ). "A defendant's appearance before a court generally indicates a submission to the court's jurisdiction. However, the mere presence in court by an attorney, retained as counsel by a person formerly a party to the lawsuit, does not constitute a general appearance, unless the attorney seeks a judgment or an adjudication on some question." *See also* **In re D.M.B.**, 467 S.W.3d 100, 103 (Tex.App.—San Antonio 2015, pet. denied).

TRCP 120a. SPECIAL APPEARANCE

1. Notwithstanding the provisions of Rules 121, 122 and 123, a special appearance may be made by any party either in person or by attorney for the purpose of objecting to the jurisdiction of the court over the person or property of the defendant on the ground that such party or property is not amenable to process issued by the courts of this State. A special appearance may be made as to an entire proceeding or as to any severable claim involved therein. Such special appearance shall be made by sworn motion filed prior to motion to transfer venue or any other plea, pleading or motion; provided however, that a motion to transfer venue and any other plea, pleading, or motion may be contained in the same instrument or filed subsequent thereto without waiver of such special appearance; and may be amended to cure defects. The issuance of process for witnesses, the taking of depositions, the serving of requests for admissions, and the use of discovery processes, shall not constitute a waiver of such special appearance. Every appearance, prior to judgment, not in compliance with this rule is a general appearance.

2. Any motion to challenge the jurisdiction provided for herein shall be heard and determined before a motion to transfer venue or any other plea or pleading may be heard. No determination of any issue of fact in connection with the objection to jurisdiction is a determination of the merits of the case or any aspect thereof.

3. The court shall determine the special appearance on the basis of the pleadings, any stipulations made by and between the parties, such affidavits and attachments as may be filed by the parties, the results of discovery processes, and any oral testimony. The affidavits, if any, shall be served at least seven days before the hearing, shall be made on personal knowledge, shall set forth specific facts as would be admissible in evidence, and shall show affirmatively that the affiant is competent to testify.

Should it appear from the affidavits of a party opposing the motion that he cannot for reasons stated present by affidavit facts essential to justify his opposition, the court may order a continuance to permit affidavits to be obtained or depositions to be taken or discovery to be had or may make such other order as is just.

Should it appear to the satisfaction of the court at any time that any of such affidavits are presented in violation of Rule 13, the court shall impose sanctions in accordance with that rule.

4. If the court sustains the objection to jurisdiction, an

appropriate order shall be entered. If the objection to jurisdiction is overruled, the objecting party may thereafter appear generally for any purpose. Any such special appearance or such general appearance shall not be deemed a waiver of the objection to jurisdiction when the objecting party or subject matter is not amenable to process issued by the courts of this State.

April 12, 1962, eff. Sept. 1, 1962. Amended by orders of July 22, 1975, eff. Jan. 1, 1976; June 15, 1983, eff. Sept. 1, 1983; April 24, 1990, eff. Sept. 1, 1990.

Comment—1990

To provide for proof by affidavit at special appearance hearings, with safeguards to responding parties. These amendments preserve Texas prior practice to place the burden of proof on the party contesting jurisdiction.

Source: New rule.

See also CPRC §§17.041, 17.042, 51.014(a)(7); **O'Connor's Texas Rules**, "Special Appearance—Challenging Personal Jurisdiction," ch. 3-B, §1 et seq.; **O'Connor's Texas Forms**, FORMS 3B.

ANNOTATIONS

Generally

Daimler AG v. Bauman, 571 U.S. 117, 137-39 (2014). "For an individual, the paradigm forum for the exercise of general jurisdiction is the individual's domicile; for a corporation, it is an equivalent place, one in which the corporation is fairly regarded as at home. With respect to a corporation, the place of incorporation and principal place of business are paradigm bases for general jurisdiction. [¶] [Ps] would have us look beyond [those paradigm bases] and approve the exercise of general jurisdiction in every State in which a corporation engages in a substantial, continuous, and systematic course of business. That formulation . . . is unacceptably grasping. [¶] [T]he inquiry . . . is not whether a foreign corporation's in-forum contacts can be said to be in some sense 'continuous and systematic,' it is whether that corporation's affiliations with the State are so 'continuous and systematic' as to render it essentially at home in the forum State. *At 139 n.19:* We do not foreclose the possibility that in an exceptional case . . . a corporation's operations in a forum other than its formal place of incorporation or principal place of business may be so substantial and of such a nature as to render the corporation at home in that state." (Internal quotes omitted.) *See also* **Searcy v. Parex Res.**, 496 S.W.3d 58, 72 (Tex.2016).

Moncrief Oil Int'l v. OAO Gazprom, 414 S.W.3d 142, 150-51 (Tex.2013). "[S]pecific jurisdiction requires us to analyze jurisdictional contacts on a claim-by-claim basis. [A] 'plaintiff bringing multiple claims that arise out of different forum contacts of the defendant must establish specific jurisdiction for each claim.' [A] court need not assess contacts on a claim-by-claim basis if all claims arise from the same forum contacts. Because we determine that the tortious interference claims arise from separate jurisdictional contacts than the trade secrets claim, we analyze those contacts separately."

PHC-Minden, L.P. v. Kimberly-Clark Corp., 235 S.W.3d 163, 169-70 (Tex.2007). "We first determine the appropriate time period for assessing contacts for purposes of general jurisdiction, an issue on which our courts of appeals are in conflict. [¶] We conclude that the relevant period ends at the time suit is filed. [G]eneral jurisdiction is dispute-blind; accordingly, and in contrast to specific jurisdiction, the incident made the basis of the suit should not be the focus in assessing continuous and systematic contacts—contacts on which jurisdiction over any claim may be based. We also agree that 'a mere one-time snapshot of the defendant's in-state activities' may not be sufficient, . . . and contacts should be assessed over a reasonable number of years, up to the date suit is filed. . . . This includes contacts at the time the cause of action arose. . . ."

Michiana Easy Livin' Country, Inc. v. Holten, 168 S.W.3d 777, 785 (Tex.2005). There are "[t]hree aspects of [the purposeful-availment requirement that] are relevant. . . . First, it is only the defendant's contacts with the forum that count. . . . [¶] Second, the acts relied on must be 'purposeful' rather than fortuitous. [¶] Third, a defendant must seek some benefit, advantage, or profit by 'availing' itself of the jurisdiction. [A] nonresident may purposefully avoid a particular jurisdiction by structuring its transactions so as neither to profit from the forum's laws nor be subject to its jurisdiction." *See also* **TV Azteca, S.A.B. de C.V. v. Ruiz**, 490 S.W.3d 29, 37-38 (Tex.2016); **Moncrief Oil Int'l v. OAO Gazprom**, 414 S.W.3d 142, 151 (Tex.2013); **Moki Mac River Expeditions v. Drugg**, 221 S.W.3d 569, 575 (Tex.2007).

BMC Software Belg., N.V. v. Marchand, 83 S.W.3d 789, 794 (Tex.2002). The "courts of appeals [should] review the trial court's factual findings for legal and factual sufficiency and review the trial court's legal conclusions *de novo*. [¶] Whether a court has personal jurisdiction over a defendant is a question of law. However, the trial court frequently must resolve questions of fact before deciding the jurisdiction question." *See also* **Zinc Nacional, S.A. v. Bouché Trucking, Inc.**, 308 S.W.3d 395, 397 (Tex.2010); **Moki Mac River Expeditions v. Drugg**, 221 S.W.3d 569, 574 (Tex.2007).

CMMC v. Salinas, 929 S.W.2d 435, 439 (Tex.1996). "[D's] mere knowledge that its winepress was to be sold and used in Texas and its wiring the machine for use in the U.S. were not sufficient to subject [D] to the jurisdiction of Texas courts. *At 440:* A manufacturer cannot fairly be expected to litigate in every part of the world where its products may end up; its contacts with the forum must be more purposeful . . . before it can constitutionally be subjected to personal jurisdiction." *See also* **CSR Ltd. v. Link**, 925 S.W.2d 591, 595-96 (Tex.1996).

Schlobohm v. Schapiro, 784 S.W.2d 355, 358 (Tex.1990). The Texas standard for jurisdiction over a nonresident defendant requires that: "(1) The nonresident defendant or foreign corporation must purposefully do some act or consummate some transaction in the forum state; (2)

The cause of action must arise from, or be connected with, such act or transaction; and (3) The assumption of jurisdiction by the forum state must not offend traditional notions of fair play and substantial justice. . . ." *See also* **Guardian Royal Exch. Assur., Ltd. v. English China Clays, P.L.C.**, 815 S.W.2d 223, 226 (Tex.1991).

Pleadings

Exito Elecs. Co. v. Trejo, 142 S.W.3d 302, 305 (Tex.2004). TRCP 120a "requires only that a special appearance be filed before any other 'plea, pleading or motion.' A [TRCP] 11 Agreement between the parties, in and of itself, is not a plea, pleading, or motion. *At 306:* [W]hile filing a Rule 11 Agreement with the trial court is a requirement for enforcement, it is not in and of itself a request for enforcement or any other affirmative action by the trial court. [A] Rule 11 Agreement that extends a defendant's time to file an initial responsive pleading and is filed in the trial court before the defendant files a special appearance, even if the agreement is not expressly made subject to the special appearance, does not violate Rule 120a's 'due-order-of-pleading' requirement and . . . does not constitute a general appearance."

Dawson-Austin v. Austin, 968 S.W.2d 319, 322-23 (Tex.1998). The Supreme Court held (1) an unverified special appearance may be amended to cure the defect, even after the trial court has overruled it, as long as the amendment is filed before the defendant enters a general appearance; and (2) it is not necessary for the answer and other motions filed in the same instrument as the special appearance to contain "subject to" language. *See also* **Horowitz v. Berger**, 377 S.W.3d 115, 123 (Tex.App.—Houston [14th Dist.] 2012, no pet.) (amended special appearance relates back, curing and replacing the original special appearance).

Casino Magic Corp. v. King, 43 S.W.3d 14, 18 (Tex.App.—Dallas 2001, pet. denied). TRCP 120a "requires special appearances to be made by 'sworn motion.' Strict compliance with the rule is required. [¶] In this case, the special appearance was not sworn or verified. Although [D] attached an affidavit to the special appearance which set out various 'jurisdictional facts,' in that affidavit [D's] general counsel stated only that the allegations in the *affidavit* were true and correct, not that the facts set out in the *special appearance* were true and correct. [W]e conclude the affidavit did not strictly comply with rule 120a and it, therefore, could not serve to verify the special appearance."

Discovery

In re Stern, 321 S.W.3d 828, 839-40 (Tex.App.—Houston [1st Dist.] 2010, orig. proceeding). "The trial court may permit a continuance so that the opposing party may obtain [any] necessary jurisdictional discovery. However, Rule 120a(3) does not authorize postponement of a special appearance hearing to allow a party to obtain discovery prior to the court's ruling on the special appearance that is unnecessary or irrelevant to the establishment of jurisdictional facts. [¶] We . . . conclude that those cases holding that 'nothing in Rule 120a specifically limits discovery to matters relating to the special appearance' are limited to those situations in which the issue is whether a defendant waives a special appearance by participating in discovery and that they do not apply when the issue is . . . whether a trial court abuses its discretion by ordering or failing to order discovery at the request of a party opposing a special appearance. Those cases are controlled by the plain language of Rule 120a(3) and by **Dawson-Austin v. Austin**[, 968 S.W.2d 319 (Tex.1998),] and its progeny."

Waiver

Exito Elecs. Co. v. Trejo, 142 S.W.3d 302, 307 (Tex.2004). "It is simply illogical to allow the parties to engage in relevant discovery, which can be a vital part of resolving a special appearance, but prohibit the nonresident defendant from seeking the trial court's ruling on disputes that may affect the evidence presented at the special appearance hearing. [A] trial court's resolution of discovery matters related to the special appearance does not amount to a general appearance by the party contesting personal jurisdiction." *See also* **Lisitsa v. Flit**, 419 S.W.3d 672, 678 (Tex.App.—Houston [14th Dist.] 2013, pet. denied); **Minucci v. Sogevalor, S.A.**, 14 S.W.3d 790, 801 (Tex.App.—Houston [1st Dist.] 2000, no pet.).

GFTA Trendanalysen v. Varme, 991 S.W.2d 785, 786 (Tex.1999). "[A] party [does not waive] a due process challenge for want of minimum contacts by challenging the method of service in the special appearance." *See also* **Moore v. Pulmosan Safety Equip. Corp.**, 278 S.W.3d 27, 33 (Tex.App.—Houston [14th Dist.] 2008, pet. denied).

Composite Cooling Solutions, L.P. v. Larrabee Air Conditioning, Inc., No. 02-17-00006-CV, 2017 WL 2979918 (Tex.App.—Fort Worth 2017, no pet.) (memo op.; 7-13-17). "A party enters a general appearance that is not in compliance with [TRCP] 120a and therefore waives the party's right to specially appear for the limited purpose of asserting a lack of personal jurisdiction by the trial court when he (1) invokes the judgment of the court on any question other than the court's jurisdiction, (2) recognizes by his acts that an action is properly pending, or (3) seeks affirmative relief from the court. [¶] After the trial court had sustained [D's] special appearance, [D] filed a motion seeking an award of 'reasonable and necessary' attorneys' fees for 'defending itself from [P's] claims pursuant to the Uniform Declaratory Judgment[s] Act [(UDJA)].' [¶] Although the trial court had sustained [D's] special appearance, [D's] subsequent motion seeking a judgment for UDJA attorneys' fees implicitly, if not explicitly, recognized that a declaratory-judgment action was or had been properly pending against [D] in the Texas trial court. Because [D] recognized by its request for UDJA attorneys' fees that a declaratory-judgment action was or had been properly pending in the trial court against [D], [D] made a general appearance, voluntarily submitted to the trial court's jurisdiction, and waived its previously-sustained special appearance."

Nationwide Distrib. Servs. v. Jones, 496 S.W.3d 221, 227-28 (Tex.App.—Houston [1st Dist.] 2016, no pet.). "The case law shows that a specially appearing party does not waive its jurisdictional challenge by: (1) serving nonjurisdictional discovery requests; (2) filing a motion to compel nonjurisdictional discovery but not scheduling a hearing or obtaining a ruling on such motion; (3) litigating a jurisdictional discovery dispute; (4) litigating other disputes that are factually related to the special appearance; or (5) litigating opposition to merits-based discovery sought by another party. To the extent each of these examples involved a defendant's 'use of discovery processes,' none of them also involved a violation of the due order of pleading."

Wakefield v. British Med. Journal Publ'g Grp., 449 S.W.3d 172, 181 (Tex.App.—Austin 2014, no pet.). "[T]he hearing on [Ds'] anti-SLAPP motion and the hearing on [Ds'] special appearances were [reset twice]. However, there is no indication that the change in settings was requested by [Ds] or otherwise required any intervention by the trial court. Further, there is no indication that the hearing on the anti-SLAPP motion was delayed for the purpose of furthering—as opposed to simply deferring—a decision from the trial court on [Ds'] anti-SLAPP motion. [W]e cannot conclude that [Ds] sought any affirmative action from the trial court or invoked the judgment of the trial court on an issue other than jurisdiction with respect to the trial court's resetting of the hearing. *At 183:* [Thus, Ds] did not waive their challenges to personal jurisdiction. . . ."

Grynberg v. M-I L.L.C., 398 S.W.3d 864, 877-78 (Tex.App.—Corpus Christi 2012, pet. denied). "[T]he mere filing of a motion for new trial or other pleadings, with or without 'subject to' language, does not necessarily waive a previously filed or a simultaneously filed special appearance. [A] defendant may include language in the motion for new trial that it is ready to proceed to trial without waiving the special appearance, as long as the motion does not acknowledge jurisdiction or ask for some action other than dismissal for lack of jurisdiction. [¶] [A]ppearing in matters ancillary and prior to the main suit does not constitute a general appearance in the main suit and will not waive a personal-jurisdiction challenge." *See also* **Carey v. State**, No. 04-09-00809-CV, 2010 WL 2838631 (Tex.App.—San Antonio 2010, pet. denied) (memo op.; 7-21-10) (Ds' agreement to extension of temporary restraining and temporary-injunction orders was not general appearance because agreement was part of ancillary proceeding). *But see* **Schoendienst v. Haug**, 399 S.W.3d 313, 321 n.8 (Tex.App.—Austin 2013, no pet.) (D appeared by agreeing to temporary injunction; categorical rule that appearing in matters "ancillary and prior to the main suit" does not constitute general appearance is overbroad oversimplification).

Milacron Inc. v. Performance Rail Tie, L.P., 262 S.W.3d 872, 875-76 (Tex.App.—Texarkana 2008, no pet.). "Rule 120a requires that the specially appearing defendant timely request a hearing, specifically bring that request to the trial court's attention, and secure a ruling on the preliminary question of personal jurisdiction. [¶] A defendant waives his special appearance by not timely pressing for a hearing. It is inappropriate, especially when considering judicial economy, to litigate the special appearance in connection with the trial of the matter." *See also* **DeGeorge v. Luedike/Fabel**, No. 09-14-00517-CV, 2016 WL 1719118 (Tex.App.—Beaumont 2016, no pet.) (memo op.; 4-28-16).

TRCP 121. ANSWER IS APPEARANCE

An answer shall constitute an appearance of the defendant so as to dispense with the necessity for the issuance or service of citation upon him.

Oct. 29, 1940, eff. Sept. 1, 1941.

ANNOTATIONS

Torres v. Johnson, 91 S.W.3d 905, 910 (Tex.App.—Fort Worth 2002, no pet.). "[N]o new service was required because [D] entered an appearance in the suit by moving for summary judgment after [P] amended his pleadings."

TRCP 122. CONSTRUCTIVE APPEARANCE

If the citation or service thereof is quashed on motion of the defendant, such defendant shall be deemed to have entered his appearance at ten o'clock a.m. on the Monday next after the expiration of twenty (20) days after the day on which the citation or service is quashed, and such defendant shall be deemed to have been duly served so as to require him to appear and answer at that time, and if he fails to do so, judgment by default may be rendered against him.

Oct. 29, 1940, eff. Sept. 1, 1941.

See also O'Connor's Texas Rules, "Motion to Quash—Challenging the Service," ch. 3-J, §1 et seq.

ANNOTATIONS

Kawasaki Steel Corp. v. Middleton, 699 S.W.2d 199, 202 (Tex.1985). "[A] non-resident defendant, like any other defendant, may move to quash the citation for defects in the process, but his only relief is additional time to answer rather than dismissal of the cause." *See also* **In re Quinones**, 557 S.W.3d 647, 649 (Tex.App.—El Paso 2017, orig. proceeding).

Ramirez v. Consolidated HGM Corp., 124 S.W.3d 914, 917 (Tex.App.—Amarillo 2004, no pet.). The trial court does not have to "resolve a motion to quash as a condition to preserving a complaint about service."

TRCP 123. REVERSAL OF JUDGMENT

Where the judgment is reversed on appeal or writ of error for the want of service, or because of defective service of

process, no new citation shall be issued or served, but the defendant shall be presumed to have entered his appearance to the term of the court at which the mandate shall be filed.

Oct. 29, 1940, eff. Sept. 1, 1941.

See also **O'Connor's Texas Rules**, "Motion to Quash—Challenging the Service," ch. 3-J, §1 et seq.

ANNOTATIONS

Boyd v. Kobierowski, 283 S.W.3d 19, 23 (Tex.App.—San Antonio 2009, no pet.). TRCP 123 "presumes the nonresident defendant's general appearance after reversal of a judgment based on defective or no service. *At 24:* [D] could have escaped Rule 123's presumption of a general appearance using [TRCP] 120a's special appearance."

TRCP 124. NO JUDGMENT WITHOUT SERVICE

In no case shall judgment be rendered against any defendant unless upon service, or acceptance or waiver of process, or upon an appearance by the defendant, as prescribed in these rules, except where otherwise expressly provided by law or these rules.

When a party asserts a counterclaim or a cross-claim against another party who has entered an appearance, the claim may be served in any manner prescribed for service of citation or as provided in Rule 21(a).

Oct. 29, 1940, eff. Sept. 1, 1941. Amended by order of Dec. 5, 1983, eff. April 1, 1984.

Source: TRCS art. 2050 (repealed).

Editor's Note: The reference to TRCP 21(a) in the second paragraph of TRCP 124 should be a reference to TRCP 21a.

See also **O'Connor's Texas Rules**, "Serving the Defendant with Suit," ch. 2-I, §1 et seq.; **O'Connor's Texas Rules**, "Default Judgment," ch. 7-A, §1 et seq.

ANNOTATIONS

Werner v. Colwell, 909 S.W.2d 866, 870 (Tex.1995). "[M]erely appearing as a witness in a cause [does not serve] as a general appearance, subjecting one to the jurisdiction of the court."

Strawder v. Thomas, 846 S.W.2d 51, 62 (Tex.App.—Corpus Christi 1992, no writ). "Rules relating to service of process are mandatory, and a failure to comply therewith, if a judgment be rendered against a party who was not served in accordance with those rules (and who did not waive service of citation or appear voluntarily) renders the judgment void." *See also* **Browserweb Media Agency v. Maxus Energy Corp.**, No. 01-14-01028-CV, 2016 WL 66540 (Tex.App.—Houston [1st Dist.] 2016, no pet.) (memo op.; 1-5-16) (D's admission that it received actual service is not substitute for service-of-process requirements).

SECTION 6. COSTS AND SECURITY THEREFOR

TRCP 125. PARTIES RESPONSIBLE

Each party to a suit shall be liable to the officers of the court for all costs incurred by himself.

Oct. 29, 1940, eff. Sept. 1, 1941.

Source: TRCS art. 2051, first sentence (repealed).

ANNOTATIONS

Borg-Warner Prot. Servs. v. Flores, 955 S.W.2d 861, 870 (Tex.App.—Corpus Christi 1997, no pet.). "[T]he right to costs is based entirely on statutes or procedural rules, and therefore the trial court is the proper authority to determine and award costs." *But see* **Bill Miller Bar-B-Q Enters. v. Gonzales**, No. 04-13-00704-CV, 2014 WL 5463951 (Tex.App.—San Antonio 2014, no pet.) (memo op.; 10-29-14) (reasonableness of amount of attorney fees awarded as costs under statute is fact issue for jury to determine).

TRCP 126. FEE FOR SERVICE OF PROCESS IN A COUNTY OTHER THAN IN THE COUNTY OF SUIT

(a) ***General Rule: Fee Due Before Service.*** A sheriff or constable may require payment before serving process in a case pending in a county other than the county in which the sheriff or constable is an officer.

(b) ***Exception: Statement of Inability to Afford Payment of Court Costs Filed.*** If a Statement of Inability to Afford Payment of Court Costs has been filed in a case in which the declarant requests service of process in a county other than in the county of suit, the clerk must indicate on the document to be served that a Statement of Inability to Afford Payment of Court Costs has been filed. The sheriff or constable must execute the service without demanding payment.

Oct. 29, 1940, eff. Sept. 1, 1941. Amended by order of Aug. 31, 2016, eff. Sept. 1, 2016.

TRCP 127. PARTIES LIABLE FOR OTHER COSTS

Each party to a suit shall be liable for all costs incurred by him. If the costs cannot be collected from the party against whom they have been adjudged, execution may issue against any party in such suit for the amount of costs incurred by such party, but no more.

Oct. 29, 1940, eff. Sept. 1, 1941.

Source: TRCS art. 2052 (repealed).

TRCP 128. REPEALED BY ORDER OF DEC. 5, 1983, EFF. APRIL 1, 1984

TRCP 129. HOW COSTS COLLECTED

If any party responsible for costs fails or refuses to pay the same within ten days after demand for payment, the clerk or justice of the peace may make certified copy of the bill of costs then due, and place the same in the hands of the sheriff or constable for collection. All taxes imposed on law proceedings shall be included in the bill of costs. Such certified bill of costs shall have the force and effect of an execution. The removal of a case by appeal shall not prevent the issuance of an execution for costs.

Oct. 29, 1940, eff. Sept. 1, 1941. Amended by order of Dec. 5, 1983, eff. April 1, 1984.

TRCP 130. OFFICER TO LEVY

The sheriff or constable upon demand and failure to pay said bill of costs, may levy upon a sufficient amount of property of the person from whom said costs are due to satisfy the same, and sell such property as under execution. Where such party is not a resident of the county where such suit is pending, the payment of such costs may be demanded of his attorney of record; and neither the clerk nor justice of the peace shall be allowed to charge any fee for making out such certified bill of costs, unless he is compelled to make a levy.

Oct. 29, 1940, eff. Sept. 1, 1941.

TRCP 131. SUCCESSFUL PARTY TO RECOVER

The successful party to a suit shall recover of his adversary all costs incurred therein, except where otherwise provided.

Oct. 29, 1940, eff. Sept. 1, 1941.

Source: TRCS art. 2056 (repealed).

See also CPRC §31.007; **O'Connor's Texas Rules**, "Judgment," ch. 9-C, §1 et seq.; **O'Connor's Texas Family Law Handbook**, "Costs," ch. 3-A, §5.4.13(4); **O'Connor's Texas Family Law Handbook**, "Award to prevailing party," ch. 4-D, §13.4.12(4)(b).

ANNOTATIONS

Furr's Supermkts., Inc. v. Bethune, 53 S.W.3d 375, 376 (Tex.2001). "Taxing costs against a successful party in the trial court . . . generally contravenes [TRCP] 131. Yet the trial court's ruling on costs under [TRCP] 141 is permitted within its sound discretion, although that discretion is not unlimited. *At 378:* Rule 131's underlying purpose is to ensure that the prevailing party is freed of the burden of court costs and that the losing party pays those costs." *See also* **Martinez v. Pierce**, 759 S.W.2d 114, 114 (Tex.1988).

Diggs v. VSM Fin., L.L.C., 482 S.W.3d 672, 674 (Tex.App.—Houston [1st Dist.] 2015, no pet.). "The trial court should state in its judgment which party is to pay costs. The judgment should not state the amount taxed as costs, but only that costs are awarded against a certain party. [¶] [T]he [TRCPs] do not require a successful party in a lawsuit to submit an accounting of its court costs to the trial court and opposing counsel *before* the entry of a judgment adjudicating costs. Instead, [CPRC] §31.007(a) requires the successful party to submit a record of its court costs to the court clerk so that the clerk can perform its ministerial duty and tax costs in accord with [TRCP] 622."

Bayer Corp. v. DX Terminals, Ltd., 214 S.W.3d 586, 611-12 (Tex.App.—Houston [14th Dist.] 2006, pet. denied). "A 'successful party' under the rules is one that obtains a judgment vindicating a civil right. [¶] Texas appellate courts have not been entirely consistent in reviewing trial courts' splitting of costs between opposing parties, particularly when claims and counterclaims are involved. Some courts have held that the party receiving the larger recovery is entitled to costs. Other courts have held that when both sides successfully prosecute their claims, a trial court can in its discretion split costs between the parties." *See also* **Mag Instr., Inc. v. G.T. Sales Inc.**, 294 S.W.3d 800, 808 (Tex.App.—Dallas 2009, pet. denied) (whether party is successful is based on merits, not on award of damages); **Imperial Lofts, Ltd. v. Imperial Woodworks, Inc.**, 245 S.W.3d 1, 8 (Tex.App.—Waco 2007, pet. denied) (D who obtains take-nothing judgment is successful party).

TRCP 132. REPEALED BY ORDER OF DEC. 5, 1983, EFF. APRIL 1, 1984

TRCP 133. COSTS OF MOTION

The court may give or refuse costs on motions at its discretion, except where otherwise provided by law or these rules.

Oct. 29, 1940, eff. Sept. 1, 1941.

TRCP 134, 135. REPEALED BY ORDER OF DEC. 5, 1983, EFF. APRIL 1, 1984

TRCP 136. DEMAND REDUCED BY PAYMENTS

Where the plaintiff's demand is reduced by payment to an amount which would not have been within the jurisdiction of the court, the defendant shall recover his costs.

Oct. 29, 1940, eff. Sept. 1, 1941.

TRCP 137. IN ASSAULT AND BATTERY, ETC.

In civil actions for assault and battery, slander and defamation of character, if the verdict or judgment shall be for the plaintiff, but for less than twenty dollars, the plaintiff shall not recover his costs, but each party shall be taxed with the costs incurred by him in such suit.

Oct. 29, 1940, eff. Sept. 1, 1941.

TRCP 138. COST OF NEW TRIALS

The costs of new trials may either abide the result of the suit or may be taxed against the party to whom the new

trial is granted, as the court may adjudge when he grants such new trial.

Oct. 29, 1940, eff. Sept. 1, 1941.

TRCP 139. ON APPEAL AND CERTIORARI

When a case is appealed, if the judgment of the higher court be against the appellant, but for less amount than the original judgment, such party shall recover the costs of the higher court but shall be adjudged to pay the costs of the court below; if the judgment be against him for the same or a greater amount than in the court below, the adverse party shall recover the costs of both courts. If the judgment of the court above be in favor of the party appealing and for more than the original judgment, such party shall recover the costs of both courts; if the judgment be in his favor, but for the same or a less amount than in the court below, he shall recover the costs of the court below, and pay the costs of the court above.

Oct. 29, 1940, eff. Sept. 1, 1941.

Source: TRCS art. 2065 (repealed).

ANNOTATIONS

Keene Corp. v. Gardner, 837 S.W.2d 224, 232 (Tex.App.—Dallas 1992, writ denied). "Because the appellate relief given [D] is *de minimis* compared to [Ps'] overall award affirmed on appeal, we assess all costs of this appeal against [D]."

TRCP 140. NO FEE FOR COPY

No fee for a copy of a paper not required by law or these rules to be copied shall be taxed in the bill of costs.

Oct. 29, 1940, eff. Sept. 1, 1941.

ANNOTATIONS

Crescendo Invs. v. Brice, 61 S.W.3d 465, 481 (Tex.App.—San Antonio 2001, pet. denied). "Transcripts 'necessarily obtained for use in the suit' seems to obviously include depositions and trial testimony used to question witnesses and prepare for argument at trial. [Ds] are not recovering for 'making copies' as prohibited by Rule 140. The expense of depositions has long been recognized as a chargeable item of court costs. Awarding costs for certified copies of depositions which may be admitted at trial does not violate Rule 140." *But see* **Gumpert v. ABF Freight Sys.**, 312 S.W.3d 237, 241 (Tex.App.—Dallas 2010, no pet.) (costs to videotape depositions and obtain copies of deposition transcripts are not recoverable as taxable costs).

TRCP 141. COURT MAY OTHERWISE ADJUDGE COSTS

The court may, for good cause, to be stated on the record, adjudge the costs otherwise than as provided by law or these rules.

Oct. 29, 1940, eff. Sept. 1, 1941.

Source: TRCS art. 2066 (repealed).

ANNOTATIONS

Roberts v. Williamson, 111 S.W.3d 113, 124 (Tex.2003). The trial court "observed that because an ad litem is there for the benefit of all parties, it is 'fair' to split costs between the losing and prevailing parties. . . . Certainly, fairness can be good cause, but the record must substantiate the connection. [¶] [T]he trial court's finding of good cause is premised on the perception that the prevailing party incidentally [benefited] from the guardian ad litem's services. . . . Rule 141 still requires that the trial court state its reasons 'on the record' and with more specificity than the court's general notion of fairness here. Grounds of perceived fairness, without more, are insufficient to constitute good cause."

Furr's Supermkts., Inc. v. Bethune, 53 S.W.3d 375, 376-77 (Tex.2001). "Rule 141 has two requirements—that there be good cause and that it be stated on the record. 'Good cause' is an elusive concept that varies from case to case. Typically though, 'good cause' has meant that the prevailing party unnecessarily prolonged the proceedings, unreasonably increased costs, or otherwise did something that should be penalized." *See also* **Diaz v. Diaz**, 350 S.W.3d 251, 256 (Tex.App.—San Antonio 2011, pet. denied) (trial courts in family-law context are not bound by good-cause requirement); **Rankin v. FPL Energy LLC**, 266 S.W.3d 506, 515 (Tex.App.—Eastland 2008, pet. denied) (party's emotional distress at having to pay costs, inability to pay, and trial court's perceived fairness do not constitute good cause).

Schreiber v. State Farm Lloyds, 474 S.W.3d 308, 319 (Tex.App.—Houston [14th Dist.] 2015, pet. denied). "[P] argues [CPRC] §31.007(b) . . . changed Texas law and gave trial courts discretion to not award the successful party all of the taxable court costs that party incurred, without any requirement that the trial court state on the record good cause for doing so. *At 320:* The statute does not address the circumstances under which a trial court may order a successful party to bear taxable court costs the party incurred. We conclude that this statute does not conflict with, supersede, or modify, [TRCP] 131 or [TRCP] 141. . . . Thus, this statute does not change the rule that the trial court must award the successful party to a suit all of its taxable court costs from the adverse party, unless the trial court finds good cause to adjudge the costs otherwise and states its reasons for finding good cause on the record."

Hatfield v. Solomon, 316 S.W.3d 50, 67 (Tex.App.—Houston [14th Dist.] 2010, no pet.). The "power to allocate costs in a manner different from the norm does not encompass the power to tax as costs items that are not normally allowed as taxable court costs." *See also* **May v. Ticor Title**

Ins., 422 S.W.3d 93, 106 (Tex.App.—Houston [14th Dist.] 2014, no pet.) (expert fees are not generally recoverable as court costs).

TRCP 142. SECURITY FOR COSTS

The clerk shall require from the plaintiff fees for services rendered before issuing any process unless filing is requested pursuant to Rule 145 of these rules.

Oct. 29, 1940, eff. Sept. 1, 1941. Amended by orders of March 31, 1941, eff. Sept. 1, 1941; July 15, 1987, eff. Jan. 1, 1988.

TRCP 143. RULE FOR COSTS

A party seeking affirmative relief may be ruled to give security for costs at any time before final judgment, upon motion of any party, or any officer of the court interested in the costs accruing in such suit, or by the court upon its own motion. If such rule be entered against any party and he failed to comply therewith on or before twenty (20) days after notice that such rule has been entered, the claim for affirmative relief of such party shall be dismissed.

Oct. 29, 1940, eff. Sept. 1, 1941. Amended by order of July 21, 1970, eff. Jan. 1, 1971.

ANNOTATIONS

TransAmerican Nat. Gas Corp. v. Mancias, 877 S.W.2d 840, 844 (Tex.App.—Corpus Christi 1994, orig. proceeding). "Rule 143 generally allows the trial court to require a party to post security for costs that have already accrued, but not to fix a specific amount for anticipated costs which a party is required to pay or post security for prematurely." *See also* **In re Pendragon Transp.**, 423 S.W.3d 537, 541 (Tex.App.—Dallas 2014, orig. proceeding); **Hager v. Apollo Paper Corp.**, 856 S.W.2d 512, 515 (Tex.App.—Houston [1st Dist.] 1993, no writ).

TRCP 143a. COSTS ON APPEAL TO COUNTY COURT

If the appellant fails to pay the costs on appeal from a judgment of a justice of the peace or small claims court within twenty (20) days after being notified to do so by the county clerk, the appeal shall be deemed not perfected and the county clerk shall return all papers in said cause to the justice of the peace having original jurisdiction and the justice of the peace shall proceed as though no appeal had been attempted.

July 22, 1975, eff. Jan. 1, 1976.

Editor's Note: Although TRCP 143a references a "small-claims court," the Texas Legislature abolished small-claims courts by repealing Gov't Code ch. 28, effective August 31, 2013. See Acts 2013, 83rd Leg., R.S., ch. 2, §2, eff. Apr. 10, 2013; Acts 2011, 82nd Leg., 1st C.S., ch. 3, §§5.06, 5.09, eff. May 1, 2013. Now small-claims proceedings must be conducted by justice courts. Gov't Code §27.060(a); see TRCP 500.3(a).

ANNOTATIONS

Farmer v. McGee Servs., 704 S.W.2d 927, 929 (Tex.App.—Tyler 1986, no writ). "Since no notice [of costs] had been given, the trial court erred in applying Rule 143a to dismiss [D's] appeal."

TRCP 144. JUDGMENT ON COST BOND

All bonds given as security for costs shall authorize judgment against all the obligors in such bond for the said costs, to be entered in the final judgment of the cause.

Oct. 29, 1940, eff. Sept. 1, 1941.

ANNOTATIONS

Mosher v. Tunnell, 400 S.W.2d 402, 404 (Tex.App.—Houston [1st Dist.] 1966, writ ref'd n.r.e.). "Rule 144 provides the bond shall authorize judgment against the obligors for said costs. This means such costs as shall be adjudged against the principal whatever be the amount."

TRCP 145. PAYMENT OF COSTS NOT REQUIRED

(a) ***General Rule.*** A party who files a Statement of Inability to Afford Payment of Court Costs cannot be required to pay costs except by order of the court as provided by this rule. After the Statement is filed, the clerk must docket the case, issue citation, and provide any other service that is ordinarily provided to a party. The Statement must either be sworn to before a notary or made under penalty of perjury. In this rule, "declarant" means the party filing the Statement.

(b) ***Supreme Court Form; Clerk to Provide.*** The declarant must use the form Statement approved by the Supreme Court, or the Statement must include the information required by the Court-approved form. The clerk must make the form available to all persons without charge or request.

(c) ***Costs Defined.*** "Costs" mean any fee charged by the court or an officer of the court that could be taxed in a bill of costs, including, but not limited to, filing fees, fees for issuance and service of process, fees for a court-appointed professional, and fees charged by the clerk or court reporter for preparation of the appellate record.

(d) ***Defects.*** The clerk may refuse to file a Statement that is not sworn to before a notary or made under penalty of perjury. No other defect is a ground for refusing to file a Statement or requiring the party to pay costs. If a defect or omission in a Statement is material, the court—on its own

motion or on motion of the clerk or any party—may direct the declarant to correct or clarify the Statement.

(e) ***Evidence of Inability to Afford Costs Required.*** The Statement must say that the declarant cannot afford to pay costs. The declarant must provide in the Statement, and, if available, in attachments to the Statement, evidence of the declarant's inability to afford costs, such as evidence that the declarant:

(1) receives benefits from a government entitlement program, eligibility for which is dependent on the recipient's means;

(2) is being represented in the case by an attorney who is providing free legal services to the declarant, without contingency, through:

(A) a provider funded by the Texas Access to Justice Foundation;

(B) a provider funded by the Legal Services Corporation; or

(C) a nonprofit that provides civil legal services to persons living at or below 200% of the federal poverty guidelines published annually by the United States Department of Health and Human Services;

(3) has applied for free legal services for the case through a provider listed in (e)(2) and was determined to be financially eligible but was declined representation; or

(4) does not have funds to afford payment of costs.

(f) ***Requirement to Pay Costs Notwithstanding Statement.*** The court may order the declarant to pay costs only as follows:

(1) *On Motion by the Clerk or a Party.* The clerk or any party may move to require the declarant to pay costs only if the motion contains sworn evidence, not merely on information or belief:

(A) that the Statement was materially false when it was made; or

(B) that because of changed circumstances, the Statement is no longer true in material respects.

(2) *On Motion by the Attorney Ad Litem for a Parent in Certain Cases.* An attorney ad litem appointed to represent a parent under Section 107.013, Family Code, may move to require the parent to pay costs only if the motion complies with (f)(1).

(3) *On Motion by the Court Reporter.* When the declarant requests the preparation of a reporter's record but cannot make arrangements to pay for it, the court reporter may move to require the declarant to prove the inability to afford costs.

(4) *On the Court's Own Motion.* Whenever evidence comes before the court that the declarant may be able to afford costs, or when an officer or professional must be appointed in the case, the court may require the declarant to prove the inability to afford costs.

(5) *Notice and Hearing.* The declarant may not be required to pay costs without an oral evidentiary hearing. The declarant must be given 10 days' notice of the hearing. Notice must either be in writing and served in accordance with Rule 21a or given in open court. At the hearing, the burden is on the declarant to prove the inability to afford costs.

(6) *Findings Required.* An order requiring the declarant to pay costs must be supported by detailed findings that the declarant can afford to pay costs.

(7) *Partial and Delayed Payment.* The court may order that the declarant pay the part of the costs the declarant can afford or that payment be made in installments. But the court must not delay the case if payment is made in installments.

(g) ***Review of Trial Court Order.***

(1) *Only Declarant May Challenge; Motion.* Only the declarant may challenge an order issued by the trial court under this rule. The declarant may challenge the order by motion filed in the court of appeals with jurisdiction over an appeal from the judgment in the case. The declarant is not required to pay any filing fees related to the motion in the court of appeals.

(2) *Time for Filing; Extension.* The motion must be filed within 10 days after the trial court's order is signed. The court of appeals may extend the deadline by 15 days if the declarant demonstrates good cause for the extension in writing.

(3) *Record.* After a motion is filed, the court of appeals must promptly send notice to the trial court clerk and the court reporter requesting preparation of the record of all trial court proceedings on the declarant's claim of indigence. The court may set a deadline for filing the record. The record must be provided without charge.

(4) *Court of Appeals to Rule Promptly.* The court of appeals must rule on the motion at the earliest practicable time.

(h) ***Judgment.*** The judgment must not require the declarant to pay costs, and a provision in the judgment purporting to do so is void, unless the court has issued an order under (f), or the declarant has obtained a monetary recovery, and the court orders the recovery to be applied toward payment of costs.

Oct. 29, 1940, eff. Sept. 1, 1941. Amended by orders of Dec. 5, 1983, eff. April 1, 1984; July 15, 1987, Jan. 1, 1988; Sept. 19, 2005, eff. Dec. 1, 2005; Aug. 31, 2016, eff. Sept. 1, 2016.

Comment—2016

The rule has been rewritten. Access to the civil justice system cannot be denied because a person cannot afford to pay court costs. Whether a particular fee is a court cost is governed by this rule, Civil Practice and Remedies Code Section 31.007, and case law.

The issue is not merely whether a person can pay costs, but whether the person can afford to pay costs. A person may have sufficient cash on hand to pay filing fees, but the person cannot afford the fees if paying them would preclude the person from paying for basic essentials, like housing or food. Experience indicates that almost all filers described in (e)(1)–(3), and most filers described in (e)(4), cannot in fact afford to pay costs.

Because costs to access the system—filing fees, fees for issuance of process and notices, and fees for service and return—are kept relatively small, the expense involved in challenging a claim of inability to afford costs often exceeds the costs themselves. Thus, the rule does not allow the clerk or a party to challenge a litigant's claim of inability to afford costs without sworn evidence that the claim is false. The filing of a Statement of Inability to Afford Payment of Court Costs—which may either be sworn to before a notary or made under penalty of perjury, as permitted by Civil Practice and Remedies Code Section 132.001—is all that is needed to require the clerk to provide ordinary services without payment of fees and costs. But evidence may come to light that the claim was false when made. And the declarant's circumstances may change, so that the claim is no longer true. Importantly, costs may increase with the appointment of officers or professionals in the case, or when a reporter's record must be prepared. The reporter is always allowed to challenge a claim of inability to afford costs before incurring the substantial expense of record preparation. The trial court always retains discretion to require evidence of an inability to afford costs.

Comment—1988

The purpose of this rule is to allow indigents to file suit and have citation issued based solely on an affidavit of indigency filed with the suit.

Source: TRCS art. 2070 (repealed).

Editor's Note: In 2020, the Supreme Court preliminarily approved amendments to TRCP 145. *See* Tex.Sup.Ct. Order, Misc. Docket No. 20-9154 (Dec. 23, 2020). These amendments are subject to change based on public comments submitted by April 2, 2021. The Court will issue a final order approving the amendments at least 60 days after their publication in the February edition of the *Texas Bar Journal*. To view the orders related to these amendments, visit the Court's website at txcourts.gov/supreme.

See also CPRC chs. 13, 14; **O'Connor's Texas Rules**, "Suit by Indigent," ch. 2-J, §1 et seq.; **O'Connor's Texas Forms**, FORMS 2J.

ANNOTATIONS

Abrigo v. Ginez, 580 S.W.3d 416, 419-20 (Tex.App.—Houston [14th Dist.] 2019, no pet.). "Although [declarant] did not use the Supreme Court-approved form, her 'Affidavit of Inability to Pay Costs' was 'sworn to before a notary or made under penalty of perjury.' The affidavit contains her monthly income from public benefits, the number of her dependents, her property, her monthly expenses, and her monthly payments to a creditor. [Declarant] stated 'I am unable to pay the court costs in this cause,' and she verified that the statements made in the affidavit were true and correct. To the extent the affidavit omits any other material information required under [TRCP 145], such a defect or omission is not a ground for refusing to file the statement or requiring [declarant] to pay costs. [Opposing party] did not request the trial court to order [declarant] to file an amended statement due to defects in form. Unless and until the trial court finds a material defect or omission in the affidavit and directs a correction or clarification, ... we conclude the affidavit in its current form is initially sufficient to invoke the protections of rule 145."

In re A.R.M., No. 05-17-00651-CV, 2017 WL 2962830 (Tex.App.—Dallas 2017, n.p.h.) (memo op.; 7-12-17). "The central inquiry under rule 145 'is not merely whether [the party] can pay costs, but whether [he] can afford to pay costs' and still pay for 'basic essentials, like housing or food.' The party is not required to show family or friends are unable to pay the costs, and he is not expected to secure the necessary funds by depriving himself and his family of the necessities of life or borrowing money he cannot repay." *See also* **Emerson v. Holly Lake Ranch Ass'n**, 603 S.W.3d 172, 174 (Tex.App.—Texarkana 2020, n.p.h.) (test for determining indigence is whether whole record shows by preponderance of evidence that party would be unable to pay costs if she made good-faith effort to do so).

In re A.M., 557 S.W.3d 607, 610 (Tex.App.—El Paso 2016, no pet.). "[T]he trial court concluded that [declarant] is above the federal poverty guidelines, and therefore, he is able to afford to pay court costs and fees. In reaching this conclusion, the trial court did not consider [declarant's] total monthly expenses or his outstanding debts. By focusing exclusively on income and disregarding expenses, the trial court did not properly consider whether [declarant] *can afford to pay costs*. Under the current version of Rule 145, this is the critical inquiry."

TRCP 146. DEPOSIT FOR COSTS

In lieu of a bond for costs, the party required to give the same may deposit with the clerk of court or the justice of the peace such sum as the court or justice from time to time may designate as sufficient to pay the accrued costs.

Oct. 29, 1940, eff. Sept. 1, 1941.

TRCP 147. APPLIES TO ANY PARTY

The foregoing rules as to security and rule for costs shall apply to any party who seeks a judgment against any other party.

Oct. 29, 1940, eff. Sept. 1, 1941. Amended by order of Dec. 5, 1983, eff. April 1, 1984.

ANNOTATIONS

Ex parte Shaffer, 649 S.W.2d 300, 302 (Tex.1983). "[O]ne who involuntarily comes into court and does not seek any affirmative relief cannot be required to post a cost bond."

TRCP 148. SECURED BY OTHER BOND

No further security shall be required if the costs are secured by the provisions of an attachment or other bond

filed by the party required to give security for costs.

Oct. 29, 1940, eff. Sept. 1, 1941.

TRCP 149. EXECUTION FOR COSTS

When costs have been adjudged against a party and are not paid, the clerk or justice of the court in which the suit was determined may issue execution, accompanied by an itemized bill of costs, against such party to be levied and collected as in other cases; and said officer, on demand of any party to whom any such costs are due, shall issue execution for costs at once. This rule shall not apply to executors, administrators or guardians in cases where costs are adjudged against the estate of a deceased person or of a ward. No execution shall issue in any case for costs until after judgment rendered therefor by the court.

Oct. 29, 1940, eff. Sept. 1, 1941.

SECTION 7. ABATEMENT AND DISCONTINUANCE OF SUIT

TRCP 150. DEATH OF PARTY

Where the cause of action is one which survives, no suit shall abate because of the death of any party thereto before the verdict or decision of the court is rendered, but such suit may proceed to judgment as hereinafter provided.

Oct. 29, 1940, eff. Sept. 1, 1941.

Source: TRCS art. 2078 (repealed).

See also **O'Connor's Texas Rules**, "Plea to the Jurisdiction—Challenging the Court," ch. 3-F, §1 et seq.; **O'Connor's Texas Rules**, "Motion to Abate—Challenging the Suit," ch. 3-I, §1 et seq.

ANNOTATIONS

Moore v. Johnson, 143 S.W.3d 339, 342 (Tex.App.—Dallas 2004, no pet.). "The probate code [now Estates Code] does not provide that letters are a prerequisite to filing or maintaining a claim on behalf of an estate. Further, under [TRCP 150 and 151], where the cause of action is one that survives, a pending suit does not abate upon the death of a party but may proceed to judgment. The heirs or executor may appear and upon suggestion of death being entered of record may be made plaintiff and suit proceed in his or their name. There is no requirement that letters testamentary be filed or any particular proof be offered with the suggestion of death."

Palomino v. Palomino, 960 S.W.2d 899, 900-01 (Tex.App.—El Paso 1997, pet. denied). "The general rule in Texas is that a cause of action for divorce is purely personal and becomes moot and abates upon the death of either spouse. . . . However, when a trial court has rendered judgment on the merits in a divorce case, the cause does not abate when a party dies, and the cause cannot be dismissed." *See also* **Pollard v. Pollard**, 316 S.W.3d 246, 250-51 (Tex.App.—Dallas 2010, no pet.).

TRCP 151. DEATH OF PLAINTIFF

If the plaintiff dies, the heirs, or the administrator or executor of such decedent may appear and upon suggestion of such death being entered of record in open court, may be made plaintiff, and the suit shall proceed in his or their name. If no such appearance and suggestion be made within a reasonable time after the death of the plaintiff, the clerk upon the application of defendant, his agent or attorney, shall issue a scire facias for the heirs or the administrator or executor of such decedent, requiring him to appear and prosecute such suit. After service of such scire facias, should such heir or administrator or executor fail to enter appearance within the time provided, the defendant may have the suit dismissed.

Oct. 29, 1940, eff. Sept. 1, 1941. Amended by order of Dec. 5, 1983, eff. April 1, 1984.

Source: TRCS arts. 2078, 2079 (repealed).

See also **O'Connor's Texas Rules**, "Estate," ch. 2-B, §4.3.2; **O'Connor's Texas Rules**, "Motion to Abate—Challenging the Suit," ch. 3-I, §1 et seq.

ANNOTATIONS

Mayhew v. Dealey, 143 S.W.3d 356, 370-71 (Tex.App.—Dallas 2004, pet. denied). "Ordinarily, only the executor or administrator may bring suit to recover property belonging to the estate, such as in a survival action. There are exceptions to this general rule. The first exception is that heirs at law may bring a survival action on behalf of the estate when no administration is pending and none is necessary. [¶] The second exception provides that heirs may bring suit when the personal representative cannot, or will not, bring the suit or when the personal representative's interests are antagonistic to those of the estate."

TRCP 152. DEATH OF DEFENDANT

Where the defendant shall die, upon the suggestion of death being entered of record in open court, or upon petition of the plaintiff, the clerk shall issue a scire facias for the administrator or executor or heir requiring him to appear and defend the suit and upon the return of such service, the suit shall proceed against such administrator or executor or heir.

Oct. 29, 1940, eff. Sept. 1, 1941.

Source: TRCS art. 2080 (repealed).

See also **O'Connor's Texas Rules**, "Estate," ch. 2-B, §4.3.2; **O'Connor's Texas Rules**, "Motion to Abate—Challenging the Suit," ch. 3-I, §1 et seq.

ANNOTATIONS

Estate of Pollack v. McMurrey, 858 S.W.2d 388, 390 n.2 (Tex.1993). "*Scire facias* . . . provides for substitution of any person or persons succeeding to the rights of the original party, whether executor, administrator, heir, or person holding the same practical relation." *See also* **Tolar v. Tolar**, No. 12-14-00228-CV, 2015 WL 2393993 (Tex.App.—Tyler 2015, no pet.) (memo op.; 5-20-15) (P has duty to cause clerk to enter scire facias).

Henson v. Estate of Crow, 734 S.W.2d 648, 649 (Tex.1987). After D died, P amended its petition naming D's estate as D. Even though an answer was filed on behalf of estate, court rendered take-nothing judgment because estate was not a legal entity; suit should have proceeded against personal representative of estate.

In re Coats, 580 S.W.3d 431, 438-39 (Tex.App.—Texarkana 2019, orig. proceeding). "[T]he remedy under Rule 152 is substitution, not dismissal. Death of the defendant does not divest the trial court of subject-matter jurisdiction, only personal jurisdiction over the deceased defendant. Rule 152 suspends the proceedings to allow for substitution of the proper party. Trial courts may dismiss cases for other reasons, such as for want of prosecution. However, Rule 152 does not provide that after a reasonable time to substitute an appropriate party for the deceased defendant, the trial court may dismiss the action; rather, it only authorizes substitution. Therefore, so long as substitution of the appropriate party for the deceased defendant is possible, dismissal is not appropriate under Rule 152."

Hegwer v. Edwards, 527 S.W.3d 337, 340-41 (Tex.App.—Dallas 2017, no pet.). TRCP 151 "governs when a plaintiff dies and [TRCP] 152 applies when a defendant dies. [R]ule 152 does not restrict who may file a suggestion of death but, upon its being entered, the 'clerk shall issue a scire facias for the administrator or executor or heir *requiring him to appear*.' Thus, the filing of the suggestion of death for a defendant cannot of itself be interpreted as a general appearance because the court is required to issue a scire facias requiring the administrator, executor or heir to appear on behalf of the deceased defendant. . . . Under rule 151, an heir, administrator, or executor of the deceased plaintiff appears by filing a suggestion of death. Thus, rules 151 and 152 have different requirements for appearances based on whether the deceased party is a plaintiff or defendant."

Roper v. CitiMortgage, Inc., No. 03-11-00887-CV, 2013 WL 6465637 (Tex.App.—Austin 2013, pet. denied) (memo op.; 11-27-13). "A suit revived by issuance of scire facias 'is merely a continuation of the original action, and the substituted party stands in the same shoes as the original party. . . .' [TRCP] 151 and 152 do not require the parties to plead or replead, and the legal representative of a decedent in a suit revived under those Rules is deemed to have adopted the pleadings of the decedent."

TRCP 153. WHEN EXECUTOR, ETC., DIES

When an executor or administrator shall be a party to any suit, whether as plaintiff or as defendant, and shall die or cease to be such executor or administrator, the suit may be continued by or against the person succeeding him in the administration, or by or against the heirs, upon like proceedings being had as provided in the two preceding rules, or the suit may be dismissed, as provided in Rule 151.

Oct. 29, 1940, eff. Sept. 1, 1941. Amended by order of Dec. 5, 1983, eff. April 1, 1984.

TRCP 154. REQUISITES OF SCIRE FACIAS

The scire facias and returns thereon, provided for in this section, shall conform to the requisites of citations and the returns thereon, under the provisions of these rules.

Oct. 29, 1940, eff. Sept. 1, 1941.

TRCP 155. SURVIVING PARTIES

Where there are two or more plaintiffs or defendants, and one or more of them die, upon suggestion of such death being entered upon the record, the suit shall at the instance of either party proceed in the name of the surviving plaintiffs or against the surviving defendants, as the case may be.

Oct. 29, 1940, eff. Sept. 1, 1941.

Source: TRCS art. 2082 (repealed).

ANNOTATIONS

First Nat'l Bank v. Hawn, 392 S.W.2d 377, 379 (Tex.App.—Dallas 1965, writ ref'd n.r.e.). "Having elected to proceed under Rule 155 against the surviving [D], approving a judgment against that [D] and that judgment having become final . . ., [P] had no right to . . . suggest [other D's] death and endeavor to reinstate the suit as to his legal representative."

TRCP 156. DEATH AFTER VERDICT OR CLOSE OF EVIDENCE

When a party in a jury case dies between verdict and judgment, or a party in a non-jury case dies after the evidence is closed and before judgment is pronounced, judgment shall be rendered and entered as if all parties were living.

Oct. 29, 1940, eff. Sept. 1, 1941. Amended by order of July 11, 1977, eff. Jan. 1, 1978.

TRCP 157. REPEALED BY ORDER OF JULY 15, 1987, EFF. JAN. 1, 1988

TRCP 158. SUIT FOR THE USE OF ANOTHER

When a plaintiff suing for the use of another shall die before verdict, the person for whose use such suit was

brought, upon such death being suggested on the record in open court, may prosecute the suit in his own name, and shall be as responsible for costs as if he brought the suit.

Oct. 29, 1940, eff. Sept. 1, 1941.

TRCP 159. SUIT FOR INJURIES RESULTING IN DEATH

In cases arising under the provisions of the title relating to injuries resulting in death, the suit shall not abate by the death of either party pending the suit, but in such case, if the plaintiff dies, where there is only one plaintiff, some one or more of the parties entitled to the money recovered may be substituted and the suit prosecuted to judgment in the name of such party or parties, for the benefit of the person entitled; if the defendant dies, his executor, administrator or heir may be made a party, and the suit prosecuted to judgment.

Oct. 29, 1940, eff. Sept. 1, 1941.

TRCP 160. DISSOLUTION OF CORPORATION

The dissolution of a corporation shall not operate to abate any pending suit in which such corporation is a defendant, but such suit shall continue against such corporation and judgment shall be rendered as though the same were not dissolved.

Oct. 29, 1940, eff. Sept. 1, 1941.

See also BOC §11.356; TRCP 29.

TRCP 161. WHERE SOME DEFENDANTS NOT SERVED

When some of the several defendants in a suit are served with process in due time and others are not so served, the plaintiff may either dismiss as to those not so served and proceed against those who are, or he may take new process against those not served, or may obtain severance of the case as between those served and those not served, but no dismissal shall be allowed as to a principal obligor without also dismissing the parties secondarily liable except in cases provided by statute. No defendant against whom any suit may be so dismissed shall be thereby exonerated from any liability, but may at any time be proceeded against as if no such suit had been brought and no such dismissal ordered.

Oct. 29, 1940, eff. Sept. 1, 1941. Amended by orders of Dec. 5, 1983, eff. April 1, 1984; April 24, 1984, eff. Oct. 1, 1984; July 15, 1987, eff. Jan. 1, 1988.

Source: TRCS art. 2087 (repealed).

See also TRCP 240.

ANNOTATIONS

Young v. Hunderup, 763 S.W.2d 611, 612-13 (Tex.App.—Austin 1989, no writ). "Where the judgment disposes of all named parties except those which have not been served and have not appeared, . . . the judgment is considered final for purposes of appeal and the case stands as if there had been a discontinuance as to those parties not served." *See also* **Osborne v. St. Luke's Episcopal Hosp.**, 915 S.W.2d 906, 908 (Tex.App.—Houston [1st Dist.] 1996, writ denied). *But see* **Reed v. Gum Keepsake Diamond Ctr.**, 657 S.W.2d 524, 525 (Tex.App.—Corpus Christi 1983, no writ) (judgment was not final because co-D was not served, did not waive service, did not make appearance, and was not dismissed).

TRCP 162. DISMISSAL OR NON-SUIT

At any time before the plaintiff has introduced all of his evidence other than rebuttal evidence, the plaintiff may dismiss a case, or take a non-suit, which shall be entered in the minutes. Notice of the dismissal or non-suit shall be served in accordance with Rule 21a on any party who has answered or has been served with process without necessity of court order.

Any dismissal pursuant to this rule shall not prejudice the right of an adverse party to be heard on a pending claim for affirmative relief or excuse the payment of all costs taxed by the clerk. A dismissal under this rule shall have no effect on any motion for sanctions, attorney's fees or other costs, pending at the time of dismissal, as determined by the court. Any dismissal pursuant to this rule which terminates the case shall authorize the clerk to tax court costs against dismissing party unless otherwise ordered by the court.

Oct. 29, 1940, eff. Sept. 1, 1941. Amended by orders of Dec. 5, 1983, eff. April 1, 1984; July 15, 1987, eff. Jan. 1, 1988.

Comment—1988

The purpose of this rule is to fix a definite time after which a party may not voluntarily dismiss or non-suit the cause of action. In addition, these amendments will not disturb any pending motions for sanctions or attorney's fees that were filed before the motion for non-suit or dismissal.

Source: TRCS art. 2089 (repealed)

See also TRCP 96; **O'Connor's Texas Rules**, "Voluntary Dismissal—Nonsuit," ch. 7-F, §1 et seq.; **O'Connor's Texas Forms**, FORMS 7F.

ANNOTATIONS

Morath v. Lewis, 601 S.W.3d 785, 787 (Tex.2020). "[D] argues that [Ps'] non-suit, filed directly in this Court, is procedurally defective and should be given no effect. As [D] sees it, Rule 162 applies only in trial courts, and there is currently a stay of all trial court proceedings during this interlocutory appeal, so the plaintiffs cannot file a non-suit in the trial court. Moreover, [D] argues, there is no mechanism in the appellate rules for a non-suit filed directly in the Supreme Court. In [D's] view, there is no procedural vehicle by which the plaintiff may accomplish a unilateral non-suit at this juncture, and [Ps] may only achieve dismissal with [D's] agreement. This is incorrect. *At 788:* We have accepted Rule 162 non-suits directly in this Court before, and we do so again in this case. . . . Because the plaintiff's non-suit 'moots his case' by 'extinguish[ing] a case or controversy,' the non-suit is not merely the end of the case. It is the end of the Court's power to decide the case, assuming there are no claims for relief against the non-suiting party. Whether or not Rule 162 formally applies in the Supreme Court, a case is generally moot once the plaintiff declares its abandonment of all claims for relief."

CTL/Thompson Tex., LLC v. Starwood Homeowner's Ass'n, 390 S.W.3d 299, 300 (Tex.2013). "A motion for sanctions is a claim for affirmative relief that survives nonsuit if the nonsuit would defeat the purpose of sanctions. For example, a sanction excluding witnesses for failure to supplement discovery does not survive nonsuit because its purpose is fully served by protecting the fairness of the trial of the action in which it is imposed. But a sanction for filing a frivolous lawsuit does survive nonsuit, else its imposition would rest completely in the plaintiff's hands, defeating its purpose."

Epps v. Fowler, 351 S.W.3d 862, 868-69 (Tex.2011). "[W]e have no doubt that a defendant who is the beneficiary of a nonsuit with prejudice would be a prevailing party [and would be entitled to attorney fees]. . . . The res judicata effect of a nonsuit with prejudice works a permanent, inalterable change in the parties' legal relationship to the defendant's benefit: the defendant can never again be sued by the plaintiff or its privies for claims arising out of the same subject matter. [¶] In contrast, a nonsuit without prejudice works no such change in the parties' legal relationship; typically, the plaintiff remains free to re-file the same claims seeking the same relief. *At 870:* [But] a defendant may be a prevailing party when a plaintiff nonsuits without prejudice if the trial court determines, on the defendant's motion, that the nonsuit was taken to avoid an unfavorable ruling on the merits."

In re Greater Houston Orthopaedic Specialists, Inc., 295 S.W.3d 323, 325 (Tex.2009). "Granting a nonsuit is a ministerial act, and a plaintiff's right to a nonsuit exists from the moment a written motion is filed or an oral motion is made in open court, unless the defendant has, prior to that time, sought affirmative relief."

Villafani v. Trejo, 251 S.W.3d 466, 469 (Tex.2008). "A nonsuit under Rule 162 . . . has 'no effect on any motion for sanctions, attorney's fees or other costs, pending at the time of dismissal.' [P] argues that since the trial court denied [D's] motion [for sanctions] before [P] filed the nonsuit, the motion was not a *pending* claim for affirmative relief[, and therefore,] Rule 162 does not protect [D's] motion from the nullifying effect of the nonsuit. [¶] We disagree. . . . Rule 162 protects a party's 'pending claim for affirmative relief' from the general rule that a party is required to get a ruling (or a refusal to rule) from a trial court to preserve a right to appeal. 'Rule 162 merely acknowledges that a nonsuit does not affect . . . a pending sanctions motion; it does not purport to limit the trial court's power to act.' *At 470:* [W]e do not read Rule 162 to mean that a nonsuit prevents a non-moving party from appealing a trial court's ruling on claims for affirmative relief merely because the ruling occurred prior to the nonsuit." *See also* **Unifund CCR Partners v. Villa**, 299 S.W.3d 92, 96 (Tex.2009); **Crites v. Collins**, 284 S.W.3d 839, 843 (Tex.2009).

Texas Mut. Ins. v. Ledbetter, 251 S.W.3d 31, 37 (Tex.2008). "Parties have an absolute right to nonsuit *their own* claims, but not *someone else's* claims they are trying to avoid. *At 38:* Rule 162 . . . provides that '[a]ny dismissal pursuant to this rule shall not prejudice the right of an adverse party to be heard on a pending claim for affirmative relief.' A claim for affirmative relief is one 'on which the claimant could recover compensation or relief even if the plaintiff abandons his cause of action.' A carrier's subrogation claim is just such a claim, as it can be prosecuted by a carrier even if an injured worker never does. [T]he carrier here sought no affirmative relief *from* [*Ps*], seeking instead reimbursement from the funds [Ds] were about to pay them. But Rule 162 is not limited to affirmative claims *against the nonsuiter*; it prohibits dismissal if the effect would be to prejudice any pending claim for affirmative relief, period. [¶] [T]he dismissal here prejudiced the carrier's pending claim for affirmative relief. . . . While [Ps] were entitled to nonsuit their own affirmative claims, they were not entitled to dismissal from the case." *See also* **General Land Office v. OXY U.S.A., Inc.**, 789 S.W.2d 569, 570 (Tex.1990).

UTMB v. Estate of Blackmon, 195 S.W.3d 98, 101 (Tex.2006). "Rule 162 permits the trial court to hold hearings and enter orders affecting costs, attorney's fees, and sanctions, even after notice of nonsuit is filed, while the court retains plenary power. Thus, the trial court has discretion to defer signing an order of dismissal so that it can 'allow a reasonable amount of time' for holding hearings on these matters which are 'collateral to the merits of the underlying case.' Although the Rule permits motions for costs, attorney's fees, and sanctions to remain viable in the trial court, it does not forestall the nonsuit's effect of rendering the merits of the case moot."

In re Bennett, 960 S.W.2d 35, 38 (Tex.1997). "[P]laintiffs have the right under [TRCP] 162 to take a nonsuit at any time until they have introduced all evidence other than rebuttal evidence. Such a nonsuit may have the effect of vitiating earlier interlocutory orders and of precluding further action by the trial court. . . . [¶] Appellate timetables do not run from the date a nonsuit is filed, but rather from the date the trial court signs an order of dismissal." *See also* **Klein v. Hernandez**, 315 S.W.3d 1, 3 (Tex.2010); **Farmer v. Ben E. Keith Co.**, 907 S.W.2d 495, 496 (Tex.1995); **Hyundai Motor Co. v. Alvarado**, 892 S.W.2d 853, 854-55 (Tex.1995).

Estate of Purgason v. Good, No. 14-14-00334-CV, 2016 WL 552149 (Tex.App.—Houston [14th Dist.] 2016, pet.

denied) (memo op.; 2-11-16). "[Ps] filed a notice of nonsuit pursuant to [TRCP] 162. . . . [Ps] subsequently refiled the suit. [T]hey . . . contend that Rule 162 authorizes the clerk to tax costs only if the dismissal 'terminates' the case, and by refiling the claim, they deprived the trial court of the ability to award the costs. [Ps] argue that the trial court *could not* award the costs as the nonsuit . . . did not 'terminate' the case because it was refiled. We disagree. [¶] The nonsuit terminated the case upon its filing."

Energy Transfer Fuel, L.P. v. Trammell, No. 12-09-00059-CV, 2010 WL 3419221 (Tex.App.—Tyler 2010, no pet.) (memo op.; 8-31-10). "A nonsuit may be taken after a temporary restraining order has been obtained but before the hearing on the temporary injunction. But the nonsuit does not defeat the right of a restrained party who is damaged by the temporary restraining order to sue for wrongful injunction."

C/S Solutions, Inc. v. Energy Maint. Servs. Grp., 274 S.W.3d 299, 306-07 (Tex.App.—Houston [1st Dist.] 2008, no pet.). "[T]reatises have drawn a distinction between a pure [TRCP] 162 nonsuit, which voluntarily dismisses the entire case, and a voluntary dismissal that abandons the case as to certain parties and/or claims. This distinction has no practical effect when a plaintiff files a written 'nonsuit' that abandons the case as to certain claims so long as the written 'nonsuit' does not run afoul of the time restrictions in [TRCP] 63. Under our liberal pleading rules, the document is in substance an amended pleading voluntarily dismissing the claims, notwithstanding the fact that the word 'nonsuit' appears. Similarly, the distinction between a pure Rule 162 nonsuit and a voluntary dismissal that abandons the case as to certain parties has no practical effect unless a plaintiff 'nonsuits' those parties in a situation in which another party is prejudiced under [TRCP] 163."

Reynolds v. Murphy, 266 S.W.3d 141, 145-46 (Tex.App.—Fort Worth 2008, pet. denied). "Although a nonsuit may have the effect of vitiating a trial court's earlier interlocutory orders, a nonsuit does not vitiate a trial court's previously-made decisions on the merits, such as a summary judgment, or even a partial summary judgment, which becomes final upon disposition of the other issues in the case. [¶] The parties disagree as to whether the trial court's rulings striking [P's] amended petition are equivalent to a decision on the merits as to the new claims in the amended petition. [D] contends that the rulings were merely incidental interlocutory rulings because they did not involve any judgments on the merits of those claims. . . . [¶] [B]y striking [P's] new causes of action in [the amended] petition, and by refusing to allow discovery on those causes of action, the trial court effected a dismissal of those causes of action with prejudice without affording [P] an opportunity to replead. In essence, . . . the trial court effected the same type of disposition as a dismissal or a partial summary judgment precluding consideration of those claims. [W]e conclude [P's] nonsuit of its sole remaining claim did not vitiate the trial court's rulings effectively barring him from pursuing his new claims. . . ." *See also* **Mobley v. Mobley**, 506 S.W.3d 87, 91-92 (Tex.App.—Texarkana 2016, no pet.); **Waterman S.S. Corp. v. Ruiz**, 355 S.W.3d 387, 400 (Tex.App.—Houston [1st Dist.] 2011, pet. denied).

Bailey v. Gardner, 154 S.W.3d 917, 920 (Tex.App.—Dallas 2005, no pet.). "[P] made a tactical decision to nonsuit his case rather than face trial without expert testimony to support his claim. Taking a voluntary nonsuit for tactical advantage will not support an equitable extension of the limitations period. [E]quitable tolling does not apply to give [P] an extension on the limitations period [to refile his suit]."

TRCP 163. DISMISSAL AS TO PARTIES SERVED, ETC.

When it will not prejudice another party, the plaintiff may dismiss his suit as to one or more of several parties who were served with process, or who have answered, but no such dismissal shall in any case, be allowed as to a principal obligor, except in the cases provided for by statute.

Oct. 29, 1940, eff. Sept. 1, 1941. Amended by orders of Dec. 5, 1983, eff. April 1, 1984; July 15, 1987, eff. Jan. 1, 1988.

See also **O'Connor's Texas Rules**, "Voluntary Dismissal—Nonsuit," ch. 7-F, §1 et seq.

ANNOTATIONS

Texas Cab Co. v. Giles, 783 S.W.2d 695, 697 (Tex.App.—El Paso 1989, no writ). "Unless the settlement with the deleted [D] was properly presented to the trial court, there generally could have been no dismissal to that [D] under [TRCP] 162 or 163, as the dismissal would have prejudiced [co-D]."

TRCP 164. REPEALED BY ORDER OF JULY 15, 1987, EFF. JAN. 1, 1988

TRCP 165. ABANDONMENT

A party who abandons any part of his claim or defense, as contained in the pleadings, may have that fact entered of record, so as to show that the matters therein were not tried.

Oct. 29, 1940, eff. Sept. 1, 1941.

See also **O'Connor's Texas Rules**, "Voluntary Dismissal—Nonsuit," ch. 7-F, §1 et seq.

ANNOTATIONS

Alan Reuber Chevrolet, Inc. v. Grady Chevrolet, Ltd., 287 S.W.3d 877, 887 (Tex.App.—Dallas 2009, no pet.). "Rule 165 permits an abandonment of a part of a claim or defense before, but not after, trial of the cause and entry of the judgment. This is the same requirement as for a nonsuit."

In re Shaw, 966 S.W.2d 174, 177 (Tex.App.—El Paso 1998, no pet.). "Whether a pleading has been abandoned is a question of law which we review de novo. Formal amendment of the pleadings is not required in order to show abandonment. Indeed, a stipulation may form the basis for abandonment."

TRCP 165a. DISMISSAL FOR WANT OF PROSECUTION

1. Failure to Appear. A case may be dismissed for want of prosecution on failure of any party seeking affirmative relief to appear for any hearing or trial of which the party had notice. Notice of the court's intention to dismiss and the date and place of the dismissal hearing shall be sent by the clerk to each attorney of record, and to each party not represented by an attorney and whose address is shown on the docket or in the papers on file, by posting same in the United States Postal Service. At the dismissal hearing, the court shall dismiss for want of prosecution unless there is good cause for the case to be maintained on the docket. If the court determines to maintain the case on the docket, it shall render a pretrial order assigning a trial date for the case and setting deadlines for the joining of new parties, all discovery, filing of all pleadings, the making of a response or supplemental responses to discovery and other pretrial matters. The case may be continued thereafter only for valid and compelling reasons specifically determined by court order. Notice of the signing of the order of dismissal shall be given as provided in Rule 306a. Failure to mail notices as required by this rule shall not affect any of the periods mentioned in Rule 306a except as provided in that rule.

2. Non-Compliance With Time Standards. Any case not disposed of within time standards promulgated by the Supreme Court under its Administrative Rules may be placed on a dismissal docket.

3. Reinstatement. A motion to reinstate shall set forth the grounds therefor and be verified by the movant or his attorney. It shall be filed with the clerk within 30 days after the order of dismissal is signed or within the period provided by Rule 306a. A copy of the motion to reinstate shall be served on each attorney of record and each party not represented by an attorney whose address is shown on the docket or in the papers on file. The clerk shall deliver a copy of the motion to the judge, who shall set a hearing on the motion as soon as practicable. The court shall notify all parties or their attorneys of record of the date, time and place of the hearing.

The court shall reinstate the case upon finding after a hearing that the failure of the party or his attorney was not intentional or the result of conscious indifference but was due to an accident or mistake or that the failure has been otherwise reasonably explained.

In the event for any reason a motion for reinstatement is not decided by signed written order within seventy-five days after the judgment is signed, or, within such other time as may be allowed by Rule 306a, the motion shall be deemed overruled by operation of law. If a motion to reinstate is timely filed by any party, the trial court, regardless of whether an appeal has been perfected, has plenary power to reinstate the case until 30 days after all such timely filed motions are overruled, either by a written and signed order or by operation of law, whichever occurs first.

4. Cumulative Remedies. This dismissal and reinstatement procedure shall be cumulative of the rules and laws governing any other procedures available to the parties in such cases. The same reinstatement procedures and timetable are applicable to all dismissals for want of prosecution including cases which are dismissed pursuant to the court's inherent power, whether or not a motion to dismiss has been filed.

Oct. 3, 1972, eff. Feb. 1, 1973. Amended by order of July 22, 1975, eff. Jan. 1, 1976; Dec. 5, 1983; July 15, 1987, eff. Jan. 1, 1988.

Source: New rule.

See also **O'Connor's Texas Rules**, "Involuntary Dismissal," ch. 7-G, §1 et seq.; **O'Connor's Texas Rules**, "Motion to Reinstate After Dismissal for Want of Prosecution," ch. 10-F, §1 et seq.; **O'Connor's Texas Forms**, FORMS 7G.

ANNOTATIONS

In re Conner, 458 S.W.3d 532, 534 (Tex.2015). "The issue here is whether a trial court abuses its discretion by refusing to grant a motion to dismiss for want of prosecution in the face of unmitigated and unexplained delay. We hold that it does. [¶] Trial courts are generally granted considerable discretion when it comes to managing their dockets. Such discretion, however, is not absolute. It has long been the case that 'a delay of an unreasonable duration . . ., if not sufficiently explained, will raise a conclusive presumption of abandonment of the plaintiff's suit.' This presumption justifies the dismissal of a suit under either a court's inherent authority or Rule 165a. . . . *At 535:* [Ps'] failure to provide good cause for their nearly decade-long delay mandates dismissal under Rule 165a(2). . . . Absent any reasonable explanation for the delay, the trial court clearly abused its discretion by disregarding the conclusive presumption of abandonment."

Alexander v. Lynda's Boutique, 134 S.W.3d 845, 849-50 (Tex.2004). "[T]he clerk has an affirmative duty under Rule 165a to give notice, but no duty to affirmatively show in the record that such notice was given. . . . [¶] [T]he fact that the record is silent about the sending of notices under Rule 165a does not establish error on the face of the

record. [M]ere silence as to whether notice was sent does not establish that notice was not sent or that it was sent to the wrong address. *At 852:* Rule 165a(1) does not preclude a trial court from scheduling a pre-trial hearing, giving notice that failure to attend that hearing may result in dismissal for want of prosecution, and also deciding at that hearing whether the case should be dismissed for want of prosecution if a party seeking relief fails to attend. All Rule 165a(1) requires is notice of intent to dismiss and of a date, time, and place for the hearing." *See also* **Roman v. Halverson**, 587 S.W.3d 509, 512-13 (Tex.App.—El Paso 2019, pet. denied).

Villarreal v. San Antonio Truck & Equip., 994 S.W.2d 628, 630 (Tex.1999). "The trial court's authority to dismiss for want of prosecution stems from two sources: (1) Rule 165a . . . and (2) the court's inherent power. [¶] [A] party must be provided with notice and an opportunity to be heard before a court may dismiss a case for want of prosecution under either Rule 165a or its inherent authority. The failure to provide adequate notice of the trial court's intent to dismiss for want of prosecution requires reversal." *See also* **Ringer v. Kimball**, 274 S.W.3d 865, 867 (Tex.App.—Fort Worth 2008, no pet.).

Smith v. Babcock & Wilcox Constr. Co., 913 S.W.2d 467, 468 (Tex.1995). "A failure to appear is not intentional or due to conscious indifference within the meaning of [TRCP 165a] merely because it is deliberate; it must also be without adequate justification. Proof of such justification—accident, mistake or other reasonable explanation—negates the intent or conscious indifference for which reinstatement can be denied. Also, conscious indifference means more than mere negligence." *See also* **Johnson v. Hawkins**, 255 S.W.3d 394, 398 (Tex.App.—Dallas 2008, pet. denied) (whether failure to appear was not intentional or result of conscious indifference is fact-finding within trial court's discretion).

Allstate Ins. v. Barnet, 589 S.W.3d 313, 319-20 (Tex.App.—El Paso 2019, no pet.). "As a prerequisite to the court's obligation to set a hearing on a motion to reinstate, the plain text of Rule 165a(3) requires . . . service of a copy of the motion on each attorney of record and each party not represented by an attorney whose address is shown on the docket or in the papers on file. [¶] On review, we note that [P's] motion for reinstatement fails to certify that [D] was served with a copy at the address shown in the papers on file as required by Rule 165a(3). When faced with a lack of verification on a motion for reinstatement, courts have held that such motion does not comply with Rule 165a(3)'s requirements. We find the lack of a certificate of service on a motion to reinstate to be analogous to a lack of proper verification given that both requirements are mandatory based on express terms of Rule 165a(3). [¶] We conclude that [P's] motion for reinstatement, which lacks a certificate of service on [D] at his address shown on the docket or in the papers on file, does not comply with Rule 165a(3)'s requirements. [¶] Given that [P's] motion to reinstate failed to meet threshold requirements of Rule 165a(3), the motion is deemed a nullity. . .."

Parker v. Cain, 505 S.W.3d 119, 123 (Tex.App.—Amarillo 2016, no pet.). "[F]or many types of motions, the movant has the responsibility and burden to set the matter for a hearing before the trial court. However, when dealing with a motion for reinstatement pursuant to Rule 165a(3), the burden falls on the trial court because of the specific language of the rule. . . . In reviewing cases from other intermediate appellate courts, we find that they have held that Rule 165a(3) requires that the court set a properly filed motion to reinstate for a hearing and that such a hearing is mandatory with the trial court."

Harris Cty. v. Gambichler, 479 S.W.3d 514, 516-17 (Tex.App.—Houston [14th Dist.] 2015, no pet.). "It is well-settled that dismissal of a case with prejudice functions as a final determination on the merits. But a dismissal for want of prosecution is not a determination on the merits, and therefore dismissal with prejudice in such circumstances is improper. An order of dismissal for want of prosecution should simply place the parties in the position they were in prior to filing the suit."

Ashley & Laird, L.C. v. Gilbert, No. 05-15-00707-CV, 2015 WL 4600245 (Tex.App.—Dallas 2015, no pet.) (memo op.; 7-31-15). " 'Rule 165a(3) sets forth a complete and exclusive remedy by way of a verified motion to reinstate.' [¶] An affidavit may satisfy the verification requirement. [W]e have also concluded that an evidentiary hearing conducted within the 30 day period for filing a verified motion for reinstatement satisfies the purposes of the rule. . . . [F]ailure to file a verified motion to reinstate may be cured if an affidavit or other evidence supporting the motion is filed within the same 30-day period required for filing the motion to reinstate. Here, however, the trial court's hearing was non-evidentiary and was conducted after the trial court's plenary power had expired, more than 30 days after the judgment dismissing the case for want of prosecution was signed. Thus, there is no basis for arguing that [Ps] made any effort to cure the defective motion to reinstate."

United Residential Props., L.P. v. Theis, 378 S.W.3d 552, 557 (Tex.App.—Houston [14th Dist.] 2012, no pet.). The 30-day deadline to file a motion to reinstate "is jurisdictional, and a trial court loses jurisdiction to reinstate a dismissed case after the deadline."

Cappetta v. Hermes, 222 S.W.3d 160, 167 (Tex.App.—San Antonio 2006, no pet.). "Several courts of appeals have concluded that Rule 165a(3)'s reinstatement standard should not apply to cases dismissed under the trial court's inherent power, but fail to explain what alternative reinstatement standard should then apply. Because a case may be dismissed for lack of diligence under either Rule 165a(2) or the court's inherent power, no purpose is served in creating two separate standards for review. The standard should be the same regardless of whether a case is dismissed pursuant to Rule 165a or the court's inherent power. [¶] We . . . hold the Rule 165a(3) standard applies to all dismissals for want of prosecution, whether rule-based or inherent power-based." *Contra* **Maida v. Fire Ins. Exch.**, under this rule.

In re Wal-Mart Stores, 20 S.W.3d 734, 740 (Tex.App.—El Paso 2000, orig. proceeding). "Rule 165a(3) requires that a case be reinstated by signed written order. . . . An oral pronouncement by the court reinstating the case, even when accompanied by a docket entry, is ordinarily inadequate to reinstate the case." *See also* **Roberts v. Franklin**, No. 01-15-01022-CV, 2016 WL 5787245 (Tex.App.—Houston [1st Dist.] 2016, no pet.) (memo op.; 10-4-16).

Maida v. Fire Ins. Exch., 990 S.W.2d 836, 840-41 (Tex.App.—Fort Worth 1999, no pet.). We agree with our sister courts that "have held [TRCP] 165a(3)'s standard for reinstatement only applies to cases dismissed for failure to appear. [¶] The standard set out in [TRCP] 165a(3) is essentially the same standard as that for setting aside a default judgment. Such a standard is well suited for analyzing specific instances of conduct. On the other hand, it does not easily lend itself to determining whether a party diligently prosecuted a case or whether the disposition of the case complies with the supreme court's time standards for disposition. [¶] Furthermore, [TRCP] 165a(4) is consistent with application of [TRCP 165a(3)] to only instances of dismissal based on a failure to appear. [TRCP] 165a(4) requires that the *procedures* and *timetable*, be applied to all dismissals for want of prosecution. Therefore, we hold that [TRCP] 165a(3)'s reinstatement standard, 'conscious indifference,' only applies to cases dismissed for failure to appear." *Contra* **Cappetta v. Hermes**, under this rule.

SECTION 8. PRE-TRIAL PROCEDURE

TRCP 166. PRE-TRIAL CONFERENCE

In an appropriate action, to assist in the disposition of the case without undue expense or burden to the parties, the court may in its discretion direct the attorneys for the parties and the parties or their duly authorized agents to appear before it for a conference to consider:

(a) All pending dilatory pleas, motions and exceptions;

(b) The necessity or desirability of amendments to the pleadings;

(c) A discovery schedule;

(d) Requiring written statements of the parties' contentions;

(e) Contested issues of fact and simplification of the issues;

(f) The possibility of obtaining stipulations of fact;

(g) The identification of legal matters to be ruled on or decided by the court;

(h) The exchange of a list of direct fact witnesses, other than rebuttal or impeaching witnesses the necessity of whose testimony cannot reasonably be anticipated before the time of trial, who will be called to testify at trial, stating their address and telephone number, and the subject of the testimony of each such witness;

(i) The exchange of a list of expert witnesses who will be called to testify at trial, stating their address and telephone number, and the subject of the testimony and opinions that will be proffered by each expert witness;

(j) Agreed applicable propositions of law and contested issues of law;

(k) Proposed jury charge questions, instructions, and definitions for a jury case or proposed findings of fact and conclusions of law for a nonjury case;

(*l*) The marking and exchanging of all exhibits that any party may use at trial and stipulation to the authenticity and admissibility of exhibits to be used at trial;

(m) Written trial objections to the opposite party's exhibits, stating the basis for each objection;

(n) The advisability of a preliminary reference of issues to a master or auditor for findings to be used as evidence when the trial is to be by jury;

(o) The settlement of the case, and to aid such consideration, the court may encourage settlement;

(p) Such other matters as may aid in the disposition of the action.

The court shall make an order that recites the action taken at the pretrial conference, the amendments allowed to the pleadings, the time within which same may be filed, and the agreements made by the parties as to any of the matters considered, and which limits the issues for trial to those not disposed of by admissions, agreements of counsel, or rulings of the court; and such order when issued shall control the subsequent course of the action, unless modified at the trial to prevent manifest injustice. The court in its discretion may establish by rule a pretrial calendar on which actions may be placed for consideration as above provided and may either confine the calendar to jury actions or extend it to all actions.

Pretrial proceedings in multidistrict litigation may also be governed by Rules 11 and 13 of the Rules of Judicial Administration.

Oct. 29, 1940, eff. Sept. 1, 1941. Amended by order of July 26, 1960, eff. Jan. 1, 1961; April 24, 1990, eff. Sept. 1, 1990; Aug. 29, 2003, eff. Sept. 1, 2003.

Comment—1990

To broaden the scope of the rule and to confirm the ability of the trial courts at pretrial hearings to encourage settlement

Source: FRCP 16. Rule gives court the power to compel appearance of parties or their agents, as well as the attorneys; case may be referred to an auditor.

See also Gov't Code §21.001(a); TRCP 248; TRJA 11, 13; **O'Connor's Texas Rules**, "Pretrial Conference," ch. 5-A, §1 et seq.; **O'Connor's Texas Rules**, "Motion to Transfer to Multidistrict Litigation Pretrial Court," ch. 5-G, §1 et seq.; **O'Connor's Texas Forms**, FORM 5A:1.

ANNOTATIONS

Koslow's v. Mackie, 796 S.W.2d 700, 703 (Tex.1990). TRCP 166 "includes the power to order the parties through their attorneys (or through themselves if appearing pro se) to confer to narrow the issues for the written pretrial conference report."

Provident Life & Acc. Ins. v. Hazlitt, 216 S.W.2d 805, 807 (Tex.1949). "The purpose of [TRCP 166] is to simplify and shorten the trial. . . . [N]o controverted issues of fact could be adjudicated at [the pretrial] conference, but orders could be entered disposing of issues which are founded upon admitted or undisputed facts."

Stamatis v. Methodist Willowbrook Hosp., No. 14-14-00492-CV, 2015 WL 3485734 (Tex.App.—Houston [14th Dist.] 2015, no pet.) (memo op.; 6-2-15). "[D]ismissal at a pretrial conference is allowed in limited situations when determination of a legal question is dispositive of a case in its entirety."

In re Estate of Henry, 250 S.W.3d 518, 526 (Tex.App.—Dallas 2008, no pet.). "Rule 166 . . . provides that an order made at a pretrial conference hearing 'shall control the subsequent course of the action.' However, the trial court retains authority under rule 166 to modify an order to prevent manifest injustice. 'Rule 166 recognizes the fundamental rule that a trial court has the inherent right to change or modify any interlocutory order or judgment until the time the judgment on the merits in the case becomes final.'"

In re Bledsoe, 41 S.W.3d 807, 812 (Tex.App.—Fort Worth 2001, orig. proceeding). "The trial court has power, implicit under rule 166, to sanction a party for failing to obey its pretrial orders." *See also* **In re Marriage of Harrison**, 557 S.W.3d 99, 123 (Tex.App.—Houston [14th Dist.] 2018, pet. denied).

Lindley v. Johnson, 936 S.W.2d 53, 55 (Tex.App.—Tyler 1996, writ denied). "When a trial court's pretrial scheduling order changes the deadlines set forth in a procedural rule, the trial court's order prevails."

TRCP 166a. SUMMARY JUDGMENT

(a) For Claimant. A party seeking to recover upon a claim, counterclaim, or cross-claim or to obtain a declaratory judgment may, at any time after the adverse party has appeared or answered, move with or without supporting affidavits for a summary judgment in his favor upon all or any part thereof. A summary judgment, interlocutory in character, may be rendered on the issue of liability alone although there is a genuine issue as to amount of damages.

(b) For Defending Party. A party against whom a claim, counterclaim, or cross-claim is asserted or a declaratory judgment is sought may, at any time, move with or without supporting affidavits for a summary judgment in his favor as to all or any part thereof.

(c) Motion and Proceedings Thereon. The motion for summary judgment shall state the specific grounds therefor. Except on leave of court, with notice to opposing counsel, the motion and any supporting affidavits shall be filed and served at least twenty-one days before the time specified for hearing. Except on leave of court, the adverse party, not later than seven days prior to the day of hearing may file and serve opposing affidavits or other written response. No oral testimony shall be received at the hearing. The judgment sought shall be rendered forthwith if (i) the deposition transcripts, interrogatory answers, and other discovery responses referenced or set forth in the motion or response, and (ii) the pleadings, admissions, affidavits, stipulations of the parties, and authenticated or certified public records, if any, on file at the time of the hearing, or filed thereafter and before judgment with permission of the court, show that, except as to the amount of damages, there is no genuine issue as to any material fact and the moving party is entitled to judgment as a matter of law on the issues expressly set out in the motion or in an answer or any other response. Issues not expressly presented to the trial court by written motion, answer or other response shall not be considered on appeal as grounds for reversal. A summary judgment may be based on uncontroverted testimonial evidence of an interested witness, or of an expert witness as to subject matter concerning which the trier of fact must be guided solely by the opinion testimony of experts, if the evidence is clear, positive and direct, otherwise credible and free from contradictions and inconsistencies, and could have been readily controverted.

(d) Appendices, References and Other Use of Discovery Not Otherwise on File. Discovery products not on file with the clerk may be used as summary judgment evidence if copies of the material, appendices containing the evidence, or a notice containing specific references to the discovery or specific references to other instruments, are filed and served on all parties together with a statement of intent to use the specified discovery as summary judgment proofs: (i) at least twenty-one days before the hearing if such proofs are to be used to support the summary judgment; or (ii) at least seven days before the hearing if such proofs are to be used to oppose the summary judgment.

(e) Case not Fully Adjudicated on Motion. If summary judgment is not rendered upon the whole case or for all the relief asked and a trial is necessary, the judge may

at the hearing examine the pleadings and the evidence on file, interrogate counsel, ascertain what material fact issues exist and make an order specifying the facts that are established as a matter of law, and directing such further proceedings in the action as are just.

(f) Form of Affidavits; Further Testimony. Supporting and opposing affidavits shall be made on personal knowledge, shall set forth such facts as would be admissible in evidence, and shall show affirmatively that the affiant is competent to testify to the matters stated therein. Sworn or certified copies of all papers or parts thereof referred to in an affidavit shall be attached thereto or served therewith. The court may permit affidavits to be supplemented or opposed by depositions or by further affidavits. Defects in the form of affidavits or attachments will not be grounds for reversal unless specifically pointed out by objection by an opposing party with opportunity, but refusal, to amend.

(g) When Affidavits Are Unavailable. Should it appear from the affidavits of a party opposing the motion that he cannot for reasons stated present by affidavit facts essential to justify his opposition, the court may refuse the application for judgment or may order a continuance to permit affidavits to be obtained or depositions to be taken or discovery to be had or may make such other order as is just.

(h) Affidavits Made in Bad Faith. Should it appear to the satisfaction of the court at any time that any of the affidavits presented pursuant to this rule are presented in bad faith or solely for the purpose of delay, the court shall forthwith order the party employing them to pay to the other party the amount of the reasonable expenses which the filing of the affidavits caused him to incur, including reasonable attorney's fees, and any offending party or attorney may be adjudged guilty of contempt.

(i) No-Evidence Motion. After adequate time for discovery, a party without presenting summary judgment evidence may move for summary judgment on the ground that there is no evidence of one or more essential elements of a claim or defense on which an adverse party would have the burden of proof at trial. The motion must state the elements as to which there is no evidence. The court must grant the motion unless the respondent produces summary judgment evidence raising a genuine issue of material fact.

Oct. 12, 1949, eff. March 1, 1950. Amended by orders of Oct. 1, 1951, eff. March 1, 1952; July 20, 1966, eff. Jan. 1, 1967; July 21, 1970, eff. Jan. 1, 1971; July 11, 1977, eff. Jan. 1, 1978; June 10, 1980, eff. Jan. 1, 1981; Dec. 5, 1983, eff. April 1, 1984; July 15, 1987, eff. Jan. 1, 1988; April 24, 1990, eff. Sept. 1, 1990; Aug. 15, 1997, eff. Sept. 1, 1997.

Comment—1997

This comment is intended to inform the construction and application of the rule. Paragraph (i) authorizes a motion for summary judgment based on the assertion that, after adequate opportunity for discovery, there is no evidence to support one or more specified elements of an adverse party's claim or defense. A discovery period set by pretrial order should be adequate opportunity for discovery unless there is a showing to the contrary, and ordinarily a motion under paragraph (i) would be permitted after the period but not before. The motion must be specific in challenging the evidentiary support for an element of a claim or defense; paragraph (i) does not authorize conclusory motions or general no-evidence challenges to an opponent's case. Paragraph (i) does not apply to ordinary motions for summary judgment under paragraphs (a) or (b), in which the movant must prove it is entitled to judgment by establishing each element of its own claim or defense as a matter of law or by negating an element of the respondent's claim or defense as a matter of law. To defeat a motion made under paragraph (i), the respondent is not required to marshal its proof; its response need only point out evidence that raises a fact issue on the challenged elements. The existing rules continue to govern the general requirements of summary judgment practice. A motion under paragraph (i) is subject to sanctions provided by existing law (Tex Civ.Prac. & Rem. Code §§9.001–10.006) and rules (Tex.R.Civ.P. 13). The denial of a motion under paragraph (i) is no more reviewable by appeal or mandamus than the denial of a motion under paragraph (c).

Comment—1990

This amendment provides a mechanism for using previously non-filed discovery in summary judgment practice. Such proofs must all be filed in advance of the hearing in accordance with Rule 166a. Paragraphs (d) through (g) are renumbered (e) through (h).

Source: FRCP 56, with changes: Substituted phrase "adverse party has appeared or answered" for the phrase "pleading in answer thereto was served" in (a).

See also **O'Connor's Texas Rules**, "Motion for Summary Judgment—General Rules," ch. 7-B, §1 et seq.; **O'Connor's Texas Rules**, "Traditional Motion for Summary Judgment," ch. 7-C, §1 et seq.; **O'Connor's Texas Rules**, "No-Evidence Motion for Summary Judgment," ch. 7-D, §1 et seq.; **O'Connor's Texas Forms**, FORMS 7B, 7C.

ANNOTATIONS

Traditional SJ

Amedisys, Inc. v. Kingwood Home Health Care, LLC, 437 S.W.3d 507, 511 (Tex.2014). "[T]he party moving for traditional summary judgment [has] the burden to submit sufficient evidence that establishe[s] on its face that 'there is no genuine issue as to any material fact' and that it is 'entitled to judgment as a matter of law.' When a movant meets that burden of establishing each element of the claim or defense on which it seeks summary judgment, the burden then shifts to the non-movant to disprove or raise an issue of fact as to at least one of those elements. But if the movant does not satisfy its initial burden, the burden does not shift and the non-movant need not respond or present any evidence." *See also* **State v. $90,235**, 390 S.W.3d 289, 292 (Tex.2013).

Frost Nat'l Bank v. Fernandez, 315 S.W.3d 494, 508 (Tex.2010). "A defendant who conclusively negates at least one of the essential elements of a cause of action or conclusively establishes an affirmative defense is entitled to summary judgment." *See also* **Stanfield v. Neubaum**, 494 S.W.3d 90, 96 (Tex.2016).

Proulx v. Wells, 235 S.W.3d 213, 215 (Tex.2007). "Our jurisprudence has at times been less than clear in explaining the summary-judgment burden that inheres when the diligent-service question is presented. *At 216:* [O]nce a defendant has affirmatively pled the limitations defense and shown that service was effected after limitations expired, the burden shifts to the plaintiff 'to explain the delay.' Thus, it is the plaintiff's burden to present evidence regarding the efforts that were made to serve the defendant, and to explain every lapse in effort or period of delay. In some instances, the plaintiff's explanation may be *legally* improper to raise the diligence issue and the defendant will bear no burden at all. In others, the plaintiff's explanation of its service efforts may demonstrate a lack of due diligence as a matter of law, as when one or more lapses between service efforts are unexplained or patently unreasonable. But if the plaintiff's explanation for the delay raises a material fact issue concerning the diligence of service efforts, the burden shifts back to the defendant to conclusively show why, as a matter of law, the explanation is insufficient." *See also* **Farmers Ins. Exch. v. Rodriguez**, 366 S.W.3d 216, 221 (Tex.App.—Houston [14th Dist.] 2012, pet. denied).

Valence Oper. Co. v. Dorsett, 164 S.W.3d 656, 661 (Tex.2005). "When both parties move for partial summary judgment on the same issues and the trial court grants one motion and denies the other . . ., the reviewing court considers the summary judgment evidence presented by both sides, determines all questions presented, and if the reviewing court determines that the trial court erred, renders the judgment the trial court should have rendered." *See also* **Texas Workforce Comm'n v. Wichita Cty.**, 548 S.W.3d 489, 492 (Tex.2018); **BCCA Appeal Grp. v. City of Houston**, 496 S.W.3d 1, 7 (Tex.2016).

Park Place Hosp. v. Estate of Milo, 909 S.W.2d 508, 510 (Tex.1995). For Ds "to prevail, they were required to prove that there was no genuine issue as to any material fact and that they were entitled to judgment as a matter of law. In reviewing a summary judgment, we must accept as true evidence favoring [P], indulging every reasonable inference and resolving all doubts in [P's] favor." *See also* **Denbury Green Pipeline-Tex., LLC v. Texas Rice Land Partners**, 510 S.W.3d 909, 914 (Tex.2017); **Cantey Hanger, LLP v. Byrd**, 467 S.W.3d 477, 481 (Tex.2015).

McConnell v. Southside ISD, 858 S.W.2d 337, 341 (Tex.1993). "In determining whether grounds are expressly presented, reliance may not be placed on briefs or summary judgment evidence."

Rush v. Barrios, 56 S.W.3d 88, 98 (Tex.App.—Houston [14th Dist.] 2001, pet. denied). "A trial court may . . . properly grant summary judgment after having previously denied [it] without a motion by or prior notice to the parties, as long as the court retains jurisdiction over the case."

Michael v. Dyke, 41 S.W.3d 746, 751 (Tex.App.—Corpus Christi 2001, no pet.). "When it is not readily apparent to the trial court that summary judgment is sought under rule 166a(i), the court should presume that it is filed under the traditional summary judgment rule and analyze it according to those well-recognized standards. [The] order granting summary judgment should clarify whether the motion is granted on no-evidence grounds or traditional grounds. When an order fails to so clarify, a motion requesting such clarification should be filed with the trial court."

No-Evidence SJ

Town of Shady Shores v. Swanson, 590 S.W.3d 544, 550 (Tex.2019). "As a procedural matter, we have held that a jurisdictional challenge, including one premised on sovereign immunity, 'may be raised by a plea to the jurisdiction, as well as by other procedural vehicles, such as a motion for summary judgment.' [¶] [T]he court of appeals in this case held that a governmental entity 'has the burden to negate the existence of jurisdictional facts before a plaintiff has any burden to produce evidence raising a fact question on jurisdiction.' In the court of appeals' view, allowing a jurisdictional challenge on immunity grounds via a no-evidence motion would improperly shift that initial burden by requiring a plaintiff to 'marshal evidence showing jurisdiction' before the governmental entity has produced evidence negating it. Consequently, the court held that a no-evidence motion for summary judgment 'may not be used by a governmental entity as a vehicle to defeat jurisdiction or otherwise circumvent its burden to disprove jurisdiction.' *At 551-52:* We cannot agree with the reasoning of the courts of appeals that have rejected no-evidence motions as vehicles to assert governmental immunity. [¶] Because jurisdiction may be challenged on evidentiary grounds and the burden to establish jurisdiction, including waiver of a government defendant's immunity from suit, is on the plaintiff, we see no reason to allow jurisdictional challenges via traditional motions for summary judgment but to foreclose such challenges via no-evidence motions. It is true that those two vehicles place different initial burdens on the movant: the former requires the movant to conclusively negate at least one element of the nonmovant's claim on which the nonmovant has the burden of proof, while the latter requires the movant to specify the elements of the nonmovant's claim for which no evidence exists. However, contrary to the court of appeals' characterization of the shifting burden, the nonmovant need not 'marshal' its evidence or prove up its case to defeat a no-evidence motion. As noted, under Rule 166a(i) the nonmovant is required only to produce enough evidence—that is, more than a scintilla—to create a genuine issue of material fact as to the challenged element. [¶] [W]hen jurisdiction is intertwined with the merits, the evidence supporting jurisdiction and the merits is necessarily intertwined as well. Thus, when a challenge to jurisdiction that implicates the merits is properly made and supported, whether by a plea to the jurisdiction or by a traditional or no-evidence motion for summary judgment, the plaintiff will be required to present sufficient evidence on the merits of her claims to create a genuine issue of material fact. The safeguards built into Rule 166a(i)—a no-

evidence motion may be filed only after an adequate time for discovery, the movant must specify the elements for which no evidence exists, the nonmovant need only present more than a scintilla of evidence supporting the challenged element, and the evidence must be viewed in the light most favorable to the nonmovant—provide a sufficient degree of protection to plaintiffs, as does the rule governing traditional motions. Accordingly, the court of appeals erred in refusing to review the trial court's denial of the . . . no-evidence motion for summary judgment challenging jurisdiction on the basis of governmental immunity."

Community Health Sys. Prof'l Servs. v. Hansen, 525 S.W.3d 671, 695-96 (Tex.2017). "Rule 166a(i) . . . requires that a no-evidence motion specifically state the element or elements for which there is no evidence. We have called for strict enforcement of this requirement. Thus, a no-evidence motion that lists each element of the plaintiff's claim and then asserts that the plaintiff has no evidence to support 'one or more' or 'any of' those elements is insufficient to support summary judgment because this language does not clearly identify which elements, whether some or all, are challenged."

Mack Trucks, Inc. v. Tamez, 206 S.W.3d 572, 581-82 (Tex.2006). A no-evidence motion for "summary judgment . . . is essentially a motion for a pretrial directed verdict. Once such a motion is filed, the burden shifts to the nonmoving party to present evidence raising an issue of material fact as to the elements specified in the motion. We review the evidence presented by the motion and response in the light most favorable to the party against whom the summary judgment was rendered, crediting evidence favorable to that party if reasonable jurors could, and disregarding contrary evidence unless reasonable jurors could not." *See also* **Timpte Indus. v. Gish**, 286 S.W.3d 306, 310 (Tex.2009).

King Ranch, Inc. v. Chapman, 118 S.W.3d 742, 751 (Tex.2003). " 'A no evidence point will be sustained when (a) there is a complete absence of evidence of a vital fact, (b) the court is barred by rules of law or of evidence from giving weight to the only evidence offered to prove a vital fact, (c) the evidence offered to prove a vital fact is no more than a mere scintilla, or (d) the evidence conclusively establishes the opposite of the vital fact.' . . . More than a scintilla of evidence exists when the evidence[] 'rises to a level that would enable reasonable and fair-minded people to differ in their conclusions.' " *See also* **Ford Motor Co. v. Ridgway**, 135 S.W.3d 598, 601 (Tex.2004) (evidence that does no more than create mere suspicion of existence of a fact is, in legal effect, no evidence).

Jatex Oil & Gas Expl. L.P. v. Nadel & Gussman Permian, L.L.C., __ S.W.3d __, 2020 WL 4873836 (Tex.App.—Eastland 2020, no pet.) (No. 11-17-00265-CV; 8-20-20). "The comment to Rule 166a(i) specifies that the nonmovant has the burden to 'point out' the evidence that defeats each challenged element of a no-evidence motion for summary judgment. . . . 'In the absence of any guidance from [the nonmovant] as to where the evidence can be found, . . . the trial court is [not] required to sift through a voluminous record in search of evidence to support [the nonmovant's] argument [that] a fact issue exists on any challenged element.' "

Neurodiagnostic Tex, L.L.C. v. Pierce, 506 S.W.3d 153, 172 (Tex.App.—Tyler 2016, no pet.). "When determining whether adequate time for discovery has elapsed, we consider (1) the nature of the cause of action; (2) the nature of the evidence necessary to controvert the no evidence motion; (3) the length of time the case has been active in the trial court; (4) the amount of time the no evidence motion has been on file; (5) whether the movant has requested stricter time deadlines for discovery; (6) the amount of discovery that has already taken place; and (7) whether the discovery deadlines that are in place are specific or vague." *See also* **McInnis v. Mallia**, 261 S.W.3d 197, 202-03 (Tex.App.—Houston [14th Dist.] 2008, no pet.) (time allocated for discovery in docket-control order is strong indicator of adequate time).

Nelson v. SCI Tex. Funeral Servs., 484 S.W.3d 248, 252 (Tex.App.—Eastland 2016), *aff'd*, 540 S.W.3d 539 (Tex.2018). "[D's] no-evidence ground . . . is not an ordinary no-evidence ground because it is premised on a legal contention concerning the law applicable to [P's] claim. [¶] '[T]he court must determine the law which is applicable to the case with respect to any no-evidence motion for summary judgment in order to determine if the summary judgment evidence raises a genuine issue of material fact. The fact that a dispute exists with respect to the applicable law does not prevent the court from performing its function of analyzing the non-movant's evidence to determine if it raises a fact issue.' Other courts have not taken this approach. They have concluded that a question of law is not a proper subject of a no-evidence motion for summary judgment."

Hybrid Motion

Merriman v. XTO Energy, Inc., 407 S.W.3d 244, 248 (Tex.2013). "[P] contends that we should treat [D's] motion as only a traditional one because [D] did not sufficiently segregate the grounds for the different types of motions. But [D] labeled its motion as a combined traditional and no-evidence motion, and as long as a motion clearly sets forth its grounds and otherwise meets the requirements of a no-evidence summary judgment motion, as [D's] did, it is sufficient as one. When a party moves for summary judgment on both traditional and no-evidence grounds as [D] did here, we first address the no-evidence grounds. That is because if the non-movant fails to produce legally sufficient evidence to meet his burden as to the no-evidence motion, there is no need to analyze whether the movant satisfied its burden under the traditional motion." *See also* **Ford Motor Co. v. Ridgway**, 135 S.W.3d 598, 600 (Tex.2004).

Binur v. Jacobo, 135 S.W.3d 646, 650-51 (Tex.2004). TRCP "166a does not prohibit a party from combining in a single motion a request for summary judgment that utilizes

the procedures under either subsection (a) or (b), with a request for summary judgment that utilizes subsection (i). . . . The fact that evidence may be attached to a motion . . . under subsection (a) or (b) does not foreclose a party from also asserting that there is no evidence with regard to a particular element. Similarly, if a motion brought solely under subsection (i) attaches evidence, that evidence should not be considered unless it creates a fact question, but such a motion should not be disregarded or treated as a motion under subsection (a) or (b). [¶] [U]sing headings to clearly delineate the basis for summary judgment under subsection (a) or (b) from the basis for summary judgment under subsection (i) would be helpful . . ., but the rule does not require it."

Waite v. Woodard, Hall & Primm, P.C., 137 S.W.3d 277, 281 (Tex.App.—Houston [1st Dist.] 2004, no pet.). "Although [TRCP] 166a does not prohibit a hybrid motion, the motion must give fair notice to the non-movant of the basis on which the summary judgment is sought. [P's] motion did not give fair notice that it was attempting to establish its entitlement to judgment as a matter of law. . . ."

SJ Evidence

Lujan v. Navistar, Inc., 555 S.W.3d 79, 87 (Tex.2018). "Rule 166a obligates Texas trial courts to distinguish genuine fact issues, which must proceed toward trial, from non-genuine fact issues, which should not survive summary judgment. Application of the sham affidavit rule is merely one way in which trial courts have gone about discharging that obligation. We affirm this approach today. Under Rule 166a(c), a trial court may conclude that a party does not raise a genuine fact issue by submitting sworn testimony that materially conflicts with the same witness's prior sworn testimony, unless there is a sufficient explanation for the conflict. We emphasize that this rule does not contravene the long-standing principle that the trial court is 'not to weigh the evidence or determine its credibility, and thus try the case on the affidavits.' Rather, the sham affidavit rule is a tool that may be used to distinguish genuine fact issues from non-genuine fact issues. . . ."

Seim v. Allstate Tex. Lloyds, 551 S.W.3d 161, 164 (Tex.2018). "Courts have held that even if a party objects to an opponent's summary-judgment evidence, the evidence 'remains part of the summary[-]judgment proof unless an order sustaining the objection is reduced to writing, signed, and entered of record.' [¶] [TRAP] 33.1(a) requires a timely and ruled-upon objection to preserve error. In 1997, language was added to the rule providing that the trial court may rule on an objection 'either expressly or implicitly.' [¶] [T]he [Second Court of Appeals has] relied on Rule 33.1's new language, construing it to mean a trial court 'implicitly' rules upon objections in summary-judgment proceedings by ruling on the merits of the summary-judgment motion. At 165: [That] court [has] held that 'error is preserved as long as the record indicates in some way that the trial court ruled on the objection either expressly or implicitly.' [¶] Other courts, however, have declined to adopt the Second Court's approach. For example, the Fourteenth Court of Appeals has held: 'We believe the better practice is for the trial court to disclose, in writing, its rulings on all objections to summary[-]judgment evidence at or before the time it enters the order granting or denying summary judgment. . . .' [¶] The Fourth Court of Appeals agreed with the Fourteenth Court, explaining that until the revision to Rule 33.1 and the . . . opinions [from the Second Court of Appeals], it was 'well settled' that trial courts must expressly rule on objections in writing for error to be preserved. *At 166:* We hold that the Fourth and the Fourteenth courts have it right. After the revisions to Rule 33.1(a) became effective, we concluded in **In re Z.L.T.** [124 S.W.3d 163 (Tex.2003),] that 'an implicit ruling may be sufficient to preserve an issue for appellate review.' In that case, we held a ruling was implied because the implication was 'clear.' But nothing in this record serves as a clearly implied ruling by the trial court on [D's] objections."

Schlumberger Tech. v. Pasko, 544 S.W.3d 830, 835 (Tex.2018). "[P] complains that the trial court improperly considered [P's] own summary judgment evidence against him. [P] argues that [D] was not entitled to rely on his summary judgment evidence because [D] did not serve it on [P] at least 21 days prior to the hearing on [D's] motion. According to [P], [D] was required to seek leave of court to submit new evidence less than 21 days before the hearing, and to reset the hearing to no sooner than 21 days after it filed its reply relying on [P's] evidence. We disagree. Rule 166a(c) plainly provides for the court to consider evidence in the record that is attached either to the motion or a response. [D] was allowed to rely on, and the trial court could consider, the evidence and pleadings [P] filed."

Wadewitz v. Montgomery, 951 S.W.2d 464, 466 (Tex.1997). "Conclusory statements by an expert are insufficient to support or defeat summary judgment." *See also* **Elizondo v. Krist**, 415 S.W.3d 259, 264 (Tex.2013); **United Blood Servs. v. Longoria**, 938 S.W.2d 29, 30 (Tex.1997).

Trico Techs. v. Montiel, 949 S.W.2d 308, 310 (Tex.1997). "The mere fact that the affidavit is self-serving does not necessarily make the evidence an improper basis for summary judgment. Summary judgment based on the uncontroverted affidavit of an interested witness is proper if the evidence is clear, positive, direct, otherwise credible, free from contradictions and inconsistencies, and could have been readily controverted. 'Could have been readily controverted' does not mean that the summary judgment evidence could have been easily and conveniently rebutted, but rather indicates that the testimony could have been effectively countered by opposing evidence." *See also* **Neely v. Wilson**, 418 S.W.3d 52, 67 n.22 (Tex.2013).

Laidlaw Waste Sys. v. City of Wilmer, 904 S.W.2d 656, 660 (Tex.1995). "Generally, pleadings are not competent evidence, even if sworn or verified."

McConathy v. McConathy, 869 S.W.2d 341, 341 (Tex.1994). "[D]eposition excerpts [and other discovery]

submitted as summary judgment evidence need not be authenticated. *At 342:* All parties have ready access to depositions taken in a cause, and thus deposition excerpts submitted with a motion for summary judgment may be easily verified as to their accuracy." *See also* **Gunville v. Gonzales**, 508 S.W.3d 547, 561-62 (Tex.App.—El Paso 2016, no pet.).

Casso v. Brand, 776 S.W.2d 551, 558 (Tex.1989). "If the credibility of the affiant . . . is likely to be a dispositive factor in the resolution of the case, then summary judgment is inappropriate. On the other hand, if the non-movant must, in all likelihood, come forth with independent evidence to prevail, then summary judgment may well be proper in the absence of such controverting proof."

Rockwall Commons Assocs. v. MRC Mortg. Grantor Trust I, 331 S.W.3d 500, 507 (Tex.App.—El Paso 2010, no pet.). "Substantive defects include affidavits that include legal or factual conclusions. Among the objections that may be raised at trial regarding the form of an affidavit are: (1) lack of personal knowledge; (2) hearsay; (3) statement of an interested witness that is not clear, positive, direct, or free from contradiction; and (4) competence."

Chau v. Riddle, 212 S.W.3d 699, 704 (Tex.App.—Houston [1st Dist.] 2006), *rev'd on other grounds*, 254 S.W.3d 453 (Tex.2008). "The affidavit of an expert who is not properly designated may not be used as evidence in a summary judgment context. Where the expert's testimony will be excluded at trial on the merits, it will be excluded from a summary judgment proceeding."

Brown v. Brown, 145 S.W.3d 745, 751 (Tex.App.—Dallas 2004, pet. denied). "Defects in the form of an affidavit must be objected to, and the opposing party must have the opportunity to amend the affidavit. The failure to obtain a ruling on an objection to the form of the affidavit waives the objection. Defects in the substance of an affidavit are not waived by the failure to obtain a ruling from the trial court on the objection, and they may be raised for the first time on appeal." *See also* **Stovall & Assocs. v. Hibbs Fin. Ctr., Ltd.**, 409 S.W.3d 790, 797 (Tex.App.—Dallas 2013, no pet.) (objection that affidavit contains hearsay is objection to defect in form of affidavit); **Vega v. Autozone W., Inc.**, No. 04-12-00724-CV, 2015 WL 4114976 (Tex.App.—San Antonio 2013, no pet.) (memo op.; 6-5-13) (objection that deposition contained hearsay statements was objection to defect in form); **Watts v. Hermann Hosp.**, 962 S.W.2d 102, 105 (Tex.App.—Houston [1st Dist.] 1997, no pet.) (without objection, defects in authentication of attachments supporting SJ motion or response are waived).

Goss v. Bobby D. Assocs., 94 S.W.3d 65, 71 (Tex.App.—Tyler 2002, no pet.). "The trial court cannot consider affidavits offered by the non-movant to contradict deemed admissions in cases involving summary judgment." *See also* **Dallas Drain Co. v. Welsh**, No. 05-14-00831-CV, 2013 WL 2446710 (Tex.App.—Dallas 2015, no pet.) (memo op.; 7-8-15).

Final vs. Partial SJ

M.O. Dental Lab v. Rape, 139 S.W.3d 671, 674 (Tex.2004). "The court of appeals . . . held that the trial court's order granting summary judgment was final for purposes of this appeal [even though it did not dispose of one D] because [that D] was never served and the record contains no pleadings or motions filed by [that D]. . . . We [previously] held [in a similar circumstance that] 'the case stands as if there had been a discontinuance as to [unserved party], and the judgment is to be regarded as final for the purposes of appeal.' [¶] [Here, P] stated '[t]he location for service of [unserved D] is unknown at this time, so no citation is requested.' [B]oth [P] and [served Ds] agreed . . . that [unserved D] was never served with process. . . . *At 675:* [W]e conclude that the trial court's order granting summary judgment is final for the purposes of this appeal." *See also* **In re Miranda**, 142 S.W.3d 354, 356-57 (Tex.App.—El Paso 2004, orig. proceeding).

Jacobs v. Satterwhite, 65 S.W.3d 653, 655 (Tex.2001). " '[I]f a defendant moves for summary judgment on only one of [multiple] claims asserted by the plaintiff, but the trial court renders judgment that the plaintiff take nothing on all claims asserted, the judgment is final—erroneous, but final.' "

McNally v. Guevara, 52 S.W.3d 195, 196 (Tex.2001). "[A] party's omission of one of his claims from a motion for summary judgment does not waive the claim because a party can always move for partial summary judgment, and thus there can be no presumption that a motion for summary judgment addresses all of the movant's claims. Nothing in the trial court's judgment, other than its award of costs to [Ds], suggests that it intended to deny [Ds'] claim for attorney fees. The award of costs, by itself, does not make the judgment final."

Lehmann v. Har-Con Corp., 39 S.W.3d 191, 192-93 (Tex.2001). "We no longer believe that a Mother Hubbard clause in an order or in a judgment issued without a full trial can be taken to indicate finality. We therefore hold that in cases in which only one final and appealable judgment can be rendered, a judgment issued without a conventional trial is final for purposes of appeal if and only if either it actually disposes of all claims and parties then before the court, regardless of its language, or it states with unmistakable clarity that it is a final judgment as to all claims and all parties." *See also* **Farm Bur. Cty. Mut. Ins. v. Rogers**, 455 S.W.3d 161, 163-64 (Tex.2015).

Pleadings in SJ Cases

Sosa v. Central Power & Light, 909 S.W.2d 893, 895 (Tex.1995). "Because [Ps] timely filed their second amended original petition, it superseded their first amended original petition containing the statements on which [Ds] based their motion for summary judgment. Contrary to state-

ments in live pleadings, those contained in superseded pleadings are not conclusive and indisputable judicial admissions. Therefore, the basis for [Ds'] motion no longer existed and summary judgment was improper."

Natividad v. Alexsis, Inc., 875 S.W.2d 695, 699 (Tex.1994). "A review of the pleadings [when an SJ is based on the pleadings] is de novo, with the reviewing court taking all allegations, facts, and inferences in the pleadings as true and viewing them in a light most favorable to the pleader. The reviewing court will affirm the summary judgment only if the pleadings are legally insufficient."

In re B.I.V., 870 S.W.2d 12, 13 (Tex.1994). "A summary judgment should not be based on a pleading deficiency that could be cured by amendment."

Burt v. Harwell, 369 S.W.3d 623, 625 (Tex.App.—Dallas 2012, no pet.). "Although summary judgment generally may not be granted on a claim not addressed in the summary judgment proceeding, it may be granted on later pleaded causes of action if the grounds asserted in the motion show that the plaintiff could not recover from the defendant on the later pleaded causes of action." *See also* **Lamell v. OneWest Bank**, 485 S.W.3d 53, 58 (Tex.App.—Houston [14th Dist.] 2015, pet. denied) (court can grant SJ on later-pleaded claims if grounds expressly presented in motion are sufficiently broad to cover claims).

Austin v. Countrywide Homes Loans, 261 S.W.3d 68, 75 (Tex.App.—Houston [1st Dist.] 2008, pet. denied). "Once the hearing date for a motion for summary judgment has passed, the movant must secure a written order granting leave in order to file an amended pleading."

Late Filings

B.C. v. Steak N Shake Opers., Inc., 598 S.W.3d 256, 259-60 (Tex.2020). " '[W]here nothing appears of record to indicate that late filing of a summary judgment response was with leave of court, it is presumed [the] trial court did not consider the response.' Courts of appeals considering whether a trial court granted leave commonly—and correctly—examine the record for 'an affirmative indication that the trial court permitted the late filing.' That indication may arise from 'a separate order, a recital in the summary judgment, or an oral ruling contained in the reporter's record of the summary judgment hearing.' So while a 'silent record' on appeal supports the presumption 'that the trial court did not grant leave,' courts should examine whether the record 'affirmatively indicates' the late-filed response was 'accepted or considered.' *At 261:* We . . . conclude that the trial court's recital that it considered the 'evidence and arguments of counsel,' without any limitation, is an 'affirmative indication' that the trial court considered [nonmovant's] response and the evidence attached to it. The court of appeals concluded this reference 'indicates nothing more than the trial court considered [movant's evidence] in conjunction with the traditional motion.' But a court's recital that it generally considered 'evidence'—especially when one party objected to the timeliness of all of the opposing party's evidence—overcomes the presumption that the court did not consider it. *At 262:* Because the trial court recited that it had considered 'the pleadings, evidence, and arguments of counsel,' the court of appeals should have considered that evidence as well in its review of the trial court's summary judgment."

Carpenter v. Cimarron Hydrocarbons Corp., 98 S.W.3d 682, 688 (Tex.2002). "[A] motion for leave to file a late summary-judgment response should be granted when a litigant establishes good cause for failing to timely respond by showing that (1) the failure to respond was not intentional or the result of conscious indifference, but the result of accident or mistake, and (2) allowing the late response will occasion no undue delay or otherwise injure the party seeking summary judgment." *See also* **Wheeler v. Green**, 157 S.W.3d 439, 442-43 (Tex.2005).

Motion for Continuance

Tenneco Inc. v. Enterprise Prods., 925 S.W.2d 640, 647 (Tex.1996). "When a party contends that it has not had an adequate opportunity for discovery before a summary judgment hearing, it must file either an affidavit explaining the need for further discovery or a verified motion for continuance. [¶] The determination to allow [Ps] more time for discovery was within the trial court's discretion." *See also* **Stierwalt v. FFE Transp. Servs.**, 499 S.W.3d 181, 192 (Tex.App.—El Paso 2016, no pet.) (affidavit should specify evidence sought and explain why it was not obtained earlier to avoid need for continuance).

Notice

Cruz v. Sanchez, 528 S.W.3d 104, 114 (Tex.App.—El Paso 2017, pet. denied). "While [P] did not properly attempt to serve [Ds] with a copy of the motion for summary judgment in compliance with [TRCP] 21a, the trial court did attempt to send out two separate notices of the hearing to [Ds'] home address before rendering summary judgment. *At 115:* 'The right to summary judgment exists only in compliance with [TRCP] 166a.' Proper notice to the nonmovant is a prerequisite to summary judgment, and it is incumbent on the *movant* to comply with notice requirements. [P] failed to properly serve the motion for summary judgment, and because it was his burden to seek summary judgment in strict compliance with [Rule 166a], the trial court's subsequent attempts to inform [Ds] about the pending summary judgment hearing could not cure the original deficiency in [P's] service of the motion."

Rorie v. Goodwin, 171 S.W.3d 579, 583 (Tex.App.—Tyler 2005, no pet.). "A trial court must give notice of the submission date for a motion for summary judgment because this date determines the date the nonmovant's response is due. The date of submission has the same meaning as the day of hearing under [TRCP] 166a(c). *At 584:* Failure to give proper notice violates the most rudimentary demands of due process of law."

TRCP 166b. REPEALED BY ORDER OF AUG. 5, 1998, AND NOV. 9, 1998, EFF. JAN. 1, 1999

TRCP 166c. REPEALED BY ORDER OF AUG. 5, 1998, AND NOV. 9, 1998, EFF. JAN. 1, 1999

TRCP 167. OFFER OF SETTLEMENT; AWARD OF LITIGATION COSTS

167.1. Generally. Certain litigation costs may be awarded against a party who rejects an offer made substantially in accordance with this rule to settle a claim for monetary damages—including a counterclaim, crossclaim, or third-party claim—except in:

(a) a class action;

(b) a shareholder's derivative action;

(c) an action by or against the State, a unit of state government, or a political subdivision of the State;

(d) an action brought under the Family Code;

(e) an action to collect workers' compensation benefits under title 5, subtitle A of the Labor Code; or

(f) an action filed in a justice of the peace court or small claims court.

167.2. Settlement Offer.

(a) ***Defendant's declaration a prerequisite; deadline.*** A settlement offer under this rule may not be made until a defendant—a party against whom a claim for monetary damages is made—files a declaration invoking this rule. When a defendant files such a declaration, an offer or offers may be made under this rule to settle only those claims by and against that defendant. The declaration must be filed no later than 45 days before the case is set for conventional trial on the merits.

(b) ***Requirements of an offer.*** A settlement offer must:

(1) be in writing;

(2) state that it is made under Rule 167 and Chapter 42 of the Texas Civil Practice and Remedies Code;

(3) identify the party or parties making the offer and the party or parties to whom the offer is made;

(4) state the terms by which all monetary claims—including any attorney fees, interest, and costs that would be recoverable up to the time of the offer—between the offeror or offerors on the one hand and the offeree or offerees on the other may be settled;

(5) state a deadline—no sooner than 14 days after the offer is served—by which the offer must be accepted;

(6) be served on all parties to whom the offer is made.

(c) ***Conditions of offer.*** An offer may be made subject to reasonable conditions, including the execution of appropriate releases, indemnities, and other documents. An offeree may object to a condition by written notice served on the offeror before the deadline stated in the offer. A condition to which no such objection is made is presumed to have been reasonable. Rejection of an offer made subject to a condition determined by the trial court to have been unreasonable cannot be the basis for an award of litigation costs under this rule.

(d) ***Non-monetary and excepted claims not included.*** An offer must not include non-monetary claims and other claims to which this rule does not apply.

(e) ***Time limitations.*** An offer may not be made:

(1) before a defendant's declaration is filed;

(2) within 60 days after the appearance in the case of the offeror or offeree, whichever is later;

(3) within 14 days before the date the case is set for a conventional trial on the merits, except that an offer may be made within that period if it is in response to, and within seven days of, a prior offer.

(f) ***Successive offers.*** A party may make an offer after having made or rejected a prior offer. A rejection of an offer is subject to imposition of litigation costs under this rule only if the offer is more favorable to the offeree than any prior offer.

167.3. Withdrawal, Acceptance, and Rejection of Offer.

(a) ***Withdrawal of offer.*** An offer can be withdrawn before it is accepted. Withdrawal is effective when written notice of the withdrawal is served on the offeree. Once an unaccepted offer has been withdrawn, it cannot be accepted or be the basis for awarding litigation costs under this rule.

(b) ***Acceptance of offer.*** An offer that has not been withdrawn can be accepted only by written notice served on the offeror by the deadline stated in the offer. When an offer is accepted, the offeror or offeree may file the offer and acceptance and may move the court to enforce the settlement.

(c) ***Rejection of offer.*** An offer that is not withdrawn or accepted is rejected. An offer may also be rejected by written notice served on the offeror by the deadline stated in the offer.

(d) ***Objection to offer made before an offeror's joinder or designation of responsible third party.*** An offer made before an offeror joins another party or designates a responsible third party may not be the basis for awarding litigation costs under this rule against an offeree

who files an objection to the offer within 15 days after service of the offeror's pleading or designation.

167.4. Awarding Litigation Costs.

(a) ***Generally.*** If a settlement offer made under this rule is rejected, and the judgment to be awarded on the monetary claims covered by the offer is significantly less favorable to the offeree than was the offer, the court must award the offeror litigation costs against the offeree from the time the offer was rejected to the time of judgment.

(b) ***"Significantly less favorable" defined.*** A judgment award on monetary claims is significantly less favorable than an offer to settle those claims if:

(1) the offeree is a claimant and the judgment would be less than 80 percent of the offer; or

(2) the offeree is a defendant and the judgment would be more than 120 percent of the offer.

(c) ***Litigation costs.*** Litigation costs are the expenditures actually made and the obligations actually incurred—directly in relation to the claims covered by a settlement offer under this rule—for the following:

(1) court costs;

(2) reasonable deposition costs, in cases filed on or after September 1, 2011;

(3) reasonable fees for not more than two testifying expert witnesses; and

(4) reasonable attorney fees.

(d) ***Limits on litigation costs.***

(1) In cases filed before September 1, 2011, the litigation costs that may be awarded under this rule must not exceed the following amount:

(A) the sum of the noneconomic damages, the exemplary or additional damages, and one-half of the economic damages to be awarded to the claimant in the judgment; minus

(B) the amount of any statutory or contractual liens in connection with the occurrences or incidents giving rise to the claim.

(2) In cases filed on or after September 1, 2011, the litigation costs that may be awarded to any party under this rule must not exceed the total amount that the claimant recovers or would recover before adding an award of litigation costs under this rule in favor of the claimant or subtracting as an offset an award of litigation costs under this rule in favor of the defendant.

(e) ***No double recovery permitted.*** A party who is entitled to recover attorney fees and costs under another law may not recover those same attorney fees and costs as litigation costs under this rule.

(f) ***Limitation on attorney fees and costs recovered by a party against whom litigation costs are awarded.*** A party against whom litigation costs are awarded may not recover attorney fees and costs under another law incurred after the date the party rejected the settlement offer made the basis of the award.

(g) ***Litigation costs to be awarded to defendant as a setoff.*** Litigation costs awarded to a defendant must be made a setoff to the claimant's judgment against the defendant.

167.5. Procedures.

(a) ***Modification of time limits.*** On motion, and for good cause shown, the court may—by written order made before commencement of trial on the merits—modify the time limits for filing a declaration under Rule 167.2(a) or for making an offer.

(b) ***Discovery permitted.*** On motion, and for good cause shown, a party against whom litigation costs are to be awarded may conduct discovery to ascertain the reasonableness of the costs requested. If the court determines the costs to be reasonable, it must order the party requesting discovery to pay all attorney fees and expenses incurred by other parties in responding to such discovery.

(c) ***Hearing required.*** The court must, upon request, conduct a hearing on a request for an award of litigation costs, at which the affected parties may present evidence.

167.6. Evidence Not Admissible. Evidence relating to an offer made under this rule is not admissible except for purposes of enforcing a settlement agreement or obtaining litigation costs. The provisions of this rule may not be made known to the jury by any means.

167.7. Other Settlement Offers Not Affected. This rule does not apply to any offer made in a mediation or arbitration proceeding. A settlement offer not made in compliance with this rule, or a settlement offer not made under this rule, or made in an action to which this rule does not apply, cannot be the basis for awarding litigation costs under this rule as to any party. This rule does not limit or affect a party's right to make a settlement offer that does not comply with this rule, or in an action to which this rule does not apply.

Oct. 9, 2003, eff. Jan. 1, 2004. Amended by order of Sept. 9, 2011, eff. Sept. 1, 2011.

Source: New rule. Former TRCP 167 repealed eff. Jan. 1, 1999, by order of Nov. 9, 1998 (977-78 S.W.2d [Tex.Cases] xxxiii). For subject matter of former TRCP 167, see TRCP 196.

Editor's Note: Although TRCP 167.1(f) references a "small-claims court," the Texas Legislature abolished small-claims courts by repealing Gov't Code ch. 28, effective August 31, 2013. See Acts 2013, 83rd Leg., R.S., ch. 2, §2, eff. Apr. 10, 2013; Acts 2011, 82nd Leg., 1st C.S., ch. 3, §§5.06, 5.09, eff. May 1, 2013. Now small-claims proceedings must be conducted by justice courts. Gov't Code §27.060(a); see TRCP 500.3(a).

See also **O'Connor's Texas Rules**, "Offer of Settlement," ch. 7-H, §1 et seq.

ANNOTATIONS

Mahaffey v. Washburne, 582 S.W.3d 527, 528-29 (Tex.App.—Fort Worth 2018, pet. denied). "In this issue of first impression, we must consider whether an order of nonsuit may trigger the shifting of litigation costs under the offer-of-settlement rule. The answer is both yes and no. [W]hile an order of nonsuit, as a 'significantly less favorable judgment,' theoretically would trigger the shifting of litigation costs under the offer-of-settlement rule, the amount that would be shifted, at least under these facts, is limited to zero. [¶] Here, there is no dispute that the declaration and offer of settlement complied with the requisites of the rule, that [D] offered [Ps] $15,100 to settle the claim, that [Ps] rejected his offer, and that their subsequent nonsuit resulted in a judgment significantly less favorable than the $15,100 [D] offered. Thus, the litigation cost-shifting mechanism of the rule was triggered. [¶] However, both [TRCP] 167 and [CPRC] ch. 42 provide limits on the amount of litigation costs that can be shifted due to an imprudent rejection of a settlement offer. Both provide that 'the litigation costs that may be awarded to any party under this rule' may not exceed 'the total amount that the claimant recovers or would recover before . . . subtracting as an offset an award of litigation costs' under this rule in favor of the defendant. [¶] Because [Ps] nonsuited their action against [D], they took nothing by way of judgment against him. Thus, . . . any litigation costs awarded could not exceed the total amount of zero (the amount that [Ps] 'recovered')."

Bobo v. Varughese, 507 S.W.3d 817, 825 (Tex.App.—Texarkana 2016, no pet.). "[W]e must determine whether prejudgment interest is included in the [TRCP] 167.4 comparison [of the settlement offer and the judgment to be awarded]. *At 828:* Since Rule 167.4 implements [CPRC] §42.004, the Supreme Court's use of 'judgment' for comparison with the offer, then, has the same meaning as the Legislature intended when it used the word 'award' in §42.004. [T]he Legislature appears to equate 'award' in §42.004 to the damages awarded by the fact-finder. Therefore, it appears that 'judgment,' as used in Rule 167.4(b)(1) and (2), means the damages awarded by the fact-finder, rather than the final judgment rendered by the trial court. This being the case, we find that prejudgment interest should not be included in the 'judgment' when comparing it with the settlement offer under Rule 167.4(b)(1) and (2)."

Note Inv. Grp. v. Associates First Capital Corp., 476 S.W.3d 463, 478 (Tex.App.—Beaumont 2015, no pet.). "[N]othing in the plain language of [TRCP 167] indicates that a claim must be formally pled when the settlement offer is made in order to be included in a settlement offer under the rule, and we decline to read any such requirement into those words when . . . there is no indication . . . that the Texas Supreme Court intended that we do so."

United Parcel Serv. v. Rankin, 468 S.W.3d 609, 628 (Tex.App.—San Antonio 2015, pet. denied). "[P] argues that 'to the time of judgment' [under TRCP 167.4(a)] includes the time until an appellate judgment is signed and thus the trial court abused its discretion by failing to award him conditional appellate attorneys' fees. [D] responds that the trial court correctly interpreted 'to the time of judgment' to mean to the time the trial court's judgment was signed. We agree with [D]. Based on the language of Rule 167 as a whole, we conclude the trial court did not abuse its discretion by failing to award conditional appellate attorneys' fees."

TRCP 167a. REPEALED BY ORDER OF AUG. 5, 1998, AND NOV. 9, 1998, EFF. JAN. 1, 1999

TRCP 168. PERMISSION TO APPEAL

On a party's motion or on its own initiative, a trial court may permit an appeal from an interlocutory order that is not otherwise appealable, as provided by statute. Permission must be stated in the order to be appealed. An order previously issued may be amended to include such permission. The permission must identify the controlling question of law as to which there is a substantial ground for difference of opinion, and must state why an immediate appeal may materially advance the ultimate termination of the litigation.

Sept. 1, 2011, eff. Sept. 1, 2011.

Comment—2011

Rule 168 is a new rule, added to implement amendments to section 51.014(d)–(f) of the Texas Civil Practice and Remedies Code. Rule 168 applies only to cases filed on or after September 1, 2011. Rule 168 clarifies that the trial court's permission to appeal should be included in the order to be appealed rather than in a separate order. Rule of Appellate Procedure 28.3 sets out the corollary requirements for permissive appeals in the courts of appeals.

Source: New rule. Former TRCP 168 repealed eff. Jan. 1, 1999, by order of Nov. 9, 1998 (977-78 S.W.2d [Tex.Cases] xxxiii). For subject matter of former TRCP 168, see TRCP 197.

ANNOTATIONS

Armour Pipe Line Co. v. Sandel Energy, Inc., No. 14-16-00010-CV, 2016 WL 514229 (Tex.App.—Houston [14th Dist.] 2016, n.p.h.) (memo op.; 2-9-16). TRCP 168 uses "the singular, 'a controlling question of law,' which arguably reflects an intent to restrict permissive appeals to interlocutory judgments that involve one controlling question of law. Even assuming that an appellate court enjoys some

measure of discretion in permitting the appeal of more than one question in appropriate circumstances, it is not clear that appropriate circumstances exist here. [The] statement of the issues . . . identifies . . . four questions (and numerous sub-issues) to be decided on appeal, which appear to encompass a number of legal points in multiple summary judgment orders. Rule 168's purpose—to provide a means for expedited appellate disposition of focused and potentially dispositive legal questions—is not served if this procedure is used to obtain piecemeal appellate review of ordinary interlocutory summary judgment orders."

TRCP 169. EXPEDITED ACTIONS

Text of Rule 169 effective for cases filed before January 1, 2021.

(a) ***Application.***

(1) The expedited actions process in this rule applies to suit in which all claimants, other than counter-claimants, affirmatively plead that they seek only monetary relief aggregating $100,000 or less, including damages of any kind, penalties, costs, expenses, pre-judgment interest, and attorney fees.

(2) The expedited actions process does not apply to a suit in which a party has filed a claim governed by the Family Code, the Property Code, the Tax Code, or Chapter 74 of the Civil Practice & Remedies Code.

(b) ***Recovery.*** In no event may a party who prosecutes a suit under this rule recover a judgment in excess of $100,000, excluding post judgment interest.

(c) ***Removal from Process.***

(1) A court must remove a suit from the expedited actions process:

(A) on motion and a showing of good cause by any party; or

(B) if any claimant, other than a counter-claimant, files a pleading or an amended or supplemental pleading that seeks any relief other than the monetary relief allowed by (a)(1).

(2) A pleading, amended pleading, or supplemental pleading that removes a suit from the expedited actions process may not be filed without leave of court unless it is filed before the earlier of 30 days after the discovery period is closed or 30 days before the date set for trial. Leave to amend may be granted only if good cause for filing the pleading outweighs any prejudice to an opposing party.

(3) If a suit is removed from the expedited actions process, the court must reopen discovery under Rule 190.2(c).

(d) ***Expedited Actions Process.***

(1) *Discovery.* Discovery is governed by Rule 190.2.

(2) *Trial Setting; Continuances.* On any party's request, the court must set the case for a trial date that is within 90 days after the discovery period in Rule 190.2(b)(1) ends. The court may continue the case twice, not to exceed a total of 60 days.

(3) *Time Limits for Trial.* Each side is allowed no more than eight hours to complete jury selection, opening statements, presentation of evidence, examination and cross-examination of witnesses, and closing arguments. On motion and a showing of good cause by any party, the court may extend the time limit to no more than twelve hours per side.

(A) The term "side" has the same definition set out in Rule 233.

(B) Time spent on objections, bench conferences, bills of exception, and challenges for cause to a juror under Rule 228 are not included in the time limit.

(4) *Alternative Dispute Resolution.*

(A) Unless the parties have agreed not to engage in alternative dispute resolution, the court may refer the case to an alternative dispute resolution procedure once, and the procedure must:

(i) not exceed a half-day in duration, excluding scheduling time;

(ii) not exceed a total cost of twice the amount of applicable civil filing fees; and

(iii) be completed no later than 60 days before the initial trial setting.

(B) The court must consider objections to the referral unless prohibited by statute.

(C) The parties may agree to engage in alternative dispute resolution other than that provided for in (A).

(5) *Expert Testimony.* Unless requested by the party sponsoring the expert, a party may only challenge the admissibility of expert testimony as an objection to summary judgment evidence under Rule 166a or during the trial on the merits. This paragraph does not apply to a motion to strike for late designation.

Text of Rule 169 effective for cases filed on or after January 1, 2021.

(a) ***Application.*** The expedited actions process in this rule applies to a suit in which all claimants, other than counter-claimants, affirmatively plead that they seek only monetary relief aggregating $250,000 or less, excluding interest, statutory or punitive damages and penalties, and attorney fees and costs.

(b) ***Recovery.*** In no event may a party who prosecutes

a suit under this rule recover a judgment in excess of $250,000, excluding interest, statutory or punitive damages and penalties, and attorney fees and costs.

(c) ***Removal from Process.***

(1) A court must remove a suit from the expedited actions process:

(A) on motion and a showing of good cause by any party; or

(B) if any claimant, other than a counter-claimant, files a pleading or an amended or supplemental pleading that seeks any relief other than the monetary relief allowed by (a).

(2) A pleading, amended pleading, or supplemental pleading that removes a suit from the expedited actions process may not be filed without leave of court unless it is filed before the earlier of 30 days after the discovery period is closed or 30 days before the date set for trial. Leave to amend may be granted only if good cause for filing the pleading outweighs any prejudice to an opposing party.

(3) If a suit is removed from the expedited actions process, the court must reopen discovery under Rule 190.2(c).

(d) ***Expedited Actions Process.***

(1) *Discovery.* Discovery is governed by Rule 190.2.

(2) *Trial Setting; Continuances.* On any party's request, the court must set the case for a trial date that is within 90 days after the discovery period in Rule 190.2(b)(1) ends. The court may continue the case twice, not to exceed a total of 60 days.

(3) *Time Limits for Trial.* Each side is allowed no more than eight hours to complete jury selection, opening statements, presentation of evidence, examination and cross-examination of witnesses, and closing arguments. On motion and a showing of good cause by any party, the court may extend the time limit to no more than twelve hours per side.

(A) The term "side" has the same definition set out in Rule 233.

(B) Time spent on objections, bench conferences, bills of exception, and challenges for cause to a juror under Rule 228 are not included in the time limit.

(4) *Alternative Dispute Resolution.*

(A) Unless the parties have agreed not to engage in alternative dispute resolution, the court may refer the case to an alternative dispute resolution procedure once, and the procedure must:

(i) not exceed a half-day in duration, excluding scheduling time;

(ii) not exceed a total cost of twice the amount of applicable civil filing fees; and

(iii) be completed no later than 60 days before the initial trial setting.

(B) The court must consider objections to the referral unless prohibited by statute.

(C) The parties may agree to engage in alternative dispute resolution other than that provided for in (A).

(5) *Expert Testimony.* Unless requested by the party sponsoring the expert, a party may only challenge the admissibility of expert testimony as an objection to summary judgment evidence under Rule 166a or during the trial on the merits. This paragraph does not apply to a motion to strike for late designation.

Adopted by order of Feb. 12, 2013, eff. March 1, 2013. Amended by order of Dec. 23, 2020, eff. Jan. 1, 2021.

Comment—2021

Rule 169 is amended to implement section 22.004(h-1) of the Texas Government Code—which calls for rules to promote the prompt, efficient, and cost-effective resolution of civil actions filed in county courts at law in which the amount in controversy does not exceed $250,000—and changes to section 22.004(h) of the Texas Government Code. To ensure uniformity, and pursuant to section 22.004(b) of the Texas Government Code, Rule 169's application is not limited to suits filed in county courts at law; any suit that falls within the definition of subsection (a) is subject to the provisions of the rule. However, certain suits are exempt from Rule 169's application by statute. *See e.g.*, Tex. Est. Code §§53.107, 1053.105. The discovery limitations for expedited actions are set out in Rule 190.2, which is also amended to implement section 22.004(h-1) of the Texas Government Code.

Comment—2013

1. Rule 169 is a new rule implementing section 22.004(h) of the Texas Government Code, which was added in 2011 and calls for rules to promote the prompt, efficient, and cost-effective resolution of civil actions when the amount in controversy does not exceed $100,000.

2. The expedited actions process created by Rule 169 is mandatory; any suit that falls within the definition of 169(a)(1) is subject to the provisions of the rule.

3. In determining whether there is good cause to remove the case from the process or extend the time limit for trial, the court should consider factors such as whether the damages sought by multiple claimants against the same defendant exceed in the aggregate the relief allowed under 169(a)(1), whether a defendant has filed a compulsory counterclaim in good faith that seeks relief other than that allowed under 169(a)(1), the number of parties and witnesses, the complexity of the legal and factual issues, and whether an interpreter is necessary.

4. Rule 169(b) specifies that a party who prosecutes a suit under this rule cannot recover a judgment in excess of $100,000. Thus, the rule in Greenhalgh v. Service Lloyds Ins. Co., 787 S.W.2d 938 (Tex. 1990), does not apply if a jury awards damages in excess of $100,000 to the party. The limitation in 169(b) does not apply to a counter-claimant that seeks relief other than that allowed under 169(a)(1).

5. The discovery limitations for expedited actions are set out in Rule 190.2, which is also amended to implement section 22.004(h) of the Texas Government Code.

Source: New rule. Former TRCP 169 repealed eff. Jan. 1, 1999, by order of Nov. 9, 1998 (977-78 S.W.2d [Tex.Cases] xxxiii). For subject matter of former TRCP 169, see TRCP 198.

See also **O'Connor's Texas Rules**, "Expedited Actions," ch. 2-C, §1 et seq.

ANNOTATIONS

Cross v. Wagner, 497 S.W.3d 611, 614 (Tex.App.—El Paso 2016, no pet.). "The gravamen of [D's] complaint is that 'any award by the jury' in excess of $100,000 is capped by Rule 169 [(pre-1-1-21 version)], and that consequently, the trial court erred in 'not capping the jury's award' at $100,000 prior to reducing the award by the proportionate responsibility of the parties. Rule 169, however, does not mandate that 'any award of the jury' be capped at $100,000. Rather, . . . Rule 169 mandates only that '[i]n no event may a party who prosecutes a suit under this rule *recover a judgment* in excess of $100,000[.]' . . . Rule 169 did not require the trial court to cap the jury's award at $100,000, but rather only required the trial court to cap its judgment to prevent an ultimate recovery of over $100,000. *At 615:* Rule 169 does not prevent a claimant from asking the jury to award damages totaling more than $100,000, nor does it bar a trial court from considering the jury's award of damages totaling more than $100,000 in reducing the claimant's recovery based on his percentage of responsibility."

TRCP 170. REPEALED BY ORDER OF DEC. 5, 1983, EFF. APRIL 1, 1984

TRCP 171. MASTER IN CHANCERY

The court may, in exceptional cases, for good cause appoint a master in chancery, who shall be a citizen of this State, and not an attorney for either party to the action, nor related to either party, who shall perform all of the duties required of him by the court, and shall be under orders of the court, and have such power as the master of chancery has in a court of equity.

The order of reference to the master may specify or limit his powers, and may direct him to report only upon particular issues, or to do or perform particular acts, or to receive and report evidence only and may fix the time and place for beginning and closing the hearings, and for the filing of the master's report. Subject to the limitations and specifications stated in the order, the master has and shall exercise the power to regulate all proceedings in every hearing before him and to do all acts and take all measures necessary or proper for the efficient performance of his duties under the order. He may require the production before him of evidence upon all matters embraced in the reference, including the production of books, papers, vouchers, documents and other writings applicable thereto. He may rule upon the admissibility of evidence, unless otherwise directed by the order of reference and has the authority to put witnesses on oath, and may, himself, examine them, and may call the parties to the action and examine them upon oath. When a party so requests, the master shall make a record of the evidence offered and excluded in the same manner as provided for a court sitting in the trial of a case.

The clerk of the court shall forthwith furnish and master with a copy of the order of reference.

The parties may procure the attendance of witnesses before the master by the issuance and service of process as provided by law and these rules.

The court may confirm, modify, correct reject, reverse or recommit the report, after it is filed, as the court may deem proper and necessary in the particular circumstances of the case. The court shall award reasonable compensation to such master to be taxed as costs of suit.

Oct. 29, 1940, eff. Sept. 1, 1941. Amended by order of Sept. 20, 1941, eff. Dec. 31, 1941.

Source: TRCS art. 2320 (repealed), FRCP 53.

See also **O'Connor's Texas Rules** "Master in Chancery," ch. 1-K, §1 et seq.

ANNOTATIONS

Simpson v. Canales, 806 S.W.2d 802, 811 (Tex.1991). "Rule 171 permits appointment of a master only 'in exceptional cases, for good cause.' [T]his requirement cannot be met merely by showing that a case is complicated or time-consuming, or that the court is busy." *See also* **Hourani v. Katzen**, 305 S.W.3d 239, 247 (Tex.App.—Houston [1st Dist.] 2009, pet. denied).

In re Harris, 315 S.W.3d 685, 705 (Tex.App.—Houston [1st Dist.] 2010, orig. proceeding). "[C]ourts have found sufficient justification for the appointment of a master to supervise 'discovery questions which require extensive examination of highly technical and complex documents by a person having both a technical and a legal background.' [¶] Here, the case is not of a 'highly technical nature.' The fact that production of some of the discovery sought by [P] might require expert forensic examination of electronic media is not sufficient to show that this is an 'exceptional case' requiring expertise in computer forensics. Electronic discovery is a common component of modern litigation, and its mere presence alone does not constitute a showing of good cause for appointing a special master." *See also* **Chapa v. Chapa**, No. 04-12-00519-CV, 2012 WL 6728242 (Tex.App.—San Antonio 2012, no pet.) (memo op.; 12-28-12) (special master's powers generally include authority to contact parties, conduct hearings, require production of evidence, and make recommendations to court).

AIU Ins. v. Mehaffy, 942 S.W.2d 796, 803 (Tex.App.—Beaumont 1997, orig. proceeding). "The cases construing Rule 171 provide that if a party timely and formally objects to a master's ruling, that party is entitled to a de novo hear-

ing before a judge or jury. We conclude this right is automatic and is not subject to a harmless error analysis."

TRCP 172. AUDIT

When an investigation of accounts or examination of vouchers appears necessary for the purpose of justice between the parties to any suit, the court shall appoint an auditor or auditors to state the accounts between the parties and to make report thereof to the court as soon as possible. The auditor shall verify his report by his affidavit stating that he has carefully examined the state of the account between the parties, and that his report contains a true statement thereof, so far as the same has come within his knowledge. Exceptions to such report or of any item thereof must be filed within 30 days of the filing of such report. The court shall award reasonable compensation to such auditor to be taxed as costs of suit.

Oct. 29, 1940, eff. Sept. 1, 1941. Amended by order of July 15, 1987, eff. Jan. 1, 1988.

See also TRE 706.

TRCP 173. GUARDIAN AD LITEM

173.1. Appointment Governed by Statute or Other Rules.

This rule does not apply to an appointment of a guardian ad litem governed by statute or other rules.

173.2. Appointment of Guardian ad Litem.

(a) ***When Appointment Required or Prohibited.*** The court must appoint a guardian ad litem for a party represented by a next friend or guardian only if:

(1) the next friend or guardian appears to the court to have an interest adverse to the party, or

(2) the parties agree.

(b) ***Appointment of the Same Person for Different Parties.*** The court must appoint the same guardian ad litem for similarly situated parties unless the court finds that the appointment of different guardians ad litem is necessary.

173.3. Procedure.

(a) ***Motion Permitted But Not Required.*** The court may appoint a guardian ad litem on the motion of any party or on its own initiative.

(b) ***Written Order Required.*** An appointment must be made by written order.

(c) ***Objection.*** Any party may object to the appointment of a guardian ad litem.

173.4. Role of Guardian ad Litem.

(a) ***Court Officer and Advisor.*** A guardian ad litem acts as an officer and advisor to the court.

(b) ***Determination of Adverse Interest.*** A guardian ad litem must determine and advise the court whether a party's next friend or guardian has an interest adverse to the party.

(c) ***When Settlement Proposed.*** When an offer has been made to settle the claim of a party represented by a next friend or guardian, a guardian ad litem has the limited duty to determine and advise the court whether the settlement is in the party's best interest.

(d) ***Participation in Litigation Limited.*** A guardian ad litem:

(1) may participate in mediation or a similar proceeding to attempt to reach a settlement;

(2) must participate in any proceeding before the court whose purpose is to determine whether a party's next friend or guardian has an interest adverse to the party, or whether a settlement of the party's claim is in the party's best interest;

(3) must not participate in discovery, trial, or any other part of the litigation unless:

(A) further participation is necessary to protect the party's interest that is adverse to the next friend's or guardian's, and

(B) the participation is directed by the court in a written order stating sufficient reasons.

173.5. Communications Privileged.

Communications between the guardian ad litem and the party, the next friend or guardian, or their attorney are privileged as if the guardian ad litem were the attorney for the party.

173.6. Compensation.

(a) ***Amount.*** If a guardian ad litem requests compensation, he or she may be reimbursed for reasonable and necessary expenses incurred and may be paid a reasonable hourly fee for necessary services performed.

(b) ***Procedure.*** At the conclusion of the appointment, a guardian ad litem may file an application for compensation. The application must be verified and must detail the basis for the compensation requested. Unless all parties agree to the application, the court must conduct an evidentiary hearing to determine the total amount of fees and expenses that are reasonable and necessary. In making this determination, the court must not consider compensation as a percentage of any judgment or settlement.

(c) ***Taxation as Costs.*** The court may tax a guardian ad litem's compensation as costs of court.

(d) ***Other Benefit Prohibited.*** A guardian ad litem

may not receive, directly or indirectly, anything of value in consideration of the appointment other than as provided by this rule.

173.7. Review.

(a) ***Right of Appeal.*** Any party may seek mandamus review of an order appointing a guardian ad litem or directing a guardian ad litem's participation in the litigation. Any party and a guardian ad litem may appeal an order awarding the guardian ad litem compensation.

(b) ***Severance.*** On motion of the guardian ad litem or any party, the court must sever any order awarding a guardian ad litem compensation to create a final, appealable order.

(c) ***No Effect on Finality of Settlement or Judgment.*** Appellate proceedings to review an order pertaining to a guardian ad litem do not affect the finality of a settlement or judgment.

June 16, 1943, eff. Dec. 31, 1943. Amended by order of Jan. 27, 2005, eff. Feb. 1, 2005.

Comment—2005

1. The rule is completely revised.

2. This rule does not apply when the procedures and purposes for appointment of guardians ad litem (as well as attorneys ad litem) are prescribed by statutes, such as the Family Code and the Probate Code, or by other rules, such as the Parental Notification Rules.

3. The rule contemplates that a guardian ad litem will be appointed when a party's next friend or guardian appears to have an interest adverse to the party because of the division of settlement proceeds. In those situations, the responsibility of the guardian ad litem as prescribed by the rule is very limited, and no reason exists for the guardian ad litem to participate in the conduct of the litigation in any other way or to review the discovery or the litigation file except to the limited extent that it may bear on the division of settlement proceeds. See Jocson v. Crabb, 133 S.W.3d 268 (Tex. 2004) (per curiam). A guardian ad litem may, of course, choose to review the file or attend proceedings when it is unnecessary, but the guardian ad litem may not be compensated for unnecessary expenses or services.

4. Only in extraordinary circumstances does the rule contemplate that a guardian ad litem will have a broader role. Even then, the role is limited to determining whether a party's next friend or guardian has an interest adverse to the party that should be considered by the court under Rule 44. In no event may a guardian ad litem supervise or supplant the next friend or undertake to represent the party while serving as guardian ad litem.

5. As an officer and advisor to the court, a guardian ad litem should have qualified judicial immunity.

6. Though an officer and adviser to the court, a guardian ad litem must not have *ex parte* communications with the court. See Tex. Code Jud. Conduct, Canon 3.

7. Because the role of guardian ad litem is limited in all but extraordinary situations, and any risk that might result from services performed is also limited, compensation, if any is sought, should ordinarily be limited.

8. A violation of this rule is subject to appropriate sanction.

Source: TRCS art. 2159 (repealed).

See also **O'Connor's Texas Rules**, "Guardian Ad Litem Under TRCP 173," ch. 1-I, §1 et seq.; **O'Connor's Texas Forms**, FORMS 1I; **O'Connor's Texas Family Law Handbook**, "Court Appointments in SAPCRs," ch. 4-C, §1 et seq.

ANNOTATIONS

Ford Motor Co. v. Stewart, Cox & Hatcher, P.C., 390 S.W.3d 294, 297 (Tex.2013). "[D] argues that the trial court abused its discretion under [TRCP] 173 by appointing a guardian ad litem when there was no apparent conflict of interest between [P-minor] and [parent-next friend]. [¶] The guardian ad litem's initial role is to 'determine and advise the court whether a party's next friend . . . has an interest adverse to the party.' The trial court should remove the guardian ad litem when the evidence presented fails to confirm that a conflict of interest exists. *At 298:* In this case, [guardian ad litem] was not specifically assigned any duties by the pretrial judge. The context of his appointment, however, indicates that [guardian ad litem] was appointed for the limited purpose of determining and advising the pretrial judge as to whether there was a conflict of interest between [P-minor] and [parent-next friend], and if so, whether the . . . settlement [with D] was in [P-minor's] best interest. [T]he pretrial judge should have removed [guardian ad litem] because there was no evidence that [parent-next friend] had an interest adverse to [P-minor]. . . . We hold that a parent's obligation to provide her child with medical care, standing alone, does not create a conflict of interest within the confines of Rule 173." *See also* **Brownsville-Valley Reg'l Med. Ctr., Inc. v. Gamez**, 894 S.W.2d 753, 755 (Tex.1995) (when conflict of interest no longer exists, trial court should remove guardian ad litem); **Owens v. Perez**, 158 S.W.3d 96, 111 (Tex.App.—Corpus Christi 2005, no pet.) (potential conflict sufficient for appointment; actual conflict not required).

Ford Motor Co. v. Chacon, 370 S.W.3d 359, 362 (Tex.2012). "A guardian ad litem has the burden to ensure that his services do not exceed the scope of the role assigned by the trial court. In the context of that appointment, a guardian ad litem 'may be reimbursed for reasonable and necessary expenses incurred and may be paid a reasonable hourly fee for necessary services performed.' The amount of the award is within the trial court's discretion. [¶] [I]n determining the nature and duties of an appointment, we look to the context of the appointment and the duties assigned to the ad litem. [¶] The context of [ad litem's] appointment as guardian ad litem clearly indicates that [ad litem] was appointed for the limited purpose of determining and advising the court whether the . . . settlement [with D1] was in [minor's] best interest. . . . After the . . . settlement [with D1] was finalized and judgment was entered, [ad litem] filed an application for compensation for guardian ad litem services he provided in connection with the [D1] settlement, which the court awarded in full. There was no subsequent motion or request for appointment of a guardian ad litem in connection with the [D2] settlement, nor did the trial court enter an order appointing one. In light of the requirements of Rule 173, we conclude that [ad litem's] work regarding the [D2] settlement was beyond the scope of his original appointment."

Ford Motor Co. v. Garcia, 363 S.W.3d 573, 580 (Tex.2012). "Rule 173.6 does not preclude awarding compensation for persons other than the person designated in the trial court's order as guardian ad litem if the evidence shows particular, unusual circumstances making services of other persons necessary for the ad litem's duties to be fulfilled. Such circumstances might exist, for example, if paralegals or other staff under the supervision of the appointed guardian ad litem could perform tasks necessary for the ad litem to properly fulfill his or her appointed role, but at a lesser hourly rate than the ad litem, or an unexpected emergency requires the guardian ad litem to miss a mandatory hearing and an associated attorney familiar with the matter appears instead. *At 580 n.5:* [A] Rule 173 guardian ad litem might need to incur unusual expenses in order to properly advise the court. For example, expenses for an actuary or accountant to evaluate the economics of a structured settlement may be necessary."

Land Rover U.K., Ltd. v. Hinojosa, 210 S.W.3d 604, 607 (Tex.2006). "A guardian ad litem is not an attorney for the child but an officer appointed by the court to assist in protecting the child's interests when a conflict of interest arises between the child and the child's guardian or next friend. As the personal representative of a minor, a guardian ad litem is required to participate in the case only to the extent necessary to protect the minor's interest and should not duplicate the work performed by the plaintiff's attorney. If a guardian ad litem performs work beyond the scope of this role, such work is non-compensable. [¶] An appointed guardian ad litem may request a reasonable fee for services performed. . . . To determine a reasonable fee for a guardian ad litem's services, a trial court applies the factors used to determine the reasonableness of attorney's fees." *See also* **Jocson v. Crabb**, 196 S.W.3d 302, 306 (Tex.App.—Houston [1st Dist.] 2006, no pet.) (guardian ad litem should not participate in litigation or review discovery unless necessary to determine division of settlement proceeds).

Jocson v. Crabb, 133 S.W.3d 268, 270 (Tex.2004). "[O]bjections to ad litem fees are timely if raised at the post-trial fee hearing. . . . [¶] While the parties would be wise to seek direction . . . when they disagree about an ad litem's role, it could be expensive and disruptive . . . to pursue every disagreement to a hearing throughout the pretrial process. The final fee hearing is an appropriate forum to assert any objections to the fee request and obtain a ruling."

In re KC Greenhouse Patio Apts., LP, 445 S.W.3d 168, 172 (Tex.App.—Houston [1st Dist.] 2012, orig. proceeding). See annotation under TRCP 44.

TRCP 174. CONSOLIDATION; SEPARATE TRIALS

(a) Consolidation. When actions involving a common question of law or fact are pending before the court, it may order a joint hearing or trial of any or all the matters in issue in the actions; it may order all the actions consolidated; and it may make such orders concerning proceedings therein as may tend to avoid unnecessary costs or delay.

(b) Separate Trials. The court in furtherance of convenience or to avoid prejudice may order a separate trial of any claim, cross-claim, counterclaim, or third-party claim, or of any separate issue or of any number of claims, cross-claims, counterclaims, third-party claims, or issues.

Oct. 29, 1940, eff. Sept. 1, 1941.

Source: FRCP 42. Supersedes TRCS art. 2160 (repealed).

See also TRCP 39–41, 51; **O'Connor's Texas Rules**, "Motions for Severance & Separate Trials," ch. 5-I, §1 et seq.; **O'Connor's Texas Rules**, "Joining Parties or Claims," ch. 5-J, §1 et seq.; **O'Connor's Texas Forms**, FORMS 5I:4, 5I:5, 5I:6, 5I:7, 5J:7, 5J:8, 5J:9.

ANNOTATIONS

Tarrant Reg'l Water Dist. v. Gragg, 151 S.W.3d 546, 556 (Tex.2004). TRCP 174(b) "allows a trial court to order a separate trial on any issue in the interest of convenience or to avoid prejudice. *At 557:* [S]eparate trials would have resulted in considerable and unnecessary evidentiary repetition. [I]t is likely that many, if not most, of the same witnesses would have been called to testify in both the liability and compensation trials had the trial court bifurcated the proceedings. '[T]here were several weeks of common questions of law and of fact involved in the matters that would have been considered in the first phase and the second phase of a bifurcated trial.' . . . Under these circumstances, we cannot say that the trial court abused its discretion in refusing to bifurcate the proceedings."

In re Ethyl Corp., 975 S.W.2d 606, 611-12 (Tex.1998). "The maximum number of claims that can be aggregated is not an absolute, and the particular circumstances determine the outer limits beyond which trial courts cannot go. [¶] While considerations of judicial economy are a factor, '[c]onsiderations of convenience and economy must yield to a paramount concern for a fair and impartial trial.'" *See also* **In re Shell Oil Co.**, 202 S.W.3d 286, 290-91 (Tex.App.—Beaumont 2006, orig. proceeding).

Liberty Nat'l Fire Ins. v. Akin, 927 S.W.2d 627, 630 (Tex.1996). "A severance may . . . be necessary in some bad faith [and contract] cases. A trial court will . . . confront instances in which evidence admissible only on the bad faith claim would prejudice the insurer to such an extent that a fair trial on the contract claim would become unlikely. One example would be when the insurer has made a settlement offer on the disputed contract claim."

Grocers Sup. v. Cabello, 390 S.W.3d 707, 726 (Tex.App.—Dallas 2012, no pet.). "An order for a separate trial leaves the lawsuit intact but enables the court to hear and determine one or more issues without trying all contro-

verted issues at the same hearing. An issue that is tried separately under rule 174 need not constitute a complete lawsuit in itself."

In re Gulf Coast Bus. Dev. Corp., 247 S.W.3d 787, 794-95 (Tex.App.—Dallas 2008, orig. proceeding). "Rule 174 give[s] the trial court broad discretion to consolidate cases with common issues of law or fact. [¶] The trial court may consolidate actions that relate to substantially the same transaction, occurrence, subject matter, or question. The actions should be so related that the evidence presented will be material, relevant, and admissible in each case. [¶] Even if the cases share common questions of law and fact, an abuse of discretion may be found if the consolidation results in prejudice to the complaining party. However, we may not presume prejudice; it must be demonstrated. Where the cases do share common questions of law and fact, and the record does not reveal actual prejudice, the consolidation does not provide a basis for reversal." *See also* **In re Woodard**, No. 12-16-00032-CV, 2016 WL 1731473 (Tex.App.—Tyler 2016, orig. proceeding) (memo op.; 4-29-16) (in deciding whether to consolidate, court must balance judicial economy and convenience gained by consolidation against possibility of delay, prejudice, or jury confusion).

TRCP 175. ISSUE OF LAW AND DILATORY PLEAS

When a case is called for trial in which there has been no pretrial hearing as provided by Rule 166, the issues of law arising on the pleadings, all pleas in abatement and other dilatory pleas remaining undisposed of shall be determined; and it shall be no cause for postponement of a trial of the issues of law that a party is not prepared to try the issues of fact.

Oct. 29, 1940, eff. Sept. 1, 1941.

ANNOTATIONS

Garcia v. Texas Empls. Ins., 622 S.W.2d 626, 630 n.3 (Tex.App.—Amarillo 1981, writ ref'd n.r.e.). "The language of Rule 175 imposes on the party relying upon a dilatory plea a duty to demand action by the court thereon at the time the rule requires action by the court, and his failure to do so is a waiver of the plea."

SECTION 9. EVIDENCE AND DISCOVERY

A. Evidence

TRCP 176. SUBPOENAS

176.1. Form. Every subpoena must be issued in the name of "The State of Texas" and must:

(a) state the style of the suit and its cause number;

(b) state the court in which the suit is pending;

(c) state the date on which the subpoena is issued;

(d) identify the person to whom the subpoena is directed;

(e) state the time, place, and nature of the action required by the person to whom the subpoena is directed, as provided in Rule 176.2;

(f) identify the party at whose instance the subpoena is issued, and the party's attorney of record, if any;

(g) state the text of Rule 176.8(a); and

(h) be signed by the person issuing the subpoena.

176.2. Required Actions. A subpoena must command the person to whom it is directed to do either or both of the following:

(a) attend and give testimony at a deposition, hearing, or trial;

(b) produce and permit inspection and copying of designated documents or tangible things in the possession, custody, or control of that person.

176.3. Limitations.

(a) ***Range.*** A person may not be required by subpoena to appear or produce documents or other things in a county that is more than 150 miles from where the person resides or is served. However, a person whose appearance or production at a deposition may be compelled by notice alone under Rules 199.3 or 200.2 may be required to appear and produce documents or other things at any location permitted under Rules 199.2(b)(2).

(b) ***Use for Discovery.*** A subpoena may not be used for discovery to an extent, in a manner, or at a time other than as provided by the rules governing discovery.

176.4. Who May Issue. A subpoena may be issued by:

(a) the clerk of the appropriate district, county, or justice court, who must provide the party requesting the subpoena with an original and a copy for each witness to be completed by the party;

(b) an attorney authorized to practice in the State of Texas, as an officer of the court; or

(c) an officer authorized to take depositions in this State, who must issue the subpoena immediately on a request accompanied by a notice to take a deposition under Rules 199[1] or 200,[2] or a notice under Rule 205.3, and who may also serve the notice with the subpoena.

[1] Vernon's Ann.Rules Civ.Proc., rule 199.1 et seq.

[2] Vernon's Ann.Rules Civ.Proc., rule 200.1 et seq.

176.5. Service.

(a) ***Manner of Service.*** A subpoena may be served at any place within the State of Texas by any sheriff or con-

stable of the State of Texas, or any person who is not a party and is 18 years of age or older. A subpoena must be served by delivering a copy to the witness and tendering to that person any fees required by law. If the witness is a party and is represented by an attorney of record in the proceeding, the subpoena may be served on the witness's attorney of record.

(b) ***Proof of Service.*** Proof of service must be made by filing either:

(1) the witness's signed written memorandum attached to the subpoena showing that the witness accepted the subpoena; or

(2) a statement by the person who made the service stating the date, time, and manner of service, and the name of the person served.

176.6. Response.

(a) ***Compliance Required.*** Except as provided in this subdivision, a person served with a subpoena must comply with the command stated therein unless discharged by the court or by the party summoning such witness. A person commanded to appear and give testimony must remain at the place of deposition, hearing, or trial from day to day until discharged by the court or by the party summoning the witness.

(b) ***Organizations.*** If a subpoena commanding testimony is directed to a corporation, partnership, association, governmental agency, or other organization, and the matters on which examination is requested are described with reasonable particularity, the organization must designate one or more persons to testify on its behalf as to matters known or reasonably available to the organization.

(c) ***Production of Documents or Tangible Things.*** A person commanded to produce documents or tangible things need not appear in person at the time and place of production unless the person is also commanded to attend and give testimony, either in the same subpoena or a separate one. A person must produce documents as they are kept in the usual course of business or must organize and label them to correspond with the categories in the demand. A person may withhold material or information claimed to be privileged but must comply with Rule 193.3. A nonparty's production of a document authenticates the document for use against the nonparty to the same extent as a party's production of a document is authenticated for use against the party under Rule 193.7.

(d) ***Objections.*** A person commanded to produce and permit inspection or copying of designated documents and things may serve on the party requesting issuance of the subpoena—before the time specified for compliance—written objections to producing any or all of the designated materials. A person need not comply with the part of a subpoena to which objection is made as provided in this paragraph unless ordered to do so by the court. The party requesting the subpoena may move for such an order at any time after an objection is made.

(e) ***Protective Orders.*** A person commanded to appear at a deposition, hearing, or trial, or to produce and permit inspection and copying of designated documents and things, and any other person affected by the subpoena, may move for a protective order under Rule 192.6(b)—before the time specified for compliance—either in the court in which the action is pending or in a district court in the county where the subpoena was served. The person must serve the motion on all parties in accordance with Rule 21a. A person need not comply with the part of a subpoena from which protection is sought under this paragraph unless ordered to do so by the court. The party requesting the subpoena may seek such an order at any time after the motion for protection is filed.

(f) ***Trial Subpoenas.*** A person commanded to attend and give testimony, or to produce documents or things, at a hearing or trial, may object or move for protective order before the court at the time and place specified for compliance, rather than under paragraphs (d) and (e).

176.7. Protection of Person from Undue Burden and Expense. A party causing a subpoena to issue must take reasonable steps to avoid imposing undue burden or expense on the person served. In ruling on objections or motions for protection, the court must provide a person served with a subpoena an adequate time for compliance, protection from disclosure of privileged material or information, and protection from undue burden or expense. The court may impose reasonable conditions on compliance with a subpoena, including compensating the witness for undue hardship.

176.8. Enforcement of Subpoena.

(a) ***Contempt.*** Failure by any person without adequate excuse to obey a subpoena served upon that person may be deemed a contempt of the court from which the subpoena is issued or a district court in the county in which the subpoena is served, and may be punished by fine or confinement, or both.

(b) ***Proof of Payment of Fees Required for Fine or Attachment.*** A fine may not be imposed, nor a person served with a subpoena attached, for failure to comply with a subpoena without proof by affidavit of the party requesting the subpoena or the party's attorney of record that all

fees due the witness by law were paid or tendered.

Aug. 5, 1998 and Nov. 9, 1998, eff. Jan. 1, 1999.

Comment—1999

1. This rule combines the former rules governing subpoenas for trial and discovery. When a subpoena is used for discovery, the protections from undue burden and expense apply, just as with any discovery.

2. Rule 176.3(b) prohibits the use of a subpoena to circumvent the discovery rules. Thus, for example, a deposition subpoena to a party is subject to the procedures of Rules 196, 199, and 200, and a deposition subpoena to a nonparty is subject to the procedures of Rule 205.

Source: New rule.

See also CPRC §22.001; **O'Connor's Texas Rules**, "Subpoenas," ch. 1-L, §1 et seq.; **O'Connor's Texas Rules**, "Depositions," ch. 6-F, §1 et seq.; **O'Connor's Texas Forms**, FORMS 1L, 6F.

ANNOTATIONS

In re FedEx Ground Package Sys., ___ S.W.3d ___, 2020 WL 2832683 (Tex.App.—Houston [14th Dist.] 2020, orig. proceeding) (No. 14-19-00861-CV; 5-28-20). "A trial court has the authority to require a witness, including a party or an officer of a party, to attend trial if the witness resides within 150 miles of the courthouse of the county in which the suit is pending or if the witness may be found within such distance at the time of trial. That [witness] is [an] employee [of D-corporation] does not change the requirement that [witness] must live within 150 miles of the . . . courthouse to be subject to the trial court's subpoena power."

St. Luke's Episcopal Hosp. v. Garcia, 928 S.W.2d 307, 310 (Tex.App.—Houston [14th Dist.] 1996, orig. proceeding). "In determining whether a deposition notice or subpoena duces tecum is unreasonable and oppressive, the following factors are relevant: '(1) the quantity of materials subpoenaed, (2) the ease or difficulty of collecting and transporting the materials, (3) the length of time before the deposition, (4) the availability of the information from other sources, and (5) the relevance of the materials.'"

TRCP 177. REPEALED BY ORDER OF AUG. 5, 1998, AND NOV. 9, 1998, EFF. JAN. 1, 1999

TRCP 177a. REPEALED BY ORDER OF AUG. 5, 1998, AND NOV. 9, 1998, EFF. JAN. 1, 1999

TRCP 178. REPEALED BY ORDER OF AUG. 5, 1998, AND NOV. 9, 1998, EFF. JAN. 1, 1999

TRCP 179. REPEALED BY ORDER OF AUG. 5, 1998, AND NOV. 9, 1998, EFF. JAN. 1, 1999

TRCP 180. REFUSAL TO TESTIFY

Any witness refusing to give evidence may be committed to jail, there to remain without bail until such witness shall consent to give evidence.

Oct. 29, 1940, eff. Sept. 1, 1941.

See also TRCP 176; **O'Connor's Texas Rules**, "Subpoenas," ch. 1-L, §1 et seq.; **O'Connor's Texas Rules**, "Depositions," ch. 6-F, §1 et seq.

TRCP 181. PARTY AS WITNESS

Either party to a suit may examine the opposing party as a witness, and shall have the same process to compel his attendance as in the case of any other witness.

Oct. 29, 1940, eff. Sept. 1, 1941.

See also TRCP 176, 199–201; **O'Connor's Texas Rules**, "Subpoenas," ch. 1-L, §1 et seq.; **O'Connor's Texas Rules**, "Depositions," ch. 6-F, §1 et seq.

TRCP 182. REPEALED BY ORDER OF JULY 15, 1987, EFF. JAN. 1, 1988

TRCP 182a. REPEALED BY ORDER OF JULY 15, 1987, EFF. JAN. 1, 1988

TRCP 183. INTERPRETERS

The court may appoint an interpreter of its own selection and may fix the interpreter's reasonable compensation. The compensation shall be paid out of funds provided by law or by one or more of the parties as the court may direct, and may be taxed ultimately as costs, in the discretion of the court.

Oct. 29, 1940, eff. Sept. 1, 1941. Amended by order of April 24, 1990, eff. Sept. 1, 1990.

Comment—1990

To adopt procedures for the appointment and compensation of interpreters. Source: Fed.R.Civ.P. 43(f). The provision regarding summoning interpreters and their conduct is deleted because it is covered by Rule 604, Texas Rules of Civil Evidence.

See also TRCP 200.4; TRE 604; **O'Connor's Texas Rules**, "Depositions," ch. 6-F, §1 et seq.

TRCP 184. REPEALED BY ORDER OF APRIL 24, 1990, EFF. SEPT. 1, 1990

TRCP 184a. REPEALED BY ORDER OF APRIL 24, 1990, EFF. SEPT. 1, 1990

TRCP 185. SUIT ON ACCOUNT

When any action or defense is founded upon an open account or other claim for goods, wares and merchandise, including any claim for a liquidated money demand based upon written contract or founded on business dealings between the parties, or is for personal service rendered, or labor done or labor or materials furnished, on which a systematic record has been kept, and is supported by the affidavit of the party, his agent or attorney taken before some officer authorized to administer oaths, to the effect that such claim is, within the knowledge of affiant, just and true, that it is due, and that all just and lawful offsets, payments and credits have been allowed, the same shall be taken as prima facie evidence thereof, unless the party resisting such claim shall file a written denial, under oath. A party resisting such

a sworn claim shall comply with the rules of pleading as are required in any other kind of suit, provided, however, that if he does not timely file a written denial, under oath, he shall not be permitted to deny the claim, or any item therein, as the case may be. No particularization or description of the nature of the component parts of the account or claim is necessary unless the trial court sustains special exceptions to the pleadings.

Oct. 29, 1940, eff. Sept. 1, 1941. Amended by orders of Oct. 12, 1949, eff. March 1, 1950; July 21, 1970, eff. Jan. 1, 1971; Dec. 5, 1983, eff. April 1, 1984.

Source: TRCS art. 3736 (repealed).

See also **O'Connor's Texas COA**, "Suit on Sworn Account," ch. 5-E, §1 et seq.; **O'Connor's Texas Forms**, FORMS 2B:3, 2B:4, 3E:3, 3E:4, 3E:10.

ANNOTATIONS

Tedder v. Gardner Aldrich, LLP, 421 S.W.3d 651, 653 (Tex.2013). "Rule 185 contemplates that the defendant has personal knowledge of the basis of the claim. . . . *At 654:* When it appears from the plaintiff's account itself that the defendant was a stranger to the account, the defendant need not file a sworn denial to contest liability. [D1] had no agreement with [law-firm-P], never promised to pay for [law-firm-P's] representation of [D2], and because of the attorney-client privilege, had no way of knowing what charges had been made or what had been paid. . . . Rule 185 does not require a party to swear to what he does not and cannot know. [T]hus [D1] was not required to deny [law-firm-P's] claim under oath in order to contest his liability for [law-firm-P's] fees."

Vance v. Holloway, 689 S.W.2d 403, 403-04 (Tex.1985). "The petition and affidavit filed by [P] clearly met the requirements of [TRCP] 185. [D] answered by way of an unverified general denial only. He failed to meet the requirements of [TRCP] 185 and 93(10) which state that a written denial of the plaintiff's action must be verified. [¶] [D], therefore, waived his right to dispute the amount and ownership of the account." *See also* **Rizk v. Financial Guardian Ins. Agency**, 584 S.W.2d 860, 862 (Tex.1979); **Day Cruises Maritime, L.L.C. v. Christus Spohn Health Sys.**, 267 S.W.3d 42, 53 (Tex.App.—Corpus Christi 2008, pet. denied).

Southern Mgmt. Servs. v. SM Energy Co., 398 S.W.3d 350, 356 (Tex.App.—Houston [14th Dist.] 2013, no pet.). "The [TRCPs] do not establish a . . . presumption that a sworn denial extends to new matters alleged in an amended pleading. This omission suggests . . . that a denial requiring verification must generally be filed again if the plaintiff amends the pleadings. [¶] [W]hen an amended account substantially differs from the original account, the party resisting the account must file another sworn denial."

Williams v. Unifund CCR Partners Assignee of Citibank, 264 S.W.3d 231, 234 (Tex.App.—Houston [1st Dist.] 2008, no pet.). "Rule 185 is a procedural tool that limits the evidence necessary to establish a prima facie right to recovery on certain types of accounts. Rule 185 applies only 'to transactions between persons, in which there is a sale upon one side and a purchase upon the other, whereby title to *personal* property passes from one to the other, and the relation of debtor and creditor is thereby created by general course of dealing. . . .' . . . A credit card issued by a financial institution is a special contract that does not create the sort of debtor-creditor relationship to bring a claim within the scope of Rule 185." *See also* **Meaders v. Biskamp**, 316 S.W.2d 75, 78 (Tex.1958).

Powers v. Adams, 2 S.W.3d 496, 498 (Tex.App.—Houston [14th Dist.] 1999, no pet.). "Under [TRCP 185], [P's] petition on sworn account must contain a systematic, itemized statement of the goods or services sold, reveal offsets made to the account, and be supported by an affidavit stating the claim is within the affiant's knowledge, and that it is 'just and true.'" *See also* **Mega Builders, Inc. v. American Door Prods.**, No. 01-12-00196-CV, 2013 WL 1136584 (Tex.App.—Houston [1st Dist.] 2013, no pet.) (memo op.; 3-19-13) (general statements without description of specific items are insufficient); **Dibco Underground, Inc. v. JCF Bridge & Concrete, Inc.**, No. 03-09-00255-CV, 2010 WL 1413071 (Tex.App.—Austin 2010, no pet.) (memo op.; 4-8-10) (account must include specifics about how figures were established).

Worley v. Butler, 809 S.W.2d 242, 245 (Tex.App.—Corpus Christi 1990, no writ). "To prevail in a cause of action on sworn account, a party must show: (1) that there was a sale and delivery of the merchandise or performance of the services; (2) that the amount of the account is just, that is, that the prices were charged in accordance with an agreement or in the absence of an agreement, they are the usual, customary and reasonable prices for that merchandise or services; and (3) that the amount is unpaid."

TRCP 186 to 186b. REPEALED BY ORDER OF DEC. 5, 1983, EFF. APRIL 1, 1984

TRCP 187. REPEALED BY ORDER OF AUG. 5, 1998, AND NOV. 9, 1998, EFF. JAN. 1, 1999

TRCP 188. REPEALED BY ORDER OF AUG. 5, 1998, AND NOV. 9, 1998, EFF. JAN. 1, 1999

TRCP 189. REPEALED BY ORDER OF DEC. 5, 1983, EFF. APRIL 1, 1984

B. Discovery

TRCP 190. DISCOVERY LIMITATIONS

190.1. Discovery Control Plan Required. Every case must be governed by a discovery control plan as provided in this Rule. A plaintiff must allege in the first numbered paragraph of the original petition whether

discovery is intended to be conducted under Level 1, 2, or 3 of this Rule.

190.2. Discovery Control Plan—Expedited Actions and Divorces Involving $50,000 or Less (Level 1).

Text of rule effective for cases filed before January 1, 2021.

(a) *Application.* This subdivision applies to:

(1) any suit that is governed by the expedited actions process in Rule 169; and

(2) unless the parties agree that Rule 190.3 should apply or the court orders a discovery control plan under Rule 190.4, any suit for divorce not involving children in which a party pleads that the value of the marital estate is more than zero but not more than $50,000.

(b) *Limitations.* Discovery is subject to the limitations provided elsewhere in these rules and to the following additional limitations:

(1) *Discovery Period.* All discovery must be conducted during the discovery period, which begins when the suit is filed and continues until 180 days after the date the first request for discovery of any kind is served on a party.

(2) *Total Time for Oral Depositions.* Each party may have no more than six hours in total to examine and cross-examine all witnesses in oral depositions. The parties may agree to expand this limit up to ten hours in total, but not more except by court order. The court may modify the deposition hours so that no party is given unfair advantage.

(3) *Interrogatories.* Any party may serve on any other party no more than 15 written interrogatories, excluding interrogatories asking a party only to identify or authenticate specific documents. Each discrete subpart of an interrogatory is considered a separate interrogatory.

(4) *Requests for Production.* Any party may serve on any other party no more than 15 written requests for production. Each discrete subpart of a request for production is considered a separate request for production.

(5) *Requests for Admissions.* Any party may serve on any other party no more than 15 written requests for admissions. Each discrete subpart of a request for admission is considered a separate request for admission.

(6) *Requests for Disclosure.* In addition to the content subject to disclosure under Rule 194.2, a party may request disclosure of all documents, electronic information, and tangible items that the disclosing party has in its possession, custody, or control and may use to support its claims or defenses. A request for disclosure made pursuant to this paragraph is not considered a request for production.

(c) *Reopening Discovery.* If a suit is removed from the expedited actions process in Rule 169 or, in a divorce, the filing of a pleading renders this subdivision no longer applicable, the discovery period reopens, and discovery must be completed within the limitations provided in Rules 190.3 or 190.4, whichever is applicable. Any person previously deposed may be redeposed. On motion of any party, the court should continue the trial date if necessary to permit completion of discovery.

190.2. Discovery Control Plan—Expedited Actions and Divorces Involving $250,000 or Less (Level 1).

Text of rule effective for cases filed on or after January 1, 2021.

(a) *Application.* This subdivision applies to:

(1) any suit that is governed by the expedited actions process in Rule 169; and

(2) unless the parties agree that rule 190.3 should apply or the court orders a discovery control plan under Rule 190.4, any suit for divorce not involving children in which a party pleads that the value of the marital estate is more than zero but not more than $250,000.

(b) *Limitations.* Discovery is subject to the limitations provided elsewhere in these rules and to the following additional limitations:

(1) *Discovery period.* All discovery must be conducted during the discovery period, which begins when the first initial disclosures are due and continues for 180 days.

(2) *Total time for oral depositions.* Each party may have no more than 20 hours in total to examine and cross-examine all witnesses in oral depositions. The court may modify the deposition hours so that no party is given unfair advantage.

(3) *Interrogatories.* Any party may serve on any other party no more than 15 written interrogatories, excluding interrogatories asking a party only to identify or authenticate specific documents. Each discrete subpart of an interrogatory is considered a separate interrogatory.

(4) *Requests for Production.* Any party may serve on any other party no more than 15 written requests for production. Each discrete subpart of a request for production is considered a separate request for production.

(5) *Requests for Admissions.* Any party may serve on any other party no more than 15 written requests for admissions. Each discrete subpart of a request for admission is considered a separate request for admission.

(c) *Reopening Discovery.* If a suit is removed from the expedited actions process in Rule 169 or, in a divorce, the filing of a pleading renders this subdivision no longer

applicable, the discovery period reopens, and discovery must be completed within the limitations provided in Rules 190.3 or 190.4, whichever is applicable. Any person previously deposed may be redeposed. On motion of any party, the court should continue the trial date if necessary to permit completion of discovery.

190.3. Discovery Control Plan—By Rule (Level 2).

(a) ***Application.*** Unless a suit is governed by a discovery control plan under Rules 190.2 or 190.4, discovery must be conducted in accordance with this subdivision.

Text of subsec. (b) effective for cases filed before January 1, 2021.

(b) ***Limitations.*** Discovery is subject to the limitations provided elsewhere in these rules and to the following additional limitations:

(1) *Discovery Period.* All discovery must be conducted during the discovery period, which begins when suit is filed and continues until:

(A) 30 days before the date set for trial, in cases under the Family Code; or

(B) in other cases, the earlier of

(i) 30 days before the date set for trial, or

(ii) nine months after the earlier of the date of the first oral deposition or the due date of the first response to written discovery.

(2) *Total Time for Oral Depositions.* Each side may have no more than 50 hours in oral depositions to examine and cross-examine parties on the opposing side, experts designated by those parties, and persons who are subject to those parties' control. "Side" refers to all the litigants with generally common interests in the litigation. If one side designates more than two experts, the opposing side may have an additional six hours of total deposition time for each additional expert designated. The court may modify the deposition hours and must do so when a side or party would be given unfair advantage.

(3) *Interrogatories.* Any party may serve on any other party no more than 25 written interrogatories, excluding interrogatories asking a party only to identify or authenticate specific documents. Each discrete subpart of an interrogatory is considered a separate interrogatory.

Text of subsec. (b) effective for cases filed on or after January 1, 2021.

(b) ***Limitations.*** Discovery is subject to the limitations provided elsewhere in these rules and to the following additional limitations:

(1) *Discovery period.* All discovery must be conducted during the discovery period, which begins when the first initial disclosures are due and continues until:

(A) 30 days before the date set for trial, in cases under the Family Code; or

(B) in other cases, the earlier of

(i) 30 days before the date set for trial, or

(ii) nine months after the first initial disclosures are due.

(2) *Total time for oral depositions.* Each side may have no more than 50 hours in oral depositions to examine and cross-examine parties on the opposing side, experts designated by those parties, and persons who are subject to those parties' control. "Side" refers to all the litigants with generally common interests in the litigation. If one side designates more than two experts, the opposing side may have an additional six hours of total deposition time for each additional expert designated. The court may modify the deposition hours and must do so when a side or party would be given unfair advantage.

(3) *Interrogatories.* Any party may serve on any other party no more than 25 written interrogatories, excluding interrogatories asking a party only to identify or authenticate specific documents. Each discrete subpart of an interrogatory is considered a separate interrogatory.

190.4. Discovery Control Plan—By Order (Level 3).

(a) ***Application.*** The court must, on a party's motion, and may, on its own initiative, order that discovery be conducted in accordance with a discovery control plan tailored to the circumstances of the specific suit. The parties may submit an agreed order to the court for its consideration. The court should act on a party's motion or agreed order under this subdivision as promptly as reasonably possible.

(b) ***Limitations.*** The discovery control plan ordered by the court may address any issue concerning discovery or the matters listed in Rule 166, and may change any limitation on the time for or amount of discovery set forth in these rules. The discovery limitations of Rule 190.2, if applicable, or otherwise of Rule 190.3 apply unless specifically changed in the discovery control plan ordered by the court. The plan must include:

(1) a date for trial or for a conference to determine a trial setting;

(2) a discovery period during which either all discovery must be conducted or all discovery requests must be sent, for the entire case or an appropriate phase of it;

(3) appropriate limits on the amount of discovery; and

(4) deadlines for joining additional parties, amending or supplementing pleadings, and designating expert witnesses.

190.5. Modification of Discovery Control Plan. The court may modify a discovery control plan at any time and must do so when the interest of justice requires. Unless a suit is governed by the expedited actions process in Rule 169, the court must allow additional discovery:

(a) related to new, amended or supplemental pleadings, or new information disclosed in a discovery response or in an amended or supplemental response, if:

(1) the pleadings or responses were made after the deadline for completion of discovery or so nearly before that deadline that an adverse party does not have an adequate opportunity to conduct discovery related to the new matters, and

(2) the adverse party would be unfairly prejudiced without such additional discovery;

(b) regarding matters that have changed materially after the discovery cutoff if trial is set or postponed so that the trial date is more than three months after the discovery period ends.

190.6. Certain Types of Discovery Excepted. This rule's limitations on discovery do not apply to or include discovery conducted under Rule 202[1] ("Depositions Before Suit or to Investigate Claims"), or Rule 621a ("Discovery and Enforcement of Judgment"). But Rule 202 cannot be used to circumvent the limitations of this rule.

Aug. 5, 1998 and Nov. 9, 1998, eff. Jan. 1, 1999. Amended by order of Feb. 12, 2013, eff. March 1, 2013; Dec. 23, 2020, eff. Jan. 1, 2021.

Comment—2021

Rule 190.2 is amended to implement section 22.004(h-1) of the Texas Government Code. Under amended Rule 190.2, Level 1 discovery limitations now apply to a broader subset of civil actions: expedited actions under Rule 169, which is also amended to implement section 22.004(h-1) of the Texas Government Code, and divorces not involving children in which the value of the marital estate is not more than $250,000. Level 1 limitations are revised to impose a twenty-hour limit on oral deposition. Disclosure requests under Rule 190.2(b)(6) and Rule 194 are now replaced by required disclosures under Rule 194, as amended. The discovery periods under Rules 190.2(b)(1) and 190.3(b)(1) are revised to reference the required disclosures.

Comment—1999

1. This rule establishes three tiers of discovery plans and requires that every case be in one at all times. A case is in Level 1 if it is pleaded by the plaintiff so as to invoke application Level 1, as provided by Rule 190.2(a). If a plaintiff does not or cannot plead the case in compliance with Rule 190.2(a) so as to invoke the application of Level 1, the case is automatically in Level 2. A case remains in Level 1 or Level 2, as determined by the pleadings, unless and until it is moved to Level 3. To be in Level 3, the court must order a specific plan for the case, either on a party's motion or on the court's own initiative. The plan may be one agreed to by the parties and submitted as an agreed order. A Level 3 plan may simply adopt Level 1 or Level 2 restrictions. Separate Level 3 plans for phases of the case may be appropriate. The initial pleading required by Rule 190.1 is merely to notify the court and other parties of the plaintiff's intention; it does not determine the applicable discovery level or bind the court or other parties. Thus, a plaintiff's failure to state in the initial pleading that the case should be in Level 1, as provided in Rule 190.1, does not alone make the case subject to Level 2 because the discovery level is determined by Rule 190.2. Likewise, a plaintiff's statement in the initial paragraph of the petition that the case is to be governed by Level 3 does not make Level 3 applicable, as a case can be in Level 3 only by court order. A plaintiff's failure to plead as required by Rule 190.1 is subject to special exception.2. Rule 190.2 does not apply to suits for injunctive relief or divorces involving children. The requirement of an affirmative pleading of limited relief (*e.g.*: "Plaintiff affirmatively pleads that he seeks only monetary relief aggregating $50,000 or less, excluding costs, pre-judgment interest and attorneys' fees") does not conflict with other pleading requirements, such as Rule 47 and Tex. Rev. Civ. Stat. Ann. art. 4590i, §5.01. In a suit to which Rule 190.2 applies, the relief awarded cannot exceed the limitations of Level 1 because the purpose of the rule, unlike Rule 47, is to bind the pleader to a maximum claim. To this extent, the rule in Greenhalgh v. Service Lloyds Ins. Co., 787 S.W.2d 938 (Tex. 1990), does not apply.

3. "Discrete subparts" of interrogatories are counted as single interrogatories, but not every separate factual inquiry is a discrete subpart. See Fed. R. Civ. P. 33(a). While not susceptible of precise definition, *see* Braden v. Downey, 811 S.W.2d 922, 927-928 (Tex. 1991), a "discrete subpart" is, in general, one that calls for information that is not logically or factually related to the primary interrogatory. The number of sets of interrogatories is no longer limited to two.

4. As other rules make clear, unless otherwise ordered or agreed, parties seeking discovery must serve requests sufficiently far in advance of the end of the discovery period that the deadline for responding will be within the discovery period. The court may order a deadline for sending discovery requests in lieu of or in addition to a deadline for completing discovery.

5. Use of forms of discovery other than depositions and interrogatories, such as requests for disclosure, admissions, or production of documents, are not restricted in Levels 1 and 2. But depositions on written questions cannot be used to circumvent the limits on interrogatories.

6. The concept of "side" in Rule 190.3(b)(2) borrows from Rule 233, which governs the allocation of peremptory strikes, and from Fed. R. Civ. P. 30(a)(2). In most cases there are only two sides—plaintiffs and defendants. In complex cases, however, there may be more than two sides, such as when defendants have sued third parties not named by plaintiffs, or when defendants have sued each other. As an example, if P1 and P2 sue D1, D2, and D3, and D1 sues D2 and D3, Ps would together be entitled to depose Ds and others permitted by the rule (*i.e.* Ds' experts and persons subject to Ds' control) for 50 hours, and Ds would together be entitled to depose Ps and others for 50 hours. D1 would also be entitled to depose D2 and D3 and others for 50 hours on matters in controversy among them, and D2 and D3 would together be entitled to depose D1 and others for 50 hours.

7. Any matter listed in Rule 166 may be addressed in an order issued under Rule 190.4. A pretrial order under Rule 166 may be used in individual cases regardless of the discovery level.

8. For purposes of defining discovery periods, "trial" does not include summary judgment.

Source: New rule.

[1]Vernon's Ann.Rules Civ.Proc., rule 202.1 et seq.

See also **O'Connor's Texas Rules**, "General Rules for Discovery," ch. 6-A, §1 et seq.; **O'Connor's Texas Forms**, FORMS 6A:6, 6A:7, 6A:8, 6A:9.

ANNOTATIONS

In re Alford Chevrolet-Geo, 997 S.W.2d 173, 181 (Tex.1999). "[C]ourts may limit discovery pending resolution of threshold issues like venue, jurisdiction, forum non conveniens, and official immunity."

Brescia v. Slack & Davis, L.L.P., No. 03-08-00042-CV, 2010 WL 4670322 (Tex.App.—Austin 2010, pet. denied) (memo op.; 11-19-10). "Rule 190.4 does not require that the court's order provide deadlines different from those under a Level-2 case. Rather, the decision to provide different deadlines is left to the court's discretion. [¶] Depending on the discovery plan level, the discovery rules establish a date certain for the completion of discovery. Under the discovery rules, no longer is there a concern that discovery will be incomplete at the summary judgment phase. The specific deadline established by the pretrial discovery rules ensures that the evidence presented at the summary judgment stage and at the trial stage remains the same."

TRCP 191. MODIFYING DISCOVERY PROCEDURES AND LIMITATIONS; CONFERENCE REQUIREMENT; SIGNING DISCLOSURES, DISCOVERY REQUESTS, RESPONSES, AND OBJECTIONS; FILING REQUIREMENTS

191.1. Modification of Procedures. Except where specifically prohibited, the procedures and limitations set forth in the rules pertaining to discovery may be modified in any suit by the agreement of the parties or by court order for good cause. An agreement of the parties is enforceable if it complies with Rule 11 or, as it affects an oral deposition, if it is made a part of the record of the deposition.

191.2. Conference. Parties and their attorneys are expected to cooperate in discovery and to make any agreements reasonably necessary for the efficient disposition of the case. All discovery motions or requests for hearings relating to discovery must contain a certificate by the party filing the motion or request that a reasonable effort has been made to resolve the dispute without the necessity of court intervention and the effort failed.

191.3. Signing of Disclosures, Discovery Requests, Notices, Responses, and Objections.

(a) ***Signature Required.*** Every disclosure, discovery request, notice, response, and objection must be signed:

(1) by an attorney, if the party is represented by an attorney, and must show the attorney's State Bar of Texas identification number, address, telephone number, and fax number, if any; or

(2) by the party, if the party is not represented by an attorney, and must show the party's address, telephone number, and fax number, if any.

(b) ***Effect of Signature on Disclosure.*** The signature of an attorney or party on a disclosure constitutes a certification that to the best of the signer's knowledge, information, and belief, formed after a reasonable inquiry, the disclosure is complete and correct as of the time it is made.

(c) ***Effect of Signature on Discovery Request, Notice, Response, or Objection.*** The signature of an attorney or party on a discovery request, notice, response, or objection constitutes a certification that to the best of the signer's knowledge, information, and belief, formed after a reasonable inquiry, the request, notice, response, or objection:

(1) is consistent with the rules of civil procedure and these discovery rules and warranted by existing law or a good faith argument for the extension, modification, or reversal of existing law;

(2) has a good faith factual basis;

(3) is not interposed for any improper purpose, such as to harass or to cause unnecessary delay or needless increase in the cost of litigation; and

(4) is not unreasonable or unduly burdensome or expensive, given the needs of the case, the discovery already had in the case, the amount in controversy, and the importance of the issues at stake in the litigation.

(d) ***Effect of Failure to Sign.*** If a request, notice, response, or objection is not signed, it must be stricken unless it is signed promptly after the omission is called to the attention of the party making the request, notice, response, or objection. A party is not required to take any action with respect to a request or notice that is not signed.

(e) ***Sanctions.*** If the certification is false without substantial justification, the court may, upon motion or its own initiative, impose on the person who made the certification, or the party on whose behalf the request, notice, response, or objection was made, or both, an appropriate sanction as for a frivolous pleading or motion under Chapter 10 of the Civil Practice and Remedies Code.

191.4. Filing of Discovery Materials.

(a) ***Discovery Materials Not to Be Filed.*** The following discovery materials must not be filed:

(1) discovery requests, deposition notices, and subpoenas required to be served only on parties;

(2) responses and objections to discovery requests and deposition notices, regardless on whom the requests or notices were served;

(3) documents and tangible things produced in discovery; and

(4) statements prepared in compliance with Rule 193.3(b) or (d).

(b) ***Discovery Materials to Be Filed.*** The following discovery materials must be filed:

(1) discovery requests, deposition notices, and subpoenas required to be served on nonparties;

(2) motions and responses to motions pertaining to discovery matters; and

(3) agreements concerning discovery matters, to the extent necessary to comply with Rule 11.

(c) ***Exceptions.*** Notwithstanding paragraph (a)—

(1) the court may order discovery materials to be filed;

(2) a person may file discovery materials in support of or in opposition to a motion or for other use in a court proceeding; and

(3) a person may file discovery materials necessary for a proceeding in an appellate court.

(d) ***Retention Requirement for Persons.*** Any person required to serve discovery materials not required to be filed must retain the original or exact copy of the materials during the pendency of the case and any related appellate proceedings begun within six months after judgment is signed, unless otherwise provided by the trial court.

(e) ***Retention Requirement for Courts.*** The clerk of the court shall retain and dispose of deposition transcripts and depositions upon written questions as directed by the Supreme Court.

191.5. Service of Discovery Materials. Every disclosure, discovery request, notice, response, and objection required to be served on a party or person must be served on all parties of record.

Added Nov. 9, 1998, eff. Jan. 1, 1999.

Comment—1999

1. Rule 191.1 preserves the ability of parties by agreement and trial courts by order to adapt discovery to different circumstances. That ability is broad but not unbounded. Parties cannot merely by agreement modify a court order without the court's concurrence. Trial courts cannot simply "opt out" of these rules by form orders or approve or order a discovery control plan that does not contain the matters specified in Rule 190.4, but trial courts may use standard or form orders for providing discovery plans, scheduling, and other pretrial matters. In individual instances, courts may order, or parties may agree, to use discovery methods other than those prescribed in these rules if appropriate. Because the general rule is stated here, it is not repeated in each context in which it applies. Thus, for example, parties can agree to enlarge or shorten the time permitted for a deposition and to change the manner in which a deposition is conducted, notwithstanding Rule 199.5, although parties could not agree to be abusive toward a witness.

2. Rule 191.2 expressly states the obligation of parties and their attorneys to cooperate in conducting discovery.

3. The requirement that discovery requests, notices, responses, and objections be signed also applies to documents used to satisfy the purposes of such instruments. An example is a statement that privileged material or information has been withheld, which may be separate from a response to the discovery request but is nevertheless part of the response.

Source: New rule.

See also CPRC §10.001; TRCP 11, 13, 57; **O'Connor's Texas Rules**, "General Rules for Discovery," ch. 6-A, §1 et seq.

ANNOTATIONS

In re BP Prods. N. Am., Inc., 244 S.W.3d 840, 846 (Tex.2008). "This Court has not previously addressed the scope of a trial court's power to set aside an otherwise enforceable Rule 191.1 agreement. Consistent with its powers over discovery, a trial court may modify discovery procedures and limitations for 'good cause.' This power, however, is not 'unbounded.' Wherever possible, a trial court should give effect to agreements between the parties. [¶] A court should be particularly reluctant to set aside a Rule 191.1 agreement after one party has acted in reliance on the agreed procedure and performed its obligations under the agreement. *At 847:* In the absence of a motion for sanctions, proper notice and opportunity to be heard, or the trial court's invocation of the court's power to sanction, the order striking the discovery agreement is not supportable as a sanctions order."

Groves v. Gabriel, 874 S.W.2d 660, 661 n.3 (Tex.1994). "[P] complains that [D's] motion to compel discovery did not contain the certificate of conference required under [TRCP 166b(7), now TRCP 191.2]. Because this rule is for the benefit of the trial court, the court's failure to require a certificate of conference does not justify mandamus relief."

TRCP 192. PERMISSIBLE DISCOVERY: FORMS AND SCOPE; WORK PRODUCT; PROTECTIVE ORDERS; DEFINITIONS

192.1. Forms of Discovery. Permissible forms of discovery are:

Text of subsec. (a) effective for cases filed before January 1, 2021.

(a) requests for disclosure;

Text of subsec. (a) effective for cases filed on or after January 1, 2021.

(a) required disclosures;

(b) requests for production and inspection of documents and tangible things;

(c) requests and motions for entry upon and examination of real property;

(d) interrogatories to a party;

(e) requests for admission;

(f) oral or written depositions; and

(g) motions for mental or physical examinations.

192.2. Sequence of Discovery.

Text of rule effective for cases filed before January 1, 2021.

The permissible forms of discovery may be combined in the same document and may be taken in any order or sequence.

192.2. Timing and Sequence of Discovery.

Text of rule effective for cases filed on or after January 1, 2021.

(a) ***Timing.*** Unless otherwise agreed to by the parties or ordered by the court, a party cannot serve discovery on another party until after the other party's initial disclosures are due.

(b) ***Sequence.*** The permissible forms of discovery may be combined in the same document and may be taken in any order or sequence.

192.3. ***Scope of Discovery.***

(a) ***Generally.*** In general, a party may obtain discovery regarding any matter that is not privileged and is relevant to the subject matter of the pending action, whether it relates to the claim or defense of the party seeking discovery or the claim or defense of any other party. It is not a ground for objection that the information sought will be inadmissible at trial if the information sought appears reasonably calculated to lead to the discovery of admissible evidence.

(b) ***Documents and Tangible Things.*** A party may obtain discovery of the existence, description, nature, custody, condition, location, and contents of documents and tangible things (including papers, books, accounts, drawings, graphs, charts, photographs, electronic or videotape recordings, data, and data compilations) that constitute or contain matters relevant to the subject matter of the action. A person is required to produce a document or tangible thing that is within the person's possession, custody, or control.

(c) ***Persons with Knowledge of Relevant Facts.*** A party may obtain discovery of the name, address, and telephone number of persons having knowledge of relevant facts, and a brief statement of each identified person's connection with the case. A person has knowledge of relevant facts when that person has or may have knowledge of any discoverable matter. The person need not have admissible information or personal knowledge of the facts. An expert is "a person with knowledge of relevant facts" only if that knowledge was obtained first-hand or if it was not obtained in preparation for trial or in anticipation of litigation.

(d) ***Trial Witnesses.*** A party may obtain discovery of the name, address, and telephone number of any person who is expected to be called to testify at trial. This paragraph does not apply to rebuttal or impeaching witnesses the necessity of whose testimony cannot reasonably be anticipated before trial.

(e) ***Testifying and Consulting Experts.*** The identity, mental impressions, and opinions of a consulting expert whose mental impressions and opinions have not been reviewed by a testifying expert are not discoverable. A party may discover the following information regarding a testifying expert or regarding a consulting expert whose mental impressions or opinions have been reviewed by a testifying expert:

(1) the expert's name, address, and telephone number;

(2) the subject matter on which a testifying expert will testify;

(3) the facts known by the expert that relate to or form the basis of the expert's mental impressions and opinions formed or made in connection with the case in which the discovery is sought, regardless of when and how the factual information was acquired;

(4) the expert's mental impressions and opinions formed or made in connection with the case in which discovery is sought, and any methods used to derive them;

(5) any bias of the witness;

(6) all documents, tangible things, reports, models, or data compilations that have been provided to, reviewed by, or prepared by or for the expert in anticipation of a testifying expert's testimony;

(7) the expert's current resume and bibliography.

(f) ***Indemnity and Insuring Agreements.*** Except as otherwise provided by law, a party may obtain discovery of the existence and contents of any indemnity or insurance agreement under which any person may be liable to satisfy part or all of a judgment rendered in the action or to indemnify or reimburse for payments made to satisfy the judgment. Information concerning the indemnity or insurance agreement is not by reason of disclosure admissible in evidence at trial.

(g) ***Settlement Agreements.*** A party may obtain discovery of the existence and contents of any relevant portions of a settlement agreement. Information concerning a settlement agreement is not by reason of disclosure admissible in evidence at trial.

(h) ***Statements of Persons with Knowledge of Relevant Facts.*** A party may obtain discovery of the state-

ment of any person with knowledge of relevant facts—a "witness statement"—regardless of when the statement was made. A witness statement is (1) a written statement signed or otherwise adopted or approved in writing by the person making it, or (2) a stenographic, mechanical, electrical, or other type of recording of a witness's oral statement, or any substantially verbatim transcription of such a recording. Notes taken during a conversation or interview with a witness are not a witness statement. Any person may obtain, upon written request, his or her own statement concerning the lawsuit, which is in the possession, custody or control of any party.

(i) ***Potential Parties.*** A party may obtain discovery of the name, address, and telephone number of any potential party.

(j) ***Contentions.*** A party may obtain discovery of any other party's legal contentions and the factual bases for those contentions.

192.4. Limitations on Scope of Discovery. The discovery methods permitted by these rules should be limited by the court if it determines, on motion or on its own initiative and on reasonable notice, that:

(a) the discovery sought is unreasonably cumulative or duplicative, or is obtainable from some other source that is more convenient, less burdensome, or less expensive; or

(b) the burden or expense of the proposed discovery outweighs its likely benefit, taking into account the needs of the case, the amount in controversy, the parties' resources, the importance of the issues at stake in the litigation, and the importance of the proposed discovery in resolving the issues.

192.5. Work Product.

(a) ***Work Product Defined.*** Work product comprises:

(1) material prepared or mental impressions developed in anticipation of litigation or for trial by or for a party or a party's representatives, including the party's attorneys, consultants, sureties, indemnitors, insurers, employees, or agents; or

(2) a communication made in anticipation of litigation or for trial between a party and the party's representatives or among a party's representatives, including the party's attorneys, consultants, sureties, indemnitors, insurers, employees, or agents.

(b) ***Protection of Work Product.***

(1) *Protection of Core Work Product-Attorney Mental Processes.* Core work product—the work product of an attorney or an attorney's representative that contains the attorney's or the attorney's representative's mental impressions, opinions, conclusions, or legal theories—is not discoverable.

(2) *Protection of Other Work Product.* Any other work product is discoverable only upon a showing that the party seeking discovery has substantial need of the materials in the preparation of the party's case and that the party is unable without undue hardship to obtain the substantial equivalent of the material by other means.

(3) *Incidental Disclosure of Attorney Mental Processes.* It is not a violation of subparagraph (1) if disclosure ordered pursuant to subparagraph (2) incidentally discloses by inference attorney mental processes otherwise protected under subparagraph (1).

(4) *Limiting Disclosure of Mental Processes.* If a court orders discovery of work product pursuant to subparagraph (2), the court must—insofar as possible—protect against disclosure of the mental impressions, opinions, conclusions, or legal theories not otherwise discoverable.

(c) ***Exceptions.*** Even if made or prepared in anticipation of litigation or for trial, the following is not work product protected from discovery:

(1) information discoverable under Rule 192.3 concerning experts, trial witnesses, witness statements, and contentions;

(2) trial exhibits ordered disclosed under Rule 166 or Rule 190.4;

(3) the name, address, and telephone number of any potential party or any person with knowledge of relevant facts;

(4) any photograph or electronic image of underlying facts (*e.g.*, a photograph of the accident scene) or a photograph or electronic image of any sort that a party intends to offer into evidence; and

(5) any work product created under circumstances within an exception to the attorney-client privilege in Rule 503(d) of the Rules of Evidence.

(d) ***Privilege.*** For purposes of these rules, an assertion that material or information is work product is an assertion of privilege.

192.6. Protective Orders.

(a) ***Motion.*** A person from whom discovery is sought, and any other person affected by the discovery request, may move within the time permitted for response to the discovery request for an order protecting that person from the discovery sought. A person should not move for protection when an objection to written discovery or an assertion of

privilege is appropriate, but a motion does not waive the objection or assertion of privilege. If a person seeks protection regarding the time or place of discovery, the person must state a reasonable time and place for discovery with which the person will comply. A person must comply with a request to the extent protection is not sought unless it is unreasonable under the circumstances to do so before obtaining a ruling on the motion.

(b) ***Order.*** To protect the movant from undue burden, unnecessary expense, harassment, annoyance, or invasion of personal, constitutional, or property rights, the court may make any order in the interest of justice and may—among other things—order that:

(1) the requested discovery not be sought in whole or in part;

(2) the extent or subject matter of discovery be limited;

(3) the discovery not be undertaken at the time or place specified;

(4) the discovery be undertaken only by such method or upon such terms and conditions or at the time and place directed by the court;

(5) the results of discovery be sealed or otherwise protected, subject to the provisions of Rule 76a.

192.7. Definitions. As used in these rules

Text of subsec. (a) effective for cases filed before January 1, 2021.

(a) *Written discovery* means requests for disclosure, requests for production and inspection of documents and tangible things, requests for entry onto property, interrogatories, and requests for admission.

Text of subsec. (a) effective for cases filed on or after January 1, 2021.

(a) *Written discovery* means required disclosures, requests for production and inspection of documents and tangible things, requests for entry onto property, interrogatories, and requests for admission.

(b) *Possession, custody, or control* of an item means that the person either has physical possession of the item or has a right to possession of the item that is equal or superior to the person who has physical possession of the item.

(c) A *testifying expert* is an expert who may be called to testify as an expert witness at trial.

(d) A *consulting expert* is an expert who has been consulted, retained, or specially employed by a party in anticipation of litigation or in preparation for trial, but who is not a testifying expert.

Aug. 5, 1998 and amended Nov. 9, 1998, eff. Jan. 1, 1999. Amended by order of Dec. 23, 2020, eff. Jan. 1, 2021.

Comment—1999

1. While the scope of discovery is quite broad, it is nevertheless confined by the subject matter of the case and reasonable expectations of obtaining information that will aid resolution of the dispute. The rule must be read and applied in that context. *See* **In re American Optical Corp.**, 988 S.W.2d 711 (Tex. 1998) (per curiam); **K-Mart v. Sanderson**, 937 S.W.2d 429 (Tex. 1996) (per curiam); **Dillard Dept. Stores v. Hall**, 909 S.W.2d 491 (Tex. 1995) (per curiam); **Texaco, Inc. v. Sanderson**, 898 S.W.2d 813 (Tex. 1995) (per curiam); **Loftin v. Martin**, 776 S.W.2d 145, 148 (Tex. 1989).

2. The definition of documents and tangible things has been revised to clarify that things relevant to the subject matter of the action are within the scope of discovery regardless of their form.

3. Rule 192.3(c) makes discoverable a "brief statement of each identified person's connection with the case." This provision does not contemplate a narrative statement of the facts the person knows, but at most a few words describing the person's identity as relevant to the lawsuit.

For instance: "treating physician," "eyewitness," "chief financial officer," "director," "plaintiff's mother and eyewitness to accident." The rule is intended to be consistent with **Axelson v. McIlhany**, 798 S.W.2d 550 (Tex. 1990).

4. Rule 192.3(g) does not suggest that settlement agreements in other cases are relevant or irrelevant.

5. Rule 192.3(j) makes a party's legal and factual contentions discoverable but does not require more than a basic statement of those contentions and does not require a marshaling of evidence.

6. The sections in former Rule 166b concerning land and medical records are not included in this rule. They remain within the scope of discovery and are discussed in other rules.

7. The court's power to limit discovery based on the needs and circumstances of the case is expressly stated in Rule 192.4. The provision is taken from Rule 26(b)(2) of the Federal Rules of Civil Procedure. Courts should limit discovery under this rule only to prevent unwarranted delay and expense as stated more fully in the rule. A court abuses its discretion in unreasonably restricting a party's access to information through discovery.

8. Work product is defined for the first time, and its exceptions stated. Work product replaces the "attorney work product" and "party communication" discovery exemptions from former Rule 166b.

9. Elimination of the "witness statement" exemption does not render all witness statements automatically discoverable but subjects them to the same rules concerning the scope of discovery and privileges applicable to other documents or tangible things.

Source: New rule.

See also **O'Connor's Texas Rules**, "General Rules for Discovery," ch. 6-A, §1 et seq.; **O'Connor's Texas Rules**, "Scope of Discovery," ch. 6-B, §1 et seq.; **O'Connor's Texas Rules**, "Electronic Discovery," ch. 6-C, §1 et seq.; **O'Connor's Texas Forms**, FORMS 6A:10, 6A:11, 6A:12, 6A:13, 6A:14.

ANNOTATIONS

Definition

In re Kuntz, 124 S.W.3d 179, 183 (Tex.2003). "[D] argues that he 'should not be ordered to produce documents in the physical possession of his corporate employer in this suit brought against him individually.' *At 184:* [D's] access is strictly limited to use of the [documents] in furtherance of

his employer's services. . . . [¶] [M]ere access to the [documents] does not constitute 'physical possession' of the documents under the definition of 'possession, custody, or control' set forth in [TRCP] 192.7(b)."

GTE Comms. Sys. v. Tanner, 856 S.W.2d 725, 729 (Tex.1993). "The phrase, 'possession, custody or control,' within the meaning of [TRCP 192.7(b)], includes not only actual physical possession, but constructive possession, and the right to obtain possession from a third party, such as an agent or representative." *See also* **In re Summersett**, 438 S.W.3d 74, 81 (Tex.App.—Corpus Christi 2013, orig. proceeding).

Scope of Discovery

In re National Lloyds Ins., 449 S.W.3d 486, 489-90 (Tex.2014). "Essentially, [the purpose of P's request for the insurance-claim files is] to compare [D's] evaluation of the damage to her home with [D's] evaluation of the damage to other homes to support her contention that her claims were undervalued. . . . Scouring claim files in hopes of finding similarly situated claimants whose claims were evaluated differently from [P's] is at best an 'impermissible fishing expedition.' [¶] [P] is correct that discovery must be reasonably limited in time and geographic scope. But such limits in and of themselves do not render the underlying information discoverable. Because the information [P] seeks is not reasonably calculated to lead to the discovery of admissible evidence, the trial court's order compelling discovery of such information is necessarily overbroad." *See also* **In re National Lloyds Ins.**, 507 S.W.3d 219, 223-25 (Tex.2016).

In re Ford Motor Co., 427 S.W.3d 396, 397 (Tex.2014). This court has "expressed concerns about allowing overly expansive discovery about testifying experts that can 'permit witnesses to be subjected to harassment and might well discourage reputable experts' from participating in the litigation process. [¶] The particular deposition notices in this case highlight the danger of permitting such expansive discovery. In his deposition notices to [experts' employers], [P] seeks detailed financial and business information for all cases the companies have handled for [D-automobile manufacturer] or any other automobile manufacturer from 2000 to 2011. Such a fishing expedition, seeking sensitive information covering twelve years, is just the type of overbroad discovery the rules are intended to prevent." *See also* **K Mart Corp. v. Sanderson**, 937 S.W.2d 429, 431 (Tex.1996); **In re Siroosian**, 449 S.W.3d 920, 923 (Tex.App.—Fort Worth 2014, orig. proceeding).

In re Dana Corp., 138 S.W.3d 298, 302 (Tex.2004). "Rule 192.3(f) does not foreclose discovery of insurance information beyond that identified in the rule; however, we also conclude that the plain language of Rule 192.3(f), by itself, does not provide a sufficient basis to order discovery beyond the production of the 'existence and contents' of the policies. [A] party may discover information beyond an insurance agreement's existence and contents only if the information is otherwise discoverable under our scope-of-discovery rule."

Ford Motor Co. v. Leggat, 904 S.W.2d 643, 649 (Tex.1995). "Settlement agreements are discoverable, to the extent they are relevant. Settlement agreements themselves, of course, are not admissible at trial to prove liability." *See also* **In re GreCon, Inc.**, 542 S.W.3d 774, 780 (Tex.App.—Houston [14th Dist.] 2018, orig. proceeding).

In re Preventative Pest Control Houston, LLC, 580 S.W.3d 455, 460 (Tex.App.—Houston [14th Dist.] 2019, orig. proceeding). "[Ds] complain that the trial court abused its discretion by ordering them to produce [documents] that do not exist. Under Texas procedure, litigants are not required to produce documents or tangible things unless those items lie within their possession, custody, or control. A document that does not exist is not within a party's possession, custody, or control. Therefore, parties cannot be forced to create documents that do not exist for the sole purpose of complying with a request for production."

Liles v. Contreras, 547 S.W.3d 280, 289-90 (Tex.App.—San Antonio 2018, pet. denied). "Rule 192.3(g) requires a party . . . to disclose not just the existence of a settlement agreement, but the contents of it. . . . Settlement agreements are discoverable for many reasons, including demonstrating bias or prejudice of a party or potential witness. Merely disclosing the names of the parties to the settlement, the amount, and that court approval was pending did not disclose 'the contents' of the settlement agreement so as to allow [P's] counsel, among other things, to determine whether there might be bias or prejudice by the settling parties based on the agreement. [O]nce the settlement agreement was complete . . . Rule 192.3(g) mandated a full and complete disclosure of the written settlement agreement."

In re Summersett, 438 S.W.3d 74, 81 (Tex.App.—Corpus Christi 2013, orig. proceeding). "Because the discovery rules often apply to reach information not within a party's physical possession, a party may often not have actual knowledge of the existence of information or documents in the possession of others 'but may be nevertheless obligated to gain knowledge of them.' Thus, in evaluating the scope of a given request to produce, the duty to produce is not always satisfied by producing the documents that are in the party's immediate physical possession but 'may often extend to documents in the possession of persons or entities that are not parties to the suit.' The party seeking production has the burden of proving that the relator has constructive possession or the right to obtain possession of the requested documents."

In re Commitment of Young, 410 S.W.3d 542, 551 (Tex.App.—Beaumont 2013, no pet.). " 'It is the discovery proponent's burden to demonstrate that the requested documents fall within the scope-of-discovery of Rule 192.3.' Trial courts have the discretion to refuse to compel discovery if the information being requested by the interrogatory or request at issue is so inclusive that responding would

require matters to be included that are unlikely to fall within the scope of discovery that governs the parties' dispute."

Experts

In re City of Dickinson, 568 S.W.3d 642, 645 (Tex.2019). "[W]e must determine whether the text of [TRCP 192.3(e)(6)] actually waives the attorney-client privilege when the client or its employee is a testifying expert witness. *At 646:* While [TRCP 192.3(e)] provides that a party 'may discover' testifying-expert materials, nothing in its language permits such discovery when the materials are attorney-client privileged. To the contrary [TRCP 192.3(a)] confirms that, absent some specific provision otherwise, Rule 192.3 does not require the disclosure of information that is attorney-client privileged. Because the rule does not specifically prohibit the use of the attorney-client privilege for testifying-expert materials, if material is privileged it may be withheld."

In re Christus Spohn Hosp. Kleberg, 222 S.W.3d 434, 439 (Tex.2007). See annotation under TRCP 193, *TRCP 193.3—Privileges.*

In re City of Georgetown, 53 S.W.3d 328, 334 (Tex.2001). "The [TRCPs] expressly provide that a party is not required to disclose the identity, mental impressions, and opinions of consulting experts. *At 337:* [I]f documents are privileged or confidential under the [TRCPs] or [TREs], they are within a 'category of information [that] is expressly made confidential under other law' within the meaning of [Gov't Code] §552.022. . . ."

In re Makris, 217 S.W.3d 521, 524 (Tex.App.—San Antonio 2006, orig. proceeding). "[P]ersonal financial records of a nonparty witness are not discoverable for the sole purpose of showing bias. [U]nder Rule 192.3(e)(5), in order to obtain discovery of personal documents from a nonparty expert solely for impeachment purposes, the party seeking the documents must first present evidence 'raising the possibility that the expert is biased.'" *See also* **In re Siroosian**, 449 S.W.3d 920, 923-24 (Tex.App.—Fort Worth 2014, orig. proceeding).

Castellanos v. Littlejohn, 945 S.W.2d 236, 239 (Tex.App.—San Antonio 1997, orig. proceeding). "The issue presented . . . is whether a party who has inadvertently listed a consulting-only expert as a testifying expert may 'de-designate' him to reflect his proper status. We believe the party can do so, as long as the 'de-designation' does not constitute 'an offensive and unacceptable use of discovery mechanisms' or 'violate[ ] the clear purpose and policy underlying the rules of discovery.'"

Work Product

In re National Lloyds Ins., 532 S.W.3d 794, 804 (Tex.2017). "Billing records constitute 'communication[s] made in anticipation of litigation or for trial between a party and the party's representatives or among a party's representatives.' Moreover, as a whole, billing records represent the mechanical compilation of information that reveals counsel's legal strategy and thought processes, at least incidentally. *At 805:* A request for all billing invoices, payment logs, payment ledgers, payment summaries, documents showing flat rates, and audits is analogous to the request in [**National Un. Fire Ins. v.**] **Valdez**[, 863 S.W.2d 458 (Tex.1993),] for an attorney's entire litigation file. . . . When a party neither seeks to recover its own attorney fees nor attempts to use its attorney-billing records to challenge the opposing party's attorney fees, the party's attorney should not be restricted in the preparation or presentment of his or her billing records by the prospect that they might have to be revealed in their entirety. Further, these billing records, which are useful to the requesting party only if they describe what the attorney has done in the case, reveal the attorney's thought processes concerning the prosecution or defense of the case. *At 806:* We therefore hold that requests for production of all billing invoices, payment logs, payment ledgers, payment summaries, documents showing flat rates, and audits invade the zone of work-product protection. Our holding does not prevent a more narrowly tailored request for information relevant to an issue in a pending case that does not invade the attorney's strategic decisions or thought processes. *At 807:* We acknowledge that an opposing party may waive its work-product privilege through offensive use—perhaps by relying on its billing records to contest the reasonableness of opposing counsel's attorney fees or to recover its own attorney fees. But in this case, [D] has stipulated it will not use its own billing records to contest [Ps'] attorney fees. Nor is [D] seeking to recover its own attorney fees from [Ps]."

In re Bexar Cty. Crim. Dist. Atty's Office, 224 S.W.3d 182, 187-88 (Tex.2007). "Rule 192.5(b)(1) distinguishes everyday work product from 'core work product' and makes clear that the latter . . . is inviolate and flatly 'not discoverable[ ]'. . . . Core work product is sacrosanct and its protection impermeable."

Occidental Chem. Corp. v. Banales, 907 S.W.2d 488, 490 (Tex.1995). "The attorney work product privilege protects two related but different concepts. First, the privilege protects the attorney's thought process, which includes strategy decisions and issue formulation, and notes or writings evincing those mental processes. Second, the privilege protects the mechanical compilation of information to the extent such compilation reveals the attorney's thought processes. The work product exemption is of continuing duration."

National Un. Fire Ins. v. Valdez, 863 S.W.2d 458, 461 (Tex.1993). "[N]o legitimate purpose is served by allowing a party to discover an opponent's litigation file. Our decision today does not prevent a party from requesting specific documents or categories of documents relevant to issues in a pending case, even though some or all of the documents may be contained in an attorney's files."

In re Fairway Methanol LLC, 515 S.W.3d 480, 490 (Tex.App.—Houston [14th Dist.] 2017, orig. proceeding).

"[A]n investigation is conducted in anticipation of litigation if (1) 'a reasonable person would have concluded from the totality of the circumstances surrounding the investigation that there was a substantial chance that litigation would ensue' (the objective prong); and (2) 'the party resisting discovery believed in good faith that there was a substantial chance that litigation would ensue and conducted the investigation for the purpose of preparing for such litigation' (the subjective prong). A 'substantial chance of litigation' does not 'refer to any particular statistical probability that litigation will occur' but 'simply means that litigation is more than merely an abstract possibility or unwarranted fear.' . . . 'It is not necessary that litigation be threatened or imminent, as long as the prospect of litigation is identifiable because of claims that have already arisen.' Nor is it necessary for the plaintiff to have manifested an intent to sue. [¶] The subjective prong does not require the investigating party to be absolutely convinced that litigation will occur; it requires only a good faith belief that there is a substantial chance that litigation will [ensue]. The subjective prong also 'requires that the investigation actually be conducted for the purpose of preparing for litigation.' However, the language of Rule 192.5 does not require that the sole or primary purpose of the material or communication be for preparing for litigation."

In re Baytown Nissan Inc., 451 S.W.3d 140, 149 (Tex.App.—Houston [1st Dist.] 2014, orig. proceeding). " 'Compelling an attorney of record involved in the litigation of the case to testify concerning the suit's subject matter generally implicates work product concerns' and 'is inappropriate under most circumstances.' [¶] Deposition questions requesting [D's attorney's] mental impressions regarding his conversation with [witness] are core work product and not discoverable. Other questions requesting factual details of [D's attorney's] conversation with [witness] are non-core work product. With respect to those questions, [P] had the burden of demonstrating the substantial need and undue hardship requirements for discovery of non-core work product. This is a particularly heavy burden when a discovery request seeks to compel the deposition of a party's attorney. . . ."

Protective Orders

In re Garza, 544 S.W.3d 836, 841-42 (Tex.2018). "While [TRCP 176.6 and 192.6] permit potential deponents to seek protection for themselves, [D] argues that [P], who is 'any other person affected' by the subpoena or the discovery request per the rules, had already sought and been denied protection as to the discovery requested from [custodians of P's medical records]. [¶] [Custodians] had independent rights to seek protection under the rules of procedure. The rules' use of 'and' means that *both* the potential deponent *and* any other person affected by the discovery request are entitled to seek protection by filing motions for protection."

General Tire, Inc. v. Kepple, 970 S.W.2d 520, 524 (Tex.1998). "To the extent that discovery, whether filed or unfiled, is a 'court record' under [TRCP] 76a, the court must follow the stricter standards of that rule to limit its dissemination. *At 525:* [W]e hold that when a party seeks a protective order under [TRCP 192.6] to restrict the dissemination of unfiled discovery, and no party or intervenor contends that the discovery is a 'court record,' a trial court need not conduct a hearing or render any findings on that issue. If a party or intervenor opposing a protective order claims that the discovery is a 'court record,' the court must make a threshold determination on that issue. However, public notice and a Rule 76a hearing are mandated only if the court finds that the documents are court records."

Crown Cent. Pet. Corp. v. Garcia 904 S.W.2d 125, 128 (Tex.1995). "When a party seeks to depose a . . . high level corporate official [i.e., an apex deposition] and that official (or the corporation) files a motion for protective order . . . denying any knowledge of relevant facts, the trial court should first determine whether the party seeking the deposition has arguably shown that the official has any unique or superior personal knowledge of discoverable information. If the party seeking the deposition cannot [so] show . . ., the trial court should grant the motion for protective order and first require the party seeking the deposition to attempt to obtain the discovery through less intrusive methods."

In re Shell E&P, Inc., 179 S.W.3d 125, 130 (Tex.App.—San Antonio 2005, orig. proceeding). "[T]he non-party owner of [a document has] the right under Rule 192.6(a) to seek protection from disclosure of its documents in the trial court, whether through an objection, assertion of privilege, motion for a protective order, or motion for enforcement of an existing protective order. The trial court's . . . order holding that [nonparty] lacks standing to object to the disclosure of its documents conflicts with Rule 192.6(a) . . .; therefore, . . . the trial court clearly abused its discretion."

TRCP 193. WRITTEN DISCOVERY: RESPONSE; OBJECTION; ASSERTION OF PRIVILEGE; SUPPLEMENTATION AND AMENDMENT; FAILURE TO TIMELY RESPOND; PRESUMPTION OF AUTHENTICITY

193.1. Responding to Written Discovery; Duty to Make Complete Response.

Text of rule effective for cases filed before January 1, 2021.

A party must respond to written discovery in writing within the time provided by court order or these rules. When responding to written discovery, a party must make a complete response, based on all information reasonably available to the responding party or its attorney at the time the response is made. The responding party's answers, objections, and other responses must be preceded by the request to which they apply.

Text of rule effective for cases filed on or after January 1, 2021.

A party must respond to written discovery in writing within the time provided by court order or these rules.

When responding to written discovery, a party must make a complete response, based on all information reasonably available to the responding party or its attorney at the time the response is made. The responding party's answers, objections, and other responses must be preceded by the request or required disclosure to which they apply.

193.2. Objecting to Written Discovery.

(a) ***Form and Time for Objections.*** A party must make any objection to written discovery in writing—either in the response or in a separate document—within the time for response. The party must state specifically the legal or factual basis for the objection and the extent to which the party is refusing to comply with the request.

(b) ***Duty to Respond When Partially Objecting; Objection to Time or Place of Production.*** A party must comply with as much of the request to which the party has made no objection unless it is unreasonable under the circumstances to do so before obtaining a ruling on the objection. If the responding party objects to the requested time or place of production, the responding party must state a reasonable time and place for complying with the request and must comply at that time and place without further request or order.

(c) ***Good Faith Basis for Objection.*** A party may object to written discovery only if a good faith factual and legal basis for the objection exists at the time the objection is made.

(d) ***Amendment.*** An objection or response to written discovery may be amended or supplemented to state an objection or basis that, at the time the objection or response initially was made, either was inapplicable or was unknown after reasonable inquiry.

(e) ***Waiver of Objection.*** An objection that is not made within the time required, or that is obscured by numerous unfounded objections, is waived unless the court excuses the waiver for good cause shown.

(f) ***No Objection to Preserve Privilege.*** A party should not object to a request for written discovery on the grounds that it calls for production of material or information that is privileged but should instead comply with Rule 193.3. A party who objects to production of privileged material or information does not waive the privilege but must comply with Rule 193.3 when the error is pointed out.

193.3. Asserting a Privilege.

Text of rule effective for cases filed before January 1, 2021.

A party may preserve a privilege from written discovery in accordance with this subdivision.

(a) ***Withholding Privileged Material or Information.*** A party who claims that material or information responsive to written discovery is privileged may withhold the privileged material or information from the response. The party must state—in the response (or an amended or supplemental response) or in a separate document—that:

(1) information or material responsive to the request has been withheld,

(2) the request to which the information or material relates, and

(3) the privilege or privileges asserted.

(b) ***Description of Withheld Material or Information.*** After receiving a response indicating that material or information has been withheld from production, the party seeking discovery may serve a written request that the withholding party identify the information and material withheld. Within 15 days of service of that request, the withholding party must serve a response that:

(1) describes the information or materials withheld that, without revealing the privileged information itself or otherwise waiving the privilege, enables other parties to assess the applicability of the privilege, and

(2) asserts a specific privilege for each item or group of items withheld.

(c) ***Exemption.*** Without complying with paragraphs (a) and (b), a party may withhold a privileged communication to or from a lawyer or lawyer's representative or a privileged document of a lawyer or lawyer's representative—

(1) created or made from the point at which a party consults a lawyer with a view to obtaining professional legal services from the lawyer in the prosecution or defense of a specific claim in the litigation in which discovery is requested, and

(2) concerning the litigation in which the discovery is requested.

(d) ***Privilege Not Waived by Production.*** A party who produces material or information without intending to waive a claim of privilege does not waive that claim under these rules or the Rules of Evidence if—within ten days or a shorter time ordered by the court, after the producing party actually discovers that such production was made—the producing party amends the response, identifying the material or information produced and stating the privilege asserted. If the producing party thus amends the response to assert a privilege, the requesting party must promptly return the specified material or information and any copies pending any ruling by the court denying the privilege.

193.3. Asserting a Privilege.

Text of rule effective for cases filed on or after January 1, 2021.

A party may preserve a privilege from written discovery in accordance with this subdivision.

(a) ***Withholding Privileged Material or Information.*** A party who claims that material or information responsive to written discovery is privileged may withhold the privileged material or information from the response. The party must state—in the response (or an amended or supplemental response) or in a separate document—that:

(1) information or material responsive to the request or required disclosure has been withheld,

(2) the request or required disclosure to which the information or material relates, and

(3) the privilege or privileges asserted.

(b) ***Description of Withheld Material or Information.*** After receiving a response indicating that material or information has been withheld from production, a party seeking discovery may serve a written request that the withholding party identify the information and material withheld. Within 15 days of service of that request, the withholding party must serve a response that:

(1) describes the information or materials withheld that, without revealing the privileged information itself or otherwise waiving the privilege, enables other parties to assess the applicability of the privilege, and

(2) asserts a specific privilege for each item or group of items withheld.

(c) ***Exemption.*** Without complying with paragraphs (a) and (b), a party may withhold a privileged communication to or from a lawyer or lawyer's representative or a privileged document of a lawyer or lawyer's representative

(1) created or made from the point at which a party consults a lawyer with a view to obtaining professional legal services from the lawyer in the prosecution or defense of a specific claim in the litigation in which discovery is requested or required, and

(2) concerning the litigation in which the discovery is requested or required.

(d) ***Privilege Not Waived by Production.*** A party who produces material or information without intending to waive a claim of privilege does not waive that claim under these rules or the Rules of Evidence if—within ten days or a shorter time ordered by the court, after the producing party actually discovers that such production was made—the producing party amends the response, identifying the material or information produced and stating the privilege asserted. If the producing party thus amends the response to assert a privilege, any party who has obtained the specific material or information must promptly return the specified material or information and any copies pending any ruling by the court denying the privilege.

193.4. Hearing and Ruling on Objections and Assertions of Privilege.

Text of rule effective for cases filed before January 1, 2021.

(a) ***Hearing.*** Any party may at any reasonable time request a hearing on an objection or claim of privilege asserted under this rule. The party making the objection or asserting the privilege must present any evidence necessary to support the objection or privilege. The evidence may be testimony presented at the hearing or affidavits served at least seven days before the hearing or at such other reasonable time as the court permits. If the court determines that an *in camera* review of some or all of the requested discovery is necessary, that material or information must be segregated and produced to the court in a sealed wrapper within a reasonable time following the hearing.

(b) ***Ruling.*** To the extent the court sustains the objection or claim of privilege, the responding party has no further duty to respond to that request. To the extent the court overrules the objection or claim of privilege, the responding party must produce the requested material or information within 30 days after the court's ruling or at such time as the court orders. A party need not request a ruling on that party's own objection or assertion of privilege to preserve the objection or privilege.

(c) ***Use of Material or Information Withheld Under Claim of Privilege.*** A party may not use—at any hearing or trial—material or information withheld from discovery under a claim of privilege, including a claim sustained by the court, without timely amending or supplementing the party's response to that discovery.

193.4. Hearing and Ruling on Objections and Assertions of Privilege.

Text of rule effective for cases filed on or after January 1, 2021.

(a) ***Hearing.*** Any party may at any reasonable time request a hearing on an objection or claim of privilege asserted under this rule. The party making the objection or asserting the privilege must present any evidence necessary to support the objection or privilege. The evidence may be testimony presented at the hearing or affidavits served at least seven days before the hearing or at such other reasonable time as the court permits. If the court determines that an *in camera* review of some or all of the requested discovery or required disclosure is necessary, that material or information must be segregated and produced to the court in a sealed wrapper within a reasonable time following the hearing.

(b) ***Ruling.*** To the extent the court sustains the objection or claim of privilege, the responding party has no further duty to respond to that request or required disclosure. To the extent the court overrules the objection or claim of privilege, the responding party must produce the requested or required material or information within 30 days after the court's ruling or at such time as the court orders. A party need not request a ruling on that party's own objection or assertion of privilege to preserve the objection or privilege.

(c) ***Use of Material or Information Withheld Under Claim of Privilege.*** A party may not use—at any hearing or trial—material or information withheld from discovery under a claim of privilege, including a claim sustained by the court, without timely amending or supplementing the party's response to that discovery.

193.5. Amending or Supplementing Responses to Written Discovery.

(a) ***Duty to Amend or Supplement.*** If a party learns that the party's response to written discovery was incomplete or incorrect when made, or, although complete and correct when made, is no longer complete and correct, the party must amend or supplement the response:

(1) to the extent that the written discovery sought the identification of persons with knowledge of relevant facts, trial witnesses, or expert witnesses, and

(2) to the extent that the written discovery sought other information, unless the additional or corrective information has been made known to the other parties in writing, on the record at a deposition, or through other discovery responses.

(b) ***Time and Form of Amended or Supplemental Response.*** An amended or supplemental response must be made reasonably promptly after the party discovers the necessity for such a response. Except as otherwise provided by these rules, it is presumed that an amended or supplemental response made less than 30 days before trial was not made reasonably promptly. An amended or supplemental response must be in the same form as the initial response and must be verified by the party if the original response was required to be verified by the party, but the failure to comply with this requirement does not make the amended or supplemental response untimely unless the party making the response refuses to correct the defect within a reasonable time after it is pointed out.

193.6. Failing to Timely Respond—Effect on Trial.

Text of subsec. (a) effective for cases filed before January 1, 2021.

(a) ***Exclusion of Evidence and Exceptions.*** A party who fails to make, amend, or supplement a discovery response in a timely manner may not introduce in evidence the material or information that was not timely disclosed, or offer the testimony of a witness (other than a named party) who was not timely identified, unless the court finds that:

(1) there was good cause for the failure to timely make, amend, or supplement the discovery response; or

(2) the failure to timely make, amend, or supplement the discovery response will not unfairly surprise or unfairly prejudice the other parties.

Text of subsec. (a) effective for cases filed on or after January 1, 2021.

(a) ***Exclusion of Evidence and Exceptions.*** A party who fails to make, amend, or supplement a discovery response, including a required disclosure, in a timely manner may not introduce in evidence the material or information that was not timely disclosed, or offer the testimony of a witness (other than a named party) who was not timely identified, unless the court finds that:

(1) there was good cause for the failure to timely make, amend, or supplement the discovery response; or

(2) the failure to timely make, amend, or supplement the discovery response will not unfairly surprise or unfairly prejudice the other parties.

(b) ***Burden of Establishing Exception.*** The burden of establishing good cause or the lack of unfair surprise or unfair prejudice is on the party seeking to introduce the evidence or call the witness. A finding of good cause or of the lack of unfair surprise or unfair prejudice must be supported by the record.

(c) ***Continuance.*** Even if the party seeking to introduce the evidence or call the witness fails to carry the burden under paragraph (b), the court may grant a continuance or temporarily postpone the trial to allow a response to be made, amended, or supplemented, and to allow opposing parties to conduct discovery regarding any new information presented by that response.

193.7. Production of Documents Self-Authenticating.

A party's production of a document in response to written discovery authenticates the document for use against that party in any pretrial proceeding or at trial unless—within ten days or a longer or shorter time ordered by the court, after the producing party has actual notice that the document will be used—the party objects to the authenticity of the document, or any part of it, stating the specific basis for objection. An objection must be either on the rec-

ord or in writing and must have a good faith factual and legal basis. An objection made to the authenticity of only part of a document does not affect the authenticity of the remainder. If objection is made, the party attempting to use the document should be given a reasonable opportunity to establish its authenticity.

Aug. 5, 1998 and amended Nov. 9, 1998, eff. Jan. 1, 1999. Amended by order of Dec. 23, 2020, eff. Jan. 1, 2021.

Comment—1999

1. This rule imposes a duty upon parties to make a complete response to written discovery based upon all information reasonably available, subject to objections and privileges.

2. An objection to written discovery does not excuse the responding party from complying with the request to the extent no objection is made. But a party may object to a request for "all documents relevant to the lawsuit" as overly broad and not in compliance with the rule requiring specific requests for documents and refuse to comply with it entirely. *See* **Loftin v. Martin**, 776 S.W.2d 145 (Tex. 1989). A party may also object to a request for a litigation file on the ground that it is overly broad and may assert that on its face the request seeks only materials protected by privilege. *See* **National Union Fire Ins. Co. v. Valdez**, 863 S.W.2d 458 (Tex. 1993). A party who objects to production of documents from a remote time period should produce documents from a more recent period unless that production would be burdensome and duplicative should the objection be overruled.

3. This rule governs the presentation of all privileges including work product. It dispenses with objections to written discovery requests on the basis that responsive information or materials are protected by a specific privilege from discovery. Instead, the rule requires parties to state that information or materials have been withheld and to identify the privilege upon which the party relies. The statement should not be made prophylactically, but only when specific information and materials have been withheld. The party must amend or supplement the statement if additional privileged information or material is found subsequent to the initial response. Thus, when large numbers of documents are being produced, a party may amend the initial response when documents are found as to which the party claims privilege. A party need not state that material created by or for lawyers for the litigation has been withheld as it can be assumed that such material will be withheld from virtually any request on the grounds of attorney-client privilege or work product. However, the rule does not prohibit a party from specifically requesting the material or information if the party has a good faith basis for asserting that it is discoverable. An example would be material or information described by Rule 503(d)(1) of the Rules of Evidence.

4. Rule 193.3(d) is a new provision that allows a party to assert a claim of privilege to material or information produced inadvertently without intending to waive the privilege. The provision is commonly used in complex cases to reduce costs and risks in large document productions. The focus is on the intent to waive the privilege, not the intent to produce the material or information. A party who fails to diligently screen documents before producing them does not waive a claim of privilege. This rule is thus broader than Tex. R. Evid. 511 and overturns **Granada Corp. v. First Court of Appeals**, 844 S.W.2d 223 (Tex. 1992), to the extent the two conflict. The ten-day period (which may be shortened by the court) allowed for an amended response does not run from the production of the material or information but from the party's first awareness of the mistake. To avoid complications at trial, a party may identify prior to trial the documents intended to be offered, thereby triggering the obligation to assert any overlooked privilege under this rule. A trial court may also order this procedure.

5. This rule imposes no duty to supplement or amend deposition testimony. The only duty to supplement deposition testimony is provided in Rule 195.6.

6. Any party can request a hearing in which the court will resolve issues brought up in objections or withholding statements. The party seeking to avoid discovery has the burden of proving the objection or privilege.

7. The self-authenticating provision is new. Authentication is, of course, but a condition precedent to admissibility and does not establish admissibility. *See* Tex. R. Evid. 901(a). The ten-day period allowed for objection to authenticity (which period may be altered by the court in appropriate circumstances) does not run from the production of the material or information but from the party's actual awareness that the document will be used. To avoid complications at trial, a party may identify prior to trial the documents intended to be offered, thereby triggering the obligation to object to authenticity. A trial court may also order this procedure. An objection to authenticity must be made in good faith.

Source: New rule.

See also **O'Connor's Texas Rules**, "General Rules for Discovery," ch. 6-A, §1 et seq.; **O'Connor's Texas Rules**, "Scope of Discovery," ch. 6-B, §1 et seq.; **O'Connor's Texas Forms**, FORMS 6A:9 6A:15, 6A:16, 6A:19, 6A:20, 6A:21, 6A:22.

ANNOTATIONS

TRCP 193.1—Duty

Lucas v. Clark, 347 S.W.3d 800, 805 (Tex.App.—Austin 2011, pet. denied). "[T]ypically any challenge to a request for admission must be in compliance with Rule 193.1, [but the] question of a deemed admission's overbreadth only arises when a request for admission has been deemed admitted, which, by definition, occurs after a party has failed to timely respond or object to the request. No request for admission would be deemed admitted if the responding party had objected in writing within the parameters of Rule 193.1. Therefore, were we to require a party to object in writing to a request for admission's overbreadth in order to preserve the issue on appeal, no appellate court would ever face the issue. [¶] [N]o objection was necessary to reach the merits of the issue in this Court. This is true because the question before us is one of evidentiary sufficiency rather than procedural error. In viewing the effect of an overly broad request for admission, our analysis centers on whether a trial court is permitted to find that the request for admission irrefutably established the facts therein such that no additional evidence is required."

TRCP 193.2—Objections

General Motors Corp. v. Tanner, 892 S.W.2d 862, 863 (Tex.1995). "As the party objecting to the request, [P] was required to provide evidence in support of his objection."

TRCP 193.3—Privileges

In re Christus Spohn Hosp. Kleberg, 222 S.W.3d 434, 439 (Tex.2007). "The snap-back provision [in TRCP 193.3(d)] has typically been applied when a party inadvertently produces privileged documents to an opposing party. In this case, however, the privileged material was produced by a party to its own testifying expert, invoking [TRCP] 192.3(e)(6)'s overlapping directive that all materials provided to a testifying expert must be produced. *At 440-41:* [TRCP] 192.3(e)(6) and 192.5(c)(1) prevail over Rule

193.3(d)'s snap-back provision so long as the expert intends to testify at trial despite the inadvertent document production. That is, once privileged documents are disclosed to a testifying expert, and the party who designated the expert continues to rely upon that designation for trial, the documents may not be retrieved even if they were inadvertently produced. Of course, inadvertently produced material that could not by its nature have influenced the expert's opinion does not evoke the concerns [TRCP 192.3(e)] was designed to prevent and the policy concerns underlying the rule's disclosure requirement would presumably never arise. In that event, there would be nothing to prevent the snap-back rule's application, although we note that a party seeking snap-back under such circumstances would bear a heavy burden in light of the ... rule's underlying purpose. *At 445:* An attorney who discovers that privileged documents have been inadvertently provided to a testifying expert may presumably withdraw the expert's designation and name another."

In re E.I. DuPont de Nemours & Co., 136 S.W.3d 218, 223 (Tex.2004). "[A]n affidavit, even if it addresses groups of documents rather than each document individually, has been held to be sufficient to make a prima facie showing of attorney-client and/or work product privilege. *At 224:* However, an affidavit is of no probative value if it merely presents global allegations that documents come within the asserted privilege. [D's affidavit] sets forth the factual basis for the applicability of the attorney-client and/or work product privileges to the documents at issue. [T]he specificity of [D's] affidavit and the log taken together are reasonably adequate to establish a prima facie case of privilege. . . ." *See also* **In re BP Prods.**, 263 S.W.3d 106, 113-14 (Tex.App.—Houston [1st Dist.] 2006, orig. proceeding).

In re Union Pac. Res., 22 S.W.3d 338, 340 (Tex.1999). "'Any party who seeks to deny the production of evidence must claim a specific privilege against such production. The burden is on the party asserting a privilege from discovery to produce evidence *concerning the applicability of a particular privilege.*'" *See also* **In re Monsanto Co.**, 998 S.W.2d 917, 926 (Tex.App.—Waco 1999, orig. proceeding).

In re FEDD Wireless, LLC, 567 S.W.3d 470, 476 (Tex.App.—Houston [14th Dist.] 2019, orig. proceeding). "[Ps] assert that [TRCP] 193.3(d) is unavailable to protect privileged information disclosed outside the written discovery context, such as when, as here, a party discloses a privileged document by relying on it to obtain traditional summary judgment. *At 477:* We disagree with [Ps] and conclude that the rule applies to the present circumstances by operation of [TRE] 511(b)(2). Rule 511 states the general rule governing when a privilege is waived by voluntary disclosure. . . . Exceptions apply, however, regardless [of] whether the disclosure occurs in the context of written discovery. . . . One of the excepted circumstances set out is inadvertent disclosure in a state civil proceeding. . .. Rule 511(b)(2) does not state that the inadvertent disclosure must occur in response to a written discovery request for the exception to apply. Thus, the exception to waiver of a lawyer-client or work-product privilege applies to any inadvertent disclosure in a state civil proceeding so long as the party asserting the privilege complies with rule 193.3(d). Accordingly, rule 193.3(d) applies with respect to the [document in this case] notwithstanding that the [document] was first disclosed as a motion for summary judgment exhibit rather than in response to a written discovery request."

In re Certain Underwriters at Lloyd's London, 294 S.W.3d 891, 902 (Tex.App.—Beaumont 2009, orig. proceeding). "Because the rules do not expressly define the term 'party who produces,' it is not clear that Rule 193.3(d) is confined to reach only parties to a suit. *At 903:* Because the law allows privileged information to be shared for certain purposes with specific others, privilege rules are necessarily designed to apply to persons other than the privilege's holder. Should the 'snap-back' provision apply only to the parties to the suit, that interpretation would effectively negate the privilege holder's enforcement rights when nonparties to the suit produce privileged information. Thus, we conclude that an interpretation of Rule 193.3(d) to read 'party who produces' as meaning 'party to the lawsuit who produces' would allow, rather than discourage, efforts to obtain privileged information from nonparties."

Warrantech Corp. v. Computer Adapters Servs., 134 S.W.3d 516, 524-25 (Tex.App.—Fort Worth 2004, no pet.). "The focus of Rule 193.3(d) is on the intent to waive the privilege, not the intent to produce the material or information. [A] party who fails to diligently screen documents before producing them does not waive a claim of privilege, and the ten-day period runs from the party's first awareness of the mistake, not from the date of production. [A] party may identify before trial the documents intended to be offered, thereby triggering the obligation to assert any overlooked privilege under this rule." *See also* **In re Certain Underwriters at Lloyd's London**, 294 S.W.3d 891, 904 (Tex.App.—Beaumont 2009, orig. proceeding).

TRCP 193.4—Hearing

In re CI Host, Inc., 92 S.W.3d 514, 517 (Tex.2002). "Our discovery rules do not require notice to third parties so that they might have an opportunity to be heard on their own objections."

TRCP 193.5—Supplementing Discovery

Titus Cty. Hosp. Dist. v. Lucas, 988 S.W.2d 740, 740 (Tex.1998). TRCP 166b(6), now 193.5, "requires supplementation of a 'response' to a 'request for discovery.' An interrogatory answer is a response to a request for discovery, but testimony in a deposition is not. A general duty to supplement deposition testimony (as opposed to a narrow duty for certain expert testimony, for example) would impose too great a burden on litigants. We therefore disapprove the court of appeals' holding that deposition testimony must be supplemented."

Exxon Corp. v. West Tex. Gathering Co., 868 S.W.2d 299, 304 (Tex.1993). "Our rules do not prevent experts from

refining calculations and perfecting reports through the time of trial. The testimony of an expert should not be barred because a change in some minor detail of the person's work has not been disclosed a month before trial. The additional supplementation requirement of [TRCP 166b(6), now TRCP 193.5,] does require that opposing parties have sufficient information about an expert's opinion to prepare a rebuttal with their own experts and cross-examination, and that they be promptly and fully advised when further developments have rendered past information incorrect or misleading."

Christus Health Gulf Coast v. Carswell, 433 S.W.3d 585, 614 (Tex.App.—Houston [1st Dist.] 2013), *rev'd in part on other grounds*, 505 S.W.3d 528 (Tex.2016). "The trial court may impose monetary sanctions on a party for its failure to supplement its discovery responses in a timely manner [under TRCP 193.5]."

Snider v. Stanley, 44 S.W.3d 713, 715 (Tex.App.—Beaumont 2001, pet. denied). "'An amended or supplemental response must be made reasonably promptly after the party discovers the necessity for such a response.' It is presumed that response made within 30 days of trial is not reasonably promptly made. [D's] response, made 30 days before trial, is not subject to the presumption. [Ps] argue that the opposite presumption applies, that is, the supplementation was made reasonably promptly. We disagree. Had such a presumption been intended, it would have been incorporated into the rules."

TRCP 193.6—Effect of Failing to Respond

Alvarado v. Farah Mfg. Co., 830 S.W.2d 911, 914 (Tex.1992). The salutary purpose of TRCP 193.6 "is to require complete responses to discovery so as to promote responsible assessment of settlement and prevent trial by ambush. The rule is mandatory, and its sole sanction—exclusion of evidence—is automatic, unless there is good cause to excuse its imposition. The good cause exception permits a trial court to excuse a failure to comply with discovery in difficult or impossible circumstances. The trial court has discretion to determine whether the offering party has met his burden of showing good cause to admit the testimony; but the trial court has no discretion to admit testimony excluded by the rule without a showing of good cause." *See also* **Hydrogeo, LLC v. Quitman ISD**, 483 S.W.3d 51, 56 (Tex.App.—Texarkana 2016, no pet.); **Reservoir Sys. v. TGS-NOPEC Geophysical Co.**, 335 S.W.3d 297, 310-11 (Tex.App.—Houston [14th Dist.] 2010, pet. denied).

TRCP 193.7—Self-Authenticating

Blanche v. First Nationwide Mortg. Corp., 74 S.W.3d 444, 451-52 (Tex.App.—Dallas 2002, no pet.). TRCP 193.7 "alleviate[s] the burden on a party receiving documents through discovery from proving the authenticity of those documents when they are used against the party who produced them. Rule 193.7 does not help [Ps] here because the documents attached to their summary judgment response were not produced to them by [D], the party against whom the documents were used. . . . A party cannot authenticate a document for use in its own favor by merely producing it in response to a discovery request."

TRCP 194. REQUIRED DISCLOSURES

194.1. Request.

Text of rule effective for cases filed before January 1, 2021.

A party may obtain disclosure from another party of the information or material listed in Rule 194.2 by serving the other party—no later than 30 days before the end of any applicable discovery period—the following request: "Pursuant to Rule 194, you are requested to disclose, within 30 days of service of this request, the information or material described in Rule [state rule, e.g., 194.2, or 194.2(a), (c), and (f), or 194.2(d)–(g)]."

194.1. Duty to Disclose; Production.

Text of rule effective for cases filed on or after January 1, 2021.

(a) ***Duty to Disclose.*** Except as exempted by Rule 194.2(d) or as otherwise agreed by the parties or ordered by the court, a party must, without awaiting a discovery request, provide to the other parties the information or material described in Rule 194.2, 194.3, and 194.4.

(b) ***Production.*** If a party does not produce copies of all responsive documents, electronically stored information, and tangible things with the response, the response must state a reasonable time and method for the production of these items. The responding party must produce the items at the time and in the method stated, unless otherwise agreed by the parties or ordered by the court, and must provide the requesting party a reasonable opportunity to inspect them.

194.2. Content.

Text of rule effective for cases filed before January 1, 2021.

A party may request disclosure of any or all of the following:

(a) the correct names of the parties to the lawsuit;

(b) the name, address, and telephone number of any potential parties;

(c) the legal theories and, in general, the factual bases of the responding party's claims or defenses (the responding party need not marshal all evidence that may be offered at trial);

(d) the amount and any method of calculating economic damages;

(e) the name, address, and telephone number of persons having knowledge of relevant facts, and a brief statement of each identified person's connection with the case;

(f) for any testifying expert:

(1) the expert's name, address, and telephone number;

(2) the subject matter on which the expert will testify;

(3) the general substance of the expert's mental impressions and opinions and a brief summary of the basis for them, or if the expert is not retained by, employed by, or otherwise subject to the control of the responding party, documents reflecting such information;

(4) if the expert is retained by, employed by, or otherwise subject to the control of the responding party:

(A) all documents, tangible things, reports, models, or data compilations that have been provided to, reviewed by, or prepared by or for the expert in anticipation of the expert's testimony; and

(B) the expert's current resume and bibliography;

(g) any indemnity and insuring agreements described in Rule 192.3(f);

(h) any settlement agreements described in Rule 192.3(g);

(i) any witness statements described in Rule 192.3(h);

(j) in a suit alleging physical or mental injury and damages from the occurrence that is the subject of the case, all medical records and bills that are reasonably related to the injuries or damages asserted or, in lieu thereof, an authorization permitting the disclosure of such medical records and bills;

(k) in a suit alleging physical or mental injury and damages from the occurrence that is the subject of the case, all medical records and bills obtained by the responding party by virtue of an authorization furnished by the requesting party;

(*l*) the name, address, and telephone number of any person who may be designated as a responsible third party.

194.2. Initial Disclosures.

Text of rule effective for cases filed on or after January 1, 2021.

(a) ***Time for Initial Disclosures.*** A party must make the initial disclosures within 30 days after the filing of the first answer or general appearance unless a different time is set by the parties' agreement or court order. A party that is first served or otherwise joined after the filing of the first answer or general appearance must make the initial disclosures within 30 days after being served or joined, unless a different time is set by the parties' agreement or court order.

(b) ***Content.*** Without awaiting a discovery request, a party must provide to the other parties:

(1) the correct names of the parties to the lawsuit;

(2) the name, address, and telephone number of any potential parties;

(3) the legal theories and, in general, the factual bases of the responding party's claims or defenses (the responding party need not marshal all evidence that may be offered at trial);

(4) the amount and any method of calculating economic damages;

(5) the name, address, and telephone number of persons having knowledge of relevant facts, and a brief statement of each identified person's connection with the case;

(6) a copy—or a description by category and location—of all documents, electronically stored information, and tangible things that the responding party has in its possession, custody, or control, and may use to support its claims or defenses, unless the use would be solely for impeachment;

(7) any indemnity and insuring agreements described in Rule 192.3(f);

(8) any settlement agreements described in Rule 192.3(g);

(9) any witness statements described in Rule 192.3(h);

(10) in a suit alleging physical or mental injury and damages from the occurrence that is the subject of the case, all medical records and bills that are reasonably related to the injuries or damages asserted or, in lieu thereof, an authorization permitting the disclosure of such medical records and bills;

(11) in a suit alleging physical or mental injury and damages from the occurrence that is the subject of the case, all medical records and bills obtained by the responding party by virtue of an authorization furnished by the requesting party; and

(12) the name, address, and telephone number of any person who may be designated as a responsible third party.

(c) ***Content in Certain Suits Under the Family Code.***

(1) In a suit for divorce, annulment, or to declare a marriage void, a party must, without awaiting a discovery

request, provide to the other party the following, for the past two years or since the date of marriage, whichever is less:

(A) all deed and lien information on any real property owned and all lease information on any real property leased;

(B) all statements for any pension plan, retirement plan, profit-sharing plan, employee benefit plan, and individual retirement plan;

(C) all statements or policies for each current life, casualty, liability, and health insurance policy; and

(D) all statements pertaining to any account at a financial institution, including banks, savings and loans institutions, credit unions, and brokerage firms.

(2) In a suit in which child or spousal support is at issue, a party must, without awaiting a discovery request, provide to the other party:

(A) information regarding all policies, statements, and the summary description of benefits for any medical and health insurance coverage that is or would be available for the child or the spouse;

(B) the party's income tax returns for the previous two years or, if no return has been filed, the party's Form W-2, Form 1099, and Schedule K-1 for such years; and

(C) the party's two most recent payroll check stubs.

(d) ***Proceedings Exempt from Initial Disclosure.*** The following proceedings are exempt from initial disclosure, but a court may order the parties to make particular disclosures and set the time for disclosure:

(1) an action for review on an administrative record;

(2) a forfeiture action arising from a state statute;

(3) a petition for habeas corpus;

(4) an action under the Family Code filed by or against the Title IV-D agency in a Title IV-D case;

(5) a child protection action under Subtitle E, Title 5 of the Family Code;

(6) a protective order action under Title 4 of the Texas Family Code;

(7) other actions involving domestic violence; and

(8) an action on appeal from a justice court.

194.3. Response.

Text of rule effective for cases filed before January 1, 2021.

The responding party must serve a written response on the requesting party within 30 days after service of the request, except that:

(a) a defendant served with a request before the defendant's answer is due need not respond until 50 days after service of the request, and

(b) a response to a request under Rule 194.2(f) is governed by Rule 195.[1]

[1] Vernon's Ann.Rules Civ.Proc., rule 195.1 et seq.

194.3. Testifying Expert Disclosures.

Text of rule effective for cases filed on or after January 1, 2021.

In addition to the disclosures required by Rule 194.2, a party must disclose to the other parties testifying expert information as provided by Rule 195.

194.4. Production.

Text of rule effective for cases filed before January 1, 2021.

Copies of documents and other tangible items ordinarily must be served with the response. But if the responsive documents are voluminous, the response must state a reasonable time and place for the production of documents. The responding party must produce the documents at the time and place stated, unless otherwise agreed by the parties or ordered by the court, and must provide the requesting party a reasonable opportunity to inspect them.

194.4. Pretrial Disclosures.

Text of rule effective for cases filed on or after January 1, 2021.

(a) ***In General.*** In addition to the disclosures required by Rule 194.2 and 194.3, a party must provide to the other parties and promptly file the following information about the evidence that it may present at trial other than solely for impeachment:

(1) the name and, if not previously provided, the address, and telephone number of each witness—separately identifying those the party expects to present and those it may call if the need arises;

(2) an identification of each document or other exhibits, including summaries of other evidence—separately identifying those items the party expects to offer and those it may offer if the need arises.

(b) ***Time for Pretrial Disclosures.*** Unless the court orders otherwise, these disclosures must be made at least 30 days before trial.

(c) ***Proceedings Exempt from Pretrial Disclosure.*** An action arising under the Family Code filed by or against the Title IV-D agency in a Title IV-D case is exempt from pretrial disclosure, but a court may order the

parties to make particular disclosures and set the time for disclosure.

194.5. No Objection or Assertion of Work Product.

Text of rule effective for cases filed before January 1, 2021.

No objection or assertion of work product is permitted to a request under this rule.

Text of rule effective for cases filed on or after January 1, 2021.

No objection or assertion of work product is permitted to a disclosure under this rule.

194.6. Certain Responses Not Admissible.

Text of rule effective for cases filed before January 1, 2021.

A response to requests under Rule 194.2(c) and (d) that has been changed by an amended or supplemental response is not admissible and may not be used for impeachment.

Text of rule effective for cases filed on or after January 1, 2021.

A disclosure under Rule 194.2(b)(3) and (4) that has been changed by an amended or supplemental response is not admissible and may not be used for impeachment.

Aug. 5, 1998 and Nov. 9, 1998, eff. Jan. 1, 1999. Amended by order of March 3, 2004, eff. March 3, 2004; Dec. 23, 2020, eff. Jan. 1, 2021.

Comment—2021

Rule 194 is amended to implement section 22.004(h-1) of the Texas Government Code. Rule 194 is amended based on Federal Rule of Civil Procedure 26(a) to require disclosure of basic discovery automatically, without awaiting a discovery request. A party is not excused from making its disclosures because it has not fully investigated the case or because it challenges the sufficiency of another party's disclosures or because another party has not made its disclosures. As with other written discovery responses, required disclosures must be signed under Rule 191.3, complete under Rule 193.1, served under Rule 191.5, and timely amended or supplemented under Rule 193.5.

Comment—1999

1. Disclosure is designed to afford parties basic discovery of specific categories of information, not automatically in every case, but upon request, without preparation of a lengthy inquiry, and without objection or assertion of work product. In those extremely rare cases when information ordinarily discoverable should be protected, such as when revealing a person's residence might result in harm to the person, a party may move for protection. A party may assert any applicable privileges other than work product using the procedures of Rule 193.3 applicable to other written discovery. Otherwise, to fail to respond fully to a request for disclosure would be an abuse of the discovery process.

2. Rule 194.2(c) and (d) permit a party further inquiry into another's legal theories and factual claims than is often provided in notice pleadings. So-called "contention interrogatories" are used for the same purpose. Such interrogatories are not properly used to require a party to marshal evidence or brief legal issues. Paragraphs (c) and (d) are intended to require disclosure of a party's basic assertions, whether in prosecution of claims or in defense. Thus, for example, a plaintiff would be required to disclose that he or she claimed damages suffered in a car wreck caused by defendant's negligence in speeding, and would be required to state how loss of past earnings and future earning capacity was calculated, but would not be required to state the speed at which defendant was allegedly driving. Paragraph (d) does not require a party, either a plaintiff or a defendant, to state a method of calculating non-economic damages, such as for mental anguish. In the same example, defendant would be required to disclose his or her denial of the speeding allegation and any basis for contesting the damage calculations.

3. Responses under Rule 194.2(c) and (d) that have been amended or supplemented are inadmissible and cannot be used for impeachment, but other evidence of changes in position is not likewise barred.

Source: New rule.

See also **O'Connor's Texas Rules**, "General Rules for Discovery," ch. 6-A, §1 et seq.; **O'Connor's Texas Rules**, "Securing Discovery from Experts," ch. 6-D, §1 et seq.; **O'Connor's Texas Rules**, "Disclosures," ch. 6-E, §1 et seq.; **O'Connor's Texas Forms**, FORMS 6D, 6E, 6J:1.

ANNOTATIONS

In re Dawson, 550 S.W.3d 625, 629 (Tex.2018). "Rule 194.2(*l*)[, now TRCP 194.2(b)(12),] required [D] to disclose 'the name, address, and telephone number of any person who may be designated as a responsible third party.' The only response [D] gave ... before limitations ran was 'Defendant will supplement.' Even after limitations had passed, [D] disclosed only [potential responsible third party's] name and phone number; the record does not show it ever provided his address. *At 630:* Perhaps the better course would've been for [P] to independently investigate the extent of [potential responsible third party's] involvement before limitations expired. But a plaintiff's determination of 'who may be designated as a responsible third party' doesn't require such an independent investigation. The [TRCPs] require the defendant to disclose that information.... [D] argues that it accomplished that disclosure by mentioning [potential responsible third party's] name in one place, including boilerplate language about unnamed 'persons or entities' it purported caused [P's] injuries in another, and [stating] 'will supplement' ... the identity of possible responsible third parties. [¶] We hold [D] did not satisfy [its] obligations under Rule 194.2(*l*). . . ."

In re Staff Care, Inc., 422 S.W.3d 876, 881 (Tex.App.—Dallas 2014, orig. proceeding). "[T]here is no presumption that an amended disclosure made more than 30 days prior to trial is timely."

TRCP 195. DISCOVERY REGARDING TESTIFYING EXPERT WITNESSES

195.1. Permissible Discovery Tools.

Text of rule effective for cases filed before January 1, 2021.

A party may request another party to designate and disclose information concerning testifying expert witnesses only through a request for disclosure under Rule 194 and through depositions and reports as permitted by this rule.

Text of rule effective for cases filed on or after January 1, 2021.

A party may obtain information concerning testifying expert witnesses only through disclosure under this rule and through depositions and reports as permitted by this rule.

195.2. Schedule for Designating Experts.

Text of undesignated paragraph effective for cases filed before January 1, 2021.

Unless otherwise ordered by the court, a party must designate experts—that is, furnish information requested under Rule 194.2(f)—by the later of the following two dates: 30 days after the request is served, or

Text of undesignated paragraph effective for cases filed on or after January 1, 2021.

Unless otherwise ordered by the court, a party must designate experts—that is, furnish information described in Rule 195.5(a)—by the following dates:

(a) with regard to all experts testifying for a party seeking affirmative relief, 90 days before the end of the discovery period;

(b) with regard to all other experts, 60 days before the end of the discovery period.

195.3. Scheduling Depositions.

(a) *Experts for Party Seeking Affirmative Relief.* A party seeking affirmative relief must make an expert retained by, employed by, or otherwise in the control of the party available for deposition as follows:

(1) *If no report furnished.* If a report of the expert's factual observations, tests, supporting data, calculations, photographs, and opinions is not produced when the expert is designated, then the party must make the expert available for deposition reasonably promptly after the expert is designated. If the deposition cannot—due to the actions of the tendering party—reasonably be concluded more than 15 days before the deadline for designating other experts, that deadline must be extended for other experts testifying on the same subject.

(2) *If report furnished.* If a report of the expert's factual observations, tests, supporting data, calculations, photographs, and opinions is produced when the expert is designated, then the party need not make the expert available for deposition until reasonably promptly after all other experts have been designated.

(b) *Other Experts.* A party not seeking affirmative relief must make an expert retained by, employed by, or otherwise in the control of the party available for deposition reasonably promptly after the expert is designated and the experts testifying on the same subject for the party seeking affirmative relief have been deposed.

195.4. Oral Deposition.

Text of rule effective for cases filed before January 1, 2021.

In addition to disclosure under Rule 194, a party may obtain discovery concerning the subject matter on which the expert is expected to testify, the expert's mental impressions and opinions, the facts known to the expert (regardless of when the factual information was acquired) that relate to or form the basis of the testifying expert's mental impressions and opinions, and other discoverable matters, including documents not produced in disclosure, only by oral deposition of the expert and by a report prepared by the expert under this rule.

Text of rule effective for cases filed on or after January 1, 2021.

In addition to the information disclosed under Rule 195.5(a), a party may obtain discovery concerning the subject matter on which the expert is expected to testify, the expert's mental impressions and opinions, the facts known to the expert (regardless of when the factual information was acquired) that relate to or form the basis of the testifying expert's mental impressions and opinions, and other discoverable matters, including documents not produced in disclosure, only by oral deposition of the expert and by a report prepared by the expert under this rule.

195.5. Court-Ordered Reports.

Text of rule effective for cases filed before January 1, 2021.

If the discoverable factual observations, tests, supporting data, calculations, photographs, or opinions of an expert have not been recorded and reduced to tangible form, the court may order these matters reduced to tangible form and produced in addition to the deposition.

195.5. Expert Disclosures and Reports.

Text of rule effective for cases filed on or after January 1, 2021.

(a) *Disclosures.* Without awaiting a discovery request, a party must provide the following for any testifying expert:

(1) the expert's name, address, and telephone number;

(2) the subject matter on which the expert will testify;

(3) the general substance of the expert's mental impressions and opinions and a brief summary of the basis for them, or if the expert is not retained by, employed by, or otherwise subject to the control of the responding party, documents reflecting such information;

(4) if the expert is retained by, employed by, or otherwise subject to the control of the responding party:

(A) all documents, tangible things, reports, models, or data compilations that have been provided to, reviewed by, or prepared by or for the expert in anticipation of the expert's testimony;

(B) the expert's current resume and bibliography;

(C) the expert's qualifications, including a list of all publications authored in the previous 10 years;

(D) except when the expert is the responding party's attorney and is testifying to attorney fees, a list of all other cases in which, during the previous four years, the expert testified as an expert at trial or by deposition; and

(E) a statement of the compensation to be paid for the expert's study and testimony in the case.

(b) ***Expert Reports.*** If the discoverable factual observations, tests, supporting data, calculations, photographs, or opinions of an expert have not been recorded and reduced to tangible form, the court may order these matters reduced to tangible form and produced in addition to the deposition.

(c) ***Expert Communications Protected.*** Communications between the party's attorney and any testifying expert witness in the case are protected from discovery, regardless of the form of the communications, except to the extent that the communications:

(1) relate to compensation for the expert's study or testimony;

(2) identify facts or data that the party's attorney provided and that the expert considered in forming the opinions to be expressed; or

(3) identify assumptions that the party's attorney provided and that the expert relied on in forming the opinions to be expressed.

(d) ***Draft Expert Reports and Disclosures Protected.*** A draft expert report or draft disclosure required under this rule is protected from discovery, regardless of the form in which the draft is recorded.

195.6. Amendment and Supplementation. A party's duty to amend and supplement written discovery regarding a testifying expert is governed by Rule 193.5. If an expert witness is retained by, employed by, or otherwise under the control of a party, that party must also amend or supplement any deposition testimony or written report by the expert, but only with regard to the expert's mental impressions or opinions and the basis for them.

195.7. Cost of Expert Witnesses. When a party takes the oral deposition of an expert witness retained by the opposing party, all reasonable fees charged by the expert for time spent in preparing for, giving, reviewing, and correcting the deposition must be paid by the party that retained the expert.

Aug. 5, 1998 and Nov. 9, 1998, eff. Jan. 1, 1999. Amended by order of Dec. 23, 2020, eff. Jan. 1, 2021.

Comment—2021

Rule 195 is amended to reflect changes to Rule 194. Amended Rule 195.5(a) lists the disclosures for any testifying expert, which are now required without awaiting a discovery request, that were formerly listed in Rule 194(f). Amended Rule 195.5(a) also includes three new disclosures based on Federal Rule of Civil Procedure 26(a)(2)(B). New Rules 195.5(b) and (c) are based on Federal Rules of Civil Procedure 26(b)(4)(B) and (C) and are added to clarify protections available.

Editor's Note: The reference to Rules 195.5(b) and (c) in the 2021 comment should be to Rules 195.5(c) and (d).

Comment—1999

1. This rule does not limit the permissible methods of discovery concerning consulting experts whose mental impressions or opinions have been reviewed by a testifying expert. See Rule 192.3(e). Information concerning purely consulting experts, of course, is not discoverable.

2. This rule and Rule 194 do not address depositions of testifying experts who are not retained by, employed by, or otherwise subject to the control of the responding party, nor the production of the materials identified in Rule 192.3(e)(5) and (6) relating to such experts. Parties may obtain this discovery, however, through Rules 176 and 205.

3. In scheduling the designations and depositions of expert witnesses, the rule attempts to minimize unfair surprise and undue expense. A party seeking affirmative relief must either produce an expert's report or tender the expert for deposition before an opposing party is required to designate experts. A party who does not wish to incur the expense of a report may simply tender the expert for deposition, but a party who wishes an expert to have the benefit of an opposing party's expert's opinions before being deposed may trigger designation by providing a report. Rule 191.1 permits a trial court, for good cause, to modify the order or deadlines for designating and deposing experts and the allocation of fees and expenses.

Source: New rule.

See also **O'Connor's Texas Rules**, "General Rules for Discovery," ch. 6-A, §1 et seq.; **O'Connor's Texas Rules**, "Securing Discovery from Experts," ch. 6-D, §1 et seq.; **O'Connor's Texas Rules**, "Disclosures," ch. 6-E, §1 et seq.; **O'Connor's Texas Rules**, "Depositions," ch. 6-F, §1 et seq.; **O'Connor's Texas Forms**, FORMS 6D, 6E, 6F:1, 6F:2, 6F:3.

ANNOTATIONS

In re Ford Motor Co., 427 S.W.3d 396, 397 (Tex.2014). "In his deposition notices to [experts' employers], [P sought] sensitive information covering 12 years, [which was an] overbroad discovery [request]. [¶] By holding that the requested discovery is impermissible in this case, we do not unduly inhibit discovery of an expert's potential bias. *At 398:* Indeed, the most probative information regarding the bias of a testifying expert comes from the expert herself. [¶] [P] argues that we have recognized at least one instance in which deposing the expert's employer was justified. In **Walker v. Packer**[, 827 S.W.2d 833 (Tex.1992)], we held that discovery beyond the individual expert's deposition might be permissible when extrinsic evidence, discovered after the expert's deposition, puts his credibility in doubt. [¶] Assuming that this aspect of our holding in **Walker** survived the adoption of Rule 195, we disagree that [it] compels the result [P] seeks. Unlike **Walker**, neither expert's credibility has been impugned in this case. And [P] has not demonstrated any other circumstance to warrant deposing the [expert] witnesses' employers' corporate representatives."

Moore v. Memorial Hermann Hosp. Sys., 140 S.W.3d 870, 875 (Tex.App.—Houston [14th Dist.] 2004, no pet.). "[P] claims that she was not required to disclose the information required under [TRCP] 194.2(f)[, now TRCP 195.5(a),] because [P's expert] was a rebuttal witness and not a

designated or retained expert. However, once [D] disclosed the opinions of . . . its testifying expert, [P] could reasonably have anticipated the need to rebut the testimony of [D's expert] at trial. Therefore, [P's expert] was simply an ordinary rebuttal witness whose use reasonably could have been anticipated; rebuttal witnesses as such are not exempt from the scope of the written discovery rules."

Snider v. Stanley, 44 S.W.3d 713, 716 (Tex.App.—Beaumont 2001, pet. denied). "[Ds] did not designate [their expert] as soon as he was retained, employed, or otherwise in their control. Instead, they waited until 30 days before trial. We hold the trial court did not abuse its discretion in finding [Ds] did not supplement their discovery responses 'reasonably promptly.'"

Castellanos v. Littlejohn, 945 S.W.2d 236, 239 (Tex.App.—San Antonio 1997, orig. proceeding). See annotation under TRCP 192, *Experts*.

TRCP 196. REQUESTS FOR PRODUCTION AND INSPECTION TO PARTIES; REQUESTS AND MOTIONS FOR ENTRY UPON PROPERTY

196.1. Request for Production and Inspection to Parties.

(a) ***Request.*** A party may serve on another party—no later than 30 days before the end of the discovery period—a request for production or for inspection, to inspect, sample, test, photograph and copy documents or tangible things within the scope of discovery.

(b) ***Contents of Request.*** The request must specify the items to be produced or inspected, either by individual item or by category, and describe with reasonable particularity each item and category. The request must specify a reasonable time (on or after the date on which the response is due) and place for production. If the requesting party will sample or test the requested items, the means, manner and procedure for testing or sampling must be described with sufficient specificity to inform the producing party of the means, manner, and procedure for testing or sampling.

(c) ***Requests for Production of Medical or Mental Health Records Regarding Nonparties.***

(1) *Service of Request on Nonparty.* If a party requests another party to produce medical or mental health records regarding a nonparty, the requesting party must serve the nonparty with the request for production under Rule 21a.

(2) *Exceptions.* A party is not required to serve the request for production on a nonparty whose medical records are sought if:

(A) the nonparty signs a release of the records that is effective as to the requesting party;

(B) the identity of the nonparty whose records are sought will not directly or indirectly be disclosed by production of the records; or

(C) the court, upon a showing of good cause by the party seeking the records, orders that service is not required.

(3) *Confidentiality.* Nothing in this rule excuses compliance with laws concerning the confidentiality of medical or mental health records.

196.2. Response to Request for Production and Inspection.

Text of subsec. (a) effective for cases filed before January 1, 2021.

(a) ***Time for Response.*** The responding party must serve a written response on the requesting party within 30 days after service of the request, except that a defendant served with a request before the defendant's answer is due need not respond until 50 days after service of the request.

Text of subsec. (a) effective for cases filed on or after January 1, 2021.

(a) ***Time for Response.*** The responding party must serve a written response on the requesting party within 30 days after service of the request.

(b) ***Content of Response.*** With respect to each item or category of items, the responding party must state objections and assert privileges as required by these rules, and state, as appropriate, that:

(1) production, inspection, or other requested action will be permitted as requested;

(2) the requested items are being served on the requesting party with the response;

(3) production, inspection, or other requested action will take place at a specified time and place, if the responding party is objecting to the time and place of production; or

(4) no items have been identified—after a diligent search—that are responsive to the request.

196.3. Production.

(a) ***Time and Place of Production.*** Subject to any objections stated in the response, the responding party must produce the requested documents or tangible things within the person's possession, custody or control at either the time and place requested or the time and place stated in the response, unless otherwise agreed by the parties or ordered by the court, and must provide the requesting party a reasonable opportunity to inspect them.

(b) ***Copies.*** The responding party may produce copies in lieu of originals unless a question is raised as to the authenticity of the original or in the circumstances it would be unfair to produce copies in lieu of originals. If originals

are produced, the responding party is entitled to retain the originals while the requesting party inspects and copies them.

(c) ***Organization.*** The responding party must either produce documents and tangible things as they are kept in the usual course of business or organize and label them to correspond with the categories in the request.

196.4. Electronic or Magnetic Data. To obtain discovery of data or information that exists in electronic or magnetic form, the requesting party must specifically request production of electronic or magnetic data and specify the form in which the requesting party wants it produced. The responding party must produce the electronic or magnetic data that is responsive to the request and is reasonably available to the responding party in its ordinary course of business. If the responding party cannot—through reasonable efforts—retrieve the data or information requested or produce it in the form requested, the responding party must state an objection complying with these rules. If the court orders the responding party to comply with the request, the court must also order that the requesting party pay the reasonable expenses of any extraordinary steps required to retrieve and produce the information.

196.5. Destruction or Alteration. Testing, sampling or examination of an item may not destroy or materially alter an item unless previously authorized by the court.

196.6. Expenses of Production. Unless otherwise ordered by the court for good cause, the expense of producing items will be borne by the responding party and the expense of inspecting, sampling, testing, photographing, and copying items produced will be borne by the requesting party.

196.7. Request or Motion for Entry Upon Property.

(a) ***Request or Motion.*** A party may gain entry on designated land or other property to inspect, measure, survey, photograph, test, or sample the property or any designated object or operation thereon by serving—no later than 30 days before the end of any applicable discovery period—

(1) a request on all parties if the land or property belongs to a party, or

(2) a motion and notice of hearing on all parties and the nonparty if the land or property belongs to a nonparty. If the identity or address of the nonparty is unknown and cannot be obtained through reasonable diligence, the court must permit service by means other than those specified in Rule 21a that are reasonably calculated to give the nonparty notice of the motion and hearing.

(b) ***Time, Place, and Other Conditions.*** The request for entry upon a party's property, or the order for entry upon a nonparty's property, must state the time, place, manner, conditions, and scope of the inspection, and must specifically describe any desired means, manner, and procedure for testing or sampling, and the person or persons by whom the inspection, testing, or sampling is to be made.

(c) ***Response to Request for Entry.***

Text of subsec. (1) effective for cases filed before January 1, 2021.

(1) *Time to Respond.* The responding party must serve a written response on the requesting party within 30 days after service of the request, except that a defendant served with a request before the defendant's answer is due need not respond until 50 days after service of the request.

Text of subsec. (1) effective for cases filed on or after January 1, 2021.

(1) *Time to Respond.* The responding party must serve a written response on the requesting party within 30 days after service of the request.

(2) *Content of Response.* The responding party must state objections and assert privileges as required by these rules, and state, as appropriate, that:

(A) entry or other requested action will be permitted as requested;

(B) entry or other requested action will take place at a specified time and place, if the responding party is objecting to the time and place of production; or

(C) entry or other requested action cannot be permitted for reasons stated in the response.

(d) ***Requirements for Order for Entry on Nonparty's Property.*** An order for entry on a nonparty's property may issue only for good cause shown and only if the land, property, or object thereon as to which discovery is sought is relevant to the subject matter of the action.

Aug. 5, 1998, Nov. 9, 1998 and Dec. 31, 1998, eff. Jan. 1, 1999. Amended by order of Dec. 23, 2020, eff. Jan. 1, 2021.

Comment—1999

1. "Document and tangible things" are defined in Rule 192.3(b).

2. A party requesting sampling or testing must describe the procedure with sufficient specificity to enable the responding party to make any appropriate objections.

3. A party requesting production of magnetic or electronic data must specifically request the data, specify the form in which it wants the data produced, and specify any extraordinary steps for retrieval and translation. Unless ordered otherwise, the responding party need only produce the data reasonably available in the ordinary course of business in reasonably usable form.

4. The rule clarifies how the expenses of production are to be allocated absent a court order to the contrary.

5. The obligation of parties to produce documents within their possession, custody or control is explained in Rule 192.3(b).

6. Parties may request production and inspection of documents and tangible things from nonparties under Rule 205.3.

7. Rule 196.3(b) is based on Tex. R. Evid. 1003.

8. Rule 196.1(c) is merely a notice requirement and does not expand the scope of discovery of a nonparty's medical records.

Source: New rule.

See also **O'Connor's Texas Rules**, "Discovery," ch. 6, §1 et seq.; **O'Connor's Texas Forms**, FORMS 6I, 6K.

ANNOTATIONS

In re State Farm Lloyds, 520 S.W.3d 595, 599-600 (Tex.2017). "Under our discovery rules, neither party may dictate the form of electronic discovery. The requesting party must specify the desired form of production, but all discovery is subject to the proportionality overlay embedded in our discovery rules and inherent in the reasonableness standard to which our electronic-discovery rule is tethered. [¶] [W]hen a party asserts that unreasonable efforts are required to produce [electronically stored information] in the requested form and a 'reasonably usable' alternative form is readily available, the trial court must balance any burden or expense of producing in the requested form against the relative benefits of doing so, the needs of the case, the amount in controversy, the parties' resources, the importance of the issues at stake in the litigation, and the importance of the requested format in resolving the issues. Even without quantifying differences in time and expense, evidence that a 'reasonably usable' alternative form is readily available gives rise to the need for balancing, and if these factors preponderate against production in the requested form, the trial court may order production as requested only if the requesting party shows a particularized need for data in that form and 'the requesting party pay[s] the reasonable expenses of any extraordinary steps required to retrieve and produce the information.'"

In re Weekley Homes, L.P., 295 S.W.3d 309, 314-15 (Tex.2009). "[E-]mail communications constitute 'electronic data,' and their characterization as such does not change when they are deleted from a party's inbox. Thus, deleted emails are within Rule 196.4's purview. . . . [I]t is a simple matter to request emails that have been deleted; knowledge as to the particular method or means of retrieving them is not necessary at the requesting stage of discovery. Once a specific request is made the parties can, and should, communicate as to the particularities of a party's computer storage system and potential methods of retrieval to assess the feasibility of their recovery. But even though it was not stated in [P's] written request that deleted emails were included within its scope, that [P] thought they were and was seeking this form of electronic information became abundantly clear in the course of discovery and before the hearing on the motion to compel. The purpose of Rule 196.4's specificity requirement is to ensure that requests for electronic information are clearly understood and disputes avoided. Because the scope of [P's] requests was understood before trial court intervention, [D] was not prejudiced by [P's] failure to follow the rule and the trial court did not abuse its discretion by ordering production of the deleted emails. To ensure compliance with the rules and avoid confusion, however, parties seeking production of deleted emails should expressly request them." *See also* **In re Shipman**, 540 S.W.3d 562, 566-67 (Tex.2018); **In re Harris**, 315 S.W.3d 685, 700-01 (Tex.App.—Houston [1st Dist.] 2010, orig. proceeding).

In re Colonial Pipeline Co., 968 S.W.2d 938, 942 (Tex.1998). "While [Ps] may be entitled to production of any relevant discovery from the related cases 'as they are kept in the usual course of business,' [Ds] cannot be forced to prepare an inventory of the documents for [Ps]."

General Motors Corp. v. Gayle, 951 S.W.2d 469, 475-76 (Tex.1997). "[Ps] rely on [TRCP] 167(1)(b) [now TRCP 196.7(a)] to support their claim to attend [D's crash] testing. . . . The rule allowing entry upon land does not render discoverable items which are privileged under [TRCP 193.3]. [TRCP 196.7(a)] does not authorize [Ps] to enter into testing facilities under [D's] control to view privileged tests."

In re Goodyear Tire & Rubber Co., 437 S.W.3d 923, 928 (Tex.App.—Dallas 2014, orig. proceeding). "Although a request for entry upon land must satisfy the general requirement of relevance, mere relevance is not sufficient to justify a request for entry upon the property of another. Discovery involving entry onto the property of another involves unique burdens and risks including, among other things, confusion and disruption of the defendant's business and employees. Thus, the trial court should conduct a 'greater inquiry into the necessity for the inspection, testing, or sampling.' In conducting such an inquiry, the court must balance the degree to which the proposed inspection will aid in the search for truth against the burdens and dangers created by the inspection. *At 929:* Rule 196.7 does not provide for the creation of new evidence for demonstrative purposes. [¶] The video [Ps] seek to record falls into the category of 'new evidence.' [It] does not attempt to document the process used in making the actual tire at issue in the case nor does it document the condition of the plant at the time that the tire was manufactured. Rather, . . . it will document work performed by different workers, using either a different machine or making a different tire, under different conditions."

In re Waste Mgmt., 392 S.W.3d 861, 874-75 (Tex.App.—Texarkana 2013, orig. proceeding). "[P's] first and third requests [for electronic discovery] contained the following instruction: 'Any and all data or information which is in electronic or magnetic form should be produced in a reasonable manner.' [¶] [D] cites [**In re Weekley Homes, L.P.**, 295 S.W.3d 309 (Tex.2009),] for the proposition that requests for production of electronic records must be 'clearly understood' so that disputes can be avoided. The Texas Supreme

Court, though, was not referring to specificity concerning the file format, but was referring to the subject matter being requested, 'deleted emails.' We do not read **Weekley Homes** as requiring . . . that the requesting party must specify the exact computer file format. [¶] A request for reasonably useable or a reasonable manner is sufficient. It provides some flexibility to the producing party. For example, a request for docx file format used by Microsoft Word 2010 might require some producing parties to purchase the specific software requested and expend resources converting files to the requested format. On the other hand, if the request was simply for a 'reasonably useable' electronic discovery, the producing party could produce files in Word Perfect X4 format instead. [I]f a party feels a request is too ambiguous, that party should contact the opposing side. A small amount of ambiguity, though, does not give the producing party *carte blanche* to do whatever it wants. [W]e have not been directed to any communication in which [P] agreed PDF files would suffice. [P's] request that the form be a 'reasonable manner' is sufficiently specific."

In re Family Dollar Stores, No. 09-11-00432-CV, 2011 WL 5299578 (Tex.App.—Beaumont 2011, orig. proceeding) (memo op.; 11-3-11). "Rule 196.4 . . . requires a specific request for production of electronic or magnetic data, and the request is required to specify the form in which the data is to be produced. [¶] [R]equiring a party to reduce raw data from an electronic database to a paper report or to a list in an electronic form requires [D] to make a list that does not currently exist. Because Rule 196.1 does not allow one party to require that others make lists, the trial court's amended discovery order is broader than the scope of discovery permitted by the [TRCPs]."

In re SWEPI L.P., 103 S.W.3d 578, 584 (Tex.App.—San Antonio 2003, orig. proceeding). "It does not appear any Texas court has directly addressed what constitutes 'good cause' for a discovery order allowing entry onto land. Generally, 'good cause' for a discovery order is shown where . . . (1) the discovery sought is relevant and material, that is, the information will in some way aid the movant in the preparation or defense of the case; and (2) the substantial equivalent of the material cannot be obtained through other means."

In re Lincoln Elec. Co., 91 S.W.3d 432, 437 (Tex.App.—Beaumont 2002, orig. proceeding). "In keeping with the overall spirit of non-waiver apparent in the . . . discovery rules . . ., we believe [TRCP 196.2(b)] permits a responding party . . . to make 'objections' to such things as vagueness, overbreadth, [and] relevance . . ., have these 'objections' ruled upon, and then make any assertions of privilege . . . at a later time."

TRCP 197. INTERROGATORIES TO PARTIES

197.1. Interrogatories. A party may serve on another party—no later than 30 days before the end of the discovery period—written interrogatories to inquire about any matter within the scope of discovery except matters covered by Rule 195.[1] An interrogatory may inquire whether a party makes a specific legal or factual contention and may ask the responding party to state the legal theories and to describe in general the factual bases for the party's claims or defenses, but interrogatories may not be used to require the responding party to marshal all of its available proof or the proof the party intends to offer at trial.

[1] Vernon's Ann.Rules Civ.Proc., rule 195.1 et seq.

197.2. Response to Interrogatories.

Text of subsec. (a) effective for cases filed before January 1, 2021.

(a) ***Time for Response.*** The responding party must serve a written response on the requesting party within 30 days after service of the interrogatories, except that a defendant served with interrogatories before the defendant's answer is due need not respond until 50 days after service of the interrogatories.

Text of subsec. (a) effective for cases filed on or after January 1, 2021.

(a) ***Time for Response.*** The responding party must serve a written response on the requesting party within 30 days after service of the interrogatories.

(b) ***Content of Response.*** A response must include the party's answers to the interrogatories and may include objections and assertions of privilege as required under these rules.

(c) ***Option to Produce Records.*** If the answer to an interrogatory may be derived or ascertained from public records, from the responding party's business records, or from a compilation, abstract or summary of the responding party's business records, and the burden of deriving or ascertaining the answer is substantially the same for the requesting party as for the responding party, the responding party may answer the interrogatory by specifying and, if applicable, producing the records or compilation, abstract or summary of the records. The records from which the answer may be derived or ascertained must be specified in sufficient detail to permit the requesting party to locate and identify them as readily as can the responding party. If the responding party has specified business records, the responding party must state a reasonable time and place for examination of the documents. The responding party must produce the documents at the time and place stated, unless otherwise agreed by the parties or ordered by the court, and must provide the requesting party a reasonable opportunity to inspect them.

(d) ***Verification Required; Exceptions.*** A responding party—not an agent or attorney as otherwise permitted by Rule 14—must sign the answers under oath except that:

(1) when answers are based on information obtained from other persons, the party may so state, and

(2) a party need not sign answers to interrogatories about persons with knowledge of relevant facts, trial witnesses, and legal contentions.

197.3. Use. Answers to interrogatories may be used only against the responding party. An answer to an interrogatory inquiring about matters described in Rule 194.2(c) and (d) that has been amended or supplemented is not admissible and may not be used for impeachment.

Aug. 5, 1998 and Nov. 9, 1998, eff. Jan. 1, 1999. Amended by order of Dec. 23, 2020, eff. Jan. 1, 2021.

Comment—1999

1. Interrogatories about specific legal or factual assertions—such as, whether a party claims a breach of implied warranty, or when a party contends that limitations began to run—are proper, but interrogatories that ask a party to state all legal and factual assertions are improper. As with requests for disclosure, interrogatories may be used to ascertain basic legal and factual claims and defenses but may not be used to force a party to marshal evidence. Use of the answers to such interrogatories is limited, just as the use of similar disclosures under Rule 194.6 is.

2. Rule 191's requirement that a party's attorney sign all discovery responses and objections applies to interrogatory responses and objections. In addition, the responding party must sign some interrogatory answers under oath, as specified by the rule. Answers in amended and supplemental responses must be signed by the party under oath only if the original answers were required to be signed under oath. The failure to sign or verify answers is only a formal defect that does not otherwise impair the answers unless the party refuses to sign or verify the answers after the defect is pointed out.

Source: New rule.

See also **O'Connor's Texas Rules**, "General Rules for Discovery," ch. 6-A, §1 et seq.; **O'Connor's Texas Rules**, "Interrogatories," ch. 6-G, §1 et seq.; **O'Connor's Texas Forms**, FORMS 6G.

ANNOTATIONS

Ticor Title Ins. v. Lacy, 803 S.W.2d 265, 266 (Tex.1991). " 'A party must be able to rely on the interrogatories and answers of other parties in the same suit. Otherwise, a multiparty case would require redundant interrogatories with identical questions and answers.' "

Palmer v. Espey Huston & Assocs., 84 S.W.3d 345, 356 (Tex.App.—Corpus Christi 2002, pet. denied). "[I]nterrogatories may be used only against the responding party."

TRCP 198. REQUESTS FOR ADMISSIONS

198.1. Request for Admissions. A party may serve on another party—no later than 30 days before the end of the discovery period—written requests that the other party admit the truth of any matter within the scope of discovery, including statements of opinion or of fact or of the application of law to fact, or the genuineness of any documents served with the request or otherwise made available for inspection and copying. Each matter for which an admission is requested must be stated separately.

198.2. Response to Requests for Admissions.

Text of subsec. (a) effective for cases filed before January 1, 2021.

(a) ***Time for Response.*** The responding party must serve a written response on the requesting party within 30 days after service of the request, except that a defendant served with a request before the defendant's answer is due need not respond until 50 days after service of the request.

Text of subsec. (a) effective for cases filed on or after January 1, 2021.

(a) ***Time for Response.*** The responding party must serve a written response on the requesting party within 30 days after service of the request.

(b) ***Content of Response.*** Unless the responding party states an objection or asserts a privilege, the responding party must specifically admit or deny the request or explain in detail the reasons that the responding party cannot admit or deny the request. A response must fairly meet the substance of the request. The responding party may qualify an answer, or deny a request in part, only when good faith requires. Lack of information or knowledge is not a proper response unless the responding party states that a reasonable inquiry was made but that the information known or easily obtainable is insufficient to enable the responding party to admit or deny. An assertion that the request presents an issue for trial is not a proper response.

(c) ***Effect of Failure to Respond.*** If a response is not timely served, the request is considered admitted without the necessity of a court order.

198.3. Effect of Admissions; Withdrawal or Amendment. Any admission made by a party under this rule may be used solely in the pending action and not in any other proceeding. A matter admitted under this rule is conclusively established as to the party making the admission unless the court permits the party to withdraw or amend the admission. The court may permit the party to withdraw or amend the admission if:

(a) the party shows good cause for the withdrawal or amendment; and

(b) the court finds that the parties relying upon the responses and deemed admissions will not be unduly prejudiced and that the presentation of the merits of the action will be subserved by permitting the party to amend or withdraw the admission.

Aug. 5, 1998 and Nov. 9, 1998, eff. Jan. 1, 1999. Amended by order of Dec. 23, 2020, eff. Jan. 1, 2021.

Source: New rule.

See also **O'Connor's Texas Rules**, "General Rules for Discovery," ch. 6-A, §1 et seq.; **O'Connor's Texas Rules**, "Requests for Admissions," ch. 6-H, §1 et seq.; **O'Connor's Texas Forms**, FORMS 6H.

ANNOTATIONS

U.S. Fid. & Guar. Co. v. Goudeau, 272 S.W.3d 603, 610 (Tex.2008). "[A] party appearing in one capacity cannot be bound by an admission sent to it in another, because admissions are binding only against 'the party making the admission.'" Held: P could not use admissions from insurance carrier in its capacity as intervenor against same insurance company in its capacity as D.

Wheeler v. Green, 157 S.W.3d 439, 442 (Tex.2005). "[W]ithdrawing deemed admissions . . . is proper upon a showing of (1) good cause, and (2) no undue prejudice. Good cause is established by showing the failure [to respond] was an accident or mistake, not intentional or the result of conscious indifference. *At 443:* Undue prejudice depends on whether withdrawing an admission . . . will delay trial or significantly hamper the opposing party's ability to prepare for [trial]." *See also* **Marino v. King**, 355 S.W.3d 629, 633 (Tex.2011); **Wal-Mart Stores v. Deggs**, 968 S.W.2d 354, 356 (Tex.1998).

In re Sewell, 472 S.W.3d 449, 456 (Tex.App.—Texarkana 2015, orig. proceeding), *disapproved on other grounds*, **In re Bayview Loan Servicing, LLC**, 532 S.W.3d 510 (Tex.App.—Texarkana 2017, orig. proceeding). "[W]here a party moves to withdraw deemed admissions that are merit-preclusive, due-process requires the party opposing withdrawal to prove that the moving party's failure to answer the admissions resulted from flagrant bad faith or callous disregard of the rules. Thus, although a party moving to withdraw admissions ordinarily must prove the requirements of Rule 198.3, when the deemed admissions are merit-preclusive, good cause exists absent bad faith or callous disregard of the rules by the party seeking the withdrawal. Moreover, in such instances, it is presumed that presentation of the merits would be served by allowing withdrawal of the deemed admissions." (Internal quotes omitted.) *See also* **Medina v. Raven**, 492 S.W.3d 53, 62 (Tex.App.—Houston [1st Dist.] 2016, no pet.).

Duff v. Spearman, 322 S.W.3d 869, 884 (Tex.App.—Beaumont 2010, pet. denied). "A party that, without objection, allows the trial court to admit evidence controverting a matter deemed admitted may waive his right to rely upon the matter."

TRCP 199. DEPOSITIONS UPON ORAL EXAMINATION

199.1. Oral Examination; Alternative Methods of Conducting or Recording.

(a) ***Generally.*** A party may take the testimony of any person or entity by deposition on oral examination before any officer authorized by law to take depositions. The testimony, objections, and any other statements during the deposition must be recorded at the time they are given or made.

(b) ***Depositions by Telephone or Other Remote Electronic Means.*** A party may take an oral deposition by telephone or other remote electronic means if the party gives reasonable prior written notice of intent to do so. For the purposes of these rules, an oral deposition taken by telephone or other remote electronic means is considered as having been taken in the district and at the place where the witness is located when answering the questions. The officer taking the deposition may be located with the party noticing the deposition instead of with the witness if the witness is placed under oath by a person who is present with the witness and authorized to administer oaths in that jurisdiction.

(c) ***Nonstenographic Recording.*** Any party may cause a deposition upon oral examination to be recorded by other than stenographic means, including videotape recording. The party requesting the nonstenographic recording will be responsible for obtaining a person authorized by law to administer the oath and for assuring that the recording will be intelligible, accurate, and trustworthy. At least five days prior to the deposition, the party must serve on the witness and all parties a notice, either in the notice of deposition or separately, that the deposition will be recorded by other than stenographic means. This notice must state the method of nonstenographic recording to be used and whether the deposition will also be recorded stenographically. Any other party may then serve written notice designating another method of recording in addition to the method specified, at the expense of such other party unless the court orders otherwise.

199.2. Procedure for Noticing Oral Deposition.

(a) ***Time to Notice Deposition.*** A notice of intent to take an oral deposition must be served on the witness and all parties a reasonable time before the deposition is taken. An oral deposition may be taken outside the discovery period only by agreement of the parties or with leave of court.

(b) ***Content of Notice.***

(1) *Identity of Witness; Organizations.* The notice must state the name of the witness, which may be either an individual or a public or private corporation, partnership, association, governmental agency, or other organization. If an organization is named as the witness, the notice must describe with reasonable particularity the matters on which examination is requested. In response,

the organization named in the notice must—a reasonable time before the deposition—designate one or more individuals to testify on its behalf and set forth, for each individual designated, the matters on which the individual will testify. Each individual designated must testify as to matters that are known or reasonably available to the organization. This subdivision does not preclude taking a deposition by any other procedure authorized by these rules.

(2) *Time and Place.* The notice must state a reasonable time and place for the oral deposition. The place may be in:

(A) the county of the witness's residence;

(B) the county where the witness is employed or regularly transacts business in person;

(C) the county of suit, if the witness is a party or a person designated by a party under Rule 199.2(b)(1);

(D) the county where the witness was served with the subpoena, or within 150 miles of the place of service, if the witness is not a resident of Texas or is a transient person; or

(E) subject to the foregoing, at any other convenient place directed by the court in which the cause is pending.

(3) *Alternative Means of Conducting and Recording.* The notice must state whether the deposition is to be taken by telephone or other remote electronic means and identify the means. If the deposition is to be recorded by nonstenographic means, the notice may include the notice required by Rule 199.1(c).

(4) *Additional Attendees.* The notice may include the notice concerning additional attendees required by Rule 199.5(a)(3).

(5) *Request for Production of Documents.* A notice may include a request that the witness produce at the deposition documents or tangible things within the scope of discovery and within the witness's possession, custody, or control. If the witness is a nonparty, the request must comply with Rule 205[1] and the designation of materials required to be identified in the subpoena must be attached to, or included in, the notice. The nonparty's response to the request is governed by Rules 176[2] and 205. When the witness is a party or subject to the control of a party, document requests under this subdivision are governed by Rules 193 and 196.[3]

[1] Vernon's Ann.Rules Civ.Proc., rule 205.1 et seq.

[2] Vernon's Ann.Rules Civ.Proc., rule 176.1 et seq.

[3] Vernon's Ann.Rules Civ.Proc., rule 193.1 et seq. and rule 196.1 et seq.

199.3. Compelling Witness to Attend. A party may compel the witness to attend the oral deposition by serving the witness with a subpoena under Rule 176. If the witness is a party or is retained by, employed by, or otherwise subject to the control of a party, however, service of the notice of oral deposition upon the party's attorney has the same effect as a subpoena served on the witness.

199.4. Objections to Time and Place of Oral Deposition. A party or witness may object to the time and place designated for an oral deposition by motion for protective order or by motion to quash the notice of deposition. If the motion is filed by the third business day after service of the notice of deposition, an objection to the time and place of a deposition stays the oral deposition until the motion can be determined.

199.5. Examination, Objection, and Conduct During Oral Depositions.

(a) ***Attendance.***

(1) *Witness.* The witness must remain in attendance from day to day until the deposition is begun and completed.

(2) *Attendance by Party.* A party may attend an oral deposition in person, even if the deposition is taken by telephone or other remote electronic means. If a deposition is taken by telephone or other remote electronic means, the party noticing the deposition must make arrangements for all persons to attend by the same means. If the party noticing the deposition appears in person, any other party may appear by telephone or other remote electronic means if that party makes the necessary arrangements with the deposition officer and the party noticing the deposition.

(3) *Other Attendees.* If any party intends to have in attendance any persons other than the witness, parties, spouses of parties, counsel, employees of counsel, and the officer taking the oral deposition, that party must give reasonable notice to all parties, either in the notice of deposition or separately, of the identity of the other persons.

(b) ***Oath; Examination.*** Every person whose deposition is taken by oral examination must first be placed under oath. The parties may examine and cross-examine the witness. Any party, in lieu of participating in the examination, may serve written questions in a sealed envelope on the party noticing the oral deposition, who must deliver them to the deposition officer, who must open the envelope and propound them to the witness.

(c) ***Time Limitation.*** No side may examine or cross-examine an individual witness for more than six hours. Breaks during depositions do not count against this limitation.

(d) ***Conduct During the Oral Deposition; Conferences.*** The oral deposition must be conducted in the same manner as if the testimony were being obtained in

court during trial. Counsel should cooperate with and be courteous to each other and to the witness. The witness should not be evasive and should not unduly delay the examination. Private conferences between the witness and the witness's attorney during the actual taking of the deposition are improper except for the purpose of determining whether a privilege should be asserted. Private conferences may be held, however, during agreed recesses and adjournments. If the lawyers and witnesses do not comply with this rule, the court may allow in evidence at trial statements, objections, discussions, and other occurrences during the oral deposition that reflect upon the credibility of the witness or the testimony.

(e) ***Objections.*** Objections to questions during the oral deposition are limited to "Objection, leading" and "Objection, form." Objections to testimony during the oral deposition are limited to "Objection, nonresponsive." These objections are waived if not stated as phrased during the oral deposition. All other objections need not be made or recorded during the oral deposition to be later raised with the court. The objecting party must give a clear and concise explanation of an objection if requested by the party taking the oral deposition, or the objection is waived. Argumentative or suggestive objections or explanations waive objection and may be grounds for terminating the oral deposition or assessing costs or other sanctions. The officer taking the oral deposition will not rule on objections but must record them for ruling by the court. The officer taking the oral deposition must not fail to record testimony because an objection has been made.

(f) ***Instructions Not to Answer.*** An attorney may instruct a witness not to answer a question during an oral deposition only if necessary to preserve a privilege, comply with a court order or these rules, protect a witness from an abusive question or one for which any answer would be misleading, or secure a ruling pursuant to paragraph (g). The attorney instructing the witness not to answer must give a concise, nonargumentative, nonsuggestive explanation of the grounds for the instruction if requested by the party who asked the question.

(g) ***Suspending the Deposition.*** If the time limitations for the deposition have expired or the deposition is being conducted or defended in violation of these rules, a party or witness may suspend the oral deposition for the time necessary to obtain a ruling.

(h) ***Good Faith Required.*** An attorney must not ask a question at an oral deposition solely to harass or mislead the witness, for any other improper purpose, or without a good faith legal basis at the time. An attorney must not object to a question at an oral deposition, instruct the witness not to answer a question, or suspend the deposition unless there is a good faith factual and legal basis for doing so at the time.

199.6. Hearing on Objections. Any party may, at any reasonable time, request a hearing on an objection or privilege asserted by an instruction not to answer or suspension of the deposition; provided the failure of a party to obtain a ruling prior to trial does not waive any objection or privilege. The party seeking to avoid discovery must present any evidence necessary to support the objection or privilege either by testimony at the hearing or by affidavits served on opposing parties at least seven days before the hearing. If the court determines that an *in camera* review of some or all of the requested discovery is necessary to rule, answers to the deposition questions may be made *in camera,* to be transcribed and sealed in the event the privilege is sustained, or made in an affidavit produced to the court in a sealed wrapper.

Aug. 5, 1998 and Nov. 9, 1998, eff. Jan. 1, 1999.

Comment—1999

1. Rule 199.2(b)(5) incorporates the procedures and limitations applicable to requests for production or inspection under Rule 196, including the 30-day deadline for responses, as well as the procedures and duties imposed by Rule 193.

2. For purposes of Rule 199.5(c), each person designated by an organization under Rule 199.2(b)(1) is a separate witness.

3. The requirement of Rule 199.5(d) that depositions be conducted in the same manner as if the testimony were being obtained in court is a limit on the conduct of the lawyers and witnesses in the deposition, not on the scope of the interrogation permitted by Rule 192.

4. An objection to the form of a question includes objections that the question calls for speculation, calls for a narrative answer, is vague, is confusing, or is ambiguous. Ordinarily, a witness must answer a question at a deposition subject to the objection. An objection may therefore be inadequate if a question incorporates such unfair assumptions or is worded so that any answer would necessarily be misleading. A witness should not be required to answer whether he has yet ceased conduct he denies ever doing, subject to an objection to form (*i.e.*, that the question is confusing or assumes facts not in evidence) because any answer would necessarily be misleading on account of the way in which the question is put. The witness may be instructed not to answer. Abusive questions include questions that inquire into matters clearly beyond the scope of discovery or that are argumentative, repetitious, or harassing.

Source: New rule.

See also CPRC §20.001; Gov't Code §52.059 (imposes joint and several liability for cost of deposition on attorney who takes deposition and attorney's firm), §§154.101, 154.112; TRE 603; **O'Connor's Texas Rules,** "General Rules for Discovery," ch. 6-A, §1 et seq.; **O'Connor's Texas Rules,** "Depositions," ch. 6-F, §1 et seq.; **O'Connor's Texas Forms,** FORMS 6F:1, 6F:2, 6F:3.

For important information about the deposition procedure, see Court Reporters Certification Board, Uniform Format Manual for Texas Reporters' Records (2010), §§3.4 cmt., 3.7 cmt., www.txcourts.gov/rules-forms/rules-standards.

ANNOTATIONS

In re Liberty Cty. Mut. Ins., 606 S.W.3d 866, 873-74 (Tex.App.—Houston [14th Dist.] 2020, orig. proceeding). "Rule 199.1(a) permits the deposition of any person or entity without any limitation that the proposed deponent have personal knowledge of the facts. [P] was not required to show that [D's] corporate representative has personal knowledge of any facts relevant to the disputed issues on liability or damages."

In re FedEx Ground Package Sys., __ S.W.3d __, 2020 WL 2832683 (Tex.App.—Houston [14th Dist.] 2020, orig. proceeding) (No. 14-19-00861-CV; 5-28-20). "[D] contends that there is no authority under which the trial court could compel [D] to produce an unnamed corporate representative to testify at trial about a list of 25 topics. [TRCP] 199.2 provides the procedure for noticing oral depositions. [¶] Rule 199.2(b)(1) is patterned after [FRCP] 30(b)(6). We may look to federal authority for guidance when the state law mirrors the federal law. In interpreting Federal Rule 30(b)(6), federal courts hold that Rule 30(b)(6) does not allow a party to subpoena a corporate representative to compel testimony at trial. Following the federal courts' interpretation of Rule 30(b)(6), we conclude that Rule 199.2(b)(1) similarly does not provide for trial subpoenas with designated topics."

In re Reaud, 286 S.W.3d 574, 580 (Tex.App.—Beaumont 2009, orig. proceeding). "The third category of nonparty witnesses [in TRCP 199.3] are those . . . 'otherwise controlled,' [a term that] is not defined by the procedural rules. [The term is limited] to include only control of the same kind, class, or nature as the types of control parties would have over employees or retained experts. . . . While [TRCP 199.3 and 205.1] contain language that allow them to reach beyond retained experts and employees, it is now clear that these two rules do not extend to nonparties over whom the party does not have the type of control as it has over an employee or a retained expert."

In re Turner, 243 S.W.3d 843, 846 (Tex.App.—Eastland 2008, orig. proceeding). "When a deposition takes place outside one of the counties specifically identified by Rule 199.2(b)(2), it must be at a *convenient place*. This imposes an additional requirement and may, therefore, alter the analysis. But because it is clearly easier for an international traveler to travel to Dallas than Stephenville, if the trial court was authorized to order [relator] to come to Stephenville for a deposition, it did not abuse its discretion by moving the deposition to Dallas." *See also* **In re Alamex, NV**, No. 01-12-00037-CV, 2012 WL 1564323 (Tex.App.—Houston [1st Dist.] 2012, orig. proceeding) (memo op.; 5-3-12) (convenience is determined from witness's viewpoint).

TRCP 200. DEPOSITIONS UPON WRITTEN QUESTIONS

200.1. Procedure for Noticing Deposition Upon Written Questions.

(a) ***Who May Be Noticed; When.*** A party may take the testimony of any person or entity by deposition on written questions before any person authorized by law to take depositions on written questions. A notice of intent to take the deposition must be served on the witness and all parties at least 20 days before the deposition is taken. A deposition on written questions may be taken outside the discovery period only by agreement of the parties or with leave of court. The party noticing the deposition must also deliver to the deposition officer a copy of the notice and of all written questions to be asked during the deposition.

(b) ***Content of Notice.*** The notice must comply with Rules 199.1(b), 199.2(b), and 199.5(a)(3). If the witness is an organization, the organization must comply with the requirements of that provision. The notice also may include a request for production of documents as permitted by Rule 199.2(b)(5), the provisions of which will govern the request, service, and response.

200.2. Compelling Witness to Attend. A party may compel the witness to attend the deposition on written questions by serving the witness with a subpoena under Rule 176. If the witness is a party or is retained by, employed by, or otherwise subject to the control of a party, however, service of the deposition notice upon the party's attorney has the same effect as a subpoena served on the witness.

200.3. Questions and Objections.

(a) ***Direct Questions.*** The direct questions to be propounded to the witness must be attached to the notice.

(b) ***Objections and Additional Questions.*** Within ten days after the notice and direct questions are served, any party may object to the direct questions and serve cross-questions on all other parties. Within five days after cross-questions are served, any party may object to the cross-questions and serve redirect questions on all other parties. Within three days after redirect questions are served, any party may object to the redirect questions and serve recross questions on all other parties. Objections to recross questions must be served within five days after the earlier of when recross questions are served or the time of the deposition on written questions.

(c) ***Objections to Form of Questions.*** Objections to the form of a question are waived unless asserted in accordance with this subdivision.

200.4. Conducting the Deposition Upon Written Questions. The deposition officer must: take the deposition on written questions at the time and place designated;

record the testimony of the witness under oath in response to the questions; and prepare, certify, and deliver the deposition transcript in accordance with Rule 203. The deposition officer has authority when necessary to summon and swear an interpreter to facilitate the taking of the deposition.

Aug. 5, 1998, Nov. 9, 1998 and Dec. 31, 1998, eff. Jan. 1, 1999.

Comment—1999

1. The procedures for asserting objections during oral depositions under Rule 199.5(e) do not apply to depositions on written questions.

2. Section 20.001 of the Civil Practice and Remedies Code provides that a deposition on written questions of a witness who is alleged to reside or to be in this state may be taken by a clerk of a district court, a judge or clerk of a county court, or a notary public of this state.

Source: New rule.

See also CPRC §20.001; Gov't Code §§154.101, 154.112; **O'Connor's Texas Rules**, "General Rules for Discovery," ch. 6-A, §1 et seq.; **O'Connor's Texas Rules**, "Depositions," ch. 6-F, §1 et seq.; **O'Connor's Texas Forms**, FORMS 6F:4, 6F:5, 6F:6.

ANNOTATIONS

In re Toyota Motor Corp., 191 S.W.3d 498, 503 (Tex.App.—Waco 2006, orig. proceeding). "[D's] counsel [was ordered not to] be present when the depositions on written questions are conducted. [D] objects to being forced to rely on 'canned interrogatory answers prepared by [P's] counsel.' However, attorneys are not to answer written depositions for their clients. Thus, a deposition officer, not [Ps'] counsel, will record [the] answers to [D's] deposition questions."

St. Luke's Episcopal Hosp. v. Garcia, 928 S.W.2d 307, 310 (Tex.App.—Houston [14th Dist.] 1996, orig. proceeding). "Because relator has no objection to the form of [the] written questions, relator claims the provision in [TRCP 200] regarding timeliness of objections is inapplicable. We agree. In its objections to the deposition notice and subpoena duces tecum, relator's primary objections are substantive objections relating to privilege. We hold that the ten-day limitation in [TRCP 200] is inapplicable to substantive objections."

TRCP 201. DEPOSITIONS IN FOREIGN JURISDICTIONS FOR USE IN TEXAS PROCEEDINGS; DEPOSITIONS IN TEXAS FOR USE IN FOREIGN PROCEEDINGS

201.1. Depositions in Foreign Jurisdictions for Use in Texas Proceedings.

(a) ***Generally.*** A party may take a deposition on oral examination or written questions of any person or entity located in another state or a foreign country for use in proceedings in this State. The deposition may be taken by:

(1) notice;

(2) letter rogatory, letter of request, or other such device;

(3) agreement of the parties; or

(4) court order.

(b) ***By Notice.*** A party may take the deposition by notice in accordance with these rules as if the deposition were taken in this State, except that the deposition officer may be a person authorized to administer oaths in the place where the deposition is taken.

(c) ***By Letter Rogatory.*** On motion by a party, the court in which an action is pending must issue a letter rogatory on terms that are just and appropriate, regardless of whether any other manner of obtaining the deposition is impractical or inconvenient. The letter must:

(1) be addressed to the appropriate authority in the jurisdiction in which the deposition is to be taken;

(2) request and authorize that authority to summon the witness before the authority at a time and place stated in the letter for examination on oral or written questions; and

(3) request and authorize that authority to cause the witness's testimony to be reduced to writing and returned, together with any items marked as exhibits, to the party requesting the letter rogatory.

(d) ***By Letter of Request or Other Such Device.*** On motion by a party, the court in which an action is pending, or the clerk of that court, must issue a letter of request or other such device in accordance with an applicable treaty or international convention on terms that are just and appropriate. The letter or other device must be issued regardless of whether any other manner of obtaining the deposition is impractical or inconvenient. The letter or other device must:

(1) be in the form prescribed by the treaty or convention under which it is issued, as presented by the movant to the court or clerk; and

(2) must state the time, place, and manner of the examination of the witness.

(e) ***Objections to Form of Letter Rogatory, Letter of Request, or Other Such Device.*** In issuing a letter rogatory, letter of request, or other such device, the court must set a time for objecting to the form of the device. A party must make any objection to the form of the device in writing and serve it on all other parties by the time set by the court, or the objection is waived.

(f) ***Admissibility of Evidence.*** Evidence obtained in response to a letter rogatory, letter of request, or other such device is not inadmissible merely because it is not a

verbatim transcript, or the testimony was not taken under oath, or for any similar departure from the requirements for depositions taken within this State under these rules.

(g) ***Deposition by Electronic Means.*** A deposition in another jurisdiction may be taken by telephone, videoconference, teleconference, or other electronic means under the provisions of Rule 199.[1]

[1]Vernon's Ann.Rules Civ.Proc., rule 199.1 et seq.

201.2. Depositions in Texas for Use in Proceedings in Foreign Jurisdictions. If a court of record of any other state or foreign jurisdiction issues a mandate, writ, or commission that requires a witness's oral or written deposition testimony in this State, the witness may be compelled to appear and testify in the same manner and by the same process used for taking testimony in a proceeding pending in this State.

Aug. 5, 1998 and Nov. 9, 1998, eff. Jan. 1, 1999.

Comment—1999

1. Rule 201.1 sets forth procedures for obtaining deposition testimony of a witness in another state or foreign jurisdiction for use in Texas court proceedings. It does not, however, address whether any of the procedures listed are, in fact, permitted or recognized by the law of the state or foreign jurisdiction where the witness is located. A party must first determine what procedures are permitted by the jurisdiction where the witness is located before using this rule.

2. Section 20.001 of the Civil Practice and Remedies Code provides a nonexclusive list of persons who are qualified to take a written deposition in Texas and who may take depositions (oral or written) in another state or outside the United States.

3. Rule 201.2 is based on Section 20.002 of the Civil Practice and Remedies Code.

See also CPRC §§20.001, 20.002; **O'Connor's Texas Rules**, "General Rules for Discovery," ch. 6-A, §1 et seq.; **O'Connor's Texas Rules**, "Depositions," ch. 6-F, §1 et seq.; **O'Connor's Texas Forms**, FORMS 6F:1, 6F:2, 6F:3, 6F:4, 6F:5, 6F:6.

ANNOTATIONS

In re Issuance of Subpoenas for the Depositions of Darrell D. Bennett et al., 502 S.W.3d 373, 377-78 (Tex.App.—Houston [14th Dist.] 2016, no pet.). "In **Ex parte Taylor**, [220 S.W. 74 (Tex.1920),] the [Supreme Court] concluded that the court with jurisdiction over the underlying case is generally charged with determining the relevancy and materiality of evidence sought by a party seeking a deposition in Texas under letters rogatory, while the Texas court has the obligation to protect the witness's legal rights, including, for example, the witness's right to avoid compelled production of privileged evidence. [¶] The trial court did not have the authority to quash or limit the depositions of the [Texas residents] based on a belief that the discovery is irrelevant. To get relief on that basis, the [Texas residents] must seek relief from the Wyoming trial court [that issued the letters rogatory]."

Kugle v. DaimlerChrysler Corp., 88 S.W.3d 355, 362 (Tex.App.—San Antonio 2002, pet. denied). "[Ps] contend that the trial court erred in admitting the deposition testimony of [three deponents] because the depositions were taken in Mexico but the witnesses were only sworn in by a Texas notary public. However, a foreign deposition may be taken by any notary public. [T]he trial court did not abuse its discretion in admitting the depositions"

TRCP 202. DEPOSITIONS BEFORE SUIT OR TO INVESTIGATE CLAIMS

202.1. Generally. A person may petition the court for an order authorizing the taking of a deposition on oral examination or written questions either:

(a) to perpetuate or obtain the person's own testimony or that of any other person for use in an anticipated suit; or

(b) to investigate a potential claim or suit.

202.2. Petition. The petition must:

(a) be verified;

(b) be filed in a proper court of any county:

(1) where venue of the anticipated suit may lie, if suit is anticipated; or

(2) where the witness resides, if no suit is yet anticipated;

(c) be in the name of the petitioner;

(d) state either:

(1) that the petitioner anticipates the institution of a suit in which the petitioner may be a party; or

(2) that the petitioner seeks to investigate a potential claim by or against petitioner;

(e) state the subject matter of the anticipated action, if any, and the petitioner's interest therein;

(f) if suit is anticipated, either:

(1) state the names of the persons petitioner expects to have interests adverse to petitioner's in the anticipated suit, and the addresses and telephone numbers for such persons; or

(2) state that the names, addresses, and telephone numbers of persons petitioner expects to have interests adverse to petitioner's in the anticipated suit cannot be ascertained through diligent inquiry, and describe those persons;

(g) state the names, addresses and telephone numbers of the persons to be deposed, the substance of the testimony that the petitioner expects to elicit from each, and the petitioner's reasons for desiring to obtain the testimony of each; and

(h) request an order authorizing the petitioner to take the depositions of the persons named in the petition.

202.3. Notice and Service.

(a) ***Personal Service on Witnesses and Persons Named.*** At least 15 days before the date of the hearing on the petition, the petitioner must serve the petition and a notice of the hearing—in accordance with Rule 21a—on all persons petitioner seeks to depose and, if suit is anticipated, on all persons petitioner expects to have interests adverse to petitioner's in the anticipated suit.

(b) ***Service by Publication on Persons Not Named.***

(1) *Manner.* Unnamed persons described in the petition whom the petitioner expects to have interests adverse to petitioner's in the anticipated suit, if any, may be served by publication with the petition and notice of the hearing. The notice must state the place for the hearing and the time it will be held, which must be more than 14 days after the first publication of the notice. The petition and notice must be published once each week for two consecutive weeks in the newspaper of broadest circulation in the county in which the petition is filed, or if no such newspaper exists, in the newspaper of broadest circulation in the nearest county where a newspaper is published.

(2) *Objection to Depositions Taken on Notice by Publication.* Any interested party may move, in the proceeding or by bill of review, to suppress any deposition, in whole or in part, taken on notice by publication, and may also attack or oppose the deposition by any other means available.

(c) ***Service in Probate Cases.*** A petition to take a deposition in anticipation of an application for probate of a will, and notice of the hearing on the petition, may be served by posting as prescribed by Section 33(f)(2) of the Probate Code. The notice and petition must be directed to all parties interested in the testator's estate and must comply with the requirements of Section 33(c) of the Probate Code insofar as they may be applicable.

(d) ***Modification by Order.*** As justice or necessity may require, the court may shorten or lengthen the notice periods under this rule and may extend the notice period to permit service on any expected adverse party.

202.4. Order.

(a) ***Required Findings.*** The court must order a deposition to be taken if, but only if, it finds that:

(1) allowing the petitioner to take the requested deposition may prevent a failure or delay of justice in an anticipated suit; or

(2) the likely benefit of allowing the petitioner to take the requested deposition to investigate a potential claim outweighs the burden or expense of the procedure.

(b) ***Contents.*** The order must state whether a deposition will be taken on oral examination or written questions. The order may also state the time and place at which a deposition will be taken. If the order does not state the time and place at which a deposition will be taken, the petitioner must notice the deposition as required by Rules 199[1] or 200.[2] The order must contain any protections the court finds necessary or appropriate to protect the witness or any person who may be affected by the procedure.

[1] Vernon's Ann.Rules Civ.Proc., rule 199.1 et seq.

[2] Vernon's Ann.Rules Civ.Proc., rule 200.1 et seq.

202.5. Manner of Taking and Use. Except as otherwise provided in this rule, depositions authorized by this rule are governed by the rules applicable to depositions of nonparties in a pending suit. The scope of discovery in depositions authorized by this rule is the same as if the anticipated suit or potential claim had been filed. A court may restrict or prohibit the use of a deposition taken under this rule in a subsequent suit to protect a person who was not served with notice of the deposition from any unfair prejudice or to prevent abuse of this rule.

Aug. 5, 1998 and Nov. 9, 1998, eff. Jan. 1, 1999.

Comment—1999

1. This rule applies to all discovery before suit covered by former rules governing depositions to perpetuate testimony and bills of discovery.

2. A deposition taken under this rule may be used in a subsequent suit as permitted by the rules of evidence, except that a court may restrict or prohibit its use to prevent taking unfair advantage of a witness or others. The bill of discovery procedure, which Rule 202 incorporates, is equitable in nature, and a court must not permit it to be used inequitably.

Editor's Note: Probate Code §33 (f)(2), as referenced in TRCP 202.3(c), is now Estates Code §51.053.

Source: New rule.

See also CPRC §20.001; **O'Connor's Texas Rules**, "General Rules for Discovery," ch. 6-A, §1 et seq.; **O'Connor's Texas Rules**, "Depositions," ch. 6-F, §1 et seq.; **O'Connor's Texas Forms**, FORMS 6F:8, 6F:9, 6F:10, 6F:11.

ANNOTATIONS

Generally

In re DePinho, 505 S.W.3d 621, 624 (Tex.2016). "Rule [202] does not broadly authorize investigation of *any* action the petitioner may have based on future events—the petition must seek 'to investigate a potential claim or suit.' [A] 'claim' denotes an *existing*—rather than future or speculative—right that may be presently asserted. [A] suit may generally be maintained (i.e., it is a '*potential* . . . suit') only when a court has jurisdiction over the matter. . . . [¶] Stated differently, a 'potential claim or suit' must be ripe."

In re Doe, 444 S.W.3d 603, 604 (Tex.2014). "Rule 202 . . . allows 'a proper court' to authorize a deposition to investigate a potential claim before suit is filed. *At 608:* While Rule 202 is silent on the subject, we think it implicit . . . that the court must have subject-matter jurisdiction over the anticipated action. The rule cannot be used, for example, to investigate a potential federal antitrust suit or patent suit, which can be brought only in federal court. We must determine whether a proper court must also have personal jurisdiction over the potential defendant. For two reasons, we think it must. [¶] *First*: To allow discovery of a potential claim against a defendant over which the court would not have personal jurisdiction denies him the protection Texas procedure would otherwise afford. *At 610: Second*: To allow a Rule 202 court to order discovery without personal jurisdiction over a potential defendant unreasonably expands the rule. [¶] The burden is on the plaintiff in an action to plead allegations showing personal jurisdiction over the defendant. The same burden should be on a potential plaintiff under Rule 202. We recognize that this burden may be heavier in a case like this, in which the potential defendant's identity is unknown and may even be impossible to ascertain. But even so, Rule 202 does not guarantee access to information for every petitioner who claims to need it." *See also* **In re City of Dallas**, 501 S.W.3d 71, 73-74 (Tex.2016).

In re Wolfe, 341 S.W.3d 932, 933 (Tex.2011). "[P]re-suit discovery 'is not an end within itself'; rather, it 'is in aid of a suit which is anticipated' and 'ancillary to the anticipated suit.' To prevent an end-run around discovery limitations that would govern the anticipated suit, Rule 202 restricts discovery in depositions to 'the same as if the anticipated suit or potential claim had been filed.' [A potential party] cannot obtain by Rule 202 what it would be denied in the anticipated action. [¶] Rule 202 is not a license for forced interrogations. Courts must strictly limit and carefully supervise pre-suit discovery to prevent abuse of the rule." *See also* **In re Akzo Nobel Chem., Inc.**, 24 S.W.3d 919, 921 (Tex.App.—Beaumont 2000, orig. proceeding) (Rule 202 does not authorize trial court, before suit is filed, to order any form of discovery but deposition).

In re Does 1&2, 337 S.W.3d 862, 863 (Tex.2011). "[A] court may not order pre-suit discovery by agreement of the witness over the objections of other interested parties without making the findings required by Rule 202.4(a). . . . *At 865:* [P] argues that compliance with Rule 202 was excused because of its agreement with [D]. . . . But [P] and [D] were not the only parties to the proceeding. Rule 202.3(a) requires that 'all persons petitioner expects to have interests adverse to petitioner's in the anticipated suit' be served with the petition and given notice of hearing. [P] asserted that relators would be defendants in the anticipated lawsuit, and by their motions to quash, relators made an appearance in the proceeding. [P] and [D] could not modify the procedures prescribed by Rule 202 by an agreement that did not include relators. [¶] Rule 202 expressly requires that discovery may be ordered 'only if' the required findings are made. The rule does not permit the findings to be implied from support in the record. [¶] The trial court clearly abused its discretion in failing to follow Rule 202." *See also* **In re Cauley**, 437 S.W.3d 650, 657-58 (Tex.App.—Tyler 2014, orig. proceeding) (memo op.; 7-23-14) (respondent does not waive appeal of Rule 202 order that lacks required findings if respondent approves form, but not substance, of order).

In re Jorden, 249 S.W.3d 416, 418 (Tex.2008). CPRC §74.351(s) "limits discovery in health-care lawsuits until the plaintiff serves an expert report summarizing how each defendant violated standards of care and caused the plaintiff injury. The issue here is whether that statute applies to presuit depositions authorized by [TRCP] 202. . . . Because the statute prohibits 'all discovery' other than three exceptions—and Rule 202 depositions are not listed among them—we hold the statute prohibits such depositions until after an expert report is served."

In re PrairieSmarts LLC, 421 S.W.3d 296, 306 (Tex.App.—Fort Worth 2014, orig. proceeding). A TRCP "202 petitioner seeking presuit discovery of information that has been proven to be trade secret information must satisfy both of the two distinct and separate burdens imposed under [TRE] 507 . . . and under rule 202. . . ."

In re Reassure Am. Life Ins., 421 S.W.3d 165, 173 (Tex.App.—Corpus Christi 2013, orig. proceeding). "A petition that merely tracks the language of Rule 202 in averring the necessity of a presuit deposition, without including any explanatory facts regarding the anticipated suit or the potential claim, is insufficient to meet the petitioner's burden."

Combs v. Texas Civil Rights Project, 410 S.W.3d 529, 533-34 (Tex.App.—Austin 2013, pet. denied). "To determine whether [Ds] have immunity from suit with regard to the rule 202 proceedings in this case, we first consider whether rule 202 proceedings generally are 'suits.' An order under rule 202, at least in certain circumstances, operates as a final, appealable order, immediately subject to appellate review. Thus, in at least those limited cases, a rule 202 proceeding seems to have characteristics of a 'suit,' in that its result is subject to appellate review. Nevertheless, a petition under rule 202 is ultimately a petition that asserts no substantive claim or cause of action upon which relief can be granted. A successful rule 202 petitioner simply acquires the right to obtain discovery—discovery that may or may not lead to a claim or cause of action. . . . Consequently, a proceeding under rule 202 'is not a separate independent lawsuit, but is in aid of and incident to an anticipated suit.' We cannot agree that a rule 202 petition is itself a 'suit,' nor can we agree that all rule 202 proceedings involving governmental entities are 'suits' that seek to control state action, as [Ds] contend. Consequently, we conclude that pre-suit depositions of governmental entities under rule 202 are not, in wholesale, barred by immunity."

Removal

Texas v. Real Parties in Interest, 259 F.3d 387, 394-95 (5th Cir.2001). When TRCP 202 is used as an inves-

tigatory tool for potential claims, the proceeding is not subject to removal. *See also* **Mayfield-George v. Texas Rehab. Comm'n**, 197 F.R.D. 280, 283 (N.D.Tex.2000).

TRCP 203. SIGNING, CERTIFICATION AND USE OF ORAL AND WRITTEN DEPOSITIONS

203.1. Signature and Changes.

(a) *Deposition Transcript to be Provided to Witness.* The deposition officer must provide the original deposition transcript to the witness for examination and signature. If the witness is represented by an attorney at the deposition, the deposition officer must provide the transcript to the attorney instead of the witness.

(b) *Changes by Witness; Signature.* The witness may change responses as reflected in the deposition transcript by indicating the desired changes, in writing, on a separate sheet of paper, together with a statement of the reasons for making the changes. No erasures or obliterations of any kind may be made to the original deposition transcript. The witness must then sign the transcript under oath and return it to the deposition officer. If the witness does not return the transcript to the deposition officer within 20 days of the date the transcript was provided to the witness or the witness's attorney, the witness may be deemed to have waived the right to make the changes.

(c) *Exceptions.* The requirements of presentation and signature under this subdivision do not apply:

(1) if the witness and all parties waive the signature requirement;

(2) to depositions on written questions; or

(3) to nonstenographic recordings of oral depositions.

203.2. Certification. The deposition officer must file with the court, serve on all parties, and attach as part of the deposition transcript or nonstenographic recording of an oral deposition a certificate duly sworn by the officer stating:

(a) that the witness was duly sworn by the officer and that the transcript or nonstenographic recording of the oral deposition is a true record of the testimony given by the witness;

(b) that the deposition transcript, if any, was submitted to the witness or to the attorney for the witness for examination and signature, the date on which the transcript was submitted, whether the witness returned the transcript, and if so, the date on which it was returned.

(c) that changes, if any, made by the witness are attached to the deposition transcript;

(d) that the deposition officer delivered the deposition transcript or nonstenographic recording of an oral deposition in accordance with Rule 203.3;

(e) the amount of time used by each party at the deposition;

(f) the amount of the deposition officer's charges for preparing the original deposition transcript, which the clerk of the court must tax as costs; and

(g) that a copy of the certificate was served on all parties and the date of service.

203.3. Delivery.

(a) *Endorsement; To Whom Delivered.* The deposition officer must endorse the title of the action and "Deposition of (name of witness)" on the original deposition transcript (or a copy, if the original was not returned) or the original nonstenographic recording of an oral deposition, and must return:

(1) the transcript to the party who asked the first question appearing in the transcript, or

(2) the recording to the party who requested it.

(b) *Notice.* The deposition officer must serve notice of delivery on all other parties.

(c) *Inspection and Copying; Copies.* The party receiving the original deposition transcript or nonstenographic recording must make it available upon reasonable request for inspection and copying by any other party. Any party or the witness is entitled to obtain a copy of the deposition transcript or nonstenographic recording from the deposition officer upon payment of a reasonable fee.

203.4. Exhibits. At the request of a party, the original documents and things produced for inspection during the examination of the witness must be marked for identification by the deposition officer and annexed to the deposition transcript or nonstenographic recording. The person producing the materials may produce copies instead of originals if the party gives all other parties fair opportunity at the deposition to compare the copies with the originals. If the person offers originals rather than copies, the deposition officer must, after the conclusion of the deposition, make copies to be attached to the original deposition transcript or nonstenographic recording, and then return the originals to the person who produced them. The person who produced the originals must preserve them for hearing or trial and make them available for inspection or copying by any other party upon seven days' notice. Copies annexed to the original deposition transcript or nonstenographic recording may be used for all purposes.

203.5. Motion to Suppress. A party may object to any errors and irregularities in the manner in which the testi-

mony is transcribed, signed, delivered, or otherwise dealt with by the deposition officer by filing a motion to suppress all or part of the deposition. If the deposition officer complies with Rule 203.3 at least one day before the case is called to trial, with regard to a deposition transcript, or 30 days before the case is called to trial, with regard to a nonstenographic recording, the party must file and serve a motion to suppress before trial commences to preserve the objections.

203.6. Use.

(a) ***Nonstenographic Recording; Transcription.*** A nonstenographic recording of an oral deposition, or a written transcription of all or part of such a recording, may be used to the same extent as a deposition taken by stenographic means. However, the court, for good cause shown, may require that the party seeking to use a nonstenographic recording or written transcription first obtain a complete transcript of the deposition recording from a certified court reporter. The court reporter's transcription must be made from the original or a certified copy of the deposition recording. The court reporter must, to the extent applicable, comply with the provisions of this rule, except that the court reporter must deliver the original transcript to the attorney requesting the transcript, and the court reporter's certificate must include a statement that the transcript is a true record of the nonstenographic recording. The party to whom the court reporter delivers the original transcript must make the transcript available, upon reasonable request, for inspection and copying by the witness or any party.

(b) ***Same Proceeding.*** All or part of a deposition may be used for any purpose in the same proceeding in which it was taken. If the original is not filed, a certified copy may be used. "Same proceeding" includes a proceeding in a different court but involving the same subject matter and the same parties or their representatives or successors in interest. A deposition is admissible against a party joined after the deposition was taken if:

(1) the deposition is admissible pursuant to Rule 804(b)(1) of the Rules of Evidence, or

(2) that party has had a reasonable opportunity to redepose the witness and has failed to do so.

(c) ***Different Proceeding.*** Depositions taken in different proceedings may be used as permitted by the Rules of Evidence.

Aug. 5, 1998 and Nov. 9, 1998, eff. Jan. 1, 1999.

Source: New rule.

See also **O'Connor's Texas Rules**, "General Rules for Discovery," ch. 6-A, §1 et seq.; **O'Connor's Texas Rules**, "Depositions," ch. 6-F, §1 et seq. For important information about the deposition procedure, see Court Reporters Certification Board, Uniform Format Manual for Texas Reporters' Records (2010), §§3.4 cmt., 3.7 cmt.

ANNOTATIONS

Jones v. Colley, 820 S.W.2d 863, 866 (Tex.App.—Texarkana 1991, writ denied). "No rule requires that a deposition be read into the record or played before the jury in chronological order. A party, as a matter of trial strategy, is entitled to present his evidence in the order he believes constitutes the most effective presentation of his case, provided that it does not convey a *distinctly false* impression."

TRCP 204. PHYSICAL AND MENTAL EXAMINATION

204.1. Motion and Order Required.

(a) ***Motion.*** A party may—no later than 30 days before the end of any applicable discovery period—move for an order compelling another party to:

(1) submit to a physical or mental examination by a qualified physician or a mental examination by a qualified psychologist; or

(2) produce for such examination a person in the other party's custody, conservatorship or legal control.

(b) ***Service.*** The motion and notice of hearing must be served on the person to be examined and all parties.

(c) ***Requirements for Obtaining Order.*** The court may issue an order for examination only for good cause shown and only in the following circumstances:

(1) when the mental or physical condition (including the blood group) of a party, or of a person in the custody, conservatorship or under the legal control of a party, is in controversy; or

(2) except as provided in Rule 204.4, an examination by a psychologist may be ordered when the party responding to the motion has designated a psychologist as a testifying expert or has disclosed a psychologist's records for possible use at trial.

(d) ***Requirements of Order.*** The order must be in writing and must specify the time, place, manner, conditions, and scope of the examination and the person or persons by whom it is to be made.

204.2. Report of Examining Physician or Psychologist.

(a) ***Right to Report.*** Upon request of the person ordered to be examined, the party causing the examination to be made must deliver to the person a copy of a detailed written report of the examining physician or psychologist setting out the findings, including results of all tests made, diagnoses and conclusions, together with like reports of all earlier examinations of the same condition. After delivery

of the report, upon request of the party causing the examination, the party against whom the order is made must produce a like report of any examination made before or after the ordered examination of the same condition, unless the person examined is not a party and the party shows that the party is unable to obtain it. The court on motion may limit delivery of a report on such terms as are just. If a physician or psychologist fails or refuses to make a report the court may exclude the testimony if offered at the trial.

(b) ***Agreements; Relationship to Other Rules.*** This subdivision applies to examinations made by agreement of the parties, unless the agreement expressly provides otherwise. This subdivision does not preclude discovery of a report of an examining physician or psychologist or the taking of a deposition of the physician or psychologist in accordance with the provisions of any other rule.

204.3. Effect of No Examination. If no examination is sought either by agreement or under this subdivision, the party whose physical or mental condition is in controversy must not comment to the court or jury concerning the party's willingness to submit to an examination, or on the right or failure of any other party to seek an examination.

204.4. Cases Arising Under Titles II or V, Family Code. In cases arising under Family Code Titles II or V, the court may—on its own initiative or on motion of a party—appoint:

(a) one or more psychologists or psychiatrists to make any and all appropriate mental examinations of the children who are the subject of the suit or of any other parties, and may make such appointment irrespective of whether a psychologist or psychiatrist has been designated by any party as a testifying expert;

(b) one or more experts who are qualified in paternity testing to take blood, body fluid, or tissue samples to conduct paternity tests as ordered by the court.

204.5. Definition. For the purpose of this rule, a psychologist is a person licensed or certified by a state or the District of Columbia as a psychologist.

Aug. 5, 1998 and Nov. 9, 1998, eff. Jan. 1, 1999.

Source: New rule.

See also TRE 510(d)(5); **O'Connor's Texas Rules**, "General Rules for Discovery," ch. 6-A, §1 et seq.; **O'Connor's Texas Rules**, "Medical Records," ch. 6-J, §1 et seq.; **O'Connor's Texas Forms**, FORMS 6J.

ANNOTATIONS

In re H.E.B. Grocery Co., 492 S.W.3d 300, 303 (Tex.2016). "The purpose of Rule 204.1's good-cause requirement is to balance the movant's right to a fair trial and the other party's right to privacy. To show good cause, the movant must (1) show that the requested examination is relevant to issues in controversy and will produce or likely lead to relevant evidence, (2) establish a reasonable nexus between the requested examination and the condition in controversy, and (3) demonstrate that the desired information cannot be obtained by less intrusive means."

In re Society of Our Lady of Most Holy Trinity, ___ S.W.3d ___, 2019 WL 3297163 (Tex.App.—Corpus Christi 2019, orig. proceeding) (No. 13-19-00064-CV; 7-23-19). "Under the majority viewpoint [of federal courts], the party requesting the presence of counsel or seeking to record or videotape the [Rule 204] examination has the burden to show a factual basis establishing special circumstances which constitute good cause for the accommodation. [¶] [G]ood cause for recording an examination is not established by the inherently adversarial nature of the examination, the fact that the examining physician was selected or paid for by opposing counsel, the theoretical potential for misconduct during the examination, the desire to obtain an accurate dispute-free version of what was said, or the fear that the examination would become a de facto deposition. [¶] The . . . federal authority requiring good cause or special circumstances for third party observations or recording an examination is consistent with Texas jurisprudence. [¶] [W]e conclude that [nonmovant] must show special circumstances or a particularized need, . . . supported by evidence including specific facts amounting to good cause, for video recording her examination."

In re Ten Hagen Excavating, Inc., 435 S.W.3d 859, 867-68 (Tex.App.—Dallas 2014, orig. proceeding). Rule 204.1's in-controversy requirement is "not met 'by mere conclusory allegations of the pleadings—nor by mere relevance to the case.' In cases involving physical injury, there are situations, however, where the pleadings alone are sufficient to place a party's physical condition in controversy. For instance, the [U.S.] Supreme Court has suggested that a plaintiff in a negligence action who claims physical injury as the result of a party's negligence places his 'physical injury clearly in controversy and provides the defendant with good cause for an examination to determine the existence and extent of such asserted injury' simply by seeking recovery for the alleged physical injury. This same precept applies equally to a defendant who asserts his physical condition as a defense to a claim."

TRCP 205. DISCOVERY FROM NONPARTIES

205.1. Forms of Discovery; Subpoena Requirement. A party may compel discovery from a nonparty—that is, a person who is not a party or subject to a party's control—only by obtaining a court order under Rules 196.7, 202, or 204, or by serving a subpoena compelling:

(a) an oral deposition;

(b) a deposition on written questions;

(c) a request for production of documents or tangible things, pursuant to Rule 199.2(b)(5) or Rule 200.1(b), served with a notice of deposition on oral examination or written questions; and

(d) a request for production of documents and tangible things under this rule.

205.2. Notice. A party seeking discovery by subpoena from a nonparty must serve, on the nonparty and all parties, a copy of the form of notice required under the rules governing the applicable form of discovery. A notice of oral or written deposition must be served before or at the same time that a subpoena compelling attendance or production under the notice is served. A notice to produce documents or tangible things under Rule 205.3 must be served at least 10 days before the subpoena compelling production is served.

205.3. Production of Documents and Tangible Things Without Deposition.

(a) ***Notice; Subpoena.*** A party may compel production of documents and tangible things from a nonparty by serving—a reasonable time before the response is due but no later than 30 days before the end of any applicable discovery period—the notice required in Rule 205.2 and a subpoena compelling production or inspection of documents or tangible things.

(b) ***Contents of Notice.*** The notice must state:

(1) the name of the person from whom production or inspection is sought to be compelled;

(2) a reasonable time and place for the production or inspection; and

(3) the items to be produced or inspected, either by individual item or by category, describing each item and category with reasonable particularity, and, if applicable, describing the desired testing and sampling with sufficient specificity to inform the nonparty of the means, manner, and procedure for testing or sampling.

(c) ***Requests for Production of Medical or Mental Health Records of Other Nonparties.*** If a party requests a nonparty to produce medical or mental health records of another nonparty, the requesting party must serve the nonparty whose records are sought with the notice required under this rule. This requirement does not apply under the circumstances set forth in Rule 196.1(c)(2).

(d) ***Response.*** The nonparty must respond to the notice and subpoena in accordance with Rule 176.6.

(e) ***Custody, Inspection and Copying.*** The party obtaining the production must make all materials produced available for inspection by any other party on reasonable notice, and must furnish copies to any party who requests at that party's expense.

(f) ***Cost of Production.*** A party requiring production of documents by a nonparty must reimburse the nonparty's reasonable costs of production.

Aug. 5, 1998, Nov. 9, 1998 and Dec. 31, 1998, eff. Jan. 1, 1999.

Comment—1999

Under this rule, a party may subpoena production of documents and tangible things from nonparties without need for a motion or oral or written deposition.

Source: New rule.

See also **O'Connor's Texas Rules**, "Securing discovery from nonparties," ch. 6-A, §9.2; **O'Connor's Texas Rules**, "Depositions," ch. 6-F, §1 et seq.; **O'Connor's Texas Rules**, "Securing Documents & Tangible Things," ch. 6-I, §1 et seq.; **O'Connor's Texas Forms**, FORM 6I:12.

ANNOTATIONS

In re University of Tex. Health Ctr., 198 S.W.3d 392, 397 (Tex.App.—Texarkana 2006, orig. proceeding). "By requiring notice of proposed testing and the manner and means of the proposed testing, the [TRCPs] clearly indicate production is available to test tangible objects beyond simple inspection. [¶] The rules expressly provide for production of a tangible item for testing, and one contemplated method by which that production may be accomplished is physically delivering possession of the item to the requesting party or that party's agent."

TRCP 206. REPEALED BY ORDER OF AUG. 5, 1998 AND NOV. 9, 1998, EFF. JAN. 1, 1999

TRCP 207. REPEALED BY ORDER OF AUG. 5, 1998 AND NOV. 9, 1998, EFF. JAN. 1, 1999

TRCP 208. REPEALED BY ORDER OF AUG. 5, 1998 AND NOV. 9, 1998, EFF. JAN. 1, 1999

TRCP 208a. REPEALED BY ORDER OF DEC. 5, 1983, EFF. APRIL 1, 1984

TRCP 209. REPEALED BY ORDER OF AUG. 5, 1998 AND NOV. 9, 1998, EFF. JAN. 1, 1999

TRCP 210 to 214. REPEALED BY ORDER OF DEC. 5, 1983, EFF. APRIL 1, 1984

TRCP 215. ABUSE OF DISCOVERY; SANCTIONS

215.1. Motion for Sanctions or Order Compelling Discovery. A party, upon reasonable notice to other parties and all other persons affected thereby, may apply for sanctions or an order compelling discovery as follows:

(a) ***Appropriate Court.*** On matters relating to a deposition, an application for an order to a party may be made to the court in which the action is pending, or to any district court in the district where the deposition is being

taken. An application for an order to a deponent who is not a party shall be made to the court in the district where the deposition is being taken. As to all other discovery matters, an application for an order will be made to the court in which the action is pending.

(b) *Motion.*

(1) If a party or other deponent which is a corporation or other entity fails to make a designation under Rules 199.2(b)(1) or 200.1(b); or

(2) If a party, or other deponent, or a person designated to testify on behalf of a party or other deponent fails:

(A) to appear before the officer who is to take his deposition, after being served with a proper notice; or

(B) to answer a question propounded or submitted upon oral examination or upon written questions; or

(3) if a party fails:

(A) to serve answers or objections to interrogatories submitted under Rule 197,[1] after proper service of the interrogatories; or

(B) to answer an interrogatory submitted under Rule 197; or

(C) to serve a written response to a request for inspection submitted under Rule 196,[2] after proper service of the request; or

(D) to respond that discovery will be permitted as requested or fails to permit discovery as requested in response to a request for inspection submitted under Rule 196;

the discovering party may move for an order compelling a designation, an appearance, an answer or answers, or inspection or production in accordance with the request, or apply to the court in which the action is pending for the imposition of any sanction authorized by Rule 215.2(b) without the necessity of first having obtained a court order compelling such discovery.

When taking a deposition on oral examination, the proponent of the question may complete or adjourn the examination before he applies for an order.

If the court denies the motion in whole or in part, it may make such protective order as it would have been empowered to make on a motion pursuant to Rule 192.6.

(c) *Evasive or Incomplete Answer.* For purposes of this subdivision an evasive or incomplete answer is to be treated as a failure to answer.

(d) *Disposition of Motion to Compel: Award of Expenses.* If the motion is granted, the court shall, after opportunity for hearing, require a party or deponent whose conduct necessitated the motion or the party or attorney advising such conduct or both of them to pay, at such time as ordered by the court, the moving party the reasonable expenses incurred in obtaining the order, including attorney fees, unless the court finds that the opposition to the motion was substantially justified or that other circumstances make an award of expenses unjust. Such an order shall be subject to review on appeal from the final judgment.

If the motion is denied, the court may, after opportunity for hearing, require the moving party or attorney advising such motion to pay to the party or deponent who opposed the motion the reasonable expenses incurred in opposing the motion, including attorney fees, unless the court finds that the making of the motion was substantially justified or that other circumstances make an award of expenses unjust.

If the motion is granted in part and denied in part, the court may apportion the reasonable expenses incurred in relation to the motion among the parties and persons in a just manner.

In determining the amount of reasonable expenses, including attorney fees, to be awarded in connection with a motion, the trial court shall award expenses which are reasonable in relation to the amount of work reasonably expended in obtaining an order compelling compliance or in opposing a motion which is denied.

(e) *Providing Person's Own Statement.* If a party fails to comply with any person's written request for the person's own statement as provided in Rule 192.3(h), the person who made the request may move for an order compelling compliance. If the motion is granted, the movant may recover the expenses incurred in obtaining the order, including attorney fees, which are reasonable in relation to the amount of work reasonably expended in obtaining the order.

[1] Vernon's Ann.Rules Civ.Proc., rule 197.1 et seq.

[2] Vernon's Ann.Rules Civ.Proc., rule 196.1 et seq.

215.2. Failure to Comply with Order or with Discovery Request.

(a) *Sanctions by Court in District Where Deposition is Taken.* If a deponent fails to appear or to be sworn or to answer a question after being directed to do so by a district court in the district in which the deposition is being taken, the failure may be considered a contempt of that court.

(b) *Sanctions by Court in Which Action is Pending.* If a party or an officer, director, or managing agent of a party or a person designated under Rules 199.2(b)(1) or 200.1(b) to testify on behalf of a party fails to

comply with proper discovery requests or to obey an order to provide or permit discovery, including an order made under Rules 204[1] or 215.1, the court in which the action is pending may, after notice and hearing, make such orders in regard to the failure as are just, and among others the following:

(1) an order disallowing any further discovery of any kind or of a particular kind by the disobedient party;

(2) an order charging all or any portion of the expenses of discovery or taxable court costs or both against the disobedient party or the attorney advising him;

(3) an order that the matters regarding which the order was made or any other designated facts shall be taken to be established for the purposes of the action in accordance with the claim of the party obtaining the order;

(4) an order refusing to allow the disobedient party to support or oppose designated claims or defenses, or prohibiting him from introducing designated matters in evidence;

(5) an order striking out pleadings or parts thereof, or staying further proceedings until the order is obeyed, or dismissing with or without prejudice the action or proceedings or any part thereof, or rendering a judgment by default against the disobedient party;

(6) in lieu of any of the foregoing orders or in addition thereto, an order treating as a contempt of court the failure to obey any orders except an order to submit to a physical or mental examination;

(7) when a party has failed to comply with an order under Rule 204 requiring him to appear or produce another for examination, such orders as are listed in paragraphs (1), (2), (3), (4) or (5) of this subdivision, unless the person failing to comply shows that he is unable to appear or to produce such person for examination.

(8) In lieu of any of the foregoing orders or in addition thereto, the court shall require the party failing to obey the order or the attorney advising him, or both, to pay, at such time as ordered by the court, the reasonable expenses, including attorney fees, caused by the failure, unless the court finds that the failure was substantially justified or that other circumstances make an award of expenses unjust. Such an order shall be subject to review on appeal from the final judgment.

(c) ***Sanction Against Nonparty For Violation of Rules 196.7 or 205.3.*** If a nonparty fails to comply with an order under Rules 196.7 or 205.3, the court which made the order may treat the failure to obey as contempt of court.

[1] Vernon's Ann.Rules Civ.Proc., rule 204.1 et seq.

215.3. Abuse of Discovery Process in Seeking, Making, or Resisting Discovery. If the court finds a party is abusing the discovery process in seeking, making or resisting discovery or if the court finds that any interrogatory or request for inspection or production is unreasonably frivolous, oppressive, or harassing, or that a response or answer is unreasonably frivolous or made for purposes of delay, then the court in which the action is pending may, after notice and hearing, impose any appropriate sanction authorized by paragraphs (1), (2), (3), (4), (5), and (8) of Rule 215.2(b). Such order of sanction shall be subject to review on appeal from the final judgment.

215.4. Failure to Comply with Rule 198.

(a) ***Motion.*** A party who has requested an admission under Rule 198 may move to determine the sufficiency of the answer or objection. For purposes of this subdivision an evasive or incomplete answer may be treated as a failure to answer. Unless the court determines that an objection is justified, it shall order that an answer be served. If the court determines that an answer does not comply with the requirements of Rule 198,[1] it may order either that the matter is admitted or that an amended answer be served. The provisions of Rule 215.1(d) apply to the award of expenses incurred in relation to the motion.

(b) ***Expenses on Failure to Admit.*** If a party fails to admit the genuineness of any document or the truth of any matter as requested under Rule 198 and if the party requesting the admissions thereafter proves the genuineness of the document or the truth of the matter, he may apply to the court for an order requiring the other party to pay him the reasonable expenses incurred in making that proof, including reasonable attorney fees. The court shall make the order unless it finds that (1) the request was held objectionable pursuant to Rule 193,[2] or (2) the admission sought was of no substantial importance, or (3) the party failing to admit had a reasonable ground to believe that he might prevail on the matter, or (4) there was other good reason for the failure to admit.

Oct. 29, 1940, eff. Sept. 1, 1941. Amended by orders of Aug. 5, 1998, and Nov. 9, 1998, eff. Jan. 1, 1999.

[1] Vernon's Ann.Rules Civ.Proc., rule 198.1 et seq.

[2] Vernon's Ann.Rules Civ.Proc., rule 193.1 et seq.

215.5. Failure of Party or Witness to Attend or to Serve Subpoena; Expenses.

(a) ***Failure of Party Giving Notice to Attend.*** If the party giving the notice of the taking of an oral deposition fails to attend and proceed therewith and another party attends in person or by attorney pursuant to the notice, the court may order the party giving the notice to pay such other party the reasonable expenses incurred by him and his attorney in attending, including reasonable attorney fees.

(b) ***Failure of Witness to Attend.*** If a party gives notice of the taking of an oral deposition of a witness and the witness does not attend because of the fault of the party giving the notice, if another party attends in person or by attorney because he expects the deposition of that witness to be taken, the court may order the party giving the notice to pay such other party the reasonable expenses incurred by him and his attorney in attending, including reasonable attorney fees.

215.6. Exhibits to Motions and Responses. Motions or responses made under this rule may have exhibits attached including affidavits, discovery pleadings, or any other documents.

Oct. 29, 1940, eff. Sept. 1, 1941. Amended by orders of Aug. 5, 1998, and Nov. 9, 1998, eff. Jan. 1, 1999.

Comment—1999

The references in this rule to other discovery rules are changed to reflect the revisions in those rules, and former Rule 203 is added as Rule 215.5 in place of the former provision, which is superseded by Rule 193.6.

Source: TRCS art. 3768 (repealed). Original TRCP 215 related to deposition of party.

See also CPRC ch. 10; **O'Connor's Texas Rules**, "Motion for Sanctions," ch. 5-K, §1 et seq.; **O'Connor's Texas Rules**, "General Rules for Discovery," ch. 6-A, §1 et seq.; **O'Connor's Texas Rules**, "Depositions," ch. 6-F, §1 et seq.; **O'Connor's Texas Rules**, "Interrogatories," ch. 6-G, §1 et seq.; **O'Connor's Texas Rules**, "Requests for Admissions," ch. 6-H, §1 et seq.; **O'Connor's Texas Rules**, "Securing Documents & Tangible Things," ch. 6-I, §1 et seq.; **O'Connor's Texas Forms**, FORMS 6A:24, 6A:25, 6A:26, 6A:27, 6A:28, 6A:29, 6A:30, 6A:31, 6A:32.

ANNOTATIONS

Nath v. Texas Children's Hosp., 576 S.W.3d 707, 708-09 (Tex.2019). "[Ds] . . . argue that a different standard of proof applies for attorney's fees awarded as sanctions because the purpose of sanctions is to punish violators and deter misconduct. Because sanctions are intended to punish, [Ds] argue they should not be held to the same evidentiary burden as in other fee-shifting cases. Indeed, some courts of appeal have not required proof of necessity or reasonableness when assessing attorney's fees as sanctions. [¶] This line of authority is premised on a misunderstanding of [an earlier] opinion from this Court. [¶] Before a court may exercise its discretion to shift attorney's fees as a sanction, there must be some evidence of reasonableness because without such proof a trial court cannot determine that the sanction is 'no more severe than necessary' to fairly compensate the prevailing party. 'Consequently, when a party seeks attorney's fees as sanctions, the burden is on that party to put forth some affirmative evidence of attorney's fees incurred and how those fees resulted from or were caused by the sanctionable conduct.'"

Petroleum Solutions, Inc. v. Head, 454 S.W.3d 482, 489 (Tex.2014). "[C]ourts generally follow a two-part test in determining whether a particular sanction for discovery abuse is just. First, a direct relationship must exist between the offensive conduct, the offender, and the sanction imposed. To meet this requirement, a sanction must be directed against the wrongful conduct and toward remedying the prejudice suffered by the innocent party. Second, a sanction must not be excessive, which means it should be no more severe than necessary to satisfy its legitimate purpose. This prong requires the trial court to consider the availability of lesser sanctions and, 'in all but the most exceptional cases, actually test the lesser sanctions.'" *See also* **CHRISTUS Health Gulf Coast v. Carswell**, 505 S.W.3d 528, 540 (Tex.2016); **Spohn Hosp. v. Mayer**, 104 S.W.3d 878, 882 (Tex.2003).

Meyer v. Cathey, 167 S.W.3d 327, 333 (Tex.2005). "[W]aiver bars a trial court from awarding posttrial sanctions based on pretrial conduct of which a party 'was aware' before trial; lack of 'conclusive evidence' is not an excuse." *See also* **Remington Arms Co. v. Caldwell**, 850 S.W.2d 167, 170 (Tex.1993).

Cire v. Cummings, 134 S.W.3d 835, 842 (Tex.2004). "Nothing . . . requires that a trial court test the effectiveness of lesser sanctions by actually implementing and ordering each and every sanction that could possibly be imposed before striking the pleadings of a disobedient party. [A] trial court [is not required] to list each possible lesser sanction in its order and then explain why each would be ineffective. [T]he record [must] reflect that the court 'consider' the availability of appropriate lesser sanctions, and cautions that in all but the most exceptional cases, the trial court must actually test the lesser sanctions before striking the pleadings. [I]n cases of exceptional misconduct . . ., the trial court is not required to test lesser sanctions before striking pleadings . . . so long as the record reflects that the trial court considered lesser sanctions before striking pleadings and the party's conduct justifies the presumption that its claims lack merit. [A] trial court must analyze the available sanctions and offer a reasoned explanation as to the appropriateness of the sanction imposed." *See also* **Low v. Henry**, 221 S.W.3d 609, 620 (Tex.2007); **Chrysler Corp. v. Blackmon**, 841 S.W.2d 844, 849 (Tex.1992); **In re F.A.V.**, 284 S.W.3d 929, 931 (Tex.App.—Dallas 2009, no pet.).

Occidental Chem. Corp. v. Banales, 907 S.W.2d 488, 490 (Tex.1995). "The sanction imposed for discovery abuse should be no more severe than necessary to satisfy the legitimate purposes of the discovery process offended. The work product privilege is essential to the attorney-client relationship. Requiring the production of the attorney's notes from interviews of witnesses is a severe sanction and should receive an appropriately strict review. Piercing the work product privilege, like the 'death penalty' sanction, should apply only when lesser sanctions are inadequate to correct the discovery abuse that has occurred, i.e., when it is the only appropriate sanction. Here the record does not reflect why lesser traditional sanctions might not cure the discovery abuse."

TransAmerican Nat. Gas Corp. v. Powell, 811 S.W.2d 913, 917 (Tex.1991). The punishment for discovery abuse "should fit the crime. *At 918:* Discovery sanctions cannot be used to adjudicate the merits of a party's claims or defenses unless a party's hindrance of the discovery process justifies a presumption that its claims or defenses lack merit." *See also* **Paradigm Oil, Inc. v. Retamco Oper., Inc.**, 372 S.W.3d 177, 184 (Tex.2012); **Hernandez v. Mid-Loop, Inc.**, 170 S.W.3d 138, 143 (Tex.App.—San Antonio 2005, no pet.).

Christus Health Gulf Coast v. Carswell, 433 S.W.3d 585, 615-16 (Tex.App.—Houston [1st Dist.] 2013), *rev'd in part on other grounds*, 505 S.W.3d 528 (Tex.2016). "When a monetary sanction awarded pursuant to Rule 215 'is not tied to any evidence in the record and the basis of calculating the amount is unknown, the sanction constitutes an impermissible arbitrary fine.' Arbitrary fines 'are not susceptible to meaningful review.' When we review a trial court's sanctions order for an abuse of discretion, 'we must be able to determine not only that the trial court's decision to sanction the conduct at issue was proper, but that the sanction the trial court chose was just.' [¶] Absent some evidence supporting the amount of the monetary sanction or some basis for calculating the amount, we have no way to determine whether the amount of the sanction is excessive. When the trial court imposes a monetary sanction, 'the sanctionable conduct alone does not prescribe the amount of the sanction.'"

JNS Enter. v. Dixie Demolition, LLC, 430 S.W.3d 444, 453 (Tex.App.—Austin 2013, no pet.). "Rule 215.3 authorizes a trial court to impose a variety of sanctions 'if the court finds a party is abusing the discovery process in seeking, making or resisting discovery.'. . . Producing false documents in discovery and then lying about those documents in deposition undoubtedly qualifies as an abuse . . . of the discovery process. . . . [¶] While it may be true that death-penalty sanctions cases in Texas *usually* involve discovery orders under rule 215, the absence of such orders does not necessarily preclude the imposition of death-penalty sanctions where . . . the objectionable discovery conduct is fabricating evidence and lying about that evidence in deposition. In most discovery disputes, the objectionable conduct is something that can be corrected using a court order. . . . But when a party fabricates evidence and lies about that evidence in deposition, these typical discovery orders would be ineffective in addressing or punishing the objectionable discovery conduct. [Thus], it is both logical and reasonable that there were no underlying discovery orders. We are not inclined to hold that, as a matter of law, there must be underlying orders that gradually lead up to the death-penalty sanction."

In re Vossdale Townhouse Ass'n, 302 S.W.3d 890, 893-94 (Tex.App.—Houston [14th Dist.] 2009, orig. proceeding). "An order directing that counsel may no longer represent his clients in the subject litigation is not among those sanctions enumerated in Rule 215.2(b). While Rule 215.2(b) does not limit the types of discovery sanctions the trial court may impose to those enumerated in the rule, the imposition of a sanction that is not specifically authorized in derogation of a clearly established legal right cannot be just. The trial court's order . . . was imposed in derogation of the clearly established right to counsel of choice." *See also* **In re White**, 227 S.W.3d 234, 236 (Tex.App.—San Antonio 2007, orig. proceeding) (Rule 215.2(b) does not authorize trial court to impose sanctions on nonparty deponents).

TRCP 215a to 215c. REPEALED BY ORDER OF DEC. 5, 1983, EFF. APRIL 1, 1984

SECTION 10. THE JURY IN COURT

TRCP 216. REQUEST AND FEE FOR JURY TRIAL

a. Request. No jury trial shall be had in any civil suit, unless a written request for a jury trial is filed with the clerk of the court a reasonable time before the date set for trial of the cause on the non-jury docket, but not less than thirty days in advance.

b. Jury Fee. Unless otherwise provided by law, a fee of ten dollars if in the district court and five dollars if in the county court must be deposited with the clerk of the court within the time for making a written request for a jury trial. The clerk shall promptly enter a notation of the payment of such fee upon the court's docket sheet.

Oct. 29, 1940, eff. Sept. 1, 1941. Amended by orders of March 31, 1941, eff. Sept. 1, 1941; Sept. 20, 1941, eff. Dec. 31, 1941; Oct. 12, 1949, eff. March 1, 1950; July 15, 1987, eff. Jan. 1, 1988; April 24, 1990, eff. Sept. 1, 1990.

Source: TRCS arts. 2124, 2125 (repealed).

See also U.S. Const. amend. 7; Tex. Const. art. 1, §15; Gov't Code §51.604; **O'Connor's Texas Rules**, "Request for Jury Trial," ch. 5-B, §1 et seq.; **O'Connor's Texas Forms**, FORMS 5B:1, 5B:2, 5B:3, 5B:4.

ANNOTATIONS

General Motors Corp. v. Gayle, 951 S.W.2d 469, 476 (Tex.1997). "Even where a party does not timely pay the jury fee, . . . a trial court should accord the right to jury trial if it can be done without interfering with the court's docket, delaying the trial, or injuring the opposing party. *At 477:* [D] established that a 30-day continuance to perfect [D's] jury trial demand would not cause [Ps] any injury or delay. [T]he trial court's seriatim trial schedule seems only a sham to hold [D] to its mistake in not paying the jury fee without penalizing the other side." *See also* **Crittenden v. Crittenden**, 52 S.W.3d 768, 769 (Tex.App.—San Antonio 2001, pet. denied).

Halsell v. Dehoyos, 810 S.W.2d 371, 371 (Tex.1991). "A [jury] request in advance of the 30-day deadline [of TRCP 216] is presumed to have been made a reasonable time before trial." *See also* **Sims v. Fitzpatrick**, 288 S.W.3d 93,

102 (Tex.App.—Houston [1st Dist.] 2009, no pet.) (party may rebut presumption by showing that granting jury trial would injure adverse party, disrupt court's docket, or impede handling of court's business); **Brockie v. Webb**, 244 S.W.3d 905, 908 (Tex.App.—Dallas 2008, pet. denied) (party may waive right to jury if request is made after case is certified for trial and less than 30 days before trial).

In re K.M.H., 181 S.W.3d 1, 8 (Tex.App.—Houston [14th Dist.] 2005, no pet.). "When a party has perfected its right to a jury trial . . . but the trial court proceeds to trial without a jury, the party must, to preserve error, either object on the record to the trial court's action or indicate affirmatively in the record it intends to stand on its perfected right to a jury trial." *See also* **Pisharodi v. Columbia Valley Healthcare Sys.**, __ S.W.3d __ n.5, 2020 WL 2213951 (Tex.App.—Corpus Christi 2020, n.p.h.) (No. 13-18-00364-CV; 5-7-20). *But see* **In re J.M.**, No. 12-19-00353-CV, 2020 WL 1528054 (Tex.App.—Tyler 2020, no pet.) (memo op.; 3-31-20) (party must simply obtain adverse ruling from trial court on jury demand; proceeding with bench trial after obtaining adverse ruling does not waive right to jury trial); **McKern v. McCann**, 675 S.W.2d 222, 223-24 (Tex.App.—Austin 1984, no writ) (same).

In re J.C., 108 S.W.3d 914, 916-17 (Tex.App.—Texarkana 2003, no pet.). "[W]hen compliance with [TRCP] 216 is made impossible by failure to give the notice required by [TRCP] 245, a demand for a jury trial made within 30 days of the trial setting will be deemed timely. Here, compliance with Rule 216 was made impossible for [D's] court-appointed attorney ad litem by the lateness of his appointment. Just as the 30-day period required by Rule 216 [has] to be expanded . . . because of the failure to give the . . . notice required by Rule 245, so must it be expanded . . . because of the late appointment of [D's] counsel."

TRCP 217. OATH OF INABILITY

The deposit for a jury fee shall not be required when the party shall within the time for making such deposit, file with the clerk his affidavit to the effect that he is unable to make such deposit, and that he can not, by the pledge of property or otherwise, obtain the money necessary for that purpose; and the court shall then order the clerk to enter the suit on the jury docket.

Oct. 29, 1940, eff. Sept. 1, 1941.

See also **O'Connor's Texas Rules**, "Request for Jury Trial," ch. 5-B, §1 et seq.

TRCP 218. JURY DOCKET

The clerks of the district and county courts shall each keep a docket, styled, "The Jury Docket," in which shall be entered in their order the cases in which jury fees have been paid or affidavit in lieu thereof has been filed as provided in the two preceding rules.

Oct. 29, 1940, eff. Sept. 1, 1941.

TRCP 219. JURY TRIAL DAY

The court shall designate the days for taking up the jury docket and the trial of jury cases. Such order may be revoked or changed in the court's discretion.

Oct. 29, 1940, eff. Sept. 1, 1941. Amended by order of Dec. 5, 1983, eff. April 1, 1984.

TRCP 220. WITHDRAWING CAUSE FROM JURY DOCKET

When any party has paid the fee for a jury trial, he shall not be permitted to withdraw the cause from the jury docket over the objection of the parties adversely interested. If so permitted, the court in its discretion may by an order permit him to withdraw also his jury fee deposit. Failure of a party to appear for trial shall be deemed a waiver by him of the right to trial by jury.

Oct. 29, 1940, eff. Sept. 1, 1941. Amended by orders of Aug. 18, 1947, eff. Dec. 31, 1947; July 21, 1970, eff. Jan. 1, 1971.

Source: TRCS art. 2130 (repealed).

See also **O'Connor's Texas Rules**, "Request for Jury Trial," ch. 5-B, §1 et seq.; **O'Connor's Texas Forms**, FORMS 5B:5, 5B:6.

ANNOTATIONS

Mercedes-Benz Credit Corp. v. Rhyne, 925 S.W.2d 664, 666 (Tex.1996). "Only when a party demands a jury *and* pays the fee can the opposing party rely on those actions. In such a case, the trial court may not remove the case from the jury docket over the objections of the opposing party." *See also* **Green v. W.E. Grace Mfg.**, 422 S.W.2d 723, 726 (Tex.1968).

In re Marriage of Harrison, 557 S.W.3d 99, 135 (Tex.App.—Houston [14th Dist.] 2018, pet. denied). "[T]he right to a jury trial may be waived or withdrawn by (a) agreeing to a bench trial, (b) failing to timely pay a jury fee, (c) failing to timely request a jury trial, (d) failing to appear for trial, or (e) failing to object to a bench trial despite a properly perfected request. *At 136-37:* A party who fails to appear at trial after filing an answer waives a right to a jury trial. At least one of our sister courts of appeals has held 'a failure to appear at the designated time constitutes a waiver of trial by jury under Rule 220.' . . . Other courts of appeals have agreed that a right to jury trial may be waived by a party's untimely appearance. [¶] [Party] failed to appear at 8:30 a.m., as ordered. The record reflects that [party] called the court clerk at approximately 9:07, but even [party's] phone call came almost forty minutes after the time the court ordered her to appear and the record does not reveal the substance of [party's] communication to the clerk. [Party] did not appear in the courtroom until approximately 10:15, over one and one-half hours late. [¶] The trial court deemed [party's] failure to appear timely as a waiver of a jury trial. . . . We . . . hold that, under the

unique facts of this case, the trial court did not abuse its discretion in deeming [party's] failure to timely appear as a waiver of her right to a jury trial. [¶] To be sure, the trial court could have declared a mistrial once [party] appeared and objected to the bench trial. But failing to start over with a jury under these facts was not an abuse of discretion. [Party] repeatedly proved herself unable or unwilling to manage her schedule or affairs in such a way as to ensure compliance with the court's orders, including orders to appear timely in court. The court was entitled to take [party's] dilatory history into account in exercising its discretion whether—and if so, for how long—to wait for [party] to appear for trial. The trial court has authority to impose consequences for a party's failure to appear timely for trial." *See also* **In re T.K.**, No. 09-09-00472-CV, 2010 WL 890657 (Tex.App.—Beaumont 2010, no pet.) (memo op.; 3-11-10) (right to jury trial can be waived if attorney is present but refuses to go forward with trial or if attorney and party arrive late).

In re J.N.F., 116 S.W.3d 426, 434-35 (Tex.App.—Houston [14th Dist.] 2003, no pet.). "'[U]nless an objection is made to the withdrawal of a case from the jury docket, the non-requesting party has no right to a jury trial.' If a party who has requested a jury trial in an initial pleading could effectively withdraw the request simply by omitting it in subsequent pleadings, the non-requesting party would be forced to scrutinize all such pleadings in order to avoid waiving a jury trial by failing to object to the withdrawal. [¶] [O]mitting a jury request from subsequent pleadings does not rise to the level of inaction that has been held to constitute the requesting party's waiver of a jury trial."

TRCP 221. CHALLENGE TO THE ARRAY

When the jurors summoned have not been selected by jury commissioners or by drawing the names from a jury wheel, any party to a suit which is to be tried by a jury may, before the jury is drawn challenge the array upon the ground that the officer summoning the jury has acted corruptly, and has wilfully summoned jurors known to be prejudiced against the party challenging or biased in favor of the adverse party. All such challenges must be in writing setting forth distinctly the grounds of such challenge and supported by the affidavit of the party or some other credible person. When such challenge is made, the court shall hear evidence and decide without delay whether or not the challenge shall be sustained.

Oct. 29, 1940, eff. Sept. 1, 1941.

See also Gov't Code §62.001; **O'Connor's Texas Rules**, "Jury Selection," ch. 8-A, §1 et seq.

TRCP 222. WHEN CHALLENGE IS SUSTAINED

If the challenge be sustained, the array of jurors summoned shall be discharged, and the court shall order other jurors summoned in their stead, and shall direct that the officer who summoned the persons so discharged, and on account of whose misconduct the challenge has been sustained, shall not summon any other jurors in the case.

Oct. 29, 1940, eff. Sept. 1, 1941.

TRCP 223. JURY LIST IN CERTAIN COUNTIES

In counties governed as to juries by the laws providing for interchangeable juries, the names of the jurors shall be placed upon the general panel in the order in which they are randomly selected, and jurors shall be assigned for service from the top thereof, in the order in which they shall be needed, and jurors returned to the general panel after service in any of such courts shall be enrolled at the bottom of the list in the order of their respective return; provided, however, after such assignment to a particular court, the trial judge of such court, upon the demand prior to voir dire examination by any party or attorney in the case reached for trial in such court, shall cause the names of all members of such assigned jury panel in such case to be placed in a receptacle, shuffled, and drawn, and such names shall be transcribed in the order drawn on the jury list from which the jury is to be selected to try such case. There shall be only one shuffle and drawing by the trial judge in each case.

Oct. 29, 1940, eff. Sept. 1, 1941. Amended by order of April 24, 1990, eff. Sept. 1, 1990.

Comment—1990

To provide uniformity in jury shuffles.

See also Gov't Code §§62.016, 62.017 (interchangeable juries in certain counties); **O'Connor's Texas Rules**, "Jury Selection," ch. 8-A, §1 et seq.

ANNOTATIONS

Rivas v. Liberty Mut. Ins., 480 S.W.2d 610, 612 (Tex.1972). "The court of civil appeals recognized the listing and reshuffle provisions of Rule 223 are designed to insure a random selection of jurors. While the method used here did not conform to the method prescribed by the rule, it did insure a degree of randomness in the listing of the jurors."

BNSF Ry. v. Wipff, 408 S.W.3d 662, 666 (Tex.App.—Fort Worth 2013, no pet.). TRCP 223 "is clear that a shuffle demand must be made before voir dire begins. [A] shuffle demand is untimely in a civil case if done after counsel reviews case-specific questionnaires that give detailed information beyond the 'name, rank, and serial number' given on information cards. [P] relies on the fact that [D] reviewed a case-specific questionnaire before demanding the shuffle. *At 667:* But it is clear that the trial court had not given the venire the prescribed instructions under [TRCP] 226a before the requested jury shuffle. The Texas Supreme Court, in ordering the form of the Rule 226a instructions, mandated that they 'shall be given by the court to the members of the jury panel after they have been sworn in as provided

in Rule 226 and *before the voir dire examination.'* [Thus], voir dire is not to begin until after the admonitory instructions are given to the venire. While true that case-specific questionnaires were completed and received by counsel, counsel had not viewed the venire, and the trial court had not given the venire the prescribed instructions. . . . Therefore, voir dire had not begun in this case even though counsel had an opportunity to review the questionnaires. *At 668:* [D's] shuffle demand was timely under Rule 223 because it was made before voir dire began."

TRCP 224. PREPARING JURY LIST

In counties not governed as to juries by the laws providing for interchangeable juries, when the parties have announced ready for trial the clerk shall write the name of each regular juror entered of record for that week on separate slips of paper, as near the same size and appearance as may be, and shall place the slips in a box and mix them well. The clerk shall draw from the box, in the presence of the court, the names of twenty-four jurors, if in the district court, or so many as there may be, if there be a less number in the box; and the names of twelve jurors if in the county court, or so many as there may be, and write the names as drawn upon two slips of paper and deliver one slip to each party to the suit or his attorney.

Oct. 29, 1940, eff. Sept. 1, 1941.

See also **O'Connor's Texas Rules**, "Jury Selection," ch. 8-A, §1 et seq.

ANNOTATIONS

Southwestern Pub. Serv. v. Morris, 380 S.W.2d 648, 649 (Tex.App.—Amarillo 1964, no writ). "[E]rror was committed by the court in refusing condemnor's request that the jury panel be drawn before the selection of the jury." Such error may be harmless.

TRCP 225. SUMMONING TALESMAN

When there are not as many as twenty-four names drawn from the box, if in the district court, or as many as twelve, if in the county court, the court shall direct the sheriff to summon such number of qualified persons as the court deems necessary to complete the panel. The names of those thus summoned shall be placed in the box and drawn and entered upon the slips as provided in the preceding rules.

Oct. 29, 1940, eff. Sept. 1, 1941.

TRCP 226. OATH TO JURY PANEL

Before the parties or their attorneys begin the examination of the jurors whose names have thus been listed, the jurors shall be sworn by the court or under its direction, as follows: "You, and each of you, do solemnly swear that you will true answers give to all questions propounded to you concerning your qualifications as a juror, so help you God."

Oct. 29, 1940, eff. Sept. 1, 1941.

See also **O'Connor's Texas Rules**, "Jury Selection," ch. 8-A, §1 et seq.

ANNOTATIONS

Barron v. State, 378 S.W.2d 144, 147 (Tex.App.—San Antonio 1964, no writ). "[F]ailure to swear the jury panel prior to the voir dire examination as required by Rule 226 . . . was waived by [the] failure to timely complain of same."

TRCP 226a. INSTRUCTIONS TO JURY PANEL AND JURY

The court must give instructions to the jury panel and the jury as prescribed by order of the Supreme Court under this rule.

Oct. 29, 1940, eff. Sept. 1, 1941. Added by order of July 20, 1966, eff. Jan. 1, 1967. Amended by order of Jan. 27, 2005, eff. Feb. 1, 2005.

Comment—2005

The rule is clarified. With these amendments, the Supreme Court has ordered changes in the prescribed jury instructions consistent with Act of June 2, 2003, 78th Leg., R.S., ch. 204, §13.04, 2003 Tex. Gen. Laws 847, 888, codified as Tex. Civ. Prac. & Rem. Code §41.003.

Source: New rule.

APPROVED INSTRUCTIONS

I.

That the following oral instructions, with such modifications as the circumstances of the particular case may require, shall be given by the court to the members of the jury panel after they have been sworn in as provided in Rule 226 and before the voir dire examination:

Members of the Jury Panel [or Ladies and Gentlemen of the Jury Panel]:

Thank you for being here. We are here to select a jury. Twelve [six] of you will be chosen for the jury. Even if you are not chosen for the jury, you are performing a valuable service that is your right and duty as a citizen of a free country.

Before we begin: Turn off all phones and other electronic devices. While you are in the courtroom, do not communicate with anyone through any electronic device. [For example, do not communicate by phone, text message, email message, chat room, blog, or social networking websites such as Facebook, Twitter, or Myspace.] [I will give you a number where others may contact you in case of an emergency.] Do not record or photograph any part of these court proceedings, because it is prohibited by law.

If you are chosen for the jury, your role as jurors will be to decide the disputed facts in this case. My role will be to ensure that this case is tried in accordance with the rules of law.

Here is some background about this case. This is a civil case. It is a lawsuit that is not a criminal case. The parties are as follows: The plaintiff is _______, and the defendant is _______. Representing the plaintiff is _______, and representing the defendant is _______. They will ask you some questions during jury selection. But before their questions begin, I must give you some instructions for jury selection.

Every juror must obey these instructions. You may be called into court to testify about any violations of these instructions. If you do not follow these instructions, you will be guilty of juror misconduct, and I might have to order a new trial and start this process over again. This would waste your time and the parties' money, and would require the taxpayers of this county to pay for another trial.

These are the instructions.

1. To avoid looking like you are friendly with one side of the case, do not mingle or talk with the lawyers, witnesses, parties, or anyone else involved in the case. You may exchange casual greetings like "hello" and "good morning." Other than that, do not talk with them at all. They have to follow these instructions too, so you should not be offended when they follow the instructions.

2. Do not accept any favors from the lawyers, witnesses, parties, or anyone else involved in the case, and do not do any favors for them. This includes favors such as giving rides and food.

3. Do not discuss this case with anyone, even your spouse or a friend, either in person or by any other means [including by phone, text message, email message, chat room, blog, or social networking websites such as Facebook, Twitter, or Myspace]. Do not allow anyone to discuss the case with you or in your hearing. If anyone tries to discuss the case with you or in your hearing, tell me immediately. We do not want you to be influenced by something other than the evidence admitted in court.

4. The parties, through their attorneys, have the right to ask you questions about your background, experiences, and attitudes. They are not trying to meddle in your affairs. They are just being thorough and trying to choose fair jurors who do not have any bias or prejudice in this particular case.

5. Remember that you took an oath that you will tell the truth, so be truthful when the lawyers ask you questions, and always give complete answers. If you do not answer a question that applies to you, that violates your oath. Sometimes a lawyer will ask a question of the whole panel instead of just one person. If the question applies to you, raise your hand and keep it raised until you are called on.

Do you understand these instructions? If you do not, please tell me now.

The lawyers will now begin to ask their questions.

II.

That the following oral and written instructions, with such modifications as the circumstances of the particular case may require, shall be given by the court to the jury immediately after the jurors are selected for the case:

Members of the Jury [or Ladies and Gentlemen]:

You have been chosen to serve on this jury. Because of the oath you have taken and your selection for the jury, you become officials of this court and active participants in our justice system.

[Hand out the written instructions.]

You have each received a set of written instructions. I am going to read them with you now. Some of them you have heard before and some are new.

1. Turn off all phones and other electronic devices. While you are in the courtroom and while you are deliberating, do not communicate with anyone through any electronic device. [For example, do not communicate by phone, text message, email message, chat room, blog, or social networking websites such as Facebook, Twitter, or Myspace.] [I will give you a number where others may contact you in case of an emergency.] Do not post information about the case on the Internet before these court proceedings end and you are released from jury duty. Do not record or photograph any part of these court proceedings, because it is prohibited by law.

2. To avoid looking like you are friendly with one side of the case, do not mingle or talk with the lawyers witnesses, parties, or anyone else involved in the case. You may exchange casual greetings like "hello" and "good morning." Other than that, do not talk with them at all. They have to follow these instructions too, so you should not be offended when they follow the instructions.

3. Do not accept any favors from the lawyers, witnesses, parties, or anyone else involved in the case, and do not do any favors for them. This includes favors such as giving rides and food.

4. Do not discuss this case with anyone, even your spouse or a friend, either in person or by any other means [including by phone, text message, email message, chat room, blog, or social networking websites such as Facebook, Twitter, or Myspace]. Do not allow anyone to discuss the case with you or in your hearing. If anyone tries to discuss the case with you or in your hearing, tell me immediately. We do not want you to be influenced by something other than the evidence admitted in court.

5. Do not discuss this case with anyone during the trial, not even with the other jurors, until the end of the trial. You should not discuss the case with your fellow jurors until the end of the trial so that you do not form opinions about the case before you have heard everything.

After you have heard all the evidence, received all of my instructions, and heard all of the lawyers' arguments, you will then go to the jury room to discuss the case with the other jurors and reach a verdict.

6. Do not investigate this case on your own. For example, do not:

a. try to get information about the case, lawyers, witnesses, or issues from outside this courtroom;

b. go to places mentioned in the case to inspect the places;

c. inspect items mentioned in this case unless they are presented as evidence in court;

d. look anything up in a law book, dictionary, or public record to try to learn more about the case;

e. look anything up on the Internet to try to learn more about the case; or

f. let anyone else do any of these things for you.

This rule is very important because we want a trial based only on evidence admitted in open court. Your conclusions about this case must be based only on what you see and hear in this courtroom because the law does not permit you to base your conclusions on information that has not been presented to you in open court. All the information must be presented in open court so the parties and their lawyers can test it and object to it. Information from other sources, like the Internet, will not go through this important process in the courtroom. In addition, information from other sources could be completely unreliable. As a result, if you investigate this case on your own, you could compromise the fairness to all parties in this case and jeopardize the results of this trial.

7. Do not tell other jurors about your own experiences or other people's experiences. For example, you may have special knowledge of something in the case, such as business, technical, or professional information. You may even have expert knowledge or opinions, or you may know what happened in this case or another similar case. Do not tell the other jurors about it. Telling other jurors about it is wrong because it means the jury will be considering things that were not admitted in court.

8. Do not consider attorneys' fees unless I tell you to. Do not guess about attorneys' fees.

9. Do not consider or guess whether any party is covered by insurance unless I tell you to.

10. During the trial, if taking notes will help focus your attention on the evidence, you may take notes using the materials the court has provided. Do not use any personal electronic devices to take notes. If taking notes will distract your attention from the evidence, you should not take notes. Your notes are for your own personal use. They are not evidence. Do not show or read your notes to anyone, including other jurors.

You must leave your notes in the jury room or with the bailiff. The bailiff is instructed not to read your notes and to give your notes to me promptly after collecting them from you. I will make sure your notes are kept in a safe, secure location and not disclosed to anyone.

[You may take your notes back into the jury room and consult them during deliberations. But keep in mind that your notes are not evidence. When you deliberate, each of you should rely on your independent recollection of the evidence and not be influenced by the fact that another juror has or has not taken notes. After you complete your deliberations, the bailiff will collect your notes.]

When you are released from jury duty, the bailiff will promptly destroy your notes so that nobody can read what you wrote.

11. I will decide matters of law in this case. It is your duty to listen to and consider the evidence and to determine fact issues that I may submit to you at the end of the trial. After you have heard all the evidence, I will give you instructions to follow as you make your decision. The instructions also will have questions for you to answer. You will not be asked and you should not consider which side will win. Instead, you will need to answer the specific questions I give you.

Every juror must obey my instructions. If you do not follow these instructions, you will be guilty of juror misconduct, and I may have to order a new trial and start this process over again. This would waste your time and the parties' money, and would require the taxpayers of this county to pay for another trial.

Do you understand these instructions? If you do not, please tell me now.

Please keep these instructions and review them as we go through this case. If anyone does not follow these instructions, tell me.

III.

COURT'S CHARGE

Before closing arguments begin, the court must give to each member of the jury a copy of the charge, which must include the following written instructions, with such modifications as the circumstances of the particular case may require:

Members of the Jury [or Ladies & Gentlemen of the Jury]:

After the closing arguments, you will go to the jury room to decide the case, answer the questions that are attached, and reach a verdict. You may discuss the case with other jurors only when you are all together in the jury room.

Remember my previous instructions: Do not discuss the case with anyone else, either in person or by any other means. Do not do any independent investigation about the case or conduct any research. Do not look up any words in dictionaries or on the Internet. Do not post information about the case on the Internet. Do not share any special knowledge or experiences with the other jurors. Do not use your phone or any other electronic device during your deliberations for any reason. [I will give you a number where others may contact you in case of an emergency.]

[Any notes you have taken are for your own personal use. You may take your notes back into the jury room and consult them during deliberations, but do not show or read your notes to your fellow jurors during your deliberations. Your notes are not evidence. Each of you should rely on your independent recollection of the evidence and not be influenced by the fact that another juror has or has not taken notes.]

[You must leave your notes with the bailiff when you are not deliberating. The bailiff will give your notes to me promptly after collecting them from you. I will make sure your notes are kept in a safe, secure location and not disclosed to anyone. After you complete your deliberations, the bailiff will collect your notes. When you are released from jury duty, the bailiff will promptly destroy your notes so that nobody can read what you wrote.]

Here are the instructions for answering the questions.

1. Do not let bias, prejudice, or sympathy play any part in your decision.

2. Base your answers only on the evidence admitted in court and on the law that is in these instructions and questions. Do not consider or discuss any evidence that was not admitted in the courtroom.

3. You are to make up your own minds about the facts. You are the sole judges of the credibility of the witnesses and the weight to give their testimony. But on matters of law, you must follow all of my instructions.

4. If my instructions use a word in a way that is different from its ordinary meaning, use the meaning I give you, which will be a proper legal definition.

5. All the questions and answers are important. No one should say that any question or answer is not important.

6. Answer "yes" or "no" to all questions unless you are told otherwise. A "yes" answer must be based on a preponderance of the evidence [unless you are told otherwise]. Whenever a question requires an answer other than "yes" or "no," your answer must be based on a preponderance of the evidence [unless you are told otherwise].

The term "preponderance of the evidence" means the greater weight of credible evidence presented in this case. If you do not find that a preponderance of the evidence supports a "yes" answer, then answer "no." A preponderance of the evidence is not measured by the number of witnesses or by the number of documents admitted in evidence. For a fact to be proved by a preponderance of the evidence, you must find that the fact is more likely true than not true.

7. Do not decide who you think should win before you answer the questions and then just answer the questions to match your decision. Answer each question carefully without considering who will win. Do not discuss or consider the effect your answers will have.

8. Do not answer questions by drawing straws or by any method of chance.

9. Some questions might ask you for a dollar amount. Do not agree in advance to decide on a dollar amount by adding up each juror's amount and then figuring the average.

10. Do not trade your answers. For example, do not say, "I will answer this question your way if you answer another question my way."

11. [Unless otherwise instructed] The answers to the questions must be based on the decision of at least 10 of the 12 [5 of the 6] jurors. The same 10 [5] jurors must agree on every answer. Do not agree to be bound by a vote of anything less than 10 [5] jurors, even if it would be a majority.

As I have said before, if you do not follow these instructions, you will be guilty of juror misconduct, and I might have to order a new trial and start this process over again. This would waste your time and the parties' money, and would require the taxpayers of this county to pay for another trial. If a juror breaks any of these rules, tell that person to stop and report it to me immediately.

[Definitions, questions, and special instructions given to the jury will be transcribed here. If exemplary damages are sought against a defendant, the jury must unanimously find, with respect to that defendant, (i) liability on at least one claim for actual damages that will support an award of exemplary damages, (ii) any additional conduct, such as malice or gross negligence, required for an award of exemplary damages, and (iii) the amount of exemplary damages to be awarded. The jury's answers to questions regarding (ii) and (iii) must be conditioned on a unanimous finding regarding (i), except in an extraordinary circumstance when the conditioning instruction would be erroneous. The jury need not be unanimous in finding the amount of actual damages. Thus, if questions regarding (ii) and (iii) are submitted to the jury for defendants D1 and D2, instructions in substantially the following form must immediately precede such questions:

Preceding question (ii):

Answer Question (ii) for D1 only if you unanimously answered "Yes" to Question[s] (i) regarding D1. Otherwise, do not answer Question (ii) for D1. [Repeat for D2.]

You are instructed that in order to answer "Yes" to [any part of] Question (ii), your answer must be unanimous. You may answer "No" to [any part of] Question (ii) only upon a vote of 10 [5] or more jurors. Otherwise, you must not answer [that part of] Question (ii).

Preceding question (iii):

Answer Question (iii) for D1 only if you answered "Yes" to Question (ii) for D1. Otherwise, do not answer Question (iii) for D1. [Repeat for D2.]

You are instructed that you must unanimously agree on the amount of any award of exemplary damages.

These examples are given by way of illustration.]

Presiding Juror:

1. When you go into the jury room to answer the questions, the first thing you will need to do is choose a presiding juror.

2. The presiding juror has these duties:

a. have the complete charge read aloud if it will be helpful to your deliberations;

b. preside over your deliberations, meaning manage the discussions, and see that you follow these instructions;

c. give written questions or comments to the bailiff who will give them to the judge;

d. write down the answers you agree on;

e. get the signatures for the verdict certificate; and

f. notify the bailiff that you have reached a verdict.

Do you understand the duties of the presiding juror? If you do not, please tell me now.

Instructions for Signing the Verdict Certificate:

1. [Unless otherwise instructed] You may answer the questions on a vote of 10 [5] jurors. The same 10 [5] jurors must agree on every answer in the charge. This means you may not have one group of 10 [5] jurors agree on one answer and a different group of 10 [5] jurors agree on another answer.

2. If 10 [5] jurors agree on every answer, those 10 [5] jurors sign the verdict.

If 11 jurors agree on every answer, those 11 jurors sign the verdict.

If all 12 [6] of you agree on every answer, you are unanimous and only the presiding juror signs the verdict.

3. All jurors should deliberate on every question. You may end up with all 12 [6] of you agreeing on some answers, while only 10 [5] or 11 of you agree on other answers. But when you sign the verdict, only those 10 [5] who agree on every answer will sign the verdict.

4. [Added if the charge requires some unanimity] There are some special instructions before Questions ____ explaining how to answer those questions. Please follow the instructions. If all 12 [6] of you answer those questions, you will need to complete a second verdict certificate for those questions.

Do you understand these instructions? If you do not, please tell me now.

____
Judge Presiding

VERDICT CERTIFICATE

Check one:

____ *Our verdict is unanimous. All 12 [6] of us have agreed to each and every answer. The presiding juror has signed the certificate for all 12 [6] of us.*

____
Signature of Presiding Juror

____
Printed Name of Presiding Juror

____ *Our verdict is not unanimous. Eleven of us have agreed to each and every answer and have signed the certificate below.*

____ *Our verdict is not unanimous. Ten [Five] of us have agreed to each and every answer and have signed the certificate below.*

	SIGNATURE	*NAME PRINTED*
1.	____________	____________
2.	____________	____________
3.	____________	____________
4.	____________	____________
5.	____________	____________
6.	____________	____________
7.	____________	____________
8.	____________	____________
9.	____________	____________
10.	____________	____________
11.	____________	____________

If you have answered Question No. ____ [the exemplary damages amount], then you must sign this certificate also.

ADDITIONAL CERTIFICATE

[Used when some questions require unanimous answers]

I certify that the jury was unanimous in answering the following questions. All 12 [6] of us agreed to each of the answers. The presiding juror has signed the certificate for all 12 [6] of us.

[Judge to list questions that require a unanimous answer, including the predicate liability question.]

____
Signature of Presiding Juror

____
Printed Name of Presiding Juror

IV.

That the following oral instructions shall be given by the court to the jury after the verdict has been accepted by the court and before the jurors are released from jury duty:

Thank you for your verdict.

I have told you that the only time you may discuss the case is with the other jurors in the jury room. I now release you from jury duty. Now you may discuss the case with anyone. But you may also choose not to discuss the case; that is your right.

After you are released from jury duty, the lawyers and others may ask you questions to see if the jury followed the instructions, and they may ask you to give a sworn statement. You are free to discuss the case with them and to give a sworn statement. But you may choose not to discuss the case and not to give a sworn statement; that is your right.

History of instructions to TRCP 226a: Amended eff. Apr. 13, 2011, by order of Apr. 13, 2011 (Tex.Sup.Ct. Order, Misc. Docket No. 11-9047a). Amended eff. Apr. 1, 2011, by order of Mar. 15, 2011 (Tex.Sup.Ct. Order, Misc. Docket No. 11-9047). Amended eff. Feb. 1, 2005, by order of Jan. 27, 2005 (Tex.Sup.Ct. Order, Misc. Docket No. 05-9022): Changed instructions from III, par. 6 to end. Amended eff. Jan. 1, 1988, by order of Jan. 28, 1988 (741-42 S.W.2d [Tex.Cases] xlv): Changed instructions from III, par. 6 to end; corrected order of Dec. 16, 1987. Amended eff. Jan. 1, 1988, by order of Dec. 16, 1987 (741-42 S.W.2d [Tex.Cases] xliv): Instructions from III, par. 6 to end changed to correct amendment of July 15, 1987, which had unintentionally included the last par. "The presiding juror . . . the juror not to do so again"; that par. deleted by this correction. Amended eff. Jan. 1, 1988, by order of July 15, 1987 (733-34 S.W.2d [Tex.Cases] lxv): Changed instructions from II, par. 10 to III, par. 6. Amended eff. Apr. 1, 1984, by orders of Dec. 5, 1983 (661-62 S.W.2d [Tex.Cases] lxxiii): Changed word "foreman" to "presiding juror." Amended eff. Feb. 1, 1973, by order of Oct. 3, 1972 (483-84 S.W.2d [Tex.Cases] xlvii): Changed instructions from III, par. 6. Amended eff. Jan. 1, 1971, by order of July 21, 1970 (455-56 S.W.2d [Tex.Cases] xxii): Changed instructions from II, par. 9. Adopted eff. Jan. 1, 1967, by order of July 20, 1966 (401-02 S.W.2d [Tex.Cases] xxxvii). Source: New rule.

See also **O'Connor's Texas Rules**, "Jury Selection," ch. 8-A, §1 et seq.; **O'Connor's Texas Rules**, "Jury Charge," ch. 8-I, §1 et seq.; **O'Connor's Texas Forms**, FORMS 8I.

ANNOTATIONS

Woods v. Crane Carrier Co., 693 S.W.2d 377, 379 (Tex.1985). "[W]hen terms requiring definitions are used more than once in a charge, it is preferable that the definition or instruction occur immediately after the general instructions required by [TRCP] 226a. . . ."

In re Commitment of Stevenson, No. 09-11-00601-CV, 2013 WL 5302591 (Tex.App.—Beaumont 2013, no pet.) (memo op.; 9-19-13). "[D] relies on Rule 226a . . . to sup-

port his argument that the trial court is prohibited from talking with the jurors. However, the instruction the Texas Supreme Court promulgated for trial courts to provide to the venire under this rule requires that trial courts instruct that members of the venire 'not mingle or talk with the lawyers, witnesses, parties, or anyone else involved in the case.' We disagree that the Texas Supreme Court has interpreted Rule 226a in a way that proscribes a trial court from communicating with potential jurors during voir dire."

TRCP 227. CHALLENGE TO JUROR

A challenge to a particular juror is either a challenge for cause or a peremptory challenge. The court shall decide without delay any such challenge, and if sustained, the juror shall be discharged from the particular case. Either such challenge may be made orally on the formation of a jury to try the case.

Oct. 29, 1940, eff. Sept. 1, 1941.

See also Gov't Code §§62.101–62.110 (juror qualifications); **O'Connor's Texas Rules**, "Jury Selection," ch. 8-A, §1 et seq.

TRCP 228. "CHALLENGE FOR CAUSE" DEFINED

A challenge for cause is an objection made to a juror, alleging some fact which by law disqualifies him to serve as a juror in the case or in any case, or which in the opinion of the court, renders him an unfit person to sit on the jury. Upon such challenge the examination is not confined to the answers of the juror, but other evidence may be heard for or against the challenge.

Oct. 29, 1940, eff. Sept. 1, 1941.

See also **O'Connor's Texas Rules**, "Challenges for cause," ch. 8-A, §6.

TRCP 229. CHALLENGE FOR CAUSE

When twenty-four or more jurors, if in the district court, or twelve or more, if in the county court, are drawn, and the lists of their names delivered to the parties, if either party desires to challenge any juror for cause, the challenge shall then be made. The name of a juror challenged and set aside for cause shall be erased from such lists.

Oct. 29, 1940, eff. Sept. 1, 1941.

See also Gov't Code §§62.101–62.110 (juror qualifications); **O'Connor's Texas Rules**, "Challenges for cause," ch. 8-A, §6.

ANNOTATIONS

Cortez v. HCCI-San Antonio, Inc., 159 S.W.3d 87, 90-91 (Tex.2005). "[T]o preserve error when a challenge for cause is denied, a party must use a peremptory challenge against the veniremember involved, exhaust its remaining challenges, and notify the trial court that a specific objectionable veniremember will remain on the jury list. [¶] While it is unclear whether [P] gave his notice to the trial court before or after he delivered his strike list, it does appear that the two events were roughly contemporaneous. More importantly, notice was given before the jury was seated. . . . We therefore hold that error was preserved. [¶] The fact that [P] prevailed at trial is not relevant [to whether any error was harmless] because . . . 'harm occurs' when 'the party uses all of his peremptory challenges and is thus prevented from striking other objectionable jurors from the list because he has no additional peremptory challenges.' . . . Here, . . . we presume harm." *See also* **Hallett v. Houston Nw. Med. Ctr.**, 689 S.W.2d 888, 890 (Tex.1985).

TRCP 230. CERTAIN QUESTIONS NOT TO BE ASKED

In examining a juror, he shall not be asked a question the answer to which may show that he has been convicted of an offense which disqualifies him, or that he stands charged by some legal accusation with theft or any felony.

Oct. 29, 1940, eff. Sept. 1, 1941.

See also **O'Connor's Texas Rules**, "Jury Selection," ch. 8-A, §1 et seq.

ANNOTATIONS

Palmer Well Servs. v. Mack Trucks, Inc., 776 S.W.2d 575, 576 (Tex.1989). Gov't Code §62.102 "disqualifies a person to serve as a petit juror if he is 'under indictment or other legal accusation of misdemeanor or felony theft, or any other felony.' "

TRCP 231. NUMBER REDUCED BY CHALLENGES

If the challenges reduce the number of jurors to less than twenty-four, if in the district court, or to less than twelve, if in the county court, the court shall order other jurors to be drawn from the wheel or from the central jury panel or summoned, as the practice may be in the particular county, and their names written upon the list instead of those set aside for cause. Such jurors so summoned may likewise be challenged for cause.

Oct. 29, 1940, eff. Sept. 1, 1941.

TRCP 232. MAKING PEREMPTORY CHALLENGES

If there remain on such lists not subject to challenge for cause, twenty-four names, if in the district court, or twelve names, if in the county court, the parties shall proceed to make their peremptory challenges. A peremptory challenge is made to a juror without assigning any reason therefor.

Oct. 29, 1940, eff. Sept. 1, 1941.

See also **O'Connor's Texas Rules**, "Peremptory challenges," ch. 8-A, §7.

ANNOTATIONS

Davis v. Fisk Elec. Co., 268 S.W.3d 508, 518-19 (Tex.2008). "Nonverbal conduct or demeanor, often elusive and always subject to interpretation, may well mask a race-based strike. For that reason, trial courts must carefully examine such rationales. . . . **Batson** requires a 'clear and reasonably specific explanation' of the legitimate reasons for a strike . . . and merely stating that a juror nonverbally 'reacted' is insufficient. *At 525:* [C]ourts must consider 'all relevant circumstances' when reviewing **Batson** challenges. And here, the relevant circumstances include many [factors], including a statistical disparity and unequal treatment of comparable jurors."

Goode v. Shoukfeh, 943 S.W.2d 441, 445-46 (Tex.1997). "At the first step of the [**Batson**] process, the opponent of the peremptory challenge must establish a prima facie case of racial discrimination. [¶] During the second step of the process, the burden shifts to the party who has exercised the strike to come forward with a race-neutral explanation. . . . The issue . . . at this juncture is the facial validity of the explanation. . . . It is not until the third step that the persuasiveness of the justification for the challenge becomes relevant. At the third step of the process, the trial court must determine if the party challenging the strike has proven purposeful racial discrimination, and the trial court may believe or not believe the explanation offered by the party who exercised the peremptory challenge. It is at this stage that implausible justifications for striking potential jurors 'may (and probably will) be found [by the trial court] to be pretexts for purposeful discrimination.'" *See also* **Jackson v. Stroud**, 539 S.W.3d 502, 507-08 (Tex.App.—Houston [1st Dist.] 2017, no pet.).

Powers v. Palacios, 813 S.W.2d 489, 491 (Tex.1991). "We hold that equal protection is denied when race is a factor in counsel's exercise of a peremptory challenge to a prospective juror."

TRCP 233. NUMBER OF PEREMPTORY CHALLENGES

Except as provided below, each party to a civil action is entitled to six peremptory challenges in a case tried in the district court, and to three in the county court.

Alignment of the Parties. In multiple party cases, it shall be the duty of the trial judge to decide whether any of the litigants aligned on the same side of the docket are antagonistic with respect to any issue to be submitted to the jury, before the exercise of peremptory challenges.

Definition of Side. The term "side" as used in this rule is not synonymous with "party," "litigant," or "person." Rather, "side" means one or more litigants who have common interests on the matters with which the jury is concerned.

Motion to Equalize. In multiple party cases, upon motion of any litigant made prior to the exercise of peremptory challenges, it shall be the duty of the trial judge to equalize the number of peremptory challenges so that no litigant or side is given unfair advantage as a result of the alignment of the litigants and the award of peremptory challenges to each litigant or side. In determining how the challenges should be allocated the court shall consider any matter brought to the attention of the trial judge concerning the ends of justice and the elimination of an unfair advantage.

Oct. 29, 1940, eff. Sept. 1, 1941. Amended by order of Dec. 5, 1983, eff. April 1, 1984.

See also **O'Connor's Texas Rules**, "Peremptory challenges," ch. 8-A, §7; **O'Connor's Texas Forms**, FORMS 8A.

ANNOTATIONS

Garcia v. Central Power & Light Co., 704 S.W.2d 734, 736 (Tex.1986). "The existence of antagonism [between litigants on the same side of a lawsuit] is a question of law. If no antagonism exists, each side must receive the same number of strikes. *At 737:* [I]n determining whether antagonism exists, the trial court must consider the pleadings, information disclosed by pretrial discovery, information and representations made during voir dire of the jury panel, and any other information brought to the attention of the trial court before the exercise of the strikes by the parties." *See also* **Moore v. Altra Energy Techs.**, 321 S.W.3d 727, 741 (Tex.App.—Houston [14th Dist.] 2010, pet. denied).

In re M.N.G., 147 S.W.3d 521, 532 (Tex.App.—Fort Worth 2004, pet. denied). "[W]hen defendants have collaborated on the exercise of their peremptory challenges so that no double strikes are made, this factor supports a finding that the defendants have used their ostensibly antagonistic positions unfairly."

TRCP 234. LISTS RETURNED TO THE CLERK

When the parties have made or declined to make their peremptory challenges, they shall deliver their lists to the clerk. The clerk shall, if the case be in the district court, call off the first twelve names on the lists that have not been erased; and if the case be in the county court, he shall call off the first six names on the lists that have not been erased; those whose names are called shall be the jury.

Oct. 29, 1940, eff. Sept. 1, 1941.

See also **O'Connor's Texas Rules**, "Jury Selection," ch. 8-A, §1 et seq.

TRCP 235. IF JURY IS INCOMPLETE

When by peremptory challenges the jury is left incomplete, the court shall direct other jurors to be drawn or sum-

moned to complete the jury; and such other jurors shall be impaneled as in the first instance.

Oct. 29, 1940, eff. Sept. 1, 1941.

See also **O'Connor's Texas Rules**, "Jury Selection," ch. 8-A, §1 et seq.

TRCP 236. OATH TO JURY

The jury shall be sworn by the court or under its direction, in substance as follows: "You, and each of you, do solemnly swear that in all cases between parties which shall be to you submitted, you will a true verdict render, according to the law, as it may be given you in charge by the court, and to the evidence submitted to you under the rulings of the court. So help you God."

Oct. 29, 1940, eff. Sept. 1, 1941.

SECTION 11. TRIAL OF CAUSES

A. Appearance and Procedure

TRCP 237. APPEARANCE DAY

If a defendant, who has been duly cited, is by the citation required to answer on a day which is in term time, such day is appearance day as to him. If he is so required to answer on a day in vacation, he shall plead or answer accordingly, and the first day of the next term is appearance day as to him.

Oct. 29, 1940, eff. Sept. 1, 1941. Amended by orders of March 31, 1941, eff. Sept. 1, 1941; July 20, 1954, eff. Jan. 1, 1955.

See also **O'Connor's Texas Rules**, "Default Judgment," ch. 7-A, §1 et seq.

ANNOTATIONS

Texas Alcoholic Bev. Comm'n v. Wilson, 573 S.W.2d 832, 835 (Tex.App.—Beaumont 1978, writ ref'd n.r.e.). "[D] had no valid notice that a hearing would be held prior to appearance day. . . . Any judgment entered before the time at which a defendant is commanded by the citation to appear and answer is erroneous and must be set aside."

TRCP 237a. CASES REMANDED FROM FEDERAL COURT

When any cause is removed to the Federal Court and is afterwards remanded to the state court, the plaintiff shall file a certified copy of the order of remand with the clerk of the state court and shall forthwith give written notice of such filing to the attorneys of record for all adverse parties. All such adverse parties shall have fifteen days from the receipt of such notice within which to file an answer. No default judgment shall be rendered against a party in a removed action remanded from federal court if that party filed an answer in federal court during removal.

July 20, 1954, eff. Jan. 1, 1955. Amended by orders of Dec. 5, 1983, eff. April 1, 1984; July 15, 1987, eff. Jan. 1, 1988; April 24, 1990, eff. Sept. 1, 1990.

Comment—1990

To expressly provide, consistent with existing law, that a default judgment cannot be taken in a case remanded from federal court if an answer was filed in federal court during removal.

Source: New rule.

ANNOTATIONS

Quaestor Invs. v. State of Chiapas, 997 S.W.2d 226, 229 (Tex.1999). "[W]e hold that jurisdiction revests in the state court when the federal district court executes the remand order and mails a certified copy to the state court. [¶] We are . . . persuaded that nothing more is required to recommence the appellate timetable than the state court's reacquiring jurisdiction over a case. . . . The court of appeals erred when it inferred from . . . rule 237a . . . that any further affirmative action was needed." *See also* **Gonzalez v. Guilbot**, 315 S.W.3d 533, 538 (Tex.2010) (jurisdiction revests when remand order hand-delivered).

Toliver v. Dallas Fort Worth Hosp. Council, 198 S.W.3d 444, 449 (Tex.App.—Dallas 2006, no pet.). "[R]ule 237a did not establish a deadline to answer in this case because [Ds] filed an answer in federal court and did not have to also file an answer in state court to avoid a default. [¶] [T]he rules that establish deadlines by which a defendant must answer a lawsuit do not provide that an answer or other pleading is waived if not filed by the deadline. Instead, the rules provide a date before which the plaintiff may not take a default judgment, even if no answer has been filed."

HBA E., Ltd. v. JEA Boxing Co., 796 S.W.2d 534, 538 (Tex.App.—Houston [1st Dist.] 1990, writ denied). "Reading [TRCP] 237a and 239 together, we conclude that a default judgment cannot be granted against a defendant following remand of a case from federal to state court until 15 days have expired from the defendant's receipt of the remand notice from the plaintiff." *See also* **Kashan v. McLane Co.**, No. 03-11-00125-CV, 2012 WL 2076821 (Tex.App.—Austin 2012, no pet.) (memo op.; 6-7-12).

TRCP 238. CALL OF APPEARANCE DOCKET

On the appearance day of a particular defendant and at the hour named in the citation, or as soon thereafter as may be practicable, the court or clerk in open court shall call, in their order, all the cases on the docket in which such day is appearance day as to any defendant, or, the court or clerk failing therein, any such case shall be so called on request of the plaintiff's attorney.

Oct. 29, 1940, eff. Sept. 1, 1941.

TRCP 239. JUDGMENT BY DEFAULT

Upon such call of the docket, or at any time after a defendant is required to answer, the plaintiff may in term

time take judgment by default against such defendant if he has not previously filed an answer, and provided that the return of service shall have been on file with the clerk for the length of time required by Rule 107.

Oct. 29, 1940, eff. Sept. 1, 1941. Amended by order of April 12, 1962, eff. Sept. 1, 1962; Dec. 12, 2011, eff. Jan. 1, 2012.

Source: TRCS art. 2154 (repealed): Added words "In term time."

See also **O'Connor's Texas Rules**, "Default Judgment," ch. 7-A, §1 et seq.; **O'Connor's Texas Rules**, "MNT after default judgment," ch. 10-B, §9; **O'Connor's Texas Forms**, FORMS 7A; **O'Connor's Texas Family Law Handbook**, "Default judgment," ch. 3-A, §13.3 (suit for divorce); **O'Connor's Texas Family Law Handbook**,"Default judgment," ch. 4-D, §10.3 (suit to dissolve marriage with children).

ANNOTATIONS

Kao Holdings, L.P. v. Young, 261 S.W.3d 60, 61 (Tex.2008). "[P] sued [limited partnership] for damages. . . . [P] did not sue [general partner] individually but served the partnership by serving him. When [limited partnership] did not answer, [P] filed a motion for default judgment stating that '[D-general partner] was properly and personally served' and had not answered. *At 65:* [TRCP] 239 . . . provides for default judgment only against 'a defendant.' [General partner] was not a defendant. [TRCP] 301 requires that '[t]he judgment of the court shall conform to the pleadings.' [P] pleaded no claim against [general partner]. [D]efault judgment against [general partner] was improper."

In re Burlington Coat Factory Whs., 167 S.W.3d 827, 830 (Tex.2005). "[A] default judgment that fails to dispose of all claims can be final only if 'intent to finally dispose of the case' is 'unequivocally expressed in the words of the order itself.'" *See also* **Lehmann v. Har-Con Corp.**, 39 S.W.3d 191, 200 (Tex.2001).

Lopez v. Lopez, 757 S.W.2d 721, 723 (Tex.1988). "Because the record here establishes that [D] had no actual or constructive notice of the trial setting, the lower courts erred in requiring him to show that he had a meritorious defense as a condition to granting his motion for new trial." *See also* **Thottumkal v. Sidhu**, No. 14-13-00966-CV, 2014 WL 6968616 (Tex.App.—Houston [14th Dist.] 2014, no pet.) (memo op.; 12-9-14).

Craddock v. Sunshine Bus Lines, Inc., 133 S.W.2d 124, 126 (Tex.1939). "A default judgment should be set aside and a new trial ordered in any case in which the failure of the defendant to answer before judgment was not intentional, or the result of conscious indifference on his part, but was due to a mistake or accident; provided the motion for a new trial sets up a meritorious defense and is filed at a time when the granting thereof will occasion no delay or otherwise work an injury to the plaintiff." *See also* **LeBlanc v. LeBlanc**, 778 S.W.2d 865, 865 (Tex.1989) (**Craddock** applies to default judgments entered on D's failure to file an answer and those entered on D's failure to appear for trial).

TRCP 239a. NOTICE OF DEFAULT JUDGMENT

At or immediately prior to the time an interlocutory or final default judgment is rendered, the party taking the same or his attorney shall certify to the clerk in writing the last known mailing address of the party against whom the judgment is taken, which certificate shall be filed among the papers in the cause. Immediately upon the signing of the judgment, the clerk shall mail written notice thereof to the party against whom the judgment was rendered at the address shown in the certificate, and note the fact of such mailing on the docket. The notice shall state the number and style of the case, the court in which the case is pending, the names of the parties in whose favor and against whom the judgment was rendered, and the date of the signing of the judgment. Failure to comply with the provisions of this rule shall not affect the finality of the judgment.

July 20, 1966, eff. Jan. 1, 1967. Amended by order of July 15, 1987, eff. Jan. 1, 1988.

Source: New rule.

See also **O'Connor's Texas Rules**, "Certificate of last known address," ch. 7-A, §3.9.2(2); **O'Connor's Texas Rules**, "Notice of default judgment," ch. 7-A, §6.

ANNOTATIONS

Campbell v. Fincher, 72 S.W.3d 723, 724 (Tex.App.—Waco 2002, no pet.). "Rule 239a is designed as an administrative convenience for the parties, and failure to give notice of the entry of a default judgment does not constitute reversible error."

TRCP 240. WHERE ONLY SOME ANSWER

Where there are several defendants, some of whom have answered or have not been duly served and some of whom have been duly served and have made default, an interlocutory judgment by default may be entered against those who have made default, and the cause may proceed or be postponed as to the others.

Oct. 29, 1940, eff. Sept. 1, 1941.

Source: TRCS art. 2155 (repealed).

See also TRCP 161; **O'Connor's Texas Rules**, "Default Judgment," ch. 7-A, §1 et seq.

ANNOTATIONS

Castano v. Foremost Cty. Mut. Ins., 31 S.W.3d 387, 388 (Tex.App.—San Antonio 2000, no pet.). "Where the

plaintiff's petition names multiple defendants . . ., and the plaintiff obtains a no-answer default judgment against one of the defendants, the default judgment is interlocutory and cannot be appealed until the trial court either renders a final judgment in the case, or signs an order of severance making the interlocutory default judgment final."

TRCP 241. ASSESSING DAMAGES ON LIQUIDATED DEMANDS

When a judgment by default is rendered against the defendant, or all of several defendants, if the claim is liquidated and proved by an instrument in writing, the damages shall be assessed by the court, or under its direction, and final judgment shall be rendered therefor, unless the defendant shall demand and be entitled to a trial by jury.

Oct. 29, 1940, eff. Sept. 1, 1941. Amended by order of Dec. 5, 1983, eff. April 1, 1984.

See also **O'Connor's Texas Rules**, "Liquidated damages—hearing not required," ch. 7-A, §3.13.1.

ANNOTATIONS

Sherman Acquisition II LP v. Garcia, 229 S.W.3d 802, 809 (Tex.App.—Waco 2007, no pet.). "A claim is liquidated if the amount of damages caused by the defendant can be accurately calculated from (1) the factual, as opposed to conclusory, allegations in the petition, and (2) an instrument in writing. Whether a claim is liquidated must be determined from the language of the petition, as a seemingly liquidated claim may be unliquidated because of pleading allegations which require proof for resolution." *See also* **Novosad v. Brian K. Cunningham, P.C.**, 38 S.W.3d 767, 773 (Tex.App.—Houston [14th Dist.] 2001, no pet.).

TRCP 242. REPEALED BY ORDER OF SEPT. 20, 1941, EFF. DEC. 31, 1941

TRCP 243. UNLIQUIDATED DEMANDS

If the cause of action is unliquidated or be not proved by an instrument in writing, the court shall hear evidence as to damages and shall render judgment therefor, unless the defendant shall demand and be entitled to a trial by jury in which case the judgment by default shall be noted, a writ of inquiry awarded, and the cause entered on the jury docket.

Oct. 29, 1940, eff. Sept. 1, 1941. Amended by order of March 31, 1941, eff. Sept. 1, 1941.

Source: TRCS art. 2157 (repealed).

See also **O'Connor's Texas Rules**, "Unliquidated damages—hearing required," ch. 7-A, §3.13.2.

ANNOTATIONS

Paradigm Oil, Inc. v. Retamco Oper., Inc., 372 S.W.3d 177, 182 (Tex.2012). "[D] does not contest the trial court's decision to strike its answer as a discovery sanction or the default judgment rendered against it on liability. [D's] appeal focuses instead on its exclusion from the trial on damages. [A] defaulted[ ] defendant has the right to participate in such a trial when, as here, the plaintiff's damages are unliquidated. *At 186:* So what kind of abuse would justify barring a defaulted defendant's participation at the hearing on unliquidated damages? [S]poliation [i]s one [possible] example[, b]ut [that] is not at issue in this case. *At 187:* Given . . . the . . . sanction that ended the liability litigation, the additional sanction . . . precluding [D's participation in] the damages trial was excessive."

Holt Atherton Indus. v. Heine, 835 S.W.2d 80, 86 (Tex.1992). "As a general matter, when we sustain a no evidence point of error after a trial on the merits, we render judgment on that point. [¶] [However,] when an appellate court sustains a no evidence point after an *uncontested* hearing on unliquidated damages following a no-answer default judgment, the appropriate disposition is a remand for a new trial on the issue of unliquidated damages."

Ingram Indus. v. U.S. Bolt Mfg., 121 S.W.3d 31, 37 (Tex.App.—Houston [1st Dist.] 2003, no pet.). "A trial court may award unliquidated damages based on affidavit testimony. [T]he trial court based the award of damages on its consideration of 'the pleadings and evidence on file.' The evidence on file contained [the affidavit of P's general manager, which] set out [P's] damages. The trial court thus considered [the] affidavit to be proof of [P's] damages. Therefore, the trial court satisfied Rule 243's hearing requirement without the need of holding an evidentiary hearing." *See also* **Texas Commerce Bank v. New**, 3 S.W.3d 515, 515-16 (Tex.1999).

TRCP 244. ON SERVICE BY PUBLICATION

Where service has been made by publication, and no answer has been filed nor appearance entered within the prescribed time, the court shall appoint an attorney to defend the suit in behalf of the defendant, and judgment shall be rendered as in other cases; but, in every such case a statement of the evidence, approved and signed by the judge, shall be filed with the papers of the cause as a part of the record thereof. The court shall allow such attorney a reasonable fee for his services, to be taxed as part of the costs.

Oct. 29, 1940, eff. Sept. 1, 1941.

Source: TRCS art. 2158 (repealed).

See also **O'Connor's Texas Rules**, "MNT after service by publication," ch. 10-B, §10; **O'Connor's Texas Forms**, FORM 10B:5.

ANNOTATIONS

Cahill v. Lyda, 826 S.W.2d 932, 933 (Tex.1992). "Rule 244 . . . requires that a trial court appoint an attorney ad

litem to represent defendants served with citation by publication who fail to file an answer or appear before the court. Rule 244 also requires that the attorney ad litem be paid a reasonable fee for his services, which is to be taxed as part of the costs. The attorney ad litem must exhaust all remedies available to his client and, if necessary, represent his client's interest on appeal." *See also* **Atlantic Shippers of Tex., Inc. v. Jefferson Cty.**, 363 S.W.3d 276, 286-87 (Tex.App.—Beaumont 2012, no pet.).

TRCP 245. ASSIGNMENT OF CASES FOR TRIAL

The Court may set contested cases on written request of any party, or on the court's own motion, with reasonable notice of not less than forty-five days to the parties of a first setting for trial, or by agreement of the parties; provided, however, that when a case previously has been set for trial, the Court may reset said contested case to a later date on any reasonable notice to the parties or by agreement of the parties. Noncontested cases may be tried or disposed of at any time whether set or not, and may be set at any time for any other time.

A request for trial setting constitutes a representation that the requesting party reasonably and in good faith expects to be ready for trial by the date requested, but no additional representation concerning the completion of pretrial proceedings or of current readiness for trial shall be required in order to obtain a trial setting in a contested case.

Oct. 29, 1940, eff. Sept. 1, 1941. Amended by orders of July 22, 1975, eff. Jan. 1, 1976; Dec. 5, 1983, eff. April 1, 1984; April 24, 1990, eff. Sept. 1, 1990.

Comment—1990

First paragraph, to harmonize a first time nonjury setting with the time for jury demand, and to set a more realistic notice for trial. Second paragraph, to standardize the readiness requirement to obtain a trial setting.

Source: FRCP 40.

See also Tex. Const. art. 1, §19; **O'Connor's Texas Rules**, "Trial setting," ch. 5-A, §3.3; **O'Connor's Texas Rules**, "Notice of trial or dispositive hearing," ch. 7-A, §4.3; **O'Connor's Texas Rules**, "Motion for New Trial," ch. 10-B, §1 et seq.

ANNOTATIONS

Morales v. Marquis, No. 13-12-00407-CV, 2013 WL 2298469 (Tex.App.—Corpus Christi 2013, no pet.) (memo op.; 5-23-13). "Notice under Rule 245 can . . . be waived if a party who is actively litigating the case did not receive the full notice but proceeded to trial without objection. In this case, nothing in the record shows that [D] had notice of the hearing in order to object, so [D] took no action whatsoever between the time she filed her answer and the time she filed her notice of restricted appeal. In these circumstances—when a defendant answers but takes no further action—many appellate courts, including this one, have held that a post-answer default should be set aside. [P] does not cite to any case where a defendant who answered but took no other action was deemed to have waived their right to notice under Rule 245, and we have found none." *See also* **Szanyi v. Gibson**, No. 01-15-00895-CV, 2016 WL 3269975 (Tex.App.—Houston [1st Dist.] 2016, no pet.) (memo op.; 6-14-16) (objection to insufficiency of notice must be made before trial; Rule 245 objection made in motion for new trial is untimely and preserves nothing for review); **Johnson v. Mohammed**, No. 03-10-00763-CV, 2013 WL 1955862 (Tex.App.—Austin 2013, pet. dism'd) (memo op.; 5-10-13) (45-day notice requirement can be waived by party's action or lack thereof).

Long v. Commission for Lawyer Discipline, No. 14-11-00059-CV, 2012 WL 5333654 (Tex.App.—Houston [14th Dist.] 2012, no pet.) (memo op.; 10-30-12). "A case is 'noncontested,' and thus is not subject to Rule 245's 45 day notice requirement, when the defendant does not file a written answer." *See also* **Templeton Mortg. Corp. v. Poenisch**, No. 04-15-00041-CV, 2015 WL 7271216 (Tex.App.—San Antonio 2015, no pet.) (memo op.; 11-18-15).

Custom-Crete, Inc. v. K-Bar Servs., 82 S.W.3d 655, 659 (Tex.App.—San Antonio 2002, no pet.). "A trial court's failure to comply with Rule 245 in a contested case deprives a party of its constitutional right to be present at the hearing, to voice its objections in an appropriate manner, and results in a violation of fundamental due process. Failure to give the required notice constitutes lack of due process and is grounds for reversal." *See also* **In re E.A.W.S.**, No. 2-06-00031-CV, 2006 WL 3525367 (Tex.App.—Fort Worth 2006, pet. denied) (memo op.; 12-7-06) (trial court abused its discretion by disregarding 45-day notice requirement, but reversal was improper because error caused no harm); **In re Brilliant**, 86 S.W.3d 680, 693 (Tex.App.—El Paso 2002, no pet.) (if respondent doesn't have notice as required by Rule 245, default judgment should be set aside because it is ineffectual).

TRCP 246. CLERK TO GIVE NOTICE OF SETTINGS

The clerk shall keep a record in his office of all cases set for trial, and it shall be his duty to inform any non-resident attorney of the date of setting of any case upon request by mail from such attorney, accompanied by a return envelope properly addressed and stamped. Failure of the clerk to furnish such information on proper request shall be sufficient ground for continuance or for a new trial when it appears to the court that such failure has prevented the attorney from preparing or presenting his claim or defense.

Oct. 29, 1940, eff. Sept. 1, 1941.

ANNOTATIONS

Bruneio v. Bruneio, 890 S.W.2d 150, 156 n.2 (Tex.App.—Corpus Christi 1994, no writ). TRCP 246 "merely

provides an additional vehicle for notice to any of the various attorneys who may be working on the case and want direct notification. . . . Accordingly, Rule 246 [expands] the requirements of notice to include non-resident attorneys who would not otherwise be entitled to direct notification of the setting under [TRCP] 245 as the attorney in charge."

TRCP 247. TRIED WHEN SET

Every suit shall be tried when it is called, unless continued or postponed to a future day or placed at the end of the docket to be called again for trial in its regular order. No cause which has been set upon the trial docket of the court shall be taken from the trial docket for the date set except by agreement of the parties or for good cause upon motion and notice to the opposing party.

Oct. 29, 1940, eff. Sept. 1, 1941. Amended by order of Dec. 5, 1983, eff. April 1, 1984.

See also **O'Connor's Texas Rules**, "Motion for Continuance," ch. 5-D, §1 et seq.

TRCP 248. JURY CASES

When a jury has been demanded, questions of law, motions, exceptions to pleadings, and other unresolved pending matters shall, as far as practicable, be heard and determined by the court before the trial commences, and jurors shall be summoned to appear on the day so designated.

Oct. 29, 1940, eff. Sept. 1, 1941. Amended by orders of Dec. 5, 1983, eff. April 1, 1984; April 24, 1990, eff. Sept. 1, 1990.

Comment—1990

To encourage resolution of matters prior to trial.

See also TRCP 166.

TRCP 249. CALL OF NON-JURY DOCKET

The non-jury docket shall be taken up at such times as not unnecessarily to interfere with the dispatch of business on the jury docket.

Oct. 29, 1940, eff. Sept. 1, 1941.

TRCP 250. REPEALED BY ORDER OF SEPT. 20, 1941, EFF. DEC. 31, 1941

B. Continuance and Change of Venue

TRCP 251. CONTINUANCE

No application for a continuance shall be heard before the defendant files his defense, nor shall any continuance be granted except for sufficient cause supported by affidavit, or by consent of the parties, or by operation of law.

Oct. 29, 1940, eff. Sept. 1, 1941.

Source: TRCS art. 2167 (repealed).

See also **O'Connor's Texas Rules**, "Motion for Continuance," ch. 5-D, §1 et seq.; **O'Connor's Texas Forms**, FORMS 5D.

ANNOTATIONS

Tenneco Inc. v. Enterprise Prods., 925 S.W.2d 640, 647 (Tex.1996). See annotation under TRCP 166a, *Motion for Continuance.*

Villegas v. Carter, 711 S.W.2d 624, 626 (Tex.1986). "Generally, when movants fail to comply with [TRCP] 251's requirement that the motion for continuance be 'supported by affidavit,' we presume that the trial court did not abuse its discretion in denying the motion. It would be unrealistic, however, to apply this presumption to lay movants who without fault have their attorney withdrawn." *See also* **Garner v. Fidelity Bank**, 244 S.W.3d 855, 858-59 (Tex.App.—Dallas 2008, no pet.) (Rule 251 does not require party opposing motion for continuance to object to lack of verification; failure to object does not preclude party from raising objection for first time on appeal).

In re Guardianship of Cantu de Villarreal, 330 S.W.3d 11, 26-27 (Tex.App.—Corpus Christi 2010, no pet.). "[A] trial court is not required to grant a motion for continuance just because a party is unable to be present at trial. When a continuance is sought because of the unavailability of a party, we examine [TRCP] 252." *See also* **Murphree v. Cooper**, No. 14-11-00416-CV, 2012 WL 2312706 (Tex.App.—Houston [14th Dist.] 2012, no pet.) (memo op.; 6-19-12).

Verkin v. Southwest Ctr. One, Ltd., 784 S.W.2d 92, 94 (Tex.App.—Houston [1st Dist.] 1989, writ denied). When a motion for continuance is (1) in substantial compliance with TRCP 251, (2) verified, and (3) uncontroverted, the court "must accept the statements in the motion as true."

TRCP 252. APPLICATION FOR CONTINUANCE

If the ground of such application be the want of testimony, the party applying therefor shall make affidavit that such testimony is material, showing the materiality thereof, and that he has used due diligence to procure such testimony, stating such diligence, and the cause of failure, if known; that such testimony cannot be procured from any other source; and, if it be for the absence of a witness, he shall state the name and residence of the witness, and what he expects to prove by him; and also state that the continuance is not sought for delay only, but that justice may be done; provided that, on a first application for a continuance, it shall not be necessary to show that the absent testimony cannot be procured from any other source.

The failure to obtain the deposition of any witness residing within 100 miles of the courthouse of the county in which the suit is pending shall not be regarded as want of diligence when diligence has been used to secure the personal attendance of such witness under the rules of law, unless by reason of age, infirmity or sickness, or official duty,

the witness will be unable to attend the court, or unless such witness is about to leave, or has left, the State or county in which the suit is pending and will not probably be present at the trial.

Oct. 29, 1940, eff. Sept. 1, 1941. Amended by order of Dec. 5, 1983, eff. April 1, 1984.

Source: TRCS art. 2168 (repealed).

See also **O'Connor's Texas Rules**, "Motion for Continuance," ch. 5-D, §1 et seq.; **O'Connor's Texas Forms**, FORMS 5D.

ANNOTATIONS

State v. Wood Oil Distrib., 751 S.W.2d 863, 865 (Tex.1988). "[T]he failure of a litigant to diligently utilize the [TRCPs] for discovery purposes will not authorize the granting of a continuance."

In re Commitment of Winkle, 434 S.W.3d 300, 306 (Tex.App.—Beaumont 2014, pet. denied). "Rule 252 implies that sworn testimony may be considered an adequate substitute for a witness's personal appearance in a civil trial."

Ramirez v. State, 973 S.W.2d 388, 391 (Tex.App.—El Paso 1998, no pet.). D's continuance "motion failed to specify the information and testimony he sought or why it was material. [D] did not state the names of the witnesses from whom he sought testimony, nor did he state what he expected to prove from said witnesses." *See also* **New York Party Shuttle, LLC v. Bilello**, 414 S.W.3d 206, 217 (Tex.App.—Houston [1st Dist.] 2013, pet. denied).

TRCP 253. ABSENCE OF COUNSEL AS GROUND FOR CONTINUANCE

Except as provided elsewhere in these rules, absence of counsel will not be good cause for a continuance or postponement of the cause when called for trial, except it be allowed in the discretion of the court, upon cause shown or upon matters within the knowledge or information of the judge to be stated on the record.

Oct. 29, 1940, eff. Sept. 1, 1941.

Source: Tex. Rules for Dist. & Cty. Cts. 49.

See also **O'Connor's Texas Rules**, "Motion for Continuance," ch. 5-D, §1 et seq.; **O'Connor's Texas Forms**, FORM 5D:2.

ANNOTATIONS

Villegas v. Carter, 711 S.W.2d 624, 626 (Tex.1986). "[T]he trial court abused its discretion because the evidence shows that [P] was not negligent or at fault in causing his attorney's withdrawal. The court granted [P's] attorney's motion to voluntarily withdraw two days before trial—too short a time for [P] to find a new attorney and for that new attorney to investigate the case and prepare for trial."

TRCP 254. ATTENDANCE ON LEGISLATURE

In all civil actions, including matters of probate, and in all matters ancillary to such suits which require action by or the attendance of an attorney, including appeals but excluding temporary restraining orders, at any time within thirty days of a date when the legislature is to be in session, or at any time the legislature is in session, or when the legislature sits as a Constitutional Convention, it shall be mandatory that the court continue the cause if it shall appear to the court, by affidavit, that any party applying for continuance, or any attorney for any party to the cause, is a member of either branch of the legislature, and will be or is in actual attendance on a session of the same. If the member of the legislature is an attorney for a party to the cause, his affidavit shall contain a declaration that it is his intention to participate actively in the preparation and/or presentation of the case. Where a party to any cause, or an attorney for any party to a cause, is a member of the legislature, his affidavit need not be corroborated. On the filing of such affidavit, the court shall continue the cause until thirty days after adjournment of the legislature and the affidavit shall be proof of the necessity for the continuance, and the continuance shall be deemed one of right and shall not be charged against the movant upon any subsequent application for continuance.

The right to a continuance shall be mandatory, except only where the attorney was employed within ten days of the date the suit is set for trial, the right to continuance shall be discretionary.

Oct. 29, 1940, eff. Sept. 1, 1941. Amended by order of June 10, 1980, eff. Jan. 1, 1981.

See also CPRC §30.003 (other requirements for legislative continuance); **O'Connor's Texas Rules**, "Motion for Continuance," ch. 5-D, §1 et seq.; **O'Connor's Texas Forms**, FORM 5D:2; **O'Connor's Texas Family Law Handbook**, "Legislator," ch. 6-C, §7.2.1(3).

ANNOTATIONS

In re Ford Motor Co., 165 S.W.3d 315, 319 (Tex.2005). " '[A] legislative continuance is mandatory except in those cases in which the party opposing the continuance alleges that a substantial existing right will be defeated or abridged by delay.' When a party opposes a legislative continuance in such circumstances, the trial court must conduct a hearing on the allegations and deny the motion if the allegations are shown to be meritorious." *See also* **Waites v. Sondock**, 561 S.W.2d 772, 776 (Tex.1977).

TRCP 255. CHANGE OF VENUE BY CONSENT

Upon the written consent of the parties filed with the papers of the cause, the court, by an order entered on the

minutes, may transfer the same for trial to the court of any other county having jurisdiction of the subject matter of such suit.

Oct. 29, 1940, eff. Sept. 1, 1941.

See also CPRC §15.020; **O'Connor's Texas Rules**, "Consent of the parties," ch. 3-C, §4; **O'Connor's Texas Forms**, FORMS 3C:10, 3C:11.

ANNOTATIONS

Farris v. Ray, 895 S.W.2d 351, 352 (Tex.1995). "[A] signed written agreement filed in the record of the *transferee* court meets all the requirements of [TRCP] 11. Such an agreement, enforceable against the signatories under the terms of the rule, operates as an express waiver of any error there may have been in the initial transfer."

TRCP 256. REPEALED BY ORDER OF MARCH 31, 1941, EFF. SEPT. 1, 1941

TRCP 257. GRANTED ON MOTION

A change of venue may be granted in civil causes upon motion of either party, supported by his own affidavit and the affidavit of at least three credible persons, residents of the county in which the suit is pending, for any following cause:

(a) That there exists in the county where the suit is pending so great a prejudice against him that he cannot obtain a fair and impartial trial.

(b) That there is a combination against him instigated by influential persons, by reason of which he cannot expect a fair and impartial trial.

(c) That an impartial trial cannot be had in the county where the action is pending.

(d) For other sufficient cause to be determined by the court.

Oct. 29, 1940, eff. Sept. 1, 1941. Amended by order of June 15, 1983, eff. Sept. 1, 1983.

See also **O'Connor's Texas Rules**, "Motion to Transfer—Challenging Venue," ch. 3-C, §1 et seq.; **O'Connor's Texas Forms**, FORMS 3C:4, 3C:8, 3C:11; **O'Connor's Texas Family Law Handbook**, "Family Code transfers," ch. 4-B, §3.2.

TRCP 258. SHALL BE GRANTED

Where such motion to transfer venue is duly made, it shall be granted, unless the credibility of those making such application, or their means of knowledge or the truth of the facts set out in the said application are attacked by the affidavit of a credible person; when thus attacked, the issue thus formed shall be tried by the judge; and the application either granted or refused. Reasonable discovery in support of, or in opposition to, the application shall be permitted, and such discovery as is relevant, including deposition testimony on file, may be attached to, or incorporated by reference in, the affidavit of a party, a witness, or an attorney who has knowledge of such discovery.

Oct. 29, 1940, eff. Sept. 1, 1941. Amended by order of June 15, 1983, eff. Sept. 1, 1983.

See also **O'Connor's Texas Rules**, "Motion to Transfer—Challenging Venue," ch. 3-C, §1 et seq.

ANNOTATIONS

In re East Tex. Med. Ctr. Athens, 154 S.W.3d 933, 935 (Tex.App.—Tyler 2005, orig. proceeding). "A trial court can deny the motion to transfer if the movant does not comply with [TRCP] 257. If the motion is challenged as permitted by [TRCP] 258, the judge must try the issue. If the motion is not challenged in the manner provided by Rule 258, transfer is mandatory." *See also* **City of Abilene v. Downs**, 367 S.W.2d 153, 155 (Tex.1963).

TRCP 259. TO WHAT COUNTY

If the motion under Rule 257 is granted, the cause shall be removed:

(a) If from a district court, to any county of proper venue in the same or an adjoining district;

(b) If from a county court, to any adjoining county of proper venue;

(c) If (a) or (b) are not applicable, to any county of proper venue;

(d) If a county of proper venue (other than the county of suit) cannot be found, then if from

(1) A district court, to any county in the same or an adjoining district or to any district where an impartial trial can be had;

(2) A county court, to any adjoining county or to any district where an impartial trial can be had;

but the parties may agree that venue shall be changed to some other county, and the order of the court shall conform to such agreement.

Oct. 29, 1940, eff. Sept. 1, 1941. Amended by order of June 15, 1983, eff. Sept. 1, 1983.

See also **O'Connor's Texas Rules**, "Motion to Transfer—Challenging Venue," ch. 3-C, §1 et seq.

TRCP 260. REPEALED BY ORDER OF APRIL 24, 1990, EFF. SEPT. 1, 1990

TRCP 261. TRANSCRIPT ON CHANGE

When a change of venue has been granted, the clerk shall immediately make out a correct transcript of all the orders made in said cause, certifying thereto officially under the

seal of the court, and send the same, with the original papers in the cause, to the clerk of the court to which the venue has been changed.

Oct. 29, 1940, eff. Sept. 1, 1941.

C. The Trial

TRCP 262. TRIAL BY THE COURT

The rules governing the trial of causes before a jury shall govern in trials by the court in so far as applicable.

Oct. 29, 1940, eff. Sept. 1, 1941.

ANNOTATIONS

Qantel Bus. Sys. v. Custom Controls Co., 761 S.W.2d 302, 304-05 (Tex.1988). "When a plaintiff rests, he indicates that he does not desire to put on further evidence, except by rebuttal testimony, and that he has fully developed his case." In a nonjury case, the court is presumed to have ruled on the sufficiency of the evidence when it grants judgment for the defendant after the plaintiff rests.

TRCP 263. AGREED CASE

Parties may submit matters in controversy to the court upon an agreed statement of facts filed with the clerk, upon which judgment shall be rendered as in other cases; and such agreed statement signed and certified by the court to be correct and the judgment rendered thereon shall constitute the record of the cause.

Oct. 29, 1940, eff. Sept. 1, 1941.

See also **O'Connor's Texas Rules**, "Motion for Judgment on Agreed Statement of Facts," ch. 7-E, §1 et seq.; **O'Connor's Texas Forms**, FORMS 7E.

ANNOTATIONS

Taylor v. First Cmty. Credit Un., 316 S.W.3d 863, 866 (Tex.App.—Houston [14th Dist.] 2010, no pet.). "Strict compliance with [TRCP 263] is not required. When . . . the record indicates that the trial court heard the case on stipulated facts, a reviewing court may treat the case as one involving an agreed statement of facts under Rule 263." *See also* **Addison Urban Dev. Partners v. Alan Ritchey Materials Co.**, 437 S.W.3d 597, 600-01 (Tex.App.—Dallas 2014, no pet.).

State Farm Lloyds v. Kessler, 932 S.W.2d 732, 735 (Tex.App.—Fort Worth 1996, writ denied). "An agreed statement of facts under rule 263 is similar to a special verdict; it is the parties' request for judgment under the applicable law. The only issue on appeal is whether the trial court properly applied the law to the agreed facts. The appellate court is limited to those facts unless other facts are necessarily implied from the express facts in the statement. In an appeal of an 'agreed' case, there are no presumed findings in favor of the judgment, and the pleadings are immaterial." *See also* **Ultrasound Tech. Servs. v. Dallas Cent. Appr. Dist.**, 357 S.W.3d 174, 176 (Tex.App.—Dallas 2011, pet. denied).

City of Galveston v. Giles, 902 S.W.2d 167, 170 n.2 (Tex.App.—Houston [1st Dist.] 1995, no writ). "Findings of fact have no place in the trial of an agreed case. Once the parties stipulate to all the facts, the court may not make additional fact findings."

TRCP 264. VIDEOTAPE TRIAL

By agreement of the parties, the trial court may allow that all testimony and such other evidence as may be appropriate be presented at trial by videotape. The expenses of such videotape recordings shall be taxed as costs. If any party withdraws agreement to a videotape trial, the videotape costs that have accrued will be taxed against the party withdrawing from the agreement.

July 15, 1987, eff. Jan. 1, 1988.

TRCP 265. ORDER OF PROCEEDINGS ON TRIAL BY JURY

The trial of cases before a jury shall proceed in the following order unless the court should, for good cause stated in the record, otherwise direct:

(a) The party upon whom rests the burden of proof on the whole case shall state to the jury briefly the nature of his claim or defense and what said party expects to prove and the relief sought. Immediately thereafter, the adverse party may make a similar statement, and intervenors and other parties will be accorded similar rights in the order determined by the court.

(b) The party upon whom rests the burden of proof on the whole case shall then introduce his evidence.

(c) The adverse party shall briefly state the nature of his claim or defense and what said party expects to prove and the relief sought unless he has already done so.

(d) He shall then introduce his evidence.

(e) The intervenor and other parties shall make their statement, unless they have already done so, and shall introduce their evidence.

(f) The parties shall then be confined to rebutting testimony on each side.

(g) But one counsel on each side shall examine and cross-examine the same witness, except on leave granted.

Oct. 29, 1940, eff. Sept. 1, 1941. Amended by orders of March 31, 1941, eff. Sept. 1, 1941; July 20, 1966, eff. Jan. 1, 1967; July 11, 1977, eff. Jan. 1, 1978.

Source: TRCS art. 2180 (repealed).

ANNOTATIONS

Sutton v. Helwig, No. 02-12-00525-CV, 2013 WL 6046533 (Tex.App.—Fort Worth 2013, no pet.) (memo op.; 11-14-13). "Although [pro se P] argues that there is no time limitation [on opening statements] in the [TRCPs] and that it would not have taken long for her to present her 21-page opening statement, rule 265 states that '[t]he party upon whom rests the burden of proof on the whole case shall state to the jury *briefly* the nature of his claim or defense. . . .' Further, . . . Rule 265(a) does not afford counsel the right to detail to the jury the evidence which he intends to offer, nor to read or describe in detail the documents he proposes to offer. The practice of detailing the expected testimony in the opening statement places matters before the jury without the trial court['s] having had an opportunity to determine the admissibility of such matters. [S]uch a practice sometimes has the effect of misleading or confusing the jurors as between the expectations of counsel and evidence actually admitted. The proper limitation of the opening statement is a matter necessarily resting in the discretion of the trial court subject to review for abuse of discretion." *See also* **In re Commitment of Dodson**, 434 S.W.3d 742, 749 (Tex.App.—Beaumont 2014, pet. denied).

TRCP 266. OPEN AND CLOSE—ADMISSION

Except as provided in Rule 269 the plaintiff shall have the right to open and conclude both in adducing his evidence and in the argument, unless the burden of proof on the whole case under the pleadings rests upon the defendant, or unless the defendant or all of the defendants, if there should be more than one, shall, after the issues of fact are settled and before the trial commences, admit that the plaintiff is entitled to recover as set forth in the petition, except so far as he may be defeated, in whole or in part, by the allegations of the answer constituting a good defense, which may be established on the trial; which admission shall be entered of record, whereupon the defendant, or the defendants, if more than one, shall have the right to open and conclude in adducing the evidence and in the argument of the cause. The admission shall not serve to admit any allegation which is inconsistent with such defense, which defense shall be one that defendant has the burden of establishing, as for example, and without excluding other defenses: accord and satisfaction, adverse possession, arbitration and award, contributory negligence, discharge in bankruptcy, duress, estoppel, failure of consideration, fraud, release, res judicata, statute of frauds, statute of limitations, waiver, and the like.

Oct. 29, 1940, eff. Sept. 1, 1941.

See also **O'Connor's Texas Rules**, "Opening Statement," ch. 8-B, §1 et seq.; **O'Connor's Texas Rules**, "Final Argument," ch. 8-J, §1 et seq.; **O'Connor's Texas Forms**, FORMS 8B, 8J.

ANNOTATIONS

4M Linen & Unif. Sup. Co. v. W.P. Ballard & Co., 793 S.W.2d 320, 324 (Tex.App.—Houston [1st Dist.] 1990, writ denied). "Rule 266 . . . provides that the plaintiff has the right to open and close argument. There are two exceptions. . . . First, a defendant has the right to open and close if the burden of proof for the entire case under the pleadings is on defendant. Second, a defendant has the right to open and close if, before trial begins, defendant admits that plaintiff is entitled to recover, subject to proof of defensive allegations. . . ."

TRCP 267. WITNESSES PLACED UNDER RULE

a. At the request of either party, in a civil case, the witnesses on both sides shall be sworn and removed out of the courtroom to some place where they cannot hear the testimony as delivered by any other witness in the cause. This is termed placing witnesses under the rule.

b. This rule does not authorize exclusion of (1) a party who is a natural person or the spouse of such natural person, or (2) an officer or employee of a party that is not a natural person and who is designated as its representative by its attorney, or (3) a person whose presence is shown by a party to be essential to the presentation of the cause.

c. If any party be absent, the court in its discretion may exempt from the rule a representative of such party.

d. Witnesses, when placed under Rule 614 of the Texas Rules of Civil Evidence, shall be instructed by the court that they are not to converse with each other or with any other person about the case other than the attorneys in the case, except by permission of the court, and that they are not to read any report of or comment upon the testimony in the case while under the rule.

e. Any witness or other person violating such instructions may be punished for contempt of court.

Oct. 29, 1940, eff. Sept. 1, 1941. Amended by order of July 15, 1987, eff. Jan. 1, 1988.

See also TRE 614; **O'Connor's Texas Rules**, "Invoking 'the Rule'," ch. 8-C, §3.

ANNOTATIONS

Drilex Sys. v. Flores, 1 S.W.3d 112, 118-19 (Tex.1999). "Although an expert witness may *typically* be found exempt under the essential presence exception, experts are not *automatically* exempt. Instead, [TRE] 614 and [TRCP] 267 vest in trial judges broad discretion to determine whether a witness is essential. *At 120:* We acknowledge that the court never expressly placed [D's expert] under [TRE 614] and

never instructed him not to discuss the case with others. However, a court may, in its discretion, exclude the testimony of a prospective witness who technically violates [TRE 614] even though the witness was never actually placed under [TRE 614]."

TRCP 268. MOTION FOR INSTRUCTED VERDICT

A motion for directed verdict shall state the specific grounds therefor.

Oct. 29, 1940, eff. Sept. 1, 1941.

Source: Last sentence of FRCP 50(a), unchanged.

See also **O'Connor's Texas Rules**, "Motion for Directed Verdict," ch. 8-G, §1 et seq.; **O'Connor's Texas Forms**, FORMS 8G.

ANNOTATIONS

City of Keller v. Wilson, 168 S.W.3d 802, 827 (Tex.2005). "As both the inclusive and exclusive standards for the scope of legal-sufficiency review have a long history in Texas, as both have been used in other contexts to review matter-of-law motions, as the federal courts have decided the differences between the two are more semantic than real, and as both—properly applied—must arrive at the same result, we see no compelling reason to choose among them. [¶] The key qualifier, of course, is 'properly applied.' The final test for legal sufficiency must always be whether the evidence at trial would enable reasonable and fair-minded people to reach the verdict under review. Whether a reviewing court begins by considering all the evidence or only the evidence supporting the verdict, legal-sufficiency review [of the denial of a directed verdict] must credit favorable evidence if reasonable jurors could, and disregard contrary evidence unless reasonable jurors could not." *See also* **Mauricio v. Castro**, 287 S.W.3d 476, 479 (Tex.App.—Dallas 2009, no pet.).

Szczepanik v. First S. Trust Co., 883 S.W.2d 648, 649 (Tex.1994). "In reviewing . . . an instructed verdict, we must determine whether there is any evidence of probative force to raise a fact issue on the material questions presented. We consider all of the evidence in a light most favorable to the party against whom the verdict was instructed and disregard all contrary evidence and inferences. . . . If there is any conflicting evidence of probative value on any theory of recovery, an instructed verdict is improper. . . ." *See also* **S.V. v. R.V.**, 933 S.W.2d 1, 8 (Tex.1996).

Johnson v. Swain, 787 S.W.2d 36, 36 n.1 (Tex.1989). "While a partial instructed verdict is not expressly contemplated by our rules, this device has been employed by trial courts as a convenient way of removing certain parts of a case from the factfinder." *See also* **In re Commitment of Scott**, No. 09-11-00555-CV, 2012 WL 5289333 (Tex.App.—Beaumont 2012, no pet.) (memo op.; 10-25-12).

Brewer v. Lowe's Home Ctrs., Inc., No. 12-14-00155-CV, 2015 WL 5965287 (Tex.App.—Tyler 2015, no pet.) (memo op.; 10-14-15). "A directed verdict is proper when (1) a defect in the opponent's pleadings makes them insufficient to support a judgment; (2) the evidence conclusively proves a fact that establishes a party's right to judgment as a matter of law; or (3) the evidence offered on a cause of action is insufficient to raise an issue of fact. Generally, a directed verdict in favor of a defendant may be proper in two situations: (1) when a plaintiff does not present evidence 'raising a fact issue essential to the plaintiff's right of recovery'; and (2) when a plaintiff 'admits or the evidence conclusively establishes a defense to the plaintiff's cause of action.' "

TRCP 269. ARGUMENT

(a) After the evidence is concluded and the charge is read, the parties may argue the case to the jury. The party having the burden of proof on the whole case, or on all matters which are submitted by the charge, shall be entitled to open and conclude the argument; where there are several parties having separate claims or defenses, the court shall prescribe the order of argument between them.

(b) In all arguments, and especially in arguments on the trial of the case, the counsel opening shall present his whole case as he relies on it, both of law and facts, and shall be heard in the concluding argument only in reply to the counsel on the other side.

(c) Counsel for an intervenor shall occupy the position in the argument assigned by the court according to the nature of the claim.

(d) Arguments on questions of law shall be addressed to the court, and counsel should state the substance of the authorities referred to without reading more from books than may be necessary to verify the statement. On a question on motions, exceptions to the evidence, and other incidental matters, the counsel will be allowed only such argument as may be necessary to present clearly the question raised, and refer to authorities on it, unless further discussion is invited by the court.

(e) Arguments on the facts should be addressed to the jury, when one is impaneled in a case that is being tried, under the supervision of the court. Counsel shall be required to confine the argument strictly to the evidence and to the arguments of opposing counsel. Mere personal criticism by counsel upon each other shall be avoided, and when indulged in shall be promptly corrected as a contempt of court.

(f) Side-bar remarks, and remarks by counsel of one side, not addressed to the court, while the counsel on the other side is examining a witness or arguing any question to the court, or addressing the jury, will be rigidly repressed by the court.

(g) The court will not be required to wait for objections to be made when the rules as to arguments are violated; but should they not be noticed and corrected by the court, opposing counsel may ask leave of the court to rise and present his point of objection. But the court shall protect counsel from any unnecessary interruption made on frivolous and unimportant grounds.

(h) It shall be the duty of every counsel to address the court from his place at the bar, and in addressing the court to rise to his feet; and while engaged in the trial of a case, he shall remain at his place in the bar.

Oct. 29, 1940, eff. Sept. 1, 1941. Amended by orders of March 31, 1941, eff. Sept. 1, 1941; April 24, 1990, eff. Sept. 1, 1990.

See also **O'Connor's Texas Rules**, "Final Argument," ch. 8-J, §1 et seq.; **O'Connor's Texas Forms**, FORMS 8J.

ANNOTATIONS

Living Ctrs. v. Peñalver, 256 S.W.3d 678, 680-81 (Tex.2008). "Error as to improper jury argument must ordinarily be preserved by a timely objection which is overruled. The complaining party must not have invited or provoked the improper argument. Typically, retraction of the argument or instruction from the court can cure any probable harm, but in rare instances the probable harm or prejudice cannot be cured. In such instances the argument is incurable and complaint about the argument may be made even though objection was not timely made. To prevail on a claim that improper argument was incurable, the complaining party generally must show that the argument by its nature, degree, and extent constituted such error that an instruction from the court or retraction of the argument could not remove its effects. [¶] [J]ury argument that strikes at the appearance of and the actual impartiality, equality, and fairness of justice rendered by courts is incurably harmful not only because of its harm to the litigants involved, but also because of its capacity to damage the judicial system. Such argument is not subject to the general harmless error analysis." *See also* **Standard Fire Ins. v. Reese**, 584 S.W.2d 835, 839 (Tex.1979); **Richmond Condos. v. Skipworth Commercial Plumbing, Inc.**, 245 S.W.3d 646, 667-68 (Tex.App.—Fort Worth 2008, pet. denied).

Jones v. Republic Waste Servs., 236 S.W.3d 390, 401 (Tex.App.—Houston [1st Dist.] 2007, pet. denied). "To obtain reversal, appellants must first prove 'an error' that was not 'invited or provoked.' Counsel must confine argument 'strictly to the evidence and to the arguments of opposing counsel.' Criticism, censure, or abuse of counsel is not permitted. Appeals to passion and prejudice are improper, as are calls to punish a litigant for the acts of counsel." *See also* **Popcap Games, Inc. v. MumboJumbo, LLC**, 350 S.W.3d 699, 721 (Tex.App.—Dallas 2011, pet. denied).

Sanchez v. Espinoza, 60 S.W.3d 392, 395 (Tex.App.—Amarillo 2001, pet. denied). In the argument, counsel "may discuss the 'environments' or circumstances of the case, the reasonableness or unreasonableness of the evidence, and the probative effect (or lack thereof) of the evidence. So too does he have the leeway to 'present his case as to make the law contained in the charge applicable to the facts of the case.' This leeway also includes the opportunity to encourage the jury to weigh, evaluate, and test the evidence before it."

TRCP 270. ADDITIONAL TESTIMONY

When it clearly appears to be necessary to the due administration of justice, the court may permit additional evidence to be offered at any time; provided that in a jury case no evidence on a controversial matter shall be received after the verdict of the jury.

Oct. 29, 1940, eff. Sept. 1, 1941. Amended by order of Dec. 5, 1983, eff. April 1, 1984.

See also **O'Connor's Texas Rules**, "Motion to Reopen for Additional Evidence," ch. 8-H, §1 et seq.; **O'Connor's Texas Forms**, FORMS 8H.

ANNOTATIONS

Holden v. Holden, 456 S.W.3d 642, 650 (Tex.App.—Tyler 2015, no pet.). "The language of [TRCP 270] does not require a motion by a party, nor have we discovered authority preventing a trial court from reopening the evidence sua sponte. Rather, the courts addressing this issue have held that the trial court may reopen the evidence on its own motion. We agree with the reasoning in those cases."

Moore v. Jet Stream Invs., 315 S.W.3d 195, 201 (Tex.App.—Texarkana 2010, pet. denied). "A trial court's discretion to permit additional evidence 'should be exercised liberally to allow both parties to fully present their case.' . . . In deciding whether to permit additional evidence, a trial court may consider (1) whether the movant showed due diligence in obtaining the evidence; (2) whether the additional evidence is decisive; (3) whether reopening the evidence will cause undue delay; and (4) whether reopening the evidence will cause injustice." *See also* **Naguib v. Naguib**, 137 S.W.3d 367, 372-73 (Tex.App.—Dallas 2004, pet. denied); **Lopez v. Lopez**, 55 S.W.3d 194, 201 (Tex.App.—Corpus Christi 2001, no pet.).

D. Charge to the Jury

TRCP 271. CHARGE TO THE JURY

Unless expressly waived by the parties, the trial court shall prepare and in open court deliver a written charge to the jury.

Oct. 29, 1940, eff. Sept. 1, 1941. Amended by orders of May 25, 1973, eff. Sept. 1, 1973; July 15, 1987, eff. Jan. 1, 1988.

See also **O'Connor's Texas Rules**, "Jury Charge," ch. 8-I, §1 et seq.

TRCP 272. REQUISITES

The charge shall be in writing, signed by the court, and filed with the clerk, and shall be a part of the record of the

cause. It shall be submitted to the respective parties or their attorneys for their inspection, and a reasonable time given them in which to examine and present objections thereto outside the presence of the jury, which objections shall in every instance be presented to the court in writing, or be dictated to the court reporter in the presence of the court and opposing counsel, before the charge is read to the jury. All objections not so presented shall be considered as waived. The court shall announce its rulings thereon before reading the charge to the jury and shall endorse the rulings on the objections if written or dictate same to the court reporter in the presence of counsel. Objections to the charge and the court's rulings thereon may be included as a part of any transcript or statement of facts on appeal and, when so included in either, shall constitute a sufficient bill of exception to the rulings of the court thereon. It shall be presumed, unless otherwise noted in the record, that the party making such objections presented the same at the proper time and excepted to the ruling thereon.

Oct. 29, 1940, eff. Sept. 1, 1941. Amended by orders of Sept. 20, 1941, eff. Dec. 31, 1941; May 25, 1973, eff. Sept. 1, 1973; July 22, 1975, eff. Jan. 1, 1976; July 15, 1987, eff. Jan. 1, 1988.

See also **O'Connor's Texas Rules**, "Jury Charge," ch. 8-I, §1 et seq.; **O'Connor's Texas Forms**, FORM 8I:1.

ANNOTATIONS

Wackenhut Corp. v. Gutierrez, 453 S.W.3d 917, 919-20 (Tex.2015). "[D] argues that, by detailing its reasons for opposing spoliation sanctions generally and a spoliation instruction in particular in its response to [P's] pretrial motion for sanctions, it timely made the trial court aware of its complaint [about the inclusion of a spoliation instruction in the jury charge]. Because the trial court ruled on the motion, [D] contends that it was not required to later object to the jury charge. [¶] [W]e have previously explained that '[t]here should be but one test for determining if a party has preserved error in the jury charge, and that is whether the party made the trial court aware of the complaint, timely and plainly, and obtained a ruling.' [¶] In light of [D's] specific reasons in its pretrial briefing for opposing a spoliation instruction and the trial court's recognition that it submitted the instruction over [D's] objection, there is no doubt that [D] timely made the trial court aware of its complaint and obtained a ruling. . . . Therefore, we conclude that [D] preserved error."

King Fisher Mar. Serv. v. Tamez, 443 S.W.3d 838, 843 (Tex.2014). Rule 272 "provides that a trial court may not consider any objections made after the charge is read to the jury. But it does not follow that a trial court is obligated to consider *every* objection made before the charge is read to the jury. Instead, the plain language of the rule sets an outside limit for charge objections. [¶] Rule 272 mandates trial courts to afford the parties a 'reasonable time' to inspect the charge and present objections outside the presence of the jury. Nothing in the rule prohibits a trial court from setting a deadline for charge objections that may expire before it charges the jury as long as the deadline affords the parties a 'reasonable time' to inspect and object to the charge. Rule 272's reliance on reasonableness invites, rather than restricts, trial-court discretion. Accordingly, while the rule strictly prohibits objections after the charge is read, it affords trial courts latitude in addressing objections made before."

Cruz v. Andrews Restoration, Inc., 364 S.W.3d 817, 829 (Tex.2012). " 'There should be but one test for determining if a party has preserved error in the jury charge, and that is whether the party made the trial court aware of the complaint, timely and plainly, and obtained a ruling.' *At 830:* A proposed charge, whether drafted by a party or by the court, may misalign the parties; misstate the burden of proof; leave out essential elements; or omit a defense, cause of action, or (as here) a line for attorney's fees. Our procedural rules require the lawyers to tell the court about such errors before the charge is formally submitted to a jury. *At 831:* Here, the parties had ample time to review the draft charge and point out discrepancies to the trial court. [P] can complain on appeal only if it made the trial court aware, timely and plainly, of the purported problem and obtained a ruling. Filing a pretrial charge that includes a question containing [a] subpart [that was omitted by the court], when no other part of the record reflects a discussion of the issue or objection to the question ultimately submitted, does not sufficiently alert the trial court to the issue." *See also* **State Dept. of Hwys. & Pub. Transp. v. Payne**, 838 S.W.2d 235, 241 (Tex.1992).

City of Brownsville v. Alvarado, 897 S.W.2d 750, 752 (Tex.1995). "Submission of an improper jury question can be harmless error if the jury's answers to other questions render the improper question immaterial. A jury question is considered immaterial when its answer can be found elsewhere in the verdict or when its answer cannot alter the effect of the verdict."

TRCP 273. JURY SUBMISSIONS

Either party may present to the court and request written questions, definitions, and instructions to be given to the jury; and the court may give them or a part thereof, or may refuse to give them, as may be proper. Such requests shall be prepared and presented to the court and submitted to opposing counsel for examination and objection within a reasonable time after the charge is given to the parties or their attorneys for examination. A request by either party for any questions, definitions, or instructions shall be made separate and apart from such party's objections to the court's charge.

Oct. 29, 1940, eff. Sept. 1, 1941. Amended by orders of Oct. 12, 1949, eff. March 1, 1950; July 15, 1987, eff. Jan. 1, 1988.

See also **O'Connor's Texas Rules**, "Jury Charge," ch. 8-I, §1 et seq.; **O'Connor's Texas Forms**, FORM 8I:1.

ANNOTATIONS

Cruz v. Andrews Restoration, Inc., 364 S.W.3d 817, 831 (Tex.2012). "A charge filed before trial begins rarely accounts fully for the inevitable developments during trial. For these reasons, [TRCP 273 requires] that requests be prepared and presented to the court 'within a reasonable time *after* the charge is given to the parties or their attorneys for examination.' Notwithstanding our rules, we have held that a party may rely on a pretrial charge as long as the record shows that the trial court knew of the written request and refused to submit it."

Alaniz v. Jones & Neuse, Inc., 907 S.W.2d 450, 451 (Tex.1995). TRCP 273 "does not prohibit including the request in a complete charge as long as it is not obscured."

TRCP 274. OBJECTIONS AND REQUESTS

A party objecting to a charge must point out distinctly the objectionable matter and the grounds of the objection. Any complaint as to a question, definition, or instruction, on account of any defect, omission, or fault in pleading, is waived unless specifically included in the objections. When the complaining party's objection, or requested question, definition, or instruction is, in the opinion of the appellate court, obscured or concealed by voluminous unfounded objections, minute differentiations or numerous unnecessary requests, such objection or request shall be untenable. No objection to one part of the charge may be adopted and applied to any other part of the charge by reference only.

Oct. 29, 1940, eff. Sept. 1, 1941. Amended by orders of Sept. 20, 1941, eff. Dec. 31, 1941; July 15, 1987, eff. Jan. 1, 1988.

Source: New rule.

See also **O'Connor's Texas Rules**, "Jury Charge," ch. 8-I, §1 et seq.

ANNOTATIONS

BP Am. Prod. v. Red Deer Res., 526 S.W.3d 389, 402 (Tex.2017). "A party need not object to an immaterial question that should not have been submitted or cannot support a judgment to preserve error. 'A jury question is considered immaterial when its answer can be found elsewhere in the verdict or when its answer cannot alter the effect of the verdict.'" *See also* **Musallam v. Ali**, 560 S.W.3d 636, 640 (Tex.2018).

Holubec v. Brandenberger, 111 S.W.3d 32, 39 (Tex.2003). "[Ds] plainly sought the submission of their statutory defense. Because the question actually submitted was defective, however, [Ds] did not have to submit their own substantially correct question. [Ds'] objection was sufficient to preserve error." *See also* **Moss v. Waste Mgmt.**, 305 S.W.3d 76, 80 (Tex.App.—Houston [1st Dist.] 2009, pet. denied).

Harris Cty. v. Smith, 96 S.W.3d 230, 236 (Tex.2002). If an element of damages in a broad-form submission is not supported by evidence, the party must object and ask the court to either (1) not include that element in the broad-form damages question or (2) submit the elements separately.

Universal Servs. Co. v. Ung, 904 S.W.2d 638, 640 (Tex.1995). A party cannot complain on appeal that the trial court did not submit an instruction or definition with the correct cluster if the party did not request it as part of that cluster.

General Chem. Corp. v. De La Lastra, 852 S.W.2d 916, 920 (Tex.1993). "[D] requested the very issues that it now seeks to avoid. Parties may not invite error by requesting an issue and then objecting to its submission."

Meyers v. 8007 Burnet Holdings, LLC, 600 S.W.3d 412, 422-23 (Tex.App.—El Paso 2020, pet. denied). "[D's] argument is that the objection made at the charge stage fails to comply with Rule 274 because it never told the trial court why the charge was wrong. And significantly, the Texas Supreme Court [has] held that an objection stating that an instruction 'may confuse the jury' or 'prejudice the defendant' was too general because it did not explain 'why the instruction [was] legally incorrect[,]' or 'how it would confuse the jury or prejudice the defendants.' Similarly, [P] here objected that a different Question Seven should be used because otherwise the question is 'confusing.' That objection, however, never explains why the question as worded is confusing. . . . We conclude that the bare objection that the charge as given was 'confusing' did not adequately preserve error. [¶] [P] responds, however, that its oral recitation of a form of the question (dictated into the record) should have alerted the trial court to the problem with the charge. . . . In effect, [F] argues that the alternate oral submission implicitly demonstrates the trial court's awareness of the complaint now urged on appeal. [¶] [T]he oral dictation of the text of a question at the same time charge objections were made did not alert the trial court to the problem with its existing question without something more. Had counsel explained why its suggested charge more closely followed the statute, we might view the situation differently. But leaving the task of discerning the differences between the two forms of the questions to the trial court simply asks too much." *See also* **Reliant Energy Servs. v. Cotton Valley Compression, L.L.C.**, 336 S.W.3d 764, 785 n.23 (Tex.App.—Houston [1st Dist.] 2011, no pet.) (general objection that instruction was "not raised by the evidence" was not specific enough complaint); **Cleveland Reg'l Med. Ctr., L.P. v. Celtic Props., L.C.**, 323 S.W.3d 322, 342 (Tex.App.—Beaumont 2010, pet. denied) (request for different instruction is generally not substitute for objection and does not preserve error).

C.M. Asfahl Agency v. Tensor, Inc., 135 S.W.3d 768, 795 (Tex.App.—Houston [1st Dist.] 2004, no pet.). "Rule

274's prohibition against adopting by reference has generally been interpreted as prohibiting one party from incorporating by reference its own objections to another portion of the charge. Yet, nothing in the rule limits its application to that context. *At 796:* [Ds] did not preserve any error premised on erroneously submitting question . . . to the jury merely by 'joining' the six substantive objections lodged by [co-D]. Instead, [Ds] were required to present their own objections."

TRCP 275. CHARGE READ BEFORE ARGUMENT

Before the argument is begun, the trial court shall read the charge to the jury in the precise words in which it was written, including all questions, definitions, and instructions which the court may give.

Oct. 29, 1940, eff. Sept. 1, 1941. Amended by order of July 15, 1987, eff. Jan. 1, 1988.

See also **O'Connor's Texas Rules**, "Jury Charge," ch. 8-I, §1 et seq.

ANNOTATIONS

Board of Regents v. S&G Constr. Co., 529 S.W.2d 90, 98-99 (Tex.App.—Austin 1975, writ ref'd n.r.e.), *overruled on other grounds*, **Federal Sign v. Texas S. Univ.**, 951 S.W.2d 401 (Tex.1997). Held: A trial court does not violate TRCP 275 by amending the written charge to correct errors after oral argument.

TRCP 276. REFUSAL OR MODIFICATION

When an instruction, question, or definition is requested and the provisions of the law have been complied with and the trial judge refuses the same, the judge shall endorse thereon "Refused," and sign the same officially. If the trial judge modifies the same the judge shall endorse thereon "Modified as follows: (stating in what particular the judge has modified the same) and given, and exception allowed" and sign the same officially. Such refused or modified instruction, question, or definition, when so endorsed shall constitute a bill of exceptions, and it shall be conclusively presumed that the party asking the same presented it at the proper time, excepted to its refusal or modification, and that all the requirements of law have been observed, and such procedure shall entitle the party requesting the same to have the action of the trial judge thereon reviewed without preparing a formal bill of exceptions.

Oct. 29, 1940, eff. Sept. 1, 1941. Amended by order of July 15, 1987, eff. Jan. 1, 1988.

Source: TRCS art. 2188 (repealed).

See also **O'Connor's Texas Rules**, "Jury Charge," ch. 8-I, §1 et seq.

ANNOTATIONS

Dallas Mkt. Ctr. Dev. Co. v. Liedeker, 958 S.W.2d 382, 386-87 (Tex.1997), *overruled on other grounds*, **Torrington Co. v. Stutzman**, 46 S.W.3d 829 (Tex.2000). Although TRCP 276 requires that the trial court endorse refused requests "Refused" and sign them officially, that is not the only way to preserve error. The court can state on the record that they are refused. *See also* **City of Lufkin v. AKJ Props., Inc.**, No. 06-12-00005-CV, 2012 WL 2393087 (Tex.App.—Texarkana 2012, no pet.) (memo op.; 6-26-12).

TRCP 277. SUBMISSION TO THE JURY

In all jury cases the court shall, whenever feasible, submit the cause upon broad-form questions. The court shall submit such instructions and definitions as shall be proper to enable the jury to render a verdict.

Inferential rebuttal questions shall not be submitted in the charge. The placing of the burden of proof may be accomplished by instructions rather than by inclusion in the question.

In any cause in which the jury is required to apportion the loss among the parties the court shall submit a question or questions inquiring what percentage, if any, of the negligence or causation, as the case may be, that caused the occurrence or injury in question is attributable to each of the persons found to have been culpable. The court shall also instruct the jury to answer the damage question or questions without any reduction because of the percentage of negligence or causation, if any, of the person injured. The court may predicate the damage question or questions upon affirmative findings of liability.

In a suit in which termination of the parent-child relationship is requested, the court shall submit separate questions for each parent and each child on (1) each individual statutory ground for termination of the parent-child relationship and (2) whether termination of the parent-child relationship is in the best interest of the child. The court shall predicate the best-interest question upon an affirmative finding of at least one termination ground.

The court may submit a question disjunctively when it is apparent from the evidence that one or the other of the conditions or facts inquired about necessarily exists.

The court shall not in its charge comment directly on the weight of the evidence or advise the jury of the effect of their answers, but the court's charge shall not be objectionable on the ground that it incidentally constitutes a comment on the weight of the evidence or advises the jury of the effect of their answers when it is properly a part of an instruction or definition.

Oct. 29, 1940, eff. Sept. 1, 1941. Amended by orders of March 31, 1941, eff. Sept. 1, 1941; May 25, 1973, eff. Sept. 1, 1973; Dec. 5, 1983, eff. April 1, 1984; July 15, 1987, eff. Jan. 1, 1988; Jan. 8, 2020, eff. May 1, 2020.

Comment—2020

Rule 277 is revised to require a jury question on each individual statutory ground for termination as to each parent and each child without requiring further granulated questions for subparts of an individual ground for termination. Rule 277 is also revised to require a separate question on best interest of the child as to each parent and each child that is predicated on an affirmative answer to at least one termination-ground question. The revisions supersede **Texas Department of Human Services v. E.B.**, 802 S.W.2d 647 (Tex. 1990).

Comment—1988

The amendment to paragraph one of Rule 277 would unify the practice of submitting broad form questions to the jury in the form approved by **Lemos v. Montez**, 680 S.W.2d 798 (Tex.1984).

The amendment to the third paragraph includes a textual change and recognizes that damage issues may be predicted on affirmative liability findings.

Source: TRCS art. 2189 (repealed).

See also **O'Connor's Texas Rules**, "Jury Charge," ch. 8-I, §1 et seq.

ANNOTATIONS

Benge v. Williams, 548 S.W.3d 466, 475 (Tex.2018). "The jury question in the present case, unlike the one in **Casteel**, did not include multiple theories, some valid and some invalid. It inquired about a single theory: negligence. But we have . . . held that when the question allows a finding of liability based on evidence that cannot support recovery, the same presumption-of-harm rule must be applied."

Bed, Bath & Beyond, Inc. v. Urista, 211 S.W.3d 753, 757 (Tex.2006). "When, as here, the broad-form questions submitted a single liability theory (negligence) to the jury, **Casteel**'s multiple-liability-theory analysis does not apply. Moreover, when a defensive theory is submitted through an inferential rebuttal instruction, **Casteel**'s solution of departing from broad-form submission and instead employing granulated submission cannot apply. Unlike alternate theories of liability and damage elements, inferential rebuttal issues cannot be submitted in the jury charge as separate questions and instead must be presented through jury instructions. Therefore, although harm can be presumed when meaningful appellate review is precluded because valid and invalid liability theories or damage elements are commingled, we are not persuaded that harm must likewise be presumed when proper jury questions are submitted along with improper inferential rebuttal instructions." *See also* **Thota v. Young**, 366 S.W.3d 678, 692-93 (Tex.2012).

Diamond Offshore Mgmt. v. Guidry, 171 S.W.3d 840, 844 (Tex.2005). "Broad-form submission does not entail omitting elements of proof from the charge. While the trial court could certainly have inquired about the separate issues . . . in a single question with proper instructions, [D] was not obligated to request such a question. It was required only to object to the absence of any inquiry, which the trial court acknowledged [D] had done with its requested questions."

Harris Cty. v. Smith, 96 S.W.3d 230, 234 (Tex.2002). "[T]he trial court erred in overruling [D's] timely and specific objection to the charge, which mixed valid and invalid elements of damages in a single broad-form submission, and that such error was harmful because it prevented the appellate court from determining 'whether the jury based its verdict on an improperly submitted invalid' element of damage. *At 236:* We hold that **Casteel**'s reasoning [as to broad-form liability questions] applies equally to broad-form damage questions, and under its rationale we conclude that the charge error in this case was harmful."

Crown Life Ins. v. Casteel, 22 S.W.3d 378, 389 (Tex.2000). "When a single broad-form liability question erroneously commingles valid and invalid liability theories and the appellant's objection is timely and specific, the error is harmful when it cannot be determined whether the improperly submitted theories formed the sole basis for the jury's finding. *At 390:* Rule 277 is not absolute; rather, it mandates broad-form submission 'whenever feasible.' [Submitting] 'alternative liability standards when the governing law is unsettled might very well be a situation where broad-form submission is not feasible.' Similarly, when the trial court is unsure whether it should submit a particular theory of liability, separating liability theories best serves the policy of judicial economy underlying Rule 277 by avoiding the need for a new trial when the basis for liability cannot be determined. Furthermore, Rule 277 mandates that '[t]he court shall submit such instructions and definitions as shall be proper to enable the jury to render a verdict.' It is implicit in this mandate that the jury be able to base its verdict on legally valid questions and instructions. Thus, it may not be feasible to submit a single broad-form liability question that incorporates wholly separate theories of liability." *See also* **Texas Comm'n on Human Rights v. Morrison**, 381 S.W.3d 533, 536-37 (Tex.2012).

Hyundai Motor Co. v. Rodriguez, 995 S.W.2d 661, 664 (Tex.1999). "[S]ubmission of a single question relating to multiple theories may be necessary to avoid the risk that the jury will become confused and answer questions inconsistently. The goal of the charge is to submit to the jury the issues for decision logically, simply, clearly, fairly, correctly, and completely." *See also* **Texas DHS v. E.B.**, 802 S.W.2d 647, 649 (Tex.1990).

H.E. Butt Grocery Co. v. Bilotto, 985 S.W.2d 22, 24 (Tex.1998). "[W]hen an instruction merely directs the jury to answer a damages question only if some condition or conditions have been met, it does not directly instruct the jury about the legal effect of its answers."

Texas Mut. Ins. v. Boetsch, 307 S.W.3d 874, 879-80 (Tex.App.—Dallas 2010, pet. denied). "An impermissible

comment on the weight of the evidence occurs when, after examining the entire charge, it is determined that the judge assumed the truth of a material controverted fact or exaggerated, minimized, or withdrew some pertinent evidence from the jury's consideration. An instruction also will be held to be an improper comment on the weight of the evidence if it suggests to the jury the trial judge's opinion concerning the matter about which the jury is asked. Reversal is required if an improper comment on the weight of the evidence is one that was calculated to cause and probably did cause the rendition of an improper judgment." *See also* **Flying J Inc. v. Meda, Inc.**, 373 S.W.3d 680, 687 (Tex.App.—San Antonio 2012, no pet.).

Valence Oper. Co. v. Anadarko Pet. Corp., 303 S.W.3d 435, 442 (Tex.App.—Texarkana 2010, no pet.). "A definition may properly be submitted to the jury if a term used in the charge has a distinct legal meaning, or if it differs in meaning from the usual and commonly accepted meaning. If the meaning that the parties intended to give to a term is a question of fact for the jury, and there is conflicting evidence before the jury as to the meaning of the term, it should not be defined, and the jury may decide the question based on its view of the evidence."

TRCP 278. SUBMISSION OF QUESTIONS, DEFINITIONS, AND INSTRUCTIONS

The court shall submit the questions, instructions and definitions in the form provided by Rule 277, which are raised by the written pleadings and the evidence. Except in trespass to try title, statutory partition proceedings, and other special proceedings in which the pleadings are specially defined by statutes or procedural rules, a party shall not be entitled to any submission of any question raised only by a general denial and not raised by affirmative written pleading by that party. Nothing herein shall change the burden of proof from what it would have been under a general denial. A judgment shall not be reversed because of the failure to submit other and various phases or different shades of the same question. Failure to submit a question shall not be deemed a ground for reversal of the judgment, unless its submission, in substantially correct wording, has been requested in writing and tendered by the party complaining of the judgment; provided, however, that objection to such failure shall suffice in such respect if the question is one relied upon by the opposing party. Failure to submit a definition or instruction shall not be deemed a ground for reversal of the judgment unless a substantially correct definition or instruction has been requested in writing and tendered by the party complaining of the judgment.

July 15, 1987, eff. Jan. 1, 1988.

Source: New rule. See former TRCP 279, first par.

See also **O'Connor's Texas Rules**, "Jury Charge," ch. 8-I, §1 et seq.; **O'Connor's Texas Forms**, FORM 8I:1.

ANNOTATIONS

Railroad Comm'n v. Gulf Energy Expl. Corp., 482 S.W.3d 559, 571 (Tex.2016). "[P] argues [D] waived any error relating to the trial court's refusal of its proposed good-faith question by failing to request a definition of good faith in conjunction with the question. We disagree. [¶] [P] does not dispute that [D's] proposed . . . question generally tracked the pertinent statutory language. [D] complied with Rule 278 and did not waive the trial court's error in refusing to submit that question by failing to request an accompanying extra-statutory definition. We are particularly loath to find waiver for failing to propose a definition of a statutory term when no case law provided explicit guidance on what the proper definition of that term should be."

Shupe v. Lingafelter, 192 S.W.3d 577, 579 (Tex.2006). "When a trial court refuses to submit a requested instruction on an issue raised by the pleadings and evidence, the question on appeal is whether the request was reasonably necessary to enable the jury to render a proper verdict. The omission of an instruction is reversible error only if the omission probably caused the rendition of an improper judgment." *See also* **Grohman v. Kahlig**, 318 S.W.3d 882, 888 (Tex.2010); **Texas Workers' Comp. Ins. Fund v. Mandlbauer**, 34 S.W.3d 909, 912 (Tex.2000).

In re S.A.P., 156 S.W.3d 574, 577 (Tex.2005). "An unpleaded issue may be tried by consent, but it still must be submitted to the jury."

Union Pac. R.R. v. Williams, 85 S.W.3d 162, 166 (Tex.2002). "A party is entitled to a jury question, instruction, or definition if the pleadings and evidence raise an issue. An instruction is proper if it (1) assists the jury, (2) accurately states the law, and (3) finds support in the pleadings and evidence." *See also* **Seger v. Yorkshire Ins. Co.**, 503 S.W.3d 388, 408 (Tex.2016); **Transcontinental Ins. v. Crump**, 330 S.W.3d 211, 221 (Tex.2010).

Triplex Comms. v. Riley, 900 S.W.2d 716, 718 (Tex.1995). "If an issue is properly pleaded and is supported by some evidence, a litigant is entitled to have controlling questions submitted to the jury." *See also* **Elbaor v. Smith**, 845 S.W.2d 240, 243 (Tex.1992).

Dernick Res. v. Wilstein, 471 S.W.3d 468, 495 (Tex.App.—Houston [1st Dist.] 2015, pet. denied). "The trial court has broad discretion in submitting the jury charge, subject only to the requirement that the questions submitted must (1) control the disposition of the case; (2) be raised by the pleadings and the evidence; and (3) properly submit the disputed issues for the jury's determination." *See also* **Texas Disposal Sys. Landfill, Inc. v. Waste Mgmt. Holdings, Inc.**, 219 S.W.3d 563, 580 (Tex.App.—Austin 2007, pet. denied).

In re F.L.R., 293 S.W.3d 278, 281 (Tex.App.—Waco 2009, no pet.). An oral request for a jury instruction, even when dictated on the record, does not satisfy TRCP 278. *See also*

Yzaguirre v. University of Tex. Health Sci. Ctr., No. 04-09-00550-CV, 2010 WL 1404620 (Tex.App.—San Antonio 2010, no pet.) (memo op.; 4-7-10) (dictating a requested instruction will not support an appeal). *But see* **In re M.P.**, 126 S.W.3d 228, 230-31 (Tex.App.—San Antonio 2003, no pet.) (allowing attorney's oral request on record).

TRCP 279. OMISSIONS FROM THE CHARGE

Upon appeal all independent grounds of recovery or of defense not conclusively established under the evidence and no element of which is submitted or requested are waived. When a ground of recovery or defense consists of more than one element, if one or more of such elements necessary to sustain such ground of recovery or defense, and necessarily referable thereto, are submitted to and found by the jury, and one or more of such elements are omitted from the charge, without request or objection, and there is factually sufficient evidence to support a finding thereon, the trial court, at the request of either party, may after notice and hearing and at any time before the judgment is rendered, make and file written findings on such omitted element or elements in support of the judgment. If no such written findings are made, such omitted element or elements shall be deemed found by the court in such manner as to support the judgment. A claim that the evidence was legally or factually insufficient to warrant the submission of any question may be made for the first time after verdict, regardless of whether the submission of such question was requested by the complainant.

Oct. 29, 1940, eff. Sept. 1, 1941. Amended by orders of March 31, 1941, eff. Sept. 1, 1941; July 15, 1987, eff. Jan. 1, 1988; Dec. 16, 1987, eff. Jan. 1, 1988.

Comment—1988

First paragraph transferred to Rule 278.

See also **O'Connor's Texas Rules**, "Jury Charge," ch. 8-I, §1 et seq.

ANNOTATIONS

DiGiuseppe v. Lawler, 269 S.W.3d 588, 599 (Tex.2008). "The purpose of the 'necessarily referable' requirement in Rule 279 is to give parties, against whom issues are to be deemed, fair notice of a partial submission, so that they have an opportunity to object to the charge or request submission of the missing issues to the ground of recovery or defense. Once a party is on notice of the independent ground of recovery or defense due to the existence of an issue necessarily referable thereto, if that party fails to object or request submission of the missing issues, he cannot be heard to complain on appeal, as he is said to have consented to the court's findings on the missing issues." (Internal quotes omitted.)

Chon Tri v. J.T.T., 162 S.W.3d 552, 558 (Tex.2005). "If one or more elements of that cause of action was omitted from the charge, and there was no request to include the omitted element or objection to its exclusion, and no written findings were made by the trial court on the omitted element, then the omitted element must be deemed found by the trial court in a manner that supports its judgment." *See also* **In re J.F.C.**, 96 S.W.3d 256, 262-63 (Tex.2002).

Gulf States Utils. Co. v. Low, 79 S.W.3d 561, 564 (Tex.2002). "Rule 279 may support a deemed finding only when it can be deemed found 'in such manner as to support the judgment.' . . . The court of appeals misapplied Rule 279 to deem a finding, not to support the trial court's judgment, but to render a new judgment for actual damages in an amount nearly 15 times the trial court's award."

E. Case to the Jury

TRCP 280. PRESIDING JUROR OF JURY

Each jury shall appoint one of their body presiding juror.

Oct. 29, 1940, eff. Sept. 1, 1941. Amended by order of Dec. 5, 1983, eff. April 1, 1984.

TRCP 281. PAPERS TAKEN TO JURY ROOM

With the court's permission, the jury may take with them to the jury room any notes they took during the trial. In addition, the jury may, and on request shall take with them in their retirement the charges and instructions, general or special, which were given and read to them, and any written evidence, except the depositions of witnesses, but shall not take with them any special charges which have been refused. Where only part of a paper has been read in evidence, the jury shall not take the same with them, unless the part so read to them is detached from that which was excluded.

Oct. 29, 1940, eff. Sept. 1, 1941. Amended by orders of Dec. 5, 1983, eff. April 1, 1984; Dec. 13, 2010, and March 15, 2011, eff. April 1, 2011.

See also **O'Connor's Texas Rules**, "Juror note-taking," ch. 8-A, §10.

ANNOTATIONS

First Empls. Ins. v. Skinner, 646 S.W.2d 170, 172 (Tex.1983). "Rule 281 is mandatory and . . . the trial court is required to send all exhibits admitted into evidence to the jury room during the deliberations of the jury. Furthermore, this rule is self-operative and requires no request from the jurors or counsel." *See also* **Formosa Plastics Corp. v. Kajima Int'l**, 216 S.W.3d 436, 464 (Tex.App.—Corpus Christi 2006, pet. denied) (any error in failing to send exhibits to jury room during deliberations is not reversible unless error probably caused rendition of improper judgment).

TRCP 282. JURY KEPT TOGETHER

The jury may either decide a case in court or retire for deliberation. If they retire, they shall be kept together in

some convenient place, under the charge of an officer, until they agree upon a verdict or are discharged by the court; but the court in its discretion may permit them to separate temporarily for the night and at their meals, and for other proper purposes.

Oct. 29, 1940, eff. Sept. 1, 1941.

TRCP 283. DUTY OF OFFICER ATTENDING JURY

The officer in charge of the jury shall not make nor permit any communication to be made to them, except to inquire if they have agreed upon a verdict, unless by order of the court; and he shall not before their verdict is rendered communicate to any person the state of their deliberations or the verdict agreed upon.

Oct. 29, 1940, eff. Sept. 1, 1941.

ANNOTATIONS

Logan v. Grady, 482 S.W.2d 313, 322 (Tex.App.—Fort Worth 1972, no writ). "[T]he jury bailiff violated [TRCP] 283 and 285 . . . when he did not make the jury's wish as communicated to him known to the court and also when he instructed the jury that its members already had in the jury room all that it needed in order to answer Issue No. 14."

TRCP 284. JUDGE TO CAUTION JURY

Immediately after jurors are selected for a case, the court must instruct them to turn off their phones and other electronic devices and not to communicate with anyone through any electronic device while they are in the courtroom or while they are deliberating. The court must also instruct them that, while they are serving as jurors, they must not post any information about the case on the Internet or search for any information outside of the courtroom, including on the Internet, to try to learn more about the case.

If jurors are permitted to separate before they are released from jury duty, either during the trial or after the case is submitted to them, the court must instruct them that it is their duty not to communicate with, or permit themselves to be addressed by, any other person about any subject relating to the case.

Oct. 29, 1940, eff. Sept. 1, 1941. Amended by orders of Dec. 13, 2010, and March 15, 2011, eff. April 1, 2011.

TRCP 285. JURY MAY COMMUNICATE WITH COURT

The jury may communicate with the court by making their wish known to the officer in charge, who shall inform the court, and they may then in open court, and through their presiding juror, communicate with the court, either verbally or in writing. If the communication is to request further instructions, Rule 286 shall be followed.

Oct. 29, 1940, eff. Sept. 1, 1941. Amended by order of Dec. 5, 1983, eff. April 1, 1984.

See also **O'Connor's Texas Rules**, "Supplemental instructions to jury," ch. 8-I, §8.

TRCP 286. JURY MAY RECEIVE FURTHER INSTRUCTIONS

After having retired, the jury may receive further instructions from the court touching any matter of law, either at their request or upon the court's own motion. For this purpose they shall appear before the judge in open court in a body, and if the instruction is being given at their request, they shall through their presiding juror state to the court, in writing, the particular question of law upon which they desire further instruction. The court shall give such instruction in writing, but no instruction shall be given except in conformity with the rules relating to the charge. Additional argument may be allowed in the discretion of the court.

Oct. 29, 1940, eff. Sept. 1, 1941. Amended by orders of Dec. 5, 1983, eff. April 1, 1984; July 15, 1987, eff. Jan. 1, 1988.

Source: TRCS art. 2198 (repealed).

See also **O'Connor's Texas Rules**, "Supplemental instructions to jury," ch. 8-I, §8.

ANNOTATIONS

Stevens v. Travelers Ins., 563 S.W.2d 223, 229 (Tex.1978). "[E]ven though there is a latent danger of coercion, supplemental, verdict-urging instructions are not, in and of themselves, erroneous, so long as the particular charge given is not otherwise objectionable."

In re E.M., 494 S.W.3d 209, 230 (Tex.App.—Waco 2015, pet. denied). "Rule 286 . . . authorizes a trial court to give further instructions to the jury during deliberations. These instructions are to be given in conformity with the rules relating to the charge, which requires submission to the parties or their attorneys for their inspection and that [there be] a reasonable time to review and object outside the presence of the jury. [¶] A party and their counsel have a right to be present in court for all proceedings. However, it is a right that can be waived. [W]hile it may be common practice to rely on the trial court or the clerk to contact the lawyers in the event of a jury note, the practice is not required or even contemplated by the [TRCPs]. Because the court remains open for all purposes, there is no requirement for additional notice to the parties not in the courtroom when issues such as the proper response to a jury note are presented to the trial court for determination, and we are not willing to impose a duty upon the trial court to provide further notice to absent parties in the absence of an agreement to do so. In such events, the court is authorized to proceed and rule on the issue."

Lochinvar Corp. v. Meyers, 930 S.W.2d 182, 187 (Tex.App.—Dallas 1996, no writ). "[R]ule 286 allow[s] a court the opportunity to correct an error by modifying its charge. [¶] The instruction was given to the jury in writing[, but the trial court did not] reassemble the jury in the courtroom. [D waived the error because it] did not object to the court's failure to reassemble the jury and read the modified charge."

TRCP 287. DISAGREEMENT AS TO EVIDENCE

If the jury disagree as to the statement of any witness, they may, upon applying to the court, have read to them from the court reporter's notes that part of such witness' testimony on the point in dispute; but, if there be no such reporter, or if his notes cannot be read to the jury, the court may cause such witness to be again brought upon the stand and the judge shall direct him to repeat his testimony as to the point in dispute, and no other, as nearly as he can in the language used on the trial; and on their notifying the court that they disagree as to any portion of a deposition or other paper not permitted to be carried with them in their retirement, the court may, in like manner, permit such portion of said deposition or paper to be again read to the jury.

Oct. 29, 1940, eff. Sept. 1, 1941.

ANNOTATIONS

Krishnan v. Ramirez, 42 S.W.3d 205, 225 (Tex.App.—Corpus Christi 2001, pet. denied). "The judge is given broad discretion in determining what portions of the testimony are relevant to the jury's request to have testimony re-read."

TRCP 288. COURT OPEN FOR JURY

The court, during the deliberations of the jury, may proceed with other business or recess from time to time, but shall be deemed open for all purposes connected with the case before the jury.

Oct. 29, 1940, eff. Sept. 1, 1941.

TRCP 289. DISCHARGE OF JURY

The jury to whom a case has been submitted may be discharged by the court when they cannot agree and the parties consent to their discharge, or when they have been kept together for such time as to render it altogether improbable that they can agree, or when any calamity or accident may, in the opinion of the court, require it, or when by sickness or other cause their number is reduced below the number constituting the jury in such court.

The cause shall again be placed on the jury docket and shall again be set for trial as the court directs.

Oct. 29, 1940, eff. Sept. 1, 1941. Amended by order of Dec. 5, 1983, eff. April 1, 1984.

See also **O'Connor's Texas Rules**, "Verdict-urging instructions," ch. 8-I, §8.3.

ANNOTATIONS

Shaw v. Greater Houston Transp., 791 S.W.2d 204, 209 (Tex.App.—Corpus Christi 1990, no writ). It was coercive for the trial court to refuse to release the jury after they stated three times that they were deadlocked.

F. Verdict

TRCP 290. DEFINITION AND SUBSTANCE

A verdict is a written declaration by a jury of its decision, comprehending the whole or all the issues submitted to the jury, and shall be either a general or special verdict, as directed, which shall be signed by the presiding juror of the jury.

A general verdict is one whereby the jury pronounces generally in favor of one or more parties to the suit upon all or any of the issues submitted to it. A special verdict is one wherein the jury finds the facts only on issues made up and submitted to them under the direction of the court.

A special verdict shall, as between the parties, be conclusive as to the facts found.

Oct. 29, 1940, eff. Sept. 1, 1941. Amended by order of Dec. 5, 1983, eff. April 1, 1984.

ANNOTATIONS

Wal-Mart Stores v. Alexander, 868 S.W.2d 322, 328 (Tex.1993). "A jury's marginal notations generally may not be considered on appeal. They reflect the jury's mental processes, but they are not part of its verdict."

Houston Fire & Cas. Ins. v. Gerhardt, 281 S.W.2d 176, 178 (Tex.App.—San Antonio 1955, orig. proceeding). "A verdict form reflecting answers to special issues but not signed by the foreman may or may not be a verdict, and presents a question which must be determined by the hearing of evidence."

TRCP 291. FORM OF VERDICT

No special form of verdict is required, and the judgment shall not be arrested or reversed for mere want of form therein if there has been substantial compliance with the requirements of the law in rendering a verdict.

Oct. 29, 1940, eff. Sept. 1, 1941. Amended by order of Oct. 3, 1972, eff. Feb. 1, 1973.

TRCP 292. VERDICT BY PORTION OF ORIGINAL JURY

(a) Except as provided in subsection (b), a verdict may be rendered in any cause by the concurrence, as to each and all answers made, of the same ten or more members of an

original jury of twelve or of the same five or more members of an original jury of six. However, where as many as three jurors die or be disabled from sitting and there are only nine of the jurors remaining of an original jury of twelve, those remaining may render and return a verdict. If less than the original twelve or six jurors render a verdict, the verdict must be signed by each juror concurring therein.

(b) A verdict may be rendered awarding exemplary damages only if the jury was unanimous in finding liability for and the amount of exemplary damages.

Oct. 29, 1940, eff. Sept. 1, 1941. Amended by order of Oct. 3, 1972, eff. Feb. 1, 1973; Oct. 7, 2004, eff. Feb. 1, 2005; Jan. 27, 2005, eff. Feb. 1, 2005.

Comment—2005

The rule is divided into two subsections. Subsection (a) is clarified. Subsection (b) is added to make the rule consistent with Act of June 2, 2003, 78th Leg., R.S., ch. 204, §13.04, 2003 Tex. Gen. Laws 847, 888, codified as Tex. Civ. Prac. & Rem. Code §41.003.

See also **O'Connor's Texas Rules**, "Verdict," ch. 8-K, §1 et seq.

ANNOTATIONS

In re M.G.N., 441 S.W.3d 246, 248 (Tex.2014). "[A] trial court may substitute a regular juror with an alternate if the regular juror is unable to fulfill or is disqualified from fulfilling his duties, but a trial court may only dismiss a juror and proceed with fewer than 12 jurors if the dismissed juror is constitutionally disabled."

Yanes v. Sowards, 996 S.W.2d 849, 850 (Tex.1999). The Texas Constitution and TRCPs "require a district-court jury to consist of 12 original jurors, but as few as 9 may render and return a verdict if the others die or become disabled from sitting. [T]rial courts have broad discretion in determining whether a juror is disabled from sitting when there is evidence of constitutional disqualification. But not just any inconvenience or delay is a disability. A constitutional disability must be in the nature of an actual physical or mental incapacity." (Internal quotes omitted.) *See also* **McDaniel v. Yarbrough**, 898 S.W.2d 251, 253 (Tex.1995).

Schlafly v. Schlafly, 33 S.W.3d 863, 870 (Tex.App.—Houston [14th Dist.] 2000, pet. denied). "The alternate juror hears the same evidence that a regular juror hears and . . . 'has the same functions, powers and privileges.' There is no reason to treat a jury comprised of 12 members, one of whom is an alternate, any differently than a jury comprised of 12 regular members. . . . We find 'original jurors' means all the jurors empaneled, both regular members and alternates."

TRCP 293. WHEN THE JURY AGREE

When the jury agree upon a verdict, they shall be brought into court by the proper officer, and they shall deliver their verdict to the clerk; and if they state that they have agreed, the verdict shall be read aloud by the clerk. If the verdict is in proper form, no juror objects to its accuracy, no juror represented as agreeing thereto dissents therefrom, and neither party requests a poll of the jury, the verdict shall be entered upon the minutes of the court.

Oct. 29, 1940, eff. Sept. 1, 1941. Amended by order of Oct. 3, 1972, eff. Feb. 1, 1973.

TRCP 294. POLLING THE JURY

Any party shall have the right to have the jury polled. A jury is polled by reading once to the jury collectively the general verdict, or the questions and answers thereto consecutively, and then calling the name of each juror separately and asking the juror if it is the juror's verdict. If any juror answers in the negative when the verdict is returned signed only by the presiding juror as a unanimous verdict, or if any juror shown by the juror's signature to agree to the verdict should answer in the negative, the jury shall be retired for further deliberation.

Oct. 29, 1940, eff. Sept. 1, 1941. Amended by orders of Oct. 3, 1972, eff. Feb. 1, 1973; Dec. 5, 1983, eff. April 1, 1984; April 24, 1990, eff. Sept. 1, 1990.

See also **O'Connor's Texas Rules**, "Request to poll jury," ch. 8-K, §6.

ANNOTATIONS

Suggs v. Fitch, 64 S.W.3d 658, 660 (Tex.App.—Texarkana 2001, no pet.). "The right to poll the jury pursuant to [TRCP] 294 is a waivable right and must be requested in order to be invoked." *See also* **Pate v. Texline Feed Mills, Inc.**, 689 S.W.2d 238, 243 (Tex.App.—Amarillo 1985, writ ref'd n.r.e.) (once proper request is made, court has no discretion but to poll jury).

TRCP 295. CORRECTION OF VERDICT

If the purported verdict is defective, the court may direct it to be reformed. If it is incomplete, or not responsive to the questions contained in the court's charge, or the answers to the questions are in conflict, the court shall in writing instruct the jury in open court of the nature of the incompleteness, unresponsiveness, or conflict, provide the jury such additional instructions as may be proper, and retire the jury for further deliberations.

Oct. 29, 1940, eff. Sept. 1, 1941. Amended by order of July 15, 1987, eff. Jan. 1, 1988.

Comment—1988

The amendment makes it clear that the court may direct a complete yet defective verdict to be reformed. The amendment also makes it clear that in the event the verdict is incomplete or otherwise improper, the court is limited to giving the jury additional instructions in writing.

See also **O'Connor's Texas Rules**, "Objections to verdict," ch. 8-K, §5.

ANNOTATIONS

USAA Tex. Lloyds Co. v. Menchaca, 545 S.W.3d 479, 526 (Tex.2018) (plurality op.). "Generally, a party should object to conflicting answers before the trial court dismisses the jury. The absence of such an objection, however, should not prohibit us from reaching the issue of irreconcilable conflicts in jury findings. *At 527:* [I]f the jury's answers conflict, the trial court *may* direct the jury to deliberate further, and if the trial court chooses to do so, additional jury instructions must be given in writing. Rule 295 does not mandate that conflicts not resolved through further deliberations are waived; the rule simply mandates written instructions in the event that the court decides to have the jury deliberate further to reform the verdict. Rule 295 does not prohibit a court from exercising another option, however: If the plaintiff insisted on submitting its claims in a way that cannot support the plaintiff's claim for recovery in light of the jury's answers, nobody objects to the jury's answers, and both parties insist there is no conflict, the trial court may enter judgment for the defendant without running afoul of the rule." *But see* **Meek v. Onstad**, 430 S.W.3d 601, 605-06 (Tex.App.—Houston [14th Dist.] 2014, no pet.) (party must raise complaint about conflicting answers before jury is discharged; otherwise, complaint is waived).

Archer Daniels Midland Co. v. Bohall, 114 S.W.3d 42, 46 (Tex.App.—Eastland 2003, no pet.). TRCP 295 "applies only to defective verdicts, not defective charges. Before Rule 295 would authorize further instruction to the jury, the verdict must be incomplete, non-responsive to the questions contained in the court's charge, or contain answers which are in conflict." *See also* **Fish v. Dallas ISD**, 170 S.W.3d 226, 229 (Tex.App.—Dallas 2005, pet. denied).

G. Findings by the Court

TRCP 296. REQUESTS FOR FINDINGS OF FACTS AND CONCLUSIONS OF LAW

In any case tried in the district or county court without a jury, any party may request the court to state in writing its findings of fact and conclusions of law. Such request shall be entitled "Request for Findings of Fact and Conclusions of Law" and shall be filed within twenty days after judgment is signed with the clerk of the court, who shall immediately call such request to the attention of the judge who tried the case. The party making the request shall serve it on all other parties in accordance with Rule 21a.

Oct. 29, 1940, eff. Sept. 1, 1941. Amended by orders of March 19, 1957, eff. Sept. 1, 1957; June 10, 1980, eff. Jan. 1, 1981; Dec. 5, 1983, eff. April 1, 1984; April 24, 1990, eff. Sept. 1, 1990.

Comment—1990

To revise the practice and times for findings of fact and conclusions of law. See also Rules 297 and 298.

Source: TRCS art. 2208 (repealed).

See also **O'Connor's Texas Rules**, "Request for Findings of Fact & Conclusions of Law," ch. 10-E, §1 et seq.; **O'Connor's Texas Forms**, FORMS 10E:1, 10E:2.

ANNOTATIONS

Black v. Dallas Cty. Child Welfare Unit, 835 S.W.2d 626, 630 n.10 (Tex.1992). "If no findings of fact or conclusions of law are filed, the reviewing court must imply all necessary fact findings in support of the trial court's judgment."

Guillory v. Dietrich, 598 S.W.3d 284, 290 (Tex.App.—Dallas 2020, pet. denied). "The purpose of requesting findings of fact and conclusions of law is to narrow the judgment's bases and thereby reduce the number of contentions the appellant must make on appeal. With this in mind, we agree with our sister courts that 'a trial court should not make findings on every disputed fact, but only those having some legal significance to an ultimate issue in the case.' [¶] Many fact findings in this case have no obvious relevance to any ultimate issue. . . . These additional findings concern evidentiary matters instead of controlling issues. As such they are unnecessary. We disregard such findings in this opinion. [¶] Moreover, the unnecessary findings made our task in resolving this appeal, and presumably appellants' task in briefing it, more difficult. A trial court should make findings as to only disputed facts significant to the case's ultimate issues. Findings that a jury would be asked to make in a case may be an appropriate guide. Although we impose no consequences for the excessive findings in this case, excessive findings that obscure rather than clarify the judgment's basis may lead to consequences such as remand for proper findings or sanctions."

Ezy-Lift v. Ezy Acquisition, LLC, No. 01-13-00058-CV, 2014 WL 1516239 (Tex.App.—Houston [1st Dist.] 2014, pet. denied) (memo op.; 4-17-14). "Parties generally may not obtain findings of fact and conclusions of law after a jury trial. Parties may be able to obtain findings, however, if fact issues were submitted to the trial court for determination without submission to the jury or if the trial court's judgment substantially differs from or exceeds the scope of the jury's verdict." *See also* **Roberts v. Roberts**, 999 S.W.2d 424, 433 (Tex.App.—El Paso 1999, no pet.).

Liberty Mut. Fire Ins. v. Laca, 243 S.W.3d 791, 794 (Tex.App.—El Paso 2007, no pet.). A party "has been harmed if, under the circumstances of the case, he is forced to guess the reason(s) why the trial court ruled against him. If there is only a single ground of recovery or a single defense in the case, the record would show that [party] has suffered no harm, because he is not forced to guess the reasons for the trial court's judgment. On the other hand, when there are multiple grounds for recovery or multiple defenses, [party] is forced to guess what the trial court's findings were, unless they are provided to him. Putting [party] in the posi-

tion of having to guess the trial court's reasons for rendering judgment against him defeats the inherent purpose of [TRCP] 296 and 297. The purpose of a request under the rules is to 'narrow the bases of the judgment to only a portion of [the multiple] claims and defenses, thereby reducing the number of contentions that . . . must [be raised] on appeal.'"

Willms v. Americas Tire Co., 190 S.W.3d 796, 810 (Tex.App.—Dallas 2006, pet. denied). "When a trial court grants summary judgment relief, . . . findings of fact are not appropriate because the summary judgment proceeding has not been 'tried' within the scope of rule 296. Findings of fact and conclusions of law have no place in a summary judgment proceeding. If summary judgment is proper, there are no facts to find, and the legal conclusions have already been stated in the motion and response." *See also* **K2M3, LLC v. Cocoon Data Holding Pty. Ltd.**, No. 13-11-00194-CV, 2012 WL 2469705 (Tex.App.—Corpus Christi 2012, pet. denied) (memo op.; 6-28-12) (term "tried" includes trial court's disposition of a case rendered after evidentiary hearing on conflicting evidence; findings and conclusions have no purpose when judgment is rendered as a matter of law); **In re Estate of Davis**, 216 S.W.3d 537, 542 (Tex.App.—Texarkana 2007, pet. denied) (no findings of fact and conclusions of law required for special appearance subject to interlocutory appeal).

TRCP 297. TIME TO FILE FINDINGS OF FACT AND CONCLUSIONS OF LAW

The court shall file its findings of fact and conclusions of law within twenty days after a timely request is filed. The court shall cause a copy of its findings and conclusions to be mailed to each party in the suit.

If the court fails to file timely findings of fact and conclusions of law, the party making the request shall, within thirty days after filing the original request, file with the clerk and serve on all other parties in accordance with Rule 21a a "Notice of Past Due Findings of Fact and Conclusions of Law" which shall be immediately called to the attention of the court by the clerk. Such notice shall state the date the original request was filed and the date the findings and conclusions were due. Upon filing this notice, the time for the court to file findings of fact and conclusions of law is extended to forty days from the date the original request was filed.

Oct. 29, 1940, eff. Sept. 1, 1941. Amended by orders of June 10, 1980, eff. Jan. 1, 1981; Dec. 5, 1983, eff. April 1, 1984; April 24, 1990, eff. Sept. 1, 1990.

Comment—1990

To revise the practice and times for findings of fact and conclusions of law. See also Rules 296 and 298.

Source: TRCS art. 2247 (repealed).

See also **O'Connor's Texas Rules**, "Request for Findings of Fact & Conclusions of Law," ch. 10-E, §1 et seq.; **O'Connor's Texas Forms**, FORM 10E:3.

ANNOTATIONS

Tenery v. Tenery, 932 S.W.2d 29, 30 (Tex.1996). "[H]arm to the complaining party is presumed unless the contrary appears on the face of the record when the party makes a proper and timely request for findings and the trial court fails to comply. Error is harmful if it prevents an appellant from properly presenting a case to the appellate court." *See also* **Cherne Indus. v. Magallanes**, 763 S.W.2d 768, 772 (Tex.1989); **Lopez v. Bailon**, No. 07-14-00442-CV, 2016 WL 4158034 (Tex.App.—Amarillo 2015, order) (memo op. 5-20-15).

Sonnier v. Sonnier, 331 S.W.3d 211, 214 (Tex.App.—Beaumont 2011, no pet.), *overruled on other grounds*, **AD Villarai, LLC v. Chan Il Pak**, 519 S.W.3d 132 (Tex.2017). "[T]he failure to file the required 'past due' notice is treated as a waiver of the right to complain of the trial court's failure to file findings. In that circumstance, when the record contains no findings of fact and conclusions of law, all necessary findings to support the judgment are implied." *See also* **Minsal v. Garcia**, No. 04-13-00593-CV, 2015 WL 1640417 (Tex.App.—San Antonio 2015, no pet.) (memo op.; 4-8-15) (premature filing of past-due notice waives right to complain about trial court's failure to file findings and conclusions); **Curtis v. Commission for Lawyer Discipline**, 20 S.W.3d 227, 232 (Tex.App.—Houston [14th Dist.] 2000, no pet.) (second request for findings and conclusions did not serve as past-due notice).

Liberty Mut. Fire Ins. v. Laca, 243 S.W.3d 791, 794 (Tex.App.—El Paso 2007, no pet.). See annotation under TRCP 296.

In re E.A.C., 162 S.W.3d 438, 443 (Tex.App.—Dallas 2005, no pet.). "When a trial court files belated findings, the only issue that arises is whether the appellant was harmed, not whether the trial court had jurisdiction to make the findings. This harm may be in two forms: (1) the litigant is unable to request additional findings, or (2) the litigant was prevented from properly presenting his appeal." *See also* **Jardon v. Pfister**, 593 S.W.3d 810, 823 (Tex.App.—El Paso 2019, n.p.h.).

TRCP 298. ADDITIONAL OR AMENDED FINDINGS OF FACT AND CONCLUSIONS OF LAW

After the court files original findings of fact and conclusions of law, any party may file with the clerk of the court a request for specified additional or amended findings or conclusions. The request for these findings shall be made within ten days after the filing of the original findings and conclusions by the court. Each request made pursuant to this rule shall be served on each party to the suit in accordance with Rule 21a.

The court shall file any additional or amended findings and conclusions that are appropriate within ten days after

such request is filed, and cause a copy to be mailed to each party to the suit. No findings or conclusions shall be deemed or presumed by any failure of the court to make any additional findings or conclusions.

Oct. 29, 1940, eff. Sept. 1, 1941. Amended by orders of March 19, 1957, eff. Sept. 1, 1957; April 24, 1990, eff. Sept. 1, 1990.

Source: TRCS art. 2247a (repealed).

See also **O'Connor's Texas Rules**, "Request for Findings of Fact & Conclusions of Law," ch. 10-E, §1 et seq.; **O'Connor's Texas Forms**, FORM 10E:4.

ANNOTATIONS

Knight Renovations, LLC v. Thomas, 525 S.W.3d 446, 454 (Tex.App.—Tyler 2017, no pet.). "The trial court is not required to make additional findings that are unsupported by the record or that relate merely to evidentiary matters other than controlling issues. Additional findings and conclusions are not required if they conflict with the original findings and conclusions made and filed by the trial court. The trial court has no duty to make additional or amended findings that are unnecessary or contrary to its judgment." *See also* **Villarreal v. Guerra**, 446 S.W.3d 404, 414 (Tex.App.—San Antonio 2014, pet. denied).

Villalpando v. Villalpando, 480 S.W.3d 801, 810 (Tex.App.—Houston [14th Dist.] 2015, no pet.). "The failure to request amended or additional findings or conclusions waives the right to complain on appeal about the trial court's failure to make the omitted findings or conclusions." *See also* **In re Marriage of C.A.S.**, 405 S.W.3d 373, 381 (Tex.App.—Dallas 2013, no pet.).

Pakdimounivong v. City of Arlington, 219 S.W.3d 401, 412 (Tex.App.—Fort Worth 2006, pet. denied). "Additional findings are not required if the original findings and conclusions properly and succinctly relate the ultimate findings of fact and law necessary to apprise the party of adequate information for the preparation of the party's appeal. An ultimate fact is one that would have a direct effect on the judgment. If the refusal to file additional findings does not prevent a party from adequately presenting an argument on appeal, there is no reversible error. If the requested findings will not result in a different judgment, the findings need not be made." *See also* **H.K. Global Trading, Ltd. v. Combs**, 429 S.W.3d 132, 141 (Tex.App.—Austin 2014, pet. denied).

Vickery v. Commission for Lawyer Discipline, 5 S.W.3d 241, 254 (Tex.App.—Houston [14th Dist.] 1999, pet. denied). "[B]efore the failure to grant additional findings will impede an appellate court from presuming implied findings, the omission must be made manifest to the trial court. . . . If the trial court is not specifically made aware of the missing element, the omission is presumed to be inadvertent."

TRCP 299. OMITTED FINDINGS

When findings of fact are filed by the trial court they shall form the basis of the judgment upon all grounds of recovery and of defense embraced therein. The judgment may not be supported upon appeal by a presumed finding upon any ground of recovery or defense, no element of which has been included in the findings of fact; but when one or more elements thereof have been found by the trial court, omitted unrequested elements, when supported by evidence, will be supplied by presumption in support of the judgment. Refusal of the court to make a finding requested shall be reviewable on appeal.

Oct. 29, 1940, eff. Sept. 1, 1941. Amended by orders of Sept. 20, 1941, eff. Dec. 31, 1941; April 24, 1990, eff. Sept. 1, 1990.

Source: New rule.

See also **O'Connor's Texas Rules**, "Request for Findings of Fact & Conclusions of Law," ch. 10-E, §1 et seq.

ANNOTATIONS

Worford v. Stamper, 801 S.W.2d 108, 109 (Tex.1990). "In this case, no findings of fact or conclusions of law were requested or filed. It is therefore implied that the trial court made all the findings necessary to support its judgment. In determining whether some evidence supports the judgment and the implied findings of fact, 'it is proper to consider only that evidence most favorable to the issue and to disregard entirely that which is opposed to it or contradictory in its nature.'" *See also* **Black v. Dallas Cty. Child Welfare Unit**, 835 S.W.2d 626, 630 n.10 (Tex.1992).

RBS Mortg., LLC v. Gonzalez, No. 04-11-00681-CV, 2013 WL 749730 (Tex.App.—San Antonio 2013, no pet.) (memo op.; 2-27-13). "When the court's findings do not address a defense and the party relying on the defense does not request additional findings, that defense is waived."

O'Brien v. Daboval, 388 S.W.3d 826, 838 (Tex.App.—Houston [1st Dist.] 2012, no pet.). "If the findings of fact and the judgment are in conflict, the unchallenged findings control over the judgment."

Vickery v. Commission for Lawyer Discipline, 5 S.W.3d 241, 252 (Tex.App.—Houston [14th Dist.] 1999, pet. denied). "When a court makes findings of fact, but inadvertently omits an essential element of a ground of recovery or defense, the presumption of validity will supply the omitted element by implication. However, if the record demonstrates the trial judge deliberately omitted the element, the presumption is refuted and the element cannot logically be supplied by implication." *See also* **Ex parte Barham**, 534 S.W.3d 547, 554 (Tex.App.—Texarkana 2017, no pet.).

TRCP 299a. FINDINGS OF FACT TO BE SEPARATELY FILED AND NOT RECITED IN A JUDGMENT

Findings of fact shall not be recited in a judgment. If there is a conflict between findings of fact recited in a judgment in violation of this rule and findings of fact made pur-

suant to Rules 297 and 298, the latter findings will control for appellate purposes. Findings of fact shall be filed with the clerk of the court as a document or documents separate and apart from the judgment.

April 24, 1990, eff. Sept. 1, 1990.

Comment—1990

To require that findings of fact be separate from the judgment and that such separate findings of fact are controlling on appeal.

Source: New rule.

See also **O'Connor's Texas Rules**, "Judgment," ch. 9-C, §1 et seq.; **O'Connor's Texas Rules**, "Request for Findings of Fact & Conclusions of Law," ch. 10-E, §1 et seq.

ANNOTATIONS

Colbert v. DFPS, 227 S.W.3d 799, 809 (Tex.App.—Houston [1st Dist.] 2006), *pet. denied sub nom.* **In re D.N.C.**, 252 S.W.3d 317 (Tex.2008). "[A] trial court's recitation in the judgment of its ground for termination of parental rights is not a fact-finding that is prohibited under rule 299a. . . . "

In re Estate of Jones, 197 S.W.3d 894, 900 n.4 (Tex.App.—Beaumont 2006, pet. denied). "[I]f findings are recited in the judgment, and no one complains or requests findings, and there is no conflict with separately filed findings of fact, the findings of fact in the judgment should not be ignored on appeal." *See also* **South Plains Lamesa R.R. v. Heinrich**, 280 S.W.3d 357, 364-65 (Tex.App.—Amarillo 2008, no pet.). *But see* **Sutherland v. Cobern**, under this rule. For a discussion of the split in the courts of appeals on this issue, see **O'Connor's Texas Rules**, "Not in judgment," ch. 10-E, §5.2.2.

Sutherland v. Cobern, 843 S.W.2d 127, 131 n.7 (Tex.App.—Texarkana 1992, writ denied). "Findings of fact contained in the body of a judgment may not be considered on appeal. Therefore, for our purposes, we review this case as one in which no findings of fact were made." *See also* **Casino Magic Corp. v. King**, 43 S.W.3d 14, 19 n.6 (Tex.App.—Dallas 2001, pet. denied). *But see* **In re Estate of Jones**, under this rule. For a discussion of the split in the courts of appeals on this issue, see **O'Connor's Texas Rules**, "Not in judgment," ch. 10-E, §5.2.2.

H. Judgments

TRCP 300. COURT TO RENDER JUDGMENT

Where a special verdict is rendered, or the conclusions of fact found by the judge are separately stated the court shall render judgment thereon unless set aside or a new trial is granted, or judgment is rendered notwithstanding verdict or jury finding under these rules.

Oct. 29, 1940, eff. Sept. 1, 1941.

ANNOTATIONS

Astec Indus. v. Suarez, 921 S.W.2d 794, 798 (Tex.App.—Fort Worth 1996, no writ). "In order for a judge's ministerial duty to render judgment under rule 300 . . . to arise, the jury must first return a sufficient verdict for the judge to receive."

TRCP 301. JUDGMENTS

The judgment of the court shall conform to the pleadings, the nature of the case proved and the verdict, if any, and shall be so framed as to give the party all the relief to which he may be entitled either in law or equity. Provided, that upon motion and reasonable notice the court may render judgment non obstante veredicto if a directed verdict would have been proper, and provided further that the court may, upon like motion and notice, disregard any jury finding on a question that has no support in the evidence. Only one final judgment shall be rendered in any cause except where it is otherwise specially provided by law. Judgment may, in a proper case, be given for or against one or more of several plaintiffs, and for or against one or more of several defendants or intervenors.

Oct. 29, 1940, eff. Sept. 1, 1941. Amended by order of July 15, 1987, eff. Jan. 1, 1988.

Source: TRCS art. 2211 (repealed).

See also **O'Connor's Texas Rules**, "Motion for JNOV," ch. 9-B, §1 et seq.; **O'Connor's Texas Rules**, "Judgment," ch. 9-C, §1 et seq.; **O'Connor's Texas Forms**, FORMS 9B, 9C:1.

ANNOTATIONS

Tiller v. McLure, 121 S.W.3d 709, 713 (Tex.2003). "A trial court may grant a [JNOV] if there is no evidence to support one or more of the jury findings on issues necessary to liability."

Spencer v. Eagle Star Ins., 876 S.W.2d 154, 157 (Tex.1994). "A trial court may disregard a jury finding only if it is unsupported by evidence . . . or if the issue is immaterial. A question is immaterial when it should not have been submitted, or when it was properly submitted but has been rendered immaterial by other findings. A question which calls for a finding beyond the province of the jury, such as a question of law, may be deemed immaterial." *See also* **Wal-Mart Stores v. McKenzie**, 997 S.W.2d 278, 280 (Tex.1999).

Stewart v. USA Custom Paint & Body Shop, Inc., 870 S.W.2d 18, 20 (Tex.1994). "A judgment must be sufficiently definite and certain to define and protect the rights of all litigants, or it should provide a definite means of ascertaining such rights, to the end that ministerial officers can carry the judgment into execution without ascertainment of facts not therein stated."

Moran v. Williamson, 498 S.W.3d 85, 93 (Tex.App.—Houston [1st Dist.] 2016, pet. denied). "In determining whether the judgment conforms to the pleadings, we must view the pleadings as a whole. A general prayer for relief will support any relief raised by the evidence that is consistent with the allegations and causes of action stated in the petition."

Pitts & Collard, L.L.P. v. Schechter, 369 S.W.3d 301, 320 (Tex.App.—Houston [1st Dist.] 2011, no pet.). "The motion [for JNOV] should be granted (1) when the evidence is conclusive, and one party is entitled to recover as a matter of law or (2) when a legal principle precludes recovery. A motion for [JNOV] based on a legal principle is appropriately granted when it is conclusively established that recovery is precluded even though all the allegations are proven." *See also* **Hampton v. Equity Trust Co.**, 607 S.W.3d 1, 5-6 (Tex.App.—Austin 2020, pet. filed 10-8-20).

Hartford Fire Ins. v. C. Springs 300, Ltd., 287 S.W.3d 771, 779-80 (Tex.App.—Houston [1st Dist.] 2009, pet. denied). "There are . . . exceptions to rule 301. Unpleaded claims or defenses that are tried by express or implied consent of the parties are treated as if they had been raised by the pleadings. The party who allows an issue to be tried by consent and who fails to raise the lack of a pleading before submission of the case cannot later raise the pleading deficiency for the first time on appeal."

TRCP 302. ON COUNTERCLAIM

If the defendant establishes a demand against the plaintiff upon a counterclaim exceeding that established against him by the plaintiff, the court shall render judgment for defendant for such excess.

Dec. 5, 1983, eff. April 1, 1984.

TRCP 303. ON COUNTERCLAIM FOR COSTS

When a counterclaim is pleaded, the party in whose favor final judgment is rendered shall also recover the costs, unless it be made to appear on the trial that the counterclaim of the defendant was acquired after the commencement of the suit, in which case, if the plaintiff establishes a claim existing at the commencement of the suit, he shall recover his costs.

Dec. 5, 1983, eff. April 1, 1984.

See also TRCP 131, 141.

ANNOTATIONS

Henry v. Masson, 453 S.W.3d 43, 50-51 (Tex.App.—Houston [1st Dist.] 2014, no pet.). "Several of our sister courts have held that when a party alleges a counterclaim[,] if neither party is wholly successful on its claims, it is within the trial court's discretion to order each party to bear its own costs. [¶] Here, neither party was wholly successful on its claims. . . . Under these facts, . . . we conclude that the trial court did not abuse its discretion when it did not assess court costs against either party."

Reyna v. First Nat'l Bank, 55 S.W.3d 58, 74 (Tex.App.—Corpus Christi 2001, no pet.). "[O]n appeal, [P] asserts that since [D] did not prevail on its counterclaim, then some of the costs should be assessed against [D]. Given that the counterclaim was . . . acquired before the suit, and [P] did not prevail on any of his claims, we conclude . . . the trial court correctly assessed all costs against [P]."

TRCP 304. JUDGMENT UPON RECORD

Judgments rendered upon questions raised upon citations, pleadings, and all other proceedings, constituting the record proper as known at common law, must be entered at the date of each term when pronounced.

Oct. 29, 1940, eff. Sept. 1, 1941.

TRCP 305. PROPOSED JUDGMENT

Any party may prepare and submit a proposed judgment to the court for signature.

Each party who submits a proposed judgment for signature shall serve the proposed judgment on all other parties to the suit who have appeared and remain in the case, in accordance with Rule 21a.

Failure to comply with this rule shall not affect the time for perfecting an appeal.

Oct. 29, 1940, eff. Sept. 1, 1941. Amended by order of April 24, 1990, eff. Sept. 1, 1990.

Comment—1990

To clarify the practice for proposed judgments and notice to other parties.

See also **O'Connor's Texas Rules**, "Judgment," ch. 9-C, §1 et seq.; **O'Connor's Texas Forms**, FORM 9C:1.

ANNOTATIONS

First Nat'l Bank v. Fojtik, 775 S.W.2d 632, 633 (Tex.1989). A party's motion asking the trial court to enter judgment does not waive the party's right to complain about that judgment. "There must be a method by which a party who desires to initiate the appellate process may move the trial court to render judgment without being bound by its terms."

Dikeman v. Snell, 490 S.W.2d 183, 185-86 (Tex.1973). Held: Even when a judgment is prepared by a party, a mistake in the rendered judgment is a judicial error.

Vann v. Brown, 244 S.W.3d 612, 617 (Tex.App.—Dallas 2008, no pet.). "We recognize that rule 305 suggests a party 'may' offer the trial court a proposed judgment, but that is not a requirement. We cannot agree with [P's] assertion that

Rule 305 suggests [D] should have supplied a proposed judgment to the trial court. The parties even acknowledge in oral argument that it is customary for the party in whose favor the verdict was returned to provide a proposed judgment to the trial judge."

TRCP 306. RECITATION OF JUDGMENT

The entry of the judgment shall contain the full names of the parties, as stated in the pleadings, for and against whom the judgment is rendered. In a suit for termination of the parent-child relationship or a suit affecting the parent-child relationship filed by a governmental entity for managing conservatorship, the judgment must state the specific grounds for termination or for appointment of the managing conservator.

July 21, 1970, eff. Jan. 1, 1971. Amended by order of Feb. 13, 2012, eff. March 1, 2012.

See also **O'Connor's Texas Rules**, "Judgment," ch. 9-C, §1 et seq.

ANNOTATIONS

Crystal City ISD v. Wagner, 605 S.W.2d 743, 747 (Tex.App.—San Antonio 1980, writ ref'd n.r.e.). "Undoubtedly, the better practice is to recite the names of all the parties in the judgment. . . . Nevertheless, when . . . the names of all the parties and the relief each is entitled to is easily ascertainable from the record, it would be a useless thing to remand the entire cause for the purpose of amending the judgment to include the names of all the parties."

TRCP 306a. PERIODS TO RUN FROM SIGNING OF JUDGMENT

1. Beginning of periods. The date of judgment or order is signed as shown of record shall determine the beginning of the periods prescribed by these rules for the court's plenary power to grant a new trial or to vacate, modify, correct or reform a judgment or order and for filing in the trial court the various documents that these rules authorize a party to file within such periods including, but not limited to, motions for new trial, motions to modify judgment, motions to reinstate a case dismissed for want of prosecution, motions to vacate judgment and requests for findings of fact and conclusions of law; but this rule shall not determine what constitutes rendition of a judgment or order for any other purpose.

2. Date to be shown. Judges, attorneys and clerks are directed to use their best efforts to cause all judgments, decisions and orders of any kind to be reduced to writing and signed by the trial judge with the date of signing stated therein. If the date of signing is not recited in the judgment or order, it may be shown in the record by a certificate of the judge or otherwise; provided, however, that the absence of a showing of the date in the record shall not invalidate any judgment or order.

3. Notice of judgment. When the final judgment or other appealable order is signed, the clerk of the court shall immediately give notice to the parties or their attorneys of record by first-class mail advising that the judgment or order was signed. Failure to comply with the provisions of this rule shall not affect the periods mentioned in paragraph (1) of this rule, except as provided in paragraph (4).

4. No notice of judgment. If within twenty days after the judgment or other appealable order is signed, a party adversely affected by it or his attorney has neither received the notice required by paragraph (3) of this rule nor acquired actual knowledge of the order, then with respect to that party all the periods mentioned in paragraph (1) shall begin on the date that such party or his attorney received such notice or acquired actual knowledge of the signing, whichever occurred first, but in no event shall such periods begin more than ninety days after the original judgment or other appealable order was signed.

5. Motion, notice and hearing. In order to establish the application of paragraph (4) of this rule, the party adversely affected is required to prove in the trial court, on sworn motion and notice, the date on which the party or his attorney first either received a notice of the judgment or acquired actual knowledge of the signing and that this date was more than twenty days after the judgment was signed.

6. Nunc pro tunc order. When a corrected judgment has been signed after expiration of the court's plenary power pursuant to Rule 316, the periods mentioned in paragraph (1) of this rule shall run from the date of signing the corrected judgment with respect to any complaint that would not be applicable to the original document.

7. When process served by publication. With respect to a motion for new trial filed more than thirty days after the judgment was signed pursuant to Rule 329 when process has been served by publication, the periods provided by paragraph (1) shall be computed as if the judgment were signed on the date of filing the motion.

June 16, 1943, eff. Dec. 31, 1943. Amended by orders of Oct. 10, 1945, eff. Feb. 1, 1946; June 10, 1980, eff. Jan. 1, 1981; Dec. 5, 1983, eff. April 1, 1984; April 10, 1986, eff. Sept. 1, 1986; July 15, 1987, eff. Jan. 1, 1988.

Comment—1988

Amended to reflect repeal of Rule 317.

See also **O'Connor's Texas Rules**, "Default Judgment," ch. 7-A, §1 et seq.; **O'Connor's Texas Rules**, "Judgment," ch. 9-C, §1 et seq.; **O'Connor's Texas Rules**, "Motion for New Trial," ch. 10-B, §1 et seq.; **O'Connor's Texas Rules**, "Motion to Reinstate After Dismissal for Want of Prosecution," ch. 10-F, §1 et seq.; **O'Connor's Texas Rules**, "Motion to Extend Postjudgment Deadlines," ch. 10-G, §1 et seq.; **O'Connor's Texas Rules**, "Motion for Judgment Nunc Pro Tunc," ch. 10-H, §1 et seq.

ANNOTATIONS

Generally

Martinez v. Humble Sand & Gravel, Inc., 875 S.W.2d 311, 312 (Tex.1994). "When . . . an otherwise final judgment fails to dispose of all parties, the court may make the judgment final for purposes of appeal by severing the causes and parties disposed of by the judgment into a different cause. *At 313:* When a severance order takes effect, the appellate timetable runs from the signing date of the order that made the judgment severed 'final' and appealable."

Wells Fargo Bank v. Erickson, 267 S.W.3d 139, 149 (Tex.App.—Corpus Christi 2008, no pet.). "[P] argues that a trial court cannot reconsider its decision to deny a rule 306a motion. We find nothing in the [TRCPs] that precludes a trial court from reconsidering its prior ruling on such a motion within its plenary power or from entertaining a second motion filed for the same purpose."

Coinmach, Inc. v. Aspenwood Apt. Corp., 98 S.W.3d 377, 378 (Tex.App.—Houston [1st Dist.] 2003, no pet.). "The issue for this Court is whether the effective date of the order granting a new trial is (1) the date the trial court signs the order or (2) the date the trial court clerk file-stamps the signed order. . . . We hold that the order granting a new trial became effective on the date signed by the trial court. . . ."

Burns v. Bishop, 48 S.W.3d 459, 465 (Tex.App.—Houston [14th Dist.] 2001, no pet.). "Signing and rendition are not synonymous. Signing an order is not among the official steps that would fall within the common meaning of 'proceedings.' Drafting and signing the judgment [are] preparatory, *administrative* acts that . . . authenticate the record of the court's rendition. Rendition occurs when the trial court officially announces its decision (1) in open court in a manner that objectively reflects its intention to render or (2) by written memorandum *filed with the clerk*."

No Notice of Judgment

Ginn v. Forrester, 282 S.W.3d 430, 433 (Tex.2009). TRCP 306a does "not impose upon the clerk an affirmative duty to record the mailing of the required notice[ ]; accordingly, the absence of proof in the record that notice was provided does not establish error on the face of the record. [¶] We . . . see [no] distinction . . . between a record that is silent and a record that contains a written notation that the record is silent; either way, proof of error is absent."

In re Lynd Co., 195 S.W.3d 682, 686 (Tex.2006). "Rule 306a does not require that the trial court issue a signed order with . . . a finding [of actual notice of final judgment]. [W]hen the trial court fails to specifically find the date of notice, the finding may be implied from the trial court's judgment, unless there is no evidence supporting the implied finding or the party challenging the judgment establishes as a matter of law an alternate notice date."

John v. Marshall Health Servs., 58 S.W.3d 738, 741 (Tex.2001). "Rule 306a(5) does not prohibit a motion from being filed at any time within the trial court's plenary jurisdiction measured from the date determined under Rule 306a(4). Rule 306a simply imposes no deadline, and none can be added by decision, other than the deadline of the expiration of the trial court's jurisdiction."

Estate of Howley v. Haberman, 878 S.W.2d 139, 140 (Tex.1994). "A party who does not have actual knowledge of an order of dismissal within 90 days of the date it is signed cannot move for reinstatement. Since [P] did not learn of the dismissal within this period, the order of dismissal for want of prosecution was final. . . . [P's] only possible recourse is a bill of review." *See also* **Levit v. Adams**, 850 S.W.2d 469, 470 (Tex.1993).

Southwest Warren, Inc. v. Crawford, 464 S.W.3d 822, 827 (Tex.App.—Houston [1st Dist.] 2015, no pet.). "Here, the trial court granted the motion to extend the post-judgment deadlines. This had the effect of establishing the new date of the judgment—for post-judgment deadline purposes—as the date that [Ds] learned of the default judgment. [T]he order 'rescinding' the grant of the motion to extend did not void or otherwise render the extension order a nullity. Because the extension order still had effect, the post-judgment deadlines continued to run from the date set by that order. To the degree that the order rescinding the grant of the extension has any legal effect, that effect cannot be to set the post-judgment deadlines at an earlier time."

TRCP 306b. REPEALED BY ORDER OF DEC. 5, 1983, EFF. APRIL 1, 1984

TRCP 306c. PREMATURELY FILED DOCUMENTS

No motion for new trial or request for findings of fact and conclusions of law shall be held ineffective because prematurely filed; but every such motion shall be deemed to have been filed on the date of but subsequent to the time of signing of the judgment the motion assails, and every such request for findings of fact and conclusions of law shall be deemed to have been filed on the date of but subsequent to the time of signing of the judgment.

Oct. 10, 1945, eff. Feb. 1, 1946. Amended by orders of April 12, 1962, eff. Sept. 1, 1962; July 22, 1975, eff. Jan. 1, 1976; Dec. 5, 1983, eff. April 1, 1984; April 10, 1986, eff. Sept. 1, 1986; April 24, 1990, eff. Sept. 1, 1990.

See also TRAP 27; **O'Connor's Texas Rules**, "Motion for New Trial," ch. 10-B, §1 et seq.; **O'Connor's Texas Rules**, "Requesting findings of fact," ch. 10-E, §3.

ANNOTATIONS

Ryland Enter. v. Weatherspoon, 355 S.W.3d 664, 666 (Tex.2011). "[T]he premature filing rules in [TRCP] 306c and

[TRAP] 27.2 apply equally to motions for new trial or to modify the judgment. [T]he filing of a motion for new trial or to modify the judgment, before the judgment is signed or within 30 days after, extends the deadline for filing a notice of appeal to 90 days."

Wilkins v. Methodist Health Care Sys., 160 S.W.3d 559, 563 (Tex.2005). "When a motion for new trial is granted, it becomes moot as to any effect it may have on a subsequent judgment. *At 564:* [A] motion for new trial that has been granted cannot 'assail' a subsequent judgment for purposes of determining the deadline for filing a notice of appeal."

Fredonia State Bank v. General Am. Life Ins., 881 S.W.2d 279, 281 (Tex.1994). "[A] motion for new trial relating to an earlier judgment may be considered applicable to a second judgment when the substance of the motion could properly be raised with respect to the corrected judgment."

TRCP 306d. REPEALED BY ORDER OF DEC. 5, 1983, EFF. APRIL 1, 1984

TRCP 307. EXCEPTIONS, ETC., TRANSCRIPT

In non-jury cases, where findings of fact and conclusions of law are requested and filed, and in jury cases, where a special verdict is returned, any party claiming that the findings of the court or the jury, as the case may be, do not support the judgment, may have noted in the record an exception to said judgment and thereupon take an appeal or writ of error, where such writ is allowed, without a statement of facts or further exceptions in the transcript, but the transcript in such cases shall contain the conclusions of law and fact or the special verdict and the judgment rendered thereon.

Oct. 29, 1940, eff. Sept. 1, 1941.

TRCP 308. COURT SHALL ENFORCE ITS DECREES

The court shall cause its judgments and decrees to be carried into execution; and where the judgment is for personal property, and it is shown by the pleadings and evidence and the verdict, if any, that such property has an especial value to the plaintiff, the court may award a special writ for the seizure and delivery of such property to the plaintiff; and in such case may enforce its judgment by attachment, fine and imprisonment.

Oct. 29, 1940, eff. Sept. 1, 1941.

ANNOTATIONS

Cook v. Stallcup, 170 S.W.3d 916, 920-21 (Tex.App.—Dallas 2005, no pet.). After the court's plenary power expired, "the trial court had power only to enforce its judgment, subject to the limitation that any enforcement may not be inconsistent with the original judgment and must not constitute a material change in substantial adjudicated portions of the judgment." *See also* **Gillet v. ZUPT, LLC**, 523 S.W.3d 749, 758-59 (Tex.App.—Houston [14th Dist.] 2017, no pet.); **Kennedy v. Hudnall**, 249 S.W.3d 520, 523 (Tex.App.—Texarkana 2008, no pet.).

TRCP 308a. IN SUITS AFFECTING THE PARENT-CHILD RELATIONSHIP

When the court has ordered child support or possession of or access to a child and it is claimed that the order has been violated, the person claiming that a violation has occurred shall make this known to the court. The court may appoint a member of the bar to investigate the claim to determine whether there is reason to believe that the court order has been violated. If the attorney in good faith believes that the order has been violated, the attorney shall take the necessary action as provided under Chapter 14,[1] Family Code. On a finding of a violation, the court may enforce its order as provided in Chapter 14,[1] Family Code.

Except by order of the court, no fee shall be charged by or paid to the attorney representing the claimant. If the court determines that an attorney's fee should be paid, the fee shall be adjudged against the party who violated the court's order. The fee may be assessed as costs of court, or awarded by judgment, or both.

Oct. 12, 1949, eff. March 1, 1950. Amended by orders of Oct. 10, 1951, eff. March 1, 1952; July 15, 1987, eff. Jan. 1, 1988; April 24, 1990, eff. Sept. 1, 1990.

Comment—1990

This rule has been completely rewritten and designed to broaden its application to cover problems dealing with possession and access to a child as well as support.

[1]Repealed; see, generally, V.T.C.A., Family Code Chapter 151 et seq.

Editor's Note: Family Code chapter 14, as referenced in the first paragraph of TRCP 308a, is now Family Code chapter 157.

TRCP 308b. DETERMINING THE ENFORCEABILITY OF A JUDGMENT OR ARBITRATION AWARD BASED ON FOREIGN LAW IN CERTAIN SUITS UNDER THE FAMILY CODE

(a) ***Definitions.*** In this rule:

(1) *Comity* means the recognition by a court of one jurisdiction of the laws and judicial decisions of another jurisdiction.

(2) *Foreign law* means a law, rule, or code of a jurisdiction outside of the states and territories of the United States.

(b) ***Applicability of This Rule.***

(1) Except as provided in (2) and (3), this rule applies to the recognition or enforcement of a judgment or arbitration award based on foreign law in a suit involving a

marriage relationship or a parent-child relationship under the Family Code.

(2) This rule does not apply to an action brought under the International Child Abduction Remedies Act (22 U.S.C. §9001 et seq.) concerning rights under the Hague Convention on the Civil Aspects of International Child Abduction.

(3) In the event of a conflict between this rule and any federal or state law, the federal or state law will prevail.

(c) ***Applicability of Texas Rule of Evidence 203.***

(1) Paragraphs (c) and (d) of Rule 203, Texas Rules of Evidence, apply to an action under this rule.

(2) Paragraphs (a) and (b) of Rule 203, Texas Rules of Evidence, do not apply to an action under this rule.

(d) ***Notice.***

(1) *Party Seeking Enforcement of a Judgment or Arbitration Award Based on Foreign Law.* Within 60 days of filing an original pleading, the party seeking enforcement must give written notice to the court and all parties that describes the court's authority to enforce or decide to enforce the judgment or award.

(2) *Party Opposing Enforcement of a Judgment or Arbitration Award Based on Foreign Law.* Within 30 days of the date that a notice under (1) is served, a party opposing enforcement must give written notice to the court and all parties that explains the basis for the party's opposition and states whether the party asserts that the judgment or award violates constitutional rights or public policy.

(e) ***Pretrial Conference.*** Within 75 days of the date that a notice under (d)(1) is served, the court must conduct a pretrial conference to set deadlines and make other appropriate orders regarding:

(1) the submission of materials for the court to consider in determining foreign law;

(2) the translation of foreign-language documents; and

(3) the designation of expert witnesses.

(f) ***Determination Hearing and Order.***

(1) At least 30 days before trial, the court must conduct a hearing on the record to determine whether to enforce the judgment or award. The parties must have timely notice of the hearing.

(2) Within 15 days of the hearing, the Court must issue a written order on the determination that includes findings of fact and conclusions of law. This deadline must not be altered absent extraordinary circumstances.

(3) The court may issue any order necessary to preserve the principles of comity or the freedom to contract for arbitration while protecting against violations of constitutional rights and public policy.

(4) The court must comply with all requirements of this paragraph and make an independent determination whether to enforce the judgment or award even if no party opposes enforcement of the judgment or award.

(g) ***Temporary Orders.*** Notwithstanding any other provision of this rule, the court may set filing deadlines and conduct the determination hearing to accommodate the circumstances of the case in connection with issuing temporary orders.

Adopted by order of Dec. 28, 2017, eff. Jan. 1, 2018.

TRCP 309. IN FORECLOSURE PROCEEDINGS

Judgments for the foreclosure of mortgages and other liens shall be that the plaintiff recover his debt, damages and costs, with a foreclosure of the plaintiff's lien on the property subject thereto, and, except in judgments against executors, administrators and guardians, that an order of sale shall issue to any sheriff or any constable within the State of Texas, directing him to seize and sell the same as under execution, in satisfaction of the judgment; and, if the property cannot be found, or if the proceeds of such sale be insufficient to satisfy the judgment, then to take the money or any balance thereof remaining unpaid, out of any other property of the defendant, as in case of ordinary executions.

July 20, 1966, eff. Jan. 1, 1967.

Source: TRCS art. 2218 (repealed), except that the order of sale is to be directed to the sheriff or constable of any county of the State, in harmony with the rules relating to executions.

ANNOTATIONS

Brown v. EMC Mortg. Corp., 326 S.W.3d 648, 653-54 (Tex.App.—Dallas 2010, pet. denied). "[T]he judgment of foreclosure in this case was not against an executor, administrator, or guardian. Thus, [TRCP] 309 requires the order of sale 'issue to any sheriff or any constable.' Instead, the trial court's order authorizes [D] to sell the property at public auction. . . . [¶] [D] argues that the trial court's order of sale is consistent with Texas law because it meets the requirements of [Prop. Code ch. 51]. [D] asks us to ignore rule 309's requirement that the property be sold by a sheriff or constable because this requirement is not also present in ch. 51. We decline to do so. [¶] The requirement that the sale of the property in a judicial foreclosure be conducted by a sheriff or constable is clear, unambiguous, and does not conflict with any provision of ch. 51. Indeed, ch. 51 distinguishes between foreclosure sales conducted under the chapter and those conducted under a court judgment foreclosing the lien. Because nothing in ch. 51 conflicts with rule

309, we must assume that the legislature intended for judicial foreclosures to continue to be conducted by sheriffs or constables even after the enactment of ch. 51. Accordingly, the order of sale in this case is not in compliance with Texas law."

TRCP 310. WRIT OF POSSESSION

When an order foreclosing a lien upon real estate is made in a suit having for its object the foreclosure of such lien, such order shall have all the force and effect of a writ of possession as between the parties to the foreclosure suit and any person claiming under the defendant to such suit by any right acquired pending such suit; and the court shall so direct in the judgment providing for the issuance of such order. The sheriff or other officer executing such order of sale shall proceed by virtue of such order of sale to place the purchaser of the property sold thereunder in possession thereof within thirty days after the day of sale.

Oct. 29, 1940, eff. Sept. 1, 1941.

Source: TRCS art. 2219 (repealed).

TRCP 311. ON APPEAL FROM PROBATE COURT

Judgment on appeal or certiorari from any county court sitting in probate shall be certified to such county court for observance.

Oct. 29, 1940, eff. Sept. 1, 1941.

TRCP 312. ON APPEAL FROM JUSTICE COURT

Judgments on appeal or certiorari from a justice court shall be enforced by the county or district court rendering the judgment.

Oct. 29, 1940, eff. Sept. 1, 1941.

TRCP 313. AGAINST EXECUTORS, ETC.

A judgment for the recovery of money against an executor, administrator or guardian, as such, shall state that it is to be paid in the due course of administration. No execution shall issue thereon, but it shall be certified to the county court, sitting in matters of probate, to be there enforced in accordance with law, but judgment against an executor appointed and acting under a will dispensing with the action of the county court in reference to such estate shall be enforced against the property of the testator in the hands of such executor, by execution, as in other cases.

Oct. 29, 1940, eff. Sept. 1, 1941.

TRCP 314. CONFESSION OF JUDGMENT

Any person against whom a cause of action exists may, without process, appear in person or by attorney, and confess judgment therefor in open court as follows:

(a) A petition shall be filed and the justness of the debt or cause of action be sworn to by the person in whose favor the judgment is confessed.

(b) If the judgment is confessed by attorney, the power of attorney shall be filed and its contents be recited in the judgment.

(c) Every such judgment duly made shall operate as a release of all errors in the record thereof, but such judgment may be impeached for fraud or other equitable cause.

Oct. 29, 1940, eff. Sept. 1, 1941.

I. Remittitur and Correction

TRCP 315. REMITTITUR

Any party in whose favor a judgment has been rendered may remit any part thereof in open court, or by executing and filing with the clerk a written remittitur signed by the party or the party's attorney of record, and duly acknowledged by the party or the party's attorney. Such remittitur shall be a part of the record of the cause. Execution shall issue for the balance only of such judgment.

July 15, 1987, eff. Jan. 1, 1988.

See also **O'Connor's Texas Rules**, "Motion for Remittitur," ch. 10-C, §1 et seq.; **O'Connor's Texas Forms**, FORMS 10C.

ANNOTATIONS

Larson v. Cactus Util. Co., 730 S.W.2d 640, 641 (Tex.1987). "A court of appeals should uphold a trial court remittitur only when the evidence is factually insufficient to support the verdict. [¶] If a court of appeals holds that there is no evidence to support a damages verdict, it should render a take nothing judgment as to that amount. If part of a damage verdict lacks sufficient evidentiary support, the proper course is to suggest a remittitur of that part of the verdict."

TRCP 316. CORRECTION OF CLERICAL MISTAKES IN JUDGMENT RECORD

Clerical mistakes in the record of any judgment may be corrected by the judge in open court according to the truth or justice of the case after notice of the motion therefor has been given to the parties interested in such judgment, as provided in Rule 21a, and thereafter the execution shall conform to the judgment as amended.

June 16, 1943, eff. Dec. 31, 1943. Amended by order of July 15, 1987, eff. Jan. 1, 1988.

Source: TRCS art. 2228 (repealed).

See also **O'Connor's Texas Rules**, "Motion for Judgment Nunc Pro Tunc," ch. 10-H, §1 et seq.; **O'Connor's Texas Forms**, FORMS 10H.

ANNOTATIONS

Texas DOT v. A.P.I. Pipe & Sup., 397 S.W.3d 162, 167 (Tex.2013). "'A clerical error is one which does not result

from judicial reasoning or determination.' Even a significant alteration to the original judgment may be accomplished through a judgment nunc pro tunc so long as it merely corrects a clerical error. If 'the signed judgment inaccurately reflects the true decision of the court,' then 'the error is clerical and may be corrected.' "

Escobar v. Escobar, 711 S.W.2d 230, 231 (Tex.1986). "After the trial court loses its jurisdiction over a judgment, it can correct only clerical errors in the judgment by judgment nunc pro tunc. In this regard, the trial court has plenary power to correct a clerical error made in *entering* final judgment. [¶] A judicial error is an error which occurs in the *rendering* as opposed to the *entering* of a judgment." *See also* **In re Daredia**, 317 S.W.3d 247, 249-50 (Tex.2010); **Andrews v. Koch**, 702 S.W.2d 584, 585 (Tex.1986).

In re Reynolds, No. 14-17-00614-CV, 2017 WL 4518602 (Tex.App.—Houston [14th Dist.] 2017, orig. proceeding) (memo op.; 10-10-17). "An application for a judgment nunc pro tunc requires 'the trial court to determine what the facts were at the time the original judgment was rendered, and a judgment nunc pro tunc should be granted only if the evidence is clear, satisfactory and convincing that a clerical error was made.' Proof of a variance between the judgment rendered and the judgment entered is not enough to require correction by judgment nunc pro tunc; there must also be a fact finding, supported by evidence or the trial judge's personal recollection, that the variance resulted from a clerical error."

In re Marriage of Snead, No. 13-11-00200-CV, 2012 WL 3537825 (Tex.App.—Corpus Christi 2012, no pet.) (memo op.; 8-16-12). "A judgment nunc pro tunc does not disturb the initial judgment rendered by the trial court; it merely brings the court records into conformity with it. Accordingly, a judgment nunc pro tunc, although signed later, relates back to the date of the original judgment and is effective as of the earlier date."

Key Fin. Corp. v. Priority Servs., No. 09-09-00531-CV, 2010 WL 3518742 (Tex.App.—Beaumont 2010, no pet.) (memo op.; 9-9-10). "Whether an error in a judgment is a judicial or clerical error is a question of law. A clerical error is a mistake preventing a judgment, as entered in the official record, from accurately reflecting the judgment that was rendered. Conceivably a judgment *nunc pro tunc* may be issued in appropriate circumstances to correct the date an order was signed if the original date is shown to have been incorrect. However, Rule 316 may not be used to simply backdate the signing of a written judgment that was not in fact signed earlier."

TRCP 317 to 319. REPEALED BY ORDER OF JULY 15, 1987, EFF. JAN. 1, 1988

J. New Trials

TRCP 320. MOTION AND ACTION OF COURT THEREON

New trials may be granted and judgment set aside for good cause, on motion or on the court's own motion on such terms as the court shall direct. New trials may be granted when the damages are manifestly too small or too large. When it appears to the court that a new trial should be granted on a point or points that affect only a part of the matters in controversy and that such part is clearly separable without unfairness to the parties, the court may grant a new trial as to that part only, provided that a separate trial on unliquidated damages alone shall not be ordered if liability issues are contested. Each motion for new trial shall be in writing and signed by the party or his attorney.

July 20, 1954, eff. Jan. 1, 1955. Amended by orders of July 22, 1975, eff. Jan. 1, 1976; July 11, 1977, eff. Jan. 1, 1978; June 10, 1980, eff. Jan. 1, 1981; Dec. 5, 1983, eff. April 1, 1984; July 15, 1987, eff. Jan. 1, 1988.

Source: TRCS art. 2232 (repealed), with changes: Inserted exceptions to harmonize with provisions for special situations.

See also **O'Connor's Texas Rules** "Motion for New Trial," ch. 10-B, §1 et seq.; **O'Connor's Texas Forms**, FORMS 10E.

ANNOTATIONS

In re Columbia Med. Ctr., 290 S.W.3d 204, 206 (Tex.2009). "The issue before us is whether, after a jury has rendered its verdict, the trial court may disregard that verdict, grant a new trial, and explain its action only as being 'in the interests of justice and fairness.' We conclude that just as appellate courts that set aside jury verdicts are required to detail reasons for doing so, trial courts must give more explanation than 'in the interest of justice' for setting aside a jury verdict. *At 212-13:* We do not retreat from the position that trial courts have significant discretion in granting new trials. However, such discretion should not, and does not, permit a trial judge to substitute his or her own views for that of the jury without a valid basis. . . . The trial court's action in failing to give its reasons for disregarding the jury verdict as to [D] was arbitrary and an abuse of discretion." *See also* **In re Bent**, 487 S.W.3d 170, 175-76 (Tex.2016); **In re Toyota Motor Sales, U.S.A., Inc.**, 407 S.W.3d 746, 756-57 (Tex.2013); **In re United Scaffolding, Inc.**, 377 S.W.3d 685, 688-89 (Tex.2012).

Old Republic Ins. v. Scott, 846 S.W.2d 832, 833 (Tex.1993). "The **filing** of a motion for new trial in order to extend the appellate timetable is a matter of right, whether or not there is any sound or reasonable basis for the conclusion that a further motion is necessary."

State Dept. of Hwys. & Pub. Transp. v. Cotner, 845 S.W.2d 818, 819 (Tex.1993). "A partial new trial may be ordered notwithstanding the prohibition in [TRCP] 41 against post-submission severances. [TRCP] 320 is thus an exception to Rule 41."

TRCP 321. FORM

Each point relied upon in a motion for new trial or in arrest of judgment shall briefly refer to that part of the ruling

of the court, charge given to the jury, or charge refused, admission or rejection of evidence, or other proceedings which are designated to be complained of, in such a way that the objection can be clearly identified and understood by the court.

June 10, 1980, eff. Jan. 1, 1981.

See also **O'Connor's Texas Rules**, "Motion for New Trial," ch. 10-B, §1 et seq.; **O'Connor's Texas Forms**, FORMS 10B.

TRCP 322. GENERALITY TO BE AVOIDED

Grounds of objections couched in general terms—as that the court erred in its charge, in sustaining or overruling exceptions to the pleadings, and in excluding or admitting evidence, the verdict of the jury is contrary to law, and the like—shall not be considered by the court.

See also **O'Connor's Texas Rules**, "Points of error," ch. 10-B, §2.3.

ANNOTATIONS

Arkoma Basin Expl. Co. v. FMF Assocs. 1990-A, Ltd., 249 S.W.3d 380, 388 (Tex.2008). "If a single jury question involves many issues, it is possible that a general objection may not tell the trial court where to start. But post-trial objections will rarely be as detailed as an appellate brief because time is short, the record may not be ready, and the trial court is already familiar with the case. In that context, an objection is not necessarily inadequate because it does not specify every reason the evidence was insufficient. Like all other procedural rules, those regarding the specificity of post-trial objections should be construed liberally so that the right to appeal is not lost unnecessarily."

TRCP 323. REPEALED BY ORDER OF JULY 11, 1977, EFF. JAN. 1, 1978

TRCP 324. PREREQUISITES OF APPEAL

(a) Motion for New Trial Not Required. A point in a motion for new trial is not a prerequisite to a complaint on appeal in either a jury or a nonjury case, except as provided in subdivision (b).

(b) Motion for New Trial Required. A point in a motion for new trial is a prerequisite to the following complaints on appeal:

(1) A complaint on which evidence must be heard such as one of jury misconduct or newly discovered evidence or failure to set aside a judgment by default;

(2) A complaint of factual insufficiency of the evidence to support a jury finding;

(3) A complaint that a jury finding is against the overwhelming weight of the evidence;

(4) A complaint of inadequacy or excessiveness of the damages found by the jury; or

(5) Incurable jury argument if not otherwise ruled on by the trial court.

(c) Judgment Notwithstanding Findings; Cross-Points. When judgment is rendered non obstante veredicto or notwithstanding the findings of a jury on one or more questions, the appellee may bring forward by cross-point contained in his brief filed in the Court of Appeals any ground which would have vitiated the verdict or would have prevented an affirmance of the judgment had one been rendered by the trial court in harmony with the verdict, including although not limited to the ground that one or more of the jury's findings have insufficient support in the evidence or are against the overwhelming preponderance of the evidence as a matter of fact, and the ground that the verdict and judgment based thereon should be set aside because of improper argument of counsel.

The failure to bring forward by cross-points such grounds as would vitiate the verdict shall be deemed a waiver thereof; provided, however, that if a cross-point is upon a ground which requires the taking of evidence in addition to that adduced upon the trial of the cause, it is not necessary that the evidentiary hearing be held until after the appellate court determines that the cause be remanded to consider such a cross-point.

March 31, 1941, eff. Sept. 1, 1941. Amended by orders of Sept. 20, 1941, eff. Dec. 31, 1941; July 20, 1954, eff. Jan. 1, 1955; March 19, 1957, eff. Sept. 1, 1957; April 12, 1962, eff. Sept. 1, 1962; July 11, 1977, eff. Jan. 1, 1978; June 10, 1980, eff. Jan. 1, 1981; Dec. 5, 1983, eff. April 1, 1984; July 15, 1987, eff. Jan. 1, 1988.

Source: Tex. Rules for Dist. & Cty. Cts. 71a, with changes: Eliminated reference to fundamental error as an exceptional situation not requiring motion for new trial; added proviso authorizing appellee, when judgment is rendered JNOV, to complain of any prejudicial error committed against him over his objection on the trial by cross-assignments of error filed in the Court of Civil Appeals, without having first presented such complaint in a motion for new trial.

See also **O'Connor's Texas Rules**, "Making & Preserving Objections," ch. 1-F, §1 et seq.; **O'Connor's Texas Rules**, "Motion for JNOV," ch. 9-B, §1 et seq.; **O'Connor's Texas Rules**, "Motion for New Trial," ch. 10-B, §1 et seq.

ANNOTATIONS

Phillips v. Bramlett, 288 S.W.3d 876, 883 (Tex.2009). "A complaint of incurable argument may be asserted and preserved in a motion for new trial, even without a complaint and ruling during the trial. Incurable jury argument is rare, however, because '[t]ypically, retraction of the argument or instruction from the court can cure any probable harm. . . .' The party claiming incurable harm must persuade the court that, based on the record as a whole, the offensive argument was so extreme that a 'juror of ordinary intelligence could have been persuaded by that argument to agree to a verdict contrary to that to which he would have agreed but for such argument.'"

Lee v. Braeburn Valley W. Civic Ass'n, 786 S.W.2d 262, 263 (Tex.1990). "[A] motion for new trial is not a prerequisite for an appeal of a summary judgment proceeding."

TRCP 325. REPEALED BY ORDER OF JULY 11, 1977, EFF. JAN. 1, 1978

TRCP 326. NOT MORE THAN TWO

Not more than two new trials shall be granted either party in the same cause because of insufficiency or weight of the evidence.

TRCP 327. FOR JURY MISCONDUCT

a. When the ground of a motion for new trial, supported by affidavit, is misconduct of the jury or of the officer in charge of them, or because of any communication made to the jury, or that a juror gave an erroneous or incorrect answer on voir dire examination, the court shall hear evidence thereof from the jury or others in open court, and may grant a new trial if such misconduct proved, or the communication made, or the erroneous or incorrect answer on voir dire examination, be material, and if it reasonably appears from the evidence both on the hearing of the motion and the trial of the case and from the record as a whole that injury probably resulted to the complaining party.

b. A juror may not testify as to any matter or statement occurring during the course of the jury's deliberations or to the effect of anything upon his or any other juror's mind or emotions as influencing him to assent to or dissent from the verdict concerning his mental processes in connection therewith, except that a juror may testify whether any outside influence was improperly brought to bear upon any juror. Nor may his affidavit or evidence of any statement by him concerning a matter about which he would be precluded from testifying be received for these purposes.

July 20, 1954, eff. Jan. 1, 1955. Amended by order of Dec. 5, 1983, eff. April 1, 1984.

Source: TRCS art. 2234 (repealed), except to impose burden on complaining party to show probability of injury.

See also TRE 606(b); **O'Connor's Texas Rules**, "MNT based on jury or bailiff misconduct," ch. 10-B, §14; **O'Connor's Texas Forms**, FORM 10B:1.

ANNOTATIONS

Ford Motor Co. v. Castillo, 279 S.W.3d 656, 666 (Tex.2009). "[B]y their plain language, [TRCP 327(b) and TRE 606(b)] apply to motions for new trials, reasons jurors voted for or against verdicts, and inquiries into the validity of verdicts or indictments. Even when those types of issues are involved, the rules specifically allow jurors to testify about outside influence brought to bear on any of them."

Golden Eagle Archery, Inc. v. Jackson, 24 S.W.3d 362, 370 (Tex.2000). "A juror may testify about jury misconduct provided it does not require delving into deliberations. [¶] [TRCP 327(b) and TRE 606(b)] contemplate that an 'outside influence' originates from sources other than the jurors themselves. *At 371:* [An] alleged conversation between [jurors] during a trial break . . . should not be considered 'deliberations' and therefore barred by Rule 606(b) and Rule 327(b)." *See also* **Vargas de Damian v. Bell Helicopter Textron, Inc.**, 352 S.W.3d 124, 161 (Tex.App.—Fort Worth 2011, pet. denied) (juror testimony that they traded answers was not evidence of outside influence); **Hutton v. AER Mfg. II, Inc.**, 224 S.W.3d 459, 463 (Tex.App.—Dallas 2007, pet. denied) (claim that jurors changed their votes or bargained away their positions because of supplemental charge was not evidence of outside influence).

Pharo v. Chambers Cty., 922 S.W.2d 945, 950 (Tex.1996). The bailiff's misconduct "justifies a new trial only if it reasonably appears from the record that injury probably resulted to the complaining party. To show probable injury, there must be some indication in the record that the alleged misconduct most likely caused a juror to vote differently than he would otherwise have done on one or more issues vital to the judgment. Determining the existence of probable injury is a question of law." (Internal quotes omitted.) *See also* **In re Health Care Unlimited, Inc.**, 429 S.W.3d 600, 603 (Tex.2014) (juror's communication with party representative about church retreat did not cause probable injury); **In re Whataburger Rests. LP**, 429 S.W.3d 597, 599 (Tex.2014) (juror's failure to disclose that she had been a D in past lawsuits did not cause probable injury).

In re Zimmer, Inc., 451 S.W.3d 893, 900 (Tex.App.—Dallas 2014, orig. proceeding). "Rule 327 . . . plainly states the trial court 'shall hear evidence [of misconduct of the jury or the officer in charge of them] from the jury or others in open court. . . .' [P] argues this evidentiary requirement applies only when one of the parties seeks to offer live testimony. He contends it exists solely so jurors or other persons who are not willing to sign affidavits may be subpoenaed and compelled to testify. We disagree. . . . *At 901-02:* A proceeding under rule 327 is not complete . . . upon the filing of the affidavits. . . . The trial court has no discretion to refuse to conduct an evidentiary hearing when a party comes forward with affidavits supporting a cognizable claim of material jury misconduct. [¶] [P] argues, however, that because here neither party sought an evidentiary hearing, the trial court was entitled to decide the question of jury misconduct on the basis of affidavits and argument alone. We disagree. [¶] [A]ffidavits attached to a motion for new trial alleging juror misconduct are 'neither evidence nor admissible as such on the hearing for a new trial on the ground of jury misconduct.' [A] trial court may properly deny a motion for new trial when a party alleging jury misconduct relies only on affidavits and fails to request a hearing on

his motion and offer live testimony proving misconduct. Similarly, a trial court properly denies a new trial when it holds a hearing and the party asserting misconduct discusses the affidavits but never attempts to admit the affidavits into evidence or present any other evidence of juror misconduct through live testimony. In such a situation there is no evidence to support the complaining party's allegations of juror misconduct. We see no reason why the evidentiary requirements of rule 327 should be interpreted any less stringently when the trial court grants new trial and sets aside the jury verdict."

Jefferson v. Fuller, No. 01-11-00199-CV, 2012 WL 2357431 (Tex.App.—Houston [1st Dist.] 2012, pet. denied) (memo op.; 6-21-12). "'A juror can commit misconduct if he lies in voir dire about a matter on which he was clearly biased or prejudiced.' For false answers to voir dire questions to entitle a party to a new trial, the concealment must be in response to a specific and direct question calling for disclosure. To establish jury misconduct on grounds that the juror concealed information during voir dire, a party must obtain proof of concealment from a source other than jury deliberations."

Brandt v. Surber, 194 S.W.3d 108, 134 (Tex.App.—Corpus Christi 2006, pet. denied). "An outside influence does not include 'information not in evidence, unknown to the jurors prior to trial, acquired by a juror and communicated to one or more other jurors between the time the jurors received their instructions from the court and the rendition of the verdict[ ]'. . . . [¶] [One juror's] affidavit stating that other jurors discussed newspaper articles during deliberations was not evidence of any outside influence, but only described matters on the minds of other jurors during deliberations. The affidavit is, therefore, incompetent to serve as evidence of juror misconduct."

TRCP 328. REPEALED BY ORDER OF JULY 15, 1987, EFF. JAN. 1, 1988

TRCP 329. MOTION FOR NEW TRIAL ON JUDGMENT FOLLOWING CITATION BY PUBLICATION

In cases in which judgment has been rendered on service of process by publication, when the defendant has not appeared in person or by attorney of his own selection:

(a) The court may grant a new trial upon petition of the defendant showing good cause, supported by affidavit, filed within two years after such judgment was signed. The parties adversely interested in such judgment shall be cited as in other cases.

(b) Execution of such judgment shall not be suspended unless the party applying therefor shall give a good and sufficient bond payable to the plaintiff in the judgment, in an amount fixed in accordance with Appellate Rule 47[1] relating to supersedeas bonds, to be approved by the clerk, and conditioned that the party will prosecute his petition for new trial to effect and will perform such judgment as may be rendered by the court should its decision be against him.

(c) If property has been sold under the judgment and execution before the process was suspended, the defendant shall not recover the property so sold, but shall have judgment against the plaintiff in the judgment for the proceeds of such sale.

(d) If the motion is filed more than thirty days after the judgment was signed, the time period shall be computed pursuant to Rule 306a(7).

June 10, 1980, eff. Jan. 1, 1981. Amended by orders of Dec. 5, 1983, eff. April 1, 1984; July 15, 1987, eff. Jan. 1, 1988.

Source: TRCS art. 2236 (repealed).

[1] See, now, Vernon's Ann.Rules App.Proc., rule 24.1 et seq.

See also **O'Connor's Texas Rules**, "MNT after service by publication," ch. 10-B, §10; **O'Connor's Texas Forms**, FORM 10B:5.

ANNOTATIONS

In re E.R., 385 S.W.3d 552, 563 (Tex.2012). "When judgment is rendered on service of process by publication, a party has two years to move for a new trial, which the trial court may grant for 'good cause.' But if service was invalid, a party is entitled to a new trial without showing good cause."

In re Boshears, No. 09-10-00187-CV, 2010 WL 2347087 (Tex.App.—Beaumont 2010, orig. proceeding) (memo op.; 6-10-10). "A bill of review filed within the time for filing a Rule 329 motion may be treated as a motion for new trial."

TRCP 329a. COUNTY COURT CASES

If a case or other matter is on trial or in the process of hearing when the term of the county court expires, such trial, hearing or other matter may be proceeded with at the next or any subsequent term of court and no motion or plea shall be considered as waived or overruled, because not acted upon at the term of court at which it was filed, but may be acted upon at any time the judge may fix or at which it may have been postponed or continued by agreement of the parties with leave of the court. This subdivision is not applicable to original or amended motions for new trial which are governed by Rule 329b.

July 20, 1954 eff. Jan. 1, 1955. Amended by orders of March 19, 1957, eff. Sept. 1, 1957; July 26, 1960, eff. Jan. 1, 1961.

TRCP 329b. TIME FOR FILING MOTIONS

The following rules shall be applicable to motions for new trial and motions to modify, correct, or reform judgments (other than motions to correct the record under Rule 316) in all district and county courts:

(a) A motion for new trial, if filed, shall be filed prior to or within thirty days after the judgment or other order complained of is signed.

(b) One or more amended motions for new trial may be filed without leave of court before any preceding motion for new trial filed by the movant is overruled and within thirty days after the judgment or other order complained of is signed.

(c) In the event an original or amended motion for new trial or a motion to modify, correct or reform a judgment is not determined by written order signed within seventy-five days after the judgment was signed, it shall be considered overruled by operation of law on expiration of that period.

(d) The trial court, regardless of whether an appeal has been perfected, has plenary power to grant a new trial or to vacate, modify, correct, or reform the judgment within thirty days after the judgment is signed.

(e) If a motion for new trial is timely filed by any party, the trial court, regardless of whether an appeal has been perfected, has plenary power to grant a new trial or to vacate, modify, correct, or reform the judgment until thirty days after all such timely-filed motions are overruled, either by a written and signed order or by operation of law, whichever occurs first.

(f) On expiration of the time within which the trial court has plenary power, a judgment cannot be set aside by the trial court except by bill of review for sufficient cause, filed within the time allowed by law; provided that the court may at any time correct a clerical error in the record of a judgment and render judgment nunc pro tunc under Rule 316, and may also sign an order declaring a previous judgment or order to be void because signed after the court's plenary power had expired.

(g) A motion to modify, correct, or reform a judgment (as distinguished from motion to correct the record of a judgment under Rule 316), if filed, shall be filed and determined within the time prescribed by this rule for a motion for new trial and shall extend the trial court's plenary power and the time for perfecting an appeal in the same manner as a motion for new trial. Each such motion shall be in writing and signed by the party or his attorney and shall specify the respects in which the judgment should be modified, corrected, or reformed. The overruling of such a motion shall not preclude the filing of a motion for new trial, nor shall the overruling of a motion for new trial preclude the filing of a motion to modify, correct, or reform.

(h) If a judgment is modified, corrected or reformed in any respect, the time for appeal shall run from the time the modified, corrected, or reformed judgment is signed, but if a correction is made pursuant to Rule 316 after expiration of the period of plenary power provided by this rule, no complaint shall be heard on appeal that could have been presented in an appeal from the original judgment.

July 20, 1954, eff. Jan. 1, 1955. Amended by orders of July 26, 1960, eff. Jan. 1, 1961; July 20, 1966, eff. Jan. 1, 1967; Oct. 3, 1972, eff. Feb. 1, 1973; July 11, 1977, eff. Jan. 1, 1978; June 10, 1980, eff. Jan. 1, 1981; Dec. 5, 1983, eff. April 1, 1984; July 15, 1987, eff. Jan. 1, 1988.

Comment—1988

Amended to conform with repeal of Rule 317.

Source: New rule. See TRCP 330(j)–(l), before Jan. 1, 1955 changes to TRCP 330.

See also **O'Connor's Texas Rules**, "Rules for Filing Documents," ch. 1-C, §1 et seq.; **O'Connor's Texas Rules**, "Motion for JNOV," ch. 9-B, §1 et seq.; **O'Connor's Texas Rules**, "Judgment," ch. 9-C, §1 et seq.; **O'Connor's Texas Rules**, "Motion for New Trial," ch. 10-B, §1 et seq.; **O'Connor's Texas Rules**, "Motion to Modify the Judgment," ch. 10-D, §1 et seq.; **O'Connor's Texas Rules**, "Motion for Judgment Nunc Pro Tunc," ch. 10-H, §1 et seq.

ANNOTATIONS

Plenary Power

In re Baylor Med. Ctr., 280 S.W.3d 227, 230-31 (Tex.2008). Rule 329b "terminates the trial court's plenary power 30 days after all timely motions for new trial are *overruled*, but there is no provision limiting its plenary power if such motions are *granted*. Under the current rules, if no judgment is signed, no plenary-power clock is ticking. [¶] When a new trial is granted, the case stands on the trial court's docket 'the same as though no trial had been had.' Accordingly, the trial court should then have the power to set aside a new trial order 'any time before a final judgment is entered.' [¶] [W]e recently clarified that 'a trial judge who modifies a judgment and then withdraws the modification has modified the judgment *twice* rather than never.' Rule 329b(h) provides that if a judgment is modified '*in any respect*' the appellate timetables are restarted. Surely a judgment that is set aside by a new trial order has been modified in *some* respect, even if it is later reinstated. Thus, if a new trial is granted and later withdrawn, the appellate deadlines run from the later order granting reinstatement rather than the earlier order. *At 232:* 'There is no sound reason why the court may not reconsider its ruling [granting] a new trial' at any time." *See also* **Hidalgo v. Hidalgo**, 310 S.W.3d 887, 889 (Tex.2010).

In re Brookshire Grocery Co., 250 S.W.3d 66, 69 (Tex.2008). "[A]n amended motion [for new trial] may be filed without leave of court when: (1) no preceding motion for new trial has been overruled *and* (2) it is filed within 30 days of judgment. 'And' is conjunctive: an amended new-trial motion is timely filed only *before* the court overrules a prior one. An amended motion filed afterwards: (1) need not be considered by the trial court and (2) does not extend the trial court's plenary power. *At 72:* [T]he trial court retains plenary power for 30 days after overruling a motion for new trial; thus, the losing party may ask the trial court

to reconsider its order denying a new trial—or the court may grant a new trial on its own initiative—so long as the court issues an order granting new trial within its period of plenary power. [¶] Additionally, under Rule 329b, a trial court's plenary power to grant a new trial expires 30 days after it overrules a motion for new trial, only provided no other *type* of 329b motion (such as a motion to modify, correct, or reform the judgment) is 'timely filed.' Thus, a party whose motion for new trial is overruled within 30 days of judgment may still file a motion to modify, correct, or reform the judgment—provided it is filed within 30 days of judgment—and thereby extend the trial court's plenary power."

Moritz v. Preiss, 121 S.W.3d 715, 720 (Tex.2003). "[A]n amended motion for new trial filed more than 30 days after the trial court signs a final judgment is untimely. [T]he trial court may, at its discretion, consider the grounds raised in an untimely motion and grant a new trial under its inherent authority before the court loses plenary power. [¶] 'If the trial court ignores the tardy motion, it is ineffectual for any purpose. [I]f the court denies a new trial, the belated motion is a nullity and supplies no basis for consideration upon appeal of grounds which were required to be set forth in a timely motion.' *At 721:* [A]n untimely amended motion for new trial does not preserve issues for appellate review, even if the trial court considers and denies the untimely motion within its plenary power period."

Lane Bank Equip. Co. v. Smith S. Equip., Inc., 10 S.W.3d 308, 312 (Tex.2000). "[A] motion made after judgment to incorporate a sanction as a part of the final judgment does propose a change to that judgment. Such a motion is, on its face, a motion to modify, correct or reform the existing judgment within the meaning of Rule 329b(g). *At 314:* We . . . hold that [such a motion] qualifies as a motion to modify under Rule 329b(g), thus extending the trial court's plenary jurisdiction and the appellate timetable." *See also* **Mann v. Kendall Home Builders Constr. Partners I, Ltd.**, 464 S.W.3d 84, 89-90 (Tex.App.—Houston [14th Dist.] 2015, no pet.).

Scott & White Mem'l Hosp. v. Schexnider, 940 S.W.2d 594, 596 (Tex.1996). "A trial court's power to decide a motion for sanctions pertaining to matters occurring before judgment is no different than its power to decide any other motion during its plenary jurisdiction. [T]he time during which the trial court has authority to impose sanctions on such a motion is limited to when it retains plenary jurisdiction. . . ." *See also* **Law Offices of Robert D. Wilson v. Texas Univest-Frisco, Ltd.**, 291 S.W.3d 110, 113 (Tex.App.—Dallas 2009, no pet.).

L.M. Healthcare, Inc. v. Childs, 929 S.W.2d 442, 443 (Tex.1996). "That the trial court overruled [P's] motion for new trial does not shorten the trial court's plenary power to resolve a motion to modify the judgment. *At 444:* [TRCP 329b(e) and (g)] provide that a timely filed motion to modify judgment extends the trial court's plenary power, separate and apart from a motion for new trial." *See also* **Board of Trs. of Bastrop ISD v. Toungate**, 958 S.W.2d 365, 367 (Tex.1997).

PNS Stores v. Rivera, 335 S.W.3d 265, 279-80 (Tex.App.—San Antonio 2010), *rev'd on other grounds*, 379 S.W.3d 267 (Tex.2012). "Generally, only a timely filed bill of review is available to set aside a judgment when the trial court's plenary power has expired. However, in **Middleton [v. Murff**, 689 S.W.2d 212 (Tex.1985)], the supreme court recognized an exception to rule 329b(f). According to the supreme court, the rule's mandate that only a timely filed bill of review is available to set aside a trial court's judgment after the court's plenary power has expired does not apply where the court had no jurisdictional power to render judgment. Importantly, however, the court specifically defined 'jurisdictional power' to mean 'jurisdiction over the subject matter, the power to hear and determine cases of the general class to which the particular one belongs.' Any other direct attack on a void judgment must comply with rule 329b(f), i.e., must be an attack by a timely filed bill of review. [¶] Accordingly, under **Middleton**, it appears that an untimely bill of review is proper only if there is an absence of subject matter jurisdiction." *See also* **Smalley v. Smalley**, 436 S.W.3d 801, 806 (Tex.App.—Houston [14th Dist.] 2014, no pet.).

Written Order

In re Lovito-Nelson, 278 S.W.3d 773, 775 (Tex.2009). "We have been clear that Rule 329b(c) requires a written order to grant a new trial. . . . Although we have never had occasion to apply the rule to scheduling orders, the courts of appeals have, and have mostly held that such orders do not grant new trials." *See also* **Faulkner v. Culver**, 851 S.W.2d 187, 188 (Tex.1993) (trial judge's oral pronouncement cannot substitute for written order).

Appellate Deadlines

Ryland Enter. v. Weatherspoon, 355 S.W.3d 664, 665-66 (Tex.2011). TRCP "329b states that a motion for new trial is timely if filed '*prior to* or within 30 days after the judgment . . . complained of is signed.' This 'prior to' language is supplemented and clarified by [TRCP] 306c, which provides that '[n]o motion for new trial . . . shall be held ineffective because prematurely filed; but every such motion shall be deemed to have been filed on the date of but subsequent to the time of signing of the judgment the motion assails.' [R]ule 329b(g) states that a 'motion to modify . . . shall be filed and determined . . . and shall extend . . . the time for perfecting an appeal in the same manner as a motion for new trial.'"

Arkoma Basin Expl. Co. v. FMF Assocs. 1990-A, Ltd., 249 S.W.3d 380, 390-91 (Tex.2008). "'If a judgment is modified in any respect,' appellate deadlines do not run from the original judgment but 'from the date when the modified judgment is signed.' [¶] [T]he deadlines are restarted by '*any* change, whether or not material or substantial.' Thus, appellate deadlines are restarted by an order that does nothing more than change the docket number or deny all relief not expressly granted." *See also* **In re J.L.**, 163 S.W.3d 79, 82 (Tex.2005) (because trial court modified and corrected

judgment while it retained plenary power, time for filing notice of appeal was calculated from date of new final judgment); **Abercia v. Kingvision Pay-Per-View, Ltd.**, 217 S.W.3d 688, 706 (Tex.App.—El Paso 2007, pet. denied) (even when later judgment differs from original judgment only by signature date, later judgment vacates former judgment).

Garza v. Garcia, 137 S.W.3d 36, 37-38 (Tex.2004). "A motion for new trial is 'conditionally filed' if tendered without the requisite fee, and appellate deadlines run from and are extended by that date: '[T]he failure to pay the fee before the motion is overruled by operation of law may forfeit altogether the movant's opportunity to have the trial court consider the motion; it does not, however, retroactively invalidate the conditional filing for purposes of the appellate timetable.' [¶] Although we have previously reserved ruling on a fee that was never paid, we now extend [this] rule in these circumstances. [¶] This is not to say filing fees are irrelevant. '[A]bsent emergency or other rare circumstances' a motion for new trial should not be considered until the filing fee is paid." *See also* **Tate v. E.I. DuPont de Nemours & Co.**, 934 S.W.2d 83, 84 (Tex.1996).

Farmer v. Ben E. Keith Co., 907 S.W.2d 495, 496 (Tex.1995). "[T]he appellate timetable runs from the signing date of whatever order that makes a judgment final and appealable, i.e. whatever *order* disposes of any parties or issues remaining before the court. Further, the appellate timetable can begin yet again with the signing of an order or judgment where there is nothing on the face of the record to indicate it was signed for the sole purpose of *extending* the appellate timetable and the order is signed within the trial court's plenary power."

K. Certain District Courts

TRCP 330. RULES OF PRACTICE AND PROCEDURE IN CERTAIN DISTRICT COURTS

The following rules of practice and procedure shall govern and be followed in all civil actions in district courts in counties where the only district court of said county vested with civil jurisdiction, or all the district courts thereof having civil jurisdiction, have successive terms in said county throughout the year, without more than two days intervening between any of such terms, whether or not any one or more of such district courts include one or more other counties within its jurisdiction.

(a) Appealed Cases. In cases appealed to said district courts from inferior courts, the appeal, including transcript, shall be filed in the district court within thirty (30) days after the rendition of the judgment or order appealed from, and the appellee shall enter his appearance on the docket or answer to said appeal on or before ten o'clock a.m. of the Monday next after the expiration of twenty (20) days from the date the appeal is filed in the district court.

(b) Repealed by order of July 22, 1975, eff. Jan. 1, 1976

(c) Postponement or Continuance. Cases may be postponed or continued by agreement with the approval of the court, or upon the court's own motion or for cause. When a case is called for trial and only one party is ready, the court may for good cause either continue the case for the term or postpone and reset it for a later day in the same or succeeding term.

(d) Cases May Be Reset. A case that is set and reached for trial may be postponed for a later day in the term or continued and reset for a day certain in the succeeding term on the same grounds as an application for continuance would be granted in other district courts. After any case has been set and reached in its due order and called for trial two (2) or more times and not tried, the court may dismiss the same unless the parties agree to a postponement or continuance but the court shall respect written agreements of counsel for postponement and continuance if filed in the case when or before it is called for trial unless to do so will unreasonably delay or interfere with other business of the court.

(e) Exchange and Transfer. Where in such county there are two or more district courts having civil jurisdiction, the judges of such courts may, in their discretion, exchange benches or districts from time to time, and may transfer cases and other proceedings from one court to another, and any of them may in his own courtroom try and determine any case or proceeding pending in another court without having the case transferred, or may sit in any other of said courts and there hear and determine any case there pending, and every judgment and order shall be entered in the minutes of the court in which the case is pending and at the time the judgment or order is rendered, and two (2) or more judges may try different cases in the same court at the same time, and each may occupy his own courtroom or the room of any other court. The judge of any such court may issue restraining orders and injunctions returnable to any other judge or court, and any judge may transfer any case or proceeding pending in his court to any other of said courts, and the judge of any court to which a case or proceeding is transferred shall receive and try the same, and in turn shall have power in his discretion to transfer any such case to any other of said courts and any other judge may in his courtroom try any case pending in any other of such courts.

(f) Cases Transferred to Judges Not Occupied. Where in such counties there are two or more district courts having civil jurisdiction, when the judge of any such court shall become disengaged, he shall notify the presiding

judge, and the presiding judge shall transfer to the court of the disengaged judge the next case which is ready for trial in any of said courts. Any judge not engaged in his own court may try any case in any other court.

(g) Judge May Hear Only Part of Case. When in such counties there are two or more district courts having civil jurisdiction, any judge may hear any part of any case or proceeding pending in any of said courts and determine the same, or may hear and determine any question in any case, and any other judge may complete the hearing and render judgment in the case.

(h) Any Judge May Hear Dilatory Pleas. Where in such county there are two or more district courts having civil jurisdiction, any judge may hear and determine motions, petitions for injunction, applications for appointment of receivers, interventions, pleas of privilege, pleas in abatement, all dilatory pleas and special exceptions, motions for a new trial and all preliminary matters, questions and proceedings and may enter judgment or order thereon in the court in which the case is pending without having the case transferred to the court of the judge acting, and the judge in whose court the case is pending may thereafter proceed to hear, complete and determine the case or other matter, or any part thereof, and render final judgment therein. Any judgment rendered or action taken by any judge in any of said courts in the county shall be valid and binding.

(i) Acts in Succeeding Terms. If a case or other matter is on trial, or in the process of hearing when the term of court expires, such trial, hearing or other matter may be proceeded with at the next or any subsequent term of court and no motion or plea shall be considered as waived or overruled, because not acted upon at the term of court at which it was filed, but may be acted upon at any time the judge may fix or at which it may have been postponed or continued by agreement of the parties with leave of the court. This subdivision is not applicable to original or amended motions for new trial which are governed by Rule 329b.

(j) Relettered to (i)

(k), (*l*) Repealed by order of July 20, 1954, eff. Jan. 1, 1955

July 20, 1954, eff. Jan. 1, 1955. Amended by orders of July 26, 1960, eff. Jan. 1, 1961; Oct. 3, 1972, eff. Feb. 1, 1973; July 22, 1975, eff. Jan. 1, 1976.

Source: TRCS art. 2092 (repealed).

See also Gov't Code §24.003.

ANNOTATIONS

In re U.S. Silica Co., 157 S.W.3d 434, 438-39 (Tex.2005). "We disagree that all orders signed by a transferring court after transfer are void; many are not. This is especially true here because the transfers involved district courts in a single county. [¶] Trial courts have broad discretion to exchange benches and enter orders on other cases in the same county, even without a formal order or transfer. Given the broad powers district courts have to act for one another, we do not agree that these [interim] orders were entered without jurisdiction."

Wilson v. Dunn, 800 S.W.2d 833, 835 n.6 (Tex.1990). "The 236th District Court and the 67th District Court both sit in Tarrant County. They are permitted to, and do, hear each other's civil cases under Rule 330." *See also* **Pinnacle Gas Treating, Inc. v. Read,** 160 S.W.3d 564, 566 (Tex.2005) (87th District Court and 278th District Court are both in Leon County and have concurrent jurisdiction).

Hull v. South Coast Catamarans, L.P., 365 S.W.3d 35, 41 (Tex.App.—Houston [1st Dist.] 2011, pet. denied). "[R]ule 330(g) does not authorize a district judge who heard none of the case to render judgment in a bench trial. *At 42:* But [this] exception to the free exchange of benches is a narrow one."

Polk v. Southwest Crossing Homeowners Ass'n, 165 S.W.3d 89, 93 (Tex.App.—Houston [14th Dist.] 2005, pet. denied). "[P] does not have a protected proprietary interest in having her case heard by a particular district judge. Counties may adopt local rules to further govern the transfer of cases from one district court to another if they are not inconsistent with Rule 330(e). *At 94:* [A] failure to comply with the local rule's *procedural* requirements does not deprive a court of its jurisdiction. While the transferring and receiving courts should have complied with their own local rules regarding the transfer of cases, their failure to do so did not deprive [the district court] of jurisdiction over [P's] case." *See also* **In re Rio Grande Valley Gas Co.,** 987 S.W.2d 167, 173 (Tex.App.—Corpus Christi 1999, orig. proceeding).

TRCP 331. REPEALED BY ORDER OF JULY 15, 1987, EFF. JAN. 1, 1988

SECTION 12. REVIEW BY DISTRICT COURTS OF COUNTY COURT RULINGS

TRCP 332 to 351. REPEALED BY ORDER OF JULY 22, 1975, EFF. JAN. 1, 1976

Part III. Rules of Procedure for the Courts of Appeals

SECTION 1. PERFECTING APPEAL

TRCP 352 to 358. REPEALED BY ORDER OF APRIL 10, 1986, EFF. SEPT. 1, 1986

TRCP 359. REPEALED BY ORDER OF DEC. 5, 1983, EFF. APRIL 1, 1984

TRCP 360. REPEALED BY ORDER OF APRIL 10, 1986, EFF. SEPT. 1, 1986

TRCP 361, 362. REPEALED BY ORDER OF DEC. 5, 1983, EFF. APRIL 1, 1984

TRCP 363 to 369a. REPEALED BY ORDER OF APRIL 10, 1986, EFF. SEPT. 1, 1986

SECTION 2. RECORD ON APPEAL

TRCP 370. REPEALED BY ORDER OF JUNE 10, 1980, EFF. JAN. 1, 1981

TRCP 371 to 373. REPEALED BY ORDER OF APRIL 10, 1986, EFF. SEPT. 1, 1986

TRCP 374. REPEALED BY ORDER OF JULY 11, 1977, EFF. JAN. 1, 1978

TRCP 375 to 382. REPEALED BY ORDER OF APRIL 10, 1986, EFF. SEPT. 1, 1986

SECTION 3. PROCEEDINGS IN THE COURTS OF APPEALS

TRCP 383 to 389a. REPEALED BY ORDER OF APRIL 10, 1986, EFF. SEPT. 1, 1986

TRCP 390. REPEALED BY ORDER OF DEC. 5, 1983, EFF. APRIL 1, 1984

TRCP 391. REPEALED BY ORDER OF OCT. 12, 1949, EFF. MARCH 1, 1950

TRCP 392. REPEALED BY ORDER OF DEC. 5, 1983, EFF. APRIL 1, 1984

TRCP 393 to 414. REPEALED BY ORDER OF APRIL 10, 1986, EFF. SEPT. 1, 1986

TRCP 415 to 417. REPEALED BY ORDER OF DEC. 5, 1983, EFF. APRIL 1, 1984

TRCP 418. REPEALED BY ORDER OF APRIL 24, 1984, EFF. OCT. 1, 1984

TRCP 419, 420. REPEALED BY ORDER OF APRIL 10, 1986, EFF. SEPT. 1, 1986

TRCP 421. REPEALED BY ORDER OF JUNE 10, 1980, EFF. JAN. 1, 1981

TRCP 422, 423. REPEALED BY ORDER OF APRIL 10, 1986, EFF. SEPT. 1, 1986

TRCP 424 to 427. REPEALED BY ORDER OF DEC. 5, 1983, EFF. APRIL 1, 1984

TRCP 428, 429. REPEALED BY ORDER OF APRIL 10, 1986, EFF. SEPT. 1, 1986

TRCP 430 to 432. REPEALED BY ORDER OF DEC. 5, 1983, EFF. APRIL 1, 1984

SECTION 4. JUDGMENT

TRCP 433 to 442. REPEALED BY ORDER OF APRIL 10, 1986, EFF. SEPT. 1, 1986

TRCP 443, 444. REPEALED BY ORDER OF DEC. 5, 1983, EFF. APRIL 1, 1984

TRCP 445. REPEALED BY ORDER OF JULY 11, 1977, EFF. JAN. 1, 1978

TRCP 446 to 448. REPEALED BY ORDER OF APRIL 10, 1986, EFF. SEPT. 1, 1986

TRCP 449, 450. REPEALED BY ORDER OF DEC. 5, 1983, EFF. APRIL 1, 1984

SECTION 5. OPINIONS

TRCP 451, 452. REPEALED BY ORDER OF APRIL 10, 1986, EFF. SEPT. 1, 1986

TRCP 453 to 455. REPEALED BY ORDER OF DEC. 5, 1983, EFF. APRIL 1, 1984

TRCP 456, 457. REPEALED BY ORDER OF APRIL 10, 1986, EFF. SEPT. 1, 1986

SECTION 6. REHEARING

TRCP 458. REPEALED BY ORDER OF APRIL 10, 1986, EFF. SEPT. 1, 1986

TRCP 459. REPEALED BY ORDER OF SEPT. 20, 1941, EFF. DEC. 31, 1941

TRCP 460. REPEALED BY ORDER OF APRIL 10, 1986, EFF. SEPT. 1, 1986

SECTION 7. CERTIFICATION OF QUESTIONS

TRCP 461, 462. REPEALED BY ORDER OF APRIL 10, 1986, EFF. SEPT. 1, 1986

TRCP 463, 464. REPEALED BY ORDER OF DEC. 5, 1983, EFF. APRIL 1, 1984

TRCP 465. RENUMBERED AS RULE 462 BY ORDER OF DEC. 5, 1983, EFF. APRIL 1, 1984

TRCP 466. REPEALED BY ORDER OF APRIL 10, 1986, EFF. SEPT. 1, 1986

SECTION 8. APPLICATION FOR WRIT OF ERROR

TRCP 467. REPEALED BY ORDER OF DEC. 5, 1983, EFF. APRIL 1, 1984

TRCP 468 to 470. REPEALED BY ORDER OF APRIL 10, 1986, EFF. SEPT. 1, 1986

TRCP 471. REPEALED BY ORDER OF DEC. 5, 1983, EFF. APRIL 1, 1984

TRCP 472. REPEALED BY ORDER OF APRIL 10, 1986, EFF. SEPT. 1, 1986

TRCP 473. REPEALED BY ORDER OF DEC. 5, 1983, EFF. APRIL 1, 1984

Part IV. Rules of Practice for the Supreme Court

TRCP 474 to 481. REPEALED BY ORDER OF APRIL 10, 1986, EFF. SEPT. 1, 1986

TRCP 482. REPEALED BY ORDER OF DEC. 5, 1983, EFF. APRIL 1, 1984

TRCP 483 to 486. REPEALED BY ORDER OF APRIL 10, 1986, EFF. SEPT. 1, 1986

TRCP 487. REPEALED BY ORDER OF OCT. 10, 1945, EFF. FEB. 1, 1946

TRCP 488 to 493. REPEALED BY ORDER OF APRIL 10, 1986, EFF. SEPT. 1, 1986

TRCP 494. REPEALED BY ORDER OF OCT. 10, 1945, EFF. FEB. 1, 1946

TRCP 495 to 499a. REPEALED BY ORDER OF APRIL 10, 1986, EFF. SEPT. 1, 1986

Part V. Rules of Practice in Justice Courts

TRCP 500. GENERAL RULES

500.1. Construction of Rules. Unless otherwise expressly provided, in Part V of these Rules of Civil Procedure:

(a) the past, present, and future tense each includes the other;

(b) the term "it" includes a person of either gender or an entity; and

(c) the singular and plural each includes the other.

500.2. Definitions. In Part V of these Rules of Civil Procedure:

(a) "Answer" is the written response that a party who is sued must file with the court after being served with a citation.

(b) "Citation" is the court-issued document required to be served upon a party to inform the party that it has been sued.

(c) "Claim" is the legal theory and alleged facts that, if proven, entitle a party to relief against another party in court.

(d) "Clerk" is a person designated by the judge as a justice court clerk, or the judge if there is no clerk available.

(e) "Counterclaim" is a claim brought by a party who has been sued against the party who filed the lawsuit, for example, a defendant suing a plaintiff.

(f) "County court" is the county court, statutory county court, or district court in a particular county with jurisdiction over appeals of civil cases from justice court.

(g) "Cross-claim" is a claim brought by one party against another party on the same side of a lawsuit. For example, if a plaintiff sues two defendants, the defendants can seek relief against each other by means of a cross-claim.

(h) "Default judgment" is a judgment awarded to a plaintiff when the defendant fails to answer and dispute the plaintiff's claims in the lawsuit.

(i) "Defendant" is a party who is sued, including a plaintiff against whom a counterclaim is filed.

(j) "Defense" is an assertion by a defendant that the plaintiff is not entitled to relief from the court.

(k) "Discovery" is the process through which parties obtain information from each other in order to prepare for trial or enforce a judgment. The term does not refer to any information that a party is entitled to under applicable law.

(*l*) "Dismissed without prejudice" means a case has been dismissed but has not been finally decided and may be refiled.

(m) "Dismissed with prejudice" means a case has been dismissed and finally decided and may not be refiled.

(n) "Judge" is a justice of the peace.

(o) "Judgment" is a final order by the court that states the relief, if any, a party is entitled to or must provide.

(p) "Jurisdiction" is the authority of the court to hear and decide a case.

(q) "Motion" is a request that the court make a specified ruling or order.

(r) "Notice" is a document prepared and delivered by the court or a party stating that something is required of the party receiving the notice.

(s) "Party" is a person or entity involved in the case that is either suing or being sued, including all plaintiffs, defendants, and third parties that have been joined in the case.

(t) "Petition" is a formal written application stating a party's claims and requesting relief from the court. It is the first document filed with the court to begin a lawsuit.

(u) "Plaintiff" is a party who sues, including a defendant who files a counterclaim.

(v) "Pleading" is a written document filed by a party, including a petition and an answer, that states a claim or defense and outlines the relief sought.

(w) "Relief" is the remedy a party requests from the court, such as the recovery of money or the return of property.

(x) "Serve" and "service" are delivery of citation as required by Rule 501.2, or of a document as required by Rule 501.4.

(y) "Sworn" means signed in front of someone authorized to take oaths, such as a notary, or signed under penalty of perjury. Filing a false sworn document can result in criminal prosecution.

(z) "Third party claim" is a claim brought by a party being sued against someone who is not yet a party to the case.

500.3. Application of Rules in Justice Court Cases.

(a) ***Small Claims Case.*** A small claims case is a lawsuit brought for the recovery of money damages, civil penalties, personal property, or other relief allowed by law. The claim can be for no more than $20,000, excluding statutory interest and court costs but including attorney fees, if any. Small claims cases are governed by Rules 500–507 of Part V of the Rules of Civil Procedure.

(b) ***Debt Claim Case.*** A debt claim case is a lawsuit brought to recover a debt by an assignee of a claim, a debt collector or collection agency, a financial institution, or a person or entity primarily engaged in the business of lending money at interest. The claim can be for no more than $20,000, excluding statutory interest and court costs but including attorney fees, if any. Debt claim cases in justice court are governed by Rules 500–507 and 508 of Part V of the Rules of Civil Procedure. To the extent of any conflict between Rule 508 and the rest of Part V, Rule 508 applies.

(c) ***Repair and Remedy Case.*** A repair and remedy case is a lawsuit filed by a residential tenant under Chapter 92, Subchapter B of the Texas Property Code to enforce the landlord's duty to repair or remedy a condition materially affecting the physical health or safety of an ordinary tenant. The relief sought can be for no more than $20,000, excluding statutory interest and court costs but including attorney fees, if any. Repair and remedy cases are governed by Rules 500–507 and 509 of Part V of the Rules of Civil Procedure. To the extent of any conflict between Rule 509 and the rest of Part V, Rule 509 applies.

(d) ***Eviction Case.*** An eviction case is a lawsuit brought to recover possession of real property under Chapter 24 of the Texas Property Code, often by a landlord against a tenant. A claim for rent may be joined with an eviction case if the amount of rent due and unpaid is not more than $20,000, excluding statutory interest and court costs but including attorney fees, if any. Eviction cases are governed by Rules 500–507 and 510 of Part V of the Rules of Civil Procedure. To the extent of any conflict between Rule 510 and the rest of Part V, Rule 510 applies.

(e) ***Application of Other Rules.*** The other Rules of Civil Procedure and the Rules of Evidence do not apply except:

(1) when the judge hearing the case determines that a particular rule must be followed to ensure that the proceedings are fair to all parties; or

(2) when otherwise specifically provided by law or these rules.

(f) ***Examination of Rules.*** The court must make the Rules of Civil Procedure and the Rules of Evidence available for examination, either in paper form or electronically, during the court's business hours.

500.4. Representation in Justice Court Cases.

(a) ***Representation of an Individual.*** An individual may:

(1) represent himself or herself;

(2) be represented by an authorized agent in an eviction case; or

(3) be represented by an attorney.

(b) ***Representation of a Corporation or Other Entity.*** A corporation or other entity may:

(1) be represented by an employee, owner, officer, or partner of the entity who is not an attorney;

(2) be represented by a property manager or other authorized agent in an eviction case; or

(3) be represented by an attorney.

(c) ***Assisted Representation.*** The court may, for good cause, allow an individual representing himself or herself to be assisted in court by a family member or other individual who is not being compensated.

500.5. Computation of Time; Timely Filing.

(a) ***Computation of Time.*** To compute a time period in these rules:

(1) exclude the day of the event that triggers the period;

(2) count every day, including Saturdays, Sundays, and legal holidays; and

(3) include the last day of the period, but

(A) if the last day is a Saturday, Sunday, or legal holiday, the time period is extended to the next day that is not a Saturday, Sunday, or legal holiday; and

(B) if the last day for filing falls on a day during which the court is closed before 5:00 p.m., the time period is extended to the court's next business day.

(b) ***Timely Filing by Mail.*** Any document required to be filed by a given date is considered timely filed if deposited in the U.S. mail on or before that date, and received within 10 days of the due date. A legible postmark affixed by the United States Postal Service is evidence of the date of mailing.

(c) *Extensions.* The judge may, for good cause shown, extend any time period under these rules except those relating to new trial and appeal.

500.6. Judge to Develop the Case. In order to develop the facts of the case, a judge may question a witness or party and may summon any person or party to appear as a witness when the judge considers it necessary to ensure a correct judgment and a speedy disposition.

500.7. Exclusion of Witnesses. The court must, on a party's request, or may, on its own initiative, order witnesses excluded so that they cannot hear the testimony of other witnesses. This rule does not authorize the exclusion of:

(a) a party who is a natural person or the spouse of such natural person;

(b) an officer or employee designated as a representative of a party who is not a natural person; or

(c) a person whose presence is shown by a party to be essential to the presentation of the party's case.

500.8. Subpoenas.

(a) *Use.* A subpoena may be used by a party or the judge to command a person or entity to attend and give testimony at a hearing or trial. A person may not be required by subpoena to appear in a county that is more than 150 miles from where the person resides or is served.

(b) *Who Can Issue.* A subpoena may be issued by the clerk of the justice court or an attorney authorized to practice in the State of Texas, as an officer of the court.

(c) *Form.* Every subpoena must be issued in the name of the "State of Texas" and must:

(1) state the style of the suit and its case number;

(2) state the court in which the suit is pending;

(3) state the date on which the subpoena is issued;

(4) identify the person to whom the subpoena is directed;

(5) state the date, time, place, and nature of the action required by the person to whom the subpoena is directed;

(6) identify the party at whose instance the subpoena is issued, and the party's attorney of record, if any;

(7) state that "Failure by any person without adequate excuse to obey a subpoena served upon that person may be deemed a contempt of court from which the subpoena is issued and may be punished by fine or confinement, or both"; and

(8) be signed by the person issuing the subpoena.

(d) *Service: Where, By Whom, How.* A subpoena may be served at any place within the State of Texas by any sheriff or constable of the State of Texas, or by any person who is not a party and is 18 years of age or older. A subpoena must be served by delivering a copy to the witness and tendering to that person any fees required by law. If the witness is a party and is represented by an attorney of record in the proceeding, the subpoena may be served on the witness's attorney of record. Proof of service must be made by filing either:

(1) the witness's signed written memorandum attached to the subpoena showing that the witness accepted the subpoena; or

(2) a statement by the person who made the service stating the date, time, and manner of service, and the name of the person served.

(e) *Compliance Required.* A person commanded by subpoena to appear and give testimony must remain at the hearing or trial from day to day until discharged by the court or by the party summoning the witness. If a subpoena commanding testimony is directed to a corporation, partnership, association, governmental agency, or other organization, and the matters on which examination is requested are described with reasonable particularity, the organization must designate one or more persons to testify on its behalf as to matters known or reasonably available to the organization.

(f) *Objection.* A person commanded to attend and give testimony at a hearing or trial may object or move for a protective order before the court at or before the time and place specified for compliance. A party causing a subpoena to issue must take reasonable steps to avoid imposing undue burden or expense on the person served. In ruling on objections or motions for protection, the court must provide a person served with a subpoena an adequate time for compliance and protection from undue burden or expense. The court may impose reasonable conditions on compliance with a subpoena, including compensating the witness for undue hardship.

(g) *Enforcement.* Failure by any person without adequate excuse to obey a subpoena served upon that person may be deemed a contempt of the court from which the subpoena is issued or of a district court in the county in which the subpoena is served, and may be punished by fine or confinement, or both. A fine may not be imposed, nor a person served with a subpoena attached, for failure to comply with a subpoena without proof of service and proof

by affidavit of the party requesting the subpoena or the party's attorney of record that all fees due the witness by law were paid or tendered.

500.9. Discovery.

(a) ***Pretrial Discovery.*** Pretrial discovery is limited to that which the judge considers reasonable and necessary. Any requests for pretrial discovery must be presented to the court for approval by written motion. The motion must be served on the responding party. Unless a hearing is requested, the judge may rule on the motion without a hearing. The discovery request must not be served on the responding party unless the judge issues a signed order approving the request. Failure to comply with a discovery order can result in sanctions, including dismissal of the case or an order to pay the other party's discovery expenses.

(b) ***Post-judgment Discovery.*** Post-judgment discovery is not required to be filed with the court. The party requesting discovery must give the responding party at least 30 days to respond to a post-judgment discovery request. The responding party may file a written objection with the court within 30 days of receiving the request. If an objection is filed, the judge must hold a hearing to determine if the request is valid. If the objection is denied, the judge must order the party to respond to the request. If the objection is upheld, the judge may reform the request or dismiss it entirely.

Adopted by order of April 15, 2013, eff. Aug. 31, 2013. Amended by order of May 26, 2020, eff. Sept. 1, 2020.

See also **O'Connor's Texas Rules**, "Justice courts," ch. 2-G, §5.

TRCP 501. CITATION AND SERVICE

501.1. Citation.

(a) ***Issuance.*** When a petition is filed with a justice court to initiate a suit, the clerk must promptly issue a citation and deliver the citation as directed by the plaintiff. The plaintiff is responsible for obtaining service on the defendant of the citation and a copy of the petition with any documents filed with the petition. Upon request, separate or additional citations must be issued by the clerk. The clerk must retain a copy of the citation in the court's file.

(b) ***Form.*** The citation must:

(1) be styled "The State of Texas";

(2) be signed by the clerk under seal of court or by the judge;

(3) contain the name, location, and address of the court;

(4) show the date of filing of the petition;

(5) show the date of issuance of the citation;

(6) show the file number and names of parties;

(7) be directed to the defendant;

(8) show the name and address of attorney for plaintiff, or if the plaintiff does not have an attorney, the address of plaintiff; and

(9) notify defendant that if the defendant fails to file an answer, judgment by default may be rendered for the relief demanded in the petition.

(c) ***Notice.*** The citation must include the following notice to the defendant in boldface type: "You have been sued. You may employ an attorney to help you in defending against this lawsuit. But you are not required to employ an attorney. You or your attorney must file an answer with the court. Your answer is due by the end of the 14th day after the day you were served with these papers. If the 14th day is a Saturday, Sunday, or legal holiday, your answer is due by the end of the first day following the 14th day that is not a Saturday, Sunday, or legal holiday. Do not ignore these papers. If you do not file an answer by the due date, a default judgment may be taken against you. For further information, consult Part V of the Texas Rules of Civil Procedure, which is available online and also at the court listed on this citation."

(d) ***Copies.*** The plaintiff must provide enough copies to be served on each defendant. If the plaintiff fails to do so, the clerk may make copies and charge the plaintiff the allowable copying cost.

501.2. Service of Citation.

(a) ***Who May Serve.*** No person who is a party to or interested in the outcome of the suit may serve citation in that suit, and, unless otherwise authorized by written court order, only a sheriff or constable may serve a citation in an eviction case, a writ that requires the actual taking of possession of a person, property or thing, or process requiring that an enforcement action be physically enforced by the person delivering the process. Other citations may be served by:

(1) a sheriff or constable;

(2) a process server certified under order of the Supreme Court;

(3) the clerk of the court, if the citation is served by registered or certified mail; or

(4) a person authorized by court order who is 18 years of age or older.

(b) ***Method of Service.*** Citation must be served by:

(1) delivering a copy of the citation with a copy of the petition attached to the defendant in person, after endorsing the date of delivery on the citation; or

(2) mailing a copy of the citation with a copy of the petition attached to the defendant by registered or certified mail, restricted delivery, with return receipt or electronic return receipt requested.

(c) ***Service Fees.*** A plaintiff must pay all fees for service unless the plaintiff has filed a Statement of Inability to Afford Payment of Court Costs with the court. If the plaintiff has filed a Statement, the plaintiff must arrange for the citation to be served by a sheriff, constable, or court clerk.

(d) ***Service on Sunday.*** A citation cannot be served on a Sunday except in attachment, garnishment, sequestration, or distress proceedings.

(e) ***Alternative Service of Citation.*** If the methods under (b) are insufficient to serve the defendant, the plaintiff, or the constable, sheriff, process server certified under order of the Supreme Court, or other person authorized to serve process, may make a request for alternative service. This request must include a sworn statement describing the methods attempted under (b) and stating the defendant's usual place of business or residence, or other place where the defendant can probably be found. The court may authorize the following types of alternative service:

(1) mailing a copy of the citation with a copy of the petition attached by first class mail to the defendant at a specified address, and also leaving a copy of the citation with petition attached at the defendant's residence or other place where the defendant can probably be found with any person found there who is at least 16 years of age; or

(2) mailing a copy of the citation with a copy of the petition attached by first class mail to the defendant at a specified address, and also serving by any other method that the court finds is reasonably likely to provide the defendant with notice of the suit.

(f) ***Service by Publication.*** In the event that service of citation by publication is necessary, the process is governed by the rules in county and district court.

501.3. Duties of Officer or Person Receiving Citation; Return of Service.

(a) ***Endorsement; Execution; Return.*** The officer or authorized person to whom process is delivered must:

(1) endorse on the process the date and hour on which he or she received it;

(2) execute and return the same without delay; and

(3) complete a return of service, which may, but need not, be endorsed on or attached to the citation.

(b) ***Contents of Return.*** The return, together with any document to which it is attached, must include the following information:

(1) the case number and case name;

(2) the court in which the case is filed;

(3) a description of what was served;

(4) the date and time the process was received for service;

(5) the person or entity served;

(6) the address served;

(7) the date of service or attempted service;

(8) the manner of delivery of service or attempted service;

(9) the name of the person who served or attempted service;

(10) if the person named in (9) is a process server certified under Supreme Court Order, his or her identification number and the expiration date of his or her certification; and

(11) any other information required by rule or law.

(c) ***Citation by Mail.*** When the citation is served by registered or certified mail as authorized by Rule 501.2(b)(2), the return by the officer or authorized person must also contain the receipt with the addressee's signature.

(d) ***Failure to Serve.*** When the officer or authorized person has not served the citation, the return must show the diligence used by the officer or authorized person to execute the same and the cause of failure to execute it, and where the defendant is to be found, if ascertainable.

(e) ***Signature.*** The officer or authorized person who serves or attempts to serve a citation must sign the return. If the return is signed by a person other than a sheriff, constable, or clerk of the court, the return must either be verified or be signed under penalty of perjury. A return signed under penalty of perjury must contain the statement below in substantially the following form:

"My name is ______ (First) ______ (Middle) ______ (Last), my date of birth is ______ (Month) ____ (Day), ____ (Year), and my address is ______ (Street), ______ (City), ______ (State) ______ (Zip Code), ______ (Country). I declare under penalty of perjury that the foregoing is true and correct.

Executed in ______ County, State of ______, on the ______ day of ______ (Month), ______ (Year).

____
Declarant"

(f) ***Alternative Service.*** Where citation is executed by an alternative method as authorized by 501.2(e), proof of service must be made in the manner ordered by the court.

(g) ***Filing Return.*** The return and any document to which it is attached must be filed with the court and may be filed electronically or by fax, if those methods of filing are available.

(h) ***Prerequisite for Default Judgment.*** No default judgment may be granted in any case until proof of service as provided by this rule, or as ordered by the court in the event citation is executed by an alternative method under 501.2(e), has been on file with the clerk of the court 3 days, exclusive of the day of filing and the day of judgment.

501.4. Service of Papers Other Than Citation.

(a) ***Method of Service.*** Other than a citation or oral motions during trial or when all parties are present, every notice required by these rules, and every pleading, plea, motion, application to the court for an order, or other form of request, must be served on all other parties in one of the following ways:

(1) *In person.* A copy may be delivered to the party to be served, or the party's duly authorized agent or attorney of record, in person or by agent.

(2) *Mail or courier.* A copy may be sent by courier-receipted delivery or by certified or registered mail, to the party's last known address. Service by certified or registered mail is complete when the document is properly addressed and deposited in the United States mail, postage prepaid.

(3) *Fax.* A copy may be faxed to the recipient's current fax number. Service by fax after 5:00 p.m. local time of the recipient will be deemed to have been served on the following day.

(4) *Email.* A copy may be sent to an email address expressly provided by the receiving party, if the party has consented to email service in writing. Service by email after 5:00 p.m. local time of the recipient will be deemed to have been served on the following day.

(5) *Other.* A copy may be delivered in any other manner directed by the court.

(b) ***Timing.*** If a document is served by mail, 3 days will be added to the length of time a party has to respond to the document. Notice of any hearing requested by a party must be served on all other parties not less than 3 days before the time specified for the hearing.

(c) ***Who May Serve.*** Documents other than a citation may be served by a party to the suit, an attorney of record, a sheriff or constable, or by any other person competent to testify.

(d) ***Certificate of Service.*** The party or the party's attorney of record must include in writing on all documents filed a signed statement describing the manner in which the document was served on the other party or parties and the date of service. A certificate by a party or the party's attorney of record, or the return of the officer, or the sworn statement of any other person showing service of a notice is proof of service.

(e) ***Failure to Serve.*** A party may offer evidence or testimony that a notice or document was not received, or, if service was by mail, that it was not received within 3 days from the date of mailing, and upon so finding, the court may extend the time for taking the action required of the party or grant other relief as it deems just.

Adopted by order of April 15, 2013, eff. Aug. 31, 2013.

Source: New rule.

TRCP 502. INSTITUTION OF SUIT

502.1. Pleadings and Motions must be Written, Signed, and Filed. Except for oral motions made during trial or when all parties are present, every pleading, plea, motion, application to the court for an order, or other form of request must be written and signed by the party or its attorney and must be filed with the court. A document may be filed with the court by personal or commercial delivery, by mail, or electronically, if the court allows electronic filing. Electronic filing is governed by Rule 21.

502.2. Petition.

(a) ***Contents.*** To initiate a lawsuit, a petition must be filed with the court. A petition must contain:

(1) the name of the plaintiff;

(2) the name, address, telephone number, and fax number, if any, of the plaintiffs attorney, if applicable, or the address, telephone number, and fax number, if any, of the plaintiff;

(3) the name, address, and telephone number, if known, of the defendant;

(4) the amount of money, if any, the plaintiff seeks;

(5) a description and claimed value of any personal property the plaintiff seeks;

(6) a description of any other relief requested;

(7) the basis for the plaintiff's claim against the defendant; and

(8) if the plaintiff consents to email service of the

answer and any other motions or pleadings, a statement consenting to email service and email contact information.

(b) [Repealed effective February 26, 2019].

502.3. Fees; Inability to Afford Fees.

(a) ***Fees and Statement of Inability to Afford Payment of Court Costs.*** On filing the petition, the plaintiff must pay the appropriate filing fee and service fees, if any, with the court. A plaintiff who is unable to afford to pay the fees must file a Statement of Inability to Afford Payment of Court Costs. The Statement must either be sworn to before a notary or made under penalty of perjury. Upon filing the Statement, the clerk must docket the action, issue citation, and provide any other customary services.

(b) ***Supreme Court Form; Contents of Statement.*** The plaintiff must use the form Statement approved by the Supreme Court, or the Statement must include the information required by the Court-approved form. The clerk must make the form available to all persons without charge or request.

(c) ***Certificate of Legal-Aid Provider.*** If the party is represented by an attorney who is providing free legal services because of the party's indigence, without contingency, and the attorney is providing services either directly or by referral from a legal-aid provider described in Rule 145(e)(2), the attorney may file a certificate confirming that the provider screened the party for eligibility under the income and asset guidelines established by the provider. A Statement that is accompanied by the certificate of a legal-aid provider may not be contested under (d).

(d) ***Contest.*** Unless a certificate is filed under (c), the defendant may file a contest of the Statement at any time within 7 days after the day the defendant's answer is due. If the Statement attests to receipt of government entitlement based on indigence, the Statement may only be contested with regard to the veracity of the attestation. If contested, the judge must hold a hearing to determine the plaintiff's ability to afford the fees. At the hearing, the burden is on the plaintiff to prove the inability to afford fees. The judge may, regardless of whether the defendant contests the Statement, examine the Statement and conduct a hearing to determine the plaintiff's ability to afford fees. If the judge determines that the plaintiff is able to afford the fees, the judge must enter a written order listing the reasons for the determination, and the plaintiff must pay the fees in the time specified in the order or the case will be dismissed without prejudice.

502.4. Venue—Where a Lawsuit May Be Brought.

(a) ***Applicable Law.*** Laws specifying the venue—the county and precinct where a lawsuit may be brought—are found in Chapter 15, Subchapter E of the Texas Civil Practice and Remedies Code, which is available online and for examination during the court's business hours.

(b) ***General Rule.*** Generally, a defendant in a small claims case as described in Rule 500.3(a) or a debt claim case as described in Rule 500.3(b) is entitled to be sued in one of the following venues:

(1) the county and precinct where the defendant resides;

(2) the county and precinct where the incident, or the majority of incidents, that gave rise to the claim occurred;

(3) the county and precinct where the contract or agreement, if any, that gave rise to the claim was to be performed; or

(4) the county and precinct where the property is located, in a suit to recover personal property.

(c) ***Non-Resident Defendant; Defendant's Residence Unknown.*** If the defendant is a non-resident of Texas, or if defendant's residence is unknown, the plaintiff may file the suit in the county and precinct where the plaintiff resides.

(d) ***Motion to Transfer Venue.*** If a plaintiff files suit in an improper venue, a defendant may challenge the venue selected by filing a motion to transfer venue. The motion must be filed before trial, no later than 21 days after the day the defendant's answer is filed, and must contain a sworn statement that the venue chosen by the plaintiff is improper and a specific county and precinct of proper venue to which transfer is sought. If the defendant fails to name a county and precinct, the court must instruct the defendant to do so and allow the defendant 7 days to cure the defect. If the defendant fails to correct the defect, the motion will be denied, and the case will proceed in the county and precinct where it was originally filed.

(1) *Procedure.*

(A) Judge to Set Hearing. If a defendant files a motion to transfer venue, the judge must set a hearing on the motion.

(B) Response. A plaintiff may file a response to a defendant's motion to transfer venue.

(C) Hearing. The parties may present evidence at the hearing. A witness may testify at a hearing, either in person or, with permission of the court, by means of telephone or an electronic communication system.

(D) Judge's Decision. If the motion is granted, the judge must sign an order designating the court to which

the case will be transferred. If the motion is denied, the case will be heard in the court in which the plaintiff initially filed suit.

(E) Review. Motions for rehearing and interlocutory appeals of the judge's ruling on venue are not permitted.

(F) Time for Trial of the Case. No trial may be held until at least the 14th day after the judge's ruling on the motion to transfer venue.

(G) Order. An order granting a motion to transfer venue must state the reason for the transfer and the name of the court to which the transfer is made. When such an order of transfer is made, the judge who issued the order must immediately make out a true and correct transcript of all the entries made on the docket in the case, certify the transcript, and send the transcript, with a certified copy of the bill of costs and the original papers in the case, to the court in the precinct to which the case has been transferred. The court receiving the case must then notify the plaintiff that the case has been received and, if the case is transferred to a different county, that the plaintiff has 14 days after receiving the notice to pay the filing fee in the new court, or file a Statement of Inability to Afford Payment of Court Costs. The plaintiff is not entitled to a refund of any fees already paid. Failure to pay the fee or file a Statement will result in dismissal of the case without prejudice.

(e) ***Fair Trial Venue Change.*** If a party believes it cannot get a fair trial in a specific precinct or before a specific judge, the party may file a sworn motion stating such, supported by the sworn statements of two other credible persons, and specifying if the party is requesting a change of location or a change of judge. Except for good cause shown, this motion must be filed no less than 7 days before trial. If the party seeks a change of judge, the judge must exchange benches with another qualified justice of the peace, or if no judge is available to exchange benches, the county judge must appoint a visiting judge to hear the case. If the party seeks a change in location, the case must be transferred to the nearest justice court in the county that is not subject to the same or some other disqualification. If there is only one justice of the peace precinct in the county, then the judge must exchange benches with another qualified justice of the peace, or if no judge is available to exchange benches, the county judge must appoint a visiting judge to hear the case. In cases where exclusive jurisdiction is within a specific precinct, as in eviction cases, the only remedy available is a change of judge. A party may apply for relief under this rule only one time in any given lawsuit.

(f) ***Transfer of Venue by Consent.*** On the written consent of all parties or their attorneys, filed with the court, venue must be transferred to the court of any other justice of the peace of the county, or any other county.

502.5. Answer.

(a) ***Requirements.*** A defendant must file with the court a written answer to a lawsuit as directed by the citation and must also serve a copy of the answer on the plaintiff. The answer must contain:

(1) the name of the defendant;

(2) the name, address, telephone number, and fax number, if any, of the defendant's attorney, if applicable, or the address, telephone number, and fax number, if any, of the defendant; and

(3) if the defendant consents to email service, a statement consenting to email service and email contact information.

(b) ***General Denial.*** An answer that denies all of the plaintiff's allegations without specifying the reasons is sufficient to constitute an answer or appearance and does not bar the defendant from raising any defense at trial.

(c) ***Answer Docketed.*** The defendant's appearance must be noted on the court's docket.

(d) ***Due Date.*** Unless the defendant is served by publication, the defendant's answer is due by the end of the 14th day after the day the defendant was served with the citation and petition, but

(1) if the 14th day is a Saturday, Sunday, or legal holiday, the answer is due on the next day that is not a Saturday, Sunday, or legal holiday; and

(2) if the 14th day falls on a day during which the court is closed before 5:00 p.m., the answer is due on the court's next business day.

(e) ***Due Date When Defendant Served by Publication.*** If a defendant is served by publication, the defendant's answer is due by the end of the 42nd day after the day the citation was issued, but

(1) if the 42nd day is a Saturday, Sunday, or legal holiday, the answer is due on the next day that is not a Saturday, Sunday, or legal holiday; and

(2) if the 42nd day falls on a day during which the court is closed before 5:00 p.m., the answer is due on the court's next business day.

502.6. Counterclaim; Cross-Claim; Third Party Claim.

(a) ***Counterclaim.*** A defendant may file a petition stating as a counterclaim any claim against a plaintiff that is within the jurisdiction of the justice court, whether or not

related to the claims in the plaintiff's petition. The defendant must file a counterclaim petition as provided in Rule 502.2, and must pay a filing fee or provide a Statement of Inability to Afford Payment of Court Costs. The court need not generate a citation for a counterclaim and no answer to the counterclaim need be filed. The defendant must serve a copy of the counterclaim as provided by Rule 501.4.

(b) ***Cross-Claim.*** A plaintiff seeking relief against another plaintiff, or a defendant seeking relief against another defendant may file a cross-claim. The filing party must file a cross-claim petition as provided in Rule 502.2, and must pay a filing fee or provide a Statement of Inability to Afford Payment of Court Costs. A citation must be issued and served as provided by Rule 501.2 on any party that has not yet filed a petition or an answer, as appropriate. If the party filed against has filed a petition or an answer, the filing party must serve the cross-claim as provided by Rule 501.4.

(c) ***Third Party Claim.*** A defendant seeking to bring another party into a lawsuit who may be liable for all or part of the plaintiff's claim against the defendant may file a petition as provided in Rule 502.2, and must pay a filing fee or provide a Statement of Inability to Afford Payment of Court Costs. A citation must be issued and served as provided by Rule 501.2.

502.7. Amending and Clarifying Pleadings.

(a) ***Amending Pleadings.*** A party may withdraw something from or add something to a pleading, as long as the amended pleading is filed and served as provided by Rule 501.4 not less than 7 days before trial. The court may allow a pleading to be amended less than 7 days before trial if the amendment will not operate as a surprise to the opposing party.

(b) ***Insufficient Pleadings.*** A party may file a motion with the court asking that another party be required to clarify a pleading. The court must determine if the pleading is sufficient to place all parties on notice of the issues in the lawsuit, and may hold a hearing to make that determination. If the court determines a pleading is insufficient, the court must order the party to amend the pleading and set a date by which the party must amend. If a party fails to comply with the court's order, the pleading may be stricken.

Adopted by order of April 15, 2013, eff. Aug. 31, 2013. Amended by order of February 26, 2019, eff. February 26, 2019.

Source: New rule.

Editor's Note: In 2020, the Supreme Court preliminarily approved amendments to TRCP 502.3. *See* Tex.Sup.Ct. Order, Misc. Docket No. 20-9154 (Dec. 23, 2020). These amendments are subject to change based on public comments submitted by April 2, 2021. The Court will issue a final order approving the amendments at least 60 days after their publication in the February edition of the *Texas Bar Journal*. To view the orders related to these amendments, visit the Court's website at txcourts.gov/supreme.

Editor's Note: Although there is a TRCP 502.4(d)(1), there is no TRCP 502.4(d)(2); the original rule includes only (d)(1).

ANNOTATIONS

Merritt v. Davis, 331 S.W.3d 857, 861 (Tex.App.—Dallas 2011, pet. denied). TRCP "18a does not apply to justice courts. . . . The justice-court rules include their own specific and simplified recusal provision. . . . We conclude that the drafters of the rules intended [TRCP 528, now 502.4(e),] to be the sole recusal mechanism in justice court."

Crowder v. Franks, 870 S.W.2d 568, 571-72 (Tex.App.—Houston [1st Dist.] 1993, no writ). "Rule 528 [now 502.4(e)] incorporates in a single procedure the legislature's decision to give a civil litigant in a justice of the peace court an absolute right to the transfer of a case to avoid the alleged prejudice of a judge or potential jury. . . . The affidavits required are sufficient even though they may be only conclusionary, albeit sworn, allegations of impartiality and residency. There is no provision in the rule for the allegations to be factually contested, nor for an eventual fact-finding made by the justice of the peace as to their accuracy."

TRCP 503. DEFAULT JUDGMENT; PRE-TRIAL MATTERS; TRIAL

503.1. If Defendant Fails to Answer.

(a) ***Default Judgment.*** If the defendant fails to file an answer by the date stated in Rule 502.5, the judge must ensure that service was proper, and may hold a hearing for this purpose. If it is determined that service was proper, the judge must render a default judgment in the following manner:

(1) *Claim Based on Written Document.* If the claim is based on a written document signed by the defendant, and a copy of the document has been filed with the court and served on the defendant, along with a sworn statement from the plaintiff that this is a true and accurate copy of the document and the relief sought is owed, and all payments, offsets or credits due to the defendant have been accounted for, the judge must render judgment for the plaintiff in the requested amount, without any necessity for a hearing. The plaintiff's attorney may also submit affidavits supporting an award of attorney fees to which the plaintiff is entitled, if any.

(2) *Other Cases.* Except as provided in (1), a

plaintiff who seeks a default judgment against a defendant must request a hearing, orally or in writing. The plaintiff must appear at the hearing and provide evidence of its damages. If the plaintiff proves its damages, the judge must render judgment for the plaintiff in the amount proven. If the plaintiff is unable to prove its damages, the judge must render judgment in favor of the defendant. With the permission of the court, a party may appear at a hearing by means of telephone or an electronic communication system.

(b) ***Appearance.*** If a defendant files an answer or otherwise appears in a case before a default judgment is signed by the judge, the judge must not enter a default judgment and the case must be set for trial as described in Rule 503.3.

(c) ***Post-Answer Default.*** If a defendant who has answered fails to appear for trial, the court may proceed to hear evidence on liability and damages and render judgment accordingly.

(d) ***Notice.*** The plaintiff requesting a default judgment must provide to the clerk in writing the last known mailing address of the defendant at or before the time the judgment is signed. When a default judgment is signed, the clerk must immediately mail written notice of the judgment to the defendant at the address provided by the plaintiff, and note the fact of such mailing on the docket. The notice must state the number and style of the case, the court in which the case is pending, the names of the parties in whose favor and against whom the judgment was rendered, and the date the judgment was signed. Failure to comply with the provisions of this rule does not affect the finality of the judgment.

503.2. Summary Disposition.

(a) ***Motion.*** A party may file a sworn motion for summary disposition of all or part of a claim or defense without a trial. The motion must set out all supporting facts. All documents on which the motion relies must be attached. The motion must be granted if it shows that:

(1) there are no genuinely disputed facts that would prevent a judgment in favor of the party;

(2) there is no evidence of one or more essential elements of a defense which the defendant must prove to defeat the plaintiff's claim; or

(3) there is no evidence of one or more essential elements of the plaintiff's claim.

(b) ***Response.*** The party opposing the motion may file a sworn written response to the motion.

(c) ***Hearing.*** The court must not consider a motion for summary disposition until it has been on file for at least 14 days. The judge may consider evidence offered by the parties at the hearing. By agreement of the parties, the judge may decide the motion and response without a hearing.

(d) ***Order.*** The judge may enter judgment as to the entire case or may specify the facts that are established and direct such further proceedings in the case as are just.

503.3. Settings and Notice; Postponing Trial.

(a) ***Settings and Notice.*** After the defendant answers, the case will be set on a trial docket at the discretion of the judge. The court must send a notice of the date, time, and place of this setting to all parties at their address of record no less than 45 days before the setting date, unless the judge determines that an earlier setting is required in the interest of justice. Reasonable notice of all subsequent settings must be sent to all parties at their addresses of record.

(b) ***Postponing Trial.*** A party may file a motion requesting that the trial be postponed. The motion must state why a postponement is necessary. The judge, for good cause, may postpone any trial for a reasonable time.

503.4. Pretrial Conference.

(a) ***Conference Set; Issues.*** If all parties have appeared in a lawsuit, the court, at any party's request or on its own, may set a case for a pretrial conference. Reasonable notice must be sent to all parties at their addresses of record. Appropriate issues for the pretrial conference include:

(1) discovery;

(2) the amendment or clarification of pleadings;

(3) the admission of facts and documents to streamline the trial process;

(4) a limitation on the number of witnesses at trial;

(5) the identification of facts, if any, which are not in dispute between the parties;

(6) mediation or other alternative dispute resolution services;

(7) the possibility of settlement;

(8) trial setting dates that are amenable to the court and all parties;

(9) the appointment of interpreters, if needed;

(10) the application of a Rule of Civil Procedure not in Part V or a Rule of Evidence; and

(11) any other issue that the court deems appropriate.

(b) ***Eviction Cases.*** The court must not schedule a pretrial conference in an eviction case if it would delay trial.

503.5. Alternative Dispute Resolution.

(a) ***State Policy.*** The policy of this state is to encourage the peaceable resolution of disputes through alternative dispute resolution, including mediation, and the early settlement of pending litigation through voluntary settlement procedures. For that purpose, the judge may order any case to mediation or another appropriate and generally accepted alternative dispute resolution process.

(b) ***Eviction Cases.*** The court must not order mediation or any other alternative dispute resolution process in an eviction case if it would delay trial.

503.6. Trial.

(a) ***Docket Called.*** On the day of the trial setting, the judge must call all of the cases set for trial that day.

(b) ***If Plaintiff Fails to Appear.*** If the plaintiff fails to appear when the case is called for trial, the judge may postpone or dismiss the suit.

(c) ***If Defendant Fails to Appear.*** If the defendant fails to appear when the case is called for trial, the judge may postpone the case, or may proceed to take evidence. If the plaintiff proves its case, judgment must be awarded for the relief proven. If the plaintiff fails to prove its case, judgment must be rendered against the plaintiff.

Adopted by order of April 15, 2013, eff. Aug. 31, 2013.

Source: New rule.

TRCP 504. JURY

504.1. Jury Trial Demanded.

(a) ***Demand.*** Any party is entitled to a trial by jury. A written demand for a jury must be filed no later than 14 days before the date a case is set for trial. If the demand is not timely, the right to a jury is waived unless the late filing is excused by the judge for good cause.

(b) ***Jury Fee.*** Unless otherwise provided by law, a party demanding a jury must pay a fee of $22.00 or must file a Statement of Inability to Afford Payment of Court Costs at or before the time the party files a written request for a jury.

(c) ***Withdrawal of Demand.*** If a party who demands a jury and pays the fee withdraws the demand, the case will remain on the jury docket unless all other parties present agree to try the case without a jury. A party that withdraws its jury demand is not entitled to a refund of the jury fee.

(d) ***No Demand.*** If no party timely demands a jury and pays the fee, the judge will try the case without a jury.

504.2. Empaneling the Jury.

(a) ***Drawing Jury and Oath.*** If no method of electronic draw has been implemented, the judge must write the names of all prospective jurors present on separate slips of paper as nearly alike as may be, place them in a box, mix them well, and then draw the names one by one from the box. The judge must list the names drawn and deliver a copy to each of the parties or their attorneys.

(b) ***Oath.*** After the draw, the judge must swear the panel as follows: "You solemnly swear or affirm that you will give true and correct answers to all questions asked of you concerning your qualifications as a juror."

(c) ***Questioning the Jury.*** The judge, the parties, or their attorneys will be allowed to question jurors as to their ability to serve impartially in the trial but may not ask the jurors how they will rule in the case. The judge will have discretion to allow or disallow specific questions and determine the amount of time each side will have for this process.

(d) ***Challenge for Cause.*** A party may challenge any juror for cause. A challenge for cause is an objection made to a juror alleging some fact, such as a bias or prejudice, that disqualifies the juror from serving in the case or that renders the juror unfit to sit on the jury. The challenge must be made during jury questioning. The party must explain to the judge why the juror should be excluded from the jury. The judge must evaluate the questions and answers given and either grant or deny the challenge. When a challenge for cause has been sustained, the juror must be excused.

(e) ***Challenges Not for Cause.*** After the judge determines any challenges for cause, each party may select up to 3 jurors to excuse for any reason or no reason at all. But no prospective juror may be excused for membership in a constitutionally protected class.

(f) ***The Jury.*** After all challenges, the first 6 prospective jurors remaining on the list constitute the jury to try the case.

(g) ***If Jury Is Incomplete.*** If challenges reduce the number of prospective jurors below 6, the judge may direct the sheriff or constable to summon others and allow them to be questioned and challenged by the parties as before, until at least 6 remain.

(h) ***Jury Sworn.*** When the jury has been selected, the judge must require them to take substantially the following oath: "You solemnly swear or affirm that you will render a true verdict according to the law and the evidence presented."

504.3. Jury Not Charged. The judge must not charge the jury.

504.4. Jury Verdict for Specific Articles. When the suit is for the recovery of specific articles and the jury finds for the plaintiff, the jury must assess the value of each article separately, according to the evidence presented at trial.

Adopted by order of April 15, 2013, eff. Aug. 31, 2013.

Source: New rule.

TRCP 505. JUDGMENT; NEW TRIAL

505.1. Judgment.

(a) ***Judgment Upon Jury Verdict.*** Where a jury has returned a verdict, the judge must announce the verdict in open court, note it in the court's docket, and render judgment accordingly. The judge may render judgment on the verdict or, if the verdict is contrary to the law or the evidence, judgment notwithstanding the verdict.

(b) ***Case Tried by Judge.*** When a case has been tried before the judge without a jury, the judge must announce the decision in open court, note the decision in the court's docket, and render judgment accordingly.

(c) ***Form.*** A judgment must:

(1) clearly state the determination of the rights of the parties in the case;

(2) state who must pay the costs;

(3) be signed by the judge; and

(4) be dated the date of the judge's signature.

(d) ***Costs.*** The judge must award costs allowed by law to the successful party.

(e) ***Judgment for Specific Articles.*** Where the judgment is for the recovery of specific articles, the judgment must order that the plaintiff recover such specific articles, if they can be found, and if not, then their value as assessed by the judge or jury with interest at the prevailing post-judgment interest rate.

505.2. Enforcement of Judgment. Justice court judgments are enforceable in the same method as in county and district court, except as provided by law. When the judgment is for personal property, the court may award a special writ for the seizure and delivery of such property to the plaintiff, and may, in addition to the other relief granted in such cases, enforce its judgment by attachment or fine.

505.3. Motion to Set Aside; Motion to Reinstate; Motion for New Trial.

(a) ***Motion to Reinstate after Dismissal.*** A plaintiff whose case is dismissed may file a motion to reinstate the case no later than 14 days after the dismissal order is signed. The plaintiff must serve the defendant with a copy of the motion no later than the next business day using a method approved under Rule 501.4. The court may reinstate the case for good cause shown.

(b) ***Motion to Set Aside Default.*** A defendant against whom a default judgment is granted may file a motion to set aside the judgment no later than 14 days after the judgment is signed. The defendant must serve the plaintiff with a copy of the motion no later than the next business day using a method approved under Rule 501.4. The court may set aside the judgment and set the case for trial for good cause shown.

(c) ***Motion for New Trial.*** A party may file a motion for a new trial no later than 14 days after the judgment is signed. The party must serve all other parties with a copy of the motion no later than the next business day using a method approved under Rule 501.4. The judge may grant a new trial upon a showing that justice was not done in the trial of the case. Only one new trial may be granted to either party.

(d) ***Motion Not Required.*** Failure to file a motion under this rule does not affect a party's right to appeal the underlying judgment.

(e) ***Motion Denied as a Matter of Law.*** If the judge has not ruled on a motion to set aside, motion to reinstate, or motion for new trial, the motion is automatically denied at 5:00 p.m. on the 21st day after the day the judgment was signed.

Adopted by order of April 15, 2013, eff. Aug. 31, 2013.

Source: New rule.

ANNOTATIONS

Pullin v. Parrish, 306 S.W.2d 241, 242 (Tex.App.—San Antonio 1957, writ ref'd). "A judgment is a prerequisite to an appeal from the justice court. [¶] The appeal must be from the judgment, and a verdict is not a judgment. Judgments, not verdicts, record the final decisions of courts. . . . An appeal from a docketed verdict, but not the judgment, is void. [¶] We do not hold that a judgment is inadequate if it is informal or merely noted on the docket sheet; . . . the record must show that it is a judgment and not a verdict."

TRCP 506. APPEAL

506.1. Appeal.

(a) ***How Taken; Time.*** A party may appeal a judgment by filing a bond, making a cash deposit, or filing a Statement of Inability to Afford Payment of Court Costs with the justice court within 21 days after the judgment is

signed or the motion to reinstate, motion to set aside, or motion for new trial, if any, is denied.

(b) ***Amount of Bond; Sureties; Terms.*** A plaintiff must file a $500 bond. A defendant must file a bond in an amount equal to twice the amount of the judgment. The bond must be supported by a surety or sureties approved by the judge. The bond must be payable to the appellee and must be conditioned on the appellant's prosecution of its appeal to effect and payment of any judgment and all costs rendered against it on appeal.

(c) ***Cash Deposit in Lieu of Bond.*** In lieu of filing a bond, an appellant may deposit with the clerk of the court cash in the amount required of the bond. The deposit must be payable to the appellee and must be conditioned on the appellant's prosecution of its appeal to effect and payment of any judgment and all costs rendered against it on appeal.

(d) ***Statement of Inability to Afford Payment of Court Costs.***

(1) *Filing.* An appellant who cannot furnish a bond or pay a cash deposit in the amount required may instead file a Statement of Inability to Afford Payment of Court Costs. The Statement must be on the form approved by the Supreme Court or include the information required by the Court-approved form and may be the same one that was filed with the petition.

(2) *Contest.* The Statement may be contested as provided in Rule 502.3(d) within 7 days after the opposing party receives notice that the Statement was filed.

(3) *Appeal If Contest Sustained.* If the contest is sustained, the appellant may appeal that decision by filing notice with the justice court within 7 days of that court's written order. The justice court must then forward all related documents to the county court for resolution. The county court must set the matter for hearing within 14 days and hear the contest de novo, as if there had been no previous hearing, and if the appeal is granted, must direct the justice court to transmit to the clerk of the county court the transcript, records, and papers of the case, as provided in these rules.

(4) *If No Appeal or If Appeal Overruled.* If the appellant does not appeal the ruling sustaining the contest, or if the county court denies the appeal, the appellant may, within five days, post an appeal bond or make a cash deposit in compliance with this rule.

(e) ***Notice to Other Parties Required.*** If a Statement of Inability to Afford Payment of Court Costs is filed, the court must provide notice to all other parties that the Statement was filed no later than the next business day. Within 7 days of filing a bond or making a cash deposit, an appellant must serve written notice of the appeal on all other parties using a method approved under Rule 501.4.

(f) ***No Default on Appeal Without Compliance With Rule.*** The county court to which an appeal is taken must not render default judgment against any party without first determining that the appellant has fully complied with this rule.

(g) ***No Dismissal of Appeal Without Opportunity for Correction.*** An appeal must not be dismissed for defects or irregularities in procedure, either of form or substance, without allowing the appellant, after 7 days' notice from the court, the opportunity to correct such defect.

(h) ***Appeal Perfected.*** An appeal is perfected when a bond, cash deposit, or Statement of Inability to Afford Payment of Court Costs is filed in accordance with this rule.

(i) ***Costs.*** The appellant must pay the costs on appeal to a county court in accordance with Rule 143a.

506.2. Record on Appeal. When an appeal has been perfected from the justice court, the judge must immediately send to the clerk of the county court a certified copy of all docket entries, a certified copy of the bill of costs, and the original papers in the case.

506.3. Trial De Novo. The case must be tried de novo in the county court. A trial de novo is a new trial in which the entire case is presented as if there had been no previous trial.

506.4. Writ of Certiorari.

(a) ***Application.*** Except in eviction cases, after final judgment in a case tried in justice court, a party may apply to the county court for a writ of certiorari.

(b) ***Grounds.*** An application must be granted only if it contains a sworn statement setting forth facts showing that either:

(1) the justice court did not have jurisdiction; or

(2) the final determination of the suit worked an injustice to the applicant that was not caused by the applicant's own inexcusable neglect.

(c) ***Bond, Cash Deposit, or Sworn Statement of Indigency to Pay Required.*** If the application is granted, a writ of certiorari must not issue until the applicant has filed a bond, made a cash deposit, or filed a Statement of Inability to Afford Payment of Court Costs that complies with Rule 145.

(d) ***Time for Filing.*** An application for writ of certiorari must be filed within 90 days after the date the final judgment is signed.

(e) *Contents of Writ.* The writ of certiorari must command the justice court to immediately make and certify a copy of the entries in the case on the docket, and immediately transmit the transcript of the proceedings in the justice court, together with the original papers and a bill of costs, to the proper court.

(f) *Clerk to Issue Writ and Citation.* When the application is granted and the bond, cash deposit, or Statement of Inability to Afford Payment of Court Costs has been filed, the clerk must issue a writ of certiorari to the justice court and citation to the adverse party.

(g) *Stay of Proceedings.* When the writ of certiorari is served on the justice court, the court must stay further proceedings on the judgment and comply with the writ.

(h) *Cause Docketed.* The action must be docketed in the name of the original plaintiff, as plaintiff, and of the original defendant, as defendant.

(i) *Motion to Dismiss.* Within 30 days after the service of citation on the writ of certiorari, the adverse party may move to dismiss the certiorari for want of sufficient cause appearing in the affidavit, or for want of sufficient bond. If the certiorari is dismissed, the judgment must direct the justice court to proceed with the execution of the judgment below.

(j) *Amendment of Bond or Oath.* The affidavit or bond may be amended at the discretion of the court in which it is filed.

(k) *Trial De Novo.* The case must be tried de novo in the county court and judgment must be rendered as in cases appealed from justice courts. A trial de novo is a new trial in which the entire case is presented as if there had been no previous trial.

Adopted by order of April 15, 2013, eff. Aug. 31, 2013. Amended by order of Aug. 31, 2016, eff. Sept. 1, 2016.

Source: New rule.

Editor's Note: In 2020, the Supreme Court preliminarily approved amendments to TRCP 506.4. *See* Tex.Sup.Ct. Order, Misc. Docket No. 20-9154 (Dec. 23, 2020). These amendments are subject to change based on public comments submitted by April 2, 2021. The Court will issue a final order approving the amendments at least 60 days after their publication in the February edition of the *Texas Bar Journal*. To view the orders related to these amendments, visit the Court's website at txcourts.gov/supreme.

ANNOTATIONS

King v. Oak Ridge Apts., No. 04-16-00667-CV, 2017 WL 2562743 (Tex.App.—San Antonio 2017, no pet.) (memo op.; 6-14-17). " 'It is not necessary in every case to set out the entire testimony on the trial in the justice court, in order to obtain a writ of certiorari.' 'But the petition must either state all the evidence, or show that a material and vital error occurred in the proceedings, or that the applicant has not been able to avail himself of a legitimate prosecution or defense, by no fault or neglect of his own.' 'One or all of these causes must be set forth, not by a general allegation of the wrong, but with sufficient detail to show a prima facie case entitling the petitioner to another hearing.' "

Rowe v. Watkins, 340 S.W.3d 860, 863 (Tex.App.—El Paso 2011, no pet.). "When the appeal bond contains defects or irregularities, either of form or substance, the case should not be dismissed without first allowing the appealing party . . ., after notice of the defect, to correct or amend the defective appeal. Although the rules do not prescribe a specific type of notice, we have held that the notice must, in the very least, conform to due process which is met if the notice affords the party a fair opportunity to appear and defend her interests. As compliance with the appellate requirements of [TRCP] 571 [now 506.1] is jurisdictional, . . . if the appealing party fails to meet any one of the rule's prerequisites, and also fails to correct the defect within [the] notice [period], the appellate court, i.e., the county court, lacks jurisdiction to hear the appeal and must dismiss the same."

TRCP 507. ADMINISTRATIVE RULES FOR JUDGES AND COURT PERSONNEL

507.1. Plenary Power. A justice court loses plenary power over a case when an appeal is perfected or if no appeal is perfected, 21 days after the later of the date judgment is signed or the date a motion to set aside, motion to reinstate, or motion for new trial, if any, is denied.

507.2. Forms. The court may provide forms to enable a party to file documents that comply with these rules. No party may be forced to use the court's forms.

507.3. Docket and Other Records.

(a) *Docket.* Each judge must keep a civil docket in a permanent record containing the following information:

(1) the title of all suits commenced before the court;

(2) the date when the first process was issued against the defendant, when returnable, and the nature of that process;

(3) the date when the parties, or either of them, appeared before the court, either with or without a citation;

(4) a description of the petition and any documents filed with the petition;

(5) every adjournment, stating at whose request and to what time;

(6) the date of the trial, stating whether the same was by a jury or by the judge;

(7) the verdict of the jury, if any;

(8) the judgment signed by the judge and the date the judgment was signed;

(9) all applications for setting aside judgments or granting new trials and the orders of the judge thereon, with the date;

(10) the date of issuing execution, to whom directed and delivered, and the amount of debt, damages and costs and, when any execution is returned, the date of the return and the manner in which it was executed; and

(11) all stays and appeals that may be taken, and the date when taken, the amount of the bond and the names of the sureties.

(b) ***Other Records.*** The judge must also keep copies of all documents filed; other dockets, books, and records as may be required by law or these rules; and a fee book in which all costs accruing in every suit commenced before the court are taxed.

(c) ***Form of Records.*** All records required to be kept under this rule may be maintained electronically.

507.4. Issuance of Writs. Every writ from the justice courts must be in writing and be issued and signed by the judge officially. The style thereof must be "The State of Texas." It must, except where otherwise specially provided by law or these rules, be directed to the person or party upon whom it is to be served, be made returnable to the court, and note the date of its issuance.

Adopted by order of April 15, 2013, eff. Aug. 31, 2013.

Source: New rule.

TRCP 508. DEBT CLAIM CASES

508.1. Application. Rule 508 applies to a claim for the recovery of a debt brought by an assignee of a claim, a financial institution, a debt collector or collection agency, or a person or entity primarily engaged in the business of lending money at interest.

508.2. Petition.

(a) ***Contents.*** In addition to the information required by Rule 502.2, a petition filed in a lawsuit governed by this rule must contain the following information:

(1) *Credit Accounts.* In a claim based upon a credit card, revolving credit, or open account, the petition must state:

(A) the account name or credit card name;

(B) the account number (which may be masked);

(C) the date of issue or origination of the account, if known;

(D) the date of charge-off or breach of the account, if known;

(E) the amount owed as of a date certain; and

(F) whether the plaintiff seeks ongoing interest.

(2) *Personal and Business Loans.* In a claim based upon a promissory note or other promise to pay a specific amount as of a date certain, the petition must state:

(A) the date and amount of the original loan;

(B) whether the repayment of the debt was accelerated, if known;

(C) the date final payment was due;

(D) the amount due as of the final payment date;

(E) the amount owed as of a date certain; and

(F) whether plaintiff seeks ongoing interest.

(3) *Ongoing Interest.* If a plaintiff seeks ongoing interest, the petition must state:

(A) the effective interest rate claimed;

(B) whether the interest rate is based upon contract or statute; and

(C) the dollar amount of interest claimed as of a date certain.

(4) *Assigned Debt.* If the debt that is the subject of the claim has been assigned or transferred, the petition must state:

(A) that the debt claim has been transferred or assigned;

(B) the date of the transfer or assignment;

(C) the name of any prior holders of the debt; and

(D) the name or a description of the original creditor.

508.3. Default Judgment.

(a) ***Generally.*** If the defendant does not file an answer to a claim by the answer date or otherwise appear in the case, the judge must promptly render a default judgment upon the plaintiff's proof of the amount of damages.

(b) ***Proof of the Amount of Damages.***

(1) *Evidence Must Be Served or Submitted.* Evidence of plaintiff's damages must either be attached to the petition and served on the defendant or submitted to the court after defendant's failure to answer by the answer date.

(2) *Form of Evidence.* Evidence of plaintiff's dam-

ages may be offered in a sworn statement or in live testimony. The evidence offered may include documentary evidence.

(3) *Establishment of the Amount of Damages.* The amount of damages is established by evidence:

(A) that the account or loan was issued to the defendant and the defendant is obligated to pay it;

(B) that the account was closed or the defendant breached the terms of the account or loan agreement;

(C) of the amount due on the account or loan as of a date certain after all payment credits and offsets have been applied; and

(D) that the plaintiff owns the account or loan and, if applicable, how the plaintiff acquired the account or loan.

(4) *Documentary Evidence Offered By Sworn Statement.* Documentary evidence may be considered if it is attached to a sworn statement made by the plaintiff or its representative, a prior holder of the debt or its representative, or the original creditor or its representative, that attests to the following:

(A) the documents were kept in the regular course of business;

(B) it was the regular course of business for an employee or representative with knowledge of the act recorded to make the record or to transmit information to be included in such record;

(C) the documents were created at or near the time or reasonably soon thereafter; and

(D) the documents attached are the original or exact duplicates of the original.

(5) *Consideration of Sworn Statement.* A judge is not required to accept a sworn statement if the source of information or the method or circumstances of preparation indicate lack of trustworthiness. But a judge may not reject a sworn statement only because it is not made by the original creditor or because the documents attested to were created by a third party and subsequently incorporated into and relied upon by the business of the plaintiff.

(c) *Hearing.* The judge may enter a default judgment without a hearing if the plaintiff submits sufficient written evidence of its damages and should do so to avoid undue expense and delay. Otherwise, the plaintiff may request a default judgment hearing at which the plaintiff must appear, in person or by telephonic or electronic means, and prove its damages. If the plaintiff proves its damages, the judge must render judgment for the plaintiff in the amount proven. If the plaintiff is unable to prove its damages, the judge must render judgment in favor of the defendant.

(d) *Appearance.* If the defendant files an answer or otherwise appears in a case before a default judgment is signed by the judge, the judge must not render a default judgment and must set the case for trial.

(e) *Post-Answer Default.* If a defendant who has answered fails to appear for trial, the court may proceed to hear evidence on liability and damages and render judgment accordingly.

Adopted by order of April 15, 2013, eff. Aug. 31, 2013.

Source: New rule.

Editor's Note: Although there is a TRCP 508.2(a), there is no TRCP 508.2(b); the original rule includes only (a).

TRCP 509. REPAIR AND REMEDY CASES

509.1. Applicability of Rule. Rule 509 applies to a lawsuit filed in a justice court by a residential tenant under Chapter 92, Subchapter B of the Texas Property Code to enforce the landlord's duty to repair or remedy a condition materially affecting the physical health or safety of an ordinary tenant.

509.2. Contents of Petition; Copies; Forms and Amendments.

(a) *Contents of Petition.* The petition must be in writing and must include the following:

(1) the street address of the residential rental property;

(2) a statement indicating whether the tenant has received in writing the name and business street address of the landlord and landlord's management company;

(3) to the extent known and applicable, the name, business street address, and telephone number of the landlord and the landlord's management company, on-premises manager, and rent collector serving the residential rental property;

(4) for all notices the tenant gave to the landlord requesting that the condition be repaired or remedied:

(A) the date of the notice;

(B) the name of the person to whom the notice was given or the place where the notice was given;

(C) whether the tenant's lease is in writing and requires written notice;

(D) whether the notice was in writing or oral;

(E) whether any written notice was given by certified mail, return receipt requested, or by registered mail; and

(F) whether the rent was current or had been timely tendered at the time notice was given;

(5) a description of the property condition materially affecting the physical health or safety of an ordinary tenant that the tenant seeks to have repaired or remedied;

(6) a statement of the relief requested by the tenant, including an order to repair or remedy a condition, a reduction in rent, actual damages, civil penalties, attorney's fees, and court costs;

(7) if the petition includes a request to reduce the rent:

(A) the amount of rent paid by the tenant, the amount of rent paid by the government, if known, the rental period, and when the rent is due; and

(B) the amount of the requested rent reduction and the date it should begin;

(8) a statement that the total relief requested does not exceed $20,000, excluding interest and court costs but including attorney's fees; and

(9) the tenant's name, address, and telephone number.

(b) ***Copies.*** The tenant must provide the court with copies of the petition and any attachments to the petition for service on the landlord.

(c) ***Forms and Amendments.*** A petition substantially in the form promulgated by the Supreme Court is sufficient. A suit may not be dismissed for a defect in the petition unless the tenant is given an opportunity to correct the defect and does not promptly correct it.

509.3. Citation: Issuance; Appearance Date; Answer.

(a) ***Issuance.*** When the tenant files a written petition with a justice court, the judge must immediately issue citation directed to the landlord, commanding the landlord to appear before such judge at the time and place named in the citation.

(b) ***Appearance Date; Answer.*** The appearance date on the citation must not be less than 10 days nor more than 21 days after the petition is filed. For purposes of this rule, the appearance date on the citation is the trial date. The landlord may, but is not required to, file a written answer on or before the appearance date.

509.4. Service and Return of Citation; Alternative Service of Citation.

(a) ***Service and Return of Citation.*** The sheriff, constable, or other person authorized by Rule 501.2 who receives the citation must serve the citation by delivering a copy of it, along with a copy of the petition and any attachments, to the landlord at least 6 days before the appearance date. At least one day before the appearance date, the person serving the citation must file a return of service with the court that issued the citation. The citation must be issued, served, and returned in like manner as ordinary citations issued from a justice court.

(b) ***Alternative Service of Citation.***

(1) If the petition does not include the landlord's name and business street address, or if, after making diligent efforts on at least two occasions, the officer or authorized person is unsuccessful in serving the citation on the landlord under (a), the officer or authorized person must serve the citation by delivering a copy of the citation, petition, and any attachments to:

(A) the landlord's management company if the tenant has received written notice of the name and business street address of the landlord's management company; or

(B) if (b)(1)(A) does not apply and the tenant has not received the landlord's name and business street address in writing, the landlord's authorized agent for service of process, which may be the landlord's management company, on-premise manager, or rent collector serving the residential rental property.

(2) If the officer or authorized person is unsuccessful in serving citation under (b)(1) after making diligent efforts on at least two occasions at either the business street address of the landlord's management company, if (b)(1)(A) applies, or at each available business street address of the landlord's authorized agent for service of process, if (b)(1)(B) applies, the officer or authorized person must execute and file in the justice court a sworn statement that the officer or authorized person made diligent efforts to serve the citation on at least two occasions at all available business street addresses of the landlord and, to the extent applicable, the landlord's management company, on-premises manager, and rent collector serving the residential rental property, providing the times, dates, and places of each attempted service. The judge may then authorize the officer or authorized person to serve citation by:

(A) delivering a copy of the citation, petition, and any attachments to someone over the age of 16 years, at any business street address listed in the petition, or, if nobody answers the door at a business street address, either placing the citation, petition, and any attachments through a door mail chute or slipping them under the front door, and if neither of these latter methods is practical, affixing the citation, petition, and any attachments to the

front door or main entry to the business street address;

(B) within 24 hours of complying with (b)(2)(A), sending by first class mail a true copy of the citation, petition, and any attachments addressed to the landlord at the landlord's business street address provided in the petition; and

(C) noting on the return of the citation the date of delivery under (b)(2)(A) and the date of mailing under (b)(2)(B).

The delivery and mailing to the business street address under (b)(2)(A)–(B) must occur at least 6 days before the appearance date. At least one day before the appearance date, a return of service must be completed and filed in accordance with Rule 501.3 with the court that issued the citation. It is not necessary for the tenant to request the alternative service authorized by this rule.

509.5. Docketing and Trial; Failure to Appear.

(a) ***Docketing and Trial.*** The case must be docketed and tried as other cases. The judge may develop the facts of the case in order to ensure justice.

(b) ***Failure to Appear.***

(1) If the tenant appears at trial and the landlord has been duly served and fails to appear at trial, the judge may proceed to hear evidence. If the tenant establishes that the tenant is entitled to recover, the judge must render judgment against the landlord in accordance with the evidence.

(2) If the tenant fails to appear for trial, the judge may dismiss the lawsuit.

509.6. Judgment: Amount; Form and Content; Issuance and Service; Failure to Comply.

(a) ***Amount.*** Judgment may be rendered against the landlord for failure to repair or remedy a condition at the residential rental property if the total judgment does not exceed $20,000, excluding interest and court costs but including attorney's fees. Any party who prevails in a lawsuit brought under these rules may recover the party's court costs and reasonable attorney's fees as allowed by law.

(b) ***Form and Content.***

(1) The judgment must be in writing, signed, and dated and must include the names of the parties to the proceeding and the street address of the residential rental property where the condition is to be repaired or remedied.

(2) In the judgment, the judge may:

(A) order the landlord to take reasonable action to repair or remedy the condition;

(B) order a reduction in the tenant's rent, from the date of the first repair notice, in proportion to the reduced rental value resulting from the condition until the condition is repaired or remedied;

(C) award a civil penalty of one month's rent plus $500;

(D) award the tenant's actual damages; and

(E) award court costs and attorney's fees, excluding any attorney's fees for a claim for damages relating to a personal injury.

(3) If the judge orders the landlord to repair or remedy a condition, the judgment must include in reasonable detail the actions the landlord must take to repair or remedy the condition and the date when the repair or remedy must be completed.

(4) If the judge orders a reduction in the tenant's rent, the judgment must state:

(A) the amount of the rent the tenant must pay, if any;

(B) the frequency with which the tenant must pay the rent;

(C) the condition justifying the reduction of rent;

(D) the effective date of the order reducing rent;

(E) that the order reducing rent will terminate on the date the condition is repaired or remedied; and

(F) that on the day the condition is repaired or remedied, the landlord must give the tenant written notice, served in accordance with Rule 501.4, that the condition justifying the reduction of rent has been repaired or remedied and the rent will revert to the rent amount specified in the lease.

(c) ***Issuance and Service.*** The judge must issue the judgment. The judgment may be served on the landlord in open court or by any means provided in Rule 501.4 at an address listed in the citation, the address listed on any answer, or such other address the landlord furnishes to the court in writing. Unless the judge serves the landlord in open court or by other means provided in Rule 501.4, the sheriff, constable, or other authorized person who serves the landlord must promptly file a return of service in the justice court.

(d) ***Failure to Comply.*** If the landlord fails to comply with an order to repair or remedy a condition or reduce the tenant's rent, the failure is grounds for citing the landlord for contempt of court under Section 21.002 of the Texas Government Code.

509.7. Counterclaims. Counterclaims and the joinder

of suits against third parties are not permitted in suits under these rules. Compulsory counterclaims may be brought in a separate suit. Any potential causes of action, including a compulsory counterclaim, that are not asserted because of this rule are not precluded.

509.8. Appeal: Time and Manner; Perfection; Effect; Costs; Trial on Appeal.

(a) ***Time and Manner.*** Either party may appeal the decision of the justice court to a statutory county court or, if there is no statutory county court with jurisdiction, a county court or district court with jurisdiction by filing a written notice of appeal with the justice court within 21 days after the date the judge signs the judgment. If the judgment is amended in any respect, any party has the right to appeal within 21 days after the date the judge signs the new judgment, in the same manner set out in this rule.

(b) ***Perfection.*** The posting of an appeal bond is not required for an appeal under this rule, and the appeal is considered perfected with the filing of a notice of appeal. Otherwise, the appeal is in the manner provided by law for appeal from a justice court.

(c) ***Effect.*** The timely filing of a notice of appeal stays the enforcement of any order to repair or remedy a condition or reduce the tenant's rent, as well as any other actions.

(d) ***Costs.*** The appellant must pay the costs on appeal to a county court in accordance with Rule 143a.

(e) ***Trial on Appeal.*** On appeal, the parties are entitled to a trial de novo. A trial de novo is a new trial in which the entire case is presented as if there had been no previous trial. Either party is entitled to trial by jury on timely request and payment of a fee, if required. An appeal of a judgment of a justice court under these rules takes precedence in the county court and may be held at any time after the eighth day after the date the transcript is filed in the county court.

509.9. Effect of Writ of Possession. If a judgment for the landlord for possession of the residential rental property becomes final, any order to repair or remedy a condition is vacated and unenforceable.

Adopted by order of April 15, 2013, eff. Aug. 31, 2013. Amended by order of May 26, 2020, eff. Sept. 1, 2020.

Source: New rule.

See also **O'Connor's Texas COA**, "Failure to Repair or Remedy," ch. 16-F, §1 et seq.

TRCP 510. EVICTION CASES

510.1. Application. Rule 510 applies to a lawsuit to recover possession of real property under Chapter 24 of the Texas Property Code.

510.2. Computation of Time for Eviction Cases. Rule 500.5 applies to the computation of time in an eviction case. But if a document is filed by mail and not received by the court by the due date, the court may take any action authorized by these rules, including issuing a writ of possession requiring a tenant to leave the property.

510.3. Petition.

(a) ***Contents.*** In addition to the requirements of Rule 502.2, a petition in an eviction case must be sworn to by the plaintiff and must contain:

(1) a description, including the address, if any, of the premises that the plaintiff seeks possession of;

(2) a description of the facts and the grounds for eviction;

(3) a description of when and how notice to vacate was delivered;

(4) the total amount of rent due and unpaid at the time of filing, if any; and

(5) a statement that attorney fees are being sought, if applicable.

(b) ***Where Filed.*** The petition must be filed in the precinct where the premises is located. If it is filed elsewhere, the judge must dismiss the case. The plaintiff will not be entitled to a refund of the filing fee, but will be refunded any service fees paid if the case is dismissed before service is attempted.

(c) ***Defendants Named.*** If the eviction is based on a written residential lease, the plaintiff must name as defendants all tenants obligated under the lease residing at the premises whom plaintiff seeks to evict. No judgment or writ of possession may issue or be executed against a tenant obligated under a lease and residing at the premises who is not named in the petition and served with citation.

(d) ***Claim for Rent.*** A claim for rent within the justice court's jurisdiction may be asserted in an eviction case.

(e) ***Only Issue.*** The court must adjudicate the right to actual possession and not title. Counterclaims and the joinder of suits against third parties are not permitted in eviction cases. A claim that is not asserted because of this rule can be brought in a separate suit in a court of proper jurisdiction.

510.4. Issuance, Service, and Return of Citation.

(a) ***Issuance of Citation; Contents.*** When a petition is filed, the court must immediately issue citation directed to each defendant. The citation must:

(1) be styled "The State of Texas";

(2) be signed by the clerk under seal of court or by the judge;

(3) contain the name, location, and address of the court;

(4) state the date of filing of the petition;

(5) state the date of issuance of the citation;

(6) state the file number and names of parties;

(7) state the plaintiff's cause of action and relief sought;

(8) be directed to the defendant;

(9) state the name and address of attorney for plaintiff, or if the plaintiff does not have an attorney, the address of plaintiff;

(10) state the day the defendant must appear in person for trial at the court issuing citation, which must not be less than 10 days nor more than 21 days after the petition is filed;

(11) notify the defendant that if the defendant fails to appear in person for trial, judgment by default may be rendered for the relief demanded in the petition;

(12) inform the defendant that, upon timely request and payment of a jury fee no later than 3 days before the day set for trial, the case will be heard by a jury;

(13) contain all warnings required by Chapter 24 of the Texas Property Code; and

(14) include the following statement: "For further information, consult Part V of the Texas Rules of Civil Procedure, which is available online and also at the court listed on this citation."

(b) *Service and Return of Citation.*

(1) *Who May Serve.* Unless otherwise authorized by written court order, citation must be served by a sheriff or constable.

(2) *Method of Service.* The constable, sheriff, or other person authorized by written court order receiving the citation must execute it by delivering a copy with a copy of the petition attached to the defendant, or by leaving a copy with a copy of the petition attached with some person, other than the plaintiff, over the age of 16 years, at the defendant's usual place of residence, at least 6 days before the day set for trial.

(3) *Return of Service.* At least one day before the day set for trial, the constable, sheriff, or other person authorized by written court order must complete and file a return of service in accordance with Rule 501.3 with the court that issued the citation.

(c) *Alternative Service by Delivery to the Premises.*

(1) *When Allowed.* The citation may be served by delivery to the premises if:

(A) the constable, sheriff, or other person authorized by written court order is unsuccessful in serving the citation under (b);

(B) the petition lists all home and work addresses of the defendant that are known to the plaintiff and states that the plaintiff knows of no other home or work addresses of the defendant in the county where the premises are located; and

(C) the constable, sheriff, or other person authorized files a sworn statement that it has made diligent efforts to serve such citation on at least two occasions at all addresses of the defendant in the county where the premises are located, stating the times and places of attempted service.

(2) *Authorization.* The judge must promptly consider a sworn statement filed under (1)(C) and determine whether citation may be served by delivery to the premises. The plaintiff is not required to make a request or motion for alternative service.

(3) *Method.* If the judge authorizes service by delivery to the premises, the constable, sheriff, or other person authorized by written court order must, at least 6 days before the day set for trial:

(A) deliver a copy of the citation with a copy of the petition attached to the premises by placing it through a door mail chute or slipping it under the front door; if neither method is possible, the officer may securely affix the citation to the front door or main entry to the premises; and

(B) deposit in the mail a copy of the citation with a copy of the petition attached, addressed to defendant at the premises and sent by first class mail.

(4) *Notation on Return.* The constable, sheriff, or other person authorized by written court order must note on the return of service the date the citation was delivered and the date it was deposited in the mail.

510.5. Request for Immediate Possession.

(a) *Immediate Possession Bond.* The plaintiff may, at the time of filing the petition or at any time prior to final judgment, file a possession bond to be approved by the judge in the probable amount of costs of suit and damages that may result to defendant in the event that the suit has been improperly instituted, and conditioned that the plaintiff will pay defendant all such costs and damages that are adjudged against plaintiff.

(b) *Notice to Defendant.* The court must notify a defendant that the plaintiff has filed a possession bond. The notice must be served in the same manner as service of citation and must inform the defendant that if the defendant does not file an answer or appear for trial, and judgment for possession is granted by default, an officer will place the plaintiff in possession of the property on or after the 7th day after the date defendant is served with the notice.

(c) *Time for Issuance and Execution of Writ.* If judgment for possession is rendered by default and a possession bond has been filed, approved, and served under this rule, a writ of possession must issue immediately upon demand and payment of any required fees. The writ must not be executed before the 7th day after the date defendant is served with notice under (b).

(d) *Effect of Appearance.* If the defendant files an answer or appears at trial, no writ of possession may issue before the 6th day after the date a judgment for possession is signed or the day following the deadline for the defendant to appeal the judgment, whichever is later.

510.6. Trial Date; Answer; Default Judgment.

(a) *Trial Date and Answer.* The defendant must appear for trial on the day set for trial in the citation. The defendant may, but is not required to, file a written answer with the court on or before the day set for trial in the citation.

(b) *Default Judgment.* If the defendant fails to appear at trial and fails to file an answer before the case is called for trial, and proof of service has been filed in accordance with Rule 510.4, the allegations of the complaint must be taken as admitted and judgment by default rendered accordingly. If a defendant who has answered fails to appear for trial, the court may proceed to hear evidence and render judgment accordingly.

(c) *Notice of Default.* When a default judgment is signed, the clerk must immediately mail written notice of the judgment by first class mail to the defendant at the address of the premises.

510.7. Trial.

(a) *Trial.* An eviction case will be docketed and tried as other cases. No eviction trial may be held less than 6 days after service under Rule 510.4 has been obtained.

(b) *Jury Trial Demanded.* Any party may file a written demand for trial by jury by making a request to the court at least 3 days before the trial date. The demand must be accompanied by payment of a jury fee or by filing a Statement of Inability to Afford Payment of Court Costs. If a jury is demanded by either party, the jury will be impaneled and sworn as in other cases; and after hearing the evidence it will return its verdict in favor of the plaintiff or the defendant. If no jury is timely demanded by either party, the judge will try the case.

(c) *Limit on Postponement.* Trial in an eviction case must not be postponed for more than 7 days total unless both parties agree in writing.

510.8. Judgment; Writ; No New Trial.

(a) *Judgment Upon Jury Verdict.* Where a jury has returned a verdict, the judge may render judgment on the verdict or, if the verdict is contrary to the law or the evidence, judgment notwithstanding the verdict.

(b) *Judgment for Plaintiff.* If the judgment is in favor of the plaintiff, the judge must render judgment for plaintiff for possession of the premises, costs, delinquent rent as of the date of entry of judgment, if any, and attorney fees if recoverable by law.

(c) *Judgment for Defendant.* If the judgment is in favor of the defendant, the judge must render judgment for defendant against the plaintiff for costs and attorney fees if recoverable by law.

(d) *Writ.* If the judgment or verdict is in favor of the plaintiff, the judge must award a writ of possession upon demand of the plaintiff and payment of any required fees.

(1) *Time to Issue.* Except as provided by Rule 510.5, no writ of possession may issue before the 6th day after the date a judgment for possession is signed or the day following the deadline for the defendant to appeal the judgment, whichever is later. A writ of possession may not issue more than 60 days after a judgment for possession is signed. For good cause, the court may extend the deadline for issuance to 90 days after a judgment for possession is signed.

(2) *Time to Execute.* A writ of possession may not be executed after the 90th day after a judgment for possession is signed.

(3) *Effect of Appeal.* A writ of possession must not issue if an appeal is perfected and, if applicable, rent is paid into the registry, as required by these rules.

(e) *No Motion For New Trial.* No motion for new trial may be filed.

510.9. Appeal.

(a) *How Taken; Time.* A party may appeal a judgment in an eviction case by filing a bond, making a cash deposit, or filing a Statement of Inability to Afford Payment of Court Costs with the justice court within 5 days after the judgment is signed.

(b) *Amount of Security; Terms.* The justice court judge will set the amount of the bond or cash deposit to

include the items enumerated in Rule 510.11. The bond or cash deposit must be payable to the appellee and must be conditioned on the appellant's prosecution of its appeal to effect and payment of any judgment and all costs rendered against it on appeal.

(c) *Statement of Inability to Afford Payment of Court Costs.*

(1) *Filing.* An appellant who cannot furnish a bond or pay a cash deposit in the amount required may instead file a Statement of Inability to Afford Payment of Court Costs. The Statement must be on the form approved by the Supreme Court or include the information required by the Court-approved form.

(2) *Contest.* The Statement may be contested as provided in Rule 502.3(d) within 5 days after the opposing party receives notice that the Statement was filed.

(3) *Appeal If Contest Sustained.* If the contest is sustained, the appellant may appeal that decision by filing notice with the justice court within 5 days of that court's written order. The justice court must then forward all related documents to the county court for resolution. The county court must set the matter for hearing within 5 days and hear the contest de novo, as if there had been no previous hearing, and, if the appeal is granted, must direct the justice court to transmit to the clerk of the county court the transcript, records, and papers of the case, as provided in these rules.

(4) *If No Appeal or If Appeal Overruled.* If the appellant does not appeal the ruling sustaining the contest, or if the county court denies the appeal, the appellant may, within one business day, post an appeal bond or make a cash deposit in compliance with this rule.

(5) *Payment of Rent in Nonpayment of Rent Appeals.*

(A) Notice. If a defendant appeals an eviction for nonpayment of rent by filing a Statement of Inability to Afford Payment of Court Costs, the justice court must provide to the defendant a written notice at the time the Statement is filed that contains the following information in bold or conspicuous type:

(i) the amount of the initial deposit of rent, equal to one rental period's rent under the terms of the rental agreement, that the defendant must pay into the justice court registry;

(ii) whether the initial deposit must be paid in cash, cashier's check, or money order, and to whom the cashier's check or money order, if applicable, must be made payable;

(iii) the calendar date by which the initial deposit must be paid into the justice court registry, which must be within 5 days of the date the Statement is filed; and

(iv) a statement that failure to pay the required amount into the justice court registry by the required date may result in the court issuing a writ of possession without hearing.

(B) Defendant May Remain in Possession. A defendant who appeals an eviction for nonpayment of rent by filing a Statement of Inability to Afford Payment of Court Costs is entitled to stay in possession of the premises during the pendency of the appeal by complying with the following procedure:

(i) Within 5 days of the date that the defendant files a Statement of Inability to Afford Payment of Court Costs, it must pay into the justice court registry the amount set forth in the notice provided at the time the defendant filed the Statement. If the defendant was provided with notice and fails to pay the designated amount into the justice court registry within 5 days, and the transcript has not been transmitted to the county clerk, the plaintiff is entitled, upon request and payment of the applicable fee, to a writ of possession, which the justice court must issue immediately and without hearing.

(ii) During the appeal process as rent becomes due under the rental agreement, the defendant must pay the designated amount into the county court registry within 5 days of the rental due date under the terms of the rental agreement.

(iii) If a government agency is responsible for all or a portion of the rent, the defendant must pay only that portion of the rent determined by the justice court to be paid during appeal. Either party may contest the portion of the rent that the justice court determines must be paid into the county court registry by filing a contest within 5 days after the judgment is signed. If a contest is filed, the justice court must notify the parties and hold a hearing on the contest within 5 days. If the defendant objects to the justice court's ruling at the hearing, the defendant is required to pay only the portion claimed to be owed by the defendant until the issue is tried in county court.

(iv) If the defendant fails to pay the designated amount into the court registry within the time limits prescribed by these rules, the plaintiff may file a sworn motion that the defendant is in default in county court. The plaintiff must notify the defendant of the motion and the hearing date. Upon a showing that the defendant is in default, the court must issue a writ of possession.

(v) The plaintiff may withdraw any or all rent in the county court registry upon sworn motion and hearing, prior to final determination of the case, showing just cause; dismissal of the appeal; or order of the court after final hearing.

(vi) All hearings and motions under this subparagraph are entitled to precedence in the county court.

(d) ***Notice to Other Parties Required.*** If a Statement of Inability to Afford Payment of Court Costs is filed, the court must provide notice to all other parties that the Statement was filed no later than the next business day. Within 5 days of filing a bond or making a cash deposit, an appellant must serve written notice of the appeal on all other parties using a method approved under Rule 501.4.

(e) ***No Default on Appeal Without Compliance With Rule.*** No judgment may be taken by default against the adverse party in the court to which the case has been appealed without first showing substantial compliance with this rule.

(f) ***Appeal Perfected.*** An appeal is perfected when a bond, cash deposit, or Statement of Inability to Afford Payment of Court Costs is filed in accordance with this rule.

510.10. Record on Appeal; Docketing; Trial De Novo.

(a) ***Preparation and Transmission of Record.*** Unless otherwise provided by law or these rules, when an appeal has been perfected, the judge must stay all further proceedings on the judgment and must immediately send to the clerk of the county court a certified copy of all docket entries, a certified copy of the bill of costs, and the original papers in the case together with any money in the court registry, including sums tendered pursuant to Rule 510.9(c)(5)(B).

(b) ***Docketing; Notice.*** The county clerk must docket the case and must immediately notify the parties of the date of receipt of the transcript and the docket number of the case. The notice must advise the defendant that it must file a written answer in the county court within 8 days if one was not filed in the justice court.

(c) ***Trial De Novo.*** The case must be tried de novo in the county court. A trial de novo is a new trial in which the entire case is presented as if there had been no previous trial. The trial, as well as any hearings and motions, is entitled to precedence in the county court.

510.11. Damages on Appeal. On the trial of the case in the county court the appellant or appellee will be permitted to plead, prove and recover his damages, if any, suffered for withholding or defending possession of the premises during the pendency of the appeal. Damages may include but are not limited to loss of rentals during the pendency of the appeal and attorney fees in the justice and county courts provided, as to attorney fees, that the requirements of Section 24.006 of the Texas Property Code have been met. Only the party prevailing in the county court will be entitled to recover damages against the adverse party. The prevailing party will also be entitled to recover court costs and to recover against the sureties on the appeal bond in cases where the adverse party has executed an appeal bond.

510.12. Judgment by Default on Appeal. An eviction case appealed to county court will be subject to trial at any time after the expiration of 8 days after the date the transcript is filed in the county court. If the defendant has filed a written answer in the justice court, it must be taken to constitute his appearance and answer in the county court and may be amended as in other cases. If the defendant made no answer in writing in the justice court and fails to file a written answer within 8 days after the transcript is filed in the county court, the allegations of the complaint may be taken as admitted and judgment by default may be entered accordingly.

510.13. Writ of Possession on Appeal. The writ of possession, or execution, or both, will be issued by the clerk of the county court according to the judgment rendered, and the same will be executed by the sheriff or constable, as in other cases. The judgment of the county court may not be stayed unless within 10 days from the judgment the appellant files a supersedeas bond in an amount set by the county court pursuant to Section 24.007 of the Texas Property Code.

Adopted by order of April 15, 2013, eff. Aug. 31, 2013. Amended by order of Aug. 31, 2016, eff. Sept. 1, 2016.

Source: New rule.

See also **O'Connor's Texas COA**, "Forcible Detainer—Eviction," ch. 16-B, §1 et seq.; **O'Connor's Texas Rules**, "Eviction," ch. 2-G, §5.2.4.

ANNOTATIONS

Norvelle v. PNC Mortg., 472 S.W.3d 444, 446 (Tex.App.—Fort Worth 2015, no pet.). "[A]lthough [Ds] refer us to the repeal of former [TRCP] 739 and its replacement with [TRCP] 510.3 and contend that there is 'no longer any provision of the applicable rules that permits a plaintiff's attorney to swear to a forcible detainer petition' and that strict compliance with the rule's language is required, they have not cited us to any authority to support the proposition that defects in an eviction petition can deprive the trial court of jurisdiction and make the resulting eviction judgment void. *At 447:* Furthermore, nothing in the applicable law invalidates [P's] petition under rule 510.3(a). *At 449:* To hold . . . that new rule 510.3(a) requires a corporation or

other entity to physically sign a petition would defy the reality that business entities operate through their agents, and it would usurp the ability of these entities to have their day in court. . . . Here, the petition filed in the justice court contained a verification sworn to by [P's] counsel, stating her authority to make the affidavit and swearing that the facts contained in the pleading were both within her personal knowledge and true and correct. As she acted as [P's] corporeal agent for purposes of instituting the action, this was sufficient to meet rule 510.3(a)'s requirements." *See also* Isaac v. CitiMortgage, Inc., 563 S.W.3d 305, 313-14 (Tex.App.—Houston [1st Dist.] 2018, pet. denied); Lenz v. Bank of Am., 510 S.W.3d 667, 668-69 (Tex.App.—San Antonio 2016, pet. denied).

Goebel v. Sharon Peters Real Estate, Inc., No. 03-14-00635-CV, 2015 WL 1778295 (Tex.App.—Austin 2015, no pet.) (memo op.; 4-16-15). "We decline to hold . . . that, despite the justice court's announcement that the security amount was zero, appellee should have filed a $500 bond under [TRCP] 506.1. Rule 506 is a general rule applying to appeals from justice court to county court. It is trumped by more specific [TRCP] 510.9, which applies in appeals from eviction cases and which states that a party may appeal by posting a security in an amount set by the justice court. In this case, that amount was initially set at zero."

Tehuti v. Trans-Atlas Fin., Inc., No. 05-14-00126-CV, 2015 WL 1111400 (Tex.App.—Dallas 2015, pet. dism'd) (memo op.; 3-12-15). In a forcible detainer action, "[t]he trial court must adjudicate the right to actual possession of the property. All other claims, including questions of title, validity of a foreclosure, counterclaims, and suits against third parties are not permitted. Those claims must be brought in separate suits. Accordingly, the only issue in a forcible detainer action is which party has the right to immediate possession of the property." *See also* **AAA Free Move Ministorage, LLC v. OIS Invs.**, 419 S.W.3d 522, 526 (Tex.App.—San Antonio 2013, pet. denied) (forcible-detainer action may only assert claims for possession and rent); **Krull v. Somoza**, 879 S.W.2d 320, 322 (Tex.App.—Houston [14th Dist.] 1994, writ denied) (damages claims related to maintaining or obtaining possession of property may be joined with forcible-detainer action).

Mohammed v. D. 1050 W. Rankin, Inc., 464 S.W.3d 737, 742-43 (Tex.App.—Houston [1st Dist.] 2014, no pet.). "The new justice court eviction procedure, contained in [TRCP] 510, does not have a specific provision addressing the timetable for an appeal when the justice court modifies its judgment in an eviction case. Generally, under [TRCP] 506, in a justice court case, a party may appeal within 21 days after the judgment is signed or motion for new [trial] is denied. This 21-day period mirrors the timetable for an appeal from an original judgment in a non-eviction justice court case. [¶] But [Rule 510's] procedure trumps the more general justice court rule when the two conflict. . . . Because [Rule 510] provides for an appellate timetable of 5 days, we conclude that the more general rule allowing 21 days for an appeal in a justice court case does not apply; in harmonizing the provisions so as not to conflict, we conclude that the 5-day timeframe applies to an appeal of an amended justice court judgment, mirroring the timeframe for an appeal from the original judgment."

Frank v. Brittany Square Apts., No. 14-09-00423-CV, 2010 WL 1544098 (Tex.App.—Houston [14th Dist.] 2010, no pet.) (memo op.; 4-20-10). "The county court's determination that a tenant has not complied with Rule 749b [now 510.9(c)(5)] is neither a final judgment nor an appealable interlocutory order. By its terms, Rule 749b addresses only entitlement to possess the premises 'during the pendency of the appeal' in the county court; it is not dispositive of that appeal itself. Consequently, a county court's order granting the landlord possession of the premises pursuant to Rule 749b is not a final order."

Mastermark Homebuilders, Inc. v. Offenburger Constr., Inc., 857 S.W.2d 765, 768 (Tex.App.—Houston [14th Dist.] 1993, no writ). TRCP 752, now TRCP 510.11, "does not require that damages in the form of attorney's fees be plead in the justice court. The rule merely states that the requirements of [Prop. Code] §24.006 . . . be satisfied."

Polk v. Braddock, 864 S.W.2d 78, 80 (Tex.App.—Dallas 1992, no writ). "[T]he proper party for a mandamus proceeding concerning the failure to file appeal papers with the county court in an appeal from the justice court under rule 751 [now 510.10] is the justice of the peace."

TRCP 511 to 513. REPEALED BY ORDER OF DEC. 5, 1983, EFF. APRIL 1, 1984

TRCP 514. REPEALED BY ORDER OF APRIL 10, 1986, EFF. SEPT. 1, 1986

TRCP 515. REPEALED BY ORDER OF APRIL 10, 1986, EFF. SEPT. 1, 1986

TRCP 516, 517. REPEALED BY ORDER OF DEC. 5, 1983, EFF. APRIL 1, 1984

TRCP 518 to 522. REPEALED BY ORDER OF OCT. 10, 1945, EFF. FEB. 1, 1946

TRCP 523 to 567. REPEALED BY ORDER OF APRIL 15, 2013, EFF. AUG. 31, 2013

TRCP 568. REPEALED BY ORDER OF JULY 15, 1987, EFF. JAN. 1, 1988

TRCP 569 to 591. REPEALED BY ORDER OF APRIL 15, 2013, EFF. AUG. 31, 2013

Part VI. Rules Relating to Ancillary Proceedings

SECTION 1. ATTACHMENT

TRCP 592. APPLICATION FOR WRIT OF ATTACHMENT AND ORDER

Either at the commencement of a suit or at any time during its progress the plaintiff may file an application for the

issuance of a writ of attachment. Such application shall be supported by affidavits of the plaintiff, his agent, his attorney, or other persons having knowledge of relevant facts. The application shall comply with all statutory requirements and shall state the grounds for issuing the writ and the specific facts relied upon by the plaintiff to warrant the required findings by the court. The writ shall not be quashed because two or more grounds are stated conjunctively or disjunctively. The application and any affidavits shall be made on personal knowledge and shall set forth such facts as would be admissible in evidence; provided that facts may be stated based upon information and belief if the grounds of such belief are specifically stated.

No writ shall issue except upon written order of the court after a hearing, which may be ex parte. The court, in its order granting the application, shall make specific findings of facts to support the statutory grounds found to exist, and shall specify the maximum value of property that may be attached, and the amount of bond required of plaintiff, and, further shall command that the attached property be kept safe and preserved subject to further orders of the court. Such bond shall be in an amount which, in the opinion of the court, will adequately compensate the defendant in the event plaintiff fails to prosecute his suit to effect, and to pay all damages and costs which may be adjudged against him for wrongfully suing out the writ of attachment. The court shall further find in its order the amount of bond required of defendant to replevy, which, unless the defendant chooses to exercise his option as provided in Rule 599, shall be the amount of plaintiff's claim, one year's accrual of interest if allowed by law on the claim, and the estimated costs of court. The order may direct the issuance of several writs at the same time, or in succession, to be sent to different counties.

July 11, 1977, eff. Jan. 1, 1978.

Source: New rule.

ANNOTATIONS

In re Argyll Equities, LLC, 227 S.W.3d 268, 271 (Tex.App.—San Antonio 2007, orig. proceeding). "The validity of a writ of attachment does not depend on the truthfulness of the allegations, but on compliance with the statute in making the affidavit. [¶] Generally, a writ of attachment is not available when the applicant's claims are for unliquidated damages. *At n.6:* When the defendant cannot be served in Texas, [however,] a writ of attachment may issue in a suit for an unliquidated claim."

TRCP 592a. BOND FOR ATTACHMENT

No writ of attachment shall issue until the party applying therefor has filed with the officer authorized to issue such writ a bond payable to the defendant in the amount fixed by the court's order, with sufficient surety or sureties as provided by statute to be approved by such officer, conditioned that the plaintiff will prosecute his suit to effect and pay to the extent of the penal amount of the bond all damages and costs as may be adjudged against him for wrongfully suing out such writ of attachment.

After notice to the opposite party, either before or after the issuance of the writ, the defendant or plaintiff may file a motion to increase or reduce the amount of such bond, or to question the sufficiency of the sureties thereon, in the court in which such suit is pending. Upon hearing, the court shall enter its order with respect to such bond and sufficiency of the sureties.

July 11, 1977, eff. Jan. 1, 1978.

TRCP 592b. FORM OF ATTACHMENT BOND

The following form of bond may be used:

"The State of Texas,

County of ______.

"We, the undersigned, ______ as principal, and ______ and ______ as sureties, acknowledge ourselves bound to pay to C.D. the sum of ______ dollars, conditioned that the above bound plaintiff in attachment against the said C.D., defendant, will prosecute his said suit to effect, and that he will pay all such damages and costs to the extent of the penal amount of this bond as shall be adjudged against him for wrongfully suing out such attachment. Witness our hands this ______ day of ______, 20____."

Renumbered from Vernon's Ann.Texas Rules Civ.Proc., rule 592 and amended by order of July 11, 1977, eff. Jan. 1, 1978.

TRCP 593. REQUISITES FOR WRIT

A writ of attachment shall be directed to the sheriff or any constable within the State of Texas. It shall command him to attach and hold, unless replevied, subject to the further order of the court, so much of the property of the defendant, of a reasonable value in approximately the amount fixed by the court, as shall be found within his county.

Amended by order of July 11, 1977, eff. Jan. 1, 1978.

TRCP 594. FORM OF WRIT

The following form of writ may be issued:

"The State of Texas.

To the Sheriff or any Constable of any County of the State of Texas, greeting:

"We command you that you attach forthwith so much of the property of C.D., if it be found in your county, repleviable on security, as shall be of value sufficient to make the sum of ________ dollars, and the probable costs of suit, to satisfy the demand of A.B., and that you keep and secure in your hands the property so attached, unless replevied, that the same may be liable to further proceedings thereon to be had before our court in ________, County of ________. You will true return make of this writ on or before 10 a.m. of Monday, the ________ day of ________, 20____, showing how you have executed the same."

TRCP 595. SEVERAL WRITS

Several writs of attachment may, at the option of the plaintiff, be issued at the same time, or in succession, and sent to different counties, until sufficient property shall be attached to satisfy the writ.

TRCP 596. DELIVERY OF WRIT

The writ of attachment shall be dated and tested as other writs, and may be delivered to the sheriff or constable by the officer issuing it, or he may deliver it to the plaintiff, his agent or attorney, for that purpose.

TRCP 597. DUTY OF OFFICER

The sheriff or constable receiving the writ shall immediately proceed to execute the same by levying upon so much of the property of the defendant subject to the writ, and found within his county, as may be sufficient to satisfy the command of the writ.

TRCP 598. LEVY, HOW MADE

The writ of attachment shall be levied in the same manner as is, or may be, the writ of execution upon similar property.

TRCP 598a. SERVICE OF WRIT ON DEFENDANT

The defendant shall be served in any manner prescribed for service of citation, or as provided in Rule 21a, with a copy of the writ of attachment, the application, accompanying affidavits, and orders of the court as soon as practicable following the levy of the writ. There shall be prominently displayed on the face of the copy of the writ served on the defendant, in ten-point type and in a manner calculated to advise a reasonably attentive person of its contents, the following:

"To ________, Defendant:

You are hereby notified that certain properties alleged to be owned by you have been attached. If you claim any rights in such property, you are advised:

"YOU HAVE A RIGHT TO REGAIN POSSESSION OF THE PROPERTY BY FILING A REPLEVY BOND. YOU HAVE A RIGHT TO SEEK TO REGAIN POSSESSION OF THE PROPERTY BY FILING WITH THE COURT A MOTION TO DISSOLVE THIS WRIT."

July 11, 1977, eff. Jan. 1, 1978.

TRCP 599. DEFENDANT MAY REPLEVY

At any time before judgment, should the attached property not have been previously claimed or sold, the defendant may replevy the same, or any part thereof, or the proceeds from the sale of the property if it has been sold under order of the court, by giving bond with sufficient surety or sureties as provided by statute, to be approved by the officer who levied the writ, payable to plaintiff, in the amount fixed by the court's order, or, at the defendant's option, for the value of the property sought to be replevied (to be estimated by the officer), plus one year's interest thereon at the legal rate from the date of the bond, conditioned that the defendant shall satisfy, to the extent of the penal amount of the bond, any judgment which may be rendered against him in such action.

On reasonable notice to the opposing party (which may be less than three days) either party shall have the right to prompt judicial review of the amount of bond required, denial of bond, sufficiency of sureties, and estimated value of the property, by the court which authorized issuance of the writ. The court's determination may be made upon the basis of affidavits, if uncontroverted, setting forth such facts as would be admissible in evidence; otherwise, the parties shall submit evidence. The court shall forthwith enter its order either approving or modifying the requirements of the officer or of the court's prior order, and such order of the court shall supersede and control with respect to such matters.

On reasonable notice to the opposing party (which may be less than three days) the defendant shall have the right to move the court for a substitution of property, of equal value as that attached, for the property attached. Provided that there has been located sufficient property of the defendants to satisfy the order of attachment, the court may authorize substitution of one or more items of defendant's property for all or for part of the property attached. The court shall first make findings as to the value of the property to be substituted. If property is substituted, the property released from attachment shall be delivered to defen-

dant, if such property is personal property, and all liens upon such property from the original order of attachment or modification thereof shall be terminated. Attachment of substituted property shall be deemed to have existed from the date of levy on the original property attached, and no property on which liens have become affixed since the date of levy on the original property may be substituted.

July 11, 1977, eff. Jan. 1, 1978.

TRCP 600. SALE OF PERISHABLE PROPERTY

Whenever personal property which has been attached shall not have been claimed or replevied, the judge, or justice of the peace, out of whose court the writ was issued, may, either in term time or in vacation, order the same to be sold, when it shall be made to appear that such property is in danger of serious and immediate waste or decay, or that the keeping of the same until the trial will necessarily be attended with such expense or deterioration in value as greatly to lessen the amount likely to be realized therefrom.

TRCP 601. TO PROTECT INTERESTS

In determining whether the property attached is perishable, and the necessity or advantage of ordering a sale thereof, the judge or justice of the peace may act upon affidavits in writing or oral testimony, and may by a preliminary order entered of record, with or without notice to the parties as the urgency of the case in his opinion requires, direct the sheriff or constable to sell such property at public auction for cash, and thereupon the officer shall sell it accordingly.

TRCP 602. BOND OF APPLICANT FOR SALE

If the application for an order of sale be filed by any person or party other than the defendant from whose possession the property was taken by levy, the court shall not grant such order unless the applicant shall file with such court a bond payable to such defendant, with two or more good and sufficient sureties, to be approved by said court, conditioned that they will be responsible to the defendant for such damages as he may sustain in case such sale be illegally and unjustly applied for, or be illegally and unjustly made.

TRCP 603. PROCEDURE FOR SALE

Such sale of attached perishable personal property shall be conducted in the same manner as sales of personal property under execution; provided, however, that the time of the sale, and at the time of advertisement thereof, may be fixed by the judge or justice of the peace at a time earlier than ten days, according to the exigency of the case, and in such event notice thereof shall be given in such manner as directed by the order.

TRCP 604. RETURN OF SALE

The officer making such sale of perishable property shall promptly pay the proceeds of such sale to the clerk of such court or justice of the peace, as the case may be, and shall make written return of the order of sale signed by him officially, stating the time and place of the sale, the name of the purchaser, and the amount of money received, with an itemized account of the expenses attending the sale. Such return shall be filed with the papers of the case.

TRCP 605. JUDGE MAY MAKE NECESSARY ORDERS

When the perishable personal property levied on under the attachment writ has not been claimed or replevied, the judge or justice of the peace may make such orders, either in term time or vacation, as may be necessary for its preservation or use.

TRCP 606. RETURN OF WRIT

The officer executing the writ of attachment shall return the writ, with his action endorsed thereon, or attached thereto, signed by him officially, to the court from which it issued, at or before 10 o'clock a.m. of the Monday next after the expiration of fifteen days from the date of issuance of the writ. Such return shall describe the property attached with sufficient certainty to identify it, and state when the same was attached, and whether any personal property attached remains still in his hands, and, if not, the disposition made of the same. When property has been replevied he shall deliver the replevy bond to the clerk or justice of the peace to be filed with the papers of the cause.

TRCP 607. REPORT OF DISPOSITION OF PROPERTY

When the property levied on is claimed, replevied or sold, or otherwise disposed of after the writ has been returned, the officer having the custody of the same shall immediately make a report in writing, signed by him officially, to the clerk, or justice of the peace, as the case may be, showing such disposition of the property. Such report shall be filed among the papers of the cause.

TRCP 608. DISSOLUTION OR MODIFICATION OF WRIT OF ATTACHMENT

A defendant whose property has been attached or any intervening party who claims an interest in such property, may by sworn written motion, seek to vacate, dissolve, or modify the writ, and the order directing its issuance, for any grounds or cause, extrinsic or intrinsic. Such motion shall admit or deny each finding of the order directing the issuance of the writ except where the movant is unable to admit or deny the finding, in which case movant shall set

forth the reasons why he cannot admit or deny. Unless the parties agree to an extension of time, the motion shall be heard promptly, after reasonable notice to the plaintiff (which may be less than three days), and the issue shall be determined not later than ten days after the motion is filed. The filing of the motion shall stay any further proceedings under the writ, except for any orders concerning the care, preservation, or sale of perishable property, until a hearing is had and the issue is determined. The writ shall be dissolved unless at such hearing, the plaintiff shall prove the grounds relied upon for its issuance, but the court may modify its previous order granting the writ and the writ issued pursuant thereto. The movant shall, however, have the burden to prove that the reasonable value of the property attached exceeds the amount necessary to secure the debt, interest for one year, and probable costs. He shall also have the burden to prove the facts to justify substitution of property.

The court's determination may be made upon the basis of affidavits, if uncontroverted, setting forth such facts as would be admissible in evidence; otherwise, the parties shall submit evidence. The court may make all such orders, including orders concerning the care, preservation, or disposition of the property (or the proceeds therefrom if the same has been sold), as justice may require. If the movant has given a replevy bond, an order to vacate or dissolve the writ shall vacate the replevy bond and discharge the sureties thereon, and if the court modifies its order or the writ issued pursuant thereto, it shall make such further orders with respect to the bond as may be consistent with its modification.

July 11, 1977, eff. Jan. 1, 1978.

TRCP 609. AMENDMENT

Clerical errors in the affidavit, bond, or writ of attachment, or the officer's return thereof, may upon application in writing to the judge or justice of the court in which the suit is filed, and after notice to the opponent, be amended in such manner and on such terms as the judge or justice shall authorize by an order entered in the minutes of the court or noted on the docket of the justice of the peace, provided the amendment does not change or add to the grounds of such attachment as stated in the affidavit, and provided such amendment appears to the judge or justice to be in furtherance of justice.

History of TRCP 609: Adopted eff. Sept. 1, 1941, by order of Oct. 29, 1940 (3 Tex.B.J. 617 [1940]). Source: New rule.

SECTION 2. DISTRESS WARRANT

TRCP 610. APPLICATION FOR DISTRESS WARRANT AND ORDER

Either at the commencement of a suit or at any time during its progress the plaintiff may file an application for the issuance of a distress warrant with the justice of the peace. Such application may be supported by affidavits of the plaintiff, his agent, his attorney, or other persons having knowledge of relevant facts, but shall include a statement that the amount sued for is rent, or advances described by statute, or shall produce a writing signed by the tenant to that effect, and shall further swear that such warrant is not sued out for the purpose of vexing and harassing the defendant. The application shall comply with all statutory requirements and shall state the grounds for issuing the warrant and the specific facts relied upon by the plaintiff to warrant the required findings by the justice of the peace. The warrant shall not be quashed because two or more grounds are stated conjunctively or disjunctively. The application and any affidavits shall be made on personal knowledge and shall set forth such facts as would be admissible in evidence provided that facts may be stated based upon information and belief if the grounds of such belief are specifically stated.

No warrant shall issue before final judgment except on written order of the justice of the peace after a hearing, which may be ex parte. Such warrant shall be made returnable to a court having jurisdiction of the amount in controversy. The justice of the peace in his order granting the application shall make specific findings of fact to support the statutory grounds found to exist, and shall specify the maximum value of property that may be seized, and the amount of bond required of plaintiff, and, further shall command that property be kept safe and preserved subject to further orders of the court having jurisdiction. Such bond shall be in an amount which, in the opinion of the court, shall adequately compensate defendant in the event plaintiff fails to prosecute his suit to effect, and pay all damages and costs as shall be adjudged against him for wrongfully suing out the warrant. The justice of the peace shall further find in his order the amount of bond required to replevy, which, unless the defendant chooses to exercise his option as provided in Rule 614, shall be the amount of plaintiff's claim, one year's accrual of interest if allowed by law on the claim, and the estimated costs of court. The order may direct the issuance of several warrants at the same time, or in succession, to be sent to different counties.

June 10, 1980, eff. Jan. 1, 1981.

TRCP 611. BOND FOR DISTRESS WARRANT

No distress warrant shall issue before final judgment until the party applying therefor has filed with the justice of the peace authorized to issue such warrant a bond payable to the defendant in an amount approved by the justice of the peace, with sufficient surety or sureties as provided by statute, conditioned that the plaintiff will prosecute his

suit to effect and pay all damages and costs as may be adjudged against him for wrongfully suing out such warrant.

After notice to the opposite party, either before or after the issuance of the warrant, the defendant or plaintiff may file a motion to increase or reduce the amount of such bond, or to question the sufficiency of the sureties thereon, in a court having jurisdiction of the subject matter. Upon hearing, the court shall enter its order with respect to such bond and sufficiency of the sureties.

June 10, 1980, eff. Jan. 1, 1981.

TRCP 612. REQUISITES FOR WARRANT

A distress warrant shall be directed to the sheriff or any constable within the State of Texas. It shall command him to attach and hold, unless replevied, subject to the further orders of the court having jurisdiction, so much of the property of the defendant, not exempt by statute, of reasonable value in approximately the amount fixed by the justice of the peace, as shall be found within his county.

June 10, 1980, eff. Jan. 1, 1981.

TRCP 613. SERVICE OF WARRANT ON DEFENDANT

The defendant shall be served in any manner prescribed for service of citation, or as provided in Rule 21a, with a copy of the distress warrant, the application, accompanying affidavits, and orders of the justice of the peace as soon as practicable following the levy of the warrant. There shall be prominently displayed on the face of the copy of the warrant served on the defendant, in 10-point type and in a manner calculated to advise a reasonably attentive person of its contents, the following:

To ______, Defendant:

You are hereby notified that certain properties alleged to be owned by you have been seized. If you claim any rights in such property, you are advised:

"YOU HAVE A RIGHT TO REGAIN POSSESSION OF THE PROPERTY BY FILING A REPLEVY BOND. YOU HAVE A RIGHT TO SEEK TO REGAIN POSSESSION OF THE PROPERTY BY FILING WITH THE COURT A MOTION TO DISSOLVE THIS WARRANT."

June 10, 1980, eff. Jan. 1, 1981.

TRCP 614. DEFENDANT MAY REPLEVY

At any time before judgment, should the seized property not have been previously claimed or sold, the defendant may replevy the same, or any part thereof, or the proceeds from the sale of the property if it has been sold under order of the court, by giving bond with sufficient surety or sureties as provided by statute, to be approved by a court having jurisdiction of the amount in controversy payable to plaintiff in double the amount of the plaintiff's debt, or, at the defendant's option for not less than the value of the property sought to be replevied, plus one year's interest thereon at the legal rate from the date of the bond, conditioned that the defendant shall satisfy to the extent of the penal amount of the bond any judgment which may be rendered against him in such action.

On reasonable notice to the opposing party (which may be less than three days) either party shall have the right to prompt judicial review of the amount of bond required, denial of bond, sufficiency of sureties, and estimated value of the property, by a court having jurisdiction of the amount in controversy. The court's determination may be made upon the basis of affidavits if uncontroverted setting forth such facts as would be admissible in evidence, otherwise the parties shall submit evidence. The court shall forthwith enter its order either approving or modifying the requirements of the order of the justice of the peace, and such order of the court shall supersede and control with respect to such matters.

On reasonable notice to the opposing party (which may be less than three days) the defendant shall have the right to move the court for a substitution of property, of equal value as that attached, for the property seized. Provided that there has been located sufficient property of the defendant's to satisfy the order of seizure, the court may authorize substitution of one or more items of defendant's property for all or part of the property seized. The court shall first make findings as to the value of the property to be substituted. If property is substituted, the property released from seizure shall be delivered to defendant, if such property is personal property, and all liens upon such property from the original order of seizure or modification thereof shall be terminated. Seizure of substituted property shall be deemed to have existed from the date of levy on the original property seized, and no property on which liens have become affixed since the date of levy on the original property may be substituted.

June 10, 1980, eff. Jan. 1, 1981.

TRCP 614a. DISSOLUTION OR MODIFICATION OF DISTRESS WARRANT

A defendant whose property has been seized or any intervening claimant who claims an interest in such property, may by sworn written motion, seek to vacate, dissolve, or modify the seizure, and the order directing its issuance,

for any grounds or cause, extrinsic or intrinsic. Such motion shall admit or deny each finding of the order directing the issuance of the warrant except where the movant is unable to admit or deny the finding, in which case movant shall set forth the reasons why he cannot admit or deny. Unless the parties agree to an extension of time, the motion shall be heard promptly, after reasonable notice to the plaintiff (which may be less than three days), and the issue shall be determined not later than 10 days after the motion is filed. The filing of the motion shall stay any further proceedings under the warrant, except for any orders concerning the care, preservation, or sale of any perishable property, until a hearing is had, and the issue is determined. The warrant shall be dissolved unless, at such hearing, the plaintiff shall prove the specific facts alleged and the grounds relied upon for its issuance, but the court may modify the order of the justice of the peace granting the warrant and the warrant issued pursuant thereto. The movant shall however have the burden to prove that the reasonable value of the property seized exceeds the amount necessary to secure the debt, interest for one year, and probable costs. He shall also have the burden to prove the facts to justify substitution of property.

The court's determination may be made upon the basis of affidavits setting forth such facts as would be admissible in evidence, but additional evidence, if tendered by either party shall be received and considered. The court may make all such orders, including orders concerning the care, preservation, or disposition of the property (or the proceeds therefrom if the same has been sold), as justice may require. If the movant has given a replevy bond, an order to vacate or dissolve the warrant shall vacate the replevy bond and discharge the sureties thereon, and if the court modifies the order of the justice of the peace or the warrant issued pursuant thereto, it shall make such further orders with respect to the bond as may be consistent with its modification.

June 10, 1980, eff. Jan. 1, 1981.

TRCP 615. SALE OF PERISHABLE PROPERTY

Whenever personal property which has been levied on under a distress warrant shall not have been claimed or replevied, the judge, or justice of the peace, to whose court such writ is made returnable may, either in term time or in vacation, order the same to be sold, when it shall be made to appear that such property is in danger of serious and immediate waste or decay, or that the keeping of the same until the trial will necessarily be attended with such expense or deterioration in value as greatly to lessen the amount likely to be realized therefrom.

History of TRCP 615: Adopted eff. Sept. 1, 1941, by order of Oct. 29, 1940 (3 Tex.B.J. 619 [1940]). Source: TRCS art. 5233 (repealed).

TRCP 616. TO PROTECT INTERESTS

In determining whether the property levied upon is perishable, and the necessity or advantage of ordering a sale thereof, the judge or justice of the peace may act upon affidavits in writing or oral testimony, and may by a preliminary order entered of record with or without notice to the parties as the urgency of the case in his opinion requires, direct the sheriff or constable to sell such property at public auction for cash, and thereupon the sheriff or constable shall sell it accordingly. If the application for an order of sale be filed by any person or party other than the defendant from whose possession the property was taken by levy, the court shall not grant such order, unless the applicant shall file with such court a bond payable to such defendant, with two or more good and sufficient sureties, to be approved by said court, conditioned that they will be responsible to the defendant for such damages as he may sustain in case such sale be illegally and unjustly applied for or be illegally and unjustly made.

History of TRCP 616: Adopted eff. Sept. 1, 1941, by order of Oct. 29, 1940 (3 Tex.B.J. 619 [1940]). Source: TRCS arts. 294, 5233 (repealed).

TRCP 617. PROCEDURE FOR SALE

Such sale of perishable personal property shall be conducted in the same manner as sales of personal property under execution; provided, however, that the time of the sale, and the time of advertisement thereof, may be fixed by the judge or justice of the peace at a time earlier than ten days, according to the exigency of the case, and in such event notice thereof shall be given in such manner as directed by the order.

History of TRCP 617: Adopted eff Sept. 1, 1941, by order of Oct. 29, 1940 (3 Tex.B.J. 619 [1940]). Source: TRCS art. 295 (repealed).

TRCP 618. RETURN OF SALE

The officer making such sale of perishable property shall promptly pay the proceeds of such sale to the clerk of such court or to the justice of the peace, as the case may be, and shall make written return of the order of sale, signed by him officially, stating the time and place of the sale, the name of the purchaser, and the amount of money received, with an itemized account of the expenses attending the sale. Such return shall be filed with the papers of the case.

History of TRCP 618: Adopted eff. Sept. 1, 1941, by order of Oct. 29, 1940 (3 Tex.B.J. 619 [1940]). Source: TRCS art. 296 (repealed).

TRCP 619. CITATION FOR DEFENDANT

The justice at the time he issues the warrant shall issue a citation to the defendant requiring him to answer before such justice at the first day of the next succeeding term of court, stating the time and place of holding the same, if he has jurisdiction to finally try the cause, and upon its being

returned served, to proceed to judgment as in ordinary cases; and, if he has not such jurisdiction, the citation shall require the defendant to answer before the court to which the warrant was made returnable at or before ten o'clock a.m. of the Monday next after the expiration of twenty days from the date of service thereof, stating the place of holding the court, and shall be returned with the other papers to such court. If the defendant has removed from the county without service, the proper officer shall state this fact in his return on the citation; and the court shall proceed to try the case ex parte, and may enter judgment.

History of TRCP 619: Adopted eff. Sept. 1, 1941, by order of Oct. 29, 1940 (3 Tex.B.J. 619 [1940]). Source: TRCS art. 5234 (repealed).

TRCP 620. PETITION

When the warrant is made returnable to the district or county court, the plaintiff shall file his petition within ten days from the date of the issuance of the writ.

History of TRCP 620: Adopted eff. Sept. 1, 1941, by order of Oct. 29, 1940 (3 Tex.B.J. 619 [1940]). Source: TRCS art. 5235 (repealed).

SECTION 3. EXECUTIONS

TRCP 621. ENFORCEMENT OF JUDGMENT

The judgments of the district, county, and justice courts shall be enforced by execution or other appropriate process. Such execution or other process shall be returnable in thirty, sixty, or ninety days as requested by the plaintiff, his agent or attorney.

History of TRCP 621: Adopted eff. Sept. 1, 1941, by order of Oct. 29, 1940 (3 Tex.B.J. 619 [1940]). Source: TRCS arts. 2445, 3784 (repealed).

TRCP 621a. DISCOVERY AND ENFORCEMENT OF JUDGMENT

At any time after rendition of judgment, and so long as said judgment has not been suspended by a supersedeas bond or by order of a proper court and has not become dormant as provided by Article 3773, V.A.T.S.,[1] the successful party may, for the purpose of obtaining information to aid in the enforcement of such judgment, initiate and maintain in the trial court in the same suit in which said judgment was rendered any discovery proceeding authorized by these rules for pre-trial matters. Also, at any time after rendition of judgment, either party may, for the purpose of obtaining information relevant to motions allowed by Texas Rules of Appellate Procedure 47 and 49[2] initiate and maintain in the trial court in the same suit in which said judgment was rendered any discovery proceeding authorized by these rules for pre-trial matters. The rules governing and related to such pre-trial discovery proceedings shall apply in like manner to discovery proceedings after judgment. The rights herein granted to the parties shall inure to their successors or assignees, in whole or in part. Judicial supervision of such discovery proceedings after judgment shall be the same as that provided by law or these rules for pre-trial discovery and proceedings insofar as applicable.

July 1, 1970, eff. Jan. 1, 1971. Amended by order of July 15, 1987, eff. Jan. 1, 1988.

Source: New rule.

[1]Repealed. See now V.T.C.A., Civil Practice & Remedies Code §34.001.
[2]So in original. Probably should be Rule 24.

ANNOTATIONS

In re Smith, 192 S.W.3d 564, 569 (Tex.2006). Judgment debtors "refused to answer much of the written post-judgment enforcement discovery. . . . Further, the parties had been engaged in post-judgment enforcement discovery for several months, and it was not until the eve of [one of their] deposition[s] that [judgment debtors] filed their cash deposits in lieu of bond and affidavits of net worth to supersede enforcement of the judgment. The trial court's conclusion that [judgment debtors] were attempting to avoid answering post-judgment enforcement discovery by filing the cash deposits in lieu of bond and affidavits of net worth was reasonable. [T]he trial court did not abuse its discretion by ordering [them] to respond to the discovery requests." *See also* **Arndt v. Farris**, 633 S.W.2d 497, 499 (Tex.1982).

Blankinship v. Brown, 399 S.W.3d 303, 312 (Tex.App.—Dallas 2013, pet. denied). "Relevance in the context of post-judgment discovery must be viewed generally in the same manner as in ordinary pretrial discovery, which includes anything reasonably calculated to lead to the discovery of material evidence. Material evidence includes any information that would aid in enforcement of the judgment."

In re Elmer, 158 S.W.3d 603, 605 (Tex.App.—San Antonio 2005, orig. proceeding). TRCP 621a "contemplates that the judgment to be enforced has at least two characteristics. First, the judgment must be of the type that it can be enforced. In order to enforce a judgment, the judgment must be final. [¶] Secondly, . . . the judgment at issue must be susceptible to being 'suspended by a supersedeas bond.' In order to suspend a judgment by a supersedeas bond, the judgment must also be final and appealable. [¶] [T]he trial court abused its discretion in compelling answers to interrogatories in aid of judgment in the absence of a final, appealable judgment."

Fisher v. P.M. Clinton Int'l Investigations, 81 S.W.3d 484, 486 (Tex.App.—Houston [1st Dist.] 2002, no pet.). "Because a post-judgment discovery order does not resolve all the disputes between the parties, a rule 621a order is not a final and appealable order." *See also* **Sintim v. Larson**, 489 S.W.3d 551, 557 (Tex.App.—Houston [14th Dist.] 2016, no pet.) (order awarding monetary sanctions issued as part of postjudgment discovery proceedings that has been reduced to judgment is final, appealable order).

TRCP 622. EXECUTION

An execution is a process of the court from which it is issued. The clerk of the district or county court or the justice

of the peace, as the case may be, shall tax the costs in every case in which a final judgment has been rendered and shall issue execution to enforce such judgment and collect such costs. The execution and subsequent executions shall not be addressed to a particular county, but shall be addressed to any sheriff or any constable within the State of Texas.

Sept. 20, 1941, eff. Dec. 31, 1941.

Source: TRCS arts. 2446, 2447, 3770, 3780–3782 (repealed).

ANNOTATIONS

In re Burlington Coat Factory Whs., 167 S.W.3d 827, 831 (Tex.2005). "[A]n interlocutory judgment may not be enforced through execution."

TRCP 623. ON DEATH OF EXECUTOR

When an executor, administrator, guardian or trustee of an express trust dies, or ceases to be such executor, administrator, guardian or trustee after judgment, execution shall issue on such judgment in the name of his successor, upon an affidavit of such death or termination being filed with the clerk of the court or the justice of the peace, as the case may be, together with the certificate of the appointment of such successor under the hand and seal of the clerk of the court wherein the appointment was made.

History of TRCP 623: Adopted eff. Sept. 1, 1941, by order of Oct. 29, 1940 (3 Tex.B.J. 620 [1940]). Source: TRCS art. 3776 (repealed).

TRCP 624. ON DEATH OF NOMINAL PLAINTIFF

When a person in whose favor a judgment is rendered for the use of another dies after judgment, execution shall issue in the name of the party for whose use the suit was brought upon an affidavit of such death being filed with the clerk of the court or the justice of the peace.

History of TRCP 624: Adopted eff. Sept. 1, 1941, by order of Oct. 29, 1940 (3 Tex.B.J. 620 [1940]). Source: TRCS art. 3777 (repealed).

TRCP 625. ON MONEY OF DECEASED

If a sole defendant dies after judgment for money against him, execution shall not issue thereon, but the judgment may be proved up and paid in due course of administration.

History of TRCP 625: Adopted eff. Sept. 1, 1941, by order of Oct. 29, 1940 (3 Tex.B.J. 620 [1940]). Source: TRCS art. 3778 (repealed).

TRCP 626. ON PROPERTY OF DECEASED

In any case of judgment other than a money judgment, where the sole defendant, or one or more of several joint defendants, shall die after judgment, upon an affidavit of such death being filed with the clerk, together with the certificate of the appointment of a representative of such decedent under the hand and seal of the clerk of the court wherein such appointment was made, the proper process on such judgment shall issue against such representative.

History of TRCP 626: Adopted eff. Sept. 1, 1941, by order of Oct. 29, 1940 (3 Tex.B.J. 620 [1940]). Source: TRCS art. 3779 (repealed).

TRCP 627. TIME FOR ISSUANCE

If no supersedeas bond or notice of appeal, as required of agencies exempt from filing bonds, has been filed and approved, the clerk of the court or justice of the peace shall issue the execution upon such judgment upon application of the successful party or his attorney after the expiration of thirty days from the time a final judgment is signed. If a timely motion for new trial or in arrest of judgment is filed, the clerk shall issue the execution upon the judgment on application of the party or his attorney after the expiration of thirty days from the time the order overruling the motion is signed or from the time the motion is overruled by operation of law.

July 22, 1975, eff. Jan. 1, 1976. Amended by orders of June 20, 1980, eff. Jan. 1, 1980; Dec. 5, 1983, eff. April 1, 1984.

Source: TRCS arts. 2448, 3771 (repealed).

See also CPRC §§65.013, 65.014.

ANNOTATIONS

Akin, Gump, Strauss, Hauer & Feld, L.L.P. v. National Dev. & Research Corp., 299 S.W.3d 106, 113 (Tex.2009). "Depending on the particular case's circumstances . . . the 30-day period [under TRCP 627] may be shortened or extended. Further, unless the judgment debtor properly supersedes the judgment, the judgment creditor is not precluded from immediately filing an abstract of judgment to aid in seeking satisfaction of its judgment."

Mackey v. Great Lakes Invs., 255 S.W.3d 243, 254 (Tex.App.—San Antonio 2008, pet. denied). Under " 'Rule 627, executions of final judgments from district courts may not issue until after 30 days have elapsed since the rendition of the final judgment or after the overruling of any motions for a new trial.' However, a prematurely issued execution of judgment is not void, only voidable." *See also* **Winkle v. Winkle**, 951 S.W.2d 80, 89 (Tex.App.—Corpus Christi 1997, pet. denied).

TRCP 628. EXECUTION WITHIN THIRTY DAYS

Such execution may be issued at any time before the thirtieth day upon the filing of an affidavit by the plaintiff in the judgment or his agent or attorney that the defendant is about to remove his personal property subject to execution by law out of the county, or is about to transfer or secrete such personal property for the purpose of defrauding his creditors.

July 22, 1975, eff. Jan. 1, 1976.

Source: TRCS arts. 2449, 3774 (repealed).

See also CPRC §§65.013, 65.014.

ANNOTATIONS

Perfection Casting Corp. v. Aluminum Alloys, Inc., 733 S.W.2d 385, 386 (Tex.App.—San Antonio 1987, no writ). Held: It was proper for the trial court to allow immediate execution on a judgment, even though the affidavit did not allege sufficient facts to warrant immediate execution, when, after the affidavit was filed and execution was granted, the party received a hearing on the sufficiency of the affidavit.

TRCP 629. REQUISITES OF EXECUTION

The style of the execution shall be "The State of Texas." It shall be directed to any sheriff or any constable within the State of Texas. It shall be signed by the clerk or justice officially, and bear the seal of the court, if issued out of the district or county court, and shall require the officer to execute it according to its terms, and to make the costs which have been adjudged against the defendant in execution and the further costs of executing the writ. It shall describe the judgment, stating the court in which, and the time when, rendered, and the names of the parties in whose favor and against whom the judgment was rendered. A correct copy of the bill of costs taxed against the defendant in execution shall be attached to the writ. It shall require the officer to return it within thirty, sixty, or ninety days, as directed by the plaintiff or his attorney.

Sept. 20, 1941, eff. Dec. 20, 1941.

TRCP 630. EXECUTION ON JUDGMENT FOR MONEY

When an execution is issued upon a judgment for a sum of money, or directing the payment simply of a sum of money, it must specify in the body thereof the sum recovered or directed to be paid and the sum actually due when it is issued and the rate of interest upon the sum due. It must require the officer to satisfy the judgment and costs out of the property of the judgment debtor subject to execution by law.

History of TRCP 630: Adopted eff. Sept. 1, 1941, by order of Oct. 29, 1940 (3 Tex.B.J. 621 [1940]). Source: TRCS art. 3783(2) (repealed).

TRCP 631. EXECUTION FOR SALE OF PARTICULAR PROPERTY

An execution issued upon a judgment for the sale of particular chattels or personal property or real estate, must particularly describe the property, and shall direct the officer to make the sale by previously giving the public notice of the time and place of sale required by law and these rules.

History of TRCP 631: Adopted eff. Sept. 1, 1941, by order of Oct. 29, 1940 (3 Tex.B.J. 621 [1940]). Source: TRCS art. 3783(3) (repealed).

TRCP 632. EXECUTION FOR DELIVERY OF CERTAIN PROPERTY

An execution issued upon a judgment for the delivery of the possession of a chattel or personal property, or for the delivery of the possession of real property, shall particularly describe the property, and designate the party to whom the judgment awards the possession. The writ shall require the officer to deliver the possession of the property to the party entitled thereto.

History of TRCP 632: Adopted eff. Sept. 1, 1941, by order of Oct. 29, 1940 (3 Tex.B.J. 621 [1940]). Source: TRCS art. 3783(4) (repealed).

TRCP 633. EXECUTION FOR POSSESSION OR VALUE OF PERSONAL PROPERTY

If the judgment be for the recovery of personal property or its value, the writ shall command the officer, in case a delivery thereof cannot be had, to levy and collect the value thereof for which the judgment was recovered, to be specified therein, out of any property of the party against whom judgment was rendered, liable to execution.

History of TRCP 633: Adopted eff. Sept. 1, 1941, by order of Oct. 29, 1940 (3 Tex.B.J. 621 [1940]). Source: TRCS art. 3783(5) (repealed).

TRCP 634. EXECUTION SUPERSEDED

The clerk or justice of the peace shall immediately issue a writ of supersedeas suspending all further proceedings under any execution previously issued when a supersedeas bond is afterward filed and approved within the time prescribed by law or these rules.

History of TRCP 634: Adopted eff. Sept. 1, 1941, by order of Oct. 29, 1940 (3 Tex.B.J. 621 [1940]). Source: TRCS art. 3772 (repealed).

See also CPRC §§65.013, 65.014.

TRCP 635. STAY OF EXECUTION IN JUSTICE COURT

At any time within ten days after the rendition of any judgment in a justice court, the justice may grant a stay of execution thereof for three months from the date of such judgment, if the person against whom such judgment was rendered shall, with one or more good and sufficient sureties, to be approved by the justice, appear before him and acknowledge themselves and each of them bound to the successful party in such judgment for the full amount thereof, with interest and costs, which acknowledgment shall be entered in writing on the docket, and signed by the persons binding themselves as sureties; provided, no such stay of execution shall be granted unless the party applying therefor shall first file an affidavit with the justice that he has not the money with which to pay such judgment, and that the enforcement of same by execution prior to three months

would be a hardship upon him and would cause a sacrifice of his property which would not likely be caused should said execution be stayed. Such acknowledgment shall be entered by the justice on his docket and shall constitute a judgment against the defendant and such sureties, upon which execution shall issue in case the same is not paid on or before the expiration of such day.

History of TRCP 635: Adopted eff. Sept. 1, 1941, by order of Oct. 29, 1940 (3 Tex.B.J. 621 [1940]). Source: TRCS art. 2453 (repealed).

See also CPRC §§65.013, 65.014.

TRCP 636. INDORSEMENTS BY OFFICER

The officer receiving the execution shall indorse thereon the exact hour and day when he received it. If he receives more than one on the same day against the same person he shall number them as received.

History of TRCP 636: Adopted eff. Sept. 1, 1941, by order of Oct. 29, 1940 (3 Tex.B.J. 622 [1940]). Source: TRCS art. 3785, first sentence and first part of second sentence (repealed in part by TRCP).

TRCP 637. LEVY OF EXECUTION

When an execution is delivered to an officer he shall proceed without delay to levy the same upon the property of the defendant found within his county not exempt from execution, unless otherwise directed by the plaintiff, his agent or attorney. The officer shall first call upon the defendant, if he can be found, or, if absent, upon his agent within the county, if known, to point out property to be levied upon, and the levy shall first be made upon the property designated by the defendant, or his agent. If in the opinion of the officer the property so designated will not sell for enough to satisfy the execution and costs of sale, he shall require an additional designation by the defendant. If no property be thus designated by the defendant, the officer shall levy the execution upon any property of the defendant subject to execution.

History of TRCP 637: Adopted eff. Sept. 1, 1941, by order of Oct. 29, 1940 (3 Tex.B.J. 622 [1940]). Source: TRCS arts. 3788–3790 (repealed).

ANNOTATIONS

Keathley v. J.J. Inv. Co., No. 06-14-00036-CV, 2015 WL 3918446 (Tex.App.—Texarkana 2015, no pet.) (memo op.; 6-26-15). Debtor "does not cite, and we have not found, any authority stating that the failure of an officer to notify the debtor before executing on his property, standing alone, is sufficient to invalidate a levy of execution. [¶] Certainly, an officer levying a writ of execution 'shall first call on the [debtor], if he can be found . . . to point out property to be levied on.' . . . The failure of an officer to make any attempt to contact the debtor and give him or her an opportunity to designate property to be levied on is an irregularity. An irregularity, however, standing alone, will not invalidate an execution sale. . . . Rather, what is required is a showing that the sale was made for a grossly inadequate price, that there were irregularities, and that the irregularities tended to contribute to the inadequate price."

TRCP 638. PROPERTY NOT TO BE DESIGNATED

A defendant in execution shall not point out property which he has sold, mortgaged or conveyed in trust, or property exempt from forced sale.

History of TRCP 638: Adopted eff. Sept. 1, 1941, by order of Oct. 29, 1940 (3 Tex.B.J. 622 [1940]). Source: TRCS art. 3791 (repealed).

TRCP 639. LEVY

In order to make a levy on real estate, it shall not be necessary for the officer to go upon the ground but it shall be sufficient for him to indorse such levy on the writ. Levy upon personal property is made by taking possession thereof, when the defendant in execution is entitled to the possession. Where the defendant in execution has an interest in personal property, but is not entitled to the possession thereof, a levy is made thereon by giving notice thereof to the person who is entitled to the possession, or one of them where there are several.

History of TRCP 639: Adopted eff. Sept. 1, 1941, by order of Oct. 29, 1940 (3 Tex.B.J. 622 [1940]). Source: TRCS art. 3793 (repealed).

ANNOTATIONS

Beaurline v. Sinclair Ref. Co., 191 S.W.2d 774, 777 (Tex.App.—San Antonio 1945, writ ref'd n.r.e.). "[W]here a levy is made on property . . . which is so cumbersome that it may not be moved except at large expense and effort, it is sufficient if the officer goes upon the premises, points out the property, asserts dominion over it and forbids its removal by the person against whom the writ has been issued. The officer in making a levy on such property must do some act which would constitute a trespass except for the immunity furnished him by the writ."

TRCP 640. LEVY ON STOCK RUNNING AT LARGE

A levy upon livestock running at large in a range, and which cannot be herded and penned without great inconvenience and expense, may be made by designating by reasonable estimate the number of animals and describing them by their marks and brands, or either; such levy shall be made in the presence of two or more credible persons, and notice thereof shall be given in writing to the owner or his herder or agent, if residing within the county and known to the officer.

History of TRCP 640: Adopted eff. Sept. 1, 1941, by order of Oct. 29,

1940 (3 Tex.B.J. 622 [1940]). Source: TRCS art. 3794 (repealed).

TRCP 641. LEVY ON SHARES OF STOCK

A levy upon shares of stock of any corporation or joint stock company for which a certificate is outstanding is made by the officer seizing and taking possession of such certificate. Provided, however, that nothing herein shall be construed as restricting any rights granted under Section 8.317 of the Texas Uniform Commercial Code.

Aug. 18, 1947, eff. Dec. 31, 1947. Amended by order of July 21, 1970, eff. Jan. 1, 1971.

Editor's Note: Texas Uniform Commercial Code §8.317, as referenced in TRCP 641, was deleted by Acts 1995, 74th Leg., ch. 962, §1, eff. Sept. 1, 1995. See Bus. & Com. Code §8.112.

Source: TRCS art. 3795 (repealed).

ANNOTATIONS

Benson v. Greenville Nat'l Exch. Bank, 253 S.W.2d 918, 928 (Tex.App.—Texarkana 1952, writ ref'd n.r.e.). "[W]hile the mere delivery of a stock certificate . . . would not transfer title, yet the mere delivery of the stock would create a right in the bank as pledgee, by virtue of which it could resort to equity if its security was in any way threatened."

TRCP 642. REPEALED JULY 22, 1975, EFFECTIVE JAN. 1, 1976

TRCP 643. LEVY ON GOODS PLEDGED OR MORTGAGED

Goods and chattels pledged, assigned or mortgaged as security for any debt or contract, may be levied upon and sold on execution against the person making the pledge, assignment or mortgage subject thereto; and the purchaser shall be entitled to the possession when it is held by the pledgee, assignee or mortgagee, on complying with the conditions of the pledge, assignment or mortgage.

History of TRCP 643: Adopted eff. Sept. 1, 1941, by order of Oct. 29, 1940 (3 Tex.B.J. 623 [1940]). Source: TRCS art. 3797 (repealed).

ANNOTATIONS

Conseco Fin. Servicing Corp. v. J&J Mobile Homes, Inc., 120 S.W.3d 878, 886 (Tex.App.—Fort Worth 2003, pet. denied). "[P] reasons that under [TRCP] 643 a tax lien is the equivalent of a judicial lien created when an officer levies upon personal property under a writ of execution. [P] argues a tax lien is therefore subordinate to a security interest noted on the certificate of title. We disagree. [P] ignores the fact that tax liens are, by statute, given express priority status over security interests noted on certificates of title."

Grocers Sup. v. Intercity Inv. Props., 795 S.W.2d 225, 227 (Tex.App.—Houston [14th Dist.] 1990, no writ). "[T]he right of . . . a prior secured creditor[ ] to take possession of its collateral was superior to the right of . . . a mere judgment creditor, and [the prior secured creditor] could regain possession of the collateral from the constable who had levied on the property."

TRCP 644. MAY GIVE DELIVERY BOND

Any personal property taken in execution may be returned to the defendant by the officer upon the delivery by the defendant to him of a bond, payable to the plaintiff, with two or more good and sufficient sureties, to be approved by the officer, conditioned that the property shall be delivered to the officer at the time and place named in the bond, to be sold according to law, or for the payment to the officer of a fair value thereof, which shall be stated in the bond.

History of TRCP 644: Adopted eff. Sept. 1, 1941, by order of Oct. 29, 1940 (3 Tex.B.J. 623 [1940]). Source: TRCS art. 3801 (repealed).

TRCP 645. PROPERTY MAY BE SOLD BY DEFENDANT

Where property has been replevied, as provided in the preceding rule, the defendant may sell or dispose of the same, paying the officer the stipulated value thereof.

History of TRCP 645: Adopted eff. Sept. 1, 1941, by order of Oct. 29, 1940 (3 Tex.B.J. 623 [1940]). Source: TRCS art. 3802 (repealed).

TRCP 646. FORFEITED DELIVERY BOND

In case of the non-delivery of the property according to the terms of the delivery bond, and non-payment of the value thereof, the officer shall forthwith indorse the bond "Forfeited" and return the same to the clerk of the court or the justice of the peace from which the execution issued; whereupon, if the judgment remain unsatisfied in whole or in part, the clerk or justice shall issue execution against the principal debtor and the sureties on the bond for the amount due, not exceeding the stipulated value of the property, upon which execution no delivery bond shall be taken, which instruction shall be indorsed by the clerk or justice on the execution.

History of TRCP 646: Adopted eff. Sept. 1, 1941, by order of Oct. 29, 1940 (3 Tex.B.J. 623 [1940]). Source: TRCS art. 3803 (repealed).

TRCP 646a. SALE OF REAL PROPERTY

Real property taken by virtue of any execution shall be sold at public auction, at the courthouse door of the county, unless the court orders that such sale be at the place where the real property is situated, on the first Tuesday of the month, between the hours of ten o'clock, a.m. and four o'clock, p.m.

July 26, 1960, eff. Jan. 1, 1961.

TRCP 647. NOTICE OF SALE OF REAL ESTATE

The time and place of sale of real estate under execution, order of sale, or venditioni exponas, shall be advertised by

the officer by having the notice thereof published in the English language once a week for three consecutive weeks preceding such sale, in some newspaper published in said county. The first of said publications shall appear not less than twenty days immediately preceding the day of sale. Said notice shall contain a statement of the authority by virtue of which the sale is to be made, the time of levy, and the time and place of sale; it shall also contain a brief description of the property to be sold, and shall give the number of acres, original survey, locality in the county, and the name by which the land is most generally known, but it shall not be necessary for it to contain field notes. Publishers of newspapers shall charge the legal rate of Two (2) Cents per word for the first insertion of such publication and One (1) Cent per word for such subsequent insertions, or such newspapers shall be entitled to charge for such publication at a rate equal to but not in excess of the published word or line rate of that newspaper for such class of advertising. If there be no newspaper published in the county, or none which will publish the notice of sale for the compensation herein fixed, the officer shall then post such notice in writing in three public places in the county, one of which shall be at the courthouse door of such county, for at least twenty days successively next before the day of sale. The officer making the levy shall give the defendant, or his attorney, written notice of such sale, either in person or by mail, which notice shall substantially conform to the foregoing requirements.

Sept. 20, 1941, eff. Dec. 31, 1941.

Source: TRCS art. 3808 (repealed).

ANNOTATIONS

Ray v. Castilian Vill. Townhouse Ass'n, No. 01-10-00937-CV, 2011 WL 1103158 (Tex.App.—Houston [1st Dist.] 2011, pet. denied) (memo op.; 3-24-11). "Although [TRCP] 647 speaks of regular mail, courts have noted that [TRCP] 21a, which applies to every notice required to be served by the [TRCPs], imposes the requirement of registered mail upon the general provisions for mail in rule 647." (Internal quotes omitted.) *See also* **Collum v. DeLoughter**, 535 S.W.2d 390, 392 (Tex.App.—Texarkana 1976, writ ref'd n.r.e.).

McCoy v. Rogers, 240 S.W.3d 267, 275 (Tex.App.—Houston [1st Dist.] 2007, pet. denied). "Compliance with the notice requirements for execution . . . is a prerequisite to the right of the trustee or sheriff to make the sale."

TRCP 648. "COURTHOUSE DOOR" DEFINED

By the term "courthouse door" of a county is meant either of the principal entrances to the house provided by the proper authority for the holding of the district court. If from any cause there is no such house, the door of the house where the district court was last held in that county shall be deemed to be the courthouse door. Where the courthouse, or house used by the court, has been destroyed by fire or other cause, and another has not been designated by the proper authority, the place where such house stood shall be deemed to be the courthouse door.

History of TRCP 648: Adopted eff. Sept. 1, 1941, by order of Oct. 29, 1940 (3 Tex.B.J. 624 [1940]). Source: TRCS art. 3809 (repealed).

ANNOTATIONS

Micrea, Inc. v. Eureka Life Ins., 534 S.W.2d 348, 358 (Tex.App.—Fort Worth 1976, writ ref'd n.r.e.). "In general the 'Courthouse Door' is either of the (several) entrances to the building provided for the holding of the district court."

TRCP 649. SALE OF PERSONAL PROPERTY

Personal property levied on under execution shall be offered for sale on the premises where it is taken in execution, or at the courthouse door of the county, or at some other place if, owing to the nature of the property, it is more convenient to exhibit it to purchasers at such place. Personal property susceptible of being exhibited shall not be sold unless the same be present and subject to the view of those attending the sale, except shares of stock in joint stock or incorporated companies, and in cases where the defendant in execution has merely an interest without right to the exclusive possession in which case the interest of defendant may be sold and conveyed without the presence or delivery of the property. When a levy is made upon livestock running at large on the range, it is not necessary that such stock, or any part thereof, be present at the place of sale, and the purchaser at such sale is authorized to gather and pen such stock and select therefrom the number purchased by him.

History of TRCP 649: Adopted eff. Sept. 1, 1941, by order of Oct. 29, 1940 (3 Tex.B.J. 624 [1940]). Source: TRCS arts. 3811, 3813, 3814 (repealed).

TRCP 650. NOTICE OF SALE OF PERSONAL PROPERTY

Previous notice of the time and place of the sale of any personal property levied on under execution shall be given by posting notice thereof for ten days successively immediately prior to the day of sale at the courthouse door of any county and at the place where the sale is to be made.

History of TRCP 650: Adopted eff. Sept. 1, 1941, by order of Oct. 29, 1940 (3 Tex.B.J. 624 [1940]). Source: TRCS art. 3812 (repealed).

TRCP 651. WHEN EXECUTION NOT SATISFIED

When the property levied upon does not sell for enough to satisfy the execution, the officer shall proceed anew, as in

the first instance, to make the residue.

History of TRCP 651: Adopted eff. Sept. 1, 1941, by order of Oct. 29, 1940 (3 Tex.B.J. 624 [1940]). Source: TRCS art. 3815 (repealed).

TRCP 652. PURCHASER FAILING TO COMPLY

If any person shall bid off property at any sale made by virtue of an execution, and shall fail to comply with the terms of the sale, he shall be liable to pay the plaintiff in execution twenty per cent on the value of the property thus bid off, besides costs, to be recovered on motion, five days notice of such motion being given to such purchaser; and should the property on a second sale bring less than on the former, he shall be liable to pay to the defendant in execution all loss which he sustains thereby, to be recovered on motion as above provided.

History of TRCP 652: Adopted eff. Sept. 1, 1941, by order of Oct. 29, 1940 (3 Tex.B.J. 625 [1940]). Source: TRCS art. 3821 (repealed).

ANNOTATIONS

Jackson v. Universal Life Ins., 582 S.W.2d 207, 209 (Tex.App.—Eastland 1979, writ ref'd n.r.e.). "[W]here a bidder fails to comply with the terms of an execution sale, he becomes liable under the express provisions of the rule, whether or not he acted in good faith."

TRCP 653. RESALE OF PROPERTY

When the terms of the sale shall not be complied with by the bidder the levying officer shall proceed to sell the same property again on the same day, if there be sufficient time; but if not, he shall re-advertise and sell the same as in the first instance.

History of TRCP 653: Adopted eff. Sept. 1, 1941, by order of Oct. 29, 1940 (3 Tex.B.J. 625 [1940]). Source: TRCS art. 3822 (repealed).

TRCP 654. RETURN OF EXECUTION

The levying officer shall make due return of the execution, in writing and signed by him officially, stating concisely what such officer has done in pursuance of the requirements of the writ and of the law. The return shall be filed with the clerk of the court or the justice of the peace as the case may be. The execution shall be returned forthwith if satisfied by the collection of the money or if ordered by the plaintiff or his attorney indorsed thereon.

History of TRCP 654: Adopted eff. Sept. 1, 1941, by order of Oct. 29, 1940 (3 Tex.B.J. 625 [1940]). Source: TRCS art. 3828 (repealed).

ANNOTATIONS

Scott v. Wilson, 231 S.W.2d 912, 913 (Tex.App.—Amarillo 1950, no writ). "[A] sheriff's return upon an execution or order of sale may be amended."

TRCP 655. RETURN OF EXECUTION BY MAIL

When an execution is placed in the hands of an officer of a county other than the one in which the judgment is rendered, return may be made by mail; but money cannot be thus sent except by direction of the party entitled to receive the same or his attorney of record.

History of TRCP 655: Adopted eff. Sept. 1, 1941, by order of Oct. 29, 1940 (3 Tex.B.J. 625 [1940]). Source: TRCS art. 3823 (repealed).

TRCP 656. EXECUTION DOCKET

The clerk of each court shall keep an execution docket in which he shall enter a statement of all executions as they are issued by him, specifying the names of the parties, the amount of the judgment, the amount due thereon, the rate of interest when it exceeds six per cent, the costs, the date of issuing the execution, to whom delivered, and the return of the officer thereon, with the date of such return. Such docket entries shall be taken and deemed to be a record. The clerk shall keep an index and cross-index to the execution docket. When execution is in favor or against several persons, it shall be indexed in the name of each person. Any clerk who shall fail to keep said execution docket and index thereto, or shall neglect to make the entries therein, shall be liable upon his official bond to any person injured for the amount of damages sustained by such neglect.

History of TRCP 656: Adopted eff. Sept. 1, 1941, by order of Oct. 29, 1940 (3 Tex.B.J. 626 [1940]). Source: TRCS art. 3831 (repealed).

SECTION 4. GARNISHMENT

TRCP 657. JUDGMENT FINAL FOR GARNISHMENT

In the case mentioned in subsection 3, section 63.001, Civil Practice and Remedies Code, the judgment whether based upon a liquidated demand or an unliquidated demand, shall be deemed final and subsisting for the purpose of garnishment from and after the date it is signed, unless a supersedeas bond shall have been approved and filed in accordance with Texas Rules of Appellate Procedure 47.[1]

June 10, 1980, eff. Jan. 1, 1981. Amended by order of July 15, 1987, eff. Jan. 1, 1988.

Source: New rule.

[1] So in original. Probably should read Rule 24.

ANNOTATIONS

Bank One v. Sunbelt Sav., 824 S.W.2d 557, 558 (Tex.1992). "Garnishment is a statutory proceeding whereby the property, money, or credits of a debtor in the possession of another are applied to the payment of the debt."

Westerman v. Comerica Bank-Tex., 928 S.W.2d 679, 682 (Tex.App.—San Antonio 1996, writ denied). "[T]he rec-

ord contains conclusive summary judgment proof showing that when the garnishment action was actually finalized, the judgment was still a 'valid subsisting judgment'. . . . The fact that the underlying judgment was reversed 14 months after the garnishment judgment was rendered does not subsequently render the garnishment proceedings wrongful."

TRCP 658. APPLICATION FOR WRIT OF GARNISHMENT AND ORDER

Either at the commencement of a suit or at any time during its progress the plaintiff may file an application for a writ of garnishment. Such application shall be supported by affidavits of the plaintiff, his agent, his attorney, or other person having knowledge of relevant facts. The application shall comply with all statutory requirements and shall state the grounds for issuing the writ and the specific facts relied upon by the plaintiff to warrant the required findings by the court. The writ shall not be quashed because two or more grounds are stated conjunctively or disjunctively. The application and any affidavits shall be made on personal knowledge and shall set forth such facts as would be admissible in evidence; provided that facts may be stated based upon information and belief if the grounds of such belief are specifically stated.

No writ shall issue before final judgment except upon written order of the court after a hearing, which may be ex parte. The court in its order granting the application shall make specific findings of facts to support the statutory grounds found to exist, and shall specify the maximum value of property or indebtedness that may be garnished and the amount of bond required of plaintiff. Such bond shall be in an amount which, in the opinion of the court, shall adequately compensate defendant in the event plaintiff fails to prosecute his suit to effect, and pay all damages and costs as shall be adjudged against him for wrongfully suing out the writ of garnishment. The court shall further find in its order the amount of bond required of defendant to replevy, which, unless defendant exercises his option as provided under Rule 664, shall be the amount of plaintiff's claim, one year's accrual of interest if allowed by law on the claim, and the estimated costs of court. The order may direct the issuance of several writs at the same time, or in succession, to be sent to different counties.

Aug. 18, 1947, eff. Dec. 31, 1947. Amended by order of July 11, 1977, eff. Jan. 1, 1978.

Source: TRCS art. 4078 (repealed).

ANNOTATIONS

El Periodico, Inc. v. Parks Oil Co., 917 S.W.2d 777, 779 (Tex.1996). Garnishor's "application did not meet the requirements of [TRCP] 658. . . . [¶] The allegation of [garnishee's] indebtedness to [judgment debtor] is made on belief of counsel, and the grounds of such belief are not specifically stated."

Simulis, L.L.C. v. G.E. Capital Corp., 276 S.W.3d 109, 115 (Tex.App.—Houston [1st Dist.] 2008, no pet.). "Although [TRCP 658's] first paragraph applies to both pre- and post-judgment garnishment proceedings, the . . . second paragraph applies only to pre-judgment proceedings. . . . Everything . . . within [the second] paragraph must be read in [the context of 'before final judgment,'] such as, for example, the requirements to obtain an order granting the application with findings of fact, to have the court determine the maximum value of property or indebtedness that may be garnished, and to set a bond for the plaintiff-creditor. . . . The reason for the bond is obviously to protect the defendant-debtor if the underlying suit for debt is not prosecuted. . . ."

TRCP 658a. BOND FOR GARNISHMENT

No writ of garnishment shall issue before final judgment until the party applying therefor has filed with the officer authorized to issue such writ a bond payable to the defendant in the amount fixed by the court's order, with sufficient surety or sureties as provided by statute, conditioned that the plaintiff will prosecute his suit to effect and pay to the extent of the penal amount of the bond all damages and costs as may be adjudged against him for wrongfully suing out such writ of garnishment.

After notice to the opposite party, either before or after the issuance of the writ, the defendant or plaintiff may file a motion to increase or reduce the amount of such bond, or to question the sufficiency of the sureties. Upon hearing, the court shall enter its order with respect to such bond and the sufficiency of the sureties.

Should it be determined from the garnishee's answer if such is not controverted that the garnishee is indebted to the defendant, or has in his hands effects belonging to the defendant, in an amount or value less than the amount of the debt claimed by the plaintiff, then after notice to the defendant the court in which such garnishment is pending upon hearing may reduce the required amount of such bond to double the sum of the garnishee's indebtedness to the defendant plus the value of the effects in his hands belonging to the defendant.

July 26, 1960, eff. Jan. 1, 1961. Amended by order of July 11, 1977, eff. Jan. 1, 1978.

TRCP 659. CASE DOCKETED

When the foregoing requirements of these rules have been complied with, the judge, or clerk, or justice of the peace, as the case may be, shall docket the case in the name of the plaintiff as plaintiff and of the garnishee as defendant;

and shall immediately issue a writ of garnishment directed to the garnishee, commanding him to appear before the court out of which the same is issued at or before 10 o'clock a.m. of the Monday next following the expiration of twenty days from the date the writ was served, if the writ is issued out of the district or county court; or the Monday next after the expiration of ten days from the date the writ was served, if the writ is issued out of the justice court. The writ shall command the garnishee to answer under oath upon such return date what, if anything, he is indebted to the defendant, and was when the writ was served, and what effects, if any, of the defendant he has in his possession, and had when such writ was served, and what other persons, if any, within his knowledge, are indebted to the defendant or have effects belonging to him in their possession.

Sept. 20, 1941, eff. Dec. 31, 1941. Amended by orders of Aug. 18, 1947, eff. Dec. 31, 1947; July 11, 1977, eff. Jan. 1, 1978.

Source: TRCS art. 4079 (repealed).

ANNOTATIONS

Cloughly v. NBC Bank-Seguin, 773 S.W.2d 652, 658 (Tex.App.—San Antonio 1989, writ denied). "Although the statute contemplates a separate docketing, we do not find harm in proceeding with a garnishment action in the same cause number. Although this was an irregularity in procedure, the validity of the judgment was not affected."

TRCP 660. REPEALED BY ORDER OF AUG. 18, 1947, EFF. DEC. 31, 1947

TRCP 661. FORM OF WRIT

The following form of writ may be used:

"The State of Texas.

To E.F., Garnishee, greeting:

"Whereas, in the _______ Court of _______ County (if a justice court, state also the number of the precinct), in a certain cause wherein A.B. is plaintiff and C.D. is defendant, the plaintiff, claiming an indebtedness against the said C.D. of _______ dollars, besides interest and costs of suit, has applied for a writ of garnishment against you, E.F.; therefore you are hereby commanded to be and appear before said court at _______ in said county (if the writ is issued from the county or district court, here proceed: 'at 10 o'clock a.m. on the Monday next following the expiration of twenty days from the date of service hereof.' If the writ is issued from a justice of the peace court, here proceed: 'at or before 10 o'clock a.m. on the Monday next after the expiration of ten days from the date of service hereof.' In either event, proceed as follows:) then and there to answer upon oath what, if anything, you are indebted to the said C.D., and were when this writ was served upon you, and what effects, if any, of the said C.D. you have in your possession, and had when this writ was served, and what other persons, if any, within your knowledge, are indebted to the said C.D. or have effects belonging to him in their possession. You are further commanded NOT to pay to defendant any debt or to deliver to him any effects, pending further order of this court. Herein fail not, but make due answer as the law directs."

Sept. 20, 1941, eff. Dec. 31, 1941. Amended by orders of Aug. 18, 1947, eff. Dec. 31, 1947; July 11, 1977, eff. Jan. 1, 1978.

Source: TRCS art. 4081 (repealed).

ANNOTATIONS

Bank One v. Sunbelt Sav., 824 S.W.2d 557, 558 (Tex.1992). "When a creditor wants to challenge title to funds held by a third party, the creditor should seek a writ of garnishment naming the nominal owner not the true owner. The court is then responsible for determining true ownership."

TRCP 662. DELIVERY OF WRIT

The writ of garnishment shall be dated and tested as other writs, and may be delivered to the sheriff or constable by the officer who issued it, or he may deliver it to the plaintiff, his agent or attorney, for that purpose.

History of TRCP 662: Adopted eff. Sept. 1, 1941, by order of Oct. 29, 1940 (3 Tex.B.J. 627 [1940]). Source: TRCS art. 4082 (repealed).

ANNOTATIONS

Moody Nat'l Bank v. Riebschlager, 946 S.W.2d 521, 523 n.1 (Tex.App.—Houston [14th Dist.] 1997, writ denied). "Private process servers are prohibited from executing writs of garnishment as only a sheriff or constable may deliver the writs to a garnishee."

TRCP 663. EXECUTION AND RETURN OF WRIT

The sheriff or constable receiving the writ of garnishment shall immediately proceed to execute the same by delivering a copy thereof to the garnishee, and shall make return thereof as of other citations.

History of TRCP 663: Adopted eff. Sept. 1, 1941, by order of Oct. 29, 1940 (3 Tex.B.J. 627 [1940]). Source: TRCS art. 4083 (repealed).

TRCP 663a. SERVICE OF WRIT ON DEFENDANT

The defendant shall be served in any manner prescribed for service of citation or as provided in Rule 21a with a copy

of the writ of garnishment, the application, accompanying affidavits and orders of the court as soon as practicable following the service of the writ. There shall be prominently displayed on the face of the copy of the writ served on the defendant, in ten-point type and in a manner calculated to advise a reasonably attentive person of its contents, the following:

"To ________, Defendant:

"You are hereby notified that certain properties alleged to be owned by you have been garnished. If you claim any rights in such property, you are advised:

"YOU HAVE A RIGHT TO REGAIN POSSESSION OF THE PROPERTY BY FILING A REPLEVY BOND. YOU HAVE A RIGHT TO SEEK TO REGAIN POSSESSION OF THE PROPERTY BY FILING WITH THE COURT A MOTION TO DISSOLVE THIS WRIT."

July 11, 1977, eff. Jan. 1, 1978.

Source: New rule.

ANNOTATIONS

Lease Fin. Grp. v. Childers, 310 S.W.3d 120, 125 (Tex.App.—Fort Worth 2010, no pet.). "Actual knowledge or a voluntary appearance by the debtor is insufficient and does not waive rule 663a's requirement of service of the writ. Although rule 663a does not entitle a debtor to a minimum of 20 days' notice as with service of an original petition, . . . the debtor does have the right to service of the writ of garnishment and related documents 'as soon as practicable following the service of the writ' on the garnishee. [¶] [P] contends there is sufficient evidence of service because the judgment recites [D] was served in compliance with rule 663a. . . . In an attack upon a default judgment, a recitation of due service in the judgment does not lead to a presumption of due service. Instead, the plaintiff must 'prove that the defendant was served in the required manner.' *At 126:* We believe the rule applicable to default judgments should apply to judgments in garnishment and hold that a recitation of due service in a judgment in garnishment does not lead to a presumption of due service. [¶] [P] next contends rule 663a does not establish a prescribed period in which a garnishor must serve a writ of garnishment on the debtor. We disagree. . . . 'As soon as practicable' is not susceptible to a definitive definition equally applicable in all cases, but we note that a 15-day delay before serving the debtor does not satisfy the strict requirements of rule 663a. *At 127:* [Here,] nothing in the record explains the 20-day delay in service. [W]e hold [P] failed to prove that it served [D] through its attorney 'as soon as practicable' as required by rule 663a."

Abdullah v. State, 211 S.W.3d 938, 943 (Tex.App.—Texarkana 2007, no pet.). "Rule 663a is unambiguous in its requirement that the debtor be given notice of the garnishment and of his rights to regain his property, and about the specific information that must be provided so that the writ may be contested. The rule makes no distinction between prejudgment and postjudgment notice to the debtor." *See also* **Zeecon Wireless Internet, LLC v. American Bank**, 305 S.W.3d 813, 817-18 (Tex.App.—Austin 2010, no pet.); **Simulis, L.L.C. v. G.E. Capital Corp.**, 276 S.W.3d 109, 115-16 (Tex.App.—Houston [1st Dist.] 2008, no pet.).

Mendoza v. Luke Fruia Invs., 962 S.W.2d 650, 652 (Tex.App.—Corpus Christi 1998, no pet.). "[R]ule 663a requires *strict compliance.* [W]hen a judgment debtor voluntarily answers and appears in a garnishment proceeding, the debtor waives only irregularities in the writ of garnishment, such as defects in the affidavit or bond. Voluntary appearance does not waive the requirements of the writ itself. [¶] Rights under a writ of garnishment are determined by priority in time, which itself is determined by service of the writ. Without proper service of the writ on the debtor, no control or custody of his property can be gained by his answer."

TRCP 664. DEFENDANT MAY REPLEVY

At any time before judgment, should the garnished property not have been previously claimed or sold, the defendant may replevy the same, or any part thereof, or the proceeds from the sale of the property if it has been sold under order of the court, by giving bond with sufficient surety or sureties as provided by statute, to be approved by the officer who levied the writ, payable to plaintiff, in the amount fixed by the court's order, or, at the defendant's option, for the value of the property or indebtedness sought to be replevied (to be estimated by the officer), plus one year's interest thereon at the legal rate from the date of the bond, conditioned that the defendant, garnishee, shall satisfy, to the extent of the penal amount of the bond, any judgment which may be rendered against him in such action.

On reasonable notice to the opposing party (which may be less than three days) either party shall have the right to prompt judicial review of the amount of bond required, denial of bond, sufficiency of sureties, and estimated value of the property, by the court which authorized issuance of the writ. The court's determination may be made upon the basis of affidavits, if uncontroverted, setting forth such facts as would be admissible in evidence; otherwise, the parties shall submit evidence. The court shall forthwith enter its order either approving or modifying the requirements of the officer or of the court's prior order, and such order of the court shall supersede and control with respect to such matters.

On reasonable notice to the opposing party (which may be less than three days) the defendant shall have the right to move the court for a substitution of property, of equal value as that garnished, for the property garnished. Provided that there has been located sufficient property of the defendant's to satisfy the order of garnishment, the court may authorize substitution of one or more items of defendant's property for all or for part of the property garnished. The court shall first make findings as to the value of the property to be substituted. If property is substituted, the property released from garnishment shall be delivered to defendant, if such property is personal property, and all liens upon such property from the original order of garnishment or modification thereof shall be terminated. Garnishment of substituted property shall be deemed to have existed from date of garnishment on the original property garnished, and no property on which liens have become affixed since the date of garnishment of the original property may be substituted.

July 11, 1977, eff. Jan. 1, 1978.

Source: TRCS art. 4084, second and third sentences (repealed in part by TRCP).

ANNOTATIONS

Woodall v. Clark, 802 S.W.2d 415, 418 (Tex.App.—Beaumont 1991, no writ). "[O]nce [D's] Replevy Bond was challenged by [P], a right provided to [P] by [TRCP] 664, the trial court was required to review, among other things, the sufficiency of the sureties."

TRCP 664a. DISSOLUTION OR MODIFICATION OF WRIT OF GARNISHMENT

A defendant whose property or account has been garnished or any intervening party who claims an interest in such property or account, may by sworn written motion, seek to vacate, dissolve or modify the writ of garnishment, and the order directing its issuance, for any grounds or cause, extrinsic or intrinsic. Such motion shall admit or deny each finding of the order directing the issuance of the writ except where the movant is unable to admit or deny the finding, in which case movant shall set forth the reasons why he cannot admit or deny. Unless the parties agree to an extension of time, the motion shall be heard promptly, after reasonable notice to the plaintiff (which may be less than three days), and the issue shall be determined not later than ten days after the motion is filed. The filing of the motion shall stay any further proceedings under the writ, except for any orders concerning the care, preservation or sale of any perishable property, until a hearing is had, and the issue is determined. The writ shall be dissolved unless, at such hearing, the plaintiff shall prove the grounds relied upon for its issuance, but the court may modify its previous order granting the writ and the writ issued pursuant thereto. The movant shall, however, have the burden to prove that the reasonable value of the property garnished exceeds the amount necessary to secure the debt, interest for one year, and probable costs. He shall also have the burden to prove facts to justify substitution of property.

The court's determination may be made upon the basis of affidavits, if uncontroverted, setting forth such facts as would be admissible in evidence; otherwise, the parties shall submit evidence. The court may make all such orders including orders concerning the care, preservation or disposition of the property (or the proceeds therefrom if the same has been sold), as justice may require. If the movant has given a replevy bond, an order to vacate or dissolve the writ shall vacate the replevy bond and discharge the sureties thereon, and if the court modifies its order or the writ issued pursuant thereto, it shall make such further orders with respect to the bond as may be consistent with its modification.

July 11, 1977, eff. Jan. 1, 1978.

Source: New rule.

ANNOTATIONS

Wease v. Bank of Am., No. 05-14-00867-CV, 2015 WL 4051974 (Tex.App.—Dallas 2015, no pet.) (memo op.; 7-2-15). "'[S]tanding under Rule 664a is a *procedural* issue; it does not affect the trial court's jurisdiction over the garnishment proceeding or over the parties.' Accordingly, lack of standing under Rule 664a must be brought to the trial court's attention before a party may complain of error on appeal."

Cadle Co. v. Davis, No. 04-09-00763-CV, 2010 WL 5545389 (Tex.App.—San Antonio 2010, pet. denied) (memo op.; 12-29-10). "Rule 664a provides a writ shall be dissolved unless at the hearing on the motion to dissolve the garnishor proves the grounds relied upon for its issuance. 'In the context of a post judgment garnishment proceeding, this means the garnishor must prove (a) it has a valid, subsisting judgment and (b) that within the garnishor's knowledge, the judgment debtor does not possess property in the state subject to execution sufficient to satisfy the judgment.'"

Simulis, L.L.C. v. G.E. Capital Corp., 276 S.W.3d 109, 115-16 (Tex.App.—Houston [1st Dist.] 2008, no pet.). The requirement in TRCP 664a to "'admit or deny each finding of the order directing the issuance of the writ' can apply only in a pre-judgment garnishment proceeding because such an order is required only at that stage."

Swiderski v. Victoria Bank & Trust Co., 706 S.W.2d 676, 678 (Tex.App.—Corpus Christi 1986, writ ref'd n.r.e.).

"A Rule 664a hearing is a distinct proceeding from the writ of garnishment proceeding between the garnishor and garnishee. . . . The issue to be determined in a Rule 664a hearing is that 'the plaintiff shall prove the grounds relied upon for its (the writ of garnishment's) issuance.' [¶] Therefore, at a Rule 664a hearing, the plaintiff does not have to prove that the garnishee is indebted to the defendant debtor. . . ."

TRCP 665. ANSWER TO WRIT

The answer of the garnishee shall be under oath, in writing and signed by him, and shall make true answers to the several matters inquired of in the writ of garnishment.

History of TRCP 665: Adopted eff. Sept. 1, 1941, by order of Oct. 29, 1940 (3 Tex.B.J. 628 [1940]). Source: TRCS art. 4085 (repealed).

See also **O'Connor's Texas Rules**, "The Answer—Denying Liability," ch. 3-E, §1 et seq.

TRCP 666. GARNISHEE DISCHARGED

If it appears from the answer of the garnishee that he is not indebted to the defendant, and was not so indebted when the writ of garnishment was served upon him, and that he has not in his possession any effects of the defendant and had not when the writ was served, and if he has either denied that any other persons within his knowledge are indebted to the defendant or have in their possession effects belonging to the defendant, or else has named such persons, should the answer of the garnishee not be controverted as hereinafter provided, the court shall enter judgment discharging the garnishee.

Aug. 18, 1947, eff. Dec. 31, 1947.

TRCP 667. JUDGMENT BY DEFAULT

If the garnishee fails to file an answer to the writ of garnishment at or before the time directed in the writ, it shall be lawful for the court, at any time after judgment shall have been rendered against the defendant, and on or after appearance day, to render judgment by default, as in other civil cases, against such garnishee for the full amount of such judgment against the defendant together with all interest and costs that may have accrued in the main case and also in the garnishment proceedings. The answer of the garnishee may be filed as in any other civil case at any time before such default judgment is rendered.

History of TRCP 667: Adopted eff. Sept. 1, 1941, by order of Oct. 29, 1940 (3 Tex.B.J. 628 [1940]). Source: TRCS art. 4087 (repealed).

See also **O'Connor's Texas Rules**, "Default Judgment," ch. 7-A, §1 et seq.

ANNOTATIONS

Invesco Inv. Servs. v. Fidelity Deposit & Disc. Bank, 355 S.W.3d 257, 259-60 (Tex.App.—Houston [1st Dist.] 2011, no pet.). "The assessment of the full amount of damages against the defaulting garnishee is premised on a presumption that the garnishee is indebted to the debtor in an amount sufficient to satisfy the claim of the garnishor."

Falderbaum v. Lowe, 964 S.W.2d 744, 747 (Tex.App.—Austin 1998, no pet.). Garnishee "cannot now claim that the district court lacks subject-matter jurisdiction *to enforce* the garnishment order when she failed to properly challenge the trial court's jurisdiction when the writ of garnishment was originally issued."

TRCP 668. JUDGMENT WHEN GARNISHEE IS INDEBTED

Should it appear from the answer of the garnishee or should it be otherwise made to appear and be found by the court that the garnishee is indebted to the defendant in any amount, or was so indebted when the writ of garnishment was served, the court shall render judgment for the plaintiff against the garnishee for the amount so admitted or found to be due to the defendant from the garnishee, unless such amount is in excess of the amount of the plaintiff's judgment against the defendant with interest and costs, in which case, judgment shall be rendered against the garnishee for the full amount of the judgment already rendered against the defendant, together with interest and costs of the suit in the original case and also in the garnishment proceedings. If the garnishee fail or refuse to pay such judgment rendered against him, execution shall issue thereon in the same manner and under the same conditions as is or may be provided for the issuance of execution in other cases.

History of TRCP 668: Adopted eff. Sept. 1, 1941, by order of Oct. 29, 1940 (3 Tex.B.J. 628 [1940]). Source: TRCS art. 4088 (repealed).

ANNOTATIONS

Wrigley v. First Nat'l Sec. Corp., 104 S.W.3d 259, 264 (Tex.App.—Beaumont 2003, no pet.). "The funds captured by the writ of garnishment are those held by the garnishee in the account of the judgment debtor on the date the writ is served, and any additional funds deposited through the date the garnishee is required to answer. [P's] right to recover those funds from the garnishee is [not necessarily] fixed by whatever judgment [P] possesses on that date. The issuance and service of the writ of garnishment fixes the trial court's jurisdiction to determine whether the garnishee holds funds belonging to the judgment debtor, and necessarily that jurisdiction extends to a determination of title and ownership of the funds, regardless of how that ownership is placed in controversy. The garnishee may deposit the funds into the court, bring in all other claimants through interpleader, and the trial court may then adjudicate the conflicting claims of the parties."

TRCP 669. JUDGMENT FOR EFFECTS

Should it appear from the garnishee's answer, or otherwise, that the garnishee has in his possession, or had when

the writ was served, any effects of the defendant liable to execution, including any certificates of stock in any corporation or joint stock company, the court shall render a decree ordering sale of such effects under execution in satisfaction of plaintiff's judgment and directing the garnishee to deliver them, or so much thereof as shall be necessary to satisfy plaintiff's judgment, to the proper officer for that purpose.

Aug. 18, 1947, eff. Dec. 31, 1947.

TRCP 670. REFUSAL TO DELIVER EFFECTS

Should the garnishee adjudged to have effects of the defendant in his possession, as provided in the preceding rule, fail or refuse to deliver them to the sheriff or constable on such demand, the officer shall immediately make return of such failure or refusal, whereupon on motion of the plaintiff, the garnishee shall be cited to show cause upon a date to be fixed by the court why he should not be attached for contempt of court for such failure or refusal. If the garnishee fails to show some good and sufficient excuse for such failure or refusal, he shall be fined for such contempt and imprisoned until he shall deliver such effects.

History of TRCP 670: Adopted eff. Sept. 1, 1941, by order of Oct. 29, 1940 (3 Tex.B.J. 628 [1940]). Source: TRCS art. 4090 (repealed).

TRCP 671. REPEALED BY ORDER OF AUG. 18, 1947, EFF. DEC. 31, 1947

TRCP 672. SALE OF EFFECTS

The sale so ordered shall be conducted in all respects as other sales of personal property under execution; and the officer making such sale shall execute a transfer of such effects or interest to the purchaser, with a brief recital of the judgment of the court under which the same was sold.

Aug. 18, 1947, eff. Dec. 31, 1947.

TRCP 673. MAY TRAVERSE ANSWER

If the plaintiff should not be satisfied with the answer of any garnishee, he may controvert the same by his affidavit stating that he has good reason to believe, and does believe, that the answer of the garnishee is incorrect, stating in what particular he believes the same to be incorrect. The defendant may also, in like manner, controvert the answer of the garnishee.

History of TRCP 673: Adopted eff. Sept. 1, 1941, by order of Oct. 29, 1940 (3 Tex.B.J. 629 [1940]). Source: TRCS art. 4094 (repealed).

TRCP 674. TRIAL OF ISSUE

If the garnishee whose answer is controverted, is a resident of the county in which the proceeding is pending, an issue shall be formed under the direction of the court and tried as in other cases.

History of TRCP 674: Adopted eff. Sept. 1, 1941, by order of Oct. 29, 1940 (3 Tex.B.J. 629 [1940]). Source: TRCS art. 4095 (repealed).

TRCP 675. DOCKET AND NOTICE

The clerk of the court or the justice of the peace, on receiving certified copies filed in the county of the garnishee's residence under the provisions of the statutes, shall docket the case in the name of the plaintiff as plaintiff, and of the garnishee as defendant, and issue a notice to the garnishee, stating that his answer has been so controverted, and that such issue will stand for trial on the docket of such court. Such notice shall be directed to the garnishee, be dated and tested as other process from such court, and served by delivering a copy thereof to the garnishee. It shall be returnable, if issued from the district or county court, at ten o'clock a.m. of the Monday next after the expiration of twenty days from the date of its service; and if issued from the justice court, to the next term of such court convening after the expiration of twenty days after the service of such notice.

Sept. 20, 1941, eff. Dec. 31, 1941.
Source: TRCS art. 4097 (repealed).

ANNOTATIONS

Atteberry, Inc. v. Standard Brass & Mfg., 270 S.W.2d 252, 255 (Tex.App.—Waco 1954, writ ref'd n.r.e.). "[T]he issuance of the writ of garnishment must come from the court where the judgment was rendered, but where the garnishee is the resident of another county and is not entitled to be discharged on its answer the cause must be docketed and tried in the court having jurisdiction of the subject matter in the county of the residence of the garnishee. ..."

TRCP 676. ISSUE TRIED AS IN OTHER CASES

Upon the return of such notice served, an issue shall be formed under the direction of the court and tried as in other cases.

History of TRCP 676: Adopted eff. Sept. 1, 1941, by order of Oct. 29, 1940 (3 Tex.B.J. 629 [1940]). Source: TRCS art. 4098 (repealed).

TRCP 677. COSTS

Where the garnishee is discharged upon his answer, the costs of the proceeding, including a reasonable compensation to the garnishee, shall be taxed against the plaintiff; where the answer of the garnishee has not been controverted and the garnishee is held thereon, such costs shall be taxed against the defendant and included in the execution provided for in this section; where the answer is contested, the costs shall abide the issue of such contest.

History of TRCP 677: Adopted eff. Sept. 1, 1941, by order of Oct. 29, 1940 (3 Tex.B.J. 629 [1940]). Source: TRCS art. 4100 (repealed).

ANNOTATIONS

General Elec. Capital Corp. v. ICO, Inc., 230 S.W.3d 702, 710 (Tex.App.—Houston [14th Dist.] 2007, pet. denied).

"The term 'costs' in [TRCP 677] has repeatedly been interpreted as including attorney's fees. [¶] Rule 677 only [gives] a garnishee the right to recover attorney's fees, and nothing in the rule allows a garnishor to recover attorney's fees from a debtor. [¶] [H]ere it is the debtor who is seeking attorney's fees under Rule 677. The rule does not provide for a debtor to recover attorney's fees, any more than it provides for a garnishor's recovery of fees."

TRCP 678. GARNISHEE DISCHARGED ON PROOF

It shall be a sufficient answer to any claim of the defendant against the garnishee founded on an indebtedness of such garnishee, or on the possession by him of any effects, for the garnishee to show that such indebtedness has been paid, or such effects, including any certificates of stock in any incorporated or joint stock company, have been delivered to any sheriff or constable as provided for in Rule 669.

Aug. 18, 1947, eff. Dec. 13, 1947.

TRCP 679. AMENDMENT

Clerical errors in the affidavit, bond, or writ of garnishment or the officer's return thereof, may upon application in writing to the judge or justice of the court in which the suit is filed, and after notice to the opponent, be amended in such manner and on such terms as the judge or justice shall authorize by an order entered in the minutes of the court (or noted on the docket of the justice of the peace), provided such amendment appears to the judge or justice to be in furtherance of justice.

History of TRCP 679: Adopted eff. Sept. 1, 1941, by order of Oct. 29, 1940 (3 Tex.B.J. 630 [1940]). Source: New rule.

ANNOTATIONS

Metroplex Factors, Inc. v. First Nat'l Bank, 610 S.W.2d 862, 866 (Tex.App.—Fort Worth 1980, writ ref'd n.r.e.). "Rule 679 authorizes correction of clerical errors (such as the missing seal) but does not apply to substantive matters, such as the sufficiency of the required supporting affidavits or other deficiencies in the application for writ of garnishment."

SECTION 5. INJUNCTIONS

TRCP 680. TEMPORARY RESTRAINING ORDER

No temporary restraining order shall be granted without notice to the adverse party unless it clearly appears from specific facts shown by affidavit or by the verified complaint that immediate and irreparable injury, loss, or damage will result to the applicant before notice can be served and a hearing had thereon. Every temporary restraining order granted without notice shall be endorsed with the date and hour of issuance; shall be filed forthwith in the clerk's office and entered of record; shall define the injury and state why it is irreparable and why the order was granted without notice; and shall expire by its terms within such time after signing, not to exceed fourteen days, as the court fixes, unless within the time so fixed the order, for good cause shown, is extended for a like period or unless the party against whom the order is directed consents that it may be extended for a longer period. The reasons for the extension shall be entered of record. No more than one extension may be granted unless subsequent extensions are unopposed. In case a temporary restraining order is granted without notice, the application for a temporary injunction shall be set down for hearing at the earliest possible date and takes precedence of all matters except older matters of the same character; and when the application comes on for hearing the party who obtained the temporary restraining order shall proceed with the application for a temporary injunction and, if he does not do so, the court shall dissolve the temporary restraining order. On two days' notice to the party who obtained the temporary restraining order without notice or on such shorter notice to that party as the court may prescribe, the adverse party may appear and move its dissolution or modification and in that event the court shall proceed to hear and determine such motion as expeditiously as the ends of justice require.

Every restraining order shall include an order setting a certain date for hearing on the temporary or permanent injunction sought.

Dec. 5, 1983, eff. April 1, 1984. Amended by order of July 15, 1987, eff. Jan. 1, 1988.

Source: FRCP 65(b), superseding TRCS art. 4654.

See also CPRC ch. 65; **O'Connor's Texas Rules**, "Injunctive Relief," ch. 2-D, §1 et seq.; **O'Connor's Texas Forms**, FORMS 2D:1, 2D:2, 2D:3; **O'Connor's Texas Family Law Handbook**, "Temporary Restraining Orders," ch. 5-B, §1 et seq.

ANNOTATIONS

In re Office of the Atty. Gen., 257 S.W.3d 695, 697 (Tex.2008). TRCP 680 and 684 "require a trial court issuing a temporary restraining order to: (1) state why the order was granted without notice if it is granted *ex parte* . . .; (2) state the reasons for the issuance of the order by defining the injury and describing why it is irreparable . . .; (3) state the date the order expires and set a hearing on a temporary injunction . . .; and (4) set a bond. . . . Orders that fail to fulfill these requirements are void."

Ex parte Lesikar, 899 S.W.2d 654, 654 (Tex.1995). "Extensions of temporary restraining orders, absent some

special statutory authority . . . must meet the limitations of [TRCP] 680, including in particular written orders and written extensions. An oral extension of a TRO is ineffective, and the contemnor must have notice of the actual written extension before he can be charged with contempt."

Davis v. Huey, 571 S.W.2d 859, 862 (Tex.1978). "At a hearing upon the request for a temporary injunction the only question before the trial court is whether the applicant is entitled to preservation of the status quo of the subject matter of the suit pending trial on the merits. On appeal the reviewing court is limited in its consideration as to whether the trial court abused its discretion in making the foregoing determination." *See also* **In re Newton**, 146 S.W.3d 648, 651 (Tex.2004) (status quo is defined as the last, actual, peaceable, noncontested status that preceded the pending controversy).

TRCP 681. TEMPORARY INJUNCTIONS: NOTICE

No temporary injunction shall be issued without notice to the adverse party.

History of TRCP 681: Adopted eff. Sept. 1, 1941, by order of Oct. 29, 1940 (3 Tex.B.J. 631 [1940]). Source: FRCP 65(a).

See also CPRC §51.014(a)(4) (interlocutory appeal of temporary injunction); **O'Connor's Texas Rules**, "Injunctive Relief," ch. 2-D, §1 et seq.; **O'Connor's Texas Family Law Handbook**, "Temporary Restraining Orders," ch. 5-B, §1 et seq.; **O'Connor's Texas Family Law Handbook**, "Temporary Injunctions," ch. 5-C, §1 et seq.

ANNOTATIONS

State v. Cook United, Inc., 469 S.W.2d 709, 712 (Tex.1971). "In the absence of notice to or service of citation upon the Attorney General of the State of Texas, . . . the temporary injunction is hereby modified to enjoin only the county and district attorneys of Tarrant and McLennan Counties [who had notice], and shall have no effect on the Attorney General . . . or the other district and county attorneys in this State."

RRE VIP Borrower, LLC v. Leisure Life Senior Apt. Hous., Ltd., No. 14-09-00923-CV, 2011 WL 1643275 (Tex.App.—Houston [14th Dist.] 2011, no pet.) (memo op.; 5-3-11). "The notice requirements of Rule 681 impliedly require that the adverse party have the right to be heard. The opportunity to be heard and present evidence must amount to more than the mere opportunity to cross-examine the other party's witnesses."

TRCP 682. SWORN PETITION

No writ of injunction shall be granted unless the applicant therefor shall present his petition to the judge verified by his affidavit and containing a plain and intelligible statement of the grounds for such relief.

March 31, 1941, eff. Sept. 1, 1941.

Source: New rule. See TRCS art. 4647 (repealed).

See also **O'Connor's Texas Rules**, "Injunctive Relief," ch. 2-D, §1 et seq.; **O'Connor's Texas Forms**, FORM 2D:1.

ANNOTATIONS

Butnaru v. Ford Motor Co., 84 S.W.3d 198, 204 (Tex.2002). "To obtain a temporary injunction, the applicant must plead and prove three specific elements: (1) a cause of action against the defendant; (2) a probable right to the relief sought; and (3) a probable, imminent, and irreparable injury in the interim."

Walling v. Metcalfe, 863 S.W.2d 56, 57 (Tex.1993). "A trial court may grant a temporary writ of injunction to preserve the status quo pending trial even though the applicant's prayer does not include a claim for equitable relief. . . . In such cases, however, a temporary injunction should only issue if the applicant establishes a probable right on final trial to the relief sought, and a probable injury in the interim."

Stewart Beach Condo. Homeowners Ass'n v. Gili N Prop Invs., 481 S.W.3d 336, 346 (Tex.App.—Houston [1st Dist.] 2015, no pet.). " '[T]he applicant for [a] temporary injunction [need not] offer evidence and persuade the judge to find from that evidence the adjudicative facts necessary for the applicant to prevail on the merits, based on probabilities.' A temporary injunction hearing is not a '*mini* trial' in which 'the judge predicts the applicant's chances of success at the real trial, based on the judge's estimate of where the truth probably lies concerning the adjudicative facts and the law made applicable thereto by the pleadings in the case.' '[T]o show a probable right of recovery,' the party applying for a temporary injunction[ ] 'must plead a cause of action and present some evidence that tends to sustain it. The evidence must be sufficient to raise a bona fide issue as to the applicant's right to ultimate relief.' "

In re MetroPCS Comms., 391 S.W.3d 329, 337 (Tex.App.—Dallas 2013, orig. proceeding). "[W]e cannot agree with [petitioner] that a temporary restraining order is not a 'writ of injunction' subject to the requirements of rule 682."

Mattox v. Jackson, 336 S.W.3d 759, 763 (Tex.App.—Houston [1st Dist.] 2011, no pet.). "A verified petition for injunctive relief is not required to grant a temporary injunction . . . when a full evidentiary hearing on evidence independent of the petition has been held."

Crystal Media, Inc. v. HCI Acquisition Corp., 773 S.W.2d 732, 734 (Tex.App.—San Antonio 1989, no writ). "If the insufficiency of the verification is not objected to prior to the introduction of evidence the defect has been waived." *See also* **Russell v. City of Dallas**, No. 05-13-00061-CV, 2014 WL 2090010 (Tex.App.—Dallas 2014, pet. denied) (memo op.; 5-16-14).

TRCP 683. FORM AND SCOPE OF INJUNCTION OR RESTRAINING ORDER

Every order granting an injunction and every restraining order shall set forth the reasons for its issuance; shall be specific in terms; shall describe in reasonable detail and not by reference to the complaint or other document, the act or acts sought to be restrained; and is binding only upon the parties to the action, their officers, agents, servants, employees, and attorneys, and upon those persons in active concert or participation with them who receive actual notice of the order by personal service or otherwise.

Every order granting a temporary injunction shall include an order setting the cause for trial on the merits with respect to the ultimate relief sought. The appeal of a temporary injunction shall constitute no cause for delay of the trial.[1]

Dec. 5, 1983, eff. April 1, 1984.

Source: FRCP 65(d).

[1]See V.T.C.A., Civil Practice and Remedies Code §51.014(b) added by Acts 1997, 75th Leg., ch. 1296, §1, effective June 20, 1997.

See also **O'Connor's Texas Rules**, "Injunctive Relief," ch. 2-D, §1 et seq.; **O'Connor's Texas Rules**, "Request for Findings of Fact & Conclusions of Law," ch. 10-E, §1 et seq.; **O'Connor's Texas Forms**, FORMS 2D:3, 2D:4; **O'Connor's Texas Family Law Handbook**, "Temporary Restraining Orders," ch. 5-B, §1 et seq.; **O'Connor's Texas Family Law Handbook**, "Temporary Injunctions," ch. 5-C, §1 et seq.

ANNOTATIONS

Qwest Comms. v. AT&T Corp., 24 S.W.3d 334, 337 (Tex.2000). The TRCPs "require that an order granting a temporary injunction set the cause for trial on the merits and fix the amount of security to be given by the applicant. These procedural requirements are mandatory, and an order granting a temporary injunction that does not meet them is subject to being declared void and dissolved." *See also* **InterFirst Bank San Felipe v. Paz Constr. Co.**, 715 S.W.2d 640, 641 (Tex.1986).

Ex parte Slavin, 412 S.W.2d 43, 44 (Tex.1967). An injunction decree "must spell out the details of compliance in clear, specific and unambiguous terms so that such person will readily know exactly what duties or obligations are imposed upon him." *See also* **RCI Entm't (San Antonio), Inc. v. City of San Antonio**, 373 S.W.3d 589, 603 (Tex.App.—San Antonio 2012, no pet.); **Murray v. Epic Energy Res.**, 300 S.W.3d 461, 470-71 (Tex.App.—Beaumont 2009, no pet.).

Livingston v. Livingston, 537 S.W.3d 578, 597 (Tex.App.—Houston [1st Dist.] 2017, no pet.). "Rule 683 'applies only to temporary injunctions, in which the relief ordered is ancillary to the ultimate relief sought, and not to permanent injunctions.' [¶] [D] asserts that Rule 683's requirement, mandating that the basis for issuance of the injunctive relief be stated in the order, applies here because the permanent-injunctive relief sought by [P] was ancillary to her request for damages. . . . However, the key to whether Rule 683 applies to a particular order is not whether the order under review is a 'final judgment[ ] whose sole object is to obtain a perpetual injunction;' rather, it is whether the injunctive relief ordered is ancillary, such as a temporary injunction."

Layton v. Ball, 396 S.W.3d 747, 753 (Tex.App.—Tyler 2013, no pet.). "Rule 683 is not violated when documents are attached to the injunction and referred to it as part of the injunction, because the attachments become part of the injunction itself."

RCI Entm't (San Antonio), Inc. v. City of San Antonio, 373 S.W.3d 589, 603 (Tex.App.—San Antonio 2012, no pet.). "An injunction should be broad enough to prevent a repetition of the wrong sought to be corrected. But, it must not be so broad as to enjoin a defendant from activities that are a lawful and proper exercise of his rights. Where a party's acts are divisible, and some acts are permissible and some are not, an injunction should not issue to restrain actions that are legal or about which there is no asserted complaint. Thus, the entry of an injunction that enjoins lawful as well as unlawful acts may constitute an abuse of discretion." *See also* **Super Starr Int'l v. Fresh Tex Produce, LLC**, 531 S.W.3d 829, 849-50 (Tex.App.—Corpus Christi 2017, no pet.).

Senter Invs. v. Veerjee, 358 S.W.3d 841, 845-46 (Tex.App.—Dallas 2012, no pet.). Appellant "asserts the temporary injunction is void because it does not contain an order setting the case for trial on the merits. [TRCP] 683 requires every order granting a temporary injunction to include such an order. However, because this case involves a temporary injunction pending arbitration, we must also consider the application of the [Texas Arbitration Act (TAA)]. [¶] Once [appellant] decided to invoke the arbitration provision and the trial court compelled arbitration, the trial proceedings were governed by the TAA as well as the rules of civil procedure. Under the TAA, the trial court was required to stay the trial proceedings pending arbitration, subject to its jurisdiction to grant orders under [CPRC] §171.086, including an injunction. [¶] The specific provisions of the TAA in this circumstance control over the rules of civil procedure; therefore, the temporary injunction order properly abated the trial court proceedings."

Intercontinental Terminals Co. v. Vopak N. Am., Inc., 354 S.W.3d 887, 899 (Tex.App.—Houston [1st Dist.] 2011, no pet.). "Rule 683 mandates that a trial court granting a temporary injunction must explain in the order its reasons for believing that the applicant has shown that it will suffer injury if interlocutory relief is not granted but does not require the trial court to provide reasons for believing that the applicant has shown a probable right to final relief. An explanation of the pending harm to the temporary injunction applicant, along with a specific recitation of the conduct enjoined, is all that is necessary to achieve Rule

683's purpose: 'to inform a party just what he is enjoined from doing and the reasons why he is so enjoined.' For these reasons, we hold that Rule 683 does not mandate that the trial court's order expressly state that the trial court found a probable right of recovery." *See also* **Johnson-Todd v. Morgan**, No. 09-15-00073-CV, 2015 WL 2255438 (Tex.App.—Beaumont 2015, pet. denied) (memo op.; 5-14-15) (specificity requirement is not satisfied by mere recital of no adequate remedy at law and irreparable harm).

Emex Holdings, LLC v. Naim, No. 13-09-591-CV, 2010 WL 2163139 (Tex.App.—Corpus Christi 2010, no pet.) (memo op.; 5-27-10). "Requiring a trial date to be placed in every injunction order prevents a temporary injunction from effectively becoming permanent without a trial. [It] also places the onus upon the party requesting injunctive relief to renew the injunction if the trial is delayed beyond the trial date set forth in the order. [¶] [R]eference to an existing docket control order is not a substitute for stating a trial date in the order itself. Logically, if a pre-existing docket control order is insufficient to comply with rule 683, then a yet to be entered docket control order . . . does not comply either." *See also* **State Bd. for Educator Certification v. Montalvo**, No. 03-12-00723-CV, 2013 WL 1405883 (Tex.App.—Austin 2013, no pet.) (memo op.; 4-3-13) (temporary injunction order without trial date is void, not voidable); **In re Marriage of Grossnickle**, 115 S.W.3d 238, 244 (Tex.App.—Texarkana 2003, no pet.) (requirement that injunction order set cause for trial on the merits is effectively same as requiring specific trial date to be set in the order).

Fasken v. Darby, 901 S.W.2d 591, 593 (Tex.App.—El Paso 1995, no writ). "An injunction that fails to identify the harm that will be suffered if it does not issue must be declared void and be dissolved. This rule operates to invalidate an injunction even when the complaining party fails to bring the error to the trial court's attention." *See also* **Big D Props., Inc. v. Foster**, 2 S.W.3d 21, 23 (Tex.App.—Fort Worth 1999, no pet.) (Rule 683's requirements cannot be waived). *But see* **Texas Tech Univ. Health Sci. Ctr. v. Rao**, 105 S.W.3d 763, 768 (Tex.App.—Amarillo 2003, pet. dism'd) (error waived). For more cases dealing with waiver of TRCP 683's requirements, see **O'Connor's Texas Rules**, "Dissolve," ch. 2-D, §8.2.2(2).

TRCP 684. APPLICANT'S BOND

In the order granting any temporary restraining order or temporary injunction, the court shall fix the amount of security to be given by the applicant. Before the issuance of the temporary restraining order or temporary injunction the applicant shall execute and file with the clerk a bond to the adverse party, with two or more good and sufficient sureties, to be approved by the clerk, in the sum fixed by the judge, conditioned that the applicant will abide the decision which may be made in the cause, and that he will pay all sums of money and costs that may be adjudged against him if the restraining order or temporary injunction shall be dissolved in whole or in part.

Where the temporary restraining order or temporary injunction is against the State, a municipality, a State agency, or a subdivision of the State in its governmental capacity, and is such that the State, municipality, State agency, or subdivision of the State in its governmental capacity, has no pecuniary interest in the suit and no monetary damages can be shown, the bond shall be allowed in the sum fixed by the judge, and the liability of the applicant shall be for its face amount if the restraining order or temporary injunction shall be dissolved in whole or in part. The discretion of the trial court in fixing the amount of the bond shall be subject to review. Provided that under equitable circumstances and for good cause shown by affidavit or otherwise the court rendering judgment on the bond may allow recovery for less than its full face amount, the action of the court to be subject to review.

June 16, 1943, eff. Dec. 31, 1943. Amended by orders of Oct. 12, 1949, eff. March 1, 1950; June 10, 1980, eff. Jan. 1, 1981.

ANNOTATIONS

In re Office of the Atty. Gen., 257 S.W.3d 695, 697 (Tex.2008). See annotation under TRCP 680.

DeSantis v. Wackenhut Corp., 793 S.W.2d 670, 685-86 (Tex.1990). To prevail in a suit on a bond, "the claimant must prove that the [TRO] or temporary injunction was issued or perpetuated when it should not have been, and that it was later dissolved. The claimant need not prove that the [TRO] or temporary injunction was obtained maliciously or without probable cause." *See also* **Duradril, L.L.C. v. Dynomax Drilling Tools, Inc.**, 516 S.W.3d 147, 167 (Tex.App.—Houston [14th Dist.] 2017, no pet.).

Hartwell v. Lone Star, PCA, 528 S.W.3d 750, 770 (Tex.App.—Texarkana 2017, pet. dism'd). "'[A]n order of injunction issued without a bond is void on its face.' A bond for a temporary restraining order does not generally continue to act as security for a temporary injunction. [¶] However, . . . the trial court may expressly provide in its order that the bond securing the temporary restraining order be continued as the bond for the temporary injunction."

TRCP 685. FILING AND DOCKETING

Upon the grant of a temporary restraining order or an order fixing a time for hearing upon an application for a temporary injunction, the party to whom the same is granted shall file his petition therefor, together with the order of the judge, with the clerk of the proper court; and, if such orders do not pertain to a pending suit in said court, the cause shall be entered on the docket of the court in its regular order in the name of the party applying for the writ

as plaintiff and of the opposite party as defendant.

History of TRCP 685: Adopted eff. Sept. 1, 1941, by order of Oct. 29, 1940 (3 Tex.B.J. 631 [1940]). Source: TRCS art. 4650, harmonized with FRCP 65(d) by minor textual change (repealed).

TRCP 686. CITATION

Upon the filing of such petition and order not pertaining to a suit pending in the court, the clerk of such court shall issue a citation to the defendant as in other civil cases, which shall be served and returned in like manner as ordinary citations issued from said court; provided, however, that when a temporary restraining order is issued and is accompanied with a true copy of plaintiff's petition, it shall not be necessary for the citation in the original suit to be accompanied with a copy of plaintiff's petition, nor contain a statement of the nature of plaintiff's demand, but it shall be sufficient for said citation to refer to plaintiff's claim as set forth in a true copy of plaintiff's petition which accompanies the temporary restraining order; and provided further that the court may have a hearing upon an application for a temporary restraining order or temporary injunction at such time and upon such reasonable notice given in such manner as the court may direct.

June 16, 1943, eff. Dec. 31, 1943. Amended by order of Aug. 18, 1947, eff. Dec. 31, 1947.

TRCP 687. REQUISITES OF WRIT

The writ of injunction shall be sufficient if it contains substantially the following requisites:

(a) Its style shall be, "The State of Texas."

(b) It shall be directed to the person or persons enjoined.

(c) It must state the names of the parties to the proceedings, plaintiff and defendant, and the nature of the plaintiff's application, with the action of the judge thereon.

(d) It must command the person or persons to whom it is directed to desist and refrain from the commission or continuance of the act enjoined, or to obey and execute such order as the judge has seen proper to make.

(e) If it is a temporary restraining order, it shall state the day and time set for hearing, which shall not exceed fourteen days from the date of the court's order granting such temporary restraining order; but if it is a temporary injunction, issued after notice, it shall be made returnable at or before ten o'clock a.m. of the Monday next after the expiration of twenty days from the date of service thereof, as in the case of ordinary citations.

(f) It shall be dated and signed by the clerk officially and attested with the seal of his office and the date of its issuance must be indorsed thereon.

April 24, 1990, eff. Sept. 1, 1990.

TRCP 688. CLERK TO ISSUE WRIT

When the petition, order of the judge and bond have been filed, the clerk shall issue the temporary restraining order or temporary injunction, as the case may be, in conformity with the terms of the order, and deliver the same to the sheriff or any constable of the county of the residence of the person enjoined, or to the applicant, as the latter shall direct. If several persons are enjoined, residing in different counties, the clerk shall issue such additional copies of the writ as shall be requested by the applicant. The clerk must retain a copy of the temporary restraining order or temporary injunction in the court's file.

Amended by order of Dec. 12, 2011, eff. Jan. 1, 2012.

TRCP 689. SERVICE AND RETURN

The officer receiving a writ of injunction shall indorse thereon the date of its receipt by him, and shall forthwith execute the same by delivering to the party enjoined a true copy thereof. The officer must complete and file a return in accordance with Rule 107.

Amended by order of Dec. 12, 2011, eff. Jan. 1, 2012.

TRCP 690. THE ANSWER

The defendant to an injunction proceeding may answer as in other civil actions; but no injunction shall be dissolved before final hearing because of the denial of the material allegations of the plaintiff's petition, unless the answer denying the same is verified by the oath of the defendant.

History of TRCP 690: Adopted eff. Sept. 1, 1941, by order of Oct. 29, 1940 (3 Tex.B.J. 632 [1940]). Source: TRCS art. 4657 (repealed).

See also **O'Connor's Texas Rules**, "Verified pleas," ch. 3-E, §4; **O'Connor's Texas Family Law Handbook**, "Temporary Injunctions," ch. 5-C, §1 et seq.

ANNOTATIONS

Executive Tele-Comm. Sys. v. Buchbaum, 669 S.W.2d 400, 403 (Tex.App.—Dallas 1984, no writ). "The only prescribed response for a defendant to a temporary injunction proceeding is pronounced in Rule 690, and the failure to answer does not impair the defendant's right to a full hearing. [A] party seeking an injunction cannot rely on the verified pleading rules to limit the defense of the nonmovant."

TRCP 691. BOND ON DISSOLUTION

Upon the dissolution of an injunction restraining the collection of money, by an interlocutory order of the court or judge, made in term time or vacation, if the petition be continued over for trial, the court or judge shall require of the defendant in such injunction proceedings a bond, with two or more good and sufficient sureties, to be approved by

the clerk of the court, payable to the complainant in double the amount of the sum enjoined, and conditioned to refund to the complainant the amount of money, interest and costs which may be collected of him in the suit or proceeding enjoined if such injunction is made perpetual on final hearing. If such injunction is so perpetuated, the court, on motion of the complainant, may enter judgment against the principal and sureties in such bond for such amount as may be shown to have been collected from such defendant.

History of TRCP 691: Adopted eff. Sept. 1, 1941, by order of Oct. 29, 1940 (3 Tex.B.J. 632 [1940]). Source: TRCS art. 4659 (repealed).

TRCP 692. DISOBEDIENCE

Disobedience of an injunction may be punished by the court or judge, in term time or in vacation, as a contempt. In case of such disobedience, the complainant, his agent or attorney, may file in the court in which such injunction is pending or with the judge in vacation, his affidavit stating what person is guilty of such disobedience and describing the acts constituting the same; and thereupon the court or judge shall cause to be issued an attachment for such person, directed to the sheriff or any constable of any county, and requiring such officer to arrest the person therein named if found within his county and have him before the court or judge at the time and place named in such writ; or said court or judge may issue a show cause order, directing and requiring such person to appear on such date as may be designated and show cause why he should not be adjudged in contempt of court. On return of such attachment or show cause order, the judge shall proceed to hear proof; and if satisfied that such person has disobeyed the injunction, either directly or indirectly, may commit such person to jail without bail until he purges himself of such contempt, in such manner and form as the court or judge may direct.

June 16, 1943, eff. Dec. 31, 1943.

ANNOTATIONS

Ex parte Jackman, 663 S.W.2d 520, 524 (Tex.App.—Dallas 1983, orig. proceeding). "The injunction must be obeyed irrespective of the ultimate validity of the order, and a defendant cannot avoid compliance with the commands, or excuse his violation, of the injunction by simply moving to dissolve it or by the pendency of a motion to modify it."

TRCP 693. PRINCIPLES OF EQUITY APPLICABLE

The principles, practice and procedure governing courts of equity shall govern proceedings in injunctions when the same are not in conflict with these rules or the provisions of the statutes.

History of TRCP 693: Adopted eff. Sept. 1, 1941, by order of Oct. 29, 1940 (3 Tex.B.J. 633 [1940]). Source: TRCS art. 4663 (repealed).

ANNOTATIONS

State v. Texas Pet Foods, Inc., 591 S.W.2d 800, 804 (Tex.1979). "[I]njunctive relief is proper when the trial court finds it justified under the rules of equity, notwithstanding a defendant's cessation of the activity or solemn promises to cease the activity. *At 805:* When it is determined that [a] statute is being violated, it is within the province of the district court to restrain it. The doctrine of balancing the equities has no application to . . . statutorily authorized injunctive relief."

TRCP 693a. BOND IN DIVORCE CASE

In a divorce case the court in its discretion may dispense with the necessity of a bond in connection with an ancillary injunction in behalf of one spouse against the other. Promulgated by order of June 16, 1943, effective December 31, 1943.

History of TRCP 693a: Adopted eff. Dec. 31, 1943, by order of June 16, 1943 (6 Tex.B.J. 436 [1943]). Source: New rule.

Source: New rule.

SECTION 6. MANDAMUS

TRCP 694. NO MANDAMUS WITHOUT NOTICE

No mandamus shall be granted by the district or county court on ex parte hearing, and any peremptory mandamus granted without notice shall be abated on motion.

History of TRCP 694: Adopted eff. Sept. 1, 1941, by order of Oct. 29, 1940 (3 Tex.B.J. 633 [1940]). Source: TRCS art. 2328 (repealed).

SECTION 7. RECEIVERS

TRCP 695. NO RECEIVER OF IMMOVABLE PROPERTY APPOINTED WITHOUT NOTICE

Except where otherwise provided by statute, no receiver shall be appointed without notice to take charge of property which is fixed and immovable. When an application for appointment of a receiver to take possession of property of this type is filed, the judge or court shall set the same down for hearing and notice of such hearing shall be given to the adverse party by serving notice thereof not less than three days prior to such hearing. If the order finds that the defendant is a non-resident or that his whereabouts is unknown, the notice may be served by affixing the same in a conspicuous manner and place upon the property or if that is impracticable it may be served in such other manner as the court or judge may require.

June 16, 1943, eff. Dec. 31, 1943.

ANNOTATIONS

Krumnow v. Krumnow, 174 S.W.3d 820, 829 (Tex.App.—Waco 2005, pet. denied). "Real estate is 'fixed

and immovable property' within the meaning of Rule 695. Appointment of a receiver without giving notice to adverse parties to be heard ***on the application*** is reversible error."

TRCP 695a. BOND, AND BOND IN DIVORCE CASE

No receiver shall be appointed with authority to take charge of property until the party applying therefor has filed with the clerk of the court a good and sufficient bond, to be approved by such clerk, payable to the defendant in the amount fixed by the court, conditioned for the payment of all damages and cost in such suit, in case it should be decided that such receiver was wrongfully appointed to take charge of such property. The amount of such bond shall be fixed at a sum sufficient to cover all such probable damages and costs. In a divorce case the court or judge, as a matter of discretion, may dispense with the necessity of a bond.

June 16, 1943, eff. Dec. 31, 1943.

ANNOTATIONS

Ahmad v. Ahmed, 199 S.W.3d 573, 575 (Tex.App.—Houston [1st Dist.] 2006, no pet.). "The applicant's bond is a prerequisite to the appointment of a receiver, and the trial court's failure to require the bond necessitates reversal of the order appointing the receiver. *At 576:* [T]he trial court's order does not require [P] to file a bond payable to [D]—nor does it indicate an appropriate amount for such a bond. . . . Although the trial court properly required the receiver to post a bond [under CPRC §64.023], it did not incorporate the additional [TRCP] 695a bond requirement into its order. [T]he record does not indicate that [P] has posted the required Rule 695a bond. Therefore, . . . the receivership must be dissolved."

In re Estate of Herring, 983 S.W.2d 61, 64 (Tex.App.—Corpus Christi 1998, no pet.). "[T]he bond requirements of Rule 695a do not apply to the appointment of a post-judgment receiver. . . ."

SECTION 8. SEQUESTRATION

TRCP 696. APPLICATION FOR WRIT OF SEQUESTRATION AND ORDER

Either at the commencement of a suit or at any time during its progress the plaintiff may file an application for a writ of sequestration. The application shall be supported by affidavits of the plaintiff, his agent, his attorney, or other persons having knowledge of relevant facts. The application shall comply with all statutory requirements and shall state the grounds for issuing the writ, including the description of the property to be sequestered with such certainty that it may be identified and distinguished from property of a like kind, giving the value of each article of the property and the county in which it is located, and the specific facts relied upon by the plaintiff to warrant the required findings by the court. The writ shall not be quashed because two or more grounds are stated conjunctively or disjunctively. The application and any affidavits shall be made on personal knowledge and shall set forth such facts as would be admissible in evidence; provided that facts may be stated based upon information and belief if the grounds of such belief are specifically stated.

No writ shall issue except upon written order of the court after a hearing, which may be ex parte. The court, in its order granting the application, shall make specific findings of facts to support the statutory grounds found to exist, and shall describe the property to be sequestered with such certainty that it may be identified and distinguished from property of a like kind, giving the value of each article of the property and the county in which it is located. Such order shall further specify the amount of bond required of plaintiff which shall be in an amount which, in the opinion of the court, shall adequately compensate defendant in the event plaintiff fails to prosecute his suit to effect and pay all damages and costs as shall be adjudged against him for wrongfully suing out the writ of sequestration including the elements of damages stated in Sections 62.044 and 62.045, Civil Practice and Remedies Code. The court shall further find in its order the amount of bond required of defendant to replevy, which shall be in an amount equivalent to the value of the property sequestered or to the amount of plaintiff's claim and one year's accrual of interest if allowed by law on the claim, whichever is the lesser amount, and the estimated costs of court. The order may direct the issuance of several writs at the same time, or in succession, to be sent to different counties.

July 11, 1977, eff. Jan. 1, 1978. Amended by order of July 15, 1987, eff. Jan. 1, 1988.

Source: TRCS art. 6841 (repealed).

See also CPRC §62.001.

ANNOTATIONS

Marrs v. South Tex. Nat'l Bank, 686 S.W.2d 675, 678 (Tex.App.—San Antonio 1985, writ ref'd n.r.e.). Held: A creditor may allege the value of the total inventory; it is not necessary to allege the value of each item.

Burnett Trailers, Inc. v. Polson, 387 S.W.2d 692, 695 (Tex.App.—San Antonio 1965, writ ref'd n.r.e.). To obtain exemplary damages, there must be "a finding that in bringing the suit and causing the writ of sequestration to issue[,

the plaintiff] was activated by malice, or that [the plaintiff] caused the writ of sequestration to issue without probable cause."

TRCP 697. PETITION

If the suit be in the district or county court, no writ of sequestration shall issue, unless a petition shall have been first filed therein, as in other suits in said courts.

History of TRCP 697: Adopted eff. Sept. 1, 1941, by order of Oct. 29, 1940 (3 Tex.B.J. 634 [1940]). Source: TRCS art. 6842 (repealed).

TRCP 698. BOND FOR SEQUESTRATION

No writ of sequestration shall issue until the party applying therefor has filed with the officer authorized to issue such writ a bond payable to the defendant in the amount fixed by the court's order, with sufficient surety or sureties as provided by statute to be approved by such officer, conditioned that the plaintiff will prosecute his suit to effect and pay to the extent of the penal amount of the bond all damages and costs as may be adjudged against him for wrongfully suing out such writ of sequestration, and plaintiff may further condition the bond pursuant to the provisions of Rule 708, in which case he shall not be required to give additional bond to replevy unless so ordered by the court.

After notice to the opposite party, either before or after the issuance of the writ, the defendant or plaintiff may file a motion to increase or reduce the amount of such bond, or to question the sufficiency of the sureties thereon, in the court in which such suit is pending. Upon hearing, the court shall enter its order with respect to such bond and sufficiency of the sureties as justice may require.

July 11, 1977, eff. Jan. 1, 1978.

Source: TRCS art. 6843 (repealed).

ANNOTATIONS

Kelso v. Hanson, 388 S.W.2d 396, 399 (Tex.1965). "[T]he sequestration bond required by [TRCP] 698 and the replevy bond required by [TRCP] 708 serve two different purposes, and are conditioned against different contingencies. The sequestration bond guarantees the payment of damages and costs in case it is decided that the sequestration was wrongfully issued."

TRCP 699. REQUISITES OF WRIT

The writ of sequestration shall be directed "To the Sheriff or any Constable within the State of Texas" (not naming a specific county) and shall command him to take into his possession the property, describing the same as it is described in the application or affidavits, if to be found in his county, and to keep the same subject to further orders of the court, unless the same is replevied. There shall be prominently displayed on the face of the writ, in ten-point type and in a manner calculated to advise a reasonably attentive person of its contents, the following:

"YOU HAVE A RIGHT TO REGAIN POSSESSION OF THE PROPERTY BY FILING A REPLEVY BOND. YOU HAVE A RIGHT TO SEEK TO REGAIN POSSESSION OF THE PROPERTY BY FILING WITH THE COURT A MOTION TO DISSOLVE THIS WRIT."

July 11, 1977, eff. Jan. 1, 1978.

Source: TRCS art. 6845 (repealed).

See also CPRC §§62.061–62.063.

ANNOTATIONS

Lindsey v. Williams, 228 S.W.2d 243, 248 (Tex.App.—Texarkana 1950, no writ). "The affidavit, the bond for sequestration, the writ, the seizure, and the officer's return are all to be read and considered together as parts of one proceeding. . . . They constitute the 'face of the record' in the sequestration proceedings."

TRCP 700. AMENDMENT

Clerical errors in the affidavit, bond, or writ of sequestration or the officer's return thereof may upon application in writing to the judge of the court in which the suit is filed and after notice to the opponent, be amended in such manner and on such terms as the judge shall authorize by an order entered in the minutes of the court, provided the amendment does not change or add to the grounds of such sequestration as stated in the affidavit, and provided such amendment appears to the judge to be in furtherance of justice.

History of TRCP 700: Adopted eff. Sept. 1, 1941, by order of Oct. 29, 1940 (3 Tex.B.J. 634 [1940]). Source: New rule.

TRCP 700a. SERVICE OF WRIT ON DEFENDANT

The defendant shall be served in any manner provided for service of citation or as provided in Rule 21a, with a copy of the writ of sequestration, the application, accompanying affidavits, and orders of the court as soon as practicable following the levy of the writ. There shall also be prominently displayed on the face of the copy of the writ served on defendant, in ten-point type and in a manner calculated to advise a reasonably attentive person of its contents, the following:

"To ________, Defendant:

You are hereby notified that certain properties alleged to be claimed by you have been sequestered. If you claim any rights in such property, you are advised:

"YOU HAVE A RIGHT TO REGAIN POSSESSION OF THE PROPERTY BY FILING A REPLEVY BOND. YOU HAVE A RIGHT TO SEEK TO REGAIN POSSESSION OF THE PROPERTY BY FILING WITH THE COURT A MOTION TO DISSOLVE THIS WRIT."

July 11, 1977, eff. Jan. 1, 1978.

TRCP 701. DEFENDANT MAY REPLEVY

At any time before judgment, should the sequestered property not have been previously claimed, replevied, or sold, the defendant may replevy the same, or any part thereof, or the proceeds from the sale of the property if it has been sold under order of the court, by giving bond, with sufficient surety or sureties as provided by statute, to be approved by the officer who levied the writ, payable to plaintiff in the amount fixed by the court's order, conditioned as provided in Rule 702 or Rule 703.

On reasonable notice to the opposing party (which may be less than three days) either party shall have the right to prompt judicial review of the amount of bond required, denial of bond, sufficiency of sureties, and estimated value of the property, by the court which authorized issuance of the writ. The court's determination may be made upon the basis of affidavits, if uncontroverted, setting forth such facts as would be admissible in evidence; otherwise, the parties shall submit evidence. The court shall forthwith enter its order either approving or modifying the requirements of the officer or of the court's prior order, and such order of the court shall supersede and control with respect to such matters.

July 11, 1977, eff. Jan. 1, 1978.

Source: TRCS art. 6849 (repealed).

ANNOTATIONS

Commercial Secs. Co. v. Thompson, 239 S.W.2d 911, 914 (Tex.App.—Fort Worth 1951, no writ). "[T]he purpose of a replevy bond is to insure that the property will be forthcoming after judgment in the same condition as when replevied."

TRCP 702. BOND FOR PERSONAL PROPERTY

If the property to be replevied be personal property, the condition of the bond shall be that the defendant will not remove the same out of the county, or that he will not waste, ill-treat, injure, destroy, or dispose of the same, according to the plaintiff's affidavit, and that he will have such property, in the same condition as when it is replevied, together with the value of the fruits, hire or revenue thereof, forthcoming to abide the decision of the court, or that he will pay the value thereof, or the difference between its value at the time of replevy and the time of judgment and of the fruits, hire or revenue of the same in case he shall be condemned to do so.

History of TRCP 702: Adopted eff. Sept. 1, 1941, by order of Oct. 29, 1940 (3 Tex.B.J. 635 [1940]). Source: TRCS art. 6850 (repealed).

ANNOTATIONS

Associates Inv. v. Soltes, 250 S.W.2d 593, 595 (Tex.App.—Dallas 1952, writ ref'd n.r.e.). "[T]he wording of Rule 702 that defendant 'will have such property, in the same condition as when it is replevied,' excludes any ordinary depreciation in market value. . . ."

TRCP 703. BOND FOR REAL ESTATE

If the property be real estate, the condition of such bond shall be that the defendant will not injure the property, and that he will pay the value of the rents of the same in case he shall be condemned so to do.

History of TRCP 703: Adopted eff. Sept. 1, 1941, by order of Oct. 29, 1940 (3 Tex.B.J. 635 [1940]). Source: TRCS art. 6851 (repealed).

TRCP 704. RETURN OF BOND AND ENTRY OF JUDGMENT

The bond provided for in the three preceding rules shall be returned with the writ to the court from whence the writ issued. In case the suit is decided against the defendant, final judgment shall be rendered against all the obligors in such bond, jointly and severally, for the value of the property replevied as of the date of the execution of the replevy bond, and the value of the fruits, hire, revenue, or rent thereof, as the case may be.

June 10, 1980, eff. Jan. 1, 1981.

Source: TRCS art. 6852 (repealed).

ANNOTATIONS

Transit Enters. v. Addicks Tire & Auto Sup., 725 S.W.2d 459, 463 (Tex.App.—Houston [1st Dist.] 1987, no writ). "The . . . cost of replacement is not evidence of the value of the fruits, hire, revenue, or rent of the property replevied, as required by Rule 704."

TRCP 705. DEFENDANT MAY RETURN SEQUESTERED PROPERTY

Within ten days after final judgment for personal property the defendant may deliver to the plaintiff, or to the of-

ficer who levied the sequestration or to his successor in office the personal property in question, and such officer shall deliver same to plaintiff upon his demand therefor; or such defendant shall deliver such property to the officer demanding same under execution issued therefor upon a judgment for the title or possession of the same; and such officer shall receipt the defendant for such property; provided, however, that such delivery to the plaintiff or to such officer shall be without prejudice to any rights of the plaintiff under the replevy bond given by the defendant. Where a mortgage or other lien of any kind is foreclosed upon personal property sequestered and replevied, the defendant shall deliver such property to the officer calling for same under order of sale issued upon a judgment foreclosing such mortgage or other lien, either in the county of defendant's residence or in the county where sequestered, as demanded by such officer; provided, however, that such delivery by the defendant shall be without prejudice to any rights of the plaintiff under the replevy bond given by the defendant.

Sept. 20, 1941, eff. Dec. 31, 1941.

TRCP 706. DISPOSITION OF THE PROPERTY BY OFFICER

When the property is tendered back by the defendant to the officer who sequestered the same or to the officer calling for same under an order of sale, such officer shall receive said property and hold or dispose of the same as ordered by the court; provided, however, that such return to and receipt of same by the officer and any sale or disposition of said property by the officer under order or judgment of the court shall not affect or limit any rights of the plaintiff under the bond provided for in Rule 702.

Sept. 20, 1941, eff. Dec. 31, 1941.

TRCP 707. EXECUTION

If the property be not returned and received, as provided in the two preceding rules, execution shall issue upon said judgment for the amount due thereon, as in other cases.

History of TRCP 707: Adopted eff. Sept. 1, 1941, by order of Oct. 29, 1940 (3 Tex.B.J. 635 [1940]). Source: TRCS art. 6855 (repealed).

TRCP 708. PLAINTIFF MAY REPLEVY

When the defendant fails to replevy the property within ten days after the levy of the writ and service of notice on defendant, the officer having the property in possession shall at any time thereafter and before final judgment, deliver the same to the plaintiff upon his giving bond payable to defendant in a sum of money not less than the amount fixed by the court's order, with sufficient surety or sureties as provided by statute to be approved by such officer. If the property to be replevied be personal property, the condition of the bond shall be that he will have such property, in the same condition as when it is replevied, together with the value of the fruits, hire or revenue thereof, forthcoming to abide the decision of the court, or that he will pay the value thereof, or the difference between its value at the time of replevy and the time of judgment (regardless of the cause of such difference in value, and of the fruits, hire or revenue of the same in case he shall be condemned to do so). If the property be real estate, the condition of such bond shall be that the plaintiff will not injure the property, and that he will pay the value of the rents of the same in case he shall be condemned to do so.

On reasonable notice to the opposing party (which may be less than three days) either party shall have the right to prompt judicial review of the amount of bond required, denial of bond, sufficiency of sureties, and estimated value of the property, by the court which authorized issuance of the writ. The court's determination may be made upon the basis of affidavits, if uncontroverted, setting forth such facts as would be admissible in evidence; otherwise, the parties shall submit evidence. The court shall forthwith enter its order either approving or modifying the requirements of the officer or of the court's prior order, and such order of the court shall supersede and control with respect to such matters.

July 11, 1977, eff. Jan. 1, 1978. Amended by order of Dec. 5, 1983, eff. April 1, 1984.

Source: TRCS art. 6856 (repealed).

ANNOTATIONS

Kelso v. Hanson, 388 S.W.2d 396, 399 (Tex.1965). See annotation under TRCP 698.

TRCP 709. WHEN BOND FORFEITED

The bond provided for in the preceding rule shall be returned by the officer to the court issuing the writ immediately after he has approved same, and in case the suit is decided against the plaintiff, final judgment shall be entered against all the obligors in such bond, jointly and severally for the value of the property replevied as of the date of the execution of the replevy bond, and the value of the fruits, hire, revenue or rent thereof as the case may be. The same rules which govern the discharge or enforcement of a judgment against the obligors in the defendant's replevy bond shall be applicable to and govern in case of a judgment against the obligors in the plaintiff's replevy bond.

History of TRCP 709: Adopted eff. Sept. 1, 1941, by order of Oct. 29, 1940 (3 Tex.B.J. 636 [1940]). Source: TRCS art. 6857, changed to harmonize with other rules (repealed).

ANNOTATIONS

Kelso v. Hanson, 388 S.W.2d 396, 399 (Tex.1965). "A plaintiff availing himself of the replevin proceeding, and those obligating themselves on the replevy bond guaranteeing the performance of its terms by the plaintiff, are bound to the conditions imposed by the rules governing the procedure."

TRCP 710. SALE OF PERISHABLE GOODS

If after the expiration of ten days from the levy of a writ of sequestration the defendant has failed to replevy the same, if the plaintiff or defendant shall make affidavit in writing that the property levied upon, or any portion thereof, is likely to be wasted or destroyed or greatly depreciated in value by keeping, and if the officer having possession of such property shall certify to the truth of such affidavit, it shall be the duty of the judge or justice of the peace to whose court the writ is returnable, upon the presentation of such affidavit and certificate, either in term time or vacation, to order the sale of said property or so much thereof as is likely to be so wasted, destroyed or depreciated in value by keeping, but either party may replevy the property at any time before such sale.

History of TRCP 710: Adopted eff. Sept. 1, 1941, by order of Oct. 29, 1940 (3 Tex.B.J. 636 [1940]). Source: TRCS art. 6859 (repealed).

TRCP 711. ORDER OF SALE FOR

The judge or justice granting the order provided for in the preceding rule shall issue an order directed to the officer having such property in possession, commanding such officer to sell such property in the same manner as under execution.

History of TRCP 711: Adopted eff. Sept. 1, 1941, by order of Oct. 29, 1940 (3 Tex.B.J. 636 [1940]). Source: TRCS art. 6860 (repealed).

TRCP 712. RETURN OF ORDER

The officer making such sale shall, within five days thereafter, return the order of sale to the court from whence the same issued, with his proceedings thereon, and shall, at the time of making such return, pay over to the clerk or justice of the peace the proceeds of such sale.

History of TRCP 712: Adopted eff. Sept. 1, 1941, by order of Oct. 29, 1940 (3 Tex.B.J. 636 [1940]). Source: TRCS art. 6861 (repealed).

TRCP 712a. DISSOLUTION OR MODIFICATION OF WRIT OF SEQUESTRATION

A defendant whose property has been sequestered or any intervening party who claims an interest in such property, may by sworn written motion, seek to vacate, dissolve, or modify the writ and the order directing its issuance, for any grounds or cause, extrinsic or intrinsic, including a motion to reduce the amount of property sequestered when the total amount described and authorized by such order exceeds the amount necessary to secure the plaintiff's claim, one year's interest if allowed by law on the claim, and costs. Such motion shall admit or deny each finding of the order directing the issuance of the writ except where the movant is unable to admit or deny the finding, in which case movant shall set forth the reasons why he cannot admit or deny. Unless the parties agree to an extension of time, the motion shall be heard promptly, after reasonable notice to the plaintiff (which may be less than three days), and the issue shall be determined not later than ten days after the motion is filed. The filing of the motion shall stay any further proceedings under the writ, except for any orders concerning the care, preservation, or sale of any perishable property, until a hearing is had, and the issue is determined. The writ shall be dissolved unless, at such hearing, the plaintiff shall prove the grounds relied upon for its issuance, but the court may modify its previous order granting the writ and the writ issued pursuant thereto. The movant shall, however, have the burden to prove that the reasonable value of the property sequestered exceeds the amount necessary to secure the debt, interest for one year, and probable costs.

The court's determination may be made upon the basis of affidavits, if uncontroverted, setting forth such facts as would be admissible in evidence; otherwise, the parties shall submit evidence. The court may make all such orders, including orders concerning the care, preservation, or disposition of the property (or the proceeds therefrom if the same has been sold) as justice may require. If the movant has given a replevy bond, an order to vacate or dissolve the writ shall vacate the replevy bond and discharge the sureties thereon, and if the court modifies its order or the writ issued pursuant thereto, it shall make such further orders with respect to the bond as may be consistent with its modification.

July 11, 1977, eff. Jan. 1, 1978.

Source: New rule.

See also CPRC §62.045.

ANNOTATIONS

Monroe v. GMAC, 573 S.W.2d 591, 594 (Tex.App.—Waco 1978, no writ). "Attorney's fees and damages against [P] are authorized only if the writ is dissolved."

TRCP 713. SALE ON DEBT NOT DUE

If the suit in which the sequestration issued be for a debt or demand not yet due, and the property sequestered be likely to be wasted, destroyed or greatly depreciated in value by keeping, the judge or justice of the peace shall,

under the regulations hereinbefore provided, order the same to be sold, giving credit on such sale until such debt or demand shall become due.

History of TRCP 713: Adopted eff. Sept. 1, 1941, by order of Oct. 29, 1940 (3 Tex.B.J. 636 [1940]). Source: TRCS art. 6862 (repealed).

See also CPRC §62.003.

TRCP 714. PURCHASER'S BOND

In the case of a sale as provided for in the preceding rule, the purchaser of the property shall execute his bond, with two or more good and sufficient sureties, to be approved by the officer making the sale, and payable to such officer, in a sum not less than double the amount of the purchase money, conditioned that such purchaser shall pay such purchase money at the expiration of the time given.

History of TRCP 714: Adopted eff. Sept. 1, 1941, by order of Oct. 29, 1940 (3 Tex.B.J. 637 [1940]). Source: TRCS art. 6863 (repealed).

TRCP 715. RETURN OF BOND

The bond provided for in the preceding rule shall be returned by the officer taking the same to the clerk or justice of the peace from whose court the order of sale issued, with such order, and shall be filed among the papers in the cause.

History of TRCP 715: Adopted eff. Sept. 1, 1941, by order of Oct. 29, 1940 (3 Tex.B.J. 637 [1940]). Source: TRCS art. 6864 (repealed).

TRCP 716. RECOVERY ON BOND

In case the purchaser does not pay the purchase money at the expiration of the time given, judgment shall be rendered against all the obligors in such bond for the amount of such purchase money, interest thereon and all costs incurred in the enforcement and collection of the same; and execution shall issue thereon in the name of the plaintiff in the suit, as in other cases, and the money when collected shall be paid to the clerk or justice of the peace to abide the final decision of the cause.

History of TRCP 716: Adopted eff. Sept. 1, 1941, by order of Oct. 29, 1940 (3 Tex.B.J. 637 [1940]). Source: TRCS art. 6864 (repealed).

SECTION 9. TRIAL OF RIGHT OF PROPERTY

TRCP 717. CLAIMANT MUST MAKE AFFIDAVIT

Whenever a distress warrant, writ of execution, sequestration, attachment, or other like writ is levied upon personal property, and such property, or any part thereof, shall be claimed by any claimant who is not a party to such writ, such claimant may make application that such claim is made in good faith, and file such application with the court in which such suit is pending. Such application may be supported by affidavits of the claimant, his agent, his attorney, or other persons having knowledge of relevant facts. The application shall comply with all statutory requirements and shall state the grounds for such claim and the specific facts relied upon by the claimant to warrant the required findings by the court.

The claim shall not be quashed because two or more grounds are stated conjunctively or disjunctively. The application and any affidavits shall be made on personal knowledge and shall set forth such facts as would be admissible in evidence; provided that facts may be stated based upon information and belief if the grounds of such belief are specifically stated.

No property shall be delivered to the claimant except on written order of the court after a hearing pursuant to Rule 718. The court in its order granting the application shall make specific findings of facts to support the statutory grounds found to exist and shall specify the amount of the bond required of the claimant.

June 10, 1980, eff. Jan. 1, 1981.

TRCP 718. PROPERTY DELIVERED TO CLAIMANT

Any claimant who claims an interest in property on which a writ has been levied may, by sworn written motion, seek to obtain possession of such property. Such motion shall admit or deny each finding of the order directing the issuance of the writ except where the claimant is unable to admit or deny the finding, in which case claimant shall set forth the reasons why he cannot admit or deny. Such motion shall also contain the reasons why the claimant has superior right or title to the property claimed as against the plaintiff in the writ. Unless the parties agree to an extension of time, the motion shall be heard promptly, after reasonable notice to the plaintiff (which may be less than three days), and the issue shall be determined not later than 10 days after the motion is filed. The filing of the motion shall stay any further proceedings under the writ, except for any orders concerning the care, preservation, or sale of any perishable property, until a hearing is had, and the issue is determined. The claimant shall have the burden to show superior right or title to the property claimed as against the plaintiff and defendant in the writ.

The court's determination may be made upon the basis of affidavits, if uncontroverted, setting forth such facts as would be admissible in evidence, but additional evidence, if tendered by either party shall be received and considered. The court may make all such orders, including orders concerning the care, preservation, or disposition of the property, or the proceeds therefrom if the same has been sold, as justice may require, and if the court modifies its order or the writ issued pursuant thereto, it shall make such further orders with respect to the bond as may be consistent with its modification.

June 10, 1980, eff. Jan. 1, 1981.

TRCP 719. BOND

No property shall be put in the custody of the claimant until the claimant has filed with the officer who made the

levy, a bond in an amount fixed by the court's order equal to double the value of the property so claimed, payable to the plaintiff in the writ, with sufficient surety or sureties as provided by statute to be approved by such officer, conditioned that the claimant will return the same to the officer making the levy, or his successor, in as good condition as he received it, and shall also pay the reasonable value of the use, hire, increase and fruits thereof from the date of said bond, or, in case he fails so to return said property and pay for the use of the same, that he shall pay the plaintiff the value of said property, with legal interest thereon from the date of the bond, and shall also pay all damages and costs that may be awarded against him for wrongfully suing out such claim.

The plaintiff or claimant may file a motion to increase or reduce the amount of such bond, or to question the sufficiency of the sureties thereon, in the court in which such suit is pending. Upon hearing, the court shall enter its order with respect to such bond and sufficiency of the sureties.

June 10, 1980, eff. Jan. 1, 1981.

TRCP 720. RETURN OF BOND

Whenever any person shall claim property and shall duly make the application and give the bond, if the writ under which the levy was made was issued by a justice of the peace or a court of the county where such levy was made, the officer receiving such application and bond shall endorse on the writ that such claim has been made and application and bond given, and by whom; and shall also endorse on such bond the value of the property as assessed by himself, and shall forthwith return such bond with a copy of the writ to the proper court having jurisdiction to try such claim.

June 10, 1980, eff. Jan. 1, 1981.

Source: New rule.

ANNOTATIONS

Sandler v. Bufkor, Inc., 658 S.W.2d 289, 292 (Tex.App.—Houston [1st Dist.] 1983, no writ). "Having waived the right to establish that the property was of lesser value than that estimated by the officer fixing the amount of the bond, [makers of the bond] became bound by the recitals of the assessed value appearing on the face of the bond they signed."

TRCP 721. OUT-COUNTY LEVY

Whenever any person shall claim property and shall make the application and give the bond as provided for herein, if the writ under which such levy was made was issued by a justice of the peace or a court of another county than that in which such levy was made, then the officer receiving such bond shall endorse on such bond the value of the property as assessed by himself, and shall forthwith return such bond with a copy of the writ, to the proper court having jurisdiction to try such claim.

June 10, 1980, eff. Jan. 1, 1981.

TRCP 722. RETURN OF ORIGINAL WRIT

The officer taking such bond shall also endorse on the original writ, if in his possession, that such claim has been made and application and bond given, stating by whom, the names of the surety or sureties, and to what justice or court the bond has been returned; and he shall forthwith return such original writ to the tribunal from which it issued.

June 10, 1980, eff. Jan. 1, 1981.

TRCP 723. DOCKETING CAUSE

Whenever any bond for the trial of the right of property shall be returned, the clerk of the court, or such justice of the peace, shall docket the same in the original writ proceeding in the name of the plaintiff in the writ as the plaintiff, and the claimant of the property as intervening claimant.

June 10, 1980, eff. Jan. 1, 1981.

TRCP 724. ISSUE MADE UP

After the claim proceedings have been docketed, and on the hearing day set by the court, then the court, or the justice of the peace, as the case may be, shall enter an order directing the making and joinder of issues by the parties. Such issues shall be in writing and signed by each party or his attorney. The plaintiff shall make a brief statement of the authority and right by which he seeks to subject the property levied on to the process, and it shall be sufficient for the claimant and other parties to make brief statements of the nature of their claims thereto.

June 10, 1980, eff. Jan. 1, 1981.

TRCP 725. JUDGMENT BY DEFAULT

If the plaintiff appears and the claimant fails to appear or neglects or refuses to join issue under the direction of the court or justice within the time prescribed for pleading, the plaintiff shall have judgment by default.

June 10, 1980, eff. Jan. 1, 1981.

TRCP 726. JUDGMENT OF NON-SUIT

If the plaintiff does not appear, he shall be non-suited.

June 10, 1980, eff. Jan. 1, 1981.

Source: New rule. See former TRCP 728, adopted eff. Sept. 1, 1941, by order of Oct., 29, 1940 (3 Tex.B.J. 638 [1940]). See TRCS art. 7414 (repealed).

ANNOTATIONS

Union Bank & Trust Co. v. Mireles, 697 S.W.2d 745, 747 (Tex.App.—Corpus Christi 1985, no writ). "When [a

plaintiff is nonsuited after failing to appear,] the claimant has possession of the property and this specialized proceeding is ended."

TRCP 727. PROCEEDINGS

The proceedings and practice on the trial shall be as nearly as may be the same as in other cases before such court or justice.

June 10, 1980, eff. Jan. 1, 1981.

TRCP 728. BURDEN OF PROOF

If the property was taken from the possession of the claimant pursuant to the original writ, the burden of proof shall be on the plaintiff in the writ. If it was taken from the possession of the defendant in such writ, or any other person than the claimant, the burden of proof shall be on the claimant.

June 10, 1980, eff. Jan. 1, 1981.

TRCP 729. COPY OF WRIT EVIDENCE

In all trials of the right of property, under the provisions of this section in any county other than that in which the writ issued under which the levy was made, the copy of the writ herein required to be returned by the officer making the levy shall be received in evidence in like manner as the original could be.

June 10, 1980, eff. Jan. 1, 1981.

TRCP 730. FAILURE TO ESTABLISH TITLE

Where any claimant has obtained possession of property, and shall ultimately fail to establish his right thereto, judgment may be rendered against him and his sureties for the value of the property, with legal interest thereon from the date of such bond. Such judgment shall be rendered in favor of the plaintiff or defendant in the writ, or of the several plaintiffs or defendants, if more than one, and shall fix the amount of the claim of each.

June 10, 1980, eff. Jan. 1, 1981.

Source: New rule. See former TRCP 732, adopted eff. Sept. 1, 1941, by order of Oct. 29, 1940 (3 Tex.B.J. 639 [1940]). See TRCS art. 7420 (repealed).

ANNOTATIONS

Sandler v. Bufkor, Inc., 658 S.W.2d 289, 292 (Tex.App.—Houston [1st Dist.] 1983, no writ). "Once [claimant] failed to establish its right to the property protected by the bond, [Ps] were entitled to judgment against [makers of the bond] and their surety for the value of the property."

TRCP 731. EXECUTION SHALL ISSUE

If such judgment should not be satisfied by a return of the property, then after the expiration of ten days from the date of the judgment, execution shall issue thereon in the name of the plaintiff or defendant for the amount of the claim, or of all the plaintiffs or defendants for the sum of their several claims, provided the amount of such judgment shall inure to the benefit of any person who shall show superior right or title to the property claimed as against the claimant; but if such judgment be for a less amount than the sum of the several plaintiffs' or defendants' claims, then the respective rights and priorities of the several plaintiffs or defendants shall be fixed and adjusted in the judgment.

June 10, 1980, eff. Jan. 1, 1981.

TRCP 732. RETURN OF PROPERTY BY CLAIMANT

If, within ten days from the rendition of said judgment, the claimant shall return such property in as good condition as he received it, and pay for the use of the same together with the damages and costs, such delivery and payment shall operate as a satisfaction of such judgment.

June 10, 1980, eff. Jan. 1, 1981.

Source: See former TRCP 734, adopted eff. Sept. 1, 1941, by order of Oct. 29, 1940 (3 Tex.B.J. 639 [1940]). See TRCS art. 7423 (repealed).

ANNOTATIONS

Sandler v. Bufkor, Inc., 658 S.W.2d 289, 292-93 (Tex.App.—Houston [1st Dist.] 1983, no writ). "Although return of the property 'in as good condition as he received it' operates as a satisfaction of the judgment, partial tender and an offer to pay for missing property does not constitute such satisfaction. . . . This is especially so where a 'substantial part' of the goods are missing."

TRCP 733. CLAIM IS A RELEASE OF DAMAGES

A claim made to the property, under the provisions of this section, shall operate as a release of all damages by the claimant against the officer who levied upon said property.

June 10, 1980, eff. Jan. 1, 1981.

TRCP 734. LEVY ON OTHER PROPERTY

Proceedings for the trial of right of property under these rules shall in no case prevent the plaintiff in the writ from having a levy made upon any other property of the defendant.

June 10, 1980, eff. June 1, 1981.

Part VII. Rules Relating to Special Proceedings

SECTION 1. PROCEDURES RELATED TO FORECLOSURES OF CERTAIN LIENS

TRCP 735. FORECLOSURES REQUIRING A COURT ORDER

735.1. Liens Affected. Rule 736 provides the procedure for obtaining a court order, when required, to allow

foreclosure of a lien containing a power of sale in the security instrument, dedicatory instrument, or declaration creating the lien, including a lien securing any of the following:

(a) a home equity loan, reverse mortgage, or home equity line of credit under article XVI, sections 50(a)(6), 50(k), and 50(t) of the Texas Constitution;

(b) a tax lien transfer or property tax loan under sections 32.06 and 32.065 of the Tax Code; or

(c) a property owners' association assessment under section 209.0092 of the Property Code.

735.2. Other Statutory and Contractual Foreclosure. A Rule 736 order does not alter any foreclosure requirement or duty imposed under applicable law or the terms of the loan agreement, contract, or lien sought to be foreclosed. The only issue to be determined in a Rule 736 proceeding is whether a party may obtain an order under Rule 736 to proceed with foreclosure under applicable law and the terms of the loan agreement, contract, or lien sought to be foreclosed.

735.3. Judicial Foreclosure Unaffected. A Rule 736 order is not a substitute for a judgment for judicial foreclosure, but any loan agreement, contract, or lien that may be foreclosed using Rule 736 procedures may also be foreclosed by judgment in an action for judicial foreclosure.

Adopted by order of Oct. 17, 2011, eff. Jan. 1, 2012. Amended by order of Dec. 12, 2011, and Dec. 30, 2011, eff. Jan. 1, 2012.

Comment—2011

Rules 735 and 736 have been rewritten and expanded to cover property owners' associations' assessment liens, in accordance with amendments to chapter 209 of the Property Code. Rule 735.1 makes the expedited procedures of Rule 736 available only when the lienholder has a power of sale but a court order is nevertheless required by law to foreclose the lien. Rule 735.2 makes clear that Rule 736 is procedural only and does not affect other contractual or legal rights or duties. Any lien which can be foreclosed under Rule 736 may also be foreclosed in an action for judicial foreclosure, as Rule 735.3 states, but no lienholder is required to obtain both a Rule 736 order and a judgment for judicial foreclosure. The requirement of conspicuousness in Rule 736.1(d)(5) has reference to section 1.201(b)(10) of the Business and Commerce Code.

Source: New rule.

See also Tex. Const. art. 16, §50; Prop. Code §51.002.

TRCP 736. EXPEDITED ORDER PROCEEDING

Source: New rule.

736.1. Application.

(a) ***Where Filed.*** An application for an expedited order allowing the foreclosure of a lien listed in Rule 735 to proceed must be filed in a county where all or part of the real property encumbered by the loan agreement, contract, or lien sought to be foreclosed is located or in a probate court with jurisdiction over proceedings involving the property.

(b) ***Style.*** An application must be styled "In re: Order for Foreclosure Concerning [state: property's mailing address] under Tex. R. Civ. P. 736."

(c) ***When Filed.*** An application may not be filed until the opportunity to cure has expired under applicable law and the loan agreement, contract, or lien sought to be foreclosed.

(d) ***Contents.*** The application must:

(1) Identify by name and last known address each of the following parties:

(A) "Petitioner"—any person legally authorized to prosecute the foreclosure;

(B) "Respondent"—according to the records of the holder or servicer of the loan agreement, contract, or lien sought to be foreclosed:

(i) for a home equity loan, reverse mortgage, or home equity line of credit, each person obligated to pay the loan agreement, contract, or lien sought to be foreclosed and each mortgagor, if any, of the loan agreement, contract, or lien sought to be foreclosed;

(ii) for a tax lien transfer or property tax loan, each person obligated to pay the loan agreement, contract, or lien sought to be foreclosed, each mortgagor, if any, of the loan agreement, contract, or lien sought to be foreclosed, each owner of the property, and the holder of any recorded preexisting first lien secured by the property;

(iii) for a property owners' association assessment, each person obligated to pay the loan agreement, contract, or lien sought to be foreclosed who has a current ownership interest in the property.

(2) Identify the property encumbered by the loan agreement, contract, or lien sought to be foreclosed by its commonly known street address and legal description.

(3) Describe or state:

(A) the type of lien listed in Rule 735 sought to be foreclosed and its constitutional or statutory reference;

(B) the authority of the party seeking foreclosure, whether as the servicer, beneficiary, lender, investor, property owners' association, or other person with authority to prosecute the foreclosure;

(C) each person obligated to pay the loan agreement, contract, or lien sought to be foreclosed;

(D) each mortgagor, if any, of the loan agreement, contract, or lien sought to be foreclosed who is not a maker or assumer of the underlying debt;

(E) as of a date that is not more than sixty days prior to the date the application is filed:

(i) if the default is monetary, the number of unpaid scheduled payments,

(ii) if the default is monetary, the amount required to cure the default,

(iii) if the default is non-monetary, the facts creating the default, and

(iv) if applicable, the total amount required to pay off the loan agreement, contract, or lien;

(F) that the requisite notice or notices to cure the default has or have been mailed to each person as required under applicable law and the loan agreement, contract, or lien sought to be foreclosed and that the opportunity to cure has expired; and

(G) that before the application was filed, any other action required under applicable law and the loan agreement, contract, or lien sought to be foreclosed was performed.

(4) For a tax lien transfer or property tax loan, state all allegations required to be contained in the application in accordance with section 32.06(c–l)(1) of the Tax Code.

(5) Conspicuously state:

(A) that legal action is not being sought against the occupant of the property unless the occupant is also named as a respondent in the application; and

(B) that if the petitioner obtains a court order, the petitioner will proceed with a foreclosure of the property in accordance with applicable law and the terms of the loan agreement, contract, or lien sought to be foreclosed.

(6) Include an affidavit of material facts in accordance with Rule 166a(f) signed by the petitioner or the servicer describing the basis for foreclosure and, depending on the type of lien sought to be foreclosed, attach a legible copy of:

(A) the note, original recorded lien, or pertinent part of a property owners' association declaration or dedicatory instrument establishing the lien, and current assignment of the lien, if assigned;

(B) each notice required to be mailed to any person under applicable law and the loan agreement, contract, or lien sought to be foreclosed before the application was filed and proof of mailing of each notice; and

(C) for a tax lien transfer or property tax loan:

(i) the property owner's sworn document required under section 32.06(a-1) of the Tax Code; and

(ii) the taxing authority's certified statement attesting to the transfer of the lien, required under section 32.06(b) of the Tax Code.

736.2. Costs.

All filing, citation, mailing, service, and other court costs and fees are costs of court and must be paid by petitioner at the time of filing an application with the clerk of the court.

736.3. Citation.

(a) ***Issuance.***

(1) When the application is filed, the clerk must issue a separate citation for each respondent named in the application and one additional citation for the occupant of the property sought to be foreclosed.

(2) Each citation that is directed to a respondent must state that any response to the application is due the first Monday after the expiration of 38 days from the date the citation was placed in the custody of the U.S. Postal Service in accordance with the clerk's standard mailing procedures and state the date that the citation was placed in the custody of the U.S. Postal Service by the clerk.

(b) ***Service and Return.***

(1) The clerk of the court must serve each citation, with a copy of the application attached, by both first class mail and certified mail. A citation directed to a respondent must be mailed to the respondent's last known address that is stated in the application. A citation directed to the occupant of the property sought to be foreclosed must be mailed to Occupant of [state: property's mailing address] at the address of the property sought to be foreclosed that is stated in the application.

(2) Concurrently with service, the clerk must complete a return of service in accordance with Rule 107, except that the return of service need not contain a return receipt. For a citation mailed by the clerk in accordance with (b)(1), the date of service is the date and time the citation was placed in the custody of the U.S. Postal Service in a properly addressed, postage prepaid envelope in accordance with the clerk's standard mailing procedures.

(3) The clerk must only charge one fee per respondent or occupant served under this rule.

736.4. Discovery.

No discovery is permitted in a Rule 736 proceeding.

736.5. Response.

(a) ***Generally.*** A respondent may file a response contesting the application.

(b) ***Due Date.*** Any response to the application is due the first Monday after the expiration of 38 days from the date the citation was placed in the custody of the U.S. Postal Service in accordance with the clerk's standard mailing procedures, as stated on the citation.

(c) ***Form.*** A response must be signed in accordance

with Rule 57 and may be in the form of a general denial under Rule 92, except that a respondent must affirmatively plead:

(1) why the respondent believes a respondent did not sign a loan agreement document, if applicable, that is specifically identified by the respondent;

(2) why the respondent is not obligated for payment of the lien;

(3) why the number of months of alleged default or the reinstatement or pay off amounts are materially incorrect;

(4) why any document attached to the application is not a true and correct copy of the original; or

(5) proof of payment in accordance with Rule 95.

(d) ***Other Claims.*** A response may not state an independent claim for relief. The court must, without a hearing, strike and dismiss any counterclaim, cross claim, third party claim, intervention, or cause of action filed by any person in a Rule 736 proceeding.

736.6. Hearing Required When Response Filed.

The court must not conduct a hearing under this rule unless a response is filed. If a response is filed, the court must hold a hearing after reasonable notice to the parties. The hearing on the application must not be held earlier than 20 days or later than 30 days after a request for a hearing is made by any party. At the hearing, the petitioner has the burden to prove by affidavits on file or evidence presented the grounds for granting the order sought in the application.

736.7. Default When No Response Filed.

(a) If no response to the application is filed by the due date, the petitioner may file a motion and proposed order to obtain a default order. For the purposes of obtaining a default order, all facts alleged in the application and supported by the affidavit of material facts constitute prima facie evidence of the truth of the matters alleged.

(b) The court must grant the application by default order no later than 30 days after a motion is filed under (a) if the application complies with the requirements of Rule 736.1 and was properly served in accordance with Rule 736.3. The petitioner need not appear in court to obtain a default order.

(c) The return of service must be on file with the clerk of the court for at least 10 days before the court may grant the application by default.

736.8. Order.

(a) The court must issue an order granting the application if the petitioner establishes the basis for the foreclosure. Otherwise, the court must deny the application.

(b) An order granting the application must describe:

(1) the material facts establishing the basis for foreclosure;

(2) the property to be foreclosed by commonly known mailing address and legal description;

(3) the name and last known address of each respondent subject to the order; and

(4) the recording or indexing information of each lien to be foreclosed.

(c) An order granting or denying the application is not subject to a motion for rehearing, new trial, bill of review, or appeal. Any challenge to a Rule 736 order must be made in a suit filed in a separate, independent, original proceeding in a court of competent jurisdiction.

736.9. Effect of the Order.

An order is without prejudice and has no res judicata, collateral estoppel, estoppel by judgment or other effect in any other judicial proceeding. After an order is obtained, a person may proceed with the foreclosure process under applicable law and the terms of the lien sought to be foreclosed.

736.10. Bankruptcy.

If a respondent provides proof to the clerk of the court that respondent filed bankruptcy before an order is signed, the proceeding under this rule must be abated so long as the automatic stay is effective.

736.11. Automatic Stay and Dismissal if Independent Suit Filed.

(a) A proceeding or order under this rule is automatically stayed if a respondent files a separate, original proceeding in a court of competent jurisdiction that puts in issue any matter related to the origination, servicing, or enforcement of the loan agreement, contract, or lien sought to be foreclosed prior to 5:00 p.m. on the Monday before the scheduled foreclosure sale.

(b) Respondent must give prompt notice of the filing of the suit to petitioner or petitioner's attorney and the foreclosure trustee or substitute trustee by any reasonable means necessary to stop the scheduled foreclosure sale.

(c) Within ten days of filing suit, the respondent must file a motion and proposed order to dismiss or vacate with the clerk of the court in which the application was filed giving notice that respondent has filed an original proceeding contesting the right to foreclose in a court of competent jurisdiction. If no order has been signed, the court must dismiss a pending proceeding. If an order has been signed, the court must vacate the Rule 736 order.

(d) If the automatic stay under this rule is in effect, any foreclosure sale of the property is void. Within 10 busi-

ness days of notice that the foreclosure sale was void, the trustee or substitute trustee must return to the buyer of the foreclosed property the purchase price paid by the buyer.

(e) The court may enforce the Rule 736 process under chapters 9 and 10 of the Civil Practices and Remedies Code.

736.12. Attachment of Order to Trustee's Deed.

A conformed copy of the order must be attached to the trustee or substitute trustee's foreclosure deed.

736.13. Promulgated Forms.

The Supreme Court of Texas may promulgate forms that conform to this rule.

Adopted by order of Oct. 17, 2011, eff. Jan. 1, 2012. Amended by order of Dec. 12, 2011, and Dec. 30, 2011, eff. Jan. 1, 2012.

Comment--2011

Rules 735 and 736 have been rewritten and expanded to cover property owners' associations' assessment liens, in accordance with amendments to chapter 209 of the Property Code. Rule 735.1 makes the expedited procedures of Rule 736 available only when the lienholder has a power of sale but a court order is nevertheless required by law to foreclose the lien. Rule 735.2 makes clear that Rule 736 is procedural only and does not affect other contractual or legal rights or duties. Any lien which can be foreclosed under Rule 736 may also be foreclosed in an action for judicial foreclosure, as Rule 735.3 states, but no lienholder is required to obtain both a Rule 736 order and a judgment for judicial foreclosure. The requirement of conspicuousness in Rule 736.1(d)(5) has reference to section 1.201(b)(10) of the Business and Commerce Code.

Editor's note: The Texas Supreme Court has approved forms for use in expedited foreclosure proceedings. See Tex.Sup.Ct. Order, Misc. Docket No. 14-9047 (eff. Feb. 10, 2014).

See also Tex. Const. art. 16, §50; CPRC §§17.031, 154.028; Prop. Code §51.002.

SECTION 2. JUSTICE COURT PROCEEDINGS TO ENFORCE LANDLORD'S DUTY TO REPAIR OR REMEDY RESIDENTIAL RENTAL PROPERTY [REPEALED BY ORDER OF APRIL 15, 2013, EFFECTIVE AUGUST 31, 2013]

TRCP 737. [DELETED]

TRCP 737.1 to 737.13. REPEALED BY ORDER OF APRIL 15, 2013, EFF. AUG. 31, 2013

SECTION 3. FORCIBLE ENTRY AND DETAINER [REPEALED BY ORDER OF APRIL 15, 2013, EFFECTIVE AUGUST 31, 2013]

TRCP 738 to 755. REPEALED BY ORDER OF APRIL 15, 2013, EFF. AUG. 31, 2013

SECTION 4. PARTITION OF REAL ESTATE

TRCP 756. PETITION

The plaintiff's petition shall state:

(a) The names and residence, if known, of each of the other joint owners, or joint claimants, of such property.

(b) The share or interest which the plaintiff and the other joint owners, or joint claimants, of same own or claim so far as known to the plaintiff.

(c) The land sought to be partitioned shall be so described as that the same may be distinguished from any other and the estimated value thereof stated.

History of TRCP 756: Adopted eff. Sept. 1, 1941, by order of Oct. 29, 1940 (3 Tex.B.J. 642 [1940]). Source: TRCS art. 6083 (repealed in part by TRCP).

See also Prop. Code §§23.001, 23.002.

ANNOTATIONS

Yoast v. Yoast, 649 S.W.2d 289, 292 (Tex.1983). "The court of appeals mischaracterized this case as a partition suit. [P's suit was for] trespass to try title. . . . Partition issues may be resolved in a trespass to try title suit once the controversy as to title or right to possession is settled. That, however, does not convert the cause of action to a partition suit. [¶] A partition suit is based on the theory of common title, rather than disputed ownership."

TRCP 757. CITATION AND SERVICE

Upon the filing of a petition for partition, the clerk shall issue citation for each of the joint owners, or joint claimants, named therein, as in other cases, and such citations shall be served in the manner and for the time provided for the service of citations in other cases.

History of TRCP 757: Adopted eff. Sept. 1, 1941, by order of Oct. 29, 1940 (3 Tex.B.J. 642 [1940]). Source: TRCS art. 6084 (repealed).

ANNOTATIONS

Carper v. Halamicek, 610 S.W.2d 556, 557 (Tex.App.—Tyler 1980, writ ref'd n.r.e.). TRCP 757 "and past cases indicate that the joinder of all owners is mandatory and that no valid, binding decree of partition can be made in their absence."

TRCP 758. WHERE DEFENDANT IS UNKNOWN OR RESIDENCE IS UNKNOWN

If the plaintiff, his agent or attorney, at the commencement of any suit, or during the progress thereof, for the partition of land, shall make affidavit that an undivided portion of the land described in plaintiff's petition in said suit is owned by some person unknown to affiant, or that the place of residence of any known party owning an interest in land sought to be partitioned is unknown to affiant, the Clerk of the Court shall issue citation for publication, conforming to the requirements of Rules 114 and 115, and served in accordance with the directions of Rule 116. In case

of unknown residence or party, the affidavit shall include a statement that after due diligence plaintiff and the affiant have been unable to ascertain the name or locate the residence of such party, as the case may be, and in such case it shall be the duty of the court trying the action to inquire into the sufficiency of the diligence so stated before granting any judgment.

July 20, 1954, eff. Jan. 1, 1955. Amended by order of Dec. 19, 1984, eff. April 1, 1985.

TRCP 759. JUDGMENT WHERE DEFENDANT CITED BY PUBLICATION

When the defendant has been duly cited by publication in accordance with the preceding rule, and no appearance is entered within the time prescribed for pleadings, the court shall appoint an attorney to defend in behalf of such owner or owners, and proceed as in other causes where service is made by publication. It shall be the special duty of the court in all cases to see that its decree protects the rights of the unknown parties thereto. The judge of the court shall fix the fee of the attorney so appointed, which shall be entered and collected as costs against said unknown owner or owners.

History of TRCP 759: Adopted eff. Sept. 1, 1941, by order of Oct. 29, 1940 (3 Tex.B.J. 642 [1940]). Caveat: [Article 6085] was amended in 1939, eff. date after the enactment of the Rule Making Statute. See **Garrett v. Mercantile Nat'l Bank**, 168 S.W.2d 636 (Tex.1943). Source: TRCS art. 6085, last two sentences (repealed).

TRCP 760. COURT SHALL DETERMINE, WHAT

Upon the hearing of the cause, the court shall determine the share or interest of each of the joint owners or claimants in the real estate sought to be divided, and all questions of law or equity affecting the title to such land which may arise.

History of TRCP 760: Adopted eff. Sept. 1, 1941, by order of Oct. 29, 1940 (3 Tex.B.J. 643 [1940]). Source: TRCS art. 6086 (repealed).

ANNOTATIONS

Johnson v. Johnson-McHenry, 978 S.W.2d 142, 144 (Tex.App.—Austin 1998, no pet.). "[I]n a partition suit, the trial court determines whether the partition will be by sale or in kind, the share or interest of the joint owners or claimants, and all questions of law or equity affecting title. The court then allocates to the parties their rightful shares or tracts. A trial court may also exercise equitable powers in a partition suit." *See also* **Carter v. Harvey**, 525 S.W.3d 420, 425 (Tex.App.—Fort Worth 2017, no pet.) (court may determine value of improvements and adjust equities between parties).

TRCP 761. APPOINTMENT OF COMMISSIONERS

The court shall determine before entering the decree of partition whether the property, or any part thereof, is susceptible of partition; and, if the court determines that the whole, or any part of such property is susceptible of partition, then the court for that part of such property held to be susceptible of partition shall enter a decree directing the partition of such real estate, describing the same, to be made in accordance with the respective shares or interests of each of such parties entitled thereto, specify in such decree the share or interest of each party, and shall appoint three or more competent and disinterested persons as commissioners to make such partition in accordance with such decree and the law, a majority of which commissioners may act.

History of TRCP 761: Adopted eff. Sept. 1, 1941, by order of Oct. 29, 1940 (3 Tex.B.J. 643 [1940]). Source: TRCS art. 6087 (repealed).

ANNOTATIONS

Goldberg v. Zinn, No. 14-11-01091-CV, 2013 WL 2456869 (Tex.App.—Houston [14th Dist.] 2013, no pet.) (memo op.; 6-6-13). "Unlike most other proceedings, a partition involves two final and appealable judgments. In the first judgment, the trial court (1) determines the interests of each of the joint owners or claimants in the real estate sought to be divided and decides all questions of law and equity affecting the title to such land; (2) determines whether the property is susceptible to partition or the subject of a sale; and (3) appoints commissioners to partition the property in accordance with the respective shares or interests of each of such parties entitled thereto. In the second judgment, the court approves of the commissioners' report and partitions the property in kind or by sale. [¶] [P] has not disputed the propriety of the appraisals in this case, and the record contains no evidence contradicting them. Without conflicting evidence, there was no need for the district court to 'try' the case for purposes of [TRCP] 296. [¶] As a result, findings of fact and conclusions of law were not required under Rule 296." *See also* **Williams v. Mai**, 471 S.W.3d 16, 18 (Tex.App.—Houston [1st Dist.] 2015, no pet.).

Benson v. Fox, 589 S.W.2d 823, 826 (Tex.App.—Tyler 1979, no writ). "Rule 761 employs the word 'partition' in a restricted sense as synonymous with the phrase 'partition in kind.' "

TRCP 762. WRIT OF PARTITION

The clerk shall issue a writ of partition, directed to the sheriff or any constable of the county, commanding such sheriff or constable to notify each of the commissioners of their appointment as such, and shall accompany such writ with a certified copy of the decree of the court directing the partition.

History of TRCP 762: Adopted eff. Sept. 1, 1941, by order of Oct. 29, 1940 (3 Tex.B.J. 643 [1940]). Source: TRCS art. 6088 (repealed).

TRCP 763. SERVICE OF WRIT OF PARTITION

The writ of partition shall be served by reading the same to each of the persons named therein as commissioners, and

by delivering to any one of them the accompanying certified copy of the decree of the court.

History of TRCP 763: Adopted eff. Sept. 1, 1941, by order of Oct. 29, 1940 (3 Tex.B.J. 643 [1940]). Source: TRCS art. 6089 (repealed).

TRCP 764. MAY APPOINT SURVEYOR

The court may, should it be deemed necessary, appoint a surveyor to assist the commissioners in making the partition, in which case the writ of partition shall name such surveyor, and shall be served upon him by reading the same to him.

History of TRCP 764: Adopted eff. Sept. 1, 1941, by order of Oct. 29, 1940 (3 Tex.B.J. 643 [1940]). Source: TRCS art. 6090 (repealed).

TRCP 765. RETURN OF WRIT

A writ of partition, unless otherwise directed by the court, shall be made returnable twenty days from date of service on the commissioner last served; and the officer serving it shall endorse thereon the time and manner of such service.

History of TRCP 765: Adopted eff. Sept. 1, 1941, by order of Oct. 29, 1940 (3 Tex.B.J. 643 [1940]). Source: TRCS art. 6091 (repealed).

TRCP 766. SHALL PROCEED TO PARTITION

The commissioners, or a majority of them, shall proceed to partition the real estate described in the decree of the court, in accordance with the directions contained in such decree and with the provisions of law and these rules.

History of TRCP 766: Adopted eff. Sept. 1, 1941, by order of Oct. 29, 1940 (3 Tex.B.J. 643 [1940]). Source: TRCS art. 6092 (repealed).

ANNOTATIONS

Goldberg v. Zinn, No. 14-11-01091-CV, 2013 WL 2456869 (Tex.App.—Houston [14th Dist.] 2013, no pet.) (memo op.; 6-6-13). See annotation under TRCP 761.

TRCP 767. MAY CAUSE SURVEY

If the commissioners deem it necessary, they may cause to be surveyed the real estate to be partitioned into several tracts or parcels.

History of TRCP 767: Adopted eff. Sept. 1, 1941, by order of Oct. 29, 1940 (3 Tex.B.J. 643 [1940]). Source: TRCS art. 6093 (repealed).

TRCP 768. SHALL DIVIDE REAL ESTATE

The commissioners shall divide the real estate to be partitioned into as many shares as there are persons entitled thereto, as determined by the court, each share to contain one or more tracts or parcels, as the commissioners may think proper, having due regard in the division to the situation, quantity and advantages of each share, so that the shares may be equal in value, as nearly as may be, in proportion to the respective interests of the parties entitled. The commissioners shall then proceed by lot to set apart to each of the parties entitled one of said shares, as determined by the decrees of the court.

History of TRCP 768: Adopted eff. Sept. 1, 1941, by order of Oct. 29, 1940 (3 Tex.B.J. 643 [1940]). Source: TRCS art. 6094 (repealed).

ANNOTATIONS

Grimes v. Hall, 211 S.W.2d 956, 958 (Tex.App.—Eastland 1948, no writ). "Where the interests of the parties in the realty to be partitioned are unequal, selection of owners of shares by lot is not required."

TRCP 769. REPORT OF COMMISSIONERS

When the commissioners have completed the partition, they shall report the same in writing and under oath to the court, which report shall show:

(a) The property divided, describing the same.

(b) The several tracts or parcels into which the same was divided by them, describing each particularly.

(c) The number of shares and the land which constitutes each share, and the estimated value of each share.

(d) The allotment of each share.

(e) The report shall be accompanied by such field notes and maps as may be necessary to make the same intelligible.

The clerk shall immediately mail written notice of the filing of the report to all parties.

April 24, 1990, eff. Sept. 1, 1990.

Comment—1990

Requirement added that clerk notify parties of the filing of the report.

TRCP 770. PROPERTY INCAPABLE OF DIVISION

Should the court be of the opinion that a fair and equitable division of the real estate, or any part thereof, cannot be made, it shall order a sale of so much as is incapable of partition, which sale shall be for cash, or upon such other terms as the court may direct, and shall be made as under execution or by private or public sale through a receiver, if the court so order, and the proceeds thereof shall be returned into court and be partitioned among the persons entitled thereto, according to their respective interests.

Oct. 12, 1949, eff. March 1, 1950.

Source: TRCS art. 6096 (repealed).

ANNOTATIONS

Bowman v. Stephens, 569 S.W.3d 210, 220 (Tex.App.—Houston [1st Dist.] 2018, no pet.). "The threshold question

in a partition suit is whether the property is 'susceptible of partition' in kind or if it is, instead, 'incapable of partition' in kind because a 'fair and equitable division' cannot be made. A tract may be incapable of partition in kind even though a partition in kind is not 'physically impossible.' The issue is whether partition in kind is so 'impractical or unfair' that 'partition by sale would best serve the parties' interest and restore or preserve the maximum value of the property.' [¶] The party seeking to obtain a partition by sale (instead of the legally favored partition in kind) has the burden to demonstrate that partition in kind is 'impractical or unfair.' *At 221:* One of the recognized factors for determining whether property is incapable of partition in kind is whether it can be divided without 'materially impairing its value.' [¶] Even if partition in kind is possible and will preserve the land's value, a trial court may reasonably conclude partition in kind is 'not feasible, fair, practical, or equitable' given the parties' interests in the property. [¶] If the trial court determines property is incapable of partition in kind, then the trial court must order partition by sale."

TRCP 771. OBJECTIONS TO REPORT

Either party to the suit may file objections to any report of the commissioners in partition within thirty days of the date the report is filed, and in such case a trial of the issues thereon shall be had as in other cases. If the report be found to be erroneous in any material respect, or unequal and unjust, the same shall be rejected, and other commissioners shall be appointed by the Court, and the same proceedings had as in the first instance.

April 24, 1990, eff. Sept. 1, 1990.

Comment—1990

To set a time within which objections to a commissioners report must be filed.

ANNOTATIONS

Williams v. Mai, 471 S.W.3d 16, 19 (Tex.App.—Houston [1st Dist.] 2015, no pet.). "Because the commissioners' report was not filed in the trial court, [D], who had objected to the preliminary replat before entry of judgment, was unable to object to the commissioners' report and have a trial of the issues as she is allowed to do under Rule 771. The trial court abused its discretion in depriving [D] of the right to object and to have a trial on the contested issues in the report."

Sand Point Ranch, Ltd. v. Smith, 363 S.W.3d 268, 272 (Tex.App.—Corpus Christi 2012, no pet.). "[A]ny complaint not made by a party in its rule 771 objection is waived on appeal." *See also* **Ellis v. First City Nat'l Bank**, 864 S.W.2d 555, 557 (Tex.App.—Tyler 1993, no writ) (objecting party has burden to prove report is materially erroneous or that partition is unequal or unjust).

SECTION 5. PARTITION OF PERSONAL PROPERTY

TRCP 772. PROCEDURE

An action seeking partition of personal property as authorized by Section 23.001, Texas Property Code, shall be commenced in the same manner as other civil suits, and the several owners or claimants of such property shall be cited as in other cases.

July 15, 1987, eff. Jan. 1, 1988.

TRCP 773. VALUE ASCERTAINED

The separate value of each article of such personal property, and the allotment in kind to which each owner is entitled, shall be ascertained by the court with or without a jury.

History of TRCP 773: Adopted eff. Sept. 1, 1941, by order of Oct. 29, 1940 (3 Tex.B.J. 644 [1940]). Source: TRCS art. 6103 (repealed).

ANNOTATIONS

Price v. Price, 394 S.W.2d 855, 858 (Tex.App.—Tyler 1965, writ ref'd n.r.e.). "The fact that the property has now been transformed into personal property in the form of money would not alter the application rule, but would only make the property more susceptible to a partition in kind."

TRCP 774. DECREE OF COURT EXECUTED

When partition in kind of personal property is ordered by the judgment of the court, a writ shall be issued in accordance with such judgment, commanding the sheriff or constable of the county where the property may be to put the parties forthwith in possession of the property allotted to each respectively.

History of TRCP 774: Adopted eff. Sept. 1, 1941, by order of Oct. 29, 1940 (3 Tex.B.J. 644 [1940]). Source: TRCS art. 6104 (repealed).

TRCP 775. PROPERTY SOLD

When personal property will not admit of a fair and equitable partition, the court shall ascertain the proportion to which each owner thereof is entitled, and order the property to be sold, and execution shall be issued to the sheriff or any constable of the county where the property may be describing such property and commanding such officer to sell the same as in other cases of execution, and pay over the proceeds of sale to the parties entitled thereto, in the proportion ascertained by the judgment of the court.

History of TRCP 775: Adopted eff. Sept. 1, 1941, by order of Oct. 29, 1940 (3 Tex.B.J. 644 [1940]). Source: TRCS art. 6105 (repealed).

SECTION 6. PARTITION: MISCELLANEOUS PROVISIONS

TRCP 776. CONSTRUCTION

No provision of the statutes or rules relating to partition shall affect the mode of proceeding prescribed by law for

the partition of estates of decedents among the heirs and legatees, nor preclude partition in any other manner authorized by the rules of equity, which rules shall govern in proceedings for partition in all respects not provided for by law or these rules.

History of TRCP 776: Adopted eff. Sept. 1, 1941, by order of Oct. 29, 1940 (3 Tex.B.J. 645 [1940]). Source: TRCS art. 6106 (repealed).

TRCP 777. PLEADING AND PRACTICE

The same rules of pleading, practice and evidence which govern in other civil actions shall govern in suits for partition, when not in conflict with any provisions of the law or these rules relating to partition.

History of TRCP 777: Adopted eff. Sept. 1, 1941, by order of Oct. 29, 1940 (3 Tex.B.J. 645 [1940]). Source: TRCS art. 6107 (repealed).

ANNOTATIONS

Rayson v. Johns, 524 S.W.2d 380, 382 (Tex.App.—Texarkana 1975, writ ref'd n.r.e.). "[I]n whatever posture the question has arisen, the courts have treated disputed issues of fact in partition proceedings as being for the jury when one has been properly demanded. *At 383:* An issue of fact was . . . raised on the question of the susceptibility of the land to division in kind, and since [Ds] properly requested it, they were entitled to a jury determination of the issue."

TRCP 778. COSTS

The court shall adjudge the costs in a partition suit to be paid by each party to whom a share has been allotted in proportion to the value of such share.

History of TRCP 778: Adopted eff. Sept. 1, 1941, by order of Oct. 29, 1940 (3 Tex.B.J. 645 [1940]). Source: TRCS art. 6109 (repealed).

SECTION 7. QUO WARRANTO

TRCP 779. JOINDER OF PARTIES

When it appears to the court or judge that the several rights of divers parties to the same office or franchise may properly be determined on one information, the court or judge may give leave to join all such persons in the same information in order to try their respective rights to such office or franchise.

History of TRCP 779: Adopted eff. Sept. 1, 1941, by order of Oct. 29, 1940 (3 Tex.B.J. 645 [1940]). Source: TRCS art. 6254 (repealed).

ANNOTATIONS

Newsom v. State, 922 S.W.2d 274, 277 (Tex.App.—Austin 1996, writ denied). "[T]he State uses quo warranto actions to challenge the authority to engage in certain practices specifically enumerated by statute. A quo warranto proceeding may be instituted by the attorney general or by a district or county attorney. The State is the real plaintiff and controls the litigation, even though in some instances the actions may be at the behest of private parties."

TRCP 780. CITATION TO ISSUE

When such information is filed, the clerk shall issue citation as in civil actions, commanding the defendant to appear and answer the relator in an information in the nature of a quo warranto.

History of TRCP 780: Adopted eff. Sept. 1, 1941, by order of Oct. 29, 1940 (3 Tex.B.J. 645 [1940]). Source: TRCS art. 6255 (repealed).

TRCP 781. PROCEEDINGS AS IN CIVIL CASES

Every person or corporation who shall be cited as hereinbefore provided shall be entitled to all the rights in the trial and investigation of the matters alleged against him, as in cases of trial in civil cases in this State. Either party may prosecute an appeal or writ of error from any judgment rendered, as in other civil cases, subject, however, to the provisions of Rule 42, Texas Rules of Appellate Procedure,[1] and the appellate court shall give preference to such case, and hear and determine the same as early as practicable.

Aug. 18, 1947, eff. Dec. 31, 1947. Amended by order of April 24, 1990, eff. Sept. 1, 1990.

Source: TRCS art. 6256 (repealed).

[1] See, now, Vernon's Ann.Texas Rules App.Proc., rules 26.1, 28.1 to 28.3, 35.1, and 38.6.

ANNOTATIONS

Beach City v. State, 473 S.W.2d 656, 659 (Tex.App.—Houston [14th Dist.] 1971, writ dism'd). "[Q]uo warranto proceedings are governed by the . . . same rules of joinder of causes of action [as] apply . . . in other civil cases."

TRCP 782. REMEDY CUMULATIVE

The remedy and mode of procedure hereby prescribed shall be construed to be cumulative of any now existing.

History of TRCP 782: Adopted eff. Sept. 1, 1941, by order of Oct. 29, 1940 (3 Tex.B.J. 645 [1940]). Source: TRCS art. 6258 (repealed).

SECTION 8. TRESPASS TO TRY TITLE

TRCP 783. REQUISITES OF PETITION

The petition shall state:

(a) The real names of the plaintiff and defendant and their residences, if known.

(b) A description of the premises by metes and bounds, or with sufficient certainty to identify the same, so that from such description possession thereof may be delivered, and state the county or counties in which the same are situated.

(c) The interest which the plaintiff claims in the

premises, whether it be a fee simple or other estate; and, if he claims an undivided interest, the petition shall state the same and the amount thereof.

(d) That the plaintiff was in possession of the premises or entitled to such possession.

(e) That the defendant afterward unlawfully entered upon and dispossessed him of such premises, stating the date, and withholds from him the possession thereof.

(f) If rents and profits or damages are claimed, such facts as show the plaintiff to be entitled thereto and the amount thereof.

(g) It shall conclude with a prayer for the relief sought.

History of TRCP 783: Adopted eff. Sept. 1, 1941, by order of Oct. 29, 1940 (3 Tex.B.J. 645 [1940]). Source: TRCS art. 7366 (repealed).

ANNOTATIONS

Yoast v. Yoast, 649 S.W.2d 289, 292 (Tex.1983). "A trespass to try title action is a procedure by which rival claims to title or right of possession may be adjudicated."

Smith v. Brooks, 825 S.W.2d 208, 210 (Tex.App.—Texarkana 1992, no writ). "In order to claim title by limitation based upon adverse possession, a party must plead it specifically."

TRCP 784. THE POSSESSOR SHALL BE DEFENDANT

The defendant in the action shall be the person in possession if the premises are occupied, or some person claiming title thereto in case they are unoccupied.

History of TRCP 784: Adopted eff. Sept. 1, 1941, by order of Oct. 29, 1940 (3 Tex.B.J. 646 [1940]). Source: TRCS art. 7370 (repealed).

TRCP 785. MAY JOIN AS DEFENDANTS, WHEN

The plaintiff may join as a defendant with the person in possession, any other person who, as landlord, remainderman, reversioner or otherwise, may claim title to the premises, or any part thereof, adversely to the plaintiff.

History of TRCP 785: Adopted eff. Sept. 1, 1941, by order of Oct. 29, 1940 (3 Tex.B.J. 646 [1940]). Source: TRCS art. 7371 (repealed).

TRCP 786. WARRANTOR, ETC., MAY BE MADE A PARTY

When a party is sued for lands, the real owner or warrantor may make himself, or may be made, a party defendant in the suit, and shall be entitled to make such defense as if he had been the original defendant in the action.

History of TRCP 786: Adopted eff. Sept. 1, 1941, by order of Oct. 29, 1940 (3 Tex.B.J. 646 [1940]). Source: TRCS art. 7368 (repealed).

ANNOTATIONS

Williams v. Ballard, 722 S.W.2d 9, 11 (Tex.App.—Dallas 1986, no writ). TRCP 786 allows the mortgagor to intervene as a matter of right.

TRCP 787. LANDLORD MAY BECOME DEFENDANT

When such action shall be commenced against a tenant in possession, the landlord may enter himself as the defendant, or he may be made a party on motion of such tenant; and he shall be entitled to make the same defense as if the suit had been originally commenced against him.

History of TRCP 787: Adopted eff. Sept. 1, 1941, by order of Oct. 29, 1940 (3 Tex.B.J. 646 [1940]). Source: TRCS art. 7369 (repealed).

TRCP 788. MAY FILE PLEA OF "NOT GUILTY" ONLY

The defendant in such action may file only the plea of "not guilty," which shall state in substance that he is not guilty of the injury complained of in the petition filed by the plaintiff against him, except that if he claims an allowance for improvements, he shall state the facts entitling him to the same.

History of TRCP 788: Adopted eff. Sept. 1, 1941, by order of Oct. 29, 1940 (3 Tex.B.J. 646 [1940]). Source: TRCS art. 7372 (repealed).

ANNOTATIONS

Cox v. Olivard, 482 S.W.2d 682, 685 (Tex.App.—Dallas 1972, writ ref'd n.r.e.). "[A] defendant in a trespass to try title action is not required to file a plea of 'not guilty' but . . . a plea of general denial has the effect of putting the plaintiff upon proof of his right to recover the land in controversy."

TRCP 789. PROOF UNDER SUCH PLEA

Under such plea of "not guilty" the defendant may give in evidence any lawful defense to the action except the defense of limitations, which shall be specially pleaded.

History of TRCP 789: Adopted eff. Sept. 1, 1941, by order of Oct. 29, 1940 (3 Tex.B.J. 646 [1940]). Source: TRCS art. 7373 (repealed).

ANNOTATIONS

Walsh v. Austin, 590 S.W.2d 612, 616 (Tex.App.—Houston [1st Dist.] 1979, writ dism'd). "Where . . . the plaintiff has established a prima facie case, whether it be at a summary judgment hearing or upon a full trial, the defendant then has the burden of introducing some defen-

sive evidence to raise an issue of material fact in order to prevent the rendition of a summary judgment or an instructed verdict."

TRCP 790. ANSWER TAKEN AS ADMITTING POSSESSION

Such plea or any other answer to the merits shall be an admission by the defendant, for the purpose of that action, that he was in possession of the premises sued for, or that he claimed title thereto at the time of commencing the action, unless he states distinctly in his answer the extent of his possession or claim, in which case it shall be an admission to such extent only.

History of TRCP 790: Adopted eff. Sept. 1, 1941, by order of Oct. 29, 1940 (3 Tex.B.J. 646 [1940]). Source: TRCS art. 7374 (repealed).

ANNOTATIONS

Brohlin v. McMinn, 341 S.W.2d 420, 422 (Tex.1960). "In an action in trespass to try title, the answer of the defendant to the merits of the case by a plea of not guilty relieves the plaintiffs of the necessity of proving a trespass, since the plea constitutes an admission by the defendant for the purpose of the action that he was in possession of or claimed title to the premises sued for by the plaintiffs."

TRCP 791. MAY DEMAND ABSTRACT OF TITLE

After answer filed, either party may, by notice in writing, duly served on the opposite party or his attorney of record, not less than ten days before the trial of the cause, demand an abstract in writing of the claim or title to the premises in question upon which he relies.

History of TRCP 791: Adopted eff. Sept. 1, 1941, by order of Oct. 29, 1940 (3 Tex.B.J. 646 [1940]). Source: TRCS art. 7376 (repealed).

ANNOTATIONS

Ramsey v. Jones Enters., 810 S.W.2d 902, 904 (Tex.App.—Beaumont 1991, writ denied). "[T]he trial court erred in allowing [P] to prove up title . . . by nothing more than the oral expert testimony of an attorney. [¶] [TRCP] 791 provides for the demanding of an abstract of title by either party. . . . *At 905:* [I]n trespass to try title actions where documents pertaining to title exist, . . . testimony of an expert witness standing alone, constitutes no evidence of titles."

TRCP 792. TIME TO FILE ABSTRACT

Such abstract of title shall be filed with the papers of the cause that within thirty days after the service of the notice, or within such further time that the court on good cause shown may grant; and in default thereof, the court may, after notice and hearing prior to the beginning of trial, order that no written instruments which are evidence of the claim or title of such opposite party be given on trial.

July 15, 1987, eff. Jan. 1, 1988. Amended by order of April 24, 1990, eff. Sept. 1, 1990.

Source: TRCS art. 7377 (repealed).

ANNOTATIONS

Hunt v. Heaton, 643 S.W.2d 677, 679 (Tex.1982). "[P] sought to prove his title by a chain of instruments beginning with a patent from the State. . . . Because of the failure to file an abstract of the chain of title, the trial court properly excluded any offer of proof by [P] relating to his claim or title. [P] failed to prove his superior title and therefore, the correct judgment is that he take nothing."

Corder v. Foster, 505 S.W.2d 645, 648 (Tex.App.—Houston [1st Dist.] 1973, writ ref'd n.r.e.). "[T]he time for filing an abstract in response to a demand will be extended where the grant of additional time will not prejudice the party making the demand and the refusal of an extension would result in injustice."

TRCP 793. ABSTRACT SHALL STATE, WHAT

The abstract mentioned in the two preceding rules shall state:

(a) The nature of each document or written instrument intended to be used as evidence and its date; or

(b) If a contract or conveyance, its date, the parties thereto and the date of the proof of acknowledgment, and before what officer the same was made; and

(c) Where recorded, stating the book and page of the record.

(d) If not recorded in the county when the trial is had, copies of such instrument, with the names of the subscribing witnesses, shall be included. If such unrecorded instrument be lost or destroyed it shall be sufficient to state the nature of such instrument and its loss or destruction.

History of TRCP 793: Adopted eff. Sept. 1, 1941, by order of Oct. 29, 1940 (3 Tex.B.J. 647 [1940]). Source: TRCS art. 7378 (repealed).

ANNOTATIONS

Walker v. Barrow, 464 S.W.2d 480, 487 (Tex.App.—Houston [1st Dist.] 1971, writ ref'd n.r.e.). "[A]ny deficiency of the description contained in the abstract filed should have been called to the attention of [receiver] by motion before trial. There was no error in its admission."

TRCP 794. AMENDED ABSTRACT

The court may allow either party to file an amended abstract of title, under the same rules, which authorize the

amendment of pleadings so far as they are applicable; but in all cases the documentary evidence of title shall at the trial be confined to the matters contained in the abstract of title.

History of TRCP 794: Adopted eff. Sept. 1, 1941, by order of Oct. 29, 1940 (3 Tex.B.J. 647 [1940]). Source: TRCS art. 7379 (repealed).

TRCP 795. RULES IN OTHER CASES OBSERVED

The trial shall be conducted according to the rules of pleading, practice and evidence in other cases in the district court and conformable to the principles of trial by ejectment, except as otherwise provided by these rules.

History of TRCP 795: Adopted eff. Sept. 1, 1941, by order of Oct. 29, 1940 (3 Tex.B.J. 647 [1940]). Source: TRCS art. 7365 (repealed).

ANNOTATIONS

Ramsey v. Jones Enters., 810 S.W.2d 902, 905 (Tex.App.—Beaumont 1991, writ denied). TRE 702, 703, and 704 do not "excuse the necessity for the production and admission of documentary evidence regarding title to real property. [TRE] 1002 . . . requires that if documentary evidence exist as to title to . . . real property, that such documentary evidence must be produced and admitted."

TRCP 796. SURVEYOR APPOINTED, ETC.

The judge of the court may, either in term time or in vacation, at his own discretion, or on motion of either party to the action appoint a surveyor, who shall survey the premises in controversy pursuant to the order of the court, and report his action under oath to such court. If said report be not rejected for good cause shown, the same shall be admitted as evidence on the trial.

History of TRCP 796: Adopted eff. Sept. 1, 1941, by order of Oct. 29, 1940 (3 Tex.B.J. 647 [1940]). Source: TRCS art. 7380 (repealed).

ANNOTATIONS

Mayflower Inv. v. Stephens, 345 S.W.2d 786, 796 (Tex.App.—Dallas 1960, writ ref'd n.r.e.). TRCP 796 "is applicable only in trespass to try title cases."

TRCP 797. SURVEY UNNECESSARY, WHEN

Where there is no dispute as to the lines or boundaries of the land in controversy, or where the defendant admits that he is in possession of the lands or tenements included in the plaintiff's claim, or title, an order of survey shall be unnecessary.

History of TRCP 797: Adopted eff. Sept. 1, 1941, by order of Oct. 29, 1940 (3 Tex.B.J. 647 [1940]). Source: TRCS art. 7381 (repealed).

TRCP 798. COMMON SOURCE OF TITLE

It shall not be necessary for the plaintiff to deraign title beyond a common source. Proof of a common source may be made by the plaintiff by certified copies of the deeds showing a chain of title to the defendant emanating from and under such common source. Before any such certified copies shall be read in evidence, they shall be filed with the papers of the suit three days before the trial, and the adverse party served with notice of such filing as in other cases. Such certified copies shall not be evidence of title in the defendant unless offered in evidence by him. The plaintiff may make any legal objection to such certified copies, or the originals thereof, when introduced by the defendant.

History of TRCP 798: Adopted eff. Sept. 1, 1941, by order of Oct. 29, 1940 (3 Tex.B.J. 647 [1940]). Source: TRCS art. 7382 (repealed).

ANNOTATIONS

Davis v. Gale, 330 S.W.2d 610, 612 (Tex.1960). "In a trespass to try title suit, where the parties agree as to a common source, it is incumbent upon the plaintiff to discharge the burden of proof resting upon him to establish a superior title from such source."

Goggins v. Leo, 849 S.W.2d 373, 377 (Tex.App.—Houston [14th Dist.] 1993, no writ). TRCP 798 applies only to trespass-to-try-title suits, not to forcible-detainer cases.

TRCP 799. JUDGMENT BY DEFAULT

If the defendant, who has been personally served with citation according to law or these rules fails to appear and answer by himself or attorney within the time prescribed by law or these rules for other actions in the district court, then judgment by default may be entered against him and in favor of the plaintiff for the title to the premises, or the possession thereof, or for both, according to the petition, and for all costs, without any proof of title by the plaintiff.

History of TRCP 799: Adopted eff. Sept. 1, 1941, by order of Oct. 29, 1940 (3 Tex.B.J. 647 [1940]). Source: TRCS art. 7383 (repealed).

TRCP 800. PROOF EX PARTE

If the defendant has been cited only by publication, and fails to appear and answer by himself, or by attorney of his own selection, or if any defendant, having answered, fails to appear by himself or attorney when the case is called for trial on its merits, the plaintiff shall make such proof as will entitle him prima facie to recover, whereupon the proper judgment shall be entered.

History of TRCP 800: Adopted eff. Sept. 1, 1941, by order of Oct. 29, 1940 (3 Tex.B.J. 647 [1940]). Source: TRCS art. 7384 (repealed).

TRCP 801. WHEN DEFENDANT CLAIMS PART ONLY

Where the defendant claims part of the premises only, the answer shall be equivalent to a disclaimer of the balance.

History of TRCP 801: Adopted eff. Sept. 1, 1941, by order of Oct. 29, 1940 (3 Tex.B.J. 647 [1940]). Source: TRCS art. 7385 (repealed).

TRCP 802. WHEN PLAINTIFF PROVES PART

Where the defendant claims the whole premises, and the plaintiff shows himself entitled to recover part, the plaintiff shall recover such part and costs.

History of TRCP 802: Adopted eff. Sept. 1, 1941, by order of Oct. 29, 1940 (3 Tex.B.J. 648 [1940]). Source: TRCS art. 7386 (repealed).

TRCP 803. MAY RECOVER A PART

When there are two or more plaintiffs or defendants any one or more of the plaintiffs may recover against one or more of the defendants the premises, or any part thereof, or any interest therein, or damages, according to the rights of the parties.

History of TRCP 803: Adopted eff. Sept. 1, 1941, by order of Oct. 29, 1940 (3 Tex.B.J. 648 [1940]). Source: TRCS art. 7387 (repealed).

TRCP 804. THE JUDGMENT

Upon the finding of the jury, or of the court where the case is tried by the court, in favor of the plaintiff for the whole or any part of the premises in controversy, the judgment shall be that the plaintiff recover of the defendant the title or possession, or both, as the case may be, of such premises, describing them, and where he recovers the possession, that he have his writ of possession.

History of TRCP 804: Adopted eff. Sept. 1, 1941, by order of Oct. 29, 1940 (3 Tex.B.J. 648 [1940]). Source: TRCS art. 7388 (repealed).

TRCP 805. DAMAGES

Where it is alleged and proved that one of the parties is in possession of the premises, the court or jury, if they find for the adverse party, shall assess the damages for the use and occupation of the premises. If special injury to the property be alleged and proved, the damages for such injury shall also be assessed, and the proper judgment shall be entered therefor, on which execution may issue.

History of TRCP 805: Adopted eff. Sept. 1, 1941, by order of Oct. 29, 1940 (3 Tex.B.J. 648 [1940]). Source: TRCS art. 7389 (repealed in part by TRCP).

TRCP 806. CLAIM FOR IMPROVEMENTS

When the defendant or person in possession has claimed an allowance for improvements in accordance with Sections 22.021–22.024, Texas Property Code, the claim for use and occupation and damages mentioned in the preceding rule shall be considered and acted on in connection with such claim by the defendant or person in possession.

Dec. 5, 1983, eff. April 1, 1984. Amended by order of July 15, 1987, eff. Jan. 1, 1988.

TRCP 807. JUDGMENT WHEN CLAIM FOR IMPROVEMENTS IS MADE

When a claim for improvements is successfully made under Sections 22.021–22.024, Texas Property Code, the judgment shall recite the estimated value of the premises without the improvements, and shall also include the conditions, stipulations and directions contained in Sections 22.021–22.024, Texas Property Code so far as applicable to the case before the court.

Dec. 5, 1983, eff. April 1, 1984. Amended by order of July 15, 1987, eff. Jan. 1, 1988.

TRCP 808. THESE RULES SHALL NOT GOVERN, WHEN

Nothing in Sections 22.001–22.045, Texas Property Code, shall be so construed as to alter, impair or take away the rights of parties, as arising under the laws in force before the introduction of the common law, but the same shall be decided by the principles of the law under which the same accrued, or by which the same were regulated or in any manner affected.

Dec. 5, 1983, eff. April 1, 1984. Amended by order of July 15, 1987, eff. Jan. 1, 1988.

TRCP 809. THESE RULES SHALL NOT GOVERN, WHEN

Nothing in these rules relating to trespass to try title shall be so construed as to alter, impair or take away the rights of parties, as arising under the laws in force before the introduction of the common law, but the same shall be decided by the principles of the law under which the same accrued, or by which the same were regulated or in any manner affected.

History of TRCP 809: Adopted eff. Sept. 1, 1941, by order of Oct. 29, 1940 (3 Tex.B.J. 648 [1940]). Source: New rule.

SECTION 9. SUITS AGAINST NON-RESIDENTS

TRCP 810. REQUISITES OF PLEADINGS

The petition in actions authorized by Section 17.003, Civil Practice and Remedies Code, shall state the real names of the plaintiff and defendant, and shall describe the property involved with sufficient certainty to identify the same, the interest which the plaintiff claims, and such proceedings shall be had in such action as may be necessary to fully settle and determine the question of right or title in and to said property between the parties to said suit, and to decree the title or right of the party entitled thereto; and the court may issue the appropriate order to carry such decree, judgment or order into effect; and whenever such petition has been duly filed and citation thereon has been duly served by publication as required by Rules 114-116, the plaintiff may, at any time prior to entering the decree by leave of court first had and obtained, file amended and supplemental pleadings that do not subject additional property to said suit without the necessity of reciting the defendants so cited as aforesaid.

Dec. 5, 1983, eff. April 1, 1984. Amended by order of July 15, 1987, eff. Jan. 1, 1988.

TRCP 811. SERVICE BY PUBLICATION IN ACTIONS UNDER SECTION 17.003, CIVIL PRACTICE AND REMEDIES CODE

In actions authorized by Section 17.003, Civil Practice and Remedies Code, service on the defendant or defendants may be made by publication as is provided by Rules 114-116 or by service of notice of the character and in the manner provided by Rule 108.

Dec. 5, 1983, eff. April 1, 1984. Amended by order of July 15, 1987, eff. Jan. 1, 1988.

TRCP 812. NO JUDGMENT BY DEFAULT

No judgment by default shall be taken in such case when service has been had by publication, but in such case the facts entitling the plaintiff to judgment shall be exhibited to the court on the trial; and a statement of facts shall be filed as provided by law and these rules in suits against nonresidents of this State served by publication, where no appearance has been made by them.

Oct. 12, 1949, eff. March 1, 1950.

TRCP 813. SUIT TO EXTINGUISH LIEN

If said suit shall be for the extinguishment of a lien or claim for money on said property that may be held by the defendant, the amount thereof, with interest, shall be ascertained by the court; and the same deposited in the registry of the court, subject to be drawn by the parties entitled thereto; but in such case no decree shall be entered until said sum is deposited; which fact shall be noted in said decree.

History of TRCP 813: Adopted eff. Sept. 1, 1941, by order of Oct. 29, 1940 (3 Tex.B.J. 649 [1940]). Source: TRCS art. 1979 (repealed).

Part VIII. Closing Rules

TRCP 814. EFFECTIVE DATE

These rules shall take effect on September 1st, 1941. They shall govern all proceedings in actions brought after they take effect, and also all further proceedings in actions then pending, except to the extent that in the opinion of the court their application in a particular action pending when the rules take effect would not be feasible or would work injustice, in which event the former procedure shall apply. All things properly done under any previously existing rule or statutes prior to the taking effect of these rules shall be treated as valid. Where citation or other process is issued and served in compliance with existing rules or laws prior to the taking effect of these rules, the party upon whom such citation or other process has been served shall have the time provided for under such previously existing rules or laws in which to comply therewith.

History of TRCP 814: Adopted eff. Sept. 1, 1941, by order of Oct. 29, 1940 (3 Tex.B.J. 649 [1940]). Source: FRCP 86.

TRCP 815. SUBSTANTIVE RIGHTS UNAFFECTED

These rules shall not be construed to enlarge or diminish any substantive rights or obligations of any parties to any civil action.

History of TRCP 815: Adopted eff. Sept. 1, 1941, by order of Oct. 29, 1940 (3 Tex.B.J. 649 [1940]). Source: TRCS art. 1731a (repealed, now Gov't Code §22.004(a)).

See also Gov't Code §22.004(a).

TRCP 816. JURISDICTION AND VENUE UNAFFECTED

These rules shall not be construed to extend or limit the jurisdiction of the courts of the State of Texas nor the venue of actions therein.

History of TRCP 816: Adopted eff. Sept. 1, 1941, by order of Oct. 29, 1940 (3 Tex.B.J. 649 [1940]). Source: FRCP 82.

TRCP 817. RENUMBERED AS VERNON'S TEXAS RULES CIV.PROC., RULE 3A BY ORDER OF DEC. 5, 1983, EFF. APRIL 1, 1984

TRCP 818. REFERENCE TO FORMER STATUTES

Wherever any statute or rule refers to any practice or procedure in any law, laws, statute or statutes, or to a title, chapter, section, or article of the statutes, or contains any reference of any such nature, and the matter referred to has been supplanted in whole or in part by these rules, every such reference shall be deemed to be to the pertinent part or parts of these rules.

History of TRCP 818: Adopted eff. Sept. 1, 1941, by order of Oct. 29, 1940 (3 Tex.B.J. 650 [1940]). Source: New rule.

TRCP 819. PROCEDURE CONTINUED

All procedure prescribed by statutes of the State of Texas not specifically listed in the accompanying enumeration of repealed articles shall, insofar as the same is not inconsistent with the provisions of these rules, continue in accordance with the provisions of such statutes as rules of court. In case of inconsistency between the provisions of these rules and any statutory procedure not specifically listed as repealed, these rules shall apply.

History of TRCP 819: Adopted eff. Sept. 1, 1941, by order of Oct. 29, 1940 (3 Tex.B.J. 650 [1940]). Source: New rule.

TRCP 820. WORKERS' COMPENSATION LAW

All portions of the Workers' Compensation Law, Articles 8306–8309-1, Revised Civil Statutes,[1] and amendments thereto, which relate to matters of practice and procedure are hereby adopted and retained in force and effect as rules of court.

Amended by order of Dec. 5, 1983, eff. April 1, 1984.

[1] Repealed, see, now, V.T.C.A., Labor Code §401.001 et seq.

TRCP 821. PRIOR COURT RULES REPEALED

These rules shall supersede all Court Rules heretofore promulgated for any court; and all of said prior Court Rules are hereby repealed; provided, however, any rules of procedure heretofore adopted by a particular county or district court or by any Court of Appeals which were not of general application but were solely to regulate procedure in the particular court promulgating such rules are to remain in force and effect insofar as they are not inconsistent with these rules.

Dec. 5, 1983, eff. April 1, 1984.

TRCP 822. TITLE

These rules may be known and cited as the Texas Rules of Civil Procedure.

History of TRCP 822: Adopted eff. Sept. 1, 1941, by order of Oct. 29, 1940 (3 Tex.B.J. 650 [1940]). Source: FRCP 85.

Appendix II. Texas Rules of Evidence

For an in-depth discussion of the Texas Rules of Evidence, see the current edition of **Texas Rules of Evidence Handbook**. To order, call 1-800-328-9352 or visit legalsolutions.thomsonreuters.com.

TABLE OF CONTENTS

Article I. General Provisions

TRE 101. TITLE, SCOPE, AND APPLICABILITY OF THE RULES; DEFINITIONS

(a) Title. These rules may be cited as the Texas Rules of Evidence.

(b) Scope. These rules apply to proceedings in Texas courts except as otherwise provided in subdivisions (d)–(f).

(c) Rules on Privilege. The rules on privilege apply to all stages of a case or proceeding.

(d) Exception for Constitutional or Statutory Provisions or Other Rules. Despite these rules, a court must admit or exclude evidence if required to do so by the United States or Texas Constitution, a federal or Texas statute, or a rule prescribed by the United States or Texas Supreme Court or the Texas Court of Criminal Appeals. If possible, a court should resolve by reasonable construction any inconsistency between these rules and applicable constitutional or statutory provisions or other rules.

(e) Exceptions. These rules—except for those on privilege—do not apply to:

(1) the court's determination, under Rule 104(a), on a preliminary question of fact governing admissibility;

(2) grand jury proceedings; and

(3) the following miscellaneous proceedings:

(A) an application for habeas corpus in extradition, rendition, or interstate detainer proceedings;

(B) an inquiry by the court under Code of Criminal Procedure article 46B.004 to determine whether evidence exists that would support a finding that the defendant may be incompetent to stand trial;

(C) bail proceedings other than hearings to deny, revoke, or increase bail;

(D) hearings on justification for pretrial detention not involving bail;

(E) proceedings to issue a search or arrest warrant; and

(F) direct contempt determination proceedings.

(f) Exception for Justice Court Cases. These rules do not apply to justice court cases except as authorized by Texas Rule of Civil Procedure 500.3.

(g) Exception for Military Justice Hearings. The Texas Code of Military Justice, Tex. Gov't Code §§432.001–432.195, governs the admissibility of evidence in hearings held under that Code.

(h) Definitions. In these rules:

(1) "civil case" means a civil action or proceeding;

(2) "criminal case" means a criminal action or proceeding, including an examining trial;

(3) "public office" includes a public agency;

(4) "record" includes a memorandum, report, or data compilation;

(5) a "rule prescribed by the United States or Texas Supreme Court or the Texas Court of Criminal Appeals" means a rule adopted by any of those courts under statutory authority;

(6) "unsworn declaration" means an unsworn declaration made in accordance with Tex. Civ. Prac. & Rem. Code §132.001; and

(7) a reference to any kind of written material or any other medium includes electronically stored information.

Eff. March 1, 1998. Amended by orders of Supreme Court March 10, 2015 and Court of Criminal Appeals March 12, 2015, eff. April 1, 2015.

Comment to 1998 change: "Criminal proceedings" rather than "criminal cases" is used since that was the terminology used in the prior Rules of Criminal Evidence. In subpart (b), the reference to "trials before magistrates" comes from prior Criminal Rule 1101(a). In the prior Criminal Rules, both Rule 101 and Rule 1101 dealt with the same thing—the applicability of the rules. Thus, Rules 101(c) and (d) have been written to incorporate the provisions of former Criminal Rule 1101 and that rule is omitted.

Comment to 2015 Restyling: The reference to "hierarchical governance" in former Rule 101(c) has been deleted as unnecessary. The textual limitation of former Rule 101(c) to criminal cases has been eliminated. Courts in civil cases must also admit or exclude evidence when required to do so by constitutional or statutory provisions or other rules that take precedence over these rules. Likewise, the title to former Rule 101(d) has been changed to more accurately indicate the purpose and scope of the subdivision.

Source: For TRE 101(a), see FRE 1103; for TRE 101(b), see FRE 101.

See also Brown & Rondon, **Texas Rules of Evidence Handbook**, Rule 101.

TRE 102. PURPOSE

These rules should be construed so as to administer every proceeding fairly, eliminate unjustifiable expense and delay, and promote the development of evidence law, to the end of ascertaining the truth and securing a just determination.

Eff. March 1, 1998. Amended by orders of Supreme Court March 10, 2015 and Court of Criminal Appeals March 12, 2015, eff. April 1, 2015.

See also Brown & Rondon, **Texas Rules of Evidence Handbook**, Rule 102.

TRE 103. RULINGS ON EVIDENCE

(a) Preserving a Claim of Error. A party may claim error in a ruling to admit or exclude evidence only if the error affects a substantial right of the party and:

(1) if the ruling admits evidence, a party, on the record:

(A) timely objects or moves to strike; and

(B) states the specific ground, unless it was apparent from the context; or

(2) if the ruling excludes evidence, a party informs the court of its substance by an offer of proof, unless the substance was apparent from the context.

(b) Not Needing to Renew an Objection. When the court hears a party's objections outside the presence of the jury and rules that evidence is admissible, a party need not renew an objection to preserve a claim of error for appeal.

(c) Court's Statement About the Ruling; Directing an Offer of Proof. The court may make any statement about the character or form of the evidence, the objection made, and the ruling. The court must allow a party to make an offer of proof as soon as practicable. In a jury trial, the court must allow a party to make the offer outside the jury's presence and before the court reads its charge to the jury. At a party's request, the court must direct that an offer of proof be made in question-and-answer form. Or the court may do so on its own.

(d) Preventing the Jury from Hearing Inadmissible Evidence. To the extent practicable, the court must conduct a jury trial so that inadmissible evidence is not suggested to the jury by any means.

(e) Taking Notice of Fundamental Error in Criminal Cases. In criminal cases, a court may take notice of a fundamental error affecting a substantial right, even if the claim of error was not properly preserved.

Eff. March 1, 1998. Amended by orders of Supreme Court March 10, 2015 and Court of Criminal Appeals March 12, 2015, eff. April 1, 2015; orders of Supreme Court May 26, 2020, and Court of Criminal Appeals June 1, 2020, eff. June 1, 2020.

Comment to 1998 change: The exception to the requirement of an offer of proof for matters that were apparent from the context within which questions were asked, found in paragraph (a)(2), is now applicable to civil as well as criminal cases.

Source: FRE 103, with changes: Party entitled to make offer in question-and-answer form.

See also TRAP 44.1; **O'Connor's Texas Rules,** "Motion in Limine," ch. 5-E, §1 et seq.; **O'Connor's Texas Rules,** "Objecting to Evidence," ch. 8-D, §1 et seq.; **O'Connor's Texas Rules,** "Offer of Proof & Bill of Exception," ch. 8-E, §1 et seq.; Brown & Rondon, **Texas Rules of Evidence Handbook**, Rule 103.

ANNOTATIONS

In re Toyota Motor Sales, U.S.A., Inc., 407 S.W.3d 746, 760 (Tex.2013). "[W]here . . . the party that requested the limine order *itself* introduces the evidence into the record, and then fails to immediately object, ask for a curative or limiting instruction or, alternatively, move for mistrial, the party waives any subsequent alleged error on the point."

PNS Stores v. Munguia, 484 S.W.3d 503, 511 (Tex.App.—Houston [14th Dist.] 2016, no pet.). "To adequately and effectively preserve error, an offer of proof must show the nature of the evidence specifically enough so that the reviewing court can determine its admissibility. The offer of proof may be made by counsel, who should reasonably and specifically summarize the evidence offered and state its relevance unless already apparent. If counsel makes such an offer, he must describe the actual content of the testimony and not merely comment on the reasons for it." *See also* **PPC Transp. v. Metcalf**, 254 S.W.3d 636, 640-41 (Tex.App.—Tyler 2008, no pet.).

Bowman v. Patel, No. 01-10-00811-CV, 2012 WL 524428 (Tex.App.—Houston [1st Dist.] 2012, no pet.) (memo op.; 2-16-12). "An offer of proof may be in the form of concise statement by counsel or in question-and-answer form. It is not required that the offer of proof show what specific facts the examination would reveal, but the appellant must clearly inform the trial court of the subject matter about which it wants to examine the witness."

Bobbora v. Unitrin Ins., 255 S.W.3d 331, 334-35 (Tex.App.—Dallas 2008, no pet.). "To preserve error concerning the exclusion of evidence, the complaining party must actually offer the evidence and secure an adverse ruling from the court. While the reviewing court may be able to discern from the record the nature of the evidence and the propriety of the trial court's ruling, without an offer of proof, we can never determine whether exclusion of the evidence was harmful. . . . An offer of proof preserves error for appeal if: (1) it is made before the court, the court reporter, and opposing counsel, outside the presence of the jury; (2) it is preserved in the reporter's record; and (3) it is made before the charge is read to the jury. When no offer of proof is made before the trial court, the party must introduce the excluded testimony into the record by a formal bill of exception. A formal bill of exception must be presented to the trial court for its approval, and, if the parties agree to the contents of the bill, the trial court must sign the bill and file it with the trial court clerk. Failure to demonstrate the substance of the excluded evidence results in waiver." *See also* **In re J.R.P.**, 526 S.W.3d 770, 780 (Tex.App.—Houston [14th Dist.] 2017, no pet.).

Benavides v. Cushman, Inc., 189 S.W.3d 875, 885 (Tex.App.—Houston [1st Dist.] 2006, no pet.). " '[A]ny error in admitting evidence is cured where the same evidence comes in elsewhere without objection.' "

Greenberg Traurig of N.Y., P.C. v. Moody, 161 S.W.3d 56, 91 (Tex.App.—Houston [14th Dist.] 2004, no pet.). "Because a trial court's ruling on a motion in limine preserves nothing for review, a party must object at trial when the testimony is offered to preserve error for appellate review. However, not all pretrial motions are motions in limine. There is a distinction between a motion in limine and a pretrial ruling on admissibility. The trial court has the authority to make a pretrial ruling on the admissibility of evidence."

Bean v. Baxter Healthcare Corp., 965 S.W.2d 656, 660 (Tex.App.—Houston [14th Dist.] 1998, no pet.). "[P] preserved error after its initial offer of the videotape. If exclusion of evidence is based on the substance of the evidence, however, the offering party must reoffer it if it again becomes relevant. This may occur when the evidence is pertinent to rebuttal. Error is waived if the offering party fails to reoffer evidence for a limited purpose after it has been excluded pursuant to a general objection."

Chance v. Chance, 911 S.W.2d 40, 52 (Tex.App.—Beaumont 1995, writ denied). "[T]he rule requiring that proffered evidence be incorporated in a bill of exception does not apply to cross examination of an adverse witness. When cross-examination testimony is excluded, [D] need not show the answer to be expected but only need show that the substance of the evidence was apparent from the context within which the question was asked."

TRE 104. PRELIMINARY QUESTIONS

(a) In General. The court must decide any preliminary question about whether a witness is qualified, a privilege exists, or evidence is admissible. In so deciding, the court is not bound by evidence rules, except those on privilege.

(b) Relevance That Depends on a Fact. When the relevance of evidence depends on whether a fact exists, proof must be introduced sufficient to support a finding that the fact does exist. The court may admit the proposed evidence on the condition that the proof be introduced later.

(c) Conducting a Hearing So That the Jury Cannot Hear It. The court must conduct any hearing on a preliminary question so that the jury cannot hear it if:

(1) the hearing involves the admissibility of a confession in a criminal case;

(2) a defendant in a criminal case is a witness and so requests; or

(3) justice so requires.

(d) Cross-Examining a Defendant in a Criminal Case. By testifying outside the jury's hearing on a preliminary question, a defendant in a criminal case does not become subject to cross-examination on other issues in the case.

(e) Evidence Relevant to Weight and Credibility. This rule does not limit a party's right to introduce before the jury evidence that is relevant to the weight or credibility of other evidence.

Eff. March 1, 1998. Amended by orders of Supreme Court March 10, 2015 and Court of Criminal Appeals March 12, 2015, eff. April 1, 2015.

See also **O'Connor's Texas Rules**, "Motion in Limine," ch. 5-E, §1 et seq.; **O'Connor's Texas Rules**, "Objecting to Evidence," ch. 8-D, §1 et seq.; Brown & Rondon, **Texas Rules of Evidence Handbook**, Rule 104.

ANNOTATIONS

E.I. du Pont de Nemours & Co. v. Robinson, 923 S.W.2d 549, 556 (Tex.1995). "The trial court is responsible for making the preliminary determination of whether the proffered testimony meets the standards set forth [for experts]." *See also* **Broders v. Heise**, 924 S.W.2d 148, 151 (Tex.1996).

TRE 105. EVIDENCE THAT IS NOT ADMISSIBLE AGAINST OTHER PARTIES OR FOR OTHER PURPOSES

(a) Limiting Admitted Evidence. If the court admits evidence that is admissible against a party or for a purpose—but not against another party or for another purpose—the court, on request, must restrict the evidence to its proper scope and instruct the jury accordingly.

(b) Preserving a Claim of Error.

(1) ***Court Admits the Evidence Without Restriction.*** A party may claim error in a ruling to admit evidence that is admissible against a party or for a purpose—but not against another party or for another purpose—only if the party requests the court to restrict the evidence to its proper scope and instruct the jury accordingly.

(2) ***Court Excludes the Evidence.*** A party may claim error in a ruling to exclude evidence that is admissible against a party or for a purpose—but not against another party or for another purpose—only if the party limits its offer to the party against whom or the purpose for which the evidence is admissible.

Eff. March 1, 1998. Amended by orders of Supreme Court March 10, 2015 and Court of Criminal Appeals March 12, 2015, eff. April 1, 2015.

See also **O'Connor's Texas Rules**, "Request for limited admissibility," ch. 8-D, §7.1.3(1); Brown & Rondon, **Texas Rules of Evidence Handbook**, Rule 105.

ANNOTATIONS

Kia Motors Corp. v. Ruiz, 432 S.W.3d 865, 879 (Tex.2014). "[W]e disagree with the court of appeals' holding that, because the portion of the spreadsheet summarizing the . . . claims was not hearsay, [D] waived its objection to the admission of the remainder of the spreadsheet by failing to request a limiting instruction. The court appeared to hold that, if one portion of a document is admissible, and another portion is inadmissible, a party must request a limiting instruction to preserve error in the admission of the improper portion. This holding mischaracterizes the nature of a limiting instruction. . . . A limiting instruction does not provide a mechanism for the admission of a document that contains both admissible evidence and inadmissible, unredacted evidence. In other words, such an instruction does not allow for admission of evidence that is otherwise inadmissible for any purpose." *See also* **U-Haul Int'l v. Waldrip**, 380 S.W.3d 118, 132 (Tex.2012).

Larson v. Cactus Util. Co., 730 S.W.2d 640, 642 (Tex.1987). "Where tendered evidence should be considered for only one purpose, it is the opponent's burden to secure a limiting instruction. Absent a requested limiting instruction, [opponent of evidence] waived his grounds for complaint." *See also* **Horizon/CMS Healthcare Corp. v. Auld**, 34 S.W.3d 887, 906 (Tex.2000).

TRE 106. REMAINDER OF OR RELATED WRITINGS OR RECORDED STATEMENTS

If a party introduces all or part of a writing or recorded statement, an adverse party may introduce, at that time, any other part—or any other writing or recorded statement—that in fairness ought to be considered at the same time. "Writing or recorded statement" includes depositions.

Eff. March 1, 1998. Amended by orders of Supreme Court March 10, 2015 and Court of Criminal Appeals March 12, 2015, eff. April 1, 2015.

Source: FRE 106. This rule is the same as FRE 106, with one modification. Under FRE 106, a party may require its opponent to introduce evidence contrary to the latter's own case. The Committee believed it was better to permit the party to introduce such evidence contemporaneously with the introduction of the incomplete evidence. TRCE 106 does not in any way circumscribe the right of a party to develop fully the matter on cross-examination or as part of his own case. Cf. Code Crim. Proc. art. 38.24. Nor does it alter the common-law doctrine that the rule of optional completeness, as to writings, oral conversations, or other matters, may take precedence over exclusionary doctrines such as the hearsay or best-evidence rule or the firsthand knowledge requirement.

See also Brown & Rondon, **Texas Rules of Evidence Handbook**, Rule 106.

ANNOTATIONS

Russell v. Beck, No. 06-11-00006-CV, 2011 WL 2225537 (Tex.App.—Texarkana 2011, no pet.) (memo op.; 6-7-11). "The rule of optional completeness only applies when one party introduces part of a statement or document, and in fairness, the opposing party is permitted to introduce as much of the balance as is necessary to explain the first part. It is permitted to correct any misleading impressions left when one party introduces only a portion of the evidence. A plain reading of [TRE] 106 and [TRE] 107 indicates their inapplicability when the same party seeks to offer an inadmissible omitted portion of a document it initially sought to introduce. [¶] Under the rule of optional completeness, additional material from a document or recording, part of which has been admitted into evidence, is admissible if that material 'ought in fairness to be considered contemporaneously.' "

Jones v. Colley, 820 S.W.2d 863, 866 (Tex.App.—Texarkana 1991, writ denied). "Rule 106 . . . is not enforced by excluding the partial statement, but by allowing the op-

posing party to contemporaneously introduce any other part of the statement that should be considered with the portion introduced by the proponent."

TRE 107. RULE OF OPTIONAL COMPLETENESS

If a party introduces part of an act, declaration, conversation, writing, or recorded statement, an adverse party may inquire into any other part on the same subject. An adverse party may also introduce any other act, declaration, conversation, writing, or recorded statement that is necessary to explain or allow the trier of fact to fully understand the part offered by the opponent. "Writing or recorded statement" includes a deposition.

Eff. March 1, 1998. Amended by orders of Supreme Court March 10, 2015 and Court of Criminal Appeals March 12, 2015,, eff. April 1, 2015.

Comment to 1998 change: This rule is the former Criminal Rule 107 except that the example regarding "when a letter is read" has been relocated in the rule so as to more accurately indicate the provision it explains. While this rule appeared only in the prior criminal rules, it is made applicable to civil cases because it accurately reflects the common law rule of optional completeness in civil cases.

See also Brown & Rondon, **Texas Rules of Evidence Handbook**, Rule 107.

ANNOTATIONS

Russell v. Beck, No. 06-11-00006-CV, 2011 WL 2225537 (Tex.App.—Texarkana 2011, no pet.) (memo op.; 6-7-11). See annotation under TRE 106.

Crosby v. Minyard Food Stores, 122 S.W.3d 899, 903 (Tex.App.—Dallas 2003, no pet.). "Rule 107 is designed to guard against the possibility of confusion, distortion, or false impression that could be created when only a portion of evidence is introduced. There are two threshold requirements for the application of the rule. First, some portion of the matter sought to be 'completed' must have actually been introduced into evidence. Merely referring to a statement does not invoke the rule. Second, the party seeking to complete the matter must show that the remainder being offered under rule 107 is on the same subject and is necessary to fully understand or explain the matter." *See also* **In re C.C.**, 476 S.W.3d 632, 636 (Tex.App.—Amarillo 2015, no pet.).

Article II. Judicial Notice

TRE 201. JUDICIAL NOTICE OF ADJUDICATIVE FACTS

(a) Scope. This rule governs judicial notice of an adjudicative fact only, not a legislative fact.

(b) Kinds of Facts That May Be Judicially Noticed. The court may judicially notice a fact that is not subject to reasonable dispute because it:

(1) is generally known within the trial court's territorial jurisdiction; or

(2) can be accurately and readily determined from sources whose accuracy cannot reasonably be questioned.

(c) Taking Notice. The court:

(1) may take judicial notice on its own; or

(2) must take judicial notice if a party requests it and the court is supplied with the necessary information.

(d) Timing. The court may take judicial notice at any stage of the proceeding.

(e) Opportunity to Be Heard. On timely request, a party is entitled to be heard on the propriety of taking judicial notice and the nature of the fact to be noticed. If the court takes judicial notice before notifying a party, the party, on request, is still entitled to be heard.

(f) Instructing the Jury. In a civil case, the court must instruct the jury to accept the noticed fact as conclusive. In a criminal case, the court must instruct the jury that it may or may not accept the noticed fact as conclusive.

Eff. March 1, 1998. Amended by orders of Supreme Court March 10, 2015 and Court of Criminal Appeals March 12, 2015, eff. April 1, 2015.

Source: FRE 201.

See also CPRC §38.004; **O'Connor's Texas Rules,** "Motion for Judicial Notice," ch. 5-M, §1 et seq.; Brown & Rondon, **Texas Rules of Evidence Handbook**, Rule 201.

See also CCP art. 21.18.

ANNOTATIONS

Freedom Comms. v. Coronado, 372 S.W.3d 621, 623 (Tex.2012). "[A] court will take judicial notice of another court's records if a party provides proof of the records."

In re J.L., 163 S.W.3d 79, 84 (Tex. 2005). "If a fact is generally known, then obviously no expert is needed. [E]xpert testimony invariably concerns matters in dispute which are not capable of accurate resolution from outside, unquestioned sources. Because [expert's] testimony concerned disputed facts and opinions, it should not have been judicially noticed."

In re Shifflet, 462 S.W.3d 528, 539 (Tex.App.—Houston [1st Dist.] 2015, orig. proceeding). "'A trial court may take judicial notice of its own records in matters that are generally known, easily proven, and not reasonably disputed.' Therefore, a court may take judicial notice that a pleading has been filed in the case, that it has signed an order, or of the law of another jurisdiction,' but '[a] court may not take judicial notice of the *truth* of allegations in its records.'" *See also* **Barnard v. Barnard**, 133 S.W.3d 782, 789 (Tex.App.—Fort Worth 2004, pet. denied).

Guyton v. Monteau, 332 S.W.3d 687, 692-93 (Tex.App.—Houston [14th Dist.] 2011, no pet.). "[T]he trial court's ruling was based on its judicial notice of all docu-

ments and testimony ever admitted in this case on any subject. [¶] Such sweeping judicial notice . . . was an abuse of discretion. . . . A judicially-noticed fact 'must be one not subject to reasonable dispute in that it is either (1) generally known within the territorial jurisdiction of the trial court or (2) capable of accurate and ready determination by resort to sources whose accuracy cannot reasonably be questioned.' But '[p]ersonal knowledge is not judicial knowledge. The judge may personally know a fact of which he cannot take judicial notice.' Moreover, the trial court may not take judicial notice of the *truth* of factual statements and allegations contained in the pleadings, affidavits, or other documents in the file. [¶] It is inappropriate for a trial judge to take judicial notice of testimony even in a retrial of the same case." *See also* **1.70 Acres v. State**, 935 S.W.2d 480, 489 (Tex.App.—Beaumont 1996, no writ) (variables such as vehicle's speed, road construction or repairs, weather, traffic, or accidents may be matters in someone's personal knowledge, but they are not necessarily matters subject to judicial review).

In re Sigmar, 270 S.W.3d 289, 302 (Tex.App.—Waco 2008, orig. proceeding). "[M]atters of legislative fact or of other non-adjudicative fact are subject to judicial notice but are not governed by Rule 201."

Sierad v. Barnett, 164 S.W.3d 471, 481 (Tex.App.—Dallas 2005, no pet.). "'It is well recognized that a trial court may take judicial notice of its own records in a cause involving the same subject matter between the same, or practically the same, parties.' A court may take judicial notice, whether requested or not. The trial court need not announce it is taking judicial notice. The court may be presumed to have taken notice of its own files." *See also* **Marble Slab Creamery, Inc. v. Wesic, Inc.**, 823 S.W.2d 436, 439 (Tex.App.—Houston [14th Dist.] 1992, no writ) (appellate court may presume trial court took judicial notice without any request or announcement). *But see* **In re C.L.**, 304 S.W.3d 512, 515-16 (Tex.App.—Waco 2009, no pet.) (appellate court held that trial court did not take judicial notice when party did not request it and trial court did not announce in open court it was taking judicial notice).

Apostolic Ch. v. American Honda Motor Co., 833 S.W.2d 553, 555-56 (Tex.App.—Tyler 1992, writ denied). "Highway nomenclature and designations within the trial court's jurisdiction are matters of common knowledge and proper subjects for judicial notice. . . . In matters involving geographical knowledge, it is not necessary that a formal request for judicial notice be made by a party."

TRE 202. JUDICIAL NOTICE OF OTHER STATES' LAW

(a) Scope. This rule governs judicial notice of another state's, territory's, or federal jurisdiction's:

- Constitution;
- public statutes;
- rules;
- regulations;
- ordinances;
- court decisions; and
- common law.

(b) Taking Notice. The court:

(1) may take judicial notice on its own; or

(2) must take judicial notice if a party requests it and the court is supplied with the necessary information.

(c) Notice and Opportunity to Be Heard.

(1) ***Notice.*** The court may require a party requesting judicial notice to notify all other parties of the request so they may respond to it.

(2) ***Opportunity to Be Heard.*** On timely request, a party is entitled to be heard on the propriety of taking judicial notice and the nature of the matter to be noticed. If the court takes judicial notice before a party has been notified, the party, on request, is still entitled to be heard.

(d) Timing. The court may take judicial notice at any stage of the proceeding.

(e) Determination and Review. The court—not the jury—must determine the law of another state, territory, or federal jurisdiction. The court's determination must be treated as a ruling on a question of law.

Eff. March 1, 1998. Amended by orders of Supreme Court March 10, 2015 and Court of Criminal Appeals March 12, 2015, eff. April 1, 2015.

See also **O'Connor's Texas Rules**, "Motion for Judicial Notice," ch. 5-M, §1 et seq.; Brown & Rondon, **Texas Rules of Evidence Handbook**, Rule 202.

ANNOTATIONS

Daugherty v. Southern Pac. Transp., 772 S.W.2d 81, 83 (Tex.1989). "The failure to plead sister-state law does not preclude a court from judicially noticing that law. . . . Rule 202 requires the moving party to furnish sufficient information to the trial court for it to determine the foreign law's applicability to the case and to furnish all parties any notice that the court finds necessary." *See also* **Colvin v. Colvin**, 291 S.W.3d 508, 514 (Tex.App.—Tyler 2009, no pet.) (preliminary motion required to assure application of laws from another jurisdiction).

Vince Poscente Int'l v. Compass Bank, 460 S.W.3d 211, 219 (Tex.App.—Dallas 2015, no pet.). "Unless a party requests the court to take judicial notice of or introduces proof of another state's law, or the court on its own motion takes judicial notice of another state's law, the court presumes the other state's law is the same as Texas law."

Burlington N. & Santa Fe Ry. v. Gunderson, Inc., 235 S.W.3d 287, 292 (Tex.App.—Fort Worth 2007, no pet.).

"Rule 202 simply provides a mechanism by which a party may compel the trial court to judicially notice the law of another state; it does not force a party to make a definitive declaration as to which state's law applies."

TRE 203. DETERMINING FOREIGN LAW

(a) Raising a Foreign Law Issue. A party who intends to raise an issue about a foreign country's law must:

(1) give reasonable notice by a pleading or other writing; and

(2) at least 30 days before trial, supply all parties a copy of any written materials or sources the party intends to use to prove the foreign law.

(b) Translations. If the materials or sources were originally written in a language other than English, the party intending to rely on them must, at least 30 days before trial, supply all parties both a copy of the foreign language text and an English translation.

(c) Materials the Court May Consider; Notice. In determining foreign law, the court may consider any material or source, whether or not admissible. If the court considers any material or source not submitted by a party, it must give all parties notice and a reasonable opportunity to comment and submit additional materials.

(d) Determination and Review. The court—not the jury—must determine foreign law. The court's determination must be treated as a ruling on a question of law.

(e) Suits Brought Under the Family Code Involving a Marriage Relationship or Parent-Child Relationship. Subsections (a) and (b) of this rule do not apply to an action to which Rule 308b, Texas Rules of Civil Procedure, applies.

Eff. March 1, 1998. Amended by orders of Supreme Court March 10, 2015 and Court of Criminal Appeals March 12, 2015, eff. April 1, 2015; order of Supreme Court Dec. 28, 2017, eff. Jan. 1, 2018.

See also **O'Connor's Texas Rules,** "Motion for Judicial Notice," ch. 5-M, §1 et seq.; Brown & Rondon, **Texas Rules of Evidence Handbook,** Rule 203.

ANNOTATIONS

Long Distance Int'l v. Telefonos de Mexico, S.A. de C.V., 49 S.W.3d 347, 351 (Tex.2001). "Rule 203 has been aptly characterized as a hybrid rule by which the presentation of the foreign law to the court resembles the presentment of evidence but which ultimately is decided as a question of law. Summary judgment is not precluded when experts disagree on the law's meaning if, as here, the parties do not dispute that all the pertinent foreign law was properly submitted in evidence. When experts disagree on how the foreign law applies to the facts, the court is presented with a question of law."

Petroleum Workers Un. v. Gomez, 503 S.W.3d 9, 33 (Tex.App.—Houston [14th Dist.] 2016, no pet.). "Rule 203 . . . contains no reference to a hearing, much less mandates one be held. [I]n interpreting Rule 203, . . . a trial court may consider any material or source, whether or not submitted by a party or admissible under the [TREs], including affidavits, testimony, briefs, and treatises. In other words, the foreign law determination can be addressed with or without an evidentiary hearing."

PennWell Corp. v. Ken Assocs., 123 S.W.3d 756, 760-61 (Tex.App.—Houston [14th Dist.] 2003, pet. denied). "Although appearing under the subtitle 'Judicial Notice' in the [TREs], the procedure established under Rule 203 for presentment of foreign law is not considered a judicial notice procedure because that term refers only to adjudicative facts and not to matters of law. Thus, the specific procedures set forth in Rule 203 must be followed for the determination of foreign law. [A] party requesting judicial notice must furnish the court with sufficient information to enable it to properly comply with the request; otherwise, the failure to provide adequate proof results in a presumption that the law of the foreign jurisdiction is identical to that of Texas." *See also* **Gerdes v. Kennamer**, 155 S.W.3d 541, 548 (Tex.App.—Corpus Christi 2004, no pet.).

TRE 204. JUDICIAL NOTICE OF TEXAS MUNICIPAL AND COUNTY ORDINANCES, TEXAS REGISTER CONTENTS, AND PUBLISHED AGENCY RULES

(a) Scope. This rule governs judicial notice of Texas municipal and county ordinances, the contents of the Texas Register, and agency rules published in the Texas Administrative Code.

(b) Taking Notice. The court:

(1) may take judicial notice on its own; or

(2) must take judicial notice if a party requests it and the court is supplied with the necessary information.

(c) Notice and Opportunity to Be Heard.

(1) ***Notice.*** The court may require a party requesting judicial notice to notify all other parties of the request so they may respond to it.

(2) ***Opportunity to Be Heard.*** On timely request, a party is entitled to be heard on the propriety of taking judicial notice and the nature of the matter to be noticed. If the court takes judicial notice before a party has been notified, the party, on request, is still entitled to be heard.

(d) Determination and Review. The court—not the jury—must determine municipal and county ordinances, the contents of the Texas Register, and published agency

rules. The court's determination must be treated as a ruling on a question of law.

Eff. March 1, 1998. Amended by orders of Supreme Court March 10, 2015 and Court of Criminal Appeals March 12, 2015, eff. April 1, 2015.

Source: New rule.

See also **O'Connor's Texas Rules,** "Motion for Judicial Notice," ch. 5-M, §1 et seq.; Brown & Rondon, **Texas Rules of Evidence Handbook,** Rule 204.

ANNOTATIONS

Eckmann v. Des Rosiers, 940 S.W.2d 394, 399 (Tex.App.—Austin 1997, no writ). "[T]he duty [to take judicial notice is] mandatory, even in the absence of a request under Rule 204, respecting administrative agency regulations published in the Texas Register and Texas Administrative Code. . . . They are legislative facts, or a part of the body of law a court is required to apply in reasoning toward a decision."

Article III. Presumptions

[No rules adopted at this time.]

Article IV. Relevance and Its Limits

TRE 401. TEST FOR RELEVANT EVIDENCE

Evidence is relevant if:

(a) it has any tendency to make a fact more or less probable than it would be without the evidence; and

(b) the fact is of consequence in determining the action.

Eff. March 1, 1998. Amended by orders of Supreme Court March 10, 2015 and Court of Criminal Appeals March 12, 2015, eff. April 1, 2015.

See also Brown & Rondon, **Texas Rules of Evidence Handbook,** Rule 401.

ANNOTATIONS

Coastal Transp. Co. v. Crown Cent. Pet. Corp., 136 S.W.3d 227, 232 (Tex.2004). "Opinion testimony that is conclusory or speculative is not relevant evidence, because it does not tend to make the existence of a material fact 'more probable or less probable.'"

E.I. du Pont de Nemours & Co. v. Robinson, 923 S.W.2d 549, 556 (Tex.1995). "[T]o constitute scientific knowledge which will assist the trier of fact, the proposed [scientific] testimony must be relevant and reliable. [¶] The requirement that the proposed testimony be relevant incorporates traditional relevancy analysis under [TRE] 401 and 402. . . . To be relevant, the proposed testimony must be 'sufficiently tied to the facts of the case that it will aid the jury in resolving a factual dispute.'"

Transportation Ins. v. Moriel, 879 S.W.2d 10, 24-25 (Tex.1994). "Simply because a piece or pieces of evidence are material in the sense that they make a 'fact that is of consequence to the determination of the action more . . . or less probable' does not render the evidence legally sufficient. As Professor McCormick succinctly put it, 'a brick is not a wall.'"

Rhey v. Redic, 408 S.W.3d 440, 460 (Tex.App.—El Paso 2013, no pet.). "To determine relevancy, the court must look at the purpose for offering the evidence. There must be some logical connection either directly or by inference between the fact offered and the fact to be proved."

TRE 402. GENERAL ADMISSIBILITY OF RELEVANT EVIDENCE

Relevant evidence is admissible unless any of the following provides otherwise:

- the United States or Texas Constitution;
- a statute;
- these rules; or
- other rules prescribed under statutory authority.

Irrelevant evidence is not admissible.

Eff. March 1, 1998. Amended by orders of Supreme Court March 10, 2015 and Court of Criminal Appeals March 12, 2015, eff. April 1, 2015.

See also Brown & Rondon, **Texas Rules of Evidence Handbook,** Rule 402.

ANNOTATIONS

E.I. du Pont de Nemours & Co. v. Robinson, 923 S.W.2d 549, 556 (Tex.1995). "Evidence that has no relationship to any of the issues in the case is irrelevant and does not satisfy [TRE] 702's requirement that the testimony be of assistance to the jury. It is thus inadmissible under Rule 702 as well as under [TRE] 401 and 402."

Lunsford v. Morris, 746 S.W.2d 471, 473 (Tex.1988), *disapproved on other grounds*, **Walker v. Packer**, 827 S.W.2d 833 (Tex.1992). The TREs do not "contemplate exclusion of otherwise relevant proof unless the evidence proffered is unfairly prejudicial, privileged, incompetent, or otherwise *legally* inadmissible."

Jampole v. Touchy, 673 S.W.2d 569, 573 (Tex.1984), *disapproved on other grounds*, **Walker v. Packer**, 827 S.W.2d 833 (Tex.1992). "To increase the likelihood that all relevant evidence will be disclosed and brought before the trier of fact, the law circumscribes a significantly larger class of discoverable evidence [than admissible evidence] to include anything reasonably calculated to lead to the discovery of material evidence."

TRE 403. EXCLUDING RELEVANT EVIDENCE FOR PREJUDICE, CONFUSION, OR OTHER REASONS

The court may exclude relevant evidence if its probative value is substantially outweighed by a danger of one or

more of the following: unfair prejudice, confusing the issues, misleading the jury, undue delay, or needlessly presenting cumulative evidence.

Eff. March 1, 1998. Amended by orders of Supreme Court March 10, 2015 and Court of Criminal Appeals March 12, 2015, eff. April 1, 2015.

Source: FRE 403.

See also **O'Connor's Texas Rules,** "Objecting to Evidence," ch. 8-D, §1 et seq.; Brown & Rondon, **Texas Rules of Evidence Handbook** Rule 403.

ANNOTATIONS

JBS Carriers, Inc. v. Washington, 564 S.W.3d 830, 836 (Tex.2018). "Testimony is not inadmissible on the sole ground that it is prejudicial because in our adversarial system, much of a proponent's evidence is legitimately intended to wound the opponent. Rather, *unfair* prejudice is the proper inquiry, and *unfair* prejudice within its context means an undue tendency to suggest a decision on an improper basis, commonly, though not necessarily, an emotional one." (Internal quotes omitted.)

Diamond Offshore Servs. v. Williams, 542 S.W.3d 539, 545 (Tex.2018). "Our sister criminal court has emphasized the importance of viewing videos before ruling on admissibility, noting it is 'difficult for a trial judge to weigh the probative value [of a video] against the potentially unfair prejudice . . . without first reviewing it.' Appellate courts around the country have similarly admonished trial courts that the proper exercise of discretion requires viewing visual evidence, particularly when balancing under Rule 403. *At 546-47:* We hold that, as a general rule, a trial court should view video evidence before ruling on admissibility when the contents of the video are at issue. We recognize circumstances might arise where viewing is unnecessary or extremely onerous. For example, '[t]here may be cases where the probative value of the evidence is so minimal that it will be obvious to the court that the potential prejudice . . . substantially outweighs any probative value the evidence might have.' Additionally, video depositions need not be viewed before ruling on objections unless the objection is specific to a visual aspect of the deposition. Exigencies of trial, moreover, could make it difficult to find time to view a late-offered video, especially if the video is lengthy. The parties could potentially address such timing issues by submitting representative excerpts for the trial court's review. In any event, trial courts should 'undertake their best efforts in attempting to view the subject visual recording prior to ruling on its admissibility.' Exceptions should be few and far between."

Owens-Corning Fiberglas Corp. v. Malone, 972 S.W.2d 35, 41 (Tex.1998). "Evidence that is not relevant, or is unduly prejudicial, and thus, not admissible to mitigate punitive damages, includes actual damage amounts paid by settlements or by judgments; the number of pending claims filed against a defendant for the same conduct; the number of anticipated claims for the same conduct; insurance coverage; unpaid punitive damages awards for the same course of conduct; and evidence of punitive damages that may be levied in the future."

Ford Motor Co. v. Miles, 967 S.W.2d 377, 389 (Tex.1998). "[R]elevant photographic evidence is admissible unless it is merely calculated to arouse the sympathy, prejudice or passion [of] the jury where the photographs do not serve to illustrate disputed issues or aid the jury in understanding the case." (Internal quotes omitted.)

In re E.A.G., 373 S.W.3d 129, 147 (Tex.App.—San Antonio 2012, pet. denied). "The relevant criteria for determining whether the prejudice of admitting the evidence substantially outweighs the probative value include, but are not limited to, the following: (1) the probative value of the evidence; (2) the potential the evidence has to impress the jury in an irrational but nevertheless indelible way; (3) the time needed to develop the evidence; and (4) the proponent's need for the evidence to prove a fact of consequence."

In re J.B.C., 233 S.W.3d 88, 94-95 (Tex.App.—Fort Worth 2007, pet. denied). "A court may consider the following factors in determining whether the probative value of photographs is substantially outweighed by the danger of unfair prejudice: (1) the number of exhibits offered, (2) their gruesomeness, (3) their detail, (4) their size, (5) whether they are offered in color or in black and white, (6) whether they are close-up, and (7) whether the body depicted is clothed or naked. Autopsy photographs are generally admissible unless they depict mutilation caused by the autopsy itself. However, photographs that depict the nature, location, and extent of a wound have been declared probative enough to outweigh any prejudicial effect. Changes rendered by the autopsy process are of minor significance if the disturbing nature of the photograph is primarily due to the injuries caused by the appellant." *See also* **In re K.Y.**, 273 S.W.3d 703, 710 (Tex.App.—Houston [14th Dist.] 2008, no pet.).

In re N.R.C., 94 S.W.3d 799, 807 (Tex.App.—Houston [14th Dist.] 2002, pet. denied). The TREs "discourage '*needless* presentation of cumulative evidence,' not cumulativeness in and of itself. The mere fact that another witness may have given the same or substantially the same testimony is not the decisive factor. Rather, we consider whether the excluded testimony would have added substantial weight to the complainant's case." *See also* **Benavides v. Cushman, Inc.**, 189 S.W.3d 875, 883-84 (Tex.App.—Houston [1st Dist.] 2006, no pet.).

TRE 404. CHARACTER EVIDENCE; CRIMES OR OTHER ACTS

(a) Character Evidence.

(1) *Prohibited Uses.* Evidence of a person's character or character trait is not admissible to prove that on a particular occasion the person acted in accordance with the character or trait.

(2) *Exceptions for an Accused.*

(A) In a criminal case, a defendant may offer evidence of the defendant's pertinent trait, and if the evidence is admitted, the prosecutor may offer evidence to rebut it.

(B) In a civil case, a party accused of conduct involving moral turpitude may offer evidence of the party's pertinent trait, and if the evidence is admitted, the accusing party may offer evidence to rebut it.

(3) *Exceptions for a Victim.*

(A) In a criminal case, subject to the limitations in Rule 412, a defendant may offer evidence of a victim's pertinent trait, and if the evidence is admitted, the prosecutor may offer evidence to rebut it.

(B) In a homicide case, the prosecutor may offer evidence of the victim's trait of peacefulness to rebut evidence that the victim was the first aggressor.

(C) In a civil case, a party accused of assaultive conduct may offer evidence of the victim's trait of violence to prove self-defense, and if the evidence is admitted, the accusing party may offer evidence of the victim's trait of peacefulness.

(4) *Exceptions for a Witness.* Evidence of a witness's character may be admitted under Rules 607, 608, and 609.

(5) *Definition of "Victim."* In this rule, "victim" includes an alleged victim.

(b) Crimes, Wrongs, or Other Acts.

(1) *Prohibited Uses.* Evidence of a crime, wrong, or other act is not admissible to prove a person's character in order to show that on a particular occasion the person acted in accordance with the character.

(2) *Permitted Uses; Notice in Criminal Case.* This evidence may be admissible for another purpose, such as proving motive, opportunity, intent, preparation, plan, knowledge, identity, absence of mistake, or lack of accident. On timely request by a defendant in a criminal case, the prosecutor must provide reasonable notice before trial that the prosecution intends to introduce such evidence—other than that arising in the same transaction—in its case-in-chief.

Eff. March 1, 1998. Amended by orders of Supreme Court March 10, 2015 and Court of Criminal Appeals March 12, 2015, eff. April 1, 2015.

Source: FRE 404.

See also Brown & Rondon, **Texas Rules of Evidence Handbook**, Rule 404.

ANNOTATIONS

Service Corp. v. Guerra, 348 S.W.3d 221, 235 (Tex.2011). "Evidence of other wrongs or acts is not admissible to prove character in order to show 'action in conformity therewith.' But it is admissible to show a party's intent, if material, provided the prior acts are 'so connected with the transaction at issue that they may all be parts of a system, scheme or plan.' This can be shown through evidence of similar acts temporally relevant and of the same substantive basis."

In re J.D., No. 03-14-00075-CV, 2016 WL 462734 (Tex.App.—Austin 2016, no pet.) (memo op.; 2-3-16). "The exceptions listed under Rule 404(b) are neither mutually exclusive nor collectively exhaustive. Rule 404(b) is a rule of inclusion rather than exclusion. The rule excludes only that evidence that is offered (or will be used) solely for the purpose of proving bad character and hence conduct in conformity with that bad character. The proponent of uncharged misconduct evidence need not stuff a given set of facts into one of the laundry-list exceptions set out in Rule 404(b), but he must be able to explain to the trial court, and to the opponent, the logical and legal rationales that support its admission on a basis other than bad character or propensity purpose." (Internal quotes omitted.)

In re V.V., 349 S.W.3d 548, 557 n.3 (Tex.App.—Houston [1st Dist.] 2010, pet. denied). "Rule 404(b) does not require a final conviction as a predicate to admission of extraneous offense evidence of other 'wrongs or acts,' if that evidence is otherwise relevant and admissible."

TRE 405. METHODS OF PROVING CHARACTER

(a) By Reputation or Opinion.

(1) *In General.* When evidence of a person's character or character trait is admissible, it may be proved by testimony about the person's reputation or by testimony in the form of an opinion. On cross-examination of the character witness, inquiry may be made into relevant specific instances of the person's conduct.

(2) *Accused's Character in a Criminal Case.* In the guilt stage of a criminal case, a witness may testify to the defendant's character or character trait only if, before the day of the offense, the witness was familiar with the defendant's reputation or the facts or information that form the basis of the witness's opinion.

(b) By Specific Instances of Conduct. When a person's character or character trait is an essential element of a charge, claim, or defense, the character or trait may also be proved by relevant specific instances of the person's conduct.

Eff. March 1, 1998. Amended by orders of Supreme Court March 10, 2015 and Court of Criminal Appeals March 12, 2015, eff. April 1, 2015.

See also Brown & Rondon, **Texas Rules of Evidence Handbook**, Rule 405.

ANNOTATIONS

In re G.M.P., 909 S.W.2d 198, 209 (Tex.App.—Houston [14th Dist.] 1995, no writ). "[W]hen a witness testifies as to the character of the accused, Rule 405(a) allows 'do you know' questions to be asked of the witness to test the basis for his personal opinion. Here, by making the statement 'My son wouldn't do that,' [D's father] became a character witness, espousing his opinion about [D's] propensity to commit the crime."

TRE 406. HABIT; ROUTINE PRACTICE

Evidence of a person's habit or an organization's routine practice may be admitted to prove that on a particular occasion the person or organization acted in accordance with the habit or routine practice. The court may admit this evidence regardless of whether it is corroborated or whether there was an eyewitness.

Eff. March 1, 1998. Amended by orders of Supreme Court March 10, 2015 and Court of Criminal Appeals March 12, 2015, eff. April 1, 2015.

Source: FRE 406.

See also Brown & Rondon, **Texas Rules of Evidence Handbook**, Rule 406; **O'Connor's Texas Forms,** FORM 5E:1.

ANNOTATIONS

Ortiz v. Glusman, 334 S.W.3d 812, 816 (Tex.App.—El Paso 2011, pet. denied). "To be admissible, the habit evidence must be 'a regular response to a repeated specific situation.' In other words, his response must be the same specific one to the same set of facts. One to two examples is insufficient to demonstrate a habit."

TRE 407. SUBSEQUENT REMEDIAL MEASURES; NOTIFICATION OF DEFECT

(a) Subsequent Remedial Measures. When measures are taken that would have made an earlier injury or harm less likely to occur, evidence of the subsequent measures is not admissible to prove:

- negligence;
- culpable conduct;
- a defect in a product or its design; or
- a need for a warning or instruction.

But the court may admit this evidence for another purpose, such as impeachment or—if disputed—proving ownership, control, or the feasibility of precautionary measures.

(b) Notification of Defect. A manufacturer's written notification to a purchaser of a defect in one of its products is admissible against the manufacturer to prove the defect.

Eff. March 1, 1998; amended by Supreme Court Aug. 29, 2003, eff. July 1, 2003. Amended by orders of Supreme Court March 10, 2015 and Court of Criminal Appeals March 12, 2015, eff. April 1, 2015.

Comment to 2015 Restyling: Rule 407 previously provided that evidence was not excluded if offered for a purpose not explicitly prohibited by the Rule. To improve the language of the Rule, it now provides that the court may admit evidence if offered for a permissible purpose. There is no intent to change the process for admitting evidence covered by the Rule. It remains the case that if offered for an impermissible purpose, it must be excluded, and if offered for a purpose not barred by the Rule, its admissibility remains governed by the general principles of Rules 402, 403, 801, etc.

See also Brown & Rondon, **Texas Rules of Evidence Handbook**, Rule 407; **O'Connor's Texas Forms,** FORM 5E:1.

ANNOTATIONS

Beavers v. Northrop Worldwide Aircraft Servs., 821 S.W.2d 669, 677 (Tex.App.—Amarillo 1991, writ denied). "[W]e hold the exclusion under Rule 407(a) does not apply to evidence of subsequent remedial measures taken by third parties when offered to show that a defendant was not the cause of plaintiff's injury."

E.V.R. II Assocs. v. Brundige, 813 S.W.2d 552, 556 (Tex.App.—Dallas 1991, no writ). "Evidence of subsequent remedial repair is inadmissible to establish negligence. The rule is one of policy and good sense to avoid discouraging safety measures. [T]he rule is inapplicable where the evidence would be valid as to other issues which also exist in the case."

TRE 408. COMPROMISE OFFERS AND NEGOTIATIONS

(a) Prohibited Uses. Evidence of the following is not admissible either to prove or disprove the validity or amount of a disputed claim:

(1) furnishing, promising, or offering—or accepting, promising to accept, or offering to accept—a valuable consideration in compromising or attempting to compromise the claim; and

(2) conduct or statements made during compromise negotiations about the claim.

(b) Permissible Uses. The court may admit this evidence for another purpose, such as proving a party's or

witness's bias, prejudice, or interest, negating a contention of undue delay, or proving an effort to obstruct a criminal investigation or prosecution.

Eff. March 1, 1998. Amended by orders of Supreme Court March 10, 2015 and Court of Criminal Appeals March 12, 2015, eff. April 1, 2015.

Comment to 2015 Restyling: Rule 408 previously provided that evidence was not excluded if offered for a purpose not explicitly prohibited by the Rule. To improve the language of the Rule, it now provides that the court may admit evidence if offered for a permissible purpose. There is no intent to change the process for admitting evidence covered by the Rule. It remains the case that if offered for an impermissible purpose, it must be excluded, and if offered for a purpose not barred by the Rule, its admissibility remains governed by the general principles of Rules 402, 403, 801, etc.

The reference to "liability" has been deleted on the ground that the deletion makes the Rule flow better and easier to read, and because "liability" is covered by the broader term "validity." Courts have not made substantive decisions on the basis of any distinction between validity and liability. No change in current practice or in the coverage of the Rule is intended.

Finally, the sentence of the Rule referring to evidence "otherwise discoverable" has been deleted as superfluous. The intent of the sentence was to prevent a party from trying to immunize admissible information, such as a pre-existing document, through the pretense of disclosing it during compromise negotiations. But even without the sentence, the Rule cannot be read to protect pre-existing information simply because it was presented to the adversary in compromise negotiations.

See also Brown & Rondon, **Texas Rules of Evidence Handbook**, Rule 408.

ANNOTATIONS

Ford Motor Co. v. Leggat, 904 S.W.2d 643, 649 (Tex.1995). "Settlement agreements are discoverable . . . to the extent they are relevant. Settlement agreements . . . are not admissible at trial to prove liability." *See also* **Birchfield v. Texarkana Mem'l Hosp.**, 747 S.W.2d 361, 365 (Tex.1987).

Lerma v. Border Demolition & Envtl., Inc., 459 S.W.3d 695, 700 (Tex.App.—El Paso 2015, pet. denied). "The central question here is whether [D's] offer . . . constituted a mitigation attempt or a settlement offer. The distinction carries a legal significance. . . . '[F]oreclosing a plaintiff from pursuing suit is not mitigation.' . . . 'If a defendant is truly offering to mitigate, the offer cannot implicitly or explicitly seek a release of the plaintiff's claims.' An offer that purports to resolve the dispute between the parties is not an unconditional mitigation offer, but an offer to settle, even where the offeror never explicitly demands release of the offeree's claims. [¶] Case law from our sister court makes clear that recasting a settlement offer as a mitigation attempt does not render the evidence admissible under other purposes grounds. [T]he Houston First Court of Appeals [has] held that a defendant who offered settlement evidence to show its 'mitigation' efforts was actually offering the evidence in an attempt to defeat its own liability and prove the invalidity of the damages amount. As such, Rule 408 prohibited its introduction. [¶] We agree with this reasoning. . . ."

Vinson Minerals, Ltd. v. XTO Energy, Inc., 335 S.W.3d 344, 351-52 (Tex.App.—Fort Worth 2010, pet. denied). "Offers of settlement are not admissible to prove liability or invalidity of a claim or its amount. In an offer of settlement or compromise, a party concedes some right to which he believes he is entitled in order to bring about a mutual settlement. But rule 408 does not bar the admission of settlement offers when offered for another relevant purpose. Thus, an offer or demand for settlement may be admissible for another purpose, such as to demonstrate bias or prejudice. [¶] The burden is on the party objecting to evidence under rule 408 to show that it was a part of settlement negotiations and not offered for another purpose."

Avary v. Bank of Am., 72 S.W.3d 779, 799 (Tex.App.—Dallas 2002, pet. denied). "[E]vidence of an offer to compromise is admissible to prove or disprove the extracontractual liability of an insurance company on a bad faith claim, even against the party making the offer. . . . [¶] Rule 408 does not prevent a party from proving a separate cause of action simply because some of the acts complained of took place during compromise negotiations." *See also* **Certain Underwriters at Lloyd's v. Chicago Bridge & Iron Co.**, 406 S.W.3d 326, 340 (Tex.App.—Beaumont 2013, pet. denied).

TRE 409. OFFERS TO PAY MEDICAL AND SIMILAR EXPENSES

Evidence of furnishing, promising to pay, or offering to pay medical, hospital, or similar expenses resulting from an injury is not admissible to prove liability for the injury.

Eff. March 1, 1998. Amended by orders of Supreme Court March 10, 2015 and Court of Criminal Appeals March 12, 2015, eff. April 1, 2015.

See also Brown & Rondon, **Texas Rules of Evidence Handbook**, Rule 409; **O'Connor's Texas Forms**, FORM 5E:1

TRE 410. PLEAS, PLEA DISCUSSIONS, AND RELATED STATEMENTS

(a) Prohibited Uses in Civil Cases. In a civil case, evidence of the following is not admissible against the defendant who made the plea or was a participant in the plea discussions:

(1) a guilty plea that was later withdrawn;

(2) a nolo contendere plea;

(3) a statement made during a proceeding on either of those pleas under Federal Rule of Criminal Procedure 11 or a comparable state procedure; or

(4) a statement made during plea discussions with an attorney for the prosecuting authority if the discussions did not result in a guilty plea or they resulted in a later-withdrawn guilty plea.

(b) Prohibited Uses in Criminal Cases. In a criminal case, evidence of the following is not admissible against the defendant who made the plea or was a participant in the plea discussions:

(1) a guilty plea that was later withdrawn;

(2) a nolo contendere plea that was later withdrawn;

(3) a statement made during a proceeding on either of those pleas under Federal Rule of Criminal Procedure 11 or a comparable state procedure; or

(4) a statement made during plea discussions with an attorney for the prosecuting authority if the discussions did not result in a guilty or nolo contendere plea or they resulted in a later-withdrawn guilty or nolo contendere plea.

(c) Exception. In a civil case, the court may admit a statement described in paragraph (a)(3) or (4) and in a criminal case, the court may admit a statement described in paragraph (b)(3) or (4), when another statement made during the same plea or plea discussions has been introduced and in fairness the statements ought to be considered together.

Eff. March 1, 1998. Amended by orders of Supreme Court March 10, 2015 and Court of Criminal Appeals March 12, 2015, eff. April 1, 2015.

See also Brown & Rondon, **Texas Rules of Evidence Handbook**, Rule 410.

TRE 411. LIABILITY INSURANCE

Evidence that a person was or was not insured against liability is not admissible to prove whether the person acted negligently or otherwise wrongfully. But the court may admit this evidence for another purpose, such as proving a witness's bias or prejudice or, if disputed, proving agency, ownership, or control.

Eff. March 1, 1998. Amended by orders of Supreme Court March 10, 2015 and Court of Criminal Appeals March 12, 2015, eff. April 1, 2015.

Source: FRE 411.

See also Brown & Rondon, **Texas Rules of Evidence Handbook**, Rule 411; **O'Connor's Texas Forms**, FORM 5E:1.

ANNOTATIONS

Canyon Vista Prop. Owners Ass'n v. Laubach, No. 03-11-00404-CV, 2014 WL 411646 (Tex.App.—Austin 2014, no pet.) (memo op.; 1-31-14). "Evidence that a person was or was not insured against liability is not admissible upon the issue of whether the person acted negligently or otherwise wrongfully. However, the mention of insurance before a jury is not always reversible error. To demonstrate reversible error, the party appealing must show: (1) that the reference to insurance probably caused the rendition of an improper judgment in the case; and (2) that the probability that the mention of insurance caused harm exceeds the probability that the verdict was grounded on proper proceedings and evidence. The record as a whole must show harm to the complaining party." *See also* **Beall v. Ditmore**, 867 S.W.2d 791, 795 (Tex.App.—El Paso 1993, writ denied).

Brownsville Pediatric Ass'n v. Reyes, 68 S.W.3d 184, 193 (Tex.App.—Corpus Christi 2002, no pet.). "[Ds] objected to the mention of insurance in the context of an insurance company issuing an annuity. The reference to insurance in this instance is not the type of injection of insurance into a case that is protected by [TRE 411]. Thus, the harm the rule was designed to prevent does not come into play."

TRE 412. EVIDENCE OF PREVIOUS SEXUAL CONDUCT IN CRIMINAL CASES

(a) In General. The following evidence is not admissible in a prosecution for sexual assault, aggravated sexual assault, or attempt to commit sexual assault or aggravated sexual assault:

(1) reputation or opinion evidence of a victim's past sexual behavior; or

(2) specific instances of a victim's past sexual behavior.

(b) Exceptions for Specific Instances. Evidence of specific instances of a victim's past sexual behavior is admissible if:

(1) the court admits the evidence in accordance with subdivisions (c) and (d);

(2) the evidence:

(A) is necessary to rebut or explain scientific or medical evidence offered by the prosecutor;

(B) concerns past sexual behavior with the defendant and is offered by the defendant to prove consent;

(C) relates to the victim's motive or bias;

(D) is admissible under Rule 609; or

(E) is constitutionally required to be admitted; and

(3) the probative value of the evidence outweighs the danger of unfair prejudice.

(c) Procedure for Offering Evidence. Before offering any evidence of the victim's past sexual behavior, the defendant must inform the court outside the jury's presence. The court must then conduct an in camera hearing, recorded by a court reporter, and determine whether the proposed evidence is admissible. The defendant may not refer to any evidence ruled inadmissible without first requesting and gaining the court's approval outside the jury's presence.

(d) Record Sealed. The court must preserve the record of the in camera hearing, under seal, as part of the record.

(e) Definition of "Victim." In this rule, "victim" includes an alleged victim.

Eff. March 1, 1998. Amended by Court of Criminal Appeals Dec. 13, 2006, eff. Jan. 1, 2007. Amended by orders of Supreme Court March 10, 2015 and Court of Criminal Appeals March 12, 2015, eff. April 1, 2015.

See also Brown & Rondon, **Texas Rules of Evidence Handbook**, Rule 412.

ANNOTATIONS

In re Doe, 22 S.W.3d 601, 611-12 (Tex.App.—Austin 2000, orig. proceeding). "[P] argues that the 'rape victims shield laws,' incorporated in [TRE] 412, should apply despite the fact that the Rule specifically applies only in criminal cases. [¶] At this early stage of the litigation and considering the fact that [P] pleads that this was a forcible assault and the grand jury indicted [D's employee] under the criminal statutes for the crime of sexual assault, we hold that until the record is more fully developed and these issues are clarified[,] the rape shield laws ought to protect the victim . . . at this time. We hold that the trial court abused its discretion by failing to issue a protective order preventing [D] from questioning [P] about her past and present sexual activity."

Article V. Privileges

TRE 501. PRIVILEGES IN GENERAL

Unless a Constitution, a statute, or these or other rules prescribed under statutory authority provide otherwise, no person has a privilege to:

(a) refuse to be a witness;

(b) refuse to disclose any matter;

(c) refuse to produce any object or writing; or

(d) prevent another from being a witness, disclosing any matter, or producing any object or writing.

Eff. March 1, 1998. Amended by orders of Supreme Court March 10, 2015 and Court of Criminal Appeals March 12, 2015, eff. April 1, 2015.

See also **O'Connor's Texas Rules,** "Scope of Discovery," ch. 6-B, §1 et seq.; Brown & Rondon, **Texas Rules of Evidence Handbook**, Rule 501; **O'Connor's Texas Family Law Handbook** (2018), "Testimony," ch. 3-A, §15.3.

ANNOTATIONS

Volkswagen, A.G. v. Valdez, 909 S.W.2d 900, 902-03 (Tex.1995). The trial court must weigh the following factors when evaluating a privilege of a foreign country: (1) the importance of the discovery request to the investigation or litigation; (2) the degree of specificity of the request; (3) whether the information originated in the U.S.; (4) the availability of alternative means of securing the information; and (5) the extent to which noncompliance with the request would undermine important interests of the U.S., or the extent to which compliance would undermine important interests of the foreign jurisdiction where the information is located.

State v. Lowry, 802 S.W.2d 669, 671 (Tex.1991). "Only in certain narrow circumstances is it appropriate to obstruct the search for truth by denying discovery. Very limited exceptions to the strongly preferred policy of openness are recognized in our state procedural rules and statutes."

Oyster Creek Fin. Corp. v. Richwood Invs., 957 S.W.2d 640, 646 (Tex.App.—Amarillo 1997, pet. denied). "[B]ecause evidence is presumed discoverable, the party resisting discovery . . . bears the burden of establishing the privilege and, therefore, must plead it and present evidence which establishes that the document(s) in question qualify for the privilege as a matter of law."

TRE 502. REQUIRED REPORTS PRIVILEGED BY STATUTE

(a) In General. If a law requiring a return or report to be made so provides:

(1) a person, corporation, association, or other organization or entity—whether public or private—that makes the required return or report has a privilege to refuse to disclose it and to prevent any other person from disclosing it; and

(2) a public officer or agency to whom the return or report must be made has a privilege to refuse to disclose it.

(b) Exceptions. This privilege does not apply in an action involving perjury, false statements, fraud in the return or report, or other failure to comply with the law in question.

Eff. March 1, 1998. Amended by orders of Supreme Court March 10, 2015 and Court of Criminal Appeals March 12, 2015, eff. April 1, 2015.

See also **O'Connor's Texas Rules,** "Scope of Discovery," ch. 6-B, §1 et seq.; Brown & Rondon, **Texas Rules of Evidence Handbook**, Rule 502; **O'Connor's Texas Family Law Handbook** (2018), "Reporting Family Violence, Child Abuse, Neglect, or History of Child Abuse," ch. 1-G, §1 et seq.

TRE 503. LAWYER-CLIENT PRIVILEGE

(a) Definitions. In this rule:

(1) A "client" is a person, public officer, or corporation, association, or other organization or entity—whether public or private—that:

(A) is rendered professional legal services by a lawyer; or

(B) consults a lawyer with a view to obtaining professional legal services from the lawyer.

(2) A "client's representative" is:

(A) a person who has authority to obtain professional legal services for the client or to act for the client on the legal advice rendered; or

(B) any other person who, to facilitate the rendition of professional legal services to the client, makes or receives a confidential communication while acting in the scope of employment for the client.

(3) A "lawyer" is a person authorized, or who the client reasonably believes is authorized, to practice law in any state or nation.

(4) A "lawyer's representative" is:

(A) one employed by the lawyer to assist in the rendition of professional legal services; or

(B) an accountant who is reasonably necessary for the lawyer's rendition of professional legal services.

(5) A communication is "confidential" if not intended to be disclosed to third persons other than those:

(A) to whom disclosure is made to further the rendition of professional legal services to the client; or

(B) reasonably necessary to transmit the communication.

(b) Rules of Privilege.

(1) ***General Rule.*** A client has a privilege to refuse to disclose and to prevent any other person from disclosing confidential communications made to facilitate the rendition of professional legal services to the client:

(A) between the client or the client's representative and the client's lawyer or the lawyer's representative;

(B) between the client's lawyer and the lawyer's representative;

(C) by the client, the client's representative, the client's lawyer, or the lawyer's representative to a lawyer representing another party in a pending action or that lawyer's representative, if the communications concern a matter of common interest in the pending action;

(D) between the client's representatives or between the client and the client's representative; or

(E) among lawyers and their representatives representing the same client.

(2) ***Special Rule in a Criminal Case.*** In a criminal case, a client has a privilege to prevent a lawyer or lawyer's representative from disclosing any other fact that came to the knowledge of the lawyer or the lawyer's representative by reason of the attorney-client relationship.

(c) Who May Claim. The privilege may be claimed by:

(1) the client;

(2) the client's guardian or conservator;

(3) a deceased client's personal representative; or

(4) the successor, trustee, or similar representative of a corporation, association, or other organization or entity—whether or not in existence.

The person who was the client's lawyer or the lawyer's representative when the communication was made may claim the privilege on the client's behalf—and is presumed to have authority to do so.

(d) Exceptions. This privilege does not apply:

(1) ***Furtherance of Crime or Fraud.*** If the lawyer's services were sought or obtained to enable or aid anyone to commit or plan to commit what the client knew or reasonably should have known to be a crime or fraud.

(2) ***Claimants Through Same Deceased Client.*** If the communication is relevant to an issue between parties claiming through the same deceased client.

(3) ***Breach of Duty By a Lawyer or Client.*** If the communication is relevant to an issue of breach of duty by a lawyer to the client or by a client to the lawyer.

(4) ***Document Attested By a Lawyer.*** If the communication is relevant to an issue concerning an attested document to which the lawyer is an attesting witness.

(5) ***Joint Clients.*** If the communication:

(A) is offered in an action between clients who retained or consulted a lawyer in common;

(B) was made by any of the clients to the lawyer; and

(C) is relevant to a matter of common interest between the clients.

Eff. March 1, 1998. Amended by orders of Supreme Court March 10, 2015 and Court of Criminal Appeals March 12, 2015, eff. April 1, 2015.

Comment to 1998 change: The addition of subsection (a)(2)(B) adopts a subject matter test for the privilege of an entity, in place of the control group test previously used. See National Tank Co. v. Brotherton, 851 S.W.2d 193, 197-198 (Tex 1993).

Source: Codification of common-law doctrine. See proposed FRE 503 (1972); Code Crim. Proc. art. 38.10 (repealed).

See also **O'Connor's Texas Rules,** "Asserting privileges," ch. 6-A, §18.2; **O'Connor's Texas Rules,** "Scope of Discovery," ch. 6-B, §1 et seq.; Brown & Rondon, **Texas Rules of Evidence Handbook,** Rule 503; **O'Connor's Texas Forms,** FORM 5E:1.

ANNOTATIONS

Generally

In re Silver, 540 S.W.3d 530, 535-37 (Tex.2018). "The definition [under Rule 503] states two requirements for a person to qualify as a lawyer. First, the person must be engaged in a particular activity—the 'practice [of] law.' Second, the person must be 'authorized' to perform the activity in a state or nation. Thus, understanding what it means to be a 'lawyer' for purposes of the rule requires determin-

ing (1) what it means to 'practice law' and (2) how one is 'authorized' to do so. [¶] Black's [Law Dictionary states services] that the 'practice of law' encompasses. . . . These types of activities are exactly what the [U.S. Patent and Trademark Office (USPTO)] says that patent agents can perform. . . . Patent agents participate in many activities that make up the practice of law. [¶] [I]n line with common understanding of what it means to practice law, . . . the practitioner [must be] providing these services directly to the client. [¶] As applied here, if a patent agent stays within the sphere of patent law, the agent can provide services directly to the client. The patent agent has no need of a supervising or intermediary attorney because the agent can provide all the same services. [¶] Registered patent agents perform the same services and are subject to the same rules and requirements as patent attorneys in the application and prosecution of patents before the USPTO. . . . Therefore, we hold that, within the scope of their practice before the USPTO, patent agents practice law. [¶] The second part of Rule 503's definition of 'lawyer' is that the individual practicing law must be authorized to do so by a state or nation. . . . Because [P's] patent agent does not have a license to practice law, [D] concludes the agent is not 'authorized' and thus not covered by Rule 503's privilege. [¶] A license is not a prerequisite to a person being classified as a 'lawyer' under the rule. At 538: '[A]uthorized' means 'sanctioned by authority' or 'approved.' The [USPTO] has approved patent agents to practice before it. The [USPTO], in turn, was given authority to do so by Congress. A registered patent agent's authority to represent clients before the USPTO therefore comes from the U.S., which is one of the sovereigns identified in our rule. And, because patent agents are authorized to practice law before the USPTO, they fall within Rule 503's definition of 'lawyer,' and, as such, their clients may invoke the lawyer-client privilege to protect communications that fall within the privilege's scope."

In re XL Specialty Ins., 373 S.W.3d 46, 50 (Tex.2012). "[T]he privilege defined in Rule 503(b)(1)(C) . . . has been variously described as the 'joint client' privilege, the 'joint defense' privilege, and the 'common interest' privilege. Courts sometimes use these terms interchangeably, but they involve distinct doctrines that serve different purposes. [¶] The joint client . . . doctrine applies '[w]hen the same attorney simultaneously represents two or more clients on the same matter.' *At 51-53:* The joint defense rule applies [only in the context of litigation and] when multiple parties to a lawsuit, each represented by different attorneys, communicate among themselves for the purpose of forming a common defense strategy. [¶] [Under t]he common interest rule[, t]he parties must share a mutual interest, but unlike the joint defense doctrine, the common interest rule applies to 'two or more separately represented persons whatever their denomination in pleadings and whether or not involved in litigation.' [¶] [Because] Texas requires that the communications be made in the context of a pending action[,] our privilege is not a 'common interest' privilege that extends beyond litigation. Nor is it a 'joint defense' privilege, as it applies not just to defendants but to any parties to a pending action. Rule 503(b)(1)(C)'s privilege is more appropriately termed an 'allied litigant' privilege. [¶] The allied litigant doctrine protects communications made between a client, or the client's lawyer, to another party's lawyer, not to the other party itself. This attorney-sharing requirement makes clear that the privilege applies only when the parties have separate counsel." *See also* **In re Park Cities Bank**, 409 S.W.3d 859, 874 (Tex.App.—Tyler 2013, orig. proceeding).

In re Rescue Concepts, Inc., 556 S.W.3d 331, 345 (Tex.App.—Houston [1st Dist.] 2017, orig. proceeding). " '[T]he subject of the information communicated between the attorney and client is of no concern in determining whether the privilege is applicable to the documents.' Rather, we must determine whether the documents constituted a communication between an attorney and client under Rule 503(b), i.e. whether they were communications that were (1) not intended to be disclosed to third parties and (2) made for the purpose of facilitating the rendition of professional legal services. If we determine that a document contains a confidential communication, the attorney-client privilege extends to the entire document, and not merely to the specific portions relating to legal advice, opinions, or mental analysis."

In re Fairway Methanol LLC, 515 S.W.3d 480, 489 (Tex.App.—Houston [14th Dist.] 2017, orig. proceeding). "[Ps] argue that for the communications at issue to be protected by the attorney-client privilege, they 'must be for the primary purpose of soliciting legal, rather than business advice'. . . . [¶] However, [Ps] cite no Texas authority for their position that the communication must have been made for the *primary* purpose of soliciting legal, rather than business advice. . . . More important, the language of Rule 503(b) does not require that the *primary* purpose of the communication be to facilitate the rendition of legal services; it only requires that the communication be made to facilitate the rendition of legal services."

In re Texas Health Res., 472 S.W.3d 895, 902 (Tex.App.—Dallas 2015, orig. proceeding). "The lawyer-client privilege protects not only confidential communications between the lawyer and client, but also the discourse among their representatives. Under Rule 503(a)(2), if a person authorized by the client to obtain legal services or act on legal advice on behalf of the client or to make or receive confidential communications with respect to legal services, that person is a client's representative even if the person is not an employee of the client. [¶] Insurance companies typically have the duty to conduct the defense of the insured under a liability policy, including the authority to select, employ, and pay the attorney. Such liability policies typically give the insurer complete and exclusive control of that defense, . . . including the ability to obtain professional legal services on behalf of the insured. For that rea-

son, under the proper circumstances, communications between an insurer and its insured may be shielded from discovery by the lawyer-client privilege." (Internal quotes omitted.)

Watson v. Kaminski, 51 S.W.3d 825, 827 (Tex.App.—Houston [1st Dist.] 2001, no pet.). "To be privileged, the communication must relate to pending or proposed litigation and must further the attorney's representation. [¶] The judge must consider the entire communication in its context and must extend the privilege to any statement that bears some relation to an existing or proposed judicial proceeding. All doubt should be resolved in favor of the communication's relation to the proceeding."

Boales v. Brighton Builders, Inc., 29 S.W.3d 159, 168 (Tex.App.—Houston [14th Dist.] 2000, pet. denied). "The [attorney-client] privilege extends to all matters concerning litigation or business transactions, regardless of whether the matters are pertinent to the matter for which the attorney was employed. The statements and advice of the attorney to the client are as protected as the communications of the client to the attorney." *See also* **In re Small**, 346 S.W.3d 657, 663 (Tex.App.—El Paso 2009, orig. proceeding).

Perez v. Kirk & Carrigan, 822 S.W.2d 261, 265 (Tex.App.—Corpus Christi 1991, writ denied). "An agreement to form an attorney-client relationship may be implied from the conduct of the parties. Moreover, the relationship does not depend upon the payment of a fee, but may exist as a result of rendering services gratuitously."

Exceptions to Privilege

Granada Corp. v. First Ct. of Appeals, 844 S.W.2d 223, 227 (Tex.1992). "The crime-fraud exception [to the attorney-client privilege in TRE 503(d)(1)] applies only if a prima facie case is made of contemplated fraud. Additionally, there must be a relationship between the document for which the privilege is challenged and the prima facie proof offered."

In re Park Cities Bank, 409 S.W.3d 859, 869 (Tex.App.—Tyler 2013, orig. proceeding). "The party seeking discovery of an otherwise privileged communication bears the burden of proving the exception. [¶] The crime-fraud exception applies only if (1) the party asserting the exception makes a prima facie showing that a crime or fraud was ongoing or about to be committed, and (2) there is a relationship between the document for which the privilege is challenged and the prima facie proof offered. The prima facie requirement is met when the proponent offers evidence establishing the elements of fraud and that the fraud was ongoing, or about to be committed, at the time the document was prepared. The fraud alleged to have occurred must have happened at or during the time the document was prepared, and the document must have been created as part of perpetrating the fraud. [¶] In addition to the prima facie showing, the party asserting the crime-fraud exception must show that a nexus exists between the privileged documents and the alleged fraud. This nexus must be established for each privileged document. Mere allegations of a connection between the alleged fraud and the document will not suffice." *See also* **In re USA Waste Mgmt. Res.**, 387 S.W.3d 92, 98 (Tex.App.—Houston [14th Dist.] 2012, orig. proceeding); **In re Small**, 346 S.W.3d 657, 666 (Tex.App.—El Paso 2009, orig. proceeding).

No Attorney-Client Privilege

Joe v. Two Thirty Nine Jt.V., 145 S.W.3d 150, 164 (Tex 2004). "Conducting legal research in preparation for a city council vote does not create an attorney-client relationship between [D] and the City, and sharing that information with fellow council members as part of deliberations does not change that conclusion. [D's] research . . . in preparation for a city council meeting [is] not part of legal services . . . and does not create an attorney-client relationship. . . ." *See also* **In re Texas Farmers Ins. Exch.**, 990 S.W.2d 337, 340 (Tex.App.—Texarkana 1999, orig. proceeding).

Huie v. DeShazo, 922 S.W.2d 920, 921 (Tex.1996). "The issue . . . is whether the attorney-client privilege protects communications between a trustee and his or her attorney relating to trust administration from discovery by a trust beneficiary. We hold . . . only the trustee, not the trust beneficiary, is the client of the trustee's attorney. The beneficiary therefore may not discover communications between the trustee and attorney otherwise protected under [TRE] 503."

In re Baytown Nissan Inc., 451 S.W.3d 140, 143 (Tex.App.—Houston [1st Dist.] 2014, orig. proceeding). "[W]e examine whether a discussion between two lawyers—one representing a trade association and the other representing one of its members—is subject to an attorney-client . . . privilege. *At 146:* [Ds] argue[ ] that the [c]onversation is privileged under Rule 503 because . . . the rule does not require an attorney-client relationship between two attorneys for it to apply. . . . [¶] [Ds'] argument, that [trade association's attorney's] status as an attorney—and not necessarily *their* attorney—is sufficient to attach attorney-client privilege disregards the purpose of the privilege: to foster open communication between clients and their attorneys so that the attorneys can best represent their clients. It is the relationship with the client that confers the privilege. [W]e reject [Ds'] request to expand the attorney-client privilege to situations outside of an attorney-client relationship."

In re Monsanto Co., 998 S.W.2d 917, 930 (Tex.App.—Waco 1999, orig. proceeding). "We recognize that it might be argued [under TRE 503(a)(2)(B)] that all communications between corporate representatives could be claimed as privileged on the basis that 'the legal department can better represent us if we keep them informed.' We reject that assertion. We do not believe that it is necessary for the legal department to be advised of every development out in the field, no matter how minute."

Offensive Use

Republic Ins. v. Davis, 856 S.W.2d 158, 163 (Tex1993). "In an instance in which the privilege is being used as a

sword rather than a shield, the privilege may be waived. [T]he following factors should guide the trial court in determining whether a waiver has occurred. [¶] First, . . . the party asserting the privilege must seek affirmative relief. Second, the privileged information sought must be such that, if believed by the fact finder, in all probability it would be outcome determinative of the cause of action asserted. Mere relevance is insufficient. A contradiction in position without more is insufficient. The confidential communication must go to the very heart of the affirmative relief sought. Third, disclosure of the confidential communication must be the only means by which the aggrieved party may obtain the evidence. If any one of these requirements is lacking, the trial court must uphold the privilege."

TRE 504. SPOUSAL PRIVILEGES

(a) Confidential Communication Privilege.

(1) ***Definition.*** A communication is "confidential" if a person makes it privately to the person's spouse and does not intend its disclosure to any other person.

(2) ***General Rule.*** A person has a privilege to refuse to disclose and to prevent any other person from disclosing a confidential communication made to the person's spouse while they were married. This privilege survives termination of the marriage.

(3) ***Who May Claim.*** The privilege may be claimed by:

(A) the communicating spouse;

(B) the guardian of a communicating spouse who is incompetent; or

(C) the personal representative of a communicating spouse who is deceased.

The other spouse may claim the privilege on the communicating spouse's behalf—and is presumed to have authority to do so.

(4) ***Exceptions.*** This privilege does not apply:

(A) ***Furtherance of Crime or Fraud.*** If the communication is made—wholly or partially—to enable or aid anyone to commit or plan to commit a crime or fraud.

(B) ***Proceeding Between Spouse and Other Spouse or Claimant Through Deceased Spouse.*** In a civil proceeding:

(i) brought by or on behalf of one spouse against the other; or

(ii) between a surviving spouse and a person claiming through the deceased spouse.

(C) ***Crime Against Family, Spouse, Household Member, or Minor Child.*** In a:

(i) proceeding in which a party is accused of conduct that, if proved, is a crime against the person of the other spouse, any member of the household of either spouse, or any minor child; or

(ii) criminal proceeding involving a charge of bigamy under Section 25.01 of the Penal Code.

(D) ***Commitment or Similar Proceeding.*** In a proceeding to commit either spouse or otherwise to place the spouse or the spouse's property under another's control because of a mental or physical condition.

(E) ***Proceeding to Establish Competence.*** In a proceeding brought by or on behalf of either spouse to establish competence.

(b) Privilege Not to Testify in a Criminal Case.

(1) ***General Rule.*** In a criminal case, an accused's spouse has a privilege not to be called to testify for the state. But this rule neither prohibits a spouse from testifying voluntarily for the state nor gives a spouse a privilege to refuse to be called to testify for the accused.

(2) ***Failure to Call Spouse.*** If other evidence indicates that the accused's spouse could testify to relevant matters, an accused's failure to call the spouse to testify is a proper subject of comment by counsel.

(3) ***Who May Claim.*** The privilege not to testify may be claimed by the accused's spouse or the spouse's guardian or representative, but not by the accused.

(4) ***Exceptions.*** This privilege does not apply:

(A) ***Certain Criminal Proceedings.*** In a criminal proceeding in which a spouse is charged with:

(i) a crime against the other spouse, any member of the household of either spouse, or any minor child; or

(ii) bigamy under Section 25.01 of the Penal Code.

(B) ***Matters That Occurred Before the Marriage.*** If the spouse is called to testify about matters that occurred before the marriage.

Eff. March 1, 1998. Amended by Court of Criminal Appeals Dec. 13, 2006, eff. January 1, 2007. Amended by orders of Supreme Court March 10, 2015 and Court of Criminal Appeals March 12, 2015, eff. April 1, 2015.

Comment to 1998 change: The rule eliminates the spousal testimonial privilege for prosecutions in which the testifying spouse is the alleged victim of a crime by the accused. This is intended to be consistent with Code of Criminal Procedure article 38.10, effective September 1, 1995.

Comment to 2015 Restyling: Previously, Rule 504(b)(1) provided that, "A spouse who testifies on behalf of an accused is subject to cross-examination as provided in Rule 611(b)." That sentence was included in the original version of Rule 504 when the Texas Rules of Criminal Evidence were promulgated in 1986 and changed the rule to a testimonial privilege held by the witness spouse. Until then, a spouse was deemed incompetent to testify against his or her defendant spouse, and when a spouse testified on behalf of a defendant spouse, the state was limited to cross-examining the spouse about matters relating to the spouse's direct testimony. The quoted sentence from the original Criminal Rule 504(b) was designed to overturn this limitation and allow the state to cross-examine a testifying spouse in the same manner as any other witness. More than twenty-five years later, it is clear that a spouse who testifies either for or against a defendant spouse may be cross-examined in the same manner as any other witness. Therefore, the continued inclusion in the rule of a provision that refers only to the cross-examination of a spouse who testifies on behalf of the accused is more confusing than helpful. Its deletion is designed to clarify the rule and does not change existing law.

See also **O'Connor's Texas Rules,** "Asserting privileges," ch. 6-A, §18.2; **O'Connor's Texas Rules,** "Scope of Discovery," ch. 6-B, §1 et seq.; Brown & Rondon, **Texas Rules of Evidence Handbook**, Rule 504; **O'Connor's Texas Family Law Handbook**, "Testimony," ch. 3-A, §15.3; **O'Connor's Texas Family Law Handbook**, "No spousal privilege," ch. 9-D, §16.6.2(5).

ANNOTATIONS

Marshall v. Ryder Sys., 928 S.W.2d 190, 195 (Tex.App.—Houston [14th Dist.] 1996, writ denied). In civil cases, "[t]he marital privilege is limited to *confidential* communications between spouses. Only in criminal cases is there a broad, general privilege protecting a person from being a witness against his or her spouse."

TRE 505. PRIVILEGE FOR COMMUNICATIONS TO A CLERGY MEMBER

(a) Definitions. In this rule:

(1) A "clergy member" is a minister, priest, rabbi, accredited Christian Science Practitioner, or other similar functionary of a religious organization or someone whom a communicant reasonably believes is a clergy member.

(2) A "communicant" is a person who consults a clergy member in the clergy member's professional capacity as a spiritual adviser.

(3) A communication is "confidential" if made privately and not intended for further disclosure except to other persons present to further the purpose of the communication.

(b) General Rule. A communicant has a privilege to refuse to disclose and to prevent any other person from disclosing a confidential communication by the communicant to a clergy member in the clergy member's professional capacity as spiritual adviser.

(c) Who May Claim. The privilege may be claimed by:

(1) the communicant;

(2) the communicant's guardian or conservator; or

(3) a deceased communicant's personal representative.

The clergy member to whom the communication was made may claim the privilege on the communicant's behalf—and is presumed to have authority to do so.

Eff. March 1, 1998. Amended by orders of Supreme Court March 10, 2015 and Court of Criminal Appeals March 12, 2015, eff. April 1, 2015.

See also **O'Connor's Texas Rules,** "Asserting privileges," ch. 6-A, §18.2; **O'Connor's Texas Rules,** "Scope of Discovery," ch. 6-B, §1 et seq.; Brown & Rondon, **Texas Rules of Evidence Handbook,** Rule 505.

ANNOTATIONS

Nicholson v. Wittig, 832 S.W.2d 681, 685 (Tex.App.—Houston [1st Dist.] 1992, orig. proceeding). The clergy-communicant "privilege attaches when a person makes a communication with a reasonable expectation of confidentiality to a member of the clergy acting in his or her professional or spiritual capacity. [¶] An individual may invoke a privilege regardless of the nature of the underlying proceeding. *At 686:* Rule 505 makes no reference to the content of the communication; rather, the rule focuses on the counseling opportunity."

TRE 506. POLITICAL VOTE PRIVILEGE

A person has a privilege to refuse to disclose the person's vote at a political election conducted by secret ballot unless the vote was cast illegally.

Eff. March 1, 1998. Amended by orders of Supreme Court March 10, 2015 and Court of Criminal Appeals March 12, 2015, eff. April 1, 2015.

Source: Elec. Code §221.009(a) (1986). See proposed FRE 507 (1972).

See also **O'Connor's Texas Rules,** "Asserting privileges," ch. 6-A, §18.2; **O'Connor's Texas Rules,** "Scope of Discovery," ch. 6-B, §1 et seq.; Brown & Rondon, **Texas Rules of Evidence Handbook,** Rule 506.

ANNOTATIONS

Oliphint v. Christy, 299 S.W.2d 933, 939 (Tex 1957). "The privilege of nondisclosure belongs only to the legal voter and the individual who votes illegally cannot be considered a 'voter' for any purpose." *See also* **Simmons v. Jones**, 838 S.W.2d 298, 300 (Tex.App.—El Paso 1992, no writ).

TRE 507. TRADE SECRETS PRIVILEGE

(a) General Rule. A person has a privilege to refuse to disclose and to prevent other persons from disclosing a trade secret owned by the person, unless the court finds that nondisclosure will tend to conceal fraud or otherwise work injustice.

(b) Who May Claim. The privilege may be claimed by the person who owns the trade secret or the person's agent or employee.

(c) Protective Measure. If a court orders a person to disclose a trade secret, it must take any protective measure required by the interests of the privilege holder and the parties and to further justice.

Eff. March 1, 1998. Amended by orders of Supreme Court March 10, 2015 and Court of Criminal Appeals March 12, 2015, eff. April 1, 2015.

Source: Common law. See proposed FRE 508 (1972).

See also Pen. Code §31.05(a)(4); **O'Connor's Texas Rules,** "Asserting privileges," ch. 6-A, §18.2; **O'Connor's Texas Rules,** "Scope of Discovery," ch. 6-B, §1 et seq.; Brown & Rondon, **Texas Rules of Evidence Handbook,** Rule 507.

ANNOTATIONS

In re Bass, 113 S.W.3d 735, 739-40 (Tex.2003). The following factors are used to "determine whether a trade secret exists . . .: '(1) the extent to which the information is known outside of his business; (2) the extent to which it is known by employees and others involved in his business; (3) the extent of the measures taken by him to guard the secrecy of the information; (4) the value of the information to him and to his competitors; (5) the amount of effort or money expended by him in developing the information; (6) the ease or difficulty with which the information could be properly acquired or duplicated by others.' [¶] Texas courts . . . are split on whether the six factors should be weighed as relevant criteria or whether a person claiming trade secret privilege must satisfy all six factors before trade secret status applies. [¶] We agree . . . that the party claiming a trade secret should not be required to satisfy all six factors because trade secrets do not fit neatly into each factor every time." *See also* **In re Union Pac. R.R.**, 294 S.W.3d 589, 592 (Tex.2009); **In re Valero Ref.-Tex., L.P.**, No. 01-14-00149-CV, 2014 WL 4115917 (Tex.App.—Houston [1st Dist.] 2014, orig. proceeding) (memo op.; 8-21-14).

In re Bridgestone/Firestone, Inc., 106 S.W.3d 730, 732-33 (Tex.2003). "Just as a party who claims the trade secret privilege cannot do so generally but must provide detailed information in support of the claim, so a party seeking such information cannot merely assert unfairness but must demonstrate with specificity exactly how the lack of the information will impair the presentation of the case on the merits to the point that an unjust result is a real, rather than a merely possible, threat." *See also* **In re Continental Gen. Tire, Inc.**, 979 S.W.2d 609, 611 (Tex.1998).

Computer Assocs. Int'l v. Altai, Inc., 918 S.W.2d 453, 455 (Tex.1996). "A trade secret is any formula, pattern, device or compilation of information which is used in one's business and presents an opportunity to obtain an advantage over competitors who do not know or use it."

In re Cooper Tire & Rubber Co., 313 S.W.3d 910, 915 (Tex.App.—Houston [14th Dist.] 2010, orig. proceeding). "The party asserting the trade secret privilege has the burden of proving that the discovery information sought qualifies as a trade secret. If the resisting party meets its burden, the burden shifts to the party seeking the trade secret discovery to establish that the information is necessary for a fair adjudication of its claim. It is an abuse of discretion for the trial court to order production once trade secret status is proven if the party seeking production has not shown necessity for the requested materials." *See also* **In re Kongsberg Inc.**, 563 S.W.3d 915, 921 (Tex.App.—Beaumont 2018, orig. proceeding).

TRE 508. INFORMER'S IDENTITY PRIVILEGE

(a) General Rule. The United States, a state, or a subdivision of either has a privilege to refuse to disclose a person's identity if:

(1) the person has furnished information to a law enforcement officer or a member of a legislative committee or its staff conducting an investigation of a possible violation of law; and

(2) the information relates to or assists in the investigation.

(b) Who May Claim. The privilege may be claimed by an appropriate representative of the public entity to which the informer furnished the information. The court in a criminal case must reject the privilege claim if the state objects.

(c) Exceptions.

(1) ***Voluntary Disclosure; Informer a Witness.*** This privilege does not apply if:

(A) the informer's identity or the informer's interest in the communication's subject matter has been disclosed—by a privilege holder or the informer's own action—to a person who would have cause to resent the communication; or

(B) the informer appears as a witness for the public entity.

(2) ***Testimony About the Merits***

(A) ***Criminal Case.*** In a criminal case, this privilege does not apply if the court finds a reasonable probability exists that the informer can give testimony necessary to a fair determination of guilt or innocence. If the court so finds and the public entity elects not to disclose the informer's identity:

(i) on the defendant's motion, the court must dismiss the charges to which the testimony would relate; or

(ii) on its own motion, the court may dismiss the charges to which the testimony would relate.

(B) ***Certain Civil Cases.*** In a civil case in which the public entity is a party, this privilege does not apply if

the court finds a reasonable probability exists that the informer can give testimony necessary to a fair determination of a material issue on the merits. If the court so finds and the public entity elects not to disclose the informer's identity, the court may make any order that justice requires.

(C) *Procedures.*

(i) If it appears that an informer may be able to give the testimony required to invoke this exception and the public entity claims the privilege, the court must give the public entity an opportunity to show in camera facts relevant to determining whether this exception is met. The showing should ordinarily be made by affidavits, but the court may take testimony if it finds the matter cannot be satisfactorily resolved by affidavits.

(ii) No counsel or party may attend the in camera showing.

(iii) The court must seal and preserve for appeal evidence submitted under this subparagraph (2)(C). The evidence must not otherwise be revealed without the public entity's consent.

(3) *Legality of Obtaining Evidence.*

(A) ***Court May Order Disclosure.*** The court may order the public entity to disclose an informer's identity if:

(i) information from an informer is relied on to establish the legality of the means by which evidence was obtained; and

(ii) the court is not satisfied that the information was received from an informer reasonably believed to be reliable or credible.

(B) *Procedures.*

(i) On the public entity's request, the court must order the disclosure be made in camera.

(ii) No counsel or party may attend the in camera disclosure.

(iii) If the informer's identity is disclosed in camera, the court must seal and preserve for appeal the record of the in camera proceeding. The record of the in camera proceeding must not otherwise be revealed without the public entity's consent.

Eff. March 1, 1998. Amended by orders of Supreme Court March 10, 2015 and Court of Criminal Appeals March 12, 2015, eff. April 1, 2015.

Source: Proposed FRE 510 (1972) and Unif. R. Evid. 509 (1974).

See also **O'Connor's Texas Rules,** "Asserting privileges," ch. 6-A, §18.2; **O'Connor's Texas Rules,** "Scope of Discovery," ch. 6-B, §1 et seq.; Brown & Rondon, **Texas Rules of Evidence Handbook,** Rule 508.

ANNOTATIONS

In re Bates, 555 S.W.2d 420, 430 (Tex.1977). When the "role of the informer was very minor and occurred quite early in the [bribery] investigation; and absent other evidence concerning the relevance of the identity of the informer; the disclosure [of the informer's identity] is not required."

Warford v. Childers, 642 S.W.2d 63, 66-67 (Tex.App.—Amarillo 1982, no writ). The rule-blocking disclosure "is a recognition of the fact that most informants relay rumor, gossip and street talk of no evidentiary value and the exceptions [to the rule] are designed for the rare case where the informant can give eyewitness testimony about the alleged crime or arrest."

TRE 509. PHYSICIAN-PATIENT PRIVILEGE

(a) Definitions. In this rule:

(1) A "patient" is a person who consults or is seen by a physician for medical care.

(2) A "physician" is a person licensed, or who the patient reasonably believes is licensed, to practice medicine in any state or nation.

(3) A communication is "confidential" if not intended to be disclosed to third persons other than those:

(A) present to further the patient's interest in the consultation, examination, or interview;

(B) reasonably necessary to transmit the communication; or

(C) participating in the diagnosis and treatment under the physician's direction, including members of the patient's family.

(b) Limited Privilege in a Criminal Case. There is no physician-patient privilege in a criminal case. But a confidential communication is not admissible in a criminal case if made:

(1) to a person involved in the treatment of or examination for alcohol or drug abuse; and

(2) by a person being treated voluntarily or being examined for admission to treatment for alcohol or drug abuse.

(c) General Rule in a Civil Case. In a civil case, a patient has a privilege to refuse to disclose and to prevent any other person from disclosing:

(1) a confidential communication between a physician and the patient that relates to or was made in connection with any professional services the physician rendered the patient; and

(2) a record of the patient's identity, diagnosis, evaluation, or treatment created or maintained by a physician.

(d) Who May Claim in a Civil Case. The privilege may be claimed by:

(1) the patient; or

(2) the patient's representative on the patient's behalf.

The physician may claim the privilege on the patient's behalf—and is presumed to have authority to do so.

(e) Exceptions in a Civil Case. This privilege does not apply:

(1) ***Proceeding Against Physician.*** If the communication or record is relevant to a claim or defense in:

(A) a proceeding the patient brings against a physician; or

(B) a license revocation proceeding in which the patient is a complaining witness.

(2) ***Consent.*** If the patient or a person authorized to act on the patient's behalf consents in writing to the release of any privileged information, as provided in subdivision (f).

(3) ***Action to Collect.*** In an action to collect a claim for medical services rendered to the patient.

(4) ***Party Relies on Patient's Condition.*** If any party relies on the patient's physical, mental, or emotional condition as a part of the party's claim or defense and the communication or record is relevant to that condition.

(5) ***Disciplinary Investigation or Proceeding.*** In a disciplinary investigation of or proceeding against a physician under the Medical Practice Act, Tex. Occ. Code §164.001 et seq., or a registered nurse under Tex. Occ. Code §301.451 et seq. But the board conducting the investigation or proceeding must protect the identity of any patient whose medical records are examined unless:

(A) the patient's records would be subject to disclosure under paragraph (e)(1); or

(B) the patient has consented in writing to the release of medical records, as provided in subdivision (f).

(6) ***Involuntary Civil Commitment or Similar Proceeding.*** In a proceeding for involuntary civil commitment or court-ordered treatment, or a probable cause hearing under Tex. Health & Safety Code:

(A) chapter 462 (Treatment of Persons With Chemical Dependencies);

(B) title 7, subtitle C (Texas Mental Health Code); or

(C) title 7, subtitle D (Persons With an Intellectual Disability Act).

(7) ***Abuse or Neglect of "Institution" Resident.*** In a proceeding regarding the abuse or neglect, or the cause of any abuse or neglect, of a resident of an "institution" as defined in Tex. Health & Safety Code §242.002.

(f) Consent for Release of Privileged Information.

(1) Consent for the release of privileged information must be in writing and signed by:

(A) the patient;

(B) a parent or legal guardian if the patient is a minor;

(C) a legal guardian if the patient has been adjudicated incompetent to manage personal affairs;

(D) an attorney appointed for the patient under Tex. Health & Safety Code title 7, subtitles C and D;

(E) an attorney ad litem appointed for the patient under Tex. Estates Code title 3, subtitle C;

(F) an attorney ad litem or guardian ad litem appointed for a minor under Tex. Fam. Code chapter 107, subchapter B; or

(G) a personal representative if the patient is deceased.

(2) The consent must specify:

(A) the information or medical records covered by the release;

(B) the reasons or purposes for the release; and

(C) the person to whom the information is to be released.

(3) The patient, or other person authorized to consent, may withdraw consent to the release of any information. But a withdrawal of consent does not affect any information disclosed before the patient or authorized person gave written notice of the withdrawal.

(4) Any person who receives information privileged under this rule may disclose the information only to the extent consistent with the purposes specified in the consent.

Eff. March 1, 1998. Amended by orders of Supreme Court March 10, 2015 and Court of Criminal Appeals March 12, 2015, eff. April 1, 2015. Amended by order of Supreme Court June 14, 2016, eff. June 14, 2016.

Comment to 1998 change: This comment is intended to inform the construction and application of this rule. Prior Criminal Rules of Evidence 509 and 510 are now in subparagraph (b) of this Rule. This rule governs disclosures of patient-physician communications only in judicial or administrative proceedings. Whether a physician may or must disclose such communications in other circumstances is governed by Tex.Rev.Civ.Stat.Ann. art. 4495b, §5.08. Former subparagraph (d)(6) of the Civil Evidence Rules, regarding disclosures in a suit affecting the parent-child relationship, is omitted, not because there should be no exception to the privilege in suits affecting the parent-child relationship, but because the exception in such suits is properly considered under subparagraph (e)(4) of the new rule (formerly subparagraph (d)(4)), as construed in **R.K. v. Ramirez**, 887 S.W.2d 836 (Tex. 1994). In determining the proper application of an exception in such suits, the trial court must ensure that the precise need for the information is not outweighed by legitimate privacy interests protected by the privilege. Subparagraph (e) of the new rule does not except from the privilege information relating to a nonparty patient who is or may be a consulting or testifying expert in the suit.

Comment to 2015 Restyling: The physician-patient privilege in a civil case was first enacted in Texas in 1981 as part of the Medical Practice Act, formerly codified in Tex. Rev. Civ. Stat. art. 4495b. That statute provided that the privilege applied even if a patient had received a physician's services before the statute's enactment. Because more than thirty years have now passed, it is no longer necessary to burden the text of the rule with a statement regarding the privilege's retroactive application. But deleting this statement from the rule's text is not intended as a substantive change in the law.

The former rule's reference to "confidentiality or" and "administrative proceedings" in subdivision (e) [Exceptions in a Civil Case] has been deleted. First, this rule is a privilege rule only. Tex. Occ. Code §159.004 sets forth exceptions to a physician's duty to maintain confidentiality of patient information outside court and administrative proceedings. Second, by their own terms the rules of evidence govern only proceedings in Texas courts. See Rule 101(b). To the extent the rules apply in administrative proceedings, it is because the Administrative Procedure Act mandates their applicability. Tex. Gov't Code §2001.083 provides that "[i]n a contested case, a state agency shall give effect to the rules of privilege recognized by law." Section 2001.091 excludes privileged material from discovery in contested administrative cases.

Statutory references in the former rule that are no longer up-to-date have been revised. Finally, reconciling the provisions of Rule 509 with the parts of Tex. Occ. Code ch. 159 that address a physician-patient privilege applicable to court proceedings is beyond the scope of the restyling project.

See also **O'Connor's Texas Rules,** "Asserting privileges," ch. 6-A, §18.2; **O'Connor's Texas Rules,** "Scope of Discovery," ch. 6-B, §1 et seq.; **O'Connor's Texas Rules,** "Medical Records," ch. 6-J, §1 et seq.; Brown & Rondon, **Texas Rules of Evidence Handbook**, Rule 509; **O'Connor's Texas Forms,** FORM 5E:1.

ANNOTATIONS

R.K. v. Ramirez, 887 S.W.2d 836, 842 (Tex.1994). "[T]he patient-litigant exception to [TRE 509 and 510] privileges applies when a party's condition relates in a significant way to a party's claim or defense. *At 843 n.7:* Whether a condition is a part of a claim or defense should be determined on the face of the pleadings, without reference to the evidence that is allegedly privileged. *At 843:* [T]he exceptions to the medical and mental health privileges apply when (1) the records sought to be discovered are relevant to the condition at issue, and (2) the condition is relied upon as a part of a party's claim or defense, meaning that the condition itself is a fact that carries some legal significance."

Groves v. Gabriel, 874 S.W.2d 660, 661 (Tex.1994). "[A] trial court's order compelling release of medical records should be restrictively drawn so as to maintain the privilege with respect to records or communications not relevant to the underlying suit. The global release in this case does not meet the **Mutter** standard." *See also* **In re Collins**, 286 S.W.3d 911, 916 (Tex.2009).

Mutter v. Wood, 744 S.W.2d 600, 600 (Tex.1988). "There are . . . eight exceptions to the [physician-patient] privilege. *At 601:* In this case, the privilege was waived completely as to the defendant doctors and partially as to the treating doctors. To the extent, however, that the treating doctors had records or communications which were not relevant to the underlying suit, they remained privileged. . . ."

In re Toyota Motor Corp., 191 S.W.3d 498, 502 (Tex.App.—Waco 2006, orig. proceeding). "A claim for mental anguish or emotional distress will not, standing alone, make a plaintiff's mental or emotional condition a part of the plaintiff's claim. [T]he allegation in [P's] petition that he suffered 'emotional shock' is not a sufficient basis to make his mental or emotional condition an issue on which the jury will be required to make a factual determination. [¶] Therefore, [P's] communications . . . are protected by the physician-patient privilege."

In re Arriola, 159 S.W.3d 670, 675-76 (Tex.App.—Corpus Christi 2004, orig. proceeding). "[Ds] contend the abuse-and-neglect exceptions [to TRE 509 and 510] apply only to proceedings brought by appropriate law enforcement agencies. [¶] However, the abuse-and-neglect exceptions . . . contain no such limitation. [R]ules 509 and 510 state that the exceptions apply in administrative proceedings and civil proceedings in court. [¶] [Ds] contend numerous state statutes and administrative rules protect the records and medical information from disclosure. . . . [¶] However, each of the confidentiality and privilege provisions [Ds cite] contains an exception to nondisclosure where release of the information is required by law or ordered by the court. *At 677:* Here, the rules of evidence are the 'law' that requires release of the information."

In re Whiteley, 79 S.W.3d 729, 732-34 (Tex.App.—Corpus Christi 2002, orig. proceeding). D-doctor in medical-malpractice case triggered the TRE 509(e)(4) exception to physician-patient privilege when he testified in deposition that he successfully performed the same surgical procedure on nonparty patients; thus, nonparty patients' medical records became discoverable by P.

James v. Kloos, 75 S.W.3d 153, 160 (Tex.App.—Fort Worth 2002, no pet.). "[A] party can be prejudiced when his doctor meets with opposing counsel, but . . . such prejudice may not be severe enough to disallow the doctor's testimony. [P]rejudice due to an improper meeting does not necessarily mean prejudice at trial, and, therefore, does not mean that an improper verdict necessarily results when a doctor is allowed to testify after such a meeting. [T]here must be a showing that the ruling probably caused the rendition of an improper judgment." *See also* **Durst v. Hill Country Mem'l Hosp.**, 70 S.W.3d 233, 237 (Tex.App.—San Antonio 2001, no pet.).

TRE 510. MENTAL HEALTH INFORMATION PRIVILEGE IN CIVIL CASES

(a) Definitions. In this rule:

(1) A "professional" is a person:

(A) authorized to practice medicine in any state or nation;

(B) licensed or certified by the State of Texas in the diagnosis, evaluation, or treatment of any mental or emotional disorder;

(C) involved in the treatment or examination of drug abusers; or

(D) who the patient reasonably believes to be a professional under this rule.

(2) A "patient" is a person who:

(A) consults or is interviewed by a professional for diagnosis, evaluation, or treatment of any mental or emotional condition or disorder, including alcoholism and drug addiction; or

(B) is being treated voluntarily or being examined for admission to voluntary treatment for drug abuse.

(3) A "patient's representative" is:

(A) any person who has the patient's written consent;

(B) the parent of a minor patient;

(C) the guardian of a patient who has been adjudicated incompetent to manage personal affairs; or

(D) the personal representative of a deceased patient.

(4) A communication is "confidential" if not intended to be disclosed to third persons other than those:

(A) present to further the patient's interest in the diagnosis, examination, evaluation, or treatment;

(B) reasonably necessary to transmit the communication; or

(C) participating in the diagnosis, examination, evaluation, or treatment under the professional's direction, including members of the patient's family.

(b) General Rule; Disclosure.

(1) In a civil case, a patient has a privilege to refuse to disclose and to prevent any other person from disclosing:

(A) a confidential communication between the patient and a professional; and

(B) a record of the patient's identity, diagnosis, evaluation, or treatment that is created or maintained by a professional.

(2) In a civil case, any person—other than a patient's representative acting on the patient's behalf—who receives information privileged under this rule may disclose the information only to the extent consistent with the purposes for which it was obtained.

(c) Who May Claim. The privilege may be claimed by:

(1) the patient; or

(2) the patient's representative on the patient's behalf.

The professional may claim the privilege on the patient's behalf—and is presumed to have authority to do so.

(d) Exceptions. This privilege does not apply:

(1) ***Proceeding Against Professional.*** If the communication or record is relevant to a claim or defense in:

(A) a proceeding the patient brings against a professional; or

(B) a license revocation proceeding in which the patient is a complaining witness.

(2) ***Written Waiver.*** If the patient or a person authorized to act on the patient's behalf waives the privilege in writing.

(3) ***Action to Collect.*** In an action to collect a claim for mental or emotional health services rendered to the patient.

(4) ***Communication Made in Court-Ordered Examination.*** To a communication the patient made to a professional during a court-ordered examination relating to the patient's mental or emotional condition or disorder if:

(A) the patient made the communication after being informed that it would not be privileged;

(B) the communication is offered to prove an issue involving the patient's mental or emotional health; and

(C) the court imposes appropriate safeguards against unauthorized disclosure.

(5) ***Party Relies on Patient's Condition.*** If any party relies on the patient's physical, mental, or emotional condition as a part of the party's claim or defense and the communication or record is relevant to that condition.

(6) ***Abuse or Neglect of "Institution" Resident.*** In a proceeding regarding the abuse or neglect, or the cause of any abuse or neglect, of a resident of an "institution" as defined in Tex. Health & Safety Code §242.002.

Eff. March 1, 1998. Amended by orders of Supreme Court March 10, 2015 and Court of Criminal Appeals March 12, 2015, eff. April 1, 2015. Amended by Supreme Court order of June 14, 2016, eff. June 14, 2016.

Comment to 1998 change: This comment is intended to inform the construction and application of this rule. This rule governs disclosures of patient-professional communications only in judicial or administrative proceedings. Whether a professional may or must disclose such communications in other circumstances is governed by Tex. Health & Safety Code §§611.001 to 611.008. Former subparagraph (d)(6) of the Civil Evidence Rules, regarding disclosures in a suit affecting the parent-child relationship, is omitted, not because there should be no exception to the privilege in suits affecting the parent-child relationship, but because the exception in such suits is properly considered under subparagraph (d)(5), as construed in R.K. v. Ramirez, 887 S.W.2d 836 (Tex. 1994). In determining the proper application of an exception in such suits, the trial court must ensure that the precise need for the information is not outweighed by legitimate privacy interests protected by the privilege. Subparagraph (d) does not except from the privilege information relating to a nonparty patient who is or may be a consulting or testifying expert in the suit.

Comment to 2015 Restyling: The mental-health-information privilege in civil cases was enacted in Texas in 1979. Tex. Rev. Civ. Stat. art. 5561h (later codified at Tex. Health & Safety Code §611.001 et seq.) provided that the privilege applied even if the patient had received the professional's services before the statute's enactment. Because more than thirty years have now passed, it is no longer necessary to burden the text of the rule with a statement regarding the privilege's retroactive application. But deleting this statement from the rule's text is not intended as a substantive change in the law.

Tex. Health & Safety Code ch. 611 addresses confidentiality rules for communications between a patient and a mental-health professional and for the professional's treatment records. Many of these provisions apply in contexts other than court proceedings. Reconciling the provisions of Rule 510 with the parts of chapter 611 that address a mental-health-information privilege applicable to court proceedings is beyond the scope of the restyling project.

See also **O'Connor's Texas Rules,** "Asserting privileges," ch. 6-A, §18.2; **O'Connor's Texas Rules,** "Scope of Discovery," ch. 6-B, §1 et seq.; **O'Connor's Texas Rules,** "Medical Records," ch. 6-J, §1 et seq.; Brown & Rondon, **Texas Rules of Evidence Handbook**, Rule 510; **O'Connor's Texas Forms,** FORM 5E:1.

ANNOTATIONS

R.K. v. Ramirez, 887 S.W.2d 836, 843 (Tex.1994). "As a general rule, a mental condition will be a 'part' of a claim or defense if the pleadings indicate that the jury must make a factual determination concerning the condition itself."

Groves v. Gabriel, 874 S.W.2d 660, 661 (Tex.1994). "Because [P] alleges severe emotional damages, including 'post-traumatic stress disorder,' [she] waived the privilege as to any medical records relevant to her claim for emotional damages." *See also* **Ginsberg v. Fifth Ct. of Appeals**, 686 S.W.2d 105, 107 (Tex.1985).

In re Arriola, 159 S.W.3d 670, 675-76 (Tex.App.—Corpus Christi 2004, orig. proceeding). See annotation under TRE 509.

TRE 511. WAIVER BY VOLUNTARY DISCLOSURE

(a) General Rule.

A person upon whom these rules confer a privilege against disclosure waives the privilege if:

(1) the person or a predecessor of the person while holder of the privilege voluntarily discloses or consents to disclosure of any significant part of the privileged matter unless such disclosure itself is privileged; or

(2) the person or a representative of the person calls a person to whom privileged communications have been made to testify as to the person's character or character trait insofar as such communications are relevant to such character or character trait.

(b) Lawyer-Client Privilege and Work Product; Limitations on Waiver.

Notwithstanding paragraph (a), the following provisions apply, in the circumstances set out, to disclosure of a communication or information covered by the lawyer-client privilege or work-product protection.

(1) ***Disclosure Made in a Federal or State Proceeding or to a Federal or State Office or Agency; Scope of a Waiver.*** When the disclosure is made in a federal proceeding or state proceeding of any state or to a federal office or agency or state office or agency of any state and waives the lawyer-client privilege or work-product protection, the waiver extends to an undisclosed communication or information only if:

(A) the waiver is intentional;

(B) the disclosed and undisclosed communications or information concern the same subject matter; and

(C) they ought in fairness to be considered together.

(2) ***Inadvertent Disclosure in State Civil Proceedings.*** When made in a Texas state proceeding, an inadvertent disclosure does not operate as a waiver if the holder followed the procedures of Rule of Civil Procedure 193.3(d).

(3) ***Controlling Effect of a Court Order.*** A disclosure made in litigation pending before a federal court or a state court of any state that has entered an order that the privilege or protection is not waived by disclosure connected with the litigation pending before that court is also not a waiver in a Texas state proceeding.

(4) ***Controlling Effect of a Party Agreement.*** An agreement on the effect of disclosure in a state proceeding of any state is binding only on the parties to the agreement, unless it is incorporated into a court order.

Eff. March 1, 1998. Amended by orders of Supreme Court March 10, 2015 and Court of Criminal Appeals March 12, 2015, eff. April 1, 2015.

Comment to 2015 Restyling: The amendments to Rule 511 are designed to align Texas law with federal law on waiver of privilege by voluntary disclosure. Subsection (a) sets forth the general rule. Subsection (b) incorporates the provisions of Federal Rule of Evidence 502. Like the federal rule, subsection (b) only addresses disclosure of communications or information covered by the lawyer-client privilege or work-product protection. These amendments do not affect the law governing waiver of other privileges or protections.

See also **O'Connor's Texas Rules,** "Waiver of objections & privileges," ch. 6-A, §25.3; Brown & Rondon, **Texas Rules of Evidence Handbook**, Rule 511; **O'Connor's Texas Forms,** FORM 6A:23.

ANNOTATIONS

In re Bexar Cty. Crim. Dist. Atty's Office, 224 S.W.3d 182, 189 (Tex.2007). "Although the DA's Office turned over its prosecution file without objection, which waived the work-product privilege as to the file's contents, the record is devoid of any indication that by doing so the DA likewise

enlisted its current and former personnel to testify in [P's] suit regarding their case materials and related impressions and communications. The DA's waiver here is limited, not limitless, and agreeing to produce a prosecution file does not in itself require the DA to produce its personnel so that their mental processes and related case preparation may be further probed."

In re Ford Motor Co., 211 S.W.3d 295, 301 (Tex.2006). "The privilege to maintain a document's confidentiality belongs to the document owner, not to the trial court. . . . Mistaken document production by a court employee in violation of a court-signed protective order cannot constitute a party's voluntary waiver of confidentiality. . . . No matter how many people eventually [see] the materials, disclosures by a third-party, whether mistaken or malevolent, do not waive the privileged nature of the information. This principle should apply with particular force when documents are entrusted to a court."

Jordan v. Fourth Ct. of Appeals, 701 S.W.2d 644, 649 (Tex.1985). "If the matter for which a privilege is sought has been disclosed to a third party, thus raising the question of waiver of the privilege, the party asserting the privilege has the burden of proving that no waiver has occurred." *See also* **In re E.C.**, 444 S.W.3d 760, 768 (Tex.App.—Fort Worth 2014, orig. proceeding).

In re Hicks, 252 S.W.3d 790, 794 (Tex.App.—Houston [14th Dist.] 2008, orig. proceeding). "An assignment of rights and claims does not automatically include a waiver of attorney-client privilege unless specifically stated in the language of the assignment." *See also* **In re General Agents Ins. Co.**, 224 S.W.3d 806, 814 (Tex.App.—Houston [14th Dist.] 2007, orig. proceeding).

TRE 512. PRIVILEGED MATTER DISCLOSED UNDER COMPULSION OR WITHOUT OPPORTUNITY TO CLAIM PRIVILEGE

A privilege claim is not defeated by a disclosure that was:

(a) compelled erroneously; or

(b) made without opportunity to claim the privilege.

Eff. March 1, 1998. Amended by orders of Supreme Court March 10, 2015 and Court of Criminal Appeals March 12, 2015, eff. April 1, 2015.

Source: Unif. R. Evid. 511 (1980).

See also Brown & Rondon, **Texas Rules of Evidence Handbook**, Rule 512.

ANNOTATIONS

In re Office of the Atty. Gen., No. 02-13-00455-CV, 2014 WL 491684 (Tex.App.—Fort Worth 2014, orig. proceeding) (memo op.; 2-6-14). "We have found no support for the trial court's reasoning that because a right *may* be waived, the trial court can *make* the party waive it. [O]nly the holder of the privilege has the power to waive it. To allow a court to compel waiver would render any privilege . . . vulnerable to forced waiver. [¶] [E]ven when a court can compel a party to produce privileged documents, it cannot waive the party's claim of privilege."

TRE 513. COMMENT ON OR INFERENCE FROM A PRIVILEGE CLAIM; INSTRUCTION

(a) Comment or Inference Not Permitted. Except as permitted in Rule 504(b)(2), neither the court nor counsel may comment on a privilege claim—whether made in the present proceeding or previously—and the factfinder may not draw an inference from the claim.

(b) Claiming Privilege Without the Jury's Knowledge. To the extent practicable, the court must conduct a jury trial so that the making of a privilege claim is not suggested to the jury by any means.

(c) Claim of Privilege Against Self-Incrimination in a Civil Case. Subdivisions (a) and (b) do not apply to a party's claim, in the present civil case, of the privilege against self-incrimination.

(d) Jury Instruction. When this rule forbids a jury from drawing an inference from a privilege claim, the court must, on request of a party against whom the jury might draw the inference, instruct the jury accordingly.

Eff. March 1, 1998. Amended by orders of Supreme Court March 10, 2015 and Court of Criminal Appeals March 12, 2015, eff. April 1, 2015.

Comment to 1998 change. Subdivision (d) regarding a party's entitlement to a jury instruction about a claim of privilege is made applicable to civil cases.

See also Brown & Rondon, **Texas Rules of Evidence Handbook**, Rule 513; **O'Connor's Texas Forms**, FORM 5E:1

ANNOTATIONS

Texas DPS Officers Ass'n v. Denton, 897 S.W.2d 757, 760 (Tex.1995). "[J]uries in civil cases [may] make negative inferences based upon the assertion of the privilege [against self-incrimination]. Also, when a plaintiff invokes the privilege, . . . the trial court can subsequently prohibit the plaintiff from introducing evidence on the subject, and such an act of judicial discretion does not constitute penalizing the plaintiff's use of the privilege." *See also* **Matbon, Inc. v. Gries**, 288 S.W.3d 471, 489-90 (Tex.App.—Eastland 2009, no pet.) (negative inference that jury may have drawn cannot rise beyond mere suspicion and cannot be considered as evidence at all, particularly under a clear-and-convincing-evidence standard); **In re Moore**, 153 S.W.3d 527, 534 (Tex.App.—Tyler 2004, orig. proceeding) (when two equally consistent inferences can be made from an assertion of the Fifth Amendment so that neither inference is more probable than the other, neither inference can be made).

In re Edge Capital Grp., 161 S.W.3d 764, 769-70 (Tex.App.—Beaumont 2005, orig. proceeding). "[W]hen a

witness invokes the Fifth Amendment in response to inquiries, '[t]he judge is entitled to determine whether the refusal to answer appears to be based upon the good faith of the witness and is justifiable under all of the circumstances.' A motion for protection should not be filed solely to avoid the assertion of the Fifth Amendment privilege in a civil case."

Wil-Roye Inv. II v. Washington Mut. Bank, 142 S.W.3d 393, 404 (Tex.App.—El Paso 2004, no pet.). "Whether [TRE] 513(c) applies to a claim of privilege by a party's agent is one of first impression in Texas. Rule 513(c) provides that Rule 513(a)'s prohibition against adverse inferences shall not apply with respect to a party's exercise of the privilege against self-incrimination, but it does not define what constitutes a party's claim . . . of privilege. . . . While it [appears] that Rule 513(c) would not apply to a non-party witness's assertion of the privilege, . . . an analogy can be drawn between admissions by an agent under [TRE] 801(e)(2) and the silence of an agent or person in some other type of special relationship with a party. *At 406-07:* [W]e conclude that the rationale for allowing introduction of an agent's admissions against the principal under [TRE 801(e)(2)(D)] also justifies admission of evidence showing that the agent/witness has exercised his Fifth Amendment privilege at least where the questions substantially relate to a party's claim or defense." (Internal quotes omitted.)

In re L.S., 748 S.W.2d 571, 575 (Tex.App.—Amarillo 1988, writ denied). TRE 513(b) "reflects a desire to protect the parties from any adverse inference drawn by the jurors who witness the invocation of the privilege against self-incrimination. 'It is reasonable to anticipate that in most instances, planned reliance upon the privilege will be known in advance and the mandate of rule 513(b) can be implemented through the use of motions in limine.'"

Article VI. Witnesses

TRE 601. COMPETENCY TO TESTIFY IN GENERAL; "DEAD MAN'S RULE"

(a) In General. Every person is competent to be a witness unless these rules provide otherwise. The following witnesses are incompetent:

(1) ***Insane Persons.*** A person who is now insane or was insane at the time of the events about which the person is called to testify.

(2) ***Persons Lacking Sufficient Intellect.*** A child—or any other person—whom the court examines and finds lacks sufficient intellect to testify concerning the matters in issue.

(b) The "Dead Man's Rule."

(1) ***Applicability.*** The "Dead Man's Rule" applies only in a civil case:

(A) by or against a party in the party's capacity as an executor, administrator, or guardian; or

(B) by or against a decedent's heirs or legal representatives and based in whole or in part on the decedent's oral statement.

(2) ***General Rule.*** In cases described in subparagraph (b)(1)(A), a party may not testify against another party about an oral statement by the testator, intestate, or ward. In cases described in subparagraph (b)(1)(B), a party may not testify against another party about an oral statement by the decedent.

(3) ***Exceptions.*** A party may testify against another party about an oral statement by the testator, intestate, ward, or decedent if:

(A) the party's testimony about the statement is corroborated; or

(B) the opposing party calls the party to testify at the trial about the statement.

(4) ***Instructions.*** If a court excludes evidence under paragraph (b)(2), the court must instruct the jury that the law prohibits a party from testifying about an oral statement by the testator, intestate, ward, or decedent unless the oral statement is corroborated or the opposing party calls the party to testify at the trial about the statement.

Eff. March 1, 1998. Amended by orders of Supreme Court March 10, 2015 and Court of Criminal Appeals March 12, 2015, eff. April 1, 2015.

Comment to 2015 Restyling: The text of the "Dead Man's Rule" has been streamlined to clarify its meaning without making any substantive changes. The text of former Rule 601(b) (as well as its statutory predecessor, Vernon's Ann. Civ. St. art. 3716) prohibits only a "party" from testifying about the dead man's statements. Despite this, the last sentence of former Rule 601(b) requires the court to instruct the jury when the rule "prohibits an interested party or witness" from testifying. Because the rule prohibits only a "party" from testifying, restyled Rule 601(b)(4) references only "a party," and not "an interested party or witness." To be sure, courts have indicated that the rule (or its statutory predecessor) may be applicable to a witness who is not nominally a party and inapplicable to a witness who is only nominally a party. *See, e.g.,* **Chandler v. Welborn**, 294 S.W.2d 801, 809 (Tex. 1956); **Ragsdale v. Ragsdale**, 179 S.W.2d 291, 295 (Tex. 1944). But these decisions are based on an interpretation of the meaning of "party." Therefore, limiting the court's instruction under restyled Rule 601(b)(4) to "a party" does not change Texas practice. In addition, restyled Rule 601(b) deletes the sentence in former Rule 601(b) that states "[e]xcept for the foregoing, a witness is not precluded from giving evidence . . . because the witness is a party to the action. . ." This sentence is surplusage. Rule 601(b) is a rule of exclusion. If the testimony falls outside the rule of exclusion, its admissibility will be determined by other applicable rules of evidence.

See also Brown & Rondon, **Texas Rules of Evidence Handbook**, Rule 601; **O'Connor's Texas Forms**, FORM 5E:1.

ANNOTATIONS

Pipkin v. Kroger Tex., L.P., 383 S.W.3d 655, 668 (Tex.App.—Houston [14th Dist.] 2012, pet. denied). "[U]nder Rule 601, a child is considered competent to testify unless, after the child is examined by the court, it appears to the

court that the child does not possess sufficient intellect to relate transactions about which he will testify. There is no age below which a child is automatically deemed incompetent to testify. When a trial court determines whether a child is competent to testify at trial, it considers (1) the competence of the child to observe intelligently the events in question at the time of the occurrence; (2) the child's capacity to recollect the events; and (3) the child's capacity to narrate the facts."

In re R.M.T., 352 S.W.3d 12, 25 (Tex.App.—Texarkana 2011, no pet.). "[T]o demonstrate incompetency under Rule 601, it must be shown that the witness lacked the ability to perceive the relevant events, recall and narrate those events at the time of trial, or that the witness lacked the capacity to understand the obligation of the oath."

Fraga v. Drake, 276 S.W.3d 55, 61 (Tex.App.—El Paso 2008, no pet.). "[C]ourts construe the Dead Man's Rule narrowly. [TRE 601(b)] does not prohibit testimony concerning statements by the deceased that are properly corroborated. Corroborating evidence must tend to support some of the material allegations or issues that are raised by the pleadings and testified to by the witness whose evidence is sought to be corroborated. It may come from any other competent witness or other legal source, including documentary evidence. Corroborating evidence . . . must tend to confirm and strengthen the testimony of the witness and show the probability of its truth. For example, it is sufficient if the corroborating evidence shows conduct by the deceased that is generally consistent with the testimony concerning the deceased's statements."

TRE 602. NEED FOR PERSONAL KNOWLEDGE

A witness may testify to a matter only if evidence is introduced sufficient to support a finding that the witness has personal knowledge of the matter. Evidence to prove personal knowledge may consist of the witness's own testimony. This rule does not apply to a witness's expert testimony under Rule 703.

Eff. March 1, 1998. Amended by orders of Supreme Court March 10, 2015 and Court of Criminal Appeals March 12, 2015, eff. April 1, 2015.

Source: FRE 602.

See also **O'Connor's Texas Rules,** "Introducing Evidence," ch. 8-C, §1 et seq.; **O'Connor's Texas Rules,** "Objecting to Evidence," ch. 8-D, §1 et seq.; Brown & Rondon, **Texas Rules of Evidence Handbook**, Rule 602.

ANNOTATIONS

Anderson Prod'g Inc. v. Koch Oil Co., 929 S.W.2d 416, 425 (Tex.1996). "[D] argues that the trial court erred [because P's attorney] failed to demonstrate personal knowledge supporting the testimony. The record reflects that [P's attorney's] testimony was based on his review of the documents executed by [D], and that [D] had ample opportunity to cross-examine [him] regarding the basis of his conclusion. Under these circumstances, the trial court did not abuse its discretion in failing to strike the testimony." *See also* **Marks v. St. Luke's Episcopal Hosp.**, 319 S.W.3d 658, 666 (Tex.2010) (affidavits based on supposition are legally insufficient).

In re Valliance Bank, 422 S.W.3d 722, 726 n.1 (Tex.App.—Fort Worth 2012, orig. proceeding). "Verification must be based on personal knowledge. A party's attorney may verify the pleading when he has personal knowledge of the facts, but he does not have authority to verify based merely on his status as counsel."

TRE 603. OATH OR AFFIRMATION TO TESTIFY TRUTHFULLY

Before testifying, a witness must give an oath or affirmation to testify truthfully. It must be in a form designed to impress that duty on the witness's conscience.

Eff. March 1, 1998. Amended by orders of Supreme Court March 10, 2015 and Court of Criminal Appeals March 12, 2015, eff. April 1, 2015.

See also Brown & Rondon, **Texas Rules of Evidence Handbook**, Rule 603.

ANNOTATIONS

Glenn v. C&G Elec., Inc., 977 S.W.2d 686, 689 (Tex.App.—Fort Worth 1998, pet. denied). The "requirement [to testify truthfully under oath] applies not only to those who will testify in person in the courtroom, but also to those whose testimony at the trial will be presented by deposition."

TRE 604. INTERPRETER

An interpreter must be qualified and must give an oath or affirmation to make a true translation.

Eff. March 1, 1998. Amended by orders of Supreme Court March 10, 2015 and Court of Criminal Appeals March 12, 2015, eff. April 1, 2015.

See also TRCP 183 (appointment and compensation of interpreters); Brown & Rondon, **Texas Rules of Evidence Handbook**, Rule 604.

ANNOTATIONS

International Commercial Bank v. Hall-Fuston Corp., 767 S.W.2d 259, 261 (Tex.App.—Beaumont 1989, writ denied). When a foreign company attempts to introduce into evidence business records that are not written in English, one of its corporate representatives can orally interpret the documents under oath after being qualified as an expert.

TRE 605. JUDGE'S COMPETENCY AS A WITNESS

The presiding judge may not testify as a witness at the trial. A party need not object to preserve the issue.

Eff. March 1, 1998. Amended by orders of Supreme Court March 10, 2015 and Court of Criminal Appeals March 12, 2015, eff. April 1, 2015.

Source: FRE 605.

See also Brown & Rondon, **Texas Rules of Evidence Handbook**, Rule 605.

ANNOTATIONS

In re M.S., 115 S.W.3d 534, 538 (Tex.2003). "A judge's findings of fact are not technically the same as testimony. . . . In this case, the orders submitted into evidence, containing findings based on pretrial evidence by the very judge presiding over the termination proceeding, could be, like a judicial comment on the weight of the evidence, a form of judicial influence no less proscribed than judicial testimony. [T]he jury was permitted to see findings of fact made by the very judge presiding over the trial, and those facts were the very ones that the jury itself was being asked to find. The fact-finding present in the orders admitted as evidence comes far too close to 'indicat[ing] the opinion of the trial judge as to the verity or accuracy of the facts in inquiry'. . . .." *See also* **In re A.T.K.**, No. 02-11-00520-CV, 2012 WL 4450361 (Tex.App.—Fort Worth 2012, no pet.) (memo op.; 9-27-12).

In re C.C.K., No. 02-12-00347-CV, 2013 WL 452163 (Tex.App.—Fort Worth 2013, no pet.) (memo op.; 2-7-13). "'The question should be whether the judge's statement of fact is essential to the exercise of some judicial function or is the functional equivalent of witness testimony.' [¶] Here, the trial judge's statement did not convey factual information not in evidence. Nor did the trial judge's statement seek to rebut any evidence adduced at trial. Instead, the trial judge's statement told the jurors what they would be asked to decide and was akin to a preview of the jury instructions that would be given at the conclusion of the trial. . . . The trial judge's instruction was not 'the functional equivalent of witness testimony,' nor did it 'convey factual information not in evidence.' The trial judge thus did not testify."

Triumph Trucking, Inc. v. Southern Corporate Ins. Managers, Inc., 226 S.W.3d 466, 472 (Tex.App.—Houston [1st Dist.] 2006, pet. denied). TRE 605 "prohibit[s] not only a judge's direct testimony, but also 'the functional equivalent of witness testimony.' [¶] [T]he documents to which [P] objected were [P's] application for turnover [of impleaded funds] and an unsigned order prepared by [P] for the judge's signature. [N]either of these documents was the functional equivalent of testimony by the judge. . . ."

O'Quinn v. Hall, 77 S.W.3d 438, 448 (Tex.App.—Corpus Christi 2002, no pet.). "Rule 605 applies not only to members of the judiciary, 'but also to those performing judicial functions that conflict with a witness's role.'"

TRE 606. JUROR'S COMPETENCY AS A WITNESS

(a) At the Trial. A juror may not testify as a witness before the other jurors at the trial. If a juror is called to testify, the court must give a party an opportunity to object outside the jury's presence.

(b) During an Inquiry into the Validity of a Verdict or Indictment.

(1) ***Prohibited Testimony or Other Evidence.*** During an inquiry into the validity of a verdict or indictment, a juror may not testify about any statement made or incident that occurred during the jury's deliberations; the effect of anything on that juror's or another juror's vote; or any juror's mental processes concerning the verdict or indictment. The court may not receive a juror's affidavit or evidence of a juror's statement on these matters.

(2) ***Exceptions.*** A juror may testify:

(A) about whether an outside influence was improperly brought to bear on any juror; or

(B) to rebut a claim that the juror was not qualified to serve.

Eff. March 1, 1998. Amended by orders of Supreme Court March 10, 2015 and Court of Criminal Appeals March 12, 2015, eff. April 1, 2015.

See also TRCP 327(b); **O'Connor's Texas Rules,** "MNT based on jury or bailiff misconduct," ch. 10-B, §14; Brown & Rondon, **Texas Rules of Evidence Handbook**, Rule 606.

ANNOTATIONS

Golden Eagle Archery, Inc. v. Jackson, 24 S.W.3d 362, 371 (Tex.2000). An "alleged conversation between [jurors] during a trial break . . . should not be considered 'deliberations' and therefore barred by [TRE] 606(b) [now TRE 606(b)(1)] and [TRCP] 327(b). [The TRCPs] use the term 'deliberations' as meaning formal jury deliberations—when the jury weighs the evidence to arrive at a verdict."

Rosell v. Central W. Motor Stages, Inc., 89 S.W.3d 643, 661 (Tex.App.—Dallas 2002, pet. denied). "The essence of the 'outside influence' rule is to prevent outside information that affects the merits of the case from reaching the jury. The only evidence here is that the jury was told that they probably would be required to deliberate another day. . . . Thus, the bailiff informing the jury of the court's schedule was not misconduct. Further, the juror testimony that jurors traded answers on issues is testimony about deliberations and is not evidence of outside influences."

Perry v. Safeco Ins., 821 S.W.2d 279, 281 (Tex.App.—Houston [1st Dist.] 1991, writ denied). "[T]he coercive influence of one juror upon the rest of the panel is not 'outside influence.' Proof of coercive statements and their effect on the jury is barred by the [TREs]."

TRE 607. WHO MAY IMPEACH A WITNESS

Any party, including the party that called the witness, may attack the witness's credibility.

Eff. March 1, 1998. Amended by orders of Supreme Court March 10, 2015 and Court of Criminal Appeals March 12, 2015, eff. April 1, 2015.

Source: FRE 607.

See also **O'Connor's Texas Rules,** "Impeaching a witness," ch. 8-C, §6; Brown & Rondon, **Texas Rules of Evidence Handbook**, Rule 607.

TRE 608. A WITNESS'S CHARACTER FOR TRUTHFULNESS OR UNTRUTHFULNESS

(a) Reputation or Opinion Evidence. A witness's credibility may be attacked or supported by testimony about the witness's reputation for having a character for truthfulness or untruthfulness, or by testimony in the form of an opinion about that character. But evidence of truthful character is admissible only after the witness's character for truthfulness has been attacked.

(b) Specific Instances of Conduct. Except for a criminal conviction under Rule 609, a party may not inquire into or offer extrinsic evidence to prove specific instances of the witness's conduct in order to attack or support the witness's character for truthfulness.

Eff. March 1, 1998. Amended by orders of Supreme Court March 10, 2015 and Court of Criminal Appeals March 12, 2015, eff. April 1, 2015.

See also **O'Connor's Texas Rules,** "Rehabilitating a witness," ch. 8-C, §7; Brown & Rondon, **Texas Rules of Evidence Handbook**, Rule 608; **O'Connor's Texas Forms,** FORM 5E:1.

ANNOTATIONS

Commerce & Indus. Ins. v. Ferguson-Stewart, 339 S.W.3d 744, 747 (Tex.App.—Houston [1st Dist.] 2011, no pet.). "Texas courts have consistently upheld the exclusion of evidence of a witness's prior drug use for general impeachment purposes."

TRE 609. IMPEACHMENT BY EVIDENCE OF A CRIMINAL CONVICTION

(a) In General. Evidence of a criminal conviction offered to attack a witness's character for truthfulness must be admitted if:

(1) the crime was a felony or involved moral turpitude, regardless of punishment;

(2) the probative value of the evidence outweighs its prejudicial effect to a party; and

(3) it is elicited from the witness or established by public record.

(b) Limit on Using the Evidence After 10 Years. This subdivision (b) applies if more than 10 years have passed since the witness's conviction or release from confinement for it, whichever is later. Evidence of the conviction is admissible only if its probative value, supported by specific facts and circumstances, substantially outweighs its prejudicial effect.

(c) Effect of a Pardon, Annulment, or Certificate of Rehabilitation. Evidence of a conviction is not admissible if:

(1) the conviction has been the subject of a pardon, annulment, certificate of rehabilitation, or other equivalent procedure based on a finding that the person has been rehabilitated, and the person has not been convicted of a later crime that was classified as a felony or involved moral turpitude, regardless of punishment;

(2) probation has been satisfactorily completed for the conviction, and the person has not been convicted of a later crime that was classified as a felony or involved moral turpitude, regardless of punishment; or

(3) the conviction has been the subject of a pardon, annulment, or other equivalent procedure based on a finding of innocence.

(d) Juvenile Adjudications. Evidence of a juvenile adjudication is admissible under this rule only if:

(1) the witness is a party in a proceeding conducted under title 3 of the Texas Family Code; or

(2) the United States or Texas Constitution requires that it be admitted.

(e) Pendency of an Appeal. A conviction for which an appeal is pending is not admissible under this rule.

(f) Notice. Evidence of a witness's conviction is not admissible under this rule if, after receiving from the adverse party a timely written request specifying the witness, the proponent of the conviction fails to provide sufficient written notice of intent to use the conviction. Notice is sufficient if it provides a fair opportunity to contest the use of such evidence.

Eff. March 1, 1998. Amended by orders of Supreme Court March 10, 2015 and Court of Criminal Appeals March 12, 2015, eff. April 1, 2015.

Source: FRE 609.

See also **O'Connor's Texas Rules,** "Impeaching by conviction," ch. 8-C, §6.4; Brown & Rondon, **Texas Rules of Evidence Handbook**, Rule 609; **O'Connor's Texas Forms,** FORM 5E:1.

ANNOTATIONS

Cortez v. Wyche, No. 02-11-00364-CV, 2012 WL 1555909 (Tex.App.—Fort Worth 2012, no pet.) (memo op.; 5-3-12). "In **Theus [v. State**, 845 S.W.2d 874 (Tex.Crim.App.1992)], the court of criminal appeals set out a nonexclusive list of factors to be considered in weighing the probative value of a conviction against its prejudicial effect under rule 609(a), including: (1) the impeachment

value of the prior crime; (2) the temporal proximity of the past crime relative to the charged offense and the witness's subsequent history; (3) the similarity between the past crime and the offense being prosecuted; (4) the importance of the defendant's testimony; and (5) the importance of the credibility issue. [¶] [As] to the first factor, if the crime involves deception, it has a higher impeachment value. The second weighs in favor of admission if the past crime is recent and the witness has shown a 'propensity for running afoul of the law.' With regard to the third factor, . . . 'in a civil case, if conduct is in issue that is similar to a past crime, then the third factor should weigh against admission.' As to the intertwined last factors, 'in a civil case, as the importance of a particular witness's testimony and credibility increases, so does the need to allow impeachment of that witness with evidence of a criminal conviction.'" *See also* **Porter v. Nemir**, 900 S.W.2d 376, 382 (Tex.App.—Austin 1995, no writ).

Taylor v. TDPRS, 160 S.W.3d 641, 653 (Tex.App.—Austin 2005, pet. denied). "[R]ule 609 is not a categorical limitation on the introduction of convictions for any purpose. Rather, it applies only to convictions offered for purposes of impeachment. Here, [P] offered [D's] convictions not solely to impeach her credibility but as relevant evidence going to the controlling issue in her case—the best interests of [child]."

U.S.A. Precision Mach. Co. v. Marshall, 95 S.W.3d 407, 410 (Tex.App.—Houston [1st Dist.] 2002, pet. denied). Held: A conviction is not final for purposes of impeachment under TRE 609 if it was reversed, it is pending on appeal, or the case was dismissed after a new trial was granted.

TRE 610. RELIGIOUS BELIEFS OR OPINIONS

Evidence of a witness's religious beliefs or opinions is not admissible to attack or support the witness's credibility.

Eff. March 1, 1998. Amended by orders of Supreme Court March 10, 2015 and Court of Criminal Appeals March 12, 2015, eff. April 1, 2015.

Comment to 1998 change: This is prior Rule of Criminal Evidence 615.

See also Brown & Rondon, **Texas Rules of Evidence Handbook**, Rule 610; **O'Connor's Texas Forms**, FORM 5E:1.

TRE 611. MODE AND ORDER OF EXAMINING WITNESSES AND PRESENTING EVIDENCE

(a) Control by the Court; Purposes. The court should exercise reasonable control over the mode and order of examining witnesses and presenting evidence so as to:

(1) make those procedures effective for determining the truth;

(2) avoid wasting time; and

(3) protect witnesses from harassment or undue embarrassment.

(b) Scope of Cross-Examination. A witness may be cross-examined on any relevant matter, including credibility.

(c) Leading Questions. Leading questions should not be used on direct examination except as necessary to develop the witness's testimony. Ordinarily, the court should allow leading questions:

(1) on cross-examination; and

(2) when a party calls a hostile witness, an adverse party, or a witness identified with an adverse party.

Eff. March 1, 1998. Amended by orders of Supreme Court March 10, 2015 and Court of Criminal Appeals March 12, 2015, eff. April 1, 2015.

See also **O'Connor's Texas Rules**, "Scope of examination," ch. 8-C, §4; Brown & Rondon, **Texas Rules of Evidence Handbook**, Rule 611.

ANNOTATIONS

State v. Gaylor Inv. Trust Prtshp., 322 S.W.3d 814, 819 (Tex.App.—Houston [14th Dist.] 2010, no pet.). "Every trial court has the inherent power to control the disposition of the cases on its docket with economy of time and effort for itself, for counsel, and for litigants. . . . The trial court's inherent power, together with applicable rules of procedure and evidence, accord trial courts broad, but not unfettered, discretion in handling trials." (Internal quotes omitted.)

Torres v. Danny's Serv. Co., 266 S.W.3d 485, 487 (Tex.App.—Eastland 2008, pet. denied). "[A] witness may be cross-examined on any issue that is probative of her credibility. [¶] Texas courts have not adopted hard and fast rules for determining whether a witness's mental health history is relevant to a credibility analysis, choosing instead to consider this evidence on an ad hoc basis. *At 488:* Because Texas follows an ad hoc approach, trial courts have broad discretion. If mental health evidence is admissible for impeachment, the trial court also has considerable discretion to limit the scope of any cross-examination. But the trial court's discretion is not limitless. The mere fact that the witness has suffered from, or received treatment for, a mental illness or disturbance is insufficient to justify its admission. The trial court must have some evidence that the illness is such that 'it might tend to reflect upon the witness's credibility.' This evidence can take many forms, but it must show that the witness's perception of events was affected or that the witness was otherwise impaired."

State Office of Risk Mgmt. v. Escalante, 162 S.W.3d 619, 628 (Tex.App.—El Paso 2005, pet. dism'd). "The right to cross examine a witness is a substantial one, and it is error to so restrict it as to prevent the cross-examining party from going fully into all matters connected with the examination in chief. Due process requires an opportunity to confront and cross-examine adverse witnesses."

Stam v. Mack, 984 S.W.2d 747, 752 (Tex.App.—Texarkana 1999, no pet.). "The trial court interrupted [P's] cross-examination because it felt that [P] was questioning the witness on immaterial issues and he was going into areas that were improper. The trial court's interruption of the

cross-examination was not improper, but was a proper action to maintain control and promote expedition."

TRE 612. WRITING USED TO REFRESH A WITNESS'S MEMORY

(a) Scope. This rule gives an adverse party certain options when a witness uses a writing to refresh memory:

(1) while testifying;

(2) before testifying, in civil cases, if the court decides that justice requires the party to have those options; or

(3) before testifying, in criminal cases.

(b) Adverse Party's Options; Deleting Unrelated Matter. An adverse party is entitled to have the writing produced at the hearing, to inspect it, to cross-examine the witness about it, and to introduce in evidence any portion that relates to the witness's testimony. If the producing party claims that the writing includes unrelated matter, the court must examine the writing in camera, delete any unrelated portion, and order that the rest be delivered to the adverse party. Any portion deleted over objection must be preserved for the record.

(c) Failure to Produce or Deliver the Writing. If a writing is not produced or is not delivered as ordered, the court may issue any appropriate order. But if the prosecution does not comply in a criminal case, the court must strike the witness's testimony or—if justice so requires—declare a mistrial.

Eff. March 1, 1998. Amended by orders of Supreme Court March 10, 2015 and Court of Criminal Appeals March 12, 2015, eff. April 1, 2015.

See also Brown & Rondon, **Texas Rules of Evidence Handbook**, Rule 612.

ANNOTATIONS

Goode v. Shoukfeh, 943 S.W.2d 441, 449 (Tex.1997). "If a witness uses the writing while testifying[,] the adverse party must be given access to it, but if the writing is used before the witness testifies, the court has the discretion to order the writing disclosed to the adverse party."

TRE 613. WITNESS'S PRIOR STATEMENT AND BIAS OR INTEREST

(a) Witness's Prior Inconsistent Statement.

(1) ***Foundation Requirement.*** When examining a witness about the witness's prior inconsistent statement—whether oral or written—a party must first tell the witness:

(A) the contents of the statement;

(B) the time and place of the statement; and

(C) the person to whom the witness made the statement.

(2) ***Need Not Show Written Statement.*** If the witness's prior inconsistent statement is written, a party need not show it to the witness before inquiring about it, but must, upon request, show it to opposing counsel.

(3) ***Opportunity to Explain or Deny.*** A witness must be given the opportunity to explain or deny the prior inconsistent statement.

(4) ***Extrinsic Evidence.*** Extrinsic evidence of a witness's prior inconsistent statement is not admissible unless the witness is first examined about the statement and fails to unequivocally admit making the statement.

(5) ***Opposing Party's Statement.*** This subdivision (a) does not apply to an opposing party's statement under Rule 801(e)(2).

(b) Witness's Bias or Interest.

(1) ***Foundation Requirement.*** When examining a witness about the witness's bias or interest, a party must first tell the witness the circumstances or statements that tend to show the witness's bias or interest. If examining a witness about a statement—whether oral or written—to prove the witness's bias or interest, a party must tell the witness:

(A) the contents of the statement;

(B) the time and place of the statement; and

(C) the person to whom the statement was made.

(2) ***Need Not Show Written Statement.*** If a party uses a written statement to prove the witness's bias or interest, a party need not show the statement to the witness before inquiring about it, but must, upon request, show it to opposing counsel.

(3) ***Opportunity to Explain or Deny.*** A witness must be given the opportunity to explain or deny the circumstances or statements that tend to show the witness's bias or interest. And the witness's proponent may present evidence to rebut the charge of bias or interest.

(4) ***Extrinsic Evidence.*** Extrinsic evidence of a witness's bias or interest is not admissible unless the witness is first examined about the bias or interest and fails to unequivocally admit it.

(c) Witness's Prior Consistent Statement. Unless Rule 801(e)(1)(B) provides otherwise, a witness's prior consistent statement is not admissible if offered solely to enhance the witness's credibility.

Eff. March 1, 1998. Amended by orders of Supreme Court March 10, 2015 and Court of Criminal Appeals March 12, 2015, eff. April 1, 2015.

Comment to 2015 Restyling: The amended rule retains the requirement that a witness be given an opportunity to explain or deny (a) a prior inconsistent statement or (b) the circumstances or a statement showing the witness's bias or interest, but this requirement is not imposed on the examining attorney. A witness may have to wait until redirect examination to explain a prior inconsistent statement or the circumstances or a statement that shows bias. But the impeaching attorney still is not permitted to introduce extrinsic evidence of the witness's prior inconsistent statement or bias unless the witness has first been examined about the statement or bias and has failed to unequivocally admit it. All other changes to the rule are intended to be stylistic only.

See also **O'Connor's Texas Rules,** "Impeaching a witness," ch. 8-C, §6; Brown & Rondon, **Texas Rules of Evidence Handbook**, Rule 613.

ANNOTATIONS

Walker v. Packer, 827 S.W.2d 833, 839 n.5 (Tex1992). "Evidence of bias is not admissible if the witness 'unequivocally admits such bias or interest' at trial. [Because D's witness] flatly denied [bias], such evidence should be discoverable."

In re Weir, 166 S.W.3d 861, 864 (Tex.App.—Beaumont 2005, orig. proceeding). "Generally, an expert witness may be questioned regarding payment received for his work as an expert witness. However, pretrial discovery of all a witness's accounting and financial records, solely for the purpose of impeachment, may be denied. *At 865:* The parties' interests in obtaining discovery solely for impeachment must be weighed against the witness's legitimate interest in protecting unrelated financial information." *See also* **In re Siroosian**, 449 S.W.3d 920, 923-26 (Tex.App.—Fort Worth 2014, orig. proceeding).

TRE 614. EXCLUDING WITNESSES

At a party's request, the court must order witnesses excluded so that they cannot hear other witnesses' testimony. Or the court may do so on its own. But this rule does not authorize excluding:

(a) a party who is a natural person and, in civil cases, that person's spouse;

(b) after being designated as the party's representative by its attorney:

(1) in a civil case, an officer or employee of a party that is not a natural person; or

(2) in a criminal case, a defendant that is not a natural person;

(c) a person whose presence a party shows to be essential to presenting the party's claim or defense; or

(d) the victim in a criminal case, unless the court determines that the victim's testimony would be materially affected by hearing other testimony at the trial.

Eff. March 1, 1998. Amended by orders of Supreme Court March 10, 2015 and Court of Criminal Appeals March 12, 2015, eff. April 1, 2015.

Source: FRE 615.

See also TRCP 267; **O'Connor's Texas Rules,** "Invoking 'the Rule'," ch. 8-C, §3; Brown & Rondon, **Texas Rules of Evidence Handbook**, Rule 614.

ANNOTATIONS

Drilex Sys. v. Flores, 1 S.W.3d 112, 118-19 (Tex1999). "Although an expert witness may typically be found exempt under the essential presence exception, experts are not automatically exempt. Instead, [TRE] 614 and [TRCP] 267 vest in trial judges broad discretion to determine whether a witness is essential."

In re A.H.J., No. 05-15-00501-CV, 2015 WL 5866256 (Tex.App.—Dallas 2015, pet. denied) (memo op.; 10-8-15). "If the Rule is violated, . . . depending on the circumstances, the trial court may allow the testimony, exclude the testimony, or hold the violator in contempt."

In re H.M.S., 349 S.W.3d 250, 253 (Tex.App.—Dallas 2011, pet. denied). "Rule 614 . . ., commonly referred to as 'the rule,' requires the exclusion of witnesses from the courtroom upon the request of a party. Although there are four classes of witnesses that are exempt from the operation of the rule, 'officers of the court' are not among those exempted. Accordingly, [Judge] erred in refusing to exclude certain witnesses on the basis that they were court employees."

TRE 615. PRODUCING A WITNESS'S STATEMENT IN CRIMINAL CASES

(a) Motion to Produce. After a witness other than the defendant testifies on direct examination, the court, on motion of a party who did not call the witness, must order an attorney for the state or the defendant and the defendant's attorney to produce, for the examination and use of the moving party, any statement of the witness that:

(1) is in their possession;

(2) relates to the subject matter of the witness's testimony; and

(3) has not previously been produced.

(b) Producing the Entire Statement. If the entire statement relates to the subject matter of the witness's testimony, the court must order that the statement be delivered to the moving party.

(c) Producing a Redacted Statement. If the party who called the witness claims that the statement contains information that does not relate to the subject matter of the witness's testimony, the court must inspect the statement in camera. After excising any unrelated portions, the court must order delivery of the redacted statement to the moving party. If a party objects to an excision, the court must

preserve the entire statement with the excised portion indicated, under seal, as part of the record.

(d) Recess to Examine a Statement. If the court orders production of a witness's statement, the court, on request, must recess the proceedings to allow the moving party time to examine the statement and prepare for its use.

(e) Sanction for Failure to Produce or Deliver a Statement. If the party who called the witness disobeys an order to produce or deliver a statement, the court must strike the witness's testimony from the record. If an attorney for the state disobeys the order, the court must declare a mistrial if justice so requires.

(f) "Statement" Defined. As used in this rule, a witness's "statement" means:

(1) a written statement that the witness makes and signs, or otherwise adopts or approves;

(2) a substantially verbatim, contemporaneously recorded recital of the witness's oral statement that is contained in any recording or any transcription of a recording; or

(3) the witness's statement to a grand jury, however taken or recorded, or a transcription of such a statement.

Eff. March 1, 1998. Amended by orders of Supreme Court March 10, 2015, and Court of Criminal Appeals March 12, 2015, eff. April 1, 2015. Amended by orders of Supreme Court February 16, 2016, and Court of Criminal Appeals Dec. 7, 2015, and February 29, 2016, eff. Jan. 1, 2016.

Comment to 1998 change: This is prior Rule of Criminal Evidence 614.

Comment to 2016 change: The Michael Morton Act, codified at Texas Code of Criminal Procedure art. 39.14, affords defendants substantial pretrial discovery, requiring the state, upon request from the defendant, to produce and permit the defendant to inspect and copy various items, including witness statements. In many instances, therefore, art. 39.14 eliminates the need, after the witness testifies on direct examination, for a defendant to request, and the court to order, production of a witness's statement.

But art. 39.14 does not entirely eliminate the need for in-trial discovery of witness statements. Art. 39.14 does not extend equivalent discovery rights to the prosecution, and so prosecutors will still need to use Rule 615 to obtain witness statements of defense witnesses. Moreover, some defendants may fail to exercise their discovery rights under art. 39.14 and so may wish to obtain a witness statement under Rule 615. In addition, the Michael Morton Act applies only to the prosecution of offenses committed after December 31, 2013. Defendants on trial for offenses committed before then have no right to pre-trial discovery of the witness statements of prosecution witnesses.

Consequently, Rule 615(a) has been amended to account for the changed pre-trial discovery regime introduced by the Michael Morton Act. If a party's adversary has already produced a witness's statement—whether through formal discovery under art. 39.14 or through more informal means—Rule 615(a) no longer gives a party the right to obtain, after the witness testifies on direct examination, a court order for production of the witness's statement. But if a party's adversary has not already produced a witness's statement, the party may still use Rule 615(a) to request and obtain a court order requiring production of the witness's statement after the witness finishes testifying on direct examination.

See also Brown & Rondon, **Texas Rules of Evidence Handbook**, Rule 615.

Article VII. Opinions and Expert Testimony

TRE 701. OPINION TESTIMONY BY LAY WITNESSES

If a witness is not testifying as an expert, testimony in the form of an opinion is limited to one that is:

(a) rationally based on the witness's perception; and

(b) helpful to clearly understanding the witness's testimony or to determining a fact in issue.

Eff. March 1, 1998. Amended by orders of Supreme Court March 10, 2015 and Court of Criminal Appeals March 12, 2015 eff. April 1, 2015.

Comment to 2015 Restyling: All references to an "inference" have been deleted because this makes the Rule flow better and easier to read, and because any "inference" is covered by the broader term "opinion." Courts have not made substantive decisions on the basis of any distinction between an opinion and an inference. No change in current practice is intended.

Source: FRE 701.

See also Brown & Rondon, **Texas Rules of Evidence Handbook**, Rule 701; **O'Connor's Texas Family Law Handbook**, "Testimony," ch. 2-A, §6.1; **O'Connor's Texas Family Law Handbook**, "Proving value of property," ch. 7-A, §5.3; **O'Connor's Texas Family Law Handbook**, "Proving value of real property," ch. 7-B, §5.3.

ANNOTATIONS

Natural Gas Pipeline Co. v. Justiss, 397 S.W.3d 150, 157 (Tex.2012). "Based on the presumption that an owner is familiar with his property and its value, the Property Owner Rule is an exception to the requirement that a witness must otherwise establish his qualifications to express an opinion on land values. Under the Rule, an owner's valuation testimony fulfills the same role that expert testimony does. *At 159:* Thus, as with expert testimony, property valuations may not be based solely on a property owner's *ipse dixit*. An owner may not simply echo the phrase 'market value' and state a number to substantiate his diminished value claim; he must provide the factual basis on which his opinion rests. [T]he owner's testimony may be challenged on cross-examination or refuted with independent evidence. But even if unchallenged, the testimony must support a verdict, and conclusory or speculative statements do not." *See also* **Jatex Oil & Gas Expl. L.P. v. Nadel & Gussman Permian, L.L.C.**, __ S.W.3d __, 2020 WL 4873836 (Tex.App.—Eastland 2020, no pet.) (No. 11-17-00265-CV; 8-20-20) (property-owner presumption does not extend to technical or specialized matters such as mineral reserves).

Reid Rd. MUD v. Speedy Stop Food Stores, 337 S.W.3d 846, 851-52 (Tex.2011). "The line between who is a [TRE] 702 expert witness and who is a [TRE] 701 witness is not always bright. But when the main substance of the witness's testimony is based on application of the witness's

specialized knowledge, skill, experience, training, or education to his familiarity with the property, then the testimony will generally be expert testimony within the scope of Rule 702. A witness giving such testimony must be properly disclosed and designated as an expert and the witness's testimony is subject to scrutiny under rules regarding experts and expert opinion. Any other principle would allow parties to conceal expert testimony by claiming the witness is one whose opinions are merely for the purpose of explaining the witness's perceptions and testimony. [¶] Accordingly, we do not categorically agree with [D's] contention that all persons with personal knowledge of real property can give opinion testimony as to the market value of that property without the testimony being considered and identified as expert testimony. Such a holding would allow circumvention of discovery and disclosure rules that allow parties to prepare for trial and protect themselves from trial by ambush. Instead, we hold that subject to the provisions of Rule 701, . . . a witness who will be giving opinion evidence about a property's fair market value must be disclosed and designated as an expert pursuant to discovery and other applicable rules."

Merrill v. Sprint Waste Servs., 527 S.W.3d 663, 670 (Tex.App.—Houston [14th Dist.] 2017, no pet.). "The requirement that an opinion be rationally based on the perceptions of the witness is composed of two parts: (1) the witness must establish personal knowledge of the events from which her opinion is drawn; and (2) the opinion drawn must be rationally based on that knowledge. [¶] An opinion will satisfy the personal knowledge requirement if it is an interpretation of the witness's objective perception of events[.] [¶] An opinion is rationally based on perception if a reasonable person could draw that opinion under the circumstances." *See also* **City of San Antonio v. Riojas**, 604 S.W.3d 432, 440 (Tex.App.—San Antonio 2020, pet. filed 5-13-20).

In re Z.R., No. 01-11-00715-CV, 2013 WL 4680241 (Tex.App.—Houston [1st Dist.] 2013, pet. denied) (memo op.; 8-29-13). "'Perceptions refer to a witness's interpretation of information acquired through his or her own senses or experiences at the time of the event (i.e., things the witness saw, heard, smelled, touched, felt, or tasted).' Thus, a Rule 701 witness may testify about his or her 'opinions, beliefs, or inferences as long as they are drawn from his or her own experiences or observations.'"

U.S. Fire Ins. v. Lynd Co., 399 S.W.3d 206, 217-18 (Tex.App.—San Antonio 2012, pet. denied). "[P] contends that lay testimony . . . cannot controvert its scientific evidence, [and that] therefore, in the absence of any scientific evidence from [D], [P] was entitled to summary judgment. . . . The question of whether hail fell on a particular location on a particular day, and whether it caused property damage, is not a matter solely within the scope of an expert's knowledge . . .; to the contrary, it is a matter of personal observation and common sense that is within the scope of lay testimony. [¶] In some areas such as medical malpractice, expert testimony is necessary to defeat a motion for summary judgment. [¶] Proof other than expert testimony will, however, constitute some evidence of causation when a layperson's general experience and common understanding would enable the layperson to determine from the evidence, with reasonable probability, the causal relationship between the event and the condition."

Kilgore Mech., LLC v. Shafiee, No. 14-10-00295-CV, 2011 WL 1849095 (Tex.App.—Houston [14th Dist.] 2011, no pet.) (memo op.; 5-12-11). "Some courts have concluded that an officer may offer a non-expert opinion as to causation where his or her testimony is rationally based on the officer's own perceptions at the scene of the accident and where the testimony aids the trier of fact in determining a fact in issue. Indeed, while police officers often qualify as expert witnesses in traffic collision cases, this qualification does not preclude them from also giving lay opinions where such opinions meet the requirements of Rule 701." *See also* **Texas DPS v. Struve**, 79 S.W.3d 796, 803 (Tex.App.—Corpus Christi 2002, pet. denied) (police officer may express opinion on whether someone is intoxicated, but if based on training and experience, TRE 702 applies).

Sierad v. Barnett, 164 S.W.3d 471, 483-84 (Tex.App.—Dallas 2005, no pet.). TRE 701 "permits a lay-witness opinion if the witness bases his opinion on his perception and if his opinion helps in determining a fact in issue. Lay witnesses can give opinions on damages as long as they testify about matters within their knowledge. A lay witness can testify about value if he has personal knowledge of facts forming the opinion, a rational connection exists between the facts and opinion, and the opinion is helpful." *See also* **Red Sea Gaming, Inc. v. Block Invs.**, 338 S.W.3d 562, 572-73 (Tex.App.—El Paso 2010, pet. denied); **Whalen v. Condominium Consulting & Mgmt.**, 13 S.W.3d 444, 448 (Tex.App.—Corpus Christi 2000, pet. denied).

City of San Antonio v. Vela, 762 S.W.2d 314, 321 (Tex.App.—San Antonio 1988, writ denied). "'In general, a witness need not be an expert in medical matters to state an opinion as to his own physical health.'"

TRE 702. TESTIMONY BY EXPERT WITNESSES

A witness who is qualified as an expert by knowledge, skill, experience, training, or education may testify in the form of an opinion or otherwise if the expert's scientific, technical, or other specialized knowledge will help the trier of fact to understand the evidence or to determine a fact in issue.

Eff. March 1, 1998. Amended by orders of Supreme Court March 10, 2015 and Court of Criminal Appeals March 12, 2015, eff. April 1, 2015.

Source: FRE 702.

See also **O'Connor's Texas Rules**, "Motion to Exclude Expert," ch. 5-N, §1 et seq.; **O'Connor's Texas Rules**, "Testimony from expert," ch. 8-C, §5.5; **O'Connor's Texas Rules**, "Objection to opinion of expert," ch. 8-D, §4.2; Brown & Rondon, **Texas Rules of Evidence Handbook**, Rule 702; **O'Connor's Texas Family Law Handbook**, "Testimony," ch. 2-A, §6.1; **O'Connor's Texas Family Law Handbook**, "Valuing assets & liabilities," ch. 7-A, §5; **O'Connor's Texas Family Law Handbook**, "Proving value of real property," ch. 7-B, §5.3.

ANNOTATIONS

Generally

Reid Rd. MUD v. Speedy Stop Food Stores, 337 S.W.3d 846, 851-52 (Tex.2011). See annotation under TRE 701.

GTE Sw., Inc. v. Bruce, 998 S.W.2d 605, 620 (Tex. 1999). "Except in highly unusual circumstances, expert testimony concerning extreme and outrageous conduct would not meet [the standards of TRE 702]. Where . . . the issue involves only general knowledge and experience rather than expertise, it is within the province of the jury to decide. . . ." *See also* **K-Mart Corp. v. Honeycutt**, 24 S.W.3d 357, 360 (Tex.2000).

Muhs v. Whataburger, Inc., No. 13-09-00434-CV, 2010 WL 4657955 (Tex.App.—Corpus Christi 2010, pet. denied) (memo op.; 11-18-10). "Accident reconstruction constitutes scientific evidence. . . . 'Texas has a long history of allowing qualified accident reconstruction experts to testify regarding the way in which an accident occurred.'"

In re G.M.P., 909 S.W.2d 198, 206 (Tex.App.—Houston [14th Dist.] 1995, no writ). "A determination of who is telling the truth is the sole province of the jury. [T]he trial court erred in allowing [expert] to testify that, in his expert opinion, [witness] was telling the truth."

Qualification of Expert

In re Commitment of Bohannan, 388 S.W.3d 296, 304-05 (Tex.2012). "That a witness has knowledge, skill, expertise, or training does not necessarily mean that the witness can assist the trier-of-fact. Expert testimony assists the trier-of-fact when the expert's knowledge and experience on a relevant issue are beyond that of the average juror and the testimony helps the trier-of-fact understand the evidence or determine a fact issue. [¶] Credentials are important, but credentials alone do not qualify an expert to testify. [F]or example, . . . a medical license does not automatically qualify the holder to testify as an expert on every medical question. Trial courts must ensure that those who purport to be experts truly have expertise concerning the actual subject about which they are offering an opinion. The test is whether the offering party has established that the expert has knowledge, skill, experience, training, or education regarding the specific issue before the court which would qualify the expert to give an opinion on that particular subject." (Internal quotes omitted.) *See also* **Broders v. Heise**, 924 S.W.2d 148, 152-53 (Tex.1996).

Havner v. E-Z Mart Stores, 825 S.W.2d 456, 460 n.4 (Tex. 1992). "An investigating officer may properly testify as to causation." *See also* **Gainsco Cty. Mut. Ins. v. Martinez**, 27 S.W.3d 97, 104 (Tex.App.—San Antonio 2000, pet. granted, judgm't vacated w.r.m.).

ExxonMobil Corp. v. Pagayon, 467 S.W.3d 36, 52 (Tex.App.—Houston [14th Dist.] 2015), *rev'd on other grounds*, 536 S.W.3d 499 (Tex.2017). "A physician from one school of practice may testify about the negligence of a physician of a different school of practice so long as the subject of inquiry is common to and equally recognized and developed in both fields. Thus, in determining whether a doctor is qualified to testify on the specific issue before it, the trial court should not focus on the specialty of the medical expert." (Internal quotes omitted.) *See also* **Puppala v. Perry**, 564 S.W.3d 190, 202 (Tex.App.—Houston [1st Dist.] 2018, no pet.).

Reliability of Opinion

Caffe Ribs, Inc. v. State, 487 S.W.3d 137, 144 (Tex.2016). "When an expert's opinion is predicated on a particular set of facts, those facts need not be undisputed. An expert's opinion is only unreliable if it is contrary to actual, undisputed facts." *See also* **Gunn v. McCoy**, 554 S.W.3d 645, 662-63 (Tex.2018).

Gharda USA, Inc. v. Control Solutions, Inc., 464 S.W.3d 338, 349 (Tex.2015). "'[E]ach material part of an expert's theory must be reliable.' [¶] Whether an expert's testimony is reliable is based on more than whether the expert's methodology satisfies the **Robinson** factors. Reliable expert testimony must be based on a probability standard, rather than on mere possibility. Expert testimony is unreliable 'if there is too great an analytical gap between the data on which the expert relies and the opinion offered.' Whether an analytical gap exists is largely determined by comparing the facts the expert relied on, the facts in the record, and the expert's ultimate opinion. Analytical gaps may include circumstances in which the expert unreliably applies otherwise sound principles and methodologies, . . . the expert's opinion is based on assumed facts that vary materially from the facts in the record, . . . or the expert's opinion is based on tests or data that do not support the conclusions reached. . . . Regardless of the manner in which we determine reliability, we do not decide whether the expert's opinions are correct; rather, we determine whether the analysis used to form those opinions is reliable." *See also* **Mack Trucks, Inc. v. Tamez**, 206 S.W.3d 572, 581 (Tex. 2006).

Transcontinental Ins. v. Crump, 330 S.W.3d 211, 215-16 (Tex.2010). "In determining whether expert testimony is reliable, a court should consider the [**Robinson**] factors . . . as well as the expert's experience, knowledge, and training. '[I]n very few cases will the evidence be such that the trial court's reliability determination can properly be based only on the experience of a qualified expert to the exclusion of factors such as those set out in **Robinson**, or, on the other hand, properly be based only on factors such as those set out in **Robinson** to the exclusion of considerations based on a qualified expert's experience.'"

Whirlpool Corp. v. Camacho, 298 S.W.3d 631, 639-40 (Tex.2009). "The proponent [of expert testimony] must satisfy its burden regardless of the quality or quantity of the opposing party's evidence on the issue and regardless of whether the opposing party attempts to conclusively prove the expert testimony is wrong. [¶] Witnesses offered as experts in an area or subject will invariably have experience in that field. If courts merely accept 'experience' as a substitute for proof that an expert's opinions are reliable and then only examine the testimony for analytical gaps in the expert's logic and opinions, an expert can effectively insulate his or her conclusions from meaningful review by filling gaps in the testimony with almost any type of data or subjective opinions. We have recognized, and do recognize, that some subjects do not lend themselves to scientific testing and scientific methodology. But given the facts in this case, the analytical gap test was not the only factor that should have been considered. . . . This is not one of the few cases in which appellate review of expert evidence should be limited to either an analysis focused solely on **Robinson**-like factors or solely on an analytical gap test. [P]roper appellate legal sufficiency review . . . requires evaluating [expert's] testimony by considering both **Robinson**-type factors and examining for analytical gaps in his testimony." *See also* **TXI Transp. v. Hughes**, 306 S.W.3d 230, 235 (Tex.2010) (factors are difficult to apply for vehicular-accident-reconstruction testimony).

Coastal Transp. Co. v. Crown Cent. Pet. Corp., 136 S.W.3d 227, 233 (Tex.2004). "When the expert's underlying methodology is challenged, the court 'necessarily looks beyond what the expert said' to evaluate the reliability of the expert's opinion. When the testimony is challenged as conclusory or speculative and therefore non-probative on its face, however, there is no need to go beyond the face of the record to test its reliability. [W]hen a reliability challenge requires the court to evaluate the underlying methodology, technique, or foundational data used by the expert, an objection must be timely made so that the trial court has the opportunity to conduct this analysis. However, when the challenge is restricted to the face of the record[,] a party may challenge the legal sufficiency of the evidence even in the absence of any objection to its admissibility." *See also* **Pike v. Texas EMC Mgmt.**, __ S.W.3d __, 2020 WL 3405812 (Tex.2020) (No. 17-0557; 6-19-20) (testimony is conclusory if no basis for opinion is offered or if basis is offered but it provides no support).

Gammill v. Jack Williams Chevrolet, Inc., 972 S.W.2d 713, 726 (Tex.1998). "Nothing in the language of [TRE 702] suggests that opinions based on scientific knowledge should be treated any differently than opinions based on technical or other specialized knowledge. It would be an odd rule of evidence that insisted that some expert opinions be reliable but not others. All expert testimony should be shown to be reliable before it is admitted." *See also* **Helena Chem. Co. v. Wilkins**, 47 S.W.3d 486, 499 (Tex.2001).

Merrell Dow Pharms. v. Havner, 953 S.W.2d 706, 714 (Tex. 1997). "If the foundational data underlying opinion testimony are unreliable, . . . any opinion drawn from that data is likewise unreliable. Further, an expert's testimony is unreliable even when the underlying data are sound if the expert draws conclusions from that data based on flawed methodology. A flaw in the expert's reasoning from the data may render reliance on a study unreasonable and render the inferences drawn therefrom dubious. Under that circumstance, the expert's scientific testimony is unreliable and, legally, no evidence." *See also* **Cooper Tire & Rubber Co. v. Mendez**, 204 S.W.3d 797, 800-01 (Tex.2006).

E.I. du Pont de Nemours & Co. v. Robinson, 923 S.W.2d 549, 557 (Tex.1995). The factors to consider in determining the admissibility of scientific knowledge include "but are not limited to: (1) the extent to which the theory has been or can be tested; (2) the extent to which the technique relies upon the subjective interpretation of the expert; (3) whether the theory has been subjected to peer review and/or publication; (4) the technique's potential rate of error; (5) whether the underlying theory or technique has been generally accepted as valid by the relevant scientific community; and (6) the non-judicial uses which have been made of the theory or technique." *See also* **Gomez v. American Honda Motor Co.**, No. 04-14-00398-CV, 2015 WL 1875954 (Tex.App.—San Antonio 2015, pet. denied) (memo op.; 4-22-15) (additional factors are whether expert has ruled out alternative causes of injury and whether expert's research and opinions were conducted and formed solely for purpose of litigation).

Taylor v. TDPRS, 160 S.W.3d 641, 650 (Tex.App.—Austin 2005, pet. denied). "[I]n fields other than the hard sciences, such as the social sciences, factors like an expert's education, training, and experience are more appropriate factors in testing reliability than the scientific method. Thus, when measuring the reliability of an expert's opinion in fields within the soft sciences, . . . courts should consider whether: (1) the field of expertise is a legitimate one; (2) the subject matter of the expert's testimony is within the scope of that field; and (3) the expert's testimony properly relies upon the principles involved in that field of study." *See also* **In re J.R.**, 501 S.W.3d 738, 748 (Tex.App.—Waco 2016, pet. denied).

Deadline to Object

General Motors Corp. v. Iracheta, 161 S.W.3d 462, 471 (Tex. 2005). "The unreliability of expert opinions may be apparent as early as the discovery process but also may not emerge until trial, during or after the expert's testimony, or even later. An objection must be timely, but it need not anticipate a deficiency before it is apparent. [W]e cannot say that [D's] objection following cross-examination came too late."

TRE 703. BASES OF AN EXPERT'S OPINION TESTIMONY

An expert may base an opinion on facts or data in the case that the expert has been made aware of, reviewed, or personally observed. If experts in the particular field would reasonably rely on those kinds of facts or data in forming an opinion on the subject, they need not be admissible for the opinion to be admitted.

Eff. March 1, 1998. Amended by orders of Supreme Court March 10, 2015 and Court of Criminal Appeals March 12, 2015, eff. April 1, 2015.

Comment to 1998 change: The former Civil Rule referred to facts or data "perceived by or reviewed by" the expert. The former Criminal Rule referred to facts or data "perceived by or made known to" the expert. The terminology is now conformed, but no change in meaning is intended.

Comment to 2015 Restyling: All references to an "inference" have been deleted because this makes the Rule flow better and easier to read, and because any "inference" is covered by the broader term "opinion." Courts have not made substantive decisions on the basis of any distinction between an opinion and an inference. No change in current practice is intended.

See also **O'Connor's Texas Rules,** "Foundation test," ch. 5-N, §2.4; Brown & Rondon, **Texas Rules of Evidence Handbook**, Rule 703.

ANNOTATIONS

Elizondo v. Krist, 415 S.W.3d 259, 263 (Tex.2013). "Under [TRE] 703, experts may base their testimony on facts or data that are 'of a type reasonably relied upon by experts in the particular field in forming opinions or inferences upon the subject.' That test is met when, in a mass tort litigation involving thousands of similar claimants and arising out of the same event, the expert measures the 'true' settlement value of a particular case by persuasively comparing all the circumstances of the case to the settlements obtained in other cases with similar circumstances arising from the event."

In re Christus Spohn Hosp. Kleberg, 222 S.W.3d 434, 440 (Tex.2007). "[I]n many instances, experts may rely on inadmissible hearsay, privileged communications, and other information that the ordinary witness may not." *See also* **Gannon v. Wyche**, 321 S.W.3d 881, 889 (Tex.App.—Houston [14th Dist.] 2010, pet. denied); **Sosa v. Koshy**, 961 S.W.2d 420, 427 (Tex.App.—Houston [1st Dist.] 1997, pet. denied).

Merrell Dow Pharms. v. Havner, 953 S.W.2d 706, 711 (Tex.1997). "The substance of the [expert's] testimony must be considered. *At 712:* [A]n expert's bald assurance of validity is not enough. *At 713:* The underlying data should be independently evaluated in determining if the opinion itself is reliable."

TRE 704. OPINION ON AN ULTIMATE ISSUE

An opinion is not objectionable just because it embraces an ultimate issue.

Eff. March 1, 1998. Amended by orders of Supreme Court March 10, 2015 and Court of Criminal Appeals March 12, 2015, eff. April 1, 2015.

See also Brown & Rondon, **Texas Rules of Evidence Handbook**, Rule 704.

ANNOTATIONS

Birchfield v. Texarkana Mem'l Hosp., 747 S.W.2d 361, 365 (Tex.1987). "Fairness and efficiency dictate that an expert may state an opinion on a mixed question of law and fact as long as the opinion is confined to the relevant issues and is based on proper legal concepts." *See also* **Dickerson v. DeBarbieris**, 964 S.W.2d 680, 690 (Tex.App.—Houston [14th Dist.] 1998, no pet.) (expert cannot state opinion or conclusion on pure question of law).

TRE 705. DISCLOSING THE UNDERLYING FACTS OR DATA AND EXAMINING AN EXPERT ABOUT THEM

(a) Stating an Opinion Without Disclosing the Underlying Facts or Data. Unless the court orders otherwise, an expert may state an opinion—and give the reasons for it—without first testifying to the underlying facts or data. But the expert may be required to disclose those facts or data on cross-examination.

(b) Voir Dire Examination of an Expert About the Underlying Facts or Data. Before an expert states an opinion or discloses the underlying facts or data, an adverse party in a civil case may—or in a criminal case must—be permitted to examine the expert about the underlying facts or data. This examination must take place outside the jury's hearing.

(c) Admissibility of Opinion. An expert's opinion is inadmissible if the underlying facts or data do not provide a sufficient basis for the opinion.

(d) When Otherwise Inadmissible Underlying Facts or Data May Be Disclosed; Instructing the Jury. If the underlying facts or data would otherwise be inadmissible, the proponent of the opinion may not disclose them to the jury if their probative value in helping the jury evaluate the opinion is outweighed by their prejudicial effect. If the court allows the proponent to disclose those facts or data the court must, upon timely request, restrict the evidence to its proper scope and instruct the jury accordingly.

Eff. March 1, 1998. Amended by orders of Supreme Court March 10, 2015 and Court of Criminal Appeals March 12, 2015, eff. April 1, 2015.

Comment to 1998 change: Paragraphs (b), (c), and (d) are based on the former Criminal Rule and are made applicable to civil cases. This rule does not preclude a party in any case from conducting a *voir dire* examination into the qualifications of an expert.

Comment to 2015 Restyling: All references to an "inference" have been deleted because this makes the Rule flow better and easier to read, and because any "inference" is covered by the broader term "opinion." Courts have not made substantive decisions on the basis of any distinction between an opinion and an inference. No change in current practice is intended.

See also **O'Connor's Texas Rules,** "Motion to Exclude Expert," ch. 5-N, §1 et seq.; Brown & Rondon, **Texas Rules of Evidence Handbook**, Rule 705.

ANNOTATIONS

Arkoma Basin Expl. Co. v. FMF Assocs. 1990-A, Ltd., 249 S.W.3d 380, 389-90 (Tex.2008). "[E]xperts are not required to introduce . . . foundational data at trial unless the opposing party or the court insists."

Kerr-McGee Corp. v. Helton, 133 S.W.3d 245, 252 (Tex.2004). "[B]ecause Rule 705(a) contemplates that the party against whom the evidence is offered may elicit testimony regarding the underlying facts or data on cross-examination, a motion to strike the testimony after such cross-examination is timely."

In re Commitment of Regalado, 598 S.W.3d 736, 742-43 (Tex.App.—Amarillo 2020, no pet.). "The 'facts and data [that the] expert admitted he did not rely upon . . . when he formulated his opinion' is the evidence in dispute. Because the expert did not rely on it, it was 'not probative' or irrelevant, according to [D]. Thus, it should have been excluded. . .. We disagree. [¶] [D]uring the preliminary hearing at which [D's] objection was addressed, the trial court had before it evidence of (1) an expert opinion, (2) the expert's reliance on offenses committed by [D] and the facts underlying those offenses, and (3) why the offenses and facts underlying them were relevant to developing the opinion ultimately voiced to the jury. This provided the trial court with the evidentiary foundation upon which to conclude that the underlying facts of ***all*** the offenses considered by the jury were relevant and, therefore, subject to disclosure under [TRE] 705(d). . .. That the disclosure included facts unknown to the expert when developing his initial opinion matters not. He knew of and had considered them by the time he informed the jury of his opinion. [¶] According to [TRE] 703, an expert 'may base an opinion on facts or data in the case that the expert has been made aware of, reviewed, or personally observed.' That language says nothing of a deadline by which the expert must discover facts which will be used as a basis for his opinion. In fact, an expert opinion may be founded on information perceived during trial. Nor does Rule 703 say anything of a deadline tied to the date on which the expert initially developed an opinion and requiring the expert to ignore information obtained later. . . . Until Rule 703 is rewritten . . . to incorporate blinders which stop the expert from seeing additional matter, we read it as permitting the continued consideration of other facts and data after development of an original opinion. And, to the extent that the additional data formed the basis of the opinion told at trial it may also be revealed to the fact-finder, if the balancing test within Rule 705(d) is otherwise met. Consequently, the trial court did not abuse its discretion by rejecting [D's] contention that facts discovered after the expert derived his initial opinion were irrelevant."

Weiss v. Mechanical Associated Servs., 989 S.W.2d 120, 124-25 (Tex.App.—San Antonio 1999, pet. denied). "The non-exclusive list of factors the court may consider in deciding admissibility [under TRE 705(c)] includes the extent to which the theory has been or can be tested, the extent to which the technique relies upon the subjective interpretation of the expert, whether the theory has been subjected to peer review and/or publication, the technique's potential rate of error, whether the underlying theory or technique has been generally accepted as valid by the relevant scientific community, and the non-judicial uses that have been made of the theory or technique."

TRE 706. AUDIT IN CIVIL CASES

Notwithstanding any other evidence rule, the court must admit an auditor's verified report prepared under Rule of Civil Procedure 172 and offered by a party. If a party files exceptions to the report, a party may offer evidence supporting the exceptions to contradict the report.

Eff. March 1, 1998. Amended by orders of Supreme Court March 10, 2015 and Court of Criminal Appeals March 12, 2015, eff. April 1, 2015.

See also Brown & Rondon, **Texas Rules of Evidence Handbook**, Rule 706.

ANNOTATIONS

Lovelace v. Sabine Consol., Inc., 733 S.W.2d 648, 656 (Tex.App.—Houston [14th Dist.] 1987, writ denied). "The audit report . . . contains no such affidavit as is required by [TRCP] 172. . . . Further, six days before trial [P] filed an objection to the audit. Therefore, the trial court did not err in admitting evidence that contradicted and supplemented the auditor's report."

Article VIII. Hearsay

TRE 801. DEFINITIONS THAT APPLY TO THIS ARTICLE; EXCLUSIONS FROM HEARSAY

(a) Statement. "Statement" means a person's oral or written verbal expression, or nonverbal conduct that a person intended as a substitute for verbal expression.

(b) Declarant. "Declarant" means the person who made the statement.

(c) Matter Asserted. "Matter asserted" means:

(1) any matter a declarant explicitly asserts; and

(2) any matter implied by a statement, if the probative value of the statement as offered flows from the declarant's belief about the matter.

(d) Hearsay. "Hearsay" means a statement that:

(1) the declarant does not make while testifying at the current trial or hearing; and

(2) a party offers in evidence to prove the truth of the matter asserted in the statement.

(e) Statements That Are Not Hearsay. A statement that meets the following conditions is not hearsay:

(1) ***A Declarant-Witness's Prior Statement.*** The declarant testifies and is subject to cross-examination about a prior statement, and the statement:

(A) is inconsistent with the declarant's testimony and:

(i) when offered in a civil case, was given under penalty of perjury at a trial, hearing, or other proceeding or in a deposition; or

(ii) when offered in a criminal case, was given under penalty of perjury at a trial, hearing, or other proceeding—except a grand jury proceeding—or in a deposition;

(B) is consistent with the declarant's testimony and is offered to rebut an express or implied charge that the declarant recently fabricated it or acted from a recent improper influence or motive in so testifying; or

(C) identifies a person as someone the declarant perceived earlier.

(2) ***An Opposing Party's Statement.*** The statement is offered against an opposing party and:

(A) was made by the party in an individual or representative capacity;

(B) is one the party manifested that it adopted or believed to be true;

(C) was made by a person whom the party authorized to make a statement on the subject;

(D) was made by the party's agent or employee on a matter within the scope of that relationship and while it existed; or

(E) was made by the party's coconspirator during and in furtherance of the conspiracy.

(3) ***A Deponent's Statement.*** In a civil case, the statement was made in a deposition taken in the same proceeding. "Same proceeding" is defined in Rule of Civil Procedure 203.6(b). The deponent's unavailability as a witness is not a requirement for admissibility.

Adopted eff. March 1, 1998. Amended eff. Jan. 1, 1999. Amended by orders of Supreme Court March 10, 2015 and Court of Criminal Appeals March 12, 2015, eff. April 1, 2015.

Comment to 2015 Restyling: Statements falling under the hearsay exclusion provided by Rule 801(e)(2) are no longer referred to as "admissions" in the title to the subdivision. The term "admissions" is confusing because not all statements covered by the exclusion are admissions in the colloquial sense—a statement can be within the exclusion even if it "admitted" nothing and was not against the party's interest when made. The term "admissions" also raises confusion in comparison with the Rule 803(24) exception for declarations against interest. No change in application of the exclusion is intended.

The deletion of former Rule 801(e)(1)(D), which cross-references Code of Criminal Procedure art. 38.071, is not intended as a substantive change. Including this cross-reference made sense when the Texas Rules of Criminal Evidence were first promulgated, but with subsequent changes to the statutory provision, its inclusion is no longer appropriate. The version of article 38.071 that was initially cross-referenced in the Rules of Criminal Evidence required the declarant-victim to be available to testify at the trial. That requirement has since been deleted from the statute, and the statute no longer requires either the availability or testimony of the declarant-victim. Thus, cross-referencing the statute in Rule 801(e)(1), which applies only when the declarant testifies at trial about the prior statement, no longer makes sense. Moreover, article 38.071 is but one of a number of statutes that mandate the admission of certain hearsay statements in particular circumstances. *See, e.g.*, Code of Criminal Procedure art. 38.072; Family Code §§54.031, 104.002, 104.006. These statutory provisions take precedence over the general rule excluding hearsay, see Rules 101(c) and 802, and there is no apparent justification for cross-referencing article 38.071 and not all other such provisions.

See also **O'Connor's Texas Rules,** "Admissibility," ch. 6-F, §12.1; Brown & Rondon, **Texas Rules of Evidence Handbook**, Rule 801; **O'Connor's Texas Forms,** FORM 5E:1.

ANNOTATIONS

TRE 801(d)

In re M.S., 115 S.W.3d 534, 543 (Tex.2003). "[T]he Agreement [between D and CPS] was not offered as proof of [D's] inability to care for her children, or as proof that her parental rights should be terminated, or as proof that termination was in the children's best interest. Rather, the Agreement was offered to show that an agreement had been made and what its terms were. The Agreement was not hearsay."

Marten v. Silva, 200 S.W.3d 297, 303 (Tex.App.—Dallas 2006, no pet.). "[N]either the document showing [car's] serial number nor the note from [D] was offered to prove the truth of the matters asserted. . . . Instead, the documents merely evidence an ongoing series of communications and faxes between [D] and [P] concerning [P's] purchase of [car]. Under these circumstances, . . . the documents were not hearsay. . . ."

City of Austin v. Houston Lighting & Power Co., 844 S.W.2d 773, 791 (Tex.App.—Dallas 1992, writ denied). "Generally, Texas courts consider newspaper articles inadmissible hearsay. [N]ewspaper articles not offered for the truth of the matters asserted but used merely to show notice of those matters are not hearsay."

TRE 801(e)

Tome v. U.S., 513 U.S. 150, 167 (1995) (criminal case interpreting federal rule). The federal rule "permits the introduction of a declarant's consistent out-of-court statements to rebut a charge of recent fabrication or improper influence or motive only when those statements were made before the charged recent fabrication or improper influence or motive."

Reid Rd. MUD v. Speedy Stop Food Stores, 337 S.W.3d 846, 858 (Tex.2011). "[A]dmissions by a party opponent can occur outside a judicial proceeding and are not inadmissible simply because they occur in an administrative hearing. . . ."

Bay Area Healthcare Grp. v. McShane, 239 S.W.3d 231, 235 (Tex.2007). "Rule 801(e)(2) is straightforward: subject to other [TREs] that may limit admissibility, *any* statement by a party-opponent is admissible against that party. [¶] Thus, the court of appeals erred in concluding that statements from [superseded] pleadings would only be admissible if they contained 'some statement relevant to a material issue in the case' that is 'inconsistent with the position taken by the party against whom it is introduced.' [T]he [TREs] no longer require inconsistency when it comes to admissibility of superseded pleadings. . . . We hold that there is no requirement that the statement be inconsistent with the party's position at trial. . . ." *See also* **Quick v. Plastic Solutions**, 270 S.W.3d 173, 185 (Tex.App.—El Paso 2008, no pet.).

Schack v. Property Owners Ass'n, 555 S.W.3d 339, 357 (Tex.App.—Corpus Christi 2018, pet. denied). " 'It has long been the rule that where a party has used a document made by a third party in such way as amounts to an approval of its contents, such statement may be received against him as an admission by adoption.' [¶] According to [Ps], [D] invited customers to leave comments on [a website where he advertised his rental operation], and he thereby 'authorized his customers to make public statements about [the rental operation]'. . . . [Ps] assert that because [D] permitted the comments to remain on his page, he thereby adopted the customer comments as his own statements and manifested his belief in the truth of these comments. *At 358:* [D] passively allowed customers to post their own remarks to [the] website. In our view, [D's] passive role in the matter does not manifest adoption or belief in the truth of the comments. [¶] [Moreover], the context does not indicate adoption[ ] because [D] apparently had no power to remove unfavorable or untrue reviews. The fact that the reviews appeared on [the] page cannot be taken as an indication of [D's] belief in their truth. *At 359:* [W]e conclude that [D] did not manifest an adoption of the customer comments."

Direct Value, L.L.C. v. Stock Bldg. Sup., 388 S.W.3d 386, 391 n.5 (Tex.App.—Amarillo 2012, no pet.), *overruled on other grounds*, **Dudley Constr., Ltd. v. ACT Pipe & Sup.**, 545 S.W.3d 532 (Tex.2018). "[E]-mail and its attachments were admissible as admissions of a party opponent."

Trencor, Inc. v. Cornech Mach. Co., 115 S.W.3d 145, 151 (Tex.App.—Fort Worth 2003, pet. denied). "A statement by a party's agent or servant concerning a matter within the scope of his agency or employment and made during the existence of the relationship may be offered as an admission by the party itself. The fact of agency must, however, be established before the declaration can be admitted."

TRE 802. THE RULE AGAINST HEARSAY

Hearsay is not admissible unless any of the following provides otherwise:

- a statute;
- these rules; or
- other rules prescribed under statutory authority.

Inadmissible hearsay admitted without objection may not be denied probative value merely because it is hearsay.

Eff. March 1, 1998. Amended by orders of Supreme Court March 10, 2015 and Court of Criminal Appeals March 12, 2015, eff. April 1, 2015.

See also Brown & Rondon, **Texas Rules of Evidence Handbook**, Rule 802; **O'Connor's Texas Forms,** FORM 5E:1.

ANNOTATIONS

Texas Commerce Bank v. New, 3 S.W.3d 515, 517 (Tex. 1999). "Nothing in rule 802 limits its application to contested hearings. The rule is not ambiguous and requires no explication." Thus, an affidavit containing unobjected-to hearsay can establish facts in a default-judgment case. *See also* **Sherman Acquisition II LP v. Garcia**, 229 S.W.3d 802, 810-11 (Tex.App.—Waco 2007, no pet.).

Lee v. Dykes, 312 S.W.3d 191, 198 (Tex.App.—Houston [14th Dist.] 2010, no pet.). "[I]nadmissible evidence is [not] necessarily probative [even] if it is admitted without objection or is uncontroverted."

TRE 803. EXCEPTIONS TO THE RULE AGAINST HEARSAY—REGARDLESS OF WHETHER THE DECLARANT IS AVAILABLE AS A WITNESS

The following are not excluded by the rule against hearsay, regardless of whether the declarant is available as a witness:

(1) ***Present Sense Impression.*** A statement describing or explaining an event or condition, made while or immediately after the declarant perceived it.

(2) ***Excited Utterance.*** A statement relating to a startling event or condition, made while the declarant was under the stress of excitement that it caused.

(3) ***Then-Existing Mental, Emotional, or Physical Condition.*** A statement of the declarant's then-existing state of mind (such as motive, intent, or plan) or emotional, sensory, or physical condition (such as mental feeling, pain, or bodily health), but not including a statement of memory or belief to prove the fact remembered or believed unless it relates to the validity or terms of the declarant's will.

(4) ***Statement Made for Medical Diagnosis or Treatment.*** A statement that:

(A) is made for—and is reasonably pertinent to—medical diagnosis or treatment; and

(B) describes medical history; past or present symptoms or sensations; their inception; or their general cause.

(5) ***Recorded Recollection.*** A record that:

(A) is on a matter the witness once knew about but now cannot recall well enough to testify fully and accurately;

(B) was made or adopted by the witness when the matter was fresh in the witness's memory; and

(C) accurately reflects the witness's knowledge, unless the circumstances of the record's preparation cast doubt on its trustworthiness.

If admitted, the record may be read into evidence but may be received as an exhibit only if offered by an adverse party.

(6) ***Records of a Regularly Conducted Activity.*** A record of an act, event, condition, opinion, or diagnosis if:

(A) the record was made at or near the time by—or from information transmitted by—someone with knowledge;

(B) the record was kept in the course of a regularly conducted business activity;

(C) making the record was a regular practice of that activity;

(D) all these conditions are shown by the testimony of the custodian or another qualified witness, or by an affidavit or unsworn declaration that complies with Rule 902(10); and

(E) the opponent fails to demonstrate that the source of information or the method or circumstances of preparation indicate a lack of trustworthiness.

"Business" as used in this paragraph includes every kind of regular organized activity whether conducted for profit or not.

(7) ***Absence of a Record of a Regularly Conducted Activity.*** Evidence that a matter is not included in a record described in paragraph (6) if:

(A) the evidence is admitted to prove that the matter did not occur or exist;

(B) a record was regularly kept for a matter of that kind; and

(C) the opponent fails to show that the possible source of the information or other circumstances indicate a lack of trustworthiness.

(8) ***Public Records.*** A record or statement of a public office if:

(A) it sets out:

(i) the office's activities;

(ii) a matter observed while under a legal duty to report, but not including, in a criminal case, a matter observed by law-enforcement personnel; or

(iii) in a civil case or against the government in a criminal case, factual findings from a legally authorized investigation; and

(B) the opponent fails to demonstrate that the source of information or other circumstances indicate a lack of trustworthiness.

(9) ***Public Records of Vital Statistics.*** A record of a birth, death, or marriage, if reported to a public office in accordance with a legal duty.

(10) ***Absence of a Public Record.*** Testimony—or a certification under Rule 902—that a diligent search failed to disclose a public record or statement if the testimony or certification is admitted to prove that:

(A) the record or statement does not exist; or

(B) a matter did not occur or exist, if a public office regularly kept a record or statement for a matter of that kind.

(11) ***Records of Religious Organizations Concerning Personal or Family History.*** A statement of birth, legitimacy, ancestry, marriage, divorce, death, relationship by blood or marriage, or similar facts of personal or family history, contained in a regularly kept record of a religious organization.

(12) ***Certificates of Marriage, Baptism, and Similar Ceremonies.*** A statement of fact contained in a certificate:

(A) made by a person who is authorized by a religious organization or by law to perform the act certified;

(B) attesting that the person performed a marriage or similar ceremony or administered a sacrament; and

(C) purporting to have been issued at the time of the act or within a reasonable time after it.

(13) ***Family Records.*** A statement of fact about personal or family history contained in a family record, such as a Bible, genealogy, chart, engraving on a ring, inscription on a portrait, or engraving on an urn or burial marker.

(14) ***Records of Documents That Affect an Interest in Property.*** The record of a document that purports to establish or affect an interest in property if:

(A) the record is admitted to prove the content of the original recorded document, along with its signing and its delivery by each person who purports to have signed it;

(B) the record is kept in a public office; and

(C) a statute authorizes recording documents of that kind in that office.

(15) ***Statements in Documents That Affect an Interest in Property.*** A statement contained in a document that purports to establish or affect an interest in property if the matter stated was relevant to the document's purpose—unless later dealings with the property are inconsistent with the truth of the statement or the purport of the document.

(16) ***Statements in Ancient Documents.*** A statement in a document that is at least 20 years old and whose authenticity is established.

(17) ***Market Reports and Similar Commercial Publications.*** Market quotations, lists, directories, or other compilations that are generally relied on by the public or by persons in particular occupations.

(18) ***Statements in Learned Treatises, Periodicals, or Pamphlets.*** A statement contained in a treatise, periodical, or pamphlet if:

(A) the statement is called to the attention of an expert witness on cross-examination or relied on by the expert on direct examination; and

(B) the publication is established as a reliable authority by the expert's admission or testimony, by another expert's testimony, or by judicial notice.

If admitted, the statement may be read into evidence but not received as an exhibit.

(19) ***Reputation Concerning Personal or Family History.*** A reputation among a person's family by blood, adoption, or marriage—or among a person's associates or in the community—concerning the person's birth, adoption, legitimacy, ancestry, marriage, divorce, death, relationship by blood, adoption, or marriage, or similar facts of personal or family history.

(20) ***Reputation Concerning Boundaries or General History.*** A reputation in a community—arising before the controversy—concerning boundaries of land in the community or customs that affect the land, or concerning general historical events important to that community, state, or nation.

(21) ***Reputation Concerning Character.*** A reputation among a person's associates or in the community concerning the person's character.

(22) ***Judgment of a Previous Conviction.*** Evidence of a final judgment of conviction if:

(A) it is offered in a civil case and:

(i) the judgment was entered after a trial or guilty plea, but not a nolo contendere plea;

(ii) the conviction was for a felony;

(iii) the evidence is admitted to prove any fact essential to the judgment; and

(iv) an appeal of the conviction is not pending; or

(B) it is offered in a criminal case and:

(i) the judgment was entered after a trial or a guilty or nolo contendere plea;

(ii) the conviction was for a criminal offense;

(iii) the evidence is admitted to prove any fact essential to the judgment;

(iv) when offered by the prosecutor for a purpose other than impeachment, the judgment was against the defendant; and

(v) an appeal of the conviction is not pending.

(23) ***Judgments Involving Personal, Family, or General History or a Boundary.*** A judgment that is admitted to prove a matter of personal, family, or general history, or boundaries, if the matter:

(A) was essential to the judgment; and

(B) could be proved by evidence of reputation.

(24) ***Statement Against Interest.*** A statement that:

(A) a reasonable person in the declarant's position would have made only if the person believed it to be true because, when made, it was so contrary to the declarant's proprietary or pecuniary interest or had so great a tendency to invalidate the declarant's claim against someone else or to expose the declarant to civil or criminal liability or to make the declarant an object of hatred, ridicule, or disgrace; and

(B) is supported by corroborating circumstances that clearly indicate its trustworthiness, if it is offered in a criminal case as one that tends to expose the declarant to criminal liability.

Eff. March 1, 1998. Amended by orders of Supreme Court March 10, 2015 and Court of Criminal Appeals March 12, 2015, eff. April 1, 2015.

Source: FRE 803. See TRCS arts. 3718–3737e (repealed).

See also Fam. Code §54.031 (statutory exceptions to hearsay rule for testimony of certain abuse victims in criminal proceedings); **O'Connor's Texas Rules**, "Introducing Evidence," ch. 8-C, §1 et seq.; Brown & Rondon, **Texas Rules of Evidence Handbook**, Rule 803.

ANNOTATIONS

Generally

Robinson v. Harkins & Co., 711 S.W.2d 619, 621 (Tex.1986). "All hearsay exceptions require a showing of trustworthiness."

Simien v. Unifund CCR Partners, 321 S.W.3d 235, 240 (Tex.App.—Houston [1st Dist.] 2010, no pet.). "The proponent of hearsay has the burden of showing that the testimony fits within an exception to the general rule prohibiting the admission of hearsay evidence." *See also* **Reed v. Cook Children's Med. Ctr., Inc.**, No. 02-13-00405-CV, 2014 WL 2462778 (Tex.App.—Fort Worth 2014, no pet.) (memo op.; 5-29-14).

TRE 803(1)

1.70 Acres v. State, 935 S.W.2d 480, 488 (Tex.App.—Beaumont 1996, no writ). "Present sense impressions are those comments made at the time the declarant is receiving the impression or immediately thereafter. They possess the following safeguards which render them reliable: (1) the report at the moment of the thing then seen, heard, etc. is safe from any error from defect of memory of the declarant; (2) there is little or no time for a calculated misstatement; (3) the statement will usually be made to another—the witness who reports it—who would have equal opportunity to observe and hence to check a misstatement." *See also* **VIA Metro. Transit Auth. v. Barraza**, No. 04-13-00035-CV, 2013 WL 6255761 (Tex.App.—San Antonio 2013, pet. denied) (memo op.; 12-4-13).

TRE 803(2)

Volkswagen v. Ramirez, 159 S.W.3d 897, 908-09 (Tex.2004). "To be admissible as an excited utterance, a statement must be (1) a spontaneous reaction (2) to a personal observance of (3) a startling event (4) made while the declarant was still under the stress of excitement caused by the event. [¶] [The statement] must occur before the declarant has the opportunity to reflect on or ponder the shocking incident. Accordingly, we also consider the lapse in time between the startling event and the statement [as well as the] declarant's tone and tenor of voice. . . ."

In re H.T.S., No. 04-11-00847-CV, 2012 WL 6743562 (Tex.App.—San Antonio 2012, pet. denied) (memo op.; 12-31-12). "To qualify as an excited utterance, the statement must be a product of a startling occurrence; the declarant must have been dominated by the emotion, excitement, fear, or pain of the occurrence; and the statement must be related to the circumstances of the startling occurrence. In determining whether a hearsay statement is admissible under the excited utterance exception, the reviewing court may look at: (1) the time that elapsed between the event and the statement, and (2) whether the statement was in response to a question. However, neither of these factors is dispositive; rather, '[t]he critical factor . . . is whether the declarant was still dominated by the emotions, fear, excitement, or pain of the event at the time of the statement.'"

Felix v. Gonzalez, 87 S.W.3d 574, 578-79 (Tex.App.—San Antonio 2002, pet. denied). "The core of the excited utterance exception is reliability—a statement made by an out-of-court declarant during a state of excitement is more reliable than a statement made after time for reflection upon a startling event. Once the timing of the state of excitement is demonstrated, so long as the statement made *relates to* the startling event, it falls within the purview of the excited utterance exception."

Almaraz v. Burke, 827 S.W.2d 80, 83 (Tex.App.—Fort Worth 1992, writ denied). "Although [**First Sw. Lloyds Ins. v. MacDowell**, 769 S.W.2d 954 (Tex.App.—Texarkana 1989, writ denied),] states that the witness's statement was a narrative account, given after he had returned to the scene of the fire, the opinion does not reflect whether the witness was still excited from the fire and the chase at the time the statement was given, nor does it state whether that mattered in reaching the result. If the witness in that case were still excited from the event at the time he told the fire marshal what had just happened, we would have held that the evidence qualified as an exception to the hearsay rule in accordance with rule 803(2). On the other hand, if there were no evidence that the witness was still under the excitement of the preceding events, we would agree with the opinion."

First Sw. Lloyds Ins. v. MacDowell, 769 S.W.2d 954, 959 (Tex.App.—Texarkana 1989, writ denied). "A statement that is simply a narrative of past acts or events, as distinguished from a spontaneous utterance, does not qualify as an excited utterance regardless of how soon after the event that it is made. The circumstances must show that it was the event speaking through the person and not the person speaking about the event."

TRE 803(3)

Power v. Kelley, 70 S.W.3d 137, 141 (Tex.App.—San Antonio 2001, pet. denied). "'Statements admitted under [TRE 803(3)] are usually spontaneous remarks about pain or some other sensation, made by the declarant while the sensation, not readily observable by a third party, is being experienced.' 'The exception does not extend to statements of past external facts or conditions.'"

TRE 803(4)

In re H.L.A., No. 01-12-00912-CV, 2014 WL 1101584 (Tex.App.—Houston [1st Dist.] 2014, no pet.) (memo op.; 3-20-14). "The witness . . . need not expressly state that the hearsay declarant recognized the need to be truthful in her statements for the medical treatment exception [in TRE 803(4)] to apply. Instead, the reviewing court must determine whether the record supports a conclusion that the declarant understood the importance of honesty in the context of medical diagnosis and treatment. [¶] The essential 'qualification' expressed in the rule is that the declarant believe that the information he conveys will ultimately be utilized in diagnosis or treatment of a condition from which the declarant is suffering, so that his selfish motive for truthfulness can be trusted. We conduct a two-part test for determining whether this requirement has been met. First, the statement must be made for the purpose of diagnosis or treatment, and the declarant must know that it is made for the purpose of diagnosis and treatment. Second, the statements must actually be pertinent to diagnosis or

treatment." (Internal quotes omitted.) *See also* **In re C.B.L.**, No. 11-15-00227-CV, 2016 WL 5853196 (Tex.App.—Eastland 2016, pet. denied) (memo op.; 9-30-16) (if identity of perpetrator is part of hearsay statement, witness must outline how identity and relationship of perpetrator to declarant is information necessary for efficacy of treatment).

TRE 803(6)

Burroughs Wellcome Co. v. Crye, 907 S.W.2d 497, 500 (Tex.1995). "The diagnoses contained in [P's] medical and hospital records are admissible. However, to constitute evidence of causation, an expert opinion must rest in reasonable medical probability. [¶] The context of the opinions contained in the medical records . . . indicates that these statements are merely recitations of medical history or opinion as to causation provided by other records, [P], or [her doctor]." Held: No evidence of causation.

Savoy v. National Collegiate Student Loan Trust, 557 S.W.3d 825, 831-32 (Tex.App.—Houston [1st Dist.] 2018, no pet.). "'A document authored or created by a third party may be admissible as business records of a different business if: (a) the document is incorporated and kept in the course of the testifying witness's business; (b) that business typically relies upon the accuracy of the contents of the document; and (c) the circumstances otherwise indicate the trustworthiness of the document.'" *See also* **Rogers v. RREF II CB Acquisitions, LLC**, 533 S.W.3d 419, 432-34 (Tex.App.—Corpus Christi 2016, no pet.).

Barnhart v. Morales, 459 S.W.3d 733, 744 (Tex.App.—Houston [14th Dist.] 2015, no pet.). "The fact that some parts of the challenged records were handwritten notes on preprinted forms designed to be filled in by the hospital's staff while evaluating and treating emergency room patients does not take them outside of the business records hearsay exception, so long as all requirements of that exception are met. [D] has not shown that the handwritten nature of these notes renders them untrustworthy."

Ortega v. CACH, LLC, 396 S.W.3d 622, 629-30 (Tex.App.—Houston [14th Dist.] 2013, no pet.). "The theory underlying the business-records exception is that there is a certain probability of trustworthiness of records regularly kept by an organization while engaged in its activities and upon which it relies in the ordinary course of its activities. Therefore, if 'the source of information or the method or circumstances of preparation indicate lack of trustworthiness,' even a properly authenticated record may be inadmissible. Lack of trustworthiness is most frequently found when the record was prepared in anticipation of litigation." *See also* **Freeman v. American Motorists Ins.**, 53 S.W.3d 710, 715 (Tex.App.—Houston [1st Dist.] 2001, no pet.).

Trantham v. Isaacks, 218 S.W.3d 750, 755 (Tex.App.—Fort Worth 2007, pet. denied). "The foundation for admission of a business record may be established by testimony or by affidavit." *See also* **Benavides v. Cushman, Inc.**, 189 S.W.3d 875, 884 n.6 (Tex.App.—Houston [1st Dist.] 2006, no pet.).

TRE 803(7)

Coleman v. United Sav. Ass'n, 846 S.W.2d 128, 131 (Tex.App.—Fort Worth 1993, no writ). "Testimony that is offered as evidence that a matter is not included in records to prove the nonoccurrence or nonexistence of the matter is inadmissible hearsay evidence unless rule 803(7) is satisfied. The initial foundational predicate of rule 803(7) is that the records that would include the matter, if it were not absent from those records, are kept in accordance with the provisions of rule 803(6). [D's] affidavit does not even attempt to satisfy the requirements of rule 803(6) and therefore cannot support the summary judgment."

TRE 803(8)

Commission for Lawyer Discipline v. Cantu, 587 S.W.3d 779, 786 (Tex.2019). "[P] argues that the trial court did not err in admitting [judge's] written Opinion denying [D's] discharge in bankruptcy. [P] is correct that the Opinion was admissible under the hearsay exception for public records found in [TRE] 803(8). . . . The Opinion sets out [judge's] legally authorized factual findings. As a court-generated document, it can qualify as a public record."

Texas DPS v. Caruana, 363 S.W.3d 558, 564 (Tex.2012). "Law enforcement investigation reports are commonly admitted in civil cases—car wrecks, for example. [¶] A report is no less admissible in a civil case merely because it is unsworn. . . ." *See also* **Texas DPS v. Todd**, No. 05-13-01198-CV, 2014 WL 2628139 (Tex.App.—Dallas 2014, no pet.) (memo op.; 6-12-14).

F-Star Socorro, L.P. v. City of El Paso, 281 S.W.3d 103, 106 (Tex.App.—El Paso 2008, no pet.). "[D] argues that the certified tax statement is not a public record under Rule 803(8). . . . The findings in the certified tax statement appear to result from the tax assessor-collector's investigation of [D], as outlined in Rule 803(8)(C) [now TRE 803(8)(A)(iii)]. Therefore, we find that the certified tax statement is a public record under the terms of Rule 803(8)."

Corrales v. TDFPS, 155 S.W.3d 478, 486 (Tex.App.—El Paso 2004, no pet.). "Generally speaking, the police reports were admissible as a public record. [¶] [T]he records also contained statements by witnesses which did not qualify as public records. Nevertheless, . . . the reports are admissible unless the sources of information indicate a lack of trustworthiness. [T]here is a presumption of admissibility and the burden is placed on the party opposing the admission of a report to show its untrustworthiness." *See also* **First Transit, Inc. v. Alfaro**, No. 14-14-00063-CV, 2015 WL 1623064 (Tex.App.—Houston [14th Dist.] 2015, pet. denied) (memo op.; 4-7-15).

TRE 803(10)

Towne Square Assocs. v. Angelina Cty. Appr. Dist., 709 S.W.2d 776, 777 (Tex.App.—Beaumont 1986, no writ).

"[Ds'] affidavits stated that, after a diligent search, [Ds] could find no notice of appeal filed in the records. [Ps] assert these affidavits are insufficient in that they contain hearsay and do not have some of the predicate language required for a business record in accordance with [TRE] 902. [Ps'] complete reliance on this rule is misplaced. The affidavits are controlled by [TRE] 803(10). . . . While it is true the affidavits do not meet the authentication requirements of Rule 902, they do contain testimony that a diligent search failed to disclose the notice of appeal."

TRE 803(14), (15)

Tri-Steel Structures, Inc. v. Baptist Found., 166 S.W.3d 443, 451 (Tex.App.—Fort Worth 2005, pet. denied). TRE 803(15) requires "that the document have some sort of official or formal nature, which an unsigned letter does not possess. [D]ealings with the property [must] not be inconsistent with the statement after it was made."

Compton v. WWV Enters., 679 S.W.2d 668, 671 (Tex.App.—Eastland 1984, no writ). "Hearsay exceptions [TRE 803(14) and (15)] must . . . be construed to relate to recitals or statements made in deeds, leases, mortgages and other such 'documents affecting an interest in property' and not to affidavits of heirship which more properly fall within the hearsay exception stated under [TRE] 804(b)(3)."

TRE 803(16)

Guthrie v. Suiter, 934 S.W.2d 820, 825 (Tex.App.—Houston [1st Dist.] 1996, no writ). "Statements contained in documents 20 years old or older qualify as an exception to the hearsay rule, provided the documents are properly authenticated. To qualify for this exception, the document must be shown (1) in such condition as to create no suspicion concerning its authenticity; (2) that it was in a place where it would likely be if it were authentic; and (3) that it has been in existence 20 years or more at the time it is offered."

TRE 803(17)

New Braunfels Factory Outlet Ctr. v. IHOP Rlty. Corp., 872 S.W.2d 303, 310 (Tex.App.—Austin 1994, no writ). "The hearsay exception provided by [TRE] 803(17) permits the admission of certain objective data. . . . At common law, survey results were also admissible *provided* that the party opposing admission was given the opportunity to cross-examine the person who had conducted the survey."

TRE 803(18)

King v. Bauer, 767 S.W.2d 197, 199-200 (Tex.App.—Corpus Christi 1989, writ denied). Under TRE 803(18), P introduced a medical textbook that was published two years after P's therapy, but the earlier edition of which was recognized by D as a learned treatise. "The fact that the third edition [of the textbook] was not published until 1980 does not serve to disqualify the evidence which was aimed at illustrating an appropriate treatment plan for [P] in 1978. Treatises which directly refer to the standard of care in use at the time of the occurrence are material, relevant and therefore admissible."

TRE 803(19)

Akers v. Stevenson, 54 S.W.3d 880, 885 (Tex.App.—Beaumont 2001, pet. denied). The hearsay exception for evidence concerning personal or family history arises "from necessity and [is] founded on the general reliability of statements by family members about family affairs when the statements by deceased persons regarding family history were made at a time when no pecuniary interest or other biased reason for the statements were present."

TRE 803(20)

Roberts v. Allison, 836 S.W.2d 185, 191 (Tex.App.—Tyler 1992, writ denied). "A reason for the exception [in TRE 803(20)] is '[t]he fact that a prolonged observation and discussion of certain matters of *general interest by a whole community will sift possible errors and bring the result down to us in a fairly trustworthy form furnishes a guarantee of correctness.*' [Ps'] proposed testimony pertains to an individual family's assertion of an easement; there is no contention of the . . . community's knowledge of [Ps'] claim to access [D's] property. . . . There was no proof of the recognized 'vehicles of reputation,' such as 'declarations of residents, old maps, surveys, deeds and leases' of the claimed easement. . . . The trial court did not abuse its discretion in excluding [the] testimony of a claimed oral agreement granting an easement to [Ps] over the subject property."

TRE 803(22)

McCormick v. Texas Commerce Bank, 751 S.W.2d 887, 890 (Tex.App.—Houston [14th Dist.] 1988, writ denied). "Where (i) the issue at stake was identical to that in the criminal case, (ii) the issue had been actually litigated, and (iii) determination of the issue was a critical and necessary part of the prior judgment, the judgment is established by offensive collateral estoppel and is within the hearsay exception of [FRE] 803(22). [¶] Applying the standards of the federal judiciary to [TRE] 803(22), we hold that the trial court did not err in refusing to permit [D] to explain the circumstances of his criminal conviction."

TRE 803(24)

State v. Arnold, 778 S.W.2d 68, 69 (Tex.1989). Under TRE 803(24), a "statement may be self-serving in one respect but contrary to another interest. The court must balance these competing interests to determine their predominant nature and ultimately the level of trustworthiness to be accorded."

Green v. Reyes, 836 S.W.2d 203, 213 (Tex.App.—Houston [14th Dist.] 1992, no writ). "[A]ffidavits of persons who . . . admit under oath an action which can subject them to criminal liability may be properly admitted at trial as an exception to the hearsay rule as statements against their interest."

TRE 804. EXCEPTIONS TO THE RULE AGAINST HEARSAY—WHEN THE DECLARANT IS UNAVAILABLE AS A WITNESS

(a) Criteria for Being Unavailable. A declarant is considered to be unavailable as a witness if the declarant:

(1) is exempted from testifying about the subject matter of the declarant's statement because the court rules that a privilege applies;

(2) refuses to testify about the subject matter despite a court order to do so;

(3) testifies to not remembering the subject matter;

(4) cannot be present or testify at the trial or hearing because of death or a then-existing infirmity, physical illness, or mental illness; or

(5) is absent from the trial or hearing and the statement's proponent has not been able, by process or other reasonable means, to procure the declarant's attendance or testimony.

But this subdivision (a) does not apply if the statement's proponent procured or wrongfully caused the declarant's unavailability as a witness in order to prevent the declarant from attending or testifying.

(b) The Exceptions. The following are not excluded by the rule against hearsay if the declarant is unavailable as a witness:

(1) ***Former Testimony.*** Testimony that:

(A) when offered in a civil case:

(i) was given as a witness at a trial or hearing of the current or a different proceeding or in a deposition in a different proceeding; and

(ii) is now offered against a party and the party—or a person with similar interest—had an opportunity and similar motive to develop the testimony by direct, cross-, or redirect examination.

(B) when offered in a criminal case:

(i) was given as a witness at a trial or hearing of the current or a different proceeding; and

(ii) is now offered against a party who had an opportunity and similar motive to develop it by direct, cross-, or redirect examination; or

(iii) was taken in a deposition under—and is now offered in accordance with—chapter 39 of the Code of Criminal Procedure.

(2) ***Statement Under the Belief of Imminent Death.*** A statement that the declarant, while believing the declarant's death to be imminent, made about its cause or circumstances.

(3) ***Statement of Personal or Family History.*** A statement about:

(A) the declarant's own birth, adoption, legitimacy, ancestry, marriage, divorce, relationship by blood, adoption or marriage, or similar facts of personal or family history, even though the declarant had no way of acquiring personal knowledge about that fact; or

(B) another person concerning any of these facts, as well as death, if the declarant was related to the person by blood, adoption, or marriage or was so intimately associated with the person's family that the declarant's information is likely to be accurate.

Eff. March 1, 1998. Amended by orders of Supreme Court March 10, 2015 and Court of Criminal Appeals March 12, 2015, eff. April 1, 2015.

Source: FRE 804.

See also Brown & Rondon, **Texas Rules of Evidence Handbook**, Rule 804.

ANNOTATIONS

Massey v. Allen Nat'l Prop., L.L.C., No. 02-11-00503-CV, 2013 WL 173737 (Tex.App.—Fort Worth 2013, no pet.) (memo op.; 1-17-13). "A party offering the prior testimony of a witness must prove the witness is unavailable. Unavailability means that the witness is dead, that he had become insane or is physically unable to testify, that he is beyond the jurisdiction of the court, that his whereabouts are unknown and that a diligent search has been made to ascertain where he is, or that he has been kept away from the trial by the adverse party. Here, [P] did not prove that [witness] was unavailable. Instead, he argued that it was impossible to procure her testimony because [TRCP] 166a(c) does not allow oral testimony at a summary judgment hearing. However, [P] could have procured [witness's] testimony in the form of an affidavit or a deposition, which would have been acceptable summary judgment evidence. Therefore, the trial court did not abuse its discretion in excluding [witness's] prior testimony because [P] did not prove [witness] was unavailable."

Fuller-Austin Insulation Co. v. Bilder, 960 S.W.2d 914, 921 (Tex.App.—Beaumont 1998, pet. granted, judgm't vacated w.r.m.). "[T]he fact that [witness] was uncooperative in attending trial did not mean he could not give his deposition. . . . Although [witness] may have been beyond the subpoena power of the court, [D] did not establish it was unable to take his deposition or otherwise procure his testimony in this cause."

Thompson v. Mayes, 707 S.W.2d 951, 957 (Tex.App.—Eastland 1986, writ ref'd n.r.e.). Under TRE 804(b)(2), "dying declarations which concern the cause or the circumstances of what the declarant believed to be his impending death are admissible as exceptions to the hearsay rule."

TRE 805. HEARSAY WITHIN HEARSAY

Hearsay within hearsay is not excluded by the rule against hearsay if each part of the combined statements conforms with an exception to the rule.

Eff. March 1, 1998. Amended by orders of Supreme Court March 10, 2015 and Court of Criminal Appeals March 12, 2015, eff. April 1, 2015.

See also Brown & Rondon, **Texas Rules of Evidence Handbook**, Rule 805.

ANNOTATIONS

Houston Lighting & Power Co. v. Klein ISD, 739 S.W.2d 508, 519 (Tex.App.—Houston [14th Dist.] 1987, writ denied). "[C]harts summarizing studies of power lines and health effects [were] objected to . . . as hearsay because the underlying studies were hearsay. [T]he error [in admitting the charts did not] cause the rendition of an improper verdict."

TRE 806. ATTACKING AND SUPPORTING THE DECLARANT'S CREDIBILITY

When a hearsay statement—or a statement described in Rule 801(e)(2)(C), (D), or (E), or, in a civil case, a statement described in Rule 801(e)(3)—has been admitted in evidence, the declarant's credibility may be attacked, and then supported, by any evidence that would be admissible for those purposes if the declarant had testified as a witness. The court may admit evidence of the declarant's statement or conduct, offered to impeach the declarant, regardless of when it occurred or whether the declarant had an opportunity to explain or deny it. If the party against whom the statement was admitted calls the declarant as a witness, the party may examine the declarant on the statement as if on cross-examination.

Eff. March 1, 1998. Amended by orders of Supreme Court March 10, 2015 and Court of Criminal Appeals March 12, 2015, eff. April 1, 2015.

Source: FRE 806.

See also Brown & Rondon, **Texas Rules of Evidence Handbook**, Rule 806.

ANNOTATIONS

Anthony Pools, Inc. v. Charles & David, Inc., 797 S.W.2d 666, 676 (Tex.App.—Houston [14th Dist.] 1990, writ denied). "Texas courts long have allowed the use of affidavits to impeach a witness. The jury could have been allowed to consider any inconsistencies between the affidavit and the deposition as damaging to the credibility of [witness's] deposition, but not as substantive evidence. [¶] Upon timely request and objection, . . . the court was required to instruct the jury of the limited use to be made of the affidavit."

Article IX. Authentication and Identification

TRE 901. AUTHENTICATING OR IDENTIFYING EVIDENCE

(a) In General. To satisfy the requirement of authenticating or identifying an item of evidence, the proponent must produce evidence sufficient to support a finding that the item is what the proponent claims it is.

(b) Examples. The following are examples only—not a complete list—of evidence that satisfies the requirement:

(1) ***Testimony of a Witness with Knowledge.*** Testimony that an item is what it is claimed to be.

(2) ***Nonexpert Opinion About Handwriting.*** A nonexpert's opinion that handwriting is genuine, based on a familiarity with it that was not acquired for the current litigation.

(3) ***Comparison by an Expert Witness or the Trier of Fact.*** A comparison by an expert witness or the trier of fact with a specimen that the court has found is genuine.

(4) ***Distinctive Characteristics and the Like.*** The appearance, contents, substance, internal patterns, or other distinctive characteristics of the item, taken together with all the circumstances.

(5) ***Opinion About a Voice.*** An opinion identifying a person's voice—whether heard firsthand or through mechanical or electronic transmission or recording—based on hearing the voice at any time under circumstances that connect it with the alleged speaker.

(6) ***Evidence About a Telephone Conversation.*** For a telephone conversation, evidence that a call was made to the number assigned at the time to:

(A) a particular person, if circumstances, including self-identification, show that the person answering was the one called; or

(B) a particular business, if the call was made to a business and the call related to business reasonably transacted over the telephone.

(7) ***Evidence About Public Records.*** Evidence that:

(A) a document was recorded or filed in a public office as authorized by law; or

(B) a purported public record or statement is from the office where items of this kind are kept.

(8) ***Evidence About Ancient Documents or Data Compilations.*** For a document or data compilation, evidence that it:

(A) is in a condition that creates no suspicion about its authenticity;

(B) was in a place where, if authentic, it would likely be; and

(C) is at least 20 years old when offered.

(9) ***Evidence About a Process or System.*** Evidence describing a process or system and showing that it produces an accurate result.

(10) ***Methods Provided by a Statute or Rule.*** Any method of authentication or identification allowed by a statute or other rule prescribed under statutory authority.

Eff. March 1, 1998. Amended by orders of Supreme Court March 10, 2015 and Court of Criminal Appeals March 12, 2015, eff. April 1, 2015.

Source: FRE 901. See TRCS arts. 3725, 3737b (repealed).

See also **O'Connor's Texas Rules,** "Authenticity," ch. 8-C, §8.4; Brown & Rondon, **Texas Rules of Evidence Handbook**, Rule 901.

ANNOTATIONS

Fleming v. Wilson, ___ S.W.3d ___, 2020 WL 5985187 (Tex.2020) (No. 19-0230; 10-9-20). "Because the copies of the ... jury verdict and final judgment attached to [D's] summary-judgment motion were not sealed or certified, they were not self-authenticating. Under [TRE] 901, [D] thus had to 'produce evidence sufficient to support a finding that' they were what [D] claimed they were. Relying on this language, the court of appeals held that rule 901 required [D] to produce *extrinsic* evidence, outside of and in addition to the documents themselves. [¶] We disagree. Rule 901 provides a non-exclusive list of examples of the type of evidence a proponent can use to authenticate an item.... Some of these examples indicate the need for *extrinsic* evidence, like opinion testimony comparing the item with a 'specimen' the court has deemed genuine or identifying a person's voice. Other examples, however, do not require or contemplate the need for extrinsic evidence. [¶] [TRE] 902 states that self-authenticating items 'require no extrinsic evidence of authenticity in order to be admitted.' But that does not mean that rule 901 *requires* extrinsic evidence. Unlike rule 901's non-exclusive list, rule 902 provides an exclusive list of items that courts must always accept as authentic, but it does not preclude courts from accepting other items that demonstrate on their face that they are what the proponent claims they are. Rule 901's route to authentication is less open-and-shut. It requires the trial court to evaluate the evidence that supports the item's authenticity—whether found within the item itself or provided by an extrinsic source. If the proponent produces only the item, but the item itself constitutes or contains evidence that it is what the proponent claims it is, the court may find it to be authentic."

General Motors Corp. v. Gayle, 951 S.W.2d 469, 475 (Tex.1997). "Any tests that a party . . . offer[s] at trial will be admissible only if the trial court determines that there is a substantial similarity between the test conditions and the accident conditions."

Kroger Co. v. Milanes, 474 S.W.3d 321, 342 (Tex.App.—Houston [14th Dist.] 2015, no pet.). "Generally, pictures or photographs relevant to any issue in a case are admissible. When a photograph or video portrays facts relevant to an issue, it is admissible if verified by a witness as being a correct representation of the facts. The verifying witness must know the object involved and be able to state that the photograph or video correctly represents it. The fact that the scene or the object portrayed in the photograph or video has changed since the time of the event in question in the litigation does not prevent the admission of the photograph or video into evidence if the changes are explained in such a manner that the photograph or video will help the jury in understanding the nature of the condition at the time of the event at issue." *See also* **Kirwan v. City of Waco**, 249 S.W.3d 544, 549 (Tex.App.—Waco 2008) (not required that witness made photographs, observed their making, or knew when they were taken), *rev'd on other grounds*, 298 S.W.3d 618 (Tex.2009).

Sanchez v. Texas State Bd. of Med. Exam'rs, 229 S.W.3d 498, 509 (Tex.App.—Austin 2007, no pet.). "[T]he predicate for admissibility under rule 901 may be proven by circumstantial evidence." *See also* **Gunville v. Gonzales**, 508 S.W.3d 547, 559 (Tex.App.—El Paso 2016, no pet.); **Nicholas v. Environmental Sys. (Int'l)**, 499 S.W.3d 888, 900 (Tex.App.—Houston [14th Dist.] 2016, pet. denied).

In re G.F.O., 874 S.W.2d 729, 731 (Tex.App.—Houston [1st Dist.] 1994, no writ). "A document is considered authentic if a sponsoring witness vouches for its authenticity. . . . [T]he confession was properly authenticated because the [arresting] officer identified [D] and his confession." *See also* **Baker v. City of Robinson**, 305 S.W.3d 783, 792 (Tex.App.—Waco 2009, pet. denied); **Durkay v. Madco Oil Co.**, 862 S.W.2d 14, 24 (Tex.App.—Corpus Christi 1993, writ denied).

TRE 902. EVIDENCE THAT IS SELF-AUTHENTICATING

The following items of evidence are self-authenticating; they require no extrinsic evidence of authenticity in order to be admitted:

(1) ***Domestic Public Documents That Are Sealed and Signed.*** A document that bears:

(A) a seal purporting to be that of the United States; any state, district, commonwealth, territory, or insular possession of the United States; the former Panama Canal Zone; the Trust Territory of the Pacific Islands; a political subdivision of any of these entities; or a department, agency, or officer of any entity named above; and

(B) a signature purporting to be an execution or attestation.

(2) ***Domestic Public Documents That Are Not Sealed But Are Signed and Certified.*** A document that bears no seal if:

(A) it bears the signature of an officer or employee of an entity named in Rule 902(1)(A); and

(B) another public officer who has a seal and official duties within that same entity certifies under seal—or its equivalent—that the signer has the official capacity and that the signature is genuine.

(3) ***Foreign Public Documents.*** A document that purports to be signed or attested by a person who is authorized by a foreign country's law to do so.

(A) ***In General.*** The document must be accompanied by a final certification that certifies the genuineness of the signature and official position of the signer or attester—or of any foreign official whose certificate of genuineness relates to the signature or attestation or is in a chain of certificates of genuineness relating to the signature or attestation. The certification may be made by a secretary of a United States embassy or legation; by a consul general, vice consul, or consular agent of the United States; or by a diplomatic or consular official of the foreign country assigned or accredited to the United States.

(B) ***If Parties Have Reasonable Opportunity to Investigate.*** If all parties have been given a reasonable opportunity to investigate the document's authenticity and accuracy, the court may, for good cause, either:

(i) order that it be treated as presumptively authentic without final certification; or

(ii) allow it to be evidenced by an attested summary with or without final certification.

(C) ***If a Treaty Abolishes or Displaces the Final Certification Requirement.*** If the United States and the foreign country in which the official record is located are parties to a treaty or convention that abolishes or displaces the final certification requirement, the record and attestation must be certified under the terms of the treaty or convention.

(4) ***Certified Copies of Public Records.*** A copy of an official record—or a copy of a document that was recorded or filed in a public office as authorized by law—if the copy is certified as correct by:

(A) the custodian or another person authorized to make the certification; or

(B) a certificate that complies with Rule 902(1), (2), or (3), a statute, or a rule prescribed under statutory authority.

(5) ***Official Publications.*** A book, pamphlet, or other publication purporting to be issued by a public authority.

(6) ***Newspapers and Periodicals.*** Printed material purporting to be a newspaper or periodical.

(7) ***Trade Inscriptions and the Like.*** An inscription, sign, tag, or label purporting to have been affixed in the course of business and indicating origin, ownership, or control.

(8) ***Acknowledged Documents.*** A document accompanied by a certificate of acknowledgment that is lawfully executed by a notary public or another officer who is authorized to take acknowledgments.

(9) ***Commercial Paper and Related Documents.*** Commercial paper, a signature on it, and related documents, to the extent allowed by general commercial law.

(10) ***Business Records Accompanied by Affidavit.*** The original or a copy of a record that meets the requirements of Rule 803(6) or (7), if the record is accompanied by an affidavit that complies with subparagraph (B) of this rule and any other requirements of law, and the record and affidavit are served in accordance with subparagraph (A). For good cause shown, the court may order that a business record be treated as presumptively authentic even if the proponent fails to comply with subparagraph (A).

(A) ***Service Requirement.*** The proponent of a record must serve the record and the accompanying affidavit on each other party to the case at least 14 days before trial. The record and affidavit may be served by any method permitted by Rule of Civil Procedure 21a.

(B) ***Form of Affidavit.*** An affidavit is sufficient if it includes the following language, but this form is not exclusive. The proponent may use an unsworn declaration made under penalty of perjury in place of an affidavit.

1. I am the custodian of records [*or* I am an employee or owner] of ________ and am familiar with the manner in which its records are created and maintained by virtue of my duties and responsibilities.

2. Attached are ____ pages of records. These are the original records or exact duplicates of the original records.

3. The records were made at or near the time of each act, event, condition, opinion, or diagnosis set forth. [*or* It is the regular practice of ________ to make this type of record at or near the time of each act, event, condition, opinion, or diagnosis set forth in the record.]

4. The records were made by, or from informa-

tion transmitted by, persons with knowledge of the matters set forth. [*or* It is the regular practice of _______ for this type of record to be made by, or from information transmitted by, persons with knowledge of the matters set forth in them.]

5. The records were kept in the course of regularly conducted business activity. [*or* It is the regular practice of _______ to keep this type of record in the course of regularly conducted business activity.]

6. It is the regular practice of the business activity to make the records.

(11) ***Presumptions Under a Statute or Rule.*** A signature, document, or anything else that a statute or rule prescribed under statutory authority declares to be presumptively or prima facie genuine or authentic.

Eff. March 1, 1998. Amended by orders of Feb. 12, 2013, and March 26, 2013, eff. March 1, 2013. Amended by orders of Supreme Court and Court of Criminal Appeals April 14, 2014, and August 19, 2014, eff. Sept. 1, 2014. Amended by order of orders of Supreme Court March 10, 2015 and Court of Criminal Appeals March 12, 2015, eff. April 1, 2015.

Comment to 2013 change: Rule 902(10)(c) is added to provide a form affidavit for proof of medical expenses. The affidavit is intended to comport with Section 41.0105 of the Civil Practice and Remedies Code, which allows evidence of only those medical expenses that have been paid or will be paid, after any required credits or adjustments. *See* Haygood v. De Escabedo, 356 S.W.3d 390 (Tex. 2011). The records attached to the affidavit must also meet the admissibility standard of *Haygood. Id.* at 399-400 ("[O]nly evidence of recoverable medical expenses is admissible at trial.").

Comment to 2014 change: At the direction of the Legislature, the requirement that records be filed with the court before trial has been removed. *See* Act of May 17, 2013, 83rd Leg., R.S., ch. 560, §3, 2013 Tex. Gen. Laws 1509, 1510 (SB 679). The word "affidavit" in this rule includes an unsworn declaration made under penalty of perjury. Tex. Civ. Prac. & Rem. Code §132.001. The reference to "any other requirements of law" incorporates the requirements of Sections 18.001 and 18.002 of the Civil Practice and Remedies Code for affidavits offered as prima facie proof of the cost or necessity of services or medical expenses. The form medical expenses affidavit that was added to this rule in 2013 has been removed as unnecessary. It can now be found in Section 18.002(b-1) of the Civil Practice and Remedies Code.

See also **O'Connor's Texas Rules,** "Documents that are self-authenticating," ch. 8-C, §8.4.4; Brown & Rondon, **Texas Rules of Evidence Handbook,** Rule 902.

ANNOTATIONS

Williams Farms Produce Sales, Inc. v. R&G Produce Co., 443 S.W.3d 250, 259 (Tex.App.—Corpus Christi 2014, no pet.). "[W]e hold that documents printed from government websites are self-authenticating under [TRE] 902(5). *At n.7:* [However], we also acknowledge that, because [the documents in this case] indicate they originated from government websites, they could also have been internally authenticated under [TRE] 901(b)(4)."

Murphy v. Countrywide Home Loans, Inc., 199 S.W.3d 441, 446 (Tex.App.—Houston [1st Dist.] 2006, pet. denied). "The deed of trust, substitute trustee's deed, and affidavit of mortgage in this case all contain file stamps which indicate that they have been filed in the [c]ounty real property records as official public records. Therefore, we hold these documents to be self-authenticated."

Texas DPS v. Silva, 988 S.W.2d 873, 877 (Tex.App.—San Antonio 1999, pet. denied). "[D] cites no authority, nor have we found any requirement that the stamp state what the document is certifying or that the stamp be from the county where the documents were prepared."

TRE 903. SUBSCRIBING WITNESS'S TESTIMONY

A subscribing witness's testimony is necessary to authenticate a writing only if required by the law of the jurisdiction that governs its validity.

Eff. March 1, 1998. Amended by orders of Supreme Court March 10, 2015 and Court of Criminal Appeals March 12, 2015, eff. April 1, 2015.

See also Brown & Rondon, **Texas Rules of Evidence Handbook,** Rule 903.

Article X. Contents of Writings, Recordings, and Photographs

TRE 1001. DEFINITIONS THAT APPLY TO THIS ARTICLE

In this article:

(a) A "writing" consists of letters, words, numbers, or their equivalent set down in any form.

(b) A "recording" consists of letters, words, numbers, or their equivalent recorded in any manner.

(c) A "photograph" means a photographic image or its equivalent stored in any form.

(d) An "original" of a writing or recording means the writing or recording itself or any counterpart intended to have the same effect by the person who executed or issued it. For electronically stored information, "original" means any printout—or other output readable by sight—if it accurately reflects the information. An "original" of a photograph includes the negative or a print from it.

(e) A "duplicate" means a counterpart produced by a mechanical, photographic, chemical, electronic, or other equivalent process or technique that accurately reproduces the original.

Eff. March 1, 1998. Amended by orders of Supreme Court March 10, 2015 and Court of Criminal Appeals March 12, 2015, eff. April 1, 2015.

See also **O'Connor's Texas Rules,** "Documents authenticated by witness," ch. 8-C, §8.4.3; Brown & Rondon, **Texas Rules of Evidence Handbook,** Rule 1001.

ANNOTATIONS

S.D.G. v. State, 936 S.W.2d 371, 381 (Tex.App.—Houston [14th Dist.] 1996, writ denied). "The predicate for

introduction of a photograph and a videotape not accompanied by a sound recording requires proof of (1) its accuracy as a correct representation of the subject at a given time, and (2) its relevance to a material issue. . . . Any witness who observed the object or the scene depicted in the photograph may lay the predicate."

TRE 1002. REQUIREMENT OF THE ORIGINAL

An original writing, recording, or photograph is required in order to prove its content unless these rules or other law provides otherwise.

Eff. March 1, 1998. Amended by orders of Supreme Court March 10, 2015 and Court of Criminal Appeals March 12, 2015, eff. April 1, 2015.

See also Brown & Rondon, **Texas Rules of Evidence Handbook**, Rule 1002.

ANNOTATIONS

White v. Bath, 825 S.W.2d 227, 231 (Tex.App.—Houston [14th Dist.] 1992, writ denied). "[O]nly when one seeks to prove the contents of a document [does] the best evidence rule [apply]. When the document and its contents are only collaterally related to the issues in the case, the best evidence rule does not apply."

Ramsey v. Jones Enters., 810 S.W.2d 902, 905 (Tex.App.—Beaumont 1991, writ denied). "The best evidence of the content of documents is the documents themselves. The trial court erred in admitting hearsay testimony to prove up the content of documents without a proper showing that the subject documents were unavailable through no fault or failure on the part of the party offering same."

TRE 1003. ADMISSIBILITY OF DUPLICATES

A duplicate is admissible to the same extent as the original unless a question is raised about the original's authenticity or the circumstances make it unfair to admit the duplicate.

Eff. March 1, 1998. Amended by orders of Supreme Court March 10, 2015 and Court of Criminal Appeals March 12, 2015, eff. April 1, 2015.

See also **O'Connor's Texas Rules,** "Copy of document," ch. 8-C, §8.4.3(2); Brown & Rondon, **Texas Rules of Evidence Handbook**, Rule 1003.

ANNOTATIONS

Ford Motor Co. v. Leggat, 904 S.W.2d 643, 646 (Tex 1995). "[I]n the absence of a challenge to the authenticity of the affidavit, submission of a copy is not grounds for rejecting it."

TRE 1004. ADMISSIBILITY OF OTHER EVIDENCE OF CONTENT

An original is not required and other evidence of the content of a writing, recording, or photograph is admissible if:

(a) all the originals are lost or destroyed, unless the proponent lost or destroyed them in bad faith;

(b) an original cannot be obtained by any available judicial process;

(c) an original is not located in Texas;

(d) the party against whom the original would be offered had control of the original; was at that time put on notice, by pleadings or otherwise, that the original would be a subject of proof at the trial or hearing; and fails to produce it at the trial or hearing; or

(e) the writing, recording, or photograph is not closely related to a controlling issue.

Eff. March 1, 1998. Amended by orders of Supreme Court March 10, 2015 and Court of Criminal Appeals March 12, 2015, eff. April 1, 2015.

See also TRCP 77; **O'Connor's Texas Rules,** "Copy of document," ch. 8-C, §8.4.3(2); Brown & Rondon, **Texas Rules of Evidence Handbook**, Rule 1004.

ANNOTATIONS

Coke v. Coke, 802 S.W.2d 270, 275 (Tex.App.—Dallas 1990, writ denied). "Under rule 1004, an original document is not required if the original is lost or destroyed without the fault of the proponent. Copies are admissible if 'there is a reasonable account for [original's] absence or if there is no question of their authenticity.' "

TRE 1005. COPIES OF PUBLIC RECORDS TO PROVE CONTENT

The proponent may use a copy to prove the content of an official record—or of a document that was recorded or filed in a public office as authorized by law—if these conditions are met: the record or document is otherwise admissible; and the copy is certified as correct in accordance with Rule 902(4) or is testified to be correct by a witness who has compared it with the original. If no such copy can be obtained by reasonable diligence, then the proponent may use other evidence to prove the content.

Eff. March 1, 1998. Amended by orders of Supreme Court March 10, 2015 and Court of Criminal Appeals March 12, 2015, eff. April 1, 2015.

See also **O'Connor's Texas Rules,** "Documents that are self-authenticating," ch. 8-C, §8.4.4; Brown & Rondon, **Texas Rules of Evidence Handbook**, Rule 1005.

ANNOTATIONS

ESIS, Inc. v. Johnson, 908 S.W.2d 554, 561 (Tex.App.—Fort Worth 1995, writ denied). "A copy of a public record is considered authentic if a sponsoring witness vouches for its

authenticity or if the document meets the certification requirements for self-authentication contained in [TRE] 902."

TRE 1006. SUMMARIES TO PROVE CONTENT

The proponent may use a summary, chart, or calculation to prove the content of voluminous writings, recordings, or photographs that cannot be conveniently examined in court. The proponent must make the originals or duplicates available for examination or copying, or both, by other parties at a reasonable time and place. And the court may order the proponent to produce them in court.

Eff. March 1, 1998. Amended by orders of Supreme Court March 10, 2015 and Court of Criminal Appeals March 12, 2015, eff. April 1, 2015.

Source: FRE 1006.

See also Brown & Rondon, **Texas Rules of Evidence Handbook**, Rule 1006; **O'Connor's Texas Family Law Handbook**, "Sworn inventory & appraisement," ch. 7-A, §3.1.

ANNOTATIONS

Aquamarine Assocs. v. Burton Shipyard, Inc., 659 S.W.2d 820, 821 (Tex.1983). "In cases involving voluminous records, the trial court has discretion to relax the best evidence rule and allow the admission of summaries. . . . The party sponsoring the summary must, however, lay the proper predicate for its admission." *See also* **Welder v. Welder**, 794 S.W.2d 420, 429 (Tex.App.—Corpus Christi 1990, no writ).

Harpst v. Fleming, 566 S.W.3d 898, 908-09 (Tex.App.—Houston [14th Dist.] 2018, no pet.). "Admissibility of summaries under rule 1006 requires that (1) the records are voluminous, (2) they have been made available to the opponent for a reasonable period of time to afford inspection and an opportunity for cross-examination, and . . . (3) the supporting documents themselves are admissible in evidence. A proper foundation for a summary 'must establish the admissibility of the underlying documents and the accuracy of the summary.'"

Shaw v. Lemon, 427 S.W.3d 536, 544-45 (Tex.App.—Dallas 2014, pet. denied). "Rule 1006 states that a summary's underlying records must have been made available to the opponent for inspection, but it does not state that the summary itself must be produced in discovery or disclosed within a certain time period of the trial. [P] has not cited, nor have we found, any case law requiring a rule 1006 summary to be produced in discovery or disclosed before trial."

TRE 1007. TESTIMONY OR STATEMENT OF A PARTY TO PROVE CONTENT

The proponent may prove the content of a writing, recording, or photograph by the testimony, deposition, or written statement of the party against whom the evidence is offered. The proponent need not account for the original.

Eff. March 1, 1998. Amended by orders of Supreme Court March 10, 2015 and Court of Criminal Appeals March 12, 2015, eff. April 1, 2015.

See also Brown & Rondon, **Texas Rules of Evidence Handbook**, Rule 1007.

TRE 1008. FUNCTIONS OF THE COURT AND JURY

Ordinarily, the court determines whether the proponent has fulfilled the factual conditions for admitting other evidence of the content of a writing, recording, or photograph under Rule 1004 or 1005. But in a jury trial, the jury determines—in accordance with Rule 104(b)—any issue about whether:

(a) an asserted writing, recording, or photograph ever existed;

(b) another one produced at the trial or hearing is the original; or

(c) other evidence of content accurately reflects the content.

Eff. March 1, 1998. Amended by orders of Supreme Court March 10, 2015 and Court of Criminal Appeals March 12, 2015, eff. April 1, 2015.

See also Brown & Rondon, **Texas Rules of Evidence Handbook**, Rule 1008.

TRE 1009. TRANSLATING A FOREIGN LANGUAGE DOCUMENT

(a) Submitting a Translation. A translation of a foreign language document is admissible if, at least 45 days before trial, the proponent serves on all parties:

(1) the translation and the underlying foreign language document; and

(2) a qualified translator's affidavit or unsworn declaration that sets forth the translator's qualifications and certifies that the translation is accurate.

(b) Objection. When objecting to a translation's accuracy, a party should specifically indicate its inaccuracies and offer an accurate translation. A party must serve the objection on all parties at least 15 days before trial.

(c) Effect of Failing to Object or Submit a Conflicting Translation. If the underlying foreign language document is otherwise admissible, the court must admit—and may not allow a party to attack the accuracy of—a translation submitted under subdivision (a) unless the party has:

(1) submitted a conflicting translation under subdivision (a); or

(2) objected to the translation under subdivision (b).

(d) Effect of Objecting or Submitting a Conflicting Translation. If conflicting translations are submitted under subdivision (a) or an objection is made under subdivision (b), the court must determine whether there is a genu-

ine issue about the accuracy of a material part of the translation. If so, the trier of fact must resolve the issue.

(e) Qualified Translator May Testify. Except for subdivision (c), this rule does not preclude a party from offering the testimony of a qualified translator to translate a foreign language document.

(f) Time Limits. On a party's motion and for good cause, the court may alter this rule's time limits.

(g) Court-Appointed Translator. If necessary, the court may appoint a qualified translator. The reasonable value of the translator's services must be taxed as court costs.

Eff. March 1, 1998. Amended by orders of Supreme Court March 10, 2015 and Court of Criminal Appeals March 12, 2015, eff. April 1, 2015.

Comment to 1998 change: This is a new rule.

Source: New rule.

See also Brown & Rondon, **Texas Rules of Evidence Handbook**, Rule 1009.

ANNOTATIONS

In re DC, No. 01-11-00387-CV, 2012 WL 682289 (Tex.App.—Houston [1st Dist.] 2012, pet. denied) (memo op.; 3-1-12). Father "complains that the initial return was in Spanish, and because it was not translated into English until after trial, it violated [TRE] 1009, which requires that all foreign documents to be admitted at trial must be translated 45 days before trial and be accompanied by an affidavit from a qualified translator. [¶] However, rule 1009 is a rule of evidence governing the admission of foreign documents of trial. [Father] has cited no cases in which rule 1009 requires the translation of foreign returns of service into English, or that such a translation could not be done in an amended return while the trial court still had plenary power. We have found no authority holding that rule 1009 trumps [TRCP] 118, which permits amended returns of service '[a]t any time.' "

Doncaster v. Hernaiz, 161 S.W.3d 594, 601 (Tex.App.—San Antonio 2005, no pet.). "[P] did file a copy of [foreign-language document] with a translation with her initial summary judgment motion, but failed to attach the translator's affidavit. Later, [P] supplemented her motion with an affidavit from the translator. . . . Because of [P's] late supplementation, the trial court provided [D] a one-week continuance before conducting the summary judgment hearing. Rule 1009 provides the court with authority to lengthen or shorten the time limits set by the rule. [A]ny error in failing to initially provide the affidavit of the translator was cured by its inclusion in the supplement, and it was therefore within the court's discretion to admit [document]."

Appendix III. Texas Rules of Appellate Procedure

To save space, we have omitted the TRAP history notes. For the complete TRAPs with annotations, see the current edition of ***O'Connor's Texas Civil Appeals***. To order, call 1-800-328-9352 or visit legalsolutions.thomsonreuters.com.

TABLE OF CONTENTS

SECTION ONE: GENERAL PROVISIONS

TRAP 1. SCOPE OF RULES; LOCAL RULES OF COURTS OF APPEALS

1.1. Scope. These rules govern procedure in appellate courts and before appellate judges and post-trial procedure in trial courts in criminal cases.

1.2. Local Rules.

(a) *Promulgation.* A court of appeals may promulgate rules governing its practice that are not inconsistent with these rules. Local rules governing civil cases must first be approved by the Supreme Court. Local rules governing criminal cases must first be approved by the Court of Criminal Appeals.

(b) *Copies.* The clerk must provide a copy of the court's local rules to anyone who requests it.

(c) *Party's Noncompliance.* A court must not dismiss an appeal for noncompliance with a local rule without giving the noncomplying party notice and a reasonable opportunity to cure the noncompliance.

TRAP 2. SUSPENSION OF RULES

On a party's motion or on its own initiative an appellate court may—to expedite a decision or for other good cause—suspend a rule's operation in a particular case and order a different procedure; but a court must not construe this rule to suspend any provision in the Code of Criminal Procedure or to alter the time for perfecting an appeal in a civil case.

TRAP 3. DEFINITIONS; UNIFORM TERMINOLOGY

3.1. Definitions.

(a) *Appellant* means a party taking an appeal to an appellate court.

(b) *Appellate court* means the courts of appeals, the Court of Criminal Appeals, and the Supreme Court.

(c) *Appellee* means a party adverse to an appellant.

(d) *Applicant* means a person seeking relief by a habeas corpus in a criminal case.

(e) *Petitioner* means a party petitioning the Supreme Court or the Court of Criminal Appeals for review.

(f) *Relator* means a person seeking relief in an original proceeding in an appellate court other than by habeas corpus in a criminal case.

(g) *Reporter* or *court reporter* means the court reporter or court recorder.

(h) *Respondent* means:

(1) a party adverse to a petitioner in the Supreme Court or the Court of Criminal Appeals; or

(2) a party against whom relief is sought in an original proceeding in an appellate court.

3.2. Uniform Terminology in Criminal Cases. In documents filed in criminal appeals, the parties are the *State* and the *appellant*. But if the State has appealed under Article 44.01 of the Code of Criminal Procedure, the defendant is the *appellee*. Otherwise, papers should use real names for parties, and such labels as *appellee, petitioner, respondent,* and *movant* should be avoided unless necessary for clarity. In habeas corpus proceedings, the person for whose relief the writ is requested is the *applicant;* Code of Criminal Procedure article 11.13.

TRAP 4. TIME AND NOTICE PROVISIONS

4.1. Computing Time.

(a) *In General.* The day of an act, event, or default after which a designated period begins to run is not included when computing a period prescribed or allowed by these rules, by court order, or by statute. The last day of the period is included, but if that day is a Saturday, Sunday, or legal holiday, the period extends to the end of the next day that is not a Saturday, Sunday, or legal holiday.

(b) *Clerk's Office Closed or Inaccessible.* If the act to be done is filing a document, and if the clerk's office where the document is to be filed is closed or inaccessible during regular hours on the last day for filing the document, the period for filing the document extends to the end of the next day when the clerk's office is open and accessible. The closing or inaccessibility of the clerk's office may be proved by a certificate of the clerk or counsel, by a party's affidavit, or by other satisfactory proof, and may be controverted in the same manner.

4.2. No Notice of Trial Court's Judgment in Civil Case.

(a) *Additional Time to File Documents.*

(1) *In general.* If a party affected by a judgment or other appealable order has not—within 20 days after the judgment or order was signed—either received the notice required by Texas Rule of Civil Procedure 306a.3 or acquired actual knowledge of the signing, then a period that, under

these rules, runs from the signing will begin for that party on the earlier of the date when the party receives notice or acquires actual knowledge of the signing. But in no event may the period begin more than 90 days after the judgment or order was signed.

(2) ***Exception for restricted appeal.*** Subparagraph (1) does not extend the time for perfecting a restricted appeal.

(b) ***Procedure to Gain Additional Time.*** The procedure to gain additional time is governed by Texas Rule of Civil Procedure 306a.5.

(c) ***The Court's Order.*** After hearing the motion, the trial court must sign a written order that finds the date when the party or the party's attorney first either received notice or acquired actual knowledge that the judgment or order was signed.

4.3. Periods Affected by Modified Judgment in Civil Case.

(a) ***During Plenary-Power Period.*** If a judgment is modified in any respect while the trial court retains plenary power, a period that, under these rules, runs from the date when the judgment is signed will run from the date when the modified judgment is signed.

(b) ***After Plenary Power Expires.*** If the trial court corrects or reforms the judgment under Texas Rule of Civil Procedure 316 after expiration of the trial court's plenary power, all periods provided in these rules that run from the date the judgment is signed run from the date the corrected judgment is signed for complaints that would not apply to the original judgment.

4.4. Periods Affected When Process Served by Publication. If process was served by publication and if a motion for new trial was filed under Texas Rule of Civil Procedure 329 more than 30 days after the judgment was signed, a period that, under these rules, runs from the date when the judgment is signed will be computed as if the judgment were signed on the date when the motion for new trial was filed.

4.5. No Notice of Judgment or Order of Appellate Court; Effect on Time to File Certain Documents.

(a) ***Additional Time to File Documents.*** A party may move for additional time to file a motion for rehearing or en banc reconsideration in the court of appeals, a petition for review, or a petition for discretionary review, if the party did not—until after the time expired for filing the document—either receive notice of the judgment or order from the clerk or acquire actual knowledge of the rendition of the judgment or order.

(b) ***Procedure to Gain Additional Time.*** The motion must state the earliest date when the party or the party's attorney received notice or acquired actual knowledge that the judgment or order had been rendered. The motion must be filed within 15 days of that date but in no event more than 90 days after the date of the judgment or order.

(c) ***Where to File.***

(1) A motion for additional time to file a motion for rehearing or en banc reconsideration in the court of appeals must be filed in and ruled on by the court of appeals in which the case is pending.

(2) A motion for additional time to file a petition for review must be filed in and ruled on by the Supreme Court.

(3) A motion for additional time to file a petition for discretionary review must be filed in and ruled on by the Court of Criminal Appeals.

(d) ***Order of the Court.*** If the court finds that the motion for additional time was timely filed and the party did not—within the time for filing the motion for rehearing or en banc reconsideration, petition for review, or petition for discretionary review, as the case may be—receive the notice or have actual knowledge of the judgment or order, the court must grant the motion. The time for filing the document will begin to run on the date when the court grants the motion.

4.6. No Notice of Trial Court's Appealable Order on a Motion for Forensic DNA Testing.

(a) ***Additional Time to File Notice of Appeal.*** If neither an adversely affected defendant nor the defendant's attorney received notice or acquired actual knowledge that the trial judge signed an order appealable under Code of Criminal Procedure Chapter 64 within twenty days after the signing, then the time periods under these rules that ordinarily run from the signing of an appealable order will begin to run on the earliest date when the defendant or the defendant's attorney received notice or acquired actual knowledge of the signing. But in no event shall such periods begin more than 120 days after the day the trial judge signed the appealable order.

(b) ***Motion to Gain Additional Time.***

(1) A defendant's motion for additional time must:

(A) Be in writing and sworn;

(B) State the defendant's desire to appeal from the appealable order;

(C) State the earliest date when the defendant

or the defendant's attorney received notice or acquired actual knowledge that the trial judge signed the appealable order; and

(D) Be filed within 120 days of the signing of the appealable order.

(2) To establish the application of paragraph (a) of this rule, the defendant adversely affected must prove in the trial court:

(A) The earliest date on which the defendant or the defendant's attorney received notice or acquired actual knowledge that the trial judge signed the appealable order; and

(B) That this date was more than twenty days after the signing of the appealable order.

(3) If the defendant's motion for additional time meets the requirements set out in paragraphs (b)(1) and (b)(2), the motion may serve as the defendant's notice of appeal.

(c) *The Court's Order.* After hearing the motion for additional time, the trial judge must sign a written order that determines the earliest date when the defendant or the defendant's attorney received notice or acquired actual knowledge that the trial judge signed the appealable order and whether this date was more than twenty days after the judge signed the appealable order.

(d) *The Clerk's Duties.* The trial court clerk must immediately (as they are filed or entered in the record) forward to all parties in the case copies of the defendant's motion for additional time, the trial judge's written order under subsection (c), the order the defendant seeks to appeal, any State's response, and any exhibits and related documents.

TRAP 5. FEES IN CIVIL CASES

A party who is not excused by statute or these rules from paying costs must pay—at the time an item is presented for filing—whatever fees are required by statute or Supreme Court order. The appellate court may enforce this rule by any order that is just.

TRAP 6. REPRESENTATION BY COUNSEL

6.1. Lead Counsel.

(a) *For Appellant.* Unless another attorney is designated, lead counsel for an appellant is the attorney whose signature first appears on the notice of appeal.

(b) *For a Party Other Than Appellant.* Unless another attorney is designated, lead counsel for a party other than an appellant is the attorney whose signature first appears on the first document filed in the appellate court on that party's behalf.

(c) *How to Designate.* The original or a new lead counsel may be designated by filing a notice stating that attorney's name, mailing address, telephone number, fax number, if any, email address, and State Bar of Texas identification number. If a new lead counsel is being designated, both the new attorney and either the party or the former lead counsel must sign the notice.

6.2. Appearance of Other Attorneys. An attorney other than lead counsel may file a notice stating that the attorney represents a specified party to the proceeding and giving that attorney's name, mailing address, telephone number, fax number, if any, email address, and State Bar of Texas identification number. The clerk will note on the docket the attorney's appearance. When a brief or motion is filed, the clerk will note on the docket the name of each attorney, if not already noted, who appears on the document.

6.3. To Whom Communications Sent. Any notice, copies of documents filed in an appellate court, or other communications must be sent to:

(a) each party's lead counsel on appeal;

(b) a party's lead counsel in the trial court if:

(1) that party was represented by counsel in the trial court;

(2) lead counsel on appeal has not yet been designated for that party; and

(3) lead counsel in the trial court has not filed a nonrepresentation notice or been allowed to withdraw;

(c) a party if the party is not represented by counsel.

6.4. Nonrepresentation Notice.

(a) *In General.* If, in accordance with paragraph 6.3(b), the lead counsel in the trial court is being sent notices, copies of documents, or other communications, that attorney may file a nonrepresentation notice in the appellate court. The notice must:

(1) state that the attorney is not representing the party on appeal;

(2) state that the court and other counsel should communicate directly with the party in the future;

(3) give the party's name and last known address and telephone number; and

(4) be signed by the party.

(b) *Appointed Counsel.* In a criminal case, an attorney appointed by the trial court to represent an indigent party cannot file a nonrepresentation notice.

6.5. Withdrawal. An appellate court may, on appropriate terms and conditions, permit an attorney to withdraw from representing a party in the appellate court.

(a) ***Contents of Motion.*** A motion for leave to withdraw must contain the following:

(1) a list of current deadlines and settings in the case;

(2) the party's name and last known address and telephone number;

(3) a statement that a copy of the motion was delivered to the party; and

(4) a statement that the party was notified in writing of the right to object to the motion.

(b) ***Delivery to Party.*** The motion must be delivered to the party in person or mailed—both by certified and by first-class mail—to the party at the party's last known address.

(c) ***If Motion Granted.*** If the court grants the motion, the withdrawing attorney must immediately notify the party, in writing, of any deadlines or settings that the attorney knows about at the time of withdrawal but that were not previously disclosed to the party. The withdrawing attorney must file a copy of that notice with the court clerk.

(d) ***Exception for Substitution of Counsel.*** If an attorney substitutes for a withdrawing attorney, the motion to withdraw need not comply with (a) but must state only the substitute attorney's name, mailing address, telephone number, fax number, if any, and State Bar of Texas identification number. The withdrawing attorney must comply with (b) but not (c).

6.6. Agreements of Parties or Counsel. To be enforceable, an agreement of parties or their counsel concerning an appellate court proceeding must be in writing and signed by the parties or their counsel. Such an agreement is subject to any appellate court order necessary to ensure that the case is properly presented.

TRAP 7. SUBSTITUTING PARTIES

7.1. Parties Who Are Not Public Officers.

(a) ***Death of a Party.***

(1) ***Civil Cases.*** If a party to a civil case dies after the trial court renders judgment but before the case has been finally disposed of on appeal, the appeal may be perfected, and the appellate court will proceed to adjudicate the appeal as if all parties were alive. The appellate court's judgment will have the same force and effect as if rendered when all parties were living. The decedent party's name may be used on all papers.

(2) ***Criminal Cases.*** If the appellant in a criminal case dies after an appeal is perfected but before the appellate court issues the mandate, the appeal will be permanently abated.

(b) ***Substitution for Other Reasons.*** If substitution of a party in the appellate court is necessary for a reason other than death, the appellate court may order substitution on any party's motion at any time.

7.2. Public Officers.

(a) ***Automatic Substitution of Officer.*** When a public officer is a party in an official capacity to an appeal or original proceeding, and if that person ceases to hold office before the appeal or original proceeding is finally disposed of, the public officer's successor is automatically substituted as a party if appropriate. Proceedings following substitution are to be in the name of the substituted party, but any misnomer that does not affect the substantial rights of the parties may be disregarded. Substitution may be ordered at any time, but failure to order substitution of the successor does not affect the substitution.

(b) ***Abatement.*** If the case is an original proceeding under Rule 52, the court must abate the proceeding to allow the successor to reconsider the original party's decision. In all other cases, the suit will not abate, and the successor will be bound by the appellate court's judgment or order as if the successor were the original party.

TRAP 8. BANKRUPTCY IN CIVIL CASES

8.1. Notice of Bankruptcy. Any party may file a notice that a party is in bankruptcy. The notice must contain:

(a) the bankrupt party's name;

(b) the court in which the bankruptcy proceeding is pending;

(c) the bankruptcy proceeding's style and case number; and

(d) the date when the bankruptcy petition was filed.

8.2. Effect of Bankruptcy. A bankruptcy suspends the appeal and all periods in these rules from the date when the bankruptcy petition is filed until the appellate court reinstates or severs the appeal in accordance with federal law. A period that began to run and had not expired at the time the proceeding was suspended begins anew when the proceeding is reinstated or severed under 8.3. A document filed by a party while the proceeding is suspended will be deemed filed on the same day, but after, the court reinstates or severs the appeal and will not be considered ineffective because it was filed while the proceeding was suspended.

8.3. Motion to Reinstate or Sever Appeal Suspended by Bankruptcy.

(a) ***Motion to Reinstate.*** If a case has been suspended by a bankruptcy filing, a party may move that the appellate court reinstate the appeal if permitted by federal

law or the bankruptcy court. If the bankruptcy court has lifted or terminated the stay, a certified copy of the order must be attached to the motion.

(b) ***Motion to Sever.*** A party may move to sever the appeal with respect to the bankrupt party and to reinstate the appeal with respect to the other parties. The motion must show that the case is severable and must comply with applicable federal law regarding severance of a bankrupt party. The court may proceed under this paragraph on its own initiative.

TRAP 9. DOCUMENTS GENERALLY

9.1. Signing.

(a) ***Represented Parties.*** If a party is represented by counsel, a document filed on that party's behalf must be signed by at least one of the party's attorneys. For each attorney whose name appears on a document as representing that party, the document must contain that attorney's State Bar of Texas identification number, mailing address, telephone number, fax number, if any, and email address.

(b) ***Unrepresented Parties.*** A party not represented by counsel must sign any document that the party files and give the party's mailing address, telephone number, fax number, if any, and email address.

(c) ***Electronic Signatures.*** A document that is electronically served, filed, or issued by a court or clerk is considered signed if the document includes:

(1) a "/s/" and name typed in the space where the signature would otherwise appear, unless the document is notarized or sworn; or

(2) an electronic image or scanned image of the signature.

9.2. Filing.

(a) ***With Whom.*** A document is filed in an appellate court by delivering it to:

(1) the clerk of the court in which the document is to be filed; or

(2) a justice or judge of that court who is willing to accept delivery. A justice or judge who accepts delivery must note on the document the date and time of delivery, which will be considered the time of filing, and must promptly send it to the clerk.

(b) ***Filing by Mail.***

(1) ***Timely Filing.*** A document received within ten days after the filing deadline is considered timely filed if:

(A) it was sent to the proper clerk by United States Postal Service or a commercial delivery service;

(B) it was placed in an envelope or wrapper properly addressed and stamped; and

(C) it was deposited in the mail or delivered to a commercial delivery service on or before the last day for filing.

(2) ***Proof of Mailing.*** Though it may consider other proof, the appellate court will accept the following as conclusive proof of the date of mailing:

(A) a legible postmark affixed by the United States Postal Service;

(B) a receipt for registered or certified mail if the receipt is endorsed by the United States Postal Service;

(C) a certificate of mailing by the United States Postal Service; or

(D) a receipt endorsed by the commercial delivery service.

(c) ***Electronic Filing.***

(1) ***Requirement.*** Attorneys in civil cases must electronically file documents. Attorneys in criminal cases must electronically file documents except for good cause shown in a motion filed in the appellate court. Unrepresented parties in civil and criminal cases may electronically file documents, but it is not required.

(2) ***Mechanism.*** Electronic filing must be done through the electronic filing manager established by the Office of Court Administration and an electronic filing service provider certified by the Office of Court Administration.

(3) ***Exceptions.*** Documents filed under seal, subject to a pending motion to seal, or to which access is otherwise restricted by law or court order must not be electronically filed. For good cause, an appellate court may permit a party to file other documents in paper form in a particular case.

(4) ***Timely Filing.*** Unless a document must be filed by a certain time of day, a document is considered timely filed if it is electronically filed at any time before midnight (in the court's time zone) on the filing deadline. An electronically filed document is deemed filed when transmitted to the filing party's electronic filing service provider, except:

(A) if a document is transmitted on a Saturday, Sunday, or legal holiday, it is deemed filed on the next day that is not a Saturday, Sunday, or legal holiday; and

(B) if a document requires a motion and an order allowing its filing, the document is deemed filed on the date the motion is granted.

(5) ***Technical Failure.*** If a document is untimely

due to a technical failure or a system outage, the filing party may seek appropriate relief from the court.

(6) ***Confirmation of Filing.*** The electronic filing manager will send a filing confirmation notice to the filing party.

(7) ***Electronic Notices From the Court.*** The clerk may send notices, orders, or other communications about the case to the party electronically. A court seal may be electronic.

9.3. Number of Copies.

(a) ***Courts of Appeals.***

(1) ***Document Filed in Paper Form.*** If a document is not electronically filed, a party must file the original and one unbound copy of the document unless otherwise required by local rule. The unbound copy of an appendix must contain a separate page before each document and must not include tabs that extend beyond the edge of the page.

(2) ***Electronically Filed Document.*** Unless required by local rule, a party need not file a paper copy of an electronically filed document.

(b) ***Supreme Court and Court of Criminal Appeals.***

(1) ***Document Filed in Paper Form.*** If a document is not electronically filed, a party must file the original and 11 copies of any document addressed to either the Supreme Court or the Court of Criminal Appeals, except that in the Supreme Court only an original and one copy must be filed of any motion, response to the motion, and reply in support of the motion, and in the Court of Criminal Appeals, only the original must be filed of a motion for extension of time or a response to the motion, or a pleading under Code of Criminal Procedure article 11.07.

(2) ***Electronically Filed Document.*** Paper copies of each document that is electronically filed with the Supreme Court or the Court of Criminal Appeals must be mailed or hand-delivered to the Supreme Court or the Court of Criminal Appeals, as appropriate, within three business days after the document is electronically filed. The number of paper copies required shall be determined, respectively, by order of the Supreme Court or the Court of Criminal Appeals.

(c) ***Exception for Record.*** Only the original record need be filed in any proceeding.

9.4. Form. Except for the record, a document filed with an appellate court, including a paper copy of an electronically filed document, must—unless the court accepts another form in the interest of justice—be in the following form:

(a) ***Printing.*** A document may be produced by standard typographic printing or by any duplicating process that produces a distinct black image. Printing must be on one side of the paper.

(b) ***Paper Type and Size.*** The paper on which a document is produced must be 8½ by 11 inches, white or nearly white, and opaque.

(c) ***Margins.*** Documents must have at least one-inch margins on both sides and at the top and bottom.

(d) ***Spacing.*** Text must be double-spaced, but footnotes, block quotations, short lists, and issues or points of error may be single-spaced.

(e) ***Typeface.*** A document produced on a computer must be printed in a conventional typeface no smaller than 14-point except for footnotes, which must be no smaller than 12-point. A typewritten document must be printed in standard 10-character-per-inch (cpi) monospaced typeface.

(f) ***Binding and Covering.*** A paper document must be bound so as to ensure that it will not lose its cover or fall apart in regular use. A paper document should be stapled once in the top left-hand corner or be bound so that it will lie flat when open. A paper petition or brief should have durable front and back covers which must not be plastic or be red, black, or dark blue.

(g) ***Contents of Cover.*** A document's front cover, if any, must contain the case style, the case number, the title of the document being filed, the name of the party filing the document, and the name, mailing address, telephone number, fax number, if any, email address, and State Bar of Texas identification number of the lead counsel for the filing party. If a party requests oral argument in the court of appeals, the request must appear on the front cover of that party's first brief.

(h) ***Appendix and Original Proceeding Record.*** A paper appendix may be bound either with the document to which it is related or separately. If separately bound, the appendix must comply with paragraph (f). A paper record in an original proceeding or a paper appendix must be tabbed and indexed. An electronically filed record in an original proceeding or an electronically filed appendix that includes more than one item must contain bookmarks to assist in locating each item.

(i) ***Length.***

(1) ***Contents Included and Excluded.*** In calculating the length of a document, every word and every part of the document, including headings, footnotes, and quotations, must be counted except the following: caption, identity of parties and counsel, statement regarding oral argument,

table of contents, index of authorities, statement of the case, statement of issues presented, statement of jurisdiction, statement of procedural history, signature, proof of service, certification, certificate of compliance, and appendix.

(2) ***Maximum Length.*** The documents listed below must not exceed the following limits:

(A) A brief and response in a direct appeal to the Court of Criminal Appeals in a case in which the death penalty has been assessed: 37,500 words if computer-generated, and 125 pages if not.

(B) A brief and response in an appellate court (other than a brief under subparagraph (A)) and a petition and response in an original proceeding in the court of appeals: 15,000 words if computer-generated, and 50 pages if not. In a civil case in the court of appeals, the aggregate of all briefs filed by a party must not exceed 27,000 words if computer-generated, and 90 pages if not.

(C) A reply brief in an appellate court and a reply to a response to a petition in an original proceeding in the court of appeals: 7,500 words if computer-generated, and 25 pages if not.

(D) A petition and response in an original proceeding in the Supreme Court and the Court of Criminal Appeals, except for petitions and responses in an original proceeding in a case in which the death penalty has been assessed, a petition for review and response in the Supreme Court, a petition for discretionary review in the Court of Criminal Appeals, and a motion for rehearing and response in an appellate court: 4,500 words if computer-generated, and 15 pages if not.

(E) A reply to a response to a petition for review in the Supreme Court, a reply to a response to a petition in an original proceeding in the Supreme Court and the Court of Criminal Appeals, except a reply to a response in an original proceeding in a case in which the death penalty has been assessed, and a reply to a petition for discretionary review in the Court of Criminal Appeals: 2,400 words if computer-generated, and 8 pages if not.

(F) A petition and response in an original proceeding in the Court of Criminal Appeals in a case in which the death penalty has been assessed: 9,000 words if computer-generated, and 30 pages if not.

(G) A reply to a response to a petition in an original proceeding in the Court of Criminal Appeals in a case in which the death penalty has been assessed: 4,800 words if computer-generated, and 16 pages if not.

(3) ***Certificate of Compliance.*** A computer-generated document that is subject to a word limit under this rule must include a certificate by counsel or an unrepresented party stating the number of words in the document. The person certifying may rely on the word count of the computer program used to prepare the document.

(4) ***Extensions.*** A court may, on motion, permit a document that exceeds the prescribed limit.

(j) ***Electronically Filed Documents.*** An electronically filed document must:

(1) be in text-searchable portable document format (PDF);

(2) be directly converted to PDF rather than scanned, if possible;

(3) not be locked;

(4) be combined with any appendix into one computer file, unless that file would exceed the size limit prescribed by the electronic filing manager; and

(5) otherwise comply with the Technology Standards set by the Judicial Committee on Information Technology and approved by the Supreme Court.

(k) ***Nonconforming Documents.*** If a document fails to conform with these rules, the court may strike the document or identify the error and permit the party to resubmit the document in a conforming format by a specified deadline.

9.5. Service.

(a) ***Service of All Documents Required.*** At or before the time of a document's filing, the filing party must serve a copy on all parties to the proceeding. Service on a party represented by counsel must be made on that party's lead counsel. Except in original proceedings, a party need not serve a copy of the record.

(b) ***Manner of Service.***

(1) ***Documents Filed Electronically.*** A document filed electronically under Rule 9.2 must be served electronically through the electronic filing manager if the email address of the party or attorney to be served is on file with the electronic filing manager. If the email address of the party or attorney to be served is not on file with the electronic filing manager, the document may be served on that party or attorney under subparagraph (2).

(2) ***Documents Not Filed Electronically.*** A document that is not filed electronically may be served in person, by mail, by commercial delivery service, by fax, or by email. Personal service includes delivery to any responsible person at the office of the lead counsel for the party served.

(c) ***When Complete.***

(1) Service by mail is complete on mailing.

(2) Service by commercial delivery service is complete when the document is placed in the control of the delivery service.

(3) Service by fax is complete on receipt.

(4) Electronic service is complete on transmission of the document to the serving party's electronic filing service provider. The electronic filing manager will send confirmation of service to the serving party.

(d) ***Proof of Service.*** A document presented for filing must contain a proof of service in the form of either an acknowledgment of service by the person served or a certificate of service. Proof of service may appear on or be affixed to the filed document. The clerk may permit a document to be filed without proof of service, but will require the proof to be filed promptly.

(e) ***Certificate Requirements.*** A certificate of service must be signed by the person who made the service and must state:

(1) the date and manner of service;

(2) the name and address of each person served; and

(3) if the person served is a party's attorney, the name of the party represented by that attorney.

9.6. Communications With the Court. Parties and counsel may communicate with the appellate court about a case only through the clerk.

9.7. Adoption by Reference. Any party may join in or adopt by reference all or any part of a brief, petition, response, motion, or other document filed in an appellate court by another party in the same case.

9.8. Protection of Minor's Identity in Parental-Rights Termination Cases and Juvenile Court Cases.

(a) ***Alias Defined.*** For purposes of this rule, an alias means one or more of a person's initials or a fictitious name, used to refer to the person.

(b) ***Parental-Rights Termination Cases.*** In an appeal or an original proceeding in an appellate court, arising out of a case in which the termination of parental rights was at issue:

(1) except for a docketing statement, in all papers submitted to the court, including all appendix items submitted with a brief, petition, or motion:

(A) a minor must be identified only by an alias unless the court orders otherwise;

(B) the court may order that a minor's parent or other family member be identified only by an alias if necessary to protect a minor's identity; and

(C) all documents must be redacted accordingly;

(2) the court must, in its opinion, use an alias to refer to a minor, and if necessary to protect the minor's identity, to the minor's parent or other family member.

(c) ***Juvenile Court Cases.*** In an appeal or an original proceeding in an appellate court, arising out of a case under Title 3 of the Family Code:

(1) except for a docketing statement, in all papers submitted to the court, including all appendix items submitted with a brief, petition, or motion:

(A) a minor must be identified only by an alias;

(B) a minor's parent or other family member must be identified only by an alias; and

(C) all documents must be redacted accordingly;

(2) the court must, in its opinion, use an alias to refer to a minor and to the minor's parent or other family member.

(d) ***No Alteration of Appellate Record.*** Nothing in this rule permits alteration of the original appellate record except as specifically authorized by court order.

9.9. Privacy Protection for Documents Filed in Civil Cases.

(a) ***Sensitive Data Defined.*** Sensitive data consists of:

(1) a driver's license number, passport number, social security number, tax identification number or similar government-issued personal identification number;

(2) a bank account number, credit card number, or other financial account number; and

(3) a birth date, home address, and the name of any person who was a minor when the underlying suit was filed.

(b) ***Filing of Documents Containing Sensitive Data Prohibited.*** Unless the inclusion of sensitive data is specifically required by a statute, court rule, or administrative regulation, an electronic or paper document containing sensitive data may not be filed with a court unless the sensitive data is redacted, except for the record in an appeal under Section Two.

(c) ***Redaction of Sensitive Data; Retention Requirement.*** Sensitive data must be redacted by using the letter "X" in place of each omitted digit or character or by removing the sensitive data in a manner indicating that the data has been redacted. The filing party must retain an unredacted version of the filed document during the pen-

dency of the appeal and any related proceedings filed within six months of the date the judgment is signed.

(d) ***Notice to Clerk.*** If a document must contain sensitive data, the filing party must notify the clerk by:

(1) designating the document as containing sensitive data when the document is electronically filed; or

(2) if the document is not electronically filed, by including, on the upper left-hand side of the first page, the phrase: "NOTICE: THIS DOCUMENT CONTAINS SENSITIVE DATA."

(e) ***Restriction on Remote Access.*** Documents that contain unredacted sensitive data in violation of this rule must not be posted on the Internet.

9.10. Privacy Protection for Documents Filed in Criminal Cases.

(a) ***Sensitive Data Defined.*** Sensitive data consists of:

(1) a driver's license number, passport number, social security number, tax identification number or similar government-issued personal identification number;

(2) bank account number, credit card number, and other financial account number;

(3) a birth date, a home address, and the name of any person who was a minor at the time the offense was committed.

(b) ***Redacted Filings.*** Unless a court orders otherwise, an electronic or paper filing with the court, including the contents of any appendices, must not contain sensitive data.

(c) ***Exemptions from the Redaction Requirement.*** The redaction requirement does not apply to the following:

(1) A court filing that is related to a criminal matter or investigation and that is prepared before the filing of a criminal charge or is not filed as part of any docketed criminal case;

(2) An arrest or search warrant;

(3) A charging document and an affidavit filed in support of any charging document;

(4) A defendant's date of birth;

(5) A defendant's address; and

(6) Any government issued number intended to identify the defendant associated with a criminal filing, except for the defendant's social security number or driver's license number.

(d) ***Redaction procedures.*** Sensitive data must be redacted by using the letter "X" in place of each omitted digit or character or by removing the sensitive data in a manner indicating that the data has been redacted. The filer must retain an unredacted version of the filed document during the pendency of the appeal and any related proceedings filed within three years of the date the judgment is signed. If a district court clerk or appellate court clerk discovers unredacted sensitive data in the record, the clerk shall notify the parties and seek a ruling from the court.

(e) ***Certification.*** The filing of a document constitutes a certification by the filer that the document complies with paragraphs (a) and (b) of this rule.

(f) ***Reference List.*** If a filer believes any information described in paragraph (a) of this rule is essential to a document or that the document would be confusing without the information, the filer may submit the information to the court in a reference list that is in paper form and under seal. The reference list must specify an appropriate identifier that corresponds uniquely to each item listed. Any reference in the document to a listed identifier will be construed to refer to the corresponding item of information. If the filer provides a reference list pursuant to this rule, the front page of the document containing the redacted information must indicate that the reference list has been, or will be, provided. On its own initiative, the court may order a sealed reference list in any case.

(g) ***Sealed materials.*** Materials that are required by statute to be sealed, redacted, or kept confidential, such as the items set out in Articles 35.29 (Personal Information About Jurors), 38.45 (Evidence Depicting or Describing Abuse of or Sexual Conduct by Child or Minor), and 42.12, §9(j), must be treated in accordance with the pertinent statutes and shall not be publicly available on the internet. A court may also order that a document be filed under seal in paper form or electronic form, without redaction. The court may later unseal the document or order the filer to provide a redacted version of the document for the public record. If a court orders material sealed, whether it be sensitive data or other materials, the court's sealing order must be affixed to the outside of the sealed container if the sealed material is filed in paper form, or be the first document that appears if filed in electronic form. Sealed portions of the clerk's and reporter's records should be clearly marked and separated from unsealed portions and tendered as separate records, whether in paper form or electronic form. Sealed material shall not be available either on the internet or in other form without court order.

(h) ***Waiver of Protection of Identifiers.*** A person waives the protection of this rule as to a person's own information by filing it without redaction and not under seal.

TRAP 10. MOTIONS IN THE APPELLATE COURTS

10.1. Contents of Motions; Response.

(a) ***Motion.*** Unless these rules prescribe another form, a party must apply by motion for an order or other relief. The motion must:

(1) contain or be accompanied by any matter specifically required by a rule governing such a motion;

(2) state with particularity the grounds on which it is based;

(3) set forth the order or relief sought;

(4) be served and filed with any brief, affidavit, or other paper filed in support of the motion; and

(5) in civil cases, except for motions for rehearing and en banc reconsideration, contain or be accompanied by a certificate stating that the filing party conferred, or made a reasonable attempt to confer, with all other parties about the merits of the motion and whether those parties oppose the motion.

(b) ***Response.*** A party may file a response to a motion at any time before the court rules on the motion or by any deadline set by the court. The court may determine a motion before a response is filed.

10.2. Evidence on Motions. A motion need not be verified unless it depends on the following types of facts, in which case the motion must be supported by affidavit or other satisfactory evidence. The types of facts requiring proof are those that are:

(a) not in the record;

(b) not within the court's knowledge in its official capacity; and

(c) not within the personal knowledge of the attorney signing the motion.

10.3. Determining Motions.

(a) ***Time for Determination.*** A court should not hear or determine a motion until 10 days after the motion was filed, unless:

(1) the motion is to extend time to file a brief, a petition for review, or a petition for discretionary review;

(2) the motion states that the parties have conferred and that no party opposes the motion; or

(3) the motion is an emergency.

(b) ***Reconsideration.*** If a motion is determined prematurely, any party adversely affected may request the court to reconsider its order.

10.4. Power of Panel or Single Justice or Judge to Entertain Motions.

(a) ***Single Justice.*** In addition to the authority expressly conferred by these rules or by law, a single justice or judge of an appellate court may grant or deny a request for relief that these rules allow to be sought by motion. But in a civil case, a single justice should not do the following:

(1) act on a petition for an extraordinary writ; or

(2) dismiss or otherwise determine an appeal or a motion for rehearing.

(b) ***Panel.*** An appellate court may provide, by order or rule, that a panel or the full court must act on any motion or class of motions.

10.5. Particular Motions.

(a) ***Motions Relating to Informalities in the Record.*** A motion relating to informalities in the manner of bringing a case into court must be filed within 30 days after the record is filed in the court of appeals. The objection, if waivable, will otherwise be deemed waived.

(b) ***Motions to Extend Time.***

(1) ***Contents of Motion in General.*** All motions to extend time, except a motion to extend time for filing a notice of appeal, must state:

(A) the deadline for filing the item in question;

(B) the length of the extension sought;

(C) the facts relied on to reasonably explain the need for an extension; and

(D) the number of previous extensions granted regarding the item in question.

(2) ***Contents of Motion to Extend Time to File Notice of Appeal.*** A motion to extend the time for filing a notice of appeal must:

(A) comply with (1)(A) and (C);

(B) identify the trial court;

(C) state the date of the trial court's judgment or appealable order; and

(D) state the case number and style of the case in the trial court.

(3) ***Contents of Motion to Extend Time to File Petition for Review or Petition for Discretionary Review.*** A motion to extend time to file a petition for review or petition for discretionary review must also specify:

(A) the court of appeals;

(B) the date of the court of appeals' judgment;

(C) the case number and style of the case in the court of appeals; and

(D) the date every motion for rehearing or en banc reconsideration was filed, and either the date and nature of the court of appeals' ruling on the motion, or that it remains pending.

(c) *Motions to Postpone Argument.* Unless all parties agree, or unless sufficient cause is apparent to the court, a motion to postpone argument of a case must be supported by sufficient cause.

TRAP 11. AMICUS CURIAE BRIEFS

An appellate clerk may receive, but not file, an amicus curiae brief. But the court for good cause may refuse to consider the brief and order that it be returned. An amicus curiae brief must:

(a) comply with the briefing rules for parties;

(b) identify the person or entity on whose behalf the brief is tendered;

(c) disclose the source of any fee paid or to be paid for preparing the brief; and

(d) certify that copies have been served on all parties.

TRAP 12. DUTIES OF APPELLATE CLERK

12.1. Docketing the Case. On receiving a copy of the notice of appeal, the petition for review, the petition for discretionary review, the petition in an original proceeding, or a certified question, the appellate clerk must:

(a) endorse on the document the date of receipt;

(b) collect any filing fee;

(c) docket the case;

(d) notify all parties of the receipt of the document; and

(e) if the document filed is a petition for review filed in the Supreme Court, notify the court of appeals clerk of the filing of the petition.

12.2. Docket Numbers. The clerk must put the case's docket number on each item received in connection with the case and must put the docket number on the envelope in which the record is stored.

(a) *Numbering System.* Each case filed in a court of appeals must be assigned a docket number consisting of the following four parts, separated by hyphens:

(1) the number of the court of appeals district;

(2) the last two digits of the year in which the case is filed;

(3) the number assigned to the case; and

(4) the designation "CV" for a civil case or "CR" for a criminal case.

(b) *Numbering Order.* Each case must be docketed in the order of its filing.

(c) *Multiple Notices of Appeal.* All notices of appeal filed in the same case must be given the same docket number.

(d) *Appeals Not Yet Filed.* A motion relating to an appeal that has been perfected but not yet filed must be docketed and assigned a docket number that will also be assigned to the appeal when it is filed.

12.3. Custody of Papers. The clerk must safeguard the record and every other item filed in a case. If the record or any part of it or any other item is missing, the court will make an order for the replacement of the record or item that is just under the circumstances.

12.4. Withdrawing Papers. The clerk may permit the record or other filed item to be taken from the clerk's office at any time, on the following conditions:

(a) the clerk must have a receipt for the record or item;

(b) the clerk should make reasonable conditions to ensure that the withdrawn record or item is preserved and returned;

(c) the clerk may demand the return of the record or item at any time;

(d) after the case is submitted to the court and before the court's decision, the record cannot be withdrawn;

(e) after the court's decision, the losing party must be given priority in withdrawing the record;

(f) the clerk may not allow original documents filed under Rule 34.5(f) or original exhibits filed under Rule 34.6(g) to be taken from the clerk's office;

(g) if the court allows an original document or exhibit to be taken by a party and it is not returned, the court may accept the opposing party's statement concerning the document's or exhibit's nature and contents;

(h) withdrawn material must not be removed from the court's jurisdiction; and

(i) the court may, on the motion of any party or its own initiative, modify any of these conditions.

12.5. Clerk's Duty to Account. The clerk of an appellate court who receives money due another court must promptly pay the money to the court to whom it is due. This rule is enforceable by the Supreme Court.

12.6. Notices of Court's Judgments and Orders. In any proceeding, the clerk of an appellate court must promptly send a notice of any judgment, mandate, or other court order to all parties to the proceeding.

TRAP 13. COURT REPORTERS AND COURT RECORDERS

13.1. Duties of Court Reporters and Recorders. The official court reporter or court recorder must:

(a) unless excused by agreement of the parties, attend court sessions and make a full record of the proceedings;

(b) take all exhibits offered in evidence during a proceeding and ensure that they are marked;

(c) file all exhibits with the trial court clerk after a proceeding ends;

(d) perform the duties prescribed by Rules 34.6 and 35; and

(e) perform other acts relating to the reporter's or recorder's official duties, as the trial court directs.

13.2. Additional Duties of Court Recorder. The official court recorder must also:

(a) ensure that the recording system functions properly throughout the proceeding and that a complete, clear, and transcribable recording is made;

(b) make a detailed, legible log of all proceedings being recorded, showing:

(1) the number and style of the case before the court;

(2) the name of each person speaking;

(3) the event being recorded such as the voir dire, the opening statement, direct and cross-examinations, and bench conferences;

(4) each exhibit offered, admitted, or excluded;

(5) the time of day of each event; and

(6) the index number on the recording device showing where each event is recorded;

(c) after a proceeding ends, file with the clerk the original log;

(d) have the original recording stored to ensure that it is preserved and is accessible; and

(e) ensure that no one gains access to the original recording without the court's written order.

13.3. Priorities of Reporters. The trial court must help ensure that the court reporter's work is timely accomplished by setting work priorities. The reporter's duties relating to proceedings before the court take preference over other work.

13.4. Report of Reporters. To aid the trial court in setting priorities under 13.3, each court reporter must give the trial court a monthly written report showing the amount and nature of the business pending in the reporter's office. A copy of this report must be filed with the appellate clerk of each district in which the court sits.

13.5. Appointing Deputy Reporter. When the official court reporter is unable to perform the duties in 13.1 or 13.2 because of illness, press of official work, or unavoidable absence or disability, the trial court may designate a deputy reporter. If the court appoints a deputy reporter, that person must file with the trial court clerk a document stating:

(a) the date the deputy worked;

(b) the court in which the deputy worked;

(c) the number and style of the case on which the deputy worked; and

(d) the deputy's name, mailing address, telephone number, fax number, if any, email address, and Certified Shorthand Reporter number.

13.6. Filing of Notes in a Criminal Case. When a defendant is convicted and sentenced, or is granted deferred adjudication for a felony other than a state jail felony, and does not appeal, the court reporter must—within 20 days after the time to perfect the appeal has expired—file the untranscribed notes or the original recording of the proceeding with the trial court clerk. The trial court clerk need not retain the notes beyond 15 years of their filing date.

TRAP 14. RECORDING AND BROADCASTING COURT PROCEEDINGS

14.1. Recording and Broadcasting Permitted. An appellate court may permit courtroom proceedings to be broadcast, televised, recorded, or photographed in accordance with this rule.

14.2. Procedure.

(a) ***Request to Cover Court Proceeding.***

(1) A person wishing to broadcast, televise, record, or photograph a court proceeding must file with the court clerk a request to cover the proceeding. The request must state:

(A) the case style and number;

(B) the date and time when the proceeding is to begin;

(C) the name of the requesting person or organization;

(D) the type of coverage requested (for example, televising or photographing); and

(E) the type and extent of equipment to be used.

(2) A request to cover argument of a case must be filed no later than five days before the date the case is set for argument and must be served on all parties to the case. A request to cover any other proceeding must be filed no later than two days before the date when the proceeding is to begin.

(b) ***Response.*** Any party may file a response to the request. If the request is to cover argument, the response must be filed no later than two days before the date set for argument. If a party objects to coverage of the argument, the response should state the injury that will allegedly result from coverage.

(c) ***Court May Shorten Time.*** The court may, in the interest of justice, shorten the time for filing a document under this rule if no party or interested person would be unduly prejudiced.

(d) ***Decision of Court.*** In deciding whether to allow coverage, the court may consider information known *ex parte* to the court. The court may allow, deny, limit, or terminate coverage for any reason the court considers necessary or appropriate, such as protecting the parties' rights or the dignity of the court and ensuring the orderly conduct of the proceedings.

14.3. Equipment and Personnel. The court may, among other things:

(a) require that a person seeking to cover a proceeding demonstrate or display the equipment that will be used;

(b) prohibit equipment that produces distracting sound or light;

(c) prohibit signal lights or devices showing when equipment is operating, or require their concealment;

(d) prohibit moving lights, flash attachments, or sudden lighting changes;

(e) require the use of the courtroom's existing video, audio, and lighting systems, if any;

(f) specify the placement of personnel and equipment;

(g) determine the number of cameras to be allowed in the courtroom; and

(h) require pooling of equipment if more than one person wishes to cover a proceeding.

14.4. Enforcement. The court may sanction a violation of this rule by measures that include barring a person or organization from access to future coverage of proceedings in that court for a defined period.

TRAP 15. ISSUANCE OF WRIT OR PROCESS BY APPELLATE COURT

15.1. In General.

(a) ***Signature Under Seal.*** A writ or process issuing from an appellate court must bear the court's seal and be signed by the clerk.

(b) ***To Whom Directed; by Whom Served.*** Unless a rule or statute provides otherwise, the writ or process must be directed to the person or court to be served. The writ or process may be served by the sheriff, constable, or other peace officer whose jurisdiction includes the county in which the person or court to be served may be found.

(c) ***Return; Lack of Execution; Simultaneous Writs.*** The writ or process must be returned to the issuing court according to the writ's direction. If the writ or process is not executed, the clerk may issue another writ or process if requested by the party who requested the former writ or process. At a party's request, the clerk may issue two or more writs simultaneously.

15.2. Appearance Without Service; Actual Knowledge. A party who appears in person or by attorney in an appellate court proceeding—or who has actual knowledge of the court's opinion, judgment, or order related to a writ or process—is bound by the opinion, judgment, or order to the same extent as if personally served under 15.1.

TRAP 16. DISQUALIFICATION OR RECUSAL OF APPELLATE JUDGES

16.1. Grounds for Disqualification. The grounds for disqualification of an appellate court justice or judge are determined by the Constitution and laws of Texas.

16.2. Grounds for Recusal. The grounds for recusal of an appellate court justice or judge are the same as those provided in the Rules of Civil Procedure. In addition, a justice or judge must recuse in a proceeding if it presents a material issue which the justice or judge participated in deciding while serving on another court in which the proceeding was pending.

16.3. Procedure for Recusal.

(a) ***Motion.*** A party may file a motion to recuse a justice or judge before whom the case is pending. The motion must be filed promptly after the party has reason to believe that the justice or judge should not participate in deciding the case.

(b) ***Decision.*** Before any further proceeding in the case, the challenged justice or judge must either remove himself or herself from all participation in the case or certify the matter to the entire court, which will decide the motion by a majority of the remaining judges sitting en banc. The challenged justice or judge must not sit with the remainder of the court to consider the motion as to him or her.

(c) ***Appeal.*** An order of recusal is not reviewable, but the denial of a recusal motion is reviewable.

TRAP 17. COURT OF APPEALS UNABLE TO TAKE IMMEDIATE ACTION

17.1. Inability to Act. A court of appeals is unable to take immediate action if it cannot—within the time when

action must be taken—assemble a panel because members of the court are ill, absent, or unavailable. A justice who is disqualified or recused is unavailable. A court of appeals' inability to act immediately may be established by certificate of the clerk, a member of the court, or a party's counsel, or by affidavit of a party.

17.2. Nearest Available Court of Appeals. If a court of appeals is unable to take immediate action, the nearest court of appeals that is able to take immediate action may do so with the same effect as the other court. The nearest court of appeals is the one whose courthouse is nearest—measured by a straight line—the courthouse of the trial court.

17.3. Further Proceedings. After acting or refusing to act, the nearest court of appeals must promptly send a copy of its order, and the original or a copy of any document presented to it, to the other court, which will conduct any further proceedings in the matter.

TRAP 18. MANDATE

18.1. Issuance. The clerk of the appellate court that rendered the judgment must issue a mandate in accordance with the judgment and send it to the clerk of the court to which it is directed and to all parties to the proceeding when one of the following periods expires:

(a) ***In the Court of Appeals.***

(1) Ten days after the time has expired for filing a motion to extend time to file a petition for review or a petition for discretionary review if:

(A) no timely petition for review or petition for discretionary review has been filed;

(B) no timely filed motion to extend time to file a petition for review or petition for discretionary review is pending; and

(C) in a criminal case, the Court of Criminal Appeals has not granted review on its own initiative.

(2) Ten days after the time has expired for filing a motion to extend time to file a motion for rehearing of a denial, refusal, or dismissal of a petition for review, or a refusal or dismissal of a petition for discretionary review, if no timely filed motion for rehearing or motion to extend time is pending.

(b) ***In the Supreme Court and the Court of Criminal Appeals.*** Ten days after the time has expired for filing a motion to extend time to file a motion for rehearing if no timely filed motion for rehearing or motion to extend time is pending.

(c) ***Agreement to Issue.*** The mandate may be issued earlier if the parties so agree, or for good cause on the motion of a party.

18.2. Stay of Mandate. A party may move to stay issuance of the mandate pending the United States Supreme Court's disposition of a petition for writ of certiorari. The motion must state the grounds for the petition and the circumstances requiring the stay. The appellate court authorized to issue the mandate may grant a stay if it finds that the grounds are substantial and that the petitioner or others would incur serious hardship from the mandate's issuance if the United States Supreme Court were later to reverse the judgment. In a criminal case, the stay will last for no more than 90 days, to permit the timely filing of a petition for writ of certiorari. After that period and others mentioned in this rule expire, the mandate will issue.

18.3. Trial Court Case Number. The mandate must state the trial court case number.

18.4. Filing of Mandate. The clerk receiving the mandate will file it with the case's other papers and note it on the docket.

18.5. Costs. The mandate will be issued without waiting for costs to be paid. If the Supreme Court declines to grant review, Supreme Court costs must be included in the court of appeals' mandate.

18.6. Mandate in Accelerated Appeals. The appellate court's judgment on an appeal from an interlocutory order takes effect when the mandate is issued. The court may issue the mandate with its judgment or delay the mandate until the appeal is finally disposed of. If the mandate is issued, any further proceeding in the trial court must conform to the mandate.

18.7. Recall of Mandate. If an appellate court vacates or modifies its judgment or order after issuing its mandate, the appellate clerk must promptly notify the clerk of the court to which the mandate was directed and all parties. The mandate will have no effect and a new mandate may be issued.

TRAP 19. PLENARY POWER OF THE COURTS OF APPEALS AND EXPIRATION OF TERM

19.1. Plenary Power of Courts of Appeals. A court of appeals' plenary power over its judgment expires:

(a) 60 days after judgment if no timely filed motion for rehearing or en banc reconsideration, or timely filed motion to extend time to file such a motion, is then pending; or

(b) 30 days after the court overrules all timely filed motions for rehearing or en banc reconsideration, and all timely filed motions to extend time to file such a motion.

19.2. Plenary Power Continues After Petition Filed. In a civil case, the court of appeals retains plenary

power to vacate or modify its judgment during the periods prescribed in 19.1 even if a party has filed a petition for review in the Supreme Court.

19.3. Proceedings After Plenary Power Expires. After its plenary power expires, the court cannot vacate or modify its judgment. But the court may:

(a) correct a clerical error in its judgment or opinion;

(b) issue and recall its mandate as these rules provide;

(c) enforce or suspend enforcement of its judgment as these rules or applicable law provide;

(d) order or modify the amount and type of security required to suspend a judgment, and decide the sufficiency of the sureties, under Rule 24[1]; and

(e) order its opinion published in accordance with Rule 47.[2]

[1] Vernon's Ann.Rules App.Proc., rule 24.1 et seq.

[2] Vernon's Ann.Rules App.Proc., rule 47.1 et seq.

19.4. Expiration of Term. The expiration of the appellate court's term does not affect the court's plenary power or its jurisdiction over a case that is pending when the court's term expires.

TRAP 20. WHEN PARTY IS INDIGENT

20.1. Civil Cases.

(a) ***Costs Defined.*** In this rule, "costs" mean filing fees charged by the appellate court. Fees charged for preparation of the appellate record are governed by Texas Rule of Civil Procedure 145.

(b) ***When a Statement Was Filed in the Trial Court.***

(1) *General Rule; Status in Trial Court Carries Forward.* A party who filed a Statement of Inability to Afford Payment of Court Costs in the trial court is not required to pay costs in the appellate court unless the trial court overruled the party's claim of indigence in an order that complies with Texas Rule of Civil Procedure 145. A party is not required to pay costs in the appellate court if the trial court ordered the party to pay partial costs or to pay costs in installments.

(2) *Establishing the Right to Proceed Under the General Rule.* To establish the right to proceed without payment of costs under (1), a party must communicate to the appellate court clerk in writing that the party is presumed indigent under this rule. In an appeal under Section Two of these rules, the applicability of the presumption should be stated in the notice of appeal and in the docketing statement.

(3) *Exception; Material Change in Circumstances.* An appellate court may permit a party who is not entitled to proceed under (1) to proceed without payment of costs if the party establishes that the party's financial circumstances have materially changed since the date of the trial court's order under Texas Rule of Civil Procedure 145.

(A) *Requirements.* The party must file a motion in the appellate court alleging that the party's financial circumstances have materially changed since the date of the trial court's order and a current Statement of Inability to Afford Payment of Court Costs that complies with Texas Rule of Civil Procedure 145. The Statement that was filed in the trial court does not meet the requirements of this rule.

(B) *Action by Appellate Court.* The appellate court may decide the motion based on the record or refer the motion to the trial court with instructions to hear evidence and issue findings of fact. If a motion is referred to the trial court, the appellate court must review the trial court's findings and the record of the hearing before ruling on the motion.

(c) ***When No Statement Was Filed in the Trial Court.*** An appellate court may permit a party who did not file a Statement of Inability to Afford Payment of Court Costs in the trial court to proceed without payment of costs. The court may require the party to file a Statement in the appellate court. If the court denies the party's request to proceed without payment of costs, it must do so in a written order.

20.2. Criminal Cases. Within the time for perfecting the appeal, an appellant who is unable to pay for the appellate record may, by motion and affidavit, ask the trial court to have the appellate record furnished without charge. If after hearing the motion the court finds that the appellant cannot pay or give security for the appellate record, the court must order the reporter to transcribe the proceedings. When the court certifies that the appellate record has been furnished to the appellant, the reporter must be paid from the general funds of the county in which the offense was committed, in the amount set by the trial court.

SECTION TWO: APPEALS FROM TRIAL COURT JUDGMENTS AND ORDERS

TRAP 21. NEW TRIALS IN CRIMINAL CASES

21.1. Definitions.

(a) *New trial* means the rehearing of a criminal action after the trial court has, on the defendant's motion, set aside a finding or verdict of guilt.

(b) *New trial on punishment* means a new hearing of the punishment stage of a criminal action after the trial

court has, on the defendant's motion, set aside an assessment of punishment without setting aside a finding or verdict of guilt.

21.2. When Motion for New Trial Required. A motion for new trial is a prerequisite to presenting a point of error on appeal only when necessary to adduce facts not in the record.

21.3. Grounds. The defendant must be granted a new trial, or a new trial on punishment, for any of the following reasons:

(a) except in a misdemeanor case in which the maximum possible punishment is a fine, when the defendant has been unlawfully tried in absentia or has been denied counsel;

(b) when the court has misdirected the jury about the law or has committed some other material error likely to injure the defendant's rights;

(c) when the verdict has been decided by lot or in any manner other than a fair expression of the jurors' opinion;

(d) when a juror has been bribed to convict or has been guilty of any other corrupt conduct;

(e) when a material defense witness has been kept from court by force, threats, or fraud, or when evidence tending to establish the defendant's innocence has been intentionally destroyed or withheld, thus preventing its production at trial;

(f) when, after retiring to deliberate, the jury has received other evidence; when a juror has talked with anyone about the case; or when a juror became so intoxicated that his or her vote was probably influenced as a result;

(g) when the jury has engaged in such misconduct that the defendant did not receive a fair and impartial trial; or

(h) when the verdict is contrary to the law and the evidence.

21.4. Time to File and Amend Motion.

(a) ***To File.*** The defendant may file a motion for new trial before, but no later than 30 days after, the date when the trial court imposes or suspends sentence in open court.

(b) ***To Amend.*** Within 30 days after the date when the trial court imposes or suspends sentence in open court but before the court overrules any preceding motion for new trial, a defendant may, without leave of court, file one or more amended motions for new trial.

21.5. State May Controvert; Effect. The State may oppose in writing any reason the defendant sets forth in the motion for new trial. The State's having opposed a motion for new trial does not affect a defendant's responsibilities under 21.6.

21.6. Time to Present. The defendant must present the motion for new trial to the trial court within 10 days of filing it, unless the trial court in its discretion permits it to be presented and heard within 75 days from the date when the court imposes or suspends sentence in open court.

21.7. Types of Evidence Allowed at Hearing. The court may receive evidence by affidavit or otherwise.

21.8. Court's Ruling.

(a) ***Time to Rule.*** The court must rule on a motion for new trial within 75 days after imposing or suspending sentence in open court.

(b) ***Ruling.*** In ruling on a motion for new trial, the court may make oral or written findings of fact. The granting of a motion for new trial must be accomplished by written order. A docket entry does not constitute a written order.

(c) ***Failure to Rule.*** A motion not timely ruled on by written order will be deemed denied when the period prescribed in (a) expires.

21.9. Granting a New Trial.

(a) A court must grant a new trial when it has found a meritorious ground for new trial, but a court must grant only a new trial on punishment when it has found a ground that affected only the assessment of punishment.

(b) Granting a new trial restores the case to its position before the former trial, including, at any party's option, arraignment or pretrial proceedings initiated by that party.

(c) Granting a new trial on punishment restores the case to its position after the defendant was found guilty. Unless the defendant, State, and trial court all agree to a change, punishment in a new trial shall be assessed in accordance with the defendant's original election under article 37.07, §2(b) of the Code of Criminal Procedure.

(d) A finding or verdict of guilt in the former trial must not be regarded as a presumption of guilt, nor may it be alluded to in the presence of the jury that hears the case on retrial of guilt. A finding of fact or an assessment of punishment in the former trial may not be alluded to in the presence of the jury that hears the case on retrial of punishment.

TRAP 22. ARREST OF JUDGMENT IN CRIMINAL CASES

22.1. Definition. *Motion in arrest of judgment* means a defendant's oral or written suggestion that, for reasons

stated in the motion, the judgment rendered against the defendant was contrary to law. Such a motion is made in the trial court.

22.2. Grounds. The motion may be based on any of the following grounds:

(a) that the indictment or information is subject to an exception on substantive grounds;

(b) that in relation to the indictment or information a verdict is substantively defective; or

(c) that the judgment is invalid for some other reason.

22.3. Time to File Motion. A defendant may file a motion in arrest of judgment before, but no later than 30 days after, the date when the trial court imposes or suspends sentence in open court.

22.4. Court's Ruling.

(a) ***Time to Rule; Form of Ruling.*** The court must rule on a motion in arrest of judgment within 75 days after imposing or suspending sentence in open court. The ruling may be oral or in writing.

(b) ***Failure to Rule.*** A motion not timely ruled on will be deemed denied when the period prescribed in (a) expires.

22.5. Effect of Denying. For purposes of the defendant's giving notice of appeal, an order denying a motion in arrest of judgment will be considered an order denying a motion for new trial.

22.6. Effect of Granting.

(a) ***Defendant Restored.*** If judgment is arrested, the defendant is restored to the position that he or she had before the indictment or information was presented.

(b) ***Defendant Discharged or Remanded.*** If the judgment is arrested, the defendant will be discharged. But the trial court may remand the defendant to custody or fix bail if the court determines, from the evidence adduced at trial, that the defendant may be convicted on a proper indictment or information, or on a proper verdict in relation to the indictment or information.

TRAP 23. NUNC PRO TUNC PROCEEDINGS IN CRIMINAL CASES

23.1. Judgment and Sentence. Unless the trial court has granted a new trial or arrested the judgment, or unless the defendant has appealed, a failure to render judgment and pronounce sentence may be corrected at any time by the court's doing so.

23.2. Credit on Sentence. When sentence is pronounced, the trial court must give the defendant credit on that sentence for:

(a) all time the defendant has been confined since the time when judgment and sentence should have been entered and pronounced; and

(b) all time between the defendant's arrest and confinement to the time when judgment and sentence should have been entered and pronounced.

TRAP 24. SUSPENSION OF ENFORCEMENT OF JUDGMENT PENDING APPEAL IN CIVIL CASES

24.1. Suspension of Enforcement.

(a) ***Methods.*** Unless the law or these rules provide otherwise, a judgment debtor may supersede the judgment by:

(1) filing with the trial court clerk a written agreement with the judgment creditor for suspending enforcement of the judgment;

(2) filing with the trial court clerk a good and sufficient bond;

(3) making a deposit with the trial court clerk in lieu of a bond; or

(4) providing alternate security ordered by the court.

(b) ***Bonds.***

(1) A bond must be:

(A) in the amount required by 24.2;

(B) payable to the judgment creditor;

(C) signed by the judgment debtor or the debtor's agent;

(D) signed by a sufficient surety or sureties as obligors; and

(E) conditioned as required by (d).

(2) To be effective a bond must be approved by the trial court clerk. On motion of any party, the trial court will review the bond.

(c) ***Deposit in Lieu of Bond.***

(1) ***Types of Deposits.*** Instead of filing a surety bond, a party may deposit with the trial court clerk:

(A) cash;

(B) a cashier's check payable to the clerk, drawn on any federally insured and federally or state-chartered bank or savings-and-loan association; or

(C) with leave of court, a negotiable obligation of the federal government or of any federally insured and federally or state-chartered bank or savings-and-loan association.

(2) ***Amount of Deposit.*** The deposit must be in the amount required by 24.2.

(3) *Clerk's Duties; Interest.* The clerk must promptly deposit any cash or a cashier's check in accordance with law. The clerk must hold the deposit until the conditions of liability in (d) are extinguished. The clerk must then release any remaining funds in the deposit to the judgment debtor.

(d) *Conditions of Liability.* The surety or sureties on a bond, any deposit in lieu of a bond, or any alternate security ordered by the court is subject to liability for all damages and costs that may be awarded against the debtor—up to the amount of the bond, deposit, or security—if:

(1) the debtor does not perfect an appeal or the debtor's appeal is dismissed, and the debtor does not perform the trial court's judgment;

(2) the debtor does not perform an adverse judgment final on appeal; or

(3) the judgment is for the recovery of an interest in real or personal property, and the debtor does not pay the creditor the value of the property interest's rent or revenue during the pendency of the appeal.

(e) *Orders of Trial Court.* The trial court may make any order necessary to adequately protect the judgment creditor against loss or damage that the appeal might cause.

(f) *Effect of Supersedeas.* Enforcement of a judgment must be suspended if the judgment is superseded. Enforcement begun before the judgment is superseded must cease when the judgment is superseded. If execution has been issued, the clerk will promptly issue a writ of supersedeas.

24.2. Amount of Bond, Deposit, or Security.

(a) *Type of Judgment.*

(1) *For Recovery of Money.* When the judgment is for money, the amount of the bond, deposit, or security must equal the sum of compensatory damages awarded in the judgment, interest for the estimated duration of the appeal, and costs awarded in the judgment. But the amount must not exceed the lesser of:

(A) 50 percent of the judgment debtor's current net worth; or

(B) 25 million dollars.

(2) *For Recovery of Property.* When the judgment is for the recovery of an interest in real or personal property, the trial court will determine the type of security that the judgment debtor must post. The amount of that security must be at least:

(A) the value of the property interest's rent or revenue, if the property interest is real; or

(B) the value of the property interest on the date when the court rendered judgment, if the property interest is personal.

(3) *Other Judgment.* When the judgment is for something other than money or an interest in property, the trial court must set the amount and type of security that the judgment debtor must post. The security must adequately protect the judgment creditor against loss or damage that the appeal might cause. But the trial court may decline to permit the judgment to be superseded if the judgment creditor posts security ordered by the trial court in an amount and type that will secure the judgment debtor against any loss or damage caused by the relief granted the judgment creditor if an appellate court determines, on final disposition, that that relief was improper. When the judgment debtor is the state, a department of this state, or the head of a department of this state, the trial court must permit a judgment to be superseded except in a matter arising from a contested case in an administrative enforcement action.

(4) *Conservatorship or Custody.* When the judgment involves the conservatorship or custody of a minor or other person under legal disability, enforcement of the judgment will not be suspended, with or without security, unless ordered by the trial court. But upon a proper showing, the appellate court may suspend enforcement of the judgment with or without security.

(5) *For a Governmental Entity.* When a judgment in favor of a governmental entity in its governmental capacity is one in which the entity has no pecuniary interest, the trial court must determine whether to suspend enforcement, with or without security, taking into account the harm that is likely to result to the judgment debtor if enforcement is not suspended, and the harm that is likely to result to others if enforcement is suspended. The appellate court may review the trial court's determination and suspend enforcement of the judgment, with or without security, or refuse to suspend the judgment. If security is required, recovery is limited to the governmental entity's actual damages resulting from suspension of the judgment.

(b) *Lesser Amount.* The trial court must lower the amount of security required by (a) to an amount that will not cause the judgment debtor substantial economic harm if, after notice to all parties and a hearing, the court finds that posting a bond, deposit, or security in the amount required by (a) is likely to cause the judgment debtor substantial economic harm.

(c) *Determination of Net Worth.*

(1) *Judgment Debtor's Affidavit Required; Contents; Prima Facie Evidence.* A judgment debtor who provides a bond, deposit, or security under (a)(1)(A) in an

amount based on the debtor's net worth must simultaneously file with the trial court clerk an affidavit that states the debtor's net worth and states complete, detailed information concerning the debtor's assets and liabilities from which net worth can be ascertained. An affidavit that meets these requirements is prima facie evidence of the debtor's net worth for the purpose of establishing the amount of the bond, deposit, or security required to suspend enforcement of the judgment. A trial court clerk must receive and file a net-worth affidavit tendered for filing by a judgment debtor.

(2) ***Contest; Discovery.*** A judgment creditor may file a contest to the debtor's claimed net worth. The contest need not be sworn. The creditor may conduct reasonable discovery concerning the judgment debtor's net worth.

(3) ***Hearing; Burden of Proof; Findings; Additional Security.*** The trial court must hear a judgment creditor's contest of the judgment debtor's claimed net worth promptly after any discovery has been completed. The judgment debtor has the burden of proving net worth. The trial court must issue an order that states the debtor's net worth and states with particularity the factual basis for that determination. If the trial court orders additional or other security to supersede the judgment, the enforcement of the judgment will be suspended for twenty days after the trial court's order. If the judgment debtor does not comply with the order within that period, the judgment may be enforced against the judgment debtor.

(d) ***Injunction.*** The trial court may enjoin the judgment debtor from dissipating or transferring assets to avoid satisfaction of the judgment, but the trial court may not make any order that interferes with the judgment debtor's use, transfer, conveyance, or dissipation of assets in the normal course of business.

24.3. Continuing Trial Court Jurisdiction; Duties of Judgment Debtor.

(a) ***Continuing Jurisdiction.*** Even after the trial court's plenary power expires, the trial court has continuing jurisdiction to do the following:

(1) order the amount and type of security and decide the sufficiency of sureties; and

(2) if circumstances change, modify the amount or type of security required to continue the suspension of a judgment's execution.

(b) ***Duties of Judgment Debtor.*** If, after jurisdiction attaches in an appellate court, the trial court orders or modifies the security or decides the sufficiency of sureties, the judgment debtor must notify the appellate court of the trial court's action.

24.4. Appellate Review.

(a) ***Motions; Review.*** A party may seek review of the trial court's ruling by motion filed in the court of appeals with jurisdiction or potential jurisdiction over the appeal from the judgment in the case. A party may seek review of the court of appeals' ruling on the motion by petition for writ of mandamus in the Supreme Court. The appellate court may review:

(1) the sufficiency or excessiveness of the amount of security, but when the judgment is for money, the appellate court must not modify the amount of security to exceed the limits imposed by Rule 24.2(a)(1);

(2) the sureties on any bond;

(3) the type of security;

(4) the determination whether to permit suspension of enforcement; and

(5) the trial court's exercise of discretion under Rule 24.3(a).

(b) ***Grounds of Review.*** Review may be based both on conditions as they existed at the time the trial court signed an order and on changes in those conditions afterward.

(c) ***Temporary Orders.*** The appellate court may issue any temporary orders necessary to preserve the parties' rights.

(d) ***Action by Appellate Court.*** The motion must be heard at the earliest practicable time. The appellate court may require that the amount of a bond, deposit, or other security be increased or decreased, and that another bond, deposit, or security be provided and approved by the trial court clerk. The appellate court may require other changes in the trial court order. The appellate court may remand to the trial court for entry of findings of fact or for the taking of evidence.

(e) ***Effect of Ruling.*** If the appellate court orders additional or other security to supersede the judgment, enforcement will be suspended for 20 days after the appellate court's order. If the judgment debtor does not comply with the order within that period, the judgment may be enforced. When any additional bond, deposit, or security has been filed, the trial court clerk must notify the appellate court. The posting of additional security will not release the previously posted security or affect any alternative security arrangements that the judgment debtor previously made unless specifically ordered by the appellate court.

TRAP 25. PERFECTING APPEAL

25.1. Civil Cases.

(a) ***Notice of Appeal.*** An appeal is perfected when a written notice of appeal is filed with the trial court clerk.

If a notice of appeal is mistakenly filed with the appellate court, the notice is deemed to have been filed the same day with the trial court clerk, and the appellate clerk must immediately send the trial court clerk a copy of the notice.

(b) ***Jurisdiction of Appellate Court.*** The filing of a notice of appeal by any party invokes the appellate court's jurisdiction over all parties to the trial court's judgment or order appealed from. Any party's failure to take any other step required by these rules, including the failure of another party to perfect an appeal under (c), does not deprive the appellate court of jurisdiction but is ground only for the appellate court to act appropriately, including dismissing the appeal.

(c) ***Who Must File Notice.*** A party who seeks to alter the trial court's judgment or other appealable order must file a notice of appeal. Parties whose interests are aligned may file a joint notice of appeal. The appellate court may not grant a party who does not file a notice of appeal more favorable relief than did the trial court except for just cause.

(d) ***Contents of Notice.*** The notice of appeal must:

(1) identify the trial court and state the case's trial court number and style;

(2) state the date of the judgment or order appealed from;

(3) state that the party desires to appeal;

(4) state the court to which the appeal is taken unless the appeal is to either the First or Fourteenth Court of Appeals, in which case the notice must state that the appeal is to either of those courts;

(5) state the name of each party filing the notice;

(6) in an accelerated appeal, state that the appeal is accelerated and state whether it is a parental termination or child protection case, as defined in Rule 28.4;

(7) in a restricted appeal:

(A) state that the appellant is a party affected by the trial court's judgment but did not participate—either in person or through counsel—in the hearing that resulted in the judgment complained of;

(B) state that the appellant did not timely file either a postjudgment motion, request for findings of fact and conclusions of law, or notice of appeal; and

(C) be verified by the appellant if the appellant does not have counsel.

(8) state, if applicable, that the appellant is presumed indigent and may proceed without paying costs under Rule 20.1.

(e) ***Notice of Notice.*** The notice of appeal must be served on all parties to the trial court's final judgment or, in an interlocutory appeal, on all parties to the trial court proceeding. At or before the time of the notice of appeal's filing, the filing party must also deliver a copy of the notice of appeal to each court reporter responsible for preparing the reporter's record.

(f) ***Trial Court Clerk's Duties.*** The trial court clerk must immediately deliver a copy of the notice of appeal to the appellate court clerk, to the trial judge, and to each court reporter responsible for preparing the reporter's record.

(g) ***Amending the Notice.*** An amended notice of appeal correcting a defect or omission in an earlier filed notice may be filed in the appellate court at any time before the appellant's brief is filed. The amended notice is subject to being struck for cause on the motion of any party affected by the amended notice. After the appellant's brief is filed, the notice may be amended only on leave of the appellate court and on such terms as the court may prescribe.

(h) ***Enforcement of Judgment Not Suspended by Appeal.*** The filing of a notice of appeal does not suspend enforcement of the judgment. Enforcement of the judgment may proceed unless:

(1) the judgment is superseded in accordance with Rule 24[1], or

(2) the appellant is entitled to supersede the judgment without security by filing a notice of appeal.

[1] Vernon's Ann.Rules App.Proc., rule 24.1 et seq.

25.2. Criminal Cases.

(a) ***Rights to Appeal.***

(1) Of the State. The State is entitled to appeal a court's order in a criminal case as provided by Code of Criminal Procedure article 44.01.

(2) Of the Defendant. A defendant in a criminal case has the right of appeal under Code of Criminal Procedure article 44.02 and these rules. The trial court shall enter a certification of the defendant's right of appeal each time it enters a judgment of guilt or other appealable order other than an order appealable under Code of Criminal Procedure Chapter 64. In a plea bargain case—that is, a case in which a defendant's plea was guilty or nolo contendere and the punishment did not exceed the punishment recommended by the prosecutor and agreed to by the defendant—a defendant may appeal only:

(A) those matters that were raised by written motion filed and ruled on before trial,

(B) after getting the trial court's permission to appeal, or

(C) where the specific appeal is expressly authorized by statute.

(b) ***Perfection of Appeal.*** In a criminal case, appeal is perfected by timely filing a sufficient notice of appeal. In a death-penalty case it is unnecessary to file a notice of appeal, but, in every death-penalty case, the clerk of the trial court shall file a notice of conviction with the Court of Criminal Appeals within thirty days after the defendant is sentenced to death.

(c) ***Form and Sufficiency of Notice.***

(1) Notice must be given in writing and filed with the trial court clerk. If the notice of appeal is received in the court of appeals, the clerk of that court shall immediately record on the notice the date that it was received and send the notice to the trial court clerk.

(2) Notice is sufficient if it shows the party's desire to appeal from the judgment or other appealable order, and, if the State is the appellant, the notice complies with Code of Criminal Procedure article 44.01.

(d) ***Certification of Defendant's Rights of Appeal.*** If the defendant is the appellant, the record must include the trial court's certification of the defendant's right of appeal under Rule 25.2(a)(2). The certification shall include a notice that the defendant has been informed of his rights concerning an appeal, as well as any right to file a *pro se* petition for discretionary review. This notification shall be signed by the defendant, with a copy given to him. The certification should be part of the record when notice is filed, but may be added by timely amendment or supplementation under this rule or Rule 34.5(c)(1) or Rule 37.1 or by order of the appellate court under Rule 34.5(c)(2). The appeal must be dismissed if a certification that shows the defendant has the right of appeal has not been made part of the record under these rules.

(e) ***Trial Court Clerk's Duties.*** The trial court clerk must note on the copies of the notice of appeal and the trial court's certification of the defendant's right of appeal the case number and the date when each was filed. The clerk must then immediately deliver one copy of each to the clerk of the appropriate court of appeals, to the trial judge, to each court reporter responsible for preparing the reporter's record, and, if the defendant is the appellant, one copy of each to the State's attorney.

(f) ***Amending the Notice or Certification.*** An amended notice of appeal or trial court's certification of the defendant's right of appeal correcting a defect or omission in an earlier filed notice or certification, including a defect in the notification of the defendant's appellate rights, may be filed in the appellate court in accordance with Rule 37.1, or at any time before the appealing party's brief is filed if the court of appeals has not used Rule 37.1. The amended notice or certification is subject to being struck for cause on the motion of any party affected by the amended notice or certification. After the appealing party's brief is filed, the notice or certification may be amended only on leave of the appellate court and on such terms as the court may prescribe.

(g) ***Effect of Appeal.*** Once the record has been filed in the appellate court, all further proceedings in the trial court—except as provided otherwise by law or by these rules—will be suspended until the trial court receives the appellate-court mandate.

(h) ***Advice of Right of Appeal.*** When a court enters a judgment or other appealable order and the defendant has a right of appeal, the court (orally or in writing) shall advise the defendant of his right of appeal and of the requirements for timely filing a sufficient notice of appeal.

TRAP 26. TIME TO PERFECT APPEAL

26.1. Civil Cases. The notice of appeal must be filed within 30 days after the judgment is signed, except as follows:

(a) the notice of appeal must be filed within 90 days after the judgment is signed if any party timely files:

(1) a motion for new trial;

(2) a motion to modify the judgment;

(3) a motion to reinstate under Texas Rule of Civil Procedure 165a; or

(4) a request for findings of fact and conclusions of law if findings and conclusions either are required by the Rules of Civil Procedure or, if not required, could properly be considered by the appellate court;

(b) in an accelerated appeal, the notice of appeal must be filed within 20 days after the judgment or order is signed;

(c) in a restricted appeal, the notice of appeal must be filed within six months after the judgment or order is signed; and

(d) if any party timely files a notice of appeal, another party may file a notice of appeal within the applicable period stated above or 14 days after the first filed notice of appeal, whichever is later.

26.2. Criminal Cases.

(a) ***By the Defendant.*** The notice of appeal must be filed:

(1) within 30 days after the day sentence is im-

posed or suspended in open court, or after the day the trial court enters an appealable order; or

(2) within 90 days after the day sentence is imposed or suspended in open court if the defendant timely files a motion for new trial.

(b) ***By the State.*** The notice of appeal must be filed within 20 days after the day the trial court enters the order, ruling, or sentence to be appealed.

26.3. Extension of Time. The appellate court may extend the time to file the notice of appeal if, within 15 days after the deadline for filing the notice of appeal, the party:

(a) files in the trial court the notice of appeal; and

(b) files in the appellate court a motion complying with Rule 10.5(b).

TRAP 27. PREMATURE FILINGS

27.1. Prematurely Filed Notice of Appeal.

(a) ***Civil Cases.*** In a civil case, a prematurely filed notice of appeal is effective and deemed filed on the day of, but after, the event that begins the period for perfecting the appeal.

(b) ***Criminal Cases.*** In a criminal case, a prematurely filed notice of appeal is effective and deemed filed on the same day, but after, sentence is imposed or suspended in open court, or the appealable order is signed by the trial court. But a notice of appeal is not effective if filed before the trial court makes a finding of guilt or receives a jury verdict.

27.2. Other Premature Actions. The appellate court may treat actions taken before an appealable order is signed as relating to an appeal of that order and give them effect as if they had been taken after the order was signed. The appellate court may allow an appealed order that is not final to be modified so as to be made final and may allow the modified order and all proceedings relating to it to be included in a supplemental record.

27.3. If Appealed Order Modified or Vacated. After an order or judgment in a civil case has been appealed, if the trial court modifies the order or judgment, or if the trial court vacates the order or judgment and replaces it with another appealable order or judgment, the appellate court must treat the appeal as from the subsequent order or judgment and may treat actions relating to the appeal of the first order or judgment as relating to the appeal of the subsequent order or judgment. The subsequent order or judgment and actions relating to it may be included in the original or supplemental record. Any party may nonetheless appeal from the subsequent order or judgment.

TRAP 28. ACCELERATED, AGREED, AND PERMISSIVE APPEALS IN CIVIL CASES

28.1. Accelerated Appeal.

(a) ***Types of Accelerated Appeals.*** Appeals from interlocutory orders (when allowed by statute), appeals in quo warranto proceedings, appeals required by statute to be accelerated or expedited, and appeals required by law to be filed or perfected within less than 30 days after the date of the order or judgment being appealed are accelerated appeals.

(b) ***Perfection of Accelerated Appeal.*** Unless otherwise provided by statute, an accelerated appeal is perfected by filing a notice of appeal in compliance with Rule 25.1 within the time allowed by Rule 26.1(b) or as extended by Rule 26.3. Filing a motion for new trial, any other post-trial motion, or a request for findings of fact will not extend the time to perfect an accelerated appeal.

(c) ***Appeals of Interlocutory Orders.*** The trial court need not file findings of fact and conclusions of law but may do so within 30 days after the order is signed.

(d) ***Quo Warranto Appeals.*** The trial court may grant a motion for new trial timely filed under Texas Rule of Civil Procedure 329b(a)–(b) until 50 days after the trial court's final judgment is signed. If not determined by signed written order within that period, the motion will be deemed overruled by operation of law on expiration of that period.

(e) ***Record and Briefs.*** In lieu of the clerk's record, the appellate court may hear an accelerated appeal on the original papers forwarded by the trial court or on sworn and uncontroverted copies of those papers. The appellate court may allow the case to be submitted without briefs. The deadlines and procedures for filing the record and briefs in an accelerated appeal are provided in Rules 35.1 and 38.6.

28.2. Agreed Interlocutory Appeals in Civil Cases.

(a) ***Perfecting Appeal.*** An agreed appeal of an interlocutory order permitted by statute must be perfected as provided in Rule 25.1. The notice of appeal must be filed no later than the 20th day after the date the trial court signs a written order granting permission to appeal, unless the court of appeals extends the time for filing pursuant to Rule 26.3.

(b) ***Other Requirements.*** In addition to perfecting appeal, the appellant must file with the clerk of the appellate court a docketing statement as provided in Rule 32.1 and pay to the clerk of the appellate court all required fees authorized to be collected by the clerk.

(c) ***Contents of Notice.*** The notice of accelerated appeal must contain, in addition to the items required by Rule 25.1(d), the following:

(1) a list of the names of all parties to the trial court proceeding and the names, addresses, and telefax numbers of all trial and appellate counsel;

(2) a copy of the trial court's order granting permission to appeal;

(3) a copy of the trial court order appealed from;

(4) a statement that all parties to the trial court proceeding agreed to the trial court's order granting permission to appeal;

(5) a statement that all parties to the trial court proceeding agreed that the order granting permission to appeal involves a controlling question of law as to which there is a substantial ground for difference of opinion;

(6) a brief statement of the issues or points presented; and

(7) a concise explanation of how an immediate appeal may materially advance the ultimate termination of the litigation.

(d) ***Determination of Jurisdiction.*** If the court of appeals determines that a notice of appeal filed under this rule does not demonstrate the court's jurisdiction, it may order the appellant to file an amended notice of appeal. On a party's motion or its own initiative, the court of appeals may also order the appellant or any other party to file briefing addressing whether the appeal meets the statutory requirements, and may direct the parties to file supporting evidence. If, after providing an opportunity to file an amended notice of appeal or briefing addressing potential jurisdictional defects, the court of appeals concludes that a jurisdictional defect exists, it may dismiss the appeal for want of jurisdiction at any stage of the appeal.

(e) ***Record; Briefs.*** The rules governing the filing of the appellate record and briefs in accelerated appeals apply. A party may address in its brief any issues related to the court of appeals' jurisdiction, including whether the appeal meets the statutory requirements.

(f) ***No Automatic Stay of Proceedings in Trial Court.*** An agreed appeal of an interlocutory order permitted by statute does not stay proceedings in the trial court except as agreed by the parties and ordered by the trial court or the court of appeals.

28.3. Permissive Appeals in Civil Cases.

(a) ***Petition Required.*** When a trial court has permitted an appeal from an interlocutory order that would not otherwise be appealable, a party seeking to appeal must petition the court of appeals for permission to appeal.

(b) ***Where Filed.*** The petition must be filed with the clerk of the court of appeals having appellate jurisdiction over the action in which the order to be appealed is issued. The First and Fourteenth Courts of Appeals must determine in which of those two courts a petition will be filed.

(c) ***When Filed.*** The petition must be filed within 15 days after the order to be appealed is signed. If the order is amended by the trial court, either on its own or in response to a party's motion, to include the court's permission to appeal, the time to petition the court of appeals runs from the date the amended order is signed.

(d) ***Extension of Time to File Petition.*** The court of appeals may extend the time to file the petition if the party:

(1) files the petition within 15 days after the deadline, and

(2) files a motion complying with Rule 10.5(b).

(e) ***Contents.*** The petition must:

(1) contain the information required by Rule 25.1(d) to be included in a notice of appeal;

(2) attach a copy of the order from which appeal is sought;

(3) contain a table of contents, index of authorities, issues presented, and a statement of facts; and

(4) argue clearly and concisely why the order to be appealed involves a controlling question of law as to which there is a substantial ground for difference of opinion and how an immediate appeal from the order may materially advance the ultimate termination of the litigation.

(f) ***Response; Reply; Cross-Petition; Time for Filing.*** If any party timely files a petition, any other party may file a response or a cross-petition within 10 days. A party may file a response to a cross-petition within 10 days of the date the cross-petition is filed. A petitioner or cross-petitioner may reply to any matter in a response within 7 days of the date the response is filed. The court of appeals may extend the time to file a response, reply, and cross-petition.

(g) ***Length of Petition, Cross-Petition, Response, and Reply.*** A petition, cross-petition, response, and reply must comply with the length limitations in Rule 9.4(i)(2)(D)–(E).

(h) ***Service.*** A petition, cross-petition, response, and reply must be served on all parties to the trial court proceeding.

(i) ***Docketing Statement.*** Upon filing the petition, the petitioner must file the docketing statement required by Rule 32.1.

(j) ***Time for Determination.*** Unless the court of ap-

peals orders otherwise, a petition, and any cross-petition, response, and reply, will be determined without oral argument, no earlier than 10 days after the petition is filed.

(k) ***When Petition Granted.*** If the petition is granted, a notice of appeal is deemed to have been filed under Rule 26.1(b) on that date, and the appeal is governed by the rules for accelerated appeals. A separate notice of appeal need not be filed. A copy of the order granting the petition must be filed with the trial court clerk.

28.4. Accelerated Appeals in Parental Termination and Child Protection Cases.

(a) ***Application and Definitions.***

(1) Appeals in parental termination and child protection cases are governed by the rules of appellate procedure for accelerated appeals, except as otherwise provided in Rule 28.4.

(2) In Rule 28.4:

(A) a "parental termination case" means a suit in which termination of the parent-child relationship is at issue.

(B) a "child protection case" means a suit affecting the parent-child relationship filed by a governmental entity for managing conservatorship.

(b) ***Appellate Record.***

(1) ***Responsibility for Preparation of Reporter's Record.*** In addition to the responsibility imposed on the trial court in Rule 35.3(c), when the reporter's responsibility to prepare, certify and timely file the reporter's record arises under Rule 35.3(b), the trial court must direct the official or deputy reporter to immediately commence the preparation of the reporter's record. The trial court must arrange for a substitute reporter, if necessary.

(2) ***Extension of Time.*** The appellate court may grant an extension of time to file a record under Rule 35.3(c); however, the extension or extensions granted must not exceed 30 days cumulatively, absent extraordinary circumstances.

(3) ***Restriction on Preparation Inapplicable.*** Section 13.003 of the Civil Practice & Remedies Code does not apply to an appeal from a parental termination or child protection case.

(c) ***Remand for New Trial.*** If the judgment of the appellate court reverses and remands a parental termination or child protection case for a new trial, the judgment must instruct the trial court to commence the new trial no later than 180 days after the mandate is issued by the appellate court.

TRAP 29. ORDERS PENDING INTERLOCUTORY APPEAL IN CIVIL CASES

29.1. Effect of Appeal. Perfecting an appeal from an order granting interlocutory relief does not suspend the order appealed from unless:

(a) the order is superseded in accordance with 29.2; or

(b) the appellant is entitled to supersede the order without security by filing a notice of appeal.

29.2. Security. The trial court may permit an order granting interlocutory relief to be superseded pending an appeal from the order, in which event the appellant may supersede the order in accordance with Rule 24.[1] If the trial court refuses to permit the appellant to supersede the order, the appellant may move the appellate court to review that decision for abuse of discretion.

[1] Vernon's Ann.Rules App.Proc., rule 24.1 et seq.

29.3. Temporary Orders of Appellate Court. When an appeal from an interlocutory order is perfected, the appellate court may make any temporary orders necessary to preserve the parties' rights until disposition of the appeal and may require appropriate security. But the appellate court must not suspend the trial court's order if the appellant's rights would be adequately protected by supersedeas or another order made under Rule 24.[1]

[1] Vernon's Ann.Rules App.Proc., rule 24.1 et seq.

29.4. Enforcement of Temporary Orders. While an appeal from an interlocutory order is pending, only the appellate court in which the appeal is pending may enforce the order. But the appellate court may refer any enforcement proceeding to the trial court with instructions to:

(a) hear evidence and grant appropriate relief; or

(b) make findings and recommendations and report them to the appellate court.

29.5. Further Proceedings in Trial Court. While an appeal from an interlocutory order is pending, the trial court retains jurisdiction of the case and unless prohibited by statute may make further orders, including one dissolving the order complained of on appeal. If permitted by law, the trial court may proceed with a trial on the merits. But the court must not make an order that:

(a) is inconsistent with any appellate court temporary order; or

(b) interferes with or impairs the jurisdiction of the appellate court or effectiveness of any relief sought or that may be granted on appeal.

29.6. Review of Further Orders.

(a) ***Motion to Review Further Orders.*** While an appeal from an interlocutory order is pending, on a party's

motion or on the appellate court's own initiative, the appellate court may review the following:

(1) a further appealable interlocutory order concerning the same subject matter; and

(2) any interlocutory order that interferes with or impairs the effectiveness of the relief sought or that may be granted on appeal.

(b) ***Record.*** The party filing the motion may rely on the original record or may file a supplemental record with the motion.

TRAP 30. RESTRICTED APPEAL TO COURT OF APPEALS IN CIVIL CASES

A party who did not participate—either in person or through counsel—in the hearing that resulted in the judgment complained of and who did not timely file a postjudgment motion or request for findings of fact and conclusions of law, or a notice of appeal within the time permitted by Rule 26.1(a), may file a notice of appeal within the time permitted by Rule 26.1(c). Restricted appeals replace writ of error appeals to the court of appeals. Statutes pertaining to writ of error appeals to the court of appeals apply equally to restricted appeals.

TRAP 31. APPEALS IN HABEAS CORPUS, BAIL, & EXTRADITION PROCEEDINGS IN CRIMINAL CASES

31.1. Filing the Record and Briefs. When written notice of appeal from a judgment or order in a habeas corpus or bail proceeding is filed, the trial court clerk must prepare and certify the clerk's record and, if the appellant requests, the court reporter must prepare and certify a reporter's record. The clerk must send the clerk's record and the court reporter must send the reporter's record to the appellate court within 15 days after the notice of appeal is filed. On reasonable explanation, the appellate court may shorten or extend the time to file the records.

(a) For an appeal from a habeas corpus proceeding challenging a conviction or an order placing the defendant on community supervision—but not challenging any particular condition of community supervision—the appellate court should use the same briefing rules, deadlines, and schedule that apply to direct appeals from criminal cases. On motion of any party, or on its own initiative, the appellate court may impose a more expedited timeline or submit the case without briefing, if necessary to do substantial justice to the parties.

(b) For an appeal from a bail proceeding or any other habeas corpus proceeding, including one that challenges a particular condition of community supervision, the court will—if it desires briefs—set the time for filing briefs.

31.2. Submission; Hearing. The applicant need not personally appear. The appellate court will not review any incidental question that might have arisen on the hearing of the application before the trial court. The sole purpose of the appeal is to do substantial justice to the parties.

(a) In an appeal from a habeas corpus proceeding challenging a conviction or an order placing the defendant on community supervision—but not challenging a particular condition of community supervision—the appellate court should use the same submission and hearing schedules that apply to direct appeals from criminal cases. On motion of any party, or on its own initiative, the appellate court may impose a more expedited timeline or submit the case without briefing, if necessary to do substantial justice to the parties.

(b) An appeal in any other habeas corpus or bail proceeding, including a challenge to a particular condition of community supervision, shall be submitted and heard at the earliest practicable time.

31.3. Orders on Appeal. The appellate court will render whatever judgment and make whatever orders the law and the nature of the case require. The court may make an appropriate order relating to costs, whether allowing costs and fixing the amount, or allowing no costs.

31.4. Stay of Mandate.

(a) ***When Motion for Stay Required.*** Despite Rule 18[1] or any other of these rules, in the following circumstances a party who in good faith intends to seek discretionary review must—within 15 days after the court of appeals renders judgment—file with the court of appeals clerk a motion for stay of mandate, to which is appended the party's petition for discretionary review showing reasons why the Court of Criminal Appeals should review the appellate court judgment:

(1) when a court of appeals affirms the judgment of the trial court in an extradition matter and thereby sanctions a defendant's extradition; or

(2) when a court of appeals reverses the trial court's judgment in a bail matter—including bail pending appeal under Code of Criminal Procedure article 44.04(g)—and thereby grants or reduces the amount of bail.

(b) ***Determination of the Motion.*** The clerk must promptly submit the motion and appendix to the court of appeals, or to one or more judges as the court deems appropriate, for immediate consideration and determination.

(1) If the motion for stay is granted, the clerk will

[1] Vernon's Ann.Rules App.Proc., rule 18.1 et seq.

immediately forward the petition for discretionary review to the clerk of the Court of Criminal Appeals.

(2) If the motion is denied, the clerk will issue a mandate in accordance with the court of appeals' judgment.

(c) ***Denial of Stay.*** If the motion for stay is denied under 31.4(b)(2), the losing party may then present the motion and appendix to the clerk of the Court of Criminal Appeals, who will promptly submit them to the Court, or to one or more judges as the Court deems appropriate, for immediate consideration and determination. The Court of Criminal Appeals may deny the motion or stay or recall the mandate. If the mandate is stayed or recalled, the clerk of the Court of Criminal Appeals will file the petition for discretionary review and process the case in accordance with Rule 68.7.

31.5. Judgment Conclusive. The court of appeals' judgment is final and conclusive if the Court of Criminal Appeals does not grant discretionary review. If the Court of Criminal Appeals grants discretionary review, that court's judgment is final and conclusive. In either case, no further application in the same case can be made for the writ unless the law provides otherwise.

31.6. Defendant Detained by Other Than Officer. If the defendant is held by a person other than an officer, the sheriff receiving the appellate court mandate so ordering must immediately cause the defendant to be discharged, for which discharge the mandate is sufficient authority.

31.7. Judgment to Be Certified. The appellate court clerk will certify the court's judgment to the officer holding the defendant in custody or, if the defendant is held by a person other than an officer, to the appropriate sheriff.

TRAP 32. DOCKETING STATEMENT

32.1. Civil Cases. Promptly upon filing the notice of appeal in a civil case, the appellant must file in the appellate court a docketing statement that includes the following information:

(a) (1) if the appellant filing the statement has counsel, the name of that appellant and the name, address, telephone number, fax number, if any, and State Bar of Texas identification number of the appellant's lead counsel; or

(2) if the appellant filing the statement is not represented by an attorney, that party's name, address, telephone number, and fax number, if any;

(b) the date the notice of appeal was filed in the trial court and, if mailed to the trial court clerk, the date of mailing;

(c) the trial court's name and county, the name of the judge who tried the case, and the date the judgment or order appealed from was signed;

(d) the date of filing of any motion for new trial, motion to modify the judgment, request for findings of fact, motion to reinstate, or other filing that affects the time for perfecting the appeal;

(e) the names of all other parties to the trial court's judgment or the order appealed from, and:

(1) if represented by counsel, their lead counsel's names, addresses, telephone numbers, and fax numbers, if any; or

(2) if not represented by counsel, the name, address, and telephone number of the party, or a statement that the appellant diligently inquired but could not discover that information;

(f) the general nature of the case—for example, personal injury, breach of contract, or temporary injunction;

(g) whether the appeal's submission should be given priority, whether the appeal is an accelerated one under Rule 28[1] or another rule or statute, and whether it is a parental termination or child protection case, as defined in Rule 28.4;

(h) whether the appellant has requested or will request a reporter's record, and whether the trial was electronically recorded;

(i) the name, mailing address, telephone number, fax number, if any, email address, and Certified Shorthand Reporter number of each court reporter responsible for preparing the reporter's record;

(j) whether the appellant intends to seek temporary or ancillary relief while the appeal is pending;

(k) if the appellant filed a Statement of Inability to Afford Payment of Court Costs in the trial court:

(1) the date that the Statement was filed;

(2) the date of filing of any motion challenging the Statement;

(3) the date of any hearing on the appellant's ability to afford costs; and

(4) if the trial court signed an order under Texas Rule of Civil Procedure 145, the court's findings regarding the appellant's ability to afford costs and the date that the order was signed;

(*l*) whether the appellant has filed or will file a supersedeas bond; and

(m) any other information the appellate court requires.

[1] Vernon's Ann.Rules App.Proc., rule 28.1 et seq.

32.2. Criminal Cases. Upon perfecting the appeal in a criminal case, the appellant must file in the appellate court a docketing statement that includes the following information:

(a) (1) if the appellant has counsel, the name of the appellant and the name, address, telephone number, fax number, if any, and State Bar of Texas identification number of the appellant's counsel, and whether the counsel is appointed or retained; or

(2) if the appellant is not represented by an attorney, that party's name, address, telephone number, and fax number, if any;

(b) the date the notice of appeal was filed in the trial court and, if mailed to the trial court clerk, the date of mailing;

(c) the trial court's name and county, and the name of the judge who tried the case;

(d) the date the trial court imposed or suspended sentence in open court, or the date the judgment or order appealed from was signed;

(e) the date of filing any motion for new trial, motion in arrest of judgment, or any other filing that affects the time for perfecting the appeal;

(f) the offense charged and the date of the offense;

(g) the defendant's plea;

(h) whether the trial was jury or nonjury;

(i) the punishment assessed;

(j) whether the appeal is from a pretrial order;

(k) whether the appeal involves the validity of a statute, ordinance, or rule;

(*l*) whether a reporter's record has been or will be requested, and whether the trial was electronically recorded;

(m) the name, mailing address, telephone number, fax number (if any), email address, and Certified Shorthand Reporter number of each court reporter responsible for preparing the reporter's record;

(n) (1) the dates of filing of any motion and affidavit of indigence;

(2) the date of any hearing;

(3) the date of any order; and

(4) whether the motion was granted or denied; and

(o) any other information the appellate court requires.

32.3. Supplemental Statements. Any party may file a statement supplementing or correcting the docketing statement.

32.4. Purpose of Statement. The docketing statement is for administrative purposes and does not affect the appellate court's jurisdiction.

TRAP 33. PRESERVATION OF APPELLATE COMPLAINTS

33.1. Preservation; How Shown.

(a) ***In General.*** As a prerequisite to presenting a complaint for appellate review, the record must show that:

(1) the complaint was made to the trial court by a timely request, objection, or motion that:

(A) stated the grounds for the ruling that the complaining party sought from the trial court with sufficient specificity to make the trial court aware of the complaint, unless the specific grounds were apparent from the context; and

(B) complied with the requirements of the Texas Rules of Evidence or the Texas Rules of Civil or Appellate Procedure; and

(2) the trial court:

(A) ruled on the request, objection, or motion, either expressly or implicitly; or

(B) refused to rule on the request, objection, or motion, and the complaining party objected to the refusal.

(b) ***Ruling by Operation of Law.*** In a civil case, the overruling by operation of law of a motion for new trial or a motion to modify the judgment preserves for appellate review a complaint properly made in the motion, unless taking evidence was necessary to properly present the complaint in the trial court.

(c) ***Formal Exception and Separate Order Not Required.*** Neither a formal exception to a trial court ruling or order nor a signed, separate order is required to preserve a complaint for appeal.

(d) ***Sufficiency of Evidence Complaints in Civil Nonjury Cases.*** In a civil nonjury case, a complaint regarding the legal or factual insufficiency of the evidence—including a complaint that the damages found by the court are excessive or inadequate, as distinguished from a complaint that the trial court erred in refusing to amend a fact finding or to make an additional finding of fact—may be made for the first time on appeal in the complaining party's brief.

33.2. Formal Bills of Exception. To complain on ap-

peal about a matter that would not otherwise appear in the record, a party must file a formal bill of exception.

(a) ***Form.*** No particular form of words is required in a bill of exception. But the objection to the court's ruling or action, and the ruling complained of, must be stated with sufficient specificity to make the trial court aware of the complaint.

(b) ***Evidence.*** When the appellate record contains the evidence needed to explain a bill of exception, the bill itself need not repeat the evidence, and a party may attach and incorporate a transcription of the evidence certified by the court reporter.

(c) ***Procedure.***

(1) The complaining party must first present a formal bill of exception to the trial court.

(2) If the parties agree on the contents of the bill of exception, the judge must sign the bill and file it with the trial court clerk. If the parties do not agree on the contents of the bill, the trial judge must—after notice and hearing—do one of the following things:

(A) sign the bill of exception and file it with the trial court clerk if the judge finds that it is correct;

(B) suggest to the complaining party those corrections to the bill that the judge believes are necessary to make it accurately reflect the proceedings in the trial court, and if the party agrees to the corrections, have the corrections made, sign the bill, and file it with the trial court clerk; or

(C) if the complaining party will not agree to the corrections suggested by the judge, return the bill to the complaining party with the judge's refusal written on it, and prepare, sign, and file with the trial court clerk such bill as will, in the judge's opinion, accurately reflect the proceedings in the trial court.

(3) If the complaining party is dissatisfied with the bill of exception filed by the judge under (2)(C), the party may file with the trial court clerk the bill that was rejected by the judge. That party must also file the affidavits of at least three people who observed the matter to which the bill of exception is addressed. The affidavits must attest to the correctness of the bill as presented by the party. The matters contained in that bill of exception may be controverted and maintained by additional affidavits filed by any party within ten days after the filing of that bill. The truth of the bill of exception will be determined by the appellate court.

(d) ***Conflict.*** If a formal bill of exception conflicts with the reporter's record, the bill controls.

(e) ***Time to File.***

(1) ***Civil Cases.*** In a civil case, a formal bill of exception must be filed no later than 30 days after the filing party's notice of appeal is filed.

(2) ***Criminal Cases.*** In a criminal case, a formal bill of exception must be filed:

(A) no later than 60 days after the trial court pronounces or suspends sentence in open court; or

(B) if a motion for new trial has been timely filed, no later than 90 days after the trial court pronounces or suspends sentence in open court.

(3) ***Extension of Time.*** The appellate court may extend the time to file a formal bill of exception if, within 15 days after the deadline for filing the bill, the party files in the appellate court a motion complying with Rule 10.5(b).

(f) ***Inclusion in Clerk's Record.*** When filed, a formal bill of exception should be included in the appellate record.

TRAP 34. APPELLATE RECORD

34.1. Contents. The appellate record consists of the clerk's record and, if necessary to the appeal, the reporter's record. Even if more than one notice of appeal is filed, there should be only one appellate record in a case.

34.2. Agreed Record. By written stipulation filed with the trial court clerk, the parties may agree on the contents of the appellate record. An agreed record will be presumed to contain all evidence and filings relevant to the appeal. To request matter to be included in the agreed record, the parties must comply with the procedures in Rules 34.5 and 34.6.

34.3. Agreed Statement of the Case. In lieu of a reporter's record, the parties may agree on a brief statement of the case. The statement must be filed with the trial court clerk and included in the appellate record.

34.4. Form. The Supreme Court and Court of Criminal Appeals will prescribe the form of the appellate record.

34.5. Clerk's Record.

(a) ***Contents.*** Unless the parties designate the filings in the appellate record by agreement under Rule 34.2, the record must include copies of the following:

(1) in civil cases, all pleadings on which the trial was held;

(2) in criminal cases, the indictment or information, any special plea or defense motion that was presented to the court and overruled, any written waiver, any written stipulation, and, in cases in which a plea of guilty or nolo contendere has been entered, any documents executed for the plea;

(3) the court's docket sheet;

(4) the court's charge and the jury's verdict, or the court's findings of fact and conclusions of law;

(5) the court's judgment or other order that is being appealed;

(6) any request for findings of fact and conclusions of law, any post-judgment motion, and the court's order on the motion;

(7) the notice of appeal;

(8) any formal bill of exception;

(9) any request for a reporter's record, including any statement of points or issues under Rule 34.6(c);

(10) any request for preparation of the clerk's record;

(11) in civil cases, a certified bill of costs, including the cost of preparing the clerk's record, showing credits for payments made;

(12) in criminal cases the trial court's certification of the defendant's right of appeal under Rule 25.2; and

(13) subject to (b), any filing that a party designates to have included in the record.

(b) *Request for Additional Items.*

(1) *Time for Request.* At any time before the clerk's record is prepared, any party may file with the trial court clerk a written designation specifying items to be included in the record.

(2) *Request Must Be Specific.* A party requesting that an item be included in the clerk's record must specifically describe the item so that the clerk can readily identify it. The clerk will disregard a general designation, such as one for "all papers filed in the case."

(3) *Requesting Unnecessary Items.* In a civil case, if a party requests that more items than necessary be included in the clerk's record or any supplement, the appellate court may—regardless of the appeal's outcome—require that party to pay the costs for the preparation of the unnecessary portion.

(4) *Failure to Timely Request.* An appellate court must not refuse to file the clerk's record or a supplemental clerk's record because of a failure to timely request items to be included in the clerk's record.

(c) *Supplementation.*

(1) If a relevant item has been omitted from the clerk's record, the trial court, the appellate court, or any party may by letter direct the trial court clerk to prepare, certify, and file in the appellate court a supplement containing the omitted item.

(2) If the appellate court in a criminal case orders the trial court to prepare and file findings of fact and conclusions of law as required by law, or certification of the defendant's right of appeal as required by these rules, the trial court clerk must prepare, certify, and file in the appellate court a supplemental clerk's record containing those findings and conclusions.

(3) Any supplemental clerk's record will be part of the appellate record.

(d) *Defects or Inaccuracies.* If the clerk's record is defective or inaccurate, the appellate clerk must inform the trial court clerk of the defect or inaccuracy and instruct the clerk to make the correction.

(e) *Clerk's Record Lost or Destroyed.* If a filing designated for inclusion in the clerk's record has been lost or destroyed, the parties may, by written stipulation, deliver a copy of that item to the trial court clerk for inclusion in the clerk's record or a supplement. If the parties cannot agree, the trial court must—on any party's motion or at the appellate court's request—determine what constitutes an accurate copy of the missing item and order it to be included in the clerk's record or a supplement.

(f) *Original Documents.* If the trial court determines that original documents filed with the trial court clerk should be inspected by the appellate court or sent to that court in lieu of copies, the trial court must make an order for the safekeeping, transportation, and return of those original documents. The order must list the original documents and briefly describe them. All the documents must be arranged in their listed sequence and bound firmly together. On any party's motion or its own initiative, the appellate court may direct the trial court clerk to send it any original document.

(g) *Additional Copies of Clerk's Record in Criminal Cases.* In a criminal case, the clerk's record must be made in duplicate, and in a case in which the death penalty was assessed, in triplicate. The trial court clerk must retain the copy or copies for the parties to use with the court's permission.

(h) *Clerk May Consult with Parties.* The clerk may consult with the parties concerning the contents of the clerk's record.

34.6. Reporter's Record.

(a) *Contents.*

(1) *Stenographic Recording.* If the proceedings were stenographically recorded, the reporter's record consists of the court reporter's transcription of so much of the proceedings, and any of the exhibits, that the parties to the appeal designate.

(2) *Electronic Recording.* If the proceedings were electronically recorded, the reporter's record consists

of certified copies of all tapes or other audio-storage devices on which the proceedings were recorded, any of the exhibits that the parties to the appeal designate, and certified copies of the logs prepared by the court recorder under Rule 13.2.

(b) ***Request for Preparation.***

(1) ***Request to Court Reporter.*** At or before the time for perfecting the appeal, the appellant must request in writing that the official reporter prepare the reporter's record. The request must designate the exhibits to be included. A request to the court reporter—but not the court recorder—must also designate the portions of the proceedings to be included.

(2) ***Filing.*** The appellant must file a copy of the request with the trial court clerk.

(3) ***Failure to Timely Request.*** An appellate court must not refuse to file a reporter's record or a supplemental reporter's record because of a failure to timely request it.

(c) ***Partial Reporter's Record.***

(1) ***Effect on Appellate Points or Issues.*** If the appellant requests a partial reporter's record, the appellant must include in the request a statement of the points or issues to be presented on appeal and will then be limited to those points or issues.

(2) ***Other Parties May Designate Additions.*** Any other party may designate additional exhibits and portions of the testimony to be included in the reporter's record.

(3) ***Costs; requesting unnecessary matter.*** Additions requested by another party must be included in the reporter's record at the appellant's cost. But if the trial court finds that all or part of the designated additions are unnecessary to the appeal, the trial court may order the other party to pay the costs for the preparation of the unnecessary additions. This paragraph does not affect the appellate court's power to tax costs differently.

(4) ***Presumptions.*** The appellate court must presume that the partial reporter's record designated by the parties constitutes the entire record for purposes of reviewing the stated points or issues. This presumption applies even if the statement includes a point or issue complaining of the legal or factual insufficiency of the evidence to support a specific factual finding identified in that point or issue.

(5) ***Criminal Cases.*** In a criminal case, if the statement contains a point complaining that the evidence is insufficient to support a finding of guilt, the record must include all the evidence admitted at the trial on the issue of guilt or innocence and punishment.

(d) ***Supplementation.*** If anything relevant is omitted from the reporter's record, the trial court, the appellate court, or any party may by letter direct the official court reporter to prepare, certify, and file in the appellate court a supplemental reporter's record containing the omitted items. Any supplemental reporter's record is part of the appellate record.

(e) ***Inaccuracies in the Reporter's Record.***

(1) ***Correction of Inaccuracies by Agreement.*** The parties may agree to correct an inaccuracy in the reporter's record, including an exhibit, without the court reporter's recertification.

(2) ***Correction of Inaccuracies by Trial Court.*** If the parties cannot agree on whether or how to correct the reporter's record so that the text accurately discloses what occurred in the trial court and the exhibits are accurate, the trial court must—after notice and hearing—settle the dispute. If the court finds any inaccuracy, it must order the court reporter to conform the reporter's record (including text and any exhibits) to what occurred in the trial court, and to file certified corrections in the appellate court.

(3) ***Correction After Filing in Appellate Court.*** If the dispute arises after the reporter's record has been filed in the appellate court, that court may submit the dispute to the trial court for resolution. The trial court must then proceed as under subparagraph (e)(2).

(f) ***Reporter's Record Lost or Destroyed.*** An appellant is entitled to a new trial under the following circumstances:

(1) if the appellant has timely requested a reporter's record;

(2) if, without the appellant's fault, a significant exhibit or a significant portion of the court reporter's notes and records has been lost or destroyed or—if the proceedings were electronically recorded—a significant portion of the recording has been lost or destroyed or is inaudible;

(3) if the lost, destroyed, or inaudible portion of the reporter's record, or the lost or destroyed exhibit, is necessary to the appeal's resolution; and

(4) if the lost, destroyed or inaudible portion of the reporter's record cannot be replaced by agreement of the parties, or the lost or destroyed exhibit cannot be replaced either by agreement of the parties or with a copy determined by the trial court to accurately duplicate with reasonable certainty the original exhibit.

(g) ***Original Exhibits.***

(1) ***Reporter May Use in Preparing Reporter's Record.*** At the court reporter's request, the trial court clerk

must give all original exhibits to the reporter for use in preparing the reporter's record. Unless ordered to include original exhibits in the reporter's record, the court reporter must return the original exhibits to the clerk after copying them for inclusion in the reporter's record. If someone other than the trial court clerk possesses an original exhibit, either the trial court or the appellate court may order that person to deliver the exhibit to the trial court clerk.

(2) ***Use of Original Exhibits by Appellate Court.*** If the trial court determines that original exhibits should be inspected by the appellate court or sent to that court in lieu of copies, the trial court must make an order for the safekeeping, transportation, and return of those exhibits. The order must list the exhibits and briefly describe them. To the extent practicable, all the exhibits must be arranged in their listed order and bound firmly together before being sent to the appellate clerk. On any party's motion or its own initiative, the appellate court may direct the trial court clerk to send it any original exhibit.

(h) ***Additional Copies of Reporter's Record in Criminal Cases.*** In a criminal case in which a party requests a reporter's record, the court reporter must prepare a duplicate of the reporter's record and file it with the trial court clerk. In a case where the death penalty was assessed, the court reporter must prepare two duplicates of the reporter's record.

(i) ***Supreme Court and Court of Criminal Appeals May Set Fee.*** From time to time, the Supreme Court and the Court of Criminal Appeals may set the fee that the court reporters may charge for preparing the reporter's record.

TRAP 35. TIME TO FILE RECORD; RESPONSIBILITY FOR FILING RECORD

35.1. Civil Cases. The appellate record must be filed in the appellate court within 60 days after the judgment is signed, except as follows:

(a) if Rule 26.1(a) applies, within 120 days after the judgment is signed;

(b) if Rule 26.1(b) applies, within 10 days after the notice of appeal is filed; or

(c) if Rule 26.1(c) applies, within 30 days after the notice of appeal is filed.

35.2. Criminal Cases. The appellate record must be filed in the appellate court:

(a) if a motion for new trial is not filed, within 60 days after the date the sentence is imposed or suspended in open court or the order appealed from is signed;

(b) if a timely motion for new trial is filed and denied, within 120 days after the date the sentence is imposed or suspended in open court; or

(c) if a motion for new trial is granted, within 60 days after the order granting the motion is signed.

35.3. Responsibility for Filing Record.

(a) ***Clerk's Record.*** The trial court clerk is responsible for preparing, certifying, and timely filing the clerk's record if:

(1) a notice of appeal has been filed, and in criminal proceedings, the trial court has certified the defendant's right of appeal, as required by Rule 25.2(d); and

(2) the party responsible for paying for the preparation of the clerk's record has paid the clerk's fee, has made satisfactory arrangements with the clerk to pay the fee, or is entitled to appeal without paying the fee.

(b) ***Reporter's Record.*** The official or deputy reporter is responsible for preparing, certifying, and timely filing the reporter's record if:

(1) a notice of appeal has been filed;

(2) the appellant has requested that the reporter's record be prepared; and

(3) the party responsible for paying for the preparation of the reporter's record has paid the reporter's fee, or has made satisfactory arrangements with the reporter to pay the fee, or is entitled to appeal without paying the fee.

(c) ***Courts to Ensure Record Timely Filed.*** The trial and appellate courts are jointly responsible for ensuring that the appellate record is timely filed. The appellate court may extend the deadline to file the record if requested by the clerk or reporter. Each extension must not exceed 30 days in an ordinary or restricted appeal, or 10 days in an accelerated appeal. The appellate court must allow the record to be filed late when the delay is not the appellant's fault, and may do so when the delay is the appellant's fault. The appellate court may enter any order necessary to ensure the timely filing of the appellate record.

TRAP 36. AGENCY RECORD IN ADMINISTRATIVE APPEALS

36.1. Scope. This rule applies only to cases involving judicial review of state agency decisions in contested cases under the Administrative Procedure Act.

36.2. Inclusion in Appellate Record. The record of an agency proceeding filed in the trial court may be included in either the clerk's record or the reporter's record.

36.3. Correcting the Record.

(a) ***Correction by Agreement.*** At any stage of the proceeding, the parties may agree to correct an agency rec-

ord filed under Section 2001.175(b) of the Government Code to ensure that the agency record accurately reflects the contested case proceedings before the agency. The court reporter need not recertify the agency record.

(b) ***Correction by Trial Court.*** If the parties cannot agree to a correction to the agency record, the appellate court must—on any party's motion or its own incentive—send the question to the trial court. After notice and hearing, the trial court must determine what constitutes an accurate copy of the agency record and order the agency to send an accurate copy to the clerk of the court in which the case is pending.

TRAP 37. DUTIES OF THE APPELLATE CLERK ON RECEIVING THE NOTICE OF APPEAL AND RECORD

37.1. On Receiving the Notice of Appeal. If the appellate clerk determines that the notice of appeal or certification of defendant's right of appeal in a criminal case is defective, the clerk must notify the parties of the defect so that it can be remedied, if possible. If a proper notice of appeal or certification of a criminal defendant's right of appeal is not filed in the trial court within 30 days of the date of the clerk's notice, the clerk must refer the matter to the appellate court, which will make an appropriate order under this rule or Rule 34.5(c)(2).

37.2. On Receiving the Record. On receiving the clerk's record or the reporter's record, the appellate clerk must determine whether each complies with the Supreme Court's and Court of Criminal Appeals' order on preparation of the record. If so, the clerk must endorse on each the date of receipt, file it, and notify the parties of the filing and the date. If not, the clerk must endorse on the clerk's record or reporter's record—whichever is defective—the date of receipt and return it to the official responsible for filing it. The appellate court clerk must specify the defects and instruct the official to correct the defects and return the record to the appellate court by a specified date. In a criminal case, the record must not be posted on the Internet.

37.3. If No Record Filed.

(a) ***Notice of Late Record.***

(1) ***Civil Cases.*** If the clerk's record or reporter's record has not been timely filed, the appellate clerk must send notice to the official responsible for filing it, stating that the record is late and requesting that the record be filed within 30 days if an ordinary or restricted appeal, or 10 days if an accelerated appeal. The appellate clerk must send a copy of this notice to the parties and the trial court. If the clerk does not receive the record within the stated period, the clerk must refer the matter to the appellate court. The court must make whatever order is appropriate to avoid further delay and to preserve the parties' rights.

(2) ***Criminal Cases.*** If the clerk's record or reporter's record has not been timely filed, the appellate court clerk must refer the matter to the appellate court. The court must make whatever order is appropriate to avoid further delay and to preserve the parties' rights.

(b) ***If No Clerk's Record Filed Due to Appellant's Fault.*** If the trial court clerk failed to file the clerk's record because the appellant failed to pay or make arrangements to pay the clerk's fee for preparing the clerk's record, the appellate court may—on a party's motion or its own initiative—dismiss the appeal for want of prosecution unless the appellant was entitled to proceed without payment of costs. The court must give the appellant a reasonable opportunity to cure before dismissal.

(c) ***If No Reporter's Record Filed Due to Appellant's Fault.*** Under the following circumstances, and if the clerk's record has been filed, the appellate court may—after first giving the appellant notice and a reasonable opportunity to cure—consider and decide those issues or points that do not require a reporter's record for a decision. The court may do this if no reporter's record has been filed because:

(1) the appellant failed to request a reporter's record; or

(2) (A) appellant failed to pay or make arrangements to pay the reporter's fee to prepare the reporter's record; and

(B) the appellant is not entitled to proceed without payment of costs.

TRAP 38. REQUISITES OF BRIEFS

38.1. Appellant's Brief. The appellant's brief must, under appropriate headings and in the order here indicated, contain the following:

(a) ***Identity of Parties and Counsel.*** The brief must give a complete list of all parties to the trial court's judgment or order appealed from, and the names and addresses of all trial and appellate counsel, except as otherwise provided in Rule 9.8.

(b) ***Table of Contents.*** The brief must have a table of contents with references to the pages of the brief. The table of contents must indicate the subject matter of each issue or point, or group of issues or points.

(c) ***Index of Authorities.*** The brief must have an index of authorities arranged alphabetically and indicating the pages of the brief where the authorities are cited.

(d) ***Statement of the Case.*** The brief must state

concisely the nature of the case (e.g., whether it is a suit for damages, on a note, or involving a murder prosecution), the course of proceedings, and the trial court's disposition of the case. The statement should be supported by record references, should seldom exceed one-half page, and should not discuss the facts.

(e) ***Any Statement Regarding Oral Argument.*** The brief may include a statement explaining why oral argument should or should not be permitted. Any such statement must not exceed one page and should address how the court's decisional process would, or would not, be aided by oral argument. As required by Rule 39.7, any party requesting oral argument must note that request on the front cover of the party's brief.

(f) ***Issues Presented.*** The brief must state concisely all issues or points presented for review. The statement of an issue or point will be treated as covering every subsidiary question that is fairly included.

(g) ***Statement of Facts.*** The brief must state concisely and without argument the facts pertinent to the issues or points presented. In a civil case, the court will accept as true the facts stated unless another party contradicts them. The statement must be supported by record references.

(h) ***Summary of the Argument.*** The brief must contain a succinct, clear, and accurate statement of the arguments made in the body of the brief. This summary must not merely repeat the issues or points presented for review.

(i) ***Argument.*** The brief must contain a clear and concise argument for the contentions made, with appropriate citations to authorities and to the record.

(j) ***Prayer.*** The brief must contain a short conclusion that clearly states the nature of the relief sought.

(k) ***Appendix in Civil Cases.***

(1) ***Necessary Contents.*** Unless voluminous or impracticable, the appendix must contain a copy of:

(A) the trial court's judgment or other appealable order from which relief is sought;

(B) the jury charge and verdict, if any, or the trial court's findings of fact and conclusions of law, if any; and

(C) the text of any rule, regulation, ordinance, statute, constitutional provision, or other law (excluding case law) on which the argument is based, and the text of any contract or other document that is central to the argument.

(2) ***Optional Contents.*** The appendix may contain any other item pertinent to the issues or points presented for review, including copies or excerpts of relevant court opinions, laws, documents on which the suit was based, pleadings, excerpts from the reporter's record, and similar material. Items should not be included in the appendix to attempt to avoid the page limits for the brief.

38.2. Appellee's Brief.

(a) ***Form of Brief.***

(1) An appellee's brief must conform to the requirements of Rule 38.1, except that:

(A) the list of parties and counsel is not required unless necessary to supplement or correct the appellant's list;

(B) the appellee's brief need not include a statement of the case, a statement of the issues presented, or a statement of facts, unless the appellee is dissatisfied with that portion of the appellant's brief; and

(C) the appendix to the appellee's brief need not contain any item already contained in an appendix filed by the appellant.

(2) When practicable, the appellee's brief should respond to the appellant's issues or points in the order the appellant presented those issues or points.

(b) ***Cross-Points.***

(1) ***Judgment Notwithstanding the Verdict.*** When the trial court renders judgment notwithstanding the verdict on one or more questions, the appellee must bring forward by cross-point any issue or point that would have vitiated the verdict or that would have prevented an affirmance of the judgment if the trial court had rendered judgment on the verdict. Failure to bring forward by cross-point an issue or point that would vitiate the verdict or prevent an affirmance of the judgment waives that complaint. Included in this requirement is a point that:

(A) the verdict or one or more jury findings have insufficient evidentiary support or are against the overwhelming preponderance of the evidence as a matter of fact; or

(B) the verdict should be set aside because of improper argument of counsel.

(2) ***When Evidentiary Hearing Needed.*** The appellate court must remand a case to the trial court to take evidence if:

(A) the appellate court has sustained a point raised by the appellant; and

(B) the appellee raised a cross-point that requires the taking of additional evidence.

38.3. Reply Brief. The appellant may file a reply brief

addressing any matter in the appellee's brief. However, the appellate court may consider and decide the case before a reply brief is filed.

38.4. REPEALED BY ORDER OF NOV. 13, 2012, EFF. DEC. 1, 2012

38.5. Appendix for Cases Recorded Electronically. In cases where the proceedings were electronically recorded, the following rules apply:

(a) ***Appendix.***

(1) ***In General.*** At or before the time a party's brief is due, the party must file one copy of an appendix containing a transcription of all portions of the recording that the party considers relevant to the appellate issues or points. Unless another party objects, the transcription will be presumed accurate.

(2) ***Repetition Not Required.*** A party's appendix need not repeat evidence included in any previously filed appendix.

(3) ***Form.*** The form of the appendix and transcription must conform to any specifications of the Supreme Court and Court of Criminal Appeals concerning the form of the reporter's record except that it need not have the reporter's certificate.

(4) ***Notice.*** At the time the appendix is filed, the party must give written notice of the filing to all parties to the trial court's judgment or order. The notice must specify, by referring to the index numbers in the court recorder's logs, those parts of the recording that are included in the appendix. The filing party need not serve a copy of the appendix but must make a copy available to all parties for inspection and copying.

(b) ***Presumptions.*** The same presumptions that apply to a partial reporter's record under Rule 34.6(c)(4) apply to the parties' appendixes. The appellate court need not review any part of the electronic recording.

(c) ***Supplemental Appendix.*** The appellate court may direct or allow a party to file a supplemental appendix containing a transcription of additional portions of the recording.

(d) ***Inability to Pay.*** A party who cannot pay the cost of an appendix must file the affidavit provided for by Rule 20.[1] The party must also state in the affidavit or a supplemental affidavit that the party has neither the access to the equipment necessary nor the skill necessary to prepare the appendix. If a contest to the affidavit is not sustained by written order, the court recorder must transcribe or have transcribed those portions of the recording that the party designates and must file the transcription as that party's appendix, along with all exhibits.

(e) ***Inaccuracies.***

(1) ***Correction by Agreement.*** The parties may agree to correct an inaccuracy in the transcription of the recording.

(2) ***Correction by Appellate or Trial Court.*** If the parties dispute whether an electronic recording or transcription accurately discloses what occurred in the trial court but cannot agree on corrections, the appellate court may:

(A) settle the dispute by reviewing the recording; or

(B) submit the dispute to the trial court, which must—after notice and hearing—settle the dispute and ensure that the recording or transcription is made to conform to what occurred in the trial court.

(f) ***Costs.*** The actual expense of preparing the appendixes or the amount prescribed for official reporters, whichever is less, is taxed as costs. The appellate court may disallow the cost of any portion of the appendixes that it considers surplusage or that does not conform to any specifications prescribed by the Supreme Court or Court of Criminal Appeals.

[1] Vernon's Ann.Rules App.Proc., rule 20.1 et seq.

38.6. Time to File Briefs.

(a) ***Appellant's Filing Date.*** Except in a habeas corpus or bail appeal, which is governed by Rule 31,[1] an appellant must file a brief within 30 days—20 days in an accelerated appeal—after the later of:

(1) the date the clerk's record was filed; or

(2) the date the reporter's record was filed.

(b) ***Appellee's Filing Date.*** The appellee's brief must be filed within 30 days—20 days in an accelerated appeal—after the date the appellant's brief was filed. In a civil case, if the appellant has not filed a brief as provided in this rule, an appellee may file a brief within 30 days—20 days in an accelerated appeal—after the date the appellant's brief was due.

(c) ***Filing Date for Reply Brief.*** A reply brief, if any, must be filed within 20 days after the date the appellee's brief was filed.

(d) ***Modifications of Filing Time.*** On motion complying with Rule 10.5(b), the appellate court may extend the time for filing a brief and may postpone submission of the case. A motion to extend the time to file a brief may be filed before or after the date the brief is due. The court may also, in the interests of justice, shorten the time for filing briefs and for submission of the case.

[1] Vernon's Ann.Rules App.Proc., rule 31.1 et seq.

38.7. Amendment or Supplementation. A brief may be amended or supplemented whenever justice requires, on whatever reasonable terms the court may prescribe.

38.8. Failure of Appellant to File Brief.

(a) ***Civil Cases.*** If an appellant fails to timely file a brief, the appellate court may:

(1) dismiss the appeal for want of prosecution, unless the appellant reasonably explains the failure and the appellee is not significantly injured by the appellant's failure to timely file a brief;

(2) decline to dismiss the appeal and give further direction to the case as it considers proper; or

(3) if an appellee's brief is filed, the court may regard that brief as correctly presenting the case and may affirm the trial court's judgment upon that brief without examining the record.

(b) ***Criminal Cases.***

(1) ***Effect.*** An appellant's failure to timely file a brief does not authorize either dismissal of the appeal or, except as provided in (4), consideration of the appeal without briefs.

(2) ***Notice.*** If the appellant's brief is not timely filed, the appellate clerk must notify counsel for the parties and the trial court of that fact. If the appellate court does not receive a satisfactory response within ten days, the court must order the trial court to immediately conduct a hearing to determine whether the appellant desires to prosecute his appeal, whether the appellant is indigent, or, if not indigent, whether retained counsel has abandoned the appeal, and to make appropriate findings and recommendations.

(3) ***Hearing.*** In accordance with (2), the trial court must conduct any necessary hearings, make appropriate findings and recommendations, and have a record of the proceedings prepared, which record—including any order and findings—must be sent to the appellate court.

(4) ***Appellate Court Action.*** Based on the trial court's record, the appellate court may act appropriately to ensure that the appellant's rights are protected, including initiating contempt proceedings against appellant's counsel. If the trial court has found that the appellant no longer desires to prosecute the appeal, or that the appellant is not indigent but has not made the necessary arrangements for filing a brief, the appellate court may consider the appeal without briefs, as justice may require.

38.9. Briefing Rules to Be Construed Liberally. Because briefs are meant to acquaint the court with the issues in a case and to present argument that will enable the court to decide the case, substantial compliance with this rule is sufficient, subject to the following.

(a) ***Formal Defects.*** If the court determines that this rule has been flagrantly violated, it may require a brief to be amended, supplemented, or redrawn. If another brief that does not comply with this rule is filed, the court may strike the brief, prohibit the party from filing another, and proceed as if the party had failed to file a brief.

(b) ***Substantive Defects.*** If the court determines, either before or after submission, that the case has not been properly presented in the briefs, or that the law and authorities have not been properly cited in the briefs, the court may postpone submission, require additional briefing, and make any other order necessary for a satisfactory submission of the case.

TRAP 39. ORAL ARGUMENT; DECISION WITHOUT ARGUMENT

39.1. Right to Oral Argument. A party who has filed a brief and who has timely requested oral argument may argue the case to the court unless the court, after examining the briefs, decides that oral argument is unnecessary for any of the following reasons:

(a) the appeal is frivolous;

(b) the dispositive issue or issues have been authoritatively decided;

(c) the facts and legal arguments are adequately presented in the briefs and record; or

(d) the decisional process would not be significantly aided by oral argument.

39.2. Purpose of Argument. Oral argument should emphasize and clarify the written arguments in the briefs. Counsel should not merely read from prepared text. Counsel should assume that all members of the court have read the briefs before oral argument and counsel should be prepared to respond to questions. A party should not refer to or comment on matters not involved in or pertaining to what is in the record.

39.3. Time Allowed. The court will set the time that will be allowed for argument. Counsel must complete argument in the time allotted and may continue after the expiration of the allotted time only with permission of the court. Counsel is not required to use all the allotted time. The appellant must be allowed to conclude the argument.

39.4. Number of Counsel. Generally, only one counsel should argue for each side. Except on leave of court, no more than two counsel on each side may argue. Only one counsel may argue in rebuttal.

39.5. Argument by Amicus. With leave of court ob-

tained before the argument and with a party's consent, an amicus curiae may share allotted time with that party. Otherwise, counsel for amicus may not argue.

39.6. When Only One Party Files a Brief. If counsel for only one party has filed a brief, the court may allow that party to argue.

39.7. Request and Waiver. A party desiring oral argument must note that request on the front cover of the party's brief. A party's failure to request oral argument waives the party's right to argue. But even if a party has waived oral argument, the court may direct the party to appear and argue.

39.8. Clerk's Notice. The clerk must send to the parties—at least 21 days before the date the case is set for argument or submission without argument—a notice telling the parties:

(a) whether the court will allow oral argument or will submit the case without argument;

(b) the date of argument or submission without argument;

(c) if argument is allowed, the time allotted for argument; and

(d) the names of the members of the panel to which the case will be argued or submitted, subject to change by the court.

A party's failure to receive the notice does not prevent a case's argument or submission on the scheduled date.

TRAP 40. ORDER OF DECISION

40.1. Civil Cases. The court of appeals may determine the order in which civil cases will be decided. But the following types of cases have precedence over all others:

(a) a case given precedence by law;

(b) an accelerated appeal; and

(c) a case that the court determines should be given precedence in the interest of justice.

40.2. Criminal Cases. In cases not otherwise given precedence by law, the court of appeals must hear and determine a criminal appeal at the earliest possible time, having due regard for the parties' rights and for the proper administration of justice.

TRAP 41. PANEL AND EN BANC DECISION

41.1. Decision by Panel.

(a) ***Constitution of Panel.*** Unless a court of appeals with more than three justices votes to decide a case en banc, a case must be assigned for decision to a panel of the court consisting of three justices, although not every member of the panel must be present for argument. If the case is decided without argument, three justices must participate in the decision. A majority of the panel, which constitutes a quorum, must agree on the judgment. Except as otherwise provided in these rules, a panel's opinion constitutes the court's opinion, and the court must render a judgment in accordance with the panel opinion.

(b) ***When Panel Cannot Agree on Judgment.*** After argument, if for any reason a member of the panel cannot participate in deciding a case, the case may be decided by the two remaining justices. If they cannot agree on a judgment, the chief justice of the court of appeals must:

(1) designate another justice of the court to sit on the panel to consider the case;

(2) request the Chief Justice of the Supreme Court to temporarily assign an eligible justice or judge to sit on the panel to consider the case; or

(3) convene the court en banc to consider the case.

The reconstituted panel or the en banc court may order the case reargued.

(c) ***When Court Cannot Agree on Judgment.*** After argument, if for any reason a member of a court consisting of only three justices cannot participate in deciding a case, the case may be decided by the two remaining justices. If they cannot agree on a judgment, that fact must be certified to the Chief Justice of the Supreme Court. The Chief Justice may then temporarily assign an eligible justice or judge to sit with the court of appeals to consider the case. The reconstituted court may order the case reargued.

41.2. Decision by En Banc Court.

(a) ***Constitution of En Banc Court.*** An en banc court consists of all members of the court who are not disqualified or recused and—if the case was originally argued before or decided by a panel—any members of the panel who are not members of the court but remain eligible for assignment to the court. A majority of the en banc court constitute a quorum. A majority of the en banc court must agree on a judgment.

(b) ***When En Banc Court Cannot Agree on Judgment.*** If a majority of an en banc court cannot agree on a judgment, that fact must be certified to the Chief Justice of the Supreme Court. The Chief Justice may then temporarily assign an eligible justice or judge to sit with the court of appeals to consider the case. The reconstituted court may order the case reargued.

(c) ***En Banc Consideration Disfavored.*** En banc consideration of a case is not favored and should not be ordered unless necessary to secure or maintain uniformity

of the court's decisions or unless extraordinary circumstances require en banc consideration. A vote to determine whether a case will be heard or reheard en banc need not be taken unless a justice of the court requests a vote. If a vote is requested and a majority of the court's members vote to hear or rehear the case en banc, the en banc court will hear or rehear the case. Otherwise, a panel of the court will consider the case.

41.3. Precedent in Transferred Cases. In cases transferred by the Supreme Court from one court of appeals to another, the court of appeals to which the case is transferred must decide the case in accordance with the precedent of the transferor court under principles of stare decisis if the transferee court's decision otherwise would have been inconsistent with the precedent of the transferor court. The court's opinion may state whether the outcome would have been different had the transferee court not been required to decide the case in accordance with the transferor court's precedent.

TRAP 42. DISMISSAL; SETTLEMENT

42.1. Voluntary Dismissal and Settlement in Civil Cases.

(a) ***On Motion or By Agreement.*** The appellate court may dispose of an appeal as follows:

(1) ***On Motion of Appellant.*** In accordance with a motion of appellant, the court may dismiss the appeal or affirm the appealed judgment or order unless such disposition would prevent a party from seeking relief to which it would otherwise be entitled.

(2) ***By Agreement.*** In accordance with an agreement signed by the parties or their attorneys and filed with the clerk, the court may:

(A) render judgment effectuating the parties' agreement;

(B) set aside the trial court's judgment without regard to the merits and remand the case to the trial court for rendition of judgment in accordance with the agreement; or

(C) abate the appeal and permit proceedings in the trial court to effectuate the agreement.

(b) ***Partial Disposition.*** A severable portion of the proceeding may be disposed of under (a) if it will not prejudice the remaining parties.

(c) ***Effect on Court's Opinion.*** In dismissing a proceeding, the appellate court will determine whether to withdraw any opinion it has already issued. An agreement or motion for dismissal cannot be conditioned on withdrawal of the opinion.

(d) ***Costs.*** Absent agreement of the parties, the court will tax costs against the appellant.

42.2. Voluntary Dismissal in Criminal Cases.

(a) At any time before the appellate court's decision, the appellate court may dismiss the appeal upon the appellant's motion. The appellant and his or her attorney must sign the written motion to dismiss and file it in duplicate with the appellate clerk, who must immediately send the duplicate copy to the trial court clerk.

(b) After the court of appeals hands down its opinion, it may not grant an appellant's motion to dismiss the appeal unless the other parties consent. If the other parties consent and the court of appeals grants the appellant's motion to dismiss the appeal, the appellate opinion must be withdrawn and the appeal dismissed. The appellate clerk must send notice of the dismissal to the trial court clerk.

42.3. Involuntary Dismissal in Civil Cases. Under the following circumstances, on any party's motion—or on its own initiative after giving ten days' notice to all parties—the appellate court may dismiss the appeal or affirm the appealed judgment or order. Dismissal or affirmance may occur if the appeal is subject to dismissal:

(a) for want of jurisdiction;

(b) for want of prosecution; or

(c) because the appellant has failed to comply with a requirement of these rules, a court order, or a notice from the clerk requiring a response or other action within a specified time.

42.4. Involuntary Dismissal in Criminal Cases. The appellate court must dismiss an appeal on the State's motion, supported by affidavit, showing that the appellant has escaped from custody pending the appeal and that to the affiant's knowledge, the appellant has not, within ten days after escaping, voluntarily returned to lawful custody within the state.

(a) ***Timely Return to Custody; Reinstatement.*** The appeal may not be dismissed—or, if dismissed, must be reinstated—if an affidavit of an officer or other credible person is filed showing that the appellant, within ten days after escaping, voluntarily returned to lawful custody within the state.

(b) ***Life Sentence.*** The appellate court may overrule the motion to dismiss—or, if the motion was granted, may reinstate the appeal—if:

(1) the appellant received a life sentence; and

(2) the appellant is recaptured or voluntarily surrenders within 30 days after escaping.

TRAP 43. JUDGMENT OF THE COURT OF APPEALS

43.1. Time. The court of appeals should render its judgment promptly after submission of a case.

43.2. Types of Judgment. The court of appeals may:

(a) affirm the trial court's judgment in whole or in part;

(b) modify the trial court's judgment and affirm it as modified;

(c) reverse the trial court's judgment in whole or in part and render the judgment that the trial court should have rendered;

(d) reverse the trial court's judgment and remand the case for further proceedings;

(e) vacate the trial court's judgment and dismiss the case; or

(f) dismiss the appeal.

43.3. Rendition Appropriate Unless Remand Necessary. When reversing a trial court's judgment, the court must render the judgment that the trial court should have rendered, except when:

(a) a remand is necessary for further proceedings; or

(b) the interests of justice require a remand for another trial.

43.4. Judgment for Costs in Civil Cases. The court of appeals' judgment should award to the prevailing party costs incurred by that party related to the appeal, including filing fees in the court of appeals and costs for preparation of the record. The court of appeals may tax costs otherwise as required by law or for good cause. But the judgment must not require the payment of costs by a party who was entitled to proceed without payment of costs under Rule 20.1, and a provision in the judgment purporting to do so is void.

43.5. Judgment Against Sureties in Civil Cases. When a court of appeals affirms the trial court judgment, or modifies that judgment and renders judgment against the appellant, the court of appeals must render judgment against the sureties on the appellant's supersedeas bond, if any, for the performance of the judgment and for any costs taxed against the appellant.

43.6. Other Orders. The court of appeals may make any other appropriate order that the law and the nature of the case require.

TRAP 44. REVERSIBLE ERROR

44.1. Reversible Error in Civil Cases.

(a) ***Standard for Reversible Error.*** No judgment may be reversed on appeal on the ground that the trial court made an error of law unless the court of appeals concludes that the error complained of:

(1) probably caused the rendition of an improper judgment; or

(2) probably prevented the appellant from properly presenting the case to the court of appeals.

(b) ***Error Affecting Only Part of Case.*** If the error affects part of, but not all, the matter in controversy and that part is separable without unfairness to the parties, the judgment must be reversed and a new trial ordered only as to the part affected by the error. The court may not order a separate trial solely on unliquidated damages if liability is contested.

44.2. Reversible Error in Criminal Cases.

(a) ***Constitutional Error.*** If the appellate record in a criminal case reveals constitutional error that is subject to harmless error review, the court of appeals must reverse a judgment of conviction or punishment unless the court determines beyond a reasonable doubt that the error did not contribute to the conviction or punishment.

(b) ***Other Errors.*** Any other error, defect, irregularity, or variance that does not affect substantial rights must be disregarded.

(c) ***Presumptions.*** Unless the following matters were disputed in the trial court, or unless the record affirmatively shows the contrary, the court of appeals must presume:

(1) that venue was proved in the trial court;

(2) that the jury was properly impaneled and sworn;

(3) that the defendant was arraigned;

(4) that the defendant pleaded to the indictment or other charging instrument; and

(5) that the court's charge was certified by the trial court and filed by the clerk before it was read to the jury.

44.3. Defects in Procedure. A court of appeals must not affirm or reverse a judgment or dismiss an appeal for formal defects or irregularities in appellate procedure without allowing a reasonable time to correct or amend the defects or irregularities.

44.4. Remediable Error of the Trial Court.

(a) ***Generally.*** A court of appeals must not affirm or reverse a judgment or dismiss an appeal if:

(1) the trial court's erroneous action or failure or refusal to act prevents the proper presentation of a case to the court of appeals; and

(2) the trial court can correct its action or failure to act.

(b) ***Court of Appeals Direction if Error Remediable.*** If the circumstances described in (a) exist, the court of appeals must direct the trial court to correct the error. The court of appeals will then proceed as if the erroneous action or failure to act had not occurred.

TRAP 45. DAMAGES FOR FRIVOLOUS APPEALS IN CIVIL CASES

If the court of appeals determines that an appeal is frivolous, it may—on motion of any party or on its own initiative, after notice and a reasonable opportunity for response—award each prevailing party just damages. In determining whether to award damages, the court must not consider any matter that does not appear in the record, briefs, or other papers filed in the court of appeals.

TRAP 46. REMITTITUR IN CIVIL CASES

46.1. Remittitur After Appeal Perfected. If the trial court suggests a remittitur but the case is appealed before the remittitur is filed, the party who would make the remittitur may do so in the court of appeals in the same manner as in the trial court. The court of appeals must then render the judgment that the trial court should have rendered if the remittitur had been made in the trial court.

46.2. Appeal on Remittitur. If a party makes the remittitur at the trial judge's suggestion and the party benefitting from the remittitur appeals, the remitting party is not barred from contending in the court of appeals that all or part of the remittitur should not have been required, but the remitting party must perfect an appeal to raise that point. If the court of appeals sustains the remitting party's contention that remittitur should not have been required, the court must render the judgment that the trial court should have rendered.

46.3. Suggestion of Remittitur by Court of Appeals. The court of appeals may suggest a remittitur. If the remittitur is timely filed, the court must reform and affirm the trial court's judgment in accordance with the remittitur. If the remittitur is not timely filed, the court must reverse the trial court's judgment.

46.4. Refusal to Remit Must Not Be Mentioned in Later Trial. If the court of appeals suggests a remittitur, but no remittitur is filed, evidence of the court's determination regarding remittitur is inadmissible in a later trial of the case.

46.5. Voluntary Remittitur. If a court of appeals reverses the trial court's judgment because of a legal error that affects only part of the damages awarded by the judgment, the affected party may—within 15 days after the court of appeals' judgment—voluntarily remit the amount that the affected party believes will cure the reversible error. A party may include in a motion for rehearing—without waiving any complaint that the court of appeals erred—a conditional request that the court accept the remittitur and affirm the trial court's judgment as reduced. If the court of appeals determines that the voluntary remittitur is not sufficient to cure the reversible error, but that remittitur is appropriate, the court must suggest a remittitur in accordance with Rule 46.3. If the remittitur is timely filed and the court of appeals determines that the voluntary remittitur cures the reversible error, then the court must accept the remittitur and reform and affirm the trial court judgment in accordance with the remittitur.

TRAP 47. OPINIONS, PUBLICATION, AND CITATION

47.1. Written Opinions. The court of appeals must hand down a written opinion that is as brief as practicable but that addresses every issue raised and necessary to final disposition of the appeal.

47.2. Designation and Signing of Opinions; Participating Justices.

(a) ***Civil and Criminal Cases.*** Each opinion of the court must be designated either an "Opinion" or a "Memorandum Opinion." A majority of the justices who participate in considering the case must determine whether the opinion will be signed by a justice or will be per curiam and whether it will be designated an opinion or memorandum opinion. The names of the participating justices must be noted on all written opinions or orders of the court or a panel of the court.

(b) ***Criminal Cases.*** In addition, each opinion and memorandum opinion in a criminal case must bear the notation "publish" or "do not publish" as determined—before the opinion is handed down—by a majority of the justices who participate in considering the case. Any party may move the appellate court to change the notation, but the court of appeals must not change the notation after the Court of Criminal Appeals has acted on any party's petition for discretionary review or other request for relief. The Court of Criminal Appeals may, at any time, order that a "do not publish" notation be changed to "publish."

(c) ***Civil Cases.*** Opinions and memorandum opinions in civil cases issued on or after January 1, 2003 shall not be designated "do not publish."

47.3. Distribution of Opinions. All opinions of the courts of appeals are open to the public and must be made available to public reporting services, print or electronic.

47.4. Memorandum Opinions. If the issues are settled, the court should write a brief memorandum opinion no longer than necessary to advise the parties of the court's decision and the basic reasons for it. An opinion may not be designated a memorandum opinion if the author of a concurrence or dissent opposes that designation. An opinion must be designated a memorandum opinion unless it does any of the following:

(a) establishes a new rule of law, alters or modifies an existing rule, or applies an existing rule to a novel fact situation likely to recur in future cases;

(b) involves issues of constitutional law or other legal issues important to the jurisprudence of Texas;

(c) criticizes existing law; or

(d) resolves an apparent conflict of authority.

47.5. Concurring and Dissenting Opinions. Only a justice who participated in the decision of a case may file or join in an opinion concurring in or dissenting from the judgment of the court of appeals. Any justice on the court may file an opinion in connection with a denial of a hearing or rehearing en banc.

47.6. Change in Designation by En Banc Court. A court en banc may change a panel's designation of an opinion.

47.7. Citation of Unpublished Opinions.

(a) ***Criminal Cases.*** Opinions and memorandum opinions not designated for publication by the court of appeals under these or prior rules have no precedential value but may be cited with the notation, "(not designated for publication)."

(b) ***Civil Cases.*** Opinions and memorandum opinions designated "do not publish" under these rules by the courts of appeals prior to January 1, 2003 have no precedential value but may be cited with the notation, "(not designated for publication)." If an opinion or memorandum opinion issued on or after that date is erroneously designated "do not publish," the erroneous designation will not affect the precedential value of the decision.

TRAP 48. COPY OF OPINION AND JUDGMENT TO INTERESTED PARTIES AND OTHER COURTS

48.1. Recipients of Opinion and Judgment in All Cases. On the date when an appellate court's opinion is handed down, the appellate clerk must send or deliver copies of the opinion and judgment to the following persons:

(a) the trial judge;

(b) the trial court clerk;

(c) the regional administrative judge; and

(d) all parties to the appeal.

48.2. Additional Recipients in Criminal Cases. In criminal cases, copies of the opinion and judgment will also be mailed or delivered to the State Prosecuting Attorney.

48.3. Filing Opinion and Judgment. The trial court clerk must file a copy of the opinion and judgment among the papers of the case in that court.

48.4. Opinion Sent to Criminal Defendant. In criminal cases, the attorney representing the defendant on appeal shall, within five days after the opinion is handed down, send his client a copy of the opinion and judgment, along with notification of the defendant's right to file a *pro se* petition for discretionary review under Rule 68. This notification shall be sent certified mail, return receipt requested, to the defendant at his last known address. The attorney shall also send the court of appeals a letter certifying his compliance with this rule and attaching a copy of the return receipt within the time for filing a motion for rehearing. The court of appeals shall file this letter in its record of the appeal.

TRAP 49. MOTION FOR REHEARING AND EN BANC RECONSIDERATION

49.1. Motion for Rehearing. A motion for rehearing may be filed within 15 days after the court of appeals' judgment or order is rendered. The motion must clearly state the points relied on for the rehearing.

49.2. Response. No response to a motion for rehearing need be filed unless the court so requests. A motion will not be granted unless a response has been filed or requested by the court.

49.3. Decision on Motion.

A motion for rehearing may be granted by a majority of the justices who participated in the decision of the case. Unless two justices who participated in the decision of the case agree on the disposition of the motion for rehearing, the chief justice of the court of appeals must assign to replace any justice who participated in the panel decision but cannot participate in deciding the motion for rehearing. If rehearing is granted, the court or panel may dispose of the case with or without rebriefing and oral argument.

49.4. Accelerated Appeals. In an accelerated appeal, the appellate court may deny the right to file a motion for rehearing or shorten the time to file such a motion.

49.5. Further Motion for Rehearing. After a motion for rehearing is decided, a further motion for rehearing may be filed within 15 days of the court's action if the court:

(a) modifies its judgment;

(b) vacates its judgment and renders a new judgment; or

(c) issues a different opinion.

49.6. Amendments. A motion for rehearing or en banc reconsideration may be amended as a matter of right anytime before the 15-day period allowed for filing the motion expires, and with leave of the court, anytime before the court of appeals decides the motion.

49.7. En Banc Reconsideration. A party may file a motion for en banc reconsideration as a separate motion, with or without filing a motion for rehearing. The motion must be filed within 15 days after the court of appeals' judgment or order, or when permitted, within 15 days after the court of appeals' denial of the party's last timely filed motion for rehearing or en banc reconsideration. While the court has plenary power, a majority of the en banc court may, with or without a motion, order en banc reconsideration of a panel's decision. If a majority orders reconsideration, the panel's judgment or order does not become final, and the case will be resubmitted to the court for en banc review and disposition.

49.8. Extension of Time. A court of appeals may extend the time for filing a motion for rehearing or en banc reconsideration if a party files a motion complying with Rule 10.5(b) no later than 15 days after the last date for filing the motion.

49.9. Not Required for Review. A motion for rehearing is not a prerequisite to filing a petition for review in the Supreme Court or a petition for discretionary review in the Court of Criminal Appeals nor is it required to preserve error.

49.10. REPEALED BY ORDER OF NOV. 13, 2012, EFF. DEC. 1, 2012

49.11. Relationship to Petition for Review. A party may not file a motion for rehearing or en banc reconsideration in the court of appeals after that party has filed a petition for review in the Supreme Court unless the court of appeals modifies its opinion or judgment after the petition for review is filed. The filing of a petition for review does not preclude another party from filing a motion for rehearing or en banc reconsideration or preclude the court of appeals from ruling on the motion. If a motion for rehearing or en banc reconsideration is timely filed after a petition for review is filed, the petitioner must immediately notify the Supreme Court clerk of the filing of the motion, and must notify the clerk when the last timely filed motion is overruled by the court of appeals.

49.12. Certificate of Conference Not Required. A certificate of conference is not required for a motion for rehearing or en banc reconsideration of a panel's decision.

Eff. Sept. 1, 1997. Amended by order of Dec. 8, 2020, eff. Jan. 1, 2021.

TRAP 50. ABOLISHED BY ORDER OF JULY 12, 2011, EFF. SEPT. 1, 2011

TRAP 51. ENFORCEMENT OF JUDGMENTS AFTER MANDATE

51.1. Civil Cases.

(a) *Statement of Costs.* The appellate clerk must prepare, and send to the trial court clerk with the mandate, a statement of costs showing:

(1) the preparation costs for the appellate record, and any court of appeals filing fees, with a notation of those items that have been paid and those that are owing; and

(2) the party or parties against whom costs have been adjudged.

(b) *Enforcement of Judgment.* When the trial court clerk receives the mandate, the appellate court's judgment must be enforced. Appellate court costs must be included with the trial court costs in any process to enforce the judgment. If all or part of the costs are collected, the trial court clerk must immediately remit to the appellate court clerk any amount due to that clerk. The trial court need not make any further order in the case, and the appellate court's judgment may be enforced as in other cases, when the appellate judgment:

(1) affirms the trial court's judgment;

(2) modifies the trial court's judgment and, as so modified, affirms that judgment; or

(3) renders the judgment the trial court should have rendered.

51.2. Criminal Cases. When the trial court clerk receives the mandate, the appellate court's judgment must be enforced as follows:

(a) *Clerk's Duties.* The trial court clerk must:

(1) send an acknowledgment to the appellate clerk of the mandate's receipt; and

(2) immediately file the mandate.

(b) *Judgment of Affirmance; Defendant Not in Custody.*

(1) *Capias to Be Issued.* If the judgment contains a sentence of confinement or imprisonment that has not been suspended, the trial court must promptly issue a capias for the defendant's arrest so that the court's sentence can be executed.

(2) *Contents of Capias.* The capias may issue to any county of this state and must be executed and returned as in felony cases, except that no bail may be taken. The capias must:

(A) recite the fact of conviction;

(B) set forth the offense and the court's judgment and sentence;

(C) state that the judgment was appealed from and affirmed, and that the mandate has been filed; and

(D) command the sheriff to arrest and take the defendant into his custody, and to place and keep the defendant in custody until delivered to the proper authorities as directed by the sentence.

(3) ***Sheriff's Duties.*** The sheriff must promptly execute the capias as directed. The sheriff must notify the trial court clerk and the appellate clerk when the mandate has been carried out and executed.

(c) ***Judgment of Reversal.***

(1) ***When New Trial Ordered.*** When the appellate court reverses the trial court's judgment and grants the defendant a new trial, the procedure is governed by Code of Criminal Procedure article 44.29. If the defendant is in custody and entitled to bail, the defendant must be released upon giving bail.

(2) ***When Case Dismissed.*** When the appellate court reverses the trial court's judgment and orders the case to be dismissed, the defendant—if in custody—must be discharged.

(d) ***Judgment of Acquittal.*** When the appellate court reverses a judgment and orders the defendant's acquittal, the defendant—if in custody—must be discharged, and no further order or judgment of the trial court is necessary.

SECTION THREE: ORIGINAL PROCEEDINGS IN THE SUPREME COURT AND THE COURTS OF APPEALS

TRAP 52. ORIGINAL PROCEEDINGS

52.1. Commencement. An original appellate proceeding seeking extraordinary relief—such as a writ of habeas corpus, mandamus, prohibition, injunction, or quo warranto—is commenced by filing a petition with the clerk of the appropriate appellate court. The petition must be captioned "*In re* [name of relator]."

52.2. Designation of Parties. The party seeking the relief is the relator. In original proceedings other than habeas corpus, the person against whom relief is sought—whether a judge, court, tribunal, officer, or other person—is the respondent. A person whose interest would be directly affected by the relief sought is a real party in interest and a party to the case.

52.3. Form and Contents of Petition. The petition must, under appropriate headings and in the order here indicated, contain the following:

(a) ***Identity of Parties and Counsel.*** The petition must give a complete list of all parties, and the names, and addresses of all counsel.

(b) ***Table of Contents.*** The petition must include a table of contents with references to the pages of the petition. The table of contents must indicate the subject matter of each issue or point, or group of issues or points.

(c) ***Index of Authorities.*** The petition must include an index of authorities arranged alphabetically and indicating the pages of the petition where the authorities are cited.

(d) ***Statement of the Case.*** The petition must contain a statement of the case that should seldom exceed one page and should not discuss the facts. The statement must contain the following:

(1) a concise description of the nature of any underlying proceeding (e.g., a suit for damages, a contempt proceeding for failure to pay child support, or the certification of a candidate for inclusion on an election ballot);

(2) if the respondent is a judge, the name of the judge, the designation of the court in which the judge was sitting, and the county in which the court is located; and if the respondent is an official other than a judge, the designation and location of the office held by the respondent;

(3) a concise description of the respondent's action from which the relator seeks relief;

(4) if the relator seeks a writ of habeas corpus, a statement describing how and where the relator is being deprived of liberty;

(5) if the petition is filed in the Supreme Court after a petition requesting the same relief was filed in the court of appeals:

(A) the date the petition was filed in the court of appeals;

(B) the district of the court of appeals and the names of the justices who participated in the decision;

(C) the author of any opinion for the court of appeals and the author of any separate opinion;

(D) the citation of the court's opinion;

(E) the disposition of the case by the court of appeals, and the date of the court of appeals' order.

(e) ***Statement of Jurisdiction.*** The petition must state, without argument, the basis of the court's jurisdiction. If the Supreme Court and the court of appeals have concurrent jurisdiction, the petition must be presented first to the court of appeals unless there is a compelling reason not to do so. If the petition is filed in the Supreme Court without

first being presented to the court of appeals, the petition must state the compelling reason why the petition was not first presented to the court of appeals.

(f) ***Issues Presented.*** The petition must state concisely all issues or points presented for relief. The statement of an issue or point will be treated as covering every subsidiary question that is fairly included.

(g) ***Statement of Facts.*** The petition must state concisely and without argument the facts pertinent to the issues or points presented. Every statement of fact in the petition must be supported by citation to competent evidence included in the appendix or record.

(h) ***Argument.*** The petition must contain a clear and concise argument for the contentions made, with appropriate citations to authorities and to the appendix or record.

(i) ***Prayer.*** The petition must contain a short conclusion that clearly states the nature of the relief sought.

(j) ***Certification.*** The person filing the petition must certify that he or she has reviewed the petition and concluded that every factual statement in the petition is supported by competent evidence included in the appendix or record.

(k) ***Appendix.***

(1) ***Necessary Contents.*** The appendix must contain:

(A) a certified or sworn copy of any order complained of, or any other document showing the matter complained of;

(B) any order or opinion of the court of appeals, if the petition is filed in the Supreme Court;

(C) unless voluminous or impracticable, the text of any rule, regulation, ordinance, statute, constitutional provision, or other law (excluding case law) on which the argument is based; and

(D) if a writ of habeas corpus is sought, proof that the relator is being restrained.

(2) ***Optional Contents.*** The appendix may contain any other item pertinent to the issues or points presented for review, including copies or excerpts of relevant court opinions, statutes, constitutional provisions, documents on which the suit was based, pleadings, and similar material. Items should not be included in the appendix to attempt to avoid the page limits for the petition. The appendix should not contain any evidence or other item that is not necessary for a decision.

52.4. Response. Any party may file a response to the petition, but it is not mandatory. The court must not grant relief—other than temporary relief—before a response has been filed or requested by the court. The response must conform to the requirements of 52.3, except that:

(a) the list of parties and counsel is not required unless necessary to supplement or correct the list contained in the petition;

(b) the response need not include a statement of the case, a statement of the issues presented, or a statement of the facts unless the responding party is dissatisfied with that portion of the petition;

(c) a statement of jurisdiction should be omitted unless the petition fails to assert valid grounds for jurisdiction, in which case the reasons why the court lacks jurisdiction must be concisely stated;

(d) the argument must be confined to the issues or points presented in the petition; and

(e) the appendix to the response need not contain any item already contained in an appendix filed by the relator.

52.5. Relator's Reply to Response. The relator may file a reply addressing any matter in the response. However, the court may consider and decide the case before a reply brief is filed.

52.6. REPEALED BY ORDER OF NOV. 13, 2012, EFF. DEC. 1, 2012

52.7. Record.

(a) ***Filing by Relator Required.*** Relator must file with the petition:

(1) a certified or sworn copy of every document that is material to the relator's claim for relief and that was filed in any underlying proceeding; and

(2) a properly authenticated transcript of any relevant testimony from any underlying proceeding, including any exhibits offered in evidence, or a statement that no testimony was adduced in connection with the matter complained.

(b) ***Supplementation Permitted.*** After the record is filed, relator or any other party to the proceeding may file additional materials for inclusion in the record.

(c) ***Service of Record on All Parties.*** Relator and any party who files materials for inclusion in the record must—at the same time—serve on each party:

(1) those materials not previously served on that party as part of the record in another original appellate proceeding in the same or another court; and

(2) an index listing the materials filed and describing them in sufficient detail to identify them.

52.8. Action on Petition.

(a) ***Relief Denied.*** If the court determines from the petition and any response and reply that the relator is not entitled to the relief sought, the court must deny the petition. If the relator in a habeas corpus proceeding has been released on bond, the court must remand the relator to custody and issue an order of commitment. If the relator is not returned to custody, the court may declare the bond to be forfeited and render judgment against the surety.

(b) ***Interim Action.*** If the court is of the tentative opinion that relator is entitled to the relief sought or that a serious question concerning the relief requires further consideration:

(1) the court must request a response if one has not been filed;

(2) the Supreme Court may request full briefing under Rule 55;

(3) in a habeas corpus proceeding, the court may order that relator be discharged on execution and filing of a bond in an amount set by the court; and

(4) the court may set the case for oral argument.

(c) ***Relief Granted.*** If the court determines that relator is entitled to relief, it must make an appropriate order. The court may grant relief without hearing oral argument.

(d) ***Opinion.*** When denying relief, the court may hand down an opinion but is not required to do so. When granting relief, the court must hand down an opinion as in any other case. Rule 47 is applicable to an order or opinion by a court of appeals except that the court of appeals may not order an unpublished opinion published after the Supreme Court or Court of Criminal Appeals has acted on any party's petition for extraordinary relief addressing the same issues.

52.9. Motion for Rehearing. Any party may file a motion for rehearing within 15 days after the final order is rendered. The motion must clearly state the points relied on for the rehearing. No response to a motion for rehearing need be filed unless the court so requests. The court will not grant a motion for rehearing unless a response has been filed or requested.

52.10. Temporary Relief.

(a) ***Motion for Temporary Relief; Certificate of Compliance.*** The relator may file a motion to stay any underlying proceedings or for any other temporary relief pending the court's action on the petition. The relator must notify or make a diligent effort to notify all parties by expedited means (such as by telephone or fax) that a motion for temporary relief has been or will be filed and must certify to the court that the relator has complied with this paragraph before temporary relief will be granted.

(b) ***Grant of Temporary Relief.*** The court—on motion of any party or on its own initiative—may without notice grant any just relief pending the court's action on the petition. As a condition of granting temporary relief, the court may require a bond to protect the parties who will be affected by the relief. Unless vacated or modified, an order granting temporary relief is effective until the case is finally decided.

(c) ***Motion to Reconsider.*** Any party may move the court at any time to reconsider a grant of temporary relief.

52.11. Groundless Petition or Misleading Statement or Record. On motion of any party or on its own initiative, the court may—after notice and a reasonable opportunity to respond—impose just sanctions on a party or attorney who is not acting in good faith as indicated by any of the following:

(a) filing a petition that is clearly groundless;

(b) bringing the petition solely for delay of an underlying proceeding;

(c) grossly misstating or omitting an obviously important and material fact in the petition or response; or

(d) filing an appendix or record that is clearly misleading because of the omission of obviously important and material evidence or documents.

SECTION FOUR: PROCEEDINGS IN THE SUPREME COURT

TRAP 53. PETITION FOR REVIEW

53.1. Method of Review. The Supreme Court may review a court of appeals' final judgment on a petition for review addressed to "The Supreme Court of Texas." A party who seeks to alter the court of appeals' judgment must file a petition for review. The petition for review procedure replaces the writ of error procedure. Statutes pertaining to the writ of error in the Supreme Court apply equally to the petition for review.

53.2. Contents of Petition. The petition for review must, under appropriate headings and in the order here indicated, contain the following items:

(a) ***Identity of Parties and Counsel.*** The petition must give a complete list of all parties to the trial court's final judgment, and the names and addresses of all trial and appellate counsel.

(b) ***Table of Contents.*** The petition must have a table of contents with references to the pages of the petition.

The table of contents must indicate the subject matter of each issue or point, or group of issues or points.

(c) ***Index of Authorities.*** The petition must have an index of authorities arranged alphabetically and indicating the pages of the petition where the authorities are cited.

(d) ***Statement of the Case.*** The petition must contain a statement of the case that should seldom exceed one page and should not discuss the facts. The statement must contain the following:

(1) a concise description of the nature of the case (e.g., whether it is a suit for damages, on a note, or in trespass to try title);

(2) the name of the judge who signed the order or judgment appealed from;

(3) the designation of the trial court and the county in which it is located;

(4) the disposition of the case by the trial court;

(5) the parties in the court of appeals;

(6) the district of the court of appeals;

(7) the names of the justices who participated in the decision in the court of appeals, the author of the opinion for the court, and the author of any separate opinion;

(8) the citation for the court of appeals' opinion; and

(9) the disposition of the case by the court of appeals, including the disposition of any motions for rehearing or en banc reconsideration, and whether any motions for rehearing or en banc reconsideration are pending in the court of appeals at the time the petition for review is filed.

(e) ***Statement of Jurisdiction.*** The petition must state, without argument, the basis of the Court's jurisdiction.

(f) ***Issues Presented.*** The petition must state concisely all issues or points presented for review. The statement of an issue or point will be treated as covering every subsidiary question that is fairly included. If the matter complained of originated in the trial court, it should have been preserved for appellate review in the trial court and assigned as error in the court of appeals.

(g) ***Statement of Facts.*** The petition must affirm that the court of appeals correctly stated the nature of the case, except in any particulars pointed out. The petition must state concisely and without argument the facts and procedural background pertinent to the issues or points presented. The statement must be supported by record references.

(h) ***Summary of the Argument.*** The petition must contain a succinct, clear, and accurate statement of the arguments made in the body of the petition. This summary must not merely repeat the issues or points presented for review.

(i) ***Argument.*** The petition must contain a clear and concise argument for the contentions made, with appropriate citations to authorities and to the record. The argument need not address every issue or point included in the statement of issues or points. Any issue or point not addressed may be addressed in the brief on the merits if one is requested by the Court. The argument should state the reasons why the Supreme Court should exercise jurisdiction to hear the case with specific reference to the factors listed in Rule 56.1(a). The petition need not quote at length from a matter included in the appendix; a reference to the appendix is sufficient. The Court will consider the court of appeals' opinion along with the petition, so statements in that opinion need not be repeated.

(j) ***Prayer.*** The petition must contain a short conclusion that clearly states the nature of the relief sought.

(k) ***Appendix.***

(1) ***Necessary Contents.*** Unless voluminous or impracticable, the appendix must contain a copy of:

(A) the judgment or other appealable order of the trial court from which relief in the court of appeals was sought;

(B) the jury charge and verdict, if any, or the trial court's findings of fact and conclusions of law, if any;

(C) the opinion and judgment of the court of appeals; and

(D) the text of any rule, regulation, ordinance, statute, constitutional provision, or other law on which the argument is based (excluding case law), and the text of any contract or other document that is central to the argument.

(2) ***Optional Contents.*** The appendix may contain any other item pertinent to the issues or points presented for review, including copies or excerpts of relevant court opinions, statutes, constitutional provisions, documents on which the suit was based, pleadings, and similar material. Items should not be included in the appendix to attempt to avoid the page limits for the petition.

53.3. Response to Petition for Review. Any other party to the appeal may file a response to the petition for review, but it is not mandatory. If no response is timely filed, or if a party files a waiver of response, the Court will consider the petition without a response. A petition will not be granted before a response has been filed or requested by the Court. The response must conform to the requirements of 53.2, except that:

(a) the list of parties and counsel is not required unless necessary to supplement or correct the list contained in the petition;

(b) a statement of the case and a statement of the facts need not be made unless the respondent is dissatisfied with that portion of the petition;

(c) a statement of the issues presented need not be made unless:

(1) the respondent is dissatisfied with the statement made in the petition;

(2) the respondent is asserting independent grounds for affirmance of the court of appeals' judgment; or

(3) the respondent is asserting grounds that establish the respondent's right to a judgment that is less favorable to the respondent than the judgment rendered by the court of appeals but more favorable to the respondent than the judgment that might be awarded to the petitioner (e.g., a remand for a new trial rather than a rendition of judgment in favor of the petitioner);

(d) a statement of jurisdiction should be omitted unless the petition fails to assert valid grounds for jurisdiction, in which case the reasons why the Supreme Court lacks jurisdiction must be concisely stated;

(e) the respondent's argument must be confined to the issues or points presented in the petition or asserted by the respondent in the respondent's statement of issues; and

(f) the appendix to the response need not contain any item already contained in an appendix filed by the petitioner.

53.4. Points Not Considered in Court of Appeals. To obtain a remand to the court of appeals for consideration of issues or points briefed in that court but not decided by that court, or to request that the Supreme Court consider such issues or points, a party may raise those issues or points in the petition, the response, the reply, any brief, or a motion for rehearing.

53.5. Petitioner's Reply to Response. The petitioner may file a reply addressing any matter in the response. However, the Court may consider and decide the case before a reply brief is filed.

53.6. REPEALED BY ORDER OF NOV. 13, 2012, EFF. DEC. 1, 2012

53.7. Time and Place of Filing.

(a) ***Petition.*** Unless the Supreme Court orders an earlier filing deadline, the petition must be filed with the Supreme Court clerk within 45 days after the following:

(1) the date the court of appeals rendered judgment, if no motion for rehearing or en banc reconsideration is timely filed; or

(2) the date of the court of appeals' last ruling on all timely filed motions for rehearing or en banc reconsideration.

(b) ***Premature Filing.*** A petition filed before the last ruling on all timely filed motions for rehearing and en banc reconsideration is treated as having been filed on the date of, but after, the last ruling on any such motion. If a party files a petition for review while a motion for rehearing or en banc reconsideration is pending in the court of appeals, the party must include that information in its petition for review.

(c) ***Petitions Filed by Other Parties.*** If a party files a petition for review within the time specified in 53.7(a)—or within the time specified by the Supreme Court in an order granting an extension of time to file a petition—any other party required to file a petition may do so within 45 days after the last timely motion for rehearing is overruled or within 30 days after any preceding petition is filed, whichever date is later.

(d) ***Response.*** Any response must be filed with the Supreme Court clerk within 30 days after the petition is filed.

(e) ***Reply.*** Any reply must be filed with the Supreme Court clerk within 15 days after the response is filed.

(f) ***Extension of Time.*** The Supreme Court may extend the time to file a petition for review if a party files a motion complying with Rule 10.5(b) no later than 15 days after the last day for filing the petition. The Supreme Court may extend the time to file a response or reply if a party files a motion complying with Rule 10.5(b) either before or after the response or reply is due.

(g) ***Petition Filed in Court of Appeals.*** If a petition is mistakenly filed in the court of appeals, the petition is deemed to have been filed the same day with the Supreme Court clerk, and the court of appeals clerk must immediately send the petition to the Supreme Court clerk.

53.8. Amendment. On motion showing good cause, the Court may allow the petition, response, or reply to be amended on such reasonable terms as the Court may prescribe.

53.9. Court May Require Revision. If a petition, response, or reply does not conform with these rules, the Supreme Court may require the document to be revised or may return the document to the party who filed it and consider the case without allowing the document to be revised.

TRAP 54. FILING THE RECORD

54.1. Request for Record. With or without granting the petition for review, the Supreme Court may request that the record from the court of appeals be filed with the clerk of the Supreme Court.

54.2. Duty of Court of Appeals Clerk.

(a) ***Request for Record.*** The court of appeals clerk must not send the record to the Supreme Court unless it is requested. Upon receiving the Supreme Court clerk's request for the record, the court of appeals clerk must promptly send to the Supreme Court clerk all of the following:

(1) the original record;

(2) any motion filed in the court of appeals;

(3) copies of all orders of the court of appeals; and

(4) copies of all opinions and the judgment of the court of appeals.

(b) ***Nondocumentary Exhibits.*** The clerk should not send any nondocumentary exhibits unless the Supreme Court specifically requests.

54.3. Expenses. The petitioner must pay to the court of appeals clerk a sum sufficient to pay the cost of mailing or shipping the record to and from the Supreme Court clerk.

54.4. Duty of Supreme Court Clerk. Upon receiving the record, the Supreme Court clerk must file it and enter the filing on the docket. The clerk may refuse the record if the charges for mailing or shipping have not been paid.

TRAP 55. BRIEFS ON THE MERITS

55.1. Request by Court. A brief on the merits must not be filed unless requested by the Court. With or without granting the petition for review, the Court may request the parties to file briefs on the merits. In appropriate cases, the Court may realign parties and direct that parties file consolidated briefs.

55.2. Petitioner's Brief on the Merits. The petitioner's brief on the merits must be confined to the issues or points stated in the petition for review and must, under appropriate headings and in the order here indicated, contain the following items:

(a) ***Identity of Parties and Counsel.*** The brief must give a complete list of all parties to the trial court's final judgment, and the names and addresses of all trial and appellate counsel.

(b) ***Table of Contents.*** The brief must have a table of contents with references to the pages of the brief. The table of contents must indicate the subject matter of each issue or point, or group of issues or points.

(c) ***Index of Authorities.*** The brief must have an index of authorities arranged alphabetically and indicating the pages of the brief where the authorities are cited.

(d) ***Statement of the Case.*** The brief must contain a statement of the case that should seldom exceed one page and should not discuss the facts. The statement must contain the following:

(1) a concise description of the nature of the case (e.g., whether it is a suit for damages, on a note, or in trespass to try title);

(2) the name of the judge who signed the order or judgment appealed from;

(3) the designation of the trial court and the county in which it is located;

(4) the disposition of the case by the trial court;

(5) the parties in the court of appeals;

(6) the district of the court of appeals;

(7) the names of the justices who participated in the decision in the court of appeals, the author of the opinion for the court, and the author of any separate opinion;

(8) the citation for the court of appeals' opinion, if available, or a statement that the opinion was unpublished; and

(9) the disposition of the case by the court of appeals.

(e) ***Statement of Jurisdiction.*** The brief must state, without argument, the basis of the Court's jurisdiction.

(f) ***Issues Presented.*** The brief must state concisely all issues or points presented for review. The statement of an issue or point will be treated as covering every subsidiary question that is fairly included. The phrasing of the issues or points need not be identical to the statement of issues or points in the petition for review, but the brief may not raise additional issues or points or change the substance of the issues or points presented in the petition.

(g) ***Statement of Facts.*** The brief must affirm that the court of appeals correctly stated the nature of the case, except in any particulars pointed out. The brief must state concisely and without argument the facts and procedural background pertinent to the issues or points presented. The statement must be supported by record references.

(h) ***Summary of the Argument.*** The brief must contain a succinct, clear, and accurate statement of the arguments made in the body of the brief. This summary must not merely repeat the issues or points presented for review.

(i) ***Argument.*** The brief must contain a clear and concise argument for the contentions made, with appropriate citations to authorities and to the record.

(j) ***Prayer.*** The brief must contain a short conclusion that clearly states the nature of the relief sought.

55.3. Respondent's Brief. If the petitioner files a brief

on the merits, any other party to the appeal may file a brief in response, which must conform to 55.2, except that:

(a) the list of parties and counsel is not required unless necessary to supplement or correct the list contained in the petitioner's brief;

(b) a statement of the case and a statement of the facts need not be made unless the respondent is dissatisfied with that portion of the petitioner's brief; and

(c) a statement of the issues presented need not be made unless:

(1) the respondent is dissatisfied with the statement made in the petitioner's brief;

(2) the respondent is asserting independent grounds for affirmance of the court of appeals' judgment; or

(3) the respondent is asserting grounds that establish the respondent's right to a judgment that is less favorable to the respondent than the judgment rendered by the court of appeals but more favorable to the respondent than the judgment that might be awarded to the petitioner (e.g., a remand for a new trial rather than a rendition of judgment in favor of the petitioner);

(d) a statement of jurisdiction should be omitted unless the petition fails to assert valid grounds for jurisdiction; and

(e) the respondent's argument must be confined to the issues or points presented in the petitioner's brief or asserted by the respondent in the respondent's statement of issues.

55.4. Petitioner's Brief in Reply. The petitioner may file a reply brief addressing any matter in the brief in response. However, the Court may consider and decide the case before a reply brief is filed.

55.5. Reliance on Prior Brief. As a brief on the merits or a brief in response, a party may file the brief that the party filed in the court of appeals.

55.6. REPEALED BY ORDER OF NOV. 13, 2012, EFF. DEC. 1, 2012

55.7. Time and Place of Filing; Extension of Time. Briefs must be filed with the Supreme Court clerk in accordance with the schedule stated in the clerk's notice that the Court has requested briefs on the merits. If no schedule is stated in the notice, petitioner must file a brief on the merits within 30 days after the date of the notice, respondent must file a brief in response within 20 days after receiving petitioner's brief, and petitioner must file any reply brief within 15 days after receiving respondent's brief. On motion complying with Rule 10.5(b) either before or after the brief is due, the Supreme Court may extend the time to file a brief.

55.8. Amendment. On motion showing good cause, the Court may allow a party to amend a brief on such reasonable terms as the Court may prescribe.

55.9. Court May Require Revision. If a brief does not conform with these rules, the Supreme Court may require the brief to be revised or may return it to the party who filed it and consider the case without further briefing by that party.

TRAP 56. ORDERS ON PETITION FOR REVIEW

56.1. Orders on Petition for Review.

(a) ***Considerations in Granting Review.*** Whether to grant review is a matter of judicial discretion. Among the factors the Supreme Court considers in deciding whether to grant a petition for review are the following:

(1) whether the justices of the court of appeals disagree on an important point of law;

(2) whether there is a conflict between the courts of appeals on an important point of law;

(3) whether a case involves the construction or validity of a statute;

(4) whether a case involves constitutional issues;

(5) whether the court of appeals appears to have committed an error of law of such importance to the state's jurisprudence that it should be corrected; and

(6) whether the court of appeals has decided an important question of state law that should be, but has not been, resolved by the Supreme Court.

(b) ***Petition Denied or Dismissed.*** When the petition has been on file in the Supreme Court for 30 days, the Court may deny or dismiss the petition—whether or not a response has been filed—with one of the following notations:

(1) ***"Denied."*** If the Supreme Court is not satisfied that the opinion of the court of appeals has correctly declared the law in all respects, but determines that the petition presents no error that requires reversal or that is of such importance to the jurisprudence of the state as to require correction, the Court will deny the petition with the notation "Denied."

(2) ***"Dismissed w.o.j."*** If the Supreme Court lacks jurisdiction, the Court will dismiss the petition with the notation "Dismissed for Want of Jurisdiction."

(c) ***Petition Refused.*** If the Supreme Court determines—after a response has been filed or requested—that the court of appeals' judgment is correct and that the legal principles announced in the opinion are likewise correct, the Court will refuse the petition with the notation

"Refused." The court of appeals' opinion in the case has the same precedential value as an opinion of the Supreme Court.

(d) ***Improvident Grant.*** If the Court has granted review but later decides that review should not have been granted, the Court may, without opinion, set aside the order granting review and dismiss the petition or deny or refuse review as though review had never been granted.

56.2. Moot Cases. If a case is moot, the Supreme Court may, after notice to the parties, grant the petition and, without hearing argument, dismiss the case or the appealable portion of it without addressing the merits of the appeal.

56.3. Settled Cases. If a case is settled by agreement of the parties and the parties so move, the Supreme Court may grant the petition if it has not already been granted and, without hearing argument or considering the merits, render a judgment to effectuate the agreement. The Supreme Court's action may include setting aside the judgment of the court of appeals or the trial court without regard to the merits and remanding the case to the trial court for rendition of a judgment in accordance with the agreement. The Supreme Court may abate the case until the lower court's proceedings to effectuate the agreement are complete. A severable portion of the proceeding may be disposed of if it will not prejudice the remaining parties. In any event, the Supreme Court's order does not vacate the court of appeals' opinion unless the order specifically provides otherwise. An agreement or motion cannot be conditioned on vacating the court of appeals' opinion.

56.4. Notice to Parties. When the Supreme Court grants, denies, refuses, or dismisses a petition for review, the Supreme Court clerk must send a written notice of the disposition to the court of appeals, the trial court, and all parties to the appeal.

56.5. Return of Documents to Court of Appeals. When the Supreme Court denies, refuses, or dismisses a petition for review, the clerk will retain the petition, together with the record and accompanying papers, for 30 days after the order is rendered. If no motion for rehearing has been filed by the end of that period or when any motion for rehearing of the order has been overruled, the clerk must send a certified copy of its order to the court of appeals and return the record and all papers (except for documents filed in the Supreme Court) to the court of appeals clerk.

TRAP 57. DIRECT APPEALS TO THE SUPREME COURT

57.1. Application. This rule governs direct appeals to the Supreme Court that are authorized by the Constitution and by statute. Except when inconsistent with a statute or this rule, the rules governing appeals to courts of appeals also apply to direct appeals to the Supreme Court.

57.2. Jurisdiction. The Supreme Court may not take jurisdiction over a direct appeal from the decision of any court other than a district court or county court, or over any question of fact. The Supreme Court may decline to exercise jurisdiction over a direct appeal of an interlocutory order if the record is not adequately developed, or if its decision would be advisory, or if the case is not of such importance to the jurisprudence of the state that a direct appeal should be allowed.

57.3. Statement of Jurisdiction. Appellant must file with the record a statement fully but plainly setting out the basis asserted for exercise of the Supreme Court's jurisdiction. Appellee may file a response to appellant's statement of jurisdiction within ten days after the statement is filed.

57.4. Preliminary Ruling on Jurisdiction. If the Supreme Court notes probable jurisdiction over a direct appeal, the parties must file briefs under Rule 38[1] as in any other case. If the Supreme Court does not note probable jurisdiction over a direct appeal, the appeal will be dismissed.

[1] Vernon's Ann.Rules App.Proc., rule 38.1 et seq.

57.5. Direct Appeal Exclusive While Pending. If a direct appeal to the Supreme Court is filed, the parties to the appeal must not, while that appeal is pending, pursue an appeal to the court of appeals. But if the direct appeal is dismissed, any party may pursue any other appeal available at the time when the direct appeal was filed. The other appeal must be perfected within ten days after dismissal of the direct appeal.

TRAP 58. CERTIFICATION OF QUESTIONS OF LAW BY UNITED STATES COURTS

58.1. Certification. The Supreme Court of Texas may answer questions of law certified to it by any federal appellate court if the certifying court is presented with determinative questions of Texas law having no controlling Supreme Court precedent. The Supreme Court may decline to answer the questions certified to it.

58.2. Contents of the Certification Order. An order from the certifying court must set forth:

(a) the questions of law to be answered; and

(b) a stipulated statement of all facts relevant to the questions certified, showing fully the nature of the controversy in which the questions arose.

58.3. Transmission of Certification Order. The

clerk of the certifying court must send to the clerk of the Supreme Court of Texas the following:

(a) the certification order under the certifying court's official seal;

(b) a list of the names of all parties to the pending case, giving the address and telephone number, if known, of any party not represented by counsel; and

(c) a list of the names, addresses, and telephone numbers of counsel for each party.

58.4. Transmission of Record. The certifying court should not send the Supreme Court of Texas the record in the pending case with the certification order. The Supreme Court may later require the original or copies of all or part of the record before the certifying court to be filed with the Supreme Court clerk.

58.5. Fees and Costs. Unless the certifying court orders otherwise in its certification order, the parties must bear equally the fees under Rule 5.

58.6. Notice. If the Supreme Court agrees to answer the questions certified to it, the Court will notify all parties and the certifying court. The Supreme Court clerk must also send a notice to the Attorney General of Texas if:

(a) the constitutionality of a Texas statute is the subject of a certified question that the Supreme Court has agreed to answer; and

(b) the State of Texas or an officer, agency, or employee of the state is not a party to the proceeding in the certifying court.

58.7. Briefs and Oral Argument.

(a) ***Briefs.*** The appealing party in the certifying court must file a brief with the Supreme Court clerk within 30 days after the date of the notice. Opposing parties must file an answering brief within 20 days after receiving the opening brief. Briefs must comply with Rule 55[1] to the extent its provisions apply. On motion complying with Rule 10.5(b), either before or after the brief is due, the Supreme Court may extend the time to file a brief.

(b) ***Oral Argument.*** Oral argument may be granted either on a party's request or on the Court's own initiative. Argument is governed by Rule 59.[2]

[1] Vernon's Ann.Rules App.Proc., rule 55.1 et seq.

[2] Vernon's Ann.Rules App.Proc., rule 59.1 et seq.

58.8. Intervention by the State. If the constitutionality of a Texas statute is the subject of a certified question that the Supreme Court has agreed to answer the State of Texas may intervene at any reasonable time for briefing and oral argument (if argument is allowed), on the question of constitutionality.

58.9. Opinion on Certified Questions. If the Supreme Court has agreed to answer a certified question, it will hand down an opinion as in any other case.

58.10. Answering Certified Questions. After all motions for rehearing have been overruled, the Supreme Court clerk must send to the certifying court the written opinion on the certified questions. The opinion must be under the Supreme Court's seal.

TRAP 59. SUBMISSION AND ARGUMENT

59.1. Submission Without Argument. If at least six members of the Court so vote, a petition may be granted and an opinion handed down without oral argument.

59.2. Submission With Argument. If the Supreme Court decides that oral argument would aid the Court, the Court will set the case for argument. The clerk will notify all parties of the submission date.

59.3. Purpose of Argument. Oral argument should emphasize and clarify the written arguments in the briefs. Counsel should not merely read from a prepared text. Counsel should assume that all Justices have read the briefs before oral argument and should be prepared to respond to the Justices' questions.

59.4. Time for Argument. Each side is allowed only as much time as the Court orders. Counsel is not required to use all the allotted time. On motion filed before the day of argument, the Court may extend the time for argument. The Court may also align the parties for purposes of presenting argument.

59.5. Number of Counsel. Generally, only one counsel should argue for each side. Except on leave of court, no more than two counsel on each side may argue. Only one counsel may argue in rebuttal.

59.6. Argument by Amicus Curiae. With leave of court obtained before the argument and with a party's consent, an amicus may share allotted time with that party. Otherwise, counsel for amicus curiae may not argue.

TRAP 60. JUDGMENTS IN THE SUPREME COURT

60.1. Announcement of Judgments. The Court's judgments will be announced by the clerk.

60.2. Types of Judgment. The Supreme Court may:

(a) affirm the lower court's judgment in whole or in part;

(b) modify the lower court's judgment and affirm it as modified;

(c) reverse the lower court's judgment in whole or in part and render the judgment that the lower court should have rendered;

(d) reverse the lower court's judgment and remand the case for further proceedings;

(e) vacate the judgments of the lower courts and dismiss the case; or

(f) vacate the lower court's judgment and remand the case for further proceedings in light of changes in the law.

60.3. Remand in the Interest of Justice. When reversing the court of appeals' judgment, the Supreme Court may, in the interest of justice, remand the case to the trial court even if a rendition of judgment is otherwise appropriate.

60.4. Judgment for Costs. The Supreme Court's judgment will award to the prevailing party the costs incurred by that party in the Supreme Court. If appropriate, the judgment may also award the prevailing party the costs—including preparation costs for the record—incurred by that party in the court of appeals and in the trial court. But the Court may tax costs otherwise as required by law or for good cause.

60.5. Judgment Against Sureties. When affirming, modifying, or rendering a judgment against the party who was the appellant in the court of appeals, the Supreme Court must render judgment against the sureties on that party's supersedeas bond, if any, for the performance of the judgment. If the Supreme Court taxes costs against the party who was the appellant in the court of appeals, the Court must render judgment for those costs against the sureties on that party's supersedeas bond, if any.

60.6. Other Orders. The Supreme Court may make any other appropriate order required by the law and the nature of the case.

TRAP 61. REVERSIBLE ERROR

61.1. Standard for Reversible Error. No judgment may be reversed on appeal on the ground that the trial court made an error of law unless the Supreme Court concludes that the error complained of:

(a) probably caused the rendition of an improper judgment; or

(b) probably prevented the petitioner from properly presenting the case to the appellate courts.

61.2. Error Affecting Only Part of the Case. If the error affects a part, but not all, of the matter in controversy, and that part is separable without unfairness to the parties, the judgment must be reversed and a new trial ordered only as to the part affected by the error. The Court may not order a separate trial solely on unliquidated damages if liability is contested.

61.3. Defects in Procedure. The Supreme Court will not affirm or reverse a judgment or dismiss a petition for review for formal defects or irregularities in appellate procedure without allowing a reasonable time to correct or amend the defects or irregularities.

61.4. Remediable Error of the Trial Court or Court of Appeals.

(a) *Generally.* The Supreme Court will not affirm or reverse a judgment or dismiss a petition for review if:

(1) the trial court's or court of appeals' erroneous action or failure or refusal to act prevents the proper presentation of a case to the Supreme Court; and

(2) the trial court or court of appeals can correct its action or failure to act.

(b) *Supreme Court Direction If Error Remediable.* If the circumstances described in (a) exist, the Supreme Court will direct the trial court or court of appeals to correct the error. The Supreme Court will then proceed as if the error had not occurred.

TRAP 62. DAMAGES FOR FRIVOLOUS APPEALS

If the Supreme Court determines that a direct appeal or a petition for review is frivolous, it may—on motion of any party or on its own initiative, after notice and a reasonable opportunity for response—award to each prevailing party just damages. In determining whether to award damages, the Court must not consider any matter that does not appear in the record, briefs, or other papers filed in the court of appeals or the Supreme Court.

TRAP 63. OPINIONS; COPY OF OPINION AND JUDGMENT TO INTERESTED PARTIES AND OTHER COURTS

The Supreme Court will hand down a written opinion in all cases in which it renders a judgment. The clerk will send a copy of the opinion and judgment to the court of appeals clerk, the trial court clerk, the regional administrative judge, and all parties to the appeal.

TRAP 64. MOTION FOR REHEARING

64.1. Time for Filing. A motion for rehearing may be filed with the Supreme Court clerk within 15 days from the date when the Court renders judgment or makes an order disposing of a petition for review. In exceptional cases, if justice requires, the Court may shorten the time within which the motion may be filed or even deny the right to file it altogether.

64.2. Contents. The motion must specify the points relied on for the rehearing.

64.3. Response and Decision. No response to a motion for rehearing need be filed unless the Court so requests. A motion will not be granted unless a response has been filed or requested by the Court. But in exceptional cases, if justice so requires, the Court may deny the right to file a response and act on a motion any time after it is filed.

64.4. Second Motion. The Court will not consider a second motion for rehearing unless the Court modifies its judgment, vacates its judgment and renders a new judgment, or issues a different opinion.

64.5. Extensions of Time. The Court may extend the time to file a motion for rehearing in the Supreme Court, if a motion complying with Rule 10.5(b) is filed with the Court no later than 15 days after the last date for filing a motion for rehearing.

64.6. REPEALED BY ORDER OF NOV. 13, 2012, EFF. DEC. 1, 2012

TRAP 65. ENFORCEMENT OF JUDGMENT AFTER MANDATE

65.1. Statement of Costs. The Supreme Court clerk will prepare, and send to the clerk to whom the mandate is directed, a statement of costs showing:

(a) the costs that were incurred in the Supreme Court, with a notation of those items that have been paid and those that are owing; and

(b) the party or parties against whom costs have been adjudged.

65.2. Enforcement of Judgment. If the Supreme Court renders judgment, the trial court need not make any further order. Upon receiving the Supreme Court's mandate, the trial court clerk must proceed to enforce the judgment of the Supreme Court's as in any other case. Appellate court costs must be included with the trial court costs in any process to enforce the judgment. If all or part of the costs are collected, the trial court clerk must immediately remit to the appellate court clerk any amount due to that clerk.

SECTION FIVE: PROCEEDINGS IN THE COURT OF CRIMINAL APPEALS

Section Five omitted by editor. For the full text, see **O'Connor's Texas Civil Appeals** (2020).

Appendix IV. Timetables

1 Special appearance

Special appearance*					
Step	**Action/Form**	**Deadline**	**Authority**	**Due**	**Done**
1	Plaintiff files suit; FORMS 2B:1 et seq., 2D:1 et seq., 2E:1	Before limitations period expires	TRCP 45–59, 78–82		
2	Defendant is served; FORMS 2I:1 et seq.	Before limitations period expires	TRCP 99, 119		
3	Deadline for defendant's answer	By 10 a.m. on the next Monday following 20 days after Step 2	TRCP 99(b)		
4	Defendant files special appearance; FORMS 3B:1, 3B:2	By Step 3 and before Step 5	TRCP 120a(1)		
5	Defendant files answer—general denial; FORMS 3E:1 et seq.	By Step 3, but after Step 4	TRCP 85, 92		
6	Plaintiff files response to special appearance; FORM 3B:3	As soon as possible, at least 7 days before Step 10	TRCP 120a(3)		
7	Plaintiff files sworn motion for continuance to secure affidavits or discovery; FORM 5D:1	As necessary, but no later than Step 9	TRCP 120a(3)		
8	Plaintiff/Defendant files discovery and stipulations	As necessary, but no later than Step 9	TRCP 120a(3)		
9	Plaintiff/Defendant files affidavits; FORM 1B:8	At least 7 days before Step 10	TRCP 120a(3)		
10	Hearing on special appearance, oral testimony permitted	Before Steps 13 and 14	TRCP 120a(2), (3)		
11	Order sustains special appearance; FORM 3B:4	None, suit dismissed	TRCP 120a(4)		
12	Order overrules special appearance; FORM 3B:4	None, suit continues	TRCP 120a(4)		
13	Hearing on other pending motions (e.g., venue, TRCP 87)	After Step 12, but before Step 14			
14	Trial	Date set by court	TRCP 247, 262–265		

* **Legend:**

FORM	***O'Connor's Texas Civil Forms*** (2020 ed.)
TRCP	Texas Rules of Civil Procedure

See "Special Appearance—Challenging Personal Jurisdiction," ch. 3-B, §1 et seq.

2 Motion to transfer venue—Wrong or inconvenient county

Motion to transfer venue—Wrong or inconvenient county*					
Step	**Action/Form**	**Deadline**	**Authority**	**Due**	**Done**
1	Plaintiff files suit; FORMS 2B:1 et seq., 2D:1 et seq., 2E:1	Before limitations period expires	TRCP 45–59, 78–82		
2	Defendant is served; FORMS 2I:1 et seq.	Before limitations period expires	TRCP 99, 119		
3	Deadline for defendant's answer	By 10 a.m. on the next Monday following 20 days after Step 2	TRCP 99(b)		
4	Defendant files motion to transfer venue to another county; FORMS 3C:1 to 3C:3	By Step 3, but after filing special appearance and before or with Step 5	CPRC §15.063; TRCP 86(1)		
5	Defendant files answer—general denial; FORMS 3E:1 et seq.	By Step 3, but with or after Step 4	TRCP 85, 92		
6	Notice of hearing; FORM 1E:1.	45 days before Step 10	TRCP 87(1)		
7	Plaintiff files response to motion to transfer; FORMS 3C:5 to 3C:7	30 days before Step 10	TRCP 87(1)		
8	Plaintiff files affidavits with discovery attached; FORM 1B:8	30 days before Step 10	TRCP 87(1), (3)(a), 88		
9	Defendant files reply to plaintiff's response, with affidavits; FORMS 1B:8, 3C:9	7 days before Step 10	TRCP 87(1)		
10	Hearing on pending motions in due order: special appearance, then venue	Promptly and a reasonable time before Step 13	TRCP 84, 87(1), 120a(2)		
11	Order grants motion to transfer; FORM 3C:11	None, suit transferred to other county	TRCP 89		
12	Order denies motion to transfer; FORM 3C:11	None, suit continues	TRCP 87(3)(c)		
13	Trial	Date set by court	TRCP 247, 262–265		

* **Legend:**

CPRC Texas Civil Practice & Remedies Code
FORM **O'Connor's Texas Civil Forms** (2020 ed.)
TRCP Texas Rules of Civil Procedure

See "Motion to Transfer—Challenging Venue," ch. 3-C, §1 et seq.

3 Motion to change venue—Local prejudice

Motion to change venue—Local prejudice*					
Step	**Action/Form**	**Deadline**	**Authority**	**Due**	**Done**
1	Plaintiff files suit; FORMS 2B:1 et seq., 2D:1 et seq., 2E:1	Before limitations period expires	TRCP 45–59, 78–82		
2	Defendant is served; FORMS 2I:1 et seq.	Before limitations period expires	TRCP 99, 119		
3	Deadline for defendant's answer	By 10 a.m. on the next Monday following 20 days after Step 2	TRCP 99(b)		
4	Defendant files answer—general denial; FORMS 3E:1 et seq.	By Step 3	TRCP 85, 92		
5	Movant (plaintiff/defendant) files motion to change venue because of local prejudice, with affidavits; FORMS 1B:8, 3C:4	As soon as prejudice becomes known	TRCP 257		
6	Nonmovant files response and controverting affidavit; FORMS 1B:8, 3C:8		TRCP 258		
7	Motion for continuance to secure discovery; FORM 5D:1	As necessary	TRCP 251, 252		
8	Hearing on pending motions in due order: special appearance, venue transfer, then venue change	Promptly and a reasonable time before Step 11	TRCP 84, 87(1), 120a(2)		
9	Order grants motion to change venue; FORM 3C:11	None, suit transferred to another county	TRCP 257–259, 261		
10	Order denies motion to change venue; FORM 3C:11	None, suit continues	TRCP 258		
11	Trial	Date set by court	TRCP 247, 262–265		

* **Legend:**

FORM — **O'Connor's Texas Civil Forms** (2020 ed.)
TRCP — Texas Rules of Civil Procedure

See "Local prejudice," ch. 3-C, §3.

4 Motion to dismiss—Code forum non conveniens

Motion to dismiss—Code forum non conveniens*					
Step	**Action/Form**	**Deadline**	**Authority**	**Due**	**Done**
1	Plaintiff files suit; FORMS 2B:1 et seq., 2D:1 et seq., 2E:1	Before limitations period expires	TRCP 45–59, 78–82		
2	Defendant is served; FORMS 2I:1 et seq.	Before limitations period expires	TRCP 99, 119		
3	Deadline for defendant's answer	By 10 a.m. on the next Monday following 20 days after Step 2	TRCP 99(b)		
4	Defendant files motion to dismiss on grounds of Code FNC; FORM 3D:1	Step 3 + 180 days	CPRC §71.051(d)		
5	Defendant files answer—general denial; FORMS 3E:1 et seq.	By Step 3, but after filing special appearance or motion to transfer venue	TRCP 85, 92		
6	Plaintiff files response to motion to dismiss, with evidence to support pleadings; FORM 3D:3	A reasonable time before Step 9			
7	Motion for continuance, for good cause; FORMS 5D:1, 5D:2	As necessary, but before Step 9	CPRC §71.051(g)		
8	Notice of hearing; FORM 1E:1	21 days before Step 9	CPRC §71.051(d)		
9	Hearing on pending motions in due order: special appearance, venue, then Code FNC	30 days before Step 12	CPRC §71.051(d); TRCP 84, 87(1), 120a(2)		
10	Order grants motion to dismiss or to stay; court has continuing jurisdiction if defendant violates court's order; FORM 3D:6	None, suit transferred to other forum	CPRC §71.051(b), (c)		
11	Order denies motion to dismiss or to stay; FORM 3D:6	None, suit continues	CPRC §71.051(e)		
12	Trial	Date set by court	TRCP 247, 262–265		

* **Legend:**

CPRC	Texas Civil Practice & Remedies Code
FNC	Forum non conveniens
FORM	**O'Connor's Texas Civil Forms** (2020 ed.)
TRCP	Texas Rules of Civil Procedure

See "Code FNC motion," ch. 3-D, §3.

5 Motion to dismiss—Common-law forum non conveniens

Motion to dismiss—Common-law forum non conveniens*					
Step	**Action/Form**	**Deadline**	**Authority**	**Due**	**Done**
1	Plaintiff files suit; FORMS 2B:1 et seq., 2D:1 et seq., 2E:1	Before limitations period expires	TRCP 45–59, 78–82		
2	Defendant is served; FORMS 2I:1 et seq.	Before limitations period expires	TRCP 99, 119		
3	Deadline for defendant's answer	By 10 a.m. on the next Monday following 20 days after Step 2	TRCP 99(b)		
4	Defendant files answer—general denial; FORMS 3E:1 et seq.	By Step 3	TRCP 85, 92		
5	Defendant files motion to dismiss on grounds of common-law FNC; FORM 3D:2	As soon as ground becomes apparent, but after filing special appearance or motion to transfer venue			
6	Defendant should file stipulation	At Step 5			
7	Plaintiff files response to motion to dismiss, with evidence to support pleadings; FORM 3D:4	Before Step 10			
8	Motion for continuance, for good cause; FORMS 5D:1, 5D:2	Before Step 10			
9	Notice of hearing; FORM 1E:1.	At least 3 days before Step 10	TRCP 21(b)		
10	Hearing on pending motions in due order: special appearance, venue, then common-law FNC	Before Step 13	TRCP 84, 87(1), 120a(2)		
11	Order grants motion to dismiss or to stay; FORM 3D:6	None, suit transferred to other forum			
12	Order denies motion to dismiss or to stay; FORM 3D:6	None, suit continues			
13	Trial	Date set by court	TRCP 247, 262–265		

* **Legend:**

FNC	Forum non conveniens
FORM	**O'Connor's Texas Civil Forms** (2020 ed.)
TRCP	Texas Rules of Civil Procedure

See "Common-Law FNC motion," ch. 3-D, §4.

6 Motion to dismiss—Baseless cause of action

Motion to dismiss—Baseless cause of action*					
Step	Action/Form	Deadline	Authority	Due	Done
1	Plaintiff files suit; FORMS 2B:1 et seq., 2D:1 et seq., 2E:1	Before limitations period expires	TRCP 45–59, 78–82		
2	Defendant is served; FORMS 2I:1 et seq.	Before limitations period expires	TRCP 99, 119		
3	Deadline for defendant's answer	By 10 a.m. on the next Monday following 20 days after Step 2	TRCP 99(b)		
4	Defendant files (as appropriate) special appearance, motion to transfer venue, and answer; FORMS 3B:1, 3B:2, 3C:1 to 3C:3, 3E:1 et seq.	By Step 3	TRCP 85, 86, 91a.8, 92, 120a(1)		
5	Defendant files motion to dismiss baseless cause of action; FORM 3H:1	Step 2 + 60 days	TRCP 91a.3(a)		
6	Plaintiff files response to motion[1]; FORM 3H:2	At least 7 days before Step 12	TRCP 91a.4		
7	Plaintiff files amended pleading[1]	At least 3 days before Step 12	TRCP 91a.5(b)		
8	Plaintiff nonsuits cause of action[1]; FORM 7F:1	At least 3 days before Step 12	TRCP 91a.5(a)		
9	Defendant withdraws motion to dismiss[2]; FORM 3H:3	If no amended pleading filed, at least 3 days before Step 12 If amended pleading filed, anytime before Step 12	TRCP 91a.5(a), (b)		
10	Defendant files amended motion to dismiss challenging amended pleading[3]	Anytime before Step 12	TRCP 91a.5(b), (d)		
11	Notice of hearing; FORM 1E:1.	At least 14 days before Step 12	TRCP 21(b), 91a.6		
12	Hearing on motion—oral hearing or on written submission	At least 21 days after Step 5 or, if defendant filed an amended motion, at least 21 days after Step 10	TRCP 91a.3(b), 91a.5(d)		
13	Order grants motion to dismiss[4]; FORM 3H:4	Step 5 + 45 days or, if defendant filed an amended motion, Step 10 + 45 days; court dismisses all or part of the suit and may award defendant attorney fees and costs[5]	GOVT §22.004(g); TRCP 91a.1, 91a.3(c), 91a.5(d), 91a.7		
14	Order denies motion to dismiss[4]; FORM 3H:4	Step 5 + 45 days or, if defendant filed an amended motion, Step 10 + 45 days; suit continues and court may award plaintiff attorney fees and costs[5]	GOVT §22.004(g); TRCP 91a.1, 91a.3(c), 91a.5(d), 91a.7		
15	Trial	Date set by court	TRCP 247, 262–265		

* **Legend:**

FORM	**O'Connor's Texas Civil Forms** (2020 ed.)
GOVT	Texas Government Code
TRCP	Texas Rules of Civil Procedure

1 The plaintiff has the option to file a response to the defendant's motion, to file an amended pleading—in addition to or instead of the response—or to nonsuit the cause of action. *See* TRCP 91a.4, 91a.5. See "Response," ch. 3-H, §3.

2 If the plaintiff does not file an amended pleading in response to the defendant's motion, the defendant can either (1) do nothing and let the court rule on the motion or (2) withdraw the motion. *See* TRCP 91a.3(c), 91a.5. If the plaintiff does file an amended pleading, the defendant should either (1) withdraw its motion or (2) file an amended motion challenging the amended pleading. TRCP 91a.5(b). See "Reply," ch. 3-H, §4.

3 If the plaintiff files an amended pleading, the defendant should either withdraw its motion or file an amended motion challenging the amended pleading. TRCP 91a.5(b). If the defendant amends the motion, all time periods in TRCP 91a are reset. TRCP 91a.5(d). See "Amend motion," ch. 3-H, §4.2.3.

4 The court cannot rule on the motion to dismiss if the plaintiff timely files a nonsuit, the defendant withdraws the motion, or the parties file an agreed motion to withdraw the motion to dismiss. *See* TRCP 91a.5. See "Ruling not permitted," ch. 3-H, §6.3.

5 For actions commenced on or after September 1, 2019, an award of attorney fees and costs is discretionary. *See* Tex. Civ. Prac. & Rem. Code §30.021; Tex. R. Civ. P. 91a.7; H.B. 3300, 86th Leg., R.S., eff. Sept. 1, 2019. For actions commenced before September 1, 2019, an award of attorney fees and costs is generally mandatory. See "Award of attorney fees & costs," ch. 3-H, §7.2.

See "Motion to Dismiss—Baseless Cause of Action," ch. 3-H, §1 et seq.

7 Motion to abate

Motion to abate*					
Step	Action/Form	Deadline	Authority	Due	Done
1	Plaintiff files suit; FORMS 2B:1 et seq., 2D:1 et seq., 2E:1	Before limitations period expires	TRCP 45–59, 78–82		
2	Defendant is served; FORMS 2I:1 et seq.	Before limitations period expires	TRCP 99, 119		
3	Deadline for defendant's answer	By 10 a.m. on the next Monday following 20 days after Step 2	TRCP 99(b)		
4	Defendant files (as appropriate) special appearance, motion to transfer venue, and answer; FORMS 3B:1, 3B:2, 3C:1 to 3C:3, 3E:1 et seq.	By Step 3	TRCP 85, 86, 92, 120a(1)		
5	Defendant files motion to abate; FORMS 3I:1, 3I:2	After Step 4, at least 3 days before Step 7, and while purpose of motion remains viable	TRCP 21(b), 85, 150–156, 158–160, 175		
6	Plaintiff files response to motion to abate; FORM 3I:3	Before Step 7			
7	Hearing on pending motions in due order: special appearance, venue, then abate	Before Step 12	TRCP 84, 87(1), 120a(2)		
8	Order grants motion to abate	None, suit abated until obstacle to its prosecution is removed			
9	Order denies motion to abate	None, suit continues			
10	Plaintiff cures defect and files motion to revive suit	After Step 8, when obstacle to suit is removed			
11	Defendant files motion to dismiss suit; FORM 7G:1	After Step 8, if defect is not cured			
12	Trial	Date set by court	TRCP 247, 262–265		

* Legend:

FORM	***O'Connor's Texas Civil Forms*** (2020 ed.)
TRCP	Texas Rules of Civil Procedure

See "Motion to Abate—Challenging the Suit," ch. 3-I, §1 et seq.

8 Pretrial motions

Pretrial motions*					
Step	**Action/Form**	**Deadline**	**Authority**	**Due**	**Done**
1	Plaintiff files suit; FORMS 2B:1 et seq., 2D:1 et seq., 2E:1	Before limitations period expires	TRCP 45–59, 78–82		
2	Jury request by either party; FORM 5B:1	At least 30 days before Step 32	TRCP 216–220		
3	Hearing on TRO, if requested	Immediately	TRCP 680		
4	Court grants TRO; FORM 2D:3		TRCP 680		
5	TRO expires	By its own terms or 14 days after Step 4	TRCP 680		
6	Hearing on temporary injunction	As soon as possible; takes precedence	TRCP 680, 681		
7	Defendant is served; FORMS 2I:1 et seq.	Before limitations period expires	TRCP 99, 119		
8	Return filed with court	After Step 7	TRCP 105, 107(g)		
9	Deadline for defendant's answer	By 10 a.m. on the next Monday following 20 days after Step 7	TRCP 99(b)		
10	Plaintiff files motion for no-answer default judgment; Timetable 11; FORM 7A:1	After Step 9 and at least 10 days after Step 8, but before defendant files answer	TRCP 107(h), 239		
11	Defendant files notice of removal to federal court; FEDFRM 4A:1	30 days after Step 7 or receipt of copy of initial pleading[1]	28 U.S.C. §1446(b)		
12	Plaintiff files motion to remand to state court; FEDFRM 4B:1	Step 11 + 30 days	28 U.S.C. §1447(c)		
13	Defendant files special appearance; Timetable 1; FORMS 3B:1, 3B:2	By Step 9 and before any other pleadings below	TRCP 120a(1)		
14	Defendant files motion to transfer venue to another county; Timetable 2; FORMS 3C:1 to 3C:3	By Step 9, after Step 13, and before Steps 15–17	TRCP 85, 86(1)		
15	Defendant files Code FNC motion to dismiss; Timetable 4; FORM 3D:1	Step 9 + 180 days	CPRC §71.051(d)		
16	Defendant files common-law FNC motion to dismiss; Timetable 5; FORM 3D:2	As soon as ground becomes apparent, but after Steps 13 and 14			
17	Defendant files motion to change venue because of local prejudice; Timetable 3; FORM 3C:4	As soon as prejudice becomes known, but at least 3 days before Step 27	TRCP 21(b), 257		
18	Defendant files answer—general denial; FORMS 3E:1 et seq.	By Step 9, but after Steps 13 and 14	TRCP 85, 92		
19	Plaintiff/Defendant files special exceptions; FORM 3G:1	At or after Step 18, but must be ruled on before Step 32	TRCP 91		
20	Defendant files motion to dismiss baseless cause of action; Timetable 6; FORM 3H:1	Step 7 + 60 days	TRCP 91a.3(a)		

Pretrial motions*					
Step	**Action/Form**	**Deadline**	**Authority**	**Due**	**Done**
21	Plaintiff/Defendant files motion to abate; Timetable 7; FORMS 3I:1, 3I:2	At or after Step 18 and at least 3 days before Step 27, but must be ruled on before Step 32	TRCP 21(b), 85		
22	Defendant files plea to the jurisdiction; FORM 3F:1	As soon as ground becomes known	TRCP 85		
23	Objection to assigned judge; FORM 5C:1	Before first hearing at which assigned judge is to preside or at least 7 days after receiving notice of assignment	GOVT §74.053(c)		
24	Motion to disqualify judge; FORM 5C:3	As soon as practicable after party learns of reason for disqualification	Tex. Const. art. 5, §11; TRCP 18a(b)(2), 18b(a)		
25	Motion to recuse judge; FORM 5C:5	At least 10 days before date set for hearing or trial[2]	TRCP 18a(b)(1), 18b(b)		
26	Plaintiff/Defendant files and serves MSJ; Timetable 12; FORMS 7C:1, 7C:2	If traditional MSJ, after Step 7 and 21 days before SJ hearing If no-evidence MSJ, after adequate time for discovery and 21 days before SJ hearing	TRCP 166a(c), (i)		
27	Hearings on pending motions in due order: special appearance, venue, FNC, abate, etc.	30 days before Step 32	CPRC §71.051(d); TRCP 84, 87(1), 120a(2)		
28	Notice of trial setting[3]	45 days before Step 32	TRCP 245		
29	Motion in limine; FORM 5E:1	Before voir dire			
30	Plaintiff files nonsuit; FORM 7F:1	Before plaintiff rests its case	TRCP 162		
31	Offer of proof	As soon as practicable; in jury trial, before jury is charged	TRE 103(c)		
32	Trial	Date set by court	TRCP 247, 262–265		

* **Legend:**

CPRC	Texas Civil Practice & Remedies Code
FEDFRM	**O'Connor's Federal Civil Forms** (2020 ed.)
FNC	Forum non conveniens
FORM	**O'Connor's Texas Civil Forms** (2020 ed.)
GOVT	Texas Government Code
MSJ	Motion for summary judgment
SJ	Summary judgment
Tex. Const.	Texas Constitution
TRCP	Texas Rules of Civil Procedure
TRE	Texas Rules of Evidence
TRO	Temporary restraining order
U.S.C.	United States Code

[1] If a suit is removable at the time it is filed, the defendant must file the notice of removal within 30 days after receiving either the summons, a copy of the complaint, or both. If a suit is not removable at the time it is initially filed, the suit must remain in state court unless a voluntary act by the plaintiff brings about a change that makes the suit removable. See "Deadlines for removal," **O'Connor's Federal Rules * Civil Trials**, ch. 4-A, §4 (2020 ed.); Appendix X, Timetable 4, Removal & Remand.

[2] In limited circumstances, the party may file a motion to recuse after the tenth day before the date set for hearing or trial. See "Motion to recuse," ch. 5-C, §4.1.6(2).

[3] In an expedited action under TRCP 169, any party can ask the court to set a trial date that is within 90 days after the discovery period ends. TRCP 169(d)(2); *see* TRCP 190.2(b)(1). A party should, however, make the request no later than 45 days after the discovery period ends. Because TRCP 245 requires that the parties have 45 days' notice of the first trial setting, any request made more than 45 days after the discovery period ends would cause the trial setting to exceed the 90-day limit under TRCP 169(d)(2). See "Trial date," ch. 2-C, §6.1.

9 Discovery schedule for Level 1

Discovery schedule for Level 1*						
Step	**Action/Form**	**Authority**	**Deadline**		**Due**	**Done**
1	Plaintiff files suit; FORMS 2B:1 et seq., 2D:1 et seq., 2E:1	TRCP 45–59, 78–82	Before limitations period expires			
2	Defendant is served; FORMS 2I:1 et seq.	TRCP 99, 119	Before limitations period expires			
3	Deadline for defendant's answer	TRCP 99(b)	By 10 a.m. on the next Monday following 20 days after Step 2			
4	Deadline for first initial disclosures	TRCP 194.2(a)	Within 30 days after Step 3 or general appearance, or as set by parties' agreement or court order			
5	Discovery period begins	TRCP 190.2(b)(1)	At Step 4			
6	Plaintiff serves discovery requests on defendant; FORMS 6F:1 et seq. to 6K:1 et seq.	TRCP 196.1(a), 196.7(a), 197.1, 198.1	No later than 30 days before Step 17	INT		
				RFP		
				RFA		
				RFE		
7	Defendant's deadline to respond or object to plaintiff's discovery requests; FORMS 6F:1 et seq. to 6K:1 et seq.	TRCP 21a(b), (c), 193.2(a), 196.2(a), 196.7(c)(1), 197.2(a), 198.2(a)	If request is served before Step 3, Step 6 + 50–53 days[1], depending on type of service If request is served after Step 3, Step 6 + 30–33 days, depending on type of service	INT		
				RFP		
				RFA		
				RFE		
8	Defendant serves discovery requests on plaintiff; FORMS 6F:1 et seq. to 6K:1 et seq.	TRCP 196.1(a), 196.7(a), 197.1, 198.1	No later than 30 days before Step 17	INT		
				RFP		
				RFA		
				RFE		
9	Plaintiff's deadline to respond or object to defendant's discovery requests; FORMS 6F:1 et seq. to 6K:1 et seq.	TRCP 21a(b), (c), 193.2(a), 196.2(a), 196.7(c)(1), 197.2(a), 198.2(a)	Step 8 + 30–33 days, depending on type of service	INT		
				RFP		
				RFA		
				RFE		
10	Plaintiff designates its testifying experts	TRCP 195.2(a), 195.5(a)	90 days before Step 17, or as ordered by court			
11	Plaintiff furnishes its retained testifying expert's report; FORM 6D:1	TRCP 195.2(a), 195.5(a)(4), (b)	At Step 10, or as ordered by court			
12	Plaintiff tenders its retained testifying expert for deposition	TRCP 195.3(a), 195.4	If plaintiff furnished expert report, reasonably promptly after Step 13 If plaintiff did not furnish expert report, reasonably promptly after Step 10			
13	Defendant designates its testifying experts	TRCP 195.2(b), 195.5(a)	60 days before Step 17, or as ordered by court			
14	Defendant furnishes its retained testifying expert's report; FORM 6D:1	TRCP 195.2(b), 195.5(a)(4), (b)	At Step 13, or as ordered by court			

Discovery schedule for Level 1*					
Step	**Action/Form**	**Authority**	**Deadline**	**Due**	**Done**
15	Defendant tenders its retained testifying expert for deposition	TRCP 195.3(b), 195.4	Reasonably promptly after Step 13 and after plaintiff's experts testifying on the same subject have been deposed		
16	Deadline to supplement discovery responses; FORMS 6A:33,, 6A:34	TRCP 193.5(b)	Reasonably promptly after discovering need and no later than 30 days before Step 22		
17	Discovery period ends	TRCP 190.2(b)(1)	180 days after Step 4		
18	Deadline for MSJ; Timetable 12	TRCP 166a(c), (i)	If date not set by court: For traditional MSJ, after Step 3 but 21 days before Step 20 For no-evidence MSJ, after adequate time for discovery but 21 days before Step 20		
19	Pretrial conference	TRCP 166	Date set by court		
20	Hearing on MSJ	TRCP 166a(c)	At least 21 days after Step 18		
21	Deadline for pretrial disclosures	TRCP 194.4	At least 30 days before Step 22, or as ordered by court		
22	Trial	TRCP 247, 262–265	Date set by court		

* **Legend:**

FORM	**O'Connor's Texas Civil Forms** (2020 ed.)
INT	Interrogatories
MSJ	Motion for summary judgment
RFA	Requests for admissions
RFE	Requests for entry on land
RFP	Requests for production of documents or things
TRCP	Texas Rules of Civil Procedure

[1] This applies to cases filed before January 1, 2021. Under the 2021 amendments to TRCP 192.2, a party cannot serve discovery requests on another party until the other party's initial disclosures required under TRCP 194 are due. *See* Tex. R. Civ. P. 190.2(b)(1), 192.2(a). These initial disclosures are generally due within 30 days after the filing of the first answer or general appearance. Tex. R. Civ. P. 194.2(a). TRCP 196, 197, and 198, which provide the response deadlines for specific types of discovery, were amended accordingly to eliminate the scenario in which a defendant was served with discovery before its answer was due and thus had 50 days to respond. *See* Tex. R. Civ. P. 196.2(a), 196.7(c)(1), 197.2(a), 198.2(a). For a detailed discussion of the changes to the disclosure procedure under the 2021 amendments, see "Disclosures," ch. 6-E, §1 et seq.

See "Computing response deadlines," ch. 1-D, §6; "Discovery," ch. 6-A, §1 et seq.

10 Discovery schedule for Level 2

Discovery schedule for Level 2*

Step	Action/Form	Authority	Deadline		Due	Done
1	Plaintiff files suit; FORMS 2B:1 et seq., 2D:1 et seq., 2E:1	TRCP 45–59, 78–82	Before limitations period expires			
2	Defendant is served; FORMS 2I:1 et seq.	TRCP 99, 119	Before limitations period expires			
3	Deadline for defendant's answer	TRCP 99(b)	By 10 a.m. on the next Monday following 20 days after Step 2			
4	Deadline for first initial disclosures	TRCP 194.2(a)	Within 30 days after Step 3 or general appearance, or as set by parties' agreement or court order			
5	Discovery period begins	TRCP 190.3(b)(1)	At Step 4			
6	Plaintiff serves discovery requests on defendant; FORMS 6F:1 et seq. to 6K:1 et seq.	TRCP 196.1(a), 196.7(a), 197.1, 198.1	No later than 30 days before Step 18	INT		
				RFP		
				RFA		
				RFE		
7	Defendant's deadline to respond or object to plaintiff's discovery requests; FORMS 6F:1 et seq. to 6K:1 et seq.	TRCP 21a(b), (c), 193.2(a), 196.2(a), 196.7(c)(1), 197.2(a), 198.2(a)	If request is served before Step 3, Step 6 + 50–53 days[1], depending on type of service If request is served after Step 3, Step 6 + 30–33 days, depending on type of service	INT		
				RFP		
				RFA		
				RFE		
8	Beginning of 9-month limitation for discovery in non-Family Code cases	TRCP 190.3(b)(1)(B)	At Step 4			
9	Defendant serves discovery requests on plaintiff; FORMS 6F:1 et seq. to 6K:1 et seq.	TRCP 196.1(a), 196.7(a), 197.1, 198.1	No later than 30 days before Step 18	INT		
				RFP		
				RFA		
				RFE		
10	Plaintiff's deadline to respond or object to defendant's discovery requests; FORMS 6F:1 et seq. to 6K:1 et seq.	TRCP 21a(b), (c), 193.2(a), 196.2(a), 196.7(c)(1), 197.2(a), 198.2(a)	Step 9 + 30–33 days, depending on type of service	INT		
				RFP		
				RFA		
				RFE		
11	Plaintiff designates its testifying experts	TRCP 195.2(a), 195.5(a)	90 days before Step 18, or as ordered by court			
12	Plaintiff furnishes its retained testifying expert's report; FORM 6D:1	TRCP 195.2(a), 195.5(a)(4), (b)	At Step 11, or as ordered by court			
13	Plaintiff tenders its retained testifying expert for deposition	TRCP 195.3(a), 195.4	If plaintiff furnished expert report, reasonably promptly after Step 14 If plaintiff did not furnish expert report, reasonably promptly after Step 11			
14	Defendant designates its testifying experts	TRCP 195.2(b), 195.5(a)	60 days before Step 18, or as ordered by court			
15	Defendant furnishes its retained testifying expert's report; FORM 6D:1	TRCP 195.2(b), 195.5(a)(4), (b)	At Step 14, or as ordered by court			

Discovery schedule for Level 2*					
Step	**Action/Form**	**Authority**	**Deadline**	**Due**	**Done**
16	Defendant tenders its retained testifying expert for deposition	TRCP 195.3(b), 195.4	Reasonably promptly after Step 14 and after plaintiff's experts testifying on the same subject have been deposed		
17	Deadline to supplement discovery responses; FORMS 6A:33,, 6A:34	TRCP 193.5(b)	Reasonably promptly after discovering need and no later than 30 days before Step 23		
18	Discovery period ends	TRCP 190.3(b)(1)	Family Code cases: 30 days before Step 23 Other cases: earlier of 30 days before Step 23, or Step 4 + 9 months		
19	Deadline for MSJ; Timetable 12	TRCP 166a(c), (i)	If date not set by court: For traditional MSJ, after Step 3 but 21 days before Step 21 For no-evidence MSJ, after adequate time for discovery but 21 days before Step 21		
20	Pretrial conference	TRCP 166	Date set by court		
21	Hearing on MSJ	TRCP 166a(c)	At least 21 days after Step 19		
22	Deadline for pretrial disclosures	TRCP 194.4	At least 30 days before Step 23, or as ordered by court		
23	Trial	TRCP 247, 262–265	Date set by court		

* **Legend:**

FORM	***O'Connor's Texas Civil Forms*** (2020 ed.)
INT	Interrogatories
MSJ	Motion for summary judgment
RFA	Requests for admissions
RFE	Requests for entry on land
RFP	Requests for production of documents or things
TRCP	Texas Rules of Civil Procedure

[1] This applies to cases filed before January 1, 2021. Under the 2021 amendments to TRCP 192.2, a party cannot serve discovery requests on another party until after the other party's initial disclosures required under TRCP 194 are due. *See* Tex. R. Civ. P. 190.3(b)(1), 192.2(a). These initial disclosures are generally due within 30 days after the filing of the first answer or general appearance. Tex R. Civ. P. 194.2(a). TRCP 196, 197, and 198, which provide the response deadlines for specific types of discovery, were amended accordingly to eliminate the scenario in which a defendant was served with discovery before its answer was due and thus had 50 days to respond. *See* Tex. R. Civ. P. 196.2(a), 196.7(c)(1), 197.2(a), 198.2(a). For a detailed discussion of the changes to the disclosure procedure under the 2021 amendments, see "Disclosures," ch. 6-E, §1 et seq.

See "Computing response deadlines," ch. 1-D, §6; "Discovery," ch. 6-A, §1 et seq.

11 No-answer default judgment

No-answer default judgment*					
Step	**Action/Form**	**Deadline**	**Authority**	**Due**	**Done**
1	Plaintiff files suit; FORMS 2B:1 et seq., 2D:1 et seq., 2E:1	Before limitations period expires	TRCP 45–59, 78–82		
2	If suit is against the State, plaintiff must send copy of petition to Attorney General by certified mail	At Step 1	CPRC §30.004(b)		
3	Defendant is served; FORMS 2I:1 et seq.	Before limitations period expires	TRCP 99, 119		
4	Return filed with court	After Step 3	TRCP 105, 107(g)		
5	Deadline for defendant's answer	By 10 a.m. on the next Monday following 20 days after Step 3	TRCP 99(b)		
6	Plaintiff files motion for default judgment; FORM 7A:1	After Step 5 and at least 10 days after Step 4	TRCP 107(h), 239		
7	If suit is against the State, plaintiff must send notice of intent to take default to Attorney General by certified mail	No later than 10 days before entry of default judgment	CPRC §39.001		
8	Plaintiff files certificate of last known address and/or servicemembers' affidavit; FORMS 7A:2, 7A:3	By Step 10	TRCP 239a; 50 U.S.C. §3931(b)(1)		
9	Hearing on motion for default judgment—unliquidated damages; FORM 7A:4	At or before Step 10	TRCP 243		
10	Default judgment signed; FORM 9C:2	At or after Step 9	TRCP 239a		
11	Clerk sends defendant notice of default judgment	After Step 10	TRCP 239a		

* **Legend:**

CPRC	Texas Civil Practice & Remedies Code
FORM	**O'Connor's Texas Civil Forms** (2020 ed.)
TRCP	Texas Rules of Civil Procedure
U.S.C.	United States Code

See "No-answer default," ch. 7-A, §3.

12 Motion for summary judgment

Motion for summary judgment*					
Step	**Action/Form**	**Deadline**	**Authority**	**Due**	**Done**
1	Plaintiff files suit; FORMS 2B:1 et seq., 2D:1 et seq., 2E:1	Before limitations period expires	TRCP 45–59, 78–82		
2	Defendant is served; FORMS 2I:1 et seq.	Before limitations period expires	TRCP 99, 119		
3	Deadline for defendant's answer	By 10 a.m. on the next Monday following 20 days after Step 2	TRCP 99(b)		
4	Defendant files answer; FORMS 3E:1 et seq.	At or before Step 3	TRCP 83–98		
5	Movant (plaintiff/defendant) files MSJ; FORMS 7C:1, 7C:2	At least 21 days before Step 15 and, if under TRCP 166a(i), after adequate time for discovery[1]	TRCP 166a(a)–(c), (i)		
6	Movant serves notice of date of SJ hearing	At or after Step 5 and at least 21 days before Step 15[1]	TRCP 166a(c)		
7	If traditional SJ, movant files evidence to support MSJ	At Step 5 and at least 21 days before Step 15[1]	TRCP 166a(c), (d)		
8	Nonmovant files response and objections to MSJ; FORMS 7C:1, 7C:2	7 days before Step 15	TRCP 166a(c), (i)		
9	Nonmovant files evidence to support response to MSJ	7 days before Step 15	TRCP 166a(c), (d), (i)		
10	Nonmovant files affidavit and motion for continuance; FORMS 7B:5, 7B:6	As soon as possible, but before Step 15	TRCP 166a(g)		
11	Nonmovant files special exceptions to challenge vague or unclear MSJ; FORM 7B:1	7 days before Step 15	TRCP 166a(c)		
12	Nonmovant files amended pleading (petition or answer) adding new claims or defenses; FORMS 2B:1 et seq., 3E:1 et seq., 5F:1	7 days before Step 15, unless leave of court obtained	TRCP 63		
13	Movant files special exceptions to challenge vague or unclear response to MSJ; FORM 7B:1	3 days before Step 15[2]	TRCP 90, 91		
14	Order on special exceptions signed; FORM 3G:2	At or before Step 15			
15	Hearing on MSJ	At least 21 days after Step 6[1]	TRCP 166a(c), (i)		
16	FORM 7C:12	As soon as practical after Step 15	TRCP 166a		
17	MNT filed; FORM 10B:6	Step 16 + 30 days	TRCP 329b		
18	MNT overruled; FORM 10B:8	Step 16 + 75 days by operation of law, or earlier by written order	TRCP 329b(c)		
19	Judgment becomes final and court loses plenary power	Step 16 + 30 days, or Step 18 + 30 days	TRCP 329b(d), (e)		

* **Legend:**

FORM **O'Connor's Texas Civil Forms** (2020 ed.)

MNT	Motion for new trial
MSJ	Motion for summary judgment
SJ	Summary judgment
TRCP	Texas Rules of Civil Procedure

[1] Depending on the type of service, the movant may need to file and serve the motion and notice of hearing more than 21 days before the hearing. *See* TRCP 21a(b), (c). See "Filing & serving motion & notice," ch. 7-B, §6.1.1.

[2] *See* **McConnell v. Southside ISD**, 858 S.W.2d 337, 343 n.7 (Tex 1993).

See "Motion for Summary Judgment—General Rules," ch. 7-B, §1 et seq.; "MNT after summary judgment," ch. 10-B, §11.

13 Offer of settlement

Offer of settlement*					
Step	**Action/Form**	**Deadline**	**Authority**	**Due**	**Done**
1	Plaintiff files suit; FORMS 2B:1 et seq., 2D:1 et seq., 2E:1	Before limitations period expires	TRCP 45–59, 78–82		
2	Defendant is served; FORMS 2I:1 et seq.	Before limitations period expires	TRCP 99, 119		
3	Deadline for defendant's answer	By 10 a.m. on the next Monday following 20 days after Step 2	TRCP 99(b)		
4	Defendant files answer; FORMS 3E:1 et seq.	At or before Step 3	TRCP 83–98		
5	Defendant files TRCP 167 declaration with court; FORM 7H:1	45 days before Step 17	TRCP 167.2(a)		
6	Offeror (plaintiff/defendant) serves settlement offer on offeree; FORM 7H:2	At least 60 days after Step 4, after Step 5, and at least 14 days before Step 17	TRCP 167.2(b)(6), (e)		
7	Deadline for offeree to accept	As stated in offer, but at least 14 days after Step 6	TRCP 167.2(b)(5)		
8	Offeree serves objections to unreasonable conditions of offer; FORM 7H:3	By Step 7	TRCP 167.2(c)		
9	Offeror serves withdrawal of offer; FORM 7H:3	Before Step 10	TRCP 167.3(a)		
10	Offeree serves acceptance of offer; FORM 7H:3	Before Steps 7 and 9	TRCP 167.2(b)(5), 167.3(b)		
11	Offeree serves rejection of offer; FORM 7H:3	Before Steps 7 and 9	TRCP 167.3(c)		
12	Offeree serves counteroffer	Within 7 days after Step 6 or at least 14 days before Step 17, whichever is later	TRCP 167.2(e)(3), (f)		
13	Offeror joins third party or designates RTP	As permitted by TRCP and CPRC[1]	CPRC §33.004; TRCP 38, 40(a), 97(f)		
14	Offeree serves objections to offer based on joinder or designation	Within 15 days after Step 13	TRCP 167.3(d)		
15	Motion to modify deadlines for Steps 5 and 6	Before Step 16	TRCP 167.5(a)		
16	Order modifying deadlines for Steps 5 and 6	Before Step 18	TRCP 167.5(a)		
17	Case set for trial on the merits		TRCP 167.2(a), 246		
18	Commencement of trial on the merits		TRCP 167.5(a), 247, 262–65		

* **Legend:**

CPRC	Texas Civil Practice & Remedies Code
FORM	***O'Connor's Texas Civil Forms*** (2020 ed.)
RTP	Responsible third party

TRCP	Texas Rules of Civil Procedure

[1] For the specific deadlines for joining a third party, see "Third-party petitions," ch. 3-E, §7.3; "RTP," ch. 3-E, §7.4.

See "Offer of Settlement," ch. 7-H, §1 et seq.

14 Offer of proof & bill of exception

Offer of proof & bill of exception*					
Step	**Action/Form**	**Deadline**	**Authority**	**Due**	**Done**
1	Offer of proof	As soon as practicable; in jury trial, before Step 2	TRE 103(c)		
2	Court reads charge to jury	After close of evidence and before closing argument	TRCP 275		
3	Jury returns verdict		TRCP 290–293		
4	Trial court signs judgment	After Step 3	TRCP 306a(1)		
5	Judgment becomes final and court loses plenary power	If no MNT, Step 4 + 30 days If MNT, 30 days after MNT is overruled by written order or by operation of law	TRCP 329b(d), (e)		
6	Movant (plaintiff/defendant) presents formal bill of exception to judge for signature; T-FORM 8E:1	As soon as possible after Step 5, but no later than Step 16 + 30 days	TRAP 33.2(c)(1), (e)(1)		
7	If parties agree to contents, judge signs and files bill with clerk	Immediately after Step 6, but no later than Step 16 + 30 days	TRAP 33.2(c)(2), (e)(1)		
8	If parties do not agree, judge notifies parties and holds hearing	As soon as possible after Step 6	TRAP 33.2(c)(2)		
9	If bill is approved, judge signs and files bill with clerk	Immediately after Step 8, but no later than Step 16 + 30 days	TRAP 33.2(c)(2)(A), (e)(1)		
10	If bill is disapproved, judge suggests changes	Immediately after Step 8	TRAP 33.2(c)(2)(B), (C)		
11	If movant agrees to changes, bill is corrected and judge signs and files bill with clerk	Immediately after Step 10, but no later than Step 16 + 30 days	TRAP 33.2(c)(2)(B), (e)(1)		
12	If movant refuses to agree to changes, judge notes bill is refused and returns it to movant	Immediately after Step 10	TRAP 33.2(c)(2)(C)		
13	Judge prepares a bill of exception that accurately reflects court proceedings and files it with clerk	Immediately after Step 12, but no later than Step 16 + 30 days	TRAP 33.2(c)(2)(C), (e)(1)		
14	If movant disagrees with judge's bill, movant may file refused bill and affidavits of 3 bystanders with clerk; T-FORMS 8E:2, 8E:3	Immediately after Step 13, but no later than Step 16 + 30 days	TRAP 33.2(c)(3), (e)(1)		
15	If nonmovant disagrees with movant's affidavits, nonmovant may file affidavits of bystanders with clerk; T-FORM 8E:3	Step 14 + 10 days	TRAP 33.2(c)(3)		
16	Movant (1) perfects appeal by filing notice of appeal in trial court and (2) files docketing statement in CA; A-FORM 5A:1	If no MNT, Step 4 + 30 days If MNT, Step 4 + 90 days	TRAP 25.1, 26.1, 32.1		
17	Movant files motion in CA for extension of time to file formal bill of exception	Last day for filing formal bill (Step 16 + 30 days) + 15 days	TRAP 10.5(b), 33.2(e)(3)		

* **Legend:**

CA	Court of appeals
FORMS	A-FORM—appeal form in **O'Connor's Texas Civil Appeals** (2020 ed.)
	T-FORM—trial form in **O'Connor's Texas Civil Forms** (2020 ed.)
MNT	Motion for new trial
TRAP	Texas Rules of Appellate Procedure
TRCP	Texas Rules of Civil Procedure
TRE	Texas Rules of Evidence

See "Offer of Proof & Bill of Exception," ch. 8-E, §1 et seq.; "Notice of Appeal," **O'Connor's Texas Civil Appeals**, ch. 5-A, §1 et seq. (2020 ed.).

15 Request for findings of fact & conclusions of law

Request for findings of fact & conclusions of law*					
Step	**Action/Form**	**Deadline**	**Authority**	**Due**	**Done**
1	Trial court signs judgment; T-FORMS 9C:1 et seq.		TRCP 306a(1)		
2	Trial-court clerk sends notice that court signed judgment	Immediately after Step 1	TRCP 306a(3)		
3	Appellant files request for FoF	Step 1 + 20 days	TRAP 26.1(a)(4); TRCP 296		
4	Appellant files notice of past-due FoF	Step 3 + 30 days	TRAP 26.1(a)(4); TRCP 297		
5	Trial court files FoF	Step 3 + 20 days, or Step 3 + 40 days, if Step 4	TRCP 297		
6	Appellant files request for additional or amended FoF	Step 5 + 10 days	TRCP 298		
7	Trial court files additional or amended FoF	Step 6 + 10 days	TRCP 298		
8	Optional—appellant files MNT; T-FORMS 10B:1 to 10B:6	Step 1 + 30 days	TRCP 324, 329b(a)		
9	MNT overruled	Step 1 + 75 days by operation of law, or earlier by written order	TRCP 329b(c)		
10	Appellant (1) perfects appeal by filing notice of appeal in trial court and (2) files docketing statement in CA; A-FORM 5A:1	If no MNT or request for FoF, Step 1 + 30 days If MNT or request for FoF, Step 1 + 90 days	TRAP 25.1, 26.1, 32.1		
11	Trial court loses plenary power over judgment	If no MNT, Step 1 + 30 days If MNT, Step 9 + 30 days	TRCP 329b(d), (e)		
For the deadlines for filing an appeal, see Timetable 18. From the timetable above, insert into Timetable 18 the dates that apply to the appeal: the date the trial court signed the judgment, the date the appeal was perfected, and the date the trial court lost plenary power.					

* **Legend:**

CA	Court of appeals
FoF	Findings of fact and conclusions of law
FORMS	A-FORM—appeal form in **O'Connor's Texas Civil Appeals** (2020 ed.)
	T-FORM—trial form in **O'Connor's Texas Civil Forms** (2020 ed.)
MNT	Motion for new trial
TRAP	Texas Rules of Appellate Procedure
TRCP	Texas Rules of Civil Procedure

See "Request for Findings of Fact & Conclusions of Law," ch. 10-E, §1 et seq.

16 Motion to reinstate after dismissal for want of prosecution

Motion to reinstate after dismissal for want of prosecution*					
Step	**Action/Form**	**Deadline**	**Authority**	**Due**	**Done**
1	Trial-court clerk sends notice of date case will be dismissed		TRCP 165a(1)		
2	Plaintiff files motion to retain on docket	Before Step 4	TRCP 165a(1)		
3	Date set for hearing on dismissal	Set by trial court	TRCP 165a(1)		
4	Trial court signs order dismissing case		TRCP 165a(1), 306a(1)		
5	Trial-court clerk sends notice of dismissal order	Immediately after Step 4	TRCP 165a(1), 306a(3)		
6	Plaintiff files VMR with affidavits; T-FORM 10F:1	Step 4 + 30 days	TRCP 165a(3), 306a		
7	Trial court sets date for hearing, with notice to parties	As soon as possible and before Step 4 + 75 days	TRCP 165a(3)		
8	Hearing on VMR	When set by court	TRCP 165a(3)		
9	VMR overruled	Step 4 + 75 days by operation of law, or earlier by written order	TRCP 165a(3), 306a		
10	Plaintiff (1) perfects appeal by filing notice of appeal in trial court and (2) files docketing statement in CA; A-FORM 5A:1	If no VMR, Step 4 + 30 days If VMR, Step 4 + 90 days	TRAP 25.1, 26.1, 32.1		
11	Trial court loses plenary power over judgment	If no VMR, Step 4 + 30 days If VMR, Step 9 + 30 days	TRCP 165a(3), 329b(d), (e)		
For the deadlines for filing an appeal, see Timetable 18. From the timetable above, insert into Timetable 18 the dates that apply to the appeal: the date of the order of dismissal, the date the appeal was perfected, and the date the trial court lost plenary power.					

* **Legend:**

CA	Court of appeals
FORMS	A-FORM—appeal form in **O'Connor's Texas Civil Appeals** (2020 ed.) T-FORM—trial form in **O'Connor's Texas Civil Forms** (2020 ed.)
TRAP	Texas Rules of Appellate Procedure
TRCP	Texas Rules of Civil Procedure
VMR	Verified motion to reinstate the case

See "Motion to Reinstate After Dismissal for Want of Prosecution," ch. 10-F, §1 et seq.

17 Motion to extend postjudgment deadlines

Motion to extend postjudgment deadlines*					
Step	Action/Form	Deadline	Authority	Due	Done
1	Trial court signs judgment; T-FORMS 9C:1 et seq.		TRCP 306a(1)		
2	Trial-court clerk sends notice that court signed judgment	Immediately after Step 1	TRCP 306a(3)		
3	Appellant receives late notice of judgment	Step 1 + 21–90 days	TRAP 4.2; TRCP 306a(4)		
4	Appellant (1) perfects appeal conditionally by filing notice of appeal in trial court and (2) files docketing statement in CA; A-FORM 5A:1	As soon as possible, but no later than— Step 3 + 30 days if no MNT, or Step 3 + 90 days if MNT	TRAP 25.1, 26.1, 32.1		
5	Appellant files MNT; T-FORMS 10B:1 to 10B:6	Step 3 + 30 days	TRCP 306a(4), 324, 329b(a)		
6	MNT overruled	Step 3 + 75 days by operation of law, or earlier by written order	TRCP 306a(4), 329b(c)		
7	Appellant files MEPD with affidavits; T-FORMS 10G:1 to 10G:3	Before Step 11	TRCP 306a(4), (5), 329b(d)		
8	Trial court conducts hearing on MEPD	As soon as possible, but before Step 11	TRCP 306a(4), (5)		
9	Court overrules MEPD; all appellate deadlines run from Step 1; T-FORM 10G:5	Enter date for judgment from Step 1	TRCP 306a(1)		
10	Court grants MEPD and makes finding of date appellant received actual notice of judgment; all appellate deadlines run from Step 10; T-FORM 10G:5	Enter new date for judgment (same as Step 3)	TRAP 4.2(c); TRCP 306a(5)		
11	Trial court loses plenary power over judgment	If no MNT, Step 3 + 30 days If MNT, Step 6 + 30 days	TRCP 306a(4), 329b(d), (e)		
For the deadlines for filing an appeal, see Timetable 18. From the timetable above, insert into Timetable 18 the dates that apply to the appeal: the new date for the judgment, the date the appeal was perfected, and the date the trial court lost plenary power.					

* **Legend:**

CA	Court of appeals
FORMS	A-FORM—appeal form in **O'Connor's Texas Civil Appeals** (2020 ed.) T-FORM—trial form in **O'Connor's Texas Civil Forms** (2020 ed.)
MEPD	Motion to extend postjudgment deadlines
MNT	Motion for new trial
TRAP	Texas Rules of Appellate Procedure
TRCP	Texas Rules of Civil Procedure

See "Motion to Extend Postjudgment Deadlines," ch. 10-G, §1 et seq.

18 Appeal to the court of appeals

Appeal to the court of appeals*					
Step	**Action/Form**	**Deadline**	**Authority**	**Due**	**Done**
1	Trial court signs judgment; T-FORMS 9C:1 et seq.		TRCP 306a(1)		
2	Appellant files MNT; T-FORMS 10B:1 to 10B:6	Step 1 + 30 days	TRCP 324, 329b(a)		
3	MNT is overruled	Step 1 + 75 days by operation of law, or earlier by written order	TRCP 329b(c)		
4	Appellant (1) perfects appeal by filing notice of appeal in trial court and (2) files docketing statement in CA; A-FORM 5A:1	If no MNT, Step 1 + 30 days If MNT, Step 1 + 90 days	TRAP 25.1, 26.1, 32.1		
5	Optional—appellant files formal bill of exception; Timetable 14; T-FORM 8E:1	Step 4 + 30 days	TRAP 33.2(e)(1)		
6	Optional—appellant files motion to stay execution of judgment in trial court; A-FORMS 4B:1 et seq.	Before execution of judgment	TRAP 24.1, 24.2; TRCP 627		
7	Appellant must arrange to pay trial-court clerk for clerk's record	Before clerk's record is prepared	TRAP 35.3(a)(2)		
8	Optional—appellant files request with trial-court clerk to include additional matters in clerk's record; A-FORM 6B:2	Before clerk's record is prepared	TRAP 34.5(b)		
9	Appellant must: (1) arrange to pay court reporter for reporter's record, (2) send written request to court reporter requesting record and list of exhibits, and (3) file copy of request in trial court; A-FORMS 6C:1 et seq.	At or before Step 4	TRAP 34.6(b), 35.3(b)(3)		
10	Judgment becomes final and court loses plenary power	If no MNT, Step 1 + 30 days If MNT, Step 3 + 30 days	TRCP 329b(d), (e)		
11	Trial-court clerk files clerk's record in CA	If no MNT, Step 1 + 60 days If MNT, Step 1 + 120 days[1]	TRAP 35.1, 35.3		
12	Court reporter files reporter's record in CA				
13	CA clerk must notify parties of dates clerk's and reporter's records filed	At Steps 11 and 12	TRAP 37.2		
14	Appellant files brief in CA; A-FORM 7B:1 et seq.	30 days after later of Step 11 or 12; if accelerated appeal, 20 days after later of Step 11 or 12	TRAP 38.1, 38.6(a), 39.7		
15	Appellee files brief in CA; A-FORMS 7B:1 to 7B:4, 7C:1 et seq.	Step 14 + 30 days; if accelerated appeal, Step 14 + 20 days	TRAP 38.2, 38.6(b), 39.7		
16	Optional—appellant files reply brief in CA	Step 15 + 20 days	TRAP 38.3, 38.6(c)		

Appeal to the court of appeals*					
Step	**Action/Form**	**Deadline**	**Authority**	**Due**	**Done**
17	CA clerk sends notice regarding oral argument to parties	21 days before Step 18	TRAP 39.8		
18	Date for oral argument or written submission in CA	As set by CA	TRAP 39.8		
19	CA renders judgment and issues opinion	Promptly after Step 18	TRAP 43.1, 47.1		
20	Optional—movant (appellant/ appellee) files MReh in CA; A-FORMS 7H:1 et seq.	Step 19 + 15 days	TRAP 49.1, 49.5, 49.8		
21	CA rules on MReh		TRAP 49.3		
22	CA may order en banc reconsideration with or without a motion	Before Step 23	TRAP 49.7		
23	CA loses plenary power over judgment	If MReh or MET, Step 21 + 30 days If MEBR or MET, Step 22 + 30 days If no MReh, MEBR, or MET, Step 19 + 60 days	TRAP 19.1		
24	For deadlines for filing a petition for review in the Texas Supreme Court, see **O'Connor's Texas Civil Appeals** (2020 ed.), Appendix IV, Timetable 9, Petition for Review to Texas Supreme Court.				
25	Mandate issues	If no MReh or petition for review filed, 10 days after deadline to file MET for filing MReh or petition for review	TRAP 18.1(a)		

* **Legend:**

CA	Court of appeals
FORMS	A-FORM—appeal form in **O'Connor's Texas Civil Appeals** (2020 ed.) T-FORM—trial form in **O'Connor's Texas Civil Forms** (2020 ed.)
MEBR	Motion for en banc reconsideration
MET	Motion to extend time
MNT	Motion for new trial
MReh	Motion for rehearing
TRAP	Texas Rules of Appellate Procedure
TRCP	Texas Rules of Civil Procedure

1 If a trial-court clerk or court reporter requests an extension of time to file the record, the appellate court may extend the deadline by no more than 30 days in an ordinary or restricted appeal or 10 days in an accelerated appeal. TRAP 35.3(c).

See "Perfecting Appeal," **O'Connor's Texas Civil Appeals**, ch. 5-A, §1 et seq. (2020 ed.); "The Court of Appeals," **O'Connor's Texas Civil Appeals**, ch. 7-A, §1 et seq. (2020 ed.); **O'Connor's Texas Civil Appeals**, Appendix IV, Timetable 1 (2020 ed.), Appeal of jury trial to court of appeals.

Index